GABRIEL MANTZ

YEARBOOK OF EUROPEAN FOOTBALL

2020-2021

British Library Cataloguing in Publication Data
A catalogue record for this book is available from the British Library

ISBN 978-1-86223-436-9

Copyright © 2020, SOCCER BOOKS LIMITED (01472 696226)
72 St. Peter's Avenue, Cleethorpes, N.E. Lincolnshire, DN35 8HU, England

Web site www.soccer-books.co.uk • e-mail info@soccer-books.co.uk

Printed in the UK by Short Run Press.

Dear Readers

The 2019/2020 season is certainly the most exceptional in the history of football, in both Europe and across the whole world. The European season began, as usual, in July 2019 with the first qualifying matches for the Champions League and Europa League. In August 2019, Liverpool FC crowned an extraordinary season by lifting the 2019 European Super Cup against Chelsea FC London, winning a penalty shoot-out 5-4 after the game had finished 2-2 following extra time. The national championships across the continent then commenced in the usual manner and nobody could have foreseen the disaster to come which would delay the end of the season until August 2020…

The last group matches for European Championship qualification were played between September and November, when 20 of the 24 final round participants were determined. There were few surprises and, in most of the groups, the favorites qualified comfortably. However, in Group B, Ukraine topped the group ahead of the reigning European champions and Nations League winners Portugal. In Group E, Croatia began the qualifiers poorly, but recovered and eventually won the group ahead of Wales who themselves profited from Hungary's poor results during autumn. The good form of the Magyars during the Spring of 2019 had put them into a strong position to earn qualification, but three defeats in their final four matches saw them drop into 4th place in the group. The big surprise of Euro 2016, Iceland, were not able to carry on such remarkable form and finished in third place in Group H behind France and Turkey. However, due to their placing in the 2018-2019 Nations League, Iceland still progressed to the Euro 2020 qualification play-offs, which were originally scheduled for early 2020. One notable success was that of Finland who finished as runners-up in Group J to qualify for a finals tournament for the first time in their footballing history!

Unfortunately, the ideal world of football, sport and life as a whole was abruptly brought back down to earth in January 2020. In a small number of weeks, a new virus originating in China quickly spread across the world and a global pandemic was declared. Nobody could have guessed what drastic measures would be necessary in an attempt to bring the number of infections and the death rate under control. In many countries around the world everyday life was completely paralysed by the COVID-19 pandemic almost overnight as people were required to stay at home, not even being allowed to visit their workplaces in many cases! Of course, football was understandably not considered as important as the attempt to save lives so, with the exception of Belarus, more or less all leagues were suspended and cup competitions were postponed or cancelled. Some countries such as Belgium, France, the Netherlands, Wales etc. ended their championships almost immediately and declared the league tables at that time to be the final tables, with relegation suspended. Other countries such as Germany and England decided to wait to see if it would be possible to continue playing at a later date, providing the pandemic could be brought under control.

Germany managed to suppress the first wave of the virus well and recommenced their season during early May, although spectators were not allowed to attend matches and players required frequent testing for the virus. At the beginning of June, Spain followed suit and resumed play as did England and Italy during mid-June. All these championships were subsequently completed. This later end of some championships had a decisive influence on other events, but more on that later. We should also not forget the financial consequences of this football lockdown and the subsequent matches without spectators, i.e. without income!

The final tournament of Euro 2020, with games scheduled to be played in 12 different cities across Europe from London to Baku, has been postponed by a year and will now hopefully be able to take place in June and July 2021. Nevertheless, the tournament will still be named "Euro 2020". The play-offs of the Nations League to determine the last four teams for the Euro 2020 finals have been postponed until Autumn 2020.

Both European cup competitions were of course suspended at the beginning of March 2020 and matches were only able to recommence in July 2020. For some clubs, instead of preparing for the new season, the European competitions were on the agenda. UEFA decided that it would be necessary to change the format of the two competitions to become more like a tournament with the games concentrated in fewer venues to reduce the risk of spreading the virus. Instead of playing home and away matches, a single game at a neutral venue instead decided who would progress to the next round. It was decided to move all games starting from the quarter-final stages of the two competitions to either Lisbon (Champions League) or the western part of Germany (Duisburg / Düsseldorf / Gelsenkirchen / Cologne – Europa League). Spectators were not allowed to attend any of these matches due to the ongoing pandemic.

The Europa League was once again won by Sevilla FC as the Spaniards defeated Internazionale Milano 3-2 in the final. Remarkably, it was the sixth win for Sevilla FC in this competition, a record, and the victory earned the club a lucrative place in the Champions League next season.

The Champions League also had a worthy winner, FC Bayern Munich, as the German Champions were crowned Champions of Europe for the sixth time in the club's history. Bayern's dominance was clear as they became the first club to win every game in the competition from their first group match through to the final itself – 13 matches played, 13 victories! The final match was decided by a single goal scored by French winger, Kingsley Coman and it is interesting to note that he began his career at Paris St. Germain before being released as a young player after just 3 senior appearances! This magnificent march through the competition by the Bavarians was undoubtedly helped by two important factors. Firstly, Hansi Flick was installed as a new trainer on 3rd November 2019, initially as an interim measure, but then permanently after he quickly impressed in the role. Secondly, Bayern benefitted from Germany's earlier restart of the season, so they were able to rest more and concentrate on preparing for the final tournament in Lisbon. Most of their opponents came to Lisbon following high workloads (the teams from Spain, England, and Italy had been playing two games each week to finish their seasons) and appeared tired and listless, while Lyon and Paris Saint Germain had only played very sporadically for months. However, that still doesn't explain quite how a team such as FC Barcelona can lose 8-2 against Bayern Munich! This is why, according to many onlookers, the German team would almost certainly have won the trophy with or without the pandemic this season!

This third edition of the Yearbook of European Football contains complete statistics for the national championships of all European countries with league results and tables. Player appearances (including substitute appearances) and goals scored are presented for all top division clubs from Europe with the unfortunate exception of those in Kosovo where it has only proved possible to obtain club squads due to a lack of available information about some championship rounds. You will also find national cup competition details including final match statistics and, of course, there are also complete statistics for national teams and the international players for each country and their clubs.

Great thanks to Mr. Dirk Karsdorp, who has once again provided full line-ups and complete statistics for both of the major European club competitions during 2019/2020.

Please enjoy the read!

The Author

FIFA COUNTRY CODES

EUROPE

ALB	Albania	GER	Germany	MKD	North Macedonia
AND	Andorra	GIB	Gibraltar	NOR	Norway
ARM	Armenia	GRE	Greece	POL	Poland
AUT	Austria	HUN	Hungary	POR	Portugal
AZE	Azerbaijan	ISL	Iceland	IRL	Republic of Ireland
BLR	Belarus	ISR	Israel	ROU	Romania
BEL	Belgium	ITA	Italy	RUS	Russia
BIH	Bosnia-Herzegovina	KAZ	Kazakhstan	SMR	San Marino
BUL	Bulgaria	KVX	Kosovo	SCO	Scotland
CRO	Croatia	LVA	Latvia	SRB	Serbia
CYP	Cyprus	LIE	Liechtenstein	SVK	Slovakia
CZE	Czech Republic	LTU	Lithuania	SVN	Slovenia
DEN	Denmark	LUX	Luxembourg	ESP	Spain
ENG	England	MLT	Malta	SWE	Sweden
EST	Estonia	MDA	Moldova	SUI	Switzerland
FRO	Faroe Islands	MNE	Montenegro	TUR	Turkey
FIN	Finland	NED	Netherlands	UKR	Ukraine
FRA	France	NIR	Northern Ireland	WAL	Wales
GEO	Georgia				

Former countries:

TCH	Czechoslovakia

YUG	Yugoslavia

ASIA

AFG	Afghanistan
AUS	Australia
CHN	China P.R.
IDN	Indonesia
IRN	Iran
IRQ	Iraq
JPN	Japan
JOR	Jordan
PRK	Korea D.P.R.
KOR	Korea Republic
KGZ	Kyrgyzstan
LIB	Lebanon
OMA	Oman
PAK	Pakistan
PLE	Palestine
PHI	Philippines
QAT	Qatar
KSA	Saudi Arabia
SYR	Syria
TJK	Tajikistan
TKM	Turkmenistan
UZB	Uzbekistan

AFRICA

ALG	Algeria
ANG	Angola
BEN	Benin
BFA	Burkina Faso
BDI	Burundi
CMR	Cameroon
CPV	Cape Verde Islands
CTA	Central African Republic
CHA	Chad
COM	Comoros Islands
CGO	Congo
COD	D.R. Congo
EGY	Egypt
EQG	Equatorial Guinea
ERI	Eritrea
GAB	Gabon
GAM	Gambia
GHA	Ghana
GUI	Guinea
GNB	Guinea-Bissau
CIV	Ivory Coast
KEN	Kenya
LBR	Liberia
LBY	Libya
MAD	Madagascar
MWI	Malawi
MLI	Mali
MTN	Mauritania
MRI	Mauritius
MAR	Morocco
MOZ	Mozambique
NAM	Namibia
NIG	Niger
NGA	Nigeria
RWA	Rwanda
STP	São Tome e Principe
SEN	Senegal
SLE	Sierra Leone
SOM	Somalia
RSA	South Africa
TAN	Tanzania
TOG	Togo
TUN	Tunisia
UGA	Uganda
WSA	West Sahara
ZAM	Zambia
ZIM	Zimbabwe

NORTH AND CENTRAL AMERICA

ARU	Aruba
BER	Bermuda
CAN	Canada
CRC	Costa Rica
CUB	Cuba
CUW	Curaçao
DOM	Dominican Republic
GYF	French Guiana
GLP	Guadeloupe
GUA	Guatemala
HAI	Haiti
HON	Honduras
JAM	Jamaica
MTQ	Martinique
MEX	Mexico
MSR	Montserrat
PAN	Panama
SKN	Saint Kitts and Nevis
SUR	Suriname
TRI	Trinidad and Tobago
USA	United States

SOUTH AMERICA

ARG	Argentina
BOL	Bolivia
BRA	Brazil
CHI	Chile
COL	Colombia
ECU	Ecuador
PAR	Paraguay
PER	Peru
URU	Uruguay
VEN	Venezuela

OCEANIA

NZL	New Zealand

OTHER ABBREVIATIONS

DOB Date of birth
M Matches played
G Goals
(F) International friendly matches
(ECQ) 2020 Euro Championship Qualifiers

SUMMARY

COMPETITIONS FOR NATIONAL TEAMS

EUROPEAN CLUB COMPETITIONS

NATIONAL ASSOCIATIONS

COMPETITIONS FOR NATIONAL TEAMS

UEFA EUROPEAN CHAMPIONSHIP 2020

QUALIFIERS

The qualifiers continued in autumn 2019 with the remaining matches and the participants of the final tournament were determined.

GROUP A

Results			
22.03.2019	Sofia	Bulgaria - Montenegro	1-1(0-0)
22.03.2019	London	England - Czech Republic	5-0(2-0)
25.03.2019	Prishtinë	Kosovo - Bulgaria	1-1(0-1)
25.03.2019	Podgorica	Montenegro - England	1-5(1-2)
07.06.2019	Praha	Czech Republic - Bulgaria	2-1(1-1)
07.06.2019	Podgorica	Montenegro - Kosovo	1-1(0-1)
10.06.2019	Sofia	Bulgaria - Kosovo	2-3(1-1)
10.06.2019	Olomouc	Czech Rep. - Montenegro	3-0(1-0)
07.09.2019	Prishtinë	Kosovo - Czech Republic	2-1(1-1)
07.09.2019	London	England - Bulgaria	4-0(1-0)
10.09.2019	Southampton	England - Kosovo	5-3(5-1)
10.09.2019	Podgorica	Montenegro - Czech Rep.	0-3(0-0)
11.10.2019	Podgorica	Montenegro - Bulgaria	0-0
11.10.2019	Praha	Czech Republic - England	2-1(1-1)
14.10.2019	Sofia	Bulgaria - England	0-6(0-4)
14.10.2019	Prishtinë	Kosovo - Montenegro	2-0(2-0)
14.11.2019	Plzeň	Czech Republic - Kosovo	2-1(0-0)
14.11.2019	London	England - Montenegro	7-0(5-0)
17.11.2019	Sofia	Bulgaria - Czech Republic	1-0(0-0)
17.11.2019	Prishtinë	Kosovo - England	0-4(0-1)

Standings								
1.	**England**	8	7	0	1	37 - 6	21
2.	**Czech Rep.**	8	5	0	3	13 - 11	15
3.	Kosovo	8	3	2	3	13 - 16	11
4.	Bulgaria	8	1	3	4	6 - 17	6
5.	Montenegro	8	0	3	5	3 - 22	3

England and Czech Republic qualified for the Final Tournament.

GROUP B

Results			
22.03.2019	Lëtzebuerg	Luxembourg - Lithuania	2-1(1-1)
22.03.2019	Lisboa	Portugal - Ukraine	0-0
25.03.2019	Lëtzebuerg	Luxembourg - Ukraine	1-2(1-1)
25.03.2019	Lisboa	Portugal - Serbia	1-1(1-1)
07.06.2019	Vilnius	Lithuania - Luxembourg	1-1(0-1)
07.06.2019	Lviv	Ukraine - Serbia	5-0(2-0)
10.06.2019	Beograd	Serbia - Lithuania	4-1(3-0)
10.06.2019	Lviv	Ukraine - Luxembourg	1-0(1-0)
07.09.2019	Vilnius	Lithuania - Ukraine	0-3(0-2)
07.09.2019	Beograd	Serbia - Portugal	2-4(0-1)
10.09.2019	Vilnius	Lithuania - Portugal	1-5(1-1)
10.09.2019	Lëtzebuerg	Luxembourg - Serbia	1-3(0-1)
11.10.2019	Lisboa	Portugal - Luxembourg	3-0(1-0)
11.10.2019	Kharkiv	Ukraine - Lithuania	2-0(1-0)
14.10.2019	Vilnius	Lithuania - Serbia	1-2(0-0)
14.10.2019	Kyiv	Ukraine - Portugal	2-1(2-0)
14.11.2019	Faro/Loulé	Portugal - Lithuania	6-0(2-0)
14.11.2019	Beograd	Serbia - Luxembourg	3-2(2-0
17.11.2019	Lëtzebuerg	Luxembourg - Portugal	0-2(0-1)
17.11.2019	Beograd	Serbia - Ukraine	2-2(1-1)

Standings								
1.	**Ukraine**	8	6	2	0	17 - 4	20
2.	**Portugal**	8	5	2	1	22 - 6	17
3.	Serbia	8	4	2	2	17 - 17	14
4.	Luxembourg	8	1	1	6	7 - 16	4
5.	Lithuania	8	0	1	7	5 - 25	1

Ukraine and Portugal qualified for the Final Tournament.

GROUP C

Results

Date	Venue	Match	Score
21.03.2019	Rotterdam	Netherlands - Belarus	4-0(2-0)
21.03.2019	Belfast	Northern Ireland - Estonia	2-0(0-0)
24.03.2019	Belfast	Northern Ireland - Belarus	2-1(1-1)
24.03.2019	Amsterdam	Netherlands - Germany	2-3(0-2)
08.06.2019	Tallinn	Estonia - Northern Ireland	1-2(1-0)
08.06.2019	Borisov	Belarus - Germany	0-2(0-1)
11.06.2019	Borisov	Belarus - Northern Ireland	0-1(0-1)
11.06.2019	Mainz	Germany - Estonia	8-0(5-0)
06.09.2019	Tallinn	Estonia - Belarus	1-2(0-0)
06.09.2019	Hamburg	Germany - Netherlands	2-4(1-0)
09.09.2019	Tallinn	Estonia - Netherlands	0-4(0-1)
09.09.2019	Belfast	Northern Ireland - Germany	0-2(0-0)
10.10.2019	Minsk	Belarus - Estonia	0-0
10.10.2019	Rotterdam	Netherlands - North. Ireland	3-1(0-0)
13.10.2019	Minsk	Belarus - Netherlands	1-2(0-2)
13.10.2019	Tallinn	Estonia - Germany	0-3(0-0)
16.11.2019	Mö-gladbach	Germany - Belarus	4-0(1-0)
16.11.2019	Belfast	North. Ireland - Netherlands	0-0
19.11.2019	Frankfurt	Germany - Northern Ireland	6-1(2-1)
19.11.2019	Amsterdam	Netherlands - Estonia	5-0(2-0)

Standings

1.	**Germany**	8	7	0	1	30	-	7	21
2.	**Netherlands**	8	6	1	1	24	-	7	19
3.	North. Ireland	8	4	1	3	9	-	13	13
4.	Belarus	8	1	1	6	4	-	16	4
5.	Estonia	8	0	1	7	2	-	26	1

Germany and Netherlands qualified for the Final Tournament.

GROUP D

Results

Date	Venue	Match	Score
23.03.2019	Tbilisi	Georgia - Switzerland	0-2(0-0)
23.03.2019	Gibraltar	Gibraltar - Rep of Ireland	0-1(0-0)
26.03.2019	Basel	Switzerland - Denmark	3-3(1-0)
26.03.2019	Dublin	Rep of Ireland - Georgia	1-0(1-0)
07.06.2019	Tbilisi	Georgia - Gibraltar	3-0(1-0)
07.06.2019	København	Denmark - Rep of Ireland	1-1(0-0)
10.06.2019	København	Denmark - Georgia	5-1(2-1)
10.06.2019	Dublin	Rep of Ireland - Gibraltar	2-0(1-0)
05.09.2019	Gibraltar	Gibraltar - Denmark	0-6(0-2)
05.09.2019	Dublin	Rep of Ireland - Switzerland	1-1(0-0)
08.09.2019	Tbilisi	Georgia - Denmark	0-0
08.09.2019	Sion	Switzerland - Gibraltar	4-0(3-0)
12.10.2019	Tbilisi	Georgia - Rep of Ireland	0-0
12.10.2019	København	Denmark - Switzerland	1-0(0-0)
15.10.2019	Gibraltar	Gibraltar - Georgia	2-3(0-2)
15.10.2019	Lancy	Switzerland - Rep of Ireland	2-0(1-0)
15.11.2019	København	Denmark - Gibraltar	6-0(1-0)
15.11.2019	St. Gallen	Switzerland - Georgia	1-0(0-0)
18.11.2019	Dublin	Rep of Ireland - Denmark	1-1(0-0)
18.11.2019	Gibraltar	Gibraltar - Switzerland	1-6(0-1)

Standings

1.	**Switzerland**	8	5	2	1	19	-	6	17
2.	**Denmark**	8	4	4	0	23	-	6	16
3.	R. of Ireland	8	3	4	1	7	-	5	13
4.	Georgia	8	2	2	4	7	-	11	8
5.	Gibraltar	8	0	0	8	3	-	31	0

Switzerland and Denmark qualified for the Final Tournament.

GROUP E

Results

Date	Venue	Match	Score
21.03.2019	Zagreb	Croatia - Azerbaijan	2-1(1-1)
21.03.2019	Trnava	Slovakia - Hungary	2-0(1-0)
24.03.2019	Cardiff	Wales - Slovakia	1-0(1-0)
24.03.2019	Budapest	Hungary - Croatia	2-1(1-1)
08.06.2019	Osijek	Croatia - Wales	2-1(1-0)
08.06.2019	Bakı	Azerbaijan - Hungary	1-3(0-1)
11.06.2019	Bakı	Azerbaijan - Slovakia	1-5(1-3)
11.06.2019	Budapest	Hungary - Wales	1-0(0-0)
06.09.2019	Trnava	Slovakia - Croatia	0-4(0-1)
06.09.2019	Cardiff	Wales - Azerbaijan	2-1(1-0)
09.09.2019	Bakı	Azerbaijan - Croatia	1-1(0-1)
09.09.2019	Budapest	Hungary - Slovakia	1-2(0-1)
10.10.2019	Split	Croatia - Hungary	3-0(3-0)
10.10.2019	Trnava	Slovakia - Wales	1-1(0-1)
13.10.2019	Budapest	Hungary - Azerbaijan	1-0(1-0)
13.10.2019	Cardiff	Wales - Croatia	1-1(1-1)
16.11.2019	Bakı	Azerbaijan - Wales	0-2(0-2)
16.11.2019	Rijeka	Croatia - Slovakia	3-1(0-1)
19.11.2019	Trnava	Slovakia - Azerbaijan	2-0(1-0)
19.11.2019	Cardiff	Wales - Hungary	2-0(1-0)

Standings

1.	**Croatia**	8	5	2	1	17	-	7	17
2.	**Wales**	8	4	2	2	10	-	6	14
3.	Slovakia	8	4	1	3	13	-	11	13
4.	Hungary	8	4	0	4	8	-	11	12
5.	Azerbaijan	8	0	1	7	5	-	18	1

Croatia and Wales qualified for the Final Tournament.

Results

23.03.2019	Attard	Malta - Faroe Islands	2-1(1-0)
23.03.2019	Stockholm	Sweden - Romania	2-1(2-0)
23.03.2019	Valencia	Spain - Norway	2-1(1-0)
26.03.2019	Cluj-Napoca	Romania - Faroe Islands	4-1(3-1)
26.03.2019	Attard	Malta - Spain	0-2(0-1)
26.03.2019	Oslo	Norway - Sweden	3-3(1-0)
07.06.2019	Tórshavn	Faroe Islands - Spain	1-4(1-3)
07.06.2019	Stockholm	Sweden - Malta	3-0(1-0)
07.06.2019	Oslo	Norway - Romania	2-2(0-0)
10.06.2019	Tórshavn	Faroe Islands - Norway	0-2(0-0)
10.06.2019	Attard	Malta - Romania	0-4(0-3)
10.06.2019	Madrid	Spain - Sweden	3-0(0-0)
05.09.2019	Tórshavn	Faroe Islands - Sweden	0-4(0-4)
05.09.2019	Oslo	Norway - Malta	2-0(2-0)
05.09.2019	Bucureşti	Romania - Spain	1-2(0-1)
08.09.2019	Ploieşti	Romania - Malta	1-0(0-0)
08.09.2019	Gijón	Spain - Faroe Islands	4-0(1-0)
08.09.2019	Stockholm	Sweden - Norway	1-1(0-1)
12.10.2019	Tórshavn	Faroe Islands - Romania	0-3(0-0)
12.10.2019	Attard	Malta - Sweden	0-4(0-1)
12.10.2019	Oslo	Norway - Spain	1-1(0-0)
15.10.2019	Tórshavn	Faroe Islands - Malta	1-0(0-0)
15.10.2019	Bucureşti	Romania - Norway	1-1(0-0)
15.10.2019	Stockholm	Sweden - Spain	1-1(0-0)
15.11.2019	Oslo	Norway - Faroe Islands	4-0(2-0)
15.11.2019	Bucureşti	Romania - Sweden	0-2(0-2)
15.11.2019	Cádiz	Spain - Malta	7-0(2-0)
18.11.2019	Attard	Malta - Norway	1-2(1-1)
18.11.2019	Madrid	Spain - Romania	5-0(4-0)
18.11.2019	Stockholm	Sweden - Faroe Islands	3-0(1-0)

Standings

1.	**Spain**	10	8	2	0	31	-	5	26
2.	**Sweden**	10	6	3	1	23	-	9	21
3.	Norway	10	4	5	1	19	-	11	17
4.	Romania	10	4	2	4	17	-	15	14
5.	Faroe Islands	10	1	0	9	4	-	30	3
6.	Malta	10	1	0	9	3	-	27	3

Spain and Sweden qualified for the Final Tournament.

Results

21.03.2019	Haifa	Israel - Slovenia	1-1(0-0)
21.03.2019	Skopje	North Macedonia - Latvia	3-1(2-0)
21.03.2019	Wien	Austria - Poland	0-1(0-0)
24.03.2019	Haifa	Israel - Austria	4-2(2-1)
24.03.2019	Warszawa	Poland - Latvia	2-0(0-0)
24.03.2019	Ljubljana	Slovenia - North Macedonia	1-1(1-0)
07.06.2019	Rīga	Latvia - Israel	0-3(0-1)
07.06.2019	Skopje	North Macedonia - Poland	0-1(0-0)
07.06.2019	Klagenfurt	Austria - Slovenia	1-0(0-0)
10.06.2019	Warszawa	Poland - Israel	4-0(1-0)
10.06.2019	Rīga	Latvia - Slovenia	0-5(0-4)
10.06.2019	Skopje	North Macedonia - Austria	1-4(1-1)
05.09.2019	Be'er Sheva	Israel - North Macedonia	1-1(0-0)
06.09.2019	W-Siezenheim	Austria - Latvia	6-0(2-0)
06.09.2019	Ljubljana	Slovenia - Poland	2-0(1-0)
09.09.2019	Rīga	Latvia - North Macedonia	0-2(0-2)
09.09.2019	Warszawa	Poland - Austria	0-0
09.09.2019	Ljubljana	Slovenia - Israel	3-2(1-0)
10.10.2019	Wien	Austria - Israel	3-1(1-1)
10.10.2019	Skopje	North Macedonia - Slovenia	2-1(0-0)
10.10.2019	Rīga	Latvia - Poland	0-3(0-2)
13.10.2019	Warszawa	Poland - North Macedonia	2-0(0-0)
13.10.2019	Ljubljana	Slovenia - Austria	0-1(0-1)
15.10.2019	Be'er Sheva	Israel - Latvia	3-1(3-1)
16.11.2019	Ljubljana	Slovenia - Latvia	1-0(0-0)
16.11.2019	Wien	Austria - North Macedonia	2-1(1-0)
16.11.2019	Jerusalem	Israel - Poland	1-2(0-1)
19.11.2019	Skopje	North Macedonia - Israel	1-0(1-0)
19.11.2019	Rīga	Latvia - Austria	1-0(0-0)
19.11.2019	Warszawa	Poland - Slovenia	3-2(1-1)

Standings

1.	**Poland**	10	8	1	1	18	-	5	25
2.	**Austria**	10	6	1	3	19	-	9	19
3.	N. Macedonia	10	4	2	4	12	-	13	14
4.	Slovenia	10	4	2	4	16	-	11	14
5.	Israel	10	3	2	5	16	-	18	11
6.	Latvia	10	1	0	9	3	-	28	3

Poland and Austria qualified for the Final Tournament.

Results

22.03.2019	Shkodër	Albania - Turkey	0-2(0-1)
22.03.2019	Andorra la V.	Andorra - Iceland	0-2(0-1)
22.03.2019	Chişinău	Moldova - France	1-4(0-3)
25.03.2019	Eskişehir	Turkey - Moldova	4-0(2-0)
25.03.2019	Andorra la V.	Andorra - Albania	0-3(0-1)
25.03.2019	Paris	France - Iceland	4-0(1-0)
08.06.2019	Reykjavík	Iceland - Albania	1-0(1-0)
08.06.2019	Chişinău	Moldova - Andorra	1-0(1-0)
08.06.2019	Konya	Turkey - France	2-0(2-0)
11.06.2019	Elbasan	Albania - Moldova	2-0(0-0)
11.06.2019	Andorra la V.	Andorra - France	0-4(0-3)
11.06.2019	Reykjavík	Iceland - Turkey	2-1(2-1)
07.09.2019	Reykjavík	Iceland - Moldova	3-0(1-0)
07.09.2019	Paris	France - Albania	4-1(2-0)
07.09.2019	İstanbul	Turkey - Andorra	1-0(0-0)
10.09.2019	Elbasan	Albania - Iceland	4-2(1-0)
10.09.2019	Paris	France - Andorra	3-0(1-0)
10.09.2019	Chişinău	Moldova - Turkey	0-4(0-1)
11.10.2019	Andorra la V.	Andorra - Moldova	1-0(0-0)
11.10.2019	Reykjavík	Iceland - France	0-1(0-1)
11.10.2019	İstanbul	Turkey - Albania	1-0(0-0)
14.10.2019	Paris	France - Turkey	1-1(0-0)
14.10.2019	Reykjavík	Iceland - Andorra	2-0(1-0)
14.10.2019	Chişinău	Moldova - Albania	0-4(0-3)
14.11.2019	İstanbul	Turkey - Iceland	0-0
14.11.2019	Elbasan	Albania - Andorra	2-2(1-1)
14.11.2019	Paris	France - Moldova	2-1(1-1)
17.11.2019	Tiranë	Albania - France	0-2(0-2)
17.11.2019	Andorra la V.	Andorra - Turkey	0-2(0-2)
17.11.2019	Chişinău	Moldova - Iceland	1-2(0-1)

Standings

1.	**France**	10	8	1	1	25	-	6	25
2.	**Turkey**	10	7	2	1	18	-	3	23
3.	Iceland	10	6	1	3	14	-	11	19
4.	Albania	10	4	1	5	16	-	14	13
5.	Andorra	10	1	1	8	3	-	20	4
6.	Moldova	10	1	0	9	4	-	26	3

France and Turkey qualified for the Final Tournament.

Results

21.03.2019	Astana	Kazakhstan - Scotland	3-0(2-0)
21.03.2019	Nicosia	Cyprus - San Marino	5-0(4-0)
21.03.2019	Bruxelles	Belgium - Russia	3-1(2-1)
24.03.2019	Nur-Sultan	Kazakhstan - Russia	0-4(0-2)
24.03.2019	Serravalle	San Marino - Scotland	0-2(0-1)
24.03.2019	Nicosia	Cyprus - Belgium	0-2(0-2)
08.06.2019	Saransk	Russia - San Marino	9-0(4-0)
08.06.2019	Bruxelles	Belgium - Kazakhstan	3-0(2-0)
08.06.2019	Glasgow	Scotland - Cyprus	2-1(0-0)
11.06.2019	Nur-Sultan	Kazakhstan - San Marino	4-0(1-0)
11.06.2019	Bruxelles	Belgium - Scotland	3-0(1-0)
11.06.2019	Nizhny Novg.	Russia - Cyprus	1-0(1-0)
06.09.2019	Nicosia	Cyprus - Kazakhstan	1-1(1-1)
06.09.2019	Serravalle	San Marino - Belgium	0-4(0-1)
06.09.2019	Glasgow	Scotland - Russia	1-2(1-1)
09.09.2019	Kaliningrad	Russia - Kazakhstan	1-0(0-0)
09.09.2019	Serravalle	San Marino - Cyprus	0-4(0-2)
09.09.2019	Glasgow	Scotland - Belgium	0-4(0-3)
10.10.2019	Nur-Sultan	Kazakhstan - Cyprus	1-2(1-0)
10.10.2019	Bruxelles	Belgium - San Marino	9-0(6-0)
10.10.2019	Moskva	Russia - Scotland	4-0(0-0)
13.10.2019	Nur-Sultan	Kazakhstan - Belgium	0-2(0-1)
13.10.2019	Nicosia	Cyprus - Russia	0-5(0-2)
13.10.2019	Glasgow	Scotland - San Marino	6-0(3-0)
16.11.2019	Nicosia	Cyprus - Scotland	1-2(0-1)
16.11.2019	St. Petersburg	Russia - Belgium	1-4(0-3)
16.11.2019	Serravalle	San Marino - Kazakhstan	1-3(0-3)
19.11.2019	Bruxelles	Belgium - Cyprus	6-1(4-1)
19.11.2019	Serravalle	San Marino - Russia	0-5(0-2)
19.11.2019	Glasgow	Scotland - Kazakhstan	3-1(0-1)

Standings

1.	**Belgium**	10	10	0	0	40	-	3	30
2.	**Russia**	10	8	0	2	33	-	8	24
3.	Scotland	10	5	0	5	16	-	19	15
4.	Cyprus	10	3	1	6	15	-	20	10
5.	Kazakhstan	10	3	1	6	13	-	17	10
6.	San Marino	10	0	0	10	1	-	51	0

Belgium and Russia qualified for the Final Tournament.

	Results		
23.03.2019	Sarajevo	Bosnia and Herz. - Armenia	2-1(1-0)
23.03.2019	Udine	Italy - Finland	2-0(1-0)
23.03.2019	Vaduz	Liechtenstein - Greece	0-2(0-1)
26.03.2019	Yerevan	Armenia - Finland	0-2(0-1)
26.03.2019	Zenica	Bosnia and Herz. - Greece	2-2(2-0)
26.03.2019	Parma	Italy - Liechtenstein	6-0(4-0)
08.06.2019	Yerevan	Armenia - Liechtenstein	3-0(2-0)
08.06.2019	Tampere	Finland - Bosnia and Herz.	2-0(0-0)
08.06.2019	Athína	Greece - Italy	0-3(0-3)
11.06.2019	Athína	Greece - Armenia	2-3(0-2)
1106.2019	Torino	Italy - Bosnia and Herz.	2-1(0-1)
11.06.2019	Vaduz	Liechtenstein - Finland	0-2(0-1)
05.09.2019	Yerevan	Armenia - Italy	1-3(1-1)
05.09.2019	Zenica	Bosnia and Herz. - Liechtenstein	5-0(1-0)
05.09.2019	Tampere	Finland - Greece	1-0(0-0)
08.09.2019	Yerevan	Armenia - Bosnia and Herz.	4-2(1-1)
08.09.2019	Tampere	Finland - Italy	1-2(0-0)
08.09.2019	Athína	Greece - Liechtenstein	1-1(1-0)
12.10.2019	Zenica	Bosnia and Herz. - Finland	4-1(2-0)
12.10.2019	Roma	Italy - Greece	2-0(0-0)
12.10.2019	Vaduz	Liechtenstein - Armenia	1-1(0-1)
15.10.2019	Turku	Finland - Armenia	3-0(1-0)
15.10.2019	Athína	Greece - Bosnia and Herz.	2-1(1-1)
15.10.2019	Vaduz	Liechtenstein - Italy	0-5(0-1)
15.11.2019	Yerevan	Armenia - Greece	0-1(0-1)
15.11.2019	Helsinki	Finland - Liechtenstein	3-0(1-0)
15.11.2019	Zenica	Bosnia and Herzegovina - Italy	0-3(0-2)
18.11.2019	Athína	Greece - Finland	2-1(0-1)
18.11.2019	Palermo	Italy - Armenia	9-1(4-0)
18.11.2019	Vaduz	Liechtenstein - Bosnia and Herz.	0-3(0-0)

	Standings								
1.	Italy	10	10	0	0	37	-	4	30
2.	Finland	10	6	0	4	16	-	10	18
3.	Greece	10	4	2	4	12	-	14	14
4.	Bosnia and H.	10	4	1	5	20	-	17	13
5.	Armenia	10	3	1	6	14	-	25	10
6.	Liechtenstein	10	0	2	8	2	-	31	2

Italy and Finland qualified for the Final Tournament.

PLAY-OFFS

Each League in the UEFA Nations League 2018/2019 will be allocated one of the four remaining final tournament spots.

Four teams from each league that have not already qualified for the European Championship finals will compete in the play-offs of their league.

The play-off berths were first allocated to each Nations League group winner, and if any of the group winners had already qualified for the European Championship finals, then to the next best ranked team of the league, etc. The matches will be played in October – November 2020. Hosts were determined by draw.

Path A	08.10.2020	Reykjavík	Iceland - Romania	(A)
	08.10.2020	Sofia	Bulgaria - Hungary	(B)
	12.11.2020		Winner **B** – Winner **A**	

Path B	08.10.2020	Sarajevo	Bosnia and Herzegovina - Northern Ireland	(A)
	08.10.2020	Bratislava	Slovakia - Republic of Ireland	(B)
	12.11.2020		Winner **A** – Winner **B**	

Path C	08.10.2020	Glasgow	Scotland - Israel	(A)
	08.10.2020	Oslo	Norway - Serbia	(B)
	12.11.2020		Winner **B** – Winner **A**	

Path D	08.10.2020	Tbilisi	Georgia - Belarus	(A)
	08.10.2020	Skopje	North Macedonia - Kosovo	(B)
	12.11.2020		Winner **A** – Winner **B**	

PRELIMINARY ROUND – SEMI-FINALS

25.06.2019. Stadiumi „Fadil Vokrri", Prishtina
Referee: Ian McNabb (NIR); Attendance: 35
SP Tre Penne – FC Santa Coloma 0-1(0-0)
SP Tre Penne: Mattia Migani, Mirko Palazzi, Davide Cesarini (46.Matteo Semprini), Alex Colonna, Nicola Chiaruzzi, Nicola Gai, Enrico Cibelli, Matteo Derjai (79.Aron Giacomoni), Federico Innocenti (58.Riccardo Innocenti), Luca Ceccaroli, Michael Angelini. Trainer: Stefano Ceci.
FC Santa Coloma: Eloy Casals, Moisés San Nicolás, Marc Rebés, Andreu Ramos, Juanma Miranda, Pedro Santos (87.Nicolás Medina), Jordi Aláez (81.Enric Pi), Loren Burón, Aleix Cistero, Javi Camochu, André Azevedo (68.Chus Sosa). Trainer: Marc Rodríguez Rebull.
Goal: 76' Javi Camochu 0-1.

25.06.2019. Stadiumi „Fadil Vokrri", Prishtina
Referee: Fedayi San (SUI); Attendance: 3,000
KF Feronikeli – Lincoln Red Imps FC 1-0(1-0)
KF Feronikeli: Deniz Troshupa, Lapidar Lladrovci, Arber Prekazi, Perparim Islami, Jean Carioca, Yll Hoxha, Albert Dabiqaj, Kastriot Rexha, Besmir Bojku (82.Astrit Thaqi), Astrit Fazliu (87.Argjend Malaj), Mendurim Hoti (74.Mevlan Zeka). Trainer: Zekirija Ramadani.
Lincoln Red Imps FC: Lolo Soler, Marcos Pérez (56.Jesús Toscano), Joseph Chipolina, Bernardo Lopes, Roy Chipolina, Borja Gil, Monti Montesinos, Gato (79.Falu Aranda), Sergio Molina, Iván Aguilar (74.Anthony Hernandez), Héctor Figueroa. Trainer: Víctor Afonso.
Goal: 3' Mendurim Hoti 1-0.

PRELIMINARY ROUND – FINALS

28.06.2019. Stadiumi „Fadil Vokrri", Prishtina
Referee: Emmanouil Skoulas (GRE); Attendance: 1,900
KF FERONIKELI – FC Santa Coloma 2-1(0-0)
KF Feronikeli: Deniz Troshupa, Lapidar Lladrovci, Arber Prekazi, Perparim Islami, Jean Carioca (67.Jetmir Topalli), Yll Hoxha, Albert Dabiqaj, Kastriot Rexha, Besmir Bojku (90+1.Arbër Potoku), Astrit Fazliu, Mevlan Zeka (79.Argjend Malaj). Trainer: Zekirija Ramadani.
FC Santa Coloma: Eloy Casals, Moisés San Nicolás, Marc Rebés (59.Enric Pi), Andreu Ramos, Juanma Miranda, Chus Sosa (82.André Azevedo), Pedro Santos, Loren Burón, Aleix Cistero, Nicolás Medina, Javi Camochu (64.Jordi Aláez). Trainer: Marc Rodríguez Rebull.
Goals: 52' Chus Sosa 0-1, 58' Mevlan Zeka 1-1, 87' Kastriot Rexha 2-1.
Sent off: 49' Yll Hoxha.

FIRST QUALIFYING ROUND

09.07.2019. Astana Arena, Nur-Sultan
Referee: Lawrence Visser (BEL); Attendance: 18,587
Astana FC – CFR Cluj 1-0(0-0)
Astana FC: Nenad Eric, Antonio Rukavina, Yuriy Logvinenko, Abzal Beysebekov, Evgeni Postnikov, Luka Simunovic, Rúnar Sigurjónsson, Marin Tomasov (58.Rangelo Janga), Ivan Maevski, Roman Murtazaev (84.Ndombe Mubele), Dorin Rotariu. Trainer: Roman Grygorchuk.
CFR Cluj: Giedrius Arlauskis, Paulo Vinícius, Mateo Susic, Camora, Andrei Burca, Emmanuel Culio, Ciprian Deac, Ovidiu Hoban (75.Mário Rondón), Mihai Bordeianu (90.Luís Aurélio), Alexandru Paun (65.Sebastian Mailat), Billel Omrani. Trainer: Dan Petrescu.
Goal: 68' Evgeni Postnikov 1-0.

17.07.2019. Stadionul "Dr. Constantin Rădulescu", Cluj-Napoca
Referee: Alexander Harkam (AUT); Attendance: 8,092
FC CFR 1907 CLUJ – Astana FC 3-1(2-1)
CFR Cluj: Giedrius Arlauskis, Paulo Vinícius, Mateo Susic, Camora, Andrei Burca, Emmanuel Culio, Ciprian Deac (86.Ovidiu Hoban), Damjan Djokovic, Mihai Bordeianu, Mário Rondón (66.Valentin Costache), Billel Omrani (84.Mickaël Pereira). Trainer: Dan Petrescu.
Astana FC: Nenad Eric, Antonio Rukavina, Yuriy Logvinenko, Abzal Beysebekov (81.Marin Anicic), Evgeni Postnikov, Luka Simunovic, Rúnar Sigurjónsson (82.Rangelo Janga), Marin Tomasov (62.Ndombe Mubele), Ivan Maevski, Roman Murtazaev, Dorin Rotariu. Trainer: Roman Grygorchuk.
Goals: 4' Roman Murtazaev 0-1, 10', 26', 73' Billel Omrani 1-1, 2-1,3-1.

09.07.2019. Yerevan Football Academy Stadium, Yerevan
Referee: Duje Strukan (CRO); Attendance: 1,497
FC Ararat-Armenia Yerevan – AIK Stockholm 2-1(2-1)
FC Ararat-Armenia: Dmitriy Abakumov, Rochdi Achenteh, Dmitri Guzj, Ângelo Meneses, Georgi Pashov, Gor Malakyan (46.Ilja Antonov), Kódjo Alphonse, Petros Avetisyan (71.Armen Ambartsumyan), Anton Kobyalko (70.Louis Ogana), Furdjel Narsingh, Zakaria Sanogo. Trainer: Vardan Minasyan.
AIK Stockholm: Oscar Linnér, Robert Lundström, Karol Mets, Daniel Granli, Panajotis Dimitriadis, Enoch Adu, Anton Salétros (84.Rasmus Lindkvist), Bilal Hussein (46.Sebastian Larsson), Tarik Elyounoussi, Henok Goitom, Chinedu Obasi (65.Kolbeinn Sigthórsson). Trainer: Rikard Norling.
Goals: 3' Petros Avetisyan 1-0 (pen), 39' Chinedu Obasi 1-1, 45' Petros Avetisyan 2-1.; Sent off: 13' Robert Lundström.

17.07.2019. Friends Arena, Stockholm
Referee: Robert Hennessy (IRL); Attendance: 11,382
AIK STOCKHOLM – FC Ararat-Armenia 3-1(0-0)
AIK Stockholm: Oscar Linnér, Per Karlsson (46.Rasmus Lindkvist), Karol Mets, Daniel Granli, Sebastian Larsson, Enoch Adu, Anton Salétros, Heradi Rashidi, Tarik Elyounoussi, Henok Goitom (90+3.Panajotis Dimitriadis), Chinedu Obasi (72.Kolbeinn Sigthórsson). Trainer: Rikard Norling.
FC Ararat-Armenia: Dmitriy Abakumov, Dmitri Guzj, Ângelo Meneses, Alex Júnior Christian, Georgi Pashov, Ilja Antonov (86.Rochdi Achenteh), Kódjo Alphonse, Petros Avetisyan (68.Armen Ambartsumyan), Anton Kobyalko, Furdjel Narsingh, Zakaria Sanogo (60.Mailson). Trainer: Vardan Minasyan.
Goals: 47', 52' Henok Goitom 1-0, 2-0, 62' Sebastian Larsson 3-0 (pen), 77' Anton Kobyalko 3-1.

09.07.2019. Kadrioru staadion, Tallinn
Referee: Donald Robertson (SCO); Attendance: 1,640
JK Nõmme Kalju – KF Shkëndija 79 0-1(0-0)
JK Nõmme Kalju: Pavel Londak, Aleksandr Kulinits, Maximiliano Uggè, Vladimir Avilov, Andriy Markovych, Nikolaj Mashichev (76.Peeter Klein), Igor Subbotin, Réginald Mbu-Alidor, Kaspar Paur, Liliu, Robert Kirss (57.Aleksandr Volkov). Trainer: Roman Kozhukhovskyi.
KF Shkëndija 79: Kostadin Zahov, Gledi Mici, Mevlan Murati, Visar Musliu, Egzon Bejtulai, Armend Alimi, Zeni Husmani, Ennur Totre (85.Arbin Zejnullai), Besart Ibraimi (77.Valjmir Nafiu), Agim Ibraimi (90+1.Omar Imeri), Marjan Radeski. (Trainer: Qatip Osmani.
Goal: 81' Agim Ibraimi 0-1 (pen).

16.07.2019. "Toše Proeski" Arena, Skopje
Referee: Alain Bieri (SUI); Attendance: 2,546
KF Shkëndija 79 – JK NÕMME KALJU 1-2(0-1)
KF Shkëndija 79: Kostadin Zahov, Gledi Mici, Mevlan Murati, Visar Musliu, Egzon Bejtulai, Armend Alimi, Zeni Husmani (46.Valjmir Nafiu), Ennur Totre, Besart Ibraimi (63.Stênio Júnior), Agim Ibraimi, Marjan Radeski. Trainer: Qatip Osmani.
JK Nõmme Kalju: Pavel Londak, Aleksandr Kulinits, Maximiliano Uggè, Vladimir Avilov, Andriy Markovych, Nikolaj Mashichev (60.Aleksandr Volkov), Igor Subbotin, Réginald Mbu-Alidor, Kaspar Paur (87.Deniss Tjapkin), Liliu, Peeter Klein. Trainer: Roman Kozhukhovskyi.
Goals: 5' Maximiliano Uggè 0-1, 62' Agim Ibraimi 1-1 (pen), 90+1' Liliu 1-2.

09.07.2019. Telia 5G -areena, Helsinki
Referee: Giorgi Kruashvili (GEO); Attendance: 4,719
HJK Helsinki – HB Tórshavn 3-0(2-0)
HJK Helsinki: Maksim Rudakov, Rafinha, Nikolai Alho, Daniel O'Shaughnessy, Faith Obilor, Riku Riski, Kaan Kairinen, Sebastian Dahlström, Lassi Lappalainen (89.Akseli Pelvas), Evans Mensah (78.Eetu Vertainen), Santeri Väänänen (33.Henri Toivomäki). Trainer: Toni Koskela.
HB Tórshav: Teitur Gestsson, Jógvan Davidsen, Bartal Wardum (82.Daniel Johansen), Lasse Andersen, Símun Samuelsen, Magnus Egilsson, Hørdur Askham, Tróndur Jensen, Dan í Soylu (81.Brynjar Hlödversson), Adrian Justinussen, Ari Olsen (46.Sebastian Pingel). Trainer: Heimir Gudjonsson.
Goals: 21' Lassi Lappalainen 1-0, 42' Daniel O'Shaughnessy 2-0, 66' Lassi Lappalainen 3-0.; Sent off: 31' Faith Obilor.

09.07.2019. Olimpijski Stadion „Asim Ferhatovic Hase", Sarajevo
Referee: Glenn Nyberg (SWE); Attendance: 24,723
FK Sarajevo – Celtic FC Glasgow 1-3(1-1)
FK Sarajevo: Vladan Kovacevic, Darko Lazic, Dusan Hodzic (87.Andrej Djokanovic), Besim Serbecic, Halid Sabanovic (66.Benjamin Tatar), Mirko Oremus, Amar Rahmanovic (78.Aladin Sisic), Anel Hebibovic, Mersudin Ahmetovic, Krste Velkoski, Slobodan Milanovic. Trainer: Husref Musemic.
Celtic FC: Scott Bain, Jozo Simunovic, Boli Bolingoli-Mbombo (57.Jonny Hayes), Kristoffer Ajer, Scott Brown, Nir Bitton, James Forrest (78.Scott Sinclair), Callum McGregor, Ryan Christie, Odsonne Édouard, Michael Johnston (65.Lewis Morgan). Trainer: Neil Lennon.
Goals: 29' Mirko Oremus 1-0, 35' Michael Johnston 1-1, 51' Odsonne Édouard 1-2, 85' Scott Sinclair 1-3.

09.07.2019. Marijampolès sporto centro stadione, Marijampolè
Referee: Jørgen Daugbjerg Burchardt (DEN); Attendance: 3,200
FK Sūduva Marijampolè – FK Crvena Zvezda Beograd 0-0
FK Sūduva Marijampolè: Ivan Kardum, Vaidas Slavickas, Algis Jankauskas, Andro Svrljuga, Aleksandar Zivanovic, Semir Kerla, Jovan Cadenovic, Ovidijus Verbickas (90+1.Eligijus Jankauskas), Giedrius Matulevicius (58.Paulius Golubickas), Josip Tadic (46.Sandro Gotal), Mihret Topcagic. Trainer: Vladimir Cheburin.
Crvena Zvezda: Milan Borjan, Nemanja Milunovic, Milan Rodic, Marko Gobeljic, Srdjan Babic, Marko Marin, Branko Jovicic (69.Cañas), Dusan Jovancic, Mirko Ivanic, Richmond Boakye (71.Milan Pavkov), Mohamed Ben Nabouhane (86.Aleksa Vukanovic). Trainer: Vladan Milojevic.

09.07.2019. Stade „Josy Barthel", Lëtzebuerg
Referee: Arnold Hunter (NIR); Attendance: 1,152
F91 Dudelange – Valletta FC 2-2(2-0)
F91 Dudelange: Tim Kips, Tom Schnell, Ricardo Delgado, Chris Stumpf, Mohamed Bouchouari, Mario Pokar, Dominik Stolz, Mickaël Garos (76.Charles Morren), Sabir Bougrine (65.Danel Sinani), Bertino Cabral Barbosa, Adel Bettaieb (84.Laurent Pomponi). Trainer: Henri Bossi.
Valletta FC: Henry Bonello, Joseph Zerafa, Steve Borg, Douglas Packer (83.Antonio Monticelli), Rowen Muscat, Kyrian Nwoko, Jean Borg, Enmy Peña, Santiago Malano (53.Nicholas Pulis), Kevin Tulimieri (62.Shaun Dimech), Mario Fontanella. Trainer: Darren Abdilla.
Goals: 26' Adel Bettaieb 1-0, 45+2' Dominik Stolz 2-0, 64' Douglas Parker 2-1, 70' Jean Borg 2-2.; Sent off: 89' Rowen Muscat.

09.07.2019. Park Hall Stadium, Oswestry
Referee: Trustin Farrugia Cann (MLT); Attendance: 1,140
The New Saints – KF Feronikeli 2-2(0-0)
The New Saints: Paul Harrison, Simon Spender, Chris Marriott (57.Ryan Harrington), Keston Davies, Aeron Edwards, Jon Routledge, Daniel Redmond, Ryan Brobbel (66.Joash Nembhard), Greg Draper (76.Kurtis Byrne), Jamie Mullan, Adrian Cieslewicz. Trainer: Scott Ruscoe.
KF Feronikeli: Deniz Troshupa, Lapidar Lladrovci, Arber Prekazi, Perparim Islami, Arbër Potoku, Jean Carioca (68.Jetmir Topalli), Albert Dabiqaj, Kastriot Rexha, Besmir Bojku (68.Argjend Malaj), Astrit Fazliu (90+4.Astrit Thaçi), Mevlan Zeka. Trainer: Zekirija Ramadani.
Goals: 49' Greg Draper 1-0 (pen), 77' Aeron Edwards 2-0, 89' Mevlan Zeka 2-1, 90+3' Astrit Fazliu 2-2 (pen).

16.07.2019. Gundadalur, Tórshavn
Referee: Goergios Kominis (GRE); Attendance: 620
HB Tórshavn – HJK HELSINKI 2-2(1-0)
HB Tórshav: Teitur Gestsson, Jógvan Davidsen, Lasse Andersen, Símun Samuelsen, Magnus Egilsson, Hørdur Askham, Tróndur Jensen, Dan í Soylu (78.Brynjar Hlödversson), Pætur Petersen, Daniel Johansen, Sebastian Pingel. Trainer: Heimir Gudjonsson.
HJK Helsinki: Maksim Rudakov, Rafinha, Henri Toivomäki, Nikolai Alho, Daniel O'Shaughnessy, Kevin Kouassivi-Benissan (46.Riku Riski), Erfan Zeneli (46.Lassi Lappalainen), Kaan Kairinen (81.Sebastian Dahlström), Evans Mensah, Santeri Väänänen, Eetu Vertainen. Trainer: Toni Koskela.
Goals: 17' Sebastian Pingel 1-0, 56' Lasse Andersen 2-0, 60', 77' Riku Riski 2-1, 2-2.

17.07.2019. Celtic Park, Glasgow
Referee: Alain Durieux (LUX); Attendance: 58,662
CELTIC FC GLASGOW – FK Sarajevo 2-1(1-0)
Celtic FC: Scott Bain, Jozo Simunovic, Boli Bolingoli-Mbombo, Kristoffer Ajer, Scott Brown, Nir Bitton, James Forrest, Callum McGregor, Ryan Christie (89.Ewan Henderson), Lewis Morgan (87.Scott Sinclair), Odsonne Édouard (78.Leigh Griffiths). Trainer: Neil Lennon.
FK Sarajevo: Vladan Kovacevic, Darko Lazic, Dusan Hodzic, Besim Serbecic, Mirko Oremus, Amar Rahmanovic (83.Gedeon Guzina), Anel Hebibovic, Mersudin Ahmetovic, Krste Velkoski, Slobodan Milanovic (60.Aladin Sisic), Benjamin Tatar (72.Andrej Djokanovic). Trainer: Husref Musemic.
Goals: 26' Ryan Christie 1-0, 62' Benjamin Tatar 1-1, 75' Callum McGregor 2-1.

16.07.2019. Stadion "Rajko Mitić", Beograd
Referee: Ádám Farkas (HUN); Attendance: 23,751
FK CRVENA ZVEZDA BEOGRAD – FK Sūduva Marijampolè 2-1(2-0)
Crvena Zvezda: Milan Borjan, Nemanja Milunovic, Milan Rodic, Marko Gobeljic, Srdjan Babic, Marko Marin (88.Milan Pavkov), Branko Jovicic, Dusan Jovancic, Mirko Ivanic (82.Aleksa Vukanovic), Richmond Boakye (62.Filip Stojkovic), Mohamed Ben Nabouhane. Trainer: Vladan Milojevic.
FK Sūduva Marijampolè: Ivan Kardum, Vaidas Slavickas (63.Ivan Hladík), Algis Jankauskas, Andro Svrljuga, Aleksandar Zivanovic, Semir Kerla, Jovan Cadenovic, Ovidijus Verbickas (76.Tosaint Ricketts), Mihret Topcagic, Sandro Gotal (51.Josip Tadic), Paulius Golubickas. Trainer: Vladimir Cheburin.
Goals: 4' Richmond Boakye 1-0, 29' Marko Marin 2-0, 90+6' Mihret Topcagic 2-1.; Sent off: 60' Marko Gobeljic.

16.07.2019. MFA Centenary Stadium, Ta'Qali
Referee: Juri Frischer (EST); Attendance: 1,512
VALLETTA FC – F91 Dudelange 1-1(1-0)
Valletta FC: Henry Bonello, Joseph Zerafa, Ryan Camilleri, Steve Borg (90+3.Juan Gill), Douglas Packer, Kyrian Nwoko (69.Shaun Dimech), Jean Borg, Enmy Peña, Kevin Tulimieri (78.Antonio Monticelli), Nicholas Pulis, Mario Fontanella. Trainer: Darren Abdilla.
F91 Dudelange: Tim Kips, Tom Schnell, Ricardo Delgado, Mehdi Kirch, Mohamed Bouchouari, Mario Pokar, Dominik Stolz, Mickaël Garos, Corenthyn Lavie (76.Bertino Cabral Barbosa), Sabir Bougrine (86.Omar Natami), Danel Sinani. Trainer: Henri Bossi.
Goals: 35' Mario Fontanella 1-0, 59' Mario Pokar 1-1.

16.07.2019. Stadiumu "Fadil Vokrri", Prishtina
Referee: Espen Eskås (NOR); Attendance: 7,800
KF Feronikeli – THE NEW SAINTS 0-1(0-0)
KF Feronikeli: Florian Smakiqi, Lapidar Lladrovci, Arber Prekazi, Perparim Islami, Yll Hoxha, Albert Dabiqaj, Kastriot Rexha, Besmir Bojku (82.Argjend Malaj), Astrit Fazliu, Mendurim Hoti (72.Jean Carioca), Mevlan Zeka (64.Jetmir Topalli). Trainer: Zekirija Ramadani.
The New Saints: Paul Harrison, Simon Spender, Keston Davies, Aeron Edwards, Jon Routledge, Daniel Redmond, Ryan Brobbel, Ryan Harrington, Greg Draper (80.Joash Nembhard), Jamie Mullan, Adrian Cieslewicz (65.Dean Ebbe). Trainer: Scott Ruscoe.
Goal: 67' Dean Ebbe 0-1.

10.07.2019. Stadiumi „Selman Stërmasi", Tiranë
Referee: Thorvaldur Árnason (ISL); Attendance: 2,210
FK Partizani Tiranë Qarabağ FK Bakı 0-0
FK Partizani: Alban Hoxha, Egzon Belica, Enea Bitri, Labinot Ibrahimi,
Esin Hakaj (80.Lorenc Trashi), Bruno Telushi, William Cordeiro (68.Ron
Broja), Esat Mala, Emmanuel Mensah (58.Brian Brown), Jasir Asani,
Eraldo Çinari. Trainer: Franco Lerda.
Qarabağ FK: Vagner, Rashad Sadigov, Maksim Medvedev, Abbas
Hüseynov, Rahil Mammadov, Míchel, Dani Quintana (62.Jaime
Romero), Richard Almeyda, Filip Ozobic (85.Gara Garayev), Abdellah
Zoubir, Mahir Emreli (73.Araz Abdullayev). Trainer: Gurban Gurbanov.

10.07.2019. Bolshaya Sportivnaya Arena, Tiraspol
Referee: Iwan Arwel Griffith (WAL); Attendance: 5,706
FC Sheriff Tiraspol – FC Saburtalo Tbilisi 0-3(0-1)
FC Sheriff Tiraspol: Zvonimir Mikulic, Veaceslav Posmac, Artem
Gordienko, Matej Palcic (69.Robert Tambe), Cristiano, Jaroslaw Jach,
Antun Palic (46.Wilfried Balima), Jury Kendysh, José Ángel Jurado
(46.Gheorghe Anton), Liridon Latifi, Gabrijel Boban.
Trainer: Zoran Zekic.
FC Saburtalo Tbilisi: Omar Migineishvili, Giorgi Rekhviashvili, Gagi
Margvelashvili, Luka Lakvekheliani, Tornike Gorgiashvili (60.Levan
Kakubava), Giorgi Diasamidze, Sandro Altunashvili, Nikoloz Mali,
Ognjen Rolovic, Vagner Gonçalves (70.Lasha Shindagoridze), Giorgi
Kokhreidze (77.Giorgi Gabedava). Trainer: Giorgi Chiabrishvili.
Goals: 30' Ognjen Rolovic 0-1, 67' Giorgi Kokhreidze 0-2, 71' Levan
Kakubava 0-3.

10.07.2019. Borisov Arena, Borisov
Referee: Mete Kalkavan (TUR); Attendance: 11,529
FC BATE Borisov – GKS Piast Gliwice 1-1(0-1)
BATE Borisov: Anton Chichkan, Egor Filipenko (10.Slobodan Simovic),
Aleksandar Filipovic, Aleksey Rios, Igor Stasevich, Dmitriy Baga,
Stanislav Dragun, Hervaine Moukam (66.Nemanja Milic), Evgeni
Yablonski, Zakhar Volkov, Bojan Dubajic (56.Maksim Skavysh).
Trainer: Aleksei Baga.
Piast Gliwice: Frantisek Plach, Uros Korun, Mikkel Kirkeskov, Jakub
Czerwinski, Martin Konczkowski, Marcin Pietrowski, Tom Hateley,
Patryk Dziczek (61.Patryk Sokolowski), Joel Valencia (90.Gerard Badía),
Piotr Parzyszek (85.Dani Aquino), Jorge Félix. Trainer: Waldemar
Fornalik.
Goals: 36' Piotr Parzyszek 0-1, 64' Stanislav Dragun 1-1.
Sent off: 89' Stanislav Dragun.

10.07.2019. Groupama Aréna, Budapest
Referee: Eitan Shemeulevitch (ISR); Attendance: 18,115
Ferencvárosi TC – PFC Ludogorets Razgrad 2-1(1-1)
Ferencvárosi TC: Dénes Dibusz, Marcel Heister, Miha Blazic, Lasha
Dvali, Michal Skvarka, Gergö Lovrencsics, Igor Kharatin (77.Dávid
Sigér), Oleksandr Zubkov, Danylo Ignatenko, Tamás Priskin (66.Davide
Lanzafame), Tokmac Nguen (83.Roland Varga). Trainer: Serhiy Rebrov.
PFC Ludogorets Razgrad: Plamen Iliev, Cosmin Moti, Georgi Terziev,
Jordan Ikoko, Anton Nedyalkov, Svetoslav Dyakov, Jacek Góralski
(78.Stéphane Badji), Dan Biton (66.Marcelinho), Jody Lukoki
(83.Jorginho), Mavis Tchibota, Jakub Swierczok. Trainer: Stoicho Stoev.
Goals: 6' Tokmac Nguen 1-0, 31' Jakub Swierczok 1-1, 65' Oleksandr
Zubkov 2-1.

10.07.2019. Národny Futbalovy Stadión, Bratislava
Referee: Vitali Meshkov (RUS); Attendance: 11,250
ŠK Slovan Bratislava – FK Sutjeska Nikšić 1-1(0-0)
Slovan Bratislava: Dominik Greif, Mitch Apau, Vasil Bozhikov, Artem
Sukhotsky, Marin Ljubicic, Kenan Bajric, "Moha" Mohammed Rharsalla
(77.Erik Daniel), Aleksandar Cavric (64.Joeri de Kamps), Andraz Sporar,
Rafael Ratão (64.Dávid Holman), Dejan Drazic. Trainer: Martin Sevela.
FK Sutjeska Nikšić: Vladan Giljen, Darko Bulatovic, Aleksandar
Sofranac, Bojan Ciger, Marko Cetkovic, Damir Kojasevic, Branislav
Jankovic, Marko Vucic (81.Milutin Osmajic), Nemanja Nedic, Novica
Erakovic, Bozo Markovic (88.Bojan Bozovic). Trainer: Nikola
Rakojevic.
Goals: 82' Andraz Sporar 1-0, 90+5' Damir Kojasevic 1-1.

17.07.2019. Dalga Arena, Bakı
Referee: Dumitru Muntean (MOL); Attendance: 5,932
QARABAĞ FK BAKI – FK Partizani Tiranë 2-0(0-0)
Qarabağ FK: Vagner, Rashad Sadigov, Maksim Medvedev, Ailton, Rahil
Mammadov, Míchel, Jaime Romero (90+4.Dani Quintana), Araz
Abdullayev (78.Mahir Emreli), Richard Almeyda, Filip Ozobic
(73.Simeon Slavchev), Abdellah Zoubir. Trainer: Gurban Gurbanov.
FK Partizani: Alban Hoxha, Egzon Belica, Enea Bitri, Labinot Ibrahimi,
Esin Hakaj (83.Brian Brown), Bruno Telushi, William Cordeiro, Esat
Mala, Jasir Asani, Eraldo Çinari (61.Lorenc Trashi), Theophilus Solomon
(75.Joseph Ekuban). Trainer: Franco Lerda.
Goals: 51' Filip Ozobic 1-0, 90+4' Dani Quintana 2-0.

16.07.2019. Mikheil Meskhis sakhelobis Stadioni, Tbilisi
Referee: Pavel Orel (CZE); Attendance: 7,560
FC SABURTALO TBILISI – FC Sheriff Tiraspol 1-3(0-3)
FC Saburtalo Tbilisi: Omar Migineishvili, Giorgi Rekhviashvili, Gagi
Margvelashvili, Luka Lakvekheliani, Tornike Gorgiashvili, Giorgi
Diasamidze, Sandro Altunashvili (70.Alwyn Tera), Nikoloz Mali, Ognjen
Rolovic (77.Giorgi Gabedava), Vagner Gonçalves (81.Lasha
Shindagoridze), Giorgi Kokhreidze. Trainer: Giorgi Chiabrishvili.
FC Sheriff Tiraspol: Zvonimir Mikulic, Artem Gordienko (69.Antun
Palic), Ousmane N'Diaye, Matej Palcic, Mateo Muzek, Cristiano, Jury
Kendysh, Gheorghe Anton (82.Jaroslaw Jach), Liridon Latifi, Gabrijel
Boban (69.Leandro Ribeiro), Robert Tambe. Trainer: Zoran Zekic.
Goals: 3' Liridon Latifi 0-1, 8' Gagi Margvelashvili 0-2 (own goal), 11'
Robert Tambe 0-3, 59' Ognjen Rolovic 1-3. Sent off: 72' Matej Palcic.

17.07.2019. Stadion Miejski, Gliwice
Referee: Antti Munukka (FIN); Attendance: 9,312
GKS Piast Gliwice – FC BATE BORISOV 1-2(1-0)
Piast Gliwice: Frantisek Plach, Uros Korun, Mikkel Kirkeskov, Jakub
Czerwinski, Martin Konczkowski (83.Gerard Badía), Marcin Pietrowski,
Tom Hateley, Patryk Dziczek, Joel Valencia, Piotr Parzyszek, Jorge Félix
(87.Dani Aquino). Trainer: Waldemar Fornalik.
BATE Borisov: Anton Chichkan, Aleksandar Filipovic, Aleksey Rios,
Igor Stasevich, Dmitriy Baga, Slobodan Simovic, Jasse Tuominen
(57.Nemanja Milic), Evgeni Yablonski, Evgeniy Berezkin (75.Hervaine
Moukam), Zakhar Volkov, Maksim Skavysh. Trainer: Aleksei Baga.
Goals: 21' Jakub Czerwinski 1-0, 82' Hervaine Moukam 1-1 (pen), 87'
Zakhar Volkov 1-2.

17.07.2019. Ludogorets Arena, Razgrad
Referee: Donatas Rumsas (LTU); Attendance: 7,365
PFC Ludogorest Razgrad – FERENCVÁROSI TC 2-3(1-2)
PFC Ludogorets Razgrad: Renan, Cosmin Moti, Georgi Terziev, Jordan
Ikoko (64.Cicinho), Anton Nedyalkov, Svetoslav Dyakov, Jacek
Góralski, Marcelinho (64.Dan Biton), Mavis Tchibota, Jakub Swierczok
(46.Claudiu Keserü), Jorginho. Trainer: Stoicho Stoev.
Ferencvárosi TC: Dénes Dibusz, Marcel Heister, Miha Blazic, Lasha
Dvali, Michal Skvarka, Gergö Lovrencsics, Igor Kharatin, Oleksandr
Zubkov, Danylo Ignatenko (57.Dávid Sigér), Tamás Priskin (73.Davide
Lanzafame), Tokmac Nguen (61.Roland Varga). Trainer: Serhiy Rebrov.
Goals: 17' Igor Kharatin 0-1, 21' Michal Skvarka 0-2, 24' Georgi Terziev
1-2, 48' Tokmac Nguen 1-3, 69' Marcel Heister 2-3 (own goal).
Sent off: 82' Cosmin Moti.

17.07.2019. Stadion Kraj Bistrice, Nikšić
Referee: Horatiu Fesnic (ROU); Attendance: 4,764
FK SUTJESKA NIKŠIĆ – ŠK Slovan Bratislava 1-1(0-0,1-1);
3-2 on penalties
FK Sutjeska Nikšić: Vladan Giljen, Darko Bulatovic, Aleksandar
Sofranac, Bojan Ciger, Marko Cetkovic (74.Stefan Nikolic), Damir
Kojasevic, Branislav Jankovic (115.Vladan Bubanja), Marko Vucic
(69.Miljan Vlaisavljevic), Nemanja Nedic, Novica Erakovic, Bozo
Markovic (86.Milutin Osmajic). Trainer: Nikola Rakojevic.
Slovan Bratislava: Dominik Greif, Vasil Bozhikov, Artem Sukhotsky,
Jurij Medvedev, Marin Ljubicic (106.Rafael Ratão), Dávid Holman
(71.Myenty Abena), Joeri de Kamps (86.Dejan Drazic), Erik Daniel
(46.Aleksandar Cavric), Kenan Bajric, "Moha" Mohammed Rharsalla,
Andraz Sporar. Trainer: Martin Sevela.
Goals: 49' Nemanja Nedic 0-1 (own goal), 90+3' Aleksandar Sofranac
1-1. Penalties: Nikolic 1-0, Drazic missed, Kojasevic missed, Bozhikov
missed, Vlaisavljevic 2-0, Rafael Ratão 2-1, Bubanja 3-1, Abena 3-2,
Bulatovic missed, Sporar missed.

10.07.2019. Windsor Park, Belfast
Referee: Ivaylo Stoyanov (BUL); Attendance: 2,710
Linfield FC – Rosenborg BK Trondheim 0-2(0-1)
Linfield FC: Gareth Deane, Chris Casement, Matthew Clarke, Mark Stafford, Niall Quinn, Jamie Mulgrew, Jimmy Callacher, Kirk Millar (68.Shayne Lavery), Bastien Héry, Andrew Waterworth, Jordan Stewart (89.Stephen Fallon). Trainer: David Healy.
Rosenborg BK: André Hansen, Tore Reginiussen, Even Hovland, Vegar Hedenstad, Birger Meling, Mike Jensen, Anders Konradsen (72.Anders Trondsen), Gjermund Åsen (70.Pål Helland), Marius Lundemo, Alexander Søderlund, Babajide Akintola (61.Yann-Erik De Lanlay). Trainer: Eirik Horneland.
Goals: 22' Mike Jensen 0-1, 69' Alexander Søderlund 0-2.

10.07.2019. Oriel Park, Dundalk
Referee: Peter Královic (SVK); Attendance: 3,100
Dundalk FC – Riga FC 0-0
Dundalk FC: Gary Rogers, Dean Jarvis, Sean Gannon, Sean Hoare, Daniel Cleary, Chris Shields (46.Andy Boyle), Patrick McEleney, John Mountney (58.Robbie Benson), Jamie McGrath (80.Daniel Kelly), Patrick Hoban, Michael Duffy. Trainer: Vinny Perth.
Riga FC: Roberts Ozols, Herdi Prenga, Antonijs Cernomordijs, Aleksejs Visnakovs, Olegs Laizāns, Ritvars Rugins, Tomislav Saric, Joël Bopesu, Roger Rodrigues Figueira (79.Deniss Rakels), Armands Pētersons, Roman Debelko. Trainer: Mihails Konevs.

10.07.2019. Vodafonevöllurinn, Reykjavík
Referee: Krzysztof Jakubik (POL); Attendance: 1,201
Valur Reykjavík – NK Maribor 0-3(0-1)
Valur Reykjavík: Hannes Halldórsson, Bjarni Eiríksson, Eidur Sigurbjörnsson, Sebastian Hedlund, Haukur Sigurdsson, Kristinn Sigurdsson, Sigurdur Lárusson (76.Kaj Leo í Bartalsstovu), Andri Adolphsson (84.Birnir Snær Ingason), Lasse Petry (78.Einar Karl Ingvarsson), Ólafur Finsen, Patrick Pedersen. Trainer: Ólafur Jóhannesson.
NK Maribor: Kenan Piric, Mitja Viler, Martin Milec, Sasa Ivkovic, Spiro Pericic, Rok Kronaveter (89.Jasmin Mesanovic), Blaz Vrhovec, Alexandru Cretu, Dino Hotic (83.Martin Kramaric), Andrej Kotnik, Marcos Tavares (75.Rudi Pozeg Vancas). Trainer: Darko Milanic.
Goals: 43' Spiro Pericic 0-1, 60' Dino Hotic 0-2, 86' Rok Kronaveter 0-3 (pen).

17.07.2019. Lerkendal Stadion, Trondheim
Referee: Enea Jorgji (ALB); Attendance: 11,904
ROSENBORG BK TRONDHEIM – Linfield FC 4-0(1-0)
Rosenborg BK: André Hansen, Tore Reginiussen, Even Hovland, Vegar Hedenstad (46.Anders Trondsen), Birger Meling, Anders Konradsen (71.Emil Ceide), Gjermund Åsen, Marius Lundemo, Pål Helland, Alexander Søderlund (58.Babajide Akintola), Yann-Erik De Lanlay. Trainer: Eirik Horneland.
Linfield FC: Gareth Deane, Chris Casement, Matthew Clarke, Niall Quinn, Jamie Mulgrew (59.Stephen Fallon), Jimmy Callacher, Daniel Kearns, Bastien Héry, Shayne Lavery (58.Andrew Waterworth), Jordan Stewart (74.Kirk Millar), Ross Larkin. Trainer: David Healy.
Goals: 20', 51' Anders Konradsen 1-0, 2-0, 69' Babajide Akintola 3-0, 85' Pål Helland 4-0.

17.07.2019. Stadions Skonto, Riga
Referee: Dimitar Meckarovski (MCD); Attendance: 6,050
Riga FC – DUNDALK FC 0-0; 4-5 on penalties
Riga FC: Roberts Ozols, Herdi Prenga, Antonijs Cernomordijs, Aleksejs Visnakovs (106.Vladislavs Gabovs), Olegs Laizāns (81.Stefan Panic), Ritvars Rugins, Tomislav Saric, Joël Bopesu (52.Deniss Rakels), Roger Rodrigues Figueira (51.Felipe Brisola), Armands Pētersons, Roman Debelko. Trainer: Mihails Konevs.
Dundalk FC: Gary Rogers, Dane Massey, Andy Boyle, Sean Gannon, Sean Hoare, Chris Shields (99.Dean Jarvis), Robbie Benson (81.Daniel Kelly), Patrick McEleney (112.Georgie Kelly), John Mountney (65.Sean Murray), Jamie McGrath, Patrick Hoban. Trainer: Vinny Perth.
Sent off: 111' Herdi Prenga.
Penalties: Debelko 1-0, Hoban 1-1, Saric 2-1, Murray 2-2, Gabovs 3-2, Jarvis 3-3, Felipe Brisola missed, Massey missed, Panic missed, Kelly missed, Rakels 4-3, McGrath 4-4, Pētersons missed, Hoare 4-5.

17.07.2019. Ljudski vrt, Maribor
Referee: João Pedro Pinheiro (POR); Attendance: 6,716
NK MARIBOR – Valur Reykjavík 2-0(2-0)
NK Maribor: Kenan Piric, Mitja Viler, Martin Milec, Sasa Ivkovic, Spiro Pericic, Rok Kronaveter (58.Rudi Pozeg Vancas), Blaz Vrhovec (73.Martin Kramaric), Alexandru Cretu, Dino Hotic, Andrej Kotnik (57.Jasmin Mesanovic), Marcos Tavares. Trainer: Darko Milanic.
Valur Reykjavík: Hannes Halldórsson, Birkir Sævarsson, Eidur Sigurbjörnsson, Orri Ómarsson, Haukur Sigurdsson (19.Lasse Petry), Kristinn Sigurdsson (77.Sebastian Hedlund), Andri Adolphsson (62.Birnir Snær Ingason), Kaj Leo í Bartalsstovu, Einar Karl Ingvarsson, Ívar Jónsson, Patrick Pedersen. Trainer: Ólafur Jóhannesson.
Goals: 11' Rok Kronaveter 1-0, 32' Marcos Tavares 2-0.

23.07.2019. Park Hall Stadium, Oswestry
Referee: Alexander Harkam (AUT); Attendance: 1,230
The New Saints – FC København 0-2(0-1)
The New Saints: Paul Harrison, Simon Spender, Keston Davies, Ryan Harrington, Aeron Edwards, Jon Routledge, Daniel Redmond, Ryan Brobbel, Jamie Mullan, Adrian Cieslewicz (75.Joash Nembhard), Dean Ebbe (56.Greg Draper). Trainer: Scott Ruscoe.
FC København: Sten Grytebust, Pierre Bengtsson, Sotirios Papagiannopoulos, Karlo Bartolec, Victor Nelsson, Rasmus Falk (35.Zeca), Robert Skov, Jens Stage, Dame N'Doye (46.Jonas Wind), Pieros Sotiriou (62.Viktor Fischer), Carlo Holse. Trainer: Ståle Solbakken.
Goals: 18' Pieros Sotiriou 0-1, 61' Robert Skov 0-2 (pen).

23.07.2019. Mikheil Meskhis sakhelobis Stadioni, Tbilisi
Referee: Petr Ardeleánu (CZE); Attendance: 15,165
FC Saburtalo Tbilisi – GNK Dinamo Zagreb 0-2(0-0)
FC Saburtalo Tbilisi: Omar Migineishvili, Giorgi Rekhviashvili, Gagi Margvelashvili, Luka Lakvekheliani, Giorgi Diasamidze (82.Dachi Tsnobiladze), Sandro Altunashvili (70.Giorgi Gabedava), Nikoloz Mali, Alwyn Tera (57.Levan Kakubava), Ognjen Rolovic, Vagner Gonçalves, Giorgi Kokhreidze. Trainer: Giorgi Chiabrishvili.
Dinamo Zagreb: Dominik Livakovic, Marin Leovac, Ivo Pinto (50.Mario Situm), Marko Leskovic, Dino Peric, Arijan Ademi, Amer Gojak (86.Ivan Sunjic), Mario Gavranovic (68.Bruno Petkovic), Mislav Orsic, Izet Hajrovic, Damian Kadzior. Trainer: Nenad Bjelica.
Goals: 67' Mislav Orsic 0-1, 78' Bruno Petkovic 0-2 (pen).

23.07.2019. Stadion Kraj Bistrice, Nikšić
Referee: István Vad (HUN); Attendance: 5,500
FK Sutjeska Nikšić – APOEL Nicosia FC 0-1(0-1)
FK Sutjeska Nikšić: Vladan Giljen, Darko Bulatovic, Aleksandar Sofranac, Bojan Ciger, Marko Cetkovic (40.Milutin Osmajic), Damir Kojasevic, Branislav Jankovic, Marko Vucic (79.Miljan Vlaisavljevic), Nemanja Nedic, Novica Erakovic, Bozo Markovic (66.Stefan Nikolic). Trainer: Nikola Rakojevic.
APOEL Nicosia: Vid Belec, Kevin Lafrance, Praxitelis Vouros, Nicholas Ioannou, Dragan Mihajlovic, Savvas Gentsoglou, Antonio Jakolis (59.Vujadin Savic), Tomás De Vincenti (90+3.Uros Matic), Lucas Souza, Musa Al-Taamari, Linus Hallenius (60.Andrija Pavlovic). Trainer: Paolo Tramezzani.
Goal: 42' Tomás De Vincenti 0-1 (pen).

24.07.2019. Borisov Arena, Borisov
Referee: Sandro Schärer (SUI); Attendance: 12,696
FC BATE Borisov – Rosenborg BK Trondheim 2-1(1-1)
BATE Borisov: Anton Chichkan, Aleksandar Filipovic, Aleksey Rios, Igor Stasevich, Dmitriy Baga, Stanislav Dragun, Slobodan Simovic, Evgeni Yablonski, Zakhar Volkov, Nemanja Milic (78.Hervaine Moukam), Maksim Skavysh (85.Jasse Tuominen). Trainer: Aleksei Baga.
Rosenborg BK: André Hansen, Tore Reginiussen, Even Hovland, Vegar Hedenstad, Birger Meling, Mike Jensen, Anders Konradsen, Marius Lundemo, Alexander Søderlund, Yann-Erik De Lanlay (77.Pål Helland), Babajide Akintola (64.Samuel Adegbenro). Trainer: Eirik Horneland.
Goals: 5' Igor Stasevich 1-0 (pen), 25' Anders Konradsen 1-1,
51' Maksim Skavysh 2-1.

24.07.2019. Stadionul "Dr. Constantin Rădulescu", Cluj-Napoca
Referee: José María Sánchez Martínez (ESP); Attendance: 11,150
FC CFR 1907 Cluj – Maccabi Tel Aviv FC 1-0(1-0)
CFR Cluj: Giedrius Arlauskis, Paulo Vinícius, Mateo Susic, Camora, Andrei Burca, Emmanuel Culio, Ciprian Deac (90+1.Mickaël Pereira), Damjan Djokovic (79.Yacouba Sylla), Mihai Bordeianu, Mário Rondón (73.Adrian Paun), Billel Omrani. Trainer: Dan Petrescu.
Maccabi Tel Aviv: Andreas Gianniotis, Ofir Davidzada, Shahar Piven-Bachtiar, Jair Amador, Maor Kandil, Avi Rikan, Dor Peretz, Dan Glazer, Itay Shechter (83.Eliran Atar), Chikeluba Ofoedu (67.Nick Blackman), Yonatan Cohen (55.Dor Micha). Trainer: Vladimir Ivic.
Goal: 22' Billel Omrani 1-0.

31.07.2019. Telia Parken, København
Referee: Karim Abed (FRA); Attendance: 12,523
FC KØBENHAVN – The New Saints 1-0(0-0)
FC København: Karl-Johan Johnsson, Pierre Bengtsson (79.Guillermo Varela), Sotirios Papagiannopoulos, Karlo Bartolec, Victor Nelsson, Zeca (60.Ahmed Daghim), Nikolaj Thomsen, Jens Stage, Pieros Sotiriou, Jonas Wind (60.Carlo Holse), Mohammed Daramy. Trainer: Ståle Solbakken.
The New Saints: Paul Harrison, Simon Spender, Chris Marriott (78.Blaine Hudson), Ryan Harrington, Aeron Edwards, Jon Routledge, Daniel Redmond, Ryan Brobbel, Jamie Mullan, Adrian Cieslewicz (59.Kane Lewis), Dean Ebbe (66.Greg Draper). Trainer: Scott Ruscoe.
Goal: 52' Zeca 1-0.

30.07.2019. Stadion Maksimir, Zagreb
Referee: Daniele Doveri (ITA); Attendance: *behind closed doors*
GNK DINAMO ZAGREB – FC Saburtalo Tbilisi 3-0(0-0)
Dinamo Zagreb: Dominik Livakovic, Marin Leovac, Ivo Pinto, Marko Leskovic, Dino Peric, Arijan Ademi, Amer Gojak (63.Bruno Petkovic), Mislav Orsic, Izet Hajrovic (84.Lovro Majer), Damian Kadzior (75.Daniel Olmo). Trainer: Nenad Bjelica.
FC Saburtalo Tbilisi: Lazare Kupatadze, Giorgi Rekhviashvili, Dachi Tsnobiladze, Gagi Margvelashvili, Grigol Chabradze (69.Jemali-Giorgi Jinjolava), Tornike Gorgiashvili (61.Giorgi Diasamidze), Levan Kakubava, Sandro Altunashvili, Nikoloz Mali (59.Iuri Tabatadze), Giorgi Gabedava, Ognjen Rolovic. Trainer: Giorgi Chiabrishvili.
Goals: 77' Mislav Orsic 1-0, 88' Bruno Petkovic 2-0, 90+4' Daniel Olmo 3-0.

30.07.2019. Neo GSP Stadium, Nicosia
Referee: Roi Reinshreiber (ISR); Attendance: 8,297
APOEL NICOSIA FC – FK Sutjeska Nikšić 3-0(2-0)
APOEL Nicosia: Vid Belec, Vujadin Savic (76.Giorgios Merkis), Praxitelis Vouros, Nicholas Ioannou, Dragan Mihajlovic, Savvas Gentsoglou (78.Alef), Antonio Jakolis, Uros Matic, Tomás De Vincenti, Musa Al-Taamari, Andrija Pavlovic (71.Roman Bezjak). Trainer: Paolo Tramezzani.
Sutjeska Nikšić: Vladan Giljen, Darko Bulatovic, Aleksandar Sofranac, Bojan Ciger, Damir Kojasevic, Branislav Jankovic, Aleksa Marusic (60.Marko Cetkovic), Nemanja Nedic, Vladan Bubanja, Milutin Osmajic (72.Miljan Vlaisavljevic), Bojan Bozovic (67.Stefan Nikolic). Trainer: Nikola Rakojevic.
Goals: 13', 25', 66' Andrija Pavlovic 1-0, 2-0, 3-0.

31.07.2019. Lerkendal Stadion, Trondheim
Referee: Marco Di Bello (ITA); Attendance: 14,875.
ROSENBORG BK TRONDHEIM – FC BATE Borisov 2-0(0-0)
Rosenborg BK: André Hansen, Tore Reginiussen, Even Hovland, Vegar Hedenstad, Birger Meling, Mike Jensen, Anders Konradsen, Anders Trondsen, Alexander Søderlund, Samuel Adegbenro (78.Yann-Erik De Lanlay), Babajide Akintola (70.Pål Helland). Trainer: Eirik Horneland.
BATE Borisov: Anton Chichkan, Aleksandar Filipovic, Aleksey Rios (62.Emil Jonassen), Igor Stasevich, Dmitriy Baga, Stanislav Dragun (87.Bojan Dubajic), Slobodan Simovic, Jasse Tuominen (76.Hervaine Moukam), Evgeni Yablonski, Zakhar Volkov, Maksim Skavysh. Trainer: Aleksei Baga.
Goals: 73' Pål Helland 1-0 (pen), 85' Alexander Søderlund 2-0.

30.07.2019. Winner Stadium, Netanya
Referee: Marco Fritz (GER); Attendance: 11,947
Maccabi Tel Aviv FC – FC CFR 1907 CLUJ 2-2(1-2)
Maccabi Tel Aviv FC: Andreas Gianniotis, Ofir Davidzada, Shahar Piven-Bachtiar, Jair Amador, Maor Kandil (59.Geraldes), Avi Rikan (46.Yonatan Cohen), Dor Micha, Dor Peretz, Dan Glazer, Nick Blackman (72.Eliran Atar), Itay Shechter. Trainer: Vladimir Ivic.
CFR Cluj: Giedrius Arlauskis, Paulo Vinícius, Mateo Susic, Camora, Andrei Burca, Emmanuel Culio, Ciprian Deac (52.Adrian Paun), Damjan Djokovic, Mihai Bordeianu, Mário Rondón (82.George Tucudean), Billel Omrani (86.Andrei Muresan). Trainer: Dan Petrescu.
Goals: 15' Nick Blackman 1-0, 19' Emmanuel Culio 1-1 (pen), 42' Mário Rondón 1-2, 48' Yonatan Cohen 2-2.

24.07.2019. Groupama Aréna, Budapest
Referee: Radu Petrescu (ROU); Attendance: 18,603
Ferencvárosi TC – Valletta FC 3-1(2-0)
Ferencvárosi TC: Dénes Dibusz, Miha Blazic, Lasha Dvali, Eldar Civic, Michal Skvarka (82.Dávid Sigér), Gergö Lovrencsics, Igor Kharatin, Oleksandr Zubkov, Danylo Ignatenko, Davide Lanzafame (66.Nikolay Signevich), Tokmac Nguen (65.Lukács Böle). Trainer: Serhiy Rebrov.
Valletta FC: Henry Bonello, Joseph Zerafa, Steve Borg, Douglas Packer (70.Yuri Messias), Rowen Muscat, Kyrian Nwoko (83.Matteo Piciollo), Jean Borg, Enmy Peña, Kevin Tulimieri, Nicholas Pulis (57.Shaun Dimech), Mario Fontanella. Trainer: Darren Abdilla.
Goals: 19' Henry Bonello 1-0 (own goal), 36', 59' Davide Lanzafame 2-0 (pen), 3-0, 85' Yuri Messias 3-1.
Sent off: 90+4' Steve Borg.

24.07.2019. Ljudski vrt, Maribor
Referee: Sascha Stegemann (GER); Attendance: 7,816
NK Maribor – AIK Stockholm 2-1(2-1)
NK Maribor: Kenan Piric, Mitja Viler, Martin Milec, Sasa Ivkovic, Spiro Pericic, Rok Kronaveter, Blaz Vrhovec, Alexandru Cretu, Dino Hotic, Andrej Kotnik (80.Rudi Pozeg Vancas), Marcos Tavares (87.Jasmin Mesanovic). Trainer: Darko Milanic.
AIK Stockholm: Oscar Linnér, Per Karlsson, Karol Mets, Daniel Granli, Sebastian Larsson, Enoch Adu, Anton Salétros (79.Rasmus Lindkvist), Heradi Rashidi, Tarik Elyounoussi, Kolbeinn Sigthórsson (62.Chinedu Obasi), Henok Goitom. Trainer: Rikard Norling.
Goals: 6' Rok Kronaveter 1-0, 28' Henok Goitom 1-1, 38' Sasa Ivkovic 2-1.

24.07.2019. Oriel Park, Dundalk
Referee: Bartosz Frankowski (POL); Attendance: 3,100
Dundalk FC – Qarabağ FK Bakı 1-1(0-1)
Dundalk FC: Gary Rogers, Dane Massey, Andy Boyle, Sean Gannon, Sean Hoare, Chris Shields, Robbie Benson (27.Sean Murray), Patrick McEleney (69.John Mountney), Jamie McGrath, Patrick Hoban (83.Georgie Kelly), Michael Duffy. Trainer: Vinny Perth.
Qarabağ FK: Vagner, Rashad Sadigov, Maksim Medvedev (53.Abbas Hüseynov), Ailton, Rahil Mammadov, Jaime Romero (87.Araz Abdullayev), Gara Garayev, Richard Almeyda, Simeon Slavchev, Abdellah Zoubir, Mahir Emreli. Trainer: Gurban Gurbanov.
Goals: 4' Mahir Emreli 0-1, 78' Patrick Hoban 1-1.

24.07.2019. Stadion „Rajko Mitić", Beograd
Referee: Pawel Gil (POL); Attendance: 36,289
Crvena Zvezda Beograd – HJK Helsinki 2-0(1-0)
Crvena Zvezda: Milan Borjan, Nemanja Milunovic, Milan Rodic, Filip Stojkovic, Srdjan Babic, Marko Marin, Branko Jovicic, Dusan Jovancic, Mirko Ivanic (63.Milan Jevtovic), Richmond Boakye (72.Milan Pavkov), Mohamed Ben Nabouhane (85.Aleksa Vukanovic). Trainer: Vladan Milojevic.
HJK Helsinki: Maksim Rudakov, Rafinha, Henri Toivomäki, Nikolai Alho, Faith Obilor, William Parra, Riku Riski, Kaan Kairinen, Sebastian Dahlström, Evans Mensah (90+1.Tim Väyrynen), Ivan Tarasov (81.Kevin Kouassivi-Benissan). Trainer: Toni Koskela.
Goals: 27' Richmond Boakye 1-0, 90' Milan Pavkov 2-0.

24.07.2019. Celtic Park, Glasgow
Referee: Jakob Kehlet (DEN); Attendance: 41,872
Celtic FC Glasgow – JK Nõmme Kalju 5-0(3-0)
Celtic FC: Scott Bain, Jozo Simunovic, Boli Bolingoli-Mbombo (37.Michael Johnston), Kristoffer Ajer, Scott Brown, Nir Bitton, James Forrest, Callum McGregor, Ryan Christie (71.Jules Olivier Ntcham), Leigh Griffiths (59.Lewis Morgan), Odsonne Édouard. Trainer: Neil Lennon.
JK Nõmme Kalju: Pavel Londak, Aleksandr Kulinits, Maximiliano Uggè, Vladimir Avilov, Andriy Markovych, Sander Puri, Igor Subbotin, Réginald Mbu-Alidor, Kaspar Paur (75.Aleksandr Volkov), Liliu (84.Nikolaj Mashichev), Peeter Klein (46.Max Mata). Trainer: Roman Kozhukhovskyi.
Goals: 36' Kristoffer Ajer 1-0, 44' Ryan Christie 2-0 (pen), 45+3' Leigh Griffiths 3-0, 65' Ryan Christie 4-0, 77' Callum McGregor 5-0.

30.07.2019. MFA Centenary Stadium, Ta'Qali
Referee: Jonathan Lardot (BEL); Attendance: 1,108
Valletta FC – FERENCVARÓSI TC 1-1(1-0)
Valletta FC: Henry Bonello, Joseph Zerafa, Ryan Camilleri, Rowen Muscat (80.Antonio Monticelli), Jean Borg, Enmy Peña, Shaun Dimech (75.Kyrian Nwoko), Matteo Piciollo (90.Ryan Tonna), Kevin Tulimieri, Yuri Messias, Mario Fontanella. Trainer: Darren Abdilla.
Ferencvárosi TC: Dénes Dibusz, Miha Blazic, Lasha Dvali, Eldar Civic, Michal Skvarka, Gergö Lovrencsics, Igor Kharatin, Oleksandr Zubkov, Danylo Ignatenko (33.Dávid Sigér), Davide Lanzafame (75.Nikolay Signevich), Tokmac Nguen (85.Roland Varga). Trainer: Serhiy Rebrov.
Goals: 27' Mario Fontanella 1-0 (pen), 60' Tokmac Nguen 1-1.

31.07.2019. Friends Arena, Solna
Referee: Adrien Jaccottet (SUI); Attendance: 19,179
AIK Stockholm – NK MARIBOR 3-2(1-0,2-1)
AIK Stockholm: Oscar Linnér, Per Karlsson, Robert Lundström (77.Heradi Rashidi), Karol Mets, Daniel Granli (105.Panajotis Dimitriadis), Sebastian Larsson (102.Bilal Hussein), Enoch Adu, Anton Salétros, Tarik Elyounoussi, Henok Goitom, Chinedu Obasi (32.Kolbeinn Sigthórsson). Trainer: Rikard Norling.
NK Maribor: Kenan Piric, Mitja Viler, Martin Milec, Sasa Ivkovic, Spiro Pericic, Rok Kronaveter (118.Aleks Pihler), Blaz Vrhovec (105.Martin Kramaric), Alexandru Cretu, Dino Hotic, Andrej Kotnik (90.Rudi Pozeg Vancas), Marcos Tavares (86.Jasmin Mesanovic). Trainer: Darko Milanic.
Goals: 4' Per Karlsson 1-0, 48' Andrej Kotnik 1-1, 61' Sebastian Larsson 2-1, 93' Tarik Elyounoussi 3-1, 117' Alexandru Cretu 3-2.

31.07.2019. Dalga Arena, Bakı
Referee: Svein Oddvar Moen (NOR); Attendance: 5,832
QARABAĞ FK BAKI – Dundalk FC 3-0(1-0)
Qarabağ FK: Vagner, Rashad Sadigov, Maksim Medvedev (82.Abbas Hüseynov), Ailton, Rahil Mammadov, Míchel (73.Simeon Slavchev), Jaime Romero, Richard Almeyda, Filip Ozobic (25.Dani Quintana), Abdellah Zoubir, Mahir Emreli. Trainer: Gurban Gurbanov.
Dundalk FC: Gary Rogers, Dane Massey, Andy Boyle, Sean Gannon, Sean Hoare (56.Sean Murray), Daniel Cleary, Chris Shields, Patrick McEleney (65.John Mountney), Jamie McGrath, Patrick Hoban, Michael Duffy (79.Daniel Kelly). Trainer: Vinny Perth.
Goals: 12' Jaime Romero 1-0, 76' Ailton 2-0, 87' Jaime Romero 3-0.

31.07.2019. Telia 5G -areena, Helsinki
Referee: Alain Bieri (SUI); Attendance: 9,107
HJK Helsinki – FK CRVENA ZVEZDA BEOGRAD 2-1(0-0)
HJK Helsinki: Maksim Rudakov, Rafinha (66.Victor Luiz Prestes Filho), Nikolai Alho, Daniel O'Shaughnessy, Faith Obilor, William Parra (77.Santeri Väänänen), Riku Riski, Kaan Kairinen, Sebastian Dahlström, Evans Mensah, Ivan Tarasov (46.Tim Väyrynen). Trainer: Toni Koskela.
Crvena Zvezda: Milan Borjan, Nemanja Milunovic, Milan Rodic, Filip Stojkovic, Srdjan Babic, Marko Marin, Cañas (88.Milos Degenek), Dusan Jovancic, Milan Jevtovic (74.Mirko Ivanic), Richmond Boakye (55.Milan Pavkov), Mohamed Ben Nabouhane.
Trainer: Vladan Milojevic.
Goals: 46' Sebastian Dahlström 1-0, 56' Dusan Jovancic 1-1, 90+2' Riku Riski 2-1.

30.07.2019. A. Le Coq Arena, Tallinn
Referee: Benoît Millot (FRA); Attendance: 4,014
JK Nõmme Kalju – CELTIC FC GLASGOW 0-2(0-1)
JK Nõmme Kalju: Pavel Londak, Aleksandr Kulinits, Maximiliano Uggè, Vladimir Avilov, Deniss Tjapkin, Andriy Markovych, Sander Puri, Igor Subbotin (79.Nikolaj Mashichev), Kaspar Paur (83.Aleksandr Ivanjusin), Liliu (38.Max Mata), Peeter Klein. Trainer: Roman Kozhukhovskyi.
Celtic FC: Craig Gordon, Jozo Simunovic, Christopher Jullien, Boli Bolingoli-Mbombo, Tony Ralston, Scott Brown, Nir Bitton (70.Marian Shved), Jules Olivier Ntcham (84.Ryan Christie), Lewis Morgan, Leigh Griffiths, Michael Johnston (61.Scott Sinclair). Trainer: Neil Lennon.
Goals: 10' Aleksandr Kulinits 0-1 (own goal), 90+3' Marian Shved 0-2.

23.07.2019. Philips Stadion, Eindhoven
Referee: Andris Treimanis (LVA); Attendance: 31,638
PSV Eindhoven – FC Basel 3-2(1-1)
PSV Eindhoven: Jeroen Zoet, Nick Viergever, Derrick Luckassen, Denzel Dumfries, Bruma (78.Cody Gakpo), Érick Gutiérrez, Michal Sadílek, Pablo Rosario, Steven Bergwijn, Hirving Lozano (82.Sam Lammers), Donyell Malen. Trainer: Mark van Bommel.
FC Basel: Jonas Omlin, Silvan Widmer, Éder Álvarez Balanta (90.Afimico Pululu), Omar Alderete, Eray Cömert, Valentin Stocker (65.Noah Okafor), Luca Zuffi, Fabian Frei, Taulant Xhaka, Ricky van Wolfswinkel, Albian Ajeti (87.Kemal Ademi). Trainer: Marcelo Koller.
Goals: 14' Bruma 1-0, 45+1' Albian Ajeti 1-1, 79' Omar Alderete 1-2, 89' Sam Lammers 2-2, 90+2' Donyell Malen 3-2.

23.07.2019. Doosan Aréna, Plzeň
Referee: Marco Guida (ITA); Attendance: 10,632
FC Viktoria Plzeň – Olympiacos SFP Peiraiás 0-0
FC Viktoria Plzeň: Ales Hruska, Adam Hlousek, Jakub Brabec (72.Lukás Hejda), Ludek Pernica, Milan Havel, Jan Kopic, Ales Cermák (83.Ondrej Mihálik), Patrik Hrosovsky, Lukás Kalvach, Joel Kayamba, Michal Krmencík (69.Tomás Chory). Trainer: Pavel Vrba.
Olympiacos Peiraiás: José Sá, Avram Papadopoulos (22.Ousseynou Ba), Omar Elabdellaoui, Rúben Semedo, Kostas Tsimikas, Mathieu Valbuena (57.Mady Camara), Guilherme, Andreas Bouchalakis, Daniel Podence, Georgios Masouras (81.Lazar Randjelovic), Guerrero. Trainer: Pedro Martins.

30.07.2019. St. Jakob-Park, Basel
Referee: Fábio Veríssimo (POR); Attendance: 29,216.
FC BASEL – PSV Eindhoven 2-1(1-1)
FC Basel: Jonas Omlin, Silvan Widmer, Éder Álvarez Balanta, Omar Alderete, Eray Cömert, Valentin Stocker, Luca Zuffi, Fabian Frei, Taulant Xhaka (81.Raoul Petretta), Ricky van Wolfswinkel, Albian Ajeti. Trainer: Marcelo Koller.
PSV Eindhoven: Jeroen Zoet, Nick Viergever, Derrick Luckassen, Denzel Dumfries, Bruma, Érick Gutiérrez, Michal Sadílek, Pablo Rosario, Steven Bergwijn, Hirving Lozano (76.Cody Gakpo), Donyell Malen. Trainer: Mark van Bommel.
Goals: 8' Eray Cömert 1-0, 23' Bruma 1-1, 68' Ricky van Wolfswinkel 2-1.

30.07.2019. Stádio „Giórgos Karaïskáki", Peiraiás
Referee: Juan Martínez Munuera (ESP); Attendance: 30,123
OLYMPIACOS SFP PEIRAIÁS – FC Viktoria Plzeň 4-0(0-0)
Olympiacos Peiraiás: José Sá, Omar Elabdellaoui, Rúben Semedo, Yassine Meriah, Kostas Tsimikas, Mathieu Valbuena (66.Mady Camara), Guilherme, Andreas Bouchalakis, Daniel Podence (85.Lazar Randjelovic), Georgios Masouras, Guerrero (80.Youssef El-Arabi). Trainer: Pedro Martins.
FC Viktoria Plzeň: Ales Hruska, Adam Hlousek, Radim Rezník, Jakub Brabec, Ludek Pernica, Jan Kopic, Patrik Hrosovsky, Lukás Kalvach (79.Dominik Janosek), Joel Kayamba (56.Jan Kovarík), Michal Krmencík, Ondrej Mihálik (74.Tomás Chory). Trainer: Pavel Vrba.
Goals: 51' Guilherme 1-0, 70' Guerrero 2-0, 73' Guilherme 3-0, 82' Rúben Semedo 4-0.

06.08.2019. Neo GSP Stadium, Nicosia
Referee: Davide Massa (ITA); Attendance: 9,481
APOEL Nicosia FC – Qarabağ FK Bakı 1-2(0-0)
APOEL Nicosia: Vid Belec, Giorgios Merkis, Praxitelis Vouros, Nicholas Ioannou, Dragan Mihajlovic, Savvas Gentsoglou (86.Linus Hallenius), Antonio Jakolis (64.André Vidigal), Uros Matic (65.Alef), Tomás De Vincenti, Musa Al-Taamari, Andrija Pavlovic. Trainer: Paolo Tramezzani.
Qarabağ FK: Vagner, Rashad Sadigov, Maksim Medvedev, Ailton, Rahil Mammadov, Míchel, Jaime Romero (85.Araz Abdullayev), Richard Almeyda (86.Gara Garayev), Simeon Slavchev, Abdellah Zoubir, Mahir Emreli (68.Magaye Gueye). Trainer: Gurban Gurbanov.
Goals: 54' Mahir Emreli 0-1, 69' Magaye Gueye 0-2, 90+5' Giorgios Merkis 1-2.

06.08.2019. Stadio Toumbas, Thessaloniki
Referee: Slavko Vinčić (SVN); Attendance: 23,418
PAOK Thessaloníki – AFC Ajax Amsterdam 2-2(2-1)
PAOK Thessaloníki: Alexandros Paschalakis, Léo Matos, José Ángel Crespo, Fernando Varela, Dimitris Giannoulis, Diego Biseswar (73.Douglas Augusto), Omar El Kaddouri, Dimitris Pelkas (65.Dimitris Limnios), Anderson Esiti, Chuba Akpom, Léo Jabá (79.Miroslav Stoch). Trainer: Abel Ferreira.
AFC Ajax: André Onana, Daley Blind, Nicolás Tagliafico, Joël Veltman, Noussair Mazraoui (82.Razvan Marin), Perr Schuurs, Lisandro Martínez, Hakim Ziyech (82.David Neres), Donny van de Beek, Dusan Tadic, Kasper Dolberg (33.Klaas Jan Huntelaar). Trainer: Erik ten Hag.
Goals: 10' Hakim Ziyech 0-1, 32' Chuba Akpom 1-1, 39' Léo Matos 2-1, 57' Klaas Jan Huntelaar 2-2.

06.08.2019. Stadion Maksimir, Zagreb
Referee: Pawel Raczkowski (POL); Attendance: 14,283
GNK Dinamo Zagreb – Ferencvárosi TC 1-1(1-0)
Dinamo Zagreb: Dominik Livakovic, Marin Leovac, Marko Leskovic, Petar Stojanovic, Dino Peric, Arijan Ademi, Amer Gojak (69.Nikola Moro), Daniel Olmo, Mislav Orsic, Izet Hajrovic (69.Lovro Majer), Bruno Petkovic (76.Mario Gavranovic). Trainer: Nenad Bjelica.
Ferencvárosi TC: Dénes Dibusz, Marcel Heister, Miha Blazic, Lasha Dvali, Michal Skvarka (89.Danylo Ignatenko), Gergő Lovrencsics, Dávid Sigér, Igor Kharatin, Oleksandr Zubkov, Nikolay Signevich (78.Davide Lanzafame), Tokmac Nguen (83.Eldar Civic). Trainer: Serhiy Rebrov.
Goals: 7' Daniel Olmo 1-0, 59' Dávid Sigér (1-1).

13.08.2019. "Tofiq Bahramov" adina Respublika stadionu, Baku
Referee: Daniel Siebert (GER); Attendance: 31,531
Qarabağ FK Bakı – APOEL NICOSIA FC 0-2(0-1)
Qarabağ FK: Vagner, Rashad Sadigov, Maksim Medvedev, Ailton (87.Araz Abdullayev), Rahil Mammadov, Míchel, Jaime Romero, Richard Almeyda, Simeon Slavchev (73.Dani Quintana), Abdellah Zoubir (80.Magaye Gueye), Mahir Emreli. Trainer: Gurban Gurbanov.
APOEL Nicosia: Vid Belec, Giorgios Merkis, Kevin Lafrance, Nicholas Ioannou, Dragan Mihajlovic, Savvas Gentsoglou, Uros Matic, Tomás De Vincenti (61.Linus Hallenius), Musa Al-Taamari, Roman Bezjak (82.Antonio Jakolis), Andrija Pavlovic (73.Lucas Souza). Trainer: Thomas Doll.
Goals: 34' Tomás De Vincenti 0-1 (pen), 68' Uros Matic 0-2.
Sent off: 90+3' Richard Almeyda.

13.08.2019. „Johan Cruijff" ArenA, Amsterdam
Referee: Craig Pawson (ENG); Attendance: 53,942
AFC AJAX AMSTERDAM – PAOK Thessaloníki 3-2(1-1)
AFC Ajax: André Onana, Daley Blind, Nicolás Tagliafico, Joël Veltman, Noussair Mazraoui, Lisandro Martínez, Hakim Ziyech, Razvan Marin (46.Sergiño Dest), Donny van de Beek (89.Dani de Wit), Dusan Tadic, David Neres (78.Klaas Jan Huntelaar). Trainer: Erik ten Hag.
PAOK Thessaloníki: Alexandros Paschalakis, Léo Matos, José Ángel Crespo, Fernando Varela, Dimitris Giannoulis, Diego Biseswar, Omar El Kaddouri, Dimitris Pelkas (63.Karol Swiderski), Anderson Esiti (82.Josip Misic), Chuba Akpom, Léo Jabá (71.Dimitris Limnios). Trainer: Abel Ferreira.
Goals: 23' Diego Biseswar 0-1, 43' Dusan Tadic 1-1 (pen), 79' Nicolás Tagliafico 2-1, 85' Dusan Tadic 3-1 (pen), 90+4' Diego Biseswar 3-2.

13.08.2019. Groupama Aréna, Budapest
Referee: Ruddy Buquet (FRA); Attendance: 20,321
Ferencvárosi TC – GNK DINAMO ZAGREB 0-4(0-1)
Ferencvárosi TC: Dénes Dibusz, Miha Blazic, Lasha Dvali, Eldar Civic, Michal Skvarka (71.Marcel Heister), Gergö Lovrencsics, Dávid Sigér, Igor Kharatin, Oleksandr Zubkov, Nikolay Signevich (84.Franck Boli), Tokmac Nguen (65.Roland Varga). Trainer: Serhiy Rebrov.
Dinamo Zagreb: Dominik Livakovic, Marin Leovac, Emir Dilaver, Petar Stojanovic, Dino Peric, Arijan Ademi (70.Amer Gojak), Nikola Moro, Daniel Olmo (84.Mario Situm), Mislav Orsic, Izet Hajrovic (77.Lovro Majer), Bruno Petkovic. Trainer: Nenad Bjelica.
Goals: 16' Arijan Ademi 0-1, 47' Bruno Petkovic 0-2, 55' Daniel Olmo 0-3, 79' Amer Gojak 0-4. Sent off: 68' Eldar Civic.

06.08.2019. Stadion „Rajko Mitić", Beograd
Referee: Tiago Bruno Lopes Martins (POR); Attendance: 40,812
FK Crvena Zvezda Beograd – FC København 1-1(1-0)
Crvena Zvezda: Milan Borjan, Nemanja Milunovic, Milan Rodic
(65.Jander), Milos Degenek, Marko Gobeljic, Marko Marin, Cañas,
Dusan Jovancic, Mirko Ivanic, Milan Pavkov (46.Richmond Boakye),
Aleksa Vukanovic (76.Mohamed Ben Nabouhane). Trainer: Vladan
Milojevic.
FC København: Sten Grytebust, Bryan Oviedo (72.Pierre Bengtsson),
Sotirios Papagiannopoulos, Guillermo Varela, Victor Nelsson, Zeca,
Viktor Fischer (64.Pep Biel Mas), Jens Stage, Dame N'Doye, Jonas
Wind, Carlo Holse (88.Karlo Bartolec). Trainer: Ståle Solbakken.
Goals: 44' Milan Pavkov 1-0, 84' Jonas Wind 1-1 (pen).

07.08.2019. Stadionul "Dr. Constantin Rădulescu", Cluj-Napoca
Referee: Srdjan Jovanovic (SRB); Attendance: 13,055
FC CFR 1907 Cluj – Celtic FC Glasgow 1-1(1-1)
CFR Cluj: Giedrius Arlauskis, Paulo Vinícius, Mateo Susic, Camora,
Andrei Burca, Ciprian Deac, Damjan Djokovic, Mihai Bordeianu, Luís
Aurélio, Mário Rondón (75.George Tucudean), Billel Omrani (66.Adrian
Paun). Trainer: Dan Petrescu.
Celtic FC: Scott Bain, Hatem Abd Elhamed (87.Nir Bitton), Jozo
Simunovic (74.Christopher Jullien), Boli Bolingoli-Mbombo, Kristoffer
Ajer, Scott Brown, James Forrest, Callum McGregor, Ryan Christie,
Lewis Morgan (67.Jules Olivier Ntcham), Odsonne Édouard. Trainer:
Neil Lennon.
Goals: 28' Mário Rondón 1-0, 37' James Forrest 1-1.

07.08.2019. Ljudski vrt, Maribor
Referee: François Letexier (FRA); Attendance: 10,316
NK Maribor – Rosenborg BK Trondheim 1-3(0-0)
NK Maribor: Kenan Piric, Mitja Viler, Martin Milec, Sasa Ivkovic, Spiro
Pericic, Rok Kronaveter, Blaz Vrhovec, Aleks Pihler, Dino Hotic
(64.Rudi Pozeg Vancas), Andrej Kotnik (85.Martin Kramaric), Marcos
Tavares. Trainer: Darko Milanic.
Rosenborg BK: André Hansen, Tore Reginiussen (14.Gustav Valsvik),
Even Hovland, Vegar Hedenstad, Birger Meling, Mike Jensen, Gjermund
Åsen (79.Anders Trondsen), Marius Lundemo, Alexander Søderlund
(68.Pål Helland), Samuel Adegbenro, Babajide Akintola. Trainer: Eirik
Horneland.
Goals: 50', 64' Alexander Søderlund 0-1, 0-2, 70' Marcos Tavares 1-2,
71' Mike Jensen 1-3.

13.08.2019. Telia Parken, København
Referee: Gediminas Mazeika (LTU); Attendance: 29,872
**FC København – FK CRVENA ZVEZDA BEOGRAD 1-1(1-1,1-1);
6-7 on penalties**
FC København: Sten Grytebust, Pierre Bengtsson, Sotirios
Papagiannopoulos, Guillermo Varela (81.Karlo Bartolec), Victor
Nelsson, Zeca, Viktor Fischer, Jens Stage (60.Rasmus Falk, 120.Pieros
Soteriou), Dame N'Doye, Jonas Wind, Carlo Holse (74.Pep Biel Mas).
Trainer: Ståle Solbakken.
Crvena Zvezda: Milan Borjan, Nemanja Milunovic, Milan Rodic
(46.Jander), Milos Degenek, Marko Gobeljic, Marko Marin, Cañas
(58.Radovan Pankov), Dusan Jovancic, Mirko Ivanic, Richmond Boakye
(81.Veljko Simic), Aleksa Vukanovic (90.Milan Jevtovic). Trainer:
Vladan Milojevic.
Goals: 17' Richmond Boakye 0-1, 45' Dame N'Doye 1-1.
Sent off: 54' Nemanja Milunovic, 112' Pep Biel Mas.
Penalties: Marin missed, Wind 1-0, Ivanic 1-1, Fischer missed, Jevtovic
missed, Soteriou 1-2, Jander 2-2, Bengtsson missed, Pankov 3-2, Zeca 3-
3, Jovancic missed, N'Doye missed, Simic missed, Bartolec missed,
Degenek 4-3, Nelsson 4-4, Gobeljic 5-4, Papagiannopoulos 5-5, Borjan
6-5, Grytebust 6-6, Pankov 7-6, Wind missed.

13.08.2019. Celtic Park, Glasgow
Referee: Andris Treimanis (LVA); Attendance: 50,964
Celtic FC Glasgow – FC CFR 1907 CLUJ 3-4(0-1)
Celtic FC: Scott Bain, Hatem Abd Elhamed, Jozo Simunovic, Kristoffer
Ajer, Scott Brown (88.Vakoun Bayo), James Forrest, Callum McGregor,
Jules Olivier Ntcham (83.Leigh Griffiths), Ryan Christie, Odsonne
Édouard, Michael Johnston (75.Lewis Morgan). Trainer: Neil Lennon.
CFR Cluj: Giedrius Arlauskis, Paulo Vinícius, Mateo Susic, Camora,
Andrei Burca, Ciprian Deac, Damjan Djokovic, Mihai Bordeianu, Luís
Aurélio (78.Adrian Paun), Mário Rondón (46.George Tucudean), Billel
Omrani (84.Andrei Muresan). Trainer: Dan Petrescu.
Goals: 27' Ciprian Deac 0-1, 51' James Forrest 1-1, 61' Odsonne
Édouard 2-1, 74' Billel Omrani 2-2 (pen), 76' Ryan Christie 3-2, 80'
Billel Omrani 3-3, 90+7' George Tucudean 3-4.

13.08.2019. Lerkendal Stadion, Trondheim
Referee: Serdar Gözübüyük (NED); Attendance: 18,564
ROSENBORG BK TRONDHEIM – NK Maribor 3-1(0-1)
Rosenborg BK: André Hansen, Tore Reginiussen, Even Hovland, Vegar
Hedenstad, Birger Meling, Mike Jensen (87.Anders Trondsen), Anders
Konradsen (90.Emil Ceide), Marius Lundemo, Alexander Søderlund,
Samuel Adegbenro (78.Gjermund Åsen), Babajide Akintola. Trainer:
Eirik Horneland.
NK Maribor: Kenan Piric, Mitja Viler, Martin Milec, Sasa Ivkovic, Spiro
Pericic, Rok Kronaveter (69.Andrej Kotnik), Blaz Vrhovec, Alexandru
Cretu, Rudi Pozeg Vancas, Dino Hotic (82.Martin Kramaric), Marcos
Tavares (69.Luka Zahovic). Trainer: Darko Milanic.
Goals: 45+2' Rudi Pozeg Vancas 0-1, 53' Alexander Søderlund 1-1, 61',
81' Anders Konradsen 2-1, 3-1.

LEAGUE PATH

06.08.2019. „Jan Breydel" Stadion, Brugge
Referee: Xavier Estrada Fernández (ESP); Attendance: 27,018
Club Brugge KV – FK Dynamo Kyiv 1-0(1-0)
Club Brugge: Simon Mignolet, Eduard Sobol, Clinton Mata, Matej
Mitrovic, Simon Deli, Ruud Vormer, Mats Rits, Hans Vanaken, Percy
Tau, David Okereke, Emmanuel Dennis Bonaventure (63.Siebe
Schrijvers). Trainer: Philippe Clement.
Dynamo Kyiv: Denis Boyko, Tamás Kádár, Tomasz Kedziora, Mykyta
Burda, Vitali Mykolenko, Sergiy Sydorchuk, Denys Garmash, Vitaliy
Buyalskiy, Benjamin Verbic (64.Carlos de Pena), Oleksandr Karavayev
(46.Viktor Tsygankov), Artem Besedin (46.Gerson Rodrigues). Trainer:
Aleksandr Khatskevich.
Goal: 37' Hans Vanaken 1-0 (pen).

13.08.2019. NSK Olimpiyskiy Stadium, Kyiv
Referee: Ivan Bebek (CRO); Attendance: 42,152
FK Dynamo Kyiv – CLUB BRUGGE KV 3-3(1-1)
Dynamo Kyiv: Denis Boyko, Tamás Kádár, Tomasz Kedziora, Mykyta
Burda, Vitali Mykolenko, Vitaliy Buyalskiy, Benjamin Verbic (69.Artem
Besedin), Oleksandr Andrievsky (46.Carlos de Pena), Viktor Tsygankov,
Volodymyr Shepelev (83.Fran Sol), Gerson Rodrigues. Trainer:
Aleksandr Khatskevich.
Club Brugge: Simon Mignolet, Eduard Sobol, Clinton Mata, Simon Deli,
Brandon Mechele, Ruud Vormer, Mats Rits, Hans Vanaken, Percy Tau,
David Okereke (81.Loïs Openda), Emmanuel Dennis Bonaventure
(52.Krépin Diatta). Trainer: Philippe Clement.
Goals: 6' Vitaliy Buyalskiy 1-0, 38' Simon Deli 1-1, 50' Volodymyr
Shepelev 2-1, 88' Ruud Vormer 2-2, 90+3' Brandon Mechele 3-2 (own
goal), 90+5' Loïs Openda 3-3.
Sent off: 82' Mykyta Burda, 84' Percy Tau.

07.08.2019. Stadion FK Krasnodar, Krasnodar
Referee: Tobias Stieler (GER); Attendance: 38,874
FK Krasnodar – FC Porto 0-1(0-0)
FK Krasnodar: Matvei Safonov, Aleksandr Martynovich, Sergej Petrov, Uros Spajic, Cristian Ramírez, Ruslan Kambolov (72.Jón Fjóluson), Rémy Cabella, Tonny Vilhena, Wamberto, Younes Namli (66.Magomed Suleymanov), Marcus Berg (62.Ari). Trainer: Sergei Matveev.
FC Porto: Agustín Marchesín, Pepe, Ivan Marcano, Alex Telles, Wilson Manafá, Sérgio Oliveira, Danilo Pereira, Romário Baró (55.Luis Díaz), Tiquinho Soares (74.Zé Luís), Jesús Corona (85.Otavinho), Moussa Marega. Trainer: Sérgio Conceição.
Goal: 89' Sérgio Oliveira 0-1.

07.08.2019. Başaksehir "Fatih Terim" Stadyumu, İstanbul
Referee: Orel Grinfeld (ISR); Attendance: 4,301
İstanbul Başaksehir FK – Olympiacos SFP Peiraiás 0-1(0-0)
İstanbul Başaksehir: Mert Günok, Gaël Clichy, Aurélien Chedjou, Júnior Caiçara, Miguel Vieira, Mahmut Tekdemir (62.Azubuike Okechukwu), Edin Visca, Irfan Kahveci, Robinho, Fredrik Gulbrandsen (69.Eljero Elia), Enzo Crivelli (81.Demba Ba). Trainer: Okan Buruk.
Olympiacos Peiraiás: José Sá, Omar Elabdellaoui, Rúben Semedo, Yassine Meriah, Kostas Tsimikas, Mathieu Valbuena (73.Mady Camara), Guilherme, Andreas Bouchalakis, Daniel Podence, Georgios Masouras (83.Bruno Souza), Guerrero (89.Youssef El-Arabi). Trainer: Pedro Martins.
Goal: 53' Georgios Masouras 0-1.
Sent off: 80' Irfan Kahveci.

07.08.2019. St. Jakob-Park, Basel
Referee: Andreas Ekberg (SWE); Attendance: 20,470
FC Basel – LASK Linz 1-2(0-0)
FC Basel: Jonas Omlin, Silvan Widmer, Éder Álvarez Balanta (76.Kevin Bua), Omar Alderete, Eray Cömert, Blas Riveros, Valentin Stocker (65.Kemal Ademi), Luca Zuffi, Fabian Frei, Ricky van Wolfswinkel, Afimico Pululu (76.Noah Okafor). Trainer: Marcelo Koller.
LASK Linz: Alexander Schlager, Christian Ramsebner (17.Emanuel Pogatetz), Gernot Trauner, Reinhold Ranftl, Philipp Wiesinger, James Holland, Thomas Goiginger (63.Dominik Frieser), Peter Michorl, René Renner, Samuel Tetteh, Klauss (83.Marko Raguz). Trainer: Valérien Ismaël.
Goals: 51' Gernot Trauner 0-1, 82' Klauss 0-2, 87' Luca Zuffi 1-2.

13.08.2019. Estádio do Dragão, Porto
Referee: Marco Guida (ITA); Attendance: 48,520
FC Porto – FK KRASNODAR 2-3(0-3)
FC Porto: Agustín Marchesín, Pepe, Ivan Marcano, Alex Telles, Renzo Saravia (38.Zé Luís), Sérgio Oliveira (49.Mateus Uribe), Danilo Pereira, Shoya Nakajima, Luis Díaz, Jesús Corona (86.Vincent Aboubakar), Moussa Marega. Trainer: Sérgio Conceição.
FK Krasnodar: Matvei Safonov, Aleksandr Martynovich, Sergej Petrov, Uros Spajic, Cristian Ramírez, Ruslan Kambolov, Rémy Cabella (80.Dmitriy Stotskiy), Tonny Vilhena, Wamberto, Marcus Berg (73.Ivan Ignatyev), Magomed Suleymanov (65.Jón Fjóluson). Trainer: Sergei Matveev.
Goals: 3' Tonny Vilhena 0-1, 13', 34' Magomed Suleymanov 0-2, 0-3, 57' Zé Luís 1-3, 76' Luis Díaz 2-3.

13.08.2019. Stádio „Giórgos Karaïskáki", Peiraiás
Referee: Bobby Madden (SCO); Attendance: 28,521
OLYMPIACOS SFP PEIRAIÁS – İstanbul Başaksehir FK 2-0(0-0)
Olympiacos Peiraiás: José Sá, Omar Elabdellaoui, Rúben Semedo, Yassine Meriah, Kostas Tsimikas, Mathieu Valbuena (82.Mady Camara), Guilherme (89.Leonardo Koutris), Andreas Bouchalakis, Daniel Podence (68.Lazar Randjelovic), Georgios Masouras, Guerrero. Trainer: Pedro Martins.
İstanbul Başaksehir: Mert Günok, Gaël Clichy, Júnior Caiçara, Miguel Vieira, Carlos Ponck, Eljero Elia, Edin Visca, Joseph Attamah (59.Demba Ba), Azubuike Okechukwu, Robinho (46.Arda Turan), Enzo Crivelli (75.Fredrik Gulbrandsen). Trainer: Okan Buruk.
Goals: 55' Rúben Semedo 1-0, 78' Mathieu Valbuena 2-0 (pen).

13.08.2019. Linzer Stadion, Linz
Referee: Aliyar Agayev (AZE); Attendance: 12,966
LASK LINZ – FC Basel 3-1(0-0)
LASK Linz: Alexander Schlager, Emanuel Pogatetz, Gernot Trauner, Reinhold Ranftl, Philipp Wiesinger, James Holland, Thomas Goiginger (90+4.Thomas Sabitzer), Peter Michorl, René Renner, Samuel Tetteh (77.Dominik Frieser), Klauss (87.Marko Raguz). Trainer: Valérien Ismaël.
FC Basel: Jonas Omlin, Silvan Widmer, Éder Álvarez Balanta (86.Afimico Pululu), Omar Alderete, Raoul Petretta, Eray Cömert, Valentin Stocker, Luca Zuffi (55.Kevin Bua), Fabian Frei, Kemal Ademi, Noah Okafor (64.Samuele Campo). Trainer: Marcelo Koller.
Goals: 59' Reinhold Ranftl 1-0, 80' Kemal Ademi 1-1, 89' Thomas Goiginger 2-1, 90+4' Marko Raguz 3-1.

PLAY-OFFS

CHAMPIONS PATH

20.08.2019. Stadionul "Dr. Constantin Rădulescu", Cluj-Napoca
Referee: Cüneyt Çakir (TUR); Attendance: 15,196
FC CFR 1907 Cluj – SK Slavia Praha 0-1(0-1)
CFR Cluj: Giedrius Arlauskis, Mateo Susic, Camora, Mike Cestor, Andrei Burca, Ciprian Deac, Damjan Djokovic, Mihai Bordeianu (87.Ovidiu Hoban), Luís Aurélio (72.Adrian Paun), George Tucudean (46.Mário Rondón), Billel Omrani. Trainer: Dan Petrescu.
Slavia Praha: Ondrej Kolár, Ondrej Kúdela, Jan Boril, Vladimír Coufal, David Hovorka, Nicolae Stanciu, Lukás Masopust (84.Tomás Holes), Peter Olayinka, Tomás Soucek, Ibrahim Traoré (64.Alex Král), Mick van Buren (68.Milan Skoda). Trainer: Jindrich Trpisovsky.
Goal: 28' Lukás Masopust 0-1.

20.08.2019. Neo GSP Stadium, Nicosia
Referee: Antonio Miguel Mateu Lahoz (ESP); Attendance: 14,549
APOEL Nicosia FC – AFC Ajax Amsterdam 0-0
APOEL Nicosia: Vid Belec, Giorgios Merkis, Joãozinho (82.André Vidigal), Nicholas Ioannou, Dragan Mihajlovic, Savvas Gentsoglou, Uros Matic, Lucas Souza, Musa Al-Taamari, Roman Bezjak (68.Antonio Jakolis), Andrija Pavlovic (68.Linus Hallenius). Trainer: Thomas Doll.
AFC Ajax: André Onana, Daley Blind, Nicolás Tagliafico, Joël Veltman, Noussair Mazraoui, Lisandro Martínez, Hakim Ziyech, Razvan Marin (62.Sergiño Dest), Donny van de Beek, Dusan Tadic, David Neres (72.Klaas Jan Huntelaar). Trainer: Erik ten Hag.
Sent off: 80' Noussair Mazraoui.

28.08.2019. Stadion Sinobo, Praha
Referee: Gianluca Rocchi (ITA); Attendance: 18,562
SK SLAVIA PRAHA – FC CFR 1907 Cluj 1-0(0-0)
Slavia Praha: Ondrej Kolár, Ondrej Kúdela, Jan Boril, Vladimír Coufal, David Hovorka, Nicolae Stanciu (90.Michal Frydrych), Lukás Masopust (84.Ibrahim Traoré), Peter Olayinka, Tomás Soucek, Alex Král, Milan Skoda (79.Abdulla Yusuf Helal). Trainer: Jindrich Trpisovsky.
CFR Cluj: Giedrius Arlauskis, Andrei Muresan, Mateo Susic, Camora, Andrei Burca, Ciprian Deac (70.Ovidiu Hoban), Damjan Djokovic, Mihai Bordeianu, Luís Aurélio (64.Adrian Paun), Mário Rondón (69.George Tucudean), Billel Omrani. Trainer: Dan Petrescu.
Goal: 66' Jan Boril 1-0.

28.08.2019. „Johan Cruijff" ArenA, Amsterdam
Referee: Felix Zwayer (GER); Attendance: 51,645
AFC AJAX AMSTERDAM – APOEL Nicosia FC 2-0(1-0)
AFC Ajax: André Onana, Daley Blind, Nicolás Tagliafico, Joël Veltman, Edson Álvarez (89.Razvan Marin), Lisandro Martínez, Sergiño Dest, Hakim Ziyech (87.Dani de Wit), Klaas Jan Huntelaar, Dusan Tadic, David Neres. Trainer: Erik ten Hag.
APOEL Nicosia: Vid Belec, Giorgios Merkis, Joãozinho, Nicholas Ioannou, Dragan Mihajlovic, Antonio Jakolis (64.Tomás De Vincenti), Uros Matic (78.Linus Hallenius), Lucas Souza, Musa Al-Taamari (72.André Vidigal), Roman Bezjak, Andrija Pavlovic. Trainer: Thomas Doll.
Goals: 43' Edson Álvarez 1-0, 80' Dusan Tadic 2-0.

21.08.2019. Stadion Maksimir, Zagreb
Referee: Daniele Orsato (ITA) ; Attendance: 23,859
GNK Dinamo Zagreb – Rosenborg BK Trondheim 2-0(2-0)
Dinamo Zagreb: Dominik Livakovic, Marin Leovac, Emir Dilaver, Petar Stojanovic, Dino Peric, Arijan Ademi, Nikola Moro, Daniel Olmo, Mislav Orsic (84.Iyayi Atiemwen), Izet Hajrovic (64.Amer Gojak), Bruno Petkovic (87.Mario Gavranovic). Trainer: Nenad Bjelica.
Rosenborg BK: André Hansen, Tore Reginiussen, Even Hovland, Vegar Hedenstad, Birger Meling, Mike Jensen, Anders Konradsen, Marius Lundemo, Alexander Søderlund, Samuel Adegbenro, Babajide Akintola (84.Pål Helland). Trainer: Eirik Horneland.
Goals: 8' Bruno Petkovic 1-0 (pen), 28' Mislav Orsic 2-0.

21.08.2019. Wankdorf Stadion, Bern
Referee: Danny Desmond Makkelie (NED); Attendance: 26,375
BSC Young Boys – FK Crvena Zvezda Beograd 2-2(1-1)
BSC Young Boys: David von Ballmoos, Fabian Lustenberger, Ulisses Garcia (67.Saidy Janko), Jordan Lotomba, Cedric Zesiger, Christopher Martins Pereira, Nicolas Moumi Ngamaleu, Vincent Sierro (57.Christian Fassnacht), Michel Aebischer (73.Guillaume Hoarau), Jean Pierre Nsamé, Roger Assalé. Trainer: Gerardo Seoane.
Crvena Zvezda: Milan Borjan, Milan Rodic, Milos Degenek, Marko Gobeljic, Radovan Pankov, Marko Marin, Cañas, Mirko Ivanic, Mateo García (55.Jander), Richmond Boakye (77.Tómané), Aleksa Vukanovic (85.Njego Petrovic). Trainer: Vladan Milojevic.
Goals: 7' Roger Assalé 1-0, 18' Milos Degenek 1-1, 46' Mateo García 1-2, 76' Guillaume Hoarau 2-2 (pen).

27.08.2019. Lerkendal Stadion, Trondheim
Referee: Ovidiu Alin Haţegan (ROU); Attendance: 18,173
Rosenborg BK Trondheim – GNK DINAMO ZAGREB 1-1(1-0)
Rosenborg BK: André Hansen, Tore Reginiussen, Even Hovland, Vegar Hedenstad (84.Emil Ceide), Birger Meling, Mike Jensen, Anders Konradsen, Marius Lundemo (74.Anders Trondsen), Alexander Søderlund, Samuel Adegbenro, Babajide Akintola (74.Yann-Erik De Lanlay). Trainer: Eirik Horneland.
Dinamo Zagreb: Dominik Livakovic, Marin Leovac, Emir Dilaver, Petar Stojanovic, Dino Peric, Arijan Ademi, Nikola Moro, Daniel Olmo (90+2.Mario Gavranovic), Mislav Orsic (81.Iyayi Atiemwen), Izet Hajrovic (66.Amer Gojak), Bruno Petkovic. Trainer: Nenad Bjelica.
Goals: 11' Babajide Akintola 1-0, 71' Amer Gojak 1-1.

27.08.2019. Stadion „Rajko Mitić", Beograd
Referee: Anthony Taylor (ENG); Attendance: 47,487
FK CRVENA ZVEZDA BEOGRAD – BSC Young Boys 1-1(0-0)
Crvena Zvezda: Milan Borjan, Nemanja Milunovic, Milan Rodic, Milos Degenek, Marko Gobeljic, Marko Marin, Cañas, Dusan Jovancic, Mateo García (69.Mohamed Ben Nabouhane), Richmond Boakye (62.Tó Mané), Aleksa Vukanovic (83.Mirko Ivanic). Trainer: Vladan Milojevic.
BSC Young Boys: David von Ballmoos, Fabian Lustenberger, Frederik Sørensen, Saidy Janko, Jordan Lotomba, Cédric Zesiger (52.Christian Fassnacht), Nicolas Moumi Ngamaleu, Vincent Sierro (65.Miralem Sulejmani), Michel Aebischer, Jean-Pierre Nsamé, Roger Assalé (65.Guillaume Hoarau). Trainer: Gerardo Seoane.
Goals: 59' Aleksa Vukanovic 1-0, 82' Mohamed Ben Nabouhane 1-1 (own goal)
Sent off: 90+6' Tó Mané.

LEAGUE PATH

20.08.2019. Linzer Stadion, Linz
Referee: Szymon Marciniak (POL); Attendance: 12,637
LASK Linz – Club Brugge KV 0-1(0-1)
LASK Linz: Alexander Schlager, Emanuel Pogatetz, Gernot Trauner, Reinhold Ranftl, Philipp Wiesinger, James Holland, Thomas Goiginger (83.Yusuf Otubanjo), Peter Michorl, René Renner (67.Marko Raguz), Samuel Tetteh (53.Dominik Frieser), Klauss. Trainer: Valérien Ismaël.
Club Brugge: Simon Mignolet, Eduard Sobol (66.Federico Ricca), Clinton Mata, Matej Mitrovic, Simon Deli, Ruud Vormer, Mats Rits, Hans Vanaken, Loïs Openda (74.Kaveh Rezaei), David Okereke (89.Krépin Diatta), Emmanuel Dennis Bonaventure. Trainer: Philippe Clement.
Goal: 10' Hans Vanaken 0-1 (pen).

21.08.2019. Stádio „Giórgos Karaïskáki", Peiraiás
Referee: Carlos del Cerro Grande (ESP); Attendance: 29,132
Olympiacos SFP Peiraiás – FK Krasnodar 4-0(1-0)
Olympiacos Peiraiás: José Sá, Omar Elabdellaoui, Rúben Semedo, Yassine Meriah, Kostas Tsimikas, Mathieu Valbuena (87.Mady Camara), Guilherme, Andreas Bouchalakis, Daniel Podence (90+2.Vasilis Torosidis), Georgios Masouras (76.Lazar Randjelovic), Guerrero. Trainer: Pedro Martins.
FK Krasnodar: Matvei Safonov, Jón Fjóluson, Sergej Petrov, Uros Spajic, Cristian Ramírez, Ruslan Kambolov, Rémy Cabella (26.Kristoffer Olsson), Tonny Vilhena, Wamberto, Younes Namli (59.Magomed Suleymanov), Marcus Berg (69.Ivan Ignatyev). Trainer: Sergei Matveev.
Goals: 30' Geurrero 1-0, 78', 85' Lazar Randjelovic 2-0, 3-0, 89' Daniel Podence 4-0.

28.08.2019. „Jan Breydel" Stadion, Brugge
Referee: Dr. Felix Brych (GER); Attendance: 25,319
CLUB BRUGGE KV – LASK Linz 2-1(0-0)
Club Brugge: Simon Mignolet, Clinton Mata, Matej Mitrovic, Simon Deli, Federico Ricca, Ruud Vormer, Mats Rits, Hans Vanaken, Loïs Openda (46.Percy Tau), David Okereke (88.Emmanuel Dennis Bonaventure), Krépin Diatta. Trainer: Philippe Clement.
LASK Linz: Alexander Schlager, Emanuel Pogatetz, Gernot Trauner, Reinhold Ranftl, Philipp Wiesinger, James Holland (90.Yusuf Otubanjo), Thomas Goiginger (72.Marko Raguz), Peter Michorl, René Renner, Dominik Frieser (62.Samuel Tetteh), Klauss. Trainer: Valérien Ismaël.
Goals: 70' Hans Vanaken 1-0, 74' Klauss 1-1 (pen), 89' Emmanuel Dennis Bonaventure 2-1.
Sent off: 81' Gernot Trauner.

27.08.2019. Stadion FK Krasnodar, Krasnodar
Referee: Damir Skomina (SVN); Attendance: 34,627
FK Krasnodar – OLYMPIACOS SFP PEIRAIÁS 1-2(1-1)
FK Krasnodar: Stanislav Kritsyuk, Jón Fjóluson, Sergej Petrov (56.Dmitriy Skopintsev), Uros Spajic, Dmitriy Stotskiy, Tonny Vilhena, Kristoffer Olsson, Wamberto, Daniil Utkin (67.Ivan Ignatyev), Marcus Berg, Magomed Suleymanov (32.Younes Namli). Trainer: Sergei Matveev.
Olympiacos Peiraiás: José Sá, Omar Elabdellaoui, Rúben Semedo (65.Pape Cissé), Yassine Meriah, Kostas Tsimikas, Mathieu Valbuena, Guilherme, Andreas Bouchalakis, Daniel Podence (84.Mady Camara), Georgios Masouras, Youssef El-Arabi (73.El Arbi Soudani). Trainer: Pedro Martins.
Goals: 10' Daniil Utkin 1-0, 11', 48' Youssef El-Arabi 1-1, 1-2.

Please note: Winners and runners-up of each group were qualified for the Round of 16. Teams ranked third were qualified for the UEFA Europa League.

GROUP A	1.	**Paris Saint-Germain FC**	6	5	1	0	17 - 2	16
	2.	**Real Madrid CF**	6	3	2	1	14 - 8	11
	3.	*Club Brugge KV*	6	0	3	3	4 - 12	3
	4.	Galatasaray SK İstanbul	6	0	2	4	1 - 14	2

18.09.2019. „Jan Breydel" Stadion, Brugge:
Referee: Slavko Vinčić (SVN); Attendance: 26,616
Club Brugge KV – Galatasaray SK İstanbul SK İstanbul 0-0
Club Brugge: Simon Mignolet, Clinton Mata, Matej Mitrovic, Simon Deli, Federico Ricca, Ruud Vormer, Mats Rits (86.Éder Balanta), Hans Vanaken, David Okereke (60.Loïs Openda), Emmanuel Dennis Bonaventure (73.Mbaye Diagne), Krépin Diatta. Trainer: Philippe Clement.
Galatasaray: Fernando Muslera, Mariano (90.Sener Özbayrakli), Yuto Nagatomo, Marcâo Teixeira, Christian Luyindama, Sofiane Féghouli, Steven N'Zonzi, Mario Lemina (60.Emre Mor), Jean Michaël Seri (90+3.Ryan Donk), Ryan Babel, Radamel Falcao. Trainer: Fatih Terim.

01.10.2019. Estadio „Santiago Bernabéu", Madrid
Referee: Georgi Kabakov (BUL); Attendance: 65,112
Real Madrid CF – Club Brugge KV 2-2(0-2)
Real Madrid: Thibaut Courtois (46.Alphonse Aréola), Sergio Ramos, Nacho (46.Marcelo), Dani Carvajal, Raphaël Varane, Luka Modric, Toni Kroos, Casemiro, Lucas Vázquez (67.Vinícius Júnior), Karim Benzema, Eden Hazard. Trainer: Zinédine Zidane.
Club Brugge: Simon Mignolet, Eduard Sobol, Clinton Mata, Simon Deli, Brandon Mechele, Ruud Vormer, Mats Rits, Hans Vanaken, Percy Tau (90+2.Siebe Schrijvers), Emmanuel Dennis Bonaventure (71.Loïs Openda, 87.Dion Cools), Krépin Diatta. Trainer: Philippe Clement.
Goals: 9', 39' Emmanuel Dennis Bonaventure 0-1, 0-2, 55' Sergio Ramos 1-2, 85' Casemiro 2-2.; Sent off: 84' Ruud Vormer.

22.10.2019. Türk Telekom Stadyumu, İstanbul
Referee: Daniele Orsato (ITA); Attendance: 48,886
Galatasaray SK İstanbul – Real Madrid CF 0-1(0-1)
Galatasaray: Fernando Muslera, Mariano, Yuto Nagatomo, Marcâo Teixeira, Christian Luyindama, Ryan Donk (46.Sofiane Féghouli), Steven N'Zonzi, Younès Belhanda (67.Ömer Bayram), Jean Michaël Seri (77.Emre Mor), Ryan Babel, Florin Andone. Trainer: Fatih Terim.
Real Madrid: Thibaut Courtois, Sergio Ramos, Marcelo, Dani Carvajal, Raphaël Varane, Toni Kroos, Casemiro, Federico Valverde (79.James Rodríguez), Karim Benzema, Eden Hazard (79.Vinícius Júnior), Rodrygo (82.Luka Jovic). Trainer: Zinédine Zidane.
Goal: 18' Toni Kroos 0-1.

06.11.2019. Estadio „Santiago Bernabéu", Madrid
Referee: Felix Zwayer (GER); Attendance: 65,492
Real Madrid CF – Galatasaray SK İstanbul 6-0(4-0)
Real Madrid: Thibaut Courtois, Sergio Ramos, Marcelo (42.Ferland Mendy), Dani Carvajal, Raphaël Varane, Toni Kroos, Casemiro (60.Luka Modric), Federico Valverde, Karim Benzema, Eden Hazard (68.Isco), Rodrygo. Trainer: Zinédine Zidane.
Galatasaray: Fernando Muslera, Mariano, Yuto Nagatomo (88.Adem Büyük), Marcâo Teixeira, Christian Luyindama, Sofiane Féghouli, Steven N'Zonzi (46.Ömer Bayram), Mario Lemina, Jean Michaël Seri, Ryan Babel, Florin Andone (46.Ryan Donk). Trainer: Fatih Terim.
Goals: 4', 7' Rodrygo 1-0, 2-0, 14' Sergio Ramos 3-0 (pen), 45', 81' Karim Benzema 4-0, 5-0, 90+2' Rodrygo 6-0.

26.11.2019. Türk Telekom Stadyumu, İstanbul
Referee: Ivan Kruzliak (SVK); Attendance: 34,500
Galatasaray SK İstanbul – Club Brugge KV 1-1(1-0)
Galatasaray: Fernando Muslera, Mariano, Yuto Nagatomo, Ömer Bayram (80.Selçuk Inan), Marcâo Teixeira, Ryan Donk, Sofiane Féghouli, Younès Belhanda (87.Emre Mor), Mario Lemina, Jean Michaël Seri (90+4.Erencan Yardimci), Adem Büyük. Trainer: Fatih Terim.
Club Brugge: Simon Mignolet, Clinton Mata, Éder Álvarez Balanta, Simon Deli, Brandon Mechele, Federico Ricca, Mats Rits (46.Charles De Ketelaere), Hans Vanaken, Loïs Openda (77.David Okereke), Emmanuel Dennis Bonaventure (58.Siebe Schrijvers), Krépin Diatta. Trainer: Philippe Clement.
Goals: 11' Adem Büyük 1-0, 90+2' Krépin Diatta 1-1.
Sent off: 90+3' Krépin Diatta, Clinton Mata.

18.09.2019. Stade Parc des Princes, Paris:
Referee: Anthony Taylor (ENG); Attendance: 46,361
Paris Saint-Germain FC – Real Madrid CF 3-0(2-0)
Paris Saint-Germain: Keylor Navas, Thiago Silva, Thomas Meunier, Marquinhos (70.Ander Herrera), Juan Bernat, Presnel Kimpembe, Ángel Di María, Marco Verratti, Idrissa Gueye, Pablo Sarabia (89.Abdou Diallo), Mauro Icardi (60.Eric Maxim Choupo-Moting). Trainer: Thomas Tuchel.
Real Madrid: Thibaut Courtois, Dani Carvajal, Raphaël Varane, Ferland Mendy, Éder Militão, Toni Kroos, James Rodríguez (70.Luka Jovic), Casemiro, Karim Benzema, Gareth Bale (79.Vinícius Júnior), Eden Hazard (70.Lucas Vázquez). Trainer: Zinédine Zidane.
Goals: 14' Ángel Di María 1-0, 33' Ángel Di María 2-0, 90+1' Thomas Meunier 3-0.

01.10.2019. Türk Telekom Stadyumu, İstanbul
Referee: Szymon Marciniak (POL); Attendance: 46,532
Galatasaray SK İstanbul – Paris Saint-Germain FC 0-1(0-0)
Galatasaray: Fernando Muslera, Mariano, Yuto Nagatomo (77.Ömer Bayram), Marcâo Teixeira, Christian Luyindama, Ryan Donk, Steven N'Zonzi, Younès Belhanda (62.Sofiane Féghouli), Jean Michaël Seri, Ryan Babel (64.Florin Andone), Radamel Falcao. Trainer: Fatih Terim.
Paris Saint-Germain: Keylor Navas, Thiago Silva, Thomas Meunier, Marquinhos, Juan Bernat, Presnel Kimpembe, Ángel Di María (83.Ander Herrera), Marco Verratti, Idrissa Gueye, Pablo Sarabia (71.Eric Maxim Choupo-Moting), Mauro Icardi (61.Kylian Mbappé). Trainer: Thomas Tuchel.
Goal: 52' Mauro Icardi 0-1.

22.10.2019. „Jan Breydel" Stadion, Brugge
Referee: Daniel Siebert (GER); Attendance: 26,946
Club Brugge KV – Paris Saint-Germain FC 0-5(0-1)
Club Brugge: Simon Mignolet, Eduard Sobol (80.Éder Álvarez Balanta), Clinton Mata, Simon Deli, Brandon Mechele, Mats Rits, Hans Vanaken, Charles De Ketelaere (57.David Okereke), Percy Tau, Emmanuel Dennis Bonaventure (76.Loïs Openda), Krépin Diatta. Trainer: Philippe Clement.
Paris Saint-Germain: Keylor Navas, Thiago Silva, Thomas Meunier, Marquinhos, Juan Bernat, Presnel Kimpembe, Ángel Di María, Ander Herrera (72.Abdou Diallo), Marco Verratti, Eric Maxim Choupo-Moting (52.Kylian Mbappé), Mauro Icardi (65.Leandro Paredes). Trainer: Thomas Tuchel.
Goals: 7' Mauro Icardi 0-1, 61' Kylian Mbappé 0-2, 63' Mauro Icardi 0-3, 79', 83' Kylian Mbappé 0-4, 0-5.

06.11.2019. Stade Parc des Princes, Paris
Referee: Bobby Madden (SCO); Attendance: 47,418
Paris Saint-Germain FC – Club Brugge KV 1-0(1-0)
Paris Saint-Germain: Keylor Navas, Thiago Silva, Marquinhos, Juan Bernat, Presnel Kimpembe, Colin Dagba, Ángel Di María, Marco Verratti (90.Pablo Sarabia), Idrissa Gueye, Mauro Icardi (72.Edinson Cavani), Kylian Mbappé (83.Julian Draxler). Trainer: Thomas Tuchel.
Club Brugge: Simon Mignolet, Éder Álvarez Balanta, Simon Deli, Brandon Mechele, Federico Ricca, Odilon Kossounou, Mats Rits (86.Charles De Ketelaere), Hans Vanaken, David Okereke (67.Mbaye Diagne), Emmanuel Dennis Bonaventure, Krépin Diatta (77.Siebe Schrijvers). Trainer: Philippe Clement.
Goal: 22' Mauro Icardi 1-0.

26.11.2019. Estadio „Santiago Bernabéu", Madrid
Referee: Artur Manuel Soares Dias (POR); Attendance: 75,534
Real Madrid CF – Paris Saint-Germain FC 2-2(1-0)
Real Madrid: Thibaut Courtois, Sergio Ramos, Marcelo, Dani Carvajal, Raphaël Varane, Toni Kroos, Casemiro, Isco (82.Rodrygo), Federico Valverde (76.Luka Modric), Karim Benzema, Eden Hazard (68.Gareth Bale). Trainer: Zinédine Zidane.
Paris Saint-Germain: Keylor Navas, Thiago Silva, Thomas Meunier, Marquinhos, Juan Bernat, Presnel Kimpembe, Ángel Di María (75.Julian Draxler), Marco Verratti, Idrissa Gueye (46.Neymar), Mauro Icardi (75.Pablo Sarabia), Kylian Mbappé. Trainer: Thomas Tuchel.
Goals: 17', 79' Karim Benzema 1-0, 2-0, 81' Kylian Mbappé 2-1, 83' Pablo Sarabia 2-2.

11.12.2019. „Jan Breydel" Stadion, Brugge
Referee: Tobias Stieler (GER); Attendance: 27,308
Club Brugge KV – Real Madrid CF 1-3(0-0)
Club Brugge: Simon Mignolet, Eduard Sobol, Éder Álvarez Balanta, Simon Deli, Brandon Mechele, Thibault Vlietinck (70.Charles De Ketelaere), Odilon Kossounou, Ruud Vormer, Hans Vanaken, Percy Tau (59.Siebe Schrijvers), Emmanuel Dennis Bonaventure. Trainer: Philippe Clement.
Real Madrid: Alphonse Aréola, Raphaël Varane, Odriozola, Ferland Mendy, Éder Militão, Luka Modric, Casemiro, Isco (84.Federico Valverde), Luka Jovic (77.Karim Benzema), Vinicíus Júnior (73.Brahim Díaz), Rodrygo. Trainer: Zinédine Zidane.
Goals: 53' Rodrygo 0-1, 55' Hans Vanaken 1-1, 64' Vinicíus Júnior 1-2, 90+1' Luka Modric 1-3.

11.12.2019. Stade Parc des Princes, Paris
Referee: István Kovács (ROU); Attendance: 46,509
Paris Saint-Germain FC – Galatarasay 5-0(2-0)
Paris Saint-Germain: Sergio Rico, Layvin Kurzawa, Marquinhos, Juan Bernat (75.Thilo Kehrer), Abdou Diallo, Nianzou Kouassi (75.Marco Verratti), Pablo Sarabia, Leandro Paredes, Neymar, Mauro Icardi (68.Edinson Cavani), Kylian Mbappé. Trainer: Thomas Tuchel.
Galatasaray: Fernando Muslera, Mariano, Yuto Nagatomo, Ömer Bayram, Marcâo Teixeira, Ryan Donk, Steven N'Zonzi (72.Sener Özbayrakli), Younès Belhanda, Mario Lemina, Jean Michaël Seri (41.Selçuk Inan), Emre Mor (62.Radamel Falcao). Trainer: Fatih Terim.
Goals: 32' Mauro Icardi 1-0, 35' Pablo Sarabia 2-0, 46' Neymar 3-0, 63' Kylian Mbappé 4-0, 84' Edinson Cavani 5-0 (pen).

GROUP B	1. **FC Bayern München**	6	6	0	0	24 - 5	18
	2. **Tottenham Hotspur FC London**	6	3	1	2	18 - 14	10
	3. *Olympiacos SFP Peiraiás*	6	1	1	4	8 - 14	4
	4. FK Crvena Zvezda Beograd	6	1	0	5	3 - 20	3

18.09.2019. Stádio „Giórgos Karaïskáki", Peiraiás
Referee: Gianluca Rocchi (ITA); Attendance: 31,001
Olympiacos SFP Peiraiás – Tottenham Hotspur FC London 2-2(1-2)
Olympiacos Peiraiás: José Sá, Omar Elabdellaoui, Rúben Semedo, Yassine Meriah, Kostas Tsimikas, Mathieu Valbuena (69.Yassine Benzia), Guilherme, Andreas Bouchalakis, Daniel Podence, Georgios Masouras (78.Lazar Randjelovic), Guerrero (89.Youssef El-Arbi). Trainer: Pedro Martins.
Tottenham Hotspur: Hugo Lloris, Jan Vertonghen, Toby Alderweireld, Ben Davies, Davinson Sánchez, Christian Eriksen, Lucas Moura (76.Érik Lamela), Dele Alli (73.Son Heung-Min), Harry Winks, Tanguy NDombèlé (62.Moussa Sissoko), Harry Kane. Trainer: Mauricio Pochettino.
Goals: 26' Harry Kane 0-1 (pen), 30' Lucas Moura 0-2, 44' Daniel Podence 1-2, 54' Mathieu Valbuena 2-2 (pen).

18.09.2019. Allianz Arena, München
Referee: Bobby Madden (SCO); Attendance: 70,000
FC Bayern München – FK Crvena Zvezda Beograd 3-0(1-0)
Bayern München: Manuel Neuer, Niklas Süle, Joshua Kimmich, Lucas Hernández, Benjamin Pavard, Ivan Perisic (66.Serge Gnabry), Thiago Alcântara, Philippe Coutinho (83.Thomas Müller), Corentin Tolisso (65.Javi Martínez), Robert Lewandowski, Kingsley Coman. Trainer: Niko Kovac.
Crvena Zvezda: Milan Borjan, Nemanja Milunovic, Jander, Milos Degenek, Marko Gobeljic, Marko Marin, Rajiv van La Parra, Cañas, Dusan Jovancic (62.Milos Vulic), Mateo García (83.Aleksa Vukanovic), Milan Pavkov (70.Richmond Boakye). Trainer: Vladan Milojevic.
Goals: 34' Kingsley Coman 1-0, 80' Robert Lewandowski 2-0, 90+1' Thomas Müller 3-0.

01.10.2019. Stadion „Rajko Mitić", Beograd
Referee: Benoît Bastien (FRA); Attendance: 43,291
FK Crvena Zvezda Beograd – Olympiacos SFP Peiraiás 3-1(0-1)
Crvena Zvezda: Milan Borjan, Nemanja Milunovic, Milan Rodic, Milos Degenek, Marko Gobeljic, Marko Marin, Rajiv van La Parra (61.Richmond Boakye), Cañas (73.Njegos Petrovic), Dusan Jovancic (55.Milos Vulic), Mateo García, Tó Mané. Trainer: Vladan Milojevic.
Olympiacos Peiraiás: José Sá, Vasilios Torosidis, Rúben Semedo, Yassine Meriah, Kostas Tsimikas, Andreas Bouchalakis, Georgios Masouras (79.Omar Elabdellaoui), Mohamed Mady Camara (89.Youssef El-Arbi), Guerrero, Yassine Benzia, Maximiliano Lovera (61.Daniel Podence). Trainer: Pedro Martins.
Goals: 37' Rúben Semedo 0-1, 62' Milos Vulic 1-1, 87' Nemanja Milunovic 2-1, 90' Richmond Boakye 3-1.
Sent off: 57' Yassine Benzia.

01.10.2019. Tottenham Hotspur Stadium, London
Referee: Clément Turpin (FRA); Attendance: 60,127
Tottenham Hotspur FC London – FC Bayern München 2-7(1-2)
Tottenham Hotspur: Hugo Lloris, Jan Vertonghen, Danny Rose, Toby Alderweireld, Serge Aurier, Moussa Sissoko, Dele Alli (71.Lucas Moura), Harry Winks (81.Érik Lamela), Tanguy NDombèlé (64.Christian Eriksen), Son Heung-Min, Harry Kane. Trainer: Mauricio Pochettino.
Bayern München: Manuel Neuer, Jérôme Boateng (72.Javi Martínez), David Alaba (46.Thiago Alcântara), Niklas Süle, Joshua Kimmich, Benjamin Pavard, Philippe Coutinho, Serge Gnabry, Corentin Tolisso, Robert Lewandowski, Kingsley Coman (71.Ivan Perisic). Trainer: Niko Kovac.
Goals: 12' Son Heung-Min 1-0, 15' Joshua Kimmich 1-1, 45' Robert Lewandowski 1-2, 53', 55' Serge Gnabry 1-3, 1-4, 61' Harry Kane 2-4 (pen), 83' Serge Gnabry 2-5, 87' Robert Lewandowski 2-6, 88' Serge Gnabry 2-7.

22.10.2019. Tottenham Hotspur Stadium, London
Referee: Marco Guida (ITA); Attendance: 51,743
Tottenham Hotspur FC London – FK Crvena Zvezda Beograd 5-0(3-0)
Tottenham Hotspur: Paulo Gazzaniga, Jan Vertonghen (73.Juan Foyth), Serge Aurier, Ben Davies, Davinson Sánchez, Moussa Sissoko, Érik Lamela, Dele Alli (79.Giovani Lo Celso), Tanguy NDombèlé, Son Heung-Min (68.Eric Dier), Harry Kane. Trainer: Mauricio Pochettino.
Crvena Zvezda: Milan Borjan, Nemanja Milunovic, Milan Rodic, Milos Degenek, Marko Gobeljic, Marko Marin, Rajiv van La Parra (82.Aleksa Vukanovic), Cañas (62.Njegos Petrovic), Milos Vulic, Mateo García, Tó Mané (62.Milan Pavkov). Trainer: Vladan Milojevic.
Goals: 9' Harry Kane 1-0, 16', 44' Son Heung-Min 2-0, 3-0, 57' Érik Lamela 4-0, 72' Harry Kane 5-0.

22.10.2019. Stádio „Giórgos Karaïskáki", Peiraiás
Referee: Danny Desmond Makkelie (NED); Attendance: 31,670.
Olympiacos SFP Peiraiás – FC Bayern München 2-3(1-1)
Olympiacos Peiraiás: José Sá, Omar Elabdellaoui, Rúben Semedo, Yassine Meriah, Kostas Tsimikas, Guilherme, Andreas Bouchalakis (69.Maximiliano Lovera), Daniel Podence, Georgios Masouras (78.Guerrero), Mohamed Mady Camara (88.Lazar Randjelovic), Youssef El-Arbi. Trainer: Pedro Martins.
Bayern München: Manuel Neuer, David Alaba, Joshua Kimmich, Lucas Hernández (59.Jérôme Boateng), Benjamin Pavard, Javi Martínez (46.Corentin Tolisso), Thiago Alcântara, Philippe Coutinho, Serge Gnabry, Thomas Müller (86.Ivan Perisic), Robert Lewandowski. Trainer: Niko Kovac.
Goals: 23' Youssef El-Arbi 1-0, 34', 62' Robert Lewandowski 1-1, 1-2, 75' Corentin Tolisso 1-3, 79' Guilherme 2-3.

06.11.2019. Allianz Arena, München
Referee: Pawel Raczkowski (POL); Attendance: 63,646.
FC Bayern München – Olympiacos SFP Peiraiás 2-0(0-0)
Bayern München: Manuel Neuer, David Alaba, Joshua Kimmich, Benjamin Pavard, Javi Martínez, Leon Goretzka (82.Corentin Tolisso), Serge Gnabry (88.Ivan Perisic), Alphonso Davies, Thomas Müller, Robert Lewandowski, Kingsley Coman (90+1.Philippe Coutinho). Trainer: Hansi Flick.
Olympiacos Peiraiás: José Sá, Omar Elabdellaoui, Rúben Semedo, Yassine Meriah, Kostas Tsimikas, Guilherme, Andreas Bouchalakis (71.Mathieu Valbuena), Daniel Podence (80.Youssef El-Arbi), Lazar Randjelovic (61.Georgios Masouras), Mohamed Mady Camara, Guerrero. Trainer: Pedro Martins.
Goals: 69' Robert Lewandowski 1-0, 89' Ivan Perisic 2-0.

26.11.2019. Tottenham Hotspur Stadium, London
Referee: Georgi Kabakov (BUL); Attendance: 57,024.
Tottenham Hotspur FC London – Olympiacos SFP Peiraiás 4-2(1-2)
Tottenham Hotspur: Paulo Gazzaniga, Danny Rose, Toby Alderweireld, Serge Aurier, Davinson Sánchez, Lucas Moura (61.Moussa Sissoko), Dele Alli (83.Tanguy NDombèlé), Eric Dier (29.Christian Eriksen), Harry Winks, Son Heung-Min, Harry Kane. Trainer: José Mourinho.
Olympiacos Peiraiás: José Sá, Omar Elabdellaoui, Rúben Semedo, Yassine Meriah, Kostas Tsimikas, Guilherme, Andreas Bouchalakis (74.Mathieu Valbuena), Daniel Podence (79.Lazar Randjelovic), Georgios Masouras, Mohamed Mady Camara, Youssef El-Arbi (85.Guerrero). Trainer: Pedro Martins.
Goals: 6' Youssef El-Arbi 0-1, 19' Rúben Semedo 0-2, 45+1' Dele Alli 1-2, 50' Harry Kane 2-2, 73' Serge Aurier 3-2, 77' Harry Kane 4-2.

11.12.2019. Stádio „Giórgos Karaïskáki", Peiraiás
Referee: Daniele Orsato (ITA); Attendance: 31,898.
Olympiacos SFP Peiraiás – FK Crvena Zvezda Beograd 1-0(0-0)
Olympiacos Peiraiás: José Sá, Omar Elabdellaoui, Rúben Semedo, Yassine Meriah, Kostas Tsimikas, Guilherme, Andreas Bouchalakis, Daniel Podence, Georgios Masouras (71.Maximiliano Lovera), Mohamed Mady Camara (61.Guerrero), Youssef El-Arbi (90.Yassine Benzia). Trainer: Pedro Martins.
Crvena Zvezda: Milan Borjan, Nemanja Milunovic, Milan Rodic (82.Jander), Milos Degenek, Marko Gobeljic, Marko Marin, Mirko Ivanic, Mateo García, Njegos Petrovic, Tó Mané (58.Rajiv van La Parra), Aleksa Vukanovic (65.Richmond Boakye). Trainer: Vladan Milojevic.
Goal: 87' Youssef El-Arbi 1-0 (pen).

06.11.2019. Stadion „Rajko Mitić", Beograd
Referee: Carlos del Cerro Grande (ESP); Attendance: 42,381.
FK Crvena Zvezda Beograd – Tottenham Hotspur FC London 0-4(0-1)
Crvena Zvezda: Milan Borjan, Nemanja Milunovic, Milan Rodic, Milos Degenek, Marko Gobeljic (46.Jander), Marko Marin, Rajiv van La Parra, Dusan Jovancic (62.Cañas), Mateo García (68.Richmond Boakye), Njegos Petrovic, Milan Pavkov. Trainer: Vladan Milojevic.
Tottenham Hotspur: Paulo Gazzaniga, Danny Rose, Davinson Sánchez, Juan Foyth, Moussa Sissoko, Dele Alli (62.Christian Eriksen), Eric Dier, Tanguy NDombèlé, Giovani Lo Celso (86.Oliver Skipp), Son Heung-Min (75.Ryan Sessegnon), Harry Kane. Trainer: Mauricio Pochettino.
Goals: 34' Giovani Lo Celso 0-1, 57', 61' Son Heung-Min 0-2, 0-3, 85' Christian Eriksen 0-4.

26.11.2019. Stadion „Rajko Mitić", Beograd
Referee: Björn Kuipers (NED); Attendance: 44,118.
FK Crvena Zvezda Beograd – FC Bayern München 0-6(0-1)
Crvena Zvezda: Milan Borjan, Nemanja Milunovic, Milan Rodic, Milos Degenek, Marko Gobeljic, Marko Marin, Cañas (61.Milos Vulic), Mateo García (69.Radovan Pankov), Njegos Petrovic (76.Mirko Ivanic), Richmond Boakye, Aleksa Vukanovic. Trainer: Vladan Milojevic.
Bayern München: Manuel Neuer, Jérôme Boateng, Benjamin Pavard, Javi Martínez (68.Joshua Kimmich), Thiago Alcântara, Philippe Coutinho (60.Ivan Perisic), Leon Goretzka, Corentin Tolisso, Alphonso Davies, Robert Lewandowski (77.Thomas Müller), Kingsley Coman. Trainer: Hansi Flick.
Goals: 14' Leon Goretzka 0-1, 53', 60', 64', 68' Robert Lewandowski 0-2 (pen), 0-3, 0-4, 0-5, 89' Corentin Tolisso 0-6.

11.12.2019. Allianz Arena, München
Referee: Gianluca Rocchi (ITA); Attendance: 66,353.
FC Bayern München – Tottenham Hotspur FC London 3-1(2-1)
Bayern München: Manuel Neuer, Jérôme Boateng, Joshua Kimmich, Benjamin Pavard, Javi Martínez (87.Leon Goretzka), Ivan Perisic (86.Joshua Zirkzee), Thiago Alcântara, Philippe Coutinho, Serge Gnabry, Alphonso Davies, Kingsley Coman (27.Thomas Müller). Trainer: Hansi Flick.
Tottenham Hotspur: Paulo Gazzaniga, Danny Rose, Toby Alderweireld, Kyle Walker-Peters, Juan Foyth, Moussa Sissoko, Christian Eriksen, Lucas Moura (65.Son Heung-Min), Eric Dier (81.Victor Wanyama), Giovani Lo Celso (65.Oliver Skipp), Ryan Sessegnon. Trainer: José Mourinho. Goals: 14' Kingsley Coman 1-0, 20' Ryan Sessegnon 1-1, 45' Thomas Müller 2-1, 64' Philippe Coutinho 3-1.

GROUP C								
1. **Manchester City FC**	6	4	2	0	16	-	4	14
2. **Atalanta Bergamasca Calcio**	6	2	1	3	8	-	12	7
3. *FK Shakhtar Donetsk*	6	1	3	2	8	-	13	6
4. GNK Dinamo Zagreb	6	1	2	3	10	-	13	5

18.09.2019. Oblasny SportKomplex Metalist, Kharkiv
Referee: Artur Manuel Soares Dias (POR); Attendance: 36,675
FK Shakhtar Donetsk – Manchester City FC 0-3(0-2)
Shakhtar Donetsk: Andriy Pyatov, Sergiy Krivtsov, Ismaily, Mykola Matvienko, Marlos, Taras Stepanenko, Taison, Alan Patrick (74.Marcos Antônio), Sergiy Bolbat, Manor Solomon (46.Yevhen Konoplyanka), Júnior Moraes (77.Dentinho). Trainer: Luís Castro.
Manchester City: Ederson Moraes, Nicolás Otamendi, Kyle Walker (81.João Cancelo), Oleksandr Zinchenko, Fernandinho, Ilkay Gündogan, Kevin De Bruyne (77.Bernardo Silva), Rodri Hernández (83.Benjamin Mendy), Riyad Mahrez, Raheem Sterling, Gabriel Jesus. Trainer: Pep Guardiola.
Goals: Manchester City FC: 24' Riyad Mahrez 0-1, 38' Ilkay Gündogan 0-2, 76' Gabriel Jesus 0-3.

01.10.2019. Stadio „Giuseppe Meazza", Milano
Referee: Tobias Stieler (GER); Attendance: 26,022
Atalanta Bergamasca Calcio – FK Shakhtar Donetsk 1-2(1-1)
Atalanta Bergamo: Pierluigi Gollini, Andrea Masiello (68.Luis Muriel), Rafael Tolói, José Palomino, Timothy Castagne, Hans Hateboer (57.Robin Gosens), Papu Gómez, Josip Ilicic (57.Ruslan Malinovskiy), Marten van Roon, Mario Pasalic, Duván Zapata. Trainer: Gian Piero Gasperini.
Shakhtar Donetsk: Andriy Pyatov, Sergiy Krivtsov, Ismaily, Mykola Matvienko, Marlos (86.Yevhen Konoplyanka), Taras Stepanenko, Taison, Alan Patrick (69.Manor Solomon), Sergiy Bolbat (90+3.Dodô), Viktor Kovalenko, Júnior Moraes. Trainer: Luís Castro.
Goals: 28' Duván Zapata 1-0, 41' Júnior Moraes 1-1, 90+5' Manor Solomon 1-2.

18.09.2019. Stadion Maksimir, Zagreb
Referee: Jesús Gil Manzano (ESP); Attendance: 28,863
GNK Dinamo Zagreb – Atalanta Bergamasca Calcio 4-0(3-0)
Dinamo Zagreb: Dominik Livakovic, Marin Leovac, Kévin Théophile-Catherine, Emir Dilaver, Petar Stojanovic, Dino Peric, Arijan Ademi, Nikola Moro (73.Amer Gojak), Daniel Olmo, Mislav Orsic (76.Luka Ivanusec), Bruno Petkovic (83.Mario Gavranovic). Trainer: Nenad Bjelica.
Atalanta Bergamo: Pierluigi Gollini, Andrea Masiello (46.Ruslan Malinovskiy), Rafael Tolói, Berat Djimsiti, Hans Hateboer, Robin Gosens, Papu Gómez, Josip Ilicic (88.Musa Barrow), Marten van Roon, Remo Freuler (46.Mario Pasalic), Duván Zapata. Trainer: Gian Piero Gasperini.
Goals: 10' Marin Leovac 1-0, 31', 42', 68' Mislav Orsic 2-0, 3-0, 4-0.

01.10.2019. Etihad Stadium, Manchester
Referee: Serdar Gözübüyük (NED); Attendance: 49,046
Manchester City FC – GNK Dinamo Zagreb 2-0(0-0)
Manchester City: Ederson Moraes, Nicolás Otamendi, João Cancelo, Benjamin Mendy, David Silva (90+1.Phil Foden), Fernandinho, Ilkay Gündogan, Bernardo Silva (56.Raheem Sterling), Rodri Hernández, Kun Agüero (89.Gabriel Jesus), Riyad Mahrez. Trainer: Pep Guardiola.
Dinamo Zagreb: Dominik Livakovic, Marin Leovac, Kévin Théophile-Catherine (76.Mario Gavranovic), Emir Dilaver, Petar Stojanovic, Dino Peric, Arijan Ademi, Nikola Moro, Daniel Olmo, Mislav Orsic (62.Amer Gojak), Bruno Petkovic (84.Iyayi Atiemwen). Trainer: Nenad Bjelica.
Goals: 66' Raheem Sterling 1-0, 90+5' Phil Foden 2-0.

22.10.2019. Oblasny SportKomplex Metalist, Kharkiv
Referee: Antonio Miguel Mateu Lahoz (ESP); Attendance: 21,526
FK Shakhtar Donetsk – GNK Dinamo Zagreb 2-2(1-1)
Shakhtar Donetsk: Andriy Pyatov, Sergiy Krivtsov, Ismaily, Mykola Matvienko, Marlos (84.Viktor Kovalenko), Taras Stepanenko, Taison, Yevhen Konoplyanka (66.Manor Solomon), Alan Patrick, Sergiy Bolbat (66.Dodô), Júnior Moraes. Trainer: Luís Castro.
Dinamo Zagreb: Dominik Livakovic, Marin Leovac, Kévin Théophile-Catherine, Emir Dilaver, Petar Stojanovic, Dino Peric, Arijan Ademi (68.Amer Gojak), Nikola Moro, Daniel Olmo, Mario Gavranovic (62.Bruno Petkovic), Mislav Orsic (90.Luka Ivanusec). Trainer: Nenad Bjelica.
Goals: 16' Yevhen Konoplyanka 1-0, 25' Daniel Olmo 1-1, 60' Mislav Orsic 1-2 (pen), 75' Dodô (75').

06.11.2019. Stadio „Giuseppe Meazza", Milano
Referee: Aleksei Kulbakov (BLR); Attendance: 34,326
Atalanta Bergamasca Calcio – Manchester City FC 1-1(0-0)
Atalanta Bergamo: Pierluigi Gollini, Rafael Tolói, José Palomino, Berat Djimsiti, Timothy Castagne (90+2.Luis Muriel), Hans Hateboer, Papu Gómez, Josip Ilicic, Marten van Roon, Remo Freuler (84.Ruslan Malinovskiy), Mario Pasalic. Trainer: Gian Piero Gasperini.
Manchester City: Ederson Moraes (46.Claudio Bravo), Nicolás Otamendi, João Cancelo, Benjamin Mendy, Fernandinho, Ilkay Gündogan, Kevin De Bruyne, Bernardo Silva, Riyad Mahrez (88.Kyle Walker), Raheem Sterling, Gabriel Jesus (73.Kun Agüero). Trainer: Pep Guardiola.
Goals: 7' Raheem Sterling 0-1, 49' Mario Pasalic 1-1.
Sent off: 81' Claudio Bravo.

26.11.2019. Etihad Stadium, Manchester
Referee: Slavko Vinčić (SVN); Attendance: 52,020
Manchester City FC – FK Shakhtar Donetsk 1-1(0-0)
Manchester City: Ederson Moraes, Nicolás Otamendi, João Cancelo, José Angeliño, Fernandinho, Ilkay Gündogan, Kevin De Bruyne (70.David Silva), Bernardo Silva, Rodri Hernández (76.Phil Foden), Raheem Sterling, Gabriel Jesus. Trainer: Pep Guardiola.
Shakhtar Donetsk: Andriy Pyatov, Sergiy Krivtsov, Ismaily, Mykola Matvienko, Dodô, Taras Stepanenko, Yevhen Konoplyanka (65.Manor Solomon), Alan Patrick, Viktor Kovalenko (81.Marcos Antônio), Mateus Martins Tetê, Júnior Moraes (90.Danylo Sikan). Trainer: Luís Castro.
Goals: 56' Ilkay Gündogan 1-0, 69' Manor Solomon 1-1.

11.12.2019. Oblasny SportKomplex Metalist, Kharkiv
Referee: Felix Zwayer (GER); Attendance: 26,536
FK Shakhtar Donetsk – Atalanta Bergamasca Calcio 0-3(0-0)
Shakhtar Donetsk: Andriy Pyatov, Sergiy Krivtsov, Ismaily, Mykola Matvienko, Dodô, Taras Stepanenko, Taison, Alan Patrick, Viktor Kovalenko (71.Manor Solomon), Mateus Martins Tetê (59.Marlos), Júnior Moraes. Trainer: Luís Castro.
Atalanta Bergamo: Pierluigi Gollini, Andrea Masiello (61.Ruslan Malinovskiy), José Palomino, Berat Djimsiti, Timothy Castagne, Robin Gosens, Papu Gómez (90.Hans Hateboer), Marten van Roon, Remo Freuler, Mario Pasalic, Luis Muriel (71.Ibañez). Trainer: Gian Piero Gasperini.
Goals: 66' Timothy Castagne 0-1, 80' Mario Pasalic 0-2, 90+4' Robin Gosens 0-3.
Sent off: 77' Dodô.

22.10.2019. Etihad Stadium, Manchester
Referee: Orel Grinfeld (ISR); Attendance: 49,308
Manchester City FC – Atalanta Bergamasca Calcio 5-1(2-1)
Manchester City: Ederson Moraes, Kyle Walker, Benjamin Mendy (71.João Cancelo), Fernandinho, Ilkay Gündogan, Kevin De Bruyne (67.Nicolás Otamendi), Rodri Hernández (41.John Stones), Phil Foden, Kun Agüero, Riyad Mahrez, Raheem Sterling. Trainer: Pep Guardiola.
Atalanta Bergamo: Pierluigi Gollini, Andrea Masiello (46.Mario Pasalic), Rafael Tolói, Berat Djimsiti, Timothy Castagne, Robin Gosens, Papu Gómez (46.Luis Muriel), Josip Ilicic (72.Hans Hateboer), Marten van Roon, Remo Freuler, Ruslan Malinovskiy. Trainer: Gian Piero Gasperini.
Goals: 28' Ruslan Malinovskiy 0-1 (pen), 34', 38' Kun Agüero 1-1, 2-1 (pen), 58', 64', 69' Raheem Sterling 3-1, 4-1, 5-1.
Sent off: 82' Phil Foden.

06.11.2019. Stadion Maksimir, Zagreb
Referee: Dr. Felix Brych (GER); Attendance: 28,316
GNK Dinamo Zagreb – FK Shakhtar Donetsk 3-3(1-1)
Dinamo Zagreb: Dominik Livakovic, Marin Leovac, Kévin Théophile-Catherine, Emir Dilaver, Petar Stojanovic (72.Luka Ivanusec), Dino Peric, Arijan Ademi, Nikola Moro, Daniel Olmo, Mislav Orsic (77.Marko Djira), Bruno Petkovic (90+1.Damian Kadzior). Trainer: Nenad Bjelica.
Shakhtar Donetsk: Andriy Pyatov, Sergiy Krivtsov, Ismaily, Mykola Matvienko (86.Dentinho), Dodô, Marlos, Taras Stepanenko (90+1.Marcos Antônio), Taison, Alan Patrick (84.Mateus Martins Tetê), Viktor Kovalenko, Júnior Moraes. Trainer: Luís Castro.
Goals: 13' Alan Patrick 0-1, 25' Bruno Petkovic 1-1, 83' Luka Ivanusec 2-1, 89' Arijan Ademi 3-1, 90+3' Júnior Moraes 3-2, 90+8' Mateus Martins Tetê 3-3 (pen).
Sent off: 74' Nikola Moro, 79' Marlos.

26.11.2019. Stadio „Giuseppe Meazza", Milano
Referee: Sergei Karasev (RUS); Attendance: 28,365
Atalanta Bergamasca Calcio – GNK Dinamo Zagreb 2-0(1-0)
Atalanta Bergamo: Pierluigi Gollini, Simon Kjær, Rafael Tolói, José Palomino, Hans Hateboer (65.Timothy Castagne), Robin Gosens, Papu Gómez (90.Ruslan Malinovskiy), Marten van Roon, Remo Freuler, Mario Pasalic, Luis Muriel (61.Josip Ilicic). Trainer: Gian Piero Gasperini.
Dinamo Zagreb: Dominik Livakovic, Marin Leovac, Kévin Théophile-Catherine, Emir Dilaver, Petar Stojanovic (75.Marko Djira), Dino Peric, Arijan Ademi, Daniel Olmo (90+2.Mario Situm), Luka Ivanusec (67.Amer Gojak), Mislav Orsic, Bruno Petkovic. Trainer: Nenad Bjelica.
Goals: 27' Luis Muriel 1-0 (pen), 47' Papu Gómez 2-0.

11.12.2019. Stadion Maksimir, Zagreb
Referee: Carlos del Cerro Grande (ESP); Attendance: 29,385
GNK Dinamo Zagreb – Manchester City FC 1-4(1-1)
Dinamo Zagreb: Dominik Livakovic, Emir Dilaver, François Moubandje, Petar Stojanovic, Arijan Ademi, Amer Gojak (81.Lovro Majer), Nikola Moro, Daniel Olmo, Mislav Orsic (81.Izet Hajrovic), Damian Kadzior (59.Marko Djira), Bruno Petkovic. Trainer: Nenad Bjelica.
Manchester City: Claudio Bravo, Nicolás Otamendi (82.Taylor Harwood-Bellis), João Cancelo, Benjamin Mendy, Eric García, Ilkay Gündogan, Bernardo Silva, Rodri Hernández (73.Raheem Sterling), Phil Foden, Riyad Mahrez, Gabriel Jesus (66.Oleksandr Zinchenko). Trainer: Pep Guardiola.
Goals: 10' Daniel Olmo 1-0, 34', 50', 54' Gabriel Jesus 1-1, 1-2, 1-3, 84' Phil Foden 1-4.

GROUP D								
1. **Juventus FC Torino**	6	5	1	0	12	-	4	16
2. **Club Atlético de Madrid**	6	3	1	2	8	-	5	10
3. *TSV Bayer 04 Leverkusen*	6	2	0	4	5	-	9	6
4. FK Lokomotiv Moskva	6	1	0	5	4	-	11	3

18.09.2019. Estadio Wanda Metropolitano, Madrid
Referee: Danny Desmond Makkelie (NED); Attendance: 66,283
Club Atlético de Madrid – Juventus FC Torino 2-2(0-0)
Atlético Madrid: Jan Oblak, Stefan Savic, Kieran Trippier, José Giménez, Renan Lodi (76.Vitolo), Saúl, Koke, Thomas Lemar (60.Ángel Correa), Thomas Partey (76.Héctor Herrera), Diego Costa, João Félix. Trainer: Diego Simeone.
Juventus: Wojciech Szczesny, Leonardo Bonucci, Danilo, Alex Sandro, Matthijs de Ligt, Blaise Matuidi, Sami Khedira (69.Rodrigo Bentancur), Miralem Pjanic (87.Aaron Ramsey), Juan Cuadrado, Cristiano Ronaldo, Gonzalo Higuaín (80.Paulo Dybala). Trainer: Maurizio Sarri.
Goals: 48' Juan Cuadrado 0-1, 65' Blaise Matuidi 0-2, 70' Stefan Savic 1-2, 90' Héctor Herrera 2-2.

01.10.2019. RZD Arena, Moskva
Referee: Orel Grinfeld (ISR); Attendance: 27,051
FK Lokomotiv Moskva – Club Atlético de Madrid 0-2(0-0)
Lokomotiv Moskva: Guilherme, Vedran Corluka, Benedikt Höwedes, Murilo Cerqueira, Maciej Rybus, Vladislav Ignatyev (80.Éder), Grzegorz Krychowiak, João Mário, Dmitry Barinov, Fyodor Smolov (83.Aleksandr Kolomeytsev), Rifat Zhemaletdinov (33.Brian Idowu). Trainer: Yuriy Semin.
Atlético Madrid: Jan Oblak, Santiago Arias, Felipe Monteiro, José Giménez, Renan Lodi, Saúl, Koke (87.Ángel Correa), Thomas Partey, Diego Costa (77.Thomas Lemar), Álvaro Morata, João Félix (84.Mario Hermoso). Trainer: Diego Simeone.
Goals: 48' João Félix 0-1, 58' Thomas Partey 0-2.

22.10.2019. Estadio Wanda Metropolitano, Madrid
Referee: Artur Manuel Soares Dias (POR); Attendance: 56,776
Club Atlético de Madrid – TSV Bayer 04 Leverkusen 1-0(0-0)
Atlético Madrid: Jan Oblak, Kieran Trippier, Felipe Monteiro, José Giménez (15.Mario Hermoso), Renan Lodi, Héctor Herrera, Saúl, Koke (70.Álvaro Morata), Thomas Partey, Diego Costa, Ángel Correa (62.Thomas Lemar). Trainer: Diego Simeone.
Bayer Leverkusen: Lukás Hrádecky, Sven Bender (90+2.Aleksandar Dragovic), Mitchell Weiser, Jonathan Tah, Lars Bender, Julian Baumgartlinger, Karim Bellarabi, Kerem Demirbay (84.Lucas Alario), Nadiem Amiri, Kai Havertz (76.Paulinho), Kevin Volland. Trainer: Peter Bosz.
Goal: 78' Álvaro Morata 1-0.

06.11.2019. RZD Arena, Moskva
Referee: Ruddy Buquet (FRA); Attendance: 26,861
FK Lokomotiv Moskva – Juventus FC Torino 1-2(1-1)
Lokomotiv Moskva: Guilherme, Vedran Corluka, Benedikt Höwedes, Maciej Rybus, Vladislav Ignatyev, Grzegorz Krychowiak, João Mário (85.Aleksandr Kolomeytsev), Dmitry Barinov, Aleksey Miranchuk, Éder, Rifat Zhemaletdinov (81.Murilo Cerqueira). Trainer: Yuriy Semin.
Juventus: Wojciech Szczesny, Leonardo Bonucci, Danilo, Alex Sandro, Daniele Rugani, Sami Khedira (70.Douglas Costa), Miralem Pjanic, Aaron Ramsey (64.Rodrigo Bentancur), Adrien Rabiot, Cristiano Ronaldo (82.Paulo Dybala), Gonzalo Higuaín. Trainer: Maurizio Sarri.
Goals: 4' Aaron Ramsey 0-1, 12' Aleksey Miranchuk 1-1, 90+3' Douglas Costa 1-2.

26.11.2019. RZD Arena, Moskva
Referee: Michael Oliver (ENG); Attendance: 25,757
FK Lokomotiv Moskva – TSV Bayer 04 Leverkusen 0-2(0-1)
Lokomotiv Moskva: Guilherme, Vedran Corluka, Benedikt Höwedes, Maciej Rybus, Vladislav Ignatyev, Grzegorz Krychowiak, Dmitry Barinov, Aleksey Miranchuk, Anton Miranchuk, Éder (77.Fedor Smolov), Rifat Zhemaletdinov (65.Daniil Kulikov). Trainer: Yuriy Semin.
Bayer Leverkusen: Lukás Hrádecky, Sven Bender, Wendell, Jonathan Tah, Panagiotis Retsos, Charles Aránguiz, Karim Bellarabi (77.Lucas Alario), Kerem Demirbay (90.Lars Bender), Kevin Volland, Leon Bailey (46.Julian Baumgartlinger), Moussa Diaby. Trainer: Peter Bosz.
Goals: 11' Rifat Zhemaletdinov 0-1 (own goal), 54' Sven Bender 0-2.

18.09.2019. BayArena, Leverkusen
Referee: Pawel Raczkowski (POL); Attendance: 26,592
TSV Bayer 04 Leverkusen – FK Lokomotiv Moskva 1-2(1-2)
Bayer Leverkusen: Lukás Hrádecky, Sven Bender, Wendell, Jonathan Tah, Lars Bender, Charles Aránguiz, Julian Baumgartlinger (71.Nadiem Amiri), Karim Bellarabi, Kai Havertz, Kevin Volland, Leon Bailey (46.Lucas Alario). Trainer: Peter Bosz.
Lokomotiv Moskva: Guilherme, Vedran Corluka, Benedikt Höwedes, Murilo Cerqueira, Maciej Rybus, Vladislav Ignatyev, Grzegorz Krychowiak, João Mário (90+3.Brian Idowu), Dmitry Barinov, Fyodor Smolov, Rifat Zhemaletdinov. Trainer: Yuriy Semin.
Goals: 16' Grzegorz Krychowiak 0-1, 25' Benedikt Höwedes 1-1 (own goal), 37' Dmitry Barinov 1-2.

01.10.2019. Allianz Stadium, Torino
Referee: William Collum (SCO); Attendance: 34,525
Juventus FC Torino – TSV Bayer 04 Leverkusen 3-0(1-0)
Juventus: Wojciech Szczesny, Leonardo Bonucci, Alex Sandro, Matthijs de Ligt, Blaise Matuidi, Sami Khedira (74.Rodrigo Bentancur), Miralem Pjanic, Juan Cuadrado, Cristiano Ronaldo, Gonzalo Higuaín (83.Paulo Dybala), Federico Bernardeschi (78.Aaron Ramsey). Trainer: Maurizio Sarri.
Bayer Leverkusen: Lukás Hrádecky, Sven Bender, Mitchell Weiser, Wendell, Jonathan Tah, Charles Aránguiz (80.Daley Sinkgraven), Julian Baumgartlinger, Kerem Demirbay (46.Nadiem Amiri), Kai Havertz, Kevin Volland, Lucas Alario (68.Paulinho). Trainer: Peter Bosz.
Goals: 17' Gonzalo Higuaín 1-0, 62' Federico Bernardeschi 2-0, 89' Cristiano Ronaldo 3-0.

22.10.2019. Allianz Stadium, Torino
Referee: Anastasios Sidiropoulos (GRE); Attendance: 38,547
Juventus FC Torino – FK Lokomotiv Moskva 2-1(0-1)
Juventus: Wojciech Szczesny, Leonardo Bonucci, Alex Sandro, Matthijs de Ligt, Blaise Matuidi (65.Adrien Rabiot), Sami Khedira (48.Gonzalo Higuaín), Miralem Pjanic, Juan Cuadrado, Rodrigo Bentancur, Cristiano Ronaldo, Paulo Dybala (81.Federico Bernardeschi). Trainer: Maurizio Sarri.
Lokomotiv Moskva: Guilherme, Vedran Corluka, Benedikt Höwedes, Brian Idowu, Murilo Cerqueira, Vladislav Ignatyev, Grzegorz Krychowiak (83.Aleksandr Kolomeytsev), João Mário, Dmitry Barinov, Aleksey Miranchuk, Éder. Trainer: Yuriy Semin.
Goals: 30' Aleksey Miranchuk 0-1, 77', 79' Paulo Dybala 1-1, 2-1.

06.11.2019. BayArena, Leverkusen
Referee: Damir Skomina (SVN); Attendance: 28,160
TSV Bayer 04 Leverkusen – Club Atlético de Madrid 2-1(1-0)
Bayer Leverkusen: Lukás Hrádecky, Sven Bender, Mitchell Weiser, Wendell (81.Panagiotis Retsos), Jonathan Tah, Charles Aránguiz (65.Julian Baumgartlinger), Karim Bellarabi, Kerem Demirbay, Nadiem Amiri, Kai Havertz (88.Aleksandar Dragovic), Kevin Volland. Trainer: Peter Bosz.
Atlético Madrid: Jan Oblak, Santiago Arias, Felipe Monteiro, Mario Hermoso, Renan Lodi (52.Thomas Lemar), Saúl, Koke, Thomas Partey, Diego Costa (61.Vitolo), Álvaro Morata, Ángel Correa (70.Héctor Herrera). Trainer: Diego Simeone.
Goals: 41' Thomas Partey 1-0 (own goal), 55' Kevin Volland 2-0, 90+4' Álvaro Morata 2-1.
Sent off: 84' Nadiem Amiri.

26.11.2019. Allianz Stadium, Torino
Referee: Anthony Taylor (ENG); Attendance: 40,486
Juventus FC Torino – Club Atlético de Madrid 1-0(1-0)
Juventus: Wojciech Szczesny, Leonardo Bonucci, Danilo, Mattia De Sciglio, Matthijs de Ligt, Blaise Matuidi, Miralem Pjanic, Aaron Ramsey (63.Federico Bernardeschi), Rodrigo Bentancur (86.Sami Khedira), Cristiano Ronaldo, Paulo Dybala (76.Gonzalo Higuaín). Trainer: Maurizio Sarri.
Atlético Madrid: Jan Oblak, Kieran Trippier, Felipe Monteiro, Mario Hermoso, Renan Lodi (64.Thomas Lemar), Héctor Herrera (60.Ángel Correa), Vitolo (54.João Félix), Saúl, Koke, Thomas Partey, Álvaro Morata. Trainer: Diego Simeone.
Goal: 45+2' Paulo Dybala 1-0.

11.12.2019. Estadio Wanda Metropolitano, Madrid
Referee: Viktor Kassai (HUN); Attendance: 58,426
Club Atlético de Madrid – FK Lokomotiv Moskva 2-0(1-0)
Atlético Madrid: Jan Oblak, Kieran Trippier, Felipe Monteiro, Mario Hermoso, Renan Lodi, Saúl, Koke (73.Thomas Lemar), Thomas Partey, Álvaro Morata, Ángel Correa (68.Héctor Herrera), João Félix (81.Marcos Llorente). Trainer: Diego Simeone.
Lokomotiv Moskva: Anton Kochenkov, Vedran Corluka (69.Stanislav Magkeev), Benedikt Höwedes, Solomon Kverkvelia, Brian Idowu, Murilo Cerqueira, Maciej Rybus, Grzegorz Krychowiak, Aleksey Miranchuk, Éder (75.Fedor Smolov), Rifat Zhemaletdinov. Trainer: Yuriy Semin.
Goals: 17' João Félix 1-0 (pen), 54' Felipe Monteiro 2-0.

11.12.2019. BayArena, Leverkusen
Referee: Benoît Bastien (FRA); Attendance: 29,542
TSV Bayer 04 Leverkusen – Juventus FC Torino 0-2(0-0)
Bayer Leverkusen: Lukás Hrádecky, Sven Bender, Aleksandar Dragovic, Daley Sinkgraven, Lars Bender, Charles Aránguiz, Karim Bellarabi (66.Leon Bailey), Kerem Demirbay (66.Julian Baumgartlinger), Kai Havertz, Lucas Alario (82.Kevin Volland), Moussa Diaby. Trainer: Peter Bosz.
Juventus: Gianluigi Buffon, Danilo, Mattia De Sciglio, Daniele Rugani, Merih Demiral, Miralem Pjanic, Juan Cuadrado (90+3.Simone Muratore), Adrien Rabiot (85.Blaise Matuidi), Cristiano Ronaldo, Gonzalo Higuaín, Federico Bernardeschi (66.Paulo Dybala). Trainer: Maurizio Sarri.
Goals: 75' Cristiano Ronaldo 0-1, 90+2' Gonzalo Higuaín 0-2.

GROUP E							
1. **Liverpool FC**	6	4	1	1	13 - 8	13
2. **SSC Napoli**	6	3	3	0	11 - 4	12
3. *FC Red Bull Salzburg*	6	2	1	3	16 - 13	7
4. KRC Genk	6	0	1	5	5 - 20	1

17.09.2019. Red Bull Arena, Wals-Siezenheim
Referee: Felix Zwayer (GER); Attendance: 29,520
FC Red Bull Salzburg – KRC Genk 6-2(5-1)
Red Bull Salzburg: Cican Stankovic, Andreas Ulmer, André Ramalho, Max Wöber, Rasmus Kristensen (83.Patrick Farkas), Zlatko Junuzovic, Antoine Bernède, Dominik Szoboszlai (62.Masaya Okugawa), Takumi Minamino, Hwang Hee-Chan, Erling Håland (72.Patson Daka). Trainer: Jesse Marsch.
KRC Genk: Gaëtan Coucke, Sebastien Dewaest, Jere Uronen, Jhon Lucumí, Joakim Mæhle, Patrik Hrosovsky, Sander Berge, Bryan Heynen (85.Paul Onuachu), Mbwana Samatta, Dieumerci Ndongala (72.Ianis Hagi), Junya Ito (46.Théo Bongonda). Trainer: Felice Mazzù.
Goals: 2', 34' Erling Håland 1-0, 2-0, 36' Hwang Hee-Chan 3-0, 40' Jhon Lucumí 3-1, 45' Erling Håland 4-1, 45+2' Dominik Szoboszlai 5-1, 52' Mbwana Samatta 5-2, 66' Andreas Ulmer 6-2.

17.09.2019. Stadio San Paolo, Napoli
Referee: Dr. Felix Brych (GER); Attendance: 38,878
SSC Napoli – Liverpool FC 2-0(0-0)
SSC Napoli: Alex Meret, Kostas Manolas, Mário Rui, Kalidou Koulibaly, Giovanni Di Lorenzo, Allan (75.Eljif Elmas), Fabián Ruiz, Dries Mertens, José Callejón, Lorenzo Insigne (66.Piotr Zielinski), Hirving Lozano (69.Llorente). Trainer: Carlo Ancelotti.
Liverpool FC: Adrián, Joel Matip, Virgil van Dijk, Andrew Robertson, Trent Alexander-Arnold, James Milner (66.Georginio Wijnaldum), Jordan Henderson (87.Xherdan Shaqiri), Fabinho, Roberto Firmino, Mohamed Salah, Sadio Mané. Trainer: Jürgen Klopp.
Goals: 82' Dries Mertens 1-0 (pen), 90+2' Llorente 2-0.

02.10.2019. Luminus Arena, Genk
Referee: István Kovács (ROU); Attendance: 19,962
KRC Genk – SSC Napoli 0-0
KRC Genk: Gaëtan Coucke, Jere Uronen, Jhon Lucumí, Carlos Cuesta, Joakim Mæhle, Patrik Hrosovsky, Ianis Hagi (90+2.Bryan Heynen), Sander Berge, Mbwana Samatta, Théo Bongonda (89.Joseph Paintsil), Junya Ito. Trainer: Felice Mazzù.
SSC Napoli: Alex Meret, Kostas Manolas, Mário Rui (33.Kévin Malcuit), Kalidou Koulibaly, Giovanni Di Lorenzo, Allan, Fabián Ruiz, Eljif Elmas (58.Dries Mertens), José Callejón, Arkadiusz Milik (72.Llorente), Hirving Lozano. Trainer: Carlo Ancelotti.

02.10.2019. Anfield Road, Liverpool
Referee: Andreas Ekberg (SWE); Attendance: 52,243
Liverpool FC – FC Red Bull Salzburg 4-3(3-1)
Liverpool FC: Adrián, Virgil van Dijk, Andrew Robertson, Joe Gomez, Trent Alexander-Arnold, Georginio Wijnaldum (64.Divock Origi), Jordan Henderson (62.James Milner), Fabinho, Roberto Firmino, Mohamed Salah (90+1.Naby Keïta), Sadio Mané. Trainer: Jürgen Klopp.
Red Bull Salzburg: Cican Stankovic, Andreas Ulmer, Jérôme Onguéné, Max Wöber, Rasmus Kristensen, Zlatko Junuzovic (78.Majeed Ashimeru), Dominik Szoboszlai (71.Masaya Okugawa), Enock Mwepu, Takumi Minamino, Hwang Hee-Chan, Patson Daka (56.Erling Håland). Trainer: Jesse Marsch.
Goals: 9' Sadio Mané 1-0, 25' Andrew Robertson 2-0, 36' Mohamed Salah 3-0, 39' Hwang Hee-Chan 3-1, 56' Takumi Minamino 3-2, 60' Erling Håland 3-3, 69' Mohamed Salah 4-3.

23.10.2019. Luminus Arena, Genk
Referee: Slavko Vinčić (SVN); Attendance: 19,626
KRC Genk – Liverpool FC 1-4(0-1)
KRC Genk: Gaëtan Coucke, Jere Uronen, Jhon Lucumí, Carlos Cuesta, Joakim Mæhle, Sander Berge, Bryan Heynen, Mbwana Samatta, Paul Onuachu (81.Stephen Odey), Théo Bongonda (66.Dieumerci Ndongala), Junya Ito (87.Ianis Hagi). Trainer: Felice Mazzù.
Liverpool FC: Alisson, Dejan Lovren, Virgil van Dijk, Andrew Robertson (63.Joe Gomez), James Milner, Alex Oxlade-Chamberlain (74.Georginio Wijnaldum), Fabinho, Naby Keïta, Roberto Firmino (80.Divock Origi), Mohamed Salah, Sadio Mané. Trainer: Jürgen Klopp.
Goals: 2', 57' Alex Oxlade-Chamberlain 0-1, 0-2, 77' Sadio Mané 0-3, 87' Mohamed Salah 0-4, 88' Stephen Odey 1-4.

23.10.2019. Red Bull Arena, Wals-Siezenheim
Referee: Clément Turpin (FRA); Attendance: 29,520
FC Red Bull Salzburg – SSC Napoli 2-3(1-1)
Red Bull Salzburg: Cican Stankovic (33.Carlos Coronel), Andreas Ulmer, André Ramalho, Max Wöber, Rasmus Kristensen, Zlatko Junuzovic, Enock Mwepu (89.Sékou Koïta), Takumi Minamino, Hwang Hee-Chan, Patson Daka (68.Majeed Ashimeru), Erling Håland. Trainer: Jesse Marsch.
SSC Napoli: Alex Meret, Kalidou Koulibaly, Kévin Malcuit, Giovanni Di Lorenzo, Sebastiano Luperto, Allan, Piotr Zielinski, Fabián Ruiz, Dries Mertens (76.Llorente), José Callejón (80.Eljif Elmas), Hirving Lozano (65.Lorenzo Insigne). Trainer: Carlo Ancelotti.
Goals: 17' Dries Mertens 0-1, 40' Erling Håland 1-1 (pen), 64' Dries Mertens 1-2, 72' Erling Håland 2-2, 73' Lorenzo Insigne 2-3.

05.11.2019. Anfield Road, Liverpool
Referee: Ivan Kruzliak (SVK); Attendance: 52,611
Liverpool FC – KRC Genk 2-1(1-1)
Liverpool FC: Alisson, Virgil van Dijk, Joe Gomez, Trent Alexander-Arnold, James Milner, Georginio Wijnaldum, Alex Oxlade-Chamberlain (75.Sadio Mané), Fabinho, Naby Keïta (74.Andrew Robertson), Mohamed Salah, Divock Origi (89.Roberto Firmino). Trainer: Jürgen Klopp.
KRC Genk: Gaëtan Coucke, Sebastien Dewaest, Casper De Norre (85.Paul Onuachu), Jhon Lucumí, Carlos Cuesta, Joakim Mæhle, Patrik Hrosovsky (85.Théo Bongonda), Sander Berge, Bryan Heynen, Mbwana Samatta, Junya Ito (68.Dieumerci Ndongala). Trainer: Felice Mazzù.
Goals: 14' Georginio Wijnaldum 1-0, 41' Mbwana Samatta 1-1, 53' Alex Oxlade-Chamberlain 2-1.

27.11.2019. Luminus Arena, Genk
Referee: Mattias Gestranius (FIN); Attendance: 17,284
KRC Genk – FC Red Bull Salzburg 1-4(0-2)
KRC Genk: Gaëtan Coucke, Sebastien Dewaest, Casper De Norre, Jhon Lucumí, Carlos Cuesta, Joakim Mæhle, Patrik Hrosovsky (59.Paul Onuachu), Sander Berge, Mbwana Samatta, Junya Ito (79.Ianis Hagi), Joseph Paintsil (65.Théo Bongonda). Trainer: Hannes Wolf.
Red Bull Salzburg: Carlos Coronel, Andreas Ulmer, Jérôme Onguéné, Max Wöber, Rasmus Kristensen, Zlatko Junuzovic, Dominik Szoboszlai (80.Masaya Okugawa), Enock Mwepu, Takumi Minamino (89.Albert Vallci), Hwang Hee-Chan, Patson Daka (62.Erling Håland). Trainer: Jesse Marsch.
Goals: 43' Patson Daka 0-1, 45' Takumi Minamino 0-2, 69' Hwang Hee-Chan 0-3, 85' Mbwana Samatta 1-3, 87' Erling Håland 1-4.

10.12.2019. Red Bull Arena, Wals-Siezenheim
Referee: Danny Desmond Makkelie (NED); Attendance: 29,520
FC Red Bull Salzburg – Liverpool FC 0-2(0-0)
Red Bull Salzburg: Cican Stankovic, Andreas Ulmer, Jérôme Onguéné, Max Wöber, Rasmus Kristensen, Zlatko Junuzovic (68.Patson Daka), Dominik Szoboszlai (90.Majeed Ashimeru), Enock Mwepu, Takumi Minamino, Hwang Hee-Chan, Erling Håland (75.Masaya Okugawa). Trainer: Jesse Marsch.
Liverpool FC: Alisson, Dejan Lovren (53.Joe Gomez), Virgil van Dijk, Andrew Robertson, Trent Alexander-Arnold, Georginio Wijnaldum, Jordan Henderson, Naby Keïta (87.Divock Origi), Roberto Firmino (75.James Milner), Mohamed Salah, Sadio Mané. Trainer: Jürgen Klopp.
Goals: 57' Naby Keïta 0-1, 58' Mohamed Salah 0-2.

05.11.2019. Stadio San Paolo, Napoli
Referee: Szymon Marciniak (POL); Attendance: 32,862
SSC Napoli – FC Red Bull Salzburg 1-1(1-1)
SSC Napoli: Alex Meret, Nikola Maksimovic, Mário Rui (46.Sebastiano Luperto), Kalidou Koulibaly, Giovanni Di Lorenzo, Piotr Zielinski, Fabián Ruiz, Dries Mertens (73.Arkadiusz Milik), José Callejón, Lorenzo Insigne, Hirving Lozano (86.Llorente). Trainer: Carlo Ancelotti.
Red Bull Salzburg: Carlos Coronel, Andreas Ulmer, Jérôme Onguéné, Max Wöber, Marin Pongracic (46.Enock Mwepu), Rasmus Kristensen, Zlatko Junuzovic, Dominik Szoboszlai, Takumi Minamino (61.Majeed Ashimeru), Hwang Hee-Chan, Erling Håland (75.Patson Daka). Trainer: Jesse Marsch.
Goals: 11' Erling Håland 0-1 (pen), 44' Hirving Lozano 1-1.

27.11.2019. Anfield Road, Liverpool
Referee: Carlos del Cerro Grande (ESP); Attendance: 52,128
Liverpool FC – SSC Napoli 1-1(0-1)
Liverpool FC: Alisson, Dejan Lovren, Virgil van Dijk, Andrew Robertson, Joe Gomez (57.Alex Oxlade-Chamberlain), James Milner (78.Trent Alexander-Arnold), Jordan Henderson, Fabinho (19.Georginio Wijnaldum), Roberto Firmino, Mohamed Salah, Sadio Mané. Trainer: Jürgen Klopp.
SSC Napoli: Alex Meret, Kostas Manolas, Nikola Maksimovic, Mário Rui, Kalidou Koulibaly, Giovanni Di Lorenzo, Allan, Piotr Zielinski (85.Amin Younes), Fabián Ruiz, Dries Mertens (81.Eljif Elmas), Hirving Lozano (72.Llorente). Trainer: Carlo Ancelotti.
Goals: 21' Dries Mertens 0-1, 65' Dejan Lovren 1-1.

10.12.2019. Stadio San Paolo, Napoli
Referee: Cüneyt Çakir (TUR); Attendance: 22,265
SSC Napoli – KRC Genk 4-0(3-0)
SSC Napoli: Alex Meret, Kostas Manolas, Mário Rui, Kalidou Koulibaly, Giovanni Di Lorenzo, Allan, Piotr Zielinski (72.Gianluca Gaetano), Fabián Ruiz, Dries Mertens, José Callejón (79.Llorente), Arkadiusz Milik (78.Hirving Lozano). Trainer: Carlo Ancelotti.
KRC Genk: Maarten Vandevoordt, Sebastien Dewaest, Casper De Norre (82.Neto Borges), Jhon Lucumí, Joakim Mæhle, Patrik Hrosovsky, Sander Berge, Mbwana Samatta (63.Théo Bongonda), Paul Onuachu, Junya Ito (72.Ianis Hagi), Joseph Paintsil. Trainer: Hannes Wolf.
Goals: 3', 26', 38' Arkadiusz Milik 1-0, 2-0, 3-0 (pen), 74' Dries Mertens 4-0 (pen).

GROUP F									
1. FC Barcelona	6	4	2	0	9	-	4		14
2. BV Borussia Dortmund	6	3	1	2	8	-	8		10
3. *FC Internazionale Milano*	6	2	1	3	10	-	9		7
4. SK Slavia Praha	6	0	2	4	4	-	10		2

17.09.2019. Stadio „Giuseppe Meazza", Milano
Referee: Ruddy Buquet (FRA); Attendance: 50,128
FC Internazionale Milano – SK Slavia Praha 1-1(0-0)
Internazionale: Samir Handanovic, Kwadwo Asamoah, Stefan de Vrij, Danilo D'Ambrosio, Milan Skriniar, Antonio Candreva (49.Valentino Lazaro), Marcelo Brozovic (71.Nicolò Barella), Roberto Gagliardini, Stefano Sensi, Romelu Lukaku, Lautaro Martínez (72.Matteo Politano). Trainer: Antonio Conte.
Slavia Praha: Ondrej Kolár, Ondrej Kúdela, Jan Boril, Vladimír Coufal, David Hovorka, Josef Husbauer, Nicolae Stanciu, Lukás Masopust (79.Abdulla Yusuf Helal), Peter Olayinka (85.Lukás Provod), Tomás Soucek, Ibrahim Traoré (60.Jaroslav Zeleny). Trainer: Jindrich Trpisovsky.
Goals: 63' Peter Olayinka 0-1, 90+2' Nicolò Barella 1-1.

02.10.2019. Stadion Sinobo, Praha
Referee: Björn Kuipers (NED); Attendance: 19,370
SK Slavia Praha – BV Borussia Dortmund 0-2(0-1)
Slavia Praha: Ondrej Kolár, Ondrej Kúdela, Jan Boril, Vladimír Coufal, David Hovorka, Nicolae Stanciu (83.Milan Skoda), Lukás Masopust (76.Jaroslav Zeleny), Petr Sevcík, Peter Olayinka, Tomás Soucek, Stanislav Tecl (59.Mick van Buren). Trainer: Jindrich Trpisovsky.
Borussia Dortmund: Roman Bürki, Mats Hummels, Lukasz Piszczek, Raphaël Guerreiro, Manuel Akanji, Achraf Hakimi (90.Dan-Axel Zagadou), Axel Witsel, Thomas Delaney, Jadon Sancho (74.Thorgan Hazard), Marco Reus, Julian Brandt (90+2.Mario Götze). Trainer: Lucien Favre.
Goals: 35', 89' Achraf Hakimi 0-1, 0-2.

17.09.2019. Signal-Iduna-Park, Dortmund
Referee: Ovidiu Alin Hațegan (ROU); Attendance: 66,099
BV Borussia Dortmund – FC Barcelona 0-0
Borussia Dortmund: Roman Bürki, Mats Hummels, Raphaël Guerreiro, Manuel Akanji, Achraf Hakimi, Axel Witsel, Thomas Delaney, Jadon Sancho, Marco Reus, Thorgan Hazard (73.Julian Brandt), Paco Alcácer (87.Jacob Bruun Larsen). Trainer: Lucien Favre.
FC Barcelona: Marc-André ter Stegen, Piqué, Jordi Alba (40.Sergi Roberto), Clément Lenglet, Nélson Semedo, Sergio Busquets (60.Ivan Rakitic), Arthur, Frenkie de Jong, Luis Suárez, Antoine Griezmann, Ansu Fati (59.Lionel Messi). Trainer: Ernesto Valverde.

02.10.2019. Estadio Camp Nou, Barcelona
Referee: Damir Skomina (SVN); Attendance: 86,141
FC Barcelona – FC Internazionale Milano 2-1(0-1)
FC Barcelona: Marc-André ter Stegen, Piqué, Sergi Roberto, Clément Lenglet, Nélson Semedo, Sergio Busquets (53.Arturo Vidal), Arthur, Frenkie de Jong, Lionel Messi, Luis Suárez, Antoine Griezmann (66.Ousmane Dembélé). Trainer: Ernesto Valverde.
Internazionale: Samir Handanovic, Diego Godín, Kwadwo Asamoah, Stefan de Vrij, Milan Skriniar, Antonio Candreva (71.Danilo D'Ambrosio), Marcelo Brozovic, Stefano Sensi (79.Matteo Politano), Nicolò Barella, Alexis Sánchez (66.Roberto Gagliardini), Lautaro Martínez. Trainer: Antonio Conte.
Goals: 3' Lautaro Martínez 0-1, 58', 84' Luis Suárez 1-1, 2-1.

23.10.2019. Stadion Sinobo, Praha
Referee: Bobby Madden (SCO); Attendance: 19,170
SK Slavia Praha – FC Barcelona 1-2(0-1)
Slavia Praha: Ondrej Kolár, Ondrej Kúdela, Jan Boril, Jaroslav Zeleny (46.Stanislav Tecl), Vladimír Coufal, David Hovorka, Nicolae Stanciu (77.Josef Husbauer), Lukás Masopust (76.Mick van Buren), Petr Sevcík, Peter Olayinka, Tomás Soucek. Trainer: Jindrich Trpisovsky.
FC Barcelona: Marc-André ter Stegen, Piqué, Jordi Alba, Clément Lenglet, Nélson Semedo, Sergio Busquets (78.Arturo Vidal), Arthur (84.Ivan Rakitic), Frenkie de Jong, Lionel Messi, Luis Suárez, Antoine Griezmann (69.Ousmane Dembélé). Trainer: Ernesto Valverde.
Goals: 3' Lionel Messi 0-1, 50' Jan Boril 1-1, 57' Peter Olayinka 1-2 (own goal).

05.11.2019. Estadio Camp Nou, Barcelona
Referee: Michael Oliver (ENG); Attendance: 67,023
FC Barcelona – SK Slavia Praha 0-0
FC Barcelona: Marc-André ter Stegen, Piqué, Jordi Alba (46.Sergi Roberto), Clément Lenglet, Nélson Semedo, Arturo Vidal, Sergio Busquets (68.Ivan Rakitic), Frenkie de Jong, Lionel Messi, Antoine Griezmann, Ousmane Dembélé (65.Ansu Fati). Trainer: Ernesto Valverde.
Slavia Praha: Ondrej Kolár, Ondrej Kúdela, Michal Frydrych, Jan Boril, Vladimír Coufal, Nicolae Stanciu (63.Josef Husbauer), Lukás Masopust (82.Lukás Provod), Petr Sevcík, Peter Olayinka, Tomás Soucek, Ibrahim Traoré (57.Stanislav Tecl). Trainer: Jindrich Trpisovsky.

27.11.2019. Stadion Sinobo, Praha
Referee: Szymon Marciniak (POL); Attendance: 19,370
SK Slavia Praha – FC Internazionale Milano 1-3(1-1)
Slavia Praha: Ondrej Kolár, Ondrej Kúdela, Michal Frydrych (83.Laco Takács), Jan Boril, Vladimír Coufal, Josef Husbauer (70.Jaroslav Zeleny), Nicolae Stanciu (58.Ibrahim Traoré), Lukás Masopust, Petr Sevcík, Peter Olayinka, Tomás Soucek. Trainer: Jindrich Trpisovsky.
Internazionale: Samir Handanovic, Diego Godín, Stefan de Vrij, Cristiano Biraghi (76.Valentino Lazaro), Milan Skriniar, Antonio Candreva, Borja Valero (76.Roberto Gagliardini), Matías Vecino (80.Sebastiano Esposito), Marcelo Brozovic, Romelu Lukaku, Lautaro Martínez. Trainer: Antonio Conte.
Goals: 19' Lautaro Martínez 0-1, 37' Tomás Soucek 1-1 (pen), 81' Romelu Lukaku 1-2, 88' Lautaro Martínez 1-3.

10.12.2019. Stadio „Giuseppe Meazza", Milano
Referee: Björn Kuipers (NED); Attendance: 71,818
FC Internazionale Milano – FC Barcelona 1-2(1-1)
Internazionale: Samir Handanovic, Diego Godín, Stefan de Vrij, Danilo D'Ambrosio (75.Matteo Politano), Cristiano Biraghi (69.Valentino Lazaro), Milan Skriniar, Borja Valero (77.Sebastiano Esposito), Matías Vecino, Marcelo Brozovic, Romelu Lukaku, Lautaro Martínez. Trainer: Antonio Conte.
FC Barcelona: Neto, Samuel Umtiti, Clément Lenglet, Junior Firpo, Moussa Wagué, Jean-Clair Todibo, Ivan Rakitic (63.Frenkie de Jong), Arturo Vidal, Carles Aleñá, Antoine Griezmann (62.Luis Suárez), Carles Pérez (85.Ansu Fati). Trainer: Ernesto Valverde.
Goals: 23' Carles Pérez 0-1, 44' Romelu Lukaku 1-1, 86' Ansu Fati 1-2.

23.10.2019. Stadio „Giuseppe Meazza", Milano
Referee: Anthony Taylor (ENG); Attendance: 65,673
FC Internazionale Milano – BV Borussia Dortmund 2-0(1-0)
Internazionale: Samir Handanovic, Diego Godín, Kwadwo Asamoah (80.Cristiano Biraghi), Stefan de Vrij, Milan Skriniar, Antonio Candreva, Marcelo Brozovic, Roberto Gagliardini, Nicolò Barella, Romelu Lukaku (62.Sebastiano Esposito), Lautaro Martínez (90+1.Borja Valero). Trainer: Antonio Conte.
Borussia Dortmund: Roman Bürki, Mats Hummels, Manuel Akanji (74.Jacob Bruun Larsen), Achraf Hakimi, Axel Witsel, Thomas Delaney (65.Mahmoud Dahoud), Nico Schulz, Julian Weigl, Jadon Sancho, Thorgan Hazard (84.Raphaël Guerreiro), Julian Brandt. Trainer: Lucien Favre.
Goals: 22' Lautaro Martínez 1-0, 89' Antonio Candreva 2-0.

05.11.2019. Signal-Iduna-Park, Dortmund
Referee: Danny Desmond Makkelie (NED); Attendance: 66,099
BV Borussia Dortmund – FC Internazionale Milano 3-2(0-2)
Borussia Dortmund: Roman Bürki, Mats Hummels, Manuel Akanji, Achraf Hakimi, Axel Witsel, Mario Götze (64.Paco Alcácer), Nico Schulz, Julian Weigl, Jadon Sancho (82.Lukasz Piszczek), Thorgan Hazard (88.Raphaël Guerreiro), Julian Brandt. Trainer: Lucien Favre.
Internazionale: Samir Handanovic, Diego Godín, Stefan de Vrij, Cristiano Biraghi (66.Valentino Lazaro), Milan Skriniar, Antonio Candreva, Matías Vecino (68.Stefano Sensi), Marcelo Brozovic, Nicolò Barella, Romelu Lukaku (73.Matteo Politano), Lautaro Martínez. Trainer: Antonio Conte.
Goals: 5' Lautaro Martínez 0-1, 40' Matías Vecino 0-2, 51' Achraf Hakimi 1-2, 64' Julian Brandt 2-2, 77' Achraf Hakimi 3-2.

27.11.2019. Estadio Camp Nou, Barcelona
Referee: Clément Turpin (FRA); Attendance: 90,071
FC Barcelona – BV Borussia Dortmund 3-1(2-0)
FC Barcelona: Marc-André ter Stegen, Sergi Roberto, Samuel Umtiti, Clément Lenglet, Junior Firpo, Ivan Rakitic (78.Arturo Vidal), Sergio Busquets, Frenkie de Jong, Lionel Messi, Luis Suárez (90+1.Moussa Wagué), Ousmane Dembélé (26.Antoine Griezmann). Trainer: Ernesto Valverde.
Borussia Dortmund: Roman Bürki, Mats Hummels, Lukasz Piszczek (76.Dan-Axel Zagadou), Raphaël Guerreiro, Manuel Akanji, Achraf Hakimi, Axel Witsel, Nico Schulz (46.Jadon Sancho), Julian Weigl (85.Mario Götze), Marco Reus, Julian Brandt. Trainer: Lucien Favre.
Goals: 29' Luis Suárez 1-0, 33' Lionel Messi 2-0, 67' Antoine Griezmann 3-0, 77' Jadon Sancho 3-1.

10.12.2019. Signal-Iduna-Park, Dortmund
Referee: Sergei Karasev (RUS); Attendance: 65,079
BV Borussia Dortmund – SK Slavia Praha 2-1(1-1)
Borussia Dortmund: Roman Bürki, Mats Hummels, Raphaël Guerreiro, Manuel Akanji, Achraf Hakimi (83.Leonardo Balerdi), Dan-Axel Zagadou, Julian Weigl, Jadon Sancho (87.Mahmoud Dahoud), Marco Reus, Thorgan Hazard (83.Lukasz Piszczek), Julian Brandt. Trainer: Lucien Favre.
Slavia Praha: Ondrej Kolár, Ondrej Kúdela, Jan Boril, Vladimír Coufal, Laco Takács (83.Josef Husbauer), Nicolae Stanciu, Lukás Masopust (72.Ibrahim Traoré), Petr Sevcík, Peter Olayinka, Tomás Soucek, Milan Skoda (65.Abdulla Yusuf Helal). Trainer: Jindrich Trpisovsky.
Goals: 10' Jadon Sancho 1-0, 43' Tomás Soucek 1-1, 61' Julian Brandt 2-1. Sent off: 77' Julian Weigl.

GROUP G	1. **RasenBallsport Leipzig**	6	3	2	1	10 - 8	11
	2. **Olympique Lyonnais**	6	2	2	2	9 - 8	8
	3. *Sport Lisboa e Benfica*	6	2	1	3	10 - 11	7
	4. FK Zenit Saint Petersburg	6	2	1	3	7 - 9	7

17.09.2019. Groupama Stadium, Décines-Charpieu
Referee: Michael Oliver (ENG); Attendance: 47,201
Olympique Lyonnais – FK Zenit Saint Petersburg 1-1(0-1)
Olympique Lyonnais: Anthony Lopes, Marcelo, Léo Dubois, Youssouf Koné, Jason Denayer, Thiago Mendes, Lucas Tousart, Jeff Reine-Adélaïde (85.Martin Terrier), Bertrand Traoré (77.Maxwel Cornet), Memphis Depay, Moussa Dembélé. Trainer: Sylvinho.
Zenit: Andrei Lunev, Branislav Ivanovic, Yaroslav Rakitskiy, Vyacheslav Karavaev (78.Oleg Shatov), Douglas Santos, Yordan Osorio, Yuriy Zhirkov (64.Daler Kuzyaev), Wilmar Barrios, Artem Dzyuba, Sardar Azmoun (47.Magomed Ozdoev), Sebastián Driussi. Trainer: Sergey Semak.
Goals: 41' Sardar Azmoun 0-1, 51' Memphis Depay 1-1 (pen).

17.09.2019. Estádio da Luz, Lisboa
Referee: Anastasios Sidiropoulos (GRE); Attendance: 46,460
Sport Lisboa e Benfica – RasenBallsport Leipzig 1-2(0-0)
Benfica: Odisseas Vlachodimos, Álex Grimaldo, Rúben Dias, "Ferro" Francisco Ferreira, Tomás Tavares, Adel Taarabt, Ljubomir Fejsa, Pizzi (76.Rafa Silva), Franco Cervi (76.Haris Seferovic), Raúl de Tomás, "Jota" João Filipe (67.David Tavares). Trainer: Bruno Lage.
RB Leipzig: Péter Gulácsi, Marcel Halstenberg (83.Lukas Klostermann), Willi Orban, Nordi Mukiele, Ibrahima Konaté, Emil Forsberg (88.Christopher Nkunku), Diego Demme, Marcel Sabitzer, Konrad Laimer (39.Amadou Haïdara), Yussuf Poulsen, Timo Werner. Trainer: Julian Nagelsmann.
Goals: 69', 78' Timo Werner 0-1, 0-2, 84' Haris Seferovic 1-2.

02.10.2019. Krestovsky Stadium, Saint Petersburg
Referee: Carlos del Cerro Grande (ESP); Attendance: 51,683
FK Zenit Saint Petersburg – Sport Lisboa e Benfica 3-1(1-0)
Zenit: Andrei Lunev, Branislav Ivanovic, Igor Smolnikov (63.Yordan Osorio), Yaroslav Rakitskiy, Douglas Santos, Oleg Shatov (68.Vyacheslav Karavaev), Magomed Ozdoev, Wilmar Barrios, Artem Dzyuba, Sardar Azmoun (81.Aleksandr Erokhin), Sebastián Driussi. Trainer: Sergey Semak.
Benfica: Odisseas Vlachodimos, Jardel, Álex Grimaldo, Rúben Dias, Tomás Tavares, Adel Taarabt, Ljubomir Fejsa (60.Caio Lucas), Pizzi (60.Carlos Vinícius), Gabriel, Rafa Silva, Haris Seferovic (81.Raúl de Tomás). Trainer: Bruno Lage.
Goals: 22' Artem Dzyuba 1-0, 70' Rúben Dias 2-0 (own goal), 78' Sardar Azmoun 3-0, 85' Raúl de Tomás 3-1.

23.10.2019. Red Bull Arena, Leipzig
Referee: Ali Palabiyik (TUR); Attendance: 41,058
RasenBallsport Leipzig – FK Zenit Saint Petersburg 2-1(0-1)
RB Leipzig: Péter Gulácsi, Willi Orban, Lukas Klostermann, Nordi Mukiele, Dayot Upamecano, Emil Forsberg, Kevin Kampl, Marcel Sabitzer, Konrad Laimer (86.Diego Demme), Timo Werner (46.Matheus Cunha), Ademola Lookman (69.Yussuf Poulsen). Trainer: Julian Nagelsmann.
Zenit: Mikhail Kerzhalov, Branislav Ivanovic, Yaroslav Rakitskiy, Vyacheslav Karavaev, Douglas Santos, Oleg Shatov (65.Yordan Osorio), Magomed Ozdoev, Wilmar Barrios, Artem Dzyuba, Sardar Azmoun (75.Daler Kuzyaev), Sebastián Driussi (82.Róbert Mak). Trainer: Sergey Semak.
Goals: 25' Yaroslav Rakitskiy 0-1, 49' Konrad Laimer 1-1, 59' Marcel Sabitzer 2-1.

05.11.2019. Krestovsky Stadium, Saint Petersburg
Referee: Orel Grinfeld (ISR); Attendance: 50,452
FK Zenit Saint Petersburg – RasenBallsport Leipzig 0-2(0-1)
Zenit: Mikhail Kerzhalov, Branislav Ivanovic (70.Sebastián Driussi), Igor Smolnikov (46.Vyacheslav Karavaev), Yaroslav Rakitskiy, Douglas Santos, Yordan Osorio, Aleksandr Erokhin (85.Daler Kuzyaev), Magomed Ozdoev, Wilmar Barrios, Artem Dzyuba, Sardar Azmoun. Trainer: Sergey Semak.
RB Leipzig: Péter Gulácsi, Marcel Halstenberg (46.Kevin Kampl), Lukas Klostermann, Nordi Mukiele, Dayot Upamecano, Emil Forsberg (76.Amadou Haïdara), Diego Demme, Marcel Sabitzer, Konrad Laimer, Christopher Nkunku (61.Timo Werner), Yussuf Poulsen. Trainer: Julian Nagelsmann.
Goals: 45+5' Diego Demme 0-1, 63' Marcel Sabitzer 0-2.

27.11.2019. Krestovsky Stadium, Saint Petersburg
Referee: Daniele Orsato (ITA); Attendance: 51,183
FK Zenit Saint Petersburg – Olympique Lyonnais 2-0(1-0)
Zenit: Mikhail Kerzhalov, Branislav Ivanovic, Yaroslav Rakitskiy, Vyacheslav Karavaev, Douglas Santos, Magomed Ozdoev, Wilmar Barrios, Daler Kuzyaev (90+2.Aleksey Sutormin), Artem Dzyuba, Sardar Azmoun (83.Aleksandr Erokhin), Sebastián Driussi (81.Yuriy Zhirkov). Trainer: Sergey Semak.
Olympique Lyonnais: Anthony Lopes, Marcelo, Fernando Marçal (58.Youssouf Koné), Joachim Andersen (83.Amine Gouiri), Léo Dubois, Jason Denayer, Lucas Tousart, Jeff Reine-Adélaïde, Bertrand Traoré, Maxwel Cornet (75.Mathis Rayan Cherki), Moussa Dembélé. Trainer: Rudi Garcia.
Goals: 42' Artem Dzyuba 1-0, 84' Magomed Ozdoev 2-0.

10.12.2019. Estádio da Luz, Lisboa
Referee: Antonio Miguel Mateu Lahoz (ESP); Attendance: 40,232
Sport Lisboa e Benfica – FK Zenit Saint Petersburg 3-0(0-0)
Benfica: Odisseas Vlachodimos, Álex Grimaldo, Rúben Dias, "Ferro" Francisco Ferreira, Tomás Tavares, Adel Taarabt, Pizzi, Gabriel (81.Andreas Samaris), Franco Cervi (81.Haris Seferovic), Chiquinho, Carlos Vinícius (89.Caio Lucas). Trainer: Bruno Lage.
Zenit: Mikhail Kerzhalov, Branislav Ivanovic, Vyacheslav Karavaev, Douglas Santos, Yordan Osorio, Oleg Shatov (90.Róbert Mak), Aleksandr Erokhin (65.Aleksey Sutormin), Magomed Ozdoev (60.Igor Smolnikov), Wilmar Barrios, Artem Dzyuba, Sardar Azmoun. Trainer: Sergey Semak.
Goals: 47' Franco Cervi 1-0, 58' Pizzi 2-0 (pen), 79' Sardar Azmoun 3-0 (own goal).
Sent off: 56' Douglas Santos.

02.10.2019. Red Bull Arena, Leipzig
Referee: Antonio Miguel Mateu Lahoz (ESP); Attendance: 40,194
RasenBallsport Leipzig – Olympique Lyonnais 0-2(0-1)
RB Leipzig: Péter Gulácsi, Marcel Halstenberg, Willi Orban, Lukas Klostermann, Dayot Upamecano (66.Christopher Nkunku), Ibrahima Konaté (23.Nordi Mukiele), Marcel Sabitzer, Konrad Laimer, Amadou Haïdara (58.Emil Forsberg), Yussuf Poulsen, Timo Werner. Trainer: Julian Nagelsmann.
Olympique Lyonnais: Anthony Lopes, Marcelo, Fernando Marçal, Joachim Andersen, Léo Dubois, Youssouf Koné, Thiago Mendes, Lucas Tousart, Martin Terrier (69.Bertrand Traoré), Houssem Aouar (87.Jean Lucas), Memphis Depay (79.Moussa Dembélé). Trainer: Sylvinho.
Goals: 11' Memphis Depay 0-1, 65' Martin Terrier 0-2.

23.10.2019. Estádio da Luz, Lisboa
Referee: Ivan Kruzliak (SVK); Attendance: 53,035
Sport Lisboa e Benfica – Olympique Lyonnais 2-1(1-0)
Benfica: Odisseas Vlachodimos, Álex Grimaldo, Rúben Dias, "Ferro" Francisco Ferreira, Tomás Tavares, Gabriel, Rafa Silva (20.Pizzi), Franco Cervi (78.Raúl de Tomás), Gedson Fernandes, Florentino Luís, Haris Seferovic (59.Carlos Vinícius). Trainer: Bruno Lage.
Olympique Lyonnais: Anthony Lopes, Marcelo, Léo Dubois, Youssouf Koné, Jason Denayer, Lucas Tousart, Martin Terrier (56.Thiago Mendes), Houssem Aouar (88.Jeff Reine-Adélaïde), Memphis Depay, Maxwel Cornet (66.Bertrand Traoré), Moussa Dembélé. Trainer: Rudi Garcia.
Goals: 4' Rafa Silva 1-0, 70' Memphis Depay 1-1, 86' Pizzi 2-1.

05.11.2019. Groupama Stadium, Décines-Charpieu
Referee: Björn Kuipers (NED); Attendance: 51,077
Olympique Lyonnais – Sport Lisboa e Benfica 3-1(2-0)
Olympique Lyonnais: Anthony Lopes, Joachim Andersen, Léo Dubois, Youssouf Koné, Jason Denayer, Thiago Mendes, Lucas Tousart, Jeff Reine-Adélaïde (73.Bertrand Traoré), Houssem Aouar (90+1.Marcelo), Memphis Depay (46.Maxwel Cornet), Moussa Dembélé. Trainer: Rudi Garcia.
Benfica: Odisseas Vlachodimos, Álex Grimaldo, Rúben Dias, "Ferro" Francisco Ferreira (16.Jardel), Tomás Tavares, Gabriel, Franco Cervi (73.Pizzi), Chiquinho, Gedson Fernandes (46.Haris Seferovic), Florentino Luís, Carlos Vinícius. Trainer: Bruno Lage.
Goals: 4' Joachim Andersen 1-0, 33' Memphis Depay 2-0, 76' Haris Seferovic 2-1, 89' Bertrand Traoré 3-1.

27.11.2019. Red Bull Arena, Leipzig
Referee: Jesús Gil Manzano (ESP); Attendance: 38,339
RasenBallsport Leipzig – Sport Lisboa e Benfica 2-2(0-1)
RB Leipzig: Péter Gulácsi (64.Yvon Mvogo), Lukas Klostermann, Dayot Upamecano, Ethan Ampadu (56.Nordi Mukiele), Emil Forsberg, Diego Demme, Marcel Sabitzer, Konrad Laimer, Christopher Nkunku, Marcelo Saracchi (70.Patrik Schick), Timo Werner. Trainer: Julian Nagelsmann.
Benfica: Odisseas Vlachodimos, André Almeida, Álex Grimaldo, Rúben Dias, "Ferro" Francisco Ferreira, Adel Taarabt, Pizzi (90+3.Caio Lucas), Gabriel, Franco Cervi (90+8."Jota" João Filipe), Chiquinho, Carlos Vinícius (82.Raúl de Tomás). Trainer: Bruno Lage.
Goals: 20' Pizzi 0-1, 59' Carlos Vinícius 0-2, 90', 90+6' Emil Forsberg 1-2 (pen), 2-2.

10.12.2019. Groupama Stadium, Décines-Charpieu
Referee: Anthony Taylor (ENG); Attendance: 53,288
Olympique Lyonnais – RasenBallsport Leipzig 2-2(0-2)
Olympique Lyonnais: Anthony Lopes, Rafael (73.Fernando Marçal), Kenny Tete, Joachim Andersen, Jason Denayer, Thiago Mendes, Lucas Tousart (64.Jeff Reine-Adélaïde), Martin Terrier (87.Marcelo), Houssem Aouar, Memphis Depay, Moussa Dembélé. Trainer: Rudi Garcia.
RB Leipzig: Péter Gulácsi, Lukas Klostermann, Nordi Mukiele, Dayot Upamecano (55.Ethan Ampadu), Emil Forsberg, Diego Demme, Christopher Nkunku (75.Konrad Laimer), Marcelo Saracchi, Amadou Haïdara, Yussuf Poulsen, Timo Werner (55.Matheus Cunha). Trainer: Julian Nagelsmann.
Goals: 9' Emil Forsberg 0-1 (pen), 33' Timo Werner 0-2 (pen), 50' Houssem Aouar 1-2, 82' Memphis Depay 2-2.

<table>
<tr><td rowspan="4">**GROUP H**</td><td>1.</td><td>**Valencia CF**</td><td>6</td><td>3</td><td>2</td><td>1</td><td>9</td><td>-</td><td>7</td><td>11</td></tr>
<tr><td>2.</td><td>**Chelsea FC London**</td><td>6</td><td>3</td><td>2</td><td>1</td><td>11</td><td>-</td><td>9</td><td>11</td></tr>
<tr><td>3.</td><td>*AFC Ajax Amsterdam*</td><td>6</td><td>3</td><td>1</td><td>2</td><td>12</td><td>-</td><td>6</td><td>10</td></tr>
<tr><td>4.</td><td>Lille OSC</td><td>6</td><td>0</td><td>1</td><td>5</td><td>4</td><td>-</td><td>14</td><td>1</td></tr>
</table>

17.09.2019. „Johan Cruijff" Arena, Amsterdam
Referee: Srdjan Jovanovic (SRB); Attendance: 51,441
AFC Ajax Amsterdam – Lille OSC 3-0(1-0)
AFC Ajax: André Onana, Daley Blind, Nicolás Tagliafico, Joël Veltman, Edson Álvarez, Lisandro Martínez (88.Jurgen Ekkelenkamp), Sergiño Dest, Hakim Ziyech (77.Noa Lang), Quincy Promes, David Neres (83.Klaas Jan Huntelaar). Trainer: Erik ten Hag.
Lille OSC: Mike Maignan, José Fonte, Mehmet Çelik, Gabriel, Domagoj Bradaric, Benjamin André, Renato Sanches (63.Luiz Araujo), Jonathan Ikoné (63.Yusuf Yazici), Boubakary Soumaré (77.Xeka), Jonathan Bamba, Victor Osimhen. Trainer: Christophe Galtier.
Goals: 18' Quincy Promes 1-0, 50' Edson Álvarez 2-0, 62' Nicolás Tagliafico 3-0.

02.10.2019. Estadio de Mestalla, Valencia
Referee: Daniele Orsato (ITA); Attendance: 44,659
Valencia CF – AFC Ajax Amsterdam 0-3(0-2)
Valencia: Jasper Cillessen, Ezequiel Garay, Jaume Costa, Gabriel Paulista, Daniel Wass, Dani Parejo, Francis Coquelin (70.Thierry Correia), Gonçalo Guedes, Ferrán Torres (76.Denis Cheryshev), Rodrigo, Maximiliano Gómez (57.Lee Kang-In). Trainer: Celades.
AFC Ajax: André Onana, Daley Blind, Nicolás Tagliafico, Joël Veltman, Edson Álvarez, Lisandro Martínez, Sergiño Dest, Hakim Ziyech (85.Klaas Jan Huntelaar), Donny van de Beek (88.Siem de Jong), Dusan Tadic, Quincy Promes (81.David Neres). Trainer: Erik ten Hag.
Goals: 8' Hakim Ziyech 0-1, 34' Quincy Promes 0-2, 67' Donny van de Beek 0-3.

23.10.2019. „Johan Cruijff" Arena, Amsterdam
Referee: Ovidiu Alin Haţegan (ROU); Attendance: 52,482
AFC Ajax Amsterdam – Chelsea FC London 0-1(0-0)
AFC Ajax: André Onana, Daley Blind, Nicolás Tagliafico, Joël Veltman (89.Klaas Jan Huntelaar), Edson Álvarez (89.Siem de Jong), Lisandro Martínez, Sergiño Dest, Hakim Ziyech, Donny van de Beek, Dusan Tadic, Quincy Promes (74.David Neres). Trainer: Erik ten Hag.
Chelsea: Kepa, Azpilicueta, Marcos Alonso, Kurt Zouma, Fikayo Tomori, Mateo Kovacic, Jorginho, Mason Mount, Willian (66.Christian Pulisic), Tammy Abraham (71.Michy Batshuayi), Callum Hudson-Odoi (90.Reece James). Trainer: Frank Lampard.
Goal: 86' Michy Batshuayi 0-1.

05.11.2019. Estadio de Mestalla, Valencia
Referee: Sergei Karasev (RUS); Attendance: 38,252
Valencia CF – Lille OSC 4-1(0-1)
Valencia: Jasper Cillessen, Ezequiel Garay, Gabriel Paulista, Gayà, Daniel Wass, Dani Parejo, Denis Cheryshev (30.Ferrán Torres), Geoffrey Kondogbia, Lee Kang-In (54.Manu Vallejo), Rodrigo (90+3.Kevin Gameiro), Maximiliano Gómez. Trainer: Celades.
Lille OSC: Mike Maignan, José Fonte, Adama Soumaoro (89.Jonathan Bamba), Mehmet Çelik, Gabriel, Domagoj Bradaric, Benjamin André (80.Luiz Araujo), Boubakary Soumaré, Yusuf Yazici (74.Renato Sanches), Loïc Rémy, Victor Osimhen. Trainer: Christophe Galtier.
Goals: 25' Victor Osimhen 0-1, 66' Dani Parejo 1-1 (pen), 82' Adama Soumaoro 2-1 (own goal), 84' Geoffrey Kondogbia 3-1, 90' Ferrán Torres 4-1.

27.11.2019. Estadio de Mestalla, Valencia
Referee: Felix Zwayer (GER); Attendance: 43,486
Valencia CF – Chelsea FC London 2-2(1-1)
Valencia: Jasper Cillessen, Ezequiel Garay, Jaume Costa (67.Kevin Gameiro), Gabriel Paulista, Gayà, Daniel Wass, Dani Parejo, Carlos Soler (78.Lee Kang-In), Ferrán Torres (74.Francis Coquelin), Rodrigo, Maximiliano Gómez. Trainer: Celades.
Chelsea: Kepa, Azpilicueta, Kurt Zouma, Andreas Christensen, Reece James, Mateo Kovacic, Jorginho (72.Emerson), N'Golo Kanté, Christian Pulisic, Willian (80.Mason Mount), Tammy Abraham (46.Michy Batshuayi). Trainer: Frank Lampard.
Goals: 40' Carlos Soler 1-0, 41' Mateo Kovacic 1-1, 50' Christian Pulisic 1-2, 82' Daniel Wass 2-2.

17.09.2019. Stamford Bridge, London
Referee: Cüneyt Çakir (TUR); Attendance: 39,469
Chelsea FC London – Valencia CF 0-1(0-0)
Chelsea: Kepa, Azpilicueta, Marcos Alonso, Kurt Zouma (73.Olivier Giroud), Andreas Christensen, Fikayo Tomori, Mateo Kovacic (80.Ross Barkley), Jorginho, Mason Mount (16.Pedro), Willian, Tammy Abraham. Trainer: Frank Lampard.
Valencia: Jasper Cillessen, Ezequiel Garay, Gabriel Paulista, Gayà, Daniel Wass, Dani Parejo, Francis Coquelin, Denis Cheryshev (90+2.Mouctar Diakhaby), Geoffrey Kondogbia, Kevin Gameiro (70.Maximiliano Gómez), Rodrigo (90.Lee Kang-In). Trainer: Celades.
Goal: 74' Rodrigo 0-1.

02.10.2019. Stade „Pierre Mauroy", Villeneuve-d'Ascq
Referee: Aleksei Kulbakov (BLR); Attendance: 48,523
Lille OSC – Chelsea FC London 1-2(1-1)
Lille OSC: Mike Maignan, José Fonte, Reinildo, Mehmet Çelik, Gabriel, Benjamin André (69.Renato Sanches), Jonathan Ikoné (62.Yusuf Yazici), Boubakary Soumaré, Luiz Araujo (75.Xeka), Jonathan Bamba, Victor Osimhen. Trainer: Christophe Galtier.
Chelsea: Kepa, Azpilicueta, Marcos Alonso, Kurt Zouma, Fikayo Tomori, Reece James (67.Callum Hudson-Odoi), Jorginho, N'Golo Kanté, Mason Mount (87.Mateo Kovacic), Willian (85.Pedro), Tammy Abraham. Trainer: Frank Lampard.
Goals: 22' Tammy Abraham 0-1, 33' Victor Osimhen 1-1, 78' Willian 1-2.

23.10.2019. Stade „Pierre Mauroy", Villeneuve-d'Ascq
Referee: Deniz Aytekin (GER); Attendance: 47,488
Lille OSC – Valencia CF 1-1(0-0)
Lille OSC: Mike Maignan, José Fonte, Mehmet Çelik, Gabriel, Tiago Djaló (87.Jonathan Bamba), Domagoj Bradaric, Benjamin André, Boubakary Soumaré, Yusuf Yazici (71.Loïc Rémy), Luiz Araujo (65.Jonathan Ikoné), Victor Osimhen. Trainer: Christophe Galtier.
Valencia: Jasper Cillessen, Jaume Costa, Gabriel Paulista, Mouctar Diakhaby, Daniel Wass, Dani Parejo, Francis Coquelin (87.Ezequiel Garay), Geoffrey Kondogbia (46.Carlos Soler), Kevin Gameiro (65.Lee Kang-In), Maximiliano Gómez. Trainer: Celades.
Goals: 63' Denis Cheryshev 0-1, 90+5' Jonathan Ikoné 1-1.
Sent off: 84' Mouctar Diakhaby.

05.11.2019. Stamford Bridge, London
Referee: Gianluca Rocchi (ITA); Attendance: 39,132
Chelsea FC London – AFC Ajax Amsterdam 4-4(1-3)
Chelsea: Kepa, Azpilicueta, Marcos Alonso (46.Reece James), Kurt Zouma, Fikayo Tomori, Mateo Kovacic (87.Michy Batshuayi), Jorginho, Mason Mount (60.Callum Hudson-Odoi), Christian Pulisic, Willian, Tammy Abraham. Trainer: Frank Lampard.
AFC Ajax: André Onana, Daley Blind, Nicolás Tagliafico, Joël Veltman, Noussair Mazraoui, Lisandro Martínez, Hakim Ziyech (72.Edson Álvarez), Donny van de Beek, Dusan Tadic, Quincy Promes, David Neres (72.Perr Schuurs). Trainer: Erik ten Hag.
Goals: 2' Tammy Abraham 0-1 (own goal), 5' Jorginho 1-1 (pen), 20' Quincy Promes 1-2, 35' Kepa 1-3 (own goal), 55' Donny van de Beek 1-4, 63' Azpilicueta 2-4, 71' Jorginho 3-4 (pen), 74' Reece James 4-4.
Sent-off: 68' Daley Blind, 69' Joël Veltman.

27.11.2019. Stade „Pierre Mauroy", Villeneuve-d'Ascq
Referee: Dr. Felix Brych (GER); Attendance: 48,612
Lille OSC – AFC Ajax Amsterdam 0-2(0-1)
Lille OSC: Mike Maignan, Reinildo, Mehmet Çelik, Gabriel, Tiago Djaló, Benjamin André (77.Renato Sanches), Jonathan Ikoné, Boubakary Soumaré, Yusuf Yazici (82.Loïc Rémy), Jonathan Bamba (72.Luiz Araujo), Victor Osimhen. Trainer: Christophe Galtier.
AFC Ajax: André Onana, Nicolás Tagliafico, Noussair Mazraoui (46.Edson Álvarez), Perr Schuurs, Lisandro Martínez, Sergiño Dest, Zakaria Labyad (45+2.Noa Lang), Hakim Ziyech (85.Siem de Jong), Donny van de Beek, Dusan Tadic, Quincy Promes. Trainer: Erik ten Hag.
Goals: 2' Hakim Ziyech 0-1, 59' Quincy Promes 0-2.

10.12.2019. „Johan Cruijff" Arena, Amsterdam
Referee: Clément Turpin (FRA); Attendance: 51,931
AFC Ajax Amsterdam – Valencia CF 0-1(0-1)
AFC Ajax: André Onana, Daley Blind, Nicolás Tagliafico (89.Siem de Jong), Joël Veltman, Noussair Mazraoui, Edson Álvarez (46.Sergiño Dest), Lisandro Martínez, Hakim Ziyech, Donny van de Beek, Noa Lang (70.Klaas Jan Huntelaar), Dusan Tadic. Trainer: Erik ten Hag.
Valencia: Jaume Doménech, Gabriel Paulista, Gayà, Mouctar Diakhaby, Daniel Wass, Dani Parejo, Francis Coquelin, Carlos Soler, Ferrán Torres (90+5.Eliaquim Mangala), Kevin Gameiro (54.Manu Vallego), Rodrigo. Trainer: Celades.
Goal: 24' Rodrigo 0-1.
Sent off: 90+3' Gabriel Paulista.

10.12.2019. Stamford Bridge, London
Referee: Anastasios Sidiropoulos (GRE); Attendance: 40,016
Chelsea FC London – Lille OSC 2-1(2-0)
Chelsea: Kepa, Azpilicueta, Kurt Zouma, Emerson, Antonio Rüdiger, Mateo Kovacic (82.Mason Mount), Jorginho, N'Golo Kanté, Christian Pulisic (62.Callum Hudson-Odoi), Willian, Tammy Abraham (72.Michy Batshuayi). Trainer: Frank Lampard.
Lille OSC: Mike Maignan (72.Léo Jardim), Jérémy Pied, Mehmet Çelik, Gabriel, Tiago Djaló, Thiago Maia (66.Jonathan Bamba), Xeka, Boubakary Soumaré, Yusuf Yazici, Loïc Rémy, Luiz Araujo (82.Renato Sanches). Trainer: Christophe Galtier.
Goals: 19' Tammy Abraham 1-0, 35' Azpilicueta 2-0, 78' Loïc Rémy 2-1.

ROUND OF 16

18.02.2020; Signal-Iduna-Park, Dortmund
Referee: Antonio Miguel Mateu Lahoz (ESP); Attendance: 66,099
BV Borussia Dortmund – Paris Saint-Germain FC 2-1(0-0)
Borussia Dortmund: Roman Bürki, Mats Hummels, Lukasz Piszczek, Raphaël Guerreiro, Achraf Hakimi, Dan-Axel Zagadou, Axel Witsel, Emre Can, Jadon Sancho (90+1.Marcel Schmelzer), Thorgan Hazard (67.Giovanni Reyna), Erling Håland. Trainer: Lucien Favre.
Paris Saint-Germain: Keylor Navas, Thiago Silva, Thomas Meunier, Layvin Kurzawa, Marquinhos, Presnel Kimpembe, Ángel Di María (76.Pablo Sarabia), Marco Verratti, Idrissa Gueye, Neymar, Kylian Mbappé. Trainer: Thomas Tuchel.
Goals: 69' Erling Håland 1-0, 75' Neymar 1-1, 77' Erling Håland 2-1.

11.03.2020; Stade Parc des Princes, Paris
Referee: Anthony Taylor (ENG)
PARIS SAINT-GERMAIN FC – BV Borussia Dortmund 2-0(2-0)
Paris Saint-Germain: Keylor Navas, Marquinhos, Juan Bernat, Presnel Kimpembe, Thilo Kehrer, Ángel Di María (79.Layvin Kurzawa), Idrissa Gueye, Pablo Sarabia (64.Kylian Mbappé), Leandro Paredes (90+2.Nianzou Kouassi), Edinson Cavani, Neymar. Trainer: Thomas Tuchel.
Borussia Dortmund: Roman Bürki, Mats Hummels, Lukasz Piszczek, Raphaël Guerreiro, Achraf Hakimi (87.Mario Götze), Dan-Axel Zagadou, Axel Witsel (71.Giovanni Reyna), Emre Can, Jadon Sancho, Thorgan Hazard (69.Julian Brandt), Erling Håland. Trainer: Lucien Favre.
Goals: 28' Neymar 1-0, 45+1' Juan Bernat 2-0.
Sent off: 89' Emre Can.

18.02.2020; Estadio Wanda Metropolitano, Madrid
Referee: Szymon Marciniak (POL); Attendance: 67,443
Club Atlético de Madrid – Liverpool FC 1-0(1-0)
Atlético Madrid: Jan Oblak, Sime Vrsaljko, Stefan Savic, Felipe Monteiro, Renan Lodi, Saúl, Koke, Thomas Lemar (46.Marcos Llorente), Thomas Partey, Álvaro Morata (70.Vitolo), Ángel Correa (77.Diego Costa). Trainer: Diego Simeone.
Liverpool FC: Alisson, Virgil van Dijk, Andrew Robertson, Joe Gomez, Trent Alexander-Arnold, Georginio Wijnaldum, Jordan Henderson (80.James Milner), Fabinho, Roberto Firmino, Mohamed Salah (72.Alex Oxlade-Chamberlain), Sadio Mané (46.Divock Origi). Trainer: Jürgen Klopp.
Goal: 4' Saúl 1-0.

11.03.2020; Anfield Road, Liverpool
Referee: Danny Desmond Makkelie (NED); Attendance: 52,267
Liverpool FC – CLUB ATLÉTICO DE MADRID 2-3(1-0,1-0)
Liverpool FC: Adrián, Virgil van Dijk, Andrew Robertson, Joe Gomez, Trent Alexander-Arnold, Georginio Wijnaldum (105.Divock Origi), Jordan Henderson (105.Fabinho), Alex Oxlade-Chamberlain (82.James Milner), Roberto Firmino (113.Takumi Minamino), Mohamed Salah, Sadio Mané. Trainer: Jürgen Klopp.
Atlético Madrid: Jan Oblak, Stefan Savic, Kieran Trippier (91.Sime Vrsaljko), Felipe Monteiro, Renan Lodi, Saúl, Koke, Thomas Partey, Diego Costa (56.Marcos Llorente), Ángel Correa (105.José Giménez), João Félix (103.Álvaro Morata). Trainer: Diego Simeone.
Goals: 43' Georginio Wijnaldum 1-0, 94' Roberto Firmino 2-0, 97', 105+1' Marcos Llorente 2-1, 2-2, 120+1' Álvaro Morata 2-3.

19.02.2020; Stadio „Giuseppe Meazza", Milano
Referee: Michael Oliver (ENG); Attendance: 44,236
Atalanta Bergamasca Calcio – Valencia CF 4-1(2-0)
Atalanta Bergamo: Pierluigi Gollini, Rafael Tolói, José Palomino, Hans Hateboer, Mattia Caldara (75.Duván Zapata), Robin Gosens, Papu Gómez (81.Ruslan Malinovskiy), Josip Ilicic, Marten van Roon, Remo Freuler, Mario Pasalic (90+2.Adrien Tameze). Trainer: Gian Piero Gasperini.
Valencia: Jaume Doménech, Eliaquim Mangala, Gayà, Mouctar Diakhaby, Daniel Wass, Dani Parejo, Geoffrey Kondogbia, Gonçalo Guedes (64.Denis Cheryshev), Carlos Soler, Ferrán Torres, Maximiliano Gómez (73.Kevin Gameiro). Trainer: Celades.
Goals: 16' Hans Hateboer 1-0, 42' Josip Ilicic 2-0, 57' Remo Freuler 3-0, 62' Hans Hateboer 4-0, 66' Denis Cheryshev 4-1.

10.03.2020; Estadio de Mestalla, Valencia
Referee: Ovidiu Alin Haţegan (ROU)
Valencia CF – ATALANTA BERGAMASCA CALCIO 3-4(1-2)
Valencia: Jasper Cillessen, Gayà, Mouctar Diakhaby (46.Gonçalo Guedes), Daniel Wass, Dani Parejo, Francis Coquelin (74.Denis Cheryshev), Geoffrey Kondogbia, Carlos Soler, Ferrán Torres, Kevin Gameiro, Rodrigo (79.Alessandro Florenzi). Trainer: Celades.
Atalanta Bergamo: Marco Sportiello, José Palomino, Berat Djimsiti, Hans Hateboer, Mattia Caldara, Robin Gosens, Papu Gómez (78.Ruslan Malinovskiy), Josip Ilicic, Marten van Roon (45.Duván Zapata), Remo Freuler, Mario Pasalic (83.Adrien Tameze). Trainer: Gian Piero Gasperini.
Goals: 3' Josip Ilicic 0-1 (pen), 21' Kevin Gameiro 1-1, 43' Josip Ilicic 1-2 (pen), 51' Kevin Gameiro 2-2, 67' Ferrán Torres 3-2, 71', 82' Josip Ilicic 3-3, 3-4.

19.02.2020; Tottenham Hotspur Stadium, London
Referee: Cüneyt Çakir (TUR); Attendance: 60,095
Tottenham Hotspur FC London – RasenBallsport Leipzig 0-1(0-0)
Tottenham Hotspur: Hugo Lloris, Toby Alderweireld, Serge Aurier, Ben Davies, Davinson Sánchez, Lucas Moura, Dele Alli (64.Érik Lamela), Harry Winks, Gedson Fernandes (64.Tanguy NDombèlé), Giovani Lo Celso, Steven Bergwijn. Trainer: José Mourinho.
RB Leipzig: Péter Gulácsi, Marcel Halstenberg, Lukas Klostermann, José Angeliño, Nordi Mukiele, Ethan Ampadu, Marcel Sabitzer, Konrad Laimer (83.Emil Forsberg), Christopher Nkunku (74.Amadou Haïdara), Timo Werner, Patrik Schick (77.Yussuf Poulsen). Trainer: Julian Nagelsmann.
Goal: 58' Timo Werner 0-1 (pen).

10.03.2020; Red Bull Arena, Leipzig
Referee: Carlos del Cerro Grande (ESP); Attendance: 42,146
RASENBALLSPORT LEIPZIG – Tottenham Hotspur FC London 3-0(2-0)
RB Leipzig: Péter Gulácsi, Marcel Halstenberg, Lukas Klostermann, José Angeliño, Nordi Mukiele (56.Tyler Adams), Dayot Upamecano, Marcel Sabitzer (87.Emil Forsberg), Konrad Laimer, Christopher Nkunku (59.Amadou Haïdara), Timo Werner, Patrik Schick. Trainer: Julian Nagelsmann.
Tottenham Hotspur: Hugo Lloris, Toby Alderweireld, Serge Aurier (90+1.Malachi Fagan-Walcott), Japhet Tanganga, Érik Lamela, Lucas Moura, Dele Alli, Eric Dier, Harry Winks, Giovani Lo Celso (80.Gedson Fernandes), Ryan Sessegnon. Trainer: José Mourinho.
Goals: 10', 21' Marcel Sabitzer 1-0, 2-0, 87' Emil Forsberg 3-0.

25.02.2020; Stamford Bridge, London
Referee: Clément Turpin (FRA); Attendance: 36,761
Chelsea FC London – FC Bayern München 0-3(0-0)
Chelsea: Willy Caballero, Azpilicueta (73.Pedro), Marcos Alonso, Antonio Rüdiger, Andreas Christensen, Reece James, Ross Barkley (61.Willian), Mateo Kovacic, Jorginho, Mason Mount, Olivier Giroud (61.Tammy Abraham). Trainer: Frank Lampard.
Bayern München: Manuel Neuer, Jérôme Boateng, David Alaba, Joshua Kimmich, Benjamin Pavard, Thiago Alcântara (90.Leon Goretzka), Serge Gnabry (85.Corentin Tolisso), Kingsley Coman (66.Philippe Coutinho), Alphonso Davies, Thomas Müller, Robert Lewandowski. Trainer: Hansi Flick.
Goals: 51', 54' Serge Gnabry 0-1, 0-2, 76' Robert Lewandowski 0-3.
Sent off: 83' Marcos Alonso.

25.02.2020; Stadio San Paolo, Naples
Referee: Dr. Felix Brych (GER); Attendance: 44,388
SSC Napoli – FC Barcelona 1-1(1-0)
SSC Napoli: David Ospina, Kostas Manolas, Nikola Maksimovic, Mário Rui, Giovanni Di Lorenzo, Diego Demme (80.Allan), Piotr Zielinski, Fabián Ruiz, Dries Mertens (54.Arkadiusz Milik), José Callejón (74.Matteo Politano), Lorenzo Insigne. Trainer: Gennaro Gattuso.
FC Barcelona: Marc-André ter Stegen, Piqué (90+3.Clément Lenglet), Samuel Umtiti, Nélson Semedo, Junior Firpo, Ivan Rakitic (56.Arthur), Arturo Vidal, Busquets, Frenkie de Jong, Lionel Messi, Antoine Griezmann (87.Ansu Fati). Trainer: Quique Setién.
Goals: 30' Dries Mertens 1-0, 57' Antoine Griezmann 1-1.
Sent off: 89' Arturo Vidal.

26.02.2020; Estadio „Santiago Bernabéu", Madrid
Referee: Daniele Orsato (ITA); Attendance: 75,615
Real Madrid CF – Manchester City FC 1-2(0-0)
Real Madrid: Thibaut Courtois, Sergio Ramos, Dani Carvajal, Raphaël Varane, Ferland Mendy, Luka Modric (84.Lucas Vázquez), Casemiro, Isco (84.Luka Jovic), Federico Valverde, Karim Benzema, Vinicíus Júnior (75.Gareth Bale). Trainer: Zinédine Zidane.
Manchester City: Ederson Moraes, Nicolás Otamendi, Kyle Walker, Benjamin Mendy, Aymeric Laporte (33.Fernandinho), Ilkay Gündogan, Kevin De Bruyne, Bernardo Silva (73.Raheem Sterling), Rodri Hernández, Riyad Mahrez, Gabriel Jesus. Trainer: Pep Guardiola.
Goals: 60' Isco 1-0, 78' Gabriel Jesus 1-1, 83' Kevin De Bruyne 1-2 (pen).
Sent off: 86' Sergio Ramos.

26.02.2020; Groupama Stadium, Décines-Charpieu
Referee: Jesús Gil Manzano (ESP); Attendance: 57,335
Olympique Lyonnais – Juventus FC Torino 1-0(1-0)
Olympique Lyonnais: Anthony Lopes, Marcelo, Fernando Marçal, Léo Dubois (78.Kenny Tete), Jason Denayer, Lucas Tousart, Bruno Guimarães, Houssem Aouar, Karl Toko Ekambi (66.Martin Terrier), Maxwel Cornet (81.Joachim Andersen), Moussa Dembélé. Trainer: Rudi García.
Juventus: Wojciech Szczesny, Leonardo Bonucci, Danilo, Alex Sandro, Matthijs de Ligt, Miralem Pjanic (62.Aaron Ramsey), Juan Cuadrado (70.Gonzalo Higuaín), Adrien Rabiot (78.Federico Bernardeschi), Rodrigo Bentancur, Cristiano Ronaldo, Paulo Dybala. Trainer: Maurizio Sarri.
Goal: 31' Lucas Tousart 1-0.

08.08.2020; Allianz Arena, München
Referee: Ovidiu Alin Haţegan (ROU)
FC BAYERN MÜNCHEN – Chelsea FC London 4-1(2-1)
Bayern München: Manuel Neuer, Jérôme Boateng (63.Niklas Süle), David Alaba, Joshua Kimmich (71.Odriozola), Ivan Perisic (64.Philippe Coutinho), Thiago Alcântara (70.Corentin Tolisso), Leon Goretzka, Serge Gnabry (81.Javi Martínez), Alphonso Davies, Thomas Müller, Robert Lewandowski. Trainer: Hansi Flick.
Chelsea: Willy Caballero, Kurt Zouma, Emerson, Andreas Christensen, Reece James, Ross Barkley, Mateo Kovacic, N'Golo Kanté, Mason Mount, Tammy Abraham (81.Olivier Giroud), Callum Hudson-Odoi. Trainer: Frank Lampard.
Goals: 10' Robert Lewandowski 1-0 (pen), 24' Ivan Perisic 2-0, 44' Tammy Abraham 2-1, 76' Corentin Tolisso 3-1, 83' Robert Lewandowski 4-1.

08.08.2020; Estadio Camp Nou, Barcelona
Referee: Cüneyt Çakir (TUR)
FC BARCELONA – SSC Napoli 3-1(3-1)
FC Barcelona: Marc-André ter Stegen, Piqué, Jordi Alba, Sergi Roberto, Clément Lenglet, Nélson Semedo, Ivan Rakitic, Frenkie de Jong, Lionel Messi, Luis Suárez (90+2.Junior Firpo), Antoine Griezmann (84.Monchu). Trainer: Quique Setién.
SSC Napoli: David Ospina, Kostas Manolas, Mário Rui, Kalidou Koulibaly, Giovanni Di Lorenzo, Diego Demme (46.Stanislav Lobotka), Piotr Zielinski (70.Hirving Lozano), Fabián Ruiz (79.Eljif Elmas), Dries Mertens, José Callejón (70.Matteo Politano), Lorenzo Insigne (79.Arkadiusz Milik). Trainer: Gennaro Gattuso.
Goals: 10' Clément Lenglet 1-0, 23' Leonel Messi 2-0, 45+1' Luis Suárez 3-0 (pen), 45+5' Lorenzo Insigne 3-1 (pen).

07.08.2020; Etihad Stadium, Manchester
Referee: Dr. Felix Brych (GER)
MANCHESTER CITY FC – Real Madrid CF 2-1(1-1)
Manchester City: Ederson Moraes, Kyle Walker, João Cancelo, Aymeric Laporte, Fernandinho, Ilkay Gündogan, Kevin De Bruyne, Rodri Hernández (89.Nicolás Otamendi), Phil Foden (67.Bernardo Silva), Raheem Sterling (81.David Silva), Gabriel Jesus. Trainer: Pep Guardiola.
Real Madrid: Thibaut Courtois, Dani Carvajal (83.Lucas Vázquez), Raphaël Varane, Ferland Mendy, Éder Militão, Luka Modric (83.Federico Valverde), Toni Kroos, Casemiro, Karim Benzema, Eden Hazard (83.Luka Jovic), Rodrygo (61.Marco Asensio). Trainer: Zinédine Zidane.
Goals: 9' Raheem Sterling 1-0, 28' Karim Benzema 1-1, 68' Gabriel Jesus 2-1.

07.08.2020; Allianz Stadium, Torino
Referee: Felix Zwayer (GER)
Juventus FC Torino – OLYMPIQUE LYONNAIS 2-1(1-1)
Juventus: Wojciech Szczesny, Leonardo Bonucci, Alex Sandro, Matthijs de Ligt, Miralem Pjanic (60.Aaron Ramsey), Juan Cuadrado (70.Danilo), Adrien Rabiot, Rodrigo Bentancur, Cristiano Ronaldo, Gonzalo Higuaín, Federico Bernardeschi (71.Paulo Dybala, 84.Marco Olivieri). Trainer: Maurizio Sarri.
Olympique Lyonnais: Anthony Lopes, Marcelo, Fernando Marçal, Léo Dubois (90+1.Kenny Tete), Jason Denayer (61.Joachim Andersen), Bruno Guimarães, Houssem Aouar (90+1.Thiago Mendes), Maxence Caqueret, Memphis Depay (67.Moussa Dembélé), Karl Toko Ekambi (67.Jeff Reine-Adélaïde), Maxwel Cornet. Trainer: Rudi García.
Goals: 12' Memphis Depay 0-1 (pen), 43', 60' Cristiano Ronaldo 1-1 (pen), 2-1.

Please note: All the matches from the quarter finals till the final were played on neutral venue in Portugal behind closed doors.

12.08.2020; Estádio da Luz, Lisboa
Referee: Anthony Taylor (ENG)
Atalanta Bergamasca Calcio – PARIS SAINT-GERMAIN FC 1-2(1-0)
Atalanta Bergamo: Marco Sportiello, Rafael Tolói, Berat Djimsiti (60.José Palomino), Hans Hateboer, Mattia Caldara, Robin Gosens (82.Timothy Castagne), Papu Gómez (59.Ruslan Malinovskiy), Marten van Roon, Remo Freuler, Mario Pasalic (70.Luis Muriel), Duván Zapata (82.Jacopo Da Riva). Trainer: Gian Piero Gasperini.
Paris Saint-Germain: Keylor Navas (79.Sergio Rico), Thiago Silva, Marquinhos, Juan Bernat, Presnel Kimpembe, Thilo Kehrer, Ander Herrera (72.Julian Draxler), Idrissa Gueye (72.Leandro Paredes), Pablo Sarabia (60.Kylian Mbappé), Neymar, Mauro Icardi (79.Eric Maxim Choupo-Moting). Trainer: Thomas Tuchel.
Goals: 27' Mario Pasalic 1-0, 90' Marquinhos 1-1, 90+3' Eric Maxim Choupo-Moting 1-2.

14.08.2020; Estádio da Luz, Lisboa
Referee: Damir Skomina (SVN)
FC Barcelona – FC BAYERN MÜNCHEN 2-8(1-4)
FC Barcelona: Marc-André ter Stegen, Piqué, Jordi Alba, Sergi Roberto (46.Antoine Griezmann), Clément Lenglet, Nélson Semedo, Arturo Vidal, Busquets (70.Ansu Fati), Frenkie de Jong, Lionel Messi, Luis Suárez. Trainer: Quique Setién.
Bayern München: Manuel Neuer, Jérôme Boateng (76.Niklas Süle), David Alaba, Joshua Kimmich, Ivan Perisic (67.Kingsley Coman), Thiago Alcântara, Leon Goretzka (84.Corentin Tolisso), Serge Gnabry (75.Philippe Coutinho), Alphonso Davies (84.Lucas Hernández), Thomas Müller, Robert Lewandowski. Trainer: Hansi Flick.
Goals: 4' Thomas Müller 0-1, 7' David Alaba 1-1 (own goal), 22' Ivan Perisic 1-2, 27' Serge Gnabry 1-3, 31' Thomas Müller 1-4, 57' Luis Suárez 2-4, 63' Joshua Kimmich 2-5, 82' Robert Lewandowski 2-6, 85', 89' Philippe Coutinho 2-7, 2-8.

13.08.2020; Estádio "José Alvalade", Lisboa
Referee: Szymon Marciniak (POL)
RASENBALLSPORT LEIPZIG – Club Atlético de Madrid 2-1(0-0)
RB Leipzig: Péter Gulácsi, Marcel Halstenberg, Lukas Klostermann, José Angeliño, Dayot Upamecano, Kevin Kampl, Marcel Sabitzer (90+2.Nordi Mukiele), Christopher Nkunku (83.Amadou Haïdara), Daniel Olmo (83.Patrik Schick), Yussuf Poulsen. Trainer: Julian Nagelsmann.
Atlético Madrid: Jan Oblak, Stefan Savic, Kieran Trippier, José Giménez, Renan Lodi, Héctor Herrera (58.João Félix), Saúl, Koke (90+2.Felipe Monteiro), Yannick Carrasco, Marcos Llorente, Diego Costa (72.Álvaro Morata). Trainer: Diego Simeone.
Goals: 51' Daniel Olmo 1-0, 71' João Félix 1-1 (pen), 88' Tyler Adams 2-1.

15.08.2020; Estádio "José Alvalade", Lisboa
Referee: Danny Desmond Makkelie (NED)
Manchester City FC – OLYMPIQUE LYONNAIS 1-3(0-1)
Manchester City: Ederson Moraes, Kyle Walker, João Cancelo, Aymeric Laporte, Eric Gacía, Fernandinho (56.Riyad Mahrez), Ilkay Gündogan, Kevin De Bruyne, Rodri Hernández (84.David Silva), Raheem Sterling, Gabriel Jesus. Trainer: Pep Guardiola.
Olympique Lyonnais: Anthony Lopes, Marcelo, Fernando Marçal, Léo Dubois (74.Kenny Tete), Jason Denayer, Bruno Guimarães (70.Thiago Mendes), Houssem Aouar, Maxence Caqueret, Memphis Depay (75.Moussa Dembélé), Karl Toko Ekambi (87.Jeff Reine-Adélaïde), Maxwel Cornet. Trainer: Rudi García.
Goals: 24' Maxwel Cornet 0-1, 69' Kevin De Bruyne 1-1, 79', 87' Moussa Dembélé 1-2, 1-3.

18.08.2020; Estádio da Luz, Lisboa
Referee: Björn Kuipers (NED)
RasenBallsport Leipzig – PARIS SAINT-GERMAIN FC 0-3(0-2)
RB Leipzig: Péter Gulácsi, Lukas Klostermann (82.Willi Orban), José Angeliño, Nordi Mukiele, Dayot Upamecano, Kevin Kampl (64.Tyler Adams), Marcel Sabitzer, Konrad Laimer (62.Marcel Halstenberg), Christopher Nkunku (46.Emil Forsberg), Daniel Olmo (46.Patrik Schick), Yussuf Poulsen. Trainer: Julian Nagelsmann.
Paris Saint-Germain: Sergio Rico, Thiago Silva, Marquinhos, Juan Bernat, Presnel Kimpembe, Thilo Kehrer, Ángel Di María (87.Pablo Sarabia), Ander Herrera (83.Marco Verratti), Leandro Paredes (83.Julian Draxler), Neymar, Kylian Mbappé (86.Eric Maxim Choupo-Moting). Trainer: Thomas Tuchel.
Goals: 13' Marquinhos 0-1, 42' Ángel Di Maria 0-2, 56' Juan Bernat 0-3.

19.08.2020; Estádio "José Alvalade", Lisboa
Referee: Antonio Miguel Mateu Lahoz (ESP)
Olympique Lyonnais – FC BAYERN MÜNCHEN 0-3(0-2)
Olympique Lyonnais: Anthony Lopes, Marcelo, Fernando Marçal (73.Mathis Rayan Cherki), Léo Dubois (67.Kenny Tete), Jason Denayer, Bruno Guimarães (46.Thiago Mendes), Houssem Aouar, Maxence Caqueret, Memphis Depay (58.Moussa Dembélé), Karl Toko Ekambi (67.Jeff Reine-Adélaïde), Maxwel Cornet. Trainer: Rudi García.
Bayern München: Manuel Neuer, Jérôme Boateng (46.Niklas Süle), David Alaba, Joshua Kimmich, Ivan Perisic (63.Kingsley Coman), Thiago Alcântara (82.Corentin Tolisso), Leon Goretzka (82.Benjamin Pavard), Serge Gnabry (75.Philippe Coutinho), Alphonso Davies, Thomas Müller, Robert Lewandowski. Trainer: Hansi Flick.
Goals: 18', 33' Serge Gnabry 0-1, 0-2, 88' Robert Lewandowski 0-3.

23.08.2020; Estádio da Luz, Lisboa: Referee: Daniele Orsato (ITA)
Paris Saint-Germain FC Paris – FC Bayern München 0-1(0-0)
Paris Saint-Germain: Keylor Antonio Navas Gamboa, Thiago Emiliano Silva, Marcos Aoás Corrêa „Marquinhos", Juan Bernat Velasco (80.Layvin Kurzawa), Presnel Kimpembe, Thilo Kehrer, Ángel Fabián Di María Hernández (80.Eric Maxim Choupo-Moting), Ander Herrera Agüera (72.Julian Draxler), Leandro Daniel Paredes (65.Marco Verratti), Kylian Sanmi Mbappé Lottin, Neymar da Silva Santos Júnior. Trainer: Thomas Tuchel.
Bayern München: Manuel Neuer, Jérôme Agyenim Boateng (25.Niklas Süle), David Olatukunbo Alaba, Joshua Walter Kimmich, Thiago Alcântara do Nascimento (86.Corentin Tolisso), Leon Christoph Goretzka, Serge David Gnabry (68.Philippe Coutinho Correia), Kingsley Junior Coman (68.Ivan Perišić), Alphonso Boyle Davies, Thomas Müller, Robert Lewandowski. Trainer: Hans-Dieter Flick.
Goal: 59' Kingsley Junior Coman 0-1.

UEFA Champions League Winner 2019/2020: **FC Bayern München** (Germany)

Best Goalscorer: Robert Lewandowski (POL, FC Bayern München) – 15 goals

EUROPEAN CHAMPION CLUBS' CUP (1955 – 1992)
UEFA CHAMPIONS LEAGUE (1992 – 2020)
TABLE OF HONOURS

1955/1956	Real Madrid CF	*Spain*
1956/1957	Real Madrid CF	*Spain*
1957/1958	Real Madrid CF	*Spain*
1958/1959	Real Madrid CF	*Spain*
1959/1960	Real Madrid CF	*Spain*
1960/1961	Sport Lisboa e Benfica	*Portugal*
1961/1962	Sport Lisboa e Benfica	*Portugal*
1962/1963	AC Milan	*Italy*
1963/1964	FC Internazionale Milano	*Italy*
1964/1965	FC Internazionale Milano	*Italy*
1965/1966	Real Madrid CF	*Spain*
1966/1967	Celtic FC Glasgow	*Scotland*
1967/1968	Manchester United FC	*England*
1968/1969	AC Milan	*Italy*
1969/1970	SC Feijenoord Rotterdam	*Netherlands*
1970/1971	AFC Ajax Amsterdam	*Netherlands*
1971/1972	AFC Ajax Amsterdam	*Netherlands*
1972/1973	AFC Ajax Amsterdam	*Netherlands*
1973/1974	FC Bayern München	*Germany*
1974/1975	FC Bayern München	*Germany*
1975/1976	FC Bayern München	*Germany*
1976/1977	Liverpool FC	*England*
1977/1978	Liverpool FC	*England*
1978/1979	Nottingham Forest FC	*England*
1979/1980	Nottingham Forest FC	*England*
1980/1981	Liverpool FC	*England*
1981/1982	Aston Villa FC Birmingham	*England*
1982/1983	Hamburger SV	*Germany*
1983/1984	Liverpool FC	*England*
1984/1985	Juventus FC Torino	*Italy*
1985/1986	FC Steaua Bucureşti	*Romania*
1986/1987	FC do Porto	*Portugal*
1987/1988	PSV Eindhoven	*Netherlands*
1988/1989	AC Milan	*Italy*
1989/1990	AC Milan	*Italy*
1990/1991	FK Crvena Zvezda Beograd	*Serbia*
1991/1992	FC Barcelona	*Spain*
1992/1993	Olympique de Marseille	*France*
1993/1994	AC Milan	*Italy*
1994/1995	AFC Ajax Amsterdam	*Netherlands*
1995/1996	Juventus FC Torino	*Italy*
1996/1997	BV Borussia 09 Dortmund	*Germany*
1997/1998	Real Madrid CF	*Spain*
1998/1999	Manchester United FC	*England*
1999/2000	Real Madrid CF	*Spain*
2000/2001	FC Bayern München	*Germany*
2001/2002	Real Madrid CF	*Spain*
2002/2003	AC Milan	*Italy*
2003/2004	FC do Porto	*Portugal*
2004/2005	Liverpool FC	*England*
2005/2006	FC Barcelona	*Spain*
2006/2007	AC Milan	*Italy*
2007/2008	Manchester United FC	*England*
2008/2009	FC Barcelona	*Spain*
2009/2010	FC Internazionale Milano	*Italy*
2010/2011	FC Barcelona	*Spain*
2011/2012	Chelsea FC London	*England*
2012/2013	FC Bayern München	*Germany*
2013/2014	Real Madrid CF	*Spain*
2014/2015	FC Barcelona	*Spain*
2015/2016	Real Madrid CF	*Spain*
2016/2017	Real Madrid CF	*Spain*
2017/2018	Real Madrid CF	*Spain*
2018/2019	Liverpool FC	*England*
2019/2020	FC Bayern München	*Germany*

PRELIMINARY ROUND

27.06.2019; Stade Parc des Sports, Differdange
Referee: Luis Teixeira (POR); Attendance: 1,984
FC Progrès Niederkorn – Cardiff Metropolitan University 1-0(0-0)
Progrès Niederkorn: Sebastian Flauss, Tom Laterza (78.Ricky Borges), Ben Vogel, Metin Karayer, Tim Hall, Aldin Skenderovic, Yann Matias Marques, Sébastien Thill, Belmin Muratovic, Mayron De Almeida, Issa Bah (60.Florik Shala). Trainer: Roland Vrabec.
Cardiff Metropolitan University: Will Fuller, Kyle McCarthy, Emlyn Lewis, Bradley Woolridge, Dylan Rees, Joel Edwards, Charlie Corsby (63.Rhydian Morgan), Will Evans (85.Tim Parker), Chris Baker, Dan Spencer (75.Jordan Lam), Eliot Evans. Trainer: Christian Edwards.
Goal: 62' Mayron De Almeida 1-0.

27.06.2019; Cardiff International Sports Stadium, Cardiff
Referee: Jason Barcelo (GIB); Attendance: 2,106
Barry Town United FC – Cliftonville FAC 0-0
Barry Town United: Mike Lewis, Luke Cummings, Luke Cooper, Chris Hugh, Jack Compton (72.Drew Fahiya), Clayton Green, Robbie Patten (72.Troy Greening), Evan Press, Kayne McLaggon, Jonathan Hood, Jordan Cotterill (82.Tom Fry). Trainer: Gavin Chesterfield.
Cliftonville FAC: Richard Brush, Garry Breen, Liam Bagnall, Conor McMenamin (83.Ryan Curran), Joe Gorman, Levi Ives, Conor McDermott (90+6.Thomas Maguire), Chris Curran, Aaron Harkin, Ronan Doherty (79.Joe Gormley), Rory Donnelly. Trainer: Paddy McLaughlin.

27.06.2019; Estadi Comunal d'Andorra la Vella, Andorra la Vella
Referee: Dragan Petrovic (BIH); Attendance: 300
UE Sant Julià – Europa FC 3-2(1-1)
UE Sant Julià: Ferran Pol, Toni Lao, Soualio Bakayoko, Nicolae Vasile, Pedro Muñoz, Jonny, Sénah Mango, Miguel Luque, Loïc Malatini (80.Walter Balufo), Fousseyni Cissé, Joel Méndez (72.Quentin Leite Pereira). Trainer: Emiliano González.
Europa FC: Javi Muñoz, Sergio Sánchez, Rahim Ayew, Olmo González, Diego Portilla, Velasco (84.Jayce Mascarenhas-Olivero), Juampe Rico, Liam Walker, Mustapha Yahaya, Marco Rosa (67.Andre Tjay de Barr), Adrián Gallardo (77.Manu Dimas). Trainer: Rafael Escobar.
Goals: 4' Adrián Gallardo 0-1, 44' Joel Méndez 1-1), 46' Sénah Mango 1-2 (own goal), 64' Joel Méndez 2-2, 90+3' Pedro Muñoz 3-2.
Sent off: 75' Fousseyni Cissé.

27.06.2019; Gundadalur, Tórshavn
Referee: Robert Jenkins (WAL); Attendance: 575
KÍ Klaksvík – SP Tre Fiori 5-1(2-0)
KÍ Klaksvík: Kristian Joensen, Jesper Brinck, Ísak Simonsen, Deni Pavlovic, Semir Hadzibulic (85.Darius Lewis), Patrik Johannesen (76.Torbjørn Grytten), Jákup Andreasen, Jóannes Bjartalíd, Simen Sandmæl, Jóannes Danielsen, Jonn Johannesen (70.Boris Dosljak). Trainer: Mikkjal Thomassen.
SP Tre Fiori: Aldo Simoncini, Enea Righetti, Leandro Carubini, Alessandro D'Addario, Claudio Cuzzilla (62.Joel Apezteguía Hijuelos), Mattia Costantini, Luca Angelini (46.Nicolo Bacchiocchi), Manolo Pestrin (75.Andrea Tamagnini), Daniele Compagno, Martin Lago Ramiro, Andrea Compagno. Trainer: Matteo Cecchetti.
Goals: 9' Patrik Johannesen 1-0, 37' Simen Sandmæl 2-0, 56' Jonn Johannesen 3-0, 73', 83' Jóannes Bjartalíd 4-0, 5-0, 90+3' Andrea Compagno 5-1.

04.07.2019; Cardiff International Sports Stadium, Cardiff
Referee: Loukas Sotiriou (CYP); Attendance: 1,316
Cardiff Metropolitan University – FC PROGRÈS NIEDERKORN 2-1(1-0)
Cardiff Metropolitan University: Will Fuller, Kyle McCarthy, Emlyn Lewis, Bradley Woolridge, Dylan Rees, Joel Edwards, Charlie Corsby (77.Dion Phillips), Will Evans, Chris Baker, Eliot Evans (56.Mael Davies), Jordan Lam (61.Tim Parker). Trainer: Christian Edwards.
Progrès Niederkorn: Sebastian Flauss, Tom Laterza, Ben Vogel, Metin Karayer, Tim Hall, Aldin Skenderovic, Yann Matias Marques (70 Yannick Bastos), Sébastien Thill, Belmin Muratovic (88.Adrien Ferino), Mayron De Almeida, Issa Bah (85.Filipe Correira Santos). Trainer: Roland Vrabec.
Goals: 2' Jordan Lam 1-0, 67' Dylan Rees 2-0 (pen) / 73 Mayron De Almeida 2-1.

04.07.2019; Solitude Stadium, Belfast
Referee: Fyodor Zammit (MLT); Attendance: 1,946
CLIFTONVILLE FAC – Barry Town United FC 4-0(2-0)
Cliftonville FAC: Richard Brush, Garry Breen, Liam Bagnall, Conor McMenamin (85.Ronan Wilson), Joe Gorman, Levi Ives, Conor McDermott, Chris Curran, Ronan Doherty, Rory Donnelly (86.Thomas Maguire), Joe Gormley (85.Jamie Harney). Trainer: Paddy McLaughlin.
Barry Town United: Mike Lewis, Paul Morgan, Luke Cooper, Chris Hugh, Troy Greening, Clayton Green, Robbie Patten (73.Tom Fry), Evan Press, Kayne McLaggon, Jonathan Hood (79.Sam Snaith), Jordan Cotterill (64.Jack Compton). Trainer: Gavin Chesterfield.
Goals: 25' Conor McMenamin 1-0, 44' Joe Gormley 2-0, 82' Conor McDermott 3-0, 84' Rory Donnelly 4-0.

04.07.2019; Victoria Stadium, Gibraltar
Referee: Matthew De Gabriele (MLT); Attendance: 1,075
EUROPA FC – UE Sant Julià 4-0(1-0)
Europa FC: Dayle Coleing, Sergio Sánchez, Rahim Ayew (79.Ethan Jolley), Olmo González, Diego Portilla (61.Jayce Mascarenhas-Olivero), Juampe Rico, Liam Walker, Mustapha Yahaya, Marco Rosa, Andre Tjay de Barr, Adrián Gallardo (70.Velasco). Trainer: Rafael Escobar.
UE Sant Julià: Anthony Kasparian, Toni Lao, Soualio Bakayoko (57.Walter Balufo), Nicolae Vasile, Pedro Muñoz, Jonny, Sénah Mango, Miguel Luque, Quentin Leite Pereira (62.Luis Blanco), Loïc Malatini, Joel Méndez. Trainer: Emiliano González.
Goals: 38' Adrián Gallardo 1-0, 48' Andre Tjay de Barr 2-0, 78' Liam Walker 3-0, 90+2' Juampe Rico 4-0.
Sent off: 83' Jonny.

04.07.2019; Stadio Olimpico di Serravalle, Serravalle
Referee: Novak Simovic (SRB); Attendance: 177
SP Tre Fiori – KÍ KLAKSVÍK 0-4(0-3)
SP Tre Fiori: Aldo Simoncini, Enea Righetti, Leandro Carubini (77.Eduardo Marconi), Alessandro D'Addario, Claudio Cuzzilla (66.Nicola Della Valle), Mattia Costantini, Luca Angelini (52.Manolo Pestrin), Daniele Compagno, Joel Apezteguía Hijuelos, Martin Lago Ramiro, Andrea Compagno. Trainer: Matteo Cecchetti.
KÍ Klaksvík: Kristian Joensen, Jesper Brinck, Ísak Simonsen, Deni Pavlovic (79.Ólavur Niclasen), Semir Hadzibulic, Patrik Johannesen (57.Páll Klettskard), Jákup Andreasen, Jóannes Bjartalíd, Simen Sandmæl, Jóannes Danielsen, Jonn Johannesen (46.Magnus Stamnestrø). Trainer: Mikkjal Thomassen.
Goals: 29' Jóannes Bjartalíd 0-1 (pen), 33' Jonn Johannesen 0-2, 45+2' Patrik Johannesen 0-3, 75' Jóannes Danielsen 0-4.

27.06.2019; Stadio Olimpico di Serravalle, Serravalle
Referee: Christophe Pires Martins (LUX); Attendance: 302
SP La Fiorita – UE Engordany 0-1(0-1)
SP La Fiorita: Gianluca Vivan, Samuele Olivi, Roberto Di Maio, Marco Gasperoni, Riccardo Mezzadri, Simone Loiodice, Armando Amati (72.Damiano Tommasi), Nicolás Castro, Andrea Bracaletti, Danilo Rinaldi (83.José Hirsch), Fabrizio Castellazzi (60.Mirco Vassallo). Trainer: Juri Tamburini.
UE Engordany: Jesús Coca, Miguel Ruiz, Rafael Brito, Aarón Sánchez, Deivis De Jesús Soares, Mario Spano, Sébastien Aguéro, Nikola Zugic (83.Jorge Sebastián Varela), Hamza Bouharma, Míguel Laborda (75.Fábio Serra Alves), Sebastián Gómez (70.Marc Ferré). Trainer: Filipe Busto.
Goal: 31' Aarón Sánchez 0-1.
Sent off: 87' Mirco Vassallo, 87' Deivis De Jesús Soares.

27.06.2019; The Showgrounds, Ballymena
Referee: Athanasios Tzilos (GRE); Attendance: 2,270
Ballymena United FC – NSÍ Runavík 2-0(0-0)
Ballymena United: Ross Glendinning, Tony Kane, Jim Ervin, Steven McCullough, Scot Whiteside, Kofi Balmer, Jude Winchester (86.Ryan Harpur), Declan Carville, Leroy Millar, Cathair Friel (79.Ryan Mayse), Adam Lecky. Trainer: David Jeffrey.
NSÍ Runavík: Tórdur Thomsen, Oddur Højgaard, Pól Justinussen, Jóhan Davidsen, Bárdur Jógvansson-Hansen, Per Langgaard (68.Betuel Hansen), Pætur Hentze, Peder Nersveen, Petur Knudsen, Klæmint Olsen, Búi Egilsson (70.Jann Benjaminsen). Trainer: Gudjón Thórdarson.
Goals: 49' Leroy Millar 1-0, 55' Jude Winchester 2-0.

27.06.2019; Stadiumi „Fadil Vokrri", Prishtina
Referee: Helgi Mikael Jónasson (ISL); Attendance: 4,000
FC Prishtina – St.Joseph's FC 1-1(1-1)
FC Prishtina: Visar Bekaj, Armend Dallku, Armend Thaçi, Leotrim Bekteshi, Abdul Bashiru, Diar Miftaraj, Kreshnik Uka (67.Meriton Korenica), Gauthier Mankenda, Endrit Krasniqi, Ergyn Ahmeti (78.Qendrim Zyba), Alban Shillova (49.Laurit Boshnjaku). Trainer: Mirel Josa.
St.Joseph's FC: Fran Mateo, Federico Villar, Pecci, Mauri Torres, Iván Lobato, Ezequiel Rojas, Domingo Ferrer (84.Andrew Hernandez), Juanma González, Pedrito, Juanfri Peña (89.Daniel Guererro), Boro (76.Ernesto Cornejo). Trainer: Raúl Procopio.
Goals: 28' Armend Dallku 1-0 (pen), 31' Juanfri Peña 1-1.

04.07.2019; Estadi Comunal d'Andorra la Vella, Andorra la Vella
Referee: Alexandru Tean (MDA); Attendance: 428
UE ENGORDANY – SP La Fiorita 2-1(1-0)
UE Engordany: Jesús Coca, Miguel Ruiz, Rafael Brito, Aarón Sánchez, Mario Spano, Sébastien Aguéro, Nikola Zugic (76.Marc Ferré), Hamza Bouharma, Míguel Laborda (56.Morgan Lafont), Sebastián Gómez, Fábio Serra Alves (86.Jorge Sebastián Varela). Trainer: Filipe Busto.
SP La Fiorita: Gianluca Vivan, Samuele Olivi, Roberto Di Maio, Marco Gasperoni, Riccardo Mezzadri, Luca Righini, José Hirsch (87.Alessandro Guidi), Simone Loiodice (63.Armando Amati), Nicolás Castro, Andrea Bracaletti (74.Fabrizio Castellazzi), Danilo Rinaldi. Trainer: Juri Tamburini.
Goals: 17' Nikola Zugic 1-0, 84' Marco Gasperoni 2-1 (own goal) / 78' Jesús Coca 1-1 (own goal).

04.07.2019; Svangaskard, Toftir
Referee: Besfort Kasumi (KVX); Attendance: 553
NSÍ Runavík – BALLYMENA UNITED FC 0-0
NSÍ Runavík: Tórdur Thomsen, Oddur Højgaard, Pól Justinussen, Jóhan Davidsen, Bárdur Jógvansson-Hansen, Pætur Hentze (85.Óli Olsen), Jann Mortensen (64.Øssur Dalbúd), Peder Nersveen, Petur Knudsen, Jann Benjaminsen (74.Búi Egilsson), Klæmint Olsen. Trainer: Gudjón Thórdarson.
Ballymena United: Ross Glendinning, Tony Kane (84.Andrew Burns), Jim Ervin, Steven McCullough, Scot Whiteside, Kofi Balmer, Jude Winchester (90+2.Ryan Harpur), Declan Carville, Leroy Millar, Cathair Friel, Adam Lecky. Trainer: David Jeffrey.

02.07.2019; Victoria Stadium, Gibraltar
Referee: Luca Barbeno (SMR); Attendance: 500
ST.JOSEPH'S FC – FC Prishtina 2-0(0-0)
St.Joseph's FC: Fran Mateo, Federico Villar, Pecci, Mauri Torres, Iván Lobato, Ezequiel Rojas, Domingo Ferrer (70.Ernesto Cornejo), Juanma González (84.Andrew Hernandez), Pedrito (87.Francisco Cano), Juanfri Peña, Boro. Trainer: Raúl Procopio.
FC Prishtina: Visar Bekaj, Armend Dallku, Armend Thaçi, Leotrim Bekteshi, Abdul Bashiru, Diar Miftaraj, Kreshnik Uka (52.Ahmet Haliti), Gauthier Mankenda, Laurit Boshnjaku (76.Meriton Korenica), Endrit Krasniqi, Ergyn Ahmeti (56.Khalid Abdul Basit). Trainer: Mirel Josa.
Goals: 75' Federico Villar 1-0, 80' Juanfri Peña 2-0.
Sent off: 48' Armend Dallku, 48' Leotrim Bekteshi, 90+3' Ezequiel Rojas.

09.07.2019; Victoria Stadium, Gibraltar
Referee: Nejc Kajtazovic (SVN); Attendance: 2,050
St.Joseph's FC – Glasgow Rangers FC 0-4(0-0)
St.Joseph's FC: Fran Mateo, Federico Villar, Pecci (70.Andrew Hernandez), Mauri Torres, Iván Lobato, Daniel Guererro, Domingo Ferrer (70.Ryan Casciaro), Pedrito (76.Sykes Garro), Juanfri Peña, Ernesto Cornejo, Boro. Trainer: Raúl Procopio.
Glasgow Rangers: Allan McGregor, James Tavernier, Connor Goldson, Borna Barisic, Nikola Katic, Steven Davis, Ryan Jack (62.Joe Aribo), Sheyi Ojo, Glen Kamara, Jordan Jones (71.Greg Stewart), Jermain Defoe (63.Alfredo Morelos). Trainer: Steven Gerrard.
Goals: 50 Ryan Jack 0-1, 56' Sheyi Ojo 0-2, 68' Connor Goldson 0-3, 77' Alfredo Morelos 0-4.

09.07.2019; MFA Centenary Stadium, Ta'Qali
Referee: Gal Leibovitz (ISR); Attendance: 683
Gzira United FC – HNK Hajduk Split 0-2(0-1)
Gzira United: Justin Haber, Arthur Henrique, Rodolfo Soares, Fernando Barbosa, Nicky Muscat (83.Sacha Borg), Hamed Koné, Gianmarco Conti (72.Andrew Cohen), Juan Corbalan, Zachary Scerri, Jefferson, Ridwaru Adeyemo (62.Elvis Sakyi). Trainer: Giovanni Tedesco.
Hajduk Split: Tomislav Duka, Oleksandr Svatok (75.Stefan Simic), Ardian Ismajli, Domagoj Bradaric (61.Ivan Dolcek), Ádám Gyurcsó (67.Francesco Tahiraj), Hamza Barry, Bassel Jradi, Stanko Juric, Darko Nejasmic, Jairo, Ivan Delic. Trainer: Sinia Orescanin.
Goals: 44' Ádám Gyurcsó 0-1, 90+6' Ivan Dolcek 0-2.

18.07.2019; Ibrox Stadium, Glasgow
Referee: Christopher Jäger (AUT); Attendance: 45,718
GLASGOW RANGERS FC – St Joseph's FC 6-0(2-0)
Glasgow Rangers: Wesley Foderingham, Connor Goldson, Matt Polster, George Edmundson, Andy Halliday, Greg Stewart, Glen Kamara, Greg Docherty (67.Josh McPake), Joe Aribo, Alfredo Morelos (67.Jermain Defoe), Jake Hastie (58.Scott Arfield). Trainer: Steven Gerrard.
St.Joseph's FC: Jamie Robba, Federico Villar, Mauri Torres, Jaime Serra, Daniel Guererro, Domingo Ferrer (79.Sykes Garro), Andrew Hernandez, Pedrito (72.José Reyes), Juanfri Peña, Ernesto Cornejo (69.Evan Green), Boro. Trainer: Raúl Procopio.
Goals: 3' Joe Aribo 1-0, 45+1', 57', 66' Alfredo Morelos 2-0, 3-0 (pen), 4-0, 77', 86' Jermain Defoe 5-0, 6-0.

18.07.2019; Stadion Poljud, Split
Referee: Nikolas Neokleous (CYP); Attendance: 18,236
HNK HAJDUK SPLIT – Gzira United FC 1-3(1-0)
Hajduk Split: Tomislav Duka, Borja López, Josip Basic, Oleksandr Svatok, Ivan Dolcek (58.Josip Juranovic), Hamza Barry, Bassel Jradi, Dino Besirovic (81.Anthony Kalik), Francesco Tahiraj (59.Stanko Juric), Jairo, Ivan Delic. Trainer: Sinia Orescanin.
Gzira United: Justin Haber, Arthur Henrique, Rodolfo Soares (77.Zachary Scerri), Fernando Barbosa, Nicky Muscat, Andrew Cohen (86.Amadou Samb), Hamed Koné, Gianmarco Conti, Juan Corbalan, Elvis Sakyi (66.Sacha Borg), Jefferson. Trainer: Giovanni Tedesco.
Goals: 7' Bassel Jradi 1-0, 57 Jefferson 1-1, 69', 90+6' Hamed Koné 1-2, 1-3.

09.07.2019; Stadion Bâlgarska Armija, Sofia
Referee: Luis Miguel Branco Godinho (POR); Attendance: 8,500
PFC CSKA Sofia – OFK Titograd Podgorica 4-0(1-0)
CSKA Sofia: Vytautas Cerniauskas, Plamen Galabov, Stoycho Atanasov, Nuno Tomás, Geferson (80.Petar Zanev), Graham Carey (60.Kristiyan Malinov), Rúben Pinto, Tiago Rodrigues, Diego Fabbrini, Ali Sowe, Evandro (73.Janio Bikel). Trainer: Dobromir Mitov.
OFK Titograd: Sasa Ivanovic, Radule Zivkovic (86.Ognjen Gasevic), Ivan Novovic, Marko Roganovic (65.Slobodan Perisic), Balsa Banovic, Ajanah-Chinedu Chukwujekwu, Mirko Raicevic, Jovan Nikolic, Vojin Pavlovic (78.Milos Brnovic), Radomir Djalovic, Mendy Mamadou. Trainer: Dragoljub Djuretic.
Goals: 40' Evandro 1-0, 53' Tiago Rodrigues 2-0, 55' Geferson 3-0, 72' Kristiyan Malinov 4-0.

10.07.2019; Stade de la Frontière, Esch-sur-Alzette
Referee: Eldorjan Hamiti (ALB); Attendance: 1,384
AS La Jeunesse d'Esch/Alzette – FC Tobol Kostanay 0-0
Jeunesse d'Esch: Kévin Sommer, Arsène Menèssou, Alessandro Fiorani, Emmanuel Lapierre (78.Clayton De Sousa Moreira), Johannes Steinbach, Halim Meddour, Yannick Makota (61.Frederick Kyereh), Milos Todorovic, Luca Duriatti, David Soares De Sousa (72.Brandon Soares Rosa), Almir Klica. Trainer: Nicolas Huysman.
Tobol Kostanay: Emil Balayev, Viktor Dmitrenko, Fernander Kassaï, Jaba Kankava, Azat Nurgaliev, Artūras Zulpa, Nika Kvekveskiri, Nikita Bocharov, Ruslan Valiullin, Mikhail Gordeychuk (59.Bauyrzhan Turysbek), Senin Sebai (60.Maxim Fedin). Trainer: Vladimir Gazzaev.

11.07.2019; Gyumri City Stadium, Gyumri
Referee: Luca Barbeno (SMR); Attendance: 2,050
FC Pyunik Yerevan – KF Shkupi Čair 3-3(1-2)
Pyunik Yerevan: Andrija Dragojevic, Antonio Stankov, Maksim Zhestokov, Kristi Marku, Armen Manucharyan, Karlen Mkrtchyan, Sergiy Shevchuk, Artem Simonyan (46.Edgar Manucharyan), Stanislav Efimov, Erik Vardanyan, Artur Miranyan. Trainer: Aleksandr Tarkhanov.
KF Shkupi: Thulio, Muharem Bajrami, Bojan Gjorgievski, Darko Ilieski, Mevlan Adili, Sabit Bilalli, Fatih Ismaili, Lamine Diack (53.Fatjon Jusufi), Marin Jurina, Serginho (83.Besart Krivanjeva), Oumar Goudiaby (69.Artan Veliu). Trainer: Recai Sahinler.
Goals: 4' Erik Vardanyan 1-0 (pen), 26' Muharem Bajrami 1-1, 43' Darko Ilieski 1-2, 60' Muharem Bajrami 1-3, 80' Maksim Zhestokov 2-3, 85' Edgar Manucharyan 3-3.

11.07.2019; Stadion Qajimuqan Muñaytpasov, Shymkent
Referee: Roomer Tarajev (EST); Attendance: 15,900
FC Ordabasy Shymkent – FC Torpedo Kutaisi 1-0(0-0)
FC Ordabasy: Dmytro Nepogodov, Pablo Fontanello, Sergiy Maliy, Mardan Tolebek (56.Ziguy Badibanga), Temirlan Yerlanov, Abdoulaye Diakhaté, May Mahlangu, Timur Dosmagambetov, Mirzad Mehanovic (67.Aleksey Shchetkin), João Paulo, Toktar Zhangylyshbay (73.Marat Bystrov). Trainer: Kakhaber Tskhadadze.
Torpedo Kutaisi: Roin Kvaskhvadze, Davit Khurtsilava, Vazha Tabatadze, Tsotne Nadaraia, Anri Chichinadze, Vakhtang Nebieridze, Mate Tsintsadze, Papuna Poniava (86.Tsotne Mosiashvili), Temur Chogadze (69.Otar Kobakhidze), Tornike Kapanadze (78.Tamaz Tsetskhladze), Zaza Tsitskishvili. Trainer: Kakhaber Chkhetiani.
Goal: 67' Temirlan Yerlanov 1-0.

11.07.2019; Olimpiskā centra Ventspils Stadionā, Ventspils
Referee: Daniyar Sakhi (KAZ); Attendance: 1,730
FK Ventspils – KF Teuta Durrës 3-0(1-0)
FK Ventspils: Konstantin Machnovskiy, Jean Alcénat (84.Ingars Stuglis), Abdoul Mamah, Giorgi Mchedlishvili, Hélio Batista, João Ananias (40.Pavel Osipov), Jevgenijs Kazacoks, Daniils Ulimbasevs, Tosin Aiyegun, Mykhaylo Sergiychuk (66.Kaspars Svārups), Lucas Villela. Trainer: Igor Klosovs.
KF Teuta Durrës: Isli Hidi, Renato Arapi, Rustem Hoxha, Alexandros Kouros, Fabjan Beqja (62.Arlind Kalaja), Gerhard Progni, Blagoja Todorovski (85.Darko Nikac), Albano Aleksi, Lancinet Sidibe, Sherif Kallaku, Tomislav Busic. Trainer: Shpëtim Kuçi.
Goals: 5' Mykhaylo Sergiychuk 1-0, 78' Daniils Ulimbasevs 2-0, 88' Tosin Aiyegun 3-0.

16.07.2019; Stadion Pod Goricom, Podgorica
Referee: Vasilis Dimitriou (CYP); Attendance: 969
OFK Titograd Podgorica – PFC CSKA SOFIA 0-0
OFK Titograd: Sasa Ivanovic, Radule Zivkovic (65.Marko Milickovic), Ivan Novovic, Marko Roganovic, Balsa Banovic, Ajanah-Chinedu Chukwujekwu, Mirko Raicevic (74.Milos Brnovic), Jovan Nikolic, Vojin Pavlovic, Radomir Djalovic, Mendy Mamadou (86.Ognjen Gasevic). Trainer: Dragoljub Djuretic.
CSKA Sofia: Vytautas Cerniauskas, Nikolay Bodurov, Kristiyan Malinov, Plamen Galabov, Geferson, Valentin Antov (67.Rúben Pinto), Graham Carey (82.Ali Sowe), Janio Bikel, Diego Fabbrini (60.Mitko Mitkov), Tony Watt, Evandro. Trainer: Dobromir Mitov.

18.07.2019; Astana Arena, Nur-Sultan
Referee: Emmanouil Skoulas (GRE); Attendance: 2,500
FC Tobol Kostanay – AS LA JEUNESSE D'ESCH/ALZETTE 1-1(1-0)
Tobol Kostanay: Emil Balayev, Viktor Dmitrenko, Fernander Kassaï, Dmitry Miroshnichenko (62.Ruslan Valiullin), Jaba Kankava, Azat Nurgaliev (82.Mikhail Gordeychuk), Artūras Zulpa, Nika Kvekveskiri, Nikita Bocharov, Bauyrzhan Turysbek (67.Maxim Fedin), Senin Sebai. Trainer: Vladimir Gazzaev.
Jeunesse d'Esch: Kévin Sommer, Arsène Menèssou, Alessandro Fiorani, Emmanuel Lapierre, Johannes Steinbach, Halim Meddour, Milos Todorovic, Luca Duriatti, David Soares De Sousa (79.Clayton De Sousa Moreira), Mehmet Arslan (72.Yannick Makota), Almir Klica. Trainer: Nicolas Huysman.
Goals: 22' Halim Meddour 1-0 (own goal), 59' Mehmet Arslan 1-1 (pen).

18.07.2019; „Toše Proeski" Arena, Skopje
Referee: Vitaliy Romanov (UKR); Attendance: 8,045
KF Shkupi Čair – FC PYUNIK YEREVAN 1-2(0-2)
KF Shkupi: Thulio, Muharem Bajrami, Bojan Gjorgievski, Darko Ilieski, Mevlan Adili, Sabit Bilalli, Fatih Ismaili (60.Besart Krivanjeva), Lamine Diack (69.Fatjon Jusufi), Marin Jurina, Serginho, Oumar Goudiaby (46.Artan Veliu). Trainer: Recai Sahinler.
Pyunik Yerevan: Andrija Dragojevic, Artak Yedigaryan, Antonio Stankov, Maksim Zhestokov, Kristi Marku, Armen Manucharyan, Karlen Mkrtchyan, Sergiy Shevchuk, Artem Simonyan (67.Steven Alfred), Erik Vardanyan, Artur Miranyan. Trainer: Aleksandr Tarkhanov.
Goals: 7' Artak Yedigaryan 0-1, 31' Artur Miranyan 0-2, 82' Marin Jurina 1-2.
Sent off: 86' Serginho.

18.07.2019; Stadioni „Mikheil Meskhi", Tbilisi
Referee: Aristotelis Diamantopoulos (GRE); Attendance: 3,753
FC Torpedo Kutaisi – FC ORDABASY SHYMKENT 0-2(0-0)
Torpedo Kutaisi: Roin Kvaskhvadze, Davit Khurtsilava, Vazha Tabatadze (80.Davit Ionanidze), Tsotne Nadaraia, Anri Chichinadze, Vakhtang Nebieridze, Grigol Dolidze (59.Zaza Tsitskishvili), Mate Tsintsadze, Papuna Poniava, Tornike Kapanadze (61.Temur Chogadze), Otar Kobakhidze. Trainer: Kakhaber Chkhetiani.
FC Ordabasy: Dmytro Nepogodov, Pablo Fontanello, Sergiy Maliy, Temirlan Yerlanov, Marat Bystrov, Kyrylo Kovalchuk (72.Mirzad Mehanovic), Abdoulaye Diakhaté, May Mahlangu, Timur Dosmagambetov, João Paulo (86.Samat Shamshi), Aleksey Shchetkin (62.Ziguy Badibanga). Trainer: Kakhaber Tskhadadze.
Goals: 81' Mirzad Mehanovic 0-1, 90+4' Ziguy Badibanga 0-2.

18.07.2019; Stadiumi „Niko Dovana", Durrës
Referee: Erez Papir (ISR); Attendance: 575
KF Teuta Durrës – FK VENTSPILS 1-0(0-0)
KF Teuta Durrës: Isli Hidi, Renato Arapi, Rustem Hoxha, Alexandros Kouros, Fabjan Beqja (76.Lorenco Vila), Albano Aleksi (57.Gerhard Progni), Lancinet Sidibe (71.Tefik Osmani), Florent Avdyli, Sherif Kallaku, Tomislav Busic, Darko Nikac. Trainer: Shpëtim Kuçi.
FK Ventspils: Konstantin Machnovskiy, Jean Alcénat, Abdoul Mamah, Giorgi Mchedlishvili, Hélio Batista, Pavel Osipov, Jevgenijs Kazacoks, Tosin Aiyegun, Kaspars Svārups, Mykhaylo Sergiychuk (85.Raens Tālbergs), Lucas Villela (90+3.Abdullahi Alfa). Trainer: Igor Klosovs.
Goal: 48' Sherif Kallaku 1-0.

11.07.2019; FFA Academy Stadium, Yerevan
Referee: Nathan Verboomen (BEL); Attendance: 1,285
FC Alashkert Yerevan – FK Makedonija Gjorče Petrov Skopje 3-1(1-0)
FC Alashkert: Ognjen Cancarevic, Hrayr Mkoyan, Gagik Dagbashyan, Hayk Ishkhanyan, Taron Voskanyan, Artak Grigoryan, Danilo Sekulic, Gustavo Marmentini dos Santos (71.Tiago Cametá), Vahagn Hayrapetyan, Uros Nenadovic (89.Mihran Manasyan), Nikita Tankov (85.Tiago Galvão). Trainer: Abraham Khashmanyan.
Makedonija: Marko Jovanovski, Filip Misevski (69.Esmin Licina), Fernando Augusto, Bianor, Bobi Bozinovski, Dejan Tanturovski, Robson, Kristijan Filipovski, Hristijan Pecov, Alen Jasaroski, Padu (89.Luka Trajkoski). Trainer: Bobi Stojkoski.
Goals: 16' Nikita Tankov 1-0, 52' Alen Jasaroski 1-1, 66' Danilo Sekulic 2-1, 82' Bianor 3-1 (own goal).

11.07.2019; Stadiumi Laçi, Laçi
Referee: Loukas Sotiriou (CYP); Attendance: 1,400
KF Laçi – Hapoel Be'er Sheva FC 1-1(1-0)
KF Laçi: Gentian Selmani, Aleksandar Ignjatovic, David Domgjoni, Eglentin Gjoni, Abdurraman Fangaj, Ardit Deliu, Regi Lushkja, Juljan Shehu, Teco, Kyrian Nwabueze (82.Elvi Berisha), Redon Xhixha (87.Ndricim Shtubina). Trainer: Sulejman Starova.
Hapoel Be'er Sheva: Ernestas Setkus, Miguel Vítor, Ben Bitton, Loai Taha, Sean Goldberg, Eden Shamir, Naor Sabag (87.Tomer Yosefi), Jimmy Marín, Ben Sahar (77.José Carrillo), Nigel Hasselbaink, Niv Zrihan (71.Gal Levi). Trainer: Barak Bakhar.
Goals: 3' Kyrian Nwabueze 1-0, 78' Gal Levi 1-1.

11.07.2019; Rakvere Linnastaadion, Rakvere
Referee: Sergey Tsinkevich (BLR); Attendance: 319
JK Narva Trans – FK Budučnost Podgorica 0-2(0-1)
JK Narva Trans: Marko Meerits, Roman Nesterovski, Tanel Tamberg, Joseph Saliste (86.Aleksei Stepanov), Irie Elysée, Dmitri Proshin, Denis Polyakov, Artjom Skinjov, Aleksandr Zakarlyuka, Nikita Mihhailov (87.Viktor Plotnikov), Eric McWoods (82.Eduard Golovljov). Trainer: Andrey Semin.
FC Budučnost Podgorica: Milos Dragojevic, Dejan Boljevic, Luka Mirkovic, Slavko Damjanovic, Stefan Milic, Drasko Bozovic (88.Vasilije Terzic), Milos Mijic, Milos Vucic, Dusan Bakic (70.Dusan Stoiljkovic), Igor Ivanovic, Mihailo Perovic (76.Aleksandar Vujacic). Trainer: Branko Brnovic.
Goals: 12' Igor Ivanovic 0-1, 88' Milos Mijic 0-2.

11.07.2019; AEK Arena, Larnaca
Referee: Michal Ocenás (SVK); Attendance: 3,561
AEK Larnaca FC – CS Petrocub Hîncești 1-0(1-0)
AEK Larnaca: Toño, Mikel González, Daniel Mojsov (85.Nacho Cases), Truyols, Thomas Ioannou (46.Tete), Ivan Trickovski, Lluis Sastre, Hector Hevel (68.Acorán), Raúl Ruiz, Apostolos Giannou, Florian Taulemesse. Trainer: Imanol Idiakez.
Petrocub Hîncești: Cristian Avram, Maxim Potîrniche, Ion Jardan, Victor Mudrac, Andrei Cojocari, Alexandru Bejan (70.Iaser Turcan), Dan Taras (62.Vlad Slivca), Jessie Guera Djou, Jacques Onana Ndzomo, Donalio Melachio Douanla, Alexandr Dedov (10.Vadim Gulceac). Trainer: Lilian Popescu.
Goal: 4' Hector Hevel 1-0.

11.07.2019; Savon Sanomat Areena, Kuopio
Referee: Danilo Grujic (SRB); Attendance: 2,560
Kuopion PS – FK Vitebsk 2-0(0-0)
Kuopion PS: Otso Virtanen, Babacar Diallo, Luis Murillo, Kalle Taimi, Vinko Soldo, Petteri Pennanen, Reuben Ayarna, Ville Saxman, Ilmari Niskanen (72.Saku Savolainen), Issa Thiaw (77.Tommi Jyry), Rangel (86.Ariel Ngueukam). Trainer: Jani Honkavaara.
FK Vitebsk: Dmitri Gushchenko, Akaki Khubutia, Oleg Karamushka, Mikhail Kozlov, Maranhão, Daniil Chalov, Artem Stargorodskiy (59.Anton Matveenko), Artem Skitov, Maksim Feshchuk, Nikolai Zolotov, Kirill Pechenin. Trainer: Sergey Yasinsky.
Goals: 61' Luis Murillo 1-0, 74' Rangel 2-0.

18.07.2019; Trening centar "Petar Miloševski", Skopje
Referee: Christophe Pires Martins (LUX); Attendance: 656
FK Makedonija Gjorče Petrov Skopje – FC ALASHKERT YEREVAN 0-3(0-1)
Makedonija GP: Marko Jovanovski, Fernando Augusto (51.Ermadin Adem), Bianor, Bobi Bozinovski, Dejan Tanturovski, Esmin Licina, Robson, Kristijan Filipovski (66.Filip Misevski), Hristijan Pecov, Alen Jasaroski, Padu (46.Benjamin Demir). Trainers: Aleksandar Tanevski & Bobi Stojkoski.
FC Alashkert: Ognjen Cancarevic, Hrayr Mkoyan, Gagik Dagbashyan, Hayk Ishkhanyan, Taron Voskanyan, Tiago Cametá, Artak Grigoryan (61.Tiago Galvão), Danilo Sekulic (77.Sargis Shahinyan), Vahagn Hayrapetyan, Uros Nenadovic, Nikita Tankov (72.Artur Avagimian). Trainer: Abraham Khashmanyan.
Goals: 21' Uros Nenadovic 0-1, 68' Tiago Galvão 0-2, 74' Taron Voskanyan 0-3.

18.07.2019; „Yaakov Turner Toto" Stadium, Beer Sheva
Referee: Tihomir Pejin (CRO); Attendance: 10,980
HAPOEL BE'ER SHEVA FC – KF Laçi 1-0(0-0)
Hapoel Be'er Sheva: Ernestas Setkus, Miguel Vítor, Ben Bitton, Loai Taha, Sean Goldberg, Ramzi Safouri (74.Niv Zrihan), Eden Shamir, Naor Sabag, Jimmy Marín, Nigel Hasselbaink (85.Marwan Kabha), José Carrillo (59.Ben Sahar). Trainer: Barak Bakhar.
KF Laçi: Gentian Selmani, Aleksandar Ignjatovic, David Domgjoni, Eglentin Gjoni, Abdurraman Fangaj (86.Rudolf Turkaj), Ardit Deliu, Regi Lushkja, Juljan Shehu, Teco (74.Elvi Berisha), Kyrian Nwabueze, Redon Xhixha. Trainer: Sulejman Starova.
Goal: 69' Naor Sabag 1-0.

18.07.2019; Stadion Pod Goricom, Podgorica:
Referee: Stefan Apostolov (BUL); Attendance: 1,700
FC BUDUČNOST PODGORICA – JK Narva Trans 4-1(1-1)
FC Budučnost Podgorica: Milos Dragojevic, Dejan Boljevic, Luka Mirkovic, Slavko Damjanovic, Stefan Milic, Drasko Bozovic (68.Milos Raickovic), Milos Mijic, Milos Vucic, Dusan Bakic, Igor Ivanovic (32.Dusan Stoiljkovic), Mihailo Perovic (77.Dejan Zarubica). Trainer: Branko Brnovic.
JK Narva Trans: Marko Meerits, Roman Nesterovski, Tanel Tamberg, Joseph Saliste, Irie Elysée, Denis Polyakov, German Slein (44.Eric McWoods), Artjom Skinjov, Aleksandr Zakarlyuka (78.Dmitri Proshin), Eduard Golovljov (63.Viktor Plotnikov), Nikita Mihhailov. Trainer: Andrey Semin.
Goals: 2' Milos Vucic 1-0, 39' Eduard Golovljov 1-1, 49' Dusan Bakic 2-1, 56' Mihailo Perovic 3-1, 78' Dejan Zarubica 4-1.

18.07.2019; Stadionul Zimbru, Chișinău
Referee: Novak Simovic (SRB); Attendance: 5,316
CS Petrocub Hîncești – AEK LARNACA FC 0-1(0-0)
Petrocub Hîncești: Cristian Avram, Maxim Potîrniche, Ion Jardan (60.Vadim Gulceac), Victor Mudrac, Vlad Slivca, Andrei Cojocari, Alexandru Bejan (82.Arcadie Rusu), Dan Taras (70.Vladimir Bogdanovic), Vladimir Ambros, Jessie Guera Djou, Jacques Onana Ndzomo. Trainer: Lilian Popescu.
AEK Larnaca: Toño, Mikel González, Daniel Mojsov, Truyols, Ivan Trickovski, Lluis Sastre, Acorán (77.Raúl Ruiz), Nacho Cases, Hector Hevel (90.Jean Luc Assoubre), Apostolos Giannou (83.Florian Taulemesse), Tete. Trainer: Imanol Idiakez.
Goal: 90+2' Maxim Potîrniche 0-1 (own goal).

18.07.2019; Stadyen Central'ny Vitsyebski, Vitebsk
Referee: Hugo Filipe Ferreira de Campos Moreira Miguel (POR); Attendance: 4,780
FK Vitebsk – KUOPION PS 1-1(1-0)
FK Vitebsk: Dmitri Gushchenko, Akaki Khubutia (65.Vladislav Fedosov), Oleg Karamushka, Anton Matveenko (85.Vladislav Ryzhkov), Mikhail Kozlov, Maranhão, Artem Stargorodskiy (76.Sergey Volkov), Artem Skitov, Maksim Feshchuk, Nikolai Zolotov, Kirill Pechenin. Trainer: Sergey Yasinsky.
Kuopion PS: Otso Virtanen, Babacar Diallo, Luis Murillo, Luc Tabi Manga (79.Kalle Taimi), Vinko Soldo, Petteri Pennanen, Reuben Ayarna, Ville Saxman, Ilmari Niskanen (90+2.Saku Savolainen), Issa Thiaw, Rangel (82.Ariel Ngueukam). Trainer: Jani Honkavaara.
Goals: 27' Artem Stargorodskiy 1-0, 53' Babacar Diallo 1-1.

11.07.2019; A. Le Coq Arena, Tallinn
Referee: Alexandru Tean (MDA); Attendance: 1,250
FC Flora Tallinn – FK Radnicki Niş 2-0(0-0)
Flora Tallinn: Matvei Igonen, Gert Kams, Märten Kuusk, Henrik Pürg, Henri Järvelaid, Konstantin Vassiljev, Mikhel Ainsalu, Martin Miller, Vladislavs Kreida, Frank Liivak, Erik Sorga (73.Mark Lepik). Trainer: Jürgen Henn.
Radnicki Niş: Nikola Petrovic, Aleksandar Todorovski, Stefan Djordjevic, Ivan Ostojic, Lazar Djordjevic, Taras Bondarenko, Nemanja Tomic (63.Veljko Batrovic), Dejan Meleg (78.Sasa Stojanovic), Ryota Noma, Erik Jirka, Milan Bojovic (70.Milan Makaric). Trainer: Simo Krunic.
Goals: 75' Mark Lepik 1-0, 89' Konstantin Vassiljev 2-0.

11.07.2019; Bayil Arena, Bakı
Referee: Fyodor Zammit (MLT); Attendance: 2,550
Sabail FK Bakı – CS Universitatea Craiova 2-3(1-1)
Sabail FK: Daniel Bozinovski, Erico, Elvin Yunuszade, Ürfan Abbasov, Mickael Essien (59.Dylan Duventru), Shahriyar Rahimov (84.Eltun Yagublu), Rahid Amirquliyev, Bilal Hamdi (72.Fahmin Muradbayli), Eugeniu Cociuc, Agabala Ramazanov, Mirabdulla Abbasov. Trainer: Aftandil Hadzhiyev.
CS Universitatea Craiova: Mirko Pigliacelli, Renato Kelic, Ivan Martic, Nicusor Bancu, Stephane Acka, Alexandru Mateiu, Bogdan Vatajelu (90.Stefan Baiaram), Kamer Qaka, Cristian Barbut (73.Alexandru Ionita), Antoni Ivanov, Mihai Roman (II) (68.Carlos Fortes). Trainer: Corneliu Papura.
Goals: 13' Alexandru Mateiu 0-1, 33' Agabala Ramazanov 1-1, 51' Nicusor Bancu 1-2, 67' Mihai Roman (II) 1-3, 82' Agabala Ramazanov 2-3.

11.07.2019; Vilniaus LFF stadionas, Vilnius
Referee: Bram Van Driessche (BEL); Attendance: 1,480
FK Riteriai Vilnius – KÍ Klaksvík 1-1(0-0)
FK Riteriai: Tomas Svedkauskas, Valdemars Borovskis, Justinas Janusevskis, Ricardas Sveikauskas, Aleksandr Levsinas, Valentin Jeriomenko, Tomas Dombrauskis, Artsem Hurenka, Dovydas Virksas (75.Dominyk Kodz), Donatas Kazlauskas, Teremas Moffi. Trainer: Aurelijus Skarbalius.
KÍ Klaksvík: Kristian Joensen, Jesper Brinck, Ísak Simonsen, Deni Pavlovic, Semir Hadzibulic, Boris Dosljak, Patrik Johannesen (89.Páll Klettskard), Jákup Andreasen (86.Torbjørn Grytten), Simen Sandmæl (90+1.Jonn Johannesen), Jóannes Danielsen. Trainer: Mikkjal Thomassen.
Goals: 46' Valdemars Borovskis 1-0, 56' Jákup Andreasen 1-1.

11.07.2019; MFA Centenary Stadium, Ta'Qali
Referee: Aleksey Matyunin (RUS); Attendance: 389
Balzan FC – NK Domžale 3-4(2-1)
Balzan FC: Kristijan Naumovski, Steven Bezzina, Aleksandar Kosoric, Ivan Bozovic, Uros Ljubomirac (82.Andrija Majdevac), Paul Fenech, Nenad Sljivic, Stefan Dimic, Ricardo Correa (86.Lydon Micallef), Alfred Effiong (69.Arthur Faría), Stephen Pisani. Trainer: Jacques Scerri.
NK Domžale: Grega Sorcan, Gaber Dobrovoljc, Gregor Sikosek, Tilen Klemencic, Senijad Ibricic, Amedej Vetrih, Josip Corluka, Adam Gnezda Cerin, Matej Podlogar (76.Ziga Repas), Slobodan Vuk (83.Dario Kolobaric), Tonci Mujan (64.Mattias Käit). Trainer: Simon Rozman.
Goals: 5' Senijad Ibricic 0-1 (pen), 34' Ricardo Correa 1-1, 38' Uros Ljubomirac 2-1, 49' Slobodan Vuk 2-2, 56' Alfred Effiong 3-2, 61' Gregor Sikosek 3-3, 76' Matej Podlogar 3-4.

11.07.2019; Futbalovy Stadión MFK Ružomberok, Ružomberok
Referee: Petri Viljanen (FIN); Attendance: 3,695
MFK Ružomberok – PFC Levski Sofia 0-2(0-1)
MFK Ružomberok: Ivan Krajcírik, Ján Maslo, Matej Curma, Michal Jonec, Alexander Mojzis, Tihomir Kostadinov, Kristi Qose, Dalibor Takác (69.Marek Zsigmund), Adam Brenkus (59.Filip Hasek), Peter Gál-Andrezly, Stefan Gerec (79.Ondrej Novotny). Trainer: Ján Haspra.
Levski Sofia: Milan Mijatovic, Zhivko Milanov, Nuno Reis, Ivan Goranov, Giannis Kargas, Martin Raynov, Davide Mariani (90+1.Franco Mazurek), Khaly Thiam, Paulinho, Iliya Yurukov (88.Zdravko Dimitrov), Stanislav Ivanov (90+3.Iliya Dimitrov). Trainer: Petar Hubchev.
Goals: 36' Davide Mariani 0-1, 51' Paulinho 0-2.

18.07.2019; Gradski Stadion Cair, Nis
Referee: Zbynek Proske (CZE); Attendance: 4,329
FK Radnicki Niş – FC FLORA TALLINN 2-2(0-0)
Radnicki Niş: Marko Knezevic, Aleksandar Todorovski, Stefan Djordjevic, Ivan Ostojic, Lazar Djordjevic, Taras Bondarenko, Sasa Stojanovic, Nemanja Tomic, Veljko Batrovic (59.Dejan Meleg), Erik Jirka (73.Nikola Cumic), Milan Bojovic (59.Stefan Mihajlovic). Trainer: Simo Krunic.
Flora Tallinn: Matvei Igonen, Gert Kams, Märten Kuusk, Henrik Pürg, Henri Järvelaid, Konstantin Vassiljev, Mikhel Ainsalu, Martin Miller (66.Vlasiy Sinyavskiy), Vladislavs Kreida, Frank Liivak, Erik Sorga (78.Mark Lepik). Trainer: Jürgen Henn.
Goals: 68' Stefan Mihajlovic 1-0, 80' Henrik Pürg 1-1, 84' Nikola Cumic 2-1, 90+3' Mark Lepik 2-2.

18.07.2019; Stadionul „Ion Oblemenco", Craiova
Referee: Helgi Mikael Jónasson (ISL); Attendance: 15,763
CS UNIVERSITATEA CRAIOVA – Sabail FK Bakı 3-2(1-0)
CS Universitatea Craiova: Mirko Pigliacelli, Renato Kelic (76.Florin Gardos), Ivan Martic, Tiago Ferreira, Nicusor Bancu, Alexandru Mateiu, Bogdan Vatajelu, Kamer Qaka (70.Vasile Constantin), Cristian Barbut, Alexandru Cicâldau (57.Antoni Ivanov), Carlos Fortes. Trainer: Corneliu Papura.
Sabail FK: Daniel Bozinovski, Erico, Elvin Yunuszade, Ürfan Abbasov (87.Eltun Yagublu), Shahriyar Rahimov, Rahid Amirquliyev, Bilal Hamdi (58.Fahmin Muradbayli), Vüqar Baybalayev, Eugeniu Cociuc, Agabala Ramazanov, Mirabdulla Abbasov (58.Dylan Duventru). Trainer: Aftandil Hadzhiyev.
Goals: 28' Alexandru Cicâldau 1-0, 54' Bogdan Vatajelu 2-0, 67' Agabala Ramazanov 2-1, 69' Dylan Duventru 2-2, 90' Carlos Fortes 3-2.

16.07.2019; Svangaskard, Toftir
Referee: Yaroslav Kozyk (UKR); Attendance: 980
KÍ KLAKSVÍK – FK Riteriai Vilnius 0-0
KÍ Klaksvík: Kristian Joensen, Jesper Brinck, Ísak Simonsen, Deni Pavlovic, Semir Hadzibulic, Boris Dosljak, Patrik Johannesen (90+4.Páll Klettskard), Jákup Andreasen, Jóannes Bjartalíd (84.Jonn Johannesen), Simen Sandmæl (90+2.Torbjørn Grytten), Jóannes Danielsen. Trainer: Mikkjal Thomassen.
FK Riteriai: Tomas Svedkauskas, Valdemars Borovskis, Justinas Janusevskis, Ricardas Sveikauskas, Aleksandr Levsinas, Valentin Jeriomenko (59.Lajo Traore), Tomas Dombrauskis, Artem Hurenka, Dovydas Virksas (62.Dominyk Kodz), Donatas Kazlauskas, Teremas Moffi. Trainer: Aurelijus Skarbalius.

18.07.2019; Sportni Park, Domžale
Referee: Marcel Bîrsan (ROU); Attendance: 1,648
NK DOMŽALE – Balzan FC 1-0(1-0)
NK Domžale: Grega Sorcan, Gaber Dobrovoljc, Gregor Sikosek, Tilen Klemencic, Senijad Ibricic, Josip Corluka, Mattias Käit (46.Ziga Repas), Adam Gnezda Cerin, Matej Podlogar (80.Sven Karic), Slobodan Vuk (66.Shamar Nicholson), Tonci Mujan. Trainer: Simon Rozman.
Balzan FC: Kristijan Naumovski, Steven Bezzina, Aleksandar Kosoric, Ivan Bozovic, Uros Ljubomirac (75.Andrija Majdevac), Augustine Loof, Paul Fenech (59.Arthur Faría), Nenad Sljivic, Stefan Dimic (62.Ricardo Correa), Alfred Effiong, Stephen Pisani. Trainer: Jacques Scerri.
Goal: 21' Slobodan Vuk 1-0.

18.07.2019; Vivacom Arena – "Georgi Asparuhov" Stadium, Sofia
Referee: Veaceslav Banari (MDA); Attendance: 17,250
PFC LEVSKI SOFIA – MFK Ružomberok 2-0(1-0)
Levski Sofia: Milan Mijatovic, Zhivko Milanov, Nuno Reis, Ivan Goranov, Giannis Kargas, Martin Raynov (78.Deni Alar), Davide Mariani, Khaly Thiam, Stanislav Kostov (58.Zdravko Dimitrov), Paulinho (72.Iliya Yurukov), Stanislav Ivanov. Trainer: Petar Hubchev.
MFK Ružomberok: Ivan Krajcírik, Ján Maslo, Matej Curma, Michal Jonec, Alexander Mojzis, Filip Twardzik (74.Ondrej Novotny), Tihomir Kostadinov (70.Filip Hasek), Kristi Qose, Dalibor Takác (67.Adam Brenkus), Peter Gál-Andrezly, Stefan Gerec. Trainer: Ján Haspra.
Goals: 33' Davide Mariani 1-0, 90+2' Deni Alar 2-0.

11.07.2019; Swedbank Stadion, Malmö
Referee: Igor Pajac (CRO); Attendance: 8,667
Malmö FF – Ballymena United FC 7-0(3-0)
Malmö FF: Johan Dahlin, Behrang Safari, Lasse Nielsen, Franz Brorsson, Søren Rieks, Fouad Bachirou (69.Bonke Innocent), Oscar Lewicki, Erdal Rakip, Markus Rosenberg (59.Marcus Antonsson), Guillermo Molins, Jo Inge Berget (59.Eric Larsson). Trainer: Uwe Rösler.
Ballymena United: Ross Glendinning, Tony Kane, Jim Ervin, Steven McCullough, Scot Whiteside, Kofi Balmer, Andy McGrory, Jude Winchester (75.Shane McGinty), Declan Carville (51.Andrew Burns), Leroy Millar, Adam Lecky (72.Cathair Friel). Trainer: David Jeffrey.
Goals: 31', 33' Markus Rosenberg 1-0, 2-0, 44' Erdal Rakip 3-0, 46' Franz Brorsson 4-0, 48' Markus Rosenberg 5-0, 54' Guillermo Molins 6-0, 74' Erdal Rakip 7-0.

11.07.2019; Gradski Stadion, Banja Luka
Referee: Volen Chinkov (BUL); Attendance: 1,500
FK Radnik Bijeljina – FC Spartak Trnava 2-0(1-0)
Radnik Bijeljina: Dalibor Kozic, Milos Simonovic, Slavisa Radovic, Velibor Djuric, Pavle Susic, Nikola Popara, Ivan Subert, Nedim Mekic (86.Vladimir Bradonjic), Dejan Maksimovic (79.Milos Plavsic), Demir Peco, Seid Zukic (66.Jovan Motika). Trainer: Mladen Zizovic.
Spartak Trnava: Dobrivoj Rusov, Matús Turna (55.Filip Orsula), Bogdan Mitrea, Jozef Menich, Lucas Lovat, Marko Tesija, Emir Halilovic, Matej Jakúbek (55.Alex Sobczyk), Filip Dangubic (79.Marko Kelemen), Kristián Mihálek, Rafael Tavares. Trainer: Ricardo Chéu.
Goals: 34' Nedim Mekic 1-0, 48' Velibor Djuric 2-0.

11.07.2019; Brann Stadion, Bergen
Referee: Juxhin Xhaja (ALB); Attendance: 4,560
SK Brann Bergen – Shamrock Rovers FC Dublin 2-2(2-1)
SK Brann: Håkon Opdal, Taijo Teniste, Bismar Acosta, Ruben Kristiansen, Christian Rismark, Fredrik Haugen, Kristoffer Løkberg (68.Petter Strand), Amer Ordagic (74.Ruben Jenssen), Veton Berisha, Gilli Rólantsson Sørensen, Gilbert Koomson (82.Daouda Bamba). Trainer: Lars Nilsen.
Shamrock Rovers: Alan Mannus, Joey O'Brien, Sean Kavanagh, Roberto Lopes, Ethan Boyle, Lee Grace, Ronan Finn (77.Aaron McEneff), Greg Bolger, Jack Byrne, Trevor Clarke (66.Dylan Watts), Aaron Greene (65.Graham Cummins). Trainer: Stephen Bradley.
Goals: 12 Taijo Teniste 1-0, 34' Amer Ordagic 1-1 (own goal), 36' Veton Berisha 2-1 (pen), 90+4' Roberto Lopes 2-2.

11.07.2019; „Boris Paichadze" Dinamo Arena, Tbilisi
Referee: Morten Krogh (DEN); Attendance: 3,680
FC Dinamo Tbilisi – UE Engordany 6-0(2-0)
Dinamo Tbilisi: José Perales, Gudzha Rukhaia, Giorgi Kimadze, Víctor Mongil, Davit Kobouri, Nika Ninua, Levan Kutalia, Giorgi Kukhianidze (76.Bakar Kardava), Giorgi Papava (57.Giorgi Zaria), Nodar Kavtaradze, Levan Shengelia (63.Arfang Daffé). Trainer: Félix Vicente Miranda.
UE Engordany: Jesús Coca, Jorge Sebastián Varela, Rafael Brito, Deivis De Jesus Soares, Mario Spano, Sébastien Aguéro, Hamza Bouharma, Míguel Laborda (71.Edu Peppe), Sebastián Gómez (90+3.Brian Mengual Maneiro), Fábio Serra Alves, Morgan Lafont (85.Rodrigo Guida). Trainer: Filipe Busto.
Goals: 6' Nika Ninua 1-0, 21' Giorgi Kukhianidze 2-0, 61' Nodar Kavtaradze 3-0, 69' Levani Kutalia 4-0 (pen), 71' Giorgi Kukhianidze 5-0, 80' Giorgi Zaria 6-0.

11.07.2019; Marijampolés sporto centro stadione, Marijampolé
Referee: Admir Sehovic (BIH); Attendance: 717
FK Kauno Žalgiris Kaunas – Apollon Limassol FC 0-2(0-1)
Kauno Žalgiris: Deividas Mikelionis, "Rudi" Rudinilson Silva (58.Edvinas Kloniūnas), Rimvydas Sadauskas, Karolis Silkaitis, Pijus Sirvys (78.Philip Otele), Dominykas Galkevicius, Yuriy Bushman, Martynas Dapkus, Daniel Romanovskij, Deividas Sesplaukis (65.Linas Pilibaitis), João Figueiredo. Trainer: Mindaugas Cepas.
Apollon Limassol: Joël Mall, Vahid Selimovic (46.Attila Szalai), Ioannis Pittas, Vincent Bessat, Héctor Yuste, Sasa Markovic, Esteban Sachetti, Emilio Zelaya, João Pedro, Fotios Papoulis (64.Serge Gakpé), Adrián Sardinero (79.Diego Aguirre). Trainer: Sofronis Avgousti.
Goals: 14' Ioannis Pittas 0-1, 90' Emilio Zelaya 0-2 (pen).

18.07.2019; The Showgrounds, Ballymena
Referee: Oskari Hämäläinen (FIN); Attendance: 1,736
Ballymena United FC – MALMÖ FF 0-4(0-1)
Ballymena United: Ross Glendinning, Andrew Burns, Jonathan Addis (75.Joshua Kelly), Steven McCullough, Kofi Balmer, Ryan Harpur (70.Ross Lavery), Andy McGrory, Shane McGinty, Leroy Millar, Ryan Mayse, Adam Lecky (71.Cathair Friel). Trainer: David Jeffrey.
Malmö FF: Dusan Melichárek, Behrang Safari, Lasse Nielsen, Franz Brorsson, Oscar Lewicki (68.Søren Rieks), Erdal Rakip (74.Anders Christiansen), Romain Gall, Bonke Innocent, Guillermo Molins (61.Tim Prica), Jo Inge Berget, Marcus Antonsson. Trainer: Uwe Rösler.
Goals: 27' Behrang Safari 0-1, 52' Guillermo Molins 0-2, 68' Erdal Rakip 0-3, 79' Romain Gall 0-4 (pen).

18.07.2019; City Arena Trnava, Trnava
Referee: Rahim Hasanov (AZE); Attendance: 4,222
FC SPARTAK TRNAVA – FK Radnik Bijeljina 2-0(1-0,2-0); 3-2 on penalties
Spartak Trnava: Dobrivoj Rusov, Bogdan Mitrea, Timotej Záhumensky, Lucas Lovat, Ivan Mesík, Marko Tesija, Emir Halilovic (93.Matús Turna), Filip Dangubic (64.Marko Kelemen), Rafael Tavares (77.Matej Jakúbek), Filip Orsula (80.Kristián Mihálek), Alex Sobczyk. Trainer: Ricardo Chéu.
Radnik Bijeljina: Dalibor Kozic, Milos Simonovic, Slavisa Radovic, Velibor Djuric (88.Vladimir Bradonjic), Pavle Susic (61.Alem Merajic), Nikola Popara, Ivan Subert, Nedim Mekic, Dejan Maksimovic (99.Milos Plavsic), Demir Peco, Seid Zukic (54.Jovan Motika). Trainer: Mladen Zizovic.; Goals: 10' Alex Sobczyk 1-0, 87' Kristián Mihálek 2-0.
Sent off: 108' Bogdan Mitrea.
Penalties: Tesija 1-0, Merajic 1-1, Sobczyk 2-1, Motika missed, Záhumensky missed, Mekic 2-2, Lucas Lovat missed, Plavsic missed, Jakúbek 3-2, Popara missed.

18.07.2019; Tallaght Stadium, Dublin
Referee: Kári Jóannesarson á Høvdanum (FRO); Attendance: 5,135
SHAMROCK ROVERS FC DUBLIN – SK Brann Bergen 2-1(0-0)
Shamrock Rovers: Alan Mannus, Joey O'Brien, Sean Kavanagh, Roberto Lopes, Ethan Boyle, Lee Grace, Ronan Finn (80.Gary O'Neill), Greg Bolger, Jack Byrne, Dylan Watts (63.Aaron McEneff), Graham Cummins (75.Daniel Carr). Trainer: Stephen Bradley.
SK Brann: Håkon Opdal, Taijo Teniste (84.Azar Karadas), Bismar Acosta, Ruben Kristiansen, Christian Rismark, Fredrik Haugen, Amer Ordagic, Petter Strand (84.Ruben Jenssen), Veton Berisha, Gilli Rólantsson Sørensen, Gilbert Koomson (46.Daouda Bamba). Trainer: Lars Nilsen.
Goals: 57' Daouda Bamba 0-1, 76' Jack Byrne 1-1, 87' Gary O'Neill 2-1.

18.07.2019; Estadi Comunal d'Andorra la Vella, Andorra la Vella
Referee: Balász Berke (HUN); Attendance: 408
UE Engordany – FC DINAMO TBILISI 0-1(0-0)
UE Engordany: Gerardo Rubio, Miguel Ruiz, Rafael Brito (89.Jorge Sebastián Varela), Deivis De Jesus Soares, Mario Spano, Marc Ferré, Sébastien Aguéro, Hamza Bouharma, Sebastián Gómez (87.Edu Peppe), Fábio Serra Alves, Morgan Lafont (72.Míguel Laborda). Trainer: Filipe Busto.
Dinamo Tbilisi: José Perales, Gudzha Rukhaia, Oleksandr Kaplienko, Davit Kobouri, Abdel Jalil Medioub, Levan Kutalia, Mychailo Shyshka (60.Nika Ninua), Arfang Daffé, Bakar Kardava, Akaki Shulaia (55.Nodar Kavtaradze), Giorgi Zaria (74.Giorgi Kukhianidze). Trainer: Félix Vicente Miranda.
Goal: 81' Abdel Jalil Medioub 0-1.

18.07.2019; Stádio Neo GSP, Nicosia
Referee: Vladimir Moskalev (RUS); Attendance: 1,427
APOLLON LIMASSOL FC – FK Kauno Žalgiris Kaunas 4-0(2-0)
Apollon Limassol: Joël Mall, Attila Szalai, Ioannis Pittas (56.Serge Gakpé), Dylan Ouédraogo, Facundo Pereyra, Giorgos Vasiliou, Sasa Markovic (69.Chambos Kyriakou), Diego Aguirre (56.Giannis Gianniotas), Esteban Sachetti, Emilio Zelaya, João Pedro. Trainer: Sofronis Avgousti.
Kauno Žalgiris: Deividas Mikelionis, Arūnas Klimavicius, "Rudi" Rudinilson Silva (60.Edvinas Kloniūnas), Karolis Silkaitis, Pijus Sirvys, Linas Pilibaitis, Dominykas Galkevicius, Yuriy Bushman, Martynas Dapkus (46.Rimvydas Sadauskas), Rokas Krusnauskas (70.Benas Anisas), João Figueiredo. Trainer: Mindaugas Cepas.
Goals: 5', 43', 60' Emilio Zelaya 1-0, 2-0 (pen), 3-0 (pen), 83' Attila Szalai 4-0.

11.07.2019; „Sammy Ofer" Stadium, Haifa
Referee: Manfredas Lukjancukas (LTU); Attendance: 16,127
Maccabi Haifa FC – NŠ Mura Murska Sobota 2-0(0-0)
Maccabi Haifa: Guy Haimov, Rami Gershon, Ernest Mabouka, Ayed Habashi, Ofri Arad (86.Allyson), Yuval Ashkenazi, Yosef Raz Meir, Neta Lavi, Maxim Plakushchenko (51.Mohammed Awaed), Dolev Haziza, Yarden Shua (72.Mohammad Abu Fani). Trainer: Marco Balbul.
NŠ Mura: Matko Obradovic, Klemen Sturm, Zan Karnicnik (74.Timo Horvat), Aleksandar Boskovic, Matic Marusko, Ziga Kous, Alen Kozar, Jon Sporn, Amadej Marosa (73.Andrija Bubnjar), Luka Bobicanec (79.Kai Cipot), Luka Susnjara. Trainer: Ante Simundza.
Goals: 64' Yuval Ashkenazi 1-0, 68' Mohammed Awaed 2-0.

11.07.2019; Nagyerdei Stadion, Debrecen
Referee: Sebastian Gishamer (AUT); Attendance: 10,250
Debreceni VSC – FK Kukësi 3-0(0-0)
Debreceni VSC: Sándor Nagy, János Ferenczi, Csaba Szatmári, Bence Pávkovics, Dániel Tözsér, Nikola Trujic (88.Richárd Csösz), Kevin Varga, Attila Haris, Erik Kusnyír (89.Ákos Kinyik), Tamás Takács (52.Haruna Garba), Márk Szécsi. Trainer: András Herczeg.
FK Kukësi: Stivi Frashëri, Ardijan Cuculi, Olsi Teqja, Tome Kitanovski, Simon Rrumbullaku, Valdet Rama, Eduart Rroca (76.Emiljano Musta), Besar Musolli, Vesel Limaj, Valon Ethemi (71.Arbër Çyrbja), Vasil Shkurti. Trainer: Ernest Gjoka.
Goals: 54' Haruna Garba 1-0, 77', 83' Kevin Varga 2-0, 3-0.

11.07.2019; Daugava Stadions, Liepāja
Referee: António Carvalho Nobre (POR); Attendance: 3,793
FK Liepāja – FC Dinamo Minsk 1-1(1-0)
FK Liepāja: Valentins Ralkevics, Vadims Zulevs, Deniss Ivanovs, Seydina Keita, Jānis Ikaunieks, Raivis Jurkovskis, Amâncio Fortes (82.Danu Spataru), Leonel Strumia, Kristers Tobers, Richard Friday, Dodô. Trainer: Aleksandrs Starkovs.
Dinamo Minsk: Maksim Plotnikov, Andrei Zaleski, Aleksey Gavrilovich, Aleksandr Chizh, Seidu Yahaya, Dinko Trebotic, Nikita Kaplenko, Vladislav Lyakh (46.Georgi Tigiev), Nikita Demchenko (72.Dmytro Bilonog), Kehinde Fatai, Yegor Zubovich (79.Kirill Vergeychik). Trainer: Sergei Gurenko.
Goals: 12' Jānis Ikaunieks 1-0 (pen), 88' Nikita Kaplenko 1-1.

11.07.2019; Seaview Stadium, Belfast
Referee: Yigal Frid (ISR); Attendance: 1,112
Crusaders FC Belfast – B36 Tórshavn 2-0(1-0)
Crusaders FC: Sean O'Neill, Billy Joe Burns, Howard Beverland, Chris Hegarty, Michael Ruddy, Declan Caddell (63.Rory Hale), Philip Lowry, Jordan Forsythe (90+9.Gary Thompson), Paul Heatley (78.David Cushley), Ross Clarke, Jordan Owens. Trainer: Stephen Baxter.
B36 Tórshavn: Hans Jørgensen, Erling Jacobsen, Alex Mellemgaard, Jónas Næs, Eli Nielsen, Árni Frederiksberg, Benjamin Heinesen (60.Stefan Radosavljevic), Andrias Eriksen, Michal Przybylski (90+1.Hannes Agnarsson), Magnus Holm Jacobsen, Lukasz Cieslewicz (90+7.Brian Jacobsen). Trainer: Jákub á Borg.
Goals: 33' Chris Hegarty 1-0, 79' Philip Lowry 2-0.

11.07.2019; Brøndby Stadion, Brøndby
Referee: Kristoffer Karlsson (SWE); Attendance: 10,296
Brøndby IF – FC Inter Turku 4-1(1-1)
Brøndby IF: Marvin Schwäbe, Paulus Arajuuri, Anthony Jung, Hjörtur Hermannsson, Dominik Kaiser (90+1.Tobias Børkeeiet), Lasse Vigen Christensen (64.Kasper Fisker), Josip Radosevic, Simon Tibbling (83.Jesper Lindstrøm), Simon Hedlund, Kamil Wilczek, Kevin Mensah. Trainer: Niels Frederiksen.
FC Inter Turku: Henrik Moisander, Niko Markkula, Luciano Balbi, Juuso Hämäläinen, Miro Tenho, Daan Klinkenberg, Álvaro Muñiz, Aleksi Paananen (81.Elias Mastokangas), Timo Furuholm, Mika Ojala (75.Mikko Kuningas), Filip Valencic. Trainer: José Riveiro.
Goals: 5' Kamil Wilczek 1-0, 2-0 Timo Furuholm 1-1, 67' Kamil Wilczek 2-1, 71' Simon Tibbling 3-1, 78' Kasper Fisker 4-1.

18.07.2019; Mestni Stadion Fazanerija, Murska Sobota
Referee: Tomasz Musial (POL); Attendance: 3,950
NŠ Mura Murska Sobota – MACCABI HAIFA FC 2-3(1-2)
NŠ Mura: Matko Obradovic, Klemen Sturm, Klemen Pucko, Aleksandar Boskovic, Matic Marusko, Alen Kozar (46.Marin Karamarko), Jon Sporn (82.Ziga Laci), Timo Horvat (45+2.Andrija Bubnjar), Amadej Marosa, Luka Bobicanec, Luka Susnjara. Trainer: Ante Simundza.
Maccabi Haifa: Guy Haimov, Rami Gershon, Ernest Mabouka, Ayed Habashi, Ofri Arad, Ikouwem Utin, Yuval Ashkenazi (77.Yanic Wildschut), Neta Lavi, Dolev Haziza (45+3.Mohammad Abu Fani), Mohammed Awaed (68.Nikita Rukavytsya), Yarden Shua. Trainer: Marco Balbul.
Goals: 6' Luka Bobicanec 1-0, 31' Mohammed Awaed 1-1, 35', 76' Yuval Ashkenazi 1-2, 1-3, 81' Jon Sporn 2-3.

18.07.2019; Elbasan Arena, Elbasan
Referee: Stanislav Todorov (BUL); Attendance: 547
FK Kukësi – DEBRECENI VSC 1-1 (1-0)
FK Kukësi: Stivi Frashëri, Ardijan Cuculi (61.Bruno Lulaj), Olsi Teqja, Tome Kitanovski, Simon Rrumbullaku, Valdet Rama, Eduart Rroca, Besar Musolli, Vesel Limaj (73.Emiljano Musta), Valon Ethemi (84.Arbër Çyrbja), Vasil Sjkurti. Trainer: Ernest Gjoka.
Debreceni VSC: Sándor Nagy, János Ferenczi, Csaba Szatmári, Bence Pávkovics, Erik Kusnyír, Dániel Tözsér, Nikola Trujic (82.Richárd Csösz), Kevin Varga, Attila Haris (90.Alex Damásdi), Márk Szécsi, Daniel Zsóri (66.Haruna Garba). Trainer: András Herczeg.
Goals: 17' Valon Ethemi 1-0, 58' Csaba Szatmári 1-1.

18.07.2019; Dynama Stadium, Minsk
Referee: Nick Walsh (SCO); Attendance: 6,705
FC Dinamo Minsk – FK LIEPĀJA 1-2(0-1)
Dinamo Minsk: Maksim Plotnikov, Andrei Zaleski (79.Nikita Demchenko), Aleksey Gavrilovich, Maksim Shvetsov, Georgi Tigiev (74.Aleksandr Ksenofontov), Aleksandr Chizh, Seidu Yahaya, Dinko Trebotic, Dmytro Bilonog, Kehinde Fatai, Yegor Zubovich (62.Kirill Vergeychik). Trainer: Sergei Gurenko.
FK Liepāja: Valentins Ralkevics, Vadims Zulevs, Deniss Ivanovs, Seydina Keita, Raivis Jurkovskis, Amâncio Fortes, Leonel Strumia, Kristers Tobers, Richard Friday (77.Vüqar Asgarov), Dodô, Danu Spataru (76.Mārtins Kigurs). Trainer: Aleksandrs Starkovs.
Goals: 10' Danu Spataru 0-1, 70' Dodô 0-2, 90+1' Valentins Ralkevics 1-2 (own goal).

18.07.2019; Gundadalur, Tórshavn
Referee: Milovan Milacic (MNE); Attendance: 1,422
B36 Tórshavn – CRUSADERS FC BELFAST 2-3(1-2)
B36 Tórshavn: Hans Jørgensen, Erling Jacobsen (62.Michal Przybylski), Jónas Næs (83.Gilli Samuelsen), Bjarni Petersen, Eli Nielsen, Árni Frederiksberg, Andrias Eriksen, Magnus Holm Jacobsen, Hugin Samuelsen (72.Hannes Agnarsson), Stefan Radosavljevic, Lukasz Cieslewicz. Trainer: Jákub á Borg.
Crusaders FC: Sean O'Neill, Billy Joe Burns, Howard Beverland, Chris Hegarty, Michael Ruddy, Declan Caddell (65.Rory Hale), Philip Lowry, Jordan Forsythe (86.Gary Thompson), Paul Heatley, Ross Clarke, Jordan Owens (83.David Cushley). Trainer: Stephen Baxter.
Goals: 3' Jordan Forsythe 0-1, 28' Paul Heatley 0-2, 37' Hugin Samuelsen 1-2, 51' Lukasz Cieslewicz 2-2, 68' Paul Heatley 2-3.

18.07.2019; Veritas Stadion, Turku
Referee: Keith Kennedy (NIR); Attendance: 3,711
FC Inter Turku – BRØNDBY IF 2-0(0-0)
FC Inter Turku: Henrik Moisander, Niko Markkula (86.Mikko Kuningas), Luciano Balbi, Juuso Hämäläinen, Miro Tenho, Arttu Hoskonen (70.Daan Klinkenberg), Álvaro Muñiz, Aleksi Paananen, Niilo Mäenpää (76.Albion Ademi), Timo Furuholm, Filip Valencic. Trainer: José Riveiro.
Brøndby IF: Marvin Schwäbe, Anthony Jung, Hjörtur Hermannsson, Jens Gammelby, Kasper Fisker (90.Paulus Arajuuri), Dominik Kaiser, Simon Tibbling, Simon Hedlund, Tobias Børkeeiet (58.Josip Radosevic), Kevin Mensah, Mikael Uhre (59.Kamil Wilczek). Trainer: Niels Frederiksen.
Goals: 52' Niko Markkula 1-0, 56' Filip Valencic 2-0.

11.07.2019; Aker Stadion, Molde
Referee: Aleksandrs Golubevs (LVA); Attendance: 3,756
Molde FK – KR Reykjavík 7-1(4-0)
Molde FK: Álex Craninx, Vegard Forren, Kristoffer Haraldseid, Kristoffer Haugen, Martin Bjørnbak, Magnus Eikrem (82.Mattias Moström), Etzaz Hussain, Eirik Hestad, Fredrik Aursnes (70.Fredrik Sjølstad), Ohi Omoijuanfo, Leke James (75.Erling Knudtzon). Trainer: Erling Moe.
KR Reykjavik: Beitir Ólafsson, Arnór Adalsteinsson, Skúli Jón Fridgeirsson, Kristinn Jónsson, Finnur Tómas Pálmason (46.Gunnar Gunnarsson), Pálmi Pálmason, Arnthór Ingi Kristinsson (78.Ægir Jónasson), Pablo Punyed, Óskar Hauksson, Kennie Chopart, Tobias Thomsen (86.Björgvin Stefánsson). Trainer: Rúnar Kristinsson.
Goals: 7' Leke James 1-0, 29' Fredrik Aursnes 2-0, 31' Leke James 3-0, 41' Leke James 4-0, 63' Vegard Forren 5-0, 66' Etzaz Hussain 6-0, 71' Tobias Thomsen 6-1, 90+3' Ohi Omoijuanfo 7-1.

11.07.2019; „Toše Proeski" Arena, Skopje
Referee: Kai Erik Steen (NOR); Attendance: 1,562
Fudbalska Akademija Pandev Strumica – HŠK Zrinjski Mostar 0-3(0-2)
Akademija Pandev: Dusan Cubrakovic, Tomislav Iliev, Dime Dimov, Ljupco Doriev, David Atanasovski, Georgi Stoilov, Stefan Kostov, Daniel Milovanovikj (78.Kristijan Velinovski), Goran Tomovski, Sasko Pandev (68.Mario Krstovski), Kristijan Stojkovski (66.Riste Temelkov). Trainer: Jugoslav Trencovski.
Zrinjski Mostar: Ivan Brkic, Tomislav Barbaric, Dario Rugasevic, Slobodan Jakovljevic, Advan Kadusic, Ivan Curjuric, Damir Sovsic (76.Semir Pezer), Edin Rustemovic, Miljan Govedarica, Stanisa Mandic (83.Marko Bencun), Irfan Hadzic (66.Ivan Lendric). Trainer: Hari Vukas.
Goals: 12' Irfan Hadzic 0-1, 28' Stanisa Mandic 0-2, 55' Miljan Govedarica 0-3.

11.07.2019; Stadyen Budaunik Stroitel, Solihorsk
Referee: Jovan Kaludjerovic (MNE); Attendance: 3,048
FC Shakhtyor Solihorsk – Hibernians FC Paola 1-0(0-0)
Shakhtyor Solihorsk: Andrey Klimovich, Sergey Matvejchik, Igor Burko, Nikola Antic, Aleksandr Sachivko, Yuri Kovalev, Július Szöke, Valeriy Gromyko, Max Ebong Ngome (46.Mykyta Tatarkov), Elis Bakaj, Vladimir Khvashchinskiy (46.Nikolai Yanush). Trainer: Sergey Tashuev.
Hibernians FC: Marko Jovicic, Andrei Agius, Márcio Silveira, Ferdinando Apap, Timothy Tabone, Bjorn Kristensen, Dunstan Vella, Jake Grech (74.Jens Wemmer), Leonardo Nanni (89.David Xuereb), Joseph Mbong, Terence Groothusen. Trainer: Stefano Sanderra.
Goal: 69' Valeriy Gromyko 1-0.

11.07.2019; Stadionul Zimbru, Chişinău
Referee: Tim Marshall (NIR); Attendance: 1,370
CSF Speranţa Nisporeni – Neftçi PFK Bakı 0-3(0-2)
Speranţa Nisporeni: Daniil Avdyushkin, Óliver Fula, Bruno Barbosa, Stefan Efros, Mihail Bolun, Fabrice Eloundou, Ichaka Tiehi, Felipe Ponce, Dayron Mosquera (46.Ion Dragan), Alisher Mirzoev (87.Ruslan Chelari), Maxim Iurcu (79.Constantin Sandu). Trainer: Cristian Efros.
Neftçi Bakı: Salahat Agayev, Kyrylo Petrov, Mamadou Mbodj, Anton Krivotsyuk, Omar Buludov, Vangelis Platellas (69.Rahman Hadzhiyev), Emin Makhmudov, Mamadou Kane, Steeven Joseph-Monrose (87.Ismayil Zülfügarli), Rauf Aliyev, Dário Júnior da Silva (80.Namiq Alasgarov). Trainer: Roberto Bordin.
Goals: 16' Emin Makhmudov 0-1 (pen), 36' Steeven Joseph-Monrose 0-2, 76' Rahman Hadzhiyev 0-3.

11.07.2019; Stade „Émile Mayrisch", Esch-sur-Alzette
Referee: Rauf Jabbarov (AZE); Attendance: 1,087
CS Fola Esch – FC Chikhura Sachkhere 1-2(1-0)
CS Fola Esch: Emanuel Cabral, Billy Bernard, Julien Klein, Cédric Sacras, Veldin Muharemovic, Dejvid Sinani (89.Jean Sylvio Ouassiero), Gérard Mersch, Bruno Freire, Gauthier Caron (75.Achraf Drif), Ken Corral (86.Zachary Hadji), Moussa Seydi. Trainer: Jeff Strasser.
Chikhura Sachkhere: Dino Hamzic, Davit Maisashvili, Lasha Chikvaidze, Revaz Chiteishvili, Oleg Mamasakhlisi, Besik Dekanoidze (90.Shota Kashia), Irakli Lekvtadze (75.Giorgi Pantsulaia), Giorgi Koripadze, Teimuraz Markozashvili, Rati Ardazishvili (65.Demur Chikhladze), Mikheil Sardalishvili. Trainer: Soso Pruidze.
Goals: 22' Dejvid Sinani 1-0 (pen), 59' Mikheil Sardalishvili 1-1, 86' Giorgi Koripadze 1-2 (pen).

18.07.2019; Alvogenvöllurinn, Reykavík
Referee: Ian McNabb (NIR); Attendance: 355
KR Reykjavík – MOLDE FK 0-0
KR Reykjavik: Beitir Ólafsson, Gunnar Gunnarsson, Arnór Adalsteinsson (46.Aron Jósepsson), Skúli Jón Fridgeirsson, Ástbjörn Thórdarson, Pálmi Pálmason (71.Atli Sigurjónsson), Finnur Margiersson (78.Kristinn Jónsson), Pablo Punyed, Kennie Chopart, Björgvin Stefánsson, Ægir Jónasson. Trainer: Rúnar Kristinsson.
Molde FK: Álex Craninx, Vegard Forren, Ruben Gabrielsen, Kristoffer Haraldseid, Kristoffer Haugen, Etzaz Hussain, Fredrik Aursnes (71.Eirik Hestad), Martin Ellingsen, Erling Knudtzon (82.Leke James), Mattias Moström, Ohi Omoijuanfo (62.Mathis Bolly). Trainer: Erling Moe.

18.07.2019; Stadion Bijeli Brijeg, Mostar
Referee: Ondrej Pechanec (CZE); Attendance: 2,500
HŠK ZRINJSKI MOSTAR – Fudbalska Akademija Pandev Strumica 3-0(0-0)
Zrinjski Mostar: Ivan Brkic, Dario Rugasevic, Slobodan Jakovljevic, Tomislav Barisic, Renato Gojkovic, Ivan Curjuric, Frane Cirjak (59.Damir Sovsic), Edin Rustemovic (79.Semir Pezer), Stanisa Mandic, Kristijan Stanic (46.Miljan Govedarica), Ivan Lendric. Trainer: Hari Vukas.
Akademija Pandev: Marko Alchevski (65.David Denkovski), Tomislav Iliev, Dime Dimov, Ljupco Doriev, Mihail Manevski, Riste Temelkov, Gjorgji Tanusev (67.Sasko Pandev), Georgi Stoilov, Stefan Kostov, Daniel Milovanovikj, Mario Krstovski (75.Vane Jovanov). Trainer: Jugoslav Trencovski.
Goals: 50' Stanisa Mandic 1-0, 79' Miljan Govedarica 2-0, 90+2' Renato Gojkovic 3-0.

18.07.2019; MFA Centenary Stadium, Ta'Qali
Referee: Furkat Atazhanov (KAZ); Attendance: 608
Hibernians FC Paola – FC SHAKHTYOR SOLIHORSK 0-1(0-0)
Hibernians FC: Marko Jovicic, Andrei Agius, Márcio Silveira (67.Jens Wemmer), Ferdinando Apap, Timothy Tabone, Bjorn Kristensen, Dunstan Vella, Jake Grech (80.Matthew Farrugia), Leonardo Nanni, Joseph Mbong (80.Connor Zammit), Terence Groothusen. Trainer: Stefano Sanderra.
Shakhtyor Solihorsk: Andrey Klimovich, Pavel Rybak, Sergey Matvejchik, Nikola Antic, Aleksandr Sachivko, Aleksandr Selyava, Yuri Kovalev, Július Szöke, Valeriy Gromyko (78.Igor Burko), Max Ebong Ngome (64.Mykyta Tatarkov), Elis Bakaj (82.Nikolai Yanush). Trainer: Sergey Tashuev.; Goal: 65' Mykyta Tatarkov 0-1.
Sent off: 33' Aleksandr Selyava, 73' Ferdinando Apap.

18.07.2019; Bakcell Arena, Bakı
Referee: Julian Weinberger (AUT); Attendance: 6,500
NEFTÇI PFK BAKI – CSF Speranţa Nisporeni 6-0(4-0)
Neftçi Bakı: Salahat Agayev, Vojislav Stankovic, Kyrylo Petrov, Anton Krivotsyuk, Omar Buludov, Vangelis Platellas (54.Rahman Hadzhiyev), Emin Makhmudov, Mamadou Kane (54.Soni Mustivar), Steeven Joseph-Monrose, Rauf Aliyev, Dário Júnior da Silva (71.Ismayil Zülfügarli). Trainer: Roberto Bordin.
Speranţa Nisporeni: Denis Macogonenco, Ion Arabadji, Óliver Fula, Bruno Barbosa, Stefan Efros, Mihail Bolun, Fabrice Eloundou (68.Luis Ferney Ríos), Felipe Ponce, Constantin Sandu (55.Ion Dragan), Ruslan Chelari (78.Dayron Mosquera), Maxim Iurcu. Trainer: Cristian Efros.
Goals: 18' Vangelis Platellas 1-0, 24' Emin Makhmudov 2-0 (pen), 40' Vangelis Platellas 3-0, 42' Dário Júnior da Silva 4-0, 67' Steeven Joseph-Monrose 5-0, 78' Ismayil Zülfügarli 6-0.

17.07.2019; „Boris Paichadze" Dinamo Arena, Tbilisi
Referee: Dragan Petrovic (BIH); Attendance: 1,458
FC CHIKHURA SACHKHERE – CS Fola Esch 2-1(1-0)
Chikhura Sachkhere: Dino Hamzic, Shota Kashia (76.Revaz Chiteishvili), Davit Maisashvili, Lasha Chikvaidze, Oleg Mamasakhlisi, Besik Dekanoidze (63.Irakli Lekvtadze), Giorgi Koripadze, Rati Ardazishvili (67.Mikheil Ergemlidze), Demur Chikhladze, Giorgi Pantsulaia, Mikheil Sardalishvili. Trainer: Soso Pruidze.
CS Fola Esch: Emanuel Cabral, Billy Bernard, Julien Klein, Cédric Sacras, Veldin Muharemovic, Dejvid Sinani, Gérard Mersch (68.Jean Sylvio Ouassiero), Bruno Freire (75.Zachary Hadji), Gauthier Caron (46.Achraf Drif), Ken Corral, Moussa Seydi. Trainer: Jeff Strasser.
Goals: 25' Rati Ardazishvili 1-0, 73' Mikheil Sardalishvili 2-0, 89' Dejvid Sinani 2-1 (pen).; Sent off: 32' Veldin Muharemovic.

11.07.2019; Stadion Stozice, Ljubljana
Referee: Urs Schnyder (SUI); Attendance: 4,200
NK Olimpija Ljubljana – FK Rīgas Futbola skola 2-3(0-0)
Olimpija Ljubljana: Nejc Vidmar, Denis Sme, Macky Frank Bagnack, Eric Boakye, Marko Putincanin (72.Luka Menalo), Asmir Suljic, Stefan Savic, Tomislav Tomic, Endri Çekiçi, Rok Kidric (63.Ante Vukusic), Mario Jurcevic. Trainer: Safet Hadzic.
FK Rīgas Futbola skola: Kaspers Ikstens, Vitalijs Jagodinskis, Edvinas Girdvainis, Vladislavs Sorokins, Tomás Simkovic (77.Tin Vukmanic), Takayuki Seto, Slavko Blagojevic, Andrejs Ciganiks (64.Alain Cedric Kouadio), Andrija Kaludjerovic (71.Glebs Kluskins), Roberts Savalnieks, Darko Lemajic. Trainer: Valdas Dambrauskas.
Goals: 52' Darko Lemajic 0-1 (pen), 81' Eric Boakye 1-1, 88' Glebs Kluskins 1-2, 90' Luka Menalo 2-2, 90+3' Tin Vukmanic 2-3.

11.07.2019; Corbett Sports Stadium, Rhyl
Referee: Erik Lambrechts (BEL); Attendance: 1,410
Connah's Quay Nomads FC – Kilmarnock FC 1-2(0-0)
Connah's Quay Nomads FC: Lewis Brass, George Horan, Danny Holmes, John Disney, Callum Roberts, Danny Harrison, Jay Owen, Michael Bakare, Callum Morris, Declan Poole, Michael Wilde. Trainer: Andy Morrison.
Kilmarnock FC: Jamie MacDonald, Kirk Broadfoot, Stephen O'Donnell, Stuart Findlay, Greg Taylor, Chris Burke, Alan Power, Gary Dicker, Dominic Thomas (78.Greg Kiltie), Rory McKenzie (64.Mohamed El Makrini), Eamonn Brophy. Trainer: Angelo Alessio.
Goals: 75' Greg Taylor 1-0 (own goal), 82' Eamonn Brophy 1-1 (pen), 90+2' Stuart Findlay 1-2.

11.07.2019; Victoria Stadium, Gibraltar
Referee: Alex Troleis (FRO); Attendance: 787
Europa FC – Legia Warszawa 0-0
Europa FC: Dayle Coleing, Sergio Sánchez, Rahim Ayew, Olmo González, Ethan Jolley, Velasco (82.Manu Dimas), Álex Quillo (59.Marco Rosa), Juampe Rico, Liam Walker, Mustapha Yahaya, Andre Tjay de Barr (88.Adrián Gallardo). Trainer: Rafael Escobar.
Legia Warszawa: Radoslaw Majecki, Artur Jedrzejczyk, William Rémy, Dominik Nagy (76.Salvador Agra), Mateusz Wieteska, Arvydas Novikovas, Marko Vesovic, André Martins, Valeriane Gvilia, Carlitos López, Vamara Sanogo (45+2.Sandro Kulenovic). Trainer: Aleksandar Vukovic.

11.07.2019; MOL Aréna, Dunajská Streda
Referee: Rade Obrenovic (SVN); Attendance: 9,860
FK DAC Dunajská Streda – KS Cracovia Kraków 1-1(1-1)
DAC Dunajská Streda: Martin Jedlicka, Éric Davis (60.César Blackman), Lubomír Satka, Dominik Kruzliak, Zsolt Kalmár, Kristián Kostrna, Kristopher Vida (71.Abdulrahman Taiwo), Máté Vida, Lukás Cmelík (76.Eric Ramírez), Connor Ronan, Marko Divkovic. Trainer: Peter Hyballa.
KS Cracovia Kraków: Michal Peskovic, Cornel Rapa, Niko Datkovic, Michal Helik, Kamil Pestka (46.Diego Ferraresso), Janusz Gol, Damian Dabrowski (84.Milan Dimun), Sergiu Hanca, Bojan Cecaric (62.Mateusz Wdowiak), Pelle van Amersfoort, "Rafa" Rafael Lopes. Trainer: Michal Probierz.
Goals: 40' Dominik Kruzliak 0-1 (own goal), 44' Marko Divkovic 1-1.

11.07.2019; Stadionul „Marin Anastasovici", Giurgiu
Referee: Kristoffer Hagenes (NOR); Attendance: 4,824
SC FCSB Bucureşti – FC Milsami Orhei 2-0(1-0)
FCSB Bucureşti: Andrei Daniel Vlad, Bogdan Planic, Claudiu Belu, Iulian Cristea, Mihai Roman (I), Dragos Nedelcu, Razvan Oaida (62.Lucian Filip), Adrian Ioan Hora, Florin Tanase, Florinel Coman (90+5.Cristián Dumitru), Dennis Man (79.Ovidiu Popescu). Trainer: Bogdan Andone.
Milsami Orhei: Anatolii Chirinciuc, Vadim Bolohan, Vasile Jardan, Artur Craciun, Alexandru Antoniuc, Alexandru Onica, Gheorghe Andronic, Andrei Rusnac, Victor Stîna (85.Maxim Antoniuc), Sergiu Platica, Sergiu Nazar (60.Veaceslav Zagaevschii). Trainer: Veaceslav Rusnac.
Goals: 12', 56' Florin Tanase 1-0, 2-0.
Sent off: 73' Lucian Filip.

18.07.2019; Daugava Stadions, Rīga
Referee: Peter Kjærsgaard-Andersen (DEN); Attendance: 3,652
FK Rīgas Futbols skola – NK OLIMPIJA LJUBLJANA 0-2(0-1)
FK Rīgas Futbola skola: Kaspers Ikstens, Vitalijs Jagodinskis, Edvinas Girdvainis, Vladislavs Sorokins, Tomás Simkovic (87.Alans Sinelnikovs), Takayuki Seto, Slavko Blagojevic, Tin Vukmanic (73.Andrejs Ciganiks), Roberts Savalnieks, Darko Lemajic, Alain Cedric Kouadio (64.Andrija Kaludjerovic). Trainer: Valdas Dambrauskas.
Olimpija Ljubljana: Nejc Vidmar, Vitalijs Maksimenko, Macky Frank Bagnack, Eric Boakye, Goran Brkic (74.Marko Putincanin), Asmir Suljic (67.Stefan Savic), Tomislav Tomic (90+5.Vitja Valencic), Endri Çekiçi, Ante Vukusic, Mario Jurcevic, Luka Menalo. Trainer: Safet Hadzic.
Goals: 45+1' Endri Çekiçi 0-1, 90+2' Stefan Savic 0-2.

18.07.2019; Rugby Park, Kilmarnock
Referee: Ferenc Karakó (HUN); Attendance: 8,306
Kilmarnock FC – CONNAH'S QUAY NOMADS FC 0-2(0-0)
Kilmarnock FC: Jamie MacDonald, Kirk Broadfoot, Stephen O'Donnell, Stuart Findlay, Greg Taylor, Chris Burke (82.Innes Cameron), Mohamed El Makrini (87.Dominic Thomas), Alan Power, Gary Dicker, Rory McKenzie, Eamonn Brophy. Trainer: Angelo Alessio.
Connah's Quay Nomads FC: Lewis Brass, George Horan, Danny Holmes, John Disney, Callum Roberts (83.Priestley Farquharson), Jay Owen, Callum Morris, Ryan Wignall, Declan Poole, Michael Wilde, Michael Bakare (70.Jamie Insall). Trainer: Andy Morrison.
Goals: 50' Ryan Wignall 0-1, 80' Callum Morris 0-2 (pen).
Sent off: 79' Stuart Findlay, 85' Ryan Wignall.

18.07.2019; Stadion "Marszalka Józefa Pilsudskiego", Warszawa
Referee: Robert Jenkins (WAL); Attendance: 14,839
LEGIA WARSZAWA – Europa FC 3-0(2-0)
Legia Warszawa: Radoslaw Majecki, Artur Jedrzejczyk, William Rémy, Mateusz Wieteska, Arvydas Novikovas, Marko Vesovic, André Martins (70.Tomasz Jodlowiec), Dominik Nagy (46.Salvador Agra), Valeriane Gvilia, Carlitos López, Sandro Kulenovic (63.Jaroslaw Niezgoda). Trainer: Aleksandar Vukovic.
Europa FC: Dayle Coleing, Sergio Sánchez, Rahim Ayew, Olmo González, Jayce Mascarenhas-Olivero, Álex Quillo (61.Marco Rosa), Juampe Rico, Liam Walker, Mustapha Yahaya, Adrián Gallardo (68.Manu Dimas), Andre Tjay de Barr (55.Velasco). Trainer: Rafael Escobar.
Goals: 7' Carlitos López 1-0, 13' Sandro Kulenovic 2-0, 60' Carlitos López 3-0;
 Sent off: 54' Sergio Sánchez.

18.07.2019; Stadion Cracovii im. "Józefa Pilsudskiego", Kraków
Referee: Athanasios Tzilos (GRE); Attendance: 13,255
KS Cracovia Kraków – FK DAC DUNAJSKÁ STREDA 2-2(1-0,1-1)
KS Cracovia Kraków: Michal Peskovic, Cornel Rapa, Diego Ferraresso, David Jablonsky, Michal Helik, Janusz Gol, Damian Dabrowski (72.Milan Dimun), Sergiu Hanca (95.Filip Piszczek), Bojan Cecaric (106.Rubio), Pelle van Amersfoort, "Rafa" Rafael Lopes (84.Mateusz Wdowiak). Trainer: Michal Probierz.
DAC Dunajská Streda: Martin Jedlicka, Éric Davis, Lubomír Satka, Kristián Kostrna, Dominik Kruzliak, Zsolt Kalmár (105.Abdulrahman Taiwo), Máté Vida, Lukás Cmelík (24.César Blackman), Connor Ronan, Eric Ramírez (98.Kristopher Vida), Marko Divkovic (120.Danilo Beskorovainyi). Trainer: Peter Hyballa.
Goals: 2' "Rafa" Rafael Lopes 1-0, 47' Connor Ronan 1-1, 94' Eric Ramírez 1-2, 120+2' Filip Piszczek 2-2.

18.07.2019; Complexul Sportiv Raional, Orhei
Referee: Timotheos Christofi (CYP); Attendance: 3,000
FC Milsami Orhei – SC FCSB BUCUREŞTI 1-2(0-2)
Milsami Orhei: Anatolii Chirinciuc, Vadim Bolohan, Vasile Jardan, Artur Craciun, Alexandru Antoniuc, Alexandru Onica, Gheorghe Andronic, Andrei Rusnac (81.Sergiu Nazar), Victor Stîna (67.Veaceslav Zagaevschii), Maxim Antoniuc, Sergiu Platica. Trainer: Veaceslav Rusnac.
FCSB Bucureşti: Andrei Daniel Vlad, Bogdan Planic, Claudiu Belu, Iulian Cristea, Mihai Roman (I), Dragos Nedelcu, Razvan Oaida, Florin Tanase (72.Ovidiu Popescu), Florinel Coman (58.Adrian Ioan Hora), Dennis Man (64.Robert Ion), Cristián Dumitru. Trainer: Bogdan Andone.
Goals: 4' Cristián Dumitru 0-1, 42' Razvan Oaida 0-2, 47' Vadim Bolohan 1-2.

11.07.2019; Stadion na Banovom brdu, Beograd
Referee: Ívar Orri Kristjánsson (ISL); Attendance: 1,203
FK Čukarički Beograd – FC Banants Erevan 3-0(1-0)
FK Čukarički Beograd: Nemanja Belic, Miroslav Bogosavac, Darko
Puskaric, Nikola Cirkovic, Luka Stojanovic (72.Aleksandar Djordjevic),
Luka Lukovic (53.Veljko Birmancevic), Marko Docic, Stefan Kovac,
Stefan Sapic, Slobodan Tedic, Milutin Vidosavljevic (82.Bojica
Nikcevic). Trainer: Aleksandar Veselinovic.
Banants Erevan: Aram Ayrapetyan, Vahagn Ayvazyan, Andranik
Voskanyan, Edward Kpodo, Narek Petrosyan, Aram Bareghamyan, Artak
Dashyan (72.Hakob Hakobyan), Pape Camara, Igor Stanojevic, Evgeni
Kobzar (68.Karen Melkonyan), Aleksandar Glisic (87.Semen
Sinyavskiy). Trainer: Ilshat Faizulin.
Goals: 43' Slobodan Tedic 1-0, 80' Stefan Kovac 2-0, 90+2' Slobodan
Tedic 3-0.

11.07.2019; Stadion Pod Goricom, Podgorica:
Referee: Georgi Vadachkoria (GEO); Attendance: 965
FK Zeta Golubovci – Fehérvár FC Székesfehérvár 1-5(1-3)
FK Zeta Golubovci: Zoran Akovic, Djordjije Vukcevic, Nemanja
Sekulic, Balsa Goranovic, Zvonko Ceklic, Armin Bosnjak, Goran
Milojko, Stefan Vukcevic (60.Alex Yamoah), Amel Tuzovic, Srdjan
Krstovic (76.Lazar Lambulic), Ivan Vukcevic (90+3.Matija Lambulic).
Trainer: Dejan Roganovic.
Fehérvár FC: Ádám Kovácsik, Roland Juhász, Attila Fiola, Loïc Négo,
Stopira, Anel Hadzic, Máté Pátkai (61.Ivan Petryak), Ákos Elek, Georgi
Milanov (64.Szabolcs Huszti), Boban Nikolov, Marko Scepovic
(80.Márkó Futács). Trainer: Marko Nikolic.
Goals: 3', 12' Loïc Négo 0-1, 0-2, 17' Balsa Goranovic 1-2, 23' Loïc
Négo 1-3, 86' Roland Juhász 1-4, 90+3' Szabolcs Huszti 1-5.

11.07.2019; Solitude Stadium, Belfast
Referee: Laurent Kopriwa (LUX); Attendance: 1,342
Cliftonville FAC – FK Haugesund 0-1(0-1)
Cliftonville FAC: Richard Brush, Garry Breen, Liam Bagnall, Conor
McMenamin, Joe Gorman (87.Thomas Maguire), Levi Ives, Conor
McDermott, Chris Curran (67.Ryan Curran), Ronan Doherty, Rory
Donnelly, Joe Gormley. Trainer: Paddy McLaughlin.
FK Haugesund: Helge Sandvik, Doug Bergqvist, Mikkel Desler,
Benjamin Tiedemann Hansen, Christian Grindheim (46.Kevin Krygård),
Sondre Tronstad, Torbjørn Kallavåg, Niklas Sandberg, Bruno Leite,
Martin Samuelsen (82.Fredrik Knudsen), Ibrahima Koné (33.Kristoffer
Velde). Trainer: Jostein Grindhaug.
Goal: 42' Christian Grindheim 0-1.
Sent off: 79' Torbjørn Kallavåg.

11.07.2019; Richmond Park, Dublin
Referee: Lionel Tschudi (SUI); Attendance: 2,389
St. Patrick's Athletic FC Dublin – IFK Norrköping 0-2(0-0)
St. Patrick's Athletic: Brendan Clarke, Ian Bermingham, Simon Madden,
Kevin Toner, Lee Desmond, Ciaran Kelly, Conor Clifford (83.Jake
Walker), Cian Coleman (64.Rhys McCabe), Jamie Lennon, Gary Shaw
(64.Dean Clarke), Michael Drennan. Trainer: Harry Kenny.
IFK Norrköping: Isak Pettersson, Lars Gerson, Kasper Larsen, Filip
Dagerstål, Rasmus Lauritsen, Gudmundur Thórarinsson (75.Sead
Haksabanovic), Simon Thern, Alexander Fransson, Christoffer Nyman
(69.Kalle Holmberg), Simon Skrabb (86.Egzon Binaku), Jordan Larsson.
Trainer: Jens Gustafsson.
Goals: 55' Simon Thern 0-1, 85' Lee Desmond 0-2 (own goal).

11.07.2019; Pittodrie Stadium, Aberdeen
Referee: Kaspar Sjöberg (SWE); Attendance: 14,377
Aberdeen FC – Rovaniemi PS 2-1(1-0)
Aberdeen FC: Joe Lewis, Andrew Considine, Shay Logan, Michael
Devlin, Scott McKenna, Niall McGinn (82.James Wilson), Lewis
Ferguson, Ryan Hedges (61.Dean Campbell), Scott Wright (74.Connor
McLennan), Sam Cosgrove, Jon Gallagher. Trainer: Derek McInnes.
Rovaniemi PS: Antonio Reguero, Taye Taïwo, Mohamadou Sissoko, Atte
Sihvonen, Juho Hyvärinen, Kalle Katz, Eetu Muinonen (57.Tarik Kada),
Sergio Llamas (76.Tommi Jäntti), Lucas Lingman, Aleksandr Kokko
(65.Niklas Jokelainen), Youness Rahimi. Trainer: Pasi Tuutti.
Goals: 36' Niall McGinn 1-0. 48' Sam Cosgrove 2-0, 90+3' Niklas
Jokelainen 2-1.

16.07.2019; Banants Stadion, Yerevan
Referee: Ioannis Papadopoulos (GRE); Attendance: 2,100
FC Banants Erevan – FK ČUKARIČKI BEOGRAD 0-5(0-2)
Banants Erevan: Aram Ayrapetyan, Vahagn Ayvazyan, Andranik
Voskanyan, Edward Kpodo, Narek Petrosyan, Aram Bareghamyan
(60.Evgeni Kobzar), Artak Dashyan, Pape Camara, Igor Stanojevic
(46.Hakob Hakobyan), Karen Melkonyan, Aleksandar Glisic (73.Semen
Sinyavskiy). Trainer: Ilshat Faizulin.
FK Čukarički Beograd: Nemanja Belic, Miroslav Bogosavac, Darko
Puskaric (73.Dimitrije Kamenovic), Nikola Cirkovic, Luka Stojanovic,
Luka Lukovic, Marko Docic (59.Aleksandar Djordjevic), Stefan Kovac,
Stefan Sapic, Slobodan Tedic (53.Veljko Birmancevic), Milutin
Vidosavljevic. Trainer: Aleksander Veselinovic.
Goals: 3' Luka Stojanovic 0-1, 31' Slobodan Tedic 0-2, 49' Luka
Lukovic 0-3, 71' Veljko Birmancevic 0-4, 75' Luka Stojanovic 0-5 (pen).

18.07.2019; Pancho Aréna, Felcsút
Referee: Paul McLaughlin (IRL) Attendance: 2,148
FEHÉRVÁR FC SZÉKESFEHÉRVÁR – FK Zeta Golubovci 0-0
Fehérvár FC: Ádám Kovácsik, Roland Juhász, Loïc Négo, Stopira,
Szabolcs Huszti, Anel Hadzic, Máté Pátkai (64.Georgi Milanov), Ákos
Elek, István Kovács, Ivan Petryak (79.Armin Hodzic), Marko Scepovic
(80.Márkó Futács). Trainer: Marko Nikolic.
FK Zeta Golubovci: Zoran Akovic, Djordjije Vukcevic, Nemanja
Sekulic, Balsa Goranovic, Zvonko Ceklic, Armin Bosnjak (89.Davor
Kontic), Goran Milojko, Stefan Vukcevic (65.Jovan Baosic), Amel
Tuzovic, Srdjan Krstovic, Ivan Vukcevic (83.Matija Lambulic). Trainer:
Dejan Roganovic.
Sent off: 74' Djordjije Vukcevic.

18.07.2019; Haugesund Stadion, Haugesund
Referee: Mario Zebec (CRO); Attendance: 2,633
FK HAUGESUND – Cliftonville FAC 5-1(3-1)
FK Haugesund: Helge Sandvik, Doug Bergqvist, Mikkel Desler,
Benjamin Tiedemann Hansen, Sondre Tronstad, Niklas Sandberg, Bruno
Leite, Kristoffer Velde, Anthony Ikedi, Martin Samuelsen (72.Eric
Ndayisenga), Ibrahima Koné (61.Kevin Krygård). Trainer: Jostein
Grindhaug.
Cliftonville FAC: Richard Brush, Garry Breen, Liam Bagnall (61.Ryan
Curran), Conor McMenamin, Joe Gorman, Levi Ives, Conor McDermott,
Chris Curran, Ronan Doherty (80.Ronan Wilson), Rory Donnelly, Joe
Gormley (70.Thomas Maguire). Trainer: Paddy McLaughlin.
Goals: 5' Kristoffer Velde 1-0, 17' Conor McMenamin 1-1, 36' Niklas
Sandberg 2-1, 45+1' Ibrahima Koné 3-1, 52' Bruno Leite 4-1, 68'
Kristoffer Velde 5-1.

18.07.2019; Östgötaporten, Norrköping
Referee: Dejan Jakimovski (MKD); Attendance: 5,925
IFK NORRKÖPING – St. Patrick's Athletic FC Dublin 2-1(1-0)
IFK Norrköping: Isak Pettersson, Lars Gerson, Kasper Larsen, Filip
Dagerstål, Rasmus Lauritsen, Gudmundur Thórarinsson, Simon Thern,
Alexander Fransson (88.Andreas Blomqvist), Christoffer Nyman
(73.Kalle Holmberg), Simon Skrabb (63.Egzon Binaku), Jordan Larsson.
Trainer: Jens Gustafsson.
St. Patrick's Athletic: Brendan Clarke, Ian Bermingham, Simon Madden,
Kevin Toner, Lee Desmond, Ciaran Kelly, Conor Clifford, Cian Coleman
(64.Darragh Markey), Jamie Lennon (73.Rhys McCabe), Gary Shaw
(52.Dean Clarke), Michael Drennan. Trainer: Harry Kenny.
Goals: 36' Jordan Larsson 1-0, 72' Conor Clifford 1-1, 85' Kalle
Holmberg 2-1.
Sent off: 89' Ciaran Kelly.

18.07.2019; Rovaniemen Keskuskenttä, Rovaniemi
Referee: Ümit Öztürk (TUR); Attendance: 2,000
Rovaniemi PS – ABERDEEN FC 1-2(1-1)
Rovaniemi PS: Antonio Reguero, Taye Taïwo, Mohamadou Sissoko, Atte
Sihvonen, Juho Hyvärinen, Kalle Katz, Eetu Muinonen (81.Tommi
Jäntti), Agnaldo Moraes (68.Youness Rahimi), Lucas Lingman, Tarik
Kada, Aleksandr Kokko (66.Niklas Jokelainen). Trainer: Pasi Tuutti.
Aberdeen FC: Joe Lewis, Andrew Considine, Shay Logan, Ash Taylor,
Scott McKenna, Niall McGinn (87.Scott Wright), Lewis Ferguson, Dean
Campbell, Ryan Hedges, Sam Cosgrove (66.Curtis Main), Jon Gallagher.
Trainer: Derek McInnes.
Goals: 2' Tarik Kada 1-0, 27' Sam Cosgrove 1-1 (pen), 90+4' Lewis
Ferguson 1-2.

11.07.2019; Turner's Cross, Cork
Referee: Aleksandrs Anufrijevs (LVA); Attendance: 3,137
Cork City FC – FC Progrès Niederkorn 0-2(0-2)
Cork City: Mark McNulty, Colm Horgan (24.Mark O'Sullivan), Dan Casey, Conor McCarthy, Ronan Hurley, Sean McLoughlin, Conor McCormack, Gearóid Morrissey, Garry Buckley (61.Gary Boylan), Karl Sheppard, Joel Coustrain (80.Darragh Crowley). Trainers: John Cotter & Frank Kelleher.
Progrès Niederkorn: Sebastian Flauss, Tom Laterza, Ben Vogel, Metin Karayer, Tim Hall, Aldin Skenderovic, Sébastien Thill (88.Adrien Ferino), Christian Silaj, Belmin Muratovic (71.Jacky Mmaee), Mayron De Almeida, Kempes Tekiela (90+3.Yann Matias Marques). Trainer: Roland Vrabec.
Goals: 11' Belmin Muratovic 0-1, 21' Mayron De Almeida 0-2 (pen).

11.07.2019; „Illovszky Rudolf" Stadion, Budapest
Referee: Boris Marhefka (SVK); Attendance: 3,622
Budapest Honvéd FC – FK Žalgiris Vilnius 3-1(1-0)
Budapest Honvéd: Rubi Levkovic, Ivan Lovric, Djordje Kamber, Bence Batik, Nikolasz Kovács, Tibor Heffler, Tonci Kukoc (74.Eke Uzoma), Dániel Gazdag, Bence Banó-Szabó (83.Dávid Kálnoki-Kis), David N'Gog (70.Dominik Cipf), Amadou Moutari. Trainer: Giuseppe Sannino.
FK Žalgiris: Martin Berkovec, Donovan Slijngard, Klemen Bolha, Rolandas Baravykas (67.Matas Vareika), Saulius Mikoliūnas (72.Karolis Uzéla), Liviu Antal, Víctor Pérez (88.Domantas Simkus), Modestas Vorobjovas, Marko Tomic, Tomislav Kis, Pau Morer. Trainer: Marek Zub.
Goals: 32' Bence Banó-Szabó 1-0, 55' David N'Gog 2-0, 69' Dániel Gazdag 3-0 (pen), 90+2' Karolis Uzéla 3-1.

11.07.2019; Stadion Pecara, Široki Brijeg
Referee: Sebastian Colțescu (ROU); Attendance: 2,436
NK Široki Brijeg – FK Kairat Almaty 1-2(1-1)
Široki Brijeg: Martin Zlomislic, Josip Kvesic, Dino Coric, Bernardo Matic, Dominik Kovacic, Mario Babic (57.Alen Jurilj), Ivan Enin, Mato Stanic (68.Boze Vukoja), Mateo Maric, Drazen Bagaric, Toni Jovic (79.Zvonimir Vukoja). Trainer: Goce Sedloski.
FK Kairat: Stas Pokatilov, Eldos Akhmetov, Gafurzhan Suyombaev, Dino Mikanovic, Rade Dugalic, Aybol Abiken (56.Islambek Kuat), Bauyrzhan Islamkhan (76.Sergey Keiler), Georgiy Zhukov, Konrad Wrzesinski, Ramazan Orazov (64.Nebojsa Kosovic), Aderinsola Eseola. Trainer: Aleksey Shpilevski.
Goals: 29' Aderinsola Eseola 0-1, 34' Ivan Enin 1-1, 58' Aderinsola Eseola 1-2.

11.07.2019; Kópavogsvöllur, Kópavogur
Referee: Nikola Popov (BUL); Attendance: 1,153
Breiðablik Kópavogur – FC Vaduz 0-0
Breiðablik: Gunnleifur Gunnleifsson, Damir Muminovic, Elfar Helgason, Arnar Geirsson, Gudjón Lydsson, Andri Yeoman, Höskuldur Gunnlaugsson (83.Brynjólfur Darri Willumsson), Viktor Örn Margeirsson, Gísli Eyjólfsson (63.Aron Bjarnason), Kolbeinn Thórdarson (73.Viktor Einarsson), Thomas Mikkelsen. Trainer: Ágúst Gylfason.
FC Vaduz: Benjamin Büchel, Denis Simani, Yannick Schmid, Berkay Sülüngöz, Gianni Antoniazzi, Cédric Gasser (76.Gabriel Lüchinger), Milan Gajic, Boris Prokopic, Sandro Wieser, Dominik Schwizer, Tunahan Çiçek (61.Mohamed Coulibaly). Trainer: Mario Frick.

11.07.2019; Samsung völlurinn, Gardabær
Referee: Denis Scherbakov (BLR); Attendance: 876
Stjarnan Garðabær – FCI Levadia Tallinn 2-1(1-0)
Stjarnan Garðabær: Haraldur Björnsson, Jósef Kristinn Jósefsson (46.Ævar Jóhannesson), Brynjar Gudjónsson, Daníel Laxdal, Jóhann Laxdal, Martin Rauschenberg Brorsen, Thorsteinn Már Ragnarsson, Heidar Ægisson (61.Eyjólfur Hédinsson), Alex Thór Hauksson, Gudmundur Hafsteinsson (90+1.Baldur Sigurdsson), Hilmar Árni Halldórsson. Trainer: Rúnar Sigmundsson.
Levadia Tallinn: Sergei Lepmets, Markus Jürgenson, Dmitri Kruglov (71.Igor Dudarev), Maksim Podholjuzin, Evgeniy Osipov, Marek Kaljumäe, Mark Roosnupp (40.Kirill Nesterov), Rasmus Peetson (79.Pavel Marin), Aime Marcelin Gando, Nikita Andreev, João Morelli. Trainer: Aleksandar Rogic.
Goals: 15', 74' Thorsteinn Már Ragnarsson 1-0, 2-0, 79' Nikita Andreev 2-1.

18.07.2019; Stade Parc des Sports, Differdange
Referee: Matthew De Gabriele (MLT); Attendance: 1,927
FC PROGRÈS NIEDERKORN – Cork City FC 1-2(0-1)
Progrès Niederkorn: Sebastian Flauss, Ben Vogel, Metin Karayer, Tim Hall, Aldin Skenderovic, Yann Matias Marques, Sébastien Thill (90+1.Adrien Ferino), Christian Silaj, Belmin Muratovic (66.Issa Bah), Mayron De Almeida, Kempes Tekiela (85.Florik Shala). Trainer: Roland Vrabec.
Cork City: Mark McNulty, Colm Horgan, Conor McCarthy, Ronan Hurley (90+6.Kevin O'Connor), Sean McLoughlin, Conor McCormack, Gearóid Morrissey, Garry Buckley, Karl Sheppard, Joel Coustrain (88.Dan Casey), Daire O'Connor (82.Shane Griffin). Trainer: Frank Kelleher.
Goals: 3' Garry Buckley 0-1, 47' Conor McCarthy 0-2, 68' Issa Bah 1-2.

18.07.2019; Vilniaus LFF stadionas, Vilnius
Referee: Rohit Saggi (NOR); Attendance: 3,725
FK Žalgiris Vilnius – BUDAPEST HONVÉD FC 1-1(1-0)
FK Žalgiris: Martin Berkovec, Donovan Slijngard, Klemen Bolha, Rolandas Baravykas (89.Domantas Simkus), Saulius Mikoliūnas, Liviu Antal, Víctor Pérez, Modestas Vorobjovas, Marko Tomic (66.Matas Vareika), Tomislav Kis, Pau Morer. Trainer: Marek Zub.
Budapest Honvéd: Rubi Levkovic, Ivan Lovric, Djordje Kamber, Dávid Kálnoki-Kis (57.Eke Uzoma), Bence Batik, Tonci Kukoc, Barna Kesztyüs (78.Mark Hegedüs), Dániel Gazdag, Bence Banó-Szabó, David N'Gog, Amadou Moutari (70.Vladyslav Kulach). Trainer: Giuseppe Sannino.
Goals: 18' Liviu Antal 1-0, 62' Djordje Kamber 1-1.

18.07.2019; Ortaliq Stadion, Almaty
Referee: Denys Shurman (UKR); Attendance: 18,500
FK KAIRAT ALMATY – NK Široki Brijeg 2-1(0-0)
FK Kairat: Stas Pokatilov, Eldos Akhmetov, Gafurzhan Suyombaev, Dino Mikanovic, Rade Dugalic, Aybol Abiken (46.Ramazan Orazov), Islambek Kuat, Bauyrzhan Islamkhan, Georgiy Zhukov, Aderinsola Eseola (79.Márton Eppel), Yerkebulan Seidakhmet (71.Konrad Wrzesinski). Trainer: Aleksey Shpilevski.
Široki Brijeg: Martin Zlomislic, Josip Kvesic, Dino Coric, Bernardo Matic, Dominik Kovacic, Petar Franjic, Mario Babic (57.Stipe Juric), Ivan Enin, Mateo Maric (46.Mato Stanic), Drazen Bagaric, Toni Jovic (65.Alen Jurilj). Trainer: Goce Sedloski.
Goals: 90' Drazen Bagaric 0-1 (pen), 90+2' Ramazan Orazov 1-1, 90+3' Islambek Kuat 2-1.

18.07.2019; Rheinpark Stadion, Vaduz
Referee: Genc Nuza (KVX); Attendance: 837
FC VADUZ – Breiðablik Kópavogur 2-1(0-0)
FC Vaduz: Benjamin Büchel, Denis Simani, Yannick Schmid, Berkay Sülüngöz, Gianni Antoniazzi, Cédric Gasser (76.Maximilian Göppel), Milan Gajic, Boris Prokopic, Dominik Schwizer, Mohamed Coulibaly (79.Noah Frick), Tunahan Çiçek (85.Aron Sele). Trainer: Mario Frick.
Breiðablik: Gunnleifur Gunnleifsson, Damir Muminovic, Elfar Helgason, Arnar Geirsson (79.Thórir Gudjónsson), Gudjón Lydsson (66.Gísli Eyjólfsson), Andri Yeoman, Höskuldur Gunnlaugsson, Viktor Örn Margeirsson, Kolbeinn Thórdarson, Thomas Mikkelsen, Alexander Sigurdarson (73.Aron Bjarnason). Trainer: Ágúst Gylfason.
Goals: 57' Mohamed Coulibaly 1-0, 79' Dominik Schwizer 2-0, 90+3' Höskuldur Gunnlaugsson 2-1.

18.07.2019; A. Le Coq Arena, Tallinn
Referee: Besfort Kasumi (KVX); Attendance: 1,446
FCI Levadia Tallinn – STJARNAN GARÐABÆR 3-2(1-1,2-1)
Levadia Tallinn: Sergei Lepmets, Dmitri Kruglov, Maksim Podholjuzin, Evgeniy Osipov, Igor Dudarev (71.Markus Jürgenson), Kirill Nesterov (80.Pavel Marin), Marek Kaljumäe, Rasmus Peetson (76.Érick Moreno), Aime Marcelin Gando, Nikita Andreev (116.Artjom Komlov), João Morelli. Trainer: Aleksandar Rogic.
Stjarnan Garðabær: Haraldur Björnsson, Jósef Kristinn Jósefsson (49.Ævar Jóhannesson), Brynjar Gudjónsson, Daníel Laxdal (93.Gudjón Baldvinsson), Jóhann Laxdal, Martin Rauschenberg Brorsen, Thorsteinn Már Ragnarsson (80.Baldur Sigurdsson), Heidar Ægisson, Alex Thór Hauksson, Gudmundur Hafsteinsson (60.Eyjólfur Hédinsson), Hilmar Árni Halldórsson. Trainer: Rúnar Sigmundsson.
Goals: 17' Evgeniy Osipov 1-0, 25' Thorsteinn Már Ragnarsson 1-1, 89' Evgeniy Osipov 2-1, 105' Dmitri Kruglov 3-1 (pen), 120+3' Brynjar Gudjónsson 3-2.

FK SARAJEVO received a bye.

23.07.2019; FFA Academy Stadium, Yerevan
Referee: Trustin Farrugia Cann (MLT); Attendance: 1,500
FC Ararat-Armenia Yerevan – Lincoln Red Imps 2-0(2-0)
FC Ararat-Armenia: Stefan Cupic, Rochdi Achenteh, Dmitri Guzj, Ângelo Meneses, Georgi Pashov, Armen Ambartsumyan (84.Gor Malakyan), Kódjo Alphonse, Petros Avetisyan, Anton Kobyalko (70.Louis Ogana), Furdjel Narsingh, Mailson (62.Zakaria Sanogo). Trainer: Vardan Minasyan.
Lincoln Red Imps: Lolo Soler, Marcos Pérez, Joseph Chipolina, Oli (46.Federico Cataruozzolo), Bernardo Lopes, Roy Chipolina, Sergio Molina (53.Jesús Toscano), Borja Gil, Anthony Hernandez, James Coombes (62.Falu Aranda), Kike Gómez. Trainer: Víctor Afonso.
Goals: 31' Anton Kobyalko 1-0, 45+2' Kódjo Alphonse 2-0.
Sent off: 49' Marcos Pérez.

23.07.2019; Gundadalur, Tórshavn
Referee: Ádám Farkas (HUN); Attendance: 751
HB Tórshavn – Linfield FC Belfast 2-2(1-1)
HB Tórshavn: Teitur Gestsson, Brynjar Hlödversson (85.Daniel Johansen), Jógvan Davidsen, Lasse Andersen, Símun Samuelsen, Magnus Egilsson, Hørdur Askham, Tróndur Jensen, Adrian Justinussen (78.Pætur Petersen), Sebastian Pingel (70.Dan í Soylu), Ari Olsen. Trainer: Heimir Gudjónsson.
Linfield FC: Rohan Ferguson, Chris Casement, Matthew Clarke, Mark Stafford, Niall Quinn (83.Joel Cooper), Jamie Mulgrew, Jimmy Callacher, Daniel Kearns (81.Shayne Lavery), Bastien Héry, Andrew Waterworth, Jordan Stewart (77.Kirk Millar). Trainer: David Healy.
Goals: 2' Andrew Waterworth 0-1, 37' Adrian Justinussen 1-1 (pen), 88' Andrew Waterworth 1-2 (pen), 89' Pætur Petersen 2-2.

23.07.2019; „Toše Proeski" Arena, Skopje
Referee: Tore Hansen (NOR); Attendance: 2,602
KF Shkëndija 79 – F91 Dudelange 1-2(1-0)
KF Shkëndija 79: Bekim Redjepi, Gledi Mici (76.Omar Imeri), Mevlan Murati, Visar Musliu, Egzon Bejtulai, Armend Alimi, Zeni Husmani (60.Ennur Totre), Agim Ibraimi, Alves, Stênio Júnior, Marjan Radeski (62.Besart Ibraimi). Trainer: Qatip Osmani.
F91 Dudelange: Tim Kips, Tom Schnell, Ricardo Delgado, Mehdi Kirch, Mohamed Bouchouari, Mario Pokar, Dominik Stolz, Mickaël Garos (80.Charles Morren), Sabir Bougrine (46.Antoine Bernier), Danel Sinani, Bertino Cabral Barbosa (64.Adel Bettaieb). Trainer: Henri Bossi.
Goals: 8' Agim Ibraimi 1-0 (pen), 64' Adel Bettaieb 1-1, 69' Danel Sinani 1-2 (pen).

23.07.2019; Estadi Comunal d'Andorra la Vella, Andorra la Vella
Referee: Robert Hennessy (IRL); Attendance: 382
FC Santa Coloma – Astana FC 0-0
FC Santa Coloma: Eloy Casals, Moisés San Nicolás, Enric Pi (58.Jordi Aláez), Marc Rebés, Chus Rubio (83.Aleix Cistero), Andreu Ramos, Juanma Miranda, Chus Sosa, Pedro Santos, André Azevedo, Diego Nájero (73.Nicolás Medina). Trainer: Marc Rodríguez Rebull.
Astana FC: Nenad Eric, Antonio Rukavina, Yuriy Logvinenko, Marin Anicic, Evgeny Postnikov, Luka Simunovic, Rúnar Sigurjónsson (64.Ndombe Mubele), Marin Tomasov, Ivan Maevski, Roman Murtazaev, Dorin Rotariu (82.Serikzhan Muzhikov). Trainer: Roman Grygorchuk.

23.07.2019; Stadio Olimpico di Serravalle, Serravalle
Referee: Krzysztof Jakubik (POL); Attendance: 354
SP Tre Penne – FK Sūdova Marijampolé 0-5(0-2)
SP Tre Penne: Mattia Migani, Mirko Palazzi, Andrea Rossi, Christofer Genestreti, Nicola Gai, Enrico Cibelli, Michael Ballistini (69.Alex Gasperoni), Luca Patregnani, Stefano Fraternali, Luca Ceccaroli (59.Matteo Semprini), Luca Sorrentino (78.Giovanni Casolla). Trainer: Stefano Ceci.
FK Sūdova Marijampolé: Ivan Kardum, Algis Jankauskas, Andro Svrljuga, Aleksandar Zivanovic, Semir Kerla, Jovan Cadjenovic, Ovidijus Verbickas, Giedrius Matulevicius (76.Povilas Leimonas), Josip Tadic (84.Tosaint Ricketts), Mihret Topcagic, Paulius Golubickas (60.Eligijus Jankasukas). Trainer: Vladimir Cheburin.
Goals: 9' Giedrius Matulevicius 0-1, 20' Mihret Topcagic 0-2, 66' Andro Svrljuga 0-3, 81' Josip Tadic 0-4, 90+1' Tosaint Ricketts 0-5.

30.07.2019; Victoria Stadium, Gibraltar
Referee: Alexandre Boucaut (BEL); Attendance: 684
Lincoln Red Imps – FC ARARAT-ARMENIA YEREVAN 1-2(0-1)
Lincoln Red Imps: Lolo Soler, Joseph Chipolina, Bernardo Lopes, Jesús Toscano, Roy Chipolina (67.Ethan Britto), Federico Cataruozzolo (46.Sergio Molina), Borja Gil, Gato, Falu Aranda, Anthony Hernandez, Kike Gómez (27.James Coombes). Trainer: Víctor Afonso.
FC Ararat-Armenia: Stefan Cupic, Rochdi Achenteh, Dmitri Guzj, Ângelo Meneses, Georgi Pashov (59.Artur Danielyan), Ilja Antonov, Kódjo Alphonse (77.Gor Malakyan), Petros Avetisyan, Furdjel Narsingh, Louis Ogana, Zakaria Sanogo (63.Alex Júnior Christian). Trainer: Vardan Minasyan.
Goals: 45+1', 58' Louis Ogana 0-1, 0-2, 74' Anthony Hernandez 1-2.

01.08.2019; Windsor Park, Belfast
Referee: Halil Umut Meler (TUR)
LINFIELD FC BELFAST – HB Tórshavn 1-0(1-0)
Linfield FC: Rohan Ferguson, Chris Casement, Mark Stafford, Niall Quinn, Jamie Mulgrew, Jimmy Callacher, Daniel Kearns (71.Shayne Lavery), Bastien Héry, Joel Cooper, Andrew Waterworth, Jordan Stewart (75.Kirk Millar). Trainer: David Healy.
HB Tórshavn: Bjarti Vitalis Mørk, Brynjar Hlödversson (61.Dan í Soylu), Jógvan Davidsen, Lasse Andersen, Símun Samuelsen, Magnus Egilsson, René Joensen (75.Pætur Petersen), Hørdur Askham, Tróndur Jensen, Adrian Justinussen, Sebastian Pingel (61.Ari Olsen). Trainer: Heimir Gudjónsson.
Goal: 20' Andrew Waterworth 1-0 (pen).

30.07.2019; Stade „Josy Barthel", Lëtzebuerg
Referee: Iwan Arwel Griffith (WAL); Attendance: 1,022
F91 DUDELANGE – KF Shkëndija 79 1-1(0-0)
F91 Dudelange: Tim Kips, Tom Schnell, Ricardo Delgado, Mehdi Kirch, Mohamed Bouchouari, Mario Pokar (90.Mickaël Garos), Dominik Stolz, Charles Morren, Danel Sinani, Adel Bettaieb (63.Laurent Pomponi), Antoine Bernier (84.Omar Natami). Trainer: Emilio Ferrera.
KF Shkëndija 79: Kostadin Zahov, Gledi Mici, Mevlan Murati (83.Konstantin Cheshmedzhiev), Visar Musliu, Egzon Bejtulai, Armend Alimi, Zeni Husmani, Besart Ibraimi (77.Omar Imeri), Agim Ibraimi, Juan Felipe Alves (66.Valjmir Nafiu), Marjan Radeski. Trainer: Qatip Osmani. Goals: 78' Ricardo Delgado 1-0, 90+2' Agim Ibraimi 1-1.
Sent off: 84' Visar Musliu, 90+4' Valjmir Nafiu, 90+5' Agim Ibraimi.

01.08.2019; Astana Arena, Astana
Referee: Giorgi Kruashvili (GEO); Attendance: 16,103
ASTANA FC – FC Santa Coloma 4-1(1-1)
Astana FC: Nenad Eric, Antonio Rukavina, Yuriy Logvinenko, Marin Anicic, Dmitriy Shomko, Evgeny Postnikov, Rúnar Sigurjónsson (63.Roman Murtazaev), Ivan Maevski, Rangelo Janga (89.Yuriy Pertsukh), Dorin Rotariu, Ndombe Mubele (60.Marin Tomasov). Trainer: Roman Grygorchuk.
FC Santa Coloma: Eloy Casals, Moisés San Nicolás, Enric Pi, Marc Rebés, Andreu Ramos (74.Nicolás Medina), Juanma Miranda, Chus Sosa (78.Diego Nájero), Pedro Santos, Jordi Aláez (80.Albert Mercadé), Aleix Cistero, André Azevedo. Trainer: Marc Rodríguez Rebull.
Goals: 7' Enric Pi 0-1, 24' Rúnar Sigurjónsson 1-1 (pen), 73', 79', 90+4' Marin Tomasov 2-1, 3-1, 4-1.

30.07.2019; Marijampolés sporto centro stadione, Marijampolé
Referee: Artyom Kuchin (KAZ); Attendance: 1,850
FK SŪDUVA MARIJAMPOLÉ – SP Tre Penne 5-0(3-0)
FK Sūdova Marijampolé: Ivan Kardum, Algis Jankauskas, Andro Svrljuga, Aleksandar Zivanovic, Semir Kerla, Jovan Cadjenovic, Ovidijus Verbickas, Giedrius Matulevicius (77.Povilas Leimonas), Josip Tadic (81.Sandro Gotal), Mihret Topcagic (64.Tosaint Ricketts), Paulius Golubickas. Trainer: Vladimir Cheburin.
SP Tre Penne: Mattia Migani, Mirko Palazzi, Andrea Rossi, Alex Gasperoni, Nicola Chiaruzzi, Enrico Cibelli, Stefano Fraternali, Matteo Semprini (87.Giacomo Zafferani), Francesco Perrotta (90+3.Simone Nanni), Luca Ceccaroli (90+2.Andrea Zanotti), Luca Sorrentino. Trainer: Stefano Ceci.
Goals: 14' Josip Tadic 1-0, 17' Semir Kerla 2-0, 39', 55' Mihret Topcagic 3-0, 4-0, 89' Sandro Gotal 5-0.

24.07.2019; Národny Futbalovy Stadión, Bratislava
Referee: Ioannis Papadopoulos (GRE); Attendance: 7,150
ŠK Slovan Bratislava – KF Feronikeli 2-1(1-0)
Slovan Bratislava: Dominik Greif, Vasil Bozhikov, Artem Sukhotskiy, Myenty Abena, Marin Ljubicic, Dávid Holman (67.Dávid Strelec), Nono Delgado (86.Joeri de Kamps), Kenan Bajric, "Moha" Mohammed Rharsalla, Andraz Sporar, Rafael Ratão (70.Erik Daniel). Trainer: Vladimir Radenkovic.
KF Feronikeli: Florian Smakiqi, Lapidar Lladrovci, Arber Prekazi, Perparim Islami, Jean Carioca (76.Mevlan Zeka), Yll Hoxha, Argjend Malaj (82.Besmir Bojku), Albert Dabiqaj, Kastriot Rexha, Astrit Fazliu, Mendurim Hoti (90+4.Jetmir Topalli). Trainer: Zekirija Ramadani.
Goals: 9' Nono Delgado 1-0, 62' Andraz Sporar 2-0 (pen), 67' Mendurim Hoti 2-1.

25.07.2019; Stadion Miejski, Gliwice
Referee: Manuel Schüttengruber (AUT); Attendance: 5,100
GKS Piast Gliwice – Rīga FC 3-2(0-1)
Piast Gliwice: Frantisek Plach, Uros Korun, Mikkel Kirkeskov, Jakub Czerwinski, Marcin Pietrowski, Tom Hateley, Gerard Badía (62.Martin Konczkowski), Patryk Dziczek, Joel Valencia (74.Patryk Sokolowski), Piotr Parzyszek (87.Dominik Steczyk), Jorge Félix. Trainer: Waldemar Fornalik.
Rīga FC: Roberts Ozols, Georgios Valerianos, Stefan Panic, Olegs Laizāns, Ritvars Rugins, Vyacheslav Sharpar, Tomislav Saric, Felipe Brisola (43.Aleksejs Visnakovs), Deniss Rakels (80.Joël Bopesu), Elvis Stuglis, Roman Debelko (84.Kamil Bilinski). Trainer: Mihails Konevs.
Goals: 22' Roman Debelko 0-1, 66' Jakub Czerwinski 1-1, 82', 85' Jorge Félix 2-1, 3-1, 86' Uros Korun 3-2 (own goal).

25.07.2019; Vodafone-Völlurin, Reykjavík
Referee: Georgios Kominis (GRE); Attendance: 802
Valur Reykjavík – PFC Ludogorets Razgrad 1-1(1-0)
Valur Reykjavík: Anton Ari Einarsson, Birkir Sævarsson, Eidur Sigurbjörnsson, Orri Ómarsson, Sebastian Hedlund, Kaj Leo í Bartalsstovu, Einar Karl Ingvarsson (67.Kristinn Sigurdsson), Lasse Petry, Kristinn Halldórsson (71.Bjarni Eiríksson), Ívar Jónsson, Patrick Pedersen (88.Birnir Snær Ingason). Trainer: Ólafur Jóhannesson.
Ludogorets Razgrad: Plamen Iliev, Cicinho (88.Jody Lukoki), Georgi Terziev, Rafael Forster, Anton Nedyalkov, Anicet Andrianantenaina, Jacek Góralski, Stéphane Badji (70.Jakub Swierczok), Claudiu Keserü, Mavis Tchibota (61.Wanderson), Jorginho. Trainer: Stoicho Stoev.
Goals: 11' Lasse Petry 1-0, 90+2' Anicet Andrianantenaina 1-1.

25.07.2019; Stadiumi „Selman Stërmasi", Tiranë
Referee: Kirill Levnikov (RUS); Attendance: 1,750
FK Partizani Tiranë – FC Sheriff Tiraspol 0-1(0-1)
FK Partizani Tiranë: Alban Hoxha (I), Egzon Belica, Enea Bitri, Libanot Ibrahimi, Esin Hakaj, Bruno Telushi (71.Aristóteles Romero), William Cordeiro, Ron Broja, Esat Mala, Eraldo Çinari (51.Jasir Asani), Theophilus Solomon (57.Joseph Ekuban). Trainer: Franco Lerda.
FC Sheriff Tiraspol: Zvonimir Mikulic, Artem Hordienko (86.Jaroslaw Jach), Ousmane N'Diaye, Mateo Muzek, Cristiano, Wilfried Balima, Jury Kendysh (90+4.Antun Palic), Gheorghe Anton, Liridon Latifi (48.Maxim Cojocaru (I)), Gabrijel Boban, Robert Tambe. Trainer: Zoran Zekic.
Goal: 24' Robert Tambe 0-1.

30.07.2019; Stadiumi „Fadil Vokrri", Prishtina
Referee: Yigal Frid (ISR); Attendance: 5,250
KF Feronikeli – ŠK SLOVAN BRATISLAVA 0-2(0-1)
KF Feronikeli: Florian Smakiqi, Lapidar Lladrovci, Arber Prekazi, Perparim Islami (68.Jetmir Topalli), Jean Carioca, Yll Hoxha, Albert Dabiqaj, Kastriot Rexha, Besmir Bojku (60.Mevlan Zeka), Astrit Fazliu, Mendurim Hoti (76.Milos Krkotic). Trainers: Zekirija Ramadani & Dejan Vukicevic.
Slovan Bratislava: Dominik Greif, Vasil Bozhikov, Vernon, Jurij Medvedev, Myenty Abena, Dávid Holman (66.Nono Delgado), Joeri de Kamps, Erik Daniel (72.Rafael Ratão), Kenan Bajric (83.Dávid Strelec), "Moha" Mohammed Rharsalla, Andraz Sporar. Trainer: Ján Kozák.
Goals: 19' Vernon 0-1, 54' Dávid Holman 0-2.
Sent off: 88' Mevlan Zeka.

01.08.2019; Skonto Stadions, Rīga
Referee: Eitan Shmuelevich (ISR); Attendance: 3,541
RĪGA FC – GKS Piast Gliwice 2-1(1-1)
Rīga FC: Roberts Ozols, Georgios Valerianos, Herdi Prenga, Stefan Panic, Aleksejs Visnakovs (67.Deniss Rakels), Vyacheslav Sharpar (61.Olegs Laizāns), Felipe Brisola, Roger, Armands Pētersons, Elvis Stuglis, Roman Debelko (80.Kamil Bilinski). Trainer: Mihails Konevs.
Piast Gliwice: Frantisek Plach, Uros Korun, Batosz Rymaniak, Mikkel Kirkeskov, Jakub Czerwinski, Martin Konczkowski, Tom Hateley (86.Aleksander Jagiello), Gerard Badía (69.Patryk Sokolowski), Patryk Dziczek, Piotr Parzyszek (58.Dominik Steczyk), Jorge Félix. Trainer: Waldemar Fornalik.
Goals: 20' Jorge Félix 0-1, 26' Armands Pētersons 1-1, 83' Kamil Bilinski 2-1.

01.08.2019; Ludogorets Arena, Razgrad
Referee: Pavel Orel (CZE); Attendance: 4,120
PFC LUDOGORETS RAZGRAD – Valur Reykjavík 4-0(2-0)
Ludogorets Razgrad: Plamen Iliev, Georgi Terziev, Rafael Forster, Jordan Ikoko, Anton Nedyalkov, Anicet Andrianantenaina, Jacek Góralski, Dan Biton, Claudiu Keserü (79' Jakub Swierczok), Mavis Tchibota (64' Wanderson), Jorginho (84' Jody Lukoki). Trainer: Stoicho Stoev.
Valur Reykjavík: Hannes Halldórsson (46' Anton Ari Einarsson), Birkir Sævarsson, Eidur Sigurbjörnsson, Sebastian Hedlund, Haukur Sigurdsson, Kristinn Sigurdsson (66' Ólafur Finsen), Kaj Leo í Bartalsstovu, Lasse Petry (72' Orri Ómarsson), Kristinn Halldórsson, Ívar Jónsson, Patrick Pedersen. Trainer: Ólafur Jóhannesson.
Goals: 7' Sebastian Hedlund 1-0 (own goal), 24' Jordan Ikoko 2-0, 82', 84' Jakub Swierczok 3-0, 4-0.

01.08.2019; Bolshaya Sportivnaya Arenan, Tiraspol
Referee: Igor Pajac (CRO); Attendance: 5,248
FC SHERIFF TIRASPOL – FK Partizani Tiranë 1-1(0-1)
FC Sheriff Tiraspol: Zvonimir Mikulic, Artem Hordienko (46.Veaceslav Posmac), Ousmane N'Diaye, Mateo Muzek, Cristiano, Wilfried Balima, Jury Kendysh, Gheorghe Anton, Liridon Latifi (84.Jaroslaw Jach), Gabrijel Boban (90+3.Maxim Cojocaru (I)), Robert Tambe. Trainer: Zoran Zekic.
FK Partizani Tiranë: Alban Hoxha (I), Egzon Belica, Lorenc Trashi (79.Eraldo Çinari), Deian Boldor, Enea Bitri, Bruno Telushi, William Cordeiro (87.Jurgen Bardhi), Ron Broja, Esat Mala, Jasir Asani (70.Brian Brown), Theophilus Solomon. Trainer: Franco Lerda.
Goals: 29' Jasir Asani 0-1, 63' Ousmane N'Diaye 1-1.

LEAGUE PATH

25.07.2019; Gyumri City Stadium, Gyumri
Referee: Fedayri San (SUI); Attendance: 1,940
FC Pyunik Yerevan – FK Jablonec 2-1(2-0)
Pyunik Yerevan: Andrija Dragojevic, Artak Yedigaryan, Antonio Stankov, Maksim Zhestokov, Kristi Marku, Armen Manucharyan, Sergiy Shevchuk, Artem Simonyan (66.Steven Alfred), Stanislav Efimov, Erik Vardanyan, Artur Miranyan (81.Aleksandr Galimov). Trainer: Aleksandr Tarkhanov.
FK Jablonec: Jan Hanus, Jakub Jugas, Tomás Brecka, Libor Holík, Tomás Hübschman, Jakub Povazanez, Jan Sykora, Milos Kratochvíl (90+2.Tomás Pilík), Jan Matousek (86.Jan Chramosta), Martin Dolezal, Vladimir Jovovic (28.Rafael Acosta). Trainer: Petr Rada.
Goals: 6', 30' Artur Miranyan 1-0, 2-0, 53' Martin Dolezal 2-1.

01.08.2019; Stadion Strelnice, Jablonec nad Nisou
Referee: Sergey Lapochkin (RUS); Attendance: 3,675
FK Jablonec – FC PYUNIK YEREVAN 0-0
FK Jablonec: Jan Hanus, Jakub Jugas, Tomás Brecka, Libor Holík, Tomás Hübschman, Jakub Povazanez, Jan Sykora, Milos Kratochvíl (54.Jan Krob), Jan Matousek (76.Tomás Pilík), Martin Dolezal, Vladimir Jovovic (66.Jan Chramosta). Trainer: Petr Rada.
Pyunik Yerevan: Andrija Dragojevic, Artak Yedigaryan (32.Artem Simonyan), Antonio Stankov, Maksim Zhestokov, Kristi Marku, Armen Manucharyan, Karlen Mkrtchyan, Sergiy Shevchuk, Stanislav Efimov, Erik Vardanyan, Artur Miranyan (90+2.Steven Alfred). Trainer: Aleksandr Tarkhanov.
Sent off: 87' Erik Vardanyan, 88' Tomás Brecka.

25.07.2019; Olimpiska centra Ventspils Stadionā, Ventspils
Referee: Dimitar Meckarovski (MKD); Attendance: 2,196
FK Ventspils – Gzira United FC 4-0(1-0)
FK Ventspils: Konstantin Machnovskiy, Jean Alcénat, Abdoul Mamah, Giorgi Mchedlishvili, Hélio Batista, Guga Palavandishvili, Jevgenijs Kazacoks (79.Ingars Stuglis), Tosin Aiyegun, Kaspars Svārups (73.Pavel Osipov), Mykhaylo Sergiychuk (89.Bekkhan Aliev), Lucas Villela. Trainer: Igor Klosovs.
Gzira United: Justin Haber, Arthur Henrique, Rodolfo Soares, Fernando Barbosa, Nicky Muscat, Andrew Cohen, Hamed Koné, Gianmarco Conti, Juan Corbalan, Zachary Scerri (80.Elvis Sakyi), Jefferson. Trainer: Giovanni Tedesco.
Goals: 41' Kaspars Svārups 1-0, 50' Hélio Batista 2-0, 83' Ingars Stuglis 3-0, 87' Tosin Aiyegun 4-0.

25.07.2019; Qäbälä Sähär stadionu, Qabala
Referee: Nick Walsh (SCO); Attendance: 2,800
Qəbələ FK – FC Dinamo Tbilisi 0-2(0-1)
Qəbələ FK: Anar Nazirov, Rasim Ramaldanov, Ivica Zunic, Yusif Nabiyev, Merab Gigauri, Amin Seydiyev, Qismat Aliyev (85.Asif Mammadov), Clésio, Fernán Ferreiro, Davit Volkovi (61.Rovlan Muradov), Ulvu Isgandarov (77.Christian Kouakou). Trainer: Zaur Hasimov.
Dinamo Tbilisi: José Perales, Giorgi Kimadze, Víctor Mongil, Nodar Iashvili, Davit Kobouri, Nika Ninua, Levan Kutalia, Giorgi Kukhianidze (65.Bakar Kardava), Giorgi Papava, Nodar Kavtaradze (74.Arfang Daffé), Levan Shengelia (86.Kwame Karikari). Trainer: Félix Vicente Miranda.
Goals: 41' Levan Kutalia 0-1, 87' Arfang Daffé 0-2.

25.07.2019; AEK Arena, Larnaca
Referee: Tiago Bruno Lopes Martins (POR); Attendance: 3,177
AEK Larnaca FC – PFC Levski Sofia 3-0(0-0)
AEK Larnaca: Toño, Mikel González, Daniel Mojsov, Truyols, Ivan Trickovski (87.Matija Spoljaric), Lluis Sastre, Acorán, Nacho Cases, Hector Hevel (76.Jean Luc Assoubre), Raúl Ruiz, Apostolos Giannou (78.Florian Taulemesse). Trainer: Imanol Idiakez.
Levski Sofia: Milan Mijatovic, Zhivko Milanov, Nuno Reis, Ivan Goranov, Giannis Kargas (46.Iliya Yurukov), Martin Raynov, Davide Mariani, Khaly Thiam, Deni Alar (46.Nasiru Mohammed), Paulinho, Stanislav Ivanov (83.Zdravko Dimitrov). Trainer: Petar Hubchev.
Goals: 67' Apostolos Giannou 1-0, 70' Raúl Ruiz 2-0, 75' Hector Hevel 3-0.; Sent off: 45+2' Zhivko Milanov.

25.07.2019; Stadion Galgenwaard, Utrecht
Referee: Aleksei Eskov (RUS); Attendance: 17,221
FC Utrecht – HŠK Zrinjski Mostar 1-1(0-1)
FC Utrecht: David Jensen, Willem Janssen, Emil Bergström, Leon Guwara, Sean Klaiber, Adam Maher, Sander van de Streek (80.Urby Emanuelson), Simon Gustafson, Justin Lonwijk (57.Nick Venema), Vaclav Cerny (62.Patrick Joosten), Gyrano Kerk. Trainer: John van den Brom.
Zrinjski Mostar: Ivan Brkic, Mario Ticinovic (57.Stanisa Mandic), Tomislav Barbaric, Dario Rugasevic, Slobodan Jakovljevic (66.Renato Gojkovic), Advan Kadusic, Damir Sovsic, Frane Cirjak, Edin Rustemovic, Miljan Govedarica, Irfan Hadzic (62.Ivan Lendric). Trainer: Hari Vukas.
Goals: 34' Miljan Govedarica 0-1, 61' Gyrano Kerk 1-1.

25.07.2019; „Boris Paichadze" Dinamo Arena, Tbilisi
Referee: Horaţiu Feşnic (ROU); Attendance: 3,218
FC Chikhura Sachkhere – Aberdeen FC 1-1(1-0)
Chikhura Sachkhere: Dino Hamzic, Shota Kashia, Davit Maisashvili, Lasha Chikvaidze, Revaz Chiteishvili (74.Demur Chikhladze), Oleg Mamasakhlisi, Besik Dekanoidze, Irakli Lekvtadze (76.Giorgi Pantsulaia), Giorgi Koripadze, Mikheil Sardalishvili, Mikheil Ergemlidze. Trainer: Soso Pruidze.
Aberdeen FC: Joe Lewis, Andrew Considine, Shay Logan, Ash Taylor (18.Craig Bryson), Scott McKenna, Funso Ojo, Lewis Ferguson, Niall McGinn, Ryan Hedges, Sam Cosgrove, Jon Gallagher (82.James Wilson). Trainer: Derek McInnes.
Goals: 41' Giorgi Koripadze 1-0 (pen), 68' Sam Cosgrove 1-1 (pen).

01.08.2019; MFA Centenary Stadium, Ta'Qali
Referee: Thorvaldur Árnason (ISL); Attendance: 332
Gzira United FC – FK VENTSPILS 2-2(1-0)
Gzira United: Justin Haber, Arthur Henrique, Rodolfo Soares, Fernando Barbosa, Nicky Muscat, Andrew Cohen, Hamed Koné, Gianmarco Conti, Juan Corbalan, Amadou Samb (80.Zachary Scerri), Jefferson. Trainer: Giovanni Tedesco.
FK Ventspils: Konstantin Machnovskiy, Jean Alcénat, Abdoul Mamah, Giorgi Mchedlishvili, Hélio Batista, Pavel Osipov (55.Lucas Villela), Eduards Tīdenbergs (69.Mykhaylo Sergiychuk), Jevgenijs Kazacoks, Abdullahi Alfa (44.Guga Palavandishvili), Tosin Aiyegun, Kaspars Svārups. Trainer: Igor Klosovs.
Goals: 15.Jefferson 1-0, 72.Jevgenijs Kazacoks 1-1, 79.Mykhaylo Sergiychuk 1-2, 90+3.Jefferson 2-2.
Sent off: 90+4' Amadou Samb, Konstantin Machnovskiy.

01.08.2019; „Boris Paichadze" Dinamo Arena, Tbilisi
Referee: Petri Viljanen (FIN); Attendance: 8,153
FC DINAMO TBILISI – Qəbələ FK 3-0(0-0)
Dinamo Tbilisi: José Perales, Giorgi Kimadze, Víctor Mongil, Nodar Iashvili (36.Gudzha Rukhaia), Davit Kobouri, Nika Ninua, Levan Kutalia (78.Kwame Karikari), Giorgi Kukhianidze, Giorgi Papava, Nodar Kavtaradze (69.Arfang Daffé), Levan Shengelia. Trainer: Félix Vicente Miranda.
Qəbələ FK: Anar Nazirov, Rasim Ramaldanov, Ivica Zunic (40.Sadig Quliyev), Asif Mammadov, Merab Gigauri, Amin Seydiyev, Qismat Aliyev, Christian Kouakou (81.Roman Hüseynov), Clésio, Fernán Ferreiro (72.Ulvu Isgandarov), Davit Volkovi. Trainer: Zaur Hasimov.
Goals: 68', 88' Levan Shengelia 1-0, 2-0, 90+3' Kwame Karikari 3-0.

01.08.2019; Vivacom Arena, Sofia
Referee: Glenn Nyberg (SWE); Attendance: 550
PFC Levski Sofia – AEK LARNACA FC 0-4(0-2)
Levski Sofia: Milan Mijatovic, Nuno Reis, Ivan Goranov, Diyan Ivanov, Martin Raynov, Khaly Thiam (5.Iliya Yurukov), Ivaylo Naydenov, Stanislav Kostov (52.Franco Mazurek), Paulinho, Nigel Robertha, Stanislav Ivanov (68.Zdravko Dimitrov). Trainer: Petar Hubchev.
AEK Larnaca: Toño, Mikel González, Daniel Mojsov, Truyols (70.Simranjit Thandi), Ivan Trickovski, Lluis Sastre, Acorán, Nacho Cases (75.Florian Taulemesse), Hector Hevel, Raúl Ruiz (54.Tete), Apostolos Giannou. Trainer: Imanol Idiakez.
Goals: 8', 29', 75', 82' Ivan Trickovski 0-1 (pen), 0-2, 0-3, 0-4.

01.08.2019; Stadion pod Bijelim Brijegom, Mostar
Referee: Antti Munukka (FIN); Attendance: 5,984
HŠK ZRINJSKI MOSTAR – FC Utrecht 2-1(0-1,1-1)
Zrinjski Mostar: Ivan Brkic, Tomislav Barbaric, Dario Rugasevic, Slobodan Jakovljevic, Advan Kadusic, Damir Sovsic, Frane Cirjak (59.Ivan Curjuric), Edin Rustemovic (78.Semir Pezer), Miljan Govedarica (87.Mario Ticinovic), Stanisa Mandic, Irfan Hadzic (103.Ivan Lendric). Trainer: Hari Vukas.
FC Utrecht: David Jensen, Willem Janssen, Emil Bergström, Leon Guwara, Sean Klaiber (87.Giovanni Troupée), Adam Maher, Sander van de Streek, Simon Gustafson, Justin Lonwijk (80.Joris van Overeem), Vaclav Cerny (66.Issah Abass), Gyrano Kerk (105.Urby Emanuelson). Trainer: John van den Brom.
Goals: 45+1' Simon Gustafson 0-1, 65' Irfan Hadzic 1-1, 111' Stanisa Mandic 2-1.

01.08.2019; Pittodrie Stadium, Aberdeen
Referee: Rade Obrenovic (SVN); Attendance: 15,167
ABERDEEN FC – FC Chikhura Sachkhere 5-0(2-0)
Aberdeen FC: Joe Lewis, Andrew Considine, Shay Logan, Gregory Leigh (67.Dean Campbell), Scott McKenna, Funso Ojo, Lewis Ferguson, Niall McGinn (62.Scott Wright), Ryan Hedges, Sam Cosgrove (82.Bruce Anderson), Jon Gallagher. Trainer: Derek McInnes.
Chikhura Sachkhere: Dino Hamzic, Shota Kashia, Davit Maisashvili, Lasha Chikvaidze, Revaz Chiteishvili (52.Teimurazi Markozashvili), Oleg Mamasakhlisi, Besik Dekanoidze (52.Giorgi Pantsulaia), Irakli Lekvtadze, Giorgi Koripadze, Mikheil Sardalishvili, Mikheil Ergemlidze (72.Demur Chikhladze). Trainer: Soso Pruidze.
Goals: 9', 20' Sam Cosgrove 1-0, 2-0, 58' Gregory Leigh 3-0, 65' Scott Wright 4-0, 80' Sam Cosgrove 5-0.

25.07.2019; ETO Park, Győr
Referee: Kevin Clancy (SCO); Attendance: 2,720
Budapest Honvéd FC – CS Universitatea Craiova 0-0
Budapest Honvéd: Rubi Levkovic, Ivan Lovric (75.MacDonald Niba
Ngwa), Djordje Kamber, Bence Batik, Eke Uzoma, Tonci Kukoc, Barna
Kesztyüs, Dániel Gazdag, Bence Banó-Szabó, David N'Gog (81.Dominik
Cipf), Amadou Moutari (65.Vladyslav Kulach). Trainer: Giuseppe
Sannino.
CS Universitatea Craiova: Mirko Pigliacelli, Renato Kelic, Ivan Martic,
Nicusor Bancu, Stephane Acka, Alexandru Mateiu, Bogdan Vatajelu,
Kamer Qaka (65.Antoni Ivanov), Cristian Barbut, Alexandru Cicâldau
(90+1.Vasile Constantin), Carlos Fortes (46.Mihai Roman (II)). Trainer:
Corneliu Papura.

25.07.2019; Haugesund Stadion, Haugesund
Referee: Donatas Rumsas (LTU); Attendance: 3,501
FK Haugesund – SK Sturm Graz 2-0(0-0)
FK Haugesund: Helge Sandvik, Doug Bergqvist, Mikkel Desler,
Benjamin Tiedemann Hansen, Sondre Tronstad, Thore Baardsen
Pedersen, Niklas Sandberg, Bruno Leite, Kristoffer Velde (90+3.Eric
Ndayisenga), Kevin Krygård, Ibrahima Koné (76.Martin Samuelsen).
Trainer: Jostein Grindhaug.
Sturm Graz: Jörg Siebenhandl, Thomas Schrammel, Anastasios
Avlonitis, Emanuel Sakic (71.Fabian Koch), Lukas Spendlhofer, Jakob
Jantscher, Juan Domínguez, Ivan Ljubic, Otar Kiteishvili, Philipp
Hosiner (71.Emeka Eze), Markus Pink (65.Michael John Lema). Trainer:
Nestor El Maestro.
Goals: 51' Kevin Krygård 1-0, 64' Niklas Sandberg 2-0.

25.07.2019; Stadion Energa Gdańsk, Gdańsk
Referee: John Beaton (SCO); Attendance: 25,875
KS Lechia Gdańsk – Brøndby IF 2-1(1-0)
Lechia Gdańsk: Dusan Kuciak, Blazej Augustyn, Zarko Udovicic, Filip
Mladenovic, Michal Nalepa, Daniel Lukasik, Lukás Haraslín
(79.Slawomir Peszko), Patryk Lipski (83.Tomasz Makowski), Jaroslaw
Kubicki, Karol Fila, Flávio Paixão (74.Artur Sobiech). Trainer: Piotr
Stokowiec.
Brøndby IF: Marvin Schwäbe, Paulus Arajuuri, Anthony Jung, Hjörtur
Hermannsson, Dominik Kaiser, Lasse Vigen Christensen, Josip
Radosevic, Simon Tibbling (75.Kasper Fisker), Simon Hedlund, Kamil
Wilczek, Kevin Mensah (81.Jens Gammelby). Trainer: Niels Frederiksen.
Goals: 26' Flávio Paixão 1-0 (pen), 59' Simon Hedlund 1-1, 63' Patryk
Lipski 2-1.

25.07.2019; Aker Stadion, Molde
Referee: Donald Robertson (SCO); Attendance: 3,198
Molde FK – FK Čukarički Beograd 0-0
Molde FK: Álex Craninx, Vegard Forren, Kristoffer Haraldseid,
Kristoffer Haugen, Martin Bjørnbak, Magnus Eikrem (77.Fredrik
Sjølstad), Etzaz Hussain, Eirik Hestad, Fredrik Aursnes, Ohi Omoijuanfo,
Leke James (66.Mathis Bolly). Trainer: Erling Moe.
FK Čukarički Beograd: Nemanja Belic, Miroslav Bogosavac, Darko
Puskaric, Nikola Cirkovic, Luka Stojanovic (62.Veljko Birmancevic),
Marko Docic, Samuel Owusu, Stefan Kovac (84.Kosta Aleksic), Stefan
Sapic, Aleksandar Djordjevic, Slobodan Tedic. Trainer: Aleksander
Veselinovic.
Sent off: 90+5' Veljko Birmancevic.

25.07.2019; Stadion Arsenal, Tula
Referee: Enea Jorgji (ALB); Attendance: 16,720
FK Arsenal Tula – Neftçi PFK Bakı 0-1(0-1)
Arsenal Tula: Mikhail Levashov, Kirill Kombarov, Gia GRīgalava,
Maxim Belyaev, Víctor Álvarez, Igor Gorbatenko, Sergey Tkachev,
Goran Causic, Daniil Lesovoy, Alexandru Tudorie (46.Evgeniy
Lutsenko), Lameck Banda (46.Georgi Kostadinov). Trainer: Igor
Cherevchenko.
Neftçi Bakı: Salahat Agayev, Vojislav Stankovic, Kyrylo Petrov, Anton
Krivotsyuk, Omar Buludov, Soni Mustivar, Emin Makhmudov
(88.Vangelis Platellas), Mamadou Kane, Steeven Joseph-Monrose, Rauf
Aliyev, Dário Júnior da Silva (73.Namiq Alasgarov). Trainer: Roberto
Bordin.
Goal: 45+1' Dário Júnior da Silva 0-1.

01.08.2019; Stadionul „Ion Oblemenco", Craiova
Referee: Arnold Hunter (NIR); Attendance: 22,134
**CS UNIVERSITATEA CRAIOVA – Budapest Honvéd FC 0-0;
3-1 on penalties**
CS Universitatea Craiova: Mirko Pigliacelli, Renato Kelic, Ivan Martic
(13.Marius Briceag), Nicusor Bancu, Stephane Acka, Alexandru Mateiu,
Bogdan Vatajelu (63.Alexandru Ionita), Cristian Barbut, Antoni Ivanov
(75.Kamer Qaka), Alexandru Cicâldau, Mihai Roman (II) (94.Carlos
Fortes). Trainer: Corneliu Papura.
Budapest Honvéd: Rubi Levkovic (40.Attila Berla), Ivan Lovric, Djordje
Kamber, Bence Batik, Patrick George Ikenne-King, Federico Moretti
(73.Eke Uzoma), Tonci Kukoc (92.MacDonald Niba Ngwa), Barna
Kesztyüs, Bence Banó-Szabó, Vladyslav Kulach (78.David N'Gog),
Amadou Moutari. Trainer: Giuseppe Sannino.
Penalties: Kamber missed, Ionita 0-1, Batik missed, Carlos Fortes 0-2,
N'Gog 1-2, Cicaldau 1-3, Banó-Szabó missed.

01.08.2019; Merkur Arena, Graz
Referee: Juri Frischer (EST); Attendance: 2,000
SK Sturm Graz – FK HAUGESUND 2-1(1-0)
Sturm Graz: Jörg Siebenhandl, Thomas Schrammel, Anastasios
Avlonitis, Emanuel Sakic, Lukas Spendlhofer, Jakob Jantscher, Philipp
Huspek (75.Michael John Lema), Juan Domínguez, Thorsten Röcher
(27.Philipp Hosiner), Ivan Ljubic (76.Christoph Leitgeb), Otar
Kiteishvili. Trainer: Nestor El Maestro.
FK Haugesund: Helge Sandvik, Doug Bergqvist, Mikkel Desler,
Benjamin Tiedemann Hansen, Sondre Tronstad, Thore Baardsen
Pedersen, Niklas Sandberg (46.Torbjørn Kallevåg), Bruno Leite
(79.Joakim Nilsen), Kristoffer Velde, Kevin Krygård, Ibrahima Koné
(90+3.Fredrik Knudsen). Trainer: Jostein Grindhaug.
Goals: 15' Niklas Sandberg 1-0 (own goal), 48' Ivan Ljubic 2-0, 68'
Kevin Krygård 2-1.

01.08.2019; Brøndby Stadion, Brøndby
Referee: Miroslav Zelinka (CZE); Attendance: 16,426
BRØNDBY IF – KS Lechia Gdańsk 4-1(1-0,2-1)
Brøndby IF: Marvin Schwäbe, Paulus Arajuuri, Anthony Jung, Hjörtur
Hermannsson, Dominik Kaiser, Lasse Vigen Christensen (78.Tobias
Børkeeiet), Josip Radosevic, Simon Tibbling (70.Mikael Uhre), Simon
Hedlund (90.Jesper Lindstrøm), Kamil Wilczek, Kevin Mensah (119.Jens
Gammelby). Trainer: Niels Frederiksen.
Lechia Gdańsk: Dusan Kuciak, Blazej Augustyn, Zarko Udovicic
(57.Slawomir Peszko), Filip Mladenovic, Michal Nalepa, Daniel Lukasik
(57.Maciej Gajos), Lukás Haraslín (97.Rafal Wolski), Patryk Lipski,
Tomasz Makowski, Karol Fila, Flávio Paixão (97.Artur Sobiech).
Trainer: Piotr Stokowiec.
Goals: 15' Paulus Arajuuri 1-0, 53' Kamil Wilczek 2-0, 67' Flávio
Paixão 2-1, 94', 118' Jesper Lindstrøm 3-1, 4-1.

31.07.2019; Stadion na Banovom brdu, Beograd
Referee: Mykola Balakin (UKR); Attendance: 3,014
FK Čukarički Beograd – MOLDE FK 1-3(0-2)
FK Čukarički Beograd: Nemanja Belic, Miroslav Bogosavac, Darko
Puskaric, Nikola Cirkovic, Luka Stojanovic (46.Milutin Vidosavljevic),
Marko Docic, Samuel Owusu, Stefan Kovac (81.Kosta Aleksic), Stefan
Sapic, Aleksandar Djordjevic (70.Asmir Kajevic), Slobodan Tedic.
Trainer: Aleksander Veselinovic.
Molde FK: Álex Craninx, Vegard Forren, Kristoffer Haraldseid,
Kristoffer Haugen, Martin Bjørnbak, Magnus Eikrem (79.Martin
Ellingsen), Etzaz Hussain, Eirik Hestad, Fredrik Aursnes, Ohi
Omoijuanfo (70.Erling Knudtzon), Leke James (87.Mathis Bolly).
Trainer: Erling Moe.
Goals: 4' Ohi Omoijuanfo 0-1, 38' Magnus Eikrem 0-2, 78' Erling
Knudtzon 0-3, 82' Asmir Kajevic 1-3.

01.08.2019; Bakcell Arena, Bakı
Referee: Alan Mario Sant (MLT); Attendance: 9,000
NEFTÇİ PFK BAKI – FK Arsenal Tula 3-0(0-0)
Neftçi Bakı: Salahat Agayev, Vojislav Stankovic, Kyrylo Petrov, Anton
Krivotsyuk, Omar Buludov, Soni Mustivar, Emin Makhmudov
(62.Namiq Alasgarov), Mamadou Kane, Steeven Joseph-Monrose, Rauf
Aliyev (77.Mamadou Mbodj), Dário Júnior da Silva (90+1.Rhman
Hadzhiyev). Trainer: Roberto Bordin.
Arsenal Tula: Mikhail Levashov, Kirill Kombarov (72.Lameck Banda),
Gia GRīgalava, Maxim Belyaev, Víctor Álvarez, Igor Gorbatenko,
Sergey Tkachev, Georgi Kostadinov (80.Alexandru Tudorie), Goran
Causic, Daniil Lesovoy, Evgeniy Lutsenko. Trainer: Igor Cherevchenko.
Goals: 49' Rauf Aliyev 1-0, 89' Dário Júnior da Silva 2-0 (pen), 90+3'
Mamadou Mbodj 3-0.

25.07.2019; Yeni Malatya Stadyumu, Malatya
Referee: João Pedro da Silva Pinheiro (POR); Attendance: 9,146
Yeni Malatya Spor Kulübü – NK Olimpija Ljubljana 2-2(1-1)
Malatya Spor Kulübü: Fabien Farnolle, Issam Chebake, Arturo Mina, Teenage Hadebe, Murat Yildirim, Mitchell Donald (64.Guilherme), Nuri Aydin (62.Ahmed Ildiz), Erkan Kas, Thievy Bifouma, Adis Jahovic, Moryké Fofana (75.Berk Yildiz). Trainer: Sergen Yalçin.
Olimpija Ljubljana: Nejc Vidmar, Miral Samardzic, Macky Frank Bagnack, Eric Boakye, Goran Brkic (70.Marko Putincanin), Asmir Suljic (73.Luka Menalo), Stefan Savic, Tomislav Tomic, Endri Çekiçi, Ante Vukusic (90+4.Haris Kadric), Mario Jurcevic. Trainer: Safet Hadzic.
Goals: 13' Ante Vukusic 0-1, 20' Arturo Mina 1-1, 66' Adis Jahovic 2-1 (pen), 74' Stefan Savic 2-2.

25.07.2019; A. Le Coq Arena, Tallinn
Referee: Ali Palabiyik (TUR); Attendance: 8,500
FC Flora Tallinn – Eintracht Frankfurt 1-2(1-1)
Flora Tallinn: Matvei Igonen, Gert Kams, Märten Kuusk, Henrik Pürg, Henri Järvelaid, Konstantin Vassiljev, Mikhel Ainsalu, Martin Miller (76.Vlasiy Sinyavskiy), Vladislavs Kreida, Frank Liivak (86.Rauno Alliku), Erik Sorga (82.Mark Lepik). Trainer: Jürgen Henn.
Eintracht Frankfurt: Felix Wiedwald, David Abraham, Danny da Costa (88.Timothy Chandler), Evan Obite N'Dicka, Makoto Hasebe, Filip Kostic, Lucas Torró, Mijat Gacinovic (64.Daichi Kamada), Dominik Kohr, Gonçalo Paciência (64.Dejan Joveljic), Ante Rebic. Trainer: Adi Hütter.
Goals: 24' Lucas Torró 0-1, 34' Mikhel Ainsalu 1-1, 71' Dejan Joveljic 1-2.

25.07.2019; Adidas Aréna, Mladá Boleslav
Referee: Sergey Tsinkevich (BLR); Attendance: 3,721
FK Mladá Boleslav – FC Ordabasy Shymkent 1-1(1-1)
FK Mladá Boleslav: Jan Seda, Daniel Pudil, Laco Takács, Antonín Krapka (62.Lukás Budínsky), Marco Tulio, Marek Matejovsky, Jakub Fulnek (75.Pavel Bucha), Michal Hubínek, Tomás Ladra, Muris Mesanovic (63.Tomás Wágner), Nikolay Komlichenko. Trainer: Jozef Weber.
FC Ordabasy: Dmytro Nepogodov, Pablo Fontanello, Sergiy Maliy, Temirlan Yerlanov, Marat Bystrov, Abdoulaye Diakhaté, May Mahlangu, Timur Dosmagambetov, Mirzad Mehanovic (72.Kyrylo Kovalchuk), João Paulo (46.Aleksey Shchetkin), Ziguy Badibanga (87.Samat Shamshi). Trainer: Kakhaber Tskhadadze.
Goals: 21' Mirzad Mehanovic 0-1, 45+2' Nikolay Komlichenko 1-1.

25.07.2019; FFA Academy Stadium, Yerevan
Referee: Robert Harvey (IRL); Attendance: 1,420
FC Alashkert Yerevan – SC FCSB Bucureşti 0-3(0-0)
FC Alashkert: Ognjen Cancarevic, Hrayr Mkoyan, Gagik Dagbashyan, Hayk Ishkhanyan, Taron Voskanyan, Tiago Cametá, Artak Grigoryan, Danilo Sekulic (65.Gustavo Marmentini Santos), Vahagn Hayrapetyan, Uros Nenadovic (72.Vardan Poghosyan), Nikita Tankov (55.Gegam Kadimyan). Trainer: Abraham Khashmanyan.
FCSB Bucureşti: Andrei Daniel Vlad, Bogdan Planic, Iulian Cristea, Lucian Filip, Ionut Vîna, Ovidiu Popescu, Dragos Nedelcu, Adrian Ioan Hora (46.Razvan Oaida), Florin Tanase, Florinel Coman (90+1.Ovidiu Perianu), Dennis Man (77.Diogo Salomão). Trainer: Bogdan Andone.
Goals: 60' Florin Tanase 0-1, 68' Iulian Cristea 0-2, 82' Florinel Coman 0-3.

25.07.2019; Stadyen Budaunik Stroitel, Solihorsk
Referee: Mete Kalkavan (TUR); Attendance: 3,050
FC Shakhtyor Solihorsk – Esbjerg fB 2-0(1-0)
Shakhtyor Solihorsk: Andrey Klimovich, Pavel Rybak, Sergey Matvejchik (52.Igor Burko), Nikola Antic, Aleksandr Sachivko, Yuri Kovalev, Július Szöke, Valeriy Gromyko (86.Nikolai Yanush), Max Ebong Ngome, Elis Bakaj, Mykyta Tatarkov (46.Sergey Balanovich). Trainer: Sergey Tashuev.
Esbjerg fB: Jeppe Højbjerg, Markus Halsti (69.Rudolph Austin), Jesper Lauridsen, Viktor Tranberg, Daniel Anyembe, Joni Kauko (46.Jacob Sørensen), Lasha Parunashvili, Mark Brink, Patrick Egelund, Pyry Soiri (69.Mathias Kristensen), Adrian Petre. Trainer: John Lammers.
Goals; 5' Elis Bakaj 1-0, 55' Pavel Rybak 2-0.

01.08.2019; Stadion Stozice, Ljubljana
Referee: Filip Glova (SVK); Attendance: 7,812
NK Olimpija Ljubljana – YENI MALATYA SPOR KULÜBÜ 0-1(0-0)
Olimpija Ljubljana: Nejc Vidmar, Miral Samardzic, Macky Frank Bagnack, Eric Boakye, Marko Putincanin (87.Goran Brkic), Asmir Suljic (16.Luka Menalo), Stefan Savic (68.Vitja Valencic), Tomislav Tomic, Endri Çekiçi, Ante Vukusic, Mario Jurcevic. Trainer: Safet Hadzic.
Malatya Spor Kulübü: Fabien Farnolle, Erkan Kas (69.Eren Tozlu), Mustafa Akbas, Issam Chebake, Arturo Mina, Murat Yildirim (61.Guilherme), Robin Yalçin, Rahman Bugra Çagiran, Adis Jahovic, Thievy Bifouma, Moryké Fofana (61.Gökhan Töre). Trainer: Sergen Yalçin.
Goal: 77' Adis Jahovic 0-1.; Sent off: 38' Endri Çekiçi.

01.08.2019; Commerzbank-Arena, Frankfurt am Main
Referee: Jørgen Daugbjerg Burchardt (DEN); Attendance: 48,000
EINTRACHT FRANKFURT – FC Flora Tallinn 2-1(1-1)
Eintracht Frankfurt: Felix Wiedwald, Makoto Hasebe, Danny da Costa (86.Erik Durm), Almamy Touré, Evan Obite N'Dicka, Filip Kostic, Lucas Torró, Dominik Kohr (75.Gelson Fernandes), Daichi Kamada, Gonçalo Paciência, Dejan Joveljic (67.Mijat Gacinovic). Trainer: Adi Hütter.
Flora Tallinn: Matvei Igonen, Gert Kams, Märten Kuusk, Henrik Pürg, Henri Järvelaid, Konstantin Vassiljev, Mihkel Ainsalu, Vlasiy Sinyavskiy, Vladislavs Kreida (78.Markus Poom), Frank Liivak (60.Rauno Alliku), Erik Sorga (70.Mark Lepik). Trainer: Jürgen Henn.
Goals: 37' Gonçalo Paciência 1-0, 40' Vlasiy Sinyavskiy 1-1, 54' Gonçalo Paciência 2-1 (pen).

01.08.2019; Stadion Qajimuqan Muñaytpasov, Shymkent
Referee: Mads-Kristoffer Kristoffersen (DEN); Attendance: 17,000
FC Ordabasy Shymkent – FK MLADÁ BOLESLAV 2-3(1-2)
FC Ordabasy: Dmytro Nepogodov, Pablo Fontanello, Sergiy Maliy (46.João Paulo), Temirlan Yerlanov, Marat Bystrov, Abdoulaye Diakhaté, May Mahlangu (59.Kyrylo Kovalchuk), Timur Dosmagambetov, Mirzad Mehanovic, Ziguy Badibanga, Aleksey Shchetkin (72.Toktar Zhangylyshbay). Trainer: Kakhaber Tskhadadze.
FK Mladá Boleslav: Jan Seda, Daniel Pudil, Laco Takács, Antonín Krapka, Marco Tulio, Marek Matejovsky, Michal Hubínek, Tomás Ladra (66.Jakub Fulnek), Pavel Bucha (83.Jonas Auer), Muris Mesanovic (90+3.Jakub Klíma), Nikolay Komlichenko. Trainer: Jozef Weber.
Goals: 8' Marek Matejovsky 0-1, 33' Nikolay Komlichenko 0-2 (pen), 45' Aleksey Shchetkin 1-2, 47' Muris Mesanovic 1-3, 56' Abdoulaye Diakhaté 2-3 (pen).

01.08.2019; Stadionul „Marin Anastasovici", Giurgiu
Referee: Peter Kralovic (SVK); Attendance: 1,828
SC FCSB BUCUREŞTI – FC Alashkert Yerevan 2-3(1-3)
FCSB Bucureşti: Andrei Daniel Vlad, Alexandru Stan (46.Diogo Salomão), Mihai Balasa, Claudiu Belu, Iulian Cristea, Thierry Moutinho (24.Florinel Coman), Lucian Filip, Ionut Vîna, Ovidiu Popescu, Razvan Oaida, Florin Tanase (82.Bogdan Planic). Trainer: Bogdan Andone.
FC Alashkert: Ognjen Cancarevic, Hrayr Mkoyan, Gagik Dagbashyan, Hayk Ishkhanyan, Taron Voskanyan, Tiago Cametá, Artak Grigoryan, Thiago Galvão (68.Nikita Tankov), Gustavo Marmentini Santos, Vahagn Hayrapetyan (68.Sargis Shahinyan), Uros Nenadovic (75.Gegam Kadimyan). Trainer: Abraham Khashmanyan.
Goals: 10' Florin Tanase 1-0 (pen), 24', 28' Gustavo Marmentini Santos 1-1, 1-2 (pen), 45' Thiago Galvão 1-3, 59' Florinel Coman 2-3.
Sent off: 27' Mihai Balasa, 63' Gustavo Marmentini Santos.

01.08.2019; Blue Water Arena, Esbjerg
Referee: Duje Strukan (CRO); Attendance: 4,517
Esbjerg fB – FC SHAKHTYOR SOLIHORSK 0-0
Esbjerg fB: Jeppe Højbjerg, Rudolph Austin (63.Mark Brink), Jesper Lauridsen, Viktor Tranberg, Daniel Anyembe, Joni Kauko, Lasha Parunashvili, Nicklas Røjkjær (63.Yury Yakovenko), Jacob Sørensen, Pyry Soiri (72.Mathias Kristensen), Adrian Petre. Trainer: John Lammers.
Shakhtyor Solihorsk: Andrey Klimovich, Pavel Rybak, Sergey Matvejchik, Igor Burko (77.Mykyta Tatarkov), Nikola Antic, Sergey Balanovich (83.Nikolai Yanush), Aleksandr Sachivko, Yuri Kovalev, Július Szöke, Max Ebong Ngome, Elis Bakaj (88.Vladimir Khvashchinskiy). Trainer: Sergey Tashuev.; Sent off: 90' Július Szöke.

25.07.2019; „Yaakov Turner Toto" Stadium, Beer Sheva
Referee: Ricardo de Burgos Bengoetxea (ESP); Attendance: 8,167
Hapoel Be'er Sheva FC – FK Kairat Almaty 2-0(1-0)
Hapoel Be'er Sheva: Ernestas Setkus, Miguel Vítor, Ben Bitton, Loai Taha, Sean Goldberg, Marwan Kabha, Ramzi Safouri (54.Ben Sahar), Eden Shamir, David Keltjens (87.Naor Sabag), Jimmy Marín, Nigel Hasselbaink (78.Niv Zrihan). Trainer: Barak Bakhar.
FK Kairat: Stas Pokatilov, Eldos Akhmetov, Gafurzhan Suyombaev, Dino Mikanovic, Rade Dugalic, Aybol Abiken (76.Ramazan Orazov), Islambek Kuat, Bauyrzhan Islamkhan (67.Márton Eppel), Georgiy Zhukov, Konrad Wrzesinski (67.Yerkebulan Seidakhmet), Aderinsola Eseola. Trainer: Aleksey Shpilevski.
Goals: 10' Ramzi Safouri 1-0 (pen), 2-0 Eden Shamir (63).

25.07.2019; Stadion Balgarska Armija, Sofia
Referee: Paolo Valeri (ITA)   Attendance: 7,500
PFC CSKA Sofia – NK Osijek 1-0(0-0)
CSKA Sofia: Vytautas Cerniauskas, Nikolay Bodurov, Petar Zanev (78.Graham Carey), Kristiyan Malinov, Nuno Tomás, Geferson, Tiago Rodrigues, Janio Bikel, Diego Fabbrini (63.Valentin Antov), Ali Sowe, Evandro (82.Bozhidar Chorbadzhiyski). Trainer: Ljubomir Petrovic.
NK Osijek: Ivica Ivusic, Tomislav Sorsa, Mile Skoric, Ante Majstorovic, Mihael Zaper (90+4.Marko Dugandzic), László Kleinheisler (83.Dmytro Lyopa), Petar Bockaj, Marin Pilj (78.Vedran Jugovic), Bosko Sutalo, Mirko Maric, Antonio Mance. Trainer: Dino Skender.
Goal: 53' Evandro 1-0.

25.07.2019; Stadion Lokomotiv, Plovdiv
Referee: Timotheos Christofi (CYP); Attendance: 5,900
PFC Lokomotiv Plovdiv – FC Spartak Trnava 2-0(1-0)
Lokomotiv Plovdiv: Martin Lukov, Milos Petrovic, Josip Tomasevic, Stephen Eze, Dimitar Iliev, Momchil Tsvetanov, Parvizchon Umarbaev (90+5.Edin Bahtic), Petar Vitanov, Birsent Karagaren (77.David Malembana), Alen Ozbolt (79.Georgi Iliev), Ante Aralica. Trainer: Bruno Akrapovic.
Spartak Trnava: Dobrivoj Rusov, Timotej Záhumensky, Jozef Menich, Lucas Lovat, Ivan Mesík, Marko Tesija, Emir Halilovic, Filip Dangubic (69.Marko Kelemen), Rafael Tavares (80.Matús Turna), Filip Orsula, Gino van Kessel (56.Matej Jakúbek). Trainer: Ricardo Chéu.
Goals: 39', 61' Dimitar Iliev 1-0 (pen), 2-0 (pen).

25.07.2019; Corbett Sports Stadium, Rhyl
Referee: Michal Ocenás (SVK); Attendance: 829
Connah's Quay Nomads FC – FK Partizan Beograd 0-1(0-0)
Connah's Quay Nomads FC: Lewis Brass, George Horan, Danny Holmes, John Disney, Callum Roberts, Jay Owen, Callum Morris, Declan Poole, Michael Wilde, Nathan Woolfe (58.Michael Bakare), Jamie Insall (73.Priestley Farquharson). Trainer: Andy Morrison.
Partizan Beograd: Vladimir Stojkovic, Bojan Ostojic, Nemanja Miletic (I), Sasa Zdjelar, Slobodan Urosevic, Strahinja Pavlovic, Zoran Tosic, Aleksandar Scekic, Seydouba Soumah, Umar Sadiq (46.Ognjen Ozegovic), Djordje Ivanovic (73.Filip Stevanovic). Trainer: Savo Milosevic.
Goal: 62' Aleksandar Scekic 0-1.

25.07.2019; Östgötaporten, Norrköping
Referee: Hüseyin Göçek (TUR); Attendance: 5,440
IFK Norrköping – FK Liepāja 2-0(1-0)
IFK Norrköping: Isak Pettersson, Lars Gerson, Kasper Larsen, Filip Dagerstål, Rasmus Lauritsen, Gudmundur Thórarinsson, Simon Thern, Alexander Fransson (72.Sead Haksabanovic), Christoffer Nyman (89.Henrik Castegren), Simon Skrabb, Kalle Holmberg (86.Andreas Blomqvist). Trainer: Jens Gustafsson.
FK Liepāja: Valentins Ralkevics, Vadims Zulevs, Deniss Ivanovs, Seydina Keita, Raivis Jurkovskis, Amâncio Fortes, Leonel Strumia, Kristers Tobers, Mārtins Kigurs (81.Cristián Torres), Richard Friday (72.Danu Spataru), Dodô. Trainer: Aleksandrs Starkovs.
Goals: 1' Simon Thern 1-0, 80' Sead Haksabanovic 2-0.

01.08.2019; Ortaliq Stadion, Almaty
Referee: Ola Hobber Nilsen (NOR); Attendance: 23,000
FK Kairat Almaty – HAPOEL BE'ER SHEVA FC 1-1(1-0)
FK Kairat: Stas Pokatilov, Eldos Akhmetov, Gafurzhan Suyombaev, Dino Mikanovic, Rade Dugalic (66.Márton Eppel), Aybol Abiken, Islambek Kuat, Bauyrzhan Islamkhan (83.Konrad Wrzesinski), Georgiy Zhukov, Aderinsola Eseola, Yerkebulan Seidakhmet (66.Ramazan Orazov). Trainer: Aleksey Shpilevski.
Hapoel Be'er Sheva: Ernestas Setkus, Miguel Vítor (46.Amit Biton), Ben Bitton, Loai Taha, Sean Goldberg, Marwan Kabha, Ramzi Safouri (67.Ben Sahar), Eden Shamir, David Keltjens, Jimmy Marín, Nigel Hasselbaink (75.Niv Zrihan). Trainer: Barak Bakhar.
Goals: 40', 63' Rade Dugalic 1-0, 1-1 (own goal).
Sent off: 55' Eldos Akhmetov, 88' Vladimir Plotnikov (*not used sub*), 90+6' Gafurzhan Suyombaev.

01.08.2019; Stadion Gradski vrt, Osijek
Referee: Robert Schörgenhofer (AUT); Attendance: 7,214
NK Osijek – PFC CSKA SOFIA 1-0(1-0,1-0); 3-4 on penalties
NK Osijek: Ivica Ivusic, Tomislav Sorsa, Mile Skoric, Ante Majstorovic, Mihael Zaper (91.Benedik Mioc), László Kleinheisler (46.Dmytro Lyopa), Petar Bockaj, Marin Pilj, Bosko Sutalo, Mirko Maric, Antonio Mance (106.Luka Marin). Trainer: Dino Skender.
CSKA Sofia: Vytautas Cerniauskas, Nikolay Bodurov, Petar Zanev (64.Ivan Turitsov), Kristiyan Malinov (80.Graham Carey), Raúl Albentosa, Nuno Tomás, Geferson, Tiago Rodrigues, Janio Bikel, Diego Fabbrini (104.Tony Watt), Ali Sowe. Trainer: Ljubomir Petrovic.
Goal: 28' Ante Majstorovic 1-0.
Penalties: Lyopa 1-0, Tiago Rodrigues 1-1, Bockaj missed, Carey 1-2, Skoric missed, Geferson missed, Pilj 2-2, Bodurov 2-3, Maric 3-3, Sowe 3-4.

01.08.2019; City Arena Trnava, Trnava
Referee: Erik Lambrechts (BEL); Attendance: 6,702
FC Spartak Trnava – PFC LOKOMOTIV PLOVDIV 3-1(1-0)
Spartak Trnava: Dobrivoj Rusov, João Diogo, Bogdan Mitrea, Timotej Záhumensky, Lucas Lovat, Ivan Mesík, Marko Tesija, Emir Halilovic (82.Marko Kelemen), Filip Dangubic (82.Matej Jakúbek), Rafael Tavares, Alex Sobczyk (72.Gino van Kessel). Trainer: Ricardo Chéu.
Lokomotiv Plovdiv: Martin Lukov, Milos Petrovic, David Malembana, Josip Tomasevic, Stephen Eze, Dimitar Iliev, Momchil Tsvetanov, Petar Vitanov (57.Parvizchon Umarbaev), Birsent Karagaren, Alen Ozbolt (89.Wiris), Ante Aralica (72.Georgi Iliev). Trainer: Bruno Akrapovic.
Goals: 16' Filip Dangubic 1-0, 53' Bogdan Mitrea 2-0 (pen), 71' Rafael Tavares 3-0, 74' Alen Ozbolt 3-1.; Sent off: 35' Timotej Záhumensky.

01.08.2019; Stadion Partizana, Beograd
Referee: Luis Miguel Branco Godinho (POR); Attendance: 8,200
FK PARTIZAN BEOGRAD – Connah's Quay Nomads FC 3-0(0-0)
Partizan Beograd: Vladimir Stojkovic, Rajko Brezancic (73.Slobodan Urosevic), Bojan Ostojic, Nemanja Miletic (I), Strahinja Pavlovic, Zoran Tosic (63.Ognjen Ozegovic), Aleksandar Scekic, Seydouba Soumah, Sasa Zdjelar, Umar Sadiq, Djordje Ivanovic (46.Filip Stevanovic). Trainer: Savo Milosevic.
Connah's Quay Nomads FC: Lewis Brass, George Horan, Danny Holmes, John Disney, Callum Roberts, Danny Harrison (63.Ryan Wignall), Jay Owen, Callum Morris, Declan Poole, Michael Wilde (74.Priestley Farquharson), Jamie Insall (81.Michael Bakare). Trainer: Andy Morrison.
Goals: 54' Zoran Tosic 1-0, 70' Ognjen Ozegovic 2-0, 73' Filip Stevanovic 3-0.

01.08.2019; Daugava Stadions, Liepāja
Referee: Marius Avram (ROU); Attendance: 4,174
FK Liepāja – IFK NORRKÖPING 0-1(0-0)
FK Liepāja: Valentins Ralkevics, Vadims Zulevs (82.Vügar Asgarov), Deniss Ivanovs, Seydina Keita, Raivis Jurkovskis, Amâncio Fortes, Leonel Strumia, Kristers Tobers, Mārtins Kigurs (70.Raivis Vilumsons), Richard Friday (68.Danu Spataru), Dodô. Trainer: Aleksandrs Starkovs.
IFK Norrköping: Isak Pettersson, Lars Gerson, Kasper Larsen, Filip Dagerstål, Rasmus Lauritsen, Gudmundur Thórarinsson (90+2.Henrik Castegren), Simon Thern (77.Andreas Blomqvist), Alexander Fransson, Christoffer Nyman, Simon Skrabb, Kalle Holmberg (56.Sead Haksabanovic). Trainer: Jens Gustafsson.
Goal: 89' Sead Haksabanovic 0-1.

25.07.2019; Pancho Aréna, Felcsút
Referee: Kai Erik Steen (NOR); Attendance: 2,224
Fehérvár FC Székesfehérvár – FC Vaduz 1-0(1-0)
Fehérvár FC: Ádám Kovácsik, Roland Juhász, Attila Fiola, Loïc Négo, Stopira, Szabolcs Huszti (57.Ivan Petryak), Anel Hadzic, Ákos Elek (46.Máté Pátkai), Georgi Milanov, Boban Nikolov, Marko Scepovic (87.Márkó Futács). Trainer: Marko Nikolic.
FC Vaduz: Benjamin Büchel, Denis Simani, Pius Dorn, Yannick Schmid, Berkay Sülüngöz, Gianni Antoniazzi (84.Maximilian Göppel), Boris Prokopic (71.Milan Gajic), Sandro Wieser, Dominik Schwizer, Manuel Sutter (66.Mohamed Coulibaly), Tunahan Çiçek. Trainer: Mario Frick.
Goal: 5' Stopira 1-0.

25.07.2019; Swissporarena, Luzern
Referee: Halis Özkahya (TUR); Attendance: 6,344
FC Luzern – KÍ Klaksvík 1-0(0-0)
FC Luzern: Marius Müller, Lazar Cirkovic, Otar Kakabadze, Marvin Schulz, Stefan Knezevic, Silvan Sidler, Idriz Voca, Christian Schneuwly, Pascal Schürpf, Shkelqim Demhasaj (55.Francesco Margiotta), Eric Tia (55.Blessing Eleke). Trainer: Thomas Häberli.
KÍ Klaksvík: Kristian Joensen, Jesper Brinck, Ísak Simonsen, Deni Pavlovic, Semir Hadzibulic (82.Steinbjørn Olsen), Patrik Johannesen, Jákup Andreasen, Jóannes Bjartalíd (72.Boris Dosljak), Simen Sandmæl, Jóannes Danielsen, Páll Klettskard (66.Torbjørn Grytten). Trainer: Mikkjal Thomassen.
Goal: 90+3' Christian Schneuwly 1-0.

25.07.2019; MOL Aréna, Dunajská Streda
Referee: Bastian Dankert (GER); Attendance: 9,980
FK DAC Dunajská Streda – APS Atromitos Athína 1-2(1-2)
DAC Dunajská Streda: Martin Jedlicka, Éric Davis (74.César Blackman), Kristián Kostrna, Dominik Kruzliak, Matej Oravec, Zsolt Kalmár, Máté Vida, Lukás Cmelík (61.Dominik Veselovsky), Connor Ronan (30.Kristopher Vida), Eric Ramírez, Marko Divkovic. Trainer: Peter Hyballa.
Atromitos Athína: Balász Megyeri, Madson, Dimitrios Goutas, Spyros Risvanis, Alexandros Katranis, Javier Umbides, Kyriakos Kivrakidis (39.Spyridon Natsos), Charilaos Charisis, Georgios Manousos, Apostolos Vellios (74.Tal Kahila), Clarck N'Sikulu (61.Farley Rosa). Trainer: Yannis Anastasiou.
Goals: 20' Javier Umbides 0-1, 35' Kristopher Vida 1-1, 43' Georgios Manousos 1-2.

25.07.2019; GHELAMCO-arena, Gent
Referee: Aleksandar Stavrev (MKD); Attendance: 13,398
KAA Gent – FC Viitorul Constanţa 6-3(5-1)
KAA Gent: Thomas Kaminski, Nana Asare, Mikael Lustig, Igor Plastun, Sigurd Rosted (70.Milad Mohammadi), Vadis Odjidja-Ofoe, Brecht Dejaegere (62.Alessio Castro-Montes), Elisha Owusu, Yuya Kubo (62.Giorgi Beridze), Roman Yaremchuk, Jonathan David. Trainer: Jess Thorup.
Viitorul Constanţa: Árpád Tordai, Sebastian Mladen, Paul Iacob (46.Virgil Ghita), Bradley de Nooijer, Vlad Achim, Bogdan Tîru, Andrei Artean, Lyes Houri, Alexandru Matan (72.Andreas Calcan), Gabriel Iancu, George Ganea (62.Denis Dragus). Trainer: Gheorghe Hagi.
Goals: 4' Nana Asare 1-0, 13' Brecht Dejaegere 2-0, 21' Sebastian Mladen 2-1, 35' Yuya Kubo 3-1, 42' Roman Yaremchuk 4-1 (pen), 45' Yuya Kubo 5-1, 50' Roman Yaremchuk 6-1, 56', 61' Bogdan Tîru 6-2, 6-3.

25.07.2019; Stádio „Kleánthis Vikelídis", Thessaloníki
Referee: Stuart Attwell (ENG); Attendance: 17,488
Aris Thessaloníki – AEL Limassol 0-0
Aris Thessaloníki: Julián Cuesta, Daniel Sundgren, Mihály Korhut, Lindsay Rose, Fran Vélez, Nicolas Diguiny, Migjen Basha (74.Lucas Sasha), Javier Matilla, Ioannis Fetfatzidis (65.Daniel Larsson), Martín Tonso (84.Nicolás Martínez), Brown Ideye. Trainer: Savvas Pantelidis.
AEL Limassol: Vózinha, Nils Teixeira, Dossa Júnior (80.Ivan Carlos), Boris Godál, André Teixeira, Christos Wheeler (88.Andreas Avraam), Adnan Aganovic, Marko Adamovic (62.Gevorg Ghazaryan), Jon Gaztañaga, Davor Zdravkovski, Rubén Jurado. Trainer: Dusan Kerkez.

01.08.2019; Rheinpark Stadion, Vaduz
Referee: Manfredas Lukjancukas (LTU); Attendance: 1,253
FC VADUZ – Fehérvár FC Székesfehérvár 2-0(0-0,1-0)
FC Vaduz: Benjamin Büchel, Maximilian Göppel, Pius Dorn, Yannick Schmid, Berkay Sülüngöz, Gianni Antoniazzi, Milan Gajic, Sandro Wieser (82.Boris Prokopic), Dominik Schwizer (114.Jens Hofer), Manuel Sutter (115.Noah Frick), Tunahan Çiçek (72.Mohamed Coulibaly). Trainer: Mario Frick.
Fehérvár FC: Ádám Kovácsik, Roland Juhász, Attila Fiola (46.Ivan Petryak), Loïc Négo, Stopira, Szabolcs Huszti (103.Armin Hodzic), Máté Pátkai, Ákos Elek, Georgi Milanov (64.István Kovács), Boban Nikolov, Marko Scepovic (83.Márkó Futács). Trainer: Marko Nikolic.
Goals: 61' Milan Gajic 1-0 (pen), 100' Mohamed Coulibaly 2-0.
Sent off: 107' Gianni Antoniazzi.

01.08.2019; Svangaskard, Toftir
Referee: Martin Strömbergsson (SWE); Attendance: 1,229
KÍ Klaksvík – FC LUZERN 0-1(0-1)
KÍ Klaksvík: Kristian Joensen, Jesper Brinck, Ísak Simonsen, Deni Pavlovic, Semir Hadzibulic (80.Torbjørn Grytten), Patrik Johannesen, Jákup Andreasen, Jóannes Bjartalíd, Simen Sandmæl (80.Jonn Johannesen), Jóannes Danielsen, Páll Klettskard. Trainer: Mikkjal Thomassen.
FC Luzern: Marius Müller, Christian Schwegler, Simon Grether, Lucas Alves "Lucão", Marvin Schulz (68.Remo Arnold), Stefan Knezevic, Idriz Voca, Pascal Schürpf (62.Otar Kakabadze), Tsiy William Ndenge, Shkelqim Demhasaj (83.Francesco Margiotta), Blessing Eleke. Trainer: Thomas Häberli.
Goal: 34' Idriz Voca 0-1.

01.08.2019; Stádio Peristeriou, Athína
Referee: Mohammed Al-Hakim (SWE); Attendance: 2,450
APS ATROMITOS ATHÍNA – FK DAC Dunajská Streda 3-2(2-0)
Atromitos Athína: Balász Megyeri, Madson, Dimitrios Goutas, Spyros Risvanis, Alexandros Katranis, Javier Umbides (86.Spyridon Natsos), Kyriakos Kivrakidis, Charilaos Charisis, Georgios Manousos, Apostolos Vellios (60.Tal Kahila), Clarck N'Sikulu (70.Farley Rosa). Trainer: Yannis Anastasiou.
DAC Dunajská Streda: Martin Jedlicka, Kristián Kostrna, Dominik Kruzliak, César Blackman (76.Marko Divkovic), Matej Oravec (62.Dominik Veselovsky), Zsolt Kalmár, Máté Vida, Lukás Cmelík (46.Kristopher Vida), Connor Ronan, Eric Ramírez, Abdulrahman Taiwo. Trainer: Peter Hyballa.
Goals: 22' Alexandros Katranis 1-0, 28' Georgios Manousos 2-0 (pen), 53' Eric Ramírez 2-1, 72' Zsolt Kalmár 2-2 (pen), 76' Spyros Risvanis 3-2.

01.08.2019; Stadionul Central, Ovidiu
Referee: José Luis Munuera Montero (ESP); Attendance: 4,088
FC Viitorul Constanţa – KAA GENT 2-1(0-1)
FC Viitorul Constanţa: Catalin Cabuz, Sebastian Mladen, Virgil Ghita, Bradley de Nooijer, Vlad Achim, Bogdan Tîru, Andrei Artean (62.Eric de Oliveira), Lyes Houri, Alexandru Matan (55.Steliano Filip), Gabriel Iancu, George Ganea (73.Andreas Calcan). Trainer: Gheorghe Hagi.
KAA Gent: Thomas Kaminski, Nana Asare, Mikael Lustig, Igor Plastun, Michael Ngadeu-Ngadjui, Vadis Odjidja-Ofoe, Brecht Dejaegere (57.Louis Verstraete), Elisha Owusu, Yuya Kubo (59.Roman Bezus), Roman Yaremchuk (88.Mamadou Sylla), Jonathan David. Trainer: Jess Thorup.
Goals: 38' Roman Yaremchuk 0-1, 47', 61' Gabriel Iancu 1-1 (pen), 2-1 (pen).

01.08.2019; AEK Arena, Larnaca
Referee: Manuel Jorge Neves Moreira Sousa (POR); Attendance: 3,346
AEL Limassol – ARIS THESSALONÍKI 0-1(0-1)
AEL Limassol: Vózinha, Nils Teixeira (65' Jarchinio Antonia), Boris Godál, André Teixeira, Christos Wheeler (52' Andreas Avraam), Adnan Aganovic, Marko Adamovic, Jon Gaztañaga, Davor Zdravkovski, Gevorg Ghazaryan, Rubén Jurado (52' Ivan Carlos). Trainer: Dusan Kerkez.
Aris Thessaloníki: Julián Cuesta, Daniel Sundgren, Mihály Korhut, Lindsay Rose, Fran Vélez, Nicolas Diguiny, Migjen Basha, Javier Matilla, Ioannis Fetfatzidis (68' Lucas Sasha), Daniel Larsson (61' Martín Tonso), Brown Ideye (86' Nicolás Martínez). Trainer: Savvas Pantelidis.
Goal: 14' Nicolas Diguiny 0-1 (pen).; Sent off: 83' Boris Godál.

25.07.2019; Stade „Josy Barthel", Lëtzebuerg
Referee: Bojan Pandžić (SWE); Attendance: 3,617
AS La Jeunesse d'Esch/Alzette – Vitória SC Guimarães 0-1(0-0)
Jeunesse d'Esch: Kévin Sommer, Arsène Menèssou, Alessandro Fiorani, Emmanuel Lapierre, Johannes Steinbach, Halim Meddour, Milos Todorovic, Luca Duriatti, David Soares De Sousa (70.Yannick Makota), Valentin Kouamé, Almir Klica (78.Mehmet Arslan). Trainer: Nicolas Huysman.
Vitória Guimarães: João Miguel Silva, Víctor García, Pedrão, Rafa Soares, Edmond Tapsoba, João Carlos Teixeira (62.Pêpê Rodrigues), Rochinha (84.João Correia), Almoatasembellah Ali Mohamed (88.Mikel Agu), Joseph Amoah, Alexandre Guedes, Davidson. Trainer: Ivo Vieira.
Goal: 90+4' Joseph Amoah 0-1.

25.07.2019; AFAS Stadion, Alkmaar
Referee: Serhiy Boyko (UKR); Attendance: 11,492
AZ Alkmaar – BK Häcken Göteborg 0-0
AZ Alkmaar: Marco Bizot, Ron Vlaar, Stijn Wuytens (59.Yukinari Sugawara), Jonas Svensson, Owen Wijndal, Fredrik Midtsjø (77.Pantelis Hatzidiakos), Teun Koopmeiners, Guus Til, Albert Gudmundsson (58.Oussama Idrissi), Myron Boadu, Calvin Stengs.
Trainer: Arne Slot.
BK Häcken: Peter Abrahamsson, Joona Toivio, Óskar Sverrisson, Elohor Ekpolo (87.Adam Andersson), Gustav Berggren, Rasmus Lindgren, Erik Friberg, Ahmed Yasin, Daleho Irandust (71.Juhani Ojala), Viktor Lundberg, Paulinho (77.Alexander Faltsetas). Trainer: Andreas Alm.

25.07.2019; Sportni Park, Domžale
Referee: Michael Fabbri (ITA); Attendance: 2,043
NK Domžale – Malmö FF 2-2(1-1)
NK Domžale: Grega Sorcan, Gaber Dobrovoljc, Gregor Sikosek, Tilen Klemencic, Senijad Ibricic (90+2.Branko Ilic), Josip Corluka, Mattias Käit, Adam Gnezda Cerin, Slobodan Vuk (37.Matej Podlogar), Tonci Mujan (89.Sven Karic), Shamar Nicholson. Trainer: Simon Rozman.
Malmö FF: Johan Dahlin, Behrang Safari, Rasmus Bengtsson, Lasse Nielsen (80.Franz Brorsson), Søren Rieks (68.Jonas Knudsen), Anders Christiansen, Fouad Bachirou, Oscar Lewicki, Markus Rosenberg, Jo Inge Berget, Marcus Antonsson (77.Guillermo Molins). Trainer: Uwe Rösler.
Goals: 37' Shamar Nicholson 1-0, 42' Rasmus Bengtsson 1-1, 48' Adam Gnezda Cerin 2-1, 52' Marcus Antonsson 2-2.

25.07.2019; Ibrox Stadium, Glasgow
Referee: Espen Eskås (NOR); Attendance: 43,629
Glasgow Rangers FC – FC Progrès Niederkorn 2-0(1-0)
Glasgow Rangers: Allan McGregor, James Tavernier, Connor Goldson, George Edmundson, Steven Davis, Scott Arfield (66.Jordan Jones), Ryan Jack, Andy Halliday, Sheyi Ojo (81.Greg Stewart), Joe Aribo, Alfredo Morelos (75.Jermain Defoe). Trainer: Steven Gerrard.
Progrès Niederkorn: Sebastian Flauss, Tom Laterza, Adrien Ferino, Ben Vogel, Metin Karayer, Tim Hall, Aldin Skenderovic (33.Yann Matias Marques), Christian Silaj, Belmin Muratovic (46.Jacky Mmaee), Mayron De Almeida, Kempes Tekiela (80.Emmanuel Françoise). Trainer: Roland Vrabec.
Goals: 20' Joe Aribo 1-0, 54' Sheyi Ojo 2-0.; Sent off: 88' Tom Laterza.

25.07.2019; Stadion Pod Goricom, Podgorica
Referee: Massimiliano Irrati (ITA); Attendance: 5,500
FC Budučnost Podgorica – FK Zorya Luhansk 1-3(0-2)
FC Budučnost Podgorica: Milos Dragojevic, Dejan Boljevic, Luka Mirkovic (77.Ivan Bojovic), Slavko Damjanovic, Stefan Milic, Drasko Bozovic (46.Milos Raickovic), Milos Mijic, Milos Vucic, Dusan Bakic (46.Dejan Zarubica), Mihailo Perovic, Dusan Stoiljkovic. Trainer: Branko Brnovic.
Zorya Luhansk: Nikita Shevchenko, Vitaliy Vernidub, Oleksandr Tymchyk, Artem Gromov (80.Levan Arveladze), Dmytro Khomchenovsky, Vladen Yurchenko (64.Maksym Lunyov), Dmitriy Ivanisenya, Bogdan Mykhaylychenko (85.Joel Abu Hanna), Yevgen Cheberko, Vladyslav Kochergin, Pylyp Budkovsky. Trainer: Viktor Skripnik.
Goals: 15', 19' Artem Gromov 0-1, 0-2, 60' Mihailo Perovic 1-2, 82' Levan Arveladze 1-3.

01.08.2019; Estádio „Dom Afonso Henriques", Guimarães
Referee: Vitali Meshkov (RUS); Attendance: 16,352
VITÓRIA SC GUIMARÃES – AS La Jeunesse d'Esch/Alzette 4-0(1-0)
Vitória Guimarães: João Miguel Silva, Pedrão, Rafa Soares, Falaye Sacko, Edmond Tapsoba, Rochinha (71.João Correia), Pêpê Rodrigues, Almoatasembellah Ali Mohamed (60.João Carlos Teixeira), Joseph Amoah, Alexandre Guedes (83.João Pedro), Davidson. Trainer: Ivo Vieira.
Jeunesse d'Esch: Kévin Sommer, Arsène Menèssou, Alessandro Fiorani, Emmanuel Lapierre, Johannes Steinbach, Halim Meddour, Yannick Makota, Milos Todorovic, Luca Duriatti (68.David Soares De Sousa), Mehmet Arslan (76.Andrea Deidda), Valentin Kouamé (68.Almir Klica). Trainer: Nicolas Huysman.
Goals: 14' Edmond Tapsoba 1-0, 63' Alexandre Guedes 2-0, 88' Edmond Tapsoba 3-0 (pen), 90+3' João Carlos Teixeira 4-0.

01.08.2019; Bravida Arena, Göteborg
Referee: Frank Schneider (FRA); Attendance: 3,845
BK Häcken Göteborg – AZ ALKMAAR 0-3(0-1)
BK Häcken: Peter Abrahamsson, Joona Toivio, Óskar Sverrisson, Elohor Ekpolo (75.Adam Andersson), Rasmus Lindgren, Erik Friberg (85.Gustav Berggren), Ahmed Yasin, Alexander Faltsetas, Daleho Irandust, Paulinho (65.Ali Youssef), Kwame Kizito. Trainer: Andreas Alm.
AZ Alkmaar: Marco Bizot, Ron Vlaar, Stijn Wuytens, Pantelis Hatzidiakos, Owen Wijndal, Fredrik Midtsjø, Teun Koopmeiners, Guus Til (73.Jordy Clasie), Oussama Idrissi (68.Thomas Ouwejan), Myron Boadu (79.Ferdy Druijf), Calvin Stengs. Trainer: Arne Slot.
Goals: 42' Myron Boadu 0-1, 56' Calvin Stengs 0-2, 67' Oussama Idrissi 0-3.

01.08.2019; Swedbank Stadion, Malmö
Referee: Amaury Delerue (FRA); Attendance: 12,348
MALMÖ FF – NK Domžale 3-2(2-2)
Malmö FF: Dusan Melichárek, Behrang Safari, Rasmus Bengtsson, Lasse Nielsen (46.Eric Larsson), Søren Rieks, Anders Christiansen, Fouad Bachirou, Oscar Lewicki, Markus Rosenberg, Jo Inge Berget (88.Franz Brorsson), Marcus Antonsson (87.Guillermo Molins). Trainer: Uwe Rösler.
NK Domžale: Grega Sorcan, Gaber Dobrovoljc, Gregor Sikosek (84.Matej Podlogar), Tilen Klemencic, Sven Karic, Senijad Ibricic, Josip Corluka (88.Branko Ilic), Mattias Käit, Adam Gnezda Cerin, Tonci Mujan (59.Slobodan Vuk), Shamar Nicholson. Trainer: Simon Rozman.
Goals: 12' Shamar Nicholson 0-1, 21' Oscar Lewicki 1-1, 32' Markus Rosenberg 2-1, 45+1' Sven Karic 2-2. 83' Rasmus Bengtsson 3-2.

01.08.2019; Stade „Josy Barthel", Lëtzebuerg
Referee: Ivaylo Stoyanov (BUL); Attendance: 3,867.
FC Progrès Niederkorn – GLASGOW RANGERS FC 0-0
Progrès Niederkorn: Sebastian Flauss, Adrien Ferino, Ben Vogel, Metin Karayer, Tim Hall, Yann Matias Marques, Emmanuel Françoise (84.Kempes Tekiela), Sébastien Thill (64.Florik Shala), Christian Silaj, Mayron De Almeida, Jacky Mmaee (70.Issa Bah). Trainer: Roland Vrabec.
Glasgow Rangers: Allan McGregor, James Tavernier, Connor Goldson, Borna Barisic (46.Andy Halliday), Nikola Katic, Scott Arfield (76.Greg Docherty), Ryan Jack, Glen Kamara, Joe Aribo, Jermain Defoe (76.Alfredo Morelos), Sheyi Ojo. Trainer: Steven Gerrard.

01.08.2019; Slavutych-Arena, Zaporizhia
Referee: Neil Doyle (IRL); Attendance: 6,158
FK ZORYA LUHANSK – FC Budučnost Podgorica 1-0(1-0)
Zorya Luhansk: Zauri Makharadze, Vitaliy Vernidub, Oleksandr Tymchyk (64.Nikita Kamenyuka), Joel Abu Hanna, Artem Gromov (61.Vladyslav Kabayev), Dmytro Khomchenovsky, Dmitriy Ivanisenya, Yevgen Cheberko, Vladyslav Kochergin (68.Igor Chaykovskiy), Bohdan Lednev, Maksym Lunyov. Trainer: Viktor Skripnik.
FC Budučnost Podgorica: Milos Dragojevic, Dejan Boljevic, Luka Mirkovic, Nikola Djuric, Stefan Milic, Drasko Bozovic, Petar Grbic (53.Milos Raickovic), Milos Mijic, Vasilije Terzic, Mihailo Perovic (37.Bojan Roganovic), Dusan Stoiljkovic (75.Dejan Zarubica). Trainer: Branko Brnovic.
Goal: 32' Artem Gromov 1-0.
Sent off: 33' Nikola Djuric, 34' Drasko Bozovic.

25.07.2019; Stade de la Meinau, Strasbourg
Referee: Kevin Blom (NED); Attendance: 20,137
Racing Club de Strasbourg – Maccabi Haifa FC 3-1(1-1)
RC Strasbourg: Matz Sels, Lamine Koné, Lionel Carole, Alexander Djiku, Ismaël Aaneba (46.Adrien Thomasson), Mohamed Simakan, Jonas Martin, Jean Ricner Bellegarde (77.Kévin Lucien Zohi), Youssouf Fofana, Nuno Da Costa (84.Dimitri Liénard), Ludovic Ajorque. Trainer: Thierry Laurey.
Maccabi Haifa: Guy Haimov, Rami Gershon, Ernest Mabouka, Ayed Habashi, Ofri Arad, Yuval Ashkenazi, Yosef Raz Meir, Neta Lavi, Maxim Plakuschenko (67.Dolev Haziza), Nikita Rukavytsya (89.Allyson), Yarden Shua (50.Sun Menachem). Trainer: Marco Balbul.
Goals: 39' Maxim Plakuschenko 0-1, 45' Ludovic Ajorque 1-1 (pen), 47' Adrien Thomasson 2-1, 61' Jonas Martin 3-1.;
Sent off: 44' Ayed Habashi.

25.07.2019; Molineux Stadium, Wolverhampton
Referee: Kristoffer Karlsson (SWE); Attendance: 29,708
Wolverhampton Wanderers FC – Crusaders FC Belfast 2-0(1-0)
Wolverhampton Wanderers: Rui Patrício, Ryan Bennett, Willy Boly, Conor Coady, Jonny Castro (64.Rúben Vinagre), João Moutinho, Leander Dendoncker, Rúben Neves (58.Raúl Jiménez), Diogo Jota, Morgan Gibbs-White (85.Romain Saïss), Adama Traoré. Trainer: Nuno Espírito Santo.
Crusaders FC: Sean O'Neill, Sean Ward, Billy Joe Burns, Chris Hegarty, Declan Caddell (67.Gary Thompson), Philip Lowry, Jordan Forsythe, Paul Heatley, Ross Clarke (61.Jordan Owens), Jarlath O'Rourke, Rory Hale (82.David Cushley). Trainer: Stephen Baxter.
Goals: 37' Diogo Jota 1-0, 90+3' Rúben Vinagre 2-0.

25.07.2019; Stadio "Giuseppe Moccagatta", Alessandria
Referee: Jens Maae (DEN); Attendance: 4,376
Torino FC – Debreceni VSC 3-0(2-0)
Torino FC: Salvatore Sirigu, Lorenzo De Silvestri, Cristian Ansaldi, Nicolas N'Koulou, Armando Izzo, Bremer, Soualiho Meïté, Daniele Baselli, Iago Falqué (75.Sasa Lukic), Andrea Belotti, Álex Berenguer (80.Simone Zaza). Trainer: Walter Mazzarri.
Debreceni VSC: Sándor Nagy, János Ferenczi, Ákos Kinyik (74.Erik Kusnyír), Csaba Szatmári, Bence Pávkovics, Dániel Tözsér, Nikola Trujic, Kevin Varga (86.Ádám Pintér), Attila Haris, Márk Szécsi, Dániel Zsóri (46.Haruna Garba). Trainer: András Herczeg.
Goals: 20' Andrea Belotti 1-0 (pen), 42' Cristian Ansaldi 2-0, 90+3' Simone Zaza 3-0.

25.07.2019; Stadion „Marszalka Józefa Pilsudskiego", Warszawa
Referee: Ivan Bebek (CRO); Attendance: 11,678
Legia Warszawa – Kuopion PS 1-0(1-0)
Legia Warszawa: Radoslaw Majecki, Artur Jedrzejczyk, Luís Rocha (81.Pawel Stolarski), Mateusz Wieteska, Arvydas Novikovas, Marko Vesovic, André Martins, Dominik Nagy (61.Luquinhas), Valeriane Gvilia (73.Domagoj Antolic), Carlitos López, Sandro Kulenovic. Trainer: Aleksandar Vukovic.
Kuopion PS: Otso Virtanen, Babacar Diallo, Luis Murillo, Luc Tabi Manga (65.Saku Savolainen), Vinko Soldo, Petteri Pennanen, Reuben Ayarna, Ville Saxman, Ilmari Niskanen, Issa Thiaw (74.Ariel Ngueukam), Rangel (80.Tommi Jyry). Trainer: Jani Honkavaara.
Goal: 9' Mateusz Wieteska 1-0.

25.07.2019; RCDE Stadium, Cornella de Llobregat
Referee: Alain Durieux (LUX); Attendance: 19,122
RCD Espanyol Barcelona – Stjarnan Garðabær 4-0(0-0)
RCD Espanyol: Diego López, Javi López, Naldo, Lluís López, Adrià Pedrosa (74.Dídac Vilà), Granero (54.Lei Wu), Víctor Sánchez (54.Marc Roca), Sergi Darder, Melendo, Facundo Ferreyra, Borja Iglesias. Trainer: David Gallego.
Stjarnan Garðabær: Haraldur Björnsson, Brynjar Gudjónsson, Daníel Laxdal (64.Thorri Geir Rúnarsson), Jóhann Laxdal, Martin Rauschenberg Brorsen, Eyjólfur Hédinsson, Thorsteinn Már Ragnarsson, Heidar Ægisson, Alex Thór Hauksson (82.Sölvi Gudbjargarson), Gudmundur Hafsteinsson (46.Gudjón Baldvinsson), Hilmar Árni Halldórsson. Trainer: Rúnar Sigmundsson.
Goals: 49', 57' Facundo Ferreyra 1-0, 2-0, 60', 68' Borja Iglesias 3-0, 4-0.

01.08.2019; „Sammy Ofer" Stadium, Haifa
Referee: Maurizio Mariani (ITA); Attendance: 23,038
Maccabi Haifa FC – RACING CLUB DE STRASBOURG 2-1(2-1)
Maccabi Haifa: Guy Haimov, Rami Gershon, Sun Menachem, Ofri Arad, Yuval Ashkenazi, Yosef Raz Meir, Allyson, Neta Lavi, Maxim Plakuschenko (72.Mohammad Abu Fani), Nikita Rukavytsya (63.Dolev Haziza), Yarden Shua (67.Muhamad Awad). Trainer: Marco Balbul.
RC Strasbourg: Matz Sels (46.Bingourou Kamara), Lamine Koné, Stefan Mitrovic, Lionel Carole, Alexander Djiku, Mohamed Simakan, Jonas Martin, Dimitri Liénard, Adrien Thomasson (72.Nuno Da Costa), Youssouf Fofana, Ludovic Ajorque (86.Ibrahima Sissoko). Trainer: Thierry Laurey.
Goals: 17' Ludovic Ajorque 0-1, 25' Yarden Shua 1-1, 40' Nikita Rukavytsya 2-1.

01.08.2019; Seaview Stadium, Belfast
Referee: Nejc Kajtazovic (SVN); Attendance: 2,700
Crusaders FC Belfast – WOLVERHAMPTON WANDERERS FC 1-4(1-3)
Crusaders FC: Sean O'Neill, Sean Ward, Billy Joe Burns, Chris Hegarty, Philip Lowry, Jordan Forsythe, Paul Heatley, Ross Clarke (78.Declan Caddell), Jarlath O'Rourke, Rory Hale (83.Gary Thompson), Jordan Owens (80.David Cushley). Trainer: Stephen Baxter.
Wolverhampton Wanderers: Rui Patrício, Ryan Bennett, Willy Boly, Conor Coady, Jonny Castro, João Moutinho, Leander Dendoncker, Rúben Neves (68.Romain Saïss), Raúl Jiménez (55.Morgan Gibbs-White), Adama Traoré, Diogo Jota (68.Rúben Vinagre). Trainer: Nuno Espírito Santo.
Goals: 13' Ryan Bennett 1-0 (own goal), 15' Raúl Jiménez 1-1, 38' Ryan Bennett 1-2, 45' Raúl Jiménez 1-3, 77' Jordan Forsythe 1-4 (own goal).

01.08.2019; Nagyerdei Stadion, Debrecen
Referee: Fran Jovic (CRO); Attendance: 15,350
Debreceni VSC – TORINO FC 1-4(0-2)
Debreceni VSC: Sándor Nagy, János Ferenczi, Csaba Szatmári, Bence Pávkovics, Erik Kusnyír, Dániel Tözsér, Nikola Trujic (90.Richárd Csösz), Kevin Varga (63.Dániel Zsóri), Attila Haris, Márk Szécsi, Haruna Garba (80.Temitope Adeniji). Trainer: András Herczeg.
Torino FC: Salvatore Sirigu, Lorenzo De Silvestri, Cristian Ansaldi, Nicolas N'Koulou, Armando Izzo (83.Wilfried Singo), Bremer, Soualiho Meïté, Daniele Baselli (45.Tomás Rincón), Simone Zaza, Andrea Belotti (76.Vincenzo Millico), Álex Berenguer. Trainer: Walter Mazzarri.
Goals: 25' Simone Zaza 0-1, 32' Armando Izzo 0-2, 52' Haruna Garba 1-2, 69' Andrea Belotti 1-3, 90+2' Vincenzo Millico 1-4.

01.08.2019; Savon Sanomat Areena, Kuopio
Referee: Lawrence Visser (BEL); Attendance: 3,200
Kuopion PS – LEGIA WARSZAWA 0-0
Kuopion PS: Otso Virtanen, Babacar Diallo, Luis Murillo, Luc Tabi Manga, Vinko Soldo, Petteri Pennanen, Reuben Ayarna, Ville Saxman (76.Ats Purje), Ilmari Niskanen, Issa Thiaw (89.Ariel Ngueukam), Rangel. Trainer: Jani Honkavaara.
Legia Warszawa: Radoslaw Majecki, Artur Jedrzejczyk, William Rémy (66.Igor Lewczuk), Luís Rocha, Arvydas Novikovas, Marko Vesovic, André Martins, Dominik Nagy (90+1.Tomasz Jodlowiec), Valeriane Gvilia, Carlitos López (61.Domagoj Antolic), Sandro Kulenovic. Trainer: Aleksandar Vukovic.

01.08.2019; Samsung völlurinn, Gardabær
Referee: Dumitri Muntean (MDA); Attendance: 1,020
Stjarnan Garðabær – RCD ESPANYOL BARCELONA 1-3(0-1)
Stjarnan Garðabær: Haraldur Björnsson, Daníel Laxdal, Jóhann Laxdal, Martin Rauschenberg Brorsen, Eyjólfur Hédinsson, Thorsteinn Már Ragnarsson (69.Gudmundur Hafsteinsson), Thorri Geir Rúnarsson (69.Baldur Sigurdsson), Heidar Ægisson, Alex Thór Hauksson, Sölvi Gudbjargarson, Hilmar Árni Halldórsson (65.Nimo Gribenco). Trainer: Rúnar Sigmundsson.
RCD Espanyol: Diego López, Bernardo Espinosa, Dídac Vilà, Javi López, Naldo, Adrià Pedrosa (70.Javi Puado), Víctor Sánchez (65.Iturraspe), Marc Roca, Melendo, Facundo Ferreyra, Borja Iglesias (65.Lei Wu). Trainer: David Gallego.
Goals: 5' Adrià Pedrosa 0-1, 52' Borja Iglesias 0-2, 79' Facundo Ferreyra 0-3, 87' Baldur Sigurdsson 1-3.

25.07.2019; Tallaght Stadium, Dublin
Referee: Stephan Klossner (SUI); Attendance: 5,396
Shamrock Rovers FC Dublin – Apollon Limassol FC 2-1(1-1)
Shamrock Rovers: Alan Mannus, Joey O'Brien, Sean Kavanagh, Roberto Lopes, Ethan Boyle, Lee Grace, Ronan Finn (77.Gary O'Neill), Greg Bolger, Aaron McEneff (85.Dylan Watts), Jack Byrne, Daniel Carr (64.Aaron Greene). Trainer: Stephen Bradley.
Apollon Limassol: Joël Mall, Attila Szalai, Ioannis Pittas (61.Serge Gakpé), Vincent Bessat, Héctor Yuste, Sasa Markovic, Esteban Sachetti, Emilio Zelaya (81.Facundo Pereyra), João Pedro, Fotios Papoulis (72.Diego Aguirre), Giannis Gianniotas. Trainer: Sofronis Avgousti.
Goals: 5' Fotios Papoulis 0-1, 14' Lee Grace 1-1, 58' Roberto Lopes 2-1.
Sent off: 83' Esteban Sachetti.

01.08.2019; Stádio Neo GSP, Nicosia
Referee: Michael Tykgaard (DEN); Attendance: 2,987
APOLLON LIMASSOL FC – Shamrock Rovers FC Dublin 3-1(1-0,2-1)
Apollon Limassol: Joël Mall, Charis Kyriakou (105' Facundo Pereyra), Héctor Yuste, Sasa Markovic, Diego Aguirre, Roger Tamba M'Pinda (58' Attila Szalai), Serge Gakpé (77' Adrián Sardinero), Emilio Zelaya, João Pedro, Fotios Papoulis, Giannis Gianniotas (90' Ioannis Pittas). Trainer: Sofronis Avgousti.
Shamrock Rovers: Alan Mannus, Joey O'Brien (83' Dylan Watts), Sean Kavanagh, Roberto Lopes, Ethan Boyle, Lee Grace, Ronan Finn (86' Daniel Carr), Greg Bolger (105' Thomas Oluwya), Aaron McEneff (75' Gary O'Neill), Jack Byrne, Aaron Greene. Trainer: Stephen Bradley.
Goals: 18' Emilio Zelaya 1-0, 64' Attila Szalai 2-0, 69' Aaron Greene 2-1, 102' Adrián Sardinero 3-1.
Sent off: 67' Fotios Papoulis, 92' Lee Grace.

THIRD QUALIFYING ROUND

CHAMPIONS PATH

06.08.2019; „Vazgen Sargsyan" anvan Hanrapetakan Marzadasht, Yerevan
Referee: Alain Bieri (SUI); Attendance: 10,500
FC Ararat-Armenia Yerevan – FC Saburtalo Tbilisi 1-2(1-0)
FC Ararat-Armenia: Stefan Cupic, Rochdi Achenteh, Dmitri Guzj, Ângelo Meneses, Georgi Pashov, Gor Malakyan (57.Ilja Antonov), Kódjo Alphonse, Petros Avetisyan (78.Zakaria Sanogo), Anton Kobyalko (71.Louis Ogana), Furdjel Narsingh, Mailson. Trainer: Vardan Minasyan.
FC Saburtalo Tbilisi: Omar Migineishvili, Giorgi Rekhviashvili, Luka Lakvekheliani, Levan Kakubava, Giorgi Diasamidze, Sandro Altunashvili, Nikoloz Mali, Alwyn Tera (71.Levan Kenia), Giorgi Gabedava, Ognjen Rolovic (57.Gagi Margvelashvili), Giorgi Kokhreidze (84.Dachi Tsnobiladze). Trainer: Giorgi Chiabrishvili.
Goals: 31' Anton Kobyalko 1-0, 72' Sandro Altunashvili 1-1, 76' Levan Kenia 1-2.

14.08.2019; Stadioni „Mikheil Meskhi", Tbilisi
Referee: Mykola Balakin (UKR); Attendance: 14,904
FC Saburtalo Tbilisi – FC ARARAT-ARMENIA YEREVAN 0-2(0-1)
FC Saburtalo Tbilisi: Omar Migineishvili, Giorgi Rekhviashvili, Gagi Margvelashvili, Luka Lakvekheliani, Levan Kakubava (69.Tornike Gorgiashvili), Giorgi Diasamidze (58.Levan Kenia), Sandro Altunashvili, Nikoloz Mali, Alwyn Tera, Giorgi Gabedava (60.Ognjen Rolovic), Giorgi Kokhreidze. Trainer: Giorgi Chiabrishvili.
FC Ararat-Armenia: Dmitriy ABakımov, Rochdi Achenteh, Dmitri Guzj, Ângelo Meneses, Georgi Pashov, Gor Malakyan (70.Ilja Antonov), Armen Ambartsumyan (57.Petros Avetisyan), Kódjo Alphonse, Anton Kobyalko (80.Aleksandar Damcevski), Furdjel Narsingh, Mailson. Trainer: Vardan Minasyan.
Goals: 10' Anton Kobyalko 0-1, 67' Petros Avetisyan 0-2 (pen).

06.08.2019; Daugava Stadions, Rīga
Referee: Kirill Levnikov (RUS); Attendance: 3,468
Rīga FC – HJK Helsinki 1-1(0-1)
Rīga FC: Roberts Ozols, Georgios Valerianos, Herdi Prenga, Stefan Panic, Tomislav Saric (76.Vyacheslav Sharpar), Felipe Brisola, Roger (74.Aleksejs Visnakovs), Armands Pētersons, Elvis Stuglis, Roman Debelko (61.Kamil Bilinski), Vladislavs Fjodorovs. Trainer: Mihails Konevs.
HJK Helsinki: Maksim Rudakov, Rafinha (58.Henri Toivomäki), Nikolai Alho, Daniel O'Shaughnessy, Faith Obilor, William Parra, Riku Riski, Kaan Kairinen, Sebastian Dahlström, Evans Mensah (67.Petteri Forsell), Tim Väyrynen (89.Erfan Zeneli). Trainer: Toni Koskela.
Goals: 7' Tim Väyrynen 0-1, 81' Kamil Bilinski 1-1.

15.08.2019; Telia 5G -areena, Helsinki
Referee: Mohammed Al-Hakim (SWE); Attendance: 6,847
HJK Helsinki – RĪGA FC 2-2(1-0)
HJK Helsinki: Maksim Rudakov, Rafinha (81.Ivan Tarasov), Nikolai Alho (77.Henri Toivomäki), Daniel O'Shaughnessy, Faith Obilor, William Parra, Riku Riski, Petteri Forsell, Kaan Kairinen (71.Sebastian Dahlström), Evans Mensah, Tim Väyrynen. Trainer: Toni Koskela.
Rīga FC: Roberts Ozols, Georgios Valerianos, Herdi Prenga, Stefan Panic, Antonijs Cernomordijs, Tomislav Saric (56.Olegs Laizāns), Felipe Brisola, Roger (90+2.Ritvars Rugins), Armands Pētersons, Roman Debelko, Vladislavs Fjodorovs (60.Deniss Rakels). Trainer: Mihails Konevs.
Goals: 5' Petteri Forsell 1-0, 62' Roman Debelko 1-1, 69' Tim Väyrynen 2-1, 80' Roman Debelko 2-2.

06.08.2019; Stadion Pod Godgom, Podgorica
Referee: Alan Mario Sant (MLT); Attendance: 3,850
FK Sutjeska Nikšić – Linfield FC Belfast 1-2(1-1)
FK Sutjeska Nikšić: Vladan Giljen, Darko Bulatovic, Aleksandar Sofranac, Bojan Ciger, Marko Cetkovic, Damir Kojasevic, Branislav Jankovic, Marko Vucic (83.Miljan Vlaisavljevic), Nemanja Nedic, Novica Erakovic (68.Vladan Bubanja), Bojan Bozovic (46.Stefan Nikolic). Trainer: Nikola Rakojevic.
Linfield FC: Rohan Ferguson, Chris Casement, Ryan McGivern, Matthew Clarke, Mark Stafford, Niall Quinn, Jamie Mulgrew, Kirk Millar (87.Jordan Stewart), Bastien Héry (90+3.Daniel Kearns), Stephen Fallon (84.Andrew Mitchell), Shayne Lavery. Trainer: David Healy.
Goals: 11' Damir Kojasevic 1-0, 38', 65' Kirk Millar 1-1, 1-2.

13.08.2019; Windsor Park, Belfast
Referee: Miroslav Zelinka (CZE); Attendance: 3,639
LINFIELD FC BELFAST – FK Sutjeska Nikšić 3-2(2-1)
Linfield FC: Rohan Ferguson, Chris Casement, Ryan McGivern, Matthew Clarke, Mark Stafford, Niall Quinn (76.Jordan Stewart), Jamie Mulgrew, Kirk Millar (67.Joel Cooper), Bastien Héry, Stephen Fallon, Shayne Lavery (79.Andrew Waterworth). Trainer: David Healy.
FK Sutjeska Nikšić: Vladan Giljen, Darko Bulatovic, Aleksandar Sofranac, Bojan Ciger, Marko Cetkovic, Damir Kojasevic, Milovan Petrovikj, Miljan Vlaisavljevic (63.Marko Vucic), Nemanja Nedic, Novica Erakovic (85.Stefan Nikolic), Bojan Bozovic (73.Bozo Markovic). Trainer: Nikola Rakojevic.
Goals: 7' Mark Stafford 1-0, 15' Bojan Bozovic 1-1, 18' Shayne Lavery 2-1, 61' Bojan Bozovic 2-2, 76' Matthew Clarke 3-2.
Sent off: 36' Aleksandar Sofranac.

07.08.2019; Národny Futbalovy Stadión, Bratislava
Referee: Frank Schneider (FRA); Attendance: 9,980
ŠK Slovan Bratislava – Dundalk FC 1-0(0-0)
Slovan Bratislava: Dominik Greif, Vasil Bozhikov, Vernon, Jurij Medvedev, Myenty Abena, Marin Ljubicic, Dávid Holman, Joeri de Kamps, "Moha" Mohammed Rharsalla (77.Erik Daniel), Andraz Sporar (80.Aleksandar Cavric), Rafael Ratão (67.Dejan Drazic). Trainer: Ján Kozák.
Dundalk FC: Gary Rogers, Dane Massey, Andrew Boyle, Sean Gannon, Daniel Cleary, Chris Shields, Sean Murray (70.Patrick McEleney), John Mountney, Jamie McGrath, Patrick Hoban (87.Cameron Dummigan), Michael Duffy (88.Daniel Kelly). Trainer: Vinny Perth.
Goal: 86' Dávid Holman 1-0.

08.08.2019; Astana Arena, Nur-Sultan
Referee: Vladislav Bezborodov (RUS); Attendance: 18,707
Astana FC – Valletta FC 5-1(3-0)
Astana FC: Nenad Eric, Antonio Rukavina, Yuriy Logvinenko, Dmitriy Shomko, Evgeny Postnikov, Luka Simunovic, Rúnar Sigurjónsson, Marin Tomasov, Ivan Maevski (63.Yuriy Pertsukh), Dorin Rotariu (87.Roman Murtazaev), Ndombe Mubele (63.Rangelo Janga). Trainer: Roman Grygorchuk.
Valletta FC: Henry Bonello, Joseph Zerafa, Ryan Camilleri, Jean Borg, Douglas Packer (78.Matteo Piciollo), Rowen Muscat, Kyrian Nwoko (61.Shaun Dimech), Enmy Peña, Kevin Tulimieri (61.Nicholas Pulis), Yuri, Mario Fontanella. Trainer: Darren Abdilla.
Goals: 8' Rúnar Sigurjónsson 1-0, 15' Yuriy Logvinenko 2-0, 35' Marin Tomasov 3-0, 57' Rúnar Sigurjónsson 4-0, 67' Mario Fontanella 4-1, 80' Rangelo Janga 5-1.

08.08.2019; Bolshaya Sportivnaya Arena, Tiraspol
Referee: Kevin Clancy (SCO); Attendance: 6,341
FC Sheriff Tiraspol – AIK Stockholm 1-2(0-2)
FC Sheriff Tiraspol: Zvonimir Mikulic, Andrej Lukic, Mateo Muzek, Cristiano, Ariel Borysiuk, Wilfried Balima (76.Maxim Cojocaru (I)), Jury Kendysh, Gheorghe Anton (46.Artem Hordienko), Liridon Latifi (87.Jaroslaw Jach), Gabrijel Boban, Robert Tambe. Trainer: Zoran Zekic.
AIK Stockholm: Oscar Linnér, Per Karlsson, Robert Lundström (90+1.Heradi Rashidi), Karol Mets, Sebastian Larsson, Panajotis Dimitriadis (73.Rasmus Lindkvist), Enoch Adu, Anton Salétros, Tarik Elyounoussi, Kolbeinn Sigthórsson (76.Nabil Bahoui), Henok Goitom. Trainer: Rikard Norling.
Goals: 12' Andrej Lukic 0-1 (own goal), 14' Kolbeinn Sigthórsson 0-2, 56' Jury Kendysh 1-2 (pen).

08.08.2019; Winner Stadium, Netanya
Referee: Neil Doyle (IRL); Attendance: 8,512
Maccabi Tel Aviv FC – FC Sūduva Marijampolė 1-2(0-1)
Maccabi Tel Aviv: Andreas Gianniotis, Saborit, Shahar Piven-Bachtiar, Jair Amador, Maor Kandil, Dor Mikha, Dor Peretz, Dan Glazer (81.Avi Rikan), Nick Blackman (63.Eliran Atar), Itay Shechter (46.Chikeluba Ofoedu), Yonatan Cohen. Trainer: Vladimir Ivic.
FK Sūduva Marijampolė: Ivan Kardum, Algis Jankauskas, Andro Svrljuga, Aleksandar Zivanovic, Semir Kerla, Jovan Cadjenovic, Ovidijus Verbickas, Giedrius Matulevicius (75.Povilas Leimonas), Josip Tadic (70.Eligijus Jankauskas), Mihret Topcagic (86.Robertas Vèzevicius), Paulius Golubickas. Trainer: Vladimir Cheburin.
Goals: 37' Semir Kerla 0-1, 76' Eligijus Jankauskas 0-2, 84' Chikeluba Ofoedu 1-2.

08.08.2019; Ludogorets Arena, Razgrad
Referee: Marius Avram (ROU); Attendance: 4,120
PFC Ludogorets Razgrad – The New Saints 5-0(3-0)
Ludogorets Razgrad: Plamen Iliev, Cosmin Moti, Rafael Forster, Jordan Ikoko, Anton Nedyalkov, Anicet Andrianantenaina (61.Stéphane Badji), Jacek Góralski, Dan Biton (77.Jakub Swierczok), Claudiu Keserü, Jody Lukoki, Mavis Tchibota (70.Wanderson). Trainer: Stoicho Stoev.
The New Saints: Paul Harrison, Simon Spender (69.Kane Lewis), Christopher Marriott, Keston Davies (46.Blaine Hudson), Ryan Harrington, Aeron Edwards, Jon Routledge, Daniel Redmond, Ryan Brobbel, Jamie Mullan, Dean Ebbe (61.Greg Draper). Trainer: Scott Ruscoe.
Goals: 10' Ryan Harrington 1-0 (own goal), 28' Mavis Tchibota 2-0, 43' Jody Lukoki 3-0, 65' Claudiu Keserü 4-0, 76' Cosmin Moti 5-0.

13.08.2019; Tallaght Stadium, Dublin
Referee: Robert Schörgenhofer (AUT); Attendance: 4,199
Dundalk FC – ŠK SLOVAN BRATISLAVA 1-3(0-2)
Dundalk FC: Gary Rogers, Dane Massey, Andrew Boyle, Sean Gannon, Daniel Cleary (46.Sean Hoare), Chris Shields, Sean Murray (46.Patrick McEleney), John Mountney, Jamie McGrath (79.Georgie Kelly), Patrick Hoban, Michael Duffy. Trainer: Vinny Perth.
Slovan Bratislava: Dominik Greif, Vasil Bozhikov, Vernon, Jurij Medvedev (65.Mitch Apau), Myenty Abena, Marin Ljubicic, Dávid Holman, Joeri de Kamps, Aleksandar Cavric (61.Erik Daniel), Andraz Sporar, Rafael Ratão (85.Artem Sukhotsky). Trainer: Ján Kozák.
Goals: 12' Rafael Ratão 0-1, 33' Aleksandar Cavric 0-2, 70' Michael Duffy 1-2, 90+3' Erik Daniel 1-3.

15.08.2019; Ta'Qali National Stadium, Attard
Referee: Stephan Klossner (SUI); Attendance: 595
Valletta FC – ASTANA FC 0-4(0-2)
Valletta FC: Yenez Cini, Joseph Zerafa (54' Eslit Sala), Ryan Camilleri, Jean Borg, Douglas Packer, Rowen Muscat, Enmy Peña, Matteo Piciollo (62' Shaun Dimech), Kevin Tulimieri (62' Nicholas Pulis), Yuri, Mario Fontanella. Trainer: Darren Abdilla.
Astana FC: Nenad Eric, Antonio Rukavina, Dmitriy Shomko (80' Abzal Beysebekov), Evgeny Postnikov, Luka Simunovic, Rúnar Sigurjónsson (68' Zarko Tomasevic), Marin Tomasov, Ivan Maevski, Serikzhan Muzhikov (76' Rangelo Janga), Roman Murtazaev, Dorin Rotariu. Trainer: Roman Grygorchuk.
Goals: 25' Roman Murtazaev 0-1, 37' Marin Tomasov 0-2, 68' Roman Murtazaev 0-3, 89' Marin Tomasov 0-4.

15.08.2019; Friends Arena, Stockholm
Referee: Roi Reinshreiber (ISR); Attendance: 13,122
AIK STOCKHOLM – FC Sheriff Tiraspol 1-1(0-0)
AIK Stockholm: Oscar Linnér, Per Karlsson, Robert Lundström, Rasmus Lindkvist, Karol Mets, Daniel Granli, Sebastian Larsson, Enoch Adu, Anton Salétros (59.Nabil Bahoui), Tarik Elyounoussi (90+1.Panajotis Dimitriadis), Henok Goitom. Trainer: Rikard Norling.
FC Sheriff Tiraspol: Zvonimir Mikulic, Ousmane N'Diaye, Matej Palcic (67.Artem Hordienko), Andrej Lukic, Mateo Muzek (90.Jaroslaw Jach), Cristiano, Ariel Borysiuk, Jury Kendysh, Liridon Latifi, Gabrijel Boban, Robert Tambe (80.Wilfried Balima). Trainer: Zoran Zekic.
Goals: 61' Nabil Bahoui 1-0, 86' Gabrijel Boban 1-1.

15.08.2019; Marijampolės sporto centro stadione, Marijampolė
Referee: Tore Hansen (NOR); Attendance: 5,337
FK SŪDUVA MARIJAMPOLĖ – Maccabi Tel Aviv FC 2-1(2-0)
FK Sūdova Marijampolė: Ivan Kardum, Algis Jankauskas, Andro Svrljuga, Aleksandar Zivanovic, Semir Kerla, Jovan Cadjenovic, Ovidijus Verbickas (68.Ivan Hladík), Giedrius Matulevicius (79.Renan Oliveira), Josip Tadic (73.Eligijus Jankauskas), Mihret Topcagic, Paulius Golubickas. Trainer: Vladimir Cheburin.
Maccabi Tel Aviv: Andreas Gianniotis, Saborit (77.Dor Peretz), Geraldes, Shahar Piven-Bachtiar, Jair Amador, Avi Rikan (58.Matan Hozez), Dor Mikha, Dan Glazer, Itay Shechter (46.Nick Blackman), Chikeluba Ofoedu, Yonatan Cohen. Trainer: Vladimir Ivic.
Goals: 12' Mihret Topcagic 1-0, 45+1' Andro Svrljuga 2-0, 86' Nick Blackman 2-1.
Sent off: 90+4' Yonatan Cohen.

15.08.2019; Racecourse Ground, Wrexham
Referee: Kristo Tohver (EST); Attendance: 712
The New Saints – PFC LUDOGORETS RAZGRAD 0-4(0-2)
The New Saints: Paul Harrison, Christopher Marriott, Blaine Hudson, Keston Davies, Kane Lewis, Ryan Harrington, Aeron Edwards, Daniel Redmond, Ryan Brobbel (78.Adrian Cieslewicz), Jamie Mullan (74.Billy Whitehouse), Dean Ebbe (68.Kurtis Byrne). Trainer: Scott Ruscoe.
Ludogorets Razgrad: Renan, Stanislav Manolev, Dragos Grigore, Cicinho, Rafael Forster, Svetoslav Dyakov, Wanderson, Jacek Góralski (68.Dan Biton), Stéphane Badji, Jody Lukoki (75.Mavis Tchibota), Jakub Swierczok (81.Claudiu Keserü). Trainer: Stoicho Stoev.
Goals: 36' Jakub Swierczok 0-1, 42' Jody Lukoki 0-2, 77' Jakub Swierczok 0-3, 90+2' Dan Biton 0-4.

08.08.2019; Stadion Bilino Polje, Zenica
Referee: Alexander Boucaut (BEL); Attendance: 7,124
FK Sarajevo – FC BATE Borisov 1-2(0-1)
FK Sarajevo: Vladan Kovacevic, Bojan Letic, Darko Lazic, Besim Serbecic, Andrej Djokanovic (58.Alen Mustafic), Nebojsa Gavric (87.Gedeon Guzina), Anel Hebibovic, Haris Handzic, Krste Velkoski, Slobodan Milanovic (74.Aladin Sisic), Benjamin Tatar. Trainer: Husref Musemic.
BATE Borisov: Anton Chichkan, Aleksander Filipovic, Aleksey Rios, Igor Stasevich, Dmitriy Baga (89.Evgeniy Berezkin), Stanislav Dragun, Slobodan Simovic, Hervaine Moukam (73.Jasse Tuominen), Evgeni Yablonski, Zakhar Volkov, Maksim Skavysh (90+1.Bojan Dubajic). Trainer: Aleksei Baga.
Goals: 19' Dmitriy Baga 0-1, 71' Hervaine Moukam 0-2 (pen), 79' Haris Handzic 1-2.

15.08.2019; Borisov Arena, Borisov
Referee: Kevin Blom (NED); Attendance: 11,876
FC BATE BORISOV – FK Sarajevo 0-0
BATE Borisov: Anton Chichkan, Aleksander Filipovic, Aleksey Rios, Igor Stasevich, Dmitriy Baga, Stanislav Dragun (90+2.Evgeniy Berezkin), Slobodan Simovic, Hervaine Moukam (68.Jasse Tuominen), Evgeni Yablonski, Zakhar Volkov, Maksim Skavysh (79.Bojan Dubajic). Trainer: Aleksei Baga.
FK Sarajevo: Vladan Kovacevic, Bojan Letic, Darko Lazic, Besim Serbecic, Andrej Djokanovic (33.Alen Mustafic), Nebojsa Gavric (73.Slobodan Milanovic), Anel Hebibovic, Aladin Sisic, Haris Handzic, Krste Velkoski, Benjamin Tatar (53.Mersudin Ahmetovic). Trainer: Husref Musemic.

08.08.2019; Stade „Josy Barthel", Lëtzebuerg
Referee: Fábio José Costa Veríssimo (POR); Attendance: 1,239
F91 Dudelange – JK Nõmme Kalju 3-1(2-1)
F91 Dudelange: Tim Kips, Tom Schnell, Ricardo Delgado, Mehdi Kirch (90+1.Thibaut Lesquoy), Mohamed Bouchouari, Mario Pokar, Ryan Klapp, Dominik Stolz (85.Omar Natami), Charles Morren, Danel Sinani, Antoine Bernier. Trainer: Emilio Ferrera.
JK Nõmme Kalju: Pavel Londak, Aleksandr Kulinits, Maximiliano Uggè, Vladimir Avilov, Deniss Tjapkin, Andriy Markovych, Sander Puri, Igor Subbotin (73.Robert Kirss), Réginald Mbu-Alidor, Kasper Paur (60.Max Mata), Peeter Klein (85.Vladyslav Khomutov). Trainer: Roman Kozhukhovskyi.
Goals: 28', 30' Dominik Stolz 1-0, 2-0, 41' Sander Puri 2-1, 75' Dominik Stolz 3-1.
Sent off: 90' Robert Kirss.

13.08.2019; A. Le Coq Arena, Tallinn
Referee: Sergey Lapochkin (RUS); Attendance: 1,202
JK Nõmme Kalju – F91 DUDELANGE 0-1(0-0)
JK Nõmme Kalju: Pavel Londak, Aleksandr Kulinits, Maximiliano Uggè, Vladimir Avilov, Deniss Tjapkin, Andriy Markovych, Sander Puri (78.Aleksandr Volkov), Igor Subbotin (65.Max Mata), Kasper Paur (55.Réginald Mbu-Alidor), Vladyslav Khomutov, Peeter Klein. Trainer: Roman Kozhukhovskyi.
F91 Dudelange: Tim Kips, Tom Schnell, Ricardo Delgado, Mehdi Kirch, Mohamed Bouchouari, Mario Pokar (78.Sabir Bougrine), Ryan Klapp (78.Mickaël Garos), Dominik Stolz, Charles Morren, Danel Sinani (88.Corenthyn Lavie), Antoine Bernier. Trainer: Emilio Ferrera.
Goal: 56' Danel Sinani 0-1.
Sent off: 34' Vladyslav Khomutov.

LEAGUE PATH

08.08.2019; AEK Arena – George Karapatakis, Larnaca
Referee: Svein Oddvar Moen (NOR); Attendance: 3,360
AEK Larnaca FC – KAA Gent 1-1(0-1)
AEK Larnaca: Toño, Mikel González, Daniel Mojsov, Truyols (48.Raúl Ruiz), Ivan Trickovski, Lluis Sastre, Acorán (82.Florian Taulemesse), Nacho Cases, Hector Hevel, Apostolos Giannou, Tete (71.Jean Luc Assoubre). Trainer: Imanol Idiakez.
KAA Gent: Thomas Kaminski, Nana Asare, Mikael Lustig, Igor Plastun, Michael Ngadeu-Ngadjui, Vadis Odjidja-Ofoe, Brecht Dejaegere (57.Louis Verstraete), Elisha Owusu, Yuya Kubo (78.Alessio Castro-Montes), Roman Yaremchuk (62.Laurent Depoitre), Jonathan David. Trainer: Jess Thorup.
Goals: 26' Roman Yaremchuk 0-1, 88' Ivan Trickovski 1-1.

15.08.2019; GHELAMCO-arena, Gent
Referee: Martin Strömbergsson (SWE); Attendance: 15,533
KAA GENT – AEK Larnaca FC 3-0(0-0)
KAA Gent: Thomas Kaminski, Nana Asare, Mikael Lustig, Igor Plastun, Michael Ngadeu-Ngadjui, Vadis Odjidja-Ofoe, Brecht Dejaegere, Elisha Owusu, Laurent Depoitre (81.Alessio Castro-Montes), Roman Yaremchuk (87.Louis Verstraete), Jonathan David. Trainer: Jess Thorup.
AEK Larnaca: Toño, Mikel González, Daniel Mojsov, Truyols (73.Raúl Ruiz), Ivan Trickovski, Lluis Sastre, Acorán, Nacho Cases (83.Jean Luc Assoubre), Hector Hevel, Apostolos Giannou, Tete (73.Florian Taulemesse). Trainer: Imanol Idiakez.
Goals: 64' Laurent Depoitre 1-0, 90+3', 90+6' Jonathan David 2-0, 3-0.

08.08.2019; „Vazgen Sargsyan" anvan Hanrapetakan Marzadasht, Yerevan
Referee: Michael Fabbri (ITA); Attendance: 13,050
FC Pyunik Yerevan – Wolverhampton Wanderers FC 0-4(0-2)
Pyunik Yerevan: Andrija Dragojevic, Antonio Stankov, Maksim Zhestokov, Kristi Marku, Armen Manucharyan, Karlen Mkrtchyan, Sergiy Shevchuk, Artem Simonyan, Stanislav Efimov (55.Marko Burzanovic), Denis Mahmudov (63.Steven Alfred), Artur Miranyan. Trainer: Aleksandr Tarkhanov.
Wolverhampton Wanderers: Rui Patrício, Ryan Bennett, Willy Boly, Matt Doherty (63.Patrick Cutrone), Conor Coady, Rúben Vinagre, João Moutinho, Romain Saïss, Leander Dendoncker, Raúl Jiménez (71.Rúben Neves), Diogo Jota (63.Jonny Castro). Trainer: Nuno Espírito Santo.
Goals: 29' Matt Doherty 0-1, 42', 46' Raúl Jiménez 0-2, 0-3, 90+1' Rúben Neves 0-4 (pen).

15.08.2019; Molineux Stadium, Wolverhampton
Referee: Donatas Rumsas (LTU); Attendance: 29,391
WOLVERHAMPTON WANDERERS FC – FC Pyunik Yerevan 4-0(0-0)
Wolverhampton Wanderers: John Rudy, Conor Coady, Vallejo, Rúben Vinagre, Max Kilman, João Moutinho (52.Leander Dendoncker), Romain Saïss, Morgan Gibbs-White, Adama Traoré, Patrick Cutrone (72.Raúl Jiménez), Pedro Neto (72.Diogo Jota). Trainer: Nuno Espírito Santo.
Pyunik Yerevan: Andrija Dragojevic, Antonio Stankov, Maksim Zhestokov, Armen Manucharyan, Anton Belov, Karlen Mkrtchyan, Sergiy Shevchuk (75.Denis Mahmudov), Artem Simonyan (71.Artak Yedigaryan), Stanislav Efimov (46.Aleksandr Galimov), Erik Vardanyan, Artur Miranyan. Trainer: Aleksandr Tarkhanov.
Goals: 54' Pedro Neto 1-0, 58' Morgan Gibbs-White 2-0, 64' Rúben Vinagre 3-0, 87' Diogo Jota 4-0.

08.08.2019; Generali Arena, Praha
Referee: José Luis Munuera Montero (ESP)
AC Sparta Praha – Trabzonspor Kulübü 2-2(1-0)
Sparta Praha: Florin Nita, Lukás Stetina, Costa Nhamoinesu, Matej Hanousek, Michal Trávník (87.David Moberg-Karlsson), Guélor Kanga, Martin Hasek, Srdjan Plavsic (90.Dávid Hancko), Michal Sácek, Ladislav Krejcí, Benjamin Tetteh (79.Libor Kozák). Trainer: Václav Jílek.
Trabzonspor: Ugurcan Çakir, João Pereira, Filip Novák, Majid Hosseini, Hüseyin Türkmen, John Obi Mikel (46.Alexander Sørloth), José Sosa, Abdülkadir Parmak, Abdülkadir Ömür (76.Donis Avdijaj), Anthony Nwakaeme, Caleb Ekuban (90+3.Dogan Erdogan). Trainer: Ünal Karaman.
Goals: 16' Costa Nhamoinesu 1-0, 68' Guélor Kanga 2-0, 84' Caleb Ekuban 2-1, 89' Alexander Sørloth 2-2.

15.08.2019; Medical Park Stadyumu, Trabzon
Referee: Jakob Kehlet (DEN); Attendance: 34,462
TRABZONSPOR KULÜBÜ – AC Sparta Praha 2-1(1-0)
Trabzonspor: Ugurcan Çakir, João Pereira, Filip Novák, Majid Hosseini, Hüseyin Türkmen, José Sosa, Abdülkadir Parmak (84' Dogan Erdogan), Abdülkadir Ömür (90+9' Yusuf Sari), Anthony Nwakaeme, Alexander Sørloth (79' John Obi Mikel), Caleb Ekuban. Trainer: Ünal Karaman.
Sparta Praha: Florin Nita, Costa Nhamoinesu (61' Dávid Hancko), Uros Radakovic (67' Libor Kozák), Matej Hanousek, Guélor Kanga, Martin Hasek (76' Georges Mandjeck), Srdjan Plavsic, Michal Sácek, Ladislav Krejcí, Benjamin Tetteh, Adam Hlozek. Trainer: Václav Jílek.
Goals: 11' Alexander Sørloth 1-0, 78' Adam Hlozek 1-1. 90+8' Filip Novák 2-1.
Sent off: 88' Srdjan Plavsic.

08.08.2019; Stadionul „Ion Oblemenco", Craiova
Referee: Dennis Higler (NED); Attendance: 2,530
CS Universitatea Craiova – AEK Athína 0-2(0-0)
CS Universitatea Craiova: Mirko Pigliacelli, Renato Kelic, Marius Briceag, Nicusor Bancu, Stephane Acka, Alexandru Mateiu, Bogdan Vatajelu, Cristian Barbut (73.Alexandru Ionita), Antoni Ivanov (66.Kamer Qaka), Alexandru Cicâldau, Mihai Roman (II) (73.Carlos Fortes). Trainer: Corneliu Papura.
AEK Athína: Vasilios Barkas, Niklas Hult, Ognjen Vranjes, Paulinho, Efstratios Svarnas, David Simão (82.Nenad Krsticic), Petros Mandalos, André Simões, Chico Geraldes, Viktor Klonaridis (39.Marko Livaja), Daniele Verde (64.Nélson Oliveira). Trainer: Miguel Cardoso.
Goals: 60' Petros Mandalos 0-1, 85' Marko Livaja 0-2.

08.08.2019; Brøndby Stadion, Brøndby
Referee: Tamás Bognár (HUN); Attendance: 15,642
Brøndby IF – Sporting Clube de Braga 2-4(1-2)
Brøndby IF: Marvin Schwäbe, Paulus Arajuuri, Anthony Jung, Hjörtur Hermannsson, Kasper Fisker (58.Simon Tibbling), Dominik Kaiser, Josip Radosevic, Simon Hedlund, Kamil Wilczek, Kevin Mensah, Mikael Uhre (67.Jesper Lindstrøm). Trainer: Niels Frederiksen.
Sporting Braga: Matheus Magalhães, Ricardo Esgaio, Nuno Sequeira, Pablo Santos, Bruno Viana, Fransérgio (68.João Novais), João Palhinha, André Horta, Wilson Eduardo (70.Murilo), Paulinho (81.Ahmed Hassan Mahgoug "Koka"), Ricardo Horta. Trainer: Sá Pinto.
Goals: 15' Dominik Kaiser 1-0, 18' Paulinho 1-1, 20' André Horta 1-2, 50' Dominik Kaiser 2-2, 90+2' Ricardo Horta 2-3, 90+4' Hjörtur Hermannsson 2-4 (own goal).

08.08.2019; Daugava Stadions, Rīga
Referee: Filip Glova (SVK); Attendance: 472
FK Ventspils – Vitória SC Guimarães 0-3(0-1)
FK Ventspils: Vjaceslavs Kudrjavcevs, Jean Alcénat, Abdoul Mamah, Giorgi Mchedlishvili (74.Raens Tālbergs), Hélio Batista, Guga Palavandishvili (66.Pavel Osipov), Jevgenijs Kazacoks, Tosin Aiyegun, Kaspars Svārups, Mykhaylo Sergiychuk (54.Daniils Ulimbasevs), Lucas Villela. Trainer: Igor Klosovs.
Vitória Guimarães: João Miguel Silva, Florent Hanin, Pedrão, Falaye Sacko, Edmond Tapsoba, Rochinha (75.André Almeida), Pêpê Rodrigues, Almoatasembellah Ali Mohamed, Joseph Amoah, Alexandre Guedes (79.João Carlos Teixeira), Davidson (85.Lucas Soares). Trainer: Ivo Vieira.
Goals: 30' Davidson 0-1, 50' Pêpê Rodrigues 0-2, 80' Joseph Amoah 0-3.

08.08.2019; Haugesund Stadion, Haugesund
Referee: Matej Jug (SVN); Attendance: 5,150
FK Haugesund – PSV Eindhoven 0-1(0-1)
FK Haugesund: Helge Sandvik, Doug Bergqvist, Mikkel Desler, Benjamin Tiedemann Hansen, Sondre Tronstad, Thore Baardsen Pedersen, Niklas Sandberg, Bruno Leite (74.Joakim Nilsen), Kristoffer Velde, Shuaibu Ibrahim (57.Ibrahima Koné), Kevin Krygård (71.Christian Grindheim). Trainer: Jostein Grindhaug.
PSV Eindhoven: Jeroen Zoet, Nick Viergever, Timo Baumgartl, Denzel Dumfries, Gastón Pereiro (59.Cody Gakpo), Érick Gutiérrez (89.Jorrit Hendrix), Michal Sadílek, Pablo Rosario, Bruma (59.Hirving Lozano), Steven Bergwijn, Donyell Malen. Trainer: Mark van Bommel.
Goal: 24' Steven Bergwijn 0-1 (pen).

08.08.2019; Aker Stadion, Molde
Referee: Maurizio Mariani (ITA); Attendance: 3,953
Molde FK – Aris Thessaloníki 3-0(2-0)
Molde FK: Álex Craninx, Ruben Gabrielsen, Kristoffer Haraldseid, Kristoffer Haugen, Martin Bjørnbak, Magnus Eikrem, Etzaz Hussain (75.Martin Ellingsen), Eirik Hestad (90+3.Mattias Mostrøm), Fredrik Aursnes, Ohi Omoijuanfo (85.Erling Knudtzon), Leke James. Trainer: Erling Moe.
Aris Thessaloníki: Julián Cuesta, Daniel Sundgren, Mihály Korhut, Lindsay Rose, Fran Vélez, Nicolas Diguiny, Migjen Basha (69.Georgios Delizisis), Javier Matilla, Lucas Sasha, Martín Tonso (75.Ioannis Fetfatzidis), Brown Ideye (81.Daniel Larsson). Trainer: Savvas Pantelidis.
Goals: 27' Magnus Eikrem 1-0, 32' Eirik Hestad 2-0, 87' Martin Ellingsen 3-0.; Sent off: 64' Fran Vélez.

15.08.2019; Stádio Olympiako „Spyros Louis", Athína
Referee: Jérôme Brisard (FRA)
AEK ATHÍNA – CS Universitatea Craiova 1-1(1-0)
AEK Athína: Vasilios Barkas, Ognjen Vranjes, Paulinho, Hélder Lopes, Efstratios Svarnas, Nenad Krsticic (58.David Simão), Petros Mandalos, André Simões (83.Konstantinos Galanopoulos), Chico Geraldes, Nélson Oliveira, Marko Livaja (58.Daniele Verde). Trainer: Miguel Cardoso.
CS Universitatea Craiova: Mirko Pigliacelli, Renato Kelic, Ivan Martic, Nicusor Bancu, Stephane Acka, Alexandru Mateiu, Cristian Barbut, Antoni Ivanov (80.Vasile Constantin), Alexandru Cicâldau, Valentin Mihaila (55.Bogdan Vatajelu), Mihai Roman (II) (64.Carlos Fortes). Trainer: Corneliu Papura.
Goals: 26' Petros Mandalos 1-0, 63' Antoni Ivanov 1-1.

15.08.2019; Estádio Municipal de Braga, Braga
Referee: Aleksei Eskov (RUS); Attendance: 11,964
SPORTING CLUBE DE BRAGA – Brøndby IF 3-1(2-0)
Sporting Braga: Matheus Magalhães, Ricardo Esgaio, Pablo Santos (71.Vítor Tormena), Caju, Bruno Viana, João Novais, João Palhinha, André Horta (59.Bruno Xadas), Wilson Eduardo (67.Francisco Trincão), Paulinho, Murilo. Trainer: Sá Pinto.
Brøndby IF: Marvin Schwäbe, Paulus Arajuuri, Anthony Jung, Hjörtur Hermannsson, Jens Gammelby, Dominik Kaiser (46.Kasper Fisker), Josip Radosevic, Simon Hedlund (73.Peter Bjur), Tobias Børkeeiet, Jesper Lindstrøm, Kamil Wilczek (46.Ante Erceg). Trainer: Niels Frederiksen.
Goals: 19' João Palhinha 1-0, 41' André Horta 2-0, 66' Paulinho 3-0, 85' Peter Bjur 3-1.

14.08.2019; Estádio „Dom Afonso Henriques", Guimarães
Referee: Halil Umut Meler (TUR); Attendance: 12,741
VITÓRIA SC GUIMARÃES – FK Ventspils 6-0(1-0)
Vitória Guimarães: João Miguel Silva, Florent Hanin, Pedrão, Falaye Sacko, Edmond Tapsoba, Rochinha, Pêpê Rodrigues, Almoatasembellah Ali Mohamed, Joseph Amoah (7.André Almeida), Alexandre Guedes (63.João Pedro), Davidson (76.João Carlos Teixeira). Trainer: Ivo Vieira.
FK Ventspils: Vjaceslavs Kudrjavcevs, Jean Alcénat (52.Pavel Osipov), Abdoul Mamah, Giorgi Mchedlishvili, Hélio Batista, Rashid Obuobi (58.Daniils Ulimbasevs), Guga Palavandishvili, Ingars Stuglis (35.Kaspars Svārups), Tosin Aiyegun, Mykhaylo Sergiychuk, Lucas Villela. Trainer: Igor Klosovs.
Goals: 28' Davidson 1-0, 48', 58' Rochinha 2-0, 3-0, 79' João Carlos Teixeira 4-0, 80' João Pedro 5-0, 86' Pêpê Rodrigues 6-0.

15.08.2019; Stadion Philips, Eindhoven
Referee: Juan Martínez Munuera (ESP); Attendance: 22,759
PSV EINDHOVEN – FK Haugesund 0-0
PSV Eindhoven: Jeroen Zoet, Nick Viergever, Timo Baumgartl, Denzel Dumfries (46.Jordan Teze), Érick Gutiérrez, Michal Sadílek, Pablo Rosario, Bruma (59.Mohammed Ihattaren), Steven Bergwijn, Donyell Malen, Cody Gakpo. Trainer: Mark van Bommel.
FK Haugesund: Helge Sandvik, Doug Bergqvist, Mikkel Desler, Benjamin Tiedemann Hansen, Sondre Tronstad, Thore Baardsen Pedersen, Niklas Sandberg, Bruno Leite (85.Joakim Nilsen), Kristoffer Velde, Kevin Krygård (75.Christian Grindheim), Ibrahima Koné (70.Martin Samuelsen). Trainer: Jostein Grindhaug.

15.08.2019; Stadio "Kleánthis Vikelídis", Thessaloníki
Referee: Robert Harvey (IRL); Attendance: 12,821
Aris Thessaloníki – MOLDE FK 3-1(2-0,3-0)
Aris Thessaloníki: Julián Cuesta, Daniel Sundgren, Mihály Korhut (104.Migjen Basha), Lindsay Rose, Georgios Delizisis, Nicolas Diguiny, Javier Matilla, Ioannis Fetfatzidis (79.Hamza Younès), Lucas Sasha, Daniel Larsson (64.Nicolás Martínez), Brown Ideye (102.Martín Tonso). Trainer: Savvas Pantelidis.
Molde FK: Álex Craninx, Ruben Gabrielsen, Kristoffer Haraldseid, Kristoffer Haugen (55.Vegard Forren), Martin Bjørnbak, Magnus Eikrem (75.Martin Ellingsen), Etzaz Hussain, Eirik Hestad (99.Erling Knudtzon), Fredrik Aursnes, Ohi Omoijuanfo (88.Mathis Bolly), Leke James. Trainer: Erling Moe.
Goals: 25' Javier Matilla 1-0, 37' Georgios Delizisis 2-0, 84' Nicolas Diguiny 3-0, 105+1' Mathis Bolly 3-1.

08.08.2019; Stadion Chornomorets, Odessa
Referee: Michael Tykgaard (DEN); Attendance: 4,426
FK Mariupol – AZ Alkmaar 0-0
FC Mariupol: Rustam Khudzhamov, Pavel Polegenko, Sergiy Chobotenko, Oleksii Bykov, Valeriy Fedorchuk, Igor Tyshchenko (86.Igor Kyryukhantsev), Vyacheslav Churko, Dmytro Myshnov, Sergiy Gorbunov (76.Joyskim Dawa), Maksym Chekh (63.Vyacheslav Tankovskiy), Vladislav Vakula. Trainer: Oleksandr Babych.
AZ Alkmaar: Marco Bizot, Ron Vlaar, Stijn Wuytens (73.Jordy Clasie), Jonas Svensson (80.Yukinari Sugawara), Thomas Ouwejan, Owen Wijndal, Fredrik Midtsjø (86.Albert Gudmundsson), Teun Koopmeiners, Oussama Idrissi, Myron Boadu, Calvin Stengs. Trainer: Arne Slot.

08.08.2019; Stockhorn Arena, Thun
Referee: Irfan Peljto (BIH); Attendance: 6,150
FC Thun – FK Spartak Moskva 2-3(0-2)
FC Thun: Guillaume Faivre, Stefan Glarner, Nikki Havenaar, Miguel Rodrigues, Sven Joss (77.Dennis Salanovic), Roy Gelmi, Miguel Castroman, Basil Stillhart, Nias Hefti, Simone Rapp, Ridge Munsy (46.Matteo Tosetti). Trainer: Marc Schneider.
Spartak Moskva: Aleksandr Maksimenko, Georgi Dzhikiya, Samuel Gigot, Ayrton, Nikolai Rasskazov, Jano Ananidze (60.André Schürrle), Roman Zobnin, Reziuan Mirzov (72.Aleksandr Tashaev), Ayaz Guliev, Zelimkhan Bakaev (87.Lorenzo Melgarejo), Ezequiel Ponce. Trainer: Oleg Kononov.
Goals: 22' Ezequiel Ponce 0-1, 29' Zelimkhan Bakaev 0-2, 52' Nias Hefti 1-2, 59' Simone Rapp 2-2, 73' Zelimkhan Bakaev 2-3.

08.08.2019; Swedbank Stadion, Malmö
Referee: Stuart Attwell (ENG); Attendance: 14,103
Malmö FF – HŠK Zrinjski Mostar 3-0(1-0)
Malmö FF: Johan Dahlin, Behrang Safari, Rasmus Bengtsson, Eric Larsson, Søren Rieks, Anders Christiansen (82.Bonke Innocent), Fouad Bachirou, Oscar Lewicki, Markus Rosenberg, Guillermo Molins (78.Marcus Antonsson), Jo Inge Berget (78.Franz Brorsson). Trainer: Uwe Rösler.
Zrinjski Mostar: Ivan Brkic, Tomislav Barbaric, Dario Rugasevic (79.Mario Ticinovic), Slobodan Jakovljevic, Advan Kadusic, Damir Sovsic (61.Damir Zlomislic), Frane Cirjak, Edin Rustemovic, Miljan Govedarica, Stanisa Mandic, Irfan Hadzic (67.Ivan Lendric). Trainer: Hari Vukas.
Goals: 36' Rasmus Bengtsson 1-0, 66' Anders Christiansen 2-0, 74' Søren Rieks 3-0.

08.08.2019; Bakcell Arena, Bakı
Referee: Karim Abed (FRA); Attendance: 10,000
Neftçi PFK Bakı – Bnei Yehuda Tel Aviv FC 2-2(1-2)
Neftçi Bakı: Salahat Agayev, Vojislav Stankovic (87.Mamadou Mbodj), Kyrylo Petrov, Anton Krivotsyuk, Omar Buludov, Soni Mustivar, Vangelis Platelas (80.Bagaliy Dabo), Emin Makhmudov, Steeven Joseph-Monrose, Rauf Aliyev (73.Namiq Alasgarov), Dário Júnior da Silva. Trainer: Roberto Bordin.
Bnei Yehuda: Emilijus Zubas, Dan Mori, Alban Pnishi, Shay Mazor (89.Paz Ben Ari), Daniel Felscher, Amir Rustom, Tamabi Sages, Ismaila Soro, Mohammad Ghadir (69.Ariel Matan Lazmi), Dor Jan (84.Dor Kochav), Avishay Cohen. Trainer: Yossi Abukasis.
Goals: 26' Tamabi Sages 0-1, 36' Mohammad Ghadir 0-2, 43' Steeven Joseph-Monrose 1-2, 90+7' Namiq Alasgarov 2-2.

08.08.2019; Stade „Roi Baudouin", Bruxelles
Referee: Jens Maae (DEN); Attendance: 15,734
Royal Antwerp FC – FC Viktoria Plzeň 1-0(1-0)
Royal Antwerp FC: Sinan Bolat, Simen Juklerød, Buta, Abdoulaye Seck, Júnior Pius (26.Dylan Batubinsika), Faris Haroun, Lior Refaelov (87.Amara Baby), Geoffry Hairemans (61.Didier Lamkel Zé), Alexis De Sart, Dieumerci Mbokani, Ivo Rodrigues. Trainer: László Bölöni.
FC Viktoria Plzeň: Ales Hruska, Radim Rezník, David Limbersky, Jakub Brabec, Lukás Hejda (46.Tomás Horava), Jan Kovarík (68.Joel Kayamba), Jan Kopic, Patrik Hrosovsky, Lukás Kalvach, Dominik Janosek, Michal Krmencík (84.Tomás Chory). Trainer: Pavel Vrba.
Goals: 29' Ivo Rodrigues 1-0.

15.08.2019; Cars Jeans Stadion, Den Haag
Referee: Bartosz Frankowski (POL); Attendance: 8,018
AZ ALKMAAR – FK Mariupol 4-0(2-0)
AZ Alkmaar: Marco Bizot, Ron Vlaar (80.Pantelis Hatzidiakos), Stijn Wuytens (75.Jordy Clasie), Jonas Svensson, Thomas Ouwejan, Owen Wijndal, Fredrik Midtsjø, Teun Koopmeiners, Oussama Idrissi, Myron Boadu (69.Ferdy Druijf), Calvin Stengs. Trainer: Arne Slot.
FC Mariupol: Rustam Khudzhamov, Sergey Yavorskiy, Pavel Polegenko, Igor Kyryukhantsev, Sergiy Chobotenko, Oleksii Bykov (46.Viktor Korniienko), Valeriy Fedorchuk, Vyacheslav Tankovskiy, Vyacheslav Churko (69.Dmytro Topalov), Dmytro Myshnov (83.Oleksii Kashchuk), Vladislav Vakula. Trainer: Oleksandr Babych.
Goals: 20' Calvin Stengs 1-0, 44' Thomas Ouwejan 2-0, 62' Stijn Wuytens 3-0, 90' Sergey Yavorskiy 4-0 (own goal).

15.08.2019; Otkrytie Arena, Moskva
Referee: Srdjan Jovanovic (SRB); Attendance: 33,076
FK SPARTAK MOSKVA – FC Thun 2-1(0-1)
Spartak Moskva: Aleksandr Maksimenko, Andrey Eshchenko, Georgi Dzhikiya, Samuel Gigot, Ayrton, André Schürrle (88.Jano Ananidze), Roman Zobnin, Reziuan Mirzov (70.Lorenzo Melgarejo), Ayaz Guliev, Zelimkhan Bakaev (77.Georgi Melkadze), Ezequiel Ponce. Trainer: Oleg Kononov.
FC Thun: Guillaume Faivre, Stefan Glarner, Nikki Havenaar, Nicola Sutter (79.Dennis Salanovic), Sven Joss (71.Ridge Munsy), Chris Kablan, Miguel Castroman, Basil Stillhart, Kenan Fatkic (63.Roy Gelmi), Nias Hefti, Simone Rapp. Trainer: Marc Schneider.
Goals: 7' Stefan Glarner 0-1, 52' Ezequiel Ponce 1-1, 58' André Schürrle 2-1.

15.08.2019; Stadion Pecara, Sikori Brijeg
Referee: Artyom Kuchin (KAZ); Attendance: 4,509
HŠK Zrinjski Mostar – MALMÖ FF 1-0(0-0)
Zrinjski Mostar: Ivan Brkic, Mario Ticinovic (72.Marko Bencun), Tomislav Barbaric, Slobodan Jakovljevic, Advan Kadusic, Ivan Curjuric (81.Frane Cirjak), Damir Sovsic, Edin Rustemovic, Miljan Govedarica, Stanisa Mandic (65.Pero Stojkic), Ivan Lendric. Trainer: Hari Vukas.
Malmö FF: Johan Dahlin, Behrang Safari, Rasmus Bengtsson, Eric Larsson, Lasse Nielsen, Jonas Knudsen, Anders Christiansen (68.Arnór Ingvi Traustason), Fouad Bachirou, Oscar Lewicki, Markus Rosenberg (87.Romain Gall), Marcus Antonsson (6.Guillermo Molins). Trainer: Uwe Rösler.
Goal: 90+1' Damir Sovsic 1-0 (pen).

15.08.2019; HaMoshava Stadium, Petah Tikva
Referee: Daniele Doveri (ITA); Attendance: 4,000
BNEI YEHUDA TEL AVIV FC – Neftçi Bakı 2-1(1-0)
Bnei Yehuda: Emilijus Zubas, Dan Mori, Alban Pnishi, Shay Mazor (74.Shimshon Tza'adon), Daniel Felscher, Amir Rustom, Tamabi Sages, Ismaila Soro, Mohammad Ghadir (78.Ariel Matan Lazmi), Dor Jan (88.Ben Shimoni), Avishay Cohen. Trainer: Yossi Abukasis.
Neftçi Bakı: Salahat Agayev, Kyrylo Petrov, Mamadou Mbodj, Anton Krivotsyuk, Omar Buludov (63.Bagaliy Dabo), Soni Mustivar, Emin Makhmudov, Mamadou Kane (46.Rahman Hadzhiyev), Steeven Joseph-Monrose, Rauf Aliyev, Dário Júnior da Silva (81.Vangelis Platelas). Trainer: Roberto Bordin.
Goals: 15' Dor Jan 1-0, 66' Tamabi Sages 2-0, 90+3' Emin Makhmudov 2-1 (pen).

15.08.2019; Doosan Aréna, Plzeň
Referee: Davide Massa (ITA); Attendance: 9,717
Viktoria Plzeň – ROYAL ANTWERP FC 2-1(0-0,1-0)
FC Viktoria Plzeň: Ales Hruska, David Limbersky, Jakub Brabec, Lukás Hejda, Milan Havel (114' Radim Rezník), Tomás Horava, Jan Kopic, Patrik Hrosovsky, Lukás Kalvach (75' Tomás Chory), Joel Kayamba (107' Adam Hlousek), Michal Krmencík (102' Ondrej Mihálik). Trainer: Pavel Vrba.
Royal Antwerp FC: Sinan Bolat, Simen Juklerød, Dylan Batubinsika, Buta, Abdoulaye Seck, Faris Haroun, Lior Refaelov, Geoffry Hairemans (94' Amara Baby), Alexis De Sart (106' Sander Coopman), Ivo Rodrigues (84' Didier Lamkel Zé), Jonathan Bolingi (45' Dieumerci Mbokani). Trainer: László Bölöni.
Goals: 81', 97' Michal Krmencík 1-0, 2-0, 113' Dieumerci Mbokani 2-1.
Sent off: 101' Abdoulaye Seck.

08.08.2019; Stadion Lokomotiv, Plovdiv
Referee: João Pedro Pinheiro (POR); Attendance: 7,600
PFC Lokomotiv Plovdiv – Racing Club de Strasbourg 0-1(0-1)
Lokomotiv Plovdiv: Martin Lukov, Milos Petrovic, Josip Tomasevic, Stephen Eze, Dimitar Iliev, Momchil Tsvetanov, Parvizchon Umarbaev (67.Wiris), Petar Vitanov (83.Georgi Iliev), Birsent Karagaren, Alen Ozbolt (67.David Malembana), Ante Aralica. Trainer: Bruno Akrapovic.
RC Strasbourg: Matz Sels, Lamine Koné, Stefan Mitrovic, Abdallah N'Dour, Alexander Djiku, Mohamed Simakan, Jonas Martin, Ibrahima Sissoko, Jean Ricner Bellegarde (83.Kévin Lucien Zohi), Youssouf Fofana (65.Kenny Lala), Nuno Da Costa (76.Ludovic Ajorque). Trainer: Thierry Laurey.
Goal: 11' Stefan Mitrovic 0-1.
Sent off: 11' Josip Tomasevic.

08.08.2019; Stadion Feijenoord, Rotterdam
Referee: Serhiy Boyko (UKR); Attendance: 36,500
Feyenoord Rotterdam – FC Dinamo Tbilisi 4-0(1-0)
Feyenoord Rotterdam: Kenneth Vermeer, Jan-Arie van der Heijden, Eric Botteghin, Ridgeciano Haps, Bart Nieuwkoop (46.Lutsharel Geertruida), Leroy Fer, Renato Tapia (77.Wouter Burger), Orkun Kökçü, Steven Berghuis, Sam Larsson, Luis Sinisterra (72.Luciano Narsingh). Trainer: Jaap Stam.
Dinamo Tbilisi: José Perales, Gudzha Rukhaia, Giorgi Kimadze, Víctor Mongil, Davit Kobouri, Nika Ninua, Levan Kutalia, Giorgi Kukhianidze (77.Bakar Kardava), Giorgi Papava, Nodar Kavtaradze (86.Kwame Karikari), Levan Shengelia (46.Akaki Shulaia). Trainer: Félix Vicente Miranda.
Goals: 43' Luis Sinisterra 1-0, 82' Davit Kobouri 2-0 (own goal), 85' Steven Berghuis 3-0 (pen), 88' Luciano Narsingh 4-0.
Sent off: 79' Akaki Shulaia.

08.08.2019; Nationalen Stadion "Vasil Levski", Sofia
Referee: Sandro Schärer (SUI); Attendance: 15,310
PFC CSKA Sofia – FK Zorya Luhansk 1-1(1-1)
CSKA Sofia: Vytautas Cerniauskas, Petar Zanev, Kristiyan Malinov, Raúl Albentosa, Nuno Tomás, Geferson (77.Viv Solomon-Otabor), Ivan Turitsov (62.Diego Fabbrini), Tiago Rodrigues, Janio Bikel, Ali Sowe, Evandro (82.Graham Carey). Trainer: Ljubomir Petrovic.
Zorya Luhansk: Mykyta Shevchenko, Vitaliy Vernidub, Dmitriy Ivanisenya (70.Levan Arveladze), Oleksandr Tymchyk, Joel Abu Hanna, Dmytro Khomchenovsky, Vladlen Yurchenko (65.Nazariy Rusyn), Bogdan Mykhaylichenko, Vladyslav Kochergin, Pylyp Budkovsky, Maksym Lunyov (65.Bohdan Lednev). Trainer: Viktor Skripnik.
Goals: 13' Evandro 1-0, 45+1' Vladlen Yurchenko 1-1 (pen).

08.08.2019; Östgötaporten, Norrköping
Referee: Pol van Boekel (NED); Attendance: 6,479
IFK Norrköping – Hapoel Be'er Sheva FC 1-1(0-0)
IFK Norrköping: Isak Pettersson, Lars Gerson, Kasper Larsen, Filip Dagerstål, Rasmus Lauritsen, Simon Thern, Alexander Fransson, Sead Haksabanovic, Maic Sema (69.Kalle Holmberg), Christoffer Nyman, Simon Skrabb (85.Gudmundur Thórarinsson). Trainer: Jens Gustafsson.
Hapoel Be'er Sheva: Ernestas Setkus, Ben Bitton, Loai Taha, Sean Goldberg, Amit Biton, Marwan Kabha, Ramzi Safouri (90.Jimmy Marín), Eden Shamir, David Keltjens, Nigel Hasselbaink (82.Ben Sahar), José Carrillo (76.Niv Zrihan). Trainer: Barak Bakhar.
Goals: 51' Maic Sema 1-0, 55' Eden Shamir 1-1.

08.08.2019; MCH Arena, Herning
Referee: Kristo Tohver (EST); Attendance: 9,322
FC Midtjylland – Glasgow Rangers FC 2-4(0-1)
FC Midtjylland: Jesper Hansen, Erik Sviatchenko, Alexander Scholz, Joel Andersson, Rasmus Nicolaisen (73.Awer Mabil), Tim Sparv (58.Júnior Brumado), Gustav Wikheim (58.Mikael Anderson), Evander, Frank Onyeka, Jens-Lys Cajuste, Sory Kaba. Trainer: Kenneth Andersen.
Glasgow Rangers: Allan McGregor, James Tavernier, Connor Goldson, John Flanagan, Nikola Katic, Scott Arfield (82.Greg Docherty), Ryan Jack, Glen Kamara, Joe Aribo, Jordan Jones (82.Sheyi Ojo), Alfredo Morelos. Trainer: Steven Gerrard.
Goals: 43' Alfredo Morelos 0-1, 52' Joe Aribo 0-2, 56' Nikola Katic 0-3, 58' Frank Onyeka 1-3, 63' Sory Kaba 2-3, 70' Scott Arfield 2-4.

15.08.2019; Stade de la Meinau, Strasbourg
Referee: John Beaton (SCO); Attendance: 19,109
RACING CLUB DE STRASBOURG – PFC Lokomotiv Plovdiv 1-0(1-0)
RC Strasbourg: Matz Sels, Lamine Koné, Stefan Mitrovic, Lionel Carole, Abdallah N'Dour, Mohamed Simakan (83.Jonas Martin), Benjamin Corgnet (77.Kenny Lala), Dimitri Liénard, Ibrahima Sissoko, Nuno Da Costa (65.Ludovic Ajorque), Kévin Lucien Zohi. Trainer: Thierry Laurey.
Lokomotiv Plovdiv: Martin Lukov, Milos Petrovic, David Malembana, Stephen Eze, Dimitar Iliev, Momchil Tsvetanov, Parvizchon Umarbaev (77.Georgi Iliev), Petar Vitanov (63.Wiris), Birsent Karagaren (83.Eliton Pardinho Junior), Alen Ozbolt, Ante Aralica. Trainer: Bruno Akrapovic.
Goal: 8' Kévin Lucien Zohi 1-0.

15.08.2019; „Boris Paichadze" Dinamo Arena, Tbilisi
Referee: Sascha Stegemann (GER)
FC Dinamo Tbilisi – FEYENOORD ROTTERDAM 1-1(0-0)
Dinamo Tbilisi: José Perales, Gudzha Rukhaia, Giorgi Kimadze (80.Irakli Azarov), Víctor Mongil, Davit Kobouri (37.Mychailo Shyshka), Nika Ninua, Abdel Jalil Medioub, Giorgi Papava, Nodar Kavtaradze (69.Nodar Iashvili), Bakar Kardava, Levan Shengelia. Trainer: Félix Vicente Miranda.
Feyenoord Rotterdam: Kenneth Vermeer, Jan-Arie van der Heijden, Eric Botteghin (70.Liam Kelly), Ridgeciano Haps (70.Tyrell Malacia), Lutsharel Geertruida, Renato Tapia, Orkun Kökçü, Wouter Burger, Luciano Narsingh, Steven Berghuis (79.Naoufal Bannis), Sam Larsson. Trainer: Jaap Stam.
Goals: 52' Levan Shengelia 1-0, 57' Eric Botteghin 1-1.

15.08.2019; Slavutych-Arena, Zaporizhia
Referee: Amaury Delerue (FRA); Attendance: 7,857
FK ZORYA LUHANSK – PFC CSKA Sofia 1-0(0-0)
Zorya Luhansk: Mykyta Shevchenko, Vitaliy Vernidub, Dmitriy Ivanisenya, Oleksandr Tymchyk, Joel Abu Hanna (4.Yevgen Cheberko), Dmytro Khomchenovsky, Vladlen Yurchenko (46.Bohdan Lednev), Bogdan Mykhaylichenko, Vladyslav Kochergin, Pylyp Budkovsky (90+4.Vladyslav Kabayev), Nazariy Rusyn. Trainer: Viktor Skripnik.
CSKA Sofia: Vytautas Cerniauskas, Petar Zanev, Kristiyan Malinov (82.Diego Fabbrini), Raúl Albentosa, Nuno Tomás, Geferson (87.Tony Watt), Ivan Turitsov, Tiago Rodrigues, Janio Bikel, Ali Sowe, Evandro (56.Mitko Mitkov). Trainer: Ljubomir Petrovic.
Goal: 89' Nazariy Rusyn 1-0.
Sent off: 22' Ivan Turitsov, 90' Nazariy Rusyn.

15.08.2019; „Yaakov Turner Toto" Stadium, Beersheva
Referee: Anastasios Papapetrou (GRE); Attendance: 10,088
HAPOEL BE'ER SHEVA FC – IFK Norrköping 3-1(0-0)
Hapoel Be'er Sheva: Ernestas Setkus, Ben Bitton, Loai Taha, Sean Goldberg, Amit Biton, Marwan Kabha, Ramzi Safouri (84' Jimmy Marín), Eden Shamir, David Keltjens, Ben Sahar (60' Niv Zrihan), Nigel Hasselbaink (78' José Carrillo). Trainer: Barak Bakhar.
IFK Norrköping: Isak Pettersson, Lars Gerson, Kasper Larsen, Filip Dagerstål, Rasmus Lauritsen, Gudmundur Thórarinsson, Simon Thern, Alexander Fransson, Sead Haksabanovic (78' Egzon Binaku), Christoffer Nyman (88' Kalle Holmberg), Simon Skrabb (78' Henrik Castegren). Trainer: Jens Gustafsson.
Goals: 67' Niv Zrihan 1-0, 72' Nigel Hasselbaink 2-0, 82' Rasmus Lauritsen 2-1, 90+4' Niv Zrihan 3-1.

15.08.2019; Ibrox Stadium, Glasgow
Referee: Marco Di Bello (ITA); Attendance: 47,184
GLASGOW RANGERS FC – FC Midtjylland 3-1(2-0)
Glasgow Rangers: Allan McGregor, James Tavernier, Connor Goldson, John Flanagan, Nikola Katic, Steven Davis, Scott Arfield, Ryan Jack (69.Greg Docherty), Glen Kamara, Sheyi Ojo (69.Jordan Jones), Alfredo Morelos (81.Jermain Defoe). Trainer: Steven Gerrard.
FC Midtjylland: Jesper Hansen, Erik Sviatchenko, Alexander Scholz, Joel Andersson, Rasmus Nicolaisen, Gustav Wikheim, Evander, Mikael Anderson (69.Tim Sparv), Frank Onyeka, Jens-Lys Cajuste (46.Awer Mabil), Sory Kaba (82.Artem Dovbyk). Trainer: Kenneth Andersen.
Goals: 14' Alfredo Morelos 1-0, 39' Sheyi Ojo 2-0, 49' Alfredo Morelos 3-0, 72' Evander 3-1.

08.08.2019; Stadion Rujevica, Rijeka
Referee: Ricardo de Burgos Bengoetxea (ESP); Attendance: 6,452
HNK Rijeka – Aberdeen FC 2-0(0-0)
NK Rijeka: Andrej Prskalo, Ivan Tomecak (75.Momcilo Raspopovic), Roberto Puncec, Dario Zuparic, Zoran Kvrzic, Luka Capan (85.Dani Iglesias), Tibor Halilovic, Stipe Loncar, Ivan Lepinjica, Antonio Colak, Boadu Maxwell Acosty (64.Robert Muric). Trainer: Igor Biscan.
Aberdeen FC: Joe Lewis, Andrew Considine, Shay Logan, Gregory Leigh, Scott McKenna, Funso Ojo, Lewis Ferguson, Niall McGinn (76.Dean Campbell), Ryan Hedges (86.Curtis Main), Sam Cosgrove, Jon Gallagher (76.Scott Wright). Trainer: Derek McInnes.
Goals: 62' Antonio Colak 1-0 (pen), 88' Robert Muric 2-0.

08.08.2019; Generali Arena, Wien
Referee: Massimoliano Irrati (ITA); Attendance: 8,165
FK Austria Wien – Apollon Limassol FC 1-2(1-1)
Austria Wien: Ivan Lucic, Michael Madl, Florian Klein, Christoph Martschinko, Maudo, Alexander Grünwald, Thomas Ebner (79.Manprit Sarkaria), James Jeggo (58.Christoph Monschein), Tarkan Serbest, Dominik Prokop, Bright Edomwonyi (68.Dominik Fitz). Trainer: Christian Ilzer.
Apollon Limassol: Joël Mall, Charis Kyriakou, Attila Szalai, Facundo Pereyra (75.Emilio N'Sue), Héctor Yuste, Sasa Markovic, Diego Aguirre (85.Giorgos Vasiliou), Serge Gakpé, João Pedro, Adrián Sardinero, Giannis Gianniotas (63.Ioannis Pittas). Trainer: Sofronis Avgousti.
Goals: 14' Sasa Markovic 0-1 (pen), 41' Florian Klein 1-1 (pen), 50' Serge Gakpé 1-2.; Sent off: 90+2' Michael Madl.

08.08.2019; Rheinpark Stadion, Vaduz
Referee: Paul Tierney (ENG); Attendance: 5,908
FC Vaduz – Eintracht Frankfurt 0-5(0-3)
FC Vaduz: Benjamin Büchel, Denis Simani, Maximilian Göppel, Pius Dorn, Yannick Schmid, Berkay Sülüngöz, Boris Prokopic, Sandro Wieser (75.Aron Sele), Mohamed Coulibaly, Manuel Sutter (46.Dominik Schwizer), Tunahan Çiçek (66.Noah Frick). Trainer: Mario Frick.
Eintracht Frankfurt: Felix Wiedwald, Makoto Hasebe, David Abraham, Martin Hinteregger, Danny da Costa, Gelson Fernandes (66.Jonathan de Guzmán), Filip Kostic, Mijat Gacinovic, Dominik Kohr, Daichi Kamada (73.Ante Rebic), Gonçalo Paciência (73.Dejan Joveljic). Trainer: Adi Hütter.
Goals: 11', 27' Filip Kostic 0-1, 0-2, 40' Dominik Kohr 0-3, 53' Gonçalo Paciência 0-4, 63' Mijat Gacinovic 0-5.

08.08.2019; Stadionul „Marin Anastasovici", Giurgiu
Referee: Adrien Jaccottet (SUI); Attendance: 2,315
SC FCSB Bucureşti – FK Mladá Boleslav 0-0
FCSB Bucureşti: Andrei Daniel Vlad, Valentin Cretu, Aristides Soiledis, Bogdan Planic, Iulian Cristea, Lucian Filip (32.Ionut Pantîru), Ionut Vîna, Ovidiu Popescu (46.Thierry Moutinho), Razvan Oaida, Florin Tanase (80.Lukasz Gikiewicz), Florinel Coman. Trainer: Vergil Andronache.
FK Mladá Boleslav: Jan Seda, Daniel Pudil, Laco Takács, Antonín Krapka, Marco Tulio, Marek Matejovsky (75.Lukás Budínsky), Michal Hubínek, Tomás Ladra (65.Jakub Fulnek), Pavel Bucha, Muris Mesanovic (88.Jonas Auer), Nikolay Komlichenko. Trainer: Jozef Weber.

08.08.2019; Stadio Olimpico Grande Torino, Torino
Referee: Daniel Stefanski (POL); Attendance: 15,977
Torino FC – FC Shakhtyor Solihorsk 5-0(2-0)
Torino FC: Salvatore Sirigu, Lorenzo De Silvestri, Cristian Ansaldi, Nicolas N'Koulou (85.Wilfried Singo), Armando Izzo (46.Kevin Bonifazi), Bremer, Soualiho Meïté, Daniele Baselli, Simone Zaza, Andrea Belotti, Álex Berenguer (77.Tomás Rincón). Trainer: Walter Mazzarri.
Shakhtyor Solihorsk: Andrey Klimovich, Pavel Rybak, Sergey Matvejchik, Igor Burko, Nikola Antic, Sergey Balanovich (73.Vladimir Khvashchinskiy), Aleksandr Sachivko, Yuri Kovalev, Ruslan Khadarkevich (66.Nikolai Yanush), Max Ebong Ngome, Elis Bakaj (77.Eduards Visnakovs). Trainer: Sergey Tashuev.
Goals: 2' Andrea Belotti 1-0, 15' Armando Izzo 2-0, 63' Andrea Belotti 3-0 (pen), 72' Lorenzo De Silvestri 4-0, 76' Kevin Bonifazi 5-0.

15.08.2019; Pittodrie Stadium, Aberdeen
Referee: Harald Lechner (AUT); Attendance: 15,246
Aberdeen FC – HNK RIJEKA 0-2(0-2)
Aberdeen FC: Joe Lewis, Andrew Considine, Shay Logan, Gregory Leigh, Scott McKenna, Funso Ojo, Lewis Ferguson, Niall McGinn (35.Dean Campbell), Ryan Hedges (75.James Wilson), Sam Cosgrove (53.Curtis Main), Jon Gallagher. Trainer: Derek McInnes.
NK Rijeka: Andrej Prskalo, Roberto Puncec, Dario Zuparic, Momcilo Raspopovic, Zoran Kvrzic, Luka Capan, Tibor Halilovic (83.Dani Iglesias), Stipe Loncar (75.Robert Muric), Ivan Lepinjica, Antonio Colak, Boadu Maxwell Acosty (82.Matej Vuk). Trainer: Igor Biscan.
Goals: 10' Stipe Loncar 0-1, 32' Antonio Colak 0-2.
Sent off: 20' Funso Ojo.

15.08.2019; Stádio Neo GSP, Nicosia
Referee: Pawel Gil (POL); Attendance: 2,750
APOLLON LIMASSOL FC – FK Austria Wien 3-1(1-1)
Apollon Limassol: Joël Mall, Charis Kyriakou (75.Emilio N'Sue), Attila Szalai, Facundo Pereyra (66.Ioannis Pittas), Héctor Yuste, Sasa Markovic, Diego Aguirre, Serge Gakpé (83.Emilio Zelaya), João Pedro, Adrián Sardinero, Giannis Gianniotas. Trainer: Sofronis Avgousti.
Austria Wien: Ivan Lucic, Florian Klein, Stephan Zwierschitz, Christoph Martschinko, Johannes Handl, Maudo, Alexander Grünwald, Maximilian Sax (63.Bright Edomwonyi), Vesel Demaku, Christoph Monschein (71.Benedikt Pichler), Dominik Fitz (63.James Jeggo). Trainer: Christian Ilzer.
Goals: 18' Maudo 0-1, 45+2' Serge Gakpé 1-1 (pen), 55' Johannes Handl 2-1 (own goal), 67' Giannis Gianniotas 3-1.

15.08.2019; Commerzbank-Arena, Frankfurt am Main
Referee: Nikola Dabanovic (MNE); Attendance: 48,000
EINTRACHT FRANKFURT – FC Vaduz 1-0(1-0)
Eintracht Frankfurt: Kevin Trapp, Marco Russ (37.Martin Hinteregger), Timothy Chandler, Erik Durm, Almamy Touré, Evan Obite N'Dicka, Jonathan de Guzmán, Sebastian Rode (72.Daichi Kamada), Lucas Torró, Mijat Gacinovic (66.Gonçalo Paciência), Dejan Joveljic. Trainer: Adi Hütter.
FC Vaduz: Benjamin Büchel, Denis Simani, Maximilian Göppel, Pius Dorn, Yannick Schmid, Berkay Sülüngöz, Boris Prokopic (74.Noah Frick), Sandro Wieser, Mohamed Coulibaly, Manuel Sutter (66.Dominik Schwizer), Tunahan Çiçek (80.Nicolae Milinceanu). Trainer: Mario Frick.
Goal: 31' Jonathan de Guzmán 1-0.

15.08.2019; Lokotrans Aréna, Mladá Boleslav
Referee: Jonathan Lardot (BEL); Attendance: 4,695
FK Mladá Boleslav – SC FCSB BUCUREŞTI 0-1(0-0)
FK Mladá Boleslav: Jan Seda, Daniel Pudil, Laco Takács, Antonín Krapka, Marco Tulio (46.Jakub Fulnek), Marek Matejovsky, Michal Hubínek (90+2.Jirí Klíma), Tomás Ladra, Pavel Bucha, Muris Mesanovic, Tomás Wágner (70.Ewerton). Trainer: Jozef Weber.
FCSB Bucureşti: Andrei Daniel Vlad, Valentin Cretu, Aristides Soiledis, Bogdan Planic, Iulian Cristea, Thierry Moutinho (63.Ionut Pantîru), Ionut Vîna, Ovidiu Popescu, Razvan Oaida, Florin Tanase, Florinel Coman. Trainer: Vergil Andronache.
Goal: 90+1' Ionut Pantîru 0-1.
Sent off: 75' Antonín Krapka.

15.08.2019; Dynama Stadium, Minsk
Referee: Radu Petrescu (ROU); Attendance: 6,154
FC Shakhtyor Solihorsk – TORINO FC 1-1(0-0)
Shakhtyor Solihorsk: Andrey Klimovich, Pavel Rybak (67.Igor Burko), Sergey Matvejchik, Nikola Antic, Sergey Balanovich (84.Darko Bodul), Aleskandr Selyava, Yuri Kovalev, Ruslan Khadarkevich, Július Szöke, Max Ebong Ngome, Elis Bakaj (76.Nikolai Yanush). Trainer: Sergey Tashuev.
Torino FC: Salvatore Sirigu, Lorenzo De Silvestri, Cristian Ansaldi (62.Ola Aina), Nicolas N'Koulou, Kevin Bonifazi (83.Wilfried Singo), Bremer, Tomás Rincón, Soualiho Meïté, Sasa Lukic, Simone Zaza, Andrea Belotti (76.Vincenzo Millico). Trainer: Walter Mazzarri.
Goals: 80' Simone Zaza 0-1, 90+1' Nikolai Yanush 1-1 (pen).

08.08.2019; Stadion "Marszalka Józefa Pilsudskiego", Warszawa
Referee: Manuel Schüttengrüber (AUT); Attendance: 15,093
Legia Warszawa – APS Atromitos Athína 0-0
Legia Warszawa: Radoslaw Majecki, Artur Jedrzejczyk, Igor Lewczuk, Luís Rocha, Arvydas Novikovas, Marko Vesovic, Domagoj Antolic, André Martins, Valeriane Gvilia, Luquinhas, Sandro Kulenovic (65.Carlitos López). Trainer: Aleksandar Vukovic.
Atromitos Athína: Balász Megyeri, Madson, Tal Kahila, Dimitrios Goutas, Spyros Risvanis, Alexandros Katranis, Javier Umbides (61.Farley Rosa), Charilaos Charisis (72.Roland Ugrai), Spyridon Natsos, Georgios Manousos (83.João Talocha), Apostolos Vellios. Trainer: Yannis Anastasiou.

08.08.2019; Stadion Partizana, Beograd
Referee: Sergey Ivanov (RUS); Attendance: 13,442
FK Partizan Beograd – Yeni Malatya Spor Kulübü 3-1(1-0)
Partizan Beograd: Vladimir Stojkovic, Bojan Ostojic (79.Igor Vujacic), Nemanja Miletic (I), Slobodan Urosevic, Strahinja Pavlovic, Zoran Tosic, Aleksandar Scekic, Seydouba Soumah, Sasa Zdjelar, Umar Sadiq (84.Ognjen Ozegovic), Filip Stevanovic (46.Takuma Asano). Trainer: Savo Milosevic.
Malatya Spor Kulübü: Fabien Farnolle, Erkan Kas, Mustafa Akbas, Issam Chebake, Arturo Mina, Robin Yalçin, Rahman Bugra Çagiran (56.Guilherme), Ghilane Chalali (71.Murat Yildirim), Adis Jahovic, Thievy Bifouma (46.Gökhan Töre), Moryké Fofana. Trainer: Sergen Yalçin.
Goals: 4' Umar Sadiq 1-0, 67' Takuma Asano 2-0, 83' Issam Chebake 2-1, 90' Seydouba Soumah 3-1 (pen).

08.08.2019; Swissporarena, Luzern
Referee: Fran Jovic (CRO); Attendance: 9,191
FC Luzern – RCD Espanyol Barcelona 0-3(0-1)
FC Luzern: Marius Müller, Christian Schwegler, Lazar Cirkovic, Otar Kakabadze, Lucas Alves "Lucão", Marvin Schulz, Silvan Sidler (61.Ibrahima Ndiaye), Idriz Voca, Tsiy William Ndenge, Shkelqim Demhasaj (78.Francesco Margiotta), Blessing Eleke (89.Eric Tia). Trainer: Thomas Häberli.
RCD Espanyol: Diego López, Dídac Vilà, Javi López, Naldo, Lluís López, Adrià Pedrosa (67.Matías Vargas), Víctor Sánchez, Marc Roca (61.Sergi Darder), Melendo, Facundo Ferreyra (71.Lei Wu), Borja Iglesias. Trainer: David Gallego.
Goals: 28' Facundo Ferreyra 0-1, 59' Dídac Vilà 0-2, 89' Matías Vargas 0-3.

14.08.2019; Stadio Peristeriou, Athína
Referee: Bas Nijhuis (NED); Attendance: 2,019
APS Atromitos Athína – LEGIA WARSZAWA 0-2(0-1)
Atromitos Athína: Balász Megyeri, Madson (69.Javier Umbides), Tal Kahila (58.Roland Ugrai), Dimitrios Goutas, Spyros Risvanis, Alexandros Katranis, Farley Rosa, Charilaos Charisis, Spyridon Natsos, Georgios Manousos, Apostolos Vellios (84.Clarck N'Sikulu). Trainer: Yannis Anastasiou.
Legia Warszawa: Radoslaw Majecki, Artur Jedrzejczyk, Igor Lewczuk, Luís Rocha (62.Mateusz Wieteska), Pawel Stolarski, Marko Vesovic (68.Dominik Nagy), André Martins, Cafú, Valeriane Gvilia, Luquinhas (77.Carlitos López), Sandro Kulenovic. Trainer: Aleksandar Vukovic.
Goals: 29' Pawel Stolarski 0-1, 51' Valeriane Gvilia 0-2.

15.08.2019; Yeni Malatya Stadyumu, Malatya
Referee: Chris Kavanagh (ENG); Attendance: 14,665
Yeni Malatya Spor Kulübü – FK PARTIZAN BEOGRAD 1-0(1-0)
Malatya Spor Kulübü: Fabien Farnolle, Erkan Kas, Mustafa Akbas, Issam Chebake (10.Rahman Bugra Çagiran), Arturo Mina, Murat Yildirim, Gökhan Töre, Guilherme (74.Eren Tozlu), Ghilane Chalali, Adis Jahovic, Thievy Bifouma (68.Moryké Fofana). Trainer: Sergen Yalçin.
Partizan Beograd: Vladimir Stojkovic, Bojan Ostojic, Nemanja Miletic (I), Slobodan Urosevic, Strahinja Pavlovic, Zoran Tosic (71.Aleksandar Lutovac), Aleksandar Scekic, Seydouba Soumah (82.Lazar Pavlovic), Sasa Zdjelar, Takuma Asano, Umar Sadiq (90+6.Ognjen Ozegovic). Trainer: Savo Milosevic.
Goal: 7' Adis Jahovic 1-0.

15.08.2019; RCDE Stadium, Cornella de Llobregat
Referee: Manuel Jorge Neves Moreira Sousa (POR); Attendance: 13,214
RCD ESPANYOL BARCELONA – FC Luzern 3-0(3-0)
RCD Espanyol: Diego López, Bernardo Espinosa, Dídac Vilà, Lluís López, Pipa Ávila, Granero, Iturraspe, Sergi Darder (52.Pol Lozano), Matías Vargas (56.Nico Melamed Ribaudo), Lei Wu, Víctor Campuzano (56.Javi Puado). Trainer: David Gallego.
FC Luzern: Marius Müller, Christian Schwegler (74.Shkelqim Demhasaj), Lazar Cirkovic, Otar Kakabadze, Lucas Alves "Lucão", Idriz Voca, Remo Arnold, Tsiy William Ndenge, Francesco Margiotta, Blessing Eleke (62.Pascal Schürpf), Ibrahima Ndiaye (65.Silvan Sidler). Trainer: Thomas Häberli.
Goals: 3' Lei Wu 1-0, 27', 38' Víctor Campuzano 2-0, 3-0.

22.08.2019; Astana Arena, Nur-Sultan
Referee: Serhiy Boyko (UKR); Attendance: 24,369
Astana FC – FC BATE Borisov 3-0(2-0)
Astana FC: Nenad Eric, Antonio Rukavina, Yuriy Logvinenko, Dmitriy Shomko, Evgeny Postnikov, Luka Simunovic, Rúnar Sigurjónsson, Marin Tomasov (82.Rangelo Janga), Ivan Maevski, Dorin Rotariu, Ndombe Mubele (46.Roman Murtazaev). Trainer: Roman Grygorchuk.
BATE Borisov: Anton Chichkan, Aleksander Filipovic, Aleksey Rios, Igor Stasevich, Dmitriy Baga (61.Willum Thór Willumsson), Stanislav Dragun, Slobodan Simovic, Hervaine Moukam (54.Jasse Tuominen), Evgeni Yablonski, Zakhar Volkov, Maksim Skavysh (79.Anton Saroka). Trainer: Aleksei Baga.
Goals: 23' Marin Tomasov 1-0, 44' Yuriy Logvinenko 2-0, 52' Rúnar Sigurjónsson 3-0 (pen).

22.08.2019; „Vazgen Sargsyan" anvan Hanrapetakan Marzadasht, Yerevan
Referee: Harald Lechner (AUT); Attendance: 11,000
FC Ararat-Armenia Yerevan – F91 Dudelange 2-1(1-0)
FC Ararat-Armenia: Dmitriy ABakımov, Rochdi Achenteh, Ângelo Meneses, Aleksandar Damcevski, Georgi Pashov, Gor Malakyan (82.Ilja Antonov), Kódjo Alphonse, Petros Avetisyan (56.Armen Ambartsumyan), Anton Kobyalko (75.Louis Ogana), Furdjel Narsingh, Mailson. Trainer: Vardan Minasyan.
F91 Dudelange: Jonathan Joubert, Tom Schnell, Ricardo Delgado, Mehdi Kirch, Mohamed Bouchouari, Mario Pokar, Ryan Klapp (78.Mickaël Garos), Dominik Stolz (54.Omar Natami), Charles Morren, Danel Sinani (90+2.Mehdi Ouamri), Antoine Bernier. Trainer: Emilio Ferrera.
Goals: 22' Mailson 1-0, 68' Danel Sinani 1-1, 90+3' Ilja Antonov 2-1.

22.08.2019; Marijampolės sporto centro stadione, Marijampolė
Referee: Manuel Schüttengruber (AUT); Attendance: 5,741
FK Sūduva Marijampolė – Ferencvárosi TC 0-0
FK Sūdova Marijampolė: Ivan Kardum, Algis Jankauskas, Andro Svrljuga, Aleksandar Zivanovic, Semir Kerla, Ivan Hladík, Renan Oliveira (78.Eligijus Jankauskas), Ovidijus Verbickas, Giedrius Matulevicius, Josip Tadic (69.Sandro Gotal), Mihret Topcagic (90+2.Robertas Vėzevicius). Trainer: Vladimir Cheburin.
Ferencvárosi TC: Dénes Dibusz, Gergö Lovrencsics, Marcel Heister, Miha Blazic, Lasha Dvali, Michal Skvarka (76.Roland Varga), Dávid Sigér, Igor Kharatin, Oleksandr Zubkov, Tokmac Nguen (87.Lukács Böle), Franck Boli (67.Tamás Priskin). Trainer: Serhiy Rebrov.

22.08.2019; Ludogorets Arena, Razgrad
Referee: Jakob Kehlet (DEN); Attendance: 6,230
PFC Ludogorets Razgrad – NK Maribor 0-0
Ludogorets Razgrad: Plamen Iliev, Cosmin Moti, Cicinho, Rafael Forster, Anton Nedyalkov, Anicet Andrianantenaina (78.Jakub Swierczok), Wanderson (72.Mavis Tchibota), Stéphane Badji, Dan Biton (65.Marcelinho), Claudiu Keserü, Jorginho. Trainer: Stoicho Stoev.
NK Maribor: Kenan Piric, Mitja Viler, Martin Milec, Sasa Ivkovic, Spiro Pericic, Rok Kronaveter (65.Marcos Tavares), Blaz Vrhovec, Alexandru Cretu, Rudi Pozeg Vancas (80.Jasmin Mesanovic), Dino Hotic, Luka Zahovic (65.Martin Kramaric). Trainer: Darko Milanic.
Sent off: 57' Dino Hotic.

29.08.2019; Borisov Arena, Borisov
Referee: Robert Madden (SCO); Attendance: 10,701
FC BATE Borisov – ASTANA FC 2-0(1-0)
BATE Borisov: Anton Chichkan, Boris Kopitovic, Aleksander Filipovic, Aleksey Rios, Igor Stasevich, Dmitriy Baga (74.Willum Thór Willumsson), Stanislav Dragun, Evgeni Yablonski, Zakhar Volkov, Maksim Skavysh (79.Jasse Tuominen), Anton Saroka (57.Hervaine Moukam). Trainer: Aleksei Baga.
Astana FC: Nenad Eric, Antonio Rukavina, Yuriy Logvinenko (87.Zarko Tomasevic), Dmitriy Shomko, Evgeny Postnikov, Luka Simunovic, Rúnar Sigurjónsson, Marin Tomasov (90+3.Abzal Beysebekov), Ivan Maevski, Roman Murtazaev (71.Rangelo Janga), Dorin Rotariu. Trainer: Roman Grygorchuk.
Goals: 6' Maksim Skavysh 1-0, 85' Evgeni Yablonski 2-0.

29.08.2019; Stade „Josy Barthel", Lëtzebuerg
Referee: Aleksandar Stavrev (MKD); Attendance: 2,874
F91 DUDELANGE – FC Ararat-Armenia Yerevan 2-1(0-1,2-1);
5-4 on penalties
F91 Dudelange: Jonathan Joubert, Tom Schnell, Ricardo Delgado (90.Kobe Cools), Mehdi Kirch, Mohamed Bouchouari, Mario Pokar (99.Sabir Bougrine), Ryan Klapp (69.Omar Natami), Dominik Stolz (110.Corenthyn Lavie), Charles Morren, Danel Sinani, Antoine Bernier. Trainer: Emilio Ferrera.
FC Ararat-Armenia: Dmitriy ABakımov, Rochdi Achenteh, Dmitri Guzj, Ângelo Meneses, Georgi Pashov, Gor Malakyan (56.Petros Avetisyan), Armen Ambartsumyan (84.Ilja Antonov), Kódjo Alphonse, Anton Kobyalko (75.Louis Ogana), Furdjel Narsingh (105.Zakaria Sanogo), Mailson. Trainer: Vardan Minasyan.
Goals: 24' Mailson 0-1, 48', 71' Danel Sinani 1-1 (pen), 2-1.
Penalties: Lavie 1-0, Avetisyan missed, Morren missed, Alphonse 1-1, Bougrine 2-1, Mailson 2-2, Natami 3-2, Ângelo Meneses 3-3, Sinani 4-3, Louis Ogana 4-4, Schnell 5-4, Pashov missed.

29.08.2019; Groupama Aréna, Budapest
Referee: Marco Guida (ITA); Attendance: 18,567
FERENCVÁROSI TC – FK Sūduva Marijampolė 4-2(2-1)
Ferencvárosi TC: Dénes Dibusz, Gergö Lovrencsics, Marcel Heister, Miha Blazic, Lasha Dvali, Dávid Sigér (71.Danylo Ignatenko), Igor Kharatin, Oleksandr Zubkov, Roland Varga (68.Isael), Tokmac Nguen, Franck Boli (80.Nikolay Signevich). Trainer: Serhiy Rebrov.
FK Sūduva Marijampolė: Ivan Kardum, Algis Jankauskas, Andro Svrljuga, Aleksandar Zivanovic, Semir Kerla, Ivan Hladík, Jovan Cadjenovic, Ovidijus Verbickas (71.Eligijus Jankauskas), Giedrius Matulevicius (88.Robertas Vėzevicius), Josip Tadic (46.Paulius Golubickas), Mihret Topcagic. Trainer: Vladimir Cheburin.
Goals: 11' Ovidijus Verbickas 0-1, 36' Roland Varga 1-1 (pen), 45+1' Franck Boli 2-1, 64' Mihret Topcagic 2-2, 66' Tokmac Nguen 3-2, 90+6' Nikolay Signevich 4-2 (pen).

29.08.2019; Ljudski vrt, Maribor
Referee: Craig Pawson (ENG); Attendance: 9,016
NK Maribor – PFC LUDOGORETS RAZGRAD 2-2(0-2)
NK Maribor: Kenan Piric, Mitja Viler, Martin Milec (46.Denis Klinar), Sasa Ivkovic, Spiro Pericic, Rok Kronaveter (60.Marcos Tavares), Blaz Vrhovec, Alexandru Cretu (86.Andrej Kotnik), Rudi Pozeg Vancas, Jasmin Mesanovic, Luka Zahovic. Trainer: Darko Milanic.
Ludogorets Razgrad: Plamen Iliev, Cosmin Moti, Cicinho, Rafael Forster, Anton Nedyalkov, Anicet Andrianantenaina, Wanderson, Stéphane Badji, Claudiu Keserü (69.Svetoslav Dyakov), Marcelinho (85.Jakub Swierczok), Jorginho (90.Dragos Grigore). Trainer: Stanislav Genchev.
Goals: 17' Marcelinho 0-1, 26' Claudiu Keserü 0-2 (pen), 65' Marcos Tavares 1-2, 72' Rudi Pozeg Vancas 2-2.

22.08.2019; Telia Parken, København
Referee: Bas Nijhuis (NED); Attendance: 13,930
FC København – Rīga FC 3-1(1-1)
FC København: Sten Grytebust, Pierre Bengtsson, Sotirios Papagiannopoulos, Karlo Bartolec, Victor Nelsson, Rasmus Falk (79.Mohammed Daramy), Zeca, Viktor Fischer, Jens Stage, Pieros Soteriou, Carlo Holse (46.Michael Santos). Trainer: Ståle Solbakken.
Rīga FC: Roberts Ozols, Stefan Panic, Antonijs Cernomordijs, Vladimirs Kamess, Ritvars Rugins, Vyacheslav Sharpar, Felipe Brisola (68.Olegs Laizāns), Roger (68.Deniss Rakels), Armands Pētersons, Elvis Stuglis, Vladislavs Fjodorovs (84.Aleksejs Visnakovs). Trainer: Mihails Konevs.
Goals: 18' Viktor Fischer 1-0, 41' Vladimirs Kamess 1-1, 62' Pieros Sotiriou 2-1 (pen), 90+3' Mohammed Daramy 3-1.

22.08.2019; Celtic Park, Glasgow
Referee: Tamás Bognár (HUN); Attendance: 40,885
Celtic FC Glasgow – AIK Stockholm 2-0(0-0)
Celtic FC: Craig Gordon, Jozo Simunovic, Christopher Jullien, Boli Bolingoli Mbombo, Kristoffer Ajer, Scott Brown, James Forrest (82.Olivier Ntcham), Callum McGregor, Ryan Christie, Odsonne Édouard (85.Vakoun Bayo), Michael Johnston (82.Lewis Morgan). Trainer: Neil Lennon.
AIK Stockholm: Oscar Linnér, Per Karlsson, Robert Lundström (87.Heradi Rashidi), Rasmus Lindkvist, Karol Mets, Daniel Granli, Sebastian Larsson, Nabil Bahoui (70.Anton Salétros), Enoch Adu, Kolbeinn Sigthórsson (72.Chinedu Obasi), Henok Goitom. Trainer: Rikard Norling.
Goals: 48' James Forrest 1-0, 73' Odsonne Édouard 2-0.

22.08.2019; Windsor Park, Belfast
Referee: Sandro Schärer (SUI); Attendance: 4,633
Linfield FC Belfast – Qarabağ FK Bakı 3-2(2-1)
Linfield FC: Rohan Ferguson, Chris Casement, Matthew Clarke, Mark Stafford, Niall Quinn, Jamie Mulgrew, Jimmy Callacher, Andrew Mitchell, Bastien Héry, Joel Cooper (90+1.Kirk Millar), Shayne Lavery (80.Andrew Waterworth). Trainer: David Healy.
Qarabağ FK: Vagner, Rashad Sadygov, Maksim Medvedev, Qara Qarayev, Fayçal Rherras, Abbas Hüseynov, Míchel, Jaime Romero, Dani Quintana (67.Magaye Gueye), Abdellah Zoubir, Mahir Emreli. Trainer: Gurban Gurbanov.
Goals: 15' Fayçal Rherras 0-1, 40' Mark Stafford 1-1, 45+1', 75' Shayne Lavery 2-1, 3-1, 90+3' Magaye Gueye 3-2 (pen).

22.08.2019; Národny Futbalovy Stadión, Bratislava
Referee: Ivan Bebek (CRO); Attendance: 20,233
ŠK Slovan Bratislava – PAOK Thessaloníki 1-0(0-0)
Slovan Bratislava: Dominik Greif, Vasil Bozhikov, Vernon, Jurij Medvedev, Myenty Abena, Marin Ljubicic, Dávid Holman, Joeri de Kamps (77.Nono Delgado), "Moha" Mohammed Rharsalla (87.Erik Daniel), Aleksandar Cavric (54.Rafael Ratão), Andraz Sporar. Trainer: Ján Kozák.
PAOK Thessaloníki: Alexandros Paschalakis, Léo Matos, José Ángel Crespo, Fernando Varela, Dimitris Giannoulis, Diego Biseswar (80.Miroslav Stoch), Omar El Kaddouri, Dimitrios Pelkas (66.Karol Swiderski), Anderson Esiti (76.Douglas Augusto), Chuba Akpom, Léo Jabá. Trainer: Abel Ferreira.
Goal: 90+4' Myenty Abena 1-0.

29.08.2019; Skonto Stadions, Rīga
Referee: Pawel Gil (POL); Attendance: 7,055
Rīga FC – FC KØBENHAVN 1-0(0-0)
Rīga FC: Roberts Ozols, Georgios Valerianos, Herdi Prenga, Stefan Panic, Antonijs Cernomordijs, Vladimirs Kamess, Vyacheslav Sharpar (66.Olegs Laizāns), Felipe Brisola, Roger (67.Deniss Rakels), Armands Pētersons (84.Miroslav Slavov), Roman Debelko. Trainer: Mihails Konevs.
FC København: Sten Grytebust, Pierre Bengtsson, Sotirios Papagiannopoulos, Karlo Bartolec, Victor Nelsson, Rasmus Falk (79.Andreas Bjelland), Zeca, Viktor Fischer (71.Michael Santos), Nikolaj Thomsen (85.Guillermo Varela), Jens Stage, Pieros Soteriou. Trainer: Ståle Solbakken.
Goal: 75' Felipe Brisola 1-0.
Sent off: 90+4' Georgios Valerianos.

29.08.2019; Friends Arena, Stockholm
Referee: Nikola Dabanovic (MNE); Attendance: 28,410
AIK Stockholm – CELTIC FC GLASGOW 1-4(1-2)
AIK Stockholm: Oscar Linnér, Per Karlsson, Robert Lundström (79.Heradi Rashidi), Karol Mets, Daniel Granli, Sebastian Larsson, Nabil Bahoui (62.Balil Hussein), Enoch Adu, Anton Salétros, Kolbeinn Sigthórsson (62.Henok Goitom), Chinedu Obasi. Trainer: Rikard Norling.
Celtic FC: Craig Gordon, Christopher Jullien, Boli Bolingoli Mbombo, Kristoffer Ajer (15.Anthony Ralston), Scott Brown, Nir Bitton, James Forrest, Callum McGregor, Ryan Christie, Odsonne Édouard (76.Vakoun Bayo), Michael Johnston (70.Lewis Morgan). Trainer: Neil Lennon.
Goals: 17' James Forrest 0-1, 33' Sebastian Larsson 1-1 (pen), 34' Michael Johnston 1-2, 87' Christopher Jullien 1-3, 90+3' Lewis Morgan 1-4.

29.08.2019; „Tofiq Bahramov" adina Respublika stadionu, Bakı
Referee: Sergey Ivanov (RUS); Attendance: 18,349
QARABAĞ FK BAKI – Linfield FC Belfast 2-1(1-0)
Qarabağ FK: Vagner, Rashad Sadygov, Maksim Medvedev, Ailton, Rahil Mammadov, Míchel (90+1.Dani Quintana), Jaime Romero, Richard Almeyda, Abdellah Zoubir (90+1.Araz Abdullayev), Magaye Gueye (85.Qara Qarayev), Mahir Emreli. Trainer: Gurban Gurbanov.
Linfield FC: Rohan Ferguson, Chris Casement, Matthew Clarke, Mark Stafford, Niall Quinn (78.Kirk Millar), Jamie Mulgrew, Jimmy Callacher, Bastien Héry, Stephen Fallon (78.Andrew Waterworth), Joel Cooper (81.Jordan Stewart), Shayne Lavery. Trainer: David Healy.
Goals: 6' Jaime Romero 1-0, 88' Abdellah Zoubir 2-0, 90+3' Shayne Lavery 2-1.

29.08.2019; Stadio Toumbas, Thessaloníki
Referee: Andreas Ekberg (SWE); Attendance: 20,776
PAOK Thessaloníki – ŠK SLOVAN BRATISLAVA 3-2(0-1)
PAOK Thessaloníki: Alexandros Paschalakis, José Ángel Crespo, Fernando Varela, Rodrigo Alves, Dimitris Giannoulis, Diego Biseswar, Omar El Kaddouri (31.Douglas Augusto), Dimitrios Pelkas (46.Karol Swiderski), Anderson Esiti (64.Josip Misic), Chuba Akpom, Dimitris Limnios. Trainer: Abel Ferreira.
Slovan Bratislava: Dominik Greif, Vasil Bozhikov, Vernon, Jurij Medvedev, Myenty Abena, Ibrahim Rabiu (68.Nono Delgado), Dávid Holman (88.Rafael Ratão), Joeri de Kamps, Kenan Bajric, "Moha" Mohammed Rharsalla (78.Artem Sukhotsky), Andraz Sporar. Trainer: Ján Kozák.
Goals: 38' Jurij Medvedev 0-1, 49' Dimitris Limnios 1-1, 50' Karol Swiderski 2-1, 62' Vernon 2-2, 87' Dimitris Giannoulis 3-2.

LEAGUE PATH

22.08.2019; Swedbank Stadion, Malmö
Referee: Pawel Raczkowski (POL); Attendance: 13,956
Malmö FF – Bnei Yehuda Tel Aviv FC 3-0(2-0)
Malmö FF: Johan Dahlin, Behrang Safari, Rasmus Bengtsson, Eric Larsson, Felix Beijmo (67.Lasse Nielsen), Søren Rieks (82.Jonas Knudsen), Anders Christiansen, Fouad Bachirou, Arnór Ingvi Traustason (60.Guillermo Molins), Oscar Lewicki, Markus Rosenberg. Trainer: Uwe Rösler.
Bnei Yehuda: Emilijus Zubas, Dan Mori, Alban Pnishi, Shay Mazor, Daniel Felscher, Matan Baltaksa, Tamabi Sages, Ismaila Soro (85.Shimshon Tza'adon), Mohammad Ghadir (67.Dor Elo), Dor Jan (73.Ariel Matan Lazmi), Avishay Cohen. Trainer: Yossi Abukasis.
Goals: 36' Markus Rosenberg 1-0, 40' Rasmus Bengtsson 2-0, 47' Oscar Lewicki 3-0.

29.08.2019; HaMoshava Stadium, Petah Tikva
Referee: Serdar Gözübüyük (NED); Attendance: 900
Bnei Yehuda Tel Aviv FC – MALMÖ FF 0-1(0-1)
Bnei Yehuda: Emilijus Zubas, Dan Mori, Alban Pnishi (46.Matan Baltaksa), Shimshon Tza'adon, Shay Mazor, Daniel Felscher, Amir Rustom, Ariel Matan Lazmi, Ismaila Soro (46.Tamabi Sages), Dor Jan (62.Amit Zaneti), Avishay Cohen. Trainer: Yossi Abukasis.
Malmö FF: Johan Dahlin, Behrang Safari, Rasmus Bengtsson (46.Felix Beijmo), Eric Larsson, Lasse Nielsen, Jonas Knudsen, Anders Christiansen (70.Marcus Antonsson), Oscar Lewicki (62.Fouad Bachirou), Romain Gall, Bonke Innocent, Guillermo Molins. Trainer: Uwe Rösler.
Goal: 7' Guillermo Molins 0-1.

22.08.2019; Stadion Feijenoord, Rotterdam
Referee: Andris Treimanis (LVA); Attendance: 35,000
Feyenoord Rotterdam – Hapoel Be'er Sheva FC 3-0(1-0)
Feyenoord Rotterdam: Kenneth Vermeer, Eric Botteghin, Edgar Ié, Ridgeciano Haps, Rick Karsdorp, Leroy Fer (88.Wouter Burger), Renato Tapia, Orkun Kökçü, Luciano Narsingh, Steven Berghuis, Sam Larsson (73.Luis Sinisterra). Trainer: Jaap Stam.
Hapoel Be'er Sheva: Ernestas Setkus, Miguel Vítor (81.Naor Sabag), Ben Bitton, Loai Taha, Sean Goldberg, Marwan Kabha, Ramzi Safouri, Eden Shamir, David Keltjens (68.Jimmy Marín), Nigel Hasselbaink, Niv Zrihan (64.Ben Sahar). Trainer: Barak Bakhar.
Goals: 33' Sam Larsson 1-0, 56', 78' Leroy Fer 2-0, 3-0.

22.08.2019; Stádio Olympiako „Spyros Louis", Athína
Referee: Daniel Siebert (GER); Attendanace: 141
AEK Athína – Trabzonspor Kulübü 1-3(1-2)
AEK Athína: Vasilios Barkas, Ognjen Vranjes, Paulinho, Hélder Lopes, Efstratios Svarnas, David Simão (63.Nenad Krsticic), Petros Mandalos, André Simões, Nélson Oliveira (84.Giorgos Giakoumakis), Marko Livaja, Daniele Verde (65.Chico Geraldes). Trainer: Miguel Cardoso.
Trabzonspor: Ugurcan Çakir, João Pereira, Filip Novák, Majid Hosseini, Hüseyin Türkmen, José Sosa, Abdülkadir Parmak, Abdülkadir Ömür, Anthony Nwakaeme (72.Donis Avdijaj), Alexander Sørloth (77.Dogan Erdogan), Caleb Ekuban (90+2.Yusuf Sari). Trainer: Ünal Karaman.
Goals: 4' Marko Livaja 1-0, 29', 44', 70' Caleb Ekuban 1-1, 1-2, 1-3.

22.08.2019; Stadion „Marszalka Józefa Pilsudskiego", Warszawa
Referee: Benoît Bastien (FRA); Attendance: 26,665
Legia Warszawa – Glasgow Rangers FC 0-0
Legia Warszawa: Radoslaw Majecki, Artur Jedrzejczyk, Igor Lewczuk, Luís Rocha, Pawel Stolarski, Marko Vesovic (84.Dominik Nagy), André Martins, Cafú (71.Domagoj Antolic), Valeriane Gvilia, Luquinhas, Sandro Kulenovic. Trainer: Aleksandar Vukovic.
Glasgow Rangers: Allan McGregor, James Tavernier, Connor Goldson, John Flanagan, Nikola Katic, Steven Davis, Scott Arfield (87.Glen Kamara), Ryan Jack, Joe Aribo, Sheyi Ojo, Alfredo Morelos (87.Jermain Defoe). Trainer: Steven Gerrard.

22.08.2019; Stadionul „Marin Anastasovici", Giurgiu
Referee: Matej Jug (SVN); Attendance: 4,518
SC FCSB Bucureşti – Vitória SC Guimarães 0-0
FCSB Bucureşti: Cristian Balgradean, Valentin Cretu, Aristides Soiledis, Bogdan Planic, Ionut Pantîru, Mihai Roman (I) (46.Adrian Popa), Mihai Pintilii (66.Razvan Oaida), Ionut Vîna (60.Harlem Gnohéré), Ovidiu Popescu, Florin Tanase, Florinel Coman. Trainer: Vergil Andronache.
Vitória Guimarães: Douglas Jesus, Florent Hanin, Valeriy Bondarenko, Falaye Sacko, Edmond Tapsoba, Rochinha (66.Rafa Soares), Pêpê Rodrigues, Almoatasembellah Ali Mohamed, André Almeida (62.Denis Poha), Davidson, Bruno Duarte (76.Alexandre Guedes). Trainer: Ivo Vieira.

22.08.2019; GHELAMCO-arena, Gent
Referee: Daniel Stefanski (POL); Attendance: 12,198
KAA Gent – HNK Rijeka 2-1(0-1)
KAA Gent: Thomas Kaminski, Nana Asare, Mikael Lustig, Igor Plastun, Michael Ngadeu-Ngadjui, Vadis Odjidja-Ofoe, Brecht Dejaegere (63.Roman Bezus), Elisha Owusu, Laurent Depoitre, Roman Yaremchuk (83.Louis Verstraete), Jonathan David (89.Yuya Kubo). Trainer: Jess Thorup.
NK Rijeka: Andrej Prskalo, Roberto Puncec, Dario Zuparic, Momcilo Raspopovic, Zoran Kvrzic (69.Darko Velkovski), Luka Capan, Tibor Halilovic, Stipe Loncar, Ivan Lepinjica, Antonio Colak (86.Jakov Puljic), Boadu Maxwell Acosty (79.Dani Iglesias). Trainer: Igor Biscan.
Goals: 39' Tibor Halilovic 0-1, 57', 71' Laurent Depoitre 1-1, 2-1.

29.08.2019; „Yaakov Turner Toto" Stadium, Beersheva
Referee: Gediminas Mazeika (LTU); Attendance: 9,107
Hapoel Be'er Sheva FC – FEYENOORD ROTTERDAM 0-3(0-0)
Hapoel Be'er Sheva: Ernestas Setkus, Miguel Vítor (50.Tomer Yosefi), Ben Bitton, Loai Taha, Sean Goldberg (45+2.David Keltjens), Hanan Maman, Marwan Kabha, Ramzi Safouri, Naor Sabag, Jimmy Marín, Ben Sahar (64.Eden Shamir). Trainer: Barak Bakhar.
Feyenoord Rotterdam: Kenneth Vermeer, Eric Botteghin, Edgar Ié, Ridgeciano Haps (77.Tyrell Malacia), Rick Karsdorp, Leroy Fer (70.Naoufal Bannis), Renato Tapia, Orkun Kökçü (59.Wouter Burger), Luciano Narsingh, Steven Berghuis, Sam Larsson. Trainer: Jaap Stam.
Goals: 46' Orkun Kökçü 0-1, 52' Steven Berghuis 0-2, 61' Wouter Burger 0-3.
Sent off: 42' Hanan Maman.

29.08.2019; Medical Park Stadyumu, Trabzon
Referee: Michael Oliver (ENG); Attendance: 30,490
TRABZONSPOR KULÜBÜ – AEK Athína 0-2(0-2)
Trabzonspor: Ugurcan Çakir, João Pereira, Filip Novák, Gastón Campi, Ivanildo Fernandes, John Obi Mikel (36.Alexander Sørloth), José Sosa, Abdülkadir Parmak, Abdülkadir Ömür (44.Yusuf Sari, 83.Dogan Erdogan), Anthony Nwakaeme, Caleb Ekuban. Trainer: Ünal Karaman.
AEK Athína: Vasilios Barkas, Dmytro Chygrynskiy, Ognjen Vranjes, Michalis Bakakis, Hélder Lopes, Marios Oikonomou (88.Viktor Klonaridis), Petros Mandalos (81.Giorgos Giakoumakis), André Simões, Konstantinos Galanopoulos (58.Nenad Krsticic), Nélson Oliveira, Marko Livaja. Trainer: Nikolaos Kostenoglou.
Goals: 24' Marko Livaja 0-1, 30' Petros Mandalos 0-2 (pen).
Sent off: 90+3' Hélder Lopes.

29.08.2019; Ibrox Stadium, Glasgow
Referee: Slavko Vincic (SVN); Attendance: 45,463
GLASGOW RANGERS FC – Legia Warszawa 1-0(0-0)
Glasgow Rangers: Allan McGregor, James Tavernier, Connor Goldson, Borna Barisic (64.John Flanagan), Nikola Katic, Steven Davis, Scott Arfield (72.Jordan Jones), Ryan Jack, Joe Aribo, Sheyi Ojo (90+5.Glen Kamara), Alfredo Morelos. Trainer: Steven Gerrard.
Legia Warszawa: Radoslaw Majecki, Artur Jedrzejczyk, Igor Lewczuk, Luís Rocha, Pawel Stolarski (73.Dominik Nagy), Marko Vesovic, André Martins, Cafú, Valeriane Gvilia, Luquinhas, Sandro Kulenovic (56.Jaroslaw Niezgoda). Trainer: Aleksandar Vukovic.
Goal: 90+1' Alfredo Morelos 1-0.

29.08.2019; Estádio „Dom Afonso Henriques", Guimarães
Referee: Irfan Peljto (BIH); Attendance: 18,352
VITÓRIA SC GUIMARÃES – SC FCSB Bucureşti 1-0(0-0)
Vitória Guimarães: Douglas Jesus, Florent Hanin, Valeriy Bondarenko, Falaye Sacko, Edmond Tapsoba, Rochinha, Pêpê Rodrigues (74.João Carlos Teixeira), Denis Poha, Almoatasembellah Ali Mohamed, Davidson (86.Rafa Soares), Bruno Duarte (78.André Pereira). Trainer: Ivo Vieira.
FCSB Bucureşti: Cristian Balgradean, Valentin Cretu (27.Mihai Roman (I)), Aristides Soiledis (72.Thierry Moutinho), Bogdan Planic, Iulian Cristea, Ionut Pantîru, Mihai Pintilii (46.Harlem Gnohéré), Ionut Vîna, Ovidiu Popescu, Florin Tanase, Florinel Coman. Trainer: Bogdan Vintila.
Goal: 53' Edmond Tapsoba 1-0 (pen).

29.08.2019; Stadion HNK Rijeka, Rijeka
Referee: François Letexier (FRA); Attendance: 7,562
HNK Rijeka – KAA GENT 1-1(1-1)
NK Rijeka: Andrej Prskalo, Ivan Tomecak, Roberto Puncec, Dario Zuparic, Momcilo Raspopovic, Luka Capan (71.Robert Muric), Tibor Halilovic (77.Alexander Gorgon), Stipe Loncar, Ivan Lepinjica, Antonio Colak (19.Jakov Puljic), Boadu Maxwell Acosty. Trainer: Igor Biscan.
KAA Gent: Thomas Kaminski, Nana Asare, Mikael Lustig, Igor Plastun, Michael Ngadeu-Ngadjui, Vadis Odjidja-Ofoe, Sven Kums (78.Alessio Castro-Montes), Brecht Dejaegere, Elisha Owusu, Laurent Depoitre (81.Giorgi Kvilitaia), Jonathan David. Trainer: Jess Thorup.
Goals: 32' Jakov Puljic 1-0, 33' Igor Plastun 1-1.

22.08.2019; Stadion Philips, Eindhoven
Referee: Aleksei Kulbakov (BLR); Attendance: 17,500
PSV Eindhoven – Apollon Limassol FC 3-0(0-0)
PSV Eindhoven: Jeroen Zoet, Nick Viergever, Timo Baumgartl, Olivier Boscagli (90.Toni Lato), Denzel Dumfries, Érick Gutiérrez, Pablo Rosario, Mohammed Ihattaren (81.Kostas Mitroglou), Steven Bergwijn, Donyell Malen, Cody Gakpo (84.Jorrit Hendrix). Trainer: Mark van Bommel.
Apollon Limassol: Joël Mall, Charis Kyriakou, Héctor Yuste, Sasa Markovic, Diego Aguirre, Esteban Sachetti, Serge Gakpé (76.Ioannis Pittas), Emilio Zelaya, João Pedro, Adrián Sardinero (67.Fotios Papoulis), Giannis Gianniotas (62.Facundo Pereyra). Trainer: Sofronis Avgousti.
Goals: 47' Mohammed Ihattaren 1-0, 56' Cody Gakpo 2-0, 61' Denzel Dumfries 3-0.

22.08.2019; Stade de la Meinau, Strasbourg
Referee: Ivan Kruzliak (SVK); Attendance: 21,708
Racing Club de Strasbourg – Eintracht Frankfurt 1-0(1-0)
RC Strasbourg: Matz Sels, Lamine Koné, Stefan Mitrovic, Lionel Carole, Kenny Lala, Alexander Djiku, Jonas Martin, Dimitri Liénard, Adrien Thomasson (77.Lebo Mothiba), Ludovic Ajorque (86.Mohamed Simakan), Kévin Lucien Zohi (64.Ibrahima Sissoko). Trainer: Thierry Laurey.
Eintracht Frankfurt: Kevin Trapp, Makoto Hasebe, David Abrahim, Martin Hinteregger, Danny da Costa, Gelson Fernandes (78.Dominik Kohr), Filip Kostic, Lucas Torró, Mijat Gacinovic (46.Sebastian Rode), Daichi Kamada, Ante Rebic (46.Gonçalo Paciência). Trainer: Adi Hütter.
Goal: 33' Kévin Lucien Zohi 1-0.

22.08.2019; De Grolsch Veste, Enschede
Referee: Srdjan Jovanovic (SRB); Attendance: 4,014
AZ Alkmaar – Royal Antwerp FC 1-1(0-1)
AZ Alkmaar: Marco Bizot, Ron Vlaar, Jonas Svensson (76.Bjørn Johnsen), Pantelis Hatzidiakos (68.Yukinari Sugawara), Thomas Ouwejan (60.Albert Gudmundsson), Owen Wijndal, Fredrik Midtsjø, Teun Koopmeiners, Oussama Idrissi, Myron Boadu, Calvin Stengs. Trainer: Arne Slot.
Royal Antwerp FC: Sinan Bolat, Ritchie De Laet, Simen Juklerød, Dylan Batubinsika, Buta, Faris Haroun, Lior Refaelov (75.Dino Arslanagic), Martin Hongla, Dieumerci Mbokani, Ivo Rodrigues (66.Geoffry Hairemans), Didier Lamkel Zé (90+4.Alexis De Sart). Trainer: László Bölöni.
Goals: 38' Dylan Batubinsika 0-1, 82' Myron Boadu 1-1.
Sent off: 73' Buta.

22.08.2019; Estádio Municipal de Braga, Braga
Referee: Xavier Estrada Fernández (ESP); Attendance: 11,667
Sporting Clube de Braga – FK Spartak Moskva 1-0(0-0)
Sporting Braga: Matheus Magalhães, Ricardo Esgaio, Nuno Sequeira, Pablo Santos (64.Vítor Tormena), Bruno Viana, Fransérgio (46.João Novais), João Palhinha, André Horta (85.Murilo), Wilson Eduardo, Paulinho, Ricardo Horta. Trainer: Sá Pinto.
Spartak Moskva: Aleksandr Maksimenko, Andrey Eshchenko, Georgi Dzhikiya, Samuel Gigot, Ayrton, André Schürrle, Roman Zobnin, Reziuan Mirzov (63.Lorenzo Melgarejo), Ayaz Guliev (85.Nail Umyarov), Zelimkhan Bakaev, Ezequiel Ponce. Trainer: Oleg Kononov.
Goal: 74' Ricardo Horta 1-0.

22.08.2019; Stadio Olimpico Grande Torino, Torino
Referee: Artur Manuel Soares Dias (POR); Attendance: 24,091
Torino FC – Wolverhampton Wanderers FC 2-3(0-1)
Torino FC: Salvatore Sirigu, Lorenzo De Silvestri, Cristian Ansaldi (71.Ola Aina), Nicolas N'Koulou, Armando Izzo, Bremer, Soualiho Meïté (64.Tomás Rincón), Daniele Baselli, Simone Zaza, Andrea Belotti, Álex Berenguer (59.Sasa Lukic). Trainer: Walter Mazzarri.
Wolverhampton Wanderers: Rui Patrício, Willy Boly, Conor Coady, Vallejo, Rúben Vinagre, João Moutinho, Romain Saïss, Leander Dendoncker, Raúl Jiménez (76.Patrick Cutrone), Adama Traoré (64.Jonny Castro), Diogo Jota (69.Pedro Neto). Trainer: Nuno Espírito Santo.
Goals: 43' Bremer 0-1 (own goal), 59' Diogo Jota 0-2, 61' Lorenzo De Silvestri 1-2, 72' Raúl Jiménez 1-3, 89' Andrea Belotti 2-3 (pen).

29.08.2019; Stádio Neo GSP, Nicosia
Referee: William Collum (SCO); Attendance: 2,004
Apollon Limassol FC – PSV EINDHOVEN 0-4(0-0)
Apollon Limassol: Joël Mall, Charis Kyriakou (61.Adrián Sardinero), Attila Szalai, Héctor Yuste, Sasa Markovic, Diego Aguirre, Serge Gakpé, Emilio Zelaya, João Pedro, Fotios Papoulis (69.Ioannis Pittas), Giannis Gianniotas (77.Roger Tamba M'Pinda). Trainer: Sofronis Avgousti.
PSV Eindhoven: Jeroen Zoet, Nick Viergever, Timo Baumgartl (81.Daniel Schwaab), Olivier Boscagli, Denzel Dumfries, Jorrit Hendrix (74.Kostas Mitroglou), Érick Gutiérrez, Pablo Rosario, Mohammed Ihattaren, Donyell Malen, Cody Gakpo (77.Amar Catic). Trainer: Mark van Bommel.
Goals: 73' Mohammed Ihattaren 0-1, 76' Kostas Mitroglou 0-2, 79', 90+4' Donyell Malen 0-3, 0-4.

29.08.2019; Commerzbank-Arena, Frankfurt am Main
Referee: Orel Grinfeld (ISR); Attendance: 47,000
EINTRACHT FRANKFURT – Racing Club de Strasbourg 3-0(1-0)
Eintracht Frankfurt: Kevin Trapp, Makoto Hasebe, Martin Hinteregger, Danny da Costa, Almamy Touré, Sebastian Rode (90.Dejan Joveljic), Filip Kostic, Dominik Kohr (75.Gelson Fernandes), Daichi Kamada, Gonçalo Paciência (83.Mijat Gacinovic), Ante Rebic. Trainer: Adi Hütter.
RC Strasbourg: Matz Sels, Lamine Koné (69.Nuno Da Costa), Stefan Mitrovic, Lionel Carole, Kenny Lala, Alexander Djiku, Jonas Martin, Dimitri Liénard, Adrien Thomasson (88.Jean Ricner Bellegarde), Ludovic Ajorque (88.Lebo Mothiba), Kévin Lucien Zohi. Trainer: Thierry Laurey.
Goals: 27' Stefan Mitrovic 1-0 (own goal), 60' Filip Kostic 2-0, 66' Danny da Costa 3-0.
Sent off: 44' Ante Rebic, 55' Dimitri Liénard.

29.08.2019; Stade „Roi Baudouin", Bruxelles
Referee: Anastasios Sidiropoulos (GRE); Attendance: 19,786
Royal Antwerp FC – AZ ALKMAAR 1-4(0-0,1-1)
Royal Antwerp FC: Sinan Bolat, Ritchie De Laet (104.Robbe Quirynen), Simen Juklerød, Dylan Batubinsika, Abdoulaye Seck, Faris Haroun, Lior Refaelov (80.Dino Arslanagic), Alexis De Sart (99.Amara Baby), Dieumerci Mbokani, Ivo Rodrigues (71.Martin Hongla), Didier Lamkel Zé. Trainer: László Bölöni.
AZ Alkmaar: Marco Bizot, Ron Vlaar, Stijn Wuytens (53.Yukinari Sugawara), Jonas Svensson (67.Ferdy Druijf), Thomas Ouwejan (46.Albert Gudmundsson), Owen Wijndal, Fredrik Midtsjø, Teun Koopmeiners, Oussama Idrissi, Myron Boadu (111.Jordy Clasie), Calvin Stengs. Trainer: Arne Slot.
Goals: 73' Didier Lamkel Zé 1-0, 90' Calvin Stengs 1-1, 96' Ferdy Druijf 1-2, 102' Teun Koopmeiners 1-3 (pen), 113' Albert Gudmundsson 1-4.
Sent off: 35' Dieumerci Mbokani, 74' Didier Lamkel Zé.

29.08.2019; Otkrytie Arena, Moskva
Referee: Davide Massa (ITA); Attendance: 38,176
FK Spartak Moskva – SPORTING CLUBE DE BRAGA 1-2(0-2)
Spartak Moskva: Aleksandr Maksimenko, Andrey Eshchenko, Georgi Dzhikiya, Samuel Gigot, Ayrton, André Schürrle, Roman Zobnin (75.Nail Umyarov), Reziuan Mirzov (46.Soltmurad Bakaev), Ayaz Guliev, Zelimkhan Bakaev, Ezequiel Ponce (62.Jano Ananidze). Trainer: Oleg Kononov.
Sporting Braga: Matheus Magalhães, Ricardo Esgaio, Nuno Sequeira, Bruno Viana, Vítor Tormena (39.Lucas "Ferrugem" Cunha), João Novais (76.Fransérgio), João Palhinha, André Horta, Wilson Eduardo (24.Galeno), Paulinho, Ricardo Horta. Trainer: Sá Pinto.
Goals: 42', 45+3' Ricardo Horta 0-1, 0-2, 89' Zelimkhan Bakaev 1-2.

29.08.2019; Molineux Stadium, Wolverhampton
Referee: Jesús Gil Manzano (ESP); Attendance: 29,222
WOLVERHAMPTON WANDERERS FC – Torino FC 2-1(1-0)
Wolverhampton Wanderers: Rui Patrício, Willy Boly, Conor Coady, Jonny Castro, Vallejo, João Moutinho (90.Rúben Neves), Romain Saïss, Leander Dendoncker, Raúl Jiménez (90+2.Pedro Neto), Adama Traoré, Diogo Jota (81.Patrick Cutrone). Trainer: Nuno Espírito Santo.
Torino FC: Salvatore Sirigu, Lorenzo De Silvestri, Armando Izzo, Ola Aina (70.Álex Berenguer), Kevin Bonifazi, Bremer, Tomás Rincón (72.Soualiho Meïté), Daniele Baselli, Sasa Lukic, Simone Zaza (82.Vincenzo Millico), Andrea Belotti. Trainer: Walter Mazzarri.
Goals: 30' Raúl Jiménez 1-0, 58' Andrea Belotti 1-1, 59' Leander Dendoncker 2-1.

22.08.2019; RCDE Stadium, Cornella de Llobregat
Referee: Tobias Stieler (GER); Attendance: 13,686
RCD Espanyol Barcelona – FK Zorya Luhansk 3-1(0-1)
RCD Espanyol: Diego López, Dídac Vilà (46.Víctor Sánchez), Javi López, Lluís López, Fernando Calero, Granero, Iturraspe (20.Marc Roca), Sergi Darder, Facundo Ferreyra, Lei Wu, Javi Puado (71.Matías Vargas). Trainer: David Gallego.
Zorya Luhansk: Mykyta Shevchenko, Dmitriy Ivanisenya (90+1.Levan Arveladze), Oleksandr Tymchyk, Joel Abu Hanna (79.Maksim Biliy), Artem Gromov, Bogdan Mykhaylichenko, Yevgen Cheberko, Vladyslav Kochergin, Bohdan Lednev, Vladyslav Kabayev, Maksym Lunyov (64.Vladlen Yurchenko). Trainer: Viktor Skripnik.
Goals: 38' Vladyslav Kochergin 0-1, 58' Facundo Ferreyra 1-1, 79' Javi López 2-1, 81' Matías Vargas 3-1.

22.08.2019; Stadion Partizana, Beograd
Referee: Viktor Kassai (HUN); Attendance: 3,157
FK Partizan Beograd – Molde FK 2-1(1-1)
Partizan Beograd: Vladimir Stojkovic, Nemanja Miletic (I), Igor Vujacic, Slobodan Urosevic, Strahinja Pavlovic, Zoran Tosic, Aleksandar Scekic, Seydouba Soumah (73.Bibras Natcho), Sasa Zdjelar, Umar Sadiq (46.Ognjen Ozegovic), Filip Stevanovic (62.Takuma Asano). Trainer: Savo Milosevic.
Molde FK: Álex Craninx, Vegard Forren, Ruben Gabrielsen, Kristoffer Haraldseid, Martin Bjørnbak, Magnus Eikrem (69.Martin Ellingsen), Etzaz Hussain, Eirik Hestad, Fredrik Aursnes, Erling Knudtzon (33.Mathis Bolly, 85.Mattias Moström), Leke James. Trainer: Erling Moe.
Goals: 44' Mathis Bolly 0-1, 45+1' Seydouba Soumah 1-1, 84' Zoran Tosic 2-1.

29.08.2019; Slavutych-Arena, Zaporizhia
Referee: Radu Petrescu (ROU); Attendance: 10,181
FK Zorya Luhansk – RCD ESPANYOL BARCELONA 2-2(0-1)
Zorya Luhansk: Mykyta Shevchenko, Dmitriy Ivanisenya, Oleksandr Tymchyk, Joel Abu Hanna, Artem Gromov (58.Nazariy Rusyn), Dmytro Khomchenovsky, Bogdan Mykhaylichenko, Yevgen Cheberko, Vladyslav Kochergin, Bohdan Lednev (68.Vladlen Yurchenko), Pylyp Budkovsky (82.Vladyslav Kabayev). Trainer: Viktor Skripnik.
RCD Espanyol: Diego López, Dídac Vilà, Javi López, Lluís López, Fernando Calero, Granero, Sergi Darder (66.Víctor Sánchez), Marc Roca, Matías Vargas (77.Víctor Campuzano), Melendo, Facundo Ferreyra (73.Lei Wu). Trainer: David Gallego.
Goals: 34' Facundo Ferreyra 0-1, 54' Bohdan Lednev 1-1, 62' Matías Vargas 1-2, 78' Nazariy Rusyn 2-2.

29.08.2019; Aker Stadion, Molde
Referee: Ruddy Buquet (FRA); Attendance: 7,102
Molde FK – FK PARTIZAN BEOGRAD 1-1(0-0)
Molde FK: Álex Craninx, Vegard Forren, Ruben Gabrielsen, Kristoffer Haraldseid, Kristoffer Haugen (84.Erling Knudtzon), Magnus Eikrem, Etzaz Hussain, Eirik Hestad, Fredrik Aursnes, Mathis Bolly (59.Ohi Omoijuanfo), Leke James. Trainer: Erling Moe.
Partizan Beograd: Vladimir Stojkovic, Bojan Ostojic, Nemanja Miletic (I), Slobodan Urosevic, Strahinja Pavlovic, Zoran Tosic (83.Aleksandar Lutovac), Aleksandar Scekic, Seydouba Soumah (66.Bibras Natcho), Sasa Zdjelar, Takuma Asano, Umar Sadiq (68.Ognjen Ozegovic). Trainer: Savo Milosevic.
Goals: 72' Leke James 1-0, 80' Nemanja Miletic (I) 1-1.

GROUP STAGE

GROUP A	1. **Sevilla FC**	6	5	0	1	14	- 3	15
	2. **APOEL Nicosia FC**	6	3	1	2	10	- 8	10
	3. Qarabağ FK Bakı	6	1	2	3	8	- 11	5
	4. F91 Dudelange	6	1	1	4	8	- 18	4

19.09.2019; „Tofiq Bahramov" adina Respublika stadionu, Bakı
Referee: Yevhen Aranovskyi (UKR); Attendance: 30,826
Qarabağ FK Bakı – Sevilla FC 0-3(0-0)
Qarabağ FK: Asmir Begovic, Maksim Medvedev, Qara Qarayev (85.Ismayil Ibrahimli), Badavi Hüseynov, Ailton, Abbas Hüseynov, Míchel, Jaime Romero (77.Dani Quintana), Richard Almeyda, Abdellah Zoubir, Magaye Gueye (67.Araz Abdullayev). Trainer: Gurban Gurbanov.
Sevilla FC: Tomás Vaclík, Escudero, Diego Carlos, Jules Koundé, Franco Vázquez, Nemanja Gudelj, Óliver Torres (86.Munas Dabour), Joan Jordán (58.Rony Lopes), Javier Hernández (72.Éver Banega), Munir, Alejandro Pozo. Trainer: Lopetegui.
Goals: 62' Javier Hernández 0-1, 78' Munir 0-2, 85' Óliver Torres 0-3.

03.10.2019; Stade „Josy Barthel", Lëtzebuerg
Referee: John Beaton (SCO); Attendance: 3,005
F91 Dudelange – Qarabağ FK Bakı 1-4(0-3)
F91 Dudelange: Jonathan Joubert, Tom Schnell, Thibaut Lesquoy, Mohamed Bouchouari, Mario Pokar (72.Kobe Cools), Ryan Klapp (56.Corenthyn Lavie), Mickaël Garos, Sabir Bougrine, Danel Sinani, Antoine Bernier, Laurent Mendy (67.Charles Morren). Trainers: Emilio Ferrera & Bertrand Crasson.
Qarabağ FK: Asmir Begovic, Rashad Sadyqov, Maksim Medvedev, Qara Qarayev (60.Simeon Slavchev), Badavi Hüseynov, Ailton, Míchel (72.Magaye Gueye), Dani Quintana (81.Araz Abdullayev), Richard Almeyda, Abdellah Zoubir, Mahir Emreli. Trainer: Gurban Gurbanov.
Goals: 11' Abdellah Zoubir 0-1, 30' Míchel 0-2, 37' Richard Almeyda 0-3 (pen), 69' Dani Quintana 0-4, 90' Antoine Bernier 1-4.
Sent off: 62' Mickaël Garos.

19.09.2019; Stádio Neo GSP, Nicosia
Referee: Dumitri Muntean (MDA); Attendance: 9,313
APOEL Nicosia FC – F91 Dudelange 3-4(0-1)
APOEL Nicosia: Vid Belec, Giorgios Merkis, Nicholas Ioannou, Dragan Mihajlovic, Savvas Gentsoglou, Antonio Jakolis (46.Moussa Al Taamari), Uros Matic, Tomás De Vincenti (76.Giorgos Efrem), Lucas Souza (46.Joãozinho), Roman Bezjak, Andrija Pavlovic. Trainer: Thomas Doll.
F91 Dudelange: Jonathan Joubert, Tom Schnell, Mehdi Kirch (63.Thibaut Lesquoy), Mohamed Bouchouari, Mario Pokar, Dominik Stolz (90+3.Kobe Cools), Mickaël Garos, Charles Morren, Danel Sinani, Antoine Bernier, Laurent Mendy (67.Corenthyn Lavie). Trainers: Emilio Ferrera & Bertrand Crasson.
Goals: 36' Danel Sinani 0-1, 51' Antoine Bernier 0-2, 54' Andrija Pavlovic 1-2, 56' Tomás De Vincenti 2-2 (pen), 58' Andrija Pavlovic 3-2, 72' Dominik Stolz 3-3, 82' Danel Sinani 3-4.

03.10.2019; Estadio „Ramón Sánchez Pizjuán", Sevilla
Referee: Bas Nijhuis (NED); Attendance: 30,008
Sevilla FC – APOEL Nicosia FC 1-0(1-0)
Sevilla FC: Yassine Bounou, Escudero, Sergi Gómez, Jules Koundé, Franco Vázquez, Nemanja Gudelj, Joan Jordán, Javier Hernández (79.Munas Dabour), Rony Lopes (72.Éver Banega), Munir (61.Bryan Gil), Alejandro Pozo. Trainer: Lopetegui.
APOEL Nicosia: Vid Belec, Vujadin Savic, Giorgios Merkis, Nicholas Ioannou, Dragan Mihajlovic, Savvas Gentsoglou (80.Giorgos Efrem), Antonio Jakolis, Uros Matic, Lucas Souza, Moussa Al Taamari (83.Stathis Aloneftis), Andrija Pavlovic (66.Linus Hallenius). Trainer: Thomas Doll.
Goal: 17' Javier Hernández 1-0.

24.10.2019; „Tofiq Bahramov" adina Respublika stadionu, Bakı
Referee: Filip Glova (SVK); Attendance: 30,824
Qarabağ FK Bakı – APOEL Nicosia FC 2-2(1-2)
Qarabağ FK: Asmir Begovic, Rashad Sadyqov, Maksim Medvedev, Qara Qarayev, Badavi Hüseynov, Ailton, Míchel, Dani Quintana, Richard Almeyda, Abdellah Zoubir, Magaye Gueye (46.Mahir Emreli). Trainer: Gurban Gurbanov.
APOEL Nicosia: Vid Belec, Vujadin Savic, Giorgios Merkis, Praxitelis Vouros, Nicholas Ioannou (67.Antonio Jakolis), Dragan Mihajlovic, Savvas Gentsoglou, Uros Matic, Lucas Souza, Linus Hallenius (76.Roman Bezjak), Andrija Pavlovic (85.Alef). Trainer: Thomas Doll.
Goals: 13' Dani Quintana 1-0, 29' Maksim Medvedev 1-1 (own goal), 45' Linus Hallenius 1-2, 58' Ailton 2-2.

07.11.2019; Stade „Josy Barthel", Lëtzebuerg
Referee: Vilhjálmur Thórarinsson (ISL); Attendance: 2.848
F91 Dudelange – Sevilla FC 2-5(0-4)
F91 Dudelange: Jonathan Joubert, Mehdi Kirch, Kobe Cools, Mohamed Bouchouari, Ryan Klapp (46.Bertino Cabral Barbosa), Dominick Stolz (86.Corenthyn Lavie), Mickaël Garos, Charles Morren, Sabir Bougrine (46.Tom Schnell), Danel Sinani, Antoine Bernier. Trainers: Emilio Ferrera & Bertrand Crasson.
Sevilla FC: Yassine Bounou, Escudero, Sergi Gómez, Nemanja Gudelj, Óliver Torres (51.Franco Vázquez), Joan Jordán (61.Fernando), Nolito (51.Luuk de Jong), Munas Dabour, Rony Lopes, Munir, Alejandro Pozo. Trainer: Lopetegui.
Goals: 17' Munas Dabour 0-1, 27', 33' Munir 0-2, 0-3, 36' Munas Dabour 0-4, 67' Munir 0-5, 69', 80' Danel Sinani 1-5, 2-5.

28.11.2019; Estadio „Ramón Sánchez Pizjuán", Sevilla
Referee: Mohammed Al-Hakim (SWE); Attendance: 19,803
Sevilla FC – Qarabağ FK Bakı 2-0(0-0)
Sevilla FC: Yassine Bounou, Daniel Carriço, Escudero, Sergi Gómez, Nemanja Gudelj, Óliver Torres (68.José Mena), Javier Hernández (62.Franco Vázquez), Munas Dabour, Rony Lopes (54.Bryan Gil), Munir, Alejandro Pozo. Trainer: Lopetegui.
Qarabağ FK: Asmir Begovic, Maksim Medvedev, Qara Qarayev, Badavi Hüseynov, Ailton, Abbas Hüseynov (69.Araz Abdullayev), Rahil Mammadov, Míchel (84.Dani Quintana), Jaime Romero (70.Mahir Emreli), Richard Almeyda, Abdellah Zoubir. Trainer: Gurban Gurbanov.
Goals: 61' Bryan Gil 10, 90+2' Munas Dabour 2-0.

12.12.2019; „Tofiq Bahramov" adina Respublika stadionu, Bakı
Referee: Kristo Tohver (EST); Attendance: 5,823
Qarabağ FK Bakı – F91 Dudelange 1-1(0-0)
Qarabağ FK: Sahrudin Mahammadaliyev, Rashad Sadyqov, Maksim Medvedev, Qara Qarayev, Badavi Hüseynov, Ailton, Míchel, Dani Quintana (64.Jaime Romero), Abdellah Zoubir, Ismayil Ibrahimli (50.Richard Almeyda), Mahir Emreli (75.Magaye Gueye). Trainer: Gurban Gurbanov.
F91 Dudelange: Jonathan Joubert, Tom Schnell, Thibaut Lesquoy, Kobe Cools, Mohamed Bouchouari, Dominick Stolz, Mickaël Garos, Charles Morren, Sabir Bougrine (84.Mario Pokar), Adel Bettaieb (86.Laurent Mendy), Antoine Bernier (78.Ryan Klapp). Trainers: Emilio Ferrera & Bertrand Crasson.
Goals: 63' Sabir Bougrine 0-1, 90+1' Magaye Gueye 1-1.
Sent off: 46' Qara Qarayev.

24.10.2019; Estadio „Ramón Sánchez Pizjuán", Sevilla
Referee: Anastasios Papapetrou (GRE); Attendance: 26,165
Sevilla FC – F91 Dudelange 3-0(0-0)
Sevilla FC: Yassine Bounou, Escudero, Sergi Gómez (70.Diego Carlos), Jules Koundé, Franco Vázquez, Nemanja Gudelj, Óliver Torres, Luuk de Jong (52.Munir), Munas Dabour, Rony Lopes (60.Bryan Gil), Alejandro Pozo. Trainer: Lopetegui.
F91 Dudelange: Jonathan Joubert, Tom Schnell, Thibaut Lesquoy, Kobe Cools, Mohamed Bouchouari, Dominick Stolz (79.Adel Bettaieb), Corenthyn Lavie, Charles Morren, Sabir Bougrine (81.Omar Natami), Danel Sinani, Antoine Bernier (76.Ryan Klapp). Trainers: Emilio Ferrera & Bertrand Crasson.
Goals: 48', 75' Franco Vázquez 1-0, 2-0, 78' Munir 3-0.

07.11.2019; Stádio Neo GSP, Nicosia
Referee: Manuel Schüttengruber (AUT); Attendance: 9,432
APOEL Nicosia FC – Qarabağ FK Bakı 2-1(0-1)
APOEL Nicosia: Vid Belec, Vujadin Savic, Joãozinho (46.Moussa Al Tamari), Praxitelis Vouros, Nicholas Ioannou, Dragan Mihajlovic, Savvas Gentsoglou (59.Roman Bezjak), Uros Matic, Lucas Souza, Linus Hallenius (75.Giorgos Efrem), Andrija Pavlovic. Trainer: Thomas Doll.
Qarabağ FK: Asmir Begovic, Rashad Sadyqov, Maksim Medvedev, Qara Qarayev, Badavi Hüseynov, Ailton, Míchel (83.Abbas Hüseynov), Dani Quintana (16.Magaye Gueye, 76.Jaime Romero), Araz Abdullayev, Richard Almeyda, Abdellah Zoubir. Trainer: Gurban Gurbanov.
Goals: 10' Maksim Medvedev 0-1, 59' Lucas Souza 1-1, 88' Nicholas Ioannou 2-1.

28.11.2019; Stade „Josy Barthel", Lëtzebuerg
Referee: Gianluca Rocchi (ITA); Attendance: 2,912
F91 Dudelange – APOEL Nicosia FC 0-2(0-2)
F91 Dudelange: Jonathan Joubert, Tom Schnell, Thibaut Lesquoy, Kobe Cools, Mohamed Bouchouari (61.Adel Bettaieb), Dominick Stolz (77.Mario Pokar), Mickaël Garos, Charles Morren, Sabir Bougrine (54.Corenthyn Lavie), Danel Sinani, Antoine Bernier. Trainers: Emilio Ferrera & Bertrand Crasson.
APOEL Nicosia: Vid Belec, Vujadin Savic, Giorgios Merkis, Praxitelis Vouros, Nicholas Ioannou (66.Antonio Jakolis), Dragan Mihajlovic, Savvas Gentsoglou (46.Alef), Uros Matic, Lucas Souza, Moussa Al Tamari, Linus Hallenius (84.Tomás De Vincenti). Trainer: Thomas Doll.
Goals: 12' Uros Matic 0-1 (pen), 43' Giorgios Merkis 0-2.
Sent off: 83' Praxitelis Vouros, 90' Danel Sinani.

12.12.2019; Stádio Neo GSP, Nicosia
Referee: Nikola Dabanovic (MNE); Attendance: 5,608
APOEL Nicosia FC – Sevilla FC 1-0(0-0)
APOEL Nicosia: Vid Belec, Vujadin Savic, Giorgios Merkis, Nicholas Ioannou, Dragan Mihajlovic, Antonio Jakolis (79.Andreas Makris), Uros Matic, Lucas Souza, Alef, Moussa Al Tamari (90+1.Giorgos Efrem), Andrija Pavlovic (70.Tomás De Vincenti). Trainer: Loukas Hatziloukas.
Sevilla FC: Yassine Bounou, Escudero, Sergi Gómez, Nemanja Gudelj, Lucas Ocampos, Joan Jordán (46.Óliver Torres), Genaro Rodríguez, Javier Hernández (46.Munas Dabour), Rony Lopes, Alejandro Pozo, Bryan Gil (68.José Mena). Trainer: Lopetegui.
Goal: 61' Vujadin Savic 1-0.

1. **Malmö FF**	6	3	2	1	8 - 6	11
2. **FC København**	6	2	3	1	5 - 4	9
3. FK Dynamo Kyiv	6	1	4	1	7 - 7	7
4. FC Lugano	6	0	3	3	2 - 5	3

19.09.2019; NSK Olimpiyskiy Stadium, Kyiv
Referee: Aleksandar Stavrev (MKD); Attendance: 17,159
FK Dinamo Kyiv – Malmö FF 1-0(0-0)
Dynamo Kyiv: Denis Boyko, Tamás Kádár, Tomasz Kedziora, Artem Shabanov, Vitali Mykolenko, Sergiy Sydorchuk, Vitaliy Buyalskiy, Benjamin Verbic, Viktor Tsygankov (90+1.Oleksandr Karavayev), Volodymyr Shepelev, Gerson Rodrigues (73.Artem Besedin). Trainer: Aleksey Mikhaylichenko.
Malmö FF: Johan Dahlin, Behrang Safari, Rasmus Bengtsson, Lasse Nielsen, Felix Beijmo (57.Eric Larsson), Søren Rieks, Anders Christiansen (73.Marcus Antonsson), Fouad Bachirou, Arnór Ingvi Traustason (86.Romain Gall), Oscar Lewicki, Markus Rosenberg. Trainer: Uwe Rösler.; Goal: 84' Vitaliy Buyalskiy 1-0.

03.10.2019; Kybunpark, St.Gallen
Referee: Karim Abed (FRA); Attendance: 1,281
FC Lugano – FK Dinamo Kyiv 0-0
FC Lugano: Noam Baumann, Mijat Maric, Fabio Daprelà, Numa Lavanchy, Eloge Yao, Marco Aratore (64.Nicola Dalmonte), Jonathan Sabbatini, Bálint Vécsei, Sandi Lovric (71.Olivier Custodio), Alexander Gerndt (78.Filip Holender), Carlinhos. Trainer: Fabio Celestini.
Dynamo Kyiv: Georgiy Bushchan, Tamás Kádár, Tomasz Kedziora, Artem Shabanov, Vitali Mykolenko, Sergiy Sydorchuk, Vitaliy Buyalskiy, Benjamin Verbic (88.Carlos de Pena), Viktor Tsygankov, Volodymyr Shepelev (84.Denys Garmash), Gerson Rodrigues (70.Artem Besedin). Trainer: Aleksey Mikhaylichenko.

24.10.2019; Swedbank Stadion, Malmö
Referee: Rob Harvey (IRL); Attendance: 16,789
Malmö FF – FC Lugano 2-1(2-0)
Malmö FF: Johan Dahlin, Eric Larsson, Lasse Nielsen, Jonas Knudsen (85.Behrang Safari), Søren Rieks, Fouad Bachirou, Arnór Ingvi Traustason, Oscar Lewicki, Bonke Innocent (68.Rasmus Bengtsson), Guillermo Molins (77.Markus Rosenberg), Jo Inge Berget. Trainer: Uwe Rösler.
FC Lugano: Noam Baumann, Mijat Maric, Fabio Daprelà, Eloge Yao (60.Marco Aratore), Linus Obexer (79.Filip Holender), Jonathan Sabbatini, Olivier Custodio, Sandi Lovric, Alexander Gerndt, Mattia Bottani (81.Francisco Rodriguez), Carlinhos. Trainer: Fabio Celestini.
Goals: 13' Jo Inge Berget 1-0 (pen), 32' Guillermo Molins 2-0, 50' Alexander Gerndt 2-1.

07.11.2019; Kybunpark, St.Gallen
Referee: Giorgi Kruashvili (GEO); Attendance: 1,875
FC Lugano – Malmö FF 0-0
FC Lugano: Noam Baumann, Mijat Maric, Fabio Daprelà, Numa Lavanchy, Eloge Yao, Marco Aratore, Bálint Vécsei, Olivier Custodio, Mattia Bottani (57.Alexander Gerndt), Filip Holender (81.Sandi Lovric), Carlinhos. Trainer: Maurizio Jacobacci.
Malmö FF: Johan Dahlin, Behrang Safari (69.Jonas Knudsen), Rasmus Bengtsson, Lasse Nielsen, Felix Beijmo (64.Guillermo Molins), Søren Rieks, Fouad Bachirou, Arnór Ingvi Traustason, Oscar Lewicki (30.Bonke Innocent), Markus Rosenberg, Jo Inge Berget. Trainer: Uwe Rösler.

28.11.2019; Swedbank Stadion, Malmö
Referee: Pavel Královec (CZE); Attendance: 19,224
Malmö FF – FK Dinamo Kyiv 4-3(1-2)
Malmö FF: Johan Dahlin, Behrang Safari (90+7.Jonas Knudsen), Rasmus Bengtsson, Eric Larsson (79.Guillermo Molins), Lasse Nielsen, Søren Rieks, Fouad Bachirou, Arnór Ingvi Traustason, Bonke Innocent (46.Erdal Rakip), Markus Rosenberg, Jo Inge Berget. Trainer: Uwe Rösler.
Dynamo Kyiv: Georgiy Bushchan, Tamás Kádár, Tomasz Kedziora, Artem Shabanov, Vitali Mykolenko, Sergiy Sydorchuk, Vitaly Buyalskiy (89.Denys Garmash), Benjamin Verbic (82.Oleksandr Karavayev), Viktor Tsygankov, Volodymyr Shepelev (71.Mykola Shaparenko), Artem Besedin. Trainer: Aleksey Mikhaylichenko.
Goals: 2.Rasmus Bengtsson 1-0, 18.Vitali Mykolenko 1-1, 39.Viktor Tsygankov 1-2, 48.Markus Rosenberg 2-2, 57.Erdal Rakip 3-2, 77.Benjamin Verbic 3-3, 90+6.Markus Rosenberg 4-3.
Sent off: 65' Sergiy Sydorchuk.

19.09.2019; Telia Parken, København
Referee: Fábio José Costa Veríssimo (POR); Attendance: 18,240
FC København – FC Lugano 1-0(0-0)
FC København: Kalle Johnsson, Pierre Bengtsson, Sotirios Papagiannopoulos, Guillermo Varela, Victor Nelsson, Rasmus Falk (79.Pep Biel Mas), Zeca, Viktor Fischer (79.Bryan Oviedo), Jens Stage, Pieros Soteriou, Michael Santos (77.Mohammed Daramy). Trainer: Ståle Solbakken.
FC Lugano: Noam Baumann, Mijat Maric, Fabio Daprelà, Numa Lavanchy, Ákos Kecskés, Eloge Yao (70.Filip Holender), Jonathan Sabbatini, Bálint Vécsei (82.Nicola Dalmonte), Olivier Custodio, Mattia Bottani (49.Marco Aratore), Carlinhos. Trainer: Fabio Celestini.
Goal: 50' Michael Santos 1-0.

03.10.2019; Swedbank Stadion, Malmö
Referee: Deniz Aytekin (GER); Attendance: 19,884
Malmö FF – FC København 1-1(0-1)
Malmö FF: Johan Dahlin, Behrang Safari, Rasmus Bengtsson, Lasse Nielsen, Søren Rieks (46.Eric Larsson), Anders Christiansen (58.Arnór Ingvi Traustason), Fouad Bachirou, Oscar Lewicki, Markus Rosenberg, Jo Inge Berget, Marcus Antonsson (78.Guillermo Molins). Trainer: Uwe Rösler.
FC København: Kalle Johnsson, Pierre Bengtsson, Andreas Bjelland, Guillermo Varela, Victor Nelsson, Rasmus Falk (85.Karlo Bartolec), Zeca, Viktor Fischer (70.Carlo Holse), Jens Stage, Pieros Soteriou, Michael Santos (86.Mohammed Daramy). Trainer: Ståle Solbakken.
Goals: 45+5' Lasse Nielsen 0-1 (own goal), 55' Markus Rosenberg 1-1.

24.10.2019; NSK Olimpiyskiy Stadium, Kyiv
Referee: Halil Umut Meler (TUR); Attendance: 21,202
FK Dinamo Kyiv – FC København 1-1(0-1)
Dynamo Kyiv: Georgiy Bushchan, Tomasz Kedziora, Artem Shabanov, Denys Popov, Vitali Mykolenko, Sergiy Sydorchuk, Benjamin Verbic, Carlos de Pena (80.Denys Garmash), Viktor Tsygankov, Volodymyr Shepelev, Artem Besedin. Trainer: Aleksey Mikhaylichenko.
FC København: Kalle Johnsson, Bryan Oviedo, Sotirios Papagiannopoulos, Karlo Bartolec, Victor Nelsson, Rasmus Falk (87.Guillermo Varela), Zeca, Viktor Fischer (75.Nicolaj Thomsen), Jens Stage, Pieros Soteriou, Michael Santos (89.Nicklas Bendtner). Trainer: Ståle Solbakken.
Goals: 2' Pieros Soteriou 0-1, 53' Artem Shabanov 1-1.

07.11.2019; Telia Parken, København
Referee: Tamás Bognár (HUN); Attendance: 23,166
FC København – FK Dinamo Kyiv 1-1(1-0)
FC København: Kalle Johnsson, Pierre Bengtsson (69.Karlo Bartolec), Sotirios Papagiannopoulos, Guillermo Varela, Victor Nelsson, Rasmus Falk (55.Mohammed Daramy), Zeca, Viktor Fischer (82.Nicolaj Thomsen), Jens Stage, Pieros Soteriou, Michael Santos. Trainer: Ståle Solbakken.
Dynamo Kyiv: Georgiy Bushchan, Tomasz Kedziora, Artem Shabanov, Denys Popov, Vitali Mykolenko, Sergiy Sydorchuk, Benjamin Verbic (89.Carlos de Pena), Oleksandr Karavayev, Viktor Tsygankov, Volodymyr Shepelev, Artem Besedin. Trainer: Aleksey Mikhaylichenko.
Goals: 4' Jens Stage 1-0, 70' Benjamin Verbic 1-1.

28.11.2019; Kybunpark, St.Gallen
Referee: Aleksei Eskov (RUS); Attendance: 1,281
FC Lugano – FC København 0-1(0-1)
FC Lugano: Noam Baumann, Fabio Daprelà, Numa Lavanchy, Ákos Kecskés, Linus Obexer, Marco Aratore (70.Franklin Sasere), Olivier Custodio, Sandi Lovric, Stefano Guidotti (76.Miroslav Covilo), Mattia Bottani, Carlinhos (62.Nicola Dalmonte). Trainer: Maurizio Jacobacci.
FC København: Kalle Johnsson, Pierre Bengtsson, Andreas Bjelland, Sotirios Papagiannopoulos, Karlo Bartolec, Victor Nelsson, Zeca, Nicolaj Thomsen (79.Robert Mudrazija), Pep Biel Mas (74.Rasmus Falk), Pieros Soteriou, Michael Santos (86.Guillermo Varela). Trainer: Ståle Solbakken.
Goal: 27' Nicolaj Thomsen 0-1.

12.12.2019; NSK Olimpiyskiy Stadium, Kyiv
Referee: Aliyar Agayev (AZE); Attendance: 15,774
FK Dinamo Kyiv – FC Lugano 1-1(0-1)
Dynamo Kyiv: Georgiy Bushchan, Tamás Kádár, Tomasz Kedziora (64.Heorhii Tsitaishvili), Denys Popov, Vitali Mykolenko, Vitaly Buyalskiy, Oleksandr Karavayev, Carlos de Pena (77.Denys Garmash), Viktor Tsygankov, Volodymyr Shepelev, Artem Besedin (81.Fran Sol). Trainer: Aleksey Mikhaylichenko.
FC Lugano: David Da Costa, Fabio Daprelà, Fulvio Sulmoni, Eloge Yao, Linus Obexer, Marco Aratore, Olivier Custodio, Sandi Lovric (84.Domen Crnigoj), Stefano Guidotti (55.Bálint Vécsei), Filip Holender, Nicola Dalmonte (64.Mijat Maric). Trainer: Maurizio Jacobacci.
Goals: 45' Marco Aratore 0-1, 90+4' Viktor Tsygankov 1-1.

12.12.2019; Telia Parken, København
Referee: Davide Massa (ITA); Attendance: 32,941
FC København – Malmö FF 0-1(0-0)
FC København: Kalle Johnsson, Pierre Bengtsson, Andreas Bjelland, Sotirios Papagiannopoulos, Guillermo Varela (84.Karlo Bartolec), Rasmus Falk, Viktor Fischer, Nicolaj Thomsen (80.Michael Santos), Robert Mudrazija (46.Carlo Holse), Dame N'Doye, Pieros Soteriou. Trainer: Ståle Solbakken.
Malmö FF: Johan Dahlin, Behrang Safari (60.Jonas Knudsen), Rasmus Bengtsson, Eric Larsson, Lasse Nielsen, Søren Rieks, Anders Christiansen (80.Oscar Lewicki), Arnór Ingvi Traustason, Erdal Rakip (68.Guillermo Molins), Bonke Innocent, Markus Rosenberg. Trainer: Uwe Rösler.
Goal: 77' Sotirios Papagiannopoulos 0-1 (own goal).

GROUP C	1. **FC Basel**	6	4	1	1	12 - 4	13
	2. **Getafe CF**	6	4	0	2	8 - 4	12
	3. FK Krasnodar	6	3	0	3	7 - 11	9
	4. Trabzonspor Kulübü	6	0	1	5	3 - 11	1

19.09.2019; Estadio Coliseum „Alfonso Pérez", Getafe
Referee: Matej Jug (SVN); Attendance: 5,786
Getafe CF – Trabzonspor Kulübü 1-0(1-0)
Getafe CF: Leandro Chichizola, Allan Nyom, Bruno, Raúl García, Djené Dakonam, Fayçal Fajr, Portillo, David Timor (90+1.Mauro Arambarri), Kenedy (77.Cucurella), Ángel, Enric Gallego (68.Mata). Trainer: José Bordalás.
Trabzonspor: Ugurcan Çakir, João Pereira, Filip Novák, Gastón Campi, Majid Hosseini, John Obi Mikel, José Sosa, Dogan Erdogan (59.Abdülkadir Parmak), Donis Avdijaj (46.Daniel Sturridge), Anthony Nwakaeme (83.Firatcan Üzüm), Alexander Sørloth. Trainer: Ünal Karaman.
Goal: 18' Ángel 1-0.

19.09.2019; St. Jakob-Park, Basel
Referee: Mattias Gestranius (FIN); Attendance: 14,127
FC Basel – FK Krasnodar 5-0(2-0)
FC Basel: Jonas Omlin, Silvan Widmer, Omar Alderete, Raoul Petretta, Eray Cömart, Valentin Stocker (58.Noah Okafor), Luca Zuffi (79.Samuele Campo), Fabian Frei, Taulant Xhaka, Kevin Bua, Arthur Cabral (66.Blas Riveros). Trainer: Marcel Koller.
FK Krasnodar: Matvei Safonov, Aleksandr Martynovich, Sergey Petrov, Uros Spajic, Cristian Ramírez, Ruslan Kambolov (46.Daniil Utkin), Tonny Vilhena, Kristoffer Olsson (60.Younes Namli), Wamberto, Magomed Suleymanov, Ivan Ignatyev (67.Marcus Berg). Trainer: Sergey Matveev.
Goals: 9', 40' Kevin Bua 1-0, 2-0, 52' Luca Zuffi 3-0, 54' Tonny Vilhena 4-0 (own goal), 79' Noah Okafor 5-0.

03.10.2019; Stadion FK Krasnodar, Krasnodar
Referee: Ivan Bebek (CRO); Attendance: 20,035
FK Krasnodar – Getafe CF 1-2(0-1)
FK Krasnodar: Matvei Safonov, Jón Fjóluson (46.Ari), Aleksandr Martynovich, Sergey Petrov, Uros Spajic, Cristian Ramírez, Tonny Vilhena, Kristoffer Olsson (74.Daniil Utkin), Younes Namli (70.Manuel Fernandes), Marcus Berg, Magomed Suleymanov. Trainer: Sergey Matveev.
Getafe CF: Leandro Chichizola, Allan Nyom, Leandro Cabrera, Bruno, Raúl García, Fayçal Fajr, Portillo (72.Jason), David Timor, Kenedy (76.Cucurella), Ángel (84.Nemanja Maksimovic), Enric Gallego. Trainer: José Bordalás.
Goals: 36', 61' Ángel 0-1, 0-2, 69' Ari 1-2.
Sent off: 81' David Timor.

03.10.2019; Medical Park Stadyumu, Trabzon
Referee: Marco Di Bello (ITA); Attendance: 23,867
Trabzonspor Kulübü – FC Basel 2-2(1-1)
Trabzonspor: Ugurcan Çakir, Filip Novák, Gastón Campi, Majid Hosseini, Hüseyin Türkmen, John Obi Mikel, Dogan Erdogan, Donis Avdijaj (46.Anthony Nwakaeme), Abdülkadir Parmak, Daniel Sturridge (81.Kâmil Çörekçi), Alexander Sørloth (65.José Sosa). Trainer: Ünal Karaman.
FC Basel: Jonas Omlin, Silvan Widmer, Omar Alderete, Raoul Petretta, Eray Cömart, Valentin Stocker, Luca Zuffi (65.Noah Okafor), Fabian Frei, Taulant Xhaka, Kevin Bua, Kemal Ademi (70.Arthur Cabral). Trainer: Marcel Koller.
Goals: 20' Silvan Widmer 0-1, 26' Abdülkadir Parmak 1-1, 78' José Sosa 2-1, 80' Noah Okafor 2-2.

24.10.2019; Medical Park Stadyumu, Trabzon
Referee: Harald Lechner (AUT); Attendance: 26,405
Trabzonspor Kulübü – FK Krasnodar 0-2(0-0)
Trabzonspor: Ugurcan Çakir, João Pereira, Filip Novák, Kâmil Çörekçi (68.Dogan Erdogan), Gastón Campi (83.Ahmet Canbaz), Ivanildo Fernandes, José Sosa, Abdülkadir Parmak (72.Donis Avdijaj), Anthony Nwakaeme, Alexander Sørloth, Yusuf Sari. Trainer: Ünal Karaman.
FK Krasnodar: Matvei Safonov, Aleksandr Martynovich, Sergey Petrov, Uros Spajic, Cristian Ramírez, Ruslan Kambolov (76.Jón Fjóluson), Dmitriy Stotskiy (62.Manuel Fernandes), Tonny Vilhena, Kristoffer Olsson, Marcus Berg (71.Ari), Magomed Suleymanov. Trainer: Sergey Matveev.
Goals: 49' Marcus Berg 0-1, 90+2' Tonny Vilhena 0-2.

24.10.2019; Estadio Coliseum „Alfonso Pérez", Getafe
Referee: Jérôme Brisard (FRA); Attendance: 6,213
Getafe CF – FC Basel 0-1(0-1)
Getafe CF: Leandro Chichizola, Allan Nyom, Bruno (14.Leandro Cabrera), Raúl García, Djené Dakonam, Fayçal Fajr, Portillo (57.Jason), Kenedy, Nemanja Maksimovic, Ángel, Jorge Molina (71.Cucurella). Trainer: José Bordalás.
FC Basel: Djordje Nikolic, Silvan Widmer, Omar Alderete, Raoul Petretta, Eray Cömart, Valentin Stocker (90+3.Afimico Pululu), Luca Zuffi, Fabian Frei, Taulant Xhaka, Kevin Bua, Kemal Ademi (69.Arthur Cabral). Trainer: Marcel Koller.
Goal: 18' Fabian Frei 0-1.;
Sent off: 73' Kevin Bua.

07.11.2019; Stadion FK Krasnodar, Krasnodar
Referee: Benoît Bastien (FRA); Attendance: 21,669
FK Krasnodar – Trabzonspor Kulübü 3-1(2-0)
FK Krasnodar: Stanislav Kritsyuk, Aleksandr Martynovich, Sergey Petrov, Uros Spajic, Cristian Ramírez, Manuel Fernandes (63.Daniil Utkin), Dmitriy Stotskiy, Tonny Vilhena, Kristoffer Olsson (77.Ruslan Kambolov), Ari (66.Ivan Ignatyev), Magomed Suleymanov. Trainer: Sergey Matveev.
Trabzonspor: Erce Kardesler, Kâmil Çörekçi (87.Yusuf Sari), Gastón Campi, Majid Hosseini, Ivanildo Fernandes, Abdurahim Dursun, Serkan Asan, Dogan Erdogan, Donis Avdijaj (65.Anthony Nwakaeme), Ahmet Canbaz, Muhammet Akpinar (72.Alexander Sørloth). Trainer: Ünal Karaman. Goals: 27' SerkanAsan 1-0 (own goal), 34' Manuel Fernandes 2-0, 90+3' Ivan Ignatyev 3-0, 90+4' Anthony Nwakaeme 3-1.

07.11.2019; St. Jakob-Park, Basel
Referee: Serhiy Boyko (UKR); Attendance: 26,298
FC Basel – Getafe CF 2-1(1-1)
FC Basel: Jonas Omlin, Silvan Widmer, Omar Alderete, Raoul Petretta, Eray Cömart, Blas Riveros, Luca Zuffi, Fabian Frei, Taulant Xhaka (64.Samuele Campo), Edon Zhegrova (88.Afimico Pululu), Arthur Cabral (73.Kemal Ademi). Trainer: Marcel Koller.
Getafe CF: Leandro Chichizola, Bruno, Raúl García, Mathías Olivera, Fayçal Fajr (79.Ángel), Portillo, David Timor (68.Allan Nyom), Nemanja Maksimovic, Mata, Enric Gallego, Hugo Duro (68.Kenedy). Trainer: José Bordalás.
Goals: 8' Arthur Cabral 1-0, 45' Mata 1-1 (pen), 60' Fabian Frei 2-1.

28.11.2019; Medical Park Stadyumu, Trabzon
Referee: Andris Treimanis (LVA); Attendance: 11,465
Trabzonspor Kulübü – Getafe CF 0-1(0-0)
Trabzonspor: Erce Kardesler, Majid Hosseini (70.Gastón Campi),
Ivanildo Fernandes, Abdurahim Dursun, Serkan Asan, Dogan Erdogan,
Donis Avdijaj (59.Behlül Aydin), Abdülkadir Parmak, Firatcan Üzüm,
Kerem Baykus (89.Kâmil Çörekçi), Muhammet Akpinar. Trainer: Ünal
Karaman.
Getafe CF: Leandro Chichizola, Allan Nyom, Bruno, Djené Dakonam,
Mathías Olivera, Fayçal Fajr, Portillo, Kenedy (86.Cucurella), Mauro
Arambarri, Jorge Molina (62.Ángel), Mata (73.David Timor). Trainer:
José Bordalás.
Goal: 50' Mata 0-1.

12.12.2019; Estadio Coliseum „Alfonso Pérez", Getafe
Referee: Daniel Siebert (GER); Attendance: 9,389
Getafe CF – FK Krasnodar 3-0(0-0)
Getafe CF: David Soria, Allan Nyom, Damián Suárez, Leandro Cabrera,
Djené Dakonam, Cucurella, Jason (68.Kenedy), Nemanja Maksimovic,
Mauro Arambarri (82.David Timor), Ángel (73.Jorge Molina), Mata.
Trainer: José Bordalás.
FK Krasnodar: Stanislav Kritsyuk, Aleksandr Martynovich, Sergey
Petrov, Uros Spajic, Cristian Ramírez (75.Dmitriy Skopintsev), Yuri
Gazinskiy, Tonny Vilhena, Wamberto, Marcus Berg, Magomed
Suleymanov (62.Younes Namli), Ivan Ignatyev (69.Daniil Utkin).
Trainer: Sergey Matveev.
Goals: 76' Leandro Cabrera 1-0, 78' Jorge Molina 2-0, 86' Kenedy 3-0.
Sent off: 88' Aleksandr Martynovich.

28.11.2019; Stadion FK Krasnodar, Krasnodar
Referee: Bobby Madden (SCO); Attendance: 22,826
FK Krasnodar – FC Basel 1-0(0-0)
FK Krasnodar: Stanislav Kritsyuk, Aleksandr Martynovich, Sergey
Petrov, Uros Spajic, Cristian Ramírez, Yuri Gazinskiy (83.Ruslan
Kambolov), Tonny Vilhena, Kristoffer Olsson (73.Daniil Utkin),
Wamberto, Ari, Magomed Suleymanov (57.Younes Namli). Trainer:
Sergey Matveev.
FC Basel: Jonas Omlin, Emil Bergström, Silvan Widmer, Omar Alderete,
Eray Cömart, Blas Riveros, Valentin Stocker (86.Afimico Pululu), Fabian
Frei, Samuele Campo, Kemal Ademi (68.Arthur Cabral), Noah Okafor
(85.Kevin Bua). Trainer: Marcel Koller.
Goal: 72' Ari 1-0 (pen).
Sent off: 90+5' Ari.

12.12.2019; St. Jakob-Park, Basel
Referee: Aleksandar Stavrev (MKD); Attendance: 17,921
FC Basel – Trabzonspor Kulübü 2-0(1-0)
FC Basel: Jonas Omlin, Silvan Widmer, Omar Alderete, Raoul Petretta,
Eray Cömart, Valentin Stocker, Luca Zuffi (78.Samuele Campo), Fabian
Frei, Taulant Xhaka, Arthur Cabral (71.Kemal Ademi), Afimico Pululu
(65.Noah Okafor). Trainer: Marcel Koller.
Trabzonspor: Erce Kardesler, Majid Hosseini (71.Gastón Campi),
Ivanildo Fernandes, Abdurahim Dursun, Serkan Asan, Ogenyi Onazi
(51.Muhammet Akpinar), Dogan Erdogan, Donis Avdijaj, Abdülkadir
Parmak, Firatcan Üzüm, Caleb Ekuban (78.Kerem Baykus). Trainer:
Ünal Karaman.
Goals: 21' Silvan Widmer 1-0, 72' Valentin Stocker 2-0.

GROUP D		1.	**LASK Linz**	6	4	1	1	11 - 4	13
		2.	**Sporting Clube de Portugal Lisboa**	6	4	0	2	11 - 7	12
		3.	PSV Eindhoven	6	2	2	2	9 - 12	8
		4.	Rosenborg BK Trondheim	6	0	1	5	3 - 11	1

19.09.2019; Stadion Philips, Eindhoven
Referee: Ivan Kruzliak (SVK); Attendance: 30,000
PSV Eindhoven – Sporting Clube de Portugal Lisboa 3-2(2-1)
PSV Eindhoven: Jeroen Zoet, Nick Viergever, Timo Baumgartl, Olivier
Boscagli, Denzel Dumfries, Jorrit Hendrix, Pablo Rosario, Mohammed
Ihattaren (64.Cody Gakpo), Bruma (78.Ritsu Doan), Steven Bergwijn,
Donyell Malen (84.Michal Sadílek). Trainer: Mark van Bommel.
Sporting: Renan Ribeiro, Neto, Sebastián Coates, Valentin Rosier, Bruno
Fernandes, Miguel Luís (80.Pedro Mendes), Idrissa Doumbia, Wendel
(90+1.Rafael Camacho), Yannick Bolasie, Marcos Acuña, Luciano Vietto
(64.Jovane Cabral). Trainer: Leonel Pontes.
Goals: 19' Donyell Malen 1-0, 25' Sebastián Coates 2-0 (own goal), 38'
Bruno Fernandes 2-1 (pen), 48' Timo Baumgartl 3-1, 82' Pedro Mendes
3-2.

03.10.2019; Lerkendal Stadion, Trondheim
Referee: Halil Umut Meler (TUR); Attendance: 10,296
Rosenborg BK Trondheim – PSV Eindhoven 1-4(0-3)
Rosenborg BK: André Hansen, Even Hovland, Gustav Valsvik, Birger
Meling, Mike Jensen, Gjermund Åsen, Anders Trondsen (79.Edvard
Tagseth), Marius Lundemo (62.Anders Konradsen), Bjørn Johnsen
(59.Alexander Søderlund), Samuel Adegbenro, Babajide Akintola.
Trainer: Eirik Horneland.
PSV Eindhoven: Robbin Ruiter, Nick Viergever, Timo Baumgartl,
Denzel Dumfries, Jorrit Hendrix (72.Érick Gutiérrez), Michal Sadílek,
Ritsu Doan (82.Bruma), Pablo Rosario, Mohammed Ihattaren (80.Kostas
Mitroglou), Steven Bergwijn, Donyell Malen. Trainer: Mark van
Bommel.;
Goals: 14' Pablo Rosario 0-1, 38' Birger Meling 0-2 (own goal), 41'
Donyell Malen 0-3, 70' Samuel Adegbenro 1-3, 79' Donyell Malen 1-4.

24.10.2019; Estádio „José Alvalade", Lisboa
Referee: Lawrence Visser (BEL); Attendance: 27,671
**Sporting Clube de Portugal Lisboa – Rosenborg BK Trondheim 1-
0(0-0)**
Sporting: Renan Ribeiro, Jérémy Mathieu, Sebastián Coates, Valentin
Rosier, Bruno Fernandes, Idrissa Doumbia, Wendel (88.Eduardo
Henrique), Yannick Bolasie, Marcos Acuña, Luciano Vietto (85.Cristian
Borja), Luiz Phellype (64.Pedro Mendes). Trainer: Emanuel Ferro.
Rosenborg BK: André Hansen, Tore Reginiussen, Even Hovland, Vegar
Hedenstad, Birger Meling, Mike Jensen, Gjermund Åsen (81.Pål André
Helland), Marius Lundemo, Alexander Søderlund, Samuel Adegbenro
(81.Bjørn Johnsen), Babajide Akintola (76.Anders Konradsen). Trainer:
Eirik Horneland.; Goal: 70' Yannick Bolasie 1-0.

19.09.2019; Linzer Stadion, Linz
Referee: Donatas Rumsas (LTU); Attendance: 12,179
LASK Linz – Rosenborg BK Trondheim 1-0(1-0)
LASK Linz: Alexander Schlager, Petar Filipovic, Reinhold Ranftl,
Markus Wostry, Philipp Wiesinger, James Holland, Thomas Goiginger
(80.Marko Raguz), Peter Michorl, René Renner (57.Marvin Potzmann),
Samuel Tetteh (40.Dominik Frieser), Klauss. Trainer: Valérien Ismaël.
Rosenborg BK: André Hansen, Tore Reginiussen, Even Hovland, Vegar
Hedenstad, Birger Meling, Mike Jensen, Anders Konradsen
(87.Gjermund Åsen), Marius Lundemo (73.Anders Trondsen), Alexander
Søderlund, Bjørn Johnsen (73.Emil Ceide), Samuel Adegbenro. Trainer:
Eirik Horneland.
Goal: 45+3' James Holland 1-0.

03.10.2019; Estádio „José Alvalade", Lisboa
Referee: Alain Durieux (LUX); Attendance: 31,225
Sporting Clube de Portugal Lisboa – LASK Linz 2-1(0-1)
Sporting: Renan Ribeiro, Jérémy Mathieu, Neto (46.Luciano Vietto),
Sebastián Coates, Bruno Fernandes, Miguel Luís, Idrissa Doumbia,
Wendel (58.Eduardo Henrique), Yannick Bolasie, Marcos Acuña
(73.Cristian Borja), Luiz Phellype. Trainer: Emanuel Ferro.
LASK Linz: Alexander Schlager, Petar Filipovic, Gernot Trauner,
Marvin Potzmann (72.René Renner), Reinhold Ranftl, Philipp Wiesinger,
James Holland, Thomas Goiginger, Peter Michorl, Dominik Frieser
(80.Thomas Sabitzer), Marko Raguz (55.Klauss). Trainer: Valérien
Ismaël.
Goals: 16' Marko Raguz 0-1, 58' Luiz Phellype 1-1, 63' Bruno
Fernandes 2-1.

24.10.2019; Stadion Philips, Eindhoven
Referee: Chris Kavanagh (ENG); Attendance: 29,000
PSV Eindhoven – LASK Linz 0-0
PSV Eindhoven: Jeroen Zoet, Daniel Schwaab, Nick Viergever, Denzel
Dumfries, Érick Gutiérrez, Michal Sadílek, Ritsu Doan (74.Bruma),
Pablo Rosario, Mohammed Ihattaren (84.Ryan Thomas), Steven
Bergwijn, Cody Gakpo (84.Kostas Mitroglou). Trainer: Mark van
Bommel.
LASK Linz: Alexander Schlager, Petar Filipovic, Gernot Trauner,
Marvin Potzmann, Reinhold Ranftl, Philipp Wiesinger, James Holland,
Thomas Goiginger, Peter Michorl, Dominik Frieser (59.Samuel Tetteh),
Marko Raguz (71.Klauss). Trainer: Valérien Ismaël.

07.11.2019; Lerkendal Stadion, Trondheim
Referee: Kevin Clancy (SCO); Attendance: 11,018
Rosenborg BK Trondheim – Sporting Clube de Portugal Lisboa 0-2(0-2)
Rosenborg BK: André Hansen, Tore Reginiussen, Even Hovland, Vegar Hedenstad, Birger Meling, Mike Jensen, Gjermund Åsen, Anders Trondsen (78.Pål André Helland), Marius Lundemo, Alexander Søderlund, Samuel Adegbenro (77.Bjørn Johnsen). Trainer: Eirik Horneland.
Sporting: Renan Ribeiro, Neto, Sebastián Coates, Tiago Ilori, Cristian Borja, Valentin Rosier, Eduardo Henrique, Bruno Fernandes (90.Pedro Mendes), Idrissa Doumbia (86.Rodrigo Fernandes), Yannick Bolasie (73.Rafael Camacho), Luciano Vietto. Trainer: Emanuel Ferro.
Goals: 16' Sebastián Coates 0-1, 38' Bruno Fernandes 0-2.

28.11.2019; Estádio „José Alvalade", Lisboa
Referee: Orel Grinfeld (ISR); Attendance: 30,146
Sporting Clube de Portugal Lisboa – PSV Eindhoven 4-0(3-0)
Sporting: Luís Maximiano, Jérémy Mathieu (73.Neto), Tiago Ilori, Valentin Rosier, Bruno Fernandes, Idrissa Doumbia, Wendel (80.Rafael Camacho), Yannick Bolasie, Marcos Acuña, Luciano Vietto, Luiz Phellype (67.Jesé). Trainer: Emanuel Ferro.
PSV Eindhoven: Lars Unnerstall, Nick Viergever, Timo Baumgartl, Denzel Dumfries, Jorrit Hendrix, Michal Sadílek, Pablo Rosario (46.Gastón Pereiro), Mohammed Ihattaren, Bruma (46.Cody Gakpo), Steven Bergwijn (79.Ryan Thomas), Donyell Malen. Trainer: Mark van Bommel.
Goals: 9' Luiz Phellype 1-0, 16' Bruno Fernandes 2-0, 43' Jérémy Mathieu 3-0, 64' Bruno Fernandes 4-0 (pen).

12.12.2019; Stadion Philips, Eindhoven
Referee: Vitali Meshkov (RUS); Attendance: 24,000
PSV Eindhoven – Rosenborg BK Trondheim 1-1(0-1)
PSV Eindhoven: Lars Unnerstall, Daniel Schwaab, Nick Viergever, Olivier Boscagli, Denzel Dumfries, Ryan Thomas (61.Pablo Rosario), Érick Gutiérrez, Mohammed Ihattaren (70.Gastón Pereiro), Bruma, Steven Bergwijn (46.Donyell Malen), Cody Gakpo. Trainer: Mark van Bommel.
Rosenborg BK: Arild Østbø, Tore Reginiussen, Even Hovland, Vegar Hedenstad, Birger Meling, Mike Jensen, Anders Trondsen, Edvard Tagseth (46.Marius Lundemo), Pål André Helland (75.Erik Botheim), Alexander Søderlund, Samuel Adegbenro (81.Emil Ceide). Trainer: Eirik Horneland.
Goals: 22' Pål André Helland 0-1, 63' Mohammed Ihattaren 1-1.

07.11.2019; Linzer Stadion, Linz
Referee: Radu Petrescu (ROU); Attendance: 12,658
LASK Linz – PSV Eindhoven 4-1(0-1)
LASK Linz: Alexander Schlager, Petar Filipovic, Gernot Trauner, Marvin Potzmann, Reinhold Ranftl (81.René Renner), Philipp Wiesinger, James Holland, Thomas Goiginger, Peter Michorl, Dominik Frieser (61.Klauss), Marko Raguz (69.Samuel Tetteh). Trainer: Valérien Ismaël.
PSV Eindhoven: Jeroen Zoet, Daniel Schwaab, Nick Viergever, Denzel Dumfries, Érick Gutiérrez, Michal Sadílek, Ritsu Doan (64.Amar Catic), Pablo Rosario, Mohammed Ihattaren, Bruma, Cody Gakpo. Trainer: Mark van Bommel.
Goals: 5' Daniel Schwaab 0-1, 56' Reinhold Ranftl 1-1, 60' Dominik Frieser (2-1), 78', 82' Klauss 3-1, 4-1.

28.11.2019; Lerkendal Stadion, Trondheim
Referee: Giorgi Kruashvili (GEO); Attendance: 9,775
Rosenborg BK Trondheim – LASK Linz 1-2(1-1)
Rosenborg BK: André Hansen, Even Hovland, Vegar Hedenstad, Gustav Valsvik, Birger Meling, Mike Jensen, Anders Trondsen, Marius Lundemo (77.Mikael Johnsen), Bjørn Johnsen (67.Erik Botheim), Samuel Adegbenro (67.Gjermund Åsen), Babajide Akintola. Trainer: Eirik Horneland.
LASK Linz: Alexander Schlager, Petar Filipovic, Gernot Trauner, Marvin Potzmann, Reinhold Ranftl, Philipp Wiesinger, James Holland, Thomas Goiginger (88.René Renner), Peter Michorl, Dominik Frieser (71.Samuel Tetteh), Klauss (71.Marko Raguz). Trainer: Valérien Ismaël.
Goals: 20' Thomas Goiginger 0-1, 45' Bjørn Johnsen 1-1, 54' Dominik Frieser 1-2.

12.12.2019; Linzer Stadion, Linz
Referee: William Collum (SCO); Attendance: 11,627
LASK Linz – Sporting Clube de Portugal Lisboa 3-0(2-0)
LASK Linz: Alexander Schlager, Petar Filipovic (88.Emanuel Pogatetz), Gernot Trauner, Marvin Potzmann, Reinhold Ranftl, Philipp Wiesinger, James Holland, Thomas Goiginger, Peter Michorl, Dominik Frieser (64.Samuel Tetteh), Klauss (71.Marko Raguz). Trainer: Valérien Ismaël.
Sporting: Renan Ribeiro, Sebastián Coates, Tiago Ilori, Cristian Borja, Valentin Rosier, Eduardo Henrique, Miguel Luís (71.Luiz Phellype), Rafael Camacho, Rodrigo Fernandes (37.Luís Maximiano goalkeeper), Jesé (46.Idrissa Doumbia), Pedro Mendes. Trainer: Emanuel Ferro.
Goals: 23' Gernot Trauner 1-0, 38' Klauss 2-0 (pen), 90+3' Marko Raguz 3-0.
Sent off: 34' Renan Ribeiro.

GROUP E	1. **Celtic FC Glasgow**	6	4	1	1	10 - 6	13
	2. **FC CFR 1907 Cluj**	6	4	0	2	6 - 4	12
	3. SS Lazio Roma	6	2	0	4	6 - 9	6
	4. Stade Rennais FC	6	1	1	4	5 - 8	4

19.09.2019; Roazhon Park, Rennes
Referee: José María Sánchez Martínez (ESP); Attendance: 27,026
Stade Rennais FC – Celtic FC Glasgow 1-1(1-0)
Stade Rennais: Edouard Mendy, Jérémy Morel, Damien Da Silva, Hamari Traoré, Joris Gnagnon, Clément Grenier (88.Theoson Siebatcheu), Jonas Martin (72.Eduardo Camavinga), Flavien Tait (72.Romain Del Castillo), Benjamin Bourigeaud, M'Baye Niang, Raphinha. Trainer: Julien Stéphane.
Celtic FC: Fraser Forster, Hatem Abd Elhamed, Christopher Jullien, Boli Bolingoli Mbombo (69.Jonny Hayes), Kristoffer Ajer, Scott Brown, James Forrest, Callum McGregor, Mohamed Elyounoussi (57.Olivier Ntcham), Ryan Christie, Odsonne Édouard (84.Vakoun Bayo). Trainer: Neil Lennon.
Goals: 38' M'Baye Niang 1-0 (pen), 59' Ryan Christie 1-1 (pen).
Sent off: 90+2' Vakoun Bayo.

19.09.2019; Stadionul Dr. Constantin Rădulescu, Cluj-Napoca
Referee: Daniel Stefanski (POL); Attendance: 9,222
FC CFR 1907 Cluj-Napoca – SS Lazio Roma 2-1(1-1)
CFR Cluj: Giedrius Arlauskis, Camora, Mike Cestor, Andrei Peteleu, Kévin Boli, Andrei Burca, Ciprian Deac (90.Catalin Golofca), Damjan Djokovic, Mihai Bordeianu, Alexandru Paun (84.Emmanuel Culio), Lacina Traoré (46.Billel Omrani). Trainer: Dan Petrescu.
Lazio Roma: Thomas Strakosha, Francesco Acerbi, Bastos (80.Bobby Adekanye), Denis Vavro, Lucas Leiva, Valon Berisha (67.Danilo Cataldi), Joaquín Correa, Manuel Lazzari, Sergej Milinkovic-Savic, Felipe Caicedo, Jony (80.Senad Lulic). Trainer: Simone Inzaghi.
Goals: 25' Bastos 0-1, 41' Ciprian Deac 1-1 (pen), 75' Billel Omrani 2-1.

03.10.2019; Stadio Olimpico, Roma
Referee: Serhiy Boyko (UKR); Attendance: 13,072
SS Lazio Roma – Stade Rennais FC 2-1(0-0)
Lazio Roma: Thomas Strakosha, Francesco Acerbi, Bastos, Denis Vavro, Senad Lulic (82.Jony), Marco Parolo, Valon Berisha (53.Luis Alberto), Manuel Lazzari, Danilo Cataldi (53.Sergej Milinkovic-Savic), Felipe Caicedo, Ciro Immobile. Trainer: Simone Inzaghi.
Stade Rennais: Edouard Mendy, Jérémy Morel, Damien Da Silva, Hamari Traoré, Souleyman Doumbia (82.Adrien Hunou), Joris Gnagnon, Clément Grenier, Jonas Martin, Flavien Tait (76.Raphinha), Eduardo Camavinga (71.Benjamin Bourigeaud), M'Baye Niang. Trainer: Julien Stéphane.
Goals: 55' Jérémy Morel 0-1, 63' Sergej Milinkovic-Savic 1-1, 75' Ciro Immobile 2-1.

24.10.2019; Celtic Park, Glasgow
Referee: Ivan Bebek (CRO); Attendance: 56,172
Celtic FC Glasgow – SS Lazio Roma 2-1(0-1)
Celtic FC: Fraser Forster, Hatem Abd Elhamed (83.Nir Bitton), Christopher Jullien, Boli Bolingoli Mbombo (85.Jonny Hayes), Kristoffer Ajer, Scott Brown, James Forrest, Callum McGregor, Mohamed Elyounoussi (66.Tom Rogic), Ryan Christie, Odsonne Édouard. Trainer: Neil Lennon.
Lazio Roma: Thomas Strakosha, Francesco Acerbi, Bastos, Denis Vavro, Lucas Leiva, Marco Parolo, Joaquín Correa (73.Ciro Immobile), Manuel Lazzari, Sergej Milinkovic-Savic, Felipe Caicedo (85.Danilo Cataldi), Jony (69.Senad Lulic). Trainer: Simone Inzaghi.
Goals: 40' Manuel Lazzari 0-1, 67' Ryan Christie 1-1, 89' Christopher Jullien 2-1.

07.11.2019; Stadio Olimpico, Roma
Referee: Tobias Stieler (GER); Attendance: 26,155
SS Lazio Roma – Celtic FC Glasgow 1-2(1-1)
Lazio Roma: Thomas Strakosha, Francesco Acerbi, Denis Vavro (82.Valon Berisha), Luiz Felipe, Lucas Leiva (58.Luis Alberto), Marco Parolo, Manuel Lazzari, Sergej Milinkovic-Savic, Felipe Caicedo, Ciro Immobile, Jony (58.Senad Lulic). Trainer: Simone Inzaghi.
Celtic FC: Fraser Forster, Hatem Abd Elhamed (83.Nir Bitton), Christopher Jullien, Kristoffer Ajer, Scott Brown, Jonny Hayes, James Forrest (89.Moritz Bauer), Callum McGregor, Mohamed Elyounoussi, Ryan Christie (77.Olivier Ntcham), Odsonne Édouard. Trainer: Neil Lennon.
Goals: 7' Ciro Immobile 1-0, 38' James Forrest 1-1, 90+5' Olivier Ntcham 1-2.

28.11.2019; Celtic Park, Glasgow
Referee: Espen Eskås (NOR); Attendance: 56,172
Celtic FC Glasgow – Stade Rennais FC 3-1(2-0)
Celtic FC: Fraser Forster, Christopher Jullien, Moritz Bauer, Kristoffer Ajer, Greg Taylor, Scott Brown (76.Nir Bitton), James Forrest (67.Mikey Johnston), Callum McGregor, Olivier Ntcham, Ryan Christie (79.Leigh Griffiths), Lewis Morgan. Trainer: Neil Lennon.
Stade Rennais: Edouard Mendy, Joris Gnagnon, Gerzino Nyamsi, Sacha Boey, Flavien Tait (80.Yann Gboho), Benjamin Bourigeaud, James Lea Siliki, Faitout Maouassa, Rafik Guitane (65.Lucas Da Cunha), Theoson Siebatcheu, Romain Del Castillo (74.Adrien Hunou). Trainer: Julien Stéphane.
Goals: 22' Lewis Morgan 1-0, 45+1' Ryan Christie 2-0, 74' Mikey Johnson 3-0, 89' Adrien Hunou 3-1.

12.12.2019; Roazhon Park, Rennes
Referee: Srdjan Jovanovic (SRB); Attendance: 25,082
Stade Rennais FC – SS Lazio Roma 2-0(1-0)
Stade Rennais: Romain Salin, Souleyman Doumbia, Joris Gnagnon, Gerzino Nyamsi, Sacha Boey, Clément Grenier, Flavien Tait, James Lea Siliki (74.Eduardo Camavinga), Lucas Da Cunha (77.Romain Del Castillo), Yann Gboho, Theoson Siebatcheu (70.M'Baye Niang). Trainer: Julien Stéphane.
Lazio Roma: Silvio Proto, Francesco Acerbi, Bastos, Denis Vavro (74.Luca Falbo), Marco Parolo, Luis Alberto (59.Valon Berisha), Manuel Lazzari, Danilo Cataldi, Felipe Caicedo, Ciro Immobile (68.Bobby Adekanye), Jony. Trainer: Simone Inzaghi.
Goals: 31', 87' Joris Gnagnon 1-0, 2-0.

03.10.2019; Celtic Park, Glasgow
Referee: Daniel Siebert (GER); Attendance: 56,172
Celtic FC Glasgow – FC CFR 1907 Cluj-Napoca 2-0(1-0)
Celtic FC: Fraser Forster, Hatem Abd Elhamed, Christopher Jullien, Boli Bolingoli Mbombo, Kristoffer Ajer, Scott Brown, James Forrest (86.Jonny Hayes), Callum McGregor, Mohamed Elyounoussi, Ryan Christie (90.Olivier Ntcham), Odsonne Édouard. Trainer: Neil Lennon.
CFR Cluj: Giedrius Arlauskis, Mateo Susic, Camora, Kévin Boli, Andrei Burca, Ciprian Deac, Damjan Djokovic (81.Catalin Golofca), Mihai Bordeianu, Luís Aurélio (57.Emmanuel Culio), Mário Rondón (70.Alexandru Paun), Billel Omrani. Trainer: Dan Petrescu.
Goals: 20' Odsonne Édouard 1-0, 59' Mohamed Elyounoussi 2-0.

24.10.2019; Roazhon Park, Rennes
Referee: Aleksei Eskov (RUS); Attendance: 27,330
Stade Rennais FC – FC CFR 1907 Cluj-Napoca 0-1(0-1)
Stade Rennais: Edouard Mendy, Jérémy Morel, Hamari Traoré, Joris Gnagnon, Benjamin Bourigeaud, Adrien Hunou, Faitout Maouassa (75.James Lea Siliki), Eduardo Camavinga, M'Baye Niang, Romain Del Castillo (8.Pépé Bonet Kapambu *goalkeeper*), Raphinha (80.Theoson Siebatcheu). Trainer: Julien Stéphane.
CFR Cluj: Giedrius Arlauskis, Mateo Susic, Camora, Kévin Boli, Andrei Burca, Emmanuel Culio, Ciprian Deac, Damjan Djokovic (70.Alexandru Paun), Mihai Bordeianu (66.Ovidiu Hoban), Lacina Traoré (84.Mike Cestor), Billel Omrani. Trainer: Dan Petrescu.
Goal: 9' Ciprian Deac 0-1.
Sent off: 5' Edouard Mendy, 46' Eduardo Camavinga, 82' Mateo Susic.

07.11.2019; Stadionul „Dr. Constantin Rădulescu", Cluj-Napoca
Referee: Tiago Bruno Lopes Martins (POR); Attendance: 11,067
FC CFR 1907 Cluj-Napoca – Stade Rennais FC 1-0(0-0)
CFR Cluj: Giedrius Arlauskis, Camora, Ionut Andrei Peteleu (74.Ovidiu Hoban), Kévin Boli, Andrei Burca, Emmanuel Culio, Ciprian Deac (89.Alexandru Paun), Damjan Djokovic, Mihai Bordeianu, Lacina Traoré (71.Mário Rondón), Billel Omrani. Trainer: Dan Petrescu.
Stade Rennais: Romain Salin, Damien Da Silva, Hamari Traoré, Joris Gnagnon, Clément Grenier, Benjamin Bourigeaud (84.Rafik Guitane), Adrien Hunou (66.Yann Gboho), Faitout Maouassa, M'Baye Niang, Romain Del Castillo (66.Theoson Siebatcheu), Raphinha. Trainer: Julien Stéphane.
Goal: 87' Mário Rondón 1-0.
Sent off: 90' Mário Rondón.

28.11.2019; Stadio Olimpico, Roma
Referee: Ali Palabiyik (TUR); Attendance: 7,604
SS Lazio Roma – FC CFR 1907 Cluj-Napoca 1-0(1-0)
Lazio Roma: Silvio Proto, Francesco Acerbi, Bastos, Denis Vavro, Marco Parolo, Luis Alberto (80.Patric), Joaquín Correa, Manuel Lazzari, Danilo Cataldi, Jony (75.Senad Lulic), Bobby Adekanye (65.Felipe Caicedo). Trainer: Simone Inzaghi.
CFR Cluj: Giedrius Arlauskis, Camora, Mike Cestor, Ionut Andrei Peteleu (73.Mateo Susic), Kévin Boli, Andrei Burca, Emmanuel Culio, Damjan Djokovic, Mihai Bordeianu (62.Ciprian Deac), Alexandru Paun (65.Lacina Traoré), Billel Omrani. Trainer: Dan Petrescu.
Goal: 24' Joaquín Correa 1-0.

12.12.2019; Stadionul „Dr. Constantin Rădulescu", Cluj-Napoca
Referee: Halis Özkahya (TUR); Attendance: 12,890
FC CFR 1907 Cluj-Napoca – Celtic FC Glasgow 2-0(0-0)
CFR Cluj: Giedrius Arlauskis, Mateo Susic, Camora, Mike Cestor, Andrei Burca, Emmanuel Culio, Ciprian Deac (85.Ovidiu Hoban), Damjan Djokovic (83.Luís Aurélio), Mihai Bordeianu, Lacina Traoré, Billel Omrani (74.Catalin Golofca). Trainer: Dan Petrescu.
Celtic FC: Craig Gordon, Christopher Jullien (46.Kristoffer Ajer), Moritz Bauer, Boli Bolingoli Mbombo, Scott Sinclair, Nir Bitton, Olivier Ntcham, Lewis Morgan (67.Vakoun Bayo), Scott Robertson, Leigh Griffiths, Mikey Johnston (72.Karamoko Dembélé). Trainer: Neil Lennon.
Goals: 49' Andrei Burca 1-0, 70' Damjan Djokovic 2-0.

GROUP F							

1. **Arsenal FC London**	6	3	2	1	14 - 7	11
2. **Eintracht Frankfurt**	6	3	0	3	8 - 10	9
3. R Standard Liège	6	2	2	2	8 - 10	8
4. Vitória SC Guimarães	6	1	2	3	7 - 10	5

19.09.2019; Commerzbank-Arena, Frankfurt am Main
Referee: Davide Massa (ITA); Attendance: 47,000
Eintracht Frankfurt – Arsenal FC London 0-3(0-1)
Eintracht Frankfurt: Kevin Trapp, Makoto Hasebe, David Abraham, Martin Hinteregger, Danny da Costa (74.Timothy Chandler), Filip Kostic, Dominik Kohr, Djibril Sow, Daichi Kamada, Bas Dost (66.Gonçalo Paciência), André Silva. Trainer: Adi Hütter.
Arsenal FC: Emiliano Martínez, David Luiz, Shkodran Mustafi, Sead Kolasinac (80.Ainsley Maitland-Niles), Calum Chambers, Granit Xhaka, Lucas Torreira, Joseph Willock (72.Dani Ceballos), Emile Smith-Rowe (60.Nicolas Pépé), Bukayo Saka, Pierre-Emerick Aubameyang. Trainer: Unai Emery.
Goals: 38' Joseph Willock 0-1, 85' Bukayo Saka 0-2, 88' Pierre-Emerick Aubameyang 0-3.;
Sent off: 79' Dominik Kohr.

03.10.2019; Estádio „Dom Afonso Henriques", Guimarães
Referee: Radu Petrescu (ROU); Attendance: 15,187
Vitória SC Guimarães – Eintracht Frankfurt 0-1(0-1)
Vitória Guimarães: João Miguel Silva, Florent Hanin, "Pedrão" Pedro Henrique, Falaye Sacko (65.Rochinha), Edmond Tapsoba, Mikel Agu, Lucas Evangelista, Denis Poha, Marcus Edwards, Léo Bonatini (65.Bruno Duarte), Davidson (78.André Pereira). Trainer: Ivo Vieira.
Eintracht Frankfurt: Frederik Rønnow, Martin Hinteregger, Erik Durm (78.Danny da Costa), Almamy Touré, Evan Obite N'Dicka, Gelson Fernandes, Sebastian Rode (60.Daichi Kamada), Filip Kostic, Djibril Sow, Gonçalo Paciência (68.Bas Dost), André Silva. Trainer: Adi Hütter.
Goal: 36' Evan Obite N'Dicka 0-1.

24.10.2019; Emirates Stadium, London
Referee: Serdar Gözübüyük (NED); Attendance: 60,195
Arsenal FC London – Vitória SC Guimarães 3-2(1-2)
Arsenal FC: Emiliano Martínez, Shkodran Mustafi, Héctor Bellerín, Kieran Tierney, Rob Holding, Ainsley Maitland-Niles (46.Mattéo Guendouzi), Lucas Torreira, Joseph Willock (46.Dani Ceballos), Emile Smith-Rowe, Alexandre Lacazette (75.Nicolas Pépé), Gabriel Martinelli. Trainer: Unai Emery.
Vitória Guimarães: João Miguel Silva, Florent Hanin, Victor García, Frederico Venâncio, Edmond Tapsoba, Mikel Agu, Denis Poha, Marcus Edwards (71.André Pereira), André Almeida (64.Pêpê Rodrigues), Davidson (87.Rochinha), Bruno Duarte. Trainer: Ivo Vieira.
Goals: 9' Marcus Edwards 0-1, 32' Gabriel Martinelli 1-1, 37' Bruno Duarte 1-2, 80', 90+3' Nicolas Pépé 2-2, 3-2.

06.11.2019; Estádio „Dom Afonso Henriques", Guimarães
Referee: Halis Özkahya (TUR); Attendance: 17,822
Vitória SC Guimarães – Arsenal FC London 1-1(0-0)
Vitória Guimarães: Douglas Jesus, Victor García, Rafa Soares, Frederico Venâncio, Edmond Tapsoba, Mikel Agu, Lucas Evangelista (82.Léo Bonatini), Pêpê Rodrigues (61.Denis Poha), Marcus Edwards, Davidson (68.Rochinha), Bruno Duarte. Trainer: Ivo Vieira.
Arsenal FC: Emiliano Martínez, Sokratis Papastathopoulos, Shkodran Mustafi, Kieran Tierney, Rob Holding, Ainsley Maitland-Niles, Dani Ceballos (54.Mattéo Guendouzi), Joseph Willock (78.Lucas Torreira), Bukayo Saka (65.Alexandre Lacazette), Nicolas Pépé, Gabriel Martinelli. Trainer: Unai Emery.
Goals: 81' Shkodran Mustafi 0-1, 90+1' Bruno Duarte 1-1.

19.09.2019; Stade „Maurice Dufrasne", Liège
Referee: Sergey Ivanov (RUS); Attendance: 13,477
R Standard Liège – Vitória SC Guimarães 2-0(0-0)
Standard Liège: Vanja Milinkovic-Savic, Kostas Laifis, Nicolas Gavory, Mergim Vojvoda, Mehdi Carcela-González (85.Aleksandar Boljevic), Gojko Cimirot, Anthony Limbombe (81.Zinho Vanheusden), Paul M'Poku, Merveille Bopé Bokadi, Samuel Bastien, Renaud Emond (68.Felipe Avenatti). Trainer: Michel Preud'homme.
Vitória Guimarães: João Miguel Silva, Florent Hanin, Valeriy Bondarenko, Falaye Sacko, Edmond Tapsoba, Mikel Agu (70.Pêpê Rodrigues), Lucas Evangelista (77.André Pereira), Rochinha, Denis Poha, Léo Bonatini (57.Bruno Duarte), Davidson. Trainer: Ivo Vieira.
Goals: 66' Florent Hanin 1-0 (own goal), 90+1' Paul M'Poku 2-0.

03.10.2019; Emirates Stadium, London
Referee: Sandro Schärer (SUI); Attendance: 58,725
Arsenal FC London – R Standard Liège 4-0(3-0)
Arsenal FC: Emiliano Martínez, Shkodran Mustafi, Héctor Bellerín, Kieran Tierney, Rob Holding, Ainsley Maitland-Niles (66.Nicolas Pépé), Dani Ceballos, Lucas Torrcira, Joseph Willock (74.Mattéo Guendouzi), Reiss Nelson (79.Pierre-Emerick Aubameyang), Gabriel Martinelli. Trainer: Unai Emery.
Standard Liège: Vanja Milinkovic-Savic, Kostas Laifis, Nicolas Gavory, Mergim Vojvoda, Zinho Vanheusden, Maxime Lestienne (80.Selim Amallah), Gojko Cimirot, Paul M'Poku, Aleksandar Boljevic (58.Mehdi Carcela-González), Samuel Bastien, Renaud Emond (73.Felipe Avenatti). Trainer: Michel Preud'homme.
Goals: 13', 16' Gabriel Martinelli 1-0, 2-0, 22' Joseph Willock 3-0, 57' Dani Ceballos 4-0.

24.10.2019; Commerzbank-Arena, Frankfurt am Main
Referee: Daniel Stefanski (POL); Attendance: 47,000
Eintracht Frankfurt – R Standard Liège 2-1(1-0)
Eintracht Frankfurt: Frederik Rønnow, Makoto Hasebe, David Abraham, Martin Hinteregger, Danny da Costa, Sebastian Rode, Filip Kostic (83.Timothy Chandler), Mijat Gacinovic (75.Dominik Kohr), Djibril Sow, Daichi Kamada (88.Gelson Fernandes), Gonçalo Paciência. Trainer: Adi Hütter.
Standard Liège: Vanja Milinkovic-Savic, Kostas Laifis, Nicolas Gavory, Collins Fai (85.Paul M'Poku), Dimitri Lavalée, Mehdi Carcela-González (75.Obbi Oularé), Gojko Cimirot, Aleksandar Boljevic, Samuel Bastien, Selim Amallah, Duje Cop (72.Maxime Lestienne). Trainer: Michel Preud'homme.
Goals: 28' David Abraham 1-0, 73' Martin Hinteregger 2-0, 82' Selim Amallah 2-1.

07.11.2019; Stade „Maurice Dufrasne", Liège
Referee: Matej Jug (SVN); Attendance: 15,952
R Standard Liège – Eintracht Frankfurt 2-1(0-0)
Standard Liège: Arnaud Bodart, Kostas Laifis, Nicolas Gavory, Collins Fai, Zinho Vanheusden, Mehdi Carcela-González (81.Maxime Lestienne), Gojko Cimirot, Samuel Bastien, Selim Amallah (73.Paul M'Poku), Duje Cop (81.Obbi Oularé), Renaud Emond. Trainer: Michel Preud'homme.
Eintracht Frankfurt: Frederik Rønnow, Makoto Hasebe, David Abraham, Martin Hinteregger, Danny da Costa (89.Timothy Chandler), Gelson Fernandes, Sebastian Rode, Filip Kostic, Djibril Sow, Gonçalo Paciência (73.Bas Dost), André Silva (62.Daichi Kamada). Trainer: Adi Hütter.
Goals: 56' Zinho Vanheusden 1-0, 65' Filip Kostic 1-1, 90+4' Maxime Lestienne 2-1.

28.11.2019; Estádio „Dom Afonso Henriques", Guimarães
Referee: Serhiy Boyko (UKR); Attendance: 11,221
Vitória SC Guimarães – R Standard Liège 1-1(1-1)
Vitória Guimarães: Douglas Jesus, Florent Hanin, "Pedrão" Pedro Henrique, Falaye Sacko, Edmond Tapsoba, Mikel Agu, Lucas Evangelista, Denis Poha, Marcus Edwards (76.Rochinha), André Pereira (86.Léo Bonatini), Bruno Duarte (45.Davidson). Trainer: Ivo Vieira.
Standard Liège: Arnaud Bodart, Kostas Laifis, Nicolas Gavory, Mergim Vojvoda, Zinho Vanheusden, Mehdi Carcela-González, Maxime Lestienne (71.Selim Amallah), Gojko Cimirot, Paul M'Poku (82.Duje Cop), Samuel Bastien, Renaud Emond (69.Obbi Oularé). Trainer: Michel Preud'homme.
Goals: 40' Maxime Lestienne 0-1 (pen), 45+2' André Pereira 1-1.

12.12.2019; Commerzbank-Arena, Frankfurt am Main
Referee: Gediminas Mazeika (LTU); Attendance: 47,000
Eintracht Frankfurt – Vitória SC Guimarães 2-3(2-1)
Eintracht Frankfurt: Frederik Rønnow, Makoto Hasebe, David Abraham, Martin Hinteregger, Danny da Costa, Sebastian Rode (78.Gelson Fernandes), Filip Kostic, Djibril Sow, Daichi Kamada, Gonçalo Paciência, André Silva (73.Mijat Gacinovic). Trainer: Adi Hütter.
Vitória Guimarães: João Miguel Silva, Florent Hanin, Victor García, "Pedrão" Pedro Henrique, Frederico Venâncio, Rochinha (70.Marcus Edwards), Pêpê Rodrigues, Denis Poha (82.Bruno Duarte), Almoatasembellah Ali Mohamed Elmusrati, Davidson, André Pereira (66.Léo Bonatini). Trainer: Ivo Vieira.
Goals: 8' Rochinha 0-1, 31' Danny da Costa 1-1, 38' Daichi Kamada 2-1, 85' Almoatasembellah Ali Mohamed Elmusrati 2-2, 87' Marcus Edwards 2-3.

28.11.2019; Emirates Stadium, London
Referee: Ruddy Buquet (FRA); Attendance: 49,419
Arsenal FC London – Eintracht Frankfurt 1-2(1-0)
Arsenal FC: Emiliano Martínez, David Luiz (31.Mattéo Guendouzi), Sokratis Papastathopoulos, Shkodran Mustafi (76.Lucas Torreira), Calum Chambers, Kieran Tierney, Granit Xhaka, Joseph Willock, Bukayo Saka, Pierre-Emerick Aubameyang, Gabriel Martinelli (60.Mesut Özil). Trainer: Unai Emery.
Eintracht Frankfurt: Frederik Rønnow, Makoto Hasebe, David Abraham, Martin Hinteregger, Danny da Costa, Gelson Fernandes (46.Dominik Kohr), Filip Kostic, Djibril Sow, Daichi Kamada, Gonçalo Paciência, André Silva (46.Mijat Gacinovic). Trainer: Adi Hütter.
Goals: 45+1' Pierre-Emerick Aubameyang 1-0, 55', 64' Daichi Kamada 1-1, 1-2.

12.12.2019; Stade „Maurice Dufrasne", Liège
Referee: Andreas Ekberg (SWE); Attendance: 21,797
R Standard Liège – Arsenal FC London 2-2(0-0)
Standard Liège: Arnaud Bodart, Kostas Laifis, Nicolas Gavory, Collins Fai, Zinho Vanheusden, Mehdi Carcela-González, Gojko Cimirot, Paul M'Poku, Samuel Bastien, Selim Amallah (85.Maxime Lestienne), Renaud Emond (46.Felipe Avenatti). Trainer: Michel Preud'homme.
Arsenal FC: Emiliano Martínez, David Luiz, Sokratis Papastathopoulos (69.Gabriel Martinelli), Konstantinos Mavropanos, Ainsley Maitland-Niles (78.Calum Chambers), Joseph Willock, Mattéo Guendouzi, Emile Smith-Rowe (85.Pierre-Emerick Aubameyang), Bukayo Saka, Alexandre Lacazette, Reiss Nelson. Trainer: Freddie Ljungberg.
Goals: 47' Samuel Bastien 1-0, 69' Selim Amallah 2-0, 78' Alexandre Lacazette 2-1, 81' Bukayo Saka 2-2.

GROUP G	1. **FC Porto**	6	3	1	2	8	-	9	10
	2. **Glasgow Rangers FC**	6	2	3	1	8	-	6	9
	3. BSC Young Boys Bern	6	2	2	2	8	-	7	8
	4. Feyenoord Rotterdam	6	1	2	3	7	-	9	5

19.09.2019; Estádio do Dragão, Porto
Referee: Andris Treimanis (LVA); Attendance: 32,929
FC Porto – BSC Young Boys Bern 2-1(2-1)
FC Porto: Agustín Marchesín, Pepe, Ivan Marcano, Alex Telles, Danilo Pereira, Mateus Uribe, Otavinho, Luis Díaz (66.Romário Baró), Tiquinho Soares (81.Fábio Silva), Jesús Corona, Moussa Marega (70.Wilson Manafá). Trainer: Sérgio Conceição.
BSC Young Boys: David von Ballmoos, Fabian Lustenberger, Frederik Sørensen, Saidy Janko, Ulisses Garcia, Nicolas Bürgy, Cédric Zesiger, Christian Fassnacht (73.Gianluca Gaudino), Vincent Sierro (69.Michel Aebischer), Jean-Pierre Nsamé (61.Guillaume Hoarau), Roger Assalé. Trainer: Gerardo Seoane.; Goals: 8' Tiquinho Soares 1-0, 15' Jean-Pierre Nsamé 1-1 (pen), 29' Tiquinho Soares 2-1.

03.10.2019; Stadion Feijenoord, Rotterdam
Referee: Sergei Karasev (RUS); Attendance: 41,000
Feyenoord Rotterdam – FC Porto 2-0(0-0)
Feyenoord Rotterdam: Kenneth Vermeer, Eric Botteghin, Edgar Ié, Ridgeciano Haps, Rick Karsdorp (85.Lutsharel Geertruida), Leroy Fer, Jens Toornstra, Renato Tapia, Steven Berghuis, Sam Larsson (83.Marcos Senesi), Luis Sinisterra (83.Luciano Narsingh). Trainer: Jaap Stam.
FC Porto: Agustín Marchesín, Pepe, Ivan Marcano, Alex Telles, Wilson Manafá, Danilo Pereira (81.Fábio Silva), Shoya Nakajima (53.Luis Díaz), Mateus Uribe, Otavinho, Zé Luís (62.Tiquinho Soares), Moussa Marega. Trainer: Sérgio Conceição.
Goals: 49' Jens Toornstra 1-0, 80' Rick Karsdorp 2-0.

24.10.2019; Stade de Suisse, Bern
Referee: Jakob Kehlet (DEN); Attendance: 27,641
BSC Young Boys Bern – Feyenoord Rotterdam 2-0(2-0)
BSC Young Boys: David von Ballmoos, Fabian Lustenberger (42.Gianluca Gaudino), Frederik Sørensen, Saidy Janko, Jordan Lotomba, Cédric Zesiger, Nicolas Moumi Ngamaleu, Christian Fassnacht (86.Ulisses Garcia), Michel Aebischer, Jean-Pierre Nsamé, Roger Assalé (66.Nicolas Bürgy). Trainer: Gerardo Seoane.
Feyenoord Rotterdam: Kenneth Vermeer, Edgar Ié (37.Eric Botteghin), Tyrell Malacia (82.Ridgeciano Haps), Marcos Senesi, Lutsharel Geertruida, Leroy Fer, Jens Toornstra, Orkun Kökçü (74.Luciano Narsingh), Steven Berghuis, Sam Larsson, Luis Sinisterra. Trainer: Jaap Stam.
Goals: 14' Roger Assalé 1-0 (pen), 28' Jean-Pierre Nsamé 2-0 (pen).

19.09.2019; Ibrox Stadium, Glasgow
Referee: Antonio Mateu Lahoz (ESP); Attendance: 46,858
Glasgow Rangers FC – Feyenoord Rotterdam 1-0(1-0)
Glasgow Rangers: Allan McGregor, James Tavernier, Connor Goldson, Filip Helander, Borna Barisic, Steven Davis, Scott Arfield (90.Andy King), Ryan Jack, Glen Kamara (82.Joe Aribo), Sheyi Ojo (74.Brandon Barker), Alfredo Morelos. Trainer: Steven Gerrard.
Feyenoord Rotterdam: Kenneth Vermeer, Eric Botteghin, Edgar Ié, Ridgeciano Haps, Rick Karsdorp, Leroy Fer, Renato Tapia, Orkun Kökçü (65.Luciano Narsingh), Steven Berghuis, Sam Larsson (78.Nicolai Jørgensen), Luis Sinisterra (86.Jens Toornstra). Trainer: Jaap Stam.
Goal: 24' Sheyi Ojo 1-0.

03.10.2019; Stade de Suisse, Bern
Referee: Manuel Schüttengruber (AUT); Attendance: 26,348
BSC Young Boys Bern – Glasgow Rangers FC 2-1(0-1)
BSC Young Boys: David von Ballmoos, Fabian Lustenberger, Frederik Sørensen, Saidy Janko, Ulisses Garcia, Cédric Zesiger, Gianluca Gaudino (73.Nicolas Moumi Ngamaleu), Christian Fassnacht, Michel Aebischer, Jean-Pierre Nsamé, Roger Assalé (67.Jordan Lotomba). Trainer: Gerardo Seoane.
Glasgow Rangers: Allan McGregor, James Tavernier, Connor Goldson, Filip Helander, Borna Barisic, Steven Davis, Scott Arfield, Ryan Jack (65.Greg Stewart), Glen Kamara, Sheyi Ojo, Alfredo Morelos. Trainer: Steven Gerrard.
Goals: 44' Alfredo Morelos 0-1, 50' Roger Assalé 1-1, 90+3' Christian Fassnacht 2-1.

24.10.2019; Estádio do Dragão, Porto
Referee: Nikola Dabanovic (MNE); Attendance: 31,307
FC Porto – Glasgow Rangers FC 1-1(1-1)
FC Porto: Agustín Marchesín, Pepe, Ivan Marcano, Alex Telles, Danilo Pereira, Mateus Uribe, Otavinho (60.Bruno Costa), Luis Díaz (63.Shoya Nakajima), Zé Luís (76.Tiquinho Soares), Jesús Corona, Moussa Marega. Trainer: Sérgio Conceição.
Glasgow Rangers: Allan McGregor, James Tavernier, Connor Goldson, Filip Helander, Borna Barisic, Steven Davis, Ryan Jack (83.Scott Arfield), Glen Kamara, Alfredo Morelos, Brandon Barker (84.Sheyi Ojo), Ryan Kent (76.Joe Aribo). Trainer: Steven Gerrard.
Goals: 36' Luis Díaz 1-0, 44' Alfredo Morelos 1-1.

07.11.2019; Stadion Feijenoord, Rotterdam
Referee: Pawel Gil (POL); Attendance: 45,022
Feyenoord Rotterdam – BSC Young Boys Bern 1-1(1-0)
Feyenoord Rotterdam: Kenneth Vermeer, Jan-Arie van der Heijden, Edgar Ié (73.Marcos Senesi), Ridgeciano Haps, Rick Karsdorp, Jens Toornstra, Renato Tapia, Orkun Kökçü, Nicolai Jørgensen, Steven Berghuis, Luis Sinisterra (73.Sam Larsson). Trainer: Dick Advocaat.
BSC Young Boys: David von Ballmoos, Fabian Lustenberger, Frederik Sørensen, Ulisses Garcia, Jordan Lotomba (68.Saidy Janko), Cédric Zesiger, Nicolas Moumi Ngamaleu (68.Marvin Spielmann), Christian Fassnacht, Michel Aebischer, Jean-Pierre Nsamé, Roger Assalé (87.Felix Mambimbi). Trainer: Gerardo Seoane.
Goals: 18' Steven Berghuis 1-0 (pen), 71' Marvin Spielmann 1-1.

28.11.2019; Stade de Suisse, Bern
Referee: Tamás Bognár (HUN); Attendance: 31,120
BSC Young Boys Bern – FC Porto 1-2(1-0)
BSC Young Boys: David von Ballmoos, Fabian Lustenberger (70.Jordan Lotomba), Frederik Sørensen, Saidy Janko (81.Guillaume Hoarau), Ulisses Garcia, Cédric Zesiger, Nicolas Moumi Ngamaleu, Christian Fassnacht, Michel Aebischer, Jean-Pierre Nsamé, Roger Assalé (57.Christopher Martins Pereira). Trainer: Gerardo Seoane.
FC Porto: Agustín Marchesín, Pepe, Ivan Marcano, Alex Telles, Chancel Mbemba (46.Wilson Manafá), Danilo Pereira, Otavinho, Mamadou Loum N'Diaye (74.Luis Díaz), Vincent Aboubakar, Jesús Corona (84.Diogo Leite), Moussa Marega. Trainer: Sérgio Conceição.
Goals: 6' Christian Fassnacht 1-0, 76', 79' Vincent Aboubakar 1-1, 1-2.

12.12.2019; Estádio do Dragão, Porto
Referee: Deniz Aytekin (GER); Attendance: 28,507
FC Porto – Feyenoord Rotterdam 3-2(3-2)
FC Porto: Agustín Marchesín, Pepe, Ivan Marcano, Alex Telles, Danilo Pereira, Mateus Uribe, Otavinho, Luis Díaz (74.Sérgio Oliveira), Tiquinho Soares (75.Zé Luís), Jesús Corona, Moussa Marega (84.Chancel Mbemba). Trainer: Sérgio Conceição.
Feyenoord Rotterdam: Nick Marsman, Eric Botteghin, Tyrell Malacia, Marcos Senesi, Lutsharel Geertruida, Leroy Fer, Jens Toornstra (72.Yassin Ayoub), Orkun Kökçü (75.Renato Tapia), Steven Berghuis, Sam Larsson, Luis Sinisterra (72.Luciano Narsingh). Trainer: Dick Advocaat.
Goals: 14' Luis Díaz 1-0, 16' Tyrell Malacia 2-0 (own goal), 19' Eric Botteghin 2-1, 22' Sam Larsson 2-2, 34' Tiquinho Soares 3-2.

07.11.2019; Ibrox Stadium, Glasgow
Referee: Davide Massa (ITA); Attendance: 49,645
Glasgow Rangers FC – FC Porto 2-0(0-0)
Glasgow Rangers: Allan McGregor, James Tavernier, Connor Goldson, Filip Helander, Borna Barisic, Steven Davis, Ryan Jack, Glen Kamara, Alfredo Morelos (85.Jermain Defoe), Brandon Barker (65.Scott Arfield), Ryan Kent (83.Joe Aribo). Trainer: Steven Gerrard.
FC Porto: Agustín Marchesín, Pepe (49.Luis Díaz), Ivan Marcano, Alex Telles, Chancel Mbemba, Wilson Manafá, Danilo Pereira, Mateus Uribe, Otavinho (74.Fábio Silva), Tiquinho Soares (64.Zé Luís), Jesús Corona. Trainer: Sérgio Conceição.
Goals: 69' Alfredo Morelos 1-0, 73' Steven Davis 2-0.

28.11.2019; Stadion Feijenoord, Rotterdam
Referee: Damir Skomina (SVN); Attendance: 47,500
Feyenoord Rotterdam – Glasgow Rangers FC 2-2(1-0)
Feyenoord Rotterdam: Nick Marsman, Eric Botteghin, Tyrell Malacia, Marcos Senesi, Lutsharel Geertruida, Leroy Fer, Jens Toornstra (85.Yassin Ayoub), Orkun Kökçü, Steven Berghuis, Sam Larsson (69.Luciano Narsingh), Luis Sinisterra. Trainer: Dick Advocaat.
Glasgow Rangers: Allan McGregor, James Tavernier, Connor Goldson, Filip Helander, Borna Barisic, Steven Davis, Ryan Jack, Glen Kamara, Sheyi Ojo (77.Scott Arfield), Alfredo Morelos, Ryan Kent. Trainer: Steven Gerrard.
Goals: 33' Jens Toornstra 1-0, 53', 65' Alfredo Morelos 1-1, 1-2, 68' Luis Sinisterra 2-2.

12.12.2019; Ibrox Stadium, Glasgow
Referee: Felix Brych (GER); Attendance: 49,015
Glasgow Rangers FC – BSC Young Boys Bern 1-1(1-0)
Glasgow Rangers: Allan McGregor, James Tavernier, Connor Goldson, Borna Barisic, Nikola Katic, Scott Arfield, Ryan Jack, Glen Kamara, Joe Aribo, Alfredo Morelos, Ryan Kent (78.Sheyi Ojo). Trainer: Steven Gerrard.
BSC Young Boys: David von Ballmoos, Frederik Sørensen, Saidy Janko, Ulisses Garcia, Nicolas Bürgy, Christopher Martins Pereira (73.Felix Mambimbi), Nicolas Moumi Ngamaleu (61.Marvin Spielmann), Christian Fassnacht, Michel Aebischer, Jean-Pierre Nsamé (61.Guillaume Hoarau), Roger Assalé. Trainer: Gerardo Seoane.
Goals: 30' Alfredo Morelos 1-0, 89' Borna Barisic 1-1 (own goal).
Sent off: 90+3' Ryan Jack.

GROUP H	1. **RCD Espanyol Barcelona**	6	3	2	1	12 - 4	11
	2. **PFC Ludogorets Razgrad**	6	2	2	2	10 - 10	8
	3. Ferencvárosi TC	6	1	4	1	5 - 7	7
	4. FK CSKA Moskva	6	1	2	3	3 - 9	5

19.09.2019; Ludogorets Arena, Razgrad
Referee: Irfan Peljto (BIH); Attendance: 8,423
PFC Ludogorets Razgrad – FK CSKA Moskva 5-1(0-1)
Ludogorets Razgrad: Renan, Dragos Grigore, Cicinho, Rafael Forster, Anton Nedyalkov, Anicet Andrianantenaina, Wanderson, Stéphane Badji, Claudiu Keserü (86.Dan Biton), Marcelinho (74.Jacek Góralski), Jody Lukoki (84.Jorginho). Trainer: Stanislav Genchev.
CSKA Moskva: Igor Akinfeev, Mário Fernandes, Hördur Magnússon, Igor Diveev, Vadim Karpov, Nikola Vlasic, Kristijan Bistrovic, Konstantin Kuchaev (71.Lucas Santos), Ivan Oblyakov, Jaka Bijol (53.Fedor Chalov), Takuma Nishimura (54.Ilzat Akhmetov). Trainer: Victor Goncharenko.
Goals: 11' Igor Diveev 0-1, 48' Wanderson 1-1, 5-0' Jody Lukoki 2-1, 52', 68', 73' Claudiu Keserü 3-1, 4-1, 5-1 (pen).

03.10.2019; Groupama Aréna, Budapest
Referee: Bartosz Frankowski (POL); Attendance: 16,163
Ferencvárosi TC – PFC Ludogorets Razgrad 0-3(0-2)
Ferencvárosi TC: Dénes Dibusz, Marcel Heister, Miha Blazic, Abraham Frimpong, Gergő Lovrencsics, Dávid Sigér (73.Nikolay Signevich), Igor Kharatin, Oleksandr Zubkov (80.Roland Varga), Isael, Tokmac Nguen, Franck Boli (73.Michal Skvarka). Trainer: Serhiy Rebrov.
Ludogorets Razgrad: Plamen Iliev, Dragos Grigore, Cicinho (69.Jordan Ikoko), Rafael Forster, Anton Nedyalkov, Anicet Andrianantenaina, Wanderson, Stéphane Badji, Claudiu Keserü, Marcelinho (46.Cosmin Moti), Jody Lukoki (57.Jacek Góralski). Trainer: Stanislav Genchev.
Goals: 1' Jody Lukoki 0-1, 40', 64' Rafael Forster 0-2, 0-3.
Sent off: 43' Dragos Grigore.

19.09.2019; RCDE Stadium, Cornellà de Llobregat
Referee: Nikola Dabanovic (MNE); Attendance: 18,125
RCD Espanyol Barcelona – Ferencvárosi TC 1-1(0-1)
RCD Espanyol: Diego López, Bernardo Espinosa, Dídac Vilà (67.Adrià Pedrosa), Javi López, Naldo, Granero, Marc Roca, Matías Vargas (74.Víctor Campuzano), Pol Lozano, Melendo (56.Jonathan Calleri), Lei Wu. Trainer: David Gallego.
Ferencvárosi TC: Dénes Dibusz, Marcel Heister, Endre Botka (66.Gergő Lovrencsics), Miha Blazic, Lasha Dvali, Dávid Sigér, Igor Kharatin, Oleksandr Zubkov, Danylo Ignatenko (85.Abraham Frimpong), Isael (65.Nikolay Signevich), Tokmac Nguen. Trainer: Serhiy Rebrov.
Goals: 10' Javi López 0-1 (own goal), 60' Matías Vargas 1-1.

03.10.2019; VEB Arena, Moskva
Referee: Ali Palabiyik (TUR); Attendance: 22,288
FK CSKA Moskva – RCD Espanyol Barcelona 0-2(0-0)
CSKA Moskva: Igor Akinfeev, Mário Fernandes, Hördur Magnússon, Zvonimir Sarlija, Igor Diveev (46.Cédric Gogoua), Nikola Vlasic, Ilzat Akhmetov (76.Jaka Bijol), Kristijan Bistrovic, Arnór Sigurdsson, Konstantin Kuchaev (67.Ivan Oblyakov), Fedor Chalov. Trainer: Victor Goncharenko.
RCD Espanyol: Diego López, Sébastien Corchia, David López, Adrià Pedrosa, Fernando Calero, Granero (90.Pol Lozano), Víctor Sánchez, Marc Roca, Matías Vargas, Lei Wu (76.Pablo Piatti), Jonathan Calleri (22.Víctor Campuzano). Trainer: David Gallego.
Goals: 64' Lei Wu 0-1, 90+5' Víctor Campuzano 0-2.

24.10.2019; VEB Arena, Moskva
Referee: Pavel Orel (CZE); Attendance: 18,518
FK CSKA Moskva – Ferencvárosi TC 0-1(0-0)
CSKA Moskva: Igor Akinfeev, Mário Fernandes, Hördur Magnússon, Igor Diveev, Vadim Karpov, Nikola Vlasic, Ilzat Akhmetov (75.Lucas Santos), Arnór Sigurdsson (80.Jaka Bijol), Konstantin Kuchaev (61.Kristijan Bistrovic), Ivan Oblyakov, Fedor Chalov. Trainer: Victor Goncharenko.
Ferencvárosi TC: Dénes Dibusz, Endre Botka, Miha Blazic, Eldar Civic, Gergö Lovrencsics, Dávid Sigér, Igor Kharatin, Oleksandr Zubkov (89.Lasha Dvali), Danylo Ignatenko, Tokmac Nguen (84.Roland Varga), Franck Boli (72.Isael). Trainer: Serhiy Rebrov.
Goal: 86' Roland Varga 0-1.

07.11.2019; Groupama Aréna, Budapest
Referee: Aleksandar Stavrev (MKD); Attendance: 18,153
Ferencvárosi TC – FK CSKA Moskva 0-0
Ferencvárosi TC: Dénes Dibusz, Endre Botka, Miha Blazic, Eldar Civic, Michal Skvarka (84.Roland Varga), Gergö Lovrencsics, Igor Kharatin, Oleksandr Zubkov, Danylo Ignatenko, Tokmac Nguen (90.Abraham Frimpong), Franck Boli (82.Isael). Trainer: Serhiy Rebrov.
CSKA Moskva: Igor Akinfeev, Mário Fernandes, Hördur Magnússon (81.Kirill Nababkin), Igor Diveev, Vadim Karpov, Nikola Vlasic, Ilzat Akhmetov (59.Kristijan Bistrovic), Arnór Sigurdsson, Ivan Oblyakov, Jaka Bijol (63.Konstantin Kuchaev), Fedor Chalov. Trainer: Victor Goncharenko.
Sent off: 90+1' Kirill Nababkin.

28.11.2019; VEB Arena, Moskva
Referee: Jakob Kehlet (DEN); Attendance: 12,948
FK CSKA Moskva – PFC Ludogorets Razgrad 1-1(0-0)
CSKA Moskva: Igor Akinfeev, Mário Fernandes, Hördur Magnússon, Igor Diveev, Vadim Karpov (76.Jaka Bijol), Nikola Vlasic, Kristijan Bistrovic, Arnór Sigurdsson (64.Ilzat Akhmetov), Konstantin Kuchaev (54.Alan Dzagoev), Ivan Oblyakov, Fedor Chalov. Trainer: Victor Goncharenko.
Ludogorets Razgrad: Plamen Iliev, Dragos Grigore, Cicinho, Georgi Terziev, Anton Nedyalkov, Anicet Andrianantenaina, Wanderson (81.Mavis Tchibota), Stéphane Badji, Claudiu Keserü (87.Jakub Swierczok), Marcelinho (76.Svetoslav Dyakov), Jody Lukoki. Trainer: Aleksi Zhelyazkov.
Goals: 66' Claudiu Keserü 0-1, 76' Fedor Chalov 1-1.

12.12.2019; Ludogorets Arena, Razgrad
Referee: Matej Jug (SVN); Attendance: 5,528
PFC Ludogorets Razgrad – Ferencvárosi TC 1-1(1-0)
Ludogorets Razgrad: Plamen Iliev, Dragos Grigore, Cicinho, Georgi Terziev, Anton Nedyalkov, Anicet Andrianantenaina, Wanderson (85.Svetoslav Dyakov), Stéphane Badji, Claudiu Keserü (90+1.Jordan Ikoko), Marcelinho, Jody Lukoki (77.Mavis Tchibota). Trainer: Aleksi Zhelyazkov.
Ferencvárosi TC: Dénes Dibusz, Marcel Heister, Endre Botka, Miha Blazic, Abraham Frimpong, Dávid Sigér (79.Michal Skvarka), Igor Kharatin (84.Danylo Ignatenko), Oleksandr Zubkov, Isael, Tokmac Nguen, Franck Boli (84.Nikolay Signevich). Trainer: Serhiy Rebrov.
Goals: 24' Jody Lukoki 1-0, 90+5' Nikolay Signevich 1-1.

24.10.2019; Ludogorets Arena, Razgrad
Referee: Aliyar Agayev (AZE); Attendance: 10,334
PFC Ludogorets Razgrad – RCD Espanyol Barcelona 0-1(0-1)
Ludogorets Razgrad: Plamen Iliev, Cosmin Moti, Cicinho, Rafael Forster, Anton Nedyalkov, Anicet Andrianantenaina (67.Dan Biton), Wanderson, Stéphane Badji, Marcelinho, Jody Lukoki (59.Jakub Swierczok), Mavis Tchibota. Trainer: Stanislav Genchev.
RCD Espanyol: Diego López, Bernardo Espinosa, Dídac Vilá, Sébastien Corchia, Javi López, Lluís López, Granero, Iturraspe, Melendo (69.Marc Roca), Lei Wu (61.Matías Vargas), Víctor Campuzano (78.Facundo Ferreyra). Trainer: Pablo Machín.
Goal: 13' Víctor Campuzano 0-1.;
Sent off: 88' Javi López.

07.11.2019; RCDE Stadium, Cornellà de Llobregat
Referee: François Letexier (FRA); Attendance: 13,963
RCD Espanyol Barcelona – PFC Ludogorets Razgrad 6-0(3-0)
RCD Espanyol: Diego López, Bernardo Espinosa (46.Adrià Pedrosa), Dídac Vilá, Sébastien Corchia, Lluís López, Fernando Calero, Granero, Matías Vargas, Pol Lozano, Melendo (72.Lei Wu), Víctor Campuzano (65.Facundo Ferreyra). Trainer: Pablo Machín.
Ludogorets Razgrad: Plamen Iliev, Cicinho, Georgi Terziev, Rafael Forster, Anton Nedyalkov, Wanderson (77.Svetoslav Dyakov), Jacek Góralski, Stéphane Badji, Claudiu Keserü (39.Anicet Andrianantenaina), Marcelinho (21.Jordan Ikoko), Jody Lukoki. Trainer: Aleksi Zhelyazkov.
Goals: 4' Melendo 1-0 19' Lluís López 2-0, 36' Matías Vargas 3-0 (pen), 52' Víctor Campuzano 4-0, 73' Adrià Pedrosa 5-0, 76' Facundo Ferreyra 6-0.; Sent off: 12' Rafael Forster, 34' Jacek Góralski.

28.11.2019; Groupama Aréna, Budapest
Referee: Tiago Bruno Lopes Martins (POR); Attendance: 19,111
Ferencvárosi TC – RCD Espanyol Barcelona 2-2(1-1)
Ferencvárosi TC: Dénes Dibusz, Miha Blazic, Abraham Frimpong, Eldar Civic, Gergö Lovrencsics, Dávid Sigér (86.Michal Skvarka), Igor Kharatin, Isael, Roland Varga (61.Oleksandr Zubkov), Tokmac Nguen, Franck Boli (83.Nikolay Signevich). Trainer: Serhiy Rebrov.
RCD Espanyol: Diego López, Dídac Vilá, Sébastien Corchia, Lluís López, Pipa Ávila, Fernando Calero, Granero (69.Mohamed Ezzarfani), Iturraspe, Pol Lozano, Melendo (81.Jonathan Calleri), Víctor Campuzano (88.Sergi Darder). Trainer: Pablo Machín.
Goals: 23' Dávid Sigér 1-0, 31' Melendo 1-1, 90+1' Michal Skvarka 2-1 (pen), 90+6' Sergi Darder 2-2.
Sent off: 90+4' Eldar Civic.

12.12.2019; RCDE Stadium, Cornellà de Llobregat
Referee: Kevin Blom (NED); Attendance: 10,615
RCD Espanyol Barcelona – FK CSKA Moskva 0-1(0-0)
RCD Espanyol: Andrés Prieto, Javi López, Naldo (86.Jonathan Calleri), Lluís López, Pipa Ávila, Adrià Pedrosa, Pablo Piatti (72.Granero), Iturraspe, Pol Lozano, Facundo Ferreyra, Víctor Campuzano (46.Lei Wu). Trainer: Pablo Machín.
CSKA Moskva: Ilya Pomazun, Mário Fernandes, Hördur Magnússon, Igor Diveev, Vadim Karpov, Nikola Vlasic (86.Jaka Bijol), Ilzat Akhmetov (81.Georgiy Shchennikov), Kristijan Bistrovic, Konstantin Kuchaev (78.Arnór Sigurdsson), Ivan Oblyakov, Fedor Chalov. Trainer: Victor Goncharenko.
Goal: 84' Nikola Vlasic 0-1.

GROUP I	1. **KAA Gent**	6	3	3	0	11 - 7	12
	2. **VfL Wolfsburg**	6	3	2	1	9 - 7	11
	3. AS Saint-Étienne	6	0	4	2	6 - 8	4
	4. FK Oleksandriya	6	0	3	3	6 - 10	3

19.09.2019; GHELAMCO-arena, Gent
Referee: Roi Reinshreiber (ISR); Attendance: 14,928
KAA Gent – AS Saint-Étienne 3-2(2-1)
KAA Gent: Thomas Kaminski, Nana Asare, Mikael Lustig, Igor Plastun, Michael Ngadeu-Ngadjui, Vadis Odjidja-Ofoe, Sven Kums (90+3.Brecht Dejaegere), Elisha Owusu, Laurent Depoitre, Roman Yaremchuk (81.Dylan Bronn), Jonathan David (90+4.Giorgi Kvilitaia). Trainer: Jess Thorup.
AS Saint-Étienne: Stéphane Ruffier, Loïc Perrin, Mathieu Debuchy, Timothée Kolodziejczak, Miguel Trauco, Harold Moukoudi (72.Robert Beric), Yohan Cabaye (65.Denis Bouanga), Yann M'Vila, Romain Hamouma (72.Arnaud Nordin), Zaydou Youssouf, Wahbi Khazri. Trainer: Ghislain Printant.
Goals: 2' Jonathan David 1-0, 38' Wahbi Khazri 1-1, 43' Jonathan David 2-1, 64' Loïc Perrin 3-1 (own goal), 75' Thomas Kaminski 3-2 (own goal).

19.09.2019; Volkswagen Arena, Wolfsburg
Referee: Halis Özkahya (TUR); Attendance: 10,112
VfL Wolfsburg – FK Oleksandriya 3-1(2-0)
VfL Wolfsburg: Pavao Pervan, Robin Knoche, Jérôme Roussillon, Marcel Tisserand (70.Jeffrey Bruma), Kevin Mbabu, Yannick Gerhardt, Admir Mehmedi (86.Renato Steffen), Josuha Guillavogui, Maximilian Arnold, Josip Brekalo (76.Lukas Nmecha), Wout Weghorst. Trainer: Oliver Glasner.
FK Oleksandriya: Yuri Pankiv, Kaspars Dubra, Pavlo Pashayev, Valeri Luchkevych (81.Yevhen Protasov), Denis Miroshnichenko, Glib Bukhal, Oleksiy Dovgiy (46.Kirilo Kovalets), Dmytro Grechyshkin, Eugene Banada, Maksym Tretyakov (65.Dmytro Shastal), Artem Sitalo. Trainer: Volodymyr Sharan.
Goals: 20' Maximilian Arnold 1-0. 24' Admir Mehmedi 2-0, 66' Eugene Banada 2-1, 67' Josip Brekalo 3-1.

03.10.2019; Arena Lviv, Lviv
Referee: Jens Maae (DEN); Attendance: 7,588
FK Oleksandriya – KAA Gent 1-1(0-1)
FK Oleksandriya: Yuri Pankiv, Kaspars Dubra, Pavlo Pashayev, Valeri Luchkevych (86.Denys Bezborodko), Denis Miroshnichenko, Glib Bukhal, Dmytro Grechyshkin, Kirilo Kovalets (75.Oleksiy Dovgiy), Eugene Banada, Maksym Tretyakov, Artem Sitalo (80.Dmytro Shastal). Trainer: Volodymyr Sharan.
KAA Gent: Thomas Kaminski, Nana Asare, Mikael Lustig, Igor Plastun, Michael Ngadeu-Ngadjui, Vadis Odjidja-Ofoe, Sven Kums, Elisha Owusu, Laurent Depoitre (85.Giorgi Kvilitaia), Roman Yaremchuk (89.Yūya Kubo), Jonathan David. Trainer: Jess Thorup.
Goals: 6' Laurent Depoitre 0-1, 60' Artem Sitalo 1-1.

24.10.2019; Stade „Geoffroy Guichard", Saint-Étienne
Referee: Espen Eskås (NOR); Attendance: 28,573
AS Saint-Étienne – FK Oleksandriya 1-1(1-1)
AS Saint-Étienne: Stéphane Ruffier, Mathieu Debuchy, Timothée Kolodziejczak, Gabriel Silva, William Saliba, Yann M'Vila, Romain Hamouma, Jean-Eudes Aholou (46.Ryad Boudebouz), Arnaud Nordin (63.Charles Abi), Zaydou Youssouf, Robert Beric (74.Denis Bouanga). Trainer: Claude Puel.
FK Oleksandriya: Yuri Pankiv, Kaspars Dubra, Pavlo Pashayev, Valeri Luchkevych (80.Dmytro Shastal), Denis Miroshnichenko, Glib Bukhal, Dmytro Grechyshkin, Kirilo Kovalets (83.Oleksiy Dovgiy), Eugene Banada, Maksym Tretyakov (90 i 3.Vladislav Baboglo), Artem Sitalo. Trainer: Volodymyr Sharan.
Goals: 8' Gabriel Silva 1-0, 14' Gabriel Silva 1-1 (own goal).

07.11.2019; Arena Lviv, Lviv
Referee: João Pedro Pinheiro (POR); Attendance: 6,361
FK Oleksandriya – AS Saint-Étienne 2-2(0-1)
FK Oleksandriya: Yuri Pankiv, Kaspars Dubra, Pavlo Pashayev, Valeri Luchkevych (78.Maksym Zaderaka), Denis Miroshnichenko, Glib Bukhal, Dmytro Grechyshkin, Kirilo Kovalets, Eugene Banada, Maksym Tretyakov (84.Timur Stetskov), Dmytro Shastal (46.Denys Bezborodko). Trainer: Volodymyr Sharan.
AS Saint-Étienne: Stéphane Ruffier, Loïc Perrin, Mathieu Debuchy, Timothée Kolodziejczak, Wesley Fofana, Jean-Eudes Aholou, Denis Bouanga, Arnaud Nordin (87.Ryad Boudebouz), Zaydou Youssouf, Wahbi Khazri (72.Gabriel Silva), Robert Beric (55.Mahdi Camara). Trainer: Claude Puel.
Goals: 24' Wahbi Khazri 0-1 (pen), 72' Mahdi Camara 0-2, 84' Denys Bezborodko 1-2, 90+1' Maksym Zaderaka 2-2.

28.11.2019; Stade „Geoffroy Guichard", Saint-Étienne
Referee: Irfan Peljto (BIH); Attendance: 25,315
AS Saint-Étienne – KAA Gent 0-0
AS Saint-Étienne: Stéphane Ruffier, Loïc Perrin, Timothée Kolodziejczak, Wesley Fofana, Yann M'Vila (80.Robert Beric), Ryad Boudebouz, Jean-Eudes Aholou (64.Arnaud Nordin), Denis Bouanga, Mahdi Camara, Loïs Diony (73.Zaydou Youssouf), Franck Honorat. Trainer: Claude Puel.
KAA Gent: Thomas Kaminski, Mikael Lustig, Igor Plastun, Michael Ngadeu-Ngadjui, Milad Mohammadi, Vadis Odjidja-Ofoe, Sven Kums, Elisha Owusu, Laurent Depoitre (78.Alessio Castro-Montes), Roman Yaremchuk (71.Giorgi Kvilitaia), Jonathan David (80.Brecht Dejaegere). Trainer: Jess Thorup.
Sent off: 76' Michael Ngadeu-Ngadjui.

12.12.2019; GHELAMCO-arena, Gent
Referee: Radu Petrescu (ROU); Attendance: 13,156
KAA Gent – FK Oleksandriya 2-1(2-0)
KAA Gent: Thomas Kaminski, Nana Asare, Mikael Lustig, Igor Plastun, Alessio Castro-Montes, Vadis Odjidja-Ofoe, Sven Kums, Roman Bezus (80.Jean-Luc Dompé), Elisha Owusu, Laurent Depoitre (90+3.Giorgi Kvilitaia), Roman Yaremchuk (73.Giorgi Chakvetadze). Trainer: Jess Thorup.
FK Oleksandriya: Yuri Pankiv, Kaspars Dubra, Pavlo Pashayev, Valeri Luchkevych, Denis Miroshnichenko, Vladislav Baboglo, Andriy Zaporozhan (46.Oleksiy Dovgiy), Dmytro Grechyshkin, Kirilo Kovalets, Maksym Tretyakov (79.Maksym Zaderaka), Denys Bezborodko (86.João Teixeira). Trainer: Volodymyr Sharan.
Goals: 7', 16' Laurent Depoitre 1-0, 2-0, 54' Denis Miroshnichenko 2-1.

03.10.2019; Stade „Geoffroy Guichard", Saint-Étienne
Referee: Craig Pawson (ENG); Attendance: 24,815
AS Saint-Étienne – VfL Wolfsburg 1-1(1-1)
AS Saint-Étienne: Jessy Moulin, Loïc Perrin, Mathieu Debuchy (60.Harold Moukoudi), Timothée Kolodziejczak, William Saliba, Yann M'Vila, Romain Hamouma, Arnaud Nordin, Zaydou Youssouf, Wahbi Khazri (86.Charles Abi), Robert Beric (65.Denis Bouanga). Trainer: Ghislain Printant.
VfL Wolfsburg: Pavao Pervan, Jeffrey Bruma, Robin Knoche, Jérôme Roussillon (83.Renato Steffen), Marcel Tisserand, William, Josuha Guillavogui, Felix Klaus, Maximilian Arnold, Josip Brekalo (72.João Victor), Wout Weghorst (60.Lukas Nmecha). Trainer: Oliver Glasner.
Goals: 13' Timothée Kolodziejczak 1-0, 15' William 1-1.

24.10.2019; GHELAMCO-arena, Gent:
Referee: Sergey Ivanov (RUS); Attendance: 15,437
KAA Gent – VfL Wolfsburg 2-2(1-2)
KAA Gent: Thomas Kaminski, Nana Asare, Mikael Lustig, Igor Plastun, Michael Ngadeu-Ngadjui, Vadis Odjidja-Ofoe, Sven Kums (87.Jean-Luc Dompé), Elisha Owusu (60.Roman Bezus), Laurent Depoitre (73.Giorgi Kvilitaia), Roman Yaremchuk, Jonathan David. Trainer: Jess Thorup.
VfL Wolfsburg: Pavao Pervan, Jeffrey Bruma, Robin Knoche, Marcel Tisserand, William (46.Kevin Mbabu), Josuha Guillavogui, Maximilian Arnold, Renato Steffen (79.Jérôme Roussillon), Josip Brekalo (66.Lukas Nmecha), Wout Weghorst, João Victor. Trainer: Oliver Glasner.
Goals: 3' Wout Weghorst 0-1, 24' João Victor 0-2, 41', 90+4' Roman Yaremchuk 1-2, 2-2.

07.11.2019; Volkswagen Arena, Wolfsburg
Referee: Massimiliano Irrati (ITA); Attendance: 11,620
VfL Wolfsburg – KAA Gent 1-3(1-0)
VfL Wolfsburg: Pavao Pervan, Jeffrey Bruma, Robin Knoche (82.Felix Klaus), Marcel Tisserand, William, Josuha Guillavogui, Maximilian Arnold (70.Lukas Nmecha), Renato Steffen, Josip Brekalo (66.Yunus Malli), Wout Weghorst, João Victor. Trainer: Oliver Glasner.
KAA Gent: Thomas Kaminski, Nana Asare, Mikael Lustig, Igor Plastun, Michael Ngadeu-Ngadjui, Vadis Odjidja-Ofoe, Sven Kums, Elisha Owusu, Laurent Depoitre (90+1.Giorgi Kvilitaia), Roman Yaremchuk (81.Alessio Castro-Montes), Jonathan David. Trainer: Jess Thorup.
Goals: 20' João Victor 1-0, 50' Roman Yaremchuk 1-1, 65' Laurent Depoitre 1-2, 76' Michael Ngadeu-Ngadjui 1-3.

28.11.2019; Arena Lviv, Lviv
Referee: Manuel Schüttengruber (AUT); Attendance: 7,118
FK Oleksandriya – VfL Wolfsburg 0-1(0-1)
FK Oleksandriya: Yuri Pankiv, Kaspars Dubra, Pavlo Pashayev, Valeri Luchkevych (86.Maksym Zaderaka), Denis Miroshnichenko, Vladislav Baboglo, Andriy Zaporozhan, Dmytro Grechyshkin, Kirilo Kovalets (39.Denys Bezborodko), Eugene Banada, Dmytro Shastal (55.Maksym Tretyakov). Trainer: Volodymyr Sharan.
VfL Wolfsburg: Koen Casteels, Jeffrey Bruma, Jérôme Roussillon, Marcel Tisserand, John Anthony Brooks, William (90+1.Kevin Mbabu), Admir Mehmedi (80.Felix Klaus), Josuha Guillavogui, Maximilian Arnold, Wout Weghorst, João Victor (61.Renato Steffen). Trainer: Oliver Glasner.
Goal: 45+1' Wout Weghorst 0-1 (pen).

12.12.2019; Volkswagen Arena, Wolfsburg
Referee: Paul Tierney (ENG); Attendance: 10,802
VfL Wolfsburg – AS Saint-Étienne 1-0(0-0)
VfL Wolfsburg: Pavao Pervan, Robin Knoche, Marcel Tisserand, Paulo Otávio (79.Jérôme Roussillon), Kevin Mbabu, Yannick Gerhardt, Renato Steffen, Xaver Schlager (64.Yunus Malli), Josip Brekalo, Elvis Rexhbeçaj, Daniel Ginczek (64.Lukas Nmecha). Trainer: Oliver Glasner.
AS Saint-Étienne: Jessy Moulin, Timothée Kolodziejczak, Sergi Palencia, Harold Moukoudi, Yann M'Vila, Romain Hamouma (55.Bilal Benkhedim), Jean-Eudes Aholou (46.Franck Honorat), Assane Dioussé (77.Gabriel Silva), Arnaud Nordin, Zaydou Youssouf, Robert Beric. Trainer: Claude Puel.
Goal: 52' Paulo Otávio 1-0.

1. İstanbul Başakşehir FK	6	3	1	2	7	-	9	10
2. AS Roma	6	2	3	1	12	-	6	9
3. Borussia VfL Mönchengladbach	6	2	2	2	6	-	9	8
4. Wolfsberger AC	6	1	2	3	7	-	8	5

GROUP J

19.09.2019; Stadio Olimpico, Roma
Referee: Xavier Estrada Fernández (ESP); Attendance: 21,348
AS Roma – İstanbul Başakşehir FK 4-0(1-0)
AS Roma: Pau López, Aleksandar Kolarov, Federico Fazio, Juan Jesus, Leonardo Spinazzola, Javier Pastore (64.Lorenzo Pellegrini), Bryan Cristante (72.Jordan Veretout), Amadou Diawara, Nicolò Zaniolo, Edin Dzeko (74.Nikola Kalinic), Justin Kluivert. Trainer: Paulo Fonseca.
İstanbul Basaksehir FK: Mert Günok, Gaël Clichy, Júnior Caiçara, Ponck, Arda Turan (64.Enzo Crivelli), Mehmet Topal, Mahmut Tekdemir, Danijel Aleksic (69.Azubuike Okechukwu), Edin Visca, Irfan Kahveci, Fredrik Gulbrandsen (77.Demba Ba). Trainer: Okan Buruk.
Goals: 42' Júnior Caiçara 1-0 (own goal), 58' Edin Dzeko 2-0, 71' Nicolò Zaniolo 3-0, 90+3' Justin Kluivert 4-0.

03.10.2019; Merkur Arena, Graz
Referee: Tiago Bruno Lopes Martins (POR); Attendance: 11,169
Wolfsberger AC – AS Roma 1-1(0-1)
Wolfsberger AC: Alexander Kofler, Nemanja Rnic, Lukas Schmitz, Michael Sollbauer, Michael Novak, Michael Liendl (88.Marc Andre Schmerböck), Mario Leitgeb, Marcel Ritzmaier (90+2.Christopher Wernitznig), Anderson Niangbo, Romano Schmid, Shon Weissman (81.Alexander Schmidt). Trainer: Gerhard Struber.
AS Roma: Antonio Miranta, Federico Fazio, Davide Santon, Leonardo Spinazzola (80.Aleksandar Kolarov), Gianluca Mancini, Javier Pastore (77.Mirko Antonucci), Bryan Cristante (82.Jordan Veretout), Amadou Diawara, Nicolò Zaniolo, Nikola Kalinic, Justin Kluivert. Trainer: Paulo Fonseca.; Goals: 27' Leonardo Spinazzola 0-1, 51' Michael Liendl 1-1.

24.10.2019; Başakşehir „Fatih Terim" Stadyumu, İstanbul
Referee: Irfan Peljto (BIH); Attendance: 4,101
İstanbul Başakşehir FK – Wolfsberger AC 1-0(0-0)
İstanbul Basaksehir FK: Mert Günok, Gaël Clichy, Martin Skrtel, Júnior Caiçara, Ponck, Mehmet Topal, Mahmut Tekdemir (46.Azubuike Okechukwu), Edin Visca (90.Ugur Uçar), Irfan Kahveci, Fredrik Gulbrandsen (64.Robinho), Enzo Crivelli. Trainer: Okan Buruk.
Wolfsberger AC: Alexander Kofler, Nemanja Rnic, Lukas Schmitz (90+1.Marc Andre Schmerböck), Michael Sollbauer, Michael Novak, Michael Liendl, Mario Leitgeb, Marcel Ritzmaier, Anderson Niangbo (76.Alexander Schmidt), Romano Schmid, Shon Weissman. Trainer: Gerhard Struber.
Goal: 78' Irfan Kahveci 1-0.

07.11.2019; Merkur Arena, Graz
Referee: Sandro Schärer (SUI); Attendance: 5,286
Wolfsberger AC – İstanbul Başakşehir FK 0-3(0-0)
Wolfsberger AC: Alexander Kofler, Nemanja Rnic, Lukas Schmitz, Michael Sollbauer, Michael Novak, Michael Liendl, Mario Leitgeb (87.Manfred Gollner), Marcel Ritzmaier, Anderson Niangbo (81.Alexander Schmidt), Romano Schmid, Shon Weissman. Trainer: Gerhard Struber.
İstanbul Basaksehir FK: Mert Günok, Gaël Clichy, Martin Skrtel, Júnior Caiçara, Ponck, Mehmet Topal, Edin Visca, Berkay Özcan (80.Arda Turan), Azubuike Okechukwu (89.Eljero Elia), Fredrik Gulbrandsen (88.Aziz Behich), Enzo Crivelli. Trainer: Okan Buruk.
Goals: 73' Edin Visca 0-1 (pen), 84', 87' Enzo Crivelli 0-2, 0-3.
Sent off: 72' Nemanja Rnic.

28.11.2019; Başakşehir „Fatih Terim" Stadyumu, İstanbul
Referee: Ovidiu Hategan (ROU); Attendance: 12,879
İstanbul Başakşehir FK – AS Roma 0-3(0-3)
İstanbul Basaksehir FK: Mert Günok, Gaël Clichy, Martin Skrtel (52.Berkay Özcan), Alexandru Epureanu (46.Robinho), Ponck, Mehmet Topal, Edin Visca, Irfan Kahveci, Azubuike Okechukwu, Fredrik Gulbrandsen (16.Aziz Behich), Enzo Crivelli. Trainer: Okan Buruk.
AS Roma: Pau López, Aleksandar Kolarov (53.Leonardo Spinazzola), Davide Santon, Chris Smalling, Gianluca Mancini, Jordan Veretout, Lorenzo Pellegrini (71.Cengiz Ünder), Amadou Diawara, Nicolò Zaniolo, Edin Dzeko (72.Henrikh Mkhitaryan), Justin Kluivert. Trainer: Paulo Fonseca.
Goals: 30' Jordan Veretout 0-1 (pen), 41' Justin Kluivert 0-2, 45+1' Edin Dzeko 0-3.

19.09.2019; Stadion im Borussia-Park, Mönchengladbach
Referee: Tamás Bornár (HUN); Attendance: 34,846
Borussia VfL Mönchengladbach – Wolfsberger AC 0-4(0-3)
Borussia Mönchengladbach: Yann Sommer, Stefan Lainer, Matthias Ginter, Nico Elvedi, Ramy Bensebaini, Christoph Kramer, László Bénes, Florian Neuhaus (46.Breel Embolo), Denis Zakaria, Alassane Pléa (72.Patrick Herrmann), Marcus Thuram (71.Raffael). Trainer: Marco Rose.
Wolfsberger AC: Alexander Kofler, Nemanja Rnic, Lukas Schmitz, Michael Sollbauer, Michael Novak, Michael Liendl, Mario Leitgeb, Marcel Ritzmaier (86.Christopher Wernitznig), Anderson Niangbo (90+1.Marc Andre Schmerböck), Romano Schmid, Shon Weissman (84.Alexander Schmidt). Trainer: Gerhard Struber.
Goals: 13' Shon Weissman 0-1, 31' Mario Leitgeb 0-2, 41' Marcel Ritzmaier 0-3, 68' Mario Leitgeb 0-4.

03.10.2019; Başakşehir „Fatih Terim" Stadyumu, İstanbul
Referee: Stuart Attwell (ENG); Attendance: 5,646
İstanbul Başakşehir FK – Borussia VfL Mönchengladbach 1-1(0-0)
İstanbul Başakşehir FK: Mert Günok, Gaël Clichy, Martin Skrtel, Júnior Caiçara, Ponck, Mahmut Tekdemir, Danijel Aleksic (46.Azubuike Okechukwu), Edin Visca, Irfan Kahveci (89.Mehmet Topal), Fredrik Gulbrandsen, Enzo Crivelli (78.Eljero Elia). Trainer: Okan Buruk.
Borussia Mönchengladbach: Yann Sommer, Oscar Wendt (76.Ramy Bensebaini), Stefan Lainer, Matthias Ginter, Nico Elvedi, Christoph Kramer (64.Patrick Herrmann), Florian Neuhaus, Denis Zakaria, Alassane Pléa (46.Raffael), Breel Embolo, Marcus Thuram. Trainer: Marco Rose.
Goals: 55' Edin Visca 1-0, 90+1' Patrick Herrmann 1-1.

24.10.2019; Stadio Olimpico, Roma
Referee: William Collum (SCO); Attendance: 29,037
AS Roma – Borussia VfL Mönchengladbach 1-1(1-0)
AS Roma: Pau López, Aleksandar Kolarov, Federico Fazio, Chris Smalling, Leonardo Spinazzola, Gianluca Mancini, Javier Pastore (62.Diego Perotti), Jordan Veretout, Nicolò Zaniolo (77.Mirko Antonucci), Edin Dzeko, Justin Kluivert (84.Alessandro Florenzi). Trainer: Paulo Fonseca.
Borussia Mönchengladbach: Yann Sommer, Tony Jantschke, Stefan Lainer, Nico Elvedi, Ramy Bensebaini, Christoph Kramer (76.László Bénes), Florian Neuhaus, Denis Zakaria, Patrick Herrmann (62.Jonas Hofmann), Breel Embolo (76.Lars Stindl), Marcus Thuram. Trainer: Marco Rose.; Goals: 32' Nicolò Zaniolo 1-0, 90+5' Lars Stindl 1-1 (pen).

07.11.2019; Stadion im Borussia-Park, Mönchengladbach
Referee: Jesús Gil Manzano (ESP); Attendance: 44,570
Borussia VfL Mönchengladbach – AS Roma 2-1(1-0)
Borussia Mönchengladbach: Yann Sommer, Oscar Wendt (85.Ramy Bensebaini), Tony Jantschke (28.Jonas Hofmann), Stefan Lainer, Matthias Ginter, Nico Elvedi, Lars Stindl, László Bénes, Florian Neuhaus (73.Alassane Pléa), Denis Zakaria, Marcus Thuram. Trainer: Marco Rose.
AS Roma: Pau López, Aleksandar Kolarov, Federico Fazio, Davide Santon, Chris Smalling, Gianluca Mancini (59.Amadou Diawara), Javier Pastore (80.Diego Perotti), Jordan Veretout, Nicolò Zaniolo (76.Cengiz Ünder), Edin Dzeko, Justin Kluivert. Trainer: Paulo Fonseca.
Goals: 35' Federico Fazio 1-0 (own goal), 64' Federico Fazio 1-1, 90+5' Marcus Thuram 2-1.

28.11.2019; Merkur Arena, Graz
Referee: Serdar Gözübüyük (NED); Attendance: 12,073
Wolfsberger AC – Borussia VfL Mönchengladbach 0-1(0-0)
Wolfsberger AC: Alexander Kofler, Lukas Schmitz, Michael Sollbauer, Manfred Gollner, Michael Novak, Michael Liendl, Mario Leitgeb, Marcel Ritzmaier, Anderson Niangbo (85.Marc Andre Schmerböck), Romano Schmid (75.Christopher Wernitznig), Shon Weissman. Trainer: Mohamed Sahli.
Borussia Mönchengladbach: Yann Sommer, Oscar Wendt, Stefan Lainer, Ramy Bensebaini, Lars Stindl (74.Breel Embolo), Tobias Strobl, Jonas Hofmann, László Bénes, Denis Zakaria, Alassane Pléa (77.Patrick Herrmann), Marcus Thuram (89.Raffael). Trainer: Marco Rose.
Goal: 60' Lars Stindl 0-1.

12.12.2019; Stadio Olimpico, Roma
Referee: Craig Pawson (ENG); Attendance: 21,672
AS Roma – Wolfsberger AC 2-2(2-1)
AS Roma: Antonio Mirante (62.Pau López), Federico Fazio, Leonardo Spinazzola, Alessandro Florenzi, Gianluca Mancini, Henrikh Mkhitaryan, Jordan Veretout, Cengiz Ünder (66.Lorenzo Pellegrini), Amadou Diawara, Edin Dzeko, Diego Perotti (67.Nicolò Zaniolo). Trainer: Paulo Fonseca.
Wolfsberger AC: Alexander Kofler, Nemanja Rnic, Lukas Schmitz, Michael Sollbauer, Michael Novak, Michael Liendl, Christopher Wernitznig (76.Lukas Schöfl), Sven Sprangler, Anderson Niangbo (90+4.Joshua Steiger), Romano Schmid, Shon Weissman (90+2.Amar Hodzic). Trainer: Mohamed Sahli.
Goals: 7' Diego Perotti 1-0 (pen), 10' Alessandro Florenzi 1-1 (own goal), 19' Edin Dzeko 2-1, 64' Shon Weissman 2-2.

12.12.2019; Stadion im Borussia-Park, Mönchengladbach
Referee: José María Sánchez Martínez (ESP); Attendance: 40,046
Borussia VfL Mönchengladbach – İstanbul Başakşehir FK 1-2(1-1)
Borussia Mönchengladbach: Yann Sommer, Oscar Wendt, Stefan Lainer, Matthias Ginter, Nico Elvedi, Christoph Kramer (90+2.Ramy Bensebaini), Florian Neuhaus (78.Lars Stindl), Denis Zakaria, Patrick Herrmann, Breel Embolo (78.Alassane Pléa), Marcus Thuram. Trainer: Marco Rose.
İstanbul Basaksehir FK: Mert Günok, Gaël Clichy, Alexandru Epureanu, Júnior Caiçara, Ponck, Eljero Elia, Mehmet Topal (88.Berkay Özcan), Danijel Aleksic (67.Demba Ba), Edin Visca, Irfan Kahveci (90+3.Azubuike Okechukwu), Enzo Crivelli. Trainer: Okan Buruk.
Goals: 33' Marcus Thuram 1-0, 44' Irfan Kahveci 1-1, 90+1' Enzo Crivelli 1-2.

GROUP K							
1. **Sporting Clube de Braga**	6	4	2	0	15 - 9	14
2. **Wolverhampton Wanderers FC**	6	4	1	1	11 - 5	13
3. ŠK Slovan Bratislava	6	1	1	4	10 - 13	4
4. Beşiktaş JK İstanbul	6	1	0	5	6 - 15	3

19.09.2019; Národny Futbalovy Stadión, Bratislava
Referee: Kristo Tohver (EST); Attendance: 5,273
ŠK Slovan Bratislava – Beşiktaş JK İstanbul 4-2(1-2)
Slovan Bratislava: Dominik Greif, Vasil Bozhikov, Vernon, Jurij Medvedev, Myenty Abena, Ibrahim Rabiu (89.Kenan Bajric), Dávid Holman, Joeri de Kamps (82.Marin Ljubicic), "Moha" Mohammed Rharsalla, Andraz Sporar, Dejan Drazic (76.Erik Daniel). Trainer: Ján Kozák.
Beşiktaş JK: Loris Karius, Domagoj Vida, Douglas Pereira, Víctor Ruíz (74.Atiba Hutchinson), Pedro Rebocho, Adem Ljajic, Mohamed Elneny, Georges-Kévin N'Koudou (82.Güven Yalçin), Dorukhan Toköz, Abdoulay Diaby (79.Jeremain Lens), Mehmet Umut Nayir. Trainer: Abdullah Avci.
Goals: 14' Andraz Sporar 1-0, 29' Adem Ljajic 1-1 (pen), 45+1' Vasil Bozhikov 1-2 (own goal), 58' Andraz Sporar 2-2, 90+3' Marin Ljubicic 3-2, 90+4' "Moha" Mohammed Rharsalla 4-2.

19.09.2019; Molineux Stadium, Wolverhampton
Referee: Jakob Kehlet (DEN); Attendance: 28,314
Wolverhampton Wanderers FC – Sporting Clube de Braga 0-1(0-0)
Wolverhampton Wanderers: Rui Patrício, Ryan Bennett, Willy Boly, Matt Doherty (80.Adama Traoré), Conor Coady, Jonny Castro, Leander Dendoncker (76.Diogo Jota), Rúben Neves, Morgan Gibbs-White (67.João Moutinho), Raúl Jiménez, Patrick Cutrone. Trainer: Nuno Espírito Santo.
Sporting Braga: Matheus Magalhães, Ricardo Esgaio, Nuno Sequeira, Pablo Santos, Bruno Viana, Fransérgio, João Palhinha, André Horta (88.Murilo), Paulinho, Ricardo Horta (86.João Novais), Galeno (84.Francisco Trincão). Trainer: Sá Pinto.
Goal: 71' Ricardo Horta 0-1.

03.10.2019; Estádio Municipal de Braga, Braga
Referee: Adrien Jaccottet (SUI); Attendance: 9,077
Sporting Clube de Braga – ŠK Slovan Bratislava 2-2(1-1)
Sporting Braga: Eduardo, Ricardo Esgaio, Nuno Sequeira, Pablo Santos, Bruno Viana, Fransérgio (88.Rui Fonte), João Palhinha, André Horta (70.João Novais), Paulinho, Ricardo Horta (71.Francisco Trincão), Galeno. Trainer: Sá Pinto.
Slovan Bratislava: Dominik Greif, Artem Sukhotskiy (80.Erik Daniel), Vernon, Jurij Medvedev, Myenty Abena, Ibrahim Rabiu, Dávid Holman (68.Dejan Drazic), Joeri de Kamps (68.Marin Ljubicic), Kenan Bajric, "Moha" Mohammed Rharsalla, Andraz Sporar. Trainer: Ján Kozák.
Goals: 31' Bruno Viana 1-0, 45+4' Andraz Sporar 1-1, 63' Galeno 2-1, 87' Bruno Viana 2-2 (own goal).

03.10.2019; Vodafone Park, İstanbul
Referee: Harald Lechner (AUT); Attendance: 22,670
Beşiktaş JK İstanbul – Wolverhampton Wanderers FC 0-1(0-0)
Beşiktaş JK: Loris Karius, Caner Erkin, Domagoj Vida, Douglas Pereira, Pedro Rebocho, Jeremain Lens (84.Gökhan Gönül), Adem Ljajic, Necip Uysal, Mohamed Elneny, Dorukhan Toköz (79.Oguzhan Özyakup), Güven Yalçin (27.Mehmet Umut Nayir). Trainer: Abdullah Avci.
Wolverhampton Wanderers: Rui Patrício, Willy Boly, Matt Doherty, Conor Coady, Jonny Castro, João Moutinho, Romain Saïss, Rúben Neves, Morgan Gibbs-White (62.Leander Dendoncker), Raúl Jiménez (79.Patrick Cutrone), Pedro Neto (46.Adama Traoré). Trainer: Nuno Espírito Santo.
Goal: 90+3' Willy Boly 0-1.

24.10.2019; Vodafone Park, İstanbul
Referee: Alejandro Hernández Hernández (ESP); Attendance: 20,956
Beşiktaş JK İstanbul – Sporting Clube de Braga 1-2(0-1)
Beşiktaş JK: Loris Karius, Caner Erkin, Domagoj Vida, Enzo Roco, Pedro Rebocho, Adem Ljajic, Necip Uysal (67.Mehmet Umut Nayir), Oguzhan Özyakup (61.Kartal Yilmaz), Mohamed Elneny, Tyler Boyd (84.Erdem Seçgin), Güven Yalçin. Trainer: Abdullah Avci.
Sporting Braga: Matheus Magalhães, Ricardo Esgaio, Nuno Sequeira, Pablo Santos, Bruno Viana, João Novais (75.Uche Agbo), João Palhinha, André Horta (75.Wilson Eduardo), Paulinho (83.Rui Fonte), Ricardo Horta, Galeno. Trainer: Sá Pinto.
Goals: 38' Ricardo Horta 0-1, 71' Mehmet Umut Nayir 1-1, 80' Wilson Eduardo 1-2.

24.10.2019; Národny Futbalovy Stadión, Bratislava
Referee: Yevhen Aranovskyi (UKR); Attendance: 20,333
ŠK Slovan Bratislava – Wolverhampton Wanderers FC 1-2(1-0)
Slovan Bratislava: Dominik Greif, Vasil Bozhikov, Vernon, Jurij Medvedev, Myenty Abena, Ibrahim Rabiu (81.Aleksandar Cavric), Dávid Holman (57.Marin Ljubicic), Joeri de Kamps, Erik Daniel (66.Rafael Ratão), "Moha" Mohammed Rharsalla, Andraz Sporar. Trainer: Ján Kozák.
Wolverhampton Wanderers: Rui Patrício, Willy Boly, Matt Doherty, Conor Coady, Rúben Vinagre, Max Kilman, João Moutinho, Romain Saïss (76.Leander Dendoncker), Morgan Gibbs-White (59.Diogo Jota), Raúl Jiménez, Patrick Cutrone (46.Adama Traoré). Trainer: Nuno Espírito Santo.
Goals: 11' Andraz Sporar 1-0, 58' Romain Saïss 1-1, 64' Raúl Jiménez 1-2 (pen).
Sent off: 87' Diogo Jota.

07.11.2019; Estádio Municipal de Braga, Braga
Referee: Gediminas Mazeika (LTU); Attendance: 8,833
Sporting Clube de Braga – Beşiktaş JK İstanbul 3-1(2-1)
Sporting Braga: Eduardo, Ricardo Esgaio, Nuno Sequeira, Wallace, Bruno Viana, Fransérgio, João Palhinha, André Horta (77.Francisco Trincão), Paulinho (67.Rui Fonte), Ricardo Horta (60.Wilson Eduardo), Galeno. Trainer: Sá Pinto.
Beşiktaş JK: Loris Karius, Caner Erkin (63.Pedro Rebocho), Domagoj Vida, Enzo Roco, Jeremain Lens, Necip Uysal, Oguzhan Özyakup, Kartal Yilmaz (72.Mohamed Elneny), Tyler Boyd, Mehmet Umut Nayir, Güven Yalçin (88.Erdem Seçgin). Trainer: Abdullah Avci.
Goals: 14' Paulinho 1-0, 29' Tyler Boyd 1-1, 37' Paulinho 2-1, 81' Wilson Eduardo 3-1.; Sent off: 44' Jeremain Lens.

28.11.2019; Vodafone Park, İstanbul
Referee: Enea Jorgji (ALB); Attendance: 11,526
Beşiktaş JK İstanbul – ŠK Slovan Bratislava 2-1(0-1)
Beşiktaş JK: Loris Karius, Caner Erkin, Domagoj Vida, Enzo Roco, Pedro Rebocho (46.Adem Ljajic), Necip Uysal, Oguzhan Özyakup (76.Güven Yalçin), Mohamed Elneny, Abdoulay Diaby, Tyler Boyd (46.Georges-Kévin N'Koudou), Mehmet Umut Nayir. Trainer: Abdullah Avci.
Slovan Bratislava: Dominik Greif, Vasil Bozhikov, Vernon, Myenty Abena, Ibrahim Rabiu, Dávid Holman (83.Marin Ljubicic), Joeri de Kamps, Erik Daniel (86.Rafael Ratão), Kenan Bajric, "Moha" Mohammed Rharsalla (76.Dejan Drazic), Andraz Sporar. Trainer: Ján Kozák.; Goals: 35' Erik Daniel 0-1, 75' Enzo Roco 1-1, 90+2' Adem Ljajic 2-1 (pen).

12.12.2019; Národny Futbalovy Stadión, Bratislava
Referee: Pawel Gil (POL); Attendance: 10,856
ŠK Slovan Bratislava – Sporting Clube de Braga 2-4(1-1)
Slovan Bratislava: Dominik Greif, Vasil Bozhikov, Vernon, Jurij Medvedev, Myenty Abena, Marin Ljubicic, Nono Delgado (76.Kenan Bajric), Erik Daniel, "Moha" Mohammed Rharsalla, Andraz Sporar, Dejan Drazic (78.Rafael Ratão). Trainer: Ján Kozák.
Sporting Braga: Tiago Sá, Ricardo Esgaio, Pablo Santos, Caju (59.Diogo Viana), Bruno Viana, Fransérgio, João Novais, Uche Agbo, Rui Fonte (82.Paulinho), Ricardo Horta, Francisco Trincão (83.Galeno). Trainer: Sá Pinto.
Goals: 42' Andraz Sporar 1-0, 44' Rui Fonte 1-1, 70' "Moha" Mohammed Rharsalla 2-1, 72' Francisco Trincão 2-2, 75' Vasil Bozhikov 2-3 (own goal), 90+3' Paulinho 2-4.

07.11.2019; Molineux Stadium, Wolverhampton
Referee: Bas Nijhuis (NED); Attendance: 29,789
Wolverhampton Wanderers FC – ŠK Slovan Bratislava 1-0(0-0)
Wolverhampton Wanderers: Rui Patrício, Matt Doherty, Conor Coady, Rúben Vinagre (90+7.Jonny Castro), Max Kilman, João Moutinho, Leander Dendoncker, Rúben Neves, Raúl Jiménez, Adama Traoré (90+10.Ryan Bennett), Pedro Neto (69.Patrick Cutrone). Trainer: Nuno Espírito Santo.
Slovan Bratislava: Dominik Greif, Vasil Bozhikov, Vernon, Jurij Medvedev, Myenty Abena, Ibrahim Rabiu (90+7.Erik Daniel), Joeri de Kamps, Kenan Bajric (89.Marin Ljubicic), Andraz Sporar, Rafael Ratão (70.Artem Sukhotskiy), Dejan Drazic. Trainer: Ján Kozák.
Goal: 90+2' Raúl Jiménez 1-0.

28.11.2019; Estádio Municipal de Braga, Braga
Referee: Aleksei Kulbakov (BLR); Attendance: 12,058
Sporting Clube de Braga – Wolverhampton Wanderers FC 3-3(1-3)
Sporting Braga: Eduardo, Ricardo Esgaio, Nuno Sequeira, Wallace (58.Wilson Eduardo), Bruno Viana, Fransérgio, João Palhinha, André Horta, Paulinho (87.Pablo Santos), Ricardo Horta (73.Rui Fonte), Galeno. Trainer: Sá Pinto.
Wolverhampton Wanderers: Rui Patrício, Matt Doherty, Conor Coady, Jonny Castro, João Moutinho, Romain Saïss, Leander Dendoncker, Rúben Neves, Raúl Jiménez (70.Pedro Neto), Adama Traoré (75.Rúben Vinagre), Diogo Jota (80.Patrick Cutrone). Trainer: Nuno Espírito Santo.
Goals: 6' André Horta 1-0, 14' Raúl Jiménez 1-1, 34' Matt Doherty 1-2, 35' Adama Traoré 1-3, 65' Paulinho 2-3, 79' Fransérgio 3-3.

12.12.2019; Molineux Stadium, Wolverhampton
Referee: Andris Treimanis (LVA); Attendance: 27,866
Wolverhampton Wanderers FC – Beşiktaş JK İstanbul 4-0(0-0)
Wolverhampton Wanderers: John Ruddy, Ryan Bennett, Conor Coady, Oskar Buur, Rúben Vinagre, Max Kilman, João Moutinho (70.Taylor Perry), Leander Dendoncker (73.Owen Otasowie), Rúben Neves (56.Diogo Jota), Patrick Cutrone, Pedro Neto. Trainer: Nuno Espírito Santo.
Beşiktaş JK: Utku Yuvakuran, Pedro Rebocho, Kerem Kalafat (76.Enzo Roco), Erdogan Kaya, Jeremain Lens (81.Abdoulay Diaby), Necip Uysal, Oguzhan Özyakup, Erdem Seçgin, Tyler Boyd, Mehmet Umut Nayir, Güven Yalçin (64.Mohamed Elneny). Trainer: Abdullah Avci.
Goals: 58', 63' Diogo Jota 1-0, 2-0, 67' Leander Dendoncker 3-0, 69' Diogo Jota 4-0.

	GROUP L								
1.	Manchester United FC	6	4	1	1	10	-	2	13
2.	AZ Alkmaar	6	2	3	1	15	-	8	9
3.	FK Partizan Beograd	6	2	2	2	10	-	10	8
4.	Astana FC	6	1	0	5	4	-	19	3

19.09.2019; Stadion Partizana, Beograd
Referee: Marco Guida (ITA); Attendance: 22,564
FK Partizan Beograd – AZ Alkmaar 2-2(1-1)
Partizan Beograd: Vladimir Stojkovic, Bojan Ostojic, Nemanja Miletic (I), Slobodan Urosevic, Strahinja Pavlovic, Bibras Natcho, Zoran Tosic (63.Lazar Markovic), Aleksandar Scekic (80.Seydouba Soumah), Sasa Zdjelar, Takuma Asano, Umar Sadiq (88.Petar Gigic). Trainer: Savo Milosevic.
AZ Alkmaar: Marco Bizot, Ron Vlaar, Stijn Wuytens (54.Pantelis Hatzidiakos), Jonas Svensson, Owen Wijndal, Fredrik Midtsjø, Dani de Wit, Teun Koopmeiners, Oussama Idrissi (31.Yukinari Sugawara), Myron Boadu, Calvin Stengs (84.Jordy Clasie). Trainer: Arne Slot.
Goals: 13' Calvin Stengs 0-1, 42', 61' Bibras Natcho 1-1 (pen), 2-1, 67' Myron Boadu 2-2.; Sent off: 27' Jonas Svensson.

03.10.2019; Astana Arena, Nur-Sultan
Referee: Mohammed Al-Hakim (SWE); Attendance: 20,137
Astana FC – FK Partizan Beograd 1-2(0-1)
Astana FC: Nenad Eric, Antonio Rukavina, Dmitriy Shomko, Zarko Tomasevic (15.Evgeny Postnikov), Abzal Beysebekov (79.Rangelo Janga), Luka Simunovic, Rúnar Sigurjónsson, Ivan Maevski, Yuri Pertsukh, Sergey Khizhnichenko (46.Roman Murtazaev), Dorin Rotariu. Trainer: Roman Grygorchuk.
Partizan Beograd: Vladimir Stojkovic, Bojan Ostojic, Nemanja Miletic (I), Slobodan Urosevic, Strahinja Pavlovic, Bibras Natcho, Zoran Tosic (77.Lazar Markovic), Seydouba Soumah (66.Aleksandar Scekic), Sasa Zdjelar, Takuma Asano (79.Rajko Brezancic), Umar Sadiq. Trainer: Savo Milosevic.
Goals: 29', 73' Umar Sadiq 0-1, 0-2, 85' Rúnar Sigurjónsson 1-2.

19.09.2019; Old Trafford, Manchester
Referee: François Letexier (FRA); Attendance: 50,783
Manchester United FC – Astana FC 1-0(0-0)
Manchester United: Sergio Romero, Marcos Rojo (78.Ashley Young), Phil Jones, Diogo Dalot, Axel Tuanzebe, Nemanja Matic, Fred, Angel Gomes (68.Mata), Marcus Rashford, Tahith Chong (68.Jesse Lingard), Mason Greenwood. Trainer: Ole Gunnar Solskjær.
Astana FC: Nenad Eric, Antonio Rukavina, Dmitriy Shomko, Zarko Tomasevic, Evgeny Postnikov, Luka Simunovic (46.Yuriy Logvinenko), Rúnar Sigurjónsson, Marin Tomasov, Ivan Maevski, Roman Murtazaev (46.Rangelo Janga), Dorin Rotariu (82.Ndombe Mubele). Trainer: Roman Grygorchuk.
Goal: 73' Mason Greenwood 1-0.

03.10.2019; Cars Jeans Stadion, Den Haag
Referee: Gediminas Mazeika (LTU); Attendance: 13,863
AZ Alkmaar – Manchester United FC 0-0
AZ Alkmaar: Marco Bizot, Ron Vlaar, Stijn Wuytens, Owen Wijndal, Yukinari Sugawara, Fredrik Midtsjø, Dani de Wit (87.Pantelis Hatzidiakos), Teun Koopmeiners, Oussama Idrissi, Myron Boadu, Calvin Stengs. Trainer: Arne Slot.
Manchester United: David de Gea, Marcos Rojo, Victor Lindelöf, Diogo Dalot, Brandon Williams, Mata (83.Scott McTominay), Nemanja Matic, Fred, Daniel James (63.Marcus Rashford), Angel Gomes, Mason Greenwood (77.Jesse Lingard). Trainer: Ole Gunnar Solskjær.

24.10.2019; Cars Jeans Stadion, Den Haag
Referee: Enea Jorgji (ALB); Attendance: 8,123
AZ Alkmaar – Astana FC 6-0(2-0)
AZ Alkmaar: Marco Bizot, Ron Vlaar (69.Pantelis Hatzidiakos), Stijn Wuytens (80.Jordy Clasie), Jonas Svensson, Owen Wijndal, Fredrik Midtsjø, Dani de Wit (71.Yukinari Sugawara), Teun Koopmeiners, Oussama Idrissi, Myron Boadu, Calvin Stengs. Trainer: Arne Slot.
Astana FC: Nenad Eric (26.Aleksandr Mokin), Yuriy Logvinenko (69.Evgeny Postnikov), Dmitriy Shomko, Abzal Beysebekov (43.Antonio Rukavina), Luka Simunovic, Ivan Maevski, Serikzhan Muzhikov, Didar Zhalmukan, Yuri Pertsukh, Rangelo Janga, Dorin Rotariu. Trainer: Roman Grygorchuk.
Goals: 39' Teun Koopmeiners 1-0 (pen), 43' Myron Boadu 2-0, 77' Calvin Stengs 3-0, 83' Teun Koopmeiners 4-0 (pen), 85' Yukinari Sugawara 5-0, 90+2' Oussama Idrissi 6-0.

07.11.2019; Astana Arena, Nur-Sultan
Referee: Mads-Kristoffer Kristoffersen (DEN); Attendance: 11,584
Astana FC – AZ Alkmaar 0-5(0-1)
Astana FC: Nenad Eric, Antonio Rukavina, Yuriy Logvinenko, Dmitriy Shomko, Abzal Beysebekov (74.Serikzhan Muzhikov), Evgeny Postnikov, Marin Tomasov, Ivan Maevski, Yuri Pertsukh, Sergey Khizhnichenko, Dorin Rotariu (71.Roman Murtazaev). Trainer: Roman Grygorchuk.
AZ Alkmaar: Marco Bizot, Stijn Wuytens, Jonas Svensson (61.Yukinari Sugawara), Pantelis Hatzidiakos, Owen Wijndal, Fredrik Midtsjø (67.Jordy Clasie), Dani de Wit, Teun Koopmeiners, Oussama Idrissi, Myron Boadu, Calvin Stengs (77.Zakaria Aboukhlal). Trainer: Arne Slot.
Goals: 29' Myron Boadu 0-1, 52' Fredrik Midtsjø 0-2, 57' Oussama Idrissi 0-3, 76' Pantelis Hatzidiakos 0-4, 77' Myron Boadu 0-5.

28.11.2019; Astana Arena, Nur-Sultan
Referee: Donatas Rumsas (LTU); Attendance: 28,949
Astana FC – Manchester United FC 2-1(0-1)
Astana FC: Nenad Eric, Antonio Rukavina, Yuriy Logvinenko, Dmitriy Shomko, Abzal Beysebekov, Evgeny Postnikov, Rúnar Sigurjónsson, Ivan Maevski, Sergey Khizhnichenko (85.Yuri Pertsukh), Roman Murtazaev (90+1.Rangelo Janga), Dorin Rotariu. Trainer: Roman Grygorchuk.
Manchester United: Lee Grant, Luke Shaw, Axel Tuanzebe, Di'Shon Bernard, Ethan Laird, Jesse Lingard, Angel Gomes (89.Ethan Galbraith), Dylan Levitt, James Garner (84.Largie Ramazani), Tahith Chong (65.D'Mani Bughail-Mellor), Mason Greenwood. Trainer: Ole Gunnar Solskjær.
Goals: 10' Jesse Lingard 0-1, 55' Dmitriy Shomko 1-1, 62' Di'Shon Bernard 2-1 (own goal).

12.12.2019; Stadion Partizana, Beograd
Referee: Filip Glova (SVK); Attendance: 8,075
FK Partizan Beograd – Astana FC 4-1(3-0)
Partizan Beograd: Vladimir Stojkovic (70.Filip Kljajic), Bojan Ostojic, Slobodan Urosevic, Strahinja Pavlovic, Zoran Tosic, Aleksandar Scekic, Seydouba Soumah (64.Lazar Pavlovic), Sasa Zdjelar, Takuma Asano, Aleksandar Lutovac, Umar Sadiq (83.Filip Stevanovic). Trainer: Savo Milosevic.
Astana FC: Nenad Eric, Antonio Rukavina, Yuriy Logvinenko, Dmitriy Shomko, Abzal Beysebekov, Evgeny Postnikov, Rúnar Sigurjónsson (85.Rangelo Janga), Ivan Maevski, Sergey Khizhnichenko, Roman Murtazaev (47.Yuri Pertsukh), Dorin Rotariu. Trainer: Roman Grygorchuk.
Goals: 4' Seydouba Soumah 1-0, 22' Umar Sadiq 2-0, 26' Takuma Asano 3-0, 76' Umar Sadiq 4-0, 79' Dorin Rotariu 4-1.

24.10.2019; Stadion Partizana, Beograd
Referee: Xavier Estrada Fernández (ESP); Attendance: 25,627
FK Partizan Beograd – Manchester United FC 0-1(0-1)
Partizan Beograd: Vladimir Stojkovic, Bojan Ostojic, Nemanja Miletic (I), Slobodan Urosevic, Strahinja Pavlovic, Bibras Natcho, Zoran Tosic (75.Filip Stevanovic), Seydouba Soumah (83.Lazar Pavlovic), Sasa Zdjelar, Takuma Asano (90+3.Djordje Ivanovic), Umar Sadiq. Trainer: Savo Milosevic.
Manchester United: Sergio Romero, Marcos Rojo, Phil Jones, Harry Maguire, Aaron Wan-Bissaka (60.Daniel James), Brandon Williams, Mata, Jesse Lingard, Scott McTominay, James Garner (82.Andreas Pereira), Anthony Martial (60.Marcus Rashford). Trainer: Ole Gunnar Solskjær.
Goal: 43' Anthony Martial 0-1 (pen).

07.11.2019; Old Trafford, Manchester
Referee: Mattias Gestranius (FIN); Attendance: 62,955
Manchester United FC – FK Partizan Beograd 3-0(2-0)
Manchester United: Sergio Romero, Ashley Young, Marcos Rojo, Harry Maguire, Aaron Wan-Bissaka, Mata, Fred (63.James Garner), Scott McTominay (75.Jesse Lingard), Anthony Martial, Marcus Rashford (67.Andreas Pereira), Mason Greenwood. Trainer: Ole Gunnar Solskjær.
Partizan Beograd: Vladimir Stojkovic, Bojan Ostojic, Nemanja Miletic (I), Slobodan Urosevic, Strahinja Pavlovic, Bibras Natcho (60.Zoran Tosic), Aleksandar Scekic, Seydouba Soumah, Sasa Zdjelar, Takuma Asano (70.Filip Stevanovic), Umar Sadiq (86.Djordje Ivanovic). Trainer: Savo Milosevic.
Goals: 22' Mason Greenwood 1-0, 33' Anthony Martial 2-0, 49' Marcus Rashford 3-0.

28.11.2019; Cars Jeans Stadion, Den Haag
Referee: Daniel Stefanski (POL); Attendance: 9,092
AZ Alkmaar – FK Partizan Beograd 2-2(0-2)
AZ Alkmaar: Marco Bizot, Stijn Wuytens (60.Yukinari Sugawara), Jonas Svensson, Pantelis Hatzidiakos (54.Ferdy Druijf), Owen Wijndal, Fredrik Midtsjø, Dani de Wit (71.Jordy Clasie), Teun Koopmeiners, Oussama Idrissi, Myron Boadu, Calvin Stengs. Trainer: Arne Slot.
Partizan Beograd: Vladimir Stojkovic, Bojan Ostojic, Nemanja Miletic (I), Slobodan Urosevic, Strahinja Pavlovic, Bibras Natcho (90+2.Igor Vujacic), Zoran Tosic (69.Rajko Brezancic), Seydouba Soumah (75.Aleksandar Scekic), Sasa Zdjelar, Takuma Asano, Umar Sadiq. Trainer: Savo Milosevic.
Goals: 16' Takuma Asano 0-1, 27' Seydouba Soumah 0-2, 88' 90+2' Ferdy Druijf 1-2, 2-2.
Sent off: 83' Myron Boadu.

12.12.2019; Old Trafford, Manchester
Referee: Sandro Schärer (SUI); Attendance: 65,773
Manchester United FC – AZ Alkmaar 4-0(0-0)
Manchester United: Sergio Romero, Ashley Young (68.Ethan Laird), Harry Maguire (68.Phil Jones), Axel Tuanzebe, Brandon Williams, Mata, Nemanja Matic, Andreas Pereira, James Garner, Anthony Martial (59.Tahith Chong), Mason Greenwood. Trainer: Ole Gunnar Solskjær.
AZ Alkmaar: Marco Bizot, Stijn Wuytens, Jonas Svensson, Owen Wijndal, Yukinari Sugawara (68.Ron Vlaar), Jordy Clasie, Fredrik Midtsjø, Dani de Wit (63.Ferdy Druijf), Teun Koopmeiners, Oussama Idrissi (77.Thomas Ouwejan), Calvin Stengs. Trainer: Arne Slot.
Goals: 53' Ashley Young 1-0, 58' Mason Greenwood 2-0, 62' Mata 3-0 (pen), 64' Mason Greenwood 4-0.

Please note: AFC Ajax Amsterdam, FC Red Bull Salzburg, FC Internazionale Milano, Sport Lisboa e Benfica, TSV Bayer 04 Leverkusen, FK Shakhtar Donetsk, SFP Olympiacos Peiraiás and Club Brugge KV entered the UEFA Europa League as the group stage third-placed teams from the UEFA Champions League.

20.02.2020; Estádio „José Alvalade", Lisboa
Referee: Anthony Taylor (ENG); Attendance: 27,392
Sporting Clube de Portugal Lisboa – İstanbul Başakşehir FK 3-1(2-0)
Sporting: Luís Maximiano, Neto, Sebastián Coates, Stefan Ristovski, Rodrigo Battaglia, Wendel, Yannick Bolasie (89.Gonzalo Plata), Marcos Acuña, Andraz Sporar (71.Pedro Mendes), Luciano Vietto, Jovane Cabral (81.Idrissa Doumbia). Trainer: Silas.
İstanbul Başakşehir: Mert Günok, Gaël Clichy, Martin Skrtel (70.Eljero Elia), Júnior Caiçara, Carlos Ponck, Mahmut Tekdemir, Edin Visca, Irfan Kahveci (81.Danijel Aleksic), Demba Ba, Fredrik Gulbrandsen (46.Berkay Özcan), Enzo Crivelli. Trainer: Okan Buruk.
Goals: 3' Sebastián Coates 1-0, 44' Andraz Sporar 2-0, 51' Luciano Vietto 3-0, 77' Edin Visca 3-1 (pen).

20.02.2020; Estadio Coliseum „Alfonso Pérez", Getafe
Referee: Ruddy Buquet (FRA); Attendance 14,039
Getafe CF – AFC Ajax Amsterdam 2-0(1-0)
Getafe CF: David Soria, Allan Nyom, Damián Suárez, Etxeita, Djené Dakonam Ortega, Cururella (88.Kenedy), Mathías Olivera, Nemanja Maksimovic, Mauro Arambarri, Mata (72.Jorge Molina), Deyverson (57.Ángel). Trainer: José Bordalás.
AFC Ajax: Bruno Varela, Daley Blind, Nicolás Tagliafico, Edson Álvarez (67.Perr Schuurs), Lisandro Martínez, Sergiño Dest, Hakim Ziyech, Donny van de Beek, Ryan Babel, Dusan Tadic, Lassina Traoré (67.Klaas Jan Huntelaar). Trainer: Erik ten Hag.
Goals: 38' Deyverson 1-0, 90+3' Kenedy 2-0.

20.02.2020; Telia Parken, København
Referee: Sergei Karasev (RUS); Attendance: 34,346
FC København – Celtic FC Glasgow 1-1(0-1)
FC København: Kalle Johnsson, Ragnar Sigurdsson (86.Sotirios Papagiannopoulos), Bryan Oviedo (73.Pierre Bengtsson), Guillermo Varela, Victor Nelsson, Rasmus Falk, Zeca, Pep Biel Mas, Jens Stage, Dame N'Doye, Michael Santos (73.Mikkel Kaufmann). Trainer: Ståle Solbakken.
Celtic FC: Fraser Forster, Christopher Jullien, Kristoffer Ajer, Jeremie Frimpong (84.Jozo Simunovic), Scott Brown (73.Nir Bitton), Jonny Hayes, James Forrest, Callum McGregor, Jules Olivier Ntcham (60.Mohamed Elyounoussi), Ryan Christie, Odsonne Édouard. Trainer: Neil Lennon.
Goals: 14' Odsonne Édouard 0-1, 52' Dame N'Doye 1-1.

20.02.2020; Stadionul „Dr. Constantin Rădulescu", Cluj-Napoca
Referee: Deniz Aytekin (GER); Attendance: 14,820
FC CFR 1907 Cluj-Napoca – Sevilla FC 1-1(0-0)
CFR Cluj: Giedrius Arlauskis, Paulo Vinícius, Camora, Andrei Burca, Cristian Manea, Ciprian Deac, Damjan Djokovic, Mihai Bordeianu, Adrian Paun (74.Ovidiu Hoban), Lacina Traoré (83.Mário Rondón), Billel Omrani (86.Catalin Golofca). Trainer: Dan Petrescu.
Sevilla FC: Tomás Vaclík, Jesús Navas (73.Youssef En-Nesyri), Escudero, Diego Carlos, Jules Koundé, Fernando, Nemanja Gudelj, Lucas Ocampos (78.Rony Lopes), Suso (90+1.Franco Vázquez), Joan Jordán, Luuk de Jong. Trainer: Lopetegui.
Goals: 59' Ciprian Deac 1-0 (pen), 82' Youssef En-Nesyri (82').

20.02.2020; „Jan Breydel" Stadion, Brugge
Referee: Aleksei Kulbakov (BLR); Attendance: 27,006
Club Brugge KV – Manchester United FC 1-1(1-1)
Club Brugge KV: Simon Mignolet, Clinton Mata, Éder Álvarez Balanta (47.Ruud Vormer), Simon Deli, Brandon Mechele, Maxim De Cuyper (73.Siebe Schrijvers), Odilon Kossounou, Mats Rits, Hans Vanaken, Percy Tau (62.Charles De Ketelaere), Emmanuel Dennis Bonaventure. Trainer: Philippe Clement.
Manchester United: Sergio Romero, Victor Lindelöf, Harry Maguire, Luke Shaw, Diogo Dalot (81.Bruno Fernandes), Brandon Williams, Mata, Nemanja Matic, Jesse Lingard, Andreas Pereira (71.Fred), Anthony Martial (67.Odion Ighalo). Trainer: Ole Gunnar Solskjær.
Goals: 15' Emmanuel Dennis Bonaventure 1-0, 36' Anthony Martial 1-1.

27.02.2020; Başakşehir „Fatih Terim" Stadyumu, İstanbul
Referee: Antonio Mateu Lahoz (ESP); Attendance: 5,892
İSTANBUL BAŞAKŞEHİR FK – Sporting Clube de Portugal Lisboa 4-1(2-0,3-1)
İstanbul Başakşehir: Mert Günok, Gaël Clichy, Martin Skrtel, Alexandru Epureanu, Júnior Caiçara, Eljero Elia (85.Fredrik Gulbrandsen), Danijel Aleksic, Edin Visca (120.Carlos Ponck), Irfan Kahveci (89.Robinho), Azubuike Okechukwu (77.Berkay Özcan), Demba Ba. Trainer: Okan Buruk
Sporting: Luís Maximiano, Sebastián Coates, Stefan Ristovski, Tiago Ilori, Rodrigo Battaglia, Wendel (90+1.Eduardo Henrique), Yannick Bolasie (60.Gonzalo Plata), Marcos Acuña, Andraz Sporar (108.Pedro Mendes), Luciano Vietto, Jovane Cabral (73.Idrissa Doumbia). Trainer: Emanuel Ferro.
Goals: 31' Martin Skrtel 1-0, 45' Danijel Aleksic 2-0, 68' Luciano Vietto 2-1, 90+2', 119' Edin Visca 3-1, 4-1 (pen).

27.02.2020; "Johan Cruijff" ArenA, Amsterdam
Referee: Anastasios Sidropoulos (GRE); Attendance: 51,487
AFC Ajax Amsterdam – GETAFE CF 2-1(1-1)
AFC Ajax: André Onana, Daley Blind, Perr Schuurs, Lisandro Martínez, Sergiño Dest, Donny van de Beek, Carel Eiting, Ryan Gravenberch (75.Klaas Jan Huntelaar), Ryan Babel, Dusan Tadic, Danilo (46.Quincy Promes). Trainer: Erik ten Hag.
Getafe CF: David Soria, Allan Nyom, Damián Suárez, Etxeita, Djené Dakonam Ortega, Cururella (90+4.Kenedy), Mathías Olivera, Nemanja Maksimovic, Mauro Arambarri, Mata (90+1.David Timor), Deyverson (70.Jorge Molina). Trainer: José Bordalás.
Goals: 5' Mata 0-1, 10' Danilo 1-1, 63' Mathías Olivera 2-1 (own goal).

27.02.2020; Celtic Park, Glasgow
Referee: Artur Manuel Soares Dias (POR); Attendance: 56,172
Celtic FC Glasgow – FC KØBENHAVN 1-3(0-0)
Celtic FC: Fraser Forster, Jozo Simunovic, Christopher Jullien, Kristoffer Ajer, Greg Taylor, Scott Brown, James Forrest, Callum McGregor, Mohamed Elyounoussi (70.Leigh Griffiths), Tom Rogic, Odsonne Édouard. Trainer: Neil Lennon.
FC København: Kalle Johnsson, Pierre Bengtsson, Ragnar Sigurdsson, Guillermo Varela, Victor Nelsson, Rasmus Falk, Zeca, Pep Biel Mas (86.Andreas Bjelland), Jens Stage, Dame N'Doye, Mikkel Kaufmann (45.Michael Santos, 88.Mohammed Daramy). Trainer: Ståle Solbakken.
Goals: 51' Michael Santos 0-1, 83' Odsonne Édouard 1-1 (pen), 85' Pep Biel Mas 1-2, 88' Dame N'Doye 1-3.

27.02.2020; Estadio „Ramón Sánchez Pizjuán", Sevilla
Referee: Andris Treimanis (LVA); Attendance: 31,338
SEVILLA FC – FC CFR 1907 Cluj-Napoca 0-0
Sevilla FC: Yassine Bounou, Jesús Navas (76.Youssef En-Nesyri), Diego Carlos, Reguilón, Jules Koundé, Fernando, Nemanja Gudelj, Lucas Ocampos, Suso (67.Nolito), Joan Jordán (57.Éver Banega), Luuk de Jong. Trainer: Lopetegui.
CFR Cluj: Giedrius Arlauskis, Paulo Vinícius, Camora, Andrei Burca (27.Kévin Boli), Cristian Manea, Ciprian Deac, Damjan Djokovic (78.Mário Rondón), Mihai Bordeianu, Adrian Paun, Lacina Traoré, Billel Omrani (84.Catalin Golofca). Trainer: Dan Petrescu.
Sent off: 90+1' Mihai Bordeianu.

27.02.2020; Old Trafford, Manchester
Referee: Serdar Gözübüyük (NED); Attendance: 70,397
MANCHESTER UNITED FC – Club Brugge KV 5-0(3-0)
Manchester United: Sergio Romero, Harry Maguire, Luke Shaw, Eric Bailly, Aaron Wan-Bissaka, Mata, Fred, Bruno Fernandes (65.Jesse Lingard), Daniel James (46.Tahith Chong), Scott McTominay (72.Mason Greenwood), Odion Ighalo. Trainer: Ole Gunnar Solskjær.
Club Brugge KV: Simon Mignolet, Clinton Mata (62.Matej Mitrovic), Simon Deli, Brandon Mechele, Federico Ricca, Maxim De Cuyper, Odilon Kossounou, Mats Rits (79.Charles De Ketelaere), Hans Vanaken, Percy Tau (61.Krépin Diatta), David Okereke. Trainer: Philippe Clement.
Goals: 27' Bruno Fernandes 1-0 (pen), 34' Odion Ighalo 2-0, 41' Scott McTominay 3-0, 82', 90+3' Fred 4-0, 5-0.
Sent off: 22' Simon Deli.

20.02.2020; Ludogorets Arena, Razgrad
Referee: Carlos del Cerro Grande (ESP); Attendance: 10,024
PFC Ludogorets Razgrad – FC Internazionale Milano 0-2(0-0)
Ludogorets Razgrad: Plamen Iliev, Dragos Grigore, Cicinho, Georgi Terziev, Anton Nedyalkov, Svetoslav Dyakov (67.Stéphane Badji), Anicet Andrianantenaina, Wanderson, Cauly (90.Dan Biton), Marcelinho, Jakub Swierczok (76.Mavis Tchibota). Trainer: Pavel Vrba.
Internazionale: Daniele Padelli, Diego Godín, Andrea Ranocchia, Danilo D'Ambrosio, Cristiano Biraghi (81.Ashley Young), Borja Valero, Victor Moses (72.Nicolò Barella), Christian Eriksen, Matías Vecino, Alexis Sánchez, Lautaro Martínez (64.Romelu Lukaku). Trainer: Antonio Conte.
Goals: 71' Christian Eriksen 0-1, 90+5' Romelu Lukaku 0-2 (pen).

20.02.2020; Commerzbank-Arena, Frankfurt am Main
Referee: Ali Palabiyik (TUR); Attendance: 47,000
Eintracht Frankfurt – FC Red Bull Salzburg 4-1(2-0)
Eintracht Frankfurt: Kevin Trapp, Makoto Hasebe, David Abraham, Almamy Touré, Evan Obite N'Dicka, Stefan Ilsanker (86.Erik Durm), Sebastian Rode, Filip Kostic, Djibril Sow, Daichi Kamada (81.Danny da Costa), André Silva (75.Gonçalo Paciência). Trainer: Adi Hütter.
Red Bull Salzburg: Cican Stankovic, Andreas Ulmer, Patrick Farkas, Jérôme Onguéné, Max Wöber, Zlatko Junuzovic, Masaya Okugawa (46.Karim Adeyemi), Dominik Szoboszlai (71.Mohamed Camara), Enock Mwepu, Hwang Hee-Chan, Patson Daka (46.Sékou Koïta). Trainer: Jesse Marsch.
Goals: 12' Daichi Kamada 1-0, 43' Daichi Kamada 2-0, 53' Daichi Kamada 3-0, 56' Filip Kostic 4-0, 85' Hwang Hee-Chan 4-1 (pen).

20.02.2020; Metalist Stadium, Kharkiv
Referee: Bobby Madden (SCO); Attendance: 24,429
FK Shakhtar Donetsk – Sport Lisboa e Benfica 2-1(0-0)
Shakhtar Donetsk: Andriy Pyatov, Sergiy Kryvtsov, Ismaily, Mykola Matviyenko, Marlos (83.Yevhen Konoplyanka), Taras Stepanenko, Taison (90+4.Tetê), Alan Patrick (80.Marcos Antônio), Sergiy Bolbat, Viktor Kovalenko, Júnior Moraes. Trainer: Luís Castro.
Benfica: Odisseas Vlachodimos, Álex Grimaldo, Rúben Dias, Francisco Reis Ferreira, Tomás Tavares, Adel Taarabt, Pizzi (90+2.Andreas Samaris), Franco Cervi, Chiquinho (79.Rafa Silva), Florentino Luís, Haris Seferovic (69.Carlos Vinícius). Trainer: Bruno Lage.
Goals: 56' Alan Patrick 1-0, 67' Pizzi 1-1 (pen), 72' Viktor Kovalenko 2-1.

20.02.2020; Molineux Stadium, Wolverhampton
Referee: Tobias Stieler (GER); Attendance: 30,435
Wolverhampton Wanderers FC – RCD Espanyol Barcelona 4-0(1-0)
Wolverhampton Wanderers: Rui Patricio, Willy Boly, Matt Doherty, Conor Coady, Jonny Castro, João Moutinho, Romain Saïss, Rúben Neves, Raúl Jiménez (75.Pedro Neto), Adama Traoré (61.Leander Dendoncker), Diogo Jota (83.Daniel Podence). Trainer: Nuno Espírito Santo.
RCD Espanyol: Andrés Prieto, Dídac Vilà, Naldo, Fernando Calero, Víctor Gómez Perea (75.Sergi Darder), Víctor Sánchez, Iturraspe (61.David López), Matías Vargas, Melendo (62.Jonathan Calleri), Facundo Ferreyra, Lei Wu. Trainer: Abelardo.
Goals: 15' Diogo Jota 1-0, 52' Rúben Neves 2-0, 67', 81' Diogo Jota 3-0, 4-0.

20.02.2020; BayArena, Leverkusen
Referee: Slavko Vincic (SVN); Attendance: 26,839
TSV Bayer 04 Leverkusen – FC Porto 2-1(1-0)
Bayer Leverkusen: Lukás Hrádecky, Sven Bender, Daley Sinkgraven, Edmond Tapsoba, Lars Bender, Charles Aránguiz (72.Julian Baumgartlinger), Kerem Demirbay, Nadiem Amiri, Kai Havertz, Kevin Volland (90+4.Paulinho), Lucas Alario (80.Leon Bailey). Trainer: Peter Bosz.
FC Porto: Agustín Marchesín, Ivan Marcano, Alex Telles, Chancel Mbemba, Wilson Manafá (61.Shoya Nakajima), Sérgio Oliveira, Mateus Uribe, Luis Díaz (77.Danilo Pereira), Tiquinho Soares (63.Zé Luís), Jesús Corona, Moussa Marega. Trainer: Sérgio Conceição.
Goals: 29' Lucas Alario 1-0, 57' Kai Havertz 2-0 (pen), 73' Luis Díaz 2-1.

27.02.2020; Stadio „Giuseppe Meazza", Milano
Referee: Daniel Siebert (GER)
FC INTERNAZIONALE MILANO – PFC Ludogorets Razgrad 2-1(2-1)
Internazionale: Daniele Padelli, Diego Godín, Andrea Ranocchia, Danilo D'Ambrosio (76.Alessandro Bastoni), Cristiano Biraghi, Borja Valero, Victor Moses, Christian Eriksen, Nicolò Barella (46.Marcelo Brozovic), Alexis Sánchez, Romelu Lukaku (62.Sebastiano Esposito). Trainer: Antonio Conte.
Ludogorets Razgrad: Plamen Iliev, Dragos Grigore, Cicinho, Georgi Terziev, Anton Nedyalkov, Svetoslav Dyakov, Wanderson (70.Mavis Tchibota), Stéphane Badji, Cauly, Claudiu Keserü (64.Jakub Swierczok), Marcelinho (83.Dan Biton). Trainer: Pavel Vrba.
Goals: 26' Cauly 0-1, 32' Cristiano Biraghi 1-1, 45+4' Romelu Lukaku 2-1.

28.02.2020; Red Bull Arena, Wals-Siezenheim
Referee: Benoît Bastien (FRA); Attendance: 29,000
FC Red Bull Salzburg – EINTRACHT FRANKFURT 2-2(1-1)
Red Bull Salzburg: Cican Stankovic, Andreas Ulmer, André Ramalho, Albert Vallci, Jérôme Onguéné, Dominik Szoboszlai (86.Antoine Bernède), Enock Mwepu (76.Mërgim Berisha), Mohamed Camara, Hwang Hee-Chan, Patson Daka, Sékou Koïta (66.Noah Okafor). Trainer: Jesse Marsch.
Eintracht Frankfurt: Kevin Trapp, David Abraham, Martin Hinteregger, Almamy Touré, Evan Obite N'Dicka, Stefan Ilsanker, Sebastian Rode, Filip Kostic (88.Timothy Chandler), Djibril Sow, Daichi Kamada (73.Danny da Costa), André Silva (88.Gonçalo Paciência). Trainer: Adi Hütter.
Goals: 10' Andreas Ulmer 1-0, 30' André Silva 1-1, 72' Jérôme Onguéné 2-1, 83' André Silva 2-2.

27.02.2020; Estádio da Luz, Lisboa
Referee: Björn Kuipers (NED); Attendance: 48,302
Sport Lisboa e Benfica – FK SHAKHTAR DONETSK 3-3(2-1)
Benfica: Odisseas Vlachodimos, Álex Grimaldo, Rúben Dias, Francisco Reis Ferreira "Ferro", Tomás Tavares, Adel Taarabt, Pizzi (79.João Filipe "Jota"), Rafa Silva, Julian Weigl, Chiquinho (67.Haris Seferovic), Dyego Sousa (79.Carlos Vinícius). Trainer: Bruno Lage.
Shakhtar Donetsk: Andriy Pyatov, Sergiy Kryvtsov, Ismaily, Mykola Matviyenko, Dodô, Marlos (62.Tetê), Taras Stepanenko, Taison (86.Yevhen Konoplyanka), Alan Patrick (90+2.Davit Khocholava), Marcos Antônio, Júnior Moraes. Trainer: Luís Castro.
Goals: 9' Pizzi 1-0, 12', 36' Rúben Dias 1-1 (own goal), 2-1, 47' Rafa Silva 3-1, 49' Taras Stepanenko 3-2, 71' Alan Patrick 3-3.

27.02.2020; RCDE Stadium, Cornellà de Llobregat
Referee: Marco Guida (ITA); Attendance: 14,525
RCD Espanyol Barcelona – WOLVERHAMPTON WANDERERS FC 3-2(1-1)
RCD Espanyol: Andrés Prieto, Naldo, David López, Adrià Pedrosa, Fernando Calero, Víctor Gómez Perea, Víctor Sánchez (61.Pol Lozano), Sergi Darder (67.Lei Wu), Matías Vargas, Melendo (75.Pipa Ávila), Jonathan Calleri. Trainer: Abelardo.
Wolverhampton Wanderers: Rui Patricio, Willy Boly, Matt Doherty, Conor Coady, Rúben Vinagre (58.Romain Saïss), Max Kilman, João Moutinho, Leander Dendoncker, Daniel Podence, Morgan Gibbs-White (64.Pedro Neto), Adama Traoré (78.Bruno Jordão). Trainer: Nuno Espírito Santo.
Goals: 16' Jonathan Calleri 1-0, 22' Adama Traoré 1-1, 57' Jonathan Calleri 2-1 (pen), 79' Matt Doherty 2-2, 90+1' Jonathan Calleri 3-2.

27.02.2020; Estádio do Dragão, Porto
Referee: István Kovács (ROU); Attendance: 30,292
FC Porto – TSV BAYER 04 LEVERKUSEN 1-3(0-1)
FC Porto: Agustín Marchesín, Ivan Marcano, Alex Telles, Chancel Mbemba, Sérgio Oliveira, Mateus Uribe (46.Pepe), Otavinho, Luis Díaz (29.Shoya Nakajima), Zé Luís (64.Tiquinho Soares), Jesús Corona, Moussa Marega. Trainer: Sérgio Conceição.
Bayer Leverkusen: Lukás Hrádecky, Sven Bender (67.Aleksandar Dragovic), Jonathan Tah, Daley Sinkgraven, Edmond Tapsoba, Lars Bender (46.Mitchell Weiser), Kerem Demirbay, Nadiem Amiri, Kai Havertz, Lucas Alario, Moussa Diaby (83.Leon Bailey). Trainer: Peter Bosz.
Goals: 10' Lucas Alario 0-1, 50' Kerem Demirbay 0-2, 58' Kai Havertz 0-3, 65' Moussa Marega 1-3.
Sent off: 85' Tiquinho Soares.

20.02.2020; Stádio Neo GSP, Nicosia
Referee: Orel Grinfeld (ISR); Attendance: 8,191
APOEL Nicosia FC – FC Basel 0-3(0-1)
APOEL Nicosia: Vid Belec, Giorgios Merkis, Praxitelis Vouros, Nicholas Ioannou (80.Christos Wheeler), Mike Jensen, Dragan Mihajlovic, Uros Matic, Tomás De Vincenti (71.Antonio Jakolis), Alef, Moussa Al Tamari, Andrija Pavlovic (56.Linus Hallenius). Trainer: Marinos Ouzounidis.
FC Basel: Jonas Omlin, Silvan Widmer, Omar Alderete, Raoul Petretta (80.Afimico Pululu), Eray Cömert, Blas Riveros, Valentin Stocker, Fabian Frei (85.Orges Bunjaku), Taulant Xhaka, Samuele Campo, Arthur Cabral (74.Kemal Ademi). Trainer: Marcel Koller.
Goals: 16' Raoul Petretta 0-1, 53' Valentin Stocker 0-2, 66' Arthur Cabral 0-3.

20.02.2020; Stádio „Giórgos Karaïskáki", Peiraiás
Referee: Felix Zwayer (GER); Attendance: 31,456
Olympiacos SFP Peiraiás – Arsenal FC London 0-1(0-0)
Olympiacos Peiraiás: José Sá, Omar Elabdellaoui, Rúben Semedo, Kostas Tsimikas, Ousseynou Ba, Mathieu Valbuena, Guilherme, Andreas Bouchalakis (65.Kostas Fortounis), Georgios Masouras (75.Maximiliano Lovera), Mady Camara, Youssef El-Arabi. Trainer: Pedro Martins.
Arsenal FC: Bernd Leno, David Luiz, Sokratis Papastathopoulos (90+2.Ainsley Maitland-Niles), Shkodran Mustafi, Granit Xhaka, Joseph Willock (75.Nicolas Pépé), Mattéo Guendouzi, Bukayo Saka, Pierre-Emerick Aubameyang, Alexandre Lacazette, Gabriel Martinelli (58.Dani Ceballos). Trainer: Mikel Arteta.
Goal: 81' Alexandre Lacazette 0-1.

20.02.2020; AFAS Stadion, Alkmaar
Referee: Mattias Gestranius (FIN); Attendance: 12,526
AZ Alkmaar – LASK Linz 1-1(0-1)
AZ Alkmaar: Marco Bizot, Ramon Leeuwin, Jonas Svensson, Owen Wijndal, Jordy Clasie, Dani de Wit, Teun Koopmeiners, Håkon Evjen (73.Yukinari Sugawara), Oussama Idrissi (81.Ferdy Druijf), Myron Boadu, Calvin Stengs. Trainer: Arne Slot.
LASK Linz: Alexander Schlager, Petar Filipovic, Gernot Trauner, Reinhold Ranftl, Philipp Wiesinger, James Holland, Thomas Goiginger, Peter Michorl, René Renner (56.Marvin Potzmann), Dominik Frieser (76.Husein Balic), Marko Raguz (56.Klauss). Trainer: Valérien Ismaël.
Goals: 26' Marko Raguz 0-1, 86' Teun Koopmeiners 1-1 (pen).

20.02.2020; Volkswagen Arena, Wolfsburg
Referee: Gediminas Mazeika (LTU); Attendance: 13,801
VfL Wolfsburg – Malmö FF 2-1(0-0)
VfL Wolfsburg: Koen Casteels, Robin Knoche, Jérôme Roussillon (46.Paulo Otávio), John Anthony Brooks, Kevin Mbabu, Yannick Gerhardt, Admir Mehmedi, Maximilian Arnold, Xaver Schlager (71.Renato Steffen), Josip Brekalo (90+3.Daniel Ginczek), Wout Weghorst. Trainer: Oliver Glasner.
Malmö FF: Johan Dahlin, Behrang Safari, Rasmus Bengtsson, Eric Larsson, Anel Ahmedhodzic, Anders Christiansen, Fouad Bachirou, Arnór Ingvi Traustason (22.Søren Rieks, 58.Jo Inge Berget), Adi Nalic, Marcus Antonsson, Isaac Kiese Thelin. Trainer: Jon Dahl Tomasson.
Goals: 47' Isaac Kiese Thelin 0-1 (pen), 49' Josip Brekalo 1-1, 62' Isaac Kiese Thelin 2-1 (own goal).

20.02.2020; Stadio Olimpico, Roma
Referee: Georgi Kabakov (BUL); Attendance: 28,248
AS Roma – KAA Gent 1-0 (1-0)
AS Roma: Pau López, Aleksandar Kolarov, Federico Fazio, Chris Smalling, Leonardo Spinazzola (69.Davide Santon), Jordan Veretout, Bryan Cristante, Lorenzo Pellegrini (79.Henrikh Mkhitaryan), Edin Dzeko, Diego Perotti (82.Justin Kluivert), Carles Pérez. Trainer: Paulo Fonseca.
KAA Gent: Thomas Kaminski, Mikael Lustig, Igor Plastun, Michael Ngadeu-Ngadjui, Milad Mohammadi, Vadis Odjidja-Ofoe, Sven Kums (90+1.Sulayman Marreh), Roman Bezus (74.Giorgi Chakvetadze), Elisha Owusu, Laurent Depoitre, Jonathan David. Trainer: Jess Thorup.
Goal: 13' Carles Pérez 1-0).

27.02.2020; St. Jakob-Park, Basel
Referee: Pavel Královcc (CZE); Attendance: 14,428
FC BASEL – APOEL Nicosia FC 1-0(1-0)
FC Basel: Djordje Nikolic, Emil Bergström, Raoul Petretta (46.Edon Zhegrova), Eray Cömart, Blas Riveros, Elis Isufi, Valentin Stocker, Fabian Frei (70.Ramires), Taulant Xhaka, Samuele Campo, Kemal Ademi (32.Arthur Cabral). Trainer: Marcel Koller.
APOEL Nicosia: Boy Waterman, Vujadin Savic, Giorgios Merkis, Praxitelis Vouros, Nicholas Ioannou, Mike Jensen, Stathis Aloneftis (62.Giorgos Efrem), Dragan Mihajlovic, Antonio Jakolis (46.Tomás De Vincenti), Uros Matic, Moussa Al Tamari (70.Andrija Pavlovic). Trainer: Marinos Ouzounidis.
Goal: 38' Fabian Frei 1-0 (pen).

27.02.2020; Emirates Stadium, London
Referee: Davide Massa (ITA); Attendance: 60,242
Arsenal FC London – OLYMPIACOS SFP PEIRAIÁS 1-2(0-0,0-1)
Arsenal FC: Bernd Leno, David Luiz, Shkodran Mustafi (103.Sokratis Papastathopoulos), Héctor Bellerín (84.Joseph Willock), Mesut Özil, Granit Xhaka, Dani Ceballos (72.Lucas Torreira), Bukayo Saka, Pierre-Emerick Aubameyang, Alexandre Lacazette (105.Gabriel Martinelli), Nicolas Pépé. Trainer: Mikel Arteta.
Olympiacos Piraeus: José Sá, Omar Elabdellaoui, Kostas Tsimikas (114.Maximiliano Lovera), Pape Cissé, Ousseynou Ba, Mathieu Valbuena (86.Bruno Gaspar), Guilherme (117.Avraam Papadopoulos), Andreas Bouchalakis, Lazar Randjelovic (77.Georgios Masouras), Mady Camara, Youssef El-Arabi. Trainer: Pedro Martins.
Goals: 53' Pape Cissé 0-1, 113' Pierre-Emerick Aubameyang 1-1, 119' Youssef El-Arabi 1-2.

27.02.2020; Linzer Stadion, Linz
Referee: Srdjan Jovanovic (SRB); Attendance: 12,855
LASK LINZ – AZ Alkmaar 2-0(1-0)
LASK Linz: Alexander Schlager, Petar Filipovic, Gernot Trauner, Reinhold Ranftl, Philipp Wiesinger, James Holland, Thomas Goiginger (89.Christian Ramsebner), Peter Michorl, René Renner, Dominik Frieser (61.Husein Balic), Marko Raguz (69.Klauss). Trainer: Valérien Ismaël.
AZ Alkmaar: Marco Bizot, Ramon Leeuwin (63.Ferdy Druijf), Jonas Svensson (76.Håkon Evjen), Owen Wijndal, Jordy Clasie, Fredrik Midtsjø, Dani de Wit, Teun Koopmeiners, Oussama Idrissi, Myron Boadu, Calvin Stengs. Trainer: Arne Slot.
Goals: 44', 50' Marko Raguz 1-0 (pen), 2-0.
Sent off: 88' Philipp Wiesinger.

27.02.2020; Swedbank Stadion Malmö
Referee: William Collum (SCO); Attendance: 20,500
Malmö FF – VFL WOLFSBURG 0-3(0-1)
Malmö FF: Johan Dahlin, Behrang Safari, Rasmus Bengtsson (76.Lasse Nielsen), Anel Ahmedhodzic, Søren Rieks, Anders Christiansen, Fouad Bachirou, Oscar Lewicki, Adi Nalic (56.Jo Inge Berget), Marcus Antonsson, Isaac Kiese Thelin. Trainer: Jon Dahl Tomasson.
VfL Wolfsburg: Koen Casteels, Robin Knoche, John Anthony Brooks, Paulo Otávio, Yannick Gerhardt, Admir Mehmedi, Maximilian Arnold, Renato Steffen, Xaver Schlager (59.João Victor), Josip Brekalo (79.Felix Klaus), Wout Weghorst (70.Daniel Ginczek). Trainer: Oliver Glasner.
Goals: 42' Josip Brekalo 0-1, 65' Yannick Gerhardt 0-2, 69' João Victor 0-3.

27.02.2020; GHELAMCO-arena, Gent
Referee: José María Sánchez Martínez (ESP); Attendance: 17,557
KAA Gent – AS ROMA 1-1(1-1)
KAA Gent: Thomas Kaminski, Igor Plastun (80.Anderson Niangbo), Michael Ngadeu-Ngadjui, Milad Mohammadi, Alessio Castro-Montes, Vadis Odjidja-Ofoe, Sven Kums, Roman Bezus (66.Giorgi Chakvetadze), Elisha Owusu, Laurent Depoitre (66.Giorgi Kvilitaia), Jonathan David. Trainer: Jess Thorup.
AS Roma: Pau López, Aleksandar Kolarov, Chris Smalling, Leonardo Spinazzola (67.Davide Santon), Gianluca Mancini, Henrikh Mkhitaryan, Jordan Veretout (78.Federico Fazio), Bryan Cristante, Edin Dzeko, Carles Pérez (83.Gonzalo Villar), Justin Kluivert. Trainer: Paulo Fonseca.
Goals: 25' Jonathan David 1-0, 29' Justin Kluivert 1-1.

20.02.2020; Ibrox Stadium, Glasgow
Referee: Xavier Estrada Fernández (ESP); Attendance: 49,378
Glasgow Rangers FC – Sporting Clube de Braga 3-2(0-1)
Glasgow Rangers: Allan McGregor, James Tavernier, Connor Goldson, Borna Barisic (73.Greg Stewart), Nikola Katic, Steven Davis, Scott Arfield, Glen Kamara (54.Joe Aribo), Ianis Hagi, Alfredo Morelos, Ryan Kent (68.Florian Kamberi). Trainer: Steven Gerrard.
Sporting Braga: Matheus Magalhães, Raúl Silva, Ricardo Esgaio, Nuno Sequeira, Wallace (12.Galeno), Bruno Viana, Fransérgio, João Palhinha (83.João Novais), Paulinho, Abel Ruiz (70.Ricardo Horta), Francisco Trincão. Trainer: Micael Sequeira.
Goals: 11' Fransérgio 0-1, 59' Abel Ruiz 0-2, 67' Ianis Hagi 1-2, 75' Joe Aribo 2-2, 82' Ianis Hagi 3-2.

26.02.2020; Estádio Municipal de Braga, Braga
Referee: Andreas Ekberg (SWE); Attendance: 18,113
Sporting Clube de Braga – GLASGOW RANGERS FC 0-1(0-0)
Sporting Braga: Matheus Magalhães, Raúl Silva (52.Galeno), Ricardo Esgaio, Nuno Sequeira, Bruno Viana, David Carmo (64.Abel Ruiz), Fransérgio, João Palhinha (46.João Novais), Paulinho, Ricardo Horta, Francisco Trincão. Trainer: Micael Sequeira.
Glasgow Rangers: Allan McGregor, James Tavernier, Connor Goldson, Borna Barisic, Samuel George Edmundson, Steven Davis, Scott Arfield, Ryan Jack, Ianis Hagi (72.Joe Aribo), Ryan Kent, Florian Kamberi (78.Sheyi Ojo). Trainer: Steven Gerrard.
Goal: 61' Ryan Kent 0-1.

ROUND OF 16

12.03.2020; Başakşehir „Fatih Terim" Stadyumu, İstanbul
Referee: William Collum (SCO); Attendance: 12,205.
İstanbul Başakşehir FK – FC København 1-0(0-0)
İstanbul Başakşehir: Mert Günok, Gaël Clichy, Martin Skrtel, Alexandru Epureanu, Júnior Caiçara, Mahmut Tekdemir (85.Fredrik Gulbrandsen), Danijel Aleksic, Edin Visca (90+1.Azubuike Okechukwu), Irfan Kahveci, Demba Ba, Enzo Crivelli (74.Robinho). Trainer: Okan Buruk.
FC København: Kalle Johnsson, Pierre Bengtsson, Andreas Bjelland, Guillermo Varela, Victor Nelsson, Rasmus Falk, Zeca, Pep Biel Mas (89.Karlo Bartolec), Jens Stage, Michael Santos (82.Viktor Fischer), Mohammed Daramy (62.Mikkel Kaufmann). Trainer: Ståle Solbakken.
Goal: 88' Edin Visca 1-0 (pen).

05.08.2020; Telia Parken, København
Referee: Daniele Orsato (ITA)
FC KØBENHAVN – İstanbul Başakşehir FK 3-0(1-0)
FC København: Kalle Johnsson, Andreas Bjelland, Nicolai Boilesen (69.Pierre Bengtsson), Guillermo Varela, Victor Nelsson, Rasmus Falk (84.Karlo Bartolec), Zeca, Pep Biel Mas (84.Bryan Oviedo), Robert Mudrazija (53.Jens Stage), Jonas Wind, Mikkel Kaufmann (53.Mohammed Daramy). Trainer: Ståle Solbakken.
İstanbul Başakşehir: Mert Günok, Gaël Clichy, Martin Skrtel, Alexandru Epurcanu, Júnior Caiçara, Mehmet Topal (54.Danijel Aleksic), Mahmut Tekdemir (54.Eljero Elia), Edin Visca, Irfan Kahveci (71.Berkay Özcan), Demba Ba, Enzo Crivelli (79.Fredrik Gulbrandsen). Trainer: Okan Buruk.
Goals: 4', 53' Jonas Wind 1-0, 2-0 (pen), 62' Rasmus Falk 3-0.

12.03.2020; Commerzbank-Arena, Frankfurt am Main
Referee: Andreas Ekberg (SWE)
Eintracht Frankfurt – FC Basel 0-3(0-1)
Eintracht Frankfurt: Kevin Trapp, Makoto Hasebe (74.Stefan Ilsanker), David Abraham, Martin Hinteregger, Almamy Touré, Evan Obite N'Dicka, Sebastian Rode, Filip Kostic, Djibril Sow (46.Gonçalo Paciência), Daichi Kamada (78.Mijat Gacinovic), André Silva. Trainer: Adi Hütter.
FC Basel: Jonas Omlin, Silvan Widmer, Omar Alderete, Raoul Petretta (68.Kevin Bua), Eray Cömart, Blas Riveros, Valentin Stocker (90+2.Edon Zhegrova), Fabian Frei, Taulant Xhaka, Samuele Campo (78.Jasper van der Werff), Arthur Cabral. Trainer: Marcel Koller.
Goals: 27' Samuele Campo 0-1, 73' Kevin Bua 0-2, 85' Fabian Frei 0-3.

06.08.2020; St. Jakob-Park, Basel
Referee: Antonio Mateu Lahoz (ESP)
FC BASEL – Eintracht Frankfurt 1-0(0-0)
FC Basel: Djordje Nikolic, Silvan Widmer, Omar Alderete, Raoul Petretta, Eray Cömart, Valentin Stocker (66.Ricky van Wolfswinkel), Fabian Frei, Taulant Xhaka (87.Yannick Marchand), Samuele Campo, Arthur Cabral (80.Kemal Ademi), Afimico Pululu (67.Jasper van der Werff). Trainer: Marcel Koller.
Eintracht Frankfurt: Kevin Trapp, David Abraham, Martin Hinteregger, Danny da Costa (67.Timothy Chandler), Evan Obite N'Dicka (46.Makoto Hasebe), Sebastian Rode (67.Stefan Ilsanker), Filip Kostic, Dominik Kohr, Daichi Kamada, Bas Dost, André Silva (46.Gonçalo Paciência). Trainer: Adi Hütter.
Goal: 88' Fabian Frei 1-0.

12.03.2020; Linzer Stadion, Linz
Referee: Artur Manuel Soares Dias (POR)
LASK Linz – Manchester United FC 0-5(0-1)
LASK Linz: Alexander Schlager, Christian Ramsebner, Gernot Trauner, Reinhold Ranftl, James Holland (76.Stefan Haudum), Peter Michorl, René Renner, Dominik Frieser (71.Husein Balic), Dominik Reiter, Samuel Tetteh (61.Marko Raguz), Klauss. Trainer: Valérien Ismaël.
Manchester United: Sergio Romero, Harry Maguire, Luke Shaw, Eric Bailly, Brandon Williams, Mata, Fred, Bruno Fernandes (78.Andreas Pereira), Daniel James (71.Tahith Chong), Scott McTominay, Odion Ighalo (85.Mason Greenwood). Trainer: Ole Gunnar Solskjær.
Goals: 28' Odion Ighalo 0-1, 58' Daniel James 0-2, 82' Mata 0-3, 90+2' Mason Greenwood
0-4, 90+3' Andreas Pereira 0-5.

05.08.2020; Old Trafford, Manchester
Referee: Anasthasios Sidiropoulos (GRE)
MANCHESTER UNITED FC – LASK Linz 2-1(0-0)
Manchester United: Sergio Romero, Harry Maguire, Eric Bailly, Timothy Fosu-Mensah (84.Teden Mengi), Brandon Williams (72.Tahith Chong), Mata, Fred (64.Andreas Pereira), Jesse Lingard (63.Paul Pogba), Daniel James (84.Anthony Martial), Scott McTominay, Odion Ighalo. Trainer: Ole Gunnar Solskjær.
LASK Linz: Alexander Schlager, Gernot Trauner, Reinhold Ranftl, Philipp Wiesinger (73.Thomas Sabitzer), Andrés Andrade (80.Petar Filipovic), James Holland, Peter Michorl, René Renner, Dominik Frieser, Husein Balic (66.Dominik Reiter), Marko Raguz. Trainer: Dominik Thalhammer
Goals: 55' Philipp Wiesinger 0-1, 57' Jesse Lingard 1-1, 88' Anthony Martial 2-1.

12.03.2020; Stádio „Giórgos Karaïskáki", Peiraiás
Referee: Clément Turpin (FRA)
Olympiacos SFP Peiraiás – Wolverhampton Wanderers FC 1-1(0-0)
Olympiacos Piraeus: José Sá, Omar Elabdellaoui, Rúben Semedo, Kostas Tsimikas, Ousseynou Ba, Mathieu Valbuena (84.Bruno Gaspar), Guilherme, Andreas Bouchalakis, Georgios Masouras (34.Pape Cissé), Mady Camara, Youssef El-Arabi (74.Kostas Fortounis). Trainer: Pedro Martins.
Wolverhampton Wanderers: Rui Patrício, Willy Boly, Matt Doherty (46.Pedro Neto), Conor Coady, Rúben Vinagre (79.Daniel Podence), João Moutinho (85.Leander Dendoncker), Romain Saïss, Rúben Neves, Raúl Jiménez, Adama Traoré, Diogo Jota. Trainer: Nuno Espírito Santo.
Goals: 54' Youssef El-Arabi 1-0, 67' Pedro Neto 1-1.
Sent off: 28' Rúben Semedo.

06.08.2020; Molineux Stadium, Wolverhampton
Referee: Szymon Marciniak (POL)
WOLVERHAMPTON WANDERERS FC – Olympiacos SFP Peiraiás 1-0(1-0)
Wolverhampton Wanderers: Rui Patrício, Willy Boly, Matt Doherty, Conor Coady, Jonny Castro (17.Rúben Vinagre), João Moutinho, Romain Saïss, Rúben Neves, Daniel Podence (71.Leander Dendoncker), Raúl Jiménez, Adama Traoré (57.Diogo Jota). Trainer: Nuno Espírito Santo.
Olympiacos Piraeus: Bobby Allain, Omar Elabdellaoui, Kostas Tsimikas, Pape Cissé, Ousseynou Ba, Mathieu Valbuena, Guilherme (82.Cafú), Andreas Bouchalakis (46.Kostas Fortounis), Georgios Masouras (46.Lazar Randjelovic), Mady Camara (65.Kouka), Youssef El-Arabi. Trainer: Pedro Martins.
Goal: 8' Raúl Jiménez 1-0 (pen).

12.03.2020; Ibrox Stadium, Glasgow
Referee: Szymon Marciniak (POL); Attendance: 47,494.
Glasgow Rangers FC – TSV Bayer 04 Leverkusen 1-3(0-1)
Glasgow Rangers: Allan McGregor, James Tavernier (85.Matt Polster), Connor Goldson, Borna Barisic, Samuel George Edmundson, Steven Davis, Scott Arfield, Glen Kamara (68.Ianis Hagi), Joe Aribo (53.Florian Kamberi), Alfredo Morelos, Ryan Kent. Trainer: Steven Gerrard.
Bayer Leverkusen: Lukás Hrádecký, Aleksandar Dragovic, Mitchell Weiser, Wendell, Jonathan Tah, Edmond Tapsoba (68.Paulinho), Charles Aránguiz, Karim Bellarabi (62.Leon Bailey), Kerem Demirbay (81.Julian Baumgartlinger), Kai Havertz, Moussa Diaby. Trainer: Peter Bosz.
Goals: 37' Kai Havertz 0-1 (pen), 67' Charles Aránguiz 0-2, 75' Samuel George Edmundson 1-2, 88' Leon Bailey 1-3.

12.03.2020; Volkswagen Arena, Wolfsburg
Referee: Damir Skomina (SVN)
VfL Wolfsburg – FK Shakhtar Donetsk 1-2(0-1)
VfL Wolfsburg: Koen Casteels, Robin Knoche, John Anthony Brooks, Paulo Otávio, Yannick Gerhardt, Admir Mehmedi (80.Daniel Ginczek), Maximilian Arnold, Renato Steffen, Xaver Schlager (73.João Victor), Josip Brekalo, Wout Weghorst. Trainer: Oliver Glasner.
Shakhtar Donetsk: Andriy Pyatov, Sergiy Kryvtsov, Ismaily (68.Davit Khocholava), Mykola Matviyenko, Dodô, Taison (88.Yevhen Konoplyanka), Alan Patrick, Viktor Kovalenko (66.Maycon), Marcos Antônio, Tetê, Júnior Moraes. Trainer: Luís Castro.
Goals: 17' Júnior Moraes 0-1, 48' John Anthony Brooks 1-1, 73' Marcos Antônio 1-2.

06.08.2020; BayArena, Leverkusen
Referee: Danny Desmond Makkelie (NED)
TSV BAYER 04 LEVERKUSEN – Glasgow Rangers 1-0(0-0)
Bayer Leverkusen: Lukás Hrádecký, Sven Bender (77.Jonathan Tah), Daley Sinkgraven, Edmond Tapsoba, Lars Bender (68.Aleksandar Dragovic), Charles Aránguiz, Exequiel Palacios (87.Adrian Stanilewicz), Kai Havertz, Florian Wirtz (68.Julian Baumgartlinger), Kevin Volland, Moussa Diaby (68.Leon Bailey). Trainer: Peter Bosz.
Glasgow Rangers: Allan McGregor, James Tavernier (77.Nathan Patterson), Connor Goldson, Filip Helander, Borna Barisic, Steven Davis (66.Scott Arfield), Ryan Jack, Joe Aribo, Alfredo Morelos (77.Greg Stewart), Brandon Barker (60.Ianis Hagi), Ryan Kent (66.Jordan Jones). Trainer: Steven Gerrard.
Goal: 51' Moussa Diaby 1-0.

05.08.2020; NSK Olimpiyskiy Stadium, Kyiv
Referee: Ivan Kruzliak (SVK)
FK SHAKHTAR DONETSK – VfL Wolfsburg 3-0(0-0)
Shakhtar Donetsk: Andriy Pyatov, Sergiy Kryvtsov, Davit Khocholava, Mykola Matviyenko, Dodô, Marlos (77.Manor Solomon), Taras Stepanenko, Taison (86.Yevhen Konoplyanka), Alan Patrick, Marcos Antônio (74.Viktor Kovalenko), Júnior Moraes. Trainer: Luís Castro.
VfL Wolfsburg: Koen Casteels, Jérôme Roussillon (83.Felix Klaus), Marcel Tisserand, John Anthony Brooks, Marin Pongracic, Maximilian Arnold, Xaver Schlager, Josip Brekalo (75.Josuha Guilavogui), Daniel Ginczek (62.Omar Marmoush), Wout Weghorst, João Victor. Trainer: Oliver Glasner.
Goals: 89' Júnior Moraes 1-0, 90+1' Manor Solomon 2-0, 90+3' Júnior Moraes 3-0.
Sent off: 67' Davit Khocholava, 70' John Anthony Brooks.

Please note: Due to the COVID-19 pandemic in Europe the competition was postponed and the remainder of the season was played later in 2020. All matches were played behind closed doors. For the two ties that had not played their first legs, the matches were instead played in a single-leg format on neutral venues in Germany.

05.08.2020; Veltins-Arena, Gelsenkirchen (GER)
Referee: Anthony Taylor (ENG)
FC INTERNAZIONALE MILANO – Getafe CF 2-0(1-0)
Internazionale: Samir Handanovic, Diego Godín, Stefan de Vrij, Alessandro Bastoni, Nicolò Barella, Roberto Gagliardini, Danilo D'Ambrosio (84.Cristiano Biraghi), Marcelo Brozovic (82.Christian Eriksen), Ashley Young, Romelu Lukaku, Lautaro Martínez (70.Alexis Sánchez). Trainer: Antonio Conte.
Getafe CF: David Soria, Damián Suárez, Djené Dakonam Ortega, Etxeita, Mathías Olivera (88.Portillo), Nemanja Maksimovic (56.Ángel), David Timor, Allan Nyom (69.Jason), Mauro Arambarri (89.Hugo Duro), Cucurella, Mata (69.Jorge Molina). Trainer: José Bordalás.
Goals: 33' Romelu Lukaku 1-0, 83' Christian Eriksen 2-0.

06.08.2020; Schauinsland-Reisen-Arena, Duisburg (GER)
Referee: Björn Kuipers (NED)
SEVILLA FC – AS Roma 2-0(2-0)
Sevilla FC: Yassine Bounou, Jesús Navas, Jules Koundé, Diego Carlos, Sergio Reguilón, Fernando, Éver Banega, Joan Jordán, Lucas Ocampos (90+6.Franco Vázquez), Youssef En-Nesyri (90+3.Luuk de Jong), Suso (67.Munir). Trainer: Lopetegui.
AS Roma: Pau López, Gianluca Mancini, Ibañez, Aleksandar Kolarov (78.Gonzalo Villar), Bruno Peres, Amadou Diawara (57.Carles Pérez), Bryan Cristante, Leonardo Spinazzola, Nicolò Zaniolo (57.Lorenzo Pellegrini), Henrikh Mkhitaryan, Edin Dzeko. Trainer: Paulo Fonseca.
Goals: 22' Sergio Reguilón 1-0, 44' Youssef En-Nesyri 2-0.
Sent off: 90+10' Gianluca Mancini.

QUARTER-FINALS

10.08.2020; RheinEnergieStadion, Köln
Referee: Clément Turpin (FRA)
MANCHESTER UNITED FC – FC København 1-0(0-0,0-0)
Manchester United: Sergio Romero, Harry Maguire, Eric Bailly (71.Victor Lindelöf), Aaron Wan-Bissaka, Brandon Williams, Paul Pogba, Fred (70.Nemanja Matic), Bruno Fernandes, Anthony Martial (120+1.Scott McTominay), Marcus Rashford (113.Jesse Lingard), Mason Greenwood (90.Mata). Trainer: Ole Gunnar Solskjær.
FC København: Kalle Johnsson, Andreas Bjelland, Nicolai Boilesen (15.Pierre Bengtsson), Guillermo Varela (105.Karlo Bartolec), Victor Nelsson, Rasmus Falk (111.William Bøving Vick), Zeca, Pep Biel Mas (57.Bryan Oviedo), Jens Stage (105.Robert Mudrazija), Mohammed Daramy (57.Mikkel Kaufmann), Jonas Wind. Trainer: Ståle Solbakken.
Goal: 95' Bruno Fernandes 1-0 (pen).

10.08.2020; Merkur Spiel-Arena, Düsseldorf
Referee: Carlos del Cerro Grande (ESP)
FC INTERNAZIONALE MILANO – TSV Bayer 04 Leverkusen 2-1(2-1)
Internazionale: Samir Handanovic, Ashley Young, Diego Godín, Stefan de Vrij, Danilo D'Ambrosio (59.Victor Moses), Alessandro Bastoni (84.Milan Skriniar), Marcelo Brozovic, Roberto Gagliardini (59.Christian Eriksen), Nicolò Barella, Romelu Lukaku, Lautaro Martínez (64.Alexis Sánchez). Trainer: Antonio Conte.
Bayer Leverkusen: Lukás Hrádecký, Jonathan Tah, Daley Sinkgraven (68.Wendell), Edmond Tapsoba, Lars Bender (85.Karim Bellarabi), Julian Baumgartlinger (68.Nadiem Amiri), Kerem Demirbay, Exequiel Palacios (59.Leon Bailey), Kai Havertz, Kevin Volland (85.Lucas Alario), Moussa Diaby. Trainer: Peter Bosz.
Goals: 15' Nicolò Barella 1-0, 21' Romelu Lukaku 2-0, 24' Kai Havertz 2-1.

11.08.2020; Veltins-Arena, Gelsenkirchen
Referee: Michael Oliver (ENG)
FK SHAKHTAR DONETSK – FC Basel 4-1(2-0)
Shakhtar Donetsk: Andriy Pyatov, Sergiy Kryvtsov, Mykola Matviyenko, Valeriy Bondar, Dodô, Marlos (72.Manor Solomon), Taras Stepanenko, Taison (85.Tetê), Alan Patrick (78.Viktor Kovalenko), Marcos Antônio (85.Maycon), Júnior Moraes (85.Fernando). Trainer: Luís Castro.
FC Basel: Djordje Nikolic, Silvan Widmer, Omar Alderete, Raoul Petretta, Jasper van der Werff (73.Ramires), Valentin Stocker (73.Ricky van Wolfswinkel), Fabian Frei, Taulant Xhaka (60.Yannick Marchand), Samuele Campo, Arthur Cabral (73.Kemal Ademi), Afimico Pululu. Trainer: Marcel Koller.
Goals: 2' Júnior Moraes 1-0, 22' Taison 2-0, 75' Alan Patrick 3-0 (pen), 88' Dodô 4-0, 90+2' Ricky van Wolfswinkel 4-1.

11.08.2020; Schauinsland-Reisen-Arena, Duisburg
Referee: Daniele Orsato (ITA)
Wolverhampton Wanderers FC – SEVILLA FC 0-1(0-0)
Wolverhampton Wanderers: Rui Patrício, Willy Boly, Matt Doherty, Conor Coady, Rúben Vinagre, João Moutinho (71.Pedro Neto), Romain Saïss, Leander Dendoncker, Rúben Neves, Raúl Jiménez, Adama Traoré (79.Diogo Jota). Trainer: Nuno Espírito Santo.
Sevilla FC: Yassine Bounou, Jesús Navas, Diego Carlos, Sergio Reguilón, Jules Koundé, Éver Banega, Fernando, Lucas Ocampos, Suso (89.Munir), Joan Jordán (85.Franco Vázquez), Youssef En-Nesyri (85.Luuk de Jong). Trainer: Lopetegui.
Goal: 88' Lucas Ocampos 0-1.

16.08.2020; RheinEnergieStadion, Köln
Referee: Dr. Felix Brych (Germany)
SEVILLA FC – Manchester United FC 2-1(1-1)
Sevilla FC: Yassine Bounou, Jesús Navas, Diego Carlos, Sergio Reguilón, Jules Koundé, Éver Banega, Fernando, Lucas Ocampos (56.Munir), Suso (75.Franco Vázquez), Joan Jordán (87.Nemanja Gudelj), Youssef En-Nesyri (56.Luuk de Jong). Trainer: Lopetegui.
Manchester United: David de Gea, Victor Lindelöf, Harry Maguire, Aaron Wan-Bissaka (87.Daniel James), Brandon Williams (87.Timothy Fosu-Mensah), Paul Pogba, Fred, Bruno Fernandes, Anthony Martial, Marcus Rashford (87.Mata), Mason Greenwood (90+3.Odion Ighalo). Trainer: Ole Gunnar Solskjær.
Goals: 9' Bruno Fernandes 0-1 (pen), 26' Suso 1-1, 78' Luuk de Jong 2-1.

17.08.2020; Merkur Spiel-Arena, Düsseldorf
Referee: Szymon Marciniak (POL)
FC INTERNAZIONALE MILANO – FK Shakhtar Donetsk 5-0(1-0)
Internazionale: Samir Handanovic, Ashley Young (66.Cristiano Biraghi), Diego Godín, Stefan de Vrij, Danilo D'Ambrosio (81.Victor Moses), Alessandro Bastoni, Marcelo Brozovic (85.Stefano Sensi), Roberto Gagliardini, Nicolò Barella, Romelu Lukaku (85.Sebastiano Esposito), Lautaro Martínez (81.Christian Eriksen). Trainer: Antonio Conte.
Shakhtar Donetsk: Andriy Pyatov, Sergiy Kryvtsov, Davit Khocholava, Mykola Matviyenko, Dodô, Marlos (75.Yevhen Konopyanka), Taras Stepanenko, Taison, Alan Patrick (59.Manor Solomon), Marcos Antônio, Júnior Moraes. Trainer: Luís Castro.
Goals: 19' Lautaro Martínez 1-0, 64' Danilo D'Ambrosio 2-0, 74' Lautaro Martínez 3-0, 78', 84' Romelu Lukaku 4-0, 5-0.

21.08.2020; RheinEnergieStadion, Köln; Referee: Danny Desmond Makkelie (Netherlands); Attendance: None
Sevilla FC – FC Internazionale Milano 3-2(2-2)
Sevilla FC: Yassine Bounou, Jesús Navas González, Diego Carlos Santos Silva (86.Nemanja Gudelj), Sergio Reguilón Rodríguez, Jules Koundé, Éver Maximiliano David Banega, Fernando Francisco Reges, Lucas Ariel Ocampos (71.Munir El Haddadi Mohamed), Jesús Joaquín Fernández Sáez de la Torre „Suso" (78.Franco Damian Vázquez), Joan Jordán Moreno, Luuk de Jong (85.Youssef En-Nesyri). Trainer: Julen Lopetegui Agote.
Internazionale: Samir Handanovic, Ashley Simon Young, Diego Roberto Godín Leal (90.Antonio Candreva), Stefan de Vrij, Danilo D'Ambrosio (78.Victor Moses), Alessandro Bastoni, Marcelo Brozović, Roberto Gagliardini (78.Christian Dannemann Eriksen), Nicolò Barella, Romelu Menama Lukaku Bolingoli, Lautaro Javier Martínez (78.Alexis Alejandro Sánchez Sánchez). Trainer: Antonio Conte.
Goals: 5' Romelu Menama Lukaku Bolingoli 0-1 (pen), 12', 33' Luuk de Jong 1-1, 2-1, 36' Diego Roberto Godín Leal 2-2, 74' Romelu Menama Lukaku Bolingoli 3-2 (own goal).

UEFA Europa League Winner 2019/2020: **Sevilla FC** (Spain)

Best Goalscorer: Bruno Miguel Borges Fernandes (Sporting Clube de Portugal Lisboa) – 8 goals

FAIRS CUP (1958-1971)
UEFA CUP (1972-2009)
UEFA EUROPA LEAGUE (2010-2020)
TABLE OF HONOURS

1955/1958	FC Barcelona	Spain
1958/1960	FC Barcelona	Spain
1960/1961	AS Roma	Italy
1961/1962	Valencia CF	Spain
1962/1963	Valencia CF	Spain
1963/1964	Real Zaragoza	Spain
1964/1965	Ferencvárosi TC	Hungary
1965/1966	FC Barcelona	Spain
1966/1967	GNK Dinamo Zagreb	Croatia
1967/1968	Leeds United FC	England
1968/1969	Newcastle United FC	England
1969/1970	Arsenal FC London	England
1970/1971	Leeds United FC	England
1971/1972	Tottenham Hotspur FC London	England
1972/1973	Liverpool FC	England
1973/1974	Feyenoord Rotterdam	Netherlands
1974/1975	Borussia VfL Mönchengladbach	Germany
1975/1976	Liverpool FC	England
1976/1977	Juventus FC Torino	Italy
1977/1978	PSV Eindhoven	Netherlands
1978/1979	Borussia VfL Mönchengladbach	Germany
1979/1980	Eintracht Frankfurt	Germany
1980/1981	Ipswich Town FC	England
1981/1982	IFK Göteborg	Sweden
1982/1983	RSC Anderlecht Bruxelles	Belgium
1983/1984	Tottenham Hotspur FC London	England
1984/1985	Real Madrid CF	Spain
1985/1986	Real Madrid CF	Spain
1986/1987	IFK Göteborg	Sweden
1987/1988	TSV Bayer 04 Leverkusen	Germany
1988/1989	SSC Napoli	Italy
1989/1990	Juventus FC Torino	Italy
1990/1991	FC Internazionale Milano	Italy
1991/1992	AFC Ajax Amsterdam	Netherlands
1992/1993	Juventus FC Torino	Italy
1993/1994	FC Internazionale Milano	Italy
1994/1995	Parma AC	Italy
1995/1996	FC Bayern München	Germany
1996/1997	FC Schalke 04 Gelsenkirchen	Germany
1997/1998	FC Internazionale Milano	Italy
1998/1999	Parma AC	Italy
1999/2000	Galatasaray SK İstanbul	Turkey
2000/2001	Liverpool FC	England
2001/2002	Feyenoord Rotterdam	Netherlands
2002/2003	FC do Porto	Portugal
2003/2004	Valencia CF	Spain
2004/2005	FK CSKA Moskva	Russia
2005/2006	Sevilla FC	Spain
2006/2007	Sevilla FC	Spain
2007/2008	FK Zenit Saint Petersburg	Russia
2008/2009	FK Shakhtar Donetsk	Ukraine
2009/2010	Club Atlético de Madrid	Spain
2010/2011	FC do Porto	Portugal
2011/2012	Club Atlético de Madrid	Spain
2012/2013	Chelsea FC London	England
2013/2014	Sevilla FC	Spain
2014/2015	Sevilla FC	Spain
2015/2016	Sevilla FC	Spain
2016/2017	Manchester United FC	England
2017/2018	Club Atlético de Madrid	Spain
2018/2019	Chelsea FC London	England
2019/2020	Sevilla FC	Spain

UEFA SUPERCUP 2019

The 2019 UEFA Super Cup was the 44th edition of the UEFA Super Cup, an annual football match organised by UEFA and contested by the winners of the two main European club competitions, the UEFA Champions League and the UEFA Europa League. The 2019 final match featured English clubs Liverpool FC (winners of the 2018/2019 UEFA Champions League) and Chelsea FC London (the winners of the 2018/2019 UEFA Europa League).

14.08.2019; Vodafone Park, İstanbul; Referee: Stéphanie Frappart (France); Attendance: 38,434
Liverpool FC – Chelsea FC London 2-2(0-1,1-1,2-2); 5-4 on penalties
Liverpool FC: Adrián San Miguel del Castillo, Joseph Dave Gomez, Job Joël André Matip, Virgil van Dijk, Andrew Robertson (91.Trent John Alexander-Arnold), James Philip Milner (64.Georginio Gregion Emile Wijnaldum), Fabio Henrique Tavares "Fabinho", Jordan Brian Henderson (Cap), Alexander Mark David Oxlade-Chamberlain (46.Roberto Firmino Barbosa de Oliveira), Mohamed Salah Ghaly, Sadio Mané (103.Divock Okoth Origi). Trainer: Jürgen Norbert Klopp (Germany).
Chelsea FC: Kepa Arrizabalaga Revuelta, César Azpilicueta Tanco (Cap), Kurt Happy Zouma, Andreas Bødtker Christensen (85.Oluwafikayomi Oluwadamilola Tomori), Emerson Palmieri dos Santos, Filho Jorge Luiz Frello „Jorginho",N'Golo Kanté, Mateo Kovačić (101.Ross Barkley), Christian Pulišić (74.Mason Tony Mount), Olivier Giroud (74.Kevin Oghenetega Tamaraebi Bakumo-Abraham), Pedro Eliezer Rodríguez Ledesma. Trainer: Frank James Lampard Junior.
Goals: 0-1 Olivier Giroud (36), 1-1 Sadio Mané (48), 2-1 Sadio Mané (95), 2-2 Filho Jorge Luiz Frello „Jorginho" (101 penalty).
Penalties: Roberto Firmino Barbosa de Oliveira 1-0; Filho Jorge Luiz Frello „Jorginho" 1-1; Fabio Henrique Tavares "Fabinho" 2-1; Ross Barkley 2-2; Divock Okoth Origi 3-2; Mason Tony Mount 3-3; Trent John Alexander-Arnold 4-3; Emerson Palmieri dos Santos 4-4; Mohamed Salah Ghaly 5-4; Kevin Oghenetega Tamaraebi Bakumo-Abraham (saved).

UEFA Supercup Winner 2019: **Liverpool FC** (England)

UEFA SUPER CUP (SINCE 1972) TABLE OF HONOURS		
1972	AFC Ajax Amsterdam (not official)	*Netherlands*
1973	AFC Ajax Amsterdam	*Netherlands*
1974	*Not played*	
1975	FK Dinamo Kyiv	*Soviet Union*
1976	RSC Anderlecht Bruxelles	*Belgium*
1977	Liverpool FC	*England*
1978	RSC Anderlecht Bruxelles	*Belgium*
1979	Nottingham Forest FC	*England*
1980	CF Valencia	*Spain*
1981	*Not played*	
1982	Aston Villa FC Birmingham	*England*
1983	Aberdeen FC	*Scotland*
1984	Juventus FC Torino	*Italy*
1985	*Not played*	
1986	FC Steaua Bucureşti	*Romania*
1987	FC do Porto	*Portugal*
1988	KV Mechelen	*Belgium*
1989	AC Milan	*Italy*
1990	AC Milan	*Italy*
1991	Manchester United FC	*England*
1992	FC Barcelona	*Spain*
1993	Parma AC	*Italy*
1994	AC Milan	*Italy*
1995	AFC Ajax Amsterdam	*Netherlands*
1996	Juventus FC Torino	*Italy*
1997	FC Barcelona	*Spain*
1998	Chelsea FC London	*England*
1999	SS Lazio Roma	*Italy*
2000	Galatasaray SK İstanbul	*Turkey*
2001	Liverpool FC	*England*
2002	Real Madrid CF	*Spain*
2003	AC Milan	*Italy*
2004	Valencia CF	*Spain*
2005	Liverpool FC	*England*
2006	Sevilla FC	*Spain*
2007	AC Milan	*Italy*
2008	FK Zenit Saint Petersburg	*Russia*
2009	FC Barcelona	*Spain*
2010	Club Atlético de Madrid	*Spain*
2011	FC Barcelona	*Spain*
2012	Club Atlético de Madrid	*Spain*
2013	FC Bayern München	*Germany*
2014	Real Madrid CF	*Spain*
2015	FC Barcelona	*Spain*
2016	Real Madrid CF	*Spain*
2017	Real Madrid CF	*Spain*
2018	Club Atlético de Madrid	*Spain*
2019	Liverpool FC	*England*

ALBANIA

The Country:
Republic of Albania (Republika e Shqipërisë)
Capital: Tiranë
Surface: 28,748 km²
Inhabitants: 2,845,955 [2020]
Time: UTC+1

The FA:
Federata Shqiptare e Futbollit
Rr. Liman Kaba 1019 Tiranë
Tel: +355 42 346601
Foundation date: 06.06.1930
Member of FIFA since: 12.06.1932
Member of UEFA since: 1954
Website: www.fshf.org

NATIONAL TEAM RECORDS

RECORDS		
First international match:	07.10.1946, Tiranë:	Albania – Yugoslavia 2-3
Most international caps:	Lorik Cana	- 93 caps (2003-2016)
Most international goals:	Erjon Bogdani	- 18 goal / 74 caps (1996-2013)

UEFA EUROPEAN CHAMPIONSHIP	
1960	Qualifiers
1964	Qualifiers
1968	Qualifiers
1972	Qualifiers
1976	Did not enter
1980	Did not enter
1984	Qualifiers
1988	Qualifiers
1992	Qualifiers
1996	Qualifiers
2000	Qualifiers
2004	Qualifiers
2008	Qualifiers
2012	Qualifiers
2016	Final Tournament (Group Stage)
2020	Qualifiers

FIFA WORLD CUP	
1930	Did not enter
1934	Did not enter
1938	Did not enter
1950	Did not enter
1954	Did not enter
1958	Did not enter
1962	Did not enter
1966	Qualifiers
1970	*Entry not accepted by FIFA*
1974	Qualifiers
1978	Did not enter
1982	Qualifiers
1986	Qualifiers
1990	Qualifiers
1994	Qualifiers
1998	Qualifiers
2002	Qualifiers
2006	Qualifiers
2010	Qualifiers
2014	Qualifiers
2018	Qualifiers

OLYMPIC TOURNAMENTS	
1908	-
1912	-
1920	-
1924	-
1928	-
1936	-
1948	-
1952	-
1956	-
1960	-
1964	-
1968	-
1972	-
1976	-
1980	-
1984	*Withdrew*
1988	-
1992	*Withdrew*
1996	-
2000	Qualifiers
2004	Qualifiers
2008	Qualifiers
2012	Qualifiers
2016	Qualifiers

UEFA NATIONS LEAGUE

2018/2019 – League C

FIFA CONFEDERATIONS CUP 1992-2017

None

ALBANIAN CLUB HONOURS IN EUROPEAN CLUB COMPETITIONS:

European Champion Clubs' Cup (1956-1992) / UEFA Champions League (1993-2020)
None

Fairs Cup (1858-1971) / UEFA Cup (1972-2009) / UEFA Europa League (2010-2020)
None

UEFA Super Cup (1972-2019)
None

European Cup Winners' Cup 1961-1999*
None

*defunct competition

NATIONAL COMPETITIONS
TABLE OF HONOURS

	CHAMPIONS	CUP WINNERS	BEST GOALSCORERS	
1930	SK Tiranë	-	-	
1931	SK Tiranë	-	Teli Samsuri (Skënderbeu Korçë)	9
1932	SK Tiranë	-	-	
1933	Skënderbeu Korçë	-	Servet Tefik Agai (Skënderbeu Korçë)	7
1934	SK Tiranë	-	Mark Gurashi (SK Tiranë)	12
1935	*No Competition*	-	*No Competition*	
1936	SK Tiranë	-	Riza Lushta (SK Tiranë)	11
1937	SK Tiranë	-	Riza Lushta (SK Tiranë)	25
1938	*No Competition*	-	*No Competition*	
1939	SK Tiranë (*unofficial*)	SK Tiranë	-	
1940	Vllaznia Shkodër (*unofficial*)	*No Competition*	-	
1941	*No Competition*	*No Competition*	*No Competition*	
1942	SK Tiranë (*unofficial*)	*No Competition*	-	
1943	*No Competition*	*No Competition*	*No Competition*	
1944	*No Competition*	*No Competition*	*No Competition*	
1945	Vllaznia Shkodër	*No Competition*	Loro Boriçi (Vllaznia Shkodër)	11
1946	Vllaznia Shkodër	*No Competition*	Xhevdet Shaqiri (Vllaznia Shkodër)	11
1947	Partizani Tiranë	*No Competition*	Hamdi Bakalli (Partizani Tiranë)	7
1948	Partizani Tiranë	Partizani Tiranë	Tish Daija (Flamurtari Vlorë) Zihni Gjinali (Partizani Tiranë)	11
1949	Partizani Tiranë	Partizani Tiranë	Zihni Gjinali (Partizani Tiranë)	14
1950	Dinamo Tiranë	Dinamo Tiranë	Refik Resmja (Partizani Tiranë)	?
1951	Dinamo Tiranë	Dinamo Tiranë	Refik Resmja (Partizani Tiranë)	59
1952	Dinamo Tiranë	Dinamo Tiranë	Refik Resmja (Partizani Tiranë)	17
1953	Dinamo Tiranë	Dinamo Tiranë	Refik Resmja (Partizani Tiranë)	9
1954	Partizani Tiranë	Dinamo Tiranë	Refik Resmja (Partizani Tiranë)	13
1955	Dinamo Tiranë	*No Competition*	Refik Resmja (Partizani Tiranë) Skënder Jareci (Dinamo Tiranë)	23
1956	Dinamo Tiranë	*No Competition*	Refik Resmja (Partizani Tiranë)	17
1957	Partizani Tiranë	Partizani Tiranë	Niko Bespalla (Teuta)	15
1958	Partizani Tiranë	Partizani Tiranë	Skënder Jareci (Dinamo Tiranë)	14
1959	Partizani Tiranë	*No Competition*	Stavri Lubonja (Dinamo Tiranë)	11
1960	Dinamo Tiranë	Dinamo Tirane	Skënder Jareci (Dinamo Tiranë)	16
1961	Partizani Tiranë	Partizani Tiranë	Panajot Pano (Partizani Tiranë)	17
1962/1963	Partizani Tiranë	*No Competition*	Robert Jashari (Partizani Tiranë)	18
1963/1964	Partizani Tiranë	17 Nëntori Tiranë	Robert Jashari (Partizani Tiranë)	9
1964/1965	17 Nëntori Tiranë	Partizani Tiranë	Robert Jashari (Partizani Tiranë)	14
1965/1966	17 Nëntori Tiranë	Vllaznia Shkodër	Sajmir Dauti (Dinamo Tiranë)	13
1966/1967	Dinamo Tiranë	Partizani Tiranë	Medin Zhega (Dinamo Tiranë)	19
1968	17 Nëntori Tiranë	Partizani Tiranë	Skënder Hyka (17 Nëntori Tiranë)	19
1969/1970	17 Nëntori Tiranë	Partizani Tiranë	Panajot Pano (Partizani Tiranë)	17
1970/1971	Partizani Tiranë	Dinamo Tiranë	Ilir Përnaska (Dinamo Tiranë)	19
1971/1972	Vllaznia Shkodër	Vllaznia Shkodër	Ilir Përnaska (Dinamo Tiranë)	17
1972/1973	Dinamo Tiranë	Partizani Tiranë	Ilir Përnaska (Dinamo Tiranë)	12
1973/1974	Vllaznia Shkodër	Dinamo Tiranë	Ilir Përnaska (Dinamo Tiranë)	19
1974/1975	Dinamo Tiranë	Elbasani	Ilir Përnaska (Dinamo Tiranë)	17
1975/1976	Dinamo Tiranë	17 Nëntori Tiranë	Ilir Përnaska (Dinamo Tiranë)	18
1976/1977	Dinamo Tiranë	17 Nëntori Tiranë	Agim Murati (Partizani Tiranë)	12
1977/1978	Vllaznia Shkodër	Dinamo Tiranë	Agim Murati (Partizani Tiranë)	14
1978/1979	Partizani Tiranë	Vllaznia Shkodër	Agim Murati (Partizani Tiranë) Petrit Dibra (17 Nëntori Tiranë)	14
1979/1980	Dinamo Tiranë	Partizani Tiranë	Përparim Kovaçi (Tomori Berat)	18
1980/1981	Partizani Tiranë	Vllaznia Shkodër	Dashnor Bajaziti (Besa Kavajë)	12
1981/1982	KF Tiranë	Dinamo Tiranë	Vasil Ruci (Flamurtari Vlorë)	12
1982/1983	Vllaznia Shkodër	17 Nëntori Tiranë	Dashnor Bajaziti (Besa Kavajë)	16
1983/1984	Elbasani	17 Nëntori Tiranë	Vasil Ruci (Flamurtari Vlorë)	12
1984/1985	17 Nëntori Tiranë	Flamurtari Vlorë	Faslli Fakja (Vllaznia Shkodër) Arben Minga (17 Nëntori Tiranë)	13
1985/1986	Dinamo Tiranë	17 Nëntori Tiranë	Kujtim Majaci (Apolonia Fier)	20
1986/1987	Partizani Tiranë	Vllaznia Shkodër	Arben Arbëri (Tomori Berat)	14
1987/1988	17 Nëntori Tiranë	Flamurtari Vlorë	Agustin Kola (17 Nëntori Tiranë)	18
1988/1989	17 Nëntori Tiranë	Dinamo Tiranë	Agustin Kola (17 Nëntori Tiranë)	19
1989/1990	Dinamo Tiranë	Dinamo Tiranë	Kujtim Majaci (Apolonia Fier)	19
1990/1991	KS Flamurtari Vlorë	FK Partizani Tiranë	Kliton Bozgo (FK Tomori Berat)	29
1991/1992	KF Vllaznia Shkodër	KF Elbasani	Edmir Bilali (KF Vllaznia Shkodër)	21
1992/1993	FK Partizani Tiranë	Partizani Tiranë	Edmond Dosti (FK Partizani Tiranë)	20
1993/1994	KF Teuta Durrës	KF Tiranë	Edi Martini (KF Vllaznia Shkodër)	14
1994/1995	KF Tiranë	KF Teuta Durrës	Arben Shehu (Luftëtari Gjirokastër FC)	21
1995/1996	KF Tiranë	KF Tiranë	Altin Çuko (FK Tomori Berat & KF Laçi)	21
1996/1997	KF Tiranë	FK Partizani Tiranë	Viktor Paço (KS Flamurtari Vlorë)	14
1997/1998	KF Vllaznia Shkodër	KF Apolonia Fier	Dorian Bubeqi (KS Shkumbini Peqin)	26

1998/1999	KF Tiranë	KF Tiranë	Artan Bano (KS Lushnja)	22
1999/2000	KF Tiranë	KF Teuta Durrës	Klodian Arbëri (FK Tomori Berat)	18
2000/2001	KF Vllaznia Shkodër	KF Tiranë	Indrit Fortuzi (KF Tiranë)	31
2001/2002	FK Dinamo Tiranë	KF Tiranë	Indrit Fortuzi (KF Tiranë)	24
2002/2003	KF Tiranë	FK Dinamo Tiranë	Mahir Halili (KF Tiranë)	20
2003/2004	KF Tiranë	FK Partizani Tiranë	Vioresin Sinani (KF Vllaznia Shkodër)	36
2004/2005	KF Tiranë	KF Teuta Durrës	Dorian Bylykbashi (FK Partizani Tiranë)	24
2005/2006	KF Elbasani	KF Tiranë	Hamdi Salihi (KF Tiranë)	29
2006/2007	KF Tiranë	KS Besa Kavajë	Vioresin Sinani (KF Tiranë)	23
2007/2008	FK Dinamo Tiranë	KF Vllaznia Shkodër	Vioresin Sinani (KF Vllaznia Shkodër)	20
2008/2009	KF Tiranë	KS Flamurtari Vlorë	Migen Memelli (KF Tiranë)	23
2009/2010	FK Dinamo Tiranë	KS Besa Kavajë	Daniel Xhafa (KS Besa Kavajë)	18
2010/2011	KF Skënderbeu Korçë	KF Tiranë	Daniel Xhafa (KS Flamurtari Vlorë)	19
2011/2012	KF Skënderbeu Korçë	KF Tiranë	Roland Dervishi (KS Shkumbini Peqin)	20
2012/2013	KF Skënderbeu Korçë	KF Laçi	Migen Memelli (KS Flamurtari Vlorë)	19
2013/2014	KF Skënderbeu Korçë	KS Flamurtari Vlorë	Pero Pejić (CRO, KF Skënderbeu Korçë)	20
2014/2015	KF Skënderbeu Korçë	KF Laçi	Pero Pejić (CRO, FK Kukësi)	31
2015/2016	KF Skënderbeu Korçë	FK Kukësi	Hamdi Salihi (KF Skënderbeu Korçë)	27
2016/2017	FK Kukësi	KF Tiranë	Pero Pejić (CRO, FK Kukësi)	28
2017/2018	KF Skënderbeu Korçë	KF Skënderbeu Korçë	Ali Sowe (GAM, KF Skënderbeu Korçë)	21
2018/2019	FK Partizani Tiranë	FK Kukësi	Reginaldo Artur Faife (MOZ, FK Kukësi)	13
2019/2020	KF Tiranë	KF Teuta Durrës	Kyrian Chinazorm Nwabueze (NGA, KF Laçi)	24

NATIONAL CHAMPIONSHIP
Albanian Superliga / Kategoria Superiore 2019/2020
(23.08.2019 – 29.07.2020)

Results

Round 1 [23-24.08.2019]
FK Kukësi - FK Partizani 1-0(1-0)
Vllaznia Shkodër - KF Laçi 1-0(1-0)
KF Tiranë - Luftëtari Gjirokastër 3-0(3-0)
Teuta Durrës - Bylis Ballsh 1-0(1-0)
Skënderbeu Korçë - Flamurtari Vlorë 1-0(0-0)

Round 2 [27-28.08.2019]
KF Tiranë - Teuta Durrës 0-0
KF Laçi - Skënderbeu Korçë 1-2(1-0)
Bylis Ballsh - Vllaznia Shkodër 0-0
Luftëtari Gjirokastër - FK Partizani 0-1(0-1)
Flamurtari Vlorë - FK Kukësi 0-3(0-1)

Round 3 [31.08.-01.09.2019]
Teuta Durrës - Luftëtari Gjirokastër 3-1(2-0)
Vllaznia Shkodër - KF Tiranë 0-2(0-0)
FK Kukësi - KF Laçi 1-1(0-0)
Skënderbeu Korçë - Bylis Ballsh 0-3(0-2)
FK Partizani - Flamurtari Vlorë 1-0(1-0)

Round 4 [14-15.09.2019]
KF Tiranë - Skënderbeu Korçë 3-1(1-0)
Teuta Durrës - Vllaznia Shkodër 0-0
Luftëtari Gjirok. - Flamurtari Vlorë 2-1(0-0)
KF Laçi - FK Partizani 1-0(0-0)
Bylis Ballsh - FK Kukësi 2-1(1-1)

Round 5 [21-22.09.2019]
Skënderbeu Korçë - Teuta Durrës 1-0(1-0)
FK Partizani - Bylis Ballsh 1-1(0-0)
FK Kukësi - KF Tiranë 2-1(1-0)
Vllaznia Shkodër - Luftëtari Gjirokastër 0-0
Flamurtari Vlorë - KF Laçi 3-3(2-1)

Round 6 [28-29.09.2019]
Teuta Durrës - FK Kukësi 1-0(0-0)
Vllaznia Shkodër - Skënderbeu Korçë 4-0(1-0)
Bylis Ballsh - Flamurtari Vlorë 5-0(3-0)
Luftëtari Gjirokastër - KF Laçi 1-1(1-0)
KF Tiranë - FK Partizani 1-2(0-2)

Round 7 [05-06.10.2019]
Skënderbeu Korçë - Luftëtari Gjirok. 2-0(0-0)
FK Partizani - Teuta Durrës 1-1(1-1)
Flamurtari Vlorë - KF Tiranë 2-2(1-2)
KF Laçi - Bylis Ballsh 0-0
FK Kukësi - Vllaznia Shkodër 1-2(0-1)

Round 8 [18-19.10.2019]
Teuta Durrës - Flamurtari Vlorë 1-0(0-0)
Luftëtari Gjirokastër - Bylis Ballsh 1-1(0-0)
KF Tiranë - KF Laçi 2-1(2-1)
Vllaznia Shkodër - FK Partizani 1-3(1-1)
Skënderbeu Korçë - FK Kukësi 0-0

Round 9 [23-24.10.2019]
FK Kukësi - Luftëtari Gjirokastër 4-1(2-0)
KF Laçi - Teuta Durrës 3-0(2-0)
Bylis Ballsh - KF Tiranë 3-1(2-0)
Flamurtari Vlorë - Vllaznia Shkodër 1-3(1-1)
FK Partizani - Skënderbeu Korçë 3-1(2-1)

Round 10 [27-28.10.2019]
Luftëtari Gjirokastër - KF Tiranë 0-3(0-2)
Bylis Ballsh - Teuta Durrës 0-0
KF Laçi - Vllaznia Shkodër 3-0(1-0)
Flamurtari Vlorë - Skënderbeu Korçë 1-1(1-1)
FK Partizani - FK Kukësi 0-0

Round 11 [02-04.11.2019]
Teuta Durrës - KF Tiranë 1-1(0-1)
Skënderbeu Korçë - KF Laçi 1-4(1-1)
FK Kukësi - Flamurtari Vlorë 1-0(0-0)
FK Partizani - Luftëtari Gjirokastër 2-0(0-0)
Vllaznia Shkodër - Bylis Ballsh 0-1(0-1)

Round 12 [08-10.11.2019]
KF Tiranë - Vllaznia Shkodër 0-0
Luftëtari Gjirokastër - Teuta Durrës 0-0
Bylis Ballsh - Skënderbeu Korçë 2-3(0-1)
KF Laçi - FK Kukësi 1-0(0-0)
Flamurtari Vlorë - FK Partizani 1-1(0-0)

Round 13 [23-25.11.2019]
FK Kukësi - Bylis Ballsh 2-1(1-1)
Flamurtari Vlorë - Luftëtari Gjirok. 1-1(0-0)
Skënderbeu Korçë - KF Tiranë 2-1(1-0)
Vllaznia Shkodër - Teuta Durrës 0-0
FK Partizani - KF Laçi 1-0(1-0)

Round 14 [07-08.12.2019]
Luftëtari Gjirok. - Vllaznia Shkodër 0-2(0-0)
Bylis Ballsh - FK Partizani 2-1(1-1)
KF Tiranë - FK Kukësi 1-3(1-0)
KF Laçi - Flamurtari Vlorë 3-0(0-0)
Teuta Durrës - Skënderbeu Korçë 1-0(0-0)

Round 15 [13-14.12.2019]
FK Partizani - KF Tiranë 1-2(1-1)
Flamurtari Vlorë - Bylis Ballsh 2-2(1-1)
KF Laçi - Luftëtari Gjirokastër 4-0(2-0)
FK Kukësi - Teuta Durrës 4-0(1-0)
Skënderbeu Korçë - Vllaznia Shkodër 0-1(0-0)

Round 16 [18.12.2019]
Luftëtari Gjirok. - Skënderbeu Korçë 2-0(1-0)
Vllaznia Shkodër - FK Kukësi 1-2(0-1)
Teuta Durrës - FK Partizani 1-0(1-0)
Bylis Ballsh - KF Laçi 1-0(0-0)
KF Tiranë - Flamurtari Vlorë 2-0(0-0)

Round 17 [22-23.12.2019]
KF Laçi - KF Tiranë 1-2(1-1)
Bylis Ballsh - Luftëtari Gjirokastër 1-0(1-0)
FK Partizani - Vllaznia Shkodër 1-0(0-0)
FK Kukësi - Skënderbeu Korçë 1-1(0-1)
Flamurtari Vlorë - Teuta Durrës 1-3(0-1)

Round 18 [21-22.01.2020]
Vllaznia Shkodër - Flamurtari Vlorë 2-0(1-0)
Skënderbeu Korçë - FK Partizani 3-2(2-1)
Teuta Durrës - KF Laçi 0-1(0-0)
Luftëtari Gjirokastër - FK Kukësi 0-0
KF Tiranë - Bylis Ballsh 2-1(1-0)

Round 19 [25-26.01.2020]
Skënderbeu Korçë - Flamurtari Vlorë 1-0(0-0)
Vllaznia Shkodër - KF Laçi 0-0
KF Tiranë - Luftëtari Gjirokastër 5-1(3-0)
Teuta Durrës - Bylis Ballsh 1-0(1-0)
FK Kukësi - FK Partizani 1-0(0-0)

Round 20 [02-03.02.2020]
Luftëtari Gjirokastër - FK Partizani 0-3(0-2)
KF Tiranë - Teuta Durrës 2-1(2-1)
Flamurtari Vlorë - FK Kukësi 1-4(0-2)
KF Laçi - Skënderbeu Korçë 1-0(0-0)
Bylis Ballsh - Vllaznia Shkodër 2-2(2-2)

Round 21 [07-08.02.2020]
Vllaznia Shkodër - KF Tiranë 0-1(0-0)
Skënderbeu Korçë - Bylis Ballsh 1-1(0-0)
FK Kukësi - KF Laçi 3-1(1-1)
Teuta Durrës - Luftëtari Gjirokastër 1-1(1-0)
FK Partizani - Flamurtari Vlorë 2-0(0-0)

Round 22 [15-16.02.2020]
KF Tiranë - Skënderbeu Korçë 1-1(0-1)
KF Laçi - FK Partizani 1-3(1-2)
Bylis Ballsh - FK Kukësi 1-1(0-1)
Luftëtari Gjirok. - Flamurtari Vlorë 0-1(0-1)
Teuta Durrës - Vllaznia Shkodër 3-1(2-1)

Round 23 [21-22.02.2020]
FK Kukësi - KF Tiranë 1-2(0-0)
Vllaznia Shkodër - Luftëtari Gjirok. 4-0(1-0)
Flamurtari Vlorë - KF Laçi 1-3(0-2)
Skënderbeu Korçë - Teuta Durrës 3-2(2-1)
FK Partizani - Bylis Ballsh 2-2(2-1)

Round 24 [28-29.02.2020]
KF Tiranë - FK Partizani 5-1(2-1)
Vllaznia Shkodër - Skënderbeu Korçë 0-1(0-0)
Bylis Ballsh - Flamurtari Vlorë 0-0
Luftëtari Gjirokastër - KF Laçi 0-2(0-0)
Teuta Durrës - FK Kukësi 2-2(1-1)

Round 25 [04.03.2020]
KF Laçi - Bylis Ballsh 2-1(0-0)
Skënderbeu Korçë - Luftëtari Gjirok. 2-0(1-0)
FK Kukësi - Vllaznia Shkodër 0-0
FK Partizani - Teuta Durrës 0-1(0-0)
Flamurtari Vlorë - KF Tiranë 0-2(0-1)

Round 26 [08-09.03.2020]
Luftëtari Gjirokastër - Bylis Ballsh 1-1(1-1)
KF Tiranë - KF Laçi 1-0(0-0)
Teuta Durrës - Flamurtari Vlorë 1-1(0-1)
Vllaznia Shkodër - FK Partizani 1-0(1-0)
Skënderbeu Korçë - FK Kukësi 2-1(2-1)

Round 27 [03.06.2020]
FK Kukësi - Luftëtari Gjirokastër 2-1(1-0)
Flamurtari Vlorë - Vllaznia Shkodër 1-3(0-0)
KF Laçi - Teuta Durrës 1-1(1-1)
Bylis Ballsh - KF Tiranë 1-3(0-2)
FK Partizani - Skënderbeu Korçë 1-2(0-2)

Round 28 [07.06.2020]
Luftëtari Gjirokastër - KF Tiranë 0-5(0-3)
Bylis Ballsh - Teuta Durrës 1-0(0-0)
KF Laçi - Vllaznia Shkodër 5-2(2-0)
Flamurtari Vlorë - Skënderbeu Korçë 0-1(0-0)
FK Partizani - FK Kukësi 1-3(0-1)

Round 29 [14-15.06.2020]
FK Partizani - Luftëtari Gjirokastër 8-1(4-1)
FK Kukësi - Flamurtari Vlorë 4-1(3-0)
Vllaznia Shkodër - Bylis Ballsh 2-2(1-1)
Skënderbeu Korçë - KF Laçi 1-1(0-1)
Teuta Durrës - KF Tiranë 1-0(1-0)

Round 30 [19-20.06.2020]
KF Tiranë - Vllaznia Shkodër 3-0(2-0)
Flamurtari Vlorë - FK Partizani 1-2(1-1)
Luftëtari Gjirokastër - Teuta Durrës 1-5(0-0)
Bylis Ballsh - Skënderbeu Korçë 1-0(0-0)
KF Laçi - FK Kukësi 2-0(1-0)

Round 31 [27-28.06.2020]
FK Partizani - KF Laçi 1-0(1-0)
Flamurtari Vlorë - Luftëtari Gjirok. 6-1(2-0)
Vllaznia Shkodër - Teuta Durrës 0-3(0-1)
FK Kukësi - Bylis Ballsh 1-0(1-0)
Skënderbeu Korçë - KF Tiranë 1-2(1-0)

Round 32 [05-06.07.2020]
Luftëtari Gjirok. - Vllaznia Shkodër 0-1(0-1)
KF Laçi - Flamurtari Vlorë 2-1(0-0)
KF Tiranë - FK Kukësi 1-2(0-0)
Bylis Ballsh - FK Partizani 1-1(1-0)
Teuta Durrës - Skënderbeu Korçë 1-0(0-0)

Round 33 [10-11.07.2020]
Flamurtari Vlorë - Bylis Ballsh 2-3(1-1)
FK Partizani - KF Tiranë 1-1(0-0)
KF Laçi - Luftëtari Gjirokastër 3-1(2-0)
FK Kukësi - Teuta Durrës 3-0(3-0)
Skënderbeu Korçë - Vllaznia Shkodër 2-1(1-0)

Round 34 [18-19.07.2020]
Luftëtari Gjirok. - Skënderbeu Korçë 0-1(0-0)
KF Tiranë - Flamurtari Vlorë 2-0(1-0)
Bylis Ballsh - KF Laçi 0-3(0-2)
Vllaznia Shkodër - FK Kukësi 1-0(0-0)
Teuta Durrës - FK Partizani 0-0

Round 35 [24.07.2020]
KF Laçi - KF Tiranë 3-1(2-0)
Flamurtari Vlorë - Teuta Durrës 2-3(2-2)
FK Partizani - Vllaznia Shkodër 3-0(2-0)
Bylis Ballsh - Luftëtari Gjirokastër 2-0(2-0)
FK Kukësi - Skënderbeu Korçë 0-0

Round 36 [29.07.2020]
Luftëtari Gjirokastër - FK Kukësi 2-5(0-2)
Vllaznia Shkodër - Flamurtari Vlorë 1-1(0-0)
KF Tiranë - Bylis Ballsh 1-1(1-0)
Skënderbeu Korçë - FK Partizani 4-1(2-0)
Teuta Durrës - KF Laçi 2-3(1-2)

Final Standings

								Home					Away				
					Total												
1.	**KF Tiranë**	36	21	7	8	67 - 35	70	11	4	3	35 - 15	10	3	5	32 - 20
2.	FK Kukësi	36	19	9	8	59 - 31	66	12	4	2	32 - 12	7	5	6	27 - 19
3.	KF Laçi	36	19	7	10	61 - 34	64	13	2	3	37 - 14	6	5	7	24 - 20
4.	KF Skënderbeu Korçë	36	17	7	12	42 - 43	58	11	3	4	27 - 20	6	4	8	15 - 23
5.	KF Teuta Durrës	36	15	12	9	41 - 34	57	10	6	2	21 - 11	5	6	7	20 - 23
6.	FK Partizani Tiranë	36	15	8	13	51 - 40	53	9	5	4	30 - 15	6	3	9	21 - 25
7.	KF Bylis Ballsh	36	12	15	9	46 - 38	51	9	6	3	25 - 16	3	9	6	21 - 22
8.	KF Vllaznia Shkodër (*Relegation Play-off*)	36	12	10	14	36 - 41	46	6	5	7	18 - 16	6	5	7	18 - 25
9.	KS Flamurtari Vlorë (*Relegated*)	36	2	9	25	32 - 72	15	1	6	11	26 - 41	1	3	14	6 - 31
10.	Luftëtari Gjirokastër FC (*Relegated*)	36	2	8	26	19 - 86	14	2	5	11	10 - 33	0	3	15	9 - 53

Top goalscorers:	
24 **Kyrian Chinazorm Nwabueze (NGA)**	*KF Laçi*
22 Vasil Shkurti	*FK Kukësi*
14 Sherif Kallaku	*KF Teuta Durrës*
13 Michael Ayodeji Ngoo (ENG)	*KF Tiranë*
12 Redon Xhixha	*KF Laçi*

Relegation Play-off [02.08.2020]

KF Vllaznia Shkodër - KS Besëlidhja Lezhë   3-1(2-1)

NATIONAL CUP
Kupa e Shqipërisë 2019/2020

First Round [18.09./01-02.10.2019]

First Leg		Second Leg	
KF Apolonia Fier - FC Kamza	3-0 *awarded*	KS Kamza - KF Apolonia Fier	0-3 *awarded*
KS Burreli - KF Vllaznia Shkodër	0-1	KF Vllaznia Shkodër - KS Burreli	2-0
KF Turbina Cërrik - Luftëtari Gjirokastër FC	0-1	Luftëtari Gjirokastër FC - Turbina Cërrik	2-1
KF Devolli - KF Skënderbeu Korçë	1-4	KF Skënderbeu Korçë - KF Devolli	0-2
KF Egnatia Rrogozhinë - KS Besa Kavajë	0-1	KS Besa Kavajë - Egnatia Rrogozhine	2-0
KF Elbasani - KF Laçi	0-0	KF Laçi - KF Elbasani	4-0
KF Erzeni Shijak - FK Dinamo Tiranë	3-0	FK Dinamo Tiranë - KF Erzeni Shijak	0-1
KS Iliria Fushë-Krujë - KS Kastrioti Krujë	2-1	KS Kastrioti Krujë - KS Iliria Fushë-Krujë	1-0
KF Veleçiku Koplik - KS Flamurtari Vlorë	3-2	KS Flamurtari Vlorë - KF Veleçiku Koplik	5-0
KF Korabi Peshkopi - KS Besëlidhja Lezhë	2-1	KS Besëlidhja Lezhë - KF Korabi Peshkopi	1-0
KS Lushnja - KF Oriku	2-1	KF Oriku - KS Lushnja	0-2
KS Pogradeci - KF Bylis Ballsh	0-4	KF Bylis Ballsh - KS Pogradeci	1-2
FK Shënkolli - KF Tiranë	0-0	KF Tiranë - FK Shënkolli	4-0
KF Shkumbini - FK Kukësi	1-3	FK Kukësi - KF Shkumbini	6-0
KF Tërbuni Pukë - KF Teuta Durrës	0-2	KF Teuta Durrës - KF Tërbuni Pukë	6-2
FK Vore - FK Partizani Tiranë	0-3	FK Partizani Tiranë - FK Vore	1-0

1/8-Finals [29-30.01./12.02.2020]

First Leg		Second Leg	
KS Besëlidhja Lezhë - FK Partizani Tiranë	3-0	FK Partizani Tiranë - KS Besëlidhja Lezhë	3-1
KF Erzeni Shijak - KF Teuta Durrës	1-3	KF Teuta Durrës - KF Erzeni Shijak	3-1
KF Vllaznia Shkodër - KS Flamurtari Vlorë	2-2	KS Flamurtari Vlorë - KF Vllaznia Shkodër	0-2
KS Kastrioti Krujë - KF Tiranë	1-3	KF Tiranë - KS Kastrioti Krujë	4-0
KS Lushnja - FK Kukësi	0-1	FK Kukësi - KS Lushnja	3-0
KS Besa Kavajë - KF Skënderbeu Korçë	0-2	KF Skënderbeu Korçë - KS Besa Kavajë	1-0
KF Apolonia Fier - Luftëtari Gjirokastër FC	3-0	Luftëtari Gjirokastër FC - KF Apolonia Fier	0-0
KF Bylis Ballsh - KF Laçi	2-0	KF Laçi - KF Bylis Ballsh	3-2

Quarter-Finals [11/24.06.2020]

First Leg		Second Leg	
KF Tiranë - KS Besëlidhja Lezhë	5-1	KS Besëlidhja Lezhë - KF Tiranë	1-1
KF Vllaznia Shkodër - KF Teuta Durrës	2-2	KF Teuta Durrës - KF Vllaznia Shkodër	1-0
KF Apolonia Fier - FK Kukësi	1-2	FK Kukësi - KF Apolonia Fier	3-1
KF Bylis Ballsh - KF Skënderbeu Korçë	1-0	KF Skënderbeu Korçë - KF Bylis Ballsh	1-1

Semi-Finals [02/15.07.2020]

First Leg		Second Leg	
KF Bylis Ballsh - KF Tiranë	2-1	KF Tiranë - KF Bylis Ballsh	2-0
FK Kukësi - KF Teuta Durrës	0-0	KF Teuta Durrës - FK Kukësi	2-1

Final

02.08.2020; Air Albania Stadium, Tiranë; Referee: Eldorjan Hamiti; Attendance: None

KF Teuta Durrës - KF Tiranë　　　　　　　　　　　　　　　　　**2-0(1-0)**

Teuta Durrës: Stivi Frashëri, Renato Arapi, Rustem Hoxha, Blagoja Todorovski, Alexandros Kouros (80.Ledjo Beqja), Emiljano Vila, Albano Aleksi, Florent Avdyli (65.Arbër Çyrbja; 72.Ildi Gruda), Sherif Kallaku, Rubin Hebaj (80.Dejvid Kapllani), Lorenco Vila. Trainer: Shpëtim Kuçi.

KF Tiranë: Ilion Lika, Marsel Ismajlgeci, Gentian Muça, Erion Hoxhallari, Kristi Vangjeli, Lancinet Sidibe (59.Erando Karabeci), Edon Hasani (50.Mario Beshiraj), Winful Cobbinah (87.Andri Stafa), Idriz Batha, Michael Ngoo, Agustin Gonzalo Torassa. Trainer: Julian Ahmataj.

Goals: 1-0 Rustem Hoxha (2), 2-0 Lorenco Vila (78).

Klubi i Futbollit Bylis Ballsh

Founded: 1972
Stadium: Stadiumi „Adush Muça", Ballsh (5,200)
Trainer: Veljko Dovedan (SRB)   01.06.1954

Goalkeepers:	DOB	M	(s)	G
Isli Hidi	15.10.1980	33		7
Festim Miraka	31.12.1987	3		
Defenders:	**DOB**	**M**	**(s)**	**G**
Ditmar Bicaj	26.02.1989	14	(1)	
Jurgen Goxha	29.12.1992	24	(1)	5
Andi Hadroj	22.02.1999	22	(1)	
Stivian Janku	23.06.1997	19	(6)	1
Eljan Mehmetaj	08.09.2001	1		
Ardit Peposhi	14.03.1993	27	(4)	2
Silvester Shkalla	10.08.1995	16		
Vicente de Paula Mercedes (BRA)	02.03.1996	5	(1)	
Vasilios Zogos (GRE)	29.07.1999	1	(1)	
Midfielders:	**DOB**	**M**	**(s)**	**G**
Kevin Aliaj	05.08.1999		(1)	
Angel González Zuluaga (ARG)	03.10.1995	1	(1)	
Fabián Nicolás Muñoz (ARG)	03.11.1991	4	(2)	
Valentino Murataj	15.08.1996	33		3
Edison Ndreca	05.07.1994	23	(2)	3
Odirah Franklin Ntephe (NGA)	26.09.1993	31	(1)	4
Fredrick Opoku (GHA)	19.09.1997		(3)	
Eridon Qardaku	10.08.2000	14	(13)	2
Daniel Saliaj	07.05.2002	1		
Alaidin Sallaku	04.02.1995	1	(5)	1
Eltun Turabov (AZE)	18.02.1997	7	(1)	
Serxho Ujka	27.08.1998	10	(14)	
Forwards:	**DOB**	**M**	**(s)**	**G**
Amos Beji Anthony (NGA)	04.01.1999	1	(2)	
Mario Barjamaj	27.06.1998	18	(7)	
Diego Adrián Celis (ARG)	22.03.1992	2	(11)	1
Saliou Guindo (MLI)	12.09.1996	26		10
Ardit Jaupaj	06.06.1996		(1)	
Flosard Malçi	23.12.1994	7	(5)	2
Michel Vaillant Mbiobe Mouegni (CMR)	03.02.1996		(3)	
Donald Mëllugja	31.05.1995	32		1
Emiliano Gastón Mozzone Sueiro (URU)	23.04.1998	8	(5)	4
Majkel Peci	29.08.1996		(12)	
Franc Ymeralilaj	14.01.1995	12		

Klubi Sportiv Flamurtari Vlorë

Founded: 23.03.1923 (*as Shoqeria Sportive Vlorë*)
Stadium: Stadiumi Flamurtari, Vlorë (8,500)
Trainer: Dritan Sadedini   24.12.1971
[24.10.2019] Luan Birçe   04.09.1961
[06.01.2020] Marcello Troisi Moreira (BRA)   09.03.1976

Goalkeepers:	DOB	M	(s)	G
Saugli Alimuçaj	03.06.2002		(1)	
Aldo Bushi	22.04.2001	1		
Shpejtim Mocka	20.10.1989	35		
Defenders:	**DOB**	**M**	**(s)**	**G**
Gerardo Ballaj	23.10.2001	2	(2)	
Vangjel Gjipali	17.11.2002		(1)	
Olsi Goçaj	30.09.1989	26		
Lirim Mema (KVX)	23.01.1998	2	(1)	
Denis Pjeshka	28.05.1995	26		2
Arinaldo Rrapaj	09.08.2001	25	(9)	
Giorgos Sarris (GRE)	08.09.1989	4	(1)	
Valto Zeqaj	24.08.1995	15		
Midfielders:	**DOB**	**M**	**(s)**	**G**
Semir Bajraktarević (BIH)	14.10.1987	5	(1)	
Carlos Henrique Ramos (BRA)	24.04.1996	8		1
Fjoralb Deliaj	04.04.1997	13	(1)	
Shaqir Haruni	27.05.1999	13	(16)	2
Odaildo Souza de Oliveira „Índio" (BRA)	01.02.1994	11		2
Kenviol Kreshpa	14.10.2000	6	(16)	
Romeo Llapi	31.01.2002		(2)	
Lucas Ramos de Oliveira (BRA)	18.01.1995	15		
Reinaldo Mukoj	05.09.2001	1	(3)	
Kreshnik Nebihu (KVX)	18.06.1997	24	(3)	1
Ansi Nika	22.08.1990	4	(3)	1
Jurgen Vrapi	14.11.1998	18	(6)	1
Forwards:	**DOB**	**M**	**(s)**	**G**
Denis Aliaj	22.01.2002	1	(3)	
Arbion Balilaj	27.07.2000	2	(11)	
Elian Çelaj	03.02.1999	1	(6)	
Gersi Diamanti	15.10.1999	3	(11)	1
Amarildo Elmazaj	04.08.2001		(1)	
Ardit Hoxhaj	20.07.1994	31	(2)	8
Altjon Kadriaj	05.05.2002	1	(3)	
Ariel Muçollari	19.04.2001	27	(3)	
Bajram Nebihi (GER)	05.08.1988	5	(2)	1
Mateo Qarri	05.05.1999	22	(1)	
Ledjon Qelaj	05.11.2001		(2)	
Andi Ribaj	21.11.1989	27		6
Xhevair Sukaj	05.10.1987	10	(1)	4
Jurgen Vatnikaj	08.08.1995	9	(6)	1
Welder de Jesus Costa (BRA)	26.12.1994	1		

Futboll Klub Kukësi

Founded: 04.03.1930
Stadium: Stadiumi Kamëz, Kukës (5,500)
Trainer: Shpëtim Duro   24.12.1959
[02.03.2020] Orges Shehi   25.09.1977

Goalkeepers:	DOB	M	(s)	G
Ilir Avdyli (KVX)	20.05.1990	7		
Dashamir Xhika	23.05.1989	29		
Defenders:	**DOB**	**M**	**(s)**	**G**
Kledis Hida	26.03.2001		(2)	
Blerim Kotobelli	10.08.1992	8	(8)	
Gëzim Krasniqi	05.01.1990	6	(5)	
Bruno Lulaj	02.04.1995	15	(16)	
Erhun Obanor (NGA)	05.09.1995	26		
Olsi Teqja	27.07.1988	29	(2)	
Midfielders:	**DOB**	**M**	**(s)**	**G**
Oumar Camara (GUI)	01.09.1998		(2)	
Valon Ethemi	03.10.1997	27	(4)	6
Enis Gavazaj	21.03.1995	27	(9)	2
Tome Kitanovski (MKD)	21.05.1992	11	(2)	
Edis Malikji (MKD)	04.05.1995	32	(1)	
Besar Musolli (KVX)	28.02.1989	31		1
Emiljano Musta	31.01.1992	23	(4)	2
Eduart Rroca	28.07.1993	29	(4)	4
Forwards:	**DOB**	**M**	**(s)**	**G**
Kristal Abazaj	06.07.1996	31	(3)	10
Marko Cema	16.01.1998		(8)	1
Godberg Cooper (ITA)	20.08.1997	3	(8)	3
Mirlind Daku (KVX)	01.01.1998	2	(11)	1
Fluturim Domi	14.10.2000		(5)	1
Vesel Limaj (GER)	01.12.1996	31	(1)	3
Arena Mateli	10.07.2000		(2)	
Vasil Shkurti	27.04.1992	29	(1)	22

Klubi i Futbollit Laçi

Founded: 1960
Stadium: Stadiumi Laçi, Laçi (2,300)
Trainer: Sulejman Starova   12.12.1955
[14.10.2019]   Armando Cungu   23.04.1973

Goalkeepers:	DOB	M	(s)	G
Edmir Sali	07.08.1997	1		
Dimitru Stajila (MDA)	02.08.1991	35		
Defenders:	**DOB**	**M**	**(s)**	**G**
Irlian Ceka	03.03.1998	1		
David Domgjonas	21.05.1997	18		
Abdurraman Fangaj	12.10.1997	29		
Eglentin Gjoni	02.12.1992	19	(1)	
Aleksandar Ignjatović (SRB)	11.04.1988	34		2
Endrit Marku	22.02.2001	2	(1)	
Donald Rapo	04.10.1990	12	(5)	3
Adolf Selmani	26.06.2000	10	(1)	1
Florian Trokthi	26.06.2001	2	(2)	
Rudolf Turkaj	03.02.1995	25	(5)	2
Midfielders:	**DOB**	**M**	**(s)**	**G**
Elvi Berisha	02.03.1999	1	(8)	
Ardit Deliu	26.10.1997	33	(2)	1
Aldo Elmazi	01.02.2000		(1)	

	DOB	M	(s)	G
Damian Gjini	06.04.1995		(2)	
Bedri Greca	23.10.1990	16	(2)	1
Regi Lushkja	17.05.1996	31	(1)	4
Albion Marku	14.10.2000	4	(6)	1
Juljan Shehu	06.09.1998	33		2
Teco (BRA)	26.06.1995	22	(4)	6
Ersil Ymeraj	06.07.1994		(5)	
Alexandros Zaimi (GRE)	19.01.1998	1	(1)	
Forwards:	**DOB**	**M**	**(s)**	**G**
Arber Bytyqi	16.10.2003		(2)	
Flosard Malçi	23.12.1994		(8)	
Kyrian Chinazorm Nwabueze (NGA)	12.11.1992	31		24
Fatmir Prengaj	01.05.2001		(12)	1
Renato Spahiu (GRE)	14.12.1998		(3)	
Uendi Veçaj	18.02.1997	1	(5)	
Redon Xhixha	14.07.1998	34	(1)	12
Dembakwi Yomba (USA)	04.09.1996	1	(1)	

Luftëtari Gjirokastër Football Club

Founded: 1929 (*as Shqiponja Gjirokastër*)
Stadium: Stadiumi Gjirokastra, Gjirokastër (8,400)
Trainer: Klevis Dalipi   13.03.1976
[23.08.2019]   Klodian Duro   21.12.1977
[06.09.2019]   Georgios Marantas (GRE)   05.08.1973
[14.12.2019]   Dritan Kristidhi   19.05.1974
[29.12.2019]   Neritan Novi   03.09.1970

Goalkeepers:	DOB	M	(s)	G
Sadik Basha	04.06.2002	3		
Panagiotis Paiteris (GRE)	14.07.1997	11		
Avernold Qyrani	20.04.1998	10	(1)	
Arlis Shala	16.07.2000	12		
Defenders:	**DOB**	**M**	**(s)**	**G**
Klaus Alinani	03.03.2002	3	(4)	
Mikel Brahilika	05.08.1999	2	(8)	
Aurel Demo	20.10.1996	16	(2)	
Redon Dragoshi	18.03.2000	21	(2)	
Cerezo Hilgen (NED)	03.05.1994	1	(1)	
Enes Isufi	14.07.2000	24	(2)	
Antonis Karabinas (GRE)	12.01.1998		(1)	
Armenis Kukaj	11.08.1997	18	(1)	
Franc Lala	11.07.1999	24	(2)	
Stiven Puci	03.05.1998	7	(11)	
Donald Rapo	04.10.1990	14	(2)	2
Kabir Tahiraga	09.06.1999		(4)	
Regild Zeneli	29.06.1996		(6)	
Midfielders:	**DOB**	**M**	**(s)**	**G**
Donaldo Açka	17.09.1997	24		1

	DOB	M	(s)	G
Alvi Ahmetaj	12.07.1998	2	(6)	
Amer Duka	21.01.1999	13		
Apostol Furxhiu (GRE)	14.12.1995		(1)	
Erald Hyseni	12.11.1999	23	(4)	
Gresild Lika	02.11.1997	27	(3)	6
Bastri Malaj	29.09.2002	4	(1)	
Muharrem Malaj	06.06.2002		(2)	
Aldrit Oshafi	26.03.2000	14	(9)	1
Paraskevas Prikas (GRE)	17.11.1998	9	(1)	
Klinti Qato	23.12.1997	20	(2)	
Forwards:	**DOB**	**M**	**(s)**	**G**
Joan Çela	06.01.2000	13	(7)	2
Elian Çelaj	03.02.1999	8	(5)	
Jurgen Dushkaj	09.06.1995	28		
Serxhio Emini	03.12.2002		(1)	
Realdo Fili	14.05.1996	11	(3)	3
Rimal Haxhiu	04.03.1999	4	(8)	2
Arber Mehmetllari	19.04.2000	14	(1)	2
Anti Renia	06.01.1993	9	(1)	
Angelmo Vyent (NED)	04.09.1991	4	(7)	
Ardit Ziaj	08.03.2000	3	(10)	

Futboll Klub Partizani Tiranë

Founded: 04.02.1946
Stadium: Stadiumi "Selman Stërmasi", Tiranë (9,600)
Trainer: Franco Lerda (ITA)   19.08.1967
[04.01.2020]   Adolfo Sormani (ITA)   11.08.1965
[13.07.2020]   Renaldo Kalari   25.06.1984

Goalkeepers:	DOB	M	(s)	G
Alban Hoxha	23.11.1987	32		
Livio Malaj	25.05.2001	1		
Aldo Teqja	04.05.1995	3		
Defenders:	**DOB**	**M**	**(s)**	**G**
Egzon Belica (MKD)	03.09.1990	32		2
Amir Bilali	15.05.1994	1	(1)	
Eneo Bitri	26.08.1996	25	(2)	3
Deian Boldor (ROU)	03.02.1995	20	(2)	
Agim Dajçi	27.07.2000	2		
Ersin Hakaj	06.12.1996	6	(5)	
Hektor Idrizaj	15.04.1989	25	(2)	
Lorenc Trashi	19.05.1992	32		2
William Cordeiro Melo (BRA)	15.07.1993	30	(1)	7
Midfielders:	**DOB**	**M**	**(s)**	**G**
Jurgen Bardhi	06.11.1997	30	(2)	3
Ron Broja (KVX)	09.04.1996	25	(5)	2

	DOB	M	(s)	G
Besnik Ferati (MKD)	19.04.2000	5	(10)	1
Alessio Hyseni	04.01.1997	1		
Eneid Kodra	04.11.1999	3	(3)	
Kristi Kote	26.09.1998	3	(7)	
Kevi Llanaj	09.04.1999	5	(4)	
Esat Mala	18.10.1998	15	(4)	1
Hermes Aristóteles Romero Espinoza (VEN)	18.10.1995	7	(7)	
Bruno Telushi	14.11.1990	30	(3)	5
Forwards:	**DOB**	**M**	**(s)**	**G**
Jasir Asani	19.05.1995	11	(3)	3
Brian Brown (JAM)	29.12.1992	8	(21)	1
Tedi Cara	15.04.2000	1	(7)	1
Eraldo Cinari	11.10.1996	27	(4)	10
Joseph Ansah Ekuban (GHA)	02.01.2000		(1)	
Dorian Kërçiku	30.08.1993		(1)	
Theophilus Solomon (NGA)	18.01.1996	16	(9)	6

Klubi Futbollistik Skënderbeu Korçë

Founded:	1925		
Stadium:	Stadiumi Skënderbeu, Korçë (12,343)		
Trainer:	Ilir Daja		20.10.1966

Goalkeepers:	DOB	M	(s)	G
Mario Dajsinani	23.12.1998		(1)	
Enea Koliçi	13.02.1986	36		
Defenders:	**DOB**	**M**	**(s)**	**G**
Eni Imami	19.12.1992	16	(1)	
Bajram Jashanica (KVX)	25.09.1990	11	(1)	1
Jorgo Meksi	21.03.1995	28		
Alfred Mensah (NED)	14.09.1996	7	(8)	2
Jean-Jacques Ndecky (SEN)	10.01.1997	13	(2)	1
Marvin Turtulli	17.10.1994	4	(2)	
Kosta Vangjeli (GRE)	21.07.2000	2	(2)	
Leonat Vitija (KVX)	22.08.2000	2	(3)	
Midfielders:	**DOB**	**M**	**(s)**	**G**
Elvi Berisha	02.03.1999	1	(5)	
Asion Daja	14.03.1990	28		
Bruno Dita	18.02.1993	32	(1)	6

Randy Dwumfour (GHA)	23.11.2000	2	(5)	
Agon Elezi (MKD)	01.03.2001	16	(6)	
Emmanuel Essien (GHA)	02.07.2001	5	(3)	
Nazmi Gripshi	05.07.1997	36		8
Uerdi Mara	30.01.1999	7	(14)	
Arbnor Muja (KVX)	29.11.1998	2	(7)	1
Gjergj Muzaka	26.09.1984	5		
Jorgo Pëllumbi	15.07.2000	29	(2)	
Artim Položani (MKD)	25.06.1982	27	(4)	1
Šçiprim Taipi	19.02.1997	20	(9)	1
Forwards:	**DOB**	**M**	**(s)**	**G**
Dejvi Bregu	24.10.1995	34		10
Otto John (NGA)	25.01.1998	5	(12)	1
Blerim Krasniqi	05.07.1996	26	(6)	8
Belajdi Pusi	23.01.1998	2	(5)	1

Klubi Futbollit Teuta Durrës

Founded:	1920		
Stadium:	Stadiumi"Niko Dovana", Durrës (13,000)		
Trainer:	Bledi Shkëmbi		13.08.1979
[15.12.2019]	Eduard Martini		02.01.1975

Goalkeepers:	DOB	M	(s)	G
Bobi Celeski (MKD)	10.06.1997	2		
Stivi Frashëri	29.08.1990	34		
Defenders:	**DOB**	**M**	**(s)**	**G**
Renato Arapi	28.09.1986	29	(1)	1
Rustem Hoxha	04.07.1991	32		2
Kenan Hreljić (BIH)	01.12.1997	6	(4)	
Artan Jazxhi	06.07.2001	1	(2)	
Alexandros Kouros (GRE)	21.08.1993	34		
Silvester Shkalla	10.08.1995	4		
Blagoja Todorovski (MKD)	11.06.1985	32		1
Midfielders:	**DOB**	**M**	**(s)**	**G**
Albano Aleksi	10.10.1992	30		1
Florent Avdyli (KVX)	10.07.1993	27	(5)	3
Fabjan Beqja	15.02.1994	8	(11)	
Ledjo Beqja	18.06.2001	1	(7)	

Arbër Çyrbja	18.09.1993	20	(4)	2
Roni Gashi (KVX)	04.06.1998	6	(6)	
Sherif Kallaku	01.03.1998	29	(3)	14
Sebastian Salillari	18.01.2001		(1)	
Emiljano Vila	12.03.1988	29	(6)	5
Forwards:	**DOB**	**M**	**(s)**	**G**
Abdul Khalid Basit (GHA)	10.08.1996	7	(2)	
Ildi Gruda	13.02.1999	1	(15)	
Rubin Hebaj	30.07.1998	9	(6)	2
Idelino Gomes Colubali (GNB)	01.01.1994	6	(2)	1
Arlind Kalaja	27.12.1995	3	(9)	
Dejvid Kapllani	03.06.2001	3	(10)	
Darko Nikač (MNE)	15.09.1990	13	(4)	1
Uendi Veçaj	18.02.1997	7	(5)	1
Lorenco Vila	14.12.1998	23	(5)	7

Klubi i Futbollit Tirana

Founded:	15.08.1920 (*as Shoqata Sportive Agimi*)		
Stadium:	Stadiumi"Selman Stërmasi", Tiranë (9,600)		
Trainer:	Ardian Mema		16.11.1971
[26.10.2019]	Julian Ahmataj		24.05.1979
[09.12.2019]	Ndubuisi Emmanuel Egbo (NGA)		25.07.1973

Goalkeepers:	DOB	M	(s)	G
Edvan Bakaj	20.07.1987	5	(1)	
Ilion Lika	17.05.1980	31		
Defenders:	**DOB**	**M**	**(s)**	**G**
Albi Doka	26.06.1997	26	(4)	
Erion Hoxhallari	15.10.1995	30		1
Eni Imami	19.12.1992	9	(2)	
Marsel Ismajlgeci	14.03.2000	13	(8)	1
Gentian Muça	13.05.1987	20	(7)	1
Tefik Osmani	08.06.1985	16	(2)	
Kristi Vangjeli	05.09.1985	30	(2)	1
Midfielders:	**DOB**	**M**	**(s)**	**G**
Idriz Batha	28.03.1992	32	(1)	10
Alban Çejku	23.07.2001		(1)	
Jurgen Çelhaka	06.12.2000	24	(4)	
Winful Cobbinah (GHA)	06.09.1991	32	(2)	7

Edon Hasani	09.01.1992	14	(11)	7
Erando Karabeci	06.09.1988	8	(7)	
Eldis Kraja	22.03.2000		(2)	
Lancinet Sidibe (GUI)	01.01.1997	3	(9)	
Andri Stafa	14.02.2002		(2)	
Forwards:	**DOB**	**M**	**(s)**	**G**
Mario Beshiraj	29.10.1999		(4)	
Élton Pereira Gomes „Calé" (BRA)	12.07.1988	27	(1)	4
Ismael Salim Dunga (KEN)	24.02.1993	3	(11)	4
Grent Halili	24.05.1998	14	(10)	3
Dorian Kërçiku	30.08.1993	2	(2)	
Mario Morina	16.10.1992		(4)	
Ernest Muci	19.03.2001	7	(13)	7
Michael Ngoo (ENG)	22.10.1992	28	(3)	13
Agustin Gonzalo Torassa (ARG)	20.10.1988	22	(3)	6

<table>
<tr><td colspan="5">

Klubi I Futbollit Vllaznia Shkodër

</td><td colspan="4">

Founded: 16.02.1919 (*as Shoqëria Sportive Vllaznia*)
Stadium: Stadiumi "Loro Boriçi", Shkodër (16,022)
Trainer: Mirsad Jonuz (MKD)   09.04.1962
[09.06.2020]   Hysen Dedja   16.10.1960

</td></tr>
</table>

Goalkeepers:	DOB	M	(s)	G				
Andreja Efremov (MKD)	02.09.1992	8			Hygor Guimarães Gonçalves (BRA)	05.01.1989	18	(3)	4
Ted Laço	01.02.1995	1			Arsid Kruja	08.06.1993	22	(8)	1
Alen Sherri	15.12.1997	27			Ardit Krymi	02.05.1996	29	(3)	3
Defenders:	**DOB**	**M**	**(s)**	**G**	Gilman Lika	13.01.1987	32	(4)	10
Mevlan Adili (MKD)	30.03.1994	15	(1)	1	Wenderson da Silva Soares „Maranhão"(BRA)	19.05.1992	3	(7)	1
Maxim Cojocaru (MDA)	29.10.1999		(4)		Herald Marku	18.05.1996	27	(6)	
Filip Gligorov (MKD)	31.07.1993	24			Behar Ramadani	06.04.1990	18	(1)	
Erdenis Gurishta	24.04.1995	32		2	Serjan Repaj	05.09.2000		(7)	
Elmir Lekaj	18.01.2000	2	(6)		Eugeniu Sidorenco (MDA)	19.03.1989	11	(5)	3
Renato Malota	24.06.1989	30		2	Silvio Zogaj	25.07.1997	16	(10)	2
Aleksandar Ristevski (MKD)	11.05.1992	1	(3)		**Forwards:**	**DOB**	**M**	**(s)**	**G**
Samet Ruqi	10.05.1995		(2)		Emerson Brito dos Santos (BRA)	08.07.1991	5	(3)	
Dajan Shehi	19.03.1997	25	(7)		Simeon Hristov (MKD)	04.09.1992	3	(1)	
Godfrey Walusimbi (UGA)	03.07.1989	5	(3)		Belajdi Pusi	23.01.1998		(4)	
Midfielders:	**DOB**	**M**	**(s)**	**G**	Ndricim Shtubina	18.03.1987	24	(9)	2
Florind Bardulla	19.11.1992	4	(11)		Sílvio Rodrigues Pereira Júnior (BRA)	04.05.1994	14	(2)	4

SECOND LEVEL
Albanian First Division / Kategoria e Parë 2019/2020

Group A

1.	KS Kastrioti Krujë	16	11	4	1	19 - 4	37
2.	KS Besëlidhja Lezhë	16	8	4	4	19 - 12	28
3.	KF Korabi Peshkopi	16	8	1	7	16 - 15	25
4.	KF Erzeni Shijak	16	7	4	5	18 - 10	25
5.	KS Burreli	16	6	6	4	17 - 16	24
6.	KF Egnatia Rrogozhinë	16	4	7	5	14 - 13	19
7.	KF Tërbuni Pukë	16	3	6	7	11 - 16	15
8.	KF Veleçiku Koplik	16	3	4	9	11 - 22	13
9.	FK Dinamo Tiranë	16	3	2	11	9 - 26	11
10.	KF Shkumbini (*Excluded from the league*)						

Please note: KF Shkumbini (3 points deducted) were excluded from the league and relegated due to violent incidents during their match in Round 11.

Group B

1.	KS Pogradeci	18	12	3	3	30 - 15	39
2.	KF Apolonia Fier	18	11	4	3	36 - 14	37
3.	KS Lushnja	18	11	2	5	30 - 18	35
4.	KS Besa Kavajë	18	8	3	7	28 - 24	27
5.	KF Oriku	18	6	6	6	12 - 15	24
6.	KF Devolli	18	7	3	8	29 - 30	24
7.	KS Iliria Fushë-Krujë	18	4	6	8	18 - 23	18
8.	KF Shënkolli	18	3	8	7	17 - 28	17
9.	KF Turbina Cërrik	18	4	4	10	14 - 26	16
10.	KF Elbasani	18	4	1	13	14 - 35	13

Top-4 of each group were qualified for the Promotion Round, while teams ranked 5-10 qualified for the Relegation Round.

Relegation Round

Group A

1.	KF Egnatia Rrogozhinë	24	7	10	7	21 - 19	31
2.	KS Burreli	24	8	7	9	23 - 25	31
3.	FK Dinamo Tiranë	24	8	3	13	20 - 29	27
4.	KF Veleçiku Koplik (*Relegation Play-off*)	24	6	7	11	21 - 30	25
5.	KF Tërbuni Pukë (*Excluded and Relegated*)	24	5	8	11	20 - 33	23

Please note: KF Tërbuni Pukë were excluded from the league and relegated due to violent incidents during their match in Round 22.

Group B

1.	KF Oriku	28	11	7	10	22 - 25	40
2.	KF Turbina Cërrik	28	11	5	12	39 - 35	38
3.	KF Elbasani	28	12	1	15	42 - 50	37
4.	KF Devolli (*Relegation Play-off*)	28	10	4	14	39 - 43	34
5.	KS Iliria Fushë-Krujë (*Relegated*)	28	9	6	13	35 - 44	33
6.	KF Shënkolli (*Relegated*)	28	3	9	16	31 - 64	18

Relegation Play-off [04-05.08.2020]

KF Veleçiku Koplik – KF Maliqi	2-1(0-0)
KF Devolli - FK Partizani Tiranë "B"	3-4(1-2,2-2)

Both KF Veleçiku Koplik and FK Partizani Tiranë "B"will play next season at Second Level.

Promotion Round

Group A

1.	KS Kastrioti Krujë (*Promoted*)	22	14	5	3	29	-	13	47
2.	KS Besëlidhja Lezhë (*Promotion Play-off*)	22	11	6	5	30	-	19	39
3.	KF Korabi Peshkopi	22	11	3	8	26	-	22	36
4.	KF Erzeni Shijak	22	7	5	10	25	-	25	26

Group B

1.	KF Apolonia Fier (*Promoted*)	24	15	6	3	55	-	26	51
2.	KS Pogradeci (*Promotion Play-off*)	24	14	4	6	39	-	24	46
3.	KS Lushnja	24	14	2	8	42	-	29	44
4.	KS Besa Kavajë	24	9	4	11	42	-	46	31

Promotion Play-off [29.07.2020, Elbasan]

KS Besëlidhja Lezhë - KS Pogradeci	3-2(1-1)

First Division Final [22.07.2020, Elbasan]

KS Kastrioti Krujë - KF Apolonia Fier	1-2(1-1)

First Division Champions 2019/2020: **KF Apolonia Fier**

NATIONAL TEAM

INTERNATIONAL MATCHES
(16.07.2019 – 15.07.2020)

07.09.2019	Paris	France - Albania	4-1(2-0)	(ECQ)
10.09.2019	Elbasan	Albania - Iceland	4-2(1-0)	(ECQ)
11.10.2019	İstanbul	Turkey - Albania	1-0(0-0)	(ECQ)
14.10.2019	Chişinău	Moldova - Albania	0-4(0-3)	(ECQ)
14.11.2019	Elbasan	Albania - Andorra	2-2(1-1)	(ECQ)
17.11.2019	Tiranë	Albania - France	0-2(0-1)	(ECQ)

07.09.2019   FRANCE - ALBANIA   **4-1(2-0)**   16th EC. Qualifiers
Stade de France, Saint-Denis, Paris, Referee: Jesús Gil Manzano (Spain); Attendance: 77,655
ALB: Thomas Strakosha, Mërgim Mavraj (Cap), Elseid Gëzim Hysaj, Berat Ridvan Gjimshiti, Ardian Ilmi Ismajli, Amir Malush Abrashi (73.Taulant Ragip Xhaka), Odise Roshi, Keidi Bare, Ylber Latif Ramadani (53.Klaus Fatmir Gjasula), Bekim Abdyl Balaj (62.Sokol Cikalleshi), Myrto Artan Uzuni. Trainer: Edoardo Reja (Italy).
Goal: Sokol Cikalleshi (90 penalty).

10.09.2019   ALBANIA - ICELAND   **4-2(1-0)**   16th EC. Qualifiers
Elbasan Arena, Elbasan; Referee: Ivan Kružliak (Slovakia); Attendance: 8,652
ALB: Thomas Strakosha, Ermir Limon Lenjani (62.Odise Roshi), Elseid Gëzim Hysaj (Cap) (72.Amir Malush Abrashi), Berat Ridvan Gjimshiti (66.Frédéric Shtjefan Veseli), Kastriot Luan Dermaku, Ardian Ilmi Ismajli, Ledian Memushaj, Klaus Fatmir Gjasula, Keidi Bare, Sokol Cikalleshi, Rey Aldo Manaj. Trainer: Edoardo Reja (Italy).
Goals: Kastriot Luan Dermaku (32), Elseid Gëzim Hysaj (52), Odise Roshi (79), Sokol Cikalleshi (83).

11.10.2019   TURKEY - ALBANIA   **1-0(0-0)**   16th EC. Qualifiers
„Şükrü Saracoğlu" Stadyumu, İstanbul; Referee: Ovidiu Alin Haţegan (Romania); Attendance: 41,438
ALB: Thomas Strakosha, Ermir Limon Lenjani (57.Odise Roshi), Frédéric Shtjefan Veseli, Berat Ridvan Gjimshiti, Kastriot Luan Dermaku, Ardian Ilmi Ismajli, Ledian Memushaj (Cap) (72.Amir Malush Abrashi), Klaus Fatmir Gjasula, Keidi Bare, Sokol Cikalleshi (84.Bekim Abdyl Balaj), Rey Aldo Manaj. Trainer: Edoardo Reja (Italy).

14.10.2019   MOLDOVA - ALBANIA   **0-4(0-3)**   16th EC. Qualifiers
Stadionul Zimbru, Chişinău; Referee: Chris Kavanagh (England); Attendance: 4,367
ALB: Thomas Strakosha, Frédéric Shtjefan Veseli, Berat Ridvan Gjimshiti, Kastriot Luan Dermaku, Lorenc Trashi, Ardian Ilmi Ismajli (89.Marash Kumbulla), Amir Malush Abrashi (Cap), Klaus Fatmir Gjasula, Keidi Bare (89.Lindon Selahi), Sokol Cikalleshi (76.Odise Roshi), Rey Aldo Manaj. Trainer: Edoardo Reja (Italy).
Goals: Sokol Cikalleshi (22), Keidi Bare (34), Lorenc Trashi (40), Rey Aldo Manaj (90).

14.11.2019   ALBANIA - ANDORRA   **2-2(1-1)**   16th EC. Qualifiers
Elbasan Arena, Elbasan; Referee: Kristo Tohver (Estonia); Attendance: 4,260
ALB: Etrit Fadil Berisha, Frédéric Shtjefan Veseli, Berat Ridvan Gjimshiti, Lorenc Trashi (46.Elseid Gëzim Hysaj), Ardian Ilmi Ismajli, Odise Roshi, Ledian Memushaj (Cap), Emanuele Ndoj (60.Keidi Bare), Ylber Latif Ramadani (73.Taulant Fatmir Seferi), Bekim Abdyl Balaj, Rey Aldo Manaj. Trainer: Edoardo Reja (Italy).
Goals: Bekim Abdyl Balaj (6), Rey Aldo Manaj (55).

17.11.2019   ALBANIA - FRANCE   **0-2(0-1)**   16th EC. Qualifiers
Air Albania Stadium, Tiranë; Referee: Slavko Vinčić (Slovenia); Attendance: 19,228
ALB: Etrit Fadil Berisha, Ermir Limon Lenjani (46.Odise Roshi), Frédéric Shtjefan Veseli, Elseid Gëzim Hysaj (Cap) (82.Lorenc Trashi), Berat Ridvan Gjimshiti, Kastriot Luan Dermaku, Klaus Fatmir Gjasula, Kristi Qose (46.Ledian Memushaj), Keidi Bare, Bekim Abdyl Balaj, Rey Aldo Manaj. Trainer: Edoardo Reja (Italy).

NATIONAL TEAM PLAYERS
(16.07.2019 – 15.07.2020)

Name	DOB	Caps	Goals	2019/2020:	Club
Goalkeepers					
Etrit Fadil BERISHA	10.03.1989	59	0	2019:	SPAL Ferrara (ITA)
Thomas STRAKOSHA	19.03.1995	12	0	2019:	SS Lazio Roma (ITA)
Defenders					
Kastriot Luan DERMAKU	15.01.1992	7	1	2019:	Parma Calcio 1913 (ITA)
Berat Ridvan GJIMSHITI	19.02.1993	29	1	2019:	Atalanta Bergamasca Calcio (ITA)
Elseid Gëzim HYSAJ	02.02.1994	52	1	2019:	SSC Napoli (ITA)
Ardian Ilmi ISMAJLI	30.09.1996	11	0	2019:	HNK Hajduk Split (CRO)
Marash KUMBULLA	08.02.2000	1	0	2019:	Hellas Verona FC (ITA)
Ermir Limon LENJANI	05.08.1989	33	3	2019:	FC Sion (SUI)
Mërgim MAVRAJ	09.06.1986	50	3	2019:	SpVgg Greuther Fürth (GER)
Lorenc TRASHI	19.05.1992	3	1	2019:	FK Partizani Tiranë
Frédéric Shtjefan VESELI	20.11.1992	26	0	2019:	Empoli FC (ITA)
Midfielders					
Amir Malush ABRASHI	27.03.1990	35	1	2019:	SC Freiburg (GER)
Keidi BARE	28.08.1997	7	1	2019:	Málaga CF (ESP)
Klaus Fatmir GJASULA	14.12.1989	5	0	2019:	SC Paderborn 07 (GER)
Ledian MEMUSHAJ	07.12.1986	40	1	2019:	Delfino Pescara 1936 (ITA)
Emanuele NDOJ	20.11.1996	6	1	2019:	Brescia Calcio (ITA)
Kristi QOSE	10.06.1995	3	0	2019:	MFK Ružomberok (SVK)
Ylber Latif RAMADANI	12.04.1996	7	1	2019:	Vejle BK (DEN)
Odise ROSHI	22.05.1991	57	5	2019:	FK Akhmat Grozny (RUS)
Lindon SELAHI	26.02.1999	1	0	2019:	FC Twente Enschede (NED)
Taulant Ragip XHAKA	28.03.1991	31	1	2019:	FC Basel (SUI)
Forwards					
Bekim Abdyl BALAJ	11.01.1991	37	7	2019:	SK Sturm Graz (AUT)
Sokol CIKALLESHI	27.07.1990	34	6	2019:	Akhisar Belediye Gençlik ve Spor Kulübü (TUR)
Rey Aldo MANAJ	24.02.1997	13	3	2019:	Albacete Balompié (ESP)
Taulant Fatmir SEFERI	15.11.1996	1	0	2019:	Neuchâtel Xamax FCS (SUI)
Myrto Artan UZUNI	31.05.1995	8	0	2019:	NK Lokomotiva Zagreb (CRO)

National team coach			
Edoardo REJA (Italy) [from 17.04.2019]	10.10.1945	8 M; 3 W; 1 D; 4 L; 13-12	

ANDORRA

The Country:
Principality of Andorra (Principat d'Andorra)
Capital: Andorra la Vella
Surface: 467,63 km²
Inhabitants: 76,543 [2020]
Time: UTC+1

The FA:
Federació Andorrana de Futbol
c/ Batlle Tomàs, 4 Baixos, AD700 Escaldes-Engordany
Tel: +376 805 830
Foundation date: 1994
Member of FIFA since: 1996
Member of UEFA since: 1996
Website: www.faf.ad

NATIONAL TEAM RECORDS

RECORDS
First international match:	13.11.1996, Andorra la Vella: Andorra – Estonia 1-6
Most international caps:	Ildefons Lima Solà - 128 caps (1997-2019)
Most international goals:	Ildefons Lima Solà - 11 goal / 128 caps (1997-2019)

UEFA EUROPEAN CHAMPIONSHIP		FIFA WORLD CUP		OLYMPIC TOURNAMENTS	
1960	-	1930	-	1908	-
1964	-	1934	-	1912	-
1968	-	1938	-	1920	-
1972	-	1950	-	1924	-
1976	-	1954	-	1928	-
1980	-	1958	-	1936	-
1984	-	1962	-	1948	-
1988	-	1966	-	1952	-
1992	-	1970	-	1956	-
1996	Did not enter	1974	-	1960	-
2000	Qualifiers	1978	-	1964	-
2004	Qualifiers	1982	-	1968	-
2008	Qualifiers	1986	-	1972	-
2012	Qualifiers	1990	-	1976	-
2016	Qualifiers	1994	Did not enter	1980	-
2020	Qualifiers	1998	Did not enter	1984	*Withdrew*
		2002	Qualifiers	1988	-
		2006	Qualifiers	1992	*Withdrew*
		2010	Qualifiers	1996	-
		2014	Qualifiers	2000	Qualifiers
		2018	Qualifiers	2004	Qualifiers
				2008	Did not enter
				2012	Qualifiers
				2016	Qualifiers

UEFA NATIONS LEAGUE
2018/2019 – League D

FIFA CONFEDERATIONS CUP 1992-2017
None

ANDORRAN CLUB HONOURS IN EUROPEAN CLUB COMPETITIONS:

European Champion Clubs.Cup (1956-1992) / UEFA Champions League (1993-2020)
None

Fairs Cup (1858-1971) / UEFA Cup (1972-2009) / UEFA Europa League (2010-2020)
None

UEFA Super Cup (1972-2019)
None

*European Cup Winners.Cup 1961-1999**
None

*defunct competition

NATIONAL COMPETITIONS
TABLE OF HONOURS

	CHAMPIONS	CUP WINNERS	BEST GOALSCORERS	
1990/1991	-	FC Santa Coloma	-	
1991/1992	-	*No competition*	-	
1992/1993	-	*No competition*	-	
1993/1994	-	CE Principat Andorra La Vella	-	
1994/1995	FC Santa Colomaa	CE Principat Andorra La Vella	-	
1995/1996	FC Encamp	CE Principat Andorra La Vella	-	
1996/1997	CE Principat Andorra La Vella	CE Principat Andorra La Vella	Patricio González Fernández (CE Principat Andorra La Vella)	25
1997/1998	CE Principat Andorra La Vella	CE Principat Andorra La Vella	Rafael Sánchez Pedrosa (ESP, FC Santa Coloma)	36
1998/1999	CE Principat Andorra La Vella	CE Principat Andorra La Vella	-	
1999/2000	Constel·lació Esportiva Andorra La Vella	Constel·lació Esportiva Andorra La Vella	-	
2000/2001	FC Santa Coloma	FC Santa Coloma	-	
2001/2002	FC Encamp	FC Lusitanos Andorra La Vella	-	
2002/2003	FC Santa Coloma	FC Santa Coloma	-	
2003/2004	FC Santa Coloma	FC Santa Coloma	Jorge Filipe Sa Silva Carneiro (POR, UE Sant Julià)	16
2004/2005	UE Sant Julià	FC Santa Coloma	-	
2005/2006	FC Rànger's Andorra La Vella	FC Santa Coloma	-	
2006/2007	FC Rànger's Andorra La Vella	FC Santa Coloma	Norberto Urbani (ARG, FC Rànger's Andorra La Vella) Joan Carles Toscano Beltrán (FC Santa Coloma)	14
2007/2008	FC Santa Coloma	UE Sant Julià	-	-
2008/2009	UE Sant Julià	FC Santa Coloma	Norberto Urbani (ARG, FC Rànger's Andorra La Vella)	22
2009/2010	FC Santa Coloma	UE Sant Julià	Gabriel Riera Lancha (UE Sant Julià)	19
2010/2011	FC Santa Coloma	UE Sant Julià	Victor Bernat Cuadros (ESP, UE Santa Coloma)	16
2011/2012	FC Lusitanos Andorra La Vella	FC Santa Coloma	Victor Bernat Cuadros (ESP, UE Santa Coloma)	14
2012/2013	FC Lusitanos Andorra La Vella	UE Santa Coloma	Bruno Filipe Raposo Fernandes "Bruninho" (POR, FC Lusitanos Andorra La Vella)	17
2013/2014	FC Santa Coloma	UE Sant Julià	Luis Miguel dos Reis (POR, FC Lusitanos Andorra La Vella)	13
2014/2015	FC Santa Coloma	UE Sant Julià	Cristian Martínez Alejo (FC Santa Coloma)	22
2015/2016	FC Santa Coloma	UE Santa Coloma	Victor Bernat Cuadros (ESP, UE Santa Coloma)	12
2016/2017	FC Santa Coloma	UE Santa Coloma	Victor Bernat Cuadros (ESP, UE Santa Coloma)	18
2017/2018	FC Santa Coloma	FC Santa Coloma	Jesús David Sosa Sebastiá "Chus Sosa" (ESP, FC Santa Coloma)	14
2018/2019	FC Santa Coloma	UE Engordany	Nicolás Estebán Medina Ríos (CHI, FC Lusitanos Andorra La Vella) Joel Méndez del Río (ESP, UE Sant Julià) Enric Pi Solá (ESP, UE Sant Julià) Genís Soldevila Solduga (ESP, Inter Club d'Escaldes)	10
2019/2020	Inter Club d'Escaldes	Inter Club d'Escaldes	Genís Soldevila Solduga (ESP, Inter Club d'Escaldes)	15

NATIONAL CHAMPIONSHIP
Primera Divisió 2019/2020
(15.09.2019 – 23.07.2020)

Regular Season - Results

Round 1 [15.09.2019]
UE Engordany - UE Sant Julià 2-5
FC Santa Coloma - AC d'Escaldes 2-0
FC Ordino - UE Santa Coloma 2-1
Inter Club d'Escaldes - CE Carroi 2-0

Round 2 [22.09.2019]
UE Santa Coloma - FC Santa Coloma 2-2
UE Sant Julià - Inter Club d'Escaldes 0-0
AC d'Escaldes - UE Engordany 2-0
CE Carroi - FC Ordino 1-1

Round 3 [29.09.2019]
Inter Club d'Escaldes - FC Ordino 1-0
UE Engordany - UE Santa Coloma 1-1
FC Santa Coloma - CE Carroi 1-0
UE Sant Julià - AC d'Escaldes 1-0

Round 4 [06.10.2019]
AC d'Escaldes - Inter Club d'Escaldes 1-3
CE Carroi - UE Engordany 0-3
UE Santa Coloma - UE Sant Julià 1-0
FC Ordino - FC Santa Coloma 0-5

Round 5 [20.10.2019]
UE Sant Julià - CE Carroi 1-0
UE Engordany - FC Ordino 3-1
Inter Club d'Escaldes - FC Santa Coloma 1-0
AC d'Escaldes - UE Santa Coloma 0-1

Round 6 [27.10.2019]
CE Carroi - AC d'Escaldes 0-0
Inter Club d'Escaldes - UE Santa Coloma 1-1
FC Ordino - UE Sant Julià 1-3
FC Santa Coloma - UE Engordany 0-1

Round 7 [03.11.2019]
UE Santa Coloma - CE Carroi 1-0
AC d'Escaldes - FC Ordino 2-0
UE Engordany - Inter Club d'Escaldes 1-1
UE Sant Julià - FC Santa Coloma 0-3

Round 8 [09-10.11.2019]
AC d'Escaldes - FC Santa Coloma 1-2
CE Carroi - Inter Club d'Escaldes 1-2
UE Sant Julià - UE Engordany 0-3
UE Santa Coloma - FC Ordino 1-0

Round 9 [24.11.2019]
FC Santa Coloma - UE Santa Coloma 2-0
Inter Club d'Escaldes - UE Sant Julià 1-0
UE Engordany - AC d'Escaldes 3-1
FC Ordino - CE Carroi 2-2

Round 10 [01.12.2019]
FC Ordino - Inter Club d'Escaldes 0-5
CE Carroi - FC Santa Coloma 0-3
AC d'Escaldes - UE Sant Julià 0-0
UE Santa Coloma - UE Engordany 0-1

Round 11 [08.12.2019]
FC Santa Coloma - FC Ordino 1-0
UE Sant Julià - UE Santa Coloma 3-0
UE Engordany - CE Carroi 3-1
Inter Club d'Escaldes - AC d'Escaldes 1-2

Round 12 [15.12.2019]
UE Santa Coloma - AC d'Escaldes 1-1
CE Carroi - UE Sant Julià 0-2
FC Santa Coloma - Inter Club d'Escaldes 1-1
FC Ordino - UE Engordany 1-2

Round 13 [02.02.2020]	Round 14 [09.02.2020]	Round 15 [16.02.2020]
UE Engordany - FC Santa Coloma 1-1	FC Ordino - AC d'Escaldes 1-1	UE Engordany - UE Sant Julià 0-1
AC d'Escaldes - CE Carroi 1-2	Inter Club d'Escaldes - UE Engordany 2-0	FC Ordino - UE Santa Coloma 0-2
UE Sant Julià - FC Ordino 3-2	CE Carroi - UE Santa Coloma 0-3	FC Santa Coloma - AC d'Escaldes 5-0
UE Santa Coloma - Inter Club d'Escaldes 0-2	FC Santa Coloma - UE Sant Julià 0-1	Inter Club d'Escaldes - CE Carroi 2-0

Round 16 [23.02.2020]	Round 17 [01.03.2020]	Round 18 [08.03.2020]
UE Sant Julià - Inter Club d'Escaldes 0-1	FC Santa Coloma - CE Carroi 4-0	AC d'Escaldes - Inter Club d'Escaldes 0-1
UE Santa Coloma - FC Santa Coloma 1-4	Inter Club d'Escaldes - FC Ordino 5-0	CE Carroi - UE Engordany 1-2
CE Carroi - FC Ordino 1-2	UE Engordany - UE Santa Coloma 1-1	UE Santa Coloma - UE Sant Julià 3-1
AC d'Escaldes - UE Engordany 1-1 [04.03.]	UE Sant Julià - AC d'Escaldes 0-4	FC Ordino - FC Santa Coloma 0-3

Round 19 [05.07.2020]	Round 20 [08-09.07.2020]	Round 21 [12.07.2020]
AC d'Escaldes - UE Santa Coloma 0-2	Inter Club d'Escaldes - UE Santa Coloma 1-3	UE Santa Coloma - CE Carroi 0-1
UE Sant Julià - CE Carroi 1-0	FC Ordino - UE Sant Julià 1-3	AC d'Escaldes - FC Ordino 4-0
UE Engordany - FC Ordino 3-1	CE Carroi - AC d'Escaldes 1-2	UE Sant Julià - FC Santa Coloma 1-1
Inter Club d'Escaldes - FC Santa Coloma 1-1	FC Santa Coloma - UE Engordany 2-0	UE Engordany - Inter Club d'Escaldes 2-3

Regular Season - League table

1.	Inter Club d'Escaldes	21	14	5	2	37	-	13	47
2.	FC Santa Coloma	21	13	5	3	43	-	11	44
3.	UE Sant Julià	21	11	3	7	26	-	23	36
4.	UE Engordany	21	10	5	6	33	-	26	35
5.	UE Santa Coloma	21	9	5	7	25	-	23	32
6.	Atlètic Club d'Escaldes Escaldes-Engordany	21	6	5	10	23	-	27	23
7.	FC Ordino	21	2	3	16	15	-	52	9
8.	CE Carroi	21	2	3	16	11	-	38	9

Top-4 teams qualified for the Championship Play-offs, while teams ranked 5-8 were qualified for the Relegation Play-offs.

Relegation Play-offs - Results

Round 22 [15.07.2020]	Round 23 [19.07.2020]	Round 24 [22.07.2020]
UE Santa Coloma - AC d'Escaldes 2-2	CE Carroi - AC d'Escaldes 0-2	AC d'Escaldes - FC Ordino 5-0
FC Ordino - CE Carroi 0-2	FC Ordino - UE Santa Coloma 0-5	UE Santa Coloma - CE Carroi 2-1

Final Standings

						Total				Home						Away			
5.	UE Santa Coloma	24	11	6	7	34 - 26	39	5	3	4	14 - 15		6	3	3	20 - 11			
6.	Atlètic Club d'Escaldes Escaldes-Engordany	24	8	6	10	32 - 29	30	4	2	6	17 - 12		4	4	4	15 - 17			
7.	CE Carroi (Relegation Play-off)	24	3	3	18	14 - 42	12	0	2	9	5 - 22		3	1	9	9 - 20			
8.	FC Ordino (Relegated)	24	2	3	19	15 - 64	9	1	2	9	8 - 34		1	1	10	7 - 30			

Championship Play-offs - Results

Round 22 [16.07.2020]	Round 23 [19.07.2020]	Round 24 [23.07.2020]
FC Santa Coloma - Inter Club d'Escaldes 1-1	UE Engordany - Inter Club d'Escaldes 0-0	Inter Club d'Escaldes - UE Sant Julià 3-0
UE Sant Julià - UE Engordany 1-2	UE Sant Julià - FC Santa Coloma 0-2	FC Santa Coloma - UE Engordany 2-0

Final Standings

						Total				Home						Away			
1.	**Inter Club d'Escaldes**	24	15	7	2	41 - 14	52	8	2	2	21 - 7		7	5	0	20 - 7			
2.	FC Santa Coloma	24	15	6	3	48 - 12	51	8	2	2	21 - 4		7	4	1	27 - 8			
3.	UE Engordany	24	11	6	7	35 - 29	39	4	5	3	20 - 17		7	1	4	15 - 12			
4.	UE Sant Julià	24	11	3	10	27 - 30	36	5	2	6	11 - 18		6	1	4	16 - 12			

Top goalscorers:	
15 Genís Soldevila Solduga (ESP)	*Inter Club d'Escaldes*
9 Bruno Mauricio Lemiechevsky Melessi (URU)	*UE Sant Julià*
8 Nicolás Estebán Medina Ríos (CHI)	*FC Santa Coloma*

Relegation Play-offs

CE Carroi - FS La Massana   4-1(1-0)

CE Carroi remains at first level for the 2020/2021 Primera Divisió.

NATIONAL CUP
Copa Constitució Final 2019/2020

First Round [19.01.2020]				
UE Engordany - FC Encamp	11-1	FC Ordino - Penya Encarnada d'Andorra	1-2
Atlètic Club d'Escaldes - FS La Massana	1-3	CE Carroi - FC Lusitanos Andorra La Vella	3-1

Quarter-Finals [25.01.-12.02.2020]			
Inter Club d'Escaldes - UE Engordany	2-1	UE Santa Coloma - Penya Encarnada d'Andorra	1-0
UE Sant Julià - FS La Massana	4-0	FC Santa Coloma - CE Carroi	3-0

Semi-Finals [26.07.2020]			
Inter Club d'Escaldes - UE Sant Julià	2-1	UE Santa Coloma - FC Santa Coloma	0-1 aet

Final

29.07.2020; Estadi Nacional, Andorra la Vella; Referee: Bruno Parentes Fernandes; Attendance: None

Inter Club d'Escaldes - FC Santa Coloma   **2-0(0-0)**

Inter Club: Josep Antoni Gomes Moreira, Rui Filipe Figueiras de Beja, Óscar Reyes Sánchez, Andrés Briñez Aranda (46.Albert Reyes Roig), Emili Josep García Miramontes, Antonio Lao Dona „Toni Lao", Marc Pujol Pons, Bruno Filipe Raposo Fernandes "Bruninho" (84.Jordi Betriu Armengol), Cristian Martínez Alejo, Sergio Moreno Marín, Genís Soldevila Soldurga. Trainer: Adolfo Baines (Spain).

FC Santa Coloma: Eloy Casals Rubio, Aleix Cístero Serna, Juan Manuel Miranda Rodríguez „Juanma",Enric Pi Sola (76.Álex Sánchez Rodríguez), Jesús Rubio Gómez, Moisés San Nicolás Schellens, Jordi Aláez Peña, Luis Blanco Coto, Pedro Santos Escolano (81.Javier López Iglesias "Camochu"), Diego Alejandro Nájera Quintero (81.Nicolás Esteban Medina Ríos), Alexandre Martínez Palau. Trainer: Marc Rodríguez Rebull.

Goals: 1-0 Bruno Filipe Raposo Fernandes "Bruninho" (70), 2-0 Genís Soldevila Soldurga (90).

THE CLUBS 2019/2020

<u>Please note</u>: matches and goals includes statistics of both regular season and Play-offs (Championship & Relegation Play-offs).

Atlètic Club d'Escaldes Escaldes-Engordany

Founded: 2002
Stadium: Camp d'Esports d'Aixovall [DEVK Arena] (900)
Trainer: *Not known*

Goalkeepers:	DOB	M	(s)	G
Friday Abidem Godswill (NGA)	02.05.1985	7		
Iván Periáñez Meca	25.01.1982	17	(2)	
Defenders:	**DOB**	**M**	**(s)**	**G**
Leonel Maciel Antunes (POR)	02.07.1982	13	(5)	1
David Maneiro Ton	16.02.1989	19	(2)	
Alagy Oliveira Diaw (ESP)	1998	9	(2)	
Christián Alexander Paredes Ponce (PER)	16.04.1987	11	(3)	
Rafael Amaral Santos Brito (POR)	06.07.1986	19	(2)	1
Adrián Rodrigues Gonçalves	14.08.1988	11		1
Sergi Suárez	02.07.1998	6		2
Midfielders:	**DOB**	**M**	**(s)**	**G**
Leandro Filipe Fernandes Gomes (POR)	06.11.1998	4	(3)	
Yael Fontan Vilches (ESP)	24.02.1980	10		1

	DOB	M	(s)	G
Gastón Rodrigo Machado López (URU)	19.01.1986	15	(2)	5
Nicolas Mariano Minutella (ARG)	23.03.1995	10	(1)	1
Richard André Hurtado Lora „Richy" (ESP)	13.11.1993	14	(4)	4
Gemelson Nayry Fay Bill Vieira (GNB)	04.08.1992	19	(1)	2
Xavier Vieira de Vasconcelos	14.01.1992	20	(2)	4
Forwards:	**DOB**	**M**	**(s)**	**G**
Fabio Felipe Serra Alves (POR)	24.08.1984	20	(2)	2
Carlos Manuel Gomes Do Nascimento	18.10.1993	11	(2)	1
Leandro Filipe Fernandes Gomes (POR)	11.06.1991	1		
Daniel Alberto Rojas Gómez (COL)	09.07.1996	10	(9)	2
Sergio Suárez Otal	02.07.1998	8	(7)	1
Estephano Brauzil Urrunaga Orellana (PER)	07.05.1998	2	(5)	2
Walter Excequiel Vázquez Bernal (URU)	11.05.1991	8		1

Club Esportiu Carroi

Founded: 2014
Stadium: Camp de Fútbol d'Aixovall (1,000)
Trainer: Hugo Gregorio Roldán

Goalkeepers:	DOB	M	(s)	G
Ilay Can Dikkaya (TUR)	04.03.1999	1		
Christopher Izaguirre Urrea (MEX)	2001	7		
Ousmane Kane (SEN)	29.05.1992	15	(1)	
Jordi Rodríguez Bertran	01.12.1993	1		
Defenders:	**DOB**	**M**	**(s)**	**G**
Rui Filipe Barroso Ribeiro (POR)	13.09.1997	6	(7)	1
Armando Avelar Castañeda	17.08.1991	19	(2)	
Renzo Alejandro Dezotti (ARG)	17.11.1990	1		
Ahmed Eid (FRA)	25.07.1998	6	(2)	1
Ramiro Fabian Ferreira Miño (PAR)	1996	10		
Ángel Ramiro Garcés Tesada (COL)	14.09.1995	9	(7)	1
David Almir Ignacio León (PER)	12.11.1985	1		
Francesc Josep Louzao Osuna	09.01.1991	3	(1)	
Alfredo Martins (POR)	1997	10	(8)	
Joao Pedro Ferreira Monteiro (POR)	11.12.1995	14	(1)	
Jorge Miquel Pinto Pedro	15.05.1994	19	(1)	

	DOB	M	(s)	G
Nicolás Alejandro Rodas Urrutia (GUA)	20.09.1998	8	(1)	
Midfielders:	**DOB**	**M**	**(s)**	**G**
Jules Bidau (FRA)	30.07.1996	15		
Eduard Carrera Turgot (ESP)	01.02.2000	3	(2)	
Hélder Jesus Teixeira (POR)	10.04.1996	20	(1)	1
Alfonso Alejandro Huerta (MEX)	19.11.1990	10		2
João Pedro da Silva Teixeira (POR)	17.07.1996	15	(4)	
José Rafael Martins Alves	07.11.1991	14	(5)	2
Daniel Pedro da Costa Silva Morais (POR)	03.02.1999	7	(2)	
Moisés Adamin Oyuela Betanco (HON)	20.08.1999	5	(6)	
Víctor Hugo Pérez Reyes (MEX)	12.11.1990	7		1
José María Ramírez Gutiérrez (MEX)	21.01.1999	23		2
Forwards:	**DOB**	**M**	**(s)**	**G**
Ronely Kingo Bonkene (FRA)	19.10.1993	7	(3)	2
Alpha Doumbia Sylla (GER)	17.09.2000	2	(1)	
Dan-Ilie Martin (ROU)	06.05.1997	5	(1)	

Unió Esportiva Engordany

Founded: 1980
Stadium: Estadi Comunal d'Andorra la Vella (1,300)
Trainer: Filipe Busto Guerra (POR) 27.12.1983

Goalkeepers:	DOB	M	(s)	G
Jesús Coca Noguerol (ESP)	22.05.1989	18		
Gerardo José Rubio Ortuna (ESP)	17.05.1987	6		
Defenders:	DOB	M	(s)	G
Sébastien Jacques Manuel Aguero (FRA)	17.08.1993	22		1
William Marcel Alexandre Boe (FRA)	16.09.1999	1	(5)	
Leandro da Silva		2	(6)	
Sergio Manuel López da Silva			(1)	
Lucas Maciel Sousa (POR)	06.03.1991	14		2
Pedro Muñoz Fontalba (ESP)	09.01.1988	17	(1)	1
Miguel Ruiz Enamorado (ESP)	16.07.1982	21	(1)	
Matías Rudler (ARG)	25.04.1988	19	(1)	
Midfielders:	DOB	M	(s)	G
Hamza Ryahi Bouharma (ESP)	11.03.1993	19	(2)	2
Marc Ferré Nazzaro	11.01.1991	17	(6)	1
Sebastián Gómez Pérez	01.11.1983	23		4
Víctor Rodríguez Soria	07.09.1987	11	(5)	1
Mario Valentín Spano (URU)	07.02.1986	21		4
Allie Thibault (FRA)	2000		(1)	
Forwards:	DOB	M	(s)	G
Junior Maxime Kobon Gneprou (CIV)	21.12.1997	9	(5)	2
Morgan Lafont (FRA)	22.11.1996	9	(12)	2
Raúl Sousa Veloso			(1)	
Gabriel Riera Lancha	05.06.1985	5	(11)	3
Aarón Sánchez Alburquerque	05.06.1996	13	(3)	2
Luigi San Nicolas Schellens	28.06.1992	15	(5)	6
Alberto López Medel "Tete" (ESP)	21.11.1998	2	(3)	2

Inter Club d'Escaldes

Founded: 1991
Stadium: Estadi Comunal d'Andorra la Vella (1,300)
Trainer: Adolfo Baines (ESP) 12.02.1972

Goalkeepers:	DOB	M	(s)	G
Josep Antoni Gomes Moreira	03.12.1985	24		
Defenders:	DOB	M	(s)	G
Rui Filipe Figueiras de Beja (POR)	14.04.1993	12	(3)	
Eric Rodríguez Barcelo „Canario"	02.04.1993	2	(2)	
Ildefons Lima Solà	10.12.1979	20		2
Xavier Moreno Marín	03.12.1990		(1)	
Óscar Reyes Sánchez (ESP)	12.03.1988	22		
Iván Vigo Babot	07.09.1986	7	(2)	
Midfielders:	DOB	M	(s)	G
Andrés Briñez Aranda (COL)	1996	3	(10)	
Emili Josep García Miramontes	11.01.1989	21		
Jordi Roca Grau	23.08.1989	9	(3)	3
Marc Pujol Pons	21.08.1982	21		5
Albert Reyes Roig	24.03.1996	3	(8)	
Antonio Lao Dona „Toni Lao" (ESP)	17.01.1984	22	(1)	
Forwards:	DOB	M	(s)	G
Jordi Betriu Armengol (ESP)	29.06.1995	15	(7)	3
Bruno Filipe Raposo Fernandes "Bruninho" (POR)	11.01.1986	13	(8)	
Cristian Martínez Alejo	16.10.1989	15	(4)	4
Sergio Moreno Marín	25.11.1987	22		3
Eugenio Else Peralta Cabrera (PAR)	16.12.1977		(11)	1
Ricardo Correia Oliveira (POR)	04.04.1996	7	(3)	1
Julià Sánchez Soto	20.06.1978	1	(5)	
Genís Soldevila Solduga (ESP)	03.03.1987	22	(1)	15
Rodrigo Armando Vergara Brango (COL)	13.06.1995	3	(5)	1

Futbol Club Ordino

Founded: 2010
Stadium: Centre Esportiu d'Ordino (200)
Trainer: Paco Domingo

Goalkeepers:	DOB	M	(s)	G
Francisco José Domingo Gil	12.02.1999	9		
Ayoub Jilali (MAR)	02.01.1998	4		
Claudio Roberto Veiga Gomes "Robi"	18.08.1987	9		
David Hidalgo Soriano (ESP)		2	(1)	
Defenders:	DOB	M	(s)	G
Akinola Akinleye	26.02.1994	6		
Alexandre Correia Alfaiate (POR)	17.08.1995	22		3
José Carlos Guerra Martins			(1)	
Levan Makharadze (UKR)	14.08.1993	18		1
Allie Thibault (FRA)	2000	3	(1)	
Rodrigo Varela		13	(2)	1
Mark Anthony Withers (USA)	10.11.1992	24		2
Jordi Xapell Flucha	1997	16	(3)	
Midfielders:	DOB	M	(s)	G
Luis Filipe Pinto Escaleira "Baixinho"	05.03.1987	6		
Sebastià Bertrán Suárez	10.12.1992	22		2
Gil Tudo Cubells	1999	2	(2)	
Marc Ferreiroa Fius	23.05.1999	2	(1)	
Juan Ezequiel García (ARG)	09.10.1991	5	(6)	
Juan Agustín López Crespo	2000	8	(1)	
Francesc Joel Martínez Vilar	31.12.1988	14	(2)	
Jean Andre Mbele Mavinga (FRA)	22.11.1993	10		
Noham Pereira Bramli	1998	11		
Jesus Santiago (FRA)	25.05.2001	9		1
Alex Villagrasa Noguera	26.03.1997	3		
Forwards:	DOB	M	(s)	G
Cheikh Ahmadou Bamba Ndiaye		9		1
Eric Marcial Cadi	11.02.1998	3	(4)	
Cristian Hidalgo González (ESP)	21.09.1983	16		3
Roger Marsal Portella	26.05.1999	5	(3)	
Miquel Torres Vila	07.10.1998	4	(3)	1

Unió Esportiva Sant Julià de Lòria

Founded: 1982
Stadium: Estadi Comunal d'Andorra la Vella (1,300)
Trainer: Luis Blanco Torrado (ESP) 27.12.1959

Goalkeepers:	DOB	M	(s)	G
Javier López Filpo (ESP)	04.05.1996	1		
Julián Lorenzo (ARG)			(6)	
Miguel Ángel Ramos Prada (ESP)	05.10.1986	23		
Defenders:	DOB	M	(s)	G
Christian Ariel Cellay (ARG)	05.09.1981	21		1
Abdallah Imamo Ahmed (COM)	19.04.1993	5	(1)	
David López Morillo (ESP)	10.01.1987	6		
Javier López Martín (ESP)	21.04.1990	6	(7)	
Daniel Sánchez Massot (ESP)	18.08.1988	11		1
Matías Nicolás Vaamonde (ARG)	30.11.1989	17	(3)	2
Jorge Sebastián Varela Delisa (URU)	23.09.1980	16	(1)	
Walter Esteban Wagner (ARG)	12.01.1981	9	(3)	
Midfielders:	DOB	M	(s)	G
Alvaro Correia	08.11.1996	1	(3)	1
Javier Lara Jiménez (ESP)	23.08.1987	9		
Ahmed Mida (TUN)	15.05.1988		(2)	
Roberto Moreno Bonilla (ESP)	04.12.1997	8	(1)	
Carlos Eduardo Peppe Britos	28.01.1983	23		1
Sergio Rodríguez Hurtado (ESP)	07.09.1992	13	(4)	2
Ignacio Rosillo López (ESP)	17.02.1988	9	(1)	3
Forwards:	DOB	M	(s)	G
Anouar Benskij (FRA)		1	(8)	1
Bruno Mauricio Lemiechevsky Melessi (URU)	03.03.1994	17	(1)	9
Maicon dos Santos Venâncio (BRA)	28.05.1983	12	(5)	1
Alberto Molina Rodríguez (ESP)	21.04.1988	20		
Víctor Hugo Moreira Teixeira	05.10.1982	7	(3)	2
Pablo Navas Alors (ESP)	04.02.1992	1	(1)	
Francesc „Fran" Piera Martínez (ESP)	19.12.1987	21		2
Sergio Urbano López (ESP)	08.12.1986	1	(8)	1
Jonathan Toledo Giráldez (ESP)	01.03.1995	4	(3)	

Futbol Club Santa Coloma

Founded: 1986
Stadium: Estadi Comunal d'Andorra la Vella (1,300)
Trainer: Marc Rodríguez Rebull

Goalkeepers:	DOB	M	(s)	G
Eloy Casals Rubio (ESP)	22.10.1982	24		
Defenders:	**DOB**	**M**	**(s)**	**G**
Aleix Cístero Serna (ESP)	25.06.1994	19	(1)	2
Juan Manuel Miranda Rodríguez „Juanma" (ESP)	01.03.1994	18	(2)	
Enric Pi Sola (ESP)	20.05.1983	12	(10)	3
Andreu Ramos Isus (ESP)	19.01.1989	16	(1)	1
Marc Rebés Ruíz	03.07.1994	20		2
Jesús Rubio Gómez	09.09.1994	14	(5)	1
Álex Sánchez Rodríguez (ESP)	19.01.1991	12	(2)	
Moisés San Nicolás Schellens	17.09.1993	15	(2)	
Jamal Zarioh Taouil	30.01.1989		(2)	

Midfielders:	DOB	M	(s)	G
Jordi Aláez Peña	23.01.1998	14	(7)	3
Luis Blanco Coto	15.01.1990	12	(7)	2
Miguel Ángel Laborda Gil (ESP)	18.02.1995	7	(3)	2
Roger Nazzaro Àlvarez	07.04.1997		(1)	
Pedro Santos Escolano (ESP)	01.06.1993	19	(1)	1
Forwards:	**DOB**	**M**	**(s)**	**G**
André Filipe Teixeira Azevedo (POR)	19.07.1990	14	(1)	
Javier López Iglesias "Camochu" (ESP)	13.04.1989	12	(7)	5
Alexandre Martínez Palau	10.10.1998	10	(1)	7
Nicolás Esteban Medina Ríos (CHI)	28.03.1987	6	(11)	8
Diego Alejandro Nájera Quintero (MEX)	11.12.1994	13	(8)	6
Jesús "Chus" David Sosa Sebastiá (ESP)	05.01.1994	7		4

Unió Esportiva Santa Coloma

Founded: 1986
Stadium: Estadi Comunal d'Andorra la Vella (1,300)
Trainer: Emilio Gómez 14.01.1958

Goalkeepers:	DOB	M	(s)	G
José Emanuel Carvalho Teixeira	10.11.2001	2	(2)	
Ricard Fernández Lizarte (ESP)	26.05.1975	2	(2)	
Ferran Pol Pérez	28.02.1983	7	(1)	1
Francisco Manuel Pires Costa „Xisco" (POR)	25.01.1998	13		
Defenders:	**DOB**	**M**	**(s)**	**G**
Eric De Pablos Sola	08.03.1999	17		
Miguel Del Castillo Somoza	30.09.1999	18	(1)	1
Christian García González	04.02.1999	16		3
André Manuel Marinho Teixeira	26.03.1993	11	(1)	
Alexandre Martínez Gutiérrez	04.03.1987	18		3
Joel Martínez Palau		7	(1)	
Cristian Orosa Lodeiro (ESP)	12.12.1990	13	(1)	1
Rubén Pinedo Rodríguez (ESP)	1996		(4)	
Midfielders:	**DOB**	**M**	**(s)**	**G**
Walid Bousenine Nafae	07.04.1993	7	(4)	1

	DOB	M	(s)	G
Alvaro Domingues Branco	01.07.1999	1	(2)	
Nourddin El Morabiti Talibe (MAR)	26.06.1994	2	(1)	1
Jordi Rubio Gómez	01.11.1987	20	(1)	7
Brian Andre Teixeira Filipe	26.06.1995	3	(6)	
Forwards:	**DOB**	**M**	**(s)**	**G**
Gerard Aloy Soler	17.04.1989	18	(2)	1
Boris Antón Codina	27.02.1987	9	(11)	1
Victor Bernat Cuadros (ESP)	17.05.1987	10	(2)	5
Eric Carmona Bonache	19.06.2001	1	(7)	1
Sergio Crespo Alonso	29.09.1992	15	(6)	1
Gabriel Fernandes Cunha	27.07.1996	3	(7)	
Roberto Carlos Gomes Rebelo	21.10.1999	16	(1)	2
Manuel Veiga Machado	15.09.1986		(1)	
Andreu Matos Muñoz	01.12.1995	19	(4)	3
Arturo Riestra Torrejón (ESP)	18.10.1999	16	(8)	1

SECOND LEVEL
Segona Divisió 2019/2020

Regular Season - League table

1. Penya Encarnada d'Andorra (*Promoted*)	17	16	1	0	56	-	8	49
2. FS La Massana (*Promotion Play-offs*)	17	15	0	2	86	-	19	45
3. FC Encamp	16	8	3	5	42	-	36	27
4. FC Rànger's Andorra la Vella	15	8	0	7	31	-	37	24
5. FC Lusitanos Andorra La Vella	15	7	2	6	48	-	22	20
6. Inter Club d'Escaldes "B"	16	6	2	8	28	-	36	20
7. UE Santa Coloma "B"	15	6	1	8	39	-	49	19
8. CF Atlètic Amèrica	16	3	0	13	30	-	64	9
9. CE Carroi "B"	16	3	1	12	25	-	53	7
10. UE Extremenya La Massana	15	2	0	13	10	-	71	3

Please note: on 05.05.2020, due to Covid-19 pandemic, the clubs and the federation agreed on how to finish the season: the two teams which remained mathematically able to qualify for promotion played each other twice to determine final places in the league.

INTERNATIONAL MATCHES
(16.07.2019 – 15.07.2020)

07.09.2019	Istanbul	Turkey - Andorra	1-0(0-0)	(ECQ)
10.09.2019	Paris	France - Andorra	3-0(1-0)	(ECQ)
11.10.2019	Andorra la Vella	Andorra - Moldova	1-0(0-0)	(ECQ)
14.10.2019	Reykjavík	Iceland - Andorra	2-0(1-0)	(ECQ)
14.11.2019	Elbasan	Albania - Andorra	2-2(1-1)	(ECQ)
17.11.2019	Andorra la Vella	Andorra - Turkey	0-2(0-2)	(ECQ)

07.09.2019   **TURKEY - ANDORRA**   **1-0(0-0)**   16th EC. Qualifiers
Vodafone Park, Istanbul; Referee: Donald Robertson (Scotland); Attendance: 42,600
AND: Josep Antoni Gómes Moreira, Ildefons Lima Solà (Cap), Marc Vales González, Moisés San Nicolás Schellens, Marc Rebés Ruiz, Max Llovera González-Adrio, Joan Cervós Moro, Víctor Rodríguez Soria (63.Marc García Renom), Márcio Vieira de Vasconcelos (87.Emili Josep García Miramontes), Cristian Martínez Alejo, Ludovic Clemente Garcés (79.Jordi Aláez Peña). Trainer: Jesús Luis Álvarez de Eulate Güergue "Koldo".

10.09.2019   **FRANCE - ANDORRA**   **3-0(1-0)**   16th EC. Qualifiers
Stade de France, Saint-Denis, Paris; Referee: Mykola Balakin (Ukraine); Attendance: 55,383
AND: Josep Antoni Gómes Moreira, Ildefons Lima Solà (Cap), Marc Vales González, Moisés San Nicolás Schellens, Marc Rebés Ruiz, Jesús Rubio Gómez, Max Llovera González-Adrio, Joan Cervós Moro, Márcio Vieira de Vasconcelos (86.Sergio Moreno Marín), Cristian Martínez Alejo (69.Jordi Aláez Peña), Ludovic Clemente Garcés (79.Jordi Rubio Gómez). Trainer: Jesús Luis Álvarez de Eulate Güergue "Koldo".

11.10.2019   **ANDORRA - MOLDOVA**   **1-0(0-0)**   16th EC. Qualifiers
Estadi Nacional, Andorra la Vella; Referee: Jonathan Lardot (Belgium); Attendance: 947
AND: Josep Antoni Gómes Moreira, Ildefons Lima Solà (Cap), Marc Vales González, Moisés San Nicolás Schellens, Jesús Rubio Gómez, Max Llovera González-Adrio, Joan Cervós Moro, Márcio Vieira de Vasconcelos, Marc Pujol Pons (83.Víctor Rodríguez Soria), Cristian Martínez Alejo (61.Jordi Aláez Peña), Ludovic Clemente Garcés (73.Marc Rebés Ruiz). Trainer: Jesús Luis Álvarez de Eulate Güergue "Koldo".
Goal: Marc Vales González (63).

14.10.2019   **ICELAND - ANDORRA**   **2-0(1-0)**   16th EC. Qualifiers
Laugardalsvöllur, Reykjavík; Referee: Bognár Tamás (Hungary); Attendance: 7,981
AND: Josep Antoni Gómes Moreira, Ildefons Lima Solà (Cap), Marc Vales González, Moisés San Nicolás Schellens, Marc Rebés Ruiz, Max Llovera González-Adrio, Joan Cervós Moro, Víctor Rodríguez Soria, Márcio Vieira de Vasconcelos (60.Ricard Fernández Betriu), Jordi Aláez Peña (87.Sebastiàn Gómez Pérez), Alexandre Martínez Palau (80.Marc García Renom). Trainer: Jesús Luis Álvarez de Eulate Güergue "Koldo".

14.11.2019   **ALBANIA - ANDORRA**   **2-2(1-1)**   16th EC. Qualifiers
Elbasan Arena, Elbasan; Referee: Kristo Tohver (Estonia); Attendance: 4,260
AND: Josep Antoni Gómes Moreira, Emili Josep García Miramontes, Marc Vales González, Moisés San Nicolás Schellens, Jesús Rubio Gómez (71.Víctor Rodríguez Soria), Max Llovera González-Adrio, Joan Cervós Moro, Sergio Moreno Marín (Cap), Jordi Aláez Peña (89.Alexandre Martínez Palau), Cristian Martínez Alejo (79.Ricard Fernández Betriu), Ludovic Clemente Garcés. Trainer: Jesús Luis Álvarez de Eulate Güergue "Koldo".
Goals: Cristian Martínez Alejo (18, 48).

17.11.2019   **ANDORRA - TURKEY**   **0-2(0-2)**   16th EC. Qualifiers
Estadi Nacional, Andorra la Vella; Referee: Ivan Kružliak (Slovakia); Attendance: 2,357
AND: Josep Antoni Gómes Moreira (87.Ferran Pol Pérez), Ildefons Lima Solà (Cap), Marc Vales González, Moisés San Nicolás Schellens, Marc Rebés Ruiz, Max Llovera González-Adrio, Joan Cervós Moro, Cristian Martínez Alejo, Jordi Aláez Peña (71.Víctor Rodríguez Soria), Alexandre Martínez Palau, Ludovic Clemente Garcés (85.Jordi Rubio Gómez). Trainer: Jesús Luis Álvarez de Eulate Güergue "Koldo".

NATIONAL TEAM PLAYERS
(16.07.2019 – 15.07.2020)

Name	DOB	Caps	Goals	2019/2020:	Club
Goalkeepers					
Josep Antoni GÓMES Moreira	03.12.1985	63	0	2019:	*Inter Club d'Escaldes*
Ferran POL Pérez	28.02.1983	27	0	2019:	*UE Santa Coloma*
Defenders					
Joan CERVÓS Moro	24.02.1998	17	0	2019:	*FC Andorra La Vella*
Emili Josep GARCÍA Miramontes	11.01.1989	46	1	2019:	*Inter Club d'Escaldes*
Ildefons LIMA Solà	10.12.1979	128	11	2019:	*Inter Club d'Escaldes*
Max LLOVERA González-Adrio	08.01.1997	36	0	2019:	*EC Granollers (ESP)*
Marc REBÉS Ruiz	03.07.1994	30	2	2019:	*FC Santa Coloma*
Jesús RUBIO Gómez	09.09.1994	25	0	2019:	*FC Santa Coloma*
Jordi RUBIO Gómez	01.11.1987	46	0	2019:	*UE Santa Coloma*
Marc VALES González	04.04.1990	67	1	2019:	*Sandefjord Fotball (NOR)*
Midfielders					
Jordi ALÁEZ Peña	23.01.1998	27	1	2019:	*FC Santa Coloma*
Marc GARCÍA Renom „Chiqui"	21.03.1988	44	0	2019:	*EC Granollers (ESP)*
Cristian MARTÍNEZ Alejo	16.10.1989	59	5	2019:	*Inter Club d'Escaldes*
Marc PUJOL Pons	21.08.1982	83	2	2019:	*Inter Club d'Escaldes*
Víctor RODRÍGUEZ Soria	07.09.1987	30	0	2019:	*FC Santa Coloma*
Moisés SAN NICOLÁS Schellens	17.09.1993	48	0	2019:	*FC Santa Coloma*
Márcio Vieira de Vasconcelos	10.10.1984	92	0	2019:	*CF Atlético de Monzón (ESP)*
Forwards					
Ludovic CLEMENTE Garcés	09.05.1986	36	0	2019:	*FC Andorra La Vella*
Ricard FERNÁNDEZ Betriu	19.03.1999	7	0	2019:	*FC Andorra La Vella*
Sebastiàn GÓMEZ Pérez	01.11.1983	32	0	2019:	*UE Engordany*
Alexandre MARTÍNEZ Palau	10.10.1998	22	1	2019:	*FC Andorra La Vella*
Sergio MORENO Marín	25.11.1987	66	0	2019:	*Inter Club d'Escaldes*
National team coach					
Jesús Luis Alvarez de Eulate „KOLDO" [from 02.02.2010]	04.09.1970		77 M; 4 W; 11 D; 62 L; 17-169		

ARMENIA

The Country:
Republic of Armenia (Hayastani Hanrapetut'yun)
Capital: Yerevan
Surface: 29,743 km²
Inhabitants: 2,974,816
Time: UTC+4

The FA:
Football Federation of Armenia
Khanjyan Street 27 0010, Yerevan
Tel: +374 10 56 88 83
Foundation date: 18.01.1992
Member of FIFA since: 1992
Member of UEFA since: 1993
Website: www.ffa.am

NATIONAL TEAM RECORDS

RECORDS		
First international match:	14.10.1992, Yerevan	Armenia – Moldova 0-0
Most international caps:	Sargis Hovsepyan	- 132 caps (1992-2012)
Most international goals:	Henrikh Mkhitaryan	- 29 goals / 86 caps (since 2007)

UEFA EUROPEAN CHAMPIONSHIP		FIFA WORLD CUP		OLYMPIC TOURNAMENTS	
1960	-	1930	-	1908	-
1964	-	1934	-	1912	-
1968	-	1938	-	1920	-
1972	-	1950	-	1924	-
1976	-	1954	-	1928	-
1980	-	1958	-	1936	-
1984	-	1962	-	1948	-
1988	-	1966	-	1952	-
1992	Did not enter	1970	-	1956	-
1996	Qualifiers	1974	-	1960	-
2000	Qualifiers	1978	-	1964	-
2004	Qualifiers	1982	-	1968	-
2008	Qualifiers	1986	-	1972	-
2012	Qualifiers	1990	-	1976	-
2016	Qualifiers	1994	Did not enter	1980	-
2020	Qualifiers	1998	Qualifiers	1984	-
		2002	Qualifiers	1988	-
		2006	Qualifiers	1992	Did not enter
		2010	Qualifiers	1996	Did not enter
		2014	Qualifiers	2000	Qualifiers
		2018	Qualifiers	2004	Qualifiers
				2008	Qualifiers
				2012	Qualifiers
				2016	Qualifiers

UEFA NATIONS LEAGUE

2018/2019 – League D

FIFA CONFEDERATIONS CUP 1992-2017

None

ARMENIAN CLUB HONOURS IN EUROPEAN CLUB COMPETITIONS:

European Champion Clubs.Cup (1956-1992) / UEFA Champions League (1993-2020)
None

Fairs Cup (1858-1971) / UEFA Cup (1972-2009) / UEFA Europa League (2010-2020)
None

UEFA Super Cup (1972-2019)
None

European Cup Winners.Cup 1961-1999*
None

*defunct competition

NATIONAL COMPETITIONS
TABLE OF HONOURS

ARMENIAN SSR (SOVIET ERA) CHAMPIONS

Year	Champion	Year	Champion	Year	Champion
1936	Dinamo Yerevan	1955	Khimik Kirovakan	1971	FIMA Yerevan
1937	Dinamo Yerevan	1956	FIMA Yerevan	1972	Zvezda Yerevan
1938	Spartak Yerevan	1957	Karmir Drosh Leninakan	1973	Kotayk Abovyan
1939	Spartak Yerevan	1958	FIMA Yerevan	1974	FIMA Yerevan
1940	Spartak Yerevan	1959	FIMA Yerevan	1975	Kotayk Abovyan
1941-44	*No competition*	1960	Tekstilshchik Leninakan	1976	Kotayk Abovyan
1945	Spartak Yerevan	1961	Tekstilshchik Leninakan	1977	Araks Yerevan
1946	Dinamo Yerevan	1962	Tekstilshchik Leninakan	1978	Kanaz Yerevan
1947	Dinamo Yerevan	1963	Lokomotiv Yerevan	1979	Aragats Leninakan
1948	Dinamo Yerevan	1964	Khimik Kirovakan	1980	Aragats Leninakan
1949	Dinamo Yerevan	1965	Araks Yerevan	1981–86	*No competition*
1950	Urozhai Yerevan	1966	Elektrotekhnik Yerevan	1987	Aragats Leninakan
1951	Shinarar Yerevan	1967	Kotayk Abovyan	1988	Elektrotekhnik Yerevan
1952	Spartak Yerevan	1968	Araks Yerevan	1989	FC Kapan
1953	Karmir Drosh Leninakan	1969	Araks Yerevan	1990	Ararat-2 Yerevan
1954	Spartak Yerevan	1970	Motor Yerevan	1991	Syunik Kapan

	CHAMPIONS	CUP WINNERS	BEST GOALSCORERS	
1992	Shirak SC Gyumri Homenetmen Yerevan (shared)	FC Banants Yerevan	Vahe Yaghmuryan (FC Ararat Yerevan)	38
1993	FC Ararat Yerevan	FC Ararat Yerevan	Andranik Hovsepyan (Banants) Gegham Hovhannisyan (Homenetmen Yerevan)	26
1994	Shirak SC Gyumri	FC Ararat Yerevan	Arsen Avetisyan (Homenetmen Yerevan)	39
1995	*Transitional Season (No Winner)*	FC Ararat Yerevan	-	
1995/1996	FC Pyunik Yerevan	FC Pyunik Yerevan	Arayik Adamyan (Shirak SC Gyumri)	28
1996/1997	FC Pyunik Yerevan	FC Ararat Yerevan	Arsen Avetisyan (FC Pyunik Yerevan)	24
1997	FC Yerevan	-	Artur Petrosyan (Shirak SC Gyumri)	18
1998	FC Tsement Ararat	FC Tsement Ararat	Ara Hakobyan (Dvin Artashat)	20
1999	Shirak SC Gyumri	FC Tsement Ararat	Shirak SC Gyumri Sarikyan (FC Tsement Ararat)	21
2000	Araks Ararat FC	FC Mika Yerevan	Ara Hakobyan (Araks Ararat FC)	21
2001	FC Pyunik Yerevan	FC Mika Yerevan	Arman Karamyan (FC Pyunik Yerevan)	21
2002	FC Pyunik Yerevan	FC Pyunik Yerevan	Arman Karamyan (FC Pyunik Yerevan)	36
2003	FC Pyunik Yerevan	FC Mika Yerevan	Ara Hakobyan (FC Banants Yerevan)	45
2004	FC Pyunik Yerevan	FC Pyunik Yerevan	Edgar Manucharyan (FC Pyunik Yerevan) Galust Petrosyan (FC Pyunik Yerevan)	21
2005	FC Pyunik Yerevan	FC Mika Yerevan	Nshan Erzrumyan (Kilikia FC Yerevan)	18
2006	FC Pyunik Yerevan	FC Mika Yerevan	Aram Hakobyan (FC Banants Yerevan)	25
2007	FC Pyunik Yerevan	FC Banants Yerevan	Marcos Pinheiro Pizzelli (Ararat Yerevan)	22
2008	FC Pyunik Yerevan	FC Ararat Yerevan	Marcos Pinheiro Pizzelli (Ararat Yerevan)	17
2009	FC Pyunik Yerevan	FC Pyunik Yerevan	Artur Kocharyan (Ulisses FC Yerevan)	15
2010	FC Pyunik Yerevan	FC Pyunik Yerevan	Marcos Pinheiro Pizzelli (FC Pyunik Yerevan) Gevorg Ghazaryan (FC Pyunik Yerevan)	16
2011	Ulisses FC Yerevan	FC Mika Yerevan	Bruno César Correa (BRA, FC Banants Yerevan)	16
2011/2012	*Transitional Season (No winner)*	Shirak SC Gyumri	-	
2012/2013	Shirak SC Gyumri	FC Pyunik Yerevan	Norayr Gyozalyan (Impuls FC Dilijan)	21
2013/2014	FC Banants Yerevan	FC Pyunik Yerevan	Mihran Manasyan (FC Alashkert Yerevan)	17
2014/2015	FC Pyunik Yerevan	FC Pyunik Yerevan	César Romero Zamora (USA, FC Pyunik Yerevan) Jean-Jacques Bougouhi (CIV, Shirak SC Gyumri)	21
2015/2016	FC Alashkert Yerevan	FC Banants Yerevan	Héber Araujo dos Santos (BRA, FC Alashkert Yerevan); Mihran Manasyan (FC Alashkert Yerevan)	16
2016/2017	FC Alashkert Yerevan	Shirak SC Gyumri	Artak Yedigaryan (FC Alashkert Yerevan) Mihran Manasyan (FC Alashkert Yerevan)	13
2017/2018	FC Alashkert Yerevan	FC Gandzasar Kapan	Artak Yedigaryan (FC Alashkert Yerevan) Gegham Harutyunyan (FC Gandzasar Kapan)	12
2018/2019	FC Ararat-Armenia Yerevan	FC Alashkert Yerevan	Jonel Désiré (HAI, Lori FC Vanadzor)	17
2019/2020	FC Ararat-Armenia Yerevan	FC Noah Yerevan	Mory Koné (CIV, Shirak SC Gyumri)	23

Please note: Homenetmen Yerevan became FC Pyunik Yerevan (1995); Tsement Ararat changed its name to Araks Ararat FC (2000).

NATIONAL CHAMPIONSHIP
Armenian Premier League 2019/2020
(02.08.2019 – 14.07.2020)

Round 1 [02-03.08.2019]
Shirak SC - FC Urartu 3-1
FC Ararat - FC Yerevan 1-0
FC Gandzasar - FC Noah 1-1
FC Pyunik - Lori FC 3-1 [26.09.]
FC Alashkert - FC Ararat-Armenia 2-1[29.10.]

Round 2 [09-11.08.2019]
FC Yerevan - FC Noah 0-2
FC Ararat - Shirak SC 2-1
FC Ararat-Armenia - FC Gandzasar 3-1
Lori FC - FC Alashkert 2-1
FC Urartu - FC Pyunik 0-3

Round 3 [16-19.08.2019]
Shirak SC - FC Yerevan 2-1
FC Alashkert - FC Urartu 2-1
FC Gandzasar - Lori FC 1-1
FC Noah - FC Ararat-Armenia 1-2
FC Pyunik - FC Ararat 1-4

Round 4 [24-26.08.2019]
Lori FC - FC Noah 1-0
FC Urartu - FC Gandzasar 1-1
Shirak SC - FC Pyunik 3-1
FC Yerevan - FC Ararat-Armenia 1-2
FC Ararat - FC Alashkert 1-1

Round 5 [29-31.08.2019]
FC Noah - FC Urartu 2-0
FC Pyunik - FC Yerevan 4-1
FC Alashkert - Shirak SC 1-2
FC Gandzasar - FC Ararat 0-1
FC Ararat-Armenia - Lori FC 0-0 [06.11.]

Round 6 [13-15.09.2019]
FC Yerevan - Lori FC 0-1
FC Urartu - FC Ararat-Armenia 1-1
FC Pyunik - FC Alashkert 0-3
Shirak SC - FC Gandzasar 0-0
FC Ararat - FC Noah 1-0

Round 7 [17-18.09.2019]
Lori FC - FC Urartu 2-1
FC Alashkert - FC Yerevan 5-1
FC Gandzasar - FC Pyunik 1-2
FC Noah - Shirak SC 0-0
FC Ararat-Armenia - FC Ararat 1-0

Round 8 [21-22.09.2019]
FC Yerevan - FC Urartu 0-1
Shirak SC - FC Ararat-Armenia 1-0
FC Alashkert - FC Gandzasar 2-0
Lori FC - FC Ararat 1-4
FC Pyunik - FC Noah 1-2

Round 9 [27-30.09.2019]
FC Gandzasar - FC Yerevan 2-0
FC Noah - FC Alashkert 1-2
FC Urartu - FC Ararat 1-0
Lori FC - Shirak SC 0-0
FC Ararat-Armenia - FC Pyunik 3-1

Round 10 [04-06.10.2019]
FC Yerevan - FC Ararat 1-3
Lori FC - FC Pyunik 2-2
FC Ararat-Armenia - FC Alashkert 2-0
FC Urartu - Shirak SC 2-2
FC Noah - FC Gandzasar 2-1

Round 11 [18-21.10.2019]
FC Noah - FC Yerevan 3-1
Shirak SC - FC Ararat 2-1
FC Alashkert - Lori FC 0-1
FC Pyunik - FC Urartu 1-2
FC Gandzasar - FC Ararat-Armenia 2-1

Round 12 [25-27.10.2019]
FC Yerevan - Shirak SC 1-4
FC Ararat - FC Pyunik 3-1
FC Urartu - FC Alashkert 2-4
Lori FC - FC Gandzasar 2-1
FC Ararat-Armenia - FC Noah 4-2

Round 13 [08-10.11.2019]
FC Gandzasar - FC Urartu 2-4
FC Pyunik - Shirak SC 1-0
FC Alashkert - FC Ararat 1-1
FC Noah - Lori FC 3-1
FC Ararat-Armenia - FC Yerevan 7-2

Round 14 [22-25.11.2019]
FC Ararat - FC Gandzasar 1-1
Shirak SC - FC Alashkert 1-3
Lori FC - FC Ararat-Armenia 2-0
FC Urartu - FC Noah 0-0
FC Yerevan - FC Pyunik 2-8

Round 15 [01-02.12.2019]
FC Alashkert - FC Pyunik 1-1
Lori FC - FC Yerevan 8-0
FC Ararat-Armenia - FC Urartu 0-0
FC Noah - FC Ararat 2-0
FC Gandzasar - Shirak SC 1-0

Round 16 [28.02.-02.03.2020]
FC Yerevan - FC Alashkert 0-3 *awarded*
Shirak SC - FC Noah 3-0
FC Pyunik - FC Gandzasar 2-0
FC Ararat - FC Ararat-Armenia 0-3
FC Urartu - Lori FC 2-0

Round 17 [06-08.03.2020]
FC Gandzasar - FC Alashkert 2-2
FC Urartu - FC Yerevan 3-0 *awarded*
FC Noah - FC Pyunik 4-2
FC Ararat-Armenia - Shirak SC 1-0
FC Ararat - Lori FC 0-0

Round 18 [23-25.05.2020]
FC Yerevan - FC Gandzasar 0-3 *awarded*
Shirak SC - Lori FC 1-2
FC Pyunik - FC Ararat-Armenia 0-3
FC Alashkert - FC Noah 0-1
FC Ararat - FC Urartu 1-0

Final Standings

1.	FC Ararat-Armenia Yerevan	18	11	3	4	33 - 15	36
2.	Lori FC Vanadzor	18	9	5	4	27 - 19	32
3.	FC Alashkert Yerevan	18	9	4	5	33 - 20	31
4.	FC Ararat Yerevan	18	9	4	5	25 - 18	31
5.	FC Noah Yerevan	18	9	3	6	25 - 19	30
6.	Shirak SC Gyumri	18	8	4	6	25 - 18	28
7.	FC Pyunik Yerevan	18	7	2	9	35 - 36	23
8.	FC Urartu Yerevan	18	6	5	7	22 - 24	23
9.	FC Gandzasar Kapan	18	4	6	8	20 - 25	18
10.	FC Yerevan	18	0	0	18	11 - 62	0

<u>Please note</u>: on 01.08.2019, FC Banants Yerevan changed its name to FC Urartu Yerevan.
Teams ranked 1-6 were qualified for the Championship Round, while teams ranked 7-9 were qualified for the Relegation Round.
FC Yerevan withdrew due to financial problems on 21.02.2020.

Championship Round

Results

Round 19 [30-31.05.2020]
Lori FC - FC Noah 2-2
FC Ararat-Armenia - Shirak SC 1-1
FC Alashkert - FC Ararat 2-1

Round 20 [03-04.06.2020]
FC Ararat-Armenia - Lori FC 0-0
Shirak SC - FC Ararat 2-0
FC Noah - FC Alashkert 1-0

Round 21 [07-08.06.2020]
FC Ararat - FC Noah 0-0
Lori FC - Shirak SC 1-1
FC Alashkert - FC Ararat-Armenia 1-2

Round 22 [11-12.06.2020]
Shirak SC - FC Noah 2-0
FC Ararat-Armenia - FC Ararat 4-2
Lori FC - FC Alashkert 0-2

Round 23 [15-16.06.2020]
FC Noah - FC Ararat-Armenia 1-1
FC Alashkert - Shirak SC 1-2
FC Ararat - Lori FC 1-1

Round 24 [20-21.06.2020]
Shirak SC - FC Ararat-Armenia 1-0
FC Noah - Lori FC 2-1
FC Ararat - FC Alashkert 1-3

Round 25 [27-28.06.2020]
FC Ararat - Shirak SC 1-4
FC Alashkert - FC Noah 0-1
Lori FC - FC Ararat-Armenia 2-1

Round 26 [02.07.2020]
Shirak SC - Lori FC 0-0
FC Noah - FC Ararat 1-0
FC Ararat-Armenia - FC Alashkert 0-0

Round 27 [06-07.07.2020]
FC Noah - Shirak SC 4-0
FC Ararat - FC Ararat-Armenia 0-1
FC Alashkert - Lori FC 5-1

Round 28 [14.07.2020]
Shirak SC - FC Alashkert 2-4
Lori FC - FC Ararat *not played*
FC Ararat-Armenia - FC Noah 2-0

Relegation Round

Results

Round 19 [01.06.2020]
FC Urartu - FC Gandzasar 1-0

Round 20 [09.06.2020]
FC Pyunik - FC Urartu 1-2

Round 21 [13.06.2020]
FC Gandzasar - FC Pyunik 1-0

Round 22 [17.06.2020]
FC Gandzasar - FC Urartu 1-1

Round 23 [28.06.2020]
FC Urartu - FC Pyunik 0-1

Round 24 [01.07.2020]
FC Pyunik - FC Gandzasar 2-3

Final Standings

								Total			Home			Away		
1.	**FC Ararat -Armenia Yerevan**	28	15	7	6	45 - 23	52	9	5	0	27 - 8	6	2	6	18 - 15
2.	FC Noah Yerevan	28	14	6	8	37 - 27	48	10	2	2	27 - 11	4	4	6	10 - 16
3.	FC Alashkert Yerevan	28	14	5	9	51 - 31	47	6	2	6	23 - 16	8	3	3	28 - 15
4.	Shirak SC Gyumri	28	13	7	8	40 - 30	46	9	2	3	23 - 13	4	5	5	17 - 17
5.	Lori FC Vanadzor	27	10	10	7	35 - 33	40	7	4	2	25 - 15	3	6	5	10 - 18
6.	FC Ararat Yerevan	27	9	6	12	31 - 36	33	5	5	4	14 - 17	4	1	8	17 - 19
7.	FC Urartu Yerevan	22	8	6	8	26 - 27	30	4	4	3	13 - 12	4	2	5	13 - 15
8.	FC Pyunik Yerevan	22	8	2	12	39 - 42	26	4	0	7	16 - 21	4	2	5	23 - 21
9.	FC Gandzasar Kapan	22	6	7	9	25 - 29	25	4	4	3	14 - 13	2	3	6	11 - 16
10.	FC Yerevan	18	0	0	18	11 - 62	0	0	0	9	5 - 27	0	0	9	6 - 35

Top goalscorers:

23	**Mory Koné (CIV)**	*Shirak SC Gyumri*
12	Jonel Désiré (HAI)	*Lori FC Vanadzor*
11	Gustavo Marmentini dos Santos (BRA)	*FC Alashkert Yerevan*
11	Aleksandar Glišić (BIH)	*FC Alashkert Yerevan*
11	Maksim Mayrovich	*FC Noah Yerevan*

NATIONAL CUP
Armenian Cup Final 2019/2020

1/8-Finals [01-03.11.2019]

Dilijan FC - Lori FC Vanadzor	0-3 *awarded*	FC Pyunik Yerevan - FC Urartu Yerevan	3-5 pen
FC Gandzasar Kapan - Shirak SC Gyumri	2-1	FC West Armenia Y. - FC Ararat-Armenia Yerevan	0-5
Sevan FC - FC Yerevan	2-0	FC Torpedo Yerevan - FC Alashkert Yerevan	1-3
FC Lokomotiv Yerevan - FC Van Charentsavan	0-1	FC Noah Yerevan - FC Ararat Yerevan	1-0

Quarter-Finals [27.11.2019]

Sevan FC - FC Ararat-Armenia Yerevan	2-11	Lori FC Vanadzor - FC Urartu Yerevan	0-1
FC Van Charentsavan - FC Noah Yerevan	0-1	FC Gandzasar Kapan - FC Alashkert Yerevan	3-1

Semi-Finals [11.03./24.06.2020]

First Leg		Second Leg	
FC Ararat-Armenia Yerevan - FC Gandzasar Kapan	1-0	FC Noah Yerevan - FC Urartu Yerevan	2-1
FC Urartu Yerevan - FC Noah Yerevan	0-1	Gandzasar Kapan - FC Ararat-Armenia Yerevan	0-2

Final

10.07.2020; Yerevan Football Academy Stadium, Yerevan; Referee: Zaven Hovhannisyan; Attendance: none
FC Noah Yerevan - FC Ararat-Armenia Yerevan   **5-5(1-4,4-4,5-5); 7-6 on penalties**

Noah Yerevan: Maksim Shvagirev, Vladislav Kryuchkov, Mikhail Kovalenko, Alan Tataev, Pavel Deobald (76.Yuri Gareginyan), Vladimir Azarov, Eduards Emsis (111.Vigen Avetisyan), Dmitri Lavrishchev (88.Rokas Krušnauskas), Helistano Ciro Manga (46.Kirill Bor), Danu Spătaru (76.Edgar Grigoryan), Maksim Mayrovich (58.Sergey Dmitriev). Trainer: Vadim Boreţ (Moldova).

Ararat-Armenia: Stefan Čupić, Rochdi Achenteh (60.Alex Júnior Christian), Serhiy Vakulenko (91.Dmitri Guzj), Ângelo Rafael Teixeira Alpoim Meneses, Artur Danielyan, Armen Ambartsumyan (74.Zakaria Sanogo), Kódjo Kassé Alphonse [*sent off 90+3*], Furdjel Narsingh (84.Armen Nahapetyan), Yusuf Olaitan Otubanjo, Ogana Louis Ugochukwu (84.Anton Kobyalko), Mailson Lima Duarte Lopes (74.Gor Malakyan). Trainer: Vardan Minasyan.

Goals: 0-1 Ogana Louis Ugochukwu (8), 0-2 Alan Tataev (23 own goal), 0-3 Yusuf Olaitan Otubanjo (29), 1-3 Maksim Mayrovich (39), 1-4 Ogana Louis Ugochukwu (40), 2-4 Vladimir Azarov (56), 3-4 Mikhail Kovalenko (60), 4-4 Danu Spătaru (67), 5-4 Vladimir Azarov (115), 5-5 Yusuf Olaitan Otubanjo (117).

Penalties: Armen Nahapetyan (saved); Kirill Bor (saved); Anton Kobyalko 0-1; Vladimir Azarov 1-1; Ângelo Rafael Teixeira Alpoim Meneses 1-2; Vigen Avetisyan (missed); Gor Malakyan (saved); Yuri Gareginyan 2-2; Yusuf Olaitan Otubanjo 2-3; Sergey Dmitriev 3-3; Zakaria Sanogo 3-4; Mikhail Kovalenko 4-4; Alex Júnior Christian 4-5; Edgar Grigoryan 5-5; Dmitri Guzj 5-6; Vladislav Kryuchkov 6-6; Artur Danielyan (missed); Rokas Krušnauskas 7-6.

THE CLUBS 2019/2020

Football Club Alashkert Yerevan

Founded:	1990
Stadium:	Alashkert Stadium, Yerevan (6,850)
Trainer:	Abraham Khashmanyan 11.11.1967
[04.09.2019]	Armen Adamyan 14.10.1967
[28.06.2020]	Yegishe Melikyan 13.08.1979

Goalkeepers:	DOB	M	(s)	G
Henri Avagyan	16.01.1996	1		
Ognjen Čančarević (SRB)	25.09.1989	26		
Defenders:	**DOB**	**M**	**(s)**	**G**
Nikita Baranov (EST)	19.08.1992	21		
Bryan Silva Garcia (BRA)	28.03.1992	8	(3)	1
Gagik Dagbashyan	19.10.1990	2	(3)	
Hayk Ishkhanyan	24.06.1989	1	(2)	
Aleksandar Miljković (SRB)	26.02.1990	13		
Risto Mitrevski (MKD)	05.10.1991	12		2
Ghukas Poghosyan	06.02.1994		(1)	
Tiago Coelho Andrade "Tiago Cametá" (BRA)	05.05.1992	25		
Taron Voskanyan	22.02.1993	24	(1)	
Midfielders:	**DOB**	**M**	**(s)**	**G**
Eduard Avagyan	21.03.1996		(3)	2

	DOB	M	(s)	G
Pape Abdou Camara (SEN)	24.09.1991	4	(6)	1
Hayk Galstyan	23.03.1998		(1)	
Wangu Batista Gome (NAM)		10	(1)	
Artak Grigoryan	19.10.1987	20	(3)	
Gustavo Marmentini dos Santos (BRA)	08.03.1994	22	(2)	11
Vahagn Hayrapetyan	14.06.1997	11	(11)	1
Sunday Umaru Ngbede (NGA)	23.04.1998	1	(1)	
Arman Sargsyan	23.07.1997		(1)	
Tiago Galvão da Silva (BRA)	24.08.1989	26	(1)	8
Forwards:	**DOB**	**M**	**(s)**	**G**
David Gatikoev (RUS)	14.09.1993		(7)	1
Aleksandar Glišić (BIH)	03.09.1992	20	(2)	11
Akhmed Jindoyan	02.10.1997	1		
Edgar Manucharyan	19.01.1987		(5)	
Nikita Tankov	29.09.1996	9	(12)	4

Football Club Ararat Yerevan

Founded: 10.05.1935
Stadium: „Vazgen Sargsyan" Stadium, Yerevan (14,403)

Trainer:	Sergey Bulatov (RUS)	21.03.1972
[29.07.2019]	Sergey Boiko (RUS)	14.09.1971
[16.09.2019]	Gagik Simonyan	21.08.1971
[14.10.2019]	Vadym Lazorenko (UKR)	01.03.1965
[01.01.2020]	Igor Kolyvanov (RUS)	06.03.1968
[04.06.2020]	Ara Abrahamyan	28.08.1971

Goalkeepers:	DOB	M	(s)	G
Evgeniy Kobozev (RUS)	11.01.1990	3		
Sergey Revyakin (RUS)	02.04.1995	24		
Defenders:	**DOB**	**M**	**(s)**	**G**
Ruslan Avagyan	24.06.1995		(1)	
David Davidyan (RUS)	14.12.1997	18	(1)	1
Rafael Henrique Milhorim „Ferrugem" (BRA)	17.03.1999	8		
James Santos das Neves (BRA)	05.02.1995	14		
Evgeni Makeev (RUS)	24.07.1989	8		
Konstantin Morozov (RUS)	13.05.1992	14	(3)	
Vahe Muradyan	28.01.1998	1		
Thomas Phibel (GLP)	21.05.1986	6	(2)	
Ivan Spychka (UKR)	18.01.1991	24	(1)	1
Pavel Stepanets (RUS)	27.05.1987	10		
Midfielders:	**DOB**	**M**	**(s)**	**G**
Petros Afajanyan	31.10.1998		(2)	
Zurab Arziani	19.10.1987	6	(6)	
Levon Badalyan	07.02.2002			
Zaven Badoyan	22.12.1989	7	(14)	3
David Baghdasaryan	08.03.1998		(3)	
Denys Dedechko (UKR)	02.07.1987	19	(1)	6
Lukman Abdulkarim Haruna (NGA)	04.12.1990	4	(1)	
Arkadi Kalaydzhyan (RUS)	01.12.1992	8	(3)	
David Khurtsidze (RUS)	04.07.1993	26		4
Aleksandr Kozlov (RUS)	19.03.1993	19		4
Albert Mnatsakanyan	09.09.1999		(1)	
Karen Shirkhanyan	06.04.2000	3		
Victor Hugo Coelho Vieira "Vitinho" (BRA)	08.09.1997	11	(2)	
Forwards:	**DOB**	**M**	**(s)**	**G**
David Arshakyan	16.08.1994	3	(2)	1
Georgi Chelidze (RUS)	20.01.2000	13	(3)	1
Igor Gabriel Aguiar (BRA)	02.01.2001		(1)	
Razmik Hakobyan	09.02.1996	1	(2)	
Ramazan Isaev (RUS)	17.01.1998		(9)	1
Ganiyu Bolaji Oseni (NGA)	19.09.1991	5	(3)	
Dmitri Ryzhov (RUS)	26.08.1989	3	(7)	1
Sancidino Malam da Silva (GNB)	05.03.1994		(2)	
Weslen Junior Faustino de Melo (BRA)	12.11.1999	15	(9)	4

Football Club Ararat-Armenia Yerevan

Founded: 2017
Stadium: Yerevan Football Academy Stadium, Yerevan (1,428)

Trainer:	Vardan Minasyan	05.01.1974

Goalkeepers:	DOB	M	(s)	G
Dmitri Abakumov (RUS)	08.07.1989	22		
Stefan Čupić (SRB)	07.05.1994	6		
Defenders:	**DOB**	**M**	**(s)**	**G**
Rochdi Achenteh (MAR)	07.03.1988	13	(1)	
Ângelo Rafael Teixeira Alpoim Meneses(POR)	03.07.1993	23	(1)	1
Alex Júnior Christian (HAI)	12.05.1993	16	(3)	
Aleksandar Damčevski (MKD)	21.11.1992	7	(3)	
Artur Danielyan	09.02.1998	15	(3)	
Dmitri Guzj (RUS)	15.05.1988	15	(6)	3
Albert Khachumyan	23.06.1999	7	(3)	
Serhiy Vakulenko (UKR)	07.09.1993	10		3
Midfielders:	**DOB**	**M**	**(s)**	**G**
Kódjo Kassé Alphonse (CIV)	28.05.1993	22		1
Armen Ambartsumyan	11.04.1994	11	(5)	3
Ilja Antonov (EST)	05.12.1992	8	(10)	
Artem Avanesyan (RUS)	17.07.1999	5		
Yoan Gouffran (FRA)	25.05.1986	7	(6)	1
Hovhannes Harutyunyan	25.05.1999	5	(4)	
Gor Malakyan	12.06.1994	15	(4)	
Armen Nahapetyan	24.07.1999	1	(7)	
Forwards:	**DOB**	**M**	**(s)**	**G**
Anton Kobyalko (RUS)	14.05.1986	9	(13)	4
Mailson Lima Duarte Lopes (CPV)	29.05.1994	20	(6)	8
Furdjel Narsingh (NED)	13.03.1988	18	(2)	4
Ogana Louis Ugochukwu (NGA)	29.12.1995	9	(11)	3
Yusuf Olaitan Otubanjo (NGA)	12.09.1992	13		7

Football Club Gandzasar Kapan

Founded: 2004
Stadium: Yerevan Football Academy Stadium, Yerevan (1,428)

Trainer:	Armen Petrosyan	26.09.1985

Goalkeepers:	DOB	M	(s)	G
Gevorg Kasparov	25.07.1980	9		
Arman Meliksetyan	01.04.2001	1		
Grigor Meliksetyan	18.08.1986	11		
Defenders:	**DOB**	**M**	**(s)**	**G**
Hamlet Asoyan	13.01.1995	5	(3)	
Hakob Hambardzumyan	26.05.1997	4		
Annan Mensah	06.07.1996	16	(1)	
Vaspurak Minasyan	29.06.1994	12		1
Gevorg Nranyan	09.03.1986	16		
Midfielders:	**DOB**	**M**	**(s)**	**G**
Adam Adamyan	22.04.1992	5	(11)	1
Grigor Aghekyan	06.04.1996	3	(2)	
Wbeymar Angulo Mosquera (COL)	06.03.1992	15	(3)	1
Narek Aslanyan	04.06.1996	7	(3)	
Artur Grigoryan	10.07.1993	15	(2)	
Alexander Hovhannisyan	20.07.1996	9		
Ivanisio de Souza Pontes Junior "Juninho" (BRA)	04.01.1992	3	(2)	
Ashot Kocharyan	13.07.1999	3	(1)	
Davit Minasyan	09.03.1993	12	(4)	2
Alen Tatintsyan	29.06.2003		(1)	
Emil Yeghiazaryan	03.11.1997	9	(10)	2
Abdoul Karim Zoko (BFA)	27.07.1993	10	(2)	1
Forwards:	**DOB**	**M**	**(s)**	**G**
Gegham Harutyunyan	23.08.1990	9	(3)	6
Andranik Kocharyan	29.01.1994	13	(5)	2
Vardan Pogosyan	08.03.1992	4	(7)	1

Lori Football Club Vanadzor

Founded: 1936
Stadium: Vanadzor Football Academy Stadium, Vanadzot (1,000)
Trainer: David Campaña Piquer (ESP) — 23.05.1974
[02.06.2020] Armen Sanamyan — 01.02.1966

Goalkeepers:	DOB	M	(s)	G
Bruno Ferreira dos Santos (BRA)	26.09.1989	2		
Diego Barrios Pérez (ESP)	30.06.1994	1		
Mickaël Meira (POR)	25.01.1994	5		
Vardan Shahatuni	13.03.1998	19		
Defenders:	**DOB**	**M**	**(s)**	**G**
Djimy Alexis (HAI)	08.10.1997	21	(1)	
Arthur Avagyan	04.07.1987	17	(4)	1
Juan David Bravo Padilla (COL)	01.04.1990	19	(2)	
Christian Jiménez (ESP)	04.07.1996	14	(2)	
Luiz Matheus Servo de Carvalho (BRA)	10.01.1993	13		2
Arman Mkrtchyan	09.07.1999	9	(8)	1
Pedro Juan Morillo Aguilar (ESP)	07.09.1998	4	(4)	
Gianni Danielle Rodríguez Fernández (URU)	07.06.1994	4	(1)	
Alexandre Primaël Yeoulé (CIV)	23.12.1995	22	(1)	1
Midfielders:	**DOB**	**M**	**(s)**	**G**
Tode Đaković (BIH)	10.01.1996	1		
Diogo Manuel Gonçalves Coelho (POR)	08.07.1992	8	(2)	1
José Luis Alfonso Gamboa Agudelo (COL)	12.04.2000		(1)	
Ugochukwu Christus Iwu (NGA)	28.10.1999	7		2
Anicet Oura (CIV)	07.12.1999	5	(4)	
David Paremuzyan	02.03.2000		(3)	
Sargis Shahinyan	10.09.1995	10	(2)	1
Julius David Ufuoma (NGA)	14.02.2000	22		
Ruslan Zaerko (RUS)	27.06.1993	16	(1)	4
Xabier "Xabi" Auzmendi Arruabarrena (ESP)	01.05.1997	19	(4)	2
Forwards:	**DOB**	**M**	**(s)**	**G**
Jonel Désiré (HAI)	12.02.1997	22	(1)	12
Enoch Darko (GHA)	09.09.2000	1	(3)	
David Ghandilyan	04.06.1993		(2)	
Mihran Manasyan	13.01.1989	3	(5)	1
Agustín Maziero (ARG)	27.11.1997	5	(2)	2
Robert Minasyan	08.04.1997	2	(12)	2

Football Club Noah Yerevan

Founded: 2017
Stadium: Alashkert Stadium, Yerevan (6,850)
Trainer: Vadim Boreț (MDA) — 05.09.1976

Goalkeepers:	DOB	M	(s)	G
Arman Meliksetyan	21.07.1995	4		
Maksim Shvagirev (RUS)	12.08.1994	2		
Valerio Vimercati (ITA)	04.03.1995	22		
Defenders:	**DOB**	**M**	**(s)**	**G**
Edgar Grigoryan	25.08.1998	1	(6)	
Karen Harutyunyan	06.07.1995	1	(3)	
Soslan Kagermazov (RUS)	20.08.1996	21	(1)	
Mikhail Kovalenko (RUS)	25.01.1995	17	(2)	2
Vladislav Kryuchkov (RUS)	24.08.1989	23		1
Vardan Movsisyan	18.08.1991	6	(4)	
Saná Gomes (GNB)	10.10.1999	1		
Alan Tataev (RUS)	03.08.1995	26		
Vitali Zaprudskikh (RUS)	01.01.1991	10	(1)	
Midfielders:	**DOB**	**M**	**(s)**	**G**
Vladimir Azarov (RUS)	19.03.1994	23	(2)	8
Pavel Deobald (RUS)	25.06.1990	18	(2)	2
Sergey Dmitriev (RUS)	14.02.1997	2	(8)	
Eduards Emsis (LVA)	23.02.1996	11	(2)	
Yuri Gareginyan	03.02.1994	12	(11)	
Helistano Ciro Manga (GNB)	20.05.1999	11	(1)	
Benik Hovhannisyan	01.05.1993	11	(7)	
Dmitri Lavrishchev (RUS)	23.12.1998	9	(15)	3
Forwards:	**DOB**	**M**	**(s)**	**G**
Vigen Avetisyan	12.01.1993	2	(8)	
Kirill Bor (RUS)	09.11.1998	14	(8)	3
Rokas Krušnauskas (LTU)	04.11.1995	4	(3)	2
Maksim Mayrovich (RUS)	06.02.1996	27		11
Danu Spătaru (MDA)	24.05.1994	13		3

Football Club Pyunik Yerevan

Founded: 1992 (*as Homenetmen Yerevan*)
Stadium: „Vazgen Sargsyan" Stadium, Yerevan (14,403)
Trainer: Aleksandr Tarkhanov (RUS) — 06.09.1954
[24.10.2019] Suren Chakhalyan — 24.08.1972
[08.01.2020] Roman Berezovskiy — 05.08.1974

Goalkeepers:	DOB	M	(s)	G
Sevak Aslanyan	17.05.1998	2		
Andrija Dragojević (MNE)	25.12.1991	17		
Vladimir Sugrobov	10.09.1996	3		
Defenders:	**DOB**	**M**	**(s)**	**G**
Serob Grigoryan	04.02.1995	15	(1)	
Robert Hakobyan	22.10.1996	7	(1)	
Artur Kartashyan	08.01.1997	7		
Armen Manucharyan	03.02.1995	14	(2)	2
Kristi Marku (ALB)	13.04.1995	5		
Guy Mfingi Magema (COD)	24.01.1996	5		
Salomon Nirisarike (RWA)	23.11.1993	10		1
Arsen Sargsyan	19.07.2000		(2)	1
Antonio Stankov (MKD)	19.02.1991	10	(3)	1
Artak Yedigaryan	18.03.1990	11	(6)	4
Midfielders:	**DOB**	**M**	**(s)**	**G**
Joseph Adah (NGA)	06.12.1997	5	(1)	1
Daniel Aghbalyan	12.03.1999	3	(1)	
Alik Arakelyan	21.05.1996	7	(2)	1
Erik Azizyan	04.03.2000	3	(2)	1
Norayr Ghazaryan	22.06.2002		(5)	
Dmitriy Malyaka (RUS)	15.01.1990	2	(1)	
Karlen Mkrtchyan	25.11.1988	6		1
Artur Nadiryan	27.03.1998		(1)	
Pertsh Poghikyan	03.02.2000		(1)	
Serhiy Shevchuk (UKR)	18.06.1985	12	(4)	1
Artem Simonyan	20.02.1995	13	(6)	3
Maksim Zhestokov (RUS)	19.06.1991	17		
Forwards:	**DOB**	**M**	**(s)**	**G**
Stephen Alfred (NGA)	11.10.1997	3	(6)	1
Denis Mahmudov (MKD)	11.06.1989	12	(4)	9
Artur Miranyan	27.12.1995	11	(2)	6
Aras Özbiliz	09.03.1990	9	(2)	5
Levon Vardanyan	02.11.2003	3	(3)	

Shirak Sports Club Gyumri

Founded: 1958
Stadium: Gyumri City Stadium, Gyumri (4,000)
Trainer: Vardan Bichakhchyan — 09.10.1977

Goalkeepers:	DOB	M	(s)	G
Vsevolod Ermakov (RUS)	06.01.1996	28		
Defenders:	**DOB**	**M**	**(s)**	**G**
Vardan Arzoyan	30.04.1995		(2)	
Aghvan Davoyan	21.03.1990	16	(1)	
Zhirayr Margaryan	13.09.1997	18	(8)	2
Artyom Mikaelyan	12.07.1991	11	(1)	
Bogdan Milićić (SRB)	06.01.1989	25	(1)	
Hrayr Mkoyan	02.09.1986	19		
Marko Prljević (SRB)	02.08.1988	24	(1)	
Midfielders:	**DOB**	**M**	**(s)**	**G**
Arman Aslanyan	30.01.1994	17	(9)	1
Edgar Malakyan	22.09.1990	19	(4)	
David Manoyan	05.07.1990	9	(4)	
Rafik Misakyan	02.01.2000	6	(5)	1
Rudik Mkrtchyan	26.10.1998	11	(6)	1
Karen Muradyan	01.11.1992	25	(2)	
Solomon Ime Udo	15.07.1995	20	(4)	2
Forwards:	**DOB**	**M**	**(s)**	**G**
Leibe Junior Avo (CIV)	20.12.1997	3	(8)	
Albert Darbinyan	02.01.2002		(1)	
Artem Gevorkyan (RUS)	21.05.1993	12	(9)	2
Mory Kone (CIV)	13.07.1995	28		23
Lyova Mryan	11.05.2000		(5)	
Aram Muradyan	14.04.1995	1	(14)	1
Uroš Nenadović (SRB)	28.01.1994	5	(5)	2
Arlen Tsaturyan	05.01.1999		(1)	

Football Club Urartu Yerevan

Founded: 20.01.1992 (*as FC Banants Yerevan*)
Stadium: Banants Stadium, Yerevan (4,860)
Trainer: Ilshat Faizulin — 05.03.1973
[25.11.2019] Aleksandr Grigoryan — 28.09.1966

Goalkeepers:	DOB	M	(s)	G
Anatoly Ayvazov	08.06.1996	8		
Arsen Beglaryan	18.02.1993	4		
Aram Hayrapetyan	22.11.1986	9		
Defenders:	**DOB**	**M**	**(s)**	**G**
Vahagn Ayvazyan	16.04.1992	1	(1)	
Ebert Cardoso da Silva (BRA)	25.05.1993	2	(1)	
Robert Darbinyan	04.10.1995	14	(1)	
Hrachya Geghamyan	02.12.1999	2	(1)	
Edward Kpodo (GHA)	14.01.1990	16		
Evgeniy Osipov (RUS)	29.10.1986	4		
Narek Petrosyan	25.01.1996	8	(3)	
Rubén Alejandro Ramírez Dos Ramos (VEN)	18.10.1995	13		
Arsen Sadoyan	16.03.1999		(1)	
Eric Simonyan	12.07.2003	1		
Midfielders:	**DOB**	**M**	**(s)**	**G**
Aram Bareghamyan	06.01.1988	14		

	DOB	M	(s)	G
Marko Brtan (CRO)	07.04.1991	9	(4)	
Jurica Grgec (CRO)	01.09.1992	19		
Hakob Hakobyan	29.03.1997	11	(6)	2
Peter Mutumosi Zilu (COD)	25.05.1998	8	(2)	
David Papikyan	08.07.2001	2	(1)	
Itoro Joseph Sunday (NGA)	23.02.2002		(2)	
Forwards:	**DOB**	**M**	**(s)**	**G**
Juan Carlos Azócar Segura (VEN)	01.10.1995	11		2
Samvel Hakobyan	30.04.2003	1		
Evgeni Kobzar (RUS)	09.08.1992	18		7
Karen Melkonyan	25.03.1999	8	(11)	1
Igor Paderin (RUS)	24.11.1989	1		1
Erik Petrosyan	19.02.1998		(3)	1
Abraham Portugalyan	08.01.1999	1	(4)	1
Semen Sinyavskiy (RUS)	30.09.1993	7	(7)	2
Gevorg Tarakhchyan	13.05.2002	4	(1)	
Taimuraz Toboev (RUS)	09.03.1995	1	(1)	

Football Club Yerevan

Founded: 1995
Stadium: Vanadzor Football Academy Stadium, Vanadzot (1,000)
Trainer: Nebojša Petrović (SRB) — 14.06.1960
[05.09.2019] Georgi Ghazaryan
[16.09.2019] Vlad Goian (MDA) — 14.11.1970
[04.10.2019] José António Caldas Oliveira (POR) — 01.05.1959

Goalkeepers:	DOB	M	(s)	G
Jānis Krūmiņš (LVA)	09.01.1992	11		
Gregory Makaryan	19.04.1995	4		
Defenders:	**DOB**	**M**	**(s)**	**G**
Pavel Demidchik (BLR)	30.01.1996	7	(4)	
Maksim Evstigneev (RUS)	29.07.1998	6		
Svyatoslav Grabchak (UKR)	04.03.1996	14		1
William Gustavo Constâncio (BRA)	09.01.1992	4		
Denis Lyubimov (RUS)	19.03.1998	5		
Argishti Petrosyan	16.10.1992	10		
Aghavard Petrosyan	16.04.1997	5	(3)	
Gegham Tumbaryan	13.05.1996	3	(4)	
Midfielders:	**DOB**	**M**	**(s)**	**G**
Vladimir Babayan	06.05.1997		(1)	
Levon Bdalyan	07.02.2002	1	(2)	
Pape Demba Dieye (SEN)	25.03.1998	8	(1)	

	DOB	M	(s)	G
Armin Mir Douraghi (IRN)	27.06.1996	4	(2)	
Elias Alves da Silva (BRA)	04.09.1981	8		
Evgeniy Evgenev (RUS)	05.05.1998	13		
Aram Hovsepyan	06.06.1991	1		
Dmytro Klimakov (UKR)	05.03.1989	3	(1)	
Antonio Tesera Georges Lokwa (COD)	26.06.2000	10	(1)	
Vahe Movsisyan	02.02.2002	2	(4)	
Roman Zavialov (RUS)	17.09.1999	8	(1)	
Forwards:	**DOB**	**M**	**(s)**	**G**
Viulen Ayvazyan	01.01.1995	3	(4)	
Jafett Del Portillo Bolaño (COL)	23.11.1991	5		
Ramazan Isaev (RUS)	17.11.1996	11	(3)	6
Jeferson Barbosa da Cruz (BRA)	08.04.1999	4	(3)	1
Sergey Lynko (BLR)	16.10.1989	5		
Edgar L. Mkrtchyan	14.07.1994	5	(4)	
Abraham Portugalyan	08.01.1999	5	(2)	3

SECOND LEVEL
Armenian First League 2019/2020

1.	FC Van Charentsavan (*Promoted*)	28	22	4	2	90 - 18	70
2.	FC Lokomotiv Yerevan	27	22	4	1	76 - 23	70
3.	FC West Armenia Yerevan	27	21	3	3	80 - 37	66
4.	BKMA Yerevan	27	16	2	9	63 - 35	50
5.	FC Ararat-Armenia-2 Yerevan	27	15	3	9	75 - 47	48
6.	FC Alashkert-2 Yerevan	27	14	5	8	69 - 39	47
7.	FC Sevan	28	14	5	9	52 - 42	47
8.	FC Urartu-2 Yerevan	28	14	3	11	72 - 40	45
9.	FC Ararat-2 Yerevan	27	11	4	12	59 - 56	37
10.	FC Torpedo Yerevan	28	8	3	17	48 - 92	27
11.	FC Aragats Ashtarak	28	7	6	15	56 - 71	27
12.	Shirak SC-2 Gyumri	29	7	6	16	41 - 72	27
13.	Lernayin Artsakh FC Stepanakert	25	6	6	13	43 - 44	24
14.	FC Ani	28	6	3	19	31 - 108	21
15.	Masis FC	27	5	5	17	44 - 82	20
16.	Dilijan FC	26	5	4	17	36 - 97	19
17.	FC Pyunik-2 Yerevan	27	5	2	20	44 - 76	17

INTERNATIONAL MATCHES
(16.07.2019 – 15.07.2020)

05.09.2019	Yerevan	Armenia - Italy	1-3(1-1)	(ECQ)
08.09.2019	Yerevan	Armenia - Bosnia and Herzegovina	4-2(1-1)	(ECQ)
12.10.2019	Vaduz	Liechtenstein - Armenia	1-1(0-1)	(ECQ)
15.10.2019	Turku	Finland - Armenia	3-0(1-0)	(ECQ)
15.11.2019	Yerevan	Armenia - Greece	0-1(0-1)	(ECQ)
18.11.2019	Palermo	Italy - Armenia	9-1(4-0)	(ECQ)

05.09.2019   ARMENIA - ITALY   **1-3(1-1)**   16th EC. Qualifiers
„Vazgen Sargsyan" Hanrapetakan Stadium, Yerevan; Referee: Daniel Siebert (Germany); Attendance: 13,680
ARM: Aram Hayrapetyan, Hovhannes Hambartsumyan, André Jack Calisir, Varazdat Haroyan, Karlen Mkrtchyan, Henrikh Mkhitaryan (Cap), Kamo Hovhannisyan, Artak Grigoryan (57.Rumyan Hovsepyan), Gevorg Ghazaryan (82.Edgar Babayan), Aleksandr Karapetyan [*sent off 45+1*], Tigran Barseghyan (57.Sargis Adamyan). Trainer: Armen Gyulbudaghyants.
Goal: Aleksandr Karapetyan (11).

08.09.2019   ARMENIA - BOSNIA AND HERZEGOVINA   4-2(1-1)   16th EC. Qualifiers
„Vazgen Sargsyan" Hanrapetakan Stadium, Yerevan; Referee: Benoît Bastien (France); Attendance: 12,457
ARM: Aram Hayrapetyan, Hovhannes Hambartsumyan, Varazdat Haroyan, Hayk Ishkhanyan, Karlen Mkrtchyan (Cap) (75.Artak Grigoryan), Henrikh Mkhitaryan, Kamo Hovhannisyan (83.Arman Hovhannisyan), Rumyan Hovsepyan (79.Erik Vardanyan), Gevorg Ghazaryan, Tigran Barseghyan, Sargis Adamyan. Trainer: Armen Gyulbudaghyants.
Goals: Henrikh Mkhitaryan (3, 66), Hovhannes Hambartsumyan (77), Stjepan Lončar (90+5 own goal).

12.10.2019   LIECHTENSTEIN - ARMENIA   **1-1(0-1)**   16th EC. Qualifiers
Rheinpark Stadion, Vaduz; Referee: István Kovács (Romania); Attendance: 2,285
ARM: Aram Hayrapetyan, Hovhannes Hambartsumyan, Varazdat Haroyan, Hayk Ishkhanyan, Arman Hovhannisyan, Rumyan Hovsepyan (83.Artur Miranyan), Marcos Pinheiro Pizzelli (60.Gor Malakyan), Aleksandr Karapetyan, Tigran Barseghyan, Gevorg Ghazaryan (Cap) (88.Aras Özbiliz), Sargis Adamyan. Trainer: Armen Gyulbudaghyants.
Goal: Tigran Barseghyan (19).

15.10.2019   FINLAND - ARMENIA   **3-0(1-0)**   16th EC. Qualifiers
Veritas Stadion, Turku; Referee: Jesús Gil Manzano (Spain); Attendance: 7,231
ARM: Aram Hayrapetyan, Hovhannes Hambartsumyan, Varazdat Haroyan, Hayk Ishkhanyan, Rumyan Hovsepyan, Arman Hovhannisyan, Artak Grigoryan (72.Gor Malakyan), Aleksandr Karapetyan, Gevorg Ghazaryan (Cap) (76.Edgar Babayan), Tigran Barseghyan (65.Aras Özbiliz), Sargis Adamyan. Trainer: Armen Gyulbudaghyants.

15.11.2019   ARMENIA - GREECE   **0-1(0-1)**   16th EC. Qualifiers
„Vazgen Sargsyan" Hanrapetakan Stadium, Yerevan; Referee: Paweł Raczkowski (Poland); Attendance: 6,450
ARM: Aram Hayrapetyan, Hovhannes Hambartsumyan (Cap), André Jack Calisir, Hayk Ishkhanyan, Taron Voskanyan (83.Petros Avetisyan), Kamo Hovhannisyan, Artak Grigoryan, Rumyan Hovsepyan (78.Artak Yedigaryan), Erik Vardanyan (59.Artur Sarkisov), Aleksandr Karapetyan, Tigran Barseghyan. Trainer: Abraham Khashmanyan.

18.11.2019   ITALY - ARMENIA   **9-1(4-0)**   16th EC. Qualifiers
Stadio "Renzo Barbera", Palermo; Referee: Tiago Bruno Lopes Martins (Portugal); Attendance: 27,752
ARM: Aram Hayrapetyan, Artak Yedigaryan (82.Petros Avetisyan), Hovhannes Hambartsumyan (Cap), André Jack Calisir, Kamo Hovhannisyan, Varazdat Haroyan, Hayk Ishkhanyan (69.Artur Sarkisov), Artak Grigoryan (60.Artem Simonyan), Edgar Babayan, Aleksandr Karapetyan, Tigran Barseghyan. Trainer: Abraham Khashmanyan.
Goal: Edgar Babayan (79).

NATIONAL TEAM PLAYERS
(16.07.2019 – 15.07.2020)

Name	DOB	Caps	Goals	2019/2020:	Club
Goalkeepers					
Aram AYRAPETYAN	22.11.1986	**11**	**0**	2019:	*FC Urartu Yerevan*
Defenders					
André Jack CALISIR	13.06.1990	**8**	**0**	2019:	*IFK Göteborg (SWE)*
Hovhannes HAMBARTSUMYAN	04.10.1990	**35**	**3**	2019:	*Enosis Neon Paralimni FC (CYP)*
Varazdat HAROYAN	24.08.1992	**50**	**2**	2019:	*FK Ural Yekaterinburg (RUS)*
Arman HOVHANNISYAN	07.07.1993	**3**	**0**	2019:	*FC Gandzasar Kapan*
Kamo HOVHANNISYAN	05.10.1990	**50**	**0**	2019:	*FC Zhetisu Taldiqorghan (KAZ)*
Hayk ISHKHANYAN	24.06.1989	**12**	**1**	2019:	*FC Alashkert Yerevan*
Taron VOSKANYAN	22.02.1993	**27**	**0**	2019:	*FC Alashkert Yerevan*
Artak YEDIGARYAN	18.03.1990	**30**	**1**	2019:	*FC Pyunik Yerevan*
Midfielders					
Petros AVETISYAN	07.01.1986	**5**	**0**	2019:	*FC Ararat-Armenia Yerevan*
Edgar BABAYAN	28.10.1995	**8**	**1**	2019:	*Hobro IK (DEN)*
Gevorg GHAZARYAN	05.04.1988	**71**	**13**	2019:	*AEL Limassol (CYP)*
Artak GRIGORYAN	19.10.1987	**26**	**1**	2019:	*FC Alashkert Yerevan*
Rumyan HOVSEPYAN	13.11.1991	**22**	**2**	2019:	*FC Arda Kardzhali (BUL)*
Gor MALAKYAN	12.06.1994	**16**	**0**	2019:	*FC Ararat-Armenia Yerevan*
Henrikh MKHITARYAN	21.01.1989	**86**	**29**	2019:	*AS Roma (ITA)*
Karlen MKRTCHYAN	25.11.1988	**56**	**2**	2019:	*FC Pyunik Yerevan*
Aras ÖZBILIZ	09.03.1990	**41**	**6**	2019:	*FC Pyunik Yerevan*
Marcos Pinheiro PIZZELLI	03.10.1984	**67**	**11**	2019:	*FC Aktobe (KAZ)*
Artem SIMONYAN	20.02.1995	**10**	**0**	2019:	*FC Pyunik Yerevan*
Erik VARDANYAN	07.06.1998	**4**	**1**	2019:	*FC Pyunik Yerevan*
Forwards					
Sargis ADAMYAN	23.05.1993	**18**	**1**	2019:	*TSG 1899 Hoffenheim (GER)*
Tigran BARSEGHYAN	22.09.1993	**28**	**5**	2019:	*FC Kaysar Kyzylorda (KAZ)*
Aleksandr KARAPETYAN	23.12.1987	**13**	**5**	2019:	*FK Sochi (RUS)*
Artur MIRANYAN	27.12.1995	**1**	**0**	2019:	*FC Pyunik Yerevan*
Artur SARKISOV	19.01.1987	**42**	**6**	2019:	*FK Yenisey Krasnoyarsk (RUS)*

National team coach

Armen GYULBUDAGHYANTS [07.10.2019 – 17.10.2019]	19.12.1966	12 M; 5 W; 2 D; 5 L; 25-20
Abraham KHASHMANYAN [06.11.2019 – 12.02.2020]	11.11.1967	2 M; 0 W; 0 D; 2 L; 1-10
Joaquín de Jesús CAPARRÓS Camino (ESP) [from 10.03.2020]	15.10.1955	-

AUSTRIA

The Country:
Republic of Austria (Republik Österreich)
Capital: Vienna
Surface: 83,879 km²
Inhabitants: 8,902,600 [2020]
Time: UTC+1

The FA:
Österreichischer Fußball-Bund
Ernst-Happel-Stadion - Sektor A/F, Meiereistrasse 7, 1021 Wien
Tel: +43 1 727 180
Foundation date: 1904
Member of FIFA since: 1905
Member of UEFA since: 1954
Website: www.oefb.at

NATIONAL TEAM RECORDS

RECORDS

First international match:	12.10.1902, Wien:	Austria – Hungary 5-0
Most international caps:	Andreas Herzog	- 103 caps (1988-2003)
Most international goals:	Anton Polster	- 44 goals / 95 caps (1982-2000)

UEFA EUROPEAN CHAMPIONSHIP		FIFA WORLD CUP		OLYMPIC TOURNAMENTS	
1960	Qualifiers	1930	*Did not enter*	1908	-
1964	Qualifiers	1934	Final Tournament (4th Place)	1912	FT/ Quarter-Finals
1968	Qualifiers	1938	*Withdrew*	1920	*Did not enter*
1972	Qualifiers	1950	*Withdrew*	1924	*Did not enter*
1976	Qualifiers	1954	Final Tournament (3rd Place)	1928	*Did not enter*
1980	Qualifiers	1958	Final Tournament (Group Stage)	1936	FT/ Runners-up
1984	Qualifiers	1962	*Withdrew*	1948	FT/ 1/8-Finals
1988	Qualifiers	1966	Qualifiers	1952	FT/ Quarter-Finals
1992	Qualifiers	1970	Qualifiers	1956	*Did not enter*
1996	Qualifiers	1974	Qualifiers	1960	Qualifiers
2000	Qualifiers	1978	Final Tournament (2nd Round)	1964	Qualifiers
2004	Qualifiers	1982	Final Tournament (2nd Round)	1968	Qualifiers
2008	Final Tournament (Group Stage)	1986	Qualifiers	1972	Qualifiers
2012	Qualifiers	1990	Final Tournament (Group Stage)	1976	Qualifiers
2016	Final Tournament (Group Stage)	1994	Qualifiers	1980	Qualifiers
2020	*Final Tournament (Qualified)*	1998	Final Tournament (Group Stage)	1984	*Did not enter*
		2002	Qualifiers	1988	Qualifiers
		2006	Qualifiers	1992	Qualifiers
		2010	Qualifiers	1996	Qualifiers
		2014	Qualifiers	2000	Qualifiers
		2018	Qualifiers	2004	Qualifiers
				2008	Qualifiers
				2012	Qualifiers
				2016	Qualifiers

UEFA NATIONS LEAGUE

2018/2019 – League B

FIFA CONFEDERATIONS CUP 1992-2017

None

AUSTRIAN CLUB HONOURS IN EUROPEAN CLUB COMPETITIONS:

European Champion Clubs.Cup (1956-1992) / UEFA Champions League (1993-2020)
None
Fairs Cup (1858-1971) / UEFA Cup (1972-2009) / UEFA Europa League (2010-2020)
None
UEFA Super Cup (1972-2019)
None
European Cup Winners.Cup 1961-1999*
None

*defunct competition

NATIONAL COMPETITIONS
TABLE OF HONOURS

	CHAMPIONS	CUP WINNERS	BEST GOALSCORERS	
1911/1912	SK Rapid Wien	-	Johann Schwarz II (First Vienna FC 1894 Wien)	22
1912/1913	SK Rapid Wien	-	Richard Kuthan (SK Rapid Wien)	16
1913/1914	Wiener AF	-	Johann Neumann (Wiener AC)	25
1914/1915	Wiener AC	-	Leopold Deutsch (Floridsdorfer AC & Wiener AC)	12
1915/1916	SK Rapid Wien	-	Richard Kuthan (SK Rapid Wien)	24
1916/1917	SK Rapid Wien	-	Eduard Bauer (SK Rapid Wien) Leopold Neubauer (Wiener AF)	21
1917/1918	Floridsdorfer AC	-	Eduard Bauer (SK Rapid Wien)	21
1918/1919	SK Rapid Wien	SK Rapid Wien	Josef Uridil (SK Rapid Wien)	16
1919/1920	SK Rapid Wien	SK Rapid Wien	Josef Uridil (SK Rapid Wien) Ernst Winkler (SpC Rudolfshügel)	21
1920/1921	SK Rapid Wien	Wiener SV Amateure	Josef Uridil (SK Rapid Wien)	35
1921/1922	Wiener Sport-Club	Wiener AF	Richard Kuthan (SK Rapid Wien)	20
1922/1923	SK Rapid Wien	Wiener Sport-Club	Ferdinand Swatosch (Wiener SV Amateure)	22
1923/1924	Wiener SV Amateure	Wiener SV Amateure	Gustav Wieser (Wiener SV Amateure)	16
1924/1925	SC Hakoah Wien	Wiener SV Amateure	Gustav Wieser (Wiener SV Amateure)	19
1925/1926	Wiener SV Amateure	Wiener SV Amateure	Gustav Wieser (Wiener SV Amateure)	25
1926/1927	SK Admira Wien	SK Rapid Wien	Anton Schall (SK Admira Wien)	27
1927/1928	SK Admira Wien	SK Admira Wien	Anton Schall (SK Admira Wien)	36
1928/1929	SK Rapid Wien	First Vienna FC 1894 Wien	Anton Schall (SK Admira Wien)	21
1929/1930	SK Rapid Wien	First Vienna FC 1894 Wien	Franz Weselik (SK Rapid Wien)	24
1930/1931	First Vienna FC 1894 Wien	Wiener AC	Anton Schall (SK Admira Wien)	25
1931/1932	SK Admira Wien	SK Admira Wien	Anton Schall (SK Admira Wien)	22
1932/1933	First Vienna FC 1894 Wien	FK Austria Wien	Franz Binder (SK Rapid Wien)	25
1933/1934	SK Admira Wien	SK Admira Wien	Josef Bican (SK Rapid Wien)	29
1934/1935	SK Rapid Wien	FK Austria Wien	Matthias Kaburek (SK Rapid Wien)	29
1935/1936	SK Admira Wien	FK Austria Wien	Wilhelm Hahnemann (SK Admira Wien)	23
1936/1937	SK Admira Wien	First Vienna FC 1894 Wien	Franz Binder (SK Rapid Wien)	29
1937/1938	SK Rapid Wien	Wiener AC – Schwarz-Rot Wien	Franz Binder (SK Rapid Wien)	22
1938/1939	SK Admira Wien	-	Franz Binder (SK Rapid Wien)	27
1939/1940	SK Rapid Wien	-	Franz Binder (SK Rapid Wien)	18
1940/1941	SK Rapid Wien	-	Franz Binder (SK Rapid Wien)	27
1941/1942	Vienna FC Wien	-	Ernst Reitermaier (SC Wacker Wien)	20
1942/1943	Vienna FC Wien	-	Karl Kerbach (Floridsdorfer AC)	31
1943/1944	Vienna FC Wien	-	Karl Decker (First Vienna FC 1894 Wien)	32
1944/1945	SK Rapid Wien	-	Richard Fischer (First Vienna FC 1894 Wien)	15
1945/1946	SK Rapid Wien	SK Rapid Wien	Ernst Stojaspal I (FK Austria Wien)	34
1946/1947	SC Wacker Wien	SC Wacker Wien	Ernst Stojaspal I (FK Austria Wien)	18
1947/1948	SK Rapid Wien	FK Austria Wien	Ernst Stojaspal I (FK Austria Wien)	24
1948/1949	FK Austria Wien	FK Austria Wien	Erich Habitzl (SK Admira Wien)	23
1949/1950	FK Austria Wien	-	Karl Decker (First Vienna FC 1894 Wien)	23
1950/1951	SK Rapid Wien	-	Robert Dienst (SK Rapid Wien)	32
1951/1952	SK Rapid Wien	-	Ernst Stojaspal I (FK Austria Wien)	31
1952/1953	FK Austria Wien	-	Ernst Stojaspal I (FK Austria Wien) Robert Dienst (SK Rapid Wien)	30
1953/1954	SK Rapid Wien	-	Robert Dienst (SK Rapid Wien)	25
1954/1955	First Vienna FC 1894 Wien	-	Richard Brousek (SC Wacker Wien)	31
1955/1956	SK Rapid Wien	-	Johann Buzek (First Vienna FC 1894 Wien)	33
1956/1957	SK Rapid Wien	-	Robert Dienst (SK Rapid Wien)	32
1957/1958	Wiener Sport-Club	-	Walter Horak (Wiener Sport-Club)	33
1958/1959	Wiener Sport-Club	Wiener AC	Erich Hof (Wiener Sport-Club)	32
1959/1960	SK Rapid Wien	FK Austria Wien	Friedrich Cejka (Wiener Sport-Club)	28
1960/1961	FK Austria Wien	SK Rapid Wien	Horst Nemec (FK Austria Wien)	31
1961/1962	FK Austria Wien	FK Austria Wien	Horst Nemec (FK Austria Wien)	24
1962/1963	FK Austria Wien	FK Austria Wien	Erich Hof (Wiener Sport-Club)	21
1963/1964	SK Rapid Wien	ESV Admira Energie Wien	Horst Nemec (FK Austria Wien)	21
1964/1965	Linzer ASK	Linzer ASK	Wolfgang Gayer (Wiener Sport-Club)	18
1965/1966	ESV Admira Energie Wien	ESV Admira Energie Wien	Johann Buzek (FK Austria Wien)	18
1966/1967	SK Rapid Wien	FK Austria Wien	August Starek (SK Rapid Wien)	21
1967/1968	SK Rapid Wien	SK Rapid Wien	Jørn Bjerregaard (DEN, SK Rapid Wien)	23
1968/1969	FK Austria Wien	SK Rapid Wien	Helmut Köglberger (FK Austria Wien)	31
1969/1970	FK Austria Wien	FC Wacker Innsbruck	Günter Kaltenbrunner (Wiener Sport-Club)	22
1970/1971	FC Wacker Innsbruck	FK Austria Wien	Wilhelm Kreuz (ESV Admira Energie Wien)	26
1971/1972	SSW Innsbruck	Wiener Sport-Club	Alfred Riedl (FK Austria Wien)	16
1972/1973	SSW Innsbruck	SSW Innsbruck	Wolfgang Breuer (SSW Innsbruck)	22
1973/1974	SK VÖEST Linz	FK Austria Wien	Johann Krankl (SK Rapid Wien)	36
1974/1975	SSW Innsbruck	SSW Innsbruck	Helmut Köglberger (FK Austria/WAC Wien - Linzer ASK)	22
1975/1976	FK Austria/WAC Wien	SK Rapid Wien	Hans Pirkner (FK Austria/WAC Wien)	21
1976/1977	SSW Innsbruck	FK Austria Wien	Johann Krankl (SK Rapid Wien)	32
1977/1978	FK Austria Wien	SSW Innsbruck	Johann Krankl (SK Rapid Wien)	32
1978/1979	FK Austria Wien	SSW Innsbruck	Walter Schachner (FK Austria Wien)	24

1979/1980	FK Austria Wien	FK Austria Wien	Walter Schachner (FK Austria Wien)	34
1980/1981	FK Austria Wien	Grazer AK	Gernot Jurtin (SK Sturm Graz)	20
1981/1982	SK Rapid Wien	FK Austria Wien	Božo Bakota (YUG, SK Sturm Graz)	24
1982/1983	SK Rapid Wien	SK Rapid Wien	Johann Krankl (SK Rapid Wien)	23
1983/1984	FK Austria Wien	SK Rapid Wien	Tibor Nyilasi (HUN, FK Austria Wien)	26
1984/1985	FK Austria Wien	SK Rapid Wien	Anton Polster (FK Austria Wien)	24
1985/1986	FK Austria Wien	FK Austria Wien	Anton Polster (FK Austria Wien)	33
1986/1987	SK Rapid Wien	SK Rapid Wien	Anton Polster (FK Austria Wien)	39
1987/1988	SK Rapid Wien	Kremser SC	Zoran Stojadinović (YUG, SK Rapid Wien)	27
1988/1989	FC Swarovski Tirol Innsbruck	FC Swarovski Tirol Innsbruck	Peter Pacult (FC Swarovski Tirol)	26
1989/1990	FC Swarovski Tirol Innsbruck	FK Austria Wien	Gerhard Rodax (FC Admira/Wacker Wien)	35
1990/1991	FK Austria Wien	SV Stockerau	Václav Daněk (TCH, FC Swarovski Tirol)	29
1991/1992	FK Austria Wien	FK Austria Wien	Christoph Westerthaler (FC Swarovski Tirol)	17
1992/1993	FK Austria Wien	FC Wacker Innsbruck	Václav Daněk (TCH, FC Wacker Tirol)	24
1993/1994	SV Austria Salzburg	FK Austria Wien	Nikola Jurčević (CRO, SV Austria Salzburg) Heimo Pfeifenberger (SV Austria Salzburg)	14
1994/1995	SV Austria Salzburg	SK Rapid Wien	Souleyman Sané (SEN, FC Tirol Innsbruck)	20
1995/1996	SK Rapid Wien	SK Sturm Graz	Ivica Vastic (SK Sturm Graz)	20
1996/1997	SV Austria Salzburg	SK Sturm Graz	René Wagner (CZE, SK Rapid Wien)	28
1997/1998	SK Sturm Graz	SV Ried im Innkreis	Geir Frigård (NOR, LASK Linz)	23
1998/1999	SK Sturm Graz	SK Sturm Graz	Eduard Glieder (SV Austria Salzburg)	22
1999/2000	FC Tirol Innsbruck	Grazer AK	Ivica Vastic (SK Sturm Graz)	32
2000/2001	FC Tirol Innsbruck	FC Kärnten	Radosław Gilewicz (POL, FC Tirol Innsbruck)	22
2001/2002	FC Tirol Innsbruck	Grazer AK	Ronald Brunmayr (Grazer AK)	27
2002/2003	FK Austria Wien	FK Austria Wien	Axel Lawarée (BEL, SC Schwarz-Weiß Bregenz)	21
2003/2004	Grazer AK	Grazer AK	Roland Kollmann (Grazer AK)	24
2004/2005	SK Rapid Wien	FK Austria Wien	Christian Mayrleb (Grazer AK)	27
2005/2006	FK Austria Wien	FK Austria Wien	Sanel Kuljic (SV Ried) Roland Linz (FK Austria Wien)	15
2006/2007	FC Red Bull Salzburg	FK Austria Wien	Alexander Zickler (GER, FC Red Bull Salzburg)	22
2007/2008	SK Rapid Wien	-	Alexander Zickler (GER, FC Red Bull Salzburg)	16
2008/2009	FC Red Bull Salzburg	FK Austria Wien	Marc Janko (FC Red Bull Salzburg)	39
2009/2010	FC Red Bull Salzburg	SK Sturm Graz	Steffen Hofmann (GER, SK Rapid Wien)	20
2010/2011	SK Sturm Graz	SV Ried im Innkreis	Roland Linz (FK Austria Wien) Roman Kienast (SK Sturm Graz)	21
2011/2012	FC Red Bull Salzburg	FC Red Bull Salzburg	Jakob Jantscher (FC Red Bull Salzburg) Stefan Maierhofer (FC Red Bull Salzburg)	14
2012/2013	FK Austria Wien	FC Pasching	Philipp Hosiner (FK Austria Wien)	32
2013/2014	FC Red Bull Salzburg	FC Red Bull Salzburg	Jonathan Soriano Casas (ESP, FC Red Bull Salzburg)	31
2014/2015	FC Red Bull Salzburg	FC Red Bull Salzburg	Jonathan Soriano Casas (ESP, FC Red Bull Salzburg)	31
2015/2016	FC Red Bull Salzburg	FC Red Bull Salzburg	Jonathan Soriano Casas (ESP, FC Red Bull Salzburg)	21
2016/2017	FC Red Bull Salzburg	FC Red Bull Salzburg	Olarenwaju Ayobami Kayode (NGA, FK Austria Wien)	17
2017/2018	FC Red Bull Salzburg	SK Sturm Graz	Moanes Dabour (ISR, FC Red Bull Salzburg)	22
2018/2019	FC Red Bull Salzburg	FC Red Bull Salzburg	Moanes Dabour (ISR, FC Red Bull Salzburg)	20
2019/2020	FC Red Bull Salzburg	FC Red Bull Salzburg	Shon Zalman Weissman (ISR, Wolfsberger AC)	30

NATIONAL CHAMPIONSHIP
Österreichische Fußballmeisterschaft – Bundesliga 2019/2020
(26.07.2019 – 05.07.2020)

Regular Season - Results

Round 1 [26-28.07.2019]
Rapid Wien - RB Salzburg 0-2(0-1)
Admira Wacker - Wolfsberger AC 0-3(0-1)
WSG Tirol - Austria Wien 3-1(1-0)
SV Mattersburg - TSV Hartberg 2-1(1-0)
Sturm Graz - SKN St. Pölten 3-0(2-0)
Linzer ASK - SCR Altach 2-0(1-0)

Round 2 [03-04.08.2019]
Austria Wien - Linzer ASK 0-3(0-1)
SCR Altach - WSG Tirol 3-2(2-2)
TSV Hartberg - FC Admira Wacker 4-1(2-0)
RB Salzburg - SV Mattersburg 4-1(3-0)
Wolfsberger AC - Sturm Graz 0-1(0-1)
SKN St. Pölten - Rapid Wien 2-2(1-1)

Round 3 [10-11.08.2019]
RB Salzburg - Wolfsberger AC 5-2(2-1)
Rapid Wien - SCR Altach 2-1(2-1)
FC Admira Wacker - Linzer ASK 0-1(0-1)
SV Mattersburg - Austria Wien 1-5(0-2)
TSV Hartberg - Sturm Graz 1-0(0-0)
WSG Tirol - SKN St. Pölten 1-1(1-0)

Round 4 [17-18.08.2019]
Linzer ASK - WSG Tirol 1-1(0-1)
Wolfsberger AC - SV Mattersburg 5-0(2-0)
SKN St. Pölten - RB Salzburg 0-6(0-2)
Austria Wien - FC Admira Wacker 1-1(1-0)
Sturm Graz - Rapid Wien 0-1(0-1)
SCR Altach - TSV Hartberg 3-3(0-3)

Round 5 [24-25.08.2019]
Rapid Wien - Linzer ASK 1-2(0-1)
Wolfsberger AC - SCR Altach 5-2(3-1)
SV Mattersburg - SKN St. Pölten 0-1(0-1)
Sturm Graz - WSG Tirol 2-0(1-0)
RB Salzburg - FC Admira Wacker 5-0(3-0)
TSV Hartberg - Austria Wien 2-2(1-0)

Round 6 [31.08.-01.09.2019]
Linzer ASK - Wolfsberger AC 0-1(0-0)
FC Admira Wacker - SV Mattersburg 1-3(1-2)
WSG Tirol - RB Salzburg 1-5(0-3)
Austria Wien - Rapid Wien 1-3(1-1)
SKN St. Pölten - TSV Hartberg 1-3(0-2)
SCR Altach - Sturm Graz 1-2(0-1)

Round 7 [14-15.09.2019]
RB Salzburg - TSV Hartberg 7-2(2-1)
Sturm Graz - Linzer ASK 0-2(0-0)
SV Mattersburg - WSG Tirol 0-2(0-1)
Rapid Wien - FC Admira Wacker 5-0(1-0)
SCR Altach - SKN St. Pölten 6-0(3-0)
Wolfsberger AC - Austria Wien 3-0(0-0)

Round 8 [21-22.09.2019]
SV Mattersburg - Sturm Graz 3-3(1-2)
FC Admira Wacker - SKN St. Pölten 1-1(1-0)
WSG Tirol - Rapid Wien 0-2(0-0)
Austria Wien - SCR Altach 2-0(0-0)
TSV Hartberg - Wolfsberger AC 0-2(0-0)
Linzer ASK - RB Salzburg 2-2(2-1)

Round 9 [28-29.09.2019]
RB Salzburg - Austria Wien 4-1(2-1)
Wolfsberger AC - WSG Tirol 2-2(0-0)
SKN St. Pölten - Linzer ASK 0-3(0-2)
Sturm Graz - FC Admira Wacker 4-1(1-0)
SCR Altach - SV Mattersburg 0-2(0-0)
Rapid Wien - TSV Hartberg 3-3(1-1)

Round 10 [05-06.10.2019]
RB Salzburg - SCR Altach 6-0(3-0)
SV Mattersburg - Rapid Wien 2-3(1-1)
FC Admira Wacker - WSG Tirol 3-1(3-1)
Wolfsberger AC - SKN St. Pölten 4-0(2-0)
TSV Hartberg - Linzer ASK 1-2(0-0)
Austria Wien - Sturm Graz 1-0(0-0)

Round 11 [19-20.10.2019]
Linzer ASK - SV Mattersburg 7-2(3-2)
Sturm Graz - RB Salzburg 1-1(1-0)
SCR Altach - FC Admira Wacker 1-4(0-3)
SKN St. Pölten - Austria Wien 2-2(0-1)
WSG Tirol - TSV Hartberg 0-1(0-0)
Rapid Wien - Wolfsberger AC 1-1(1-0)

Round 12 [26-27.10.2019]
Austria Wien - WSG Tirol 2-3(0-2)
TSV Hartberg - SV Mattersburg 3-1(1-0)
SKN St. Pölten - Sturm Graz 0-4(0-0)
Wolfsberger AC - Admira Wacker 2-2(0-1)
SCR Altach - Linzer ASK 0-1(0-1)
RB Salzburg - Rapid Wien 3-2(2-1)

Round 13 [02-03.11.2019]
SV Mattersburg - RB Salzburg 0-3(0-2)
Sturm Graz - Wolfsberger AC 0-4(0-3)
Rapid Wien - SKN St. Pölten 0-1(0-0)
WSG Tirol - SCR Altach 0-4(0-1)
FC Admira Wacker - TSV Hartberg 0-1(0-0)
Linzer ASK - Austria Wien 2-0(1-0)

Round 14 [09-10.11.2019]
SCR Altach - Rapid Wien 0-3(0-3)
Sturm Graz - TSV Hartberg 3-1(0-0)
SKN St. Pölten - WSG Tirol 5-1(3-1)
Linzer ASK - FC Admira Wacker 1-0(1-0)
Austria Wien - SV Mattersburg 2-1(1-0)
Wolfsberger AC - RB Salzburg 0-3(0-1)

Round 15 [23-24.11.2019]
RB Salzburg - SKN St. Pölten 2-2(2-1)
WSG Tirol - Linzer ASK 0-2(0-0)
SV Mattersburg - Wolfsberger AC 1-4(0-2)
FC Admira Wacker - Austria Wien 0-0
TSV Hartberg - SCR Altach 2-1(1-1)
Rapid Wien - Sturm Graz 1-1(1-0)

Round 16 [30.11.-01.12.2019]
SKN St. Pölten - SV Mattersburg 0-0
WSG Tirol - Sturm Graz 1-5(0-2)
Austria Wien - TSV Hartberg 5-0(3-0)
SCR Altach - Wolfsberger AC 2-1(2-0)
FC Admira Wacker - RB Salzburg 1-1(1-0)
Linzer ASK - Rapid Wien 0-4(0-1)

Round 17 [07-08.12.2019]
Wolfsberger AC - Linzer ASK 1-3(0-2)
RB Salzburg - WSG Tirol 5-1(3-0)
TSV Hartberg - SKN St. Pölten 3-2(2-0)
SV Mattersburg - FC Admira Wacker 1-2(0-0)
Sturm Graz - SCR Altach 1-2(1-0)
Rapid Wien - Austria Wien 2-2(1-2)

Round 18 [14-15.12.2019]
TSV Hartberg - RB Salzburg 2-2(1-1)
FC Admira Wacker - Rapid Wien 0-3(0-2)
SKN St. Pölten - SCR Altach 0-3(0-0)
Austria Wien - Wolfsberger AC 1-1(1-0)
WSG Tirol - SV Mattersburg 1-3(0-1)
Linzer ASK - Sturm Graz 3-3(2-3)

Round 19 [14-16.02.2020]
RB Salzburg - Linzer ASK 2-3(1-2)
SCR Altach - Austria Wien 2-2(2-1)
Wolfsberger AC - TSV Hartberg 3-0(0-0)
Sturm Graz - SV Mattersburg 1-2(0-2)
SKN St. Pölten - FC Admira Wacker 2-2(0-0)
Rapid Wien - WSG Tirol 2-0(2-0)

Round 20 [22-23.02.2020]
WSG Tirol - Wolfsberger AC 2-0(2-0)
FC Admira Wacker - Sturm Graz 0-2(0-1)
SV Mattersburg - SCR Altach 0-0
Linzer ASK - SKN St. Pölten 4-1(3-1)
TSV Hartberg - Rapid Wien 2-2(1-1)
Austria Wien - RB Salzburg 2-2(0-1)

Round 21 [01-02.03.2020]
SKN St. Pölten - Wolfsberger AC 0-4(0-1)
Sturm Graz - Austria Wien 1-1(0-0)
Rapid Wien - SV Mattersburg 3-1(1-1)
WSG Tirol - FC Admira Wacker 1-1(0-0)
Linzer ASK - TSV Hartberg 5-1(0-1)
SCR Altach - RB Salzburg 3-2(1-0)

Round 22 [07-08.03.2020]
Austria Wien - SKN St. Pölten 0-0
Wolfsberger AC - Rapid Wien 2-2(1-1)
FC Admira Wacker - SCR Altach 2-0(0-0)
TSV Hartberg - WSG Tirol 0-3(0-0)
SV Mattersburg - Linzer ASK 0-1(0-1)
RB Salzburg - Sturm Graz 2-0(0-0)

Final Standings

1.	FC Red Bull Salzburg	22	14	6	2	74	- 26	48
2.	Linzer ASK*	22	17	3	2	50	- 20	42
3.	SK Rapid Wien	22	11	7	4	47	- 26	40
4.	Wolfsberger AC	22	11	5	6	50	- 27	38
5.	SK Sturm Graz	22	9	5	8	37	- 28	32
6.	TSV Hartberg	22	8	5	9	36	- 50	29
7.	FK Austria Wien	22	5	10	7	33	- 36	25
8.	SC Rheindorf Altach	22	7	3	12	34	- 44	24
9.	FC Admira Wacker Mödling	22	4	7	11	22	- 43	19
10.	WSG Swarovski Tirol Wattens	22	5	4	13	26	- 50	19
11.	SV Mattersburg	22	5	3	14	26	- 52	18
12.	SKN St. Pölten	22	3	8	11	21	- 54	17

*Please note: Linzer ASK were deducted 12 points for violating regulations concernic the Covid-19 pandemic. The punishment was later reduced to 4 points. Teams ranked 1-6 were qualified for the Championship Round, while teams ranked 7-12 were qualified for the Relegation Round.

The points obtained during the regular season were halved (and rounded down) before the start of the play-offs.
As a result, the teams started with the following points:
Championship Round: FC Red Bull Salzburg 24, Linzer ASK 21 points, SK Rapid Wien 20, Wolfsberger AC 19, SK Sturm Graz 16, TSV Hartberg 14.
Relegation Round: FK Austria Wien 12, SC Rheindorf Altach 12, FC Admira Wacker Mödling 9, WSG Swarovski Tirol Wattens 9, SV Mattersburg 9, SKN St. Pölten 8.

Championship Round

Results

Round 23 [03.06.2020]
Linzer ASK - TSV Hartberg 1-2(1-1)
Sturm Graz - Wolfsberger AC 1-2(0-1)
RB Salzburg - Rapid Wien 2-0(1-0)

Round 24 [07.06.2020]
Wolfsberger AC - Linzer ASK 3-3(0-1)
TSV Hartberg - RB Salzburg 0-6(0-4)
Rapid Wien - Sturm Graz 4-0(2-0)

Round 25 [10.06.2020]
Wolfsberger AC - TSV Hartberg 2-4(2-1)
Linzer ASK - Rapid Wien 0-1(0-0)
Sturm Graz - RB Salzburg 1-5(1-4)

Round 26 [14.06.2020]
Rapid Wien - Wolfsberger AC 2-1(1-0)
TSV Hartberg - Sturm Graz 1-2(1-0)
RB Salzburg - Linzer ASK 3-1(2-0)

Round 27 [17.06.2020]
Wolfsberger AC - RB Salzburg 0-0
TSV Hartberg - Rapid Wien 0-1(0-1)
Linzer ASK - Sturm Graz 4-0(3-0)

Round 28 [21.06.2020]
RB Salzburg - Wolfsberger AC 2-2(1-0)
Rapid Wien - TSV Hartberg 0-1(0-1)
Sturm Graz - Linzer ASK 0-2(0-1)

Round 29 [24.06.2020]
TSV Hartberg - Linzer ASK 1-5(0-0)
Wolfsberger AC - Sturm Graz 2-0(0-0)
Rapid Wien - RB Salzburg 2-7(1-4)

Round 30 [28.06.2020]
Linzer ASK - Wolfsberger AC 0-1(0-0)
RB Salzburg - TSV Hartberg 3-0(1-0)
Sturm Graz - Rapid Wien 2-3(2-0)

Round 31 [01-02.07.2020]
RB Salzburg - Sturm Graz 5-2(1-0)
Rapid Wien - Linzer ASK 3-1(2-0)
TSV Hartberg - Wolfsberger AC 3-3(1-0)

Round 32 [05.07.2020]
Sturm Graz - TSV Hartberg 1-4(1-3)
Linzer ASK - RB Salzburg 0-3(0-0)
Wolfsberger AC - Rapid Wien 3-1(2-0)

Final Standings

										Home				Away	
1. **FC Red Bull Salzburg**	32	22	8	2	110 - 34	50	13	2	1	60 - 19	9	6	1	50 - 15
2. SK Rapid Wien	32	17	7	8	64 - 43	38	7	4	5	31 - 24	10	3	3	33 - 19
3. Wolfsberger AC	32	15	9	8	69 - 43	35	7	5	4	37 - 23	8	4	4	32 - 20
4. Linzer ASK*	32	20	4	8	67 - 37	33	7	3	6	32 - 22	13	1	2	35 - 15
5. TSV Hartberg	32	12	6	14	52 - 74	27	5	4	7	25 - 35	7	2	7	27 - 39
6. SK Sturm Graz	32	10	5	17	46 - 60	19	4	2	10	21 - 31	6	3	7	25 - 29

TSV Hartberg qualified for the Europa League Play-offs Finals.
*Please note: Linzer ASK were deducted 4 points (see above).

Relegation Round

Results

Round 23 [02.06.2020]
SV Mattersburg - SCR Altach 1-1(1-1)
WSG Tirol - SKN St. Pölten 0-5(0-3)
Austria Wien - FC Admira Wacker 1-0(0-0)

Round 24 [06.06.2020]
SCR Altach - WSG Tirol 1-1(0-0)
SKN St. Pölten - Austria Wien 1-1(0-1)
FC Admira Wacker - SV Mattersburg 0-2(0-2)

Round 25 [09.06.2020]
SKN St. Pölten - FC Admira Wacker 0-3(0-1)
WSG Tirol - SV Mattersburg 1-1(1-1)
Austria Wien - SCR Altach 0-2(0-1)

Round 26 [13.06.2020]
SCR Altach - SKN St. Pölten 2-0(1-0)
SV Mattersburg - Austria Wien 1-4(1-2)
FC Admira Wacker - WSG Tirol 0-3(0-1)

Round 27 [16.06.2020]
SKN St. Pölten - SV Mattersburg 1-0(1-0)
FC Admira Wacker - SCR Altach 1-1(1-1)
Austria Wien - WSG Tirol 1-0(1-0)

Round 28 [20.06.2020]
WSG Tirol - Austria Wien 1-2(1-1)
SV Mattersburg - SKN St. Pölten 2-0(1-0)
SCR Altach - FC Admira Wacker 1-1(0-0)

Round 29 [23.06.2020]
SCR Altach - SV Mattersburg 1-1(1-1)
FC Admira Wacker - Austria Wien 0-2(0-1)
SKN St. Pölten - WSG Tirol 1-1(1-0)

Round 30 [27.06.2020]
Austria Wien - SKN St. Pölten 2-5(2-2)
SV Mattersburg - FC Admira Wacker 1-2(1-0)
WSG Tirol - SCR Altach 0-1(0-1)

Round 31 [30.06.2020]
SCR Altach - Austria Wien 1-2(1-0)
SV Mattersburg - WSG Tirol 4-1(2-0)
FC Admira Wacker - SKN St. Pölten 0-3(0-0)

Round 32 [04.07.2020]
SKN St. Pölten - SCR Altach 2-0(0-0)
Austria Wien - SV Mattersburg 1-0(0-0)
WSG Tirol - FC Admira Wacker 0-0

Final Standings

										Home				Away	
1. FK Austria Wien	32	12	11	9	49 - 47	34	7	4	5	22 - 21	5	7	4	27 - 26
2. SC Rheindorf Altach	32	10	8	14	45 - 53	26	5	5	6	27 - 27	5	3	8	18 - 26
3. SKN St. Pölten	32	8	10	14	39 - 65	25	3	6	7	17 - 35	5	4	7	22 - 30
4. SV Mattersburg	32	8	6	18	39 - 64	21	3	3	10	19 - 33	5	3	8	20 - 31
5. FC Admira Wacker Mödling	32	6	10	16	29 - 57	18	2	4	10	9 - 27	4	6	6	20 - 30
6. WSG Swarovski Tirol Wattens**	32	6	8	18	34 - 66	16	2	4	10	12 - 34	4	4	8	22 - 32
(Relegated)															

FK Austria Wien and SC Rheindorf Altach qualified for the Europa League Play-offs Semi-Final.
**On 05.08.2020, SV Mattersburg filed for insolvency and withdrew from the Bundesliga, sparing WSG Swarovski Tirol Wattens from relegation.

<table>
<tr><td colspan="2" align="center">**Top goalscorers:**</td></tr>
<tr><td>30 **Shon Zalman Weissman (ISR)**</td><td>*Wolfsberger AC*</td></tr>
<tr><td>24 Patson Daka (ZAM)</td><td>*FC Red Bull Salzburg*</td></tr>
<tr><td>19 Taxiarchis Fountas (GRE)</td><td>*SK Rapid Wien*</td></tr>
<tr><td>17 Christoph Monschein</td><td>*FK Austria Wien*</td></tr>
<tr><td>17 Dario Tadić</td><td>*TSV Hartberg*</td></tr>
<tr><td>16 Erling Braut Håland (NOR)</td><td>*FC Red Bull Salzburg*</td></tr>
</table>

Europa League Play-offs – Semi-Finals [08.07.2020]

FK Austria Wien - SC Rheindorf Altach	1-0(1-0)

Europa League Play-offs – Final [11-15.07.2020]

FK Austria Wien - **TSV Hartberg**	2-3(0-1)	0-0

NATIONAL CUP
ÖFB Cup 2019/2020

First Round [19-21.07.2019]

USK Anif - SK Sturm Graz	1-4(1-2)	SC Wiener Viktoria - TSV Hartberg	2-2 aet; 5-3 pen
SK Treibach - WSG Swarovski Tirol Wattens	1-2(0-0)	SV Gloggnitz - SKN St. Pölten	1-2(0-1)
FC Langenegg - SK Austria Klagenfurt	1-4(1-1)	ASKÖ Köttmannsdorf - FK Austria Wien	0-9(0-4)
ASK-BSC Bruck/Leitha - SV Ried	0-4(0-3)	SC Pinkafeld - SV Mattersburg	0-10(0-3)
ATSV Wolfsberg - AS Koma Elektra	4-1(3-0)	WSC Hertha Wels - VfB Hohenems	1-0(1-0)
FC Kitzbühel - FC Wacker Innsbruck	0-7(0-1)	ATSV Stadl-Paura - SC Austria Lustenau	0-5(0-2)
SV Hall - FC Juniors OÖ Pasching	1-5(0-2)	FC Kufstein - SC Rheindorf Altach	1-6(1-2)
ASK Ebreichsdorf - SV Lafnitz	2-1(1-0,1-1)	SAK Klagenfurt - Wolfsberger AC	0-9(0-4)
TuS Bad Gleichenberg - SK Vorwärts Steyr	2-3(1-1)	USV St. Anna - SC Kalsdorf	1-0(1-0)
FC Gleisdorf 09 - ASV Draßburg	4-0(1-0)	Union Edelweiß Linz - FC Admira Wacker Mödling	0-5(0-3)
Union Gurten - FC Zell am See	1-0(1-0)	FCM Traiskirchen - SV Horn	1-5(0-3)
SV Seekirchen - SKU Amstetten	1-4(1-1)	SV Leobendorf - FC Blau Weiß Linz	0-5(0-0)
Wiener Sport-Club - FC Dornbirn	2-6(0-2)	Union Vöcklamarkt - Linzer ASK	2-6(1-1)
FC Mauerwerk - FC Mannsdorf/Großenzersdorf	1-2(0-1)	SC Neusiedl/See 1919 - Grazer AK	1-6(1-2)
SC/ESV Parndorf - FC Red Bull Salzburg	1-7(0-3)	USV Allerheiligen - SK Rapid Wien	1-9(0-3)
FC Wolfurt - Floridsdorfer AC	0-3(0-2)	SC Schwaz - Kapfenberger SV 1919	1-3(0-1)

Second Round [24-25.09.2019]

SC Austria Lustenau - Floridsdorfer AC	2-1(1-1,1-1)	SKN St. Pölten - SV Mattersburg	2-1(0-0)
Grazer AK - FC Wacker Innsbruck	1-2(0-2)	SC Wiener Viktoria - Linzer ASK	1-4(0-1)
ASK Ebreichsdorf - FC Admira Wacker Mödling	2-1(2-0)	SK Austria Klagenfurt - SK Sturm Graz	2-4(1-1,2-2)
Union Gurten - SV Horn	2-0(0-0)	WSG Swarovski Tirol Wattens - FK Austria Wien	5-2(2-1)
FC Gleisdorf 09 - FC Juniors OÖ Pasching	3-0(0-0)	ATSV Wolfsberg - Wolfsberger AC	0-6(0-2)
USV St. Anna - FC Dornbirn	2-0(1-0)	WSC Hertha Wels - SC Rheindorf Altach	1-4(0-2)
FC Mannsdorf/Großenzersdorf - Kapfenberger SV	1-2(0-2)	SK Vorwärts Steyr - SV Ried	3-4(0-2)
SKU Amstetten - FC Blau Weiß Linz	4-1(0-1,1-1)	SK Rapid Wien - FC Red Bull Salzburg	1-2(0-0,1-1)

1/8-Finals [29-30.10.2019]

SKN St. Pölten - SV Ried	1-0(1-0)	Kapfenberger SV 1919 - SK Sturm Graz	0-2(0-0)
Union Gurten - SC Austria Lustenau	2-3(0-1)	ASK Ebreichsdorf - FC Red Bull Salzburg	0-5(0-3)
USV St. Anna - SKU Amstetten	0-3(0-2)	FC Wacker Innsbruck - Wolfsberger AC	1-0(1-0)
FC Gleisdorf 09 - WSG Swarovski Tirol Wattens	1-4(0-1,1-1)	Linzer ASK - SC Rheindorf Altach	3-1(3-0)

Quarter-Finals [07-09.02.2020]

SKN St. Pölten - FC Wacker Innsbruck	3-3 aet; 3-5 pen	Linzer ASK - SK Sturm Graz	2-0(0-0)
SC Austria Lustenau - WSG Swarovski Tirol Wattens	2-2 aet; 5-4 pen	SKU Amstetten - FC Red Bull Salzburg	0-3(0-1)

Semi-Finals [04-05.03.2020]

SC Austria Lustenau - FC Wacker Innsbruck	1-0(1-0)	FC Red Bull Salzburg - Linzer ASK	1-0(0-0)

Final

29.05.2020; Wörthersee Stadion, Klagenfurt; Referee: Dieter Muckenhammer; Attendance: none

FC Red Bull Salzburg – SC Austria Lustenau   **5-0(2-0)**

FC Red Bull: Cican Stanković, Albert Vallci, André Ramalho da Silva, Andreas Ulmer (86.Patrick Farkas), Max Wöber (78.Jérôme Onguéné), Majeed Ashimeru, Dominik Szoboszlai, Zlatko Junuzović (68.Antoine Bernède), Hwang Hee-chan (68.Sékou Koïta), Patson Daka (78.Karim Adeyemi), Noah Okafor. Trainer: Jesse Alan Marsch (United States).

Austria Lustenau: Florian Ereš, Dominik Štumberger, Christian Schilling (75.Bojan Avramović), Sebastian Feyrer, Michael Lageder, Alexander Ranacher, Christoph Freitag, Pius Grabher (62.Daniel Steinwender), Daniel Tiefenbach (55.Wallace Menezes dos Santos), Thomas Mayer (55.Lukas Katnik), Ronivaldo Bernardo Sales. Trainer: Roman Mählich.

Goals: 1-0 Dominik Szoboszlai (19), 2-0 Dominik Štumberger (21 own goal), 3-0 Noah Okafor (53), 4-0 Majeed Ashimeru (65), 5-0 Sékou Koïta (79).

Fußballclub Admira Wacker Mödling

Founded:	1905	
Stadium:	BSFZ-Arena, Maria Enzersdorf – Südstadt (10,600)	
Trainer:	Reiner Geyer (GER)	20.04.1964
[02.09.2019]	Klaus Schmidt	21.10.1967
[23.02.2020]	Michael Horvath	05.02.1982
[25.02.2020]	Zvonimir Soldo (CRO)	02.11.1967

Goalkeepers:	DOB	M	(s)	G
Andreas Leitner	25.03.1994	32		
Defenders:	**DOB**	**M**	**(s)**	**G**
Emanuel Aiwu	25.12.2000	25	(1)	
Sebastian Bauer	07.11.1992	18	(1)	
Leonardo Lukačević	21.01.1999	17	(2)	
Fabian Menig (GER)	26.02.1994	16		
Mario Pavelić	19.09.1993	11	(3)	1
Pascal Petlach	18.01.1999	3	(5)	1
Christoph Schösswendter	16.07.1988	25		1
Miloš Spasić (SRB)	29.01.1998	4		
Fabio Strauss	06.08.1994	3	(1)	
Bjarne Thoelke (GER)	11.04.1992	1	(2)	
Midfielders:	**DOB**	**M**	**(s)**	**G**
Onurhan Babuscu	05.09.2003		(2)	
Morten Hjulmand (DEN)	25.06.1999	27	(3)	1
Marco Kadlec	28.02.2000	8	(10)	1
Roman Kerschbaum	19.01.1994	28	(1)	3
Kim Jung-min (KOR)	13.11.1999	1	(2)	
Markus Lackner	05.04.1991	25	(2)	1
Marcus Maier	18.12.1995	14	(3)	
Kolja Pusch (GER)	12.02.1993	15	(2)	3
Muhammed-Cham Saracevic	26.09.2000	7	(9)	
Jonathan Scherzer	22.07.1995	7	(1)	
Daniel Toth	10.06.1987	7	(9)	1
Wilhelm Vorsager	29.06.1997	1	(1)	
Forwards:	**DOB**	**M**	**(s)**	**G**
Sinan Bakış (TUR)	22.04.1994	22	(3)	12
Boris Cmiljanić (MNE)	17.03.1996	4	(4)	1
Erwin Hoffer	14.04.1987	10	(15)	2
Seth Paintsil (GHA)	20.05.1996	9	(13)	
Markus Pink	24.02.1991	5	(5)	1
Patrick Schmidt	22.07.1998	2		
Dominik Starkl	06.11.1993	5	(5)	

Fußballklub Austria Wien

Founded:	15.03.1911	
Stadium:	Generali Arena, Wien (17,500)	
Trainer:	Christian Ilzer	21.10.1997

Goalkeepers:	DOB	M	(s)	G
Mirko Kos	12.04.1997	1		
Ivan Lučić	23.03.1995	18		
Patrick Pentz	02.01.1997	13		
Defenders:	**DOB**	**M**	**(s)**	**G**
Alexandar Borković	11.06.1999	15	(4)	
Caner Çavlan (NED)	05.02.1992	7		
Johannes Handl	07.05.1998	3	(1)	
Florian Klein	17.11.1986	28	(1)	
Michael Madl	21.03.1988	23	(1)	
Christoph Martschinko	13.02.1994	13		
Maudo Lamine Jarjué (GNB)	30.09.1997	4	(2)	
Erik Palmer-Brown (USA)	24.04.1997	19	(3)	2
Andreas Poulsen (DEN)	13.10.1999	5		
Stephan Zwierschitz	17.09.1990	13	(2)	1
Midfielders:	**DOB**	**M**	**(s)**	**G**
Vesel Demaku	05.02.2000	5	(4)	
Thomas Ebner	22.02.1992	16	(6)	1
Dominik Fitz	16.06.1999	23	(2)	4
Alexander Grünwald	01.05.1989	26	(3)	7
Niels Hahn	24.05.2001		(1)	
James Alexander Jeggo (AUS)	12.02.1992	21	(6)	
Aleksandar Jukić	26.07.2000	1		
Dominik Prokop	02.06.1997	7	(8)	
Manprit Sarkaria	26.08.1996	18	(3)	4
Maximilian Sax	22.11.1992	10	(11)	2
Tarkan Serbest (TUR)	02.05.1994	13	(2)	
Alon Turgeman (ISR)	09.06.1991	3	(5)	3
Patrick Wimmer	30.05.2001	4	(12)	
Forwards:	**DOB**	**M**	**(s)**	**G**
Bright Osagie Edomwonyi (NGA)	24.07.1994	4	(21)	2
Christoph Monschein	22.10.1992	30	(2)	17
Benedikt Pichler	20.07.1997	9	(7)	4
Sterling Yatéké (CTA)	15.09.1999		(3)	

Linzer Athletik-Sport-Klub

Founded:	07.08.1908	
Stadium:	TGW Arena [Waldstadion], Pasching (7,870)	
Trainer:	Valérien Ismaël (FRA)	28.09.1975

Goalkeepers:	DOB	M	(s)	G
Alexander Schlager	01.02.1996	32		
Defenders:	**DOB**	**M**	**(s)**	**G**
Andrés Alberto Andrade Cedeño (PAN)	16.10.1998	4	(6)	
Petar Filipović (CRO)	14.09.1990	19	(2)	2
Emanuel Pogatetz	16.01.1983	1	(4)	
Marvin Potzmann	07.12.1993	9	(7)	1
Christian Ramsebner	26.03.1989	8		1
Reinhold Ranftl	24.01.1992	28		5
David Schnegg	29.09.1998	1	(1)	
Gernot Trauner	25.03.1992	28		3
Philipp Wiesinger	23.05.1994	26	(1)	1
Markus Wostry	19.07.1992	8	(3)	1
Midfielders:	**DOB**	**M**	**(s)**	**G**
Nemanja Celic	26.04.1999	1		
Dominik Frieser	09.09.1993	26	(4)	8
Thomas Goiginger	15.03.1993	14	(5)	5
Stefan Haudum	27.11.1994	5	(5)	1
James Robert Holland (AUS)	15.05.1989	28	(1)	2
Peter Michorl	09.05.1995	29	(1)	5
Valentino Müller	19.01.1999	3	(4)	1
René Renner	29.11.1993	22	(4)	
Forwards:	**DOB**	**M**	**(s)**	**G**
Husein Balić (BIH)	15.02.1996	8	(3)	3
João Klauss de Mello (BRA)	01.03.1997	15	(13)	12
Yusuf Olaitan Otubanjo (NGA)	12.09.1992		(2)	
Marko Raguž	10.06.1998	17	(10)	7
Dominik Reiter	04.01.1998	3	(9)	1
Thomas Sabitzer	12.10.2000	3	(7)	
Samuel Tetteh (GHA)	28.07.1996	14	(15)	7

Sportklub Rapid Wien

Founded: 1899
Stadium: Allianz Stadion, Wien (28,000)
Trainer: Dietmar Kühbauer   04.04.1971

Goalkeepers:	DOB	M	(s)	G
Paul Gartler	10.03.1997	2		
Tobias Knoflach	30.12.1993	10	(2)	
Richard Strebinger	14.02.1993	20		
Defenders:	**DOB**	**M**	**(s)**	**G**
Stephan Auer	11.01.1991	7	(8)	
Mateo Barać (CRO)	20.07.1994	17	(1)	3
Christopher Dibon	02.11.1990	22		2
Paul Gobara	26.03.2000		(1)	
Leo Greiml	03.07.2001	9		
Adrian Hajdari (MKD)	31.05.2000		(2)	
Maximilian Hofmann	07.08.1993	16	(2)	1
Mert Müldür	03.04.1999	4		1
Mario Sonnleitner	08.10.1986	4	(3)	
Filip Stojković (MNE)	22.01.1993	19		
Maximilian Ullmann	17.06.1996	31		3
Midfielders:	**DOB**	**M**	**(s)**	**G**
Srđan Grahovac (BIH)	19.09.1992	13	(6)	
Melih Ibrahimoglu	17.07.2000		(4)	
Christoph Knasmüllner	30.04.1992	24	(4)	4
Dejan Ljubicic	08.10.1997	21	(1)	2
Manuel Martić	15.08.1995		(1)	
Thomas Murg	14.11.1994	15	(5)	3
Dejan Petrović (SVN)	12.01.1998	9	(5)	
Thorsten Schick	19.05.1990	9	(8)	
Lion Schuster	09.08.2000		(1)	
Stefan Schwab	27.09.1990	30		8
Dalibor Velimirovic	13.02.2001	4	(2)	
Nicholas Wunsch	05.10.2000		(1)	
Forwards:	**DOB**	**M**	**(s)**	**G**
Kelvin Arase	15.01.1999	15	(10)	5
Aliou Badji (SEN)	10.10.1997	9	(7)	3
Yusuf Demir	02.06.2003	1	(5)	
Taxiarchis Fountas (GRE)	04.09.1995	23	(4)	19
Ercan Kara	03.01.1996	5	(4)	3
Koya Kitagawa (JPN)	26.07.1996	6	(13)	2
Dragoljub Savić (SRB)	25.04.2001		(1)	
Philipp Schobesberger	10.12.1993	7	(4)	2

Football Club Red Bull Salzburg

Founded: 13.09.1933 (*as SV Austria Salzburg*)
Stadium: Red Bull Arena, Wals-Siezenheim (31,895)
Trainer: Jesse Alan Marsch (USA)   08.11.1973

Goalkeepers:	DOB	M	(s)	G
Carlos Miguel Coronel (BRA)	29.12.1996	5		
Cican Stanković	04.11.1992	27		
Defenders:	**DOB**	**M**	**(s)**	**G**
André Ramalho da Silva (BRA)	16.02.1992	26		6
Patrick Farkas	09.09.1992	12	(6)	
Rasmus Kristensen (DEN)	11.07.1997	10	(2)	
Jérôme Onguéné (FRA)	22.12.1997	20	(3)	1
Marin Pongračić (CRO)	11.09.1997	4	(1)	
Andreas Ulmer	30.10.1985	27	(2)	2
Albert Vallci	02.07.1995	15	(3)	2
Max Wöber	04.02.1998	21	(3)	
Midfielders:	**DOB**	**M**	**(s)**	**G**
Majeed Ashimeru (GHA)	10.10.1997	15	(5)	2
Antoine Bernède (FRA)	26.05.1999	8	(2)	
Mohamed Camara (MLI)	06.01.2000	11	(2)	1
Zlatko Junuzović	26.09.1987	19	(4)	3
Enock Mwepu (ZAM)	01.01.1998	16	(9)	4
Masaya Okugawa (JPN)	14.04.1996	17	(6)	9
Diadié Samassékou (MLI)	11.01.1996	1		
Dominik Szoboszlai (HUN)	25.10.2000	18	(9)	9
Forwards:	**DOB**	**M**	**(s)**	**G**
Karim Adeyemi (GER)	18.01.2002	1	(8)	1
Mërgim Berisha (GER)	11.05.1998	3	(5)	1
Patson Daka (ZAM)	09.10.1998	21	(10)	24
Erling Braut Håland (NOR)	21.07.2000	11	(3)	16
Hwang Hee-chan (KOR)	26.01.1996	17	(10)	11
Sékou Koïta (MLI)	28.11.1999	8	(9)	8
Takumi Minamino (JPN)	16.01.1995	11	(3)	5
Noah Okafor (SUI)	24.05.2000	5	(6)	3
Smail Prevljak (BIH)	10.05.1995	3	(1)	1

Sportclub Rheindorf Altach

Founded: 26.12.1929
Stadium: Stadion Schnabelholz, Altach (8,500)
Trainer: Alexander Anton Aiko Pastoor (NED)   26.10.1966

Goalkeepers:	DOB	M	(s)	G
Reuf Duraković	21.03.1994	2		
Martin Kobras	19.06.1986	29		
Benjamin Ožegović	09.08.1999	1	(1)	
Defenders:	**DOB**	**M**	**(s)**	**G**
Anderson dos Santos Gomes (BRA)	03.01.1998	17	(2)	
Berkay Dabanlı (GER)	27.06.1990	12		
Emir Karic	09.06.1997	27		1
Matthias Maak	12.05.1992	8	(8)	1
Philipp Netzer	02.10.1985	3		
Philipp Schmiedl	23.07.1997	18	(3)	1
Emanuel Schreiner	02.02.1989	21	(4)	5
Manuel Thurnwald	16.07.1998	22	(5)	
Jan Zwischenbrugger	16.06.1990	24	(2)	5
Midfielders:	**DOB**	**M**	**(s)**	**G**
Aljaz Casar (SVN)	17.09.2000		(3)	
Ousmane Diakité (MLI)	25.07.2000	9		
Manfred Fischer	06.08.1995	19	(7)	3
Christian Gebauer	20.12.1993	26	(5)	5
Samuel Yves Oum Gouet (CMR)	14.12.1997	23	(6)	1
Florian Jamnig	03.11.1990	5	(6)	1
Marco Meilinger	03.08.1991	9	(4)	
Lars Nussbaumer	31.01.2001	6	(4)	
Matthias Puschl	09.06.1996	2	(1)	
Sidney Sam (GER)	31.01.1988	16	(5)	6
Johannes Tartarotti	02.08.1999	21	(5)	2
Alain Wiss (SUI)	21.08.1990	7	(2)	
Forwards:	**DOB**	**M**	**(s)**	**G**
Mërgim Berisha (KVX)	11.05.1998	15	(2)	7
Bernd Gschweidl	08.09.1995		(6)	
Daniel Nussbaumer	29.11.1999	8	(9)	4
Frantz Pangop T'chidjui (CMR)	18.05.1993	1	(6)	1
Julio César Villalba Gaona (PAR)	17.09.1998	1	(7)	

Sportklub Niederösterreich St. Pölten

Founded: 2000
Stadium: NV Arena, Sankt Pölten (8,000)
Trainer: Alexander Schmidt (GER)   23.10.1968
[09.03.2020]   Robert Ibertsberger   20.01.1977

Goalkeepers:	DOB	M	(s)	G
Christoph Riegler	30.03.1992	26		
Thomas Vollnhofer	02.09.1984	6	(1)	
Defenders:	**DOB**	**M**	**(s)**	**G**
Daniel Drescher	07.10.1989	14	(3)	
Manuel Haas	07.05.1996	4	(5)	
Sandro Ingolitsch	18.04.1997	22	(5)	1
Christoph Klarer	14.06.2000	12	(1)	
Luan Leite Da Silva (BRA)	31.05.1996	24		1
Luca Meisl	04.03.1999	14	(3)	
Ahmet Muhamedbegovic	30.10.1998	18	(2)	1
Danijel Petrović (SRB)	27.11.1992	4	(2)	
Michael Schimpelsberger	12.02.1991	2		
Kofi Schulz (GER)	21.07.1989	10		1
Stefan Stangl	20.10.1991	1	(1)	
Noah Steiner	26.02.1999	3	(2)	
Midfielders:	**DOB**	**M**	**(s)**	**G**
Michael Ambichl	26.04.1991	19	(3)	1
Husein Balić (BIH)	15.02.1996	18		4
George Davies (SLE)	16.11.1996	15	(8)	2
Nico Gorzel (GER)	29.07.1998	5	(4)	
Dominik Hofbauer	19.09.1990	16	(3)	1
Alan Lima Carius (BRA)	04.04.1997	10	(3)	2
Robert Ljubičić (CRO)	14.07.1999	23	(6)	3
Daniel Luxbacher	13.03.1992	24	(1)	3
Christoph Messerer	10.11.2001	3	(8)	1
Martin Rasner	18.05.1995	12	(8)	
Daniel Schütz	19.06.1991	7	(7)	4
Forwards:	**DOB**	**M**	**(s)**	**G**
Cory Burke (JAM)	28.12.1991	9	(2)	4
René Gartler	21.10.1985	6	(8)	2
Lorenz Grabovac	25.07.1997		(1)	
Nicolas Meister	28.09.1999	2	(8)	
Issiaka Ouédraogo (BFA)	19.08.1988	3	(10)	3
Pak Kwang-Ryong (PRK)	27.09.1992	12	(1)	5
Roope Riski (FIN)	16.08.1991	6	(2)	
Marcel Tanzmayr	13.01.2002		(1)	
Aleksandar Vucenovic	10.10.1997	2		

Sportklub Sturm Graz

Founded: 1909
Stadium: Merkur-Arena, Graz (15,323)
Trainer: Nestor El Maestro (Jevtić) (SRB)   25.03.1983

Goalkeepers:	DOB	M	(s)	G
Jörg Siebenhandl	18.01.1990	32		
Defenders:	**DOB**	**M**	**(s)**	**G**
Anastasios Avlonitis (GRE)	01.01.1990	28		1
Isaac Donkor (GHA)	15.08.1995	11	(1)	
Niklas Geyrhofer	11.02.2000	6		
Fabian Koch	24.06.1989	2	(1)	
Dario Maresić	29.09.1999		(1)	
Emanuel Sakić	25.01.1991	26	(2)	
Thomas Schrammel	05.09.1987	12	(4)	
Lukas Spendlhofer	02.06.1993	24		
Vincent Trummer	18.05.2000	8	(3)	
Midfielders:	**DOB**	**M**	**(s)**	**G**
Stefan Hierländer	03.02.1991	22	(4)	4
Philipp Huspek	05.02.1991	13	(9)	3
Lukas Jäger	12.02.1994	10	(3)	
Jakob Jantscher	08.01.1989	7	(15)	5
Juan Domínguez Lamas (ESP)	08.01.1990	25	(3)	4
Otar Kiteishvili (GEO)	26.03.1996	31		6
Tobias Koch	06.04.2001	1	(1)	
Christoph Leitgeb	14.04.1985	5	(18)	
Michael John Lema	13.09.1999	3	(3)	
Ivan Ljubić	07.07.1996	25	(4)	1
Thorsten Röcher	11.06.1991	19	(4)	5
Dardan Shabanhaxhaj (KVX)	23.04.2001		(2)	
Forwards:	**DOB**	**M**	**(s)**	**G**
Winfred Amoah (GHA)	18.05.2000		(1)	
Bekim Balaj (ALB)	11.01.1991	23	(5)	6
Kiril Despodov (BUL)	11.11.1996	16	(3)	8
Emeka Friday Eze (NGA)	26.09.1996		(1)	
Kevin Friesenbichler	06.05.1994	3	(9)	
Markus Pink	24.02.1991		(9)	

Sportverein Mattersburg

Founded: 1922
Stadium: Pappelstadion, Mattersburg (17,100)
Trainer: Franz Ponweiser   15.09.1975

Goalkeepers:	DOB	M	(s)	G
Tino Casali	14.11.1995	4		
Markus Kuster	22.02.1994	27		
Bernhard Unger	23.04.1999	1		
Defenders:	**DOB**	**M**	**(s)**	**G**
Raffael Behounek	16.04.1997	4	(2)	
Philipp Erhardt	10.09.1993	29		
Florian Hart	11.05.1990	11	(2)	1
Alois Höller	15.03.1989	15	(6)	1
Michael Lercher	04.01.1996	20	(4)	1
Thorsten Mahrer	22.01.1990	27	(1)	1
Martin Majnovics (HUN)	26.10.2000	1	(2)	
Nedeljko Malić (BIH)	15.05.1988	14	(1)	1
David Nemeth	18.03.2001	12		
Lukas Rath	18.01.1992	19	(3)	
Michael Steinwender	04.05.2000	1	(3)	
Midfielders:	**DOB**	**M**	**(s)**	**G**
Julius Ertlthaler	25.04.1997	4	(2)	
Andreas Gruber	29.06.1995	18	(2)	12
Christoph Halper	21.05.1998	17	(7)	1
Alejandro Velasco Fariñas „Jano" (ESP)	23.12.1986	22	(5)	3
Andreas Kuen	24.03.1995	25	(3)	4
Fabian Miesenböck	07.07.1993	9	(7)	1
Luca Pichler	02.03.1998	1	(1)	
Nico Pichler	02.03.1998	1	(4)	
Patrick Salomon	10.06.1988	29	(1)	
Stefan Schimandl	30.03.2001	5	(4)	1
Forwards:	**DOB**	**M**	**(s)**	**G**
Filip Borsos (HUN)	22.06.2000	1	(1)	
Patrick Bürger	27.06.1987	11	(15)	4
Marko Kvasina	20.12.1996	6	(13)	2
Victor Oluyemi Olatunji (NGA)	05.09.1999	5	(9)	
Martin Pušić	24.10.1987	13	(7)	5

Turn- und Sportverein Hartberg

Founded: 29.04.1946
Stadium: Profertil Arena, Hartberg (4,500)
Trainer: Markus Schopp — 22.02.1974

Goalkeepers:	DOB	M	(s)	G
Florian Faist	10.04.1989	1		
Raphael Sallinger	08.12.1995	1		
Rene Swete	01.06.1990	30		
Defenders:	**DOB**	**M**	**(s)**	**G**
Amadou Dante (MLI)	07.10.2000	7	(1)	1
Michael Huber	14.01.1990	27	(4)	2
Tobias Kainz	31.10.1992	21	(7)	2
Dominik Kirnbauer	28.08.2002		(2)	
Christian Klem	21.04.1991	30		1
Andreas Lienhart	28.01.1986	17	(4)	3
Felix Luckeneder	21.03.1994	29		2
Patrick Obermüller	17.02.1999	3	(1)	
Siegfried Rasswalder	13.05.1987	3	(6)	
Thomas Rotter	27.01.1992	8	(10)	1
Midfielders:	**DOB**	**M**	**(s)**	**G**
David Cancola	23.10.1996	22	(6)	1
Jodel Dossou (BEN)	17.03.1992	17	(12)	6
Lukas Gabbichler	12.05.1998	5	(7)	1
Jürgen Heil	04.04.1997	13	(9)	
Michael John Lema	13.09.1999	1	(1)	
Bakary Nimaga (MLI)	06.12.1994	22	(1)	1
Tomáš Ostrák (CZE)	05.02.2000	4	(7)	1
Stefan Rakowitz	03.04.1990	10	(2)	2
Lukas Ried	10.10.1995	13	(12)	1
Marcel Schantl	17.08.2000	1	(1)	
Tino-Sven Sušić (BIH)	13.02.1992	1	(1)	
Peter Tschernegg	23.07.1992	4	(3)	
Forwards:	**DOB**	**M**	**(s)**	**G**
Sandro Gotal	09.09.1991	2	(7)	
Christoph Kröpfl	04.05.1990	3	(8)	
Rajko Rep (SVN)	20.06.1990	31		8
Dario Tadić	11.05.1990	26	(4)	17

Wolfsberger Athletik Club

Founded: 1931
Stadium: Lavanttal-Arena, Wolfsberg (7,300)
Trainer: Gerhard Struber — 24.01.1977
[20.11.2019] Mohamed Sahli — 24.03.1978
[01.01.2020] Ferdinand Feldhofer — 23.10.1979

Goalkeepers:	DOB	M	(s)	G
Alexander Kofler	06.11.1986	28		
Manuel Kuttin	17.12.1993	4		
Defenders:	**DOB**	**M**	**(s)**	**G**
Dominik Baumgartner	20.07.1996	11	(1)	
Stefan Gölles	04.10.1991	1	(11)	
Manfred Gollner	22.12.1990	10	(7)	2
Luís Miguel Vieira Silva (POR)	08.10.1990	5	(2)	
Michael Novak	30.12.1990	29	(2)	4
Stefan Perić	13.02.1997		(1)	
Nemanja Rnić (SRB)	30.09.1984	25		
Lukas Schmitz (GER)	13.10.1988	29	(2)	1
Michael Sollbauer	15.05.1990	29	(2)	4
Midfielders:	**DOB**	**M**	**(s)**	**G**
Cheikhou Dieng (SEN)	23.11.1993	6	(6)	1
Miloš Jojić (SRB)	19.03.1992	14		1
Mario Leitgeb	30.06.1988	28	(2)	3
Michael Liendl	25.10.1985	31	(1)	8
Marcel Ritzmaier	22.04.1993	28	(2)	3
Marc Andre Schmerböck	01.04.1994	6	(11)	2
Romano Schmid	27.01.2000	24	(1)	2
Lukas Schöfl	11.02.2001	1	(6)	
Sven Sprangler	27.03.1995	3	(10)	
Kai Stratznig	15.04.2002	2	(2)	
Christopher Wernitznig	24.02.1990	9	(20)	4
Forwards:	**DOB**	**M**	**(s)**	**G**
Marcel Holzer	06.10.1998	1	(5)	
Dogbole Franck Anderson Niangbo (CIV)	06.10.1999	25		
Alexander Schmidt	19.01.1998	7	(13)	
Shon Zalman Weissman (ISR)	14.02.1996	30	(1)	30

Wattener Sportgemeinschaft Tirol Swarovski Innsbruck

Founded: 1930
Stadium: Tivoli-Neu Stadion, Innsbruck (16,000)
Trainer: Thomas Silberberger — 03.06.1973
[01.06.2020] Martin Švejnoha (CZE) — 25.11.1977
[13.06.2020] Thomas Silberberger — 03.06.1973

Goalkeepers:	DOB	M	(s)	G
Simon Beccari (ITA)	18.11.1998	1		
Ferdinand Oswald (GER)	05.10.1990	31		
Defenders:	**DOB**	**M**	**(s)**	**G**
Felix Adjei (GHA)	17.12.1990	17	(4)	
Bruno Gabriel Soares (BRA)	21.08.1988	10		
Florian Buchacher	28.09.1987	12	(5)	1
Julian Gölles	22.09.1999	8	(7)	
David Gugganig	10.02.1997	21	(2)	
Stefan Hager	25.01.1995	24	(5)	2
Ione Agoney Jiménez Cabrera (ESP)	13.10.1985	12	(1)	
Fabian Koch	24.06.1989	11		1
Sandro Neurauter	21.03.1992	10	(9)	
Michael Svoboda	15.10.1998	26	(7)	1
Midfielders:	**DOB**	**M**	**(s)**	**G**
Lukas Grgic	17.08.1995	18	(1)	
Dino Kovačec (CRO)	27.12.1993	6	(2)	
Florian Mader	14.09.1982	7	(2)	
Kevin Nitzlnader	03.02.1993	4	(5)	
Thanos Petsos (GRE)	05.06.1991	14		1
Benjamin Pranter	22.09.1989	21	(1)	3
Florian Rieder	16.05.1996	19	(9)	
Sebastian Santin	15.06.1994	10	(13)	1
Florian Toplitsch	07.09.1991	7	(6)	
Clemens Walch	10.07.1987	9	(8)	2
Forwards:	**DOB**	**M**	**(s)**	**G**
Zlatko Dedič (SVN)	05.10.1984	27	(4)	12
Milan Jurdík (CZE)	08.11.1991		(9)	
Lukas Katnik	31.07.1989		(2)	
Felix Kerber	25.10.2002		(1)	
Stefan Maierhofer	16.08.1982	12	(1)	2
Kelvin Kwarteng Yeboah (ITA)	06.05.2000	15	(10)	4

1.	SV Ried im Innkreis (*Promoted*)	30	20	4	6	73	-	39	64
2.	SK Austria Klagenfurt	30	19	7	4	65	-	36	64
3.	FC Liefering	30	15	8	7	73	-	47	53
4.	FK Austria Wien II	30	14	6	10	62	-	44	48
5.	SKU Amstetten	30	12	9	9	51	-	47	45
6.	FC Wacker Innsbruck	30	13	5	12	44	-	49	44
7.	SK Vorwärts Steyr	30	11	8	11	42	-	36	41
8.	SV Lafnitz	30	9	12	9	42	-	42	39
9.	FC Juniors OÖ Pasching	30	10	8	12	50	-	63	38
10.	FC Blau-Weiß Linz	30	10	7	13	51	-	57	37
11.	SC Austria Lustenau	30	10	5	15	57	-	58	35
12.	FC Dornbirn 1913	30	8	10	12	40	-	59	34
13.	SV Horn	30	8	8	14	58	-	67	32
14.	Floridsdorfer AC Wien	30	7	11	12	32	-	51	32
15.	Grazer AK	30	7	10	13	40	-	50	31
16.	Kapfenberger SV	30	6	4	20	34	-	69	22

NATIONAL TEAM

INTERNATIONAL MATCHES
(16.07.2019 – 15.07.2020)

06.09.2019	Wals-Siezenheim	Austria - Latvia	6-0(2-0)	(ECQ)
09.09.2019	Warszawa	Poland - Austria	0-0	(ECQ)
10.10.2019	Wien	Austria - Israel	3-1(1-1)	(ECQ)
13.10.2019	Ljubljana	Slovenia - Austria	0-1(0-1)	(ECQ)
16.11.2019	Wien	Austria - North Macedonia	2-1(1-0)	(ECQ)
19.11.2019	Rīga	Latvia - Austria	1-0(0-0)	(ECQ)

06.09.2019   AUSTRIA - LATVIA   **6-0(2-0)**   16th EC. Qualifiers

Stadion Wals-Siezenheim [Red Bull Arena], Wals-Siezenheim; Referee: Robert Hennessy (Republic of Ireland); Attendance: 16,300

AUT: Cican Stanković, Andreas Ulmer, Aleksandar Dragović (81.Florian Grillitsch), David Olatukunbo Alaba, Stefan Lainer, Martin Hinteregger, Julian Baumgartlinger (Cap) (75.Stefan Ilsanker), Marcel Sabitzer, Valentino Lando Lazaro (69.Michael Gregoritsch), Konrad Laimer, Marko Arnautović. Trainer: Franco Foda (Germany).

Goals: Marko Arnautović (7), Marcel Sabitzer (13), Marko Arnautović (53 penalty), Pāvels Šteinbors (76 own goal), Konrad Laimer (80), Michael Gregoritsch (85).

09.09.2019   POLAND - AUSTRIA   **0-0**   16th EC. Qualifiers

Stadion PGE Narodowy, Warszawa; Referee: Viktor Kassai (Hungary); Attendance: 56,788

AUT: Cican Stanković, Andreas Ulmer, Aleksandar Dragović, David Olatukunbo Alaba, Stefan Lainer, Stefan Posch, Julian Baumgartlinger (Cap), Marcel Sabitzer, Valentino Lando Lazaro (77.Stefan Ilsanker), Konrad Laimer (89.Michael Gregoritsch), Marko Arnautović. Trainer: Franco Foda (Germany).

10.10.2019   AUSTRIA - ISRAEL   **3-1(1-1)**   16th EC. Qualifiers

"Ernst Happel" Stadion, Wien; Referee: William Collum (Scotland); Attendance: 26,200

AUT: Cican Stanković, Andreas Ulmer, Aleksandar Dragović, Martin Hinteregger, Stefan Posch (63.Christopher Trimmel), Julian Baumgartlinger (Cap), Stefan Ilsanker, Marcel Sabitzer, Valentino Lando Lazaro, Konrad Laimer (59.Louis Schaub), Marko Arnautović (82.Michael Gregoritsch). Trainer: Franco Foda (Germany).

Goals: Valentino Lando Lazaro (41), Martin Hinteregger (56), Marcel Sabitzer (88).

13.10.2019   SLOVENIA - AUSTRIA   **0-1(0-1)**   16th EC. Qualifiers

Stadion Stožice, Ljubljana; Referee: Cüneyt Çakır (Turkey); Attendance: 15,108

AUT: Cican Stanković, Andreas Ulmer, Aleksandar Dragović, Martin Hinteregger, Stefan Posch, Julian Baumgartlinger (Cap), Stefan Ilsanker, Michael Gregoritsch (83.Karim Onisiwo), Valentino Lando Lazaro (88.Christopher Trimmel), Konrad Laimer, Marcel Sabitzer (90+2.Florian Kainz). Trainer: Franco Foda (Germany).

Goal: Stefan Posch (21).

16.11.2019   AUSTRIA - NORTH MACEDONIA   **2-1(1-0)**   16th EC. Qualifiers

"Ernst Happel" Stadion, Wien; Referee: Michael Oliver (England); Attendance: 41,100

AUT: Alexander Schlager, Andreas Ulmer, Aleksandar Dragović, David Olatukunbo Alaba (90+2.Michael Gregoritsch), Stefan Lainer, Martin Hinteregger, Julian Baumgartlinger (Cap), Marcel Sabitzer, Valentino Lando Lazaro (79.Christopher Trimmel), Konrad Laimer (90.Stefan Ilsanker), Marko Arnautović. Trainer: Franco Foda (Germany).

Goals: David Olatukunbo Alaba (7), Stefan Lainer (48).

19.11.2019   LATVIA - AUSTRIA   **1-0(0-0)**   16th EC. Qualifiers

Daugava Stadions, Rīga; Referee: Alejandro José Hernández Hernández (Spain); Attendance: 2,781

AUT: Pavao Pervan, Aleksandar Dragović, Christopher Trimmel, Stefan Posch, Maximilian Wöber, Julian Baumgartlinger (Cap) (46.Karim Onisiwo), Stefan Ilsanker (77.Reinhold Ranftl), Michael Gregoritsch, Louis Schaub, Thomas Goiginger (69.Lukas Hinterseer), Florian Grillitsch. Trainer: Franco Foda (Germany).

NATIONAL TEAM PLAYERS
(16.07.2019 – 15.07.2020)

Name	DOB	Caps	Goals	2019/2020:	Club
Goalkeepers					
Pavao PERVAN	13.11.1987	1	0	2019:	*VfL Wolfsburg (GER)*
Alexander SCHLAGER	01.02.1996	1	0	2019:	*Linzer ASK*
Cican STANKOVIĆ	04.11.1992	4	0	2019:	*FC Red Bull Salzburg*
Defenders					
David Olatukunbo ALABA	24.06.1992	72	14	2019:	*FC Bayern München (GER)*
Aleksandar DRAGOVIĆ	06.03.1991	80	1	2019:	*TSV Bayer 04 Leverkusen (GER)*
Martin HINTEREGGER	07.09.1992	45	4	2019:	*Eintracht Frankfurt (GER)*
Stefan LAINER	27.08.1992	18	1	2019:	*Borussia VfL Mönchengladbach (GER)*
Stefan POSCH	14.05.1997	5	1	2019:	*TSG 1899 Hoffenheim (GER)*
Christopher TRIMMEL	24.02.1987	7	0	2019:	*1. FC Union Berlin (GER)*
Andreas ULMER	30.10.1985	17	0	2019:	*FC Red Bull Salzburg*
Maximilian WÖBER	04.02.1998	6	0	2019:	*FC Red Bull Salzburg*
Midfielders					
Julian BAUMGARTLINGER	02.01.1988	74	1	2019:	*TSV Bayer 04 Leverkusen (GER)*
Thomas GOIGINGER	15.03.1993	1	0	2019:	*Linzer ASK*
Florian GRILLITSCH	07.08.1995	16	1	2019:	*TSG 1899 Hoffenheim (GER)*
Stefan ILSANKER	18.05.1989	42	0	2019:	*RasenBallsport Leipzig (GER)*
Florian KAINZ	24.10.1992	16	0	2019:	*1.FC Köln (GER)*
Konrad LAIMER	27.05.1997	7	1	2019:	*RasenBallsport Leipzig (GER)*
Valentino Lando LAZARO	24.03.1996	28	3	2019:	*FC Internazionale Milano (ITA)*
Reinhold RANFTL	24.01.1992	1	0	2019:	*Linzer ASK*
Louis SCHAUB	29.12.1994	14	5	2019:	*1.FC Köln (GER)*
Forwards					
Marko ARNAUTOVIĆ	19.04.1989	85	26	2019:	*Shanghai SIPG FC (ENG)*
Michael GREGORITSCH	18.04.1994	17	2	2019:	*FC Augsburg (GER)*
Lukas HINTERSEER	28.03.1991	13	0	2019:	*Hamburger SV (GER)*
Karim ONISIWO	17.03.1992	6	0	2019:	*1.FSV Mainz 05 (GER)*
Marcel SABITZER	17.03.1994	42	7	2019:	*RasenBallsport Leipzig (GER)*
National team coach					
Franco FODA (Germany) [from 14.11.2017]	23.04.1966			22 M; 14 W; 2 D; 6 L; 36-18	

AZERBAIJAN

AFFA
Azərbaycan Futbol
Federasiyaları Assosiasiyası

The Country:
Republic of Azerbaijan (Azərbaycan Respublikası)
Capital: Bakı
Surface: 86,600 km²
Inhabitants: 10,127,874 [2019]
Time: UTC+4

The FA:
Azərbaycan Futbol Federasiyaları Assosiasiyası
2208 Nobel prospekti 1025, Bakı
Tel: +994 12 404 27 77
Foundation date: 1992
Member of FIFA since: 1994
Member of UEFA since: 1994
Website: www.affa.az

NATIONAL TEAM RECORDS

RECORDS
First international match:	17.09.1992, Gurdzhaani:	Georgia – Azerbaijan 6-3
Most international caps:	Rəşad Ferhad Sadıqov	- 111 caps (2001-2017)
Most international goals:	Qurban Osman Qurbanov	- 12 goals / 65 caps (1992-2005)

UEFA EUROPEAN CHAMPIONSHIP		FIFA WORLD CUP		OLYMPIC TOURNAMENTS	
1960	-	1930	-	1908	-
1964	-	1934	-	1912	-
1968	-	1938	-	1920	-
1972	-	1950	-	1924	-
1976	-	1954	-	1928	-
1980	-	1958	-	1936	-
1984	-	1962	-	1948	-
1988	-	1966	-	1952	-
1992	-	1970	-	1956	-
1996	Qualifiers	1974	-	1960	-
2000	Qualifiers	1978	-	1964	-
2004	Qualifiers	1982	-	1968	-
2008	Qualifiers	1986	-	1972	-
2012	Qualifiers	1990	-	1976	-
2016	Qualifiers	1994	*Did not enter*	1980	-
2020	Qualifiers	1998	Qualifiers	1984	-
		2002	Qualifiers	1988	-
		2006	Qualifiers	1992	-
		2010	Qualifiers	1996	Qualifiers
		2014	Qualifiers	2000	Qualifiers
		2018	Qualifiers	2004	Qualifiers
				2008	Qualifiers
				2012	Qualifiers
				2016	Qualifiers

UEFA NATIONS LEAGUE
2018/2019 – League D

FIFA CONFEDERATIONS CUP 1992-2017
None

AZERBAIJAN CLUB HONOURS IN EUROPEAN CLUB COMPETITIONS:

European Champion Clubs' Cup (1956-1992) / UEFA Champions League (1993-2020)
None

Fairs Cup (1858-1971) / UEFA Cup (1972-2009) / UEFA Europa League (2010-2020)
None

UEFA Super Cup (1972-2019)
None

*European Cup Winners' Cup 1961-1999**
None

*defunct competition

NATIONAL COMPETITIONS
TABLE OF HONOURS

AZERBAIJAN SSR (SOVIET ERA) CHAMPIONS

Year	Champion	Year	Champion	Year	Champion
1928	Progress-2 Baku	1954	Zavod S.M. Budennogo Baku	1973	Araz Baku
1929–33	*Not known*	1955	Ordjonikidzeneft Baku	1974	Araz Baku
1934	Profsoyuz Baku	1956	NPU Ordgonikidzeneft Baku	1975	Araz Baku
1935	Stroitel Yuga Baku	1957	NPU Ordjonikidzeneft Baku	1976	Araz Baku
1936	Stroitel Yuga Baku	1958	NPU Ordjonikidzeneft Baku	1977	Karabakh Khankendi
1937	Lokomotiv Baku	1959	Baku Teams (Spartakiada)	1978	SKIF Baku
1938	Lokomotiv Baku	1960	SKA Baku	1979	SKA Baku
1939	Lokomotiv Baku	1961	Spartak Guba	1980	Energetik Ali-Bayramly
1940	Lokomotiv Baku	1962	SKA Baku	1981	Gandjlik Baku
1941–43	*Not known*	1963	Araz Baku	1982	Tokhudju Baku
1944	Dinamo Baku	1964	Polad Sumgait	1983	Termist Baku
1945	*No competition*	1965	Vostok Baku	1984	Termist Baku
1946	Lokomotiv Baku	1966	Vostok Baku	1985	Khazar Sumgayit
1947	Trudovye Rezervy Baku	1967	Araz Baku	1986	Göyəzən
1948	KKF Baku	1968	SKA Baku	1987	Araz Naxçıvan
1949	KKF Baku	1969	Araz Baku	1988	Qarabağ Ağdam
1950	Iskra Baku	1970	SKA Baku	1989	Stroitel Sabirabad
1951	Ordjonikidzeneft Baku	1971	Khimik Salyany	1990	Qarabağ Ağdam
1952	Ordjonikidzeneft Baku	1972	Surahanets Baku	1991	Khazar Sumgayit
1953	Ordjonikidzeneft Baku				

	CHAMPIONS	CUP WINNERS	BEST GOALSCORERS	
1992	Neftçi PFK Bakı	İnşaatçı Bakı FK	Nazim Aliyev (FK Xəzər Lənkəran Sumqayit)	39
1993	Qarabağ FK Ağdam	Qarabağ FK Ağdam	Samir Alakbarov (Neftçi PFK Bakı)	16
1993/1994	FK Turan Tovuz	Kəpəz FK Gəncə	Musa Gurbanov (FK Turan Tovuz)	35
1994/1995	Kəpəz FK Gəncə	Neftçi PFK Bakı	Nazim Aliyev (Neftçi PFK Bakı)	26
1995/1996	Neftçi PFK Bakı	Neftçi PFK Bakı	Fazil Parvarov (Kəpəz FK Gəncə) Rovshan Ahmadov (Kəpəz FK Gəncə)	23
1996/1997	Neftçi PFK Bakı	Kəpəz FK Gəncə	Gurban Gurbanov (Neftçi PFK Bakı)	34
1997/1998	Kəpəz FK Gəncə	Kəpəz FK Gəncə	Nazim Aliyev (Bakı FK)	23
1998/1999	Kəpəz FK Gəncə	Neftçi PFK Bakı	Alay Bahramov (FK Viləş Masallı)	24
1999/2000	FK Şəmkir	Kəpəz FK Gəncə	Badri Kvaratskhelia (FK Şəmkir)	16
2000/2001	FK Şəmkir	Şəfa Bakı FK	Pasha Aliyev (Bakılı PFK Bakı)	12
2001/2002	*Championship abandoned*	Neftçi PFK Bakı	-	
2002/2003	*No competition*	*No competition*	-	
2003/2004	Neftçi PFK Bakı	Neftçi PFK Bakı	Samir Musayev (Qarabağ FK Ağdam)	20
2004/2005	Neftçi PFK Bakı	Bakı FK	Zaur Ramazanov (Karvan FK)	21
2005/2006	Bakı FK	Qarabağ FK Bakı	Yacouba Bamba (CIV, Karvan FK)	16
2006/2007	Xəzər Lənkəran FK	Xəzər Lənkəran FK	Zaur Ramazanov (Xəzər Lənkəran FK)	20
2007/2008	İnter PİK Bakı	Xəzər Lənkəran FK	Khagani Mammadov (İnter PİK Bakı)	19
2008/2009	Bakı FK	Qarabağ FK Bakı	Walter Guglielmone Gómez (URU, İnter PİK Bakı)	17
2009/2010	İnter PİK Bakı	Bakı FK	Farid Guliyev (Standard FK Sumqayit)	16
2010/2011	Neftçi PFK Bakı	Xəzər Lənkəran FK	Georgi Adamia (GEO, Qarabağ FK Bakı)	18
2011/2012	Neftçi PFK Bakı	Bakı FK	Bahodir Nasimov (UZB, Neftçi PFK Bakı)	16
2012/2013	Neftçi PFK Bakı	Neftçi PFK Bakı	Nicolás Sebastián Canales Calas (CHI, Neftçi PFK Bakı)	26
2013/2014	Qarabağ FK Bakı	Neftçi PFK Bakı	Reynaldo dos Santos Silva (Qarabağ FK Bakı)	22
2014/2015	Qarabağ FK Bakı	Qarabağ FK Bakı	Nurlan Novruzov (Bakı FK)	15
2015/2016	Qarabağ FK Bakı	Qarabağ FK Bakı	Daniel Quintana Sosa "Dani Quintana" (ESP, Qarabağ FK Bakı)	15
2016/2017	Qarabağ FK Bakı	Qarabağ FK Bakı	Filip Ozobić (CRO, Qəbələ FK) Rauf Aliyev (İnter PİK Bakı)	11
2017/2018	Qarabağ FK Bakı	Keşlə FK Bakı	Bagaliy Dabo (FRA, Qəbələ FK)	13
2018/2019	Qarabağ FK Bakı	Qəbələ FK	Mahir Anar Mədətov (Qarabağ FK Bakı)	16
2019/2020	Qarabağ FK Bakı	*Competition cancelled*	Peyman Babaei (IRN, Sumqayıt FK) Steeven Joseph-Monrose (FRA, Neftçi PFK Bakı) Bagaliy Dabo (FRA, Neftçi PFK Bakı) Mahir Anar Emreli (Qarabağ FK Bakı)	7

Please note: Qarabağ FK moved 1993 from Ağdam to Bakı.

NATIONAL CHAMPIONSHIP
Azerbaijan Premier League – Azərbaycan Premyer Liqası 2019/2020
(16.08.2019 – 08.03.2020)

Results

Round 1 [16-19.08.2019]
Keşlə FK Bakı - Qarabağ FK 0-1(0-0)
Qəbələ FK - Sumqayıt FK 0-2(0-2)
Səbail FK Bakı - Zirə FK Bakı 1-0(0-0)
Neftçi PFK Bakı - Sabah FC Bakı 1-1(1-1)

Round 2 [24-26.08.2019]
Sumqayıt FK - Səbail FK Bakı 0-3(0-1)
Sabah FC Bakı - Keşlə FK Bakı 0-1(0-1)
Qarabağ FK - Qəbələ FK 3-0(0-0)
Zirə FK Bakı - Neftçi PFK Bakı 1-0(1-0)

Round 3 [31.08.-01.09.2019]
Qəbələ FK - Keşlə FK Bakı 0-4(0-3)
Zirə FK Bakı - Sabah FC Bakı 1-1(0-1)
Neftçi PFK Bakı - Sumqayıt FK 2-1(0-1)
Səbail FK Bakı - Qarabağ FK 0-4(0-2)

Round 4 [14-15.09.2019]
Sumqayıt FK - Zirə FK Bakı 1-2(1-1)
Sabah FC Bakı - Qəbələ FK 0-1(0-0)
Keşlə FK Bakı - Səbail FK Bakı 1-2(0-2)
Qarabağ FK - Neftçi PFK Bakı 2-0(1-0)

Round 5 [21-23.09.2019]
Sumqayıt FK - Sabah FC Bakı 1-0(1-0)
Səbail FK Bakı - Qəbələ FK 1-1(0-1)
Neftçi PFK Bakı - Keşlə FK Bakı 0-0
Zirə FK Bakı - Qarabağ FK 1-3(0-3)

Round 6 [27-29.09.2019]
Qarabağ FK - Sumqayıt FK 2-0(1-0)
Qəbələ FK - Neftçi PFK Bakı 0-3(0-0)
Sabah FC Bakı - Səbail FK Bakı 3-0(0-0)
Keşlə FK Bakı - Zirə FK Bakı 2-0(0-0)

Round 7 [05-06.10.2019]
Sumqayıt FK - Keşlə FK Bakı 0-0
Neftçi PFK Bakı - Səbail FK Bakı 2-1(2-0)
Zirə FK Bakı - Qəbələ FK 1-1(0-0)
Qarabağ FK - Sabah FC Bakı 2-0(1-0)

Round 8 [19-20.10.2019]
Qəbələ FK - Qarabağ FK 1-1(1-1)
Keşlə FK Bakı - Sabah FC Bakı 1-1(1-0)
Neftçi PFK Bakı - Zirə FK Bakı 3-0(1-0)
Səbail FK Bakı - Sumqayıt FK 0-2(0-0)

Round 9 [26-28.10.2019]
Keşlə FK Bakı - Qəbələ FK 2-1(2-0)
Sabah FC Bakı - Zirə FK Bakı 2-2(2-1)
Sumqayıt FK - Neftçi PFK Bakı 2-4(1-2)
Qarabağ FK - Səbail FK Bakı 1-0(0-0)

Round 10 [01-03.11.2019]
Neftçi PFK Bakı - Qarabağ FK 0-0
Səbail FK Bakı - Keşlə FK Bakı 0-0
Zirə FK Bakı - Sumqayıt FK 2-2(1-1)
Qəbələ FK - Sabah FC Bakı 1-2(1-0)

Round 11 [09-10.11.2019]
Qəbələ FK - Səbail FK Bakı 3-0(2-0)
Keşlə FK Bakı - Neftçi PFK Bakı 2-1(0-1)
Sabah FC Bakı - Sumqayıt FK 1-3(1-0)
Qarabağ FK - Zirə FK Bakı 1-1(1-0)

Round 12 [22-24.11.2019]
Sumqayıt FK - Qarabağ FK 2-1(0-1)
Səbail FK Bakı - Sabah FC Bakı 1-3(0-0)
Zirə FK Bakı - Keşlə FK Bakı 3-1(3-1)
Neftçi PFK Bakı - Qəbələ FK 4-1(3-0)

Round 13 [30.11.-02.12.2019]
Qəbələ FK - Zirə FK Bakı 3-0(2-0)
Keşlə FK Bakı - Sumqayıt FK 2-1(1-0)
Səbail FK Bakı - Neftçi PFK Bakı 0-0
Sabah FC Bakı - Qarabağ FK 0-1(0-0)

Round 14 [06-08.12.2019]
Qarabağ FK - Keşlə FK Bakı 2-2(2-1)
Sumqayıt FK - Qəbələ FK 1-1(1-1)
Zirə FK Bakı - Səbail FK Bakı 4-1(2-0)
Sabah FC Bakı - Neftçi PFK Bakı 0-2(0-1)

Round 15 [01-02.02.2020]
Zirə FK Bakı - Sabah FC Bakı 2-0(1-0)
Neftçi PFK Bakı - Sumqayıt FK 1-1(0-1)
Qəbələ FK - Keşlə FK Bakı 1-2(0-2)
Səbail FK Bakı - Qarabağ FK 0-1(0-0)

Round 16 [07-08.02.2020]
Sabah FC Bakı - Qəbələ FK 3-2(2-1)
Keşlə FK Bakı - Səbail FK Bakı 0-1(0-0)
Sumqayıt FK - Zirə FK Bakı 2-1(1-1)
Qarabağ FK - Neftçi PFK Bakı 0-0

Round 17 [15-16.02.2020]
Zirə FK Bakı - Qarabağ FK 0-6(0-4)
Sumqayıt FK - Sabah FC Bakı 1-2(0-0)
Səbail FK Bakı - Qəbələ FK 3-1(0-1)
Neftçi PFK Bakı - Keşlə FK Bakı 3-1(2-0)

Round 18 [22-23.02.2020]
Qəbələ FK - Neftçi PFK Bakı 0-2(0-2)
Keşlə FK Bakı - Zirə FK Bakı 4-0(2-0)
Sabah FC Bakı - Səbail FK Bakı 0-0
Qarabağ FK - Sumqayıt FK 1-0(0-0)

Round 19 [29.02.-01.03.2020]
Sumqayıt FK - Keşlə FK Bakı 2-2(1-1)
Qarabağ FK - Sabah FC Bakı 0-0
Zirə FK Bakı - Qəbələ FK 1-2(1-0)
Neftçi PFK Bakı - Səbail FK Bakı 1-1(0-0)

Round 20 [07-08.03.2020]
Qəbələ FK - Sumqayıt FK 5-0(2-0)
Neftçi PFK Bakı - Sabah FC Bakı 4-0(1-0)
Səbail FK Bakı - Zirə FK Bakı 1-3(1-1)
Keşlə FK Bakı - Qarabağ FK 0-2(0-1)

On 19.06.2020, the AFFA announced that the Azerbaijan Premier League was officially ended without the resumption of the remains matches due to the escalating situation of the Covid-19 pandemic in Azerbaijan. As a result Qarabağ were crowned champions. No team were relegated.

Final Standings

								Home				Away			
1. **Qarabağ FK Bakı**	20	13	6	1	34 - 7	45	6	4	0	14 - 3	7	2	1	20 - 4
2. Neftçi PFK Bakı	20	10	7	3	33 - 14	37	6	5	0	21 - 7	4	2	3	12 - 7
3. Keşlə FK Bakı	20	8	6	6	27 - 21	30	5	1	4	14 - 10	3	5	2	13 - 11
4. Sumqayıt FK	20	6	5	9	24 - 32	23	3	3	4	12 - 16	3	2	5	12 - 16
5. Zirə FK Bakı	20	6	5	9	25 - 37	23	4	3	3	16 - 17	2	2	6	9 - 20
6. Sabah FC Bakı	20	5	6	9	19 - 27	21	2	2	5	9 - 12	3	4	4	10 - 15
7. Səbail FK Bakı	20	5	5	10	16 - 30	20	2	3	5	7 - 15	3	2	5	9 - 15
8. Qəbələ FK	20	5	4	11	25 - 35	19	3	1	6	14 - 16	2	3	5	11 - 19

Top goalscorers:

7	**Peyman Babaei (IRN)**	*Sumqayıt FK*
7	Steeven Joseph-Monrose (FRA)	*Neftçi PFK Bakı*
7	Bagaliy Dabo (FRA)	*Neftçi PFK Bakı*
7	Mahir Anar Emreli	*Qarabağ FK Bakı*
6	Lorenzo Rodrigo Frutos Britos (PAR)	*Keşlə FK Bakı*
6	Aghabala Ramazanov	*Səbail FK Bakı / Zirə FK Bakı*
6	Davit Volkovi (GEO)	*Qəbələ FK / Zirə FK Bakı*

NATIONAL CUP
Azərbaycan Kuboku 2019/2020

First Round [03-04.12.2019]				
Keşlə FK Bakı - Kəpəz FK Gəncə	3-1	Sabah FC Bakı - Ağsu FK	5-0	
Zirə FK Bakı - Qaradağ Lökbatan FK	4-0	Sumqayıt FK - Zaqatala PFK	2-0	

Quarter-Finals [15-20.12.2019]				
First Leg		**Second Leg**		
Qəbələ FK - Sabah FC Bakı	3-0	Sabah FC Bakı - Qəbələ FK	2-3	
Səbail FK - Zirə FK Bakı	0-0	Zirə FK Bakı - Səbail FK	1-0	
Neftçi PFK - Sumqayıt FK	0-1	Sumqayıt FK - Neftçi PFK	0-0	
Qarabağ FK Bakı - Keşlə FK Bakı	1-0	Keşlə FK Bakı - Qarabağ FK Bakı	1-3	

The Semi-Finals (scheduled on 22-29.04.2020) and Final match (16.05.2020) were cancelled. No title was awarded.

THE CLUBS 2019/2020

Keşlə Futbol Klubu Bakı

Founded: 1997
Stadium: ASK Arena, Keşlə (8,125)
Trainer: Tərlan Musa Əhmədov   17.11.1971

Goalkeepers:	DOB	M	(s)	G
Stanislav Namaşco (MDA)	10.11.1986	20		
Defenders:	**DOB**	**M**	**(s)**	**G**
Slavik Həsrət Alxasov	06.02.1993	19		2
Mijuško Bojović (MNE)	09.08.1988	19		2
Franco Valentin Flores (ARG)	28.05.1993	17	(1)	1
İkin Qırtımov	04.11.1990	15	(1)	
Tərlan Şahmurad Quliyev	19.04.1992	5	(2)	
Azər Vəlhəd Salahlı	11.04.1994	3	(2)	
Cabir Əmirli	06.01.1997	7	(11)	
Midfielders:	**DOB**	**M**	**(s)**	**G**
Parviz Azadov	19.10.2000	1	(3)	1
Tural Bayramlı	07.01.1998	19		2

	DOB	M	(s)	G
Orkhan Fərəcov	07.01.2001		(1)	
Shokhrukh Gadoev (UZB)	31.12.1991	4	(2)	2
Əfran İsmayılov	08.10.1988	3	(12)	
John Bankolé Kamara (SLE)	05.12.1988	18		
Xəzər Mahmudov	23.11.2000	1		
Emin Mehdiyev	22.09.1991		(7)	
Rəşad Əbülfəz Sadiqov	08.10.1983		(6)	
Forwards:	**DOB**	**M**	**(s)**	**G**
Alexander Domingos Christovão M'Futila (ANG)	14.03.1993	4	(2)	
Vüsal Mahmud İsgəndərli	03.11.1995	20		4
Lorenzo Rodrigo Frutos Britos (PAR)	04.06.1989	15	(2)	6
Ruslan Qurbanov	12.09.1991	14	(2)	2
César Meza Colli (PAR)	05.10.1991	16		4

Neftçi Peşəkar Futbol Klubu Bakı

Founded: 18.03.1937
Stadium: Bakcell Arena, Bakı (10,500)
Trainer: Roberto Bordin (ITA)   10.01.1965
[18.01.2020] Fuzuli Mammadov   08.09.1977

Goalkeepers:	DOB	M	(s)	G
Səlahət Nüsrət Ağayev	04.01.1991	15	(1)	
Aqil Məmmədov	01.05.1989	5	(1)	
Defenders:	**DOB**	**M**	**(s)**	**G**
Tural Axundov	01.08.1988	12		1
Ömər Fuad Buludov	15.12.1998	11	(2)	1
Wilde-Donald Guerrier (HAI)	31.03.1989	13		1
Anton Viktor Krivotsyuk	20.08.1998	16		4
Pape Mamadou Mbodj (SEN)	12.03.1993	3	(6)	1
Kyrylo Petrov (UKR)	22.06.1990	10	(1)	
Vojislav Stanković (SRB)	22.09.1987	16		
İsmayil Zülfüqarlı	16.04.2001		(3)	
Midfielders:	**DOB**	**M**	**(s)**	**G**
Rəhman Xudayət Hacıyev	25.07.1993	8	(7)	

	DOB	M	(s)	G
Mamadou Kane (GUI)	22.01.1997	16		
Emin Cəbrayıl Mahmudov	27.04.1992	19		3
Soni Mustivar (HAI)	12.02.1990	10	(4)	2
Vangelis Platellas (GRE)	01.12.1988	5	(7)	1
Turan Vəlizadə	01.01.2001		(1)	
Namiq Əvəz Ələsgərov	03.02.1995	11	(7)	
Forwards:	**DOB**	**M**	**(s)**	**G**
Mirabdulla Miryavər Abassov	27.04.1995		(3)	1
Bagaliy Dabo (FRA)	27.07.1988	13	(2)	7
Dário Frederico da Silva (BRA)	11.09.1991	10	(7)	1
Steeven Joseph-Monrose (FRA)	20.07.1990	17	(2)	7
Saman Nariman Jahan (IRN)	18.04.1991	6		1
Rauf Səhraman Əliyev	12.02.1989	4	(5)	1

Qarabağ Futbol Klubu Bakı

Founded: 1951
Stadium: Azersun Arena, Bakı (5,800)
Trainer: Qurban Osman Qurbanov   13.04.1992

Goalkeepers:	DOB	M	(s)	G
Asmir Begović (BIH)	20.06.1987	10		
Şahrudin Məhəmmədəliyev	12.06.1994	10		
Defenders:	**DOB**	**M**	**(s)**	**G**
Aílton Ferreira Silva (BRA)	16.03.1995	13	(2)	1
Toral Bayramov	23.02.2001	1	(1)	
Abbas İsrafil Hüseynov	13.06.1995	11	(4)	1
Bədavi Ruslan Hüseynov	11.07.1991	14		1
Rahil Məmmədov	24.11.1995	8		
Maksim Boris Medvedev	20.09.1989	16	(1)	
Faycal Rherras (MAR)	07.04.1993	6		
Rəşad Farhad Sadıqov	16.06.1982	10		
Midfielders:	**DOB**	**M**	**(s)**	**G**
Richard Almeida de Oliveira	20.03.1989	12	(2)	1

	DOB	M	(s)	G
Daniel Quintana Sosa "Dani Quintana" (ESP)	08.03.1987	9	(2)	3
Hacıağa Hacılı	30.01.1998	5	(2)	
İsmayıl İbrahimli	13.02.1998	15	(1)	4
Miguel Marcos Madera "Míchel" (ESP)	08.11.1985	9	(3)	
Filip Ozobić (CRO)	08.04.1991	3	(2)	1
Qara Elxan Qarayev	12.10.1992	13	(3)	1
Simeon Slavchev (BUL)	25.09.1993	2		
Forwards:	**DOB**	**M**	**(s)**	**G**
Araz Abdulla Abdullayev	18.04.1992	6	(5)	
Mahir Anar Emreli	01.07.1997	12	(4)	7
Magaye Gueye (SEN)	06.07.1990	9	(9)	5
Jaime Romero Gómez (ESP)	31.07.1990	10	(3)	3
Owusu Kwabena (GHA)	18.06.1997	2	(3)	
Abdellah Zoubir (FRA)	05.12.1991	14	(5)	5

Qəbələ Futbol Klubu

Founded:	01.09.1955		
Stadium:	Qabala City Stadium, Qabala (4,500)		
Trainer:	Sənan Şamil Qurbanov		04.08.1980
[02.09.2019]	Elmar Baxşiyev		03.08.1980
[02.10.2019]	Azar Bagyrov		17.04.1984

Goalkeepers:	DOB	M	(s)	G
Anar Nazirov	08.09.1985	15		
Tarlan Əhmədli	21.11.1994	5	(2)	
Defenders:	**DOB**	**M**	**(s)**	**G**
Faiq Hacıyev	22.05.1999	1	(3)	
Murad Musayev	13.06.1994	6	(2)	
Yusif Nəbiyev	03.09.1997	12	(2)	
Sadiq Quliyev	09.03.1995	5	(4)	
Rasim Əsədulla Ramaldanov	24.01.1986	5		
Amin Seydiyev	15.11.1998	19		1
Ivan Žunić (CRO)	11.09.1988	17		2
Midfielders:	**DOB**	**M**	**(s)**	**G**
Yaovi Akakpo (TOG)	03.11.1999		(1)	
Qismat Aliyev	24.10.1996	18	(1)	1
Fernán Ferreiroá López (ESP)	10.02.1995	18		3
Abdelrafik Gérard (FRA)	08.06.1993	2	(2)	
Merib Gigauri (GEO)	05.01.1993	18		
Roman Hüseynov	26.12.1997	10	(3)	1
İdris İnqilablı	06.10.2001	1	(2)	
Ibrahima Niasse (SEN)	18.04.1988	2	(1)	
Asif Məmmədov	05.08.1986	12	(1)	
Forwards:	**DOB**	**M**	**(s)**	**G**
Clésio Palmirim David Baúque (MOZ)	11.10.1994	18		
Rodrigo Pablo Gattas Bertoni (CHI)	02.12.1991		(2)	
Ülvi İsgəndərov	17.04.1998	6	(12)	3
Christian Kouakou Yao (CIV)	01.03.1991	1	(3)	
Rövlan Muradov	28.03.1998	10	(8)	4
Nicolas Rajsel (SVN)	31.05.1993	3	(1)	4
Ehtiram Etibar Şahverdiyev	01.10.1996	2	(3)	
Davit Volkovi (GEO)	03.06.1995	14		5

Sabah Football Club Bakı

Founded:	2016		
Stadium:	Bank Respublika Arena, Masazır (13,000)		
Trainer:	Elşad Əhmədov		11.09.1970
[19.09.2019]	Igor Ponomaryov		24.02.1960
[27.11.2019]	Željko Sopić (CRO)		26.07.1974

Goalkeepers:	DOB	M	(s)	G
Dmytro Bezruk (UKR)	30.03.1996	3		
Sasa Stamenković (SRB)	05.01.1985	17		
Defenders:	**DOB**	**M**	**(s)**	**G**
Ruslan Abışov	10.10.1987	8		
Arsen Ağcabəyov	11.09.2000	1		
Kərim Şahin Diniyev	05.09.1993	7	(2)	
Filip Ivanović (SRB)	13.02.1992	13	(1)	
Məqsəd İsayev	07.06.1994	14	(1)	
Mahammad Mirzəbəyov	16.11.1990	16		
Bəhlul Ələmdar Mustafazadə	27.02.1997	18		
Təmkin Şaiq Xəlilzadə	06.08.1993	14	(3)	
Midfielders:	**DOB**	**M**	**(s)**	**G**
Vadim Vaqif Abdullayev	17.12.1994	1	(2)	
Abbas Ağazadə	10.02.1999	2	(1)	
Eugeniu Cociuc (MDA)	11.05.1993	3	(1)	
Coşqun Şahin Diniyev	13.09.1995	11	(3)	1
Hendrick Ekstein (RSA)	01.01.1991	10	(3)	3
Rəşad Elman Eyyubov	03.12.1992	7	(4)	1
Cavid Əbdirəhman İmamverdiyev	08.01.1990	10	(4)	2
Mario Marina (CRO)	03.08.1989	6		1
Şakir Seyidov	31.12.2000	10	(6)	2
Cavid Tağıyev	22.07.1992	1	(3)	
Forwards:	**DOB**	**M**	**(s)**	**G**
Amadou Diallo (FRA)	21.06.1994	13	(6)	3
Ulysse Diallo (MLI)	26.10.1992	9	(5)	3
Marko Dević (UKR)	27.10.1983	3		1
Ozan Kökcü	18.08.1998	14	(1)	1
Emil Qasımov	09.04.2000		(1)	
Julio César Rodríguez Giménez (PAR)	05.12.1990	5	(1)	
Róger Fabricio Rojas Lazo (HON)	09.06.1990	4	(7)	
Ramil Şeydayev	15.03.1996		(3)	

Səbail Futbol Klubu Bakı

Founded:	2016		
Stadium:	Bayil Arena, Bakı (5,000)		
Trainer:	Aftandil Sabir Hacıyev		13.08.1981

Goalkeepers:	DOB	M	(s)	G
Kamal Bayramov	19.08.1985	11		
Oleksandr Rybka (UKR)	10.04.1987	9		
Defenders:	**DOB**	**M**	**(s)**	**G**
Ürfan Abbasov	14.10.1992	20		
Erico Constantino da Silva (BRA)	20.07.1989	8		1
Peyman Keshavarz (IRN)	03.03.1996	2		
Ihor Korotetskyi (UKR)	13.09.1987		(1)	
Adil Nağıyev	11.09.1995	13	(2)	
Şəhriyar Ağali Rəhimov	06.04.1989	18		1
Eltun Sifik Yagublu	19.08.1991	7	(2)	
Elvin Qərib Yunuszadə	22.08.1992	11		
Midfielders:	**DOB**	**M**	**(s)**	**G**
Vüqar Bəybala Bəybalayev	05.08.1993	4	(2)	
Eugeniu Cociuc (MDA)	11.05.1993	12		1
Hendrick Ekstein (RSA)	01.01.1991	5	(1)	2
Michaël Kojo Essien (GHA)	03.12.1982	5	(5)	
Ruslan Hacıyev	26.03.1998	5	(2)	
Chikito Lema Mabidi (COD)	11.06.1993		(2)	
Turan Manafov	19.09.1998	15	(1)	
Ədilkhan Qarahmadov	05.06.2001	1	(8)	
Aqşin Həsən Qurbanlı	15.07.1996		(2)	
Orxan Nizami Qurbanlı	12.07.1995		(4)	
Elchin Rəhimli	17.06.1991	7	(4)	
Əli Sadıxov	13.08.1999		(6)	
Rahid Ələkbər Əmirquliyev	01.09.1989	20		
Forwards:	**DOB**	**M**	**(s)**	**G**
Mirabdulla Miryavər Abbasov	27.04.1995	9	(2)	
Mirsahib Abbasov	19.01.1993	7	(7)	1
Bahadur Həziyev	26.03.1999		(1)	
Fəhmin Muradbəyli	16.03.1996	13	(5)	
Ağabala Ramazanov	20.01.1993	13		3
Rauf Əliyev	12.02.1989	5		3

Sumqayıt Futbol Klubu

Founded: 1961 (*as Metallurg Sumqayıt*)
Stadium: Kapital Bank Arena, Sumqayit (1,500)
Trainer: Ayxan Abbasov   25.08.1981

Goalkeepers:	DOB	M	(s)	G
Mehdi Cənnətov	26.01.1992	20		
Defenders:	**DOB**	**M**	**(s)**	**G**
Rüfat Abdullazadə	17.01.2001		(4)	
Elvin Bədəlov	14.06.1995	11	(5)	
Vurğun Tofiq Hüseynov	25.04.1988	11		
Dzhamaldin Khodzhaniyazov (RUS)	18.07.1996	16		
Rail Nadiroğlu Məlikov	18.12.1985	3		
İlqar Qurbanov	25.04.1986		(4)	
Sertan Taşqın	08.10.1997	16	(2)	1
Şariyar Əliyev	25.12.1992	16		
Midfielders:	**DOB**	**M**	**(s)**	**G**
Sabuhi Abdullazadə	18.12.2001	8	(4)	
Elvin Cəfərquliyev	26.10.2000	15	(2)	2

	DOB	M	(s)	G
Aleksey Isaev	09.11.1995	11		
Murad Khachayev	14.04.1998	2		
Vüqar Mustafayev	05.08.1994	15		
Nabi Məmmədov	20.08.1999		(1)	
Xəyal Nazim Nəcəfov	19.12.1997	5	(4)	1
Ragim Sadikhov (RUS)	18.07.1996	13	(2)	3
Forwards:	**DOB**	**M**	**(s)**	**G**
Amir Agayev (ISR)	10.02.1992	18	(1)	4
Peyman Babaei (IRN)	14.02.1994	16	(3)	7
Mehdi Sharifi (IRN)	16.08.1992	12	(4)	5
Ehtiram Etibar Şahverdiyev	01.10.1996		(1)	
Elgün Tağıyev	04.01.1996		(3)	
Amil Yunanov	06.01.1993	2	(14)	
Süleyman Əhmədov	25.11.1999	10	(6)	

Zirə Futbol Klubu Bakı

Founded: 28.07.2014
Stadium: Zirə Olympic Spot Complex Stadium, Bakı (1,400)
Trainer: Samir Abbasov   01.02.1978

Goalkeepers:	DOB	M	(s)	G
Emil Balayev	17.04.1994	1		
Orxan Mehdi Sadıqlı	19.05.1993	11		
Bojan Zogović (MNE)	16.02.1989	8		
Defenders:	**DOB**	**M**	**(s)**	**G**
Álvaro Francisco Ampuero García-Rosell (PER)	25.09.1992	15	(1)	
Miloš Bakrač (MNE)	25.02.1992	9	(2)	
Rauf Hüseynli	25.01.2000	3		
Bəxtiyar Bəyqulu Həsənalızadə	29.12.1992	9	(2)	
Jovan Krneta (SRB)	04.05.1992	2		
Rafael Maharramli	01.10.1999	6	(3)	
Tellur Mütəllimov	08.04.1995	8	(5)	1
Anastasios Papazoglou (GRE)	24.09.1988	9	(1)	
Adrian Manuel Scarlatache (ROU)	05.12.1986	14	(1)	1
Alie Sesay (SLE)	02.08.1994	6		
Əli Şirinov	09.08.1998		(1)	

Midfielders:	DOB	M	(s)	G
Gheorghe Anton (MDA)	27.01.1993	5	(1)	
Elvin Sərkər Camalov	04.02.1995	18		
Cavid Şakir Hüseynov	09.03.1988	15	(1)	2
İlkin Muradov	05.03.1996	13	(2)	2
Sony Nordé (HAI)	27.70.1989	6	(5)	1
Nicat Süleymanov	15.11.1998	11	(2)	4
Chafik Tigroudja (FRA)	16.01.1992	10	(2)	2
Forwards:	**DOB**	**M**	**(s)**	**G**
Richard Gadze (GHA)	23.08.1994	11		3
Rudolph Mpho Kgaswane (BOT)	13.06.1994	5	(7)	1
Elvin Nəsrəddin Məmmədov	18.07.1988	4	(6)	
Robin Ngalande Junior (MWI)	02.11.1992	2	(3)	
Agabala Ramazanov	20.01.1993	4		3
Julio César Rodríguez Giménez (PAR)	05.12.1990	9	(2)	4
Davit Volkovi (GEO)	03.06.1995	6		1

SECOND LEVEL
First Division - Azərbaycan Birinci Divizionu 2019/2020

1.	Turan Tovuz IK	17	12	1	4	29	-	18	37
2.	Səbail FK-2 Bakı	18	10	6	2	30	-	11	36
3.	Zaqatala PFK	17	11	2	4	36	-	16	35
4.	Sabah FC-2 Bakı	18	10	2	6	29	-	19	32
5.	Neftçi PFK-2 Bakı	18	8	5	5	27	-	15	29
6.	Kəpəz FK Gəncə	18	8	4	6	23	-	19	28
7.	Keşla FK-2 Bakı	17	7	4	6	28	-	22	25
8.	Sumqayıt FK-2	17	7	3	7	19	-	24	24
9.	Qarabağ FK-2 Bakı	17	7	3	7	36	-	21	24
10.	MOIK Bakı	16	5	4	7	19	-	22	19
11.	Ağsu FK	18	4	1	13	13	-	45	13
12.	Zirə FK-2 Bakı	17	3	2	12	18	-	41	11
13.	Qaradağ Lökbatan FK	18	2	1	15	10	-	44	7

The league was cancelled due to Covid-19 pandemic. No teams were promoted.

INTERNATIONAL MATCHES
(16.07.2019 – 15.07.2020)

06.09.2019	Cardiff	Wales - Azerbaijan	2-1(1-0)	(ECQ)
09.09.2019	Bakı	Azerbaijan - Croatia	1-1(0-1)	(ECQ)
09.10.2019	Riffa	Bahrain - Azerbaijan	2-3(1-1)	(F)
13.10.2019	Budapest	Hungary - Azerbaijan	1-0(1-0)	(ECQ)
16.11.2019	Bakı	Azerbaijan - Wales	0-2(0-2)	(ECQ)
19.11.2019	Trnava	Slovakia - Azerbaijan	2-0(1-0)	(ECQ)

06.09.2019   WALES - AZERBAIJAN   **2-1(1-0)**   16th EC. Qualifiers
Cardiff City Stadium, Cardiff; Referee: Trustin Farrugia Cann (Malta); Attendance: 28,385
AZE: Səlahət Nüsrat Ağayev, Pavel Vaqif Paşayev, Maksim Boris Medvedev (Cap), Qara Elxan Qarayev, Anton Viktor Krivotsyuk, Bəhlul Ələmdar Mustafazadə, Şəhriyar Ağəli Rəhimov (73.Təmkin Şaiq Xəlilzadə), Richard Almeida de Oliveira (69.Rəşad Elman Eyyubov), Dmitriy Valentin Nazarov (86.Ağabala Ramazanov), Ramil Teymur Şeydayev, Mahir Anar Emreli. Trainer: Nikola Jurčević (Croatia).
Goal: Mahir Anar Emreli (59).

09.09.2019   AZERBAIJAN - CROATIA   **1-1(0-1)**   16th EC. Qualifiers
Bakcell Arena, Bakı; Referee: Sandro Schärer (Switzerland); Attendance: 9,150
AZE: Emil Nazim Balayev, Pavel Vaqif Paşayev (46.Təmkin Şaiq Xəlilzadə), Şəhriyar Ağəli Rəhimov, Maksim Boris Medvedev (Cap) , Qara Elxan Qarayev, Bəhlul Ələmdar Mustafazadə, Cavid Şakir Hüseynov (60.Emin Cəbrayıl Mahmudov), Anton Viktor Krivotsyuk, Dmitriy Valentin Nazarov (90.Rəşad Elman Eyyubov), Ramil Teymur Şeydayev, Mahir Anar Emreli. Trainer: Nikola Jurčević (Croatia).
Goal: Təmkin Şaiq Xəlilzadə (72).

09.10.2019   BAHRAIN - AZERBAIJAN   **2-3(1-1)**   Friendly International
Bahrain National Stadium, Riffa; Referee: Ahmed Abu Bakar Said Al Kaf (Oman); Attendance: 500
AZE: Emil Nazim Balayev, Abbas İsrafil Hüseynov (46.Təmkin Şaiq Xəlilzadə), Bəhlul Ələmdar Mustafazadə, Eddi Silvestre Pascual İsrafilov, Bədavi Ruslan Hüseynov (Cap), Şəhriyar Ağəli Rəhimov (68.Araz Abdulla Abdullayev), Richard Almeida de Oliveira (77.Cavid Şakir Hüseynov), Emin Cəbrayıl Mahmudov (46.Rəşad Elman Eyyubov), Ramil Teymur Şeydayev (72.Renat Oleq Dadaşov), Ağabala Ramazanov, Rüfət Oleq Dadaşov (46.Təmkin Şaiq Xəlilzadə). Trainer: Nikola Jurčević (Croatia).
Goals: Rüfət Oleq Dadaşov (41), Təmkin Şaiq Xəlilzadə (62), Ramil Teymur Şeydayev (70).

13.10.2019   HUNGARY - AZERBAIJAN   **1-0(1-0)**   16th EC. Qualifiers
Groupama Arena, Budapest; Referee: Dennis Higler (Netherlands); Attendance: 11,300
AZE: Emil Nazim Balayev, Pavel Vaqif Paşayev, Qara Elxan Qarayev (Cap), Bədavi Ruslan Hüseynov, Bəhlul Ələmdar Mustafazadə, Şəhriyar Ağəli Rəhimov, Richard Almeida de Oliveira (58.Araz Abdulla Abdullayev), Eddi Silvestre Pascual Israfilov, Təmkin Şaiq Xəlilzadə (66.Cavid Şakir Hüseynov), Ağabala Ramazanov (85.Renat Oleq Dadaşov), Ramil Teymur Şeydayev. Trainer: Nikola Jurčević (Croatia).

16.11.2019   AZERBAIJAN - WALES   **0-2(0-2)**   16th EC. Qualifiers
Bakcell Arena, Bakı; Referee: Deniz Aytekin (Germany); Attendance: 8,622
AZE: Emil Nazim Balayev, Pavel Vaqif Paşayev, Qara Elxan Qarayev (Cap), Bədavi Ruslan Hüseynov, Bəhlul Ələmdar Mustafazadə, Anton Viktor Krivotsyuk (46.Təmkin Şaiq Xəlilzadə), Şəhriyar Ağəli Rəhimov, Richard Almeida de Oliveira, Araz Abdulla Abdullayev (64.Ağabala Ramazanov), Dmitriy Valentin Nazarov (82.Cavid Şakir Hüseynov), Ramil Teymur Şeydayev. Trainer: Nikola Jurčević (Croatia).

19.11.2019   SLOVAKIA - AZERBAIJAN   **2-0(1-0)**   16th EC. Qualifiers
Štadión "Antona Malatinského", Trnava; Referee: Serhiy Boyko (Ukraine); Attendance: 7,825
AZE: Emil Nazim Balayev, Qara Elxan Qarayev (Cap), Bədavi Ruslan Hüseynov, Bəhlul Ələmdar Mustafazadə, Şəhriyar Ağəli Rəhimov, Abbas İsrafil Hüseynov, Anton Viktor Krivotsyuk (72.Təmkin Şaiq Xəlilzadə), Cavid Şakir Hüseynov (79.Renat Oleq Dadaşov), Eddi Silvestre Pascual İsrafilov (46.Elvin Sərkər Camalov), Vüsal Mahmud İsgəndərli, Ramil Teymur Şeydayev. Trainer: Nikola Jurčević (Croatia).

NATIONAL TEAM PLAYERS
(16.07.2019 – 15.07.2020)

Name	DOB	Caps	Goals	2019/2020:	Club
Goalkeepers					
Səlahət Nüsrat AĞAYEV	04.01.1991	19	0	2019:	*Neftçi PFK Bakı*
Emil Nazim BALAYEV	17.04.1994	5	0	2019:	*FC Tobol Kostanay (KAZ)*
Defenders					
Ömər Fuad BULUDOV	15.12.1998	1	0	2019:	*Neftçi PFK Bakı*
Abbas İsrafil HÜSEYNOV	13.06.1995	3	0	2019:	*Qarabağ FK Bakı*
Bədavi Ruslan HÜSEYNOV	11.07.1991	49	0	2019:	*Qarabağ FK Bakı*
Anton Viktor KRIVOTSYUK	20.08.1998	7	0	2019:	*Neftçi PFK Bakı*
Maksim Boris MEDVEDEV	29.05.1989	60	3	2019:	*Qarabağ FK Bakı*
Bəhlul Ələmdar MUSTAFAZADƏ	27.02.1997	6	0	2019:	*Sabah FC Bakı*
Pavel Vaqif PAŞAYEV	04.01.1988	21	0	2019:	*FK Oleksandriya (UKR)*
Şəhriyar Ağəli RƏHIMOV	06.04.1989	9	0	2019:	*Səbail FK Bakı*
Təmkin Şaiq XƏLILZADƏ	06.08.1993	17	3	2019:	*Sabah FC Bakı*
Midfielders					
Araz Abdulla ABDULLAYEV	18.04.1992	38	3	2019:	*Qarabağ FK Bakı*
Richard ALMEIDA de Oliveira	20.03.1989	22	3	2019:	*Qarabağ FK Bakı*
Elvin Sərkər CAMALOV	04.02.1995	1	0	2019:	*Zirə FK Bakı*
Rəşad Elman EYYUBOV	03.12.1992	7	0	2019:	*Sabah FC Bakı*
Cavid Şakir HÜSEYNOV	09.03.1988	59	2	2019:	*Zirə FK Bakı*
Emin Cəbrayıl MAHMUDOV	27.04.1992	14	1	2019:	*Neftçi PFK Bakı*
Qara Elxan QARAYEV	12.10.1992	57	0	2019:	*Qarabağ FK Bakı*
Ağabala RAMAZANOV	20.01.1993	18	1	2019:	*Səbail FK Bakı*
Vüsal Mahmud İSGƏNDƏRLI	03.11.1995	1	0	2019:	*Keşlə FK Bakı*
Eddi Silvestre Pascual İSRAFILOV	02.08.1992	13	0	2019:	*Albacete Balompié (ESP)*
Forwards					
Renat Oleq DADAŞOV	17.05.1999	6	0	2019:	*FC Paços de Ferreira (POR)*
Rüfət Oleq DADAŞOV	29.09.1991	24	5	2019:	*SC Preußen Münster (GER)*
Mahir Anar EMRELI	01.07.1997	19	4	2019:	*Qarabağ FK Bakı*
Dmitriy Valentin NAZAROV	04.04.1990	43	8	2019:	*FC Erzgebirge Aue (GER)*
Ramil Teymur ŞEYDAYEV	15.03.1996	26	4	2019:	*FK Dinamo Moskva (RUS)*

National team coach

Nikola JURČEVIĆ (CRO) [11.02.2019 – 13.12.2019]	14.09.1966	10 M; 1 W; 2 D; 7 L; 8-20
Giovanni Girolamo DE BIASI (ITA) [from 11.07.2020]	16.06.1956	-

BELARUS

The Country:
Рэспубліка Беларусь (Republic of Belarus)
Capital: Minsk
Surface: 207,595 km^2
Inhabitants: 9,413,446 [2019]
Time: UTC+3

The FA:
Belaruskaya Federatiya Futbola
Prospekt Pobeditelei, 20/3 220020, Minsk
Tel: +375 17 254 56 00
Foundation date: 1889
Member of FIFA since: 1992
Member of UEFA since: 1993
Website: www.bff.by

NATIONAL TEAM RECORDS

RECORDS

First international match:	28.10.1992, Minsk: Belarus – Ukraine 1-1
Most international caps:	Alyaksandr Kulchy - 102 caps (1996-2012)
Most international goals:	Maxym Romashchenko - 20 goal / 64 caps (1998-2008)

UEFA EUROPEAN CHAMPIONSHIP		FIFA WORLD CUP		OLYMPIC TOURNAMENTS	
1960	-	1930	-	1908	-
1964	-	1934	-	1912	-
1968	-	1938	-	1920	-
1972	-	1950	-	1924	-
1976	-	1954	-	1928	-
1980	-	1958	-	1936	-
1984	-	1962	-	1948	-
1988	-	1966	-	1952	-
1992	-	1970	-	1956	-
1996	Qualifiers	1974	-	1960	-
2000	Qualifiers	1978	-	1964	-
2004	Qualifiers	1982	-	1968	-
2008	Qualifiers	1986	-	1972	-
2012	Qualifiers	1990	-	1976	-
2016	Qualifiers	1994	*Did not enter*	1980	-
2020	Qualifiers	1998	Qualifiers	1984	-
		2002	Qualifiers	1988	-
		2006	Qualifiers	1992	-
		2010	Qualifiers	1996	Qualifiers
		2014	Qualifiers	2000	Qualifiers
		2018	Qualifiers	2004	Qualifiers
				2008	Qualifiers
				2012	Final Tournament (Group Stage)
				2016	Qualifiers

Please note: *was part of Soviet Union until 1990.*

UEFA NATIONS LEAGUE
2018/2019 – League D (promoted to League C)

FIFA CONFEDERATIONS CUP 1992-2017
None

BELARUSIAN CLUB HONOURS IN EUROPEAN CLUB COMPETITIONS:

European Champion Clubs.Cup (1956-1992) / UEFA Champions League (1993-2020)
None

Fairs Cup (1858-1971) / UEFA Cup (1972-2009) / UEFA Europa League (2010-2020)
None

UEFA Super Cup (1972-2019)
None

*European Cup Winners.Cup 1961-1999**
None

*defunct competition

BELARUS SSR (SOVIET ERA) CHAMPIONS

Year	Champion	Year	Champion	Year	Champion
1922	Minsk (city team)	1949	Traktor MTZ Minsk	1970	Torpedo Zhodino
1923	*Not known*	1950	ODO Minsk	1971	Torpedo Zhodino
1924	Minsk (city team)	1951	Dinamo Minsk	1972	Stroitel.Bobruisk
1925	*Not known*	1952	ODO Minsk	1973	Stroitel.Bobruisk
1926	Bobruisk (city team)	1953	Spartak Minsk	1974	BATE Borisov
1927	Unknown	1954	ODO Minsk	1975	Dinamo Minsk
1928	Gomel (city team)	1955	FSM Minsk	1976	BATE Borisov
1929–32	*Not known*	1956	Spartak Minsk	1977	Sputnik Minsk
1933	Gomel (city team)	1957	Sputnik Minsk	1978	Shinnik Bobruisk
1934	BVO Minsk	1958	Spartak Bobruisk	1979	BATE Borisov
1935	BVO Minsk	1959	Minsk (city team)	1980	Torpedo Zhodino
1936	BVO Minsk	1960	Sputnik Minsk	1981	Torpedo Zhodino
1937	Dinamo Minsk	1961	Volna Pinsk	1982	Torpedo Mogilev
1938	Dinamo Minsk	1962	Torpedo Minsk	1983	Obuvschik Lida
1939	Dinamo Minsk	1963	Naroch.Molodechno	1984	Orbita Minsk
1940	DKA Minsk	1964	SKA Minsk	1985	Obuvschik Lida
1941–44	*Not known*	1965	SKA Minsk	1986	Obuvschik Lida
1945	Dinamo Minsk	1966	Torpedo Minsk	1987	Shinnik Bobruisk
1946	ODO Minsk	1967	Torpedo Minsk	1988	Sputnik Minsk
1947	Torpedo Minsk	1968	Sputnik Minsk	1989	Obuvschik Lida
1948	Traktor MTZ Minsk	1969	Torpedo Minsk	1990	Sputnik Minsk
				1991	Metallurg Molodechno

	CHAMPIONS	CUP WINNERS	BEST GOALSCORERS	
1992	FC Dinamo Minsk	FC Dinamo Minsk	Andrey Skorobogatko (FC Dnepr Mogilev)	11
1992/1993	FC Dinamo Minsk	FC Neman Grodno	Syarhey Baranovsky (FC Dinamo Minsk) Miroslav Romaschenko (FC Vedrich Rechitsa / FC Dnepr Mogilev)	19
1993/1994	FC Dinamo Minsk	FC Dinamo Minsk	Pyotr Kachuro (FC Dinamo-93 Minsk / FC Dinamo Minsk)	21
1994/1995	FC Dinamo Minsk	-	Pavel Shavrov (FC Dinamo-93 Minsk)	19
1995	FC Dinamo Minsk	FC Dinamo-93 Minsk	Syarhey Yaromko (MPKC Mozyr)	16
1996	MPKC Mozyr	MPKC Mozyr	Andrey Khlebasolaw (FC Belshina Bobruisk)	34
1997	FC Dinamo Minsk	FC Belshina Bobruisk	Andrey Khlebasolaw (FC Belshina Bobruisk)	19
1998	FC Dnepr Mogilev	FC Lokomotiv-96 Vitebsk	Syarhey Yaromko (FC Torpedo Minsk)	19
1999	FC BATE Borisov	FC Belshina Bobruisk	Valery Strypeykis (FC Slavia Mozyr)	21
2000	FC Slavia Mozyr	FC Slavia Mozyr	Raman Vasilyuk (FC Slavia Mozyr)	31
2001	FC Belshina Bobruisk	FC Belshina Bobruisk	Sergei Davydov (RUS, FC Neman Grodno)	25
2002	FC BATE Borisov	FC Gomel	Valery Strypeykis (FC Belshina Bobruisk)	18
2003	FC Gomel	FC Dinamo Minsk	Gennadi Bliznyuk (FC Gomel)	18
2004	FC Dinamo Minsk	FC Shakhtyor Solihorsk	Valery Strypeykis (Naftan Novopolotsk)	18
2005	FC Shakhtyor Solihorsk	MTZ-RIPO Minsk	Valery Strypeykis (Naftan Novopolotsk)	16
2006	FC BATE Borisov	FC BATE Borisov	Alyaksandr Klimenka (FC Shakhtyor Solihorsk)	17
2007	FC BATE Borisov	FC Dynamo Brest	Raman Vasilyuk (FC Gomel)	24
2008	FC BATE Borisov	MTZ-RIPO Minsk	Gennadi Bliznyuk (FC BATE Borisov) Vitali Rodionov (FC BATE Borisov)	16
2009	FC BATE Borisov	FC Naftan Novopolotsk	Maycon Rogério Silva Calijuri (BRA, FC Gomel)	15
2010	FC BATE Borisov	FC BATE Borisov	Renan Bardini Bressan (BRA, FC BATE Borisov)	15
2011	FC BATE Borisov	FC Gomel	Renan Bardini Bressan (BRA, FC BATE Borisov)	13
2012	FC BATE Borisov	FC Naftan Novopolotsk	Dzmitry Asipenka (FC Shakhtyor Solihorsk)	14
2013	FC BATE Borisov	FC Minsk	Vitali Rodionov (FC BATE Borisov)	14
2014	FC BATE Borisov	FC Shakhtyor Solihorsk	Mikalay Yanush (FC Shakhtyor Solihorsk)	15
2015	FC BATE Borisov	FC BATE Borisov	Mikalay Yanush (FC Shakhtyor Solihorsk)	15
2016	FC BATE Borisov	FC Torpedo-BelAZ Zhodino	Vitali Rodionov (FC BATE Borisov) Mikhayl Gordeichuk (FC BATE Borisov)	16
2017	FC BATE Borisov	FC Dinamo Brest	Mikhayl Gordeichuk (FC BATE Borisov)	18
2018	FC BATE Borisov	FC Dinamo Brest	Pavel Savitski (FC Dinamo Brest)	15
2019	FC Dinamo Brest	FC Shakhtyor Solihorsk	Ilya Shkurin (FC Energetik-BGU Minsk)	19

Please note: In spring 2019, FC Luch Minsk merged with FC Dnepr Mogilev. The united club was named FC Dnyapro Mogilev. It inherited FC Luch Minsk 's Premier League spot and licence, their sponsorships and most of the squad, while keeping only a few of FC Dnepr Mogilev players and relocating to Mogilev.

Results

Round 1 [29-31.03.2019]
FC Minsk - FC Vitebsk 0-0
FC Gomel - Neman Grodno 2-3(1-3)
Isloch Minsk - FC Gorodeya 2-0(1-0)
Shakhtyor Solih. - Torpedo Minsk 1-0(0-0)
BATE Borisov - Dnyapro Mogilev 2-0(1-0)
Dinamo Minsk - FC Slavia Mozyr 1-0(0-0)
Torpedo-BelAZ - Dinamo Brest 1-2(0-0)
FC Slutsk - Energetik-BGU 0-0

Round 2 [05-07.04.2019]
FC Minsk - Dinamo Minsk 0-0
FC Gorodeya - FC Vitebsk 1-1(0-0)
Energetik-BGU - BATE Borisov 0-4(0-2)
FC Slutsk - FC Gomel 0-6(0-1)
Neman Grodno - Shakhtyor Solih. 0-3(0-0)
Torpedo Minsk - Isloch Minsk 1-0(0-0)
FC Slavia Mozyr - Torpedo-BelAZ 1-2(0-2)
Dinamo Brest - Dnyapro Mogilev 3-1(1-0)

Round 3 [12-15.04.2019]
Dnyapro Mogilev - FC Slavia Mozyr 1-2(1-0)
Torpedo-BelAZ - FC Minsk 1-1(0-0)
FC Gomel - Energetik-BGU 3-0(2-0)
BATE Borisov - Dinamo Brest 0-1(0-0)
Isloch Minsk - Neman Grodno 1-0(0-0)
FC Vitebsk - Torpedo Minsk 1-1(1-0)
Dinamo Minsk - FC Gorodeya 1-0(1-0)
Shakhtyor Solihorsk - FC Slutsk 1-0(1-0)

Round 4 [19-21.04.2019]
FC Minsk - Dnyapro Mogilev 0-0
Neman Grodno - FC Vitebsk 1-0(1-0)
FC Slavia Mozyr - BATE Borisov 1-2(1-0)
Torpedo Minsk - Dinamo Minsk 0-1(0-0)
FC Gorodeya - Torpedo-BelAZ 0-3(0-1)
FC Slutsk - Isloch Minsk 1-3(1-0)
Energetik-BGU - Dinamo Brest 1-1(1-0)
FC Gomel - Shakhtyor Solihorsk 0-1(0-0)

Round 5 [25-27.04.2019]
Torpedo-BelAZ - Torpedo Minsk 2-0(2-0)
Dinamo Brest - FC Slavia Mozyr 0-0
FC Vitebsk - FC Slutsk 2-0(2-0)
Dinamo Minsk - Neman Grodno 0-1(0-0)
BATE Borisov - FC Minsk 1-0(1-0)
Isloch Minsk - FC Gomel 3-1(1-1)
Shakhtyor Solih. - Energetik-BGU 3-4(1-0)
Dnyapro Mogilev - FC Gorodeya 0-0

Round 6 [04-06.05.2019]
Torpedo Minsk - Dnyapro Mogilev 0-1(0-0)
Neman Grodno - Torpedo-BelAZ 0-0
Energetik-BGU - FC Slavia Mozyr 1-2(0-1)
FC Slutsk - Dinamo Minsk 2-1(0-0)
FC Minsk - Dinamo Brest 1-2(1-0)
FC Gomel - FC Vitebsk 1-2(0-2)
FC Gorodeya - BATE Borisov 1-0(0-0)
Shakhtyor Solihorsk - Isloch Minsk 1-0(1-0)

Round 7 [10-12.05.2019]
FC Slavia Mozyr - FC Minsk 4-3(2-0)
Isloch Minsk - Energetik-BGU 2-1(2-1)
Dnyapro Mogilev - Neman Grodno 0-3(0-1)
Dinamo Brest - FC Gorodeya 4-0(2-0)
Torpedo-BelAZ - FC Slutsk 1-0(0-0)
Dinamo Minsk - FC Gomel 3-1(1-0)
FC Vitebsk - Shakhtyor Solihorsk 1-0(1-0)
BATE Borisov - Torpedo Minsk 1-0(1-0)

Round 8 [17-19.05.2019]
Energetik-BGU - FC Minsk 3-3(1-0)
Neman Grodno - BATE Borisov 0-1(0-1)
FC Gorodeya - FC Slavia Mozyr 1-0(0-0)
Isloch Minsk - FC Vitebsk 3-0(1-0)
FC Gomel - Torpedo-BelAZ 2-3(1-1)
Shakhtyor Solih. - Dinamo Minsk 3-0(0-0)
Torpedo Minsk - Dinamo Brest 0-1(0-0)
FC Slutsk - Dnyapro Mogilev 2-2(1-1)

Round 9 [22-25.05.2019]
FC Vitebsk - Energetik-BGU 3-0(1-0)
Torpedo-BelAZ - Shakhtyor Solih. 0-1(0-1)
Dinamo Minsk - Isloch Minsk 1-0(0-0)
BATE Borisov - FC Slutsk 3-0(0-0)
Dnyapro Mogilev - FC Gomel 1-1(1-1)
FC Minsk - FC Gorodeya 0-3(0-1)
FC Slavia Mozyr - Torpedo Minsk 2-0(1-0)
Dinamo Brest - Neman Grodno 6-1(2-0)

Round 10 [31.05.-02.06.2019]
Isloch Minsk - Torpedo-BelAZ 1-0(0-0)
Shakhtyor Solih. - Dnyapro Mogilev 3-1(1-1)
Energetik-BGU - FC Gorodeya 0-0
FC Vitebsk - Dinamo Minsk 1-3(1-1)
FC Gomel - BATE Borisov 0-2(0-1)
Torpedo Minsk - FC Minsk 0-0
FC Slutsk - Dinamo Brest 1-3(0-1)
Neman Grodno - FC Slavia Mozyr 0-1(0-1)

Round 11 [14-16.06.2019]
FC Minsk - Neman Grodno 2-1(1-0)
FC Gorodeya - Torpedo Minsk 0-0
Dnyapro Mogilev - Isloch Minsk 3-0(1-0)
FC Slavia Mozyr - FC Slutsk 1-1(1-1)
Torpedo-BelAZ - FC Vitebsk 1-0(1-0)
BATE Borisov - Shakhtyor Solih. 3-1(0-0)
Dinamo Minsk - Energetik-BGU 6-1(2-1)
Dinamo Brest - FC Gomel 3-0(1-0)

Round 12 [21-23.06.2019]
Energetik-BGU - Torpedo Minsk 2-1(0-0)
Neman Grodno - FC Gorodeya 1-3(0-1)
Isloch Minsk - BATE Borisov 0-0
Dinamo Minsk - Torpedo-BelAZ 0-3(0-2)
Shakhtyor Solihorsk - Dinamo Brest 0-0
FC Slutsk - FC Minsk 1-0(1-0)
FC Vitebsk - Dnyapro Mogilev 2-1(0-1)
FC Gomel - FC Slavia Mozyr 2-2(1-0)

Round 13 [28-30.06.2019]
Torpedo Minsk - Neman Grodno 0-3(0-3)
Torpedo-BelAZ - Energetik-BGU 3-3(2-3)
FC Minsk - FC Gomel 3-2(1-1)
FC Gorodeya - FC Slutsk 1-0(0-0)
Dinamo Brest - Isloch Minsk 5-1(2-0)
FC Slavia Mozyr - Shakhtyor Solih. 0-1(0-0)
Dnyapro Mogilev - Dinamo Minsk 0-2(0-2)
BATE Borisov - FC Vitebsk 3-0(3-0)

Round 14 [05-07.07.2019]
Dinamo Minsk - BATE Borisov 1-2(0-1)
Torpedo-BelAZ - Dnyapro Mogilev 1-0(0-0)
Energetik-BGU - Neman Grodno 2-4(0-4)
Shakhtyor Solihorsk - FC Minsk 3-2(2-2)
FC Vitebsk - Dinamo Brest 0-1(0-0)
Isloch Minsk - FC Slavia Mozyr 2-1(1-0)
FC Slutsk - Torpedo Minsk 1-0(1-0)
FC Gomel - FC Gorodeya 0-0

Round 15 [12-14.07.2019]
Dnyapro Mogilev - Energetik-BGU 3-4(2-2)
FC Minsk - Isloch Minsk 3-3(2-1)
Torpedo Minsk - FC Gomel 1-2(0-2)
Neman Grodno - FC Slutsk 0-0
BATE Borisov - Torpedo-BelAZ 4-1(2-0)
Dinamo Brest - Dinamo Minsk 1-2(0-0)
Slavia Mozyr - FC Vitebsk 0-1(0-0) [25.09.]
FC Gorodeya - Shakhtyor Solih. 0-0 [25.09.]

Round 16 [19-21.07.2019]
Energetik-BGU - FC Slutsk 0-1(0-1)
Neman Grodno - FC Gomel 1-1(0-0)
FC Gorodeya - Isloch Minsk 1-2(0-1)
Dinamo Brest - Torpedo-BelAZ 4-1(1-1)
FC Vitebsk - FC Minsk 1-1(1-0)
Torpedo Minsk - Shakhtyor Sol. 0-3 *Awarded*
Slavia Mozyr - Din. Minsk 1-1(0-1) [30.10.]
Dnyapro Mogilev - BATE B. 0-1(0-1) [30.10.]

Round 17 [09-12.08.2019]
Isloch Minsk - Torpedo Minsk 3-0 *Awarded*
Torpedo-BelAZ - FC Slavia Mozyr 1-1(0-0)
FC Gomel - FC Slutsk 3-4(1-3)
Dnyapro Mogilev - Dinamo Brest 0-1(0-1)
FC Vitebsk - FC Gorodeya 0-2(0-0)
BATE Borisov - Energetik-BGU 4-1(4-1)
Dinamo Minsk - FC Minsk 3-2(1-1)
Shakhtyor Solihorsk - Neman Grodno 6-0(4-0)

Round 18 [16-19.08.2019]
Energetik-BGU - FC Gomel 1-1(1-0)
Neman Grodno - Isloch Minsk 1-1(0-0)
FC Slavia Mozyr - Dnyapro Mogilev 1-0(1-0)
FC Minsk - Torpedo-BelAZ 2-0(0-0)
Torpedo Minsk - FC Vitebsk 0-3 *Awarded*
FC Gorodeya - Dinamo Minsk 3-1(2-0)
FC Slutsk - Shakhtyor Solihorsk 0-5(0-3)
Dinamo Brest - BATE Boris. 1-1(0-0) [25.09.]

Round 19 [23-25.08.2019]
Isloch Minsk - FC Slutsk 0-1(0-0)
Dnyapro Mogilev - FC Minsk 1-0(0-0)
FC Vitebsk - Neman Grodno 0-0
Dinamo Brest - Energetik-BGU 6-2(5-1)
Dinamo Minsk - Torpedo Minsk 3-0 *Awarded*
Torpedo-BelAZ - FC Gorodeya 1-1(0-1)
Shakhtyor Solihorsk - FC Gomel 3-1(2-1)
BATE Borisov - FC Slavia Mozyr 4-0(1-0)

Round 20 [30.08.-01.09.2019]
Torp. Minsk - Torpedo-BelAZ 0-3 *Awarded*
FC Gorodeya - Dnyapro Mogilev 3-2(1-1)
FC Slavia Mozyr - Dinamo Brest 2-4(1-2)
FC Slutsk - FC Vitebsk 3-0(3-0)
FC Gomel - Isloch Minsk 2-2(1-1)
Neman Grodno - Dinamo Minsk 0-1(0-0)
Energetik-BGU - Shakhtyor Solih. 1-2(1-2)
FC Minsk - BATE Borisov 3-2(3-0)

Round 21 [13-16.09.2019]
Dnyapro Mogil - Torpedo Minsk 3-0 *Awarded*
Torpedo-BelAZ - Neman Grodno 1-0(1-0)
Dinamo Brest - FC Minsk 3-0(0-0)
BATE Borisov - FC Gorodeya 2-1(0-0)
FC Slavia Mozyr - Energetik-BGU 2-2(2-1)
Isloch Minsk - Shakhtyor Solihorsk 0-1(0-0)
Dinamo Minsk - FC Slutsk 2-1(0-0)
FC Vitebsk - FC Gomel 1-2(1-1)

Round 22 [20-22.09.2019]
FC Minsk - FC Slavia Mozyr 1-0(0-0)
FC Gorodeya - Dinamo Brest 1-3(0-1)
FC Slutsk - Torpedo-BelAZ 1-2(1-1)
Neman Grodno - Dnyapro Mogilev 1-0(0-0)
Shakhtyor Solihorsk - FC Vitebsk 4-0(3-0)
Torpedo Minsk - BATE Borisov 0-3 *Awarded*
Energetik-BGU - Isloch Minsk 1-2(0-1)
FC Gomel - Dinamo Minsk 0-1(0-0)

Round 23 [27-29.09.2019]
Dinamo Brest - Torpedo Minsk 3-0 *Awarded*
FC Minsk - Energetik-BGU 1-6(1-2)
Dnyapro Mogilev - FC Slutsk 2-0(0-0)
Torpedo-BelAZ - FC Gomel 2-0(1-0)
BATE Borisov - Neman Grodno 1-0(1-0)
FC Slavia Mozyr - FC Gorodeya 0-1(0-0)
FC Vitebsk - Isloch Minsk 2-0(0-0)
Dinamo Minsk - Shakhtyor Solihorsk 1-1(0-1)

Round 24 [04-06.10.2019]
Torpedo Minsk - Slavia Mozyr 0-3 *Awarded*
FC Gorodeya - FC Minsk 1-2(1-0)
FC Slutsk - BATE Borisov 0-3(0-1)
Shakhtyor Solih. - Torpedo-BelAZ 3-0(1-0)
Neman Grodno - Dinamo Brest 0-1(0-0)
Isloch Minsk - Dinamo Minsk 1-1(0-1)
Energetik-BGU - FC Vitebsk 2-0(1-0)
FC Gomel - Dnyapro Mogilev 0-0

Round 25 [18-21.10.2019]
FC Minsk - Torpedo Minsk 3-0 *Awarded*
FC Slavia Mozyr - Neman Grodno 0-1(0-0)
BATE Borisov - FC Gomel 1-1(0-1)
Dinamo Minsk - FC Vitebsk 0-2(0-1)
Torpedo-BelAZ - Isloch Minsk 1-3(0-1)
Dnyapro Mogilev - Shakhtyor Solih. 2-0(0-0)
Dinamo Brest - FC Slutsk 3-2(0-1)
FC Gorodeya - Energetik-BGU 1-0(1-0)

Round 26 [25-27.10.2019]
Neman Grodno - FC Minsk 1-0(1-0)
Torpedo Minsk - FC Gorodeya 0-3 *Awarded*
Energetik-BGU - Dinamo Minsk 3-3(2-2)
FC Slutsk - FC Slavia Mozyr 0-0
FC Gomel - Dinamo Brest 1-2(1-0)
Isloch Minsk - Dnyapro Mogilev 1-1(1-0)
FC Vitebsk - Torpedo-BelAZ 0-0
Shakhtyor Solihorsk - BATE Borisov 2-2(0-1)

Round 27 [01-04.11.2019]
Torpedo Minsk - Energetik-BGU 0-3 *Awarded*
FC Minsk - FC Slutsk 1-0(1-0)
FC Gorodeya - Neman Grodno 1-0(0-0)
Torpedo-BelAZ - Dinamo Minsk 4-0(1-0)
Dnyapro Mogilev - FC Vitebsk 2-0(1-0)
Dinamo Brest - Shakhtyor Solihorsk 1-1(1-1)
BATE Borisov - Isloch Minsk 2-4(2-1)
FC Slavia Mozyr - FC Gomel 3-2(0-2)

Round 28 [08-10.11.2019]
Neman Grodno - Torpedo Minsk 3-0 *Awarded*
Dinamo Minsk - Dnyapro Mogilev 3-0(1-0)
FC Slutsk - FC Gorodeya 0-0
Shakhtyor Solih. - FC Slavia Mozyr 5-1(2-0)
FC Gomel - FC Minsk 1-0(0-0)
Energetik-BGU - Torpedo-BelAZ 2-1(0-1)
Isloch Minsk - Dinamo Brest 1-1(1-1)
FC Vitebsk - BATE Borisov 1-2(0-0)

Round 29 [23-24.11.2019]
Torpedo Minsk - FC Slutsk 0-3 *Awarded*
Neman Grodno - Energetik-BGU 1-1(0-0)
FC Gorodeya - FC Gomel 2-3(0-3)
FC Minsk - Shakhtyor Solihorsk 1-0(0-0)
FC Slavia Mozyr - Isloch Minsk 2-0(0-0)
Dinamo Brest - FC Vitebsk 1-0(1-0)
BATE Borisov - Dinamo Minsk 3-0(2-0)
Dnyapro Mogilev - Torpedo-BelAZ 2-1(0-0)

Round 30 [01.12.2019]
Energetik-BGU - Dnyapro Mogilev 5-3(2-1)
Torpedo-BelAZ - BATE Borisov 1-2(1-1)
Dinamo Minsk - Dinamo Brest 1-3(0-1)
FC Vitebsk - FC Slavia Mozyr 0-2(0-0)
Isloch Minsk - FC Minsk 1-0(0-0)
Shakhtyor Solihorsk - FC Gorodeya 1-0(1-0)
FC Gomel - Torpedo Minsk 3-0 *Awarded*
FC Slutsk - Neman Grodno 2-1(2-0)

Final Standings

					Total					Home					Away		
1. **FC Dinamo Brest**	30	23	6	1	70 - 22	75	11	3	1	44 - 12	12	3	0	26 - 10
2. FC BATE Borisov	30	22	4	4	61 - 21	70	12	1	2	34 - 10	10	3	2	27 - 11
3. FC Shakhtyor Solihorsk	30	20	5	5	59 - 21	65	12	2	1	39 - 11	8	3	4	20 - 10
4. FC Dinamo Minsk	30	15	5	10	43 - 39	50	9	1	5	26 - 17	6	4	5	17 - 22
5. FC Isloch Minsk Raion	30	13	8	9	42 - 36	47	8	5	2	21 - 9	5	3	7	21 - 27
6. FC Torpedo-BelAZ Zhodino	30	13	6	11	41 - 36	45	7	4	4	21 - 14	6	2	7	20 - 22
7. FC Gorodeya	30	12	8	10	31 - 29	44	7	3	5	17 - 17	5	5	5	14 - 12
8. FC Slavia Mozyr	30	10	7	13	35 - 40	37	5	3	7	20 - 21	5	4	6	15 - 19
9. FC Minsk	30	9	9	12	36 - 44	36	8	4	3	21 - 19	1	5	9	15 - 25
10. FC Neman Grodno	30	10	6	14	28 - 37	36	4	5	6	10 - 13	6	1	8	18 - 24
11. FC Slutsk	30	9	7	14	29 - 46	34	5	4	6	14 - 26	4	3	8	15 - 20
12. FC Energetik-BGU Minsk	30	8	9	13	52 - 66	33	4	5	6	24 - 28	4	4	7	28 - 38
13. FC Vitebsk	30	8	7	15	24 - 39	31	4	5	6	15 - 17	4	2	9	9 - 22
14. FC Dnyapro Mogilev *(Relegation Play-offs)*	30	8	6	16	32 - 42	30	7	2	6	20 - 15	1	4	10	12 - 27
15. FC Gomel *(Relegated)*	30	7	8	15	44 - 50	29	3	4	8	20 - 22	4	4	7	24 - 28
16. FC Torpedo Minsk *(Relegated)*	30	1	3	26	4 - 63	6	1	1	13	2 - 32	0	2	13	2 - 31

Please note: FC Torpedo Minsk withdrew from the league after the end of the first half of the season due to financial problems. Their matches of the second half were forfeited 0–3 in favor of their opponents.

Top goalscorers:	
19 **Ilya Shkurin**	*FC Energetik-BGU Minsk*
14 Stanislav Dragun	*FC BATE Borisov*
14 Vitaliy Kvashuk (UKR)	*FC Gomel*
12 Dzyanis Laptsev	*FC Dinamo Brest*
12 Pavel Nyakhaychyk	*FC Dinamo Brest*
11 Momo Yansane (GUI)	*FC Isloch Minsk Raion*
11 Mikalay Yanush	*FC Shakhtyor Solihorsk*

Relegation Play-offs

FC Rukh Brest - FC Dnyapro Mogilev 2-1(0-0) 1-2 aet; 5-4 pen

FC Rukh Brest promoted for the Belarusian Premier League 2020.

NATIONAL CUP
Kubak Belarusi 2018/2019

First Round [12-13.05.2018]

Sdiušor-MTZ-Siabar - FC Ivatsevichi	1-0	FC Pripyat - FC Gomel	4-1

Second Round [11-13.06.2018]

FC Montazhnik Mozyr - FC Naftan Novopolotsk	0-0; 1-4 pen	FC SMI Autotrans - FC Baranovichi	0-0; 4-3 pen
Sdiušor-MTZ-Siabar - FC Belita-Vitex Uzda	0-3(0-1)	FC Polotsk - FC Orsha	2-3(1-0)
FC Energosbyt-BSATU - FC Khimik Svetlogorsk	0-0; 6-5 pen	FC Krumkachy Minsk - FC AUS Zhitkovichi	0-1(0-1)
FC Victoria Maryina Gorka - FC Lida	0-6(0-1)	FC Kletsk - FC Granit Mikashevichi	1-0(0-0,0-0)
Oshmyany FC - FC Energetik-BGU Minsk	0-0; 1-3 pen	FC Gorki - FC Slonim-2017	0-2(0-1)
FC Pripyat - FC Belshina Bobruisk	0-8(0-3)	FC Molodechno - FC Čisť	1-3(0-2)
FC Sputnik Rechytsa - FC Smorgon	0-0; 3-4 pen	FC Neman-Agro Stoŭbcy - FC Lokomotiv Gomel	1-3(1-1)
FC Osipovichi - FC Slavia Mozyr	2-3(0-1)	FC Tsementnik Krasnoselsky - FC Volna Pinsk	0-5(0-2)

1/8-Finals [11.07./24-29.07.2018]

FC Energetik-BGU Minsk - FC BATE Borisov	1-2(0-1,1-1)	FC Naftan Novopolotsk - FC Slutsk	0-1(0-1)
FC Orsha - FC Vitebsk	0-4(0-1)	FC SMI Autotrans - FC Gomel	1-6(1-2)
FC Lida - FC Minsk	0-3(0-2)	FC Smorgon - FC Torpedo Minsk	0-4(0-2)
FC Volna Pinsk - FC Torpedo-BelAZ Zhodino	0-2(0-0,0-0)	FC AUS Zhitkovichi - FC Isloch Minsk	0-5(0-1)
FC Lokomotiv Gomel - FC Dnyapro Mogilev	3-2(2-1)	FC Slavia Mozyr - FC Luch Minsk	3-2(2-0)
FC Belshina Bobruisk - FC Neman Grodno	3-1(1-0)	FC Kletsk - Dinamo Brest	2-2; 0-2 pen
FC Belita-Vitex Uzda - FC Smolevichy-STI	2-3(0-2)	FC Čisť - FC Shakhtyor Solihorsk	0-11(0-9)
FC Slonim-2017 - FC Gorodeya	1-2(1-0)	FC Energosbyt-BSATU - FC Dinamo Minsk	0-7(0-3)

1/8-Finals [11-12.08./26.09./03.10./17.11.2018]

FC Lokomotiv Gomel - FC Smolevichy-STI	3-0(1-0)	FC Dinamo Minsk - FC Minsk	2-0(1-0)
FC Vitebsk - FC Torpedo-BelAZ Zhodino	0-0; 5-4 pen	FC Shakhtyor Solihorsk - Dinamo Brest	0-0; 4-2 pen
FC Torpedo Minsk - FC Slutsk	0-2(0-1)	FC Slavia Mozyr - FC Belshina Bobruisk	0-0; 3-4 pen
FC Gomel - FC Isloch Minsk	0-2(0-2)	FC BATE Borisov - FC Gorodeya	0-0; 4-2 pen

Quarter-Finals [09-10/14-16.03.2019]

First Leg		Second Leg	
FC BATE Borisov - FC Isloch Minsk	1-1(1-1)	FC Isloch Minsk - FC BATE Borisov	1-0(1-0)
FC Vitebsk - FC Lokomotiv Gomel	1-0(0-0)	FC Lokomotiv Gomel - FC Vitebsk	1-2(1-0)
FC Shakhtyor Solihorsk - FC Belshina Bobruisk	5-0(2-0)	FC Belshina Bobruisk - FC Shakhtyor Solihorsk	0-1(0-0)
FC Dinamo Minsk - FC Slutsk	2-0(0-0)	FC Slutsk - FC Dinamo Minsk	1-0(1-0)

Semi-Finals [10.04./30.04.-01.05.2019]

First Leg		Second Leg	
FC Isloch Minsk - FC Shakhtyor Solihorsk	2-2(2-0)	FC Shakhtyor Solihorsk - FC Isloch Minsk	4-2(2-1,2-2)
FC Vitebsk - FC Dinamo Minsk	1-0(1-0)	FC Dinamo Minsk - FC Vitebsk	0-0

Final

26.05.2019; Vitebsky CSK, Vitebsk; Referee: Andrey Vasilevich; Attendance: 7,954
FC Shakhtyor Solihorsk - FC Vitebsk   **2-0(1-0)**

Shakhtyor Solihorsk: Andrey Klimovich, Syarhey Matvejchik, Pavel Rybak, Alyaksandr Sachywka, Nikola Antić, Alyaksandr Selyava, Afrid Max Ebong Ngome, Yury Kavalyow, Valeriy Gromyko (90.Vasyl Pryima), Mykyta Tatarkov (64.Ihar Burko), Darko Bodul (70.Mikalay Yanush). Trainer: Sergey Tashuev (Russia).

FC Vitebsk: Dmitri Gushchenko, Artem Skitov, Akaki Khubutia, Daniil Chalov (74.Vladislav Ryzhkov), Kiryl Pyachenin, Mikalay Zolataw, Wanderson Calvacante Melo, Mikhail Kozlov, Anton Matveenko, Artem Stargorodskiy (86.Syarhey Volkaw), Maksim Feshchuk (86.Ilmir Nurisov). Trainer: Syarhey Yasinsky.

Goals: 1-0 Darko Bodul (45), 2-0 Nikola Antić (80).

THE CLUBS 2019

Football Club BATE Borisov				**Founded**: 1996 **Stadium**: Borisov Arena, Borisov (13,126) **Trainer**: Aleksei Baga 04.02.1981

Goalkeepers:	DOB	M	(s)	G					
Syarhey Chernik	20.07.1988	7			Stanislaw Drahun	04.06.1988	27		14
Anton Chichkan	10.07.1995	12			Aliaksandr Hleb	01.05.1981		(1)	
Dzyanis Scherbitski	14.04.1996	10			Alyaksey Rios	14.05.1987	16	(1)	
Defenders:	**DOB**	**M**	**(s)**	**G**	Slobodan Simović (SRB)	22.05.1989	6		
Ihar Filipenko	10.04.1988	23			Ihar Stasevich	21.10.1985	28		10
Aleksander Filipović (SRB)	20.12.1994	29		1	Willum Thór Willumsson (ISL)	23.10.1998	7	(12)	1
Boris Kopitović (MNE)	17.09.1994	12			Yawhen Yablonski	10.05.1995	24	(1)	2
Emil Jonassen (NOR)	17.02.1993	4			**Forwards:**	**DOB**	**M**	**(s)**	**G**
Dzhamaldin Khodzhaniyazov (RUS)	18.07.1996	2			Bojan Dubajić (SRB)	01.09.1990	14	(7)	6
Zakhar Volkov	12.08.1997	22		1	Nemanja Milić (SRB)	25.05.1990	14	(6)	4
Midfielders:	**DOB**	**M**	**(s)**	**G**	Hervaine Moukam (FRA)	24.05.1994	8	(12)	1
Dzmitry Baha	04.01.1990	15	(5)	1	Anton Saroka	05.03.1992	8	(4)	2
Yawhen Berezkin	05.07.1996	9	(8)	2	Maksim Skavysh	13.11.1989	12	(13)	10
Dzmitryi Bessmertny	03.01.1997	7	(1)		Jasse Tuominen (FIN)	12.11.1995	3	(4)	1

Football Club Dinamo Brest

Founded: 1960
Stadium: Regional Sport Complex Brestsky (10,600)
Trainer: Marcel Lička (CZE)   17.07.1977

Goalkeepers:	DOB	M	(s)	G
Alyaksandr Hutar	18.04.1989	25		
Pavel Pawlyuchenka	01.01.1998	4		
Defenders:	DOB	M	(s)	G
Dénis Paulo Duarte (POR)	04.05.1994	18	(2)	2
Giorgios Katsikas (GRE)	14.06.1990	6		
Gaby Kiki (CMR)	15.02.1995	25		1
Alyaksandar Pawlavets	13.08.1996	17	(6)	
Aleh Veratsila	10.07.1988	28		
Maksim Vitus	11.02.1989	20	(1)	
Midfielders:	DOB	M	(s)	G
Saliw Babawo (GHA)	03.02.1999		(3)	
Artem Bykov	19.10.1992	8	(3)	
Syarhey Kislyak	06.08.1987	26		2
Syarhey Krivets	08.06.1986	1	(1)	1

	DOB	M	(s)	G
Pavel Nyakhaychyk	17.05.1988	23	(1)	12
Aleh Nikiforenko	17.03.2001		(3)	
Oleksandr Noyok (UKR)	15.05.1992	23	(1)	6
Chidi Ema Osuchukwu (NGA)	11.10.1993	1	(1)	
Vladislav Vasiliev (KAZ)	10.04.1997	4	(4)	
Raman Yuzapchuk	24.07.1997	2	(13)	1
Forwards:	DOB	M	(s)	G
Ihar Bogomolskiy	03.06.2000		(1)	
Joel Fameyeh (GHA)	14.05.1997	7	(3)	5
Mikhail Gordeychuk	23.10.1989	9	(2)	4
Oleksiy Khoblenko (UKR)	04.04.1994	12	(13)	9
Dzyanis Laptsew	01.08.1991	23	(6)	12
Artem Milevskiy (UKR)	12.01.1985	23	(3)	4
Kirill Polkhovski	09.01.2002		(2)	
Pavel Savitski	12.07.1994	14	(10)	8

Football Club Dinamo Minsk

Founded: 18.06.1927
Stadium: Dinamo National Olympic Stadium, Minsk (22,246)
Trainer: Roman Pylypchuk (UKR)   27.07.1967
[01.06.2019]   Radislav Orlovskiy   09.03.1970
[06.06.2019]   Sergei Gurenko   30.09.1972

Goalkeepers:	DOB	M	(s)	G
Syarhey Ignatovich	29.06.1992	5		
Maksim Plotnikaw	29.01.1998	23		
Dzyanis Shpakovski	26.05.2001	1		
Defenders:	DOB	M	(s)	G
Alyaksandr Chyzh	10.02.1997	8		2
Vitaliy Dyakov (RUS)	31.01.1989	10		1
Nino Galović (CRO)	06.07.1992	14		1
Alyaksey Gavrilovich	05.01.1990	18	(4)	
Nikita Khalimonchik	03.01.2000	1	(1)	
Valeriy Kiçin (KGZ)	12.10.1992	11	(1)	
Vladislav Lyakh	18.03.1999	3	(1)	
Ihar Shitov	24.10.1986	13		1
Maksim Shvyatsow	02.04.1998	21	(1)	
Georgi Tigiev (RUS)	26.05.1995	11	(1)	
Dmitriy Yatchenko (RUS)	25.08.1986	12	(1)	2
Andrei Zaleskiy	20.01.1991	12		
Midfielders:	DOB	M	(s)	G
Dmytro Bilonoh (UKR)	26.05.1995	13	(11)	7
Alan Chochiev (RUS)	07.09.1991	10		

	DOB	M	(s)	G
Richard Danilo Maciel Sousa Campos (BEL)	13.01.1990	19	(3)	6
Enis Gavazaj (ALB)	21.03.1995		(5)	
Mikalay Ivanov	02.01.2000		(2)	
Nikita Kaplenko	18.09.1995	13	(1)	
Alyaksandr Ksenofontov	05.05.1999	4		
Sulley Muniru (GHA)	25.10.1992	8	(2)	
Edgar Olekhnovich	17.05.1987	12	(1)	
Aleksandr Pejović (SRB)	28.12.1990	6	(3)	1
Anton Susha	25.01.2000	1		
Dinko Trebotić (CRO)	30.07.1990	5	(4)	3
Seidu Yahaya (GHA)	31.12.1989	20	(3)	1
Forwards:	DOB	M	(s)	G
Dmitri Antilevski	12.06.1997	3	(2)	
Ihar Bogomolskiy	03.06.2000	2	(5)	
Kehinde Abdul Feyi Fatai (NGA)	19.02.1990	11	(12)	3
Filipp Ivanov	21.07.1990	7	(5)	2
Vladislav Lozhkin	25.03.2002		(1)	
Kirill Vergeychik	23.08.1991	7	(4)	1
Ihar Zubovich	01.06.1989	15	(12)	8

Football Club Dnyapro Mogilev

Founded: 04.01.1960
Stadium: Spartak Stadium, Mogilev (7,990)
Trainer: Ivan Bionchik   07.10.1985

Goalkeepers:	DOB	M	(s)	G
Arsen Beglaryan (ARM)	18.02.1993	9		
Artem Soroko	01.04.1992	20		
Defenders:	DOB	M	(s)	G
Arseni Bondarenko	09.10.1995	28		1
Pavel Chikida	21.06.1995	11	(5)	
Mikhail Kalugin (UKR)	20.11.1994		(3)	
Valeri Karshakevich	15.02.1988	6	(2)	
Artur Kats	26.12.1994	2	(10)	
Ihar Khvalko	18.02.1997	11	(3)	
Mikita Stsyapanaw	06.04.1996	25	(2)	1
Dmitriy Yashin (RUS)	25.04.1993	23	(3)	
Alyaksey Zaleskiy	07.10.1994	25	(1)	5
Midfielders:	DOB	M	(s)	G
Oleksandr Batyshchev (UKR)	14.09.1991	13		
Nikita Bobchenok	04.09.1999		(1)	

	DOB	M	(s)	G
El Moustapha Diaw (MTN)	31.12.1996	3		
Dzmitry Ignatenko	24.10.1988	5		1
Artyom Kontsevoj	26.08.1999	4	(1)	
Yuri Kozlov	21.05.1991	11	(8)	2
Timofei Lukashevich	21.03.1997	6	(2)	
Zoran Marušić (SRB)	29.11.1993	14	(11)	4
Vadim Pobudei	17.12.1994	28		4
Yawhen Savostyanov	30.01.1988		(6)	
Maksim Shilo	17.04.1993	24	(2)	
Eugen Zasaviţchi (MDA)	24.11.1992	6	(5)	
Forwards:	DOB	M	(s)	G
Raman Gribovskiy	17.07.1995	14	(3)	6
Leonid Khankevich	21.08.1995	6	(6)	1
Dzmitry Padstrelaw	06.09.1998	15	(7)	4
Yawhen Veljko	23.02.1997	10	(6)	

Football Club Energetik-BGU Minsk

Founded: 1996
Stadium: RCOP BGU Stadium, Minsk (1,500)
Trainer: Vladimir Belyavskiy   27.06.1962

Goalkeepers:	DOB	M	(s)	G
Alyaksey Kharitonovich	30.04.1995	16		
Artur Lesko	25.04.1984	13	(1)	
Defenders:	**DOB**	**M**	**(s)**	**G**
Alex Flávio Santos Luz (BRA)	21.01.1993	5	(1)	
Eugene Chouchou Swen (LBR)	18.11.1999	11		
Ivan Kisel	28.05.1998	1	(2)	
Daniil Miroshnikov	01.11.2000	1		
Artyom Shkurdyuk	20.08.1998	28		1
Pavel Shorats	30.01.1998	5	(2)	
Evgeny Voina	12.01.2000	1		
Yawhen Yudchits	25.11.1996	22	(4)	3
Midfielders:	**DOB**	**M**	**(s)**	**G**
Andrey Alshanik	03.05.1999	2	(2)	
Pavel Grechishko	23.03.1989	7	(4)	
Arseny Kontsedaylov	15.07.1997	1	(9)	1
Maksim Kovalchuk	05.03.2000		(2)	
Jérémy Mawatu (FRA)	12.08.1997	28	(1)	1

	DOB	M	(s)	G
Alyaksey Nosko	15.08.1996	17	(1)	1
Nemanja Obrenovic (SRB)	11.07.1995	1	(1)	
Raman Plekhov	10.09.1997	2	(11)	1
Danil Poluboyarinov (RUS)	04.02.1997	8	(1)	
Vasili Sovpel	23.03.1999	11	(10)	1
Aliaksandr Svirepa	24.08.1999	6	(5)	1
David Teklo Tweh (LBR)	25.12.1998	28		4
Vladislav Vasiliev (KAZ)	10.04.1997	15		2
Daniil Vigovski (RUS)	27.03.2001	1	(4)	
Wictor Dias (BRA)	23.08.2000	2	(4)	
Dzyanis Yaskovich	30.08.1995	14		
Forwards:	**DOB**	**M**	**(s)**	**G**
Atay Dzhumashev (KGZ)	15.09.1998	6	(1)	
Dmitri Girs	11.06.1997	6	(2)	1
Zhakhongir Khodzhamov (KAZ)	24.05.1996	4	(3)	
Aik Musahagian	20.03.1998	13	(11)	3
Vsevolod Sadovskiy	04.10.1996	22		9
Ilya Shkurin	17.08.1999	22	(4)	19

Football Club Gomel

Founded: 1959
Stadium: Central Stadium, Gomel (14,037)
Trainer: Alyaksey Merkulov   17.11.1972
[04.09.2019] Aliaksandr Kulchiy   01.11.1973

Goalkeepers:	DOB	M	(s)	G
Dmitri Dudar	08.11.1991	1		
Denis Kavlinov (RUS)	10.01.1995	21		
Aleh Kovalyov	24.05.1987	7		
Defenders:	**DOB**	**M**	**(s)**	**G**
Badri Akubardia (UKR)	11.01.1993	21	(1)	2
Ilya Gultyaev (RUS)	05.09.1988	18		1
Dmitri Ignatenko	01.02.1995	5	(4)	
Andrey Ivanov (RUS)	02.09.1994	12		
Terentiy Lutsevich	19.04.1991	11	(13)	3
Artem Sokol	30.03.1994	4	(7)	
Guram Tetrashvili (RUS)	02.08.1988	13		1
Andrey Vasilyev (RUS)	11.02.1992	14		
Ruslan Yudenkov	28.04.1987	19	(2)	1
Midfielders:	**DOB**	**M**	**(s)**	**G**
Milovan Kapor (CAN)	05.08.1991	9	(1)	

	DOB	M	(s)	G
Dzmitry Malyaka (RUS)	15.01.1990	10		
Yawhen Milevskiy	14.01.1995	9	(7)	1
Alyaksandr Nemirko	08.02.2000	1	(1)	
Ihar Rozhkov	24.06.1981		(2)	
Yevhen Smirnov (UKR)	16.04.1993	7		
Eduard Sukhanov (RUS)	22.04.1991	10		
Dmitriy Tereshchenko (UKR)	04.04.1987	4	(9)	
Ivan Zhestkin	08.05.1991	11	(9)	1
Forwards:	**DOB**	**M**	**(s)**	**G**
Ruslan Bolov (RUS)	07.05.1994	28	(1)	9
Syarhey Glebko	23.08.1992	7	(6)	1
Vitaliy Kvashuk (UKR)	01.04.1993	27		14
Nivaldo Rodriguez Ferreira (BRA)	22.06.1988	27		3
Anton Shramchenko	12.02.1993	23	(4)	2
Petr Zgurski	12.07.2001		(1)	

Football Club Gorodeya

Founded: 2004
Stadium: Gorodeya Stadium, Gorodeya (2,100)
Trainer: Syarhey Yaromko   07.04.1967
[26.06.2019] Aleh Radushko   10.01.1967

Goalkeepers:	DOB	M	(s)	G
Ihar Dovgyallo	17.07.1985	26		
Maksim Vysotsky	29.01.1995	3	(1)	
Defenders:	**DOB**	**M**	**(s)**	**G**
Dmitri Bayduk	03.08.1996	8	(12)	1
Milan Joksimović (SRB)	09.02.1990	27		
Kirill Pavlyuchek	27.06.1984	25		1
Alyaksandr Paznyak	23.07.1994	4	(2)	
Syarhey Pushnyakov	08.02.1993	26	(1)	4
Stanislav Sazonovich	06.03.1992	21	(1)	1
Semen Shestilovski	30.05.1994	15	(1)	
Andrey Sorokin (RUS)	28.03.1996	13	(7)	2
Syarhey Usenya	04.03.1988	3	(5)	
Edgaras Žarskis (LTU)	04.05.1994	14	(3)	2

Midfielders:	DOB	M	(s)	G
Martin Artyukh	06.05.1996	1	(1)	
Mikhail Bashilov (RUS)	12.01.1993	19	(5)	
Dzmitry Lebedev	13.05.1986	22	(3)	4
Filipp Rudik	22.03.1987	6	(1)	
Syarhey Tikhonovskiy	26.06.1990	4	(2)	
Artiom Vaskov	21.10.1988	5	(12)	
Yuri Volovik	19.06.1993	22	(2)	
Forwards:	**DOB**	**M**	**(s)**	**G**
Artem Arkhipov (RUS)	15.12.1996	12	(1)	8
Leonid Khankevich	21.08.1995	1	(1)	
Artem Mitasov (RUS)	12.03.1990	17	(4)	1
Lazar Sajčić (SRB)	24.09.1996	15	(4)	1
Mikhail Sorokin (RUS)	20.02.1992		(2)	
Raman Volkov	08.01.1987	10	(11)	2

Football Club Isloch Minsk Raion

Founded: 2007
Stadium: FC Minsk Stadium, Minsk (3,000)
Trainer: Vitali Zhukovski   17.05.1984

Goalkeepers:	DOB	M	(s)	G
Yahor Hatkevich	09.07.1988	29		
Defenders:	**DOB**	**M**	**(s)**	**G**
Layonel Adams (RUS)	09.08.1994	15	(2)	
Weslie John (TRI)	29.07.1991	3	(2)	
Syarhey Karpovich	29.03.1994	27		1
Syarhey Kontsevoy	21.06.1986	23	(2)	
Oleksandr Papush (UKR)	14.01.1985	5	(4)	
Artem Rakhmanov	10.07.1990	10	(1)	
Artur Slabashevich	09.02.1989	4	(4)	
Godfrey Stephen (NGA)	22.08.2000	20	(4)	5
Alyaksey Yanushkevich	15.01.1986	26		
Midfielders:	**DOB**	**M**	**(s)**	**G**
Mikhail Afanasiev	04.11.1986	6	(4)	
Igor Banović (CRO)	12.05.1987	5	(6)	

	DOB	M	(s)	G
Alyaksandr Bychenok	30.05.1985	12	(6)	
Aliaksandr Hleb	01.05.1981	8	(5)	
Yawhen Krasnov	09.02.1998	3	(3)	
Sergey Makarov (RUS)	03.10.1996	28		1
Aleh Patotskiy	24.06.1991	2	(2)	
Dzmitry Rekish	14.09.1988	5	(17)	1
Alyaksandr Shagoyko	27.07.1980	18	(1)	
Theo Maia Marques de Oliveira (BRA)	29.01.1998	10	(4)	
Forwards:	**DOB**	**M**	**(s)**	**G**
Grigor Aghekyan (ARM)	07.04.1996	1	(4)	1
Alyaksandr Kholodinsky	16.10.1991		(1)	
Dzmitry Komarovskiy	10.10.1986	17	(1)	8
Alyaksandr Makas	08.10.1991	17	(4)	10
Alyaksey Rudenok	25.02.1993		(4)	
Momo Yansane (GUI)	29.07.1997	25	(3)	11

Football Club Minsk

Founded: 2006
Stadium: FC Minsk Stadium, Minsk (3,000)
Trainer: Andrey Razin   12.08.1979

Goalkeepers:	DOB	M	(s)	G
Pavel Golovenko	12.01.1997	3		
Artyom Leonov (RUS)	28.06.1994	11		
Syarhey Veremko	16.10.1982	15		
Defenders:	**DOB**	**M**	**(s)**	**G**
Yevhen Chagovets (UKR)	24.03.1998	12		2
Hleb Gurban	15.05.2001		(1)	
Alyaksey Ivanov	19.02.1997	7	(1)	
Dmitry Klimovich	09.02.1984	25		1
Aleksei Lavrik	07.08.2000		(1)	
Yuriy Ostroukh	21.01.1988	4		
Dmitry Pryshchepa	21.06.2001	7	(6)	
Aleksa Vidić (SRB)	29.09.1994	25		
Gleb Zherdev	18.05.2000		(8)	
Dmitri Zinovich	29.03.1995	2	(2)	
Midfielders:	**DOB**	**M**	**(s)**	**G**
Ilya Aleksievich	10.02.1991	12	(2)	
Vladislav Nasibulin (UKR)	06.07.1989	23	(1)	1
Nemanja Nikolić (MNE)	01.01.1988	7	(2)	
Syarhey Sazonchik	20.10.2000	11	(1)	
Mikhail Shibun	01.01.1996	2	(3)	
Viktor Svezhov (RUS)	17.05.1991	5	(8)	
Oleksandr Vasyliev (UKR)	27.04.1994	25		10
Yaroslav Yarotski	28.03.1996	16	(7)	1
Yevhen Zubeyko (UKR)	30.09.1989	20	(1)	2
Forwards:	**DOB**	**M**	**(s)**	**G**
Ivan Bakhar	10.07.1998	29		7
Pavel Gorbach	13.03.2000	1	(3)	
Filipp Ivanov	21.07.1990	5	(1)	1
Leonid Kovel	29.07.1986	8	(15)	
Vadim Larionov (RUS)	22.10.1996		(2)	
Anton Novik	23.07.1998		(1)	
Andrey Shemruk	27.04.1994	12	(5)	
Yawhen Shawchenka	06.06.1996	25	(4)	4
Dzimitryi Tshihamirau	21.04.1999		(2)	
Artem Vasilyev	23.01.1997	7	(7)	4

Football Club Neman Grodno

Founded: 1964
Stadium: Neman Stadium, Grodno (8,479)
Trainer: Ihar Kovalevich   03.02.1968

Goalkeepers:	DOB	M	(s)	G
Dzmitry Dudar	08.11.1991	14		
Syarhey Kurganski	15.05.1986	13		
Maksim Shishlov	17.02.1996	2	(1)	
Defenders:	**DOB**	**M**	**(s)**	**G**
Paul Bebey Kingue (CMR)	09.11.1986	24		
Andrey Gorbach	20.05.1985	10	(1)	
Giorgi Kantaria (GEO)	27.04.1997	21		1
Yawhen Leshko	24.06.1996	13	(2)	
Oleg Murachev (RUS)	22.02.1995	9	(1)	
Alexandr Poznyak	23.07.1994	1	(1)	
Artur Slabashevich	09.02.1989	14		
Danijel Stojković (SRB)	14.08.1990	7	(2)	1
Raman Vyahera	14.07.2000	6	(4)	
Patrick Wessely (AUT)	27.03.1994	6		
Pavel Zabelin	30.06.1995	9	(8)	
Midfielders:	**DOB**	**M**	**(s)**	**G**
Mikhail Babichev	02.02.1995	10	(4)	1
Dzmitry Borisov	08.01.1995	2		
Aleh Evdokimov	25.02.1994	26	(1)	1
Daniil Kopach	17.02.2000	1		
Alyaksey Legchilin	11.04.1992	23	(1)	2
Filipp Rudik	22.03.1987		(4)	
Pavel Tseslyukevich	11.05.1995	6	(5)	
Maksim Yablonski	15.08.1996	16		3
Andrey Yakimov	17.11.1989	22	(2)	3
Vladislav Yatskevich	29.09.1998	1	(5)	
Valeriy Zhukovskiy	21.05.1984	12	(13)	4
Forwards:	**DOB**	**M**	**(s)**	**G**
Jesús Alberto Alvarado Morín (MEX)	04.10.1988	5	(2)	
Gulzhygit Alykulov (KGZ)	25.11.2000	13	(10)	4
Junior Atemengue (CMR)	01.07.1995	8	(10)	
Artem Kontsevoj	20.05.1983	4	(4)	
Maksim Lukashevich	28.03.1992	1	(3)	
Joseph Yannick N'Djeng (CMR)	11.03.1990	8	(1)	1
Gleb Rassadkin	05.04.1995	12	(2)	3

Football Club Shakhtyor Solihorsk

Founded: 1961
Stadium: Stroitel Stadium, Solihorsk (4,200)
Trainer: Sergey Tashuev (RUS)   01.01.1959
[05.11.2019] Syarhey Nikiforenko   18.02.1978
[10.11.2019] Yuriy Vernydub   22.01.1966

Goalkeepers:	DOB	M	(s)	G
Pavel Chesnovskiy	04.03.1986	11		
Aleksandr Filtsov (RUS)	02.01.1990	1		
Andrey Klimovich	27.08.1988	17		
Defenders:	**DOB**	**M**	**(s)**	**G**
Nikola Antić (SRB)	04.01.1994	25		3
Ihar Burko	08.09.1988	7	(8)	1
Ruslan Khadarkevich	18.06.1993	3	(4)	
Zarija Lambulić (SRB)	25.05.1998	2		
Syarhey Matvejchik	05.06.1988	28		
Vasyl Pryima (UKR)	10.06.1991	3	(3)	
Pavel Rybak	11.09.1983	23		2
Alyaksandr Sachywka	05.01.1986	25		2
Midfielders:	**DOB**	**M**	**(s)**	**G**
Syarhey Balanovich	29.08.1987	23	(1)	3
Afrid Max Ebong Ngome	26.08.1999	11	(6)	
Valeriy Gromyko	23.01.1997	9	(1)	4
Yury Kavalyow	27.01.1993	27		6
Alyaksandr Selyava	17.05.1992	24	(5)	
Július Szöke (SVK)	01.08.1995	26		1
Mykyta Tatarkov (UKR)	04.01.1995		(8)	
Forwards:	**DOB**	**M**	**(s)**	**G**
Elis Bakaj (ALB)	25.06.1987	21	(1)	10
Darko Bodul (CRO)	11.01.1989	14	(3)	8
Vladimir Khvashchinskiy	10.05.1990	2	(10)	1
Anton Kavalyow	19.04.2000		(1)	
Azdren Llullaku (ALB)	15.02.1988	2	(4)	1
Ion Nicolăescu (MDA)	07.09.1998	2	(3)	
Lasha Shindagoridze (GEO)	30.01.1993	2	(8)	2
Eduards Višņakovs (LVA)	10.05.1990	1	(2)	
Mikalay Yanush	09.09.1984	10	(16)	11

Football Club Slavia Mozyr

Founded: 1987
Stadium: Yunost [Junactva] Stadium, Mozyr (5,300)
Trainer: Mikhail Martinovich 14.09.1979

Goalkeepers:	DOB	M	(s)	G
Mikhail Baranovskiy (RUS)	04.01.1983	13		
Rodion Syamuk	11.03.1989	16		
Yawhen Ivanenko	22.12.1995		(1)	
Defenders:	**DOB**	**M**	**(s)**	**G**
Andrey Chukhley	02.10.1987	22	(3)	5
Ruslan Khadarkevich	18.06.1993	10	(1)	
Mikhail Kolyadko	21.11.1988	1	(1)	
Dzyanis Kovalevski	02.05.1992	21	(1)	1
Yuri Nedashkovskiy (RUS)	11.04.1986	24		1
Yurii Pantia (UKR)	05.04.1990	25		
Egor Potapov (RUS)	21.09.1993	7	(1)	1
Alyaksandr Raevskiy	19.06.1988	8	(2)	
Gleb Shevchenko	17.02.1999	17	(5)	
Andrei Sorokin (UKR)	01.01.1991	1	(1)	

Midfielders:	DOB	M	(s)	G
Alyaksandr Anufriev	21.07.1995	8	(17)	4
Igor Kostrov (MDA)	03.08.1987	27		1
Dmitri Krivosheev	19.09.1998		(3)	
Vadim Kurlovich	30.10.1992	7	(8)	
Redvan Memeshev (UKR)	15.08.1993	5	(3)	1
Ihar Rozhkov	24.06.1981	6	(4)	1
Igor Voronkov (UKR)	24.04.1981	19	(2)	
Vladislav Zhuk	11.06.1994	14	(3)	
Forwards:	**DOB**	**M**	**(s)**	**G**
Nikita Melnikov (RUS)	28.02.1997	20	(6)	2
Francis Narh (GHA)	18.04.1994	15		2
Artyom Petrenko	01.03.2000	10	(4)	4
Maksim Sliusar (UKR)	01.07.1997	20	(8)	4
Dennis Tetteh (GHA)	06.03.1997	2	(7)	2
Dzyanis Trapashko	17.05.1990	1	(3)	

Football Club Slutsk

Founded: 1998
Stadium: City Stadium, Slutsk (2,150)
Trainer: Vitaly Pavlov 21.08.1965

Goalkeepers:	DOB	M	(s)	G
Ilya Branovets	16.04.1990	11		
Boris Pankratov	30.12.1982	18		
Defenders:	**DOB**	**M**	**(s)**	**G**
Aliyu Audu Abubakar (NGA)	15.06.1996	12		
Alyaksandr Anyukevich	10.04.1992	22	(3)	
Aleh Chmyrikov	08.02.1996	3	(2)	
Ihar Gubanov (RUS)	04.02.1992	8	(1)	
Raman Krivulkin	18.02.1996	12	(1)	1
Oleksiy Kurilov (RUS)	24.04.1988	8		
Pavel Nazarenko	20.01.1995	24	(1)	1
Dzyanis Obrazov	24.04.1988	11		
Soslan Takulov (RUS)	28.04.1995	8	(2)	
Alyaksey Timoshenko	09.12.1986	10	(5)	
Vitaliy Trubilo	07.01.1985	19	(1)	1
Midfielders:	**DOB**	**M**	**(s)**	**G**
Yacouba Bamba (CIV)	30.11.1991	4	(1)	2

	DOB	M	(s)	G
Ihar Bobko	09.09.1985	5	(3)	
Marat Buraev (RUS)	22.10.1995	8	(4)	2
Adakh Oma Dzhozef (NGA)	06.12.1997	17	(7)	1
Murat Khotov (RUS)	02.06.1987	7	(1)	3
Vladimir Medved	04.11.1999	1	(3)	
Abdullahi Oyedele (NGA)	15.07.1999	4	(6)	
Alyaksey Pustozerov (RUS)	21.09.1988	11	(3)	1
Yawhen Savostyanov	30.01.1988	12		1
Ihar Semenov	06.01.1988	17	(4)	1
Yuriy Teterenko (UKR)	22.01.1997	15	(6)	
Forwards:	**DOB**	**M**	**(s)**	**G**
Fanen Akiam (NGA)	14.04.2000	7	(3)	
Artem Dudik (UKR)	02.01.1997	23	(4)	4
Vitaliy Kibuk	07.01.1989	2	(13)	1
Cédric Khaleb Kouadio (CIV)	25.07.1997	7	(1)	1
Artem Serdyuk (RUS)	22.01.1990	10	(1)	4
Alyaksandr Yatskevich	04.01.1985	3	(7)	

Football Club Torpedo-BelAZ Zhodino

Founded: 1961
Stadium: Torpedo Stadium, Zhodino (6,524)
Trainer: Vadim Skripchenko 26.11.1975
[10.09.2019] Syarhey Zenevich 23.01.1976
[24.09.2019] Yuri Puntus 08.10.1960

Goalkeepers:	DOB	M	(s)	G
Vladimir Bushma	24.11.1983	23		
Andrey Gorbunov	29.05.1983	6		
Defenders:	**DOB**	**M**	**(s)**	**G**
Yann Affi (CIV)	11.11.1995	22	(1)	
Dzmitry Aliseyko	28.08.1992	10		
Raman Begunov	22.03.1993	10	(1)	
Vitaly Gayduchik	12.07.1989	16		1
Ihar Kuzmenok	06.07.1990	11		2
Mikhail Mishchenko (RUS)	27.06.1989	4		
Dennis Olsson (SWE)	03.10.1994	6	(1)	
Vladimir Shcherbo	01.04.1986	13	(1)	
Midfielders:	**DOB**	**M**	**(s)**	**G**
Stefan Bukorac (SRB)	15.02.1991	22	(1)	2
Andrey Khachaturyan	02.09.1987	24	(1)	

	DOB	M	(s)	G
Bogdan Myshenko (UKR)	29.12.1994	23	(5)	7
Nikita Nikolaevich	11.09.1997	12	(9)	2
Kirill Premudrov	11.06.1992	13	(7)	1
Artem Shchadin (RUS)	01.11.1992	5	(4)	1
Mikhail Shibun	01.01.1996	1		
Artem Solovey	01.11.1990	9	(8)	2
Dzyanis Yaskovich	30.08.1995	1	(2)	
Forwards:	**DOB**	**M**	**(s)**	**G**
Valery Gorbachik	19.01.1995	23	(2)	5
Uladzislaw Klimovich	12.06.1996	22	(5)	2
Alyaksandr Kotlyarov	30.01.1993	1	(5)	
Dzyanis Levitskiy	05.02.1997	14	(1)	
Marko Obradović (SRB)	30.06.1991	14	(6)	5
JeanMorel Poé (CIV)	15.12.1996	7	(15)	1
Dmytro Yusov (UKR)	11.05.1993	7	(11)	7

Football Club Torpedo Minsk

Founded: 1947
Stadium: SOK Olimpiysky Stadium, Minsk (1,530)
Trainer: Vladimir Nevinski 14.09.1973

Goalkeepers:	DOB	M	(s)	G
Artyom Leonov (RUS)	28.04.1994	9		
Raman Stepanov	06.08.1991	6		
Defenders:	**DOB**	**M**	**(s)**	**G**
Raman Gaev	20.01.1989	1	(2)	
Vladislav Glinskiy	29.05.2000	13	(1)	
Igor Gubanov (RUS)	04.02.1992	12		
Vyacheslav Krivulets	27.02.1998		(1)	
Raman Krivulkin	18.02.1996	3	(2)	
Andrei Pilipovets	17.02.1999	4	(1)	
Vladislav Rubin	22.03.1999		(1)	
Ihar Shumilov	20.10.1993	12		
Andrey Vasilyev (RUS)	11.02.1992	13		
Midfielders:	**DOB**	**M**	**(s)**	**G**
Oleksandr Batyshchev (UKR)	14.09.1991	13		

	DOB	M	(s)	G
Alyaksey Butarevich	12.01.1997	5	(3)	
Alyaksandr Dzhigero	15.04.1996	15		1
Yawhen Elesarenko	04.07.1993	11		
Dmitri Lisakovich	10.10.1999		(6)	1
Kirill Orekhov (RUS)	27.01.1999		(1)	
Dmitri Tamelo	08.11.1992	11	(2)	
Forwards:	**DOB**	**M**	**(s)**	**G**
Hicham El Hamdaoui (FRA)	18.11.1995		(1)	
Syarhey Glebko	23.08.1992	11	(2)	
Konstantin Kazakov	14.06.1999	1	(1)	
Pavel Klenyo	28.04.1999	5	(7)	1
Cédric Kouadio (CIV)	25.07.1997	8	(3)	1
Syarhey Lynko	16.10.1989	11	(1)	
Oleksiy Zbun (UKR)	09.06.1997	1	(8)	

Football Club Vitebsk

Founded:	1960		
Stadium:	Vitebsky Central Sport Complex, Vitebsk (8,100)		
Trainer:	Syarhey Yasinsky		07.01.1965

Goalkeepers:	DOB	M	(s)	G
Dmitri Gushchenko	12.05.1988	24		
Vladimir Zhurov	09.03.1991	5		
Defenders:	**DOB**	**M**	**(s)**	**G**
Daniil Chalov (RUS)	17.06.1994	22	(3)	
Oleh Karamushka (UKR)	30.04.1984	17	(2)	1
Akaki Khubutia (GEO)	17.03.1986	20	(2)	
Yawhen Klopotskiy	12.08.1993	10		
Kiryl Pyachenin	18.03.1997	27	(2)	2
Artem Skitov	21.01.1991	21		
Mikalay Zolataw	11.11.1994	24	(1)	2
Midfielders:	**DOB**	**M**	**(s)**	**G**
Nika Basariya	21.09.1999		(5)	
Maksim Drobysh	30.01.2001		(1)	
Mikhail Kozlov	12.02.1990	24	(2)	

	DOB	M	(s)	G
Yan Mosesov	31.03.2000		(3)	
Vladislav Ryzhkov (RUS)	28.02.1990	8	(4)	1
Artem Stargorodskiy (UKR)	17.01.1982	22	(5)	2
Syarhey Volkaw	27.01.1999	8	(9)	1
Wanderson Calvacante Melo (BRA)	27.06.1994	26		
Forwards:	**DOB**	**M**	**(s)**	**G**
Diego Silva Nascimento Santos „Carioca" (BRA)	06.02.1998	6	(9)	
Vladislav Fedosov	05.05.1998	5	(10)	3
Maksim Feshchuk (UKR)	25.11.1985	9	(2)	1
Artem Gurenko	18.06.1994	10	(3)	2
Anton Matveenko	03.09.1986	23	(2)	4
Ilmir Nurisov (RUS)	05.08.1996	1	(8)	
Aleksandr Prudnikov (RUS)	26.02.1989	6	(2)	1
Ruslan Teverov	01.05.1994	1	(5)	1

SECOND LEVEL
First League 2019

1. FC Belshina Bobruisk (*Promoted*)	28	21	5	2	74 - 22	68
2. FC Smolevichi (*Promoted*)	28	19	7	2	60 - 15	64
3. FC Rukh Brest (*Promotion Play-offs*)	28	15	11	2	65 - 26	56
4. FC Lokomotiv Gomel	28	17	5	6	60 - 24	56
5. FC Naftan Novopolotsk	28	13	8	7	58 - 43	47
6. FC Sputnik Rechitsa	28	13	6	9	46 - 36	45
7. FC Lida	28	12	8	8	49 - 32	44
8. FC NFK Minsk	28	11	7	10	41 - 38	40
9. FC Granit Mikashevichi	28	9	8	11	38 - 41	35
10. FC Orsha	28	9	4	15	33 - 61	31
11. FC Khimik Svetlogorsk	28	7	5	16	26 - 59	26
12. FC Volna Pinsk	28	5	6	17	29 - 48	21
13. FC Slonim-2017	28	4	9	15	18 - 47	21
14. FC Smorgon	28	4	6	18	27 - 63	18
15. FC Baranovichi (*Relegated*)	28	2	3	23	12 - 80	9

NATIONAL TEAM

INTERNATIONAL MATCHES
(16.07.2019 – 15.07.2020)

06.09.2019	Tallinn	Estonia - Belarus	1-2(0-0)	(ECQ)
09.09.2019	Cardiff	Wales - Belarus	1-0(1-0)	(F)
10.10.2019	Minsk	Belarus - Estonia	0-0	(ECQ)
13.10.2019	Minsk	Belarus - Netherlands	1-2(0-2)	(ECQ)
16.11.2019	Mönchengladbach	Germany - Belarus	4-0(1-0)	(ECQ)
19.11.2019	Podgorica	Montenegro - Belarus	2-0(2-0)	(F)
23.02.2020	Sharjah	Uzbekistan - Belarus	0-1(0-1)	(F)
26.02.2020	Sofia	Bulgaria - Belarus	0-1(0-1)	(F)

06.09.2019   ESTONIA - BELARUS   1-2(0-0)   16th EC. Qualifiers
A. Le Coq Arena, Tallinn; Referee: Alain Durieux (Luxembourg); Attendance: 7,314
BLR: Alyaksandr Hutar, Syarhey Palitsevich, Dzyanis Palyakow, Syarhey Matveichyk, Mikita Navumaw, Ihar Stasevich (Cap), Stanislaw Drahun, Ivan Maewski, Yury Kavalyow (77.Maksim Skavysh), Yawhen Yablonski, Mikalay Signevich (64.Ivan Bakhar). Trainer: Mikhail Markhel.
Goals: Mikita Navumaw (48), Maksim Skavysh (90+2).

09.09.2019   WALES - BELARUS   1-0(1-0)   Friendly International
Cardiff City Stadium, Cardiff; Referee: William Collum (Scotland); Attendance: 7,666
BLR: Maksim Plotnikaw, Syarhey Palitsevich (Cap), Dzyanis Palyakow, Zakhar Volkov, Dzmitry Baha (71.Stanislaw Drahun), Yury Kavalyow (46.Afrid Max Ebong Ngome), Yawhen Yablonski (46.Ivan Maewski), Ivan Bakhar (84.Uladislaw Klimovich), Maksim Skavysh (76.Kiryl Pyachenin), Mikalay Signevich (70.Ihar Stasevich), Mikalay Zolataw. Trainer: Mikhail Markhel.

10.10.2019   BELARUS - ESTONIA   0-0   16th EC. Qualifiers
Stadion Dynama, Minsk; Referee: Ricardo de Burgos Bengoetxea (Spain); Attendance: 11,300
BLR: Alyaksandr Hutar, Syarhey Palitsevich, Dzyanis Palyakow, Syarhey Matveichyk, Alyaksandr Martynovich (Cap), Ihar Stasevich, Stanislaw Drahun, Ivan Maewski, Pavel Savitski (59.Ivan Bakhar), Yawhen Yablonski (83.Vital Lisakovich), Maksim Skavysh (64.Dzyanis Laptsew). Trainer: Mikhail Markhel.

13.10.2019   BELARUS - NETHERLANDS   1-2(0-2)   16th EC. Qualifiers
Stadion Dynama, Minsk; Referee: Anastasios Sidiropoulos (Greece); Attendance: 21,639
BLR: Alyaksandr Hutar, Dzyanis Palyakow, Aleh Veratsila, Alyaksandr Martynovich (Cap), Mikita Navumaw, Ihar Stasevich, Stanislaw Drahun, Yury Kavalyow (60.Maksim Skavysh), Yawhen Yablonski, Ivan Bakhar (70.Afrid Max Ebong Ngome), Dzyanis Laptsew (83.Yawhen Shawchenka). Trainer: Mikhail Markhel.
Goal: Stanislaw Drahun (53).

16.11.2019 GERMANY - BELARUS   4-0(1-0)   16th EC. Qualifiers

Stadion im Borussia-Park, Mönchengladbach; Referee: Orel Greenfield (Israel); Attendance: 33,164
BLR: Alyaksandr Hutar, Dzyanis Palyakow, Syarhey Matveichyk, Alyaksandr Martynovich (Cap), Mikita Navumaw, Pavel Nyakhaychyk (84.Dzmitryi Bessmertny), Ihar Stasevich, Stanislaw Drahun, Ivan Maewski, Yury Kavalyow (78.Maksim Skavysh), Dzyanis Laptsew (68.Vital Lisakovich). Trainer: Mikhail Markhel.

19.11.2019 MONTENEGRO - BELARUS   2-0(2-0)   Friendly International

Stadion Pod Goricom, Podgorica; Referee: Trustin Farrugia Cann (Malta); Attendance: 1,000
BLR: Syarhey Chernik, Dzyanis Palyakow (46.Mikalay Zolataw), Aleh Veratsila, Alyaksandr Martynovich (Cap) (46.Alyaksandar Pawlavets), Alyaksandr Sachywka, Ihar Stasevich (46.Dzmitryi Bessmertny), Stanislaw Drahun (46.Ivan Maewski), Syarhey Kislyak, Yawhen Yablonski, Maksim Skavysh (75.Dzyanis Laptsew), Vital Lisakovich (58.Pavel Nyakhaychyk). Trainer: Mikhail Markhel.

23.02.2020 UZBEKISTAN - BELARUS   0-1(0-1)   16th EC. Qualifiers

Al Hamriya Sports Club Stadium, Sharjah (United Arab Emirates); Referee: Omar Mohamed Ahmed Hassan Al Ali (United Arab Emirates); Attendance: n/a
BLR: Pavel Pawlyuchenka, Syarhey Palitsevich, Syarhey Matveichyk, Ihar Burko (90.Maksim Shvyatsow), Alyaksandar Pawlavets, Pavel Nyakhaychyk (90.Syarhey Karpovich), Ihar Stasevich (Cap), Stanislaw Drahun, Yury Kendysh, Mikita Korzun (67.Vital Lisakovich), Dzyanis Laptsew (78.Dzmitry Padstrelaw). Trainer: Mikhail Markhel.
Goal: Pavel Nyakhaychyk (26).

26.02.2020 BULGARIA - BELARUS   0-1(0-1)   16th EC. Qualifiers

Nationalen Stadion "Vasil Levski", Sofia; Referee: Trustin Farrugia Cann (Malta); Attendance: 250
BLR: Yahor Hatkevich, Syarhey Karpovich (90+3.Raman Vyahera), Alyaksandr Paznyak, Maksim Shvyatsow, Mikita Korzun (Cap), Mikita Stsyapanaw, Yawhen Yablonski, Raman Yuzapchuk (60.Yawhen Shawchenka; 78.Syarhey Volkaw), Dzmitry Padstrelaw, Uladislaw Klimovich, Vital Lisakovich (69.Kiryl Pyachenin). Trainer: Mikhail Markhel.
Goal: Dzmitry Padstrelaw (15).

NATIONAL TEAM PLAYERS (16.07.2019 – 15.07.2020)					
Name	**DOB**	**Caps**	**Goals**	**2019/2020:**	***Club***
Goalkeepers					
Syarhey CHERNIK	20.07.1988	19	0	2019/2020:	*FC BATE Borisov*
Yahor HATKEVICH	09.07.1988	1	0	2020:	*FC Isloch Minsk Raion*
Alyaksandr HUTAR	18.04.1989	16	0	2019:	*FC Dinamo Brest*
Pavel PAWLYUCHENKA	01.01.1998	2	0	2020:	*FC Dinamo Brest*
Maksim PLOTNIKAW	29.01.1998	1	0	2019:	*FC Dinamo Minsk*
Defenders					
Ihar BURKO	08.09.1988	6	0	2020:	*FC Shakhtyor Solihorsk*
Dzmitryi BESSMERTNY	03.01.1997	2	0	2019:	*FC BATE Borisov*
Syarhey KARPOVICH	29.03.1994	2	0	2020:	*FC Isloch Minsk Raion*
Alyaksandr MARTYNOVICH	26.08.1987	71	2	2019:	*FK Krasnodar (RUS)*
Syarhey MATVEICHYK	05.06.1988	15	0	2019/2020:	*FC Shakhtyor Solihorsk*
Mikita NAVUMAW	15.11.1989	6	1	2019:	*FC Zhetisu Taldiqorghan (KAZ)*
Syarhey PALITSEVICH	09.04.1990	33	1	2019: 16.01.2020->	*FC Kairat Almaty (KAZ)* *FC Shakhtyor Solihorsk*
Dzyanis PALYAKOW	17.04.1991	42	1	2019:	*FK Ural Yekaterinburg (RUS)*
Alyaksandar PAWLAVETS	13.08.1996	6	0	2019/2020:	*FC Dinamo Brest*
Alyaksandr PAZNYAK	23.07.1994	1	0	2020:	*FC Gorodeya*
Kiryl PYACHENIN	18.03.1997	2	0	2019: 05.01.2020->	*FC Vitebsk* *FC Dinamo Brest*
Alyaksandr SACHYWKA	05.01.1986	5	0	2019:	*FC Shakhtyor Solihorsk*
Pavel SAVITSKI	12.07.1994	19	4	2019:	*FC Dinamo Brest*
Maksim SHVYATSOW	02.04.1998	2	0	2020:	*FC Dinamo Minsk*
Mikita STSYAPANAW	06.04.1996	1	0	2020:	*FC Torpedo-BelAZ Zhodino*
Aleh VERATSILA	10.07.1988	20	0	2019:	*FC Dinamo Brest*
Zakhar VOLKOV	12.08.1997	1	0	2019:	*FC BATE Borisov*
Raman VYAHERA	14.07.2000	1	0	2020:	*FC Neman Grodno*
Mikalay ZOLATAW	11.11.1994	2	0	2019:	*FC Vitebsk*

Midfielders

Dzmitry BAHA	04.01.1990	3	0	2019:	FC BATE Borisov
Ivan BAKHAR	10.07.1998	4	0	2019:	FC Minsk
Stanislaw DRAHUN	04.06.1988	66	11	2019/2020:	FC BATE Borisov
Afrid Max EBONG Ngome	26.08.1999	2	0	2019:	FC Shakhtyor Solihorsk
Yury KAVALYOW	27.01.1993	16	1	2019/2020:	FC Shakhtyor Solihorsk
Yury KENDYSH	10.06.1990	9	0	2020:	FC Shakhtyor Solihorsk
Syarhey KISLYAK	06.08.1987	71	9	2019:	FC Dinamo Brest
Uladislaw KLIMOVICH	12.06.1996	4	0	2019:	FC Torpedo-BelAZ Zhodino
				28.01.2020->	FC Dinamo Minsk
Mikita KORZUN	06.03.1995	16	0	2020:	UD Vilafranquense (POR)
Ivan MAEWSKI	05.05.1988	34	0	2019:	FK Astana (KAZ)
Pavel NYAKHAYCHYK	15.07.1988	33	3	2019:	FC Dinamo Brest
				04.01.2020->	FC BATE Borisov
Ihar STASEVICH	21.10.1985	54	5	2019/2020:	FC BATE Borisov
Syarhey VOLKAW	27.01.1999	1	0	2020:	FC Vitebsk
Yawhen YABLONSKI	10.05.1995	6	0	2019/2020:	FC BATE Borisov
Raman YUZAPCHUK	24.07.1997	1	0	2020:	FC Dinamo Brest

Forwards

Dzyanis LAPTSEW	01.08.1991	24	0	2019/2020:	FC Dinamo Brest
Vital LISAKOVICH	08.02.1998	5	0	2019:	NK Varaždin (CRO)
				06.02.2020->	FC Shakhtyor Solihorsk
Dzmitry PADSTRELAW	06.09.1998	2	1	2020:	FC Shakhtyor Solihorsk
Yawhen SHAWCHENKA	06.06.1996			2019:	FC Minsk
				01.01.2020->	FC Dinamo Brest
Mikalay SIGNEVICH	20.02.1992	18	1	2019:	Ferencvárosi TC (HUN)
Maksim SKAVYSH	13.11.1989	19	2	2019:	FC BATE Borisov

National team coach

Mikhail MARKHEL [from 20.06.2019]	10.03.1966	8 M; 3 W; 1 D; 4 L; 5-10

BELGIUM

ROYAL BELGIAN FA·1895

The Country:
Royaume de Belgique / Koninkrijk België (Kingdom of Belgium)
Capital: Bruxelles
Surface: 30,528 km²
Inhabitants: 11,492,641 [2020]
Time: UTC+1

The FA:
Union royale belge des sociétés de football association / Koninklijke Belgische Voetbalbond
145, Avenue Houba de Strooper, 1020 Bruxelles
Tel: +32 2 477 1211
Foundation date: 1895
Member of FIFA since: 1904
Member of UEFA since: 1954
Website: www.belgianfootball.be

NATIONAL TEAM RECORDS

RECORDS
First international match:	01.05.1994, Bruxelles: Belgium – France 3-3
Most international caps:	Jan Bert Lieve Vertonghen - 118 caps (since 2007)
Most international goals:	Romelu Menama Lukaku Bolingoli - 52 goals / 84 caps (since 2010)

UEFA EUROPEAN CHAMPIONSHIP
1960	*Did not enter*
1964	Qualifiers
1968	Qualifiers
1972	Final Tournament (3rd Place)
1976	Qualifiers
1980	Final Tournament (Runners-up)
1984	Final Tournament (Group Stage)
1988	Qualifiers
1992	Qualifiers
1996	Qualifiers
2000	Final Tournament (Group Stage)
2004	Qualifiers
2008	Qualifiers
2012	Qualifiers
2016	Final Tournament (Quarter-Finals)
2020	*Final Tournament (Qualified)*

FIFA WORLD CUP
1930	Final Tournament (Group Stage)
1934	Final Tournament (1st Round)
1938	Final Tournament (1st Round)
1950	*Withdrew*
1954	Final Tournament (Group Stage)
1958	Qualifiers
1962	Qualifiers
1966	Qualifiers
1970	Final Tournament (Group Stage)
1974	Qualifiers
1978	Qualifiers
1982	Final Tournament (2nd Round)
1986	Final Tournament (4th Place)
1990	Final Tournament (2nd Round of 16)
1994	Final Tournament (2nd Round of 16)
1998	Final Tournament (Group Stage)
2002	Final Tournament (2nd Round of 16)
2006	Qualifiers
2010	Qualifiers
2014	Final Tournament (Quarter-Finals)
2018	Final Tournament (3rd Place)

OLYMPIC TOURNAMENTS
1908	-
1912	-
1920	**Winners**
1924	TF / 1/8-Finals
1928	Quarter-Finals
1936	*Did not enter*
1948	*Did not enter*
1952	*Did not enter*
1956	*Did not enter*
1960	*Did not enter*
1964	*Did not enter*
1968	*Did not enter*
1972	*Did not enter*
1976	*Did not enter*
1980	Qualifiers
1984	Qualifiers
1988	Qualifiers
1992	Qualifiers
1996	Qualifiers
2000	Qualifiers
2004	Qualifiers
2008	FT / 4th Place
2012	Qualifiers
2016	Qualifiers

UEFA NATIONS LEAGUE
2018/2019 – League A

FIFA CONFEDERATIONS CUP 1992-2017
None

BELGIAN CLUB HONOURS IN EUROPEAN CLUB COMPETITIONS:

European Champion Clubs' Cup (1956-1992) / UEFA Champions League (1993-2020)		
None		
Fairs Cup (1858-1971) / UEFA Cup (1972-2009) / UEFA Europa League (2010-2020)		
RSC Anderlecht Bruxelles	1	1982/1983
UEFA Super Cup (1972-2019)		
RSC Anderlecht Bruxelles	2	1976, 1978
KV Mechelen	1	1988
European Cup Winners' Cup 1961-1999*		
RSC Anderlecht Bruxelles	2	1975/1976, 1977/1978
KV Mechelen	1	1987/1988

*defunct competition

NATIONAL COMPETITIONS
TABLE OF HONOURS

	CHAMPIONS	CUP WINNERS	BEST GOALSCORERS	
1895/1896	FC Liégeois	-	Samuel Hickson (ENG, FC Liégeois)	?
1896/1897	Racing Club de Bruxelles	-	Samuel Hickson (ENG, FC Liégeois)	?
1897/1898	FC Liégeois	-	Franz König (SUI, Racing Club de Bruxelles)	?
1898/1899	FC Liégeois	-	Franz König (SUI, Racing Club de Bruxelles)	?
1899/1900	Racing Club de Bruxelles	-	Charles Richard Atkinson-Grimshaw (ENG, Racing Club de Bruxelles)	?
1900/1901	Racing Club de Bruxelles	-	Herbert Alfred Potts (ENG, K Beerschot VAC)	26
1901/1902	Racing Club de Bruxelles	-	Herbert Alfred Potts (ENG, K Beerschot VAC)	16
1902/1903	Racing Club de Bruxelles	-	Gustave Vanderstappen (Royale Union Saint-Gilloise)	?
1903/1904	Royale Union Saint-Gilloise	-	Gustave Vanderstappen (Royale Union Saint-Gilloise)	30
1904/1905	Royale Union Saint-Gilloise	-	Robert De Veen (FC Brugeois)	?
1905/1906	Royale Union Saint-Gilloise	-	Robert De Veen (FC Brugeois)	26
1906/1907	Royale Union Saint-Gilloise	-	Maurice Vertongen (Racing Club de Bruxelles)	29
1907/1908	Racing Club de Bruxelles	-	Maurice Vertongen (Racing Club de Bruxelles)	23
1908/1909	Royale Union Saint-Gilloise	-	Vahram Kevorkian (RUS, Racing Club de Bruxelles)	30
1909/1910	Royale Union Saint-Gilloise	-	Maurice Vertongen (Royale Union Saint-Gilloise)	36
1910/1911	CS Brugeois	-	Alphonse Six (CS Brugeois)	40
1911/1912	Daring Club de Bruxelles	Racing Club de Bruxelles	Maurice Taylor Bunyan (ENG, Racing Club de Bruxelles)	35
1912/1913	Royale Union Saint-Gilloise	Royale Union Saint-Gilloise	Sylva Brébart (Daring Club de Bruxelles)	31
1913/1914	Daring Club de Bruxelles	Royale Union Saint-Gilloise	Maurice Bunyan (ENG, Racing Club de Bruxelles)	28
1915-1919	*No competition*	*No competition*	-	
1919/1920	FC Brugeois	*No competition*	Honoré Vlamynck (Daring Club de Bruxelles)	26
1920/1921	Daring Club de Bruxelles	*No competition*	Ivan Thys (K Beerschot VAC)	23
1921/1922	K Beerschot VAC	*No competition*	Ivan Thys (K Beerschot VAC)	21
1922/1923	Royale Union Saint-Gilloise	*No competition*	Achille Meyskens (Royale Union Saint-Gilloise)	24
1923/1924	K Beerschot VAC	*No competition*	Charles Jooris (Racing Club de Bruxelles)	18
1924/1925	K Beerschot VAC	*No competition*	Joseph Taeymans (K Berchem Sport)	20
1925/1926	K Beerschot VAC	*No competition*	Laurent Grimmonprez (RC Gent)	28
1926/1927	RCS Brugeois	RCS Brugeois	Lucien Fabry (R Standard Liège)	28
1927/1928	K Beerschot VAC	*No competition*	Raymond Braine (K Beerschot VAC)	35
1928/1929	R Antwerp FC	*No competition*	Raymond Braine (K Beerschot VAC)	30
1929/1930	RCS Brugeois	*No competition*	Pierre De Vidts (Daring Club de Bruxelles)	26
1930/1931	R Antwerp FC	*No competition*	Jacques Secretin (RCFC Montegnée) Joseph Van Beeck (R Antwerp FC)	21
1931/1932	K Lierse SK	*No competition*	Bernard Delmez (K Lierse SK)	26
1932/1933	Royale Union Saint-Gilloise	*No competition*	Willy Ulens (R Antwerp FC)	26
1933/1934	Royale Union Saint-Gilloise	*No competition*	Vital Van Landeghem (Royale Union Saint-Gilloise)	29
1934/1935	Royale Union Saint-Gilloise	Daring Club de Bruxelles	Marius Mondelé (Daring Club de Bruxelles)	28
1935/1936	Daring Club de Bruxelles SR	*No competition*	Flor Lambrechts (R Antwerp FC)	37
1936/1937	Daring Club de Bruxelles SR	*No competition*	Jean Collet (White Star WAC Bruxelles)	22
1937/1938	R Beerschot AC Antwerp	*No competition*	Marius Mondelé (Daring Club de Bruxelles)	32
1938/1939	R Beerschot AC Antwerp	*No competition*	Jozef Wagner (R Antwerp FC)	31
1939-1941	*No competition*	*No competition*	-	
1941/1942	K Liersche SK	*No competition*	Bert De Cleyn (R Antwerp FC)	34
1942/1943	RFC Malinois	*No competition*	Arthur Ceuleers (K Beerschot VAC) Jules Van Craen (K Lierse SK)	41
1943/1944	R Antwerp FC	*No competition*	Jan Goossens (ROC Charleroi)	34
1944/1945	*No competition*	*No competition*	-	
1945/1946	RFC Malinois	*No competition*	-	
1946/1947	RSC Anderlecht Bruxelles	*No competition*	Jef Mermans (RSC Anderlecht Bruxelles)	39
1947/1948	RFC Malinois	*No competition*	Jef Mermans (RSC Anderlecht Bruxelles)	23
1948/1949	RSC Anderlecht Bruxelles	*No competition*	René Thirifays (R Charleroi SC)	26
1949/1950	RSC Anderlecht Bruxelles	*No competition*	Jef Mermans (RSC Anderlecht Bruxelles)	37
1950/1951	RSC Anderlecht Bruxelles	*No competition*	Albert Dehert (K Berchem Sport)	27
1951/1952	RFC Liégeois	*No competition*	Jozef Mannaerts (KRC Mechelen)	25
1952/1953	RFC Liégeois	*No competition*	Rik Coppens (K Beerschot VAC)	35
1953/1954	RSC Anderlecht Bruxelles	R Standard Liège	Hippolyte Van Den Bosch (RSC Anderlecht Bruxelles)	29
1954/1955	RSC Anderlecht Bruxelles	R Antwerp FC	Rik Coppens (K Beerschot VAC)	35
1955/1956	RSC Anderlecht Bruxelles	RRC Tournaisien	Jean Mathonet (R Standard Liège)	26
1956/1957	R Antwerp FC	*No competition*	Maurice Willems (KAA Gent)	35
1957/1958	R Standard Liège	*No competition*	Jef Vliers (K Beerschot VAC)	25
1958/1959	RSC Anderlecht Bruxelles	*No competition*	Victor Wegria (RFC Liégeois)	26
1959/1960	K Lierse SK	*No competition*	Victor Wegria (RFC Liégeois)	21
1960/1961	R Standard Liège	*No competition*	Victor Wegria (RFC Liégeois)	23
1961/1962	RSC Anderlecht Bruxelles	*No competition*	Jacky Stockman (RSC Anderlecht Bruxelles)	29
1962/1963	R Standard Liège	*No competition*	Victor Wegria (RFC Liégeois)	29
1963/1964	RSC Anderlecht Bruxelles	ARA La Gantoise	Paul Van Himst (RSC Anderlecht Bruxelles)	26
1964/1965	RSC Anderlecht Bruxelles	RSC Anderlecht Bruxelles	Jean-Paul Colonval (RFC Tilleur Saint-Nicolas)	25
1965/1966	RSC Anderlecht Bruxelles	R Standard Liège	Paul Van Himst (RSC Anderlecht Bruxelles)	25

1966/1967	RSC Anderlecht Bruxelles	R Standard Liège	Johan Mulder (NED, RSC Anderlecht Bruxelles)	20
1967/1968	RSC Anderlecht Bruxelles	Club Brugge KV	Roger Claessen (R Standard Liège Liège) Paul Van Himst (RSC Anderlecht Bruxelles)	20
1968/1969	R Standard Liège	K Lierse SK	Antal Nagy (HUN, R Standard Liège Liège)	20
1969/1970	R Standard Liège	Club Brugge KV	Lothar Emmerich (GER, K Beerschot VAC)	29
1970/1971	R Standard Liège	K Beerschot VAV	Erwin Kostedde (GER, R Standard Liège Liège)	26
1971/1972	RSC Anderlecht Bruxelles	RSC Anderlecht Bruxelles	Raoul Lambert (Club Brugge KV)	17
1972/1973	Club Brugge KV	RSC Anderlecht Bruxelles	Pieter Robert Rensenbrink (NED, RSC Anderlecht Bruxelles) Alfred Riedl (AUT, K Sint-Truidense VV)	16
1973/1974	RSC Anderlecht Bruxelles	KSV Waregem	Attila Ladynski (HUN, RSC Anderlecht Bruxelles)	22
1974/1975	R White Daring Molenbeek	RSC Anderlecht Bruxelles	Alfred Riedl (AUT, R Antwerp FC)	28
1975/1976	Club Brugge KV	RSC Anderlecht Bruxelles	Hans Posthumus (K Lierse SK)	26
1976/1977	Club Brugge KV	Club Brugge KV	François Van Der Elst (RSC Anderlecht Bruxelles)	21
1977/1978	Club Brugge KV	KSK Beveren	Harald Nickel (R Standard Liège Liège)	22
1978/1979	KSK Beveren	K Beerschot VAV	Erwin Albert (KSK Beveren)	28
1979/1980	Club Brugge KV	K Waterschei SV Thor Genk	Erwin Vandenbergh (K Lierse SK)	39
1980/1981	RSC Anderlecht Bruxelles	R Standard Liège	Erwin Vandenbergh (K Lierse SK)	24
1981/1982	R Standard Liège	K Waterschei SV Thor Genk	Erwin Vandenbergh (K Lierse SK)	25
1982/1983	R Standard Liège	KSK Beveren	Erwin Vandenbergh (RSC Anderlecht Bruxelles)	20
1983/1984	KSK Beveren	KAA Gent	Nicolaas Pieter Claesen (RFC Seraing)	27
1984/1985	RSC Anderlecht Bruxelles	Cercle Brugge KSV	Ronny Martens (KAA Gent)	23
1985/1986	RSC Anderlecht Bruxelles	Club Brugge KV	Erwin Vandenbergh (RSC Anderlecht Bruxelles)	27
1986/1987	RSC Anderlecht Bruxelles	KV Mechelen	Arnór Guðjohnsen (ISL, RSC Anderlecht Bruxelles)	19
1987/1988	Club Brugge KV	RSC Anderlecht Bruxelles	Francis Severeyns (R Antwerp FC)	24
1988/1989	KV Mechelen	RSC Anderlecht Bruxelles	Edward Krncevic (AUS, RSC Anderlecht Bruxelles)	23
1989/1990	Club Brugge KV	RFC Liégeois	Frank Farina (AUS, Club Brugge KV)	24
1990/1991	RSC Anderlecht Bruxelles	Club Brugge KV	Erwin Vandenbergh (KAA Gent)	23
1991/1992	Club Brugge KV	Royal Antwerp F.C.	Josip Weber (CRO, Cercle Brugge KSV)	26
1992/1993	RSC Anderlecht Bruxelles	R Standard Liège	Josip Weber (CRO, Cercle Brugge KSV)	31
1993/1994	RSC Anderlecht Bruxelles	RSC Anderlecht Bruxelles	Josip Weber (Cercle Brugge KSV)	31
1994/1995	RSC Anderlecht Bruxelles	Club Brugge KV	Aurelio Vidmar (AUS, R Standard Liège Liège)	22
1995/1996	Club Brugge KV	Club Brugge KV	Mario Stanić (CRO, Club Brugge KV)	20
1996/1997	K Lierse SK	KFC Germinal Ekeren	Robert Špehar (CRO, Club Brugge KV)	26
1997/1998	Club Brugge KV	KRC Genk	Branko Strupar (KRC Genk)	22
1998/1999	KRC Genk	Lierse S.K.	Jan Koller (CZE, Lokeren)	24
1999/2000	RSC Anderlecht Bruxelles	KRC Genk	Ole Martin Årst (NOR, KAA Gent) Antonio Brogno (KVC Westerlo)	30
2000/2001	RSC Anderlecht Bruxelles	KVC Westerlo	Tomasz Radzinski (CAN, RSC Anderlecht Bruxelles)	23
2001/2002	KRC Genk	Club Brugge KV	Wesley Sonck (KRC Genk)	30
2002/2003	Club Brugge KV	RAA La Louvière	Cédric Roussel (RAEC Mons) Wesley Sonck (KRC Genk)	22
2003/2004	RSC Anderlecht Bruxelles	Club Brugge KV	Luigi Pieroni (Mouscron)	28
2004/2005	Club Brugge KV	KFC Germinal Beerschot	Nenad Jestrović (SRB, RSC Anderlecht Bruxelles)	18
2005/2006	RSC Anderlecht Bruxelles	SV Zulte-Waregem	Tosin Dosunmu (NGA, KFC Germinal Beerschot Antwerpen)	18
2006/2007	RSC Anderlecht Bruxelles	Club Brugge KV	François Sterchele (KFC Germinal Beerschot Antwerpen)	21
2007/2008	R Standard Liège	RSC Anderlecht Bruxelles	Joseph Eneojo Akpala (NGA, R Charleroi SC)	18
2008/2009	R Standard Liège	KRC Genk	Jaime Alfonso Ruiz (COL, KVC Westerlo)	18
2009/2010	RSC Anderlecht Bruxelles	KAA Gent	Romelu Menama Lukaku Bolingoli (RSC Anderlecht Bruxelles)	15
2010/2011	KRC Genk	R Standard Liège	Ivan Perišić (CRO, Club Brugge KV)	22
2011/2012	RSC Anderlecht Bruxelles	KSC Lokeren	Jérémy Perbet (FRA, RAEC Mons)	25
2012/2013	RSC Anderlecht Bruxelles	KRC Genk	Carlos Arturo Bacca Ahumada (COL, Club Brugge KV)	25
2013/2014	RSC Anderlecht Bruxelles	KSC Lokeren	Hamdi Harbaoui (TUN, KSC Lokeren Oost-Vlaanderen)	22
2014/2015	KAA Gent	Club Brugge KV	Aleksandar Mitrović (SRB, RSC Anderlecht Bruxelles)	20
2015/2016	Club Brugge KV	R Standard Liège	Jérémy Perbet (FRA, R Charleroi SC)	22
2016/2017	RSC Anderlecht Bruxelles	SV Zulte Waregem	Łukasz Teodorczyk (POL, RSC Anderlecht Bruxelles)	22
2017/2018	Club Brugge KV	R Standard Liège	Hamdi Harbaoui (TUN, SV Zulte Waregem)	22
2018/2019	KRC Genk	KV Mechelen	Hamdi Harbaoui (TUN, SV Zulte Waregem)	25
2019/2020	Club Brugge KV	Royal Antwerp FC	Dieudonné Mbokani Bezua (COD, R Antwerp FC) Jonathan Christian David (CAN, KAA Gent)	18

NATIONAL CHAMPIONSHIP
Eerste Divisie / Jupiler Pro League - 2019/2020
(26.07.2019 – 07.03.2020)

Regular Season - Results

Round 1 [26-28.07.2019]
KRC Genk - KV Kortrijk 2-1(0-1)
Cercle Brugge - Standard Liège 0-2(0-0)
Sint-Truidense VV - Excel Mouscron 0-1(0-1)
SV Zulte Waregem - KV Mechelen 0-2(0-1)
Waasland-Beveren - Club Brugge 1-3(1-1)
Anderlecht - KV Oostende 1-2(1-1)
Charleroi - KAA Gent 1-1(0-0)
KAS Eupen - Antwerp FC 1-4(1-1)

Round 2 [02-04.08.2019]
Club Brugge - Sint-Truidense VV 6-0(4-0)
Standard Liège - SV Zulte Waregem 4-0(2-0)
KV Kortrijk - Charleroi 1-1(0-1)
KV Oostende - Cercle Brugge 3-1(2-1)
KV Mechelen - KRC Genk 3-1(1-1)
KAA Gent - KAS Eupen 6-1(4-0)
Excel Mouscron - Anderlecht 0-0
Antwerp FC - Waasland-Beveren 4-1(2-1)

Round 3 [09-11.08.2019]
Anderlecht - KV Mechelen 0-0
KV Oostende - Club Brugge 0-2(0-0)
KAS Eupen - Waasland-Beveren 1-1(0-1)
Cercle Brugge - KV Kortrijk 1-3(1-0)
KRC Genk - SV Zulte Waregem 0-2(0-1)
Sint-Truidense VV - Standard Liège 2-1(2-0)
Charleroi - Antwerp FC 2-1(0-0)
Excel Mouscron - KAA Gent 2-1(2-1)

Round 4 [16-19.08.2019]
Club Brugge - KAS Eupen 0-0
KV Kortrijk - Anderlecht 4-2(0-1)
KV Mechelen - Cercle Brugge 3-1(1-0)
Waasland-Beveren - KRC Genk 0-4(0-1)
Standard Liège - Excel Mouscron 4-1(2-0)
Antwerp FC - Sint-Truidense VV 2-0(1-0)
KAA Gent - KV Oostende 2-0(0-0)
SV Zulte Waregem - Charleroi 3-1(1-0)

Round 5 [23-25.08.2019]
KRC Genk - Anderlecht 1-0(0-0)
Cercle Brugge - Waasland-Beveren 1-0(0-0)
Sint-Truidense VV - SV Zulte Waregem 0-0
KV Oostende - KV Mechelen 2-0(1-0)
Standard Liège - KV Kortrijk 2-1(0-1)
Excel Mouscron - KAS Eupen 2-0(1-0)
Antwerp FC - KAA Gent 3-2(2-1) [21.11.]
Charleroi - Club Brugge 0-0 [29.01.2020]

Round 6 [30.08.-01.09.2019]
KV Mechelen - Excel Mouscron 2-2(2-1)
KAS Eupen - Sint-Truidense VV 0-2(0-1)
KV Kortrijk - KV Oostende 2-2(0-1)
Waasland-Beveren - Charleroi 0-4(0-1)
Club Brugge - KRC Genk 1-1(1-0)
Anderlecht - Standard Liège 1-0(1-0)
KAA Gent - Cercle Brugge 3-2(3-1)
SV Zulte Waregem - Antwerp FC 2-0(2-0)

Round 7 [13-15.09.2019]
Charleroi - KRC Genk 2-1(2-0)
KV Oostende - Standard Liège 1-4(1-1)
KAS Eupen - SV Zulte Waregem 1-1(0-1)
Sint-Truidense VV - Waasland-Bev. 1-1(0-0)
Cercle Brugge - Club Brugge 0-2(0-1)
Anderlecht - Antwerp FC 1-2(0-0)
KAA Gent - KV Mechelen 3-0(3-0)
Excel Mouscron - KV Kortrijk 2-0(1-0)

Round 8 [20-22.09.2019]
KV Kortrijk - KV Mechelen 2-3(1-0)
Charleroi - Sint-Truidense VV 0-3(0-1)
Antwerp FC - Cercle Brugge 3-1(1-1)
Waasland-Beveren - Excel Mouscron 1-1(0-1)
KRC Genk - KV Oostende 3-1(2-1)
Standard Liège - KAS Eupen 3-0(2-0)
Club Brugge - Anderlecht 2-1(1-1)
SV Zulte Waregem - KAA Gent 2-2(1-1)

Round 9 [28-29.09.2019]
KV Mechelen - Club Brugge 0-5(0-1)
KAA Gent - KV Kortrijk 2-0(0-0)
Excel Mouscron - SV Zulte Waregem 2-2(1-0)
Cercle Brugge - KAS Eupen 1-2(1-0)
Sint-Truidense VV - KRC Genk 3-3(0-1)
Anderlecht - Waasland-Beveren 0-0
Standard Liège - Charleroi 1-1(0-1)
KV Oostende - Antwerp FC 1-1(0-1)

Round 10 [04-06.10.2019]
Charleroi - Anderlecht 1-2(1-1)
KAS Eupen - KV Mechelen 0-2(0-1)
SV Zulte Waregem - Cercle Brugge 6-0(2-0)
Waasland-Beveren - KV Oostende 3-1(2-1)
KV Kortrijk - Sint-Truidense VV 4-0(3-0)
Club Brugge - KAA Gent 4-0(2-0)
Antwerp FC - Standard Liège 2-2(1-0)
KRC Genk - Excel Mouscron 2-1(0-0)

Round 11 [18-20.10.2019]
Excel Mouscron - Club Brugge 0-1(0-1)
Standard Liège - KRC Genk 1-0(0-0)
KV Kortrijk - SV Zulte Waregem 2-0(1-0)
KV Oostende - KAS Eupen 2-3(2-1)
KAA Gent - Waasland-Beveren 2-0(1-0)
KV Mechelen - Antwerp FC 3-1(2-1)
Anderlecht - Sint-Truidense VV 4-1(2-0)
Cercle Brugge - Charleroi 0-3(0-3)

Round 12 [25-27.10.2019]
KAS Eupen - Anderlecht 0-0
Charleroi - Excel Mouscron 1-0(0-0)
SV Zulte Waregem - KV Oostende 2-0(0-0)
Antwerp FC - KV Kortrijk 3-1(1-0)
KRC Genk - Cercle Brugge 1-0(1-0)
Club Brugge - Standard Liège 1-1(0-1)
Sint-Truidense VV - KAA Gent 0-0
Waasland-Beveren - KV Mechelen 1-3(0-1)

Round 13 [29-31.10.2019]
KV Kortrijk - KAS Eupen 1-2(0-2)
KV Oostende - Charleroi 0-1(0-0)
Cercle Brugge - Excel Mouscron 2-2(1-1)
Standard Liège - Waasland-Beveren 2-0(1-0)
KRC Genk - Antwerp FC 2-2(0-1)
SV Zulte Waregem - Club Brugge 0-2(0-1)
KV Mechelen - Sint-Truidense VV 1-2(1-0)
Anderlecht - KAA Gent 3-3(1-1)

Round 14 [02-03.11.2019]
KAS Eupen - KRC Genk 2-0(2-0)
Excel Mouscron - Antwerp FC 3-1(0-1)
Waasland-Bev. - SV Zulte Waregem 1-2(0-1)
Sint-Truidense VV - KV Oostende 1-0(0-0)
Club Brugge - KV Kortrijk 3-0(2-0)
Anderlecht - Cercle Brugge 2-1(2-1)
KAA Gent - Standard Liège 3-1(0-1)
KV Mechelen - Charleroi 2-2(2-2)

Round 15 [08-10.11.2019]
SV Zulte Waregem - Anderlecht 1-2(0-1)
Charleroi - KAS Eupen 1-0(0-0)
KV Kortrijk - Waasland-Beveren 1-3(0-2)
Cercle Brugge - Sint-Truidense VV 2-1(1-0)
KV Oostende - Excel Mouscron 2-2(1-0)
Antwerp FC - Club Brugge 2-1(0-1)
KRC Genk - KAA Gent 0-2(0-1)
Standard Liège - KV Mechelen 1-2(0-1)

Round 16 [22-24.11.2019]
Club Brugge - KV Oostende 2-0(1-0)
KAS Eupen - Standard Liège 1-2(0-1)
KV Mechelen - SV Zulte Waregem 0-2(0-1)
Waasland-Beveren - Cercle Brugge 1-1(1-0)
Excel Mouscron - KRC Genk 2-2(1-1)
KAA Gent - Antwerp FC 1-1(1-0)
Anderlecht - KV Kortrijk 0-0
Sint-Truidense VV - Charleroi 1-3(0-0)

Round 17 [29.11.-01.12.2019]
Antwerp FC - KV Mechelen 1-0(0-0)
Club Brugge - Excel Mouscron 1-0(1-0)
SV Zulte Waregem - KAS Eupen 1-0(1-0)
Charleroi - Waasland-Beveren 2-0(2-0)
KRC Genk - Sint-Truidense VV 1-2(1-2)
KV Oostende - Anderlecht 3-2(2-0)
Standard Liège - Cercle Brugge 2-1(1-0)
KV Kortrijk - KAA Gent 0-2(0-1)

Round 18 [06-08.12.2019]
Waasland-Beveren - Antwerp FC 0-4(0-1)
KV Mechelen - KV Kortrijk 1-1(0-0)
KAA Gent - SV Zulte Waregem 2-0(2-0)
Cercle Brugge - KRC Genk 1-2(0-1)
Sint-Truidense VV - Club Brugge 1-2(1-1)
Excel Mouscron - Standard Liège 2-2(1-1)
Anderlecht - Charleroi 0-0
KAS Eupen - KV Oostende 1-0(0-0)

Round 19 [13-15.12.2019]
KV Kortrijk - Excel Mouscron 1-2(1-0)
Antwerp FC - KAS Eupen 1-0(0-0)
SV Zulte Waregem - Sint-Truidense 5-1(2-1)
Charleroi - Cercle Brugge 3-0(1-0)
KRC Genk - Waasland-Beveren 4-1(3-0)
Standard Liège - Anderlecht 1-1(1-0)
Club Brugge - KV Mechelen 3-0(2-0)
KV Oostende - KAA Gent 2-1(1-1)

Round 20 [20-22.12.2019]
KV Mechelen - KV Oostende 1-0(0-0)
Excel Mouscron - Charleroi 1-1(1-0)
KAS Eupen - KV Kortrijk 1-2(1-1)
Cercle Brugge - SV Zulte Waregem 2-0(1-0)
Waasland-Beveren - Standard Liège 2-1(0-1)
KAA Gent - Club Brugge 1-1(0-0)
Sint-Truidense VV - Antwerp FC 1-1(0-0)
Anderlecht - KRC Genk 2-0(0-0)

Round 21 [26-27.12.2019]
KRC Genk - KAS Eupen 2-1(1-0)
KV Kortrijk - Cercle Brugge 1-0(0-0)
Excel Mouscron - KV Mechelen 1-2(0-2)
Waasland-Beveren - Sint-Truidense 1-0(1-0)
Club Brugge - SV Zulte Waregem 4-0(1-0)
Standard Liège - KAA Gent 0-1(0-0)
Charleroi - KV Oostende 5-0(1-0)
Antwerp FC - Anderlecht 0-0

Round 22 [17-19.01.2020]
KV Mechelen - Standard Liège 2-3(0-1)
KAS Eupen - Charleroi 1-1(1-1)
KV Oostende - Waasland-Beveren 0-1(0-1)
Sint-Truidense VV - KV Kortrijk 2-0(0-0)
KAA Gent - Excel Mouscron 3-1(1-0)
Cercle Brugge - Antwerp FC 1-2(1-1)
Anderlecht - Club Brugge 1-2(1-1)
SV Zulte Waregem - KRC Genk 0-3(0-1)

Round 23 [24-26.01.2020]
Standard Liège - KV Oostende 2-1(0-0)
Excel Mouscron - Sint-Truidense VV 1-3(0-1)
Waasland-Beveren - KAS Eupen 0-1(0-1)
KAA Gent - KRC Genk 4-1(1-1)
Cercle Brugge - Anderlecht 1-2(1-0)
KV Kortrijk - Club Brugge 2-2(1-2)
Antwerp FC - SV Zulte Waregem 2-1(1-1)
Charleroi - KV Mechelen 2-1(0-0) [11.02.]

Round 24 [31.01.-02.02.2020]
KV Kortrijk - Standard Liège 3-1(0-0)
KRC Genk - Charleroi 1-0(1-0)
KAS Eupen - Cercle Brugge 1-0(1-0)
KV Oostende - Sint-Truidense VV 1-0(0-0)
KV Mechelen - KAA Gent 0-3(0-1)
Club Brugge - Antwerp FC 1-0(0-0)
Anderlecht - Excel Mouscron 1-0(0-0)
Zulte Waregem - Waasland-Beveren 5-0(3-0)

Round 25 [07-13.02.2020]
KAA Gent - Anderlecht 1-1(1-1)
Charleroi - SV Zulte Waregem 4-0(1-0)
Cercle Brugge - KV Mechelen 3-2(2-1)
Sint-Truidense VV - KAS Eupen 5-2(3-2)
Excel Mouscron - KV Oostende 3-1(0-1)
Standard Liège - Club Brugge 0-0
Waasland-Beveren - KV Kortrijk 1-2(1-1)
Antwerp FC - KRC Genk 1-1(1-1)

Round 26 [14-16.02.2020]
KAS Eupen - KAA Gent 2-3(2-2)
Club Brugge - Waasland-Beveren 2-1(1-0)
KV Oostende - KV Kortrijk 0-3(0-0)
Sint-Truidense VV - Cercle Brugge 0-1(0-0)
KV Mechelen - Anderlecht 2-0(0-0)
Antwerp FC - Charleroi 1-1(1-0)
KRC Genk - Standard Liège 1-3(0-2)
SV Zulte Waregem - Excel Mouscron 1-2(0-1)

Round 27 [21-23.02.2020]
KV Kortrijk - KRC Genk 0-1(0-0)
Standard Liège - Antwerp FC 1-0(1-0)
Excel Mouscron - Cercle Brugge 0-1(0-0)
KV Oostende - SV Zulte Waregem 1-1(1-1)
KV Mechelen - Waasland-Beveren 4-0(2-0)
Club Brugge - Charleroi 1-0(1-0)
Anderlecht - KAS Eupen 6-1(4-0)
KAA Gent - Sint-Truidense VV 4-1(3-0)

Round 28 [28.02.-01.03.2020]
Sint-Truidense VV - KV Mechelen 0-3(0-0)
Waasland-Beveren - Anderlecht 0-3(0-1)
KAS Eupen - Excel Mouscron 2-1(1-1)
SV Zulte Waregem - KV Kortrijk 2-2(2-0)
Antwerp FC - KV Oostende 3-1(2-0)
KRC Genk - Club Brugge 1-2(1-1)
Charleroi - Standard Liège 2-0(1-0)
Cercle Brugge - KAA Gent 1-0(1-0)

Round 29 [07.03.2020]
Club Brugge - Cercle Brugge 2-1(1-0)
Anderlecht - SV Zulte Waregem 7-0(2-0)
Standard Liège - Sint-Truidense VV 0-0
KAA Gent - Charleroi 1-4(0-2)
KV Kortrijk - Antwerp FC 0-1(0-0)
Excel Mouscron - Waasland-Beveren 1-0(0-0)
KV Oostende - KRC Genk 2-4(1-0)
KV Mechelen - KAS Eupen 1-1(1-0)

The saison was interrupted after 29 Rounds due to Covid-19 pandemic. On 02.04.2020, the Jupiler Pro League's board of directors proposed to cancel the season early during the COVID-19 pandemic. The proposal to vote about this decision was postponed three times. Finally, the proposal was accepted by the General Assembly on 15.05.2020, confirming Club Brugge KV as 2019/2020 champions. Both Championship and Relegation Play-offs were cancelled.

Final Standings

					Total			Home					Away				
1.	**Club Brugge KV**	29	21	7	1	58 - 14	70	12	3	0	33 - 5	9	4	1	25 - 9
2.	KAA Gent	29	16	7	6	59 - 34	55	11	3	1	38 - 14	5	4	5	21 - 20
3.	R Charleroi SC	29	15	9	5	49 - 23	54	10	2	2	26 - 9	5	7	3	23 - 14
4.	Antwerp FC	29	15	8	6	49 - 32	53	10	4	0	28 - 12	5	4	6	21 - 20
5.	R Standard Liège	29	14	7	8	47 - 32	49	9	4	2	24 - 9	5	3	6	23 - 23
6.	KV Mechelen	29	13	5	11	46 - 43	44	6	4	5	25 - 24	7	1	6	21 - 19
7.	KRC Genk	29	13	5	11	45 - 42	44	8	1	5	21 - 18	5	4	6	24 - 24
8.	RSC Anderlecht Bruxelles	29	11	10	8	45 - 29	43	7	5	3	29 - 12	4	5	5	16 - 17
9.	SV Zulte Waregem	29	10	6	13	41 - 49	36	7	2	5	30 - 17	3	4	8	11 - 32
10.	Royal Excel Mouscron	29	9	9	11	38 - 40	36	6	5	4	22 - 17	3	4	7	16 - 23
11.	KV Kortrijk	29	9	6	14	40 - 44	33	5	3	7	24 - 22	4	3	7	16 - 22
12.	Sint-Truidense VV	29	9	6	14	33 - 50	33	4	5	5	17 - 18	5	1	9	16 - 32
13.	KAS Eupen	29	8	6	15	28 - 51	30	4	4	6	14 - 19	4	2	9	14 - 32
14.	Cercle Brugge KSV	29	7	2	20	27 - 54	23	5	1	8	16 - 23	2	1	12	11 - 31
15.	KV Oostende	29	6	4	19	29 - 58	22	5	3	7	20 - 27	1	1	12	9 - 31
16.	KVRS Waasland-Beveren (*Relegated*)*	29	5	5	19	21 - 60	20	3	2	9	12 - 30	2	3	10	9 - 30

Top goalscorers:	
18 Dieudonné Mbokani Bezua (COD)	*R Antwerp FC*
18 Jonathan Christian David (CAN)	*KAA Gent*
13 Hans Vanaken	*Club Brugge KV*
12 Kaveh Rezaei (IRN)	*R Charleroi SC*
11 Lior Refaelov (ISR)	*R Antwerp FC*

*Please note: Finishing last, KVRS Waasland-Beveren have been relegated, however following legal proceedings the Belgian Pro League eventually voted in favour of expanding the 2020/2021 Eerste Divisie to 18 teams. Due to this fact, KVRS Waasland-Beveren remains at first level and both Oud-Heverle Leuven and K Beerschot VA were promoted for next saison's first level.

NATIONAL CUP
Coupe de Belgique / Beker van België Final 2019/2020

Fifth Round [23-25.08.2019]				
Royal Cercle Sportif de Verlaine - KRC Bambrugge	4-2 pen		UR La Louvière Centre - KVC Westerlo	1-2
Oud-Heverlee Leuven - Standaard Wetteren	6-0		KSK Heist - KSC Lokeren	0-4
KFCO Beerschot Wilrijk - SC Dikkelvenne	6-1		Rupel Boom FC - KVV Vosselaar	6-4 pen
KFC Dessel Sport - Royal Excelsior Virton	3-1		KFC Duffel - Royal Knokke FC	2-1
RFC Seraing - KSV Roeselare	1-0		R. Cappellen FC - KFC VW Hamme	1-0
CS Onhaye - SC Eendracht Aalst	0-1		RUS Rebecquoise - Royal Tilleur FC	2-1
KFC Mandel United - FC Gullegem	1-0 n.V.		Royal Francs Borains - Torhout 1992 KM	6-1
Lommel SK - KSV Temse	4-0		KSK Ronse - Olympia Wijgmaal	4-2

Sixth Round [24-26.09.2019]				
Cercle Brugge KSV - RUS Rebecquoise	0-1(0-1)		KFC Mandel United - KV Oostende	0-2(0-1)
KVRS Waasland-Beveren - KVC Westerlo	3-4(3-1)		Royal Francs Borains - Club Brugge KV	0-3(0-0)
KSK Ronse - KRC Genk	0-3(0-0)		Sint-Truidense VV - Oud-Heverlee Leuven	2-0(0-0,0-0)
R. Cappellen FC - KAS Eupen	0-0 aet; 3-5 pen		SC Eendracht Aalst - KAA Gent	0-4(0-1)
SV Zulte Waregem - KFC Duffel	4-2(1-1)		KFC Dessel Sport - Royal Excel Mouscron	0-1(0-1)
Rupel Boom FC - R Charleroi SC	2-3(1-1)		KFCO Beerschot Wilrijk - RSC Anderlecht Bruxelles	2-3(1-1,2-2)
Union St. Gilloise - Royal Cercle Sportif de Verlaine	3-0(1-0)		Royal Antwerp FC - KSC Lokeren	4-2(2-1,2-2)
RFC Seraing - KV Kortrijk	1-3(1-2)		R Standard Liège - Lommel SK	2-1(1-0)

1/8-Finals [03-05.12.2019]				
Royal Antwerp FC - KRC Genk	3-3 aet; 4-3 pen		Union St. Gilloise - KVC Westerlo	0-0 aet; 4-1 pen
SV Zulte Waregem - Sint-Truidense VV	3-0(1-0)		KV Oostende - Club Brugge KV	1-1 aet; 2-4 pen
KV Kortrijk - KAS Eupen	2-1(0-1)		R Charleroi SC - KAA Gent	1-0(0-0)
R Standard Liège - RUS Rebecquoise	3-0(1-0)		Royal Excel Mouscron - RSC Anderlecht Bruxelles	2-3(1-2)

Quarter-Finals [17-19.12.2019]				
SV Zulte Waregem - R Charleroi SC	2-0(0-0)		R Standard Liège - Royal Antwerp FC	1-3(1-0)
Union St. Gilloise - KV Kortrijk	0-1(0-0)		RSC Anderlecht Bruxelles - Club Brugge KV	0-2(0-0)

Semi-Finals [22-23.01./05-06.02.2020]				
First Leg			**Second Leg**	
Club Brugge KV - SV Zulte Waregem	1-1(0-0)		SV Zulte Waregem - Club Brugge KV	1-2(0-0)
Royal Antwerp FC - KV Kortrijk	1-1(0-0)		KV Kortrijk - Royal Antwerp FC	0-1(0-1)

Final

01.08.2020; Stade "Roi Baudouin", Bruxelles; Referee: Nicolas Laforge; Attendance: none
Club Brugge KV - Royal Antwerp FC **0-1(0-1)**

Club Brugge: Simon Mignolet, Clinton Mukoni Mata Pedro Lourenço, Brandon Mechele, Simon Deli, Krépin Diatta, Ruud Vormer (Cap), Hans Vanaken, Éder Fabián Álvarez Balanta (75.Mats Rits), Eduard Sobol (75.Siebe Schrijvers), Charles De Ketelaere, David Chidozie Okereke (52.Youssouph Mamadou Badji). Trainer: Philippe Clement.

Antwerp FC: Davor Matijaš, Abdoulaye Seck, Junior Udeme Pius, Ritchie De Laet, Didier Lamkel Zé (90.Ivo Tiago dos Santos Rodrigues), Aurélio Gabriel Ulineia Buta, Faris Haroun (Cap), Martin Hongla Yma, Simen Juklerød, Lior Refaelov (90+1.Bruny Nsimba), Manuel Benson. Trainer: Ivan Leko (CRO).

Goal: 0-1 Lior Refaelov (25).

THE CLUBS 2019/2020

Royal Sporting Club Anderlecht Bruxelles

Founded:	27.05.1908	
Stadium:	Stade "Constant Vanden Stock", Bruxelles (21,500)	
Trainer:	Simon Ithel Davies &	23.04.1974
	Vincent Jean Mpoy Kompany	10.04.1986
[03.10.2019]	Jonas De Roeck	20.12.1979
[07.10.2019]	François Vercauteren	28.10.1956

Goalkeepers:	DOB	M	(s)	G
Thomas Didillon (FRA)	28.11.1995	1		
Hendrik Van Crombrugge	30.04.1993	28		
Defenders:	**DOB**	**M**	**(s)**	**G**
Sebastiaan Bornauw	22.03.1999	1		
Elias Cobbaut	24.11.1997	22	(2)	
Hotman El Kababri (MAR)	24.01.2000	1		
Marco Kana	08.08.2002	12	(3)	1
Vincent Jean Mpoy Kompany	10.04.1986	15		1
Kemar Michael Lawrence (JAM)	17.09.1992		(1)	
Derrick Luckassen (NED)	03.07.1995	18		
Thierry Lutonda	27.10.2000		(1)	
Michael Amir Murillo Bermúdez (PAN)	11.02.1996	8		1
Alexis Saelemaekers	27.06.1999	14	(2)	2
Philippe Sandler (NED)	10.02.1997	9		
Killian Sardella	02.05.2002	15	(3)	
Midfielders:	**DOB**	**M**	**(s)**	**G**
Anouar Ait El Hadj	20.04.2002		(2)	
Sieben Dewaele	02.02.1999	14	(1)	

Pieter Gerkens	13.08.1995	5	(2)	
Edo Kayembe (COD)	03.06.1998	9	(9)	
Samir Nasri (FRA)	26.06.1987	5	(2)	1
Albert Sambi Lokonga	22.10.1999	22	(1)	
Adrien Trebel (FRA)	03.03.1991	3	(1)	
Yari Verschaeren	12.07.2001	17	(4)	2
Michel Vlap (NED)	02.06.1997	18	(5)	11
Peter Žulj (AUT)	09.06.1993	16	(6)	
Forwards:	**DOB**	**M**	**(s)**	**G**
Luka Adžić (SRB)	17.09.1998	1	(4)	
Francis Amuzu	23.08.1999	11	(9)	3
Zakaria Bakkali	26.01.1996		(4)	1
Nacer Chadli	02.08.1989	15	(2)	8
Antoine Colassin	26.02.2001	4		3
Jérémy Doku	27.05.2002	14	(7)	3
Dejan Joveljić (SRB)	07.08.1999	4	(1)	
Marko Pjaca (CRO)	06.05.1995	2	(2)	1
Kemar Roofe (ENG)	06.01.1993	13		6
Isaac Kiese Thelin (SWE)	24.06.1992	2	(8)	

Royal Antwerp Football Club

Founded: 1880
Stadium: Bosuilstadion, Antwerp (12,975)
Trainer: Ladislau Bölöni (ROU)　　　　11.03.1953

Goalkeepers:	DOB	M	(s)	G
Sinan Bolat (TUR)	03.09.1988	27		
Jens Teunckens	30.01.1998	2		
Defenders:	**DOB**	**M**	**(s)**	**G**
Dino Arslanagić	24.04.1993	21		
Dylan Batubinsika (FRA)	15.02.1996	4		
Aurélio Gabriel Ulineia Buta (POR)	10.02.1997	28		2
Ritchie De Laet	28.11.1988	19	(3)	
Wesley Hoedt (NED)	06.03.1994	21		
Simen Juklerød (NOR)	18.05.1994	11	(3)	
Robbe Quirynen	03.11.2001	2	(1)	
Abdoulaye Seck (SEN)	04.06.1992	10	(3)	
Midfielders:	**DOB**	**M**	**(s)**	**G**
Sander Coopman	12.03.1995	3	(7)	
Alexis De Sart	12.11.1996	20	(3)	1

	DOB	M	(s)	G
Steven Defour	15.04.1988	9	(2)	
Geoffry Hairemans	21.10.1991	3	(1)	
Faris Haroun	22.09.1985	24	(1)	
Martin Hongla Yma (CMR)	16.03.1998	3	(6)	
Koji Miyoshi (JPN)	26.03.1997	4	(10)	1
Lior Refaelov (ISR)	26.04.1986	21	(3)	11
Forwards:	**DOB**	**M**	**(s)**	**G**
Amara Baby (SEN)	23.02.1989	3	(6)	
Jonathan Bolingi Mpangi Merikani (COD)	30.06.1994		(3)	
Zinho Gano	13.10.1993	1	(10)	2
Ivo Tiago dos Santos Rodrigues (POR)	30.03.1995	17	(5)	4
Didier Lamkel Zé (CMR)	17.09.1996	21	(4)	6
Manuel Benson	28.03.1997	6	(5)	
Dieudonné Mbokani Bezua (COD)	22.11.1985	28		18
Kevin Antonio Joel Gislain Mirallas y Castillo	05.10.1987	11	(7)	2

Cercle Brugge Koninklijke Sportvereniging

Founded: 1899
Stadium: "Jan Breydel" Stadium, Brugge (29,042)
Trainer: Fabien Mercadal (FRA)　　　　29.02.1972
[12.10.2019]　Bernd Storck (GER)　　　　25.01.1963

Goalkeepers:	DOB	M	(s)	G
Loïc Badiashile Mukinayi (FRA)	05.02.1998	10		
Moucz Hassen (TUN)	05.03.1995	4		
Guillaume Hubert	11.01.1994	8		
Lennart Moser (GER)	06.12.1999	7		
Defenders:	**DOB**	**M**	**(s)**	**G**
Giulian Biancone (FRA)	31.03.2000	24	(1)	1
Arne Cassaert	20.11.2000	1		
Dimitrios Chatziisaias (GRE)	21.09.1992	8		
Kouadio-Yves Dabila (CIV)	01.01.1997	21		1
Corentin Fiore	24.03.1995	3	(2)	
Rominigue Kouamé N'Guessan (CIV)	17.12.1996	11	(2)	
Jonathan Panzo (ENG)	25.10.2000	17		
Julien Serrano (FRA)	13.02.1998	5	(2)	
Jérémy Taravel (FRA)	17.04.1987	10		
Naomichi Ueda (JPN)	24.10.1994	18	(1)	
Dimitar Velkovski (BUL)	22.01.1995	6		
Midfielders:	**DOB**	**M**	**(s)**	**G**
Lassana Coulibaly (MLI)	10.04.1996	14	(2)	
Calvin Dekuyper	24.02.2000	8		

	DOB	M	(s)	G
Olivier Deman	06.04.2000		(3)	
Aldom Deuro (MLI)	20.12.2000	1		
Godfred Donsah (GHA)	07.06.1996	15	(4)	
Kylian Hazard	05.08.1995	19	(8)	1
Kévin Hoggas (FRA)	16.11.1991	16	(2)	6
Dino Hotič (BIH)	26.07.1995	6	(1)	1
Johanna Ochieng Omolo (KEN)	31.07.1989	8	(4)	1
Stéphane Richi Oméonga	27.03.1996	1	(2)	
Stef Peeters	09.02.1992	24		6
Thibo Somers	16.03.1999	5	(8)	1
Forwards:	**DOB**	**M**	**(s)**	**G**
William Balikwisha	12.05.1999		(3)	
Adrien Bongiovanni	20.09.1999	1	(2)	
Dylan De Belder	03.04.1992	10	(1)	1
Márton Eppel (HUN)	26.10.1991	5	(3)	1
Lyle Brent Foster (RSA)	03.09.2000	8	(10)	1
Alimani Gory (FRA)	30.08.1996	13	(6)	2
Aboubakary Kanté (GAM)	11.08.1994		(3)	
Jordi Mboula Queralt (ESP)	16.03.1999	3	(4)	
Idriss Saâdi (ALG)	08.02.1992	9	(7)	3

Royal Charleroi Sporting Club

Founded: 01.01.1904
Stadium: Stade du Pays de Charleroi, Charleroi (14,000)
Trainer: Karim Belhocine (FRA)　　　　02.04.1978

Goalkeepers:	DOB	M	(s)	G
Rémy Descamps (FRA)	25.06.1996		(1)	
Nicolas Penneteau (FRA)	20.02.1981	29		
Defenders:	**DOB**	**M**	**(s)**	**G**
Maxime Busi	14.10.1999	19	(2)	
Dorian Dessoleil	07.08.1992	28		1
Modou Diagne (SEN)	03.01.1994	14	(2)	1
Stergos Marinos (GRE)	17.09.1987	9	(2)	
Núrio Domingos Matias Fortuna (POR)	24.03.1995	28		1
Steeven Willems (FRA)	31.08.1990	16	(3)	
Gjoko Zajkov (MKD)	10.02.1995	1		
Midfielders:	**DOB**	**M**	**(s)**	**G**
Massimo Bruno	17.09.1993	25		4
Christophe Diandy	25.11.1990	13		

	DOB	M	(s)	G
Gaëtan Hendrickx	30.03.1995	2	(11)	
Marco Ilaimaharitra (MAD)	26.07.1995	27		2
Ryota Morioka (JPN)	12.04.1991	29		6
Forwards:	**DOB**	**M**	**(s)**	**G**
Chris Bedia (CIV)	05.03.1996	1	(2)	
Mamadou Fall (SEN)	31.12.1991	22	(4)	7
Ali Gholizadeh (IRN)	10.03.1996	18	(4)	3
David Henen	19.04.1996	2	(14)	1
Joris Kayembe	08.08.1994	3	(5)	
Adama Niane (MLI)	16.06.1993	3	(1)	
Shamar Nicholson (JAM)	16.03.1997	12	(13)	8
Jérémy Perbet (FRA)	12.12.1984		(3)	1
Kaveh Rezaei (IRN)	05.04.1992	18	(3)	12
Frank Tsadjout (ITA)	28.07.1999		(10)	1

Club Brugge Koninklijke Voetbalvereniging

Founded: 13.11.1891
Stadium: "Jan Breydel" Stadium, Brugge (29,042)
Trainer: Philippe Clement　　　　22.03.1974

Goalkeepers:	DOB	M	(s)	G
Ethan Horvath (USA)	09.06.1995	2		
Simon Mignolet	06.03.1988	27		
Defenders:	**DOB**	**M**	**(s)**	**G**
Clinton Mata Pedro Lourenço (ANG)	07.11.1992	24	(1)	
Dion Cools	04.06.1996	1	(1)	
Simon Deli (CIV)	27.10.1991	26		2
Odilon Kossounou (CIV)	04.01.2001	4	(3)	
Brandon Mechele	28.01.1993	24		
Matej Mitrović (CRO)	10.11.1993	6	(1)	
Federico Ricca Rostagnol (URU)	01.12.1994	7	(1)	2
Eduard Sobol (UKR)	20.04.1995	23	(3)	
Ignace Van Der Brempt	01.04.2002		(1)	
Midfielders:	**DOB**	**M**	**(s)**	**G**
Éder Fabián Álvarez Balanta (COL)	28.02.1993	13	(3)	2
Sofyan Amrabat (MAR)	21.08.1996	1		

	DOB	M	(s)	G
Charles De Ketelaere	10.03.2001	8	(5)	1
Mats Rits	18.07.1993	17	(3)	5
Hans Vanaken	24.08.1992	28	(1)	13
Ruud Vormer (NED)	11.05.1988	26	(1)	1
Forwards:	**DOB**	**M**	**(s)**	**G**
Emmanuel Dennis Bonaventure (NGA)	15.11.1997	15	(5)	5
Arnaut Danjuma (NED)	31.01.1997	1		
Mbaye Diagne (SEN)	28.10.1991	1	(5)	4
Krépin Diatta (SEN)	25.02.1999	19	(3)	6
Michal Krmenčík (CZE)	15.03.1993	2	(4)	
David Chidozie Okereke (NGA)	29.08.1997	13	(9)	9
Loïs Openda	16.02.2000	3	(12)	
Siebe Schrijvers	18.07.1996	13	(9)	4
Percy Tau (RSA)	13.05.1994	12	(6)	3
Thibault Vlietinck	19.08.1997	2	(3)	
Jelle Vossen	22.03.1989	1	(1)	

Königliche Allgemeine Sportvereinigung Eupen

Goalkeepers:	DOB	M	(s)	G
Ortwin De Wolf	23.04.1997	28		
Hendrik Van Crombrugge	30.04.1993	1		
Defenders:	**DOB**	**M**	**(s)**	**G**
Emmanuel Adjei (GHA)	16.01.1998	2	(1)	
Francesc Xavier Molina Arias (ESP)	19.07.1986	2		
Andreas Beck (GER)	13.03.1987	27		1
Siebe Blondelle	20.04.1986	24	(1)	1
Silas Gnaka (CIV)	18.12.1998	10	(1)	
Jordi Amat Maas (ESP)	21.03.1992	23	(1)	2
Menno Koch (NED)	02.07.1994	14	(9)	1
Olivier Verdon (BEN)	05.10.1995	21	(1)	
Francesc Xavier Molina Arias "Xavi" (ESP)	19.07.1986	1	(1)	
Midfielders:	**DOB**	**M**	**(s)**	**G**
Jean Thierry Lazare Amani (CIV)	07.03.1998	4	(3)	1
Carlos Apna Embalo (GNB)	25.11.1994	2	(14)	1
Jens Cools	16.10.1990	26		1

Founded: 1945
Stadium: Kehrwegstadion, Eupen (8,363)
Trainer: Beñat San José Gil (ESP)   24.09.1979

	DOB	M	(s)	G
Omid Ebrahimi (IRN)	16.09.1987	18		
Saeid Ezatolahi (IRN)	01.10.1996	2	(2)	
Sibiry Keita (MLI)	30.01.2001	3		
Mégan Laurent	24.03.1992	2	(2)	
Sulayman Marreh (GAM)	15.01.1996	7	(4)	
Danijel Miličević (BIH)	05.01.1986	21	(2)	5
Konan N'Dri (CIV)	27.10.2000		(3)	
Leonardo Miramar Rocha (POR)	23.05.1997	1	(5)	
Nils Schouterden	14.12.1988	17	(7)	1
Yuta Toyokawa (JPN)	09.09.1994	8	(8)	1
Forwards:	**DOB**	**M**	**(s)**	**G**
Jonathan Bolingi (COD)	30.06.1994	14	(4)	4
Flavio Germán Ciampichetti (ARG)	07.03.1988	5	(9)	
Jon Bautista Orgilles (ESP)	03.07.1995	20	(6)	3
Knowledge Musona (ZIM)	21.06.1990	7		2
Adalberto Peñaranda Maestre (VEN)	31.05.1997	4	(1)	
Smail Prevljak (BIH)	10.05.1995	5		4

Koninklijke Racing Club Genk

Goalkeepers:	DOB	M	(s)	G
Gaëtan Coucke	03.12.1998	18		
Thomas Didillon (FRA)	28.11.1995	6		
Maarten Vandevoordt	26.02.2002	4		
Danny Vuković (AUS)	27.03.1985	1		
Defenders:	**DOB**	**M**	**(s)**	**G**
Carlos Cuesta (COL)	09.03.1999	20		
Sebastien Dewaest	27.05.1991	24		4
Jhon Janer Lucumi Bonilla (COL)	26.06.1998	21	(1)	1
Joakim Mæhle (DEN)	20.05.1997	23	(2)	
Vivaldo Borges dos Santos Neto (BRA)	13.09.1996	3	(2)	
Jere Uronen (FIN)	13.07.1994	17		
Dries Wouters	28.01.1997	9	(4)	1
Midfielders:	**DOB**	**M**	**(s)**	**G**
Manuel Benson Hedilazio	28.03.1997	1	(2)	
Sander Berge (NOR)	14.02.1998	22	(1)	4
Casper De Norre	07.02.1997	10	(3)	

Founded: 1988
Stadium: Luminus Arena, Genk (24,956)
Trainer: Felice Mazzù   12.03.1966
[18.11.2019]   Hannes Wolf (GER)   15.04.1981

	DOB	M	(s)	G
Kouassi Eboue (CIV)	13.12.1997	3	(1)	
Ianis Hagi (ROU)	22.10.1998	6	(8)	3
Bryan Heynen	06.02.1997	11	(3)	
Patrik Hrošovský (SVK)	22.04.1992	16	(5)	1
Mats Møller Dæhli (NOR)	02.03.1995	2	(1)	1
Joseph Paintsil (GHA)	01.02.1998	10	(8)	1
Jakub Piotrowski (POL)	04.10.1997	4	(2)	
Kristian Thorstvedt (NOR)	13.03.1999	5	(3)	1
Forwards:	**DOB**	**M**	**(s)**	**G**
Théo Bongonda	20.11.1995	15	(7)	5
Junya Ito (JPN)	09.03.1993	26	(3)	5
Bryan Limbombe	14.05.2001		(5)	
Dieumerci Ndongala (COD)	14.06.1991	5	(6)	
Benjamin Nygren (SWE)	08.07.2001	2		1
Stephen Pius Odey (NGA)	15.01.1998	1	(10)	
Ebere Paul Onuachu (NGA)	28.05.1994	17	(5)	9
Mbwana Aly Samatta (TAN)	23.12.1992	17	(3)	7

Koninklijke Atletiek Associatie Gent

Goalkeepers:	DOB	M	(s)	G
Colin Coosemans	03.08.1992		(1)	
Thomas Kaminski	23.10.1992	29		
Defenders:	**DOB**	**M**	**(s)**	**G**
Nana Asare (GHA)	11.07.1986	12		
Bruno Godeau	10.05.1992		(1)	
Mikael Lustig (SWE)	13.12.1986	14	(2)	
Milad Mohammadi (IRN)	29.09.1993	17	(1)	1
Michael Ngadeu-Ngadjui (CMR)	23.11.1990	29		3
Igor Plastun (UKR)	20.08.1990	28		1
Dylan Bronn (TUN)	19.06.1995	2	(3)	
Midfielders:	**DOB**	**M**	**(s)**	**G**
Roman Bezus (UKR)	26.09.1990	14	(7)	7
Alessio Castro-Montes	17.05.1997	14	(7)	2
Giorgi Chakvetadze (GEO)	29.08.1999	2	(7)	
Brecht Dejaegere	29.05.1991	6	(8)	

Founded: 1900
Stadium: Ghelamco Arena, Gent (20,000)
Trainer: Jess Thorup (DEN)   21.02.1970

	DOB	M	(s)	G
Sven Kums	26.02.1988	22		1
Sulayman Marreh (GAM)	15.01.1996	1	(3)	
Vadis Odjidja-Ofoe	21.02.1989	26		3
Elisha Owusu (FRA)	07.11.1997	27		
Louis Verstraete	04.05.1999	3	(2)	
Forwards:	**DOB**	**M**	**(s)**	**G**
Giorgi Beridze (GEO)	12.05.1997		(1)	
Jonathan Christian David (CAN)	14.01.2000	24	(3)	18
Laurent Depoitre	07.12.1988	19	(3)	8
Jean-Luc Dompé (FRA)	12.08.1995		(6)	
Yūya Kubo (JPN)	24.12.1993	2	(4)	
Giorgi Kvilitaia (GEO)	01.10.1993	8	(15)	1
Dylan Mbayo	11.10.2001		(4)	
Anderson Niangbo (CIV)	06.10.1999	1	(6)	3
Mamadou Sylla Diallo (SEN)	20.03.1994	1		
Roman Yaremchuk (UKR)	27.11.1995	18		10

Koninklijke Voetbalclub Kortrijk

Goalkeepers:	DOB	M	(s)	G
Sébastien Bruzzese	01.03.1989	15		
Adam Jakubech (SVK)	02.01.1997	14		
Defenders:	**DOB**	**M**	**(s)**	**G**
Andriy Batsula (UKR)	06.02.1992	4	(4)	
Timothy Derijck	25.05.1987	7		
Petar Golubović (SRB)	13.07.1994	20	(1)	
Brendan Hines-Ike (USA)	07.04.1994	14	(1)	
Gary Christofer Kagelmacher Pérez (URU)	21.04.1988	19		2
Vladimir Kovačević (SRB)	11.11.1992	4	(1)	
Evgen Makarenko (UKR)	21.05.1991	4		
Nihad Mujakić (BIH)	15.04.1998	1		
Lucas Rougeaux (FRA)	10.03.1994	7	(1)	
Lucas Silva Melo „Tuta" (BRA)	04.07.1999	14		1
Midfielders:	**DOB**	**M**	**(s)**	**G**
Abdul Jeleel Ajagun (NGA)	10.02.1993	9	(9)	1
Larry Francis Abdel Azouni (FRA)	23.03.1994	12	(5)	

Founded: 1901
Stadium: Guldensporen Stadion, Kortrijk (9,399)
Trainer: Yves Vanderhaeghe   30.01.1970

	DOB	M	(s)	G
Kristof D'Haene	06.06.1990	29		1
Julien De Sart	23.12.1994	27	(1)	4
Tyron Ivanof	17.07.1997	2		
Hervé Kage (COD)	10.04.1989	9	(9)	2
Christophe Lepoint	24.10.1984	13	(8)	1
Elohim Rolland (FRA)	03.03.1989	3	(3)	
Jovan Stojanović (SRB)	21.04.1992	7	(13)	2
Hannes Van der Bruggen	01.04.1993	24	(1)	3
Forwards:	**DOB**	**M**	**(s)**	**G**
Imoh Ezekiel (NGA)	24.10.1993	5	(7)	2
Pape Gueye (SEN)	20.09.1999		(4)	1
Fraser Hornby (SCO)	13.09.1999	9	(3)	3
Pelé M'Boyo	22.04.1987	24	(3)	8
Teremas Igoboras Moffi (NGA)	25.05.1999	4	(3)	4
Eric Ocansey (GHA)	22.08.1997	17	(5)	2
Faïz Selemani (COM)	14.11.1993	2	(5)	1

Koninklijke Voetbalclub Mechelen

Founded:	1904		
Stadium:	AFAS-stadion Achter de Kazerne, Mechelen (1904)		
Trainer:	Wouter Vrancken		03.02.1979

Goalkeepers:	DOB	M	(s)	G
Sofiane Bouzian	13.07.2000		(1)	
Bram Castro	30.09.1982	7	(1)	
Yannick Thoelen	18.07.1990	22		
Defenders:	**DOB**	**M**	**(s)**	**G**
Sheldon Michael Louis Bateau (TRI)	29.01.1991	6	(5)	
Lucas Bijker (NED)	04.03.1993	12	(6)	
Alexander Corryn	03.01.1994	19	(4)	
Issa Kabore (BFA)	12.05.2001	5		
Thibault Peyre (FRA)	03.10.1992	29		
Arjan Swinkels (NED)	15.10.1984	24		
Jules van Cleemput	04.02.1997	23		
Alec Van Hoorenbeeck	30.12.1998	1		

Midfielders:	DOB	M	(s)	G
Geoffry Hairemans	21.10.1991	11	(6)	1
Onur Kaya	20.04.1986	23	(1)	3
Rob Schoofs	23.03.1994	24	(2)	3
Joachim Van Damme	23.07.1991	18	(2)	3
Jordi Vanlerberghe	27.06.1996	13	(4)	3
Aster Vranckx	04.10.2002	7	(2)	1
Forwards:	**DOB**	**M**	**(s)**	**G**
Igor de Camargo	12.05.1983	19	(8)	10
Gustav Engvall (SWE)	29.04.1996	7	(2)	2
Nikola Storm	30.09.1994	25	(2)	4
Clément Tainmont (FRA)	03.12.1986	3	(18)	
William Togui (CIV)	07.08.1996	11	(15)	9
Dante Vanzeir	16.04.1998	10	(8)	3

Royal Excel Mouscron

Founded:	1922 (*as RRC Péruwelz*)		
Stadium:	Stade Le Canonnier, Mouscron (10,571)		
Trainer:	Bernd Hollerbach (GER)		08.12.1969
[05.02.2020]	Philippe Saint-Jean		13.05.1954
[25.02.2020]	Bernd Hollerbach (GER)		08.12.1969

Goalkeepers:	DOB	M	(s)	G
Jean Butez (FRA)	08.06.1995	16		
Vaso Vasić (SRB)	26.04.1990	13		
Defenders:	**DOB**	**M**	**(s)**	**G**
Nemanja Antonov (SRB)	06.05.1995	5	(12)	2
Joan Vidal Campins (ESP)	24.06.1995	9	(1)	1
Alessandro Ciranni	28.06.1996	15	(3)	2
Nathan De Medina	08.10.1997	20	(2)	1
Diogo Lucas Queirós (POR)	05.01.1999	19		1
Noë Dussenne	07.04.1992	2		
Bruno Godeau	10.05.1992	16	(4)	1
Jérémy Huyghebaert	07.01.1989		(5)	
Rafał Pietrzak (POL)	30.01.1992	13	(2)	
Lasse Sobiech (GER)	18.01.1991	6		1
Kevin Wimmer (AUT)	15.11.1992	17		
Midfielders:	**DOB**	**M**	**(s)**	**G**
Aleix García Serrano (ESP)	28.06.1997	22	(1)	5
Marko Bakić (MNE)	01.11.1993	8	(5)	

	DOB	M	(s)	G
Frank Thierry Boya (CMR)	01.07.1996	28		2
Jonathan Buatu Mananga (ANG)	27.09.1993		(2)	
Deni Hočko (MNE)	22.04.1994	24		
Dimitri Mohamed (FRA)	11.06.1989	11	(5)	1
Sebastjan Spahiu	30.10.1999		(2)	
Benjamin Van Durmen	20.03.1997	11	(13)	
Forwards:	**DOB**	**M**	**(s)**	**G**
Sami Allagui (TUN)	28.05.1986	10	(2)	2
Zakaria Atteri	15.02.2001		(1)	
Babacar Dione	22.03.1997		(2)	
Alexandre Ippolito	05.01.1999		(3)	
Fabrice Olinga Essono (CMR)	12.05.1996	23	(2)	3
Cedric Omoigui (NGA)	11.11.1994	3	(3)	1
Jonah Osabutey (GHA)	08.10.1998	19	(3)	5
Stipe Perica (CRO)	07.07.1995	9	(6)	7
Frantzdy Pierrot (HAI)	07.01.1997		(3)	
Dylan Seys	26.09.1996		(1)	

Koninklijke Voetbalclub Oostende

Founded:	1904		
Stadium:	Versluys Arena, Ostend (8,432)		
Trainer:	Kåre Hedley Ingebrigtsen (NOR)		11.11.1965
[31.12.2019]	Dennis Johannes van Wijk (NED)		16.12.1962
[03.03.2020]	Adnan Čustović (BIH)		16.04.1978

Goalkeepers:	DOB	M	(s)	G
William Dutoit (FRA)	18.09.1988	24		
Joseph Fabrice Ondoa Ebogo (CMR)	24.12.1995	5		
Defenders:	**DOB**	**M**	**(s)**	**G**
Jelle Bataille	20.05.1999	23	(1)	2
Brecht Capon	24.04.1988	13	(3)	
Wout Faes	03.04.1998	28		
Goran Milović (CRO)	29.01.1989	28		
Logan Ndenbe	09.02.2000	7		
Yakhya Sané (SEN)	04.08.1989	4	(1)	
Bubacarr Sanneh (GAM)	14.11.1994	3		
Ari Skúlason (ISL)	14.05.1987	22		3
Midfielders:	**DOB**	**M**	**(s)**	**G**
Indy Boonen	04.01.1999	2	(10)	
Robbie D'Haese	25.02.1999	9	(5)	
Fernando Canesin Matos (BRA)	27.02.1992	11	(5)	1

	DOB	M	(s)	G
Andrew Hjulsager (DEN)	15.01.1995	16	(3)	2
Michiel Jonckheere	03.01.1990	10	(8)	1
François Marquet	17.04.1995	3	(4)	1
Ante Palaversa (CRO)	06.04.2000	19		
Renato Cardoso Porto Neto (BRA)	27.09.1991	7	(3)	
Anton Tanghe	28.01.1999		(1)	
Kévin Vandendriessche (FRA)	07.08.1989	24	(2)	2
Ronald Alejandro Vargas Aranguren (VEN)	02.12.1986	10	(8)	3
Louis Verstraete	04.05.1999	3	(1)	
Forwards:	**DOB**	**M**	**(s)**	**G**
Joseph Akpala (NGA)	24.08.1986	5	(1)	1
Sindri Guri (ALB)	23.10.1993	3	(12)	2
Adama Niane (MLI)	16.06.1993	4	(1)	
Nicolas Antoine Rajsel (SVN)	31.05.1993	1	(1)	
Fashion Sakala (ZAM)	14.03.1997	24	(4)	8
Idrissa Sylla (GUI)	03.12.1990	11	(6)	2

Koninklijke Sint-Truidense Voetbalvereniging

Founded:	1924		
Stadium:	Stayen Stadium, Sint-Truiden (14,600)		
Trainer:	Marc Brys	10.05.1962	
[26.11.2019]	Nicky Hayen	16.08.1980	
[03.01.2020]	Miloš Kostić (SVN)	23.11.1971	
[05.06.2020]	Kevin Vincent Muscat (AUS)	07.08.1973	

Goalkeepers:	DOB	M	(s)	G
Daniel Yuji Yakubi Schmidt (JPN)	03.02.1992	20		
Kenny Steppe	14.11.1988	9		
Defenders:	**DOB**	**M**	**(s)**	**G**
Rocky Bushiri	30.11.1999	6	(1)	
Thibault De Smet	05.06.1998	12		
Wataru Endo (JPN)	09.02.1993	1	(2)	
Avelino Jorge Filipe Teixeira (POR)	27.08.1986	8		1
Mory Konaté (GUI)	01.01.1993	2		1
Ko Matsubara (JPN)	30.08.1996	1		
Samy Mmaee	08.09.1996	21	(1)	
Pol García Tena (ESP)	18.02.1995	20	(1)	1
Midfielders:	**DOB**	**M**	**(s)**	**G**
Allan Gonçalves Sousa (BRA)	27.01.1997	9	(14)	
Samuel Asamoah (GHA)	23.03.1994	20	(7)	4
Jordan Botaka (COD)	24.06.1993	25	(3)	3
Santiago Colombatto (ARG)	17.01.1997	18	(1)	
Alexandre De Bruyn	04.06.1994	24	(1)	3

	DOB	M	(s)	G
Steve De Ridder	25.02.1987	8	(4)	
Chris Durkin (USA)	08.02.2000	10	(3)	1
Hamza Masoudi	24.01.2000	5	(1)	1
Ibrahima Sankhon (GUI)	01.01.1996	25		
Stan Van Dessel	24.07.2001	1	(4)	
Forwards:	**DOB**	**M**	**(s)**	**G**
Elton Acolatse (NED)	25.07.1995	10	(8)	
Nelson Balongo (COD)	15.04.1999	5	(2)	
Yohan Boli (FRA)	17.11.1993	15	(2)	10
Facundo Colidio (ARG)	04.01.2000	7	(5)	1
Công Phượng Nguyễn (VIE)	21.01.1995		(1)	
Tatsuya Ito (JPN)	26.06.1997		(7)	
Wolke Janssens	01.08.1995	15	(3)	
Lee Seung-woo (KOR)	06.01.1998	2	(2)	
Duckens Moses Nazon (HAI)	07.04.1994		(1)	
Yuma Suzuki (JPN)	26.04.1996	20	(4)	7
Mathieu Troonbeeckx	16.02.1998		(3)	

Royal Standard de Liège

Founded:	1898	
Stadium:	Stade "Maurice Dufrasne", Liège (27,670)	
Trainer:	Michel Jean Georges Ghislain Preud'homme	24.01.1959

Goalkeepers:	DOB	M	(s)	G
Arnaud Bodart	11.03.1998	29		
Defenders:	**DOB**	**M**	**(s)**	**G**
Noë Dussenne	07.04.1992	1	(1)	
Collins Fai (CMR)	13.08.1992	5	(3)	
Nicolas Gavory (FRA)	16.02.1995	29		
Réginal Goreux (HAI)	31.12.1987	1		
Miloš Kosanović (SRB)	28.05.1990	3		
Kostas Laifis (CYP)	19.05.1993	28		3
Dimitri Lavalée	13.01.1997	3	(2)	
Senna Miangue	05.02.1997		(4)	
Zinho Vanheusden	29.07.1999	20		1
Mergim Vojvoda (KVX)	01.02.1995	24	(1)	1
Midfielders:	**DOB**	**M**	**(s)**	**G**
Selim Amallah	15.11.1996	21	(4)	7
Samuel Bastien	26.09.1996	26		4

Bopé Bokadi (COD)	21.05.1996	5	(1)	
Joachim Carcela-González	16.12.1999		(1)	
Gojko Cimirot (BIH)	19.12.1992	27		1
Nicolas Raskin	23.02.2001	1	(1)	
Eden Shamir (ISR)	25.06.1995	2	(1)	
Forwards:	**DOB**	**M**	**(s)**	**G**
Felipe Nicolás Avenatti Dovillabichus (URU)	26.04.1993	5	(13)	2
Aleksandar Boljević (MNE)	12.12.1995	7	(14)	3
Mehdi Carcela-González (MAR)	01.07.1989	17	(9)	3
Duje Čop (CRO)	01.02.1990	5	(7)	1
Denis Mihai Drăguş (ROU)	06.07.1999		(2)	
Renaud Emond	05.12.1991	10	(4)	7
Maxime Lestienne	17.06.1992	24	(3)	7
Anthony Limbombe Ekango	15.07.1994	2	(4)	1
Paul-José Mpoku Ebunge (COD)	19.04.1992	15	(3)	3
Obbi Oularé	08.01.1996	9	(5)	2

Koninklijke Voetbalclub Red Star Waasland-Sportkring-Beveren

Founded:	2010 (*merged with KSK Beveren*)		
Stadium:	Freethiel Stadion, Beveren (8,190)		
Trainer:	Adnan Čustović (BIH)	16.04.1978	
[26.08.2019]	Dirk Geeraerd	02.12.1963	
[02.09.2019]	Arnauld Mercier (FRA)	04.06.1972	
[23.02.2020]	Dirk Geeraerd	02.12.1963	

Goalkeepers:	DOB	M	(s)	G
Brent Gabriël	27.01.1999	3		
Nordin Jackers	05.09.1997	16		
Lucas Pirard	10.03.1995	10		
Defenders:	**DOB**	**M**	**(s)**	**G**
Maximiliano Caufriez	16.02.1997	29		
Daam Foulon	23.03.1999	21	(2)	
Alexis Yohaslin Gamboa Rojas (CRC)	20.03.1999	3	(2)	
Valtteri Moren (FIN)	15.06.1991	5		
Jur Schryvers	11.03.1997	27	(1)	1
Andrija Vukčević (MNE)	11.10.1996	8	(3)	
Aleksandar Vukotić (SRB)	22.07.1995	26	(1)	2
Andreas Wiegel (GER)	21.07.1991	23		1
Midfielders:	**DOB**	**M**	**(s)**	**G**
Djihad Bizimana (RWA)	12.12.1996	13	(2)	
Fiorin Durmishaj (ALB)	14.11.1996	5	(3)	
Xian Emmers	20.07.1999	5	(3)	

Daan Heymans	15.06.1999	2	(3)	
Denzel Jubitana	06.05.1999	8	(7)	
Paul Keita (SEN)	23.06.1992	1		
Yuki Kobayashi (JPN)	24.04.1992	14	(6)	2
Jakub Piotrowski (POL)	04.10.1997	3	(2)	
Aaron Tshibola (ENG)	02.01.1995	8		
Matthias Verreth	20.02.1998	10	(8)	1
Forwards:	**DOB**	**M**	**(s)**	**G**
Thomas Agyepong (GHA)	10.10.1995	5	(9)	
Eric Asomani (GHA)	08.11.1999		(1)	
Beni Badibanga	19.02.1996	22	(6)	2
Olivier Dhauholou (CIV)	06.06.1997		(1)	
Tuur Dierckx	09.05.1995	13	(4)	3
Francesco Forte (ITA)	01.05.1993	4		1
Aboubakary Koita	20.09.1998	19	(3)	2
Stefan Milošević (MNE)	23.06.1996	9	(9)	3
Din Sula (ALB)	02.03.1998	7	(11)	2

Sportvereniging Zulte Waregem

Founded:	01.07.2001		
Stadium:	Regenboogstadion, Waregem (12,250)		
Trainer:	Francky Dury		11.10.1957

Goalkeepers:	DOB	M	(s)	G
Eike Bansen (GER)	21.02.1998	6		
Sammy Bossut	11.08.1985	23		
Defenders:	**DOB**	**M**	**(s)**	**G**
Marvin Baudry (CGO)	26.01.1990	5	(3)	
Marco Bürki (SUI)	10.07.1993	12	(4)	
Davy De fauw	08.07.1981	29		6
Olivier Deschacht	16.02.1981	24		
Cameron Humphreys Grant (ENG)	22.08.1998	1	(2)	
Gideon Mensah (GHA)	18.07.1998	19		
Ewoud Pletinckx	10.10.2000	19	(2)	
George Christos Timotheou (AUS)	29.07.1997		(1)	
Sandy Walsh (NED)	14.03.1995	6	(3)	
Midfielders:	**DOB**	**M**	**(s)**	**G**
Mathieu De Smet	27.04.2000		(3)	
Omar Nicolás Govea García (MEX)	18.01.1996	19	(2)	2

	DOB	M	(s)	G
Damien Marcq (FRA)	08.12.1988	13	(3)	1
Ibrahima Seck (SEN)	10.08.1989	21		2
Abdoulaye Sissako (FRA)	26.05.1998	14	(6)	1
Bassem Srarfi (TUN)	25.06.1997		(4)	
Jannes Van Hecke	15.01.2002	1	(1)	
Forwards:	**DOB**	**M**	**(s)**	**G**
Saido Berahino (BDI)	04.08.1993	17	(1)	6
Henrik Bjørdal (NOR)	04.02.1997	12	(8)	2
Gianni Bruno	19.08.1991	23	(4)	9
Jean-Luc Dompé (FRA)	12.08.1995	2	(4)	
Nikolaos Kenourgios (GRE)	08.09.1998	2	(1)	
Cyle Larin (CAN)	17.04.1995	28	(1)	7
Dimitri Oberlin (SUI)	27.09.1997	6	(12)	2
Mikael Soisalo (FIN)	24.04.1998		(2)	
Jelle Vossen	22.03.1989	6		2
Luka Zarandia (GEO)	17.02.1996	11	(7)	

SECOND LEVEL
First Division B 2019/2020

Opening Tournament

1.	Oud-Heverle Leuven	14	9	2	3	22	-	10	29
2.	Royal Excelsior Virton	14	9	0	5	26	-	10	27
3.	KVC Westerlo	14	8	2	4	21	-	10	26
4.	Royale Union Saint-Gilloise	14	6	5	3	18	-	15	23
5.	K Beerschot VA	14	5	2	7	13	-	19	17
6.	KSC Lokeren	14	3	4	7	13	-	23	13
7.	KSV Roeselare	14	3	2	9	15	-	31	11
8.	Lommel SK	14	2	5	7	9	-	19	11

Oud-Heverle Leuven were qualified for the Promotion Play-offs.

Closing Tournament

1.	K Beerschot VA	13	7	5	1	18	-	8	26
2.	KVC Westerlo	14	7	2	5	24	-	20	23
3.	Royale Union Saint-Gilloise	14	5	7	2	25	-	17	22
4.	Royal Excelsior Virton	13	5	5	3	18	-	11	20
5.	Oud-Heverle Leuven	14	5	2	7	23	-	30	17
6.	Lommel SK	14	4	4	6	12	-	18	16
7.	KSV Roeselare	14	2	9	3	22	-	23	15
8.	KSC Lokeren	14	1	4	9	11	-	26	7

K Beerschot VA were qualified for the Promotion Play-offs.

Aggregate Table

1.	KVC Westerlo	28	15	4	9	45	-	30	49
2.	Royal Excelsior Virton[1] (*Relegated*)	27	14	5	8	44	-	21	47
3.	**Oud-Heverle Leuven**	28	14	4	10	45	-	40	46
4.	Royale Union Saint-Gilloise	28	11	12	5	43	-	32	45
5.	**K Beerschot VA**	27	12	7	8	31	-	27	43
6.	Lommel SK	28	6	9	13	21	-	37	27
7.	KSV Roeselare[2] (*Relegated*)	28	5	11	12	37	-	54	26
8.	KSC Lokeren (dissolved)	28	4	8	16	24	-	49	20

[1]Royal Excelsior Virton were refused on 12.05.2020 a professional license and were relegated.
[2] KSV Roeselare were refused on 11.05.2020 a professional license and were relegated.

KSC Lokeren went bankrupt and was dissolved at the end of Closing Tournament.

Promotion Play-off [08.03.-02.08.2020]

K Beerschot VA - Oud-Heverle Leuven	1-0(1-0)	4-1(1-0)

Please note: both Oud-Heverle Leuven and K Beerschot VA were promoted for next saison's first level as Belgian Pro League voted in favour of expanding the 2020/2021 Eerste Divisie to 18 teams.

BELGIUM NATIONAL TEAM

INTERNATIONAL MATCHES
(16.07.2019 – 15.07.2020)

06.09.2019	Serravalle	San Marino - Belgium	0-4(0-1)	(ECQ)
09.09.2019	Glasgow	Scotland - Belgium	0-4(0-3)	(ECQ)
10.10.2019	Bruxelles	Belgium - San Marino	9-0(6-0)	(ECQ)
13.10.2019	Nur-Sultan	Kazakhstan - Belgium	0-2(0-1)	(ECQ)
16.11.2019	Saint Petersburg	Russia - Belgium	1-4(0-3)	(ECQ)
19.11.2019	Bruxelles	Belgium - Cyprus	6-1(4-1)	(ECQ)

06.09.2019   SAN MARINO - BELGIUM   0-4(0-1)   16th EC. Qualifiers
San Marino Stadium, Serravalle; Referee: Horațiu Feșnic (Romania); Attendance: 2,523
BEL: Thibaut Nicolas Marc Courtois, Thomas Meunier, Jan Bert Lieve Vertonghen, Tobias Albertine Maurits Alderweireld, Yannick Ferreira Carrasco, Jason Grégory Marianne Denayer, Kevin De Bruyne (Cap) (76.Dennis Pierre Jacques Albert Praet), Adnan Januzaj (56.Nacer Chadli), Youri Tielemans, Michy Batshuayi-Atunga, Divock Okoth Origi (55.Dries Mertens). Trainer: Roberto Martínez Montoliu (Spain).
Goals: Michy Batshuayi-Atunga (43 penalty), Dries Mertens (57), Nacer Chadli (63), Michy Batshuayi-Atunga (90+2).

09.09.2019   SCOTLAND - BELGIUM   0-4(0-3)   16th EC. Qualifiers
Hampden Park, Glasgow; Referee: Paweł Gil (Poland); Attendance: 25,524
BEL: Thibaut Nicolas Marc Courtois, Thomas Meunier (90.Benito Raman), Tobias Albertine Maurits Alderweireld, Thomas Vermaelen, Jan Bert Lieve Vertonghen, Nacer Chadli (77.Yannick Ferreira Carrasco), Kevin De Bruyne (Cap), Leander Dendoncker, Youri Tielemans (86.Yari Verschaeren), Dries Mertens, Romelu Menama Lukaku Bolingoli. Trainer: Roberto Martínez Montoliu (Spain).
Goals: Romelu Menama Lukaku Bolingoli (9), Thomas Vermaelen (24), Tobias Albertine Maurits Alderweireld (32), Kevin De Bruyne (82).

10.10.2019   BELGIUM - SAN MARINO   9-0(6-0)   16th EC. Qualifiers
Stade "Roi Baudouin", Bruxelles; Referee: Anastasios Papapetrou (Greece); Attendance: 34,504
BEL: Thibaut Nicolas Marc Courtois, Thomas Vermaelen, Jan Bert Lieve Vertonghen, Tobias Albertine Maurits Alderweireld, Timothy Castagne, Nacer Chadli, Hans Vanaken, Youri Tielemans, Eden Michael Hazard (Cap) (63.Yannick Ferreira Carrasco), Dries Mertens (63.Yari Verschaeren), Romelu Menama Lukaku Bolingoli (76.Christian Benteke Liolo). Trainer: Roberto Martínez Montoliu (Spain).
Goals: Romelu Menama Lukaku Bolingoli (28), Nacer Chadli (31), Cristian Brolli (35 own goal), Romelu Menama Lukaku Bolingoli (41), Tobias Albertine Maurits Alderweireld (43), Youri Tielemans (45+1), Christian Benteke Liolo (79), Yari Verschaeren (84 penalty), Timothy Castagne (90).

13.10.2019   KAZAKHSTAN - BELGIUM   0-2(0-1)   16th EC. Qualifiers
Astana Arena, Nur-Sultan; Referee: Gediminas Mažeika (Lithuania); Attendance: 26,801
BEL: Thibaut Nicolas Marc Courtois, Thomas Meunier, Thomas Vermaelen (90+2.Brandon Mechele), Jan Bert Lieve Vertonghen, Tobias Albertine Maurits Alderweireld, Axel Tomas Laurent Angel Lambert Witsel, Dennis Pierre Jacques Albert Praet, Eden Michael Hazard (Cap), Thorgan Ganael Francis Hazard, Dries Mertens (78.Yannick Ferreira Carrasco), Michy Batshuayi-Atunga (78.Christian Benteke Liolo). Trainer: Roberto Martínez Montoliu (Spain).
Goals: Michy Batshuayi-Atunga (21), Thomas Meunier (53).

16.11.2019   RUSSIA - BELGIUM   1-4(0-3)   16th EC. Qualifiers
Krestovsky Stadium, Saint Petersburg; Referee: Artur Manuel Soares Dias (Portugal); Attendance: 53,317
BEL: Thibaut Nicolas Marc Courtois, Thomas Vermaelen (67.Jason Grégory Marianne Denayer), Tobias Albertine Maurits Alderweireld, Anga Dedryck Boyata, Timothy Castagne, Axel Tomas Laurent Angel Lambert Witsel, Kevin De Bruyne, Eden Michael Hazard (Cap),Thorgan Ganael Francis Hazard, Dries Mertens (52.Youri Tielemans), Romelu Menama Lukaku Bolingoli (77.Michy Batshuayi-Atunga). Trainer: Roberto Martínez Montoliu (Spain).
Goals: Thorgan Ganael Francis Hazard (19), Eden Michael Hazard (33, 40), Romelu Menama Lukaku Bolingoli (72).

19.11.2019   BELGIUM - CYPRUS   6-1(4-1)   16th EC. Qualifiers
Stade "Roi Baudouin", Bruxelles; Referee: Jørgen Burchardt (Denmark); Attendance: 40,568
BEL: Simon Mignolet, Tobias Albertine Maurits Alderweireld, Jason Grégory Marianne Denayer, Elias Cobbaut, Kevin De Bruyne (68.Dennis Pierre Jacques Albert Praet), Hans Vanaken, Yannick Ferreira Carrasco, Youri Tielemans, Eden Michael Hazard (Cap) (64.Yari Verschaeren), Thorgan Ganael Francis Hazard, Christian Benteke Liolo (79.Divock Okoth Origi). Trainer: Roberto Martínez Montoliu (Spain).
Goals: Christian Benteke Liolo (16), Kevin De Bruyne (36), Kevin De Bruyne (41), Yannick Ferreira Carrasco (44), Kypros Hristoforo (51 own goal), Christian Benteke Liolo 68).

NATIONAL TEAM PLAYERS
(16.07.2019 – 15.07.2020)

Name	DOB	Caps	Goals	2019/2020:	Club
Goalkeepers					
Thibaut Nicolas Marc COURTOIS	11.05.1992	79	0	2019:	*Real Madrid CF (ESP)*
Simon Luc Hildebert MIGNOLET	06.03.1988	23	0	2019:	*Club Brugge KV*
Defenders					
Tobias Albertine Maurits ALDERWEIRELD	02.03.1989	98	5	2019:	*Tottenham Hotspur FC London (ENG)*
Anga Dedryck BOYATA	28.11.1990	17	0	2019:	*Hertha BSC Berlin (GER)*
Timothy CASTAGNE	05.12.1995	7	2	2019:	*Atalanta Bergamasca Calcio (ITA)*
Elias COBBAUT	24.11.1997	1	0	2019:	*RSC Anderlecht Bruxelles*
Jason Grégory Marianne DENAYER	28.06.1995	13	0	2019:	*Olympique Lyonnais (FRA)*
Leander DENDONCKER	15.04.1995	9	0	2019:	*Wolverhampton Wanderers FC (ENG)*
Brandon MECHELE	28.01.1993	1	0	2019:	*Club Brugge KV*
Thomas MEUNIER	12.09.1991	40	7	2019:	*Paris Saint-Germain FC (FRA)*
Thomas VERMAELEN	14.11.1985	78	2	2019:	*Vissel Kobe (JPN)*
Jan Bert Lieve VERTONGHEN	24.04.1987	118	9	2019:	*Tottenham Hotspur FC London (ENG)*
Midfielders					
Yannick Ferreira CARRASCO	04.09.1993	41	6	2019:	*Dalian Yifang FC (CHN)*
Nacer CHADLI	02.08.1989	59	8	2019:	*RSC Anderlecht Bruxelles*
Kevin DE BRUYNE	28.06.1991	74	19	2019:	*Manchester City FC (ENG)*
Adnan JANUZAJ	05.02.1995	12	1	2019:	*Real Sociedad San Sebastián (ESP)*
Dennis Pierre Jacques Albert PRAET	14.05.1994	6	0	2019:	*Leicester City FC (ENG)*
Youri TIELEMANS	07.05.1997	28	2	2019:	*Leicester City FC (ENG)*
Hans VANAKEN	24.08.1992	4	0	2019:	*Club Brugge KV*
Yari Verschaeren	12.07.2001	3	1	2019:	*RSC Anderlecht Bruxelles*
Axel Tomas Laurent Angel Lambert WITSEL	12.01.1989	103	9	2019:	*BV Borussia 09 Dortmund (GER)*
Forwards					
Michy BATSHUAYI-Atunga	02.10.1993	29	16	2019:	*Chelsea FC London (ENG)*
Christian BENTEKE Liolo	03.12.1990	37	15	2019:	*Crystal Palace FC London (ENG)*
Eden Michael HAZARD	07.01.1991	106	32	2019:	*Real Madrid CF (ESP)*
Thorgan Ganael Francis HAZARD	29.03.1993	23	3	2019:	*BV Borussia 09 Dortmund (GER)*
Romelu Menama LUKAKU Bolingoli	13.05.1993	84	52	2019:	*FC Internazionale Milano (ITA)*
Dries MERTENS	06.05.1987	90	18	2019:	*SSC Napoli (ITA)*
Divock Okoth ORIGI	18.04.1995	28	3	2019:	*Liverpool FC (ENG)*
Benito RAMAN	07.11.1994	1	0	2019:	*FC Schalke 04 Gelsenkirchen (GER)*
National team coach					
Roberto MARTÍNEZ Montoliu (Spain) [from 03.06.2016]	13.07.1973			43 M; 34 W; 6 D; 3 L; 134-33	

BOSNIA AND HERZEGOVINA

The Country:
Bosnia and Herzegovina (Bosna i Hercegovina / Босна и Херцеговина)
Capital: Sarajevo
Surface: 51,197 km²
Inhabitants: 3,301,000 [2019]
Time: UTC+1

The FA:
Nogometni/Fudbalski Savez Bosne i Hercegovine
Bulevar Meše Selimovica 95 71000, Sarajevo
Tel: +387 33 276 660
Foundation date: 1920 / 1992
Member of FIFA since: 1996
Member of UEFA since: 1998
Website: www.nfsbih.ba

NATIONAL TEAM RECORDS

RECORDS	
First international match:	30.11.1995, Tiranë Albania - Bosnia and Herzegovina 2-0
Most international caps:	Edin Džeko - 107 caps (since 2007)
Most international goals:	Edin Džeko - 58 goals / 107 caps (since 2007)

UEFA EUROPEAN CHAMPIONSHIP	
1960	-
1964	-
1968	-
1972	-
1976	-
1980	-
1984	-
1988	-
1992	-
1996	Did not enter
2000	Qualifiers
2004	Qualifiers
2008	Qualifiers
2012	Qualifiers
2016	Qualifiers
2020	*To be determined*

FIFA WORLD CUP	
1930	-
1934	-
1938	-
1950	-
1954	-
1958	-
1962	-
1966	-
1970	-
1974	-
1978	-
1982	-
1986	-
1990	-
1994	-
1998	Qualifiers
2002	Qualifiers
2006	Qualifiers
2010	Qualifiers
2014	Final Tournament (Group Stage)
2018	Qualifiers

OLYMPIC TOURNAMENTS	
1908	-
1912	-
1920	-
1924	-
1928	-
1936	-
1948	-
1952	-
1956	-
1960	-
1964	-
1968	-
1972	-
1976	-
1980	-
1984	-
1988	-
1992	-
1996	-
2000	Qualifiers
2004	Qualifiers
2008	Qualifiers
2012	Qualifiers
2016	Qualifiers

was part of Yugoslavia until 01.03.1992

UEFA NATIONS LEAGUE
2018/2019 – League B (promoted to League A)

FIFA CONFEDERATIONS CUP 1992-2017
None

BOSNIAN CLUB HONOURS IN EUROPEAN CLUB COMPETITIONS:

European Champion Clubs' Cup (1956-1992) / UEFA Champions League (1993-2020)
None

Fairs Cup (1858-1971) / UEFA Cup (1972-2009) / UEFA Europa League (2010-2020)
None

UEFA Super Cup (1972-2019)
None

*European Cup Winners' Cup 1961-1999**
None

defunct competition

NATIONAL COMPETITIONS
TABLE OF HONOURS

FIRST LEAGUE OF BOSNIA AND HERZEGOVINA CHAMPIONS	
1994/1995	NK Čelik Zenica
1995/1996	NK Čelik Zenica
1996/1997	NK Čelik Zenica
1997/1998	NK Bosna Visoko
1998/1999	FK Sarajevo
1999/2000	NK Jedinstvo Bihać

FIRST LEAGUE OF HERZEG-BOSNIA CHAMPIONS	
1993/1994	NK Široki Brijeg
1994/1995	NK Široki Brijeg
1995/1996	NK Široki Brijeg
1996/1997	NK Široki Brijeg
1997/1998	NK Široki Brijeg
1998/1999	NK Posušje
1999/2000	NK Posušje

FIRST LEAGUE OF THE REPUBLIKA SRPSKA CHAMPIONS	
1995/1996	FK Boksit Milići
1996/1997	FK Rudar Ugljevik
1997/1998	FK Rudar Ugljevik
1998/1999	FK Radnik Bijeljina
1999/2000	FK Boksit Milići
2000/2001	FK Borac Banja Luka
2001/2002	FK Leotar Trebinje

BOSNIA AND HERZEGOVINA CUP WINNERS	
1994/1995	NK Čelik Zenica
1995/1996	NK Čelik Zenica
1996/1997	FK Sarajevo
1997/1998	FK Sarajevo
1998/1999	NK Bosna Visoko

HERZEG-BOSNIA CUP WINNERS	
1994/1995	NK Bigeste Ljubuški
1995/1996	NK Bigeste Ljubuški
1996/1997	NK Troglav 1918 Livno
1997/1998	HNK Orašje
1998/1999	NK Brotnjo
1999/2000	HNK Orašje

REPUBLIKA SRPSKA CUP WINNERS	
1993/1994	FK Kozara Gradiška
1994/1995	FK Borac Banja Luka
1995/1996	FK Borac Banja Luka
1996/1997	FK Sloga Trn
1997/1998	FK Rudar Ugljevik
1998/1999	FK Rudar Ugljevik
1999/2000	FK Kozara Gradiška

	PLAYOFF CHAMPIONS	CUP WINNERS	BEST GOALSCORERS	
1997/1998	FK Željezničar Sarajevo	FK Sarajevo	Stanko Bubalo (CRO, NK Široki Brijeg) Hadis Zubanović (FK Željezničar Sarajevo)	3
1998/1999	FK Sarajevo (Regional NK Posušje winners FK Radnik Bijeljina shared)	No competition	-	
1999/2000	NK Brotnjo	FK Željezničar Sarajevo	Zikret Kuljaninović (FK Budućnost Banovići) Alen Škoro (FK Sarajevo) Halim Stupac (NK Jedinstvo Bihać)	5
	PREMIER LEAGUE			
2000/2001	FK Željezničar Sarajevo	FK Željezničar Sarajevo	Dželaludin Muharemović (FK Željezničar Sarajevo)	31
2001/2002	FK Željezničar Sarajevo	FK Sarajevo	Ivica Huljev (FK Željezničar Sarajevo)	15
2002/2003	FK Leotar Trebinje	FK Željezničar Sarajevo	Emir Obuća (FK Sarajevo)	24
2003/2004	NK Široki Brijeg	FK Modriča	Alen Škoro (FK Sarajevo)	20
2004/2005	HŠK Zrinjski Mostar	FK Sarajevo	Zoran Rajović (SRB, HŠK Zrinjski Mostar)	17
2005/2006	NK Široki Brijeg	HNK Orašje	Petar Jelić (FK Modriča)	19
2006/2007	FK Sarajevo	NK Široki Brijeg	Stevo Nikolić (FK Modriča) Dragan Benić (FK Borac Banja Luka)	19
2007/2008	FK Modriča	HŠK Zrinjski Mostar	Darko Spalević (SRB, FK Slavija Sarajevo)	18
2008/2009	HŠK Zrinjski Mostar	FK Slavija Sarajevo	Darko Spalević (SRB, FK Slavija Sarajevo)	17
2009/2010	FK Željezničar Sarajevo	FK Borac Banja Luka	Feđa Dudić (NK Travnik)	16
2010/2011	FK Borac Banja Luka	FK Željezničar Sarajevo	Ivan Lendrić (CRO, HŠK Zrinjski Mostar)	16
2011/2012	FK Željezničar Sarajevo	FK Željezničar Sarajevo	Eldin Adilović (FK Željezničar Sarajevo)	19
2012/2013	FK Željezničar Sarajevo	NK Široki Brijeg	Emir Hadžić (FK Sarajevo)	20
2013/2014	HŠK Zrinjski Mostar	FK Sarajevo	Wagner Santos Lago (BRA, NK Široki Brijeg)	18
2014/2015	FK Sarajevo	FK Olimpik Sarajevo	Riad Bajić (FK Željezničar Sarajevo)	15
2015/2016	HŠK Zrinjski Mostar	FK Radnik Bijeljina	Leon Benko (CRO, FK Sarajevo)	17
2016/2017	HŠK Zrinjski Mostar	NK Široki Brijeg	Ivan Lendrić (CRO, FK Željezničar Sarajevo)	19
2017/2018	HŠK Zrinjski Mostar	FK Željezničar Sarajevo	Miloš Filipović (SRB, HŠK Zrinjski Mostar)	16
2018/2019	FK Sarajevo	FK Sarajevo	Sulejman Krpić (FK Sarajevo)	16
2019/2020	FK Sarajevo	Competition cancelled	Mersudin Ahmetović (FK Sarajevo)	13

Results

Round 1 [20-22.07.2019]
Velež Mostar - FK Mladost 1-3(0-1)
FK Zvijezda 09 - FK Tuzla City 1-5(0-3)
FK Željezničar - Borac Banja Luka 0-0
FK Sarajevo - Zrinjski Mostar 1-0(0-0)
Sloboda Tuzla - Radnik Bijeljina 2-1(1-0)
Široki Brijeg - Čelik Zenica 0-1(0-0)

Round 2 [27-28.07.2019]
FK Mladost - FK Željezničar 0-2(0-0)
Radnik Bijeljina - FK Tuzla City 3-0(3-0)
Borac Banja Luka - FK Zvijezda 09 1-0(1-0)
Sloboda Tuzla - Široki Brijeg 2-2(1-1)
Zrinjski Mostar - Velež Mostar 1-0(0-0)
Čelik Zenica - FK Sarajevo 0-0

Round 3 [03-04.08.2019]
Velež Mostar - Čelik Zenica 1-2(1-0)
FK Zvijezda 09 - FK Mladost 1-1(1-0)
FK Tuzla City - Borac Banja Luka 2-1(0-0)
FK Sarajevo - Sloboda Tuzla 3-0(1-0)
FK Željezničar - Zrinjski Mostar 1-0(0-0)
Široki Brijeg - Radnik Bijeljina 3-0(2-0)

Round 4 [10.08.2019]
FK Mladost - FK Tuzla City 0-1(0-0)
Radnik Bijeljina - Borac Banja Luka 1-2(1-0)
Čelik Zenica - FK Željezničar 0-2(0-0)
Sloboda Tuzla - Velež Mostar 0-0
Zrinjski Mostar - Zvijezda 09 3-0(2-0) [28.08.]
Široki Brijeg - FK Sarajevo 0-0 [28.08.]

Round 5 [17-19.08.2019]
Velež Mostar - Široki Brijeg 1-0(1-0)
FK Zvijezda 09 - Čelik Zenica 2-2(1-0)
Borac Banja Luka - FK Mladost 0-0
FK Željezničar - Sloboda Tuzla 2-2(2-1)
FK Tuzla City - Zrinjski Mostar 0-0
FK Sarajevo - Radnik Bijeljina 2-1(1-0)

Round 6 [24.08.2019]
Čelik Zenica - FK Tuzla City 0-0
Radnik Bijeljina - FK Mladost 3-0(1-0)
FK Sarajevo - Velež Mostar 2-1(0-1)
Sloboda Tuzla - FK Zvijezda 09 1-0(0-0)
Široki Brijeg - FK Željezničar 3-3(3-1)
Zrinjski Mostar - Borac Banja Luka 4-0(0-0)

Round 7 [31.08.-01.09.2019]
FK Mladost - Zrinjski Mostar 0-2(0-0)
Velež Mostar - Radnik Bijeljina 0-1(0-0)
FK Zvijezda 09 - Široki Brijeg 0-0
FK Željezničar - FK Sarajevo 5-2(2-2)
FK Tuzla City - Sloboda Tuzla 2-1(0-0)
Borac Banja Luka - Čelik Zenica 3-1(2-1)

Round 8 [14-15.09.2019]
Čelik Zenica - FK Mladost 1-0(0-0)
Radnik Bijeljina - Zrinjski Mostar 1-0(0-0)
Velež Mostar - FK Željezničar 1-1(1-0)
Sloboda Tuzla - Borac Banja Luka 3-1(2-1)
FK Sarajevo - FK Zvijezda 09 2-0(1-0)
Široki Brijeg - FK Tuzla City 1-3(1-1)

Round 9 [21-22.09.2019]
FK Mladost - Sloboda Tuzla 2-0(1-0)
FK Tuzla City - FK Sarajevo 2-1(1-0)
Borac Banja Luka - Široki Brijeg 1-1(0-1)
FK Željezničar - Radnik Bijeljina 1-0(0-0)
Zrinjski Mostar - Čelik Zenica 3-0(2-0)
FK Zvijezda 09 - Velež Mostar 1-2(0-0)

Round 10 [25.09.2019]
Radnik Bijeljina - Čelik Zenica 2-1(2-1)
Sloboda Tuzla - Zrinjski Mostar 0-3(0-1)
Velež Mostar - FK Tuzla City 2-1(0-1)
FK Sarajevo - Borac Banja Luka 1-0(0-0)
Široki Brijeg - FK Mladost 3-2(1-2)
FK Željezničar - FK Zvijezda 09 6-0(3-0)

Round 11 [28-29.09.2019]
FK Tuzla City - FK Željezničar 2-2(1-1)
FK Zvijezda 09 - Radnik Bijeljina 1-4(1-0)
Čelik Zenica - Sloboda Tuzla 0-0
FK Mladost - FK Sarajevo 0-3(0-2)
Zrinjski Mostar - Široki Brijeg 1-3(1-1)
Borac Banja Luka - Velež Mostar 3-1(1-1)

Round 12 [05-06.10.2019]
FK Tuzla City - FK Zvijezda 09 3-0(0-0)
Čelik Zenica - Široki Brijeg 2-0(0-0)
Radnik Bijeljina - Sloboda Tuzla 3-2(2-2)
Zrinjski Mostar - FK Sarajevo 0-0
FK Mladost - Velež Mostar 2-2(2-0)
Borac Banja Luka - FK Željezničar 3-0(1-0)

Round 13 [18-20.10.2019]
FK Sarajevo - Čelik Zenica 2-0(0-0)
Velež Mostar - Zrinjski Mostar 1-0(0-0)
FK Tuzla City - Radnik Bijeljina 0-3(0-0)
FK Zvijezda 09 - Borac Banja Luka 0-2(0-1)
FK Željezničar - FK Mladost 2-1(0-1)
Široki Brijeg - Sloboda Tuzla 2-0(1-0)

Round 14 [25-27.10.2019]
FK Mladost - FK Zvijezda 09 1-0(0-0)
Čelik Zenica - Velež Mostar 0-2(0-0)
Zrinjski Mostar - FK Željezničar 2-1(1-0)
Radnik Bijeljina - Široki Brijeg 0-0
Sloboda Tuzla - FK Sarajevo 1-1(0-1)
Borac Banja Luka - FK Tuzla City 2-0(1-0)

Round 15 [02-03.11.2019]
Velež Mostar - Sloboda Tuzla 2-2(1-1)
FK Zvijezda 09 - Zrinjski Mostar 2-0(1-0)
FK Tuzla City - FK Mladost 1-0(1-0)
FK Sarajevo - Široki Brijeg 3-0(2-0)
FK Željezničar - Čelik Zenica 3-0 *awarded*
Borac Banja Luka - Radnik Bijeljina 2-0(0-0)

Round 16 [09-10.11.2019]
Čelik Zenica - FK Zvijezda 09 2-1(2-1)
Radnik Bijeljina - FK Sarajevo 1-1(0-0)
Zrinjski Mostar - FK Tuzla City 4-0(2-0)
Sloboda Tuzla - FK Željezničar 0-4(0-1)
FK Mladost - Borac Banja Luka 1-1(0-1)
Široki Brijeg - Velež Mostar 1-0(1-0)

Round 17 [23-24.11.2019]
FK Zvijezda 09 - Sloboda Tuzla 1-1(1-0)
Velež Mostar - FK Sarajevo 1-2(0-1)
FK Mladost - Radnik Bijeljina 0-4(0-3)
FK Tuzla City - Čelik Zenica 1-0(1-0)
Borac Banja Luka - Zrinjski Mostar 0-0
FK Željezničar - Široki Brijeg 1-2(1-1)

Round 18 [30.11.-01.12.2019]
Sloboda Tuzla - FK Tuzla City 1-1(1-0)
FK Sarajevo - FK Željezničar 1-3(1-1)
Zrinjski Mostar - FK Mladost 1-1(0-0)
Čelik Zenica - Borac Banja Luka 1-2(1-0)
Radnik Bijeljina - Velež Mostar 0-1(0-1)
Široki Brijeg - FK Zvijezda 09 4-0(2-0)

Round 19 [07-08.12.2019]
FK Tuzla City - Široki Brijeg 1-0(0-0)
FK Zvijezda 09 - FK Sarajevo 1-1(0-0)
Zrinjski Mostar - Radnik Bijeljina 1-0(0-0)
FK Mladost - Čelik Zenica 4-2(1-1)
FK Željezničar - Velež Mostar 0-2(0-1)
Borac Banja Luka - Sloboda Tuzla 2-1(1-0)

Round 20 [22-23.02.2020]
Radnik Bijeljina - FK Željezničar 0-0
Velež Mostar - FK Zvijezda 09 2-0(1-0)
FK Sarajevo - FK Tuzla City 6-2(2-1)
Sloboda Tuzla - FK Mladost 0-0
Čelik Zenica - Zrinjski Mostar 0-2(0-1)
Široki Brijeg - Borac Banja Luka 2-2(0-2)

Round 21 [28.02.-01.03.2020]
FK Tuzla City - Velež Mostar 0-0
FK Zvijezda 09 - FK Željezničar 0-3(0-2)
FK Mladost - Široki Brijeg 2-3(1-1)
Borac Banja Luka - FK Sarajevo 0-2(0-1)
Zrinjski Mostar - Sloboda Tuzla 2-0(2-0)
Čelik Zenica - Radnik Bijeljina 1-1(0-1)

Round 22 [07-08.03.2020]
Radnik Bijeljina - FK Zvijezda 09 5-1(2-0)
Sloboda Tuzla - Čelik Zenica 2-1(2-0)
FK Sarajevo - FK Mladost 2-1(1-1)
Velež Mostar - Borac Banja Luka 1-0(0-0)
FK Željezničar - FK Tuzla City 1-0(0-0)
Široki Brijeg - Zrinjski Mostar 1-1(1-1)

The season was interrupted on 08.03.2020 due to Covid-19 pandemic. On 01.06.2020, the competition was ended and FK Sarajevo declared champions.

Final Standings

			Total					Home					Away			
1. **FK Sarajevo**	22	13	6	3	38 - 19	45	10	0	1	25 - 8		3	6	2	13 - 11
2. FK Željezničar Sarajevo	22	12	6	4	43 - 21	42	7	2	2	22 - 9		5	4	2	21 - 12
3. HŠK Zrinjski Mostar	22	11	5	6	30 - 12	38	8	2	1	22 - 5		3	3	5	8 - 7
4. FK Borac Banja Luka	22	10	6	6	29 - 23	36	7	3	1	17 - 6		3	3	5	12 - 17
5. FK Tuzla City	22	10	5	7	27 - 29	35	7	3	1	14 - 8		3	2	6	13 - 21
6. FK Radnik Bijeljina	22	10	4	8	34 - 21	34	6	3	2	19 - 8		4	1	6	15 - 13
7. NK Široki Brijeg	22	8	8	6	31 - 26	32	5	4	2	20 - 12		3	4	4	11 - 14
8. FK Velež Mostar	22	9	5	8	25 - 23	32	5	2	4	14 - 13		4	3	4	11 - 10
9. FK Sloboda Tuzla	22	4	9	9	21 - 35	21	4	5	2	12 - 14		0	4	7	9 - 21
10. FK Mladost Doboj Kakanj	22	4	6	12	21 - 35	18	3	2	6	12 - 20		1	4	6	9 - 15
11. NK Čelik Zenica (*Relegated*)*	22	5	5	12	17 - 33	17	3	4	4	7 - 10		2	1	8	10 - 23
12. FK Zvijezda 09 Bijeljina (*Relegated*)	22	1	5	16	12 - 51	8	1	5	5	10 - 21		0	0	11	2 - 30

*<u>Please note</u>: NK Čelik Zenica (3 points deducted) were excluded from professional football and relegated to fourth level.

Top goalscorers:	
13 **Mersudin Ahmetović**	***FK Sarajevo***
12 Sulejman Krpić	*FK Željezničar Sarajevo*
12 Vojislav Ubiparip (SRB)	*FK Tuzla City*
12 Stojan Vranješ	*FK Borac Banja Luka*
10 Ubiratan Brandao de Souza (BRA)	*FK Velež Mostar*

NATIONAL CUP
Kup Bosne i Hercegovine u nogometu 2019/2020

First Round [18.09.2019]

FK Krupa na Vrbasu - FK Tuzla City	6-7 pen	FK Modriča - FK Zvijezda 09 Bijeljina	0-3
NK Bratstvo Gračanica - FK Velež Mostar	2-3	NK Jedinstvo - FK Mladost Doboj-Kakanj	1-2
FK Kozara Gradiška - Sloboda Tuzla	3-5 pen	FK Budućnost Banovići - NK Široki Brijeg	1-4 pen
NK GOŠK Gabela - FK Radnik Bijeljina	4-2 pen	NK Zvijezda Gradačac - HŠK Zrinjski Mostar	0-4
NK Sloga Ljubuški - FK Sarajevo	2-4	FK Rudar Kakanj - FK Slavija Sarajevo	4-1
FK Tekstilac Kort - FK Željezničar Sarajevo	0-3	FK Olimpik Sarajevo - FK Radnik Hadžići	2-1
HNK Orašje - FK Borac Banja Luka	0-4	FK Ljubić Prnjavor - NK Travnik	5-4 pen
FK Rudar Kakanj - NK Čelik Zenica	3-0	FK Skugrić 1964 - NK TOŠK Tešanj	0-10

1/8-Finals [02.10.2019]

HŠK Zrinjski Mostar - Sloboda Tuzla	2-0	FK Zvijezda 09 Bijeljina - FK Borac Banja Luka	0-6
FK Olimpik Sarajevo - NK TOŠK Tešanj	3-0	FK Tuzla City - FK Velež Mostar	1-0
FK Ljubić Prnjavor - NK GOŠK Gabela	0-2	FK Željezničar Sarajevo - FK Mladost Doboj-Kakanj	6-1
FK Rudar - FK Rudar Kakanj	4-5 pen	NK Široki Brijeg - FK Sarajevo	3-2

Quarter-Finals [04.03.2020]

FK Rudar Kakanj - NK GOŠK Gabela	0-3 (0-1)	NK Široki Brijeg - FK Olimpik Sarajevo	1-1 aet; 5-4 pen
HŠK Zrinjski Mostar - FK Tuzla City	2-1 (1-0)	FK Borac Banja Luka - FK Željezničar Sarajevo	0-2 (0-0)

Semi-Finals and Finals were cancelled due to Covid-19 pandemic. No title was awarded.

THE CLUBS 2019/2020

Fudbalski klub Borac Banja Luka

Founded:	04.07.1926	
Stadium:	Gradski stadion Banja Luka, Banja Luka (10,030)	
Trainer:	Branislav Krunic	28.01.1979
[05.03.2019]	Vlado Jagodić	22.03.1964

Goalkeepers:	DOB	M	(s)	G
Mladen Kukrika	11.01.1991	1	(1)	
Mladen Lučić	06.07.1985	21		
Defenders:	**DOB**	**M**	**(s)**	**G**
Denis Čomor	03.01.1990	5		
Đorđe Ćosić	11.09.1995	21	(1)	
Siniša Dujaković	22.11.1991	16		
Marin Galić	21.09.1995	1	(1)	
Nemanja Janičić (SRB)	13.07.1986	15		
Marko Jovanović (SRB)	26.03.1988	20		2
Nebojša Runić	12.10.1992	2	(2)	
Aleksandar Subić	27.09.1993	3		
Vladimir Volkov (MNE)	06.06.1986	5	(2)	
Midfielders:	**DOB**	**M**	**(s)**	**G**
Dejan Bosančić	02.06.1998	4	(2)	
David Čavić	21.11.2002		(1)	
Ivan Crnov (CRO)	01.02.1990	13	(6)	2
Vladan Danilović	27.07.1999	18	(2)	
Zoran Milutinović	01.03.1988	16	(4)	2
Aleksandar Radulović	09.02.1987	10	(9)	
Nikola Turanjanin	12.04.2001		(1)	
Stojan Vranješ	11.10.1986	22		12
Goran Zakarić	07.11.1992	2	(1)	1
Forwards:	**DOB**	**M**	**(s)**	**G**
Demir Jakupović	16.02.1996	2	(6)	1
Saša Kajkut	07.07.1984	12	(6)	5
Bojan Marković	13.11.1999		(3)	
Marko Mirić (SRB)	26.03.1987	14	(4)	1
Srđan Vujaklija (SRB)	23.03.1988	8	(9)	2
Dino Ziljkic (SRB)	25.02.1996	11	(3)	

Nogometni klub Čelik Zenica

Founded:	16.06.1945	
Stadium:	Stadion Bilino Polje, Zenica (15,292)	
Trainer:	Hasan Özer (TUR)	01.10.1974
[28.08.2019]	Almir Seferović	04.08.1976
[30.09.2019]	Marko Babić (CRO)	28.01.1981
[03.12.2019]	Slaviša Božičić	08.01.1966
[15.12.2019]	Igor Jović (AUT)	07.01.1975

Goalkeepers:	DOB	M	(s)	G
Bojan Pavlović (SRB)	08.11.1986	21		
Defenders:	**DOB**	**M**	**(s)**	**G**
Ante Blažević (CRO)	05.05.1996	10	(2)	
Slavko Brekalo	25.02.1990	7	(2)	
Almir Ćubara	21.11.1997	10		
Kenan Horić	13.09.1990	1		
Tarik Isić	08.10.1994	7	(2)	
Carlos Fabián León Filipetto (PAR)	06.02.1998	6	(2)	2
Azur Mahmić	06.05.2003	1	(1)	
Ljubiša Pecelj	29.09.1993	12	(1)	
Petar Raguž (CRO)	05.10.1996	3		
Emirhan Topçu (TUR)	11.10.2000	1		
Vedran Vrhovac	20.11.1998	19	(1)	1
Mladen Zeljković (SRB)	18.11.1987	3		
Midfielders:	**DOB**	**M**	**(s)**	**G**
Nikola Baban	29.09.1998		(1)	
Semir Bajraktarević	14.10.1987	2		
Nikola Bjeloš	03.08.1998		(2)	
Anel Dedić	02.05.1991	13	(1)	2
Vladimir Grahovac	12.01.1995	15	(4)	1
Nermin Jamak	25.08.1986	14	(1)	
Semir Musić	20.07.1995		(1)	
Marko Perišić	25.01.1991	19		
Ševkija Resić	04.12.1999	5	(7)	1
Fenan Salčinović	26.06.1987	7	(1)	
Selim Zuna	02.08.2000	6	(9)	
Forwards:	**DOB**	**M**	**(s)**	**G**
Almir Aganspahić	12.09.1996	5	(6)	
Drilon Cenaj	12.09.1997	1	(2)	
Mario Crnički (CRO)	04.02.1998		(1)	1
Haris Dilaver	06.02.1990	12	(2)	2
Volkan Egri (TUR)	02.04.1998	1		
Ermin Huseinbašić	11.07.1993	14	(3)	2
Ajdin Mahmutović	06.04.1986	5	(9)	5
Ševko Okić	26.07.1988	11	(2)	

Fudbalski klub Mladost Doboj Kakanj

Founded:	25.05.1959	
Stadium:	MGM Farm Arena, Doboj (3,000)	
Trainer:	Elvedin Beganović	07.11.1971
[02.09.2019]	Ibro Rahimić	17.04.1963
[27.11.2019]	Fahrudin Solbić	23.10.1958

Goalkeepers:	DOB	M	(s)	G
Tarik Abdulahović	18.04.1998	4		
Semir Bukvić	21.05.1991	9		
Emil Velić (SVN)	06.02.1995	9		
Defenders:	**DOB**	**M**	**(s)**	**G**
Branko Bajić	04.06.1998	13	(2)	
Arnel Delić	13.02.1992	6	(1)	
Ivan Dujmović	19.04.1998	9	(1)	
Aladin Isaković	28.07.1985	18		
Kenan Hreljic	01.12.1997	8	(1)	
Miloš Nikolić (SRB)	03.10.1994	1	(2)	
Nemanja Nikolić	21.02.2001	8		
Rijad Sadiku	18.01.2000	3		
Burak Yamaç (TUR)	29.03.1998		(2)	
Midfielders:	**DOB**	**M**	**(s)**	**G**
Amar Begić	07.08.2000	14	(1)	
Edin Biber	06.01.1999	10	(7)	
Anel Dedić	02.05.1991	1	(1)	
Benaris Duraković	16.03.2001	1	(1)	
Matthias Fanimo (ENG)	28.01.1994	17		5
Šerif Hasić	07.01.1988	14	(1)	
Amer Hiroš	10.06.1996	16	(1)	1
Kenan Horić	13.09.1990	14		1
Anes Hrustanović	13.03.2002	1	(3)	
Aleksandar Mirkov (SRB)	08.01.1996	1		
Kemal Mujarić	12.09.1999	3	(4)	
Semir Pezer	18.08.1992	1		
Anes Vazda	24.07.1997	11	(8)	4
Anes Vehab	28.09.1996	4	(3)	
Forwards:	**DOB**	**M**	**(s)**	**G**
Bahrudin Atajić	16.11.1993	13	(6)	2
Mario Daniel Crnički (CRO)	04.02.1998	10	(1)	2
Nemanja Dragutinović	09.04.1999	2	(4)	2
Nedim Hadžić	19.03.1999	8	(1)	3
Nikola Marić (CRO)	04.08.1997	2		
Mustafa Mušija	22.03.1998	1	(4)	1
Semir Smajlagić	18.09.1998	10	(6)	
Andrej Todorović	18.09.1998		(2)	

Fudbalski klub Radnik Bijeljina

Founded: 14.06.1945
Stadium: Stadion Gradski, Bijeljina (6,000)
Trainer: Mladen Žižović — 27.12.1980
[11.11.2019] Slobodan Starčević — 14.08.1971
[13.01.2020] Slavko Petrović (SRB) — 10.08.1958

Goalkeepers:	DOB	M	(s)	G
Luka Bilobrk	08.12.1985	18		
Dalibor Kozić	10.02.1988	4		
Defenders:	**DOB**	**M**	**(s)**	**G**
Srđan Bečelić (SRB)	08.06.1992	9	(4)	
Marko Despotović	20.10.1998	2	(1)	
Alem Merajić	04.02.1994	3	(2)	
Saša Novaković (CRO)	27.05.1991	2		
Slaviša Radović (SRB)	08.10.1993	19		
Miloš Simonović (SRB)	28.05.1990	19		
Ivan Šubert (SRB)	14.10.1993	21		
Pavle Sušić (SRB)	15.04.1988	2	(10)	1
Aleksandar Vasić	04.01.1985	12	(3)	
Midfielders:	**DOB**	**M**	**(s)**	**G**
Velibor Đurić	05.05.1982	21		7
Faruk Gogić	04.10.1999		(1)	
Eldar Hasanović	12.01.1990	5	(3)	
Stefan Janjić	11.02.1996		(1)	1
Dejan Maksimović	11.10.1995	14	(4)	6
Nedim Mekić	15.04.1995	18	(2)	1
Demir Peco	31.07.1996	21		3
Miloš Plavšić (SRB)	04.04.1990	7	(1)	2
Nikola Popara	08.03.1992	12	(1)	
Vilim Posinković (CRO)	10.01.1991	2	(3)	1
Forwards:	**DOB**	**M**	**(s)**	**G**
Vladimir Bradonjić	11.12.1999	9	(7)	7
Mahir Karić	14.12.1986	18	(1)	3
Jovan Motika	11.09.1998	1	(12)	1
Ševko Okić	26.07.1988	1	(1)	
Seid Zukić	09.04.1994	2	(7)	

Fudbalski klub Sarajevo

Founded: 24.10.1946
Stadium: Stadion "Asim Ferhatović Hase", Sarajevo (35,630)
Trainer: Husref Musemić — 04.07.1961
[30.12.2019] Vinko Marinović — 03.02.1971

Goalkeepers:	DOB	M	(s)	G
Elvis Džafić (SVN)	19.12.1990	2		
Vladan Kovačević	11.04.1998	20		
Defenders:	**DOB**	**M**	**(s)**	**G**
Amer Dupovac	29.05.1991	5		
Dušan Hodžić	31.10.1993	11	(4)	1
Numan Kurdić	01.07.1999	2	(1)	
Darko Lazić (SRB)	19.07.1994	15		
Bojan Letić	21.12.1992	12	(1)	
Hrvoje Miličević (CRO)	20.04.1993	3		1
Halid Šabanović	22.08.1999	10	(3)	
Besim Šerbečić	01.05.1998	20		2
Midfielders:	**DOB**	**M**	**(s)**	**G**
Andrej Đokanović	01.03.2001	11	(6)	
Nebojša Gavrić (SRB)	27.08.1991	15	(1)	
Gedeon Guzina	26.12.1993	5	(5)	
Anel Hebibović	07.07.1990	15		3
Ivan Jukić	21.06.1996	3		
Alen Mustafić	05.07.1999	5	(2)	1
Zinedin Mustedanagić	01.08.1998		(2)	
Mirko Oremuš (CRO)	06.09.1988	6	(2)	
Amar Rahmanović	13.05.1994	8	(4)	3
Đani Salčin	19.03.2000	3		
Miloš Stanojević (SRB)	20.11.1993	1	(5)	
Tino-Sven Sušić	13.02.1992	1	(1)	1
Aladin Šišić	28.09.1991	3	(5)	
Forwards:	**DOB**	**M**	**(s)**	**G**
Mersudin Ahmetović	19.03.1985	20		13
Haris Handžić	20.06.1990	3	(8)	2
Slobodan Milanović	27.08.1992	15	(2)	1
Nathan Crepaldi da Cruz (BRA)	28.05.1999		(3)	
Benjamin Tatar	18.05.1994	14	(3)	6
Krste Velkoski (MKD)	20.02.1988	14	(5)	2

Fudbalski Klub Sloboda Tuzla

Founded: 10.10.1919
Stadium: Stadion Tušanj, Tuzla (7,200)
Trainer: Mile Lazarević — 16.08.1960
[07.10.2019] Marijan Bloudek (SVN) — 23.08.1951
[18.10.2019] Milenko Bošnjaković — 04.03.1968
[18.12.2019] Gradimir Crnogorac — 14.11.1982

Goalkeepers:	DOB	M	(s)	G
Irfan Fejzić	01.07.1986	1		
Adnan Golubović (SVN)	22.07.1995	2		
Nikola Lakić	01.10.1995	19		
Anes Mehić	10.07.2002		(1)	
Defenders:	**DOB**	**M**	**(s)**	**G**
Amar Beganović	25.11.1999	19		
Almir Bekić	01.06.1989	18		
Perica Ivetić	28.11.1986	16	(1)	
Emir Jusić	13.06.1986	15	(1)	
Marko Marinković (SRB)	06.01.1994	2		
Asim Muratović	07.05.2001	3	(2)	
Marinko Rastoka	03.10.1991		(4)	
Adnan Salihović	18.10.1992	9	(2)	
Miloš Stojanović (SRB)	18.01.1997	2		
Dejan Uzelac (SRB)	29.11.1993	10	(1)	1
Midfielders:	**DOB**	**M**	**(s)**	**G**
Samir Bekrić	20.10.1984	18	(3)	4
Adnan Buljić	08.07.1997	3	(3)	
Haris Hajdarević	07.10.1998	3		
Elvedin Herić	09.02.1997	1	(1)	
Armin Hodžić	29.02.2000	8	(5)	1
Said Husejinović	17.05.1988	2	(1)	
Saša Maksimović	18.12.1999	12	(6)	2
Yoann Martelat (FRA)	16.01.1997	9	(1)	
Fedor Predragović	08.04.1991	1	(1)	
Omar Pršeš	07.05.1995	19		2
Dušan Ristić (SRB)	24.09.1997	8	(3)	
Edis Smajič	10.09.1999	5	(6)	1
Forwards:	**DOB**	**M**	**(s)**	**G**
Adi Alić	05.03.2002		(1)	
Amer Bekić	05.08.1992	11	(1)	7
Toni Livančić (CRO)	11.12.1994	15	(5)	1
Abid Mujagić	05.08.1993	10	(9)	
Eldin Omerović	26.05.2000		(1)	
Adnan Osmanović	20.03.1997	1	(5)	
Semir Smajlagić	18.09.1998		(2)	

Nogometni klub Široki Brijeg

Founded: 1948
Stadium: Stadion Pecara, Široki Brijeg (5,628)
Trainer: Denis Ćorić (CRO) — 10.12.1977
[16.09.2019] Toni Karačić — 06.12.1974

Goalkeepers:	DOB	M	(s)	G
Dario Miškić (CRO)	18.04.1996	3		
Martin Zlomislić	16.08.1998	19		
Defenders:	**DOB**	**M**	**(s)**	**G**
Josip Barišić	12.08.1983	9	(3)	
Branimir Cipetić (CRO)	24.05.1995	18		
Marko Jurić (CRO)	07.10.1994	2		
Josip Kvesič	21.09.1990	14	(1)	1
Bernardo Matić (CRO)	27.07.1994	18		1
Toni Nikić	27.03.1998	1		
Stjepan Radeljić	05.09.1997	3		1
Midfielders:	**DOB**	**M**	**(s)**	**G**
Mario Babić (CRO)	03.07.1992	1	(1)	
Zvonimir Begić	22.09.1990		(3)	
Dino Ćorić	30.06.1990	19		6
Ivan Enin (RUS)	06.02.1994	17		1
Petar Franjić (CRO)	21.08.1991	4	(7)	1
Marin Glavaš (CRO)	17.03.1992	2		
Ante Hrkać	11.03.1992	17	(2)	1
Dominik Kovačić (CRO)	05.01.1994	18		
Mateo Marić	18.03.1998	16	(1)	2
Marko Pervan (CRO)	04.04.1996	2	(1)	1
Mato Stanić	11.01.1998	9	(5)	
Bože Vukoja	03.04.1998	7	(6)	
Forwards:	**DOB**	**M**	**(s)**	**G**
Viktor Angelov (MKD)	27.03.1994	7	(1)	3
Dražen Bagarić (AUT)	12.11.1992	18		6
Toni Jović (CRO)	02.09.1992	13		5
Stipe Jurić	19.11.1998	1	(12)	1
Alen Jurilj	07.03.1996	4	(13)	1
Luka Knežević	14.03.1999		(2)	
Zvonimir Vukoja (CRO)	29.07.1997		(6)	

Fudbalski klub Tuzla City

Founded: 1955 (*as FK Sloga Simin Han*)
Stadium: Stadion Tušanj, Tuzla (7,200)
Trainer: Milenko Bošnjaković — 04.03.1968
[02.10.2019] Elvir Baljić — 08.07.1974

Goalkeepers:	DOB	M	(s)	G
Nevres Fejzić	04.11.1990	13	(1)	
Azir Muminović	18.04.1997	9	(1)	
Defenders:	**DOB**	**M**	**(s)**	**G**
Samir Efendić	10.05.1991	17		
Mirsad Hasanović (SUI)	03.07.1995	13	(1)	1
Jovo Kojić	08.04.1988	20		1
Ivan Kostić (SRB)	24.06.1989	2		
Nikola Leković (SRB)	19.12.1989	3		
Darrick-Kobie Morris (CRO)	15.07.1995	8	(1)	
Ermin Musić	28.05.1997	1		
Borislav Terzić	01.11.1991	13	(2)	
Nemanja Zlatković (SRB)	21.08.1988	14		
Midfielders:	**DOB**	**M**	**(s)**	**G**
Filip Arežina	08.11.1992	3		
Samir Burić	08.06.1998	1	(4)	1
Nermin Crnkić	31.08.1992	14	(4)	4
Adis Hadžanović	02.01.1993	8	(5)	
Said Huso Husejinović	17.05.1988	14	(2)	1
Muzafer Ivkovic	02.04.1998		(1)	
Huso Karjašević	10.07.1997		(5)	
Amar Kovčić	27.11.2000		(1)	
Belmin Mešinović	06.12.2001		(3)	
Ajdin Nukic	26.11.1997	17	(2)	1
Ivan Sesar	29.08.1989	20	(1)	
Nemanja Stjepanović (SRB)	07.02.1984	7	(9)	
Nassim Farouk Zitouni (ALG)	31.03.1994	1	(6)	
Forwards:	**DOB**	**M**	**(s)**	**G**
Badara Badji (SEN)	24.02.1994	1		
Dženis Beganović	23.03.1996	7	(2)	1
Vedin Kulović	12.12.1995	2		
Mirsad Ramić	06.12.1992	7	(13)	2
Budimir Šarčević (SRB)	05.01.1996	7	(2)	1
Vojislav Ubiparip (SRB)	10.05.1988	20		12

Fudbalski klub Velež Mostar

Founded: 26.06.1922
Stadium: Stadion Rođeni, Mostar (7,000)
Trainer: Ibro Rahimić — 17.04.1963
[05.08.2019] Feđa Dudić — 01.02.1983

Goalkeepers:	DOB	M	(s)	G
Adnan Bobić	04.02.1987	21		
Slaviša Bogdanović	11.10.1993	1		
Defenders:	**DOB**	**M**	**(s)**	**G**
Faruk Bihorać (SRB)	12.05.1996		(1)	
Muharem Čivić	04.01.1993	15	(4)	2
Fernando Darío Ferreyra	19.01.1997	15	(3)	
Elmir Kuduzović	28.02.1985		(3)	
Kosta Manev (FIN)	07.04.1993	19		
Uirá de Oliveira Marques (BRA)	22.07.1993	1		
Yani Urdinov (MKD)	28.03.1991	11		
Denis Zvonić	08.02.1992	20	(2)	2
Midfielders:	**DOB**	**M**	**(s)**	**G**
Nermin Alagić	03.05.2001		(2)	
Seid Behram	12.07.1998	8	(10)	1
Mehmed Ćosić	25.06.1997	20	(1)	1
Dino Hasanović	21.01.1996	18		
Vasko Kalezić (MNE)	14.03.1994	3	(7)	
Melvin Osmić	16.02.1999	2	(5)	
Omar Pršeš	07.05.1995	3		
Samir Radovac	25.01.1996	1	(1)	
Sinan Samardžić	27.01.1997	2	(4)	
Edo Vehabović	01.05.1995	17	(4)	3
Samir Zeljković	04.09.1997	17		1
Forwards:	**DOB**	**M**	**(s)**	**G**
Valmir Berisha (SWE)	06.06.1996	4	(5)	1
Ubiratan Brandao de Souza (BRA)	01.11.1995	22		10
Berin Ćatić	30.01.2000		(1)	
Obren Cvijanović	30.08.1994	1	(9)	1
Nusmir Fajić	12.01.1987	18	(1)	4
Haris Ovcina	24.10.1996	3	(2)	

Hrvatski športski klub Zrinjski Mostar

Founded:	1905			
Stadium:	Stadion pod Bijelim Brijegom, Mostar (20,000)			
Trainer:	Hari Vukas (CRO)			06.10.1972
[12.11.2019]	Mladen Žižović			27.12.1980

Goalkeepers:	DOB	M	(s)	G
Ivan Brkić (CRO)	29.06.1995	16		
Dinko Horkaš (CRO)	10.03.1999	3		
Antonio Soldo	12.01.1988	3		
Kenan Topolović	03.03.1998		(1)	
Defenders:	**DOB**	**M**	**(s)**	**G**
Tomislav Barbarić (CRO)	29.03.1989	15		1
Tomislav Barišić	06.03.1993	8	(2)	
Gabrijel Čoko	03.07.2001		(7)	
Josip Čorluka (CRO)	03.03.1995		(1)	
Renato Gojković	10.09.1995	11	(2)	1
Luis Ezequiel Ibáñez (ARG)	15.07.1988	5	(2)	
Slobodan Jakovljević (SRB)	26.05.1989	15		1
Advan Kadušić	14.10.1996	14	(1)	
Dario Rugašević (CRO)	29.01.1991	11	(1)	
Pero Stojkić	09.12.1986	8	(2)	1
Mario Tičinović (CRO)	20.08.1991	7		
Midfielders:	**DOB**	**M**	**(s)**	**G**
Jasmin Čeliković	07.01.1999	1		
Frane Čirjak (CRO)	23.06.1995	6	(10)	1
Ivan Ćurjurić (CRO)	30.11.1988	15	(4)	3
Miloš Filipović (SRB)	09.05.1990	3		1
Ivan Jajalo (CRO)	14.07.1998		(1)	
Robert Mišković (GER)	20.10.1999		(2)	
Semir Pezer	18.08.1992	2	(5)	
Edin Rustemović	06.01.1993	16		2
Damir Šovšić (CRO)	05.02.1990	12	(1)	2
Damir Zlomislić	20.07.1991	14	(1)	
Forwards:	**DOB**	**M**	**(s)**	**G**
Marko Bencun (CRO)	09.01.1992	2	(4)	
Nemanja Bilbija	02.11.1990	3		2
Miljan Govedarica	26.05.1994	10	(1)	3
Irfan Hadžić	15.06.1993	1	(1)	
Petar Kunić	15.07.1993	9	(5)	2
Ivan Lendrić (CRO)	08.08.1991	11	(5)	3
Staniša Mandić (MNE)	27.01.1995	15	(1)	1
Miljan Škrbić (SRB)	18.09.1995	2	(1)	1
Kristijan Stanić	20.04.2001	1	(4)	1
Asim Zec	23.01.1994	3		1

Fudbalski klub Zvijezda 09 Bijeljina

Founded:	2009		
Stadium:	Stadion u Ugljeviku, Ugljevik (5,000)		
Trainer:	Boris Savić		18.01.1988
[06.09.2019]	Slavoljub Bubanja (MNE)		12.07.1967
[09.10.2019]	Adnan Zildžović		28.10.1969

Goalkeepers:	DOB	M	(s)	G
Milun Avramovic	16.07.1998	5		
Strahinja Manojlović	11.08.2002	14		
Nikola Vujanac (SRB)	22.06.1991	3		
Defenders:	**DOB**	**M**	**(s)**	**G**
Dušan Babić (SRB)	07.01.1994	7		
Vukašin Benović	31.07.1986	17		
Luka Janković	20.08.2002	3	(1)	
Nikola Janković (SRB)	07.06.1993	3		
Slavko Lukić (SRB)	14.03.1989	1		
Vladan Mandić	10.04.1999	1		
Bojan Marković	12.11.1985	10	(3)	1
Danijel Matić	29.11.2000	1	(2)	
Haris Mehmedagić (CRO)	29.03.1988	15		
Kristijan Tojčić	06.12.1999	18	(1)	
Aleksandar Vojinović	03.10.1996	21		
Midfielders:	**DOB**	**M**	**(s)**	**G**
Esmir Ahmetovic (SRB)	17.01.1991	1		
Srđan Ajković (MNE)	13.10.1991		(7)	
Igor Blagojević (SRB)	18.01.2000	8	(9)	1
Caique Augusto Correia Chagas (BRA)	26.04.1994	19		
Ognjen Đelmić	18.08.1988	19	(2)	5
Ismar Hairlahović	04.03.1996	9		
Harun Karić	30.11.2002		(1)	
Aleksa Kovačević	05.06.2002		(1)	
Nemanja Parmaković (SRB)	24.06.1999	1	(5)	
Dejan Popara	10.03.2003	3		
Fedor Predragović	08.04.1995	16	(2)	2
Nemanja Rakić	19.06.2001	1		
Nikola Stanisić	22.02.2001	1		
Slaven Stjepanović (MNE)	02.11.1987	19		2
Christantus Ejike Uzoenyi (NGA)	23.03.1988	2		
Forwards:	**DOB**	**M**	**(s)**	**G**
Badara Badji (SEN)	24.02.1994	16		
Mohamed Malela Bangoura (GUI)	22.10.1998		(2)	
Nermin Haljeta (SVN)	07.06.1997	3		
Milivoje Lazić	19.09.1992	1		
Lucas Júnior Silva Santos (BRA)	16.02.1996		(6)	
Sreten Milošević	27.01.2002		(5)	
Edin Murga	21.12.1994	1		
Stefan Rakić	16.06.1998	1	(7)	
David Rukavina	21.02.2001		(2)	
Goran Šujić	20.01.2000	1	(2)	
Antonio Vidović	25.07.1989		(1)	
Dejan Zivković	21.08.2000	1	(5)	

Fudbalski klub Željezničar Sarajevo

Founded:	19.09.1921		
Stadium:	Stadion Grbavica, Sarajevo (14,000)		
Trainer:	Amar Osim		18.07.1967

Goalkeepers:	DOB	M	(s)	G
Filip Erić (SRB)	10.10.1994	16		
Vedran Kjosevski	22.05.1995	5		
Defenders:	**DOB**	**M**	**(s)**	**G**
Jadranko Bogičević	11.03.1983	5		1
Frane Ikić (CRO)	19.06.1994	2		
Aleksandar Jovanović (AUS)	04.08.1989	1		
Aleksandar Kosorić	30.01.1987	3		
Mustafa Mujezinović	06.05.1993	2	(9)	
Kemal Osmanković	04.03.1997	16		1
Antonio Pavić (CRO)	18.11.1994	14	(1)	
Siniša Stevanović (SRB)	12.01.1989	18		
Eldar Šehić	28.04.2000	1		
Enes Šipović	11.09.1990	15		1
Midfielders:	**DOB**	**M**	**(s)**	**G**
Mehmed Alispahić	24.11.1987	18	(1)	2
Petar Bojo	08.01.1998	14	(5)	2
Semir Dacić	10.04.1999		(3)	
Haris Hajdarević	07.10.1998	1	(5)	1
Nermin Jamak	25.08.1986	1	(1)	
Sinan Ramović	13.10.1992	9	(6)	1
Damir Sadiković	07.04.1995	20		2
Srđan Stanić	06.07.1989	9	(3)	
Semir Štilić	08.10.1987	9	(5)	8
Mladen Veselinović	04.01.1993	14	(4)	1
Forwards:	**DOB**	**M**	**(s)**	**G**
Sulejman Krpić	01.01.1991	18		12
Ivan Lendrić (CRO)	08.08.1991	3		1
Sedad Subašić	16.02.2001		(2)	
Dženan Zajmović	11.11.1994	3	(11)	2
Asim Zec	23.01.1994	6	(2)	2
Ermin Zec	18.02.1988	8	(3)	1

First League of the Federation of Bosnia and Herzegovina

1.	FK Olimpik Sarajevo (*Promoted*)	16	11	4	1	28 - 13	37
2.	NK TOŠK Tešanj	16	10	1	5	27 - 21	31
3.	FK Goražde	16	8	4	4	27 - 15	28
4.	NK GOŠK Gabela	16	8	4	4	30 - 25	28
5.	HNK Čapljina	16	7	3	6	19 - 15	24
6.	FK Rudar Kakanj	16	7	2	7	26 - 21	23
7.	NK Travnik	16	7	2	7	23 - 21	23
8.	FK Igman Konjic	16	7	2	7	17 - 18	23
9.	NK Zvijezda Gradačac	16	6	4	6	23 - 26	22
10.	NK Metalleghe-BSI Jajce*	16	5	6	5	23 - 26	21
11.	FK Budućnost Banovići	16	5	5	6	26 - 22	20
12.	NK Bratstvo Gračanica	16	6	2	8	24 - 29	20
13.	HNK Orašje	16	5	3	8	24 - 32	18
14.	NK Jedinstvo Bihać	16	5	2	9	20 - 30	17
15.	NK Slaven Živinice	16	4	1	11	15 - 24	13
16.	FK Radnik Hadžići	16	4	1	11	17 - 31	13

*Please note: NK Metalleghe-BSI Jajce were excluded from professional football due to financial difficulties and relegated to fourth level.

First League of of the Republika Srpska

1.	FK Krupa na Vrbasu (*Promoted*)	14	12	2	0	34 - 6	38
2.	FK Rudar Prijedor	14	8	3	3	20 - 7	27
3.	FK Kozara Gradiška	14	6	4	4	15 - 16	22
4.	FK Željezničar Banja Luka	13	4	4	5	10 - 12	16
5.	FK Alfa Modriča	13	4	2	7	15 - 15	14
6.	FK Slavija Sarajevo	13	2	7	4	14 - 20	13
7.	FK Tekstilac Derventa	13	3	4	6	14 - 20	13
8.	FK Podrinje Janja Bijeljina	13	3	4	6	10 - 20	13
9.	FK Jedinstvo Brčko	13	2	2	9	12 - 28	8
10.	FK Sloga Gornje Crnjelovo (*Relegated*)	(*withdrew*)					

NATIONAL TEAM

INTERNATIONAL MATCHES
(16.07.2019 – 15.07.2020)

05.09.2019	Zenica	Bosnia and Herzegovina - Liechtenstein	5-0(1-0)	(ECQ)
08.09.2019	Yerevan	Armenia - Bosnia and Herzegovina	4-2(1-1)	(ECQ)
12.10.2019	Zenica	Bosnia and Herzegovina - Finland	4-1(2-0)	(ECQ)
15.10.2019	Athína	Greece - Bosnia and Herzegovina	2-1(1-1)	(ECQ)
15.11.2019	Zenica	Bosnia and Herzegovina - Italy	0-3(0-2)	(ECQ)
18.11.2019	Vaduz	Liechtenstein - Bosnia and Herzegovina	0-3(0-0)	(ECQ)

05.09.2019 BOSNIA AND HERZEGOVINA - LIECHTENSTEIN 5-0(1-0)   16th EC. Qualifiers
Stadion Bilino Polje, Zenica; Referee: Glenn Nyberg (Sweden); Attendance: 3,825
BIH: Ibrahim Šehić, Toni Šunjić (25.Marko Mihojević), Ervin Zukanović, Sead Kolašinac, Darko Todorović, Miralem Pjanić (83.Stjepan Lončar), Edin Višća, Deni Milošević (55.Haris Duljević), Rade Krunić, Amer Gojak, Edin Džeko (Cap). Trainer: Robert Prosinečki (Croatia).
Goals: Amer Gojak (11), Andreas Malin (80 own goal), Edin Džeko (85), (87), Amer Gojak (89).

08.09.2019 ARMENIA - BOSNIA AND HERZEGOVINA 4-2(1-1)   16th EC. Qualifiers
„Vazgen Sargsyan" Hanrapetakan Stadium, Yerevan; Referee: Benoît Bastien (France); Attendance: 12,457
BIH: Ibrahim Šehić, Ervin Zukanović, Ermin Bičakčić, Sead Kolašinac, Darko Todorović (85.Riad Bajić), Miralem Pjanić, Edin Višća (64.Haris Duljević), Gojko Cimirot, Muhamed Bešić (80.Stjepan Lončar), Amer Gojak, Edin Džeko (Cap). Trainer: Robert Prosinečki (Croatia).
Goals: Edin Džeko (13), Amer Gojak (70).

12.10.2019 BOSNIA AND HERZEGOVINA - FINLAND 4-1(2-0)   16th EC. Qualifiers
Stadion Bilino Polje, Zenica; Referee: Ivan Kružliak (Slovakia); Attendance: 8,193
BIH: Ibrahim Šehić, Ermin Bičakčić, Adnan Kovačević, Sead Kolašinac, Miralem Pjanić (Cap) (76.Rade Krunić), Edin Višća (18.Izet Hajrović), Gojko Cimirot, Zoran Kvržić, Elvis Sarić (71.Mato Jajalo), Amer Gojak, Armin Hodžić. Trainer: Robert Prosinečki (Croatia).
Goals: Izet Hajrović (29), Miralem Pjanić (37 penalty, 58), Armin Hodžić (73).

15.10.2019 GREECE - BOSNIA AND HERZEGOVINA 2-1(1-1)   16th EC. Qualifiers
Stádio Olympiako „Spiros Louis", Athína; Referee: Felix Zwayer (Germany); Attendance: 4,512
BIH: Ibrahim Šehić, Ermin Bičakčić, Adnan Kovačević, Sead Kolašinac, Miralem Pjanić (Cap), Gojko Cimirot (46.Mato Jajalo), Zoran Kvržić, Elvis Sarić (63.Haris Duljević), Izet Hajrović, Amer Gojak, Armin Hodžić (71.Riad Bajić). Trainer: Robert Prosinečki (Croatia).
Goal: Amer Gojak (35).

15.11.2019   **BOSNIA AND HERZEGOVINA - ITALY**   **0-3(0-2)**   16th EC. Qualifiers
Stadion Bilino Polje, Zenica; Referee: Glenn Nyberg (Sweden); Attendance: 3,825
BIH: Ibrahim Šehić, Ermin Bičakčić, Adnan Kovačević, Sead Kolašinac, Miralem Pjanić (77.Mato Jajalo), Edin Višća (61.Armin Hodžić), Gojko Cimirot, Zoran Kvržić, Muhamed Bešić (61.Elvis Sarić), Rade Krunić, Edin Džeko (Cap). Trainer: Robert Prosinečki (Croatia).

18.11.2019   **LIECHTENSTEIN - BOSNIA AND HERZEGOVINA**   **0-3(0-0)**   16th EC. Qualifiers
Rheinpark Stadion, Vaduz Referee: Halis Özkahya (Turkey); Attendance: 2,993
BIH: Kenan Pirić, Ermin Bičakčić (Cap), Marko Mihojević (70.Edin Džeko), Eldar Čivić, Samir Memišević, Mato Jajalo, Elvis Sarić, Haris Hajradinović (65.Muhamed Bešić), Izet Hajrović, Armin Hodžić, Haris Duljević (46.Dino Hotič). Trainer: Robert Prosinečki (Croatia).
Goals: Eldar Čivić (57), Armin Hodžić (64, 72).

NATIONAL TEAM PLAYERS
(16.07.2019 – 15.07.2020)

Name	DOB	Caps	Goals	2019/2020:	Club
Goalkeepers					
Kenan PIRIĆ	07.07.1994	2	0	2019:	*NK Maribor (SVN)*
Ibrahim ŠEHIĆ	02.09.1988	27	0	2019:	*Büyükşehir Belediye Erzurumspor (TUR)*
Defenders					
Ermin BIČAKČIĆ	24.01.1990	34	3	2019:	*TSG 1899 Hoffenheim (GER)*
Eldar ČIVIĆ	28.05.1996	9	0	2019:	*Ferencvárosi TC (HUN)*
Sead KOLAŠINAC	20.06.1993	30	0	2019:	*Arsenal FC London (GER)*
Adnan KOVAČEVIĆ	09.09.1993	3	0	2019:	*Korona Kielce (POL)*
Zoran KVRŽIĆ	07.08.1988	6	0	2019:	*HNK Rijeka (CRO)*
Samir MEMIŠEVIĆ	13.08.1993	3	0	2019:	*FC Groningen (NED)*
Marko MIHOJEVIĆ	21.04.1996	3	0	2019:	*FC Erzgebirge Aue (GER)*
Toni ŠUNJIĆ	15.12.1988	40	1	2019:	*FK Dinamo Moskva (RUS)*
Darko TODOROVIĆ	05.05.1997	10	0	2019:	*KSV Holstein Kiel (GER)*
Midfielders					
Muhamed BEŠIĆ	10.09.1992	43	0	2019:	*Sheffield United FC (ENG)*
Gojko CIMIROT	19.12.1992	22	0	2019:	*R Standard Liège (BEL)*
Haris DULJEVIĆ	16.11.1993	23	1	2019:	*Nîmes Olympique FC (FRA)*
Amer GOJAK	13.02.1997	10	4	2019:	*GNK Dinamo Zagreb (CRO)*
Haris HAJRADINOVIĆ	18.02.1994	1	0	2019:	*Kasımpaşa Spor Kulübü (TUR)*
Izet HAJROVIĆ	04.08.1991	27	6	2019:	*GNK Dinamo Zagreb (CRO)*
Dino HOTIČ	26.07.1995	1	0	2019:	*NK Maribor (SVN)*
Mato JAJALO	25.05.1988	11	0	2019:	*Udinese Calcio (ITA)*
Rade KRUNIĆ	07.10.1993	13	1	2019:	*AC Milan (ITA)*
Stjepan LONČAR	10.11.1996	4	0	2019:	*HNK Rijeka (CRO)*
Forwards					
Riad BAJIĆ	06.05.1994	12	0	2019:	*Konyaspor Kulübü*
Edin DŽEKO	17.03.1986	107	58	2019:	*AS Roma (ITA)*
Armin HODŽIĆ	17.11.1994	9	3	2019:	*MOL Fehérvár FC Székesfehérvár (HUN)*
Deni MILOŠEVIĆ	09.03.1995	7	1	2019:	*Konyaspor Kulübü (TUR)*
Miralem PJANIĆ	02.04.1990	92	15	2019:	*Juventus FC Torino (ITA)*
Elvis SARIĆ	21.07.1990	18	1	2019:	*Al Ahli SC Jeddah (KSA)*
Edin VIŠĆA	17.02.1990	50	10	2019:	*İstanbul Başakşehir FK (TUR)*
Ervin ZUKANOVIĆ	11.02.1987	39	0	2019:	*Al Ahli SC Jeddah (KSA)*

National team coach			
Robert PROSINEČKI (Croatia) [04.01.2019 - 27.11.2019]	12.01.1969	22 M; 9 W; 6 D; 7 L; 29-21	
Dušan BAJEVIĆ [from 21.12.2019]	10.12.1948	-	

BULGARIA

The Country:
Република България (Republic of Bulgaria)
Capital: Sofia
Surface: 110,994 km^2
Inhabitants: 6,951,482 [2019]
Time: UTC+2

The FA:
Български футболен съюз (Bulgarian Football Union)
18 Vitoshko lale Str. BG - 1616, Sofia
Tel: +359 2 9426 202
Foundation date: 1923
Member of FIFA since: 1924
Member of UEFA since: 1954
Website: www.bfunion.bg

NATIONAL TEAM RECORDS

RECORDS
First international match:	21.05.1924, Wien	Austria – Bulgaria 6-0
Most international caps:	Stilian Petrov	- 105 caps (1998-2011)
Most international goals:	Dimitar Berbatov	- 48 goals / 78 caps (1999-2010)

UEFA EUROPEAN CHAMPIONSHIP		FIFA WORLD CUP		OLYMPIC TOURNAMENTS	
1960	Qualifiers	1930	Did not enter	1908	*Did not enter*
1964	Qualifiers	1934	Qualifiers	1912	*Did not enter*
1968	Qualifiers	1938	Qualifiers	1920	*Did not enter*
1972	Qualifiers	1950	Did not enter	1924	1st Round
1976	Qualifiers	1954	Qualifiers	1928	*Did not enter*
1980	Qualifiers	1958	Qualifiers	1936	*Did not enter*
1984	Qualifiers	1962	Final Tournament (Group Stage)	1948	*Did not enter*
1988	Qualifiers	1966	Final Tournament (Group Stage)	1952	1st Round
1992	Qualifiers	1970	Final Tournament (Group Stage)	1956	Semi-Finals
1996	Final Tournament (Group Stage)	1974	Final Tournament (Group Stage)	1960	Group Stage
2000	Qualifiers	1978	Qualifiers	1964	Qualifiers
2004	Final Tournament (Group Stage)	1982	Qualifiers	1968	Runners-up
2008	Qualifiers	1986	Final Tournament (2nd Round of 16)	1972	Qualifiers
2012	Qualifiers	1990	Qualifiers	1976	Qualifiers
2016	Qualifiers	1994	Final Tournament (4th Place)	1980	Qualifiers
2020	*To be determined*	1998	Final Tournament (Group Stage)	1984	Qualifiers
		2002	Qualifiers	1988	Qualifiers
		2006	Qualifiers	1992	Qualifiers
		2010	Qualifiers	1996	Qualifiers
		2014	Qualifiers	2000	Qualifiers
		2018	Qualifiers	2004	Qualifiers
				2008	Qualifiers
				2012	Qualifiers
				2016	Qualifiers

UEFA NATIONS LEAGUE
2018/2019 – League C (promoted to League B)

FIFA CONFEDERATIONS CUP 1992-2017
None

BULGARIAN CLUB HONOURS IN EUROPEAN CLUB COMPETITIONS:

European Champion Clubs' Cup (1956-1992) / UEFA Champions League (1993-2020)
None

Fairs Cup (1858-1971) / UEFA Cup (1972-2009) / UEFA Europa League (2010-2020)
None

UEFA Super Cup (1972-2019)
None

European Cup Winners' Cup 1961-1999*
None

defunct competition

NATIONAL COMPETITIONS
TABLE OF HONOURS

	STATE CHAMPIONSHIPS CHAMPIONS	CUP WINNERS*	BEST GOALSCORERS	
1924	*Not finished*	-	-	
1925	Vladislav Varna	-	-	
1926	Vladislav Varna	-	-	
1927	*No competition*	-	-	
1928	Slavia Sofia	-	-	
1929	Botev Plovdiv	-	-	
1930	SK Slavia Sofia	-	-	
1931	AS 23 Sofia	-	-	
1932	Spartak Varna	-	-	
1933	SK Levski Sofia	-	-	
1934	Vladislav Varna	-	-	
1935	Sportklub Sofia	-	-	
1936	SK Slavia Sofia	-	-	
1937	SK Levski Sofia	-	-	
1937/1938	Ticha Varna	FC 13 Sofia	Krum Milev (Slavia Sofia)	12
1938/1939	SK Slavia Sofia	Shipka Sofia	Georgi Pachedzhiev (AS 23 Sofia)	14
1939/1940	Lokomotiv Sofia	FC 13 Sofia	-	
1941	SK Slavia Sofia	AS 23 Sofia	-	
1942	SK Levski Sofia	Levski Sofia	-	
1943	Slavia Sofia	-	-	
1944	*Not finished*	-	-	

*called between 1938-1942 Tsar's Cup.

	REPUBLIC CHAMPIONSHIPS CHAMPIONS	CUP WINNERS**	BEST GOALSCORERS
1945	Lokomotiv Sofia	-	-
1946	SK Levski Sofia	SK Levski Sofia	-
1947	SK Levski Sofia	SK Levski Sofia	-
1948	CDNV Sofia	Lokomotiv Sofia	-

	„A" GROUP CHAMPIONS	CUP WINNERS**	BEST GOALSCORERS	
1948/1949	SK Levski Sofia	SK Levski Sofia	Dimitar Milanov (CSKA Sofia)	
			Nedko Nedev (Cherno More Varna)	11
1950	SK Levski Sofia	SK Levski Sofia	Lyubomir Hranov (SK Levski Sofia)	13
1951	CDNA Sofia	CDNA Sofia	Dimitar Milanov (CDNA Sofia)	14
1952	CDNA Sofia	GUTP-DSO Udarnik Sofia	Dimitar Isakov (GUTP-DSO Udarnik Sofia)	
			Dobromir Tashkov (Spartak Sofia)	10
1953	SK Levski Sofia	Lokomotiv Sofia	Dimitar Minchev (Spartak Pleven / VVS Sofia)	15
1954	CDNA Sofia	CDNA Sofia	Dobromir Tashkov (GUTP-DSO Udarnik Sofia)	25
1955	CDNA Sofia	CDNA Sofia	Todor Diev (Spartak Plovdiv)	13
1956	CDNA Sofia	SK Levski Sofia	Pavel Vladimirov (Minyor Pernik)	16
1957	CDNA Sofia	SK Levski Sofia	Hristo Iliev (SK Levski Sofia)	
			Dimitar Milanov (CDNA Sofia)	14
1958	CDNA Sofia	Spartak Plovdiv	Dobromir Tashkov (FD Slavia Sofia)	
			Georgi Arnaudov (Spartak Varna)	9
1958/1959	CDNA Sofia	SK Levski Sofia	Aleksandar Vasilev (FD Slavia Sofia)	13
1959/1960	CDNA Sofia	Septemvri Sofia	Dimitar Yordanov (SK Levski Sofia)	
			Lyuben Kostov (Spartak Varna)	12
1960/1961	CDNA Sofia	CDNA Sofia	Ivan Sotirov (Botev Plovdiv)	20
1961/1962	CDNA Sofia	Botev Plovdiv	Nikola Yordanov (Dunav Ruse)	
			Todor Diev (Spartak Plovdiv)	23
1962/1963	Spartak Plovdiv	FD Slavia Sofia	Todor Diev (Spartak Plovdiv)	26
1963/1964	Lokomotiv Sofia	FD Slavia Sofia	Nikola Tsanev (CDNA Sofia)	26
1964/1965	SK Levski Sofia	CSKA Cerveno Zname Sofia	Georgi Asparuhov (SK Levski Sofia)	27
1965/1966	CSKA Cerveno Zname Sofia	FD Slavia Sofia	Traycho Spasov (Marek Dupnitsa)	21
1966/1967	Botev Plovdiv	SK Levski Sofia	Petar Zhekov (Beroe Stara Zagora)	21
1967/1968	SK Levski Sofia	Spartak Sofia	Petar Zhekov (Beroe Stara Zagora)	31
1968/1969	CSKA Septemvrijsko Zname Sofia	CSKA Septemvrijsko Zname Sofia	Petar Zhekov (CSKA Septemvrijsko Zname Sofia)	36
1969/1970	DFS Levski-Spartak Sofia	DFS Levski-Spartak Sofia	Petar Zhekov (CSKA Septemvrijsko Zname Sofia)	31
1970/1971	CSKA Septemvrijsko Zname Sofia	DFS Levski-Spartak Sofia	Dimitar Yakimov (CSKA Septemvrijsko Zname Sofia)	26
1971/1972	CSKA Septemvrijsko Zname Sofia	CSKA Septemvrijsko Zname Sofia	Petar Zhekov (CSKA Septemvrijsko Zname Sofia)	27
1972/1973	CSKA Septemvrijsko Zname Sofia	CSKA Septemvrijsko Zname Sofia	Petar Zhekov (CSKA Septemvrijsko Zname Sofia)	29
1973/1974	DFS Levski-Spartak Sofia	CSKA Septemvrijsko Zname Sofia	Petko Petkov (Beroe Stara Zagora)	
			Kiril Milanov (DFS Levski-Spartak Sofia)	19
1974/1975	CSKA Septemvrijsko Zname Sofia	DFS Slavia Sofia	Ivan Pritargov (Botev Plovdiv)	20
1975/1976	CSKA Septemvrijsko Zname Sofia	DFS Levski-Spartak Sofia	Petko Petkov (Beroe Stara Zagora)	
			Pavel Panov (DFS Levski-Spartak Sofia)	18
1976/1977	DFS Levski-Spartak Sofia	DFS Levski-Spartak Sofia	Pavel Panov (DFS Levski-Spartak Sofia)	20
1977/1978	Lokomotiv Sofia	Marek Dupnitsa	Stoycho Mladenov (Beroe Stara Zagora)	21

1978/1979	DFS Levski-Spartak Sofia	DFS Levski-Spartak Sofia	Rusi Gochev (Chernomorets Burgas / DFS Levski-Spartak Sofia)	19
1979/1980	CSKA Septemvrijsko Zname Sofia	DFS Slavia Sofia	Spas Dzhevizov (CSKA Sofia)	23
1980/1981	CSKA Septemvrijsko Zname Sofia	Botev Plovdiv	Georgi Slavkov (Botev Plovdiv)	31
1981/1982	CSKA Septemvrijsko Zname Sofia	Lokomotiv Sofia	Mihail Valchev (DFS Levski-Spartak Sofia)	24
1982/1983	CSKA Septemvrijsko Zname Sofia	CSKA Septemvrijsko Zname Sofia	Antim Pehlivanov (Botev Plovdiv)	20
1983/1984	DFS Levski-Spartak Sofia	DFS Levski-Spartak Sofia	Eduard Eranosyan (Lokomotiv Plovdiv) Emil Spasov (DFS Levski-Spartak Sofia)	19
1984/1985	DFS Levski-Spartak Sofia	CSKA Septemvrijsko Zname Sofia	Plamen Getov (Spartak Pleven)	26
1985/1986	Beroe Stara Zagora	FK Vitosha Sofia	Atanas Pashev (Botev Plovdiv)	30
1986/1987	FK Sredets Sofia	FK Sredets Sofia	Nasko Sirakov (FK Vitosha Sofia)	36
1987/1988	FK Vitosha Sofia	FK Sredets Sofia	Nasko Sirakov (FK Vitosha Sofia)	28
1988/1989	CFKA Sredets Sofia	FK Sredets Sofia	Hristo Stoichkov (CFKA Sredets Sofia)	23
1989/1990	CFKA Sofia	FC Sliven	Hristo Stoichkov (CFKA Sofia)	38
1990/1991	FC Etar Veliko Tarnovo	PFC Levski Sofia	Ivaylo Yordanov (FC Lokomotiv Gorna Oryahovitsa)	21
1991/1992	PFC CSKA Sofia	PFC Levski Sofia	Nasko Sirakov (PFC Levski Sofia)	26
1992/1993	PFC Levski Sofia	PFC CSKA Sofia	Plamen Getov (PFC Levski Sofia)	26
1993/1994	PFC Levski Sofia	PFC Levski Sofia	Nasko Sirakov (PFC Levski Sofia)	30
1994/1995	PFC Levski Sofia	PFC Lokomotiv Sofia	Petar Mihtarski (PFC CSKA Sofia)	24
1995/1996	PFC Slavia Sofia	PFC Slavia Sofia	Ivo Georgiev (FC Spartak Varna)	21
1996/1997	PFC CSKA Sofia	PFC CSKA Sofia	Todor Pramatarov (PFC Slavia Sofia)	26
1997/1998	PFC Litex Lovech	PFC Levski Sofia	Anton Spasov (PFC Naftex Burgas) Bontcho Guentchev (PFC CSKA Sofia)	17
1998/1999	PFC Litex Lovech	PFC CSKA Sofia	Dimcho Belyakov (PFC Litex Lovech)	21
1999/2000	PFC Levski Sofia	PFC Levski Sofia	Mihail Mihaylov (FC Velbazhd Kyustendil)	20
2000/2001	PFC Levski Sofia	PFC Litex Lovech	Georgi Ivanov (PFC Levski Sofia)	22
2001/2002	PFC Levski Sofia	PFC Levski Sofia	Vladimir Manchev (PFC CSKA Sofia)	21
2002/2003	PFC CSKA Sofia	PFC Levski Sofia	Georgi Chilikov (PFC Levski Sofia)	23
2003/2004	PFC Lokomotiv Plovdiv	PFC Litex Lovech	Martin Kamburov (PFC Lokomotiv Plovdiv)	25
2004/2005	PFC CSKA Sofia	PFC Levski Sofia	Martin Kamburov (PFC Lokomotiv Plovdiv)	27
2005/2006	PFC Levski Sofia	PFC CSKA Sofia	Milivoje Novaković (SVN, Litex Lovech) José Emílio Robalo Furtado (CPV, OFC Vihren Sandanski / PFC CSKA Sofia)	16
2006/2007	PFC Levski Sofia	PFC Levski Sofia	Tsvetan Genkov (PFC Lokomotiv Sofia)	27
2007/2008	PFC CSKA Sofia	PFC Litex Lovech	Georgi Hristov (PFC Botev Plovdiv)	19
2008/2009	PFC Levski Sofia	PFC Litex Lovech	Martin Kamburov (PFC Lokomotiv Sofia)	17
2009/2010	PFC Litex Lovech	PFC Beroe Stara Zagora	Wilfried Niflore (FRA, PFC Litex Lovech)	19
2010/2011	PFC Litex Lovech	PFC CSKA Sofia	Garra Dembélé (MLI, PFC Levski Sofia)	26
2011/2012	PFC Ludogorets Razgrad	PFC Ludogorets Razgrad	Ivan Stoyanov (PFC Ludogorets Razgrad) Aluísio Chaves Ribeiro Moraes Júnior (BRA, PFC CSKA Sofia)	16
2012/2013	PFC Ludogorets Razgrad	PFC Beroe Stara Zagora	Basile Salomon Pereira de Carvalho (GNB, PFC Levski Sofia)	19
2013/2014	PFC Ludogorets Razgrad	PFC Ludogorets Razgrad	Wilmar Jordán Gil (COL, PFC Litex Lovech) Martin Kamburov (PFC Lokomotiv Plovdiv)	20
2014/2015	PFC Ludogorets Razgrad	PFC Cherno More Varna	Antonio Salas Quinta „Añete" (ESP, PFC Levski Sofia)	14
2015/2016	PFC Ludogorets Razgrad	PFC CSKA Sofia	Martin Kamburov (PFC Lokomotiv Plovdiv)	18
2016/2017	PFC Ludogorets Razgrad	PFC Botev Plovdiv	Claudiu Andrei Keşerü (ROU, PFC Ludogorets Razgrad)	22
2017/2018	PFC Ludogorets Razgrad	PFC Slavia Sofia	Claudiu Andrei Keşerü (ROU, PFC Ludogorets Razgrad)	26
2018/2019	PFC Ludogorets Razgrad	PFC Lokomotiv Plovdiv	Stanislav Kostov (PFC Levski Sofia)	24
2019/2020	PFC Ludogorets Razgrad	PFC Lokomotiv Plovdiv	Martin Kamburov (PFC Beroe Stara Zagora)	18

**called "Cup of the Soviet Army" (between 1945 - 1982) and Bulgarian Cup (from 1982 until today).

Please note:

FC CSKA Sofia changed several times its name as following: 1948 CDNV Sofia, 1949 NV Sofia, 1950 NA Sofia, 1951 CDNA Sofia, 1953 Sofijski Garnizon Sofia, 1953 CDNA Sofia, 1964 CSKA Cerveno Zname Sofia, 1968 CSKA Septemvrijsko Zname Sofia, 1985 FK Sredets Sofia, 1987 CFKA Sredets Sofia, November 1989 CFKA Sofia, 1st january 1990 PFC CSKA Sofia.

FC Levski Sofia changed several times its name as following: 1914 CS Levski Sofia, SK Levski Sofia, 1949 Dinamo Sofia, 1957 FD Levski Sofia, 1969 DFS Levski-Spartak Sofia, 1985 FK Vitosha Sofia, 1990 FK Levski-1914 Sofia, 1998 PFC Levski Sofia.

FC Slavia Sofia changed several times its name as following: 1913 Botev Sofia, 1915 SK Slavia Sofia, 1945 NFD Slavia Sofia, 1949 DSO Strojtel Sofia, 1951 USS-DSO Udarnik Sofia, 1952 GUTP-DSO Udarnik Sofia, 1957 FD Slavia Sofia, 1969 ZSK Slavia Sofia, 1971 DFS Slavia Sofia, 1986 FC Slavia Sofia; 1990 PFC Slavia Sofia.

Regular Season - Results

Round 1 [12-15.07.2019]
Botev Vratsa - Beroe Stara Zagora 1-3(0-1)
CSKA Sofia - Etar Tarnovo 2-2(1-0)
Arda Kardzhali - Botev Plovdiv 0-0
PFC Ludogorets - Tsarsko Selo 2-0(1-0)
Slavia Sofia - Vitosha Bistritsa 3-2(1-2)
Cherno More V. - Lokomotiv Plovdiv 3-1(1-1)
Dunav Ruse - Levski Sofia 1-4(0-2)

Round 2 [19-22.07.2019]
Tsarsko Selo - Arda Kardzhali 0-0
Lokomotiv Plovdiv - Slavia Sofia 3-2(3-1)
CSKA Sofia - Cherno More Varna 1-3(0-2)
Beroe Stara Zagora - PFC Ludogorets 2-4(1-2)
Botev Plovdiv - Dunav Ruse 3-1(1-1)
Etar Tarnovo - Levski Sofia 0-0
Vitosha Bistritsa - Botev Vratsa 0-2(0-1)

Round 3 [26-29.07.2019]
Dunav Ruse - Tsarsko Selo 3-1(2-0)
Cherno More Varna - Etar Tarnovo 1-1(1-0)
Arda Kardzhali - Beroe Stara Zagora 3-1(1-1)
Botev Vratsa - Lokomotiv Plovdiv 1-4(0-2)
Slavia Sofia - CSKA Sofia 1-2(0-0)
Levski Sofia - Botev Plovdiv 3-1(1-1)
PFC Ludogorets - Vitosha Bistritsa 2-0(0-0)

Round 4 [02-05.08.2019]
Vitosha Bistritsa - Arda Kardzhali 1-3(1-1)
Cherno More Varna - Slavia Sofia 0-0
Etar Tarnovo - Botev Plovdiv 2-2(1-2)
Beroe Stara Zagora - Dunav Ruse 2-0(2-0)
CSKA Sofia - Botev Vratsa 1-0(0-0)
Lokomotiv Plovdiv - PFC Ludogorets 1-1(0-0)
Tsarsko Selo - Levski Sofia 0-2(0-0)

Round 5 [09-12.08.2019]
Botev Vratsa - Cherno More Varna 1-1(0-1)
Slavia Sofia - Etar Tarnovo 2-1(1-0)
Botev Plovdiv - Tsarsko Selo 0-2(0-0)
Levski Sofia - Beroe Stara Zagora 1-3(0-1)
Arda Kardzhali - Lokomotiv Plovdiv 2-5(0-3)
PFC Ludogorets - CSKA Sofia 0-0
Dunav Ruse - Vitosha Bistritsa 2-0(1-0)

Round 6 [16-19.08.2019]
Slavia Sofia - Botev Vratsa 2-2(1-0)
Etar Tarnovo - Tsarsko Selo 1-1(1-1)
Beroe Stara Zagora - Botev Plovdiv 2-0(0-0)
Vitosha Bistritsa - Levski Sofia 0-4(0-1)
CSKA Sofia - Arda Kardzhali 3-2(1-1)
Cherno More V. - PFC Ludogorets 1-2(1-1)
Lokomotiv Plovdiv - Dunav Ruse 3-1(2-1)

Round 7 [23-26.08.2019]
Tsarsko Selo - Beroe Stara Zagora 2-1(1-1)
Arda Kardzhali - Cherno More Varna 0-0
Botev Plovdiv - Vitosha Bistritsa 2-1(1-1)
Levski Sofia - Lokomotiv Plovdiv 1-0(0-0)
Dunav Ruse - CSKA Sofia 1-1(1-0)
PFC Ludogorets - Slavia Sofia 0-0
Botev Vratsa - Etar Tarnovo 2-1(0-1)

Round 8 [30.08.-01.09.2019]
Cherno More Varna - Dunav Ruse 1-1(0-1)
Slavia Sofia - Arda Kardzhali 2-3(1-2)
Lokomotiv Plovdiv - Botev Plovdiv 1-1(0-1)
Etar Tarnovo - Beroe Stara Zagora 2-1(1-0)
Vitosha Bistritsa - Tsarsko Selo 3-2(1-1)
CSKA Sofia - Levski Sofia 2-2(0-2)
Botev Vratsa - PFC Ludogorets 0-1(0-1)

Round 9 [13-16.09.2019]
Tsarsko Selo - Lokomotiv Plovdiv 2-3(0-1)
Arda Kardzhali - Botev Vratsa 2-1(1-0)
Botev Plovdiv - CSKA Sofia 0-1(0-0)
PFC Ludogorets - Etar Tarnovo 2-0(0-0)
Dunav Ruse - Slavia Sofia 0-0
Levski Sofia - Cherno More Varna 3-0(3-0)
Beroe Stara Zag. - Vitosha Bistritsa 1-0(0-0)

Round 10 [20-23.09.2019]
Cherno More Varna - Botev Plovdiv 2-0(0-0)
CSKA Sofia - Tsarsko Selo 3-0(0-0)
Botev Vratsa - Dunav Ruse 0-0
Slavia Sofia - Levski Sofia 0-2(0-0)
Lokomotiv Plovdiv - Beroe Stara Z. 3-0(2-0)
PFC Ludogorets - Arda Kardzhali 2-0(1-0)
Etar Tarnovo - Vitosha Bistritsa 1-0(1-0)

Round 11 [27-30.09.2019]
Tsarsko Selo - Cherno More Varna 1-1(0-0)
Levski Sofia - Botev Vratsa 3-1(2-0)
Botev Plovdiv - Slavia Sofia 0-1(0-1)
Dunav Ruse - PFC Ludogorets 0-1(0-1)
Beroe Stara Zagora - CSKA Sofia 2-1(1-0)
Arda Kardzhali - Etar Tarnovo 2-1(0-0)
Vitosha Bistritsa - Lokomotiv Plovd. 2-3(0-1)

Round 12 [04-06.10.2019]
Slavia Sofia - Tsarsko Selo 1-0(1-0)
Cherno More Varna - Beroe Stara Z. 2-0(1-0)
Botev Vratsa - Botev Plovdiv 3-0(0-0)
Etar Tarnovo - Lokomotiv Plovdiv 0-5(0-3)
CSKA Sofia - Vitosha Bistritsa 4-0(3-0)
Arda Kardzhali - Dunav Ruse 0-2(0-1)
PFC Ludogorets - Levski Sofia 2-0(1-0)

Round 13 [18-21.10.2019]
Vitosha Bistritsa - Cherno More V. 0-2(0-0)
Dunav Ruse - Etar Tarnovo 0-2(0-0)
Botev Plovdiv - PFC Ludogorets 0-1(0-1)
Levski Sofia - Arda Kardzhali 2-1(0-0)
Lokomotiv Plovdiv - CSKA Sofia 1-0(1-0)
Tsarsko Selo - Botev Vratsa 3-0(1-0)
Beroe Stara Zagora - Slavia Sofia 1-2(0-0)

Round 14 [29-31.10.2019]
Beroe Stara Zagora - Botev Vratsa 4-0(1-0)
Lokomotiv Plovdiv - Cherno More V. 1-0(1-0)
Tsarsko Selo - PFC Ludogorets 0-2(0-1)
Botev Plovdiv - Arda Kardzhali 1-1(0-0)
Etar Tarnovo - CSKA Sofia 0-4(0-0)
Vitosha Bistritsa - Slavia Sofia 0-1(0-0)
Levski Sofia - Dunav Ruse 2-0(2-0)

Round 15 [02-07.11.2019]
PFC Ludogorets - Beroe Stara Zagora 3-1(1-1)
Botev Vratsa - Vitosha Bistritsa 1-1(1-0)
Slavia Sofia - Lokomotiv Plovdiv 1-1(0-0)
Cherno More Varna - CSKA Sofia 0-2(0-0)
Dunav Ruse - Botev Plovdiv 1-2(0-1)
Levski Sofia - Etar Tarnovo 3-0(1-0)
Arda Kardzhali - Tsarsko Selo 0-2(0-0)

Round 16 [08-11.11.2019]
Lokomotiv Plovdiv - Botev Vratsa 2-0(1-0)
Etar Tarnovo - Cherno More Varna 1-0(1-0)
CSKA Sofia - Slavia Sofia 1-0(0-0)
Beroe Stara Zagora - Arda Kardzhali 0-1(0-1)
Botev Plovdiv - Levski Sofia 1-0(0-0)
Vitosha Bistritsa - PFC Ludogorets 0-1(0-0)
Tsarsko Selo - Dunav Ruse 1-2(1-1)

Round 17 [22-25.11.2019]
Arda Kardzhali - Vitosha Bistritsa 2-0(1-0)
Slavia Sofia - Cherno More Varna 0-1(0-0)
Botev Vratsa - CSKA Sofia 0-3(0-2)
PFC Ludogorets - Lokomotiv Plovdiv 2-1(2-1)
Dunav Ruse - Beroe Stara Zagora 0-3(0-0)
Levski Sofia - Tsarsko Selo 2-0(2-0)
Botev Plovdiv - Etar Tarnovo 2-0(0-0)

Round 18 [29.11.-01.12.2019]
Etar Tarnovo - Slavia Sofia 0-2(0-2)
Cherno More Varna - Botev Vratsa 4-1(2-0)
Tsarsko Selo - Botev Plovdiv 0-3(0-2)
Beroe Stara Zagora - Levski Sofia 1-1(1-1)
Lokomotiv Plovdiv - Arda Kardzhali 0-0
Vitosha Bistritsa - Dunav Ruse 1-1(0-0)
CSKA Sofia - PFC Ludogorets 0-0

Round 19 [06-09.12.2019]
Tsarsko Selo - Etar Tarnovo 2-2(0-0)
Botev Plovdiv - Beroe Stara Zagora 3-1(1-1)
PFC Ludogorets - Cherno More V. 1-1(0-1)
Botev Vratsa - Slavia Sofia 0-2(0-1)
Arda Kardzhali - CSKA Sofia 0-0
Levski Sofia - Vitosha Bistritsa 2-0(1-0)
Dunav Ruse - Lokomotiv Plovdiv 0-3(0-2)

Round 20 [13-15.12.2019]
Etar Tarnovo - Botev Vratsa 1-1(1-0)
Beroe Stara Zagora - Tsarsko Selo 2-0(0-0)
Cherno More Varna - Arda Kardzhali 1-1(0-1)
CSKA Sofia - Dunav Ruse 4-0(1-0)
Vitosha Bistritsa - Botev Plovdiv 0-2(0-0)
Lokomotiv Plovdiv - Levski Sofia 0-0
Slavia Sofia - PFC Ludogorets 1-1(0-1)

Round 21 [14-17.02.2020]
Tsarsko Selo - Vitosha Bistritsa 1-0(0-0)
Levski Sofia - CSKA Sofia 0-0
PFC Ludogorets - Botev Vratsa 6-0(2-0)
Beroe Stara Zagora - Etar Tarnovo 2-0(0-0)
Botev Plovdiv - Lokomotiv Plovdiv 0-0
Dunav Ruse - Cherno More Varna 0-2(0-1)
Arda Kardzhali - Slavia Sofia 0-1(0-1)

Round 22 [22-24.02.2020]
Botev Vratsa - Arda Kardzhali 3-1(2-1)
Cherno More Varna - Levski Sofia 2-2(1-1)
CSKA Sofia - Botev Plovdiv 1-0(1-0)
Vitosha Bistritsa - Beroe Stara Z. 1-2(1-1)
Lokomotiv Plovdiv - Tsarsko Selo 4-0(1-0)
Etar Tarnovo - PFC Ludogorets 1-1(0-0)
Slavia Sofia - Dunav Ruse 3-1(2-1)

Round 23 [28.02.-02.03.2020]
Beroe Stara Z. - Lokomotiv Plovdiv 2-0(2-0)
Dunav Ruse - Botev Vratsa 0-0
Botev Plovdiv - Cherno More Varna 1-1(0-0)
Tsarsko Selo - CSKA Sofia 2-1(2-1)
Levski Sofia - Slavia Sofia 1-2(1-1)
Vitosha Bistritsa - Etar Tarnovo 2-6(1-4)
Arda Kardzhali - Ludogorets 1-1(1-1) [10.06.]

Round 24 [06-08.03.2020]
Cherno More Varna - Tsarsko Selo 1-0(1-0)
Etar Tarnovo - Arda Kardzhali 1-1(0-0)
Lokomotiv Plovd. - Vitosha Bistritsa 1-1(1-0)
CSKA Sofia - Beroe Stara Zagora 2-0(0-0)
Slavia Sofia - Botev Plovdiv 2-1(0-0)
Botev Vratsa - Levski Sofia 0-0
PFC Ludogorets - Dunav Ruse 5-1(4-1)

Round 25 [05-08.06.2020]
| |
Lokomotiv Plovdiv - Etar Tarnovo 2-0(0-0)
Levski Sofia - PFC Ludogorets 0-1(0-0)
Dunav Ruse - Arda Kardzhali 0-0
Botev Plovdiv - Botev Vratsa 0-1(0-1)
Vitosha Bistritsa - CSKA Sofia 0-1(0-0)
Beroe Stara Z. - Cherno More Varna 3-0(2-0)
Tsarsko Selo - Slavia Sofia 1-3(0-1)

Round 26 [11-14.06.2020]
Etar Tarnovo - Dunav Ruse 5-3(2-1)
Botev Vratsa - Tsarsko Selo 0-1(0-0)
Cherno More V. - Vitosha Bistritsa 2-0(1-0)
Slavia Sofia - Beroe Stara Zagora 2-4(2-2)
Arda Kardzhali - Levski Sofia 1-3(1-1)
PFC Ludogorets - Botev Plovdiv 2-1(0-1)
CSKA Sofia - Lokomotiv Plovdiv 1-1(0-1)

Final Standings

1.	PFC Ludogorets Razgrad	26	18	8	0	46	-	12	62
2.	PFC Lokomotiv Plovdiv	26	14	8	4	49	-	23	50
3.	PFC CSKA Sofia	26	14	8	4	41	-	17	50
4.	PFC Levski Sofia	26	14	7	5	43	-	19	49
5.	PFC Slavia Sofia	26	13	6	7	36	-	28	45
6.	PFC Beroe Stara Zagora	26	14	1	11	44	-	34	43
7.	PFC Cherno More Varna	26	10	10	6	32	-	24	40
8.	FC Arda 1924 Kardzhali	26	7	10	9	27	-	33	31
9.	PFC Botev Plovdiv	26	8	6	12	26	-	30	30
10.	SFC Etar Veliko Tarnovo	26	6	9	11	31	-	45	27
11.	FC Tsarsko Selo Sofia	26	7	4	15	24	-	42	25
12.	POFC Botev Vratsa	26	5	7	14	21	-	46	22
13.	FC Dunav Ruse 2010	26	4	7	15	21	-	49	19
14.	FC Vitosha Bistritsa	26	1	3	22	15	-	54	6

Teams ranked 1-6 were qualified for the Championship Round, while teams ranked 7-14 were qualified for the Relegation Round.

Relegation Round

Results

Round 27 [19-22.06.2020]
Cherno More V. - Vitosha Bistritsa 1-0(1-0)
Botev Plovdiv - Botev Vratsa 3-2(0-1)
Arda Kardzhali - Dunav Ruse 0-2(0-2)
Etar Tarnovo - Tsarsko Selo 0-1(0-1)

Round 28 [26-29.06.2020]
Cherno More Varna - Etar Tarnovo 2-2(1-0)
Vitosha Bistritsa - Tsarsko Selo 0-1(0-0)
Dunav Ruse - Botev Vratsa 1-3(0-1)
Arda Kardzhali - Botev Plovdiv 1-0(0-0)

Round 29 [02-03.07.2020]
Etar Tarnovo - Vitosha Bistritsa 1-0(1-0)
Tsarsko Selo - Cherno More Varna 1-4(1-2)
Botev Vratsa - Arda Kardzhali 0-0
Botev Plovdiv - Dunav Ruse 3-1(1-1)

Final Standings

Group A

					Total			Home					Away			
1.	PFC Cherno More Varna	29	12	11	6	39 - 27	47	7	6	2	23 - 13	5	5	4	16 - 14
2.	SFC Etar Veliko Tarnovo	29	7	10	12	34 - 48	31	5	6	4	16 - 22	2	4	8	18 - 26
3.	FC Tsarsko Selo Sofia	29	9	4	16	27 - 46	31	4	3	7	16 - 24	5	1	9	11 - 22
	(*Relegation Play-offs*)														
4.	FC Vitosha Bistritsa (*Relegated*)	29	1	3	25	15 - 57	6	1	1	12	10 - 31	0	2	13	5 - 26

Group B

					Total			Home					Away			
1.	PFC Botev Plovdiv	29	10	6	13	32 - 34	36	7	3	5	19 - 14	3	3	8	13 - 20
2.	FC Arda 1924 Kardzhali	29	8	11	10	28 - 35	35	5	4	6	14 - 19	3	7	4	14 - 16
3.	POFC Botev Vratsa	29	6	8	15	26 - 50	26	3	5	6	12 - 18	3	3	9	14 - 32
	(*Relegation Play-offs*)														
4.	FC Dunav Ruse 2010	29	5	7	17	25 - 55	22	2	4	8	9 - 22	3	3	9	16 - 33
	(*Relegation Play-offs*)														

Teams ranked 1-2 in both groups were qualified for the European play-offs Quarter-Finals.

European Play-offs

Quarter-Finals [07.07.2020]	PFC Cherno More Varna - FC Arda 1924 Kardzhali	1-0(1-0)
	PFC Botev Plovdiv - SFC Etar Veliko Tarnovo	1-0(1-0)
Semi-Finals [11.07.2020]	PFC Cherno More Varna - PFC Botev Plovdiv	0-1(0-0)
Final [19.07.2020]	PFC Slavia Sofia - PFC Botev Plovdiv	2-1(1-0)

Championship Round

Results

Round 27 [20-21.06.2020]
CSKA Sofia - Levski Sofia 3-3(1-2)
Lokomotiv Plovdiv - Slavia Sofia 0-1(0-0)
PFC Ludogorets - Beroe Stara Zagora 2-1(0-1)

Round 28 [27-28.06.2020]
Slavia Sofia - CSKA Sofia 0-0
PFC Ludogorets - Lokomotiv Plovdiv 6-1(4-0)
Beroe Stara Zagora - Levski Sofia 1-2(1-1)

Round 29 [04-05.07.2020]
Levski Sofia - Slavia Sofia 1-2(1-0)
Lokomotiv Plovdiv - Beroe Stara Z. 0-2(0-0)
CSKA Sofia - PFC Ludogorets 1-1(0-0)

Round 30 [08-09.07.2020]
PFC Ludogorets - Levski Sofia 3-0(1-0)
Beroe Stara Zagora - Slavia Sofia 2-0(1-0)
Lokomotiv Plovdiv - CSKA Sofia 1-2(0-0)

Round 31 [12.07.2020]
CSKA Sofia - Beroe Stara Zagora 5-0(2-0)
Levski Sofia - Lokomotiv Plovdiv 1-2(1-1)
Slavia Sofia - PFC Ludogorets 3-1(3-0)

Final Standings

				Total				Home					Away				
1. **PFC Ludogorets Razgrad**	31	21	9	1	59 - 18	72	13	3	0	40 - 7	8	6	1	19 - 11
2. PFC CSKA Sofia	31	16	11	4	52 - 22	59	9	6	1	34 - 14	7	5	3	18 - 8
3. PFC Slavia Sofia	31	16	7	8	42 - 32	55	6	4	5	23 - 22	10	3	3	19 - 10
4. PFC Levski Sofia	31	15	8	8	50 - 30	53	9	1	5	25 - 13	6	7	3	25 - 17
5. PFC Lokomotiv Plovdiv	31	15	8	8	53 - 35	53	8	5	3	23 - 11	7	3	5	30 - 24
6. PFC Beroe Stara Zagora	31	16	1	14	50 - 43	49	10	1	4	27 - 11	6	0	10	23 - 32

PFC Slavia Sofia wer equalifeid for the European Play-off Final.

Top goalscorers:

18	**Martin Kamburov**	*PFC Beroe Stara Zagora*
13	Ali Sowe (GAM)	*PFC CSKA Sofia*
13	Ismail Isa Mustafa	*PFC Cherno More Varna*
12	Dimitar Iliev	*PFC Lokomotiv Plovdiv*
12	Claudiu Andrei Keşerü (ROU)	*PFC Ludogorets Razgrad*
11	Nigel Robertha (CUW)	*PFC Levski Sofia*

Relegation Play-offs

Results

POFC Botev Vratsa - FC Dunav Ruse 2010	0-0
FC Tsarsko Selo Sofia - POFC Botev Vratsa	0-3(0-0)
FC Dunav Ruse 2010 - FC Tsarsko Selo Sofia	1-0(0-0)

1. POFC Botev Vratsa	2	1	1	0	3 - 0	4
2. FC Dunav Ruse 2010	2	1	1	0	1 - 0	4
3. FC Tsarsko Selo Sofia	2	0	0	2	0 - 4	0

Relegation Finals [17-18.07.2020]

FC Dunav Ruse 2010 - FC Montana	1-4(0-2)
FC Tsarsko Selo Sofia - PFC Septemvri Sofia	2-0(1-0)

FC Montana and FC Tsarsko Selo Sofia will play 2020/2021 at first level.

First Round [24-26.09.2019]				
OFC Botev Ihtiman - PFC Cherno More Varna	0-3(0-0)	PFC Neftochimic Burgas - PFC Ludogorets Razgrad	1-4(1-0)
FC Kariana Erden - FC Tsarsko Selo Sofia	3-0(2-0)	FC Balkan Botevgrad - PFC Lokomotiv Plovdiv	0-3(0-2)
FC Lokomotiv Gorna Oryahov. - PFC CSKA Sofia	0-3(0-1)	FC Hebar Pazardzhik - FC Arda 1924 Kardzhali	0-2(0-1)
FC Dobrudzha Dobrich - POFC Botev Vratsa	0-4(0-0)	OFC Pomorie - PFC Beroe Stara Zagora	0-2(0-1)
FC Minyor Pernik - PFC Botev Plovdiv	1-2(1-1)	OFC Spartak Pleven - PFC Septemvri Sofia	3-4(1-3)
FC Spartak Varna - PFC Levski Sofia	1-5(0-2)	FC Chernomorets Balchik - FC Vitosha Bistritsa	0-4(0-3)
FC Zagorets Nova Zagora - PFC Slavia Sofia	0-4(0-2)	FC Botev Galabovo - SFC Etar Veliko Tarnovo	2-1(0-0)
PFC Litex Lovech - FC Montana	3-0(1-0)	FC CSKA 1948 Sofia - FC Dunav Ruse 2010	2-1(1-1)

1/8-Finals [03-05.12.2019]			
PFC Beroe Stara Zagora - FC CSKA 1948 Sofia	3-4(2-3)	POFC Botev Vratsa - FC Kariana Erden	4-0(3-0)
PFC Slavia Sofia - PFC Botev Plovdiv	1-2(0-2)	PFC Levski Sofia - PFC Cherno More Varna	1-0(1-0)
PFC Septemvri Sofia - PFC Ludogorets Razgrad	0-3(0-2)	FC Arda 1924 Kardzhali - PFC CSKA Sofia	0-1(0-1)
FC Botev Galabovo - FC Vitosha Bistritsa	2-1(0-0)	PFC Lokomotiv Plovdiv - PFC Litex Lovech	2-1(0-0)

Quarter-Finals [03-05.03.2020]			
PFC Lokomotiv Plovdiv - FC CSKA 1948 Sofia	2-0(1-0)	FC Botev Galabovo - PFC Botev Plovdiv	0-1(0-0,0-0)
PFC CSKA Sofia - POFC Botev Vratsa	2-1(0-1)	PFC Levski Sofia - PFC Ludogorets Razgrad	0-0 aet; 6-5 pen

Semi-Finals [09-10/23-24.06.2020]			
First Leg		**Second Leg**	
PFC Lokomotiv Plovdiv - PFC Levski Sofia	2-0(2-0)	PFC Levski Sofia - PFC Lokomotiv Plovdiv	0-0
PFC Botev Plovdiv - PFC CSKA Sofia	0-0	PFC CSKA Sofia - PFC Botev Plovdiv	2-0(1-0)

Final

01.07.2020; Nationalen Stadion "Vasil Levski", Sofia; Referee: Georgi Kabakov; Attendance: 12,000
PFC Lokomotiv Plovdiv - PFC CSKA Sofia   **0-0; 5-3 on penalties**

Lokomotiv Plovdiv: Martin Lukov (120+1.Ilko Pirgov), Dinis Costa Lima Almeida, Lucas Gabriel Masoero Masi, Miloš Petrović, Birsent Hamdi Karagaren, Parvizchon Umarbaev (110.Dominique Sossorobla Malonga), Petar Vitanov, Josip Tomašević, Lucas Spinola Salinas (88.Momchil Tsvetanov), Dimitar Iliev (Cap), Ante Aralica. Trainer: Bruno Akrapović (Bosnia and Herzegovina).

CSKA Sofia: Gustavo Busatto, Ivan Turitsov, Valentin Antov, Petar Zanev (Cap), Bradley Mazikou, Kristiyan Malinov [*sent off 115*], Rúben Rafael Melo Silva Pinto (117.Plamen Galabov), Graham Carey, Tiago Filipe Sousa Nóbrega Rodrigues (88.Stefano Beltrame), Evandro da Silva (57.Henrique Roberto Rafael; 111.Geferson Cerqueira Teles), Ali Sowe. Trainer: Miloš Kruščić (Serbia).

Penalties: Dimitar Iliev 1-0; Petar Zanev 1-1; Dinis Costa Lima Almeida 2-1; Ali Sowe (saved); Birsent Hamdi Karagaren 3-1; Geferson Cerqueira Teles 3-2; Dominique Sossorobla Malonga 4-2; Graham Carey 4-3; Momchil Tsvetanov 5-3.

THE CLUBS 2019/2020

Please <u>note</u>: matches and goals includes statistics of regular season and play-offs (Championship Round and Relegation Round).

Professional Football Club Arda 1924 Kardzhali

Founded:	10.08.1924	
Stadium:	Arena Arda, Arda (15,000)	
Trainer:	Stamen Belchev	07.05.1969
[21.04.2020]	Nikolai Kirov	12.06.1975

Goalkeepers:	DOB	M	(s)	G
Nikolay Bankov	19.11.1990	3		
Ivan Karadzhov	12.07.1989	23	(1)	
Mesut Yusuf	14.01.1992	3		
Defenders:	**DOB**	**M**	**(s)**	**G**
Stoycho Atanasov	14.05.1997	3	(1)	
Zoran Gajić (SRB)	18.05.1990	22		
Darko Glisić (MKD)	23.09.1991	12		
Ilias Hassani (FRA)	08.11.1995	11	(1)	1
Martin Kostadinov	13.05.1996	4	(1)	
Atanasav Kratsev	01.02.1993	7	(8)	
Plamen Krumov	04.11.1985	15	(2)	1
Matheus Izidorio Leoni (BRA)	20.09.1991	15		
Connor Randall (ENG)	21.10.1995	7	(3)	
Alie Sesay (SLE)	02.08.1994		(1)	
Darren Sidoel (NED)	10.03.1998	11	(5)	
Ventsislav Vasilev	08.07.1988	2		
Midfielders:	**DOB**	**M**	**(s)**	**G**
Ventsislav Bengyuzov	22.01.1991	1	(4)	

	DOB	M	(s)	G
Aleksandar Georgiev	10.10.1997	10	(8)	
Rumyan Hovsepyan (ARM)	13.11.1991	20	(4)	1
Ivan Kokonov	17.08.1991	22	(3)	5
João Carlos Nogueira Amorim (POR)	11.02.1992	13	(1)	1
Deyan Lozev	26.10.1993	19		1
Lucas Willian Cruzeiro Martins (BRA)	12.05.1995	2	(9)	
Emil Martinov	18.03.1992	25	(3)	
Rumen Rumenov	07.06.1993	7		
Milen Stoev	29.09.1999	8	(2)	
Forwards:	**DOB**	**M**	**(s)**	**G**
Spas Delev	22.09.1989	15	(3)	1
Petar Hristov	25.06.1999		(1)	
Eray Karadayi	19.05.1995	1	(2)	
Svetoslav Kovachev	14.03.1998	7	(1)	2
Veselin Marchev	07.02.1990	3		1
Ahmed Osman	23.04.1985		(7)	
Elisha Sam (BEL)	31.03.1997	6	(12)	3
Radoslav Vasilev	12.10.1990	22	(4)	10

Professional Football Club Beroe Stara Zagora

Founded:	06.05.1916
Stadium:	Stadion Beroe, Stara Zagora (12,128)
Trainer:	Aleksandar Tomovski — 02.09.1978
[29.11.2019]	Dimitar Dimitrov — 09.06.1959

Goalkeepers:	DOB	M	(s)	G
Gennady Ganev (UKR)	15.05.1990	3		
Ivan Goshev	01.01.2000	1		
Plamen Kolev	09.02.1988	1		
Dušan Perniš (SVK)	28.11.1984	26		
Defenders:	**DOB**	**M**	**(s)**	**G**
Erol Alkan (TUR)	16.02.1994	15	(1)	
Ivan Bandalovski	23.11.1986	14		
Nikita Baranov (EST)	19.08.1992	3		
Pedro Miguel Pina Eugénio (POR)	26.06.1990	12	(2)	3
Steeve Furtado (FRA)	22.11.1994	9		
Victor Genev	27.10.1988	5	(2)	
Georgi Madzharov	22.03.2002		(1)	
Teddy Mézague (FRA)	27.05.1990	11		
Yaya Omnibes (CIV)	25.09.1997	5	(7)	
Krum Stoyanov	01.08.1991	11		1
Ahmed Touba (BEL)	13.03.1998	16		
Aleksandar Vasilev	27.04.1995	22	(2)	
Milen Zhelev	17.07.1993	10	(3)	1

Midfielders:	DOB	M	(s)	G
Georgi Angelov	12.11.1990	14	(2)	
Ruben Luís Maurício Brígido (POR)	23.06.1991	17	(3)	2
Ibrahima Conté (GUI)	03.04.1991	18	(6)	7
Gaïus Makouta (CGO)	25.07.1997	11		2
Ivan Minchev	28.05.1991	24	(5)	3
Octávio Merlo Manteca (BRA)	29.12.1993	4	(7)	1
Carlos Ohene (GHA)	21.07.1993	13	(4)	
Petko Tsankov	19.12.1995	1	(1)	
Aleksandar Tsvetkov	31.08.1990	29		1
Forwards:	**DOB**	**M**	**(s)**	**G**
Alioune Fall (SEN)	24.12.1994	10	(1)	5
Pierre Xavier Fonkeu (CMR)	10.07.1997	1	(2)	
Zoran Josipović (SUI)	25.08.1995	9	(10)	6
Martin Kamburov	13.10.1980	20	(9)	18
Nikola Marinov	30.07.2002		(8)	
Yulian Nenov	17.11.1994	1	(6)	
Wanderson Costa Viana (BRA)	07.02.1994	5	(7)	

Professional Football Club Botev Plovdiv

Founded:	12.03.1912
Stadium:	Botev 1912 Football Complex, Plovdiv (4,000)
Trainer:	Željko Petrović (MNE) — 13.11.1965
[08.10.2019]	Ferario Spasov — 20.02.1962

Goalkeepers:	DOB	M	(s)	G
Georgi Argilashki	13.06.1991	9		
Yanko Georgiev	22.10.1988	20		
Defenders:	**DOB**	**M**	**(s)**	**G**
Ivan Bandalovski	23.11.1986	9		
Kristian Dimitrov	27.02.1997	18		
Ebert Cardoso da Silva (BRA)	25.05.1993	10	(1)	1
Filip Filipov	02.08.1988	22	(5)	1
Johnathan Carlos Pereira (BRA)	04.04.1995	13	(7)	
Rodney Klooster (NED)	26.11.1996	3	(2)	
Lazar Marin	09.02.1994	18		2
Kostadin Nichev	22.07.1987	4	(4)	
Dimitar Pirgov	23.10.1989	23		
Radoslav Terziev	06.08.1994	20	(4)	1
Midfielders:	**DOB**	**M**	**(s)**	**G**
Lachezar Baltanov	11.07.1988	23	(2)	2
Biser Bonev	04.06.2003		(4)	
Petr Itov	12.02.2002		(1)	
Todor Nedelev	07.02.1993	26	(1)	9

	DOB	M	(s)	G
Marko Pervan (CRO)	04.04.1996	10	(8)	3
Dimitar Proychev	10.09.2001		(1)	
Stanislav Rabotov	14.06.2002	7		
Stanislav Shopov	23.02.2002	16	(8)	1
Atanas Stoimenov	25.09.2002		(3)	
Dimitar Tonev	15.10.2001	4	(7)	
Philippe van Arnhem	24.08.1996	8	(3)	
Antonio Vutov	06.06.1996	13	(6)	5
Forwards:	**DOB**	**M**	**(s)**	**G**
Anderson Pinto Ferreira Barbosa (BRA)	17.03.1999		(2)	
Fáider Fabio Burbano Castillo (COL)	12.06.1992	3	(2)	
Kristian Dobrev	27.04.2001	1	(5)	
Fernando Viana Jardim Silva (BRA)	20.02.1992	12	(2)	4
Nikola Iliev	06.06.2004	1	(1)	
Anton Karachanakov	17.01.1992	1		
Ivo Kazakov	30.01.2002		(2)	
Taylon Nicolas Correa Marcolino (BRA)	16.03.1995	4	(1)	
Aleksandar Tonev	03.02.1990	21	(2)	2
Ivan Vasilev	16.05.2001		(2)	

Professional Football Club Botev Vratsa

Founded:	1921
Stadium:	Stadion "Hristo Botev", Vratsa (12,000)
Trainer:	Sasho Angelov — 15.08.1969
[07.11.2019]	Stoycho Dramov
[10.11.2019]	Antoni Zdravkov — 20.08.1964

Goalkeepers:	DOB	M	(s)	G
Krasimir Kostov	11.02.1995	25		
Hristo Mitov	24.01.1985	4		
Defenders:	**DOB**	**M**	**(s)**	**G**
Petko Ganev	17.09.1996	8		1
Deyan Ivanov	12.04.1996	7	(1)	
Ventsislav Kerchev	02.06.1997	26	(1)	1
Angel Lyaskov	18.03.1998	18	(1)	
Ratko Mandić (SRB)	11.10.1992	1		
Simeon Mechev	16.03.1990	6	(5)	
Iliya Milanov	19.02.1992	25	(1)	2
Apostol Popov	22.12.1982	8		
Filip Žderić (GER)	11.12.1991	2		
Midfielders:	**DOB**	**M**	**(s)**	**G**
Petar Atanasov	13.10.1990	20	(7)	5
Daniel Gadzhev	21.06.1985	13	(6)	
Daniel Genov	19.05.1989	19	(4)	3

	DOB	M	(s)	G
Chavdar Ivaylov	09.07.1996	3	(1)	
Ivaylo Mihaylov	18.01.1991	8	(11)	
Alassane N'Diaye (FRA)	25.02.1990	8		1
Wellington Brito da Silva Tom (BRA)	23.07.1985	6	(2)	
Vladislav Uzunov	25.05.1991	3	(1)	
Georgi Valchev	07.03.1991	17	(1)	1
Milan Vušurović (MNE)	18.04.1995	2	(3)	
Dominik Yankov	28.07.2000	12	(10)	3
Atanas Zehirov	13.02.1989	5	(2)	
Hristo Zlatinski	22.01.1985	15	(1)	
Forwards:	**DOB**	**M**	**(s)**	**G**
Valeri Bojinov	15.02.1986	5	(4)	
Miroslav Budinov	23.01.1986	3	(12)	2
David Ribeiro Pereira (BRA)	23.04.1998	3	(2)	
Valeri Domovchiyski	05.10.1986	24	(3)	7
Andreas Vasev	01.03.1991	23	(4)	

Professional Football Club Cherno More Varna

Founded: 03.03.1913
Stadium: Stadion Ticha, Varna (8,250)
Trainer: Ilian Iliev   02.07.1968

Goalkeepers:	DOB	M	(s)	G
Ivan Dichevski	24.04.2001	1		
Ivan Dyulgerov	15.07.1999	9		
Miodrag Mitrovič (SUI)	14.07.1991	19		
Defenders:	**DOB**	**M**	**(s)**	**G**
Fahd Aktaou (MAR)	13.01.1993	2	(2)	1
Dimitrios Chantakias (GRE)	04.01.1995	16	(5)	1
Daniel Dimov	21.01.1989	18	(1)	1
Miroslav Enchev	08.08.1991	14	(1)	1
Tsvetomir Panov	17.04.1989	27		
Viktor Popov	05.03.2000	26		
Stefan Stanchev	26.04.1989	17	(2)	
Emil Yanchev	08.02.1999	2	(7)	
Midfielders:	**DOB**	**M**	**(s)**	**G**
Mehdi Boukassi (ALG)	15.06.1996	5	(5)	1
Pavel Georgiev			(1)	
Dani Kiki	08.01.1988	7	(7)	1
Ionuţ Neagu (ROU)	26.10.1989		(5)	
Vasil Panayotov	16.07.1990	26	(2)	
Erickson Patrick Correia Andrade (CPV)	09.02.1993	22	(2)	1
Petar Vutsov	07.08.2000	1	(1)	
Lachezar Yordanov	31.05.2000		(3)	
Forwards:	**DOB**	**M**	**(s)**	**G**
Denislav Angelov	05.01.2001		(9)	
Mathias Coureur (MTQ)	22.03.1988	8		3
Ilian Iliev	20.08.1999	11	(9)	3
Ismail Isa	26.06.1989	22		13
Álvaro Jordão Pinto da Silva Cardoso (POR)	14.10.1996	4	(15)	
Jorge Vinícius Oliveira Alves „Jorginho"(BRA)	03.05.1988	3	(3)	
Martin Minchev	22.04.2001	24	(1)	6
Aristote N'Dongala Fundu (COD)	19.01.1994	10	(7)	1
Rodrigo Henrique Santana da Silva (BRA)	02.07.1993	25	(1)	5
Velislav Vasilev	08.05.2001		(3)	

Professional Football Club Centralen Sporten Klub na Armiyata (CSKA) Sofia

Founded: 05.05.1948
Stadium: Balgarska Armiya Stadion, Sofia (18,495)
Trainer: Ljupko Petrović (SRB)   15.05.1947
[03.10.2019] Miloš Kruščić (SRB)   03.10.1976
[02.07.2020] Stamen Belchev   07.05.1969

Goalkeepers:	DOB	M	(s)	G
Gustavo Busatto (BRA)	23.10.1990	24		
Vytautas Černiauskas (LTU)	12.03.1989	7		
Defenders:	**DOB**	**M**	**(s)**	**G**
Valentin Antov	09.11.2000	17		1
Stoycho Atanasov	14.05.1997	2		
Nikolaj Bodurov	30.05.1986	2		
Bozhidar Chorbadzhiyski	08.08.1995	3		
Plamen Galabov	02.11.1995	17		1
Geferson Cerqueira Teles (BRA)	13.05.1994	9	(10)	1
Bradley Mazikou (FRA)	02.06.1996	23	(2)	
Mitko Mitkov	28.08.2000		(2)	1
Nuno Miguel Adro Tomás (POR)	15.09.1995	4		
Raúl Albentosa Redal (ESP)	07.09.1988	15		2
Ivan Turitsov	18.07.1999	19		
Petar Zanev	18.10.1985	26		1
Midfielders:	**DOB**	**M**	**(s)**	**G**
Ahmed Ahmedov	04.03.1995	2	(4)	
Vurnon Anita (NED)	04.04.1989	1	(1)	
Yoan Baurenski	25.10.2001		(1)	
Stefano Beltrame (ITA)	08.02.1993	6	(1)	2
Graham Carey (IRL)	20.05.1989	16	(9)	4
Diego Fabbrini (ITA)	31.07.1990	3	(2)	
Janio Bikel Figueiredo da Silva (POR)	28.06.1995	12	(2)	
Kristiyan Malinov	16.07.1994	21	(6)	2
Rúben Rafael Melo Silva Pinto (POR)	24.04.1992	15	(4)	1
Viv Solomon-Otabor (NGA)	02.01.1996	13	(6)	1
Tiago Filipe Sousa Nóbrega Rodrigues (POR)	29.01.1992	18	(6)	8
Forwards:	**DOB**	**M**	**(s)**	**G**
Denis Davydov (RUS)	22.03.1995		(3)	
Evandro da Silva (BRA)	14.01.1997	22	(8)	10
Edwin Gyasi (GHA)	01.07.1991	6	(3)	
Henrique Roberto Rafael (BRA)	23.08.1993	4	(7)	
Tomi Jurić (AUS)	22.07.1991		(7)	
Martin Smolenski	08.03.2003		(1)	
Ali Sowe (GAM)	14.06.1994	27	(3)	13
Anthony Paul Watt (SCO)	29.12.1993	7	(8)	3

Football Club Dunav Ruse 2010

Founded: 16.02.1949
Stadium: Stadion Gradski, Ruse (12,400)
Trainer: Ljudmil Kirov   16.02.1976

Goalkeepers:	DOB	M	(s)	G
Vincenzo Angelov	24.11.2000		(1)	
Hugo Chiusoli Gumiero (BRA)	01.01.1993	2		
Blagoy Makendzhiev	11.07.1988	27		
Defenders:	**DOB**	**M**	**(s)**	**G**
Georgi Dinkov	20.05.1991	2		1
Aleksandar Isaevski (MKD)	19.05.1995	19	(4)	
Rosen Kolev	04.07.1990	13	(2)	
Martin Kostadinov	13.05.1996	12	(4)	
Martin Kovachev	12.03.1982	16	(1)	1
Mihail Milchev	18.06.1988	26	(1)	
Mitko Mitkov	28.08.2000	3	(1)	
Iliya Munin	16.01.1993	2		
Lyuben Nikolov	08.09.1985	21	(1)	
Preslav Paparkov	30.01.2001	1		
Dimitar Todorov	19.09.2003	3		
Midfielders:	**DOB**	**M**	**(s)**	**G**
Ahmed Ahmedov	04.03.1995	18		6
Samir Ahmed Ayass (LIB)	24.12.1990	8	(7)	
Diyan Dimov	27.09.1985	22	(2)	
Samuel Eboue Inkoom (GHA)	01.06.1989	9	(1)	
Ivaylo Lazarov	11.04.1992	23	(3)	2
Mitko Rusanov	08.03.2001	4	(4)	
Sandro Emanuel Gonçalves Reis Pires Semedo (POR)	03.12.1996		(4)	
Svilen Shterev	14.12.1992	18	(7)	2
Alber Silviev	02.03.2002	1		
Atanas Stambolov	09.01.2003		(3)	
Mert Tasim	23.10.2002		(1)	
Petko Tsankov	19.12.1995	7		
Kristian Varbanov	01.01.2001	1	(1)	
Forwards:	**DOB**	**M**	**(s)**	**G**
Boris Dimitrov	29.03.2004		(2)	
Grigor Dolapchiev	23.02.1994	5	(3)	2
Stefan Hristov	28.08.1989	26	(1)	7
Simeon Ivanov	04.11.2002		(4)	
Valeri Ivanov	06.01.2002		(1)	
Konstantin Mitev			(3)	
Daudet N'Dongala (FRA)	16.09.1994	1	(4)	1
Yulian Nenov	17.11.1994	8		
Fernando Henrique Quintela (BRA)	03.05.1990	15	(9)	1
Ivan Selemenev (RUS)	24.12.1996	6	(7)	1

Sports Football Club Etar Veliko Tarnovo

Founded: 17.07.2013
Stadium: Stadion Ivaylo, Veliko Tarnovo (18,000)
Trainer: Rosen Kirilov   04.01.1973
[10.12.2019]   Petko Petkov   29.03.1968

Goalkeepers:	DOB	M	(s)	G
Anatoliy Gospodinov	21.03.1994	2		
Hristo Ivanov	06.04.1982	27		
Defenders:	DOB	M	(s)	G
Yordan Apostolov	30.11.1989	2	(3)	
Artjom Artjunin (EST)	24.01.1990	8	(4)	
Alexander Dyulgerov	19.04.1990	23		2
Hristofor Hubchev	24.11.1995	5	(1)	
Zdravko Iliev	19.10.1984	26		1
Ivan Ivanov	25.02.1988	11		
Georgi Kupenov	24.02.1997	4		
Ivan Skerlev	28.01.1986	10		
Krum Stoyanov	01.08.1991	18		
Midfielders:	DOB	M	(s)	G
Stelian Dobrev	13.09.2002	1	(3)	
Erol Dost	29.05.1999	2	(3)	
Nikola Kolev	06.06.1995	16	(4)	
Dino Martinović (SVN)	20.07.1990	3	(9)	1

	DOB	M	(s)	G
Daniel Mladenov	25.05.1987	15		8
Anton Ognyanov	30.06.1988	9		
Pedro Manuel Grácio Lagoa (POR)	21.08.1997	2	(4)	
Yani Pehlivanov	14.07.1988	16	(4)	3
Rumen Rumenov	07.06.1993	16	(1)	2
Kolyo Stanev	10.10.2001	2	(5)	
Krasimir Stanoev	14.09.1994	23		2
Forwards:	DOB	M	(s)	G
Milcho Angelov	02.01.1995	15	(5)	4
Florent Bojaj (ENG)	13.04.1996	20	(2)	3
Ivailo Dimitrov	26.03.1989	5	(6)	
Chris Gadi N'Kiasala (FRA)	09.04.1992	4	(1)	
Toni Ivanov	21.03.1999		(2)	
Bozhidar Katsarov	30.12.1993	8		
Svetoslav Kovachev	14.03.1998	12	(7)	
Ivan Petkov	22.01.1982		(3)	
Ivan Stoyanov	24.07.1983	8	(15)	2
Tonislav Yordanov	27.11.1998	6	(1)	5

Professional Football Club Levski Sofia

Founded: 24.05.1914
Stadium: Stadion Vivacom Arena „Georgi Asparuhov", Sofia (25,000)
Trainer: Petar Hubchev   26.02.1974

Goalkeepers:	DOB	M	(s)	G
Georgi Georgiev	12.10.1988	5		
Milan Mijatović (SRB)	26.07.1987	26		
Defenders:	DOB	M	(s)	G
Hólmar Eyjólfsson (ISL)	06.08.1990	20	(3)	3
Ivan Goranov	10.06.1992	28		2
Kostadin Iliev	21.02.2002	1		
Deyan Ivanov	12.04.1996	1		
Giannis Kargas (GRE)	09.12.1994	19	(2)	
Zhivko Milanov	15.07.1984	23		
Nuno Miguel Pereira Reis (POR)	31.01.1991	18	(1)	
Midfielders:	DOB	M	(s)	G
Asen Chandarov	13.11.1998		(3)	
Zdravko Dimitrov	24.08.1998	6	(5)	
Deyan Lozev	26.10.1993	4	(2)	
Franco Eduardo Mazurek (ARG)	24.09.1993	14	(11)	1
Filipe Guterres Nascimento (POR)	07.01.1995	10	(3)	2

	DOB	M	(s)	G
Davide Mariani (SUI)	19.05.1991	3		4
Ivaylo Naydenov	22.03.1998	8	(4)	
Martin Raynov	25.04.1992	28	(2)	
Simeon Slavchev	25.09.1993	1	(2)	1
Stijn Spierings (NED)	12.03.1996	7	(2)	2
Khaly Iyane Thiam (SEN)	07.01.1994	21		2
Iliya Yurukov	22.09.1999	7	(2)	
Forwards:	DOB	M	(s)	G
Deni Alar (AUT)	18.01.1990	12	(10)	2
Iliya Dimitrov	10.07.1996		(1)	
Stanislav Ivanov	16.04.1999	25	(2)	9
Stanislav Kostov	02.10.1991	6	(8)	
Mohammed Nasiru (GHA)	06.06.1994	1	(10)	1
Paulo Victor de Menezes Melo „Paulinho" (BRA)	29.05.1993	30		8
Marin Petkov	02.10.2003		(4)	
Martin Petkov	15.08.2002		(16)	1
Nigel Robertha (CUW)	13.02.1998	17	(2)	11

Professional Football Club Lokomotiv Plovdiv

Founded: 25.07.1926
Stadium: Stadion Lokomotiv, Plovdiv (13,000)
Trainer: Bruno Akrapović (BIH)   26.09.1967

Goalkeepers:	DOB	M	(s)	G
Martin Lukov	05.07.1993	26		
Ilko Pirgov	23.05.1986	5		
Defenders:	DOB	M	(s)	G
Mustapha Abdullahi (NGA)	18.01.1996		(1)	
Shola Akinyemi (NOR)	03.07.1993	8	(1)	
Dinis Costa Lima Almeida (POR)	28.05.1995	21	(2)	3
Stephen Eze (NGA)	08.03.1994	19		3
Arhan Isuf	25.01.1999	1		
Mihovil Klapan (CRO)	27.03.1995	1	(5)	
David Malembana (GER)	11.10.1995	19	(5)	1
Lucas Gabriel Masoero Masi (ARG)	01.02.1995	12		
Petar Petrov			(3)	
Miloš Petrović (SRB)	05.05.1990	19	(3)	
Josip Tomašević (CRO)	04.03.1994	25	(3)	2
Midfielders:	DOB	M	(s)	G
Edin Bahtic (AUT)	14.07.1996	3	(12)	1
Eliton Pardinho Toreta Junior (BRA)	28.01.1998	1	(1)	

	DOB	M	(s)	G
Georgi Iliev	05.09.1981	13	(6)	4
Lucas Spinola Salinas (BRA)	14.10.1995	10		2
Valentino Pugliese (SUI)	18.07.1997	2	(2)	
Parvizchon Umarbaev (TJK)	01.11.1994	24	(2)	
Petar Vitanov	10.03.1995	19	(7)	
Wiris Gustavo de Oliveira (BRA)	04.07.2000	4	(3)	1
Forwards:	DOB	M	(s)	G
Ante Aralica (CRO)	23.07.1996	14	(11)	5
Mirza Hasanbegovic (BIH)	19.07.2001		(1)	
Dimitar Iliev	25.09.1988	27		12
Birsent Hamdi Karagaren	06.12.1992	25	(3)	7
Dominique Sossorobla Malonga (CGO)	08.01.1989	4	(3)	3
Kenan Muslimović (AUT)	13.02.1997	1	(1)	1
Nikolay Nikolaev	01.10.1992	6	(7)	
Alen Ožbolt (SVN)	24.06.1996	18	(2)	6
Stoimen Totkov	03.01.2000			
Momchil Tsvetanov	03.12.1990	14	(10)	

Professional Football Club Ludogorets Razgrad

Founded:	1945		
Stadium:	Ludogorets Arena, Razgrad (10,442)		
Trainer:	Stoycho Stoev		15.07.1962
[09.09.2019]	Stanislav Genchev		20.03.1981
[01.01.2020]	Pavel Vrba (CZE)		06.12.1963

Goalkeepers:	DOB	M	(s)	G
Plamen Iliev	30.11.1991	16		
Renan dos Santos (BRA)	18.05.1989	8		
Vladislav Stoyanov	08.06.1987	7		
Defenders:	**DOB**	**M**	**(s)**	**G**
Neuciano de Jesus Gusmão „Cicinho" (BRA)	26.12.1988	17	(1)	
Dragoş Grigore (ROU)	07.09.1986	17		
Jordan Ikoko (COD)	03.02.1994	15	(3)	1
Stanislav Manolev	16.12.1985	8	(7)	1
Cosmin Iosif Moţi (ROU)	03.12.1984	11	(1)	2
Anton Nedyalkov	30.04.1993	23	(3)	
Rafael Forster (BRA)	23.07.1990	8		
Taleb Tawatha (ISR)	21.06.1992	4	(2)	
Georgi Terziev	18.04.1992	22	(2)	
Midfielders:	**DOB**	**M**	**(s)**	**G**
Stéphane Badji (SEN)	18.01.1990	17	(4)	
Dan Biton (ISR)	20.07.1995	14	(7)	5
Cauly Oliveira-Souza (BRA)	15.09.1995	9	(1)	3
Svetoslav Dyakov	31.05.1984	15	(7)	
Jacek Góralski (POL)	21.09.1992	8	(3)	
Jorge Fernando Barbosa Intima „Jorghinho"(GNB)	21.09.1995	17	(5)	7
Marcelo Nascimento da Costa „Marcelinho"	24.08.1984	12	(4)	5
Dominik Yankov	28.07.2000	1		
Ivan Yordanov	07.11.2000		(2)	
Serkan Yusein	31.03.1996	2	(1)	
Forwards:	**DOB**	**M**	**(s)**	**G**
Anicet Andrianantenaina Abel (MAD)	13.03.1990	19	(3)	1
Dimo Bakalov	19.12.1988	4	(14)	1
Claudiu Andrei Keşerü (ROU)	02.12.1986	13	(6)	12
Jody Lukoki (COD)	15.11.1992	7	(4)	3
Jakub Świerczok (POL)	28.12.1992	11	(10)	6
Mavis Tchibota Dufounou (CGO)	07.05.1996	19	(6)	7
Wanderson Cristaldo Farias (BRA)	02.01.1988	17	(5)	5

Professional Football Club Slavia Sofia

Founded:	10.04.1913		
Stadium:	Stadion Slavia, Sofia (25,556)		
Trainer:	Zlatomir Zagorčić		15.06.1971

Goalkeepers:	DOB	M	(s)	G
Georgi Georgiev	12.10.1988	17		
Georgi Petkov	14.03.1976	1	(1)	
Antonis Stergiakis (GRE)	16.03.1999	13		
Defenders:	**DOB**	**M**	**(s)**	**G**
Martin Achkov	10.07.1999	1		
Martin Atanasov	19.01.2002		(4)	
David Humanes Muñoz (ESP)	13.11.1996	4		
Venelin Filipov	20.08.1990	2	(2)	
Andrea Hristov	01.03.1999	17		
Petar Patev	21.05.1993	17	(2)	
Hristo Popadiyn	06.01.1994	26	(1)	1
Ertan Tombak	30.05.1999		(3)	
Emil Viyachki	18.05.1990	23	(2)	1
Midfielders:	**DOB**	**M**	**(s)**	**G**
Ventsislav Bengyuzov	22.01.1991	12	(6)	
Nikolay Dyulgerov	10.03.1988	6	(2)	
Milen Gamakov	12.04.1994	27	(1)	
Galin Ivanov	15.04.1988	26		7
Yanis Karabelyov	23.01.1996	22		3
Nediljko Kovačević (CRO)	16.10.1995		(1)	
Filip Krastev	15.10.2001	13	(2)	3
Emil Stoev	17.01.1996	15	(11)	4
Slavcho Shokolarov	20.08.1989	12	(1)	1
Dimitar Stoyanov	14.04.2001		(2)	
Darko Tasevski (MKD)	20.05.1984	7	(4)	1
Vladislav Uzunov	24.05.1991	7	(7)	2
Georgi Valchev	07.03.1991	1	(5)	
Dimitar Velkovski	22.01.1995	12	(1)	1
Forwards:	**DOB**	**M**	**(s)**	**G**
Tsvetelin Chunchukov	26.12.1994	19	(3)	3
Ivailo Dimitrov	26.03.1989	3	(7)	3
Radoslav Kirilov	29.06.1992	18	(4)	4
Kaloyan Krastev	24.01.1999	4	(16)	2
Ilian Micanski	20.12.1985	1	(2)	1
Georgi Yomov	06.07.1997	15	(8)	4

Football Club Tsarko Selo Sofia

Founded:	01.07.2015		
Stadium:	Arena Tsarko Selo, Sofia (1,550)		
Trainer:	Nikola Spasov		15.12.1958
[30.04.2020]	Luboslav Penev		31.08.1966

Goalkeepers:	DOB	M	(s)	G
Ivan Čvorović	21.09.1985	4		
Martin Dimitrov	20.03.1996	7		
Johny Placide (HAI)	29.01.1988	18		
Defenders:	**DOB**	**M**	**(s)**	**G**
Charleston Silva dos Santos „Charles" (BRA)	23.09.1996	1	(2)	
Dilyan Georgiev	23.06.1905		(1)	
Gustavo Carbonieri Santa Rosa (BRA)	04.03.1992	14	(1)	1
Rumen Gyonov	09.05.1992	8		
Georgi Hashev	26.03.1990	3	(6)	
Ivailo Ivanov	11.01.2001	2	(4)	
Julio César Rodríguez López (ESP)	07.12.1995	5	(1)	
Martin Kavdanski	13.02.1987	24	(3)	
Leonardo Savicius Raimundo Fioravanti(BRA)	26.11.1992	2	(2)	
Ivaylo Markov	05.06.1997	17	(1)	
Simeon Mechev	16.03.1990	2	(3)	1
Veselin Minev	14.10.1980	17		
Yordan Minev	14.10.1980	12	(1)	
Midfielders:	**DOB**	**M**	**(s)**	**G**
Dylan Bahamboula (FRA)	22.05.1995	12	(3)	2
Edin Bahtic (AUT)	14.07.1996	1		
Reyan Daskalov	10.02.1995	26	(1)	
Svetoslav Dikov	18.04.1992		(4)	
Iliya Dzhamov	11.06.1998		(4)	
Everton Macedo Dias (BRA)	04.06.1990	4		
Antonio Georgiev	26.10.1997	14	(3)	2
Emanuil Manev	19.04.1992	4	(4)	
Toma Ushagelov	17.04.2001		(4)	1
Serkan Kadir Yusein	31.03.1996	9	(2)	
Forwards:	**DOB**	**M**	**(s)**	**G**
Anderson Cordeiro Costa (BRA)	10.10.1998	12	(7)	1
Rodney Antwi (NED)	03.11.1995	20		9
Borislav Baldzhiyski	12.10.1990		(2)	
Miroslav Budinov	23.01.1986	8		1
Sergey Georgiev	05.05.1992		(3)	
Ventsislav Hristov	09.11.1988	6	(5)	
Vladislav Ivanov			(2)	
Anton Karachanakov	17.01.1992	8	(5)	2
Bozhidar Katsarov	30.12.1993	10	(2)	
Ludcinio Marengo (NED)	14.09.1991	4		
Damien Clément Marie (FRA)	19.06.1994	1	(4)	
Georgi Minchev	20.04.1995	18	(5)	3
Wesley Natã Wachholz (BRA)	18.04.1995	26		3

Football Club Vitosha Bistritsa

Founded:	1958	
Stadium:	Stadion Bistritsa, Bistritsa (2,500)	
Trainer:	Engibar Engibarov	05.09.1971
[17.01.2020]	Asen Bukarev	07.02.1979

Goalkeepers:	DOB	M	(s)	G
Nikolaj Georgiev	06.09.1998	2		
Kristiyan Katsarev	07.08.1995	5	(1)	
Nikolai Krastev	06.12.1996	6		
Hristiyan Vasilev	05.12.1997	16		
Defenders:	**DOB**	**M**	**(s)**	**G**
Ventzislav Bonev	08.05.1980	27		1
Nikolay Borisov	21.11.2000		(1)	
Mario Dilchovski	28.08.2001	3		
Bogomil Dyakov	04.12.1984	8		
Todor Gochev	15.04.1993	18		
Rumen Gyonov	09.05.1992	12		
Teodor Kostadinov	08.05.2001		(4)	
Theofilos Kouroupis (GRE)	11.04.1990	4	(5)	
Georgi Kupenov	24.02.1997	12	(1)	1
Veselin Minev	14.10.1980	4		
Yordan Minev	14.10.1980	2		
Zdravko Panev	11.09.2001		(1)	
Apostol Popov	22.12.1982	1	(1)	1
Kristian Uzunov	04.02.1989	2	(6)	
Midfielders:	**DOB**	**M**	**(s)**	**G**
Georgi Amzin	18.04.1992	24	(1)	2

	DOB	M	(s)	G
Emil Gargorov	15.02.1981	11	(3)	3
Alexander Hristev	07.04.1997	3	(1)	
Kristiyan Kochilov	03.04.1990	14	(4)	1
Vasil Prvanov	13.07.2001		(6)	
Chetin Sadula	16.06.1987	21	(3)	1
Georgi Sarmov	07.09.1985	1	(1)	
Martin Stankev	29.07.1989	8	(3)	
Alex Terziiski	09.06.2001		(4)	
Evgeni Zyumbyulev	02.02.1989	19	(1)	
Forwards:	**DOB**	**M**	**(s)**	**G**
Iliya Dimitrov	10.07.1996	14	(1)	3
Zapro Dinev	25.09.1999	7	(15)	1
Grigor Dolapchiev	23.02.1994	6	(6)	
Alexey Georgiev	21.11.2001		(1)	
Hristo Ivanov	16.12.2000	7	(6)	
Vanyo Ivanov	09.05.2000	7	(1)	
Atanas Kabov	11.04.1999	20	(4)	1
Daniel Kutev	06.03.1991	7	(5)	
Aristote Madiani (FRA)	22.08.1995		(1)	
Stanislav Malamov	10.11.1989	4		
Andreas David Palomike Sánchez (COL)	30.09.1998		(1)	
Mohammed Sila (MLI)	01.11.1998	2	(2)	

SECOND LEVEL
Second Professional Football League 2019/2020

1.	FC CSKA 1948 Sofia (*Promoted*)	21	18	1	2	59	-	18	55
2.	PFC Septemvri Sofia (*Promotion Play-offs*)	20	17	1	2	47	-	19	52
3.	FC Montana (*Promotion Play-offs*)	21	13	3	5	40	-	17	42
4.	FC Lokomotiv 1929 Sofia	21	12	3	6	34	-	18	39
5.	PFC Neftochimic Burgas	21	10	3	8	35	-	29	33
6.	FC Hebar Pazardzhik	21	10	3	8	35	-	30	33
7.	PFC Litex Lovech	20	9	5	6	29	-	15	32
8.	FC Kariana Erden	20	9	5	6	30	-	24	32
9.	FC Lokomotiv Gorna Oryahovitsa	21	8	5	8	32	-	30	29
10.	FC Botev Galabovo*	21	6	7	8	23	-	32	25
11.	OFC Pirin Blagoevgrad	20	6	7	7	24	-	29	25
12.	PFC Ludogorets Razgrad II	21	5	9	7	20	-	25	24
13.	FC Strumska Slava Radomir	21	7	1	13	21	-	34	22
14.	FC Chernomorets Balchik*	20	6	4	10	15	-	27	22
15.	FC Spartak Varna (*Relegated*)	21	2	4	15	6	-	42	10
16.	OFC Spartak Pleven (*Relegated*)	21	2	4	15	10	-	41	7
17.	OFC Pomorie*	21	2	3	16	15		45	6

*Disqualified and relegated to the Third League.

INTERNATIONAL MATCHES
(16.07.2019 – 15.07.2020)

07.09.2019	London	England - Bulgaria	4-0(1-0)	(ECQ)
10.09.2019	Dublin	Republic of Ireland - Bulgaria	3-1(0-0)	(F)
11.10.2019	Podgorica	Montenegro - Bulgaria	0-0	(ECQ)
14.10.2019	Sofia	Bulgaria - England	0-6(0-4)	(ECQ)
14.11.2019	Sofia	Bulgaria - Paraguay	0-1(0-0)	(F)
17.11.2019	Sofia	Bulgaria - Czech Republic	1-0(0-0)	(ECQ)
26.02.2020	Sofia	Bulgaria - Belarus	0-1(0-1)	(F)

07.09.2019 ENGLAND - BULGARIA 4-0(1-0) 16th EC. Qualifiers

Wembley Stadium, London; Referee: Marco Guida (Italy); Attendance: 82,605
BUL: Plamen Iliev, Nikolay Bodurov (65.Kristian Dimitrov), Strahil Popov, Vasil Bozhikov, Anton Nedyalkov, Georgi Sarmov, Ivelin Popov (Cap), Galin Ivanov (83.Daniel Mladenov), Kristiyan Malinov, Wanderson Cristaldo Farias, Marcelo Nascimento da Costa "Marcelinho" (67.Kiril Despodov). Trainer: Krasimir Balakov.

10.09.2019 REPUBLIC OF IRELAND - BULGARIA 3-1(0-0) Friendly International

Aviva Stadium, Dublin; Referee: Tobias Welz (Germany); Attendance: 18,259
BUL: Hristo Ivanov, Ivan Goranov, Anton Nedyalkov (Cap) (59.Vasil Bozhikov), Kristian Dimitrov (80.Vasil Panayotov), Nikolay Dimitrov (59.Wanderson Cristaldo Farias), Georgi Milanov (46.Ivelin Popov), Daniel Mladenov (68.Kiril Despodov), Georgi Pashov, Kristiyan Malinov (81.Georgi Terziev), Simeon Slavchev, Bozhidar Kraev. Trainer: Krasimir Balakov.
Goal: Ivelin Popov (67 penalty).

11.10.2019 MONTENEGRO - BULGARIA 0-0 16th EC. Qualifiers

Stadion pod Goricom, Podgorica; Referee: Andreas Ekberg (Sweden); Attendance: 2,743
BUL: Plamen Iliev, Petar Zanev, Kristiyan Malinov, Anton Nedyalkov, Kristian Dimitrov, Galin Ivanov, Ivelin Popov (Cap) (63.Georgi Kostadinov), Georgi Pashov, Wanderson Cristaldo Farias (77.Bircent Hamdi Karagaren), Marcelo Nascimento da Costa "Marcelinho" (70.Ismail Isa Mustafa), Bozhidar Kraev. Trainer: Krasimir Balakov.

14.10.2019 BULGARIA - ENGLAND 0-6(0-4) 16th EC. Qualifiers

Nationalen Stadion "Vasil Levski", Sofia; Referee: Referee: Ivan Bebek (Croatia); Attendance: 17,481
BUL: Plamen Iliev, Petar Zanev, Georgi Terziev, Kamen Hadzhiev, Georgi Sarmov (46.Bozhidar Kraev), Ivelin Popov (Cap), Georgi Pashov, Georgi Kostadinov, Wanderson Cristaldo Farias (76.Kristiyan Malinov), Ismail Isa Mustafa (68.Galin Ivanov), Kiril Despodov. Trainer: Krasimir Balakov.

14.11.2019 BULGARIA - PARAGUAY 0-1(0-0) Friendly International

Nationalen Stadion "Vasil Levski", Sofia; Referee: Inácio Altino da Costa Pereira (Portugal); Attendance: 500
BUL: Georgi Georgiev, Strahil Popov (84.Viktor Popov), Georgi Terziev (63.Kristian Dimitrov), Ivan Goranov, Bozhidar Chorbadzhiyski, Ivelin Popov (Cap), Kristiyan Malinov, Wanderson Cristaldo Farias (69.Galin Ivanov), Georgi Kostadinov (80.Aleksandar Tsvetkov), Todor Nedelev (46.Bozhidar Kraev), Marcelo Nascimento da Costa "Marcelinho" (46.Kiril Despodov). Trainer: Georgi Dermendzhiev.

17.11.2019 BULGARIA - CZECH REPUBLIC 1-0(0-0) 16th EC. Qualifiers

Nationalen Stadion "Vasil Levski", Sofia; Referee: Referee: Sergei Karasev (Russia); Attendance: *played behind closed doors*
BUL: Georgi Georgiev, Petar Zanev, Strahil Popov, Vasil Bozhikov, Georgi Terziev, Ivelin Popov (Cap), Georgi Kostadinov, Kristiyan Malinov (88.Aleksandar Tsvetkov), Wanderson Cristaldo Farias (73.Todor Nedelev), Marcelo Nascimento da Costa "Marcelinho", Kiril Despodov (69.Bozhidar Kraev). Trainer: Georgi Dermendzhiev.
Goal: Vasil Bozhikov (56).

26.02.2020 BULGARIA - BELARUS 0-1(0-1) Friendly International

Nationalen Stadion "Vasil Levski", Sofia; Referee: Trustin Farrugia Cann (Malta); Attendance: 250
BUL: Georgi Georgiev, Petar Zanev (Cap), Ivan Goranov, Stefan Velkov (77.Valentin Antov), Ivan Turitsov, Georgi Milanov (76.Aleksandar Tsvetkov), Kristiyan Malinov, Ismail Isa Mustafa (68.Svetoslav Kovachev), Dimitar Iliev (46.Todor Nedelev), Spas Delev (89.Viktor Popov), Aleksandar Tonev (83.Martin Minchev). Trainer: Georgi Dermendzhiev.

NATIONAL TEAM PLAYERS
(16.07.2019 – 15.07.2020)

Name	DOB	Caps	Goals	2019/2020:	Club
Goalkeepers					
Georgi GEORGIEV	12.10.1988	3	0	2019/2020:	*PFC Slavia Sofia*
Plamen ILIEV	30.11.1991	16	0	2019:	*PFC Ludogorets Razgrad*
Hristo IVANOV	06.04.1982	1	0	2019:	*SFC Etar Veliko Tarnovo*
Defenders					
Valentin ANTOV	09.11.2000	2	0	2019/2020:	*PFC CSKA Sofia*
Nikolay BODUROV	30.05.1986	50	2	2019:	*PFC CSKA Sofia*
Vasil BOZHIKOV	02.06.1988	26	2	2019:	*ŠK Slovan Bratislava (SVK)*
Bozhidar CHORBADZHIYSKI	01.08.1995	9	0	2019:	*FCSB Bucureşti (ROU)*
Kristian DIMITROV	27.02.1997	6	1	2019:	*PFC Botev Plovdiv*
Ivan GORANOV	10.06.1992	6	0	2019/2020:	*PFC Levski Sofia*
Anton NEDYALKOV	30.04.1993	14	0	2019:	*PFC Ludogorets Razgrad*
Georgi PASHOV	04.03.1990	1	0	2019:	*FC Ararat-Armenia Yerevan (ARM)*
Strahil POPOV	31.08.1990	29	0	2019:	*Kasımpaşa SK Beyoğlu (TUR)*
Viktor POPOV	05.03.2000	2	0	2019/2020:	*PFC Cherno More Varna*
Georgi TERZIEV	18.04.1992	14	0	2019:	*PFC Ludogorets Razgrad*
Ivan TURITSOV	18.07.1999	1	0	2020:	*PFC CSKA Sofia*
Stefan VELKOV	12.12.1996	1	0	2020:	*RKC Waalwijk (NED)*
Petar ZANEV	18.10.1985	43	0	2019/2020:	*PFC CSKA Sofia*
Midfielders					
Nikolay DIMITROV	15.10.1987	10	1	2019:	*FK Ural Yekaterinburg (RUS)*
Kamen HADZHIEV	22.09.1991	1	0	2019:	*Puskás Ferenc Labdarugó Akadémia Felcsút (HUN)*
Dimitar ILIEV	25.09.1988	1	0	2020:	*PFC Lokomotiv Plovdiv*
Galin IVANOV	15.04.1988	10	1	2019:	*PFC Slavia Sofia*
Georgi KOSTADINOV	07.09.1990	23	3	2019:	*FK Arsenal Tula (RUS)*
Bozhidar KRAEV	23.06.1997	14	2	2019:	*Gil Vicente FC Barcelos (POR)*
Kristiyan MALINOV	30.03.1994	12	0	2019/2020:	*PFC CSKA Sofia*
Marcelo Nascimento da Costa "MARCELINHO"	24.08.1984	11	2	2019:	*PFC Ludogorets Razgrad*
Georgi MILANOV	19.02.1992	43	2	2019/2020:	*MOL Fehérvár FC Székesfehérvár (HUN)*
Todor NEDELEV	07.02.1993	28	2	2019/2020:	*PFC Botev Plovdiv*
Vasil PANAYOTOV	16.07.1990	1	0	2019:	*PFC Cherno More Varna*
Georgi SARMOV	07.09.1985	15	0	2019:	*Chemnitzer FC (GER)*
Simeon SLAVCHEV	25.09.1993	25	0	2019:	*Qarabağ FK Bakı (AZE)*
Aleksandar TONEV	03.02.1990	29	5	2020:	*PFC Botev Plovdiv*
Aleksandar TSVETKOV	31.08.1990	5	0	2019/2020:	*PFC Beroe Stara Zagora*
WANDERSON Cristaldo Farias	02.01.1988	6	0	2019:	*PFC Ludogorets Razgrad*
Forwards					
Spas DELEV	22.09.1989	25	2	2020:	*FC Arda Kardzhali*
Kiril DESPODOV	11.08.1996	12	1	2019:	*SK Sturm Graz (AUT)*
Ismail ISA Mustafa	26.06.1989	5	1	2019/2020:	*PFC Cherno More Varna*
Bircent Hamdi KARAGAREN	06.12.1992	1	0	2019:	*PFC Lokomotiv Plovdiv*
Svetoslav KOVACHEV	14.03.1998	1	0	2020:	*FC Arda Kardzhali*
Martin MINCHEV	22.04.2001	4	0	2020:	*PFC Cherno More Varna*
Daniel MLADENOV	25.05.1987	2	0	2019:	*SFC Etar Veliko Tarnovo*
Ivelin POPOV	26.10.1987	90	16	2019:	*FK Rostov-na-Donu (RUS)*

National team coach		
Krasimir BALAKOV [01.06. – 18.10.2019]	29.03.1966	6 M; 1 W; 1 D; 4 L; 5-17
Georgi DERMENDZHIEV [from 28.10.20199	04.01.1955	3 M; 1 W; 0 D; 2 L; 1-2

CROATIA

The Country:
Republika Hrvatska (Republic of Croatia)
Capital: Zagreb
Surface: 56,594 km²
Inhabitants: 4,076,246 [2019]
Time: UTC+1

The FA:
Hrvatski nogometni savez
Vukovarska 269A, 10000 Zagreb
Tel: +385 1 2361 555
Foundation date: 16.07.1941 (as Independent State of Croatia); 03.07.1992 (as Croatia)
Member of FIFA since: 1992
Member of UEFA since: 1993
Website: www.hns-cff.hr

NATIONAL TEAM RECORDS

RECORDS		
First international match:	02.04.1940, Zagreb:	Croatia – Switzerland 4-0
Most international caps:	Darijo Srna	- 134 caps (2002-2016)
Most international goals:	Davor Šuker	- 45 goals / 69 caps (1990-2002)

UEFA EUROPEAN CHAMPIONSHIP	
1960	-
1964	-
1968	-
1972	-
1976	-
1980	-
1984	-
1988	-
1992	-
1996	Final Tournament (Quarter-Finals)
2000	Qualifiers
2004	Final Tournament (Group Stage)
2008	Final Tournament (Quarter-Finals)
2012	Final Tournament (Group Stage)
2016	Final Tournament (Group Stage)
2020	*Final Tournament (Qualified)*

FIFA WORLD CUP	
1930	-
1934	-
1938	-
1950	-
1954	-
1958	-
1962	-
1966	-
1970	-
1974	-
1978	-
1982	-
1986	-
1990	-
1994	Did not enter
1998	Final Tournament (3rd Place)
2002	Final Tournament (Group Stage)
2006	Final Tournament (Group Stage)
2010	Qualifiers
2014	Final Tournament (Group Stage)
2018	Final Tournament (Runners-up)

OLYMPIC TOURNAMENTS	
1908	-
1912	-
1920	-
1924	-
1928	-
1936	-
1948	-
1952	-
1956	-
1960	-
1964	-
1968	-
1972	-
1976	-
1980	-
1984	-
1988	-
1992	-
1996	Qualifiers
2000	Qualifiers
2004	Qualifiers
2008	Qualifiers
2012	Qualifiers
2016	Qualifiers

UEFA NATIONS LEAGUE

2018/2019 – League A

FIFA CONFEDERATIONS CUP 1992-2017

None

CROATIAN CLUB HONOURS IN EUROPEAN CLUB COMPETITIONS:

European Champion Clubs' Cup (1956-1992) / UEFA Champions League (1993-2020)		
None		

Fairs Cup (1858-1971) / UEFA Cup (1972-2009) / UEFA Europa League (2010-2020)		
GNK Dinamo Zagreb*	1	1966/1967

represented Yugoslavia

UEFA Super Cup (1972-2019)		
None		

*European Cup Winners' Cup 1961-1999**		
None		

defunct competition

	CHAMPIONS	CUP WINNERS	BEST GOALSCORERS	
1992	HNK Hajduk Split	NK Inter Zaprešić	Ardian Kozniku (HNK Hajduk Split)	12
1992/1993	NK Croatia Zagreb	HNK Hajduk Split	Goran Vlaović (NK Croatia Zagreb)	23
1993/1994	HNK Hajduk Split	NK Croatia Zagreb	Goran Vlaović (NK Croatia Zagreb)	29
1994/1995	HNK Hajduk Split	HNK Hajduk Split	Robert Špehar (NK Osijek)	23
1995/1996	NK Croatia Zagreb	NK Croatia Zagreb	Igor Cvitanović (NK Croatia Zagreb)	19
1996/1997	NK Croatia Zagreb	NK Croatia Zagreb	Igor Cvitanović (NK Croatia Zagreb)	20
1997/1998	NK Croatia Zagreb	NK Croatia Zagreb	Mate Baturina (NK Zagreb)	18
1998/1999	NK Croatia Zagreb	NK Osijek	Joško Popović (HNK Šibenik)	21
1999/2000	GNK Dinamo Zagreb	HNK Hajduk Split	Tomo Šokota (GNK Dinamo Zagreb)	21
2000/2001	HNK Hajduk Split	GNK Dinamo Zagreb	Tomo Šokota (GNK Dinamo Zagreb)	20
2001/2002	NK Zagreb	GNK Dinamo Zagreb	Ivica Olić (NK Zagreb)	21
2002/2003	GNK Dinamo Zagreb	HNK Hajduk Split	Ivica Olić (GNK Dinamo Zagreb)	16
2003/2004	HNK Hajduk Split	GNK Dinamo Zagreb	Robert Špehar (NK Osijek)	18
2004/2005	HNK Hajduk Split	HNK Rijeka	Tomislav Erceg (HNK Rijeka)	17
2005/2006	GNK Dinamo Zagreb	HNK Rijeka	Ivan Bošnjak (GNK Dinamo Zagreb)	22
2006/2007	GNK Dinamo Zagreb	GNK Dinamo Zagreb	Eduardo (GNK Dinamo Zagreb)	34
2007/2008	GNK Dinamo Zagreb	GNK Dinamo Zagreb	Želimir Terkeš (BIH, NK Zadar)	21
2008/2009	GNK Dinamo Zagreb	GNK Dinamo Zagreb	Mario Mandžukić (GNK Dinamo Zagreb)	16
2009/2010	GNK Dinamo Zagreb	HNK Hajduk Split	Davor Vugrinec (NK Zagreb)	18
2010/2011	GNK Dinamo Zagreb	GNK Dinamo Zagreb	Ivan Krstanović (BIH, NK Zagreb)	19
2011/2012	GNK Dinamo Zagreb	GNK Dinamo Zagreb	Fatos Bećiraj (MNE, GNK Dinamo Zagreb)	15
2012/2013	GNK Dinamo Zagreb	HNK Hajduk Split	Leon Benko (HNK Rijeka)	19
2013/2014	GNK Dinamo Zagreb	HNK Rijeka	Duje Čop (GNK Dinamo Zagreb)	22
2014/2015	GNK Dinamo Zagreb	GNK Dinamo Zagreb	Andrej Kramarić (HNK Rijeka)	21
2015/2016	GNK Dinamo Zagreb	GNK Dinamo Zagreb	Ilija Nestorovski (MKD, NK Inter Zaprešić)	25
2016/2017	HNK Rijeka	HNK Rijeka	Márkó Futács (HUN, HNK Hajduk Split)	18
2017/2018	GNK Dinamo Zagreb	GNK Dinamo Zagreb	El Arabi Hillel Soudani (ALG, GNK Dinamo Zagreb)	17
2018/2019	GNK Dinamo Zagreb	HNK Rijeka	Mijo Caktaš (HNK Hajduk Split)	19
2019/2020	GNK Dinamo Zagreb	HNK Rijeka	Antonio Čolak (HNK Rijeka) Mijo Caktaš (HNK Hajduk Split) Mirko Marić (NK Osijek)	20

Please note: GNK Dinamo Zagreb were called NK Croatia Zagreb between 1993 and 2000.

NATIONAL CHAMPIONSHIP
Hrvatski Telekom Prva liga 2019/2020
(19.07.2019 – 25.07.2020)

Results

Round 1 [19-21.07.2019]
NK Osijek - Slaven Belupo 2-0(1-0)
Dinamo Zagreb - Lokomotiva Zagreb 3-0(2-0)
HNK Rijeka - NK Varaždin 2-1(1-1)
HNK Gorica - Inter Zaprešić 1-1(1-0)
Hajduk Split - NK Istra 1961 2-0(1-0)

Round 2 [26-28.07.2019]
Inter Zaprešić - NK Istra 1961 0-2(0-0)
Slaven Belupo - Dinamo Zagreb 0-3(0-2)
Lokomotiva Zagreb - HNK Rijeka 0-1(0-0)
HNK Gorica - NK Osijek 3-1(1-0)
NK Varaždin - Hajduk Split 0-3(0-0)

Round 3 [02-04.08.2019]
Dinamo Zagreb - HNK Gorica 3-1(1-0)
NK Istra 1961 - NK Varaždin 3-1(1-0)
HNK Rijeka - Slaven Belupo 3-1(2-0)
Hajduk Split - Lokomotiva Zagreb 3-0(2-0)
NK Osijek - Inter Zaprešić 3-1(0-1)

Round 4 [09-11.08.2019]
NK Osijek - Dinamo Zagreb 0-0
Inter Zaprešić - NK Varaždin 2-2(2-1)
Lokomotiva Zagreb - NK Istra 1961 4-1(2-0)
Slaven Belupo - Hajduk Split 2-1(1-0)
HNK Gorica - HNK Rijeka 2-0(1-0)

Round 5 [16-18.08.2019]
Inter Zaprešić - Dinamo Zagreb 1-2(1-1)
NK Varaždin - Lokomotiva Zagreb 1-1(1-0)
NK Istra 1961 - Slaven Belupo 2-3(2-2)
Hajduk Split - HNK Gorica 3-0(1-0)
HNK Rijeka - NK Osijek 1-1(1-0)

Round 6 [24-25.08.2019]
Slaven Belupo - NK Varaždin 1-1(0-0)
Inter Zaprešić - Lokomotiva Zagreb 1-2(0-1)
HNK Gorica - NK Istra 1961 1-1(0-1)
NK Osijek - Hajduk Split 1-0(1-0)
Dinamo Zagreb - Rijeka 3-0(2-0) [18.12.]

Round 7 [30.08.-01.09.2019]
Lokomotiva Zagreb - Slaven Belupo 6-1(2-0)
Hajduk Split - Dinamo Zagreb 1-0(0-0)
NK Istra 1961 - NK Osijek 0-0
NK Varaždin - HNK Gorica 1-3(1-1)
HNK Rijeka - Inter Zaprešić 1-1(1-1)

Round 8 [13-15.09.2019]
Dinamo Zagreb - NK Istra 1961 1-0(0-0)
Inter Zaprešić - Slaven Belupo 3-1(0-0)
HNK Gorica - Lokomotiva Zagreb 0-0
NK Osijek - NK Varaždin 2-2(2-0)
HNK Rijeka - Hajduk Split 1-1(1-0)

Round 9 [20-22.09.2019]
Lokomotiva Zagreb - NK Osijek 2-1(1-1)
Slaven Belupo - HNK Gorica 2-0(1-0)
NK Varaždin - Dinamo Zagreb 1-0(0-0)
Hajduk Split - Inter Zaprešić 3-1(1-0)
NK Istra 1961 - HNK Rijeka 0-3(0-2)

Round 10 [27-29.09.2019]
Lokomotiva Zagreb - Dinamo Zagreb 0-4(0-1)
NK Varaždin - HNK Rijeka 0-2(0-2)
Slaven Belupo - NK Osijek 0-4(0-3)
Inter Zaprešić - HNK Gorica 0-2(0-1)
NK Istra 1961 - Hajduk Split 1-1(0-1)

Round 11 [04-06.10.2019]
NK Istra 1961 - Inter Zaprešić 2-2(0-1)
Hajduk Split - NK Varaždin 2-0(1-0)
Dinamo Zagreb - Slaven Belupo 1-0(1-0)
NK Osijek - HNK Gorica 2-1(0-0)
HNK Rijeka - Lokomotiva Zagreb 1-1(1-0)

Round 12 [18-20.10.2019]
HNK Gorica - Dinamo Zagreb 2-4(0-2)
NK Varaždin - NK Istra 1961 1-0(0-0)
Slaven Belupo - HNK Rijeka 1-2(1-0)
Inter Zaprešić - NK Osijek 3-3(2-1)
Lokomotiva Zagreb - Hajduk Split 0-0

Round 13 [25-27.10.2019]
NK Varaždin - Inter Zaprešić 0-1(0-1)
Hajduk Split - Slaven Belupo 2-0(1-0)
HNK Rijeka - HNK Gorica 1-2(0-0)
NK Istra 1961 - Lokomotiva Zagreb 0-2(0-0)
Dinamo Zagreb - NK Osijek 1-0(1-0)

Round 14 [02-04.11.2019]
Dinamo Zagreb - Inter Zaprešić 1-0(0-0)
HNK Gorica - Hajduk Split 2-1(1-1)
Slaven Belupo - NK Istra 1961 0-0
NK Osijek - HNK Rijeka 3-2(0-2)
Lokomotiva Zagreb - NK Varaždin 2-1(1-1)

Round 15 [08-10.11.2019]
NK Istra 1961 - HNK Gorica 2-2(1-1)
Lokomotiva Zagreb - Inter Zaprešić 3-1(1-0)
NK Varaždin - Slaven Belupo 0-0
Hajduk Split - NK Osijek 3-2(2-1)
HNK Rijeka - Dinamo Zagreb 0-5(0-4)

Round 16 [22-24.11.2019]
Dinamo Zagreb - Hajduk Split 1-1(1-1)
HNK Gorica - NK Varaždin 1-0(0-0)
Slaven Belupo - Lokomotiva Zagreb 1-0(1-0)
NK Osijek - NK Istra 1961 1-0(0-0)
Inter Zaprešić - HNK Rijeka 1-4(0-4)

Round 17 [29.11.-01.12.2019]
Slaven Belupo - Inter Zaprešić 3-0(2-0)
Lokomotiva Zagreb - HNK Gorica 4-0(2-0)
NK Varaždin - NK Istra 1961 1-0(0-1)
NK Istra 1961 - Dinamo Zagreb 1-2(0-1)
Hajduk Split - HNK Rijeka 0-4(0-1)

Round 18 [06-08.12.2019]
Dinamo Zagreb - NK Varaždin 1-0(0-0)
HNK Gorica - Slaven Belupo 2-0(2-0)
Inter Zaprešić - Hajduk Split 1-1(1-1)
NK Osijek - Lokomotiva Zagreb 4-0(0-0)
HNK Rijeka - NK Istra 1961 2-0(2-0)

Round 19 [13-15.12.2019]
HNK Gorica - Inter Zaprešić 1-1(1-0)
HNK Rijeka - NK Varaždin 3-1(1-0)
Dinamo Zagreb - Lokomotiva Zagreb 1-0(0-0)
NK Osijek - Slaven Belupo 3-2(1-0)
Hajduk Split - NK Istra 1961 2-1(0-1

Round 20 [31.01.-01.02.2020]
Inter Zaprešić - NK Istra 1961 2-0(2-0)
Lokomotiva Zagreb - HNK Rijeka 2-1(1-0)
Slaven Belupo - Dinamo Zagreb 0-2(0-1)
NK Varaždin - Hajduk Split 0-3(0-1)
HNK Gorica - NK Osijek 0-0

Round 21 [07-09.02.2020]
NK Istra 1961 - NK Varaždin 1-0(1-0)
NK Osijek - Inter Zaprešić 1-1(1-1)
Hajduk Split - Lokomotiva Zagreb 1-0(1-0)
HNK Rijeka - Slaven Belupo 1-0(1-0)
Dinamo Zagreb - HNK Gorica 2-0(0-0)

Round 22 [14-16.02.2020]
Lokomotiva Zagreb - NK Istra 1961 2-0(0-0)
Inter Zaprešić - NK Varaždin 1-2(1-0)
Slaven Belupo - Hajduk Split 2-1(1-1)
NK Osijek - Dinamo Zagreb 1-0(0-0)
HNK Gorica - HNK Rijeka 0-0

Round 23 [21-23.02.2020]
NK Varaždin - Lokomotiva Zagreb 0-2(0-2)
Hajduk Split - HNK Gorica 6-0(3-0)
HNK Rijeka - NK Osijek 1-0(1-0)
Dinamo Zagreb - Inter Zaprešić 3-2(1-1)
NK Istra 1961 - Slaven Belupo 1-1(1-1)

Round 24 [27-29.02.2020]
Inter Zaprešić - Lokomotiva Zagreb 0-2(0-1)
Slaven Belupo - NK Varaždin 0-0
HNK Gorica - NK Istra 1961 3-0(0-0)
NK Osijek - Hajduk Split 0-0
Dinamo Zagreb - HNK Rijeka 4-0(1-0)

Round 25 [03-04.03.2020]
Lokomotiva Zagreb - Slaven Belupo 3-0(0-0)
HNK Rijeka - Inter Zaprešić 4-1(2-0)
NK Istra 1961 - NK Osijek 1-0(1-0)
NK Varaždin - HNK Gorica 2-2(2-0)
Hajduk Split - Dinamo Zagreb 0-2(0-0)

Round 26 [07-09.03.2020]
Inter Zaprešić - Slaven Belupo 0-2(0-2)
NK Osijek - NK Varaždin 2-0(2-0)
Dinamo Zagreb - NK Istra 1961 2-0(1-0)
HNK Rijeka - Hajduk Split 2-0(0-0)
HNK Gorica - Lokomotiva Zagreb 1-3(0-0)

Round 27 [05-07.06.2020]
Hajduk Split - Inter Zaprešić 2-1(0-1)
Slaven Belupo - HNK Gorica 0-0
NK Varaždin - Dinamo Zagreb 1-3(0-2)
NK Istra 1961 - HNK Rijeka 1-3(0-1)
Lokomotiva Zagreb - NK Osijek 0-1(0-1)

Round 28 [11-13.06.2020]
Inter Zaprešić - HNK Gorica 0-3(0-0)
NK Istra 1961 - Hajduk Split 0-1(0-1)
NK Varaždin - HNK Rijeka 0-0
Lokomotiva Zagreb - Dinamo Zagreb 1-0(0-0)
Slaven Belupo - NK Osijek 0-0

Round 29 [16-17.06.2020]
Hajduk Split - NK Varaždin 2-3(0-3)
NK Istra 1961 - Inter Zaprešić 2-0(2-0)
HNK Rijeka - Lokomotiva Zagreb 2-2(0-1)
Dinamo Zagreb - Slaven Belupo 3-2(2-1)
NK Osijek - HNK Gorica 2-1(1-0)

Round 30 [20-21.06.2020]
Inter Zaprešić - NK Osijek 0-1(0-0)
HNK Gorica - Dinamo Zagreb 0-0
NK Varaždin - NK Istra 1961 3-0(0-0)
Slaven Belupo - HNK Rijeka 1-0(1-0)
Lokomotiva Zagreb - Hajduk Split 3-2(1-2)

Round 31 [25-27.06.2020]
NK Istra 1961 - Lokomotiva Zagreb 1-1(1-1)
NK Varaždin - Inter Zaprešić 1-0(1-0)
HNK Rijeka - HNK Gorica 1-2(0-1)
Hajduk Split - Slaven Belupo 2-1(1-1)
Dinamo Zagreb - NK Osijek 0-0

Round 32 [30.06.-01.07.2020]
Lokomotiva Zagreb - NK Varaždin 2-0(1-0)
Slaven Belupo - NK Istra 1961 3-0(3-0)
HNK Gorica - Hajduk Split 3-1(2-1)
Inter Zaprešić - Dinamo Zagreb 0-1(0-0)
NK Osijek - HNK Rijeka 1-0(0-0)

Round 33 [04-05.07.2020]
NK Istra 1961 - HNK Gorica 2-2(1-0)
Lokomotiva Zagreb - Inter Zaprešić 3-1(1-0)
NK Varaždin - Slaven Belupo 1-0(0-0)
Hajduk Split - NK Osijek 0-1(0-1)
HNK Rijeka - Dinamo Zagreb 2-0(1-0)

Round 34 [10-12.07.2020]
HNK Gorica - NK Varaždin 0-1(0-0)
Inter Zaprešić - HNK Rijeka 0-1(0-0)
NK Osijek - NK Istra 1961 2-0(1-0)
Slaven Belupo - Lokomotiva Zagreb 1-1(0-0)
Dinamo Zagreb - Hajduk Split 2-3(1-1)

Round 35 [17-19.07.2020]
Slaven Belupo - Inter Zaprešić 3-1(1-1)
NK Varaždin - NK Osijek 1-0(1-0)
NK Istra 1961 - Dinamo Zagreb 0-0
Lokomotiva Zagreb - HNK Gorica 1-1(1-0)
Hajduk Split - HNK Rijeka 2-3(1-2)

Round 36 [24-25.07.2020]
Dinamo Zagreb - NK Varaždin 2-0(2-0)
HNK Gorica - Slaven Belupo 0-0
Inter Zaprešić - Hajduk Split 1-4(0-0)
NK Osijek - Lokomotiva Zagreb 1-2(0-0)
HNK Rijeka - NK Istra 1961 4-2(3-0)

Final Standings

					Total			Home					Away			
1. **GNK Dinamo Zagreb**	36	25	5	6	62 - 20	80	15	2	1	34 - 9		10	3	5	28 - 11
2. NK Lokomotiva Zagreb	36	19	8	9	57 - 38	65	13	2	3	38 - 16		6	6	6	19 - 22
3. HNK Rijeka	36	19	7	10	58 - 42	64	10	5	3	32 - 21		9	2	7	26 - 21
4. NK Osijek	36	17	11	8	47 - 29	62	13	4	1	31 - 12		4	7	7	16 - 17
5. HNK Hajduk Split	36	18	6	12	60 - 41	60	13	0	5	36 - 19		5	6	7	24 - 22
6. HNK Gorica	36	12	13	11	44 - 48	49	7	8	3	22 - 14		5	5	8	22 - 34
7. NK Slaven Belupo Koprivnica	36	10	9	17	34 - 51	39	8	6	4	20 - 16		2	3	13	14 - 35
8. NK Varaždin	36	9	9	18	29 - 50	36	6	5	7	14 - 21		3	4	11	15 - 29
9. NK Istra 1961 Pula (*Relegation Play-offs*)	36	5	10	21	27 - 59	25	4	8	6	20 - 24		1	2	15	7 - 35
10. HNK Inter Zaprešić (*Relegated*)	36	3	8	25	32 - 72	17	2	3	13	16 - 35		1	5	12	16 - 37

Top goalscorers:		
20	Antonio Čolak	*HNK Rijeka*
20	Mijo Caktaš	*HNK Hajduk Split*
20	Mirko Marić	*NK Osijek*
14	Kristijan Lovrić	*HNK Gorica*
13	Mislav Oršić	*GNK Dinamo Zagreb*
12	Ivan Krstanović	*NK Slaven Belupo Koprivnica*

Relegation Play-offs [02-05.08.2020]

HNK Orijent 1919 Sušak - NK Istra 1961 Pula   0-3(0-1)   1-0(0-0)

NK Istra 1961 Pula remains at First Level.

NATIONAL CUP
Hrvatski nogometni kup 2019/2020

First Round [14/27/28.08.2019]

HNK Suhopolje Virovitica - NK Oriolik Oriovac	2-6(0-5)	NK Bjelovar - NK Opatija	0-3(0-1)
NK Hrvace - HNK Segesta	3-1(1-0)	NK Maksimir Zagreb - NK Varaždin ŠN	2-6(0-2)
NK Mladost Kloštar Podr. - NK Sloga Nova Gradiška	1-4(0-1)	NK Zagora Unešić - NK Papuk Orahovica	5-1(4-0)
NK Nehaj Senj - NK Karlovac	0-2(0-1)	NK Belišće - NK Jadran Luka Ploče	0-0 aet; 4-2 pen
HNK Primorac Biograd/Moru - NK BSK Bijelo Brdo	1-3(1-3)	NK Borac Imbriovec - NK Jadran Poreč	1-3(0-0)
NK Dinamo Predavac - NK Kurilovec Velika Gorica	1-3(1-1,1-1)	NK Nedelišće - NK Slavonija Požega	0-2(0-1)
NK Slavonac Komletinci - NK Buje	2-2 aet; 3-4 pen	NK Mladost Petrinja - NK Međimurje Čakovec	3-0(2-0)
NK Bednja Beletinec - NK Vuteks-Sloga	1-2(1-0, 1-1)	HNK Gorica - NK Zagorec Krapina	10-0(3-0)

Second Round [24-25.09./01.10.2019]

NK Hrvace - NK Slaven Belupo Koprivnica	1-2(1-1)	NK Jadran Poreč - NK Inter Zaprešić	3-7(1-2)
NK Karlovac - GNK Dinamo Zagreb	0-7(0-4)	NK Slavonija Požega - HNK Šibenik	1-5(1-3)
NK Oriolik Oriovac - NK Lokomotiva Zagreb	0-3(0-0)	NK Sloga Nova Gradiška - NK Vinogradar	1-2(0-1)
NK Vuteks-Sloga - NK Osijek	0-8(0-2)	NK Kurilovec Velika Gorica - NK Istra 1961 Pula	2-3(2-1,2-2)
NK Belišće - RNK Split	3-1(0-0,0-0)	NK Zagora Unešić - NK Zadar	1-2(1-0,1-1)
NK BSK Bijelo Brdo - HNK Cibalia Vinkovci	1-0(1-0)	HNK Gorica - NK Zagreb	8-0(4-0)
NK Mladost Petrinja - HNK Hajduk Split	0-2(0-1)	NK Varaždin ŠN - NK Rudeš	4-2(2-0)
NK Opatija - NK Novigrad	3-1(2-0)	NK Buje - HNK Rijeka	0-11(0-5)

1/8-Finals [23/30.10.2019]

NK Zadar - NK Osijek	0-3(0-2)	NK Istra 1961 Pula - NK Inter Zaprešić	1-2(1-1)
NK BSK Bijelo Brdo - NK Slaven Belupo Koprivn.	0-2(0-0)	HNK Gorica - HNK Hajduk Split	2-1(0-0)
HNK Šibenik - NK Belišće	2-1(1-1)	NK Opatija - GNK Dinamo Zagreb	0-3(0-3)
NK Vinogradar - NK Lokomotiva Zagreb	0-3(0-1)	NK Varaždin ŠN - HNK Rijeka	1-2(0-0)

Quarter-Finals [03-04.12.2019/05.02.2020]

HNK Šibenik - NK Lokomotiva Zagreb	0-4(0-1)	HNK Gorica - NK Slaven Belupo Koprivnica	1-2(0-1)
NK Inter Zaprešić - NK Osijek	0-2(0-1)	HNK Rijeka - GNK Dinamo Zagreb	1-0(1-0)

Semi-Finals [30-31.05.2020]

NK Slaven Belupo Kopriv. - NK Lokomotiva Zagreb	1-3(1-0)	HNK Rijeka - NK Osijek	3-2(0-1)

Final

01.08.2020; Stadion Šubićevac, Šibenik, City; Referee: Tihomir Pejin; Attendance: None
HNK Rijeka - NK Lokomotiva Zagreb   1-0(0-0)

HNK Rijeka: Ivor Pandur, Darko Velkovski, Nino Galović, João Rodrigo Pereira Escoval, Daniel Štefulj (90+5.Ivan Tomečak), Filip Braut, Domagoj Pavičić (89.Luka Capan), Stjepan Lončar, Tibor Halilović, Franko Andrijašević (46.Ivan Lepinjica), Antonio Čolak. Trainer: Simon Rožman (Slovenia).

Lokomotiva Zagreb: Ivo Grbić, Fran Karačić, Dominik Kovačić, Denis Kolinger, Ivan Čeliković (85.Stipo Marković), Oliver Petrak (77.Jorge Sammir Cruz Campos), Jon Mersinaj (78.Mario Budimir), Enis Çokaj (71.Kristijan Jakić), Marko Tolić, Lirim Kastrati, Myrto Uzuni. Trainer: Goran Tomić.

Goal: 1-0 Tibor Halilović (77).

Građanski nogometni klub Dinamo Zagreb

Founded:	09.06.1945	
Stadium:	Stadion Maksimir, Zagreb (35,123)	
Trainer:	Nenad Bjelica	20.08.1971
[22.04.2020]	Igor Jovićević	30.11.1973
[07.07.2020]	Zoran Mamić	30.09.1971

Goalkeepers:	DOB	M	(s)	G
Renato Josipović	12.06.2001		(1)	
Dominik Livaković	09.01.1995	26		
Daniel Zagorac	07.02.1987	10		
Defenders:	**DOB**	**M**	**(s)**	**G**
Emir Dilaver (AUT)	07.05.1991	19	(2)	1
Bartol Franjić	14.01.2000	3	(1)	
Joško Gvardiol	23.01.2002	9	(2)	1
Tin Hrvoj	06.06.2001	2		
Marin Leovac	07.08.1988	18	(1)	1
Marko Lešković	27.04.1991	4	(1)	
Sadegh Moharrami (IRN)	01.03.1996	9		
François Moubandje (SUI)	21.06.1990	13	(1)	
Dino Perić	12.07.1994	15	(2)	
Petar Stojanović (SVN)	07.10.1995	15	(2)	1
Josip Šutalo	28.02.2000	3	(1)	
Kévin Théophile-Catherine (MTQ)	28.10.1989	21		1
Midfielders:	**DOB**	**M**	**(s)**	**G**
Arijan Ademi (MKD)	29.05.1991	16	(3)	3
Daniel Olmo Carvajal „Dani Olmo" (ESP)	07.05.1998	9		3
Marko Đira	05.05.1999	5	(10)	

	DOB	M	(s)	G
Amer Gojak (BIH)	13.02.1997	19	(8)	2
Luka Ivanušec	26.11.1998	14	(10)	4
Ivo Daniel Ferreira Mendonça Pinto (POR)	07.01.1990	6		
Tomislav Krizmanić	21.04.2001		(1)	
Lovro Majer	17.01.1998	14	(7)	2
Nikola Moro	12.03.1998	27	(1)	2
Forwards:	**DOB**	**M**	**(s)**	**G**
Iyayi Believe Atiemwen (NGA)	24.01.1996	6	(5)	3
Bartol Barišić	01.01.2003		(1)	
Roko Baturina	20.06.2000		(1)	
Mario Čuže	24.04.1999	5	(7)	2
Mario Gavranović (SUI)	24.11.1989	9	(10)	4
Izet Hajrović (BIH)	04.08.1991	3	(8)	
Damian Kądzior (POL)	16.06.1992	27	(3)	10
Sandro Kulenović	04.12.1999	7	(9)	
Antonio Marin	09.01.2001	6	(7)	1
Mislav Oršić	29.12.1992	25	(3)	13
Bruno Petković	16.09.1994	20	(5)	7
Leon Šipoš	28.02.2000		(1)	
Mario Šitum	04.04.1992	9	(4)	

Hrvatski Nogometni Klub Gorica

Founded:	16.07.2009 (*as merger of NK Radnik Velika Gorica and NK Polet Buševec*)	
Stadium:	Stadion Gradski, Velika Gorica (5,000)	
Trainer:	Sergej Jakirović (BIH)	23.12.1976
[25.02.2020]	Valdas Dambrauskas (LTU)	07.01.1977

Goalkeepers:	DOB	M	(s)	G
Kristijan Kahlina (SVN)	24.07.1992	36		
Defenders:	**DOB**	**M**	**(s)**	**G**
Marijan Čabraja	25.02.1997	33		1
Maks Čelić	08.03.1996	6	(1)	
Aleksandar Jovičić (BIH)	18.07.1995	34		1
Krešimir Krizmanić	03.07.2000	8	(3)	
Nemanja Ljubisavljević (SRB)	26.11.1996	2	(1)	
Nasiru Moro (GHA)	24.09.1996	2		
Musa Muhammed Shehu (NGA)	31.10.1996	31		
Patrik Periša	25.03.1996	2	(3)	
Matthew Steenvoorden (NED)	09.01.1993	24	(2)	1
Midfielders:	**DOB**	**M**	**(s)**	**G**
Hrvoje Babec	28.07.1999	17	(8)	
Dario Čanađija	17.04.1994	17	(5)	
Gojko Gadže	10.01.2000	1	(3)	
Jiloan Hamad (SWE)	06.11.1990	19	(6)	3

	DOB	M	(s)	G
Anthony Kalik (AUS)	05.11.1997	6	(3)	
Martin Maloča	21.03.1990	1	(2)	
Mario Marina (BIH)	03.08.1989	12	(1)	
Michał Masłowski (POL)	19.12.1989	11	(11)	2
Farouk Miya (UGA)	26.11.1997	2	(1)	1
Joey Suk (NED)	08.07.1989	27	(3)	4
Matija Špičić	24.02.1988	1		
Forwards:	**DOB**	**M**	**(s)**	**G**
Matija Dvorneković	01.01.1989	16	(13)	2
Paulius Golubickas (LTU)	19.08.1999	3	(2)	
Kristijan Lovrić	01.12.1995	31		14
Justin Mathieu (NED)	12.04.1996	6	(10)	
Ognjen Mudrinski (SRB)	15.11.1991	3	(9)	4
Cherif Ndiaye (SEN)	23.01.1996	30	(3)	7
Dario Špikić	22.03.1999	5	(10)	
Martin Šroler (SVN)	02.11.1998		(5)	
Łukasz Zwoliński (POL)	24.02.1993	10	(7)	4

Hrvatski nogometni klub Hajduk Split

Founded:	13.02.1911	
Stadium:	Stadion Poljud, Split (34,198)	
Trainer:	Damir Burić	07.07.1964
[23.12.2019]	Igor Tudor	16.04.1978

Goalkeepers:	DOB	M	(s)	G
Tomislav Duka	07.09.1992	2		
Marin Ljubić	18.10.1997	8		
Josip Posavec	10.03.1996	26		
Defenders:	**DOB**	**M**	**(s)**	**G**
Josip Bašić	02.03.1996	3		
David Čolina	19.07.2000	18	(4)	
Kristian Dimitrov (BUL)	27.02.1997	12	(2)	1
Ardian Ismajli (ALB)	30.09.1996	28		
Josip Juranović	16.08.1995	32		2
Nihad Mujakić (BIH)	15.04.1998	9		
Stipe Radić	10.06.2000	4	(4)	
Stefan Simić (CZE)	20.01.1995	16		1
Oleksandr Svatok (UKR)	27.09.1994	5	(1)	
Stipe Vučur (AUT)	22.05.1992	1	(1)	
Mario Vušković	16.11.2001	8	(2)	1
Midfielders:	**DOB**	**M**	**(s)**	**G**
Hamza Barry (GAM)	15.10.1994	24	(3)	1
Jakov Blagaić	08.02.2000	1	(8)	

	DOB	M	(s)	G
Dino Beširević (BIH)	31.01.1994		(2)	
Filip Bradarić	11.01.1992	9		
Mijo Caktaš	08.05.1992	32		20
Mario Čuić	22.04.2001	6	(2)	2
Bassel Jradi (DEN)	06.07.1993	26	(7)	3
Stanko Jurić	16.08.1996	15	(7)	1
Anthony Kalik (AUS)	05.11.1997	4	(5)	
Darko Nejašmić	25.01.1999	20	(5)	2
Forwards:	**DOB**	**M**	**(s)**	**G**
Ivan Brnić	23.08.2001	3	(4)	
Ivan Delić	29.09.1998		(5)	
Ivan Dolček	24.04.2000	12	(9)	1
Samuel Emem Eduok (NGA)	31.01.1994	20	(10)	11
Ádám Gyurcsó (HUN)	06.03.1991	1		
Jairo De Macedo Da Silva (BRA)	06.05.1992	33		9
Marin Jakoliš	26.12.1996	6	(10)	1
Leon Kreković	07.05.2000	4	(11)	1
Francesco Tahiraj (ALB)	21.09.1996	8	(2)	
Tonio Teklić	09.09.1999		(13)	1

Nogometni Klub Inter Zaprešić

Founded: 25.06.1929 (*as NK Sava*)
Stadium: Stadion ŠRC Zaprešić, Zaprešić (5,228)

Trainer:	Samir Toplak	23.04.1970
[04.01.2020]	Željko Petrović (MNE)	13.11.1965
[26.04.2020]	Tomislav Ivković	11.08.1960

Goalkeepers:	DOB	M	(s)	G
Žiga Frelih (SVN)	06.02.1998	22		1
Osman Hadžikić (AUT)	12.03.1996	5		
Mladen Matković	12.05.1989	9		
Defenders:	**DOB**	**M**	**(s)**	**G**
Gordan Barić	11.08.1994	8	(4)	
Antonio Bosec	28.08.1997	30	(3)	3
Ivan Čeliković	10.04.1989	13	(1)	
Marin Galić	21.09.1995	8	(2)	
Damir Grgić	18.05.1992	18	(2)	1
Manuel Haas (AUT)	07.05.1996	1	(1)	
Ivan Nekić	24.12.2000	3	(1)	
Matija Rom (SVN)	01.11.1998	11		
Milan Savić (SRB)	04.04.1994	12	(1)	
Nikola Soldo	25.01.2001	21	(6)	1
Ivan Tatomirović (SRB)	11.01.1989	18	(1)	
Damian van Bruggen (NED)	18.03.1996	16		
Stjepan Vego	09.07.1997	12	(1)	
Midfielders:	**DOB**	**M**	**(s)**	**G**
Valon Ahmedi (ALB)	07.10.1994	5		

	DOB	M	(s)	G
Juraj Ljubić	26.05.2000	3	(7)	
Sacha Marasovic (FRA)	06.01.1998	7	(4)	
Manuel Martić (AUT)	15.08.1995	3	(1)	
Tomislav Mazalović	10.06.1990	24	(2)	
Frano Mlinar	30.03.1992	30		1
Todor Petrović (SRB)	18.08.1994	1	(2)	
Igor Postonjski	04.02.1995	25	(5)	
Borislav Tsonev (BUL)	29.04.1995	20	(3)	4
Forwards:	**DOB**	**M**	**(s)**	**G**
Komnen Andrić (SRB)	01.07.1995	12	(2)	3
Mihael Benčić	25.06.2001	3	(6)	
Borna Bilobrk	20.01.2001	1	(6)	
Ivan Mamut	30.04.1997	20	(10)	6
Josip Mitrović	11.06.2000	12	(15)	1
Mateo Plehan	13.03.2003		(2)	
Serder Serderov (RUS)	10.03.1994	21	(1)	9
William Tchuameni (CMR)	25.12.1996		(9)	
Mario Vasilj (SVN)	25.01.1995		(1)	
Moreno Vušković	21.04.2003		(3)	
Oussama Zamouri (NED)	18.02.1996	2	(8)	

Nogometni Klub Istra 1961 Pula

Founded: 1948
Stadium: Stadion "Aldo Drosina", Pula (9,800)

Trainer:	Ivan Prelec	24.07.1987

Goalkeepers:	DOB	M	(s)	G
Josip Čondrić	27.08.1993	27		
Tomislav Duka	07.09.1992	8		
Lovro Majkić	08.10.1999	1	(1)	
Defenders:	**DOB**	**M**	**(s)**	**G**
Petar Bosančić	19.04.1996	29	(1)	2
Einar Galilea Azaceta (ESP)	22.05.1994	29	(2)	
Martin Franić	13.01.1997	9	(5)	
Marin Grujević	23.12.1991	27	(1)	
Markus Pavic (AUT)	26.03.1995	28	(1)	
Rafa Páez Cardona (ESP)	10.08.1994	6	(2)	1
Petar Rubić	03.07.1998	1	(4)	
Agron Rufati (MKD)	06.04.1999	4	(2)	
Sergio González Testón „Sergi" (ESP)	26.05.1995	8	(1)	
Josip Tomašević	26.09.1993	31		
Midfielders:	**DOB**	**M**	**(s)**	**G**
Slavko Blagojević	21.03.1987	14		
Denis Bušnja	14.04.2000	6	(9)	
Matija Fintić	12.06.1997	8	(8)	1

	DOB	M	(s)	G
Antonio Ivančić	25.05.1995	24	(6)	2
Mateo Lisica	09.07.2003	1	(3)	
Stefan Lončar (MNE)	19.02.1996	23	(9)	1
Ivan Močinić	30.04.1993	10	(9)	1
Octavio Andrés Páez Gil (VEN)	28.02.2000		(2)	
Obeng Regan (GHA)	15.08.1994	15	(5)	1
Drilon Sadiku (BEL)	27.05.2000		(1)	
Forwards:	**DOB**	**M**	**(s)**	**G**
Adrián Fuentes González (ESP)	17.07.1996	4	(4)	
Mario Čuže	24.04.1999	16	(2)	7
Ivan Delić	29.09.1998	10	(4)	2
Šime Gržan	06.04.1994	31	(2)	4
Gedeon Guzina (BIH)	26.12.1993	12	(2)	3
Karolis Laukžemis (LTU)	11.03.1992	3		1
Josip Maganjić	06.01.1999	2	(7)	
Vice Miljanić	30.05.1998	1	(1)	
Mario Munivrana	12.05.1995		(7)	
Robert Perić-Komšić	30.03.1999	7	(18)	1
Arona Sané (SEN)	21.06.1995	1	(3)	

Nogometni klub Lokomotiva Zagreb

Founded: 01.05.1914 (*as ŽSK Victoria Zagreb*)
Stadium: Stadion u Kranjčevićevoj ulici, Zagreb (8,850)

Trainer:	Goran Tomić	18.03.1977

Goalkeepers:	DOB	M	(s)	G
Ivo Grbić	18.01.1996	35		
Krunoslav Hendija	19.03.1989	1		
Defenders:	**DOB**	**M**	**(s)**	**G**
Ivan Čeliković	10.04.1989	5	(1)	
Toni Datković	06.11.1993	7		1
Petar Gluhaković (AUT)	25.03.1996	2	(3)	
Luka Hujber	16.06.1999	1		
Fran Karačić (AUS)	12.05.1996	30		2
Denis Kolinger	14.01.1994	32		2
Dominik Kovačić	05.01.1994	9		
Stipo Marković (BIH)	03.12.1993	29	(3)	1
Jon Mersinaj (ALB)	08.02.1999	24	(1)	
Midfielders:	**DOB**	**M**	**(s)**	**G**
Filip Arežina (BIH)	08.11.1992	2	(3)	
Pape Assane (SEN)	20.09.1997	4	(3)	
Enis Çokaj (ALB)	23.02.1999	26	(4)	1
Domagoj Drožđek	20.03.1996	6	(9)	2

	DOB	M	(s)	G
Emerson Santana Deocleciano (BRA)	27.07.1999	1	(2)	
Dino Halilović	08.02.1998	7	(14)	1
Luka Ivanušec	26.11.1998	3		1
Kristijan Jakić	14.05.1997	22	(5)	4
Bojan Knežević	28.01.1997		(2)	
Sadegh Moharrami (IRN)	01.03.1996	7		
Jorge Sammir Cruz Campos	23.04.1987	10	(4)	
Oliver Petrak	06.02.1991	15	(4)	1
Marko Tolić	05.07.1996	20	(11)	11
Frane Vojković	20.12.1996		(1)	
Forwards:	**DOB**	**M**	**(s)**	**G**
Iyayi Believe Atiemwen (NGA)	24.01.1996	6	(4)	1
Mario Budimir	12.02.1986	15	(9)	2
Lirim Kastrati (KVX)	16.01.1999	34		11
Josip Majic	05.07.1994	1	(7)	
Đorđe Rakić (SRB)	31.10.1985	1	(4)	
Indrit Tuci (ALB)	14.09.2000	11	(14)	4
Myrto Uzuni (ALB)	31.05.1995	30	(2)	9

Nogometni klub Osijek

Founded: 27.02.1947
Stadium: Stadion Gradski vrt, Osijek (18,856)
Trainer: Dino Skender   10.12.1983
[23.09.2019] Ivica Kuleševic   31.10.1969

Goalkeepers:	DOB	M	(s)	G
Ivica Ivušić	01.02.1995	36		
Defenders:	**DOB**	**M**	**(s)**	**G**
Petar Bočkaj	23.07.1996	22	(2)	4
Gutieri Tomelin „Guti" (BRA)	29.06.1991	4	(4)	
Igor Silva de Almeida „Igor Carioca" (BRA)	21.08.1996	24	(3)	1
Ante Majstorović	06.11.1993	33		
Luka Marin	16.03.1998	1		
Mile Škorić	19.06.1991	31		1
Tomislav Šorša	11.05.1989	8		
Talys Alves Pereira Oliveira (BRA)	10.02.1999	26	(5)	
Todor Todoroski (MKD)	26.02.1999	3	(1)	
Andrej Šimunec	02.03.1995	1		
Boško Šutalo	01.01.2000	16		
Midfielders:	**DOB**	**M**	**(s)**	**G**
Mihail Caimacov (MDA)	22.07.1998		(1)	
Vedran Jugović	31.07.1989	9	(5)	

	DOB	M	(s)	G
Karlo Kamenar	15.03.1994	1	(1)	
László Kleinheisler (HUN)	08.04.1994	22	(2)	3
Danijel Lončar	26.06.1997	10	(6)	1
Dmytro Lyopa (UKR)	23.11.1988	16	(11)	4
Benedik Mioč	06.10.1994	1	(3)	
Merveil Ndockyt (CGO)	20.07.1998	14	(13)	
Marin Pilj	03.12.1996	19	(8)	1
Mihael Žaper	11.08.1998	29	(1)	4
Forwards:	**DOB**	**M**	**(s)**	**G**
Dion Beljo	01.03.2002		(6)	
Marko Dugandžić	07.04.1994	1	(2)	
Eros Grezda (ALB)	15.04.1995	6	(4)	
Alen Grgić	10.08.1994	1	(2)	
Antonio Mance	07.08.1995	24	(6)	7
Mirko Marić (BIH)	16.05.1995	34	(1)	20
Jerry Uche Mbakogu (NGA)	01.10.1992	1	(6)	
Josip Špoljarić	05.01.1997	3	(16)	1

Hrvatski Nogometni Klub Rijeka

Founded: 29.07.1946 (as Sportsko Društvo Kvarner)
Stadium: Stadion Rujevica, Rijeka (8,279)
Trainer: Igor Bišćan   04.05.1978
[23.09.2019] Simon Rožman (SVN)   06.04.1983

Goalkeepers:	DOB	M	(s)	G
Ivor Pandur	25.03.2000	18		
Andrej Prskalo	01.05.1987	18		
Defenders:	**DOB**	**M**	**(s)**	**G**
Filip Braut	05.06.2002	5	(3)	
Niko Galešić	26.03.2001		(1)	
Nino Galović	06.07.1992	9	(1)	2
João Rodrigo Pereira Escoval (POR)	08.05.1997	23	(4)	1
Roberto Punčec	27.10.1991	9		
Momcilo Raspopović (MNE)	18.03.1994	14	(7)	1
Hrvoje Smolčić	17.08.2000	23	(1)	
Daniel Štefulj	08.11.1999	9		
Darko Velkovski (MKD)	21.06.1995	17	(1)	
Dario Župarić	03.05.1992	17		1
Midfielders:	**DOB**	**M**	**(s)**	**G**
Franko Andrijašević	22.06.1991	25	(1)	5
Denis Bušnja	14.04.2000	1	(2)	
Luka Capan	06.04.1995	13	(7)	
Jasmin Čeliković (BIH)	07.01.1999		(1)	

	DOB	M	(s)	G
Daniel „Dani" Iglesias Gago (ESP)	18.08.1995	3	(6)	
Tibor Halilović	18.03.1995	27	(1)	2
Ivan Lepinjica	09.07.1999	21	(6)	1
Stjepan Lončar (BIH)	10.11.1996	24	(8)	4
Petar Mamić	06.03.1996	1		
Domagoj Pavičić	09.03.1994	12	(12)	
Jakov Puljić	04.08.1993	5	(3)	
Ivan Tomečak	07.12.1989	20	(3)	2
Forwards:	**DOB**	**M**	**(s)**	**G**
Boadu Maxwell Acosty (GHA)	10.09.1991	9	(8)	3
Matko Babić	28.07.1998		(2)	
Antonio Čolak	17.09.1993	27	(5)	20
Felipe Augusto Rodrigues Pires (BRA)	18.04.1995		(5)	1
Alexander Gorgon (AUT)	28.10.1988	20	(6)	7
Zoran Kvržić (BIH)	07.08.1988	10	(5)	
Robert Murić	12.03.1996	13	(11)	6
Matej Vuk	10.06.2000	1	(1)	
Sterling Yatéké (CTA)	15.09.1999	2	(8)	1

Nogometni klub Slaven Belupo Koprivnica

Founded: 1907
Stadium: Gradski Stadion "Ivan Kušek Apaš", Koprivnica (3,205)
Trainer: Ivica Sertić   14.05.1973
[08.10.2019] Tommy Stipić   01.08.1979

Goalkeepers:	DOB	M	(s)	G
Ivan Filipović	13.11.1994	18		
Antonio Ježina	05.06.1989	18		
Defenders:	**DOB**	**M**	**(s)**	**G**
Tomislav Božić	01.11.1987	23	(1)	1
Bruno Čovo	19.09.2000		(2)	
Marko Čovo	07.04.1999		(3)	
Bruno Goda	17.04.1998	22	(6)	
Marko Iharoš	23.06.1996	3		
Vinko Međimorec	01.06.1996	8	(4)	1
Krystian Nowak (POL)	01.04.1994	9	(5)	2
Miloš Radivojević (SRB)	05.04.1990	8	(1)	1
Vinko Soldo	15.02.1998	6		
Matko Žirdum	21.07.1998	14	(5)	1
Midfielders:	**DOB**	**M**	**(s)**	**G**
Stipe Bačelić-Grgić	16.02.1988	23	(2)	2
Arijan Brković	03.02.2001	8	(8)	
Dario Čanađija	17.04.1994	3		
Nemanja Glavčić (SRB)	19.02.1997	31	(3)	
Robin Kamber (SUI)	15.02.1996	3	(1)	
Marko Karamarko	27.03.1993	3	(2)	

	DOB	M	(s)	G
Ko Myeong-jin (KOR)	09.01.1988	3	(1)	
Luka Liklin	21.02.2001		(3)	
Davor Lovren	03.10.1998	2	(3)	
Karlo Lulić	10.05.1996	21	(3)	2
Goran Paracki	21.01.1987	31		
Karlo Plantak	11.11.1997		(1)	
David Puclin	17.06.1992	12	(1)	2
Forwards:	**DOB**	**M**	**(s)**	**G**
Festim Alidema (KVX)	05.10.1997		(5)	
Bruno Bogojević	29.06.1996	29	(3)	2
Mateas Delić	17.06.1988	12	(5)	
Muzafer Ejupi (MKD)	16.09.1988	9	(4)	1
Franck Etoundi (CMR)	30.08.1990	3	(3)	1
Niko Havelka	17.12.1999	1		
Ivan Jajalo (AUT)	22.07.1993	3	(2)	
Jeffrén Isaac Suárez Bermúdez (VEN)	20.01.1988	7	(4)	1
Ivan Krstanović (BIH)	05.01.1983	30	(3)	12
Mateus Lima Cruz (BRA)	18.01.1993	18	(12)	2
Božo Mikulić	29.01.1997	14	(3)	1
Mihael Mladen	28.09.1999		(2)	
Michele Šego	05.08.2000	1	(7)	

Nogometni klub Varaždin

Founded:	01.07.2012	
Stadium:	Stadion „Anđelko Herjavec", Varaždin (8,850)	
Trainer:	Borimir Perković	25.09.1967
[09.10.2019]	Luka Bonačić	21.03.1955
[10.02.2020]	Samir Toplak	23.04.1970

Goalkeepers:	DOB	M	(s)	G
Ivan Nevistić	31.07.1998	36		
Defenders:	**DOB**	**M**	**(s)**	**G**
Vladan Adžić (MNE)	05.07.1987	12		
Petar Mamić	06.03.1996	13		1
Ivan Miličević (BIH)	16.07.1998	8		
Ivan Novoselec	19.06.1995	6	(6)	
Dominik Perković	06.09.1996	3	(3)	
Franjo Prce	07.01.1996	8		
Matej Rodin	13.02.1996	11	(2)	
Karlo Sambolec	29.05.1995	2	(2)	
Matej Senić	21.02.1995	23	(3)	
Marko Stolnik	08.07.1996	30		2
Daniel Štefulj	08.11.1999	11	(2)	
Nikola Tkalčić	03.12.1989	28		
Midfielders:	**DOB**	**M**	**(s)**	**G**
Jamal Bajandouh (KSA)	22.08.1992	5	(4)	
Fran Cerovčec	06.02.2001		(1)	
Domagoj Drožđek	20.03.1996	14	(1)	6
Neven Đurasek	15.08.1998	28	(1)	1
Dejan Glavica	20.08.1991	4	(15)	4

	DOB	M	(s)	G
Denis Glavina	03.03.1986	3	(1)	
Jessie Guera Djou (CMR)	03.05.1997	15	(1)	1
Dario Jertec	05.09.1985	5	(1)	
Matija Kolaric	14.04.1996	16	(8)	1
Luka Mezga	29.01.2001		(1)	
Duje Ninčević	03.05.1997		(2)	
Jorge Leonardo Obregón Rojas (COL)	29.03.1997	10	(1)	3
Ivan Posavec	05.07.1998	27	(5)	
Ivan Roca	31.03.1996	7		
Matija Špičić	24.02.1988	4	(3)	
Tonio Teklić	09.09.1999	11	(1)	
Karlo Težak	30.10.1993	6	(3)	
Forwards:	**DOB**	**M**	**(s)**	**G**
Leon Benko	11.11.1983	23	(6)	5
Kristian Fućak	14.11.1998		(2)	
Dominik Glavina	06.12.1992	7	(12)	1
Vitali Lisakovich (BLR)	08.02.1998	6	(5)	1
Mehdi Mehdikhani (IRN)	28.07.1997	5	(14)	
Vinko Petković	01.10.1995	6	(9)	2
Tomislav Turčin	31.05.1997	3	(1)	
Leonard Vuk	23.05.1995		(6)	

SECOND LEVEL
FavBet Druga liga 2019/2020

1.	HNK Šibenik (*Promoted*)	19	13	2	4	26	-	15	41
2.	NK Croatia Zmijavci	19	10	3	6	28	-	17	33
3.	HNK Orijent 1919 Sušak (*Promotion Play-offs*)	19	9	6	4	26	-	23	33
4.	NK Sesvete	19	8	5	6	28	-	22	29
5.	NK Rudeš	19	8	5	6	25	-	20	29
6.	HNK Hajduk Split II*	19	7	6	6	29	-	23	27
7.	NK Osijek II*	19	7	5	7	26	-	19	26
8.	GNK Dinamo Zagreb II*	19	7	5	7	20	-	21	26
9.	NK Hrvatski Dragovoljac Zagreb	19	7	5	7	21	-	26	26
10.	NK Dugopolje	19	7	4	8	30	-	31	25
11.	NK Međimurje Čakovec	19	6	5	8	26	-	26	23
12.	NK Dubrava Zagreb	19	6	5	8	21	-	24	23
13.	NK Kustošija	19	6	5	8	19	-	27	23
14.	NK BSK Bijelo Brdo	19	6	4	9	18	-	23	22
15.	NK Solin	19	5	4	10	22	-	27	19
16.	HNK Cibalia Vinkovci	19	2	7	10	13	-	34	13

*Please note: reserve teams are ineligible for promotion to the Croatian First Football League!
The league was cancelled after 19 Rounds due to Covid-19 pandemic. No teams were relegated.

INTERNATIONAL MATCHES
(16.07.2019 – 15.07.2020)

06.09.2019	Trnava	Slovakia - Croatia	0-4(0-1)	(ECQ)
09.09.2019	Bakı	Azerbaijan - Croatia	1-1(0-1)	(ECQ)
10.10.2019	Split	Croatia - Hungary	3-0(3-0)	(ECQ)
13.10.2019	Cardiff	Wales - Croatia	1-1(1-1)	(ECQ)
16.11.2019	Rijeka	Croatia - Slovakia	3-1(0-1)	(ECQ)
19.11.2019	Pula	Croatia - Georgia	2-1(1-1)	(F)

06.09.2019   SLOVAKIA - CROATIA   **0-4(0-1)**   16th E.C. Qualifiers

Štadión „Antona Malatinského", Trnava; Referee: Dr. Felix Brych (Germany); Attendance: 18,098

CRO: Dominik Livaković, Karlo Bartolec, Domagoj Vida, Dejan Lovren, Borna Barišić, Luka Modrić (Cap), Marcelo Brozović, Nikola Vlašić (82.Milan Badelj), Ivan Perišić, Ante Rebić (70.Josip Brekalo), Bruno Petković (83.Mario Pašalić). Trainer: Zlatko Dalić.

Goals: Nikola Vlašić (45), Ivan Perišić (46), Bruno Petković (72), Dejan Lovren (89).

09.09.2019   AZERBAIJAN - CROATIA   **1-1(0-1)**   16th EC. Qualifiers

Bakcell Arena, Bakı; Referee: Sandro Schärer (Switzerland); Attendance: 9,150

CRO: Dominik Livaković, Karlo Bartolec (76.Josip Brekalo), Dejan Lovren, Domagoj Vida, Borna Barišić, Luka Modrić (Cap), Marcelo Brozović, Nikola Vlašić, Ivan Perišić, Ante Rebić (86.Mislav Oršić), Bruno Petković. Trainer: Zlatko Dalić.

Goal: Luka Modrić (11 penalty).

10.10.2019   CROATIA - HUNGARY   **3-0(3-0)**   16th EC. Qualifiers

Stadion Poljud, Split; Referee: Daniele Orsato (Italy); Attendance: 32,110

CRO: Dominik Livaković, Tin Jedvaj, Borna Barišić, Dejan Lovren, Domagoj Vida, Ivan Rakitić (74.Nikola Vlašić), Luka Modrić (Cap) (67.Mateo Kovačić), Marcelo Brozović, Ivan Perišić (60.Josip Brekalo), Ante Rebić, Bruno Petković. Trainer: Zlatko Dalić.

Goals: Luka Modrić (5), Bruno Petković (24, 42).

13.10.2019   WALES - CROATIA   **1-1(1-1)**   16th EC. Qualifiers

Cardiff City Stadium, Cardiff; Referee: Björn Kuipers (Netherlands); Attendance: 31,745

CRO: Dominik Livaković, Tin Jedvaj, Domagoj Vida, Dejan Lovren, Borna Barišić, Luka Modrić (Cap) (90.Milan Badelj), Mateo Kovačić (46.Ivan Rakitić), Nikola Vlašić, Ivan Perišić, Josip Brekalo, Bruno Petković (64.Ante Rebić). Trainer: Zlatko Dalić.

Goal: Nikola Vlašić (9).

16.11.2019   CROATIA - SLOVAKIA   **3-1(0-1)**   16th EC. Qualifiers

Stadion Rujevica, Rijeka; Referee: Clément Turpin (France); Attendance: 8,212

CRO: Dominik Livaković, Tin Jedvaj, Duje Ćaleta-Car, Dino Perić, Borna Barišić, Luka Modrić (Cap), Marcelo Brozović, Nikola Vlašić (75.Mateo Kovačić), Ivan Perišić (81.Mislav Oršić), Ante Rebić (54.Josip Brekalo), Bruno Petković. Trainer: Zlatko Dalić.

Goals: Nikola Vlašić (56), Bruno Petković (60), Ivan Perišić (74).

19.11.2019   CROATIA - GEORGIA   **2-1(1-1)**   Friendly International

Stadion "Aldo Drosina", Pula; Referee: Alan Mario Sant (Malta); Attendance: 5,072

CRO: Lovre Kalinić (46.Simon Sluga), Karlo Bartolec (46.Josip Juranović), Tin Jedvaj (46.Duje Ćaleta-Car), Dario Melnjak, Mile Škorić, Mateo Kovačić (65.Nikola Vlašić), Mislav Oršić (46.Marko Rog), Mario Pašalić, Milan Badelj, Ivan Perišić (Cap) (75.Dino Perić), Ante Rebić. Trainer: Zlatko Dalić.

Goals: Guram Kashia (25 own goal), Ivan Perišić (54).

NATIONAL TEAM PLAYERS
(16.07.2019 – 15.07.2020)

Name	DOB	Caps	Goals	2019:	Club
Goalkeepers					
Lovre KALINIĆ	03.04.1990	19	0	2019:	*Aston Villa FC Birmingham (ENG)*
Dominik LIVAKOVIĆ	09.01.1995	9	0	2019:	*GNK Dinamo Zagreb*
Simon SLUGA	17.03.1993	2	0	2019:	*Luton Town FC (ENG)*
Defenders					
Borna BARIŠIĆ	10.11.1992	12	1	2019:	*Rangers FC Glasgow (SCO)*
Karlo BARTOLEC	20.04.1995	5	0	2019:	*FC København (DEN)*
Duje ĆALETA-CAR	17.09.1996	5	0	2019:	*Olympique de Marseille (FRA)*
Tin JEDVAJ	28.11.1995	24	2	2019:	*FC Augsburg (GER)*
Josip JURANOVIĆ	16.08.1995	2	0	2019:	*HNK Hajduk Split*
Dejan LOVREN	05.07.1989	57	3	2019:	*Liverpool FC (ENG)*
Dino PERIĆ	12.07.1994	2	0	2019:	*GNK Dinamo Zagreb*
Mile ŠKORIĆ	19.06.1991	3	0	2019:	*NK Osijek*
Domagoj VIDA	29.04.1989	79	4	2019:	*Beşiktaş JK Istanbul (TUR)*
Midfielders					
Milan BADELJ	25.02.1989	50	2	2019:	*ACF Fiorentina (ITA)*
Marcelo BROZOVIĆ	16.11.1992	51	6	2019:	*FC Internazionale Milano (ITA)*
Mateo KOVAČIĆ	06.05.1994	56	1	2019:	*Chelsea FC London (ENG)*
Luka MODRIĆ	09.09.1985	127	16	2019:	*Real Madrid CF (ESP)*
Mario PAŠALIĆ	09.02.1995	12	0	2019:	*Atalanta Bergamasca Calcio (ITA)*
Ivan PERIŠIĆ	02.02.1989	88	26	2019:	*FC Bayern München (GER)*
Ivan RAKITIĆ	10.03.1988	106	15	2019:	*FC Barcelona (ESP)*
Marko ROG	19.07.1995	17	0	2019:	*Cagliari Calcio (ITA)*
Nikola VLAŠIĆ	04.10.1997	11	3	2019:	*FK CSKA Moskva (RUS)*
Forwards					
Josip BREKALO	23.06.1998	11	0	2019:	*VfL Wolfsburg (GER)*
Dario MELNJAK	31.10.1992	2	0	2019:	*Çaykur Rizespor Kulübü (TUR)*
Mislav ORŠIĆ	29.12.1992	3	0	2019:	*GNK Dinamo Zagreb*
Bruno PETKOVIĆ	16.09.1994	8	5	2019:	*GNK Dinamo Zagreb*
Ante REBIĆ	21.09.1993	34	3	2019:	*AC Milan (ITA)*
National team coach					
Zlatko DALIĆ [from 07.10.2017]		26.10.1966	30 M; 16 W; 7 D; 7 L; 50-37		

CYPRUS

The Country:
Κυπριακή Δημοκρατία (Republic of Cyprus)
Capital: Nicosia
Surface: 9,251 km²
Inhabitants: 1,189,265 [2019]
Time: UTC+2

The FA:
Cyprus Football Association
10 Achaion Street 2413 Engomi, PO Box 25071 1306 Nicosia
Tel: +357 22 352 341
Foundation date: 23.09.1934
Member of FIFA since: 1948
Member of UEFA since: 1962
Website: www.cfa.com.cy

NATIONAL TEAM RECORDS

RECORDS

First international match:	13.11.1960, Nicosia:	Cyprus – Israel 1-1
Most international caps:	Yiannakis Okkas	- 103 caps (1997-2011)
Most international goals:	Michalis Konstantinou	- 32 goals / 84 caps (1997-2012)

UEFA EUROPEAN CHAMPIONSHIP		FIFA WORLD CUP		OLYMPIC TOURNAMENTS	
1960	Did not enter	1930	Did not enter	1908	-
1964	Did not enter	1934	Did not enter	1912	-
1968	Qualifiers	1938	Did not enter	1920	-
1972	Qualifiers	1950	Did not enter	1924	-
1976	Qualifiers	1954	Did not enter	1928	-
1980	Qualifiers	1958	Did not enter	1936	-
1984	Qualifiers	1962	Qualifiers	1948	-
1988	Qualifiers	1966	Qualifiers	1952	-
1992	Qualifiers	1970	Qualifiers	1956	-
1996	Qualifiers	1974	Qualifiers	1960	-
2000	Qualifiers	1978	Qualifiers	1964	-
2004	Qualifiers	1982	Qualifiers	1968	-
2008	Qualifiers	1986	Qualifiers	1972	-
2012	Qualifiers	1990	Qualifiers	1976	-
2016	Qualifiers	1994	Qualifiers	1980	-
2020	Qualifiers	1998	Qualifiers	1984	-
		2002	Qualifiers	1988	-
		2006	Qualifiers	1992	Qualifiers
		2010	Qualifiers	1996	Qualifiers
		2014	Qualifiers	2000	Qualifiers
		2018	Qualifiers	2004	Qualifiers
				2008	Qualifiers
				2012	Qualifiers
				2016	Qualifiers

UEFA NATIONS LEAGUE

2018/2019 – League C

FIFA CONFEDERATIONS CUP 1992-2017

None

CYPRIOT CLUB HONOURS IN EUROPEAN CLUB COMPETITIONS:

European Champion Clubs' Cup (1956-1992) / UEFA Champions League (1993-2020)
None

Fairs Cup (1858-1971) / UEFA Cup (1972-2009) / UEFA Europa League (2010-2020)
None

UEFA Super Cup (1972-2019)
None

*European Cup Winners' Cup 1961-1999**
None

*defunct competition

NATIONAL COMPETITIONS
TABLE OF HONOURS

	CHAMPIONS	CUP WINNERS	BEST GOALSCORERS	
1934/1935	Enosis Neon Trust Nicosia	Enosis Neon Trust Nicosia	-	
1935/1936	APOEL FC Nicosia	Enosis Neon Trust Nicosia	-	
1936/1937	APOEL FC Nicosia	APOEL FC Nicosia	-	
1937/1938	APOEL FC Nicosia	Enosis Neon Trust Nicosia	-	
1938/1939	APOEL FC Nicosia	AEL Limassol	-	
1939/1940	APOEL FC Nicosia	AEL Limassol	-	
1940/1941	AEL Limassol	APOEL FC Nicosia	-	
1941-1944	*No competition*	*No competition*	-	
1944/1945	EPA Larnaca FC	EPA Larnaca FC	-	
1945/1946	EPA Larnaca FC	EPA Larnaca FC	-	
1946/1947	APOEL FC Nicosia	APOEL FC Nicosia	-	
1947/1948	APOEL FC Nicosia	AEL Limassol	-	
1948/1949	APOEL FC Nicosia	Anorthosis Famagusta FC	-	
1949/1950	Anorthosis Famagusta FC	EPA Larnaca FC	-	
1950/1951	Çetinkaya Türk Spor Kulübü	APOEL FC Nicosia	-	
1951/1952	APOEL FC Nicosia	Çetinkaya Türk Spor Kulübü	-	
1952/1953	AEL Limassol	EPA Larnaca FC	-	
1953/1954	Pezoporikos Larnaca FC	Çetinkaya Türk Spor Kulübü	-	
1954/1955	AEL Limassol	EPA Larnaca FC	-	
1955/1956	AEL Limassol	*No competition*	-	
1956/1957	Anorthosis Famagusta FC	*No competition*	-	
1957/1958	Anorthosis Famagusta FC	*No competition*	-	
1958/1959	*No competition*	Anorthosis Famagusta FC	-	
1959/1960	Anorthosis Famagusta FC	*No competition*	-	
1960/1961	AC Omonia Nicosia	*No competition*	Panikos Krystallis (Apollon Limassol FC)	26
1961/1962	Anorthosis Famagusta FC	Anorthosis Famagusta FC	Michalis Shialis (Anorthosis Famagusta FC)	22
1962/1963	Anorthosis Famagusta FC	APOEL FC Nicosia	Panikos Papadopoulos (AEL Limassol)	24
1963/1964	*Championship Abandoned*	Anorthosis Famagusta FC	*Championship abandoned*	
1964/1965	APOEL FC Nicosia	AC Omonia Nicosia	Kostakis Pieridis (Olympiakos Nicosia FC)	21
1965/1966	AC Omonia Nicosia	Apollon Limassol FC	Panikos Efthymiades (Olympiakos Nicosia FC)	20
1966/1967	Olympiakos Nicosia FC	Apollon Limassol FC	Andreas Stylianou (APOEL FC Nicosia)	29
1967/1968	AEL Limassol	APOEL FC Nicosia	Charalambos Papadopoulos (AEL Limassol)	31
1968/1969	Olympiakos Nicosia FC	APOEL FC Nicosia	Panikos Efthymiades (Olympiakos Nicosia FC)	17
1969/1970	EPA Larnaca FC	Pezoporikos Larnaca FC	Tasos Constantinou (EPA Larnaca FC)	24
1970/1971	Olympiakos Nicosia FC	Anorthosis Famagusta FC	Andreas Stylianou (APOEL FC Nicosia) Kostas Vasiliades (Apollon Limassol FC) Panikos Efthymiades (Olympiakos Nicosia FC)	11
1971/1972	AC Omonia Nicosia	AC Omonia Nicosia	Sotiris Kaiafas (AC Omonia Nicosia)	24
1972/1973	APOEL FC Nicosia	APOEL FC Nicosia	Lakis Theodorou (EPA Larnaca FC)	17
1973/1974	AC Omonia Nicosia	AC Omonia Nicosia	Sotiris Kaiafas (AC Omonia Nicosia)	20
1974/1975	AC Omonia Nicosia	Anorthosis Famagusta FC	Andros Savva (AC Omonia Nicosia)	21
1975/1976	AC Omonia Nicosia	APOEL FC Nicosia	Sotiris Kaiafas (AC Omonia Nicosia)	39
1976/1977	AC Omonia Nicosia	Olympiakos Nicosia FC	Sotiris Kaiafas (AC Omonia Nicosia)	44
1977/1978	AC Omonia Nicosia	APOEL FC Nicosia	Andreas Kanaris (AC Omonia Nicosia)	20
1978/1979	AC Omonia Nicosia	APOEL FC Nicosia	Sotiris Kaiafas (AC Omonia Nicosia)	28
1979/1980	APOEL FC Nicosia	AC Omonia Nicosia	Sotiris Kaiafas (AC Omonia Nicosia)	23
1980/1981	AC Omonia Nicosia	AC Omonia Nicosia	Sotiris Kaiafas (AC Omonia Nicosia)	14
1981/1982	AC Omonia Nicosia	AC Omonia Nicosia	Sotiris Kaiafas (AC Omonia Nicosia)	19
1982/1983	AC Omonia Nicosia	AC Omonia Nicosia	Panikos Hatziloizou (Aris Limassol FC)	17
1983/1984	AC Omonia Nicosia	APOEL FC Nicosia	Sylvester Vernon (Pezoporikos Larnaca FC) Lenos Kittos (Ermis Aradippou FC)	14
1984/1985	AC Omonia Nicosia	AEL Limassol	Giorgos Savvidis (AC Omonia Nicosia)	24
1985/1986	APOEL FC Nicosia	Apollon Limassol FC	Yiannos Ioannou (APOEL FC Nicosia)	22
1986/1987	AC Omonia Nicosia	AEL Limassol	Spas Dzhevizov (BUL, AC Omonia Nicosia)	32
1987/1988	Pezoporikos Larnaca FC	AC Omonia Nicosia	Tasos Zouvanis (Enosis Neon Paralimni FC)	23
1988/1989	AC Omonia Nicosia	AEL Limassol	Nigel McNeal (ENG, Nea Salamis Famagusta FC)	19
1989/1990	APOEL FC Nicosia	Nea Salamis Famagusta FC	Siniša Gogić (YUG, APOEL FC Nicosia)	19
1990/1991	Apollon Limassol FC	AC Omonia Nicosia	Suad Beširević (YUG, Apollon Limassol FC) Panikos Xiourouppas (AC Omonia Nicosia)	19
1991/1992	APOEL FC Nicosia	Apollon Limassol FC	József Dzurják (HUN, AC Omonia Nicosia)	21
1992/1993	AC Omonia Nicosia	APOEL FC Nicosia	Slađan Šćepović (YUG, Apollon Limassol FC)	25
1993/1994	Apollon Limassol FC	AC Omonia Nicosia	Siniša Gogić (YUG, Anorthosis Famagusta FC)	26
1994/1995	Anorthosis Famagusta FC	APOEL FC Nicosia	Pambis Andreou (Nea Salamis Famagusta FC)	25
1995/1996	APOEL FC Nicosia	APOEL FC Nicosia	József Kiprich (HUN, APOEL FC Nicosia)	25
1996/1997	Anorthosis Famagusta FC	APOEL FC Nicosia	Michalis Konstantinou (Enosis Neon Paralimni FC)	17
1997/1998	Anorthosis Famagusta FC	Anorthosis Famagusta FC	Rainer Rauffmann (GER, AC Omonia Nicosia)	42
1998/1999	Anorthosis Famagusta FC	APOEL FC Nicosia	Rainer Rauffmann (GER, AC Omonia Nicosia)	35
1999/2000	Anorthosis Famagusta FC	AC Omonia Nicosia	Rainer Rauffmann (GER, AC Omonia Nicosia)	34
2000/2001	AC Omonia Nicosia	Apollon Limassol FC	Rainer Rauffmann (GER, AC Omonia Nicosia)	30
2001/2002	APOEL FC Nicosia	Anorthosis Famagusta FC	Wojciech Kowalczyk (POL, Anorthosis Famagusta FC)	22
2002/2003	AC Omonia Nicosia	Anorthosis Famagusta FC	Marios Neophytou (Anorthosis Famagusta FC)	33

2003/2004	APOEL FC Nicosia	AEK Larnaca FC	Łukasz Sosin (POL, Apollon Limassol FC)	
			Jozef Kožlej (SVK, AC Omonia Nicosia)	21
2004/2005	Anorthosis Famagusta FC	AC Omonia Nicosia	Łukasz Sosin (POL, Apollon Limassol FC)	21
2005/2006	Apollon Limassol FC	APOEL FC Nicosia	Łukasz Sosin (POL, Apollon Limassol FC)	28
2006/2007	APOEL FC Nicosia	Anorthosis Famagusta FC	Esteban Andrés Solari Poggio (ARG, APOEL FC Nicosia)	20
2007/2008	Anorthosis Famagusta FC	APOEL FC Nicosia	David Pereira da Costa (BRA, Doxa Katokopias FC)	
			Łukasz Sosin (POL, Anorthosis Famagusta FC)	16
2008/2009	APOEL FC Nicosia	APOP Kinyras Peyias FC	Sérgio Luis Gardino da Silva "Serjão"	
			(BRA, Doxa Katokopias FC)	24
2009/2010	AC Omonia Nicosia	Apollon Limassol FC	Joeano Pinto Chaves (BRA, Ermis Aradippou FC)	
			José Filipe CorreiaSemedo (CPV, APOP Kinyras)	22
2010/2011	APOEL FC Nicosia	AC Omonia Nicosia	Miljan Mrdaković (SRB, Apollon Limassol FC)	21
2011/2012	AEL Limassol	AC Omonia Nicosia	Frederico Castro Roque dos Santos "Freddy"	
			(ANG, AC Omonia Nicosia)	17
2012/2013	APOEL FC Nicosia	Apollon Limassol FC	Bernardo Lino Castro Paes Vasconcelos	
			(POR, Alki Larnaca FC)	18
2013/2014	APOEL FC Nicosia	APOEL FC Nicosia	Gastón Maximiliano Sangoy (ARG, Apollon Limassol FC)	
			Marco Tagbajumi (NGA, Ermis Aradippou FC)	
			Jorge Filipe Monteiro dos Santos Lourenço	
			(POR, AEL Limassol)	18
2014/2015	APOEL FC Nicosia	APOEL FC Nicosia	Mickaël Poté (BEN, AC Omonia Nicosia)	17
2015/2016	APOEL FC Nicosia	Apollon Limassol FC	Fernando Ezequiel Cavenaghi (ARG, APOEL FC Nicosia)	
			André Alves dos Santos (BRA, AEK Larnaca FC)	
			Dimitar Makriev (BUL, Nea Salamis Famagusta FC)	19
2016/2017	APOEL FC Nicosia	Apollon Limassol FC	Matthew Anthony Derbyshire (ENG, AC Omonia Nicosia)	24
2017/2018	APOEL FC Nicosia	AEK Larnaca FC	Matthew Anthony Derbyshire (ENG, AC Omonia Nicosia)	23
2018/2019	APOEL FC Nicosia	AEL Limassol	Adam Nemec (SVK, Pafos FC Paphos)	16
2019/2020	*Championship abandoned*	*Competition abandoned*	-	

NATIONAL CHAMPIONSHIP
Cypriot First Division 2019/2020
(23.08.2019 – 09.03.2020)

Regular Season - Results

Round 1 [23-26.08.2019]
Nea Salamina - Pafos FC 1-2(0-1)
Doxa Katokopias - AC Omonia 0-2(0-1)
AEL Limassol - Anorthosis 0-0
Neon Paralimni - Ethnikos Achna 3-4(2-3)
AEK Larnaca - Apollon 0-0 [27.09.]
APOEL - Olympiakos 4-2(0-1) [08.01.2020]

Round 2 [30.08.-01.09.2019]
Pafos FC - AEK Larnaca 0-2(0-0)
AC Omonia - Nea Salamina 2-0(2-0)
AEL Limassol - Neon Paralimni 2-0(0-0)
Olympiakos - Doxa Katokopias 1-1(0-1)
Anorthosis - Apollon 3-1(2-0) [02.10.]
Ethnikos Achna - APOEL 0-0 [15.01.2020]

Round 3 [14-16.09.2019]
APOEL Nicosia - AEL Limassol 3-0(2-0)
Apollon - Pafos FC 3-2(1-1)
AEK Larnaca - AC Omonia 2-2(1-1)
Doxa Katokopias - Ethnikos Achna 1-1(0-1)
Neon Paralimni - Anorthosis 1-2(0-1)
Nea Salamina - Olympiakos Nicosia 3-2(1-1)

Round 4 [20-23.09.2019]
Olympiakos Nicosia - AEK Larnaca 2-2(1-2)
AC Omonia - Apollon 1-0(0-0)
AEL Limassol - Doxa Katokopias 1-0(0-0)
Anorthosis - Pafos FC 2-0(1-0)
Ethnikos Achna - Nea Salamina 2-0(0-0)
Neon Paralimni - APOEL Nicosia 2-3(0-1)

Round 5 [04-06.10.2019]
AEK Larnaca - Ethnikos Achna 5-1(2-1)
Pafos FC - AC Omonia 2-1(0-0)
Doxa Katokopias - Neon Paralimni 1-3(1-2)
Nea Salamina - AEL Limassol 3-2(1-1)
Apollon - Olympiakos Nicosia 3-1(1-0)
APOEL Nicosia - Anorthosis 0-0 [05.02.2020]

Round 6 [19-21.10.2019]
APOEL Nicosia - Doxa Katokopias 2-0(1-0)
Ethnikos Achna - Apollon 1-0(0-0)
Neon Paralimni - Nea Salamina 0-1(0-1)
Anorthosis - AC Omonia 0-0
Olympiakos Nicosia - Pafos FC 1-1(0-0)
AEL Limassol - AEK Larnaca 1-1(0-0)

Round 7 [25-28.10.2019]
AC Omonia - Olympiakos Nicosia 1-1(0-0)
Pafos FC - Ethnikos Achna 1-1(0-0)
Apollon - AEL Limassol 1-2(1-1)
AEK Larnaca - Neon Paralimni 4-4(1-3)
Doxa Katokopias - Anorthosis 0-6(0-2)
Nea Salamina - APOEL Nicosia 0-3(0-0)

Round 8 [01-04.11.2019]
Doxa Katokopias - Nea Salamina 0-0
APOEL Nicosia - AEK Larnaca 0-0
Ethnikos Achna - AC Omonia 1-2(1-1)
Neon Paralimni - Apollon 0-3(0-1)
Anorthosis - Olympiakos Nicosia 4-0(1-0)
AEL Limassol - Pafos FC 2-0(0-0)

Round 9 [08-10.11.2019]
AEK Larnaca - Doxa Katokopias 2-1(1-0)
AC Omonia - AEL Limassol 1-0(1-0)
Nea Salamina - Anorthosis 2-2(1-1)
Pafos FC - Neon Paralimni 1-1(1-0)
Olympiakos - Ethnikos Achna 4-0(2-0)
Apollon - APOEL Nicosia 1-1(0-0)

Round 10 [23-25.11.2019]
Nea Salamina - AEK Larnaca 1-0(0-0)
APOEL Nicosia - Pafos FC 3-0(2-0)
Neon Paralimni - AC Omonia 0-2(0-1)
AEL Limassol - Olympiakos Nicosia 0-0
Anorthosis - Ethnikos Achna 2-1(2-0)
Doxa Katokopias - Apollon 0-1(0-1)

Round 11 [29.11.-02.12.2019]
Olympiakos Nicosia - Neon Paralimni 0-0
AEK Larnaca - Anorthosis 1-2(0-1)
Ethnikos Achna - AEL Limassol 0-1(0-1)
Pafos FC - Doxa Katokopias 0-1(0-0)
Apollon - Nea Salamina 4-1(3-0)
AC Omonia - APOEL Nicosia 0-0

Round 12 [06-09.12.2019]
Pafos FC - Nea Salamina 1-0(0-0)
Anorthosis - AEL Limassol 2-0(2-0)
Olympiakos - APOEL Nicosia 2-0(1-0)
AC Omonia - Doxa Katokopias 2-0(2-0)
Apollon - AEK Larnaca 3-1(0-0)
Ethnikos Achna - Neon Paralimni 2-2(0-1)

Round 13 [13-16.12.2019]
Doxa Katokopias - Olympiakos 2-6(1-1)
AEK Larnaca - Pafos FC 1-0(1-0)
Apollon - Anorthosis 2-0(0-0)
Neon Paralimni - AEL Limassol 2-2(1-2)
Nea Salamina - AC Omonia 0-3(0-2)
APOEL Nicosia - Ethnikos Achna 2-0(1-0)

Round 14 [20-22.12.2019]
Anorthosis - Neon Paralimni 5-1(4-1)
AEL Limassol - APOEL Nicosia 2-1(0-0)
Olympiakos Nicosia - Nea Salamina 0-3(0-0)
AC Omonia - AEK Larnaca 3-2(2-1)
Ethnikos Achna - Doxa Katokopias 1-1(1-0)
Pafos FC - Apollon 3-2(2-2) [12.02.2020]

Round 15 [03-06.01.2020]
Doxa Katokopias - AEL Limassol 2-2(2-1)
AEK Larnaca - Olympiakos Nicosia 0-0
Apollon - AC Omonia 2-1(1-0)
APOEL Nicosia - Neon Paralimni 4-0(2-0)
Nea Salamina - Ethnikos Achna 3-2(3-2)
Pafos FC - Anorthosis 0-3(0-2)

Round 16 [10-13.01.2020]
AC Omonia - Pafos FC 0-0
AEL Limassol - Nea Salamina 1-2(0-1)
Ethnikos Achna - AEK Larnaca 2-5(2-0)
Anorthosis - APOEL Nicosia 1-0(0-0)
Olympiakos Nicosia - Apollon 0-2(0-1)
Neon Paralimni - Doxa Katokopias 1-0(1-0)

Round 17 [25-26.01.2020]
Pafos FC - Olympiakos Nicosia 1-1(0-0)
AEK Larnaca - AEL Limassol 3-1(1-1)
Doxa Katokopias - APOEL Nicosia 0-3(0-3)
Apollon - Ethnikos Achna 3-2(3-1)
AC Omonia - Anorthosis 1-0(0-0)
Nea Salamina - Neon Paralimni 1-1(0-0)

Round 18 [01-03.02.2020]
Ethnikos Achna - Pafos FC 0-3(0-1)
Anorthosis - Doxa Katokopias 3-0(1-0)
Olympiakos Nicosia - AC Omonia 0-2(0-2)
AEL Limassol - Apollon 2-0(0-0)
APOEL Nicosia - Nea Salamina 2-1(0-0)
Neon Paralimni - AEK Larnaca 2-1(1-1)

Round 19 [08-10.02.2020]
Olympiakos Nicosia - Anorthosis 2-1(1-0)
AEK Larnaca - APOEL Nicosia 1-0(1-0)
AC Omonia - Ethnikos Achna 1-2(0-0)
Apollon - Neon Paralimni 0-1(0-0)
Pafos FC - AEL Limassol 2-0(1-0)
Nea Salamina - Doxa Katokopias 0-1(0-0)

Round 20 [14-16.02.2020]
Ethnikos Achna - Olympiakos 0-1(0-0)
APOEL Nicosia - Apollon 4-1(1-0)
Neon Paralimni - Pafos FC 1-1(1-1)
AEL Limassol - AC Omonia 1-1(1-1)
Anorthosis - Nea Salamina 3-2(2-2)
Doxa Katokopias - AEK Larnaca 0-1(0-0)

Round 21 [22-23.02.2020]
AC Omonia - Neon Paralimni 3-0(1-0)
Apollon - Doxa Katokopias 3-2(3-1)
Ethnikos Achna - Anorthosis 5-0(3-0)
Pafos FC - APOEL Nicosia 2-0(0-0)
AEK Larnaca - Nea Salamina 0-0
Olympiakos Nicosia - AEL Limassol 1-1(0-1)

Round 22 [29.02.-02.03.2020]
AEL Limassol - Ethnikos Achna 4-1(2-0)
Doxa Katokopias - Pafos FC 0-4(0-1)
Nea Salamina - Apollon 1-3(0-1)
Anorthosis - AEK Larnaca 1-2(0-1)
Neon Paralimni - Olympiakos 3-0(0-0)
APOEL Nicosia - AC Omonia 0-0

Final Standings

1.	AC Omonia Nicosia	22	12	7	3	31	-	13	43
2.	Anorthosis Famagusta FC	22	13	4	5	42	-	21	43
3.	APOEL FC Nicosia	22	11	6	5	35	-	15	39
4.	Apollon Limassol FC	22	12	2	8	38	-	29	38
5.	AEK Larnaca FC	22	9	8	5	36	-	26	35
6.	AEL Limassol	22	8	7	7	27	-	26	31
7.	Pafos FC Paphos	22	8	6	8	26	-	26	30
8.	Nea Salamis Famagusta FC	22	7	4	11	25	-	36	25
9.	Olympiakos Nicosia FC	22	5	9	8	27	-	34	24
10.	Enosis Neon Paralimni FC	22	5	7	10	28	-	42	22
11.	Ethnikos Achna FC	22	5	5	12	29	-	44	20
12.	Doxa Katokopias FC	22	2	5	15	13	-	45	11

Teams ranked 1-6 were qualified for the Championship Round, while teams ranked 7-12 were qualified for the Relegation Round.

Relegation Round

Results

Round 23 [07-09.03.2020]
Nea Salamina - Ethnikos Achna 2-2(1-0)
Neon Paralimni - Olympiakos 1-1(0-0)
Doxa Katokopias - Pafos FC 2-0(0-0)

Standings

			Total							Home						Away				
7.	Pafos FC Paphos	23	8	6	9	26	-	28	30	5	3	3	13	-	12	3	3	6	13	-	16
8.	Nea Salamis Famagusta FC	23	7	5	11	27	-	38	26	4	3	5	17	-	23	3	2	6	10	-	15
9.	Olympiakos Nicosia FC	23	5	10	8	28	-	35	25	3	5	3	13	-	13	2	5	5	15	-	22
10.	Enosis Neon Paralimni FC	23	5	8	10	29	-	43	23	3	3	6	16	-	20	2	5	4	13	-	23
11.	Ethnikos Achna FC	23	5	6	12	31	-	46	21	3	3	5	14	-	15	2	3	7	17	-	31
12.	Doxa Katokopias FC	23	3	5	15	15	-	45	14	1	3	8	8	-	29	2	2	7	7	-	16

Results

Round 23 [07-08.03.2020]
AEL Limassol - AC Omonia 0-3(0-1)
Anorthosis - AEK Larnaca 3-0(1-0)
Apollon - APOEL Nicosia 1-1(1-0)

Standings

					Total				Home				Away		
1. AC Omonia Nicosia	23	13	7	3	34 - 13	46	7	3	1	15 - 5	6	4	2	19 - 8
2. Anorthosis Famagusta FC	23	14	4	5	45 - 21	46	10	1	1	29 - 7	4	3	4	16 - 14
3. APOEL FC Nicosia	23	11	7	5	36 - 16	40	8	3	0	24 - 4	3	4	5	12 - 12
4. Apollon Limassol FC	23	12	3	8	39 - 30	39	8	2	2	26 - 15	4	1	6	13 - 15
5. AEK Larnaca FC	23	9	8	6	36 - 29	35	5	5	1	19 - 11	4	3	5	17 - 18
6. AEL Limassol	23	8	7	8	27 - 29	31	6	4	2	16 - 9	2	3	6	11 - 20

Both Relegation and Championship Play-offs were interrupted on 09.03.2020 due to Covid-19 pandemic.
The league was abandoned on 15.05.2020. No title was awarded and no teams were relegated. The league will be expanded to 14 teams next season (for a transitional year!).

Top goalscorers:

20	Ivan Tričkovski (MKD)	*AEK Larnaca FC*
14	Kingsley Onuegbu (NGA)	*Nea Salamis Famagusta FC*
14	Rubén Rayo Serna (ESP)	*Anorthosis Famagusta FC*
13	Matthew Anthony Derbyshire (ENG)	*AC Omonia Nicosia*

NATIONAL CUP
Kypello Kyprou 2019/2020

1/8-Finals [08.01.-05.02.2020]

First Leg		Second Leg	
AEK Larnaca FC - Karmiotissa Pano Polemidia FC	3-0(0-0)	Karmiotissa Pano Polemidia FC - AEK Larnaca FC	0-1(0-0)
Enosis Neon Paralimni FC - Doxa Katokopias FC	0-2(0-1)	Doxa Katokopias FC - Enosis Neon Paralimni FC	1-1(0-0)
Alki Oroklini FC - AEL Limassol	1-5(1-2)	AEL Limassol - Alki Oroklini FC	2-1(0-1)
Pafos FC Paphos - Nea Salamis Famagusta FC	0-1(0-1)	Nea Salamis Famagusta FC - Pafos FC Paphos	2-1(1-1)
Olympiakos Nicosia FC - Anorthosis Famagusta FC	0-0	Anorthosis Famagusta FC - Olympiakos Nicosia FC	3-0(2-0)
Ermis Aradippou FC - AC Omonia Nicosia	0-5(0-3)	AC Omonia Nicosia - Ermis Aradippou FC	3-0(2-0)
Apollon Limassol FC - APOEL Nikosia	1-0(1-0)	APOEL Nikosia - Apollon Limassol FC	1-2(0-1)
Digenis Akritas Morphou FC - Ethnikos Achna FC	0-3(0-1)	Ethnikos Achna FC - Digenis Akritas Morphou FC	3-0(1-0)

Quarter-Finals [06-26.02.2020]

First Leg		Second Leg	
AC Omonia Nicosia - Doxa Katokopias FC	4-1(2-0)	Doxa Katokopias FC - AC Omonia Nicosia	1-1(0-1)
AEL Limassol - AEK Larnaca FC	0-0	AEK Larnaca FC - AEL Limassol	1-1(1-1)
Anorthosis Famagusta FC - Nea Salamis Famagusta	1-1(0-0)	Nea Salamis Famagusta - Anorthosis Famagusta FC	0-2(0-1)
Apollon Limassol FC - Ethnikos Achna FC	2-0(1-0)	Ethnikos Achna FC - Apollon Limassol FC	2-1(1-0,2-0)

Semi-Finals [scheduled 22-29.04.2020]

First Leg		Second Leg	
Apollon Limassol FC - AEL Limassol	*Not played*	AEL Limassol - Apollon Limassol FC	*Not played*
AC Omonia Nicosia - Anorthosis Famagusta FC	*Not played*	Anorthosis Famagusta FC - AC Omonia Nicosia	*Not played*

On 15.05.2020, the competition was abandoned due to Covid-19 pandemic. No title was awarded.

Athletiki Enosi Kition Larnakas (AEK Larnaca)

Founded:	18.07.1994		
Stadium:	AEK Arena, Larnaca (7,400)		
Trainer:	Joseba Imanol Idiakez Barkaiztegui(ESP)	14.03.1972	
[09.12.2019]	Ilias Charalampous	25.09.1980	
[26.02.2020]	David Caneda Pérez (ESP)	30.01.1970	

Goalkeepers:	DOB	M	(s)	G
Antonio Ramírez Martínez „Toño" (ESP)	23.11.1986	23		
Defenders:	**DOB**	**M**	**(s)**	**G**
Carles Planas Antolínez (ESP)	04.03.1991	12	(1)	1
José Manuel Fernández Reyes (ESP)	18.11.1989	5		
Thomas Ioannou	19.07.1995	10	(3)	1
Mikel González de Martín Martínez (ESP)	24.09.1985	22		
Daniel Mojsov (MKD)	25.12.1987	7		
Raúl Ruiz Matarín (ESP)	25.03.1990	7	(5)	
Román Golobart Benet (ESP)	21.03.1992	3	(2)	
Simranjit Singh Thandi (ENG)	11.10.1999	10	(3)	
Joan Guillem Truyols Mascaró (ESP)	11.11.1989	19	(1)	2
Midfielders:	**DOB**	**M**	**(s)**	**G**
Abraham González Casanova (ESP)	16.07.1985	3	(2)	
Konstantinos Anastasiou	05.07.1999		(5)	
Ivan Fiolić (CRO)	29.04.1996	8	(5)	3

	DOB	M	(s)	G
Facundo García (ARG)	16.12.1999	11	(3)	1
Hector Hevel (NED)	15.05.1996	13	(4)	1
Ignacio Cases Mora „Nacho Cases" (ESP)	22.12.1987	13	(1)	2
Lluís Sastre Reus (ESP)	26.03.1986	16		
Matija Špoljarić (SRB)	02.04.1997	8	(4)	
Alberto Sansimena Chamorro „Tete" (ESP)	26.05.1985	16	(1)	
Forwards:	**DOB**	**M**	**(s)**	**G**
Acorán Barrera Reyes (ESP)	31.01.1983	4	(5)	1
Apostolos Giannou (AUS)	25.01.1990	18	(1)	1
Jozsef Keaveny (ENG)	12.10.1999		(9)	1
Konstantinos Konstantinou	08.10.1999		(5)	
José Manuel García Naranjo (ESP)	28.07.1994	5		1
Dimitris Raspas	01.04.2001		(1)	
Thierry Alain Florian Taulemesse (FRA)	31.01.1986	2	(5)	1
Ivan Tričkovski (MKD)	18.04.1987	18	(1)	20

Athlitiki Enosi Lemesou (AEL Limassol)

Founded:	04.10.1930		
Stadium:	Stádio Tsirion, Limassol (13,331)		
Trainer:	Dušan Kerkez (BIH)	01.05.1976	

Goalkeepers:	DOB	M	(s)	G
Michalis Kyriakou	30.12.2002	1		
Josimar Diaz Vózinha (CPV)	03.06.1986	23		
Defenders:	**DOB**	**M**	**(s)**	**G**
André Ferreira Teixeira (POR)	14.08.1993	22		3
Andreas Avraam	06.06.1987	18	(1)	1
Dossa Júnior	28.07.1986	5		
Boris Godál (SVK)	27.05.1987	7	(2)	1
Charalambos Kyriakou	15.10.1989	13	(1)	
Momčilo Rašo (MNE)	06.02.1997	14	(2)	
Nils Teixeira (GER)	10.07.1990	7	(1)	1
Christos Wheeler	29.06.1997	10	(4)	
Midfielders:	**DOB**	**M**	**(s)**	**G**
Marko Adamović (SRB)	11.03.1991	4	(5)	
Adnan Aganović (CRO)	03.10.1987	15	(1)	3

	DOB	M	(s)	G
Jon Gaztañaga Arrospide (ESP)	28.06.1991	14		
Giannis Gerolemou	27.01.2000	8	(3)	
Manuel Torres Jiménez (ESP)	05.01.1991	5	(8)	1
Slobodan Medojević (SRB)	20.11.1990	14	(1)	
Stylianos Panteli	07.08.1999		(4)	
Davor Zdravkovski (MKD)	20.03.1998	17	(2)	
Forwards:	**DOB**	**M**	**(s)**	**G**
Minas Antoniou	22.02.1994	13	(5)	
Gevorg Ghazaryan (ARM)	05.04.1988	5	(8)	
Ivan Carlos França Coelho (BRA)	06.12.1989	7	(4)	3
Andrija Majdevac (SRB)	07.08.1997	4	(2)	3
Ryan Mmaee (BEL)	01.11.1997	16	(4)	5
Kire Markoski (MKD)	20.02.1995		(6)	
Rubén Jurado Fernández (ESP)	25.04.1986	11	(5)	5

Anorthosis Famagusta Football Club

Founded:	30.01.1911		
Stadium:	Stádio "Antonis Papadopoulos", Larnaca (10,230)		
Trainer:	Temur Ketsbaia (GEO)	18.03.1968	

Goalkeepers:	DOB	M	(s)	G
Giorgi Loria (GEO)	27.01.1986	21		
Georgios Papadopoulos	24.04.1991	2		
Defenders:	**DOB**	**M**	**(s)**	**G**
Panagiotis Artymatas	12.11.1998	1	(3)	
Georgios Galitsios (GRE)	06.07.1986	19		4
Erwin Koffi (FRAU)	10.01.1995	1	(2)	
Gordon Schildenfeld (CRO)	18.03.1985	23		4
Evgen Selin (UKR)	09.05.1988	18	(2)	1
Branko Vrgoč (CRO)	18.12.1989	23		
Midfielders:	**DOB**	**M**	**(s)**	**G**
Jano Ananidze (GEO)	10.10.1992	2	(4)	
Kostakis Artymatas	15.04.1993	20	(2)	
Dimitris Christofi	28.09.1988	1	(3)	1

	DOB	M	(s)	G
Murtaz Daushvili (GEO)	01.05.1989	14	(7)	1
Michalis Ioannou	30.06.2000	4	(4)	
Margaça	17.07.1985	9	(2)	
Tornike Okriashvili (GEO)	12.02.1992	13	(1)	3
Rubén Rayo Serna (ESP)	21.06.1986	23		14
Theodoros Vasilakakis (GRE)	20.07.1988	5	(6)	1
Forwards:	**DOB**	**M**	**(s)**	**G**
Michal Ďuriš (SVK)	01.06.1988	11	(9)	5
Nikos Englezou	11.07.1993	4	(1)	
Nika Kacharava (GEO)	13.01.1994	11	(7)	6
Nikolaos Kaltsas (GRE)	03.05.1990	17	(1)	4
Georgios Manthatis (GRE)	11.05.1997	8	(10)	
Berat Sadik (FIN)	14.09.1986	3	(5)	

Athletikos Podosferikos Omilos Ellinon Lefkosias (APOEL Football Club Nicosia)

Founded:	08.11.1926	
Stadium:	Stádio GSP, Nicosia (22,859)	
Trainer:	Paolo Tramezzani (ITA)	30.07.1970
[08.08.2019]	Thomas Jens-Uwe Doll (GER)	09.04.1966
[09.12.2019]	Loukas Chatziloukas	06.06.1967
[28.12.2019]	Kare Ingebrigtsen (NOR)	11.11.1965
[12.02.2020]	Marinos Ouzounidis	10.10.1968

Goalkeepers:	DOB	M	(s)	G
Vid Belec (SVN)	06.06.1990	21		
Boy Waterman (NED)	24.01.1984	2		
Defenders:	**DOB**	**M**	**(s)**	**G**
Nicholas Ioannou	10.11.1995	19		
João Carlos Reis Graça „Joãozinho" (POR)	02.07.1989	5		
Giorgios Merkis	30.07.1984	17	(1)	6
Vujadin Savić (SRB)	01.07.1990	17		1
Christos Shelis	02.02.2000	2	(1)	
Praxitelis Vouros (GRE)	05.05.1995	15	(1)	
Christos Wheeler	29.06.1997	2	(1)	
Midfielders:	**DOB**	**M**	**(s)**	**G**
Musa Suliman Al Taamari (JOR)	10.06.1997	18	(3)	3
Omar Hani Ismail Al Zebdieh (JOR)	27.06.1999		(1)	
Alef dos Santos Saldanha (BRA)	28.01.1995	12	(5)	
Tomás Sebastián De Vincenti (ARG)	09.02.1989	13	(4)	4
Giorgos Efrem	05.07.1989	10	(4)	1
Savvas Gentsoglou (GRE)	19.09.1990	2		
Antonio Jakoliš (CRO)	28.02.1992	5	(9)	
Mike Jensen (DEN)	19.02.1988	6	(1)	1
Lucas Vieira de Souza (BRA)	04.06.1990	16	(1)	4
Uroš Matić (SRB)	23.05.1990	15	(4)	1
Dragan Mihajlović (SUI)	22.08.1991	19		2
Forwards:	**DOB**	**M**	**(s)**	**G**
Stathis Aloneftis	29.03.1983		(6)	
André Filipe Cunha Vidigal (POR)	17.08.1998	7	(6)	1
Roman Bezjak (SVN)	21.02.1989	1	(3)	
Linus Hallenius (SWE)	01.04.1989	10	(4)	6
Milan Jevtović (SRB)	13.06.1993	4	(2)	
Andreas Makris	27.11.1995	3	(2)	
Andrija Pavlović (SRB)	16.11.1993	12	(9)	5

Apollon Lemesou (Apollon Football Club Limassol)

Founded:	14.04.1954	
Stadium:	Stádio Tsirion, Limassol (13,331)	
Trainer:	Sofronis Avgousti	09.03.1977
[09.09.2019]	Ivan Vukomanović (SRB)	19.06.1977
[04.10.2019]	Sofronis Avgousti	09.03.1977

Goalkeepers:	DOB	M	(s)	G
Dimitris Dimitriou	15.01.1999	3		
Joël Mall (SUI)	05.04.1991	20		
Defenders:	**DOB**	**M**	**(s)**	**G**
Marios Antoniades	14.05.1990	3	(4)	
Héctor Yuste Canton (ESP)	12.01.1988	13	(1)	
Emilio N'Sue López (EQG)	30.09.1989	11	(3)	1
Valentin Sébastien Roger Roberge (FRA)	09.06.1987	2		
Vahid Selimović (LUX)	03.04.1997	12	(1)	
Attila Szalai (HUN)	20.01.1998	14		
Midfielders:	**DOB**	**M**	**(s)**	**G**
Đorđe Denić (SRB)	01.04.1996	7		
Diego Aguirre Parra (ESP)	17.10.1990	16	(2)	1
Demetris Erodotou	20.04.2002		(1)	
João Pedro Guerra Cunha (POR)	04.05.1986	21		1
Chambos Kyriakou	09.02.1995	15	(1)	
Saša Marković (SRB)	13.03.1991	9	(4)	1
Florentin Matei (ROU)	15.04.1993	3	(5)	2
Ioannis Pittas	10.07.1996	6	(13)	2
Esteban Fernando Sachetti (ARG)	21.11.1985	15	(1)	1
Roger Tamba M'Pinda (FRA)	13.08.1998	2	(2)	
Giorgos Vasiliou	12.06.1984	6	(3)	
Forwards:	**DOB**	**M**	**(s)**	**G**
Daniel Clive Carr (TRI)	29.05.1994	2	(2)	1
Adrián Sardinero Corpa (ESP)	13.10.1990	8	(7)	1
Charlison Benschop (CUW)	21.08.1989	7		3
Serge Gakpé (TOG)	07.05.1987	9	(4)	6
Giannis Gianniotas (GRE)	29.04.1993	13	(3)	3
Fotios Papoulis (GRE)	22.01.1985	17	(3)	5
Facundo Abel Pereyra (ARG)	03.09.1987	8	(6)	3
Matías Roskopf (ARG)	14.01.1998		(1)	
Emilio José Zelaya (ARG)	30.07.1987	11	(1)	8

Doxa Katokopias Football Club

Founded:	1954	
Stadium:	Stádio "Makario", Nicosia (16,000)	
Trainer:	Loukas Hatziloukas	06.06.1967
[30.10.2019]	Eduard Eranosyan (BUL)	08.01.1961
[26.02.2020]	Kostas Sakkas	1973

Goalkeepers:	DOB	M	(s)	G
Armin Gremsl (AUT)	18.08.1994	14		
Antreas Paraskevas	15.09.1998	3		
Thierry Ramos Graça (CPV)	27.01.1995	6		
Defenders:	**DOB**	**M**	**(s)**	**G**
Alfonso Artabe Meca (ESP)	18.08.1988	2		
Martinos Christofi	26.07.1993	11	(2)	
Dorian Dervite (FRA)	25.07.1988	20		1
Mladen Jutrić (AUT)	19.04.1996	4		1
Andreas Michael	24.03.2003		(2)	
Konstantinos Mintikkis	14.07.1989	15	(3)	
Stephanos Mouktaris	10.07.1994	11	(1)	
Nélson Barbosa Conceição "Nelsinho" (BRA)	01.01.1988	5		
Midfielders:	**DOB**	**M**	**(s)**	**G**
Benjamin Akoto Asamoah (GHA)	04.01.1994	15	(4)	2
Vladimir Boljević (MNE)	17.01.1988	20	(3)	
Carlos Miguel Tavares de Oliveira „Carlitos" (POR)	09.03.1993	10	(7)	1
Marko Charalampous	11.01.1993	6	(3)	1
Fidelis Christopher Irhene (NGA)	20.01.1996	2	(2)	
Luís Carlos Eneas da Conceição Lima (BRA)	15.06.1987	14	(5)	2
Lukas Pivetta Brambilla (BRA)	04.01.1995	5	(8)	
Vasilios Papafotis	10.08.1995	16	(3)	4
Duško Trajčevski (MKD)	01.11.1990	15	(3)	
José Pedro Magalhães Valente „Zé Valente" (POR)	14.05.1994	11	(5)	
Forwards:	**DOB**	**M**	**(s)**	**G**
Nektarios Alexandrou	19.12.1983	6		
Carlos Alexandre Souza Silva „Carlão" (BRA)	01.08.1986	7	(1)	1
Italo de Carvalho Rocha Lima (BRA)	07.11.1996	7	(11)	1
Jorge Vinícius Oliveira Alves „Jorginho" (BRA)	03.05.1988	7	(1)	
Buomesca Tue Na Bangna „Mesca" (GNB)	06.05.1993	21		

Enosi Neon Paralimniou
(Enosis Neon Paralimni Football Club)

Founded: 1936
Stadium: Stádio "Tasos Markou", Paralimni (5,800)
Trainer: Giorgos Kosma
[30.09.2019]   Gustavo Lionel Siviero (ARG)   13.09.1969
[20.01.2020]   Čedomir Janevski (MKD)   30.07.1961

Goalkeepers:	DOB	M	(s)	G
Boris Kleiman (ISR)	26.10.1990	21		
Konstantinos Petrou	23.09.1997	2		
Defenders:	DOB	M	(s)	G
Angelis Angeli	31.05.1989	10		
Gregor Balažic (SVN)	12.02.1988	8		
Diego Martín Barboza González (URU)	09.01.1991	8		
Hovhannes Hambardzumyan (ARM)	04.10.1990	17	(1)	3
Antonis Koumis	11.02.1997	4	(6)	
Andreas Kyriakou	05.02.1994	11	(1)	1
Risto Mitrevski (MKD)	05.10.1991	7	(1)	1
Demetris Moulazimis	15.01.1992	4	(1)	
Orlin Starokin (BUL)	08.01.1987	9	(4)	
Midfielders:	DOB	M	(s)	G
Ernest Agyiri (GHA)	06.03.1998	10	(9)	3

	DOB	M	(s)	G
Carlos Alberto Matos Rodrigues „Cal" (BRA)	14.03.1996	2	(4)	
Shaloze Chigozie Udoji (NGA)	16.07.1986	17	(3)	2
Loizos Kosmas	25.01.1995	9	(4)	
Irakli Maisuradze (GEO)	22.08.1988	14	(2)	
Danilo Spoljaric	14.07.1999	16		
Nicolás Varela Batista (URU)	19.01.1991	12	(8)	5
Vasilios Vallianos (GRE)	11.09.1988	15	(2)	1
Forwards:	DOB	M	(s)	G
Kristis Andreou	12.08.1994		(2)	
Theodoros Kolokoudias	06.07.1999		(3)	
Onisiforos Roushias	15.07.1992	8	(10)	1
Berat Sadik (FIN)	14.09.1986	2	(4)	2
Llorenc Riera Ortega „Sito Riera" (ESP)	05.01.1987	18		1
Mateusz Szczepaniak (POL)	23.01.1991	8	(3)	2
Dimitris Theodorou	10.09.1997	21	(1)	7

Ethnikos Achnas Football Club

Founded: 1968
Stadium: Stádio Dasaki, Achna (7,000)
Trainer: Panagiotis Egomitis   26.05.1972
[01.01.2020]   Dean Klafurić (CRO)   26.07.1972

Goalkeepers:	DOB	M	(s)	G
Martin Bogatinov (MKD)	26.04.1986	22		
Kyriakos Stratilatis (GRE)	05.01.1988	1	(1)	
Defenders:	DOB	M	(s)	G
Deyvison Denílson de Sousa Bessas (BRA)	18.10.1988	12		
Yiannis Efstathiou	14.02.1992	8	(2)	
Sotiris Finiris	07.09.1991	7	(6)	
Christopher Glombard (MTQ)	05.06.1989	20		
Petros Ioannou	10.01.1999	4	(3)	
Pavlos Korrea	14.07.1998	5		
Bojan Markoski (MKD)	08.08.1983	15	(1)	
Josip Projić (SRB)	23.08.1987	2		
Midfielders:	DOB	M	(s)	G
Stjepan Babić (CRO)	04.12.1988	2		

	DOB	M	(s)	G
Dimitris Charalambous	09.04.1997	6	(9)	
Christoforos Christofi	23.03.1991	14	(1)	2
Konstantinos Ilia	25.10.2000	1	(3)	
Igor Khudobyak (UKR)	20.02.1985	16	(2)	3
Vincent Laban	09.09.1984	14	(1)	2
Luís Miguel Teixeira Ribeiro „Miguelito" (POR)	09.03.1990	20	(3)	4
Giorgos Papageorgiou	07.06.1997	13	(4)	
Forwards:	DOB	M	(s)	G
Andreas Elia	09.08.1997	1	(4)	
Marios Elia	19.05.1996	9	(7)	3
Ibrahim Koneh (CMR)	09.09.1994	17	(5)	6
Jovan Kostovski (MKD)	19.04.1987	17	(2)	6
Dimitris Kyprianou	02.02.1993	18	(2)	
Ilya Markovskyy (UKR)	06.06.1997	9	(10)	4

Nea Salamis Famagusta Football Club

Founded: 07.03.1948
Stadium: Stádio Ammochostos, Famagusta (5,500)
Trainer: Savvas Poursaitidis   23.06.1976

Goalkeepers:	DOB	M	(s)	G
Tasos Kissas	18.01.1988	17	(1)	
Robert Veselovsky (SVK)	02.09.1985	6		
Defenders:	DOB	M	(s)	G
Anderson Correia de Barros (BRA)	06.05.1991	23		1
Rolandas Baravykas (LTU)	23.08.1995	3		
Kypros Christoforou	23.04.1993	20	(1)	
David Omar Rodríguez Barrera „Deivid"(ESP)	27.01.1989	4		
Ivan Fuštar (CRO)	18.08.1989	7	(1)	
Jordi César López Delgado (ESP)	27.03.1992	4	(1)	
Benjamin Lambot (BEL)	02.05.1987	23		2
Timotheus Pavlou	08.09.1994		(1)	
José Ignacio San Román Canciani (ARG)	17.08.1988	17		
Savvas Tsabouris (GRE)	16.07.1986	9	(1)	

Midfielders:	DOB	M	(s)	G
Charles Betrand Etoundi Eloundou (CMR)	04.12.1994	20	(2)	2
Ioannis Kosti	17.03.2000	17	(4)	1
Saša Marjanović (SRB)	13.11.1987	15	(6)	1
Farshad Noor (AFG)	02.10.1994	14	(3)	1
Alasdair David Reynolds (SCO)	02.09.1996	7	(5)	
Ryan Telfer (TRI)	04.03.1994	1	(2)	
Tonia Tisdell (LBR)	20.03.1992	8	(7)	1
Forwards:	DOB	M	(s)	G
Maurício Plenckauskas Cordeiro (BRA)	31.12.1992	1	(9)	
Kingsley Onuegbu (NGA)	05.03.1986	22	(1)	14
Theodosis Siathas	16.12.1998	3	(14)	2
Jay Simpson (ENG)	01.12.1988	12	(8)	2

Olympiakos Nicosia Football Club

Founded: 1931
Stadium: Stádio Makario, Nicosia (16,000=
Trainer: Pampos Christodoulou   17.10.1967

Goalkeepers:	DOB	M	(s)	G
Pavol Bajza (SVK)	04.09.1991	12		
Mario Kirev (BUL)	15.08.1989	4		
Markos Vellidis (GRE)	04.04.1987	7		
Defenders:	DOB	M	(s)	G
Francisco Manuel Geraldo Rosa „Kiko" (POR)	20.01.1993	21		2
Erwin Koffi (FRA)	10.01.1995	5	(3)	1
Stephanos Mouktaris	10.07.1994		(1)	
Nanísio Justino Mendes Soares (GNB)	17.09.1991	11	(5)	
Paris Psaltis	12.11.1996	21	(1)	1
Mamadu Samba Candé „Sambinha" (POR)	23.09.1992	20		
Ousmane Sidibé (GUI)	23.04.1985	7	(1)	
Midfielders:	DOB	M	(s)	G
Rafael Eduardo Acosta Cammarota (VEN)	13.02.1989	15	(2)	1

	DOB	M	(s)	G
Eyong Tarkang Enoh (CMR)	23.03.1986	6	(2)	
Bilal Hamdi (ALG)	01.05.1991	13	(1)	
Evangelos Kyriakou	03.02.1994	5	(1)	
Giorgos Oikonomides	10.04.1990	17	(4)	1
Andreas Pachipis	16.12.1994	1	(2)	
Konstantinos Sotiriou	21.06.1996	9	(4)	1
Vinicius Oliveira Franco (BRA)	16.05.1986	16	(3)	
Forwards:	DOB	M	(s)	G
Jonathan Serge Folly Ayité (TOG)	22.07.1985	15	(6)	5
Dylan Duventru (MTQ)	03.01.1989	15	(5)	4
Fabrice Kah Nkwoh (CMR)	09.03.1996	8	(12)	3
Rogério Miguel Reis Silva (POR)	05.04.1997	4	(5)	
Tiago Lima Leal „Tiago Azulão" (BRA)	26.03.1988	8	(4)	
Pangiotis Zachariou	26.02.1996	13	(5)	6

Athlitikos Sillogos Omonia Lefkosias
(Athletic Club Omonia Nicosia)

Founded: 04.06.1948
Stadium: Stádio GSP, Nicosia (22,859)
Trainer: Henning Stille Berg (NOR)   01.09.1969

Goalkeepers:	DOB	M	(s)	G
Fabiano Ribeiro de Freitas (BRA)	29.02.1988	11		
Charalambos Kyriakides	30.11.1998	1		
Costel Fane Pantilimon (ROU)	01.02.1987	6		
Francis Odinaka Uzoho (NGA)	28.10.1998	5		
Defenders:	DOB	M	(s)	G
Tomáš Hubočan (SVK)	17.09.1985	6	(5)	
Joel Vieira Pereira (POR)	28.09.1996	1		
Ioannis Kousoulos	14.06.1996	6	(4)	1
Ádám Lang (HUN)	17.01.1993	22		
Jan Lecjaks (CZE)	09.08.1990	23		
Michael Lüftner (CZE)	14.03.1994	22		
Midfielders:	DOB	M	(s)	G
David Babajide Akintola (NGA)	13.01.1996	4	(2)	
Charalampos Charalampous	04.04.2002		(1)	

	DOB	M	(s)	G
Dimitris Christofi	28.09.1988	2	(4)	1
Jordi Gómez García-Penche (ESP)	24.05.1985	20		3
Fanos Katelaris	26.08.1996	3		
Charis Mavrias (GRE)	21.02.1994	21		1
Michael Javier Ortega Dieppa (COL)	06.04.1991	12	(2)	2
Thiago Ferreira Dos Santos (BRA)	12.07.1987	23		4
Marinos Tzionis	16.07.2001		(5)	
Vítor Hugo Gomes da Silva (POR)	25.12.1987	17	(2)	1
Forwards:	DOB	M	(s)	G
Éric Bauthéac (FRA)	24.08.1987	17	(1)	4
Matt Derbyshire (ENG)	14.04.1986	21	(1)	13
Hen Ezra (ISR)	19.01.1989	6	(2)	
Nicolás Ladislao Fedor Flores (VEN)	19.08.1985	2	(7)	
Andronikos Kakouli	03.05.2001	2	(12)	2
Loizos Loizou	18.07.2003		(1)	1

Pafos Football Club Paphos

Founded: 10.06.2014 (after the merger of AEK Kouklia and AEP Paphos)
Stadium: Stádio „Stelios Kyriakides", Paphos (9,394)
Trainer: Željko Kopić (CRO)   10.09.1977
[06.11.2019] Jeremy Steele (ENG)
[13.12.2019] Jon Cameron Toshack (WAL)   07.03.1970

Goalkeepers:	DOB	M	(s)	G
Evgenios Petrou	06.09.1997	2	(1)	
Artur Rudko (UKR)	07.05.1992	21		
Defenders:	DOB	M	(s)	G
Kyriakos Antoniou	03.05.2001	10	(2)	1
Paulus Arajuuri (FIN)	15.06.1988	17		2
Kevin Lafrance (HAI)	13.01.1990	15	(1)	1
Pavel Lelyukhin (RUS)	23.04.1998	4	(6)	
Andreas Panayiotou	31.05.1995	13	(4)	1
Mickaël Panos (FRA)	10.02.1997	18	(2)	
Matija Širok (SVN)	31.05.1991	20		
Georgios Valerianos (GRE)	13.02.1992	13		
Midfielders:	DOB	M	(s)	G
Brayan Angulo Mosquera (COL)	19.07.1993	1	(1)	
Nahir Besara (SWE)	25.02.1991	20	(2)	1
Zdeněk Folprecht (CZE)	01.07.1991	7	(1)	
Gerasimos Fylaktou	24.07.1991	2		

	DOB	M	(s)	G
Cy Goddard (JPN)	02.04.1997	2	(4)	
Abdisalam Ibrahim (NOR)	01.05.1991	2		
Luis Marcelo Morais dos Reis „Lulinha"(BRA)	10.04.1990	1	(6)	1
Jason Puncheon (ENG)	26.06.1986	15	(1)	
Bakary Sako (MLI)	26.04.1988	6		1
Stephen Obayan Sunday (NGA)	17.09.1988	2	(3)	
Onni Valakari (FIN)	18.08.1999	6		5
Daniel Williams (USA)	08.03.1989	9	(2)	
Forwards:	DOB	M	(s)	G
Kévin Bérigaud (FRA)	09.05.1988	6	(1)	2
Jerson Cabral (CPV)	03.01.1991	8	(3)	3
Alexandros Konstantinou	11.04.1992		(7)	
Adam Nemec (SVK)	02.09.1985	12	(2)	1
Deniss Rakels (LVA)	20.08.1992	4	(4)	1
Federico Iván Rasic (ARG)	24.03.1992	2	(2)	1
Marcelo Luis Torres (ARG)	06.11.1997	2	(3)	2
Vladimiro Etson António Félix „Vá" (ANG)	24.04.1998	13	(3)	2

SECOND LEVEL
Cypriot Second Division 2019/2020

First Phase

Group A

1.	Aris Limassol FC	14	9	3	2	24 - 10	30
2.	Karmiotissa Pano Polemidia FC	14	10	0	4	25 - 16	30
3.	Athlitikos Omilos Ayia Napa FC	14	8	3	3	20 - 12	27
4.	ASIL Lysi	14	8	3	3	24 - 14	27
5.	Alki Oroklini FC	14	4	3	7	19 - 14	15
6.	Omonia Aradippou FC	14	3	4	7	9 - 14	13
7.	EN Ypsona-Digenis Ipsona	14	3	3	8	9 - 21	12
8.	Omonia Psevda FD	14	2	1	11	12 - 41	7

Group B

1.	Ermis Aradippou FC	14	12	2	0	31 - 8	38
2.	Onisilos Sotira 2014	14	7	5	2	24 - 14	26
3.	AC Othellos Athienou	14	6	2	6	21 - 17	20
4.	Anagennisi Deryneia FC	14	4	3	7	12 - 13	15
5.	Digenis Akritas Morphou FC	14	5	3	6	18 - 20	15
6.	Akritas Chlorakas FC	14	3	6	5	19 - 26	15
7.	Podosfairikos Omilos Xylotymbou 2006	14	3	4	7	14 - 22	13
8.	Athletic Union of Zakaki	14	2	3	9	11 - 30	9

Top-4 of each were qualified for the Second Phase Premier Group, while teams ranked 5-8 were qualified for the Second Phase Standard Group.

Please note: teams lost half their points (rounded downwards) from first stage. League was abandoned after 20 Rounds.

	Premier Group								
1.	Karmiotissa Pano Polemidia FC (*Promoted*)	20	15	0	5	40	-	23	30
2.	Ermis Aradippou FC (*Promoted*)	20	15	3	2	40	-	16	29
3.	Aris Limassol FC	20	13	2	5	31	-	14	27
4.	Athlitikos Omilos Ayia Napa FC	20	11	5	4	24	-	14	25
5.	Onisilos Sotira 2014	20	9	6	5	30	-	22	20
6.	ASIL Lysi	20	9	5	6	27	-	19	19
7.	AC Othellos Athienou	20	7	3	10	28	-	30	14
8.	Anagennisi Deryneia FC	20	5	3	12	20	-	25	11

	Standard Group								
1.	Alki Oroklini FC	20	8	3	9	31	-	19	20
2.	Podosfairikos Omilos Xylotymbou 2006	20	6	6	8	22	-	28	18
3.	Omonia Aradippou FC	20	6	6	8	18	-	20	18
4.	Digenis Akritas Morphou FC	20	8	3	9	24	-	27	17
5.	Athletic Union of Zakaki (*Relegated*)	20	5	6	9	16	-	31	17
6.	Akritas Chlorakas FC (*Relegated*)	20	5	7	8	25	-	33	15
7.	EN Ypsona-Digenis Ipsona (*Relegated*)	20	4	5	11	14	-	32	11
8.	Omonia Psevda FD (*Relegated*)	20	2	1	17	18	-	55	4

NATIONAL TEAM

INTERNATIONAL MATCHES
(16.07.2019 – 15.07.2020)

06.09.2019	Nicosia	Cyprus - Kazakhstan	1-1(1-1)	(ECQ)
09.09.2019	Serravalle	San Marino - Cyprus	0-4(0-2)	(ECQ)
10.10.2019	Nur-Sultan	Kazakhstan - Cyprus	1-2(1-0)	(ECQ)
13.10.2019	Nicosia	Cyprus - Russia	0-5(0-2)	(ECQ)
16.11.2019	Nicosia	Cyprus - Scotland	1-2(0-1)	(ECQ)
19.11.2019	Brussels	Belgium - Cyprus	6-1(4-1)	(ECQ)

06.09.2019   CYPRUS - KAZAKHSTAN   1-1(1-1)   16th EC. Qualifiers
Stádio GSP, Nicosia; Referee: Mattias Gestranius (Finland); Attendance: 5,639
CYP: Constantinos Panayi, Giorgos Merkis (Cap), Konstantinos Mintikkis, Konstantinos Laifis, Charalambos Kyriakou, Nicholas Ioannou, Ioannis Kousoulos, Georgios Efrem (73.Ioannis Kosti), Grigoris Kastanos (58.Anthony Georgiou), Fotios Papoulis (90.Ioannis Pittas), Pieros Sotiriou. Trainer: Ran Ben Shimon (Israel).
Goal: Pieros Sotiriou (39).

09.09.2019   SAN MARINO - CYPRUS   0-4(0-2)   16th EC. Qualifiers
San Marino Stadium, Serravalle; Referee: Iwan Arwel Griffith (Wales); Attendance: 662
CYP: Constantinos Panayi, Konstantinos Laifis, Charalambos Kyriakou, Nicholas Ioannou, Ioannis Kousoulos, Ioannis Pittas (74.Grigoris Kastanos), Ioannis Kosti, Kostakis Artymatas, Fotios Papoulis (46.Anthony Georgiou), Matija Špoljarić (62.Mihalis Ioannou), Pieros Sotiriou (Cap). Trainer: Ran Ben Shimon (Israel).
Goals: Ioannis Kousoulos (2), Fotios Papoulis (38), Ioannis Kousoulos (73), Kostakis Artymatas (75).

10.10.2019   KAZAKHSTAN - CYPRUS   1-2(1-0)   16th EC. Qualifiers
Astana Arena, Nur-Sultan; Referee: Craig Pawson (England); Attendance: 11,769
CYP: Constantinos Panayi, Giorgos Merkis (Cap) (62.Matija Špoljarić), Konstantinos Mintikkis (46.Panayiotis Zachariou), Konstantinos Laifis, Charalambos Kyriakou, Nicholas Ioannou, Ioannis Kousoulos, Ioannis Kosti, Kostakis Artymatas, Fotios Papoulis (88.Renato João Inácio Margaça), Pieros Sotiriou. Trainer: Ran Ben Shimon (Israel).
Goals: Pieros Sotiriou (73), Nicholas Ioannou (84).

13.10.2019   CYPRUS - RUSSIA   0-5(0-2)   16th EC. Qualifiers
Stádio GSP, Nicosia; Referee: Srđan Jovanović (Serbia); Attendance: 9,439
CYP: Constantinos Panayi (40.Urko Rafael Pardo Goas), Giorgos Merkis (Cap), Konstantinos Laifis [*sent off 27*], Charalambos Kyriakou, Nicholas Ioannou, Ioannis Kousoulos, Ioannis Kosti, Kostakis Artymatas, Panayiotis Zachariou (36.Renato João Inácio Margaça), Mihalis Ioannou, Matija Špoljarić (79.Fotios Papoulis). Trainer: Ran Ben Shimon (Israel).

16.11.2019   CYPRUS - SCOTLAND   1-2(0-1)   16th EC. Qualifiers
Stádio GSP, Nicosia; Referee: Harald Lechner (Austria); Attendance: 7,595
CYP: Urko Rafael Pardo Goas, Giorgos Merkis (Cap), Charalambos Kyriakou (77.Dimitris Theodorou), Andreas Karo (42.Grigoris Kastanos), Nicholas Ioannou, Ioannis Kousoulos, Ioannis Kosti, Georgios Efrem (74.Matija Špoljarić), Jason Dimitriou, Fotios Papoulis, Pieros Sotiriou. Trainer: Ran Ben Shimon (Israel).
Goal: Georgios Efrem (47).

19.11.2019   BELGIUM - CYPRUS   6-1(4-1)   16th EC. Qualifiers
Stade "Roi Baudouin", Bruxelles; Referee: Jørgen Burchardt (Denmark); Attendance: 40,568
CYP: Neofytos Michael, Giorgos Merkis (Cap), Charalambos Kyriakou, Hristos Wheeler, Nicholas Ioannou (67.Ioannis Kousoulos), Kypros Hristoforou, Ioannis Kosti (81.Fotios Papoulis), Kostakis Artymatas, Grigoris Kastanos, Matija Špoljarić (79.Georgios Efrem), Pieros Sotiriou. Trainer: Ran Ben Shimon (Israel).
Goal: Nicholas Ioannou (14).

NATIONAL TEAM PLAYERS
(16.07.2019 – 15.07.2020)

Name	DOB	Caps	Goals	2019/2020:	Club
Goalkeepers					
Neofytos MICHAEL	16.12.1993	1	0	2019:	*AGS Asteras Tripolis (GRE)*
Constantinos PANAYI	08.10.1994	22	0	2019:	*AC Omonia Nicosia*
Urko Rafael PARDO Goas	28.01.1983	9	0	2019:	*Alki Oroklini FC*
Defenders					
Jason DEMETRIOU	18.11.1987	51	1	2019:	*Southend United FC (ENG)*
Kypros HRISTOFOROU	23.04.1993	2	0	2019:	*Nea Salamis Famagusta FC*
Nicholas IOANNOU	10.11.1995	19	2	2019:	*APOEL FC Nicosia*
Andreas KARO	09.09.1996	1	0	2019:	*US Salernitana 1919 (ITA)*
Ioannis KOUSOULOS	14.06.1996	18	4	2019:	*AC Omonia Nicosia*
Konstantinos LAIFIS	19.04.1993	34	3	2019:	*R Standard Liège (BEL)*
Giorgos MERKIS	30.07.1984	54	1	2019:	*APOEL FC Nicosia*
Hristos WHEELER	29.06.1997	1	0	2019:	*AEL Limassol*
Midfielders					
Kostakis ARTYMATAS	15.04.1993	38	1	2019:	*Anorthosis Famagusta FC*
Georgios EFREM	05.07.1989	48	5	2019:	*APOEL FC Nicosia*
Anthony GEORGIOU	24.02.1997	8	0	2019:	*Ipswich Town FC (ENG)*
Grigoris KASTANOS	30.01.1998	23	1	2019:	*Delfino Pescara 1936 (ITA)*
Ioannis KOSTI	17.03.2000	8	0	2019:	*Nea Salamis Famagusta FC*
Charalambos KYRIAKOU	09.02.1995	26	0	2019:	*Apollon Limassol FC*
Renato João Inácio MARGAÇA	17.07.1985	21	0	2019:	*Anorthosis Famagusta FC*
Fotios PAPOULIS	22.01.1985	12	2	2019:	*Apollon Limassol FC*
Ioannis PITTAS	10.07.1996	4	0	2019:	*Apollon Limassol FC*
Matija ŠPOLJARIĆ	02.04.1997	9	0	2019:	*AEK Larnaca FC*
Dimitris THEODOROU	10.09.1997	1	0	2019:	*Enosis Neon Paralimni FC*
Forwards					
Pieros SOTIRIOU	13.01.1993	40	10	2019:	*FC København (DEN)*
Panayiotis ZACHARIOU	26.02.1996	4	1	2019:	*Olympiakos Nicosia FC*
National team coach					
Ran BEN SHIMON (Israel) [05.07.2017 – 30.11.2019]	28.11.1970	24 M; 3 W; 3 D; 12 L; 17-30			
Johan WALEM (Belgium) [from 25.01.2020]	01.02.1972	-			

CZECH REPUBLIC

The Country:
Česká republika (Czech Republic)
Capital: Praha
Surface: 78,866 km^2
Inhabitants: 10,693,939 [2020]
Time: UTC+1

The FA:
Fotbalová asociace České republiky
Atletická 2474/8 169 00, Praha
Tel: +420 233 029 111
Foundation date: 1901 (as Bohemia)
Member of FIFA since: 1907 (as Bohemia)
Member of UEFA since: 1954 (as Czechoslovakia)
Website: www.fotbal.cz

NATIONAL TEAM RECORDS

RECORDS

First international match:	28.08.1920, Antwerpen: Czechoslovakia - Yugoslavia 7-0
Most international caps:	Petr Čech - 124 caps (2002-2016)
Most international goals:	Jan Koller - 55 goals / 91 caps (1999-2009)

UEFA EUROPEAN CHAMPIONSHIP

1960	Final Tournament (3rd Place)
1964	Qualifiers
1968	Qualifiers
1972	Qualifiers
1976	**Final Tournament (Winners)**
1980	Final Tournament (3rd Place)
1984	Qualifiers
1988	Qualifiers
1992	Qualifiers
1996	Final Tournament (Runners-up)
2000	Final Tournament (Group Stage)
2004	Final Tournament (Semi-Finals)
2008	Final Tournament (Group Stage)
2012	Final Tournament (Quarter-Finals)
2016	Final Tournament (Qualified)
2020	*Final Tournament (Qualified)*

FIFA WORLD CUP

1930	Did not enter
1934	Final Tournament (Runners-up)
1938	Final Tournament (Quarter-Finals)
1950	Did not enter
1954	Final Tournament (Group Stage)
1958	Final Tournament (Group Stage)
1962	Final Tournament (Runners-up)
1966	Qualifiers
1970	Final Tournament (Group Stage)
1974	Qualifiers
1978	Qualifiers
1982	Final Tournament (Group Stage)
1986	Qualifiers
1990	Final Tournament (Quarter-Finals)
1994	Qualifiers
1998	Qualifiers
2002	Qualifiers
2006	Final Tournament (Group Stage)
2010	Qualifiers
2014	Qualifiers
2018	Qualifiers

OLYMPIC TOURNAMENTS

1908	-
1912	-
1920	Runners-up
1924	1/8 Finals
1928	Did not enter
1936	Did not enter
1948	Did not enter
1952	Did not enter
1956	Did not enter
1960	Qualifiers
1964	Runners-up
1968	Group Stage
1972	Did not enter
1976	Qualifiers
1980	**Winners**
1984	Did not enter
1988	Qualifiers
1992	Qualifiers
1996	Qualifiers
2000	Group Stage
2004	Qualifiers
2008	Qualifiers
2012	Qualifiers
2016	Qualifiers

UEFA NATIONS LEAGUE

2018/2019 – League B

FIFA CONFEDERATIONS CUP 1992-2017

1997 (3rd Place)

CZECH CLUB HONOURS IN EUROPEAN CLUB COMPETITIONS:

European Champion Clubs' Cup (1956-1992) / UEFA Champions League (1993-2020)
None

Fairs Cup (1858-1971) / UEFA Cup (1972-2009) / UEFA Europa League (2010-2020)
None

UEFA Super Cup (1972-2019)
None

European Cup Winners' Cup 1961-1999*
None

*defunct competition

NATIONAL COMPETITIONS
TABLE OF HONOURS

CZECHOSLOVAKIA 1925-1938 / BOHEMIA-MORAVIA 1938-1944 / CZECHOSLOVAKIA 1945-1993

	CHAMPIONS	CUP WINNERS	BEST GOALSCORERS	
1925	SK Slavia Praha	-	Jan Vaník (SK Slavia Praha)	13
1925/1926	AC Sparta Praha	-	Jan Dvořáček (AC Sparta Praha)	32
1927	AC Sparta Praha	-	Antonín Puč (SK Slavia Praha) Josef Šíma (AC Sparta Praha)	13
1927/1928	SK Viktoria Žižkov	-	Karel Meduna (SK Viktoria Žižkov)	12
1928/1929	SK Slavia Praha	-	Antonín Puč (SK Slavia Praha)	13
1929/1930	SK Slavia Praha	-	František Kloz (SK Kladno)	15
1930/1931	SK Slavia Praha	-	Josef Silný (AC Sparta Praha)	18
1931/1932	AC Sparta Praha	-	Raymond Braine (AC Sparta Praha)	16
1932/1933	SK Slavia Praha	-	Gejza Kocsis (Teplitzer FK / Bohemians AFK Vršovice)	23
1933/1934	SK Slavia Praha	-	Raymond Braine (AC Sparta Praha) Jiří Sobotka (SK Slavia Praha)	18
1934/1935	SK Slavia Praha	-	František Svoboda (SK Slavia Praha)	27
1935/1936	AC Sparta Praha	-	Vojtěch Bradáč (SK Slavia Praha)	42
1936/1937	SK Slavia Praha	-	František Kloz (SK Kladno)	28
1937/1938	AC Sparta Praha	-	Josef Bican (SK Slavia Praha)	22
1938/1939	AC Sparta Praha	-	Josef Bican (SK Slavia Praha)	29
1939/1940	SK Slavia Praha	-	Josef Bican (SK Slavia Praha)	50
1940/1941	SK Slavia Praha	-	Josef Bican (SK Slavia Praha)	38
1941/1942	SK Slavia Praha	-	Josef Bican (SK Slavia Praha)	45
1942/1943	SK Slavia Praha	-	Josef Bican (SK Slavia Praha)	39
1943/1944	AC Sparta Praha	-	Josef Bican (SK Slavia Praha)	57
1944/1945	*No competition*	-	-	
1945/1946	AC Sparta Praha	-	Josef Bican (SK Slavia Praha)	31
1946/1947	SK Slavia Praha	-	Josef Bican (SK Slavia Praha)	43
1947/1948	AC Sparta Praha	-	Jaroslav Cejp (AC Sparta Praha)	21
1948	*Championship abandoned*	-	Josef Bican (Sokol Slavia Praha)	21
1949	ŠK NV Bratislava	-	Ladislav Hlaváček (ZSJ Dynamo Slavia Praha)	28
1950	ŠK NV Bratislava	-	Josef Bican (Sokol Vítkovice Železárny)	22
1951	ŠK NV Bratislava	-	Alois Jaroš (ZSJ Vodotechna Teplice)	16
1952	Sparta ČKD Sokolovo	-	Miroslav Wiecek (OKD Ostrava)	20
1953	ÚDA Praha	-	Josef Majer (DSO Baník Kladno)	13
1954	TJ Spartak Praha Sokolovo	-	Jiří Pešek (TJ Spartak Praha Sokolovo)	13
1955	ŠK Slovan Bratislava	-	Emil Pažický (ÚNV Slovan Bratislava / Jiskra Slovena Žilina)	9
1956	AS Dukla Praha	-	Milan Dvořák (AS Dukla Praha) Miroslav Wiecek (DSO Baník Ostrava)	15
1957/1958	AS Dukla Praha	-	Miroslav Wiecek (DSO Baník Ostrava)	25
1958/1959	ČH Bratislava	-	Miroslav Wiecek (DSO Baník Ostrava)	20
1959/1960	DSO Spartak Hradec Králové	-	Michal Pucher (TJ Slovan Nitra)	18
1960/1961	AS Dukla Praha	AS Dukla Praha	Rudolf Kučera (AS Dukla Praha) Ladislav Pavlovič (TJ Tatran Prešov)	17
1961/1962	AS Dukla Praha	Slovan CHZJD Bratislava	Adolf Scherer (TJ Červená Hviezda Bratislava)	24
1962/1963	AS Dukla Praha	Slovan CHZJD Bratislava	Karel Petroš (TJ Tatran Prešov)	19
1963/1964	AS Dukla Praha	Spartak Praha Sokolovo	Ladislav Pavlovič (TJ Tatran Prešov)	21
1964/1965	TJ Spartak Praha Sokolovo	AS Dukla Praha	Pavol Bencz (Jednota Trenčín)	21
1965/1966	AS Dukla Praha	AS Dukla Praha	Ladislav Michalík (TJ Baník Ostrava)	15
1966/1967	TJ Sparta ČKD Praha	Spartak Trnava	Jozef Adamec (Spartak Trnava)	21
1967/1968	Spartak TAZ Trnava	Slovan CHZJD Bratislava	Jozef Adamec (Spartak TAZ Trnava)	18
1968/1969	Spartak TAZ Trnava	AS Dukla Praha	Ladislav Petráš (AS Dukla Banská Bystrica)	20
1969/1970	Slovan CHZJD Bratislava	TJ Gottwaldov	Jozef Adamec (Spartak TAZ Trnava)	18
1970/1971	Spartak TAZ Trnava	Spartak TAZ Trnava	Jozef Adamec (Spartak TAZ Trnava) Zdeněk Nehoda (TJ Gottwaldov)	16
1971/1972	Spartak TAZ Trnava	TJ Sparta ČKD Praha	Ján Čapkovič (Slovan CHZJD Bratislava)	19
1972/1973	Spartak TAZ Trnava	TJ Baník Ostrava OKD	Ladislav Józsa (TJ Lokomotíva Košice)	21
1973/1974	Slovan CHZJD Bratislava	Slovan CHZJD Bratislava	Ladislav Józsa (TJ Lokomotíva Košice) Přemysl Bičovský (TJ Sklo Union Teplice)	17
1974/1975	Slovan CHZJD Bratislava	Spartak TAZ Trnava	Ladislav Petráš (TJ Internacionál Slovnaft Bratislava)	20
1975/1976	TJ Baník Ostrava OKD	TJ Sparta ČKD Praha	Dušan Galis (TJ VSS Košice)	21
1976/1977	ASVS Dukla Praha	TJ Lokomotíva Košice	Ladislav Józsa (TJ Lokomotíva Košice)	18
1977/1978	Zbrojovka Brno	TJ Baník Ostrava OKD	Karel Kroupa (Zbrojovka Brno)	20
1978/1979	ASVS Dukla Praha	TJ Lokomotíva Košice	Karel Kroupa (Zbrojovka Brno) Zdeněk Nehoda (ASVS Dukla Praha)	17
1979/1980	TJ Baník Ostrava OKD	TJ Sparta ČKD Praha	Werner Lička (TJ Baník Ostrava OKD)	18
1980/1981	TJ Baník Ostrava OKD	ASVS Dukla Praha	Marián Masný (Slovan CHZJD Bratislava)	16
1981/1982	ASVS Dukla Praha	Slovan CHZJD Bratislava	Peter Herda (SK Slavia IPS Praha) Ladislav Vízek (ASVS Dukla Praha)	15
1982/1983	Bohemians ČKD Praha	ASVS Dukla Praha	Pavel Chaloupka (Bohemians ČKD Praha)	17
1983/1984	TJ Sparta ČKD Praha	AC Sparta Praha	Werner Lička (TJ Baník Ostrava OKD)	20

1984/1985	TJ Sparta ČKD Praha	ASVS Dukla Praha	Ivo Knoflíček (SK Slavia IPS Praha)	21
1985/1986	TJ Vítkovice	Spartak TAZ Trnava	Stanislav Griga (TJ Sparta ČKD Praha)	19
1986/1987	TJ Sparta ČKD Praha	DAC Dunajská Streda	Václav Daněk (TJ Baník Ostrava OKD)	24
1987/1988	TJ Sparta ČKD Praha	TJ Sparta ČKD Praha	Milan Luhový (ASVS Dukla Praha)	24
1988/1989	TJ Sparta ČKD Praha	TJ Sparta ČKD Praha	Milan Luhový (ASVS Dukla Praha)	25
1989/1990	TJ Sparta ČKD Praha	ASVS Dukla Praha	Ľubomír Luhový (TJ Internacionál Slovnaft ZŤS Bratislava)	20
1990/1991	TJ Sparta Praha	FC Baník Ostrava	Roman Kukleta (TJ Sparta Praha)	17
1991/1992	ŠK Slovan Bratislava	AC Sparta Praha	Peter Dubovský (ŠK Slovan Bratislava)	27
1992/1993	AC Sparta Praha	1. FC Košice	Peter Dubovský (ŠK Slovan Bratislava)	24

CZECH REPUBLIC (Since 1993)

1993/1994	AC Sparta Praha	FK Viktoria Žižkov	Horst Siegl (AC Sparta Praha)	20
1994/1995	AC Sparta Praha	SK Hradec Králové	Radek Drulák (FK Drnovice)	15
1995/1996	SK Slavia Praha	AC Sparta Praha	Radek Drulák (FK Drnovice)	22
1996/1997	AC Sparta Praha	SK Slavia Praha	Horst Siegl (AC Sparta Praha)	19
1997/1998	AC Sparta Praha	FK Jablonec 97	Horst Siegl (AC Sparta Praha)	13
1998/1999	AC Sparta Praha	SK Slavia Praha	Horst Siegl (AC Sparta Praha)	18
1999/2000	AC Sparta Praha	FC Slovan Liberec	Vratislav Lokvenc (AC Sparta Praha)	22
2000/2001	AC Sparta Praha	FK Viktoria Žižkov	Vítězslav Tuma (FK Drnovice)	15
2001/2002	FC Slovan Liberec	SK Slavia Praha	Jiří Štajner (FC Slovan Liberec)	15
2002/2003	AC Sparta Praha	FK Teplice	Jiří Kowalík (1. FC Synot Uherské Hradiště)	16
2003/2004	FC Baník Ostrava	AC Sparta Praha	Marek Heinz (FC Baník Ostrava)	19
2004/2005	AC Sparta Praha	FC Baník Ostrava	Tomáš Jun (AC Sparta Praha)	14
2005/2006	FC Slovan Liberec	AC Sparta Praha	Milan Ivana (FC Slovácko Uherské Hradiště)	11
2006/2007	AC Sparta Praha	AC Sparta Praha	Luboš Pecka (FK Mladá Boleslav)	16
2007/2008	SK Slavia Praha	AC Sparta Praha	Václav Svěrkoš (FC Baník Ostrava)	15
2008/2009	SK Slavia Praha	FK Teplice	Andrej Kerić (FC Slovan Liberec)	15
2009/2010	AC Sparta Praha	FC Viktoria Plzeň	Michal Ordoš (Sigma Olomouc)	12
2010/2011	FC Viktoria Plzeň	FK Mladá Boleslav	David Lafata (FK Baumit Jablonec)	19
2011/2012	FC Slovan Liberec	SK Sigma Olomouc	David Lafata (FK Baumit Jablonec)	25
2012/2013	FC Viktoria Plzeň	FK Baumit Jablonec	David Lafata (FK Baumit Jablonec / AC Sparta Praha)	20
2013/2014	AC Sparta Praha	AC Sparta Praha	Josef Hušbauer (AC Sparta Praha)	18
2014/2015	FC Viktoria Plzeň	FC Slovan Liberec	David Lafata (AC Sparta Praha)	20
2015/2016	FC Viktoria Plzeň	FK Mladá Boleslav	David Lafata (AC Sparta Praha)	20
2016/2017	SK Slavia Praha	FC Fastav Zlín	Milan Škoda (SK Slavia Praha) David Lafata (AC Sparta Praha)	15
2017/2018	FC Viktoria Plzeň	SK Slavia Praha	Michael Krmenčík (FC Viktoria Plzeň)	16
2018/2019	SK Slavia Praha	SK Slavia Praha	Nikolay Komlichenko (RUS, FK Mladá Boleslav)	29
2019/2020	SK Slavia Praha	AC Sparta Praha	Petar Musa (CRO, FC Slovan Liberec / SK Slavia Praha) Libor Kozák (AC Sparta Praha)	14

Name changements for most important Czech clubs:

AC Sparta Praha:
1893 - Athletic Club Královské Vinohrady; 1894 - Athletic Club Sparta Praha; 1948 - Athletic Club Sparta Bubeneč; 1949 - Sokol Bratrství Sparta Praha; 1951 - Sparta ČKD Sokolovo Praha; 1953 - TJ Spartak Praha Sokolovo; 1965 - TJ Sparta ČKD Praha; 1990 - TJ Sparta Praha; 1991 - AC Sparta Praha; 1993 - AC Sparta Praha fotbal, a.s.

SK Slavia Praha:
1892 - SK ACOS Praha (Sportovní klub Akademický cyklistický odbor Slavia Praha); 1893 - SK Slavia Praha (Sportovní klub Slavia Praha); 1948 - Sokol Slavia Praha; 1949 - ZSJ Dynamo Slavia Praha (Základní sportovní jednota Dynamo Slavia Praha); 1953 - DSO Dynamo Praha (Dobrovolná sportovní organizace Dynamo Praha); 1954 - TJ Dynamo Praha (Tělovýchovná jednota Dynamo Praha); 1965 - SK Slavia Praha (Sportovní klub Slavia Praha); 1973 - TJ Slavia Praha (Tělovýchovná jednota Slavia Praha); 1977 - TJ Slavia IPS Praha (Tělovýchovná jednota Slavia Inženýrské průmyslové stavby Praha); 1978 - SK Slavia IPS Praha (Sportovní klub Slavia Inženýrské průmyslové stavby Praha); 1991 - SK Slavia Praha (Sportovní klub Slavia Praha - fotbal, a.s.)

FK Viktoria Žižkov:
1903 - Sportovní kroužek Viktoria Žižkov; 1904 - SK Viktoria Žižkov; 1950 - Sokol Viktoria Žižkov; 1951 - Sokol ČSAD Žižkov; 1952 - TJ Slavoj Žižkov (after merger with Avia Čakovice); 1965 - TJ Viktoria Žižkov; 1973 - TJ Viktoria Žižkov Strojimport; 1982 - TJ Viktoria Žižkov PSO; 1992 - FK Viktoria Žižkov.

MFK Vítkovice:
1919 - SK Slavoj Vítkovice; 1922 - SK Vítkovice; 1923 - SSK Vítkovice; 1937 - SK Železárny Vítkovice; 1939 - ČSK Vítkovice; 1945 - SK Vítkovice Železárny; 1948 - Sokol Vítkovice Železárny; 1953 - Baník Vítkovice; 1957 - TJ VŽKG Ostrava; 1979 - TJ Vítkovice; 1993 - FC Vítkovice Kovkor; 1994 - FC Karviná-Vítkovice (after merger with Kovona Karviná); 1995 - FC Vítkovice (after spliting); 2012 - MFK Vítkovice.

FK Teplice:
1945 - SK Teplice-Šanov (Sportovní klub Teplice-Šanov); 1948 - Sokol Teplice; 1949 - ZSJ Technomat Teplice (Základní sportovní jednota Technomat Teplice); 1951 - ZSJ Vodotechna Teplice; 1952 - ZSJ Ingstav Teplice; 1953 - DSO Tatran Teplice (Dobrovolná sportovní organizace Tatran Teplice); 1960 - TJ Slovan Teplice (Tělovýchovná jednota Slovan Teplice); 1966 - TJ Sklo Union Teplice; 1991 - TFK VTJ Teplice (Tělovýchovný fotbalový klub Vojenská tělovýchovná jednota Teplice); 1993 - FK Frydrych Teplice (Fotbalový klub Frydrych Teplice); 1994 - FK Teplice (Fotbalový klub Teplice, a.s.).

FK Dukla Praha:
1948 - ATK Praha (Armádní tělovýchovný klub Praha); 1953 - ÚDA Praha (Ústřední dům armády Praha); 1956 - AS Dukla Praha (Armádní středisko Dukla Praha); 1976 - ASVS Dukla Praha (Armádní středisko vrcholového sportu Dukla Praha); 1991 - FC Dukla Praha (Football Club Dukla Praha); 1994 - FK Dukla Praha (Fotbalový klub Dukla Praha); 1996 - FK Marila Příbram (after merger between FC Příbram and FC Dukla Praha); 1998 - FK Dukla Praha, o.s. (Fotbalový klub Dukla Praha, občanské sdružení); 2007 - FK Dukla Praha, a.s. (Fotbalový klub Dukla Praha, akciová společnost).

FC Baník Ostrava:
1922 - SK Slezská Ostrava (Sportovní klub Slezská Ostrava); 1945 - SK Ostrava; 1948 - Sokol Trojice Ostrava; 1951 - Sokol OKD Ostrava (Sokol Ostravsko-karvinské doly Ostrava); 1952 - DSO Baník Ostrava (Dobrovolná sportovní organizace Baník Ostrava); 1961 - TJ Baník Ostrava (Tělovýchovná jednota Baník Ostrava); 1970 - TJ Baník Ostrava OKD; 1990 - FC Baník Ostrava (Football Club Baník Ostrava, a.s.).

FC Zbrojovka Brno:
1913 - SK Židenice; 1951 - Zbrojovka Brno; 1956 - Spartak ZJŠ Brno; 1968 - Zbrojovka Brno; 1992 - Boby Brno; 2000 - Stavo Artikel Brno; 2002 - 1.FC Brno; 2010 - FC Zbrojovka Brno.

Bohemians Praha 1905:
1905 - AFK Vršovice; 1927 - Bohemians AFK Vršovice; 1941 - Bohemia AFK Vršovice; 1945 - Bohemians AFK Vršovice; 1948 - Sokol Vršovice Bohemians; 1949 - Sokol Železničáři Bohemians Praha; 1950 - Sokol Železničáři Praha; 1951 - Sokol ČKD Stalingrad Praha; 1953 - Spartak Praha Stalingrad; 1962 - ČKD Praha; 1965 - Bohemians ČKD Praha; 1993 - Bohemians Praha; 1999 - CU Bohemians Praha; 2001 - FC Bohemians Praha; 2005 - Bohemians 1905; 2013 - Bohemians Praha 1905.

Name changements for most important Slovak clubs:

FK Inter Bratislava:
1940 - ŠK Apollo Bratislava; 1945 - TKNB Bratislava; 1948 - Sokol SNB Bratislava; 1952 - TJ Červená Hviezda Bratislava; 1962 - TJ Iskra Slovnaft Bratislava; 1965 - TJ Internacionál Slovnaft Bratislava; 1986 - TJ Internacionál Slovnaft ZŤS Bratislava (after merge with TJ ZŤS Petržalka); 1991 - AŠK Inter Slovnaft Bratislava; 2004 - FK Inter Bratislava; 2009 - Sold club license to FK Senica; 2009 - Inter Bratislava; 2014 - FK Inter Bratislava a.s.

ŠK Slovan Bratislava:
1919 - 1. ČsŠK Bratislava; 1939 - ŠK Bratislava; 1948 - Sokol ŠK NV Bratislava; 1953 - ÚNV Slovan Bratislava; 1961 - Slovan CHZJD Bratislava; 1990 - ŠK Slovan Bratislava.

FC Lokomotíva Košice:
1946 - ŠK Železničiari Košice; 1946 - ŠK Železničiari Sparta Košice (Merge with ŠK Sparta Košice); 1949 - ZSJ Dynamo ČSD Košice (Merge with Sokol Jednota Dynamo Košice); 1952 - TJ Lokomotíva Košice; 1965 - TJ Lokomotíva VSŽ Košice (Merge with TJ VSŽ Košice); 1967 - TJ Lokomotíva Košice (End of merge with TJ VSŽ Košice); 1990 - FK Lokomotíva Košice; 1994 - FK Lokomotíva Energogas Košice; 1999 - FK Lokomotíva PČSP Košice; 2003 - FC Lokomotíva Košice.

FC Spartak Trnava:
1923 - ŠK Rapid Trnava; 1939 - TSS Trnava; 1948 - Sokol NV Trnava; 1949 - ZTJ Kovosmalt Trnava; 1953 - Spartak Trnava; 1967 - Spartak TAZ Trnava; 1988 - Spartak ZTS Trnava; 1993 - FC Spartak Trnava.

NATIONAL CHAMPIONSHIP
Czech First League / Fortuna Liga 2019/2020
(12.07.2019 - 08.07.2020)

Regular Season - Results

Round 1 [12-15.07.2019]
FK Jablonec - Bohemians 1905 2-0(1-0)
Baník Ostrava - Slovan Liberec 1-2(1-0)
1. FK Příbram - FK Teplice 1-1(1-0)
Viktoria Plzeň - Sigma Olomouc 3-1(1-1)
SK Dynamo - SFC Opava 0-1(0-1)
Mladá Boleslav - MFK Karviná 1-0(0-0)
Sparta Praha - 1. FC Slovácko 0-2(0-2)
FC Fastav Zlín - Slavia Praha 0-1(0-0)

Round 2 [19-22.07.2019]
Slovan Liberec - Viktoria Plzeň 1-2(0-0)
SFC Opava - 1. FK Příbram 1-0(0-0)
Sigma Olomouc - FC Fastav Zlín 1-0(0-0)
1. FC Slovácko - SK Dynamo 0-2(0-1)
Sparta Praha - FK Jablonec 2-0(0-0)
Bohemians 1905 - Mladá Boleslav 3-0(3-0)
FK Teplice - Slavia Praha 1-5(0-3)
MFK Karviná - Baník Ostrava 1-2(0-1)

Round 3 [26-29.07.2019]
Baník Ostrava - FK Teplice 0-1(0-1)
1. FK Příbram - Bohemians 1905 3-2(1-0)
FC Fastav Zlín - Slovan Liberec 2-1(1-0)
Viktoria Plzeň - MFK Karviná 3-2(1-0)
FK Jablonec - 1. FC Slovácko 6-0(1-0)
Mladá Boleslav - SFC Opava 4-1(2-1)
Slavia Praha - Sigma Olomouc 1-0(1-0)
SK Dynamo - Sparta Praha 2-2(2-0)

Round 4 [02-04.08.2019]
SFC Opava - Baník Ostrava 0-2(0-1)
Slovan Liberec - Sigma Olomouc 0-1(0-1)
1. FC Slovácko - FC Fastav Zlín 1-0(1-0)
Bohemians 1905 - Viktoria Plzeň 0-0
SK Dynamo - FK Jablonec 1-1(0-1)
MFK Karviná - Slavia Praha 0-0
Sparta Praha - 1. FK Příbram 3-0(2-0)
FK Teplice - Mladá Boleslav 2-0(2-0) [18.09.]

Round 5 [09-11.08.2019]
FC Fastav Zlín - FK Teplice 1-0(0-0)
Baník Ostrava - Bohemians 1905 4-2(2-1)
1. FK Příbram - SK Dynamo 2-0(2-0)
Sigma Olomouc - MFK Karviná 1-1(1-0)
Slavia Praha - Slovan Liberec 1-0(1-0)
FK Jablonec - SFC Opava 2-1(0-0)
Viktoria Plzeň - 1. FC Slovácko 0-2(0-1)
Mladá Boleslav - Sparta Praha 4-3(2-1)

Round 6 [16-18.08.2019]
SK Dynamo - Slavia Praha 0-3(0-0)
SFC Opava - FC Fastav Zlín 0-3(0-1)
1. FC Slovácko - 1. FK Příbram 2-0(0-0)
Bohemians 1905 - Sigma Olomouc 3-2(0-1)
Sparta Praha - Baník Ostrava 2-0(2-0)
FK Jablonec - Mladá Boleslav 2-1(1-0)
MFK Karviná - Slovan Liberec 0-1(0-1)
FK Teplice - Viktoria Plzeň 1-1(0-1)

Round 7 [23-25.08.2019]
Baník Ostrava - 1. FC Slovácko 3-0(2-0)
Sigma Olomouc - FK Teplice 2-0(1-0)
FC Fastav Zlín - MFK Karviná 1-4(0-1)
1. FK Příbram - FK Jablonec 4-0(2-0)
Slavia Praha - Bohemians 1905 4-0(1-0)
Mladá Boleslav - SK Dynamo 4-2(2-2)
Viktoria Plzeň - SFC Opava 4-0(2-0)
Slovan Liberec - Sparta Praha 3-1(1-0)

Round 8 [31.08.-01.09.2019]
Bohemians 1905 - Slovan Liberec 2-1(0-0)
1. FC Slovácko - Mladá Boleslav 1-1(1-0)
1. FK Příbram - Viktoria Plzeň 1-2(1-1)
SK Dynamo - FC Fastav Zlín 2-0(1-0)
FK Jablonec - Baník Ostrava 2-1(2-0)
SFC Opava - Slavia Praha 1-1(0-1)
FK Teplice - MFK Karviná 0-0
Sparta Praha - Sigma Olomouc 3-3(1-2)

Round 9 [13-16.09.2019]
Sigma Olomouc - SFC Opava 2-0(0-0)
Slovan Liberec - FK Teplice 1-1(1-1)
Mladá Boleslav - 1. FK Příbram 6-0(3-0)
Slavia Praha - 1. FC Slovácko 3-0(2-0)
MFK Karviná - Bohemians 1905 0-0
FC Fastav Zlín - Sparta Praha 0-2(0-2)
Baník Ostrava - SK Dynamo 2-1(1-0)
Viktoria Plzeň - FK Jablonec 3-2(1-1)

Round 10 [20-23.09.2019]
Bohemians 1905 - FC Fastav Zlín 2-2(1-2)
SFC Opava - Slovan Liberec 1-1(0-0)
1. FK Příbram - MFK Karviná 0-2(0-1)
1. FC Slovácko - FK Teplice 1-1(1-1)
SK Dynamo - Viktoria Plzeň 0-3(0-2)
Mladá Boleslav - Baník Ostrava 2-0(1-0)
Sparta Praha - Slavia Praha 0-3(0-1)
FK Jablonec - Sigma Olomouc 2-2(1-1)

Round 11 [27-30.09.2019]
FK Teplice - Bohemians 1905 1-0(0-0)
Sigma Olomouc - 1. FC Slovácko 2-2(0-1)
FC Fastav Zlín - FK Jablonec 0-1(0-1)
Slavia Praha - Mladá Boleslav 1-0(1-0)
MFK Karviná - SFC Opava 1-1(1-0)
Viktoria Plzeň - Sparta Praha 1-0(0-0)
Slovan Liberec - SK Dynamo 4-2(2-2)
Baník Ostrava - 1. FK Příbram 3-0(3-0)

Round 12 [04-06.10.2019]
1. FC Slovácko - Slovan Liberec 3-1(2-1)
SFC Opava - FK Teplice 0-1(0-0)
Baník Ostrava - FC Fastav Zlín 4-0(4-0)
1. FK Příbram - Sigma Olomouc 0-0
Sparta Praha - MFK Karviná 4-0(1-0)
SK Dynamo - Bohemians 1905 3-2(1-0)
Mladá Boleslav - Viktoria Plzeň 2-1(0-1)
FK Jablonec - Slavia Praha 0-2(0-0)

Round 13 [19-20.10.2019]
Slovan Liberec - FK Jablonec 2-2(0-1)
Sigma Olomouc - SK Dynamo 1-3(0-1)
FC Fastav Zlín - Mladá Boleslav 0-2(0-1)
Slavia Praha - 1. FK Příbram 3-1(0-1)
Bohemians 1905 - SFC Opava 1-0(0-0)
MFK Karviná - 1. FC Slovácko 0-2(0-1)
Viktoria Plzeň - Baník Ostrava 3-0(0-0)
FK Teplice - Sparta Praha 1-1(0-0)

Round 14 [25-27.10.2019]
FK Jablonec - FK Teplice 4-1(2-0)
Baník Ostrava - Sigma Olomouc 2-2(2-1)
1. FK Příbram - FC Fastav Zlín 0-0
1. FC Slovácko - SFC Opava 4-0(1-0)
Sparta Praha - Bohemians 1905 4-0(2-0)
SK Dynamo - MFK Karviná 3-0(2-0)
Mladá Boleslav - Slovan Liberec 1-3(0-1)
Viktoria Plzeň - Slavia Praha 0-1(0-1)

Round 15 [01-04.11.2019]
Bohemians 1905 - 1. FC Slovácko 0-0
Sigma Olomouc - Mladá Boleslav 2-2(1-0)
Slavia Praha - Baník Ostrava 4-0(1-0)
MFK Karviná - FK Jablonec 0-1(0-0)
Slovan Liberec - 1. FK Příbram 3-2(2-1)
FK Teplice - SK Dynamo 1-3(0-3)
SFC Opava - Sparta Praha 0-1(0-1)
FC Fastav Zlín - Viktoria Plzeň 1-1(0-0)

Round 16 [08-10.11.2019]
Mladá Boleslav - Bohemians 1905 2-1(0-1)
Baník Ostrava - MFK Karviná 3-0(1-0)
1. FK Příbram - SFC Opava 0-0
FC Fastav Zlín - Sigma Olomouc 1-0(0-0)
FK Jablonec - Sparta Praha 2-2(0-2)
SK Dynamo - 1. FC Slovácko 2-0(1-0)
Viktoria Plzeň - Slovan Liberec 4-1(2-1)
Slavia Praha - FK Teplice 3-0(1-0)

Round 17 [22-25.11.2019]
Sparta Praha - SK Dynamo 3-3(1-2)
Bohemians 1905 - 1. FK Příbram 1-0(0-0)
Slovan Liberec - FC Fastav Zlín 5-0(3-0)
SFC Opava - Mladá Boleslav 1-0(1-0)
Sigma Olomouc - Slavia Praha 0-0
FK Teplice - Baník Ostrava 1-1(0-0)
MFK Karviná - Viktoria Plzeň 1-1(1-0)
1. FC Slovácko - FK Jablonec 1-1(1-1)

Round 18 [29.11.-01.12.2019]
Baník Ostrava - SFC Opava 0-0
Sigma Olomouc - Slovan Liberec 1-0(1-0)
FC Fastav Zlín - 1. FC Slovácko 2-1(1-0)
1. FK Příbram - Sparta Praha 0-1(0-1)
FK Jablonec - SK Dynamo 0-1(0-0)
Mladá Boleslav - FK Teplice 3-0(0-0)
Viktoria Plzeň - Bohemians 1905 1-0(1-0)
Slavia Praha - MFK Karviná 2-0(0-0)

Round 19 [06-08.12.2019]
Bohemians 1905 - Baník Ostrava 0-2(0-0)
Slovan Liberec - Slavia Praha 0-3(0-2)
SFC Opava - FK Jablonec 1-2(0-0)
FK Teplice - FC Fastav Zlín 2-1(0-0)
1. FC Slovácko - Viktoria Plzeň 2-1(1-1)
SK Dynamo - 1. FK Příbram 2-0(1-0)
MFK Karviná - Sigma Olomouc 1-1(0-1)
Sparta Praha - Mladá Boleslav 5-2(2-1)

Round 20 [13-15.12.2019]
Mladá Boleslav - FK Jablonec 2-3(1-3)
Slovan Liberec - MFK Karviná 3-0(0-0)
1. FK Příbram - 1. FC Slovácko 1-4(0-3)
Sigma Olomouc - Bohemians 1905 1-1(0-1)
FC Fastav Zlín - SFC Opava 2-0(0-0)
Baník Ostrava - Sparta Praha 0-0
Viktoria Plzeň - FK Teplice 1-1(1-1)
Slavia Praha - SK Dynamo 4-1(3-0)

Round 21 [14-17.02.2020]
SK Dynamo - Mladá Boleslav 3-0(3-0)
MFK Karviná - FC Fastav Zlín 2-0(1-0)
1. FC Slovácko - Baník Ostrava 0-1(0-0)
FK Teplice - Sigma Olomouc 1-3(0-3)
Sparta Praha - SFC Opava 3-0(0-0)
SFC Opava - Viktoria Plzeň 0 3(0-0)
Bohemians 1905 - Slavia Praha 1-0(0-0)
FK Jablonec - 1. FK Příbram 4-0(1-0)

Round 22 [22-24.02.2020]
Slovan Liberec - Bohemians 1905 3-1(2-1)
Mladá Boleslav - 1. FC Slovácko 0-0
Slavia Praha - SFC Opava 2-0(1-0)
Viktoria Plzeň - 1. FK Příbram 4-0(2-0)
MFK Karviná - FK Teplice 3-0(3-0)
FC Fastav Zlín - SK Dynamo 2-3(0-2)
Sigma Olomouc - Sparta Praha 1-0(1-0)
Baník Ostrava - FK Jablonec 1-1(1-1)

Round 23 [28.02.-01.03.2020]
SK Dynamo - Baník Ostrava 0-2(0-1)
FK Jablonec - Viktoria Plzeň 1-2(0-2)
SFC Opava - Sigma Olomouc 2-1(2-0)
1. FK Příbram - Mladá Boleslav 0-0
Sparta Praha - FC Fastav Zlín 2-2(0-0)
1. FC Slovácko - Slavia Praha 2-0(1-0)
Bohemians 1905 - MFK Karviná 0-0
FK Teplice - Slovan Liberec 2-0(1-0) [23,05,]

Round 24 [07-09.03.2020]
Sigma Olomouc - FK Jablonec 1-1(1-0)
FC Fastav Zlín - Bohemians 1905 2-3(1-2)
Viktoria Plzeň - SK Dynamo 1-0(0-0)
MFK Karviná - 1. FK Příbram 2-0(1-0)
Slovan Liberec - SFC Opava 4-0(2-0)
FK Teplice - 1. FC Slovácko 0-0
Slavia Praha - Sparta Praha 1-1(0-0)
Baník Ostrava - Mladá Boleslav 2-3(1-2)

Round 25 [26-27.05.2020]
FK Jablonec - FC Fastav Zlín 1-0(1-0)
1. FK Příbram - Baník Ostrava 0-0
1. FC Slovácko - Sigma Olomouc 2-0(0-0)
Mladá Boleslav - Slavia Praha 0-1(0-1)
Bohemians 1905 - FK Teplice 4-0(2-0)
SK Dynamo - Slovan Liberec 0-1(0-0)
SFC Opava - MFK Karviná 0-0
Sparta Praha - Viktoria Plzeň 1-2(0-1)

Round 26 [30-31.05.2020]
Sigma Olomouc - 1. FK Příbram 1-2(1-1)
Slovan Liberec - 1. FC Slovácko 3-1(1-1)
FC Fastav Zlín - Baník Ostrava 1-0(1-0)
Viktoria Plzeň - Mladá Boleslav 7-1(4-0)
Slavia Praha - FK Jablonec 5-0(2-0)
FK Teplice - SFC Opava 2-2(1-1)
Bohemians 1905 - SK Dynamo 3-2(2-0)
MFK Karviná - Sparta Praha 1-4(1-0)

Round 27 [02-03.06.2020]
FK Jablonec - Slovan Liberec 0-1(0-0)
Mladá Boleslav - FC Fastav Zlín 1-1(1-1)
1. FK Příbram - Slavia Praha 0-1(0-0)
SK Dynamo - Sigma Olomouc 2-0(0-0)
SFC Opava - Bohemians 1905 0-1(0-0)
Baník Ostrava - Viktoria Plzeň 0-2(0-1)
1. FC Slovácko - MFK Karviná 2-0(2-0)
Sparta Praha - FK Teplice 3-0(3-0)

Round 28 [06-07.06.2020]
FC Fastav Zlín - 1. FK Příbram 1-0(1-0)
Slovan Liberec - Mladá Boleslav 2-2(1-1)
Bohemians 1905 - Sparta Praha 0-1(0-0)
MFK Karviná - SK Dynamo 0-0
SFC Opava - 1. FC Slovácko 1-1(1-0)
Sigma Olomouc - Baník Ostrava 2-3(1-3)
FK Teplice - FK Jablonec 1-2(0-1)
Slavia Praha - Viktoria Plzeň 0-0

Round 29 [10.06.2020]
SK Dynamo - FK Teplice 3-1(0-0)
FK Jablonec - MFK Karviná 1-0(0-0)
Mladá Boleslav - Sigma Olomouc 0-2(0-1)
Baník Ostrava - Slavia Praha 2-2(1-1)
Viktoria Plzeň - FC Fastav Zlín 3-0(2-0)
1. FK Příbram - Slovan Liberec 2-1(2-1)
1. FC Slovácko - Bohemians 1905 1-2(1-2)
Sparta Praha - SFC Opava 2-0(1-0)

Round 30 [14.06.2020]
Bohemians 1905 - FK Jablonec 3-0(2-0)
MFK Karviná - Mladá Boleslav 2-2(2-1)
Slovan Liberec - Baník Ostrava 0-0
SFC Opava - SK Dynamo 2-0(0-0)
Sigma Olomouc - Viktoria Plzeň 0-1(0-1)
Slavia Praha - FC Fastav Zlín 1-0(0-0)
1. FC Slovácko - Sparta Praha 0-2(0-0)
FK Teplice - 1. FK Příbram 4-0(2-0)

Final Standings

		Total							Home					Away				
1.	SK Slavia Praha	30	22	6	2	58	-	10	72	13	2	0	35 - 3	9	4	2	23 - 7
2.	FC Viktoria Plzeň	30	20	6	4	60	-	22	66	12	1	2	38 - 11	8	5	2	22 - 11
3.	AC Sparta Praha	30	14	8	8	55	-	35	50	8	3	4	34 - 19	6	5	4	21 - 16
4.	FK Jablonec	30	14	7	9	46	-	41	49	9	2	4	29 - 14	5	5	5	17 - 27
5.	FC Slovan Liberec	30	14	5	11	50	-	38	47	8	4	3	34 - 18	6	1	8	16 - 20
6.	FC Baník Ostrava	30	12	9	9	42	-	34	45	6	5	4	27 - 16	6	4	5	15 - 18
7.	SK Dynamo České Budějovice	30	13	4	13	46	-	45	43	8	2	5	23 - 16	5	2	8	23 - 29
8.	Bohemians Praha 1905	30	12	6	12	38	-	41	42	9	4	2	23 - 10	3	2	10	15 - 31
9.	1. FC Slovácko Uherské Hradiště	30	11	9	10	35	-	35	42	7	4	4	20 - 12	4	5	6	15 - 23
10.	FK Mladá Boleslav	30	11	7	12	48	-	52	40	9	2	4	32 - 19	2	5	8	16 - 33
11.	SK Sigma Olomouc	30	8	12	10	36	-	37	36	5	6	4	18 - 16	3	6	6	18 - 21
12.	FK Teplice	30	7	10	13	29	-	49	31	5	6	4	20 - 19	2	4	9	9 - 30
13.	FC Fastav Zlín	30	7	6	17	25	-	47	27	6	2	7	16 - 20	1	4	10	9 - 27
14.	MFK Karviná	30	5	11	14	23	-	39	26	3	7	5	14 - 15	2	4	9	9 - 24
15.	Slezský FC Opava	30	5	8	17	16	-	47	23	4	4	7	10 - 17	1	4	10	6 - 30
16.	1. FK Příbram	30	5	6	19	19	-	54	21	4	6	5	14 - 14	1	0	14	5 - 40

Teams ranked 1-6 were qualified for the Championship Play-offs, teams ranked 7-10 were qualified for the Europa League Play-offs and teams ranked 11-16 were qualified for the Relegation Play-offs.

Relegation Play-offs

Results

Round 31 [20.06.2020]
FC Fastav Zlín - SFC Opava 3-1(2-1)
1. FK Příbram - Sigma Olomouc 2-0(1-0)
FK Teplice - MFK Karviná 4-1(2-0)

Round 32 [23.06.2020]
FC Fastav Zlín - 1. FK Příbram 1-0(0-0)
MFK Karviná - SFC Opava 0-0
Sigma Olomouc - FK Teplice 0-0

Round 33 [28.06.2020]
FK Teplice - FC Fastav Zlín 4-1(1-1)
Sigma Olomouc - MFK Karviná 3-1(2-0)
SFC Opava - 1. FK Příbram 0-0

Round 34 [23.07.2020]
FC Fastav Zlín - MFK Karviná *not played*
1. FK Příbram - FK Teplice *not played*
SFC Opava - Sigma Olomouc *not played*

Round 35 [26.07.2020]
FK Teplice - SFC Opava *not played*
MFK Karviná - 1. FK Příbram *not played*
Sigma Olomouc - FC Fastav Zlín *not played*

Please note: one player from Slezský FC Opava was testing positive for Covid-19. As a consequence, the last two Rounds was not played.
No teams were relegated, the next season's First League teams number being increased to 18.

Final Standings

		Total							Home					Away				
11.	SK Sigma Olomouc	33	9	13	11	39	-	40	40	6	7	4	21 - 17	3	6	7	18 - 23
12.	FK Teplice	33	9	11	13	37	-	51	38	7	6	4	28 - 21	2	5	9	9 - 39
13.	FC Fastav Zlín	33	9	6	18	30	-	52	33	8	2	7	20 - 21	1	4	11	10 - 31
14.	MFK Karviná	33	5	12	16	25	-	46	27	3	8	5	14 - 15	2	4	11	11 - 31
15.	Slezský FC Opava	33	5	10	18	17	-	50	25	4	5	7	10 - 17	1	5	11	7 - 33
16.	1. FK Příbram	33	6	7	20	21	-	55	25	5	6	5	16 - 14	1	1	15	5 - 41

Championship Play-offs

Results

Round 31 [20-21.06.2020]
Sparta Praha - Slovan Liberec 4-1(2-1)
Baník Ostrava - Slavia Praha 1-3(0-2)
Viktoria Plzeň - FK Jablonec 2-0(1-0)

Round 32 [23-24.06.2020]
Sparta Praha - Baník Ostrava 3-2(3-1)
FK Jablonec - Slovan Liberec 1-1(0-1)
Slavia Praha - Viktoria Plzeň 1-0(0-0)

Round 33 [27-28.06.2020]
Slovan Liberec - Baník Ostrava 2-1(0-0)
Viktoria Plzeň - Sparta Praha 2-1(0-0)
Slavia Praha - FK Jablonec 4-0(2-0)

Round 34 [05.07.2020]
Baník Ostrava - Viktoria Plzeň 0-0
Slovan Liberec - Slavia Praha 1-3(0-2)
Sparta Praha - FK Jablonec 3-0(1-0)

Round 35 [08.07.2020]
FK Jablonec - Baník Ostrava 1-1(1-0)
Slavia Praha - Sparta Praha 0-0
Viktoria Plzeň - Slovan Liberec 4-0(2-0)

Final Standings

		Total							Home					Away				
1.	**SK Slavia Praha**	35	26	7	2	69	-	12	85	15	3	0	40 - 3	11	4	2	29 - 9
2.	FC Viktoria Plzeň	35	23	7	5	68	-	24	76	15	1	2	46 - 12	8	6	3	22 - 12
3.	AC Sparta Praha	35	17	9	9	66	-	40	60	11	3	4	44 - 22	6	6	5	22 - 18
4.	FK Jablonec	35	14	9	12	48	-	52	51	9	4	4	31 - 16	5	5	8	17 - 36
5.	FC Slovan Liberec	35	15	6	14	55	-	51	51	9	4	4	37 - 22	6	2	10	18 - 29
6.	FC Baník Ostrava	35	12	11	12	47	-	43	47	6	6	5	28 - 19	6	5	7	19 - 24

Top goalscorers:	
14 Petar Musa (CRO)	*FC Slovan Liberec / SK Slavia Praha*
14 Libor Kozák	*AC Sparta Praha*
13 Lukáš Budínský	*FK Mladá Boleslav*
12 Guélor Kanga Kaku (GAB)	*AC Sparta Praha*
12 Jakub Řezníček	*FK Teplice*

Europa League Play-offs [21.06.-12.07.2020]

First Round	FK Mladá Boleslav - SK Dynamo České Budějovice	2-1(0-1)	2-0(1-0)
	1. FC Slovácko Uherské Hradiště - Bohemians Praha 1905	1-2(1-1)	1-2(1-0)
Second Round	FK Mladá Boleslav - Bohemians Praha 1905	3-0(1-0)	1-2(1-1)
Europa League Play-off Final	**FC Slovan Liberec** - FK Mladá Boleslav	2-0(0-0)	

NATIONAL CUP
Pohár Českomoravského fotbalového svazu / MOL Cup 2019/2020

First Round [07/13-14/20.08.2019]

FK Náchod - FK Viktoria Žižkov	0-5	1. FC Olešnice u Bouzova - FC Viktoria Otrokovice	2-1
SK Kladno - FK TJ Štěchovice	1-2	FC Slovan Rosice - FC Velké Meziríčí	4-2
FK Brandýs nad Labem - FK Ústí nad Labem	0-10	TJ Jiskra Rýmařov - SK Uničov	2-3
FK Olympie Březová - FC Viktoria Mariánské Lázně	0-3	TJ Tatran Sedlčany - FK MAS Táborsko	0-4
FK Meteor Praha VIII - MFK Chrudim	1-3	TJ Skaštice - SK Líšeň	3-5
FK Přepeře - TJ Dvůr Králové	6-2	FK Spartak Soběslav - SK Benešov	0-2
SK Aritma Praha - FK Admira Praha	0-1	FK Baník Souš - FK Baník Sokolov	0-3
Český lev - Union Beroun - FK Dukla Praha	0-7	TJ Sokol Srbice - FK Králův Dvůr	1-2
SK Český Brod - FC Slovan Velvary	1-3	FC Strání - SK Prostějov	1-3
SK Dětmarovice - FK Fotbal Třinec	1-7	TJ Valašské Meziříčí - FC Slavičín	4-2 aet
FK Komarov - FK Loko Vltavín	0-1	TJ Sokol Velké Hamry - FK Varnsdorf	0-4
SK Beskyd Frenštát pod Radhoštěm - FC Hlučín	1-2	TJ Tatran Všechovice - FC Odra Petřkovice	0-4
TJ Unie Hlubina - FC Dolní Benešov	1-2	FK Zbuzany - TJ Jiskra Domažlice	1-3
Sokol Hostouň - FC Slavia Karlovy Vary	2-1	SK Ždírec nad Doubravou - FSC Stará Říše	3-1 aet
AFC Humpolec - FC Vysočina Jihlava	0-9	1. HFK Olomouc - FC Zbrojovka Brno	0-3
FK Kolín - TJ Jiskra Ústí nad Orlicí	0-1	SS Ostrá - FC Sellier & Bellot Vlašim	1-3
SK Hanácká Slávia Kroměříž - MFK Vítkovice	3-4 pcn	SK Slany - FC Slavoj Vyšehrad	0-4
TJ Sokol Lanžhot - 1. SC Znojmo	3-1 pen	SK Libčany - FK Chlumec nad Cidlinou	0-3
FK OEZ Letohrad - FC Hradec Králové	0-3	MFK Dobříš - FC Písek	0-2
TJ Sokol Libiš - TJ Sokol Zápy	0-2	TJ Sokol Tasovice - SFK Vrchovina	0-1
SK Motorlet Praha - FC Chomutov	4-0	SK Vysoké Mýto - FK Pardubice	0-2
TJ Nový Jičín - FK Frýdek-Místek	2-3		

Second Round [27-28.08./03-04/10.09.2019]

FC Slovan Rosice - SK Sigma Olomouc	1-5	TJ Jiskra Domažlice - FK Ústí nad Labem	4-3 pen
FC Dolní Benešov - SK Prostějov	2-3	FK Králův Dvůr - FK Dukla Praha	0-2
TJ Valašské Meziříčí - FK Fotbal Třinec	0-5	TJ Sokol Lanžhot - FC Baník Ostrava	1-3
SFK Vrchovina - 1. FC Slovácko Uherské Hradiště	0-5	FC Odra Petřkovice - FC Zbrojovka Brno	3-4 aet
FK MAS Táborsko - FK Varnsdorf	3-5 pen	FK Frýdek-Místek - MFK Karvina	1-3
SK Motorlet Praha - FC Slavoj Vyšehrad	0-5	SK Uničov - FC Fastav Zlín	1-4
FK Přepeře - MFK Chrudim	0-1	1. FC Olešnice u Bouzova - SFC Opava	0-6
FC Viktoria Mariánské Lázně - FC Slovan Liberec	2-5	SK Ždírec nad Doubravou - SK Líšeň Brno	0-4
FC Slovan Velvary - FK Viktoria Žižkov	0-1	FK TJ Štěchovice - FK Baník Sokolov	1-4
FK Chlumec nad Cidlinou - 1. FK Příbram	2-1	SK Benešov - FK Pardubice	2-1
FK Loko Vltavín - FC Sellier & Bellot Vlašim	2-1	FK Admira Praha - FC Hradec Králové	1-2
TJ Jiskra Ústí nad Orlicí - SK Dynamo České Buděj.	0-2	Sokol Hostouň - FC Vysočina Jihlava	1-6
FC Písek - FK Teplice	1-3	FC Hlučín - MFK Vítkovice	4-2
TJ Sokol Zápy - Bohemians Praha 1905	2-3		

Third Round [24-25.09./01-02.10.2019]

SK Benešov - 1. FC Slovácko Uherské Hradiště	1-3(1-1)	FC Vysočina Jihlava - AC Sparta Praha	1-2(1-1)
FK Baník Sokolov - SFC Opava	0-1(0-0)	FC Slovan Liberec - SK Prostějov	3-1(2-0)
FK Varnsdorf - FC Fastav Zlín	1-2(1-1)	FC Baník Ostrava - FC Hradec Králové	2-0(1-0)
FK Loko Vltavín - SK Dynamo České Budějovice	1-4(1-2)	FK Mladá Boleslav - MFK Chrudim	4-2(0-0)
TJ Jiskra Domažlice - FK Dukla Praha	1-3(0-1)	FK Jablonec - FC Zbrojovka Brno	3-2(1-1)
SK Slavia Praha - FC Slavoj Vyšehrad	8-0(5-0)	FK Teplice - FK Fotbal Třinec	2-1(1-1)
MFK Karvina - FK Viktoria Žižkov	0-2(0-1)	SK Sigma Olomouc - SK Líšeň Brno	4-2(2-0)
FC Hlučín - FC Viktoria Plzeň	1-3(0-2)	FK Chlumec nad Cidlinou - Bohemians Praha 1905	2-1(1-0)

1/8-Finals [29-30.10./06.11.2019]

SFC Opava - FK Jablonec	0-2(0-0,0-0)	SK Dynamo České Budějovice - AC Sparta Praha	0-4(0-2)
SK Sigma Olomouc - FK Dukla Praha	4-0(2-0)	FC Baník Ostrava - SK Slavia Praha	2-0(0-0,0-0)
FK Chlumec nad Cidlinou - FC Viktoria Plzeň	3-4(1-0,3-3)	FC Slovan Liberec - FK Teplice	2-0(0-0)
FK Mladá Boleslav - FC Fastav Zlín	3-1(1-1)	1. FC Slovácko Uher. Hradiště - FK Viktoria Žižkov	3-1(0-0,1-1)

Quarter-Finals [04.03.2020]				
SK Sigma Olomouc - FK Jablonec	3-1(1-0)	1. FC Slovácko Uher. Hradiště - FC Slovan Liberec	0-0 aet; 2-4 pen
FC Viktoria Plzeň - FK Mladá Boleslav	4-2(3-0)	AC Sparta Praha - FC Baník Ostrava	5-0(1-0)

Semi-Finals [17.06.2020]			
SK Sigma Olomouc - FC Slovan Liberec	1-2(0-2)	AC Sparta Praha - FC Viktoria Plzeň	2-1(2-0)

Final

01.07.2020; Stadion u Nisy, Liberec; Referee: Pavel Královec; Attendance: None

AC Sparta Praha - FC Slovan Liberec   **2-1(0-0)**

Sparta Praha: Milan Heča, Lukáš Štetina, Dávid Hancko, Guélor Kanga Kaku, Bořek Dočkal (90.Michal Trávník), Michal Sáček, Martin Frýdek, Ladislav Krejčí, David Moberg-Karlsson, Libor Kozák (85.Matěj Hanousek), Adam Hložek (61.Benjamin Tetteh). Trainer: Václav Kotal.

Slovan Liberec: Milan Knobloch, Jan Mikula, Ondřej Karafiát, Taras Kacharaba, Tomáš Malínský, Alexandru Mihail Băluță (84.Michal Beran), Martin Koscelník, Kamso Mara, Jakub Hromada (70.Akhmed Alibekov), Jakub Pešek (90.Martin Zeman), Imad Rondić [*sent off 90*]. Trainer: Pavel Hoftych.

Goals: 0-1 Jakub Pešek (50), 1-1 David Moberg-Karlsson (65), 2-1 Guélor Kanga Kaku (74 penalty).

THE CLUBS 2019/2020

Please note: matches and goals includes statistics of both regular season and play-offs (Championship Round, Relegation Round and Europa League Play-offs).

Football Club Baník Ostrava

Founded:	1922 (*as SK Slezská Ostrava*)	
Stadium:	Městský stadion, Ostrava (15,123)	
Trainer:	Bohumil Páník	31.12.1956
[01.01.2020]	Luboš Kozel	16.03.1971

Goalkeepers:	DOB	M	(s)	G
Viktor Budinský (SVK)	09.05.1993	12	(1)	
Jan Laštůvka	07.07.1982	23		
Defenders:	**DOB**	**M**	**(s)**	**G**
Josef Celba	30.01.1995	1		
Jiří Fleišman	02.10.1984	30	(1)	2
Denis Granečný	07.09.1998	3	(9)	
Lukáš Pazdera	06.03.1987	1		
Jakub Pokorný	11.09.1996	21	(1)	3
Václav Procházka	08.05.1984	16	(6)	
Patrizio Stronati	17.11.1994	30		4
Jaroslav Svozil	09.09.1993	8	(1)	2
Martin Šindelář	22.01.1991	6	(4)	1
Midfielders:	**DOB**	**M**	**(s)**	**G**
David Buchta	27.06.1999	2	(7)	1
Jakub Drozd	13.06.2003	1	(4)	
Martin Fillo	07.02.1986	28	(1)	2
Daniel Holzer	18.08.1995	9	(10)	
Robert Hrubý	27.04.1994	22	(3)	1
Adam Jánoš	20.07.1992	24		1
Milan Jirásek	14.05.1992	21	(5)	3
Filip Kaloč	27.02.2000	5	(6)	
Milan Lalkovič (SVK)	09.12.1992	4	(6)	
Rudolf Reiter	28.09.1994	21	(9)	1
Forwards:	**DOB**	**M**	**(s)**	**G**
Dyjan Carlos De Azevedo (BRA)	23.06.1991	12	(6)	2
Milan Baroš	28.10.1981	2	(15)	1
Dame Diop (SEN)	15.02.1993	13	(6)	6
Nemanja Kuzmanović (SRB)	27.05.1989	29	(3)	9
Roman Potočný	25.04.1991	13		1
Tomáš Smola	19.01.1989	16	(14)	4
Ondřej Šašinka	21.03.1998	12	(1)	1

Bohemians Praha 1905

Founded:	1905	
Stadium:	Stadion Ďolíček, Praha (5,000)	
Trainer:	Martin Hašek	11.10.1969
[10.10.2019]	Luděk Klusáček	09.02.1967

Goalkeepers:	DOB	M	(s)	G
Tomáš Fryšták	18.08.1987	7		
Patrik Lé Giang (SVK)	08.09.1992	15		
Roman Valeš	06.03.1990	12		
Defenders:	**DOB**	**M**	**(s)**	**G**
Jiří Bederka	18.02.1995	10	(3)	
Martin Dostál	23.09.1989	6	(4)	1
Milan Havel	07.08.1994	11		3
Lukáš Hůlka	31.03.1995	34		1
Daniel Köstl	23.05.1998	18	(4)	
Daniel Krch	20.03.1992	16	(3)	1
Jakub Podaný	15.06.1987	19	(2)	2
Lukáš Pokorný	05.07.1993	12		
Till Schumacher (GER)	10.12.1997	11	(2)	1
Michal Šmíd	20.10.1986	6	(2)	
Midfielders:	**DOB**	**M**	**(s)**	**G**
David Bartek	13.02.1988	22	(3)	3
Petr Hronek	04.07.1993	22	(1)	5
Josef Jindřišek	14.02.1981	32		2
Roman Květ	17.12.1997	3	(8)	1
Vladislav Levin (RUS)	28.03.1995	8		
Vojtěch Novák	20.01.2002		(1)	
Jakub Rada	05.05.1987	4	(4)	1
Kamil Vacek	18.05.1987	19	(4)	4
Antonín Vaníček	22.04.1998	13	(14)	1
Jan Vodháněl	25.04.1997	28	(4)	5
Jan Záviška	21.08.1995	1	(8)	
Forwards:	**DOB**	**M**	**(s)**	**G**
Ibrahim Keïta (FRA)	18.01.1996	14	(8)	2
Matěj Koubek	10.01.2000		(2)	
Jhon Édison Mosquera Rebolledo (COL)	06.06.1990	4	(6)	3
Jakub Nečas	26.01.1995	10	(15)	1
Pavel Osmančík	26.02.2000		(1)	
Matěj Pulkrab	23.05.1997	8		5
David Puškáč	14.05.1993	4	(5)	1
Michael Junior Ugwu (NGA)	10.01.1999	5	(14)	

Sportovní klub Dynamo České Budějovice

Founded: 1905
Stadium: Stadion Střelecký ostrov, České Budějovice (6,681)
Trainer: David Horejš   19.05.1977

Goalkeepers:	DOB	M	(s)	G
Jaroslav Drobný	18.10.1979	18		
Zdeněk Křížek	16.01.1983	3		
Jindřich Staněk	27.04.1996	11		
Defenders:	**DOB**	**M**	**(s)**	**G**
Benjamin Čolić (BIH)	23.07.1991	28		2
Denis Granečný	07.09.1998		(1)	
Lukáš Havel	06.06.1996	30	(2)	6
Matěj Helešic	12.11.1996	2	(6)	
Jiří Kladrubský	19.11.1985	15	(6)	2
Miloš Kopečný	26.12.1993	1	(3)	
Pavel Novák	30.11.1989	24	(2)	1
Maksym Taloverov (UKR)	28.06.2000	5	(2)	
Midfielders:	**DOB**	**M**	**(s)**	**G**
Patrik Čavoš	07.01.1995	24	(4)	3
Filip Havelka	21.01.1998	24	(1)	1
Petr Javorek	09.02.1986	24	(3)	1
Jiří Kulhánek	08.03.1996	8	(7)	
Matej Mršić (CRO)	13.01.1994	21	(7)	2
Zinedin Mustedanagić (BIH)	01.08.1998	2	(3)	
Tomáš Sivok	15.09.1983	19		1
Pavel Šulc	29.12.2000	7	(4)	2
Forwards:	**DOB**	**M**	**(s)**	**G**
Patrik Brandner	04.01.1994	22	(6)	5
Dzon Delarge (CGO)	24.06.1990	1	(2)	
Ubong Moses Ekpai (NGA)	17.10.1995	1	(4)	1
David Ledecký	24.07.1993	18	(7)	5
Ladislav Martan	02.10.1989		(2)	
Karol Mészáros (SVK)	25.07.1993	6	(5)	
Lukáš Provod	23.10.1996	7		2
Michael Rabušic	17.09.1989	2	(4)	2
Ivan Schranz (SVK)	13.09.1993	29	(1)	9
Ivo Taborský	10.05.1985		(17)	2

Fotbalový Klub Jablonec

Founded: 1945
Stadium: Stadion Střelnice, Jablonec nad Nisou (6,108)
Trainer: Petr Rada   21.08.1958

Goalkeepers:	DOB	M	(s)	G
Jan Hanuš	28.04.1988	1	(1)	
Vlastimil Hrubý	21.02.1985	34		
Defenders:	**DOB**	**M**	**(s)**	**G**
Tomáš Břečka	12.05.1994	18		2
Libor Holík	12.05.1998	31		2
Michal Jeřábek	10.09.1993	9	(3)	1
Jakub Jugas	05.05.1992	16		
Jan Krob	27.04.1987	30	(2)	2
Dominik Plechatý	18.04.1999	26	(2)	
David Štěpánek	30.03.1997	4	(1)	1
Jiří Váňa	05.07.1989	1		
Midfielders:	**DOB**	**M**	**(s)**	**G**
Alejandro Rafael Acosta Cabrera (URU)	02.10.1990	5	(5)	
Kasper Hämäläinen (FIN)	08.08.1986	3	(12)	2
Tomáš Hübschman	04.09.1981	25		1
Miloš Kratochvíl	26.04.1996	16	(7)	3
Vojtěch Kubista	19.03.1993	7	(6)	2
David Macháček	14.06.2000		(2)	
Jan Matoušek	09.05.1998	18	(5)	6
Tomáš Pilík	20.12.1988	11	(19)	
Dominik Pleštil	09.08.1999	8	(8)	2
Jakub Považanec (SVK)	31.01.1991	34		
Jan Sýkora	29.12.1993	29		8
Forwards:	**DOB**	**M**	**(s)**	**G**
Dominik Breda	27.02.1998		(1)	
Michal Černák	01.09.2003	1	(4)	
Jan Chramosta	12.10.1990	5	(22)	2
Tomáš Dočekal	24.05.1989	1	(3)	
Martin Doležal	03.05.1990	33		10
Vladimir Jovović (MNE)	26.10.1994	19		4
Zoran Petrović (MNE)	14.07.1997		(2)	
Oliver Velich	12.06.2001		(5)	

Městský fotbalový klub Karviná

Founded: 2003
Stadium: Stadion Městský, Karviná (4,833)
Trainer: František Straka   28.05.1958
[14.11.2019]   Juraj Jarábek (SVK)   03.10.1962

Goalkeepers:	DOB	M	(s)	G
Petr Bolek	13.06.1984	12		
Libor Hrdlička	02.01.1986	12		
Vladimir Neuman	10.02.2000	1		
Martin Pastornický	18.03.1996	8		
Defenders:	**DOB**	**M**	**(s)**	**G**
Matúš Čonka (SVK)	15.10.1990	23	(3)	
Soufiane Dramé (FRA)	27.02.1996		(1)	
Pavel Dreksa	17.09.1989	5	(1)	
Eduardo Gonzaga Mendes Santos (BRA)	28.11.1997	5	(4)	
Martin Kouřil	24.02.1991	13	(1)	
Ján Krivák (SVK)	10.11.1993	6	(2)	
Gigli Ndefe (NED)	03.02.1994	30		1
Oliver Putyera	21.08.1997	3	(6)	
Milan Rundić (SRB)	29.03.1992	28	(1)	2
Daniel Stropek	03.03.1998	1	(1)	
Martin Šindelář	22.01.1991	13		
Midfielders:	**DOB**	**M**	**(s)**	**G**
Martin Bukata (SVK)	02.10.1993	8	(10)	1
Marek Hanousek	06.08.1991	19	(9)	1
Marek Janečka (SVK)	09.06.1983	20	(6)	1
Jean Mangabeira da Silva (BRA)	10.03.1997	5		
Ondřej Lingr	07.10.1998	28	(1)	7
Jan Moravec	13.07.1987	10	(3)	
Erik Puchel	15.05.1996	2	(2)	1
Kristi Qose (ALB)	10.06.1995	11	(1)	1
Vojtěch Smrž	20.01.1997	22	(5)	3
Tomáš Weber	26.05.1996	1	(1)	
Ivan Zhelizko (UKR)	12.02.2001		(3)	
Forwards:	**DOB**	**M**	**(s)**	**G**
Adriel D'Avila Ba Loua (CIV)	25.07.1996	23	(4)	1
Petr Galuška	08.07.1996	5	(2)	
Dávid Guba (SVK)	29.06.1991	2	(10)	
Filip Kubala	02.09.1999	1	(2)	
Steven Petkov (BUL)	07.05.1995	4	(7)	
Michal Petráň	26.06.1992	17	(3)	3
Jakub Šašinka	02.10.1995	2	(4)	
Abdulrahman Taiwo (NGA)	05.08.1998	12	(1)	3
Muhamed Tijani (NGA)	26.07.2000	1	(4)	
Vukadin Vukadinović (SRB)	14.12.1990	10	(12)	

Fotbalový klub Mladá Boleslav

Founded: 1902
Stadium: Stadion Městský, Mladá Boleslav (5,000)
Trainer: Jozef Weber 25.12.1970

Goalkeepers:	DOB	M	(s)	G
Jan Šeda	17.12.1985	22		
Jan Stejskal	14.02.1997	13		
Defenders:	**DOB**	**M**	**(s)**	**G**
Anderson Arroyo Córdoba (COL)	27.09.1999		(2)	
Dominik Hašek	19.07.1998	1	(2)	
Jakub Klíma	28.08.1998	26	(2)	1
Antonín Křapka	22.01.1994	21	(3)	
Marco Tulio De Paula Medeiros (BRA)	31.05.1998	17	(4)	
Ondřej Mazuch	15.03.1989	4	(6)	
Daniel Pudil	27.09.1985	25	(3)	
Aleksey Tataev (RUS)	08.10.1998	23		1
Tomáš Wiesner	17.07.1997	2		
Jaroslav Zelený	20.08.1992	12	(1)	1
Midfielders:	**DOB**	**M**	**(s)**	**G**
Jonas Auer (AUT)	05.08.2000	2	(4)	
Pavel Bucha	11.03.1998	17	(2)	6
Lukáš Budínský	27.03.1992	31	(3)	13
David Douděra	31.05.1998	7	(7)	
Ewerton Paixao da Silva (BRA)	28.12.1996		(1)	
Michael Hönig	13.01.2000		(2)	
Michal Hubínek	10.11.1994	28	(2)	1
Dominik Janošek	13.06.1998	14		
Dominik Mašek	10.07.1995	1	(7)	2
Marek Matějovský	20.12.1981	16	(2)	
David Pech	22.02.2002		(5)	
Laco Takács	15.07.1996	7		1
Forwards:	**DOB**	**M**	**(s)**	**G**
An Jae-joon (KOR)	13.04.2001		(1)	
Jakub Fulnek	26.04.1994	27	(7)	2
Jiří Klíma	05.01.1997	14	(18)	7
Nikolay Komlichenko (RUS)	29.06.1995	15		10
Ladislav Krobot	01.04.2001		(6)	
Tomáš Ladra	24.04.1997	21	(11)	3
Muris Mešanović (BIH)	06.07.1990	15	(3)	8
Vojtěch Stránský	13.03.2003		(3)	
Tomáš Wágner	06.03.1990	4	(10)	

Slezský fotbalový club Opava

Founded: 1907
Stadium: Stadion v Městských sadech, Opava (7,758)
Trainer: Ivan Kopecký 10.06.1970
[26.09.2019] Alois Grussmann 06.09.1964
[12.11.2019] Jiří Balcárek 29.04.1973
[11.06.2020] Radoslav Kováč 27.11.1979

Goalkeepers:	DOB	M	(s)	G
Vilém Fendrich	22.01.1991	29		
Vojtěch Šrom	03.05.1988	4		
Defenders:	**DOB**	**M**	**(s)**	**G**
Štěpán Harazim	13.07.2000	6	(1)	
Matěj Helebrand	19.06.1997	4	(2)	
Matěj Helešic	12.11.1996	9		
Josef Hnaníček	28.12.1986	8	(1)	
Jan Hošek	01.04.1989	4	(2)	
Matěj Hrabina	29.04.1993	26	(1)	
Adam Rychlý	25.09.1998	7	(2)	
Dominik Simerský	29.09.1992	20		
Martin Sus	15.03.1990	9	(6)	1
Jan Žídek	04.07.1985	32		3
Midfielders:	**DOB**	**M**	**(s)**	**G**
Bojan Đorđić (SRB)	26.05.1994	13		2
Václav Jurečka	26.06.1994	7		1
Tomáš Jursa	09.03.1989	17	(8)	
Jan Řezníček	22.11.1992	15	(5)	1
Jan Schaffartzik	15.12.1987	16	(8)	
Filip Souček	18.09.2000	15	(6)	1
Jaroslav Svozil	09.09.1993	15		
Bronislav Stáňa	12.11.1993	1	(9)	
Adam Ščudla	28.12.2001		(1)	
Pavel Šulc	29.12.2000	9	(6)	
Jiří Texl	03.01.1993	7	(5)	
Petr Zapalač	30.04.1987	7	(10)	
Pavel Zavadil	30.04.1978	24		1
Forwards:	**DOB**	**M**	**(s)**	**G**
Endy Bernadina (NED)	03.05.1995		(5)	
René Dedič (SVK)	07.08.1993	19	(3)	4
Václav Juřena	02.02.1991	11	(10)	1
Dominik Kuča	11.02.2002		(2)	
Budge Manzia (COD)	24.09.1994	3	(3)	
Karol Mondek (SVK)	02.06.1991	20	(10)	1
Lukáš Železník	18.06.1990	6	(4)	1

1. Fotbalový Klub Příbram

Founded: 1928
Stadium: Stadion Na Litavce, Příbram (9,100)
Trainer: Roman Nádvorník 21.03.1973
[25.02.2020] Petr Cuhel 04.01.1965
[11.03.2020] Pavel Horvath 22.04.1975

Goalkeepers:	DOB	M	(s)	G
Marek Boháč	31.10.1988	10		
Ondřej Kočí	07.04.1995	14		
Martin Melichár	06.07.2000	9		
Defenders:	**DOB**	**M**	**(s)**	**G**
Mihailo Cmiljanović (SRB)	15.06.1994	21	(3)	
Soufiane Dramé (FRA)	27.02.1996	15	(6)	1
Tomáš Jablonský	21.06.1987		(2)	
Petr Janota	23.03.2000		(1)	
Juan Olivier Simo Kingue (CMR)	20.02.1996	11		
Peter Kleščík (SVK)	18.09.1988	4	(2)	
Marek Kodr	17.08.1996	20		2
Jan Kvída	17.01.1991	9	(1)	
Jiří Mezera	21.07.2000	1		
Martin Nový	23.06.1993	17	(1)	2
Lukáš Pazdera	06.03.1987	4	(8)	
David Šimek	15.02.1998	19	(1)	
Jaroslav Tregler	20.01.1995	29	(1)	1
Stefan Vilotic (SRB)	16.10.1999		(1)	
Midfielders:	**DOB**	**M**	**(s)**	**G**
Marko Alvir (CRO)	19.04.1994	17	(1)	2
Emmanuel Antwi (GHA)	05.05.1996	11	(4)	1
Pavel Hájek	03.08.2001	1	(9)	
Dominik Kříž	25.09.1999	2	(8)	
Roman Květ	17.12.1997	2	(1)	
Paulo Manuel Neves Alves „Paulinho" (POR)	25.12.1997		(1)	
Adam Petrák	20.08.1999	3		1
Karel Soldát	07.11.1993	21	(5)	
Martin Zeman	28.03.1989	16	(1)	
Filip Zorvan	07.04.1996	12	(1)	
Forwards:	**DOB**	**M**	**(s)**	**G**
Sunday Damilare Adetunji (NGA)	10.12.1997	1		
Jan Díl	28.02.1997		(2)	
Martin Jindráček	29.11.1989	3	(4)	
Dušan Pinc	01.05.1998	2	(3)	
Matěj Polidar	20.12.1999	31	(1)	1
Jan Rezek	05.05.1982	28		1
Miroslav Slepička	10.11.1981	5	(10)	
Filip Stuparević (SRB)	30.08.2000		(9)	
Jakub Šašinka	02.10.1995		(2)	
Michal Škoda	01.03.1988	20	(8)	7
Radek Voltr	28.11.1991	5	(11)	1

Sportovní Klub Sigma Olomouc

Founded: 1919 (*as FK Hejčín Olomouc*)
Stadium: Stadion Andrův, Olomouc (12,483)
Trainer: Radoslav Látal   06.01.1970

Goalkeepers:	DOB	M	(s)	G
Miloš Buchta	19.07.1980	4		
Aleš Mandous	21.04.1992	16		
Michal Reichl	14.09.1992	13		
Defenders:	**DOB**	**M**	**(s)**	**G**
Vít Beneš	12.08.1988	24		1
Václav Jemelka	23.06.1995	31		3
Milan Kerbr	10.09.1989	8	(4)	1
Martin Sladký	01.03.1992	18	(3)	
Jan Štěrba	08.07.1994	10	(4)	
Michal Vepřek	17.06.1985	23		1
David Zima	08.11.2000	1	(1)	
Midfielders:	**DOB**	**M**	**(s)**	**G**
Radim Breite	10.08.1989	9	(1)	
Kryštof Daněk	05.01.2003	1	(2)	
Šimon Falta	24.03.1993	26	(5)	2
Lukáš Greššák (SVK)	23.01.1989	19	(3)	

	DOB	M	(s)	G
Martin Hála	24.03.1992	17	(7)	2
David Houska	29.06.1993	31	(1)	3
Radek Látal	16.12.1997	5	(5)	
Václav Pilař	13.10.1988	10	(5)	1
Jakub Plšek	13.12.1993	20		7
Jiří Texl	03.01.1993	2	(11)	
Tomáš Zahradníček	11.08.1993	12	(13)	1
Tomáš Zlatohlávek	22.05.2000		(1)	
Ondřej Zmrzlý	22.04.1999	9	(10)	
Forwards:	**DOB**	**M**	**(s)**	**G**
Mojmír Chytil	29.04.1999	12	(6)	1
Lukáš Juliš	02.12.1994	10	(2)	8
Martin Nešpor	05.06.1990	6	(5)	3
Pablo González Juárez (ESP)	12.05.1993	16	(6)	1
Ismar Tandir (BIH)	19.08.1995		(4)	
Jakub Yunis	25.03.1996	10	(10)	

Sportovní klub Slavia Praha

Founded: 02.11.1902 (*as Akademický cyklistický odbor Slavia*)
Stadium: Stadion Sinobo, Praha (19,370)
Trainer: Jindřich Trpišovský   27.02.1976

Goalkeepers:	DOB	M	(s)	G
Ondřej Kolář	17.10.1994	32		
Přemysl Kovář	14.10.1985	1		
Jakub Markovič	13.07.2001	2		
Defenders:	**DOB**	**M**	**(s)**	**G**
Jan Bořil	11.01.1991	28		1
Vladimír Coufal	22.08.1992	32		3
Michal Frydrych	27.02.1990	13	(10)	1
Tomáš Holeš	31.03.1993	12	(3)	1
David Hovorka	07.08.1993	9		
Ondřej Kúdela	26.03.1987	30		2
Mohamed Tijani (CIV)	10.07.1997	2		
Jaroslav Zelený	20.08.1992	5	(2)	
David Zima	08.11.2000	12		1
Midfielders:	**DOB**	**M**	**(s)**	**G**
Alexandru Mihail Băluță (ROU)	13.09.1993	1		
Lukáš Červ	10.04.2001		(1)	
Oscar Dorley (LBR)	19.07.1998	3	(3)	
Patrik Hellebrand	16.05.1999	2	(8)	
Jakub Hora	23.02.1991	1	(3)	

	DOB	M	(s)	G
Josef Hušbauer	16.03.1990	18		5
Daniel Kosek	19.05.2001	1		
Alex Král	19.05.1998	2	(4)	
Lukáš Masopust	12.02.1993	21	(6)	6
Tomáš Souček	27.02.1995	17		8
Petr Ševčík	04.05.1994	22	(2)	6
Nicolae Claudiu Stanciu (ROU)	07.05.1993	25	(6)	4
Laco Takács	15.07.1996	9	(4)	1
Ibrahim Traoré (CIV)	16.09.1988	13	(12)	3
Jaromír Zmrhal	02.08.1993	3		1
Forwards:	**DOB**	**M**	**(s)**	**G**
João Felipe Silva Estevam Aguiar (BRA)	24.06.2001		(1)	
Petar Musa (CRO)	04.03.1998	7	(7)	7
Peter Oladeji Olayinka (NGA)	16.11.1995	17	(3)	4
Lukáš Provod	23.10.1996	14	(6)	2
Milan Škoda	16.01.1986	5	(9)	5
Stanislav Tecl	01.09.1990	14	(9)	3
Mick van Buren (NED)	24.08.1992	6	(8)	1
Abdulla Yusuf (BHR)	12.06.1993	6	(11)	2

1. Fudbalový Klub Slovácko Uherské Hradiště

Founded: 1927 (*as SK Staré Město*)
Stadium: Městský fotbalový stadion "Miroslava Valenty", Uherské Hradiště (8,000)
Trainer: Martin Svědík   27.06.1974

Goalkeepers:	DOB	M	(s)	G
Vít Nemrava	09.01.1996	1		
Radek Porcal	05.02.1988	4	(1)	
Matouš Trmal	02.10.1998	27		
Defenders:	**DOB**	**M**	**(s)**	**G**
Josef Divíšek	24.09.1990	21	(3)	
Stanislav Hofmann	17.06.1990	27		2
Michal Kadlec	13.12.1984	26	(1)	
Jiří Krejčí	22.03.1986	2	(9)	
Petr Reinberk	23.05.1989	27	(1)	2
Patrik Šimko (SVK)	08.07.1991	7	(6)	1
Tomáš Vincour	02.01.2001		(1)	
Ondřej Zahustel	18.06.1991		(6)	1
Midfielders:	**DOB**	**M**	**(s)**	**G**
Vlastimil Daníček	15.07.1991	29		3
Marek Havlík	08.07.1995	31	(1)	3

	DOB	M	(s)	G
Patrik Hellebrand	16.05.1999	3	(8)	1
Jan Juroška	02.03.1993	11	(7)	1
Michal Kohút	04.06.2000	3	(5)	
Daniel Mareček	30.05.1998	1	(3)	
Jan Navrátil	13.04.1990	30	(1)	
Milan Petržela	19.06.1983	25	(2)	4
Marek Polášek	18.05.2001		(1)	
Lukáš Sadílek	23.05.1996	13	(10)	1
Tomáš Vasiljev	11.07.1994		(2)	
Forwards:	**DOB**	**M**	**(s)**	**G**
Pavel Dvořák	19.02.1989	9	(8)	
Václav Jurečka	26.06.1994	5	(4)	1
Jan Kalabiška	22.12.1986	12	(15)	4
Jan Kliment	01.09.1993	1	(2)	
Ondřej Šašinka	21.03.1998	14	(2)	5
Tomáš Zajíc	12.08.1996	23	(4)	7

Football Club Slovan Liberec

Founded: 1958
Stadium: Stadion u Nisy, Liberec (9,900)
Trainer: Pavel Hoftych   09.05.1967

Goalkeepers:	DOB	M	(s)	G
Milan Knobloch	23.08.1992	3		
Filip Nguyen	14.09.1992	33		
Defenders:	**DOB**	**M**	**(s)**	**G**
Matěj Chaluš	02.02.1998	7	(2)	
Miroslav Dvořák	18.12.1998	1	(2)	
Michal Fukala	22.10.2000	9	(6)	
Matěj Hybš	03.01.1993	25		
Taras Kacharaba (UKR)	07.01.1995	31	(1)	
Ondřej Karafiát	01.12.1994	28	(1)	
Jan Mikula	05.01.1992	33		1
Midfielders:	**DOB**	**M**	**(s)**	**G**
Akhmed Alibekov (UKR)	29.05.1998	9	(5)	
Alexandru Mihail Băluță (ROU)	13.09.1993	21		4
Radim Breite	10.08.1989	15	(2)	2
Michal Beran	22.08.2000	4	(8)	1
Radim Černický	18.02.2001	1	(3)	
Oscar Murphy Dorley (LBR)	19.07.1998	13	(2)	1
Bojan Đorđić (SRB)	26.05.1994		(4)	

	DOB	M	(s)	G
Jakub Hromada (SVK)	25.05.1996	10	(3)	
Martin Koscelník (SVK)	02.03.1995	12	(4)	1
Tomáš Malínský	25.08.1991	28	(4)	7
Kamso Mara (GUI)	24.12.1994	31	(3)	7
Kristian Michal	26.11.2000	3	(4)	
Aleš Nešický	01.06.1992	1	(4)	
Martin Zeman	28.03.1989	5	(8)	
Forwards:	**DOB**	**M**	**(s)**	**G**
Dominik Gembický	26.07.1999		(2)	
Milan Králíček	18.07.2001		(3)	1
Jan Kuchta	08.01.1997	15	(8)	6
Petar Musa (CRO)	04.03.1998	11	(6)	7
Jan Pázler	10.01.1991	1	(1)	
Jakub Pešek	24.06.1993	23	(11)	7
Roman Potočný	25.04.1991	19		9
Imad Rondić (BIH)	16.02.1999	3	(12)	
Elvis Sukisa (COD)	06.06.1994	1	(4)	
Yoo Kang-hyun (KOR)	27.04.1996		(2)	

Athletic Club Sparta Praha

Founded: 16.11.1893
Stadium: Generali Arena, Praha (18,887)
Trainer: Václav Jílek   16.05.1976
[18.02.2020]   Václav Kotal   02.10.1952

Goalkeepers:	DOB	M	(s)	G
Milan Heča	23.03.1991	24		
Florin Constantin Niță (ROU)	03.07.1987	11		
Defenders:	**DOB**	**M**	**(s)**	**G**
Dávid Hancko (SVK)	13.12.1997	18	(1)	2
Matěj Hanousek	02.06.1993	18	(8)	
Daniel Horák	10.10.2000		(1)	
Semih Kaya (TUR)	24.02.1991	9	(1)	2
David Lischka	15.08.1997	13	(1)	
Costa Nhamoinesu (ZIM)	06.01.1986	7	(2)	1
Vojtěch Patrák	13.03.2000		(1)	
Uroš Radaković (SRB)	31.03.1994	3		
Lukáš Štetina (SVK)	28.07.1991	16	(1)	
Andreas Vindheim (NOR)	04.08.1995	12	(9)	2
Ondřej Zahustel	18.06.1991	1		
Midfielders:	**DOB**	**M**	**(s)**	**G**
Bořek Dočkal	30.09.1988	12	(1)	1

	DOB	M	(s)	G
Martin Frýdek	24.03.1992	20	(5)	2
Martin Hašek	03.10.1995	14	(2)	5
Guélor Kanga Kaku (GAB)	01.09.1990	28	(3)	12
Adam Karabec	02.07.2003	4	(6)	1
Ladislav Krejčí	20.04.1999	19	(4)	1
Georges Mandjeck (CMR)	09.12.1988	11	(5)	
Michal Sáček	19.09.1996	32	(3)	2
Michal Trávník	17.05.1994	18	(10)	
Forwards:	**DOB**	**M**	**(s)**	**G**
Václav Drchal	25.07.1999	2	(1)	
Martin Graiciar	11.04.1999	1	(7)	
Adam Hložek	25.07.2002	33	(1)	7
Lukáš Juliš	02.12.1994		(4)	
Libor Kozák	30.05.1989	19	(12)	14
David Moberg-Karlsson (SWE)	20.03.1994	13	(4)	4
Srđan Plavšić (SRB)	03.12.1995	14	(6)	1
Benjamin Tetteh (GHA)	10.07.1997	13	(20)	8

Fotbalový klub Teplice

Founded: 1945
Stadium: Stadion Na Stínadlech, Teplice (18,221)
Trainer: Stanislav Hejkal   03.01.1970

Goalkeepers:	DOB	M	(s)	G
Tomáš Grigar	01.02.1983	33		
Defenders:	**DOB**	**M**	**(s)**	**G**
Pavel Čmovš	29.06.1990	26	(1)	
Matěj Hýbl	24.08.1994	3	(1)	
Alois Hyčka	22.07.1990	13	(5)	
Michal Jeřábek	10.09.1993	10		
Jan Knapík	11.12.2000	8	(3)	1
Manel Royo Castell (ESP)	28.02.1994	1	(3)	
Evgeniy Nazarov (RUS)	07.04.1997	9	(7)	
Igor Paradin (RUS)	10.09.1998	12	(5)	
Tomáš Vondrášek	26.10.1987	24	(2)	2
Midfielders:	**DOB**	**M**	**(s)**	**G**
Jakub Emmer	30.03.2001		(1)	
Jakub Hora	23.02.1991	6		1
Petr Kodeš	31.01.1996	17	(2)	

	DOB	M	(s)	G
Tomáš Kučera	20.07.1991	29	(3)	1
Admir Ljevakovič (BIH)	07.08.1984	5	(9)	
Lukáš Mareček	17.04.1990	8	(1)	
Petr Mareš	17.01.1991	17	(5)	2
Matěj Radosta	10.05.2001	3	(10)	
Jan Shejbal	20.04.1994	23	(1)	3
Daniel Trubač	17.07.1997	15	(3)	3
Patrik Žitný	21.01.1999	25	(5)	4
Forwards:	**DOB**	**M**	**(s)**	**G**
David Černý	10.12.1995	3	(7)	
Martin Jindráček	29.11.1989	1	(7)	
Jakub Mareš	26.01.1987	26	(3)	7
Pavel Moulis	07.04.1991	17	(7)	1
Jakub Řezníček	26.05.1988	25		12
Martins Toutou (FRA)	13.03.1996		(2)	
Pavel Vyhnal	25.05.1990	4	(10)	

Football Club Viktoria Plzeň

Founded: 11.06.1911
Stadium: Doosan Arena, Plzeň (11,700)
Trainer: Pavel Vrba   06.12.1963
[01.01.2020] Adrian Gula (SVK)   29.06.1975

Goalkeepers:	DOB	M	(s)	G
Aleš Hruška	23.11.1985	34		
Jindřich Staněk	27.04.1996	1		
Defenders:	**DOB**	**M**	**(s)**	**G**
Jakub Brabec	06.08.1992	32		1
Milan Havel	07.08.1994	8	(4)	2
Lukáš Hejda	09.03.1990	27	(1)	1
Adam Hloušek	20.12.1988	13	(5)	1
Roman Hubník	06.06.1984	1	(4)	
David Limberský	06.10.1983	20		1
Luděk Pernica	16.06.1990	10	(7)	2
Radim Řezník	20.01.1989	28	(2)	
Midfielders:	**DOB**	**M**	**(s)**	**G**
Marko Alvir (CRO)	19.04.1994		(2)	
Pavel Bucha	11.03.1998	12	(2)	4
Aleš Čermák	01.10.1994	20		8
Iván Santiago Díaz (ARG)	23.01.1993		(1)	
Christián Herc (SVK)	30.09.1998		(1)	
Tomáš Hořava	29.05.1988	19	(7)	2
Patrik Hrošovský (SVK)	22.04.1992	4		
Dominik Janošek	13.06.1998	2	(8)	
Lukáš Kalvach	19.07.1995	33		5
Jan Kopic	04.06.1990	24	(5)	7
Jan Kovařík	19.06.1988	21	(7)	4
Roman Procházka (SVK)	14.03.1989	12		3
Forwards:	**DOB**	**M**	**(s)**	**G**
Jean-David Beauguel (FRA)	21.03.1992	10	(11)	6
Tomáš Chorý	26.01.1995	6	(26)	6
Joel Ngandu Kayamba (COD)	17.04.1992	23	(3)	1
Michal Krmenčík	15.03.1993	19	(1)	10
Ondřej Mihálik	02.04.1997	6	(17)	4

Football Club Fastav Zlín

Founded: 1919
Stadium: Stadion Letná, Zlín (5,783)
Trainer: Josef Csaplár   29.10.1962
[07.10.2019] Jan Kameník   25.01.1982
[10.03.2020] Bohumil Páník   31.12.1956

Goalkeepers:	DOB	M	(s)	G
Stanislav Dostál	20.06.1991	19		
Matej Rakovan (SVK)	14.03.1990	14		
Defenders:	**DOB**	**M**	**(s)**	**G**
Oleksandr Azatskyi (UKR)	13.01.1994	11	(3)	
Ondřej Bačo	25.03.1996	2	(3)	
Lukáš Bartošák	03.07.1990	19	(7)	
Petr Buchta	15.07.1992	32	(1)	
Martin Cedidla	22.11.2001	15	(8)	
Andro Giorgadze (GEO)	03.05.1996	1	(1)	
Jakub Kolar	16.01.2000	1	(1)	1
Róbert Matejov (SVK)	05.07.1988	24	(2)	2
Dominik Simerský	29.09.1992	13		2
Midfielders:	**DOB**	**M**	**(s)**	**G**
Vakhtang Chanturishvili (GEO)	05.08.1993	21	(4)	
Cheick Conde (GUI)	26.07.2000	6	(5)	
Adnan Džafić (BIH)	10.05.1990	16	(13)	3
Antonín Fantiš	15.04.1992	25	(5)	3
Zdeněk Folprecht	01.07.1991	8		
Marek Hlinka (SVK)	04.10.1990	24		
Josef Hnaníček	28.12.1986	7	(4)	
Jakub Janetzký	12.06.1997	11	(11)	1
Petr Jiráček	02.03.1986	28	(2)	2
Dominik Mašek	10.07.1995	11	(2)	2
Martin Nečas	04.09.1998	2	(4)	
Pedro Martínez García (ESP)	09.02.1996		(4)	
Pablo Joaquín Podio (ARG)	07.08.1989	11	(1)	1
Forwards:	**DOB**	**M**	**(s)**	**G**
Šimon Chwaszcz	28.05.1996		(1)	
Dāvis Ikaunieks (LVA)	07.01.1994		(2)	
Lamin Jawo (GAM)	15.03.1995	6	(7)	1
Petr Pejša	13.08.1997		(1)	
Tomáš Poznar	27.09.1988	26	(2)	9
Patrik Slaměna	07.07.2000		(1)	
Tomáš Wágner	06.03.1990	8	(2)	2
Lukáš Železník	18.06.1990	2	(13)	

SECOND LEVEL
Czech National Football League 2019/2020

1.	FK Pardubice (*Promoted*)	30	22	4	4	55	-	19	70
2.	FC Zbrojovka Brno (*Promoted*)	30	20	7	3	75	-	29	67
3.	FK Dukla Praha	30	19	2	9	62	-	40	59
4.	FC Hradec Králové	30	15	9	6	54	-	29	54
5.	FK Viktoria Žižkov	30	15	4	11	45	-	40	49
6.	FC Vysočina Jihlava	30	14	7	9	59	-	46	49
7.	FK Ústí nad Labem	30	11	8	11	46	-	47	41
8.	FC Sellier & Bellot Vlašim	30	11	4	15	32	-	43	37
9.	SK Líšeň Brno	30	8	12	10	49	-	47	36
10.	MFK Chrudim	30	10	6	14	44	-	61	36
11.	1. SK Prostějov	30	8	11	11	33	-	42	35
12.	FC Slavoj Vyšehrad	30	9	6	15	40	-	55	33
13.	FK Fotbal Třinec	30	7	10	13	40	-	55	31
14.	FK Varnsdorf	30	6	8	16	37	-	65	26
15.	FK Baník Sokolov (*Relegated*)	30	7	5	18	34	-	51	26
16.	MFK Vítkovice (*Relegated*)	30	4	5	21	35	-	71	17

NATIONAL TEAM

INTERNATIONAL MATCHES
(16.07.2019 – 15.07.2020)

07.09.2019	Pristina	Kosovo - Czech Republic	2-1(1-1)	(ECQ)
10.09.2019	Podgorica	Montenegro - Czech Republic	0-3(0-0)	(ECQ)
11.10.2019	Praha	Czech Republic - England	2-1(1-1)	(ECQ)
14.10.2019	Praha	Czech Republic - Northern Ireland	2-3(0-3)	(F)
14.11.2019	Plzeň	Czech Republic - Kosovo	2-1(0-0)	(ECQ)
17.11.2019	Sofia	Bulgaria - Czech Republic	1-0(0-0)	(ECQ)

07.09.2019   KOSOVO - CZECH REPUBLIC   **2-1(1-1)**   16th EC. Qualifiers

Stadiumi „Fadil Vokrri", Prishtinë; Referee: Danny Desmond Makkelie (Netherlands); Attendance: 12,678
CZE: Tomáš Vaclík, Marek Suchý (Cap), Ondřej Čelůstka, Jan Bořil, Pavel Kadeřábek, Vladimír Darida, Lukáš Masopust (80.Martin Doležal), Tomáš Souček, Alex Král (72.Josef Hušbauer), Jakub Jankto, Patrik Schick (61.Michael Krmenčík). Trainer: Jaroslav Šilhavý.
Goal: Patrik Schick (16).

10.09.2019   MONTENEGRO - CZECH REPUBLIC   **0-3(0-0)**   16th EC. Qualifiers

Stadion pod Goricom, Podgorica; Referee: Ali Palabıyık (Turkey); Attendance: 5,951
CZE: Tomáš Vaclík, Marek Suchý (46.Jakub Brabec), Ondřej Čelůstka, Jan Bořil, Vladimír Coufal, Vladimír Darida, Lukáš Masopust (77.Jan Kopic), Tomáš Souček, Alex Král, Jakub Jankto, Patrik Schick (90+2.Michael Krmenčík). Trainer: Jaroslav Šilhavý.
Goals: Tomáš Souček (54), Lukáš Masopust (58), Vladimír Darida (90+5 penalty).

11.10.2019   CZECH REPUBLIC - ENGLAND   **2-1(1-1)**   16th EC. Qualifiers

Stadion Sinobo, Praha; Referee: Damir Skomina (Slovenia); Attendance: 18,651
CZE: Tomáš Vaclík, Ondřej Čelůstka, Jakub Brabec, Jan Bořil, Vladimír Coufal, Vladimír Darida (Cap), Lukáš Masopust (90.Jaromír Zmrhal), Tomáš Souček, Alex Král, Jakub Jankto (82.Jan Kopic), Patrik Schick (65.Zdenek Ondrášek). Trainer: Jaroslav Šilhavý.
Goals: Jakub Brabec (9), Zdenek Ondrášek (85).

14.10.2019   CZECH REPUBLIC - NORTHERN IRELAND   **2-3(0-3)**   Friendly International

Stadion Letná, Praha; Referee: Ivan Kružliak (Slovakia); Attendance: 9,139
CZE: Jiří Pavlenka, Ondřej Kúdela, Radim Řezník, Stefan Simić (46.Ondřej Čelůstka), Jan Kopic, Josef Hušbauer (Cap) (66.Patrik Schick), Ladislav Krejčí (75.Lukáš Masopust), Jaromír Zmrhal (46.Jan Bořil), Lukáš Kalvach (46.Vladimír Darida), Alex Král, Michael Krmenčík (46.Zdenek Ondrášek). Trainer: Jaroslav Šilhavý.
Goals: Vladimír Darida (67), Alex Král (68).

14.11.2019   CZECH REPUBLIC - KOSOVO   **2-1(0-0)**   16th EC. Qualifiers

Štruncovy sady Stadion, Plzeň; Referee: Gianluca Rocchi (Italy); Attendance: 10,986
CZE: Tomáš Vaclík, Ondřej Čelůstka, Jakub Brabec, Jan Bořil, Vladimír Coufal, Vladimír Darida (Cap), Lukáš Masopust (76.Petr Ševčík), Tomáš Souček, Alex Král, Jakub Jankto (90+1.Pavel Kadeřábek), Michael Krmenčík (61.Zdenek Ondrášek). Trainer: Jaroslav Šilhavý.
Goals: Alex Král (71), Ondřej Čelůstka (79).

17.11.2019   BULGARIA - CZECH REPUBLIC   **1-0(0-0)**   16th EC. Qualifiers

Nationalen Stadion "Vasil Levski", Sofia; Referee: Referee: Sergei Karasev (Russia); Attendance: *played behind closed doors*
CZE: Ondřej Kolář, Ondřej Kúdela, Ondřej Čelůstka, Jan Bořil, Pavel Kadeřábek, Vladimír Darida (Cap), Petr Ševčík (66.Lukáš Masopust), Tomáš Souček, Alex Král (71.Josef Hušbauer), Jakub Jankto, Zdenek Ondrášek (79.Martin Doležal). Trainer: Jaroslav Šilhavý.

NATIONAL TEAM PLAYERS
(16.07.2019 – 15.07.2020)

Name	DOB	Caps	Goals	2019/2020:	Club
Goalkeepers					
Ondřej KOLÁŘ	17.10.1994	1	0	2019:	SK Slavia Praha
Jiří PAVLENKA	14.04.1992	11	0	2019:	SV Werder Bremen (GER)
Tomáš VACLÍK	29.03.1989	29	0	2019:	Sevilla FC (ESP)
Defenders					
Jan BOŘIL	11.01.1991	15	0	2019:	SK Slavia Praha
Jakub BRABEC	06.08.1992	17	1	2019:	FC Viktoria Plzeň
Vladimír COUFAL	22.08.1992	7	0	2019:	SK Slavia Praha
Ondřej ČELŮSTKA	18.06.1989	18	2	2019:	Antalyaspor Kulübü (TUR)
Pavel KADEŘÁBEK	25.04.1992	42	3	2019:	TSG 1899 Hoffenheim (GER)
Ondřej KÚDELA	26.03.1987	3	0	2019:	SK Slavia Praha
Radim ŘEZNÍK	20.01.1989	3	0	2019:	FC Viktoria Plzeň
Stefan SIMIĆ	20.01.1995	2	0	2019:	HNK Hajduk Split (CRO)
Marek SUCHÝ	29.03.1988	44	1	2019:	FC Augsburg (GER)
Midfielders					
Vladimír DARIDA	08.08.1990	61	6	2019:	Hertha BSC Berlin (GER)
Josef HUŠBAUER	16.03.1990	21	1	2019:	SK Slavia Praha
Jakub JANKTO	19.01.1996	26	3	2019:	UC Sampdoria Genova (ITA)
Lukáš KALVACH	19.07.1995	1	0	2019:	FC Viktoria Plzeň
Jan KOPIC	04.06.1990	19	3	2019:	FC Viktoria Plzeň
Alex KRÁL	19.05.1998	9	2	2019:	FK Spartak Moskva (RUS)
Ladislav KREJČÍ	05.07.1992	41	5	2019:	Bologna FC 1909 (ITA)
Lukáš MASOPUST	12.02.1993	11	1	2019:	SK Slavia Praha
Tomáš SOUČEK	27.02.1995	25	3	2019:	SK Slavia Praha
Petr ŠEVČÍK	04.05.1994	2	0	2019:	SK Slavia Praha
Jaromír ZMRHAL	02.08.1993	15	1	2019:	Brescia Calcio (ITA)
Forwards					
Martin DOLEŽAL	03.05.1990	5	0	2019:	FK Jablonec
Michael KRMENČÍK	15.03.1993	23	8	2019:	FC Viktoria Plzeň
Zdenek ONDRÁŠEK	22.12.1988	4	1	2019:	FC Dallas (USA)
Patrik SCHICK	24.01.1996	22	9	2019:	RasenBallsport Leipzig (GER)
National team coach					
Jaroslav ŠILHAVÝ [from 18.09.2019]	03.11.1961	14 M; 8 W; 0 D; 6 L; 20-19			

DENMARK

The Country:
Kongeriget Danmark (Kingdom of Denmark)
Capital: København
Surface: 42,925 km^2
Inhabitants: 5,814,461 [2019]
Time: UTC+1

The FA:
Dansk Boldspil-Union
House of Football, DBU Allé 1, 2605 Brøndby
Tel: +45 43 262 222
Foundation date: 18.05.1889
Member of FIFA since: 1904
Member of UEFA since: 1954
Website: www.dbu.dk

NATIONAL TEAM RECORDS

RECORDS

First international match:	19.10.1908, London:	France – Denmark 0-9 (5th OG. 1st Round)
Most international caps:	Peter Schmeichel	- 129 caps (1987-2001)
Most international goals:	Jon Dahl Tomasson	- 52 goals / 112 caps (1997-2008)
	Poul "Tist" Nielsen	- 52 goals / 38 caps (1910-1925)

UEFA EUROPEAN CHAMPIONSHIP

1960	Qualifiers
1964	Final Tournament (4th Place)
1968	Qualifiers
1972	Qualifiers
1976	Qualifiers
1980	Qualifiers
1984	Final Tournament (Semi-Finals)
1988	Final Tournament (Group Stage)
1992	**Final Tournament (Winners)**
1996	Final Tournament (Group Stage)
2000	Final Tournament (Group Stage)
2004	Final Tournament (Quarter-Finals)
2008	Qualifiers
2012	Final Tournament (Group Stage)
2016	Qualifiers
2020	*Final Tournament (Qualified)*

FIFA WORLD CUP

1930	Did not enter
1934	Did not enter
1938	Did not enter
1950	Did not enter
1954	Did not enter
1958	Qualifiers
1962	Did not enter
1966	Qualifiers
1970	Qualifiers
1974	Qualifiers
1978	Qualifiers
1982	Qualifiers
1986	Final Tournament (2nd Round of 16)
1990	Qualifiers
1994	Qualifiers
1998	Final Tournament (Quarter-Finals)
2002	Final Tournament (2nd Round of 16)
2006	Qualifiers
2010	Final Tournament (Group Stage)
2014	Qualifiers
2018	Final Tournament (2nd Round of 16)

OLYMPIC TOURNAMENTS

1908	Runners-up
1912	Runners-up
1920	First Round
1924	Did not enter
1928	Did not enter
1936	Did not enter
1948	3rd Place
1952	Quarter-Finals
1956	Did not enter
1960	Runners-up
1964	Qualifiers
1968	Did not enter
1972	Second Round
1976	Qualifiers
1980	Qualifiers
1984	Qualifiers
1988	Qualifiers
1992	Group Stage
1996	Qualifiers
2000	Qualifiers
2004	Qualifiers
2008	Qualifiers
2012	Qualifiers
2016	Quarter-Finals

UEFA NATIONS LEAGUE

2018/2019 – League B (promoted to League A)

FIFA CONFEDERATIONS CUP 1992-2017

1995 (Winners)

DANISH CLUB HONOURS IN EUROPEAN CLUB COMPETITIONS:

European Champion Clubs' Cup (1956-1992) / UEFA Champions League (1993-2020)
None

Fairs Cup (1858-1971) / UEFA Cup (1972-2009) / UEFA Europa League (2010-2020)
None

UEFA Super Cup (1972-2019)
None

*European Cup Winners' Cup 1961-1999**
None

defunct competition

NATIONAL COMPETITIONS
TABLE OF HONOURS

		CHAMPIONS	CUP WINNERS*	BEST GOALSCORERS	
1912/1913		Kjøbenhavns Boldklub	-	-	
1913/1914		Kjøbenhavns Boldklub	-	-	
1914/1915		*No competition*	-	-	
1915/1916		B 93 København	-	-	
1916/1917		Kjøbenhavns Boldklub	-	-	
1917/1918		Kjøbenhavns Boldklub	-	-	
1918/1919		Akademisk BK København	-	-	
1919/1920		B 1903 København	-	-	
1920/1921		Akademisk BK København	-	-	
1921/1922		Kjøbenhavns Boldklub	-	-	
1922/1923		BK Frem København	-	-	
1923/1924		B 1903 København	-	-	
1924/1925		Kjøbenhavns Boldklub	-	-	
1925/1926		B 1903 København	-	-	
1926/1927		B 93 København	-	-	
1927/1928		*No competition*	-		
1928/1929		B 93 København	-	*Not available*	
1929/1930		B 93 København	-	*Not available*	
1930/1931		BK Frem København	-	*Not available*	
1931/1932		Kjøbenhavns Boldklub	-	*Not available*	
1932/1933		BK Frem København	-	*Not available*	
1933/1934		B 93 København	-	*Not available*	
1934/1935		B 93 København	-	*Not available*	
1935/1936		BK Frem København	-	*Not available*	
1936/1937		Akademisk BK København	-	Pauli Jørgensen (BK Frem København)	19
1937/1938		B 1903 København	-	Knud Andersen (B 1903 København)	23
1938/1939		B 93 København	-	Erik Petersen (B 93 København)	27
1939/1940		Kjøbenhavns Boldklub	-	Frede Jensen (Køge BK) Kaj Hansen (B 93 København)	12
1940/1941		BK Frem København	-	-	
1941/1942		B 93 København	-	-	
1942/1943		Akademisk BK København	-	-	
1943/1944		BK Frem København		-	
1944/1945		Akademisk BK København	-	-	
1945/1946		B 93 København	-	Jørgen Leschly Sørensen (B 93 København)	16
1946/1947		Akademisk BK København	-	Helge Broneé (Østerbros Boldklub)	21
1947/1948		Kjøbenhavns Boldklub	-	John Hansen (BK Frem København)	20
1948/1949		Kjøbenhavns Boldklub	-	Jørgen Leschly Sørensen (Odense Boldklub)	16
1949/1950		Kjøbenhavns Boldklub	-	James Rønvang (Akademisk BK København)	15
1950/1951		Akademisk BK København	-	James Rønvang (Akademisk BK København) Henning Bjerregaard (B 93 København) Jens Peter Hansen (Esbjerg fB)	11
1951/1952		Akademisk BK København	-	Valdemar Kendzior (Skovshoved IF) Poul Erik Petersen (Køge BK)	13
1952/1953		Kjøbenhavns Boldklub	-	Valdemar Kendzior (Skovshoved IF)	17
1953/1954		Køge BK	-	Jens-Carl Kristensen (Akademisk BK København)	12
1954/1955		AGF Aarhus	AGF Aarhus	Henning Jensen (BK Frem København)	17
1955/1956		AGF Aarhus	BK Frem København	Gunnar Kjeldberg (AGF Aarhus)	18
1956/1957		AGF Aarhus	AGF Aarhus	Søren Andersen (BK Frem København)	27
1958		Vejle Boldklub	Vejle Boldklub	Henning Enoksen (Vejle Boldklub)	27
1959		B 1909 Odense	Vejle Boldklub	Per Jensen (Kjøbenhavns Boldklub)	20
1960		AGF Aarhus	AGF Aarhus	Harald Nielsen (Frederikshavn fI)	19
1961		Esbjerg fB	AGF Aarhus	Jørgen Ravn (Kjøbenhavns Boldklub)	26
1962		Esbjerg fB	B 1909 Odense	Henning Enoksen (AGF Aarhus) Carl Emil Christiansen (Esbjerg fB)	24
1963		Esbjerg fB	B 1913 Odense	Mogens Haastrup (B 1909 Odense)	21
1964		B 1909 Odense	Esbjerg fB	Jørgen Ravn (Kjøbenhavns Boldklub)	21
1965		Esbjerg fB	AGF Aarhus	Per Petersen (B 1903 København)	18
1966		Hvidovre IF	Aalborg BK	Henning Enoksen (AGF Aarhus)	16
1967		Akademisk BK København	Randers Freja	Leif Nielsen (BK Frem København)	15
1968		Kjøbenhavns Boldklub	Randers Freja	Niels-Christian Holmstrøm (Kjøbenhavns Boldklub)	23
1969		B 1903 København	Kjøbenhavns Boldklub	Steen Rømer Larsen (B 1903 København)	15
1970		B 1903 København	Aalborg BK	Ole Forsing (B 1903 København)	18
1971		Vejle Boldklub	B 1909 Odense	Uffe Brage (Kjøbenhavns Boldklub) John Nielsen (B 1901 Nykøbing)	19
1972		Vejle Boldklub	Vejle Boldklub	Karsten Lund (Vejle Boldklub) John Nielsen (B 1901 Nykøbing)	16
1973		Hvidovre IF	Randers Freja	Hans Aabech (Hvidovre IF)	28
1974		Kjøbenhavns Boldklub	Vanløse IF	Niels-Christian Holmstrøm (Kjøbenhavns Boldklub)	24
1975		Køge BK	Vejle Boldklub	Bjarne Petersen (Kjøbenhavns Boldklub)	25
1976		B 1903 København	Esbjerg fB	Mogens Jespersen (Aalborg BK)	22

1977	Odense Boldklub	Vejle Boldklub	Allan Hansen (Odense Boldklub)	23
1978	Vejle Boldklub	BK Frem København	John Eriksen (Odense Boldklub)	22
1979	Esbjerg fB	B 1903 København	John Eriksen (Odense Boldklub)	20
1980	Kjøbenhavns Boldklub	Hvidovre IF	Hans Aabech (Kjøbenhavns Boldklub)	19
1981	Hvidovre IF	Vejle Boldklub	Allan Hansen (Odense Boldklub)	28
1982	Odense Boldklub	B 93 København	Ib Jacquet (Vejle Boldklub)	20
1983	Lyngby Boldklub	Odense Boldklub	Vilhelm Munk Nielsen (Odense Boldklub)	20
1984	Vejle Boldklub	Lyngby Boldklub	Steen Thychosen (Vejle Boldklub)	24
1985	Brøndby IF	Lyngby Boldklub	Lars Bastrup (Ikast FS)	20
1986	AGF Aarhus	B 1903 København	Claus Nielsen (Brøndby IF)	16
1987	Brøndby IF	AGF Aarhus	Claus Nielsen (Brøndby IF)	20
1988	Brøndby IF	AGF Aarhus	Bent Christensen (Brøndby IF)	21
1989	Odense Boldklub	Brøndby IF	Miklos Molnar (BK Frem København) Flemming Christensen (Lyngby Boldklub) Lars Jakobsen (Odense Boldklub)	14
1990	Brøndby IF	Lyngby Boldklub	Bent Christensen (Brøndby IF)	17
1991	Brøndby IF	Odense Boldklub	Bent Christensen (Brøndby IF)	11
1991/1992	Lyngby Boldklub	AGF Aarhus	Peter Møller (Aalborg BK)	17
1992/1993	FC København	Odense Boldklub	Peter Møller (Aalborg BK)	22
1993/1994	Silkeborg IF	Brøndby IF	Søren Frederiksen (Silkeborg IF)	18
1994/1995	Aalborg BK	FC København	Erik Bo Andersen (Aalborg BK)	24
1995/1996	Brøndby IF	AGF Aarhus	Thomas Thorninger (AGF Aarhus)	20
1996/1997	Brøndby IF	FC København	Miklos Molnar (Lyngby Boldklub)	26
1997/1998	Brøndby IF	Brøndby IF	Ebbe Sand (Brøndby IF)	28
1998/1999	Aalborg BK	Akademisk BK København	Heine Fernandez (Viborg FF)	23
1999/2000	Herfølge BK	Viborg FF	Peter Lassen (Silkeborg IF)	16
2000/2001	FC København	Silkeborg IF	Peter Graulund (Brøndby IF)	21
2001/2002	Brøndby IF	Odense Boldklub	Peter Madsen (Brøndby IF) Kaspar Dalgas (Odense Boldklub)	22
2002/2003	FC København	Brøndby IF	Søren Frederiksen (Viborg FF) Jan Kristiansen (Esbjerg fB)	18
2003/2004	FC København	FC København	Steffen Højer (Odense Boldklub) Mohamed Zidan (EGY, FC Midtjylland Herning) Tommy Bechmann (Esbjerg fB) Mwape Miti (ZAM, Odense Boldklub)	19
2004/2005	Brøndby IF	Brøndby IF	Steffen Højer (Odense Boldklub)	20
2005/2006	FC København	Randers FC	Steffen Højer (Viborg FF)	16
2006/2007	FC København	Odense Boldklub	Rade Prica (SWE, Aalborg BK)	19
2007/2008	Aalborg BK	Brøndby IF	Jeppe Lund Curth (Aalborg BK)	17
2008/2009	FC København	FC København	Morten Nordstrand (FC København) Marc Nygaard (Randers FC)	16
2009/2010	FC København	FC Nordsjælland Farum	Peter Maduabuchi Utaka (NGA, Odense Boldklub)	18
2010/2011	FC København	FC Nordsjælland Farum	Dame N'Doye (SEN, FC København)	25
2011/2012	FC Nordsjælland Farum	FC København	Dame N'Doye (SEN, FC København)	18
2012/2013	FC København	Esbjerg fB	Andreas Evald Cornelius (FC København)	18
2013/2014	Aalborg BK	Aalborg BK	Thomas Dalgaard (Viborg FF)	18
2014/2015	FC Midtjylland Herning	FC København	Martin Pušić (AUT, Esbjerg fB / FC Midtjylland Herning)	17
2015/2016	FC København	FC København	Lukas Spalvis (LTU, Aalborg BK)	18
2016/2017	FC København	FC København	Marcus Ingvartsen (FC Nordsjælland Farum)	23
2017/2018	FC Midtjylland Herning	Brøndby IF	Pål Alexander Kirkevold (NOR, Hobro IK)	22
2018/2019	FC København	FC Midtjylland Herning	Robert Skov (FC København)	29
2019/2020	FC Midtjylland Herning	Sønderjysk Elitesport	Ronnie Schwartz (Silkeborg IF / FC Midtjylland Herning)	18

*Cup competition called Landspokalturneringen (1954-1989), Giro Cup (1898-1996), Compaq Cup (1996-1999), DONG Cup (1999-2004), Landspokalturneringen (2004-2008), Ekstra Bladet Cup (2008-2011) and DBU Pokalen (since 2011).

NATIONAL CHAMPIONSHIP
Alka Superligaen 2019/2020
(12.07.2019 – 26.07.2020)

Regular Season - Results

Round 1 [12-15.07.2019]
FC Midtjylland - Esbjerg fB 1-0(0-0)
SønderjyskE - Randers FC 2-1(1-0)
AC Horsens - FC Nordsjælland 0-3(0-1)
Lyngby BK - Aalborg BK 2-0(1-0)
Odense BK - FC København 2-3(2-1)
Brøndby IF - Silkeborg IF 3-0(2-0)
Hobro IK - AGF Aarhus 1-1(0-0)

Round 2 [19-22.07.2019]
FC København - AGF Aarhus 2-1(1-0)
Silkeborg IF - AC Horsens 0-3(0-2)
Aalborg BK - SønderjyskE 1-1(0-0)
Esbjerg fB - Hobro IK 1-1(1-0)
Randers FC - Brøndby IF 2-2(1-1)
FC Midtjylland - FC Nordsjælland 2-1(1-1)
Odense BK - Lyngby BK 4-1(1-1)

Round 3 [26-29.07.2019]
Lyngby BK - SønderjyskE 0-3(0-0)
AC Horsens - FC København 0-2(0-0)
Hobro IK - Randers FC 2-2(1-1)
FC Nordsjælland - Esbjerg fB 2-0(0-0)
AGF Aarhus - FC Midtjylland 0-1(0-0)
Brøndby IF - Odense BK 3-2(1-1)
Aalborg BK - Silkeborg IF 3-1(3-0)

Round 4 [02-05.08.2019]
Silkeborg IF - Hobro IK 2-3(1-1)
SønderjyskE - FC København 1-2(0-1)
Randers FC - FC Nordsjælland 3-1(3-0)
Esbjerg fB - Odense BK 0-1(0-0)
Brøndby IF - AC Horsens 1-2(1-1)
FC Midtjylland - Aalborg BK 1-0(0-0)
Lyngby BK - AGF Aarhus 2-1(0-1)

Round 5 [09-12.08.2019]
FC København - Lyngby BK 2-0(0-0)
Odense BK - Randers FC 1-0(0-0)
FC Nordsjælland - Silkeborg IF 2-2(0-2)
Aalborg BK - Esbjerg fB 4-0(4-0)
AC Horsens - FC Midtjylland 0-2(0-1)
Hobro IK - Brøndby IF 0-2(0-0)
SønderjyskE - AGF Aarhus 0-0

Round 6 [16-19.08.2019]
Randers FC - FC København 0-1(0-0)
FC Nordsjælland - Odense BK 2-0(1-0)
Silkeborg IF - SønderjyskE 3-3(1-0)
Esbjerg fB - Lyngby BK 1-0(1-0)
FC Midtjylland - Hobro IK 1-1(0-0)
Brøndby IF - Aalborg BK 2-1(1-0)
AGF Aarhus - AC Horsens 2-0(1-0)

Round 7 [23-26.08.2019]
Hobro IK - Odense BK 0-0
Lyngby BK - Randers FC 2-0(1-0)
Esbjerg fB - Silkeborg IF 2-2(1-1)
SønderjyskE - FC Midtjylland 0-2(0-1)
Brøndby IF - AGF Aarhus 0-3(0-0)
FC København - FC Nordsjælland 3-1(1-1)
AC Horsens - Aalborg BK 0-5(0-2)

Round 8 [30.08.-01.09.2019]
Odense BK - SønderjyskE 0-0
FC Nordsjælland - Hobro IK 2-1(2-1)
AGF Aarhus - Esbjerg fB 1-0(1-0)
Randers FC - Silkeborg IF 2-0(1-0)
AC Horsens - Lyngby BK 2-1(0-1)
Aalborg BK - FC København 1-0(1-0)
FC Midtjylland - Brøndby IF 1-0(1-0)

Round 9 [13-16.09.2019]
SønderjyskE - AC Horsens 0-0
AGF Aarhus - Aalborg BK 3-0(2-0)
Esbjerg fB - Randers FC 0-3(0-1)
Lyngby BK - FC Midtjylland 0-3(0-1)
Hobro IK - FC København 2-1(2-1)
Brøndby IF - FC Nordsjælland 4-2(2-0)
Silkeborg IF - Odense BK 0-3(0-2)

Round 10 [20-23.09.2019]
Odense BK - AGF Aarhus 1-2(0-1)
Hobro IK - SønderjyskE 1-1(0-1)
FC Nordsjælland - Aalborg BK 2-1(2-0)
Silkeborg IF - Lyngby BK 2-3(2-1)
Esbjerg fB - Brøndby IF 3-1(2-1)
FC København - FC Midtjylland 0-0
Randers FC - AC Horsens 2-1(2-1)

Round 11 [27-30.09.2019]
Lyngby BK - Hobro IK 2-1(1-0)
FC København - Silkeborg IF 4-2(4-0)
AGF Aarhus - FC Nordsjælland 3-1(1-1)
Aalborg BK - Randers FC 0-3(0-1)
FC Midtjylland - Odense BK 0-1(0-0)
SønderjyskE - Brøndby IF 2-1(1-0)
AC Horsens - Esbjerg fB 1-1(1-0)

Round 12 [04-06.10.2019]
FC Nordsjælland - Lyngby BK 1-1(1-0)
Hobro IK - Aalborg BK 0-2(0-1)
Esbjerg fB - SønderjyskE 1-2(0-0)
Brøndby IF - FC København 3-1(2-1)
Odense BK - AC Horsens 3-0(2-0)
Randers FC - AGF Aarhus 2-0(0-0)
Silkeborg IF - FC Midtjylland 1-2(0-1)

Round 13 [18-21.10.2019]
Aalborg BK - Odense BK 1-0(1-0)
AC Horsens - Hobro IK 1-0(0-0)
SønderjyskE - FC Nordsjælland 1-4(1-1)
AGF Aarhus - Silkeborg IF 3-4(2-2)
FC København - Esbjerg fB 3-1(1-0)
Lyngby BK - Brøndby IF 0-3(0-1)
FC Midtjylland - Randers FC 2-1(0-0)

Round 14 [25-28.10.2019]
Esbjerg fB - FC Midtjylland 1-2(0-0)
Hobro IK - Silkeborg IF 1-1(1-1)
Odense BK - FC Nordsjælland 3-1(2-0)
Lyngby BK - AC Horsens 2-1(0-1)
Brøndby IF - Randers FC 5-2(3-2)
SønderjyskE - Aalborg BK 1-3(1-0)
AGF Aarhus - FC København 1-2(0-1)

Round 15 [01-04.11.2019]
Esbjerg fB - AC Horsens 1-1(1-1)
Randers FC - Lyngby BK 2-1(1-0)
Odense BK - Hobro IK 2-1(2-1)
FC Nordsjælland - AGF Aarhus 0-1(0-0)
Aalborg BK - FC Midtjylland 0-1(0-1)
FC København - SønderjyskE 3-0(1-0)
Silkeborg IF - Brøndby IF 0-1(0-1)

Round 16 [08-10.11.2019]
Randers FC - Aalborg BK 3-3(2-1)
AC Horsens - Silkeborg IF 2-1(1-1)
Hobro IK - FC Nordsjælland 2-2(1-1)
AGF Aarhus - SønderjyskE 4-2(2-0)
Lyngby BK - Odense BK 4-3(2-1)
Brøndby IF - Esbjerg fB 2-1(2-0)
FC Midtjylland - FC København 4-1(2-0)

Round 17 [22-25.11.2019]
FC Nordsjælland - Randers FC 3-0(0-0)
SønderjyskE - Lyngby BK 2-2(1-1)
Aalborg BK - AC Horsens 4-0(0-0)
Silkeborg IF - Esbjerg fB 1-2(1-0)
FC København - Hobro IK 2-1(0-1)
AGF Aarhus - Brøndby IF 2-1(1-0)
Odense BK - FC Midtjylland 1-2(0-2)

Round 18 [29.11.-02.12.2019]
Lyngby BK - FC Nordsjælland 1-1(0-1)
FC København - Brøndby IF 2-1(1-1)
Randers FC - SønderjyskE 3-0(1-0)
AC Horsens - Odense BK 2-1(0-1)
Esbjerg fB - AGF Aarhus 1-2(0-1)
Aalborg BK - Hobro IK 1-1(1-1)
FC Midtjylland - Silkeborg IF 2-1(1-0)

Round 19 [06-09.12.2019]
Hobro IK - AC Horsens 0-0
Silkeborg IF - Randers FC 2-1(1-1)
SønderjyskE - Esbjerg fB 2-1(0-1)
AGF Aarhus - Lyngby BK 1-1(1-1)
FC Nordsjælland - FC København 0-1(0-1)
Brøndby IF - FC Midtjylland 1-2(0-0)
Odense BK - Aalborg BK 0-0

Round 20 [13-16.12.2019]
Aalborg BK - FC Nordsjælland 1-3(0-2)
AC Horsens - SønderjyskE 2-1(2-0)
Randers FC - Esbjerg fB 3-0(2-0)
Lyngby BK - Silkeborg IF 1-0(0-0)
Brøndby IF - Hobro IK 1-1(1-1)
FC Midtjylland - AGF Aarhus 1-3(1-0)
FC København - Odense BK 2-1(0-1)

Round 21 [14-19.02.2020]
Esbjerg fB - FC København 1-0(1-0)
SønderjyskE - Hobro IK 3-1(2-0)
Silkeborg IF - Aalborg BK 0-2(0-0)
Odense BK - Brøndby IF 0-2(0-1)
FC Midtjylland - Lyngby BK 2-0(1-0)
FC Nordsjælland - AC Horsens 6-0(2-0)
AGF Aarhus - Randers FC 1-1(0-1) [28.05.]

Round 22 [21-24.02.2020]
Hobro IK - FC Midtjylland 0-2(0-0)
FC Nordsjælland - SønderjyskE 2-1(0-1)
Randers FC - Odense BK 0-0
Lyngby BK - Esbjerg fB 2-0(1-0)
Silkeborg IF - FC København 1-1(1-0)
Aalborg BK - Brøndby IF 3-2(0-0)
AC Horsens - AGF Aarhus 1-2(1-1)

Round 23 [28.02.-02.03.2020]
AGF Aarhus - Hobro IK 0-0
Esbjerg fB - FC Nordsjælland 1-2(1-2)
AC Horsens - Randers FC 1-2(1-1)
Odense BK - Silkeborg IF 1-1(1-0)
Brøndby IF - Lyngby BK 1-0(0-0)
FC København - Aalborg BK 3-2(0-0)
FC Midtjylland - SønderjyskE 3-0(3-0)

Round 24 [08.03.2020]
Hobro IK - Esbjerg fB 1-1(0-0)
SønderjyskE - Odense BK 1-1(0-1)
Aalborg BK - Lyngby BK 3-0(3-0)
FC København - AC Horsens 0-1(0-0)
FC Nordsjælland - Brøndby IF 2-2(1-2)
Randers FC - FC Midtjylland 0-2(0-2)
Silkeborg IF - AGF Aarhus 2-1(2-0)

Round 25 [29.05.-02.06.2020]
Silkeborg IF - FC Nordsjælland 0-2(0-2)
Esbjerg fB - Aalborg BK 1-1(0-0)
Randers FC - Hobro IK 0-1(0-1)
FC Midtjylland - AC Horsens 0-1(0-1)
Lyngby BK - FC København 1-4(0-1)
AGF Aarhus - Odense BK 1-0(0-0)
Brøndby IF - SønderjyskE 1-0(0-0)

Round 26 [07.06.2020]
FC København - Randers FC 2-1(2-0)
SønderjyskE - Silkeborg IF 2-2(1-1)
Aalborg BK - AGF Aarhus 2-3(0-1)
Odense BK - Esbjerg fB 3-1(3-0)
AC Horsens - Brøndby IF 3-2(0-1)
FC Nordsjælland - FC Midtjylland 0-1(0-1)
Hobro IK - Lyngby BK 2-2(0-1)

Final Standings

1.	FC Midtjylland Herning	26	21	2	3	42	-	14	65
2.	FC København	26	18	2	6	47	-	29	56
3.	AGF Aarhus	26	14	5	7	42	-	28	47
4.	Brøndby IF	26	13	3	10	47	-	37	42
5.	FC Nordsjælland Farum	26	12	5	9	48	-	35	41
6.	Aalborg BK	26	11	5	10	44	-	33	38
7.	Randers FC	26	10	5	11	39	-	35	35
8.	AC Horsens	26	10	4	12	25	-	44	34
9.	Odense Boldklub	26	9	6	11	34	-	30	33
10.	Lyngby Boldklub	26	9	5	12	31	-	45	32
11.	Sønderjysk Elitesport	26	6	9	11	31	-	44	27
12.	Hobro IK	26	3	14	9	25	-	35	23
13.	Esbjerg fB	26	4	6	16	22	-	44	18
14.	Silkeborg IF	26	3	7	16	31	-	55	16

Teams ranked 1-6 were qualified for the Championship Round, while teams ranked 7-14 were qualified for the Relegation Round.

Championship Round

Results

Round 27 [14.06.2020]
Aalborg BK - FC Midtjylland 0-2(0-2)
FC Nordsjælland - FC København 1-1(0-1)
Brøndby IF - AGF Aarhus 0-0

Round 28 [17-18.06.2020]
AGF Aarhus - FC Nordsjælland 2-1(2-0)
FC København - Aalborg BK 2-0(2-0)
FC Midtjylland - Brøndby IF 0-0

Round 29 [20-21.06.2020]
Aalborg BK - FC Nordsjælland 0-4(0-2)
Brøndby IF - FC København 1-1(0-0)
FC Midtjylland - AGF Aarhus 3-4(1-1)

Round 30 [26-28.06.2020]
AGF Aarhus - Aalborg BK 1-4(1-3)
FC Nordsjælland - Brøndby IF 0-2(0-1)
FC København - FC Midtjylland 1-2(0-1)

Round 31 [05.07.2020]
FC Nordsjælland - FC Midtjylland 0-1(0-0)
Aalborg BK - Brøndby IF 2-0(1-0)
AGF Aarhus - FC København 1-0(0-0)

Round 32 [09.07.2020]
Brøndby IF - FC Nordsjælland 4-0(2-0)
Aalborg BK - AGF Aarhus 1-0(1-0)
FC Midtjylland - FC København 3-1(0-1)

Round 33 [12.07.2020]
FC Nordsjælland - Aalborg BK 0-0
FC København - Brøndby IF 0-0
AGF Aarhus - FC Midtjylland 3-0(1-0)

Round 34 [17-19.07.2020]
FC Midtjylland - FC Nordsjælland 6-3(1-2)
Brøndby IF - Aalborg BK 0-1(0-1)
FC København - AGF Aarhus 2-4(1-2)

Round 35 [22-23.07.2020]
FC Nordsjælland - AGF Aarhus 1-1(0-0)
Brøndby IF - FC Midtjylland 1-1(1-1)
Aalborg BK - FC København 0-1(0-0)

Round 36 [26.07.2020]
FC Midtjylland - Aalborg BK 1-2(0-2)
FC København - FC Nordsjælland 2-1(1-1)
AGF Aarhus - Brøndby IF 0-1(0-0)

Final Standings

		Total								Home							Away					
1.	**FC Midtjylland Herning**	36	26	4	6	61	-	29	82	11	2	5	33	-	20	15	2	1	28	-	9
2.	FC København	36	21	5	10	58	-	42	68	13	2	3	35	-	19	8	3	7	23	-	23
3.	AGF Aarhus	36	19	7	10	58	-	41	64	10	3	5	29	-	19	9	4	5	29	-	22
4.	Brøndby IF	36	16	8	12	56	-	42	56	10	4	4	33	-	20	6	4	8	23	-	22
5.	Aalborg BK	36	16	6	14	54	-	44	54	9	2	7	27	-	22	7	4	7	27	-	22
6.	FC Nordsjælland Farum	36	13	8	15	59	-	54	47	7	6	5	26	-	16	6	2	10	33	-	38

Relegation Round

Group A - Results

Round 27 [14-15.06.2020]
SønderjyskE - Lyngby BK 1-0(0-0)
Silkeborg IF - Odense BK 6-0(2-0)

Round 28 [16.06.2020]
Odense BK - SønderjyskE 2-0(2-0)
Lyngby BK - Silkeborg IF 0-0

Round 29 [21-22.06.2020]
Silkeborg IF - SønderjyskE 1-2(1-0)
Lyngby BK - Odense BK 1-2(1-1)

Round 30 [27-29.06.2020]
SønderjyskE - Silkeborg IF 1-0(0-0)
Odense BK - Lyngby BK 3-1(0-1)

Round 31 [04.07.2020]
Silkeborg IF - Lyngby BK 2-0(0-0)
SønderjyskE - Odense BK 1-1(0-0)

Round 32 [08.07.2020]
Odense BK - Silkeborg IF 1-3(0-2)
Lyngby BK - SønderjyskE 1-1(0-1)

Group B - Results

Round 27 [12-13.06.2020]
Esbjerg fB - Randers FC 4-2(3-2)
Hobro IK - AC Horsens 1-1(1-1)

Round 28 [18.06.2020]
AC Horsens - Esbjerg fB 2-2(1-1)
Randers FC - Hobro IK 4-0(2-0)

Round 29 [20-21.06.2020]
AC Horsens - Randers FC 0-0
Esbjerg fB - Hobro IK 1-3(1-0)

Round 30 [28.06.2020]
Randers FC - AC Horsens 0-3(0-1)
Hobro IK - Esbjerg fB 2-1(0-1)

Round 31 [03-05.07.2020]
Esbjerg fB - AC Horsens 1-2(1-1)
Hobro IK - Randers FC 2-3(1-2)

Round 32 [08.07.2020]
Randers FC - Esbjerg fB 3-1(0-1)
AC Horsens - Hobro IK 3-2(1-2)

Final Standings

Group A

				Total			Home					Away				
1. Odense Boldklub	32	12	7	13	43 - 42	43	8	3	5	27 - 18		4	4	8	16 - 24
2. Sønderjysk Elitesport	32	9	11	12	37 - 49	38	6	6	4	20 - 21		3	5	8	17 - 28
3. Lyngby Boldklub (*Relegation Play-offs*)	32	9	7	16	34 - 54	34	8	3	5	21 - 23		1	4	11	13 - 31
4. Silkeborg IF (*Relegated*)	32	6	8	18	43 - 59	26	4	2	10	23 - 29		2	6	8	20 - 30

Group B

				Total			Home					Away				
1. AC Horsens	32	13	7	12	36 - 50	46	7	3	6	20 - 27		6	4	6	16 - 23
2. Randers FC	32	13	6	13	51 - 45	45	9	3	4	29 - 16		4	3	9	22 - 29
3. Hobro IK (*Relegation Play-offs*)	32	5	15	12	35 - 48	30	2	10	4	17 - 22		3	5	8	18 - 26
4. Esbjerg fB (*Relegated*)	32	5	7	20	32 - 58	22	4	4	8	20 - 25		1	3	12	12 - 33

<u>Please note</u>: Winners and runners-up of both groups were qualified for the European Play-offs.

Top goalscorers:	
18 Ronnie Schwartz	***Silkeborg IF / FC Midtjylland Herning***
17 Kamil Wilczek (POL)	*Brøndby IF*
17 Patrick Mortensen	*AGF Aarhus*
12 Sander Svendsen (NOR)	*Odense Boldklub*
11 Mohammed Kudus (GHA)	*FC Nordsjælland Farum*
10 Mikkel Damsgaard	*FC Nordsjælland Farum*

Europa League Play-offs [11-29.07.2020]

First Round	Randers FC - Odense Boldklub	2-1(0-1)	0-2(0-1)
Second Round	Odense Boldklub - AC Horsens	3-1(1-0)	1-1(0-0)
Europa League Play-off Final	AGF Aarhus - Odense Boldklub	2-1(1-0)	

Relegation Play-offs [13-20.07.2020]

Hobro IK - Lyngby Boldklub	1-2(1-0)	2-2(1-1)

Lyngby Boldklub remains at first level for 2020/2021.

NATIONAL CUP
DBU Pokalen / Sydbank Pokalen 2019/2020

First Round [06-08/13-14/28.08.2019]

Marstal/Rise - Kolding Boldklub	5-3 aet		Dalum IF - Kolding IF	0-3
Nørresundby BK - IF Lyseng	2-1		Hatting-Torsted Fodbold - FC Fredericia	0-5
Aarhus Fremad - Brabrand IF	2-3 aet		Allesø GF - Vejle BK	0-6
Fuglebakken KFUM - Vatanspor	3-1 aet		OKS Odense - FC Sydvest 05	1-2
Vildbjerg SF - Vejgaard BK	2-3 aet		FC Rudersdal - Hillerød GI	0-5
Sædding/Guldager - Tarup-Paarup IF	1-6		Frederiksberg BK - KFUMs BK København	3-2 aet
Flemløse/Hårby BK - Otterup B&IK	1-2		Holbæk B&I - Nykøbing FC	1-2
Chang Odense - FC Sønderborg	2-3 pen		Advedøre IF - Slagelse B&I	0-1
FC Sunshine - BK Frem København	0-3		Dronninglund IF - FC Djursland	0-3
BK Union København - B.93 København	1-0		Holstebro BK - Odder IGF	3-0
Herlev IF - Karlslunde IF	4-1		BK Skjold - BK Fremad Amager	0-1
Herstedøster IC - Taastrup FC	1-0		Lystrup IF - Skive IK	1-16
Eskilstrup BK - KFUMs BK Roskilde	0-12		Skagen IK - Thisted FC	0-8
FC Helsingør - AB Gladsaxe	0-2		BK Avarta - Skovshoved IF	4-2
Jammerbugt FC - Viborg FF	1-2 aet		Nordfalsters FB - FC Roskilde	1-7
BK Marienlyst - Hedensted IF	3-1		Vordingborg IK - Næstved BK	1-3
SfB-Oure FA - Middelfart Fodbold	0-1 aet		Skjold Birkerød - Vanløse IF	1-4
Jaegersborg BK - Hellerup IK	1-2 aet		Fårvang IF - Viby IF	2-3
FC 77 Næstved - Ledøje-Smørum Fodbold	0-8		Toreby-Grænge BK - HB Køge	0-9
Rønne IK - B 1908 Amager	0-2		BK Viktoria - Hundested IK	3-1
Ringkøbing IF - VSK Aarhus	0-1		Kjellerup IF - Vendsyssel FF Hjørring	0-9
KE Fodbold - Varde IF	2-3		Brønshøj BK - Hvidovre IF	1-2 aet

Second Round [03-05./10-11.09.2019]

Otterup B&IK - FC Sydvest 05	4-0		BK Avarta - BK Frem København	2-1
Vejgaard BK - Hobro IK	2-1		BK Union København - AC Horsens	0-2
FC Djursland - VSK Aarhus	1-4		Kolding IF - Randers FC	0-4
Fuglebakken KFUM - Viby IF	0-3		Slagelse B&I - AB Gladsaxe	1-2
Hillerød GI - Næstved BK	1-0		BK Viktoria - Sønderjysk Elitesport	0-5
Herstedøster IC - Hellerup IK	4-7		Middelfart Fodbold - Skive IK	0-2
Ledøje-Smørum Fodbold - Nykøbing FC	1-4		Varde IF - Thisted FC	3-4
Tarup-Paarup IF - FC Roskilde	0-3		B 1908 Amager - Hvidovre IF	2-5
KFUMs BK Roskilde - HB Køge	1-3		FC Sønderborg - Viborg FF	0-4
BK Marienlyst - Holstebro BK	2-1		Vendsyssel FF Hjørring - Vejle BK	1-0
Frederiksberg BK - Vanløse IF	2-3		Nørresundby FB - Aalborg BK	0-8
Brabrand IF - FC Fredericia	1-4		Marstal/Rise - AGF Aarhus	2-6 aet
Herlev IF - Silkeborg IF	1-3		BK Fremad Amager - Lyngby BK	5-4 pen

Third Round [24-26.09./01-03.10./09.10.2019]

Otterup B&IK - Odense Boldklub	0-2(0-1)		Skive IK - Brøndby IF	2-3(0-0,1-1)
Vejgaard BK - Aalborg BK	0-6(0-0)		VSK Aarhus - AGF Aarhus	1-3(1-0,1-1)
BK Avarta - FC Fredericia	2-4(2-2)		FC Roskilde - Randers FC	1-2(0-1)
Hillerød GI - FC København	1-1 aet; 2-4 pen		BK Fremad Amager - FC Midtjylland Herning	1-0(0-0)
BK Marienlyst - Esbjerg fB	2-5(1-1)		Viby IF - Vanløse IF	1-0(0-0)
AB Gladsaxe - Viborg FF	3-1(0-1,1-1)		Hellerup IK - Silkeborg IF	0-1(0-1)
Hvidovre IF - Sønderjysk Elitesport	2-4(0-2,2-2)		Thisted FC - AC Horsens	1-2(0-1)
HB Køge - Nykøbing FC	1-0(0-0)		Vendsyssel FF Hjørring - FC Nordsjælland	0-2(0-1)

1/8-Finals [11/30/31.10.-06/27.11.2019]

FC Fredericia - Silkeborg IF	3-4(2-1,3-3)		AGF Aarhus - Odense Boldklub	1-0(0-0)
Viby IF - Randers FC	0-2(0-0)		AB Gladsaxe - Esbjerg fB	1-2(1-0)
Brøndby IF - Sønderjysk Elitesport	0-1(0-0)		BK Fremad Amager - AC Horsens	0-3(0-1)
FC København - FC Nordsjælland	4-1(1-1)		HB Køge - Aalborg BK	0-3(0-1)

Quarter-Finals [03-05.03.2020]

Esbjerg fB - AGF Aarhus	1-4(0-2)		Randers FC - Sønderjysk Elitesport	1-2(1-0)
Aalborg BK - FC København	2-0(1-0)		AC Horsens - Silkeborg IF	1-1 aet; 8-7 pen

Semi-Finals [10.06.2020]

Sønderjysk Elitesport - AC Horsens	2-1(0-0)		Aalborg BK - AGF Aarhus	3-2(1-0)

Final

01.07.2020; Blue Water Arena, Esbjerg; Referee: Jørgen Daugbjerg Burchardt; Attendance: 1,750

Sønderjysk Elitesport - Aalborg BK   **2-0(1-0)**

Sønderjysk: Sebastian Mielitz, Pierre Kanstrup, Stefan Gartenmann, Eggert Jónsson (63.Patrick Banggaard), Mads Albæk (87.Emil Frederiksen), Christian Jakobsen (76.Rilwan Hassan), Julius Eskesen [sent off 65], Alexander Bah, Victor Sylvestre Mpindi Ekani (87.Rasmus Vinderslev), Johan Absalonsen, Anders Jacobsen. Trainer: Glen Riddersholm.

Aalborg BK: Andreas Hansen, Jakob Ahlmann Nielsen (59.Frederik Børsting), Rasmus Thelander, Jores Okore, Kristoffer Pallesen (81.Patrick Kristensen), Kasper Kusk, Patrick Olsen, Lucas Andersen (42.Søren Tengstedt), Iver Fossum, Magnus Christensen (46.Robert Kakeeto), Tom van Weert (59.Mathias Ross). Trainer: Jacob Friis.

Goals: 1-0 Anders Jacobsen (38), 2-0 Anders Jacobsen (56).

Please note: matches and goals includes statistics of both regular season and play-offs (Championship Round & Relegation Round).

Aalborg Boldspilklub

Founded: 13.05.1985
Stadium: Aalborg Portland Park (13,797)
Trainer: Jacob Friis   11.12.1976

Goalkeepers:	DOB	M	(s)	G
Andreas Hansen	11.08.1995	2	(1)	
Jacob Rinne (SWE)	20.06.1993	34		
Defenders:	**DOB**	**M**	**(s)**	**G**
Jakob Ahlmann	18.01.1991	23	(5)	
Anders Bærtelsen	09.05.2000	1	(1)	
Lukas Klitten	01.05.2000	6	(5)	
Patrick Kristensen	28.04.1987	13	(10)	
Jores Okore	11.08.1992	35		1
Kristoffer Pallesen	30.04.1990	30	(4)	2
Kasper Pedersen	13.01.1991	13	(5)	
Mathias Ross	15.01.2001	18	(5)	
Rasmus Thelander	09.07.1991	15	(5)	1
Midfielders:	**DOB**	**M**	**(s)**	**G**
Oliver Abildgaard Nielsen	10.06.1996	2	(9)	1
Frederik Børsting	13.02.1995	21	(9)	4
Magnus Christensen	20.08.1997	20	(7)	1
Iver Fossum (NOR)	15.07.1996	28	(1)	2
Malthe Højholt	16.04.2001	2	(2)	
Robert Kakeeto (UGA)	19.05.1995	9	(6)	
Kasper Kusk	10.11.1991	20	(12)	5
Patrick Olsen	23.04.1994	35		7
Jeppe Pedersen	03.03.2001		(2)	
Rasmus Thellufsen Pedersen	09.01.1997		(2)	
Forwards:	**DOB**	**M**	**(s)**	**G**
Wessam Abou Ali	04.01.1999		(2)	
Lucas Andersen	13.09.1994	24	(3)	10
Mikkel Kaufmann	03.01.2001	15	(2)	7
Oliver Klitten	01.05.2000	8	(11)	
Søren Tengstedt	30.06.2000	4	(8)	2
Tom van Weert (NED)	07.06.1990	18	(6)	10

Aarhus Gymnastikforening

Founded: 1880
Stadium: Ceres Park, Aarhus (20,032)
Trainer: David Nielsen   01.12.1976

Goalkeepers:	DOB	M	(s)	G
William Eskelinen (SWE)	03.09.1996	28		
Aleksandar Jovanović (SRB)	06.12.1992	6		
Kasper Kristensen	04.08.1999		(1)	
Óscar Alexander Whalley Guardado (ESP)	29.03.1994	2		
Defenders:	**DOB**	**M**	**(s)**	**G**
Magnus Anbo	18.09.2000		(4)	
Niklas Backman (SWE)	13.11.1988	21		
Kevin Diks (NED)	06.10.1996	9	(9)	1
Alexander Joseph Gersbach (AUS)	08.05.1997		(4)	
Sebastian Hausner	11.04.2000	17	(1)	
Casper Højer Nielsen	20.11.1994	35		4
Jesper Juelsgård	26.01.1989	8	(3)	1
Alexander Munksgaard	13.12.1997	28	(5)	1
Midfielders:	**DOB**	**M**	**(s)**	**G**
Mustafa Amini (AUS)	20.04.1993	19	(6)	2
Jakob Ankersen	22.09.1990	25	(10)	6
Bror Blume	22.01.1992	33	(2)	5
Zachary Duncan (AUS)	31.05.2000	7	(8)	
Albert Grønbæk Erlykke	23.05.2001	1	(7)	
Benjamin Hvidt	12.03.2000	14	(1)	
Kasper Lunding	17.07.1999	2	(1)	
Nikolai Poulsen	15.08.1993	29		
Tobias Sana	11.07.1989	1	(3)	
Frederik Tingager	22.02.1993	26	(1)	
Jón Dagur Þorsteinsson (ISL)	26.11.1998	22	(8)	8
Forwards:	**DOB**	**M**	**(s)**	**G**
Alexander Ballegaard Ammitzbøll	17.02.1999	1	(2)	
Mustapha Bundu (SLE)	27.02.1997	24	(3)	8
Nicklas Helenius	08.05.1991	7	(22)	3
Gift Links (RSA)	02.10.1998	1	(13)	
Patrick Mortensen	13.07.1989	30	(4)	17

Brøndbyernes Idrætsforening

Founded: 03.12.1964
Stadium: Brøndby Stadion, Brøndby (29,000)
Trainer: Niels Frederiksen   11.09.1968

Goalkeepers:	DOB	M	(s)	G
Marvin Schwäbe (GER)	25.04.1995	36		
Defenders:	**DOB**	**M**	**(s)**	**G**
Paulus Arajuuri (FIN)	15.06.1988	4		1
Andreas Bruus	16.01.1999	8	(4)	
Jens Gammelby	05.02.1995	14	(2)	
Hjörtur Hermannsson (ISL)	08.02.1995	22	(2)	
Anthony Jung (GER)	03.11.1991	32		3
Johan Erik Larsson (SWE)	05.05.1990	7	(2)	
Andreas Maxsø	18.03.1994	28		1
Kevin Mensah	15.05.1991	23	(3)	
Sigurd Rosted (NOR)	22.07.1994	23	(2)	1
Anton Skipper Hendriksen	31.03.2000	9	(2)	
Midfielders:	**DOB**	**M**	**(s)**	**G**
Anis Ben Slimane (TUN)	16.03.2001	10	(6)	1
Peter Bjur	02.02.2000		(3)	
Tobias Børkeeiet (NOR)	18.04.1999	1	(5)	
Kasper Fisker	22.05.1988	3	(7)	
Morten Frendrup	07.04.2001	19	(7)	
Dominik Kaiser (GER)	16.09.1988	20		8
Hany Mukhtar (GER)	21.03.1995	9	(3)	2
Josip Radošević (CRO)	03.04.1994	22	(5)	1
Simon Tibbling (SWE)	07.09.1994	8	(16)	1
Lasse Vigen	15.08.1994	17	(10)	1
Forwards:	**DOB**	**M**	**(s)**	**G**
Ante Erceg (CRO)	12.12.1989		(2)	
Simon Hedlund (SWE)	11.03.1993	30	(1)	5
Jesper Lindstrøm	29.02.2000	14	(14)	3
Samuel Mráz (SVK)	13.05.1997	10	(11)	4
Mikkel Uhre	30.09.1994	9	(16)	6
Kamil Wilczek (POL)	14.01.1988	18		17

Esbjerg forenede Boldklubber

Founded: 23.07.1924
Stadium: Blue Water Arena, Esbjerg (16,942)
Trainer: John Lammers (NED) 11.09.1973
[16.09.2019] Claus Nörgaard 17.12.1979
[28.10.2019] Lars Olsen 02.02.1961
[10.06.2020] Troels Bech 29.07.1966

Goalkeepers:	DOB	M	(s)	G
Jeppe Højbjerg	30.04.1995	20		
Vito Mannone (ITA)	02.03.1988	12		
Defenders:	**DOB**	**M**	**(s)**	**G**
Daniel Anyembe	22.07.1998	24	(3)	1
Rodolph Austin (JAM)	01.06.1985	27		1
Jeppe Brinch	08.05.1995	17	(6)	
Franz Brorsson (SWE)	30.01.1996	3	(4)	1
Kevin Conboy	15.10.1987	11		1
Markus Halsti (FIN)	19.03.1984	17	(1)	1
Jesper Lauridsen	27.03.1991	19		
Jonas Mortensen	16.01.2001	2	(1)	
Noah Nurmi (FIN)	06.02.2001		(1)	
Søren Reese	29.07.1993	10		
Viktor Tranberg	26.02.1997	1	(3)	
Midfielders:	**DOB**	**M**	**(s)**	**G**
Mark Brink	15.03.1998	3	(7)	
Joni Kauko (FIN)	12.07.1990	29	(1)	6
Matthias Kristensen	21.03.1997	16	(3)	
Mads Larsen	20.09.2001	1	(8)	1
Lasha Parunashvili (GEO)	14.02.1993	30	(1)	
Jacob Sørensen	03.03.1998	29		1
Forwards:	**DOB**	**M**	**(s)**	**G**
Mohammed Dauda (GHA)	20.02.1998	16	(6)	4
Patrick Egelund	02.08.2000	2	(14)	2
Ante Erceg (CRO)	12.12.1989	4	(3)	
Rafał Kurzawa (POL)	29.01.1993	12		2
Adrian Petre (ROU)	11.02.1998	9	(7)	3
Nicklas Røjkjær	24.07.1998	2	(7)	
Pyry Soiri (FIN)	22.09.1994	15	(9)	1
Yuriy Yakovenko (UKR)	03.09.1993	21	(4)	7

Hobro Idræts Klub

Founded: 13.06.1913
Stadium: DS Arena, Hobro (10,700)
Trainer: Peter Sørensen 24.03.1973

Goalkeepers:	DOB	M	(s)	G
Adrian Kappenberger	25.08.1996	1		
Jesper Rask	18.07.1988	31		
Defenders:	**DOB**	**M**	**(s)**	**G**
Anel Ahmedhodžić (SWE)	26.03.1999	19		1
Jesper Bøge	22.02.1990	28		
Nicholas Gotfredsen	05.02.1989	4	(8)	
Mathias Haarup	10.02.1996	23	(3)	
Simon Jakobsen	17.11.1990	9	(1)	1
Kerim Memija (BIH)	06.01.1996		(2)	
Rasmus Minor Petersen	13.09.1988	31	(1)	2
Brandon Onkony (SUI)	12.02.1997	4	(7)	
Jacob Tjørnelund	31.12.1991	6	(8)	1
Midfielders:	**DOB**	**M**	**(s)**	**G**
Jonas Brix-Damborg	17.04.1986	18	(3)	
Christian Cappis (USA)	13.08.1999	24	(4)	1
Hamse Hussein	07.01.2000	1	(3)	
Mikkel Mejlstrup Pedersen	07.01.1996	28	(3)	1
Emmanuel Sabbi (USA)	24.12.1997	26	(1)	7
Mathies Skjellerup	23.05.1996	1	(2)	1
Forwards:	**DOB**	**M**	**(s)**	**G**
Edgar Babayan	28.10.1995	29		4
Alexander Baun	18.11.1995		(1)	
Louicius Don Deedson (HAI)	11.02.2001		(7)	1
Mads Hvilsom	23.08.1992	3	(2)	1
Pål Kirkevold (NOR)	10.11.1990	24	(7)	6
Julian Kristoffersen (NOR)	10.05.1997	11	(10)	2
Imed Louati (TUN)	11.10.1993	18	(5)	5
Frans Dhia Putros (IRQ)	14.07.1993	6	(4)	
Yosef Samuel (USA)	03.07.1997		(5)	
Oliver Thychosen	17.01.1993	6	(11)	

Alliance Club Horsens

Founded: 1994
Stadium: CASA Arena, Horsens (10,400)
Trainer: Bo Henriksen 07.02.1975

Goalkeepers:	DOB	M	(s)	G
Matej Delač (CRO)	20.08.1992	18	(1)	
Michael Lansing (USA)	13.06.1994	14		
Defenders:	**DOB**	**M**	**(s)**	**G**
Sebastian Avanzini (ITA)	01.04.1995		(3)	
Rune Frantsen	15.10.1991	20	(9)	2
James Gomez (GAM)	14.11.2001		(2)	
Magnus Jensen	27.10.1996		(2)	
Malte Kiilerich	16.10.1995	30		2
Thomas Kortegaard	02.07.1984		(3)	
Alexander Ludwig	30.06.1993	24	(2)	2
Erhan Mašović (SRB)	22.11.1998	1	(17)	
Peter Nymann	22.08.1982	29		
Mikkel Qvist	22.04.1993	1	(4)	
Midfielders:	**DOB**	**M**	**(s)**	**G**
Jonas Gemmer	31.01.1996	2	(5)	
Hállur Hansson (FRO)	08.07.1992	25	(1)	6
Bjarke Jacobsen	21.08.1993	29		1
Jacob Dyrberg Linnet	17.04.1995		(4)	
Michael Lumb	09.01.1988	31		3
Sivert Nilsen (NOR)	02.10.1991	5		
Ayo Simon Okosun	21.07.1993	23		3
Matthias Præst	21.06.2000		(1)	
Peter Therkildsen	13.06.1998	11	(16)	3
Jonas Thorsen	19.04.1990	31	(1)	3
Forwards:	**DOB**	**M**	**(s)**	**G**
Nicolai Brock-Madsen	09.01.1993	22	(2)	3
Oliver Drost	04.11.1995		(6)	
Jeppe Kjær Jensen	01.03.2004	2	(5)	1
Kasper Junker	05.03.1994	1	(2)	
Jannik Pohl	06.04.1996	5	(3)	
Louka Prip Andreassen	29.06.1997	28	(3)	5

Football Club København

Founded: 01.07.1992
Stadium: Telia Parken, København (38,065)
Trainer: Ståle Solbakken (NOR) 27.02.1968

Goalkeepers:	DOB	M	(s)	G
Sten Grytebust (NOR)	25.10.1989	7		
Kalle Johnsson (SWE)	28.01.1990	29		
Defenders:	**DOB**	**M**	**(s)**	**G**
Karlo Bartolec (CRO)	20.04.1995	13	(11)	1
Pierre Bengtsson (SWE)	12.04.1988	28	(3)	1
Andreas Bjelland	11.07.1988	18	(3)	
Nicolai Boilesen	16.02.1992		(2)	
Victor Nelsson	14.10.1998	34		
Bryan Josué Oviedo Jiménez (CRC)	18.02.1990	5	(10)	
Sotirios Papagiannopoulos (SWE)	05.09.1990	19	(8)	
Ragnar Sigurðsson (ISL)	19.06.1986	2	(1)	
Guillermo Varela Olivera (URU)	24.03.1993	26	(1)	
Midfielders:	**DOB**	**M**	**(s)**	**G**
Rasmus Falk	15.01.1992	31		1
Viktor Fischer	09.06.1994	17	(3)	2
Robert Mudražija (CRO)	05.05.1997		(10)	
Pep Biel Mas Jaume (ESP)	05.09.1996	21	(8)	4
Jens Stage	08.11.1996	23	(8)	5
Nicolaj Thomsen	08.05.1993	6	(7)	
José Carlos Gonçalves Rodrigues „Zeca" (GRE)	31.08.1988	34	(1)	2
Forwards:	**DOB**	**M**	**(s)**	**G**
Nicklas Bendtner	16.01.1988	2	(4)	
Mohammed Daramy	07.01.2002	18	(11)	4
Carlo Holse	02.06.1999	2	(7)	
Mikkel Kaufmann	03.01.2001	10	(5)	1
Dame N'Doye (SEN)	21.02.1985	13	(1)	9
Michael Nicolás Santos Rosadilla (URU)	13.03.1993	16	(7)	7
Robert Skov	20.05.1996	2		
Pieros Sotiriou (CYP)	13.01.1993	9	(9)	9
Jonas Wind	07.02.1999	11	(2)	7

Lyngby Boldklub

Founded: 30.03.1921
Stadium: Lyngby Stadion, Lyngby (8,000)
Trainer: Christian Nielsen   09.01.1974

Goalkeepers:	DOB	M	(s)	G
Thomas Mikkelsen	27.08.1983	31		
Frederik Schram (ISL)	19.01.1995	1		
Defenders:	**DOB**	**M**	**(s)**	**G**
Patrick da Silva	23.10.1994	29		2
Kasper Enghardt	27.05.1992	26	(4)	1
Nicolai Geertsen	19.06.1991	27	(1)	2
Pascal Gregor	18.02.1994	12		
Kasper Jørgensen	07.11.1999	7	(12)	
Lasse Nielsen	03.03.1987	2	(7)	
Adam Sørensen	11.11.2000		(1)	
Kevin Tshiembe	31.03.1997	17	(4)	1
Frederik Winther	04.01.2001	27	(1)	
Midfielders:	**DOB**	**M**	**(s)**	**G**
Jesper Christjansen	20.12.1987	12	(7)	1
Frederik Gytkjær	16.03.1993	17	(5)	6

	DOB	M	(s)	G
Mathias Hebo Rasmussen	02.08.1995	10	(1)	1
Martin Ørnskov	10.10.1985	8	(3)	
Marcel Rømer	08.08.1991	20	(2)	2
Emilio Stuberg Simonsen	31.10.1999	1	(5)	1
Magnus Westergaard	27.05.1998	4	(15)	
Adnan Mohammad Yaqoob (PAK)	02.07.1996	3	(3)	
Forwards:	**DOB**	**M**	**(s)**	**G**
Rezan Corlu	07.08.1997	20	(5)	6
Lasse Fosgaard	06.09.1986	26		1
Emil Kornvig	28.04.2000		(2)	
Gustav Marcussen	12.06.1998	14	(12)	3
Emil Nielsen	08.11.1993	23	(4)	2
André Riel	21.10.1989	11	(7)	3
Ertuğrul Tekşen (TUR)	25.04.2000	1	(4)	
Magnus Warming	08.06.2000	2	(6)	2

Football Club Midtjylland Herning

Founded: 02.02.1999
Stadium: MCH Arena, Herning (11,800)
Trainer: Kenneth Andersen   23.10.1967
[19.08.2019] Brian Priske   14.05.1977

Goalkeepers:	DOB	M	(s)	G
Mikkel Andersen	17.12.1988	2	(1)	
Jesper Hansen	31.03.1985	34		
Defenders:	**DOB**	**M**	**(s)**	**G**
Joel Andersson (SWE)	11.11.1996	31		1
Dion Cools (BEL)	04.06.1996	2	(3)	
Kian Hansen	03.03.1989	1		
Marc Hende	06.11.1990	7	(2)	
Manjrekar James (CAN)	05.08.1993	3	(2)	
Rasmus Nicolaisen	16.03.1997	8	(8)	1
Paulo Victor da Silva „Paulinho" (BRA)	03.01.1991	15	(4)	1
Alexander Scholz	24.10.1992	34		3
Erik Sviatchenko	04.10.1991	32		7
Midfielders:	**DOB**	**M**	**(s)**	**G**
Mikael Anderson (ISL)	01.07.1998	21	(10)	4
Jens Cajuste (SWE)	10.08.1999	14	(10)	1
Nikolas Dyhr	18.06.2001	13	(2)	
Evander Da Silva Ferreira (BRA)	09.06.1998	29	(1)	8

	DOB	M	(s)	G
Awer Mabil (AUS)	15.09.1995	30	(4)	8
Nicolas Madsen	17.03.2000	2	(7)	
Emiliano Marcondes Camargo Hansen	09.03.1995	12		2
Ayo Simon Okosun	21.07.1993	4	(1)	1
Frank Ogochukwu Onyeka (NGA)	01.01.1998	30	(2)	3
Jakob Poulsen	07.07.1983		(1)	
Oliver Sørensen Jensen	10.03.2002		(2)	
Tim Sparv (FIN)	20.02.1987	8	(8)	
Lasse Vibe	22.02.1987	3	(10)	2
Gustav Wikheim (NOR)	18.03.1993	5	(2)	
Forwards:	**DOB**	**M**	**(s)**	**G**
Artem Dovbyk (UKR)	21.06.1997		(3)	
Anders Dreyer	02.05.1998	14	(2)	4
Gustav Isaksen	19.04.2001	5	(9)	
José Francisco dos Santos Júnior "Brumado" (BRA)	15.05.1999	8	(9)	
Sory Kaba (GUI)	28.07.1995	22	(8)	7
Ronnie Schwartz	29.08.1989	7	(8)	6
Aral Simsir	19.06.2002		(3)	

Football Club Nordsjælland Farum

Founded: 01.07.2003
Stadium: Right to Dream Park, Farum (9,900)
Trainer: Flemming Pedersen   30.06.1963

Goalkeepers:	DOB	M	(s)	G
Nicolai Larsen	09.03.1991	27		
Peter Vindahl Jensen	16.02.1998	9	(1)	
Defenders:	**DOB**	**M**	**(s)**	**G**
Clinton Antwi (GHA)	06.11.1999	11	(5)	
Kian Hansen	03.03.1989	30		2
Abdel Mumin (GHA)	06.06.1998	19	(7)	1
Mathias Rasmussen (NOR)	25.11.1997	10	(7)	3
Oliver Rose-Villadsen	16.11.2001	3	(8)	
Mads Thychosen	27.06.1997	28		2
Maxwell Woledzi (GHA)	02.07.2001	2	(2)	
Ulrik Yttergård Jenssen (NOR)	17.07.1996	31	(1)	1
Midfielders:	**DOB**	**M**	**(s)**	**G**
Mads Aaquist	31.12.1994	5		
Oliver Antman (FIN)	15.08.2001	1	(4)	1
Tochi Chukwuani	24.03.2003	2	(5)	1
Mikkel Damsgaard	03.07.2000	31	(4)	10

	DOB	M	(s)	G
Abu Francis (GHA)	27.04.2001	8	(12)	3
Martin Frese	04.01.1998	1	(6)	
Magnus Kofod Andersen	10.05.1999	35	(1)	1
Mohammed Kudus (GHA)	02.08.2000	22	(3)	11
Ivan Mesík (SVK)	01.06.2001	9	(2)	
Mikkel Rygaard	25.12.1990	26	(4)	5
Jacob Steen Christensen	25.06.2001	21	(11)	1
Nicklas Strunck Jakobsen	17.08.1999		(1)	
Forwards:	**DOB**	**M**	**(s)**	**G**
Jonathan Amon (USA)	30.04.1999		(2)	
Isaac Atanga (GHA)	29.07.2000	26	(8)	7
Mohammed Diomande (GHA)	30.10.2001	12	(3)	
Godsway Donyoh (GHA)	14.10.1994	2	(4)	1
Joachim Rothmann	29.06.2000	2	(10)	
Ibrahim Sadiq (GHA)	07.05.2000	17	(9)	3
Kamal Sulemana (GHA)	15.02.2002	6	(7)	4

Odense Boldklub

Founded: 12.07.1887
Stadium: Nature Energy Park, Odense (15,633)
Trainer: Jakob Michelsen   30.09.1980

Goalkeepers:	DOB	M	(s)	G
Hans Christian Bernat	13.11.2000	1		
Oliver Christensen	22.03.1999	29		
Mandé Sayouba (CIV)	15.06.1993	2		
Defenders:	**DOB**	**M**	**(s)**	**G**
Ryan Johnson Laursen	14.04.1992	19	(1)	1
Alexander Juel Andersen	29.01.1991	12	(3)	
Kasper Larsen	25.01.1993	6	(1)	
Jacob Laursen	17.11.1994	20	(6)	1
Ramon Leeuwin (NED)	01.09.1987	17		
Alexander Ludwig	30.06.1993	1	(1)	
Marco Lund	30.06.1996	23		
Oliver Lund	21.08.1990	19	(4)	1
Kingsley Madu (NGA)	12.12.1995	1		
Daniel Obbekjær	16.07.2002	2	(4)	
Robin Østrøm (NOR)	09.08.2002	1	(3)	
Jørgen Skjelvik (NOR)	05.07.1991	4	(1)	
Jeppe Tverskov	12.03.1993	25		1
Midfielders:	**DOB**	**M**	**(s)**	**G**
Mathias Brems	13.03.2002		(2)	
Jakob Breum	17.11.2003	1	(2)	
Janus Drachmann	11.05.1988	25	(2)	
Julius Eskesen	16.03.1999		(5)	
Mads Frøkjær-Jensen	29.07.1999	14	(6)	2
Mathias Greve	11.02.1995	4	(9)	1
Jonathan Harboe	24.05.2000	1		
Tarik Ibrahimagić	23.01.2001		(2)	
Troels Kløve	23.10.1990	22	(1)	5
Anders Klynge	14.10.2000	1	(3)	
Moses Opondo (UGA)	28.10.1997	11	(11)	1
Jens Thomasen	25.06.1996	18	(5)	
Aron Þrándarson (ISL)	10.11.1994	6	(2)	1
Forwards:	**DOB**	**M**	**(s)**	**G**
Max Fenger	07.08.2001	5	(1)	
Mikkel Hyllegaard	03.04.1999	1	(7)	2
Anders Jacobsen	27.10.1989	4	(8)	2
Issam Jebali (TUN)	25.12.1991	11	(8)	3
Bashkim Kadrii	09.07.1991	20		10
Mart Lieder (NED)	01.05.1990	2	(2)	
Sander Svendsen (NOR)	06.08.1997	23	(4)	12

Randers Football Club

Founded: 01.01.2003
Stadium: BioNutria Park, Randers (12,000)
Trainer: Thomas Thomasberg   15.10.1974

Goalkeepers:	DOB	M	(s)	G
Patrik Carlgren (SWE)	08.01.1992	29		
Jonas Dakir	18.04.1997	3	(1)	
Defenders:	**DOB**	**M**	**(s)**	**G**
Kevin Conboy	15.10.1987	15	(1)	
Tobias Damsgaard	03.08.1998		(3)	
Simon Graves	22.03.1999	5	(4)	
Björn Kopplin (GER)	07.01.1989	29	(2)	3
Jesper Lauridsen	27.03.1991	4		
Erik Marxen	02.12.1990	25	(1)	1
Mathias Nielsen	02.03.1991	12	(12)	1
Johnny Thomsen	26.02.1982	16	(8)	
Midfielders:	**DOB**	**M**	**(s)**	**G**
Oliver Bundgaard Kristensen	15.06.2001	1	(4)	
Vito Hammershøy-Mistrati	15.06.1992	19	(12)	8
Oliver Jensen	30.04.2002		(1)	
Mikkel Kallesøe	20.04.1997	26	(2)	2
Frederik Lauenborg	18.05.1997	18	(11)	
Saba Lobzhanidze (GEO)	18.12.1994	13	(2)	8
Simon Piesinger (AUT)	13.05.1992	26		2
André Rømer	18.07.1993	26	(3)	2
Issah Salou (NIG)	04.02.1999	1		
Laurs Skjellerup		1	(1)	
Forwards:	**DOB**	**M**	**(s)**	**G**
Marvin Egho (AUT)	09.05.1994	27	(1)	7
Mathias Greve	11.02.1995	7	(2)	1
Kasper Høgh	06.12.2000	1	(7)	
Alhaji Kamara (SLE)	16.04.1994	10	(9)	4
Tosin Kehinde (NGA)	18.06.1998	9	(9)	1
Tobias Klysner	03.07.2001	2	(5)	
Emil Riis Jakobsen	24.06.1998	27	(4)	8
Benjamin Stokke (NOR)	20.08.1990		(4)	

Silkeborg Idrætsforening

Founded: 26.04.1917
Stadium: JYSK Park, Silkeborg (10,000)
Trainer: Kent Nielsen   28.12.1961

Goalkeepers:	DOB	M	(s)	G
Oscar Hedvall	09.08.1998	9		
Rafael Enrique Romo Pérez (VEN)	25.02.1990	23		
Defenders:	**DOB**	**M**	**(s)**	**G**
Frederik Alves Ibsen	08.11.1999	21	(1)	
Svenn Crone	20.05.1995	24	(2)	1
Dennis Flinta	14.11.1983	7	(3)	
Jeppe Gertsen	09.02.1997	11		
Anders Hagelskjær	16.02.1997	21	(3)	2
Simon Skov Jakobsen	17.11.1990	5		
Kees Luijckx (NED)	11.02.1986	8		
Frederik Møller	08.07.1993	26	(1)	
Midfielders:	**DOB**	**M**	**(s)**	**G**
Mark Brink	15.03.1998	3	(7)	
Gustav Dahl	21.01.1996	1	(1)	
Andreas Heimer Hansen	10.12.1997		(2)	
Sebastian Jørgensen	31.12.2000		(8)	
Mads Kaalund	16.08.1996	16	(6)	2
Filip Lesniak (SVK)	14.05.1996	27	(5)	
Mads Madsen	14.01.1998	30		2
Pelle Mattsson	04.08.2001	1		
Vegard Moberg (NOR)	23.01.1991	10	(1)	1
Valance Nambishi (ZAM)	30.11.1997	3	(7)	
Mathias Hebo Rasmussen	02.08.1995	11	(1)	1
Forwards:	**DOB**	**M**	**(s)**	**G**
Rasmus Carstensen	11.10.2000	9	(5)	1
Oliver Haurits	12.12.2000		(1)	
Emil Holten	08.08.1996	5	(18)	5
José Francisco dos Santos Júnior "Brumado" (BRA)	15.05.1999	9		2
Alexander Lind Rasmussen	26.06.2002		(9)	2
Shkodran Maholi (SWE)	10.04.1993	6	(10)	2
Jeppe Okkels	27.07.1999	20	(9)	3
Ronnie Schwartz	29.08.1989	20		12
Marc Rochester Sørensen	13.12.1992	3	(5)	
Nicolai Vallys	04.09.1996	23	(6)	6

Sønderjysk Elitesport

Founded:	01.01.2004			
Stadium:	Sydbank Park, Haderslev (10,000)			
Trainer:	Glen Riddersholm			24.04.1972

Goalkeepers:	DOB	M	(s)	G
Sebastian Mielitz (GER)	18.07.1989	28		
Nikola Mirković (SRB)	26.07.1991	4		
Defenders:	**DOB**	**M**	**(s)**	**G**
Patrick Banggaard	04.04.1994	23	(1)	1
Stefan Gartenmann	02.02.1997	29		1
João Duarte Vieira Pereira (POR)	10.05.1990	4		1
Pierre Kanstrup	21.02.1989	9		
Kees Luijckx (NED)	11.02.1986	14	(1)	
Nicholas Marfelt	15.09.1994	10	(6)	
Theofanis Mavromatis (GRE)	16.01.1997	2		
Ísak Óli Ólafsson (ISL)	30.06.2000	1	(1)	
Jeppe Simonsen	21.11.1995	9	(8)	1
Midfielders:	**DOB**	**M**	**(s)**	**G**
Mads Albæk	14.01.1990	22	(3)	2
Danny Amankwaa	30.01.1994	1	(10)	
Victor Sylvestre Mpindi Ekani (CMR)	27.02.1997	11	(6)	

Julius Eskesen	16.03.1999	6	(4)	
Emil Frederiksen	05.09.2000	5	(6)	
Mads Hansen	10.04.2001	1	(4)	
Christian Jakobsen	27.03.1993	25	(4)	8
Eggert Jónsson (ISL)	18.08.1988	20	(7)	1
Marco Rodrigo Rojas (NZL)	05.11.1991	15	(4)	2
Marcel Rømer	08.08.1991		(1)	
Rasmus Vinderslev	12.08.1997	6	(4)	
Forwards:	**DOB**	**M**	**(s)**	**G**
Johan Absalonsen	16.09.1985	21	(2)	3
Alexander Bah	09.12.1997	28	(1)	1
Peter Christiansen	02.12.1999	2	(16)	3
Artem Dovbyk (UKR)	21.06.1997	1	(17)	2
Rilwan Hassan (NGA)	09.02.1991	24	(3)	1
Anders Jacobsen	27.10.1989	11		3
Mart Lieder (NED)	01.05.1990	20		6

SECOND LEVEL
1. division - NordicBet Liga 2019/2020

1.	Vejle Boldklub (*Promoted*)	33	20	8	5	63	-	31	68
2.	Viborg FF	33	17	8	8	66	-	44	59
3.	FC Fredericia	33	15	7	11	60	-	51	52
4.	BK Fremad Amager	33	13	10	10	45	-	45	49
5.	Skive IK	33	13	9	11	46	-	46	48
6.	Kolding IF	33	13	8	12	50	-	49	47
7.	Vendsyssel FF Hjørring	33	12	8	13	35	-	39	44
8.	Hvidovre IF	33	10	11	12	46	-	46	41
9.	HB Køge	33	9	13	11	43	-	47	40
10.	Nykøbing FC (*Relegated*)	33	7	12	14	46	-	63	33
11.	FC Roskilde (*Relegated*)	33	8	7	18	43	-	61	31
12.	Næstved Boldklub (*Relegated*)	33	5	11	17	29		50	26

INTERNATIONAL MATCHES
(16.07.2019 – 15.07.2020)

05.09.2019	Gibraltar	Gibraltar - Denmark	0-6(0-2)	(ECQ)
08.09.2019	Tbilisi	Georgia - Denmark	0-0	(ECQ)
12.10.2019	København	Denmark - Switzerland	1-0(0-0)	(ECQ)
15.10.2019	Aalborg	Denmark - Luxembourg	4-0(2-0)	(F)
15.11.2019	København	Denmark - Gibraltar	6-0(1-0)	(ECQ)
18.11.2019	Dublin	Republic of Ireland - Denmark	1-1(0-0)	(ECQ)

05.09.2019 GIBRALTAR - DENMARK **0-6(0-2)** 16th EC. Qualifiers
Victoria Stadium, Gibraltar; Referee: Jonathan Lardot (Belgium); Attendance: 2,076
DEN: Kasper Peter Schmeichel, Simon Thorup Kjær (Cap) (63.Mathias Jattah-Njie Jørgensen), Jens Stryger Larsen, Andreas Bødtker Christensen, Daniel Wass, Thomas Joseph Delaney (77.Lasse Schøne), Christian Dannemann Eriksen, Pierre-Emile Kordt Højbjerg, Robert Skov, Christian Lund Gytkjær, Yussuf Yurary Poulsen (63.Martin Braithwaite Christensen). Trainer: Åge Fridtjof Hareide (Norway).
Goals: Robert Skov (6), Christian Dannemann Eriksen (34 penalty, 50 penalty), Thomas Joseph Delaney (69), Christian Lund Gytkjær (73, 78).

08.09.2019 GEORGIA - DENMARK **0-0** 16th EC. Qualifiers
„Boris Paichadze" Dinamo Arena, Tbilisi; Referee: Referee: François Letexier (France); Attendance: 21,456
DEN: Kasper Peter Schmeichel, Simon Thorup Kjær (Cap), Jens Stryger Larsen, Andreas Bødtker Christensen, Henrik Dalsgaard, Thomas Joseph Delaney, Christian Dannemann Eriksen, Pierre-Emile Kordt Højbjerg (73.Lasse Schøne), Martin Braithwaite Christensen, Yussuf Yurary Poulsen, Kasper Dolberg Rasmussen (67.Christian Lund Gytkjær). Trainer: Åge Fridtjof Hareide (Norway).

12.10.2019 DENMARK - SWITZERLAND **1-0(0-0)** 16th EC. Qualifiers
Parken Stadium, København; Referee: Aleksei Kulbakov (Belarus); Attendance: 35,964
DEN: Kasper Peter Schmeichel, Simon Thorup Kjær (Cap), Henrik Dalsgaard, Jens Stryger Larsen (80.Peter Svarrer Ankersen), Andreas Bødtker Christensen (87.Mathias Jattah-Njie Jørgensen), Lasse Schøne (65.Pierre-Emile Kordt Højbjerg), Thomas Joseph Delaney, Christian Dannemann Eriksen, Martin Braithwaite Christensen, Yussuf Yurary Poulsen, Andreas Evald Cornelius. Trainer: Åge Fridtjof Hareide (Norway).
Goal: Yussuf Yurary Poulsen (84).

15.10.2019 DENMARK - LUXEMBOURG **4-0(2-0)** Friendly International
Portland park, Aalborg; Referee: Bojan Pandžić (Sweden); Attendance: 9,043
DEN: Kasper Peter Schmeichel, Simon Thorup Kjær (Cap) (83.Joachim Christian Andersen), Mathias Jattah-Njie Jørgensen, Henrik Dalsgaard (67.Jonas Hjort Knudsen), Peter Svarrer Ankersen, Daniel Wass, Christian Dannemann Eriksen (46.Lukas Reiff Lerager), Pierre-Emile Kordt Højbjerg, Robert Skov, Martin Braithwaite Christensen (61.Lucas Qvistorff Andersen), Kasper Dolberg Rasmussen (61.Christian Lund Gytkjær). Trainer: Åge Fridtjof Hareide (Norway).
Goals: Martin Braithwaite Christensen (13), Kasper Dolberg Rasmussen (21, 59), Christian Lund Gytkjær (67).

15.11.2019 DENMARK - GIBRALTAR **6-0(1-0)** 16th EC. Qualifiers
Parken Stadium, København; Referee: István Vad (Hungary); Attendance: 24,033
DEN: Kasper Peter Schmeichel, Simon Thorup Kjær (Cap), Mathias Jattah-Njie Jørgensen, Jens Stryger Larsen (78.Andreas Bødtker Christensen), Daniel Wass, Lasse Schøne (54.Pierre-Emile Kordt Højbjerg), Thomas Joseph Delaney, Christian Dannemann Eriksen, Robert Skov, Christian Lund Gytkjær, Martin Braithwaite Christensen (54.Kasper Dolberg Rasmussen). Trainer: Åge Fridtjof Hareide (Norway).
Goals: Robert Skov (12), Christian Lund Gytkjær (47), Martin Braithwaite Christensen (51), Robert Skov (64), Christian Dannemann Eriksen (85, 90+4).

18.11.2019 REPUBLIC OF IRELAND - DENMARK **1-1(0-0)** 16th EC. Qualifiers
Aviva Stadium, Dublin; Referee: Dr. Felix Brych (Germany); Attendance: 51,700
DEN: Kasper Peter Schmeichel, Simon Thorup Kjær (Cap), Mathias Jattah-Njie Jørgensen, Jens Stryger Larsen, Henrik Dalsgaard, Lasse Schøne (84.Andreas Bødtker Christensen), Thomas Joseph Delaney (13.Pierre-Emile Kordt Højbjerg), Christian Dannemann Eriksen, Martin Braithwaite Christensen, Yussuf Yurary Poulsen, Andreas Evald Cornelius (33.Kasper Dolberg Rasmussen). Trainer: Åge Fridtjof Hareide (Norway).
Goal: Martin Braithwaite Christensen (73).

Name	DOB	Caps	Goals	2019/2020:	Club
Goalkeepers					
Kasper Peter SCHMEICHEL	05.11.1986	53	0	2019:	Leicester City FC (ENG)
Defenders					
Joachim Christian ANDERSEN	10.04.1996	1	0	2019:	Olympique Lyonnais (FRA)
Peter Svarrer ANKERSEN	22.09.1990	27	1	2019:	Genoa C&FC (ITA)
Andreas Bødtker CHRISTENSEN	10.04.1996	31	1	2019:	Chelsea FC London (ENG)
Henrik DALSGAARD	27.07.1989	25	1	2019:	Brentford FC London (ENG)
Mathias Jattah-Njie JØRGENSEN	23.04.1990	28	2	2019:	Fenerbahçe SK İstanbul (TUR)
Simon Thorup KJÆR	26.03.1989	95	3	2019:	Atalanta Bergamasca Calcio (ITA)
Jonas Hjort KNUDSEN	16.09.1992	7	0	2019:	Malmö FF (SWE)
Jens STRYGER Larsen	21.02.1991	29	1	2019:	Udinese Calcio (ITA)
Midfielders					
Thomas Joseph DELANEY	03.09.1991	43	5	2019:	BV Borussia 09 Dortmund (GER)
Christian Dannemann ERIKSEN	14.02.1992	95	31	2019:	Tottenham Hotspur FC London (ENG)
Pierre-Emile Kordt HØJBJERG	05.08.1995	33	3	2019:	Southampton FC (ENG)
Lukas Reiff LERAGER	12.07.1993	10	1	2019:	Genoa C&FC (ITA)
Lasse SCHØNE	27.05.1986	50	3	2019:	Genoa C&FC (ITA)
Daniel WASS	31.05.1989	20	0	2019:	Valencia CF (ESP)
Forwards					
Lucas Qvistorff ANDERSEN	13.09.1994	4	0	2019:	Aalborg BK
Martin BRAITHWAITE Christensen	05.06.1991	39	7	2019:	CD Leganés (ESP)
Andreas Evald CORNELIUS	16.03.1993	25	4	2019:	Parma Calcio 1913 (ITA)
Kasper Dolberg RASMUSSEN	06.10.1997	17	5	2019:	OGC Nice (FRA)
Christian Lund GYTKJÆR	06.05.1990	9	5	2019:	KKS Lech Poznań (POL)
Yussuf Yurary POULSEN	15.06.1994	43	7	2019:	RasenBallsport Leipzig (GER)
Robert SKOV	20.05.1996	4	3	2019:	TSG 1899 Hoffenheim (GER)
National team coach					
Åge Fridtjof HAREIDE (Norway) [from 01.03.2016]	23.09.1953	42 M; 21 W; 18 D; 3 L; 81-26			

ENGLAND

The Country:
England
Capital: London
Surface: 130,279 km^2
Inhabitants: 56,286,961 [2019]
Time: UTC

The FA:
The Football Association
Wembley Stadium, P.O. Box 1966, SWIP 9EQ, London
Tel: +44 844 980 8200
Foundation date: 1863
Member of FIFA: 1905-1918, 1924-1928, since 1946
Member of UEFA since: 1954
Website: www.thefa.com

NATIONAL TEAM RECORDS

RECORDS		
First international match:	30.11.1872, Glasgow:	Scotland – England 0-0
Most international caps:	Peter Leslie Shilton	- 125 caps (1970-1990)
Most international goals:	Wayne Mark Rooney	- 53 goals / 120 caps (2003-2018)

UEFA EUROPEAN CHAMPIONSHIP		FIFA WORLD CUP		OLYMPIC TOURNAMENTS	
1960	Did not enter	1930	Did not enter	1908	-
1964	Qualifiers	1934	Did not enter	1912	-
1968	Final Tournament (3rd Place)	1938	Did not enter	1920	-
1972	Qualifiers	1950	Final Tournament (Group Stage)	1924	-
1976	Qualifiers	1954	Final Tournament (Quarter-Finals)	1928	-
1980	Final Tournament (Group Stage)	1958	Final Tournament (Group Stage)	1936	-
1984	Qualifiers	1962	Final Tournament (Quarter-Finals)	1948	-
1988	Final Tournament (Group Stage)	1966	**Final Tournament (Winners)**	1952	-
1992	Final Tournament (Group Stage)	1970	Final Tournament (Quarter-Finals)	1956	-
1996	Final Tournament (Semi-Finals)	1974	Qualifiers	1960	-
2000	Final Tournament (Group Stage)	1978	Qualifiers	1964	-
2004	Final Tournament (Quarter-Finals)	1982	Final Tournament (2nd Round)	1968	-
2008	Qualifiers	1986	Final Tournament (Quarter-Finals)	1972	-
2012	Final Tournament (Quarter-Finals)	1990	Final Tournament (4th Place)	1976	-
2016	Final Tournament (2nd Round of 16)	1994	Qualifiers	1980	-
2020	*Final Tournament (Qualified)*	1998	Final Tournament (2nd Round of 16)	1984	-
		2002	Final Tournament (Quarter-Finals)	1988	-
		2006	Final Tournament (Quarter-Finals)	1992	-
		2010	Final Tournament (2nd Round of 16)	1996	-
		2014	Final Tournament (Group Stage)	2000	-
		2018	Final Tournament (4th Place)	2004	-
				2008	-
				2012	-
				2016	-

UEFA NATIONS LEAGUE

2018/2019 – League A (Final Tournament – 3rd Place)

FIFA CONFEDERATIONS CUP 1992-2017

None

ENGLISH CLUB HONOURS IN EUROPEAN CLUB COMPETITIONS:

European Champion Clubs' Cup (1956-1992) / UEFA Champions League (1993-2020)		
Liverpool FC	6	1976/1977, 1977/1978, 1980/1981, 1983/1984, 2004/2005, 2018/2019
Manchester United FC	3	1967/1968, 1998/1999, 2007/2008
Notthingam Forest FC	2	1978/1979, 1979/1980
Aston Villa FC Birmingham	1	1981/1982
Chelsea FC London	1	2011/2012
Fairs Cup (1858-1971) / UEFA Cup (1972-2009) / UEFA Europa League (2010-2020)		
Liverpool FC	3	1972/1973, 1975/1976, 2000/2001
Leeds United FC	2	1967/1968, 1970/1971
Tottenham Hotspur FC London	2	1971/1972, 1983/1984
Chelsea FC London	2	2012/2013, 2018/2019
Newcastle United FC	1	1968/1969
Arsenal FC London	1	1969/1970

Ipswich Town FC	1	1980/1981	
Manchester United FC	1	2016/2017	

UEFA Super Cup (1972-2019)		
Liverpool FC	4	1977, 2001, 2005, 2019
Notthingam Forest FC	1	1979
Aston Villa FC Birmingham	1	1982
Manchester United FC	1	1991
Chelsea FC London	1	1998

European Cup Winners' Cup 1961-1999*		
Chelsea FC London	2	1970/1971, 1997/1998
Tottenham Hotspur FC London	1	1962/1963
West Ham United FC London	1	1964/1965
Manchester City FC	1	1969/1970
Everton FC Liverpool	1	1984/1985
Manchester United FC	1	1990/1991
Arsenal FC London	1	1993/1994

defunct competition

NATIONAL COMPETITIONS
TABLE OF HONOURS

	CHAMPIONS	CUP WINNERS	BEST GOALSCORERS	
1871/1872	-	Wanderers FC London	-	
1872/1873	-	Wanderers FC London	-	
1873/1874	-	Oxford University AFC	-	
1874/1875	-	Royal Engineers AFC	-	
1875/1876	-	Wanderers FC London	-	
1876/1877	-	Wanderers FC London	-	
1877/1878	-	Wanderers FC London	-	
1878/1879	-	Old Etonians AFC	-	
1879/1880	-	Clapham Rovers FC	-	
1880/1881	-	Old Carthusians FC	-	
1881/1882	-	Old Etonians AFC	-	
1882/1883	-	Blackburn Olympic FC	-	
1883/1884	-	Blackburn Rovers FC	-	
1884/1885	-	Blackburn Rovers FC	-	
1885/1886	-	Blackburn Rovers FC	-	
1886/1887	-	Aston Villa FC Birmingham	-	
1887/1888	-	West Bromwich Albion FC	-	
1888/1889	Preston North End FC	Preston North End FC	John Goodall (Preston North End FC)	21
1889/1890	Preston North End FC	Blackburn Rovers FC	Jimmy Ross (SCO, Preston North End FC)	24
1890/1891	Everton FC Liverpool	Blackburn Rovers FC	Jack Southworth (Blackburn Rovers FC)	26
1891/1892	Sunderland AFC	West Bromwich Albion FC	John Campbell (SCO, Sunderland AFC)	32
1892/1893	Sunderland AFC	Wolverhampton Wanderers FC	John Campbell (SCO, Sunderland AFC)	31
1893/1894	Aston Villa FC Birmingham	Notts County FC	Jack Southworth (Everton FC Liverpool)	27
1894/1895	Sunderland AFC	Aston Villa FC Birmingham	John Campbell (SCO, Sunderland AFC)	22
1895/1896	Aston Villa FC Birmingham	The Wednesday Sheffield FC	John James Campbell (SCO, Aston Villa FC Birmingham) Stephen Bloomer (Derby County FC)	20
1896/1897	Aston Villa FC Birmingham	Aston Villa FC Birmingham	Stephen Bloomer (Derby County FC)	22
1897/1898	Sheffield United FC	Nottingham Forest FC	Fred Wheldon (Aston Villa FC Birmingham)	21
1898/1899	Aston Villa FC Birmingham	Sheffield United FC	Stephen Bloomer (Derby County FC)	23
1899/1900	Aston Villa FC Birmingham	Bury FC	Billy Garraty (Aston Villa FC Birmingham)	27
1900/1901	Liverpool FC	Tottenham Hotspur FC London	Stephen Bloomer (Derby County FC)	23
1901/1902	Sunderland AFC	Sheffield United FC	Jimmy Settle (Everton FC Liverpool)	18
1902/1903	The Wednesday Sheffield FC	Bury FC	Sam Raybould (Liverpool FC)	31
1903/1904	The Wednesday Sheffield FC	Manchester City FC	Stephen Bloomer (Derby County FC)	20
1904/1905	Newcastle United FC	Aston Villa FC Birmingham	Arthur Brown (Sheffield United FC)	22
1905/1906	Liverpool FC	Everton FC Liverpool	Albert Shepherd (Bolton Wanderers FC)	26
1906/1907	Newcastle United FC	The Wednesday Sheffield FC	Alex Young (SCO, Everton FC Liverpool)	30
1907/1908	Manchester United FC	Wolverhampton Wanderers FC	Enoch West (Nottingham Forest FC)	27
1908/1909	Newcastle United FC	Manchester United FC	Bert Freeman (Everton FC Liverpool)	38
1909/1910	Aston Villa FC Birmingham	Newcastle United FC	Jack Parkinson (Liverpool FC)	30
1910/1911	Manchester United FC	Bradford City AFC	Albert Shepherd (Newcastle United FC)	25
1911/1912	Blackburn Rovers FC	Barnsley FC	Harry Hampton (Aston Villa FC Birmingham) George Holley (Sunderland AFC) David McLean (The Wednesday Sheffield FC)	25
1912/1913	Sunderland AFC	Aston Villa FC Birmingham	David McLean (SCO, The Wednesday Sheffield FC)	30
1913/1914	Blackburn Rovers FC	Burnley FC	George Elliot (Middlesbrough FC)	32
1914/1915	Everton FC Liverpool	Sheffield United FC	Bobby Parker (SCO, Everton FC Liverpool)	35
1915-1919	*No competition*	*No competition*	-	
1919/1920	West Bromwich Albion FC	Aston Villa FC Birmingham	Fred Morris (West Bromwich Albion FC)	37
1920/1921	Burnley FC	Tottenham Hotspur FC London	Joe Smith (Bolton Wanderers FC)	38
1921/1922	Liverpool FC	Huddersfield Town AFC	Andy Wilson (SCO, Middlesbrough FC)	31
1922/1923	Liverpool FC	Bolton Wanderers FC	Charles Murray Buchan (SCO, Sunderland AFC)	30

1923/1924	Huddersfield Town AFC	Newcastle United FC	Wilf Chadwick (Everton FC Liverpool)	28
1924/1925	Huddersfield Town AFC	Sheffield United FC	Frank Roberts (Manchester City FC)	31
1925/1926	Huddersfield Town AFC	Bolton Wanderers FC	Ted Harper (Blackburn Rovers FC)	43
1926/1927	Newcastle United FC	Cardiff City FC (WAL)	Jimmy Trotter (The Wednesday Sheffield FC)	37
1927/1928	Everton FC Liverpool	Blackburn Rovers FC	William Ralph Dean (Everton FC Liverpool)	60
1928/1929	The Wednesday Sheffield FC	Bolton Wanderers FC	Dave Halliday (SCO, Sunderland AFC)	43
1929/1930	Sheffield Wednesday FC	Arsenal FC London	Victor Martin Watson (West Ham United FC)	41
1930/1931	Arsenal FC London	West Bromwich Albion FC	Thomas Waring (Aston Villa FC Birmingham)	49
1931/1932	Everton FC Liverpool	Newcastle United FC	William Ralph Dean (Everton FC Liverpool)	44
1932/1933	Arsenal FC London	Everton FC Liverpool	John William Anslow Bowers (Derby County FC)	35
1933/1934	Arsenal FC London	Manchester City FC	John William Anslow Bowers (Derby County FC)	34
1934/1935	Arsenal FC London	Sheffield Wednesday FC	Edward Joseph Drake (Arsenal FC London)	42
1935/1936	Sunderland AFC	Arsenal FC London	William "Ginger" Richardson (West Bromwich Albion FC)	39
1936/1937	Manchester City FC	Sunderland AFC	Frederick Charles Steele (Stoke City FC)	33
1937/1938	Arsenal FC London	Preston North End FC	Thomas Lawton (Everton FC Liverpool)	28
1938/1939	Everton FC Liverpool	Portsmouth FC	Thomas Lawton (Everton FC Liverpool)	35
1939-1945	*No competition*	*No competition*	-	
1945/1946	*No competition*	Derby County FC	-	
1946/1947	Liverpool FC	Charlton Athletic FC	Dennis Westcott (Wolverhampton Wanderers FC)	37
1947/1948	Arsenal FC London	Manchester United FC	Ronald Leslie Rooke (Arsenal FC London)	33
1948/1949	Portsmouth FC	Wolverhampton Wanderers FC	William Moir (SCO, Bolton Wanderers FC)	25
1949/1950	Portsmouth FC	Arsenal FC London	Richard Daniel Davis (Sunderland AFC)	25
1950/1951	Tottenham Hotspur FC London	Newcastle United FC	Stanley Harding Mortensen (Blackpool FC)	30
1951/1952	Manchester United FC	Newcastle United FC	Jorge Robledo Oliver (CHI, Newcastle United FC)	33
1952/1953	Arsenal FC London	Blackpool FC	Charles Wayman (Preston North End FC)	24
1953/1954	Wolverhampton Wanderers FC	West Bromwich Albion FC	Jimmy Glazzard (Huddersfield Town AFC)	29
1954/1955	Chelsea FC London	Newcastle United FC	Ronald Allen (West Bromwich Albion FC)	27
1955/1956	Manchester United FC	Manchester City FC	Nathaniel Lofthouse (Bolton Wanderers FC)	33
1956/1957	Manchester United FC	Aston Villa FC Birmingham	William John Charles (WAL, Leeds United FC)	38
1957/1958	Wolverhampton Wanderers FC	Bolton Wanderers FC	Robert Alfred Smith (Tottenham Hotspur FC)	36
1958/1959	Wolverhampton Wanderers FC	Nottingham Forest FC	James Peter Greaves (Chelsea FC London)	33
1959/1960	Burnley FC	Wolverhampton Wanderers FC	Dennis Sydney Viollet (Manchester United FC)	32
1960/1961	Tottenham Hotspur FC London	Tottenham Hotspur FC London	James Peter Greaves (Chelsea FC London)	41
1961/1962	Ipswich Town FC	Tottenham Hotspur FC London	Raymond Crawford (Ipswich Town FC) Derek Tennyson Kevan (West Bromwich Albion FC)	33
1962/1963	Everton FC Liverpool	Manchester United FC	James Peter Greaves (Tottenham Hotspur FC)	37
1963/1964	Liverpool FC	West Ham United FC London	James Peter Greaves (Tottenham Hotspur FC)	35
1964/1965	Manchester United FC	Liverpool FC	Andrew McEvoy (IRL, Blackburn Rovers FC) James Peter Greaves (Tottenham Hotspur FC)	29
1965/1966	Liverpool FC	Everton FC Liverpool	William John Irvine (NIR, Burnley FC)	29
1966/1967	Manchester United FC	Tottenham Hotspur FC London	Ron Davies (WAL, Southampton FC)	37
1967/1968	Manchester City FC	West Bromwich Albion FC	George Best (NIR, Manchester United FC) Ronald Tudor Davies (WAL, Southampton FC)	28
1968/1969	Leeds United FC	Manchester City FC	James Peter Greaves (Tottenham Hotspur FC)	27
1969/1970	Everton FC Liverpool	Chelsea FC London	Jeffrey Astle (West Bromwich Albion FC)	25
1970/1971	Arsenal FC London	Arsenal FC London	Anthony Brown (West Bromwich Albion FC)	28
1971/1972	Derby County FC	Leeds United FC	Francis Henry Lee (Manchester City FC)	33
1972/1973	Liverpool FC	Sunderland AFC	Bryan Stanley Robson (West Ham United FC)	28
1973/1974	Leeds United FC	Liverpool FC	Michael Roger Channon (Southampton FC)	21
1974/1975	Derby County FC	West Ham United FC London	Malcolm Ian Macdonald (Newcastle United FC)	21
1975/1976	Liverpool FC	Southampton FC	Edward John MacDougall (SCO, Norwich City FC)	23
1976/1977	Liverpool FC	Manchester United FC	Malcolm Ian Macdonald (Arsenal FC London) Andrew Mullen Gray (SCO, Aston Villa FC)	25
1977/1978	Nottingham Forest FC	Ipswich Town FC	Robert Dennis Latchford (Everton FC Liverpool)	30
1978/1979	Liverpool FC	Arsenal FC London	Frank Stewart Worthington (Bolton Wanderers FC)	24
1979/1980	Liverpool FC	West Ham United FC London	Philip John Boyer (Southampton FC)	23
1980/1981	Aston Villa FC Birmingham	Tottenham Hotspur FC London	Peter Withe (Aston Villa FC Birmingham) Steven Archibald (SCO, Tottenham Hotspur FC)	20
1981/1982	Liverpool FC	Tottenham Hotspur FC London	Joseph Kevin Keegan (Southampton FC)	26
1982/1983	Liverpool FC	Manchester United FC	Luther Loide Blissett (Watford FC)	27
1983/1984	Liverpool FC	Everton FC Liverpool	Ian James Rush (WAL, Liverpool FC)	32
1984/1985	Everton FC Liverpool	Manchester United FC	Kerry Michael Dixon (Chelsea FC London) Gary Winston Lineker (Leicester City FC)	24
1985/1986	Liverpool FC	Liverpool FC	Gary Winston Lineker (Everton FC Liverpool)	30
1986/1987	Everton FC Liverpool	Coventry City FC	Clive Darren Allen (Tottenham Hotspur FC London)	33
1987/1988	Liverpool FC	Wimbledon	John William Aldridge (IRL, Liverpool FC)	26
1988/1989	Arsenal FC London	Liverpool FC	Alan Martin Smith (Arsenal FC London)	23
1989/1990	Liverpool FC	Manchester United FC	Gary Winston Lineker (Tottenham Hotspur FC)	24
1990/1991	Arsenal FC London	Tottenham Hotspur FC London	Alan Martin Smith (Arsenal FC London)	22
1991/1992	Leeds United FC	Liverpool FC	Ian Edward Wright (Crystal Palace FC London/Arsenal FC London)	29
1992/1993	Manchester United FC	Arsenal FC London	Edward Paul Sheringham (Nottingham Forest FC/Tottenham Hotspur FC London)	22
1993/1994	Manchester United FC	Manchester United FC	Andrew Alexander Cole (Newcastle United FC)	34
1994/1995	Blackburn Rovers FC	Everton FC Liverpool	Alan Shearer (Blackburn Rovers FC)	34
1995/1996	Manchester United FC	Manchester United FC	Alan Shearer (Blackburn Rovers FC)	31
1996/1997	Manchester United FC	Chelsea FC London	Alan Shearer (Newcastle United FC)	25

1997/1998	Arsenal FC London	Arsenal FC London	Christopher Roy Sutton (Blackburn Rovers FC) Dion Dublin (Coventry City FC) Michael James Owen (Liverpool FC)	18
1998/1999	Manchester United FC	Manchester United FC	Jimmy Floyd Hasselbaink (NED, Leeds United FC) Michael James Owen (Liverpool FC) Dwight Eversley Yorke (TRI, Manchester United)	18
1999/2000	Manchester United FC	Chelsea FC London	Kevin Mark Phillips (Sunderland AFC)	30
2000/2001	Manchester United FC	Liverpool FC	Jimmy Floyd Hasselbaink (NED, Chelsea FC London)	23
2001/2002	Arsenal FC London	Arsenal FC London	Thierry Daniel Henry (FRA, Arsenal FC London)	24
2002/2003	Manchester United FC	Arsenal FC London	Rutgerus Johannes Martinus "Ruud" van Nistelrooy (NED, Manchester United FC)	25
2003/2004	Arsenal FC London	Manchester United FC	Thierry Daniel Henry (FRA, Arsenal FC London)	30
2004/2005	Chelsea FC London	Arsenal FC London	Thierry Daniel Henry (FRA, Arsenal FC London)	25
2005/2006	Chelsea FC London	Liverpool FC	Thierry Daniel Henry (FRA, Arsenal FC London)	27
2006/2007	Manchester United FC	Chelsea FC London	Didier Yves Drogba Tébily (CIV, Chelsea FC London)	20
2007/2008	Manchester United FC	Portsmouth FC	Cristiano Ronaldo dos Santos Aveiro (POR, Manchester United FC)	31
2008/2009	Manchester United FC	Chelsea FC London	Nicolas Sébastien Anelka (FRA, Chelsea FC London)	19
2009/2010	Chelsea FC London	Chelsea FC London	Didier Yves Drogba Tébily (CIV, Chelsea FC London)	29
2010/2011	Manchester United FC	Manchester City FC	Dimitar Berbatov (BUL, Manchester United FC) Carlos Alberto Martínez Tevez (ARG, Manchester City FC)	20
2011/2012	Manchester City FC	Chelsea FC London	Robin van Persie (NED, Arsenal FC London)	30
2012/2013	Manchester United FC	Wigan Athletic FC	Robin van Persie (NED, Manchester United FC)	26
2013/2014	Manchester City FC	Arsenal FC London	Luis Alberto Suárez Díaz (URU, Liverpool FC)	31
2014/2015	Chelsea FC London	Arsenal FC London	Sergio Leonel Agüero del Castillo (ARG, Manchester City FC)	26
2015/2016	Leicester City FC	Manchester United FC	Harry Edward Kane (Tottenham Hotspur FC)	25
2016/2017	Chelsea FC London	Arsenal FC London	Harry Edward Kane (Tottenham Hotspur FC)	29
2017/2018	Manchester City FC	Chelsea FC London	Mohamed Salah Ghaly (EGY, Liverpool FC)	32
2018/2019	Manchester City FC	Manchester City FC	Pierre-Emerick Emiliano François Aubameyang (GAB, Arsenal FC London) Sadio Mané (SEN, Liverpool FC) Mohamed Salah Ghaly (EGY, Liverpool FC)	22
2019/2020	Liverpool FC	Arsenal FC London	Jamie Richard Vardy (Leicester City FC)	23

Please note: the championship was called Football League (1888–1892), Football League First Division (1892–1992) and Premier League (1992–present).

EFL (LEAGUE) CUP WINNERS

1960/1961	Aston Villa FC Birmingham	1980/1981	Liverpool FC	2000/2001	Liverpool FC
1961/1962	Norwich City FC	1981/1982	Liverpool FC	2001/2002	Blackburn Rovers FC
1962/1963	Birmingham City FC	1982/1983	Liverpool FC	2002/2003	Liverpool FC
1963/1964	Leicester City FC	1983/1984	Liverpool FC	2003/2004	Middlesbrough FC
1964/1965	Chelsea FC London	1984/1985	Norwich City FC	2004/2005	Chelsea FC London
1965/1966	West Bromwich Albion FC	1985/1986	Oxford United FC	2005/2006	Manchester United FC
1966/1967	Queens Park Rangers FC	1986/1987	Arsenal FC London	2006/2007	Chelsea FC London
1967/1968	Leeds United FC	1987/1988	Luton Town FC	2007/2008	Tottenham Hotspur FC London
1968/1969	Swindon Town FC	1988/1989	Nottingham Forest FC	2008/2009	Manchester United FC
1969/1970	Manchester City FC	1989/1990	Nottingham Forest FC	2009/2010	Manchester United FC
1970/1971	Tottenham Hotspur FC London	1990/1991	Sheffield Wednesday FC	2010/2011	Birmingham City FC
1971/1972	Stoke City FC	1991/1992	Manchester United FC	2011/2012	Liverpool FC
1972/1973	Tottenham Hotspur FC London	1992/1993	Arsenal FC London	2012/2013	Swansea City AFC
1973/1974	Wolverhampton Wanderers FC	1993/1994	Aston Villa FC Birmingham	2013/2014	Manchester City FC
1974/1975	Aston Villa FC Birmingham	1994/1995	Liverpool FC	2014/2015	Chelsea FC London
1975/1976	Manchester City FC	1995/1996	Aston Villa FC Birmingham	2015/2016	Manchester City FC
1976/1977	Aston Villa FC Birmingham	1996/1997	Leicester City FC	2016/2017	Manchester United FC
1977/1978	Nottingham Forest FC	1997/1998	Chelsea FC London	2017/2018	Manchester City FC
1978/1979	Nottingham Forest FC	1998/1999	Tottenham Hotspur FC London	2018/2019	Manchester City FC
1979/1980	Wolverhampton Wanderers FC	1999/2000	Leicester City FC	2019/2020	Manchester City FC

NATIONAL CHAMPIONSHIP
Premier League 2019/2020
(09.08.2019 – 26.07.2020)

Results

Round 1 [09-11.08.2019]
Liverpool FC - Norwich City 4-1(4-0)
West Ham - Manchester City 0-5(0-1)
AFC Bournemouth - Sheffield United 1-1(0-0)
Burnley - Southampton 3-0(0-0)
Crystal Palace - Everton 0-0
Watford - Brighton & Hove 0-3(0-1)
Tottenham Hotspur - Aston Villa 3-1(0-1)
Leicester City - Wolverhampton 0-0
Newcastle United - Arsenal 0-1(0-0)
Manchester United - Chelsea 4-0(1-0)

Round 2 [17-19.08.2019]
Arsenal - Burnley 2-1(1-1)
Aston Villa - AFC Bournemouth 1-2(0-2)
Brighton & Hove - West Ham 1-1(0-0)
Everton - Watford 1-0(1-0)
Norwich City - Newcastle United 3-1(1-0)
Southampton - Liverpool FC 1-2(0-1)
Manchester City - Tottenham Hots. 2-2(2-1)
Sheffield United - Crystal Palace 1-0(0-0)
Chelsea - Leicester City 1-1(1-0)
Wolverhampton - Manchester United 1-1(0-1)

Round 3 [23-25.08.2019]
Aston Villa - Everton 2-0(1-0)
Norwich City - Chelsea 2-3(2-2)
Brighton & Hove - Southampton 0-2(0-0)
Manchester United - Crystal Palace 1-2(0-1)
Sheffield United - Leicester City 1-2(0-1)
Watford - West Ham 1-3(1-1)
Liverpool FC - Arsenal 3-1(1-0)
AFC Bournemouth - Manchester City 1-3(1-2)
Tottenham Hots. - Newcastle United 0-1(0-1)
Wolverhampton - Burnley 1-1(0-1)

Round 4 [31.08.-01.09.2019]
Southampton - Manchester United 1-1(0-1)
Chelsea - Sheffield United 2-2(2-0)
Crystal Palace - Aston Villa 1-0(0-0)
Leicester City - AFC Bournemouth 3-1(2-1)
Manchester City - Brighton & Hove 4-0(2-0)
Newcastle United - Watford 1-1(1-1)
West Ham - Norwich City 2-0(1-0)
Burnley - Liverpool FC 0-3(0-2)
Everton - Wolverhampton 3-2(2-1)
Arsenal - Tottenham Hotspur 2-2(1-2)

Round 5 [14-16.09.2019]
Liverpool FC - Newcastle United 3-1(2-1)
Brighton & Hove - Burnley 1-1(0-1)
Manchester United - Leicester City 1-0(1-0)
Sheffield United - Southampton 0-1(0-0)
Tottenham Hotspur - Crystal Palace 4-0(4-0)
Wolverhampton - Chelsea 2-5(0-3)
Norwich City - Manchester City 3-2(2-1)
AFC Bournemouth - Everton 3-1(1-1)
Watford - Arsenal 2-2(0-2)
Aston Villa - West Ham 0-0

Round 6 [20-22.09.2019]
Southampton - AFC Bournemouth 1-3(0-2)
Leicester City - Tottenham Hotspur 2-1(0-1)
Burnley - Norwich City 2-0(2-0)
Everton - Sheffield United 0-2(0-1)
Manchester City - Watford 8-0(5-0)
Newcastle United - Brighton & Hove 0-0
Crystal Palace - Wolverhampton 1-1(0-0)
West Ham - Manchester United 2-0(1-0)
Arsenal - Aston Villa 3-2(0-1)
Chelsea - Liverpool FC 1-2(0-2)

Round 7 [28-30.09.2019]
Sheffield United - Liverpool FC 0-1(0-0)
AFC Bournemouth - West Ham 2-2(1-1)
Aston Villa - Burnley 2-2(1-0)
Chelsea - Brighton & Hove 2-0(0-0)
Crystal Palace - Norwich City 2-0(1-0)
Tottenham Hotspur - Southampton 2-1(2-1)
Wolverhampton - Watford 2-0(1-0)
Everton - Manchester City 1-3(1-1)
Leicester City - Newcastle United 5-0(1-0)
Manchester United - Arsenal 1-1(1-0)

Round 8 [05-06.10.2019]
Brighton & Hove - Tottenham Hots. 3-0(2-0)
Burnley - Everton 1-0(0-0)
Liverpool FC - Leicester City 2-1(1-0)
Norwich City - Aston Villa 1-5(0-2)
Watford - Sheffield United 0-0
West Ham - Crystal Palace 1-2(0-0)
Arsenal - AFC Bournemouth 1-0(1-0)
Manchester City - Wolverhampton 0-2(0-0)
Southampton - Chelsea 1-4(1-3)
Newcastle United - Manchester Unit. 1-0(0-0)

Round 9 [19-21.10.2019]
Everton - West Ham 2-0(1-0)
AFC Bournemouth - Norwich City 0-0
Aston Villa - Brighton & Hove 2-1(1-1)
Chelsea - Newcastle United 1-0(0-0)
Leicester City - Burnley 2-1(1-1)
Tottenham Hotspur - Watford 1-1(0-1)
Wolverhampton - Southampton 1-1(0-0)
Crystal Palace - Manchester City 0-2(0-2)
Manchester United - Liverpool FC 1-1(1-0)
Sheffield United - Arsenal 1-0(1-0)

Round 10 [25-27.10.2019]
Southampton - Leicester City 0-9(0-5)
Manchester City - Aston Villa 3-0(0-0)
Brighton & Hove - Everton 3-2(1-1)
Watford - AFC Bournemouth 0-0
West Ham - Sheffield United 1-1(1-0)
Burnley - Chelsea 2-4(0-2)
Newcastle United - Wolverhampton 1-1(1-0)
Arsenal - Crystal Palace 2-2(2-1)
Liverpool FC - Tottenham Hotspur 2-1(0-1)
Norwich City - Manchester United 1-3(0-2)

Round 11 [02-03.11.2019]
AFC Bournemouth - Manchester Unit 1-0(1-0)
Arsenal - Wolverhampton 1-1(1-0)
Aston Villa - Liverpool FC 1-2(1-0)
Brighton & Hove - Norwich City 2-0(0-0)
Manchester City - Southampton 2-1(0-1)
Sheffield United - Burnley 3-0(3-0)
West Ham - Newcastle United 2-3(0-2)
Watford - Chelsea 1-2(0-1)
Crystal Palace - Leicester City 0-2(0-0)
Everton - Tottenham Hotspur 1-1(0-0)

Round 12 [08-10.11.2019]
Norwich City - Watford 0-2(0-1)
Chelsea - Crystal Palace 2-0(0-0)
Burnley - West Ham 3-0(2-0)
Newcastle United - Bournemouth 2-1(1-1)
Southampton - Everton 1-2(0-1)
Tottenham Hotspur - Sheffield Unit. 1-1(0-0)
Leicester City - Arsenal 2-0(0-0)
Manchester Unit. - Brighton & Hove 3-1(2-0)
Wolverhampton - Aston Villa 2-1(1-0)
Liverpool FC - Manchester City 3-1(2-0)

Round 13 [23-25.11.2019]
West Ham - Tottenham Hotspur 2-3(0-2)
AFC Bournemouth - Wolverhampton 1-2(0-2)
Arsenal - Southampton 2-2(1-1)
Brighton & Hove - Leicester City 0-2(0-0)
Crystal Palace - Liverpool FC 1-2(0-0)
Everton - Norwich City 0-2(0-0)
Watford - Burnley 0-3(0-0)
Manchester City - Chelsea 2-1(2-1)
Sheffield United - Manchester United 3-3(1-0)
Aston Villa - Newcastle United 2-0(2-0)

Round 14 [30.11.-01.12.2019]
Newcastle United - Manchester City 2-2(1-1)
Burnley - Crystal Palace 0-2(0-1)
Chelsea - West Ham 0-1(0-0)
Liverpool FC - Brighton & Hove 2-1(2-0)
Tottenham Hotspur - Bournemouth 3-2(1-0)
Southampton - Watford 2-1(0-1)
Norwich City - Arsenal 2-2(2-1)
Wolverhampton - Sheffield United 1-1(0-1)
Leicester City - Everton 2-1(0-1)
Manchester United - Aston Villa 2-2(1-1)

Round 15 [03-05.12.2019]
Crystal Palace - AFC Bournemouth 1-0(0-0)
Burnley - Manchester City 1-4(0-1)
Leicester City - Watford 2-0(0-0)
Wolverhampton - West Ham 2-0(1-0)
Manchester United - Tottenham Hots. 2-1(1-1)
Chelsea - Aston Villa 2-1(1-1)
Southampton - Norwich City 2-1(2-0)
Liverpool FC - Everton 5-2(4-2)
Sheffield United - Newcastle United 0-2(0-1)
Arsenal - Brighton & Hove 1-2(0-1)

Round 16 [07-09.12.2019]
Everton - Chelsea 3-1(1-0)
AFC Bournemouth - Liverpool FC 0-3(0-2)
Tottenham Hotspur - Burnley 5-0(3-0)
Watford - Crystal Palace 0-0
Manchester City - Manchester United 1-2(0-2)
Aston Villa - Leicester City 1-4(1-2)
Newcastle United - Southampton 2-1(0-0)
Norwich City - Sheffield United 1-2(1-0)
Brighton & Hove - Wolverhampton 2-2(2-2)
West Ham - Arsenal 1-3(1-0)

Round 17 [14-16.12.2019]
Liverpool FC - Watford 2-0(1-0)
Burnley - Newcastle United 1-0(0-0)
Chelsea - AFC Bournemouth 0-1(0-0)
Leicester City - Norwich City 1-1(1-1)
Sheffield United - Aston Villa 2-0(0-0)
Southampton - West Ham 0-1(0-1)
Manchester United - Everton 1-1(0-1)
Wolverhampton - Tottenham Hotspur 1-2(0-1)
Arsenal - Manchester City 0-3(0-3)
Crystal Palace - Brighton & Hove 1-1(0-0)

Round 18 [21-22.12.2019]
Everton - Arsenal 0-0
AFC Bournemouth - Burnley 0-1(0-0)
Aston Villa - Southampton 1-3(0-2)
Brighton & Hove - Sheffield United 0-1(0-1)
Newcastle United - Crystal Palace 1-0(0-0)
Norwich City - Wolverhampton 1-2(1-0)
Manchester City - Leicester City 3-1(2-1)
Watford - Manchester United 2-0(0-0)
Tottenham Hotspur - Chelsea 0-2(0-2)
West Ham - Liverpool 0-2(0-1) [29.01.2020]

Round 19 [26-27.12.2019]	Round 20 [28-29.12.2019]	Round 21 [01-02.01.2020]
Tottenham Hots. - Brighton & Hove 2-1(0-1)	Brighton & Hove - Bournemouth 2-0(1-0)	Brighton & Hove - Chelsea 1-1(0-1)
AFC Bournemouth - Arsenal 1-1(1-0)	Newcastle United - Everton 1-2(0-1)	Burnley - Aston Villa 1-2(0-2)
Aston Villa - Norwich City 1-0(0-0)	Southampton - Crystal Palace 1-1(0-0)	Newcastle United - Leicester City 0-3(0-2)
Chelsea - Southampton 0-2(0-1)	Watford - Aston Villa 3-0(1-0)	Southampton - Tottenham Hotspur 1-0(1-0)
Crystal Palace - West Ham 2-1(0-0)	Norwich City - Tottenham Hotspur 2-2(1-0)	Watford - Wolverhampton 2-1(1-0)
Everton - Burnley 1-0(0-0)	West Ham - Leicester City 1-2(1-1)	Manchester City - Everton 2-1(0-0)
Sheffield United - Watford 1-1(1-1)	Burnley - Manchester United 0-2(0-1)	Norwich City - Crystal Palace 1-1(0-0)
Manchester Unit. - Newcastle United 4-1(3-1)	Arsenal - Chelsea 1-2(1-0)	West Ham - AFC Bournemouth 4-0(3-0)
Leicester City - Liverpool FC 0-4(0-1)	Liverpool FC - Wolverhampton 1-0(1-0)	Arsenal - Manchester United 2-0(2-0)
Wolverhampton - Manchester City 3-2(0-1)	Manchester City - Sheffield United 2-0(0-0)	Liverpool FC - Sheffield United 2-0(1-0)

Round 22 [10-12.01.2020]	Round 23 [18-19.01.2020]	Round 24 [21-23.01.2020]
Sheffield United - West Ham 1-0(0-0)	Watford - Tottenham Hotspur 0-0	Bournemouth - Brighton & Hove 3-1(2-0)
Crystal Palace - Arsenal 1-1(0-1)	Arsenal - Sheffield United 1-1(1-0)	Aston Villa - Watford 2-1(0-1)
Chelsea - Burnley 3-0(2-0)	Brighton & Hove - Aston Villa 1-1(1-0)	Everton - Newcastle United 2-2(1-0)
Everton - Brighton & Hove 1-0(1-0)	Manchester City - Crystal Palace 2-2(0-1)	Sheffield United - Manchester City 0-1(0-0)
Leicester City - Southampton 1-2(1-1)	Norwich City - AFC Bournemouth 1-0(1-0)	Crystal Palace - Southampton 0-2(0-1)
Manchester United - Norwich City 4-0(1-0)	Southampton - Wolverhampton 2-3(2-0)	Chelsea - Arsenal 2-2(1-0)
Wolverhampton - Newcastle United 1-1(1-1)	West Ham - Everton 1-1(1-1)	Leicester City - West Ham 4-1(2-0)
Tottenham Hotspur - Liverpool FC 0-1(0-1)	Newcastle United - Chelsea 1-0(0-0)	Tottenham Hotspur - Norwich City 2-1(1-0)
AFC Bournemouth - Watford 0-3(0-1)	Burnley - Leicester City 2-1(0-1)	Manchester United - Burnley 0-2(0-1)
Aston Villa - Manchester City 1-6(0-4)	Liverpool FC - Manchester United 2-0(1-0)	Wolverhampton - Liverpool FC 1-2(0-1)

Round 25 [01-02.02.2020]	Round 26 [08-09.02./14-19.02.2020]	Round 27 [22-24.02.2020]
Leicester City - Chelsea 2-2(0-0)	Everton - Crystal Palace 3-1(1-0)	Chelsea - Tottenham Hotspur 2-1(1-0)
AFC Bournemouth - Aston Villa 2-1(2-0)	Brighton & Hove - Watford 1-1(0-1)	Burnley - AFC Bournemouth 3-0(0-0)
Crystal Palace - Sheffield United 0-1(0-0)	Sheffield United - AFC Bournemouth 2-1(1-1)	Crystal Palace - Newcastle United 1-0(1-0)
Liverpool FC - Southampton 4-0(0-0)	Wolverhampton - Leicester City 0-0	Sheffield United - Brighton & Hove 1-1(1-1)
Newcastle United - Norwich City 0-0	Southampton - Burnley 1-2(1-1)	Southampton - Aston Villa 2-0(1-0)
Watford - Everton 2-3(2-2)	Norwich City - Liverpool FC 0-1(0-0)	Leicester City - Manchester City 0-1(0-0)
West Ham - Brighton & Hove 3-3(2-0)	Aston Villa - Tottenham Hotspur 2-3(1-2)	Manchester United - Watford 3-0(1-0)
Manchester United - Wolverhampton 0-0	Arsenal - Newcastle United 4-0(0-0)	Wolverhampton - Norwich City 3-0(2-0)
Burnley - Arsenal 0-0	Chelsea - Manchester United 0-2(0-1)	Arsenal - Everton 3-2(2-2)
Tottenham Hotsp. - Manchester City 2-0(0-0)	Manchester City - West Ham 2-0(1-0)	Liverpool FC - West Ham 3-2(1-1)

Round 28 [28.02.-01.03.2020]	Round 29 [07-09.03.2020]	Round 30 [19-22.06.2020]
Norwich City - Leicester City 1-0(0-0)	Liverpool FC - AFC Bournemouth 2-1(2-1)	Norwich City - Southampton 0-3(0-0)
Brighton & Hove - Crystal Palace 0-1(0-0)	Arsenal - West Ham 1-0(0-0)	Tottenham Hots. - Manchester United 1-1(1-0)
AFC Bournemouth - Chelsea 2-2(0-1)	Crystal Palace - Watford 1-0(1-0)	Watford - Leicester City 1-1(0-0)
Newcastle United - Burnley 0-0	Sheffield United - Norwich City 1-0(1-0)	Brighton & Hove - Arsenal 2-1(0-0)
West Ham - Southampton 3-1(2-1)	Southampton - Newcastle United 0-1(0-0)	West Ham - Wolverhampton 0-2(0-0)
Watford - Liverpool FC 3-0(0-0)	Wolverhampton - Brighton & Hove 0-0	AFC Bournemouth - Crystal Palace 0-2(0-2)
Everton - Manchester United 1-1(1-1)	Burnley - Tottenham Hotspur 1-1(1-0)	Newcastle United - Sheffield United 3-0(0-0)
Tottenham Hotspur - Wolverhampton 2-3(2-1)	Chelsea - Everton 4-0(2-0)	Aston Villa - Chelsea 1-2(1-0)
Aston Villa - Sheffield United 0-0 [17.06.]	Manchester United - Manchester City 2-0(1-0)	Everton - Liverpool FC 0-0
Manchester City - Arsenal 3-0(1-0) [17.06.]	Leicester City - Aston Villa 4-0(1-0)	Manchester City - Burnley 5-0(3-0)

Round 31 [23-25.06.2020]	Round 32 [27.06.-02.07.2020]	Round 33 [04-06.07.2020]
Leicester City - Brighton & Hove 0-0	Aston Villa - Wolverhampton 0-1(0-0)	Norwich City - Brighton & Hove 0-1(0-1)
Tottenham Hotspur - West Ham 2-0(0-0)	Watford - Southampton 1-3(0-1)	Leicester City - Crystal Palace 3-0(0-0)
Manchester United - Sheffield United 3-0(2-0)	Crystal Palace - Burnley 0-1(0-0)	Manchester United - Bournemouth 5-2(3-1)
Newcastle United - Aston Villa 1-1(0-0)	Brighton & Hove - Manchester Unit. 0-3(0-2)	Wolverhampton - Arsenal 0-2(0-1)
Norwich City - Everton 0-1(0-0)	Bournemouth - Newcastle United 1-4(0-2)	Chelsea - Watford 3-0(2-0)
Wolverhampton - AFC Bournemouth 1-0(0-0)	Arsenal - Norwich City 4-0(2-0)	Burnley - Sheffield United 1-1(1-0)
Liverpool FC - Crystal Palace 4-0(2-0)	Everton - Leicester City 2-1(2-0)	Newcastle United - West Ham 2-2(1-1)
Burnley - Watford 1-0(0-0)	West Ham - Chelsea 3-2(1-1)	Liverpool FC - Aston Villa 2-0(0-0)
Southampton - Arsenal 0-2(0-1)	Sheffield United - Tottenham Hots. 3-1(1-0)	Southampton - Manchester City 1-0(1-0)
Chelsea - Manchester City 2-1(1-0)	Manchester City - Liverpool FC 4-0(3-0)	Tottenham Hotspur - Everton 1-0(1-0)

Round 34 [07-09.07.2020]	Round 35 [11-13.07.2020]	Round 36 [14-17.07.2020]
Crystal Palace - Chelsea 2-3(1-2)	Norwich City - West Ham 0-4(0-2)	Chelsea - Norwich City 1-0(1-0)
Watford - Norwich City 2-1(1-1)	Watford - Newcastle United 1-2(0-1)	Burnley - Wolverhampton 1-1(0-0)
Arsenal - Leicester City 1-1(1-0)	Liverpool FC - Burnley 1-1(1-0)	Manchester City - AFC Bournemouth 2-1(2-0)
Manchester City - Newcastle United 5-0(2-0)	Sheffield United - Chelsea 3-0(2-0)	Newcastle United - Tottenham Hots. 1-3(0-1)
Sheffield United - Wolverhampton 1-0(0-0)	Brighton & Hove - Manchester City 0-5(0-2)	Arsenal - Liverpool FC 2-1(2-1)
West Ham - Burnley 0-1(0-1)	Wolverhampton - Everton 3-0(1-0)	Everton - Aston Villa 1-1(0-0)
Brighton & Hove - Liverpool FC 1-3(1-2)	Aston Villa - Crystal Palace 2-0(1-0)	Leicester City - Sheffield United 2-0(1-0)
AFC Bournemouth - Tottenham Hotspur 0-0	Tottenham Hotspur - Arsenal 2-1(1-1)	Crystal Palace - Manchester United 0-2(0-1)
Everton - Southampton 1-1(1-1)	AFC Bournemouth - Leicester City 4-1(0-1)	Southampton - Brighton & Hove 1-1(0-1)
Aston Villa - Manchester United 0-3(0-2)	Manchester United - Southampton 2-2(2-1)	West Ham - Watford 3-1(3-0)

Round 37 [18-22.07.2020]
Norwich City - Burnley 0-2(0-1)
AFC Bournemouth - Southampton 0-2(0-1)
Tottenham Hotspur - Leicester City 3-0(3-0)
Brighton & Hove - Newcastle United 0-0
Sheffield United - Everton 0-1(0-0)
Wolverhampton - Crystal Palace 2-0(1-0)
Watford - Manchester City 0-4(0-2)
Aston Villa - Arsenal 1-0(1-0)
Manchester United - West Ham 1-1(0-1)
Liverpool FC - Chelsea 5-3(3-1)

Round 38 [26.07.2020]
Arsenal - Watford 3-2(3-1)
Burnley - Brighton & Hove 1-2(1-1)
Chelsea - Wolverhampton 2-0(2-0)
Crystal Palace - Tottenham Hotspur 1-1(0-1)
Everton - AFC Bournemouth 1-3(1-2)
Leicester City - Manchester United 0-2(0-0)
Manchester City - Norwich City 5-0(2-0)
Newcastle United - Liverpool FC 1-3(1-1)
Southampton - Sheffield United 3-1(0-1)
West Ham - Aston Villa 1-1(0-0)

Final Standings

						Total				Home					Away		
1.	**Liverpool FC**	38	32	3	3	85 - 33	99	18	1	0	52 - 16	14	2	3	33 - 17
2.	Manchester City FC	38	26	3	9	102 - 35	81	15	2	2	57 - 13	11	1	7	45 - 22
3.	Manchester United FC	38	18	12	8	66 - 36	66	10	7	2	40 - 17	8	5	6	26 - 19
4.	Chelsea FC London	38	20	6	12	69 - 54	66	11	3	5	30 - 16	9	3	7	39 - 38
5.	Leicester City FC	38	18	8	12	67 - 41	62	11	4	4	35 - 17	7	4	8	32 - 24
6.	Tottenham Hotspur FC London	38	16	11	11	61 - 47	59	12	3	4	36 - 17	4	8	7	25 - 30
7.	Wolverhampton Wanderers FC	38	15	14	9	51 - 40	59	8	7	4	27 - 19	7	7	5	24 - 21
8.	Arsenal FC London	38	14	14	10	56 - 48	56	10	6	3	36 - 24	4	8	7	20 - 24
9.	Sheffield United FC	38	14	12	12	39 - 39	54	10	3	6	24 - 15	4	9	6	15 - 24
10.	Burnley FC	38	15	9	14	43 - 50	54	8	4	7	24 - 23	7	5	7	19 - 27
11.	Southampton FC	38	15	7	16	51 - 60	52	6	3	10	21 - 35	9	4	6	30 - 25
12.	Everton FC Liverpool	38	13	10	15	44 - 56	49	8	7	4	24 - 21	5	3	11	20 - 35
13.	Newcastle United FC	38	11	11	16	38 - 58	44	6	8	5	20 - 21	5	3	11	18 - 37
14.	Crystal Palace FC London	38	11	10	17	31 - 50	43	6	5	8	15 - 20	5	5	9	16 - 30
15.	Brighton & Hove Albion FC	38	9	14	15	39 - 54	41	5	7	7	20 - 27	4	7	8	19 - 27
16.	West Ham United FC London	38	10	9	19	49 - 62	39	6	4	9	30 - 33	4	5	10	19 - 29
17.	Aston Villa FC Birmingham	38	9	8	21	41 - 67	35	7	3	9	22 - 30	2	5	12	19 - 37
18.	AFC Bournemouth (Relegated)	38	9	7	22	40 - 65	34	5	6	8	22 - 30	4	1	14	18 - 35
19.	Watford FC (Relegated)	38	8	10	20	36 - 64	34	6	6	7	22 - 27	2	4	13	14 - 37
20.	Norwich City FC (Relegated)	38	5	6	27	26 - 75	21	4	3	12	19 - 37	1	3	15	7 - 38

Top goalscorers:	
23 Jamie Richard Vardy	*Leicester City FC*
22 Pierre-Emerick Emiliano François Aubameyang (GAB)	*Arsenal FC London*
22 Daniel William John Ings	*Southampton FC*
20 Raheem Shaquille Sterling	*Manchester City FC*
19 Mohamed Salah Ghaly (EGY)	*Liverpool FC*
18 Harry Edward Kane	*Tottenham Hotspur FC London*
18 Sadio Mané (SEN)	*Liverpool FC*

EFL (League) Cup Final 2019/2020

01.03.2020; Wembley Stadium, London; Referee: Lee Stephen Mason; Attendance: 82,145
Manchester City FC - Aston Villa FC Birmingham   **2-1(2-1)**

Manchester City: Claudio Andrés Bravo Muñoz, Kyle Andrew Walker, John Stones, Oleksandr Zinchenko, Fernando Luiz Roza „Fernandinho", İlkay Gündoğan (58.Kevin De Bruyne), Rodrigo Hernández Cascante „Rodri", Philip Walter Foden, David Josué Jiménez Silva (Cap) (77.Bernardo Mota Veiga de Carvalho e Silva), Raheem Shaquille Sterling, Sergio Leonel Agüero del Castillo (84.Gabriel Fernando de Jesus). Trainer: Josep "Pep" Guardiola Sala (Spain).

Aston Villa: Ørjan Håskjold Nyland, Frédéric Guilbert, Björn Lionel Engels, Tyrone Deon Mings, Matthew Robert Targett, Douglas Luiz Soares de Paulo, Marvelous Nakamba, Ahmed Eissa Elmohamady Abdel Fattah (70.Conor Hourihane), Jack Peter Grealish (Cap), Anwar El Ghazi (70.Mahmoud Ahmed Ibrahim Hassan „Trezeguet"), Mbwana Ally Samatta (80.Keinan Vincent Joseph Davis). Trainer: Dean Smith.

Goals: 1-0 Sergio Leonel Agüero del Castillo (20), 2-0 Rodrigo Hernández Cascante „Rodri" (30), 2-1 Mbwana Ally Samatta (41).

NATIONAL CUP
FA Cup 2019/2020

Second Round [29-30.11./01-02/10/16-17.12.2019]			
Maldon & Tiptree FC - Newport County AFC	0-1(0-0)	Peterborough United FC - Dover Athletic FC	3-0(1-0)
Portsmouth FC - Altrincham FC	2-1(0-0)	Crawley Town FC - Fleetwood Town FC	1-2(1-1)
Shrewsbury Town FC - Mansfield Town FC	2-0(0-0)	Northampton Town FC - Notts County FC	3-1(2-0)
Kingstonian FC - AFC Fylde	0-2(0-2)	Bristol Rovers FC - Plymouth Argyle FC	1-1(0-0)
Walsall FC - Oxford United FC	0-1(0-0)	Tranmere Rovers FC - Chichester City FC	5-1(0-0)
Forest Green Rovers FC - Carlisle United FC	2-2(1-1)	Solihull Moors FC - Rotherham United FC	3-4(2-0)
Oldham Athletic AFC - Burton Albion FC	0-1(0-1)	*Replay*:	
Cheltenham Town FC - Port Vale FC Burslem	1-3(1-0)	Plymouth Argyle FC - Bristol Rovers FC	0-1(0-0)
Eastleigh FC - Crewe Alexandra FC	1-1(0-1)	Carlisle United FC - Forest Green Rovers FC	1-0(1-0)
Blackpool FC - Maidstone United FC	3-1(0-1)	Crewe Alexandra FC - Eastleigh FC	3-1(1-0)
Coventry City FC - Ipswich Town FC	1-1(0-0)	Ipswich Town FC - Coventry City FC	1-2(0-2)
Exeter City FC - Hartlepool United FC	2-2(2-0)	Boston United FC - Rochdale AFC	1-2(0-1)
Gillingham FC - Doncaster Rovers FC	3-0(2-0)	Hartlepool United FC - Exeter City FC	1-0(0-0,0-0)
Rochdale AFC - Boston United FC	0-0		

Third Round [04-06/14-15/23.01.2020]				
Rochdale AFC - Newcastle United FC	1-1(0-1)		Chelsea FC London - Nottingham Forest FC	2-0(2-0)
Bristol City FC - Shrewsbury Town FC	1-1(1-0)		Charlton Athletic - West Bromwich Albion FC	0-1(0-1)
Millwall FC - Newport County AFC	3-0(1-0)		Sheffield United FC - AFC Fylde	2-1(1-0)
Rotherham United FC - Hull City AFC	2-3(2-1)		Bristol Rovers FC - Coventry City FC	2-2(2-1)
Burnley FC - Peterborough United FC	4-2(3-1)		Crewe Alexandra FC - Barnsley FC	1-3(0-1)
Birmingham City FC - Blackburn Rovers FC	2-1(1-0)		Middlesbrough FC - Tottenham Hotspur FC London	1-1(0-0)
Fulham FC London - Aston Villa FC Birmingham	2-1(0-0)		Crystal Palace FC London - Derby County FC	0-1(0-1)
Cardiff City FC - Carlisle United FC	2-2(0-2)		Burton Albion FC - Northampton Town FC	2-4(1-3)
Oxford United FC - Hartlepool United FC	4-1(0-1)		Liverpool FC - Everton FC Liverpool	1-0(0-0)
Southampton FC - Huddersfield Town AFC	2-0(0-0)		Gillingham FC - West Ham United FC London	0-2(0-0)
Brighton & Hove Albion - Sheffield Wednesday FC	0-1(0-0)		Arsenal FC London - Leeds United FC	1-0(0-0)
Reading FC - Blackpool FC	2-2(0-1)		*Replay*:	
Watford FC - Tranmere Rovers FC	3-3(3-0)		Newcastle United FC - Rochdale AFC	4-1(3-0)
Preston North End FC - Norwich City FC	2-4(0-3)		Shrewsbury Town FC - Bristol City FC	1-0(0-0)
Brentford FC - Stoke City FC	1-0(1-0)		Carlisle United FC - Cardiff City FC	3-4(1-2)
Leicester City FC - Wigan Athletic FC	2-0(2-0)		Blackpool FC - Reading FC	0-2(0-1)
Wolverhampton Wanderers - Manchester United FC	0-0		Tranmere Rovers FC - Watford FC	2-1(1-0,1-1)
AFC Bournemouth - Luton Town FC	4-0(1-0)		Manchester United FC - Wolverhampton Wanderers	1-0(0-0)
Manchester City FC - Port Vale FC Burslem	4-1(2-1)		Coventry City FC - Bristol Rovers FC	3-0(1-0)
Fleetwood Town FC - Portsmouth FC	1-2(0-0)		Tottenham Hotspur FC London - Middlesbrough FC	2-1(2-0)
Queens Park Rangers FC - Swansea City AFC	5-1(3-0)			

Fourth Round [24-27.01./04-05.02.2020]				
Queens Park Rangers FC - Sheffield Wednesday FC	1-2(0-1)		Manchester City FC - Fulham FC London	4-0(2-0)
Northampton Town FC - Derby County FC	0-0		Tranmere Rovers FC - Manchester United FC	0-6(0-5)
Brentford FC - Leicester City FC	0-1(0-1)		Shrewsbury Town FC - Liverpool FC	2-2(0-1)
Southampton FC - Tottenham Hotspur FC London	1-1(0-0)		AFC Bournemouth - Arsenal FC London	1-2(0-2)
Millwall FC - Sheffield United FC	0-2(0-0)		*Replay*:	
Reading FC - Cardiff City FC	1-1(1-1)		Cardiff City FC - Reading FC	3-3 aet; 1-4 pen
West Ham United FC - West Bromwich Albion FC	0-1(0-1)		Derby County FC - Northampton Town FC	4-2(2-0)
Burnley FC - Norwich City FC	1-2(0-0)		Birmingham City FC - Coventry City FC	2-2 aet; 4-1 pen
Coventry City FC - Birmingham City FC	0-0		Liverpool FC - Shrewsbury Town FC	1-0(0-0)
Newcastle United FC - Oxford United FC	0-0		Oxford United FC - Newcastle United FC	2-3(0-2,2-2)
Portsmouth FC - Barnsley FC	4-2(2-0)		Tottenham Hotspur FC London - Southampton FC	3-2(1-1)
Hull City AFC - Chelsea FC London	1-2(0-1)			

1/8-Finals [02-05.03.2020]				
Portsmouth FC - Arsenal FC London	0-2(0-1)		Sheffield Wednesday FC - Manchester City FC	0-1(0-0)
Chelsea FC London - Liverpool FC	2-0(1-0)		Leicester City FC - Birmingham City FC	1-0(0-0)
Reading FC - Sheffield United FC	1-2(1-1,1-1)		Tottenham Hotspur FC London - Norwich City FC	1-1 aet; 2-3 pen
West Bromwich Albion FC - Newcastle United FC	2-3(0-2)		Derby County FC - Manchester United FC	0-3(0-2)

Quarter-Finals [27-28.06.2020]				
Norwich City FC - Manchester United FC	1-2(0-0,1-1)		Leicester City FC - Chelsea FC London	0-1(0-0)
Sheffield United FC - Arsenal FC London	1-2(0-1)		Newcastle United FC - Manchester City FC	0-2(0-1)

Semi-Finals [18-19.07.2020]				
Arsenal FC London - Manchester City FC	2-0(1-0)		Manchester United FC - Chelsea FC London	1-3(0-1)

Final

01.08.2020; Wembley Stadium, London; Referee: Anthony Taylor; Attendance: None

Arsenal FC London - Chelsea FC London　　　　　　　　　　　　　　　　**2-1(1-1)**

Arsenal: Emiliano Martínez, Robert Samuel Holding, David Luiz Moreira Marinho (88.Sokratis Papastathopoulos), Kieran Tierney (90+13.Sead Kolašinac), Héctor Bellerín Moruno, Daniel „Dani" Ceballos Fernández, Granit Xhaka, Ainsley Maitland-Niles, Nicolas Pépé, Alexandre Lacazette (82.Edward Keddar Nketiah), Pierre Emerick François Aubameyang (Cap). Trainer: Mikel Amatriain Arteta (Spain).

Chelsea: Wilfredo Daniel Caballero Lazcano, César Azpilicueta Tanco (Cap) (35.Andreas Bødtker Christensen), Kurt Happy Zouma, Antonio Rüdiger (78.Ross Barkley), Reece James, Filho Jorge Luiz Frello „Jorginho",Mateo Kovačić [*sent off 73*], Marcos Alonso Mendoza, Mason Tony Mount (78.Callum James Hudson-Odoi), Olivier Giroud (78.Kevin Oghenetega Tamaraebi Bakumo-Abraham), Christian Pulišić (49.Pedro Eliezer Rodríguez Ledesma). Trainer: Frank James Lampard Junior.

Goals: 0-1 Christian Pulišić (5), 1-1 Pierre Emerick François Aubameyang (28 penalty), 2-1 Pierre Emerick François Aubameyang (67).

Arsenal Football Club London

Founded:	1886
Stadium:	Emirates Stadium, London (60,704)
Trainer:	Unai Emery Etxegoien (ESP) 03.11.1971
[29.11.2019]	Karl Fredrik Ljungberg (SWE) 16.04.1977
[22.12.2019]	Mikel Amatriain Arteta (ESP) 26.03.1982

Goalkeepers:	DOB	M	(s)	G
Bernd Leno (GER)	04.03.1992	30		
Emiliano Martínez (ARG)	02.09.1992	8	(1)	
Defenders:	**DOB**	**M**	**(s)**	**G**
Cédric Ricardo Alves Soares (POR)	31.08.1991	3	(2)	1
Calum Chambers	20.01.1995	13	(1)	1
David Luiz Moreira Marinho (BRA)	22.04.1987	32	(1)	2
Héctor Bellerín Moruno (ESP)	19.03.1995	13	(2)	1
Robert Samuel Holding	20.09.1995	6	(2)	
Sead Kolašinac (BIH)	20.06.1993	19	(7)	
Ainsley Maitland-Niles	29.08.1997	15	(5)	
Shkodran Mustafi (GER)	17.04.1992	13	(2)	
Ignacio Monreal Eraso „Nacho Monreal"(ESP)	26.02.1986	3		
Pablo Marí Villar (ESP)	31.08.1993	2		
Sokratis Papastathopoulos (GRE)	09.06.1988	19		2
Kieran Tierney (SCO)	05.06.1997	12	(3)	1

Midfielders:	DOB	M	(s)	G
Daniel „Dani" Ceballos Fernández (ESP)	07.08.1996	18	(6)	
Mattéo Guendouzi (FRA)	14.04.1999	19	(5)	
Henrikh Mkhitaryan (ARM)	21.01.1989	1	(2)	
Mesut Özil (GER)	15.10.1988	18		1
Emile Smith-Rowe	28.07.2000	1	(1)	
Lucas Sebastián Torreira Di Pascua (URU)	11.02.1996	17	(12)	1
Joseph George Willock	20.08.1999	8	(21)	1
Granit Xhaka (SUI)	27.09.1992	30	(1)	1
Forwards:	**DOB**	**M**	**(s)**	**G**
Pierre Emerick François Aubameyang (GAB)	18.06.1989	35	(1)	22
Gabriel Teodoro Martinelli Silva (BRA)	18.06.2001	6	(8)	3
Alexandre Lacazette (FRA)	28.05.1991	22	(8)	10
Reiss Nelson	10.12.1999	7	(10)	1
Edward Keddar Nketiah	30.05.1999	7	(6)	2
Nicolas Pépé (CIV)	29.05.1995	22	(9)	5
Bukayo Saka	05.09.2001	19	(7)	1

Aston Villa Football Club Birmingham

Founded:	21.11.1874
Stadium:	Villa park, Birmingham (42,875)
Trainer:	Dean Smith 19.03.1971

Goalkeepers:	DOB	M	(s)	G
Thomas David Heaton	15.04.1986	20		
Ørjan Håskjold Nyland (NOR)	10.09.1990	5	(2)	
José Manuel "Pepe" Reina Páez (ESP)	31.08.1982	12		
Jed John Steer	23.09.1992	1		
Defenders:	**DOB**	**M**	**(s)**	**G**
Ahmed Eissa Elmohamady Abdel Fattah(EGY)	09.09.1987	11	(7)	1
Björn Lionel Engels (BEL)	15.09.1994	15	(2)	1
Frédéric Guilbert (FRA)	24.12.1994	22	(3)	
Kortney Paul Duncan Hause	16.07.1995	17	(1)	1
Ezri Konsa Ngoyo	23.10.1997	24	(1)	1
Tyrone Deon Mings	13.03.1993	33		2
Matthew Robert Targett	18.09.1995	27	(1)	1
Neil John Taylor (WAL)	07.02.1989	11	(3)	
Midfielders:	**DOB**	**M**	**(s)**	**G**
Douglas Luiz Soares de Paulo (BRA)	09.05.1998	28	(8)	3

	DOB	M	(s)	G
Daniel Noel Drinkwater	05.03.1990	4		
Anwar El Ghazi (NED)	03.05.1995	26	(8)	4
Jack Peter Grealish	10.09.1995	36		8
Conor Hourihane (IRL)	02.02.1991	18	(9)	3
José Ignacio Peleteiro Ramallo „Jota" (ESP)	16.06.1991	4	(6)	
Henri George Lansbury	12.10.1990	2	(8)	
John McGinn (SCO)	18.10.1994	27	(1)	3
Marvelous Nakamba (ZIM)	19.01.1994	19	(10)	
Forwards:	**DOB**	**M**	**(s)**	**G**
Borja González Tomás „Borja Bastón" (ESP)	25.08.1992		(2)	
Keinan Vincent Joseph Davis	13.02.1998	4	(14)	
Jonathan Adjo Kodjia (IRL)	22.10.1989		(6)	
Mbwana Ally Samatta (TAN)	23.12.1992	11	(3)	1
Mahmoud Ahmed Ibrahim Hassan (EGY)	01.10.1994	20	(14)	6
Indiana Denchev Vassilev (USA)	16.02.2001		(4)	
Wesley Moraes Ferreira da Silva (BRA)	26.11.1996	21		5

Athletic Football Club Bournemouth

Founded:	1899
Stadium:	Vitality Stadium, Bournemouth (11,329)
Trainer:	Edward Howe 29.11.1977

Goalkeepers:	DOB	M	(s)	G
Aaron Ramsdale	14.05.1998	37		
Mark Travers (IRL)	18.05.1999	1		
Defenders:	**DOB**	**M**	**(s)**	**G**
Nathan Benjamin Aké (NED)	18.02.1995	29		2
Steve Cook	19.04.1991	28	(1)	1
Charlie Daniels	07.09.1986	2		
Diego Rico Salguero (ESP)	23.02.1993	27		
Simon Francis	16.02.1985	10	(5)	
Lloyd Kelly	06.10.1998	7	(1)	
Christopher James Mepham (WAL)	05.11.1997	10	(2)	1
Jack Benjamin Simpson	08.01.1997	1	(3)	
Adam James Smith	29.04.1991	24		
Jack Stacey	06.04.1996	17	(2)	
Midfielders:	**DOB**	**M**	**(s)**	**G**
Philip Billing (DEN)	11.06.1996	29	(5)	1

	DOB	M	(s)	G
David Robert Brooks (WAL)	08.07.1997	8	(1)	1
Lewis John Cook	03.02.1997	14	(13)	
Daniel Gosling	02.02.1990	14	(10)	3
Jefferson Andrés Lerma Solís (COL)	25.10.1994	31	(2)	1
Andrew Ronald Edward Surman (RSA)	20.08.1986	2	(3)	
Forwards:	**DOB**	**M**	**(s)**	**G**
Arnaut Danjuma (NED)	31.01.1997	6	(8)	
Ryan Fraser (SCO)	24.02.1994	21	(7)	1
Jordon Femi Ashley Ibe	08.12.1995		(2)	
Joshua Christian Kojo King (NOR)	15.01.1992	24	(2)	6
Dominic Solanke	14.09.1997	17	(15)	3
Junior Stanislas	26.11.1989	7	(8)	3
Sam Surridge	28.07.1998		(4)	
Callum Eddie Graham Wilson	27.02.1992	32	(3)	8
Harry Wilson (WAL)	22.03.1997	20	(11)	7

Brighton & Hove Albion Football Club

Founded:	24.06.1901
Stadium:	Falmer Stadium, Brighton and Hove (30,666)
Trainer:	Graham Stephen Potter 20.05.1975

Goalkeepers:	DOB	M	(s)	G
Mathew David Ryan (AUS)	08.04.1992	38		
Defenders:	**DOB**	**M**	**(s)**	**G**
Bernardo Fernandes da Silva Junior (BRA)	14.05.1995	7	(7)	
Gaëtan Bong Songo (CMR)	25.04.1988		(4)	
Daniel Johnson Burn	09.05.1992	33	(1)	
Shane Patrick Michael Duffy (IRL)	01.01.1992	12	(7)	1
Lewis Carl Dunk	21.11.1991	36		3
Tariq Kwame Nii-Lante Lamptey	30.09.2000	7	(1)	
Martín Montoya Torralbo (ESP)	14.04.1991	23	(4)	
Ezequiel Schelotto (ITA)	23.05.1989	4	(4)	
Adam Harry Webster	04.01.1995	31		3
Midfielders:	**DOB**	**M**	**(s)**	**G**
Steven Alzate (COL)	08.09.1998	12	(7)	
Yves Bissouma (MLI)	30.08.1996	15	(7)	1

	DOB	M	(s)	G
Pascal Groß (GER)	15.06.1991	22	(7)	2
Alexis Mac Allister (ARG)	24.12.1998	4	(5)	
Solomon Benjamin March	20.07.1994	11	(8)	
Aaron Frank Mooy (AUS)	15.09.1990	25	(6)	2
David Petrus Wenceslaus Henri Pröpper(NED)	02.09.1991	32	(3)	1
Dale Christopher Stephens	12.06.1989	28	(5)	
Leandro Trossard (BEL)	04.12.1994	22	(9)	5
Forwards:	**DOB**	**M**	**(s)**	**G**
Florin Andone (ROU)	11.04.1993	1	(2)	1
Aaron Anthony Connolly (IRL)	28.01.2000	14	(10)	3
Alireza Jahanbakhsh (IRN)	11.08.1993	3	(7)	2
Jürgen Leonardo Locadia (NED)	07.11.1993	1	(1)	
Neal Maupay (FRA)	14.08.1996	30	(7)	10
Glenn Murray	25.09.1983	7	(16)	1

Burnley Football Club

Founded: 18.05.1882
Stadium: Turf Moor, Burnley (21,944)
Trainer: Sean Mark Dyche 28.06.1971

Goalkeepers:	DOB	M	(s)	G
Nicholas David Pope	19.04.1992	38		
Defenders:	**DOB**	**M**	**(s)**	**G**
Phillip Anthony Bardsley (SCO)	28.06.1985	21		
Kevin Finbarr Long (IRL)	18.08.1990	6	(2)	
Matthew John Lowton	09.06.1989	17		
Benjamin Mee	21.09.1989	32		1
Erik Pieters (NED)	07.08.1988	21	(3)	
James Alan Tarkowski	19.11.1992	38		2
Charles James Taylor	18.09.1993	22	(2)	
Midfielders:	**DOB**	**M**	**(s)**	**G**
Robert Brady (IRL)	14.01.1992	5	(12)	1
Joshua Brownhill	19.12.1995	9	(1)	
Jack Frank Porteous Cork	25.06.1989	30		
Daniel Noel Drinkwater	05.03.1990	1		
Jóhann Guðmundsson (ISL)	27.10.1990	6	(6)	1
Jeffrey Patrick Hendrick (IRL)	31.01.1992	22	(2)	2
Aaron Justin Lennon	16.04.1987	4	(12)	
Ashley Roy Westwood	01.04.1990	35		2
Forwards:	**DOB**	**M**	**(s)**	**G**
Ashley Luke Barnes	30.10.1989	17	(2)	6
Dwight James Matthew McNeil	22.11.1999	38		2
Jay Enrique Rodriguez	29.07.1989	20	(16)	8
Max Thompson	09.02.2002		(1)	
Matěj Vydra (CZE)	01.05.1992	7	(12)	2
Christopher Grant Wood (NZL)	07.12.1991	29	(3)	14

Chelsea Football Club London

Founded: 10.03.1905
Stadium: Stamford Bridge, London (40,853)
Trainer: Frank James Lampard Junior 20.06.1978

Goalkeepers:	DOB	M	(s)	G
Wilfredo Daniel Caballero Lazcano (ARG)	28.09.1981	5		
Kepa Arrizabalaga Revuelta (ESP)	03.10.1994	33		
Defenders:	**DOB**	**M**	**(s)**	**G**
César Azpilicueta Tanco (ESP)	28.08.1989	36		2
Andreas Bødtker Christensen (DEN)	10.04.1996	21		
Emerson Palmieri dos Santos (ITA)	03.08.1994	13	(2)	
Reece James	08.12.1999	16	(8)	
Tariq Kwame Nii-Lante Lamptey	30.09.2000		(1)	
Marcos Alonso Mendoza (ESP)	28.12.1990	15	(3)	4
Antonio Rüdiger (GER)	03.03.1993	19	(1)	2
Oluwafikayomi Oluwadamilola Tomori	19.12.1997	15		1
Kurt Happy Zouma (FRA)	27.10.1994	25	(3)	
Midfielders:	**DOB**	**M**	**(s)**	**G**
Faustino Adebola Rasheed Anjorin	23.11.2001		(1)	
Ross Barkley	05.12.1993	13	(8)	1
Billy Clifford Gilmour (SCO)	11.06.2001	2	(4)	
Filho Jorge Luiz Frello „Jorginho" (ITA)	20.12.1991	27	(4)	4
N'Golo Kanté (FRA)	29.03.1991	20	(2)	3
Mateo Kovačić (CRO)	06.05.1994	23	(8)	1
Ruben Ira Loftus-Cheek	23.01.1996	2	(5)	
Mason Tony Mount	10.01.1999	32	(5)	7
Forwards:	**DOB**	**M**	**(s)**	**G**
Kevin Oghenetega Tamaraebi Bakumo-Abraham	02.10.1997	25	(9)	15
Michy Batshuayi-Atunga (BEL)	02.10.1993	1	(15)	1
Armando Broja (ALB)	10.09.2001		(1)	
Olivier Giroud (FRA)	30.09.1986	12	(6)	8
Callum James Hudson-Odoi	07.11.2000	7	(15)	1
Pedro Eliezer Rodríguez Ledesma (ESP)	28.07.1987	8	(3)	1
Christian Pulišić (USA)	18.09.1998	19	(6)	9
Willian Borges da Silva (BRA)	09.08.1988	29	(7)	9

Crystal Palace Football Club London

Founded: 10.09.1905
Stadium: Selhurst Park, London (26,074)
Trainer: Roy Hodgson 09.08.1947

Goalkeepers:	DOB	M	(s)	G
Vicente Guaita Panadero (ESP)	10.01.1987	35		
Wayne Robert Hennessey (WAL)	24.01.1987	3		
Defenders:	**DOB**	**M**	**(s)**	**G**
Gary James Cahill	19.12.1985	25		
Scott Dann	14.02.1987	14	(2)	
Martin Ronald Kelly	27.04.1990	17	(2)	
Tyrick Mitchell	01.09.1999	2	(2)	
Mamadou Sakho (FRA)	13.02.1990	11	(3)	
James Oliver Charles Tomkins	29.03.1989	18		1
Patrick John Miguel van Aanholt (NED)	29.08.1990	29		3
Joel Edward Philip Ward	29.10.1989	27	(2)	
Midfielders:	**DOB**	**M**	**(s)**	**G**
Pierrick Brandon Leroy Keutcha	10.12.2001		(2)	
Cheikhou Kouyaté (SEN)	21.12.1989	29	(6)	1
James McFarlane McArthur (SCO)	07.10.1987	37		
James Patrick McCarthy (IRL)	12.11.1990	16	(17)	
Max Meyer (GER)	18.09.1995	6	(11)	
Luka Milivojević (SRB)	07.04.1991	28	(3)	3
Jaïro Jocquim Riedewald (NED)	09.09.1996	7	(10)	
Jeffrey Schlupp (GHA)	23.12.1992	11	(6)	3
Andros Darryl Townsend	16.07.1991	14	(10)	1
Forwards:	**DOB**	**M**	**(s)**	**G**
Jordan Pierre Ayew (GHA)	11.09.1991	37		9
Christian Benteke Liolo (BEL)	03.12.1990	13	(11)	2
Cenk Tosun (TUR)	07.06.1991	2	(3)	1
Victor Camarasa Ferrando (ESP)	28.05.1994		(1)	
Connor Neil Ralph Wickham	31.03.1993		(6)	1
Dazet Wilfried Armel Zaha (CIV)	10.11.1992	37	(1)	4

Everton Football Club Liverpool

Founded: 1878
Stadium: Goodison Park, Liverpool (39,414)
Trainer: Marco Alexandre Saraiva da Silva (POR) 12.07.1977
[05.12.2019] Duncan Cowan Ferguson (SCO) 27.12.1971
[22.12.2019] Carlo Ancelotti (ITA) 10.06.1959

Goalkeepers:	DOB	M	(s)	G
Jordan Lee Pickford	07.03.1994	38		
Defenders:	**DOB**	**M**	**(s)**	**G**
Leighton John Baines	11.12.1984	4	(4)	
Jarrad Paul Branthwaite	27.06.2002	2	(2)	
Séamus Coleman (IRL)	11.10.1988	21	(6)	
Lucas Digne (FRA)	20.07.1993	35		
Mason Anthony Holgate	22.10.1996	24	(3)	
Michael Vincent Keane	11.01.1993	28	(3)	2
Yerry Fernando Mina González (COL)	23.09.1994	25	(4)	2
Djibril Sidibé (FRA)	29.07.1992	18	(7)	
Midfielders:	**DOB**	**M**	**(s)**	**G**
André Filipe Tavares Gomes (POR)	30.07.1993	17	(2)	
Bernard Anício Caldeira Duarte (BRA)	08.09.1992	15	(12)	3
Thomas Davies	30.06.1998	23	(7)	1
Fabian Delph	21.11.1989	13	(3)	
Jean-Philippe Gbamin (CIV)	25.09.1995	1	(1)	
Alexander Chuka Iwobi (NGA)	03.05.1996	19	(6)	1
Morgan Fernand Gérard Schneiderlin (FRA)	08.11.1989	12	(3)	
Gylfi Sigurðsson (ISL)	08.09.1989	28	(7)	2
Forwards:	**DOB**	**M**	**(s)**	**G**
Dominic Calvert-Lewin	16.03.1997	30	(6)	13
Anthony Michael Gordon	24.02.2001	4	(7)	
Bioty Moise Kean (ITA)	28.02.2000	6	(23)	2
El Hadji Baye Oumar Niasse (SEN)	18.04.1990		(3)	
Richarlison de Andrade (BRA)	10.05.1997	36		13
Cenk Tosun (TUR)	07.06.1991	2	(3)	1
Theo James Walcott	16.03.1989	17	(8)	2

Leicester City Football Club

Founded: 1884
Stadium: King Power Stadium, Leicester (32,243)
Trainer: Brendan Rodgers (NIR)　　26.01.1973

Goalkeepers:	DOB	M	(s)	G
Kasper Peter Schmeichel (DEN)	05.11.1986	38		
Defenders:	**DOB**	**M**	**(s)**	**G**
Ryan Bennett	06.03.1990	3	(2)	
Benjamin James Chilwell	21.12.1996	27		3
Jonathan Grant Evans (NIR)	03.01.1988	38		1
Christian Fuchs (AUT)	07.04.1986	8	(3)	
James Michael Justin	11.07.1999	11	(2)	
Westley Nathan Morgan (JAM)	21.01.1984	4	(7)	
Çağlar Söyüncü (TUR)	23.05.1996	34		1
Midfielders:	**DOB**	**M**	**(s)**	**G**
Marc Kevin Albrighton	18.11.1989	9	(11)	
Harvey Lewis Barnes	09.12.1997	24	(12)	6

	DOB	M	(s)	G
Hamza Dewan Choudhury	01.10.1997	10	(10)	1
Demarai Remelle Gray	28.06.1996	3	(18)	2
Matthew Lee James	22.07.1991		(1)	
James Daniel Maddison	23.11.1996	29	(2)	6
Nampalys Mendy (FRA)	23.06.1992	4	(3)	
Onyinye Wilfred Ndidi (NGA)	16.12.1996	29	(3)	2
Dennis Praet (BEL)	14.05.1994	12	(15)	1
Ricardo Domingos Barbosa Pereira (POR)	06.10.1993	28		3
Youri Marion Tielemans (BEL)	07.05.1997	32	(5)	3
Forwards:	**DOB**	**M**	**(s)**	**G**
Ayoze Pérez Gutiérrez (ESP)	23.07.1993	26	(7)	8
Kelechi Promise Iheanacho (NGA)	03.10.1996	12	(8)	5
Jamie Richard Vardy	11.01.1987	34	(1)	23

Liverpool Football Club

Founded: 03.06.1892
Stadium: Anfield Road, Liverpool (53,394)
Trainer: Jürgen Norbert Klopp (GER)　　16.06.1967

Goalkeepers:	DOB	M	(s)	G
Adrián San Miguel del Castillo (ESP)	03.01.1987	9	(2)	
Alisson Ramses Becker (BRA)	02.10.1992	29		
Defenders:	**DOB**	**M**	**(s)**	**G**
Trent John Alexander-Arnold	07.10.1998	35	(3)	4
Joseph Dave Gomez	23.05.1997	22	(6)	
Dejan Lovren (CRO)	05.07.1989	9	(1)	
Job Joël André Matip (CMR)	08.08.1991	8	(1)	1
Andrew Robertson (SCO)	11.03.1994	34	(2)	2
Virgil van Dijk (NED)	08.07.1991	38		5
Neco Shay Williams (WAL)	13.04.2001	3	(3)	
Midfielders:	**DOB**	**M**	**(s)**	**G**
Harvey Scott Elliott	04.04.2003		(2)	
Fabio Henrique Tavares "Fabinho" (BRA)	23.10.1993	22	(6)	2

	DOB	M	(s)	G
Jordan Brian Henderson	17.06.1990	26	(4)	4
Curtis Julian Jones	30.01.2001	1	(5)	1
Naby Keïta (GUI)	10.02.1995	9	(9)	2
Adam David Lallana	10.05.1988	3	(12)	1
James Philip Milner	04.01.1986	9	(13)	2
Alexander Mark David Oxlade-Chamberlain	15.08.1993	17	(13)	4
Georginio Gregion Emile Wijnaldum (NED)	11.11.1990	35	(2)	4
Forwards:	**DOB**	**M**	**(s)**	**G**
Sadio Mané (SEN)	10.04.1992	31	(4)	18
Takumi Minamino (JPN)	16.01.1995	2	(8)	
Divock Okoth Origi (BEL)	18.04.1995	7	(21)	4
Roberto Firmino Barbosa de Oliveira (BRA)	02.10.1991	34	(4)	9
Mohamed Salah Ghaly (EGY)	15.06.1992	33	(1)	19
Xherdan Shaqiri (SUI)	10.10.1991	2	(5)	1

Manchester City Football Club

Founded: 1880
Stadium: Etihad (City of Manchester) Stadium, Manchester (55,017)
Trainer: Josep "Pep" Guardiola Sala (ESP)　　18.01.1971

Goalkeepers:	DOB	M	(s)	G
Claudio Andrés Bravo Muñoz (CHI)	13.04.1983	3	(1)	
Ederson Santana de Moraes (BRA)	17.08.1993	35		
Defenders:	**DOB**	**M**	**(s)**	**G**
Eric García Martret (ESP)	09.01.2001	8	(5)	
João Pedro Cavaco Cancelo (POR)	27.05.1994	13	(4)	
Aymeric Jean Louis Gerard Alphonse Laporte (FRA)	27.05.1994	14	(1)	1
Benjamin Mendy (FRA)	17.07.1994	18	(1)	
Nicolás Hernán Gonzalo Otamendi (ARG)	12.02.1988	18	(6)	2
John Stones	28.05.1994	12	(4)	
Kyle Andrew Walker	28.05.1990	28	(1)	1
Oleksandr Zinchenko (UKR)	15.12.1996	13	(6)	
Midfielders:	**DOB**	**M**	**(s)**	**G**
José Ángel Esmorís Tasende „Angeliño" (ESP)	04.01.1997	4	(2)	

	DOB	M	(s)	G
David Josué Jiménez Silva (ESP)	08.01.1986	22	(5)	6
Kevin De Bruyne (BEL)	28.06.1991	32	(3)	13
Thomas Doyle	17.10.2001		(1)	
Fernando Luiz Roza „Fernandinho" (BRA)	04.05.1985	26	(4)	
Philip Walter Foden	28.05.2000	9	(14)	5
İlkay Gündoğan (GER)	24.10.1990	21	(10)	2
Riyad Karim Mahrez (ALG)	21.02.1991	21	(12)	11
Rodrigo Hernández Cascante „Rodri" (ESP)	22.06.1996	29	(6)	3
Forwards:	**DOB**	**M**	**(s)**	**G**
Sergio Leonel Agüero del Castillo (ARG)	02.06.1988	18	(6)	16
Bernardo Mota Veiga de Carvalho e Silva (POR)	10.08.1994	23	(11)	6
Gabriel Fernando de Jesus (BRA)	03.04.1997	21	(13)	14
Leroy Aziz Sané (GER)	11.01.1996		(1)	
Raheem Shaquille Sterling	08.12.1994	30	(3)	20

Manchester United Football Club

Founded: 1878
Stadium: Old Trafford, Manchester (74,879)
Trainer: Ole Gunnar Solskjær (NOR)　　26.02.1973

Goalkeepers:	DOB	M	(s)	G
David de Gea Quintana (ESP)	07.11.1990	38		
Defenders:	**DOB**	**M**	**(s)**	**G**
Eric Bertrand Bailly (CIV)	12.04.1994	1	(3)	
José Diogo Dalot Teixeira (POR)	18.03.1999	1	(3)	
Evans Timothy Fosu Fosu-Mensah (NED)	02.01.1998	2	(1)	
Philip Anthony Jones	21.02.1992	2		
Victor Jörgen Nilsson Lindelöf (SWE)	17.07.1994	35		1
Jacob Harry Maguire	05.03.1993	38		1
Faustino Marcos Alberto Rojo (ARG)	20.03.1990	1	(2)	
Luke Paul Hoare Shaw	12.07.1995	20	(4)	
Axel Tuanzebe	14.11.1997	2	(3)	
Aaron Wan-Bissaka	26.11.1997	34	(1)	
Brandon Paul Brian Williams	03.09.2000	11	(6)	1
Ashley Simon Young	09.07.1985	10	(2)	
Midfielders:	**DOB**	**M**	**(s)**	**G**
Andreas Hugo Hoelgebaum Pereira (BRA)	01.01.1996	18	(7)	1

	DOB	M	(s)	G
Bruno Miguel Borges Fernandes (POR)	08.09.1994	14		8
Frederico Rodrigues de Paula Santos "Fred"(BRA)	05.03.1993	23	(6)	
James David Garner	13.03.2001		(1)	
Adilson Angel Abreu de Almeida Gomes	31.08.2000		(2)	
Daniel Owen James (WAL)	10.11.1997	26	(7)	3
Jesse Ellis Lingard	15.12.1992	9	(13)	1
Juan Manuel Mata García (ESP)	28.04.1988	8	(11)	
Nemanja Matić (SRB)	01.08.1988	18	(3)	
Scott Francis McTominay (SCO)	08.12.1996	20	(7)	3
Paul Labile Pogba (FRA)	15.03.1993	13	(3)	1
Forwards:	**DOB**	**M**	**(s)**	**G**
Tahith Chong (NED)	04.12.1999		(3)	
Mason Will John Greenwood	01.10.2001	12	(19)	10
Odion Jude Ighalo (NGA)	16.06.1989		(11)	
Anthony Joran Martial (FRA)	05.12.1995	31	(1)	17
Marcus Rashford	31.10.1997	31		17

Newcastle United Football Club

Founded: 09.12.1892
Stadium: St James' Park, Newcastle upon Tyne (52,388)
Trainer: Stephen Roger Bruce 31.12.1960

Goalkeepers:	DOB	M	(s)	G
Martin Dúbravka (SVK)	15.01.1989	38		
Defenders:	**DOB**	**M**	**(s)**	**G**
Ciaran Clark (IRL)	26.09.1989	14		2
Paul Dummett (WAL)	26.09.1991	14	(2)	
Emil Henry Kristoffer Krafth (SWE)	02.08.1994	11	(6)	
Jamaal Lascelles	11.11.1993	24		1
Florian Gregoire Claude Lejeune (FRA)	20.05.1991	4	(2)	2
Javier Manquillo Gaitán (ESP)	05.05.1994	18	(3)	
Daniel Lee Rose	02.07.1990	10	(1)	
Fabian Schär (SUI)	20.12.1991	18	(4)	2
Jetro Danovich Sexer Willems (NED)	30.03.1994	18	(1)	2
Kelland John William James Watts	03.11.1999		(1)	
DeAndre Roselle Yedlin (USA)	09.07.1993	10	(6)	1
Midfielders:	**DOB**	**M**	**(s)**	**G**
Miguel Ángel Almiron Rejala (PAR)	10.02.1994	35	(1)	4
Nabil Bentaleb (ALG)	24.11.1994	8	(4)	
Federico Fernández (ARG)	21.02.1989	29	(3)	2
Isaac Scot Hayden	22.03.1995	26	(3)	1
Ki Sung-yueng (KOR)	24.01.1989	1	(2)	
Valentino Lando Lazaro (AUT)	24.03.1996	4	(9)	1
Matthew Longstaff	21.03.2000	6	(3)	2
Sean David Longstaff	30.10.1997	14	(9)	1
Matthew Thomas Ritchie (SCO)	10.09.1989	14	(4)	2
Allan Irénée Saint-Maximin (FRA)	12.03.1997	23	(3)	3
Jonjo Shelvey	27.02.1992	25	(1)	6
Forwards:	**DOB**	**M**	**(s)**	**G**
Christian Atsu Twasam (GHA)	10.01.1992	6	(13)	
Andrew Thomas Carroll	06.01.1989	4	(15)	
Dwight Devon Boyd Gayle	17.10.1990	10	(10)	4
Joelinton Cássio Apolinário de Lira (BRA)	14.08.1996	32	(6)	2
Yoshinori Mutō (JPN)	15.07.1992	2	(6)	

Norwich City Football Club

Founded: 17.06.1902
Stadium: Carrow Road, Norwich (27,244)
Trainer: Daniel Farke (GER) 30.10.1976

Goalkeepers:	DOB	M	(s)	G
Ralf Fährmann (GER)	27.09.1988	1		
Timothy Michael Krul (NED)	03.04.1988	36		
Michael McGovern (NIR)	12.07.1984	1	(1)	
Defenders:	**DOB**	**M**	**(s)**	**G**
Maximillian James Aarons	04.01.2000	36		
Samuel Mark Byram	16.09.1993	15	(2)	
Akinlolu Richard Olamide Famewo	09.11.1998		(1)	
Benjamin Matthew Godfrey	15.01.1998	30		
Grant Campbell Hanley (SCO)	20.11.1991	14	(1)	
Timm Klose (SUI)	09.05.1988	7		
Jordan James Chattenton Thomas	02.01.2001		(1)	
Christoph Zimmermann (GER)	12.01.1993	16	(1)	
Midfielders:	**DOB**	**M**	**(s)**	**G**
Ibrahim Amadou (FRA)	06.04.1993	8	(3)	
Emiliano Buendia Stati (ARG)	25.12.1996	28	(8)	1
Todd Owen Cantwell	27.02.1998	30	(7)	6
Ondrej Duda (SVK)	05.12.1994	9	(1)	
Onel Lázaro Hernández Mayea (CUB)	01.02.1993	14	(12)	1
Moritz Leitner (GER)	08.12.1992	7	(2)	
Jamal Piaras Lewis (NIR)	25.01.1998	25	(3)	1
Kenneth McLean (SCO)	08.01.1992	32	(5)	1
Patrick John Joseph Roberts	05.02.1997		(3)	
Lukas Peter Rupp (GER)	08.01.1991	8	(4)	
Marco Stiepermann (GER)	09.02.1991	14	(10)	
Alexander Banor Tettey (NOR)	04.04.1986	28	(2)	1
Tom Trybull (GER)	09.03.1993	14	(2)	
Mario Vrančić (BIH)	23.05.1989	6	(14)	1
Forwards:	**DOB**	**M**	**(s)**	**G**
Josip Drmić (SUI)	08.08.1992	5	(16)	1
Adam Idah (IRL)	11.02.2001	1	(11)	
Joshua Saul Martin	09.09.2001		(5)	
Teemu Eino Antero Pukki (FIN)	29.03.1990	33	(3)	11
Dennis Srbeny	05.05.1994		(8)	1

Sheffield United Football Club

Founded: 22.03.1889
Stadium: Bramall Lane, Sheffield (32,125)
Trainer: Christopher John Wilder 23.09.1967

Goalkeepers:	DOB	M	(s)	G
Dean Bradley Henderson	12.03.1997	36		
Simon William Moore	19.05.1990	2		
Defenders:	**DOB**	**M**	**(s)**	**G**
George Henry Ivor Baldock	09.03.1993	38		2
Christopher Paul Basham	20.07.1988	38		
John Egan (IRL)	20.10.1992	36		2
Kieron Samuel Freeman (WAL)	21.03.1992		(2)	
Philip Nikodem Jagielka	17.08.1982	2	(4)	
Jack William O'Connell	29.03.1994	32	(1)	
Jack Robinson	01.09.1993	6		
Jack Christian Rodwell	11.03.1991		(1)	
Enda John Stevens (IRL)	09.07.1990	38		2
Midfielders:	**DOB**	**M**	**(s)**	**G**
Sander Gard Bolin Berge (NOR)	14.02.1998	12	(2)	1
Muhamed Bešić (BIH)	10.09.1992	2	(7)	
John Alexander Fleck (SCO)	24.08.1991	28	(2)	5
Luke Anthony Freeman	22.03.1992	3	(8)	
John David Lundstram	18.02.1994	26	(8)	5
Ravel Ryan Morrison	02.02.1993		(1)	
Oliver James Norwood (NIR)	12.04.1991	37	(1)	1
Benjamin Jarrod Osborn	05.08.1994	6	(7)	
Forwards:	**DOB**	**M**	**(s)**	**G**
Leon Marvin Clarke	10.02.1985		(2)	
Oliver Robert McBurnie (SCO)	04.06.1996	24	(12)	6
David James McGoldrick (IRL)	29.11.1987	22	(6)	2
Lys Émilien Mousset (FRA)	08.02.1996	11	(19)	6
Callum Jack Robinson (IRL)	02.02.1995	9	(7)	1
Billy Louis Sharp	05.02.1986	10	(15)	3
Richairo Juliano Živković (NED)	05.09.1996		(5)	

Southampton Football Club

Founded: 21.11.1885
Stadium: St. Mary's Stadium, Southampton (32,384)
Trainer: Ralph Hasenhüttl (AUT) 09.08.1967

Goalkeepers:	DOB	M	(s)	G
Angus Fraser James Gunn	22.01.1996	10		
Alex Simon McCarthy	03.12.1989	28		
Defenders:	**DOB**	**M**	**(s)**	**G**
Jan Bednarek (POL)	12.04.1996	34		1
Ryan Dominic Bertrand	05.08.1989	31	(1)	1
Cédric Ricardo Alves Soares (POR)	31.08.1991	16		
Kevin Danso (AUT)	19.09.1998	3	(3)	
Jack Stephens	27.01.1994	27	(1)	1
Yan Valery (FRA)	22.02.1999	10	(1)	
Jannik Vestergaard (DEN)	03.08.1992	17	(2)	1
Jake Vokins	17.03.2000	1		
Kyle Leonardus Walker-Peters	13.04.1997	7	(3)	
Maya Yoshida (JPN)	24.08.1988	6	(2)	
Midfielders:	**DOB**	**M**	**(s)**	**G**
Stuart Armstrong (SCO)	30.03.1992	19	(11)	5
Sofiane Boufal (MAR)	17.09.1993	8	(12)	
Pierre-Emile Kordt Højbjerg (DEN)	05.08.1995	30	(3)	
Oriol Romeu Vidal (ESP)	24.09.1991	20	(10)	
Nathan Daniel Jerome Redmond	06.03.1994	32		4
William Anthony Patrick Smallbone (IRL)	21.02.2000	4	(5)	
James Michael Edward Ward-Prowse	01.11.1994	38		5
Forwards:	**DOB**	**M**	**(s)**	**G**
Ché Zach Everton Fred Adams	13.07.1996	12	(18)	4
Moussa Djénépo (MLI)	15.06.1998	10	(8)	2
Daniel William John Ings	23.07.1992	32	(6)	22
Shane Patrick Long (IRL)	22.01.1987	15	(11)	2
Michael Oluwadurotimi Obafemi (IRL)	06.07.2000	8	(13)	3
Nathan Adewale Temitayo Tella	05.07.1999		(1)	

Tottenham Hotspur Football Club London

Founded:	05.09.1882			
Stadium:	Tottenham Hotspur Stadium, London (62,303)			
Trainer:	Mauricio Roberto Pochettino Trossero (ARG)		02.03.1972	
[20.11.2019]	José Mário dos Santos Mourinho Félix (POR)		26.01.1963	

Goalkeepers:	DOB	M	(s)	G
Paulo Dino Gazzaniga (ARG)	02.01.1992	17	(1)	
Hugo Lloris (FRA)	26.12.1986	21		
Defenders:	**DOB**	**M**	**(s)**	**G**
Tobias Albertine Maurits Alderweireld (BEL)	02.03.1989	33		2
Serge Alain Stephane Aurier (CIV)	24.12.1992	31	(2)	1
Benjamin Thomas Davies (WAL)	24.04.1993	16	(2)	
Juan Marcos Foyth (ARG)	12.01.1998	1	(3)	
Dávinson Sánchez Mina (COL)	12.06.1996	27	(2)	
Daniel Lee Rose	02.07.1990	10	(2)	
Japhet Manzambi Tanganga	31.03.1999	6		
Jan Bert Lieve Vertonghen (BEL)	24.04.1987	19	(4)	1
Kyle Leonardus Walker-Peters	13.04.1997	3		
Midfielders:	**DOB**	**M**	**(s)**	**G**
Bamidele Jermaine "Dele" Alli	11.04.1996	21	(4)	8
Eric Jeremy Edgar Dier	15.01.1994	15	(4)	
Christian Dannemann Eriksen (DEN)	14.02.1992	10	(10)	2
Gedson Carvalho Fernandes (POR)	09.01.1999		(7)	
Érik Manuel Lamela (ARG)	04.03.1992	12	(13)	2
Giovani Lo Celso (ARG)	09.04.1996	15	(13)	
Lucas Rodrigues Moura da Silva (BRA)	13.08.1992	25	(10)	4
Tanguy Ndombele Alvaro (FRA)	28.12.1996	12	(9)	2
Georges-Kévin N'Koudou Mbida (FRA)	13.02.1995		(1)	
Moussa Sissoko (FRA)	16.08.1989	28	(1)	2
Oliver William Skipp	16.09.2000	1	(6)	
Victor Mugubi Wanyama (KEN)	25.06.1991		(2)	
Harry Billy Winks	02.02.1996	26	(5)	
Forwards:	**DOB**	**M**	**(s)**	**G**
Steven Charles Bergwijn (NED)	08.10.1997	8	(6)	3
Harry Edward Kane	28.07.1993	29		18
Troy Daniel Parrott (IRL)	04.02.2002		(2)	
Kouassi Ryan Sessegnon	18.05.2000	4	(2)	
Son Heung-min (KOR)	08.07.1992	28	(2)	11

Watford Football Club

Founded:	1881		
Stadium:	Vicarage Road, Watford (20,220)		
Trainer:	Javier Gracia Carlos (ESP)		01.05.1970
[07.09.2019]	Quique Sánchez Flores (ESP)		02.02.1965
[02.12.2019]	Hayden Ian Mullins		27.03.1979
[09.12.2019]	Nigel Graham Pearson		21.08.1963
[19.07.2020]	Hayden Ian Mullins		27.03.1979

Goalkeepers:	DOB	M	(s)	G
Benjamin Anthony Foster	03.04.1983	38		
Defenders:	**DOB**	**M**	**(s)**	**G**
Craig George Cathcart (NIR)	06.02.1989	28	(1)	
Craig Dawson	06.05.1990	26	(3)	2
Dimitri Christophe Foulquier (FRA)	23.03.1993	1	(2)	
José Lloyd Holebas (GRE)	27.06.1984	11	(3)	
Daryl Janmaat (NED)	22.07.1989	7	(1)	
Christian Kabasele (BEL)	24.02.1991	26	(1)	
Adrian Joseph Mariappa (JAM)	03.10.1986	15	(5)	
Adam Masina (ITA)	02.01.1994	20	(6)	1
Sebastian Prödl (AUT)	21.06.1987	1		
Midfielders:	**DOB**	**M**	**(s)**	**G**
Étienne Capoue (FRA)	11.07.1988	30		
Nathaniel Nyakie Chalobah	12.12.1994	10	(12)	
Thomas William Cleverley	12.08.1989	11	(7)	1
Domingos Quina (POR)	18.11.1999		(4)	
Abdoulaye Doucouré (FRA)	01.01.1993	36	(1)	4
William James Hughes	07.04.1995	27	(3)	1
Francisco Femenía Far "Kiko Femenía" (ESP)	02.02.1991	26	(2)	
Roberto Maximiliano Pereyra (ARG)	07.01.1991	17	(11)	3
Forwards:	**DOB**	**M**	**(s)**	**G**
Troy Matthew Deeney	29.06.1988	26	(1)	10
Gerard Deulofeu Lázaro (ESP)	13.03.1994	25	(3)	4
Andre Anthony Gray	26.06.1991	7	(16)	2
João Pedro Junqueira de Jesus (BRA)	26.09.2001		(3)	
Ignacio Pussetto (ARG)	21.12.1995		(7)	
Ismaïla Sarr (SEN)	25.02.1998	22	(6)	5
Isaac Ajayi Success (NGA)	07.01.1996		(5)	
Daniel Nii Tackie Mensah Welbeck	26.11.1990	8	(10)	2

West Ham United Football Club London

Founded:	29.06.1895		
Stadium:	London Stadium, London (60,000)		
Trainer:	Manuel Luis Pellegrini Ripamonti (CHI)		16.09.1953
[29.12.2019]	David William Moyes (SCO)		25.04.1963

Goalkeepers:	DOB	M	(s)	G
Łukasz Fabiański (POL)	18.04.1985	25		
David Edward Martin	22.01.1986	4	(1)	
Darren Edward Andrew Randolph (IRL)	12.05.1987	2		
Roberto Jiménez Gago (ESP)	10.02.1986	7	(1)	
Defenders:	**DOB**	**M**	**(s)**	**G**
Fabián Cornelio Balbuena González (PAR)	23.08.1991	13	(4)	1
Aaron William Cresswell	15.12.1989	31		3
Issa Diop (FRA)	09.01.1997	31	(1)	3
Ryan Marlow Fredericks	10.10.1992	25	(2)	
Benjamin Anthony Johnson	24.01.2000	3		
Fuka-Arthur Masuaku Kawela (COD)	07.11.1993	10	(7)	
Jeremy Ngakia	07.09.2000	5		
Obinze Angelo Ogbonna (ITA)	23.05.1988	31		2
Pablo Javier Zabaleta Girod (ARG)	16.01.1985	6	(4)	
Midfielders:	**DOB**	**M**	**(s)**	**G**
Michail Gregory Antonio	28.03.1990	19	(5)	10
Felipe Anderson Pereira Gomes (BRA)	15.04.1993	20	(5)	1
Nathan Elliot Holland	19.06.1998		(2)	
Manuel Lanzini (ARG)	15.02.1993	14	(10)	
Mark James Noble	08.05.1987	32	(1)	4
Pablo Fornals Malla (ESP)	22.02.1996	24	(12)	2
Declan Rice	14.01.1999	38		1
Carlos Alberto Sánchez Moreno (COL)	06.02.1986	1	(5)	
Robert Snodgrass (SCO)	07.09.1987	17	(7)	5
Tomáš Souček (CZE)	27.02.1995	12	(1)	3
Jack Andrew Garry Wilshere	01.01.1992	2	(6)	
Forwards:	**DOB**	**M**	**(s)**	**G**
Albian Ajeti (SUI)	26.02.1997		(9)	
Jarrod Bowen	20.12.1996	11	(2)	1
Sébastien Romain Teddy Haller (FRA)	22.06.1994	24	(8)	7
Javier Hernández Balcázar (MEX)	01.06.1988	1	(1)	1
Andrey Yarmolenko (UKR)	23.10.1989	10	(13)	5

Wolverhampton Wanderers Football Club

Founded:	1877 (*as St. Luke's FC*)
Stadium:	Molineux Stadium, Wolverhampton (32,050)
Trainer:	Nuno Herlander Simões do Espírito Santo (POR) 25.01.1974

Goalkeepers:	DOB	M	(s)	G
Rui Pedro dos Santos Patrício (POR)	15.02.1988	38		
Defenders:	**DOB**	**M**	**(s)**	**G**
Ryan Bennett	06.03.1990	7	(4)	
Willy Arnaud Zobo Boly (FRA)	03.02.1991	22		
Conor David Coady	25.02.1993	38		
Matthew James Doherty (IRL)	16.01.1992	32	(4)	4
Jesús Vallejo Lázaro (ESP)	05.01.1997	1	(1)	
Jonathan Castro Otto "Jonny" (ESP)	03.03.1994	33	(2)	2
Maximilian William Kilman	23.05.1997	2	(1)	
Rúben Gonçalo Silva Nascimento Vinagre (POR)	09.04.1999	6	(10)	
Romain Saïss (MAR)	26.03.1990	31	(2)	2

Midfielders:	DOB	M	(s)	G
Bruno André Cavaco Jordão (POR)	12.10.1998		(1)	
Leander Dendoncker (BEL)	15.04.1995	32	(6)	4
Diogo José Teixeira da Silva „Diogo Jota" (POR)	04.12.1996	27	(7)	7
Morgan Anthony Gibbs-White	27.01.2000	1	(6)	
João Filipe Iria Santos Moutinho (POR)	08.09.1986	34	(4)	1
Rúben Diogo da Silva Neves (POR)	13.03.1997	35	(3)	2
Forwards:	**DOB**	**M**	**(s)**	**G**
Patrick Cutrone (ITA)	03.01.1998	3	(9)	2
Daniel Castelo Podence (POR)	21.10.1995	3	(6)	1
Raúl Alonso Jiménez Rodríguez (MEX)	05.05.1991	37	(1)	17
Pedro Lomba Neto (POR)	09.03.2000	9	(20)	3
Adama Traoré Diarra (ESP)	25.01.1996	27	(10)	4

SECOND LEVEL
EFL Championship 2019/2020

1.	Leeds United FC (*Promoted*)	46	28	9	9	77	-	35	93
2.	West Bromwich Albion FC (*Promoted*)	46	22	17	7	77	-	45	83
3.	Brentford FC	46	24	9	13	80	-	38	81
4.	Fulham FC London	46	23	12	11	64	-	48	81
5.	Cardiff City FC	46	19	16	11	68	-	58	73
6.	Swansea City AFC	46	18	16	12	62	-	53	70
7.	Nottingham Forest FC	46	18	16	12	58	-	50	70
8.	Millwall FC London	46	17	17	12	57	-	51	68
9.	Preston North End FC	46	18	12	16	59	-	54	66
10.	Derby County FC	46	17	13	16	62	-	64	64
11.	Blackburn Rovers FC	46	17	12	17	66	-	63	63
12.	Bristol City FC	46	17	12	17	60	-	65	63
13.	Queens Park Rangers FC London	46	16	10	20	67	-	76	58
14.	Reading FC	46	15	11	20	59	-	58	56
15.	Stoke City FC	46	16	8	22	62	-	68	56
16.	Sheffield Wednesday FC	46	15	11	20	58	-	66	56
17.	Middlesbrough FC	46	13	14	19	48	-	61	53
18.	Huddersfield Town AFC	46	13	12	21	52	-	70	51
19.	Luton Town FC	46	14	9	23	54	-	82	51
20.	Birmingham City FC	46	12	14	20	54	-	75	50
21.	Barnsley FC	46	12	13	21	49	-	69	49
22.	Charlton Athletic FC London (*Relegated*)	46	12	12	22	50	-	65	48
23.	Wigan Athletic FC* (*Relegated*)	46	15	14	17	57	-	56	47
24.	Hull City AFC (*Relegated*)	46	12	9	25	57	-	87	45

*12 points deducted
Clubs ranked 3-6 were qualified for the Promotion Play-offs.

Promotion Play-offs [26.07.-04.08.2020]			
Play-off Semi-Finals	Swansea City AFC - Brentford FC	1-0(0-0)	1-3(0-2)
	Cardiff City FC - Fulham FC London	0-2(0-0)	2-1(1-1)
Play-off Finals	Brentford FC - Fulham FC London	1-2(0-0,0-0)	

Fulham FC London promoted to the 2020/2021 Premier League.

INTERNATIONAL MATCHES
(16.07.2019 – 15.07.2020)

07.09.2019	London	England - Bulgaria	4-0(1-0)	(ECQ)
10.09.2019	Southampton	England - Kosovo	5-3(5-1)	(ECQ)
11.10.2019	Praha	Czech Republic - England	2-1(1-1)	(ECQ)
14.10.2019	Sofia	Bulgaria - England	0-6(0-4)	(ECQ)
14.11.2019	London	England - Montenegro	7-0(5-0)	(ECQ)
17.11.2019	Prishtinë	Kosovo - England	0-4(0-1)	(ECQ)

07.09.2019   ENGLAND - BULGARIA   **4-0(1-0)**   16th EC. Qualifiers
Wembley Stadium, London; Referee: Marco Guida (Italy); Attendance: 82,605
ENG: Jordan Lee Pickford, Daniel Lee Rose, Kieran John Trippier, Jacob Harry Maguire, Michael Vincent Keane, Jordan Brian Henderson (67.Mason Tony Mount), Ross Barkley, Declan Rice, Raheem Shaquille Sterling (71.Jadon Malik Sancho), Harry Edward Kane (Cap) (77.Alexander Mark David Oxlade-Chamberlain) , Marcus Rashford. Trainer: Gareth Southgate.
Goals: Harry Edward Kane (24, 50 penalty), Raheem Shaquille Sterling (55), Harry Edward Kane (73 penalty).

10.09.2019   ENGLAND - KOSOVO   **5-3(5-1)**   16th EC. Qualifiers
St. Mary's Stadium, Southampton; Referee: Felix Zwayer (Germany); Attendance: 30,155
ENG: Jordan Lee Pickford, Trent John Alexander-Arnold, Jacob Harry Maguire, Michael Vincent Keane, Benjamin James Chilwell, Jordan Brian Henderson, Ross Barkley (83.Mason Tony Mount), Declan Rice, Jadon Malik Sancho (85.Marcus Rashford), Harry Edward Kane (Cap), Raheem Shaquille Sterling. Trainer: Gareth Southgate.
Goals: Raheem Shaquille Sterling (8), Harry Edward Kane (19), Mërgim Vojvoda (38 own goal), Jadon Malik Sancho (44, 45+1).

11.10.2019   CZECH REPUBLIC - ENGLAND   **2-1(1-1)**   16th EC. Qualifiers
Stadion Sinobo, Praha; Referee: Damir Skomina (Slovenia); Attendance: 18,651
ENG: Jordan Lee Pickford, Daniel Lee Rose, Kieran John Trippier, Jacob Harry Maguire, Michael Vincent Keane, Jordan Brian Henderson, Mason Tony Mount (72.Ross Barkley), Declan Rice (88.Kevin Oghenetega Tamaraebi Bakumo-Abraham), Jadon Malik Sancho (73.Marcus Rashford), Harry Edward Kane (Cap), Raheem Shaquille Sterling. Trainer: Gareth Southgate.
Goal: Harry Edward Kane (5 penalty).

14.10.2019   BULGARIA - ENGLAND   **0-6(0-4)**   16th EC. Qualifiers
Nationalen Stadion "Vasil Levski", Sofia; Referee: Referee: Ivan Bebek (Croatia); Attendance: 17,481
ENG: Jordan Lee Pickford, Kieran John Trippier, Jacob Harry Maguire, Tyrone Deon Mings, Benjamin James Chilwell, Jordan Brian Henderson, Ross Barkley (72.Mason Tony Mount), Harry Billy Winks, Harry Edward Kane (Cap), Raheem Shaquille Sterling (73.Jadon Malik Sancho), Marcus Rashford (76.Callum Eddie Graham Wilson). Trainer: Gareth Southgate.
Goals: Marcus Rashford (7), Ross Barkley (20, 32), Raheem Shaquille Sterling (45+3, 69), Harry Edward Kane (85).

14.11.2019   ENGLAND - MONTENEGRO   **7-0(5-0)**   16th EC. Qualifiers
Wembley Stadium, London; Referee: Antonio Miguel Mateu Lahoz (Spain); Attendance: 77,277
ENG: Jordan Lee Pickford, Trent John Alexander-Arnold, Jacob Harry Maguire, John Stones, Benjamin James Chilwell, Alexander Mark David Oxlade-Chamberlain (56.James Daniel Maddison), Harry Billy Winks, Mason Tony Mount (70.Joseph Dave Gomez), Jadon Malik Sancho, Harry Edward Kane (Cap) (57.Kevin Oghenetega Tamaraebi Bakumo-Abraham), Marcus Rashford. Trainer: Gareth Southgate.
Goals: Alexander Mark David Oxlade-Chamberlain (11), Harry Edward Kane (19, 24), Marcus Rashford (30), Harry Edward Kane (37), Aleksandar Šofranac (66 own goal), Kevin Oghenetega Tamaraebi Bakumo-Abraham (84).

17.11.2019   KOSOVO - ENGLAND   **0-4(0-1)**   16th EC. Qualifiers
Stadiumi "Fadil Vokrri", Prishtinë; Referee: Paweł Gil (Poland); Attendance: 12,326
ENG: Nicholas David Pope, Trent John Alexander-Arnold (84.Oluwafikayomi Oluwadamilola Tomori), Jacob Harry Maguire, Tyrone Deon Mings, Benjamin James Chilwell, Alexander Mark David Oxlade-Chamberlain (73.Mason Tony Mount), Harry Billy Winks, Declan Rice, Harry Edward Kane (Cap), Raheem Shaquille Sterling, Callum James Hudson-Odoi (59.Marcus Rashford). Trainer: Gareth Southgate.
Goals: Harry Billy Winks (32), Harry Edward Kane (79), Marcus Rashford (83), Mason Tony Mount (90+1).

NATIONAL TEAM PLAYERS
(16.07.2019 – 15.07.2020)

Name	DOB	Caps	Goals	2019/2020:	Club
Goalkeepers					
Jordan Lee PICKFORD	07.03.1994	24	0	2019:	*Everton FC Liverpool*
Nicholas David POPE	19.04.1992	2	0	2019:	*Burnley FC*
Defenders					
Trent John ALEXANDER-ARNOLD	07.10.1998	9	1	2019:	*Liverpool FC*
Benjamin James CHILWELL	21.12.1996	11	0	2019:	*Leicester City FC*
Joseph Dave GOMEZ	23.05.1997	8	0	2019:	*Liverpool FC*
Michael Vincent KEANE	11.01.1993	10	1	2019:	*Everton FC Liverpool*
Jacob Harry MAGUIRE	05.03.1993	26	1	2019:	*Manchester United FC*
Tyrone Deon MINGS	13.03.1993	2	0	2019:	*Aston Villa FC Birmingham*
Daniel Lee ROSE	02.07.1990	29	0	2019:	*Tottenham Hotspur FC London*
John STONES	28.05.1994	39	2	2019:	*Manchester City FC*
Oluwafikayomi Oluwadamilola TOMORI	19.12.1997	1	0	2019:	*Chelsea FC London*
Kieran John TRIPPIER	19.09.1990	19	1	2019:	*Club Atlético de Madrid (ESP)*
Midfielders					
Ross BARKLEY	05.12.1993	33	6	2019:	*Chelsea FC London*
Jordan Brian HENDERSON	17.06.1990	55	0	2019:	*Liverpool FC*
James Daniel MADDISON	23.11.1996	1	0	2019:	*Leicester City FC*
Mason Tony MOUNT	10.01.1999	6	1	2019:	*Chelsea FC London*
Alexander Mark David OXLADE-CHAMBERLAIN	15.08.1993	35	7	2019:	*Liverpool FC*
Declan RICE	14.01.1999	7	0	2019:	*West Ham United FC London*
Harry Billy WINKS	02.02.1996	6	1	2019:	*Tottenham Hotspur FC London*
Forwards					
Kevin Oghenetega Tamaraebi BAKUMO-ABRAHAM	02.10.1997	4	1	2019:	*Chelsea FC London*
Callum James HUDSON-ODOI	07.11.2000	3	0	2019:	*Chelsea FC London*
Harry Edward KANE	28.07.1993	45	32	2019:	*Tottenham Hotspur FC London*
Marcus RASHFORD	31.10.1997	38	10	2019:	*Manchester United FC*
Jadon Malik SANCHO	25.03.2000	11	2	2019:	*BV Borussia 09 Dortmund (GER)*
Raheem Shaquille STERLING	08.12.1994	56	12	2019:	*Manchester City FC*
Callum Eddie Graham WILSON	27.02.1992	4	1	2019:	*AFC Bournemouth*
National team coach					
Gareth SOUTHGATE [from 30.11.2016]	03.09.1970	41 M; 24 W; 9 D; 8 L; 87-33			

ESTONIA

The Country:
Eesti Vabariik (Republic of Estonia)
Capital: Tallinn
Surface: 45,339 km²
Inhabitants: 1,328,360 [2020]
Time: UTC+2

The FA:
Eesti Jalgpalli Liit
A. Le Coq Arena, Asula 4c, 11312 Tallinn
Tel: +372 627 9960
Foundation date: 14.12.1921
Member of FIFA since: 1923
Member of UEFA since: 1992
Website: www.jalgpall.ee

NATIONAL TEAM RECORDS

First international match:	20.10.1920, Helsinki:	Finland – Estonia 6-0
Most international caps:	Martin Reim	- 157 caps (1991-2009)
Most international goals:	Andres Oper	- 38 goals / 134 caps (1995-2014)

UEFA EUROPEAN CHAMPIONSHIP		FIFA WORLD CUP		OLYMPIC TOURNAMENTS	
1960	-	1930	-	1908	-
1964	-	1934	Qualifiers	1912	-
1968	-	1938	Qualifiers	1920	-
1972	-	1950	-	1924	-
1976	-	1954	-	1928	-
1980	-	1958	-	1936	-
1984	-	1962	-	1948	-
1988	-	1966	-	1952	-
1992	-	1970	-	1956	-
1996	Qualifiers	1974	-	1960	-
2000	Qualifiers	1978	-	1964	-
2004	Qualifiers	1982	-	1968	-
2008	Qualifiers	1986	-	1972	-
2012	Qualifiers	1990	-	1976	-
2016	Qualifiers	1994	Qualifiers	1980	-
2020	Qualifiers	1998	Qualifiers	1984	-
		2002	Qualifiers	1988	-
		2006	Qualifiers	1992	-
		2010	Qualifiers	1996	Qualifiers
		2014	Qualifiers	2000	Qualifiers
		2018	Qualifiers	2004	Qualifiers
				2008	Qualifiers
				2012	Qualifiers
				2016	Qualifiers

Please note: *was part of Soviet Union from 1945 to 1991.*

UEFA NATIONS LEAGUE
2018/2019 – League C (relegated to League D)

FIFA CONFEDERATIONS CUP 1992-2017
None

ESTONIAN CLUB HONOURS IN EUROPEAN CLUB COMPETITIONS:

European Champion Clubs' Cup (1956-1992) / UEFA Champions League (1993-2020)
None

Fairs Cup (1858-1971) / UEFA Cup (1972-2009) / UEFA Europa League (2010-2020)
None

UEFA Super Cup (1972-2019)
None

*European Cup Winners' Cup 1961-1999**
None

*defunct competition

NATIONAL COMPETITIONS
TABLE OF HONOURS

ESTONIAN SSR (SOVIET ERA) CHAMPIONS

Year	Champion	Year	Champion	Year	Champion
1945	Dünamo Tallinn	1961	Kalev Kopli	1977	Baltika Narva
1946	BL Tallinn	1962	Kalev Ülemiste	1978	Dünamo Tallinn
1947	Dünamo Tallinn	1963	Tempo Tallinn	1979	Norma Tallinn
1948	Balti Laevastik Tallinn	1964	Norma Tallinn	1980	Dünamo Tallinn
1949	Dünamo Tallinn	1965	Balti Laevastik Tallinn	1981	Dünamo Tallinn
1950	Dünamo Tallinn	1966	Balti Laevastik Tallinn	1982	Tempo Tallinn
1951	Balti Laevastik Tallinn	1967	Norma Tallinn	1983	Dünamo Tallinn
1952	Balti Laevastik Tallinn	1968	Balti Laevastik Tallinn	1984	Estonia Jõhvi
1953	Dünamo Tallinn	1969	Dvigatel Tallinn	1985	Kalakombinaat/MEK Pärnu
1954	Dünamo Tallinn	1970	Norma Tallinn	1986	Zvezda Tallinn
1955	Kalev Tallinn	1971	Tempo Tallinn	1987	Tempo Tallinn
1956	Balti Laevastik Tallinn	1972	Balti Laevastik Tallinn	1988	Norma Tallinn
1957	Kalev Ülemiste	1973	Kreenholm Narva	1989	Zvezda Tallinn
1958	Kalev Ülemiste	1974	Baltika Narva	1990	Tallinna VMK
1959	Kalev Ülemiste	1975	Baltika Narva	1991	Tallinna VMK
1960	Balti Laevastik Tallinn	1976	Dvigatel Tallinn		

	CHAMPIONS	CUP WINNERS	BEST GOALSCORERS	
1921	Sport Tallinn	-	-	
1922	Sport Tallinn	-	-	
1923	Kalev Tallinn	-	-	
1924	Sport Tallinn	-	-	
1925	Sport Tallinn	-	-	
1926	Jalgpalliklubi Tallinn	-	-	
1927	Sport Tallinn	-	-	
1928	Jalgpalliklubi Tallinn	-	-	
1929	Sport Tallinn	-	-	
1930	Kalev Tallinn	-	-	
1931	Sport Tallinn	-	-	
1932	Sport Tallinn	-	-	
1933	Sport Tallinn	-	-	
1934	Tallinn	-	-	
1935	Tallinn	-	-	
1936	Tallinn	-	-	
1937/1938	Tallinn	SK Tallinna Sport	-	
1938/1939	Tallinn	Jalgpalliklubi Tallinn	-	
1939/1940	Olümpia Tartu	-	-	
1941	*Championship not finished*	-	-	
1942	PSR Tartu *(unofficial)*	-	-	
1943	Tallinn *(unofficial)*	-	-	
1944	*Championship not finished*	-	-	
1992	FC Norma Tallinn	-	Sergei Bragin (FC Norma Tallinn)	18
1992/1993	FC Norma Tallinn	FC Nikol Tallinn	Sergei Bragin (FC Norma Tallinn)	27
1993/1994	FC Flora Tallinn	FC Norma Tallinn	Maksim Gruznov (JK Narva Trans/Tevalte Tallinn)	21
1994/1995	FC Flora Tallinn	FC Flora Tallinn	Serhiy Morozov (UKR, FC Lantana Tallinn)	25
1995/1996	FC Lantana Tallinn	JK Tallinna Sadam	Lembit Rajala (FC Flora Tallinn)	16
1996/1997	FC Lantana Tallinn	JK Tallinna Sadam	Sergei Bragin (FC Lantana Tallinn)	18
1997/1998	FC Flora Tallinn	-	Konstantin Kolbassenko (JK Tallinna Sadam)	18
1998	FC Flora Tallinn	FC Flora Tallinn	Konstantin Kolbassenko (JK Tallinna Sadam)	13
1999	FC Levadia Maardu	FC Levadia Maardu	Toomas Krõm (FC Levadia Maardu)	19
2000	FC Levadia Maardu	FC Levadia Maardu	Egidijus Juška (LTU, FC Tallinna VMK) / Toomas Krõm (FC Levadia Maardu)	24
2001	FC Flora Tallinn	JK Narva Trans	Maksim Gruznov (JK Narva Trans)	37
2002	FC Flora Tallinn	FC Levadia Maardu	Andrei Krõlov (FC Tallinna VMK)	37
2003	FC Flora Tallinn	FC Tallinna VMK	Tor Henning Hamre (NOR, FC Flora Tallinn)	39
2004	FC Levadia Maardu	FC Levadia Maardu	Vjatšeslav Zahovaiko (FC Flora Tallinn)	28
2005	FC Tallinna VMK	FC Levadia Tallinn	Tarmo Neemelo (FC Tallinna VMK)	41
2006	FC Levadia Tallinn	FC Tallinna VMK	Maksim Gruznov (JK Narva Trans)	31
2007	FC Levadia Tallinn	FC Levadia Tallinn	Russia Dmitri Lipartov (JK Narva Trans)	30
2008	FC Levadia Tallinn	FC Flora Tallinn	Ingemar Teever (Nõmme Kalju FC Tallinn)	23
2009	FC Levadia Tallinn	FC Flora Tallinn	Vitali Gussev (FC Levadia Tallinn)	26
2010	FC Flora Tallinn	FC Levadia Tallinn	Sander Post (FC Flora Tallinn)	24
2011	FC Flora Tallinn	FC Flora Tallinn	Latvia Aleksandrs Čekulajevs (JK Narva Trans)	46
2012	Nõmme Kalju FC Tallinn	FC Levadia Tallinn	Vladislav Ivanov (RUS, JK Sillamäe Kalev / JK Narva Trans)	23
2013	FC Levadia Tallinn	FC Flora Tallinn	Vladimir Voskoboinikov (Nõmme Kalju FC Tallinn)	23
2014	FC Levadia Tallinn	FC Levadia Tallinn	Russia Yevgeni Kabaev (JK Sillamäe Kalev)	36
2015	FC Flora Tallinn	Nõmme Kalju FC Tallinn	Ingemar Teever (FC Levadia Tallinn)	24

2016	FC Infonet Tallinn	FC Flora Tallinn	Russia Yevgeni Kabaev (JK Sillamäe Kalev)	25
2017	FC Flora Tallinn	FC Infonet Tallinn	Albert Prosa (FC Infonet Tallinn)	
			Rauno Sappinen (FC Flora Tallinn)	27
2018	Nõmme Kalju FC Tallinn	FCI Levadia Tallinn	Ellinton Antonio Costa Morais "Liliu"	31
			(BRA, Nõmme Kalju FC Tallinn)	
2019	FC Flora Tallinn	JK Narva Trans	Erik Sorga (FC Flora Tallinn)	31

NATIONAL CHAMPIONSHIP
Meistriliiga 2019
(08.03.2019 – 09.11.2019)

Results

Round 1 [08-10.03.2019]
JK Nõmme - Paide Linnameeskond 0-2(0-1)
Narva Trans - FC Kuressaare 0-0
FCI Levadia - Tallinna Kalev 5-1(2-1)
JK Tammeka - Maardu Linnamees. 2-2(0-1)
FC Flora - Viljandi JK 2-0(1-0)

Round 2 [16-17.03.2019]
FC Kuressaare - FCI Levadia 0-1(0-1)
Viljandi JK - JK Tammeka 0-4(0-3)
Tallinna Kalev - Narva Trans 0-4(0-2)
Paide Linnameeskond - FC Flora 0-1(0-0)
Maardu Linnameeskond - JK Nõmme 0-5(0-2)

Round 3 [30-31.03.2019]
Paide Linnamees. - Tallinna Kalev 2-0(1-0)
Narva Trans - JK Nõmme 0-0
FC Flora - JK Tammeka 4-1(1-0)
FCI Levadia - Maardu Linnamees. 8-0(3-0)
Viljandi JK - FC Kuressaare 1-2(1-0)

Round 4 [02-03.04.2019]
JK Tammeka - Paide Linnameeskond 0-3(0-0)
JK Nõmme - FC Flora 0-3(0-0)
Maardu Linnamees. - FC Kuressaare 1-0(1-0)
Tallinna Kalev - Viljandi JK 0-2(0-0)
Narva Trans - FCI Levadia 1-2(0-2)

Round 5 [06-07.04.2019]
Paide Linnameeskond - Narva Trans 0-0
JK Tammeka - FCI Levadia 1-2(0-1)
Viljandi JK - JK Nõmme 2-3(2-3)
FC Kuressaare - Tallinna Kalev 2-0(0-0)
FC Flora - Maardu Linnameeskond 6-0(4-0)

Round 6 [13-14.04.2019]
Tallinna Kalev - Maardu Linnamees. 2-0(2-0)
FCI Levadia - Viljandi JK 5-2(3-1)
Narva Trans - FC Flora 0-1(0-0)
FC Kuressaare - Paide Linnamees. 0-1(0-0)
JK Nõmme - JK Tammeka 2-0(1-0)

Round 7 [20-21.04.2019]
Maardu Linnameeskond - Viljandi JK 0-0
JK Nõmme - Tallinna Kalev 2-2(0-0)
JK Tammeka - Narva Trans 1-2(1-0)
FC Flora - FC Kuressaare 5-0(2-0)
Paide Linnameeskond - FCI Levadia 0-2(0-1)

Round 8 [27-28.04.2019]
Tallinna Kalev - JK Tammeka 0-4(0-1)
Maardu Linnamees. - Narva Trans 0-1(0-0)
FC Kuressaare - JK Nõmme 0-0
Viljandi JK - Paide Linnameeskond 2-2(0-1)
FCI Levadia - FC Flora 1-2(0-1)

Round 9 [03-05.05.2019]
JK Tammeka - FC Kuressaare 1-1(1-1)
FC Flora - Tallinna Kalev 6-0(4-0)
Paide Linnamees. - Maardu Linnam. 2-0(1-0)
Narva Trans - Viljandi JK 0-1(0-1)
JK Nõmme - FCI Levadia 2-1(1-0)

Round 10 [10-12.05.2019]
FC Kuressaare - Maardu Linnamees. 1-0(1-0)
FCI Levadia - JK Tammeka 7-0(2-0)
Narva Trans - Paide Linnameeskond 0-1(0-0)
Viljandi JK - FC Flora 1-3(0-1)
Tallinna Kalev - JK Nõmme 0-1(0-0)

Round 11 [17-19.05.2019]
JK Nõmme - FC Kuressaare 3-2(2-1)
Viljandi JK - FCI Levadia 0-3(0-3)
FC Flora - Narva Trans 2-2(1-1)
Paide Linnameeskond - JK Tammeka 2-1(1-1)
Maardu Linnameeskond - Tallinna Kalev 0-0

Round 12 [21-24.05.2019]
FCI Levadia - JK Nõmme 0-0
Narva Trans - Maardu Linnamees. 5-1(1-1)
JK Tammeka - FC Flora 0-2(0-1)
Tallinna Kalev - Paide Linnamees. 0-3(0-1)
FC Kuressaare - Viljandi JK 1-0(0-0)

Round 13 [28-29.05.2019]
Maardu Linnamees. - JK Tammeka 2-1(1-1)
Tallinna Kalev - FC Kuressaare 3-0(1-0)
Viljandi JK - Narva Trans 1-1(0-0)
Paide Linnameeskond - JK Nõmme 0-2(0-1)
FC Flora - FCI Levadia 1-3(1-1)

Round 14 [31.05.-02.06.2019]
Narva Trans - Tallinna Kalev 2-2(1-1)
JK Nõmme - Maardu Linnameeskond 6-0(3-0)
JK Tammeka - Viljandi JK 0-1(0-0)
FC Kuressaare - FC Flora 0-4(0-1)
FCI Levadia - Paide Linnameeskond 1-1(0-0)

Round 15 [14-15.06.2019]
Tallinna Kalev - FCI Levadia 1-6(1-2)
Paide Linnameeskond - Viljandi JK 6-0(1-0)
Maardu Linnameeskond - FC Flora 3-8(0-3)
JK Nõmme - Narva Trans 3-2(1-2)
FC Kuressaare - JK Tammeka 1-1(0-1)

Round 16 [18-19.06.2019]
JK Tammeka - Tallinna Kalev 2-0(1-0)
Viljandi JK - Maardu Linnameeskond 2-0(2-0)
FC Flora - JK Nõmme 0-1(0-1)
Paide Linnamees. - FC Kuressaare 7-0(4-0)
FCI Levadia - Narva Trans 2-0(0-0)

Round 17 [21-22.06.2019]
Tallinna Kalev - FC Flora 0-2(0-2)
FCI Levadia - FC Kuressaare 5-0(1-0)
JK Nõmme - Viljandi JK 2-1(1-1)
Maardu Linnamees. - Paide Linnam. 1-4(0-3)
Narva Trans - JK Tammeka 2-5(1-4)

Round 18 [28-30.06.2019]
JK Tammeka - JK Nõmme 0-0
Maardu Linnamees. - FCI Levadia 1-6(0-3)
FC Kuressaare - Narva Trans 1-1(0-1)
FC Flora - Paide Linnameeskond 4-1(1-1)
Viljandi JK - Tallinna Kalev 1-2(1-2)

Round 19 [05-07.07.2019]
Paide Linnamees. - FC Kuressaare 6-1(4-0)
Narva Trans - JK Nõmme 1-1(0-1)
FCI Levadia - FC Flora 1-2(0-1)
Viljandi JK - JK Tammeka 0-1(0-0)
Tallinna Kalev - Maardu Linnamees. 1-4(1-1)

Round 20 [19-21.07.2019]
JK Nõmme - Paide Linnameeskond 1-1(0-1)
JK Tammeka - Tallinna Kalev 2-2(0-2)
Narva Trans - Viljandi JK 3-2(3-1)
FC Kuressaare - FCI Levadia 0-3(0-2)
FC Flora - Maardu Linnameeskond 3-0(2-0)

Round 21 [26-28.07.2019]
Paide Linnameeskond - JK Tammeka 2-0(1-0)
Maardu Linnamees. - Narva Trans 1-3(0-2)
Viljandi JK - FCI Levadia 0-3(0-3)
FC Kuressaare - FC Flora 0-3(0-1) [13.08.]
Tallinna Kalev - JK Nõmme 2-3(1-0) [24.09.]

Round 22 [02-03.08.2019]
JK Tammeka - Maardu Linnamees. 2-0(0-0)
Paide Linnameeskond - Narva Trans 1-0(1-0)
FCI Levadia - Tallinna Kalev 7-0(3-0)
JK Nõmme - FC Kuressaare 7-2(4-1)
FC Flora - Viljandi JK 3-0(2-0) [25.09.]

Round 23 [09-11.08.2019]
FC Kuressaare - Tallinna Kalev 0-1(0-0)
FC Flora - JK Tammeka 0-1(0-0)
Narva Trans - FCI Levadia 1-3(0-2)
Viljandi JK - Paide Linnameeskond 1-2(0-1)
Maardu Linna. - JK Nõmme 1-4(1-2) [01.10.]

Round 24 [16-18.08.2019]
JK Tammeka - Narva Trans 6-4(4-1)
Tallinna Kalev - FC Flora 0-2(0-1)
Maardu Linnamees. - FC Kuressaare 2-1(1-0)
FCI Levadia - Paide Linnameeskond 3-2(1-0)
JK Nõmme - Viljandi JK 2-2(1-0)

Round 25 [23-25.08.2019]
FC Kuressaare - JK Tammeka 0-1(0-1)
JK Nõmme - FCI Levadia 2-1(2-1)
Narva Trans - FC Flora 0-1(0-0)
Paide Linnamees. - Maardu Linnam. 5-0(3-0)
Viljandi JK - Tallinna Kalev 1-1(1-1)

Round 26 [27-28.08.2019]
JK Tammeka - FCI Levadia 1-1(0-0)
Maardu Linnameeskond - Viljandi JK 2-2(1-1)
Narva Trans - FC Kuressaare 4-2(1-1)
Tallinna Kalev - Paide Linnamees. 0-2(0-2)
FC Flora - JK Nõmme 1-1(0-0)

Round 27 [31.08.-01.09.2019]
Tallinna Kalev - Narva Trans 0-3(0-1)
JK Tammeka - JK Nõmme 1-2(1-0)
Viljandi JK - FC Kuressaare 3-0(1-0)
Paide Linnameeskond - FC Flora 1-1(1-0)
FCI Levadia - Maardu Linnamees. 3-1(3-1)

Round 28 [13-15.09.2019]
FC Flora - Tallinna Kalev 5-0(1-0)
FC Kuressaare - Paide Linnames. 0-3(0-0)
FCI Levadia - Viljandi JK 1-1(0-0)
JK Nõmme - Narva Trans 2-2(1-1)
Maardu Linnamees. - JK Tammeka 0-1(0-0)

Round 29 [17-18.09.2019]
Viljandi JK - JK Nõmme 0-3(0-1)
Tallinna Kalev - FC Kuressaare 2-1(1-1)
Maardu Linnamees. - Paide Linnam. 2-4(1-1)
Narva Trans - JK Tammeka 3-2(1-1)
FC Flora - FCI Levadia 2-1(1-1)

Round 30 [21-22.09.2019]
JK Nõmme - Tallinna Kalev 6-0(3-0)
Paide Linnameeskond - Viljandi JK 4-0(1-0)
FCI Levadia - Narva Trans 1-0(1-0)
FC Kuressaare - Maardu Linnamees. 1-0(0-0)
JK Tammeka - FC Flora 1-6(0-1)

Round 31 [28-29.09.2019]
Tallinna Kalev - FCI Levadia 0-1(0-1)
JK Nõmme - Maardu Linnameeskond 4-0(1-0)
Narva Trans - Paide Linnameeskond 0-1(0-0)
Viljandi JK - FC Flora 0-3(0-3)
JK Tammeka - FC Kuressaare 4-0(2-0)

Round 32 [05-06.10.2019]
FC Kuressaare - Viljandi JK 4-1(4-1)
Maardu Linnamees. - Tallinna Kalev 2-2(1-0)
FC Flora - Narva Trans 1-0(0-0)
Paide Linnameeskond - JK Nõmme 0-1(0-1)
FCI Levadia - JK Tammeka 1-1(0-0)

Round 33 [19-20.10.2019]
FCI Levadia - FC Kuressaare 2-1(1-0)
Paide Linnamees. - Tallinna Kalev 2-1(0-0)
Narva Trans - Maardu Linnamees. 5-2(3-1)
JK Tammeka - Viljandi JK 1-3(1-0)
JK Nõmme - FC Flora 2-1(0-0)

Round 34 [26-28.10.2019]
Tallinna Kalev - JK Tammeka 1-2(0-2)
Viljandi JK - Narva Trans 0-2(0-1)
Maardu Linnamees. - FCI Levadia 1-4(0-2)
FC Flora - Paide Linnameeskond 1-0(0-0)
FC Kuressaare - JK Nõmme 0-3(0-1)

Round 35 [02-03.11.2019]
Narva Trans - Tallinna Kalev 2-0(0-0)
FCI Levadia - JK Nõmme 1-1(1-1)
Viljandi JK - Maardu Linnameeskond 2-1(1-0)
FC Flora - FC Kuressaare 7-0(2-0)
JK Tammeka - Paide Linnameeskond 3-2(0-1)

Round 36 [09.11.2019]
FC Kuressaare - Narva Trans 0-1(0-0)
Maardu Linnameeskond - FC Flora 0-12(0-4)
Tallinna Kalev - Viljandi JK 3-0(1-0)
JK Nõmme - JK Tammeka 2-3(0-1)
Paide Linnameeskond - FCI Levadia 3-1(1-1)

Final Standings

									Home					Away				
1.	**FC Flora Tallinn**	36	29	3	4	110	-	21	90	13	2	3	53	- 11	16	1	1	57	- 10
2.	FCI Levadia Tallinn	36	24	6	6	98	-	32	78	11	5	2	54	- 15	13	1	4	44	- 17
3.	Nõmme Kalju FC Tallinn	36	22	11	3	79	-	34	77	11	4	3	48	- 25	11	7	0	31	- 9
4.	Paide Linnameeskond	36	23	5	8	78	-	30	74	12	2	4	43	- 11	11	3	4	35	- 19
5.	Tartu JK Tammeka	36	14	7	15	57	-	62	49	5	5	8	28	- 33	9	2	7	29	- 29
6.	JK Narva Trans	36	13	9	14	57	-	49	48	6	4	8	29	- 27	7	5	6	28	- 22
7.	Viljandi JK Tulevik	36	7	7	22	35	-	75	28	3	3	12	17	- 36	4	4	10	18	- 39
8.	JK Tallinna Kalev	36	6	6	24	29	-	89	24	4	0	14	15	- 40	2	6	10	14	- 49
9.	FC Kuressaare (*Relegation Play-offs*)	36	6	5	25	24	-	87	23	5	3	10	11	- 24	1	2	15	13	- 63
10.	Maardu Linnameeskond (*Relegated*)	36	4	5	27	30	-	118	17	3	4	11	19	- 58	1	1	16	11	- 60

Top goalscorers:

31	**Erik Sorga**	*FC Flora Tallinn*
13	Nikita Andreev (RUS)	*FCI Levadia Tallinn*
13	Alassana Jatta (GAM)	*Paide Linnameeskond*
13	Eric McWoods (USA)	*JK Narva Trans*
13	Kaimar Saag	*Viljandi JK Tulevik*
12	Herol Riiberg	*FC Flora Tallinn*
12	Konstantin Vassiljev	*FC Flora Tallinn*

Relegation Play-offs [16-23.11.2019]

Pärnu JK Vaprus - FC Kuressaare   1-4(1-1)   2-1(0-1)
FC Kuressaare remains at first level.

NATIONAL CUP
Eesti Karikas 2019

First Round [05/12/14/17/21/26.06.2018]

Põhja-Sakala Suure-Jaani - Tallinna JK Legion	1-3	Koeru JK - Viimsi Lõvid	3-2
FC Mulgi - Ambla Vallameeskond	1-2	Maardu Linnameeskond - Viljandi JK Tulevik	3-0
Maardu United II - JK Mauruse Saurused	21-2	Paide Linnameeskond U-21 - Tabasalu JK	0-3
FC Sillamäe - Anija JK	3-1 pen	SK Imavere - Rasmus Värki Jalgpallikool	4-3
Rumori Calcio Tallinn - Raplamaa JK	3-0	JK Loo - Pärnu JK Vaprus	1-2
JK Tallinna Kalev II - Läänemaa JK Haapsalu	3-5 pen	FC Npm Silmet - FC Tallinn	w/o
Valga FC Warrior - FC Viking	5-1	Tõrva JK - Kohtla-Järve JK Järve	1-3
Paide Linnameeskond III - JK Püsivus Kohila	6-1	FC Kuressaare - Põlva FC Lootos	22-0
Tallinna FC Ararat TTÜ - Maarjamäe FC Igiliikur	1-4 pen	Märjamaa Kompanii - FC Tallinna Wolves	10-0
Vaimastvere SK Illi - JK Raudteetöölised	8-0	Viljandi JK Tulevik II - FC Jõgeva Wolves	4-3
Viimsi JK II - Pärnu JK Poseidon II	3-0	FC Puhkus Mehhikos - Põhja-Tallinna JK Volta II	2-9
Põhja-Tallinna JK Volta - Tartu JK Tammeka	0-3	Tallinna FC TransferWise - Kohtla-Nõmme	2-3
Kadrina SK Moe - FCP Pärnu	3-0	Tallinna FC Soccernet - FCI Levadia Tallinn	0-12
Tallinna FC Olympic - FC Flora Tallinn	0-16		

Second Round [28-29.06. & 04/07/08/13/16/17/18/19/24/25.07.2018]

FC Sillamäe - Nõmme Kalju FC Tallinn	0-16	Tabasalu JK - FC Lelle	6-0
SK Imavere - JK Narva Trans	0-10	Ambla Vallameeskond - Viimsi JK	1-6
Tartu FC Helios - FC Flora Tallinn	0-13	Jõgeva Wolves - Maardu United II	10-0
FCI Levadia Tallinn - FC Nõmme United	4-1	FC Flora Tallinn II - Maardu United II	10-0
JK Jalgpallihaigla - Valga FC Warrior	0-7	FC Vastseliina - Tartu FC Santos	2-5
Tallinna JK Augur - Paide Linnameeskond	1-15	Viimsi JK II - FC Maksatransport	3-2
Tartu JK Welco - FC Flora Tallinn III	1-0	Märjamaa Kompanii - FC Zenit Tallinn	2-3 pen
FC Teleios - Kohtla-Nõmme	4-1	FC Npm Silmet - Pärnu JK Vaprus	1-2
JK Sillamäe Kalev - Viljandi JK Tulevik II	4-2	Rakvere JK Tarvas - Tallinna JK Legion	0-3
Rumori Calcio Tallinn - JK Tallinna Kalev	1-8	Jõgeva SK Noorus-69 - FC Otepää	7-3
FC Kose - Koeru JK	w/o	Maardu Linnameeskond - Põhja-Tallinna JK Volta II	5-1
Läänemaa JK Haapsalu - Nõmme Kalju FC III	6-0	Maarjamäe FC Igiliikur - Kohtla-Järve JK Järve II	1-2
Kohtla-Järve JK Järve - Tartu JK Tammeka	0-2	Tallinna JK Piraaja - Tartu FC Helios II	7-0
FC Järva-Jaani - Tallinna FC Zapoos	3-1	FC Kuressaare - Vaimastvere SK Illi	15-0
Tallinna FC Eston Villa - FC Elva	0-4	Paide Linnameeskond III - JK Kernu Kadakas	10-4(3-2, 4-4)
Kadrina SK Moe - Tallinna Depoo	2-0	Raasiku FC Joker - Pärnu JK Poseidon Nirvaana	4-4 aet; 1-3 pen

Third Round [08/14/16/21/22/23.08.2018]

JK Tallinna Kalev - Tartu FC Santos	3-0(0-0)	FC Järva-Jaani - Jõgeva Wolves	5-0(3-0)
FC Kuressaare - Nõmme Kalju FC Tallinn	2-3(0-1)	Kadrina SK Moe - JK Narva Trans	0-7(0-3)
Tartu JK Tammeka - FC Flora Tallinn II	1-0(1-0)	Maardu Linnameeskond - JK Sillamäe Kalev	4-0(2-0)
Viimsi JK - FC Elva	2-3(1-1)	Viimsi JK II - Kohtla-Järve JK Järve II	3-2(0-2,2-2)
Paide Linnameeskond - Paide Linnameeskond III	2-1(1-0)	FC Zenit Tallinn - FC Kose	4-2
FC Flora Tallinn - Valga FC Warrior	13-0(4-0)	Pärnu JK Poseidon Nirvaana - Tabasalu JK	0-3(0-1)
Tallinna JK Legion - Pärnu JK Vaprus	3-0(1-0)	Tartu JK Welco - FCI Levadia Tallinn	0-5(0-1)
Läänemaa JK Haapsalu - FC Teleios	14-1(4-0)	Tallinna JK Piraaja - Jõgeva SK Noorus-69	3-4(2-2)

1/8-Finals [05/06/25/26.09.2018]

Maardu Linnameeskond - Läänemaa JK Haapsalu	4-0(3-0)	Paide Linnameeskond - Tallinna JK Legion	2-1(0-1)
FC Järva-Jaani - Tartu JK Tammeka	0-6(0-1)	Tabasalu JK - FC Zenit Tallinn	6-1(1-0)
FCI Levadia Tallinn - FC Flora Tallinn	2-1(1-1)	Nõmme Kalju FC Tallinn - JK Tallinna Kalev	3-0(0-0,0-0)
JK Narva Trans - Jõgeva SK Noorus-69	8-0(3-0)	Viimsi JK II - FC Elva	0-3(0-0)

Quarter-Finals [23-24.04.2019]

Tabasalu JK - FC Elva	1-5(1-2)	JK Narva Trans - Maardu Linnameeskond	2-0(0-0)
Nõmme Kalju FC Tallinn - Tartu JK Tammeka	2-1(0-0,0-0)	Paide Linnameeskond - FCI Levadia Tallinn	1-4(1-0,1-1)

Semi-Finals [07-08.05.2019]

JK Narva Trans - FC Elva	5-0(1-0)	Nõmme Kalju FC Tallinn - FCI Levadia Tallinn	3-2(1-1,2-2)

Final

25.05.2019; A. Le Coq Arena, Tallinn; Referee: Grigori Ošomkov; Attendance: 956
JK Narva Trans - Nõmme Kalju FC Tallinn   **2-1(1-1,1-1)**

Narva Trans: Marko Meerits, Abdoulaye Diallo, Roman Nesterovski, Joseph Saliste, Aleksandr Zakarlyuka, Dmitri Proshin, Artjom Škinjov (91.Markas Beneta), Elysée Irié Bi Séhi, Denis Polyakov (105.Nikita Mihhailov), Eric McWoods, Eduard Golovljov (76.Viktor Plotnikov). Trainer: Dmitrijs Kalašņikovs (Latvia).

Nõmme Kalju: Vitali Teleš, Aleksandr Kulinitš, Mikk Reintam, Maximiliano Uggè [*sent off 68*], Andriy Markovych, Réginald Mbu Alidor, Sander Puri (73.Peeter Klein), Ellinton Antonio Costa Morais „Liliu" (70.Vladimir Avilov), Igor Subbotin, Robert Kirss (87.Nikolai Mašitšev), Kaspar Paur (106.Roman Sobtšenko). Trainer: Roman Kozhukhovskiy (Ukraine)

Goals: 0-1 Ellinton Antonio Costa Morais „Liliu" (32), 1-1 Aleksandr Zakarlyuka (44), 2-1 Viktor Plotnikov (93).

THE CLUBS 2019

Football Club Flora Tallinn

Founded: 10.03.1990
Stadium: A. Le Coq Arena, Tallinn (14,336)
Trainer: Jürgen Henn   02.06.1987

Goalkeepers:	DOB	M	(s)	G
Richard Aland	15.03.1994	17		
Matvei Igonen	02.10.1996	16		
Kristen Lapa	11.02.2000	1		
Ingmar Paplavskis	17.05.1999	2		
Defenders:	**DOB**	**M**	**(s)**	**G**
Enar Jääger	18.11.1984	5		
Gert Kams	25.05.1985	29	(2)	3
Märten Kuusk	05.04.1996	32		4
Michael Lilander	10.06.1997	11	(1)	
Marco Lukka	04.12.1996	4		
Anselmi Nurmela (FIN)	22.11.1996	7	(7)	2
Henrik Pürg	03.06.1996	29		6
Markkus Seppik	16.04.2001	2		

Midfielders:	DOB	M	(s)	G
Mihkel Ainsalu	08.03.1996	21	(5)	5
Pavel Dõmov	31.12.1993	2	(5)	1
Henri Järvelaid	11.12.1998	25	(1)	3
Vladislavs Kreida	25.09.1999	31		
Martin Miller	25.09.1997	21	(5)	5
Markus Poom	27.02.1999	7	(12)	5
Herol Riiberg	14.04.1997	17	(8)	12
Vlasiy Sinyavskiy	27.11.1996	29	(7)	6
Konstantin Vassiljev	16.08.1984	31	(1)	12
Forwards:	**DOB**	**M**	**(s)**	**G**
Rauno Alliku	02.03.1990	16	(11)	5
Mark Anders Lepik	10.09.2000		(4)	
Frank Liivak	07.07.1996	14	(17)	8
Erik Sorga	08.07.1999	27	(7)	31

FCI Levadia Tallinn

Founded: 22.10.1998
Stadium: A. Le Coq Arena, Tallinn (14,336)
Trainer: Aleksandar Rogić (SRB)   03.08.1981
[16.09.2019] Vladimir Vassiljev   13.02.1988

Goalkeepers:	DOB	M	(s)	G
Artur Kotenko	20.08.1981	4		
Sergei Lepmets	05.04.1987	32		
Defenders:	**DOB**	**M**	**(s)**	**G**
Igor Dudarev (RUS)	12.08.1993	13	(6)	1
Markus Jürgenson	09.09.1987	31	(1)	8
Dmitri Kruglov	24.05.1984	30	(1)	
Marko Lipp	19.03.1999	13	(3)	1
Evgeniy Osipov (RUS)	29.10.1986	30		6
Maksim Podholjuzin	13.11.1992	25	(2)	2
Morits Veering	26.12.1999		(1)	
Midfielders:	**DOB**	**M**	**(s)**	**G**
Aimé Marcelin Gando Biala (CMR)	27.02.1997	28	(3)	9
Marek Kaljumäe	18.02.1991	20	(7)	1
Artjom Komlov	09.09.2002	2	(4)	2

	DOB	M	(s)	G
Pavel Marin	14.06.1995	10	(18)	2
Kirill Nesterov (RUS)	21.07.1989	17	(7)	6
Rasmus Peetson	03.05.1995	18	(7)	5
Yuriy Tkachuk (UKR)	18.04.1995	25	(3)	1
Bogdan Vaštšuk	04.10.1995	2	(4)	
Ihor Zhurakhovskyi (UKR)	19.09.1994	6	(1)	2
Forwards:	**DOB**	**M**	**(s)**	**G**
Nikita Andreev (RUS)	22.09.1988	28	(6)	13
Evgen Budnik (UKR)	04.09.1990	12	(2)	11
João Morelli Neto (BRA)	11.03.1996	27	(3)	11
Evgeny Kabaev (RUS)	28.02.1988	2		1
Anton Krutogolov	05.04.2001		(1)	
Érick Andrés Moreno Serna (COL)	24.11.1991	2	(7)	1
Karl Õigus	05.11.1998	1	(5)	1
Mark Roosnupp	12.05.1997	18	(7)	11

Football Club Kuressaare

Founded: 14.03.1997
Stadium: Kuressaare linnastaadion, Kuressaare (1,000)
Trainer: Jan Važinski   10.08.1964
[22.08.2019] Dmitrijs Kalašņikovs (LVA)   11.12.1983

Goalkeepers:	DOB	M	(s)	G
Magnus Karofeld	20.08.1996	30		
Roland Kütt	22.04.1987	6	(1)	
Defenders:	**DOB**	**M**	**(s)**	**G**
Ranon Kriisa	28.01.1996	27	(3)	1
Mairo Miil	15.02.2000	31		
Märten Pajunurm	29.04.1993	34		7
Mario Pruul	10.09.1990	11	(1)	
Elari Valmas	02.07.1988	23	(4)	
Reivo Vinter	02.02.1997	1	(3)	
Midfielders:	**DOB**	**M**	**(s)**	**G**
Nikita Komissarov	25.04.2000	15	(1)	
Sander Laht	26.09.1991	31	(2)	5
Amor Luup	18.02.1992	3	(3)	
Karl Maar	26.02.1993	5	(8)	1

	DOB	M	(s)	G
Kristjan Moorats	24.11.2000		(1)	
Märten Opp	15.09.1999	21	(6)	1
Karmo Paju	12.09.1999	10	(10)	
Oliver Rass	25.05.2000	26	(4)	
Alari Saar	28.03.1996	2	(3)	
Rasmus Saar	02.03.2000	21	(3)	
Sander Seeman	12.09.1992	27		
Rauno Tutk	10.04.1988	31		2
Forwards:	**DOB**	**M**	**(s)**	**G**
Silver Kelder	22.10.1995	8	(14)	
OttoRobert Lipp	02.12.2000	13	(7)	4
Sten Penzev	13.12.2001	1	(4)	
Joonas Soomre	17.05.2000	8		1
Mario Stern	26.07.1997	2	(4)	
Maarek Suursaar	16.07.1997	10	(10)	1

Maardu Linnameeskond

Founded: 1997
Stadium: Maardu linnastaadion, Maardu (500)
Trainer: Andrei Borissov   01.08.1969
[03.10.2019] Mark Kolk   03.02.1994

Goalkeepers:	DOB	M	(s)	G
Artjom Jakovlev	28.08.1998	1		
Ilja Kassjantsuk	06.02.1986	34		
Maksim Zelentsov	03.08.1995	1		
Defenders:	**DOB**	**M**	**(s)**	**G**
Anton Aristov	22.08.1986	16	(8)	1
Klimentii Boldyrev (UKR)	20.03.1992	30	(1)	
Yaroslav Dmitriev (RUS)	25.06.1988	8	(10)	
Alger Džumadil	29.07.1996	24	(4)	1
Erik Grigorjev	31.12.1986	15	(2)	
Deniss Kovtun	16.09.1989	17	(5)	
Deniss Malov	08.06.1980	20	(4)	1
Vladislav Tšurilkin	30.05.1989	8		
Midfielders:	**DOB**	**M**	**(s)**	**G**
Rain Aasmäe	15.01.1992	12	(8)	
Domantas Antanavičius (LTU)	18.11.1998	12	(1)	1

	DOB	M	(s)	G
Vadim Aksjonov	20.11.1996	29	(1)	2
Kotaro Amemiya (JPN)	16.04.1994	24	(3)	3
Nikita Brõlin	17.08.1995	1	(1)	
Sho Hayasaka (JPN)	23.09.1995	35		4
Martin Jaagumets	17.04.2002	1	(3)	
Alan Mones	18.06.1998	2	(6)	
Vladislav Ogorodnik	18.03.1995	25		1
Vadim Šalabai	16.04.1992	6	(16)	1
Deniss Suvorikov	28.12.1986	1	(4)	
Stanislav Tsõmbaljuk	25.11.2002	1	(2)	
Ilja Zelentsov	02.08.1992	31		4
Forwards:	**DOB**	**M**	**(s)**	**G**
Vitali Gussev	16.03.1983	33		5
Maksim Krivošein	03.06.1983		(4)	
Jasper Chibueze Uwaegbulam (NGA)	12.12.1994	5	(2)	5

Jalgpalliklubi Narva Trans

Founded: 1979 (*as Avtomobilist Narva*)
Stadium: Narva Kreenholm staadion, Narva (1,065)
Trainer: Dmitrijs Kalašņikovs (LVA)   11.12.1983
[01.06.2019] Valeri Bondarenko (RUS)   22.04.1953
[01.06.2019] Andrey Semin (RUS)   26.08.1969
[23.08.2019] Oleg Kurotskin   11.05.1971

Goalkeepers:	DOB	M	(s)	G
Aleksei Matrossov	06.04.1991	6		
Marko Meerits	26.04.1992	30		
Defenders:	**DOB**	**M**	**(s)**	**G**
Markas Beneta (LTU)	08.07.1993	23		4
Abdoulaye Diallo (SEN)	21.10.1992	10		2
Sergei Kondrattsev	23.09.2001		(4)	
Roman Nesterovski	09.06.1989	28		
Joseph Saliste	10.04.1995	35		5
Nikita Savenkov	28.07.1998	7		
Tanel Tamberg	06.06.1992	16	(4)	
Maksim Tšerezov	26.03.2001	2	(3)	
Midfielders:	**DOB**	**M**	**(s)**	**G**
Elysée Irié Bi Séhi (CIV)	13.09.1989	30		1

	DOB	M	(s)	G
Arseni Kovaltšuk	07.01.2001		(1)	
Vadim Mihailov	06.06.1998	25	(9)	2
Denis Polyakov (RUS)	21.02.1992	24	(1)	
Dmitri Proshin (RUS)	06.01.1984	13	(1)	
Artjom Škinjov	30.01.1996	19	(6)	2
Aleksandr Zakarlyuka (RUS)	24.06.1995	26	(9)	9
Forwards:	**DOB**	**M**	**(s)**	**G**
Eduard Golovljov	25.01.1997	15	(4)	7
Aleksandr Jurõšev	14.03.2001		(3)	
Julius Kasparavičius (LTU)	03.04.1995	27	(2)	5
Eric McWoods (USA)	21.10.1995	30	(1)	13
Nikita Mihhailov	20.06.2002	15	(8)	2
Viktor Plotnikov	14.07.1989	14	(11)	4
Aleksei Stepanov	13.02.2002	1	(6)	

Nõmme Kalju Football Club Tallinn

Founded: 1923 (Re-established in 1997)
Stadium: Hiiu staadion, Tallinn (650)
Trainer: Sergey Frantsev (RUS)   17.03.1959
[25.04.2019] Roman Kozhukhovskiy (UKR)   24.01.1979

Goalkeepers:	DOB	M	(s)	G
Pavel Londak	14.05.1980	20		
Vitali Teleš	17.10.1983	16	(1)	
Defenders:	**DOB**	**M**	**(s)**	**G**
Vladimir Avilov	10.03.1995	25		1
Aleksandr Kulinitš	24.05.1992	29	(2)	3
Ivan Lobay (UKR)	21.05.1996	10		1
Andriy Markovych (UKR)	25.06.1995	33		1
Mikk Reintam	22.05.1990	22	(1)	3
Maximiliano Uggè (ITA)	24.09.1991	21	(2)	6
Midfielders:	**DOB**	**M**	**(s)**	**G**
Aleksandr Ivanjushin (RUS)	07.09.1995	2	(2)	
Vladyslav Khomutov (UKR)	04.06.1998	11	(1)	5
Nikolai Mašitšev (RUS)	05.12.1988	4	(6)	1
Réginald Mbu Alidor (FRA)	19.05.1993	28	(1)	
Sander Puri	07.05.1988	24	(4)	5

	DOB	M	(s)	G
Kirill Šustov	15.11.2001		(1)	
Deniss Tjapkin	30.01.1991	15	(6)	3
Eugen Zasaviţchi (MDA)	24.11.1992	3		
Forwards:	**DOB**	**M**	**(s)**	**G**
Jevgeni Demidov	11.02.2000		(3)	
Robert Kirss	03.09.1994	21	(8)	6
Peeter Klein	28.01.1997	6	(8)	2
Ellinton Antonio Costa Morais „Liliu" (BRA)	30.03.1990	18	(2)	9
Max Andrew Mata (NZL)	10.07.2000	11	(3)	9
Héctor Núñez Segovia (CHI)	15.04.1992	3	(3)	1
Kaspar Paur	16.02.1995	32	(3)	5
Roman Sobtšenko	25.01.1994		(5)	
Igor Subbotin	26.06.1990	32	(1)	9
Alex Tamm	24.07.2001	3	(11)	1
Aleksandr Volkov	11.10.1994	7	(10)	5

Paide Linnameeskond

Founded: 2004
Stadium: Paide linnastaadion, Paide (268)
Trainer: Vjatšeslav Zahovaiko   29.12.1981

Goalkeepers:	DOB	M	(s)	G
Mait Toom	07.05.1990	36		
Defenders:	**DOB**	**M**	**(s)**	**G**
Siim Aer	22.07.2001	1	(1)	1
Mikel Gurrutxaga Barruetabeña (ESP)	22.08.1996	30		5
Sören Kaldma	03.07.1996	19	(3)	
Martin Kase	02.09.1993	27		1
Karl Mööl	04.03.1992	34		2
Tanel Neubauer	22.02.2000	1		
Kristjan Pelt	12.07.2001	14	(3)	
Rico Reinoja	16.07.2000		(1)	
Muhammed Sanneh (GAM)	07.11.2000	31	(1)	
Edgar Tur	28.12.1996	13	(3)	2
Midfielders:	**DOB**	**M**	**(s)**	**G**
Bruno Souza Caprioli (BRA)	21.02.1996	10	(4)	
Andre Frolov	18.04.1988	35		7

	DOB	M	(s)	G
Rasmus Kallas	18.11.2003	1	(1)	
Joel Kokla	20.06.2001	2	(8)	
Siim Luts	12.03.1989	4	(1)	
Sander Sinilaid	07.10.1990	29	(6)	9
Henri Välja	04.11.2001	29	(2)	9
Yann Michael Yao (CIV)	20.06.1997	27	(2)	11
Vladislav Zanfirov	01.02.1999	2	(2)	
Forwards:	**DOB**	**M**	**(s)**	**G**
Andre Järva	21.11.1996	4	(5)	1
Alassana Jatta (GAM)	12.01.1999	14	(3)	13
Kevin Kauber	23.03.1995	6		3
Tarmo Neemelo	10.02.1982	6	(15)	2
Kristofer Piht	24.04.2001	2	(7)	2
Patrick Sylva (GAM)	22.12.2000		(2)	
Ander Ott Valge	20.10.1998	19	(10)	9

Jalgpalliklubi Tallinna Kalev Tallinn

Founded: 1909 (*as Meteor Tallinn*); Re-established on 01.09.2002
Stadium: Kalev Keskstaadion, Tallinn (11,500)
Trainer: Aleksandr Dmitrijev   18.02.1982

Goalkeepers:	DOB	M	(s)	G
Daniil Koroljov	11.12.1999	5		
Karl Vallner	28.02.1998	31		
Defenders:	**DOB**	**M**	**(s)**	**G**
Markus Allast	05.09.2000	17	(4)	
Kaspar Laur	08.04.2000	34		
Roger Colville Lee (BER)	01.07.1991	23	(1)	
Denis Maksimenko	12.08.1998	22	(3)	
Andreas Raudsepp	13.12.1993	34	(1)	4
Daniil Sheviakov (RUS)	29.07.1999	23	(1)	4
Jakob Tamberg	16.06.2003	1	(1)	
Kaspar Tilga	24.10.1998	2		
Midfielders:	**DOB**	**M**	**(s)**	**G**
Wale Musa Alli (NGA)	31.12.2000	28	(5)	7
Sandor Dino Franch	29.09.2002	1	(2)	
Watson Fabrice Hounkpe (BEN)	31.07.2001	3	(1)	1

	DOB	M	(s)	G
Bangaly Kouyaté (CAN)	13.06.1995	23	(3)	
Mikk Kruusalu	06.12.2000	3	(5)	
Reinhard Reimaa	12.11.1998	29	(5)	4
Mikk Johannes Siitam	25.12.2003		(4)	
Tristan Teeväli	19.05.2003	17	(6)	
Martin Vetkal	21.02.2004	4	(4)	1
Forwards:	**DOB**	**M**	**(s)**	**G**
Hannes Anier	16.01.1993	12	(8)	3
Brandon Bachmann	28.02.2000	6	(12)	
Artjom Ostrovski	24.05.2000	5	(5)	
Mark Petrov	03.04.2002	15	(12)	1
Kevin Rääbis	02.01.1994	17	(2)	1
Karl Sõerde	06.04.1996	1	(2)	
Daniil Sõtšugov	15.01.2003	13	(5)	
Markus Vaherna	27.01.1999	27	(5)	2

Jalgpallikool Tammeka Tartu

Founded: 13.06.1989
Stadium: Tartu Tamme staadion, Tartu (1,500)
Trainer: Kaido Koppel   09.05.1988

Goalkeepers:	DOB	M	(s)	G
Carl Kiidjärv	05.12.2001	2		
Karl Pechter	02.03.1996	34		
Defenders:	**DOB**	**M**	**(s)**	**G**
Kevin Aloe	07.05.1995	30	(1)	1
Kevin Anderson	10.11.1993	20	(3)	
Daaniel Maanas	05.01.2000	1	(2)	
Frankline Okoye (NGA)	06.05.1999	20	(7)	3
Akim Sairinen (FIN)	22.05.1994	36		1
Mikhail Slashchyov (RUS)	21.06.1997	29	(1)	1
Ats Toomsalu	17.08.2002	1		
Midfielders:	**DOB**	**M**	**(s)**	**G**
Joonas Kartsep	13.11.1997	4	(9)	
Reio Laabus	14.03.1990	14	(6)	1
Dominic Laaneots	16.06.2001		(2)	

	DOB	M	(s)	G
Andre Paju	05.01.1995	22	(3)	4
Markus Soomets	02.03.2000	3		2
Tauno Tekko	14.12.1994	30	(3)	6
Artur Uljanov	25.03.1999	18	(17)	2
Forwards:	**DOB**	**M**	**(s)**	**G**
Mikhel Järviste	28.05.2000	30	(3)	4
Martin Jõgi	05.01.1995	6	(4)	2
Sander Kapper	08.12.1994	30	(3)	4
Tristan Koskor	28.11.1995	14	(2)	5
Erki Mõttus	15.01.1997		(1)	
Mart Preiman	01.05.1997	1	(9)	1
Albert Prosa	01.10.1990	10		3
Sten Reinkort	29.04.1998	25	(11)	11
Rasmus Tauts	07.01.1997	1	(5)	
Patrik Veelma	15.04.2002	15	(10)	5

Viljandi Jalgpalliklubi Tulevik

Founded: 1912
Stadium: Viljandi linnastaadion, Viljandi (1,084)
Trainer: Sander Post   10.09.1984

Goalkeepers:	DOB	M	(s)	G
Andreas Kallaste	29.06.2000	8		
KarlRomet Nõmm	04.01.1998	16		
Ingmar Krister Paplavskis	17.05.1999	12		
Defenders:	**DOB**	**M**	**(s)**	**G**
Martin Allik	13.08.1994	21	(4)	
Ridwan Babatunde (NGA)	05.05.2001	10		
Mark Edur	11.12.1998	31		
Gerdo Juhkam	19.06.1994	12		
Janar Õunap	09.09.1994	32	(1)	2
Siim Saar	09.07.1995	1		
Gustav Hendrik Seeder	29.11.2000	19	(5)	
Midfielders:	**DOB**	**M**	**(s)**	**G**
Rasmus Alles	02.01.1992	12	(5)	1
Arlet Hunt	23.04.2000	1	(4)	
Indrek Ilves	27.04.1990	19	(7)	5

	DOB	M	(s)	G
Kristjan Kask	05.07.1999	30		2
Tanel Lang	15.08.1995	34		2
Illimar Loigo	14.08.1998	31	(2)	2
Ifeanyi David Onyeanula (NGA)	13.07.2000	8		
Karl Org	15.05.2001	1	(4)	
Alex Roosalu	04.05.1999	27	(2)	
Kaur Tomson	28.11.1992	11	(9)	1
Herbert Velleste	17.01.2001		(2)	
Vladislav Zanfirov	01.02.1999	5	(7)	
Forwards:	**DOB**	**M**	**(s)**	**G**
Kossi Romeo Stephane Da-Costa (BEN)	25.02.2001	6	(1)	
Lauri Elur	20.02.1999	4	(6)	
Kristen Kähr	05.10.1989	2		
Rainer Peips	11.08.1990	10	(13)	5
Kaimar Saag	05.08.1988	33	(1)	13

SECOND LEVEL
Esiliiga 2019

1.	Tallinna JK Legion (*Promoted*)	36	28	5	3	127	-	35	89
2.	FC Flora U-21 Tallinn*	36	22	7	7	85	-	37	73
3.	Pärnu JK Vaprus (*Promotion Play-offs*)	36	21	4	11	73	-	48	67
4.	Tartu JK Tammeka U-21*	36	18	4	14	59	-	55	58
5.	FC Elva	36	18	2	16	67	-	63	56
6.	FC Levadia U-21 Tallinn*	36	16	5	15	78	-	65	53
7.	Kothla-Järve JK	36	12	4	20	51	-	82	40
8.	Rakvere JK Tarvas (*Relegation Play-offs*)	36	8	4	24	35	-	96	28
9.	JK Tallinna Kalev U-21 (*Relegated*)	36	8	4	24	38	-	82	28
10.	Tartu Jalgpalliklubi Welco (*Relegated*)	36	6	6	24	39	-	89	24

*as reserve team, not eligible for promotion.

Relegation Play-offs (2ⁿᵈ/3ʳᵈ Level) [17-23.11.2019]

Pärnu JK - Rakvere JK Tarvas   3-2(1-0)   4-0(2-0)
Pärnu JK promoted for the 2020 Esiliiga.

INTERNATIONAL MATCHES
(16.07.2019 – 15.07.2020)

06.09.2019	Tallinn	Estonia - Belarus	1-2(0-0)	(ECQ)
09.09.2019	Tallinn	Estonia - Netherlands	0-4(0-1)	(ECQ)
10.10.2019	Minsk	Belarus - Estonia	0-0	(ECQ)
13.10.2019	Tallinn	Estonia - Germany	0-3(0-0)	(ECQ)
14.11.2019	Zaporizhya	Ukraine - Estonia	1-0(0-0)	(F)
19.11.2019	Amsterdam	Netherlands - Estonia	5-0(2-0)	(ECQ)

06.09.2019   ESTONIA - BELARUS   **1-2(0-0)**   16th EC. Qualifiers
A. Le Coq Arena, Tallinn; Referee: Alain Durieux (Luxembourg); Attendance: 7,314
EST: Sergei Lepmets, Ragnar Klavan (Cap), Taijo Teniste, Joonas Tamm, Karol Mets, Artur Pikk, Konstantin Vassiljev (77.Artjom Dmitrijev), Mattias Käit, Sergei Zenjov, Henrik Ojamaa (86.Vlasiy Sinyavskiy), Erik Sorga (83.Rauno Sappinen). Trainer: Karel Voolaid.
Goal: Erik Sorga (54).

09.09.2019   ESTONIA - NETHERLANDS   **0-4(0-1)**   16th EC. Qualifiers
A. Le Coq Arena, Tallinn; Referee: Serhiy Boyko (Ukraine); Attendance: 11,006
EST: Sergei Lepmets, Ragnar Klavan (Cap), Taijo Teniste, Ken Kallaste, Joonas Tamm, Karol Mets, Mihkel Ainsalu (87.Aleksandr Dmitrijev), Mattias Käit, Sergei Zenjov (60.Frank Liivak), Henrik Ojamaa (85.Rauno Sappinen), Erik Sorga. Trainer: Karel Voolaid.

10.10.2019   BELARUS - ESTONIA   **0-0**   16th EC. Qualifiers
Stadion Dynama, Minsk; Referee: Ricardo de Burgos Bengoetxea (Spain); Attendance: 11,300
EST: Sergei Lepmets, Taijo Teniste, Ken Kallaste, Nikita Baranov, Karol Mets, Konstantin Vassiljev (Cap), Mattias Käit, Vladislav Kreida, Sergei Zenjov (59.Frank Liivak), Henrik Ojamaa (89.Martin Miller), Erik Sorga (80.Rauno Sappinen). Trainer: Karel Voolaid.

13.10.2019   ESTONIA - GERMANY   **0-3(0-0)**   16th EC. Qualifiers
A. Le Coq Arena, Tallinn; Referee: Georgi Kabakov (Bulgaria); Attendance: 12,062
EST: Sergei Lepmets, Gert Kams, Joonas Tamm, Nikita Baranov, Karol Mets, Artur Pikk, Konstantin Vassiljev (Cap) (61.Mattias Käit), Ilja Antonov, Mihkel Ainsalu, Rauno Sappinen (56.Sergei Zenjov), Frank Liivak (77.Henrik Ojamaa). Trainer: Karel Voolaid.

14.11.2019   UKRAINE - ESTONIA   **1-0(0-0)**   Friendly International
Slavutych Arena, Zaporizhya; Referee: Juan Martínez Munuera (Spain); Attendance: 11,756
EST: Matvei Igonen, Gert Kams (Cap) (46.Taijo Teniste), Nikita Baranov, Artur Pikk, Märten Kuusk, Sander Puri (82.Ken Kallaste), Mihkel Ainsalu (62.Ilja Antonov), Mattias Käit (70.Konstantin Vassiljev), Vladislav Kreida, Henri Anier (70.Erik Sorga), Frank Liivak (62.Sergei Zenjov). Trainer: Karel Voolaid.

19.11.2019   NETHERLANDS - ESTONIA   **5-0(2-0)**   16th EC. Qualifiers
"Johann Cruijff ArenA", Amsterdam; Referee: Davide Massa (Italy); Attendance: 50,386
EST: Sergei Lepmets, Taijo Teniste (61.Nikita Baranov), Ken Kallaste, Joonas Tamm, Karol Mets, Konstantin Vassiljev (Cap), Ilja Antonov, Mihkel Ainsalu, Sergei Zenjov (76.Frank Liivak), Henrik Ojamaa (83.Mattias Käit), Erik Sorga. Trainer: Karel Voolaid.

NATIONAL TEAM PLAYERS
(16.07.2019 – 15.07.2020)

Name	DOB	Caps	Goals	2019/2020:	Club
Goalkeepers					
Matvei IGONEN	02.10.1996	3	0	2019:	FC Flora Tallinn
Sergei LEPMETS	05.04.1987	12	0	2019:	FCI Levadia Tallinn
Defenders					
Nikita BARANOV	19.08.1992	38	0	2019:	FC Alashkert Yerevan (ARM)
Ken KALLASTE	31.08.1988	45	0	2019:	GKS Tychy (POL)
Gert KAMS	25.05.1985	60	3	2019:	FC Flora Tallinn
Ragnar KLAVAN	30.10.1985	127	3	2019:	Cagliari Calcio (ITA)
Märten KUUSK	05.04.1996	2	0	2019:	FC Flora Tallinn
Karol METS	16.05.1993	61	0	2019:	AIK Stockholm (SWE)
Hindrek OJAMAA	12.06.1995	5	0	2019:	Vaasan Palloseura (FIN)
Artur PIKK	05.03.1993	36	1	2019:	MKS Miedź Legnica (POL)
Joonas TAMM	02.02.1992	35	3	2019:	Lillestrøm SK (NOR)
Taijo TENISTE	31.01.1988	77	0	2019:	SK Brann Bergen (NOR)
Midfielders					
Mihkel AINSALU	08.03.1996	7	0	2019:	FC Flora Tallinn
Ilja ANTONOV	05.12.1992	50	2	2019:	FC Ararat-Armenia Yerevan (ARM)
Aleksandr DMITRIJEV	18.02.1982	107	0	2019:	FC Okzhetpes Kokshetau (KAZ)
Vladislav KREIDA	25.09.1999	3	0	2019:	FC Flora Tallinn
Mattias KÄIT	29.06.1998	26	5	2019:	NK Domžale (SVN)
Martin MILLER	25.09.1997	9	1	2019:	FC Flora Tallinn
Sander PURI	07.05.1988	78	4	2019:	Nõmme Kalju FC Tallinn
Konstantin VASSILJEV	16.08.1984	119	25	2019:	FC Flora Tallinn
Forwards					
Henri ANIER	17.12.1990	61	13	2019:	Suwon FC (KOR)
Frank LIIVAK	07.07.1996	17	2	2019:	FC Flora Tallinn
Henrik OJAMAA	20.05.1991	43	1	2019:	MKS Miedź Legnica (POL)
Rauno SAPPINEN	23.01.1996	25	2	2019:	NK Domžale (SVN)
Vlasiy SINYAVSKIY	27.11.1996	2	0	2019:	FC Flora Tallinn
Erik SORGA	08.07.1999	6	1	2019:	FC Flora Tallinn
Sergei ZENJOV	20.04.1989	84	13	2019:	FC Shakhter Karagandy (KAZ)
National team coach					
Karel VOOLAID [since 03.07.2019]	04.07.1977	6 M; 0 W; 1 D; 5 L; 1-48			

FAROE ISLANDS

The Country:
Faroe Islands (Føroyar)
Capital: Tórshavn
Surface: 1,399 km²
Inhabitants: 52,110 [2020]
Time: UTC

The FA:
Fótbóltssamband Føroya
Gundadalur P.O. Box 3028, 110 Tórshavn
Tel: +298 351 979
Foundation date: 1979
Member of FIFA since: 1988
Member of UEFA since: 1990
Website: www.football.fo

NATIONAL TEAM RECORDS

RECORDS		
First international match:	24.08.1988, Akranes:	Iceland – Faroe Islands 1-0
Most international caps:	Fróði Benjaminsen	- 95 caps (1999-2017)
Most international goals:	Rógvi Jacobsen	- 10 goals / 53 caps (1999-2009)

UEFA EUROPEAN CHAMPIONSHIP	
1960	-
1964	-
1968	-
1972	-
1976	-
1980	-
1984	-
1988	-
1992	Qualifiers
1996	Qualifiers
2000	Qualifiers
2004	Qualifiers
2008	Qualifiers
2012	Qualifiers
2016	Qualifiers
2020	Qualifiers

FIFA WORLD CUP	
1930	-
1934	-
1938	-
1950	-
1954	-
1958	-
1962	-
1966	-
1970	-
1974	-
1978	-
1982	*Did not enter*
1986	*Did not enter*
1990	*Did not enter*
1994	Qualifiers
1998	Qualifiers
2002	Qualifiers
2006	Qualifiers
2010	Qualifiers
2014	Qualifiers
2018	Qualifiers

OLYMPIC TOURNAMENTS	
1908	-
1912	-
1920	-
1924	-
1928	-
1936	-
1948	-
1952	-
1956	-
1960	-
1964	-
1968	-
1972	-
1976	-
1980	-
1984	*Did not enter*
1988	*Did not enter*
1992	*Did not enter*
1996	*Did not enter*
2000	*Did not enter*
2004	*Did not enter*
2008	*Did not enter*
2012	Qualifiers
2016	Qualifiers

UEFA NATIONS LEAGUE

2018/2019 – League D

FIFA CONFEDERATIONS CUP 1992-2017

None

FAROE ISLANDS CLUB HONOURS IN EUROPEAN CLUB COMPETITIONS:

European Champion Clubs' Cup (1956-1992) / UEFA Champions League (1993-2020)
None

Fairs Cup (1858-1971) / UEFA Cup (1972-2009) / UEFA Europa League (2010-2020)
None

UEFA Super Cup (1972-2019)
None

*European Cup Winners' Cup 1961-1999**
None

defunct competition

NATIONAL COMPETITIONS
TABLE OF HONOURS

	CHAMPIONS	CUP WINNERS	BEST GOALSCORERS	
1942	KÍ Klaksvík	-	-	
1943	TB Tvøroyri	-	-	
1944	No competition	-	-	
1945	KÍ Klaksvík	-	-	
1946	B36 Tórshavn	-	-	
1947	SÍ Sørvágur	-	-	
1948	B36 Tórshavn	-	-	
1949	TB Tvøroyri	-	-	
1950	B36 Tórshavn	-	-	
1951	TB Tvøroyri	-	-	
1952	KÍ Klaksvík	-	-	
1953	KÍ Klaksvík	-	-	
1954	KÍ Klaksvík	-	-	
1955	HB Tórshavn	HB Tórshavn	-	
1956	KÍ Klaksvík	TB Tvøroyri	-	
1957	KÍ Klaksvík	HB Tórshavn	-	
1958	KÍ Klaksvík	TB Tvøroyri	-	
1959	B36 Tórshavn	HB Tórshavn	-	
1960	HB Tórshavn	TB Tvøroyri	-	
1961	KÍ Klaksvík	TB Tvøroyri	-	
1962	B36 Tórshavn	HB Tórshavn	-	
1963	HB Tórshavn	HB Tórshavn	-	
1964	HB Tórshavn	HB Tórshavn	-	
1965	HB Tórshavn	B36 Tórshavn	-	
1966	KÍ Klaksvík	KÍ Klaksvík	-	
1967	KÍ Klaksvík	KÍ Klaksvík	-	
1968	KÍ Klaksvík	HB Tórshavn	-	
1969	KÍ Klaksvík	HB Tórshavn	-	
1970	KÍ Klaksvík	Cup Final not played	-	
1971	HB Tórshavn	HB Tórshavn	-	
1972	KÍ Klaksvík	HB Tórshavn	-	
1973	HB Tórshavn	HB Tórshavn	-	
1974	HB Tórshavn	VB Vágur	-	
1975	HB Tórshavn	HB Tórshavn	-	
1976	TB Tvøroyri	HB Tórshavn	-	
1977	TB Tvøroyri	TB Tvøroyri	-	
1978	HB Tórshavn	HB Tórshavn	-	
1979	ÍF Fuglafjørður	HB Tórshavn	-	
1980	TB Tvøroyri	HB Tórshavn	Jóan Petur Olgarsson (TB Tvøroyri)	18
1981	HB Tórshavn	HB Tórshavn	Jóannes Jakobsen (HB Tórshavn)	14
1982	HB Tórshavn	HB Tórshavn	Jóannes Jakobsen (HB Tórshavn)	9
1983	Gøtu Ítróttarfelag	Gøtu Ítróttarfelag	Petur Hans Hansen (B68 Toftir) Hans Leo í Bartalsstovu (Gøtu Ítróttarfelag)	10
1984	B68 Toftir	HB Tórshavn	Aksel Højgaard (B68 Toftir) Erling Jacobsen (HB Tórshavn)	10
1985	B68 Toftir	Gøtu Ítróttarfelag	Símun Petur Justinussen (Gøtu Ítróttarfelag)	10
1986	Gøtu Ítróttarfelag	NSÍ Runavík	Jesper Wiemer (DEN, B68 Toftir) Símun Petur Justinussen (Gøtu Ítróttarfelag)	13
1987	TB Tvøroyri	HB Tórshavn	Símun Petur Justinussen (Gøtu Ítróttarfelag)	10
1988	HB Tórshavn	HB Tórshavn	Jógvan Petersen (B68 Toftir)	9
1989	B71 Sandoy	HB Tórshavn	Egill Steinþórsson (ISL, VB Vágur)	16
1990	HB Tórshavn	KÍ Klaksvík	Gunnar Mohr (HB Tórshavn) Jens Erik Rasmussen (MB Miðvágur)	10
1991	Klaksvíkar Ítróttarfelag	B36 Tórshavn	Símun Petur Justinussen (Gøtu Ítróttarfelag)	15
1992	B68 Toftir	HB Tórshavn	Símun Petur Justinussen (Gøtu Ítróttarfelag)	14
1993	Gøtu Ítróttarfelag	B71 Sandur	Uni Arge (HB Tórshavn)	11
1994	Gøtu Ítróttarfelag	KÍ Klaksvík	John Petersen (Gøtu Ítróttarfelag)	21
1995	Gøtu Ítróttarfelag	HB Tórshavn	Súni Fríði Johannesen (B68 Toftir)	24
1996	Gøtu Ítróttarfelag	Gøtu Ítróttarfelag	Kurt Mørkøre (KÍ Klaksvík)	20
1997	B36 Tórshavn	Gøtu Ítróttarfelag	Uni Arge (HB Tórshavn)	24
1998	HB Tórshavn	HB Tórshavn	Jákup á Borg (B36 Tórshavn)	20
1999	Klaksvíkar Ítróttarfelag	KÍ Klaksvík	Jákup á Borg (B36 Tórshavn)	17
2000	VB Vágur	Gøtu Ítróttarfelag	Súni Fríði Johannesen (B36 Tórshavn)	16
2001	B36 Tórshavn	B36 Tórshavn	Helgi L. Petersen (Gøtu Ítróttarfelag)	19
2002	HB Tórshavn	NSÍ Runavík	Andrew av Fløtum (HB Tórshavn)	18
2003	HB Tórshavn	B36 Tórshavn	Hjalgrím Elttør (KÍ Klaksvík)	13
2004	HB Tórshavn	HB Tórshavn	Sonni L. Petersen (EB/Streymur)	13
2005	B36 Tórshavn	Gøtu Ítróttarfelag	Christian Høgni Jacobsen (NSÍ Runavík)	18
2006	HB Tórshavn	B36 Tórshavn	Christian Høgni Jacobsen (NSÍ Runavík)	18
2007	NSÍ Runavík	EB/Streymur	Amed Davy Sylla (FRA, B36 Tórshavn)	18
2008	EB/Streymur	EB/Streymur	Arnbjørn Hansen (EB/Streymur)	20

2009	HB Tórshavn	Víkingur Gøta	Finnur Justinussen (Víkingur Gøta)	19
2010	HB Tórshavn	EB/Streymur	Arnbjørn Hansen (EB/Streymur) Christian Høgni Jacobsen (NSÍ Runavík)	22
2011	B36 Tórshavn	EB/Streymur	Finnur Justinussen (Víkingur Gøta)	21
2012	EB/Streymur	Víkingur Gøta	Clayton Soares do Nascimento (BRA, ÍF Fuglafjørður) Páll Klettskarð (KÍ Klaksvík)	22
2013	HB Tórshavn	Víkingur Gøta	Klæmint Andrasson Olsen (NSÍ Runavík)	21
2014	B36 Tórshavn	Víkingur Gøta	Klæmint Andrasson Olsen (NSÍ Runavík)	22
2015	B36 Tórshavn	Víkingur Gøta	Klæmint Andrasson Olsen (NSÍ Runavík)	21
2016	Víkingur Gøta	KÍ Klaksvík	Klæmint Andrasson Olsen (NSÍ Runavík)	23
2017	Víkingur Gøta	NSÍ Runavík	Adeshina Abayomi Lawal (NGA, (Víkingur Gøta)	17
2018	HB Tórshavn	B36 Tórshavn	Adrian Justinussen (HB Tórshavn)	20
2019	KÍ Klaksvík	HB Tórshavn	Klæmint Andrasson Olsen (NSÍ Runavík)	26

NATIONAL CHAMPIONSHIP
Faroe Islands Premier League - Effodeildin 2019
(10.03.2019 – 26.10.2019)

Results

Round 1 [10.03.2019]
B36 Tórshavn - Skála ÍF 1-0(1-0)
KÍ Klaksvík - HB Tórshavn 0-0
NSÍ Runavík - EB/Streymur 1-0(0-0)
TB Tvøroyri - AB Argir 2-1(1-0)
Víkingur Gøta - ÍF Fuglafjørður 3-0(0-0)

Round 2 [17.03.2019]
HB Tórshavn - NSÍ Runavík 1-1(0-1)
Skála ÍF - TB Tvøroyri 2-0(2-0)
EB/Streymur - B36 Tórshavn 1-2(0-1)
Víkingur Gøta - KÍ Klaksvík 2-2(0-0)
AB Argir - ÍF Fuglafjørður 2-1(0-0)

Round 3 [30-31.03.2019]
AB Argir - B36 Tórshavn 1-2(1-0)
Skála ÍF - NSÍ Runavík 2-0(2-0)
HB Tórshavn - Víkingur Gøta 3-1(2-1)
KÍ Klaksvík - EB/Streymur 2-1(1-1)
ÍF Fuglafjørður - TB Tvøroyri 2-2(0-1)

Round 4 [06-07.04.2019]
NSÍ Runavík - Víkingur Gøta 4-2(4-0)
B36 Tórshavn - HB Tórshavn 2-1(1-0)
TB Tvøroyri - EB/Streymur 1-0(1-0)
ÍF Fuglafjørður - KÍ Klaksvík 2-3(0-3)
AB Argir - Skála ÍF 0-1(0-0)

Round 5 [14.04.2019]
ÍF Fuglafjørður - Skála ÍF 0-3(0-2)
KÍ Klaksvík - NSÍ Runavík 2-0(2-0)
TB Tvøroyri - HB Tórshavn 1-1(0-0)
EB/Streymur - AB Argir 5-1(2-1)
Víkingur G. - B36 Tórshavn 1-0(0-0) [26.04.]

Round 6 [18.04.2019]
B36 Tórshavn - KÍ Klaksvík 0-3(0-1)
Skála ÍF - EB/Streymur 1-2(1-0)
TB Tvøroyri - Víkingur Gøta 1-2(0-0)
HB Tórshavn - AB Argir 4-3(2-1)
NSÍ Runavík - ÍF Fuglafjørður 3-1(0-1)

Round 7 [28-30.04.2019]
HB Tórshavn - Skála ÍF 0-2(0-1)
KÍ Klaksvík - TB Tvøroyri 7-0(4-0)
EB/Streymur - ÍF Fuglafjørður 0-2(0-1)
AB Argir - Víkingur Gøta 1-3(1-2)
NSÍ Runavík - B36 Tórshavn 2-1(0-1)

Round 8 [05.05.2019]
AB Argir - KÍ Klaksvík 0-4(0-1)
B36 Tórshavn - ÍF Fuglafjørður 3-0(1-0)
Skála ÍF - Víkingur Gøta 2-3(0-1)
EB/Streymur - HB Tórshavn 0-3(0-0)
TB Tvøroyri - NSÍ Runavík 0-3(0-2)

Round 9 [12-13.05.2019]
B36 Tórshavn - TB Tvøroyri 1-0(1-0)
ÍF Fuglafjørður - HB Tórshavn 0-2(0-0)
NSÍ Runavík - AB Argir 5-1(2-0)
Skála ÍF - KÍ Klaksvík 0-1(0-1)
Víkingur Gøta - EB/Streymur 1-1(0-1)

Round 10 [17-19.05.2019]
Skála ÍF - B36 Tórshavn 1-2(1-1)
ÍF Fuglafjørður - Víkingur Gøta 0-4(0-3)
HB Tórshavn - KÍ Klaksvík 4-1(3-1)
EB/Streymur - NSÍ Runavík 1-8(1-5)
AB Argir - TB Tvøroyri 2-2(1-2)

Round 11 [26-27.05.2019]
B36 Tórshavn - AB Argir 4-1(2-0)
KÍ Klaksvík - EB/Streymur 4-0(2-0)
TB Tvøroyri - ÍF Fuglafjørður 1-0(0-0)
Víkingur Gøta - HB Tórshavn 1-0(1-0)
NSÍ Runavík - Skála ÍF 3-0(3-0)

Round 12 [01-02.06.2019]
NSÍ Runavík - TB Tvøroyri 3-1(2-0)
HB Tórshavn - EB/Streymur 6-4(3-3)
ÍF Fuglafjørður - B36 Tórshavn 1-3(0-2)
Víkingur Gøta - Skála ÍF 2-1(0-1)
KÍ Klaksvík - AB Argir 2-1(0-0)

Round 13 [14-16.06.2019]
Skála ÍF - KÍ Klaksvík 0-2(0-2)
EB/Streymur - Víkingur Gøta 1-4(0-1)
NSÍ Runavík - AB Argir 2-0(0-0)
ÍF Fuglafjørður - HB Tórshavn 1-5(0-3)
TB Tvøroyri - B36 Tórshavn 0-1(0-0)

Round 14 [22-23.06.2019]
B36 Tórshavn - NSÍ Runavík 1-1(1-0)
TB Tvøroyri - KÍ Klaksvík 1-0(0-0)
AB Argir - Víkingur Gøta 0-3(0-1)
Skála ÍF - HB Tórshavn 0-3(0-3)
EB/Streymur - ÍF Fuglafjørður 0-0

Round 15 [28-29.06.2019]
HB Tórshavn - AB Argir 5-0(1-0)
EB/Streymur - Skála ÍF 0-1(0-0)
Víkingur Gøta - TB Tvøroyri 3-1(1-0)
Fuglafjørður - NSÍ Runavík 2-4(2-1) [14.08.]
KÍ Klaksvík - B36 Tórshavn 0-2(0-0) [21.08.]

Round 16 [27-28.07.2019]
HB Tórshavn - TB Tvøroyri 3-0(0-0)
Skála ÍF - ÍF Fuglafjørður 2-1(1-1)
AB Argir - EB/Streymur 1-1(1-0)
B36 Tórshavn - Víkingur Gøta 2-1(1-1)
NSÍ Runavík - KÍ Klaksvík 0-1(0-0) [18.09.]

Round 17 [04-05.08.2019]
Skála ÍF - AB Argir 0-1(0-0)
EB/Streymur - TB Tvøroyri 0-2(0-1)
Víkingur Gøta - NSÍ Runavík 2-3(2-0)
HB Tórshavn - B36 Tórshavn 0-0
ÍF Fuglafjørður - KÍ Klaksvík 0-3(0-2)

Round 18 [09-11.08.2019]
KÍ Klaksvík - Víkingur Gøta 2-0(0-0)
AB Argir - ÍF Fuglafjørður 3-1(0-0)
B36 Tórshavn - EB/Streymur 3-0(1-0)
TB Tvøroyri - Skála ÍF 0-2(0-1)
NSÍ Runavík - HB Tórshavn 1-1(0-1)

Round 19 [17-18.08.2019]
B36 Tórshavn - TB Tvøroyri 3-1(2-1)
KÍ Klaksvík - Skála ÍF 2-2(2-2)
AB Argir - NSÍ Runavík 1-5(1-1)
HB Tórshavn - ÍF Fuglafjørður 6-0(2-0)
Víkingur Gøta - EB/Streymur 2-1(0-0)

Round 20 [25.08.2019]
HB Tórshavn - Víkingur Gøta 3-1(0-1)
ÍF Fuglafjørður - TB Tvøroyri 1-1(1-1)
Skála ÍF - NSÍ Runavík 1-2(0-1)
EB/Streymur - KÍ Klaksvík 0-1(0-1)
AB Argir - B36 Tórshavn 1-2(1-1)

Round 21 [01.09.2019]
B36 Tórshavn - Skála ÍF 1-0(0-0)
KÍ Klaksvík - HB Tórshavn 3-1(1-0)
TB Tvøroyri - AB Argir 0-1(0-0)
Víkingur Gøta - ÍF Fuglafjørður 3-2(1-2)
NSÍ Runavík - EB/Streymur 3-0(2-0)

Round 22 [15.09.2019]
HB Tórshavn - Skála ÍF 3-0(2-0)
Víkingur Gøta - AB Argir 1-1(1-1)
KÍ Klaksvík - TB Tvøroyri 3-0(2-0)
ÍF Fuglafjørður - EB/Streymur 2-3(1-2)
NSÍ Runavík - B36 Tórshavn 0-3(0-2)

Round 23 [22-25.09.2019]
TB Tvøroyri - NSÍ Runavík 1-4(0-1)
B36 Tórshavn - ÍF Fuglafjørður 7-2(4-1)
AB Argir - KÍ Klaksvík 0-2(0-2)
Skála ÍF - Víkingur Gøta 0-1(0-0)
EB/Streymur - HB Tórshavn 1-0(0-0)

Round 24 [29.09.2019]
TB Tvøroyri - EB/Streymur 1-2(1-1)
AB Argir - Skála ÍF 0-2(0-2)
B36 Tórshavn - HB Tórshavn 2-2(0-1)
KÍ Klaksvík - ÍF Fuglafjørður 3-0(1-0)
NSÍ Runavík - Víkingur Gøta 0-2(0-1)

Round 25 [05-08.10.2019]		Round 26 [20.10.2019]		Round 27 [26.10.2019]	
Skála ÍF - TB Tvøroyri	5-1(3-0)	HB Tórshavn - TB Tvøroyri	3-0(2-0)	AB Argir - HB Tórshavn	1-2(1-0)
HB Tórshavn - NSÍ Runavík	0-2(0-1)	ÍF Fuglafjørður - Skála ÍF	1-3(0-0)	Skála ÍF - EB/Streymur	5-0(2-0)
ÍF Fuglafjørður - AB Argir	4-6(0-4)	KÍ Klaksvík - NSÍ Runavík	3-2(2-1)	NSÍ Runavík - ÍF Fuglafjørður	3-1(2-0)
EB/Streymur - B36 Tórshavn	0-4(0-2)	EB/Streymur - AB Argir	1-2(1-1)	TB Tvøroyri - Víkingur Gøta	0-2(0-2)
Víkingur Gøta - KÍ Klaksvík	1-3(0-0)	Víkingur Gøta - B36 Tórshavn	0-1(0-1)	B36 Tórshavn - KÍ Klaksvík	0-3(0-2)

Final Standings

									Total					Home					Away			
1.	**KÍ Klaksvík**	27	21	3	3	62	-	19	66	10	2	1	33	-	9	11	1	2	29	-	10
2.	B36 Tórshavn	27	20	3	4	53	-	23	63	10	2	2	30	-	15	10	1	2	23	-	8
3.	NSÍ Runavík	27	18	3	6	65	-	31	57	10	1	3	30	-	14	8	2	3	35	-	17
4.	HB Tórshavn	27	15	6	6	62	-	28	51	10	2	2	41	-	15	5	4	4	21	-	13
5.	Víkingur Gøta	27	16	3	8	51	-	35	51	7	3	3	22	-	16	9	0	5	29	-	19
6.	Skála ÍF	27	12	1	14	38	-	32	37	5	0	9	21	-	19	7	1	5	17	-	13
7.	AB Argir	27	6	3	18	32	-	66	21	2	2	10	13	-	31	4	1	8	19	-	35
8.	TB Tvøroyri*	27	5	4	18	20	-	57	19	4	1	8	9	-	19	1	3	10	11	-	38
9.	EB/Streymur	27	5	3	19	25	-	63	18	2	1	10	10	-	30	3	2	9	15	-	33
10.	ÍF Fuglafjarðar	27	1	3	23	27	-	81	6	0	2	11	16	-	42	1	1	12	11	-	39

Please note: there was no relegation this season as three reserve teams finished in the top three in 1. Deild (Seconfd Level).
*until end of last season's end, TB/FC Suðuroy/Royn played at first level. After two years the three clubs ended the co-operation and TB Tvøroyri continued to play with their licence which was for the Faroe Islands Premier League.

Top goalscorers:

26	**Klæmint Andrasson Olsen**	*NSÍ Runavík*
18	Jóannes Bjartalíð	*KÍ Klaksvík*
16	Adrian Justinussen	*HB Tórshavn*
13	Patrik Johannesen	*KÍ Klaksvík*
12	Ari Olsen	*HB Tórshavn*

NATIONAL CUP
Løgmanssteypid 2019

First Round [30.03.2019]

Royn Hvalba - FC Hoyvík	2-1

1/8-Finals [10.04.2019]

Royn Hvalba - B68 Toftir	0-4	Skála ÍF - AB Argir	1-0
HB Tórshavn - NSÍ Runavík	2-1	B71 Sandoy - ÍF Fuglafjarðar	1-0
Undrið FF - KÍ Klaksvík	1-13	EB/Streymur - Víkingur Gøta	2-6
TB Tvøroyri - FC Suðuroy	2-1	B36 Tórshavn - 07 Vestur Sørvágur	4-0

Quarter-Finals [22.04.2019]

B36 Tórshavn - KÍ Klaksvík	3-4(2-0,2-2)	Skála ÍF - TB Tvøroyri	5-1(3-0)
Víkingur Gøta - B68 Toftir	10-0(4-0)	HB Tórshavn - B71 Sandoy	4-0(0-0)

Semi-Finals [08-23.05.2019]

First Leg		Second Leg	
HB Tórshavn - KÍ Klaksvík	1-1(0-1)	KÍ Klaksvík - HB Tórshavn	0-1(0-0)
Skála ÍF - Víkingur Gøta	1-1(1-0)	Víkingur Gøta - Skála ÍF	0-0

Final

21.09.2019; Tórsvøllur, Tórshavn; Referee: Dagfinn Forná; Attendance: 2,962
HB Tórshavn - Víkingur Gøta   **3-1(1-0)**

HB Tórshavn: Teitur Gestsson, Brynjar Hlöðversson, Bartal Wardum (83.Jógvan Davidsen), Lasse Andersen, Daniel Johansen, Magnus Egilsson (68.Sebastian Pingel), René Shaki Joensen, Dan í Soylu, Símun Samuelsen, Adrian Justinussen, Ari Olsen (90.Pætur Petersen). Trainer: Heimir Guðjónsson (Iceland).

Víkingur: Elias Rasmussen, Atli Gregersen, Hanus Jacobsen, Vukašin Tomić, Sølvi Vatnhamar, Bogi Petersen (59.Filip Đorđević), Gunnar Vatnhamar, Heðin Hansen, Arnbjørn Svensson (59.Elias Jóhannesson Lervig), Andreas Olsen, Adeshina Lawal. Trainer: Sámal Erik Hentze.

Goals: 1-0 Adrian Justinussen (40), 2-0 Símun Samuelsen (52), 2-1 Andreas Olsen (62), 3-1 Sebastian Pingel (71).

Argja Bóltfelag Argir

Founded: 15.08.1973
Stadium: Skansi Arena, Argir (2,000)
Trainer: Sorin Vasile Anghel Olaru (ROU) 16.07.1979

Goalkeepers:	DOB	M	(s)	G
Mattias Lamhauge	02.08.1999	8		
Tobias Larsen (DEN)	10.03.1994	12		
Sverri Petersen	25.10.2001	3		
Heðin Stenberg	14.01.1989	4		
Defenders:	**DOB**	**M**	**(s)**	**G**
Jákup Pauli Breckmann	16.04.1998	1	(2)	
Lukas Grenaa Giessing	09.05.2000	12		5
Beinir Henriksen	16.02.1997	14	(2)	
Leivur Joensen	08.01.1988	15	(3)	
Tóki Rasmussen	31.03.1999		(1)	
Sørin Samuelsen	29.04.1992	25		2
Jónas Stenberg	07.04.1987	12	(10)	
Hørður Tórsson	29.08.1998	2	(2)	
Midfielders:	**DOB**	**M**	**(s)**	**G**
Tóki á Lofti	06.12.1993	15	(8)	4

Eli Christiansson	12.04.1998	16	(2)	3
Gert Schrøter Drangastein	25.08.1994	4		
Jobin Drangastein	01.11.1990	11	(1)	1
Mikkjal Hentze	08.12.1986	18	(5)	
Filip í Líða	06.11.2000	14	(9)	3
Ari Johannesen	15.09.1992		(1)	
Heri Mohr	13.05.1997	27		3
Bárður Olsen	05.12.1985	20		3
Bartal Petersen	22.11.2000	4	(8)	
Rógvi Poulsen	31.10.1989	13	(3)	1
Bjarni Skála	14.11.1997	16	(5)	
Ragnar Skála	05.09.2000	4	(5)	
Forwards:	**DOB**	**M**	**(s)**	**G**
Hans Jákup Annfinsson	19.03.1999	3	(9)	1
Bjarki Nielsen	02.11.1998	24		6

Bóltfelagið 1936 Tórshavn

Founded: 28.03.1936
Stadium: Gundadalur, Tórshavn (5,000)
Trainer: Jákup á Borg 26.10.1979

Goalkeepers:	DOB	M	(s)	G
Trygvi Askham	28.03.1988	1		
Símun Rógvi Hansen	10.04.1987	5		
Hans Jørgensen	13.08.1990	21		
Defenders:	**DOB**	**M**	**(s)**	**G**
Andrias Eriksen	22.02.1994	27		
Erling Jacobsen	14.02.1990	15	(1)	1
Mattias Weihe Joensen	15.02.2003		(2)	
Alex Mellemgaard	27.11.1991	22		6
Sveinur Lava Olsen	14.01.2001		(1)	
Bjarni Petersen	12.08.1998	13	(7)	
Andreas Thomsen	04.10.2001		(2)	
Midfielders:	**DOB**	**M**	**(s)**	**G**
Hannes Agnarsson	26.02.1999	1	(10)	

Árni Frederiksberg	13.06.1992	27		8
Benjamin Heinesen	26.03.1996	21	(4)	7
Brian Jacobsen	04.11.1991	17	(3)	7
Magnus Holm Jacobsen	23.05.2000	17	(1)	
Jónas Næs	27.12.1986	26		2
Eli Falkvard Nielsen	23.09.1992	24	(1)	
Gilli Samuelsen	12.02.1999	5	(8)	
Hugin Samuelsen	12.02.1999	7	(7)	4
Ragnar Samuelsen	23.08.1999	6	(4)	1
Forwards:	**DOB**	**M**	**(s)**	**G**
Łukasz Cieślewicz (POL)	15.11.1987	18	(7)	5
Andrass Johansen	16.11.2001	1	(9)	1
Michał Przybylski (POL)	29.12.1997	16	(7)	7
Stefan Radosavljević	08.09.2000	7	(5)	3

Eiðis Bóltfelag / Streymur

Founded: 1993
Stadium: Við Margáir, Streymnes (2,000)
Trainer: Jákup Joensen 07.05.1976

Goalkeepers:	DOB	M	(s)	G
Jákup Højgaard	06.02.1994	8	(2)	
Rói Zachariasen	12.10.1998	19		
Defenders:	**DOB**	**M**	**(s)**	**G**
Gestur Dam	17.09.1994	11	(1)	1
Ragnar Danielsen	24.02.1992	22	(3)	2
Mikkjal Hellisá	18.02.2002	5	(4)	
Sveinur Magnussen	26.03.1999	21	(6)	1
Rógvi Nielsen	07.12.1992	25		3
Poul Olsen	30.09.1991	24		2
Rói Olsen	03.03.1997	9	(7)	
Sveinur Lava Olsen	14.01.2001		(1)	
Teitur Olsen	04.02.1992	7	(4)	
Petur Zachariassen	19.04.1995	22		
Midfielders:	**DOB**	**M**	**(s)**	**G**
Gutti Dahl-Olsen	19.01.2002	1	(5)	

Magnus Jarnskor	14.12.1995	17	(4)	1
Tóki Johannesen	17.03.1997	9	(5)	
Fríði Johansen	17.05.2000		(1)	
Jónstein Magnussen	21.05.1990	10	(3)	
Høgni Midjord	04.02.1991	3	(1)	
Árni Olsen	13.09.1993	24		
Ragnar Samuelsen	23.08.1999	13		2
Forwards:	**DOB**	**M**	**(s)**	**G**
Arnar Dam	18.10.1991	3	(3)	
Arnbjørn Hansen	27.02.1986	6	(10)	7
Høgni Hummeland	14.07.1996		(2)	
Jens Jensen	24.01.1991		(3)	
Niklas Kruse	11.05.1999	12	(6)	2
Steffan Abrahamsson Løkin	13.11.2000	21	(2)	4
Hans Pauli Samuelsen	18.10.1984	5	(2)	

Havnar Bóltfelag Tórshavn

Founded: 04.10.1904
Stadium: Gundadalur, Tórshavn (5,000)
Trainer: Heimir Guðjónsson (ISL) 03.04.1969

Goalkeepers:	DOB	M	(s)	G
Teitur Gestsson	19.08.1992	27		
Defenders:	**DOB**	**M**	**(s)**	**G**
Lasse Andersen (DEN)	24.05.1995	24		
Jógvan Davidsen	09.10.1991	19	(4)	
Magnus Egilsson	19.03.1994	24	(1)	1
Brynjar Hlöðversson (ISL)	03.04.1989	17	(1)	1
Daniel Johansen	09.07.1998	13	(11)	2
Bartal Wardum	03.05.1997	18	(4)	1
Midfielders:	**DOB**	**M**	**(s)**	**G**
Hørður Heðinsson Askham	22.09.1994	21		3
Andreas Breimyr (NOR)	02.04.1996	4	(4)	

Dan í Soylu	09.07.1996	21	(3)	6
Tróndur Jensen	06.02.1993	14	(2)	1
René Shaki Joensen	08.02.1993	6	(2)	
Jógvan Andrias Nolsøe	20.05.1992	1	(5)	
Pætur Petersen	29.03.1998	15	(11)	6
Símun Sólheim	25.02.2001	1	(1)	
Forwards:	**DOB**	**M**	**(s)**	**G**
Samuel Johansen Chukwudi	25.06.2003	2	(1)	
Adrian Justinussen	21.07.1998	24	(2)	16
Ari Olsen	16.12.1997	22	(3)	12
Sebastian Pingel (DEN)	11.05.1993	8	(12)	5
Simun Samuelsen	21.05.1985	16	(6)	5

Ítróttarfelag Fuglafjarðar

Founded: 25.03.1946
Stadium: Í Fløtugerði, Fuglafjørður (3,000)
Trainer: Jógvan Hendrik Samuelsen 09.06.1973
[18.04.2019] Ólavur Larsen 13.10.1983
[28.04.2019] Kári Reynheim 15.02.1964

Goalkeepers:	DOB	M	(s)	G
Petur Magnussen	26.03.1990	24	(1)	
Jákup Olsen	03.01.1999	2		
Tóri Traðará	16.07.1996	1		
Defenders:	**DOB**	**M**	**(s)**	**G**
Alex José Dos Santos (BRA)	28.03.1981	2	(6)	
Gunnar Christiansen	08.08.1992	4	(1)	
Jan Ellingsgaard	26.06.1990	23		6
Poul Mikkelsen	19.04.1995	6		
Gundur Petersen	15.02.2001	9	(11)	3
Midfielders:	**DOB**	**M**	**(s)**	**G**
Dánjal á Lakjuni	22.09.1990	7	(3)	1
Ari Ellingsgaard	03.02.1993	24		2
Sverri Ellingsgaard	16.04.1985	7	(2)	
Bjarti J. Højbro	13.06.2003		(1)	
Sámal Joensen	15.09.1997	11	(5)	
Dávid Langgaard	30.03.1995	24		4

	DOB	M	(s)	G
Hans Jákup Lervig	26.02.1997	14		4
Karl Løkin	19.04.1991	24		1
Pól Jákup Lundsbjerg	22.12.2000	9	(8)	
Høgni Madsen	02.04.1985	21	(2)	1
Jóhan Petersen	13.08.1998	8	(6)	1
Frank Poulsen	03.11.1988	6	(3)	
Rói Róin	31.10.2001	2	(4)	
Milan Svojić (SRB)	09.10.1985	9		
Høgni Zachariassen	26.08.1982	5	(3)	
Forwards:	**DOB**	**M**	**(s)**	**G**
Holgar Durhuus	29.10.1992	17	(3)	
Sunnvar Hansen	28.03.1997		(2)	
Henry Heinesen	01.06.1988	2		
Dánjal Pauli Højgaard	27.12.1983	10	(2)	2
Arnold Kristiansen	24.03.1995		(1)	
Andy Olsen	03.12.1984	26		2
Tóri Olsen	24.10.2001		(5)	

Klaksvíkar Ítróttarfelag

Founded: 24.08.1904
Stadium: Við Djúpumýrar, Klaksvík (4,000)
Trainer: Mikkjal Thomassen 12.01.1976

Goalkeepers:	DOB	M	(s)	G
Kristian Joensen	21.12.1992	24		
Meinhardt Joensen	27.11.1979	3		
Defenders:	**DOB**	**M**	**(s)**	**G**
Mikkjal á Bergi	03.02.1997		(3)	
Jesper Brinck (DEN)	22.03.1989	25		
Ólavur Niclasen	07.07.1998	14	(3)	
Deni Pavlović (SRB)	01.09.1993	15		2
Børge Petersen	24.04.2002		(6)	
Ísak Simonsen	12.10.1993	20	(2)	
Midfielders:	**DOB**	**M**	**(s)**	**G**
Jákup Andreasen	31.05.1998	26		2
Aksel Danielsen	03.04.1999		(2)	
Jóannes Danielsen	10.09.1997	27		

	DOB	M	(s)	G
Boris Došljak (MNE)	04.06.1989	19	(6)	5
Semir Hadžibulić (SRB)	16.08.1986	7	(3)	1
Jonn Johannesen	30.12.2001	10	(12)	2
Takuya Matsunaga (JPN)	10.06.1990	3	(3)	
Steinbjørn Olsen	11.09.1996	7	(13)	1
Óli Poulsen	30.05.2001	1		
Simen Sandmæl (NOR)	04.08.1990	21		3
Magnus Stamnestrø (NOR)	18.04.1992	8	(1)	1
Forwards:	**DOB**	**M**	**(s)**	**G**
Jóannes Bjartalíð	10.07.1996	27		18
Torbjørn Grytten (NOR)	06.04.1995	5	(8)	3
Patrik Johannesen	07.09.1995	25		13
Páll Klettskarð	17.05.1990	7	(7)	6
Darius Lewis (USA)	20.11.1999	3	(9)	3

Nes Sóknar Ítróttarfelag Runavík

Founded: 1957
Stadium: Við Løkin, Runavík (2,000)
Trainer: Gudjón Thórdarson (ISL) 14.09.1955

Goalkeepers:	DOB	M	(s)	G
Eli Joensen	01.10.1998	1		
Tórður Thomsen	11.06.1986	26		
Defenders:	**DOB**	**M**	**(s)**	**G**
Jóhan Davidsen	31.01.1988	26		
Meinhard Debes Geyti	03.05.2001		(1)	
Pætur Hentze	06.11.1999	14		
Oddur Højgaard	12.09.1989	25		1
Pól Justinussen	13.01.1989	25		7
Per Langgaard	30.05.1991	3	(3)	
Sjúrður Nielsen	18.04.2000		(1)	
Einar Tróndargjógv	02.04.1988	11		
Midfielders:	**DOB**	**M**	**(s)**	**G**
Andri Benjaminsen	12.01.1999	1	(4)	2

	DOB	M	(s)	G
Jann Benjaminsen	02.03.1997	15	(10)	3
Bárður Hansen	13.03.1992	19	(2)	2
Betuel Hansen	14.03.1997	5	(17)	
Petur Knudsen	21.04.1998	19	(1)	8
Jann Mortensen	18.07.1989	24	(2)	5
Mórits Heini Mortensen	25.03.1999		(1)	
Peder Nersveen (NOR)	03.12.1992	27		1
Jannik Mathias Olsen	28.12.1998	1	(2)	
Magnus Olsen	26.10.1986	3	(4)	1
Forwards:	**DOB**	**M**	**(s)**	**G**
Øssur Dalbúð	28.03.1989	4	(8)	3
Búi Egilsson	04.01.1996	22	(4)	4
Klæmint Andrasson Olsen	17.07.1990	26	(1)	26
Óli Olsen	24.11.1985		(8)	

Skála Ítróttarfelag

Founded: 1965
Stadium: Undir Mýruhjalla, Skála (1,500)
Trainer: Eyðun Klakstein 28.11.1972

Goalkeepers:	DOB	M	(s)	G
Karstin Hansen	05.10.1997	27		
Defenders:	**DOB**	**M**	**(s)**	**G**
Erland Danielsen	16.05.1990	3	(2)	
Jákup Jakobsen	22.11.1992	26		
Poul Kallsberg	04.02.2003		(2)	
Hanus Mikkelsen	28.11.2002		(1)	
Petur Mikkelsen	20.06.1990	7	(1)	
Djóni Petersen	09.10.1999	2	(8)	
Teitur Poulsen	22.07.2000		(1)	
Midfielders:	**DOB**	**M**	**(s)**	**G**
Fróði Benjaminsen	14.12.1977	23	(1)	2
Aksel Bjartalíð Danielsen	03.04.1999	3	(9)	2
Niels Pauli Danielsen	18.01.1989	11	(8)	1
Jan Hansen	08.10.1997		(4)	

	DOB	M	(s)	G
Haraldur Højgaard	21.03.1995	21	(4)	4
Edvin Jacobsen	12.04.1991	6		
Pætur Jacobsen	05.12.1982	21	(1)	3
Teitur Joensen	10.11.1986	22	(1)	1
Dávid Johansen	08.02.1997		(3)	
Heðin Klakstein	30.04.1992	26		3
Ólavur Mikkelsen	11.01.1992	5	(7)	
Ari Olsen	09.09.1998	27		
Janus Samuelsen	27.09.1998	11	(12)	1
Forwards:	**DOB**	**M**	**(s)**	**G**
Andreas Jacobsen	25.11.1999	6	(9)	3
Jákup Johansen	27.04.1993	22	(3)	7
Ronny Møller-Iversen (DEN)	17.07.1994	26		8
Søren Nielsen (DEN)	03.11.1990	2		1
Rói Olsen	28.04.2001		(2)	

Tvøroyrar Bóltfelag

Founded: 13.05.1892
Stadium: Við Stórá Stadium, Trongisvágur (4,000)
Trainer: Zoran Pavlović (SRB)   04.09.1966
[01.10.2019] Karl Öster   18.02.1976

Goalkeepers:	DOB	M	(s)	G
Miloš Budaković (SRB)	10.07.1991	27		
Bárður Dimon	18.08.1999		(1)	
Defenders:	**DOB**	**M**	**(s)**	**G**
Tórmóður Djurhuus	02.09.2000	7	(5)	
Eirikur Ellendersen	05.03.1994	12		1
Dánjal Godtfred	07.03.1996	27		
Regin í Lágabø	05.08.1998	11		
Bartal Olsen	27.10.1998		(1)	
Niklas Olsen	29.04.1999		(1)	
Teitur Olsen	10.05.1995	9		1
Martin Tausen	04.05.1990	11		
Midfielders:	**DOB**	**M**	**(s)**	**G**
Hávar Albinus	19.02.1998		(4)	
Jens Bruhn	12.05.2002	6	(13)	
Jannik Dalfoss	18.03.2003		(3)	
Ndende Adama Guéye (SEN)	05.01.1983	26		2
Ivan Ivanović (MNE)	14.09.1989	19	(3)	2

	DOB	M	(s)	G
Luc Jeggo (AUS)	25.05.1994	12		2
Rógvi Joensen	14.07.1993	8		1
Nikolei Johannesen	15.05.2001	20	(5)	
John Villi Leo	13.08.1997	26		1
Heine Mortensen	26.02.1991	2	(2)	
Arthur Poulsen	29.12.1992		(3)	
Stefan Radosavljević	08.09.2000	13		6
Ólavur av Fløtum Reginsson	21.12.1998		(1)	
Andrias Sørensen	17.02.2000	2	(3)	
Ári Thomassen	21.07.2003	2	(2)	
Jóhan Thomsen	14.05.2002		(3)	
Einar Thorsteinsson	07.10.2000		(1)	
Forwards:	**DOB**	**M**	**(s)**	**G**
Ken Fagerberg (SWE)	09.01.1989	8	(2)	
Poul Ingason	28.09.1995	16		2
Aron Sørensen	22.11.1988	11	(5)	
Ragnar Tausen	06.09.1994	4	(3)	1
Veljko Vuković (SRB)	14.07.1989	18		1

Víkingur Gøta

Founded: 14.01.2008 (*after the merger of GÍ Gøta and Leirvík ÍF*)
Stadium: Sarpugerði, Norðragøta (3,000)
Trainer: Sámal Erik Hentze   27.01.1972

Goalkeepers:	DOB	M	(s)	G
Bárður á Reynatrøð	08.01.2000	1		
Elias Rasmussen	13.05.1996	26		
Defenders:	**DOB**	**M**	**(s)**	**G**
Atli Gregersen	15.06.1982	24		
Bergur Gregersen	11.09.1994	5	(8)	
Gert Aage Hansen	25.07.1984	1	(4)	
Pól Enok Hansen	18.06.1997		(1)	
Hanus Jacobsen	25.05.1985	25	(1)	1
Óla Kristian Skála Jacobsen	07.07.1997		(1)	
Noah Mneney	06.12.2002		(3)	
Jákup Olsen	30.05.1996	1	(7)	
Vukašin Tomić (SRB)	08.04.1987	26		2
Midfielders:	**DOB**	**M**	**(s)**	**G**
Dion Jacobsen	05.06.1989	18	(3)	5

	DOB	M	(s)	G
Elias Jóhannesson Lervig	26.02.1997	20	(1)	
Hans Jákup Jóhannesson Lervig	26.02.1997		(2)	
Bogi Petersen	20.02.1993	7	(3)	2
Hjalti Strømsten	21.01.1997		(1)	
Arnbjørn Svensson	01.07.1999	8	(12)	2
Milan Svojić (SRB)	09.10.1985	4	(1)	
Gunnar Vatnhamar	29.03.1995	26		7
Sølvi Vatnhamar	05.05.1986	24		9
Forwards:	**DOB**	**M**	**(s)**	**G**
Filip Đorđević (SRB)	07.03.1994	20	(6)	5
Heðin Hansen	30.07.1993	25		5
Ingi Jonhardsson	11.09.2001		(6)	
Adeshina Lawal (NGA)	17.10.1984	19	(2)	7
Andreas Olsen	09.10.1987	17	(3)	4
Tonni Thomsen	05.02.1999		(1)	

SECOND LEVEL
1.deild 2019

1.	KÍ Klaksvík II	27	18	3	6	75 - 37	57
2.	Víkingur Gøta II	27	16	7	4	51 - 27	55
3.	NSÍ Runavík II	27	16	5	6	68 - 40	53
4.	07 Vestur Sørvágur	27	13	5	9	57 - 48	44
5.	B68 Toftir	27	9	8	10	44 - 44	35
6.	B36 Tórshavn II	27	8	6	13	52 - 53	30
7.	B71 Sandoy	27	8	6	13	49 - 72	30
8.	HB Tórshavn II	27	8	5	14	40 - 44	29
9.	Skála ÍF II (*Relegated*)	27	5	13	9	37 - 47	28
10.	EB/Streymur II (*Relegated*)	27	2	6	19	31 - 92	12

NATIONAL TEAM

INTERNATIONAL MATCHES
(16.07.2019 – 15.07.2020)

05.09.2019	Tórshavn	Faroe Islands - Sweden	0-4(0-4)	(ECQ)
08.09.2019	Gijón	Spain - Faroe Islands	4-0(1-0)	(ECQ)
12.10.2019	Tórshavn	Faroe Islands - Romania	0-3(0-0)	(ECQ)
15.10.2019	Tórshavn	Faroe Islands - Malta	1-0(0-0)	(ECQ)
15.11.2019	Oslo	Norway - Faroe Islands	4-0(2-0)	(ECQ)
18.11.2019	Stockholm	Sweden - Faroe Islands	3-0(1-0)	(ECQ)

05.09.2019　**FAROE ISLANDS - SWEDEN**　　　　**0-4(0-4)**　　　　　　　16th EC. Qualifiers
Tórsvøllur, Tórshavn; Referee: Tiago Bruno Lopes Martins (Portugal); Attendance: 3,108
FRO: Gunnar Nielsen, Atli Gregersen (Cap), Viljormur í Heiðunum Davidsen, Rógvi Asmundur Baldvinsson, Hørður Heðinsson Askham, Jóan Símun Edmundsson, Sølvi Vatnhamar, Hallur Hansson, Árni Frederiksberg (63.Jóannes Bjartalíð), Brandur Hendriksson Olsen (76.Meinhard Egilsson Olsen), René Shaki Joensen (46.Heini Vatnsdal). Trainer: Lars Christian Olsen (Denmark).

08.09.2019　**SPAIN - FAROE ISLANDS**　　　　**4-0(1-0)**　　　　　　　16th EC. Qualifiers
Estadio Municipal El Molinón, Gijón; Referee: Krzysztof Jakubik (Poland); Attendance: 23,644
FRO: Gunnar Nielsen, Atli Gregersen (Cap), Heini Vatnsdal, Viljormur í Heiðunum Davidsen, Rógvi Asmundur Baldvinsson (55.Andrias Høgnason Eriksen), Jóan Símun Edmundsson (65.Kaj Leo í Bartalsstovu), Sølvi Vatnhamar, Hallur Hansson, Brandur Hendriksson Olsen, Jóannes Bjartalíð, Klæmint Andrasson Olsen (87.Magnus Egilsson). Trainer: Lars Christian Olsen (Denmark).

12.10.2019　**FAROE ISLANDS - ROMANIA**　　　　**0-3(0-0)**　　　　　　　16th EC. Qualifiers
Tórsvøllur, Tórshavn; Referee: Əliyar Ağayev (Azerbaijan); Attendance: 2,381
FRO: Gunnar Nielsen, Atli Gregersen (Cap), Heini Vatnsdal, Viljormur í Heiðunum Davidsen, Rógvi Asmundur Baldvinsson (78.Eli Falkvard Nielsen), Sølvi Vatnhamar, Hallur Hansson, Brandur Hendriksson Olsen (71.Andrias Høgnason Eriksen), Jóannes Bjartalíð, Klæmint Andrasson Olsen (75.Jóan Símun Edmundsson), Gilli Rólantsson Sørensen. Trainer: Lars Christian Olsen (Denmark).

15.10.2019　**FAROE ISLANDS - MALTA**　　　　**1-0(0-0)**　　　　　　　16th EC. Qualifiers
Tórsvøllur, Tórshavn; Referee: José María Sánchez Martínez (Spain); Attendance: 2,677
FRO: Gunnar Nielsen, Atli Gregersen (Cap), Heini Vatnsdal, Viljormur í Heiðunum Davidsen (85.Árni Frederiksberg), Rógvi Asmundur Baldvinsson, Jóannes Danielsen, Jóan Símun Edmundsson (90+3.Magnus Egilsson), Sølvi Vatnhamar, Hallur Hansson, Brandur Hendriksson Olsen, Jóannes Bjartalíð (65.Klæmint Andrasson Olsen). Trainer: Lars Christian Olsen (Denmark).
Goal: Rógvi Asmundur Baldvinsson (71).

15.11.2019　**NORWAY - FAROE ISLANDS**　　　　**4-0(2-0)**　　　　　　　16th EC. Qualifiers
Ullevaal Stadion, Oslo; Referee: Fran Jović (Croatia); Attendance: 10,400
FRO: Gunnar Nielsen, Odmar Færø, Atli Gregersen (Cap), Heini Vatnsdal, Rógvi Asmundur Baldvinsson, Ári Mohr Jónsson, Jóan Símun Edmundsson (71.Klæmint Andrasson Olsen), Sølvi Vatnhamar (78.Kaj Leo í Bartalsstovu), Brandur Hendriksson Olsen, Jóannes Bjartalíð (71.Árni Frederiksberg), Gilli Rólantsson Sørensen. Trainer: Lars Christian Olsen (Denmark).

18.11.2019　**SWEDEN - FAROE ISLANDS**　　　　**3-0(1-0)**　　　　　　　16th EC. Qualifiers
Friends Arena, Stockholm; Referee: Matej Jug (Slovenia); Attendance: 19,500
FRO: Gunnar Nielsen, Atli Gregersen (Cap), Heini Vatnsdal, Viljormur í Heiðunum Davidsen, Rógvi Asmundur Baldvinsson, Jóan Símun Edmundsson (89.Árni Frederiksberg), Sølvi Vatnhamar, Brandur Hendriksson Olsen, Jóannes Bjartalíð (46.Kaj Leo í Bartalsstovu), Klæmint Andrasson Olsen (74.Patrik Johannesen), Gilli Rólantsson Sørensen. Trainer: Lars Christian Olsen (Denmark).

NATIONAL TEAM PLAYERS
(16.07.2019 – 15.07.2020)

Name	DOB	Caps	Goals	2019:	Club
Goalkeepers					
Gunnar NIELSEN	07.10.1986	**58**	**0**	2019:	*FH Hafnarfjarðar (ISL)*
Defenders					
Hørður Heðinsson ASKHAM	22.09.1994	1	0	2019:	*HB Tórshavn*
Rógvi Asmundur BALDVINSSON	06.12.1989	45	4	2019:	*Bryne FK (NOR)*
Viljormur í Heiðunum DAVIDSEN	19.07.1991	38	1	2019:	*Vejle BK (DEN)*
Magnus EGILSSON	19.03.1994	2	0	2019:	*HB Tórshavn*
Andrias Høgnason ERIKSEN	22.02.1994	2	0	2019:	*B36 Tórshavn*
Odmar FÆRØ	01.11.1989	29	0	2019:	*Hamarkameratene (NOR)*
Atli GREGERSEN	15.06.1982	59	1	2019:	*Víkingur Gøta*
Heini VATNSDAL	18.10.1991	19	0	2019:	*BK Fremad Amager (DEN)*
Midfielders					
Kaj Leo í BARTALSSTOVU	23.06.1991	27	1	2019:	*Valur Reykjavík (ISL)*
Jóannes BJARTALÍÐ	10.07.1996	6	0	2019:	*KÍ Klaksvík*
Jóannes DANIELSEN	10.09.1997	1	0	2019:	*KÍ Klaksvík*
Hallur HANSSON	08.07.1992	47	5	2019:	*AC Horsens (DEN)*
René Shaki JOENSEN	08.02.1993	26	3	2019:	*HB Tórshavn*
Patrik JOHANNESEN	07.09.1995	6	0	2019:	*KÍ Klaksvík*
Brandur Hendriksson OLSEN	19.12.1995	32	3	2019:	*FH Hafnarfjörður (ISL)*
Ári Mohr JÓNSSON	22.07.1994	4	0	2019:	*Sandnes Ulf (NOR)*
Eli Falkvard NIELSEN	23.09.1992	1	0	2019:	*B36 Tórshavn*
Gilli Rólantsson SØRENSEN	11.08.1992	36	1	2019:	*SK Brann Bergen (NOR)*
Sølvi VATNHAMAR	05.05.1986	37	1	2019:	*Víkingur Gøta*
Forwards					
Jóan Símun EDMUNDSSON	26.07.1991	58	7	2019:	*DSC Arminia Bielefeld (GER)*
Árni FREDERIKSBERG	13.06.1992	11	0	2019:	*B36 Tórshavn*
Klæmint Andrasson OLSEN	17.07.1990	28	1	2019:	*NSÍ Runavík*
Meinhard Egilsson OLSEN	10.04.1997	2	0	2019:	*Kristiansund BK (NOR)*

National team coach

Lars Christian OLSEN (Denmark) [01.12.2011-18.11.2019]	02.02.1961	55 M; 9 W; 7 D; 39 L; 32-108
Håkan ERICSON (Sweden) [since 16.12.2019]	29.05.1960	-

FINLAND

The Country:
Suomen tasavalta (Republic of Finland)
Capital: Helsinki
Surface: 338,424 km^2
Inhabitants: 5,520,535 [2018]
Time: UTC+2

The FA:
Suomen Palloliitto
Urheilukatu 1 PO Box 191, 00251 Helsinki
Tel: +358 9 7421 51
Foundation date: 1907
Member of FIFA since: 1908
Member of UEFA since: 1954
Website:

NATIONAL TEAM RECORDS

RECORDS
First international match:	22.10.1911, Helsinki:	Finland – Sweden 2-5
Most international caps:	Jari Olavi Litmanen	- 137 caps (1989-2010)
Most international goals:	Jari Olavi Litmanen	- 32 goals / 137 caps (1989-2010)

UEFA EUROPEAN CHAMPIONSHIP		FIFA WORLD CUP		OLYMPIC TOURNAMENTS	
1960	Did not enter	1930	Did not enter	1908	-
1964	Did not enter	1934	Did not enter	1912	-
1968	Qualifiers	1938	Qualifiers	1920	-
1972	Qualifiers	1950	*Withdrew*	1924	-
1976	Qualifiers	1954	Qualifiers	1928	-
1980	Qualifiers	1958	Qualifiers	1936	Qualifiers
1984	Qualifiers	1962	Qualifiers	1948	-
1988	Qualifiers	1966	Qualifiers	1952	Round 1
1992	Qualifiers	1970	Qualifiers	1956	-
1996	Qualifiers	1974	Qualifiers	1960	Qualifiers
2000	Qualifiers	1978	Qualifiers	1964	Qualifiers
2004	Qualifiers	1982	Qualifiers	1968	Qualifiers
2008	Qualifiers	1986	Qualifiers	1972	*Withdrew*
2012	Qualifiers	1990	Qualifiers	1976	Qualifiers
2016	Qualifiers	1994	Qualifiers	1980	Group Stage
2020	*Final Tournament (Qualified)*	1998	Qualifiers	1984	Qualifiers
		2002	Qualifiers	1988	Qualifiers
		2006	Qualifiers	1992	Qualifiers
		2010	Qualifiers	1996	Qualifiers
		2014	Qualifiers	2000	Qualifiers
		2018	Qualifiers	2004	Qualifiers
				2008	Qualifiers
				2012	Qualifiers
				2016	Qualifiers

UEFA NATIONS LEAGUE
2018/2019 – League C (promoted to League B)

FIFA CONFEDERATIONS CUP 1992-2017
None

FINNISH CLUB HONOURS IN EUROPEAN CLUB COMPETITIONS:

European Champion Clubs.Cup (1956-1992) / UEFA Champions League (1993-2020)
None

Fairs Cup (1858-1971) / UEFA Cup (1972-2009) / UEFA Europa League (2010-2020)
None

UEFA Super Cup (1972-2019)
None

*European Cup Winners.Cup 1961-1999**
None

defunct competition

NATIONAL COMPETITIONS
TABLE OF HONOURS

	CHAMPIONS	CUP WINNERS	BEST GOALSCORERS	
1908	Unitas Helsinki	-	-	
1909	PUS Helsinki	-	-	
1910	Åbo IFK Turku	-	-	
1911	HJK Helsinki	-	-	
1912	HJK Helsinki	-	-	
1913	KIF Helsinki	-	-	
1914	*No competition*	-	-	
1915	KIF Helsinki	-	-	
1916	KIF Helsinki	-	-	
1917	HJK Helsinki	-	-	
1918	HJK Helsinki	-	-	
1919	HJK Helsinki	-	-	
1920	Åbo IFK Turku	-	-	
1921	Helsingin Palloseura	-	-	
1922	Helsingin Palloseura	-	-	
1923	HJK Helsinki	-	-	
1924	Åbo IFK Turku	-	-	
1925	HJK Helsinki	-	-	
1926	Helsingin Palloseura	-	-	
1927	Helsingin Palloseura	-	-	
1928	TPS Turku	-	-	
1929	Helsingin Palloseura	-	-	
1930	IFK Helsingfors	-	Holger Salin (IFK Helsingfors)	
			Olof Strömsten (KIF Helsinki)	9
1931	IFK Helsingfors	-	Holger Salin (IFK Helsingfors)	11
1932	Helsingin Palloseura	-	Lauri Lehtinen (TPS Turku)	13
1933	IFK Helsingfors	-	Olof Strömsten (IFK Helsingfors)	18
1934	Helsingin Palloseura	-	Olof Strömsten (IFK Helsingfors)	15
1935	Helsingin Palloseura	-	Aatos Lehtonen (HJK Helsinki)	
			Nuutti Lintamo (VPS Vaasa)	13
1936	HJK Helsinki	-	Aatos Lehtonen (HJK Helsinki)	14
1937	IFK Helsingfors	-	Aatos Lehtonen (HJK Helsinki)	25
1938	HJK Helsinki	-	Aatos Lehtonen (HJK Helsinki)	14
1939	TPS Turku	-	Aatos Lehtonen (HJK Helsinki)	15
1940	Sudet Viipuri	-	*Not known*	
1941	TPS Turku	-	Jussi Valtonen (TPS Turku)	14
1942	HT Helsinki	-	*Not known*	
1943	*No competition*	-	-	
1944	VIFK Vaasa	-	Urho Teräs (TPS Turku)	
			Leo Turunen (Sudet Viipuri)	9
1945	VPS Vaasa	-	*Not known*	
1946	VIFK Vaasa	-	*Not known*	
1947	IFK Helsingfors	-	*Not known*	
1948	VPS Vaasa	-	Stig-Göran Myntti (VIFK Vaasa)	15
1949	TPS Turku	-	Yrjö Asikainen (Ilves-Kissat Tampere)	
			Kaimo Lintamo (VPS Vaasa)	20
1950	Ilves-Kissat Tampere	-	Yrjö Asikainen (Ilves-Kissat Tampere)	
			Jorma Saarinen (VPS Vaasa)	15
1951	KTP Kotka	-	Åke Forsberg (KIF Helsinki)	16
1952	KTP Kotka	-	Mauri Vanhanen (KTP Kotka)	16
1953	VIFK Vaasa	-	Rainer Forss (Pyrkivä Turku)	15
1954	Pyrkivä Turku	-	Eino Koskinen (TuTo Turku)	16
1955	KIF Helsinki	FC Haka Valkeakoski	Yrjö Asikainen (KIF Helsinki)	12
1956	KuPS Kuopio	PPojat Helsinki	Pentti Styck (HJK Helsinki)	20
1957	Helsingin Palloseura	Drott Pietarsaari	Matti Sundelin (TPS Turku)	21
1958	KuPS Kuopio	KTP Kotka	Kalevi Lehtovirta (TPS Turku)	
			Kai Pahlman (Helsingin Palloseura)	17
1959	IFK Helsingfors	FC Haka Valkeakoski	Matti Sundelin (TPS Turku)	21
1960	FC Haka Valkeakoski	FC Haka Valkeakoski	Matti Sundelin (TPS Turku)	30
1961	IFK Helsingfors	KTP Kotka	Kai Pahlman (Helsingin Palloseura)	20
1962	FC Haka Valkeakoski	Helsingin Palloseura	Tor Österlund (HIK Hanko)	22
1963	Reipas Lahti	FC Haka Valkeakoski	Juha Lyytikäinen (IFK Helsingfors)	16
1964	HJK Helsinki	Reipas Lahti	Arto Tolsa (KTP Kotka)	26
1965	FC Haka Valkeakoski	Åbo IFK Turku	Kai Pahlman (HJK Helsinki)	22
1966	KuPS Kuopio	HJK Helsinki	Markku Hyvärinen (KuPS Kuopio)	16
1967	Reipas Lahti	KTP Kotka	Tommy Lindholm (TPS Turku)	22
1968	TPS Turku	KuPS Kuopio	Tommy Lindholm (TPS Turku)	23
1969	KPV Kokkola	FC Haka Valkeakoski	Hannu Lamberg (KPV Kokkola)	
			Pekka Talaslahti (HJK Helsinki)	18
1970	Reipas Lahti	MP Mikkeli	Matti Paatelainen (IFK Helsingfors)	20
1971	TPS Turku	MP Mikkeli	Pentti Toivola (MP Mikkeli)	17
1972	TPS Turku	Reipas Lahti	Matti Paatelainen (IFK Helsingfors)	

Year	Champion	Runner-up	Top scorer	Goals
			Heikki Suhonen (TPS Turku)	16
1973	HJK Helsinki	Reipas Lahti	Hannu Lamberg (KPV Kokkola)	13
1974	KuPS Kuopio	Reipas Lahti	Erkki Salo (TPS Turku)	17
1975	TPS Turku	Reipas Lahti	Reijo Rantanen (MiPK Mikkeli)	16
1976	KuPS Kuopio	Reipas Lahti	Matti Paatelainen (FC Haka Valkeakoski)	17
1977	FC Haka Valkeakoski	FC Haka Valkeakoski	Matti Paatelainen (FC Haka Valkeakoski)	20
1978	HJK Helsinki	Reipas Lahti	Atik Ismail (HJK Helsinki)	20
1979	OPS Oulu	FC Ilves Tampere	Atik Ismail (HJK Helsinki) Heikki Suhonen (TPS Turku)	15
1980	OPS Oulu	KTP Kotka	Hannu Rajaniemi (Sepsi-78 Seinäjoki)	19
1981	HJK Helsinki	HJK Helsinki	Juhani Himanka (OPS Oulu)	22
1982	FC Kuusysi Lahti	FC Haka Valkeakoski	Atik Ismail (HJK Helsinki)	19
1983	FC Ilves Tampere	FC Kuusysi Lahti	Mika Lipponen (TPS Turku)	22
1984	FC Kuusysi Lahti	HJK Helsinki	Mika Lipponen (TPS Turku)	25
1985	HJK Helsinki	FC Haka Valkeakoski	Ismo Lius (FC Kuusysi Lahti)	19
1986	FC Kuusysi Lahti	RoPS Rovaniemi	Ismo Lius (FC Kuusysi Lahti) Jari Niinimäki (FC Ilves Tampere)	13
1987	HJK Helsinki	FC Kuusysi Lahti	Ari Hjelm (FC Ilves Tampere)	20
1988	HJK Helsinki	FC Haka Valkeakoski	Ismo Lius (FC Kuusysi Lahti)	22
1989	FC Kuusysi Lahti	KuPS Kuopio	Ismo Lius (FC Kuusysi Lahti)	15
1990	HJK Helsinki	FC Ilves Tampere	Marek Czakon (POL, FC Ilves Tampere) Kimmo Tarkkio (HJK Helsinki)	16
1991	FC Kuusysi Lahti	TPS Turku	Kimmo Tarkkio (FC Haka Valkeakoski)	23
1992	HJK Helsinki	MyPa Myllykoski	Luiz Antônio Moraes (BRA, FC Jazz Pori)	21
1993	FC Jazz Pori	HJK Helsinki	Antti Sumiala (FC Jazz Pori)	20
1994	TPV Tampere	TPS Turku	Dionísio Domingos Rangel (BRA, TPV Tampere)	17
1995	FC Haka Valkeakoski	MyPa Myllykoski	Valeri Popovitch (RUS, FC Haka Valkeakoski)	21
1996	FC Jazz Pori	HJK Helsinki	Luiz Antônio Moraes (BRA, FC Jazz Pori)	17
1997	HJK Helsinki	FC Haka Valkeakoski	Rafael Pires Vieira (BRA, HJK Helsinki)	11
1998	FC Haka Valkeakoski	HJK Helsinki	Matti Hiukka (RoPS Rovaniemi)	11
1999	FC Haka Valkeakoski	Jokerit Helsinki	Valeri Popovitch (FC Haka Valkeakoski)	23
2000	FC Haka Valkeakoski	HJK Helsinki	Shefki Kuqi (Jokerit Helsinki)	19
2001	TamU Tampere	Atlantis Helsinki	Paulus Roiha (HJK Helsinki)	22
2002	HJK Helsinki	FC Haka Valkeakoski	Mika Kottila (HJK Helsinki)	18
2003	HJK Helsinki	HJK Helsinki	Saku Puhakainen (MyPa Myllykoski)	14
2004	FC Haka Valkeakoski	MyPa Myllykoski	Antti Pohja (TamU Tampere)	16
2005	MyPa Myllykoski	FC Haka Valkeakoski	Juho Mäkelä (HJK Helsinki)	16
2006	TamU Tampere	HJK Helsinki	Hermanni Vuorinen (FC Honka Espoo)	16
2007	TamU Tampere	TamU Tampere	Rafael Pires Vieira (BRA, FC Lahti)	14
2008	FC Inter Turku	HJK Helsinki	Aleksandr Kokko (FC Honka Espoo) Henri Myntti (TamU Tampere)	13
2009	HJK Helsinki	FC Inter Turku	Hermanni Vuorinen (FC Honka Espoo)	16
2010	HJK Helsinki	TPS Turku	Juho Mäkelä (HJK Helsinki)	16
2011	HJK Helsinki	HJK Helsinki	Timo Furuholm (FC Inter Turku)	22
2012	HJK Helsinki	FC Honka Espoo	Irakli Sirbiladze (GEO, FC Inter Turku)	17
2013	HJK Helsinki	RoPS Rovaniemi	Tim Väyrynen (FC Honka Espoo)	17
2014	HJK Helsinki	HJK Helsinki	Jonas Emet (FF Jaro Pietarsaari) Luis Emilio Solignac (ARG, IFK Mariehamn)	14
2015	SJK Seinäjoki	IFK Mariehamn	Aleksandr Kokko (RoPS Rovaniemi)	17
2016	IFK Mariehamn	SJK Seinäjoki	Roope Riski (SJK Seinäjoki)	17
2017	HJK Helsinki	HJK Helsinki	Aleksei Kangaskolkka (IFK Mariehamn)	16
2018	HJK Helsinki	FC Inter Turku	João Klauss De Mello (BRA, HJK Helsinki)	21
2019	Kuopion Palloseura	FC Ilves Tampere	Filip Valenčić (SVN, FC Inter Turku)	17

NATIONAL CHAMPIONSHIP
Veikkausliiga 2019
(07.04.2019 – 19.10.2019)

Regular Season - Results

Date	Match	Result
03.04.2019	Kuopion PS - Rovaniemi PS	2-2(0-1)
	HJK Helsinki - FC Inter Turku	2-1(0-0)
06.04.2019	SJK Seinäjoki - Helsingin IFK	1-0(0-0)
07.04.2019	Rovaniemi PS - FC Honka	1-2(0-0)
	Kokkolan Palloveikot - FC Ilves Tampere	0-2(0-1)
	FC Lahti - Kuopion PS	3-3(0-3)
08.04.2019	HJK Helsinki - IFK Mariehamn	2-1(0-0)
	Vaasan PS - FC Inter Turku	1-2(0-1)
13.04.2019	FC Inter Turku - SJK Seinäjoki	1-2(0-2)
	Kokkolan Palloveikot - Rovaniemi PS	0-1(0-0)
	Kuopion PS - HJK Helsinki	0-0
14.04.2019	FC Ilves Tampere - Vaasan PS	0-0
15.04.2019	FC Honka - IFK Mariehamn	1-3(1-1)
	Helsingin IFK - FC Lahti	0-1(0-0)
18.04.2019	SJK Seinäjoki - HJK Helsinki	0-0
19.04.2019	FC Lahti - FC Inter Turku	1-1(0-1)
20.04.2019	Vaasan PS - Kokkolan Palloveikot	2-2(1-0)
	Kuopion PS - FC Honka	0-3(0-1)
	IFK Mariehamn - Rovaniemi PS	2-0(1-0)
22.04.2019	SJK Seinäjoki - FC Ilves Tampere	0-1(0-0)
23.04.2019	HJK Helsinki - Helsingin IFK	1-1(0-0)
25.04.2019	FC Honka - FC Inter Turku	3-2(1-1)
	Kokkolan Palloveikot - IFK Mariehamn	0-4(0-2)
26.04.2019	Vaasan PS - SJK Seinäjoki	1-1(1-0)
	FC Ilves Tampere - FC Lahti	1-0(1-0)
	Rovaniemi PS - Kuopion PS	0-1(0-0)
29.04.2019	Helsingin IFK - FC Honka	2-0(0-0)
	FC Inter Turku - HJK Helsinki	4-1(2-1)
30.04.2019	FC Lahti - Vaasan PS	1-1(0-1)
	SJK Seinäjoki - Kokkolan Palloveikot	1-0(0-0)
01.05.2019	IFK Mariehamn - Kuopion PS	3-4(3-0)
03.05.2019	Rovaniemi PS - Helsingin IFK	1-0(1-0)
	HJK Helsinki - FC Ilves Tampere	0-0
05.05.2019	FC Lahti - SJK Seinäjoki	1-1(0-0)
	Kuopion PS - Kokkolan Palloveikot	3-1(0-1)
07.05.2019	FC Inter Turku - Rovaniemi PS	3-0(3-0)
	FC Ilves Tampere - FC Honka	1-1(0-0)
	Vaasan PS - HJK Helsinki	1-1(0-0)
08.05.2019	Helsingin IFK - IFK Mariehamn	1-1(1-0)
11.05.2019	FC Honka - Vaasan PS	1-1(1-1)
	Kokkolan Palloveikot - FC Lahti	0-0
	HJK Helsinki - SJK Seinäjoki	2-2(1-0)
12.05.2019	Rovaniemi PS - FC Ilves Tampere	0-1(0-1)
	IFK Mariehamn - FC Inter Turku	1-2(0-2)
	Helsingin IFK - Kuopion PS	1-1(1-1)
17.05.2019	FC Inter Turku - Kuopion PS	1-0(1-0)
18.05.2019	SJK Seinäjoki - FC Honka	1-2(1-0)
20.05.2019	Vaasan PS - Rovaniemi PS	0-1(0-0)
	Kokkolan Palloveikot - Helsingin IFK	1-1(0-1)
	FC Ilves Tampere - IFK Mariehamn	0-0
	FC Lahti - HJK Helsinki	3-0(2-0)
24.05.2019	Kuopion PS - FC Ilves Tampere	1-0(0-0)
25.05.2019	Helsingin IFK - FC Inter Turku	1-1(1-0)
	Rovaniemi PS - SJK Seinäjoki	1-1(0-1)
26.05.2019	IFK Mariehamn - Vaasan PS	1-0(1-0)
	HJK Helsinki - Kokkolan Palloveikot	3-1(2-0)
27.05.2019	FC Honka - FC Lahti	2-0(1-0)
31.05.2019	Rovaniemi PS - HJK Helsinki	0-1(0-0)
	Helsingin IFK - Vaasan PS	2-1(1-0)
	FC Inter Turku - FC Ilves Tampere	2-3(2-2)
02.06.2019	FC Honka - Kokkolan Palloveikot	0-1(0-1)
	IFK Mariehamn - FC Lahti	0-1(0-0)
	Kuopion PS - SJK Seinäjoki	0-1(0-1)
16.06.2019	Kokkolan Palloveikot - FC Inter Turku	1-3(1-1)
17.06.2019	Vaasan PS - Kuopion PS	1-2(0-2)
18.06.2019	FC Lahti - Rovaniemi PS	1-2(0-1)
	Helsingin IFK - SJK Seinäjoki	1-0(1-0)
19.06.2019	HJK Helsinki - FC Honka	0-1(0-0)
25.06.2019	IFK Mariehamn - HJK Helsinki	0-2(0-1)
	FC Honka - Rovaniemi PS	1-0(0-0)
	FC Inter Turku - Vaasan PS 1-1(1-0)	
	Kuopion PS - FC Lahti	5-1(1-0)
	FC Ilves Tampere - Kokkolan Palloveikot	4-2(1-1)
29.06.2019	Vaasan PS - FC Ilves Tampere	1-2(1-2)
	HJK Helsinki - Kuopion PS	1-1(0-0)
	Rovaniemi PS - Kokkolan Palloveikot	0-0
30.06.2019	FC Lahti - Helsingin IFK	0-0
	IFK Mariehamn - FC Honka	2-2(0-2)
01.07.2019	SJK Seinäjoki - FC Inter Turku	2-1(0-0)
04.07.2019	Helsingin IFK - HJK Helsinki	0-2(0-2)
05.07.2019	FC Inter Turku - FC Lahti	2-0(2-0)
06.07.2019	Kokkolan Palloveikot - Vaasan PS	2-1(1-0)
	Rovaniemi PS - IFK Mariehamn	1-2(0-2)
	FC Honka - Kuopion PS	1-2(0-1)
07.07.2019	FC Ilves Tampere - SJK Seinäjoki	3-0(2-0)
13.07.2019	FC Honka - Helsingin IFK	3-0(1-0)
	SJK Seinäjoki - Vaasan PS	1-0(0-0)
14.07.2019	IFK Mariehamn - Kokkolan Palloveikot	3-0(1-0)
	FC Lahti - FC Ilves Tampere	1-0(1-0)
20.07.2019	Kokkolan Palloveikot - SJK Seinäjoki	1-2(0-1)
	Vaasan PS - FC Lahti	1-1(1-1)
	FC Ilves Tampere - HJK Helsinki	1-1(0-0)
21.07.2019	FC Inter Turku - FC Honka	3-1(1-0)
	Helsingin IFK - Rovaniemi PS	1-0(1-0)
	Kuopion PS - IFK Mariehamn	0-0
26.07.2019	SJK Seinäjoki - FC Lahti	0-2(0-0)
27.07.2019	FC Honka - FC Ilves Tampere	1-2(1-0)
	HJK Helsinki - Vaasan PS	1-1(0-1)
28.07.2019	Kokkolan Palloveikot - Kuopion PS	2-1(0-0)
	Rovaniemi PS - FC Inter Turku	0-2(0-1)
	IFK Mariehamn - Helsingin IFK	1-3(1-1)
03.08.2019	Vaasan PS - FC Honka	2-3(1-0)
04.08.2019	FC Lahti - Kokkolan Palloveikot	1-0(0-0)
	FC Ilves Tampere - Rovaniemi PS	2-2(0-1)
	Kuopion PS - Helsingin IFK	1-1(0-1)
	FC Inter Turku - IFK Mariehamn	1-0(0-0)
09.08.2019	Helsingin IFK - Kokkolan Palloveikot	3-2(0-2)
10.08.2019	FC Honka - SJK Seinäjoki	0-0
	HJK Helsinki - FC Lahti	4-0(3-0)
	Kuopion PS - FC Inter Turku	2-0(0-0)
11.08.2019	IFK Mariehamn - FC Ilves Tampere	0-1(0-0)
	Rovaniemi PS - Vaasan PS	2-1(1-1)
15.08.2019	SJK Seinäjoki - IFK Mariehamn	0-2(0-0)
16.08.2019	FC Ilves Tampere - Kuopion PS	0-2(0-0)
	FC Inter Turku - Helsingin IFK	3-2(2-2)
18.08.2019	Kokkolan Palloveikot - HJK Helsinki	2-1(1-0)
19.08.2019	SJK Seinäjoki - Rovaniemi PS	0-0
	Vaasan PS - IFK Mariehamn	2-1(1-0)
	FC Lahti - FC Honka	3-2(3-0)
23.08.2019	Helsingin IFK - FC Ilves Tampere	2-2(1-1)
24.08.2019	FC Honka - HJK Helsinki	0-1(0-0)
	Kuopion PS - Vaasan PS	5-0(4-0)
25.08.2019	IFK Mariehamn - SJK Seinäjoki	1-0(0-0)
	Rovaniemi PS - FC Lahti	3-0(3-0)
26.08.2019	FC Inter Turku - Kokkolan Palloveikot	2-1(1-0)
27.08.2019	FC Ilves Tampere - Helsingin IFK	3-1(0-0)
31.08.2019	Kokkolan Palloveikot - FC Honka	0-1(0-0)
	SJK Seinäjoki - Kuopion PS	1-3(0-0)
	FC Ilves Tampere - FC Inter Turku	0-1(0-0)
	Vaasan PS - Helsingin IFK	3-2(1-1)
01.09.2019	FC Lahti - IFK Mariehamn	0-1(0-0)
	HJK Helsinki - Rovaniemi PS	2-2(1-1)

1.	FC Inter Turku	22	13	3	6	39	-	25	42
2.	Kuopion Palloseura	22	11	7	4	39	-	23	40
3.	FC Ilves Tampere	22	11	7	4	29	-	18	40
4.	HJK Helsinki	22	8	10	4	28	-	22	34
5.	FC Honka Espoo	22	10	4	8	31	-	27	34
6.	IFK Mariehamn	22	9	4	9	29	-	23	31
7.	SJK Seinäjoki	22	7	7	8	17	-	23	28
8.	FC Lahti	22	7	7	8	21	-	29	28
9.	Helsingin IFK	22	6	8	8	25	-	29	26
10.	Rovaniemen Palloseura	22	6	6	10	19	-	25	24
11.	Kokkolan Palloveikot	22	4	4	14	19	-	39	16
12.	Vaasan Palloseura	22	2	9	11	22	-	35	15

Teams ranked 1-6 were qualified for the Championship Round, while teams ranked 7-12 were qualified for the Relegation Round.

Championship Round

Results

Round 23 [15.09.2019]
FC Inter Turku - IFK Mariehamn 2-0(0-0)
Kuopion PS - HJK Helsinki 1-0(1-0)
FC Ilves Tampere - FC Honka 0-2(0-1)

Round 24 [21-22.09.2019]
FC Honka - HJK Helsinki 3-1(0-1)
IFK Mariehamn - Kuopion PS 0-1(0-0)
FC Ilves Tampere - FC Inter Turku 1-0(0-0)

Round 25 [27-28.09.2019]
Kuopion PS - FC Ilves Tampere 2-0(0-0)
FC Inter Turku - FC Honka 0-1(0-1)
HJK Helsinki - IFK Mariehamn 3-0(0-0)

Round 26 [06.10.2019]
HJK Helsinki - FC Inter Turku 0-1(0-0)
Kuopion PS - FC Honka 1-1(1-0)
IFK Mariehamn - FC Ilves Tampere 2-2(0-0)

Round 27 [19.10.2019]
FC Inter Turku - Kuopion PS 0-2(0-0)
FC Ilves Tampere - HJK Helsinki 2-1(0-1)
FC Honka - IFK Mariehamn 3-0(1-0)

Relegation Round

Results

Round 23 [13-14.09.2019]
SJK Seinäjoki - Vaasan PS 1-1(0-1)
Helsingin IFK - Kokkolan Palloveik. 3-1(0-0)
FC Lahti - Rovaniemi PS 3-0(1-0)

Round 24 [20-21.09.2019]
Vaasan PS - FC Lahti 1-2(1-0)
Kokkolan Palloveik. - Rovaniemi PS 4-1(1-1)
Helsingin IFK - SJK Seinäjoki 2-0(2-0)

Round 25 [27-28.09.2019]
SJK Seinäjoki - Kokkolan Palloveik. 0-2(0-2)
FC Lahti - Helsingin IFK 2-2(1-0)
Rovaniemi PS - Vaasan PS 2-1(0-0)

Round 26 [06.10.2019]
Rovaniemi PS - SJK Seinäjoki 1-0(1-0)
FC Lahti - Kokkolan Palloveikot 1-4(1-0)
Vaasan PS - Helsingin IFK 2-3(1-0)

Round 27 [19.10.2019]
SJK Seinäjoki - FC Lahti 0-0
Helsingin IFK - Rovaniemi PS 2-0(1-0)
Kokkolan Palloveikot - Vaasan PS 2-3(1-1)

Final Standings

									Total							Home							Away	
1.	**Kuopion Palloseura**	27	15	8	4	46	-	24	53	7	5	2	23	-	10	8	3	2	23	-	14			
2.	FC Inter Turku	27	15	3	9	42	-	29	48	9	1	4	25	-	14	6	2	5	17	-	15			
3.	FC Honka Espoo	27	14	5	8	41	-	29	47	6	2	5	19	-	13	8	3	3	22	-	16			
4.	FC Ilves Tampere	27	13	8	6	34	-	25	47	6	5	3	18	-	13	7	3	3	16	-	12			
5.	HJK Helsinki	27	9	10	8	33	-	29	37	5	6	2	21	-	12	4	4	6	12	-	17			
6.	IFK Mariehamn	27	9	5	13	31	-	34	32	4	2	7	16	-	18	5	3	6	15	-	16			
7.	Helsingin IFK	27	10	9	8	37	-	34	39	8	4	2	21	-	12	2	5	6	16	-	22			
8.	FC Lahti	27	9	9	9	29	-	36	36	5	6	3	21	-	17	4	3	6	8	-	19			
9.	SJK Seinäjoki	27	7	9	11	18	-	29	30	4	4	6	8	-	14	3	5	5	10	-	15			
10.	Rovaniemen Palloseura	27	8	6	13	23	-	35	30	5	2	6	12	-	12	3	4	7	11	-	23			
11.	Kokkolan Palloveikot (Relegation Play-offs)	27	7	4	16	32	-	47	25	4	2	7	15	-	21	3	2	9	17	-	26			
12.	Vaasan Palloseura (Relegated)	27	3	10	14	30	-	45	19	2	4	7	18	-	23	1	6	7	12	-	22			

Top goalscorers:

17	**Filip Valenčič (SVN)**	**FC Inter Turku**
13	Borjas Martín González (ESP)	FC Honka Espoo
12	Lauri Ala-Myllymäki	FC Ilves Tampere
10	Erikson Carlos Batista dos Santos „Tiquinho" (BRA)	Helsingin IFK
10	Timo Furuholm	FC Inter Turku

Relegation Play-offs [24-27.10.2019]

Turun Palloseura Turku - Kokkolan Palloveikot   0-0   3-0(1-0)
Turun Palloseura Turku promoted for the 2020 Veikkausliiga.

| Semi-Finals [23.10.2019] | HJK Helsinki - FC Lahti | 2-2(2-0,2-2,2-2); 4-2 pen |
| | IFK Mariehamn - Helsingin IFK | 0-0; 4-2 pen |

| Semi-Final [27.10.2019] | HJK Helsinki - IFK Mariehamn | 1-2(1-0,1-1) |

| Final [30.10.-03.11.2019] | IFK Mariehamn - FC Honka Espoo | 1-2(1-2) | 0-1(0-1) |

NATIONAL CUP
Suomen cup 2019

Group Stage [18.01.-03.03.2019]

Group A

FC Honka Espoo - FC Lahti	0-1
FC Inter Turku - IFK Mariehamn	2-1
HJK Helsinki - Helsingin IFK	1-0
HJK Helsinki - IFK Mariehamn	2-2
FC Lahti - Helsingin IFK	2-1
FC Inter Turku - HJK Helsinki	1-0
Helsingin IFK - FC Honka Espoo	1-2
IFK Mariehamn - FC Lahti	1-0
FC Inter Turku - FC Lahti	1-2
HJK Helsinki - FC Honka Espoo	2-3
Helsingin IFK - FC Inter Turku	1-3
FC Honka Espoo - IFK Mariehamn	0-0
FC Lahti - HJK Helsinki	1-4
FC Honka Espoo - FC Inter Turku	2-0
IFK Mariehamn - Helsingin IFK	3-0

Qualified: FC Honka Espoo, FC Inter Turku, FC Lahti, IFK Mariehamn

Group B

FC Ilves Tampere - Kuopion Palloseura	4-1
Kokkolan Palloveikot - Kuopion Palloseura	1-1
SJK Seinäjoki - Vaasan Palloseura	1-2
FC Ilves Tampere - Rovaniemen Palloseura	1-1
FC Ilves Tampere - SJK Seinäjoki	2-1
Vaasan Palloseura - Kuopion Palloseura	1-0
Kokkolan Palloveikot - FC Ilves Tampere	1-2
Kuopion Palloseura - SJK Seinäjoki	2-2
Vaasan Palloseura - Rovaniemen Palloseura	2-1
Rovaniemen Palloseura - SJK Seinäjoki	3-2
Vaasan Palloseura - Kokkolan Palloveikot	0-1
SJK Seinäjoki - Kokkolan Palloveikot	1-1
FC Ilves Tampere - Vaasan Palloseura	3-0
Rovaniemen Palloseura - Kokkolan Palloveikot	0-2
Rovaniemen Palloseura - Kuopion Palloseura	3-2

Qualified: FC Ilves Tampere, Vaasan Palloseura, Kokkolan Palloveikot, Rovaniemen Palloseura

Group C

FC Haka Valkeakoski - Myllykosken Pallo−47	2-2
Musan Salama Pori - FF Jaro Jakobstad	1-1
Myllykosken Pallo−47 - FF Jaro Jakobstad	0-0
FC Haka Valkeakoski - AC Oulu	2-1
FF Jaro Jakobstad - AC Oulu	1-3
Myllykosken Pallo−47 - Musan Salama Pori	1-4
Musan Salama Pori - FC Haka Valkeakoski	2-0
FF Jaro Jakobstad - FC Haka Valkeakoski	0-3
AC Oulu - Musan Salama Pori	0-0
AC Oulu - Myllykosken Pallo−47	4-0

Qualified: AC Oulu, FC Haka Valkeakoski

Group D

Turun Palloseura Turku - Tampereen Pallo-Veikot	2-0
FC Kotkan Työväen Palloilijat - AC Kajaani	4-1
Turun Palloseura Turku - Ekenäs IF	3-1
Tampereen Pallo-Veikot - AC Kajaani	6-0
FC Kotkan Työväen Palloilijat - Turun Palloseura Turku	3-2
Ekenäs IF - Tampereen Pallo-Veikot	3-5
Ekenäs IF - FC Kotkan Työväen Palloilijat	1-0
AC Kajaani - Turun Palloseura Turku	2-1
Tampereen Pallo-Veikot - FC Kotkan Työväen Palloilijat	1-1
AC Kajaani - Ekenäs IF	2-1

Qualified: Tampereen Pallo-Veikot, FC Kotkan Työväen Palloilijat

1/8-Finals [15-17.03.2019]

VJS - Kokkolan Palloveikot	0-3(0-1)	AC Oulu - FC Honka Espoo	0-1(0-0)
IF Gnistan - Vaasan Palloseura	1-3(0-0,1-1)	FC Kiisto - FC Lahti	0-5(0-1)
FC Haka Valkeakoski - Rovaniemen Palloseura	0-1(0-0)	Tampereen Pallo-Veikot - IFK Mariehamn	0-2(0-0)
FC Kotkan Työväen Palloilijat - FC Ilves Tampere	0-2(0-2)	JS Hercules - FC Inter Turku	0-2(0-1)

Quarter-Finals [30-31.03.2019]

| FC Inter Turku - Vaasan Palloseura | 1-2(1-0) | FC Honka Espoo - FC Ilves Tampere | 1-1 aet; 3-4 pen |
| Rovaniemen Palloseura - Kokkolan Palloveikot | 1-2(0-1) | IFK Mariehamn - FC Lahti | 3-1(0-1,1-1) |

Semi-Finals [16.05.2019]

| Kokkolan Palloveikot - FC Ilves Tampere | 2-3(2-1) | Vaasan Palloseura - IFK Mariehamn | 1-3(1-2) |

Final

15.06.2019; Wiklöf Holding Arena, Mariehamn; Referee: Toni Pohjoismäki; Attendance: 3,250

FC Ilves Tampere - IFK Mariehamn   **2-0(2-0)**

FC Ilves Tampere: Mika Hilander, David Addy, Felipe Aspegren, Baba Mensah, Tatu Miettunen, Matias Ojala (86.Diogo Tomas), Lauri Ala-Myllymäki, Jair Tavares da Silva, Yussif Daouda Moussa (77.Iiro Järvinen), Ilari Mettälä, Tiémoko Fofana (70.Emile Tendeng). Trainer: Jarkko Wiss.

IFK Mariehamn: Oskari Forsman, Robin Buwalda, Dylan Murnane, Aapo Mäenpää (89.Amos Ekhalie), Rick Ketting, Daniel Sjölund, Robin Sid, Robert David Crawford, Keaton Isaksson (59.Simon Silverholt), Hampus Lönn (67.Riku Sjöroos), Aristote Mboma. Trainer: Peter Lundberg.

Goals: 1-0 Matias Ojala (33), 2-0 Tatu Miettunen (44).

THE CLUBS 2019

Football Club Honska Espoo

Founded: 1957
Stadium: Tapiolan Urheilupuisto, Espoo (6,000)
Trainer: Vesa Vasara   16.08.1976

Goalkeepers:	DOB	M	(s)	G
Tim Murray (USA)	30.07.1987	27		
Defenders:	**DOB**	**M**	**(s)**	**G**
Henri Aalto	20.04.1989	20	(1)	1
Gideon Baah (GHA)	01.10.1991	17		1
Nasiru Banahene (HUN)	08.07.2000		(1)	
Robert Ivanov	21.07.1993	26	(1)	2
Joona Rahikka	29.01.1999		(1)	
Tommi Saarinen	31.01.1995	7	(2)	
Mikko Sumusalo	12.03.1990	22		3
Midfielders:	**DOB**	**M**	**(s)**	**G**
Abel Miguel Suárez Torres (ESP)	11.04.1991	5	(7)	2
Erik Bakker (NED)	21.03.1990	1	(2)	
Duarte Cartaxo-Tammilehto	15.02.1990	15		
Javier Hervás Salmoral „Javi Hervás" (ESP)	09.06.1989	22	(1)	1

	DOB	M	(s)	G
Armend Kabashi	04.12.1995	1	(4)	
Jonas Levänen	12.01.1994	1	(2)	
Lucas Paz Kaufmann (BRA)	26.03.1991	26		2
Joel Perovuo	11.08.1985	10	(11)	
Konsta Rasimus	15.12.1990	20	(1)	
Martin Salin	02.01.2002	2	(6)	1
Arlind Sejdiu	11.08.2001	2	(14)	2
Luis Saúl Silva López (MEX)	12.10.1988	10	(3)	3
Forwards:	**DOB**	**M**	**(s)**	**G**
Robbie Azodo	23.04.2001		(1)	
Borjas Martín González (ESP)	28.06.1987	26		13
Juha Hakola	27.10.1987	23	(1)	4
Elmo Heinonen	02.04.1997	1		
Macoumba Kandji (SEN)	02.08.1985	1	1	1
Demba Savage (GAM)	17.06.1988	12	(13)	4

Football Club International Turku

Founded: 1990
Stadium: Veritas Stadion, Turku (10,000)
Trainer: José Riveiro (ESP)   15.09.1975

Goalkeepers:	DOB	M	(s)	G
Aati Marttinen	26.12.1997	6		
Henrik Moisander	29.09.1985	21		
Defenders:	**DOB**	**M**	**(s)**	**G**
Luciano Damián Balbi (ARG)	04.04.1989	11		
Juuso Hämäläinen	30.11.1992	23		1
Arttu Hoskonen	16.04.1997	9	(7)	
Daniel Kamy Ntankeu Yves (CMR)	08.03.1996	4	(5)	1
Daan Klinkenberg (NED)	12.01.1996	22	(1)	1
Niko Markkula	27.06.1990	23	(1)	
Connor James Ruane (ENG)	15.11.1993	6	(1)	1
Miro Tenho	02.04.1995	23	(1)	1
Midfielders:	**DOB**	**M**	**(s)**	**G**
Álvaro Muñiz Cegarra (ESP)	07.09.1988	22	(1)	
Anthony Gildas Kofi Annan (GHA)	21.07.1986	3	(3)	

	DOB	M	(s)	G
Mikko Kuningas	30.07.1997	16	(8)	
Mikke Louhela	29.05.1997		(2)	
Niilo Mäenpää	14.01.1998	9	(12)	1
Elias Mastokangas	01.02.2001	4	(6)	
Aleksi Paananen	25.01.1993	20		2
Filip Valenčič (SVN)	07.01.1992	27		17
Forwards:	**DOB**	**M**	**(s)**	**G**
Albion Ademi (ALB)	19.02.1999	1	(10)	1
Hanson Tamba Boakai (CAN)	28.10.1996		(2)	
Timo Furuholm	11.10.1987	21	(4)	10
Joona Järvistö	29.12.1996	1	(3)	
Mika Ojala	21.06.1988	21	(3)	6
Eero Tamminen	19.05.1995	4	(3)	
Lassi Viholainen	16.06.1999		(2)	

Football Club Lahti

Founded: 1996
Stadium: Lahden Stadion, Lahti (15,000)
Trainer: Sami Ristilä   15.08.1974

Goalkeepers:	DOB	M	(s)	G
Patrick Rakovsky (CZE)	02.06.1993	26		
Joona Tiainen	07.05.2000	1		
Defenders:	**DOB**	**M**	**(s)**	**G**
Jean-Christophe Coubronne (FRA)	30.07.1989	23		
Lassi Forss	15.01.2002	1		
Mikko Hauhia	03.09.1984	24	(3)	
Josué Currais Prieto „Josu" (ESP)	27.02.1993	25	(1)	6
Jani Tanska	29.07.1988	18	(3)	1
Mikko Viitikko	18.04.1995	21	(2)	
Midfielders:	**DOB**	**M**	**(s)**	**G**
Teemu Jäntti	02.03.2000	9	(9)	1
Matti Klinga	10.12.1994	22	(2)	1
Pekka Lagerblom	19.10.1982	6	(6)	
Brent Lepistu (EST)	26.03.1993	7	(1)	

	DOB	M	(s)	G
Tim Martinen	28.11.1999		(5)	
Matias Niuta	09.03.2001		(1)	
Teemu Penninkangas	24.07.1992	22	(1)	1
Eemeli Virta	28.09.2000	21	(1)	1
Forwards:	**DOB**	**M**	**(s)**	**G**
Jerónimo Arturo Amione Cevallos (MEX)	31.03.1990	10	(4)	4
Jasin Assehnoun	26.12.1998	18	(8)	2
Gaël Junior Etock (CMR)	05.07.1993	15	(2)	5
Tomi Kult	04.07.2000	1	(9)	1
Pyry Lampinen	07.03.2002	7	(3)	2
Irfan Sadik	12.01.1999		(1)	
Ville Salmikivi	20.05.1992	10	(5)	
Drilon Shala	20.03.1987		(2)	
Erik Törnros (SWE)	11.06.1993	9	(7)	2
Altin Zeqiri	01.03.2000	1	(5)	1

Helsingin Idrottsföreningen Kamraterna

Founded: 1897
Stadium: Telia 5G-areena, Helsinki (10,770)
Trainer: Tor Thodesen (NOR)   03.03.1966

Goalkeepers:	DOB	M	(s)	G
Daniel Kollár	29.03.1994	15	(1)	
Arnold Origi Otieno (KEN)	15.11.1983	12		
Defenders:	**DOB**	**M**	**(s)**	**G**
Tuukka Andberg	01.05.1998	7	(5)	
Tero Mäntylä	18.04.1991	22		
Tino Palmasto	09.10.1998		(2)	1
Hannu Patronen	23.05.1984	20	(1)	
Hassan Sesay (SLE)	22.10.1987	20		1
Tobias Vibe (NOR)	19.08.1990	6	(2)	
Midfielders:	**DOB**	**M**	**(s)**	**G**
Jani Bäckman	20.03.1988	20	(2)	1
Jakob Dunsby (NOR)	13.03.2000	11	(1)	3
Xhevdet Gela (KVX)	14.11.1989	3	(2)	
Jukka Halme	30.11.1984	15	(1)	1
Matias Hänninen	15.03.1991	11	(4)	
Macario Hing-Glover (USA)	04.04.1995	9		
Robert Kakeeto (UGA)	19.05.1995	5		

	DOB	M	(s)	G
Fernando Cózar Torres „Nando Cózar" (ESP)	02.03.1991	1	(1)	
Riku Selander	22.11.1994	20	(2)	
Rafael Ferreira Francisco „Toró" (BRA)	13.04.1986	14		
Forwards:	**DOB**	**M**	**(s)**	**G**
Samuel Haglund	04.03.1997		(2)	
Njazi Kuqi	25.03.1983		(6)	
Kevin Larsson	15.09.2001	4	(13)	
Luis Henrique Farinhas Taffner (BRA)	17.03.1998	12	(1)	8
Elsaad Maher Taher Mohamed (EGY)	04.03.1991		(3)	
Foday Manneh (GAM)	14.01.2000		(4)	
Joel Mattsson	17.03.1999	20	(2)	4
Xusen Cabdikariim Maxamed (SOM)	20.03.1997		(3)	
Thais Damgaard Nielsen (DEN)	23.03.2000	1	(1)	-
Nikolas Saira	11.02.1999	10	(2)	
Jabar Sharza (AFG)	06.04.1994	8	(2)	2
Erikson Carlos Batista dos Santos „Tiquinho" (BRA)	26.02.1995	23	(3)	10
Sakari Ilmari Tukiainen	02.10.1991	8	(4)	5

Helsingin Jalkapalloklubi

Founded: 19.06.1907
Stadium: Telia 5G–areena, Helsinki (10,770)
Trainer: Mika Lehkosuo 08.01.1970
[23.05.2019] Toni Koskela 16.02.1983

Name	DOB	M	(s)	G
Goalkeepers:				
Maksim Rudakov (RUS)	22.01.1996	26		
Markus Uusitalo	15.05.1997	1		
Defenders:				
Elderson Uwa Echiéjilé (NGA)	20.01.1988	5		2
Kevin Kouassivi-Benissan	25.01.1999	4	(4)	
Samu Laitinen	13.08.1999		(1)	
Daniel O'Shaughnessy	14.09.1994	21	(3)	2
Faith Obilor (NGA)	05.03.1991	21		
Roni Peiponen	09.04.1997	6	(3)	
Rafinha Scapini de Almeida (BRA)	29.06.1982	20	(5)	1
Henri Toivomäki	21.02.1991	14	(3)	
Victor Luiz Prestes Filho (BRA)	05.12.1997	4		
Midfielders:				
Sebastian Dahlström	05.11.1996	21		2
Kaan Kairinen	22.12.1998	21	(1)	2
William Parra Sinisterra (COL)	01.03.1995	8		1
Matti Peltola	03.07.2002	1		
Riku Riski	16.08.1989	15	(2)	7
Harmeet Singh (NOR)	12.11.1990	8	(3)	
Santeri Väänänen	01.01.2002	6	(3)	
Joonas Vahtera	06.01.1996	2	(5)	
Eetu Vertainen	11.05.1999	13	(10)	2
Erfan Zeneli (KVX)	28.12.1986	3	(4)	
Forwards:				
Nikolai Alho	12.03.1993	20		
Marco Antonio Bueno Ontiveros (MEX)	31.03.1994	7	(2)	
Sekou Camara (ALB)	20.07.1997	1	(2)	
Jani Petteri Forsell	16.10.1990	7	(2)	1
Lassi Lappalainen	24.08.1998	15	(1)	3
Evans Mensah (GHA)	09.02.1998	14	(5)	6
Akseli Pelvas	08.02.1989	2	(6)	1
Ivan Tarasov (RUS)	30.01.2000	5	(7)	
Tim Väyrynen	30.03.1993	6	(4)	2

Idrottsföreningen Kamraterna Mariehamn

Founded: 1919
Stadium: Wiklöf Holding Arena, Mariehamn (4,000)
Trainer: Peter Lundberg 15.04.1981

Name	DOB	M	(s)	G
Goalkeepers:				
Oskari Forsman	28.01.1988	27		
Defenders:				
Robin Buwalda (NED)	17.08.1994	22		1
Tarik Hamza (SWE)	23.02.1997	7	(3)	
Lassi Järvenpää	28.10.1996	11	(4)	
Rick Ketting (NED)	15.11.1996	24	(1)	4
Aapo Mäenpää	14.01.1998	18	(2)	
Dylan Murnane (AUS)	18.01.1995	25		2
Midfielders:				
Gustaf Backaliden (SWE)	15.09.1997	15	(2)	2
Robert David Crawford (SCO)	19.03.1993	24		1
Amos Ekhalie (KEN)	08.07.1988	9	(11)	3
Keaton Isaksson	21.04.1994	19	(4)	6
Joel Karlstrom	17.05.2001	1	(7)	
Robin Sid	21.09.1994	21	(2)	2
Simon Silverholt (SWE)	17.06.1993	11	(6)	3
Daniel Sjölund	22.04.1983	16	(4)	
Forwards:				
Hampus Lönn (SWE)	28.10.1991	16	(8)	1
Aristote Mboma (COD)	30.06.1994	20	(2)	6
Riku Sjöroos	10.03.1995	11	(12)	

Tampereen Ilves

Founded: 1931
Stadium: Tammelan Stadion, Tampere (5,040)
Trainer: Jarkko Wiss 17.04.1972

Name	DOB	M	(s)	G
Goalkeepers:				
Mika Hilander	17.08.1983	27		
Defenders:				
David Addy (GHA)	21.02.1990	19		
Felipe Aspegren	12.02.1994	22	(1)	
Tariq Kazi	06.10.2000	2	(1)	
Baba Mensah (GHA)	20.08.1994	26		1
Tatu Miettunen	24.04.1995	25	(1)	2
Janne Saksela	14.03.1993	1	(1)	
Diogo Tomas	31.07.1997	9	(8)	1
Midfielders:				
Lauri Ala-Myllymäki	04.06.1997	24		12
Jair Tavares da Silva (BRA)	03.08.1994	25	(1)	2
Iiro Järvinen	03.11.1996	15	(7)	1
Janne-Pekka Laine	25.01.2001		(1)	
Yussif Daouda Moussa (NIG)	04.09.1998	16	(7)	2
Matias Ojala	28.02.1995	12	(1)	
Tuure Siira	25.10.1994	13	(7)	
Naatan Skyttä	07.05.2002	5	(6)	2
Emile Tendeng (SEN)	09.03.1992	14	(5)	1
Forwards:				
Samuel Afum (GHA)	24.12.1990	1	(1)	
Tiémoko Fofana (CIV)	22.10.1999	18	(7)	5
Jacques Haman (CMR)	30.08.1994	1	(6)	
Ilari Mettälä	26.04.1994	11	(9)	4
Eetu Mömmö	04.05.2002	1		
Eemeli Raittinen	03.02.2000	2	(5)	
Eero Tamminen	19.05.1995	5	(3)	
Aleksi Tarvonen	19.07.1994	3	(3)	

Kokkolan Palloveikot

Founded: 1930
Stadium: Kokkolan Keskuskenttä, Kokkola (2,000)
Trainer: Jarmo Korhonen 28.06.1964
[29.05.2019] Niko Kalliokoski 26.05.1982
[22.07.2019] Jani Uotinen 17.05.1978

Name	DOB	M	(s)	G
Goalkeepers:				
Teppo Marttinen	06.05.1997	21		
Joonas Myllymäki	09.09.1989	6		
Defenders:				
Miloš Josimov (SRB)	27.09.1984	21		2
El-Hadji Kane (SEN)	11.04.1995	5		
Juri Kinnunen	09.03.1990	21	(1)	
Ville Koskimaa	21.05.1983	25		1
Hysen Memolla (ALB)	03.07.1992	8		3
Juhani Pikkarainen	30.07.1998	9	(4)	
Timo Rauhala	07.09.1989	16	(3)	
Stefan Umjenovic (AUT)	11.08.1995	3	(1)	
Midfielders:				
Patrick Byskata	13.08.1990	11	(3)	
Maksim Gussev (EST)	20.07.1994	2	(8)	
Harri Heiermann	08.09.1996	11	(7)	2
Hendrik Helmke (GER)	13.07.1987	23		4
Sebastian Mannström	29.10.1988	18	(2)	2
Patrick Poutiainen	14.06.1991	3	(6)	
Isaac Shaze (GHA)	25.06.1989	14		
Adam Vidjeskog	07.07.1998	9	(5)	2
Ishmael Yartey (GHA)	11.01.1990	11		6
Forwards:				
Enoch Banza	04.02.2000	15	(9)	3
Filip Ivanovski (MKD)	01.05.1985	1	(3)	
Joni Mäkelä	28.09.1993	15	(6)	3
Yessy Ferley Mena Palacios (COL)	05.07.1989	6	(10)	
Simo Roiha	27.12.1990	18	(7)	4
Taiki Kagayama (JPN)	14.05.1996	5	(1)	

Kuopion Palloseura

Founded: 1923
Stadium: Savon Sanomat Areena, Kuopio (5,000)
Trainer: Jani Honkavaara 02.02.1976

Goalkeepers:	DOB	M	(s)	G
Miika Töyräs	05.06.1999	2		
Otso Virtanen	03.04.1994	25		
Defenders:	**DOB**	**M**	**(s)**	**G**
Babacar Diallo (SEN)	25.03.1989	18		3
Luc Landry Tabi Manga (CMR)	17.11.1994	15	(4)	
Luis Carlos Murillo (COL)	16.10.1990	23	(3)	
Jiri Nissinen	30.05.1997	2	(2)	
Juho Pirttijoki	30.07.1996	6	(5)	
Vinko Soldo (CRO)	15.02.1998	19	(2)	
Kalle Taimi	27.01.1992	12	(4)	
Midfielders:	**DOB**	**M**	**(s)**	**G**
Reuben Ayarna (GHA)	22.10.1985	15	(6)	2
Arttu Heinonen	22.04.1999		(8)	
Jere Hiltunen	11.06.1999	2	(2)	
Tommi Jyry	16.08.1999	18	(4)	1
Petteri Pennanen	19.09.1990	26	(1)	6
Ville Saxman	15.11.1989	25		6
Issa Thiaw (SEN)	12.10.1992	7	(5)	2
Forwards:	**DOB**	**M**	**(s)**	**G**
Rasmus Karjalainen	04.04.1996	10	(2)	3
Ariel Thierry Ngueukam (CMR)	15.11.1988	11	(1)	4
Ilmari Niskanen	27.10.1997	26		5
Eetu Pellikka	23.02.2000		(1)	
Ats Purje (EST)	03.08.1985	9	(7)	5
Lucas Rangel Nunes Gonvalves (BRA)	29.12.1994	8	(8)	8
Eetu Rissanen	15.10.2002	1	(3)	
Saku Savolainen	13.08.1996	17	(1)	

Rovaniemen Palloseura

Founded: 1950
Stadium: Rovaniemen keskuskenttä, Rovaniemi (4,000)
Trainer: Toni Koskela 16.02.1983
[23.05.2019] Pasi Tuutti 21.03.1979

Goalkeepers:	DOB	M	(s)	G
Antonio Reguero Chapinal (ESP)	04.07.1982	22		
Damjan Siskovski (MKD)	18.03.1995	5		
Defenders:	**DOB**	**M**	**(s)**	**G**
Juho Hyvärinen	27.03.2000	25	(1)	2
Kalle Katz	04.01.2000	16	(1)	
Kevin Kouassivi-Benissan	25.01.1999	5	(3)	1
Samuel Olawunmi Olabisi (NGA)	17.11.1993	2		
Henrik Ölander	29.10.1997	5	(9)	
Atte Sihvonen	18.02.1996	24	(2)	2
Mohamadou Sissoko (FRA)	08.08.1988	24		
Taye Ismaila Taïwo (NGA)	16.04.1985	27		1
Midfielders:	**DOB**	**M**	**(s)**	**G**
Agnaldo Pinto de Moraes Júnior (BRA)	11.03.1994	16	(3)	
Jagoba Beobide Larrañaga (ESP)	19.02.1987	10		
Tommi Jäntti	07.03.2000	8	(11)	1
Tuomas Kaukua	13.10.2000	3	(2)	
Lucas Lingman	25.01.1998	25	(1)	3
Eetu Muinonen	05.04.1986	18	(5)	2
Sergio Llamas Pardo (ESP)	06.03.1993	8	(1)	
Forwards:	**DOB**	**M**	**(s)**	**G**
Sampo Ala	18.01.2002	3	(5)	1
Santeri Haarala	17.12.1999		(1)	
Niklas Jokelainen	30.03.2000	7	(13)	2
Tarik Kada (NED)	26.05.1996	8	(4)	
Aleksandr Kokko	04.06.1987	7	(4)	1
Youness Rahimi	13.02.1995	21	(4)	5
Matias Tamminen	21.11.2001	8	(6)	2

Seinäjoen Jalkapallokerho

Founded: 05.11.2007
Stadium: OmaSP Stadion, Seinäjoki (6,000)
Trainer: Alexey Eremenko 17.01.1964
[16.08.2019] Brian Page (SCO) 24.07.1980

Goalkeepers:	DOB	M	(s)	G
Mihkel Aksalu (EST)	07.11.1984	15		
Jesse Öst	20.10.1990	12		
Defenders:	**DOB**	**M**	**(s)**	**G**
Samba Seynabou Benga (SEN)	24.11.1996	2		
Trevor Elhi (EST)	11.04.1993	14	(2)	
Dani Hatakka	12.03.1994	19	(2)	1
Jarkko Hurme	04.06.1986	7	(1)	
Didier Boris Kadio (CIV)	05.04.1990	15		
Joona Lautamaja	12.07.1995	2	(3)	
Joel Mero	07.02.1995	9	(3)	
José Nadson Ferreira (BRA)	18.10.1984	18		1
Joonas Sundman	20.01.1998	14	(2)	
Ville Tikkanen	08.08.1999	6	(1)	
Midfielders:	**DOB**	**M**	**(s)**	**G**
Jude Arthur (GHA)	08.06.1999	15	(6)	1
Zakaria Beglarishvili (GEO)	30.04.1990	2	(3)	
Sergey Eremenko (RUS)	06.01.1999	12	(2)	
Mehmet Hetemaj	08.12.1987	21	(1)	2
Obed Malolo	18.04.1997	11	(4)	
Moshtagh Yaghoubi	08.11.1994	15		1
Forwards:	**DOB**	**M**	**(s)**	**G**
Dion Jeremy Acoff (USA)	23.09.1991	11	(4)	
Arttu Aromaa	05.01.1995	1		
Serge Atakayi	30.01.1999	8	(2)	1
Daniel Håkans	26.10.2000		(2)	
William Greenwell Ions (ENG)	11.03.1994	6	(2)	
Jyri Kiuru	09.02.2000	3	(1)	
Joonas Lepistö	22.06.1998	2		
Matheus dos Santos Batista (BRA)	16.06.1995	8	(10)	2
Denys Oliynyk (UKR)	16.06.1987	24	(1)	8
Jesse Sarajärvi	20.05.1995	11	(7)	
Jeremiah Streng	08.11.2001	10	(7)	
Maximo Tolonen	04.03.2001	4	(12)	1

Vaasan Palloseura

Founded: 1924
Stadium: Elisa Stadion, Vaasa (6,000)
Trainer: Petri Vuorinen 31.08.1972
[08.07.2019] Christian Sund 28.12.1978

Goalkeepers:	DOB	M	(s)	G
Martin Kompalla (GER)	26.08.1992	23		
Valeriy Voskonyan (ARM)	06.04.1994	4		
Defenders:	**DOB**	**M**	**(s)**	**G**
Eero-Matti Auvinen	05.03.1996	17	(1)	1
Jesper Engström	24.04.1992	9		
Jonas Häkkinen (CAN)	21.03.1999	24	(2)	
Martti Haukioja	06.10.1999	16	(1)	
Hampus Holmgren	14.11.1995	13	(3)	
Timi Lahti	28.06.1990	20		2
Giuseppe Lo Giudice	18.12.2000	1		
Hindrek Ojamaa (EST)	12.06.1995	14	(4)	1
Midfielders:	**DOB**	**M**	**(s)**	**G**
Fabrice Gatambiye	19.01.2000	2	(6)	1
Aatu Kujanpää	27.07.1998	1	(2)	
Aatu Laatikainen	03.01.1997	8	(8)	
Juho Lähde	11.02.1991	13	(2)	1
Valtteri Lehtonen	30.04.2001	5	(1)	
Ricardo Wayne Morris (JAM)	11.02.1992	3	(5)	
Samba Sillah	10.01.1999	10	(7)	1
Sebastian Strandvall	16.09.1986	17	(3)	2
Jerry Voutilainen	29.03.1995	21		1
Forwards:	**DOB**	**M**	**(s)**	**G**
Samu Alanko	16.05.1998	10	(6)	2
Alain Richard Ebwelle (CMR)	28.09.1995	20	(1)	5
Steven Morrissey (JAM)	25.07.1986	21	(5)	7
Momodou Sarr	31.03.2000	20	(6)	4
Kostas Stavrothanasopoulos (GRE)	06.02.1992	5	(9)	1

SECOND LEVEL
Ykkönen 2019

1.	FC Haka Valkeakoski (*Promoted*)	27	24	2	1	76	-	22	74
2.	Turun Palloseura Turku (*Promotion Play-offs*)	27	16	7	4	45	-	23	55
3.	FF Jaro Jakobstad	27	12	7	8	53	-	40	43
4.	FC Kotkan Työväen Palloilijat	27	13	3	11	46	-	44	42
5.	Musan Salama Pori	27	11	5	11	40	-	54	38
6.	Ekenäs IF	27	9	3	15	42	-	55	30
7.	AC Oulu	27	7	8	12	34	-	30	29
8.	AC Kajaani	27	6	6	15	40	-	52	24
9.	Myllykosken Pallo-47	27	5	7	15	30	-	62	22
10.	Tampereen Pallo-Veikot (*Relegated*)	27	5	6	16	30	-	54	21

NATIONAL TEAM

INTERNATIONAL MATCHES
(16.07.2019 – 15.07.2020)

05.09.2019	Tampere	Finland - Greece	1-0(0-0)	(ECQ)
08.09.2019	Tampere	Finland - Italy	1-2(0-0)	(ECQ)
12.10.2019	Zenica	Bosnia and Herzegovina - Finland	4-1(2-0)	(ECQ)
15.10.2019	Turku	Finland - Armenia	3-0(1-0)	(ECQ)
15.11.2019	Helsinki	Finland - Liechtenstein	3-0(1-0)	(ECQ)
18.11.2019	Athína	Greece - Finland	2-1(0-1)	(ECQ)

05.09.2019   FINLAND - GREECE   **1-0(0-0)**   16th EC. Qualifiers

Ratinan Stadion, Tampere; Referee: Juan Martínez Munuera (Spain); Attendance: 16,163
FIN: Lukáš Hrádecký, Jukka Raitala, Paulus Verneri Arajuuri, Joona Marko Aleksi Toivio, Jere Uronen, Tim Sparv (Cap), Robin Lod, Pyry Henri Hidipo Soiri (90+3.Rasmus Schüller), Glen Kamara, Jasse Tuominen (87.Fredrik Jensen), Teemu Eino Antero Pukki (85.Rasmus Karjalainen). Trainer: Markku Kanerva.
Goal: Teemu Eino Antero Pukki (52 penalty).

08.09.2019   FINLAND - ITALY   **1-2(0-0)**   16th EC. Qualifiers

Ratinan Stadion, Tampere; Referee: Robert Madden (Scotland); Attendance: 16,292
FIN: Lukáš Hrádecký (Cap), Paulus Verneri Arajuuri, Joona Marko Aleksi Toivio, Albin Granlund (82.Pyry Henri Hidipo Soiri), Jere Uronen, Sauli Aapo Kasperi Väisänen, Rasmus Schüller (87.Joni Kauko), Robin Lod, Glen Kamara, Lassi Lappalainen (75.Jasse Tuominen), Teemu Eino Antero Pukki. Trainer: Markku Kanerva.
Goal: Teemu Eino Antero Pukki (72 penalty).

12.10.2019   BOSNIA AND HERZEGOVINA - FINLAND   **4-1(2-0)**   16th EC. Qualifiers

Stadion Bilino Polje, Zenica; Referee: Ivan Kružliak (Slovakia); Attendance: 8,193
FIN: Lukáš Hrádecký, Jukka Raitala, Paulus Verneri Arajuuri (5.Sauli Aapo Kasperi Väisänen), Joona Marko Aleksi Toivio, Jere Uronen, Tim Sparv (Cap) (71.Joni Kauko), Robin Lod, Glen Kamara, Pyry Henri Hidipo Soiri (46.Joel Pohjanpalo), Jasse Tuominen, Teemu Eino Antero Pukki. Trainer: Markku Kanerva.
Goal: Joel Pohjanpalo (79).

15.10.2019   FINLAND - ARMENIA   **3-0(1-0)**   16th EC. Qualifiers

Veritas Stadion, Turku; Referee: Jesús Gil Manzano (Spain); Attendance: 7,231
FIN: Lukáš Hrádecký (Cap), Jukka Raitala, Joona Marko Aleksi Toivio, Jere Uronen, Sauli Aapo Kasperi Väisänen, Joni Kauko, Robin Lod, Glen Kamara (87.Rasmus Schüller), Fredrik Jensen (53.Joel Pohjanpalo), Lassi Lappalainen (61.Pyry Henri Hidipo Soiri), Teemu Eino Antero Pukki. Trainer: Markku Kanerva.
Goals: Fredrik Jensen (31), Teemu Eino Antero Pukki (61, 88).

15.11.2019   FINLAND - LIECHTENSTEIN   **3-0(1-0)**   16th EC. Qualifiers

Telia 5G-areena, Helsinki; Referee: Benoît Bastien (France); Attendance: 9,804
FIN: Lukáš Hrádecký, Jukka Raitala, Juha Pirinen, Paulus Verneri Arajuuri, Joona Marko Aleksi Toivio, Tim Sparv (Cap) (71.Joni Kauko), Robin Lod, Glen Kamara, Pyry Henri Hidipo Soiri (78.Simon Skrabb), Jasse Tuominen, Teemu Eino Antero Pukki (84.Rasmus Karjalainen). Trainer: Markku Kanerva.
Goals: Jasse Tuominen (21), Teemu Eino Antero Pukki (64 penalty, 75).

18.11.2019   GREECE - FINLAND   **2-1(0-1)**   16th EC. Qualifiers

Stádio Olympiako „Spiros Louis", Athína; Referee: Aleksei Eskov (Russia); Attendance: 5,453
FIN: Jesse Joronen, Jukka Raitala, Joona Marko Aleksi Toivio (Cap) (59.Thomas Lam), Sauli Aapo Kasperi Väisänen, Leo Väisänen, Rasmus Schüller (77.Fredrik Jensen), Joni Kauko, Robin Lod, Glen Kamara, Simon Skrabb (77.Pyry Henri Hidipo Soiri), Teemu Eino Antero Pukki. Trainer: Markku Kanerva.
Goal: Teemu Eino Antero Pukki (27).

NATIONAL TEAM PLAYERS
(16.07.2019 – 15.07.2020)

Name	DOB	Caps	Goals	2019/2020:	Club
Goalkeepers					
Lukáš HRÁDECKÝ	24.11.1989	58	0	2019:	*TSV Bayer 04 Leverkusen (GER)*
Jesse JORONEN	21.03.1993	8	0	2019:	*Brescia Calcio (ITA)*
Defenders					
Paulus Verneri ARAJUURI	15.06.1988	43	3	2019:	*Pafos FC Paphos (CYP)*
Albin GRANLUND	01.09.1989	17	0	2019:	*Örebro SK (SWE)*
Juha PIRINEN	22.10.1991	18	0	2019:	*Tromsø IL (NOR)*
Jukka RAITALA	15.09.1988	51	0	2019:	*Montréal Impact FC (CAN)*
Joona Marko Aleksi TOIVIO	10.03.1988	65	3	2019:	*BK Häcken Göteborg (SWE)*
Jere URONEN	13.07.1994	40	1	2019:	*KRC Genk (BEL)*
Leo VÄISÄNEN	23.07.1997	2	0	2019:	*FC Den Bosch (NED)*
Sauli Aapo Kasperi VÄISÄNEN	05.06.1994	19	0	2019:	*AC Chievo Verona (ITA)*
Midfielders					
Fredrik JENSEN	09.09.1997	11	4	2019:	*FC Augsburg (GER)*
Glen KAMARA	28.10.1995	19	1	2019:	*Rangers FC Glasgow (SCO)*
Joni KAUKO	12.07.1990	18	0	2019:	*Esbjerg fB (DEN)*
Thomas LAM	18.12.1993	22	0	2019:	*PEC Zwolle (NED)*
Robin LOD	17.04.1993	39	3	2019:	*Minnesota United FC (USA)*
Rasmus SCHÜLLER	18.06.1991	40	0	2019:	*Minnesota United FC (USA)*
Simon SKRABB	19.01.1995	14	0	2019:	*IFK Norrköping (SWE)*
Pyry Henri Hidipo SOIRI	22.09.1994	22	5	2019:	*Esbjerg fB (DEN)*
Tim SPARV	20.02.1987	74	1	2019:	*FC Midtjylland Herning (DEN)*
Forwards					
Rasmus KARJALAINEN	04.04.1996	9	1	2019:	*Fortuna Sittard (NED)*
Lassi LAPPALAINEN	24.08.1998	7	0	2019:	*Montréal Impact FC (CAN)*
Joel POHJANPALO	13.09.1994	32	7	2019:	*TSV Bayer 04 Leverkusen (GER)*
Teemu Eino Antero PUKKI	29.03.1990	80	25	2019:	*Norwich City FC (ENG)*
Jasse TUOMINEN	12.11.1995	15	1	2019:	*FC BATE Borisov (BLR)*

National team coach

Markku KANERVA [from 12.12.2016]   24.05.1964   34 M; 18 W; 5 D; 11 L; 44-29
Complete record as trainer of Finland:
40 M; 20 W; 8 D; 12 L; 49-34
(09.02.2011 – 29.03.2011) & (04.09.2015 – 11.10.2015) &
(09.01.2017 – 18.11.2019)

FRANCE

FFF

The Country:
French Republic (République française)
Capital: Paris
Surface: 643,801 km²
Inhabitants: 67,186,638 [2017]
Time: UTC+1

The FA:
Fédération Française de Football
87, Boulevard de Grenelle, 75738 Paris Cedex 15
Tel: +33 1 4431 7300
Foundation date: 07.04.1919
Member of FIFA since: 1907
Member of UEFA since: 1954
Website: www.fff.fr

NATIONAL TEAM RECORDS

RECORDS		
First international match:	01.05.1994, Bruxelles:	Belgium – France 3-3
Most international caps:	Lilian Thuram	- 142 caps (1994-2008)
Most international goals:	Thierry Daniel Henry	- 51 goals / 123 caps (1997-2010)

UEFA EUROPEAN CHAMPIONSHIP

1960	Final Tournament (4th Place)
1964	Qualifiers
1968	Qualifiers
1972	Qualifiers
1976	Qualifiers
1980	Qualifiers
1984	**Final Tournament (Winners)**
1988	Qualifiers
1992	Final Tournament (Group Stage)
1996	Final Tournament (Semi-Finals)
2000	**Final Tournament (Winners)**
2004	Final Tournament (Quarter-Finals)
2008	Final Tournament (Group Stage)
2012	Final Tournament (Quarter-Finals)
2016	Final Tournament (Runners-up)
2020	*Final Tournament (Qualified)*

FIFA WORLD CUP

1930	Final Tournament (Group Stage)
1934	Final Tournament (1st Round)
1938	Final Tournament (Quarter-Finals)
1950	*Withdrew*
1954	Final Tournament (Group Stage)
1958	Final Tournament (3rd Place)
1962	Qualifiers
1966	Final Tournament (Group Stage)
1970	Qualifiers
1974	Qualifiers
1978	Final Tournament (Group Stage)
1982	Final Tournament (4th Place)
1986	Final Tournament (3rd Place)
1990	Qualifiers
1994	Qualifiers
1998	**Final Tournament (Winners)**
2002	Final Tournament (Group Stage)
2006	Final Tournament (Runners-up)
2010	Final Tournament (Group Stage)
2014	Final Tournament (Quarter-Finals)
2018	**Final Tournament (Winners)**

OLYMPIC TOURNAMENTS

1908	Final Tournament
1912	-
1920	Semi-Finals
1924	Quarter-Finals
1928	1/8-Finals
1936	-
1948	Quarter-Finals
1952	Qualifiers
1956	-
1960	Group Stage
1964	Qualifiers
1968	Quarter-Finals
1972	Qualifiers
1976	Quarter-Finals
1980	Qualifiers
1984	**Winners**
1988	Qualifiers
1992	Qualifiers
1996	Quarter-Finals
2000	Qualifiers
2004	Qualifiers
2008	Qualifiers
2012	Qualifiers
2016	Qualifiers

UEFA NATIONS LEAGUE

2018/2019 – League A

FIFA CONFEDERATIONS CUP 1992-2017

2001 (Winners), 2003 (Winners)

FRENCH CLUB HONOURS IN EUROPEAN CLUB COMPETITIONS:

European Champion Clubs' Cup (1956-1992) / UEFA Champions League (1993-2020)		
Olympique de Marseille	1	1992/1993
Fairs Cup (1858-1971) / UEFA Cup (1972-2009) / UEFA Europa League (2010-2020)		
None		
UEFA Super Cup (1972-2019)		
None		
European Cup Winners' Cup 1961-1999		
Paris Saint-Germain FC	1	1995/1996

defunct competition

NATIONAL COMPETITIONS
TABLE OF HONOURS

	CHAMPIONS	CUP WINNERS	BEST GOALSCORERS	
1893/1894	Standard Athletic Club Paris	-	-	
1894/1895	Standard Athletic Club Paris	-	-	
1895/1896	Club Français Paris	-	-	
1896/1897	Standard Athletic Club Paris	-	-	
1897/1898	Standard Athletic Club Paris	-	-	
1898/1899	Le Havre AC	-	-	
1899/1900	Le Havre AC	-	-	
1900/1901	Standard Athletic Club Paris	-	-	
1901/1902	Racing Club de Roubaix	-	-	
1902/1903	Racing Club de Roubaix	-	-	
1903/1904	Racing Club de Roubaix	-	-	
1904/1905	Gallia Club Paris	-	-	
1905/1906	Racing Club de Roubaix	-	-	
1906/1907	Racing Club de France Paris	-	-	
1907/1908	Racing Club de Roubaix	-	-	
1908/1909	Stade Helvétique de Marseille	-	-	
1909/1910	US Tourcoing	-	-	
1910/1911	Stade Helvétique de Marseille	-	-	
1911/1912	Stade Saint-Raphaëlois	-	-	
1912/1913	Stade Helvétique de Marseille	-	-	
1913/1914	Olympique Lillois	-	-	
1914/1915	*No competition*	-	-	
1915/1916	*No competition*	-	-	
1916/1917	*No competition*	-	-	
1917/1918	*No competition*	Olympique de Pantin	-	
1918/1919	Le Havre AC	CASG Paris	-	
1919/1920	*No competition*	Cercle Athlétique de Paris	-	
1920/1921	*No competition*	Red Star FC Paris	-	
1921/1922	*No competition*	Red Star FC Paris	-	
1922/1923	*No competition*	Red Star FC Paris	-	
1923/1924	*No competition*	Olympique de Marseille	-	
1924/1925	*No competition*	CASG Paris	-	
1925/1926	*No competition*	Olympique de Marseille	-	
1926/1927	Cercle Athlétique de Paris	Olympique de Marseille	-	
1927/1928	Stade Français Paris	Red Star FC Paris	-	
1928/1929	Olympique de Marseille	Montpellier Hérault Sport Club	-	
1929/1930	*No competition*	FC Sète	-	
1930/1931	*No competition*	Club Français Paris	-	
1931/1932	*No competition*	AS Cannes	-	
1932/1933	Olympique Lillois	Excelsior Athlétic Club de Roubaix	Walter Kaiser (GER, Stade Rennais FC) Robert Mercier (Club Français Paris)	15
1933/1934	FC Sète	FC Sète	István Lukács (HUN, FC Sète)	28
1934/1935	Sochaux	Olympique de Marseille	André Abegglen (SUI, FC Sochaux-Montbéliard)	30
1935/1936	Racing Club de France Paris	RC Paris	Roger Courtois (FC Sochaux-Montbéliard)	34
1936/1937	Olympique de Marseille	FC FC Sochaux-Montbéliard	Oskar Rohr (GER, Racing Club de Strasbourg)	30
1937/1938	FC Sochaux-Montbéliard	Olympique de Marseille	Jean Nicolas (FC Rouen)	26
1938/1939	FC Sète	Racing Club de France Paris	Roger Courtois (FC Sochaux-Montbéliard) Désiré Koranyi (FC Sète)	27
1939/1940	*No competition*	Racing Club de France Paris	-	
1940/1941	*No competition*	FC Girondins de Bordeaux	-	
1941/1942	*No competition*	Red Star FC Paris	-	
1942/1943	*No competition*	Olympique de Marseille	-	
1943/1944	*No competition*	Équipe fédérale Nancy-Lorraine	-	
1944/1945	*No competition*	Racing Club de France Paris	-	
1945/1946	Lille OSC	Lille OSC	René Bihel (Lille OSC)	28
1946/1947	Racing Club de Roubaix–Tourcoing	Lille OSC	Pierre Sinibaldi (Stade de Reims)	33
1947/1948	Olympique de Marseille	Lille OSC	Jean Baratte (Lille OSC)	31
1948/1949	Stade de Reims	Racing Club de France Paris	Jean Baratte (Lille OSC) Josef Humpál (CZE, FC Sochaux-Montbéliard)	26
1949/1950	FC Girondins de Bordeaux	Stade de Reims	Jean Grumellon (Stade Rennais FC)	25
1950/1951	OGC Nice	Racing Club de Strasbourg	Roger Piantoni (AS Nancy-Lorraine) Jean Courteaux (OGC Nice)	27
1951/1952	OGC Nice	OGC Nice	Gunnar Andersson (SWE, Olympique de Marseille)	31
1952/1953	Stade de Reims	Lille OSC	Gunnar Andersson (SWE, Olympique de Marseille)	35
1953/1954	Lille OSC	OGC Nice	Édouard Kargu (FC Girondins de Bordeaux)	27
1954/1955	Stade de Reims	Lille OSC	René Bliard (Stade de Reims)	30
1955/1956	OGC Nice	CS Sedan	Thadée Cisowski (Racing Club de France Paris)	31
1956/1957	AS Saint-Étienne	Toulouse FC	Thadée Cisowski (Racing Club de France Paris)	33
1957/1958	Stade de Reims	Stade de Reims	Just Fontaine (Stade de Reims)	34
1958/1959	OGC Nice	Le Havre AC	Thadée Cisowski (Racing Club de France Paris)	30
1959/1960	Stade de Reims	AS Monaco FC	Just Fontaine (Stade de Reims)	28

1960/1961	AS Monaco FC	CS Sedan	Roger Piantoni (Stade de Reims)	28
1961/1962	Stade de Reims	AS Saint-Étienne	Sékou Touré (CIV, Montpellier Hérault Sport Club)	25
1962/1963	AS Monaco FC	AS Monaco FC	Serge Masnaghetti (USVA Valenciennes)	35
1963/1964	AS Saint-Étienne	Olympique Lyonnais	Ahmed Oudjani (ALG, Racing Club de Lens)	30
1964/1965	FC Nantes	Stade Rennais FC	Jacques Simon (FC Nantes)	24
1965/1966	FC Nantes	Racing Club de Strasbourg	Philippe Gondet (FC Nantes)	36
1966/1967	AS Saint-Étienne	Olympique Lyonnais	Hervé Revelli (AS Saint-Étienne)	31
1967/1968	AS Saint-Étienne	AS Saint-Étienne	Étienne Sansonetti (AC Ajaccio)	26
1968/1969	AS Saint-Étienne	Olympique de Marseille	André Guy (Olympique Lyonnais)	25
1969/1970	AS Saint-Étienne	AS Saint-Étienne	Hervé Revelli (AS Saint-Étienne)	28
1970/1971	Olympique de Marseille	Stade Rennais FC	Josip Skoblar (YUG, Olympique de Marseille)	44
1971/1972	Olympique de Marseille	Olympique de Marseille	Josip Skoblar (YUG, Olympique de Marseille)	30
1972/1973	FC Nantes	Olympique Lyonnais	Josip Skoblar (YUG, Olympique de Marseille)	26
1973/1974	AS Saint-Étienne	AS Saint-Étienne	Carlos Arcecio Bianchi (ARG, Stade de Reims)	30
1974/1975	AS Saint-Étienne	AS Saint-Étienne	Delio Onnis (ARG, AS Monaco FC)	30
1975/1976	AS Saint-Étienne	Olympique de Marseille	Carlos Arcecio Bianchi (ARG, Stade de Reims)	34
1976/1977	FC Nantes	AS Saint-Étienne	Carlos Arcecio Bianchi (ARG, Stade de Reims)	28
1977/1978	AS Monaco FC	AS Nancy-Lorraine	Carlos Arcecio Bianchi (ARG, Paris Saint-Germain FC)	37
1978/1979	Racing Club de Strasbourg	FC Nantes	Carlos Arcecio Bianchi (ARG, Paris Saint-Germain FC)	27
1979/1980	FC Nantes	AS Monaco FC	Erwin Kostedde (GER, Stade Lavallois) Delio Onnis (ARG, AS Monaco FC)	21
1980/1981	AS Saint-Étienne	SC Bastia	Delio Onnis (ARG, Tours FC)	24
1981/1982	AS Monaco FC	Paris Saint-Germain FC	Delio Onnis (ARG, Tours FC)	29
1982/1983	FC Nantes	Paris Saint-Germain FC	Vahid Halilhodžić (YUG, FC Nantes)	27
1983/1984	FC Girondins de Bordeaux	FC Metz	Patrice Garande (AJ Auxerre) Delio Onnis (ARG, Sporting Club Toulon)	21
1984/1985	FC Girondins de Bordeaux	AS Monaco FC	Vahid Halilhodžić (YUG, FC Nantes)	28
1985/1986	Paris Saint-Germain FC	FC Girondins de Bordeaux	Jules François Bocandé (SEN, FC Metz)	23
1986/1987	FC Girondins de Bordeaux	FC Girondins de Bordeaux	Bernard Zénier (FC Metz)	18
1987/1988	AS Monaco FC	FC Metz	Jean-Pierre Papin (Olympique de Marseille)	19
1988/1989	Olympique de Marseille	Olympique de Marseille	Jean-Pierre Papin (Olympique de Marseille)	22
1989/1990	Olympique de Marseille	Montpellier Hérault Sport Club	Jean-Pierre Papin (Olympique de Marseille)	30
1990/1991	Olympique de Marseille	AS Monaco FC	Jean-Pierre Papin (Olympique de Marseille)	23
1991/1992	Olympique de Marseille	Not played to end	Jean-Pierre Papin (Olympique de Marseille)	27
1992/1993	No winner was declared by FFF	Paris Saint-Germain FC	Alen Bokšić (CRO, Olympique de Marseille)	22
1993/1994	Paris Saint-Germain FC	AJ Auxerre	Roger Zokou Boli (Racing Club de Lens) Youri Djorkaeff (AS Monaco FC) Nicolas Pierre Ouédec (FC Nantes)	20
1994/1995	FC Nantes	Paris Saint-Germain FC	Patrice Loko (FC Nantes)	22
1995/1996	AJ Auxerre	AJ Auxerre	Anderson da Silva (BRA, AS Monaco FC)	21
1996/1997	AS Monaco FC	OGC Nice	Stéphane Pierre Yves Guivarc'h (Stade Rennais FC)	21
1997/1998	Racing Club de Lens	Paris Saint-Germain FC	Stéphane Pierre Yves Guivarc'h (AJ Auxerre)	21
1998/1999	FC Girondins de Bordeaux	FC Nantes	Sylvain Wiltord (FC Girondins de Bordeaux)	22
1999/2000	AS Monaco FC	FC Nantes	Anderson da Silva (BRA, Olympique Lyonnais)	23
2000/2001	FC Nantes	Racing Club de Strasbourg	Anderson da Silva (BRA, Olympique Lyonnais)	22
2001/2002	Olympique Lyonnais	FC Lorient	Djibril Cissé (AJ Auxerre) Pedro Miguel Carreiro Resendes "Pauleta" (POR, FC Girondins de Bordeaux)	22
2002/2003	Olympique Lyonnais	AJ Auxerre	Shabani Christophe Nonda (COD, AS Monaco FC)	26
2003/2004	Olympique Lyonnais	Paris Saint-Germain FC	Djibril Cissé (AJ Auxerre)	26
2004/2005	Olympique Lyonnais	AJ Auxerre	Alexander Frei (SUI, Stade Rennais FC)	20
2005/2006	Olympique Lyonnais	Paris Saint-Germain FC	Pedro Miguel Carreiro Resendes "Pauleta" (POR, Paris Saint-Germain FC)	21
2006/2007	Olympique Lyonnais	FC Sochaux-Montbéliard	Pedro Miguel Carreiro Resendes "Pauleta" (POR, Paris Saint-Germain FC)	15
2007/2008	Olympique Lyonnais	Olympique Lyonnais	Karim Mostafa Benzema (Olympique Lyonnais)	20
2008/2009	FC Girondins de Bordeaux	En Avant de Guingamp	André-Pierre Christian Gignac (Toulouse FC)	24
2009/2010	Olympique de Marseille	Paris Saint-Germain FC	Mamadou Hamidou Niang (SEN, Olympique de Marseille)	18
2010/2011	Lille OSC	Lille OSC	Moussa Sow (SEN, Lille OSC)	25
2011/2012	Montpellier Hérault Sport Club	Olympique Lyonnais	Olivier Giroud (Montpellier Hérault Sport Club) Anderson Luiz de Carvalho "Nenê" (BRA, Paris Saint-Germain FC)	21
2012/2013	Paris Saint-Germain FC	FC Girondins de Bordeaux	Zlatan Ibrahimović (SWE, Paris Saint-Germain FC)	30
2013/2014	Paris Saint-Germain FC	En Avant de Guingamp	Zlatan Ibrahimović (SWE, Paris Saint-Germain FC)	26
2014/2015	Paris Saint-Germain FC	Paris Saint-Germain FC	Alexandre Lacazette (Olympique Lyonnais)	27
2015/2016	Paris Saint-Germain FC	Paris Saint-Germain FC	Zlatan Ibrahimović (SWE, Paris Saint-Germain FC)	38
2016/2017	AS Monaco FC	Paris Saint-Germain FC	Edinson Roberto Cavani Gómez (URU, Paris Saint-Germain FC)	35
2017/2018	Paris Saint-Germain FC	Paris Saint-Germain FC	Edinson Roberto Cavani Gómez (URU, Paris Saint-Germain FC)	28
2018/2019	Paris Saint-Germain FC	Stade Rennais FC	Kylian Sanmi Mbappé Lottin (Paris Saint-Germain FC)	33
2019/2020	Paris Saint-Germain FC	Paris Saint-Germain FC	Wissam Ben Yedder (AS Monaco FC) Kylian Sanmi Mbappé Lottin (Paris Saint-Germain FC)	18

1963/1964	Racing Club de Strasbourg	1998/1999	Racing Club de Lens	2009/2010	Olympique de Marseille
1964/1965	FC Nantes	1999/2000	FC Gueugnon	2010/2011	Olympique de Marseille
1981/1982	Stade Lavallois	2000/2001	Olympique Lyonnais	2011/2012	Olympique de Marseille
1983/1984	Stade Lavallois	2001/2002	FC Girondins de Bordeaux	2012/2013	AS Saint-Étienne
1985/1986	FC Metz	2002/2003	AS Monaco FC	2013/2014	Paris Saint-Germain FC
1990/1991	Stade de Reims	2003/2004	FC Sochaux-Montbéliard	2014/2015	Paris Saint-Germain FC
1991/1992	Montpellier Hérault Sport Club	2004/2005	Racing Club de Strasbourg	2015/2016	Paris Saint-Germain FC
1993/1994	Racing Club de Lens	2005/2006	AS Nancy-Lorraine	2016/2017	Paris Saint-Germain FC
1994/1995	Paris Saint-Germain FC	2006/2007	FC Girondins de Bordeaux	2017/2018	Paris Saint-Germain FC
1995/1996	FC Metz	2007/2008	Paris Saint-Germain FC	2018/2019	Racing Club de Strasbourg
1996/1997	Racing Club de Strasbourg	2008/2009	FC Girondins de Bordeaux	2019/2020	Paris Saint-Germain FC
1997/1998	Paris Saint-Germain FC				

*Competition called: Coupe de la Ligue (1963–1965), Coupe d'Été/Coupe de la Ligue (1982–1994) and Coupe de la Ligue (since 1994).

NATIONAL CHAMPIONSHIP
Ligue 1 2019/2020
(09.08.2019 – 08.03.2020)

Results

Round 1 [09-11.08.2019]
AS Monaco - Olympique Lyon 0-3(0-2)
Olympique Marseille - Stade Reims 0-2(0-0)
Angers SCO - Bordeaux 3-1(3-1)
Dijon FCO - Saint-Étienne 1-2(1-2)
Montpellier - Stade Rennais 0-1(0-1)
OGC Nice - Amiens SC 2-1(1-0)
Stade Brestois - Toulouse FC 1-1(1-0)
Lille OSC - FC Nantes 2-1(1-0)
RC Strasbourg - FC Metz 1-1(1-0)
Paris Saint-Germain - Nîmes Olymp. 3-0(1-0)

Round 2 [16-18.08.2019]
Olympique Lyon - Angers SCO 6-0(3-0)
FC Nantes - Olympique Marseille 0-0
FC Metz - AS Monaco 3-0(1-0)
Toulouse FC - Dijon FCO 1-0(0-0)
Bordeaux - Montpellier 1-1(0-1)
Nîmes Olympique - OGC Nice 1-2(1-2)
Amiens SC - Lille OSC 1-0(0-0)
Saint-Étienne - Stade Brestois 1-1(0-1)
Stade Reims - RC Strasbourg 0-0
Stade Rennais - Paris Saint-Germain 2-1(1-1)

Round 3 [24-28.08.2019]
Dijon FCO - Bordeaux 0-2(0-1)
Amiens SC - FC Nantes 1-2(0-0)
Angers SCO - FC Metz 3-0(2-0)
Stade Brestois - Stade Reims 1-0(0-0)
AS Monaco - Nîmes Olympique 2-2(2-0)
RC Strasbourg - Stade Rennais 0-2(0-1)
Paris Saint-Germain - Toulouse FC 4-0(0-0)
Montpellier - Olympique Lyon 1-0(1-0)
Lille OSC - Saint-Étienne 3-0(1-0)
OGC Nice - Olympique Marseille 1-2(0-1)

Round 4 [30.08.-01.09.2019]
FC Metz - Paris Saint-Germain 0-2(0-2)
Olympique Lyon - Bordeaux 1-1(1-0)
FC Nantes - Montpellier 1-0(0-0)
Toulouse FC - Amiens SC 2-0(0-0)
Nîmes Olympique - Stade Brestois 3-0(2-0)
Angers SCO - Dijon FCO 2-0(0-0)
Stade Reims - Lille OSC 2-0(0-0)
Stade Rennais - OGC Nice 1-2(1-0)
RC Strasbourg - AS Monaco 2-2(1-2)
Olympique Marseille - Saint-Étienne 1-0(1-0)

Round 5 [13-15.09.2019]
Lille OSC - Angers SCO 2-1(1-0)
Amiens SC - Olympique Lyon 2-2(1-2)
Paris Saint-Germain - RC Strasbourg 1-0(0-0)
Dijon FCO - Nîmes Olympique 0-0
Bordeaux - FC Metz 2-0(2-0)
Montpellier - OGC Nice 2-1(1-1)
Stade Brestois - Stade Rennais 0-0
FC Nantes - Stade Reims 1-0(0-0)
Saint-Étienne - Toulouse FC 2-2(1-2)
AS Monaco - Olympique Marseille 3-4(2-2)

Round 6 [20-22.09.2019]
RC Strasbourg - FC Nantes 2-1(0-1)
Olympique Marseille - Montpellier 1-1(0-1)
FC Metz - Amiens SC 1-2(0-1)
Bordeaux - Stade Brestois 2-2(1-2)
OGC Nice - Dijon FCO 2-1(1-1)
Nîmes Olympique - Toulouse FC 1-0(1-0)
Stade Reims - AS Monaco 0-0
Stade Rennais - Lille OSC 1-1(0-0)
Angers SCO - Saint-Étienne 4-1(0-1)
Olympique Lyon - Paris St-Germain 0-1(0-0)

Round 7 [24-25.09.2019]
Dijon FCO - Olympique Marseille 0-0
AS Monaco - OGC Nice 3-1(1-0)
Saint-Étienne - FC Metz 1-0(0-0)
FC Nantes - Stade Rennais 1-0(0-0)
Toulouse FC - Angers SCO 0-2(0-0)
Montpellier - Nîmes Olympique 1-0(1-0)
Lille OSC - RC Strasbourg 2-0(1-0)
Amiens SC - Bordeaux 1-3(1-2)
Stade Brestois - Olympique Lyon 2-2(1-1)
Paris Saint-Germain - Stade Reims 0-2(0-1)

Round 8 [28-29.09.2019]
Olympique Lyon - FC Nantes 0-1(0-0)
Bordeaux - Paris Saint-Germain 0-1(0-0)
AS Monaco - Stade Brestois 4-1(1-0)
FC Metz - Toulouse FC 2-2(1-0)
OGC Nice - Lille OSC 1-1(1-1)
Angers SCO - Amiens SC 1-1(0-1)
Stade Reims - Dijon FCO 1-2(1-1)
RC Strasbourg - Montpellier 1-0(1-0)
Nîmes Olympique - Saint-Étienne 0-1(0-0)
Olympique Marseille - Stade Rennais 1-1(0-1)

Round 9 [04-06.10.2019]
Amiens SC - Olympique Marseille 3-1(2-1)
Paris Saint-Germain - Angers SCO 4-0(2-0)
Dijon FCO - RC Strasbourg 1-0(1-0)
FC Nantes - OGC Nice 1-0(0-0)
Toulouse FC - Bordeaux 1-3(0-2)
Montpellier - AS Monaco 3-1(2-0)
Stade Brestois - FC Metz 2-0(2-0)
Lille OSC - Nîmes Olympique 2-2(1-1)
Stade Rennais - Stade Reims 0-1(0-0)
Saint-Étienne - Olympique Lyon 1-0(0-0)

Round 10 [18-20.10.2019]
OGC Nice - Paris Saint-Germain 1-4(0-2)
Olympique Lyon - Dijon FCO 0-0
FC Metz - FC Nantes 1-0(0-0)
Toulouse FC - Lille OSC 2-1(0-0)
Nîmes Olympique - Amiens SC 1-1(1-0)
Angers SCO - Stade Brestois 0-1(0-0)
Stade Reims - Montpellier 1-0(1-0)
Bordeaux - Saint-Étienne 0-1(0-0)
AS Monaco - Stade Rennais 3-2(1-1)
Olympique Marseille - Strasbourg 2-0(1-0)

Round 11 [25-27.10.2019]
FC Nantes - AS Monaco 0-1(0-1)
Lille OSC - Bordeaux 3-0(1-0)
Montpellier - Angers SCO 0-0
Olympique Lyon - FC Metz 2-0(2-0)
RC Strasbourg - OGC Nice 1-0(1-0)
Stade Brestois - Dijon FCO 2-0(0-0)
Stade Reims - Nîmes Olympique 0-0
Stade Rennais - Toulouse FC 3-2(2-1)
Saint-Étienne - Amiens SC 2-2(1-0)
Paris St-Germain - Olymp. Marseille 4-0(4-0)

Round 12 [01-03.11.2019]
Dijon FCO - Paris Saint-Germain 2-1(1-1)
Olympique Marseille - Lille OSC 2-1(0-0)
FC Metz - Montpellier 2-2(1-0)
Toulouse FC - Olympique Lyon 2-3(1-1)
Amiens SC - Stade Brestois 1-0(1-0)
Angers SCO - RC Strasbourg 1-0(1-0)
Bordeaux - FC Nantes 2-0(1-0)
OGC Nice - Stade Reims 2-0(2-0)
Saint-Étienne - AS Monaco 1-0(0-0)
Nîmes - Stade Rennais 0-1(0-0) [15.01.2020]

Round 13 [08-10.11.2019]
OGC Nice - Bordeaux 1-1(1-0)
Stade Brestois - Paris Saint-Germain 1-2(0-1)
AS Monaco - Dijon FCO 1-0(1-0)
Lille OSC - FC Metz 0-0
RC Strasbourg - Nîmes Olympique 4-1(2-0)
Stade Reims - Angers SCO 0-0
Stade Rennais - Amiens SC 3-1(1-1)
FC Nantes - Saint-Étienne 2-3(2-2)
Montpellier - Toulouse FC 3-0(1-0)
Olymp. Marseille - Olympique Lyon 2-1(2-0)

Round 14 [22-24.11.2019]
Paris Saint-Germain - Lille OSC 2-0(2-0)
Olympique Lyon - OGC Nice 2-1(2-0)
Dijon FCO - Stade Rennais 2-1(0-0)
FC Metz - Stade Reims 1-1(0-1)
Amiens SC - RC Strasbourg 0-4(0-1)
Angers SCO - Nîmes Olympique 1-0(0-0)
Stade Brestois - FC Nantes 1-1(0-1)
Bordeaux - AS Monaco 2-1(1-1)
Saint-Étienne - Montpellier 0-0
Toulouse FC - Olympique Marseille 0-2(0-0)

Round 15 [29.11.-01.12.2019]
Olympique Marseille - Stade Brestois 2-1(0-0)
RC Strasbourg - Olympique Lyon 1-2(1-1)
Montpellier - Amiens SC 4-2(1-1)
OGC Nice - Angers SCO 3-1(1-1)
Nîmes Olympique - FC Metz 1-1(0-1)
Lille OSC - Dijon FCO 1-0(1-0)
Stade Reims - Bordeaux 1-1(0-1)
FC Nantes - Toulouse FC 2-1(1-0)
Stade Rennais - Saint-Étienne 2-1(1-1)
AS Monaco - Paris SG 1-4(0-2) [15.01.2020]

Round 16 [03-04.12.2019]
Bordeaux - Nîmes Olympique 6-0(2-0)
Angers SCO - Olympique Marseille 0-2(0-2)
Stade Brestois - RC Strasbourg 5-0(2-0)
Olympique Lyon - Lille OSC 0-1(0-0)
Saint-Étienne - OGC Nice 4-1(3-1)
Dijon FCO - Montpellier 2-2(1-2)
FC Metz - Stade Rennais 0-1(0-1)
Toulouse FC - AS Monaco 1-2(1-1)
Paris Saint-Germain - FC Nantes 2-0(0-0)
Amiens - Stade Reims 1-1(0-1) [15.01.2020]

Round 17 [06-08.12.2019]
Lille OSC - Stade Brestois 1-0(1-0)
Nîmes Olympique - Olympique Lyon 0-4(0-1)
Montpellier - Paris Saint-Germain 1-3(1-0)
AS Monaco - Amiens SC 3-0(0-0)
OGC Nice - FC Metz 4-1(3-1)
RC Strasbourg - Toulouse FC 4-2(2-1)
Stade Rennais - Angers SCO 2-1(1-0)
Stade Reims - Saint-Étienne 3-1(1-0)
FC Nantes - Dijon FCO 1-0(0-0)
Olympique Marseille - Bordeaux 3-1(0-1)

Round 18 [13-15.12.2019]
Lille OSC - Montpellier 2-1(1-0)
FC Metz - Olympique Marseille 1-1(1-0)
Toulouse FC - Stade Reims 0-1(0-1)
Nîmes Olympique - FC Nantes 0-1(0-1)
Amiens SC - Dijon FCO 1-1(1-1)
Angers SCO - AS Monaco 0-0
Stade Brestois - OGC Nice 0-0
Bordeaux - RC Strasbourg 0-1(0-1)
Olympique Lyon - Stade Rennais 0-1(0-0)
Saint-Étienne - Paris Saint-Germain 0-4(0-2)

Round 19 [21.12.2019]
AS Monaco - Lille OSC 5-1(2-1)
Dijon FCO - FC Metz 2-2(2-1)
FC Nantes - Angers SCO 2-1(1-0)
Montpellier - Stade Brestois 4-0(2-0)
OGC Nice - Toulouse FC 3-0(3-0)
Olympique Marseille - Nîmes Olymp. 3-1(0-0)
Paris Saint-Germain - Amiens SC 4-1(1-0)
RC Strasbourg - Saint-Étienne 2-1(1-0)
Stade Reims - Olympique Lyon 1-1(1-1)
Stade Rennais - Bordeaux 1-0(0-0)

Round 20 [10-12.01.2020]
Stade Rennais - Olympique Marseille 0-1(0-0)
Bordeaux - Olympique Lyon 1-2(1-0)
FC Metz - RC Strasbourg 1-0(0-0)
Toulouse FC - Stade Brestois 2-5(2-1)
Nîmes Olympique - Stade Reims 2-0(1-0)
Amiens SC - Montpellier 1-2(1-0)
Angers SCO - OGC Nice 1-1(1-1)
Saint-Étienne - FC Nantes 0-2(0-1)
Dijon FCO - Lille OSC 1-0(0-0)
Paris Saint-Germain - AS Monaco 3-3(3-2)

Round 21 [24-26.01.2020]
OGC Nice - Stade Rennais 1-1(0-0)
Olympique Marseille - Angers SCO 0-0
AS Monaco - RC Strasbourg 1-3(0-1)
Saint-Étienne - Nîmes Olympique 2-1(2-1)
Montpellier - Dijon FCO 2-1(0-0)
Stade Brestois - Amiens SC 2-1(0-0)
Stade Reims - FC Metz 0-1(0-1)
Olympique Lyon - Toulouse FC 3-0(1-0)
FC Nantes - Bordeaux 0-1(0-0)
Lille OSC - Paris Saint-Germain 0-2(0-1)

Round 22 [31.01.-02.02.2020]
Stade Rennais - FC Nantes 3-2(0-0)
Paris Saint-Germain - Montpellier 5-0(3-0)
Dijon FCO - Stade Brestois 3-0(2-0)
Nîmes Olympique - AS Monaco 3-1(1-1)
RC Strasbourg - Lille OSC 1-2(1-0)
Amiens SC - Toulouse FC 0-0
Angers SCO - Stade Reims 1-4(1-1)
OGC Nice - Olympique Lyon 2-1(1-1)
FC Metz - Saint-Étienne 3-1(1-0)
Bordeaux - Olympique Marseille 0-0

Round 23 [04-05.02.2020]
AS Monaco - Angers SCO 1-0(1-0)
Lille OSC - Stade Rennais 1-0(1-0)
FC Nantes - Paris Saint-Germain 1-2(0-1)
Toulouse FC - RC Strasbourg 0-1(0-0)
Montpellier - FC Metz 1-1(1-0)
Nîmes Olympique - Dijon FCO 2-0(2-0)
Olympique Lyon - Amiens SC 0-0
Stade Brestois - Bordeaux 1-1(0-1)
Stade Reims - OGC Nice 1-1(0-0)
Saint-Étienne - Olympique Marseille 0-2(0-1)

Round 24 [07-09.02.2020]
Angers SCO - Lille OSC 0-2(0-1)
Olympique Marseille - Toulouse FC 1-0(0-0)
Dijon FCO - FC Nantes 3-3(2-2)
FC Metz - Bordeaux 1-2(1-0)
OGC Nice - Nîmes Olympique 1-3(1-1)
Amiens SC - AS Monaco 1-2(1-0)
Stade Rennais - Stade Brestois 0-0
Montpellier - Saint-Étienne 1-0(1-0)
RC Strasbourg - Stade Reims 3-0(0-0)
Paris St-Germain - Olympique Lyon 4-2(2-0)

Round 25 [14-16.02.2020]
AS Monaco - Montpellier 1-0(0-0)
Amiens SC - Paris Saint-Germain 4-4(3-1)
FC Nantes - FC Metz 0-0
Toulouse FC - OGC Nice 0-2(0-1)
Bordeaux - Dijon FCO 2-2(1-1)
Nîmes Olympique - Angers SCO 1-0(0-0)
Olympique Lyon - RC Strasbourg 1-1(1-1)
Stade Brestois - Saint-Étienne 3-2(3-0)
Stade Reims - Stade Rennais 1-0(0-0)
Lille OSC - Olympique Marseille 1-2(0-0)

Round 26 [21-23.02.2020]
OGC Nice - Stade Brestois 2-2(2-1)
FC Metz - Olympique Lyon 0-2(0-1)
Olympique Marseille - FC Nantes 1-3(1-1)
Dijon FCO - AS Monaco 1-0(0-0)
Lille OSC - Toulouse FC 3-0(2-0)
RC Strasbourg - Amiens SC 0-0
Angers SCO - Montpellier 1-0(0-0)
Saint-Étienne - Stade Reims 1-1(0-0)
Stade Rennais - Nîmes Olympique 2-1(1-1)
Paris Saint-Germain - Bordeaux 4-3(2-2)

Round 27 [28.02.-01.03.2020]
Nîmes Olymp. - Olympique Marseille 2-3(1-2)
Paris Saint-Germain - Dijon FCO 4-0(1-0)
AS Monaco - Stade Reims 1-1(1-0)
Toulouse FC - Stade Rennais 0-2(0-1)
Montpellier - RC Strasbourg 3-0(0-0)
Amiens SC - FC Metz 0-1(0-1)
Stade Brestois - Angers SCO 0-1(0-1)
FC Nantes - Lille OSC 0-1(0-0)
Bordeaux - OGC Nice 1-1(1-0)
Olympique Lyon - Saint-Étienne 2-0(1-0)

Round 28 [06-08.03.2020]
Olympique Marseille - Amiens SC 2-2(1-0)
Strasbourg - Paris Saint-Germain *not played*
Dijon FCO - Toulouse FC 2-1(1-1)
FC Metz - Nîmes Olympique 2-1(1-0)
OGC Nice - AS Monaco 2-1(0-1)
Angers SCO - FC Nantes 2-0(0-0)
Stade Reims - Stade Brestois 1-0(1-0)
Saint-Étienne - Bordeaux 1-1(0-0)
Stade Rennais - Montpellier 5-0(2-0)
Lille OSC - Olympique Lyon 1-0(1-0)

On 13.03.2020, the LFP suspended Ligue 1 (and Ligue 2, see pages below) indefinitely following the outbreak of COVID-19 in France. On 28.04.2020, it was announced that Ligue 1 and Ligue 2 campaigns would not resume, after the country banned all sporting events until September 2020.
Following the cancellation of the 2019–20 season, on 30.04.2020, Paris Saint-Germain were awarded the championship.

Final Standings

#	Team	(avg)	P	W	D	L	GF	-	GA	Pts	W	D	L	GF	-	GA	W	D	L	GF	-	GA
							Total					Home						Away				
1.	**Paris Saint-Germain FC**	**(2,52)**	27	22	2	3	75	-	24	68	12	1	1	44	-	11	10	1	2	31	-	13
2.	Olympique de Marseille	(2,00)	28	16	8	4	41	-	29	56	8	4	2	21	-	14	8	4	2	20	-	15
3.	Stade Rennais FC	(1.79)	28	15	5	8	38	-	24	50	9	2	3	25	-	14	6	3	5	13	-	10
4.	Lille OSC	(1.75)	28	15	4	9	35	-	27	49	11	2	2	24	-	9	4	2	7	11	-	18
5.	OGC Nice	(1.46)	28	11	8	9	41	-	38	41	8	4	3	28	-	20	3	4	6	13	-	18
6.	Stade de Reims	(1.46)	28	10	11	7	26	-	21	41	5	7	2	12	-	7	5	4	5	14	-	14
7.	Olympique Lyonnais	(1.43)	28	11	7	10	42	-	27	40	5	4	4	17	-	7	6	3	6	25	-	20
8.	Montpellier Hérault SC	(1.43)	28	11	7	10	35	-	34	40	10	2	2	26	-	10	1	5	8	9	-	24
9.	AS Monaco FC	(1.43)	28	11	7	10	44	-	44	40	8	2	4	29	-	22	3	5	6	15	-	22
10.	Racing Club de Strasbourg	(1.41)	27	11	5	11	32	-	32	38	7	3	3	22	-	14	4	2	8	10	-	18
11.	Angers SCO	(1.39)	28	11	6	11	28	-	33	39	8	3	4	20	-	13	3	3	7	8	-	20
12.	Girondins de Bordeaux FC	(1.32)	28	9	10	9	40	-	34	37	4	5	4	19	-	12	5	5	5	21	-	22
13.	FC Nantes	(1.32)	28	11	4	13	28	-	31	37	6	2	6	11	-	11	5	2	7	17	-	20
14.	Stade Brestois 29	(1.21)	28	8	10	10	34	-	37	34	6	6	2	21	-	11	2	4	8	13	-	26
15.	FC Metz	(1.21)	28	8	10	10	27	-	35	34	5	4	5	18	-	17	3	6	5	9	-	18
16.	Dijon FCO	(1.07)	28	7	9	12	27	-	37	30	6	6	2	20	-	15	1	3	10	7	-	22
17.	AS Saint-Étienne	(1.07)	28	8	6	14	29	-	45	30	4	6	4	15	-	18	4	0	10	14	-	27
18.	Nîmes Olympique	(0.96)	28	7	6	15	29	-	44	27	6	2	6	17	-	15	1	4	9	12	-	29
19.	Amiens SC (*Relegated*)*	(0.82)	28	4	11	13	31	-	50	23	3	5	6	17	-	23	1	6	7	14	-	27
20.	Toulouse FC (*Relegated*)*	(0.46)	28	3	4	21	22	-	58	13	3	0	10	11	-	24	0	4	11	11	-	34

The final standings were based on an average of points earned per matches played. In case of a tied average, head-to-head results were used to ranked them if both matches between them were played.

*On 09.06.2020, France's highest administrative court ruled that relegation for Amiens SC and Toulouse FC was suspended for this season. On 23.06.2020, this decision was overruled and both clubs were relegated to Ligue 2.

Top goalscorers:	
18 Wissam Ben Yedder	*AS Monaco FC*
18 Kylian Sanmi Mbappé Lottin	*Paris Saint-Germain FC*
16 Moussa Dembélé	*Olympique Lyonnais*
13 Neymar da Silva Santos Júnior (BRA)	*Paris Saint-Germain FC*
13 Victor James Osimhen	*Lille OSC*
12 Habibou Mouhamadou Diallo (SEN)	*FC Metz*
12 Mauro Icardi	*Paris Saint-Germain FC*

NATIONAL CUP
Coupe de France 2019/2020

Round of 64 [04-05.01.2020]

Girondins de Bordeaux FC - Le Mans FC	2-0(0-0)		Red Star FC Paris - FC Chambly Oise	2-1(0-1)
AS Fabrègues - Paris FC	0-2(0-1)		FC Bourg-en-Presse Péronnas 01 - Olympique Lyon.	0-7(0-2)
Aviron Bayonnais FC - FC Nantes	0-2(0-1)		FC Bastia-Borgo - AS Saint-Étienne	0-3(0-2)
Chamois Niortais FC - JS Saint-Pierroise	1-2(0-0)		ES Reims Sainte-Anne CC - Montpellier Hérault SC	0-1(0-1)
FC Versailles 78 - US Granville	1-2(1-1)		Trélissac FC - Olympique de Marseille	1-1 aet; 2-4 pen
FC Guichen - Stade Malherbe Caen	1-2(0-2)		US Raon-l'Etape - Lille OSC	2-3(0-1)
AS Monaco FC - Stade de Reims	2-1(0-0)		FC Lorient-Bretagne Sud - Stade Brestois 29	2-1(1-1,1-1)
Tours FC - Nîmes Olympique	2-2 aet; 2-4 pen		OGC Nice - Étoile FC Fréjus Saint-Raphaël	2-0(0-0)
Stade Portelois - Racing Club de Strasbourg	1-4(1-1)		FC Limonest Saint-Didier - Le Puy Foot 43 Auvergne	1-1 aet; 3-1 pen
Stade Briochin St-Brieuc – ESM Gonfreville-l'Orch.	1-1 aet; 3-4 pen		Olympique Grande-Synthe - AS Nancy-Lorraine	0-1(0-0)
Athletico Marseille - Rodez Aveyron Football	2-1(1-0)		SSEP Hombourg-Haut - AS Prix-lès-Mézières	0-3(0-2)
ASM Belfort FC - FC Montceau Bourgogne	3-0(0-0)		L'Entente Sannois Saint-Gratien - SAS Épinal	0-1(0-0)
Saint-Pryvé Sainte Hilaire FC - Toulouse FC	1-0(0-0)		Valenciennes FC - Dijon FCO	1-2(1-1)
Sablé FC - Pau FC	2-2 aet; 2-4 pen		FC Dieppe - Angers SCO	1-3(0-0)
Angoulême-Soyaume Charente - FC Challans	3-1(1-1)		ESA Linas-Montlhéry - Paris Saint-Germain FC	0-6(0-2)
Stade Rennais FC - Amiens SC	0-0 aet; 5-4 pen		FC Rouen 1899 - FC Metz	3-0(1-0)

Round of 32 [16-30.01.2020]

Pau FC - Girondins de Bordeaux FC	3-2(2-1,2-2)		Angoulême-Soyaume Charente - RC de Strasbourg	1-5(1-4)
US Granville - Olympique de Marseille	0-3(0-0)		FC Nantes - Olympique Lyonnais	3-4(1-3)
AS Prix-lès-Mézières - FC Limonest	0-1(0-0)		Athletico Marseille - Stade Rennais FC	0-2(0-2)
SAS Épinal - JS Saint-Pierroise	1-0(0-0,0-0)		Dijon FCO - Nîmes Olympique	5-0(1-0)
OGC Nice - Red Star FC Paris	2-1(2-0)		FC Rouen 1899 - Angers SCO	1-4(1-3)
ASM Belfort FC - AS Nancy-Lorraine	3-1(1-1)		Montpellier Hérault SC - Stade Malherbe Caen	5-0(3-0)
ESM Gonfreville-l'Orcher - Lille OSC	0-2(0-0)		FC Lorient-Bretagne Sud - Paris Saint-Germain FC	0-1(0-0)
Paris FC - AS Saint-Étienne	2-3(1-1)		Saint-Pryvé Sainte Hilaire FC - AS Monaco FC	1-3(0-3)

Round of 16 [28-30.01.2020]

ASM Belfort FC - Montpellier Hérault SC	0-0 aet; 5-4 pen		SAS Épinal - Lille OSC	2-1(0-1)
Angers SCO - Stade Rennais FC	4-5(0-2,3-3)		Pau FC - Paris Saint-Germain FC	0-2(0-1)
FC Limonest - Dijon FCO	1-2(0-0,1-1)		Olympique de Marseille - Racing Club de Strasbourg	3-1(2-0)
AS Monaco FC - AS Saint-Étienne	0-1(0-1)		OGC Nice - Olympique Lyonnais	1-2(0-1)

Quarter-Finals [11-13.02.2019]

ASM Belfort FC - Stade Rennais FC	0-3(0-1)		Olympique Lyonnais - Olympique de Marseille	1-0(0-0)
Dijon FCO - Paris Saint-Germain FC	1-6(1-2)		SAS Épinal - AS Saint-Étienne	1-2(0-1)

Semi-Finals [04-05.03.2020]

Olympique Lyonnais - Paris Saint-Germain FC	1-5(1-1)		AS Saint-Étienne - Stade Rennais FC	2-1(1-1)

Final

24.07.2020; Stade de France, Saint-Denis, Paris; Referee: Amaury Delerue; Attendance: 2,805
Paris Saint-Germain FC - AS Saint-Étienne   **1-0(1-0)**

Paris Saint-Germain: Keylor Antonio Navas Gamboa, Thilo Kehrer (20.Colin Dagba), Thiago Emiliano Silva (Cap), Marcos Aoás Corrêa „Marquinhos", Mitchel Bakker, Ángel Fabián Di María Hernández, Leandro Daniel Paredes (75.Marco Verratti), Idrissa Gana Gueye, Neymar da Silva Santos Júnior, Kylian Sanmi Mbappé Lottin (33.Pablo Sarabia García), Mauro Icardi. Trainer: Thomas Tuchel (Germany).

Saint-Étienne: Jessy Moulin, Mathieu Debuchy (83.Jean-Philippe Krasso), Wesley Fofana, Loïc Perrin (Cap) [*sent off 31*], Timothée Kolodziejczak, Mahdi Camara (46.Yvan Neyou Noupa), Yann Gérard M'Vila, Yvann Maçon (34.Harold Moukoudi), Ryad Boudebouz (75.Arnaud Nordin), Denis Bouanga, Romain Hamouma (46.Wahbi Khazri). Trainer: Claude Jacques Puel.

Goal: 1-0 Neymar da Silva Santos Júnior (14).

Coupe de la Ligue Final 2019/2020

Please note: the LFP voted in September 2019 to abolish the Coupe de la Ligue for the following season, this edition was the last in the competition's history.

31.07.2020; Stade de France, Saint-Denis, Paris; Referee: Jérôme Brisard; Attendance: 3,500
Paris Saint-Germain FC - Olympique Lyonnais   **0-0; 6-5 on penalties**

Paris Saint-Germain: Keylor Antonio Navas Gamboa, Layvin Kurzawa (70.Thilo Kehrer), Thiago Emiliano Silva (Cap) (90.Leandro Daniel Paredes), Presnel Kimpembe, Marco Verratti, Marcos Aoás Corrêa „Marquinhos" (114.Abdou Diallo), Idrissa Gana Gueye (58.Pablo Sarabia García), Ángel Fabián Di María Hernández, Mauro Icardi (58.Ander Herrera Agüera), Neymar da Silva Santos Júnior. Trainer: Thomas Tuchel (Germany).

Olympique Lyonnais: Anthony Lopes, Jason Denayer, Marcelo Antônio Guedes Filho (81.Joachim Andersen), Fernando Marçal de Oliveira, Léo Dubois (86.Rafael Pereira da Silva [*sent off 119*]), Gnaly Albert Maxwel Cornet, Bruno Guimarães Rodriguez Moura (65.Thiago Henrique Mendes Ribeiro), Maxence Caqueret, Houssem Aouar, Moussa Dembélé (80.Karl Toko Ekambi), Memphis Depay (Cap) (80.Bertrand Traoré). Trainer: Rudi García.

Penalties: Joachim Andersen 0-1; Ángel Fabián Di María Hernández 1-1; Karl Toko Ekambi 1-2; Marco Verratti 2-2; Maxence Caqueret 1-3; Leandro Daniel Paredes 3-3; Thiago Henrique Mendes Ribeiro 3-4; Ander Herrera Agüera 4-4; Houssem Aouar 4-5; Neymar da Silva Santos Júnior 5-5; Bertrand Traoré (saved); Pablo Sarabia García 6-5.

THE CLUBS 2019/2020

Amiens Sporting Club

Founded:	1901		
Stadium:	Stade de la Licorne, Amiens (12,097)		
Trainer:	Luka Elsner (SVN)		02.08.1982

Goalkeepers:	DOB	M	(s)	G
Régis Gurtner	08.12.1986	28		
Defenders:	**DOB**	**M**	**(s)**	**G**
Haitam Aleesami (NOR)	31.07.1991	21	(1)	1
Arturo Calabresi (ITA)	17.03.1996	21		1
Aurélien Bayard Chedjou Fongang (CMR)	20.06.1985	22		
Bakaye Dibassy (MLI)	11.08.1989	22		2
Prince Gouano	24.12.1993	3		
Christophe Jallet	31.10.1983	10	(2)	1
Jordan Lefort	09.08.1993	8	(2)	
Nicholas Opoku (GHA)	08.11.1997	7		
Midfielders:	**DOB**	**M**	**(s)**	**G**
Alexis Blin	19.09.1996	21	(3)	
Mathieu Bodmer	22.11.1982		(9)	1
Vhakka Eddy Stelh Gnahoré	14.11.1993	14	(3)	
Gaël Kakuta (COD)	21.06.1991	23	(1)	2

	DOB	M	(s)	G
Thomas Monconduit	10.02.1991	15	(4)	
Mahdi Talal	17.08.1997		(2)	
Cheick Timite (CIV)	20.11.1997	2	(1)	
Bongani Zungu (RSA)	09.10.1992	10	(11)	1
Forwards:	**DOB**	**M**	**(s)**	**G**
Chadrac Akolo Ababa (COD)	01.04.1995	5	(10)	2
Quentin Cornette	17.01.1994	3	(10)	
Fousséni Diabaté (MLI)	18.10.1995	15	(5)	1
Saman Ghoddos (IRN)	06.09.1993	2	(3)	1
Serhou Guirassy	12.03.1996	23		9
Moussa Konaté	03.04.1993	6	(6)	2
Jack Lahne (SWE)	24.10.2001		(1)	1
Isaac Mbenza (BEL)	08.03.1996	1	(2)	
John Stiven Mendoza Valencia (COL)	27.06.1992	12	(3)	5
Juan Ferney Otero Tovar (COL)	26.05.1995	14	(4)	1

Angers Sporting Club de l'Ouest

Founded:	1919		
Stadium:	Stade "Raymond Kopa", Angers (17,835)		
Trainer:	Stéphane Moulin		04.08.1967

Goalkeepers:	DOB	M	(s)	G
Ludovic Butelle	13.04.1983	26		
Danijel Petković (MNE)	25.05.1993	2		
Defenders:	**DOB**	**M**	**(s)**	**G**
Rayan Aït Nouri	06.06.2001	16	(1)	
Abdoulaye Bamba (CIV)	25.04.1990	7	(1)	
Ibrahim Cissé	02.05.1996	1		
Souleyman Doumbia (CIV)	24.09.1996	5		
Vincent Manceau	10.07.1989	21		
Mateo Pavlović (CRO)	09.06.1990	8	(3)	
Théo Pellenard	04.03.1994	4	(4)	
Romain Thomas	12.06.1988	27		1
Ismaël Traoré (CIV)	18.08.1986	23		
Midfielders:	**DOB**	**M**	**(s)**	**G**
Antonin Bobichon	14.09.1995	8	(3)	2

	DOB	M	(s)	G
Pierrick Capelle	15.04.1987	20	(4)	1
Angelo Fulgini	20.08.1996	19	(1)	1
Thomas Mangani	29.04.1987	21	(3)	2
Zinédine Ould Khaled	14.01.2000	1		
Mathias Pereira Lage (POR)	30.11.1996	17	(8)	1
Vincent Pajot	19.08.1990	1	(5)	
Jeff Reine-Adélaïde	17.01.1998	1		1
Baptiste Santamaría	09.03.1995	28		1
Forwards:	**DOB**	**M**	**(s)**	**G**
Rachid Alioui (MAR)	18.06.1992	17	(11)	6
Stéphane Bahoken	28.05.1992	10	(10)	4
Farid El Melali (ALG)	05.05.1997	4	(4)	3
Aka Kanga	21.02.1998		(4)	
Casimir Ninga (CHA)	17.05.1993	6	(10)	3
Sada Thioub	01.06.1995	15	(8)	1

Football Club des Girondins de Bordeaux

Founded:	1881		
Stadium:	Matmut Atlantique, Bordeaux (42,115)		
Trainer:	Paulo Manuel Carvalho Sousa (POR)		30.08.1970

Goalkeepers:	DOB	M	(s)	G
Benoît Costil	03.07.1987	28		
Defenders:	**DOB**	**M**	**(s)**	**G**
Raoul Bellanova (ITA)	17.05.2000	1		
Loris Benito (SUI)	07.01.1992	21	(2)	1
Vukašin Jovanović (SRB)	17.05.1996	5	(4)	
Laurent Koscielny	10.09.1985	25		
Enock Kwateng	09.04.1997	13	(1)	
Edson André Sitoe „Mexer" (MOZ)	08.09.1988	16	(3)	
Pablo Nascimento Castro (BRA)	21.06.1991	25		4
Maxime Poundje	16.08.1992		(2)	
Youssouf Sabaly (SEN)	05.03.1993	10	(2)	
Midfielders:	**DOB**	**M**	**(s)**	**G**
Yacine Adli	29.07.2000	11	(10)	3
Youssef Aït Bennasser (MAR)	07.07.1996	6	(6)	

	DOB	M	(s)	G
Yassine Benrahou	24.01.1999	1	(5)	
Toma Bašić (CRO)	25.11.1996	11	(4)	1
Albert Lottin	29.08.2001	1		
Otavio Henrique Passos Santos (BRA)	04.05.1994	25		2
Rubén Pardo Gutiérrez (ESP)	22.10.1992	1	(5)	1
Aurélien Tchouaméni	27.01.2000	13	(2)	
Forwards:	**DOB**	**M**	**(s)**	**G**
Jimmy Briand	02.08.1985	18	(4)	7
Jonathan Renato Barbosa „Cafú" (BRA)	10.07.1991	2	(1)	
Nicolas de Préville	08.01.1991	23	(1)	6
Hwang Ui-jo (KOR)	28.08.1992	19	(5)	6
Samuel Kalu Ojim (NGA)	26.08.1997	15	(5)	
François Kamano (GUI)	01.05.1996	7	(4)	1
Joshua Erowoli Oluwaseun Maja (NGA)	27.12.1998	6	(15)	6
Rémi Oudin	18.11.1996	5	(3)	1

Stade Brestois 29

Founded:	1950		
Stadium:	Stade „Francis-Le Blé", Brest (15,931)		
Trainer:	Olivier Dall'Oglio		16.05.1964

Goalkeepers:	DOB	M	(s)	G
Gautier Larsonneur	23.02.1997	27		
Donovan Léon (GYF)	03.11.1992	1	(1)	
Defenders:	**DOB**	**M**	**(s)**	**G**
Ludovic Baal (GYF)	24.05.1986	9	(2)	
Denys Bain	02.07.1993	13	(2)	1
Gaëtan Belaud	16.09.1986	6	(1)	
Jean-Charles Castelletto (CMR)	26.01.1995	22		1
Brendan Chardonnet	22.12.1994	9	(3)	
Jean-Kevin Duverne	12.07.1997	13	(1)	
Julien Faussurier	14.01.1987	22		2
Romain Perraud	22.09.1997	19	(1)	
Midfielders:	**DOB**	**M**	**(s)**	**G**
Cristian Battocchio (ITA)	10.02.1992	16	(8)	3

	DOB	M	(s)	G
Haris Belkebla (ALG)	28.01.1994	20	(3)	
Yoann Court	14.01.1990	18	(5)	3
Ibrahima Diallo	08.03.1999	18	(1)	
Paul Lasne	16.01.1989	14	(5)	2
Hugo Magnetti	30.05.1998	2	(6)	
Hiang'a Mbock	28.12.1999	1	(1)	1
Ferris N'Goma	15.06.1993		(4)	1
Forwards:	**DOB**	**M**	**(s)**	**G**
Mathias Autret	01.03.1991	14	(9)	2
Irvin Cardona	08.08.1997	15	(6)	6
Gaëtan Charbonnier	27.12.1988	23	(3)	4
Samuel Grandsir	14.08.1996	17	(7)	3
Kévin Mayi	14.01.1993		(2)	
Alexandre Mendy	20.03.1994	9	(11)	3

Dijon Football Côte d'Or

Founded: 1998
Stadium: Stade „Gaston Gérard", Dijon (18,376)
Trainer: Stéphane Jobard   21.02.1971

Goalkeepers:	DOB	M	(s)	G
Amigo Alfred Junior Gomis (SEN)	05.09.1993	19		
Rúnar Rúnarsson (ISL)	18.02.1995	9	(2)	
Defenders:	**DOB**	**M**	**(s)**	**G**
Nayef Aguerd (MAR)	30.03.1996	11		1
Mickaël Alphonse (GPE)	12.07.1989	15	(2)	
Fouad Chafik (MAR)	16.10.1986	18	(2)	
Senou Coulibaly	04.09.1994	9	(1)	
Bruno Écuélé (GAB)	16.07.1988	28		
Wesley Lautoa	25.08.1987	21	(2)	
Hamza Mendyl (MAR)	21.10.1997	16	(2)	1
Glody Ngonda Muzinga (COD)	31.12.1994	6		
Ahmad Toure Ngouyamsa Nounchil (CMR)	21.12.2000		(1)	
Midfielders:	**DOB**	**M**	**(s)**	**G**
Romain Amalfitano	27.08.1989	18	(8)	1
Mama Samba Baldé (GNB)	06.11.1995	20	(4)	6
Florent Balmont	02.02.1980	4	(7)	
Mounir Chouiar	23.01.1999	18	(2)	4
Benjamin Jeannot	22.01.1992	2		
Enzo Loiodice	27.11.2000	2	(3)	
Jordan Marié	29.09.1991	1	(7)	
Didier Ndong (GAB)	17.06.1994	27		
Frédéric Sammaritano	23.03.1986	6	(4)	1
Bryan Soumaré	11.02.1999	4	(8)	
Forwards:	**DOB**	**M**	**(s)**	**G**
Yassine Benzia (ALG)	08.09.1994	2	(1)	
Jhonder Leonel Cádiz Fernández (VEN)	29.07.1995	7	(10)	2
Júlio Tavares (CPV)	19.11.1988	22	(1)	5
Abdoulaye Jules Keita (GUI)	20.07.1998	1	(2)	
Matheus Pereira da Silva (BRA)	25.02.1998	6	(4)	
Stephy Mavididi (ENG)	31.05.1998	16	(8)	5
Rayan Philippe	23.10.2000		(1)	

Lille Olympique Sporting Club

Founded: 23.09.1944
Stadium: Stade "Pierre Mauroy", Villeneuve-d'Ascq (50,157)
Trainer: Christophe Galtier   26.08.1966

Goalkeepers:	DOB	M	(s)	G
Mike Maignan	03.07.1995	28		
Defenders:	**DOB**	**M**	**(s)**	**G**
Domagoj Bradarić (CRO)	10.12.1999	16	(2)	
Mehmet Çelik (TUR)	17.02.1997	23		
Gabriel dos Santos Magalhaes (BRA)	19.12.1997	23	(1)	1
José Miguel da Rocha Fonte (POR)	22.12.1983	25		1
Jérémy Pied	23.02.1989	5		
Reinildo Isnard Mandava (MOZ)	21.01.1994	12	(4)	
Adama Soumaoro	18.06.1992	4	(2)	1
Tiago Emanuel Embaló Djaló (POR)	09.04.2000	8		
Midfielders:	**DOB**	**M**	**(s)**	**G**
Benjamin André	03.08.1990	23	(3)	2
Osvaldo Nicolás Fabián Gaitán (ARG)	23.02.1988		(4)	
Nanitamo Jonathan Ikoné	02.05.1998	26	(2)	3
Cheikh Ahmet Tidian Niasse (SEN)	19.01.2000		(1)	
Jean Emile Junior Onana Onana (CMR)	08.01.2000	1		
Renato Júnior Luz Sanches (POR)	18.08.1997	16	(3)	3
Thiago Maia Alencar (BRA)	23.03.1997		(3)	
Boubakary Soumaré	27.02.1999	15	(5)	
Miguel Ângelo da Silva Rocha „Xeka" (POR)	10.11.1994	8	(9)	
Yusuf Yazıcı (TUR)	29.01.1997	9	(9)	1
Forwards:	**DOB**	**M**	**(s)**	**G**
Jonathan Bamba	26.03.1996	22	(4)	1
Luiz Araujo Guimarães Neto (BRA)	02.06.1996	7	(14)	2
Victor James Osimhen (NGA)	29.12.1998	25	(2)	13
Abou Ben Qadir Abou Ouattara (BFA)	26.12.1999		(1)	
Loïc Rémy	02.01.1987	11	(9)	7
Timothy Tarpeh Weah (USA)	22.02.2000	1	(2)	

Olympique Lyonnais

Founded: 1950
Stadium: Groupama Stadium, Décines-Charpieu, Lyon (59,186)
Trainer: Sylvio Mendes Campos Júnior "Sylvinho" (BRA)   12.04.1974
[14.10.2019] Rudi García   20.02.1964

Goalkeepers:	DOB	M	(s)	G
Anthony Lopes (POR)	01.10.1990	26		
Ciprian Anton Tătăruşanu (ROU)	09.02.1986	2		
Defenders:	**DOB**	**M**	**(s)**	**G**
Joachim Andersen (DEN)	31.05.1996	17	(1)	1
Melvin Bard	06.11.2000		(1)	
Jason Denayer (BEL)	28.06.1995	24	(1)	
Léo Dubois	14.09.1994	15	(1)	
Youssouf Koné (MLI)	05.07.1995	10	(1)	
Fernando Marçal de Oliveira (BRA)	19.02.1989	11		
Marcelo Antônio Guedes Filho (BRA)	25.05.1987	17		
Rafael Pereira da Silva (BRA)	09.07.1990	9	(4)	
Oumar Solet	07.02.2000		(1)	
Kenny Joelle Tete (NED)	09.10.1995	9	(9)	
Midfielders:	**DOB**	**M**	**(s)**	**G**
Houssem Aouar	30.06.1998	23	(2)	3
Bruno Guimarães Rodriguez Moura (BRA)	16.11.1997	3		
Maxence Caqueret	15.02.2000	7	(1)	
Jean Lucas de Souza Oliveira (BRA)	22.06.1998	1	(10)	1
Jeff Reine-Adélaïde	17.01.1998	11	(3)	2
Thiago Henrique Mendes Ribeiro (BRA)	15.03.1992	21	(1)	
Lucas Tousart	29.04.1997	19	(5)	2
Forwards:	**DOB**	**M**	**(s)**	**G**
Rayan Cherki	17.08.2003	1	(5)	
Maxwel Cornet (CIV)	27.09.1996	14	(8)	4
Moussa Dembélé	12.07.1996	24	(3)	16
Memphis Depay (NED)	13.02.1994	12	(1)	9
Amine Gouiri	16.02.2000		(1)	
Martin Terrier	04.03.1997	13	(10)	1
Karl Toko Ekambi (CMR)	14.09.1992	5	(3)	2
Bertrand Traoré (BFA)	06.09.1995	14	(9)	1

Olympique de Marseille

Founded: 31.08.1899
Stadium: Stade Orange Vélodrome, Marseille (67,394)
Trainer: Luís André de Pina Cabral e Villas-Boas   17.10.1977

Goalkeepers:	DOB	M	(s)	G
Steve Mandanda Mpidi	28.03.1985	27		
Yohann Pelé	04.11.1982	1	(1)	
Defenders:	**DOB**	**M**	**(s)**	**G**
Álvaro González Soberón (ESP)	08.01.1990	19	(1)	
Jordan Amavi	09.03.1994	24	(2)	1
Duje Ćaleta-Car (CRO)	17.09.1996	20	(3)	1
Boubacar Kamara	23.11.1999	24		1
Lucas Perrin	19.11.1998	4		
Hiroki Sakai (JPN)	12.04.1990	19	(2)	
Bouna Sarr (GUI)	31.01.1992	25	(2)	1
Midfielders:	**DOB**	**M**	**(s)**	**G**
Florian Chabrolle	07.04.1998		(1)	
Saîf-Eddine Khaoui (TUN)	27.04.1995		(7)	
Maxime Lopez	04.12.1997	13	(10)	
Luiz Gustavo Dias (BRA)	23.07.1987	2	(1)	
Florent Dimitri Payet	29.03.1987	22		9
Valentin Rongier	07.12.1994	20	(3)	
Morgan Sanson	18.08.1994	26	(1)	5
Kevin Strootman (NED)	13.02.1990	15	(10)	2
Forwards:	**DOB**	**M**	**(s)**	**G**
Marley Aké	05.01.2001		(9)	
Darío Ismael Benedetto (ARG)	17.05.1990	25	(1)	11
Valère Germain	17.04.1990	14	(11)	2
Isaac Lihadji	10.04.2002		(2)	
Nemanja Radonjić (SRB)	15.02.1996	8	(13)	4
Florian Thauvin	26.01.1993		(2)	

Football Club de Metz

Founded: 1932
Stadium: Stade Municipal Saint-Symphorien, Metz (25,636)
Trainer: Vincent Hognon   16.08.1974

Goalkeepers:	DOB	M	(s)	G
Paul Delecroix	14.10.1988	1	(1)	
Alexandre Oukidja	19.07.1988	27		
Defenders:	**DOB**	**M**	**(s)**	**G**
John Boye (GHA)	23.04.1987	24		2
Dylan Bronn (TUN)	19.06.1995	9		
Manuel Cabit (MTQ)	03.06.1993	3		
Fabien Centonze	16.01.1996	28		
Thomas Delaine	24.03.1992	14	(2)	
Mamadou Fofana (MLI)	21.01.1998	18	(2)	
Félix Stoppila Sunzu (ZAM)	22.06.1989	14	(3)	
Matthieu Udol	20.03.1996	12	(1)	
Midfielders:	**DOB**	**M**	**(s)**	**G**
Farid Boulaya (ALG)	25.02.1993	8	(11)	2
Renaud Cohade	29.09.1984	9	(3)	1

	DOB	M	(s)	G
Marvin Gakpa (ALG)	01.11.1993	4	(9)	
Habib Maïga (CIV)	01.01.1996	26		1
Kévin N'Doram	22.01.1996	19	(1)	
Vincent Pajot	19.08.1990	7		
Adama Traoré II (MLI)	28.06.1995	12	(2)	1
Papa Ndiaga Yade (SEN)	05.01.2000		(2)	
Forwards:	**DOB**	**M**	**(s)**	**G**
Thierry Ambrose	28.03.1997	4	(14)	
Victorien Angban (CIV)	29.09.1996	11	(9)	
Habibou Mouhamadou Diallo (SEN)	18.06.1995	26		12
Georges Mikautadze	31.10.2000		(1)	
Opa Nguette	08.07.1994	23	(3)	5
Ibrahima Niane (SEN)	11.03.1999	9	(12)	3
Adama Malouda Traoré (MLI)	05.06.1995		(1)	

Association Sportive de Monaco Football Club

Founded: 23.08.1924
Stadium: Stade „Louis II", Monaco (18,523)
Trainer: José Leonardo Nunes Alves Sousa (POR)   01.08.1974
[28.12.2019]   Robert Moreno González (ESP)   19.09.1977

Goalkeepers:	DOB	M	(s)	G
Benjamin Lecomte	26.04.1991	28		
Defenders:	**DOB**	**M**	**(s)**	**G**
Ruben Aguilar	26.04.1993	11	(8)	
Benoît Badiashile	26.03.2001	16		
Fodé Ballo-Touré	03.01.1997	18	(3)	
Kamil Glik (POL)	03.02.1988	23		1
Benjamin Henrichs (GER)	23.02.1997	10	(3)	
Jemerson de Jesus Nascimento (BRA)	24.08.1992	13		
Guillermo Alfonso Maripán Loayza (CHI)	06.05.1994	20		2
Jonathan Panzo (ENG)	25.10.2000	1	(1)	
Midfielders:	**DOB**	**M**	**(s)**	**G**
Adrien Sebastian Perruchet Silva (POR)	15.03.1989	13	(9)	
Tiemoué Bakayoko	17.08.1994	20		1
Gabriel Boschilia (BRA)	05.03.1996	1	(4)	
Francesc „Cesc" Fàbregas Soler (ESP)	04.05.1987	12	(6)	

	DOB	M	(s)	G
Youssouf Fofana	10.01.1999	7		
Gil Bastião Dias (POR)	28.09.1996	12	(2)	
Aleksandr Golovin (RUS)	30.05.1996	24	(1)	3
Marcos Paulo Mesquita Lopes „Rony"(POR)	28.12.1995	1		
Aurélien Tchouaméni	27.01.2000		(3)	
Adama Noss Traoré (MLI)	28.06.1995		(2)	
Forwards:	**DOB**	**M**	**(s)**	**G**
Jean-Kévin Augustin	16.06.1997	2	(8)	
Keita Baldé Diao	08.03.1995	9	(12)	4
Wissam Ben Yedder	12.08.1990	25	(1)	18
Lyle Brent Foster (RSA)	03.09.2000	1	(1)	
Gelson Dany Batalha Martins (POR)	11.05.1995	20	(1)	4
Stevan Jovetić (MNE)	02.11.1989	5	(4)	2
Henry Chukwuemeka Onyekuru (NGA)	05.06.1997	2	(2)	
Islam Slimani (ALG)	18.06.1988	14	(4)	9
Moussa Sylla	25.11.1999		(1)	

Montpellier Hérault Sport Club

Founded: 1919
Stadium: Stade de la Mosson, Montpellier (32,939)
Trainer: Michel Der Zakarian   18.02.1963

Goalkeepers:	DOB	M	(s)	G
Dimitry Bertaud	06.06.1998	3		
Mathis Carvalho (POR)	28.04.1999		(1)	
Gerónimo Rulli (ARG)	20.05.1992	25		
Defenders:	**DOB**	**M**	**(s)**	**G**
Daniel Congré	05.04.1985	23	(1)	
Nicolas Cozza	08.01.1999	6	(1)	
Vitorino Hilton de Silva (BRA)	13.09.1977	28		
Damien Le Tallec	19.04.1990	28		2
Ambroise Oyongo Bitolo (CMR)	22.06.1991	21		
Pedro Filipe Teodosio Mendes (POR)	01.10.1990	16		1
Mihailo Ristić (SRB)	31.10.1995	8	(10)	
Arnaud Souquet	12.02.1992	22	(2)	2
Mathías Sebastián Suárez Suárez (URU)	24.06.1996	1		
Clément Vidal	18.06.2000	1		
Thibaut Vargas	22.05.2000	2	(1)	

Midfielders:	DOB	M	(s)	G
Bilal Boutobba	29.08.1998		(1)	
Joris Chotard	24.09.2001	13	(7)	
Keagan Larenzo Dolly (RSA)	22.01.1993	1	(5)	
Jordan Ferri	12.03.1992	13	(3)	
Florent Mollet	19.11.1991	19	(6)	6
Junior Sambia	07.09.1996	5	(12)	1
Téji Savanier	22.12.1991	18	(1)	6
Forwards:	**DOB**	**M**	**(s)**	**G**
Bastian Badu	02.02.2000		(1)	
Souleymane Camara (SEN)	22.12.1982		(13)	
Andy Delort (ALG)	09.10.1991	26		9
Gaëtan Laborde	03.05.1994	27	(1)	6
Petar Škuletić (SRB)	29.06.1990	1	(4)	
Yun il-lok (KOR)	07.03.1992	1	(4)	

Football Club de Nantes

Founded: 1943
Stadium: Stade de la Beaujoire, Nantes (37,473)
Trainer: Christian Jean Gourcuff   05.04.1955

Goalkeepers:	DOB	M	(s)	G
Alban Lafont	23.01.1999	27		
Denis Petrić (SRB)	24.05.1988	1		
Defenders:	**DOB**	**M**	**(s)**	**G**
Dennis Appiah	09.06.1992	18	(1)	
Thomas Basila	30.04.1999	3	(4)	
Fábio Pereira da Silva (BRA)	09.07.1990	10		
Josué Homawoo (TOG)	12.11.1997		(1)	
Lucas Pedro Alves de Lima (BRA)	10.10.1991	3		
Wesley Moustache	26.02.1999	1		
Nicolas Pallois	19.09.1987	21		
Charles Traoré (MLI)	01.01.1992	20		
Molla Wagué (MLI)	21.02.1991	8	(1)	
Midfielders:	**DOB**	**M**	**(s)**	**G**
Mehdi Abeid	06.08.1992	20	(5)	1
Andrei Girotto (BRA)	17.02.1992	25		1
Abdoul Bamba	25.05.1994	16	(11)	1

	DOB	M	(s)	G
Cristián Benavente Bristol (PER)	19.05.1994	4	(8)	
Ludovic Blas	31.12.1997	22	(2)	5
Marcus Coco	24.06.1996	1		
Rene Krhin (SVN)	21.05.1990	4	(4)	
Imran Louza	01.05.1999	22	(2)	2
Samuel Moutoussamy	12.08.1996	3	(15)	
Roli Pereira de Sa	10.12.1996		(1)	
Valentin Rongier	07.12.1994	3		
Percy Prado Ruiz (PER)	14.01.1996	2	(1)	
Abdoulaye Touré	03.03.1994	24	(3)	3
Forwards:	**DOB**	**M**	**(s)**	**G**
Kalifa Coulibaly (MLI)	21.08.1991	18	(3)	4
Renaud Emond (BEL)	05.12.1991	3	(3)	
Anthony Limbombe (BEL)	15.07.1994	2	(2)	1
Moses Daddy-Ayala Simon (NGA)	12.07.1995	25	(1)	5
Thody Élie Youan	07.04.1999	2	(3)	

Olympique Gymnaste Club Nice Côte d'Azur

Founded: 09.07.1904 (*as Le Gymnaste Club de Nice*)
Stadium: Allianz Riviera, Nice (35,624)
Trainer: Patrick Vieira   23.06.1976

Goalkeepers:	DOB	M	(s)	G
Walter Daniel Benítez (ARG)	19.01.1993	26		
Yannis Clementia (MTQ)	05.07.1997	2		
Defenders:	**DOB**	**M**	**(s)**	**G**
Youcef Atal (ALG)	17.05.1996	12	(1)	1
Patrick Burner	11.04.1996	15	(5)	1
Ibrahim Cissé (CIV)	11.01.1999		(2)	
Racine Coly (SEN)	08.12.1995	8	(2)	1
Bonfim Costa Santos Dante (BRA)	18.10.1983	21		1
Riza Durmisi (DEN)	08.01.1994	2	(2)	
Christophe Hérelle	22.08.1992	13	(2)	3
Gautier Lloris	18.07.1995	3		
Stanley N'Soki	09.04.1999	14	(3)	
Andy Pelmard	12.03.2000	8	(2)	
Malang Sarr	23.01.1999	16	(3)	1
Moussa Wagué (SEN)	04.10.1998	2	(3)	
Midfielders:	**DOB**	**M**	**(s)**	**G**
Hichem Boudaoui (ALG)	23.09.1999	6	(3)	1
Alexis Claude-Maurice	06.06.1998	19	(3)	1
Wylan Cyprien	28.01.1995	20		7
Danilo Barbosa da Silva (BRA)	28.02.1996	12	(4)	
Pierre Lees-Melou	25.05.1993	25	(1)	5
Arnaud Lusamba	04.01.1997	11	(4)	1
Bassem Srarfi (TUN)	25.06.1997	1	(2)	
Eddy Sylvestre	29.08.1999		(1)	
Adrien Tameze	04.02.1994	6	(2)	1
Khéphren Thuram	26.03.2001	7	(7)	
Rémi Walter	26.04.1995	1		
Forwards:	**DOB**	**M**	**(s)**	**G**
Kasper Dolberg (DEN)	06.10.1997	22	(1)	11
Ignatius Kpene Ganago (CMR)	16.02.1999	12	(14)	3
Mickaël Le Bihan	16.05.1990	1	(1)	
Myziane Maolida	14.02.1999	7	(11)	1
Adam Ounas (ALG)	11.11.1996	14	(2)	2
Ihsan Sacko	19.07.1997	2	(1)	

Nîmes Olympique

Founded: 10.04.1937 (*as Le Gymnaste Club de Nice*)
Stadium: Stade des Costières, Nîmes (18,482)
Trainer: Bernard Blaquart   16.08.1957

Goalkeepers:	DOB	M	(s)	G
Paul Bernardoni	18.04.1997	25		
Lucas Lionel Dias	22.05.1999	3	(1)	
Defenders:	**DOB**	**M**	**(s)**	**G**
Sofiane Alakouch	29.07.1998	17		
Anthony Briançon	28.11.1994	20	(2)	1
Lucas Buades	28.12.1997	1	(5)	
Loïck Landré	05.05.1992	10	(1)	1
Pablo Martinez	21.02.1989	26		2
Florian Miguel	01.09.1996	23	(1)	1
Gaëtan Paquiez	15.02.1994	17	(4)	
Midfielders:	**DOB**	**M**	**(s)**	**G**
Yassine Benrahou	24.01.1999	9		2
Antonin Bobichon	14.09.1995	2		
Lucas Deaux	26.12.1988	15	(2)	2
Zinedine Ferhat (ALG)	01.03.1993	25	(1)	3
Lamine Fomba	26.01.1998	15	(5)	
Romain Philippoteaux	02.03.1988	23	(4)	5
Renaud Ripart	14.03.1993	23	(1)	4
Theo Sainte-Luce	20.10.1998		(3)	
Sidy Sarr (SEN)	05.06.1996	12	(10)	
Pierrick Valdivia	18.04.1988	1	(1)	
Antoine Valério	11.12.1999	1	(4)	
Lucas Valls	25.09.1998		(1)	
Theo Valls	18.12.1995	20	(3)	1
Forwards:	**DOB**	**M**	**(s)**	**G**
Sami Ben Amar (MAR)	02.03.1998		(2)	
Kevin Denkey (TOG)	30.11.2000	6	(11)	3
Haris Duljević (BIH)	16.11.1993	5	(9)	
Moussa Koné (SEN)	30.12.1996	1	(4)	2
Nolan Roux	01.03.1988	7		2
Vlatko Stojanovski	23.04.1997	1	(5)	

Paris Saint-Germain Football Club

Founded: 12.08.1970
Stadium: Stade Parc des Princes, Paris (48,583)
Trainer: Thomas Tuchel (GER)   29.08.1973

Goalkeepers:	DOB	M	(s)	G
Alphonse Aréola	27.02.1993	3		
Marcin Bułka (POL)	04.10.1999	1		
Keylor Antonio Navas Gamboa (CRC)	15.12.1986	21		
Sergio Rico González (ESP)	01.09.1993	2		
Defenders:	**DOB**	**M**	**(s)**	**G**
Mitchel Bakker (NED)	20.06.2000	1		
Colin Dagba	09.09.1998	7	(3)	
Abdou Diallo	04.05.1996	14	(2)	
Juan Bernat Velasco (ESP)	01.03.1993	16	(2)	
Thilo Kehrer (GER)	21.09.1996	5	(2)	1
Presnel Kimpembe	13.08.1995	14	(2)	
Nianzou Kouassi	07.06.2002	4	(2)	2
Layvin Kurzawa	04.09.1992	9	(5)	1
Marcos Aoás Corrêa „Marquinhos" (BRA)	14.05.1994	15	(4)	3
Loïc Mbe Soh	13.06.2001	1		
Thomas Meunier (BEL)	12.09.1991	14	(2)	
Thiago Emiliano Silva (BRA)	22.09.1984	20	(1)	
Arthur Zagre	04.10.2001		(1)	
Midfielders:	**DOB**	**M**	**(s)**	**G**
Ander Herrera Agüera (ESP)	14.08.1989	6	(2)	1
Adil Aouchiche	15.07.2002	1		
Idrissa Gana Gueye (SEN)	26.09.1989	19	(1)	1
Pablo Sarabia García (ESP)	11.05.1992	13	(8)	4
Leandro Daniel Paredes (ARG)	29.06.1994	8	(9)	
Marco Verratti (ITA)	05.11.1992	15	(5)	
Forwards:	**DOB**	**M**	**(s)**	**G**
Edinson Roberto Cavani Gómez (URU)	14.02.1987	7	(7)	4
Eric Maxim Choupo-Moting (CMR)	23.03.1989	5	(4)	3
Ángel Fabián Di María Hernández (ARG)	14.02.1988	23	(3)	8
Julian Draxler (GER)	20.09.1993	7	(4)	
Mauro Icardi (ARG)	19.02.1993	14	(6)	12
Jesé Rodríguez Ruíz (ESP)	26.02.1993		(1)	
Kylian Sanmi Mbappé Lottin	20.12.1998	17	(3)	18
Neymar da Silva Santos Júnior (BRA)	05.02.1992	15		13

Stade de Reims

Founded: 1931 (*as Société Sportive du Parc Pommery*)
Stadium: Stade „Auguste Delaune", Reims (21,684)
Trainer: David Guion   30.09.1967

Goalkeepers:	DOB	M	(s)	G
Nicolas Lemaître	12.01.1997	1		
Predrag Rajković (SRB)	31.10.1995	27		
Defenders:	**DOB**	**M**	**(s)**	**G**
Yunis Abdelhamid (MAR)	28.09.1987	28		3
Axel Disasi	11.03.1998	27		1
Thomas Foket (BEL)	25.09.1994	27		
Ghislain N'Clomandès Konan (CIV)	27.12.1995	15	(1)	
Dario Maresić (AUT)	29.09.1999	1		
Midfielders:	**DOB**	**M**	**(s)**	**G**
Mathieu Cafaro	25.03.1997	12	(1)	1
Xavier Chavalerin	07.03.1991	24		1
Tristan Dingomé	17.02.1991	12	(3)	
Moussa Doumbia (MLI)	15.08.1994	22	(4)	2
Hassane Kamara (GAM)	05.03.1994	18	(5)	2
Dereck Kutesa (SUI)	06.12.1997	4	(10)	1
Moreto Moro Cassamá (GNB)	16.02.1998	7		
Marshall Munetsi (ZIM)	22.06.1996	8	(9)	
Jacques Alaixys Romao (TOG)	18.01.1984	21	(1)	
Sambou Sissoko	27.04.1999		(3)	
Forwards:	**DOB**	**M**	**(s)**	**G**
Boulaye Dia	16.11.1996	21	(3)	7
Anastasios Donis (GRE)	29.08.1996	6	(9)	
Nathanaël Mbuku	16.03.2002	3	(8)	
Timothé Nkada	20.07.1999		(8)	
Rémi Oudin	18.11.1996	16	(2)	3
Kaj Sierhuis (NED)	27.04.1998	1		
Suk Hyun-jun (KOR)	29.06.1991	1	(12)	1
El Bilal Touré (MLI)	03.10.2001	6	(1)	3
Arber Zeneli (KVX)	25.02.1995		(1)	

Stade Rennais Football Club

Founded: 10.03.1901
Stadium: Roazhon Park, Rennes (29,778)
Trainer: Julien Stéphan   18.09.1980

Goalkeepers:	DOB	M	(s)	G
Edouard Mendy	01.03.1992	24		
Romain Salin	29.07.1984	4		
Defenders:	**DOB**	**M**	**(s)**	**G**
Sacha Boey	13.09.2000	1	(4)	
Damien Da Silva	17.05.1988	25		1
Souleyman Doumbia (CIV)	24.09.1996	1		
Jérémy Gelin	24.04.1997	10	(4)	
Joris Gnagnon	13.01.1997	14	(5)	
Faitout Maouassa	06.07.1998	23		3
Jérémy Morel (MAD)	02.04.1984	20	(1)	1
Gerzino Nyamsi	22.01.1997		(4)	
Hamari Traoré (MLI)	27.01.1992	27		
Midfielders:	**DOB**	**M**	**(s)**	**G**
Benjamin Bourigeaud	14.01.1994	21	(4)	2
Eduardo Camavinga	10.11.2002	24	(1)	1
Yann Gboho	14.01.2001	2	(6)	1
Clément Grenier	07.01.1991	10	(1)	1
Rafik Guitane	26.05.1999		(2)	
Adrien Hunou	19.01.1994	13	(10)	8
James Lea Siliki	12.06.1996	12	(8)	
Jonas Martin	09.04.1990	1	(2)	
Steven N'Zonzi	15.12.1988	4	(1)	
Flavien Tait	02.02.1993	9	(8)	2
Forwards:	**DOB**	**M**	**(s)**	**G**
Lucas Da Cunha	09.06.2001	1	(1)	
Romain Del Castillo	29.03.1996	14	(7)	2
M'Baye Niang (SEN)	19.12.1994	24	(2)	10
Raphael Dias Belloli „Raphinha" (BRA)	14.12.1996	20	(2)	5
Theoson Siebatcheu	26.04.1996	4	(10)	

Association Sportive de Saint-Étienne Loire

Founded: 1919
Stadium: Stade „Geoffroy Guichard", Saint-Étienne (41,965)
Trainer: Ghislain Printant   13.05.1961
[04.10.2019] Claude Jacques Puel   02.09.1961

Goalkeepers:	DOB	M	(s)	G
Stefan Bajic	23.12.2001	1		
Jessy Moulin	13.01.1986	5		
Stéphane Ruffier	27.09.1986	22		
Defenders:	**DOB**	**M**	**(s)**	**G**
Mathieu Debuchy	28.07.1985	20	(1)	1
Wesley Fofana	17.12.2000	13	(1)	1
Gabriel Moisés Antunes da Silva (BRA)	13.05.1991	3	(1)	
Timothée Kolodziejczak	01.10.1991	14	(1)	
Harold Moukoudi (CMR)	27.11.1997	11		
Loïc Perrin	07.08.1985	20	(1)	
William Saliba	24.03.2001	11	(1)	
Sergi Palencia Hurtado (ESP)	23.03.1996	6		
Miguel Angel Trauco Saavedra (PER)	25.08.1992	17	(2)	1
Midfielders:	**DOB**	**M**	**(s)**	**G**
Jean-Eudes Aholou (CIV)	20.03.1994	8	(3)	1
Bilal Benkhedim	20.04.2001	1	(2)	
Denis Bouanga (GAB)	11.11.1994	23	(3)	10
Ryad Boudebouz (ALG)	19.02.1990	20	(4)	1
Yohan Cabaye	14.01.1986	12	(3)	
Mahdi Camara	30.06.1998	10	(?)	
Assane Dioussé El Hadji (SEN)	20.09.1997	1	(3)	
Edmilson Indjai Correia (GNB)	06.06.2000		(4)	
Wahbi Khazri (TUN)	08.02.1991	13	(3)	3
Yann Gérard M'Vila	29.06.1990	21	(2)	
Yvann Maçon	01.10.1998	2		
Arnaud Nordin	17.06.1998	9	(9)	1
Zaydou Youssouf	11.07.1999	9	(7)	
Forwards:	**DOB**	**M**	**(s)**	**G**
Charles Abi	12.04.2000	6	(9)	
Robert Berić (SVN)	17.06.1991	4	(7)	1
Loïs Diony	20.12.1992	8	(4)	2
Romain Hamouma	29.03.1987	9	(5)	6
Franck Honorat	11.08.1996	9	(3)	
Maxence Rivera	30.05.2002		(1)	

Racing Club de Strasbourg Alsace

Founded: 1906
Stadium: Stade de la Meinau, Strasbourg (29,230)
Trainer: Thierry Laurey   14.02.1964

Goalkeepers:	DOB	M	(s)	G
Matz Willy Sels (BEL)	26.02.1992	27		
Defenders:	**DOB**	**M**	**(s)**	**G**
Anthony Caci	01.07.1997	8		1
Lionel Carole	12.04.1991	14	(4)	
Alexander Djiku	09.08.1994	23	(2)	1
Lamine Koné (CIV)	01.02.1989	17	(1)	1
Kenny Lala	03.10.1991	22	(3)	2
Adrien Lebeau	26.01.1998		(2)	
Stefan Mitrović (SRB)	22.05.1990	23		1
Abdallah N'Dour (SEN)	20.12.1993	4	(2)	
Mohamed Simakan	03.05.2000	17	(2)	
Moataz Zemzemi (TUN)	07.08.1999	1		
Midfielders:	**DOB**	**M**	**(s)**	**G**
Jean Bellegarde	27.06.1998	16	(8)	
Benjamin Corgnet	06.04.1987	3	(3)	
Youssouf Fofana	10.01.1999	12	1	1
Jérémy Grimm	27.03.1987		(1)	
Dimitri Liénard	13.02.1988	16	(6)	2
Jonas Martin	09.04.1990	3		
Sanjin Prcić (BIH)	20.11.1993	1	(2)	
Ibrahima Sissoko	27.10.1997	18	(5)	
Adrien Thomasson	10.12.1993	24	(1)	8
Forwards:	**DOB**	**M**	**(s)**	**G**
Ludovic Ajorque	25.02.1994	24	(2)	8
Lebogang Mothiba (RSA)	28.01.1996	12	(9)	3
Nuno Miguel da Costa Jóia (CPV)	10.02.1991	4	10	1
Majeed Waris (GHA)	19.09.1991	4	(3)	2
Kévin Lucien Zohi (CIV)	19.12.1996	5	(12)	1

Toulouse Football Club

Founded:	1970	
Stadium:	Stadium Municipal, Toulouse (33,150)	
Trainer:	Alain Casanova	18.09.1961
[14.10.2019]	Antoine Krilone Kombouaré	16.11.1963
[06.01.2020]	Denis Zanko	13.04.1964

Goalkeepers:	DOB	M	(s)	G
Mauro Daniel Goicoechea Furia (URU)	27.03.1988	2		
Lovre Kalinić (CRO)	03.04.1990	4		
Baptiste Reynet	28.10.1990	22	(1)	
Defenders:	**DOB**	**M**	**(s)**	**G**
Kelvin Amian Adou	08.02.1998	17	(3)	
Bafodé Diakité	06.01.2001	16		2
Moussa Diarra	10.11.2000	1		
Ruben Gabrielsen (NOR)	10.03.1992	8		
Mathieu Goncalves	08.06.2001	3	(1)	
Nicolas Isimat-Mirin	15.11.1991	14		1
Steven Moreira	13.08.1994	16	(1)	
Agustín Maximiliano Rogel Paita (URU)	17.10.1997	9	(1)	
Gen Shōji (JPN)	11.12.1992	1		
Issiaga Sylla (GUI)	01.01.1994	28		
Midfielders:	**DOB**	**M**	**(s)**	**G**
Amine Adli	10.05.2000		(4)	

	DOB	M	(s)	G
Quentin Boisgard	17.03.1997	13	(7)	1
Mathieu Dossevi (TOG)	12.02.1988	20	(6)	1
Kouadio Koné	17.05.2001	11	(2)	
Jean-Victor Makengo	12.06.1998	12	(7)	2
Nathan Ngoumou	14.03.2000		(1)	
Ibrahim Sangaré (CIV)	02.12.1997	25		
Kalidou Sidibé	28.01.1999		(4)	
Adil Taoui	10.08.2001		(2)	
William Vainqueur	19.11.1988	21		
Forwards:	**DOB**	**M**	**(s)**	**G**
Janis Antiste	18.08.2002		(1)	
Max-Alain Gradel (CIV)	30.11.1987	19	(2)	3
Corentin Jean	15.07.1995		(1)	
Efthimios Koulouris (GRE)	06.03.1996	17	(7)	4
Aaron Leya Iseka (BEL)	15.11.1997	6	(16)	2
Wesley Saïd	19.04.1995	14	(9)	2
Yaya Sanogo	27.01.1993	9	(6)	3

SECOND LEVEL
Ligue 2 2019/2020

1.	FC Lorient-Bretagne Sud (*Promoted*)	28	17	3	8	45 - 25		54
2.	Racing Club de Lens (*Promoted*)	28	15	8	5	39 - 24		53
3.	AC Ajaccio	28	15	7	6	38 - 22		52
4.	ES Troyes Aube Champagne	28	16	3	9	34 - 25		51
5.	Clermont Foot 63	28	14	8	6	35 - 25		50
6.	Le Havre AC	28	11	11	6	38 - 25		44
7.	Valenciennes FC	28	11	9	8	24 - 20		42
8.	En Avant de Guingamp	28	10	9	9	40 - 33		39
9.	Grenoble Foot 38	28	7	14	7	27 - 29		35
10.	FC Chambly Oise	28	9	8	11	26 - 32		35
11.	AJ Auxerre	28	8	10	10	31 - 30		34
12.	AS Nancy-Lorraine	28	6	16	6	27 - 26		34
13.	Stade Malherbe Caen	28	8	10	10	33 - 34		34
14.	FC Sochaux-Montbéliard	28	8	10	10	28 - 30		34
15.	La Berrichonne de Châteauroux	28	9	7	12	22 - 38		34
16.	Rodez Aveyron Football	28	8	8	12	31 - 34		32
17.	Paris FC	28	7	7	14	22 - 40		28
18.	Chamois Niortais FC	28	6	8	14	30 - 41		26
19.	Le Mans FC (*Relegated*)*	28	7	5	16	30 - 45		26
20.	US Orléans Loiret Football (*Relegated*)*	28	4	7	17	21 - 43		19

Please note: the season was suspended indefinitely on 12 March 2020 due to the COVID-19 pandemic.

On 28.04.2020, the French Prime Minister Édouard Philippe announced that there would be no sporting events, even behind closed doors, before September 2020, thus in effect ending the season. On 30 April 2020, the LFP announced that FC Lorient were declared champions of Ligue 2, and both winners and runners-up would be promoted to Ligue 1 2020/2021.

*On 27.05.2020, the executive committee of the FFF rejected a proposal by the LFP to have 22 clubs in the 2020/2021 competition, so both teams were relegated to Championat de France National (Third Level).

INTERNATIONAL MATCHES
(16.07.2019 – 15.07.2020)

07.09.2019	Paris	France - Albania	4-1(2-0)	(ECQ)
10.09.2019	Paris	France - Andorra	3-0(1-0)	(ECQ)
11.10.2019	Reykjavík	Island - France	0-1(0-0)	(ECQ)
14.10.2019	Paris	France - Turkey	1-1(0-0)	(ECQ)
14.11.2019	Paris	France - Moldova	2-1(1-1)	(ECQ)
17.11.2019	Tiranë	Albania - France	0-2(0-1)	(ECQ)

07.09.2019   FRANCE - ALBANIA   4-1(2-0)   16th EC. Qualifiers
Stade de France, Saint-Denis, Paris; Referee: Jesús Gil Manzano (Spain); Attendance: 77,655
FRA: Hugo Lloris (Cap), Benjamin Jacques Marcel Pavard, Raphaël Varane, Clément Nicolas Laurent Lenglet, Lucas François Bernard Hernández (80.Lucas Digne), Blaise Matuidi, Thomas Lemar (84.Nabil Fekir), Corentin Tolisso, Olivier Giroud, Antoine Griezmann, Kingsley Junior Coman (77.Nanitamo Jonathan Ikoné). Trainer: Didier Claude Deschamps.
Goals: Kingsley Junior Coman (8), Olivier Giroud (27), Kingsley Junior Coman (68), Nanitamo Jonathan Ikoné (85).

10.09.2019   FRANCE - ANDORRA   3-0(1-0)   16th EC. Qualifiers
Stade de France, Saint-Denis, Paris; Referee: Mykola Balakin (Ukraine); Attendance: 55,383
FRA: Hugo Lloris (Cap), Lucas Digne, Raphaël Varane, Clément Nicolas Laurent Lenglet, Léo Dubois, Moussa Sissoko, Corentin Tolisso, Nanitamo Jonathan Ikoné (63.Thomas Lemar), Olivier Giroud (72.Wissam Ben Yedder), Antoine Griezmann, Kingsley Junior Coman (85.Nabil Fekir). Trainer: Didier Claude Deschamps.
Goals: Kingsley Junior Coman (18), Clément Nicolas Laurent Lenglet (52), Wissam Ben Yedder (90+1).

11.10.2019   ISLAND - FRANCE   0-1(0-0)   16th EC. Qualifiers
Laugardalsvöllur, Reykjavík; Referee: Gianluca Rocchi (Italy); Attendance: 9,719
FRA: Steve Mandanda Mpidi, Benjamin Jacques Marcel Pavard, Lucas Digne, Raphaël Varane (Cap), Clément Nicolas Laurent Lenglet, Blaise Matuidi, Moussa Sissoko, Corentin Tolisso, Olivier Giroud (78.Wissam Ben Yedder), Antoine Griezmann, Kingsley Junior Coman (88.Nanitamo Jonathan Ikoné). Trainer: Didier Claude Deschamps.
Goal: Olivier Giroud (66 penalty).

14.10.2019   FRANCE - TURKEY   1-1(0-0)   16th EC. Qualifiers
Stade de France, Saint-Denis, Paris; Referee: Dr. Felix Brych (Germany); Attendance: 72,154
FRA: Steve Mandanda Mpidi, Benjamin Jacques Marcel Pavard, Raphaël Varane (Cap), Clément Nicolas Laurent Lenglet, Lucas François Bernard Hernández, Blaise Matuidi (77.Thomas Lemar), Moussa Sissoko, Corentin Tolisso, Antoine Griezmann, Wissam Ben Yedder (72.Olivier Giroud), Kingsley Junior Coman (87.Nanitamo Jonathan Ikoné). Trainer: Didier Claude Deschamps.
Goal: Olivier Giroud (76).

14.11.2019   FRANCE - MOLDOVA   2-1(1-1)   16th EC. Qualifiers
Stade de France, Saint-Denis, Paris; Referee: Gediminas Mažeika (Lithuania); Attendance: 64,367
FRA: Steve Mandanda Mpidi, Benjamin Jacques Marcel Pavard, Lucas Digne, Raphaël Varane (Cap), Clément Nicolas Laurent Lenglet, N'Golo Kanté, Corentin Tolisso, Olivier Giroud, Kylian Sanmi Mbappé Lottin, Antoine Griezmann, Kingsley Junior Coman (88.Thomas Lemar).Trainer: Didier Claude Deschamps.
Goals: Raphaël Varane (35), Olivier Giroud (79 penalty).

17.11.2019   ALBANIA - FRANCE   0-2(0-1)   16th EC. Qualifiers
Air Albania Stadium, Tiranë; Referee: Slavko Vinčić (Slovenia); Attendance: 19,228
FRA: Steve Mandanda Mpidi, Raphaël Varane (Cap), Benjamin Mendy (75.Lucas Digne), Clément Nicolas Laurent Lenglet, Presnel Kimpembe, Léo Dubois (88.Benjamin Jacques Marcel Pavard), Moussa Sissoko, Corentin Tolisso, Olivier Giroud, Antoine Griezmann, Wissam Ben Yedder (85.Nabil Fekir). Trainer: Didier Claude Deschamps.
Goals: Corentin Tolisso (9), Antoine Griezmann (30).

NATIONAL TEAM PLAYERS
(16.07.2019 – 15.07.2020)

Name	DOB	Caps	Goals	2019/2020:	Club
Goalkeepers					
Hugo LLORIS	26.12.1986	**114**	**0**	2019:	*Tottenham Hotspur FC London (ENG)*
Steve MANDANDA Mpidi	28.03.1985	**32**	**0**	2019:	*Olympique de Marseille*
Defenders					
Lucas DIGNE	20.07.1993	**30**	**0**	2019:	*Everton FC Liverpool (ENG)*
Léo DUBOIS	14.09.1994	**4**	**0**	2019:	*Olympique Lyonnais*
Lucas François Bernard HERNÁNDEZ	14.02.1996	**17**	**0**	2019:	*FC Bayern München (GER)*
Presnel KIMPEMBE	13.08.1995	**9**	**0**	2019:	*Paris Saint-Germain FC*
Clément Nicolas Laurent LENGLET	17.06.1995	**7**	**1**	2019:	*FC Barcelona (ESP)*
Benjamin MENDY	17.07.1994	**10**	**0**	2019:	*Manchester City FC (ENG)*
Benjamin Jacques Marcel PAVARD	28.03.1996	**27**	**1**	2019:	*FC Bayern München (GER)*
Raphaël Xavier VARANE	25.04.1993	**64**	**5**	2019:	*Real Madrid CF (ESP)*
Midfielders					
N'Golo KANTÉ	29.03.1991	**39**	**1**	2019:	*Chelsea FC London (ENG)*
Blaise MATUIDI	09.04.1987	**84**	**9**	2019:	*Juventus FC Torino (ITA)*
Moussa SISSOKO	16.08.1989	**62**	**2**	2019:	*Tottenham Hotspur FC London (ENG)*
Corentin TOLISSO	03.08.1994	**21**	**1**	2019:	*FC Bayern München (GER)*
Forwards					
Wissam BEN YEDDER	12.08.1990	**8**	**2**	2019:	*AS Monaco FC*
Kingsley Junior COMAN	13.06.1996	**22**	**4**	2019:	*FC Bayern München (GER)*
Nabil FEKIR	18.07.1993	**24**	**2**	2019:	*Real Betis Balompié Sevilla (ESP)*
Olivier GIROUD	30.09.1986	**97**	**39**	2019:	*Chelsea FC London (ENG)*
Antoine GRIEZMANN	21.03.1991	**78**	**30**	2019:	*FC Barcelona (ESP)*
Nanitamo Jonathan IKONÉ	02.05.1998	**4**	**1**	2019:	*Lille OSC*
Thomas LEMAR	12.11.1995	**22**	**4**	2019:	*Club Atlético de Madrid (ESP)*
Kylian Sanmi MBAPPÉ Lottin	20.12.1998	**34**	**13**	2019:	*Paris Saint-Germain FC*
National team coach					
Didier Claude DESCHAMPS [from 08.07.2012]	15.10.1968	100 M; 65 W; 18 D; 17 L; 196-83			

GEORGIA

The Country:
Georgia (საქართველო)
Capital: Tbilisi
Surface: 69,700 km²
Inhabitants: 3,716,858 [2020]
Time: UTC+4

The FA:
Georgian Football Federation
76a Chavchavadze Avenue, 0162 Tbilisi
Tel: +995 32 912 680
Founded: 1936/re-founded 1990
Member of FIFA since: 1992
Member of UEFA since: 1992
Website: www.gff.ge

NATIONAL TEAM RECORDS

RECORDS

First international match:	27.05.1990, Tbilisi:	Georgia – Lithuania 2-2
Most international caps:	Levan Kobiashvili	- 100 caps (1996-2011)
Most international goals:	Shota Arveladze	- 26 goals / 61 caps (1992-2007)

UEFA EUROPEAN CHAMPIONSHIP		FIFA WORLD CUP		OLYMPIC TOURNAMENTS	
1960	-	1930	-	1908	-
1964	-	1934	-	1912	-
1968	-	1938	-	1920	-
1972	-	1950	-	1924	-
1976	-	1954	-	1928	-
1980	-	1958	-	1936	-
1984	-	1962	-	1948	-
1988	-	1966	-	1952	-
1992	-	1970	-	1956	-
1996	Qualifiers	1974	-	1960	-
2000	Qualifiers	1978	-	1964	-
2004	Qualifiers	1982	-	1968	-
2008	Qualifiers	1986	-	1972	-
2012	Qualifiers	1990	-	1976	-
2016	Qualifiers	1994	Did not enter	1980	-
2020	*To be determined*	1998	Qualifiers	1984	-
		2002	Qualifiers	1988	-
		2006	Qualifiers	1992	-
		2010	Qualifiers	1996	Qualifiers
		2014	Qualifiers	2000	Qualifiers
		2018	Qualifiers	2004	Qualifiers
				2008	Qualifiers
				2012	Qualifiers
				2016	Qualifiers

was part of Soviet Union between 1930-1990

UEFA NATIONS LEAGUE

2018/2019 – League D (promoted to League C)

FIFA CONFEDERATIONS CUP 1992-2017

None

GEORGIAN CLUB HONOURS IN EUROPEAN CLUB COMPETITIONS:

European Champion Clubs.Cup (1956-1992) / UEFA Champions League (1993-2020)		
None		
Fairs Cup (1858-1971) / UEFA Cup (1972-2009) / UEFA Europa League (2010-2020)		
None		
UEFA Super Cup (1972-2019)		
None		
European Cup Winners.Cup 1961-1999*		
FC Dinamo Tbilisi*	1	1980/1981
represented the Soviet Union		

defunct competition

NATIONAL COMPETITIONS
TABLE OF HONOURS

GEORGIAN SSR (SOVIET ERA) CHAMPIONS

1927	Batumi XI	1953	TTU Tbilisi	1972	Lokomotivi FC Samtredia
1928	Tbilisi XI	1954	TTU Tbilisi	1973	Dinamo Zugdidi
1929-1935	*No competition*	1955	Dinamo Kutaisi	1974	Metallurg Rustavi
1936	ZII Tbilisi	1956	FC FC Lokomotivi Tbilisi	1975	Magaroeli Chiatura
1937	FC FC Lokomotivi Tbilisi	1957	TTU Tbilisi	1976	SKIF Tbilisi
1938	FC FC Dinamo Batumi	1958	TTU Tbilisi	1977	Mziuri Gali
1939	Nauka Tbilisi	1959	Metallurg Rustavi	1978	Kolheti Poti
1940	FC FC Dinamo Batumi	1960	Imereti Kutaisi	1979	Metallurg Rustavi
1941-1942	*No competition*	1961	FC Guria Lanchkhuti	1980	Meshakhte Tkibuli
1943	ODKA Tbilisi	1962	Imereti Kutaisi	1981	Meshakhte Tkibuli
1944	*No competition*	1963	Imereti Kutaisi	1982	Mertskhali Makharadze
1945	FC FC Lokomotivi Tbilisi	1964	IngurGES Zugdidi	1983	Samgulari Tskhaltubo
1946	Dinamo Kutaisi	1965	Tolia Tbilisi	1984	Metallurg Rustavi
1947	FC Dinamo Sokhumi	1966	FC Guria Lanchkhuti	1985	Shadrevani-83 Tskhaltubo
1948	FC Dinamo Sokhumi	1967	Mertskhali Makharadze	1986	Shevardeni-1906 Tbilisi
1949	FC FC Torpedo Kutaisi	1968	SKA Tbilisi	1987	Mertskhali Makharadze
1950	TODO Tbilisi	1969	Sulori Vani	1988	Kolheti Poti
1951	TODO Tbilisi	1970	SKIF Tbilisi	1989	Shadrevani-83 Tskhaltubo
1952	TTU Tbilisi	1971	FC Guria Lanchkhuti		

	CHAMPIONS	CUP WINNERS	BEST GOALSCORERS	
1990	FC Iberia Tbilisi	FC Guria Lanchkhuti	Gia Guruli (FC Iberia Tbilisi)	
			Mamuka Pantsulaia (FC Gorda Rustavi)	23
1991	FC Iberia Tbilisi	FC Dinamo Tbilisi	Otar Korgalidze (FC Guria Lanchkhuti)	14
1991/1992	FC Dinamo Tbilisi	FC Dinamo Tbilisi	Otar Korgalidze (FC Guria Lanchkhuti)	40
1992/1993	FC Dinamo Tbilisi	FC Dinamo Tbilisi	Merab Megreladze (Samgurali Tskhaltubo)	41
1993/1994	FC Dinamo Tbilisi	FC Dinamo Tbilisi	Merab Megreladze (FC Margveti Zestafoni)	31
1994/1995	FC Dinamo Tbilisi	FC Dinamo Tbilisi	Giorgi Daraselia (FC Kolkheti-1913 Poti)	26
1995/1996	FC Dinamo Tbilisi	FC Dinamo Tbilisi	Zviad Endeladze (FC Margveti Zestafoni)	40
1996/1997	FC Dinamo Tbilisi	FC Dinamo Batumi	Giorgi Demetradze (FC Dinamo Tbilisi)	
			David Ujmajuridze (FC Dinamo Batumi)	26
1997/1998	FC Dinamo Tbilisi	FC Torpedo Kutaisi	Levan Khomeriki (FC Dinamo Tbilisi)	23
1998/1999	FC Dinamo Tbilisi	FC Lokomotivi Tbilisi	Mikheil Ashvetia (FC Dinamo Tbilisi)	26
1999/2000	FC Torpedo Kutaisi	FC Torpedo Kutaisi	Zurab Ionanidze (FC Torpedo Kutaisi)	24
2000/2001	FC Torpedo Kutaisi	FC Lokomotivi Tbilisi	Zaza Zirakishvili (FC Dinamo Tbilisi)	21
2001/2002	FC Torpedo Kutaisi	FC Dinamo Tbilisi	Suliko Davitashvili	
			(FC Lokomotivi Tbilisi / FC Merani Tbilisi)	18
2002/2003	FC Dinamo Tbilisi	FC Dinamo Tbilisi	Zurab Ionanidze (FC Torpedo Kutaisi)	26
2003/2004	FC WIT Georgia Tbilisi	FC Lokomotivi Tbilisi	Suliko Davitashvili (FC Torpedo Kutaisi)	20
2004/2005	FC Dinamo Tbilisi	FC Ameri Tbilisi	Levani Melkadze (FC Dinamo Tbilisi)	27
2005/2006	FC Sioni Bolnisi	FC Ameri Tbilisi	Jaba Dvali (FC Dinamo Tbilisi)	21
2006/2007	FC Olimpi Rustavi	FC Zestafoni	Sandro Iashvili (FC Dinamo Tbilisi)	27
2007/2008	FC Dinamo Tbilisi	FC Dinamo Tbilisi	Mikheil Khutsishvili (FC Dinamo Tbilisi)	16
2008/2009	FC WIT Georgia Tbilisi	FC WIT Georgia Tbilisi	Nikoloz Gelashvili (FC Zestafoni)	20
2009/2010	FC Olimpi Rustavi	FC Gagra	Brazil Anderson Aquino (FC Metalurgi Rustavi)	26
2010/2011	FC Zestafoni	FC Dila Gori	Nikoloz Gelashvili (FC Zestafoni)	18
2011/2012	FC Zestafoni	FC Dinamo Tbilisi	Jaba Dvali (FC Zestafoni)	20
2012/2013	FC Dinamo Tbilisi	FC Dinamo Tbilisi	Spain Xisco (FC Dinamo Tbilisi)	24
2013/2014	FC Dinamo Tbilisi	FC Dinamo Tbilisi	Spain Xisco (FC Dinamo Tbilisi)	19
2014/2015	FC Dila Gori	FC Dinamo Tbilisi	Irakli Modebadze (FC Dila Gori)	16
2015/2016	FC Dinamo Tbilisi	FC Torpedo Kutaisi	Giorgi Kvilitaia (FC Dinamo Tbilisi)	24
2016	FC Samtredia	FC Chikhura Sachkhere	Budu Zivzivadze (FC Samtredia)	11
2017	FC Torpedo Kutaisi	FC Guria Lanchkhuti	Irakli Sikharulidze (FC Lokomotivi Tbilisi)	25
2018	FC Saburtalo Tbilisi	FC Torpedo Kutaisi	Giorgi Gabedava (FC Chikhura Sachkhere)	
			Budu Zivzivadze (FC Dinamo Tbilisi)	22
2019	FC Dinamo Tbilisi	FC Saburtalo Tbilisi	Levan Kutalia (FC Dinamo Tbilisi)	20

Please note: FC Dinamo Tbilisi changed its name to FC Iberia Tbilisi between 1990-1992; FC Olimpi Rustavi became FC Metalurgi Rustavi (2011-2015) and later FC Rustavi (since 2011).

NATIONAL CHAMPIONSHIP
Erovnuli Liga 2019
(01.03.2019 – 01.12.2019)

Results

Round 1 [01-03.03.2019]
FC Saburtalo - Dinamo Batumi 1-0(0-0)
Lokomotivi Tbilisi - FC Rustavi 4-1(2-1)
Torpedo Kutaisi - Sioni Bolnisi 3-2(2-1)
Dinamo Tbilisi - Chikhura Sachkhere 2-0(1-0)
Dila Gori - WIT Georgia 0-1(0-0)

Round 2 [05-06.03.2019]
Lokomotivi Tbilisi - FC Saburtalo 1-3(1-1)
Dinamo Batumi - Torpedo Kutaisi 0-2(0-2)
Sioni Bolnisi - Dinamo Tbilisi 2-1(1-1)
FC Rustavi - WIT Georgia 0-0
Chikhura Sachkhere - Dila Gori 1-1(1-0)

Round 3 [09-11.03.2019]
Torpedo Kutaisi - Lokomotivi Tbilisi 0-2(0-0)
Dinamo Tbilisi - Dinamo Batumi 0-1(0-1)
FC Saburtalo - FC Rustavi 2-1(0-1)
WIT Georgia - Chikhura Sachkhere 1-1(1-0)
Dila Gori - Sioni Bolnisi 0-0

Round 4 [15-17.03.2019]
FC Saburtalo - Torpedo Kutaisi 3-0(3-0)
FC Rustavi - Chikhura Sachkhere 1-1(1-1)
Dinamo Batumi - Dila Gori 1-0(0-0)
Sioni Bolnisi - WIT Georgia 1-0(0-0)
Lokomotivi Tbilisi - Dinamo Tbilisi 0-4(0-1)

Round 5 [30-31.03.2019]
Chikhura Sachkhere - Sioni Bolnisi 5-0(4-0)
Dila Gori - Lokomotivi Tbilisi 3-1(2-1)
WIT Georgia - Dinamo Batumi 0-1(0-0)
Torpedo Kutaisi - FC Rustavi 2-0(1-0)
Dinamo Tbilisi - FC Saburtalo 4-2(2-2)

Round 6 [02-03.04.2019]
Lokomotivi Tbilisi - WIT Georgia 0-1(0-0)
Dinamo Batumi - Chikhura Sachkhere 0-0
Torpedo Kutaisi - Dinamo Tbilisi 0-0
FC Rustavi - Sioni Bolnisi 1-1(1-1)
FC Saburtalo - Dila Gori 2-1(1-0)

Round 7 [06-08.04.2019]
Chikhura Sachkhere - Lokom. Tbilisi 1-0(0-0)
Sioni Bolnisi - Dinamo Batumi 2-4(1-2)
Dinamo Tbilisi - FC Rustavi 3-1(2-0)
Dila Gori - Torpedo Kutaisi 0-2(0-0)
WIT Georgia - FC Saburtalo 0-3(0-0)

Round 8 [12-13.04.2019]
Dinamo Tbilisi - Dila Gori 1-0(1-0)
Lokomotivi Tbilisi - Sioni Bolnisi 1-2(0-1)
Torpedo Kutaisi - WIT Georgia 2-1(1-0)
FC Rustavi - Dinamo Batumi 0-2(0-1)
FC Saburtalo - Chikhura Sachkhere 2-3(1-3)

Round 9 [20-21.04.2019]
Sioni Bolnisi - FC Saburtalo 2-3(0-1)
Dila Gori - FC Rustavi 2-1(1-0)
Dinamo Batumi - Lokomotivi Tbilisi 2-1(1-1)
Chikhura Sachkhere - Torpedo Kutaisi 0-0
WIT Georgia - Dinamo Tbilisi 1-0(0-0)

Round 10 [24-25.04.2019]
FC Rustavi - Lokomotivi Tbilisi 0-2(0-1)
Dinamo Batumi - FC Saburtalo 4-2(3-2)
Sioni Bolnisi - Torpedo Kutaisi 2-1(1-1)
Chikhura Sachkhere - Dinamo Tbilisi 2-2(0-0)
WIT Georgia - Dila Gori 0-1(0-0)

Round 11 [04-05.05.2019]
Torpedo Kutaisi - Dinamo Batumi 3-2(2-1)
Dinamo Tbilisi - Sioni Bolnisi 5-1(2-1)
WIT Georgia - FC Rustavi 2-3(2-0)
Dila Gori - Chikhura Sachkhere 2-0(2-0)
FC Saburtalo - Lokomotivi Tbilisi 1-0(0-0)

Round 12 [10-11.05.2019]
Lokomotivi Tbilisi - Torpedo Kutaisi 1-3(0-2)
FC Rustavi - FC Saburtalo 3-1(0-0)
Sioni Bolnisi - Dila Gori 2-1(1-1)
Chikhura Sachkhere - WIT Georgia 1-0(0-0)
Dinamo Batumi - Dinamo Tbilisi 3-2(2-0)

Round 13 [14-15.05.2019]
Torpedo Kutaisi - FC Saburtalo 2-3(1-2)
WIT Georgia - Sioni Bolnisi 0-1(0-0)
Chikhura Sachkhere - FC Rustavi 0-0
Dila Gori - Dinamo Batumi 1-0(0-0)
Dinamo Tbilisi - Lokomotivi Tbilisi 1-3(0-1)

Round 14 [19-20.05.2019]
Sioni Bolnisi - Chikhura Sachkhere 0-5(0-4)
Lokomotivi Tbilisi - Dila Gori 1-0(1-0)
Dinamo Batumi - WIT Georgia 2-0(1-0)
FC Rustavi - Torpedo Kutaisi 2-4(0-0)
FC Saburtalo - Dinamo Tbilisi 2-0(0-0)

Round 15 [23-24.05.2019]
Chikhura Sachkh. - Dinamo Batumi 1-2(1-1)
WIT Georgia - Lokomotivi Tbilisi 0-3(0-1)
Sioni Bolnisi - FC Rustavi 3-3(0-2)
Dinamo Tbilisi - Torpedo Kutaisi 2-1(1-0)
Dila Gori - FC Saburtalo 1-1(0-0)

Round 16 [28-29.05.2019]
Torpedo Kutaisi - Dila Gori 3-3(3-1)
FC Rustavi - Dinamo Tbilisi 0-1(0-1)
FC Saburtalo - WIT Georgia 3-0(1-0)
Lokomotivi Tbilisi - Chikhura Sach. 2-0(0-0)
Dinamo Batumi - Sioni Bolnisi 5-1(1-0)

Round 17 [01-02.06.2019]
Dila Gori - Dinamo Tbilisi 2-3(1-3)
WIT Georgia - Torpedo Kutaisi 3-0(1-0)
Sioni Bolnisi - Lokomotivi Tbilisi 0-0
Dinamo Batumi - FC Rustavi 2-1(1-1)
Chikhura Sachkhere - FC Saburtalo 0-0

Round 18 [14-16.06.2019]
FC Rustavi - Dila Gori 2-1(2-0)
FC Saburtalo - Sioni Bolnisi 2-1(1-0)
Torpedo Kutaisi - Chikhura Sachkh. 5-3(4-1)
Lokomotivi Tbilisi - Dinamo Batumi 1-0(0-0)
Dinamo Tbilisi - WIT Georgia 2-1(1-1)

Round 19 [22-23.06.2019]
Torpedo Kutaisi - Sioni Bolnisi 7-0(4-0)
Lokomotivi Tbilisi - FC Rustavi 1-1(1-1)
FC Saburtalo - Dinamo Batumi 0-0
Dinamo Tbilisi - Chikhura Sachkhere 1-0(0-0)
Dila Gori - WIT Georgia 2-0(0-0)

Round 20 [25-27.06.2019]
Lokomotivi Tbilisi - FC Saburtalo 1-0(0-0)
Dinamo Batumi - Torpedo Kutaisi 2-2(2-1)
Chikhura Sachkhere - Dila Gori 4-1(2-1)
Sioni Bolnisi - Dinamo Tbilisi 0-3(0-1)
FC Rustavi - WIT Georgia 1-0(0-0)

Round 21 [02-03.07.2019]
Torpedo Kutaisi - Lokomotivi Tbilisi 0-2(0-0)
WIT Georgia - Chikhura Sachkhere 0-0
FC Saburtalo - FC Rustavi 2-2(1-2)
Dila Gori - Sioni Bolnisi 2-0(1-0)
Dinamo Tbilisi - Dinamo Batumi 2-1(1-1)

Round 22 03-06.08.2019 [ ]
Sioni Bolnisi - WIT Georgia 1-0(0-0)
Dinamo Batumi - Dila Gori 0-0
Lokomotivi Tbilisi - Dinamo Tbilisi 0-6(0-4)
FC Rustavi - Chikhura Sachkhere 1-0(1-0)
Saburtalo - Torpedo Kutaisi 1-1(0-1) [16.09.]

Round 23 [10-11.08.2019]
Dila Gori - Lokomotivi Tbilisi 0-1(0-0)
WIT Georgia - Dinamo Batumi 0-3(0-2)
Chikhura Sachkhere - Sioni Bolnisi 2-2(1-0)
Torpedo Kutaisi - FC Rustavi 0-1(0-0)
Dinamo Tbilisi - Saburtalo 2-1(0-1) [02.10.]

Round 24 [16-20.08.2019]
Lokomotivi Tbilisi - WIT Georgia 1-1(1-0)
FC Rustavi - Sioni Bolnisi 2-1(1-1)
Dinamo Batumi - Chikhura Sachkh. 2-0(0-0)
Torpedo Kutaisi - Dinamo Tbilisi 0-1(0-1)
FC Saburtalo - Dila Gori 3-0(1-0)

Round 25 [23-25.08.2019]
Sioni Bolnisi - Dinamo Batumi 0-4(0-0)
Chikhura Sachk. - Lokomotivi Tbilisi 3-2(1-1)
Dila Gori - Torpedo Kutaisi 2-2(1-2)
WIT Georgia - FC Saburtalo 0-0
Dinamo Tbilisi - FC Rustavi 2-2(1-0)

Round 26 [29.08.-01.09.2019]
Dinamo Tbilisi - Dila Gori 5-0(2-0)
Lokomotivi Tbilisi - Sioni Bolnisi 1-1(0-0)
Torpedo Kutaisi - WIT Georgia 1-0(0-0)
FC Rustavi - Dinamo Batumi 0-2(0-2)
FC Saburtalo - Chikhura Sachkhere 1-0(0-0)

Round 27 [12-15.09.2019]
Sioni Bolnisi - FC Saburtalo 1-3(0-3)
Chikhura Sachkh. - Torpedo Kutaisi 1-1(0-0)
Dila Gori - FC Rustavi 0-0
Dinamo Batumi - Lokomotivi Tbilisi 2-1(1-0)
WIT Georgia - Dinamo Tbilisi 0-3(0-1)

Round 28 [20-21.09.2019]
Sioni Bolnisi - Torpedo Kutaisi 2-0(1-0)
FC Rustavi - Lokomotivi Tbilisi 2-1(0-0)
Dinamo Batumi - FC Saburtalo 1-0(0-0)
Chikhura Sachkhere - Dinamo Tbilisi 0-2(0-0)
WIT Georgia - Dila Gori 0-2(0-1)

Round 29 [28-29.09.2019]
FC Saburtalo - Lokomotivi Tbilisi 4-0(2-0)
Dinamo Tbilisi - Sioni Bolnisi 1-1(0-0)
Torpedo Kutaisi - Dinamo Batumi 1-2(1-2)
WIT Georgia - FC Rustavi 0-0
Dila Gori - Chikhura Sachkhere 2-1(1-1)

Round 30 [05-06.10.2019]
Sioni Bolnisi - Dila Gori 0-4(0-0)
Lokomotivi Tbilisi - Torpedo Kutaisi 2-0(1-0)
Chikhura Sachkhere - WIT Georgia 2-1(1-0)
FC Rustavi - FC Saburtalo 0-3(0-1)
Dinamo Batumi - Dinamo Tbilisi 1-1(0-0)

Round 31 [19-20.10.2019]
Torpedo Kutaisi - FC Saburtalo 0-2(0-0)
Dinamo Tbilisi - Lokomotivi Tbilisi 0-1(0-0)
Chikhura Sachkhere - FC Rustavi 3-2(1-2)
WIT Georgia - Sioni Bolnisi 0-0
Dila Gori - Dinamo Batumi 0-0

Round 32 [25-27.10.2019]
Dinamo Batumi - WIT Georgia 1-1(1-0)
Sioni Bolnisi - Chikhura Sachkhere 2-1(0-1)
FC Rustavi - Torpedo Kutaisi 2-0(1-0)
FC Saburtalo - Dinamo Tbilisi 0-0
Lokomotivi Tbilisi - Dila Gori 1-0(0-0)

Round 33 [01-03.11.2019]
Chikhura Sachkh. - Dinamo Batumi 2-0(0-0)
Sioni Bolnisi - FC Rustavi 2-1(2-1)
WIT Georgia - Lokomotivi Tbilisi 0-2(0-0)
Dila Gori - FC Saburtalo 2-0(0-0)
Dinamo Tbilisi - Torpedo Kutaisi 2-1(2-0)

Round 34 [08-10.11.2019]
Dinamo Batumi - Sioni Bolnisi 2-0(1-0)
FC Rustavi - Dinamo Tbilisi 0-2(0-0)
FC Saburtalo - WIT Georgia 3-1(0-0)
Lokomotivi Tbilisi - Chikhura Sachk. 0-2(0-1)
Torpedo Kutaisi - Dila Gori 1-1(1-0)

Round 35 [24.11.2019]
Sioni Bolnisi - Lokomotivi Tbilisi 1-2(0-2)
Chikhura Sachkhere - FC Saburtalo 1-3(0-1)
Dila Gori - Dinamo Tbilisi 1-2(0-2)
Dinamo Batumi - FC Rustavi 2-1(1-1)
WIT Georgia - Torpedo Kutaisi 0-2(0-0)

Round 36 [30.11.-01.12.2019]
FC Rustavi - Dila Gori 2-2(0-2)
FC Saburtalo - Sioni Bolnisi 5-1(1-1)
Torpedo Kutaisi - Chikhura Sachkh. 1-2(1-1)
Dinamo Tbilisi - WIT Georgia 2-0(1-0)
Lokomotivi Tbilisi - Dinamo Batumi 2-1(0-0)

Final Standings

								Total			Home				Away		
1.	**FC Dinamo Tbilisi**	36	23	6	7	70 - 31	75	13	2	3	37 - 17	10	4	4	33 - 14
2.	FC Dinamo Batumi	36	21	7	8	57 - 31	70	12	5	1	32 - 15	9	2	7	25 - 16
3.	FC Saburtalo Tbilisi	36	21	7	8	67 - 36	70	13	4	1	37 - 11	8	3	7	30 - 25
4.	FC Lokomotivi Tbilisi	36	17	4	15	44 - 46	55	8	3	7	20 - 26	9	1	8	24 - 20
5.	FC Chikhura Sachkhere	36	12	11	13	48 - 44	47	8	7	3	29 - 19	4	4	10	19 - 25
6.	FC Torpedo Kutaisi	36	12	8	16	53 - 54	44	7	3	8	31 - 27	5	5	8	22 - 27
7.	FC Dila Gori	36	11	10	15	40 - 44	43	8	5	5	22 - 15	3	5	10	18 - 29
8.	FC Rustavi (*Relegation Play-offs*)	36	9	11	16	40 - 56	38	7	4	7	19 - 24	2	7	9	21 - 32
9.	FC Sioni Bolnisi (*Relegation Play-offs*)	36	10	8	18	38 - 80	38	8	2	8	23 - 36	2	6	10	15 - 44
10.	FC WIT Georgia Tbilisi (*Relegated*)	36	4	8	24	15 - 50	20	2	5	11	7 - 25	2	3	13	8 - 25

Top goalscorers:	
20 **Levan Kutalia**	*FC Dinamo Tbilisi*
17 Jovinho Flamarion Filho (BRA)	*FC Dinamo Batumi*
16 Irakli Sikharulidze	*FC Lokomotivi Tbilisi*
13 Budu Zivzivadze	*FC Torpedo Kutaisi*
12 Levan Shengelia	*FC Dinamo Tbilisi*

Relegation Play-offs [05-11.12.2019]

FC Telavi - FC Rustavi	1-0(0-0)	2-1(2-1)
FC Sioni Bolnisi – **FC Samtredia**	0-0	1-4(0-2)

FC Rustavi and FC Samtredia promoted for the Erovnuli Liga 2020.

NATIONAL CUP
Georgian Cup - Sakartvelos tasi 2019

Second Round [27-29.03.2019]

Lazika Zugdidi - FC Betlemi Keda	0-3	FC Chiatura - FC Dusheti	1-0
Senakuri Senaki – FC Samgurali Tskhaltubo	2-0	FC Tori Borjomi - FC Borjomi	2-5
FC Dinamo Batumi II - FC Saburtalo II	1-0 aet	FC Iberia Tbilisi – FC Samegrelo Chkhorotsku	3-2
FC Gareji Sagarejo - Bakhmaro Chokhatauri	1-0	FC Legioni - Gori FC	3-2 pen
FC Merani Martvili - FC Meshakhte Tkibuli	1-0	FC Algeti Marneuli - Spaeri FC	0-3
FC Zestafoni - FC Khobi	2-0	FC Sulori Vani – FC Tbilisi City	3-4 pen

Third Round [16-17.04.2019]

FC Samtredia – FC Dila Gori	3-2	FC Gagra - FC Kobuleti	2-0
FC Gareji Sagarejo - FC Chiatura	2-0	FC Telavi - FC WIT Georgia Tbilisi	3-0
FC Iberia Tbilisi - FC Merani Martvili	0-2	FC Zugdidi - FC Tskhinvali Gori	3-2 aet
FC Legioni – FC Tbilisi City	1-2	FC Betlemi Keda - FC Guria Lanchkhuti	1-2
FC Shevardeni-1906 Tbilisi - FC Sioni Bolnisi	1-2	FC Borjomi - FC Torpedo Kutaisi	1-4
FC Senakuri Senaki - FC Dinamo Tbilisi	1-4	FC Zestafoni - FC Merani Tbilisi	0-2
FC Saburtalo - FC Dinamo Batumi	1-0	Spaeri FC - FC Kolkheti-1913 Poti	5-1
FC Dinamo Batumi II - FC Rustavi	0-2	FC Lokomotivi Tbilisi – FC Chikhura Sachkhere	1-0

1/8-Finals [18-19.06.2019]

FC Gareji Sagarejo - Spaeri FC	3-3 aet; 4-2 pen	FC Gagra - FC Torpedo Kutaisi	2-3
FC Tbilisi City - FC Zugdidi	3-1	FC Telavi - FC Lokomotivi Tbilisi	0-1
FC Merani Martvili - FC Guria Lanchkhuti	3-0	FC Merani Tbilisi - FC Dinamo Tbilisi	1-0 aet
FC Samtredia - FC Saburtalo	1-2	FC Rustavi - FC Sioni Bolnisi	2-0

Quarter-Finals [24-25.09.2019]

FC Merani Martvili - FC Lokomotivi Tbilisi	1-2 aet	FC Gareji Sagarejo – FC Tbilisi City	2-1
FC Merani Tbilisi - FC Saburtalo	1-2 aet	FC Rustavi - FC Torpedo Kutaisi	2-4 pen

Semi-Finals [23.10.2019]				
FC Gareji Sagarejo - FC Lokomotivi Tbilisi	2-3		FC Saburtalo - FC Torpedo Kutaisi	2-0

Final

08.12.2019; Stadioni "Tengiz Burjanadze", Gori; Referee: Irakli Kvirikashvili; Attendance: 3,000
FC Saburtalo Tbilisi - FC Lokomotivi Tbilisi   **3-1(2-0)**

FC Saburtalo: Lazare Kupatadze, Giorgi Rekhviashvili, Gagi Margvelashvili, Tornike Gorgiashvili (61.Levan Kenia), Levan Kakubava, Sandro Altunashvili, Nikoloz Mali, Alwyn Tera, Iuri Tabatadze (86.Dachi Tsnobiladze), Giorgi Gabedava, Giorgi Kokhreidze (67.Lasha Kokhreidze). Trainer: Giorgi Chiabrishvili.

FC Lokomotivi: Demetre Buliskeria, Nika Tchanturia, Aleksandre Gureshidze, Davit Ubilava, Temuri Shonia, Davit Kirkitadze (77.Lasha Gvalia), Irakli Komakhidze, Davit Samurkasovi, Beka Dartsmelia (82.Davit Jikia), Tornike Kirkitadze (30.Revaz Injgia), Irakli Sikharulidze. Trainer: Levan Korgalidze.

Goals: 1-0 Giorgi Kokhreidze (12), 2-0 Giorgi Gabedava (19), 2-1 Irakli Sikharulidze (52 penalty), 3-1 Levan Kakubava (89).

THE CLUBS 2019

Football Club Chikhura Sachkhere

Founded: 1938
Stadium: Stadioni Central, Sachkere (2,000)
Trainer: Samson Pruidze   06.10.1957

Goalkeepers:	DOB	M	(s)	G
Dino Hamzić (BIH)	22.01.1988	36		
Defenders:	**DOB**	**M**	**(s)**	**G**
Lasha Chikvaidze	04.10.1989	25	(1)	3
Revaz Chiteishvili	30.01.1994	22	(6)	
Irakli Kamladze	18.02.1997	8	(11)	1
Giorgi Koripadze	03.10.1989	35		6
Shota Kashia	22.10.1984	29		
Davit Maisashvili	18.02.1989	33		2
Davit Megrelishvili	25.09.1991	13	(10)	
Midfielders:	**DOB**	**M**	**(s)**	**G**
Rati Ardazishvili	27.01.1998	7	(2)	1
Demur Chikhladze	23.09.1996	26	(9)	2

	DOB	M	(s)	G
Beso Dekanoidze	01.03.1992	26	(4)	5
Zurab Kapanadze	02.01.2001		(2)	
Irakli Lekvtadze	30.08.1991	19	(3)	2
Bidzina Makharoblidze	10.10.1992	17	(3)	9
Oleg Mamasakhlisi	25.11.1995	24	(1)	1
Teimuraz Markozashvili	09.08.1994	21	(9)	1
Mikheil Sardalishvili	17.09.1992	32	(2)	8
Forwards:	**DOB**	**M**	**(s)**	**G**
Mikheil Ergemlidze	28.09.1999	3	(8)	
Davit Ionanidze	05.08.1998		(9)	
Tornike Mumladze	23.07.1992	5	(13)	1
Giorgi Pantsulaia	06.01.1994	15	(5)	5

Football Club Dila Gori

Founded: 1949
Stadium: Stadioni „Tengiz Burjanadze", Gori (8,230)
Trainer: Giorgi Dekanosidze   02.01.1981
[01.07.2019] Irakli Modebadze   04.10.1984
[17.07.2019] Giorgi Nemsadze   10.05.1972

Goalkeepers:	DOB	M	(s)	G
Giorgi Begashvili	12.02.1991	4		
Giorgi Chochishvili	07.05.1998	14		
Luka Gugeshashvili	29.04.1999	17		
Lasha Titvinidze	12.02.2002	1	(1)	
Defenders:	**DOB**	**M**	**(s)**	**G**
Alef Santos de Araujo (BRA)	06.11.1996	5	(3)	1
Gia Chaduneli	15.05.1994	24		1
Eriks de Souza Santos Pereira (BRA)	23.02.1996	23		
Guram Giorbelidze	25.02.1996	32		
Tornike Grigalashvili	28.01.1993	15		
Levan Kurdadze	03.09.1990	5	(3)	
Goderdzi Machaidze	17.07.1992	1		
Bakar Mirtskhulava	24.05.1992	28	(2)	
Balgou Yendountie (TOG)	24.12.1999	10		
Midfielders:	**DOB**	**M**	**(s)**	**G**
Giorgi Alimbarashvili	01.09.2001		(1)	

	DOB	M	(s)	G
Nika Gagnidze	20.03.2001	4	(11)	
Zaur Kereleishvili	25.09.1998	6	(4)	
Giorgi Kutsia	27.10.1999	27	(3)	4
Issifu Lamptey (GHA)	01.06.1995	2	(14)	
Levan Nonikashvili	05.04.1995	31	(2)	4
Amos Nondi Obiero (KEN)	10.02.1999	27	(4)	
Luka Razmadze	30.12.1983	24	(5)	
Tengiz Tsikaridze	21.12.1995	3	(4)	1
Forwards:	**DOB**	**M**	**(s)**	**G**
Alvin Mateus Fortes (NED)	25.05.1994	32	(2)	8
Felipe Vasconcelos Paim (BRA)	23.05.1997	7	(14)	1
Guram Goshteliani	05.01.1997	24	(3)	7
Didier Kougbenya (TOG)	12.11.1995	8	(3)	4
Mykola Kovtaliuk (UKR)	26.04.1995	5	(3)	3
Jacob Njoku (NGA)	16.11.1997	2	(6)	1
Fabian Reid (JAM)	06.08.1991	3		
Nugzar Spanderashvili	16.01.1999	12	(17)	3

Football Club Dinamo Batumi

Founded: 1923
Stadium: Chele Arena, Kobuleti (6,000)
Trainer: George Geguchadze   20.06.1965

Goalkeepers:	DOB	M	(s)	G
Mikheil Alavidze	05.11.1987	36		
Defenders:	**DOB**	**M**	**(s)**	**G**
Guram Adamadze	21.08.1988	15		
Alef Santos de Araujo (BRA)	06.11.1996	5	(1)	
Lasha Chaladze	11.05.1987	10	(8)	1
Giorgi Gadrani	30.09.1994	4	(1)	1
Malkhaz Gagoshidze	20.02.1993	34		1
Levan Gegetchkori	05.06.1994	12		
Mamuka Kobakhidze	23.08.1992	17		
Kichi Meliava	14.04.1992	18		
Giorgi Navalovski	28.06.1986	26	(1)	
Vazha Patsatsia	29.01.1992	2		
Midfielders:	**DOB**	**M**	**(s)**	**G**
Tornike Gaprindashvili	20.07.1997		(26)	3

	DOB	M	(s)	G
Giorgi Janelidze	25.09.1989	17	(5)	1
Jaba Jigauri	08.07.1992	12	(2)	6
Vladimer Mamuchashvili	28.08.1997	32	(2)	5
Giuli Mandzhgaladze	09.09.1992	28	(2)	3
Benjamin Teidi (NGA)	07.05.1994	24	(5)	3
Valerian Tevdoradze	11.10.1993	8	(25)	1
Rati Tsatskrialashvili	11.10.1993	1	(3)	
Forwards:	**DOB**	**M**	**(s)**	**G**
Vladimer Dvalishvili	20.04.1986	12	(2)	3
Flamarion Jovinho Filho (BRA)	30.07.1996	28	(2)	17
Giorgi Iluridze	20.02.1992	1	(8)	
Gabriel Ramos da Penha (BRA)	20.03.1996	33	(2)	4
Nikoloz Sabanadze	02.05.1991	18	(2)	5
Roman Tchanturia	09.02.1996	3	(7)	2

Football Club Dinamo Tbilisi

Founded: 1925
Stadium: „Boris Paichadze" Dinamo Arena, Tbilisi (54,549)
Trainer: Félix Vicente Miranda (ESP)   16.06.1978

Goalkeepers:	DOB	M	(s)	G
José Perales Nájera (ESP)	25.05.1993	34	(1)	
Ştefan Sicaci (MDA)	08.09.1988	2		
Defenders:	**DOB**	**M**	**(s)**	**G**
Nodar Iashvili	24.01.1993	30	(3)	
Oleksandr Kapliyenko (UKR)	07.03.1996	11	(1)	
Giorgi Kimadze	11.02.1992	14		
Davit Kobouri	24.01.1998	18	(5)	
Abdel Medioub (FRA)	28.08.1997	19		1
Guja Rukhaia	22.07.1987	17	(2)	1
Sergio Jesús Noche Márquez (ESP)	22.12.1992	3		
Víctor Mongil Adeva (ESP)	21.07.1992	36		1
Midfielders:	**DOB**	**M**	**(s)**	**G**
Giorgi Abuashvili	08.02.2003		(1)	
Irakli Azarovi	21.01.2002	1	(6)	
Arfang Boubacar Daffé (SEN)	24.06.1991	5	(8)	1
Dmytro Ivanisenya (UKR)	11.01.1994	13	(3)	3
Bakar Kardava	04.10.1994	7	(14)	1
Nodar Kavtaradze	02.01.1993	13		5
Giorgi Kukhianidze	01.07.1992	14	(9)	1
Mate Kvirkvia	14.06.1996		(1)	
Nika Ninua	22.06.1999	28	(3)	8
Giorgi Papava	16.02.1993	32	(2)	2
Akaki Shulaia	06.09.1996	23	(6)	3
Mykhaylo Shyshka (UKR)	05.07.1994	1	(6)	1
Giorgi Zaria	14.07.1997	8	(14)	1
Forwards:	**DOB**	**M**	**(s)**	**G**
Kwame Karikari (GHA)	21.01.1992	5	(3)	2
Levan Kutalia	19.07.1989	32	(1)	20
Levan Mchedlidze	24.03.1990		(5)	1
Levan Shengelia	27.10.1995	23	(1)	12
Antonio Raúl Rojano (ARG)	27.04.1991	2	(7)	

Football Club Lokomotivi Tbilisi

Founded: 1936
Stadium: Stadioni „Mikheil Meskhi", Tbilisi (27,223)
Trainer: Lasha Chagiashvili   17.02.1981
[09.04.2019] Levan Korgalidze   21.02.1980

Goalkeepers:	DOB	M	(s)	G
Demetre Buliskeria	09.01.2000	34		
Luka Sherozia	11.08.1997	2		
Defenders:	**DOB**	**M**	**(s)**	**G**
Beqa Buighlishvili	27.09.2000	1		
Giorgi Gabadze	02.03.1995	6	(1)	
Aleksandre Gureshidze	23.04.1995	34		
Luka Japaridze	21.02.2000		(1)	
Tornike Kirkitadze	23.07.1996	18	(3)	3
Nika Tchanturia	19.01.1995	35		
Davit Ubilava	27.01.1994	34		1
Midfielders:	**DOB**	**M**	**(s)**	**G**
Aleksandre Andronikashvili	09.04.1999	3	(3)	
Rati Ardazishvili	27.01.1998	7	(2)	1
Beka Dartsmelia	21.03.2000	6	(2)	
Zurab Davitashvili	15.02.2001	7	(3)	
Tornike Dzebniauri	27.11.1999	21	(1)	1
Giorgi Gorozia	26.03.1995	5	(9)	
Lasha Gvalia	06.10.1991	13	(14)	1
Luka Kikabidze	21.01.1995	3	(4)	1
Irakli Komakhidze	26.03.1997	26	(2)	
Bidzina Makharoblidze	10.10.1992	6		
Davit Samurkasovi	05.02.1998	25	(6)	2
Temuri Shonia	28.05.1990	35		7
Forwards:	**DOB**	**M**	**(s)**	**G**
Giorgi Iakobidze	27.02.2001		(2)	
Revaz Injgia	31.12.2000	4	(9)	2
Davit Jikia	10.01.1995	11	(17)	2
Davit Kirkitadze	03.09.1992	12	(2)	3
Otar Kobakhidze	29.02.1996	13	(5)	1
Lasha Ozbetelashvili	20.01.1999		(1)	
Shota Shekiladze	14.02.2000		(19)	1
Irakli Sikharulidze	18.07.1990	35	(1)	16

Football Club Rustavi

Founded: 1948
Stadium: Stadioni Poladi, Rustavi (10,720)
Trainer: Ucha Sosiashvili   26.07.1989
[23.04.2019] Varlam Kilasonia   13.08.1967

Goalkeepers:	DOB	M	(s)	G
Giorgi Kulua	19.07.1997	8		
Giorgi Mamardashvili	29.09.2000	28		
Defenders:	**DOB**	**M**	**(s)**	**G**
Luka Asatiani	22.04.1999		(1)	
Georgi Bugulov (RUS)	17.03.1993	15	(2)	
Otar Chichagua	08.08.1996	1		
Luka Gadrani	12.04.1997	14	(3)	
Zurab Japiashvili	26.05.1996	14	(3)	
Tsotne Kapanadze	30.08.2001	30	(2)	
Akaki Khubutia	17.03.1986	3		
Giorgi Latsabidze	15.05.1995	11	(1)	1
Giorgi Narimanidze	25.11.1993	4		
Luka Nozadze	25.12.1996	15		
Soslan Takulov	28.04.1995	13	(2)	
Giorgi Tevzadze	25.08.1996	3	(6)	
Oleg Tolmasov (RUS)	23.04.1991	1		
Midfielders:	**DOB**	**M**	**(s)**	**G**
Fuad Bayramov (AZE)	30.11.1994	5	(1)	1
Temur Chogadze	05.05.1998	11	(10)	4
Avtandil Gujabidze	06.07.1997	21	(5)	1
Farkhad Gystarov (RUS)	21.11.1994	12		2
Nikolay Kipiani (RUS)	25.01.1997	10	(3)	3
Paata Kiteishvili	16.01.1999	11	(10)	1
Lasha Kochladze	22.08.1995	28	(2)	3
Konstantin Pavlov (RUS)	21.01.1989	2	(1)	
Papuna Poniava	10.03.1994	18	(2)	
Revaz Salukvadze	11.09.1999		(2)	
Luka Silagadze	21.04.1990	35		5
Data Sichinava	21.03.1989	5	(9)	2
Giorgi Vasadze	14.06.1989	11	(2)	
Luka Zviadadze	20.05.1999		(5)	1
Forwards:	**DOB**	**M**	**(s)**	**G**
Nika Dzalamidze	06.01.1992	2	(8)	
Luka Imnadze	26.08.1997	25	(8)	2
Beka Kavtaradze	15.06.1999	19	(3)	8
Lasha Lezhava	11.01.1998	2	(6)	
Tornike Metreveli	22.06.1998		(1)	
Zaza Tsitskishvili	04.07.1995	19	(2)	5

Football Club Saburtalo Tbilisi

Founded: 20.08.1999
Stadium: Stadioni „Mikheil Meskhi", Tbilisi (27,223)
Trainer: Giorgi Chiabrishvili   07.10.1979

Goalkeepers:	DOB	M	(s)	G
Lazare Kupatadze	01.01.1996	11		
Omar Migineishvili	02.06.1984	24		
Denys Shelikhov	23.06.1989	1		
Defenders:	**DOB**	**M**	**(s)**	**G**
Grigol Chabradze	20.04.1996	21	(2)	1
Tedore Grigalashvili	12.05.1993	1	(3)	
Jemali-Giorgi Jinjolava	28.01.2000	1		
Luka Lakvekheliani	20.10.1998	19	(8)	1
Gagi Margvelashvili	30.10.1996	30	(2)	
Tsotne Nadaraia	21.02.1997	4		
Giorgi Rekhviashvili	01.02.1988	13	(1)	1
Nika Sandokhadze	20.02.1994	11		
Giorgi Tevzadze	25.08.1996	2	(1)	
Dachi Tsnobiladze	28.01.1994	18	(4)	1
Midfielders:	**DOB**	**M**	**(s)**	**G**
Sandro Altunashvili	19.05.1997	25	(4)	2
Giorgi Diasamidze	08.05.1992	22	(3)	1

	DOB	M	(s)	G
Tornike Gorgiashvili	27.04.1988	17	(11)	2
Inters Gui	08.08.1992	13	(8)	2
Beka Gvaradze	11.08.1997	2	(6)	
Levan Kakubava	15.10.1990	25	(2)	1
Levan Kenia	18.10.1990	3	(4)	
Nikoloz Mali	27.01.1999	19	(5)	1
Iuri Tabatadze	29.11.1999	6	(2)	2
Alwyn Tera (KEN)	18.01.1997	19	(3)	
Forwards:	**DOB**	**M**	**(s)**	**G**
Vladimer Dvalishvili	20.04.1986	11	(3)	3
Giorgi Gabedava	03.10.1989	12	(5)	6
Vagner Gonçalves Nogueira de Souza (FRA)	27.04.1996	8	(2)	1
Guram Goshteliani	05.01.1997	1		
Giorgi Guliashvili	05.09.2001	2	(2)	
Giorgi Kokhreidze	18.11.1998	20	(5)	8
Lasha Kokhreidze	18.11.1998	1	(1)	3
Ognjen Rolović (MNE)	25.08.1993	16	(18)	8
Lasha Shindagoridze	03.10.1989	18	(3)	1

Football Club Sioni Bolnisi

Founded: 1936
Stadium: Stadioni „Tamaz Stephania", Bolnisi (3,242)
Trainer: Temur Shalamberidze   08.12.1969

Goalkeepers:	DOB	M	(s)	G
Oto Goshadze	13.10.1997	15		
Levan Isiani	30.04.1998	8	(2)	
Tornike Zarkua	01.09.1990	13		
Defenders:	**DOB**	**M**	**(s)**	**G**
Nikoloz Apakidze	04.04.1992	30		
Roman Chachua	01.11.1997	18	(3)	1
Zurab Japiashvili	26.05.1996	13		1
Givi Khetsuriani	02.07.1999	2	(1)	
Gulverd Tomashvili	13.10.1988	16	(6)	
Archil Tvildiani	31.01.1993	14	(7)	
Aleksandre Saganelidze	09.08.1999		(1)	
Anzor Sukhiashvili	28.01.1988	32	(2)	
Lasha Ugrekhelidze	25.08.1999	20	(2)	
Midfielders:	**DOB**	**M**	**(s)**	**G**
Beka Gvaradze	11.08.1997	13	(4)	3
Giorgi Ivanishvili	18.10.1989	15		1
Levan Khmaladze	06.04.1985	30		3
Giorgi Khvadagiani	03.10.2001		(1)	

	DOB	M	(s)	G
Vazha Kikava	28.12.1995	7	(6)	
Lasha Managadze	11.11.1994	1	(6)	
Archil Meskhi	02.11.1995	1	(2)	
Davit Razhamashvili	28.10.1988	4	(7)	
Ilia Sabiashvili	25.02.1998		(1)	
Zviad Sikharulia	01.08.1992	9	(8)	2
Sandro Shinjikashvili	01.09.1997		(2)	
David Targamadze	22.08.1989	17	(9)	1
Tornike Tarkhnishvili	07.03.1990	28	(4)	
Rati Tsatskrialashvili	11.10.1993	10	(2)	1
Giorgi Ugrekhelidze I	26.06.1997		(2)	
Forwards:	**DOB**	**M**	**(s)**	**G**
Vili Isiani	22.03.1991	16	(2)	6
Kakhaber Kakhabrishvili	08.07.1993	9	(3)	1
Davit Kirkitadze	03.09.1992	21		4
Lasha Lezhava	11.01.1998		(2)	
Tamaz Makatsaria	03.10.1995	2	(9)	
Dimitri Tatanashvili	19.10.1983	11	(3)	4
Jaba Ugulava	08.04.1992	21	(8)	9

Football Club Torpedo Kutaisi

Founded: 1946
Stadium: Stadioni „Ramaz Shengelia", Kutaisi (19,400)
Trainer: Kakhaber Shkhetiani   24.02.1978

Goalkeepers:	DOB	M	(s)	G
David Asatiani	05.09.2003	4		
Roin Kvaskhvadze	31.05.1989	19		
Maksime Kvilitaia	17.09.1985	7		
Levan Shovnadze	19.11.1997	6	(1)	
Defenders:	**DOB**	**M**	**(s)**	**G**
Giorgi Abzianidze	27.07.2001	1		
Otar Apridonidze	10.02.2003	1		
Oleksandr Azatskyi (UKR)	13.01.1994	17		2
Vakhtang Botchorishvili	21.08.2001	2	(1)	
Anri Chichinadze	05.10.1997	19	(8)	
Ukwubile Raphael Chukwurah (NGA)	17.05.1992	14		3
Giorgi Gadrani	30.09.1994	3	(1)	
Levan Gegetchkori	05.06.1994	17		2
Merab Gigauri	05.01.1993	19		
Tornike Grigalashvili	28.01.1993	7	(1)	
Davit Khurtsilava	09.03.1988	25		
Giorgi Kimadze	11.02.1992	13	(3)	2
Mamuka Kobakhidze	23.08.1992	16		
Goderdzi Machaidze	17.07.1992	8	(1)	
Tsotne Nadaraia	21.02.1997	12		
Vakhtang Nebieridze	09.07.1999	4	(3)	
Luka Pipia	26.04.1998	1		
Nikola Stijepović (MNE)	02.11.1993	6		
Vazha Tabatadze	01.02.1991	9	(4)	1
Midfielders:	**DOB**	**M**	**(s)**	**G**
Mate Abuladze	30.06.2000	1	(2)	

	DOB	M	(s)	G
Sergi Babunashvili	31.03.2003		(1)	
Ambrosiy Chachua	02.04.1994	4	(5)	
Guram Deisadze	01.01.2003	1		
Grigol Dolidze	25.10.1982	20	(11)	3
Luka Elbakidze	16.03.2004		(1)	
Giorgi Kiknadze	27.09.1997		(5)	1
Nika Koridze	04.01.1997	1	(2)	
Iakob Maglaperidze	07.01.2000		(1)	
Tsotne Mosiashvili	14.02.1995	10	(3)	1
Givi Mukbaniani	20.12.2001		(3)	
Saba Piranishvili	19.10.1999		(1)	
Papuna Poniava	10.03.1994	8		
Murtaz Saneblidze	05.09.2002	1		
Tamaz Sharvashidze	06.12.2000	2	(3)	
Tamaz Tsetskhladze	08.12.1996	9	(3)	
Tengiz Tsikaridze	21.12.1995	8	(8)	3
Mate Tsintsadze	07.01.1995	17		
Forwards:	**DOB**	**M**	**(s)**	**G**
Temur Chogadze	05.05.1998	5	(7)	1
Davit Ionanidze	05.08.1998	1	(9)	
Tornike Kapanadze	04.06.1992	18	(10)	6
Nodar Kavtaradze	02.01.1993	20		7
Akaki Meladze	22.04.2003	1		
Richard Luca Rosa Da Silva Sousa (BRA)	06.01.1998	7	(6)	3
Zaza Tsitskishvili	04.07.1995	13		2
Budu Zivzivadze	10.03.1994	19	(1)	13

Football Club WIT Georgia Tbilisi

Founded:	1997
Stadium:	Mtskheta Park, Mtskheta (2,000)
Trainer:	Vladimer Khachidze 01.06.1951

Goalkeepers:	DOB	M	(s)	G
Levan Isergishvili	08.03.1994	20		
Nika Kavtaradze	17.06.1998	4		
Joni Sherozia	09.09.1990	12		
Defenders:	**DOB**	**M**	**(s)**	**G**
Shota Avlokhashvili	10.05.1998		(1)	
Aliko Chakvetadze	28.03.1995	16		
Revaz Chitishvili	19.05.1994	15	(1)	
Giorgi Getiashvili	07.03.1990	14		1
Luka Janelidze	02.08.1998	7	(4)	
Davit Kikalishvili	19.03.1999	11	(1)	
Nodar Kiknavelidze	25.04.1993	5	(2)	
Vasil Kisievi	22.02.1996	18		
Giorgi Latsabidze	15.05.1995	13	(5)	
Andro Nemsadze	15.08.1997	14		
Moris Nusuev (SVN)	28.06.1997	4		
Davit Sajaia	23.08.1993	8	(3)	
Zurab Sekhniashvili	24.06.1996	27		2
Luka Tatkhashvili	18.02.1993	11	(4)	
Midfielders:	**DOB**	**M**	**(s)**	**G**
Nikoloz Abuladze	02.03.1998		(2)	
Beka Ashordia	03.03.2001		(5)	

	DOB	M	(s)	G
Giorgi Gaprindashvili	06.05.1995	13	(2)	
Kakhaber Kakashvili	26.06.1993	16	(1)	2
Vano Kurdghelashvili	17.10.1995	6	(6)	
Nikoloz Maisuradze	29.05.1989	6	(2)	
Tsotne Mosiashvili	14.02.1995	16	(3)	2
Zviad Nachkebia	19.08.1999	4	(3)	
Lasha Nanobashvili	03.05.2000	11	(4)	
Luka Vardzelashvili	09.03.1998	12	(2)	
Giorgi Vasadze	14.06.1989	18	(3)	
Giorgi Vazagashvili	08.04.1995	1	(6)	
Giorgi Vekua	24.08.1996		(1)	
Forwards:	**DOB**	**M**	**(s)**	**G**
Zurab Ghirdaladze	09.06.1994	8	(3)	
Giorgi Gvasalia	19.08.1998		(2)	
Paata Gudushauri	07.06.1997	12	(1)	1
Beka Gugberidze	16.06.2001		(3)	
Dimitri Khutsianidze	23.04.1998	7	(5)	
Tamaz Makatsaria	03.10.1995	8	(3)	
David Mujiri	28.01.1999	7	(4)	
Zurab Museliani	17.09.1999	27	(8)	6
Tornike Muzashvili	25.07.1998	9	(7)	
Irakli Zaridze	03.01.1999	16	(4)	1

SECOND LEVEL
Erovnuli Liga 2 2019

1.	FC Merani Tbilisi (*Promoted*)	36	25	6	5	87	-	35	81
2.	FC Samtredia (*Promotion Play-offs*)	36	23	8	5	63	-	28	77
3.	FC Telavi (*Promotion Play-offs*)	36	19	6	11	70	-	36	63
4.	FC Shevardeni-1906 Tbilisi	36	14	10	12	47	-	48	52
5.	FC Gagra	36	13	8	15	46	-	42	47
6.	FC Shukura Kobuleti	36	13	7	16	36	-	46	46
7.	FC Zugdidi	36	13	1	22	38	-	54	40
8.	FC Guria Lanchkhuti* (*Relegation Play-offs*)	36	10	6	20	39	-	64	33
9.	FC Kolkheti-1913 Poti** (*Relegation Play-offs*)	36	10	4	22	31	-	80	28
10.	FC Tskhinvali Gori** (*Relegated*)	36	8	8	20	38	-	62	26

*3 points deducted
**6 points deducted

Relegation Play-offs (2nd / 3rd Level)

FC Aragvi Dusheti - FC Guria Lanchkhuti	0-1(0-1)	2-0(1-0,1-0)
FC Kolkheti-1913 Poti - **FC Samgurali Tskhaltubo**	0-3(0-2)	0-6(0-2)

INTERNATIONAL MATCHES
(16.07.2019 – 15.07.2020)

05.09.2019	İstanbul	Korea Republic - Georgia	2-2(0-1)	(F)
08.09.2019	Tbilisi	Georgia - Denmark	0-0	(ECQ)
12.10.2019	Tbilisi	Georgia - Republic of Ireland	0-0	(ECQ)
15.10.2019	Gibraltar	Gibraltar - Georgia	2-3(0-2)	(ECQ)
15.11.2019	St. Gallen	Switzerland - Georgia	1-0(0-0)	(ECQ)
19.11.2019	Pula	Croatia - Georgia	2-1(1-1)	(F)

05.09.2019   KOREA REPUBLIC - GEORGIA   2-2(0-1)   Friendly International
"Başakşehir Fatih Terim" Stadium, İstanbul (Turkey); Referee: Hüseyin Göçek (Turkey); Attendance: 750
GEO: Giorgi Makaridze, Guram Kashia (Cap), Otar Kakabadze, Jemal Tabidze, Levan Kharabadze, Jano Ananidze (57.Giorgi Papunishvili), Tornike Okriashvili (57.Giorgi Kvilitaia), Valeri Qazaishvili (84.Jaba Kankava), Giorgi Aburjania (57.Valerian Gvilia), Otar Kiteishvili (71.Murtaz Daushvili), Zuriko Davitashvili (73.Saba Lobjanidze). Trainer: Vladimír Weiss (Slovakia).
Goals: Jano Ananidze (40), Giorgi Kvilitaia (90).

08.09.2019   GEORGIA - DENMARK   0-0   16th EC. Qualifiers
„Boris Paichadze" Dinamo Arena, Tbilisi; Referee: Referee: François Letexier (France); Attendance: 21,456
GEO: Giorgi Loria, Gia Grigalava, Guram Kashia (Cap), Otar Kakabadze, Jemal Tabidze, Jano Ananidze, Tornike Okriashvili, Valeri Qazaishvili, Giorgi Aburjania (86.Valerian Gvilia), Otar Kiteishvili, Giorgi Kvilitaia (90.Murtaz Daushvili). Trainer: Vladimír Weiss (Slovakia).

12.10.2019   GEORGIA - REPUBLIC OF IRELAND   0-0   16th EC. Qualifiers
„Boris Paichadze" Dinamo Arena, Tbilisi; Referee: Marco Guida (Italy); Attendance: 24,835
GEO: Giorgi Loria, Gia Grigalava, Guram Kashia, Otar Kakabadze, Jemal Tabidze, Jaba Kankava (Cap), Jano Ananidze, Tornike Okriashvili (79.Elguja Lobjanidze), Valeri Qazaishvili, Otar Kiteishvili (90.Giorgi Aburjania), Giorgi Kvilitaia (73.Levan Shengelia). Trainer: Vladimír Weiss (Slovakia).

15.10.2019   GIBRALTAR - GEORGIA   2-3(0-2)   16th EC. Qualifiers
Victoria Stadium, Gibraltar; Referee: Paolo Valeri (Italy); Attendance: 1,455
GEO: Giorgi Loria, Giorgi Navalovski (90+3.Solomon Kvirkvelia), Gia Grigalava, Davit Khocholava, Otar Kakabadze, Jaba Kankava (Cap), Jano Ananidze, Valeri Qazaishvili, Levan Shengelia, Elguja Lobjanidze (68.Giorgi Kvilitaia), Giorgi Kharaishvili (60.Otar Kiteishvili). Trainer: Vladimír Weiss (Slovakia).
Goals: Giorgi Kharaishvili (10), Jaba Kankava (21), Giorgi Kvilitaia (84).

15.11.2019   SWITZERLAND - GEORGIA   1-0(0-0)   16th EC. Qualifiers
kybunpark Stadion, St. Gallen; Referee: Danny Desmond Makkelie (Netherlands); Attendance: 16,400
GEO: Giorgi Loria, Gia Grigalava, Guram Kashia, Davit Khocholava, Otar Kakabadze, Jaba Kankava (Cap), Valeri Qazaishvili, Levan Shengelia, Otar Kiteishvili (84.Giorgi Papunashvili), Zuriko Davitashvili (85.Valerian Gvilia), Giorgi Kvilitaia (82.Elguja Lobjanidze). Trainer: Vladimír Weiss (Slovakia).

19.11.2019   CROATIA - GEORGIA   2-1(1-1)   Friendly International
Stadion "Aldo Drosina", Pula; Referee: Alan Mario Sant (Malta); Attendance: 5,072
GEO: Giorgi Makaridze, Giorgi Navalovski, Guram Kashia (Cap), Davit Khocholava (80.Gia Grigalava), Otar Kakabadze (39.Levan Shengelia), Valeri Qazaishvili (87.Giorgi Kharaishvili), Giorgi Aburjania, Jambul Jighauri, Giorgi Papunashvili (65.Otar Kiteishvili), Valerian Gvilia (83.Giorgi Kvilitaia), Elguja Lobjanidze (51.Bachana Arabuli). Trainer: Vladimír Weiss (Slovakia).
Goal: Giorgi Papunashvili (19).

NATIONAL TEAM PLAYERS
(16.07.2019 – 15.07.2020)

Name	DOB	Caps	Goals	2019/2020:	Club
Goalkeepers					
Giorgi LORIA	27.01.1986	56	0	2019:	*Anorthosis Famagusta FC (CYP)*
Giorgi MAKARIDZE	31.03.1990	15	0	2019:	*Vitória FC Setúbal (POR)*
Defenders					
Gia GRIGALAVA	05.08.1989	31	0	2019:	*FK Arsenal Tula (RUS)*
Otar KAKABADZE	27.06.1995	33	0	2019:	*FC Luzern (SUI)*
Guram KASHIA	04.07.1987	79	2	2019:	*San Jose Earthquakes (USA)*
Levan KHARABADZE	26.01.2000	3	0	2019:	*FC Zürich (SUI)*
Davit KHOCHOLAVA	08.02.1993	21	0	2019:	*FK Shakhtar Donetsk (UKR)*
Solomon KVIRKVELIA	06.02.1992	36	0	2019:	*FK Lokomotiv Moskva (RUS)*
Giorgi NAVALOVSKI	28.06.1986	38	0	2019:	*FC Dinamo Batumi*
Jemal TABIDZE	18.03.1996	11	1	2019:	*FK Ufa (RUS)*
Midfielders					
Giorgi ABURJANIA	02.01.1995	16	0	2019:	*FC Twente Enschede (NED)*
Jano ANANIDZE	10.10.1992	45	7	2019:	*FK Spartak Moskva (RUS)*
Murtaz DAUSHVILI	01.05.1989	36	0	2019:	*Anorthosis Famagusta FC (CYP)*
Zuriko DAVITASHVILI	15.02.2001	2	0	2019:	*FK Rubin Kazan (RUS)*
Valerian GVILIA	24.05.1994	27	3	2019:	*Legia Warszawa (POL)*
Jambul „Jaba" JIGHAURI	08.07.1992	14	0	2019:	*FC Dinamo Batumi*
Jaba KANKAVA	18.03.1986	86	10	2019:	*FC Tobol Kostanay (KAZ)*
Giorgi KHARAISHVILI	29.07.1996	6	1	2019:	*IFK Göteborg (SWE)*
Otar KITEISHVILI	26.03.1996	16	0	2019:	*SK Sturm Graz (SUI)*
Saba LOBJANIDZE	18.12.1994	8	2	2019:	*Randers FC (DEN)*
Tornike OKRIASHVILI	12.02.1992	40	9	2019:	*Anorthosis Famagusta FC (CYP)*
Giorgi PAPUNASHVILI	02.09.1995	14	3	2019:	*Real Zaragoza (ESP)*
Valeri QAZAISHVILI	29.01.1993	47	10	2019:	*San Jose Earthquakes (USA)*
Levan SHENGELIA	27.10.1995	4	0	2019:	*Konyaspor Kulübü (TUR)*
Forwards					
Bachana ARABULI	05.01.1994	7	0	2019:	*Panionios GSS Athína (GRE)*
Giorgi KVILITAIA	01.10.1993	23	6	2019:	*KAA Gent (BEL)*
Elguja LOBJANIDZE	17.09.1992	6	0	2019:	*FC Taraz (KAZ)*

National team coach		
Vladimír WEISS (Slovakia) [from 14.03.2016]	22.09.1964	40 M; 14 W; 12 D; 14 L; 54-46

GERMANY

The Country:
Bundesrepublik Deutschland (Federal Republic of Germany)
Capital: Berlin
Surface: 357,168 km²
Inhabitants: 83,166,711 [2019]
Time: UTC+1

The FA:
Deutscher Fußball-Bund
Otto-Fleck-Schneise 6, Postfach 710265, 60492 Frankfurt am Main
Tel: +49 69 678 80
Foundation date: 28.01.1900
Member of FIFA since: 1904
Member of UEFA since: 1954
Website: www.dfb.de

NATIONAL TEAM RECORDS

RECORDS

First international match:	05.04.1908, Basel:	Switzerland – Germany 5-3
Most international caps:	Lothar Herbert Matthäus	- 150 caps (1980-2000)
Most international goals:	Miroslav Klose	- 71 goals / 137 caps (2001-2014)

UEFA EUROPEAN CHAMPIONSHIP

1960	Did not enter
1964	Did not enter
1968	Qualifiers
1972	**Final Tournament (Winners)**
1976	Final Tournament (Runners-up)
1980	**Final Tournament (Winners)**
1984	Final Tournament (Group Stage)
1988	Final Tournament (Semi-Finals)
1992	Final Tournament (Runners-up)
1996	**Final Tournament (Winners)**
2000	Final Tournament (Group Stage)
2004	Final Tournament (Group Stage)
2008	Final Tournament (Runners-up)
2012	Final Tournament (Semi-Finals)
2016	Final Tournament (Semi-Finals)
2020	*Final Tournament (Qualified)*

FIFA WORLD CUP

1930	Did not enter
1934	Final Tournament (3rd Place)
1938	Final Tournament (1st Round)
1950	*Banned*
1954	**Final Tournament (Winners)**
1958	Final Tournament (3rd Place)
1962	Final Tournament (Quarter-Finals)
1966	Final Tournament (Runners-up)
1970	Final Tournament (3rd Place)
1974	**Final Tournament (Winners)**
1978	Final Tournament (Second Round)
1982	Final Tournament (Runners-up)
1986	Final Tournament (Runners-up)
1990	**Final Tournament (Winners)**
1994	Final Tournament (Quarter-Finals)
1998	Final Tournament (Quarter-Finals)
2002	Final Tournament (Runners-up)
2006	Final Tournament (3rd Place)
2010	Final Tournament (3rd Place)
2014	**Final Tournament (Winners)**
2018	Final Tournament (Group Stage)

OLYMPIC TOURNAMENTS

1908	-
1912	1st Round
1920	-
1924	-
1928	Quarter-Finals
1936	Quarter-Finals
1948	-
1952	4th Place
1956	1st Round
1960	Qualifiers
1964	Qualifiers
1968	-
1972	Second Round
1976	Qualifiers
1980	Qualifiers
1984	Quarter-Finals
1988	3rd Place
1992	Qualifiers
1996	Qualifiers
2000	Qualifiers
2004	Qualifiers
2008	Qualifiers
2012	Qualifiers
2016	Runners-up

UEFA NATIONS LEAGUE

2018/2019 – League A

FIFA CONFEDERATIONS CUP 1992-2017

1999 (Group Stage), 2005 (3rd Place), **2017 (Winners)**

GERMAN CLUB HONOURS IN EUROPEAN CLUB COMPETITIONS:

European Champion Clubs' Cup (1956-1992) / UEFA Champions League (1993-2020)		
FC Bayern München	6	1973/1974, 1974/1975, 1975/1976, 2000/2001, 2012/2013, 2019/2020
Hamburger SV	1	1982/1983
BV Borussia Dortmund	1	1996/1997
Fairs Cup (1858-1971) / UEFA Cup (1972-2009) / UEFA Europa League (2010-2020)		
Borussia VfL Mönchengladbach	2	1974/1975, 1978/1979
Eintracht Frankfurt	1	1979/1980
TSV Bayer 04 Leverkusen	1	1987/1988
FC Bayern München	1	1995/1996
FC Schalke 04 Gelsenkirchen	1	1996/1997
UEFA Super Cup (1972-2019)		
FC Bayern München	1	2013

European Cup Winners' Cup 1961-1999*		
BV Borussia Dortmund	1	1965/1966
Hamburger SV	1	1976/1977
FC Bayern München	1	1966/1967
SV Werder Bremen	1	1991/1992

defunct competition

NATIONAL COMPETITIONS
TABLE OF HONOURS

	CHAMPIONS	CUP WINNERS	BEST GOALSCORERS	
1902/1903	VfB Leipzig	-	-	
1903/1904	*No champions (final not played)*	-	-	
1904/1905	Berliner TuFC Union 1892	-	-	
1905/1906	VfB Leipzig	-	-	
1906/1907	Freiburger FC	-	-	
1907/1908	Berliner TuFC Viktoria 1889	-	-	
1908/1909	FC Phönix Karlsruhe	-	-	
1909/1910	Karlsruher FV	-	-	
1910/1911	Berliner TuFC Viktoria 1889	-	-	
1911/1912	Holstein Kiel	-	-	
1912/1913	VfB Leipzig	-	-	
1913/1914	SpVgg Fürth	-	-	
1914-1919	*No competition*	-	-	
1919/1920	1. FC Nürnberg	-	-	
1920/1921	1. FC Nürnberg	-	-	
1921/1922	*No champions (title declined by DFB)*	-	-	
1922/1923	Hamburger SV	-	-	
1923/1924	1. FC Nürnberg	-	-	
1924/1925	1. FC Nürnberg	-	-	
1925/1926	SpVgg Fürth	-	-	
1926/1927	1. FC Nürnberg	-	-	
1927/1928	Hamburger SV	-	-	
1928/1929	SpVgg Fürth	-	-	
1929/1930	Hertha BSC Berlin	-	-	
1930/1931	Hertha BSC Berlin	-	-	
1931/1932	FC Bayern München	-	-	
1932/1933	TSV Fortuna Düsseldorf	-	-	
1933/1934	FC Schalke 04 Gelsenkirchen	-	-	
1934/1935	FC Schalke 04 Gelsenkirchen	1. FC Nürnberg	-	
1935/1936	1. FC Nürnberg	VfB Leipzig	-	
1936/1937	FC Schalke 04 Gelsenkirchen	FC Schalke 04 Gelsenkirchen	-	
1937/1938	SV Hannover 96	SK Rapid Wien	-	
1938/1939	FC Schalke 04 Gelsenkirchen	1. FC Nürnberg	-	
1939/1940	FC Schalke 04 Gelsenkirchen	Dresdner SC	-	
1940/1941	SK Rapid Wien	Dresdner SC	-	
1941/1942	FC Schalke 04 Gelsenkirchen	TSV 1860 München	-	
1942/1943	Dresdner SC	1894 First Vienna FC	-	
1943/1944	Dresdner SC	*No competition*	-	
1944/1945	*No competition*	*No competition*	-	
1945/1946	VfB Stuttgart	*No competition*	-	
1946/1947	1. FC Nürnberg	*No competition*	-	
1947/1948	1. FC Nürnberg	*No competition*	-	
1948/1949	VfR Mannheim	*No competition*	-	
1949/1950	VfB Stuttgart	*No competition*	-	
1950/1951	1. FC Kaiserslautern	*No competition*	-	
1951/1952	VfB Stuttgart	*No competition*	-	
1952/1953	1. FC Kaiserslautern	Rot-Weiss Essen	-	
1953/1954	SV Hannover 96	VfB Stuttgart	-	
1954/1955	Rot-Weiss Essen	Karlsruher SC	-	
1955/1956	BV Borussia 09 Dortmund	Karlsruher SC	-	
1956/1957	BV Borussia 09 Dortmund	FC Bayern München	-	
1957/1958	FC Schalke 04 Gelsenkirchen	VfB Stuttgart	-	
1958/1959	Eintracht Frankfurt	TB Schwarz-Weiß Essen	-	
1959/1960	Hamburger SV	Borussia VfL Mönchengladbach	-	
1960/1961	1. FC Nürnberg	SV Werder Bremen	-	
1961/1962	1. FC Köln	1. FC Nürnberg	-	
1962/1963	BV Borussia 09 Dortmund	Hamburger SV	-	
1963/1964	1. FC Köln	TSV 1860 München	Uwe Seeler (Hamburger SV)	30
1964/1965	SV Werder Bremen	BV Borussia 09 Dortmund	Rudolf Brunnenmeier (TSV 1860 München)	24
1965/1966	TSV 1860 München	FC Bayern München	Lothar Emmerich (BV Borussia 09 Dortmund)	31
1966/1967	TSV Eintracht Braunschweig	FC Bayern München	Lothar Emmerich (BV Borussia 09 Dortmund) Gerhard Müller (FC Bayern München)	28
1967/1968	1. FC Nürnberg	1. FC Köln 1. FC Köln	Johannes Löhr (1. FC Köln)	27
1968/1969	FC Bayern München	FC Bayern München	Gerhard Müller (FC Bayern München)	30
1969/1970	Borussia VfL Mönchengladbach	Kickers Offenbach FC	Gerhard Müller (FC Bayern München)	38

1970/1971	Borussia VfL Mönchengladbach	FC Bayern München	Lothar Kobluhn (SC Rot-Weiß Oberhausen)	24
1971/1972	FC Bayern München	FC Schalke 04 Gelsenkirchen	Gerhard Müller (FC Bayern München)	40
1972/1973	FC Bayern München	Borussia VfL Mönchengladbach	Gerhard Müller (FC Bayern München)	36
1973/1974	FC Bayern München	Eintracht Frankfurt	Gerhard Müller (FC Bayern München) Josef Heynckes (Borussia VfL Mönchengladbach)	30
1974/1975	Borussia VfL Mönchengladbach	Eintracht Frankfurt	Josef Heynckes (Borussia VfL Mönchengladbach)	27
1975/1976	Borussia VfL Mönchengladbach	Hamburger SV	Klaus Fischer (FC Schalke 04 Gelsenkirchen)	29
1976/1977	Borussia VfL Mönchengladbach	1. FC Köln	Dieter Müller (1. FC Köln)	34
1977/1978	1. FC Köln	1. FC Köln	Dieter Müller (1. FC Köln) Gerhard Müller (FC Bayern München)	24
1978/1979	Hamburger SV	TSV Fortuna Düsseldorf	Klaus Allofs (TSV TSV Fortuna Düsseldorf)	22
1979/1980	FC Bayern München	TSV Fortuna Düsseldorf	Karl-Heinz Rummenigge (FC Bayern München)	26
1980/1981	FC Bayern München	Eintracht Frankfurt	Karl-Heinz Rummenigge (FC Bayern München)	29
1981/1982	Hamburger SV	FC Bayern München	Horst Hrubesch (Hamburger SV)	27
1982/1983	Hamburger SV	1. FC Köln	Rudolf Völler (SV Werder Bremen)	23
1983/1984	VfB Stuttgart	FC Bayern München	Karl-Heinz Rummenigge (FC Bayern München)	26
1984/1985	FC Bayern München	FC Bayer 05 Uerdingen	Klaus Allofs (1. FC Köln)	26
1985/1986	FC Bayern München	FC Bayern München	Stefan Kuntz (VfL Bochum)	22
1986/1987	FC Bayern München	Hamburger SV	Uwe Rahn (Borussia VfL Mönchengladbach)	24
1987/1988	SV Werder Bremen	Eintracht Frankfurt	Jürgen Klinsmann (VfB Stuttgart)	19
1988/1989	FC Bayern München	BV Borussia 09 Dortmund	Thomas Allofs (1. FC Köln) Roland Wohlfarth (FC Bayern München)	17
1989/1990	FC Bayern München	1. FC Kaiserslautern	Jørn Andersen (NOR, Eintracht Frankfurt)	18
1990/1991	1. FC Kaiserslautern	SV Werder Bremen	Roland Wohlfarth (FC Bayern München)	21
1991/1992	VfB Stuttgart	SV Hannover 96	Fritz Walter (VfB Stuttgart)	22
1992/1993	SV Werder Bremen	TSV Bayer 04 Leverkusen	Ulf Kirsten (TSV Bayer 04 Leverkusen) Anthony Yeboah (GHA, Eintracht Frankfurt)	20
1993/1994	FC Bayern München	SV Werder Bremen	Stefan Kuntz (1. FC Kaiserslautern) Anthony Yeboah (GHA, Eintracht Frankfurt)	18
1994/1995	BV Borussia 09 Dortmund	Borussia VfL Mönchengladbach	Mario Basler (SV Werder Bremen) Heiko Herrlich (Borussia VfL Mönchengladbach)	20
1995/1996	BV Borussia 09 Dortmund	1. FC Kaiserslautern	Fredi Bobič (VfB Stuttgart)	17
1996/1997	FC Bayern München	VfB Stuttgart	Ulf Kirsten (TSV Bayer 04 Leverkusen)	22
1997/1998	1. FC Kaiserslautern	FC Bayern München	Ulf Kirsten (TSV Bayer 04 Leverkusen)	22
1998/1999	FC Bayern München	SV Werder Bremen	Michael Preetz (Hertha BSC Berlin)	23
1999/2000	FC Bayern München	FC Bayern München	Martin Max (TSV 1860 München)	19
2000/2001	FC Bayern München	FC Schalke 04 Gelsenkirchen	Sergej Barbarez (BIH, Hamburger SV) Ebbe Sand (DEN, FC Schalke 04 Gelsenkirchen)	22
2001/2002	BV Borussia 09 Dortmund	FC Schalke 04 Gelsenkirchen	Márcio Amoroso dos Santos (BRA, BV Borussia 09 Dortmund) Martin Max (TSV 1860 München)	18
2002/2003	FC Bayern München	FC Bayern München	Thomas Christiansen Tarín (DEN, VfL Bochum) Giovane Élber de Souza (BRA, FC Bayern München)	21
2003/2004	SV Werder Bremen	SV Werder Bremen	Aílton Gonçalves da Silva (BRA, SV Werder Bremen)	28
2004/2005	FC Bayern München	FC Bayern München	Marek Mintál (SVK, 1. FC Nürnberg)	24
2005/2006	FC Bayern München	FC Bayern München	Miroslav Klose (SV Werder Bremen)	25
2006/2007	VfB Stuttgart	1. FC Nürnberg	Theofanis Gekas (GRE, VfL Bochum)	20
2007/2008	FC Bayern München	FC Bayern München	Luca Toni Varchetta (ITA, FC Bayern München)	24
2008/2009	VfL Wolfsburg	SV Werder Bremen	Edinaldo Batista Libânio "Grafite" (BRA, VfL Wolfsburg)	28
2009/2010	FC Bayern München	FC Bayern München	Edin Džeko (BIH, VfL Wolfsburg)	22
2010/2011	BV Borussia 09 Dortmund	FC Schalke 04 Gelsenkirchen	Mario Gómez García (FC Bayern München)	28
2011/2012	BV Borussia 09 Dortmund	BV Borussia 09 Dortmund	Dirk Jan Klaas Huntelaar (NED, FC Schalke 04 Gelsenkirchen)	29
2012/2013	FC Bayern München	FC Bayern München	Stefan Kießling (TSV Bayer 04 Leverkusen)	25
2013/2014	FC Bayern München	FC Bayern München	Robert Lewandowski (POL, BV Borussia 09 Dortmund)	20
2014/2015	FC Bayern München	VfL Wolfsburg	Alexander Meier (Eintracht Frankfurt)	19
2015/2016	FC Bayern München	FC Bayern München	Robert Lewandowski (POL, FC Bayern München)	30
2016/2017	FC Bayern München	BV Borussia 09 Dortmund	Pierre-Emerick Emiliano François Aubameyang (GAB, BV Borussia 09 Dortmund)	31
2017/2018	FC Bayern München	Eintracht Frankfurt	Robert Lewandowski (POL, FC Bayern München)	29
2018/2019	FC Bayern München	FC Bayern München	Robert Lewandowski (POL, FC Bayern München)	22
2019/2020	FC Bayern München	FC Bayern München	Robert Lewandowski (POL, FC Bayern München)	34

Please note: the Bundesliga was introduced at the start of the 1963/1964 season.

NATIONAL CHAMPIONSHIP
Bundesliga 2019/2020
(18.08.2019 – 27.06.2020)

Results

Round 1 [16-18.08.2019]
Bayern München - Hertha BSC 2-2(1-2)
Borussia Dortmund - FC Augsburg 5-1(1-1)
Bayer Leverkusen - SC Paderborn 3-2(2-2)
VfL Wolfsburg - FC Köln 2-1(1-0)
Werder Bremen - Fortuna Düsseldorf 1-3(0-1)
SC Freiburg - FSV Mainz 05 3-0(0-0)
Mönchengladbach - Schalke 04 0-0
Eintracht Frankfurt - Hoffenheim 1-0(1-0)
Union Berlin - RB Leipzig 0-4(0-3)

Round 2 [23-25.08.2019]
FC Köln - Borussia Dortmund 1-3(1-0)
Hoffenheim - Werder Bremen 3-2(0-1)
Fortuna Düsseldorf - Bay.Leverkusen 1-3(0-3)
FSV Mainz 05 - Mönchengladbach 1-3(1-1)
FC Augsburg - Union Berlin 1-1(0-0)
SC Paderborn - SC Freiburg 1-3(1-2)
Schalke 04 - Bayern München 0-3(0-1)
RB Leipzig - Eintracht Frankfurt 2-1(1-0)
Hertha BSC - VfL Wolfsburg 0-3(0-1)

Round 3 [30.08.-01.09.2019]
Mönchengladbach - RB Leipzig 1-3(0-1)
Bayern München - FSV Mainz 05 6-1(2-1)
Bayer Leverkusen - Hoffenheim 0-0
VfL Wolfsburg - SC Paderborn 1-1(0-1)
SC Freiburg - FC Köln 1-2(1-0)
Schalke 04 - Hertha BSC 3-0(1-0)
Union Berlin - Borussia Dortmund 3-1(1-1)
Werder Bremen - FC Augsburg 3-2(2-1)
Eintracht Frank. - Fortuna Düsseldorf 2-1(0-1)

Round 4 [13-15.09.2019]
Fortuna Düsseldorf - VfL Wolfsburg 1-1(1-1)
Borussia Dortmund - Leverkusen 4-0(1-0)
FSV Mainz 05 - Hertha BSC 2-1(1-0)
FC Augsburg - Eintracht Frankfurt 2-1(2-0)
FC Köln - Mönchengladbach 0-1(0-1)
Union Berlin - Werder Bremen 1-2(1-1)
RB Leipzig - Bayern München 1-1(1-1)
Hoffenheim - SC Freiburg 0-3(0-2)
SC Paderborn - Schalke 04 1-5(1-1)

Round 5 [20-23.09.2019]
Schalke 04 - FSV Mainz 05 2-1(1-0)
Bayern München - FC Köln 4-0(1-0)
Bayer Leverkusen - Union Berlin 2-0(2-0)
Hertha BSC - SC Paderborn 2-1(1-0)
SC Freiburg - FC Augsburg 1-1(1-1)
Werder Bremen - RB Leipzig 0-3(0-2)
Mönchengladbach - Fortuna Düsseld. 2-1(0-1)
Eintracht Frankfurt - Bor. Dortmund 2-2(1-1)
VfL Wolfsburg - Hoffenheim 1-1(1-1)

Round 6 [27-29.09.2019]
Union Berlin - Eintracht Frankfurt 1-2(0-0)
RB Leipzig - Schalke 04 1-3(0-2)
Hoffenheim - Mönchengladbach 0-3(0-1)
FSV Mainz 05 - VfL Wolfsburg 0-1(0-1)
FC Augsburg - Bayer Leverkusen 0-3(0-1)
SC Paderborn - Bayern München 2-3(0-1)
Borussia Dortmund - Werder Bremen 2-2(2-1)
Fortuna Düsseldorf - SC Freiburg 1-2(1-1)
FC Köln - Hertha BSC 0-4(0-1)

Round 7 [04-06.10.2019]
Hertha BSC - Fortuna Düsseldorf 3-1(2-1)
Bayern München - Hoffenheim 1-2(0-0)
Bayer Leverkusen - RB Leipzig 1-1(0-0)
SC Freiburg - Borussia Dortmund 2-2(0-1)
SC Paderborn - FSV Mainz 05 1-2(1-2)
Schalke 04 - FC Köln 1-1(0-0)
Mönchengladbach - FC Augsburg 5-1(4-0)
VfL Wolfsburg - Union Berlin 1-0(0-0)
Eintracht Frankfurt - Werder Bremen 2-2(0-1)

Round 8 [18-20.10.2019]
Eintracht Frankfurt - Leverkusen 3-0(2-0)
RB Leipzig - VfL Wolfsburg 1-1(0-0)
Werder Bremen - Hertha BSC 1-1(1-0)
Fortuna Düsseldorf - FSV Mainz 05 1-0(0-0)
FC Augsburg - Bayern München 2-2(1-1)
Union Berlin - SC Freiburg 2-0(1-0)
Bor. Dortmund - Mönchengladbach 1-0(0-0)
FC Köln - SC Paderborn 3-0(1-0)
Hoffenheim - Schalke 04 2-0(0-0)

Round 9 [25-27.10.2019]
FSV Mainz 05 - FC Köln 3-1(1-1)
Bayern München - Union Berlin 2-1(1-0)
Hertha BSC - Hoffenheim 2-3(0-2)
SC Freiburg - RB Leipzig 2-1(1-0)
Schalke 04 - Borussia Dortmund 0-0
SC Paderborn - Fortuna Düsseldorf 2-0(1-0)
Bayer Leverkusen - Werder Bremen 2-2(1-1)
VfL Wolfsburg - FC Augsburg 0-0
Mönchengladbach - Eintracht Frank. 4-2(2-0)

Round 10 [01-03.11.2019]
Hoffenheim - SC Paderborn 3-0(3-0)
Borussia Dortmund - VfL Wolfsburg 3-0(0-0)
RB Leipzig - FSV Mainz 05 8-0(5-0)
Leverkusen - Mönchengladbach 1-2(1-2)
Eintracht Frank. - Bayern München 5-1(2-1)
Werder Bremen - SC Freiburg 2-2(1-1)
Union Berlin - Hertha BSC 1-0(0-0)
Fortuna Düsseldorf - FC Köln 2-0(1-0)
FC Augsburg - Schalke 04 2-3(1-1)

Round 11 [08-10.11.2019]
FC Köln - Hoffenheim 1-2(1-0)
Hertha BSC - RB Leipzig 2-4(1-2)
FSV Mainz 05 - Union Berlin 2-3(0-2)
Schalke 04 - Fortuna Düsseldorf 3-3(1-0)
SC Paderborn - FC Augsburg 0-1(0-1)
Bayern München - Bor. Dortmund 4-0(1-0)
Mönchengladbach - Werder Bremen 3-1(2-0)
VfL Wolfsburg - Bayer Leverkusen 0-2(0-1)
SC Freiburg - Eintracht Frankfurt 1-0(0-0)

Round 12 [22-24.11.2019]
Borussia Dortmund - SC Paderborn 3-3(0-3)
Bayer Leverkusen - SC Freiburg 1-1(1-1)
Eintracht Frankfurt - VfL Wolfsburg 0-2(0-1)
Werder Bremen - Schalke 04 1-2(0-1)
Fortuna Düssel. - Bayern München 0-4(0-3)
Union Berlin - Mönchengladbach 2-0(1-0)
RB Leipzig - FC Köln 4-1(3-1)
FC Augsburg - Hertha BSC 4-0(2-0)
Hoffenheim - FSV Mainz 05 1-5(0-1)

Round 13 [29.11.-02.12.2019]
Schalke 04 - Union Berlin 2-1(1-1)
Hoffenheim - Fortuna Düsseldorf 1-1(1-0)
Hertha BSC - Borussia Dortmund 1-2(1-2)
FC Köln - FC Augsburg 1-1(0-1)
SC Paderborn - RB Leipzig 2-3(0-3)
Bayern München - Bayer Leverkusen 1-2(1-2)
Mönchengladbach - SC Freiburg 4-2(1-1)
VfL Wolfsburg - Werder Bremen 2-3(1-2)
FSV Mainz 05 - Eintracht Frankfurt 2-1(0-1)

Round 14 [06-08.12.2019]
Eintracht Frankfurt - Hertha BSC 2-2(0-1)
Bor. Dortmund - Fortuna Düsseldorf 5-0(1-0)
RB Leipzig - Hoffenheim 3-1(1-0)
Mönchengladbach - Bayern München 2-1(0-0)
SC Freiburg - VfL Wolfsburg 1-0(0-0)
FC Augsburg - FSV Mainz 05 2-1(1-1)
Bayer Leverkusen - Schalke 04 2-1(1-0)
Union Berlin - FC Köln 2-0(1-0)
Werder Bremen - SC Paderborn 0-1(0-0)

Round 15 [13-15.12.2019]
Hoffenheim - FC Augsburg 2-4(1-1)
Bayern München - Werder Bremen 6-1(2-1)
Hertha BSC - SC Freiburg 1-0(0-0)
FSV Mainz 05 - Borussia Dortmund 0-4(0-1)
FC Köln - Bayer Leverkusen 2-0(1-0)
SC Paderborn - Union Berlin 1-1(1-1)
Fortuna Düsseldorf - RB Leipzig 0-3(0-1)
VfL Wolfsburg - Mönchengladbach 2-1(1-1)
Schalke 04 - Eintracht Frankfurt 1-0(0-0)

Round 16 [17-18.12.2019]
Werder Bremen - FSV Mainz 05 0-5(0-4)
Borussia Dortmund - RB Leipzig 3-3(2-0)
FC Augsburg - Fortuna Düsseldorf 3-0(1-0)
Union Berlin - Hoffenheim 0-2(0-0)
Bayer Leverkusen - Hertha BSC 0-1(0-0)
Mönchengladbach - SC Paderborn 2-0(0-0)
VfL Wolfsburg - Schalke 04 1-1(0-0)
Eintracht Frankfurt - FC Köln 2-4(2-1)
SC Freiburg - Bayern München 1-3(0-1)

Round 17 [20-22.12.2019]
Hoffenheim - Borussia Dortmund 2-1(0-1)
Bayern München - VfL Wolfsburg 2-0(0-0)
RB Leipzig - FC Augsburg 3-1(0-1)
FSV Mainz 05 - Bayer Leverkusen 0-1(0-0)
Schalke 04 - SC Freiburg 2-2(1-0)
FC Köln - Werder Bremen 1-0(1-0)
Hertha BSC - Mönchengladbach 0-0
Fortuna Düsseldorf - Union Berlin 2-1(1-0)
SC Paderborn - Eintracht Frankfurt 2-1(2-0)

Round 18 [17-19.01.2020]
Schalke 04 - Mönchengladbach 2-0(0-0)
FC Augsburg - Borussia Dortmund 3-5(1-0)
FC Köln - VfL Wolfsburg 3-1(2-0)
Hoffenheim - Eintracht Frankfurt 1-2(0-1)
Fortuna Düsseldorf - Werder Bremen 0-1(0-0)
FSV Mainz 05 - SC Freiburg 1-2(0-2)
RB Leipzig - Union Berlin 3-1(0-1)
Hertha BSC - Bayern München 0-4(0-0)
SC Paderborn - Bayer Leverkusen 1-4(0-3)

Round 19 [24-26.01.2020]
Borussia Dortmund - FC Köln 5-1(2-0)
Eintracht Frankfurt - RB Leipzig 2-0(0-0)
VfL Wolfsburg - Hertha BSC 1-2(0-0)
Mönchengladbach - FSV Mainz 05 3-1(1-1)
Union Berlin - FC Augsburg 2-0(0-0)
SC Freiburg - SC Paderborn 0-2(0-0)
Bayern München - Schalke 04 5-0(2-0)
Werder Bremen - Hoffenheim 0-3(0-0)
Leverkusen - Fortuna Düsseldorf 3-0(1-0)

Round 20 [31.01.-02.02.2020]
Hertha BSC - Schalke 04 0-0
FSV Mainz 05 - Bayern München 1-3(1-3)
Hoffenheim - Bayer Leverkusen 2-1(1-1)
Fortuna Düsseldorf - Eintracht Frank. 1-1(0-0)
FC Augsburg - Werder Bremen 2-1(0-1)
Borussia Dortmund - Union Berlin 5-0(2-0)
RB Leipzig - Mönchengladbach 2-2(0-2)
FC Köln - SC Freiburg 4-0(1-0)
SC Paderborn - VfL Wolfsburg 2-4(1-2)

Round 21 [07-09.02.2020]
Eintracht Frankfurt - FC Augsburg 5-0(1-0)
SC Freiburg - Hoffenheim 1-0(1-0)
VfL Wolfsburg - Fortuna Düsseldorf 1-1(0-1)
Hertha BSC - FSV Mainz 05 1-3(0-1)
Schalke 04 - SC Paderborn 1-1(0-0)
Werder Bremen - Union Berlin 0-2(0-0)
Leverkusen - Borussia Dortmund 4-3(2-2)
Bayern München - RB Leipzig 0-0
Mönchengladbach - FC Köln 2-1(1-0) [11.03.]

Round 22 [14-15.02.2020]
Bor. Dortmund - Eintracht Frankfurt 4-0(1-0)
Union Berlin - Bayer Leverkusen 2-3(1-1)
Hoffenheim - VfL Wolfsburg 2-3(1-1)
RB Leipzig - Werder Bremen 3-0(2-0)
SC Paderborn - Hertha BSC 1-2(0-1)
FC Augsburg - SC Freiburg 1-1(1-0)
Fortuna Düsseld. - Mönchengladbach 1-4(1-1)
FC Köln - Bayern München 1-4(0-3)
FSV Mainz 05 - Schalke 04 0-0

Round 23 [21-24.02.2020]
Bayern München - SC Paderborn 3-2(1-1)
Werder Bremen - Borussia Dortmund 0-2(0-0)
Mönchengladbach - Hoffenheim 1-1(1-0)
SC Freiburg - Fortuna Düsseldorf 0-2(0-1)
Hertha BSC - FC Köln 0-5(0-3)
Schalke 04 - RB Leipzig 0-5(0-1)
Bayer Leverkusen - FC Augsburg 2-0(1-0)
VfL Wolfsburg - FSV Mainz 05 4-0(2-0)
Eintracht Frankfurt - Union Berlin 1-2(0-0)

Round 24 [28.02.-01.03.2020]
Fortuna Düsseldorf - Hertha BSC 3-3(3-0)
Hoffenheim - Bayern München 0-6(0-4)
FC Augsburg - Mönchengladbach 2-3(0-0)
Borussia Dortmund - SC Freiburg 1-0(1-0)
FSV Mainz 05 - SC Paderborn 2-0(2-0)
FC Köln - Schalke 04 3-0(2-0)
Union Berlin - VfL Wolfsburg 2-2(1-0)
RB Leipzig - Bayer Leverkusen 1-1(1-1)
Werder Bremen - Eintracht F. 0-3(0-0)[03.06.]

Round 25 [06-08.03.2020]
SC Paderborn - FC Köln 1-2(0-2)
VfL Wolfsburg - RB Leipzig 0-0
Leverkusen - Eintracht Frankfurt 4-0(2-0)
Hertha BSC - Werder Bremen 2-2(1-2)
Schalke 04 - Hoffenheim 1-1(1-0)
SC Freiburg - Union Berlin 3-1(1-0)
Mönchengladbach - Bor. Dortmund 1-2(0-1)
Bayern München - FC Augsburg 2-0(0-0)
FSV Mainz 05 - Fortuna Düsseldorf 1-1(0-0)

Round 26 [16-18.05.2020]
FC Augsburg - VfL Wolfsburg 1-2(0-1)
Hoffenheim - Hertha BSC 0-3(0-0)
RB Leipzig - SC Freiburg 1-1(0-1)
Borussia Dortmund - Schalke 04 4-0(2-0)
Fortuna Düsseldorf - SC Paderborn 0-0
Eintracht Frank. - Mönchengladbach 1-3(0-2)
FC Köln - FSV Mainz 05 2-2(1-0)
Union Berlin - Bayern München 0-2(0-1)
Werder Bremen - Bayer Leverkusen 1-4(1-2)

Round 27 [22-24.05.2020]
Hertha BSC - Union Berlin 4-0(0-0)
VfL Wolfsburg - Borussia Dortmund 0-2(0-1)
Mönchengladbach - Leverkusen 1-3(0-1)
SC Freiburg - Werder Bremen 1-0(0-1)
SC Paderborn - Hoffenheim 1-1(1-1)
Bayern München - Eintracht Frank. 5-2(2-0)
Schalke 04 - FC Augsburg 0-3(0-1)
FSV Mainz 05 - RB Leipzig 0-5(0-3)
FC Köln - Fortuna Düsseldorf 2-2(0-1)

Round 28 [26-27.05.2020]
Bor. Dortmund - Bayern München 0-1(0-1)
Werder Bremen - Mönchengladbach 0-0
Bayer Leverkusen - VfL Wolfsburg 1-4(0-1)
Eintracht Frankfurt - SC Freiburg 3-3(1-1)
RB Leipzig - Hertha BSC 2-2(1-1)
Union Berlin - FSV Mainz 05 1-1(1-1)
Fortuna Düsseldorf - Schalke 04 2-1(0-0)
Hoffenheim - FC Köln 3-1(1-0)
FC Augsburg - SC Paderborn 0-0

Round 29 [29.05.-01.06.2020]
SC Freiburg - Bayer Leverkusen 0-1(0-0)
VfL Wolfsburg - Eintracht Frankfurt 1-2(0-1)
Schalke 04 - Werder Bremen 0-1(0-1)
FSV Mainz 05 - Hoffenheim 0-1(0-1)
Hertha BSC - FC Augsburg 2-0(1-0)
Bayern München - Fortuna Düssel. 5-0(3-0)
Mönchengladbach - Union Berlin 4-1(2-0)
SC Paderborn - Borussia Dortmund 1-6(0-0)
FC Köln - RB Leipzig 2-4(1-2)

Round 30 [05-07.06.2020]
SC Freiburg - Mönchengladbach 1-0(0-0)
Bayer Leverkusen - Bayern München 2-4(1-3)
Fortuna Düsseldorf - Hoffenheim 2-2(1-1)
Eintracht Frankfurt - FSV Mainz 05 0-2(0-1)
RB Leipzig - SC Paderborn 1-1(1-0)
Borussia Dortmund - Hertha BSC 1-0(0-0)
Werder Bremen - VfL Wolfsburg 0-1(0-0)
Union Berlin - Schalke 04 1-1(1-1)
FC Augsburg - FC Köln 1-1(0-0)

Round 31 [12-14.06.2020]
Hoffenheim - RB Leipzig 0-2(0-2)
Fortuna Düsseldorf - Bor. Dortmund 0-1(0-0)
Hertha BSC - Eintracht Frankfurt 1-4(1-0)
SC Paderborn - Werder Bremen 1-5(0-3)
VfL Wolfsburg - SC Freiburg 2-2(2-1)
FC Köln - Union Berlin 1-2(0-1)
Bayern München - Mönchengladbach 2-1(1-1)
FSV Mainz 05 - FC Augsburg 0-1(0-1)
Schalke 04 - Bayer Leverkusen 1-1(0-0)

Round 32 [16-17.06.2020]
Mönchengladbach - VfL Wolfsburg 3-0(2-0)
Werder Bremen - Bayern München 0-1(0-1)
SC Freiburg - Hertha BSC 2-1(0-0)
Union Berlin - SC Paderborn 1-0(1-0)
Eintracht Frankfurt - Schalke 04 2-1(1-0)
FC Augsburg - Hoffenheim 1-3(0-0)
RB Leipzig - Fortuna Düsseldorf 2-2(0-0)
Borussia Dortmund - FSV Mainz 05 0-2(0-1)
Bayer Leverkusen - FC Köln 3-1(2-0)

Round 33 [20.06.2020]
RB Leipzig - Borussia Dortmund 0-2(0-1)
Hertha BSC - Bayer Leverkusen 2-0(1-0)
SC Paderborn - Mönchengladbach 1-3(0-1)
Schalke 04 - VfL Wolfsburg 1-4(0-1)
FC Köln - Eintracht Frankfurt 1-1(1-0)
FSV Mainz 05 - Werder Bremen 3-1(2-0)
Bayern München - SC Freiburg 3-1(3-1)
Fortuna Düsseldorf - FC Augsburg 1-1(1-1)
Hoffenheim - Union Berlin 4-0(3-0)

Round 34 [27.06.2020]
VfL Wolfsburg - Bayern München 0-4(0-2)
FC Augsburg - RB Leipzig 1-2(0-1)
Borussia Dortmund - Hoffenheim 0-4(0-2)
Union Berlin - Fortuna Düsseldorf 3-0(1-0)
Mönchengladbach - Hertha BSC 2-1(1-0)
Bayer Leverkusen - FSV Mainz 05 1-0(1-0)
SC Freiburg - Schalke 04 4-0(2-0)
Werder Bremen - FC Köln 6-1(3-0)
Eintracht Frankfurt - SC Paderborn 3-2(2-0)

Final Standings

					Total				Home					Away					
1.	**FC Bayern München**	34	26	4	4	100	-	32	82	13	2	2	53 - 15	13	2	2	47 - 17
2.	BV Borussia 09 Dortmund	34	21	6	7	84	-	41	69	11	3	3	46 - 17	10	3	4	38 - 24
3.	RasenBallsport Leipzig	34	18	12	4	81	-	37	66	7	8	2	38 - 21	11	4	2	43 - 16
4.	Borussia VfL Mönchengladbach	34	20	5	9	66	-	40	65	12	2	3	40 - 21	8	3	6	26 - 19
5.	TSV Bayer 04 Leverkusen	34	19	6	9	61	-	44	63	9	4	4	32 - 22	10	2	5	29 - 22
6.	TSG 1899 Hoffenheim	34	15	7	12	53	-	53	52	7	1	9	26 - 37	8	6	3	27 - 16
7.	VfL Wolfsburg	34	13	10	11	48	-	46	49	4	7	6	19 - 23	9	3	5	29 - 23
8.	SC Freiburg	34	13	9	12	48	-	47	48	9	2	6	23 - 17	4	7	6	25 - 30
9.	Eintracht Frankfurt	34	13	6	15	59	-	60	45	8	4	5	36 - 27	5	2	10	23 - 33
10.	Hertha BSC Berlin	34	11	8	15	48	-	59	41	6	3	8	23 - 32	5	5	7	25 - 27
11.	1. FC Union Berlin	34	12	5	17	41	-	58	41	8	3	6	24 - 20	4	2	11	17 - 38
12.	FC Schalke 04 Gelsenkirchen	34	9	12	13	38	-	58	39	5	7	5	20 - 27	4	5	8	18 - 31
13.	1. FSV Mainz 05	34	11	4	19	44	-	65	37	5	2	10	18 - 29	6	2	9	26 - 36
14.	1. FC Köln	34	10	6	18	51	-	69	36	6	4	7	28 - 27	4	2	11	23 - 42
15.	FC Augsburg	34	9	9	16	45	-	63	36	5	5	7	28 - 29	4	4	9	17 - 34
16.	SV Werder Bremen (*Relegation Play-offs*)	34	8	7	19	42	-	69	31	2	3	12	15 - 36	6	4	7	27 - 33
17.	TSV Fortuna Düsseldorf (*Relegated*)	34	6	12	16	36	-	67	30	4	6	7	18 - 28	2	6	9	18 - 39
18.	SC Paderborn 07 (*Relegated*)	34	4	8	22	37	-	74	20	2	2	13	21 - 46	2	6	9	16 - 28

Top goalscorers:

34	**Robert Lewandowski (POL)**	*FC Bayern München*
28	Timo Werner	*RasenBallsport Leipzig*
17	Jadon Malik Sancho (ENG)	*BV Borussia 09 Dortmund*
16	Wout Weghorst (NED)	*VfL Wolfsburg*
15	Rouwen Hennings	*TSV Fortuna Düsseldorf*
13	Jhon Andrés Córdoba Copete (COL)	*1. FC Köln*
13	Erling Braut Håland (NOR)	*BV Borussia 09 Dortmund*
13	Florian Niederlechner	*FC Augsburg*
13	Robin Kwamina Quaison (SWE)	*1. FSV Mainz 05*

Relegation Play-offs (02-06.07.2020)

SV Werder Bremen - 1. FC Heidenheim		0-0	2-2(1-0)

SV Werder Bremen remains at first level for 2020/2021.

NATIONAL CUP
DFB Pokal 2019/2020

First Round [09-12.08.2019]

KFC Uerdingen 05 - BV Borussia 09 Dortmund	0-2(0-0)		FSV Salmrohr - SV Holstein Kiel	0-6(0-1)
FC Ingolstadt 04 - 1. FC Nürnberg	0-1(0-0)		Germania Halberstadt - 1. FC Union Berlin	0-6(0-1)
SV Sandhausen - Borussia VfL Mönchengladbach	0-1(0-1)		SV Rödinghausen - SC Paderborn 07	3-3 aet; 2-4 pen
1. FC Kaiserslautern - 1. FSV Mainz 05	2-0(0-0)		SV Waldhof Mannheim - Eintracht Frankfurt	3-5(2-2)
Alemannia 1900 Aachen - TSV Bayer 04 Leverkusen	1-4(0-2)		FC Oberneuland - SV Darmstadt 98	1-6(0-3)
TuS Dassendorf - SG Dynamo Dresden	0-3(0-1)		1. FC Saarbrücken - SSV Jahn Regensburg	3-2(0-0)
FC 08 Villingen - TSV Fortuna Düsseldorf	1-3(1-0,1-1)		VfB Lübeck - FC St. Pauli Hamburg	3-3 aet; 3-4 pen
SV Drochtersen/Assel - FC Schalke 04 Gelsenkirchen	0-5(0-1)		VfB Eichstätt - Hertha BSC Berlin	1-5(0-3)
FC Viktoria 1889 Berlin - DSC Arminia Bielefeld	0-1(0-1)		VfL Osnabrück - RasenBallsport Leipzig	2-3(1-3)
SC Verl - FC Augsburg	2-1(2-0)		Chemnitzer FC - Hamburger SV	2-2 aet; 5-6 pen
Wacker Nordhausen - FC Erzgebirge Aue	1-4(1-1)		MSV Duisburg - SpVgg Greuther Fürth	2-0(2-0)
1. FC Magdeburg - SC Freiburg	0-1(0-0,0-0)		SV Wehen Wiesbaden - 1. FC Köln	3-3 aet; 2-3 pen
Würzburger Kickers - TSG 1899 Hoffenheim	3-3 aet; 4-5 pen		Hallescher FC - VfL Wolfsburg	3-5(1-1,3-3)
KSV Baunatal - VfL Bochum	2-3(2-1)		Karlsruher SC - SV Hannover 96	2-0(0-0)
SSV Ulm 1846 - 1. FC Heidenheim 1846	0-2(0-1)		FC Hansa Rostock - VfB Stuttgart	0-1(0-1)
Atlas Delmenhorst - SV Werder Bremen	1-6(1-4)		FC Energie Cottbus - FC Bayern München	1-3(0-1)

Second Round [29-30.10.2019]

MSV Duisburg - TSG 1899 Hoffenheim	0-2(0-0)		1. FC Kaiserslautern - 1. FC Nürnberg	2-2 aet; 6-5 pen
1. FC Saarbrücken - 1. FC Köln	3-2(0-0)		SC Verl - SV Holstein Kiel	1-1 aet; 8-7 pen
SC Freiburg - 1. FC Union Berlin	1-3(1-1)		VfL Wolfsburg - RasenBallsport Leipzig	1-6(0-1)
Hamburger SV - VfB Stuttgart	1-2(1-1,1-1)		SV Werder Bremen - 1. FC Heidenheim 1846	4-1(4-1)
VfL Bochum - FC Bayern München	1-2(1-0)		TSV Fortuna Düsseldorf - FC Erzgebirge Aue	2-1(1-1)
SV Darmstadt 98 - Karlsruher SC	0-1(0-0)		Borussia Dortmund - Borussia Mönchengladbach	2-1(1-0)
TSV Bayer 04 Leverkusen - SC Paderborn 07	1-0(1-0)		Hertha BSC Berlin - SG Dynamo Dresden	3-3 aet; 5-4 pen
DSC Arminia Bielefeld - FC Schalke 04 Gelsenk.	2-3(0-3)		FC St. Pauli Hamburg - Eintracht Frankfurt	1-2(1-2)

Third Round [04-05.02.2020]				
Eintracht Frankfurt - RasenBallsport Leipzig	3-1(1-0)		TSV Bayer 04 Leverkusen - VfB Stuttgart	2-1(0-0)
1. FC Kaiserslautern - TSV Fortuna Düsseldorf	2-5(2-1)		SC Verl - 1. FC Union Berlin	0-1(0-0)
FC Schalke 04 Gelsenkirchen - Hertha BSC Berlin	3-2(0-2,2-2)		FC Bayern München - TSG 1899 Hoffenheim	4-3(3-1)
SV Werder Bremen - BV Borussia 09 Dortmund	3-2(2-0)		1. FC Saarbrücken - Karlsruher SC	0-0 aet; 5-3 pen

Quarter-Finals [03-04.03.2020]				
1. FC Saarbrücken - TSV Fortuna Düsseldorf	1-1 aet; 7-6 pen		TSV Bayer 04 Leverkusen - 1. FC Union Berlin	3-1(0-1)
FC Schalke 04 Gelsenkirchen - FC Bayern München	0-1(0-1)		Eintracht Frankfurt - SV Werder Bremen	2-0(1-0)

Semi-Finals [09-10.06.2020]				
1. FC Saarbrücken - TSV Bayer 04 Leverkusen	0-3(0-2)		FC Bayern München - Eintracht Frankfurt	2-1(1-0)

Final

04.07.2020; Olympiastadion, Berlin; Referee: Tobias Welz; Attendance: none
FC Bayern München – TSV Bayer 04 Leverkusen   **4-2(2-0)**

Bayern München: Manuel Neuer (Cap), Benjamin Jacques Marcel Pavard, Jérôme Agyenim Boateng (69.Lucas François Bernard Hernández), David Olatukunbo Alaba, Alphonso Boyle Davies, Joshua Walter Kimmich, Leon Christoph Goretzka, Serge David Gnabry (87.Thiago Alcântara do Nascimento), Thomas Müller (87.Philippe Coutinho Correia), Robert Lewandowski, Kingsley Junior Coman (64.Ivan Perišić). Trainer: Hans-Dieter Flick.

Leverkusen: Lukáš Hrádecký, Lars Bender (Cap) (82.Mitchell Weiser), Sven Bender, Edmond Tapsoba, Wendell Nascimento Borges, Charles Mariano Aránguiz Sandoval, Julian Baumgartlinger (46.Kerem Demirbay), Nadiem Amiri (46.Kevin Volland), Moussa Diaby, Leon Bailey Butler (76.Karim Bellarabi), Kai Havertz. Trainer: Peter Sylvester Bosz (Netherlands).

Goals: 1-0 David Olatukunbo Alaba (16), 2-0 Serge David Gnabry (24), 3-0 Robert Lewandowski (59), 3-1 Sven Bender (64), 4-1 Robert Lewandowski (89), 4-2 Kai Havertz (90+5 penalty).

THE CLUBS 2019/2020

Fußball-Club Augsburg 1907

Founded:	08.08.1907
Stadium:	WWK Arena, Augsburg (30,660)
Trainer:	Martin Schmidt (SUI) 12.04.1967
[09.03.2020]	Heiko Herrlich 03.12.1971

Goalkeepers:	DOB	M	(s)	G
Tomáš Koubek (CZE)	26.08.1992	24		
Andreas Luthe	10.03.1987	10		
Defenders:	**DOB**	**M**	**(s)**	**G**
Raphael Framberger	06.09.1995	12	(6)	
Jeffrey Gouweleeuw (NED)	10.07.1991	18	(3)	
Iago Amaral Borduchi (BRA)	23.03.1997	7	(3)	1
Tin Jedvaj (CRO)	28.11.1995	30	(1)	2
Stephan Lichtsteiner (SUI)	16.01.1984	17	(3)	
Philipp Max	30.09.1993	31		8
Reece Joel Oxford (ENG)	16.12.1998	2	(10)	
Mads Giersing Valentin Pedersen (DEN)	01.09.1996	1	(1)	
Marek Suchý (CZE)	29.03.1988	4	(3)	
Felix Uduokhai	09.09.1997	21	(5)	
Midfielders:	**DOB**	**M**	**(s)**	**G**
Daniel Baier	18.05.1984	22	(1)	1

Carlos Armando Gruezo Arboleda (ECU)	19.04.1995	10	(1)	
Fredrik Jensen (FIN)	09.09.1997	5	(5)	1
Rani Khedira	27.01.1994	32		
Eduard Löwen	28.01.1997	7	(9)	2
Jan Morávek (CZE)	01.11.1989	4	(7)	
Georg Teigl (AUT)	09.02.1991	1	(2)	
Forwards:	**DOB**	**M**	**(s)**	**G**
Sergio Duvan Cordóva Lezama (VEN)	09.07.1997	4	(12)	2
Alfreð Finnbogason (ISL)	01.02.1989	10	(11)	3
Michael Gregoritsch (AUT)	18.04.1994	4	(2)	
André Hahn	13.08.1990	8	(7)	1
Florian Niederlechner	24.10.1990	31	(2)	13
Marco Richter	24.11.1997	26	(5)	4
Noah Sarenren Bazee (NGA)	21.08.1996	4	(6)	1
Julian Schieber	13.02.1989		(2)	
Rubén Estephan Vargas Martínez (SUI)	05.08.1998	29	(4)	6

Bayer 04 Leverkusen Fußball GmbH

Founded:	01.07.1904
Stadium:	BayArena, Leverkusen (30,210)
Trainer:	Peter Sylvester Bosz (NED) 21.11.1963

Goalkeepers:	DOB	M	(s)	G
Lukáš Hrádecký (FIN)	24.11.1989	34		
Defenders:	**DOB**	**M**	**(s)**	**G**
Sven Bender	27.04.1989	33		2
Aleksandar Dragović (AUT)	06.03.1991	10	(5)	
Panagiotis Retsos (GRE)	09.08.1998	1	(2)	
Daley Sinkgraven (NED)	04.07.1995	11	(2)	
Jonathan Tah	11.02.1996	22	(3)	
Edmond Tapsoba (BFA)	02.02.1999	12	(2)	
Wendell Nascimento Borges (BRA)	20.07.1993	21	(3)	
Midfielders:	**DOB**	**M**	**(s)**	**G**
Nadiem Amiri	27.10.1996	22	(8)	1
Charles Mariano Aránguiz Sandoval (CHI)	17.04.1989	23	(4)	1
Julian Baumgartlinger (AUT)	02.01.1988	20	(7)	2

Karim Bellarabi	08.04.1990	17	(9)	4
Lars Bender	27.04.1989	16	(2)	2
Kerem Demirbay	03.07.1993	18	(7)	1
Kai Havertz	11.06.1999	29	(1)	12
Exequiel Alejandro Palacios (ARG)	05.10.1998	2	(1)	
Mitchell Weiser	21.04.1994	14	(4)	1
Florian Wirtz	03.05.2003	3	(4)	1
Forwards:	**DOB**	**M**	**(s)**	**G**
Lucas Nicolás Alario (ARG)	08.10.1992	11	(13)	7
Leon Bailey Butler (JAM)	09.08.1997	12	(10)	5
Moussa Diaby (FRA)	07.07.1999	18	(10)	5
Paulo Henrique Sampaio Filho „Paulinho" (BRA)	15.07.2000	1	(12)	3
Joel Pohjanpalo (FIN)	13.09.1994		(1)	
Kevin Volland	30.07.1992	24	(3)	10

Fußball-Club Bayern München

Founded:	27.02.1900		
Stadium:	Allianz Arena, München (75,000)		
Trainer:	Niko Kovač (CRO)		15.10.1971
[03.11.2019]	Hans-Dieter Flick		24.02.1965

Goalkeepers:	DOB	M	(s)	G
Manuel Neuer	27.03.1986	33		
Sven Ulreich	03.08.1988	1		
Defenders:	**DOB**	**M**	**(s)**	**G**
David Olatukunbo Alaba (AUT)	24.06.1992	27	(1)	1
Jérôme Agyenim Boateng	03.09.1988	23	(1)	
Alphonso Boyle Davies (CAN)	02.11.2000	24	(5)	3
Lucas François Bernard Hernández (FRA)	14.02.1996	10	(9)	
Joshua Walter Kimmich	08.02.1995	32	(1)	4
Álvaro Odriozola Arzallus (ESP)	14.12.1995	2	(1)	
Benjamin Jacques Marcel Pavard (FRA)	28.03.1996	31	(1)	4
Christopher Jeffrey Richards (USA)	28.03.2000		(1)	
Niklas Süle	03.09.1995	8		
Midfielders:	**DOB**	**M**	**(s)**	**G**
Mickaël Cuisance (FRA)	16.08.1999	3	(6)	1
Leon Christoph Goretzka	06.02.1995	17	(7)	6
Javier Martínez Aginaga „Javi Martínez"(ESP)	02.09.1988	6	(10)	
Jamal Musiala (ENG)	26.02.2003		(1)	
Philippe Coutinho Correia (BRA)	12.06.1992	15	(8)	8
Renato Júnior Luz Sanches (POR)	18.08.1997		(1)	
Sarpreet Singh (NZL)	20.02.1999	1	(1)	
Thiago Alcântara do Nascimento (ESP)	11.04.1991	20	(4)	3
Corentin Tolisso (FRA)	03.08.1994	7	(6)	1
Forwards:	**DOB**	**M**	**(s)**	**G**
Oliver Batista-Meier	16.02.2001		(1)	
Kingsley Junior Coman (FRA)	13.06.1996	17	(7)	4
Leon Dajaku	12.04.2001		(2)	
Serge David Gnabry	14.07.1995	26	(5)	12
Robert Lewandowski (POL)	21.08.1988	31		34
Thomas Müller	13.09.1989	26	(7)	8
Ivan Perišić (CRO)	02.02.1989	11	(11)	4
Kwasi Okyere Wriedt (GHA)	10.07.1994		(1)	
Joshua Orobosa Zirkzee (NED)	22.05.2001	3	(6)	4

Ballspielverein Borussia 09 Dortmund

Founded:	19.12.1909		
Stadium:	Signal Iduna Park, Dortmund (81,360)		
Trainer:	Lucien Favre (SUI)		02.11.1957

Goalkeepers:	DOB	M	(s)	G
Roman Bürki (SUI)	14.11.1990	31		
Marwin Hitz (SUI)	18.09.1987	3	(1)	
Defenders:	**DOB**	**M**	**(s)**	**G**
Manuel Akanji (SUI)	19.07.1995	25	(4)	
Leonardo Julián Balerdi Rosa (ARG)	26.01.1999	1	(6)	
Achraf Hakimi (MAR)	04.11.1998	29	(4)	5
Mats Julian Hummels	16.12.1988	31		1
Mateu Jaume Morey Bauzà (ESP)	02.03.2000	2	(3)	
Łukasz Piszczek (POL)	03.06.1985	25	(4)	1
Marcel Schmelzer	22.01.1988		(7)	1
Nico Schulz	01.04.1993	7	(4)	1
Dan-Axel Zagadou (FRA)	03.06.1999	10	(5)	1
Midfielders:	**DOB**	**M**	**(s)**	**G**
Julian Brandt	02.05.1996	25	(8)	3
Emre Can	12.01.1994	10	(2)	2
Mahmoud Dahoud	01.01.1996	6	(6)	
Thomas Joseph Delaney (DEN)	03.09.1991	11		
Mario Götze	03.06.1992	5	(10)	3
Raphaël Adelino José Guerreiro (POR)	22.12.1993	26	(3)	8
Tobias Raschl	21.02.2000		(1)	
Giovanni Alejandro Reyna (USA)	13.11.2002	2	(13)	
Julian Weigl	08.09.1995	12	(1)	1
Axel Laurent Angel Lambert Witsel (BEL)	12.01.1989	25	(3)	4
Forwards:	**DOB**	**M**	**(s)**	**G**
Jacob Bruun Larsen (DEN)	19.09.1998		(4)	
Erling Braut Håland (NOR)	21.07.2000	11	(4)	13
Thorgan Hazard (BEL)	29.03.1993	28	(5)	7
Francisco „Paco" Alcácer García (ESP)	30.08.1993	6	(5)	5
Marco Reus	31.05.1989	18	(1)	11
Jadon Malik Sancho (ENG)	25.03.2000	25	(7)	17

Borussia Verein für Leibesübungen 1900 Mönchengladbach

Founded:	01.08.1900		
Stadium:	Borussia-Park, Mönchengladbach (54,014)		
Trainer:	Marco Rose		11.09.1976

Goalkeepers:	DOB	M	(s)	G
Yann Sommer (SUI)	17.12.1988	34		
Defenders:	**DOB**	**M**	**(s)**	**G**
Ramy Bensebaini (ALG)	16.04.1995	16	(3)	5
Jordan Beyer	19.05.2000		(3)	
Mamadou Doucouré (FRA)	21.05.1998		(2)	
Nico Elvedi (SUI)	30.09.1996	30	(2)	1
Matthias Ginter	19.01.1994	31		1
Tony Jantschke	07.04.1990	11	(6)	
Stefan Lainer (AUT)	27.08.1992	31		1
Oscar Wendt (SWE)	24.10.1985	18	(7)	2
Midfielders:	**DOB**	**M**	**(s)**	**G**
László Bénes (SVK)	09.09.1997	10	(12)	
Patrick Herrmann	12.02.1991	16	(11)	6
Jonas Hofmann	14.07.1992	18	(6)	5
Fabian Marco Johnson (USA)	11.12.1987	3	(3)	
Christoph Kramer	19.02.1991	17	(5)	
Torben Müsel	25.07.1999		(1)	
Florian Neuhaus	16.03.1997	26	(4)	4
Tobias Strobl	12.05.1990	6	(4)	
Ibrahima Traoré (GUI)	21.04.1988	1	(6)	
Denis Zakaria (SUI)	20.11.1996	22	(1)	2
Forwards:	**DOB**	**M**	**(s)**	**G**
Keanan Bennetts (ENG)	09.03.1999		(1)	
Breel-Donald Embolo (SUI)	14.02.1997	17	(11)	8
Alassane Pléa (FRA)	10.03.1993	25	(2)	10
Raffael Caetano de Araújo (BRA)	28.03.1985		(8)	
Lars Stindl	26.08.1988	14	(11)	9
Marcus Lilian Thuram-Ulien (FRA)	06.08.1997	28	(3)	10

Eintracht Frankfurt

Founded:	08.03.1899		
Stadium:	Commerzbank-Arena, Frankfurt (51,500)		
Trainer:	Adolf Hütter (AUT)		11.02.1970

Goalkeepers:	DOB	M	(s)	G
Frederik Riis Rønnow (DEN)	04.08.1992	9		
Kevin Trapp	08.07.1990	22		
Felix Wiedwald	15.03.1990	3		
Defenders:	**DOB**	**M**	**(s)**	**G**
David Ángel Abraham (ARG)	15.07.1986	19	(1)	2
Timothy Chandler (USA)	29.03.1990	12	(10)	5
Danny da Costa	13.07.1993	15	(4)	1
Erik Durm	12.05.1992	6	(3)	
Simon Falette (GUI)	19.02.1992	1		
Martin Hinteregger (AUT)	07.09.1992	30	(1)	8
Evan N'Dicka (FRA)	20.08.1999	20	(2)	1
Almamy Touré (FRA)	28.04.1996	18	(1)	1
Midfielders:	**DOB**	**M**	**(s)**	**G**
Jonathan de Guzmán (NED)	13.09.1987		(8)	
Gélson da Conceição Tavares Fernandes (SUI)	02.09.1986	10	(1)	
Mijat Gaćinović (SRB)	08.02.1995	11	(12)	
Makoto Hasebe (JPN)	18.01.1984	21	(2)	
Stefan Ilsanker (AUT)	18.05.1989	9	(3)	2
Daichi Kamada (JPN)	05.08.1996	22	(6)	2
Dominik Kohr	31.01.1994	16	(10)	
Filip Kostić (SRB)	01.11.1992	33		4
Lucas Torró Marset (ESP)	19.07.1994	4	(3)	
Sebastian Rode	11.10.1990	25	(4)	3
Djibril Sow (SUI)	06.02.1997	18	(11)	1
Forwards:	**DOB**	**M**	**(s)**	**G**
André Miguel Valente da Silva (POR)	06.11.1995	16	(9)	12
Bas Dost (NED)	31.05.1989	16	(8)	8
Dejan Joveljić (SRB)	07.08.1999	2	(2)	
Gonçalo Mendes Paciência (POR)	01.08.1994	15	(8)	7
Ante Rebić (CRO)	21.09.1993	1		

Düsseldorfer Turn- und Sportverein Fortuna 1895

Founded: 05.05.1895
Stadium: Merkur Spiel-Arena, Düsseldorf (54,600)
Trainer: Friedhelm Funkel — 10.12.1953
[29.01.2020] Uwe Rösler — 15.11.1968

Goalkeepers:	DOB	M	(s)	G
Florian Kastenmeier	28.06.1997	17		
Zackary Thomas Steffen (USA)	02.04.1995	17		
Defenders:	**DOB**	**M**	**(s)**	**G**
Kasim Adams (GHA)	22.06.1995	11	(2)	1
Kaan Ayhan (TUR)	10.11.1994	31		2
Robin Bormuth	19.09.1995	2	(1)	
Niko Gießelmann	26.09.1991	22	(3)	1
Mathias Jattah-Njie Jørgensen (DEN)	23.04.1990	5	(4)	
Markus Suttner (AUT)	16.04.1987	16	(5)	
Jean Zimmer	06.12.1993	8	(9)	
Midfielders:	**DOB**	**M**	**(s)**	**G**
Lewis Renard Baker (ENG)	25.04.1995	7	(1)	
Aymane Barkok	21.05.1998	1	(2)	
Valon Berisha (KVX)	07.02.1993	12	(1)	
Adam Bodzek	07.09.1985	22	(6)	
Oliver Fink	06.06.1982	8	(6)	
André Hoffmann	28.02.1993	27	(2)	2
Alfredo Morales (USA)	12.05.1990	18	(9)	1
Kelvin Ofori (GHA)	27.07.2001		(2)	
Thomas Pledl	23.05.1994		(5)	
Marcel Sobottka	25.04.1994	8	(10)	
Kevin Stöger (AUT)	27.08.1993	14	(3)	
Erik Thommy	20.08.1994	25	(9)	6
Matthias Zimmermann	16.06.1992	33	(1)	1
Forwards:	**DOB**	**M**	**(s)**	**G**
Nana Ampomah (GHA)	02.01.1996	5	(7)	
Rouwen Hennings	28.08.1987	27	(5)	15
Kenan Karaman (TUR)	05.03.1994	16	(4)	6
Dawid Kownacki (POL)	14.03.1997	11	(9)	
Steven Skrzybski	18.11.1992	6	(5)	1
Bernard Tekpetey (GHA)	03.09.1997	5	(4)	

Sport-Club Freiburg

Founded: 1904
Stadium: Schwarzwald-Stadion, Freiburg (24,000)
Trainer: Christian Streich — 11.06.1965

Goalkeepers:	DOB	M	(s)	G
Mark Flekken (NED)	13.06.1993	10		
Alexander Schwolow	02.06.1992	24		
Niclas Thiede	14.04.1999		(1)	
Defenders:	**DOB**	**M**	**(s)**	**G**
Manuel Gulde	12.02.1991	15	(2)	1
Christian Günter	28.02.1993	34		2
Dominique Heintz	15.08.1993	27	(1)	
Gian-Luca Itter	05.01.1999		(3)	
Robin Koch	17.07.1996	31	(1)	1
Lukas Kübler	30.08.1992	3	(2)	
Philipp Lienhart (AUT)	11.07.1996	20	(2)	
Nico Schlotterbeck	01.12.1999	4	(9)	
Midfielders:	**DOB**	**M**	**(s)**	**G**
Amir Abrashi (ALB)	27.03.1990	8	(5)	
Mike Frantz	14.10.1986	3	(15)	
Jérôme Gondorf	26.06.1988	2		
Vincenzo Grifo (ITA)	07.04.1993	17	(9)	4
Janik Haberer	02.04.1994	20	(6)	2
Nicolas Höfler	09.03.1990	31	(1)	1
Yannik Keitel	15.02.2000	2	(1)	
Kwon Chang-hoon (KOR)	30.06.1994	6	(17)	2
Roland Sallai (HUN)	22.05.1997	15	(6)	2
Jonathan Schmid (FRA)	26.06.1990	31	(2)	5
Lino Tempelmann	02.02.1999	1		
Forwards:	**DOB**	**M**	**(s)**	**G**
Brandon Joel Gaetano Borrello (AUS)	25.07.1995	4	(3)	
Lucas Höler	10.07.1994	28	(6)	8
Nils Petersen	06.12.1988	24	(10)	11
Luca Waldschmidt	19.05.1996	14	(9)	7

Hertha Berliner Sport-Club

Founded: 25.07.1892
Stadium: Olympiastadion, Berlin (74,475)
Trainer: Ante Čović (CRO) — 31.08.1975
[27.11.2019] Jürgen Klinsmann — 30.07.1964
[11.02.2020] Alexander Nouri — 20.08.1979
[09.04.2018] Bruno Labbadia — 08.02.1966

Goalkeepers:	DOB	M	(s)	G
Rune Jarstein (NOR)	29.09.1984	29		
Thomas Kraft	22.07.1988	4		
Dennis Smarsch	14.01.1999	1	(1)	
Defenders:	**DOB**	**M**	**(s)**	**G**
Dedryck Boyata (BEL)	28.11.1990	28		4
Lukas Klünter	26.05.1996	20	(3)	
Maximilian Mittelstädt	18.03.1997	19	(7)	1
Peter Pekarík (SVK)	30.10.1986	9		
Marvin Plattenhardt	26.01.1992	17		
Karim Rekik (NED)	02.12.1994	14		1
Niklas Stark	14.04.1995	20	(1)	1
Jordan Torunarigha	07.08.1997	16	(2)	1
Midfielders:	**DOB**	**M**	**(s)**	**G**
Santiago Lionel Ascacíbar (ARG)	25.02.1997	7	(1)	
Vladimír Darida (CZE)	08.08.1990	25	(3)	3
Ondrej Duda (SVK)	05.12.1994	6	(1)	
Marko Grujić (SRB)	13.04.1996	29		4
Eduard Löwen	28.01.1997	2	(5)	
Arne Maier	08.01.1999	5	(9)	
Lazar Samardžić	24.02.2002		(3)	
Per Skjelbred (NOR)	16.06.1987	21	(3)	
Forwards:	**DOB**	**M**	**(s)**	**G**
Javairô Dilrosun (NED)	22.06.1998	16	(7)	4
Alexander Esswein	25.03.1990	1	(6)	
Vedad Ibišević (BIH)	06.08.1984	15	(10)	7
Salomon Kalou (CIV)	05.08.1985	1	(4)	1
Pascal Köpke	03.09.1995	1	(3)	
Mathew Allan Leckie (AUS)	04.02.1991	1	(6)	
Dodi Lukebakio Ngandoli (BEL)	24.09.1997	24	(6)	7
Matheus Santos Carneiro da Cunha (BRA)	27.05.1999	9	(2)	5
Jessic Ngankam	20.07.2000		(4)	
Krzysztof Piątek (POL)	01.07.1995	9	(6)	4
Daishawn Orpheo Marvin Redan (DEN)	02.02.2001		(1)	
Davie Selke	20.01.1995	10	(9)	1
Marius Wolf	27.05.1995	15	(6)	1

Turn- und Sportgemeinschaft 1899 Hoffenheim

Founded:	01.07.1899	
Stadium:	Rhein-Neckar-Arena, Sinsheim (30,150)	
Trainer:	Alfred Schreuder (NED)	02.11.1972
[09.06.2020]	Marcel Rapp	16.04.1979

Goalkeepers:	DOB	M	(s)	G
Oliver Baumann	02.06.1990	30		
Philipp Pentke	01.05.1985	4		
Defenders:	**DOB**	**M**	**(s)**	**G**
Kevin Akpoguma	19.04.1995	12	(6)	
Ermin Bičakčić (BIH)	24.01.1990	13	(8)	2
Melayro Bogarde (NED)	28.05.2002	1	(1)	
Benjamin Hübner	04.07.1989	25		1
Pavel Kadeřábek (CZE)	25.04.1992	28	(2)	2
Lucas Ribeiro dos Santos (BRA)	19.01.1999		(2)	1
Stefan Posch (AUT)	14.05.1997	27	(1)	
Kostas Stafylidis (GRE)	02.12.1993	4	(3)	1
Kevin Vogt	23.09.1991	11		
Midfielders:	**DOB**	**M**	**(s)**	**G**
Christoph Baumgartner (AUT)	01.08.1999	17	(9)	7
Leonardo Jesus Loureiro Bittencourt	19.12.1993		(1)	
Ilay Elmkies (ISR)	10.03.2000		(1)	
Dennis Geiger	10.06.1998	13	(8)	
Vincenzo Grifo (ITA)	07.04.1993		(1)	
Florian Grillitsch (AUT)	07.08.1995	28	(3)	
Håvard Nordtveit (NOR)	21.06.1990	7	(4)	
Sebastian Rudy	28.02.1990	31	(1)	1
Lukas Rupp	08.01.1991	4	(3)	
Diadié Samassékou (MLI)	11.01.1996	16	(5)	
Robert Skov (DEN)	20.05.1996	29	(2)	4
Steven Zuber (SUI)	17.08.1991	10	(4)	2
Forwards:	**DOB**	**M**	**(s)**	**G**
Sargis Adamyan (ARM)	23.05.1993	6	(9)	5
Ihlas Bebou (TOG)	23.04.1994	20	(12)	6
Maximilian Beier	17.10.2002		(6)	
Ishak Belfodil (ALG)	15.01.1992	3	(2)	
Jacob Bruun Larsen (DEN)	19.09.1998	5	(6)	
Munas Dabbur (ISR)	14.05.1992	11	(3)	4
Andrej Kramarić (CRO)	19.06.1991	14	(5)	12
Jürgen Leonardo Locadia (NED)	07.11.1993	5	(6)	4

1. Fußball-Club Köln 01/07

Founded:	13.02.1948	
Stadium:	RheinEnergieStadion, Köln (49,698)	
Trainer:	Achim Beierlorzer	20.11.1967
[18.11.2019]	Markus Gisdol (NED)	17.08.1969

Goalkeepers:	DOB	M	(s)	G
Timo Horn	12.05.1993	34		
Defenders:	**DOB**	**M**	**(s)**	**G**
Matthias Bader	17.06.1997		(1)	
Sebastiaan Bornauw (BEL)	22.03.1999	28		6
Rafael Czichos	14.05.1990	26		1
Kingsley Ehizibue (NGA)	25.05.1995	29	(2)	1
Jonas Hector	27.05.1990	28	(1)	4
Ismail Jakobs	17.08.1999	20		2
Jorge Meré Pérez (ESP)	17.04.1997	5	(6)	1
Noah Katterbach	13.04.2001	16	(2)	
Toni Leistner	19.08.1990	11	(2)	
Benno Schmitz	17.11.1994	13	(5)	
Lasse Sobiech	18.01.1991	1		
Midfielders:	**DOB**	**M**	**(s)**	**G**
Darko Churlinov (MKD)	11.07.2000		(1)	
Christian Clemens	04.08.1991		(1)	
Dominick Drexler	26.05.1990	18	(9)	3
Marco Höger	16.09.1989	6	(9)	
Florian Kainz (AUT)	24.10.1992	16	(12)	5
Elvis Rexhbeçaj	01.11.1997	7	(6)	
Marcel Risse	17.12.1989		(6)	
Louis Schaub	29.12.1994	7	(2)	1
Kingsley Schindler	12.07.1993	9	(4)	
Ellyes Skhiri (TUN)	10.05.1995	31	(1)	1
Birger Verstraete (BEL)	16.04.1994	7	(2)	
Forwards:	**DOB**	**M**	**(s)**	**G**
Jhon Andrés Córdoba Copete (COL)	11.05.1993	23	(6)	13
Tim Lemperle	05.02.2002		(1)	
Anthony Mbu Agogo Modeste (FRA)	14.04.1988	11	(16)	4
Simon Terodde	02.03.1988	7	(16)	3
Jan Thielmann	26.05.2002	7	(5)	
Mark-Alexander Uth	24.08.1991	14	(1)	5

RasenBallsport Leipzig

Founded:	19.05.2009	
Stadium:	Red Bull Arena, Leipzig (42,558)	
Trainer:	Julian Nagelsmann	23.07.1987

Goalkeepers:	DOB	M	(s)	G
Péter Gulácsi (HUN)	06.05.1990	32		
Yvon Mvogo (SUI)	06.06.1994	2		
Defenders:	**DOB**	**M**	**(s)**	**G**
Ethan Kwame Colm Raymond Ampadu (WAL)	14.09.2000		(3)	
Marcel Halstenberg	27.09.1991	28	(1)	3
José Ángel Esmorís Tasende (ESP)	04.01.1997	12	(1)	1
Lukas Manuel Klostermann	03.06.1996	31		3
Ibrahima Konaté (FRA)	25.05.1999	6	(2)	
Nordi Mukiele Mulere (FRA)	01.11.1997	21	(4)	3
Willi Orban (HUN)	03.11.1992	9	(3)	1
Marcelo Josemir Saracchi Pintos (URU)	23.04.1998	1	(3)	1
Dayotchanculle Upamecano (FRA)	27.10.1998	27	(1)	
Midfielders:	**DOB**	**M**	**(s)**	**G**
Tyler Shaan Adams (USA)	14.02.1999	10	(4)	
Daniel Olmo Carvajal „Dani Olmo" (ESP)	07.05.1998	9	(3)	3
Diego Demme	21.11.1991	14	(3)	
Emil Forsberg (SWE)	23.10.1991	14	(8)	5
Amadou Haïdara (MLI)	31.01.1998	5	(14)	
Stefan Ilsanker (AUT)	18.05.1989	5	(1)	
Kevin Kampl (SVN)	09.10.1990	8	(3)	2
Tom Krauß	22.06.2001		(1)	
Konrad Laimer (AUT)	27.05.1997	26	(3)	2
Christopher Nkunku (FRA)	14.11.1997	21	(11)	5
Marcel Sabitzer (AUT)	17.03.1994	30	(2)	9
Forwards:	**DOB**	**M**	**(s)**	**G**
Dennis Borkowski	26.01.2002		(1)	
Ademola Lookman (ENG)	20.10.1997	1	(10)	
Matheus Santos Carneiro da Cunha (BRA)	27.05.1999	2	(8)	
Yussuf Yurary Poulsen (DEN)	15.06.1994	12	(10)	5
Patrik Schick (CZE)	24.01.1996	15	(7)	10
Timo Werner	06.03.1996	33	(1)	28
Hannes Wolf (AUT)	16.04.1999		(5)	

1. Fußball- und Sportverein Mainz 05

Founded: 16.03.1905
Stadium: Opel Arena, Mainz (34,000)
Trainer: Sandro Schwarz   17.10.1978
[18.11.2019] Achim Beierlorzer   20.11.1967

Goalkeepers:	DOB	M	(s)	G
Florian Müller	13.11.1997	12	(1)	
Robin Zentner	28.10.1994	22		
Defenders:	**DOB**	**M**	**(s)**	**G**
Aarón Martín Caricol (ESP)	22.04.1997	21	(1)	
Daniel Brosinski	17.07.1988	16	(10)	2
Jeffrey Kevin van Homoet Bruma (NED)	13.11.1991	8		
Alexander Hack	08.09.1993	9	(5)	
Phillipp Mwene (AUT)	29.01.1994	4		
Moussa Niakhaté (FRA)	08.03.1996	33		1
Ronaël Pierre-Gabriel (FRA)	13.06.1998	8		
Jerry St. Juste (NED)	19.10.1996	24	(1)	2
Midfielders:	**DOB**	**M**	**(s)**	**G**
Ridle Baku	08.04.1998	26	(4)	1
Leandro Barreiro (LUX)	03.01.2000	11	(7)	

	DOB	M	(s)	G
Edimilson Fernandes Ribeiro (SUI)	15.04.1996	18	(6)	1
Danny Latza	07.12.1989	15	(8)	
Pierre Malong (CMR)	26.07.1995	22	(6)	4
Alexandru Iulian Maxim (ROU)	08.07.1990		(5)	
Levin Öztunali	15.03.1996	19	(8)	4
Robin Kwamina Quaison (SWE)	09.10.1993	31	(1)	13
Forwards:	**DOB**	**M**	**(s)**	**G**
Taiwo Michael Awoniyi (NGA)	12.08.1997	5	(7)	1
Jean-Paul Boëtius (NED)	22.03.1994	26	(2)	4
Jonathan Burkardt	11.07.2000	3	(5)	1
Dong-won Ji (KOR)	28.05.1991	1	(3)	
Jean-Philippe Mateta (FRA)	28.06.1997	12	(6)	3
Karim Onisiwo (AUT)	17.03.1992	16	(16)	4
Ádám Csaba Szalai (HUN)	09.12.1987	12	(15)	1

Sport-Club Paderborn 07

Founded: 1907
Stadium: Benteler-Arena, Paderborn (15,000)
Trainer: Steffen Baumgart   05.01.1972

Goalkeepers:	DOB	M	(s)	G
Jannik Huth	15.04.1994	6		
Leopold Zingerle	10.04.1994	28		
Defenders:	**DOB**	**M**	**(s)**	**G**
Jamilu Collins (NGA)	05.08.1994	30		1
Uwe Hünemeier	09.01.1986	13	(3)	1
Laurent Jans (LUX)	05.08.1992	19	(3)	
Luca Kilian	01.09.1999	14	(1)	
Jan-Luca Rumpf	08.07.1999	1		
Sebastian Schonlau	05.08.1994	23		2
Christian Strohdiek	22.01.1988	16		1
Midfielders:	**DOB**	**M**	**(s)**	**G**
Christopher Antwi-Adjei (GHA)	07.02.1994	28	(6)	1
Cauly Oliveira-Souza (BRA)	15.09.1995	8	(5)	2
Mohamed Dräger (TUN)	25.06.1996	16	(2)	1
Antony Evans (ENG)	23.09.1998	2	(4)	

	DOB	M	(s)	G
Samúel Kári Friðjónsson (ISL)	22.02.1996	2	(3)	
Klaus Gjasula	14.12.1989	28	(1)	2
Gerrit Holtmann	25.03.1995	13	(11)	1
Kai Pröger	15.05.1992	22	(9)	2
Abdelhamid Sabiri	28.11.1996	9	(15)	4
Sebastian Vasiliadis (GRE)	04.10.1997	32		1
Forwards:	**DOB**	**M**	**(s)**	**G**
Babacar Gueye (SEN)	31.12.1994	1	(2)	
Dennis Jastrzembski	20.02.2000	1	(5)	
Streli Mamba	17.06.1994	18	(6)	5
Sven Michel	15.07.1990	13	(16)	5
Marlon Ritter	15.10.1994	3	(8)	
Khiry Lamar Shelton (USA)	26.06.1993		(2)	
Dennis Srbeny	05.05.1994	14	(3)	5
Ben Zolinski	03.05.1992	14	(14)	3

Fußballclub Gelsenkirchen-Schalke 04

Founded: 04.05.1904
Stadium: Veltins-Arena, Gelsenkirchen (62,271)
Trainer: David Wagner (USA)   19.10.1971

Goalkeepers:	DOB	M	(s)	G
Alexander Nübel	30.09.1996	26		
Markus Schubert	12.06.1998	8	(1)	
Defenders:	**DOB**	**M**	**(s)**	**G**
Timo Becker	25.03.1997	4	(6)	
Juan Miranda González (ESP)	19.01.2000	8	(3)	
Ozan Kabak (TUR)	25.03.2000	21	(5)	3
Jonjoe Kenny (ENG)	15.03.1997	31		2
Matija Nastasić (SRB)	28.03.1993	15	(1)	
Bastian Oczipka	12.01.1989	33	(1)	
Salif Sané (SEN)	25.08.1990	13	(2)	2
Benjamin Stambouli (FRA)	13.08.1990	9		
Malick Thiaw (FIN)	08.08.2001		(4)	
Jean-Clair Todibo (FRA)	30.12.1999	4	(4)	
Midfielders:	**DOB**	**M**	**(s)**	**G**
Nassim Boujellab	20.06.1999	3	(8)	
Can Bozdogan	05.04.2001	3		

	DOB	M	(s)	G
Daniel Caligiuri	15.01.1988	26	(2)	2
Amine Harit (MAR)	18.06.1997	24	(1)	6
Jonas Hofmann	07.02.1997		(1)	
Omar Mascarell González (ESP)	02.02.1993	23		
Weston McKennie (USA)	28.08.1998	24	(4)	3
Levent Mercan	10.12.2000	1	(4)	
Alessandro Schöpf (AUT)	07.02.1994	15	(7)	
Suat Serdar	11.04.1997	19	(1)	7
Forwards:	**DOB**	**M**	**(s)**	**G**
Guido Burgstaller (AUT)	29.04.1989	13	(8)	
Michael Gregoritsch (AUT)	18.04.1994	10	(4)	1
Ahmed Kutucu (TUR)	01.03.2000	3	(22)	3
Rabbi Matondo (WAL)	09.09.2000	14	(6)	2
Benito Raman (BEL)	07.11.1994	19	(6)	4
Fabian Reese	29.11.1997	1	(1)	
Mark Alexander Uth	24.08.1991	4	(4)	

1. Fußballclub Union Berlin

Founded: 20.01.1966
Stadium: Stadion An der Alten Försterei, Berlin (22,012)
Trainer: Urs Fischer (SUI)   20.02.1966

Goalkeepers:	DOB	M	(s)	G
Rafał Gikiewicz (POL)	26.10.1987	33		
Moritz Nicolas	21.10.1997	1		
Defenders:	**DOB**	**M**	**(s)**	**G**
Marvin Friedrich	13.12.1995	31		2
Florian Hübner	01.03.1991	9	(2)	
Christopher Lenz	22.09.1994	26		
Michael Parensen	24.06.1986	6	(3)	1
Ken Reichel	19.12.1986	6	(1)	
Keven Schlotterbeck	28.04.1997	23		
Neven Subotić (SRB)	10.12.1988	23		1
Christopher Trimmel (AUT)	24.02.1987	32		
Midfielders:	**DOB**	**M**	**(s)**	**G**
Robert Andrich	22.09.1994	30		1
Christian Gentner	14.08.1985	29	(2)	3

	DOB	M	(s)	G
Akaki Gogia	18.01.1992	1	(2)	
Felix Kroos	12.03.1991	3	(12)	
Yunus Mallı (TUR)	24.02.1992	9	(4)	
Grischa Prömel	09.01.1995	9	(7)	
Julian Ryerson (NOR)	17.11.1997	3	(11)	
Manuel Schmiedebach	05.12.1988	2	(3)	
Forwards:	**DOB**	**M**	**(s)**	**G**
Suleiman Abdullahi (NGA)	10.12.1996	1	(5)	1
Sebastian Andersson (SWE)	15.07.1991	31	(2)	12
Sheraldo Becker (NED)	09.02.1995	5	(8)	
Marius Bülter	29.03.1993	28	(4)	7
Marcus Ingvartsen (DEN)	04.01.1996	20	(8)	5
Joshua Mees	15.04.1996	1	(14)	
Sebastian Polter	01.04.1991	2	(11)	2
Anthony Ujah (NGA)	14.10.1990	10	(14)	3

Sportverein Werder Bremen von 1899

Founded: 04.02.1899
Stadium: Weser-Stadion, Bremen (42,100)
Trainer: Florian Kohfeldt — 05.10.1982

Goalkeepers:	DOB	M	(s)	G
Stefanos Kapino (GRE)	18.03.1994	1		
Jiří Pavlenka (CZE)	14.04.1992	33		

Defenders:	DOB	M	(s)	G
Hans Carl Ludwig Augustinsson (SWE)	21.04.1994	10	(2)	
Marco Friedl (AUT)	16.03.1998	24	(3)	1
Theodor Gebre Selassie (CZE)	24.12.1986	28		2
Michael Lang (SUI)	08.02.1991	6	(3)	
Sebastian Langkamp	15.01.1988	3	(2)	
Niklas Moisander (FIN)	29.09.1985	22		
Ömer Toprak (TUR)	21.07.1989	9	(1)	
Miloš Veljković (SRB)	26.09.1995	23	(1)	
Kevin Vogt	23.09.1991	14		

Midfielders:	DOB	M	(s)	G
Philipp Bargfrede	03.03.1989	6	(9)	
Fin Bartels	07.02.1987	1	(13)	
Leonardo Jesus Loureiro Bittencourt	19.12.1993	23	(5)	4
Maximilian Eggestein	08.12.1996	32		1
Benjamin Goller	01.01.1999	2	(8)	
Christian Groß	08.02.1989	10	(4)	
Davy Klaassen (NED)	21.02.1993	33		7
Kevin Möhwald	03.07.1993		(1)	
Nuri Şahin (TUR)	05.09.1988	16		

Forwards:	DOB	M	(s)	G
Johannes Eggestein	08.05.1998	4	(10)	1
Niclas Füllkrug	09.02.1993	4	(4)	4
Martin Harnik (AUT)	10.06.1987		(2)	
Luc Ihorst	07.03.2000		(1)	
Yuya Osako (JPN)	18.05.1990	22	(6)	8
Claudio Miguel Pizarro Bossio (PER)	03.10.1978		(18)	
Milot Rashica (KVX)	28.06.1996	27	(1)	8
Joshua Thomas Sargent (USA)	20.02.2000	15	(13)	4
Davie Selke	20.01.1995	5	(6)	
Nick Woltemade	14.02.2002	1	(4)	

Verein für Leibesübungen Wolfsburg

Founded: 12.09.1945
Stadium: Volkswagen Arena, Wolfsburg (30,000)
Trainer: Oliver Glasner (AUT) — 28.08.1974

Goalkeepers:	DOB	M	(s)	G
Koen Casteels (BEL)	25.06.1992	26		
Pavao Pervan (AUT)	13.11.1987	8		

Defenders:	DOB	M	(s)	G
John Anthony Brooks (USA)	28.01.1993	25		
Jeffrey Kevin van Homoet Bruma (NED)	13.11.1991	9		
Robin Knoche	22.05.1992	17	(4)	1
Melingo Kevin Mbabu (SUI)	19.04.1995	18	(2)	3
Paulo Otávio Rosa da Silva (BRA)	23.11.1994	4	(1)	
Marin Pongračić (CRO)	11.09.1997	11		2
Jérôme Roussillon (FRA)	06.01.1993	27	(2)	1
Marcel Tisserand (COD)	10.01.1993	14	(1)	1
William de Asevedo Furtado (BRA)	03.04.1995	16		1

Midfielders:	DOB	M	(s)	G
Maximilian Arnold	27.05.1994	32	(1)	4
Josip Brekalo (CRO)	23.06.1998	19	(11)	3
Yannick Gerhardt	13.03.1994	7	(11)	2
Josuha Guilavogui (FRA)	19.09.1990	23	(2)	
Luca Horn	19.12.1998		(1)	
João Victor Santos Sá (BRA)	27.03.1994	18	(14)	2
Felix Klaus	13.09.1992	6	(17)	
Xaver Schlager (AUT)	28.09.1997	21	(2)	1
Renato Steffen (SUI)	03.11.1991	19	(8)	6

Forwards:	DOB	M	(s)	G
Daniel Ginczek	13.04.1991	9	(9)	3
Mamoudou Karamoko (FRA)	08.09.1999		(1)	
Omar Marmoush (EGY)	07.02.1999		(5)	
Admir Mehmedi (SUI)	16.03.1991	14	(7)	2
Lukas Nmecha	14.12.1998	1	(5)	
Wout Weghorst (NED)	07.08.1992	30	(2)	16

SECOND LEVEL
2. Bundesliga 2019/2020

1.	DSC Arminia Bielefeld (*Promoted*)	34	18	14	2	65 - 30	68
2.	VfB Stuttgart (*Promoted*)	34	17	7	10	62 - 41	58
3.	1. FC Heidenheim (*Promotion Play-offs*)	34	15	10	9	45 - 36	55
4.	Hamburger SV	34	14	12	8	62 - 46	54
5.	SV Darmstadt 98	34	13	13	8	48 - 43	52
6.	SV Hannover 96	34	13	9	12	54 - 49	48
7.	FC Erzgebirge Aue	34	13	8	13	46 - 48	47
8.	VfL Bochum	34	11	13	10	53 - 51	46
9.	SpVgg Greuther Fürth	34	11	11	12	46 - 45	44
10.	SV Sandhausen	34	10	13	11	43 - 45	43
11.	SV Holstein Kiel	34	11	10	13	53 - 56	43
12.	SSV Jahn Regensburg	34	11	10	13	50 - 56	43
13.	VfL Osnabrück	34	9	13	12	46 - 48	40
14.	FC St. Pauli Hamburg	34	9	12	13	41 - 50	39
15.	Karlsruher SC	34	8	13	13	45 - 56	37
16.	1. FC Nürnberg (*Relegation Play-offs*)	34	8	13	13	45 - 58	37
17.	SV Wehen Wiesbaden (*Relegated*)	34	9	7	18	45 - 65	34
18.	SG Dynamo Dresden (*Relegated*)	34	8	8	18	32 - 58	32

Relegation Play-offs (07-11.07.2019)

1. FC Nürnberg - FC Ingolstadt 04   2-0(2-0)   1-3(0-0)

INTERNATIONAL MATCHES
(16.07.2019 – 15.07.2020)

06.09.2019	Hamburg	Germany - Netherlands	2-4(1-0)	(ECQ)
09.09.2019	Belfast	Northern Ireland - Germany	0-2(0-0)	(ECQ)
09.10.2019	Dortmund	Germany - Argentina	2-2(2-0)	(F)
13.10.2019	Tallinn	Estonia - Germany	0-3(0-0)	(ECQ)
16.11.2019	Mönchengladbach	Germany - Belarus	4-0(1-0)	(ECQ)
19.11.2019	Frankfurt am Main	Germany - Northern Ireland	6-1(2-1)	(ECQ)

06.09.2019 GERMANY - NETHERLANDS 2-4(1-0) 16th EC. Qualifiers
Volksparkstadion, Hamburg; Referee: Artur Manuel Soares Dias (Portugal); Attendance: 51,299
GER: Manuel Peter Neuer (Cap), Lukas Manuel Klostermann, Matthias Lukas Ginter, Niklas Süle, Jonathan Glao Tah, Joshua Walter Kimmich, Toni Kroos, Nico Schulz, Marco Reus (61.İlkay Gündoğan), Serge David Gnabry, Timo Werner (61.Kai Havertz). Trainer: Trainer: Joachim Löw.
Goals: Serge David Gnabry (9), Toni Kroos (73 penalty).

09.09.2019 NORTHERN IRELAND - GERMANY 0-2(0-0) 16th EC. Qualifiers
Windsor Park, Belfast; Referee: Daniele Orsato (Italy); Attendance: 18,326
GER: Manuel Peter Neuer (Cap), Lukas Manuel Klostermann, Matthias Lukas Ginter (40.Jonathan Glao Tah), Niklas Süle, Marcel Halstenberg, Joshua Walter Kimmich, Toni Kroos, Marco Reus (85.Emre Can), Julian Brandt, Serge David Gnabry, Timo Werner (68.Kai Havertz). Trainer: Trainer: Joachim Löw.
Goals: Marcel Halstenberg (48), Serge David Gnabry (90+3).

09.10.2019 GERMANY - ARGENTINA 2-2(2-0) Friendly International
Signal Iduna Park, Dortmund, Referee: Clément Turpin (France); Attendance: 45,197
GER: Marc-André ter Stegen, Lukas Manuel Klostermann, Robin Koch, Niklas Süle, Marcel Halstenberg, Joshua Walter Kimmich (Cap), Emre Can, Kai Havertz (83.Sebastian Rudy), Julian Brandt (66.Nadiem Amiri), Serge David Gnabry (72.Suat Serdar), Gian-Luca Waldschmidt. Trainer: Trainer: Joachim Löw.
Goals: Serge David Gnabry (15), Kai Havertz (22).

13.10.2019 ESTONIA - GERMANY 0-3(0-0) 16th EC. Qualifiers
A. Le Coq Arena, Tallinn; Referee: Georgi Kabakov (Bulgaria); Attendance: 12,062
GER: Manuel Peter Neuer (Cap), Lukas Manuel Klostermann, Niklas Süle, Marcel Halstenberg, Joshua Walter Kimmich, Emre Can [*sent off 14*], İlkay Gündoğan, Kai Havertz, Julian Brandt (86.Nadiem Amiri, Gian-Luca Waldschmidt (66.Timo Werner), Marco Reus (77.Suat Serdar). Trainer: Trainer: Joachim Löw.
Goals: İlkay Gündoğan (51, 57), Timo Werner (71).

16.11.2019 GERMANY - BELARUS 4-0(1-0) 16th EC. Qualifiers
Stadion im Borussia-Park, Mönchengladbach; Referee: Orel Greenfield (Israel); Attendance: 33,164
GER: Manuel Peter Neuer (Cap), Lukas Manuel Klostermann, Matthias Lukas Ginter, Robin Koch, Nico Schulz, Joshua Walter Kimmich, İlkay Gündoğan, Leon Christoph Goretzka, Toni Kroos, Serge David Gnabry (84.Gian-Luca Waldschmidt; 90+1.Sebastian Rudy), Timo Werner (68.Julian Brandt). Trainer: Trainer: Joachim Löw.
Goals: Matthias Lukas Ginter (41), Leon Christoph Goretzka (49), Toni Kroos (55, 83).

19.11.2019 GERMANY - NORTHERN IRELAND 6-1(2-1) 16th EC. Qualifiers
Commerzbank-Arena, Frankfurt am Main; Referee: Carlos del Cerro Grande (Spain); Attendance: 42,855
GER: Marc-André ter Stegen, Lukas Manuel Klostermann (65.Niklas Stark), Jonathan Glao Tah, Jonas Armin Hector, Joshua Walter Kimmich, Emre Can, İlkay Gündoğan, Leon Christoph Goretzka (73.Suat Serdar), Toni Kroos (Cap), Julian Brandt, Serge David Gnabry (80.Nadiem Amiri). Trainer: Trainer: Joachim Löw.
Goals: Serge David Gnabry (19), Leon Christoph Goretzka (43), Serge David Gnabry (47, 60), Leon Christoph Goretzka (73), Julian Brandt (90+1).

NATIONAL TEAM PLAYERS
(16.07.2019 – 15.07.2020)

Name	DOB	Caps	Goals	2019/2020:	Club
Goalkeepers					
Manuel Peter NEUER	27.03.1986	92	0	2019:	*FC Bayern München*
Marc-André TER STEGEN	30.04.1992	24	0	2019:	*FC Barcelona (ESP)*
Defenders					
Matthias Lukas GINTER	19.01.1994	29	1	2019:	*Borussia VfL Mönchengladbach*
Marcel HALSTENBERG	27.09.1991	6	1	2019:	*RasenBallsport Leipzig*
Jonas Armin HECTOR	27.05.1990	43	3	2019:	*1. FC Köln*
Lukas Manuel KLOSTERMANN	03.06.1996	8	0	2019:	*RasenBallsport Leipzig*
Robin KOCH	17.07.1996	2	0	2019:	*SC Freiburg*
Nico SCHULZ	01.04.1993	10	2	2019:	*BV Borussia 09 Dortmund*
Niklas STARK	14.04.1995	1	0	2019:	*Hertha BSC Berlin*
Niklas SÜLE	03.09.1995	24	1	2019:	*FC Bayern München*
Jonathan Glao TAH	11.02.1996	9	0	2019:	*TSV Bayer 04 Leverkusen*
Midfielders					
Nadiem AMIRI	27.10.1996	3	0	2019:	*TSV Bayer 04 Leverkusen*
Julian BRANDT	02.05.1996	31	3	2019:	*BV Borussia 09 Dortmund*
Emre CAN	12.01.1994	25	1	2019:	*Juventus FC Torino (ITA)*
Leon Christoph GORETZKA	06.02.1995	25	11	2019:	*FC Bayern München*
İlkay GÜNDOĞAN	24.10.1990	37	7	2019:	*Manchester City FC (ENG)*
Kai HAVERTZ	11.06.1999	7	1	2019:	*TSV Bayer 04 Leverkusen*
Joshua Walter KIMMICH	08.02.1995	48	3	2019:	*FC Bayern München*
Toni KROOS	04.01.1990	96	17	2019:	*Real Madrid CF (ESP)*
Marco REUS	31.05.1989	44	13	2019:	*BV Borussia 09 Dortmund*
Sebastian RUDY	28.02.1990	29	1	2019:	*TSG 1899 Hoffenheim*
Suat SERDAR	11.04.1997	3	0	2019:	*FC Schalke 04 Gelsenkirchen*
Forwards					
Serge David GNABRY	14.07.1995	13	13	2019:	*FC Bayern München*
Gian-Luca Waldschmidt	19.05.1996	3	0	2019:	*SC Freiburg*
Timo WERNER	06.03.1996	29	11	2019:	*RasenBallsport Leipzig*
National team coach					
Joachim LÖW [from 12.07.2006]	03.02.1960	181 M; 117 W; 34 D; 30 L; 434-173			

GIBRALTAR

The Country:
Gibraltar [*British Overseas Territory*]
Capital: Gibraltar
Surface: 6,8 km²
Inhabitants: 34,003 [2020]
Time: UTC+1

The FA:
Gibraltar Football Association
2nd Floor, 62-64 Irish town, P.O. Box 513 GX11, 1AA Gibraltar
Tel: +350 200 42 941
Foundation date: 1895
Member of FIFA since: 13.05.2016
Member of UEFA since: 24.05.2013
Website: www.gibraltarfa.com

NATIONAL TEAM RECORDS

RECORDS

First international match:	19.11.2013, Faro/Loulé (POR):	Gibraltar – Slovakia 0-0
Most international caps:	Liam Walker	- 44 caps (since 2013)
Most international goals:	Lee Henry Casciaro	- 3 goals / 33 caps (since 2014)

UEFA EUROPEAN CHAMPIONSHIP

1960	Not a UEFA member
1964	Not a UEFA member
1968	Not a UEFA member
1972	Not a UEFA member
1976	Not a UEFA member
1980	Not a UEFA member
1984	Not a UEFA member
1988	Not a UEFA member
1992	Not a UEFA member
1996	Not a UEFA member
2000	Not a UEFA member
2004	Not a UEFA member
2008	Not a UEFA member
2012	Not a UEFA member
2016	Qualifiers
2020	Qualifiers

FIFA WORLD CUP

1930	Not a FIFA member
1934	Not a FIFA member
1938	Not a FIFA member
1950	Not a FIFA member
1954	Not a FIFA member
1958	Not a FIFA member
1962	Not a FIFA member
1966	Not a FIFA member
1970	Not a FIFA member
1974	Not a FIFA member
1978	Not a FIFA member
1982	Not a FIFA member
1986	Not a FIFA member
1990	Not a FIFA member
1994	Not a FIFA member
1998	Not a FIFA member
2002	Not a FIFA member
2006	Not a FIFA member
2010	Not a FIFA member
2014	Not a FIFA member
2018	Qualifiers

OLYMPIC TOURNAMENTS

1908	Not a FIFA member
1912	Not a FIFA member
1920	Not a FIFA member
1924	Not a FIFA member
1928	Not a FIFA member
1936	Not a FIFA member
1948	Not a FIFA member
1952	Not a FIFA member
1956	Not a FIFA member
1960	Not a FIFA member
1964	Not a FIFA member
1968	Not a FIFA member
1972	Not a FIFA member
1976	Not a FIFA member
1980	Not a FIFA member
1984	Not a FIFA member
1988	Not a FIFA member
1992	Not a FIFA member
1996	Not a FIFA member
2000	Not a FIFA member
2004	Not a FIFA member
2008	Not a FIFA member
2012	Not a FIFA member
2016	Not a FIFA member

UEFA NATIONS LEAGUE

2018/2019 – League D

FIFA CONFEDERATIONS CUP 1992-2017

None

GIBRALTARIAN CLUB HONOURS IN EUROPEAN CLUB COMPETITIONS:

European Champion Clubs' Cup (1956-1992) / UEFA Champions League (1993-2020)
None

Fairs Cup (1858-1971) / UEFA Cup (1972-2009) / UEFA Europa League (2010-2020)
None

UEFA Super Cup (1972-2019)
None

*European Cup Winners' Cup 1961-1999**
None

*defunct competition

NATIONAL COMPETITIONS
TABLE OF HONOURS

	CHAMPIONS	CUP WINNERS
1894/1895	-	Gibraltar FC
1895/1896	Gibraltar FC	*Not known*
1896/1897	Jubilee FC	*Not known*
1897/1898	Jubilee FC	*Not known*
1898/1899	Albion FC	*Not known*
1899/1900	Exiles FC	*Not known*
1900/1901	Prince of Wales FC	*Not known*
1901/1902	Exiles FC	*Not known*
1902/1903	Prince of Wales FC	*Not known*
1903/1904	Prince of Wales FC	*Not known*
1904/1905	Athletic FC	*Not known*
1905/1906	Prince of Wales FC	*Not known*
1906/1907	*No competition*	*Not known*
1907/1908	FC Britannia XI	*Not known*
1908/1909	Prince of Wales FC	*Not known*
1909/1910	South United FC	*Not known*
1910/1911	South United FC	*Not known*
1911/1912	FC Britannia XI	*Not known*
1912/1913	FC Britannia XI	*Not known*
1913/1914	Prince of Wales FC	*Not known*
1914/1915	Royal Sovereign	*Not known*
1915/1916	*No competition*	*Not known*
1916/1917	Prince of Wales FC	*Not known*
1917/1918	FC Britannia XI	*Not known*
1918/1919	Prince of Wales FC	*Not known*
1919/1920	FC Britannia XI	*Not known*
1920/1921	Prince of Wales FC	*Not known*
1921/1922	Prince of Wales FC	*Not known*
1922/1923	Prince of Wales FC	*Not known*
1923/1924	Gibraltar FC	*Not known*
1924/1925	Prince of Wales FC	*Not known*
1925/1926	Prince of Wales FC	*Not known*
1926/1927	Prince of Wales FC	*Not known*
1927/1928	Prince of Wales FC	*Not known*
1928/1929	Europa FC	*Not known*
1929/1930	Europa FC	*Not known*
1930/1931	Prince of Wales FC	*Not known*
1931/1932	Europa FC	*Not known*
1932/1933	Europa FC	*Not known*
1933/1934	Commander of the Yard FC	*Not known*
1934/1935	Chief Construction FC	*Not known*
1935/1936	Chief Constructor FC	HMS Hood
1936/1937	FC Britannia XI	FC Britannia XI
1937/1938	Europa FC	Europa FC
1938/1939	Prince of Wales FC	2nd Battalion The King's Regiment
1939/1940	Prince of Wales FC	FC Britannia XI
1940/1941	FC Britannia XI	*No competition*
1941/1942	*No competition*	A.A.R.A.
1942/1943	*No competition*	Royal Air Force New Camp
1943/1944	*No competition*	4th Btallion Royal Scott
1944/1945	*No competition*	*No competition*
1945/1946	*No competition*	Europa FC
1946/1947	Gibraltar United FC	Gibraltar United FC
1947/1948	Gibraltar United FC	FC Britannia XI
1948/1949	Gibraltar United FC	Prince of Wales FC
1949/1950	Gibraltar United FC	Europa FC
1950/1951	Gibraltar United FC	Europa FC
1951/1952	Europa FC	Europa FC
1952/1953	Prince of Wales FC	*Not known*
1953/1954	Gibraltar United FC	*Not known*
1954/1955	FC Britannia XI	*Not known*
1955/1956	FC Britannia XI	*Not known*
1956/1957	FC Britannia XI	*Not known*
1957/1958	FC Britannia XI	*Not known*
1958/1959	FC Britannia XI	*Not known*
1959/1960	Gibraltar United FC	*Not known*
1960/1961	FC Britannia XI	*Not known*
1961/1962	Gibraltar United FC	*Not known*
1962/1963	FC Britannia XI	*Not known*
1963/1964	Gibraltar United FC	*Not known*
1964/1965	Gibraltar United FC	*Not known*
1965/1966	Glacis United FC	*Not known*

1966/1967	Glacis United FC	*Not known*
1967/1968	Glacis United FC	*Not known*
1968/1969	Glacis United FC	*Not known*
1969/1970	Glacis United FC	*Not known*
1970/1971	Glacis United FC	*Not known*
1971/1972	Glacis United FC	*Not known*
1972/1973	Glacis United FC	*Not known*
1973/1974	Glacis United FC	Manchester United FC
1974/1975	Manchester United FC	Glacis United FC
1975/1976	Glacis United FC	2nd Battalion Royal Green Jackets
1976/1977	Manchester United FC	Manchester United FC
1977/1978	*No competition*	*Not known*
1978/1979	Manchester United FC	St Joseph's FC
1979/1980	Manchester United FC	Manchester United FC
1980/1981	Glacis United FC	Glacis United FC
1981/1982	Glacis United FC	Glacis United FC
1982/1983	Glacis United FC	St Joseph's FC
1983/1984	Manchester United FC	St Joseph's FC
1984/1985	Glacis United FC & Lincoln Red Imps FC	St Joseph's FC
1985/1986	Lincoln Red Imps FC	Lincoln Red Imps FC
1986/1987	St Theresa's FC	St Joseph's FC
1987/1988	St Theresa's FC	Royal Air Force Gibraltar
1988/1989	Glacis United FC	Lincoln Red Imps FC
1989/1990	Lincoln Red Imps FC	Lincoln Red Imps FC
1990/1991	Lincoln Red Imps FC	*Not known*
1991/1992	Lincoln Red Imps FC	St Joseph's FC
1992/1993	Lincoln Red Imps FC	Lincoln Red Imps FC
1993/1994	Lincoln Red Imps FC	Lincoln Red Imps FC
1994/1995	Manchester United FC	St Theresa's FC
1995/1996	St Joseph's FC	St Joseph's FC
1996/1997	Glacis United FC	Manchester United FC
1997/1998	St Theresa's FC	Glacis United FC
1998/1999	Manchester United FC	Gibraltar United FC
1999/2000	Glacis United FC	Gibraltar United FC
2000/2001	Lincoln Red Imps FC	Gibraltar United FC
2001/2002	Gibraltar United FC	Lincoln Red Imps FC
2002/2003	Lincoln Red Imps FC	Manchester United FC
2003/2004	Lincoln Red Imps FC	Newcastle FC
2004/2005	Lincoln Red Imps FC	Newcastle FC
2005/2006	Lincoln Red Imps FC	Newcastle FC
2006/2007	Lincoln Red Imps FC	Newcastle FC
2007/2008	Lincoln Red Imps FC	Lincoln Red Imps FC
2008/2009	Lincoln Red Imps FC	Lincoln Red Imps FC
2009/2010	Lincoln Red Imps FC	Lincoln Red Imps FC
2010/2011	Lincoln Red Imps FC	Lincoln Red Imps FC
2011/2012	Lincoln Red Imps FC	St Joseph's FC
2012/2013	Lincoln Red Imps FC	St Joseph's FC
2013/2014	Lincoln Red Imps FC	Lincoln Red Imps FC
2014/2015	Lincoln Red Imps FC	Lincoln Red Imps FC
2015/2016	Lincoln Red Imps FC	Lincoln Red Imps FC
2016/2017	Europa FC	Europa FC
2017/2018	Lincoln Red Imps FC	Europa FC
2018/2019	Lincoln Red Imps FC	Europa FC
2019/2020	*Championship cancelled*	*Competition cancelled*

Please note: Manchester United FC changed its name to Manchester 62 FC (2013); Newcastle FC was a temporary name for Lincoln Red Imps FC.

Please note: Gibraltar Phoenix FC withdrew on 09.08.2019; Gibraltar United FC were excluded for failure to repay debts on 12.08.2019; Leo FC withdrew on 13.08.2019; FC Olympique Gibraltar 13 were excluded on 11.09.2019 after forfeiting their match against Europa FC.

Regular Stage - Results

Date	Match	Score
12.08.2019	Lynx FC - Mons Calpe SC	5-1
13.08.2019	Manchester 62 FC - FC Boca Gibraltar	0-0
14.08.2019	Lions Gibraltar FC - Europa Point FC	0-0
15.08.2019	Glacis United FC - FCB Magpies	0-9
16.08.2019	Europa FC - Lincoln Red Imps	4-1
19.08.2019	St. Joseph's FC - College 1975 FC	7-0
21.08.2019	Europa Point FC - Lynx FC	0-5
22.08.2019	Lincoln Red Imps - Glacis United FC	8-0
23.08.2019	FCB Magpies - Lions Gibraltar FC	2-0
24.08.2019	College 1975 FC - Mons Calpe SC	1-9
	St. Joseph's FC - Manchester 62 FC	3-0
12.09.2019	Lions Gibraltar FC - Lynx FC	0-0
13.09.2019	Glacis United FC - Mons Calpe SC	0-5
14.09.2019	St. Joseph's FC - FC Boca Gibraltar	2-0
15.09.2019	College 1975 FC - FCB Magpies	1-3
	Europa FC - Europa Point FC	1-0
19.09.2019	Lincoln Red Imps - College 1975 FC	9-1
	FC Boca Gibraltar - Lynx FC	1-3
20.09.2019	FCB Magpies - Europa FC	0-6
22.09.2019	Europa Point FC - Glacis United FC	0-3
	Mons Calpe SC - Lions Gibraltar FC	1-1
25.09.2019	Europa FC - St. Joseph's FC	2-2
29.09.2019	Lions Gibraltar FC - Lincoln Red Imps	1-7
	Lynx FC - FCB Magpies	2-0
	FC Boca Gibraltar - Mons Calpe SC	1-1
30.09.2019	College 1975 FC - Manchester 62 FC	0-3
05.10.2019	Mons Calpe SC - Europa Point FC	0-2
19.10.2019	FC Boca Gibraltar - Europa Point FC	1-1
	FCB Magpies - Mons Calpe SC	1-3
20.10.2019	St. Joseph's FC - Glacis United FC	8-1
	Manchester 62 FC - Europa FC	0-7
21.10.2019	Lincoln Red Imps - Lynx FC	4-0
24.10.2019	College 1975 FC - FC Boca Gibraltar	0-4
25.10.2019	Europa Point FC - FCB Magpies	2-3
26.10.2019	Glacis United FC - Manchester 62 FC	2-3
	Lions Gibraltar FC - St. Joseph's FC	0-4
27.10.2019	Mons Calpe SC - Lincoln Red Imps	0-2
31.10.2019	Manchester 62 FC - Lions Gibraltar FC	0-3
01.11.2019	College 1975 FC - Europa FC	0-12
03.11.2019	Lincoln Red Imps - Europa Point FC	3-0
	St. Joseph's FC - Lynx FC	1-1
04.11.2019	FC Boca Gibraltar - FCB Magpies	1-2
21.11.2019	Lynx FC - Manchester 62 FC	5-0
22.11.2019	Glacis United FC - College 1975 FC	4-0
23.11.2019	FCB Magpies - Lincoln Red Imps	0-3
	Europa FC - FC Boca Gibraltar	6-1
24.11.2019	Mons Calpe SC - St. Joseph's FC	0-6
27.11.2019	FC Boca Gibraltar - Lincoln Red Imps	1-8
28.11.2019	College 1975 FC - Lions Gibraltar FC	1-6
29.11.2019	Europa FC - Glacis United FC	6-2
30.11.2019	Manchester 62 FC - Mons Calpe SC	1-4
	St. Joseph's FC - Europa Point FC	5-0
04.12.2019	Lions Gibraltar FC - Europa FC	2-5
05.12.2019	Glacis United FC - FC Boca Gibraltar	0-2
06.12.2019	Lynx FC - College 1975 FC	4-0
07.12.2019	FCB Magpies - St. Joseph's FC	0-3
	Europa Point FC - Manchester 62 FC	1-3
10.12.2019	Glacis United FC - Lions Gibraltar FC	1-3
11.12.2019	Europa FC - Lynx FC	2-0
12.12.2019	Manchester 62 FC - FCB Magpies	0-2
13.12.2019	St. Joseph's FC - Lincoln Red Imps	2-1
16.12.2019	Europa Point FC - College 1975 FC	6-1
17.12.2019	Mons Calpe SC - Europa FC	0-7
	Lions Gibraltar FC - FC Boca Gibraltar	6-4
18.12.2019	Lynx FC - Glacis United FC	3-2
19.12.2019	Lincoln Red Imps - Manchester 62 FC	2-0

Final Standings

1.	Europa FC	11	10	1	0	58	-	8	31
2.	St. Joseph's FC	11	9	2	0	43	-	5	29
3.	Lincoln Red Imps FC	11	9	0	2	48	-	9	27
4.	Lynx FC	11	7	2	2	28	-	11	23
5.	FC Bruno's Magpies	11	6	0	5	22	-	21	18
6.	Lions Gibraltar FC	11	4	3	4	22	-	25	15
7.	Mons Calpe SC	11	4	2	5	24	-	27	14
8.	Manchester 62 FC	11	3	1	7	10	-	29	10
9.	FC Boca Juniors Gibraltar	11	2	3	6	16	-	29	9
10.	Europa Point FC	11	2	2	7	12	-	25	8
11.	Glacis United FC	11	2	0	9	15	-	47	6
12.	College 1975 FC	11	0	0	11	5	-	67	0

Teams ranked 1-6 were qualified for the Championship Round, while teams ranked 7-12 were qualified for the Challenge (Relegation) Round.

Please note: the season was suspended on 14.03.2020 due to Covid-19 pandemic. The Challenge Group was abandoned, while the Gibraltar FA attempted to continue the Championship Group. On 01.05.2020, the season was cancelled, no title was awarded.

Challenge Round

Results

Round 1 [14-16.01.2020]
FC Boca Gibraltar - Europa Point FC 2-4
Manchester 62 FC - Glacis United FC 1-0
Mons Calpe SC - College 1975 FC 1-0

Round 2 [21-23.01.2020]
Mons Calpe SC - Manchester 62 FC 3-0
Glacis United FC - FC Boca Gibraltar 2-2
College 1975 FC - Europa Point FC 2-6

Round 3 [28-30.01.2020]
FC Boca Gibraltar - Mons Calpe SC 0-2
Manchester 62 FC - College 1975 FC 5-0
Europa Point FC - Glacis United FC 2-1

Round 4 [02-08.02.2020]
Manchester 62 FC - FC Boca Gibraltar 1-2
College 1975 FC - Glacis United FC 1-2
Mons Calpe SC - Europa Point FC 1-1

Round 5 [19-22.02.2020]
Europa Point FC - Manchester 62 FC 3-1
FC Boca Gibraltar - College 1975 FC 7-5
Glacis United FC - Mons Calpe SC 0-1

Round 6 [25-27.02.2020]
Europa Point FC - FC Boca Gibraltar 2-1
College 1975 FC - Mons Calpe SC 0-6
Glacis United FC - Manchester 62 FC 1-2

Final Standings

				Total				Home				Away		
7. Mons Calpe SC	18	10	3	5	49 - 29	33	2	2	4	6 - 19	8	1	1	43 - 10
8. Europa Point FC	18	7	4	7	35 - 38	25	4	1	4	21 - 23	3	3	3	14 - 15
9. Manchester 62 FC	18	6	1	11	21 - 49	19	2	1	6	9 - 29	4	0	5	12 - 20
10. FC Boca Juniors Gibraltar	17	4	4	9	30 - 45	16	1	2	5	14 - 26	3	2	4	16 - 19
11. Glacis United FC	17	3	1	13	21 - 56	10	1	1	7	10 - 27	2	0	6	11 - 29
12. College 1975 FC	18	0	1	17	18 - 99	1	0	0	9	6 - 51	0	1	8	12 - 48

Championship Round

Results

Round 1 [17-18.01.2020]
Europa FC - Lions Gibraltar FC 5-0
St. Joseph's FC - FCB Magpies 3-1
Lincoln Red Imps - Lynx FC 5-0

Round 2 [24-25.01.2020]
FCB Magpies - Lincoln Red Imps 1-5
Lions Gibraltar FC - Lynx FC 2-3
Europa FC - St. Joseph's FC 3-1

Round 3 [31.01.-01.02.2020]
St. Joseph's FC - Lions Gibraltar FC 5-3
Lincoln Red Imps - Europa FC 0-2
Lynx FC - FCB Magpies 3-1

Round 4 [07-08.02.2020]
Europa FC - Lynx FC 5-0
St. Joseph's FC - Lincoln Red Imps 1-0
Lions Gibraltar FC - FCB Magpies 2-3

Round 5 [21-22.02.2020]
Lincoln Red Imps - Lions Gibraltar FC 7-1
Lynx FC - St. Joseph's FC 2-3
FCB Magpies - Europa FC 0-5

Round 6 [28-29.02.2020]
Lynx FC - Lincoln Red Imps 1-3
Lions Gibraltar FC - Europa FC 0-7
FCB Magpies - St. Joseph's FC 1-2

Final Standings

				Total				Home				Away		
1. Europa FC	17	16	1	0	85 - 9	49	8	1	0	34 - 7	8	0	0	51 - 2
2. St. Joseph's FC	17	14	2	1	58 - 15	44	9	1	0	37 - 7	5	1	1	21 - 8
3. Lincoln Red Imps FC	17	13	0	4	68 - 15	39	7	0	1	38 - 4	6	0	3	30 - 11
4. Lynx FC	17	9	2	6	37 - 30	29	6	0	2	25 - 10	3	2	4	12 - 20
5. FC Bruno's Magpies	17	7	0	10	29 - 41	21	1	0	7	5 - 27	6	0	3	24 - 14
6. Lions Gibraltar FC	17	4	3	10	30 - 55	15	1	2	6	13 - 33	3	1	4	17 - 22

Top goalscorers:

24	**Juan Francisco García Peña "Juanfri" (ESP)**	*St. Joseph's FC*
21	Liam Walker	*Europa FC*
15	Enrique "Kike" Gómez Bernal (PHI)	*Lincoln Red Imps FC*
15	Juan Pedro Rico Domínguez "Juanpe" (ESP)	*Europa FC*

NATIONAL CUP
Rock Cup 2019/2020

First Round [14-16.02.2020]

FC Hound Dogs - Europa Point FC	0-10		Manchester 62 FC - Mons Calpe SC	1-2
Europa FC - Glacis United FC	12-0		Lynx FC - FC Bruno's Magpies	0-1
Lincoln Red Imps FC - College 1975 FC	15-0			

Quarter-Finals [06-08.03.2020]

Mons Calpe SC - Europa Point FC	3-1		Europa FC -	2-0
St. Joseph's FC - FC Bruno's Magpies	1-0		Lincoln Red Imps FC -	6-0

The competition was cancelled due to Covid-19 pandemic. No title was awarded.

Football Club Boca Juniors Gibraltar

Founded:	2012
Stadium:	Victoria Stadium, Gibraltar (2,800)
Trainer:	Christian Ressa

Trainer:	Christian Ressa	19.01.1978
[18.10.2019]	Juan Maria Sánchez Fernández (ESP)	07.12.1971
[12.11.2019]	Juan Carlos Camacho Contreras (ESP)	16.05.1978
[09.01.2020]	Craig Cowell (ENG)	04.03.1970

Goalkeepers:	DOB	M	(s)	G
Albert Chichon	01.12.1980	4	(1)	
Jordan López Pérez	13.11.1986	7		
Daniel Tudela Barreira (ESP)	09.03.1999	6		1
Defenders:	**DOB**	**M**	**(s)**	**G**
Federico Acosta (ARG)	30.03.1996	9		1
Erin Anthony Barnett	02.09.1996	1		
Francisco Carlos Belmonte Rodríguez (ESP)	15.07.1985	11	(1)	1
José Maria Arana Triviño "Chema" (ESP)	26.04.1991	4		
Jamie Campoy González (ESP)	20.02.1997	1		
Kyle Falero	29.10.2000		(1)	
Juan José Fernández Jiménez (ESP)	29.11.1988	1		
Steven González García (ESP)	18.02.1986	4		
Elias Juel-Saleh	06.05.2003	5	(1)	
Gerardo López Rico (ESP)	18.10.1994	4		
Ashley Joseph Pérez	23.02.1989	5	(1)	
Guillermo Pérez Sánchez (ESP)	12.07.1989	13		
Daniel Quiñones Campos (ESP)	10.04.1984	2	(2)	

Midfielders:	DOB	M	(s)	G
Julio Gil Bado	03.06.1983	10		
Carlos Martín Briones "Charly" (EQG)	18.02.1990	9		
José Antonio Rubio Quirós "Chico" (ESP)	11.07.1996	10		3
James Chiles-Cowell	14.02.2003	8	(6)	
Jayce Nicholas Consigliero	03.08.1997	5	(1)	1
Haitam Fakir Sellam	09.04.1994	1		
Antonio Fernández Sabastro (ESP)	17.07.1996	1		
Felix Formica-Corsi	25.01.1977	3	(6)	2
Sean Gilbert	14.11.1992	9	(3)	
Yannick Luib	20.06.2003	3		
Francisco Javier Moreno Jiménez (ESP)	18.09.1990	3	(2)	
Forwards:	**DOB**	**M**	**(s)**	**G**
James Edouard Adams (FRA)	05.01.1998	5	(5)	4
Ardi Ahmeti (AUS)	26.06.2000	1	(2)	
Germán Cortés Narváez (ESP)	03.02.1994	13		12
Evan James Green (ENG)	13.03.1993	5		
José Luís Reyes Verdejo (ESP)	05.10.1981	6	(1)	
Nathan Albert Santos	11.10.1988	16	(1)	4

Football Club Bruno's Magpies

Founded:	2013
Stadium:	Victoria Stadium, Gibraltar (2,800)

Trainer:	David Wilson (SCO)	22.02.1974
[18.10.2019]	Alfonso Cortijo Cabrera (ESP)	14.09.1966
[03.01.2020]	Juan Maria Sánchez Fernández (ESP)	07.12.1971

Goalkeepers:	DOB	M	(s)	G
Matthew Paul Cafer	27.09.1994	11		
Conor Peter O'Keefe (ENG)	26.09.1995	4		
Iván Villanueva Ramírez (ESP)	28.02.1996	2		
Defenders:	**DOB**	**M**	**(s)**	**G**
Daniel Bent (ENG)	10.01.1996	12		
Shea Kevin Luke Breakspear	22.11.1991	10		
Jared Buhagiar	20.10.1992	7		
José Maria Arana Triviño "Chema" (ESP)	26.04.1991	4	(1)	
Tamupiwa Dimairo (NZL)	22.03.1996	10	(3)	1
Jamie Fortuna	07.07.1995	7		1
Javier "Javi" Gallardo (ESP)	30.09.1988	6		
Jean-Carlos Anthony Garcia	05.07.1992	14	(2)	
Ross Gray (SCO)	12.09.1994	1		
Enrique Linares Fernández (ESP)	12.07.1999	3		
Harrison Turner	03.03.2003	1		
Francisco Javier Gil Zúñiga (MEX)	22.12.1990	5		1
Midfielders:	**DOB**	**M**	**(s)**	**G**
Chase Covello (USA)	02.08.1997	8	(3)	

	DOB	M	(s)	G
Luis Ignacio Fernández Ríos (ESP)	28.01.1988	14	(1)	1
Juan Sebastián Pegalajar Valero "Juanse"(ESP)	19.04.1989	12	(3)	3
Kye William Livingstone	09.03.2003		(5)	
Matheus Assumpção (BRA)	26.06.1995	8	(5)	7
Aaron Payas	24.05.1985	3	(1)	
Brian Perez	16.09.1986	9	(1)	2
Ashley Rodriguez	13.11.1989		(1)	
Tyson Ruiz	10.03.1988	2	(1)	
Aaron Splaine (SCO)	13.10.1996	5	(1)	2
Stefan Thorne	28.03.2003		(2)	
Jaron Vinet	12.12.1997	4	(1)	
Forwards:	**DOB**	**M**	**(s)**	**G**
John-Paul Duarte	13.12.1986	6	(1)	3
Oliver Ford (ENG)	11.03.1997	11	(4)	6
Ronan Kearney (SCO)	22.08.1999	2	(5)	
Lython Marquez	06.02.1995		(4)	
Kelvin Morgan	14.11.1997	3	(2)	
Dylan Peacock	24.08.2001	4		1

College 1975 Football Club

Founded:	1975
Stadium:	Victoria Stadium, Gibraltar (2,800)
Trainer:	Bernardo Andres Cano (ESP)
[01.02.2020]	Ángel Espinosa (ESP)

Goalkeepers:	DOB	M	(s)	G
Victor Manuel Ayala Orrillo (ESP)	01.01.1999	11		
Kaydon Migge	16.08.2002	5		
Mark Warwick	21.04.2003	2	(1)	
Defenders:	**DOB**	**M**	**(s)**	**G**
Damien Francisco Beldi Leon (ESP)	12.11.1992	2	(2)	
Angel Field	19.08.2002	6		
Joanthan Field	25.06.1989	7		
Dario Guerrero Alconchel (ESP)	01.01.1999	7		
Dion Hammond	18.08.1994	5	(2)	
Zac Olivero	11.01.2002	1		
Thomas Palao	27.10.1995	4	(2)	
Ilias Rahmouni	18.11.1988	6		
Midfielders:	**DOB**	**M**	**(s)**	**G**
Antonio Bermúdez Sánchez (ESP)	30.09.1999	11	(1)	1
Dylan Borrell	23.03.1998	5	(7)	1
Nacho Callejón Lucena (ESP)	26.07.1997	2		
Daniel Ceballo Sánchez (ESP)	13.08.1995		(1)	
Brandon Desoiza	19.01.2002	1		
Antonio Fernández Sabastro (ESP)	17.07.1996	1		
Kaylan Franco	13.08.2001	3	(4)	
Kaine Grech	09.03.2002	1	(2)	

	DOB	M	(s)	G
Cristian Guerrero Alconchel (ESP)	25.03.1998	8	(1)	1
Alejandro Herrera López (ESP)	30.09.1997	1		
Zane Holgado	16.10.1995	2		
Nazim Hughes	08.10.1992	16		1
Duncan Lamont (SCO)	20.05.1996	3	(7)	
Francisco Marín (ESP)	07.11.1986	7	(4)	
Jemar Matto	19.01.2001	15	(2)	
Francisco Luis Morales Sánchez (ESP)	07.01.1994	9	(1)	
Christian Pacheco López (ESP)	19.11.1998	16	(2)	1
Karim Dechraqui Piñero (ESP)	30.04.1992	3		
Liam Roche	11.12.1985		(1)	
Pablo Ruiz López (ESP)	09.02.1998	1	(7)	
Francis Seidu (GHA)	22.09.1986	4		
Adam Zammitt	19.10.2001		(1)	
Forwards:	**DOB**	**M**	**(s)**	**G**
Yuri Ruh Dos Santos (POR)	07.02.1998	5		1
Juan Francisco Ruiz Rincón „Juanfri" (ESP)	01.05.1998	5		2
José Oncala Rojas (ESP)	27.05.1999	2	(3)	6
Mariano Nicolás Pereira (ARG)	27.03.1990	7		
José Luis Romero (ESP)	19.07.1992	4		2
Antonio Jesús Urenda Aranda (ESP)	27.12.1995	10		1

Europa Football Club

Founded: 1925
Stadium: Victoria Stadium, Gibraltar (2,800)
Trainer: Rafael Escobar Obrero (ESP) 12.08.1969

Goalkeepers:	DOB	M	(s)	G
Dayle Edward Coleing	23.10.1996	11		
Javier Muñoz Arévalo	27.01.1982	6	(1)	
Daniel Tudela Barreira (ESP)	09.03.1999		(1)	
Defenders:	**DOB**	**M**	**(s)**	**G**
Ibrahim Ayew (GHA)	16.04.1988	4	(8)	
Ethan Terence Jolley	29.03.1997	9	(4)	
Olmo González Casado (ESP)	15.06.1987	15		
Sergio Jiménez Sánchez (ESP)	22.08.1987	12	(1)	4
Jayce Lee Mascarenhas-Olivero	02.07.1998	16	(1)	
Diego Portilla Rodríguez (ESP)	28.04.1994	4	(4)	1
Midfielders:	**DOB**	**M**	**(s)**	**G**
Alejandro Rodríguez Rivas "Álex Quillo" (ESP)	07.10.1986	7	(7)	3

	DOB	M	(s)	G
Luke Bautista	09.11.2001	1	(2)	2
Alejandro Carrascal Avilés (ESP)	24.04.1995	13		3
Marco Rosa Blanco (ESP)	30.11.1995	11	(2)	2
John Iain Stephen Sergeant	27.02.1995	8	(1)	1
Liam Walker	13.04.1988	16		21
Forwards:	**DOB**	**M**	**(s)**	**G**
Manuel "Manu" Dimas Suárez Arbelo (ESP)	18.04.1992	10	(5)	11
Adrián Gallardo Valdés (ESP)	20.11.1987	5	(2)	4
Juan Pedro Rico Domínguez "Juanpe" (ESP)	24.05.1984	17		15
Juan Manuel Labrador Aguilar „Labra" (ESP)	24.06.1995	3	(6)	8
Fernando Velasco Salazar (ESP)	08.01.1985	6	(4)	
Juan Luis Becerra Gallego „Willy" (ESP)	08.09.1989	5		3
Michael Thomas Yome	29.08.1994	8	(2)	5

Europa Point Football Club

Founded: 2014
Stadium: Victoria Stadium, Gibraltar (2,800)
Trainer: Allen Bula 04.01.1965
[26.11.2019] Ian Michael Hendon (ENG) 05.12.1971

Goalkeepers:	DOB	M	(s)	G
Jorge Manuel Avellano	15.12.2000	1	(1)	
Conor O'Keefe (ENG)	26.09.1995	11		
Martin Tsvetanov (BUL)	01.03.2000	6		
Defenders:	**DOB**	**M**	**(s)**	**G**
Aiden Antony Casey	17.08.1990	5		
Tarik Chrayeh	05.11.1986	1		
Cian Collins (IRL)	13.06.1999	4	(1)	
Archie Harvey (LBR)	03.11.1992	7		
TomTom Johnson (USA)	17.06.1995	2	(1)	
Carl Derek Machin	29.07.1993	2		
Antony Moulds	04.02.1988	15		
Stefan Oliva	26.07.1992	5	(2)	
Oliver Alfred Leesley Pritchard (ENG)	24.08.2000	10		
Jason Pusey	18.02.1989	4		1
Shohei Tsurumi (JPN)	12.06.1989	11		2
Samuel François Vermeeren (NED)	29.01.1998		(1)	
Midfielders:	**DOB**	**M**	**(s)**	**G**
Marcus Birkelund (NOR)	05.06.1999	5	(1)	
Lukas Lindholm Corner (SWE)	14.01.1999	6	(1)	5
Tito De Torres	27.11.1997	5	(2)	

	DOB	M	(s)	G
Omar El Yettefti	23.11.2002	13		
Aaron Fleming (ENG)	16.05.1995	5		3
Christian Gonzalez	22.10.1992		(1)	
Bradley Hockin (ENG)	26.06.1993	14	(3)	1
Jeremy Joseph Lopez	09.07.1989	12	(3)	4
Kaylan Muscat	17.10.1989	3	(4)	
Bryan Orta (USA)	09.08.1992	1	(1)	
Aaron Splaine (SCO)	13.10.1996	3	(1)	
Jack Royston (ENG)	25.10.1996		(3)	
Diego Vera Idoate (ESP)	08.03.1983	13	(1)	5
Forwards:	**DOB**	**M**	**(s)**	**G**
Iljas Ahmedov (SWE)	13.08.1992	5	(4)	3
Stefan Balev (BUL)	01.05.1997	11	(6)	4
José Antonio Campoy López (ESP)	09.02.1995	2	(2)	
Dean Dillon (IRL)	08.06.1999	5	(1)	5
Byron Manuel Espinosa	15.03.1999	2		
Panashe Kuzamba (AUS)	03.07.2001		(1)	
Jerome Martelli (ENG)	20.01.1996		(1)	
Josh Moody (USA)	26.08.1999		(2)	1
Samir Omari	28.08.1993	7	(1)	
Jonathan Sánchez Muñoz (ESP)	24.01.1990	1		

Glacis United Football Club

Founded: 1965
Stadium: Victoria Stadium, Gibraltar (2,800)
Trainer: Bennie Brinkman (NED) 01.11.1963
[17.09.2019] Michele Di Piedi (ITA) 04.12.1980

Goalkeepers:	DOB	M	(s)	G
Ivan Moreno	05.02.1998	13		
Denzel Navarro	28.04.1994	2		
Fernando Sánchez Díaz (ESP)	24.03.1988	2		
Defenders:	**DOB**	**M**	**(s)**	**G**
Sean Borg	04.06.2001		(2)	
Kaydan Byrne	13.10.1996	5	(2)	
Sebastián Cardozo Coitinho (URU)	09.09.1995	3		
James Castle	13.06.1997	5	(2)	1
Yassin El Melki (MAR)	01.01.1998	4		
Quentin Kaleba (FRA)	03.09.1997	2	(1)	
Miguel Londero (ARG)	03.01.1989	14		2
Jorge Andrés Luna Aguilar (VEN)	26.01.1994	3		
Jordan McGrail	21.09.2000	6	(1)	
José Manuel Muñoz Oña (ESP)	17.02.1992	1		
Nicholas Perera	17.08.2001		(1)	
Aidan Plows	10.05.1994	2		
Niall Serra	03.05.2001	1	(2)	
Mauro Zardetto (ARG)	01.01.1991	13		1
Midfielders:	**DOB**	**M**	**(s)**	**G**
Julian Brinkman	02.01.2003	12	(2)	1

	DOB	M	(s)	G
Nicholas Castle	18.01.1994	13		
Aaron Champion	07.05.1997	8	(3)	1
Jonathan Rodolfo Di Toro (ARG)	22.12.1984	7		
Unai Gutiérrez Albizu (ESP)	15.02.1991	4		
Matthew Lopez	08.04.2000	1	(3)	
Jamie Muir	08.04.2001	3	(1)	
Kevin Poggio	15.11.2000	2	(6)	
José Manuel Rodríguez Candón (ESP)	31.10.1996	12	(1)	
Hatim Smith	25.12.2000	4		
Forwards:	**DOB**	**M**	**(s)**	**G**
Michele Di Piedi (ITA)	04.12.1980	9	(3)	1
Salvatore Gallo (ITA)	19.08.2001	13	(1)	2
Charlie Kendall (ENG)	01.01.1999		(1)	
Julian Lopez	14.09.1991	1	(2)	1
Sidi Mahamud Buna (WSA)	05.05.1993	2	(1)	1
Jerome Martelli (ENG)	20.01.1996	4		1
Declan Pizarro	21.09.2000	1		
Daniel Pratts	06.06.1998	1	(1)	
Michael Ruiz	07.12.2000	7	(2)	2
Joao De Carvalho Goncalves „Joao Serra" (POR)	31.12.1995			
Pietro Terranova (ITA)	10.08.1994	7		5

Lincoln Red Imps Football Club

Founded:	1976		
Stadium:	Victoria Stadium, Gibraltar (2,800)		
Trainer:	Víctor Manuel Afonso Mateo (ESP)	27.08.1971
[04.01.2020]	Germán Crespo Sánchez (ESP)	19.11.1975

Goalkeepers:	DOB	M	(s)	G
Kyle Albert Goldwin	24.04.1985	12		
Manuel Soler Ortuño (ESP)	17.09.1986	5		
Defenders:	**DOB**	**M**	**(s)**	**G**
Ethan Britto	30.11.2000	13		3
Joseph Luis Chipolina	14.12.1987	8	(1)	2
Roy Alan Chipolina	20.01.1983	3		
Ethan Thorne-Llambias	23.11.2000		(3)	
Bernardo Morgado Gaspar Lopes (POR)	30.07.1993	16		2
Álvaro Oliver París (ESP)	25.01.1992	5		
Marcos Luis Pérez Trujillo (ESP)	30.09.1989	12		
Jesús Toscano Serrano (ESP)	13.12.1990	11	(1)	
Midfielders:	**DOB**	**M**	**(s)**	**G**
Blas Álvarez Cortés (ESP)	19.07.1995	8	(4)	1
Federico Cataruozzolo	08.09.1987	6	(2)	
Craig Galliano	23.04.2002	1	(4)	
Borja Gil Albarracín (ESP)	04.12.1990	14	(1)	1
Andrew Albert Hernandez	03.02.1995	5	(3)	4
Shay Jones	24.02.2002		(1)	
Sergio Molina Rivero (ESP)	14.11.1983	7		9
Mustapha Yahaya (GHA)	09.01.1994	3	(2)	
Forwards:	**DOB**	**M**	**(s)**	**G**
Dylan Borge	15.10.2003		(1)	
Kyle Casciaro	02.12.1987	2	(1)	1
Lee Henry Casciaro	29.09.1981	12	(2)	2
Idelino Gomes Colubali „Idé Colubali" (GNB)	01.01.1994	2	(3)	5
James Timothy Barry Coombes	27.05.1996	10	(2)	3
Julian Del Rio	15.02.2002	4	(10)	6
Sunday Chukuamaka Emmanuel (NGA)	25.02.1992	3	(1)	3
Antonio Jesús Ramos Rincón "Gato" (ESP)	22.02.1989	12	(1)	9
Enrique "Kike" Gómez Bernal (PHI)	04.05.1994	12	(1)	15
Juan Pablo Pereira Sastre (ARG)	02.07.1987	1	(6)	1

Lions Gibraltar Football Club

Founded:	1966	
Stadium:	Victoria Stadium, Gibraltar (2,800)	
Trainer:	Albert Ferri Sola (ESP)	24.02.1970

Goalkeepers:	DOB	M	(s)	G
John Paul Hernandez	08.03.2002	7		
Álvaro Pérez Pichardo (ESP)	13.12.1996	10		
Defenders:	**DOB**	**M**	**(s)**	**G**
Craig Bossano-Anes	22.10.2002	4	(4)	
James Bosio	27.03.1991	14		
Jared Buhagiar	20.10.1992	4		
Lee Coombes	20.06.1996	4	(2)	
Nathan Fortunato	16.06.2003		(2)	
Thomas Hastings	23.09.1992	14		
James Michael Parkinson	21.05.2000	6	(6)	
Kaylan Alfred Rumbo	12.12.1990	13		
Adrián Vera Tovar (ESP)	21.02.1990	13		
Midfielders:	**DOB**	**M**	**(s)**	**G**
Antonio Cintas Sánchez (ESP)	11.05.1995	14		2
John Charles Gaivizo	27.07.1993	1	(2)	1
Julian Grech	15.04.2003		(1)	
Aiman Mkerreff	11.12.1996	1	(1)	
Louis Parral	13.03.2002	4	(5)	
Richard Louis Parral	23.03.1999		(1)	
Iván Ruiz Pecino (ESP)	16.09.1990	16		2
Stefan Thorne	28.03.2003		(1)	
Forwards:	**DOB**	**M**	**(s)**	**G**
Alberto Caravaca Castro (ESP)	23.03.1990	14		12
Luis Manuel Casas Domínguez (ESP)	06.09.1996	14	(1)	7
Martin Gándara (ITA)	25.03.1996	3	(2)	
Raymond Gomez	06.07.2002		(4)	
Jonay López Luque (ESP)	17.01.1991	13	(2)	
Alan Parker	15.05.1996	6	(3)	1
Sergio Pérez Benítez (ESP)	16.01.1990	1	(3)	
Abraham Pomares Fernández (ESP)	13.09.1992	10	(3)	4
Brendan Ramagge	29.05.2002		(5)	

Lynx Football Club

Founded:	2007	
Stadium:	Victoria Stadium, Gibraltar (2,800)	
Trainer:	Albert Parody	30.08.1968

Goalkeepers:	DOB	M	(s)	G
Bradley James Banda	20.01.1998	16		
Adrián Pacheco Mariscal (ESP)	30.09.1992	1		
Defenders:	**DOB**	**M**	**(s)**	**G**
David Alberto Bautista Martos „Bauti" (ESP)	27.02.1992	13	(1)	3
Hrvoje Bukvić (CRO)	26.01.1995	11		
Ryan John Dean	18.07.1998	3	(2)	
Gabriel González (ARG)	16.07.1991	4	(3)	
Brad Philip Power	29.10.1992	15	(1)	2
Mario Ruesca Torres (ESP)	17.11.1993	7	(4)	
Andrés Salas Trenas (ESP)	07.05.1985	6		
Midfielders:	**DOB**	**M**	**(s)**	**G**
Alisson Vieira Rasquinha (BRA)	29.01.1999	3	(1)	
Mohamed Badr Hassan	18.11.1996	16	(1)	6
Estivien Morente Vélez „Estiven" (ESP)	16.02.1991	6	(5)	1
Antonio González García (ESP)	06.05.1996	12	(2)	2
Ed Kevin Kokorović (CRO)	04.01.1995	10	2	
Kevin Morán Blanco (ARG)	24.05.1997	6	(5)	
Dexter Panzavechia	30.12.1990	3	(1)	
Jaydan Parody	08.05.1998	12	(4)	4
Aidan Serra	28.12.1994	3		
Alexandre Bernardo Teixeira Gomez (BRA)	21.06.1988	1	(3)	1
Carl Thomas	06.07.1988	3		
Jesse Victory	02.04.1996	9	(5)	
Forwards:	**DOB**	**M**	**(s)**	**G**
Michael Gracia	25.11.1992		(4)	
Dylan Hernández Orribo (ESP)	20.04.1996	5		4
Marko Marcius (CRO)	24.03.1995	8		2
Michael Ruiz	07.12.2000	2		
Leone Seatory	21.06.1997	1	(3)	3
Antonio Jesús Urenda Aranda (ESP)	27.12.1995		(3)	
José Alberto Mateos Valdivia (ESP)	18.01.1996	11	(3)	7

Manchester 62 Football Club

Founded: 1962
Stadium: Victoria Stadium, Gibraltar (2,800)
Trainer: Jeffrey Reginald Wood (ENG) — 04.02.1954
[06.11.2019] David Wilson (SCO) — 22.02.1974

Goalkeepers:	DOB	M	(s)	G
Christian Lopez	10.02.2001	3		
Takumi Tomizawa (JPN)	25.11.1996	7		
Frank Warwick	15.03.1994	8		
Defenders:	**DOB**	**M**	**(s)**	**G**
Liam Asquez	02.04.2003		(1)	
Karl Baldachino	21.11.1995	1	(1)	
Jaydan Catania	06.03.1993	15		1
Matthew Clenahan (ENG)	11.02.1996	14		2
Liam Crisp	23.09.1999	3	(1)	
Ryan Dean	18.07.1998	2		
Tom Farmer (WAL)	11.12.1996	13	(1)	
Ross Gray (SCO)	12.09.1994		(1)	
Mickey Johnson (USA)	22.05.1998	2	(2)	
Stefan Ramirez	18.11.1998	1	(1)	
Peter Sardena	03.03.1996	13		1
Jermain Sodi	01.01.2002		(1)	
Sean Wyan	15.04.1999		(2)	
Midfielders:	**DOB**	**M**	**(s)**	**G**
Scott Ballantine	12.04.1996	8		1
Evan Coleing	10.10.1994	7	(1)	1
Dylan De Los Santos	27.06.2002	3	(5)	
Shaun De Los Santos	26.01.1998	12	(4)	2
Kieron Garcia	04.08.1998	11		
Daniel Herbert	19.12.1993	1	(1)	
Matthew Langtry	06.09.1994		(2)	
Jamie-Luke McCarthy	21.07.1992	2	(2)	
Luis McCoy	02.09.1994	4	(8)	
Michael Negrette	14.09.1998	2	(2)	
Kian Ronan	09.03.2001	13		6
Carl Thomas	06.07.1988	5	(1)	
Daylian Victor	18.01.1996	1	(1)	
Etien Victory	21.09.1999	4	(6)	
Jack Thomas Willbye (ENG)	09.01.1996	10		
Forwards:	**DOB**	**M**	**(s)**	**G**
Mark Chichon	24.12.1994	2	(1)	
Yuri Ruh Dos Santos (POR)	07.02.1998	8	(1)	2
Robert Montovio	03.08.1984	12		4
Mariano Nicolás Pereira (ARG)	27.03.1990	7		
Luis Miguel Pérez Lobato (ESP)	05.02.1992	5	(2)	2

Mons Calpe Sports Club

Founded: 2013
Stadium: Victoria Stadium, Gibraltar (2,800)
Trainer: Loren Morón Vizcaíno (ESP) — 16.02.1970
[18.10.2019] Leonardo Federico Vela (ARG) — 05.12.1982
[01.01.2020] Luis Manuel Blanco (ARG) — 13.12.1953

Goalkeepers:	DOB	M	(s)	G
Leandro Evangelisti (ARG)	25.01.1982	3		
Christian Hernán Fraiz García (ARG)	22.02.1988	14		
Ezequiel Muth (GER)	14.06.1999	1		
Defenders:	**DOB**	**M**	**(s)**	**G**
André Luiz Dos Santos (BRA)	19.02.1992	16		7
Diego Martín Caballero Manzanares (URU)	13.06.1991	3		
Maximiliano Continente Minguit (ARG)	21.05.1988	4		
David Gallardo	04.05.1991	3		
Esteban Goicoechea (ARG)	22.09.1986	9		
Antonio González Moreno (ESP)	19.06.2000		(1)	
Pedro León Expósito (ESP)	27.02.1996	2	(1)	
Juan Carlos Medina (VEN)	14.08.1991	1		
Renan Bernardes (BRA)	21.03.1992	4	(3)	
Sean Robba	26.08.1992		(1)	
Diego Martín Sabatel (URU)	24.08.1999	2		
Andrés Salas Trenas (ESP)	07.05.1985	10		1
Ethan James Santos	22.12.1998	14	(1)	
Richard Silva	19.05.2000	1		
Francisco Javier Gil Zúñiga (MEX)	22.12.1990	2	(1)	
Midfielders:	**DOB**	**M**	**(s)**	**G**
Hugo Colace (ARG)	06.01.1984	7		1
Max Cottrell	15.09.1999	1		
Diego Martínez Macarro "Dieguito" (ESP)	20.03.1989	8	(1)	
Naoufal El Andaloussi	07.04.1991	4		1
Ayoub El Hmidi	30.09.2000	10	(3)	5
Ilyias El Ouahabi	20.06.1999	1	(4)	
Juan Matias Etchegoyen (ARG)	24.02.1995	1	(1)	
Hamza Abdel-Lah Hamed "Majuda" (ESP)	12.03.1997		(2)	
Juan Mattea (ARG)	02.05.1996	3	(1)	3
Kaylan Muscat	17.10.1989	1	(1)	
Mikel Pérez (ESP)	15.04.1992		(2)	
Karim Dechraqui Piñero (ESP)	30.04.1992	4		
Kevagn Robba	20.09.1994	4		2
Ashley Rodriguez	13.11.1989	2	(1)	
Tyson Ruiz	10.03.1988	5	(2)	
Daniel Segui	11.06.2000		(1)	
Nahuel Martín Sendín Saldaña (ARG)	12.01.1993	3		1
Juan Pablo Sosa (ITA)	26.08.1999	2	(2)	
Jaron Vinet	12.12.1997	10		4
Forwards:	**DOB**	**M**	**(s)**	**G**
Oulid Ben Abdel Hanin	07.01.2002	3	(2)	
Leonardo Ezequiel Carboni (ARG)	04.11.1984	6	(2)	4
Franco Nicolás Carella (ARG)	14.03.1992	7	(3)	7
Kivan Castle	21.02.1990	10	(2)	
Diego Diaz (ARG)	01.12.1991	4		3
Kelvin Morgan	14.11.1997	3	(5)	1
Lee Muscat	23.09.1988	3		4
Santiago Pastorini Terán (ARG)	17.07.1997	1	(1)	3
Kevagn Ronco	20.04.1998	2		
Ernest Tomsett	16.11.1998	2	(1)	
Jorge Yepes Roda (ESP)	25.02.1989	1	(1)	

St. Joseph's Football Club

Founded: 1912
Stadium: Victoria Stadium, Gibraltar (2,800)
Trainer: Raúl Procopio Baizán (ESP) — 10.07.1968

Goalkeepers:	DOB	M	(s)	G
Jamie Kevagn Robba	26.10.1991	14		
Francisco Javier Mateo Vera (ESP)	14.08.1990	3		
Defenders:	**DOB**	**M**	**(s)**	**G**
Francisco José Cano Hernández (ESP)	01.03.1991	6		
Ryan Casciaro	11.05.1984		(3)	
Kenneth Chipolina	08.04.1994	1		
Daniel Guerrero Heredia (ESP)	08.07.1983		(1)	
Iván Lobato González (ESP)	28.05.1991	1	(1)	
Aymen Mouelhi	14.09.1986	13		1
Jaime Serra	30.10.1998	8	(2)	
Mauricio "Mauri" Torres Fernández (ESP)	26.02.1988		(1)	
Federico Martin Villar (ARG)	24.11.1985	7	(2)	1
Midfielders:	**DOB**	**M**	**(s)**	**G**
Leon Clinton	19.07.1998		(1)	
Domingo Jesús Ferrer López (ESP)	10.04.1989	15	(2)	7
Sykes Garro	26.02.1993	6	(5)	1
Andrew Hernandez	10.01.1999	12	(1)	
Juan Manuel Gonzáles Pérez "Juanma" (ESP)	02.05.1991	10	(5)	2
Kohei Kato (JPN)	14.06.1989	4	(2)	
Cristian Pecci Macías (ESP)	10.05.1988	15		3
Pedro Jesús Fernández Martínez „Pedrito" (ESP)	28.11.1990		(9)	2
Alain Pons	16.09.1995	13		
Kevagn Robba	20.09.1994		(1)	
Forwards:	**DOB**	**M**	**(s)**	**G**
Salvador Manuel Alegre Delgado "Boro"(ESP)	04.05.1991	15		12
Leonardo Ezequiel Carboni (ARG)	04.11.1984		(2)	
Kyle Casciaro	02.12.1987	2	(5)	1
Ernesto Cornejo Sánchez (ESP)	25.03.1993	4	(9)	2
Ángel Guirado Aldeguer (PHI)	09.12.1984	1	(2)	
Juan Francisco García Peña "Juanfri" (ESP)	01.10.1989	17		24
Ezequiel Rojas Piñer (ESP)	22.06.1990	16	(1)	2

INTERNATIONAL MATCHES
(16.07.2019 – 15.07.2020)

05.09.2019	Gibraltar	Gibraltar - Denmark	0-6(0-2)	(ECQ)
08.09.2019	Sion	Switzerland - Gibraltar	4-0(3-0)	(ECQ)
10.10.2019	Prishtina	Kosovo - Gibraltar	1-0(0-0)	(F)
15.10.2019	Gibraltar	Gibraltar - Georgia	2-3(0-2)	(ECQ)
15.11.2019	København	Denmark - Gibraltar	6-0(1-0)	(ECQ)
18.11.2019	Gibraltar	Gibraltar - Switzerland	1-6(0-1)	(ECQ)

05.09.2019   GIBRALTAR - DENMARK   **0-6(0-2)**   16th EC. Qualifiers
Victoria Stadium, Gibraltar; Referee: Jonathan Lardot (Belgium); Attendance: 2,076
GIB: Dayle Edward Coleing, Joseph Luis Chipolina, Jayce Lee Mascarenhas-Olivero, Roy Alan Chipolina (Cap), Ethan Britto (46.Alain Anthony Pons), Louie John Annesley (46.Erin Anthony Barnett), Liam Walker, Jack Sergeant (83.Ethan Terence Jolley), Andrew Albert Hernandez, Anthony Alland Hernandez, Andre Tjay De Barr. Trainer: Julio César Ribas Vlacovich (Uruguay).

08.09.2019   SWITZERLAND - GIBRALTAR   **4-0(3-0)**   16th EC. Qualifiers
Stade Tourbillon, Sion; Referee: Pavel Orel (Czech Republic); Attendance: 8,318
GIB: Dayle Edward Coleing (25.Kyle Albert Goldwin), Joseph Luis Chipolina, Jayce Lee Mascarenhas-Olivero, Roy Alan Chipolina (Cap), Ethan Britto (67.Alain Anthony Pons), Louie John Annesley, Liam Walker, Jack Sergeant, Andrew Albert Hernandez (58.Jamie Timothy Barry Coombes), Anthony Alland Hernandez, Andre Tjay De Barr. Trainer: Julio César Ribas Vlacovich (Uruguay).

10.10.2019   KOSOVO - GIBRALTAR   **1-0(0-0)**   Friendly International
Stadiumi „Fadil Vokrri", Prishtina; Referee: Junxhin Xhaja (Albania); Attendance: 12,142
GIB: Kyle Albert Goldwin (46.Dayle Edward Coleing; 77.Matthew Paul Cafer), Jack Sergeant, Jayce Lee Mascarenhas-Olivero, Mohamed Badr Hassan, Lee Henry Casciaro (58.Alain Anthony Pons), Ethan Britto (58.Andrew Albert Hernandez), Joseph Luis Chipolina, Roy Alan Chipolina (Cap), Aymen Mouelhi (75.Ethan Terence Jolley), Anthony Alland Hernandez, Andre Tjay De Barr (58.Jamie Timothy Barry Coombes). Trainer: Julio César Ribas Vlacovich (Uruguay).

15.10.2019   GIBRALTAR - GEORGIA   **2-3(0-2)**   16th EC. Qualifiers
Victoria Stadium, Gibraltar; Referee: Paolo Valeri (Italy); Attendance: 1,455
GIB: Kyle Albert Goldwin, Joseph Luis Chipolina (82.Erin Anthony Barnett), Aymen Mouelhi, Jayce Lee Mascarenhas-Olivero, Roy Alan Chipolina (Cap), Ethan Britto, Liam Walker (90.Alain Anthony Pons), Jack Sergeant, Mohamed Badr Hassan (81.Andrew Albert Hernandez), Lee Henry Casciaro, Andre Tjay De Barr. Trainer: Julio César Ribas Vlacovich (Uruguay).
Goals: Lee Henry Casciaro (66), Roy Alan Chipolina (74).

15.11.2019   DENMARK - GIBRALTAR   **6-0(1-0)**   16th EC. Qualifiers
Parken Stadium, København; Referee: István Vad (Hungary); Attendance: 24,033
GIB: Kyle Albert Goldwin, Joseph Luis Chipolina, Aymen Mouelhi (65.Erin Anthony Barnett), Jayce Lee Mascarenhas-Olivero, Roy Alan Chipolina (Cap), Ethan Britto, Liam Walker, Jack Sergeant, Mohamed Badr Hassan (65.Andrew Albert Hernandez), Lee Henry Casciaro, Andre Tjay De Barr (72.Reece Styche). Trainer: Julio César Ribas Vlacovich (Uruguay).

18.11.2019   GIBRALTAR - SWITZERLAND   **1-6(0-1)**   16th EC. Qualifiers
Victoria Stadium, Gibraltar; Referee: Benoît Millot (France); Attendance: 2,079
GIB: Dayle Edward Coleing, Joseph Luis Chipolina, Aymen Mouelhi, Erin Anthony Barnett, Roy Alan Chipolina (Cap), Ethan Britto, Liam Walker, Jack Sergeant, Mohamed Badr Hassan (85.Alain Anthony Pons), Lee Henry Casciaro (61.Reece Styche), Andre Tjay De Barr (61.Jamie Timothy Barry Coombes). Trainer: Julio César Ribas Vlacovich (Uruguay).
Goal: Reece Styche (74).

NATIONAL TEAM PLAYERS
(16.07.2019 – 15.07.2020)

Name	DOB	Caps	Goals	2019/2020:	Club
Goalkeepers					
Matthew Paul CAFER	27.09.1994	2	0	2019:	*FC Bruno's Magpies*
Dayle Edward COLEING	23.10.1996	4	0	2019:	*Europa FC*
Kyle Albert GOLDWIN	24.04.1985	14	0	2019:	*Lincoln Red Imps FC*
Defenders					
Erin Anthony BARNETT	02.09.1996	19	0	2019:	*FC Boca Juniors Gibraltar*
Ethan BRITTO	30.11.2000	8	0	2019:	*Lincoln Red Imps FC*
Joseph Luis CHIPOLINA	14.12.1987	42	2	2019:	*Lincoln Red Imps FC*
Roy Alan CHIPOLINA	20.01.1983	42	2	2019:	*Lincoln Red Imps FC*
Ethan Terence JOLLEY	29.03.1997	4	0	2019:	*Europa FC*
Aymen MOUELHI	14.09.1986	7	0	2019:	*St. Joseph's FC*
Jayce Lee MASCARENHAS-OLIVERO	02.07.1998	27	0	2019:	*Europa FC*
John Iain Stephen SERGEANT	27.02.1995	28	0	2019:	*Europa FC*
Midfielders					
Louie John ANNESLEY	03.05.2000	9	0	2019:	*Blackburn Rovers FC (ENG)*
Mohamed BADR Hassan	25.11.1989	4	0	2019:	*Lynx FC*
Andrew Albert HERNANDEZ	10.01.1999	10	0	2019:	*St. Joseph's FC*
Anthony Alland HERNANDEZ	03.02.1995	23	1	2019:	*Lincoln Red Imps FC*
Alain Anthony PONS	16.09.1995	18	0	2019:	*Lincoln Red Imps FC*
Reece STYCHE	03.05.1989	7	1	2019:	*Hereford FC (ENG)*
Liam WALKER	13.04.1988	44	2	2019:	*Europa FC*
Forwards					
Lee Henry CASCIARO	29.09.1981	33	3	2019:	*Lincoln Red Imps FC*
James Timothy Barry COOMBES	27.05.1996	16	0	2019:	*Lincoln Red Imps FC*
Andre Tjay DE BARR	13.03.2000	16	1	2019:	*Real Oviedo"B" (ESP)*

National team coach

Julio César RIBAS Vlacovich (Uruguay) [from 01.07.2019]	08.01.1957	16 M; 2 W; 0 D; 14 L; 8-48

GREECE

The Country:
Ελληνική Δημοκρατία (Hellenic Republic)
Capital: Athína
Surface: 131,957 km²
Inhabitants: 10,724,599 [2019]
Time: UTC+2

The FA:
Hellenic Football Federation
Goudi Park P.O. Box 14161, 11510 Athens
Tel: +30 21 0930 6000
Foundation date: 1926
Member of FIFA since: 1927
Member of UEFA since: 1954
Website: www.epo.gr

NATIONAL TEAM RECORDS

RECORDS

First international match:	07.04.1929, Athína:	Greece – Italy "B" 1-4
Most international caps:	Georgios Karagoúnis	- 139 caps (1999-2014)
Most international goals:	Nikolaos Anastopoulos	- 29 goals / 74 caps (1977-1988)

UEFA EUROPEAN CHAMPIONSHIP

1960	Qualifiers
1964	Did not enter
1968	Qualifiers
1972	Qualifiers
1976	Qualifiers
1980	Final Tournament (Group Stage)
1984	Qualifiers
1988	Qualifiers
1992	Qualifiers
1996	Qualifiers
2000	Qualifiers
2004	**Final Tournament (Winners)**
2008	Final Tournament (Group Stage)
2012	Final Tournament (Quarter-Finals)
2016	Qualifiers
2020	Qualifiers

FIFA WORLD CUP

1930	Did not enter
1934	Qualifiers
1938	Qualifiers
1950	Did not enter
1954	Qualifiers
1958	Qualifiers
1962	Qualifiers
1966	Qualifiers
1970	Qualifiers
1974	Qualifiers
1978	Qualifiers
1982	Qualifiers
1986	Qualifiers
1990	Qualifiers
1994	Final Tournament (Group Stage)
1998	Qualifiers
2002	Qualifiers
2006	Qualifiers
2010	Final Tournament (Group Stage)
2014	Final Tournament (2nd Round of 16)
2018	Qualifiers

OLYMPIC TOURNAMENTS

1908	-
1912	-
1920	Quarter-Finals
1924	-
1928	-
1936	-
1948	-
1952	Preliminary Round
1956	-
1960	Qualifiers
1964	Qualifiers
1968	Qualifiers
1972	Qualifiers
1976	Qualifiers
1980	Group Stage
1984	Qualifiers
1988	Qualifiers
1992	Qualifiers
1996	Qualifiers
2000	Qualifiers
2004	Group Stage
2008	Qualifiers
2012	Qualifiers
2016	Qualifiers

UEFA NATIONS LEAGUE

2018/2019 – League C

FIFA CONFEDERATIONS CUP 1992-2017

2005 (Group Stage)

GREEK CLUB HONOURS IN EUROPEAN CLUB COMPETITIONS:

European Champion Clubs' Cup (1956-1992) / UEFA Champions League (1993-2020)
None

Fairs Cup (1858-1971) / UEFA Cup (1972-2009) / UEFA Europa League (2010-2020)
None

UEFA Super Cup (1972-2019)
None

*European Cup Winners' Cup 1961-1999**
None

defunct competition

NATIONAL COMPETITIONS
TABLE OF HONOURS

	CHAMPIONS	CUP WINNERS	BEST GOALSCORERS	
1905/1906	Ethnikos GS Athína	-	-	
1906/1907	Ethnikos GS Athína	-	-	
1907/1908	FC Goudi Athína	-	-	
1908/1909	Peiraikos Syndesmos	-	-	
1909/1910	FC Goudi Athína	-	-	
1910/1911	Podosferikos Omilos Athinon	-	-	
1911/1912	FC Goudi Athína	-	-	
1912/1913	*No competition*	-	-	
1913/1914	*No competition*	-	-	
1914/1915	*No competition*	-	-	
1915/1916	*No competition*	-	-	
1916/1917	*Championship not finished*	-	-	
1917/1918	*No competition*	-	-	
1918/1919	*No competition*	-	-	
1919/1920	*No competition*	-	-	
1920/1921	*No competition*	-	-	
1921/1922	Panellinios Podosferikos Omilos	-	-	
1922/1923	Peiraikos Syndesmos	-	-	
1923/1924	Apollonas Athína (Athína champions) APS Peiraiás (Athína/Peiraiás champions) Aris Thessaloníki (Thessaloníki champions)	-	-	
1924/1925	PAE Panathinaïkos Athína (Athína champions) Olympiacos SFP Peiraiás (Athína/Peiraiás champions)	-	-	
1925/1926	PAE Panathinaïkos Athína (Athína champions) Olympiacos SFP Peiraiás (Athína/Peiraiás champions) Aris Thessaloníki (Thessaloníki champions)	-	-	
1926/1927	PAE Panathinaïkos Athína (Athína champions) Olympiacos SFP Peiraiás (Athína/Peiraiás champions) Iraklis Thessaloníki (Thessaloníki champions)	-	-	
1927/1928	Aris Thessaloníki	-	-	
1928/1929	*No competition*	-	-	
1929/1930	PAE Panathinaïkos Athína	-	-	
1930/1931	Olympiacos SFP Peiraiás	-	-	
1931/1932	Aris Thessaloníki	AEK Athína	-	
1932/1933	Olympiacos SFP Peiraiás	Ethnikos Peiraiás	-	
1933/1934	Olympiacos SFP Peiraiás	*No competition*	-	
1934/1935	*Championship not finished*	*No competition*	-	
1935/1936	Olympiacos SFP Peiraiás	*No competition*	-	
1936/1937	Olympiacos SFP Peiraiás	*No competition*	-	
1937/1938	Olympiacos SFP Peiraiás	*No competition*	-	
1938/1939	AEK Athína	AEK Athína	-	
1939/1940	AEK Athína	PAE Panathinaïkos Athína	-	
1940/1941	*Championship not finished*	*No competition*	-	
1941/1942	*No competition*	*No competition*	-	
1942/1943	*Championship not finished*	*No competition*	-	
1943/1944	*No competition*	*No competition*	-	
1944/1945	*No competition*	*No competition*	-	
1945/1946	Aris Thessaloníki	*No competition*	-	
1946/1947	Olympiacos SFP Peiraiás	Olympiacos SFP Peiraiás	-	
1947/1948	Olympiacos SFP Peiraiás	PAE Panathinaïkos Athína	-	
1948/1949	PAE Panathinaïkos Athína	AEK Athína	-	
1949/1950	*No competition*	AEK Athína	-	
1950/1951	Olympiacos SFP Peiraiás	Olympiacos SFP Peiraiás	-	
1951/1952	*No competition*	Olympiacos SFP Peiraiás	-	
1952/1953	PAE Panathinaïkos Athína	Olympiacos SFP Peiraiás	-	
1953/1954	Olympiacos SFP Peiraiás	Olympiacos SFP Peiraiás	-	
1954/1955	Olympiacos SFP Peiraiás	PAE Panathinaïkos Athína	-	
1955/1956	Olympiacos SFP Peiraiás	AEK Athína	-	
1956/1957	Olympiacos SFP Peiraiás	Olympiacos SFP Peiraiás	-	
1957/1958	Olympiacos SFP Peiraiás	Olympiacos SFP Peiraiás	-	
1958/1959	Olympiacos SFP Peiraiás	Olympiacos SFP Peiraiás	-	
1959/1960	PAE Panathinaïkos Athína	Olympiacos SFP Peiraiás	Konstantinos Nestoridis (AEK Athína)	30
1960/1961	PAE Panathinaïkos Athína	Olympiacos SFP Peiraiás	Konstantinos Nestoridis (AEK Athína)	27
1961/1962	PAE Panathinaïkos Athína	*Final abandoned, no winner*	Konstantinos Nestoridis (AEK Athína)	29
1962/1963	AEK Athína	Olympiacos SFP Peiraiás	Konstantinos Nestoridis (AEK Athína)	23
1963/1964	PAE Panathinaïkos Athína	AEK Athína	Dimitrios Papaioannou (AEK Athína)	29
1964/1965	PAE Panathinaïkos Athína	Olympiacos SFP Peiraiás	Giorgos Sideris (Olympiacos SFP Peiraiás)	29
1965/1966	Olympiacos SFP Peiraiás	AEK Athína	Dimitrios Papaioannou (AEK Athína)	23

1966/1967	Olympiacos SFP Peiraiás	PAE Panathinaïkos Athína	Giorgos Sideris (Olympiacos SFP Peiraiás)	24
1967/1968	AEK Athína	Olympiacos SFP Peiraiás	Thanasis Intzoglou (Panionios GSS Athína)	24
1968/1969	PAE Panathinaïkos Athína	PAE Panathinaïkos Athína	Giorgos Sideris (Olympiacos SFP Peiraiás)	35
1969/1970	PAE Panathinaïkos Athína	Aris Thessaloníki	Antonis Antoniadis (PAE Panathinaïkos Athína)	25
1970/1971	AEK Athína	Olympiacos SFP Peiraiás	Giorgos Dedes (Panionios GSS Athína)	28
1971/1972	PAE Panathinaïkos Athína	PAOK Thessaloníki	Antonis Antoniadis (PAE Panathinaïkos Athína)	39
1972/1973	Olympiacos SFP Peiraiás	Olympiacos SFP Peiraiás	Antonis Antoniadis (PAE Panathinaïkos Athína)	22
1973/1974	Olympiacos SFP Peiraiás	PAOK Thessaloníki	Antonis Antoniadis (PAE Panathinaïkos Athína)	26
1974/1975	Olympiacos SFP Peiraiás	Olympiacos SFP Peiraiás	Antonis Antoniadis (PAE Panathinaïkos Athína) Roberto Calcadera (URU, Ethnikos Peiraiás)	20
1975/1976	PAOK Thessaloníki	Iraklis Thessaloníki	Giorgos Dedes (AEK Athína)	15
1976/1977	PAE Panathinaïkos Athína	PAE Panathinaïkos Athína	Thanasis Intzoglou (Ethnikos Peiraiás) Dimitrios Papadopoulos (OFI Heraklion)	22
1977/1978	AEK Athína	AEK Athína	Thomas Mavros (AEK Athína)	22
1978/1979	AEK Athína	Panionios GSS Athína	Thomas Mavros (AEK Athína)	31
1979/1980	Olympiacos SFP Peiraiás	AGSK Kastoria	Dušan Bajević (YUG, AEK Athína)	25
1980/1981	Olympiacos SFP Peiraiás	Olympiacos SFP Peiraiás	Dinos Kouis (Aris Thessaloníki)	21
1981/1982	Olympiacos SFP Peiraiás	PAE Panathinaïkos Athína	Grigoris Charalampidis (PAE Panathinaïkos Athína)	21
1982/1983	Olympiacos SFP Peiraiás	AEK Athína	Nikolaos Anastopoulos (Olympiacos SFP Peiraiás)	29
1983/1984	PAE Panathinaïkos Athína	PAE Panathinaïkos Athína	Nikolaos Anastopoulos (Olympiacos SFP Peiraiás)	18
1984/1985	PAOK Thessaloníki	AE Lárissa	Thomas Mavros (AEK Athína)	27
1985/1986	PAE Panathinaïkos Athína	PAE Panathinaïkos Athína	Nikolaos Anastopoulos (Olympiacos SFP Peiraiás)	19
1986/1987	Olympiacos SFP Peiraiás	OFI Heraklion	Nikolaos Anastopoulos (Olympiacos SFP Peiraiás)	16
1987/1988	AE Lárissa	PAE Panathinaïkos Athína	Henrik Nielsen (DEN, AEK Athína)	20
1988/1989	AEK Athína	PAE Panathinaïkos Athína	Imre Boda (HUN, Olympiakos Vólos)	20
1989/1990	PAE Panathinaïkos Athína	Olympiacos SFP Peiraiás	Thomas Mavros (Panionios GSS Athína)	22
1990/1991	PAE Panathinaïkos Athína	PAE Panathinaïkos Athína	Dimitrios Saravakos (PAE Panathinaïkos Athína)	23
1991/1992	AEK Athína	Olympiacos SFP Peiraiás	Vasilios Dimitriadis (AEK Athína)	28
1992/1993	AEK Athína	PAE Panathinaïkos Athína	Vasilios Dimitriadis (AEK Athína)	33
1993/1994	AEK Athína	PAE Panathinaïkos Athína	Alexandros Alexandris (AEK Athína) Krzysztof Warzycha (POL, PAE Panathinaïkos Athína)	24
1994/1995	PAE Panathinaïkos Athína	PAE Panathinaïkos Athína	Krzysztof Warzycha (POL, PAE Panathinaïkos Athína)	29
1995/1996	PAE Panathinaïkos Athína	AEK Athína	Vassilis Tsiartas (AEK Athína)	26
1996/1997	Olympiacos SFP Peiraiás	AEK Athína	Alexandros Alexandris (Olympiacos SFP Peiraiás)	23
1997/1998	Olympiacos SFP Peiraiás	Panionios GSS Athína	Krzysztof Warzycha (POL, PAE Panathinaïkos Athína)	32
1998/1999	Olympiacos SFP Peiraiás	Olympiacos SFP Peiraiás	Themistoklis Nikolaidis (AEK Athína)	22
1999/2000	Olympiacos SFP Peiraiás	AEK Athína	Dimitrios Nalitzis (Panionios, PAOK Thessaloníki)	24
2000/2001	Olympiacos SFP Peiraiás	PAOK Thessaloníki	Alexandros Alexandris (Olympiacos SFP Peiraiás)	19
2001/2002	Olympiacos SFP Peiraiás	AEK Athína	Alexandros Alexandris (Olympiacos SFP Peiraiás)	19
2002/2003	Olympiacos SFP Peiraiás	PAOK Thessaloníki	Nikolaos Liberopoulos (PAE Panathinaïkos Athína)	16
2003/2004	PAE Panathinaïkos Athína	PAE Panathinaïkos Athína	Giovanni Silva de Oliveira (BRA, Olympiacos SFP Peiraiás)	21
2004/2005	Olympiacos SFP Peiraiás	Olympiacos SFP Peiraiás	Theofanis Gekas (PAE Panathinaïkos Athína)	18
2005/2006	Olympiacos SFP Peiraiás	Olympiacos SFP Peiraiás	Dimitrios Salpingidis (PAOK Thessaloníki)	17
2006/2007	Olympiacos SFP Peiraiás	AE Lárissa	Nikolaos Liberopoulos (AEK Athína)	18
2007/2008	Olympiacos SFP Peiraiás	Olympiacos SFP Peiraiás	Ismael Alfonso Blanco (ARG, AEK Athína)	19
2008/2009	Olympiacos SFP Peiraiás	Olympiacos SFP Peiraiás	Ismael Alfonso Blanco (ARG, AEK Athína) Luciano Martín Galletti (ARG, Olympiacos SFP Peiraiás)	14
2009/2010	PAE Panathinaïkos Athína	PAE Panathinaïkos Athína	Djibril Cissé (FRA, PAE Panathinaïkos Athína)	23
2010/2011	Olympiacos SFP Peiraiás	AEK Athína	Djibril Cissé (FRA, PAE Panathinaïkos Athína)	20
2011/2012	Olympiacos SFP Peiraiás	Olympiacos SFP Peiraiás	Kevin Antonio Joel Gislain Mirallas y Castillo (BEL, Olympiacos SFP Peiraiás)	22
2012/2013	Olympiacos SFP Peiraiás	Olympiacos SFP Peiraiás	Rafik Djebbour (ALG, Olympiacos SFP Peiraiás)	20
2013/2014	Olympiacos SFP Peiraiás	PAE Panathinaïkos Athína	Esteban Andrés Solari Poggio (ARG, Skoda Xanthi AC)	16
2014/2015	Olympiacos SFP Peiraiás	Olympiacos SFP Peiraiás	Jerónimo Barrales (ARG, AGS Asteras Tripoli)	17
2015/2016	Olympiacos SFP Peiraiás	AEK Athína	Konstantinos Fortounis (Olympiacos SFP Peiraiás)	18
2016/2017	Olympiacos SFP Peiraiás	PAOK Thessaloníki	Bengt Erik Markus Berg (SWE, PAE Panathinaïkos Athína)	22
2017/2018	AEK Athína	PAOK Thessaloníki	Aleksandar Prijović (SRB, PAOK Thessaloníki)	19
2018/2019	PAOK Thessaloníki	PAOK Thessaloníki	Efthymis Koulouris (APS Atromitos Athína)	19
2019/2020	Olympiacos SFP Peiraiás	Olympiacos SFP Peiraiás	Youssef El-Arabi (MAR, Olympiacos SFP Peiraiás)	20

NATIONAL CHAMPIONSHIP
Super League 1 2019/2020
(24.08.2019 – 19.07.2020)

Results

Round 1 [24-25.08.2019]
Lamia - Panathinaïkos 1-1(1-1)
Aris Thessaloníki - OFI Heraklion 1-1(0-1)
Olympiacos Peiraiás - Asteras Trip. 1-0(1-0)
Atromitos - AE Lárissa 1-1(1-1)
Panionios - Vólos 1-2(0-1)
PAOK Thessaloníki - Panetolikos 2-1(1-0)
AEK Athína - AO Xanthi 1-2(0-0)

Round 2 [31-01.09.08.2019]
Panetolikos - AO Xanthi 1-2(0-0)
Panathinaïkos - OFI Heraklion 1-3(0-1)
Vólos - Aris Thessaloníki 1-0(0-0)
PAOK Thessaloníki - Panionios 2-1(1-0)
AE Lárissa - Olympiacos Peiraiás 0-1(0-1)
Lamia - Atromitos 2-2(1-1)
Asteras Tripolis - AEK Athína 2-3(1-1)

Round 3 [14-15.09.2019]
Atromitos - PAOK Thessaloníki 2-3(1-2)
OFI Heraklion - Panetolikos 3-1(0-0)
Olympiacos Peiraiás - Vólos 5-0(1-0)
AO Xanthi - Asteras Tripolis 2-1(1-0)
AEK Athína - Lamia 2-0(2-0)
Panionios - AE Lárissa 1-0(0-0)
Aris Thessaloníki - Panathinaïkos 4-0(2-0)

Round 4 [21-22.09.2019]
Vólos - OFI Heraklion 1-0(0-0)
Asteras Tripolis - Atromitos 2-1(2-0)
Panetolikos - AEK Athína 0-1(0-0)
AE Lárissa - AO Xanthi 3-0(1-0)
PAOK Thessaloníki - Aris Thessal. 2-2(1-1)
Lamia - Panionios 1-1(0-0)
Panathinaïkos - Olympiacos Peiraiás 1-1(0-1)

Round 5 [28-29.09.2019]
Aris Thessaloníki - AE Lárissa 2-3(2-2)
Atromitos - Panetolikos 2-0(1-0)
Olympiacos Peiraiás - Lamia 2-0(0-0)
OFI Heraklion - Asteras Tripolis 3-1(0-0)
AO Xanthi - Vólos 3-1(1-0)
Panionios - Panathinaïkos 0-1(0-1)
AEK Athína - PAOK Thessaloníki 2-2(0-1)

Round 6 [05-07.10.2019]
Panathinaïkos - AO Xanthi 0-1(0-0)
AE Lárissa - AEK Athína 0-0
Vólos - Atromitos 2-3(2-2)
Asteras Trip. - PAOK Thessaloníki 1-2(0-1)
OFI Heraklion - Panionios 4-1(1-1)
Aris Thessal. - Olympiacos Peiraiás 1-2(1-2)
Lamia - Panetolikos 0-0

Round 7 [19-20.10.2019]
Olympiacos Peiraiás - OFI Heraklion 2-1(1-1)
Panetolikos - AE Lárissa 2-2(1-1)
Panionios - Asteras Tripolis 0-1(0-1)
AO Xanthi - Aris Thessaloníki 0-1(0-1)
PAOK Thessaloníki - Lamia 3-0(3-0)
AEK Athína - Vólos 3-2(1-1)
Atromitos - Panathinaïkos 0-1(0-1)

Round 8 [26-28.10.2019]
OFI Heraklion - AO Xanthi 2-0(0-0)
Vólos - PAOK Thessaloníki 0-2(0-1)
Panathinaïkos - AE Lárissa 1-2(0-1)
Atromitos - Panionios 4-0(3-0)
Aris Thessaloníki - Panetolikos 2-0(2-0)
Olympiacos Peiraiás - AEK Athína 2-0(1-0)
Asteras Tripolis - Lamia 4-1(2-1)

Round 9 [02-04.11.2019]
Panionios - Aris Thessaloníki 1-1(0-0)
AO Xanthi - Olympiacos Peiraiás 0-0
AE Lárissa - OFI Heraklion 3-2(1-2)
Panetolikos - Asteras Tripolis 1-1(1-1)
AEK Athína - Atromitos 3-2(0-1)
PAOK Thessaloníki - Panathinaïkos 2-2(0-1)
Lamia - Vólos 1-0(0-0)

Round 10 [09-11.11.2019]
Vólos - Panetolikos 3-2(0-1)
OFI Heraklion - PAOK Thessaloníki 0-1(0-0)
Aris Thessaloníki - Asteras Tripolis 2-1(2-1)
AO Xanthi - Panionios 1-2(0-0)
Olympiacos Peiraiás - Atromitos 2-0(0-0)
Panathinaïkos - AEK Athína 3-2(0-2)
AE Lárissa - Lamia 0-3(0-1)

Round 11 [23-24.11.2019]
Panionios - Olympiacos Peiraiás 1-1(0-0)
Lamia - AO Xanthi 1-0(0-0)
Atromitos - OFI Heraklion 2-1(1-1)
Asteras Tripolis - Vólos 0-0
PAOK Thessaloníki - AE Lárissa 1-0(1-0)
AEK Athína - Aris Thessaloníki 1-1(0-0)
Panetolikos - Panathinaïkos 0-0

Round 12 [30.11.-01.12.2019]
AE Lárissa - Vólos 2-1(0-1)
Panionios - Panetolikos 3-0(1-0)
OFI Heraklion - AEK Athína 1-0(0-0)
Panathinaïkos - Asteras Tripolis 1-0(1-0)
AO Xanthi - Atromitos 1-0(0-0)
Aris Thessaloníki - Lamia 1-1(1-1)
Olympiacos Peiraiás - PAOK Thessal 1-1(0-1)

Round 13 [07-08.12.2019]
PAOK Thessaloníki - AO Xanthi 2-0(0-0)
AEK Athína - Panionios 5-0(2-0)
Panetolikos - Olympiacos Peiraiás 0-3(0-3)
Lamia - OFI Heraklion 2-1(1-1)
Asteras Tripolis - AE Lárissa 1-1(1-0)
Atromitos - Aris Thessaloníki 2-2(1-1)
Vólos - Panathinaïkos 1-1(1-1)

Round 14 [14-15.12.2019]
OFI Heraklion - Aris Thessaloníki 3-1(1-1)
Panathinaïkos - Lamia 2-0(1-0)
AO Xanthi - AEK Athína 0-1(0-0)
AE Lárissa - Atromitos 1-2(1-2)
Vólos - Panionios 2-1(0-1)
Asteras Trip. - Olympiacos Peiraiás 0-5(0-4)
Panetolikos - PAOK Thessaloníki 0-3(0-1)

Round 15 [18-19.12.2019]
AO Xanthi - Panetolikos 0-0
Olympiacos Peiraiás - AE Lárissa 4-1(4-0)
OFI Heraklion - Panathinaïkos 1-1(0-0)
AEK Athína - Asteras Tripolis 2-1(1-0)
Atromitos - Lamia 1-1(0-0)
Aris Thessaloníki - Vólos 4-0(3-0)
Panionios - PAOK Thessaloníki 0-2(0-0)

Round 16 [21-23.12.2019]
Asteras Tripolis - AO Xanthi 5-0(2-0)
Lamia - AEK Athína 0-0
AE Lárissa - Panionios 2-0(2-0)
Panetolikos - OFI Heraklion 2-0(0-0)
Vólos - Olympiacos Peiraiás 0-0
Panathinaïkos - Aris Thessaloníki 0-0
PAOK Thessaloníki - Atromitos 5-1(3-0)

Round 17 [04-05.01.2020]
OFI Heraklion - Vólos 1-2(0-1)
Aris Thessal. - PAOK Thessaloníki 4-2(2-1)
Atromitos - Asteras Tripolis 2-1(0-0)
AEK Athína - Panetolikos 3-1(1-1)
AO Xanthi - AE Lárissa 2-1(0-0)
Panionios - Lamia 0-1(0-1)
Olympiacos Peiraiás - Panathinaïkos 1-0(0-0)

Round 18 [11-12.01.2020]
Vólos - AO Xanthi 1-3(0-1)
AE Lárissa - Aris Thessaloníki 0-0
Panetolikos - Atromitos 0-1(0-0)
Asteras Tripolis - OFI Heraklion 2-0(1-0)
Lamia - Olympiacos Peiraiás 0-4(0-1)
Panathinaïkos - Panionios 3-0(2-0)
PAOK Thessaloníki - AEK Athína 1-0(0-0)

Round 19 [18-19.01.2020]
Panionios - OFI Heraklion 1-2(0-1)
Panetolikos - Lamia 1-1(0-1)
AO Xanthi - Panathinaïkos 0-1(0-0)
AEK Athína - AE Lárissa 3-0(1-0)
Atromitos - Vólos 0-0
PAOK Thessaloníki - Asteras Trip. 3-1(1-0)
Olympiacos Peiraiás - Aris Thessal. 4-2(3-1)

Round 20 [22-23.01.2020]
AE Lárissa - Panetolikos 2-2(0-1)
Vólos - AEK Athína 1-3(0-2)
OFI Heraklion - Olympiacos Peiraiás 0-1(0-1)
Panathinaïkos - Atromitos 3-0(1-0)
Asteras Tripolis - Panionios 2-0(1-0)
Lamia - PAOK Thessaloníki 0-1(0-1)
Aris Thessaloníki - AO Xanthi 1-0(0-0)

Round 21 [25-27.01.2020]
AE Lárissa - Panathinaïkos 0-2(0-1)
AO Xanthi - OFI Heraklion 2-2(0-1)
Panionios - Atromitos 1-0(0-0)
Panetolikos - Aris Thessaloníki 2-0(0-0)
AEK Athína - Olympiacos Peiraiás 0-0
PAOK Thessaloníki - Vólos 1-0(0-0)
Lamia - Asteras Tripolis 1-1(0-0)

Round 22 [01-02.02.2020]
Vólos - Lamia 1-0(0-0)
OFI Heraklion - AE Lárissa 0-0
Olympiacos Peiraiás - AO Xanthi 3-1(2-0)
Aris Thessaloníki - Panionios 2-0(2-0)
Asteras Tripolis - Panetolikos 2-1(0-0)
Atromitos - AEK Athína 0-1(0-0)
Panathinaïkos - PAOK Thessaloníki 2-0(0-0)

Round 23 [08-10.02.2020]
Panionios - AO Xanthi 0-0
Lamia - AE Lárissa 0-0
Asteras Tripolis - Aris Thessaloníki 1-1(1-1)
Atromitos - Olympiacos Peiraiás 0-1(0-0)
PAOK Thessaloníki - OFI Heraklion 4-0(0-0)
AEK Athína - Panathinaïkos 1-0(1-0)
Panetolikos - Vólos 1-1(1-0)

Round 24 [15-17.02.2020]
AE Lárissa - PAOK Thessaloníki 1-2(0-2)
Olympiacos Peiraiás - Panionios 4-0(4-0)
Panathinaïkos - Panetolikos 3-1(2-0)
AO Xanthi - Lamia 0-0
Vólos - Asteras Tripolis 0-1(0-0)
Aris Thessaloníki - AEK Athína 0-1(0-1)
OFI Heraklion - Atromitos 1-0(0-0)

Round 25 [22-23.02.2020]
Asteras Tripolis - Panathinaïkos 1-1(0-0)
Lamia - Aris Thessaloníki 2-2(1-0)
Panetolikos - Panionios 1-0(0-0)
Atromitos - AO Xanthi 1-0(1-0)
Vólos - AE Lárissa 0-0
AEK Athína - OFI Heraklion 3-0(3-0)
PAOK Thessal - Olympiacos Peiraiás 0-1(0-0)

Round 26 [01.03.2020]
AE Lárissa - Asteras Tripolis 3-0(3-0)
AO Xanthi - PAOK Thessaloníki 1-1(1-1)
Aris Thessaloníki - Atromitos 1-2(0-0)
Olympiacos Peiraiás - Panetolikos 2-0(0-0)
OFI Heraklion - Lamia 3-0(3-0)
Panathinaïkos - Vólos 4-1(2-0)
Panionios - AEK Athína 1-1(1-0)

Final Standings

1.	Olympiacos SFP Peiraiás	26	20	6	0	53 - 9	66
2.	PAOK Thessaloníki	26	18	5	3	50 - 23	59
3.	AEK Athína	26	15	6	5	42 - 22	51
4.	PAE Panathinaïkos Athína	26	12	8	6	35 - 23	44
5.	OFI Heraklion	26	10	4	12	35 - 35	34
6.	Aris Thessaloníki	26	8	10	8	38 - 32	34
7.	APS Atromitos Athína	26	9	5	12	31 - 36	32
8.	AE Lárissa	26	7	9	10	28 - 33	30
9.	AO Xanthi	26	8	6	12	21 - 32	30
10.	AGS Asteras Tripolis	26	8	6	12	33 - 37	30
11.	PAS Lamia	26	5	12	9	19 - 33	27
12.	Vólos NPS	26	7	6	13	23 - 42	27
13.	Panetolikos GPS Agrinio	26	3	8	15	20 - 42	17
14.	Panionios GSS Athína*	26	4	5	17	16 - 45	11

*6 points deducted for non-licensing.
Teams ranked 1-6 were qualified for the Championship Round, while teams ranked 7-14 were qualified for the Relegation Round.

Relegation Round

Results

Round 27 [06-08.06.2020]
Panionios - Vólos 1-0(0-0)
AE Lárissa - Asteras Tripolis 1-2(1-1)
Lamia - Panetolikos 2-0(1-0)
AO Xanthi - Atromitos 1-0(0-0) [24.06.]

Round 28 [13-15.06.2020]
Vólos - AO Xanthi 1-0(1-0)
Atromitos - Lamia 1-1(1-1)
Asteras Tripolis - Panionios 0-0
Panetolikos - AE Lárissa 3-0(0-0)

Round 29 [21-22.06.2020]
Asteras Tripolis - Atromitos 1-1(1-1)
AO Xanthi - Panetolikos 1-1(0-0)
AE Lárissa - Vólos 3-1(1-1)
Lamia - Panionios 0-1(0-1)

Round 30 [27-29.06.2020]
Panionios - AO Xanthi 2-1(1-0)
Panetolikos - Asteras Tripolis 1-1(1-1)
Vólos - Lamia 0-0
Atromitos - AE Lárissa 3-0(1-0)

Round 31 [04-05.07.2020]
Asteras Tripolis - Vólos 4-0(2-0)
Lamia - AO Xanthi 0-0
AE Lárissa - Panionios 0-0
Atromitos - Panetolikos 2-2(1-1)

Round 32 [11.07.2020]
Lamia - AE Lárissa 0-0
Panionios - Panetolikos 0-2(0-1)
Vólos - Atromitos 2-3(0-3)
AO Xanthi - Asteras Tripolis 1-2(0-1)

Round 33 [18.07.2020]
AE Lárissa - AO Xanthi 0-0
Asteras Tripolis - Lamia 1-1(1-0)
Atromitos - Panionios 0-0
Panetolikos - Vólos 1-0(1-0)

Final Standings

		Total						Home					Away				
7.	AGS Asteras Tripolis	33	11	10	12	44 - 42	43	7	7	3	29 - 18	4	3	9	15 - 24
8.	APS Atromitos Athína	33	11	9	13	41 - 43	42	6	7	4	23 - 15	5	2	9	18 - 28
9.	AE Lárissa	33	8	12	13	32 - 42	36	6	5	6	21 - 18	2	7	7	11 - 24
10.	PAS Lamia	33	6	17	10	23 - 36	35	4	10	3	13 - 14	2	7	7	10 - 22
11.	Vólos NPS	33	8	7	18	27 - 54	31	6	4	6	16 - 19	2	3	12	11 - 35
12.	Panetolikos GPS Agrinio	33	6	11	16	30 - 48	29	5	6	5	16 - 16	1	5	11	14 - 32
13.	AO Xanthi (Relegation Play-offs)	33	9	9	15	25 - 38	24	5	6	5	15 - 14	4	3	10	10 - 24
14.	Panionios GSS Athína (Relegated)	33	7	8	18	20 - 48	23	5	4	7	13 - 15	2	4	11	7 - 33

Results

Round 27 [06-07.06.2020]
Aris Thessaloníki - OFI Heraklion 3-1(1-1)
PAOK Thessal - Olympiacos Peiraiás 0-1(0-1)
AEK Athína - Panathinaïkos 1-1(0-0)

Round 28 [13-14.06.2020]
Panathinaïkos - PAOK Thessaloníki 0-0
OFI Heraklion - AEK Athína 0-2(0-1)
Olympiacos Peiraiás - Aris Thessal. 3-1(3-0)

Round 29 [20-21.06.2020]
PAOK Thessaloníki - OFI Heraklion 3-1(0-0)
AEK Athína - Aris Thessaloníki 2-2(0-0)
Olympiacos Peiraiás - Panathinaïkos 3-0(2-0)

Round 30 [27-28.06.2020]
OFI Heraklion - Panathinaïkos 0-0
Aris Thessaloníki - PAOK Thessal. 0-2(0-2)
AEK Athína - Olympiacos Peiraiás 1-2(0-2)

Round 31 [01.07.2020]
Panathinaïkos - Aris Thessaloníki 2-0(1-0)
PAOK Thessaloníki - AEK Athína 0-2(0-1)
Olympiacos Peiraiás - OFI Heraklion 2-1(1-1)

Round 32 [04-05.07.2020]
OFI Heraklion - PAOK Thessaloníki 2-2(2-1)
Aris Thessaloníki - AEK Athína 1-4(1-1)
Panathinaïkos - Olympiacos Peiraiás 0-0

Round 33 [08.07.2020]
Aris Thessal. - Olympiacos Peiraiás 2-4(0-2)
PAOK Thessaloníki - Panathinaïkos 0-0
AEK Athína - OFI Heraklion 2-0(2-0)

Round 34 [11-12.07.2020]
OFI Heraklion - Aris Thessaloníki 0-1(0-1)
Panathinaïkos - AEK Athína 1-3(1-2)
Olympiacos Peiraiás - PAOK Thessal 0-1(0-0)

Round 35 [15.07.2020]
Aris Thessaloníki - Panathinaïkos 0-1(0-0)
OFI Heraklion - Olympiacos Peiraiás 1-3(0-2)
AEK Athína - PAOK Thessaloníki 0-0

Round 36 [19.07.2020]
Olympiacos Peiraiás - AEK Athína 3-0(2-0)
Panathinaïkos - OFI Heraklion 3-2(3-2)
PAOK Thessaloníki - Aris Thessaloníki 0-0

Final Standings

				Total				Home				Away			
1.	**Olympiacos SFP Peiraiás**	36	28	7	1	74 - 16	91	16	1	1	44 - 9	12	6	0	30 - 7
2.	PAOK Thessaloníki	36	21	10	5	58 - 29	73	11	4	3	31 - 13	10	6	2	27 - 16
3.	AEK Athína	36	20	9	7	59 - 32	69	10	6	2	35 - 16	10	3	5	24 - 16
4.	PAE Panathinaïkos Athína	36	15	13	8	43 - 32	58	10	4	4	30 - 16	5	9	4	13 - 16
5.	Aris Thessaloníki	36	10	12	14	48 - 51	42	8	2	8	31 - 25	2	10	6	17 - 26
6.	OFI Heraklion	36	10	6	20	43 - 56	36	8	4	6	25 - 17	2	2	14	18 - 39

Top goalscorers:

20	**Youssef El-Arabi (MAR)**	*Olympiacos SFP Peiraiás)*
14	Nélson Miguel Castro Oliveira (POR)	*AEK Athína*
14	Georgios Manousos	*APS Atromitos Athína*
14	Federico Macheda (ITA)	*PAE Panathinaïkos Athína*
12	Bruno Alexandre Vilela Gama (POR)	*Aris Thessaloníki*

Relegation Play-offs [26-29.08.2020]

AO Xanthi - GS Apollon Smyrna   0-1(0-0)   1-3(0-2)

GS Apollon Smyrna promoted to the Super League 2020/2021.

NATIONAL CUP
Greek Football Cup - Kypello Elladas 2019/2020

Fourth Round [24-26.09./02.10./09.10./23.10.2019]

AO Trikala - GS Doxa Drama	1-0		Panthiraikos AO Santorini - AO Platanias	1-2
PAE Ionikos Nikea - Panachaiki 1891 FC Patras	1-2		PAE Ialyssos Rhodos - AOK Kerkyra	1-0
PAE Veria - APO Levadiakos	3-0		Enosis Panaspropyrgiakou - PAS Giannina	0-2
PS Kalamata - AE Karaiskakis Arta	4-3 pen		AS Aetos Orfano - PAE Apollon Larissa	0-1
PAE Aigaleo Athína - GS Ergotelis Heraklion	0-2		Olympiacos Vólos - PAE Apollon Pontus Kalamaria	1-0
AO Kavala - AO Chania Kissamikos PAE	2-0		AEPS Aiolikos Mytilinis - GS Apollon Smyrna	1-0

Fifth Round [29-31.10./03-05.12.2019]

First Leg			Second Leg	
PAE Apollon Larissa - AO Xanthi	2-1(0-1)		AO Xanthi - PAE Apollon Larissa	3-0(2-0)
Panserraikos Serres - Vólos NPS	1-1(0-0)		Vólos NPS - Panserraikos Serres	1-1 aet; 4-2pen
PAS Giannina - PAE Veria	1-0(0-0)		PAE Veria - PAS Giannina	1-2(1-1)
PAE AS Olympiacos Vólos - Panionios GSS Athína	0-3(0-0)		Panionios GSS Athína - PAE AS Olympiacos Vólos	6-0(3-0)
PS Kalamata - AE Lárissa	3-0(1-0)		AE Lárissa - PS Kalamata	1-0(0-0)
AO Kavala - OFI Heraklion	2-0(2-0)		OFI Heraklion - AO Kavala	4-0(1-0)
Panachaiki 1891 Patras - PAE Panathinaïkos Athína	1-3(0-2)		PAE Panathinaïkos Athína - Panachaiki 1891 Patras	2-0(0-0)
AO Platanias - AGS Asteras Tripolis	0-1(0-0)		AGS Asteras Tripolis - AO Platanias	3-2(0-1,0-1)
PAE Ialyssos Rhodos - Panetolikos GPS Agrinio	0-4(0-1)		Panetolikos GPS Agrinio - PAE Ialyssos Rhodos	5-1(0-0)
AEPS Aiolikos Mytilinis - PAS Lamia	0-3(0-2)		PAS Lamia - AEPS Aiolikos Mytilinis	3-0(2-0)
AO Trikala - GS Ergotelis Heraklion	3-2(0-0)		GS Ergotelis Heraklion - AO Trikala	0-1(0-1)

1/8-Finals [07-16./14-30.01.2020]

First Leg			Second Leg	
Vólos NPS - APS Atromitos Athína	0-3(0-1)		APS Atromitos Athína - Vólos NPS	0-2(0-2)
OFI Heraklion - PAOK Thessaloníki	0-3(0-2)		PAOK Thessaloníki - OFI Heraklion	4-1(2-1)
PS Kalamata - Olympiacos SFP Peiraiás	0-2(0-1)		Olympiacos SFP Peiraiás - PS Kalamata	4-1(2-0)
PAS Giannina - PAE Panathinaïkos Athína	1-0(1-0)		PAE Panathinaïkos Athína - PAS Giannina	3-1(0-1)
Panetolikos GPS Agrinio - Panionios GSS Athína	0-0		Panionios GSS Athína - Panetolikos GPS Agrinio	1-1(0-0,0-0)
AO Xanthi - Aris Thessaloníki	0-1(0-1)		Aris Thessaloníki - AO Xanthi	2-1(1-1)
AO Trikala - PAS Lamia	0-1(0-0)		PAS Lamia - AO Trikala	1-1(1-1)
AGS Asteras Tripolis - AEK Athína	1-1(1-1)		AEK Athína - AGS Asteras Tripolis	2-0(2-0)

Quarter-Finals [04-06/12-19.02.2020]

First Leg			Second Leg	
PAS Lamia - Olympiacos SFP Peiraiás	0-0		Olympiacos SFP Peiraiás - PAS Lamia	3-2(0-1)
Panetolikos GPS Agrinio - AEK Athína	1-1(0-1)		AEK Athína - Panetolikos GPS Agrinio	4-0(2-0)
PAOK Thessaloníki - PAE Panathinaïkos Athína	2-0(1-0)		PAE Panathinaïkos Athína - PAOK Thessaloníki	0-1(0-1)
Aris Thessaloníki - APS Atromitos Athína	0-0		APS Atromitos Athína - Aris Thessaloníki	0-1(0-1)

Semi-Finals [04.03./24.06.2020]

First Leg			Second Leg	
AEK Athína - Aris Thessaloníki	2-1(1-1)		Aris Thessaloníki - AEK Athína	2-2(0-0,2-1)
PAOK Thessaloníki - Olympiacos SFP Peiraiás	3-2(2-2)		Olympiacos SFP Peiraiás - PAOK Thessaloníki	2-0(0-0)

Final

12.09.2020; Stádio Panthessaliko, Vólos; Referee: Björn Kuipers (Netherlands); Attendance: None

Olympiacos SFP Peiraiás - AEK Athína   **1-0(1-0)**

Olympiacos: Konstantinos Tzolakis, Ousseynou Ba, Vasilios Torosidis (80.Rúben Afonso Borges Semedo), Pape Cissé, Mohamed Mady Camara, Andreas Bouchalakis, Georgios Masouras, Mathieu Valbuena (76.Carlos Miguel Ribeiro Dias „Cafú"), Lazar Ranđelović, Youssef El-Arabi (90.Kostas Fortounis), Bruno Felipe Souza da Silva. Trainer: Pedro Rui da Mota Vieira Martins (Portugal).

AEK: Panagiotis Tsintotas, Michalis Bakakis (62.Paulo Sérgio Mota „Paulinho"), Hélder Filipe Oliveira Lopes, Dmitro Chigrinskiy, Stratos Svarnas, Nenad Krstičić, André Luis Gomes Simões (80.Theodosis Machairas), Petros Mantalos, Daniele Verde (62.Christos Albanis), Marko Livaja, Nélson Miguel Castro Oliveira. Trainer: Massimo Carrera (Italy).

Goal: 1-0 Lazar Ranđelović (9).

Athlitikí Énosis Konstantinoupóleos Athína

Founded: 13.04.1924
Stadium: Stádio Olympiako „Spiros Louis", Athína (69,618)
Trainer: José Miguel Azevedo Cardoso (POR) 28.05.1972
[26.08.2019] Nikolaos Kostenoglou 03.10.1970
[08.12.2019] Massimo Carrera (ITA) 22.04.1964

Goalkeepers:	DOB	M	(s)	G
Vassilis Barkas	30.09.1994	28		
Panagiotis Tsintotas	04.07.1993	8	(1)	
Defenders:	**DOB**	**M**	**(s)**	**G**
Michalis Bakakis	18.03.1991	27		1
Dmitro Chigrinskiy (UKR)	07.11.1986	20	(1)	3
Hélder Filipe Oliveira Lopes (POR)	04.01.1989	23		1
Niklas Hult (SWE)	13.02.1990	13	(1)	
Žiga Laci (SVN)	20.07.2002	1		
Marios Oikonomou	06.10.1992	18	(7)	1
Paulo Sérgio Mota „Paulinho" (POR)	13.07.1991	17	(4)	
Stratos Svarnas	11.11.1997	19	(2)	1
Stavros Vasilantonopoulos	28.01.1992		(2)	
Ognjen Vranješ (BIH)	24.10.1989	18		1
Midfielders:	**DOB**	**M**	**(s)**	**G**
André Luis Gomes Simões (POR)	16.12.1989	24	(4)	3
Giannis-Fivos Botos	20.12.2000		(2)	
Francisco Oliveira „Chico" Geraldes (POR)	18.04.1995	2	(1)	

	DOB	M	(s)	G
David Martins Simão (POR)	15.05.1990	1	(3)	
Konstantinos Galanopoulos	28.12.1997	9	(4)	1
Christos Giousis	08.02.1999		(1)	
Viktor Klonaridis (BEL)	28.07.1992	2	(5)	2
Nenad Krstičić (SRB)	03.07.1990	28	(2)	1
Petros Mantalos	31.08.1991	27	(3)	6
Anel Šabanadžović (BIH)	24.05.1999	4	(7)	
Damian Szymański (POL)	16.06.1995	12	(4)	1
Forwards:	**DOB**	**M**	**(s)**	**G**
Christos Albanis	05.11.1994	13	(13)	2
Sergio Ezequiel Araujo (ARG)	28.01.1992	6	(9)	3
Efthymios Christopoulos	20.09.2000		(1)	
Miloš Deletić (SRB)	14.10.1993	4	(5)	1
Georgios Giakoumakis	09.12.1994	2	(11)	
Marko Livaja (CRO)	26.08.1993	30	(2)	9
Theodosis Machairas	06.05.2000		(2)	
Nélson Miguel Castro Oliveira (POR)	08.08.1991	21	(5)	14
Daniele Verde (ITA)	20.06.1996	19	(11)	6

Athlitiki Enosi Lárissa

Founded: 17.05.1964
Stadium: AEL FC Arena, Larissa (16,118)
Trainer: Gordan Petrić (SRB) 01.07.2019
[09.08.2019] Michalis Grigoriou 19.12.1973

Goalkeepers:	DOB	M	(s)	G
Ögmundur Kristinsson (ISL)	19.06.1989	32		
Gergely Nagy (HUN)	27.05.1994	1		
Defenders:	**DOB**	**M**	**(s)**	**G**
Manolis Bertos	13.05.1989	21	(2)	1
Slavko Bralić (CRO)	15.12.1992	16		
Steliano Filip (ROU)	15.05.1994	3	(4)	
Aleksandar Gojković (SRB)	10.08.1988		(1)	
Theocharis Iliadis	05.09.1996	4	(4)	1
Nikos Karanikas	04.03.1992	14	(2)	
Svetozar Marković (SRB)	23.03.2000	7	(1)	
Alexandros Michail	18.08.1986	27	(2)	1
Vangelis Moras	26.08.1981	25	(1)	2
Mateo Mužek (CRO)	29.04.1995	10	(2)	
Nikola Stanković (SRB)	18.12.1993	14		
Stefan Živković (SRB)	01.06.1990	3		
Nikola Žižić (CRO)	23.01.1988	7	(3)	
Midfielders:	**DOB**	**M**	**(s)**	**G**
Fatjon Andoni (ALB)	19.06.1991	9	(6)	3

	DOB	M	(s)	G
Jean Assoubre (CIV)	08.08.1992	4	(9)	1
Panagiotis Ballas	06.09.1993	1	(7)	
Jonathan Ezequiel Bustos (ARG)	29.06.1994	7	(15)	1
Bruno Araújo Chalkiadakis	07.04.1993		(3)	
Miloš Filipović (SRB)	09.05.1990		(5)	
Aly Ahmed Aly Mohamed (EGY)	01.02.1992	9	(2)	
Ergys Kaçe (ALB)	08.07.1993	18	(1)	
Giannis Masouras	24.08.1996	1		
Radomir Milosavljević (SRB)	28.07.1992	29	(1)	9
Dimitrios Pinakas	01.09.2001	3	(5)	
Adnan Šećerović (BIH)	01.12.1991	27	(3)	
Gabriel Andrei Torje (ROU)	22.11.1989	9	(1)	2
Forwards:	**DOB**	**M**	**(s)**	**G**
Abiola Adedeji Dauda (NGA)	03.02.1988	7	(5)	2
Dimitrios Loufakis	01.04.2000		(3)	
Marko Nunič (SVN)	16.03.1993	12	(9)	2
Thanasis Papazoglou	30.03.1988	11	(2)	
Vinícius Santos Silva (BRA)	03.08.1993	10	(4)	
Amr Warda (EGY)	17.09.1993	22		6

Aris Thessaloníki

Founded: 25.03.1914
Stadium: Stádio " Kleanthis Vikelidis", Thessaloníki (22,800)
Trainer: Savvas Pantelidis 07.04.1965
[02.09.2019] Apostolos Terzis 13.03.1971
[14.10.2019] Michael Oenning (GER) 27.09.1965

Goalkeepers:	DOB	M	(s)	G
Fabian Ehmann (AUT)	28.08.1998	11	(1)	
Julián Cuesta Díaz (ESP)	28.03.1991	23		
Apostolos Tsilingiris	06.09.2000	2	(1)	
Defenders:	**DOB**	**M**	**(s)**	**G**
Petros Bagalianis	06.02.2001	6	(1)	1
Georgios Delizisis	01.12.1987	23	(1)	
Francisco "Fran" Manuel Vélez Jiménez (ESP)	23.06.1991	24		4
Hugo Filipe Gonçalves Martins de Sousa(POR)	04.06.1992	6	(8)	
Mihály Korhut (HUN)	01.12.1988	28		1
Lindsay Rose (MRI)	08.02.1992	34		3
Daniel Sundgren (SWE)	22.11.1990	14		
Panagiotis Tsagalidis	05.03.2001		(1)	
Midfielders:	**DOB**	**M**	**(s)**	**G**
Abou Ba (FRA)	29.07.1998	8	(10)	
Petros Bakoutsis	29.06.2001	5	(3)	

	DOB	M	(s)	G
Lerin Duarte (NED)	11.08.1990	1	(2)	
Ioannis Fetfatzidis	21.12.1990	32		5
Javier Magro Matilla (ESP)	01.01.1988	33		1
Daniel Mancini (ARG)	11.11.1996	12	(13)	
Nicolás Martínez (ARG)	25.09.1987	7	(16)	1
Lucas Pacheco Affini „Sasha" (BRA)	01.03.1990	34		3
Martín Tonso (ARG)	19.10.1989	3	(13)	
Forwards:	**DOB**	**M**	**(s)**	**G**
Bruno Alexandre Vilela Gama (POR)	15.11.1987	33	(1)	12
Dimitrios Diamantopoulos	18.11.1988	2	(4)	
Nicolas Diguiny (FRA)	31.05.1988	15	(9)	5
Fiorin Durmishaj (ALB)	14.11.1996	1	(5)	
Aide Brown Ideye (NGA)	10.10.1988	22		8
Daniel Larsson (SWE)	25.01.1987	17	(9)	4
Hamza Younès (TUN)	16.04.1986		(1)	

Athletic Gymnastics Society Asteras Tripolis

Founded:	26.03.1931
Stadium:	Stádio "Theodoros Kolokotronis", Tripolis (7,616)
Trainer:	Borja Jiménez Sáez (ESP) 21.01.1985
[05.12.2019]	Milan Rastavac 01.11.1973

Goalkeepers:	DOB	M	(s)	G
Neofytos Michail (CYP)	16.12.1993	1		
Nikolaos Papadopoulos	11.04.1990	30		
Antonis Tsiftsis	21.07.1999	2		
Defenders:	**DOB**	**M**	**(s)**	**G**
Oluwatobiloba Adefunyibomi Alagbe (NGA)	24.04.2000		(3)	
Ángel Martínez Ortega (ESP)	15.05.1991	14	(2)	
Georgios Antzoulas	04.02.2000	7	(3)	
Giannis Christopoulos	22.07.2000	1		
Daniel „Dani" Suárez García-Osorio (ESP)	05.07.1990	20		3
Giannis Kotsiras	16.12.1992	27	(3)	
Giorgos Kyriakopoulos	05.02.1996	2		
Patricio Matricardi (ARG)	07.01.1994	15		
Triantafyllos Pasalidis	19.07.1996	19	(1)	1
Christos Tasoulis	03.05.1991	18	(4)	2
Valentinos Vlachos	14.02.1992	5	(1)	
Midfielders:	**DOB**	**M**	**(s)**	**G**
Franco Bellocq (ARG)	15.10.1993	3	(3)	

	DOB	M	(s)	G
Borja Fernández Fernández (ESP)	16.08.1995	11	(16)	
Eneko Capilla González (ESP)	13.06.1995	14	(2)	1
Walter Matías Iglesias (ARG)	18.04.1985	9	(8)	2
José Luis Valiente Giménez (ESP)	18.05.1991	22	(5)	
Georgios Kanellopoulos	29.01.2000		(1)	
Juan Manuel Munafo Horta (ARG)	20.03.1988	25	(1)	1
Panagiotis Tzimas	12.03.2001		(5)	
Forwards:	**DOB**	**M**	**(s)**	**G**
Adrián Riera Torrecillas (ESP)	19.04.1996	14	(10)	
Sudais Ali Baba (NGA)	25.08.2000	2	(2)	
Jerónimo Barrales (ARG)	28.01.1986	19	(5)	11
Miloš Deletić (SRB)	14.10.1993	8	(1)	2
Anastasios Douvikas	02.08.1999		(2)	
Eneko Jauregi Escobar (ESP)	13.07.1996	8	(6)	1
Luis Fernández Teijeiro (ESP)	27.09.1993	22	(3)	10
Marc Fernández Gràcia (ESP)	29.04.1990	23	(3)	6
Andrés Pascual Santoja „Sito" (ESP)	18.11.1996	12	(11)	2
Francesc "Xesc" Regis Crespi (ESP)	30.09.1996	10	(6)	2

PAE APS Atromitos Athinon

Founded:	30.04.1923
Stadium:	Stádio Peristeri, Athína (10,005)
Trainer:	Giannis Anastasiou 05.03.1973
[16.11.2019]	Georgios Korakakis 09.02.1976
[05.12.2019]	Savvas Pantelidis 07.04.1965

Goalkeepers:	DOB	M	(s)	G
Christos Mandas	17.09.2001	12		
Balázs Megyeri (HUN)	31.03.1990	19		
Christos Theodorakis	17.09.1996	2	(1)	
Defenders:	**DOB**	**M**	**(s)**	**G**
Dimitrios Goutas	04.04.1994	30		1
João Carlos Araújo Fonseca Silva (POR)	30.08.1989	9		
Tal Kachila (ISR)	26.06.1992	4		
Alexandros Katranis	04.05.1998	21	(1)	
Kyriakos Kivrakidis	21.07.1992	13	(2)	
Spyros Natsos	09.06.1998	12	(2)	1
Spyros Risvanis	03.01.1994	27		2
Rodrigo Galo Brito (BRA)	19.09.1986	20	(2)	3
Stefanos Stroungis	09.10.1997	7	(3)	
Midfielders:	**DOB**	**M**	**(s)**	**G**
Athanasios Androutsos	06.05.1997	20	(7)	4

	DOB	M	(s)	G
Azer Bušuladžić (BIH)	12.11.1991	13	(1)	
Charilaos Charisis	12.01.1995	24	(1)	
Nill De Pauw (BEL)	06.01.1990	7	(2)	
Iraklis Garoufalias	01.05.1993	1		
Madson Henrique Nascimento Santos (BRA)	09.05.1991	11	(5)	
Bryan Martín Rabello Mella (CHI)	16.05.1994	5	(4)	
José Raúl Baena Urdiales (ESP)	02.03.1989	9	(8)	
Javier Horacio Umbides (ARG)	09.02.1982	10	(15)	2
Forwards:	**DOB**	**M**	**(s)**	**G**
Georgios Daviotis	29.06.1998	4	(8)	
Farley Vieira Rosa (BRA)	14.01.1994	9	(5)	
Petros Giakoumakis	03.07.1992	8	(15)	3
Georgios Manousos	03.12.1987	31		14
Clarck N'Sikulu (COD)	10.07.1992	17	(9)	2
Roland Ugrai (HUN)	13.11.1992	3	(6)	2
Apostolos Vellios	08.01.1992	15	(12)	6

PAS Lamia 1964 Football Club

Founded:	01.06.1964
Stadium:	Stádio Dimotiko, Lamia (6,000)
Trainer:	Ioakeim Chavos 05.09.1969
[06.08.2019]	Sotiris Antoniou 10.09.1975
[24.10.2019]	Apostolos Mantzios 21.10.1969
[25.06.2020]	Georgios Petrakis 08.02.1988

Goalkeepers:	DOB	M	(s)	G
Damir Kahriman (SRB)	05.11.1984	4		
Panagiotis Katsikas	10.03.1999	1	(1)	
Devis Mboka (FRA)	02.02.1993	5		
Konstantinos Theodoropoulos	27.03.1990	16		
Markos Vellidis	04.04.1987	7		
Defenders:	**DOB**	**M**	**(s)**	**G**
Daniel Adejo (NGA)	07.08.1989	31		1
Mark Nyaaba Asigba (GHA)	07.07.1990	9	(2)	1
Patrick Bahanack (CMR)	03.08.1997	2		
Vasilios Pliatsikas	14.04.1988	20	(2)	
Manolis Saliakas	12.09.1996	9	(15)	1
Giannis Skondras	21.02.1990	28	(3)	2
Adam Tzanetopoulos	10.02.1995	3	(5)	
Vanderson Scardovelli (BRA)	27.09.1984	31		
Loukas Vyntra	05.02.1981	22	(7)	
Midfielders:	**DOB**	**M**	**(s)**	**G**
Danny Bryan Bejarano Yañez (BOL)	03.01.1994	27	(1)	3

	DOB	M	(s)	G
Kostas Bouloulis	07.12.1993	3	(12)	
Elini Dimoutsos	18.08.1988	26	(1)	1
Christoforos Karagiannis	09.12.1999		(1)	
Lucas Ramos de Oliveira (BRA)	18.01.1995		(1)	
Ibrahima Niasse (SEN)	18.04.1988	6	(2)	
Ismaïl Sassi (TUN)	24.12.1991	2	(8)	
Tyronne Gustavo del Pino Ramos (ESP)	27.01.1991	12	(5)	
Andreas Vasilogiannis	21.02.1991	15	(14)	
Leonardo Enrique Villalba (ARG)	29.09.1994	6	(2)	1
Forwards:	**DOB**	**M**	**(s)**	**G**
Christos Aravidis	13.03.1987	5	(1)	2
Anastasios Karamanos	21.09.1990	27	(3)	1
Miguel Antonio Bianconi Kohl (BRA)	14.05.1992	4	(5)	3
Konstantinos Nikolopoulos	13.07.2002		(1)	
Lazar Romanić (SRB)	23.03.1998	30	(2)	1
Rogerio Conceicão do Rosario „Thuram" (BRA)	01.02.1991	11	(4)	6
Nikos Tsoukalos	23.03.1992		(2)	
Anestis Vlachomitros	06.11.2001	1	(2)	

Ómilos Filáthlon Heraklíou

Founded: 1925
Stadium: Stádio „Theodoros Vardinogiannis", Heraklion (9,088)
Trainer: Georgios Simos   29.03.1978

Goalkeepers:	DOB	M	(s)	G
Giannis Dermitzakis	05.11.1992	1		
Óscar Alexander Whalley Guardado (ESP)	29.03.1994	10		
Dimitrios Sotiriou	13.09.1987	25		
Defenders:	**DOB**	**M**	**(s)**	**G**
Manolis Bolakis	20.10.1994	1		
Christopher Braun (GER)	15.07.1991	18	(10)	
Panagiotis Deligiannidis	29.08.1996	3	(3)	1
Konstantinos Giannoulis	09.12.1987	33	(1)	
Georgios Koutroumpis	10.02.1991	21	(5)	
Nikolaos Marinakis	12.09.1993	27	(2)	
Anestis Nastos	28.04.1989	11	(9)	
Manolis Perdikis	29.08.1999	1	(1)	
Nikos Vafeas	21.02.1997	5	(1)	
Midfielders:	**DOB**	**M**	**(s)**	**G**
Athanasios Dinas	12.11.1989		(1)	
João Victor de Albuquerque Bruno (BRA)	07.11.1988	8	(3)	

	DOB	M	(s)	G
Nikos Korovesis	10.08.1991	30	(1)	
Miguel Alberto Mellado (ARG)	18.03.1993	20	(2)	1
Theodoros Mingos	06.02.1998		(1)	
Adil Nabi (ENG)	28.02.1994	20	(5)	4
Juan Ángel Neira (ARG)	21.02.1989	28	(2)	5
Vajebah Sakor (NOR)	14.04.1996	15	(4)	2
Ismaïl Sassi (TUN)	24.12.1991		(1)	
Georgios Sournakis	07.11.1999		(4)	
Paschalis Staikos	08.02.1996	14	(12)	
Forwards:	**DOB**	**M**	**(s)**	**G**
Felipe Souza Ferreyra (BRA)	21.05.1998	2	(6)	1
João Vitor Brandão Figueiredo (BRA)	27.05.1996	23	(10)	11
Lisandro Pedro Varela Semedo (POR)	12.03.1996	27	(1)	7
Dimitrios Manos	16.09.1994	13	(16)	3
Vangelis Nikokyrakis	04.10.2001	2	(8)	
Ricardo Alvares Guedes Vaz (POR)	26.11.1994	15	(8)	2
Kosmas Tsilianidis	09.05.1994	23		6

Olympiakós Sýndesmos Filáthlon Peiraiós

Founded: 10.03.1925
Stadium: Stádio „Giórgos Karaïskáki", Peiraiás (32,115)
Trainer: Pedro Rui da Mota Vieira Martins (POR)   17.07.1970

Goalkeepers:	DOB	M	(s)	G
Bobby Allain (FRA)	28.11.1991	3		
José Pedro Malheiro de Sá (POR)	17.01.1993	33		
Ilias Karargyris	29.06.2002		(1)	
Konstantinos Tzolakis	08.11.2002		(1)	
Defenders:	**DOB**	**M**	**(s)**	**G**
Ousseynou Ba (SEN)	11.11.1995	22		
Bruno Miguel Boialvo Gaspar (POR)	21.04.1993	10	(5)	
Pape Cissé (SEN)	14.09.1995	10	(3)	
Omar Elabdellaoui (NOR)	05.12.1991	27	(1)	1
Leonardo Koutris	23.07.1995	4	(2)	
Apostolos-Ilias Martinis	08.01.2001		(1)	
Yassine Meryah (TUN)	02.07.1993	4	(1)	
Avraam Papadopoulos	03.12.1984	9	(3)	
Rúben Afonso Borges Semedo (POR)	04.04.1994	27		1
Vasilios Torosidis	10.06.1985	3	(3)	
Kostas Tsimikas	12.05.1996	27		
Midfielders:	**DOB**	**M**	**(s)**	**G**
Andreas Bouchalakis	05.04.1993	29	(4)	1

	DOB	M	(s)	G
Carlos Miguel Ribeiro Dias „Cafú" (POR)	26.02.1993	3	(4)	1
Mady Camara (GUI)	28.02.1997	27	(4)	6
Kostas Fortounis	16.10.1992	7	(6)	3
Guilherme dos Santos Torres (BRA)	05.04.1991	27		3
Maximiliano Alberto Lovera (ARG)	09.03.1999	5	(14)	
Georgios Masouras	01.01.1994	23	(9)	9
Lazar Ranđelović (SRB)	05.08.1997	7	(8)	2
Vasilios Sourlis	16.11.2002		(1)	
Mathieu Valbuena (FRA)	28.09.1984	20	(6)	7
Georgios Xenitidis	04.09.1999		(1)	
Forwards:	**DOB**	**M**	**(s)**	**G**
Yassine Benzia (ALG)	08.09.1994	1	(4)	
Bruno Felipe Souza da Silva (BRA)	26.05.1994	2	(5)	
Lazaros Christodoulopoulos	19.12.1986		(6)	
Daniel Castelo Podence (POR)	21.10.1995	15		3
Youssef El-Arabi (MAR)	03.02.1987	30	(4)	20
Ahmed Hassan Mahgoub Abdelmoneim (EGY)	05.03.1993	5	(9)	6
Miguel Ángel Guerrero Martín (ESP)	12.07.1990	3	(11)	2
El Arbi Soudani (ALG)	25.11.1987	13	(6)	7

Panathinaïkós Athlitikós Ómilos Athína

Founded: 03.02.1908
Stadium: Stádio Olympiako „Spiros Louis", Athína (69,618)
Trainer: Georgios Donis   22.10.1969

Goalkeepers:	DOB	M	(s)	G
Nikolaos Christogeorgos	03.01.2000	1		
Sokratis Dioudis	03.02.1993	32		
Vasilis Xenopoulos	20.05.1998	3		
Defenders:	**DOB**	**M**	**(s)**	**G**
Ilias Chatzitheodoridis	05.11.1997	15	(8)	
Emanuel Mariano Insúa Zapata (ARG)	10.04.1991	20		1
João Aniceto Grandela Nunes (POR)	19.11.1995	5	(6)	
Mattias Johansson (SWE)	16.02.1992	23		
Dimitrios Kolovetsios	16.10.1991	15	(5)	2
Theofanis Mavromatis	16.01.1997	1		
Achilleas Poungouras	13.12.1995	24		
Bart Schenkeveld (NED)	28.08.1991	29		1
Georgios Vagiannidis	12.09.2001	1		1
Vasilios Zagaritis	04.05.2001	5	(2)	
Midfielders:	**DOB**	**M**	**(s)**	**G**
Sotirios Alexandropoulos	26.11.2001	4	(6)	
Kostas Apostolakis	28.05.1999	5	(1)	
Andreas Athanasakopoulos	27.11.2001	1	(2)	

	DOB	M	(s)	G
Yassin Ayoub (MAR)	06.03.1994	4	(2)	
Giannis Bouzoukis	27.03.1998	26	(7)	1
Christos Donis	09.10.1994	26		1
Dimitrios Kolovos	27.04.1993	7	(14)	1
Dimitrios Kourbelis	02.11.1993	31		3
Yohan Albert Pierre Stéphane Mollo (FRA)	18.07.1989	1	(4)	1
Dimitrios Serpezis	14.03.2001	1	(5)	
Vangelis Theocharis	06.07.1998	6	(1)	
Anuar Tuhami (MAR)	15.01.1995	10	(6)	
Ghayas Zahid (NOR)	08.09.1994	22	(3)	4
Forwards:	**DOB**	**M**	**(s)**	**G**
Uffe Manich Bech (DEN)	13.01.1993	3	(11)	1
Anastasios Chatzigiovannis	31.05.1997	30	(2)	8
Anargyros Kampetsis	06.05.1999	8	(10)	
Federico Macheda (ITA)	22.08.1991	29	(4)	14
Dominik Nagy (HUN)	08.05.1995	4	(5)	1
Juan José Perea Mendoza (COL)	23.02.2000	4	(19)	3
Spyros Tzavidas	21.08.2001		(1)	

Panaetolikos Gymnastikos Philekpaideutikos Syllogos Agrinio

Founded: 09.03.1926
Stadium: Stádio Panetolikos, Agrinio (7,000)
Trainer: Luís Manuel Ferreira de Castro (POR) — 07.05.1980
[15.10.2019] Makis Chavos — 05.09.1969

Goalkeepers:	DOB	M	(s)	G
Nikos Giannakopoulos	19.02.1993	5	(2)	
Jesús Fernández Collado (ESP)	11.06.1988	10	(1)	
Christopher Knett (AUT)	01.08.1990	18		
Defenders:	**DOB**	**M**	**(s)**	**G**
Luciano Damián Balbi (ARG)	04.04.1989	4	(1)	
Igor Jovanović (CRO)	03.05.1989	20		
Kevin Martín García Martínez (ESP)	08.09.1989	15		
Apostolos Konstantopoulos	02.08.2002	3		1
Alexandros Malis	19.03.1997	13	(2)	
Johan Martial (FRA)	30.05.1991	14	(2)	1
Alexandros Parras	12.05.1998	3	(1)	
Pierre Sagna (SEN)	21.08.1990	18		1
Manolis Tzanakakis	30.04.1992	12	(1)	1
Midfielders:	**DOB**	**M**	**(s)**	**G**
Gregory Ariyibi (USA)	18.01.1995	10	(9)	1
Euciodálcio Gomes „Dálcio" (POR)	22.05.1996	26	(4)	1
Dimitrios Fytopoulos	11.02.2000	4	(5)	
Georgios Liavas	12.02.2001	16	(3)	
Atair Mimito Rocha Biai (GUI)	12.12.1997	8	(10)	
Anthony Mounier (FRA)	27.09.1987	9	(3)	4
Rasmus Sjöstedt (SWE)	28.02.1992	17	(1)	
Aymen Tahar (ALG)	02.10.1989	19	(4)	
Angelos Tsigaras	24.07.1999	12	(11)	
Forwards:	**DOB**	**M**	**(s)**	**G**
Juan Ignacio Álvarez Moringo (ARG)	27.10.1997	11	(2)	
Admir Bajrović (SWE)	06.08.1995	13	(11)	5
Abiola Adedeji Dauda (NGA)	03.02.1988	11	(1)	6
Jorge Luis Díaz Gutiérrez (URU)	28.06.1989	30		2
Farley Vieira Rosa (BRA)	14.01.1994	14		3
Frederico Duarte (POR)	30.03.1999	6	(17)	2
Joan Ángel Román i Ollè (ESP)	18.05.1993	3	(4)	
Alexandros Kavvadias	10.05.2000		(5)	
Óscar Adrián Lucero (ARG)	16.08.1985	14	(5)	
Vlad Călin Morar (ROU)	01.08.1993	5	(2)	1

Paniónios Gymnastikós Sýllogos Smýrnis Athína

Founded: 14.09.1890
Stadium: Stádio Nea Smyrni, Athína (11,700)
Trainer: Apostolos Mantzios — 21.10.1969
[03.09.2019] Nikodimos Papavasiliou (CYP) — 31.08.1970
[21.02.2020] Dimitrios Koropoulis — 30.01.1979
[26.02.2020] Leonidas Vokolos — 31.08.1970

Goalkeepers:	DOB	M	(s)	G
Matic Kotnik (SVN)	23.07.1990	22		
Jérémy Malherbe (FRA)	15.03.1991	11	(1)	
Defenders:	**DOB**	**M**	**(s)**	**G**
Luiz Gustavo Domingues (BRA)	28.09.1988	18		
Stefanos Evangelou	12.05.1998	16	(2)	
Ioannis Kiakos	14.02.1998	5	(1)	
Odysseas Lymperakis	05.06.1998	17	(3)	
Antonio Mico	27.01.2000		(1)	
Athanasios Papageorgiou	09.05.1987	17	(8)	
Giorgos Saramantas	29.01.1992	21	(4)	
Dimitrios Stavropoulos	01.05.1997	31		1
Midfielders:	**DOB**	**M**	**(s)**	**G**
Pedro Arce Latapí (MEX)	25.11.1991	11	(4)	2
Frixos Grivas	23.09.2000	3	(8)	
Panagiotis Korbos	11.09.1985	29		
Novica Maksimović (SRB)	04.04.1988	13	(2)	2
Ioannis Maniatis	12.10.1986	3	(1)	
Giannis Masouras	24.08.1996	12	(1)	
Giannis Oikonomidis	03.01.1998	20	(4)	
Giannis Papanikolaou	18.11.1998	23	(7)	
Vasilios Rentzas	16.04.1992	18	(3)	
Christos Retsos	02.05.2001	1	(2)	
Sotiris Tsiloulis	14.02.1995	22	(7)	4
Forwards:	**DOB**	**M**	**(s)**	**G**
Bachana Arabuli (GEO)	05.01.1994	26	(2)	6
Oumar Camara (FRA)	19.08.1992	5	(7)	
Konstantinos Doumtsios	20.09.1997	3	(10)	
Dimitrios Emmanouilidis	24.10.2000	11	(8)	4
Nemanja Milojević	23.02.1998	5	(12)	1
Sofiane Sidi Ali (FRA)	14.07.1995		(3)	

Panthessaloníkios Athlitikós Ómilos Konstantinoupolitón

Founded: 20.04.1926
Stadium: Stádio Toumba, Thessaloníki (28,703)
Trainer: Abel Fernando Moreira Ferreira (POR) — 22.12.1978

Goalkeepers:	DOB	M	(s)	G
Alexandros Paschalakis	28.07.1989	16		
Živko Živković (SRB)	14.04.1989	20		
Defenders:	**DOB**	**M**	**(s)**	**G**
José Ángel Crespo Rincón (ESP)	09.02.1987	15	(1)	2
Fernando Lopes dos Santos Varela (CPV)	26.11.1987	27	(1)	1
Dimitris Giannoulis	17.10.1995	34		
Sverrir Ingason (ISL)	05.08.1993	27	(1)	4
Leonardo de Matos Cruz "Léo Matos" (BRA)	02.04.1986	26	(4)	4
Giannis Michailidis	18.02.2000	4	(3)	1
Enea Mihaj (ALB)	05.07.1998	3	(1)	1
Rodrigo Alves Soares (BRA)	26.12.1992	7	(7)	
Adelino André Vieira de Freitas „Vieirinha"(POR)	24.01.1986	14	(6)	5
Midfielders:	**DOB**	**M**	**(s)**	**G**
Diego Marvin Biseswar (SUR)	08.03.1988	24	(7)	2
Douglas Augusto Soares Gomes (BRA)	13.01.1997	15	(3)	2
Omar El Kaddouri (MAR)	21.08.1990	16	(7)	1
Anderson Esiti (NGA)	24.05.1994	12	(9)	
Maurício José Da Silveira Junior (BRA)	21.10.1988	18	(9)	
Josip Mišić (CRO)	28.06.1994	25	(1)	5
Dimitrios Pelkas	26.10.1993	11	(8)	3
Theocharis Tsiggaras	20.08.2000		(2)	
Forwards:	**DOB**	**M**	**(s)**	**G**
Chuba Amechi Akpom (ENG)	09.10.1995	14	(19)	8
Lazaros Lamprou	19.12.1997	4	(6)	2
Leonardo Rodrigues Lima "Léo Jabá" (BRA)	02.08.1998	2	(4)	
Dimitris Limnios	27.05.1998	27	(8)	4
Miroslav Stoch (SVK)	19.10.1989	6	(5)	
Karol Świderski (POL)	23.01.1997	23	(11)	11
Christos Tzolis	30.01.2002	6	(3)	1

Vólos Néos Podosfairikós Sýllogos

Founded: 02.06.2017
Stadium: Stádio Panthessaliko, Vólos (22,700)
Trainer: Juan Ferrando Fenoll (ESP)   02.01.1981

Goalkeepers:	DOB	M	(s)	G
Athanasios Garavelis	06.08.1992	22	(1)	
Anastasios Karagiozis	20.06.1997	3		
Nikolaos Melissas	24.02.1993	8		
Defenders:	**DOB**	**M**	**(s)**	**G**
Sébastien Aymer Bassong N'Guema (CMR)	09.07.1986	3		
Liassine Cadamuro (FRA)	05.03.1988	5		
Antonis Dentakis	13.03.1995	23	(1)	
Apostolos Diamantis	20.05.2000	13	(2)	
Stergios Dimopoulos	25.05.1990	25	(3)	2
Franco Ferrari (ARG)	09.05.1992	31		
Vangelis Ikonomou	18.07.1987	8	(1)	
Lefteris Lyratzis	22.02.2000	13	(11)	1
Gerasimos Mitoglou	20.10.1999	3	(1)	
Sergio Chica Villares (ESP)	11.07.1996	16		
Marios Tsaousis	11.05.2000	6	(7)	1
Anastasios Tsokanis	02.05.1991	31		3

Midfielders:	DOB	M	(s)	G
Konstantinos Balogiannis	08.02.1999	13	(9)	
Fernando Rubén Joao (ARG)	26.05.1994	22	(4)	1
Kostas Korelas	01.03.2000		(2)	
Augusto Max (ARG)	10.08.1992	18	(6)	
Juan Muñiz Gallego (ESP)	14.03.1992	27	(1)	5
Ignacio Cases Mora „Nacho Cases" (ESP)	22.12.1987	1	(5)	
Brian Óscar Sarmiento (ARG)	22.04.1990		(1)	
Joaquin Torres (ARG)	28.01.1997	15	(9)	5
Forwards:	**DOB**	**M**	**(s)**	**G**
Yahia Attiyat Allah (MAR)	02.03.1995	3	(5)	1
Georgios Ballas	07.04.2001		(3)	
Iker Guarrotxena Vallejo (ESP)	06.12.1992	14		1
Konstantinos Iliopoulos	15.03.1989		(3)	
Erik Jendrišek (SVK)	26.10.1986	19	(5)	4
Alexandros Kyziridis	16.09.2000	3	(3)	1
Vasilios Mantzis	04.12.1991	13	(9)	2
Ioannis Mystakidis	07.12.1994	5	(3)	

Athlitikos Omilos Xanthi

Founded: 01.01.1967
Stadium: AO Xanthi Arena, Xanthi (7,422)
Trainer: Francisco "Kiko" Ramírez González (ESP)   14.07.1970
[25.11.2019]   Georgios Koltsis   22.10.1974
[08.12.2019]   Georgios Paraschos   23.08.1952
[07.03.2020]   Nikolaos Karageorgiou   08.12.1962

Goalkeepers:	DOB	M	(s)	G
Carlos Javier Abad Hernández Trujillo (ESP)	28.06.1995	28		
Vítor Emanuel Gonçalves São Bento (POR)	09.08.1992	5		
Defenders:	**DOB**	**M**	**(s)**	**G**
Dimosthenis Baxevanidis	14.04.1988	17		1
Mikael Dyrestam (GUI)	10.12.1991	6	(2)	
Jorge Casado Rodríguez (ESP)	26.06.1989	17		
Aristotelis Karasalidis	03.05.1991	31	(1)	
Christos Lisgaras	12.02.1986	25	(1)	3
Stelios Malezas	11.03.1985	10	(1)	
Luis Leandro Sosa Otermin (URU)	18.03.1991	19	(6)	
Dimosthenis Teuekes	03.01.2001			
Konstantinos Thymianis	28.02.2001	1	(2)	
Midfielders:	**DOB**	**M**	**(s)**	**G**
Jean Pierre Agustin Barrientos Díaz (URU)	16.09.1990	11	(12)	2
Khassa Camara (MTN)	22.10.1992	11	(3)	
Pablo de Lucas Torres (ESP)	20.09.1986	2	(4)	

	DOB	M	(s)	G
Petar Đuričković (SRB)	20.06.1991	19	(10)	2
Fábio Miguel dos Santos Sturgeon (POR)	04.02.1994	26	(5)	1
Sofiane Khadda (FRA)	23.12.1991			
Aleksandar Kovačević (SRB)	09.01.1992	26	(2)	
Lucas Poletto Costa (BRA)	29.03.1995		(1)	
Thibault Moulin (FRA)	13.01.1990	9	(8)	
Medhi Terki (FRA)	27.09.1991	25	(4)	
Forwards:	**DOB**	**M**	**(s)**	**G**
Matías Gastón Castro (ARG)	18.12.1991	10	(4)	1
Eduardo Antonio Machado Teixeira (BRA)	07.06.1993	20	(6)	4
Ioannis Fakis	14.04.2001			
Vasilios Fasidis	22.06.1996	9	(5)	
Jordan Faucher (FRA)	06.11.1991	12	(14)	7
Alexandros Gargkalatzidis	12.04.2000	1	(4)	
Vincenzo Rennella (FRA)	08.10.1988	8	(4)	
William Douglas De Amorim (BRA)	15.12.1991	15	(11)	2

SECOND LEVEL
Super League 2 2019/2020

1. PAS Giannina (*Promoted*)	20	15	4	1	44	-	11	49
2. GS Apollon Smyrna (*Promotion Play-offs*)	20	13	3	4	36	-	13	42
3. AO Chania Kissamikos PAE	20	11	5	4	33	-	9	38
4. APO Levadiakos	20	11	5	4	27	-	15	38
5. AE Karaiskakis Arta	20	9	4	7	32	-	29	31
6. PAE Apollon Lárissa	20	9	3	8	27	-	25	30
7. GS Ergotelis Heraklion	20	9	2	9	31	-	33	29
8. Panachaiki 1891 FC Patras	20	8	4	8	34	-	19	28
9. AO Platanias	20	8	2	10	26	-	32	26
10. GS Doxa Drama	20	6	6	8	25	-	25	24
11. AOK Kerkyra* (*Relegated*)	20	1	0	19	6	-	52	0
12. PAE Apollon Pontus Kalamaria** (*Relegated*)	20	1	0	19	5	-	61	−3

*3 points deducted
**6 points deducted
The League was abandoned after 20 Rounds due to Covid-19 pandemic.

INTERNATIONAL MATCHES
(16.07.2019 – 15.07.2020)

05.09.2019	Tampere	Finland - Greece	1-0(0-0)	(ECQ)
08.09.2019	Athína	Greece - Liechtenstein	1-1(1-0)	(ECQ)
12.10.2019	Rome	Italy - Greece	2-0(0-0)	(ECQ)
15.10.2019	Athína	Greece - Bosnia and Herzegovina	2-1(1-1)	(ECQ)
15.11.2019	Yerevan	Armenia - Greece	0-1(0-1)	(ECQ)
18.11.2019	Athína	Greece - Finland	2-1(0-1)	(ECQ)

05.09.2019   FINLAND - GREECE   **1-0(0-0)**   16th EC. Qualifiers
Ratinan Stadion, Tampere; Referee: Juan Martínez Munuera (Spain); Attendance: 16,163
GRE: Vasilios Barkas, Vasilios Torosidis (Cap) (70.Michalis Bakakis), Sokratis Papastathopoulos, Konstantinos Manolas, Konstantinos Stafylidis, Andreas Bouchalakis, Dimitrios Kolovos (60.Dimitrios Pelkas), Dimitrios Kourbelis, Giorgos Masouras, Efthimis Koulouris (76.Vangelis Pavlidis), Marios Vrousai. Trainer: Johannes Nicolaas van 't Schip (Netherlands).

08.09.2019   GREECE - LIECHTENSTEIN   **1-1(1-0)**   16th EC. Qualifiers
Stádio Olympiako „Spiros Louis", Athína; Referee: Alexander Harkam (Austria); Attendance: 3,445
GRE: Vasilios Barkas, Sokratis Papastathopoulos (Cap), Konstantinos Manolas, Michalis Bakakis, Konstantinos Tsimikas, Ioannis Fetfatzidis (68.Vangelis Pavlidis), Andreas Samaris, Andreas Bouchalakis (62.José Carlos Gonçalves Rodrigues "Zeca"), Giorgos Masouras (86.Dimitrios Hristos Giannoulis), Efthimis Koulouris, Marios Vrousai. Trainer: Johannes Nicolaas van 't Schip (Netherlands).
Goal: Giorgos Masouras (33).

12.10.2019   ITALY - GREECE   **2-0(0-0)**   16th EC. Qualifiers
Stadio Olimpico, Roma; Referee: Sergei Karasev (Russia); Attendance: 56,274
GRE: Alexandros Paschalakis, Dimitrios Siovas, Michalis Bakakis, Konstantinos Stafylidis (Cap), Pantelis Hatzidiakos, José Carlos Gonçalves Rodrigues "Zeca", Andreas Bouchalakis (75.Dimitrios Hristos Giannoulis), Dimitrios Kourbelis, Anastasios Bakasetas (80.Petros Mantalos), Efthimis Koulouris (67.Anastasios Donis), Dimitrios Limnios. Trainer: Johannes Nicolaas van 't Schip (Netherlands).

15.10.2019   GREECE - BOSNIA AND HERZEGOVINA   **2-1(1-1)**   16th EC. Qualifiers
Stádio Olympiako „Spiros Louis", Athína; Referee: Felix Zwayer (Germany); Attendance: 4,512
GRE: Alexandros Paschalakis, Michalis Bakakis, Konstantinos Stafylidis (Cap), Dimitrios Hristos Giannoulis, Pantelis Hatzidiakos, Petros Mantalos (60.Giorgos Masouras), Dimitrios Kourbelis, Konstantinos Galanopoulos, Anastasios Bakasetas, Vangelis Pavlidis (70.Efthimis Koulouris), Dimitrios Limnios (84.Ioannis Fetfatzidis). Trainer: Johannes Nicolaas van 't Schip (Netherlands).
Goals: Vangelis Pavlidis (30), Adnan Kovačević (88 own goal).

15.11.2019   ARMENIA - GREECE   **0-1(0-1)**   16th EC. Qualifiers
„Vazgen Sargsyan" Hanrapetakan Stadium, Yerevan; Referee: Paweł Raczkowski (Poland); Attendance: 6,450
GRE: Odisseas Vlachodimos, Michalis Bakakis, Konstantinos Stafylidis (Cap), Dimitrios Hristos Giannoulis, Pantelis Hatzidiakos, Petros Mantalos (66.Giorgos Masouras), Dimitrios Kourbelis, Konstantinos Galanopoulos, Anastasios Bakasetas (81.Anastasios Donis), Vangelis Pavlidis (74.Efthimis Koulouris), Dimitrios Limnios. Trainer: Johannes Nicolaas van 't Schip (Netherlands).
Goal: Dimitrios Limnios (35).

18.11.2019   GREECE - FINLAND   **2-1(0-1)**   16th EC. Qualifiers
Stádio Olympiako „Spiros Louis", Athína; Referee: Aleksei Eskov (Russia); Attendance: 5,453
GRE: Odisseas Vlachodimos, Michalis Bakakis, Konstantinos Stafylidis (Cap), Dimitrios Hristos Giannoulis, Pantelis Hatzidiakos, Petros Mantalos (90+3.Giorgos Masouras), Dimitrios Kourbelis, Konstantinos Galanopoulos (73.Andreas Bouchalakis), Anastasios Bakasetas, Vangelis Pavlidis (64.Efthimis Koulouris), Dimitrios Limnios. Trainer: Johannes Nicolaas van 't Schip (Netherlands).
Goals: Petros Mantalos (47), Konstantinos Galanopoulos (70).

NATIONAL TEAM PLAYERS
(16.07.2019 – 15.07.2020)

Name	DOB	Caps	Goals	2019/2020:	Club
Goalkeepers					
Vasilios BARKAS	30.05.1994	**10**	**0**	2019:	*AEK Athína*
Alexandros PASCHALAKIS	28.07.1989	**3**	**0**	2019:	*PAOK Thessaloníki*
Odisseas VLACHODIMOS	26.04.1994	**6**	**0**	2019:	*Sport Lisboa e Benfica (POR)*
Defenders					
Michalis BAKAKIS	18.04.1991	**15**	**0**	2019:	*AEK Athína*
Dimitrios Hristos GIANNOULIS	17.10.1995	**7**	**0**	2019:	*APS Atromitos Athína*
Pantelis HATZIDIAKOS	18.01.1997	**4**	**0**	2019:	*AZ Alkmaar (NED)*
Konstantinos MANOLAS	14.06.1991	**42**	**1**	2019:	*SSC Napoli (ITA)*
Sokratis PAPASTATHOPOULOS	09.06.1988	**90**	**3**	2019:	*Arsenal FC London (ENG)*
Dimitrios SIOVAS	16.09.1988	**18**	**0**	2019:	*CD Leganés (ESP)*
Konstantinos STAFYLIDIS	02.12.1993	**31**	**2**	2019:	*TSG Hoffenheim 1899 (GER)*
Vasilios TOROSIDIS	10.06.1985	**101**	**10**	2019:	*Olympiacos SFP Peiraiás*
Konstantinos TSIMIKAS	12.05.1996	**3**	**0**	2019:	*Olympiacos SFP Peiraiás*
Midfielders					
Andreas BOUCHALAKIS	05.04.1993	**10**	**0**	2019:	*Olympiacos SFP Peiraiás*
Ioannis FETFATZIDIS	21.12.1990	**27**	**3**	2019:	*Aris Thessaloníki*
Konstantinos GALANOPOULOS	28.12.1997	**4**	**1**	2019:	*AEK Athína*
Dimitrios KOLOVOS	27.04.1993	**9**	**1**	2019:	*PAE Panathinaïkos Athína*
Dimitrios KOURBELIS	02.11.1993	**16**	**1**	2019:	*PAE Panathinaïkos Athína*
Petros MANTALOS	31.08.1991	**27**	**3**	2019:	*AEK Athína*
Dimitrios PELKAS	26.10.1993	**15**	**0**	2019:	*PAOK Thessaloníki*
Andreas SAMARIS	13.06.1989	**39**	**1**	2019:	*Sport Lisboa e Benfica (POR)*
José Carlos Gonçalves Rodrigues "ZECA"	31.08.1988	**19**	**2**	2019:	*FC København (DEN)*
Forwards					
Anastasios BAKASETAS	28.06.1993	**25**	**0**	2019:	*Alanyaspor (TUR)*
Anastasios DONIS	29.08.1996	**11**	**1**	2019:	*Stade de Reims (FRA)*
Efthimis KOULOURIS	06.03.1996	**15**	**0**	2019:	*Toulouse FC (FRA)*
Dimitrios LIMNIOS	27.05.1998	**5**	**1**	2019:	*PAOK Thessaloníki*
Giorgos MASOURAS	01.01.1994	**11**	**1**	2019:	*Olympiacos SFP Peiraiás*
Vangelis PAVLIDIS	21.11.1998	**5**	**1**	2019:	*Willem II Tilburg (NED)*
Marios VROUSAI	02.07.1998	**2**	**0**	2019:	*Willem II Tilburg (NED)*

National team coach

Johannes Nicolaas "John" van 't SCHIP (Netherlands)   30.12.1963   6 M; 3 W; 1 D; 2 L; 6-6
[from 31.07.2019]

HUNGARY

The Country:
Magyarország (Hungary)
Capital: Budapest
Surface: 93,030 km²
Inhabitants: 9,772,756 [2019]
Time: UTC+1

The FA:
Magyar Labdarúgó Szövetség
1112 Budapest, Kánai út 2.D
Tel: +36 1 577 9500
Foundation date: 00.00.1900
Member of FIFA since: 1901
Member of UEFA since: 1954
Website: www.mlsz.hu

NATIONAL TEAM RECORDS

RECORDS

First international match:	12.10.1902, Wien: Austria – Hungary 5-0	
Most international caps:	Gábor Király	- 108 caps (1998-2016)
	Balázs Dzsudzsák	- 108 caps (since 2007)
Most international goals:	Ferenc Puskás	- 84 goals / 85 caps (1945-1956)

UEFA EUROPEAN CHAMPIONSHIP		FIFA WORLD CUP		OLYMPIC TOURNAMENTS	
1960	Qualifiers	1930	Did not enter	1908	Did not enter
1964	Final Tournament (3rd Place)	1934	Final Tournament (Quarter-Finals)	1912	Quarter-Finals
1968	Qualifiers	1938	Final Tournament (Runners-up)	1920	Did not enter
1972	Final Tournament (4th Place)	1950	Did not enter	1924	1/8-Finals
1976	Qualifiers	1954	Final Tournament (Runners-up)	1928	Did not enter
1980	Qualifiers	1958	Final Tournament (Group Stage)	1936	1/8-Finals
1984	Qualifiers	1962	Final Tournament (Quarter-Finals)	1948	Did not enter
1988	Qualifiers	1966	Final Tournament (Quarter-Finals)	1952	**Winners**
1992	Qualifiers	1970	Qualifiers	1956	Did not enter
1996	Qualifiers	1974	Qualifiers	1960	3rd Place
2000	Qualifiers	1978	Final Tournament (Group Stage)	1964	**Winners**
2004	Qualifiers	1982	Final Tournament (Group Stage)	1968	**Winners**
2008	Qualifiers	1986	Final Tournament (Group Stage)	1972	Runners-up
2012	Qualifiers	1990	Qualifiers	1976	Qualifiers
2016	Final Tournament (2nd Round of 16)	1994	Qualifiers	1980	Qualifiers
2020	*To be determined*	1998	Qualifiers	1984	Qualifiers
		2002	Qualifiers	1988	Qualifiers
		2006	Qualifiers	1992	Qualifiers
		2010	Qualifiers	1996	Group Stage
		2014	Qualifiers	2000	Qualifiers
		2018	Qualifiers	2004	Qualifiers
				2008	Qualifiers
				2012	Qualifiers
				2016	Qualifiers

UEFA NATIONS LEAGUE
2018/2019 – League C (promoted to League B)

FIFA CONFEDERATIONS CUP 1992-2017
None

HUNGARIAN CLUB HONOURS IN EUROPEAN CLUB COMPETITIONS:

European Champion Clubs' Cup (1956-1992) / UEFA Champions League (1993-2020)		
None		
Fairs Cup (1858-1971) / UEFA Cup (1972-2009) / UEFA Europa League (2010-2020)		
Ferencvárosi TC	1	1964/1965
UEFA Super Cup (1972-2019)		
None		
European Cup Winners' Cup 1961-1999*		
None		

*defunct competition

NATIONAL COMPETITIONS
TABLE OF HONOURS

	CHAMPIONS	CUP WINNERS	BEST GOALSCORERS	
1901	Budapesti Torna Club	-	Miltiades Manno (Budapesti Torna Club)	17
1902	Budapesti Torna Club	-	Miltiades Manno (Budapesti Torna Club)	10
1903	Ferencvárosi TC	-	Jenő Károly (MTK Budapest)	15
1904	MTK Budapest	-	József Pokorny (Ferencvárosi TC)	12
1905	Ferencvárosi TC	-	Jenő Károly (MTK Budapest)	13
1906/1907	Ferencvárosi TC	-	Béla Kelemen (Magyar Atlétikai Club)	21
1907/1908	MTK Budapest	-	Gyula Vangel (Magyar Atlétikai Club)	21
1908/1909	Ferencvárosi TC	-	Imre Schlosser (Ferencvárosi TC)	30
1909/1910	Ferencvárosi TC	MTK Budapest	Imre Schlosser (Ferencvárosi TC)	18
1910/1911	Ferencvárosi TC	MTK Budapest	Imre Schlosser (Ferencvárosi TC)	38
1911/1912	Ferencvárosi TC	MTK Budapest	Imre Schlosser (Ferencvárosi TC)	34
1912/1913	Ferencvárosi TC	Ferencvárosi TC	Imre Schlosser (Ferencvárosi TC)	33
1913/1914	MTK Budapest	MTK Budapest	Imre Schlosser (Ferencvárosi TC)	21
1914/1915	*No competition*	*No competition*	-	
1915/1916	*No competition*	*No competition*		
1916/1917	MTK Budapest	*No competition*	Imre Schlosser (MTK Budapest)	38
1917/1918	MTK Budapest	*No competition*	Alfréd Schaffer (MTK Budapest)	46
1918/1919	MTK Budapest	*No competition*	Alfréd Schaffer (MTK Budapest)	41
1919/1920	MTK Budapest	*No competition*	György Orth (MTK Budapest)	28
1920/1921	MTK Budapest	*No competition*	György Orth (MTK Budapest)	21
1921/1922	MTK Budapest	Ferencvárosi TC	György Orth (MTK Budapest)	26
1922/1923	MTK Budapest	MTK Budapest	István Priboj (Újpesti TE)	25
1923/1924	MTK Budapest	*No competition*	József Jeszmás (Újpesti TE)	15
1924/1925	MTK Budapest	MTK Budapest	György Molnár (MTK Budapest)	21
1925/1926	Ferencvárosi TC	Kispest AC	József Takács (Vasas SC Budapest)	29
1926/1927	Ferencvárosi TC	Ferencvárosi TC	László Horváth (Ferencvárosi TC)	14
1927/1928	Ferencvárosi TC	Ferencvárosi TC	József Takács (Ferencvárosi TC)	31
1928/1929	Hungária MTK FC Budapest	*No competition*	József Takács (Ferencvárosi TC)	41
1929/1930	Újpesti TE	Debreceni Bocskai FC	József Takács (Ferencvárosi TC)	40
1930/1931	Újpesti TE	III. Kerületi TVE	Jenő Vincze (Debreceni Bocskai FC)	20
1931/1932	Ferencvárosi TC	Hungária MTK FC Budapest	József Takács (Ferencvárosi TC)	42
1932/1933	Újpesti TE	Ferencvárosi TC	Pál Jávor (Újpesti TE)	31
1933/1934	Ferencvárosi TC	Soroksár FC	Géza Toldi (Ferencvárosi TC)	27
1934/1935	Újpesti TE	Ferencvárosi TC	László Cseh II (MTK Budapest)	23
1935/1936	Hungária MTK FC Budapest	*No competition*	György Sárosi dr. (Ferencvárosi TC)	36
1936/1937	Hungária MTK FC Budapest	*No competition*	László Cseh II (MTK Budapest)	36
1937/1938	Ferencvárosi TC	*No competition*	Gyula Zsengellér (Újpesti TE)	31
1938/1939	Újpesti TE	*No competition*	Gyula Zsengellér (Újpesti TE)	56
1939/1940	Ferencvárosi TC	*No competition*	György Sárosi dr. (Ferencvárosi TC)	23
1940/1941	Ferencvárosi TC	Szolnoki MÁV SE	György Sárosi dr. (Ferencvárosi TC)	29
1941/1942	Csepel SC Budapest	Ferencvárosi TC	György Kalmár (Szegedi AK)	35
1942/1943	Csepel SC Budapest	Ferencvárosi TC	Gyula Zsengellér (Újpesti TE) Jenő Jenőfi (Vasas SC Budapest)	26
1943/1944	Nagyváradi AC	Ferencvárosi TC	Gyula Zsengellér (Újpesti TE)	33
1945	Újpesti TE	*No competition*	Gyula Zsengellér (Újpesti TE)	36
1945/1946	Újpesti TE	*No competition*	Ferenc Deák (Szentlőrinci AC)	66
1946/1947	Újpesti TE	*No competition*	Ferenc Deák (Szentlőrinci AC)	48
1947/1948	Csepel SC Budapest	*No competition*	Ferenc Puskás (Budapest Honvéd SE)	50
1948/1949	Ferencvárosi TC	*No competition*	Ferenc Deák (Ferencvárosi TC)	59
1949/1950	Budapest Honvéd SE	*No competition*	Ferenc Puskás (Budapest Honvéd SE)	31
1950	Budapest Honvéd SE	*No competition*	Ferenc Puskás (Budapest Honvéd SE)	25
1951	Budapesti Textiles SE	*No competition*	Sándor Kocsis (Budapest Honvéd SE)	30
1952	Budapest Honvéd SE	Budapesti Bástya SE	Sándor Kocsis (Budapest Honvéd SE)	36
1953	Budapesti Vörös Lobogó SE	*No competition*	Ferenc Puskás (Budapest Honvéd SE)	27
1954	Budapest Honvéd SE	*No competition*	Sándor Kocsis (Budapest Honvéd SE)	33
1955	Budapest Honvéd SE	Vasas SC Budapest	Zoltán Czibor (Budapest Honvéd SE) Ferenc Machos (Budapest Honvéd SE)	20
1956	*No competition*	*No competition*	-	
1957	Vasas SC Budapest	*No competition*	Gyula Szilágyi (Vasas SC Budapest)	17
1957/1958	MTK Budapest	Ferencvárosi TC	Zoltán Friedmanszky (Ferencvárosi TC) János Molnár (MTK Budapest)	16
1958/1959	Csepel SC Budapest	*No competition*	Róbert Kisuczky (Csepel) Tivadar Monostori (Dorog) Lajos Tichy (Honvéd)	15
1959/1960	Újpesti Dózsa SC	*No competition*	Flórián Albert (Ferencvárosi TC)	27
1960/1961	Vasas SC Budapest	*No competition*	Flórián Albert (Ferencvárosi TC) Lajos Tichy (Budapest Honvéd SE)	21
1961/1962	Vasas SC Budapest	*No competition*	Lajos Tichy (Budapest Honvéd SE)	23
1962/1963	Ferencvárosi TC	*No competition*	Ferenc Bene (Újpesti Dózsa SC)	23
1963	Győri Vasas ETO	*No competition*	Lajos Tichy (Budapest Honvéd SE)	13
1964	Ferencvárosi TC	Budapest Honvéd SE	Lajos Tichy (Budapest Honvéd SE)	28

Year	Champions	Cup Winners	Top Scorer	Goals
1965	Vasas SC Budapest	Rába Vasas ETO Győr	Flórián Albert (Ferencvárosi TC)	27
1966	Vasas SC Budapest	Rába Vasas ETO Győr	János Farkas (Vasas SC Budapest)	25
1967	Ferencvárosi TC	Rába Vasas ETO Győr	Antal Dunai II (Újpesti Dózsa SC)	36
1968	Ferencvárosi TC	MTK Budapest	Antal Dunai II (Újpesti Dózsa SC)	31
1969	Újpesti Dózsa SC	Újpesti Dózsa SC	Ferenc Bene (Újpesti Dózsa SC)	27
1970	Újpesti Dózsa SC	Újpesti Dózsa SC	Antal Dunai II (Újpesti Dózsa SC)	14
1970/1971	Újpesti Dózsa SC	*No competition*	Mihály Kozma (Budapest Honvéd SE)	25
1971/1972	Újpesti Dózsa SC	Ferencvárosi TC	Ferenc Bene (Újpesti Dózsa SC)	29
1972/1973	Újpesti Dózsa SC	Vasas Budapest SC	Ferenc Bene (Újpesti Dózsa SC)	23
1973/1974	Újpesti Dózsa SC	Ferencvárosi TC	Mihály Kozma (Budapest Honvéd SE)	27
1974/1975	Újpesti Dózsa SC	Újpesti Dózsa SC	Mihály Kozma (Budapest Honvéd SE) Ferenc Bene (Újpesti Dózsa SC)	20
1975/1976	Ferencvárosi TC	Ferencvárosi TC	László Fazekas (Újpesti Dózsa SC)	19
1976/1977	Vasas SC Budapest	Diósgyőri VTK	Béla Várady (Vasas SC Budapest)	36
1977/1978	Újpesti Dózsa SC	Ferencvárosi TC	László Fazekas (Újpesti Dózsa SC)	24
1978/1979	Újpesti Dózsa SC	Rába Vasas ETO Győr	László Fekete (Újpesti Dózsa SC)	31
1979/1980	Budapest Honvéd SE	Diósgyőri VTK	László Fekete (Újpesti Dózsa SC)	36
1980/1981	Ferencvárosi TC	Vasas Budapest SC	Tibor Nyilasi (Ferencvárosi TC)	30
1981/1982	Rába Vasas ETO Győr	Újpesti Dózsa SC	Péter Hannich (Rába Vasas ETO Győr)	22
1982/1983	Rába Vasas ETO Győr	Újpesti Dózsa SC	Lajos Dobány (Pécsi MSC / Szombathely)	23
1983/1984	Budapest Honvéd SE	Siófoki Bányász SK	József Szabó (Videoton SC Székesfehérvár)	19
1984/1985	Budapest Honvéd SE	Budapest Honvéd SE	Lajos Détári (Budapest Honvéd SE) József Kiprich (Tatabányai Bányász)	18
1985/1986	Budapest Honvéd SE	Vasas Budapest SC	Lajos Détári (Budapest Honvéd SE)	27
1986/1987	MTK-VM Budapest	Újpesti Dózsa SC	Lajos Détári (Budapest Honvéd SE)	19
1987/1988	Budapest Honvéd SE	Békéscsabai Előre SSC	Béla Melis (Debreceni VSC)	19
1988/1989	Budapest Honvéd SE	Budapest Honvéd SE	Tamás Petres (Videoton SC Székesfehérvár)	19
1989/1990	Újpesti TE	Pécsi MSC	József Dzurják (Ferencvárosi TC)	18
1990/1991	Budapest Honvéd SE	Ferencvárosi TC	József Gregor (Budapest Honvéd SE)	19
1991/1992	Ferencvárosi TC	Újpesti TE	Pál Fischer (Siófoki Bányász SK) Ferenc Orosz (Vác FC)	16
1992/1993	Kispest Honvéd FC	Ferencvárosi TC	László Répási (Vác FC)	16
1993/1994	Vác FC	Ferencvárosi TC	Béla Illés (Kispest Honvéd FC)	17
1994/1995	Ferencvárosi TC	Ferencvárosi TC	Sándor Preisinger (Zalaegerszeg)	21
1995/1996	Ferencvárosi TC	Kispest Honvéd FC	Ihor Nichenko (UKR, Stadler FC / Ferencvárosi TC)	18
1996/1997	MTK Budapest FC	MTK Budapest FC	Béla Illés (MTK Budapest FC)	23
1997/1998	Újpesti TE	MTK Budapest FC	Krisztián Tiber (Gázszer FC Gárdony)	20
1998/1999	MTK Hungária FC Budapest	Debreceni VSC	Béla Illés (MTK Hungária FC Budapest)	22
1999/2000	Dunaferr SE Dunaújváros	MTK Hungária FC Budapest	Attila Tököli (Dunaferr SE Dunaújváros)	22
2000/2001	Ferencvárosi TC	Debreceni VSC	Péter Kabát (Vasas SC Budapest)	24
2001/2002	Zalaegerszegi TE FC	Újpesti TE	Attila Tököli (Dunaferr SE Dunaújváros)	28
2002/2003	MTK Hungária FC Budapest	Ferencvárosi TC	Krisztián Kenesei (Zalaegerszegi TE FC)	23
2003/2004	Ferencvárosi TC	Ferencvárosi TC	Mihály Tóth (Soproni VSE)	17
2004/2005	Debreceni VSC	Sopron FC	Tomáš Medveď (SVK, Pápai FC)	18
2005/2006	Debreceni VSC	FC Fehérvár Székesfehérvár	Péter Rajczi (Újpest FC)	23
2006/2007	Debreceni VSC	Budapest Honvéd FC	Ibrahim Sidibe (SEN, Debreceni VSC) Péter Bajzát (Győri ETO FC)	18
2007/2008	MTK Budapest FC	Debreceni VSC	Róbert Waltner (Zalaegerszegi TE FC)	18
2008/2009	Debreceni VSC	Budapest Honvéd FC	Péter Bajzát (Győri ETO FC)	20
2009/2010	Debreceni VSC	Debreceni VSC	Nemanja Nikolić (SRB, Videoton FC Székesfehérvár)	18
2010/2011	Videoton FC Székesfehérvár	Kecskeméti TE	André Alves dos Santos (BRA, Videoton FC Székesfehérvár)	24
2011/2012	Debreceni VSC	Debreceni VSC	Adamo Coulibaly (FRA, Debreceni VSC)	20
2012/2013	Győri ETO FC	Debreceni VSC	Adamo Coulibaly (FRA, Debreceni VSC)	18
2013/2014	Debreceni VSC	Újpest FC	Nemanja Nikolić (Videoton FC Székesfehérvár) Attila Simon (Paksi FC)	21
2014/2015	Videoton FC Székesfehérvár	Ferencvárosi TC	Nemanja Nikolić (Videoton FC Székesfehérvár)	21
2015/2016	Ferencvárosi TC	Ferencvárosi TC	Dániel Böde (Ferencvárosi TC)	17
2016/2017	Budapest Honvéd FC	Ferencvárosi TC	Márton Eppel (Budapest Honvéd FC)	16
2017/2018	Videoton FC Székesfehérvár	Újpest FC	Davide Lanzafame (ITA, Budapest Honvéd FC)	18
2018/2019	Ferencvárosi TC	MOL Vidi FC Székesfehérvár	Davide Lanzafame (ITA, Budapest Honvéd FC) Filip Holender (Budapest Honvéd FC)	16
2019/2020	Ferencvárosi TC	Budapest Honvéd FC	András Radó (Zalaegerszegi TE FC)	13

NATIONAL CHAMPIONSHIP
Nemzeti Bajnokság I 2019/2020
(03.08.2019 – 27.06.2020)

Results

Round 1 [03-04.08.2019]
Mezőkövesd - Zalaegerszeg 1-0(1-0)
Kisvárda FC - Paksi FC 1-0(0-0)
Újpest FC - Puskás Akadémia 1-3(0-2)
Diósgyőri VTK - Budapest Honvéd 2-1(1-1)
Fehérvár FC - Kaposvár 4-2(3-2)
Ferencváros - Debrecen 2-1(2-1) [23.05.2020]

Round 2 [10-11.08.2019]
Kaposvár - Mezőkövesd 1-2(1-2)
Diósgyőri VTK - Újpest FC 1-2(1-1)
Paksi FC - Budapest Honvéd 3-1(2-0)
Debreceni VSC - Kisvárda FC 4-1(2-1)
Puskás Akadémia - Fehérvár FC 0-2(0-0)
Zalaegerszeg - Ferencváros 1-2(1-0) [22.09.]

Round 3 [17.08.2019]
Debreceni VSC - Zalaegerszeg 3-2(2-1)
Újpest FC - Paksi FC 1-1(0-0)
Ferencvárosi TC - Kaposvár 1-0(1-0)
Fehérvár FC - Diósgyőri VTK 5-1(1-1)
Mezőkövesd - Puskás Akadémia 1-0(0-0)
Budapest Honvéd - Kisvárda FC 1-3(0-1)

Round 4 [24-25.08.2019]
Kaposvár - Zalaegerszeg 0-4(0-2)
Budapest Honvéd - Debreceni VSC 2-3(1-1)
Diósgyőri VTK - Mezőkövesd 0-3(0-0)
Kisvárda FC - Újpest FC 2-0(1-0)
Paksi FC - Fehérvár FC 0-2(0-1)
Puskás Akadémia - Ferencvárosi TC 4-1(1-1)

Round 5 [31.08.-01.09.2019]
Zalaegerszeg - Puskás Akadémia 1-1(1-1)
Mezőkövesd - Paksi FC 0-2(0-1)
Újpest FC - Budapest Honvéd 2-3(1-3)
Fehérvár FC - Kisvárda FC 3-0(1-0)
Debreceni VSC - Kaposvár 0-1(0-1)
Ferencvárosi TC - Diósgyőri VTK 1-0(1-0)

Round 6 [14.09.2019]
Diósgyőri VTK - Zalaegerszeg 1-0(1-0)
Kisvárda FC - Mezőkövesd 1-2(0-1)
Újpest FC - Debreceni VSC 3-2(0-1)
Puskás Akadémia - Kaposvár 2-0(0-0)
Budapest Honvéd - Fehérvár FC 0-1(0-0)
Paksi FC - Ferencvárosi TC 0-4(0-3)

Round 7 [28-29.09.2019]
Kaposvár - Diósgyőri VTK 2-0(1-0)
Mezőkövesd - Budapest Honvéd 1-2(0-1)
Zalaegerszeg - Paksi FC 3-1(2-1)
Debreceni VSC - Puskás Akadémia 1-2(0-2)
Fehérvár FC - Újpest FC 0-2(0-0)
Ferencvárosi TC - Kisvárda FC 1-0(0-0)

Round 8 [05-06.10.2019]
Újpest FC - Mezőkövesd 1-2(0-1)
Paksi FC - Kaposvár 2-1(0-1)
Kisvárda FC - Zalaegerszeg 3-3(0-2)
Diósgyőri VTK - Puskás Akadémia 1-1(0-0)
Fehérvár FC - Debreceni VSC 2-1(1-1)
Budapest Honvéd - Ferencvárosi TC 0-0

Round 9 [19.10.2019]
Kaposvár - Kisvárda FC 0-2(0-1)
Debreceni VSC - Diósgyőri VTK 2-1(1-0)
Puskás Akadémia - Paksi FC 4-2(2-1)
Mezőkövesd - Fehérvár FC 0-0
Zalaegerszeg - Budapest Honvéd 0-1(0-0)
Ferencvárosi TC - Újpest FC 1-0(1-0)

Round 10 [26-27.10.2019]
Mezőkövesd - Debreceni VSC 3-1(1-0)
Kisvárda FC - Puskás Akadémia 0-1(0-0)
Újpest FC - Zalaegerszeg 0-0
Paksi FC - Diósgyőri VTK 1-2(0-1)
Budapest Honvéd - Kaposvár 2-0(2-0)
Fehérvár FC - Ferencvárosi TC 1-2(0-1)

Round 11 [02.11.2019]
Puskás Akadémia - Budapest Honvéd 1-2(1-1)
Diósgyőri VTK - Kisvárda FC 3-1(1-0)
Kaposvár - Újpest FC 2-3(1-2)
Ferencvárosi TC - Mezőkövesd 1-1(1-0)
Zalaegerszeg - Fehérvár FC 3-3(2-0)
Debreceni VSC - Paksi FC 3-1(2-0)

Round 12 [09-10.11.2019]
Puskás Akadémia - Újpest FC 1-3(1-2)
Zalaegerszeg - Mezőkövesd 1-1(0-1)
Kaposvár - Fehérvár FC 0-2(0-1)
Paksi FC - Kisvárda FC 1-1(0-0)
Budapest Honvéd - Diósgyőri VTK 1-0(1-0)
Debreceni VSC - Ferencvárosi TC 1-6(0-2)

Round 13 [23-24.11.2019]
Mezőkövesd - Kaposvár 2-0(1-0)
Fehérvár FC - Puskás Akadémia 1-3(0-2)
Kisvárda FC - Debreceni VSC 1-0(1-0)
Budapest Honvéd - Paksi FC 2-1(0-0)
Újpest FC - Diósgyőri VTK 0-2(0-2)
Ferencvárosi TC - Zalaegerszeg 3-2(3-1)

Round 14 [30.11.-01.12.2019]
Zalaegerszeg - Debreceni VSC 0-2(0-1)
Puskás Akadémia - Mezőkövesd 1-1(1-0)
Paksi FC - Újpest FC 2-4(0-1)
Kisvárda FC - Budapest Honvéd 2-0(1-0)
Diósgyőri VTK - Fehérvár FC 1-3(1-2)
Kaposvár - Ferencvárosi TC 2-3(1-2)

Round 15 [07-08.12.2019]
Mezőkövesd - Diósgyőri VTK 0-1(0-0)
Újpest FC - Kisvárda FC 1-0(1-0)
Zalaegerszeg - Kaposvár 2-0(2-0)
Debreceni VSC - Budapest Honvéd 1-1(0-1)
Fehérvár FC - Paksi FC 0-2(0-0)
Ferencvárosi TC - Puskás Akadémia 2-2(2-0)

Round 16 [14-15.12.2019]
Kisvárda FC - Fehérvár FC 0-2(0-1)
Paksi FC - Mezőkövesd 1-0(1-0)
Kaposvár - Debreceni VSC 4-1(2-0)
Puskás Akadémia - Zalaegerszeg 0-1(0-0)
Budapest Honvéd - Újpest FC 0-0
Diósgyőri VTK - Ferencvárosi TC 0-1(0-1)

Round 17 [25.01.2020]
Ferencvárosi TC - Paksi FC 4-0(2-0)
Fehérvár FC - Budapest Honvéd 0-0
Zalaegerszeg - Diósgyőri VTK 1-3(0-0)
Kaposvár - Puskás Akadémia 1-1(1-1)
Mezőkövesd - Kisvárda FC 1-0(1-0)
Debreceni VSC - Újpest FC 4-0(0-0)

Round 18 [01.02.2020]
Puskás Akadémia - Debreceni VSC 0-0
Diósgyőri VTK - Kaposvár 2-0(2-0)
Budapest Honvéd - Mezőkövesd 1-2(1-1)
Paksi FC - Zalaegerszeg 2-0(1-0)
Kisvárda FC - Ferencvárosi TC 1-2(1-1)
Újpest FC - Fehérvár FC 0-1(0-0)

Round 19 [04-05.02.2020]
Mezőkövesd - Újpest FC 2-2(0-1)
Zalaegerszeg - Kisvárda FC 1-1(0-1)
Kaposvár - Paksi FC 0-3(0-2)
Puskás Akadémia - Diósgyőri VTK 2-2(0-0)
Debreceni VSC - Fehérvár FC 1-1(0-1)
Ferencvárosi TC - Budapest Honvéd 0-0

Round 20 [08.02.2020]
Budapest Honvéd - Zalaegerszeg 2-0(1-0)
Diósgyőri VTK - Debreceni VSC 1-2(1-2)
Fehérvár FC - Mezőkövesd 2-1(2-1)
Kisvárda FC - Kaposvár 5-3(1-1)
Paksi FC - Puskás Akadémia 0-2(0-1)
Újpest FC - Ferencvárosi TC 0-1(0-1) [27.05.]

Round 21 [15.02.2020]
Puskás Akadémia - Kisvárda FC 3-1(1-0)
Kaposvár - Budapest Honvéd 0-1(0-1)
Zalaegerszeg - Újpest FC 2-1(1-1)
Diósgyőri VTK - Paksi FC 2-0(1-0)
Debreceni VSC - Mezőkövesd 1-3(0-2)
Ferencvárosi TC - Fehérvár FC 1-0(0-0)

Round 22 [22.02.2020]
Paksi FC - Debreceni VSC 4-2(2-1)
Kisvárda FC - Diósgyőri VTK 2-2(1-0)
Budapest Honvéd - Puskás Akadémia 1-1(0-0)
Fehérvár FC - Zalaegerszeg 4-1(1-0)
Újpest FC - Kaposvár 1-0(1-0)
Mezőkövesd - Ferencvárosi TC 3-0(3-0)

Round 23 [29.02.2020]
Budapest Honvéd - Diósgyőri VTK 0-4(0-0)
Mezőkövesd - Zalaegerszeg 1-2(0-1)
Fehérvár FC - Kaposvár 3-0(3-0)
Kisvárda FC - Paksi FC 2-0(0-0)
Újpest FC - Puskás Akadémia 2-3(1-2)
Ferencvárosi TC - Debreceni VSC 2-0(2-0)

Round 24 [07.03.2020]
Kaposvár - Mezőkövesd 0-4(0-1)
Puskás Akadémia - Fehérvár FC 1-4(1-0)
Diósgyőri VTK - Újpest FC 2-1(1-0)
Paksi FC - Budapest Honvéd 0-0
Debreceni VSC - Kisvárda FC 1-0(0-0)
Zalaegerszeg - Ferencvárosi TC 1-1(0-1)

Round 25 [14.03.2020]
Debreceni VSC - Zalaegerszeg 0-3(0-2)
Budapest Honvéd - Kisvárda FC 1-5(0-2)
Újpest FC - Paksi FC 1-1(0-0)
Mezőkövesd - Puskás Akadémia 0-0
Ferencvárosi TC - Kaposvár 5-0(1-0)
Fehérvár FC - Diósgyőri VTK 1-1(0-0)

Round 26 [29-31.05.2020]
Kaposvár - Zalaegerszeg 0-6(0-5)
Kisvárda FC - Újpest FC 1-0(0-0)
Diósgyőri VTK - Mezőkövesd 1-0(0-0)
Paksi FC - Fehérvár FC 0-0
Budapest Honvéd - Debreceni VSC 3-1(1-0)
Puskás Akadémia - Ferencvárosi TC 1-1(1-1)

Round 27 [05-07.06.2020]
Debreceni VSC - Kaposvár 1-1(1-0)
Mezőkövesd - Paksi FC 0-2(0-0)
Fehérvár FC - Kisvárda FC 2-0(1-0)
Újpest FC - Budapest Honvéd 1-0(1-0)
Zalaegerszeg - Puskás Akadémia 2-0(0-0)
Ferencvárosi TC - Diósgyőri VTK 3-0(0-0)

Round 28 [09-10.06.2020]
Kisvárda FC - Mezõkövesd 1-1(1-1)
Újpest FC - Debreceni VSC 3-1(1-0)
Budapest Honvéd - Fehérvár FC 1-1(0-1)
Diósgyõri VTK - Zalaegerszeg 1-1(0-0)
Puskás Akadémia - Kaposvár 2-1(1-1)
Paksi FC - Ferencvárosi TC 2-2(0-0)

Round 29 [12-14.06.2020]
Mezõkövesd - Budapest Honvéd 1-2(0-2)
Ferencvárosi TC - Kisvárda FC 1-0(0-0)
Debreceni VSC - Puskás Akadémia 2-2(1-1)
Zalaegerszeg - Paksi FC 3-3(1-1)
Kaposvár - Diósgyõri VTK 3-0(1-0)
Fehérvár FC - Újpest FC 2-2(1-0)

Round 30 [16-17.06.2020]
Kisvárda FC - Zalaegerszeg 0-1(0-0)
Budapest Honvéd - Ferencvárosi TC 0-2(0-0)
Paksi FC - Kaposvár 3-0(2-0)
Diósgyõri VTK - Puskás Akadémia 1-2(1-1)
Fehérvár FC - Debreceni VSC 1-0(0-0)
Újpest FC - Mezõkövesd 1-1(0-0)

Round 31 [19-21.06.2020]
Zalaegerszeg - Budapest Honvéd 2-0(0-0)
Mezõkövesd - Fehérvár FC 2-1(1-1)
Puskás Akadémia - Paksi FC 3-1(2-0)
Ferencvárosi TC - Újpest FC 1-0(0-0)
Kaposvár - Kisvárda FC 1-2(1-2)
Debreceni VSC - Diósgyõri VTK 4-0(3-0)

Round 32 [23-24.06.2020]
Fehérvár FC - Ferencvárosi TC 1-0(1-0)
Újpest FC - Zalaegerszeg 2-1(1-0)
Mezõkövesd - Debreceni VSC 0-1(0-0)
Kisvárda FC - Puskás Akadémia 1-1(0-0)
Budapest Honvéd - Kaposvár 4-2(1-0)
Paksi FC - Diósgyõri VTK 4-2(1-0)

Round 33 [27.06.2020]
Zalaegerszeg - Fehérvár FC 1-1(0-1)
Újpest FC - Kaposvár 5-0(3-0)
Diósgyõri VTK - Kisvárda FC 0-2(0-2)
Debreceni VSC - Paksi FC 1-1(0-1)
Puskás Akadémia - Budapest Honvéd 2-1(1-1)
Ferencvárosi TC - Mezõkövesd 1-0(1-0)

Final Standings

									Home				Away		
				Total												
1.	**Ferencvárosi TC**	33	23	7	3	58 - 24	76	14	3	0	30 - 6	9	4	3	28 - 18
2.	Fehérvár FC Székesfehérvár	33	18	9	6	56 - 29	63	10	3	4	32 - 18	8	6	2	24 - 11
3.	Puskás Ferenc Labdarugó Akadémia Felcsút	33	14	12	7	52 - 41	54	7	4	5	27 - 23	7	8	2	25 - 18
4.	Mezõkövesdi SE	33	14	8	11	42 - 31	50	7	3	7	18 - 16	7	5	4	24 - 15
5.	Budapest Honvéd FC	33	12	8	13	36 - 44	44	6	4	7	21 - 26	6	4	6	15 - 18
6.	Újpest FC	33	12	7	14	45 - 45	43	6	4	7	24 - 22	6	3	7	21 - 23
7.	Zalaegerszegi TE FC	33	11	10	12	51 - 44	43	5	7	4	24 - 21	6	3	8	27 - 23
8.	Kisvárda FC	33	12	6	15	42 - 43	42	7	4	5	23 - 18	5	2	10	19 - 25
9.	Diósgyõri VTK	33	12	5	16	40 - 52	41	7	2	7	19 - 20	5	3	9	21 - 32
10.	Paksi FC	33	11	8	14	46 - 53	41	7	4	5	25 - 23	4	4	9	21 - 30
11.	Debreceni VSC (*Relegated*)	33	11	6	16	48 - 57	39	7	5	5	30 - 26	4	1	11	18 - 31
12.	Kaposvári Rákóczi FC (*Relegated*)	33	4	2	27	27 - 80	14	3	1	12	16 - 35	1	1	15	11 - 45

Please <u>note</u>: MOL Vidi FC Székesfehérvár changed its name to Fehérvár FC Székesfehérvár.

Top goalscorers:

13	**András Radó**	*Zalaegerszegi TE FC*
11	Norbert Könyves	*Paksi FC*
11	Davide Lanzafame (ITA)	*Budapest Honvéd FC*
11	David Vaněček (CZE)	*Puskás Ferenc Labdarugó Akadémia Felcsút*
10	Gergely Bobál	*Zalaegerszegi TE FC*
10	Bi Sylvestre Franck Fortune Boli	*Ferencvárosi TC*
10	Armin Hodžić (BIH)	*Fehérvár FC Székesfehérvár*

NATIONAL CUP
Magyar Kupa 2019/2020

Seventh Round [29-30.10.2019]

FC Ajka - Újpest FC	2-5	Mosonmagyaróvári TE - Tállya KSE	4-1
Kozármisleny SE - Kisvárda FC	1-2	Sárbogárd SE - Vác FC	1-3
Budaörsi SC - Zalaegerszegi TE FC	3-7	Vép VSE - Szeged 2011 FC	1-4
Kazincbarcikai SC - Budapest Honvéd FC	0-2 aet	Szegedi VSE - Ózdi FC	2-4
Sényő FC - Mezőkövesdi SE	1-2	Ménfőcsanak ESK - Szombathelyi Haladás	0-2
BKV Előre SC Budapest - Ferencvárosi TC	1-3	III. Kerületi TVE - Nyíregyháza Spartacus FC	5-0
Dabas FC - Diósgyőri VTK	0-3	Balatoni Vasas SE - Dabas-Gyón FC	0-4
Maglódi TC - Puskás Ferenc Labdarugó Akadémia	0-15	Füzesgyarmati SK - Békéscsaba 1912 Előre SE	0-1
FC Tiszaújváros - Fehérvár FC Székesfehérvár	0-3	Pécsi MFC - Rákosmenti KSK	2-0
Salgótarjani BTC - Paksi SE	1-7	FC Tatabánya - Debreceni VSC	0-2
Debreceni EAC - MTK Budapest FC	0-3	Tiszakécske FC - Kaposvári RFC	0-1
Tamási 2009 FC - Monori SE	0-2	SC Sopron - Budafoki MTE	1-2 pen
ASR Gázgyár - Győri ETO FC	1-4	Pálhalma SE - Nagykanizsai ULE	2-1 aet
Nagybajomi AC - Dorogi FC	0-5	Gyirmót SE - Soroksár SC	3-0
Berettyóújfalui SE - Bodajk FC Siófok	0-4	Kecskeméti TE - Lipót Pékség SE	0-1
Szarvasi FC - Balkányi SE	2-1	Pápai PFC - Vasas FC Budapest	3-4 aet

Eighth Round [03-04/11/31.12.2019]

MTK Budapest FC - Diósgyőri VTK	1-0 aet	III. Kerületi TVE - Vasas FC Budapest	2-1 aet
Szeged 2011 FC - Fehérvár FC Székesfehérvár	0-1 aet	Szombathelyi Haladás - Budafoki MTE	2-1
Monori SE - Budapest Honvéd FC	1-3	Győri ETO FC - Mezőkövesdi SE	2-3 aet
Pécsi MFC - Kisvárda FC	1-0	Pálhalma SE - Bodajk FC Siófok	2-1
Szarvasi FC - Zalaegerszegi TE FC	0-2	Békéscsaba 1912 Előre SE - Ferencvárosi TC	2 0
Dabas-Gyón FC - Puskás Ferenc Labdarugó Akad.	0-3	Vác FC - Újpest FC	0-3
Mosonmagyaróvári TE - Paksi SE	0-4	Dorogi FC - Debreceni VSC	5-4 pen
Lipót Pékség SE - Gyirmót SE	3-1 aet	Ózdi FC - Kaposvári RFC	*not played*

1/8-Finals [11/12-19.02.2020]

First Leg		Second Leg	
Újpest FC - Fehérvár FC Székesfehérvár	0-0	Fehérvár FC Székesfehérvár - Újpest FC	1-0(0-0)
Lipót Pékség SE - Zalaegerszegi TE FC	3-1(1-0)	Zalaegerszegi TE FC - Lipót Pékség SE	5-1(2-0)
Pécsi MFC - Paksi SE	1-2(1-0)	Paksi SE - Pécsi MFC	1-0(0-0)
Dorogi FC - III. Kerületi TVE	4-1(3-1)	III. Kerületi TVE - Dorogi FC	0-2(0-0)
Mezőkövesdi SE - Kaposvári RFC	2-1(0-0)	Kaposvári RFC - Mezőkövesdi SE	1-3(0-1)
Békéscsaba 1912 Előre SE - Puskás Ferenc La. Akad.	0-3(0-2)	Puskás Ferenc La.Akad. - Békéscsaba 1912 Előre SE	3-0(1-0)
MTK Budapest FC - Pálhalma SE	3-0(2-0)	Pálhalma SE - MTK Budapest FC	0-2(0-1)
Budapest Honvéd FC - Szombathelyi Haladás	1-0(0-0)	Szombathelyi Haladás - Budapest Honvéd FC	2-1(1-0,1-0)

Quarter-Finals [03/04-11.03.2020]

First Leg		Second Leg	
Puskás Ferenc Labdarugó Akad. - Mezőkövesdi SE	0-1(0-0)	Mezőkövesdi SE - Puskás Ferenc Labdarugó Akad.	1-1(0-0)
Dorogi FC - MTK Budapest FC	0-1(0-1)	MTK Budapest FC - Dorogi FC	3-0(2-0)
Paksi SE - Budapest Honvéd FC	0-0	Budapest Honvéd FC - Paksi SE	2-0(1-0)
Zalaegerszegi TE FC - Fehérvár FC Székesfehérvár	2-0(0-0)	Fehérvár FC Székesfehérvár - Zalaegerszegi TE FC	5-0(3-0)

Semi-Finals [23-26.05.2020]

First Leg		Second Leg	
Mezőkövesdi SE - Fehérvár FC Székesfehérvár	1-1(0-1)	Fehérvár FC Székesfehérvár - Mezőkövesdi SE	2-2(0-1)
MTK Budapest FC - Budapest Honvéd FC	0-0	Budapest Honvéd FC - MTK Budapest FC	0-0 aet; 5-4 pen

Final

03.06.2020; Puskás Aréna, Budapest; Referee: Tamás Bognár; Attendance: 10,000
Budapest Honvéd FC - Mezőkövesdi SE   **2-1(1-1)**

Budapest Honvéd: Tomáš Tujvel, Eke Uzoma, Bence Batik, Ivan Lovrić, Dániel Gazdag (85.Naser Aliji), Patrik Hidi, Đorđe Kamber, Patrick George Ikenne-King (85.Gergő Nagy). Davide Lanzafame (85.Mayron Antonio George Clayton), Roland Ugrai (79.Barna Kesztyűs), Norbert Szendrei. Trainer: István Pisont.

Mezőkövesd: Péter Szappanos, Gábor Eperjesi (70.Danijel Farkaš), Andriy Nesterov, Róbert Pillár, Erik Silye (70.Dániel Vadnai), Dino Beširović, László Pekár (79.Marin Jurina), Zsombor Berecz, Aleksandr Karnitskiy, Budu Zivzivadze, Tamás Cseri. Trainer: Attila Kuttor.

Goals: 1-0 Ivan Lovrić (33), 1-1 László Pekár (37), 2-1 Đorđe Kamber (56).

THE CLUBS 2019/2020

Debreceni Vasutas Sport Club

Founded:	12.03.1902		
Stadium:	Nagyerdei Stadion, Debrecen (20,340)		
Trainer:	András Herczeg	11.07.1956	
[30.12.2019]	Zoltán Vitelki	13.09.1970	
[07.06.2020]	Elemér Kondás	11.09.1963	

Goalkeepers:	DOB	M	(s)	G
Tomáš Košický (SVK)	11.03.1986	16	(1)	
Oleksandr Nad (UKR)	02.09.1985	17		
Defenders:	**DOB**	**M**	**(s)**	**G**
Szabolcs Barna	27.04.1996	1	(3)	
Csaba Belényesi	03.03.1994		(1)	
Balázs Bényei	10.01.1990	15	(4)	
Ákos Kinyik	12.05.1993	22	(4)	1
Bence Pávkovics	27.03.1997	28	(2)	1
Csaba Szatmári	14.06.1994	22	(1)	2
Midfielders:	**DOB**	**M**	**(s)**	**G**
Péter Baráth	21.02.2002	1	(6)	
Ádám Bódi	18.10.1990	15	(2)	3
Richárd Csősz	22.04.1997	9	(9)	
János Ferenczi	03.04.1991	32		
Yuriy Habovda (UKR)	06.05.1989	5	(1)	
Attila Haris	23.01.1997	23	(1)	1
Erik Kusnyír	07.02.2000	27	(2)	1
Bence Szabó	16.01.1998	2	(2)	1
Dániel Tőzsér	12.05.1985	21		2
Forwards:	**DOB**	**M**	**(s)**	**G**
Babatunde Temitope Adeniji (NGA)	17.09.1995	18	(11)	9
Dániel Bereczki	02.06.1995		(2)	
Haruna Zumbak Garba (NGA)	17.01.1994	16	(12)	7
Norbert Kundrák	18.05.1999	5	(14)	2
Luka Milunović (SRB)	21.12.1992	1	(7)	
Ádám Pintér	25.12.2001		(4)	
Márk Szécsi	22.05.1994	27	(4)	9
Nikola Trujić (SRB)	14.04.1992	12	(12)	3
Kevin Varga	30.03.1996	27	(2)	4
Dániel Zsóri	14.10.2000	1	(1)	

Diósgyőr-Vasgyári Testgyakorlók Köre

Founded:	06.02.1910		
Stadium:	Diósgyőri Stadion, Miskolc (15,325)		
Trainer:	Fernando Miguel Fernández Escribano (ESP)	02.06.1979	
[04.09.2019]	Tamás Feczkó	08.09.1977	

Goalkeepers:	DOB	M	(s)	G
Botond Antal	22.08.1991	1		
Erik Bukrán	06.12.1996	2		
Branislav Danilović (SRB)	24.06.1988	30		
Defenders:	**DOB**	**M**	**(s)**	**G**
Dušan Brković (SRB)	20.01.1989	25		3
Dejan Karan (SRB)	25.08.1988	12		
Hysen Memolla (ALB)	03.07.1992	4	(1)	
Yannick Ndzoumou (CMR)	18.05.1996	1		
Donát Orosz	28.07.2002	4	(1)	
Kristóf Polgár	28.11.1996	31	(1)	1
Kornél Szűcs	24.09.2001	5		
Márk Tamás	28.10.1993	16	(1)	
András Vági	25.12.1988	20	(5)	
Midfielders:	**DOB**	**M**	**(s)**	**G**
Joachim Adukor (GHA)	02.05.1993	4	(3)	
Tamás Egerszegi	02.08.1991	1	(9)	1
Florent Hasani (KVX)	30.03.1997	25	(8)	3
Bence Iszlai	29.05.1990	26		6
Dávid Márkvárt	20.09.1994	30	(1)	2
Sergiy Shestakov (UKR)	12.04.1990	23	(3)	3
Bence Szabó	16.01.1998	2	(6)	
Mátyás Tajti	02.06.1998	4		2
Patrik Ternován	10.06.1997	2		
Barnabás Tóth	28.07.1994	1	(2)	
Forwards:	**DOB**	**M**	**(s)**	**G**
Patrik Bacsa	03.06.1992	1	(8)	1
Gábor Boros	26.09.1997		(1)	
José Ricardo Córtes (COL)	08.09.1994	2	(8)	
Mirko Ivanovski (MKD)	31.10.1989	21	(2)	6
Martin Juhár (SVK)	09.03.1988	1	(1)	
Tamás Kiss	24.11.2000	15	(1)	
Kristof Korbely	26.05.2000	9	(9)	
Gábor Makrai	26.06.1996		(4)	
Gábor Molnár	16.05.1994	2	(13)	4
Dániel Prosser	15.06.1994	13	(3)	1
Rui Pedro Couto Ramalho (POR)	02.07.1988	25	(1)	3
Haris Tabaković (SUI)	20.06.1994	4	(16)	2
Richard Tibor Zsolnai	28.03.1995	1		

Fehérvár Football Club Székesfehérvár

Founded:	1941		
Stadium:	MOL Aréna Sóstó, Székesfehérvár (14,201)		
Trainer:	Marko Nikolić (SRB)	20.07.1979	
[25.11.2019]	Joan Antoni Carrillo Milán (ESP)	08.09.1968	

Goalkeepers:	DOB	M	(s)	G
Dániel Kovács	16.01.1994	1		
Adam Kovacsik	04.04.1991	32		
Defenders:	**DOB**	**M**	**(s)**	**G**
Attila Fiola	17.02.1990	14	(3)	
Szilveszter Hangya	02.01.1994	19	(2)	
Roland Juhász	01.07.1983	19	(1)	3
Visar Musliu (MKD)	13.11.1994	24	(2)	2
Loïc Négo (FRA)	15.01.1991	23	(3)	3
Paulo Vinicius Souza Dos Santos	21.02.1990	7	(3)	
Adrián Rus (ROU)	18.03.1996	10	(1)	
Ianique dos Santos Tavares „Stopira" (CPV)	20.05.1988	21		3
Olivér Tamás	14.04.2001	1		
Midfielders:	**DOB**	**M**	**(s)**	**G**
Ákos Elek	21.07.1988	17	(6)	1
Lyes Houri (FRA)	19.01.1996	13	(4)	1
Anel Hadžić (BIH)	16.08.1989	5	(5)	
Szabolcs Huszti	18.04.1983	5	(2)	1
István Kovács	27.03.1992	25	(5)	2
Georgi Milanov (BUL)	19.02.1992	9	(9)	3
Boban Nikolov (MKD)	28.07.1994	13	(9)	1
Patrik Nyári	09.04.2001	1	(2)	
Danilo Pantić (SRB)	26.10.1996	3	(5)	
Máté Pátkai	06.03.1988	22	(3)	1
Ivan Petryak (UKR)	13.03.1994	29	(4)	6
Forwards:	**DOB**	**M**	**(s)**	**G**
Funsho Ibrahim Bamgboye (NGA)	09.01.1999	8	(8)	2
Márkó Futács	22.02.1990	15	(9)	9
Armin Hodžić (BIH)	17.11.1994	19	(8)	10
Nemanja Nikolić	31.12.1987	8	(6)	5
Levente Szabó	06.06.1999		(3)	
Marko Šćepović (SRB)	23.05.1991		(1)	
Dániel Zsóri	14.10.2000		(5)	

Ferencvárosi Torna Club

Founded: 03.05.1899
Stadium: Groupama Aréna, Budapest (23,700)
Trainer: Serhiy Rebrov (UKR)   03.06.1974

Goalkeepers:	DOB	M	(s)	G
Dénes Dibusz	16.11.1990	26		
Dávid Gróf	17.04.1989	7		
Defenders:	**DOB**	**M**	**(s)**	**G**
Miha Blažič (SVN)	08.05.1993	30	(1)	3
Endre Botka	25.08.1994	17	(5)	1
Eldar Čivić (BIH)	28.05.1996	24	(1)	
Lasha Dvali (GEO)	14.05.1995	3		
Abraham Frimpong (GHA)	06.04.1993	11	(8)	
Marcel Heister (GER)	29.07.1992	12	(4)	
Kenneth Otigba	29.08.1992	12		
Dominik Zoltán	11.08.2002		(2)	
Midfielders:	**DOB**	**M**	**(s)**	**G**
Lukács Bőle	27.03.1990	3	(3)	1
András Csonka	01.05.2000	3	(2)	
Danylo Ignatenko	13.03.1997	9	(4)	1
Isael da Silva Barbosa (BRA)	13.05.1988	25	(2)	7
Igor Kharatin (UKR)	02.02.1995	27	(3)	1

	DOB	M	(s)	G
Leandro Marcolini Pedroso de Almeida	19.03.1982	3	(6)	2
Gastón Andrés Lódico (ARG)	28.05.1998	1	(4)	
Tokmac Chol Nguen (NOR)	20.10.1993	25	(5)	8
Ammar Ramadan (SYR)	05.01.2001		(1)	
Dávid Sigér	30.11.1990	24	(3)	5
Michal Škvarka (SVK)	19.08.1992	5	(10)	1
Wergiton do Rosario Calmon „Somália"(BRA)	28.09.1988	2	(4)	
Stefan Spirovski (MKD)	23.08.1990	1		1
Bálint Vécsei	13.07.1993	3	(9)	
Oleksandr Zubkov (UKR)	03.08.1996	25	(3)	9
Forwards:	**DOB**	**M**	**(s)**	**G**
Bi Sylvestre Franck Fortune Boli (CIV)	07.12.1993	24	(4)	10
Gergő Lovrencsics	01.09.1988	24	(3)	
Tamás Priskin	27.09.1986	1	(1)	
Nikolay Signevich (BLR)	20.02.1992	6	(15)	1
Regő Szánthó	22.11.2000		(1)	
Krisztofer Szerető	10.01.2000	1		
Roland Varga	23.01.1990	9	(12)	6

Budapest Honvéd Football Club

Founded: 03.08.1909
Stadium: "Bozsik József" Stadion, Budapest (10,000)
Trainer: Giuseppe Sannino (UTA)   30.04.1957
[20.03.2020] István Pisont   16.05.1970

Goalkeepers:	DOB	M	(s)	G
Attila Berla	08.04.1999	2		
András Horváth	03.02.1988	2		
Rubi Levkovich (ISR)	31.08.1988	3	(1)	
Tomáš Tujvel (SVK)	19.09.1983	26		
Defenders:	**DOB**	**M**	**(s)**	**G**
Naser Aliji (SUI)	27.12.1993	19	(2)	1
Bence Batik	08.11.1993	30		1
Gábor Buna	24.05.2002		(1)	
Dávid Kálnoki	06.08.1991	4	(4)	1
Tonči Kukoč (CRO)	25.09.1990	3	(11)	1
Ivan Lovrić (CRO)	11.07.1985	27	(2)	
Mohamed Mezghrani (BEL)	02.06.1994	9	(2)	
MacDonald Ngwa Niba (CMR)	08.08.1994	7	(1)	
Eke Uzoma (NGA)	11.08.1989	22	(5)	1
Midfielders:	**DOB**	**M**	**(s)**	**G**
Moutari Amadou (NIG)	19.01.1994	17	(13)	4
Bence Banó-Szabó	25.07.1999	11	(7)	1
Änis Ben-Hatira (TUN)	18.07.1988	5	(3)	1
Tamás Egerszegi	02.08.1991		(1)	

	DOB	M	(s)	G
Dániel Gazdag	02.03.1996	23	(1)	5
Patrik Hidi	27.11.1990	15		1
Patrick George Ikenne-King (NGA)	29.10.1991	11	(2)	
Gergő Irimiás	08.09.2001	1	(3)	
Đorđe Kamber (BIH)	20.11.1983	31	(1)	1
Barna Kesztyűs	04.09.1993	19	(10)	
Federico Moretti (ITA)	28.10.1988	1		
Gergő Nagy	07.01.1993	18	(7)	
Péter Tóth	10.04.2001		(1)	
Krisztián Vadócz	03.05.1985	9	(2)	
Forwards:	**DOB**	**M**	**(s)**	**G**
Dominik Cipf	31.01.2001	2	(12)	
Mayron Antonio George Clayton (CRC)	23.10.1993	3	(3)	1
Nikolasz Kovács	27.02.1999		(1)	
Vladyslav Kulach (UKR)	07.05.1993	2	(1)	
Davide Lanzafame (ITA)	09.02.1987	21	(2)	11
Dávid László	25.04.2002		(4)	
David N'Gog (FRA)	01.04.1989	3	(2)	2
Norbert Szendrei	27.03.2000	8		1
Roland Ugrai	13.11.1992	9	(4)	3

Kaposvári Rákoczi Football Club

Founded: 15.08.1923
Stadium: Rákóczi Stadion, Kaposvár (7,000)
Trainer: Róbert Waltner   20.09.1977
[04.12.2019] László Disztl   04.06.1962

Goalkeepers:	DOB	M	(s)	G
Márk Bonnyai	28.06.1999		(1)	
László Laky	06.02.2000	1		
Krisztián Pogacsics	17.10.1985	28		
Balázs Slakta	01.12.1994	4	(3)	
Defenders:	**DOB**	**M**	**(s)**	**G**
Marcell Fodor	27.10.1987	24	(3)	1
János Nagy	07.08.1992	27	(6)	2
Tamás Nagy	18.01.1988	15	(6)	1
Alex Szabó	26.08.1998	12		
Igors Tarasovs (LVA)	16.10.1988	7		
László Ur	05.03.1988	14	(3)	
Csaba Vachtler	16.03.1993	27	(4)	
Midfielders:	**DOB**	**M**	**(s)**	**G**
Zsombor Bévárdi	30.01.1999	5	(2)	3
Ákos Borbély	12.06.2000	4	(8)	1
Norbert Csíki	21.05.1991	20	(5)	2
Aurél Farkas	31.03.1994	1	(2)	
Valentin Hadaró	08.06.1995	12	(4)	

	DOB	M	(s)	G
Dávid Hegedűs	06.06.1985	18	(2)	2
Vanja Marković (SRB)	20.06.1994		(1)	
Krisztián Nagy	18.07.1995	7	(10)	1
Richárd Nagy	08.04.1994	25	(4)	3
Antun Palić (CRO)	25.06.1988	6	(3)	
Attila Szakály	30.06.1992	29	(2)	2
Dinko Trebotić (CRO)	30.07.1990	6	(5)	
Aljoša Vojnović (CRO)	24.10.1985	1	(1)	
Andriy Yakimov (UKR)	15.06.1997	12	(3)	
Forwards:	**DOB**	**M**	**(s)**	**G**
Martin Ádám	06.11.1994	30		5
Zsolt Balázs	11.08.1988	11	(11)	2
Gergő Beliczky	03.07.1990	9	(4)	
Dominik Bíró	25.06.1998		(3)	
Zalán Keresztes	17.06.2001	1	(1)	
Ádám Pintér	25.12.2001	5	(5)	
Matej Poplatnik (SVN)	15.07.1992	1	(5)	
Bálint Tömösvári	14.06.1998		(1)	1
Ervin Zsiga	11.07.1991	1	(4)	

Kisvárda Futball Club

Founded:	1911	
Stadium:	Várkerti Stadion, Kisvárda (2,850)	
Trainer:	Vasile Miriuță	19.09.1968
[16.10.2019]	László Dajka	29.04.1959
[06.02.2020]	Tamás Bódog	27.09.1970

Goalkeepers:	DOB	M	(s)	G
Abov Avetisyan (UKR)	03.10.2001		(1)	
Dávid Dombó	26.02.1993	16		
Luiz Felipe Ventura dos Santos (BRA)	22.02.1984	12		
Mihai Adrian Mincă (ROU)	08.10.1984	3		
Illés Zöldesi	09.02.1998	2		
Defenders:	**DOB**	**M**	**(s)**	**G**
Anderson „Pico" da Silveira Ribeiro (BRA)	04.11.1988		(1)	
Ádám Baranyai	05.03.1993	3	(2)	
Theodoros Berios (GRE)	21.03.1989	17	(1)	
Cornel Ene (ROU)	21.07.1993	12	(2)	1
Anton Kravchenko (UKR)	23.03.1991	17		2
Bogdan Melnyk (UKR)	04.01.1997	24	(2)	2
Radoš Protić (SRB)	31.01.1987	29		
Tamás Rubus	13.07.1989	19	(3)	1
Czene Zalán	22.12.2002		(2)	
Midfielders:	**DOB**	**M**	**(s)**	**G**
Roland Biró	30.05.2003		(1)	
Claudiu Vasile Bumba (ROU)	05.01.1994	18	(5)	3

	DOB	M	(s)	G
Gheorghe Teodor Grozav (ROU)	29.09.1990	14		7
Viktor Hei (UKR)	02.02.1996	15	(4)	
Hugo André Rodrigues Seco (POR)	17.06.1988	9	(5)	
Roman Karasyuk (UKR)	27.03.1991	18	(3)	
Lucas Marcolini Dantas Bertucci (BRA)	06.05.1989	31		4
Sergiu Negruț (ROU)	01.04.1993		(1)	
Viktor Riznicsenko	21.06.2002		(1)	
Slobodan Simović (SRB)	22.05.1989	4	(5)	
Stavros Tsoukalas (GRE)	28.05.1988	25	(2)	3
Forwards:	**DOB**	**M**	**(s)**	**G**
Fernando Viana Jardim Silva (BRA)	20.02.1992	13	(2)	4
András Gosztonyi	07.11.1990	13	(10)	4
Richárd Jelena	08.01.1998	1	(3)	
Vasyl Khymich	17.05.2001		(1)	
Márk Kovácsréti	01.09.2000	17	(6)	1
Nemanja Obradović (SRB)	29.05.1989	6	(3)	2
Jefferson Gomes de Oliveira „Sassá" (BRA)	26.01.1988	8	(19)	3
Levente Szőr	14.01.2001	1	(1)	
Patrik Tischler	30.07.1991	7	(20)	5

Mezőkövesdi Sport Egyesület

Founded:	31.01.1975	
Stadium:	Városi Stadion, Mezőkövesd (4,183)	
Trainer:	Attila Kuttor	29.05.1970

Goalkeepers:	DOB	M	(s)	G
Danylo Ryabenko (UKR)	09.10.1998	1		
Péter Szappanos	14.11.1990	32		
Defenders:	**DOB**	**M**	**(s)**	**G**
Gábor Eperjesi	12.01.1994	9	(6)	
Danijel Farkaš (SRB)	13.01.1993	23	(2)	
Richárd Guzmics	16.04.1987	3		
Andriy Nesterov (UKR)	02.07.1990	20	(1)	1
Róbert Pillár (SVK)	27.05.1991	22	(1)	1
Erik Silye	12.06.1996	17	(4)	2
Matija Katanec (CRO)	04.05.1990	16	(1)	
Dániel Vadnai	19.02.1988	16	(6)	
Midfielders:	**DOB**	**M**	**(s)**	**G**
Zsombor Berecz	13.12.1995	27	(1)	4
Lajos Bertus	26.09.1990	2	(1)	

	DOB	M	(s)	G
Dino Beširović (BIH)	31.01.1994	14	(2)	5
Aleksandr Karnitskiy (BLR)	14.02.1989	30	(1)	3
Mykhailo Meskhi (UKR)	26.02.1997	6	(5)	1
Dániel Nagy	15.03.1991	25	(7)	4
László Pekár	20.01.1993	19	(7)	1
Tamás Szeles	07.12.1993	3		
Sándor Vajda	14.12.1991	8	(18)	1
Forwards:	**DOB**	**M**	**(s)**	**G**
Tamás Cseri	15.01.1988	29	(3)	7
Filip Dragóner	12.03.1998		(4)	1
Marin Jurina (BIH)	26.11.1993	7	(7)	2
Gábor Molnár	16.05.1994	4	(3)	
Máté Sajbán	19.12.1995		(7)	1
Tamás Takács	20.02.1991	2	(13)	
Budu Zivzivadze (GEO)	10.03.1994	28	(4)	8

Paksi Futball Club

Founded:	28.11.1952	
Stadium:	Fehérvári úti Stadion, Paks (6,150)	
Trainer:	Tomislav Sivić (SRB)	29.08.1966
[05.11.2019]	Gábor Osztermajer	12.03.1978

Goalkeepers:	DOB	M	(s)	G
Ádám Holczer	28.03.1988	12		
Gergő Rácz	20.11.1995	21		
Defenders:	**DOB**	**M**	**(s)**	**G**
Támas Báló	12.01.1984		(2)	
András Fejes	26.08.1988	10		
Zsolt Gévay	19.11.1987	13	(1)	1
Dávid Kelemen	24.05.1992	10		1
Dávid Kulcsár	25.02.1988	6	(11)	1
Bence Lenzsér	09.04.1996	20	(1)	
Attila Osváth	10.12.1995	27	(1)	
Patrik Poór	15.11.1993	10	(5)	
János Szabó	11.07.1989	31	(1)	2
Midfielders:	**DOB**	**M**	**(s)**	**G**
Balász Balogh	11.06.1990	27	(3)	1
Lajos Bertus	26.09.1990	11	(4)	
Benjámin Cseke	22.07.1994		(2)	
Tamás Kecskés	15.01.1986	6	(12)	

	DOB	M	(s)	G
Kristóf Papp	14.05.1993	12	(2)	1
Mohamed Remili	31.05.1985	5	(7)	2
Ádám Simon	30.03.1990	6	(2)	
Dénes Szakály	15.03.1988	13	(3)	
Norbert Szélpál	03.03.1996	13	(1)	
József Windecker	02.12.1992	17	(9)	6
Forwards:	**DOB**	**M**	**(s)**	**G**
László Bartha	09.02.1987	5	(6)	
Dániel Böde	24.10.1986	24	(3)	6
Dávid Bor	10.12.1994		(2)	1
Áron Fejős	17.04.1997	4	(6)	
János Hahn	15.05.1995	25	(5)	7
Zsolt Haraszti	04.11.1991	5	(5)	2
Norbert Könyves	10.06.1989	26	(2)	11
Róbert Kővári	23.11.1995		(1)	
Máté Sajbán	19.12.1995	3	(10)	4
András Simon	30.03.1990	1		
Ákos Szendrei	23.01.2003		(3)	

Puskás Ferenc Labdarugó Akadémia Felcsút

Founded: 2005
Stadium: Pancho Aréna, Felcsút (3,816)
Trainer: Zsolt Hornyák (SVK)   01.05.1973

Goalkeepers:	DOB	M	(s)	G
Lajos Hegedüs	19.12.1987	25		
Balázs Tóth	04.09.1997	8	(1)	
Defenders:	**DOB**	**M**	**(s)**	**G**
László Deutsch	09.03.1999	10	(1)	1
Kamen Hadzhiev (BUL)	22.09.1991	28		
András Huszti	29.01.2001	2		
Thomas Meißner (GER)	26.03.1991	32		1
Zsolt Nagy	25.05.1993	22	(3)	1
Csaba Spandler	07.03.1996	8	(10)	
Roland Szolnoki	21.01.1992	27		1
Midfielders:	**DOB**	**M**	**(s)**	**G**
Artem Favorov (UKR)	19.03.1994	5	(5)	1
Lóránd Levente Fülöp (ROU)	24.07.1997	1		
Josip Knežević (CRO)	03.10.1988	30		8

Jakub Plšek (CZE)	13.12.1993	10	(5)	
Márton Radics	02.12.2001	9	(4)	
Bence Sós	10.05.1994	11	(17)	1
Jozef Urblík (SVK)	22.08.1996	18	(5)	4
Yoëll van Nieff (NED)	17.06.1993	27	(1)	2
József Varga	06.06.1988	2	(2)	
Ján Vlasko (SVK)	11.01.1990		(3)	1
Forwards:	**DOB**	**M**	**(s)**	**G**
Ádám Gyurcsó	06.03.1991	27	(2)	7
Ezekiel Isoken Henty (NGA)	13.05.1993	11	(1)	7
Tamás Kiss	24.11.2000	1	(9)	
Gol-Gol Tedros Mebrahtu (AUS)	28.08.1990	6	(11)	1
Luciano Slagveer (NED)	05.10.1993	13	(3)	2
Nandor Támas (ROU)	24.10.2000		(7)	1
David Vaněček (CZE)	09.03.1991	30	(2)	11

Újpest Football Club

Founded: 16.06.1885
Stadium: "Szusza Ferenc" Stadion, Budapest (13,501)
Trainer: Nebojša Vignjević (SRB)   15.04.1968
[01.06.2020] Predrag Rogan (SRB)   02.08.1974

Goalkeepers:	DOB	M	(s)	G
Dávid Banai	09.05.1994	23		
Filip Pajović (SRB)	30.07.1993	10		
Defenders:	**DOB**	**M**	**(s)**	**G**
Dženan Bureković (BIH)	29.05.1995	25	(2)	
Jonathan Heris (BEL)	03.09.1990	25	(1)	1
Róbert Litauszki	15.03.1990	11		1
Zsolt Máté	14.09.1997	3		1
Branko Pauljević (SRB)	12.06.1989	26		1
Kire Ristevski (MKD)	22.10.1990	29		2
Midfielders:	**DOB**	**M**	**(s)**	**G**
Benjámin Balázs	26.04.1990	17	(6)	1
Mátyás Katona	30.12.1999		(2)	
Lóránt Kovács (ROU)	06.06.1993	1	(2)	
Obinna Nwobodo (NGA)	29.11.1996	32		3
Vincent Onovo (NGA)	10.12.1995	29	(3)	2

Barnabás Rácz	26.04.1996	7	(2)	
Bojan Sanković (CRO)	21.11.1993	16		1
Péter Szakály	17.08.1986	5	(15)	
Donát Zsótér	06.01.1996	21	(6)	3
Forwards:	**DOB**	**M**	**(s)**	**G**
Patrik Bacsa	03.06.1992	2	(12)	2
Aron Bjarnason (ISL)	14.10.1995	5	(11)	
Andreiaş Cristian Calcan (ROU)	09.04.1994	6	(3)	2
Aron Csongvai	31.10.2000	4	(6)	
Róbert Feczesin	22.02.1986	12		8
Márk Koszta	26.09.1996	2	(16)	3
Karol Mészáros (SVK)	25.07.1993		(3)	
Soma Novothny	16.06.1994	16	(1)	6
Antonio Perošević (CRO)	06.03.1992	10	(6)	
Jakub Sedláček (SVK)	09.03.1998	2		
Krisztián Simon	10.06.1991	24	(5)	5

Zalaegerszegi Torna Egylet Football Club

Founded: 1920
Stadium: ZTE Aréna, Zalaegerszeg (11,200)
Trainer: Barna Dobos   12.05.1970
[10.02.2020] Gábor Márton   15.10.1966

Goalkeepers:	DOB	M	(s)	G
Patrik Demjén	22.03.1998	33		
Defenders:	**DOB**	**M**	**(s)**	**G**
Bence Bedi	14.11.1996	30	(1)	2
Dávid Bobál	31.08.1995	18	(7)	1
Bendegúz Bolla	22.11.1999	26	(1)	1
Szilárd Devecseri	13.02.1990	8	(2)	1
Bence Gergényi	16.03.1998	3	(3)	
Matija Katanec (CRO)	04.05.1990	8	(1)	
Gergő Kocsis	07.03.1994	21	(5)	
Zoran Lesjak (CRO)	01.02.1988	25		3
János Szépe (SVK)	15.03.1996	14	(1)	
Krisztián Tamás	18.04.1995	17		
Midfielders:	**DOB**	**M**	**(s)**	**G**
Dávid Barczi	01.02.1989	11	(6)	2

Lukács Bőle	27.03.1990	9	(2)	3
Oleg Golodyuk (UKR)	02.01.1988	2	(3)	
Martin Hudák	22.02.1994		(9)	
Fanos Katelaris (CYP)	26.08.1996	8	(5)	
Máté Kiss	30.04.1991	1	(1)	
Nikola Mitrović (SRB)	02.01.1987	29	(2)	3
Stjepan Ostrek (CRO)	09.08.1996	2	(5)	
Zoltán Stieber	16.10.1988	20	(2)	2
Forwards:	**DOB**	**M**	**(s)**	**G**
Benjamin Babati	29.11.1995	10	(11)	3
Gergely Bobál	31.08.1995	20	(9)	10
Miroslav Grumić (SRB)	29.06.1984	3	(6)	
Eduvie Ikoba (USA)	26.10.1997	11	(14)	4
Eric Lemond McWoods (USA)	21.10.1995	3	(3)	1
András Radó	09.09.1993	31	(2)	13

1.	MTK Budapest FC (*Promoted*)	27	18	5	4	60	-	33	59
2.	Budafoki MTE (*Promoted*)	27	16	6	5	42	-	23	54
3.	Vasas FC Budapest	27	14	5	8	55	-	39	47
4.	Aqvital FC Csákvár	26	13	4	9	40	-	43	43
5.	Bodajk FC Siófok	26	11	9	6	40	-	31	42
6.	Győri ETO FC	27	11	8	8	36	-	32	41
7.	Gyirmót FC Győr	27	10	8	9	32	-	29	38
8.	Nyíregyháza Spartacus FC	27	11	2	14	45	-	45	35
9.	FC Ajka	26	10	5	11	41	-	40	35
10.	Soroksár SC	26	10	5	11	38	-	44	35
11.	Budaörsi SC	26	10	4	12	38	-	37	34
12.	Szeged-Csanád Grosics Akadémia	26	8	10	8	31	-	29	34
13.	Dorogi FC	26	9	6	11	29	-	29	33
14.	Kazincbarcikai SC	27	8	9	10	33	-	38	33
15.	Békéscsaba 1912 Előre SE	26	8	8	10	30	-	35	32
16.	Szolnoki MÁV FC	26	7	10	9	22	-	27	31
17.	Szombathelyi Haladás	27	7	9	11	32	-	34	30
18.	Tiszakécske FC (*Relegated*)	27	7	5	15	25	-	50	26
19.	Vác FC (*Relegated*)	27	2	6	19	17	-	48	12
20.	Balmazújvárosi FC (*Relegated*)	(*Suspended*)							

Please note: on 04.05.2020, the season was suspended due to Covid-19 pandemic.

NATIONAL TEAM

INTERNATIONAL MATCHES
(16.07.2019 – 15.07.2020)

05.09.2019	Podgorica	Montenegro - Hungary	2-1(1-1)	(F)
09.09.2019	Budapest	Hungary - Slovakia	1-2(0-1)	(ECQ)
10.10.2019	Split	Croatia - Hungary	3-0(3-0)	(ECQ)
13.10.2019	Budapest	Hungary - Azerbaijan	1-0(1-0)	(ECQ)
15.11.2019	Budapest	Hungary - Uruguay	1-2(1-2)	(F)
19.11.2019	Cardiff	Wales - Hungary	2-0(1-0)	(ECQ)

05.09.2019   **MONTENEGRO - HUNGARY**   **2-1(1-1)**   Friendly International
Stadion pod Goricom, Podgorica; Referee: Dimitar Mečkarovski (North Macedonia); Attendance: 3,370
HUN: Dénes Dibusz, Botond Baráth (46.Vilmos Tamás Orbán), Ádám Lang, Barnabás Bese, Mihály Korhut (61.János Ferenczi), Dávid Holman, László Kleinheisler (46.Dávid Sigér), Dániel Gazdag (46.István Kovács), Dominik Nagy (69.Balázs Dzsudzsák), Krisztián Németh (Cap), Filip Holender (64.Roland Varga). Trainer: Marco Rossi (Italy).
Goal: Filip Holender (2).

09.09.2019   **HUNGARY - SLOVAKIA**   **1-2(0-1)**   16th EC. Qualifiers
Groupama Arena, Budapest; Referee: Antonio Miguel Mateu Lahoz (Spain); Attendance: 21,700
HUN: Péter Gulácsi, Botond Baráth [*sent off 90+5*], Vilmos Tamás Orbán, Tamás Kádár, Gergő Lovrencsics (30.Barnabás Bese), László Kleinheisler (85.Filip Holender), Ádám Nagy (65.Máté Pátkai), Dominik Szoboszlai, Balázs Dzsudzsák (Cap), Ádám Csaba Szalai, Roland Sallai. Trainer: Marco Rossi (Italy).
Goal: Dominik Szoboszlai (50).

10.10.2019   **CROATIA - HUNGARY**   **3-0(3-0)**   16th EC. Qualifiers
Stadion Poljud, Split; Referee: Daniele Orsato (Italy); Attendance: 32,110
HUN: Péter Gulácsi, Gergő Lovrencsics, Mihály Korhut, Vilmos Tamás Orbán, Tamás Kádár (46.Ádám Lang), László Kleinheisler [*sent off 56*], Dávid Holman, Máté Vida, Balázs Dzsudzsák (Cap) (60.Dominik Nagy), Ádám Csaba Szalai, Roland Sallai (76.Roland Varga). Trainer: Marco Rossi (Italy).

13.10.2019   **HUNGARY - AZERBAIJAN**   **1-0(1-0)**   16th EC. Qualifiers
Groupama Arena, Budapest; Referee: Dennis Higler (Netherlands); Attendance: 11,300
HUN: Péter Gulácsi, Botond Baráth, Vilmos Tamás Orbán, Mihály Korhut, Gergő Lovrencsics, István Kovács (86.Sigér Dávid), Máté Vida, Dominik Szoboszlai (76.Dávid Holman), Balázs Dzsudzsák (Cap) (71.Dominik Nagy), Ádám Csaba Szalai, Roland Sallai. Trainer: Marco Rossi (Italy).
Goal: Mihály Korhut (10).

15.11.2019   **HUNGARY - URUGUAY**   **1-2(1-2)**   Friendly International
Puskás Aréna, Budapest; Referee: Damir Skomina (Slovenia); Attendance: 65,114
HUN: Dénes Dibusz, Botond Baráth (72.Attila Szalai), Barnabás Bese, Ádám Lang, Mihály Korhut (75.Zsolt Nagy), Máté Vida, Zsolt Kalmár (83.Dávid Holman), Dominik Szoboszlai (68.Ádám Nagy), Balázs Dzsudzsák (Cap) (54.István Kovács), Ádám Csaba Szalai (60.Róbert Feczesin), Roland Varga. Trainer: Marco Rossi (Italy).
Goal: Ádám Csaba Szalai (24).

19.11.2019   **WALES - HUNGARY**   **2-0(1-0)**   16th EC. Qualifiers
Cardiff City Stadium, Cardiff; Referee: Ovidiu Alin Haţegan (Romania); Attendance: 31,762
HUN: Péter Gulácsi, Botond Baráth, Ádám Lang, Zsolt Nagy, Máté Pátkai, Gergő Lovrencsics, Ádám Nagy (60.István Kovács), Dominik Szoboszlai, Balázs Dzsudzsák (Cap) (72.Roland Varga), Ádám Csaba Szalai, Roland Sallai (83.Filip Holender). Trainer: Marco Rossi (Italy).

NATIONAL TEAM PLAYERS
(16.07.2019 – 15.07.2020)

Name	DOB	Caps	Goals	2019/2020:	Club
Goalkeepers					
Dénes DIBUSZ	16.11.1990	9	0	2019:	*Ferencvárosi TC*
Péter GULÁCSI	06.05.1990	31	0	2019:	*RasenBallsport Leipzig (GER)*
Defenders					
Botond BARÁTH	21.04.1992	11	0	2019:	*Sporting Kansas City (USA)*
Barnabás BESE	06.05.1994	20	0	2019:	*AC Le Havre (FRA)*
János FERENCZI	03.04.1991	1	0	2019:	*Debreceni VSC*
Tamás KÁDÁR	14.03.1990	57	1	2019:	*FK Dynamo Kyiv (UKR)*
Mihály KORHUT	01.12.1988	22	1	2019:	*Aris Thessaloníki (GRE)*
Ádám LANG	17.01.1993	30	1	2019:	*AC Omonia Nicosia (CYP)*
Gergő LOVRENCSICS	01.09.1988	36	1	2019:	*Ferencvárosi TC*
Zsolt NAGY	25.05.1993	2	0	2019:	*Puskás Ferenc Labdarugó Akadémia Felcsút*
Vilmos Tamás „Willi" ORBÁN	03.11.1992	12	3	2019:	*RasenBallsport Leipzig (GER)*
Midfielders					
Balázs DZSUDZSÁK	23.12.1986	108	21	2019:	*Al-Ittihad Kalba SC (UAE)*
Dániel GAZDAG	02.03.1996	1	0	2019:	*Budapest Honvéd FC*
Dávid HOLMAN	17.03.1993	5	1	2019:	*ŠK Slovan Bratislava (SVK)*
Zsolt KALMÁR	09.06.1995	16	0	2019:	*FC DAC 1904 Dunajská Streda (SVK)*
László KLEINHEISLER	08.04.1994	29	2	2019:	*NK Osijek (CRO)*
István KOVÁCS	27.03.1992	15	0	2019:	*Fehérvár FC Székesfehérvár*
Dominik NAGY	08.05.1995	10	1	2019:	*Legia Warszawa (POL)*
Ádám NAGY	17.06.1995	36	1	2019:	*Bristol City FC (ENG)*
Máté PÁTKAI	06.03.1988	23	2	2019:	*Fehérvár FC Székesfehérvár*
Dávid SIGÉR	30.11.1990	2	0	2019:	*Ferencvárosi TC*
Dominik SZOBOSZLAI	25.10.2000	8	1	2019:	*FC Red Bull Salzburg (AUT)*
Máté VIDA	08.03.1996	6	0	2019:	*FC DAC 1904 Dunajská Streda (SVK)*
Forwards					
Róbert FECZESIN	22.02.1986	12	4	2019:	*Újpest FC*
Filip HOLENDER	27.07.1994	6	1	2019:	*FC Lugano (SUI)*
Krisztián NÉMETH	05.01.1989	37	4	2019:	*Sporting Kansas City (USA)*
Roland SALLAI	22.05.1997	16	1	2019:	*SC Freiburg (GER)*
Ádám Csaba SZALAI	09.12.1987	61	21	2019:	*1. FSV Mainz 05 (GER)*
Roland VARGA	23.01.1990	19	3	2019:	*Ferencvárosi TC*
National team coach					
Marco ROSSI (Italy) [from 19.06.2019]	09.09.1964	16 M; 7 W; 1 D; 8 L; 19-21			

ICELAND

The Country:
Ísland (Iceland)
Capital: Reykjavík
Surface: 102,775 km²
Inhabitants: 360,390 [2019]
Time: UTC

The FA:
Knattspyrnusamband Íslands
Laugardal 104, Reykjavík
Tel: +354 510 2900
Foundation date: 1947
Member of FIFA since: 1947
Member of UEFA since: 1954
Website: www.ksi.is

NATIONAL TEAM RECORDS

RECORDS

First international match:	17.07.1946, Reykjavík:	Iceland – Denmark 0-3
Most international caps:	Rúnar Kristinsson	- 104 caps (1987-2004)
Most international goals:	Eiður Smári Guðjohnsen	- 26 goals / 88 caps (1996-2016)
	Kolbeinn Sigþórsson	- 26 goals / 57 caps (2010-2020)

UEFA EUROPEAN CHAMPIONSHIP		FIFA WORLD CUP		OLYMPIC TOURNAMENTS	
1960	Did not enter	1930	-	1908	-
1964	Qualifiers	1934	-	1912	-
1968	Did not enter	1938	-	1920	-
1972	Did not enter	1950	-	1924	-
1976	Qualifiers	1954	*Entry not accepted by FIFA*	1928	-
1980	Qualifiers	1958	Qualifiers	1936	-
1984	Qualifiers	1962	Did not enter	1948	-
1988	Qualifiers	1966	Did not enter	1952	-
1992	Qualifiers	1970	Did not enter	1956	-
1996	Qualifiers	1974	Qualifiers	1960	Qualifiers
2000	Qualifiers	1978	Qualifiers	1964	Qualifiers
2004	Qualifiers	1982	Qualifiers	1968	Qualifiers
2008	Qualifiers	1986	Qualifiers	1972	Qualifiers
2012	Qualifiers	1990	Qualifiers	1976	Did not enter
2016	Final Tournament (Quarter-Finals)	1994	Qualifiers	1980	Did not enter
2020	*To be determined*	1998	Qualifiers	1984	Did not enter
		2002	Qualifiers	1988	Qualifiers
		2006	Qualifiers	1992	Qualifiers
		2010	Qualifiers	1996	Qualifiers
		2014	Qualifiers	2000	Qualifiers
		2018	Final Tournament (Group Stage)	2004	Qualifiers
				2008	Qualifiers
				2012	Qualifiers
				2016	Qualifiers

UEFA NATIONS LEAGUE

2018/2019 – League A (relegated to League B)

FIFA CONFEDERATIONS CUP 1992-2017

None

ICELANDIAN CLUB HONOURS IN EUROPEAN CLUB COMPETITIONS:

European Champion Clubs' Cup (1956-1992) / UEFA Champions League (1993-2020)
None

Fairs Cup (1858-1971) / UEFA Cup (1972-2009) / UEFA Europa League (2010-2020)
None

UEFA Super Cup (1972-2019)
None

*European Cup Winners' Cup 1961-1999**
None

*defunct competition

NATIONAL COMPETITIONS
TABLE OF HONOURS

	CHAMPIONS	CUP WINNERS	BEST GOALSCORERS	
1912	KR Reykjavík	-	-	
1913	Fram Reykjavík	-	-	
1914	Fram Reykjavík	-	-	
1915	Fram Reykjavík	-	-	
1916	Fram Reykjavík	-	-	
1917	Fram Reykjavík	-	-	
1918	Fram Reykjavík	-	-	
1919	KR Reykjavík	-	-	
1920	Víkingur Reykjavík	-	-	
1921	Fram Reykjavík	-	-	
1922	Fram Reykjavík	-	-	
1923	Fram Reykjavík	-	-	
1924	Víkingur Reykjavík	-	-	
1925	Fram Reykjavík	-	-	
1926	KR Reykjavík	-	-	
1927	KR Reykjavík	-	-	
1928	KR Reykjavík	-	-	
1929	KR Reykjavík	-	-	
1930	Valur Reykjavík	-	-	
1931	KR Reykjavík	-	-	
1932	KR Reykjavík	-	-	
1933	Valur Reykjavík	-	-	
1934	KR Reykjavík	-	-	
1935	Valur Reykjavík	-	-	
1936	Valur Reykjavík	-	-	
1937	Valur Reykjavík	-	-	
1938	Valur Reykjavík	-	-	
1939	Fram Reykjavík	-	-	
1940	Valur Reykjavík	-	-	
1941	KR Reykjavík	-	-	
1942	Valur Reykjavík	-	-	
1943	Valur Reykjavík	-	-	
1944	Valur Reykjavík	-	-	
1945	Valur Reykjavík	-	-	
1946	Fram Reykjavík	-	-	
1947	Fram Reykjavík	-	-	
1948	KR Reykjavík	-	-	
1949	KR Reykjavík	-	-	
1950	KR Reykjavík	-	-	
1951	ÍA Akranes	-	-	
1952	KR Reykjavík	-	-	
1953	ÍA Akranes	-	-	
1954	ÍA Akranes	-	-	
1955	KR Reykjavík	-	-	
1956	Valur Reykjavík	-	-	
1957	ÍA Akranes	-	-	
1958	ÍA Akranes	-	-	
1959	KR Reykjavík	-	-	
1960	ÍA Akranes	KR Reykjavík	-	
1961	KR Reykjavík	KR Reykjavík	-	
1962	Fram Reykjavík	KR Reykjavík	-	
1963	KR Reykjavík	KR Reykjavík	-	
1964	Keflavík ÍF	KR Reykjavík	-	
1965	KR Reykjavík	Valur Reykjavík	-	
1966	Valur Reykjavík	KR Reykjavík	-	
1967	Valur Reykjavík	KR Reykjavík	-	
1968	KR Reykjavík	ÍBV Vestmannaeyjar	-	
1969	Keflavík ÍF	KA Akureyrar	-	
1970	ÍA Akranes	Fram Reykjavík	-	
1971	Keflavík ÍF	Víkingur Reykjavík	-	
1972	Fram Reykjavík	ÍBV Vestmannaeyjar	-	
1973	Keflavík ÍF	Fram Reykjavík	-	
1974	ÍA Akranes	Valur Reykjavík	-	
1975	ÍA Akranes	Keflavík ÍF	-	
1976	Valur Reykjavík	Valur Reykjavík	-	
1977	ÍA Akranes	Valur Reykjavík	-	
1978	Valur Reykjavík	ÍA Akranes	-	
1979	ÍBV Vestmannaeyjar	Fram Reykjavík	-	
1980	Valur Reykjavík	Fram Reykjavík	Matthias Hallgrimsson (Valur Reykjavík)	15
1981	Víkingur Reykjavík	ÍBV Vestmannaeyjar	Sigurlás Þorleifsson (ÍBV Vestmannaeyjar)	
			Larus Gudmundsson (Víkingur Reykjavík)	12

1982	Víkingur Reykjavík	ÍA Akranes	Sigurlás Þorleifsson (ÍBV Vestmannaeyjar)	
			Heimir Karlsson (Víkingur Reykjavík)	10
1983	ÍA Akranes	ÍA Akranes	Ingi Björn Albertsson (Valur Reykjavík)	14
1984	ÍA Akranes	ÍA Akranes	Guðmundur Steinsson (Fram Reykjavík)	10
1985	Valur Reykjavík	Fram Reykjavík	Ómar Torfason (Fram Reykjavík)	13
1986	Fram Reykjavík	ÍA Akranes	Gudmundur Torfason (Fram Reykjavík)	19
1987	Valur Reykjavík	Fram Reykjavík	Petur Ormslev (Fram Reykjavík)	12
1988	Fram Reykjavík	Valur Reykjavík	Sigurjón Kristjánsson (Valur Reykjavík)	13
1989	KA Akureyri	Fram Reykjavík	Hörður Magnússon (FH Hafnarfjörður)	12
1990	Fram Reykjavík	Valur Reykjavík	Hörður Magnússon (FH Hafnarfjörður)	13
1991	Víkingur Reykjavík	Valur Reykjavík	Hörður Magnússon (FH Hafnarfjörður)	
			Guðmundur Steinsson (Víkingur Reykjavík)	13
1992	ÍA Akranes	Valur Reykjavík	Arnar Gunnlaugsson (ÍA Akranes)	15
1993	ÍA Akranes	ÍA Akranes	Þórður Guðjónsson (ÍA Akranes)	19
1994	ÍA Akranes	KR Reykjavík	Mihajlo Biberčić (SRB, ÍA Akranes)	14
1995	ÍA Akranes	KR Reykjavík	Arnar Gunnlaugsson (ÍA Akranes)	15
1996	ÍA Akranes	ÍA Akranes	Ríkharður Daðason (KR Reykjavík)	14
1997	ÍBV Vestmannaeyjar	Keflavík ÍF	Tryggvi Guðmundsson (ÍBV Vestmannaeyjar)	19
1998	ÍBV Vestmannaeyjar	ÍBV Vestmannaeyjar	Steingrímur Jóhannesson (ÍBV Vestmannaeyjar)	16
1999	KR Reykjavík	KR Reykjavík	Steingrímur Jóhannesson (ÍBV Vestmannaeyjar)	12
2000	KR Reykjavík	ÍA Akranes	Guðmundur Steinarsson (Keflavík ÍF)	
			Andri Sigþórsson (KR Reykjavík)	14
2001	ÍA Akranes	Fylkir Reykjavík	Hjörtur Hjartarson (ÍA Akranes)	15
2002	KR Reykjavík	Fylkir Reykjavík	Grétar Hjartarson (UMF Grindavík)	13
2003	KR Reykjavík	ÍA Akranes	Björgólfur Takefusa (Þróttur Reykjavík)	10
2004	FH Hafnarfjörður	Keflavík ÍF	Gunnar Heiðar Þorvaldsson (ÍBV Vestmannaeyjar)	12
2005	FH Hafnarfjörður	Valur Reykjavík	Tryggvi Guðmundsson (FH Hafnarfjörður)	16
2006	FH Hafnarfjörður	Keflavík ÍF	Marel Baldvinsson (Breiðablik Kópavogur)	11
2007	Valur Reykjavík	FH Hafnarfjörður	Jónas Grani Garðarsson (Fram Reykjavík)	13
2008	FH Hafnarfjörður	KR Reykjavík	Guðmundur Steinarsson (Keflavík ÍF)	16
2009	FH Hafnarfjörður	Breiðablik Kópavogur	Björgólfur Takefusa (KR Reykjavík)	16
2010	Breiðablik Kópavogur	FH Hafnarfjörður	Gilles Mbang Ondo (GAB, UMF Grindavík)	14
2011	KR Reykjavík	KR Reykjavík	Garðar Jóhannsson (Stjarnan Garðabær)	15
2012	FH Hafnarfjörður	KR Reykjavík	Atli Guðnason (FH Hafnarfjörður)	12
2013	KR Reykjavík	Fram Reykjavík	Atli Viðar Björnsson (FH Hafnarfjörður)	
			Viðar Örn Kjartansson (Fylkir Reykjavík)	
			Gary Martin (ENG, KR Reykjavík)	13
2014	Stjarnan Garðabær	KR Reykjavík	Gary Martin (ENG, KR Reykjavík)	13
2015	FH Hafnarfjörður	Valur Reykjavík	Patrick Pedersen (DEN, Valur Reykjavík)	13
2016	FH Hafnarfjörður	Valur Reykjavík	Garðar Gunnlaugsson (ÍA Akranes)	14
2017	Valur Reykjavík	ÍBV Vestmannaeyjar	Andri Rúnar Bjarnason (UMF Grindavík)	19
2018	Valur Reykjavík	Stjarnan Garðabær	Patrick Pedersen (DEN, Valur Reykjavík)	17
2019	KR Reykjavík	Víkingur Reykjavík	Gary John Martin	
			(ENG, Valur Reykjavík / ÍBV Vestmannaeyjar)	14

NATIONAL CHAMPIONSHIP
Úrvalsdeild karla 2019
(26.04.2019 – 28.09.2019)

Results

Round 1 [26-27.04.2019]
Valur Reykjavik - Víkingur 3-3(0-1)
Grindavík - Breiðablik 0-2(0-0)
ÍBV Vestmannaeyjar - Fylkir Reyk. 0-3(0-2)
ÍA Akranes - KA Akureyri 3-1(2-1)
FH Hafnarfjörður - Kópavogur 2-0(1-0)
Stjarnan - KR Reykjavík 1-1(1-0)

Round 2 [04-06.05.2019]
Kópavogur - Breiðablik 2-2(0-0)
KA Akureyri - Valur Reykjavík 1-0(0-0)
KR Reykjavík - ÍBV Vestmannaeyjar 3-0(0-0)
Fylkir Reykjavík - ÍA Akranes 2-2(0-1)
Grindavík - Stjarnan 1-1(0-1)
Víkingur - FH Hafnarfjörður 1-1(1-0)

Round 3 [10-12.05.2019]
FH Hafnarfjörður - KA Akureyri 3-2(1-0)
Stjarnan - Kópavogur 1-0(0-0)
Breiðablik - Víkingur 3-1(2-1)
ÍBV Vestmannaeyjar - Grindavík 2-2(2-1)
Valur Reykjavík - ÍA Akranes 1-2(0-2)
KR Reykjavík - Fylkir Reykjavík 1-1(1-0)

Round 4 [15-16.05.2019]
ÍA Akranes - FH Hafnarfjörður 2-0(1-0)
KA Akureyri - Breiðablik 0-1(0-1)
Víkingur - Stjarnan 3-4(0-2)
Kópavogur - ÍBV Vestmannaeyjar 2-0(2-0)
Fylkir Reykjavík - Valur Reykjavík 0-1(0-1)
Grindavík - KR Reykjavík 2-1(2-0)

Round 5 [19-20.05.2019]
ÍBV Vestmannaeyjar - Víkingur 1-1(0-0)
Stjarnan - KA Akureyri 0-2(0-0)
Breiðablik - ÍA Akranes 0-1(0-0)
Grindavík - Fylkir Reykjavík 1-0(0-0)
FH Hafnarfjörður - Valur Reykjavík 3-2(1-0)
KR Reykjavík - Kópavogur 3-2(2-0)

Round 6 [25-26.05.2019]
Kópavogur - Grindavík 0-0
KA Akureyri - ÍBV Vestmannaeyjar 2-0(0-0)
Víkingur - KR Reykjavík 0-1(0-1)
ÍA Akranes - Stjarnan 2-0(0-0)
Fylkir Reykjavík - FH Hafnarfjörður 2-2(1-1)
Valur Reykjavík - Breiðablik 0-1(0-0)

Round 7 [01-02.06.2019]
Grindavík - Víkingur 0-0
KR Reykjavík - KA Akureyri 1-0(0-0)
ÍBV Vestmannaeyjar - ÍA Akranes 3-2(2-1)
Breiðablik - FH Hafnarfjörður 4-1(0-0)
Kópavogur - Fylkir Reykjavík 1-2(1-0)
Stjarnan - Valur Reykjavík 2-1(0-1)

Round 8 [14-15.06.2019]
Fylkir Reykjavík - Breiðablik 4-3(2-1)
FH Hafnarfjörður - Stjarnan 2-2(0-1)
Víkingur - Kópavogur 2-1(2-1)
ÍA Akranes - KR Reykjavík 1-3(0-2)
Valur Reyk. - ÍBV Vestmannaeyjar 5-1(1-0)
KA Akureyri - Grindavík 2-1(1-0)

Round 9 [18-19.06.2019]
Stjarnan - Breiðablik 1-3(0-0)
KR Reykjavík - Valur Reykjavík 3-2(0-1)
ÍBV Vestm. - Hafnarfjörður 1-2(0-1) [13.07.]
Kópavogur - KA Akureyri 2-1(1-1) [14.07.]
Grindavík - ÍA Akranes 1-1(1-1) [15.07.]
Víkingur - Fylkir Reykjavík 1-1(1-1) [15.07.]

Round 10 [22-23.06.2019]
Breiðablik - ÍBV Vestmannaeyjar 3-1(1-1)
ÍA Akranes - Kópavogur 0-2(0-1)
Stjarnan - Fylkir Reykjavík 5-1(1-1)
Valur Reykjavík - Grindavík 1-0(0-0)
KA Akureyri - Víkingur 3-4(1-2)
FH Hafnarfjörður - KR Reykjavík 1-2(0-1)

Round 11 [30.06.-01.07.2019]
ÍBV Vestmannaeyjar - Stjarnan 0-2(0-0)
Fylkir Reykjavík - KA Akureyri 3-2(1-1)
Kópavogur - Valur Reykjavík 1-2(0-0)
Grindavík - FH Hafnarfjörður 0-0
KR Reykjavík - Breiðablik 2-0(1-0)
Víkingur - ÍA Akranes 0-0

Round 12 [04-08.07.2019]
Valur Reykjavík - KA Akureyri 3-1(1-0)
Stjarnan - Grindavík 0-0
ÍA Akranes - Fylkir Reykjavík 2-0(1-0)
ÍBV Vestmannaeyjar - KR Reykjavík 1-2(0-1)
Breiðablik - Kópavogur 1-2(0-1)
FH Hafnarfjörður - Víkingur 1-0(0-0)

Round 13 [21-22.07.2019]
Fylkir Reykj. - ÍBV Vestmannaeyjar 3-0(2-0)
KA Akureyri - ÍA Akranes 1-1(0-1)
Víkingur - Valur Reykjavík 2-2(0-1)
KR Reykjavík - Stjarnan 2-2(0-1)
Breiðablik - Grindavík 0-0
Kópavogur - FH Hafnarfjörður 2-0(2-0)

Round 14 [28-29.07.2019]
Grindavík - ÍBV Vestmannaeyjar 2-1(0-1)
KA Akureyri - FH Hafnarfjörður 1-0(0-0)
ÍA Akranes - Valur Reykjavík 1-2(1-1)
Fylkir Reykjavík - KR Reykjavík 1-4(0-3)
Kópavogur - Stjarnan 1-1(1-1)
Víkingur - Breiðablik 3-2(1-0)

Round 15 [03-07.08.2019]
ÍBV Vestmannaeyjar - Kópavogur 0-1(0-0)
FH Hafnarfjörður - ÍA Akranes 1-0(0-0)
KR Reykjavík - Grindavík 5-2(1-0)
Breiðablik - KA Akureyri 4-0(2-0)
Stjarnan - Víkingur 2-1(0-0)
Valur Reykjavík - Fylkir Reykjavík 1-0(1-0)

Round 16 [11-12.08.2019]
ÍA Akranes - Breiðablik 1-2(1-2)
KA Akureyri - Stjarnan 4-2(2-1)
Kópavogur - KR Reykjavík 4-1(3-1)
Víkingur - ÍBV Vestmannaeyjar 3-1(1-0)
Valur Reykjavík - FH Hafnarfjörður 2-3(0-0)
Fylkir Reykjavík - Grindavík 2-1(2-0)

Round 17 [18-19.08.2019]
ÍBV Vestmannaeyjar - KA Akureyri 1-1(0-1)
Grindavík - Kópavogur 1-1(0-1)
FH Hafnarfjörður - Fylkir Reykjavík 2-1(0-0)
Stjarnan - ÍA Akranes 3-1(1-1)
KR Reykjavík - Víkingur 1-0(1-0)
Breiðablik - Valur Reykjavík 3-3(2-2)

Round 18 [24-26.08.2019]
ÍA Akranes - ÍBV Vestmannaeyjar 2-1(1-0)
KA Akureyri - KR Reykjavík 0-0
Víkingur - Grindavík 1-0(0-0)
FH Hafnarfjörður - Breiðablik 2-4(2-1)
Fylkir Reykjavík - Kópavogur 3-2(2-1)
Valur Reykjavík - Stjarnan 2-2(1-1)

Round 19 [31.08.-01.09.2019]
Grindavík - KA Akureyri 0-2(0-0)
Stjarnan - FH Hafnarfjörður 1-3(1-0)
Kópavogur - Víkingur 1-3(0-1)
ÍBV Vestmannaeyjar - Valur Reykj. 2-1(1-1)
KR Reykjavík - ÍA Akranes 2-0(1-0)
Breiðablik - Fylkir Reykjavík 4-3(3-0)

Round 20 [15-18.09.2019]
KA Akureyri - Kópavogur 1-1(1-0)
ÍA Akranes - Grindavík 1-1(1-0)
Breiðablik - Stjarnan 1-1(0-1)
Valur Reykjavík - KR Reykjavík 0-1(0-1)
FH Hafnarfjörður - Vestmannaeyjar 6-4(4-1)
Fylkir Reykjavík - Víkingur 3-1(1-0)

Round 21 [22.09.2019]
Fylkir Reykjavík - Stjarnan 1-4(0-0)
Grindavík - Valur Reykjavík 2-2(1-1)
Kópavogur - ÍA Akranes 1-1(0-0)
KR Reykjavík - FH Hafnarfjörður 3-2(2-1)
ÍBV Vestmannaeyjar - Breiðablik 1-1(1-1)
Víkingur - KA Akureyri 2-3(0-1)

Round 22 [28.09.2019]
ÍA Akranes - Víkingur 1-5(1-2)
Breiðablik - KR Reykjavík 1-2(0-2)
FH Hafnarfjörður - Grindavík 3-0(1-0)
KA Akureyri - Fylkir Reykjavík 4-2(2-1)
Stjarnan - ÍBV Vestmannaeyjar 3-2(1-0)
Valur Reykjavík - Kópavogur 2-0(2-0)

Final Standings

					Total				Home				Away		
1. **KR Reykjavík**	22	16	4	2	44 - 23	52	9	2	0	26 - 11	7	2	2	18 - 12
2. Breiðablik Kópavogur	22	11	5	6	45 - 31	38	5	3	3	24 - 15	6	2	3	21 - 16
3. FH Hafnarfjörður	22	11	4	7	40 - 36	37	8	1	2	26 - 17	3	3	5	14 - 19
4. Stjarnan Garðabær	22	9	8	5	40 - 34	35	6	2	3	19 - 15	3	6	2	21 - 19
5. KA Akureyri	22	9	4	9	34 - 34	31	6	3	2	19 - 12	3	1	7	15 - 22
6. Valur Reykjavík	22	8	5	9	38 - 34	29	5	2	4	20 - 14	3	3	5	18 - 20
7. Víkingur Reykjavík	22	7	7	8	37 - 35	28	4	4	3	18 - 16	3	3	5	19 - 19
8. Fylkir Reykjavík	22	8	4	10	38 - 44	28	6	2	3	24 - 22	2	2	7	14 - 22
9. HK Kópavogur	22	7	6	9	29 - 29	27	4	4	3	17 - 13	3	2	6	12 - 16
10. ÍA Akranes	22	7	6	9	27 - 32	27	5	1	5	16 - 17	2	5	4	11 - 15
11. UMF Grindavík (*Relegated*)	22	3	11	8	17 - 28	20	3	6	2	10 - 11	0	5	6	7 - 17
12. ÍBV Vestmannaeyjar (*Relegated*)	22	2	4	16	23 - 52	10	2	4	5	12 - 18	0	0	11	11 - 34

Top goalscorers:	
14 Gary John Martin (ENG)	*Valur Reykjavík / ÍBV Vestmannaeyjar*
13 Steven Lennon (SCO)	*FH Hafnarfjörður*
13 Thomas Mikkelsen (DEN)	*Breiðablik Kópavogur*
13 Elfar Árni Aðalsteinsson	*KA Akureyri*
13 Hilmar Árni Halldórsson	*Stjarnan Garðabær*
10 Geoffrey Wynton Mandelano Castillion (NED)	*Fylkir Reykjavík*
10 Hallgrímur Mar Steingrímsson	*KA Akureyri*

First Round [10-15.04.2019]

Kári - Hamar	5-1		Dalvík/Reynir - Samherjar	6-0
Elliði - Álafoss	8-1		Huginn/Höttur - UMF Einherji	3-1
Afturelding - Léttir	6-0		UMF Tindastóll - Æskan	5-0
ÍR Reykjavík - SR	5-0		Kórdrengir - KM Reykjavík	7-0
Grótta - Álftanes	8-2		IF Vestri - Víðir Garður	1-0
Fram Reykjavík - GG Grindavík	2-1		Haukar Hafnarfjörður - KFS Vestmannaeyjar	5-2
Ýmir - Afríka	6-1		Nökkvi - KF Fjallabyggðar	2-4
Vængir Júpiters - Kóngarnir	9-0		Hvíti riddarinn - Kormákur/Hvöt	4-1
Kría - KÁ Ásvellir	1-2		Hörður Í. - KF Berserkir	1-5
Fenrir - Ægir	0-2		KFR Hvolsvöllur - KH Hlídarendi	1-0
KF Garðabæjar - Reynir Árskógsströnd	1-2 aet		UMF Skallagrímur - KV Vesturbæjar	1-4
Mídas - Ísbjörninn	1-0		Úlfarnir - Vatnaliljur	6-1
ÍH Hafnarfjörður - Björninn	3-0		UMF Selfoss - Þróttur Vogar	3-0
Augnablik - Árborg	8-1		KB Breiðholt - UMF Snæfell	2-1

Second Round [13-24.04.2019]

Sindri Höfn - Leiknir Fáskrúðsfirði	5-1		KB Breiðholt - Ægir	1-2 aet
Leiknir Reykjavík - Fjölnir Reykjavík	1-4		ÍR Reykjavík - KV Vesturbæjar	3-0
Fram Reykjavík - Ýmir	6-0		Víkingur Ólafsvík - Úlfarnir	2-6
KÁ Ásvellir - KF Berserkir	4-2		ÍH Hafnarfjörður - Augnablik	0-3
Þróttur Reykjavík - Reynir Sandgerði	2-0		Hvíti riddarinn - UMF Njarðvík	0-6
Afturelding - UMF Selfoss	3-2		Þór Akureyri - Dalvík/Reynir	2-3
Elliði - Mídas	1-2 aet		Huginn/Höttur - KF Fjarðabyggðar	0-2
Keflavík ÍF - Haukar Hafnarfjörður	1-0		KF Fjallabyggðar - ÍF Magni	0-4
Grótta - KFR Hvolsvöllur	10-0		IF Vestri - Kári	3-1
Kórdrengir - Vængir Júpiters	1-0		ÍF Völsungur - UMF Tindastóll	3-1

Third Round [28.04.-01.05.2019]

IF Vestri - Úlfarnir	2-1 aet		Augnablik - ÍA Akranes	0-3
ÍR Reykjavík - Fjölnir Reykjavík	1-3		HK Kópavogur - KF Fjarðabyggðar	5-1
Ægir - Þróttur Reykjavík	0-4		KR Reykjavík - Dalvík/Reynir	5-0
Fram Reykjavík - UMF Njarðvík	1-3		Sindri Höfn - KA Akureyri	0-5
UMF Grindavík - Afturelding	4-1		ÍF Magni - Breiðablik Kópavogur	1-10
Keflavík ÍF - Kórdrengir	1-0		ÍBV Vestmannaeyjar - UMF Stjarnan	1-0
KÁ Ásvellir - Víkingur Reykjavík	1-2		ÍF Völsungur - Mídas	4-0
Fylkir Reykjavík - Grótta	2-1		Valur Reykjavík - FH Hafnarfjörður	1-2

1/8-Finals [28-30.05.2019]

Víkingur Reykjavík - KA Akureyri	5-4 pen		ÍF Völsungur - KR Reykjavík	0-2
UMF Grindavík - IF Vestri	3-1		FH Hafnarfjörður - ÍA Akranes	2-1
Keflavík ÍF - UMF Njarðvík	0-1		Þróttur Reykjavík - Fylkir Reykjavík	1-3
ÍBV Vestmannaeyjar - Fjölnir Reykjavík	2-0		Breiðablik Kópavogur - HK Kópavogur	3-1

Quarter-Finals [26-27.06.2019]

ÍBV Vestmannaeyjar - Víkingur Reykjavík	2-3		Breiðablik Kópavogur - Fylkir Reykjavík	4-2 aet
FH Hafnarfjörður - UMF Grindavík	7-1		KR Reykjavík - UMF Njarðvík	3-0

Semi-Finals [14-15.08.2019]

FH Hafnarfjörður - KR Reykjavík	3-1		Víkingur Reykjavík - Breiðablik Kópavogur	3-1

Final

14.09.2019; Laugardalsvöllur, Reykjavík; Referee: Petur Gudmundsson; Attendance: 4,257

Víkingur Reykjavík - FH Hafnarfjörður   **1-0(0-0)**

Víkingur Reykjavík: Þórður Ingason, Sölvi Ottesen, Halldór Sigurðsson, Júlíus Magnússon, Erlingur Agnarsson (72.Viktor Örlygur Andrason), Ágúst Eðvald Hlynsson, Guðmundur Andri Tryggvason (88.Atli Hrafn Andrason), Logi Tómasson, Davíð Atlason, Nikolaj Hansen (71.Örvar Eggertsson). Trainer: Arnar Gunnlaugsson.

FH Hafnarfjörður: Daði Arnarsson, Pétur Viðarsson [*sent off 60*], Cédric D'Ulivo (88.Halldór Björnsson), Davíð Viðarsson, Guðmundur Kristjánsson, Björn Sverrisson, Brandur Hendriksson, Þórður Þorsteinn Þórðarson (81.Þórir Jóhann Helgason), Steven Lennon, Morten Beck Guldsmed, Jónatan Jónsson (62.Guðmann Þórisson). Trainer: Ólafur Helgi Kristjánsson.

Goal: 1-0 Ágúst Eðvald Hlynsson (58 penalty).

Breiðablik Kópavogur

Founded: 12.04.1950
Stadium: Kópavogsvöllur, Kópavogur (5,501)
Trainer: Ágúst Þór Gylfason   01.08.1971

Goalkeepers:	DOB	M	(s)	G
Gunnleifur Gunnleifsson	14.07.1975	22		
Hlynur Hlöðversson	12.05.1996		(1)	
Defenders:	**DOB**	**M**	**(s)**	**G**
Guðmundur Guðjónsson	03.08.1989	1	(5)	
Elfar Helgason	27.07.1989	18		
Jonathan Hendrickx (BEL)	25.12.1993	9		
Viktor Örn Margeirsson	22.07.1994	21		2
Damir Muminović (SRB)	13.05.1990	20	(1)	1
Alfons Sampsted	06.04.1998	8		1
Midfielders:	**DOB**	**M**	**(s)**	**G**
Viktor Einarsson	30.01.1997	5	(9)	1
Gísli Eyjólfsson	31.05.1994	5	(5)	
Höskuldur Gunnlaugsson	26.09.1994	18	(2)	7

	DOB	M	(s)	G
Kristian Nökkvi Hlynsson	23.01.2004		(1)	
Davíð Ingvarsson	25.04.1999	14	(1)	
Guðjón Lýðsson	28.12.1987	21		1
Kwame Quee (SLE)	07.09.1996		(1)	
Brynjólfur Darri Willumsson	12.08.2000	5	(12)	3
Kolbeinn Þórðarson	12.03.2000	10	(3)	4
Forwards:	**DOB**	**M**	**(s)**	**G**
Aron Bjarnason	14.10.1995	7	(3)	4
Arnar Geirsson	30.08.1991	9	(2)	
Þórir Guðjónsson	07.04.1991	1	(5)	1
Karl Gunnarsson	06.07.2001	1	(1)	
Thomas Mikkelsen (DEN)	19.01.1990	20		13
Alexander Sigurðarson	08.04.1996	12	(4)	2
Andri Yeoman	18.04.1992	15	(4)	4

Fimleikafélag Hafnarfjarðar

Founded: 15.10.1929
Stadium: Kaplakriki, Hafnarfjörður (6,738)
Trainer: Ólafur Helgi Kristjánsson   20.05.1968

Goalkeepers:	DOB	M	(s)	G
Daði Arnarsson	23.09.1998	15		
Vignir Jóhannesson	06.09.1990	4	(1)	
Gunnar Nielsen (FRO)	07.10.1986	3		
Defenders:	**DOB**	**M**	**(s)**	**G**
Cédric D'Ulivo (FRA)	29.08.1989	9	(3)	
Logi Hrafn Róbertsson	22.07.2004		(1)	
Hjörtur Valgarðsson	27.09.1988	17		1
Pétur Viðarsson	25.11.1987	18		1
Midfielders:	**DOB**	**M**	**(s)**	**G**
Brynjar Ásgeir Guðmundsson	22.06.1992	5	(6)	1
Þórir Jóhann Helgason	28.09.2000	10	(6)	
Guðmundur Kristjánsson	01.03.1989	19		

	DOB	M	(s)	G
Brandur Olsen (FRO)	19.12.1995	17	(1)	6
Kristinn Steindórsson	29.04.1990	10	(2)	
Björn Sverrisson	29.05.1990	22		3
Davíð Viðarsson	24.04.1984	11	(5)	
Þórður Þorsteinn Þórðarson	22.02.1995	6	(3)	
Guðmann Þórisson	30.01.1987	14	(4)	
Forwards:	**DOB**	**M**	**(s)**	**G**
Halldór Björnsson	02.03.1987	7	(11)	3
Atli Guðnason	28.09.1984	10	(7)	1
Morten Beck Guldsmed (DEN)	02.01.1988	8		8
Jónatan Jónsson	15.03.1999	16	(5)	1
Steven Lennon (SCO)	20.01.1988	15	(4)	13
Jákup Thomsen (FRO)	23.11.1997	6	(5)	1

Íþróttafélagið Fylkir Reykjavík

Founded: 28.05.1967
Stadium: Floridana völlurinn, Reykjavík (5,000)
Trainer: Helgi Sigurðsson   17.09.1974

Goalkeepers:	DOB	M	(s)	G
Aron Snær Friðriksson	29.01.1997	10		
Ólafur Helgason	24.10.2002	1		
Stefán Logi Magnússon	05.09.1980	10		
Kristófer Leví Sigtryggsson	31.07.2000	1	(1)	
Defenders:	**DOB**	**M**	**(s)**	**G**
Ásgeir Eyþórsson	29.04.1993	21	(1)	3
Birkir Eyþórsson	22.06.1905	3	(2)	
Valdimar Þór Ingimundarson	28.04.1999	17	(4)	6
Andrés Jóhannesson	21.12.1988	15	(2)	
Hákon Ingi Jónsson	10.11.1995	12	(9)	4
Midfielders:	**DOB**	**M**	**(s)**	**G**
Davíð Þór Ásbjörnsson	24.02.1992		(1)	
Emil Ásmundsson	08.01.1995	4	(4)	1

	DOB	M	(s)	G
Helgi Daníelsson	13.07.1981	20		4
Kolbeinn Finnsson	25.08.1999	11	(2)	2
Oddur Guðmundsson	28.01.1989	1		
Sam Hewson (ENG)	28.11.1988	13	(7)	1
Ari Leifsson	19.04.1998	21	(1)	
Daði Ólafsson	05.01.1994	17	(2)	
Leonard Sigurðsson	30.04.1996	1	(3)	
Ólafur Skúlason	01.04.1983	19		2
Orri Sveinn Stefánsson	20.02.1996	11	(6)	1
Forwards:	**DOB**	**M**	**(s)**	**G**
Geoffrey Wynton Mandelano Castillion (NED)	25.05.1991	18	(1)	10
Andri Jónsson	24.02.1991		(3)	
Arnór Gauti Ragnarsson	04.02.1997	5	(11)	
Ragnar Sveinsson	18.12.1994	12	(2)	

Ungmennafélag Grindavíkur

Founded: 1935
Stadium: Grindavíkurvöllur, Grindavík (1,750)
Trainer: Srdjan Tufegdzić (SRB)   06.04.1980

Goalkeepers:	DOB	M	(s)	G
Vladan Đogatović (SRB)	03.11.1984	21		
Maciej Majewski (POL)	24.01.1989	1		
Defenders:	**DOB**	**M**	**(s)**	**G**
Hermann Björnsson	12.07.1992	1	(10)	
Jón Ingason	21.09.1995		(6)	
Marc McAusland (SCO)	13.08.1988	22		
Sigurjón Rúnarsson	02.10.2000	11	(3)	1
Elias Alexander Tamburini (FIN)	01.02.1995	22		
Josip Zeba (CRO)	20.04.1990	22		2
Midfielders:	**DOB**	**M**	**(s)**	**G**
Sigurður Hallsson	01.09.1999	8	(8)	2
Marinó Axel Helgason	04.01.1997	16	(2)	
René Shaki Joensen (FRO)	08.02.1993	6	(1)	

	DOB	M	(s)	G
Aron Jóhannsson	11.01.1994	20	(2)	3
Nemanja Latinovic	10.10.1995		(1)	
Diego Diz Martínez (ESP)	12.11.1991	6	(5)	
Rodrigo Gomes Mateo „Rodri" (ESP)	09.02.1989	20		
Símon Logi Thasaphong	13.02.2001		(1)	
Alexander Þórarinsson	14.12.1988	12	(2)	2
Gunnar Þorsteinsson	01.02.1994	20		
Forwards:	**DOB**	**M**	**(s)**	**G**
Dagur Gunnarsson	02.07.2000	1	(11)	
Stefan Alexander Ljubicic	05.10.1999	6	(2)	1
Patrick N'Koyi-Kiabu (COD)	01.01.1990	5	(3)	1
Óscar Manuel Conde Cruz (ESP)	24.06.1993	11	(1)	3
Vladimir Tufegdžić (SRB)	12.06.1991	11	(1)	1

Íþróttabandalag Vestmannaeyja

Founded: 1903
Stadium: Hásteinsvöllur, Vestmannaeyjar (3,034)
Trainer: Pedro Manuel da Cunha Hipólito (POR)   16.09.1978
[01.07.2019]   Ian David Jeffs (ENG)   12.10.1982

Goalkeepers:	DOB	M	(s)	G
Halldór Geirsson	21.07.1994	15		
Rafael Henriques Vasquez Veloso (POR)	03.11.1993	7		
Defenders:	DOB	M	(s)	G
Gilson Correia (GNB)	05.04.1997	8		
Diogo Manuel Gonçalves Coelho (POR)	08.07.1992	17		
Felix Örn Friðriksson	16.03.1999	15	(5)	
Matt Garner (ENG)	09.04.1984	14	(2)	
Oran Egypt Jackson (ENG)	16.10.1998	9		
Sigurður Arnar Magnússon	30.06.1999	16	(2)	2
Nökkvi Már Nökkvason	02.07.2000	2	(1)	
Midfielders:	DOB	M	(s)	G
Sindri Björnsson	29.03.1995	3	(2)	
Róbert Eysteinsson	17.06.1999	6	(7)	
Priestley Griffiths (ENG)	11.06.1996	16	(3)	

	DOB	M	(s)	G
Eyþór Daði Kjartansson	20.06.2000		(1)	
Sindri Snær Magnússon	18.02.1992	6	(2)	
Tómas Bent Magnússon	14.08.2002	1	(1)	
Evariste Ngolok (CMR)	15.11.1988	5	(2)	
Breki Ómarsson	10.08.1998	5	(7)	1
Eyþór Orri Ómarsson	08.07.2003		(7)	
Benjamin Prah (GHA)	05.07.1994	2	(4)	
Telmo Ferreira Castanheira (POR)	13.04.1992	21		2
Forwards:	DOB	M	(s)	G
Jonathan Ian Franks (ENG)	06.04.1990	18	(2)	
Jonathan Ricardo Glenn (TRI)	27.08.1987	9	(5)	2
Guðmundur Magnússon	10.06.1991	6	(4)	1
Gary John Martin (ENG)	10.10.1990	12		12
Óskar Óskarsson	04.11.1995	8	(6)	
Víðir Þorvarðarson	07.07.1992	21		2

Knattspyrnufélag Akureyrar

Founded: 1928
Stadium: Akureyrarvöllur, Akureyri (1,770)
Trainer: Óli Stefán Flóventsson   07.12.1975

Goalkeepers:	DOB	M	(s)	G
Aron Dagur Birnuson	03.07.1999	12		
Kristijan Jajalo (BIH)	04.03.1993	10	(1)	
Defenders:	DOB	M	(s)	G
Ívar Örn Árnason	12.04.1996	3	(1)	
Alexander Groven (NOR)	02.01.1992	9	(4)	1
Haukur Hauksson	01.09.1991	11		
Hallgrímur Jónasson	04.05.1986	11	(1)	
Andri Stefánsson	22.04.1991	12	(7)	1
Hrannar Björn Steingrímsson	19.06.1992	17	(1)	1
Midfielders:	DOB	M	(s)	G
Bjarni Aðalsteinsson	01.09.1999	2	(5)	
Brynjar Ingi Bjarnason	06.12.1999	7	(5)	
David Cuerva Barroso (ESP)	06.04.1991	4	(2)	
Ýmir Már Geirsson	11.11.1997	11	(1)	

	DOB	M	(s)	G
Torfi Gunnarsson	31.01.1999	12	(3)	1
Daníel Hafsteinsson	12.11.1999	12		1
Iosu Villar Vidal (ESP)	16.02.1987	10		
Almarr Ormarsson	25.02.1988	20		1
Ólafur Aron Pétursson	17.07.1995		(3)	1
Hallgrímur Mar Steingrímsson	02.10.1990	22		10
Callum Williams (ENG)	08.11.1994	17		
Þorri Mar Þórisson	13.08.1999		(2)	
Steinþór Þorsteinsson	29.07.1985	7	(3)	
Forwards:	DOB	M	(s)	G
Elfar Aðalsteinsson	12.08.1990	20		13
Sæþór Olgeirsson	06.04.1998	1	(5)	
Ásgeir Sigurgeirsson	11.12.1996	11	(4)	1
Nökkvi Þórisson	13.08.1999	1	(16)	2

Knattspyrnufélag Reykjavíkur

Founded: 16.02.1899
Stadium: Alvogenvöllurinn, Reykjavík (3,333)
Trainer: Rúnar Kristinsson   05.09.1969

Goalkeepers:	DOB	M	(s)	G
Beitir Ólafsson	02.07.1986	22		
Defenders:	DOB	M	(s)	G
Arnór Aðalsteinsson	26.01.1986	21		
Skúli Jón Friðgeirsson	30.07.1988	7	(5)	
Gunnar Gunnarsson	04.10.1985	6	(1)	
Kristinn Jónsson	04.08.1990	18	(1)	3
Aron Jósepsson	21.11.1989	1	(4)	
Finnur Tómas Pálmason	12.02.2001	17		1
Midfielders:	DOB	M	(s)	G
Kristján Flóki Finnbogason	12.01.1995	8		3
Óskar Hauksson	22.08.1984	22		7

	DOB	M	(s)	G
Alex Freyr Hilmarsson	26.07.1993	5	(2)	2
Ægir Jónasson	08.03.1998	3	(15)	
Arnþór Ingi Kristinsson	15.03.1990	12	(4)	2
Finnur Margeirsson	08.03.1991	7	(7)	
Pálmi Pálmason	09.11.1984	22		8
Pablo Oshan Battuto Punyed (SLV)	18.04.1990	13	(9)	3
Atli Sigurjónsson	01.07.1991	14	(3)	1
Björgvin Stefánsson	20.12.1994	5	(6)	4
Ástbjörn Þórðarson	26.07.1999		(4)	
Forwards:	DOB	M	(s)	G
Kennie Knak Chopart (DEN)	01.06.1990	18	(2)	2
Tobias Thomsen (DEN)	19.10.1992	21		7

Handknattleiksfélag Kópavogs

Founded: 26.01.1970
Stadium: Kórinn, Kopavogur (1,452)
Trainer: Brynjar Björn Gunnarsson   16.10.1975

Goalkeepers:	DOB	M	(s)	G
Arnar Freyr Ólafsson	06.03.1993	22		
Defenders:	DOB	M	(s)	G
Aron Kári Aðalsteinsson	09.07.1999	1	(2)	
Hörður Árnason	19.05.1989	21		
Björn Bryde	08.07.1992	17		2
Daníel Ingi Egilsson	16.08.2000		(1)	
Birnir Snær Ingason	04.12.1996	6	(2)	1
Andri Jónasson	14.09.1994		(1)	
Birkir Valur Jónsson	02.11.1998	21		2
Leifur Andri Leifsson	11.10.1989	22		
Alexander Freyr Sindrason	31.07.1993	4	(2)	
Midfielders:	DOB	M	(s)	G
Ásgeir Ásgeirsson	16.04.1987	17	(2)	1

	DOB	M	(s)	G
Hafsteinn Briem	28.02.1991		(1)	
Ólafur Örn Eyjólfsson	14.10.1994	5		
Máni Hilmarsson	02.06.1998	3	(5)	
Ásgeir Marteinsson	07.07.1994	19	(1)	5
Valgeir Valgeirsson	22.09.2002	14	(6)	3
Forwards:	DOB	M	(s)	G
Atli Arnarson	29.11.1993	18		5
Arnþór Ari Atlason	12.10.1993	18		2
Emil Atlason	22.07.1993	11	(10)	3
Bjarni Gunnarsson	29.01.1993	15	(2)	3
Brynjar Jónasson	14.09.1994	5	(8)	1
Kári Pétursson	01.10.1996	3	(6)	1
Ari Sigurpálsson	17.03.2003		(2)	

Íþróttabandalag Akraness

Founded: 1946
Stadium: Norðurálsvöllurinn, Akranes (3,054)
Trainer: Jóhannes Karl Guðjónsson 25.05.1980

Goalkeepers:	DOB	M	(s)	G
Árni Ólafsson	16.08.1991	22		
Defenders:	**DOB**	**M**	**(s)**	**G**
Jón Gíslason	25.02.2002	8	(2)	
Arnór Snær Guðmundsson	20.04.1993	6	(7)	
Marcus Johansson (SWE)	24.08.1993	19		
Aron Kristófer Lárusson	17.09.1998	5	(2)	1
Midfielders:	**DOB**	**M**	**(s)**	**G**
Bjarki Steinn Bjarkason	11.05.2000	9	(11)	3
Einar Einarsson	24.11.1991	19		3
Hallur Flosason	01.05.1993	12	(2)	1
Óttar Bjarni Guðmundsson	15.04.1990	20		2
Hörður Ingi Gunnarsson	14.08.1998	21		2

	DOB	M	(s)	G
Albert Hafsteinsson	05.06.1996	6	(9)	
Tryggvi Hrafn Haraldsson	30.09.1996	20	(2)	7
Hlynur Sævar Jónsson	29.03.1999	1		
Sindri Snær Magnússon	18.02.1992	7		
Brynjar Pálsson	11.11.2001		(1)	
Þórður Þórðarson	22.02.1995	1	(3)	
Sigurður Hrannar Þorsteinsson	19.04.2000		(1)	
Steinar Þorsteinsson	06.12.1997	9	(11)	2
Forwards:	**DOB**	**M**	**(s)**	**G**
Gonzalo Zamorano Léon (ESP)	11.06.1995	10	(10)	
Arnar Guðjónsson	20.02.1987	13		1
Viktor Jónsson	23.06.1994	15	(3)	4
Stefán Teitur Þórðarson	16.10.1998	19	(1)	1

Ungmennafélagið Stjarnan Garðabær

Founded: 1960
Stadium: Samsung völlurinn, Garðabær (2,300)
Trainer: Rúnar Páll Sigmundsson 05.05.1974

Goalkeepers:	DOB	M	(s)	G
Haraldur Björnsson	11.01.1989	22		
Guðjón Sigurjónsson	21.10.1992		(2)	
Defenders:	**DOB**	**M**	**(s)**	**G**
Heiðar Ægisson	10.08.1995	13	(1)	
Brynjar Guðjónsson	27.02.1992	17	(2)	
Jósef Kristinn Jósefsson	12.09.1989	14	(1)	2
Daníel Laxdal	22.09.1986	11	(2)	
Jóhann Laxdal	27.01.1990	7	(1)	
Martin Rauschenberg Brorsen (DEN)	15.01.1992	19		1
Þórarinn Valdimarsson	23.04.1990	7	(1)	
Midfielders:	**DOB**	**M**	**(s)**	**G**
Elís Rafn Björnsson	13.10.1992	3	(1)	
Sölvi Guðbjargarson	25.07.2001	12	(6)	5

	DOB	M	(s)	G
Alex Þór Hauksson	26.11.1999	17	(2)	3
Eyjólfur Héðinsson	01.01.1985	16	(3)	
Ævar Jóhannesson	31.01.1995	4	(2)	2
Þorsteinn Már Ragnarsson	19.04.1990	19	(1)	4
Þorri Geir Rúnarsson	24.04.1995	7	(6)	1
Baldur Sigurðsson	24.04.1985	14	(4)	3
Forwards:	**DOB**	**M**	**(s)**	**G**
Guðjón Baldvinsson	15.02.1986	11	(3)	3
Adolf Daði Birgisson	03.06.2004		(1)	
Nimo Gribenco (DEN)	23.01.1997	3	(9)	
Guðmundur Hafsteinsson	14.06.1989	5	(13)	3
Hilmar Árni Halldórsson	14.02.1992	21	(1)	13
Óli Ómarsson	09.01.2003		(1)	

Knattspyrnufélagið Valur Reykjavík

Founded: 11.05.1911
Stadium: Valsvöllur, Reykjavík (2,465)
Trainer: Ólafur Jóhannesson 30.06.1957

Goalkeepers:	DOB	M	(s)	G
Anton Ari Einarsson	25.08.1994	3		
Hannes Halldórsson	27.04.1984	19		
Defenders:	**DOB**	**M**	**(s)**	**G**
Bjarni Eiríksson	28.03.1982	18		
Sebastian Hedlund (SWE)	05.04.1995	16	(3)	
Birnir Snær Ingason	04.12.1996		(10)	1
Sigurður Lárusson	22.01.1992	16		3
Birkir Sævarsson	11.11.1984	22		2
Eiður Sigurbjörnsson	26.02.1990	21		1
Midfielders:	**DOB**	**M**	**(s)**	**G**
Sindri Björnsson	29.03.1995	1		
Ólafur Finsen	30.03.1992	9	(3)	5
Kristinn Halldórsson	08.04.1989	4	(10)	

	DOB	M	(s)	G
Einar Karl Ingvarsson	08.10.1993	12	(5)	
Orri Ómarsson	18.02.1995	10	(2)	1
Lasse Petry (DEN)	19.09.1992	12		3
Haukur Sigurðsson	05.08.1987	19		2
Kristinn Sigurðsson	25.12.1991	15	(3)	3
Forwards:	**DOB**	**M**	**(s)**	**G**
Andri Adolphsson	01.12.1992	21		5
Valgeir Friðriksson	24.09.2001		(1)	
Garðar Gunnlaugsson	24.04.1983		(4)	
Kaj Leo í Bartalsstovu (FRO)	23.06.1991	4	(12)	
Ívar Jónsson	02.02.1994	3	(3)	
Emil Lyng (DEN)	03.08.1989	3	(7)	1
Gary John Martin (ENG)	10.10.1990	3		2
Patrick Pedersen (DEN)	25.11.1991	11		8

Knattspyrnufélagið Víkingur Reykjavík

Founded: 21.04.1908
Stadium: Víkingsvöllur, Reykjavík (1,848)
Trainer: Arnar Gunnlaugsson 06.03.1973

Goalkeepers:	DOB	M	(s)	G
Francisco Marmolejo Mancilla „Fran" (ESP)	19.01.1988	2		
Þórður Ingason	30.03.1988	20		
Defenders:	**DOB**	**M**	**(s)**	**G**
Mohamed Fofana (GUI)	08.04.1998	7	(1)	
Gunnlaugur Guðmundsson	17.07.1994	1	(1)	
Sölvi Ottesen	18.02.1984	20		2
Dofri Snorrason	21.07.1990	9	(3)	
Halldór Þórðarson	12.07.1996		(2)	
Midfielders:	**DOB**	**M**	**(s)**	**G**
Erlingur Agnarsson	05.03.1998	14	(1)	2
Atli Hrafn Andrason	04.01.1999	12	(6)	1
Kári Árnason	13.10.1982	10		2
Ágúst Eðvald Hlynsson	28.03.2000	21		4
James Charles Mack III (USA)	10.08.1988		(5)	

	DOB	M	(s)	G
Júlíus Magnússon	28.06.1998	17		1
Kwame Quee (SLE)	07.09.1996	9	(3)	4
Bjarni Páll Runólfsson	10.09.1996		(2)	
Halldór Sigurðsson	04.10.1988	21		
Logi Tómasson	13.09.2000	8	(8)	2
Guðmundur Andri Tryggvason	04.11.1999	16		7
Þórir Rafn Þórisson	23.05.2001		(1)	
Forwards:	**DOB**	**M**	**(s)**	**G**
Viktor Örlygur Andrason	05.02.2000	6	(9)	
Davíð Atlason	18.08.1994	20		
Örvar Eggertsson	28.02.1999	3	(9)	1
Nikolaj Hansen (DEN)	15.03.1993	14	(2)	4
Óttar Magnús Karlsson	21.02.1997	8		5
Rick ten Voorde (NED)	20.06.1991	4	(4)	1

Yearbook of European Football-368

SECOND LEVEL
1. deild karla 2019

1.	IF Grótta Seltjarnarnes (*Promoted*)	22	12	7	3	45	-	31	43
2.	Fjölnir Reykjavík (*Promoted*)	22	12	6	4	49	-	22	42
3.	Leiknir Reykjavík	22	12	4	6	37	-	28	40
4.	Víkingur Ólafsvík	22	9	7	6	28	-	20	34
5.	Keflavík	22	10	4	8	31	-	27	34
6.	Þór Akureyri	22	9	7	6	31	-	30	34
7.	Fram Reykjavík	22	10	3	9	33	-	32	33
8.	UMF Afturelding Mosfellsbær	22	6	5	11	30	-	37	23
9.	IF Magni Grenivík	22	6	5	11	27	-	49	23
10.	Þróttur Reykjavík	22	6	4	12	36	-	40	22
11.	Haukar Hafnarfjörður (*Relegated*)	22	5	7	10	31	-	41	22
12.	UMF Njarðvík (*Relegated*)	22	4	3	15	23	-	44	15

NATIONAL TEAM

INTERNATIONAL MATCHES
(16.07.2019 – 15.07.2020)

07.09.2019	Reykjavík	Iceland - Moldova	3-0(1-0)	(ECQ)
10.09.2019	Elbasan	Albania - Iceland	4-2(1-0)	(ECQ)
11.10.2019	Reykjavík	Iceland - France	0-1(0-0)	(ECQ)
14.10.2019	Reykjavík	Iceland - Andorra	2-0(1-0)	(ECQ)
14.11.2019	İstanbul	Turkey - Iceland	0-0	(ECQ)
17.11.2019	Chişinău	Moldova - Iceland	1-2(0-1)	(ECQ)
15.01.2020	Irvine	Canada - Iceland	0-1(0-1)	(F)
19.01.2020	Carson	El Salvador - Iceland	0-1(0-0)	(F)

07.09.2019   ICELAND - MOLDOVA   **3-0(1-0)**   16th EC. Qualifiers
Laugardalsvöllur, Reykjavík; Referee: João Pedro Silva Pinheiro (Portugal); Attendance: 8,338
ISL: Hannes Þór Halldórsson, Ragnar Sigurðsson, Ari Freyr Skúlason, Kári Árnason, Hjörtur Hermannsson, Birkir Bjarnason (78.Rúnar Már Sigurjónsson), Aron Einar Gunnarsson (Cap), Gylfi Þór Sigurðsson, Arnór Ingvi Traustason, Kolbeinn Sigþórsson (63.Emil Hallfreðsson), Jón Daði Böðvarsson (84.Viðar Örn Kjartansson). Trainer: Erik Anders Hamrén (Sweden).
Goals: Kolbeinn Sigþórsson (31), Birkir Bjarnason (55), Jón Böðvarsson (77).

10.09.2019   ALBANIA - ICELAND   **4-2(1-0)**   16th EC. Qualifiers
Elbasan Arena, Elbasan; Referee: Ivan Kružliak (Slovakia); Attendance: 8,652
ISL: Hannes Þór Halldórsson, Ragnar Sigurðsson, Ari Freyr Skúlason, Kári Árnason, Hjörtur Hermannsson, Birkir Bjarnason (71.Hörður Björgvin Magnússon), Emil Hallfreðsson (56.Kolbeinn Sigþórsson), Aron Einar Gunnarsson (Cap), Rúnar Már Sigurjónsson, Gylfi Þór Sigurðsson, Jón Daði Böðvarsson (83.Viðar Örn Kjartansson). Trainer: Erik Anders Hamrén (Sweden).
Goals: Gylfi Þór Sigurðsson (47), Kolbeinn Sigþórsson (58).

11.10.2019   ICELAND - FRANCE   **0-1(0-0)**   16th EC. Qualifiers
Laugardalsvöllur, Reykjavík; Referee: Gianluca Rocchi (Italy); Attendance: 9,719
ISL: Hannes Þór Halldórsson, Ragnar Sigurðsson, Ari Freyr Skúlason, Kári Árnason, Birkir Bjarnason, Jóhann Berg Guðmundsson (15.Jón Daði Böðvarsson), Rúnar Már Sigurjónsson (73.Alfreð Finnbogason), Gylfi Þór Sigurðsson (Cap), Guðlaugur Victor Pálsson, Arnór Ingvi Traustason (81.Arnór Sigurðsson), Kolbeinn Sigþórsson. Trainer: Erik Anders Hamrén (Sweden).

14.10.2019   ICELAND - ANDORRA   **2-0(1-0)**   16th EC. Qualifiers
Laugardalsvöllur, Reykjavík; Referee: Bognár Tamás (Hungary); Attendance: 7,981
ISL: Hannes Þór Halldórsson, Ragnar Sigurðsson (68.Sverrir Ingi Ingason), Jón Guðni Fjóluson, Ari Freyr Skúlason, Birkir Bjarnason (70.Emil Hallfreðsson), Gylfi Þór Sigurðsson (Cap), Guðlaugur Victor Pálsson, Arnór Ingvi Traustason, Arnór Sigurðsson, Kolbeinn Sigþórsson, Alfreð Finnbogason (64.Jón Daði Böðvarsson). Trainer: Erik Anders Hamrén (Sweden).
Goals: Arnór Sigurðsson (38), Kolbeinn Sigþórsson (65).

14.11.2019   TURKEY - ICELAND   **0-0**   16th EC. Qualifiers
Türk Telekom Arena, İstanbul; Referee: Anthony Taylor (England); Attendance: 48,329
ISL: Hannes Þór Halldórsson, Ragnar Sigurðsson, Ari Freyr Skúlason (85.Mikael Neville Anderson), Kári Árnason, Birkir Bjarnason, Gylfi Þór Sigurðsson (Cap), Guðlaugur Victor Pálsson, Kolbeinn Sigþórsson, Arnór Ingvi Traustason (63.Hörður Björgvin Magnússon), Alfreð Finnbogason (24.Arnór Sigurðsson), Jón Daði Böðvarsson. Trainer: Erik Anders Hamrén (Sweden).

17.11.2019   MOLDOVA - ICELAND   **1-2(0-1)**   16th EC. Qualifiers
Stadionul Zimbru, Chişinău; Referee: Pavel Královec (Czech Republic); Attendance: 6,742
ISL: Hannes Þór Halldórsson, Ragnar Sigurðsson (Cap), Ari Freyr Skúlason, Sverrir Ingi Ingason, Birkir Bjarnason (87.Hörður Björgvin Magnússon), Gylfi Þór Sigurðsson, Guðlaugur Victor Pálsson, Arnór Sigurðsson, Mikael Neville Anderson (55.Samúel Kári Friðjónsson), Kolbeinn Sigþórsson (29.Viðar Örn Kjartansson), Jón Daði Böðvarsson. Trainer: Erik Anders Hamrén (Sweden).
Goals: Birkir Bjarnason (17), Gylfi Þór Sigurðsson (65).

15.01.2020   CANADA - ICELAND   **0-1(0-1)**   Friendly International
Championship Soccer Stadium, Irvine (United States); Referee: Rubiel Vazquez (United States); Attendance: 20
ISL: Hannes Þór Halldórsson, Hólmar Örn Eyjólfsson, Kári Árnason (Cap) (46.Birkir Már Sævarsson) , Daníel Leó Grétarsson, Davíð Kristján Ólafsson, Aron Elís Þrándarson (73.Stefán Teitur Þórðarson), Höskuldur Gunnlaugsson (81.Bjarni Mark Antonsson), Alex Þór Hauksson, Mikael Neville Anderson (89.Alfons Sampsted), Kjartan Henry Finnbogason (60.Óttar Magnús Karlsson), Viðar Örn Kjartansson (60.Kristján Flóki Finnbogason). Trainer: Erik Anders Hamrén (Sweden).
Goal: Hólmar Eyjólfsson (21).

19.01.2020   EL SALVADOR - ICELAND   0-1(0-0)   Friendly International

Dignity Health Sports Park, Carson (United States); Referee: Alejandro Mariscal (United States); Attendance: 500

ISL: Hannes Þór Halldórsson, Birkir Már Sævarsson (46.Alfons Sampsted), Kári Árnason (Cap) (61.Hólmar Örn Eyjólfsson), Óskar Tor Sverrisson, Ari Leifsson, Bjarni Mark Antonsson, Tryggvi Hrafn Haraldsson (61.Mikael Neville Anderson), Kjartan Henry Finnbogason (74.Kolbeinn Sigþórsson), Kristján Flóki Finnbogason (46.Viðar Örn Kjartansson), Óttar Magnús Karlsson, Stefán Teitur Þórðarson (78.Alex Þór Hauksson). Trainer: Erik Anders Hamrén (Sweden).

Goal: Kjartan Finnbogason (65).

NATIONAL TEAM PLAYERS
(16.07.2019 – 15.07.2020)

Name	DOB	Caps	Goals	2019/2020:	Club
Goalkeepers					
Hannes Þór HALLDÓRSSON	27.04.1984	69	0	2019/2020:	Valur Reykjavík
Defenders					
Kári ÁRNASON	13.10.1982	83	6	2019/2020:	Víkingur Reykjavík
Hólmar Örn EYJÓLFSSON	06.08.1990	14	2	2019/2020:	PFC Levski Sofia (BUL)
Jón Guðni FJÓLUSON	10.04.1989	16	1	2019:	FK Krasnodar (RUS)
Samúel Kári FRIDJÓNSSON	22.02.1996	8	0	2019:	Viking FK Stavanger (NOR)
Daníel Leó GRÉTARSSON	02.10.1995	1	0	2020:	Aalesunds FK (NOR)
Iljörtur HERMANNSSON	08.02.1995	14	1	2019:	Brøndby IF (DEN)
Sverrir Ingi INGASON	05.05.1993	29	3	2019:	PAOK Thessaloníki (GRE)
Ari LEIFSSON	19.08.1998	1	0	2020:	Fylkir Reykjavík
Hörður Björgvin MAGNÚSSON	11.02.1993	28	2	2019:	FK CSKA Moskva (RUS)
Davíð Kristján ÓLAFSSON	15.05.1995	2	0	2020:	Aalesunds FK (NOR)
Alfons SAMPSTED	06.04.1998	2	0	2020:	IFK Norrköping (SWE)
Ragnar SIGURÐSSON	19.06.1986	94	5	2019:	FK Rostov (RUS)
Ari Freyr SKÚLASON	14.05.1987	72	0	2019:	KV Oostende (BEL)
Óskar Tor SVERRISSON	26.11.1992	1	0	2020:	BK Häcken Göteborg (SWE)
Birkir Már SÆVARSSON	11.11.1984	92	1	2020:	Valur Reykjavík
Midfielders					
Mikael Neville ANDERSON	01.07.1998	5	0	2019/2020:	FC Midtjylland Herning (DEN)
Bjarni Mark ANTONSSON	27.12.1995	2	0	2020:	IK Brage Borlänge (SWE)
Birkir BJARNASON	27.05.1988	84	13	2019: 15.10.2019->	Unattached Al-Arabi SC Doha (QAT)
Höskuldur GUNNLAUGSSON	26.09.1994	1	0	2020:	Halmstads BK (SWE)
Aron Einar GUNNARSSON	22.04.1989	87	2	2019:	Al-Arabi SC Doha (QAT)
Jóhann Berg GUÐMUNDSSON	27.10.1990	75	7	2019:	Burnley FC (ENG)
Emil HALLFREÐSSON	29.06.1984	71	1	2019:	Unattached
Alex Þór HAUKSSON	26.11.1999	3	0	2020:	Stjarnan Garðabær
Guðlaugur Victor PÁLSSON	30.04.1991	15	0	2019:	SV Darmstadt 98 (GER)
Rúnar Már SIGURJÓNSSON	18.06.1990	22	1	2019:	Astana FC (KAZ)
Arnór SIGURÐSSON	15.05.1999	8	1	2019:	FK CSKA Moskva (RUS)
Gylfi Þór SIGURÐSSON	08.09.1989	74	22	2019:	Everton FC Liverpool (ENG)
Arnór Ingvi TRAUSTASON	30.04.1993	33	5	2019:	Malmö FF (SWE)
Aron Elís ÞRÁNDARSON	10.11.1994	5	0	2020:	Odense BK (DEN)
Forwards					
Jón Daði BÖÐVARSSON	25.05.1992	48	3	2019:	Millwall FC London (ENG)
Alfreð FINNBOGASON	01.02.1989	57	15	2019:	FC Augsburg (GER)
Kjartan Henry FINNBOGASON	09.07.1986	13	3	2020:	Vejle BK (DEN)
Kristján Flóki FINNBOGASON	12.01.1995	6	1	2020:	KR Reykjavík
Tryggvi Hrafn HARALDSSON	30.09.1996	4	1	2020:	ÍA Akranes
Óttar Magnús KARLSSON	21.02.1997	9	2	2020:	Víkingur Reykjavík
Viðar Örn KJARTANSSON	11.03.1990	26	3	2019: 11.01.2020->	FK Rubin Kazan (RUS) FK Rostov (RUS)
Kolbeinn SIGÞÓRSSON	14.03.1990	57	26	2019/2020:	AIK Stockholm (SWE)
Stefán Teitur ÞÓRÐARSON	16.10.1998	2	0	2020:	ÍA Akranes
National team coach					
Erik Anders HAMRÉN (Sweden) [from 08.08.2018]	27.06.1957		20 M; 8 W; 5 D; 7 L; 23-30		

ISRAEL

The Country:
יִשְׂרָאֵל מְדִינַת (State of Israel)
Capital: Jerusalem
Surface: 20,770–22,072 km²
Inhabitants: 9,245,550 [2020]
Time: UTC+2

The FA:
Israel Football Association
Ramat Gan Stadium 299, Aba Hilell Street, P.O. Box 3591, 52134 Ramat Gan, Tel Aviv
Tel: +972 3 617 1500
Foundation date: 18.07.1928
Member of FIFA since: 1929
Member of UEFA since: 1994
Website: www.football.org.il

NATIONAL TEAM RECORDS

RECORDS
First international match:	16.03.1934, Cairo: Egypt – Palestina 7-1
Most international caps:	Yosef Shay Benayoun - 102 caps (1998-2017)
Most international goals:	Mordechai Spiegler - 83 goals / 32 caps (1963-1977)

UEFA EUROPEAN CHAMPIONSHIP
1960	-
1964	-
1968	-
1972	-
1976	-
1980	-
1984	-
1988	-
1992	-
1996	Qualifiers
2000	Qualifiers
2004	Qualifiers
2008	Qualifiers
2012	Qualifiers
2016	Qualifiers
2020	Qualifiers

FIFA WORLD CUP
1930	Did not enter
1934	Qualifiers
1938	Qualifiers
1950	Qualifiers
1954	Qualifiers
1958	Qualifiers
1962	Qualifiers
1966	Qualifiers
1970	Final Tournament (Group Stage)
1974	Qualifiers
1978	Qualifiers
1982	Qualifiers
1986	Qualifiers
1990	Qualifiers
1994	Qualifiers
1998	Qualifiers
2002	Qualifiers
2006	Qualifiers
2010	Qualifiers
2014	Qualifiers
2018	Qualifiers

OLYMPIC TOURNAMENTS
1908	-
1912	-
1920	-
1924	-
1928	-
1936	-
1948	-
1952	Qualifiers
1956	Qualifiers
1960	Qualifiers
1964	Qualifiers
1968	FT/Quarter-Finals
1972	Qualifiers
1976	FT/Quarter-Finals
1980	*Withdrew*
1984	Qualifiers
1988	Qualifiers
1992	Qualifiers
1996	Qualifiers
2000	Qualifiers
2004	Qualifiers
2008	Qualifiers
2012	Qualifiers
2016	Qualifiers

UEFA NATIONS LEAGUE
2018/2019 – League C

FIFA CONFEDERATIONS CUP 1992-2017
None

ISRAELI CLUB HONOURS IN EUROPEAN CLUB COMPETITIONS:

European Champion Clubs' Cup (1956-1992) / UEFA Champions League (1993-2020)
None

Fairs Cup (1858-1971) / UEFA Cup (1972-2009) / UEFA Europa League (2010-2020)
None

UEFA Super Cup (1972-2019)
None

*European Cup Winners' Cup 1961-1999**
None

defunct competition

NATIONAL COMPETITIONS
TABLE OF HONOURS

	CHAMPIONS	CUP WINNERS	BEST GOALSCORERS	
1927/1928	–	Hapoel Tel Aviv FC Maccabi Hasmonean Jerusalem FC (*shared*)	–	
1928/1929	–	Maccabi Tel Aviv FC	–	
1929/1930	–	Maccabi Tel Aviv FC	–	
1930/1931	–	*No competition*	–	
1931/1932	United Kingdom British Police	United Kingdom British Police	–	
1932/1933	*No Championship*	Maccabi Tel Aviv FC	–	
1933/1934	Hapoel Tel Aviv FC	Hapoel Tel Aviv FC	–	
1934/1935	Hapoel Tel Aviv FC	Maccabi Petah Tikva FC	–	
1935/1936	Maccabi Tel Aviv FC	*No competition*	–	
1936/1937	Maccabi Tel Aviv FC	Hapoel Tel Aviv FC	–	
1937/1938	Hapoel Tel Aviv FC	Hapoel Tel Aviv FC	–	
1938/1939	*No Championship*	Hapoel Tel Aviv FC	–	
1939/1940	Hapoel Tel Aviv FC	Beitar Tel Aviv FC	–	
1940/1941	*No Championship*	Maccabi Tel Aviv FC	–	
1941/1942	Maccabi Tel Aviv FC	Beitar Tel Aviv FC	–	
1942/1943	*Championship not finished*	*No competition*	–	
1943/1944	Hapoel Tel Aviv FC	*No competition*	–	
1944/1945	Hapoel Tel Aviv FC Beitar Tel Aviv FC (*shared*)	*No competition*	–	
1945/1946	*No Championship*	Maccabi Tel Aviv FC	–	
1946/1947	Maccabi Tel Aviv FC	Maccabi Tel Aviv FC	–	
1947/1948	*Championship not finished*	*No competition*	–	
1948	*Championship not finished*	*No competition*	–	
1949/1950	Maccabi Tel Aviv FC	*No competition*	Yosef Merimovich (Maccabi Tel Aviv FC)	25
1950/1951	*No Championship*	*No competition*	–	–
1951/1952	Maccabi Tel Aviv FC	Maccabi Petah Tikva FC	Yehoshua Glazer (Maccabi Tel Aviv FC)	24
1952/1953	*No Championship*	*No competition*	–	–
1953/1954	Maccabi Tel Aviv FC	Maccabi Tel Aviv FC	Eliezer Spiegel (Maccabi Petah Tikva FC)	16
1954/1955	Hapoel Petah Tikva FC	Maccabi Tel Aviv FC	Nisim Elmaliah (Beitar Tel Aviv FC)	30
1955/1956	Maccabi Tel Aviv FC	*No competition*	Avraham Levi (Beitar Tel Aviv FC) Michael Michaelov (Beitar Tel Aviv FC)	16
1956/1957	Hapoel Tel Aviv FC	Hapoel Petah Tikva FC	Avraham Ginzburg (Hapoel Haifa FC)	16
1957/1958	Maccabi Tel Aviv FC	Maccabi Tel Aviv FC	Rafi Levi (Maccabi Tel Aviv FC)	14
1958/1959	Hapoel Petah Tikva FC	Maccabi Tel Aviv FC	Aharon Amar (Maccabi Haifa FC)	17
1959/1960	Hapoel Petah Tikva FC	*No competition*	Rafi Levi (Maccabi Tel Aviv FC)	19
1960/1961	Hapoel Petah Tikva FC	Hapoel Tel Aviv FC	Shlomo Levi (Hapoel Tel Aviv FC) Zharia Ratzabi (Hapoel Petah Tikva FC)	15
1961/1962	Hapoel Petah Tikva FC	Maccabi Haifa FC	Shlomo Levi (Maccabi Haifa FC) Itzhak Nizri (Hapoel Tiberias)	16
1962/1963	Hapoel Petah Tikva FC	Hapoel Haifa FC	Zharia Ratzabi (Hapoel Petah Tikva FC)	12
1963/1964	Hapoel Haifa FC	Maccabi Tel Aviv FC	Israel Ashkenazi (Maccabi Jaffa FC)	21
1964/1965	Hakoah Ramat Gan FC	Maccabi Tel Aviv FC	Israel Ashkenazi (Maccabi Jaffa FC) Itzhak Mizrahi (Bnei Yehuda Tel Aviv FC)	18
1965/1966	Hapoel Tel Aviv FC	Hapoel Haifa FC	Moshe Romano (Shimshon Tel Aviv FC) Mordechai Spiegler (Maccabi Netanya FC)	17
1966/1967	-	Maccabi Tel Aviv FC		
1967/1968	Maccabi Tel Aviv FC [1966-1968]	Bnei Yehuda Tel Aviv FC	Mordechai Spiegler (Maccabi Netanya FC)	38
1968/1969	Hapoel Tel Aviv FC	Hakoah Ramat Gan FC	Mordechai Spiegler (Maccabi Netanya FC)	25
1969/1970	Maccabi Tel Aviv FC	Maccabi Tel Aviv FC	Moshe Romano (Shimshon Tel Aviv FC)	15
1970/1971	Maccabi Netanya FC	Hakoah Ramat Gan FC	Eli Ben Rimoz (Hapoel Jerusalem FC)	20
1971/1972	Maccabi Tel Aviv FC	Hapoel Tel Aviv FC	Yehouda Shaharabani (Hakoah Ramat Gan FC)	21
1972/1973	Hakoah Ramat Gan FC	Hapoel Jerusalem FC	Moshe Romano (Beitar Tel Aviv FC)	18
1973/1974	Maccabi Netanya FC	Hapoel Haifa FC	Benny Alon (Hapoel Haifa FC)	15
1974/1975	Hapoel Be'er Sheva FC	Hapoel Kfar Saba FC	Moshe Romano (Shimshon Tel Aviv FC)	17
1975/1976	Hapoel Be'er Sheva FC	Beitar Jerusalem FC	Oded Machnes (Maccabi Netanya FC)	21
1976/1977	Maccabi Tel Aviv FC	Maccabi Tel Aviv FC	Vicky Peretz (Maccabi Tel Aviv FC)	17
1977/1978	Maccabi Netanya FC	Maccabi Netanya FC	David Lavi (Maccabi Netanya FC)	16
1978/1979	Maccabi Tel Aviv FC	Beitar Jerusalem FC	Oded Machnes (Maccabi Netanya FC) Eli Miali (Beitar Jerusalem FC)	18
1979/1980	Maccabi Netanya FC	Hapoel Kfar Saba FC	David Lavi (Maccabi Netanya FC)	18
1980/1981	Hapoel Tel Aviv FC	Bnei Yehuda Tel Aviv FC	Hertzel Fitusi (Maccabi Petah Tikva FC)	22
1981/1982	Hapoel Kfar Saba FC	Hapoel Yehud	Oded Machnes (Maccabi Netanya FC)	26
1982/1983	Maccabi Netanya FC	Hapoel Tel Aviv FC	Oded Machnes (Maccabi Netanya FC)	22
1983/1984	Maccabi Haifa FC	Hapoel Lod	David Lavi (Maccabi Netanya FC)	16
1984/1985	Maccabi Haifa FC	Beitar Jerusalem FC	David Lavi (Maccabi Netanya FC)	18
1985/1986	Hapoel Tel Aviv FC	Beitar Jerusalem FC	Uri Malmilian (Beitar Jerusalem FC) Doron Rabinzon (Maccabi Petah Tikva FC)	14
1986/1987	Beitar Jerusalem FC	Maccabi Tel Aviv FC	Eli Yani (Hapoel Kfar Saba FC)	16
1987/1988	Hapoel Tel Aviv FC	Maccabi Tel Aviv FC	Zahi Armeli (Maccabi Haifa FC)	25

1988/1989	Maccabi Haifa FC	Beitar Jerusalem FC	Benny Tabak (Maccabi Tel Aviv FC)	18
1989/1990	Bnei Yehuda Tel Aviv FC	Hapoel Kfar Saba FC	Uri Malmilian (Maccabi Tel Aviv FC)	16
1990/1991	Maccabi Haifa FC	Maccabi Haifa FC	Nir Levine (Hapoel Petah Tikva FC)	20
1991/1992	Maccabi Tel Aviv FC	Hapoel Petah Tikva FC	Alon Mizrahi (Bnei Yehuda Tel Aviv FC)	20
1992/1993	Beitar Jerusalem FC	Maccabi Haifa FC	Alon Mizrahi (Bnei Yehuda Tel Aviv FC)	26
1993/1994	Maccabi Haifa FC	Maccabi Tel Aviv FC	Alon Mizrahi (Maccabi Haifa FC)	28
1994/1995	Maccabi Tel Aviv FC	Maccabi Haifa FC	Haim Revivo (Maccabi Haifa FC) Amir Turgeman (Maccabi Ironi Ashdod FC FC)	17
1995/1996	Maccabi Tel Aviv FC	Maccabi Tel Aviv FC	Haim Revivo (Maccabi Haifa FC)	26
1996/1997	Beitar Jerusalem FC	Hapoel Be'er Sheva FC	Motti Kakoun (Hapoel Petah Tikva FC)	21
1997/1998	Beitar Jerusalem FC	Maccabi Haifa FC	Alon Mizrahi (Maccabi Tel Aviv FC)	18
1998/1999	Hapoel Haifa FC	Hapoel Tel Aviv FC	Andrzej Kubica (Maccabi Tel Aviv FC)	21
1999/2000	Hapoel Tel Aviv FC	Hapoel Tel Aviv FC	Assi Tubi (Maccabi Petah Tikva FC)	27
2000/2001	Maccabi Haifa FC	Maccabi Tel Aviv FC	Avi Nimni (Maccabi Tel Aviv FC)	25
2001/2002	Maccabi Haifa FC	Maccabi Tel Aviv FC	Kobi Refua (Maccabi Petah Tikva FC)	18
2002/2003	Maccabi Tel Aviv FC	Hapoel Haifa FC	Yaniv Abargil (Hapoel Kfar Saba FC) Shay Holtzman (Ironi Rishon LeZion FC / FC Ashdod)	18
2003/2004	Maccabi Haifa FC	Bnei Sakhnin FC	Ofir Haim (Hapoel Be'er Sheva FC) Shay Holtzman (FC Ashdod)	16
2004/2005	Maccabi Haifa FC	Maccabi Tel Aviv FC	Roberto Colautti (Maccabi Haifa FC)	19
2005/2006	Maccabi Haifa FC	Hapoel Tel Aviv FC	Shay Holtzman (FC Ashdod)	18
2006/2007	Beitar Jerusalem FC	Hapoel Tel Aviv FC	Yaniv Azran (FC Ashdod)	15
2007/2008	Beitar Jerusalem FC	Beitar Jerusalem FC	Samuel Yeboah (Hapoel Kfar Saba FC)	15
2008/2009	Maccabi Haifa FC	Beitar Jerusalem FC	Barak Yitzhaki (Beitar Jerusalem FC) Shimon Abuhatzira (Hapoel Petah Tikva FC) Eliran Atar (Bnei Yehuda Tel Aviv FC)	14
2009/2010	Hapoel Tel Aviv FC	Hapoel Tel Aviv FC	Shlomi Arbeitman (Maccabi Haifa FC)	28
2010/2011	Maccabi Haifa FC	Hapoel Tel Aviv FC	Toto Tamuz (Hapoel Tel Aviv FC)	21
2011/2012	Ironi Kiryat	Hapoel Tel Aviv FC	Achmad Saba'a (Maccabi Netanya FC)	20
2012/2013	Maccabi Tel Aviv FC	Hapoel Haifa FC	Eliran Atar (Maccabi Tel Aviv FC)	22
2013/2014	Maccabi Tel Aviv FC	Hapoel Ironi Kiryat Shmona FC	Eran Zahavi (Maccabi Tel Aviv FC)	29
2014/2015	Maccabi Tel Aviv FC	Maccabi Haifa FC	Eran Zahavi (Maccabi Tel Aviv FC)	27
2015/2016	Hapoel Be'er Sheva FC	Maccabi Haifa FC	Eran Zahavi (Maccabi Tel Aviv FC)	35
2016/2017	Hapoel Be'er Sheva FC	Bnei Yehuda Tel Aviv FC	Viðar Örn Kjartansson (ISL, Maccabi Tel Aviv FC)	19
2017/2018	Hapoel Be'er Sheva FC	Hapoel Haifa FC	Dia Saba (Maccabi Netanya FC)	24
2018/2019	Maccabi Tel Aviv FC	Bnei Yehuda Tel Aviv FC	Ben Sahar (Hapoel Be'er Sheva FC)	15
2019/2020	Maccabi Tel Aviv FC	Hapoel Be'er Sheva FC	Nikita Rukavytsya (AUS, Maccabi Haifa FC)	22

NATIONAL CHAMPIONSHIP
Israeli Premier League (Ligat Winner) 2019/2020
(24.08.2019 – 07.07.2020)

Regular Season - Results

Round 1 [24-26.08.2019]
Maccabi Haifa - Hapoel Ra'anana 4-3(2-2)
Hapoel Hadera - FC Ashdod 1-1(0-1)
Sektzia Nes Tz. - Maccabi Tel Aviv 0-2(0-2)
Hapoel Kfar Saba - Hapoel Haifa 0-1(0-0)
Bnei Yehuda - Hapoel Ironi 2-1(0-1)
Beitar Jerusalem - Hapoel Be'er Sheva 0-0
Hapoel Tel Aviv - Maccabi Netanya 0-0

Round 2 [31.08.-02.09.2019]
FC Ashdod - Hapoel Tel Aviv 2-1(0-0)
Maccabi Netanya - Sektzia Nes Tz. 3-0(2-0)
Hapoel Haifa - Maccabi Haifa 0-0
Hapoel Be'er Sheva - Hapoel Hadera 3-0(1-0)
Hapoel Ra'anana - Beitar Jerusalem 2-1(1-0)
Maccabi Tel Aviv - Bnei Yehuda 0-0
Hapoel Ironi - Hapoel Kfar Saba 1-3(0-2)

Round 3 [14-16.09.2019]
Maccabi Haifa - Hapoel Ironi 2-0(0-0)
Hapoel Tel Aviv - Sektzia Nes Tz. 1-1(1-0)
Hapoel Hadera - Hapoel Ra'anana 4-0(1-0)
Hapoel Kfar Saba - Maccabi T. Aviv 0-1(0-1)
Bnei Yehuda - Maccabi Netanya 0-0
FC Ashdod - Hapoel Be'er Sheva 2-2(1-1)
Beitar Jerusalem - Hapoel Haifa 0-2(0-1)

Round 4 [21-23.09.2019]
Maccabi Netanya - Hapoel Kfar Saba 2-2(0-0)
Sektzia Nes Tziona - Bnei Yehuda 0-1(0-1)
Hapoel Ironi - Beitar Jerusalem 0-2(0-0)
Maccabi Tel Aviv - Maccabi Haifa 1-0(1-0)
Hapoel Ra'anana - FC Ashdod 1-1(1-0)
Hapoel Haifa - Hapoel Hadera 1-2(0-1)
Hapoel Be'er Sheva - Hapoel T. Aviv 3-0(1-0)

Round 5 [25-28.09.2019]
Hapoel Kfar Saba - Sektzia Nes Tz. 1-1(1-1)
Maccabi Haifa - Maccabi Netanya 3-0(2-0)
Hapoel Hadera - Hapoel Ironi 2-2(1-1)
FC Ashdod - Hapoel Haifa 1-1(0-0)
Hapoel Tel Aviv - Bnei Yehuda 1-1(0-1)
Beitar Jerusalem - Maccabi Tel Aviv 0-4(0-1)
Hapoel Be'er Sh. - Hapoel Ra'anana 1-0(1-0)

Round 6 [05-07.10.2019]
Maccabi Tel Aviv - Hapoel Hadera 0-0
Sektzia Nes Tziona - Maccabi Haifa 0-3(0-0)
Hapoel Haifa - Hapoel Be'er Sheva 0-3(0-1)
Bnei Yehuda - Hapoel Kfar Saba 0-1(0-1)
Hapoel Ra'anana - Hapoel Tel Aviv 2-2(1-1)
Maccabi Netanya - Beitar Jerusalem 0-3(0-3)
Hapoel Ironi - FC Ashdod 2-0(2-0)

Round 7 [19-21.10.2019]
Hapoel Tel Aviv - Hapoel Kfar Saba 2-1(0-1)
Hapoel Hadera - Maccabi Netanya 1-0(0-0)
Hapoel Be'er Sheva - Hapoel Ironi 2-1(1-0)
Sektzia Nes Tz. - Beitar Jerusalem 0-4(0-2)
Hapoel Ra'anana - Hapoel Haifa 0-0
FC Ashdod - Maccabi Tel Aviv 0-1(0-0)
Maccabi Haifa - Bnei Yehuda 1-1(0-0)

Round 8 [26-28.10.2019]
Hapoel Haifa - Hapoel Tel Aviv 3-0(2-0)
Hapoel Ironi - Hapoel Ra'anana 2-1(1-0)
Maccabi Netanya - FC Ashdod 2-4(1-2)
Hapoel Kfar Saba - Maccabi Haifa 0-3(0-1)
Sektzia Nes Tziona - Hapoel Hadera 2-2(1-1)
Bnei Yehuda - Beitar Jerusalem 0-2(0-1)
Maccabi T. Aviv - Hapoel Be'er Sh. 2-0(1-0)

Round 9 [02-04.11.2019]
Hapoel Haifa - Hapoel Ironi 2-1(2-1)
Hapoel Ra'anana - Maccabi Tel Aviv 0-2(0-1)
Hapoel Hadera - Bnei Yehuda 0-0
Beitar Jerusalem - Hapoel Kfar Saba 1-0(0-0)
FC Ashdod - Sektzia Nes Tziona 2-2(0-1)
Hapoel Be'er Sh. - Maccabi Netanya 2-0(1-0)
Hapoel Tel Aviv - Maccabi Haifa 1-2(1-0)

Round 10 [09-10.11.2019]
Hapoel Ironi - Hapoel Tel Aviv 0-1(0-1)
Sektzia Nes Tz. - Hapoel Be'er Sheva 2-1(0-0)
Maccabi Netanya - Hapoel Ra'anana 1-0(0-0)
Maccabi Tel Aviv - Hapoel Haifa 3-0(1-0)
Hapoel Kfar Saba - Hapoel Hadera 0-0
Bnei Yehuda - FC Ashdod 2-0(1-0)
Maccabi Haifa - Beitar Jerusalem 3-1(0-1)

Round 11 [30.11.-01.12.2019]
Hapoel Ra'anana - Sektzia Nes Tziona 0-0
Hapoel Haifa - Maccabi Netanya 1-3(0-1)
Hapoel Ironi - Maccabi Tel Aviv 0-1(0-1)
FC Ashdod - Hapoel Kfar Saba 0-0
Hapoel Be'er Sheva - Bnei Yehuda 1-2(1-0)
Hapoel Hadera - Maccabi Haifa 0-3(0-2)
Hapoel Tel Aviv - Beitar Jerusalem 0-1(0-1)

Round 12 [03-04.12.2019]
Bnei Yehuda - Hapoel Ra'anana 1-1(0-1)
Maccabi Netanya - Hapoel Ironi 1-0(1-0)
Hapoel Kfar Saba - Hapoel Be'er Sh. 0-1(0-1)
Sektzia Nes Tziona - Hapoel Haifa 1-2(1-1)
Beitar Jerusalem - Hapoel Hadera 2-0(2-0)
Maccabi Haifa - FC Ashdod 3-3(0-1)
Hapoel Tel Aviv - Maccabi Tel Aviv 0-3(0-1)

Round 13 [07-09.12.2019]
Hapoel Ra'anana - Hapoel Kfar Saba 1-1(1-0)
Hapoel Haifa - Bnei Yehuda 3-0(1-0)
Hapoel Ironi - Sektzia Nes Tziona 1-0(0-0)
Maccabi Tel Aviv - Maccabi Netanya 0-0
Hapoel Hadera - Hapoel Tel Aviv 0-1(0-1)
FC Ashdod - Beitar Jerusalem 2-2(1-1)
Hapoel Be'er Sheva - Maccabi Haifa 0-2(0-2)

Round 14 [14-16.12.2019]
Maccabi Tel Aviv - Sektzia Nes Tz. 1-1(1-1)
Hapoel Ironi - Bnei Yehuda 2-1(2-0)
Hapoel Haifa - Hapoel Kfar Saba 0-2(0-1)
Hapoel Ra'anana - Maccabi Haifa 0-0
FC Ashdod - Hapoel Hadera 0-2(0-1)
Maccabi Netanya - Hapoel Tel Aviv 4-0(2-0)
Hapoel Be'er Sh. - Beitar Jerusalem 0-1(0-1)

Round 15 [24-25.12.2019]
Hapoel Kfar Saba - Hapoel Ironi 0-3(0-1)
Hapoel Hadera - Hapoel Be'er Sheva 0-1(0-0)
Maccabi Haifa - Hapoel Haifa 3-0(0-0)
Bnei Yehuda - Maccabi Tel Aviv 0-3(0-2)
Sektzia Nes Tz. - Maccabi Netanya 1-0(1-0)
Hapoel Tel Aviv - FC Ashdod 0-0
Beitar Jerusalem - Hapoel Ra'anana 2-0(1-0)

Round 16 [28-30.12.2019]
Maccabi T. Aviv - Hapoel Kfar Saba 4-0(1-0)
Hapoel Ironi - Maccabi Haifa 1-2(0-1)
Hapoel Ra'anana - Hapoel Hadera 1-1(1-0)
Hapoel Be'er Sheva - FC Ashdod 2-1(0-1)
Maccabi Netanya - Bnei Yehuda 0-3(0-2)
Sektzia Nes Tz. - Hapoel Tel Aviv 0-1(0-1)
Hapoel Haifa - Beitar Jerusalem 1-4(0-3)

Round 17 [04-06.01.2020]
Hapoel Kfar Saba - Maccabi Netanya 1-2(0-0)
Hapoel Hadera - Hapoel Haifa 2-0(0-0)
Beitar Jerusalem - Hapoel Ironi 2-2(1-2)
FC Ashdod - Hapoel Ra'anana 3-0(1-0)
Hapoel T. Aviv - Hapoel Be'er Sheva 1-0(1-0)
Bnei Yehuda - Sektzia Nes Tziona 1-2(0-0)
Maccabi Haifa - Maccabi Tel Aviv 3-4(0-1)

Round 18 [11-13.01.2020]
Hapoel Haifa - FC Ashdod 1-0(0-0)
Hapoel Ra'anana - Hapoel Be'er Sh. 2-1(0-0)
Hapoel Ironi - Hapoel Hadera 0-1(0-1)
Maccabi Netanya - Maccabi Haifa 0-2(0-0)
Sektzia Nes Tz. - Hapoel Kfar Saba 0-1(0-1)
Bnei Yehuda - Hapoel Tel Aviv 1-2(1-1)
Maccabi Tel Aviv - Beitar Jerusalem 0-0

Round 19 [18-20.01.2020]
FC Ashdod - Hapoel Ironi 1-0(1-0)
Maccabi Haifa - Sektzia Nes Tziona 4-0(0-0)
Hapoel Hadera - Maccabi Tel Aviv 0-3(0-1)
Hapoel Tel Aviv - Hapoel Ra'anana 3-1(1-1)
Hapoel Kfar Saba - Bnei Yehuda 0-1(0-0)
Hapoel Be'er Sheva - Hapoel Haifa 1-0(0-0)
Beitar Jerusalem - Maccabi Netanya 3-1(1-1)

Round 20 [25-27.01.2020]
Hapoel Kfar Saba - Hapoel Tel Aviv 1-2(1-1)
Hapoel Ironi - Hapoel Be'er Sheva 0-0
Hapoel Haifa - Hapoel Ra'anana 2-2(0-2)
Maccabi Tel Aviv - FC Ashdod 2-0(1-0)
Maccabi Netanya - Hapoel Hadera 1-0(0-0)
Beitar Jerusalem - Sektzia Nes Tz. 1-0(1-0)
Bnei Yehuda - Maccabi Haifa 1-3(0-2)

Round 21 [29.01.-02.02.2020]
Hapoel Ra'anana - Hapoel Ironi 1-1(1-0)
Hapoel Be'er Sh. - Maccabi T. Aviv 1-1(0-1)
FC Ashdod - Maccabi Netanya 0-0
Maccabi Haifa - Hapoel Kfar Saba 0-1(0-0)
Hapoel Hadera - Sektzia Nes Tziona 1-0(0-0)
Hapoel Tel Aviv - Hapoel Haifa 0-1(0-1)
Beitar Jerusalem - Bnei Yehuda 1-3(1-0)

Round 22 [03-05.02.2020]
Maccabi Tel Aviv - Hapoel Ra'anana 2-1(0-0)
Sektzia Nes Tziona - FC Ashdod 0-2(0-1)
Hapoel Ironi - Hapoel Haifa 1-2(0-0)
Maccabi Haifa - Hapoel Tel Aviv 5-0(3-0)
Bnei Yehuda - Hapoel Hadera 0-1(0-1)
Maccabi Netanya - Hapoel Be'er Sh. 1-1(1-1)
Hapoel Kfar Saba - Beitar Jerusalem 2-1(1-1)

Round 23 [08-10.02.2020]
Hapoel Tel Aviv - Hapoel Ironi 2-0(0-0)
Hapoel Ra'anana - Maccabi Netanya 1-2(1-0)
Hapoel Hadera - Hapoel Kfar Saba 2-0(1-0)
Hapoel Haifa - Maccabi Tel Aviv 1-1(0-1)
FC Ashdod - Bnei Yehuda 0-1(0-1)
Hapoel Be'er Sheva - Sektzia Nes Tz. 3-0(2-0)
Beitar Jerusalem - Maccabi Haifa 2-0(1-0)

Round 24 [15-17.02.2020]
Maccabi Netanya - Hapoel Haifa 0-0
Bnei Yehuda - Hapoel Be'er Sheva 0-1(0-0)
Hapoel Kfar Saba - FC Ashdod 1-3(0-2)
Maccabi Haifa - Hapoel Hadera 1-0(0-0)
Sektzia Nes Tz. - Hapoel Ra'anana 3-0(1-0)
Maccabi Tel Aviv - Hapoel Ironi 3-0(0-0)
Beitar Jerusalem - Hapoel Tel Aviv 0-1(0-1)

Round 25 [22-24.02.2020]
Hapoel Ironi - Maccabi Netanya 3-0(2-0)
FC Ashdod - Maccabi Haifa 1-2(1-1)
Hapoel Haifa - Sektzia Nes Tziona 2-0(2-0)
Hapoel Hadera - Beitar Jerusalem 1-4(1-1)
Hapoel Ra'anana - Bnei Yehuda 0-1(0-0)
Hapoel Be'er Sheva - Hapoel Kfar S. 3-1(2-1)
Maccabi Tel Aviv - Hapoel Tel Aviv 3-0(1-0)

Round 26 [29.02.-01.03.2020]
Hapoel Kfar Saba - Hapoel Ra'anana 3-0(2-0)
Maccabi Netanya - Maccabi Tel Aviv 0-1(0-1)
Hapoel Tel Aviv - Hapoel Hadera 2-1(1-1)
Bnei Yehuda - Hapoel Haifa 0-0
Sektzia Nes Tziona - Hapoel Ironi 1-0(0-0)
Beitar Jerusalem - FC Ashdod 2-1(1-0)
Maccabi Haifa - Hapoel Be'er Sheva 4-0(2-0)

Final Standings

1.	Maccabi Tel Aviv FC	26	19	7	0	48 - 7	64
2.	Maccabi Haifa FC	26	18	4	4	58 - 20	58
3.	Beitar Jerusalem FC	26	15	4	7	42 - 25	49
4.	Hapoel Be'er Sheva FC	26	13	5	8	33 - 23	44
5.	Hapoel Tel Aviv FC	26	11	5	10	24 - 36	38
6.	Hapoel Haifa FC	26	10	7	9	26 - 30	37
7.	Bnei Yehuda Tel Aviv FC	26	9	7	10	23 - 26	34
8.	Hapoel Hadera–Giv'at Olga "Shulem Schwarz"	26	9	7	10	24 - 28	34
9.	Maccabi Netanya FC	26	8	7	11	23 - 32	31
10.	FC Ashdod	26	6	10	10	30 - 33	28
11.	Hapoel Kfar Saba FC	26	7	5	14	22 - 35	26
12.	Hapoel Ironi Kiryat Shmona FC	26	6	4	16	24 - 35	22
13.	Sektzia Nes Tziona FC	26	5	6	15	17 - 40	21
14.	Hapoel Ra'anana AFC	26	2	10	14	20 - 44	16

Teams ranked 1-6 were qualified for the Championship Round, while teams ranked 7-14 were qualified for the Relegation Round.

Results

Round 27 [30.05.2020]
Maccabi Tel Aviv - Hapoel Haifa 2-0(1-0)
Beitar Jerusalem - Hapoel Be'er Sh. 1-1(0-0)
Maccabi Haifa - Hapoel Tel Aviv 1-2(0-1)

Round 28 [02-03.06.2020]
Hapoel Tel Aviv - Beitar Jerusalem 3-0(2-0)
Hapoel Haifa - Hapoel Be'er Sheva 1-1(0-0)
Maccabi Tel Aviv - Maccabi Haifa 2-0(1-0)

Round 29 [06-08.06.2020]
Hapoel Be'er Sheva - Hapoel Tel Aviv 0-0
Maccabi Haifa - Hapoel Haifa 2-2(1-0)
Beitar Jerusalem - Maccabi Tel Aviv 0-0

Round 30 [13-15.06.2020]
Maccabi Haifa - Beitar Jerusalem 0-0
Hapoel Haifa - Hapoel Tel Aviv 4-0(1-0)
Maccabi Tel Aviv - Hapoel Be'er Sh. 1-1(1-0)

Round 31 [17-20.06.2020]
Beitar Jerusalem - Hapoel Haifa 1-1(1-0)
Hapoel Be'er Sheva - Maccabi Haifa 0-1(0-0)
Hapoel Tel Aviv - Maccabi Tel Aviv 0-2(0-0)

Round 32 [23.06.2020]
Hapoel Be'er Sh. - Beitar Jerusalem 2-2(1-1)
Hapoel Haifa - Maccabi Tel Aviv 0-3(0-2)
Hapoel Tel Aviv - Maccabi Haifa 1-3(0-2)

Round 33 [27-28.06.2020]
Maccabi Haifa - Hapoel Be'er Sheva 2-1(1-0)
Maccabi Tel Aviv - Hapoel Tel Aviv 3-0(0-0)
Hapoel Haifa - Beitar Jerusalem 0-0

Round 34 [30.06.-01.07.2020]
Hapoel Tel Aviv - Hapoel Be'er Sh. 1-0(0-0)
Hapoel Haifa - Maccabi Haifa 1-4(0-4)
Maccabi Tel Aviv - Beitar Jerusalem 1-0(0-0)

Round 35 [04.07.2020]
Beitar Jerusalem - Hapoel Tel Aviv 3-0(2-0)
Hapoel Be'er Sheva - Hapoel Haifa 3-1(1-0)
Maccabi Haifa - Maccabi Tel Aviv 0-1(0-1)

Round 36 [07.07.2020]
Hapoel Tel Aviv - Hapoel Haifa 0-3(0-1)
Hapoel Be'er Sh. - Maccabi Tel Aviv 2-0(2-0)
Beitar Jerusalem - Maccabi Haifa 2-2(0-1)

Final Standings

								Home				Away			
1. **Maccabi Tel Aviv FC**	36	26	9	1	63 - 10	87	12	6	0	30 - 3	14	3	1	33 - 7
2. Maccabi Haifa FC	36	22	7	7	73 - 32	73	10	4	4	41 - 19	12	3	3	32 - 13
3. Beitar Jerusalem FC	36	16	11	9	51 - 35	59	8	6	4	23 - 18	8	5	5	28 - 17
4. Hapoel Be'er Sheva FC	36	15	10	11	44 - 33	55	11	3	4	29 - 13	4	7	7	15 - 20
5. Hapoel Tel Aviv FC	36	14	6	16	31 - 55	48	7	4	7	18 - 20	7	2	9	13 - 35
6. Hapoel Haifa FC	36	12	11	13	39 - 46	47	6	5	7	23 - 26	6	6	6	16 - 20

Round 27 [01-03.06.2020]
Bnei Yehuda - Hapoel Kfar Saba 0-0
FC Ashdod - Hapoel Ra'anana 3-2(0-1)
Maccabi Netanya - Hapoel Ironi 3-1(2-0)
Hapoel Hadera - Sektzia Nes Tziona 2-2(0-0)

Round 28 [06-07.06.2020]
Hapoel Ironi - FC Ashdod 3-0(2-0)
Bnei Yehuda - Hapoel Hadera 5-0(3-0)
Hapoel Kfar Saba - Hapoel Ra'anana 2-0(0-0)
Sektzia Nes Tz. - Maccabi Netanya 1-0(0-0)

Round 29 [13-15.06.2020]
Hapoel Hadera - Hapoel Kfar Saba 0-0
Hapoel Ra'anana - Hapoel Ironi 0-1(0-0)
FC Ashdod - Sektzia Nes Tziona 2-0(1-0)
Maccabi Netanya - Bnei Yehuda 1-3(1-1)

Round 30 [18-21.06.2020]
Sektzia Nes Tz. - Hapoel Ra'anana 2-1(1-0)
Hapoel Hadera - Maccabi Netanya 1-2(0-0)
Hapoel Kfar Saba - Hapoel Ironi 0-0
Bnei Yehuda - FC Ashdod 3-3(1-2)

Round 31 [23-24.06.2020]
Hapoel Ra'anana - Maccabi Netanya 2-4(0-2)
FC Ashdod - Hapoel Kfar Saba 2-3(1-2)
Sektzia Nes Tziona - Bnei Yehuda 0-0
Hapoel Ironi - Hapoel Hadera 0-3(0-1)

Round 32 [27-28.06.2020]
Hapoel Hadera - Hapoel Ra'anana 2-2(2-1)
Hapoel Kfar Saba - Sektzia Nes Tz. 0-1(0-1)
Bnei Yehuda - Hapoel Ironi 2-0(0-0)
Maccabi Netanya - FC Ashdod 2-5(1-3)

Round 33 [01-02.07.2020]
Hapoel Ra'anana - Bnei Yehuda 0-4(0-2)
Maccabi Netanya - Hapoel Kfar Saba 0-1(0-1)
FC Ashdod - Hapoel Hadera 3-1(2-0)
Hapoel Ironi - Sektzia Nes Tziona 1-0(0-0)

Final Standings

								Home				Away			
7. Bnei Yehuda Tel Aviv FC	33	13	10	10	40 - 30	49	4	5	8	18 - 20	9	5	2	22 - 10
8. FC Ashdod	33	10	11	12	48 - 47	41	6	6	5	24 - 20	4	5	7	24 - 27
9. Hapoel Hadera–Giv'at Olga "Shulem Schwarz"	33	10	10	13	33 - 42	40	5	6	6	19 - 21	5	4	7	14 - 21
10. Maccabi Netanya FC	33	11	7	15	35 - 46	40	6	3	8	21 - 26	5	4	7	14 - 20
11. Hapoel Kfar Saba FC	33	10	8	15	28 - 38	38	3	3	10	11 - 20	7	5	5	17 - 18
12. Hapoel Ironi Kiryat Shmona FC	33	9	5	19	30 - 43	32	7	1	8	17 - 17	2	4	11	13 - 26
13. Sektzia Nes Tziona FC (*Relegated*)	33	8	8	17	23 - 46	32	6	2	8	13 - 20	2	6	9	10 - 26
14. Hapoel Ra'anana AFC (*Relegated*)	33	2	11	20	27 - 62	17	2	8	6	13 - 22	0	3	14	14 - 40

Top goalscorers:

22	**Nikita Rukavytsya (AUS)**	*Maccabi Haifa FC*
13	Ben Sahar	*Hapoel Be'er Sheva FC*
12	Yonatan Cohen	*Maccabi Tel Aviv FC*
11	Omri Altman	*Hapoel Tel Aviv FC*
11	Dean David	*FC Ashdod*

NATIONAL CUP
Israel State Cup (Gvia HaMedina) 2019/2020

Eighth Round [19-22.12.2019]

Maccabi Bnei Raina FC - Maccabi Ironi Sderot FC	2-0		FC Tira - Maccabi Netanya FC	0-4
FC Kafr Qasim - Hapoel Kfar Saba FC	1-0		Hapoel Bnei Lod Rakevet FC - Hapoel Haifa FC	1-5
Hapoel Afula FC - Hapoel Ashkelon FC	2-1		Maccabi Petah Tikva - Hapoel Ironi Kiryat Shmona	3-2 aet
Bnei Sakhnin FC - Hapoel Nir Ramat HaSharon FC	3-2 aet		Maccabi Haifa FC - Sektzia Nes Tziona FC	3-1 aet
Bnei Yehuda Tel Aviv FC - Hapoel Hadera FC	2-0 aet		FC Ashdod - Hapoel Be'er Sheva FC	3-4
Agudat Sport Ashdod - Hapoel Petah Tikva FC	1-0 aet		Hapoel Umm al-Fahm FC - Maccabi Tel Aviv FC	3-2
Hapoel Nof HaGalil FC - Hapoel Ironi Marmorek FC	3-1		Hapoel Tel Aviv FC - Hapoel Katamon Jerusalem FC	2-0 aet
Maccabi Ironi Kiry. Malakhi - Hapoel Ra'anana AFC	1-4		Beitar Jerusalem FC - Hapoel Rishon LeZion FC	5-0

1/8-Finals [14-16.01.2020]

Hapoel Nof HaGalil F.C - Maccabi Petah Tikva FC	0-1		Bnei Yehuda Tel Aviv FC - Hapoel Afula FC	1-0
Hapoel Umm al-Fahm FC - Maccabi Haifa FC	0-1		Bnei Sakhnin FC - Hapoel Tel Aviv FC	0-3
Hapoel Haifa FC - FC Kafr Qasim	1-0		Beitar Jerusalem FC - Maccabi Bnei Raina FC	3-1
Agudat Sport Ashdod - Hapoel Ra'anana AFC	2-4		Maccabi Netanya FC - Hapoel Be'er Sheva FC	1-2

Quarter-Finals [03-09.03.2020]

Hapoel Haifa FC - Bnei Yehuda Tel Aviv FC	0-2		Beitar Jerusalem FC - Maccabi Petah Tikva FC	3-5 pen
Hapoel Tel Aviv FC - Hapoel Ra'anana AFC	2-1 aet		Maccabi Haifa FC - Hapoel Be'er Sheva FC	1-2

Semi-Finals [09-10.06.2020]

Hapoel Tel Aviv FC - Maccabi Petah Tikva FC	0-2		Hapoel Be'er Sheva FC - Bnei Yehuda Tel Aviv FC	1-1 aet; 6-5 pen

Final

13.07.2020, Bloomfield Stadium, Tel Aviv; Referee: Orel Grinfeld; Attendance: None

Hapoel Be'er Sheva FC - Maccabi Petah Tikva FC   **2-0(0-0)**

Hapoel Be'er Sheva: Ohad Levita, Ben Bitton, Miguel Ângelo Leonardo Vítor, Sean Goldberg, Loai Taha, Marwan Kabha (90.Shir Tzedek), Josué Filipe Soares Pesqueira (90.Oren Biton), Tomer Yosefi (67.Or Dadia), David Martins Simão, Elton Acolatse (90.Naor Sabag), Ben Sahar (82.Qays Ganem). Trainer: Yosef Abukasis.

Maccabi Petah Tikva: Dor Hevron, Or Blorian, Dudu Twito, Daniel Pelshar, Tomer Levy (73.Omar Danino), Muhamad Sarsur (53.Lidor Cohen), Arad Bar, Guy Hadida (63.Ethane Azoulay), Lior Inbrum (73.Ido Davidov), Liel Abada (73.Thai Baribo), Dor Hugy. Trainer: Guy Luzon.

Goals: 1-0 Ben Sahar (49), 2-0 Josué Filipe Soares Pesqueira (61).

THE CLUBS 2019/2020

Please note: matches and goals includes statistics of both regular season and play-offs (Championship Round and Relegation Round).

Beitar Jerusalem Football Club				

Founded:	1936		
Stadium:	Teddy Stadium, Jerusalem (31,733)		
Trainer:	Ronny Levy		14.11.1966

Goalkeepers:	DOB	M	(s)	G
Netanel Daloya	14.07.1998	2	(1)	
Itamar Nitzan	23.06.1987	34		
Defenders:	**DOB**	**M**	**(s)**	**G**
Tal Ben Haim	31.03.1982	15	(1)	
Antoine Conte (FRA)	29.01.1994	22	(1)	2
Diogo Sousa Verdasca (POR)	26.10.1996	32		
Maksim Grechkin	04.03.1996	23		
Shay Konstantini	27.06.1996	21	(5)	2
Uri Magbo	12.09.1987	13	(9)	2
Or Zahavi	23.04.1996	16	(3)	1
Midfielders:	**DOB**	**M**	**(s)**	**G**
Tamir Adi	02.05.1993	13	(6)	1
David Dego	09.05.2001		(2)	
Shalom Edri	07.04.1994	2	(26)	1

Dan Einbinder	16.02.1989	26	(4)	1
Gadi Kinda	17.05.1994	16		7
Ofir Kriaf	17.03.1991	11	(7)	1
Hanan Maman	28.08.1989	12	(1)	1
Ali Muhammad (NIG)	07.10.1995	34		1
Liran Rotman	07.06.1996	8	(12)	
Aviel Zargary	11.12.2002	1	(3)	
Forwards:	**DOB**	**M**	**(s)**	**G**
Eliran Atar	17.02.1987	5		4
Shlomi Azulay	18.10.1989	27	(5)	9
Roy Doga	23.07.2002		(3)	
Levi Samuel García (TRI)	20.11.1997	28	(2)	5
Ange-Freddy Plumain (FRA)	02.03.1995	21	(6)	6
Gaëtan Antony Varenne	24.06.1990	6	(14)	4
Idan Vered	25.05.1989	8	(8)	3

Bnei Yehuda Football Club

Founded: 1936
Stadium: Bloomfield Stadium, Tel Aviv (29,150)
Trainer: Yosef Abukasis — 10.09.1970
[08.01.2020] Elisha Levy — 18.11.1957

Goalkeepers:	DOB	M	(s)	G
Omer Niron	17.04.2001	3		
Yonathan Shabi	24.12.1996	3		
Emilijus Zubas (LTU)	10.07.1990	27		
Defenders:	**DOB**	**M**	**(s)**	**G**
Allyson Aires dos Santos (BRA)	23.10.1990	29		
Netanel Amoyal	28.09.2000		(2)	
Matan Baltaxa	20.09.1995	30	(1)	1
Paz Ben Ari	10.12.1996		(2)	
Avishai Cohen	19.05.1995	24	(5)	
Dor Elo	26.09.1993	12	(3)	
Daniel Pelshar	26.07.1997	3		
Dan Mori	08.11.1988	32		1
Alban Pnishi (KVX)	20.10.1990	9	(1)	1
Amir Rustum	18.10.1998	7	(5)	
Midfielders:	**DOB**	**M**	**(s)**	**G**
Shay Golan	17.10.1998	2	(2)	
Ronen Gradashov	29.01.2003		(1)	
Dor Kochav	06.05.1993	6	(8)	1
Ariel Lazmi	17.04.1994	8	(12)	4
Matija Ljujić (SRB)	28.10.1993	25	(2)	4
Shay Mazor	14.06.1993	18	(4)	3
Ismaila Wafougossani Soro (CIV)	07.05.1998	17		
Sagas Tambi	21.10.1994	29	(1)	1
Eitan Velblum	27.02.1997	2	(12)	
Forwards:	**DOB**	**M**	**(s)**	**G**
Ben Azubel	19.09.1993	2	(8)	
Roei Ben Shimon	04.12.2000	6	(2)	4
Mohammad Ghadir	21.01.1991	19	(5)	2
Dor Jan	16.12.1994	18	(14)	10
Ayi Silva Kangani	15.05.2003	5	(1)	2
Mihlali Mayambela	25.08.1996	5	(2)	1
Joseph Mensah (GHA)	29.09.1994	1	(5)	1
Amit Zenati	02.04.1997	21	(11)	4

Football Club Ashdod

Founded: 1999
Stadium: Yud-Alef Stadium, Ashdod (8,200)
Trainer: Ronny Awat — 01.08.1968
[21.01.2020] Ran Ben Shimon — 28.11.1970

Goalkeepers:	DOB	M	(s)	G
Omer Egozi	13.06.1997		(1)	
Roi Mishpati	23.11.1992	30		
Ron Shushan	11.06.1993	3		
Defenders:	**DOB**	**M**	**(s)**	**G**
Timothy Dennis Awany (UGA)	06.08.1996	32		1
Nir Bardea	25.01.1996	24	(2)	2
Tom Ben Zaken	29.10.1994	6	(2)	
Gil Cohen	08.11.2000	23	(1)	
Montari Kamaheni (GHA)	01.02.2000	12	(2)	1
David Tiram	16.09.1993	5	(2)	
Zohar Zasano	21.11.2001	6	(3)	
Midfielders:	**DOB**	**M**	**(s)**	**G**
Fares Abu Akel	08.02.1997	18	(7)	
Naor Aboudi	17.07.1993	4	(3)	
Samuel Alabi Borquaye (GHA)	06.05.2000	13	(10)	1
Yitzhak Asefa	19.11.1998	11		
Gal Aviv	22.08.1998		(2)	
Shlomi Azulay	30.03.1990	26	(5)	8
Oz Bilu	16.01.2001	1	(5)	
Mor Edri	18.08.2000	2	(2)	
Roei Gordana	06.07.1990	23	(4)	3
Shalev Harush	08.05.2002		(1)	
Nir Hasson	19.12.2001	1	(1)	
Jimmy Marín Vílchez (CRC)	08.10.1997	1	(2)	1
Leonard Owusu (GHA)	03.06.1997	17		
Renan Carvalho Areias (BRA)	18.01.1998	2	(8)	
Yoni Sisay	16.11.2000	1		
Forwards:	**DOB**	**M**	**(s)**	**G**
Yaakov Brihon	06.07.1993	9	(8)	2
Idan Dahan	07.03.2001	1	(4)	3
Dean David	14.03.1996	27	(3)	11
Shoval Gozlan	25.04.1994	7	(11)	4
Mohamad Kna'an	14.01.2000	13	(12)	4
Benzion Moshel	31.07.1993	16	(3)	
Hamza Mowasi	09.02.2001		(3)	1
Jakub Sylvestr (SVK)	02.02.1989	6	(2)	1
Sagiv Yehezkel	21.03.1995	23	(4)	7

Hapoel Be'er Sheva Football Club

Founded: 01.05.1949
Stadium: Turner Stadium, Be'er Sheva (16,126)
Trainer: Barak Bakhar — 21.09.1979
[08.01.2020] Yosef Abukasis — 10.09.1970

Goalkeepers:	DOB	M	(s)	G
Ohad Levita	17.02.1986	15	(1)	
Ernestas Šetkus (LTU)	25.05.1985	21		
Defenders:	**DOB**	**M**	**(s)**	**G**
Oren Biton	16.06.1994	23	(3)	1
Amit Bitton	24.07.1996	15		
Ben Bitton	03.01.1991	27	(4)	
Liran Cohen	06.05.2001	1		
Or Dadia	12.07.1997	11	(5)	1
Sean Goldberg	13.06.1995	13	(2)	
Miguel Ângelo Leonardo Vítor (POR)	30.06.1989	29		3
Loai Taha	26.11.1989	16	(2)	
Shir Tzedek	22.08.1989	11	(1)	
Midfielders:	**DOB**	**M**	**(s)**	**G**
Netanel Askias	01.05.2001	2	(2)	
David Martins Simão (POR)	15.05.1990	9	(1)	
Josué Filipe Soares Pesqueira (POR)	17.09.1990	22	(6)	4
Marwan Kabha	23.02.1991	19	(4)	1
David Keltjens	11.06.1995	14	(3)	
Gal Levi	09.02.1994		(2)	
Ilay Madmon	23.02.1993	3		
Hanan Maman	28.08.1989	7	(9)	
Jimmy Marín Vílchez (CRC)	08.10.1997	7	(6)	1
Naor Sabag	23.05.1993	14	(10)	1
Eden Shamir	25.06.1995	17		1
Tomer Yosefi	02.02.1999	11	(6)	2
Forwards:	**DOB**	**M**	**(s)**	**G**
Abdallah Abu Abaid	14.12.2001		(2)	
Elton Acolatse (NED)	25.07.1995	9	(1)	
Roei Avitan	29.09.2000		(1)	
Qays Ganem	31.12.1997	4	(9)	1
Nigel Hasselbaink (NED)	21.11.1990	15	(6)	7
José Ángel Carrillo Casamayor (ESP)	07.01.1994	1		
Maor Melikson	30.10.1984		(2)	
Ramzi Safuri	21.10.1995	16	(12)	3
Ben Sahar	10.08.1989	28	(5)	13
Gaëtan Antony Varenne	24.06.1990	2	(4)	
Niv Zrihen	24.05.1994	14	(13)	3

Hapoel Hadera–Giv'at Olga "Shulem Schwarz" Football Club

Founded: 1936
Stadium: Netanya Stadium, Netanya (13,610)
Trainer: Ori Guttman 13.07.1985
[10.12.2019] Sharon Mimer 06.09.1973

Goalkeepers:	DOB	M	(s)	G
Augustine Amamchukwu Ejide (NGA)	08.04.1984	30		
Adi Tabachnik	16.11.1998	3	(1)	
Defenders:	DOB	M	(s)	G
Gilad Avramov	30.03.2000	8	(10)	1
Jonathan Cissé (CIV)	18.05.1997	11	(1)	
Hagai Goldenberg	15.09.1990	30	(1)	2
Yahav Gurfinkel	27.06.1998	26	(2)	
Yarin Hassan	22.03.1994	21	(4)	
Dia Lababidi	26.07.1992	22	(3)	
Dan Lugasi	27.02.2001		(2)	
Ashraf Rabah	10.02.1994	2		
Wassem Rabah	13.03.1994	30	(1)	
Sagiv Solomon	30.12.1995	1		
Midfielders:	DOB	M	(s)	G
Mohammed Abu Fani	27.04.1998	27	(1)	4
Alon Deri	04.06.2000		(6)	
George Fochive (USA)	24.03.1992	24	(1)	1
Eliel Peretz	18.11.1996	15	(7)	9
Yehonatan Levi	25.08.1999	5	(10)	
Amit Mor	14.09.2000		(6)	
Daniel Solomon	21.07.1991	12	(8)	
Menashe Zalka	01.07.1990	16	(4)	1
Forwards:	DOB	M	(s)	G
Salim Amash	05.07.1994	2	(10)	
Sagi Dror	07.08.1995	4	(10)	1
Didier Kougbenya (TOG)	12.11.1995	15	(5)	1
Lucielmo Palhano Soares "Lúcio Maranhão" (BRA)	28.09.1988	27	(4)	7
Junior Ogedi-Uzokwe (ENG)	03.03.1994	3	(2)	
Omar Younes	03.01.2003		(2)	
Ben Yosefi	13.06.1998		(4)	
Roei Zikri	13.10.1992	29	(2)	6

Hapoel Haifa Football Club

Founded: 24.04.1924
Stadium: „Sammy Ofer" Stadium, Haifa (30,870)
Trainer: Haim Silvas 21.11.1975

Goalkeepers:	DOB	M	(s)	G
Jasmin Burić (BIH)	18.02.1987	34		
Ran Kadosh	04.10.1985	2		
Defenders:	DOB	M	(s)	G
Eli Balilti	23.02.1994	23	(6)	1
Ofek Fishler	24.08.1996		(1)	
Nikola Gulan (SRB)	23.03.1989	20	(5)	
Nisso Kapiloto	10.01.1989	18	(1)	1
Dor Malul	30.04.1989	33	(1)	
Guy Mishpati	21.06.1990	18	(1)	2
Michael Siroshten	25.04.1989	17		
Ben Vahaba	27.03.1992	15		
Midfielders:	DOB	M	(s)	G
Tomer Altman	08.02.1998	11	(4)	
Gal Arel	09.07.1989	11	(11)	6
Francisco Santos da Silva Júnior (GNB)	18.01.1992	19	(4)	
Guy Hadida	23.07.1995		(2)	
Afik Katan	30.08.2000		(1)	
Gidi Kanyuk	11.02.1993	26	(2)	4
Yarin Sardal	13.02.2001	1	(2)	
Liran Serdal	02.07.1994	25	(3)	2
Snir Talias	26.07.1999	1	(2)	
Kevin Tapoko (FRA)	13.04.1994	19	(3)	1
Gil Vermouth	05.08.1985	5	(15)	
Forwards:	DOB	M	(s)	G
Maaran Al Lala	07.03.1982	6	(18)	1
Dudu Altrovich	12.07.1999		(2)	
Eden Ben Basat	08.09.1986	20	(3)	4
Almog Buzaglo	08.12.1992	13	(6)	1
Saar Fadida	04.01.1997	17	(4)	2
Ofir Mizrahi	04.12.1993	3	(6)	1
Aner Schechter	29.04.1997		(3)	
Jakub Sylvestr (SVK)	02.02.1989	12	(5)	5
Emery Welshman	09.11.1991	3	(5)	
Ness Zamir	31.10.1990	24	(9)	7

Hapoel Ironi Kiryat Shmona Football Club

Founded: 2000
Stadium: Kiryat Shmona Municipal Stadium, Kiryat Shmona (5,300)
Trainer: Messay Dego 15.02.1986
[21.10.2019] Kobi Refua 03.09.1974

Goalkeepers:	DOB	M	(s)	G
Gad Amos	24.12.1988	8		
Dziugas Bartkus (LTU)	07.11.1989	25		
Defenders:	DOB	M	(s)	G
Iyad Abu Abaid	31.12.1994	1	(1)	
Amir Ben Shimon	14.12.1993	12	(4)	
Uri Dahan	07.12.1999	20	(1)	1
Yuval Levin	13.02.2000	3		
Uri Magbo	12.09.1987		(1)	
Marcus Plínio Diniz Paixão (BRA)	01.08.1987	31		1
Ziv Morgan	19.01.2000	20	(1)	
Idan Nachmias	17.03.1997	31		1
Idan Rata	13.08.1999	2	(5)	
Samuel Scheimann	03.11.1987	4	(3)	
Gal Shish	28.01.1989	2		
Ori Tza'adon	17.05.1994	11	(3)	
Midfielders:	DOB	M	(s)	G
Samuel Bar-On	03.03.1998	21	(7)	
Maalique Nathanael Foster (JAM)	05.11.1996	2	(11)	
Radu Gînsari (MDA)	10.12.1991	4		1
Shay Golan	17.10.1998	4	(3)	
Eden Karzev	11.04.2000	23	(3)	1
Omer Lakau	27.02.1998	20	(11)	2
Yadin Lugasi	04.04.1999		(1)	
Silas Araújo da Silva (BRA)	30.05.1996	16	(3)	
Forwards:	DOB	M	(s)	G
Ahmed Abed	30.03.1990	11	(2)	
Yoel Abuhatzira	12.07.1996	8	(7)	1
Segun James Adeniyi (NGA)	20.12.1992	15	(4)	3
Guy Ben Lulu	19.05.2000	3	(2)	
Abdallah Khalaihal	11.01.2001	2	(6)	3
John Jairo Ruiz Barrantes (CRC)	10.01.1994	4	(3)	1
Ismail Ryan	24.04.1994	21	(7)	4
Mohammed Shakar	14.11.1996	23	(6)	5
Cillian Sheridan (IRL)	23.02.1989	16	(3)	4

Hapoel Kfar Saba Football Club

	Founded:	1928			
	Stadium:	HaMoshava Stadium, Petah Tikva (11,500)			
	Trainer:	Ofir Haim		21.04.1975	
	[26.02.2020]	Amir Turgeman		05.10.1972	

Goalkeepers:	DOB	M	(s)	G
Yigal Becker	09.09.1999	3		
Itamar Israeli	22.03.1992	30		
Defenders:	**DOB**	**M**	**(s)**	**G**
Sodiq Atanda (NGA)	26.08.1993	27		
Evgeniy Berkman	29.09.1991	20	(7)	
Noam Gamon	08.03.1997	13	(3)	
Tal Machluf	31.08.1991	30		
Niran Rotshtein	14.06.1993	1		
Tom Shelach	10.07.1996	20	(1)	
Itay Shor	18.02.2001	1	(1)	
Aviv Solomon	10.01.1995	27	(2)	2
Midfielders:	**DOB**	**M**	**(s)**	**G**
Dan Azaria	29.08.1995	16	(11)	
Noor Bisan	17.01.1995	1	(5)	
Triko Gateon	01.01.1995	8	(3)	1
Ben Hayun	08.11.2000		(3)	

Gershon Koffie (GHA)	25.08.1991	24	(5)	1
Ben Reichert	04.03.1994	11	(2)	1
Kevin Rainstein	22.02.1991	6	(3)	
Adrian Rochet	26.05.1987	15	(12)	
Liroy Zhairi	02.03.1989	4	(3)	
Forwards:	**DOB**	**M**	**(s)**	**G**
Yahav Afriat	25.01.1997	11	(15)	3
Sagi Dror	07.08.1995	3	(6)	
Omer Fadida	17.07.1990	24	(5)	10
Luwagga William Kizito (UGA)	20.12.1993	7	(4)	2
Benjamin Kuku (NGA)	08.03.1995	18	(2)	1
Ben Mizan	19.02.1995	3	(4)	
Amadou Soukouna (FRA)	21.06.1992	10	(2)	2
Boubacar Faye Traoré (SEN)	26.07.1997	24	(6)	3
Richárd Vernes (HUN)	24.02.1992	2	(2)	
Mahmoud Yousef (PLE)	30.07.1997	4	(3)	1

Hapoel Ra'anana Association Football Club

	Founded:	1972			
	Stadium:	HaMoshava Stadium, Petah Tikva (11,500)			
	Trainer:	Menahem Koretski		04.04.1974	
	[10.12.2019]	Nisso Avitan		29.09.1971	
	[19.02.2020]	Gal Cohen		14.08.1982	
	[24.05.2020]	Eyal Lahman		29.09.1965	

Goalkeepers:	DOB	M	(s)	G
Niv Antman	02.08.1992	3	(1)	
Roy Leib	07.05.2001	1		
Assaf Tsur	28.08.1998	29		
Defenders:	**DOB**	**M**	**(s)**	**G**
Amit Cohen	21.11.1998	27	(2)	1
Yarden Cohen	26.03.1997	24	(2)	
David Mateos Ramajo (ESP)	22.04.1987	26	(1)	1
Vitali Ganon	11.11.1991	1		
Maor Gerassi	03.10.1994		(1)	
Roy Herman	21.06.2000	3	(2)	
Sean Klimkin	16.09.1999	14	(3)	
Darryl Brian Ricky Lachman (CUW)	11.11.1989	4	(2)	
Ido Levy	31.07.1990	28		2
Adi Nimni	27.08.1991	21		1
Midfielders:	**DOB**	**M**	**(s)**	**G**
Ido Ben Yosef	03.10.2000	1	(1)	
Lior Berkovich	04.03.1998	1	(6)	

Ben Binyamin	17.12.1985	21	(2)	
Benny Golan	31.10.2000	1	(3)	2
Itay Katzav	21.02.2000	6	(1)	
Divine Naah	20.04.1996	13	(6)	
Ben Savir	05.03.1998	7	(8)	
Snir Shoker	08.05.1989	14	(3)	1
Avihai Yadin	26.10.1986	14	(5)	
Forwards:	**DOB**	**M**	**(s)**	**G**
Eugene Ansah (GHA)	16.12.1994	29	(2)	5
Karem Arshid	24.01.1995	17	(9)	2
Or Dasa	20.09.1998	22	(5)	4
Qays Ghanem	31.12.1997	17	(3)	1
Yaya Kone (CIV)	28.11.1998		(3)	
Roy Levy	13.01.2000	2	(13)	
Carlos Augusto Rivas Murillo (COL)	15.04.1994	2	(1)	
Idan Shemesh	06.08.1990	5	(14)	2
Elia Soriano (ITA)	26.06.1989		(1)	
Yoav Tomer	17.01.1998	10	(9)	5

Hapoel Tel Aviv Football Club

	Founded:	1923			
	Stadium:	Bloomfield Stadium, Tel Aviv (29,150)			
	Trainer:	Nisso Avitan		29.09.1971	
	[05.11.2019]	Nir Klinger		25.05.1966	

Goalkeepers:	DOB	M	(s)	G
Yoav Gerafi	29.08.1993	22		
Ido Sharon	06.06.2002		(1)	
Arik Yanko	21.12.1991	14		
Defenders:	**DOB**	**M**	**(s)**	**G**
Iyad Abu Abaid	31.12.1994	30	(1)	1
Idan Cohen	06.01.1996	12	(4)	
Orel Dgani	08.01.1989	27		1
Abdi Farhat	03.06.1996	4	(5)	
Doron Leidner	26.04.2002	7	(3)	
Tom Ahi Mordechai	09.05.2001	1		
Marvin Peersman (BEL)	10.02.1991	30	(3)	1
Raz Shlomo	13.08.1999	35	(1)	1
Midfielders:	**DOB**	**M**	**(s)**	**G**
Omri Altman	23.03.1994	30	(2)	11
Moti Barshazky	06.09.1996	14	(12)	2
Emmanuel Boateng (GHA)	17.06.1997	22	(4)	
Claudemir Ferreira da Silva (BRA)	17.08.1984	2		
Raz Cohen	11.11.1994	7	(5)	

Danny Gruper	16.03.1999	8	(13)	1
Shay Lee Izan	27.08.2000	23	(2)	
Nir Lax	10.08.1994	12	(5)	
Amit Meir	07.01.2001	6	(3)	
Stefan Spirovski (MKD)	23.08.1990	20	(1)	3
Ilay Tamam	07.05.2001	4	(4)	
Forwards:	**DOB**	**M**	**(s)**	**G**
Maor Buzaglo	14.01.1988	12	(9)	3
Demba Camara (GUI)	07.11.1994	11		2
Omer Damari	24.03.1989	8	(13)	2
Osher Davida	18.02.2001	2	(8)	
Shahar Hirsh	13.02.1993	3	(3)	1
Or Inbrum	12.01.1996	9	(2)	1
Ali Kna'ana	18.07.1996		(3)	
Francis Kyeremeh (GHA)	23.06.1997	5	(4)	1
Shavit Mazal	29.11.2001	2	(4)	
Michael Olaha	04.07.1996	9	(6)	
Ofek Ovadia	30.01.2001	2		
Felipe Jorge Rodríguez Valla (URU)	26.05.1990	3	(4)	

Maccabi Haifa Football Club

Founded: 1913
Stadium: "Sammy Ofer" Stadium, Haifa (30,870)
Trainer: Marco Balbul — 13.07.1967

Goalkeepers:	DOB	M	(s)	G
Joshua Cohen (USA)	18.08.1992	30	(1)	
Guy Haimov	09.03.1986	6		
Gil Ofek	09.01.1986		(1)	
Defenders:	**DOB**	**M**	**(s)**	**G**
Allyson Aires dos Santos (BRA)	23.10.1990	1		
Ofri Arad	11.09.1998	31	(2)	2
Rami Gershon	12.08.1988	2	(2)	
Ayid Habashi	10.05.1995	14	(3)	1
Manuel Castellano Castro "Lillo" (ESP)	27.03.1989	1		
Ernest Mabouka (CMR)	16.06.1988	33	(1)	1
Raz Meir	30.11.1996	4	(10)	
Sun Menahem	07.09.1993	33		1
Trent Lucas Sainsbury (AUS)	05.01.1992	29	(2)	2
Ikouwem Udo Utin (NGA)	11.11.1999	1	(6)	

Midfielders:	DOB	M	(s)	G
Yuval Ashkenazi	13.02.1992	26		7
Tjaronn Chery (NED)	04.06.1988	34	(2)	10
Jeando Pourrat Fuchs (CMR)	11.10.1997	1	(5)	
Dolev Haziza	05.07.1995	24	(7)	6
Neta Lavi	25.08.1996	33		2
Maor Levi	18.06.2000		(4)	
Maxim Plakuschenko	04.01.1996	10	(16)	1
Sintyahu Sallalich	20.06.1991	13	(9)	5
Forwards:	**DOB**	**M**	**(s)**	**G**
Mohamad Awad	09.06.1997	3	(23)	5
Stav Nachmani	06.10.2002		(1)	
Suf Podgoreanu	20.01.2002		(5)	
Nikita Rukavytsya (AUS)	22.06.1987	36		22
Yarden Shua	16.06.1999	4	(16)	2
Yanic Wildschut (NED)	01.11.1991	27	(5)	5

Maccabi Netanya Football Club

Founded: 1934
Stadium: Netanya Stadium, Netanya (13,610)
Trainer: Slobodan Drapić (SRB) — 28.02.1965

Goalkeepers:	DOB	M	(s)	G
Dani Amos	02.02.1987	30		
Roy Beigel	05.07.1999	1	(1)	
Raz Karmi	27.01.1996	2		
Defenders:	**DOB**	**M**	**(s)**	**G**
Dolev Azulay	09.10.1997	27	(1)	
Borja Herrera González (ESP)	08.01.1993	4		
Lazar Ćirković (SRB)	22.08.1992	4		
Tim Heubach (GER)	12.04.1988	18		2
Karem Jaber	31.10.2000	17	(2)	
Viki Kahlon	15.01.1993	15	(3)	
Rotem Keller	09.11.2002	3	(1)	
Matan Levy	19.02.2002	4	(1)	
Tzlil Nehemia	02.03.1995	5	(1)	1
Román Golobart Benet	21.03.1992	9	(1)	2
Yuval Sade	10.05.2000	1		
Zlatko Šehović (SRB)	08.08.2000	9	(1)	
Ben Turgeman	09.01.1989	6		
Muhammed Zubeidat	15.11.1991	8	(2)	

Midfielders:	DOB	M	(s)	G
Aviv Avraham	30.03.1996	17	(7)	2
Almog Cohen	01.09.1988	24		
Stav Finish	26.03.1992	7	(10)	
Omri Gandelman	16.05.2000	4	(2)	
Jahmir Hyka (ALB)	08.03.1988	7	(10)	
Gavriel Kanichowsky	24.08.1997	31		3
Roi Kehat	12.05.1992	23	(5)	4
Moshe Mula	29.02.2000	1	(3)	
Konstantin Oykin	30.06.2002		(1)	
Nicolas Olsak	25.11.1991	16	(4)	1
Forwards:	**DOB**	**M**	**(s)**	**G**
Ron Ashkenazi	20.08.1998	3	(16)	
Fatos Bećiraj (MNE)	05.05.1988	18	(6)	7
Hen Ezra	19.01.1989	9	(3)	2
Roy Korine	10.09.2002	3	(4)	
Yonas Malede	14.11.1999	20	(12)	2
Guy Melamed	21.12.1992	17	(13)	8

Maccabi Tel Aviv Football Club

Founded: 1906 (*as HaRishon LeZion-Yaffo*)
Stadium: Bloomfield Stadium, Tel Aviv (29,150)
Trainer: Vladimir Ivić (SRB)

Goalkeepers:	DOB	M	(s)	G
Daniel Miller Tenenbaum (BRA)	19.04.1995	33		
Andreas Gianniotis (GRE)	18.12.1992	3		
Defenders:	**DOB**	**M**	**(s)**	**G**
Ofir Davidzada	05.05.1991	6	(2)	
André Geraldes de Barros (POR)	02.05.1991	32	(1)	
Jair Amador Silos (POR)	21.08.1989	31	(1)	
Maor Kandil	27.11.1993	4	(2)	
Shahar Piven-Bachtiar	21.09.1995	9	(5)	1
Enric Saborit Teixidor (ESP)	27.04.1992	32	(1)	1
Eitan Tibi	16.11.1987	29		3
Sheran Yeini	08.12.1986	7	(3)	
Midfielders:	**DOB**	**M**	**(s)**	**G**
Roslan Barsky	03.01.1992	7	(9)	1
Dan Glazer	20.09.1996	32	(1)	
Eyal Golasa	07.10.1991	23	(7)	4

	DOB	M	(s)	G
Parfait Guiagon (CIV)	22.02.2001	1	(2)	
Dor Micha	02.03.1992	17	(11)	3
Nadav Aviv Nidam	11.04.2001		(1)	
Uroš Nikolić (SRB)	14.12.1993		(2)	
Dor Peretz	17.05.1995	12	(3)	1
Avi Rikan	10.09.1988	16	(11)	3
Forwards:	**DOB**	**M**	**(s)**	**G**
Eylon Almog	08.01.1999	9	(12)	4
Eliran Atar	17.02.1987	3	(2)	1
Omer Atzili	27.07.1993	17	(4)	8
Nick Blackman	11.11.1989	9	(9)	1
Yonatan Cohen	29.06.1996	28	(5)	12
Matan Hozez	12.08.1996	7	(4)	2
Chikeluba Francis Ofoedu (NGA)	12.11.1992	12	(9)	9
Aaron Schoenfeld	17.04.1990	2	(2)	1
Itay Shechter	22.02.1987	15	(17)	6

Football Section Sektia Nes Tziona

Founded:	1955; Refounded 2005		
Stadium:	HaMoshava Stadium, Petah Tikva (11,500)		
Trainer:	Amir Turgeman		05.10.1972
[07.02.2020]	Erez Belfer		17.06.1972
[17.02.2020]	Lior Zada		26.12.1978

Goalkeepers:	DOB	M	(s)	G
Omri Glazer	11.03.1996	33		
Matan Zalmanovich	13.08.1994		(1)	
Defenders:	**DOB**	**M**	**(s)**	**G**
Osher Abu	15.01.1993	5	(2)	
Noam Cohen	06.01.1999	16	(6)	
Francisco Dutari (ARG)	03.03.1988	22	(4)	
Ramaric Etou (CGO)	25.01.1995	18	(1)	
Yonatan Levi	02.01.1998	3	(3)	
Raz Nahmias	06.05.1996	32	(1)	
Itay Ozeri	24.05.1990	25		
Ben Sitelkol	12.04.1992	3		
Dries Wuytens (BEL)	18.03.1991	25	(3)	
Midfielders:	**DOB**	**M**	**(s)**	**G**
Guy Badash	24.05.1994	9	(13)	
Ofek Biton	27.09.1999	21		
Shay Elias	25.02.1999	13	(3)	

	DOB	M	(s)	G
Jahmir Hyka (ALB)	08.03.1988	6	(5)	1
Dor Kochav	06.05.1993	5	(5)	2
Sahar Levy	26.10.1985		(6)	
Sabien Lilaj (ALB)	18.02.1989	28	(2)	1
Elad Shahaf	13.01.1998	18	(11)	2
Amnon Tadela	19.11.1997	1	(7)	
Saikou Touray (GAM)	06.06.2000	22	(1)	2
Eylon Yerushalmi	10.03.1997	3	(5)	
Forwards:	**DOB**	**M**	**(s)**	**G**
David Boysen (DEN)	30.04.1991	1	(4)	1
Dor Galili	14.04.1997	1	(6)	
Moussa Maazou (NIG)	25.08.1988	19	(6)	4
Ofir Mizrahi	04.12.1993	5	(2)	
Raz Stain	23.02.1994	23	(4)	9
Eden Shrem	09.03.1993	3	(4)	
Eyal Strahman	21.06.1989	3	(4)	1

SECOND LEVEL
Liga Leumit 2019/2020

Regular Season

1.	Maccabi Petah Tikva FC	30	19	7	4	62 - 28	64
2.	Hapoel Rishon LeZion FC	30	15	9	6	43 - 29	54
3.	Hapoel Katamon Jerusalem FC	30	14	7	9	37 - 30	49
4.	Bnei Sakhnin FC	30	13	9	8	46 - 30	48
5.	Hapoel Nir Ramat HaSharon FC	30	13	7	10	42 - 43	46
6.	Hapoel Ramat Gan Givatayim FC	30	12	8	10	37 - 29	44
7.	FC Kafr Qasim	30	12	8	10	41 - 40	44
8.	Beitar Tel Aviv Bat Yam FC	30	12	7	11	40 - 40	43
9.	Hapoel Umm al-Fahm FC	30	10	9	11	35 - 38	39
10.	Hapoel Petah Tikva FC	30	9	11	10	42 - 43	38
11.	Hapoel Nof HaGalil FC	30	9	10	11	36 - 37	37
12.	Hapoel Acre FC	30	8	10	12	24 - 27	34
13.	Maccabi Ahi Nazareth FC	30	7	10	13	31 - 42	31
14.	Hapoel Bnei Lod Rakevet FC	30	7	5	18	26 - 59	26
15.	Hapoel Ashkelon FC	30	9	6	15	31 - 38	24
16.	Hapoel Afula FC	30	4	11	15	21 - 41	23

Promotion Play-offs

1.	Maccabi Petah Tikva FC (*Promoted*)	37	21	8	8	66 - 37	71
2.	Bnei Sakhnin FC (*Promoted*)	37	19	10	8	60 - 32	67
3.	Hapoel Ramat Gan Givatayim FC	37	17	9	11	51 - 36	60
4.	Hapoel Katamon Jerusalem FC	37	16	11	10	42 - 33	59
5.	Hapoel Rishon LeZion FC	37	16	10	11	55 - 42	58
6.	FC Kafr Qasim	37	16	8	13	53 - 48	56
7.	Beitar Tel Aviv Bat Yam FC	37	15	7	15	51 - 54	52
8.	Hapoel Nir Ramat HaSharon FC	37	14	7	16	50 - 60	49

Relegation Play-offs

9.	Hapoel Umm al-Fahm FC	36	13	10	13	45 - 44	49
10.	Hapoel Petah Tikva FC	36	12	11	13	52 - 54	47
11.	Hapoel Nof HaGalil FC	37	11	12	14	45 - 48	45
12.	Hapoel Acre FC	37	10	13	14	30 - 32	43
13.	Maccabi Ahi Nazareth FC	37	10	13	14	42 - 48	43
14.	Hapoel Afula FC (*Relegation Play-off*)	37	8	12	17	36 - 54	36
15.	Hapoel Bnei Lod Rakevet FC (*Relegated*)	35	9	6	20	34 - 69	33
16.	Hapoel Ashkelon FC* (*Relegated*)	37	9	9	19	37 - 51	27

9 points deducted

Relegation Play-off: Hapoel Afula FC – Hapoel Ironi Marmorek Rehovot FC   2-0(0-0)

Hapoel Afula FC remains at Second Level.

NATIONAL TEAM

INTERNATIONAL MATCHES
(16.07.2019 – 15.07.2020)

05.09.2019	Beersheba	Israel - North Macedonia	1-1(0-0)	(ECQ)
09.09.2019	Ljubljana	Slovenia - Israel	3-2(1-0)	(ECQ)
10.10.2019	Wien	Austria - Israel	3-1(1-1)	(ECQ)
15.10.2019	Beersheba	Israel - Latvia	3-1(3-1)	(ECQ)
16.11.2019	Jerusalem	Israel - Poland	1-2(0-1)	(ECQ)
19.11.2019	Skopje	North Macedonia - Israel	1-0(1-0)	(ECQ)

05.09.2019 ISRAEL - NORTH MACEDONIA 1-1(0-0) 16th EC. Qualifiers
"Yaakov Turner Toto" Stadium, Beersheba; Referee: Andreas Ekberg (Sweden); Attendance: 15,200
ISR: Ofir Meir Marciano, Orel Dgani, Omri Ben Harush (60.Beram Kayal), Hatem Abd Elhamed, Loai Taha, Elazar Dasa, Bibras Natkho (Cap), Dor Peretz, Manor Solomon, Eran Zahavi, Moanes Dabour (75.Tomer Hemed). Trainer: Andreas Herzog (Austria).
Goal: Eran Zahavi (55).

09.09.2019 SLOVENIA - ISRAEL 3-2(1-0) 16th EC. Qualifiers
Stadion Stožice, Ljubljana; Referee: Anthony Taylor (England); Attendance: 10,669
ISR: Ofir Meir Marciano, Orel Dgani, Omri Ben Harush (46.Beram Kayal), Hatem Abd Elhamed, Loai Taha, Elazar Dasa, Bibras Natkho (Cap), Manor Solomon, Dor Peretz (77.Dan Leon Glazer), Eran Zahavi, Shon Weissman (61.Moanes Dabour). Trainer: Andreas Herzog (Austria).
Goals: Bibras Natkho (50), Eran Zahavi (63).

10.10.2019 AUSTRIA - ISRAEL 3-1(1-1) 16th EC. Qualifiers
"Ernst Happel" Stadion, Wien; Referee: William Collum (Scotland); Attendance: 26,200
ISR: Ofir Meir Marciano, Taleb Tawatha (54.Omri Ben Harush), Eitan Tibi, Hatem Abd Elhamed, Loai Taha (76.Yonatan Cohen), Elazar Dasa, Bibras Natkho (Cap), Nir Biton, Manor Solomon, Eran Zahavi, Moanes Dabour (70.Shon Weissman). Trainer: Andreas Herzog (Austria).
Goal: Eran Zahavi (34).

15.10.2019 ISRAEL - LATVIA 3-1(3-1) 16th EC. Qualifiers
"Yaakov Turner Toto" Stadium, Beersheba; Referee: Arnold Hunter (Northern Ireland); Attendance: 9,150
ISR: Ofir Meir Marciano, Taleb Tawatha (78.Sun Menahem), Hatem Abd Elhamed, Loai Taha, Elazar Dasa, Bibras Natkho (Cap), Nir Biton, Dia Saba (76.Ilay Eliyau Elmkies), Dan Leon Glazer, Eran Zahavi, Moanes Dabour (76.Shon Weissman). Trainer: Andreas Herzog (Austria).
Goals: Moanes Dabour (16), Eran Zahavi (26), Moanes Dabour (42).

16.11.2019 ISRAEL - POLAND 1-2(0-1) 16th EC. Qualifiers
Teddy Stadium, Jerusalem; Referee: Mattias Gestranius (Finland); Attendance: 16,700
ISR: Ofir Meir Marciano, Omri Ben Harush (65.Sun Menahem), Eitan Tibi, Loai Taha (42.Dolev Haziza), Elazar Dasa, Bibras Natkho (Cap), Beram Kayal (79.Ilay Eliyau Elmkies), Nir Biton, Dan Leon Glazer, Eran Zahavi, Moanes Dabour. Trainer: Andreas Herzog (Austria).
Goal: Moanes Dabour (88).

19.11.2019 NORTH MACEDONIA - ISRAEL 1-0(1-0) 16th EC. Qualifiers
"Toše Proeski" Arena, Skopje; Referee: Paolo Valeri (Italy); Attendance: 5,573
ISR: Ariel Harush, Eitan Tibi, Elazar Dasa (41.Orel Dgani), Sun Menahem, Bibras Natkho (Cap), Nir Biton, Dia Saba (68.Shon Weissman), Dan Leon Glazer, Ilay Eliyau Elmkies (59.Dolev Haziza), Eran Zahavi, Moanes Dabour. Trainer: Andreas Herzog (Austria).

NATIONAL TEAM PLAYERS
(16.07.2019 – 15.07.2020)

Name	DOB	Caps	Goals	2019/2020:	Club
Goalkeepers					
Ariel HARUSH	25.05.1988	20	0	2019:	*Sparta Rotterdam (NED)*
Ofir Meir MARCIANO	07.10.1989	16	0	2019:	*Hibernian FC Edinburgh (SCO)*
Defenders					
Omri BEN HARUSH	07.03.1990	27	0	2019:	*KSC Lokeren (BEL)*
Elazar DASA	03.12.1992	25	0	2019: 09.09.2019->	*Unattached; SBV Vitesse Arnhem (NED)*
Orel DGANI	08.01.1989	12	0	2019:	*Hapoel Tel Aviv FC*
Hatem Abd ELHAMED	18.03.1991	5	0	2019:	*Celtic FC Glasgow (SCO)*
Sun MENAHEM	07.09.1993	3	0	2019:	*Maccabi Haifa FC*
Loai TAHA	26.11.1989	12	0	2019:	*Hapoel Be'er Sheva FC*
Eitan TIBI	16.11.1987	41	1	2019:	*Maccabi Tel Aviv FC*
Taleb TAWATHA	21.06.1992	18	1	2019:	*PFC Ludogorets Razgrad (BUL)*
Midfielders					
Nir BITTON	30.10.1991	27	2	2019:	*Celtic FC Glasgow (SCO)*
Yonatan COHEN	29.06.1996	4	0	2019:	*Maccabi Tel Aviv FC*
Ilay Eliyau ELMKIES	10.03.2000	3	0	2019:	*TSG 1899 Hoffenheim (GER)*
Dan Leon GLAZER	20.09.1996	7	0	2019:	*Maccabi Tel Aviv FC*
Dolev HAZIZA	05.07.1995	2	0	2019:	*Maccabi Haifa FC*
Beram KAYAL	02.05.1988	46	2	2019:	*Charlton Athletic FC London (ENG)*
Bibras NATKHO	18.02.1988	66	2	2019:	*FK Partizan Beograd (SRB)*
Dor PERETZ	17.05.1995	14	1	2019:	*Maccabi Tel Aviv FC*
Eran ZAHAVI	25.07.1987	52	19	2019:	*Guangzhou R&F FC (CHN)*
Forwards					
Moanes DABOUR	14.05.1992	21	7	2019:	*Sevilla FC (ESP)*
Tomer HEMED	02.05.1987	37	17	2019:	*Charlton Athletic FC London (ENG)*
Dia SABA	18.11.1992	10	3	2019:	*Guangzhou R&F FC (CHN)*
Manor SOLOMON	24.07.1999	7	0	2019:	*FK Shakhtar Donetsk (UKR)*
Shon WEISSMAN	14.02.1996	4	0	2019:	*Wolfsberger AC (AUT)*
National team coach					
Andreas HERZOG (Austria) [01.08.2019 – 24.06.2020]	10.09.1968	16 M; 6 W; 2 D; 8 L; 29-26			

ITALY

The Country:
Repubblica Italiana (Italian Republic)
Capital: Roma
Surface: 301,338 km²
Inhabitants: 60,317,116 [2020]
Time: UTC+1

The FA:
Federazione Italiana Giuoco Calcio
Via Gregorio Allegri 14, CP 2450 00198, Roma
Tel: +39 06 84 912553
Foundation date: 1898
Member of FIFA since: 1905
Member of UEFA since: 1954
Website: www.figc.it

NATIONAL TEAM RECORDS

RECORDS
First international match:	15.05.1910, Milano:	Italy – France 6-2
Most international caps:	Gianluigi Buffon	- 176 caps (1997-2018)
Most international goals:	Luigi Riva	- 35 goals / 42 caps (1965-1974)

UEFA EUROPEAN CHAMPIONSHIP
1960	Did not enter
1964	Qualifiers
1968	**Final Tournament (Winners)**
1972	Qualifiers
1976	Qualifiers
1980	Final Tournament (4th Place)
1984	Qualifiers
1988	Final Tournament (Semi-Finals)
1992	Qualifiers
1996	Final Tournament (Group Stage)
2000	Final Tournament (Runners-up)
2004	Final Tournament (Group Stage)
2008	Final Tournament (Quarter-Finals)
2012	Final Tournament (Runners-up)
2016	Final Tournament (Quarter-Finals)
2020	*Final Tournament (Qualified)*

FIFA WORLD CUP
1930	Did not enter
1934	**Final Tournament (Winners)**
1938	**Final Tournament (Winners)**
1950	Final Tournament (Group Stage)
1954	Final Tournament (Group Stage)
1958	Qualifiers
1962	Final Tournament (Group Stage)
1966	Final Tournament (Group Stage)
1970	Final Tournament (Runners-up)
1974	Final Tournament (Group Stage)
1978	Final Tournament (4th Place)
1982	**Final Tournament (Winners)**
1986	Final Tournament (Second Round of 16)
1990	Final Tournament (3rd Place)
1994	Final Tournament (Runners-up)
1998	Final Tournament (Quarter-Finals)
2002	Final Tournament (Second Round of 16)
2006	**Final Tournament (Winners)**
2010	Final Tournament (Group Stage)
2014	Final Tournament (Group Stage)
2018	Qualifiers

OLYMPIC TOURNAMENTS
1908	-
1912	Round 1
1920	Quarter-Finals
1924	Quarter-Finals
1928	3rd Place
1936	**Winners**
1948	Quarter-Finals
1952	Round 1
1956	Did not enter
1960	4th Place
1964	Qualifiers
1968	*Withdrew*
1972	Qualifiers
1976	Did not enter
1980	Group Stage
1984	4th Place
1988	4th Place
1992	Quarter-Finals
1996	Group Stage
2000	Quarter-Finals
2004	3rd Place
2008	Quarter-Finals
2012	Qualifiers
2016	Qualifiers

UEFA NATIONS LEAGUE
2018/2019 – League A (Final Tournament – 3rd Place)

FIFA CONFEDERATIONS CUP 1992-2017
2009 (Group Stage), 2013 (3rd Place)

ITALIAN CLUB HONOURS IN EUROPEAN CLUB COMPETITIONS:

European Champion Clubs' Cup (1956-1992) / UEFA Champions League (1993-2020)		
AC Milan	7	1962/1963, 1968/1969, 1988/1989, 1989/1990, 1993/1994, 2002/2003, 2006/2007
FC Internazionale Milano	3	1963/1964, 1964/1965, 2009/2010
Juventus FC Torino	2	1984/1985, 1995/1996
Fairs Cup (1858-1971) / UEFA Cup (1972-2009) / UEFA Europa League (2010-2020)		
Juventus FC Torino	3	1976/1977, 1989/1990, 1992/1993
FC Internazionale Milano	3	1990/1991, 1993/1994, 1997/1998
AC Parma	2	1994/1995, 1998/1999
AS Roma	1	1960/1961
SSC Napoli	1	1988/1989

UEFA Super Cup (1972-2019)		
AC Milan	5	1989, 1990, 1994, 2003, 2007
Juventus FC Torino	2	1984, 1996
AC Parma	1	1993
SS Lazio Roma	1	1999
European Cup Winners' Cup 1961-1999*		
AC Milan	2	1967/1968, 1972/1973
AC Fiorentina	1	1960/1961
Juventus FC Torino	1	1983/1984
UC Sampdoria Genova	1	1989/1990
AC Parma	1	1992/1993

defunct competition

NATIONAL COMPETITIONS
TABLE OF HONOURS

	CHAMPIONS	CUP WINNERS	BEST GOALSCORERS	
1898	Genoa CFC	-	-	
1899	Genoa CFC	-	-	
1900	Genoa CFC	-	-	
1901	AC Milan	-	-	
1902	Genoa CFC	-	-	
1903	Genoa CFC	-	-	
1904	Genoa CFC	-	-	
1905	Juventus FC Torino	-	-	
1906	AC Milan	-	-	
1907	AC Milan	-	-	
1908	FC Pro Vercelli	-	-	
1909	FC Pro Vercelli	-	-	
1909/1910	FC Internazionale Milano	-	-	
1910/1911	FC Pro Vercelli	-	-	
1911/1912	FC Pro Vercelli	-	-	
1912/1913	FC Pro Vercelli	-	-	
1913/1914	Casale FBC	-	-	
1914/1915	Genoa CFC	-	-	
1915/1916	*No competition*	-	-	
1916/1917	*No competition*	-	-	
1917/1918	*No competition*	-	-	
1918/1919	*No competition*	-	-	
1919/1920	FC Internazionale Milano	-	-	
1920/1921	FC Pro Vercelli	-		
1921/1922	USD Novese Novi Ligure (FIGC) FC Pro Vercelli (CCI)	FC Vado	-	
1922/1923	Genoa CFC	*No competition*	-	
1923/1924	Genoa CFC	*No competition*	Heinrich Schönfeld (AUT, FBC Torino)	22
1924/1925	Bologna SC	*No competition*	Mario Magnozzi (AS Livorno Calcio)	19
1925/1926	Juventus FC Torino	*No competition*	Ferenc Hirzer (HUN, Juventus FC Torino)	35
1926/1927	*Not awarded*	*No competition*	Anton Powolny (FC Internazionale Milano)	22
1927/1928	FBC Torino	*No competition*	Julio Libonatti (ARG, FBC Torino)	35
1928/1929	Bologna SC	*No competition*	Gino Rossetti (FBC Torino)	36
1929/1930	Ambrosiana-Inter Milano	*No competition*	Giuseppe Meazza (Ambrosiana-Inter Milano)	31
1930/1931	Juventus FC Torino	*No competition*	Rodolfo Volk (AS Roma)	29
1931/1932	Juventus FC Torino	*No competition*	Pedro Petrone Schiavione (URU, ACF Fiorentina) Angelo Schiavio (Bologna SC)	25
1932/1933	Juventus FC Torino	*No competition*	Felice Placido Borel (Juventus FC Torino)	29
1933/1934	Juventus FC Torino	*No competition*	Felice Placido Borel (Juventus FC Torino)	31
1934/1935	Juventus FC Torino	*No competition*	Enrico Guaita (ARG, AS Roma)	31
1935/1936	Bologna AGC	FBC Torino	Giuseppe Meazza (Ambrosiana-Inter Milano)	25
1936/1937	Bologna AGC	Genoa CFC	Silvio Piola (SS Lazio Roma)	21
1937/1938	Ambrosiana-Inter Milano	Juventus FC Torino	Giuseppe Meazza (Ambrosiana-Inter Milano)	20
1938/1939	Bologna AGC	FC Internazionale Milano	Aldo Boffi (AC Milan) Héctor Puricelli (URU, Bologna AGC)	19
1939/1940	Ambrosiana-Inter Milano	ACF Fiorentina	Aldo Boffi (AC Milan)	24
1940/1941	Bologna AGC	Venezia FBC	Héctor Puricelli (URU, Bologna AGC)	22
1941/1942	AS Roma	Juventus FC Torino	Aldo Boffi (AC Milan)	22
1942/1943	AC Torino	AC Torino	Silvio Piola (SS Lazio Roma)	21
1944	AC Spezia *(honorific title awarded in 2002)*	*No competition*	-	
1944/1945	*No competition*	*No competition*	-	
1945/1946	AC Torino	*No competition*	Guglielmo Gabetto (AC Torino)	22
1946/1947	AC Torino	*No competition*	Valentino Mazzola (AC Torino)	29
1947/1948	AC Torino	*No competition*	Giampiero Boniperti (Juventus FC Torino)	27
1948/1949	AC Torino	*No competition*	István Nyers (HUN, FC Internazionale Milano)	26

Season	Champion	Cup Winner	Top Scorer	Goals
1949/1950	Juventus FC Torino	*No competition*	Gunnar Nordahl (SWE, AC Milan)	35
1950/1951	AC Milan	*No competition*	Gunnar Nordahl (SWE, AC Milan)	34
1951/1952	Juventus FC Torino	*No competition*	John Hansen (DEN, Juventus FC Torino)	30
1952/1953	FC Internazionale Milano	*No competition*	Gunnar Nordahl (SWE, AC Milan)	26
1953/1954	FC Internazionale Milano	*No competition*	Gunnar Nordahl (SWE, AC Milan)	23
1954/1955	AC Milan	*No competition*	Gunnar Nordahl (SWE, AC Milan)	26
1955/1956	ACF Fiorentina	*No competition*	Gino Pivatelli (Bologna FC)	29
1956/1957	AC Milan	*No competition*	Dino da Costa (BRA, AS Roma)	22
1957/1958	Juventus FC Torino	SS Lazio Roma	William John Charles (WAL, Juventus FC Torino)	28
1958/1959	AC Milan	Juventus FC Torino	Antonio Valentin Angelillo (ARG, FC Internazionale Milano)	33
1959/1960	Juventus FC Torino	Juventus FC Torino	Enrique Omar Sivori (ARG, Juventus FC Torino)	28
1960/1961	Juventus FC Torino	ACF Fiorentina	Sergio Brighenti (Sampdoria UC Genova)	27
1961/1962	AC Milan	SSC Napoli	José João Altafini "Mazzola" (BRA, AC Milan) Aurelio Milani (ACF Fiorentina)	22
1962/1963	FC Internazionale Milano	Atalanta Bergamasca Calcio	Harald Nielsen (DEN, Bologna FC) Pedro Waldemar Manfredini (ARG, AS Roma)	19
1963/1964	Bologna FC	AS Roma	Harald Nielsen (DEN, Bologna FC)	21
1964/1965	FC Internazionale Milano	Juventus FC Torino	Alessandro Mazzola (FC Internazionale Milano) Alberto Orlando (ACF Fiorentina)	17
1965/1966	FC Internazionale Milano	ACF Fiorentina	Luis Vinicio (Lanerossi Vicenza)	25
1966/1967	Juventus FC Torino	AC Milan	Luigi Riva (US Cagliari)	18
1967/1968	AC Milan	AC Torino	Pierino Prati (AC Milan)	15
1968/1969	ACF Fiorentina	AS Roma	Luigi Riva (US Cagliari)	21
1969/1970	US Cagliari	Bologna FC	Luigi Riva (US Cagliari)	21
1970/1971	FC Internazionale Milano	AC Torino	Roberto Boninsegna (FC Internazionale Milano)	24
1971/1972	Juventus FC Torino	AC Milan	Roberto Boninsegna (FC Internazionale Milano)	22
1972/1973	Juventus FC Torino	AC Milan	Giuseppe Savoldi (Bologna FC) Paolino Pulici (AC Torino) Gianni Rivera (AC Milan)	17
1973/1974	SS Lazio Roma	Bologna FC	Giorgio Chinaglia (SS Lazio Roma)	24
1974/1975	Juventus FC Torino	ACF Fiorentina	Paolino Pulici (AC Torino)	18
1975/1976	AC Torino	SSC Napoli	Paolino Pulici (AC Torino)	21
1976/1977	Juventus FC Torino	AC Milan	Francesco Graziani (AC Torino)	21
1977/1978	Juventus FC Torino	FC Internazionale Milano	Paolo Rossi (Lanerossi Vicenza)	24
1978/1979	AC Milan	Juventus FC Torino	Bruno Giordano (SS Lazio Roma)	19
1979/1980	FC Internazionale Milano	AS Roma	Roberto Bettega (Juventus FC Torino)	16
1980/1981	Juventus FC Torino	AS Roma	Roberto Pruzzo (AS Roma)	18
1981/1982	Juventus FC Torino	FC Internazionale Milano	Roberto Pruzzo (AS Roma)	15
1982/1983	AS Roma	Juventus FC Torino	Michel Platini (FRA, Juventus FC Torino)	16
1983/1984	Juventus FC Torino	AS Roma	Michel Platini (FRA, Juventus FC Torino)	20
1984/1985	AC Hellas Verona	Sampdoria UC Genova	Michel Platini (FRA, Juventus FC Torino)	18
1985/1986	Juventus FC Torino	AS Roma	Roberto Pruzzo (AS Roma)	19
1986/1987	SSC Napoli	SSC Napoli	Pietro Paolo Virdis (AC Milan)	17
1987/1988	AC Milan	Sampdoria UC Genova	Diego Armando Maradona (ARG, SSC Napoli)	15
1988/1989	FC Internazionale Milano	Sampdoria UC Genova	Aldo Serena (FC Internazionale Milano)	22
1989/1990	SSC Napoli	Juventus FC Torino	Marcel van Basten (NED, AC Milan)	19
1990/1991	Sampdoria UC Genova	AS Roma	Gianluca Vialli (Sampdoria UC Genova)	19
1991/1992	AC Milan	AC Parma	Marcel van Basten (NED, AC Milan)	25
1992/1993	AC Milan	Torino Calcio	Giuseppe Signori (SS Lazio Roma)	26
1993/1994	AC Milan	Sampdoria UC Genova	Giuseppe Signori (SS Lazio Roma)	23
1994/1995	Juventus FC Torino	Juventus FC Torino	Gabriel Omar Batistuta (ARG, ACF Fiorentina)	26
1995/1996	AC Milan	ACF Fiorentina	Igor Protti (AS Bari) Giuseppe Signori (SS Lazio Roma)	24
1996/1997	Juventus FC Torino	Vicenza Calcio	Filippo Inzaghi (Atalanta Bergamasca Calcio)	24
1997/1998	Juventus FC Torino	SS Lazio Roma	Oliver Bierhoff (GER, Udinese Calcio)	27
1998/1999	AC Milan	AC Parma	Márcio Amoroso dos Santos (BRA, Udinese Calcio)	22
1999/2000	SS Lazio Roma	SS Lazio Roma	Andriy Shevchenko (UKR, AC Milan)	24
2000/2001	AS Roma	ACF Fiorentina	Hernán Jorge Crespo (ARG, SS Lazio Roma)	26
2001/2002	Juventus FC Torino	AC Parma	David Sergio Trezeguet (FRA, Juventus FC Torino) Dario Hübner (Piacenza Calcio)	24
2002/2003	Juventus FC Torino	AC Milan	Christian Vieri (FC Internazionale Milano)	24
2003/2004	AC Milan	SS Lazio Roma	Andriy Shevchenko (UKR, AC Milan)	24
2004/2005	*Not awarded*	FC Internazionale Milano	Cristiano Lucarelli (AS Livorno Calcio)	24
2005/2006	FC Internazionale Milano	FC Internazionale Milano	Luca Toni (ACF Fiorentina)	31
2006/2007	FC Internazionale Milano	AS Roma	Francesco Totti (AS Roma)	26
2007/2008	FC Internazionale Milano	AS Roma	Alessandro Del Piero (Juventus FC Torino)	21
2008/2009	FC Internazionale Milano	SS Lazio Roma	Zlatan Ibrahimović (SWE, FC Internazionale Milano)	25
2009/2010	FC Internazionale Milano	FC Internazionale Milano	Antonio Di Natale (Udinese Calcio)	29
2010/2011	AC Milan	FC Internazionale Milano	Antonio Di Natale (Udinese Calcio)	28
2011/2012	Juventus FC Torino	SSC Napoli	Zlatan Ibrahimović (SWE, AC Milan)	28
2012/2013	Juventus FC Torino	SS Lazio Roma	Edinson Roberto Cavani Gómez (URU, SSC Napoli)	29
2013/2014	Juventus FC Torino	SSC Napoli	Ciro Immobile (Torino FC)	22
2014/2015	Juventus FC Torino	Juventus FC Torino	Mauro Emanuel Icardi (ARG, FC Internazionale Milano) Luca Toni (Hellas Verona FC)	22
2015/2016	Juventus FC Torino	Juventus FC Torino	Gonzalo Gerardo Higuaín (ARG, SSC Napoli)	36
2016/2017	Juventus FC Torino	Juventus FC Torino	Edin Džeko (BIH, AS Roma)	29

2017/2018	Juventus FC Torino	Juventus FC Torino	Mauro Emanuel Icardi (ARG, FC Internazionale Milano) Ciro Immobile (SS Lazio Roma)	29
2018/2019	Juventus FC Torino	SS Lazio Roma	Fabio Quagliarella (Sampdoria UC Genova)	26
2019/2020	Juventus FC Torino	SSC Napoli	Ciro Immobile (SS Lazio Roma)	36

NATIONAL CHAMPIONSHIP
Serie A 2019/2020
(24.08.2019 – 02.08.2020)

Results

Round 1 [24-26.08.2019]
Parma - Juventus 0-1(0-1)
Fiorentina - SSC Napoli 3-4(1-2)
Udinese - AC Milan 1-0(0-0)
Cagliari - Brescia 0-1(0-0)
Hellas Verona - Bologna FC 1-1(1-1)
AS Roma - Genoa CFC 3-3(2-2)
Sampdoria - Lazio Roma 0-3(0-1)
SPAL Ferrara - Atalanta 2-3(2-1)
Torino FC - US Sassuolo 2-1(1-0)
Internazionale - US Lecce 4-0(2-0)

Round 2 [30.08.-01.09.2019]
Bologna FC - SPAL Ferrara 1-0(0-0)
AC Milan - Brescia 1-0(1-0)
Juventus - SSC Napoli 4-3(2-0)
Lazio Roma - AS Roma 1-1(0-1)
Atalanta - Torino FC 2-3(1-1)
Cagliari - Internazionale 1-2(0-1)
Genoa CFC - Fiorentina 2-1(1-0)
US Lecce - Hellas Verona 0-1(0-0)
US Sassuolo - Sampdoria 4-1(3-0)
Udinese - Parma 1-3(1-1)

Round 3 [14-16.09.2019]
Fiorentina - Juventus 0-0
SSC Napoli - Sampdoria 2-0(1-0)
Internazionale - Udinese 1-0(1-0)
Genoa CFC - Atalanta 1-2(0-0)
Brescia - Bologna FC 3-4(3-1)
Parma - Cagliari 1-3(0-2)
SPAL Ferrara - Lazio Roma 2-1(0-1)
AS Roma - US Sassuolo 4-2(4-0)
Hellas Verona - AC Milan 0-1(0-0)
Torino FC - US Lecce 1-2(0-1)

Round 4 [20-22.09.2019]
Cagliari - Genoa CFC 3-1(0-0)
Udinese - Brescia 0-1(0-0)
Juventus - Hellas Verona 2-1(1-1)
AC Milan - Internazionale 0-2(0-0)
US Sassuolo - SPAL Ferrara 3-0(2-0)
Bologna FC - AS Roma 1-2(0-0)
US Lecce - SSC Napoli 1-4(0-2)
Sampdoria - Torino FC 1-0(0-0)
Atalanta - Fiorentina 2-2(0-1)
Lazio Roma - Parma 2-0(1-0)

Round 5 [24-26.09.2019]
Hellas Verona - Udinese 0-0
Brescia - Juventus 1-2(1-1)
AS Roma - Atalanta 0-2(0-0)
Fiorentina - Sampdoria 2-1(1-0)
Genoa CFC - Bologna FC 0-0
Internazionale - Lazio Roma 1-0(1-0)
SSC Napoli - Cagliari 0-1(0-0)
Parma - US Sassuolo 1-0(0-0)
SPAL Ferrara - US Lecce 1-3(1-1)
Torino FC - AC Milan 2-1(0-1)

Round 6 [28-30.09.2019]
Juventus - SPAL Ferrara 2-0(1-0)
Sampdoria - Internazionale 1-3(0-2)
US Sassuolo - Atalanta 1-4(0-4)
SSC Napoli - Brescia 2-1(2-0)
Lazio Roma - Genoa CFC 4-0(2-0)
US Lecce - AS Roma 0-1(0-0)
Udinese - Bologna FC 1-0(1-0)
Cagliari - Hellas Verona 1-1(1-0)
AC Milan - Fiorentina 1-3(0-1)
Parma - Torino FC 3-2(2-2)

Round 7 [05-06.10.2019]
SPAL Ferrara - Parma 1-0(1-0)
Hellas Verona - Sampdoria 2-0(1-0)
Genoa CFC - AC Milan 1-2(1-0)
Fiorentina - Udinese 1-0(0-0)
Atalanta - US Lecce 3-1(2-0)
Bologna FC - Lazio Roma 2-2(2-2)
AS Roma - Cagliari 1-1(1-1)
Torino FC - SSC Napoli 0-0
Internazionale - Juventus 1-2(1-1)
Brescia - US Sassuolo 0-2(0-1) [18.12.]

Round 8 [19-21.10.2019]
Lazio Roma - Atalanta 3-3(0-3)
SSC Napoli - Hellas Verona 2-0(1-0)
Juventus - Bologna FC 2-1(1-1)
US Sassuolo - Internazionale 3-4(1-3)
Cagliari - SPAL Ferrara 2-0(1-0)
Sampdoria - AS Roma 0-0
Udinese - Torino FC 1-0(1-0)
Parma - Genoa CFC 5-1(3-0)
AC Milan - US Lecce 2-2(1-0)
Brescia - Fiorentina 0-0

Round 9 [25-27.10.2019]
Hellas Verona - US Sassuolo 0-1(0-0)
US Lecce - Juventus 1-1(0-0)
Internazionale - Parma 2-2(1-2)
Genoa CFC - Brescia 3-1(0-1)
Bologna FC - Sampdoria 2-1(0-0)
Atalanta - Udinese 7-1(3-1)
SPAL Ferrara - SSC Napoli 1-1(1-1)
Torino FC - Cagliari 1-1(0-1)
AS Roma - AC Milan 2-1(1-0)
Fiorentina - Lazio Roma 1-2(1-1)

Round 10 [29-31.10.2019]
Parma - Hellas Verona 0-1(0-1)
Brescia - Internazionale 1-2(0-1)
SSC Napoli - Atalanta 2-2(1-1)
Cagliari - Bologna FC 3-2(0-1)
Juventus - Genoa CFC 2-1(1-1)
Lazio Roma - Torino FC 4-0(2-0)
Sampdoria - US Lecce 1-1(0-1)
US Sassuolo - Fiorentina 1-2(1-0)
Udinese - AS Roma 0-4(0-1)
AC Milan - SPAL Ferrara 1-0(0-0)

Round 11 [02-04.11.2019]
AS Roma - SSC Napoli 2-1(1-0)
Bologna FC - Internazionale 1-2(0-0)
Torino FC - Juventus 0-1(0-0)
Atalanta - Cagliari 0-2(0-1)
Genoa CFC - Udinese 1-3(1-1)
Hellas Verona - Brescia 2-1(0-0)
US Lecce - US Sassuolo 2-2(2-1)
Fiorentina - Parma 1-1(0-1)
AC Milan - Lazio Roma 1-2(1-1)
SPAL Ferrara - Sampdoria 0-1(0-0)

Round 12 [08-10.11.2019]
US Sassuolo - Bologna FC 3-1(1-0)
Brescia - Torino FC 0-4(0-2)
Internazionale - Hellas Verona 2-1(0-1)
SSC Napoli - Genoa CFC 0-0
Cagliari - Fiorentina 5-2(3-0)
Lazio Roma - US Lecce 4-2(1-1)
Sampdoria - Atalanta 0-0
Udinese - SPAL Ferrara 0-0
Parma - AS Roma 2-0(0-0)
Juventus - AC Milan 1-0(0-0)

Round 13 [23-25.11.2019]
Atalanta - Juventus 1-3(0-0)
AC Milan - SSC Napoli 1-1(1-1)
Torino FC - Internazionale 0-3(0-2)
Bologna FC - Parma 2-2(1-1)
Hellas Verona - Fiorentina 1-0(0-0)
AS Roma - Brescia 3-0(0-0)
US Sassuolo - Lazio Roma 1-2(1-1)
Sampdoria - Udinese 2-1(1-1)
US Lecce - Cagliari 2-2(0-1)
SPAL Ferrara - Genoa CFC 1-1(0-0)

Round 14 [30.11.-02.12.2019]
Brescia - Atalanta 0-3(0-1)
Genoa CFC - Torino FC 0-1(0-0)
Fiorentina - US Lecce 0-1(0-0)
Juventus - US Sassuolo 2-2(1-1)
Internazionale - SPAL Ferrara 2-1(2-0)
Lazio Roma - Udinese 3-0(3-0)
Parma - AC Milan 0-1(0-0)
SSC Napoli - Bologna FC 1-2(1-0)
Hellas Verona - AS Roma 1-3(1-2)
Cagliari - Sampdoria 4-3(0-1)

Round 15 [06-08.12.2019]
Internazionale - AS Roma 0-0
Atalanta - Hellas Verona 3-2(1-1)
Udinese - SSC Napoli 1-1(1-0)
Lazio Roma - Juventus 3-1(1-1)
US Lecce - Genoa CFC 2-2(0-2)
US Sassuolo - Cagliari 2-2(2-0)
SPAL Ferrara - Brescia 0-1(0-0)
Torino FC - Fiorentina 2-1(1-0)
Sampdoria - Parma 0-1(0-1)
Bologna FC - AC Milan 2-3(1-2)

Round 16 [14-16.12.2019]
Brescia - US Lecce 3-0(2-0)
SSC Napoli - Parma 1-2(0-1)
Genoa CFC - Sampdoria 0-1(0-0)
Hellas Verona - Torino FC 3-3(0-1)
Bologna FC - Atalanta 2-1(1-0)
Juventus - Udinese 3-1(3-0)
AC Milan - US Sassuolo 0-0
AS Roma - SPAL Ferrara 3-1(0-1)
Fiorentina - Internazionale 1-1(0-1)
Cagliari - Lazio Roma 1-2(1-0)

Round 17 [18-22.12.2019]
Sampdoria - Juventus 1-2(1-2)
Fiorentina - AS Roma 1-4(1-2)
Udinese - Cagliari 2-1(1-0)
Internazionale - Genoa CFC 4-0(2-0)
Torino FC - SPAL Ferrara 1-2(1-1)
Atalanta - AC Milan 5-0(1-0)
US Lecce - Bologna FC 2-3(0-1)
Parma - Brescia 1-1(0-1)
US Sassuolo - SSC Napoli 1-2(1-0)
Lazio Roma - Hellas Verona 0-0 [05.02.2020]

Round 18 [05-06.01.2020]
Brescia - Lazio Roma 1-2(1-1)
SPAL Ferrara - Hellas Verona 0-2(0-1)
Genoa CFC - US Sassuolo 2-1(1-1)
AS Roma - Torino FC 0-2(0-1)
Bologna FC - Fiorentina 1-1(0-1)
Atalanta - Parma 5-0(3-0)
Juventus - Cagliari 4-0(0-0)
AC Milan - Sampdoria 0-0
US Lecce - Udinese 0-1(0-0)
SSC Napoli - Internazionale 1-3(1-2)

Round 19 [11-13.01.2020]
Cagliari - AC Milan 0-2(0-0)
Lazio Roma - SSC Napoli 1-0(0-0)
Internazionale - Atalanta 1-1(1-0)
Udinese - US Sassuolo 3-0(1-0)
Fiorentina - SPAL Ferrara 1-0(0-0)
Sampdoria - Brescia 5-1(2-1)
Torino FC - Bologna FC 1-0(1-0)
Hellas Verona - Genoa CFC 2-1(0-1)
AS Roma - Juventus 1-2(0-2)
Parma - US Lecce 2-0(0-0)

Round 20 [18-20.01.2020]
Lazio Roma - Sampdoria 5-1(3-0)
US Sassuolo - Torino FC 2-1(0-1)
SSC Napoli - Fiorentina 0-2(0-1)
AC Milan - Udinese 3-2(0-1)
Brescia - Cagliari 2-2(1-1)
Bologna FC - Hellas Verona 1-1(1-0)
US Lecce - Internazionale 1-1(0-0)
Genoa CFC - AS Roma 1-3(1-2)
Juventus - Parma 2-1(1-0)
Atalanta - SPAL Ferrara 1-2(1-0)

Round 21 [24-26.01.2020]
Brescia - AC Milan 0-1(0-0)
SPAL Ferrara - Bologna FC 1-3(1-1)
Fiorentina - Genoa CFC 0-0
Torino FC - Atalanta 0-7(0-3)
Internazionale - Cagliari 1-1(1-0)
Hellas Verona - US Lecce 3-0(2-0)
Sampdoria - US Sassuolo 0-0
Parma - Udinese 2-0(2-0)
AS Roma - Lazio Roma 1-1(1-1)
SSC Napoli - Juventus 2-1(0-0)

Round 22 [01-03.02.2020]
Bologna FC - Brescia 2-1(1-1)
Cagliari - Parma 2-2(1-1)
US Sassuolo - AS Roma 4-2(3-0)
Juventus - Fiorentina 3-0(1-0)
Atalanta - Genoa CFC 2-2(2-2)
AC Milan - Hellas Verona 1-1(1-1)
Lazio Roma - SPAL Ferrara 5-1(4-0)
US Lecce - Torino FC 4-0(2-0)
Udinese - Internazionale 0-2(0-0)
Sampdoria - SSC Napoli 2-4(1-2)

Round 23 [07-09.02.2020]
AS Roma - Bologna FC 2-3(1-2)
Fiorentina - Atalanta 1-1(1-1)
Torino FC - Sampdoria 1-3(0-0)
Hellas Verona - Juventus 2-1(0-0)
SPAL Ferrara - US Sassuolo 1-2(1-0)
Genoa CFC - Cagliari 1-0(1-0)
SSC Napoli - US Lecce 2-3(0-1)
Brescia - Udinese 1-1(0-0)
Parma - Lazio Roma 0-1(0-1)
Internazionale - AC Milan 4-2(0-2)

Round 24 [15-17.02.2020]
US Lecce - SPAL Ferrara 2-1(1-0)
Bologna FC - Genoa CFC 0-3(0-2)
Atalanta - AS Roma 2-1(0-1)
Udinese - Hellas Verona 0-0
Juventus - Brescia 2-0(1-0)
Sampdoria - Fiorentina 1-5(0-3)
US Sassuolo - Parma 0-1(0-1)
Cagliari - SSC Napoli 0-1(0-0)
Lazio Roma - Internazionale 2-1(0-1)
AC Milan - Torino FC 1-0(1-0)

Round 25 [21-23.02.2020/20-21.06.2020*]
Brescia - SSC Napoli 1-2(1-0)
Bologna FC - Udinese 1-1(0-1)
SPAL Ferrara - Juventus 1-2(0-1)
Fiorentina - AC Milan 1-1(0-0)
Genoa CFC - Lazio Roma 2-3(0-1)
AS Roma - US Lecce 4-0(2-0)
Torino FC - Parma 1-1(1-1)*
Hellas Verona - Cagliari 2-1(2-1)*
Atalanta - US Sassuolo 4-1(3-0)*
Internazionale - Sampdoria 2-1(2-0)*

Round 26 [29.02.-08.03.2020]
Lazio Roma - Bologna FC 2-0(2-0)
SSC Napoli - Torino FC 2-1(1-0)
US Lecce - Atalanta 2-7(2-2)
Cagliari - AS Roma 3-4(1-2)
Parma - SPAL Ferrara 0-1(0-0)
AC Milan - Genoa CFC 1-2(0-2)
Sampdoria - Hellas Verona 2-1(0-1)
Udinese - Fiorentina 0-0
Juventus - Internazionale 2-0(0-0)
US Sassuolo - Brescia 3-0(1-0)

Round 27 [22-24.06.2020]
Fiorentina - Brescia 1-1(1-1)
US Lecce - AC Milan 1-4(0-1)
Bologna FC - Juventus 0-2(0-2)
SPAL Ferrara - Cagliari 0-1(0-0)
Hellas Verona - SSC Napoli 0-2(0-1)
Genoa CFC - Parma 1-4(0-2)
Torino FC - Udinese 1-0(1-0)
Internazionale - US Sassuolo 3-3(2-1)
Atalanta - Lazio Roma 3-2(1-2)
AS Roma - Sampdoria 2-1(0-1)

Round 28 [26-28.06.2020]
Juventus - US Lecce 4-0(0-0)
Brescia - Genoa CFC 2-2(2-1)
Cagliari - Torino FC 4-2(2-0)
Lazio Roma - Fiorentina 2-1(0-1)
AC Milan - AS Roma 2-0(0-0)
Udinese - Atalanta 2-3(1-1)
Sampdoria - Bologna FC 1-2(0-0)
US Sassuolo - Hellas Verona 3-3(0-0)
SSC Napoli - SPAL Ferrara 3-1(2-1)
Parma - Internazionale 1-2(1-0)

Round 29 [30.06.-02.07.2020]
Torino FC - Lazio Roma 1-2(1-0)
Genoa CFC - Juventus 1-3(0-0)
Internazionale - Brescia 6-0(3-0)
Bologna FC - Cagliari 1-1(1-0)
SPAL Ferrara - AC Milan 2-2(2-0)
Hellas Verona - Parma 3-2(1-1)
US Lecce - Sampdoria 1-2(0-1)
Fiorentina - US Sassuolo 1-3(0-2)
Atalanta - SSC Napoli 2-0(0-0)
AS Roma - Udinese 0-2(0-1)

Round 30 [04-05.07.2020]
Juventus - Torino FC 4-1(2-1)
US Sassuolo - US Lecce 4-2(1-1)
Lazio Roma - AC Milan 0-3(0-2)
Internazionale - Bologna FC 1-2(1-0)
Cagliari - Atalanta 0-1(0-1)
Parma - Fiorentina 1-2(0-2)
Udinese - Genoa CFC 2-2(1-0)
Brescia - Hellas Verona 2-0(0-0)
Sampdoria - SPAL Ferrara 3-0(3-0)
SSC Napoli - AS Roma 2-1(0-0)

Round 31 [07-09.07.2020]
US Lecce - Lazio Roma 2-1(1-1)
AC Milan - Juventus 4-2(0-0)
Fiorentina - Cagliari 0-0
Genoa CFC - SSC Napoli 1-2(0-1)
Torino FC - Brescia 3-1(0-1)
AS Roma - Parma 2-1(1-1)
Atalanta - Sampdoria 2-0(0-0)
Bologna FC - US Sassuolo 1-2(0-1)
SPAL Ferrara - Udinese 0-3(0-2)
Hellas Verona - Internazionale 2-2(1-0)

Round 32 [11-13.07.2020]
Lazio Roma - US Sassuolo 1-2(1-0)
Brescia - AS Roma 0-3(0-0)
Juventus - Atalanta 2-2(0-1)
Genoa CFC - SPAL Ferrara 2-0(1-0)
Parma - Bologna FC 2-2(0-2)
Fiorentina - Hellas Verona 1-1(0-1)
Cagliari - US Lecce 0-0
Udinese - Sampdoria 1-3(1-1)
SSC Napoli - AC Milan 2-2(1-1)
Internazionale - Torino FC 3-1(0-1)

Round 33 [14-16.07.2020]
Atalanta - Brescia 6-2(4-1)
Sampdoria - Cagliari 3-0(2-0)
Bologna FC - SSC Napoli 1-1(0-1)
AC Milan - Parma 3-1(0-1)
US Lecce - Fiorentina 1-3(0-3)
AS Roma - Hellas Verona 2-1(2-0)
US Sassuolo - Juventus 3-3(1-2)
Udinese - Lazio Roma 0-0
Torino FC - Genoa CFC 3-0(1-0)
SPAL Ferrara - Internazionale 0-4(0-1)

Round 34 [18-20.07.2020]
Hellas Verona - Atalanta 1-1(0-0)
Cagliari - US Sassuolo 1-1(0-1)
AC Milan - Bologna FC 5-1(2-1)
Parma - Sampdoria 2-3(2-0)
Genoa CFC - US Lecce 2-1(1-0)
Brescia - SPAL Ferrara 2-1(0-1)
Fiorentina - Torino FC 2-0(1-0)
SSC Napoli - Udinese 2-1(1-1)
AS Roma - Internazionale 2-2(1-1)
Juventus - Lazio Roma 2-1(0-0)

Round 35 [21-23.07.2020]
Atalanta - Bologna FC 1-0(0-0)
US Sassuolo - AC Milan 1-2(1-2)
Parma - SSC Napoli 2-1(1-0)
US Lecce - Brescia 3-1(2-0)
Internazionale - Fiorentina 0-0
Sampdoria - Genoa CFC 1-2(1-1)
Torino FC - Hellas Verona 1-1(0-0)
SPAL Ferrara - AS Roma 1-6(1-2)
Udinese - Juventus 2-1(0-1)
Lazio Roma - Cagliari 2-1(0-1)

Round 36 [24-26.07.2020]
AC Milan - Atalanta 1-1(1-1)
Brescia - Parma 1-2(0-0)
Genoa CFC - Internazionale 0-3(0-1)
SSC Napoli - US Sassuolo 2-0(1-0)
Bologna FC - US Lecce 3-2(2-1)
AS Roma - Fiorentina 2-1(1-0)
Hellas Verona - Lazio Roma 1-5(1-1)
SPAL Ferrara - Torino FC 1-1(0-0)
Cagliari - Udinese 0-1(0-1)
Juventus - Sampdoria 2-0(1-0)

Round 37 [28-29.07.2020]
Parma - Atalanta 1-2(1-0)
Internazionale - SSC Napoli 2-0(1-0)
Lazio Roma - Brescia 2-0(1-0)
US Sassuolo - Genoa CFC 5-0(2-0)
Udinese - US Lecce 1-2(1-1)
Sampdoria - AC Milan 1-4(0-1)
Hellas Verona - SPAL Ferrara 3-0(2-0)
Fiorentina - Bologna FC 4-0(0-0)
Cagliari - Juventus 2-0(2-0)
Torino FC - AS Roma 2-3(1-2)

Round 38 [01-02.08.2020]
Brescia - Sampdoria 1-1(0-1)
AC Milan - Cagliari 3-0(1-0)
Atalanta - Internazionale 0-2(0-2)
SSC Napoli - Lazio Roma 3-1(1-1)
Juventus - AS Roma 1-3(1-2)
SPAL Ferrara - Fiorentina 1-3(1-1)
Genoa CFC - Hellas Verona 3-0(3-0)
US Lecce - Parma 3-4(2-2)
Bologna FC - Torino FC 1-1(1-0)
US Sassuolo - Udinese 0-1(0-0)

Final Standings

							Total			Home					Away				
1.	**Juventus FC Torino**	38	26	5	7	76 - 43	83	16	2	1	46 - 17	10	3	6	30 - 26
2.	FC Internazionale Milano	38	24	10	4	81 - 36	82	11	6	2	40 - 17	13	4	2	41 - 19
3.	Atalanta Bergamasca Calcio	38	23	9	6	98 - 48	78	12	2	5	51 - 26	11	7	1	47 - 22
4.	SS Lazio Roma	38	24	6	8	79 - 42	78	14	3	2	46 - 17	10	3	6	33 - 25
5.	AS Roma	38	21	7	10	77 - 51	70	10	4	5	36 - 27	11	3	5	41 - 24
6.	AC Milan	38	19	9	10	63 - 46	66	9	6	4	31 - 20	10	3	6	32 - 26
7.	SSC Napoli	38	18	8	12	61 - 50	62	10	3	6	31 - 24	8	5	6	30 - 26
8.	US Sassuolo Calcio	38	14	9	15	69 - 63	51	8	3	8	44 - 33	6	6	7	25 - 30
9.	Hellas Verona FC	38	12	13	13	47 - 51	49	9	5	5	29 - 25	3	8	8	18 - 26
10.	ACF Fiorentina	38	12	13	13	51 - 48	49	5	8	6	22 - 22	7	5	7	29 - 26
11.	Parma Calcio 1913	38	14	7	17	56 - 57	49	7	2	10	26 - 24	7	5	7	30 - 33
12.	Bologna FC 1909	38	12	11	15	52 - 65	47	5	8	6	25 - 29	7	3	9	27 - 36
13.	Udinese Calcio	38	12	9	17	37 - 51	45	6	6	7	18 - 23	6	3	10	19 - 28
14.	Cagliari Calcio	38	11	12	15	52 - 56	45	7	4	8	32 - 28	4	8	7	20 - 28
15.	Sampdoria UC Genova	38	12	6	20	48 - 65	42	6	4	9	25 - 30	6	2	11	23 - 35
16.	Torino FC	38	11	7	20	46 - 68	40	7	4	8	23 - 30	4	3	12	23 - 38
17.	Genoa C&FC	38	10	9	19	47 - 73	39	7	1	11	24 - 31	3	8	8	23 - 42
18.	US Lecce (*Relegated*)	38	9	8	21	52 - 85	35	4	5	10	30 - 41	5	3	11	22 - 44
19.	Brescia Calcio (*Relegated*)	38	6	7	25	35 - 79	25	3	5	11	21 - 34	3	2	14	14 - 45
20.	SPAL Ferrara (*Relegated*)	38	5	5	28	27 - 77	20	2	4	13	16 - 40	3	1	15	11 - 37

Top goalscorers:	
36 **Ciro Immobile**	*SS Lazio Roma*
31 Cristiano Ronaldo dos Santos Aveiro (POR)	*Juventus FC Torino*
23 Romelu Menama Lukaku Bolingoli (BEL)	*FC Internazionale Milano*
21 Francesco Caputo	*US Sassuolo Calcio*
18 João Pedro Geraldino dos Santos Galvão (BRA)	*Cagliari Calcio*
18 Luis Fernando Muriel Fruito (COL)	*Atalanta Bergamasca Calcio*
18 Duván Esteban Zapata Banguero (COL)	*Atalanta Bergamasca Calcio*

NATIONAL CUP
Coppa Italia 2019/2020

First Round [03-06.08.2019]

Virtus Francavilla Calcio - Novara Calcio	2-1(1-1)	US Catanzaro 1929 - Casertana FC	4-1(0-0,1-1)
FC Pro Vercelli 1892 - Rende Calcio 1968	2-0(0-0,0-0)	US Triestina Calcio 1918 - Cavese 1919	3-1(2-1)
FC Südtirol Bolzano - USD Città di Fasano	4-2(1-0)	Robur Siena - Mantova 1911 SSD	0-2(0-1)
Ravenna FC - SSD San Remo Calcio	1-0(1-0)	Imolese Calcio 1919 - SS Sambenedettese	3-3 aet; 4-3 pen
USD Adriese 1906 - Feralpisalò	0-1(0-0)	Calcio Catania - ASD Fanfulla	3-0(2-0)
Carrarese Calcio 1908 - Fermana FC	1-1 aet; 5-4 pen	SS Monopoli 1966 - FC Ponsacco 1920	4-1(3-1)
Piacenza Calcio 1919 - AS Viterbese Calcio	1-1 aet; 3-2 pen	SS Arezzo - SS Turris Calcio	1-0(1-0)
Aurora Pro Patria 1919 - SS Matelica Calcio 1921	1-0(0-0)	Potenza Calcio - Lanusei Calcio	2-0(0-0)
AC Monza - US Alessandria Calcio 1912	2-0(2-0)	Reggina 1914 - LR Vicenza Virtus	3-2(1-1)

Second Round [10-11.08.2019]

Ascoli Calcio 1898 FC - FC Pro Vercelli 1892	5-1(2-1)	Trapani Calcio - Piacenza Calcio 1919	3-1(1-1)
Spezia Calcio - Aurora Pro Patria 1919 Busto Arsizio	5-0(2-0)	Frosinone Calcio - Carrarese Calcio	4-0(2-0)
AC Chievo Verona - Ravenna FC	1-1 aet; 3-1 pen	SS Monopoli 1966 - Cosenza Calcio	1-0(0-0)
Venezia FC - Calcio Catania	2-1(1-1)	Virtus Entella - FC Südtirol Bolzano	1-2(1-1)
AC Perugia Calcio - US Triestina Calcio 1918	1-0(1-0)	Pordenone Calcio - Feralpisalò	1-2(1-1)
US Cremonese - Virtus Francavilla Calcio	4-0(2-0)	AS Livorno - Carpi FC 1909	0-1(0-0)
Empoli FC - Reggina 1914	2-1(1-1)	FC Crotone - SS Arezzo	4-3(3-3)
Delfino Pescara 1936 - Mantova 1911 SSD	3-2(1-0)	US Salernitana 1919 - US Catanzaro 1929	3-1(2-0)
Benevento Calcio - AC Monza	3-4(0-2)	SS Juve Stabia - Imolese Calcio 1919	1-1 aet; 2-3 pen
AS Cittadella - Calcio Padova	3-0(2-0)	AC Pisa 1909 - Potenza Calcio	3-0(1-0)

Third Round [16-18.08.2019]

Genoa C&FC - Imolese Calcio 1919	4-1(3-0)	Ascoli Calcio 1898 FC - Trapani Calcio	2-0(0-0)
Parma Calcio 1913 - Venezia FC	3-1(2-1)	Frosinone Calcio - SS Monopoli 1966	5-1(2-0)
AC Perugia Calcio - Brescia Calcio	2-1(0-1,1-1)	Udinese Calcio - FC Südtirol Bolzano	3-1(0-0)
ACF Fiorentina - AC Monza	3-1(0-1)	Sassuolo Calcio - Spezia Calcio	1-0(1-0)
Hellas Verona FC - US Cremonese	1-2(1-0,1-1)	SPAL 2013 Ferrara - Feralpisalò	3-1(3-1)
Empoli FC - Delfino Pescara 1936	2-1(1-1,1-1)	US Lecce - US Salernitana 1919	4-0(1-0)
AS Cittadella - Carpi FC 1909	3-3 aet; 5-4 pen	AC Pisa 1909 - Bologna FC 1909	0-3(0-1)
Cagliari Calcio - AC Chievo Verona	2-1(2-1)	FC Crotone - Sampdoria UC Genova	1-3(1-2)

Fourth Round [03-05.12.2019]

US Cremonese - Empoli FC	1-0(1-0)	SPAL 2013 Ferrara - US Lecce	5-1(4-0)
Genoa C&FC - Ascoli Calcio 1898 FC	3-2(1-0)	Udinese Calcio - Bologna FC 1909	4-0(2-0)
ACF Fiorentina - AS Cittadella	2-0(1-0)	Parma Calcio 1913 - Frosinone Calcio	2-1(1-0)
Sassuolo Calcio - AC Perugia Calcio	1-2(0-2)	Cagliari Calcio - Sampdoria UC Genova	2-1(1-0)

1/8-Finals [09/14-16.01.2020]

Torino FC - Genoa C&FC	1-1 aet; 5-3 pen	ACF Fiorentina - Atalanta Bergamasca Calcio	2-1(1-0)
SSC Napoli - AC Perugia Calcio	2-0(2-0)	AC Milan - SPAL 2013 Ferrara	3-0(2-0)
SS Lazio Roma - US Cremonese	4-0(2-0)	Juventus FC Torino - Udinese Calcio	4-0(2-0)
FC Internazionale Milano - Cagliari Calcio	4-1(2-0)	Parma Calcio 1913 - AS Roma	0-2(0-0)

Quarter-Finals [21-22/28-29.01.2020]

SSC Napoli - SS Lazio Roma	1-0(1-0)	AC Milan - Torino FC	4-2(1-1,2-2)
Juventus FC Torino - AS Roma	3-1(3-0)	FC Internazionale Milano - ACF Fiorentina	2-1(1-0)

Semi-Finals [12-13.02./12-13.06.2020]

First Leg		Second Leg	
FC Internazionale Milano - SSC Napoli	0-1(0-0)	SSC Napoli - FC Internazionale Milano	1-1(1-1)
AC Milan - Juventus FC Torino	1-1(0-0)	Juventus FC Torino - AC Milan	0-0

Final

17.06.2020; Stadio Olimpico, Roma; Referee: Daniele Doveri; Attendance: None
SSC Napoli - Juventus FC Torino   **0-0; 4-2 on penalties**

SSC Napoli: Alex Meret, Mário Rui Silva Duarte (81.Elseid Hysaj), Nikola Maksimović, Giovanni Di Lorenzo, Kalidou Koulibaly, Diego Demme, Fabián Ruiz Peña (80.Allan Marques Loureiro), Piotr Zieliński (88.Eljif Elmas), José María Callejón Bueno (66.Matteo Politano), Dries Mertens (67.Arkadiusz Milik), Lorenzo Insigne. Trainer: Gennaro Gattuso.

Juventus FC: Gianluigi Buffon, Matthijs de Ligt, Alex Sandro Lobo Silva, Leonardo Bonucci, Miralem Pjanić (74.Federico Bernardeschi), Blaise Matuidi, Rodrigo Bentancur Colmán, Cristiano Ronaldo dos Santos Aveiro, Douglas Costa de Souza (66.Danilo Luiz da Silva), Paulo Bruno Exequiel Dybala, Juan Guillermo Cuadrado Bello (85.Aaron James Ramsey). Trainer: Maurizio Sarri.

Penalties: Paulo Bruno Exequiel Dybala (saved); Lorenzo Insigne 1-0; Danilo Luiz da Silva (missed); Matteo Politano 2-0; Leonardo Bonucci 2-1; Nikola Maksimović 3-1; Aaron James Ramsey 3-2; Arkadiusz Milik 4-2.

Atalanta Bergamasca Calcio

Founded: 17.10.1907
Stadium: Stadio Atleti Azzurri d'Italia, Bergamo (21,300)
Trainer: Gian Piero Gasperini   26.01.1958

Goalkeepers:	DOB	M	(s)	G
Pierluigi Gollini	18.03.1995	33		
Francesco Rossi	27.04.1991		(1)	
Marco Sportiello	10.05.1992	5	(1)	
Defenders:	**DOB**	**M**	**(s)**	**G**
Raoul Bellanova	17.05.2000		(1)	
Mattia Caldara	05.05.1994	11	(3)	
Timothy Castagne (BEL)	05.12.1995	19	(8)	1
Lennart Czyborra (GER)	03.05.1999		(1)	
Berat Djimsiti (ALB)	19.02.1993	32	(2)	2
Robin Gosens (GER)	05.07.1994	31	(3)	9
Guilherme Antonio Arana Lopes (BRA)	14.04.1997		(4)	
Hans Hateboer (NED)	09.01.1994	25	(7)	
Simon Thorup Kjær (DEN)	26.03.1989	3	(2)	
Andrea Masiello	05.02.1986	7		
José Luis Palomino (ARG)	05.01.1990	28	(2)	2
Boško Šutalo (CRO)	01.01.2000	3	(4)	
Rafael Tolói (BRA)	10.10.1990	29	(4)	2
Midfielders:	**DOB**	**M**	**(s)**	**G**
Ebrima Colley (GAM)	01.02.2000		(5)	
Jacopo Da Riva	27.10.2000		(1)	
Marten Elco de Roon (NED)	29.03.1991	29	(6)	2
Remo Freuler (SUI)	15.04.1992	28	(3)	2
Ruslan Malinovskiy (UKR)	04.05.1993	12	(22)	8
Mario Pašalić (CRO)	09.02.1995	30	(5)	9
Adrien Tameze (FRA)	04.02.1994	2	(5)	
Forwards:	**DOB**	**M**	**(s)**	**G**
Musa Barrow (GAM)	14.11.1998	1	(6)	
Alejandro Darío Gómez (ARG)	15.02.1988	34	(2)	7
Josip Iličić (SVN)	29.01.1988	21	(5)	15
Luis Fernando Muriel Fruito (COL)	16.04.1991	10	(24)	18
Roberto Piccoli	27.01.2001		(1)	
Amad Traoré (CIV)	11.07.2002		(3)	1
Duván Esteban Zapata Banguero (COL)	01.04.1991	25	(3)	18

Bologna Football Club 1909

Founded: 03.10.1909
Stadium: Stadio "Renato Dall'Ara", Bologna (38,279)
Trainer: Siniša Mihajlović (SRB)   20.02.1969

Goalkeepers:	DOB	M	(s)	G
Angelo Esmael da Costa Júnior (BRA)	12.11.1983	1		
Łukasz Skorupski (POL)	05.05.1991	37		
Defenders:	**DOB**	**M**	**(s)**	**G**
Mattia Bani	10.12.1993	26	(1)	4
Federico Bonini	06.08.2001		(1)	
Gabriele Corbo	11.01.2000	1	(1)	
Danilo Larangeira (BRA)	10.05.1984	30		2
Stefano Denswil (NED)	07.05.1993	25	(1)	
Mitchell Dijks (NED)	09.02.1993	12	(1)	
Ibrahima M'Baye (SEN)	19.11.1994	16	(4)	
Nehuén Mario Paz (ARG)	28.04.1993	1	(2)	
Takehiro Tomiyasu (JPN)	05.11.1998	29		1
Midfielders:	**DOB**	**M**	**(s)**	**G**
Andri Baldursson (ISL)	10.01.2002		(7)	
Nicolás Martín Domínguez (ARG)	28.06.1998	7	(9)	
Blerim Džemaili (SUI)	12.04.1986	8	(6)	1
Gary Alexis Medel Soto (CHI)	03.08.1987	22	(1)	
Andrea Poli	29.09.1989	22	(6)	2
Dion Ruffo Luci	12.07.2001		(1)	
Kingsley Dogo Michael (NGA)	26.08.1999	1		
Jerdy Schouten (NED)	12.01.1997	13	(6)	
Roberto Soriano	08.02.1991	29		5
Mattias Svanberg (SWE)	05.01.1999	12	(13)	1
Forwards:	**DOB**	**M**	**(s)**	**G**
Musa Barrow (GAM)	14.11.1998	14	(4)	9
Gianmarco Cangiano	16.11.2001		(3)	
Mattia Destro	20.03.1991	2	(3)	
Musa Juwara (GAM)	26.12.2001	1	(6)	1
Ladislav Krejčí (CZE)	05.07.1992	11	(3)	1
Riccardo Orsolini	24.01.1997	32	(5)	8
Rodrigo Sebastián Palacio Alcalde (ARG)	05.02.1982	28	(7)	7
Nicola Sansone	10.09.1991	26	(7)	4
Federico Javier Santander Mereles (PAR)	04.06.1991	5	(19)	1
Andreas Skov Olsen (DEN)	29.12.1999	7	(19)	1

Brescia Calcio

Founded: 1911
Stadium: Stadio „Mario Rigamonti", Brescia (19,500)
Trainer: Eugenio Corini   30.07.1970
[05.02.2020] Luis Diego López Breijo (URU)   22.08.1974

Goalkeepers:	DOB	M	(s)	G
Enrico Alfonso	04.05.1988	4		
Lorenzo Andrenacci	02.01.1995	5	(1)	
Jesse Joronen (FIN)	21.03.1993	29		
Defenders:	**DOB**	**M**	**(s)**	**G**
Jhon Carlos Chancellor Cedeño (VEN)	02.01.1992	26		3
Andrea Cistana	01.04.1997	21		1
Felipe Castaldo Curcio (BRA)	08.06.1993		(1)	
Daniele Gastaldello	25.06.1983	4	(4)	
Giangiacomo Magnani	04.10.1995	1	(1)	
Massimiliano Mangraviti	24.01.1998	11	(2)	
Aleš Matějů (CZE)	03.06.1996	28	(3)	
Andrea Papetti	03.07.2002	10	(1)	1
Stefano Sabelli	13.01.1993	36		
Alessandro Semprini	24.02.1998	6	(6)	1
Midfielders:	**DOB**	**M**	**(s)**	**G**
Dimitri Bisoli	25.03.1994	24	(1)	1
Birkir Bjarnason (ISL)	27.05.1988	9	(4)	
Daniele Dessena	10.05.1987	22	(2)	2
Bruno Martella	14.08.1992	13	(11)	
Leonardo Morosini	13.10.1995		(3)	
Emanuele Ndoj (ALB)	20.11.1996	6	(12)	
Rômulo Souza Orestes Caldeira	22.05.1987	19	(3)	1
Nikolas Špalek (SVK)	12.02.1997	20	(5)	2
Sandro Tonali	08.05.2000	34	(1)	1
Luca Tremolada	25.11.1991		(1)	
Mattia Viviani	04.09.2000	3	(5)	
Jaromír Zmrhal (CZE)	02.08.1993	11	(10)	2
Forwards:	**DOB**	**M**	**(s)**	**G**
Florian Ayé (FRA)	19.01.1997	15	(7)	
Mario Balotelli	12.08.1990	16	(3)	5
Alfredo Donnarumma	30.11.1990	20	(11)	7
Andrea Ghezzi	02.03.2001		(5)	
Alessandro Matri	19.08.1984		(8)	
Simon Skrabb (FIN)	19.01.1995	3	(7)	
Ernesto Torregrossa	28.06.1992	22	(3)	7

Cagliari Calcio

Founded:	30.05.1920	
Stadium:	Sardegna Arena, Cagliari (16,233)	
Trainer:	Rolando Maran	14.07.1963
[03.03.2020]	Walter Zenga	28.04.1960

Goalkeepers:	DOB	M	(s)	G
Alessio Cragno	28.06.1994	16		
Robin Patrick Olsen (SWE)	08.01.1990	17		
Rafael De Andrade Bittencourt Pinheiro (BRA)	03.03.1982	5	(1)	
Defenders:	DOB	M	(s)	G
Fabrizio Cacciatore	08.10.1986	14	(2)	
Andrea Carboni	04.02.2001	5	(2)	
Luca Ceppitelli	11.08.1989	15	(1)	2
Ragnar Klavan (EST)	30.10.1985	26	(5)	
Charalampos Lykogiannis (GRE)	22.10.1993	14	(6)	
Luca Pellegrini	07.03.1999	22	(2)	
Simone Pinna	17.10.1997	1		
Fabio Pisacane	28.01.1986	28	(2)	1
Sebastian Walukiewicz (POL)	05.04.2000	13	(1)	
Midfielders:	DOB	M	(s)	G
Valter Birsa (SVN)	07.08.1986	4	(9)	
Luca Cigarini	20.06.1986	19	(3)	
Lucas Nahuel Castro (ARG)	09.04.1989	6	(9)	2

Alessandro Deiola	01.08.1995		(1)	
Paolo Faragò	12.02.1993	14	(7)	1
Artur Ioniță (MDA)	17.08.1990	21	(13)	
João Pedro Geraldino dos Santos Galvão(BRA)	09.03.1992	35	(1)	18
Riccardo Ladinetti	20.12.2000	1	(2)	
Federico Mattiello	14.07.1995	9	(9)	
Radja Nainggolan (BEL)	04.05.1988	25	(1)	6
Nahitan Michel Nández Acosta (URU)	28.12.1995	32	(3)	2
Christian Gabriel Oliva Giménez (URU)	01.06.1996	4	(7)	1
Gastón Rodrigo Pereiro López (URU)	11.06.1995	4	(6)	1
Marko Rog (CRO)	19.07.1995	28	(2)	1
Forwards:	DOB	M	(s)	G
Alberto Cerri	16.04.1996	1	(10)	1
Luca Gagliano	14.07.2000	1	(1)	1
Alberto Paloschi	04.01.1990	1	(6)	
Leonardo Pavoletti	26.11.1988	1	(1)	
Daniele Ragatzu	21.09.1991	2	(11)	1
Giovanni Simeone (ARG)	05.07.1995	34	(3)	12

Associazione Calcio Fiorentina Firenze

Founded:	29.08.1926 (re-founded 01.08.2002)	
Stadium:	Stadio "Artemio Franchi", Firenze (43,147)	
Trainer:	Vincenzo Montella	18.06.1974
[23.12.2019]	Giuseppe Iachini	07.05.1964

Goalkeepers:	DOB	M	(s)	G
Federico Brancolini	14.07.2001		(1)	
Bartłomiej Drągowski (POL)	19.08.1997	31		
Pietro Terracciano	08.03.1990	7		
Defenders:	DOB	M	(s)	G
José Martín Cáceres Silva (URU)	07.04.1987	27		1
Federico Ceccherini	11.05.1992	8	(7)	
Dalbert Henrique Chagas Estevão (BRA)	08.09.1993	29	(2)	
Christian Dalle Mura	02.02.2002		(1)	
Igor Julio dos Santos de Paulo (BRA)	07.02.1998	6	(3)	
Pol Mikel Lirola Kosok (ESP)	13.08.1997	30	(5)	
Nikola Milenković (SRB)	12.10.1997	36	(1)	5
Maximiliano Martín Olivera de Andrea (URU)	05.03.1992		(1)	
Germán Alejo Pezzella (ARG)	27.06.1991	33		3
Luca Ranieri	23.04.1999	2	(1)	
Aleksa Terzić (SRB)	17.08.1999		(2)	
Lorenzo Venuti	12.04.1995	10	(6)	
Midfielders:	DOB	M	(s)	G
Kevin Andrés Agudelo Ardila (COL)	14.11.1998	1	(2)	

Milan Badelj (CRO)	25.02.1989	20	(2)	1
Marco Benassi	08.09.1994	10	(8)	1
Kevin-Prince Boateng (GHA)	06.03.1987	6	(8)	1
Gaetano Castrovilli	17.02.1997	31	(2)	3
Federico Chiesa	25.10.1997	31	(3)	10
Sebastián Carlos Cristóforo Pepe (URU)	23.08.1993	1		
Alfred Duncan (GHA)	10.03.1993	10	(3)	1
Valentin Eysseric (FRA)	25.03.1992		(3)	
Erick Antonio Pulgar Farfán (CHI)	15.01.1994	32	(5)	7
Franck Bilal Ribéry (FRA)	07.04.1983	19	(2)	3
Szymon Żurkowski (POL)	25.09.1997		(2)	
Forwards:	DOB	M	(s)	G
Patrick Cutrone	03.01.1998	9	(10)	4
Rachid Ghezzal (ALG)	09.05.1992	9	(10)	1
Christian Kouamé (CIV)	06.12.1997	3	(4)	1
Pedro Guilherme Abreu dos Santos (ESP)	20.06.1997		(4)	
Riccardo Sottil	03.06.1999	4	(14)	
Dušan Vlahović (SRB)	28.01.2000	13	(17)	6

Genoa Cricket and Football Club

Founded:	07.09.1893	
Stadium:	Stadio „Luigi Ferraris", Genova (36,685)	
Trainer:	Aurelio Andreazzoli	05.11.1953
[28.08.1982]	Thiago Motta Santon Olivares (BRA)	22.10.2019
[28.12.2019]	Davide Nicola	05.03.1973

Goalkeepers:	DOB	M	(s)	G
Mattia Perin	10.11.1992	21		
Ionuț Andrei Radu (ROU)	28.05.1997	17		
Defenders:	DOB	M	(s)	G
Peter Ankersen (DEN)	22.09.1990	11	(8)	
Antonio Barreca	18.03.1995	11	(7)	
Davide Biraschi	02.07.1994	22	(2)	
Domenico Criscito	30.12.1986	24	(2)	8
Edoardo Goldaniga	02.11.1993	8	(5)	1
Jawad El Yamiq (MAR)	29.02.1992	2	(1)	
Andrea Masiello	05.02.1986	15		
Cristian Gabriel Romero (ARG)	27.04.1998	30		1
Adama Soumaoro (FRA)	18.06.1992	7	(1)	1
Cristián Eduardo Zapata Valencia (COL)	30.09.1986	19	(1)	1
Midfielders:	DOB	M	(s)	G
Kevin Andrés Agudelo Ardila (COL)	14.11.1998	7	(3)	1
Valon Behrami (SUI)	19.04.1985	13	(4)	
Francesco Cassata	16.07.1997	18	(6)	2
Paolo Ghiglione	02.02.1997	20	(5)	

Sinan Gümüş (GER)	15.01.1994	1	(2)	
Filip Jagiełło (POL)	08.08.1997	6	(5)	
Lukas Lerager (DEN)	12.07.1993	15	(6)	1
Marko Pajač (CRO)	11.05.1993	8	(3)	
Ivan Radovanović (SRB)	29.08.1988	15	(4)	
Rômulo Souza Orestes Caldeira (BRA)	22.05.1987		(1)	
Nicolò Rovella	04.12.2001	1	(1)	
Riccardo Saponara	21.12.1991	2	(2)	
Lasse Schöne (DEN)	27.05.1986	29	(3)	2
Stefano Sturaro	09.03.1993	15	(1)	1
Forwards:	DOB	M	(s)	G
Denilho Cleonise (NED)	08.12.2001		(4)	
Mattia Destro	20.03.1991	1	(7)	
Andrea Favilli	17.05.1997	7	(13)	
Iago Falqué Silva (ESP)	04.01.1990	6	(4)	2
Cristhian Kouamé (CIV)	06.12.1997	10	(1)	5
Goran Pandev (MKD)	27.07.1983	18	(16)	9
Andrea Pinamonti	19.05.1999	23	(9)	5
Arnaldo Antonio Sanabria Ayala (PAR)	04.03.1996	16	(8)	6

Hellas Verona Football Club

Founded: 1903 (*as AC Hellas Verona*; re-founded 1995)
Stadium: Stadio „Marc'Antonio Bentegodi", Verona (39,211)
Trainer: Ivan Jurić (CRO)   25.08.1975

Goalkeepers:	DOB	M	(s)	G
Boris Radunović (SRB)	26.05.1996	3		
Marco Silvestri	02.03.1991	35		
Defenders:	**DOB**	**M**	**(s)**	**G**
Claud Adjapong (GHA)	06.05.1998	2	(3)	
Alan Pereira Empereur (BRA)	10.03.1994	8	(5)	
Salvatore Bocchetti	30.11.1986	3	(2)	
Paweł Dawidowicz (POL)	20.05.1995	7	(8)	1
Federico Dimarco	10.11.1997	5	(8)	
Davide Faraoni	25.10.1991	36		5
Koray Günter (GER)	16.08.1994	31	(1)	
Marash Kumbulla (ALB)	08.02.2000	25		1
Matteo Lovato	14.02.2000		(1)	
Amir Rrahmani (KVX)	24.02.1994	36		
Midfielders:	**DOB**	**M**	**(s)**	**G**
Emmanuel Agyemang-Badu (GHA)	02.12.1990	2	(8)	
Sofyan Amrabat (MAR)	21.08.1996	33	(1)	1

	DOB	M	(s)	G
Andrea Danzi	25.02.1999		(1)	
Valentin Eysseric (FRA)	25.03.1992	3	(3)	
Liam Henderson (SCO)	25.04.1996	2	(2)	
Darko Lazović (SRB)	15.09.1990	37	(1)	3
Lucas Felippe Martello Nascimento (BRA)	03.05.2000		(2)	
Miguel Luís Pinto Veloso (POR)	11.05.1986	32	(2)	3
Matteo Pessina	21.04.1997	27	(8)	7
Valerio Verre	11.01.1994	22	(10)	3
Luigi Vitale	05.10.1987		(2)	
Mattia Zaccagni	16.06.1995	26	(8)	2
Forwards:	**DOB**	**M**	**(s)**	**G**
Fabio Borini	29.03.1991	9	(5)	3
Samuel Di Carmine	29.09.1988	17	(5)	8
Giampaolo Pazzini	02.08.1984	1	(14)	4
Eddie Salcedo	01.10.2001	7	(10)	1
Mariusz Stępiński (POL)	12.05.1995	7	(14)	3
Gennaro Tutino	20.08.1996	2	(4)	

Football Club Internazionale Milano

Founded: 09.03.1908
Stadium: Stadio "Giuseppe Meazza", Milano (80,018)
Trainer: Antonio Conte   31.07.1969

Goalkeepers:	DOB	M	(s)	G
Samir Handanovič (SVN)	14.07.1984	35		
Daniele Padelli	25.10.1985	3		
Defenders:	**DOB**	**M**	**(s)**	**G**
Alessandro Bastoni	13.04.1999	21	(4)	2
Cristiano Biraghi	01.09.1992	18	(8)	2
Danilo D'Ambrosio	09.09.1988	15	(7)	4
Stefan de Vrij (NED)	05.02.1992	32	(2)	4
Federico Dimarco	10.11.1997		(3)	
Diego Roberto Godín Leal (URU)	16.02.1986	18	(5)	1
Lorenzo Pirola	20.02.2002		(1)	
Andrea Ranocchia	16.02.1988	5	(2)	
Milan Škriniar (SVK)	11.02.1995	30	(2)	
Ashley Simon Young (ENG)	09.07.1985	13	(5)	4
Midfielders:	**DOB**	**M**	**(s)**	**G**
Lucien Agoumé (FRA)	09.02.2002		(3)	
Kwadwo Asamoah (GHA)	09.12.1988	7	(1)	

	DOB	M	(s)	G
Nicolò Barella	07.02.1997	23	(4)	1
Borja Valero Iglesias (ESP)	12.01.1985	9	(10)	2
Marcelo Brozović (CRO)	16.11.1992	30	(2)	3
Antonio Candreva	28.02.1987	24	(8)	5
Christian Dannemann Eriksen (DEN)	14.02.1992	8	(9)	1
Roberto Gagliardini	07.04.1994	21	(3)	4
Valentino Lando Lazaro (AUT)	24.03.1996	3	(3)	
Victor Moses (NGA)	12.12.1990	4	(8)	
Stefano Sensi	05.08.1995	9	(3)	3
Matías Vecino Falero (URU)	24.08.1991	14	(6)	2
Forwards:	**DOB**	**M**	**(s)**	**G**
Sebastiano Esposito	02.07.2002	2	(5)	1
Romelu Menama Lukaku Bolingoli (BEL)	13.05.1993	33	(3)	23
Lautaro Javier Martínez (ARG)	22.08.1997	29	(6)	14
Matteo Politano	03.08.1993	2	(9)	
Alexis Alejandro Sánchez Sánchez (CHI)	19.12.1988	10	(12)	4

Juventus Football Club Torino

Founded: 01.11.1897
Stadium: Allianz Stadium, Torino (41,507)
Trainer: Maurizio Sarri   10.01.1959

Goalkeepers:	DOB	M	(s)	G
Gianluigi Buffon	28.01.1978	9		
Carlo Pinsoglio	16.03.1990		(1)	
Wojciech Szczęsny (POL)	18.04.1990	29		
Defenders:	**DOB**	**M**	**(s)**	**G**
Alex Sandro Lobo Silva (BRA)	26.01.1991	27	(2)	1
Leonardo Bonucci	01.05.1987	35		3
Giorgio Chiellini	14.08.1984	3	(1)	1
Danilo Luiz da Silva (BRA)	15.07.1991	16	(6)	2
Matthijs de Ligt (NED)	12.08.1999	26	(3)	4
Mattia De Sciglio	20.10.1992	6	(3)	
Merih Demiral (TUR)	05.03.1998	5	(1)	1
Daniele Rugani	29.07.1994	7	(3)	
Midfielders:	**DOB**	**M**	**(s)**	**G**
Rodrigo Bentancur Colmán (URU)	05.06.1997	25	(5)	
Emre Can (GER)	12.01.1994	2	(6)	
Sami Khedira (GER)	04.04.1987	9	(3)	

	DOB	M	(s)	G
Blaise Matuidi (FRA)	09.04.1987	23	(12)	
Simone Muratore	30.05.1998	2	(2)	
Daouda Peeters (BEL)	26.01.1999		(1)	
Miralem Pjanić (BIH)	02.04.1990	28	(2)	3
Adrien Rabiot-Provost (FRA)	03.04.1995	21	(7)	1
Aaron James Ramsey (WAL)	26.12.1990	11	(13)	3
Forwards:	**DOB**	**M**	**(s)**	**G**
Federico Bernardeschi	16.02.1994	19	(10)	1
Cristiano Ronaldo dos Santos Aveiro (POR)	05.02.1985	33		31
Juan Guillermo Cuadrado Bello (COL)	26.05.1988	28	(5)	2
Douglas Costa de Souza (BRA)	14.09.1990	7	(16)	1
Paulo Bruno Exequiel Dybala (ARG)	15.11.1993	25	(8)	11
Gonzalo Gerardo Higuaín (ARG)	10.12.1987	20	(12)	8
Marco Olivieri	30.06.1999		(3)	
Giacomo Vrioni (ALB)	15.10.1998		(1)	
Luca Zanimacchia	19.07.1998	1	(1)	

Società Sportiva Lazio Roma

Founded: 09.01.1900
Stadium: Stadio Olimpico, Roma (70,634)
Trainer: Simone Inzaghi   05.04.1976

Goalkeepers:	DOB	M	(s)	G
Thomas Strakosha (ALB)	19.03.1995	38		
Defenders:	**DOB**	**M**	**(s)**	**G**
Francesco Acerbi	10.02.1988	36		2
Djavan Anderson (NED)	21.04.1995	2	(4)	
Nicolò Armini	07.03.2001		(1)	
Bartolomeu Jacinto Quissanga „Bastos" (ANG)	23.11.1991	6	(10)	1
Luca Falbo	21.02.2000		(1)	
Luiz Felipe Ramos Marchi (BRA)	22.03.1997	24	(2)	1
Jordan Zacharie Lukaku Menama Mokelenge (BEL)	25.07.1994	1	(12)	
Patricio Gabarrón Gil „Patric" (ESP)	17.04.1993	19	(2)	
Stefan Daniel Radu (ROU)	22.10.1986	28	(1)	1
Denis Vavro (SVK)	10.04.1996	1	(10)	
Midfielders:	**DOB**	**M**	**(s)**	**G**
André Anderson Pomilio Lima	23.09.1999		(6)	

	DOB	M	(s)	G
Valon Berisha (KVX)	07.02.1993		(3)	
Danilo Cataldi	06.08.1994	3	(18)	1
Carlos Joaquín Correa (ARG)	13.08.1994	22	(8)	9
Jonathan Rodríguez Menéndez „Jony" (ESP)	09.07.1991	14	(10)	
Manuel Lazzari	29.11.1993	29	(3)	
Lucas Pezzini Leiva (BRA)	09.01.1987	23	(2)	
Senad Lulić (BIH)	18.01.1986	20		
Adam Marušić (MNE)	17.10.1992	10	(5)	2
Sergej Milinković-Savić (SRB)	27.02.1995	35	(2)	7
Marco Parolo	25.01.1985	17	(12)	1
Forwards:	**DOB**	**M**	**(s)**	**G**
Bobby Adekanye (NED)	14.02.1999		(11)	1
Felipe Salvador Caicedo Corozo (ECU)	05.09.1988	18	(12)	9
Ciro Immobile	20.02.1990	36	(1)	36
Luis Alberto Romero Alconchel (ESP)	28.11.1992	36		6

Unione Sportiva Lecce

Founded: 17.03.1908 (re-founded 1934)
Stadium: Stadio „Ettore Giardiniero" - Via del Mare, Lecce (31,533)
Trainer: Fabio Liverani   29.04.1976

Goalkeepers:	DOB	M	(s)	G
Gabriel Vasconcelos Ferreira (BRA)	27.09.1992	34		
Mauro Vigorito	22.05.1990	4	(1)	
Defenders:	**DOB**	**M**	**(s)**	**G**
Romario Sandu Benzar (ROU)	26.03.1992	1	(2)	
Marco Calderoni	18.02.1989	24	(2)	3
Cristian Dell'Orco	10.02.1994	11	(3)	
Giulio Donati	05.02.1990	20		1
Fabio Lucioni	25.09.1987	36		3
Biagio Meccariello	27.03.1991	8	(6)	1
Nehuén Mario Paz (ARG)	28.04.1993	10	(3)	
Davide Riccardi	09.04.1996		(1)	
Andrea Rispoli	29.09.1988	20	(8)	
Luca Rossettini	09.05.1985	25	(1)	
Brayan Emanuel Vera Ramírez (COL)	15.01.1999	1	(7)	
Midfielders:	**DOB**	**M**	**(s)**	**G**
Antonín Barák (CZE)	03.12.1994	15	(1)	2

	DOB	M	(s)	G
Alessandro Deiola	01.08.1995	8	(2)	1
Filippo Falco	11.02.1992	24	(6)	4
Gilbert Giannelli Imbula Wanga (FRA)	12.09.1992	1	(2)	
Žan Majer (SVN)	25.07.1992	19	(8)	1
Marco Mancosu	22.08.1988	28	(5)	14
Ilario Monterisi	19.12.2001		(1)	
Jacopo Petriccione	22.02.1995	24	(7)	
Riccardo Saponara	21.12.1991	11	(2)	2
Yevhen Shakhov (UKR)	30.11.1990	9	(15)	1
Andrea Tabanelli	02.02.1990	11	(2)	1
Panagiotis Tachtsidis (GRE)	15.02.1991	24	(4)	
Forwards:	**DOB**	**M**	**(s)**	**G**
Khouma Babacar (SEN)	17.03.1993	17	(8)	3
Diego Farias da Silva (BRA)	10.05.1990	7	(11)	2
Edgaras Dubickas (LTU)	09.07.1998		(1)	
Andrea La Mantia	06.05.1991	6	(6)	2
Gianluca Lapadula	07.02.1990	20	(5)	11

Associazione Calcio Milan

Founded: 16.12.1899
Stadium: Stadio "Giuseppe Meazza", Milano (80,018)
Trainer: Marco Giampaolo   02.08.1967
[09.10.2019]   Stefano Pioli   20.10.1965

Goalkeepers:	DOB	M	(s)	G
Asmir Begović (BIH)	20.06.1987	1	(1)	
Gianluigi Donnarumma	25.02.1999	36		
José Manuel „Pepe" Reina Páez (ESP)	31.08.1982	1		
Defenders:	**DOB**	**M**	**(s)**	**G**
Davide Calabria	06.12.1996	16	(9)	1
Andrea Conti	02.03.1994	21	(2)	
Matteo Gabbia	21.10.1999	6	(3)	
Theo Bernard François Hernández (FRA)	06.10.1997	32	(1)	6
Simon Thorup Kjær (DEN)	26.03.1989	15		
Diego Sebastián Laxalt Suárez (URU)	07.02.1993	1	(3)	
Leonardo Campos „Léo" Duarte Da Silva (BRA)	17.07.1996	4	(2)	
Mateo Pablo Musacchio (ARG)	26.08.1990	17	(1)	
Ricardo Iván Rodríguez Araya (SUI)	25.08.1992	5		
Alessio Romagnoli	12.01.1995	35		1
Midfielders:	**DOB**	**M**	**(s)**	**G**
Ismaël Bennacer (FRA)	01.12.1997	28	(3)	1
Lucas Rodrigo Biglia (ARG)	30.01.1986	8	(6)	

	DOB	M	(s)	G
Giacomo Bonaventura	22.08.1989	13	(16)	3
Marco Brescianini	20.01.2000		(1)	
Hakan Çalhanoğlu (TUR)	08.02.1994	34	(1)	9
Franck Yannick Kessié (CIV)	19.12.1996	33	(2)	4
Rade Krunić (BIH)	07.10.1993	4	(11)	
Lucas "Paquetá" Tolentino Coelho de Lima (BRA)	27.08.1997	12	(12)	
Daniel Maldini	11.10.2001		(2)	
Alexis Saelemaekers (BEL)	27.06.1999	6	(7)	1
Forwards:	**DOB**	**M**	**(s)**	**G**
André Miguel Valente da Silva (POR)	06.11.1995	1		
Fabio Borini	23.03.1991	1	(1)	
Lorenzo Colombo	08.03.2002		(1)	
Zlatan Ibrahimović (SWE)	03.10.1981	16	(2)	10
Rafael Alexandre da Conceição Leão (POR)	10.06.1999	12	(19)	6
Krzysztof Piątek (POL)		14	(4)	4
Ante Rebić (CRO)	21.09.1993	15	(11)	11
Samuel Castillejo Azuaga (ESP)	18.01.1995	16	(6)	2
Jesús Joaquín Fernández Sáenz de la Torre „Suso" (ESP)	19.11.1993	15	(1)	1

Società Sportiva Calcio Napoli

Founded: 01.08.1926 (*as Associazione Calcio Napoli*)
Stadium: Stadio San Paolo, Napoli (60,240)
Trainer: Carlo Ancelotti   10.06.1959
[11.12.2019]   Gennaro Gattuso   09.01.1978

Goalkeepers:	DOB	M	(s)	G
Alex Meret	22.03.1997	21	(1)	
David Ospina Ramírez (COL)	31.08.1988	17		
Defenders:	**DOB**	**M**	**(s)**	**G**
Giovanni Di Lorenzo	04.08.1993	33		3
Faouzi Ghoulam (ALG)	01.02.1991	3	(6)	
Elseid Hysaj (ALB)	02.02.1994	17	(3)	1
Kalidou Koulibaly (SEN)	20.06.1991	24	(1)	
Sebastiano Luperto	06.09.1996	5	(4)	
Nikola Maksimović (SRB)	25.11.1991	20	(2)	1
Kévin Malcuit (FRA)	31.07.1991	3	(1)	
Kostas Manolas (GRE)	14.06.1991	25	(1)	4
Mário Rui Silva Duarte (POR)	27.05.1991	22	(2)	
Midfielders:	**DOB**	**M**	**(s)**	**G**
Allan Marques Loureiro (BRA)	08.01.1991	16	(7)	2

	DOB	M	(s)	G
Diego Demme (GER)	21.11.1991	10	(5)	1
Eljif Elmas (MKD)	24.09.1999	12	(14)	1
Fabián Ruiz Peña (ESP)	03.04.1996	30	(3)	3
Stanislav Lobotka (SVK)	25.11.1994	9	(5)	
Amin Younes (GER)	06.08.1993	1	(8)	1
Piotr Zieliński (POL)	20.05.1994	32	(5)	2
Forwards:	**DOB**	**M**	**(s)**	**G**
Lorenzo Insigne	04.06.1991	34	(3)	8
José María Callejón Bueno (ESP)	11.02.1987	25	(8)	4
Fernando Llorente Torres (ESP)	26.02.1985	3	(14)	3
Hirving Rodrigo Lozano Bahena (MEX)	30.07.1995	10	(16)	4
Dries Mertens (BEL)	06.05.1987	18	(13)	9
Arkadiusz Milik (POL)	28.02.1994	19	(7)	11
Matteo Politano	03.08.1993	9	(6)	2

Parma Calcio 1913

Founded: 16.12.1913 (*as Parma Foot Ball Club*)
Stadium: Stadio „Ennio Tardini", Parma (27,906)
Trainer: Roberto D'Aversa   12.08.1975

Goalkeepers:	DOB	M	(s)	G
Simone Colombi	01.07.1991	4		
Luigi Sepe	08.05.1991	34		
Defenders:	**DOB**	**M**	**(s)**	**G**
Bruno Eduardo Regufe Alves (POR)	27.11.1981	31	(2)	
Matteo Darmian	02.12.1989	30	(3)	1
Kastriot Dermaku (KVX)	15.01.1992	10	(6)	
Riccardo Gagliolo (SWE)	28.04.1990	31	(1)	3
Simone Iacoponi	30.04.1987	34	(2)	2
Vincent Laurini (FRA)	10.06.1989	10	(5)	
Giuseppe Pezzella	29.11.1997	8	(14)	
Vasco Regini	09.09.1990		(2)	
Midfielders:	**DOB**	**M**	**(s)**	**G**
Antonino Barillà	01.04.1988	20	(6)	1
Gastón Brugman Duarte (URU)	07.09.1992	17	(6)	

	DOB	M	(s)	G
Alberto Grassi	07.03.1995	6	(10)	1
Hernani Azevedo Junior (BRA)	27.03.1994	27	(5)	
Juraj Kucka (SVK)	26.02.1987	22	(4)	6
Dejan Kulusevski (SWE)	25.04.2000	33	(3)	10
Jasmin Kurtić (SVN)	10.01.1989	18	(2)	2
Matteo Scozzarella	05.06.1988	12	(4)	
Forwards:	**DOB**	**M**	**(s)**	**G**
Gianluca Caprari	30.07.1993	7	(5)	2
Andreas Cornelius (DEN)	16.03.1993	17	(9)	12
Gervais Lombe Yao Kouassi „Gervinho" (CIV)	27.05.1987	27	(4)	7
Roberto Inglese	12.11.1991	8	(9)	4
Yann Karamoh (FRA)	08.07.1998	5	(9)	1
Luca Siligardi	26.01.1988	3	(9)	
Mattia Sprocati	28.04.1993	4	(16)	

Associazione Sportiva Roma

Founded: 07.06.1927
Stadium: Stadio Olimpico, Roma (70,634)
Trainer: Paulo Alexandre Rodrigues Fonseca (POR)　　05.03.1973

Goalkeepers:	DOB	M	(s)	G
Daniel Cerantola Fuzato (BRA)	04.07.1997	1		
Antonio Mirante	08.07.1983	5		
Pau López Sabata (ESP)	13.12.1994	32		
Defenders:	**DOB**	**M**	**(s)**	**G**
Bruno da Silva Peres (BRA)	01.03.1990	12	(4)	2
Riccardo Calafiori	19.05.2002	1		
Yıldırım Mert Çetin (TUR)	01.01.1997	2	(4)	
Federico Julián Fazio (ARG)	17.03.1987	14	(2)	1
Roger Ibanez da Silva „Ibañez" (BRA)	23.11.1998	7	(2)	
Juan Guilherme Nunes Jesus (BRA)	10.06.1991	1	(3)	
Aleksandar Kolarov (SRB)	10.11.1985	30	(2)	7
Gianluca Mancini	17.04.1996	31	(1)	1
Davide Santon	02.01.1991	7	(8)	
Christopher Lloyd Smalling (ENG)	22.11.1989	29	(1)	3
Davide Zappacosta	11.06.1992	3	(6)	
Midfielders:	**DOB**	**M**	**(s)**	**G**
Bryan Cristante	03.03.1995	18	(8)	1
Amadou Diawara (GUI)	17.07.1997	19	(3)	1
Alessandro Florenzi	11.03.1991	12	(2)	
Gonzalo Villar del Fraile (ESP)	23.03.1998	2	(7)	
Henrikh Mkhitaryan (ARM)	21.01.1989	16	(6)	9
Javier Matías Pastore (ARG)	20.06.1989	5	(6)	
Lorenzo Pellegrini	19.06.1996	26	(1)	1
Diego Perotti (ARG)	26.07.1988	10	(11)	5
Leonardo Spinazzola	25.03.1993	18	(6)	1
Cengiz Ünder (TUR)	14.07.1997	10	(8)	3
Jordan Veretout (FRA)	01.03.1993	30	(3)	6
Nicolò Zaniolo	02.07.1999	16	(10)	6
Forwards:	**DOB**	**M**	**(s)**	**G**
Mirko Antonucci	11.03.1999		(2)	
Carles Pérez Sayol (ESP)	16.02.1998	5	(9)	1
Edin Džeko (BIH)	17.03.1986	31	(4)	16
Nikola Kalinić (CRO)	05.01.1988	6	(9)	5
Justin Kluivert (NED)	05.05.1999	19	(3)	4

Unione Calcio Sampdoria Genova

Founded: 12.08.1946
Stadium: Stadio "Luigi Ferraris", Genova (36,685)
Trainer: Eusebio Di Francesco　　08.09.1969
[12.10.2019]　Claudio Ranieri　　20.10.1951

Goalkeepers:	DOB	M	(s)	G
Emil Audero	18.01.1997	36		
Wladimiro Falcone	12.04.1995	2		
Defenders:	**DOB**	**M**	**(s)**	**G**
Tommaso Augello	30.08.1994	12	(5)	
Bartosz Bereszyński (POL)	12.07.1992	27	(1)	
Julian Chabot (GER)	12.02.1998	7	(1)	1
Omar Colley (GAM)	24.10.1992	30	(1)	
Alex Ferrari	01.07.1994	11	(1)	
Jeison Fabián Murillo Cerón (COL)	27.05.1992	7	(3)	
Nicola Murru	16.12.1994	26	(2)	
Vasco Regini	09.09.1990	2	(1)	
Lorenzo Tonelli	17.01.1990	9		
Maya Yoshida (JPN)	24.08.1988	13	(1)	
Midfielders:	**DOB**	**M**	**(s)**	**G**
Kristoffer Askildsen (NOR)	09.01.2001		(4)	1
Edgar Osvaldo Barreto Cáceres (PAR)	15.07.1984	1	(1)	
Andrea Bertolacci	11.01.1991	8	(4)	
Felice D'Amico	22.08.2000		(2)	
Fabio Depaoli	24.04.1997	21	(8)	
Albin Ekdal (SWE)	28.07.1989	27	(5)	
Jakub Jankto (CZE)	19.01.1996	25	(5)	2
Mehdi Léris (FRA)	23.05.1998	3	(12)	1
Karol Linetty (POL)	02.02.1995	22	(6)	4
Gonzalo Maroni (ARG)	18.03.1999	1	(4)	
Gastón Exequiel Ramírez Pereyra (URU)	02.12.1990	19	(7)	7
Emiliano Ariel Rigoni (ARG)	04.02.1993	4	(4)	
Morten Thorsby (NOR)	05.05.1996	21	(3)	1
Ronaldo Vieira (ENG)	19.07.1998	20	(7)	
Forwards:	**DOB**	**M**	**(s)**	**G**
Federico Bonazzoli	21.05.1997	7	(12)	6
Gianluca Caprari	30.07.1993	5	(13)	3
Manolo Gabbiadini	26.11.1991	24	(9)	11
Antonino La Gumina	06.03.1996	2	(3)	
Fabio Quagliarella	31.01.1983	26	(2)	11

Unione Sportiva Sassuolo Calcio

Founded: 17.07.1920
Stadium: Mapei Stadium – Città del Tricolore, Reggio Emilia (23,717)
Trainer: Roberto De Zerbi　　06.06.1979

Goalkeepers:	DOB	M	(s)	G
Andrea Consigli	27.01.1987	31		
Gianluca Pegolo	25.03.1981	5		
Stefano Turati	05.09.2001	2		
Defenders:	**DOB**	**M**	**(s)**	**G**
Vlad Iulian Chiricheş (ROU)	14.11.1989	8	(1)	
Gianmarco Ferrari	15.02.1992	21	(2)	
Giorgos Kyriakopoulos (GRE)	05.02.1996	17	(9)	
Giangiacomo Magnani	04.10.1995	1	(7)	1
Marlon Santos da Silva Barbosa (BRA)	07.09.1995	21	(2)	
Mert Müldür (TUR)	03.04.1999	13	(11)	2
Federico Peluso	20.01.1984	17	(6)	
Stefano Piccinini	31.12.2002		(1)	
Rogério Oliveira da Silva (BRA)	13.01.1998	12	(3)	1
Filippo Romagna	26.05.1997	16	(2)	
Jeremy Toljan (GER)	08.08.1994	25	(4)	1
Alessandro Tripaldelli	09.02.1999	1	(1)	
Midfielders:	**DOB**	**M**	**(s)**	**G**
Jérémie Boga (CIV)	03.01.1997	28	(6)	11
Mehdi Bourabia (FRA)	07.08.1991	10	(7)	1
Alfred Duncan (GHA)	10.03.1993	10	(3)	1
Filip Đuričić (SRB)	30.01.1992	19	(10)	5
Andrea Ghion	23.02.2000		(3)	
Manuel Locatelli	08.01.1998	31	(2)	
Francesco Magnanelli	12.11.1984	15	(7)	
Luca Mazzitelli	15.11.1995		(1)	
Pedro Obiang (EQG)	27.03.1992	18	(7)	1
Hamed Traorè (CIV)	16.02.2000	20	(11)	4
Forwards:	**DOB**	**M**	**(s)**	**G**
Domenico Berardi	01.08.1994	29	(2)	14
Francesco Caputo	06.08.1987	33	(3)	21
Grégoire Defrel (MTQ)	17.06.1991	9	(8)	3
Lukáš Haraslín (SVK)	26.05.1996	4	(7)	1
Giacomo Raspadori	18.02.2000	2	(9)	2

Società Polisportiva Ars et Labor Ferrara

Founded:	1907 (re-founded 2005 and 2012)		
Stadium:	Stadio "Paolo Mazza", Ferrara (13,020)		
Trainer:	Leonardo Semplici		18.07.1967
[10.02.2020]	Luigi Di Biagio		03.06.1971

Goalkeepers:	DOB	M	(s)	G
Etrit Berisha (ALB)	10.03.1989	26		
Karlo Letica (CRO)	11.02.1997	10		
Demba Thiam (SEN)	09.03.1998	2		
Defenders:	**DOB**	**M**	**(s)**	**G**
Kevin Bonifazi	19.05.1996	13	(1)	1
Thiago Rangel Cionek (POL)	21.04.1986	23	(5)	
Felipe Dias da Silva dal Belo (BRA)	31.07.1984	11	(4)	
Arkadiusz Reca (POL)	17.06.1995	22	(3)	
Jacopo Sala	05.12.1991	9	(7)	
Bartosz Salamon (POL)	01.05.1991	3	(4)	
Nenad Tomović (SRB)	30.08.1987	20	(3)	
Francesco Vicari	03.08.1994	33	(1)	
Ervin Zukanović (BIH)	11.02.1987	2	(1)	
Midfielders:	**DOB**	**M**	**(s)**	**G**
Lucas Nahuel Castro (ARG)	09.04.1989	6	(1)	
Marco D'Alessandro	17.02.1991	10	(5)	2
Bryan Dabo (BFA)	18.02.1992	13	(3)	1

	DOB	M	(s)	G
Mohamed Fares (ALG)	15.02.1996	5	(3)	
Gabriel Tadeu Strefezza Rebecato (BRA)	18.04.1997	24	(8)	1
Igor Julio dos Santos de Paulo (BRA)	07.02.1998	15	(2)	
Jasmin Kurtić (SVN)	10.01.1989	16		2
Simone Missiroli	23.05.1986	31	(3)	1
Alessandro Murgia	09.08.1996	19	(6)	
Georgi Tunjov (EST)	17.04.2001	3	(7)	
Mirko Valdifiori	21.04.1986	15	(7)	
Mattia Valoti	06.09.1993	18	(9)	3
Forwards:	**DOB**	**M**	**(s)**	**G**
Alberto Cerri	16.04.1996	5	(3)	1
Jaume Alberto Cuéllar Mendoza (BOL)	23.08.2001	1	(1)	
Federico Di Francesco	14.06.1994	13	(7)	2
Sergio Floccari	12.11.1981	9	(15)	1
Marko Janković (MNE)	09.07.1995	1	(5)	
Gabriele Moncini	26.04.1996	2	(2)	
Alberto Paloschi	04.01.1990	5	(5)	
Andrea Petagna	30.06.1995	33	(3)	12

Torino Football Club

Founded:	03.12.1906		
Stadium:	Stadio Olimpico Grande Torino, Torino (27,994)		
Trainer:	Walter Mazzarri		01.10.1961
[04.02.2020]	Moreno Longo		14.02.1976

Goalkeepers:	DOB	M	(s)	G
Antonio Rosati	26.03.1983	1		
Salvatore Sirigu	12.01.1987	36		
Samir Ujkani (KVX)	05.07.1988	1		
Defenders:	**DOB**	**M**	**(s)**	**G**
Temitayo Olufisayo Olaoluwa Aina (NGA)	08.10.1996	20	(12)	
Cristian Daniel Ansaldi (ARG)	20.09.1986	21	(6)	4
Kevin Bonifazi	19.05.1996	3		1
Gleison Bremer Silva Nascimento (BRA)	18.03.1997	27		3
Christian Celesia	22.01.2002		(1)	
Lorenzo De Silvestri	23.05.1988	28	(1)	
Koffi Djidji (CIV)	30.11.1992	9	(8)	
Armando Izzo	02.03.1992	30	(1)	1
Diego Sebastián Laxalt Suárez (URU)	07.02.1993	4	(12)	
Lyanco Evangelista Silveira Neves Vojnović(SRB)	01.02.1997	15	(2)	
Nicolas Alexis Julio Nkoulou Ndoubena (CMR)	27.03.1990	30	(1)	1

	DOB	M	(s)	G
Wilfried Singo (CIV)	25.12.2000	1	(3)	1
Midfielders:	**DOB**	**M**	**(s)**	**G**
Michel Adopo (FRA)	19.07.2000		(2)	
Daniele Baselli	12.03.1992	16		
Saša Lukić (SRB)	13.08.1996	20	(10)	1
Soualiho Meïté (FRA)	17.03.1994	23	(10)	
Tomás Eduardo Rincón Hernández (VEN)	13.01.1988	31	(1)	1
Forwards:	**DOB**	**M**	**(s)**	**G**
Alejandro Berenguer Remiro „Álex" (ESP)	04.07.1995	21	(8)	6
Andrea Belotti	20.12.1993	34	(2)	16
Simone Edera	09.01.1997	4	(9)	1
Iago Falqué Silva (ESP)	04.01.1990	1	(3)	
Vincenzo Millico	12.08.2000		(11)	
Simone Verdi	12.07.1992	26	(7)	2
Simone Zaza	25.06.1991	16	(8)	6

Udinese Calcio

Founded:	1896		
Stadium:	Stadio Friuli, Udine (25,144)		
Trainer:	Igor Tudor (CRO)		16.04.1978
[01.11.2019]	Luca Gotti		13.09.1967

Goalkeepers:	DOB	M	(s)	G
Juan Agustín Musso (ARG)	06.05.1994	38		
Defenders:	**DOB**	**M**	**(s)**	**G**
Marco Ballarini	28.03.2001		(1)	
Antonín Barák (CZE)	03.12.1994	1	(7)	
Sebastien De Maio (FRA)	05.03.1987	17	(4)	
Bram Nuytinck (NED)	04.05.1990	26		
Nicholas Opoku (GHA)	08.11.1997	6	(1)	
Giuseppe Pezzella	29.11.1997	1		
Rodrigo Nascimento Franca „Rodrigo Becão" (BRA)	19.01.1996	24	(5)	1
Samir Caetano de Souza Santos (BRA)	05.12.1994	16	(5)	1
Jens Stryger Larsen (DEN)	21.02.1991	32	(1)	1
Hidde ter Avest (NED)	20.05.1997	6	(14)	
William Troost-Ekong (NGA)	01.09.1993	29	(1)	
Marvin Zeegelaar (NED)	12.08.1990	6	(7)	

Midfielders:	DOB	M	(s)	G
Rodrigo Javier de Paul (ARG)	24.05.1994	33	(1)	7
Seko Fofana (CIV)	07.05.1995	24	(8)	3
Mato Jajalo (BIH)	24.05.1988	19	(7)	
Rolando Mandragora	29.06.1997	24	(2)	
Martin Palumbo (NOR)	05.03.2002		(1)	
Ken Nlata Sema (SWE)	30.09.1993	30	(2)	2
Walace Souza Silva (BRA)	04.04.1995	12	(8)	
Forwards:	**DOB**	**M**	**(s)**	**G**
Kevin Lasagna	10.08.1992	28	(8)	10
Ilija Nestorovski (MKD)	12.03.1990	15	(13)	3
Stefano Okaka	09.08.1989	28	(5)	8
Ignacio Pussetto (ARG)	21.12.1995	2	(10)	1
Łukasz Teodorczyk (POL)	03.06.1991	1	(13)	

SECOND LEVEL
Serie B 2019/2020

1.	Benevento Calcio (*Promoted*)	38	26	8	4	67	-	27	86
2.	FC Crotone (*Promoted*)	38	20	8	10	63	-	40	68
3.	Spezia Calcio (*Promotion Play-offs*)	38	17	10	11	54	-	40	61
4.	Pordenone Calcio (*Promotion Play-offs*)	38	16	10	12	48	-	46	58
5.	AS Cittadella (*Promotion Play-offs*)	38	17	7	14	49	-	49	58
6.	AC Chievo Verona (*Promotion Play-offs*)	38	14	14	10	48	-	38	56
7.	Empoli FC (*Promotion Play-offs*)	38	14	12	12	47	-	48	54
8.	Frosinone Calcio (*Promotion Play-offs*)	38	14	12	12	41	-	38	54
9.	AC Pisa 1909	38	14	12	12	49	-	45	54
10.	US Salernitana 1919	38	14	10	14	53	-	50	52
11.	Venezia FC	38	12	14	12	37	-	40	50
12.	US Cremonese	38	12	13	13	42	-	43	49
13.	Virtus Entella Chiavari	38	12	12	14	46	-	50	48
14.	Ascoli Calcio 1898 FC	38	13	7	18	50	-	58	46
15.	Cosenza Calcio	38	12	10	16	50	-	49	46
16.	AC Perugia Calcio (*Relegation Play-out*)	38	12	9	17	38	-	49	45
17.	Delfino Pescara 1936 (*Relegation Play-out*)	38	12	9	17	48	-	55	45
18.	Trapani Calcio* (*Relegated*)	38	11	13	14	48	-	60	44
19.	SS Juve Stabia (*Relegated*)	38	11	8	19	47	-	63	41
20.	AS Livorno Calcio (*Relegated*)	38	5	6	27	30	-	67	21

*2 points deducted for administral irregularities.

Relegation Play-out [10-14.08.2020]

Delfino Pescara 1936 - AC Perugia Calcio	2-1(0-1)	1-2 aet; 4-2 pen

Delfino Pescara 1936 remains at Second Level.

Promotion Play-offs [04-20.08.2020]

Preliminary Round	AC Chievo Verona - Empoli FC	1-1(0-0,0-0)	
	AS Cittadella - Frosinone Calcio	2-3(2-1,2-2)	
Semi-Finals	AC Chievo Verona - Spezia Calcio	2-0(2-0)	1-3(0-1)
	Frosinone Calcio - Pordenone Calcio	0-1(0-0)	2-0(2-0)
Finals	Frosinone Calcio - Spezia Calcio	0-1(0-1)	1-0(0-0)

Spezia Calcio promoted to 2020/2021 Serie A.

NATIONAL TEAM

INTERNATIONAL MATCHES
(16.07.2019 – 15.07.2020)

05.09.2019	Yerevan	Armenia - Italy	1-3(1-1)	(ECQ)
08.09.2019	Tampere	Finland - Italy	1-2(0-0)	(ECQ)
12.10.2019	Roma	Italy - Greece	2-0(0-0)	(ECQ)
15.10.2019	Vaduz	Liechtenstein - Italy	0-5(0-1)	(ECQ)
15.11.2019	Zenica	Bosnia and Herzegovina - Italy	0-3(0-2)	(ECQ)
18.11.2019	Palermo	Italy - Armenia	9-1(4-0)	(ECQ)

05.09.2019 ARMENIA - ITALY   **1-3(1-1)**   16th EC. Qualifiers
„Vazgen Sargsyan" Hanrapetakan Stadium, Yerevan; Referee: Daniel Siebert (Germany); Attendance: 13,680
ITA: Gianluigi Donnarumma, Leonardo Bonucci (Cap), Emerson Palmieri dos Santos, Alessandro Florenzi, Alessio Romagnoli, Marco Verratti, Jorge Luiz Frello Filho „Jorginho", Nicolò Barella (69.Stefano Sensi), Andrea Belotti, Federico Bernardeschi (83.Kevin Lasagna), Federico Chiesa (61.Lorenzo Pellegrini). Trainer: Roberto Mancini.
Goals: Andrea Belotti (28), Lorenzo Pellegrini (77), Aram Hayrapetyan (80 own goal).

08.09.2019 FINLAND - ITALY   **1-2(0-0)**   16th EC. Qualifiers
Ratinan Stadion, Tampere; Referee: Robert Madden (Scotland); Attendance: 16,292
ITA: Gianluigi Donnarumma, Leonardo Bonucci (Cap), Francesco Acerbi, Emerson Palmieri dos Santos (8.Alessandro Florenzi), Armando Izzo, Jorge Luiz Frello Filho „Jorginho", Stefano Sensi, Nicolò Barella, Lorenzo Pellegrini, Ciro Immobile (76.Andrea Belotti), Federico Chiesa (72.Federico Bernardeschi). Trainer: Roberto Mancini.
Goals: Ciro Immobile (59), Jorge Luiz Frello Filho "Jorginho" (79 penalty).

12.10.2019 ITALY - GREECE   **2-0(0-0)**   16th EC. Qualifiers
Stadio Olimpico, Roma; Referee: Sergei Karasev (Russia); Attendance: 56,274
ITA: Gianluigi Donnarumma, Leonardo Bonucci (Cap), Danilo D'Ambrosio, Francesco Acerbi, Leonardo Spinazzola, Marco Verratti, Jorge Luiz Frello Filho „Jorginho", Nicolò Barella (87.Nicolò Zaniolo), Ciro Immobile (79.Andrea Belotti), Lorenzo Insigne, Federico Chiesa (39.Federico Bernardeschi). Trainer: Roberto Mancini.
Goals: Jorge Luiz Frello Filho "Jorge Luiz Frello Filho „Jorginho"" (63 penalty), Federico Bernardeschi (78).

15.10.2019 LIECHTENSTEIN - ITALY   **0-5(0-1)**   16th EC. Qualifiers
Rheinpark Stadion, Vaduz; Referee: Andris Treimanis (Latvia); Attendance: 5,087
ITA: Salvatore Sirigu, Cristiano Biraghi (88.Leonardo Bonucci), Giovanni Di Lorenzo, Alessio Romagnoli, Gianluca Mancini, Marco Verratti (Cap), Bryan Cristante, Vincenzo Grifo, Nicolò Zaniolo (63.Stephan Kareem El Shaarawy), Andrea Belotti, Federico Bernardeschi (74.Sandro Tonali). Trainer: Roberto Mancini.
Goals: Federico Bernardeschi (2), Andrea Belotti (70), Alessio Romagnoli (77), Stephan Kareem El Shaarawy (82), Andrea Belotti (90+2).

15.11.2019 BOSNIA AND HERZEGOVINA - ITALY   **0-3(0-2)**   16th EC. Qualifiers
Stadion Bilino Polje, Zenica; Referee: Glenn Nyberg (Sweden); Attendance: 3,825
ITA: Gianluigi Donnarumma (88.Pierluigi Gollini), Leonardo Bonucci (Cap), Francesco Acerbi, Emerson Palmieri dos Santos, Alessandro Florenzi, Jorge Luiz Frello Filho „Jorginho", Nicolò Barella, Sandro Tonali, Lorenzo Insigne (86.Gaetano Castrovilli), Andrea Belotti, Federico Bernardeschi (75.Stephan Kareem El Shaarawy). Trainer: Roberto Mancini.
Goals: Francesco Acerbi (21), Lorenzo Insigne (37), Andrea Belotti (52).

18.11.2019 ITALY - ARMENIA   **9-1(4-0)**   16th EC. Qualifiers
Stadio "Renzo Barbera", Palermo; Referee: Tiago Bruno Lopes Martins (Portugal); Attendance: 27,752
ITA: Salvatore Sirigu (77.Alex Meret), Leonardo Bonucci (Cap) (69.Armando Izzo) , Giovanni Di Lorenzo, Cristiano Biraghi, Alessio Romagnoli, Jorge Luiz Frello Filho „Jorginho", Nicolò Barella (46.Riccardo Orsolini), Nicolò Zaniolo, Sandro Tonali, Ciro Immobile, Federico Chiesa. Trainer: Roberto Mancini.
Goals: Ciro Immobile (8), Nicolò Zaniolo (9), Nicolò Barella (29), Ciro Immobile (33), Nicolò Zaniolo (64), Alessio Romagnoli (72), Jorge Luiz Frello Filho "Jorginho" (75 penalty), Riccardo Orsolini (78), Federico Chiesa (81).

NATIONAL TEAM PLAYERS
(16.07.2019 – 15.07.2020)

Name	DOB	Caps	Goals	2019/2020:	Club
Goalkeepers					
Gianluigi DONNARUMMA	25.02.1999	16	0	2019:	*AC Milan*
Pierluigi GOLLINI	18.03.1995	1	0	2019:	*Atalanta Bergamasca Calcio*
Alex MERET	22.03.1997	1	0	2019:	*SSC Napoli*
Salvatore SIRIGU	12.01.1987	24	0	2019:	*Torino FC*
Defenders					
Francesco ACERBI	10.08.1988	6	1	2019:	*SS Lazio Roma*
Cristiano BIRAGHI	01.09.1992	7	1	2019:	*FC Internazionale Milano*
Leonardo BONUCCI	01.05.1987	95	7	2019:	*Juventus FC Torino*
Danilo D'AMBROSIO	09.09.1988	3	0	2019:	*FC Internazionale Milano*
Giovanni DI LORENZO	04.08.1993	2	0	2019:	*SSC Napoli*
EMERSON Palmieri dos Santos	03.08.1994	7	0	2019:	*Chelsea FC London (ENG)*
Alessandro FLORENZI	11.03.1991	35	2	2019:	*AS Roma*
Armando IZZO	02.03.1992	3	0	2019:	*Torino FC*
Gianluca MANCINI	17.04.1996	3	0	2019:	*AS Roma*
Alessio ROMAGNOLI	12.01.1995	12	2	2019:	*AC Milan*
Leonardo SPINAZZOLA	25.03.1993	8	0	2019:	*AS Roma*
Midfielders					
Nicolò BARELLA	07.02.1997	12	3	2019:	*FC Internazionale Milano*
Gaetano CASTROVILLI	17.02.1997	1	0	2019:	*ACF Fiorentina*
Bryan CRISTANTE	03.03.1995	7	0	2019:	*AS Roma*
Jorge Luiz Frello Filho "JORGINHO"	20.12.1991	22	4	2019:	*Chelsea FC London (ENG)*
Lorenzo PELLEGRINI	19.06.1996	12	1	2019:	*AS Roma*
Stefano SENSI	05.08.1995	4	1	2019:	*FC Internazionale Milano*
Sandro TONALI	08.05.2000	3	0	2019:	*Brescia Calcio*
Marco VERRATTI	05.11.1992	36	3	2019:	*Paris Saint-Germain FC (FRA)*
Nicolò ZANIOLO	02.07.1999	5	2	2019:	*AS Roma*
Forwards					
Andrea BELOTTI	20.12.1993	27	9	2019:	*Torino FC*
Federico BERNARDESCHI	16.02.1994	24	4	2019:	*Juventus FC Torino*
Federico CHIESA	25.10.1997	17	1	2019:	*ACF Fiorentina*
Stephan Kareem EL SHAARAWY	27.10.1992	25	4	2019:	*Shanghai Greenland Shenhua FC (CHN)*
Vincenzo GRIFO	07.04.1993	2	0	2019:	*SC Freiburg (GER)*
Ciro IMMOBILE	20.02.1990	39	10	2019:	*SS Lazio Roma*
Lorenzo INSIGNE	04.06.1991	34	7	2019:	*SSC Napoli*
Kevin LASAGNA	10.08.1992	4	0	2019:	*Udinese Calcio*
Riccardo ORSOLINI	24.01.1997	1	0	2019:	*Bologna FC 1909*
National team coach					
Roberto MANCINI [from 14.05.2019]	27.11.1964		19 M; 13 W; 4 D; 2 L; 45-12		

KAZAKHSTAN

The Country:
Қазақстан Республикасы (Republic of Kazakhstan)
Capital: Nur-Sultan
Surface: 2,724,900 km²
Inhabitants: 18,708,352 [2020]
Time: UTC+5/+6

The FA:
Қазақстанның Футбол Федерациясы (Football Federation of Kazakhstan)
5a, Momyshuly Avenue, 010000 Nur-Sultan
Tel: +7 7172 790780
Foundation date: 1914
Member of FIFA since: 1994
Member of UEFA since: 2002
Website: www.kff.kz

NATIONAL TEAM RECORDS

RECORDS

First international match:	01.06.1992, Almaty:	Kazakhstan – Turkmenistan 1-0
Most international caps:	Samat Smakov	- 76 caps (2000-2016)
Most international goals:	Ruslan Baltiyev	- 13 goals / 73 caps (1997-2009)

UEFA EUROPEAN CHAMPIONSHIP		FIFA WORLD CUP		OLYMPIC TOURNAMENTS	
1960	-*	1930	-*	1908	-*
1964	-	1934	-	1912	-
1968	-	1938	-	1920	-
1972	-	1950	-	1924	-
1976	-	1954	-	1928	-
1980	-	1958	-	1936	-
1984	-	1962	-	1948	-
1988	-	1966	-	1952	-
1992	-	1970	-	1956	-
1996	-	1974	-	1960	-
2000	-	1978	-	1964	-
2004	-	1982	-	1968	-
2008	Qualifiers	1986	-	1972	-
2012	Qualifiers	1990	-	1976	-
2016	Qualifiers	1994	Did not enter	1980	-
2020	Qualifiers	1998	Qualifiers	1984	-
		2002	Qualifiers	1988	-
		2006	Qualifiers	1992	-
		2010	Qualifiers	1996	Qualifiers
		2014	Qualifiers	2000	Qualifiers
		2018	Qualifiers	2004	Did not enter
				2008	Qualifiers
				2012	Qualifiers
				2016	Qualifiers

*was part of Soviet Union until 1990

UEFA NATIONS LEAGUE

2018/2019 – League D (promoted to League C)

FIFA CONFEDERATIONS CUP 1992-2017

None

KAZAKH CLUB HONOURS IN EUROPEAN CLUB COMPETITIONS:

European Champion Clubs' Cup (1956-1992) / UEFA Champions League (1993-2020)
None
Fairs Cup (1858-1971) / UEFA Cup (1972-2009) / UEFA Europa League (2010-2020)
None
UEFA Super Cup (1972-2019)
None
*European Cup Winners' Cup 1961-1999**
None

*defunct competition

KAZAKH SSR (SOVIET ERA) CHAMPIONS

Year	Champion		Year	Champion		Year	Champion
1936	Sbornaya Alma-Aty		1960	Yenbek Guryev		1977	Khimik Stepnogorsk
1937	Dinamo Alma-Ata		1961	Avangard Petropavlovsk		1978	Trud Shevchenko
1938	Dinamo Alma-Ata		1962	ADK Alma-Ata		1979	Khimik Stepnogorsk
1939/1945	*No Championship*		1963	Tselinnik Semipalatinsk		1980	Meliorator Chimkent
1946	Dinamo Alma-Ata		1964	ADK Alma-Ata		1981	Burevestnik Kustanay
1947	Lokomotiv Jambul		1965	ADK Alma-Ata		1980	Traktor Pavlodar
1948	Trudovye Rezervy Alma-Ata		1966	Aktyubinets Aktyubinsk		1981	Aktyubinets Aktyubinsk
1949	Dinamo Karaganda		1967	Torpedo Kokchetav		1982	Shakhtyor Karaganda
1950	Sbornaya Alma-Aty		1968	Gornyak Jezkangan		1983	Shakhtyor Karaganda
1951	Meliorator Chimkent		1969	Shakhtyor Saran'		1984	Tselinnik Tselinograd
1952	Meliorator Chimkent		1970	Stroitel Temir-Tau		1985	Meliorator Chimkent
1953	Meliorator Chimkent		1971	Yenbek Jezkangan		1986	Meliorator Chimkent
1954	Dinamo Alma-Ata		1972	Traktor Pavlodar		1987	Meliorator Chimkent
1955	Dinamo Alma-Ata		1973	Yenbek Jezkangan		1988	Traktor Pavlodar
1956	Sbornaya Alma-Aty		1974	Gornyak Nikol'sky		1989	Traktor Pavlodar
1957	Stroitel Alma-Ata		1975	Meliorator Chimkent		1990	Vostok Ust'-Kamenogorsk
1958	Spartak Alma-Ata		1976	Khimik Stepnogorsk		1991	Aktyubinets Aktyubinsk
1959	Spartak Alma-Ata						

	CHAMPIONS	CUP WINNERS	BEST GOALSCORERS	
1992	FC Kairat Almaty	FC Kairat Almaty	Sergey Kogai (FC Kaysar Kyzylorda)	21
1993	FC Irtysh Pavlodar	FC Dostyk Almaty	Aleksandr Shmarikov (FC Taraz)	28
1994	FC Spartak Semey	FC Vostok Oskemen	Oleg Litvinenko (FC Taraz)	20
1995	FC Spartak Semey	FC Spartak Semey	Andrei Miroshnichenko (FC Spartak Semey)	23
1996	FC Taraz	-	Viktor Antonov (FC Irtysh Pavlodar)	21
1997	FC Irtysh Pavlodar	FC Kairat Almaty (1996/97)	Nurken Mazbaev (FC Taraz)	16
1998	FC Spartak Semey	FC Irtysh Pavlodar (1997/98)	Oleg Litvinenko (FC Spartak Semey)	14
1999	FC Irtysh Pavlodar	FC Kaysar Kyzylorda (1998/99)	Rejepmyrat Agabaýew (TKM, FC Kairat Almaty)	24
2000	FC Astana-64	FC Kairat Almaty (1999/2000)	Nilton Pereira Mendes (BRA, FC Irtysh Pavlodar)	21
#	-	FC Astana-64 (2000/2001)		
2001	FC Astana-64	FC Kairat Almaty	Arsen Tlekhugov (FC Astana-64)	30
2002	FC Irtysh Pavlodar	FC Astana-64	Evgeniy Lunev (FC Shakhter Karagandy)	16
2003	FC Irtysh Pavlodar	FC Kairat Almaty	Andrei Finonchenko (FC Shakhter Karagandy)	18
2004	FC Kairat Almaty	FC Taraz	Ulugbek Bakaev (UZB, FC Tobol Kostanay) Arsen Tlekhugov (FC Kairat Almaty)	22
2005	FC Aktobe	FC Astana-64	Murat Tleshev (FC Irtysh Pavlodar)	20
2006	FC Astana-64	FC Alma-Ata	Jafar Irismetov (UZB, FC Alma-Ata)	17
2007	FC Aktobe	FC Tobol Kostanay	Jafar Irismetov (UZB, FC Alma-Ata)	17
2008	FC Aktobe	FC Aktobe	Murat Tleshev (FC Irtysh Pavlodar)	13
2009	FC Aktobe	FC Atyrau	Murat Tleshev (FC Aktobe) Wladimir Baýramow (TKM, FC Tobol Kostanay)	20
2010	FC Tobol Kostanay	FC Lokomotiv Astana	Ulugbek Bakaev (UZB, FC Tobol Kostanay)	16
2011	FC Shakhter Karagandy	FC Ordabasy	Ulugbek Bakaev (UZB, FC Zhetysu Taldykorgan)	18
2012	FC Shakhter Karagandy	Astana FC	Ulugbek Bakaev (UZB, FC Irtysh Pavlodar)	14
2013	FC Aktobe	FC Shakhter Karagandy	Ihar Zenkovich (BLR, FC Shakhter Karagandy)	15
2014	Astana FC	FC Kairat Almaty	Foxi Kéthévoama (CTA, Astana FC)	16
2015	Astana FC	FC Kairat Almaty	Gerard Bi Goua Gohou (CIV, FC Kairat Almaty)	22
2016	Astana FC	Astana FC	Gerard Bi Goua Gohou (CIV, FC Kairat Almaty)	22
2017	Astana FC	FC Kairat Almaty	Gerard Bi Goua Gohou (CIV, FC Kairat Almaty)	24
2018	Astana FC	FC Kairat Almaty	Marcos Pinheiro Pizzelli (FC Aktobe)	18
2019	Astana FC	FC Kaysar Kyzylorda	Marin Tomasov (CRO, Astana FC) Aderinsola Habib Eseola (UKR, FC Kairat Almaty)	19

Please note: FC Lokomotiv Astana changed its name to Astana FC in 2011.

Results

Round 1 [09-10.03.2019]
FC Ordabasy - Shakhter Karagandy 3-0(0-0)
FC Zhetysu - FC Okzhetpes 5-1(3-0)
Tobol Kostanay - Irtysh Pavlodar 3-0(2-0)
FC Kairat - FC Taraz 2-0(1-0)
Kaysar Kyzylorda - FC Atyrau 0-1(0-1)
Astana FC - FC Aktobe 4-1(3-1)

Round 2 [15.03.2019]
FC Atyrau - Irtysh Pavlodar 1-3(1-3)
FC Ordabasy - FC Aktobe 1-0(0-0)
Kaysar Kyzylorda - FC Zhetysu 0-1(0-1)
Tobol Kostanay - FC Taraz 4-1(1-0)
FC Kairat - Shakhter Karagandy 2-1(1-0)
Astana FC - FC Okzhetpes 2-1(0-0)

Round 3 [30-31.03.2019]
Irtysh Pavlodar - Kaysar Kyzylorda 0-1(0-0)
FC Taraz - FC Atyrau 2-0(0-0)
FC Zhetysu - Astana FC 0-2(0-1)
FC Aktobe - FC Kairat 1-3(0-3)
Shakhter Karagan. - Tobol Kostanay 0-1(0-0)
FC Okzhetpes - FC Ordabasy 0-0

Round 4 [06-07.04.2019]
Irtysh Pavlodar - FC Taraz 2-0(1-0)
Tobol Kostanay - FC Aktobe 2-1(1-0)
FC Ordabasy - FC Zhetysu 1-0(0-0)
FC Kairat - FC Okzhetpes 4-1(3-1)
Kaysar Kyzylorda - Astana FC 0-0
FC Atyrau - Shakhter Karagandy 0-0

Round 5 [14.04.2019]
FC Aktobe - FC Atyrau 2-0(2-0)
FC Okzhetpes - Tobol Kostanay 1-2(0-1)
Shakhter Karagandy - Irtysh Pavlodar 4-0(3-0)
FC Taraz - Kaysar Kyzylorda 1-2(1-1)
FC Zhetysu - FC Kairat 3-0(1-0)
Astana FC - FC Ordabasy 2-1(1-1)

Round 6 [20.04.2019]
FC Atyrau - FC Okzhetpes 1-2(0-2)
Irtysh Pavlodar - FC Aktobe 0-1(0-1)
FC Kairat - Astana FC 0-1(0-1)
Kaysar Kyzylorda - FC Ordabasy 0-0
FC Taraz - Shakhter Karagandy 1-2(1-2)
Tobol Kostanay - FC Zhetysu 0-0

Round 7 [27.04.2019]
FC Okzhetpes - Irtysh Pavlodar 1-0(1-0)
Shakhter Karag. - Kaysar Kyzylorda 0-1(0-1)
FC Ordabasy - FC Kairat 0-0
FC Zhetysu - FC Atyrau 0-0
FC Aktobe - FC Taraz 2-3(0-2)
Astana FC - Tobol Kostanay 2-1(0-1)

Round 8 [01.05.2019]
Shakhter Karagandy - FC Aktobe 3-0(0-0)
FC Taraz - FC Okzhetpes 2-6(2-2)
Tobol Kostanay - FC Ordabasy 1-1(0-0)
FC Atyrau - Astana FC 0-3(0-1)
Kaysar Kyzylorda - FC Kairat 2-1(0-1)
Irtysh Pavlodar - FC Zhetysu 0-3(0-1)

Round 9 [05.05.2019]
FC Okzhetpes - Shakhter Karagandy 2-2(0-0)
FC Ordabasy - FC Atyrau 1-1(0-0)
FC Zhetysu - FC Taraz 1-0(0-0)
FC Kairat - Tobol Kostanay 0-1(0-0)
FC Aktobe - Kaysar Kyzylorda 1-3(1-3)
Astana FC - Irtysh Pavlodar 0-1(0-0)

Round 10 [11-12.05.2019]
FC Taraz - Astana FC 2-0(0-0)
Irtysh Pavlodar - FC Ordabasy 0-2(0-1)
Shakhter Karagandy - FC Zhetysu 2-0(1-0)
Kaysar Kyzylorda - Tobol Kostanay 5-1(3-0)
FC Aktobe - FC Okzhetpes 0-2(0-1)
FC Atyrau - FC Kairat 2-1(1-1)

Round 11 [18-19.05.2019]
FC Okzhetpes - Kaysar Kyzylorda 1-2(1-1)
Tobol Kostanay - FC Atyrau 3-0(1-0)
FC Zhetysu - FC Aktobe 1-1(1-0)
FC Ordabasy - FC Taraz 3-0(2-0)
Astana FC - Shakhter Karagandy 1-2(1-0)
FC Kairat - Irtysh Pavlodar 2-1(2-1)

Round 12 [26.05.2019]
FC Taraz - Tobol Kostanay 0-1(0-0)
FC Okzhetpes - Astana FC 1-1(0-1)
FC Zhetysu - Kaysar Kyzylorda 1-0(0-0)
Irtysh Pavlodar - FC Atyrau 1-0(0-0)
Shakhter Karagandy - FC Kairat 1-2(1-0)
FC Aktobe - FC Ordabasy 0-3(0-2)

Round 13 [31.05.2019]
FC Atyrau - FC Taraz 1-1(0-0)
FC Ordabasy - FC Okzhetpes 3-0(3-0)
Astana FC - FC Zhetysu 1-0(1-0)
FC Kairat - FC Aktobe 3-0(0-0)
Kaysar Kyzylorda - Irtysh Pavlodar 2-0(0-0)
Tobol Kostanay - Shakhter Karagan. 2-0(1-0)

Round 14 [15 16.06.2019]
FC Aktobe - Tobol Kostanay 0-1(0-0)
FC Okzhetpes - FC Kairat 1-2(0-1)
FC Taraz - Irtysh Pavlodar 0-0
FC Zhetysu - FC Ordabasy 1-1(1-1)
Astana FC - Kaysar Kyzylorda 4-1(2-0)
Shakhter Karagandy - FC Atyrau 1-1(1-0)

Round 15 [23.06.2019]
Irtysh Pavlodar - Shakhter Karagandy 0-0
FC Kairat - FC Zhetysu 0-0
Kaysar Kyzylorda - FC Taraz 1-1(1-1)
FC Ordabasy - Astana FC 3-2(2-1)
Tobol Kostanay - FC Okzhetpes 2-0(0-0)
FC Atyrau - FC Aktobe 1-1(1-1)

Round 16 [30.06.2019]
FC Okzhetpes - FC Atyrau 3-0(1-0)
FC Zhetysu - Tobol Kostanay 0-1(0-1)
FC Ordabasy - Kaysar Kyzylorda 1-2(1-1)
Shakhter Karagandy - FC Taraz 1-0(1-0)
FC Aktobe - Irtysh Pavlodar 2-1(0-1)
Astana FC - FC Kairat 0-2(0-0)

Round 17 [05-06.07.2019]
FC Kairat - FC Ordabasy 0-1(0-0)
Tobol Kostanay - Astana FC 0-2(0-0)
FC Taraz - FC Aktobe 1-1(1-0)
Irtysh Pavlodar - FC Okzhetpes 2-1(0-0)
FC Atyrau - FC Zhetysu 2-1(1-0)
Kaysar Kyzylorda - Shakhter Karag. 2-2(2-1)

Round 18 [13-14.07.2019]
Astana FC - FC Atyrau 3-1(2-0) [03.04.]
FC Zhetysu - Irtysh Pavlodar 4-0(2-0)
FC Aktobe - Shakhter Karagandy 2-2(0-2)
FC Okzhetpes - FC Taraz 3-1(0-1)
FC Kairat - Kaysar Kyzylorda 5-1(1-0)
FC Ordabasy - Tobol Kostanay 0-0

Round 19 [20-21.07.2019]
Irtysh Pavlodar - Astana FC 0-4(0-1) [15.05.]
Shakhter Karagandy - FC Okzhetpes 1-0(0-0)
Kaysar Kyzylorda - FC Aktobe 0-1(0-1)
Tobol Kostanay - FC Kairat 3-5(2-1)
FC Taraz - FC Zhetysu 2-0(0-0)
FC Atyrau - FC Ordabasy 1-0(0-0)

Round 20 27-28.07.2019 [ ]
FC Kairat - FC Atyrau 2-0(1-0) [24.04.]
FC Okzhetpes - FC Aktobe 4-0(1-0)
FC Zhetysu - Shakhter Karagandy 2-0(2-0)
Astana FC - FC Taraz 4-0(1-0)
Tobol Kostanay - Kaysar Kyzylorda 0-2(0-2)
FC Ordabasy - Irtysh Pavlodar 1-0(0-0)

Round 21 [03-04.08.2019]
FC Aktobe - FC Zhetysu 1-2(0-1)
Kaysar Kyzylorda - FC Okzhetpes 0-1(0-1)
Irtysh Pavlodar - FC Kairat 0-2(0-1)
Shakhter Karagandy - Astana FC 1-0(1-0)
FC Taraz - FC Ordabasy 1-0(1-0)
FC Atyrau - Tobol Kostanay 0-1(0-1)

Round 22 [10-11.08.2019]
FC Okzhetpes - FC Zhetysu 0-1(0-1)
FC Atyrau - Kaysar Kyzylorda 1-3(1-2)
Irtysh Pavlodar - Tobol Kostanay 0-2(0-0)
Shakhter Karagandy - FC Ordabasy 1-2(0-1)
FC Taraz - FC Kairat 0-1(0-0)
FC Aktobe - Astana FC 2-3(0-1)

Round 23 [17-18.08.2019]
FC Okzhetpes - FC Ordabasy 0-4(0-2)
Irtysh Pavlodar - Tobol Kostanay 0-0
FC Taraz - FC Kairat 0-2(0-0)
FC Zhetysu - FC Aktobe 5-0(2-0)
Shakhter Karag. - Kaysar Kyzylorda 3-0(0-0)
FC Atyrau - Astana FC 1-4(0-4) [25.09.]

Round 24 [24-25.08.2019]
FC Ordabasy - Shakhter Karagandy 3-2(1-0)
Tobol Kostanay - FC Atyrau 2-0(1-0)
Astana FC - FC Taraz 5-0(1-0)
Kaysar Kyzylorda - FC Zhetysu 0-2(0-1)
FC Aktobe - Irtysh Pavlodar 1-1(0-0)
FC Kairat - FC Okzhetpes 0-1(0-1)

Round 25 [31.08.2019]
FC Zhetysu - FC Ordabasy 0-1(0-1)
Shakhter Karagandy - FC Kairat 0-4(0-1)
FC Taraz - Tobol Kostanay 0-5(0-3)
Kaysar Kyzylorda - FC Aktobe 1-3(0-1)
FC Atyrau - Irtysh Pavlodar 0-3(0-1)
FC Okzhetpes - Astana FC 0-1(0-1) [30.10.]

Round 26 [15.09.2019]
Irtysh Pavlodar - FC Taraz 1-0(1-0)
FC Ordabasy - Kaysar Kyzylorda 0-2(0-2)
Tobol Kostanay - FC Okzhetpes 1-0
FC Aktobe - FC Atyrau 3-2(1-2)
Astana FC - Shakhter Karagandy 2-1(0-1)
FC Kairat - FC Zhetysu 4-1(3-0)

Round 27 [21-22.09.2019]
FC Okzhetpes - Irtysh Pavlodar 1-0(0-0)
Kaysar Kyzylorda - FC Kairat 0-1(0-0)
FC Taraz - FC Atyrau 2-2(0-0)
Shakhter Karagan. - Tobol Kostanay 0-1(0-0)
FC Zhetysu - Astana FC 2-1(0-1)
FC Ordabasy - FC Aktobe 4-1(2-0)

Round 28 [28-29.09.2019]
Irtysh Pavlodar - Shakhter Karagandy 4-2(0-2)
Tobol Kostanay - FC Zhetysu 0-0
FC Atyrau - FC Okzhetpes 2-2(2-1)
FC Aktobe - FC Taraz 2-2(0-1)
Astana FC - Kaysar Kyzylorda 3-0(2-0)
FC Kairat - FC Ordabasy 4-1(2-0)

Round 29 [05-06.10.2019]
FC Okzhetpes - FC Taraz 2-3(2-1)
FC Zhetysu - Irtysh Pavlodar 2-1(0-1)
FC Kairat - FC Aktobe 6-0(2-0)
FC Ordabasy - Astana FC 1-1(0-1)
Kaysar Ky. - Tobol Kostanay 1-1(1-0) [30.10.]
Shakhter Karag. - FC Atyrau 0-1(0-1) [30.10.]

Round 30 [19-20.10.2019]
FC Atyrau - FC Zhetysu 0-3(0-3)
Irtysh Pavlodar - Kaysar Kyzylorda 2-1(1-0)
Tobol Kostanay - FC Ordabasy 1-2(1-1)
FC Taraz - Shakhter Karagandy 0-0
FC Aktobe - FC Okzhetpes 1-2(1-1)
Astana FC - FC Kairat 3-1(1-0)

Round 31 [25-27.10.2019]
Kaysar Kyzylorda - FC Atyrau 0-1(0-1)
FC Ordabasy - Irtysh Pavlodar 2-0(0-0)
Shakhter Karagandy - FC Okzhetpes 2-2(1-1)
FC Kairat - Tobol Kostanay 2-0(0-0)
FC Zhetysu - FC Taraz 0-0
Astana FC - FC Aktobe 5-0(2-0)

Round 32 [03.11.2019]
FC Aktobe - Shakhter Karagandy 3-2(2-0)
FC Atyrau - FC Ordabasy 1-3(1-1)
Irtysh Pavlodar - FC Kairat 5-0(1-0)
FC Okzhetpes - FC Zhetysu 1-1(0-0)
FC Taraz - Kaysar Kyzylorda 2-1(2-1)
Tobol Kostanay - Astana FC 0-1(0-1)

Round 33 [10.11.2019]
Astana FC - Irtysh Pavlodar 0-2(0-1)
FC Kairat - FC Atyrau 2-1(1-0)
Kaysar Kyzylorda - FC Okzhetpes 1-1(1-0)
FC Ordabasy - FC Taraz 3-0(1-0)
Tobol Kostanay - FC Aktobe 2-1(1-1)
FC Zhetysu - Shakhter Karagandy 3-2(2-1)

Final Standings

						Total					Home					Away		
1.	**Astana FC**	33	22	3	8	67 - 28	69	13	0	4	41 - 15	9	3	4	26 - 13
2.	FC Kairat Almaty	33	22	2	9	65 - 32	68	12	1	4	38 - 11	10	1	5	27 - 21
3.	FC Ordabasy Shymkent	33	19	8	6	52 - 24	65	11	4	2	30 - 11	8	4	4	22 - 13
4.	FC Tobol Kostanay	33	19	6	8	45 - 27	63	9	3	5	26 - 16	10	3	3	19 - 11
5.	FC Zhetysu Taldiqorghan	33	16	8	9	45 - 25	56	10	4	3	30 - 11	6	4	6	15 - 14
6.	FC Kaysar Kyzylorda	33	12	6	15	37 - 43	42	3	6	8	15 - 18	9	0	7	22 - 25
7.	FC Okzhetpes Kokshetau	33	11	7	15	44 - 49	40	5	4	7	21 - 20	6	3	8	23 - 29
8.	FC Irtysh Pavlodar	33	11	4	18	30 - 45	37	7	2	7	17 - 19	4	2	11	13 - 26
9.	FC Shakhter Karagandy	33	9	8	16	40 - 47	35	7	2	7	20 - 15	2	6	9	20 - 32
10.	FC Taraz (Relegation Play-offs)	33	7	8	18	28 - 60	29	5	4	7	16 - 23	2	4	11	12 - 37
11.	FC Atyrau (Relegated)	33	6	8	19	25 - 58	26	3	4	9	14 - 31	3	4	10	11 - 27
12.	FC Aktobe* (Relegated)	33	7	6	20	35 - 75	15	4	3	9	23 - 32	3	3	11	12 - 43

*Please note: 12 points deducted due to unpaid debts.

Top goalscorers:	
19 Marin Tomasov (CRO)	*Astana FC*
19 Aderinsola Habib Eseola (UKR)	*FC Kairat Almaty*
16 Abat Aimbetov	*FC Aktobe*
16 Márton Eppel (HUN)	*FC Kairat Almaty*
15 João Paulo da Silva Araújo (BRA)	*FC Ordabasy Shymkent*
12 Tigran Barseghyan (ARM)	*FC Kaysar Kyzylorda*
10 Azat Nurgaliev	*FC Tobol Kostanay*

Relegation Play-offs [15-18.11.2019]

FC Akzhayik Oral - FC Taraz   0-0   1-3(1-3)
FC Taraz remains at first level.

NATIONAL CUP
Kazakhstan Kubok 2019

1/8 - Finals [10.04.2019]

FC Aktobe - FC Irtysh Pavlodar	1-3 pen		FC Kaspiy Aqtau - FC Kairat Almaty	5-6 pen
Akademiya Ontustik - FC Kaysar Kyzylorda	1-2 aet		FC Aksu - FC Tobol Kostanay	0-3
FC Okzhetpes Kokshetau - FC Ordabasy Shymkent	0-1		FC Taraz - FC Shakhter Karagandy	2-0
FC Altay Semey - Astana FC	15-14 pen		FC Atyrau - FC Zhetysu Taldiqorghan	1-0

Quarter-Finals [08.05.2019]

FC Altay Semey - FC Atyrau	1-3 pen		FC Irtysh Pavlodar - FC Kaysar Kyzylorda	1-2
FC Taraz - FC Ordabasy Shymkent	0-1		FC Kairat Almaty - FC Tobol Kostanay	1-5

Semi-Finals [22.05./19.06.2019]

First Leg			Second Leg	
FC Ordabasy Shymkent - FC Atyrau	1-1		FC Atyrau - FC Ordabasy Shymkent	0-0
FC Tobol Kostanay - FC Kaysar Kyzylorda	1-0		FC Kaysar Kyzylorda - FC Tobol Kostanay	3-1

Final

06.10.2019; Astana Arena, Nur-Sultan; Referee: Timur Kumashev; Attendance: 4,500
FC Kaysar Kyzylorda - FC Atyrau   **2-1(0-0,1-1)**

Kaysar Kyzylorda: Aleksandr Grigorenko, Ilyas Amirseitov (86.Ivan Sadovnichiy), Abdel Lamanje, Ivan Graf, Aleksandr Marochkin, Clarence Junior Bitang (84.Igor Zenkovich), Askhat Tagybergen [*sent off 70*], Duman Narzildaev, Joshua John (72.André Watshini Bukia), Tigran Barseghyan (120+4.Mark Gurman), Richard Kule Mbombo. Trainer: Stoicho Mladenov (Bulgaria).

FC Atyrau: Antun Marković, Andrey Shabaev, Mikhail Gabyshev (74.Boubacar Mansaly; 113.Ivan Antipov), Rizvan Ablitarov, Kuanysh Kalmuratov, Eldar Abdrakhmanov (90+3.Aybolat Makuov), Jacques Alberto Ngwem Ngwem [*sent off 93*], Aléx Bruno de Souza Silva, Rafail Ospanov, Piotr Grzelczak, Islamnur Abdulavov (51.Rinat Dzumatov). Trainer: Kuanysh Kabdulov.

Goals: 0-1 Piotr Grzelczak (67), 1-1 Igor Zenkovich (88), 2-1 Duman Narzildaev (120+3).

THE CLUBS 2019

Football Club Aktobe

Founded: 1967 (*as Aktyubinets*)
Stadium: Aktobe Central Stadium, Aktobe (15,000)
Trainer: Aleksandr Sednev   16.08.1973

Goalkeepers:	DOB	M	(s)	G
Ramil Nurmukhametov	21.12.1987	14		
Mukhambet Tamabay	28.07.1996	3		
Igor Trofimets	20.08.1996	16	(1)	
Defenders:	**DOB**	**M**	**(s)**	**G**
Bagdat Kairov	27.04.1993	29		
Adilkhan Tanzharikov	25.11.1996	30		
Rustam Uksumbayev	18.01.1996		(5)	
Vitaliy Volkov (RUS)	22.03.1981	32		1
Sayat Zhumagali	25.04.1995	10	(4)	
Midfielders:	**DOB**	**M**	**(s)**	**G**
Alisher Azhimov	29.05.2001	16	(13)	2
Nurbolat Batyrkhanov	11.02.1998		(7)	
Aslanbek Kakimov	02.10.1993	27	(6)	4
Oleksandr Kitsak (UKR)	23.06.1996	17		1
Zhambyl Kukeyev	20.09.1988	17	(7)	

	DOB	M	(s)	G
Saša Marjanović (SRB)	13.11.1987	15		
Hrvoje Miličević (CRO)	20.04.1993	8		1
Alisher Nazarov	01.05.1999	1		
Milan Radin (SRB)	25.06.1991	10	(1)	1
Ardak Saulet	12.01.1997	25	(6)	3
Anton Shurygin	03.12.1988	10	(7)	1
Rustam Temirkhan	10.08.1997	20	(4)	1
Esen Zhasanov	24.04.1998	21	(7)	1
Forwards:	**DOB**	**M**	**(s)**	**G**
Abilkhan Abdukarimov	07.04.1998		(2)	
Abat Aimbetov	07.08.1995	28	(1)	16
Marcos Pinheiro Pizzelli	03.10.1984	9	(2)	2
Rustam Sakhibov	28.04.1996	6	(16)	
Maksim Samorodov	29.06.2002		(3)	
Ulykbek Syrlybaev	30.06.1996		(2)	

Astana Football Club

Founded: 2009 (*as FC Lokomotiv Astana*)
Stadium: Astana Arena, Nur-Sultan (30,000)
Trainer: Roman Hryhorchuk (UKR)   22.03.1965

Goalkeepers:	DOB	M	(s)	G
Nenad Erić	26.05.1982	28		
Aleksandr Mokin	19.06.1981	5		
Defenders:	**DOB**	**M**	**(s)**	**G**
Marin Aničić (BIH)	17.08.1989	14		2
Abzal Beysebekov	30.11.1992	21	(9)	2
Yuriy Logvinenko	22.07.1988	14	(1)	3
Evgeni Postnikov (RUS)	16.04.1986	30	(1)	1
Antonio Rukavina (SRB)	26.01.1984	28		
Dmitriy Shomko	19.03.1990	26	(5)	
Luka Šimunović (CRO)	24.05.1997	16	(2)	
Žarko Tomašević (MNE)	22.02.1990	2		
Midfielders:	**DOB**	**M**	**(s)**	**G**
Ivan Maevskiy (BLR)	05.05.1988	26		2

	DOB	M	(s)	G
Serikzhan Muzhikov	17.06.1989	10	(8)	2
Yuriy Pertsukh	13.05.1996	20	(9)	2
Rúnar Már Sigurjónsson (ISL)	18.06.1990	9	(2)	2
Marin Tomasov (CRO)	31.08.1987	29	(2)	19
Didar Zhalmukan	22.05.1996	2	(5)	2
Forwards:	**DOB**	**M**	**(s)**	**G**
Rangelo Maria Janga (CUW)	16.04.1992	8	(22)	6
Junior Kabananga Kalonji (COD)	04.04.1989	12	(2)	2
Sergey Khizhnichenko	17.07.1991	7	(3)	4
Firmin Ndombe Mubele (COD)	17.04.1994	2	(3)	1
Roman Murtazayev	10.09.1993	26	(6)	7
Vladislav Prokopenko	01.07.2000		(1)	
Dorin Rotariu (ROU)	29.07.1995	28	(3)	7

Football Club Atyrau

Founded: 1980
Stadium: Munaishy Stadium, Atyrau (8,690)
Trainer: Viktor Kumykov   25.06.1963
[28.04.2019] Kuanysh Kabdulov   09.07.1987
[03.05.2019] Oleg Dulub (BLR)   20.09.1965
[17.09.2019] Kuanysh Kabdulov   09.07.1987
[16.10.2019] Askar Kozhabergenov   20.09.1965

Goalkeepers:	DOB	M	(s)	G
Nurbolat Kalmenov	15.09.1990	5		
Vladimir Loginovskiy	08.10.1985	16		
Antun Marković (CRO)	04.07.1992	10		
Aleksandr Zarutskiy	26.08.1993	2		
Defenders:	**DOB**	**M**	**(s)**	**G**
Rizvan Ablitarov (UKR)	18.04.1989	29	(1)	2
Kuanysh Eltezerov	22.09.1995		(1)	
Mikhail Gabyshev	02.01.1990	8	(1)	
Kuanysh Kalmuratov	27.08.1996	31		2
Dauren Mazhitov	03.03.1996	15	(3)	1
Andrey Shabaev	15.02.1987	28	(2)	
Vitali Ustinov (RUS)	03.05.1991	5	(1)	
Adilbek Zhumakhanov	27.12.2002	1		
Ivica Žunić (CRO)	11.09.1988	18		2
Midfielders:	**DOB**	**M**	**(s)**	**G**
Eldar Abdrakhmanov	16.01.1987	13	(4)	
Aléx Bruno de Souza Silva (BRA)	07.10.1993	8	(3)	
Ivan Antipov	14.01.1996	5	(5)	1
Rinat Dzumatov	13.10.1997	10	(7)	1
Željko Filipović (SVN)	03.10.1988	8	(1)	
Dauren Kayralliev	15.05.1992	3	(6)	
František Kubik (SVK)	14.03.1989	7	(1)	
Boubacar Mansaly (SEN)	04.02.1988	6	(1)	
Aibar Nurybekov	29.08.1992	2		
Jacques Alberto Ngwem Ngwem (CMR)	03.08.1992	11		
Rafail Ospanov	05.11.1997	13	(10)	
Sanzhar Satanov	21.09.2001		(1)	
Eduard Sergienko	18.02.1983	23	(4)	1
Andriy Tkachuk (UKR)	18.11.1987	15	(2)	
Sergiy Zagynaylov (UKR)	03.01.1991	9	(5)	
Forwards:	**DOB**	**M**	**(s)**	**G**
Islamnur Abdulavov (RUS)	07.03.1994	13		5
Darko Bjedov (SRB)	28.03.1989	11	(3)	2
Piotr Grzelczak (POL)	02.03.1988	7	(1)	4
Josip Ivančić (CRO)	29.03.1991	4	(3)	1
Aybolat Makuov	16.02.1997	10	(2)	
Malick Mané (SEN)	14.10.1988	4		
Aleksey Rodionov	29.03.1994	10	(16)	1
Vladimir Vomenko	22.05.1995	3	(6)	1

Football Club Irtysh Pavlodar

Founded: 1965
Stadium: Pavlodar Central Stadium, Pavlodar (15,000)
Trainer: Dimitar Dimitrov (BUL)   09.06.1959
[01.05.2019] Sergey Klimov   16.01.1960
[07.06.2019] Milan Milanović (SRB)   10.01.1963

Goalkeepers:	DOB	M	(s)	G
Nikita Kalmykov	24.08.1989	5		
Andrey Pasechenko	09.08.1987	9		
Anton Tsirin	10.08.1987	12		
Aleksandr Zarutskiy	26.08.1993	7		
Defenders:	**DOB**	**M**	**(s)**	**G**
Rafkat Aslan	02.02.1994	15	(4)	1
Kaspars Dubra (LVA)	20.12.1990	12		
Stanislav Lunin	02.05.1993	3	(1)	
Dmitri Shmidt	17.11.1993	32		
Aleksandr Sokolenko	23.11.1996	4	(2)	
Miloš Stamenković (SRB)	01.06.1990	16		1
Bauyrzhan Tanirbergenov	11.02.1995		(3)	
Sagadat Tursynbay	26.03.1999	9	(3)	
Uroš Vitas (SRB)	06.07.1992	20		2
Ruslan Yesimov	28.04.1990	19	(3)	2
Midfielders:	**DOB**	**M**	**(s)**	**G**
Oybek Baltabaev	13.06.1994	1	(2)	
Róger Cañas Henao (COL)	27.03.1990	15		3
Aslan Darabaev	21.01.1989	7		1
Carlos Manuel Costa Fernandes Fonseca(POR)	23.08.1987	22	(3)	2
Patrik Hidi (HUN)	27.11.1990	33		1
Arman Kenesov	04.09.2000	2	(10)	1
Jérémy Manzorro (FRA)	11.11.1991	24	(2)	6
Magomed Paragulgov	26.03.1994	20	(4)	
Artem Popov	17.01.1998	8	(5)	
Madiyar Raiymbek	15.08.1995	2	(8)	
Sultan Sagnaev	14.01.2000	3	(3)	1
Pavel Shabalin	23.10.1988	1	(5)	
Marko Stanojević (SRB)	22.06.1988	14		2
Forwards:	**DOB**	**M**	**(s)**	**G**
Momodou Ceesay (GAM)	24.12.1988	2	(7)	
Dejan Georgijević (SRB)	19.01.1994	11	(5)	2
Ruslan Mingazov (TKM)	23.11.1991	6	(5)	2
Milan Mirosavljev (SRB)	24.04.1995	6	(5)	
Timur Muldinov	19.09.1993	10	(7)	1
Arman Nusip	22.01.1994	13	(9)	
Reynaldo dos Santos Silva (BRA)	24.08.1989		(1)	

Football Club Kairat Almaty

Founded: 1954 (*as Lokomotiv Alma-Ata*)
Stadium: Almaty Central Stadium, Almaty (25,057)
Trainer: Aleksey Shpilevski   17.02.1988

Goalkeepers:	DOB	M	(s)	G
Vladimir Plotnikov	03.04.1986	2		
Stanislav Pokatilov	08.12.1992	31		
Defenders:	**DOB**	**M**	**(s)**	**G**
Aybol Abiken	01.06.1996	22	(6)	4
Yeldos Akhmetov	01.06.1990	7		
Nuray Alip	22.12.1999	19	(1)	
Rade Dugalić (SRB)	05.11.1992	30		5
Sergey Keiler	08.11.1994	9	(4)	
Dino Mikanović (CRO)	07.05.1994	31		1
Sergey Politsevich (BLR)	09.04.1990	10		
Gafurzhan Suyumbayev	19.08.1990	22	(2)	2
Midfielders:	**DOB**	**M**	**(s)**	**G**
Adam Adakhadzhiev	23.11.1998		(1)	
Han Jeong-uh (KOR)	26.12.1998	2	(3)	
Bauyrzhan Islamkhan	23.02.1993	18	(4)	7
Nebojša Kosović (MNE)	24.02.1995	8	(9)	
Islambek Kuat	12.01.1993	21	(5)	
Ramazan Orazov	30.01.1998	12	(8)	
Yerkebulan Tungyshbaev	14.01.1995	4	(10)	
Yan Vorogovskiy	07.08.1996	10	(2)	
Konrad Wrzesiński (POL)	19.08.1996	23	(2)	3
Georgiy Zhukov	19.11.1994	25	(1)	2
Forwards:	**DOB**	**M**	**(s)**	**G**
Sultanbek Astanov	23.03.1999	6	(4)	1
Márton Eppel (HUN)	26.10.1991	19	(9)	16
Aderinsola Habib Eseola (UKR)	28.06.1991	21	(6)	19
Rifat Nurmugamet	22.05.1996	1		1
Samat Sarsenov	19.08.1996	1	(4)	
Yerkebulan Seydakhmet	04.02.2000	9	(3)	1
Artur Shushenachev	07.04.1998		(3)	1
Vyacheslav Shvyrev	07.01.2001		(10)	2

Football Club Kaysar Kyzylorda

Founded: 1968
Stadium: "Gany Muratbayev" Stadium, Kyzylorda (7,500)
Trainer: Stoicho Mladenov (BUL) 12.04.1957

Goalkeepers:	DOB	M	(s)	G
Aleksandr Grigorenko	06.02.1985	19		
Marsel Islamkulov	18.04.1994	14		
Defenders:	**DOB**	**M**	**(s)**	**G**
Olzhas Altaev	15.07.1989		(1)	
Ilyas Amirseitov	22.10.1989	29		
Ivan Graf (CRO)	17.06.1987	30		2
Abdel Lamanje (CMR)	27.07.1990	29		2
Aleksandr Marochkin	14.07.1990	30		2
Ivan Sadovnichiy (BLR)	11.05.1987	4	(10)	
Midfielders:	**DOB**	**M**	**(s)**	**G**
Maksat Bayzhanov	06.08.1984	13	(6)	1
Samat Balymbetov	10.04.1994		(3)	
Clarence Junior Bitang (CMR)	02.09.1992	10	(3)	
Carlos Miguel Tavares de Oliveira (POR)	09.03.1993		(5)	

	DOB	M	(s)	G
Valentin Chureyev	29.08.1986	7	(2)	
Mark Gurman	09.02.1989	20	(6)	
Marat Khayrullin	26.04.1984	9	(7)	
Bekzat Kurmanbekuly	14.04.2000		(1)	
Duman Narzildaev	06.09.1993	29		
Askhat Tagybergen	09.08.1990	29	(1)	4
Forwards:	**DOB**	**M**	**(s)**	**G**
Shokan Abzalov	11.09.1993	3	(8)	1
Tigran Barseghyan	22.09.1993	29		12
André Watshini Bukia (COD)	03.03.1995	7	(8)	1
Joshua John (ARU)	01.10.1988	19	(2)	1
Orken Makhan	27.01.1998		(10)	1
Richard Kule Mbombo (COD)	10.05.1996	25	(1)	9
Bratislav Punoševac (SRB)	09.07.1987	5	(8)	1
Igor Zenkovich	17.09.1987	3	(15)	

Football Club Okzhetpes Kokshetau

Founded: 1957
Stadium: „Alisher Sagynbayev" Stadium, Kokshetau (4,158)
Trainer: Andrey Karpovich 18.01.1981

Goalkeepers:	DOB	M	(s)	G
Ruslan Abzhanov	28.04.1990	9	(1)	
Dzhurakhon Babakhanov	31.10.1991	11		
Yaroslav Baginskiy	03.10.1987	13	(1)	
Defenders:	**DOB**	**M**	**(s)**	**G**
Renat Abdulin	14.04.1982	4	(2)	
Ivan Bobko (UKR)	10.12.1990	11		
Nurlan Dairov	26.06.1995	24	(1)	
Plamen Dimov (BUL)	29.10.1990	15		
Azat Ersalimov	19.07.1988	21	(5)	
Niyaz Idrisov	21.07.1999			
Aleksandr Kislitsyn	08.03.1986	29	(1)	1
Vladislav Kosmynin (BLR)	17.01.1990	12		1
Ulanbek Kuanyshbekov	16.07.1998			
Roderick Alonso Miller Molina (PAN)	03.04.1992	3	(1)	
Timur Rudoselskiy	21.12.1994	11		1
Timur Zhakupov	06.09.1995	4	(11)	

Midfielders:	DOB	M	(s)	G
Evgeniy Ashikhmin	02.12.1998	1	(1)	
Artjom Dmitrijev (EST)	14.11.1988	28	(1)	5
Aslan Dzhanuzakov	06.01.1993			
Ilya Kalinin	03.02.1992	29	(2)	
Ulan Konysbaev	28.05.1989		(3)	
Altynbek Saparov	26.04.1995	11	(12)	1
Milan Stojanović (SRB)	10.05.1988	29	(1)	7
Miras Tuliev	30.08.1994	2	(13)	
Forwards:	**DOB**	**M**	**(s)**	**G**
Danilo Almeida Alves (BRA)	11.04.1991	25	(2)	6
Deimantas Petravičius (LTU)	02.09.1995	1	(4)	
Zhasulan Moldakaraev	07.05.1987	18	(7)	5
Tanat Nuserbayev	01.01.1987	8	(6)	5
Sanat Zhumakhanov	30.01.1988	15	(14)	5
Darko Zorić (MNE)	12.09.1993	29		4

Football Club Ordabasy Shymkent

Founded: 2000
Stadium: "Kazhymukan Munaitpasov" Stadium, Shymkent (20,000)
Trainer: Kakhaber Tskhadadze (GEO) 07.09.1968

Goalkeepers:	DOB	M	(s)	G
Dmitriy Nepogodov	17.02.1988	29		
Bekkhan Shayzada	28.02.1998	4		
Defenders:	**DOB**	**M**	**(s)**	**G**
Marat Bystrov	19.06.1992	21	(2)	
Damir Dautov	03.03.1990	12	(2)	
Temirlan Erlanov	09.07.1993	23	(2)	2
Pablo Ezequiel Fontanello (ARG)	26.09.1984	31	(2)	1
Sergey Maliy	05.06.1990	28	(1)	1
Mardan Tolebek	18.12.1990	11	(2)	1
Ular Zhaksybayev	20.10.1994	1	(2)	
Midfielders:	**DOB**	**M**	**(s)**	**G**
Elkhan Astanov	21.05.2000	1	(2)	
Abdoulaye Diakhaté (SEN)	16.01.1988	29		5
Adilkhan Dobay	02.06.2002		(2)	

	DOB	M	(s)	G
Timur Dosmagambetov	01.05.1989	30		2
Asludin Khadzhiev	24.10.2000	1	(3)	
Kyrylo Kovalchuk (UKR)	11.06.1986	9	(13)	1
Valeriy Korobkin	02.07.1984	5	(4)	
May Sphiwe Mahlangu (RSA)	01.05.1989	27	(2)	3
Mirzad Mehanovič (BIH)	05.01.1993	24	(3)	3
Samat Shamshi	05.12.1996	4	(13)	
Forwards:	**DOB**	**M**	**(s)**	**G**
Ziguy Badibanga (BEL)	26.11.1991	10	(14)	3
João Paulo da Silva Araújo (BRA)	02.06.1988	25	(6)	15
Vitali Li	13.03.1994	2	(2)	
Aleksey Shchetkin	21.05.1991	16	(6)	7
Maksim Vaganov	08.08.2000		(2)	
Toktar Zhangylyshbay	25.05.1993	20	(10)	8

Football Club Shakhter Karagandy

Founded: 1958
Stadium: Shakhter Stadium, Karaganda (20,000)
Trainer: Nikolai Kostov (BUL) 02.07.1963

Goalkeepers:	DOB	M	(s)	G
Igor Shatskiy	11.05.1989	33		
Defenders:	**DOB**	**M**	**(s)**	**G**
Ruslan Alimbayev	02.03.1997	2		
Artem Baranovskiy (UKR)	17.03.1990	33		1
Anton Chichulin	27.10.1984	7	(4)	
Stanislav Lunin	02.05.1993	3	(1)	
Berik Shaykhov	20.02.1994	15		
Niyaz Shugaev	14.09.1998	7	(9)	
Yevgeniy Tarasov	16.04.1985	2	(7)	
Evhen Tkachuk (UKR)	27.06.1991	24		2
Midfielders:	**DOB**	**M**	**(s)**	**G**
Lukas Droppa (CZE)	22.04.1989	9	(1)	
Gevorg Najaryan	06.01.1998	20	(8)	
Yerkebulan Nurgaliev	12.09.1993	22	(6)	4

	DOB	M	(s)	G
Ivan Pešić (CRO)	06.04.1992	33		8
Donjet Shkodra (KVX)	30.04.1989	28		4
Sergey Skorykh	25.05.1984	7	(2)	
Miloš Vidović (SRB)	25.05.1984	10	(3)	
Forwards:	**DOB**	**M**	**(s)**	**G**
Dmitri Bachek	13.12.2000		(6)	
Bauyrzhan Baytana	06.05.1992	5	(7)	
Luwagga William Kizito (UGA)	20.12.1993	17	(7)	5
Oralkhan Omirtayev	16.07.1998	6	(14)	2
Zhan-Ali Payruz	12.08.1990	16	(13)	1
Reginaldo Artur Faife (MOZ)	14.06.1990	8	(6)	3
Marat Shakhmetov	06.02.1989	27		2
Sergey Vetrov	11.11.1994		(2)	
Sergei Zenjov	12.08.1999	29	(1)	8

Football Club Taraz

Founded: 1960
Stadium: „Yerkebulan Babayev" Stadium, Taraz (11,525)
Trainer: Vakhid Masudov   10.10.1959
[05.09.2019]   Nurmat Mirzabaev   11.11.1972

Goalkeepers:	DOB	M	(s)	G
Almaz Khamytbekov	29.09.1991	1		
Samat Otarbaev	18.02.1990	14		
Mukhamedzhan Seysen	14.02.1999	17		
Timurbek Zakirov	01.03.1996	1		
Defenders:	**DOB**	**M**	**(s)**	**G**
Berik Aytbaev	26.06.1991	19	(1)	
Mihailo Jovanović (SRB)	15.02.1989	12	(2)	
Lasha Kasradze (GEO)	28.07.1989	17		
Viktor Kryukov	30.06.1990	3	(1)	
Madiyar Nuraly	20.01.1995	2	(10)	
Bekzat Shadmanov	12.08.1997	24	(6)	1
Aleksandar Simčević (SRB)	15.02.1987	14		
Midfielders:	**DOB**	**M**	**(s)**	**G**
Maksat Amirkhanov	10.02.1992	27	(1)	
Bekzat Beysenov	18.02.1988		(6)	

	DOB	M	(s)	G
Elivelton Ribeiro Dantas (BRA)	02.01.1992	23	(4)	4
Gian dos Santos Martins (BRA)	02.04.1993	31		
Zhakyp Kozhamberdy	26.02.1992	13	(7)	
Sheykhislam Kulakhmetov	15.01.1996		(1)	
Igor Pikalkin	19.03.1992	17	(4)	
Rakhimzhan Rozybakiev	02.01.1991	14	(5)	
Abzal Taubay	18.02.1995	17	(8)	3
Nemanja Subotić (SRB)	23.01.1992	25	(7)	
Forwards:	**DOB**	**M**	**(s)**	**G**
Gavril Kan	10.01.1999		(6)	
Dinmukhamed Karaman	26.06.2000	3	(6)	
Elguja Lobjanidze (GEO)	17.09.1992	22	(2)	8
Serge Komla Nyuiadzi (TOG)	17.09.1991	23	(3)	8
Samat Sarsenov	19.08.1996	5	(6)	
Alisher Suley	01.11.1995	18	(9)	4
Abylaykhan Zhumabek	19.10.2001	1	(1)	

Football Club Tobol Kostanay

Founded: 1967
Stadium: „Bauyrzhan Sagintayev" Stadium, Kostanay (10,500)
Trainer: Vladimir Gazzaev (RUS)   01.07.1980
[20.07.2019]   Evgeni Antonov   17.04.1977
[28.07.2019]   Nurbol Zhumaskaliev   11.05.1981

Goalkeepers:	DOB	M	(s)	G
Emil Balayev	17.04.1994	31		
Sultan Busurmanov	10.05.1996	1		
Zhasur Narzikulov	13.04.1984	1		
Andrey Pasechenko	09.08.1987		(1)	
Defenders:	**DOB**	**M**	**(s)**	**G**
Vytautas Andriuškevičius (LTU)	08.10.1990	12		
Viktor Dmitrenko	04.04.1991	25	(6)	
Fernander Kassaï (CTA)	01.07.1987	27	(1)	2
Aleksandr Kleshchenko	02.11.1990	12		
Dmitry Miroshnichenko	26.02.1992	22	(2)	2
Midfielders:	**DOB**	**M**	**(s)**	**G**
Sultan Abilgazy	22.02.1997	10	(5)	1
Nikita Bocharov	12.06.1992	12	(3)	1

	DOB	M	(s)	G
Maxim Fedin	08.06.1996	32	(1)	5
Jaba Kankava (GEO)	18.03.1986	28	(1)	
Nika Kvekveskiri (GEO)	29.05.1992	18	(4)	2
Azat Nurgaliev	30.06.1986	30	(2)	10
Daniyar Semchenkov	12.02.1997		(3)	
Ruslan Valiullin	09.09.1994	32		1
Samat Zharynbetov	04.01.1994	2	(13)	
Artūras Žulpa (LTU)	10.06.1990	29		2
Forwards:	**DOB**	**M**	**(s)**	**G**
Mikhail Gordeychuk (BLR)	23.10.1989	10	(4)	2
Senin Sebai (CIV)	18.12.1993	14	(12)	8
Artem Sherstov	16.10.1998		(13)	1
Bauyrzhan Turysbek	15.10.1991	15	(15)	8

Football Club Zhetysu Taldykorgan

Founded: 1981
Stadium: „Samat Suyumbayev" Stadium, Taldykorgan (4,000)
Trainer: Dmitriy Ogai   14.05.1960

Goalkeepers:	DOB	M	(s)	G
Nurlybek Ayazbaev	24.01.1991	2		
Almat Bekbaev	14.07.1984	20		
Andrey Shabanov	17.11.1986	11	(1)	
Defenders:	**DOB**	**M**	**(s)**	**G**
Olzhas Kerymzhanov	16.05.1989	21		1
Andrey Kharabara (RUS)	01.09.1985		(3)	
Ermek Kuantayev	13.10.1990	25	(2)	
Andrey Lebedev (BLR)	01.02.1991	13	(4)	
David Mawutor (GHA)	12.04.1992	29		
Nikita Naumov (BLR)	15.11.1989	30		4
Miram Sapanov	12.03.1986	16	(2)	
Midfielders:	**DOB**	**M**	**(s)**	**G**
Nenad Adamović (SRB)	12.01.1989	28	(3)	5
Ivan Antipov	14.01.1996	2	(3)	
Aslan Darabaev	21.01.1989	16	(1)	2

	DOB	M	(s)	G
Raul Dzhalilov (KGZ)	20.07.1994	2	(6)	
Kamo Hovhannisyan (ARM)	05.10.1992	24	(3)	5
Sabyrkhan Ibraev	22.03.1988	2	(1)	
Mantas Kuklys (LTU)	10.06.1987	22	(2)	2
Almir Mukhutdinov	09.06.1985	12	(3)	
Erkin Tapalov	03.09.1993	17	(4)	
Forwards:	**DOB**	**M**	**(s)**	**G**
Elzhas Altynbekov	22.11.1993	16	(11)	5
Ivaylo Dimitrov (BUL)	26.03.1989	4	(2)	
Oleg Khromtsov (MDA)	30.05.1981	1	(13)	1
Abylaykhan Makhambetov	03.08.1991	3	(1)	1
Rifat Nurmugamet	22.05.1996		(1)	
Ruslan Stepanyuk (UKR)	16.01.1992	30	(2)	4
Martin Toshev (BUL)	17.04.1990	13	(1)	9
Aybar Zhaksylykov	24.07.1997	4	(20)	6

1. FC Kyzylzhar SK Petropavlovsk (*Promoted*)	26	17	7	2	58	-	15	58
2. FC Kaspiy Aqtau (*Promoted*)	26	17	5	4	48	-	21	56
3. FC Akzhayik Oral (*Promotion Play-off*)	26	16	7	3	45	-	21	55
4. FC Altay Semey	26	16	5	5	43	-	14	53
5. FC Zhetisu II Taldiqorghan	26	10	12	4	42	-	23	42
6. FC Maqtaaral Jetisay	26	13	2	11	37	-	34	41
7. Sport Academy Kayrat Almaty	26	11	4	11	49	-	36	37
8. FC Baykonur Kyzylorda	26	10	7	9	37	-	43	37
9. FK Akademiya Ontustik	26	10	3	13	28	-	38	33
10. FC Kyran Shimkent	26	7	6	13	45	-	55	27
11. FC Shakhtar-Bulat Temirtau	26	6	5	15	24	-	47	23
12. FC Ekibastuz	26	6	4	16	22	-	42	22
13. Astana FC II	26	6	4	16	32	-	60	22
14. FC Aktobe Jas* (*Relegation*)	26	0	3	23	11	-	72	-3

*6 points deducted

NATIONAL TEAM

INTERNATIONAL MATCHES
(16.07.2019 – 15.07.2020)

06.09.2019	Nicosia	Cyprus - Kazakhstan	1-1(1-1)	(ECQ)
09.09.2019	Kaliningrad	Russia - Kazakhstan	1-0(0-0)	(ECQ)
10.10.2019	Nur-Sultan	Kazakhstan - Cyprus	1-2(1-0)	(ECQ)
13.10.2019	Nur-Sultan	Kazakhstan - Belgium	0-2(0-1)	(ECQ)
16.11.2019	Serravalle	San Marino - Kazakhstan	1-3(0-3)	(ECQ)
19.11.2019	Glasgow	Scotland - Kazakhstan	3-1(0-1)	(ECQ)

06.09.2019 CYPRUS - KAZAKHSTAN 1-1(1-1) 16th EC. Qualifiers
Stádio GSP, Nicosia; Referee: Mattias Gestranius (Finland); Attendance: 5,639
KAZ: Dmytro Nepohodov, Sergey Malyi, Gafurzhan Suyumbayev, Temirlan Yerlanov, Aleksandr Marochkin, Islambek Kuat, Bauyrzhan Islamkhan (Cap) (65.Maxim Fedin), Askat Tagybergen (82.Georgiy Zhukov), Yan Vorogovskiy, Yuriy Pertsukh, Aleksey Shchetkin (87.Abat Aymbetov). Trainer: Michal Bílek (Czech Republic).
Goal: Aleksey Shchetkin (2).

09.09.2019 RUSSIA - KAZAKHSTAN 1-0(0-0) 16th EC. Qualifiers
Kaliningrad Stadium, Kaliningrad; Referee: Nikola Dabanović (Montenegro); Attendance: 31,818
KAZ: Dmytro Nepohodov, Dmitriy Shomko (Cap), Sergey Malyi, Abzal Beysebekov, Temirlan Yerlanov, Aleksandr Marochkin, Aybol Abiken, Georgiy Zhukov (61.Bauyrzhan Islamkhan), Maxim Fedin (77.Serikzhan Muzhikov), Yuriy Pertsukh, Aleksey Shchetkin (90.Abat Aymbetov). Trainer: Michal Bílek (Czech Republic).

10.10.2019 KAZAKHSTAN - CYPRUS 1-2(1-0) 16th EC. Qualifiers
Astana Arena, Nur-Sultan; Referee: Craig Pawson (England); Attendance: 11,769
KAZ: Dmytro Nepohodov, Sergey Malyi, Gafurzhan Suyumbayev, Temirlan Yerlanov, Aleksandr Marochkin, Aybol Abiken (80.Maxim Fedin), Islambek Kuat (90.Askat Tagybergen), Bauyrzhan Islamkhan (Cap), Yan Vorogovskiy, Yuriy Pertsukh, Toktar Zhangylyshbay (61.Sergey Khizhnichenko). Trainer: Michal Bílek (Czech Republic).
Goal: Temirlan Yerlanov (34).

13.10.2019 KAZAKHSTAN - BELGIUM 0-2(0-1) 16th EC. Qualifiers
Astana Arena, Nur-Sultan; Referee: Gediminas Mažeika (Lithuania); Attendance: 26,801
KAZ: Dmytro Nepohodov, Dmitriy Shomko, Sergey Malyi, Abzal Beysebekov, Olzhas Kerymzhanov, Gafurzhan Suyumbayev (61.Yan Vorogovskiy), Aleksandr Marochkin, Aybol Abiken, Bauyrzhan Islamkhan (Cap), Georgiy Zhukov (84.Toktar Zhangylyshbay), Maxim Fedin (71.Yuriy Pertsukh). Trainer: Michal Bílek (Czech Republic).

16.11.2019 SAN MARINO - KAZAKHSTAN 1-3(0-3) 16th EC. Qualifiers
San Marino Stadium, Serravalle; Referee: Ali Palabıyık (Turkey); Attendance: 643
KAZ: Dmytro Nepohodov, Dmitriy Shomko, Sergey Malyi, Gafurzhan Suyumbayev, Aleksandr Marochkin, Islambek Kuat, Bauyrzhan Islamkhan (Cap), Askat Tagybergen (66.Maxim Fedin), Yan Vorogovskiy (18.Dmitriy Miroshnichenko), Baktiyor Zainutdinov, Aleksey Shchetkin (73.Abat Aymbetov). Trainer: Michal Bílek (Czech Republic).
Goals: Baktiyor Zainutdinov (6), Gafurzhan Suyumbayev (23), Aleksey Shchetkin (27).

19.11.2019 SCOTLAND - KAZAKHSTAN 3-1(0-1) 16th EC. Qualifiers
Hampden Park, Glasgow; Referee: Hendrikus Sebastian "Bas" Nijhuis (Netherlands); Attendance: 19,515
KAZ: Dmytro Nepohodov, Yuriy Logvinenko, Dmitriy Shomko, Sergey Malyi, Gafurzhan Suyumbayev, Aleksandr Marochkin, Aybol Abiken, Bauyrzhan Islamkhan (Cap) (74.74.Maxim Fedin), Baktiyor Zainutdinov, Yuriy Pertsukh (74.Islambek Kuat), Aleksey Shchetkin (83.Abat Aymbetov). Trainer: Michal Bílek (Czech Republic).
Goal: Baktiyor Zainutdinov (34).

NATIONAL TEAM PLAYERS
(16.07.2019 – 15.07.2020)

Name	DOB	Caps	Goals	2019/2020:	Club
Goalkeepers					
Dmytro NEPOHODOV	17.02.1988	12	0	2019:	*FC Ordabasy Shymkent*
Defenders					
Abzal BEYSEBEKOV	30.11.1992	28	0	2019:	*Astana FC*
Olzhas KERYMZHANOV	16.05.1989	1	0	2019:	*FC Zhetisu Taldiqorghan*
Yuriy LOGVINENKO	22.07.1988	51	5	2019:	*Astana FC*
Sergey MALYI	05.06.1990	41	0	2019:	*FC Ordabasy Shymkent*
Aleksandr MAROCHKIN	14.07.1990	7	0	2019:	*FC Kaysar Kyzylorda*
Dmitriy MIROSHNICHENKO	26.02.1992	10	0	2019:	*FC Tobol Kostanay*
Dmitriy SHOMKO	19.03.1990	45	2	2019:	*Astana FC*
Gafurzhan SUYUMBAYEV	19.08.1990	34	4	2019:	*FC Kairat Almaty*
Temirlan YERLANOV	09.07.1993	7	1	2019:	*FC Ordabasy Shymkent*
Midfielders					
Aybol ABIKEN	01.06.1996	4	0	2019:	*FC Kairat Almaty*
Bauyrzhan ISLAMKHAN	23.02.1993	44	3	2019:	*FC Kairat Almaty*
Islambek KUAT	12.01.1993	31	4	2019:	*FC Kairat Almaty*
Serikzhan MUZHIKOV	07.08.1989	23	1	2019:	*Astana FC*
Askat TAGYBERGEN	09.08.1990	23	0	2019:	*FC Kaysar Kyzylorda*
Yan VOROGOVSKIY	07.08.1996	11	1	2019:	*K Beerschot VA (BEL)*
Baktiyor ZAYNUTDINOV	02.04.1998	13	6	2019:	*FK Rostov-na-Donu (RUS)*
Toktar ZHANGYLYSHBAY	25.05.1993	5	0	2019:	*FC Ordabasy Shymkent*
Georgiy ZHUKOV	19.11.1994	15	0	2019:	*FC Kairat Almaty*
Forwards					
Abat AYMBETOV	07.08.1995	6	0	2019:	*FC Aktobe*
Maxim FEDIN	08.06.1996	13	1	2019:	*FC Tobol Kostanay*
Sergey KHIZHNICHENKO	17.07.1991	48	8	2019:	*Astana FC*
Yuriy PERTSUKH	13.05.1996	13	1	2019:	*Astana FC*
Aleksey SHCHETKIN	21.05.1991	31	3	2019:	*FC Ordabasy Shymkent*

National team coach		
Michal BÍLEK (Czech Republic) [since 18.01.2019]	13.04.1965	11 M; 4 W; 1 D; 6 L; 14-17

KOSOVO

The Country:
Republika e Kosovës (Republic of Kosovo)
Capital: Prishtina
Surface: 10,908 km²
Inhabitants: 1,810,463 [2020]
Time: UTC+1

The FA:
Federata e Futbollit e Kosovës
Rruga "28 Nëntori", nr. 171, Prishtina / Kosovë 10000
Tel: +383 38 600 220
Foundation date: 1946
Member of FIFA since: 2016
Member of UEFA since: 2016
Website: www.ffk-kosova.com

NATIONAL TEAM RECORDS

RECORDS
First international match:	05.03.2014, Mitrovicë:	Kosovo – Haiti 0-0
Most international caps:	Amir Kadri Rrahmani	- 29 caps (since 2014)
Most international goals:	Vedat Muriqi	- 8 goals / 23 caps (since 2016)

UEFA EUROPEAN CHAMPIONSHIP		FIFA WORLD CUP		OLYMPIC TOURNAMENTS	
1960	-	1930	-	1908	-
1964	-	1934	-	1912	-
1968	-	1938	-	1920	-
1972	-	1950	-	1924	-
1976	-	1954	-	1928	-
1980	-	1958	-	1936	-
1984	-	1962	-	1948	-
1988	-	1966	-	1952	-
1992	-	1970	-	1956	-
1996	-	1974	-	1960	-
2000	-	1978	-	1964	-
2004	-	1982	-	1968	-
2008	-	1986	-	1972	-
2012	-	1990	-	1976	-
2016	-	1994	-	1980	-
2020	*To be determined*	1998	-	1984	-
		2002	-	1988	-
		2006	-	1992	-
		2010	-	1996	-
		2014	-	2000	-
		2018	Qualifiers	2004	-
				2008	-
				2012	-
				2016	-

Please note: was part of Yugoslavia / Serbia and Montenegro / Serbia until 17.02.2008

UEFA NATIONS LEAGUE
2018/2019 – League D (promoted to League C)

OLYMPIC FOOTBALL TOURNAMENTS 1908-2016
None

FIFA CONFEDERATIONS CUP 1992-2017
None

KOSOVO CLUB HONOURS IN EUROPEAN CLUB COMPETITIONS:

European Champion Clubs' Cup (1956-1992) / UEFA Champions League (1993-2020)
None

Fairs Cup (1858-1971) / UEFA Cup (1972-2009) / UEFA Europa League (2010-2020)
None

UEFA Super Cup (1972-2019)
None

European Cup Winners' Cup 1961-1999*
None

*defunct competition

NATIONAL COMPETITIONS
TABLE OF HONOURS

Kosovo Province League (within F.R. Yugoslavia)

	CHAMPIONS	CUP WINNERS
1945	Jedinstvo Prishtina	-
1946	Jedinstvo Prishtina	-
1947	KF Trepça Mitrovicë	-
1947/1948	Proleteri Prishtina	-
1948/1949	KF Trepça Mitrovicë	-
1950	KF Trepça Mitrovicë	-
1951	Kosova Prishtina	-
1952	KF Trepça Mitrovicë	-
1953/1954	Kosova Prishtina	-
1954/1955	KF Trepça Mitrovicë	-
1955/1956	Rudari Stantërg	-
1956/1957	Rudniku Hajvali	-
1957/1958	Rudari Stantërg	-
1958/1959	FC Prishtina	-
1959/1960	Rudari Stantërg	-
1960/1961	FC Prishtina	-
1961/1962	Buduqnosti Pejë	-
1962/1963	Crvena zvezda Gjilani	-
1963/1964	Slloga Lipyan	-
1964/1965	Slloga Lipyan	-
1965/1966	Buduqnosti Pejë	-
1966/1967	Obiliqi Kastriot	-
1967/1968	FC Vëllaznimi Gjakovë	-
1968/1969	FC Vëllaznimi Gjakovë	-
1969/1970	FC Vëllaznimi Gjakovë	-
1970/1971	FC Vëllaznimi Gjakovë	-
1971/1972	FC Obiliqi	-
1972/1973	KF Fushë Kosova	-
1973/1974	FC Vëllaznimi Gjakovë	-
1974/1975	KF Liria Prizreni	-
1975/1976	RHMK Obilić	-
1976/1977	FC Prishtina	-
1977/1978	Buduqnosti Pejë	-
1978/1979	FC Prishtina	-
1979/1980	FC Vëllaznimi Gjakovë	-
1980/1981	KF Liria Prizreni	-
1981/1982	FC Vëllaznimi Gjakovë	-
1982/1983	KNI Ramiz Sadiku	-
1983/1984	KF Liria Prizreni	-
1984/1985	Crvena zvezda Gjilani	FC Vëllaznimi Gjakovë
1985/1986	FC Vëllaznimi Gjakovë	FC Vëllaznimi Gjakovë
1986/1987	KF Liria Prizreni	FC Vëllaznimi Gjakovë
1987/1988	Crvena zvezda Gjilani	*No competition*
1988/1989	Buduqnosti Pejë	*No competition*
1989/1990	FC Vëllaznimi Gjakovë	*No competition*

Independent League of Kosovo

	CHAMPIONS	CUP WINNERS
1990/1991	KF Fushë-Kosova	*No competition*
1991/1992	FC Prishtina	KF Trepça Mitrovicë
1992/1993	KF Trepça Mitrovicë	KF Flamurtari Prishtina
1993/1994	KF Dukagjini Klinë	FC Prishtina
1994/1995	KF Liria Prizreni	KF Liria Prizreni
1995/1996	FC Prishtina	KF Flamurtari Prishtina
1996/1997	FC Prishtina	*Final not played*
1997/1998	*Tournament abandoned*	*No competition*
1998/1999	*No competition*	*No competition*

Establishment as top-league after UNMIK* take-over of Kosovo

	CHAMPIONS	CUP WINNERS
1999/2000	FC Prishtina	SC Gjilani
2000/2001	FC Prishtina	FC Drita Gjilani
2001/2002	KF Besiana Podujevë	KF Besiana Podujevo
2002/2003	FC Drita Gjilani	KF KEK-u Obilić
2003/2004	FC Prishtina	KF Kosova Prishtina
2004/2005	KF Besa Pejë Peć	KF Besa Pejë Peć
2005/2006	KF Besa Pejë Peć	FC Prishtina
2006/2007	KF Besa Pejë Peć	KF Liria Prizreni
2007/2008	FC Prishtina	FC Vëllaznimi Gjakovë

After proclamation of independence

	CHAMPIONS	CUP WINNERS
2008/2009	FC Prishtina	KF Hysi Podujevo
2009/2010	KF Trepça Mitrovicë	KF Liria Prizreni
2010/2011	KF Hysi Milloshevë	FC Prishtina
2011/2012	FC Prishtina	KF Trepça'89 Mitrovicë
2012/2013	FC Prishtina	FC Prishtina
2013/2014	KF Vushtria	KF Hajvalia
2014/2015	KF Feronikeli Glogovac	KV Feronikeli Glogovac
2015/2016	KF Feronikeli Glogovac	FC Prishtina

United Nations Mission in Kosovo

Please note: Jedinstvo Prishtina changed its name to Proleteri Prishtina, Kosova Prishtina and finally to FC Prishtina.
Buduqnosti Pejë became KF Besa Pejë Peć; FC Obiliqi changed its name to RHMK Obilić and later KF KEK-u Obilić

After membership in UEFA and FIFA

	CHAMPIONS	CUP WINNERS	BEST GOALSCORERS	
2016/2017	KF Trepça'89 Mitrovicë	KF Llapi Podujevë	John Otto John (NGA, KF Trepça'89 Mitrovicë)	24
2017/2018	FC Drita Gjilan	FC Vëllaznimi Gjakovë	John Otto John (NGA, KF Trepça'89 Mitrovicë) Mirlind Daku (KF Llapi Podujevë)	17
2018/2019	KF Feronikeli Glogovac	KF Feronikeli Glogovac	Kastriot Rexha (KF Feronikeli Glogovac)	21
2019/2020	FC Drita Gjilan	FC Prishtina	Blendi Baftiu (KF Ballkani Suva Reka) Arb Manaj (KF Trepça'89 Mitrovicë)	19

NATIONAL CHAMPIONSHIP
Football Superleague of Kosovo 2019/2020
(17.08.2019 – 26.07.2020)

Results

Round 1 [17-18.08.2019]
KF Flamurtari - FC Prishtina 1-1
KF Feronikeli - KF Drenica 4-1
KF Llapi - KF Vushtrria 4-1
FC Drita Gjilan - KF Ferizaj 0-1
KF Dukagjini - KF Ballkani 0-0
KF Trepça'89 - KF Gjilani 4-1

Round 2 [23-25.08.2019]
KF Drenica - KF Llapi 3-0
KF Ferizaj - KF Gjilani 0-3
KF Ballkani - KF Feronikeli 3-1
FC Drita Gjilan - KF Flamurtari 3-0
KF Vushtrria - KF Trepça'89 1-1
FC Prishtina - KF Dukagjini 2-0 [25.09.]

Round 3 [31.08.-01.09.2019]
KF Flamurtari - KF Ferizaj 1-0
KF Dukagjini - FC Drita Gjilan 0-4
KF Feronikeli - FC Prishtina 1-0
KF Llapi - KF Ballkani 0-0
KF Trepça'89 - KF Drenica 1-1
KF Gjilani - KF Vushtrria 2-0

Round 4 [13-15.09.2019]
KF Ballkani - KF Trepça'89 3-2
FC Prishtina - KF Llapi 0-1
KF Drenica - KF Gjilani 0-2
FC Drita Gjilan - KF Feronikeli 1-0
KF Ferizaj - KF Vushtrria 0-1
KF Flamurtari - KF Dukagjini 2-0

Round 5 [18-19.09.2019]
KF Gjilani - KF Ballkani 1-0
KF Trepça'89 - FC Prishtina 0-1
KF Llapi - FC Drita Gjilan 2-2
KF Vushtrria - KF Drenica 2-2
KF Feronikeli - KF Flamurtari 2-1
KF Dukagjini - KF Ferizaj 0-1

Round 6 [22-23.09.2019]
FC Drita Gjilan - KF Trepça'89 1-1
KF Dukagjini - KF Feronikeli 0-2
FC Prishtina - KF Gjilani 2-1
KF Ferizaj - KF Drenica 0-1
KF Ballkani - KF Vushtrria 5-2
KF Flamurtari - KF Llapi 1-5

Round 7 [28-29.09.2019]
KF Feronikeli - KF Ferizaj 5-0
KF Llapi - KF Dukagjini 2-1
KF Trepça'89 - KF Flamurtari 5-1
KF Drenica - KF Ballkani 0-1
KF Gjilani - FC Drita Gjilan 0-1
KF Vushtrria - FC Prishtina 0-3

Round 8 [02-03.10.2019]
KF Ferizaj - KF Ballkani 1-2
KF Dukagjini - KF Trepça'89 1-0
KF Feronikeli - KF Llapi 1-2
FC Drita Gjilan - KF Vushtrria 5-1
KF Flamurtari - KF Gjilani 1-4
FC Prishtina - KF Drenica 0-0 [16.10.]

Round 9 [05-08.10.2019]
KF Llapi - KF Ferizaj 2-4
KF Trepça'89 - KF Feronikeli 1-1
KF Vushtrria - KF Flamurtari 2-2
KF Ballkani - FC Prishtina 1-0
KF Gjilani - KF Dukagjini 1-0
KF Drenica - FC Drita Gjilan 1-1

Round 10 [18-20.10.2019]
KF Dukagjini - KF Vushtrria 1-0
KF Feronikeli - KF Gjilani 1-2
KF Llapi - KF Trepça'89 4-1
KF Flamurtari - KF Drenica 0-0
KF Ferizaj - FC Prishtina 0-2
FC Drita Gjilan - KF Ballkani 2-0

Round 11 [22-24.10.2019]
KF Vushtrria - KF Feronikeli 0-1
KF Trepça'89 - KF Ferizaj 1-0
KF Gjilani - KF Llapi 3-0
KF Drenica - KF Dukagjini 3-0
KF Ballkani - KF Flamurtari 3-1
FC Prishtina - FC Drita Gjilan 1-0

Round 12 [26-28.10.2019]
KF Vushtrria - KF Llapi 1-0
KF Drenica - KF Feronikeli 1-0
KF Ballkani - KF Dukagjini 3-0
KF Gjilani - KF Trepça'89 0-2
KF Ferizaj - FC Drita Gjilan 0-2
FC Prishtina - KF Flamurtari 2-0

Round 13 [01-03.11.2019]
KF Llapi - KF Drenica 1-0
KF Trepça'89 - KF Vushtrria 1-0
KF Feronikeli - KF Ballkani 0-2
KF Dukagjini - FC Prishtina 0-0
KF Gjilani - KF Ferizaj 4-0
KF Flamurtari - FC Drita Gjilan 1-0

Round 14 [06-07.11.2019]
KF Ballkani - KF Llapi 1-1
KF Drenica - KF Trepça'89 3-2
FC Drita Gjilan - KF Dukagjini 1-0
FC Prishtina - KF Feronikeli 2-3
KF Ferizaj - KF Flamurtari 1-0
KF Vushtrria - KF Gjilani 1-3

Round 15 [09-11.11.2019]
KF Feronikeli - FC Drita Gjilan 0-0
KF Llapi - FC Prishtina 1-4
KF Gjilani - KF Drenica 1-1
KF Trepça'89 - KF Ballkani 0-0
KF Dukagjini - KF Flamurtari 1-2
KF Vushtrria - KF Ferizaj 3-1

Round 16 [22-24.11.2019]
KF Ballkani - KF Gjilani 2-1
KF Drenica - KF Vushtrria 3-0
KF Flamurtari - KF Feronikeli 2-2
FC Drita Gjilan - KF Llapi 2-0
FC Prishtina - KF Trepça'89 1-0
KF Ferizaj - KF Dukagjini 2-0

Round 17 [01-02.12.2019]
KF Gjilani - FC Prishtina 0-0
KF Llapi - KF Flamurtari 1-4
KF Trepça'89 - FC Drita Gjilan 3-1
KF Drenica - KF Ferizaj 0-2
KF Feronikeli - KF Dukagjini 4-2
KF Vushtrria - KF Ballkani 1-0

Round 18 [15-16.02.2020]
KF Ballkani - KF Drenica 3-0
FC Prishtina - KF Vushtrria 4-0
KF Ferizaj - KF Feronikeli 1-1
FC Drita Gjilan - KF Gjilani 2-0
KF Flamurtari - KF Trepça'89 4-3
KF Dukagjini - KF Llapi 0-0

Round 19 [21-23.02.2020]
KF Vushtrria - FC Drita Gjilan 2-3
KF Drenica - FC Prishtina 1-3
KF Llapi - KF Feronikeli 2-1
KF Gjilani - KF Flamurtari 2-0
KF Ballkani - KF Ferizaj 3-0
KF Trepça'89 - KF Dukagjini 2-1

Round 20 [28.02.-02.03.2020]
FC Drita Gjilan - KF Drenica 4-1
KF Ferizaj - KF Llapi 2-0
KF Feronikeli - KF Trepça'89 3-0
KF Dukagjini - KF Gjilani 0-4
FC Prishtina - KF Ballkani 0-0
KF Flamurtari - KF Vushtrria 2-0

Round 21 [04-05.03.2020]
KF Ballkani - FC Drita Gjilan 2-0
KF Gjilani - KF Feronikeli 2-1
KF Trepça'89 - KF Llapi 1-2
FC Prishtina - KF Ferizaj 3-2
KF Drenica - KF Flamurtari 3-1
KF Vushtrria - KF Dukagjini 3-3

Round 22 [07-09.03.2020]
KF Ferizaj - KF Trepça'89 4-0
FC Drita Gjilan - FC Prishtina 2-1
KF Llapi - KF Gjilani 2-1
KF Flamurtari - KF Ballkani 2-1
KF Feronikeli - KF Vushtrria 2-0
KF Dukagjini - KF Drenica 1-3

Round 23 [05-07.06.2020]
KF Llapi - KF Dukagjini 4-1
FC Drita Gjilan - KF Flamurtari 1-0
KF Feronikeli - KF Vushtrria 3-1
KF Ballkani - KF Drenica 0-0
KF Gjilani - KF Trepça'89 1-1
FC Prishtina - KF Ferizaj 8-1

Round 24 [12-14.06.2020]
KF Dukagjini - KF Feronikeli 0-2
KF Flamurtari - KF Ballkani 0-0
KF Llapi - KF Drenica 0-2
KF Vushtrria - FC Prishtina 0-2
KF Ferizaj - KF Gjilani 0-3
KF Trepça'89 - FC Drita Gjilan 0-2

Round 25 [19-21.06.2020]
FC Drita Gjilan - KF Ferizaj 2-0
KF Drenica - KF Flamurtari 1-2
KF Gjilani - KF Vushtrria 3-0
FC Prishtina - KF Dukagjini 4-1
KF Ballkani - KF Trepça'89 3-1
KF Feronikeli - KF Llapi 2-1

Round 26 [24-25.06.2020]
KF Dukagjini - KF Gjilani 1-3
KF Vushtrria - FC Drita Gjilan 0-4
KF Trepça'89 - KF Flamurtari 1-1
KF Feronikeli - KF Drenica 0-0
KF Llapi - FC Prishtina 1-1
KF Ferizaj - KF Ballkani 1-1

Round 27 [28-29.06.2020]
KF Drenica - KF Trepça'89 2-4
KF Flamurtari - KF Ferizaj 3-2
FC Drita Gjilan - KF Dukagjini 2-0
KF Ballkani - KF Vushtrria 3-1
KF Gjilani - KF Llapi 2-2
FC Prishtina - KF Feronikeli 3-1

Round 28 [03-05.07.2020]	
KF Vushtrria - KF Flamurtari	2-2
FC Prishtina - KF Drenica	1-0
KF Feronikeli - KF Gjilani	0-2
KF Dukagjini - KF Ballkani	1-5
KF Llapi - FC Drita Gjilan	0-4
KF Ferizaj - KF Trepça'89	2-5

Round 29 [08-09.07.2020]	
KF Drenica - KF Ferizaj	3-0
KF Ballkani - KF Llapi	5-1
KF Gjilani - FC Prishtina	2-1
KF Trepça'89 - KF Vushtrria	1-1
KF Flamurtari - KF Dukagjini	4-3
FC Drita Gjilan - KF Feronikeli	2-1

Round 30 [12-13.07.2020]	
KF Gjilani - KF Drenica	2-0
FC Prishtina - FC Drita Gjilan	1-1
KF Feronikeli - KF Ballkani	0-1
KF Llapi - KF Flamurtari	1-0
KF Dukagjini - KF Trepça'89	3-2
KF Vushtrria - KF Ferizaj	1-3

Round 31 [18.07.2020]	
KF Drenica - KF Vushtrria	2-1
KF Ferizaj - KF Dukagjini	0-4
KF Trepça'89 - KF Llapi	5-4
KF Flamurtari - KF Feronikeli	1-0
KF Ballkani - FC Prishtina	2-2
FC Drita Gjilan - KF Gjilani	0-2

Round 32 [21-22.07.2020]	
FC Drita Gjilan - KF Drenica	1-0
KF Gjilani - KF Ballkani	2-2
FC Prishtina - KF Flamurtari	3-0
KF Feronikeli - KF Trepça'89	1-2
KF Llapi - KF Ferizaj	2-1
KF Dukagjini - KF Vushtrria	2-1

Round 33 [26.07.2020]	
KF Drenica - KF Dukagjini	1-0
KF Vushtrria - KF Llapi	5-3
KF Ferizaj - KF Feronikeli	2-4
KF Trepça'89 - FC Prishtina	2-1
KF Flamurtari - KF Gjilani	0-1
KF Ballkani - FC Drita Gjilan	2-1

Final Standings

						Total					Home					Away		
1.	**FC Drita Gjilan**	33	21	5	7	57 - 23	68	14	1	2	31 - 8		7	4	5	26 - 15
2.	SC Gjilani	33	21	5	7	61 - 27	68	10	5	2	28 - 11		11	0	5	33 - 16
3.	KF Ballkani Suva Reka	33	19	10	4	59 - 25	67	14	3	0	44 - 14		5	7	4	15 - 11
4.	FC Prishtina	33	18	8	7	59 - 25	62	12	3	2	37 - 11		6	5	5	22 - 14
5.	KF Feronikeli Glogovac	33	14	5	14	50 - 40	47	9	2	6	29 - 17		5	3	8	21 - 23
6.	KF Llapi Podujevë	33	13	6	14	51 - 62	45	9	3	5	29 - 28		4	3	9	22 - 34
7.	KF Trepça'89 Mitrovicë	33	12	8	13	55 - 55	44	8	5	3	28 - 18		4	3	10	27 - 37
8.	KF Drenica Skenderaj	33	12	8	13	39 - 40	44	9	1	6	27 - 19		3	7	7	12 - 21
9.	KF Flamurtari Prishtina (*Relegated*)	33	12	7	14	42 - 56	43	9	4	3	25 - 22		3	3	11	17 - 34
10.	KF Ferizaj (*Relegated*)	33	9	2	22	34 - 70	29	4	2	10	16 - 29		5	0	12	18 - 41
11.	KF Vushtrria (*Relegated*)	33	5	6	22	34 - 76	21	4	5	7	24 - 33		1	1	15	10 - 43
12.	KF Dukagjini Klinë (*Relegated*)	33	5	4	24	27 - 69	19	4	3	9	11 - 29		1	1	15	16 - 40

Top goalscorers:

19	**Blendi Baftiu**	*KF Ballkani Suva Reka*
19	**Arb Manaj**	*KF Trepça'89 Mitrovicë*
14	Ahmed Januzi (ALB)	*FC Prishtina*
13	Kastriot Rexha	*FC Drita Gjilan*
12	Gerhard Progni (ALB)	*SC Gjilani*

NATIONAL CUP
Kosovo Cup / Kupa e Kosovës 2019/2020

Second Round [28.11.2019]

KF 2 Korriku Prishtina - KF Istogu	1-0		KF Ballkani Suva Reka - FC Drita Gjilan	1-1 aet; 5-4 p
KF Dukagjini Klinë - KF Besa Pejë Peć	2-1		KF Dardanët Gjakovë - KF Trepça'89 Mitrovicë	0-5
KF Vëllaznimi Gjakovë - KF Ferizaj	2-4		KF Flamurtari Prishtina - KF Vushtrria	1-3
KF Vitia - KF Ramiz Sadiku Prishtina	5-1		KF Minatori - FC Prishtina	0-4
KF Ulpiana Lipljan - KF Liria Prizren	1-3		KF Drenica Skenderaj - KF Fushë Kosova	3-1
KF UV Malisheva - SC Gjilani	0-3		KF Trepça Mitrovicë - KF Drenasi Glogovac	2-1 aet
KF Feronikeli Glogovac - KF Llapi Podujevë	1-0		KF A&N Prizren - KF KEK-u Obilić	4-1
KF Dardana - KF Vllaznia Požaranje	4-3 aet		KF Arbëria Lipljan - KF Onix-Banjë	1-0

1/8-Finals [07-08.12.2019]

KF Ballkani Suva Reka - KF Trepça'89 Mitrovicë	3-0		KF Arbëria Lipljan - FC Prishtina	0-1
KF Drenica Skenderaj - KF Dardana	5-0		KF Trepça Mitrovicë - KF Vushtrria	2-4
KF Feronikeli Glogovac - KF A&N Prizren	4-0		KF Liria Prizren - KF Ferizaj	1-0
KF Vitia - KF Dukagjini Klinë	1-2		SC Gjilani - KF 2 Korriku Prishtina	6-1

Quarter-Finals [08/09.12.02.2020]

KF Drenica Skenderaj - SC Gjilani	2-1 aet		KF Dukagjini Klinë - KF Ballkani Suva Reka	0-2
FC Prishtina - KF Vushtrria	4-1		KF Liria Prizren - KF Feronikeli Glogovac	0-2

Semi-Finals [02/17.06.2020]

First Leg			Second Leg	
FC Prishtina - KF Drenica Skenderaj	3-0		KF Drenica Skenderaj - FC Prishtina	2-3
KF Ballkani Suva Reka - KF Feronikeli Glogovac	0-0		KF Feronikeli Glogovac - KF Ballkani Suva Reka	1-1

Final

29.07.2020; Stadiumi „Fadil Vokrri", Prishtina; Referee: Genc Nuza; Attendance: None
FC Prishtina - KF Ballkani Suva Reka   1-0(1-0)

FC Prishtina: Visar Bekaj, Armend Thaqi (Cap), Diar Miftaraj (84.Ahmet Haliti), Leotrim Bekteshi, Leonit Abazi, Endrit Krasniqi (76.Ardit Hila), Lorik Boshnjaku, Qëndrim Zyba, Meriton Korenica (76.Labinot Ibrahimi), John Otto John, Gauthier Mankenda (60.Kreshnik Uka). Trainer: Armend Dallku (Albania).

KF Ballkani: Armend Rugji, Besnik Krasniqi (75.Liridon Fetahaj), Visar Berisha (Cap) (72.Egzon Sinani), Arber Potoku, Arbër Prekazi, Roni Gashi, Edvin Kuc, Jetmir Topalli, Blend Baftiu, Ermal Krasniqi (63.Artur Magani), Mirlind Daku. Trainer: Ismet Munishi.

Goal: 1-0 John Otto John (20).

THE CLUBS 2019/2020

Please note: the squads on the following pages contain lists of players who were used in the 2019/2020 season. FC Drita Gjilani is presented with complete statistics. The rest of the data was also transmitted, unfortunately not completely, because these data did not include game days 29-30-31 and partially 28 & 32. Thus this data became unusable and the entire number of matches / subs / goals was completely removed. We ask for your understanding.

Klubi Futbollistik Ballkani Suva Reka

Founded:	1947
Stadium:	Stadiumi i Qytetit të Suharekës, Suva Reka (1,500)
Trainer:	Ismet Munishi 03.10.1974

Goalkeepers:	DOB
Flamur Gashi	06.06.2000
Armend Rugji	30.12.1985
Defenders:	**DOB**
Visar Berisha	07.12.1986
Ramiz Bytyqi	10.01.1999
Elbasan Gashi	22.05.1992
Dardan Jashari	28.03.1990
Albin Kapra	07.06.2000
Besnik Krasniqi	01.02.1990
Arber Potoku	19.04.1994
Arbër Prekazi	11.10.1989
Egzon Sinani	07.06.1994
Edmond Turku	06.01.1989
Uran Shala	
Midfielders:	**DOB**
Endrit Asllanaj	16.05.2001

Blend Baftiu	17.02.1998
Liridon Fetahaj	21.09.1991
Roni Gashi	04.06.1998
Edvin Kuc (MNE)	27.10.1993
Kushtrim Gashi	05.11.1992
Forwards:	**DOB**
Albin Berisha	14.01.2001
Mirlind Daku	01.01.1998
Durim Gashi	14.06.1992
Leutrim Gashi	13.05.1996
Arbër Hoxha	06.10.1998
Ermal Krasniqi	07.09.1998
Artur Magani (ALB)	08.07.1994
Edi Maksutaj	04.10.2000
Bleon Sekiraqa	17.10.2000
Jetmir Topalli	07.02.1998

Klubi Futbollistik Drenica Skenderaj

Founded:	1958
Stadium:	Stadiumi"Bajram Aliu", Skenderaj (3,000)
Trainer:	Tahir Lushtaku
[03.01.2020]	Gani Sejdiu

Goalkeepers:	DOB
Mikel Kaloshi (ALB)	16.06.1993
Arion Ymeri	30.03.1995
Defenders:	**DOB**
Prince Balde (LBR)	23.03.1998
Azem Bejta	03.08.1990
Souleymane Coulibaly (FRA)	26.01.1998
Drilon Lladrovci	27.07.1994
Shkelzen Lushtaku	22.06.1990
Armin Mujkić (BIH)	10.03.1994
Muharrem Musa	25.06.1994
Përparim Osmani	27.03.1988
Edon Pasoma	21.08.1992
Arsen Sykaj (ALB)	16.04.1990
Edmond Turku	06.01.1989
Midfielders:	**DOB**
Armend Abazi	17.08.1994

Argjend Bardhi	28.04.1993
Qemail Elshani	28.06.1991
Genc Hamiti	21.09.1993
Hasan Hyseni	14.04.1997
Flamur Muleci	28.03.1995
Argjend Mustafa	30.08.1992
Dijar Mustafa	07.11.1993
Arbios Thaçi	13.10.1993
Forwards:	**DOB**
Van-Dave Harmon (LBR)	22.09.1995
Vilfor Hysa (ALB)	09.09.1989
Vildan Kerim (MKD)	04.08.1994
Osman Mëziu	05.09.1999
Diar Prokshi	27.08.1998
Alban Shillova	13.08.1992
Hysen Tahiri	28.09.1992

Football Club Drita Gjilan

Founded:	1947
Stadium:	Stadiumi i Qytetit, Gjilan (15,000)
Trainer:	Ardijan Nuhiji (MKD) 07.12.1978

Goalkeepers:	DOB	M	(s)	G
Faton Maloku	14.06.1991	15		
Darko Tofiloski (MKD)	13.01.1986	18	(1)	
Defenders:	**DOB**	**M**	**(s)**	**G**
Sedat Berisha (MKD)	03.09.1989	3	(3)	
Ilir Blakçori	01.02.1993	18	(3)	
Ardian Cuculi (MKD)	19.07.1987	29		2
Fidan Gërbeshi	19.05.1985	30	(1)	2
Liridon Leci	11.02.1985	16		2
Ardian Limani	18.11.1993	31		
Lirim Mema	23.01.1998	2	(1)	
Midfielders:	**DOB**	**M**	**(s)**	**G**
Astrit Fazliu	28.10.1987	13	(3)	5
Donat Hasanaj	18.09.1998	2	(3)	
Drilon Islami	18.07.2000		(7)	

Albin Krasniqi	03.06.2001	3	(3)	
Olti Mehmeti	29.04.2002		(1)	
Hamdi Namani	16.10.1994	26	(4)	1
Bujar Shabani	11.10.1990	27	(1)	1
Erjon Vucaj (ALB)	25.12.1990	19	(10)	4
Forwards:	**DOB**	**M**	**(s)**	**G**
Almir Ajzeraj	05.10.1997	2	(12)	
Izair Emini (MKD)	04.10.1985	17	(10)	6
Gilberto Valdensio Fortunato (BRA)	11.07.1987	10	(4)	5
Betim Haxhimusa	14.04.1992	23	(9)	10
Lucas Ferreira Cardoso (BRA)	07.04.1994	1	(11)	1
Ardit Mustafa	06.10.2001		(1)	
Kastriot Rexha	27.09.1988	11	(2)	8
Bunjamin Shabani (MKD)	30.01.1991	16	(12)	1
Xhevdet Shabani	10.10.1986	31		7

Klubi Futbollistik Dukagjini Klinë

Founded: 1958
Stadium: Stadiumi 18 Qershor, Klinë (2,000)
Trainer: Xhengiz Rexhepi

Goalkeepers:	DOB
Burim Bojaj	
Drin Hodaj	27.02.1997
Altik Muhaxhiri	09.01.1992
Flamur Neziri	22.05.1987
Art Zenunaj	
Defenders:	**DOB**
Elton Basriu (ALB)	03.08.1987
Leutrim Beqiri	05.04.1990
Bujar Gojani	28.03.1993
Denis Haliti	31.01.1997
Muharrem Musa	25.06.1994
Liridon Palushaj	
Arbër Shala	23.12.1991
Ilir Syla	
Midfielders:	**DOB**
Diellor Beseni	31.05.2002
Lulzim Doshlaku	28.01.1991
Jeton Dushi	06.03.1996

	DOB
Drilon Elshani	
Orgest Gava (ALB)	29.03.1990
Mhill Grabanica	17.04.1996
Labinot Jashanica	16.04.1997
Fuad Karabegu	01.02.1994
Altin Loga (ALB)	10.11.1989
Leorant Marmullaku	24.09.2002
Blendi Memaj	02.01.1995
Abedin Merlaku	
Mark Milicaj	15.01.1987
Erblind Mulaj	25.09.1995
Ilir Mustafa	07.08.1996
Forwards:	**DOB**
Granit Arifaj	29.11.1990
Husein Demiri (MKD)	06.09.1995
Granit Elezaj	
Abu Kamara (LBR)	01.04.1997
Altin Merlaku	07.03.1993
Albion Osmani	15.12.2001

Klubi Futbollistik Ferizaj

Founded:	1923	
Stadium:	Stadiumi "Ismet Shabani", Ferizaj (2,000)	
Trainer:	Bylbyl Sokoli	19.12.1958
[05.08.2019]	Bekim Isufi	02.01.1976

Goalkeepers:	DOB
Armend Blakqori	06.08.1990
Donat Kaqiu	20.09.1993
Defenders:	**DOB**
Bujamin Asani (MKD)	10.08.1988
Behar Bardhi (MKD)	24.03.1993
Dardan Cerkini	27.09.1991
Gentrit Halili	14.12.2001
Gentian Hazizi	
Ergon Hyseni	18.01.1994
Dardan Jashari	28.03.1990
Viktor Kuka	25.06.1990
Veton Shabani	05.05.1990
Ardian Shaljani	20.02.2000
Filip Stojanovski (MKD)	01.12.1996
Midfielders:	**DOB**
Genc Berisha	
Taulant Dajaku	09.01.1987
Altin Ibrahimi	14.07.2000
Granit Jashari	20.08.1998

	DOB
Albin Krasniqi	03.06.2001
Euren Krasniqi	14.04.2001
Përparim Livoreka	28.06.1987
Blerton Mehmeti	
Zgjim Mustafa	22.11.1994
Kenan Orana	
Kastriot Rexhepi	
Edon Sadriu	20.05.1997
Egzon Shabani	27.08.1989
Filonit Shaqiri	29.05.1993
Forwards:	**DOB**
Shpend Asani (MKD)	14.11.1996
Erli Çupi	03.02.1997
Dren Gashi	25.01.1994
Durim Gashi	14.06.1992
Nermin Hajdarević (BIH)	10.02.1999
Fatih Karahoda	07.04.1987
Aurel Idrizi	07.02.2001
Alban Rexhepi	15.12.1995
Adenis Shala	23.10.1998

Klubi Futbollistik Feronikeli Glogovac

Founded:	1974	
Stadium:	Stadiumi "Rexhep Rexhepi", Glogovac (2,000)	
Trainer:	Dejan Vukičević (MNE)	27.04.1968
[01.11.2019]	Agim Sopi (MKD)	28.10.1969
[05.03.2020]	Afrim Tovërlani	17.01.1967

Goalkeepers:	DOB
Florjan Smakiqi	10.08.1998
Jacek Troshupa (POL)	04.10.1993
Defenders:	**DOB**
Prince Balde (LBR)	23.03.1998
Ilir Berisha	25.06.1991
Keith Groeneveld (RSA)	24.06.1999
Yll Hoxha	26.12.1987
Perparim Islami	01.05.1995
Lapidar Lladrovci	15.12.1990
Simon Loshi (NED)	16.02.2000
Arbër Prekazi	11.10.1989
Astrit Thaqi	20.04.1993
Midfielders:	**DOB**
Besmir Bojku (MKD)	03.01.1995
Albert Dabiqaj	10.07.1996
Mirlind Demaku	

	DOB
Lulzim Doshlaku	28.01.1991
Astrit Fazliu	28.10.1987
Medjon Hoxha	27.07.1999
Jean Agostinho da Silva "Jean Carioca" (BRA)	01.06.1988
Miloš Krkotić (MNE)	29.09.1987
Kristi Kullaj (ALB)	02.01.1999
Argjend Malaj	16.10.1993
Met Millaku	15.11.1997
Albutrint Morina	20.02.1993
Haxhi Neziraj (ALB)	16.03.1993
Forwards:	**DOB**
Nicholas Andrews (LBR)	04.08.1998
Van-Dave Harmon (LBR)	22.09.1995
Mendurim Hoti	23.02.1996
Kastriot Rexha	27.09.1988
Mevlan Zeka	28.05.1994

Klubi Futbollistik Flamurtari Prishtina

Founded:	1968
Stadium:	Stadiumi "Xhemail Ibishi", Prishtina (5,000)
Trainer:	Arsim Thaqi

Goalkeepers:	DOB		Ersin Fetahi (MKD)	01.08.1996
Ardit Nika	17.02.1998		Donat Hasanaj	18.09.1998
Erind Selimaj (ALB)	22.05.1989		Ernes Isljami (MNE)	22.09.1993
Defenders:	DOB		Albinot Kozmaqi	12.01.2000
Gentrit Dumani	13.07.1993		Egzon Krasniqi	27.04.1991
Angel Granchov (BUL)	16.10.1992		Arnis Latifaj (BEL)	11.09.1998
Lyubomir Gutsev (BUL)	18.03.1990		Altin Loga (MKD)	10.11.1989
Riste Ilijovski (MKD)	27.09.1994		Bashkim Shala	05.04.1991
Veton Kabashi			Danin Talović (MNE)	08.03.1995
Valdrin Kaqiku	02.06.1995		Liridon Voca	
Lorik Maxhuni	02.07.1992		Arbnor Zeqiri	02.08.1996
Donart Vitija			Edon Zeqiri	04.06.1990
Melos Zenunaj	29.08.2000		Forwards:	DOB
Valdo Zeqaj (ALB)	24.08.1995		Gentrit Begolli	21.02.1992
Midfielders:	DOB		Shend Kelmendi	21.09.1994
Shqipdon Ademi	03.04.1992		Festim Krasniqi	12.07.1991
Mërgim Boshnjaku			Adem Maliqi	17.07.1997
Agron Bruqi			Torvioll Stullqaku	

Soccer Club Gjilani

Founded:	1945	
Stadium:	Stadiumi i Qytetit, Gjilan (15,000)	
Trainer:	Gentian Mezani (ALB)	13.10.1975

Goalkeepers:	DOB		Fjoart Jonuzi (ALB)	09.07.1996
Kenan Haxhihamza	28.12.1996		Kushtrim Shabani	08.02.1997
Shkëlzen Ruçi (ALB)	01.07.1992		Muamer Svraka (BIH)	14.02.1988
Defenders:	DOB		Muhamed Useini (MKD)	21.11.1988
Erlis Frashëri (ALB)	13.05.1988		Forwards:	DOB
Armend Halili	22.06.1997		Tomislav Bušić (CRO)	02.02.1986
Jackson Ferreira Silvério (BRA)	12.04.1991		Bedri Greca (ALB)	23.10.1990
Ylber Kastrati	09.04.1987		Fiton Hajdari	19.09.1991
Edison Kqiku	16.01.1999		Darko Nikač (MNE)	15.09.1990
Oltion Rapa (ALB)	30.09.1989		Sebino Plaku (ALB)	20.05.1985
Franc Veliu (ALB)	11.11.1988		Gerhard Progni (ALB)	06.11.1986
Midfielders:	DOB		Keita Alassane Razak (CIV)	28.09.1996
Keita Lanzeni Aziz (CIV)	28.12.1996		Adenis Shala	23.10.1998
Qendrim Dautaj	26.09.1998			

Klubi Futbollistik Llapi Podujevë

Founded:	1932	
Stadium:	Stadiumi „Zahir Pajaziti", Podujevë (10,000)	
Trainer:	Xhengiz Rexhepi (MKD)	
[01.07.2020]	Tahir Batatina	12.07.1977

Goalkeepers:	DOB		Egzon Krasniqi	27.04.1991
Afrim Ademi	19.05.1989		Behar Maliqi	22.09.1986
Bledar Hajdini	16.06.1995		Blendi Memaj	02.01.1995
Donat Mehmeti	06.07.1999		Albutrint Morina	20.02.1993
Giacomo Nava (ITA)	27.01.1997		Argjend Mustafa	22.10.1993
Defenders:	DOB		Mergim Pefqeli	25.11.1993
Xhelil Abdulla (MKD)	25.09.1991		Arbnor Ramadani	03.06.1994
Florian Daci (ALB)	02.04.1991		Kastriot Selmani	08.07.1999
Benjamin Emini	20.07.1992		Alban Shabani	18.05.2000
Ardian Hoti	14.09.1996		Ersil Ymeri (ALB)	06.07.1994
Nertil Hoxhaj (ALB)	21.05.1997		Mentor Zhdrella	06.10.1990
Senad Hušić (BIH)	12.04.1990		Forwards:	DOB
Bujar Idrizi	11.12.1991		Muhamet Hyseni	06.02.2001
Leutrim Kadriu	01.04.1994		Bekim Maliqi	26.07.2001
Armin Mujkić (BIH)	10.03.1994		Mentor Mazrekaj (ALB)	08.02.1989
Florent Murseli	28.10.1999		Labinot Osmani	15.07.1985
Elvis Prençi (ALB)	26.06.1993		Sebino Plaku (ALB)	20.05.1985
Hajdin Salihu	18.01.2002		Blerand Qitaku	13.12.2000
Midfielders:	DOB		Jasmin Raboshta (ALB)	30.04.1990
Lis Behrami	27.08.2002		Valmir Veliu	04.06.2000
Gentrit Duriqi	22.02.2001		Enis Zabërgja	22.06.1985

Football Club Prishtina

Founded:	1922
Stadium:	Stadiumi "Fadil Vokrri", Prishtina (13,500)

Trainer:	Mirel Josa (ALB)	01.06.1963
[04.09.2019]	Bylbyl Sokoli	19.12.1958
[21.09.2019]	Armend Dallku (ALB)	16.06.1983

Goalkeepers:	DOB
Visar Bekaj	24.05.1997
Eglant Haxho (ALB)	11.11.1988
Alban Muqiqi	10.11.1995
Defenders:	**DOB**
Leonit Abazi (ALB)	05.07.1993
Tun Bardhoku	12.09.1993
Leotrim Bekteshi	21.04.1992
Erdin Dushi	07.10.2002
Ahmet Haliti	01.10.1988
Labinot Ibrahimi	25.06.1986
Armend Thaqi	10.10.1992
Ermal Vitija	28.01.2001
Leonat Vitija	22.08.2000
Midfielders:	**DOB**
Ergyn Ahmeti	21.12.1995

	DOB
Lorik Boshnjaku	07.07.1995
Ardit Hila (ALB)	06.01.1993
Endrit Krasniqi	26.10.1994
Gauthier Mankenda (COD)	20.07.1997
Diar Miftaraj	20.10.1990
Qëndrim Zyba	03.01.2001
Forwards:	**DOB**
Ahmed Januzi (ALB)	08.07.1988
John Otto John (NGA)	25.01.1998
Meriton Korenica	15.12.1996
Max Rugova	17.02.2000
Trimror Selimi	06.09.2000
Alban Shillova	13.08.1992
Kreshnik Uka	07.01.1995
Dhurim Zhuri	20.09.2002

Klubi Futbollistik Trepça'89 Mitrovicë

Founded:	1992
Stadium:	Stadiumi "Riza Lushta", Mitrovicë (12,000)

Trainer:	Shpëtim Idrizi	12.11.1981

Goalkeepers:	DOB
Arben Beqiri	02.06.1988
Ardit Hyseni	28.12.1999
Auron Loxha	15.11.2001
Januz Miftari	30.10.2003
Erkan Spahija (ALB)	03.04.1994
Defenders:	**DOB**
Richard Asare (GHA)	08.03.1995
Milot Kamberi	05.08.1997
Albert Kaqiku	21.01.1995
Ylber Maloku	04.01.1996
Ergis Mersini (ALB)	30.09.1989
Edon Pasoma	21.08.1992
Arbër Pira	09.02.1995
Albion Pllana	20.08.2000
Bujar Pllana	29.10.2001
Robert Rrahmani	28.01.2001
Rron Statovci	18.01.1997
Walter Ventura (BRA)	09.02.1990

Midfielders:	DOB
Zeki Ademi	
Berat Ahmeti	26.01.1995
Milot Avdyli	28.07.2002
Taulant Avdyli	22.10.1998
Tarik Cmajcanin (SRB)	18.06.1994
Valon Dedia	
Engjëll Hoti (GER)	26.02.1997
Muharrem Jashari	21.02.1998
Joe Jeanjacques (FRA)	
Gzim Rusi	29.11.1994
Lassine Traoré (MLI)	06.10.2000
Forwards:	**DOB**
Ardian Berisha (SWE)	07.05.1998
Djibril Diawara (MLI)	07.07.1999
Leart Emini	24.11.1992
Arb Manaj	23.07.1998
Arbnor Muja	29.11.1998
Ardian Muja	09.12.1997

Klubi Futbollistik Vushtrria Vučitrn

Founded:	1922
Stadium:	Stadiumi „Ferki Aliu", Vushtrri (6,000)

Trainer:	Bekim Shotani	06.12.1974
[08.09.2019]	Antonio Toma (ITA)	19.08.1963

Goalkeepers:	DOB
Erdin Bajrami (ALB)	06.10.1998
Fabio Gjonikaj (ALB)	25.05.1995
Marly Koubassanath (CGO)	10.04.1999
Enes Manxholli	14.07.1986
Petrit Tahiri	06.02.1993
Defenders:	**DOB**
Liridon Ahmeti	16.07.1985
Etrit Halimi	06.05.1994
Muhamet Haradinaj	10.06.1995
Nertil Hoxhaj (ALB)	21.05.1997
Bler Istrefi	20.05.1999
Ilir Izmaku	17.05.1983
Kadri Kodrolli	02.04.2000
Klevis Lushaku (ALB)	04.10.2000
Adnard Mehmeti	
Clinton Nnorom (GHA)	16.09.1997
Kujtim Pantina	
Midfielders:	**DOB**
Dren Ahmeti	08.06.1998
Valmir Azemi	24.04.1998
Besfort Dervishaj	24.09.1998
Djellon Dragusha	
Kushtrim Fazliu	16.09.2001

	DOB
Qendrim Feka	25.01.1999
Alush Gavazaj	24.03.1995
Ian Augusto de Almeida Ribeiro (BRA)	29.11.1995
Çlirim Imeri	04.01.2000
Forwards:	**DOB**
Daut Maxhuni	09.12.1990
Ledion Muçaj (ALB)	04.09.1992
Joseph Okonkwo	05.04.2000
Evan Salines (FRA)	26.03.1998
Bashkim Shala	05.04.1991
Dior Zabërgja	
Rinor Karaqa	
Naoufal Boumina (BEL)	15.11.1993
Sekou Doumbia	27.11.1999
Drilon Fazliu	17.11.2000
Qendrim Gashi	27.03.1995
Eri Lamçja (ALB)	10.03.1994
Matheus Henrique de Paula (BRA)	06.04.1995
Jasmin Raboshta (ALB)	30.04.1990
Bismark Charles Sie (GHA)	26.05.2001
Ygor Vinicius de Souza (BRA)	31.05.1992
Baton Zabergja	18.04.2001
Bajram Zuqaku	26.07.1989

SECOND LEVEL
First Football of Kosovo - Liga e Parë 2019/2020

1.	KF Besa Pejë Peć (*Promoted*)	20	12	4	4	29	-	11	40
2.	KF Arbëria Lipljan (*Promoted*)	20	10	6	4	34	-	26	36
3.	KF Liria Prizren	20	8	7	5	23	-	15	31
4.	KF Istogu	20	8	7	5	22	-	18	31
5.	KF Drenasi Glogovac	20	8	6	6	25	-	18	30
6.	KF 2 Korriku Prishtina	20	9	3	8	31	-	26	30
7.	KF UV Malisheva	20	9	3	8	23	-	18	30
8.	KF Dardana Kamenicë	20	8	6	6	22	-	23	30
9.	KF Onix-Banjë	20	8	5	7	25	-	16	29
10.	KF KEK-u Obilić	20	7	7	6	23	-	19	28
11.	KF Trepça Mitrovicë	20	6	5	9	25	-	35	23
12.	KF Ulpiana Lipljan	20	5	7	8	22	-	26	22
13.	KF Vllaznia Požaranje	20	6	3	11	27	-	42	21
14.	KF Ramiz Sadiku Prishtina	20	5	5	10	22	-	29	20
15.	KF Vitia	20	3	8	9	20	-	33	17
16.	KF Vëllaznimi Gjakovë	20	3	8	9	20	-	38	17

Please note: the league was suspended on 09.03.2020 due to Covid-19 pandemic. On 27.05.2020, the league was cancelled with no teams relegated.

NATIONAL TEAM

INTERNATIONAL MATCHES
(16.07.2019 – 15.07.2020)

07.09.2019	Prishtina	Kosovo - Czech Republic	2-1(1-1)	(ECQ)
10.09.2019	Southampton	England - Kosovo	5-3(5-1)	(ECQ)
10.10.2019	Prishtina	Kosovo - Gibraltar	1-0(0-0)	(F)
14.10.2019	Prishtina	Kosovo - Montenegro	2-0(2-0)	(ECQ)
14.11.2019	Plzeň	Czech Republic - Kosovo	2-1(0-0)	(ECQ)
17.11.2019	Prishtina	Kosovo - England	0-4(0-1)	(ECQ)
12.01.2020	Doha	Sweden - Kosovo	1-0(0-0)	(F)

07.09.2019   KOSOVO - CZECH REPUBLIC   **2-1(1-1)**   16th EC. Qualifiers
Stadiumi „Fadil Vokrri", Prishtina; Referee: Danny Desmond Makkelie (Netherlands); Attendance: 12,678
KVX: Arijanet Anan Muriqi, Fidan Aliti, Amir Kadri Rrahmani (Cap), Florent Hadergjonaj, Mërgim Vojvoda, Idriz Voca, Elbasan Rashani (51.Valon Berisha), Besar Halimi (87 Anel Rashkaj), Bersant Celina, Vedat Muriqi, Edon Zhegrova (56.Florent Muslija). Trainer: Bernard Challandes (Switzerland).
Goals: Vedat Muriqi (20), Mërgim Vojvoda (66).

10.09.2019   ENGLAND - KOSOVO   **5-3(5-1)**   16th EC. Qualifiers
St. Mary's Stadium, Southampton; Referee: Felix Zwayer (Germany); Attendance: 30,155
KVX: Arijanet Anan Muriqi, Fidan Aliti, Amir Kadri Rrahmani (Cap), Florent Hadergjonaj, Mërgim Vojvoda, Idriz Voca (59.Anel Rashkaj), Valon Berisha (85.Florent Hasani), Besar Halimi, Bersant Celina, Florent Muslija (46.Leart Paqarada), Vedat Muriqi. Trainer: Bernard Challandes (Switzerland).
Goals: Valon Berisha (1, 49), Vedat Muriqi (55 penalty).

10.10.2019   KOSOVO - GIBRALTAR   **1-0(0-0)**   Friendly International
Stadiumi „Fadil Vokrri", Prishtina; Referee: Junxhin Xhaja (Albania); Attendance: 12,142
KVX: Samir Ujkani (Cap), Benjamin Kololli (46.Leart Paqarada), Arbenit Xhemajli, Ibrahim Dreshaj, Florent Hadergjonaj, Anel Rashkaj, Valon Berisha (63.Idriz Voca), Bernard Berisha (46.Elbasan Rashani), Florent Muslija (46.Florent Hasani), Edon Zhegrova (46.Lirim Kastrati), Atdhe Nuhiu. Trainer: Bernard Challandes (Switzerland).
Goal: Florent Hasani (69).

14.10.2019   KOSOVO - MONTENEGRO   **2-0(2-0)**   16th EC. Qualifiers
Stadiumi „Fadil Vokrri", Prishtina; Referee: Artur Manuel Soares Dias (Portugal); Attendance: 12,494
KVX: Arijanet Anan Muriqi, Fidan Aliti, Amir Kadri Rrahmani (Cap), Florent Hadergjonaj, Mërgim Vojvoda (88.Edon Zhegrova), Herolind Shala (82.Anel Rashkaj), Valon Berisha, Bersant Celina (90+2.Florent Hasani), Benjamin Kololli, Milot Rashica, Vedat Muriqi. Trainer: Bernard Challandes (Switzerland).
Goals: Amir Kadri Rrahmani (10), Vedat Muriqi (35).

14.11.2019   CZECH REPUBLIC - KOSOVO   **2-1(0-0)**   16th EC. Qualifiers
Štruncovy sady Stadion, Plzeň; Referee: Gianluca Rocchi (Italy); Attendance: 10,986
KVX: Arijanet Anan Muriqi, Fidan Aliti, Amir Kadri Rrahmani (Cap), Florent Hadergjonaj (77.Edon Zhegrova), Mërgim Vojvoda, Anel Rashkaj (46.Besar Halimi), Valon Berisha, Bersant Celina (85.Elbasan Rashani), Benjamin Kololli, Milot Rashica, Atdhe Nuhiu. Trainer: Bernard Challandes (Switzerland).
Goal: Atdhe Nuhiu (50).

17.11.2019   KOSOVO - ENGLAND   **0-4(0-1)**   16th EC. Qualifiers
Stadiumi "Fadil Vokrri", Prishtina; Referee: Paweł Gil (Poland); Attendance: 12,326
KVX: Arijanet Anan Muriqi, Fidan Aliti, Amir Kadri Rrahmani (Cap), Florent Hadergjonaj (73.Edon Zhegrova), Mërgim Vojvoda, Ibrahim Dreshaj, Valon Berisha (65.Besar Halimi), Bersant Celina, Benjamin Kololli, Milot Rashica, Atdhe Nuhiu (82.Elbasan Rashani). Trainer: Bernard Challandes (Switzerland).

12.01.2020   SWEDEN - KOSOVO   **1-0(0-0)**   Friendly International
"Hamad bin Khalifa" Stadium, Doha (Qatar); Referee: Mohammed Ahmed Al Shammari (Qatar); Attendance: 75
KVX: Visar Bekaj, Fidan Aliti (Cap), Armend Thaqi, Leotrim Bekteshi (46.Lapidar Lladrovci), Herolind Shala (46.Valmir Veliu), Florian Loshaj (32.Ismet Lushaku; 64.Rron Broja), Flamur Kastrati (46.Jetmir Topalli), Ylldren Ibrahimaj (46.Blendi Baftiu), Lirim Kastrati II (46.Anel Rashkaj), Zymer Bytyqi (46.Arbër Hoxha), Elbasan Rashani (84.Arb Manaj). Trainer: Bernard Challandes (Switzerland).

NATIONAL TEAM PLAYERS
(16.07.2019 – 15.07.2020)

Name	DOB	Caps	Goals	2019/2020:	*Club*
Goalkeepers					
Visar BEKAJ	24.05.1997	2	0	2020:	*FC Prishtina*
Arijanet Anan MURIQI	07.11.1998	10	0	2019:	*Nottingham Forest FC (ENG)*
Samir UJKANI	05.07.1988	26	0	2019:	*Torino FC (ITA)*
Defenders					
Fidan ALITI	03.10.1993	21	0	2019/2020:	*Kalmar FF (SWE)*
Leotrim BEKTESHI	21.04.1992	1	0	2020:	*FC Prishtina*
Ibrahim DRESHAJ	24.01.1997	2	0	2019:	*SC Heerenveen (NED)*
Florent HADERGJONAJ	31.07.1994	7	0	2019:	*Huddersfield Town FC (ENG)*
Lirim KASTRATI	16.01.1999	3	0	2019:	*NK Lokomotiva Zagreb (CRO)*
Lapidar LLADROVCI	15.12.1990	1	0	2020:	*KF Feronikeli Glogovac*
Leart PAQARADA	10.08.1994	19	1	2019:	*SV Sandhausen (GER)*
Amir Kadri RRAHMANI	24.02.1994	29	5	2019:	*Hellas Verona FC (ITA)*
Armend THAQI	10.10.1992	2	0	2020:	*FC Prishtina*
Mërgim VOJVODA	01.02.1995	24	1	2019:	*R Standard Liège (BEL)*
Arbenit XHEMAJLI	23.04.1998	1	0	2019:	*Neuchâtel Xamax FCS (SUI)*
Midfielders					
Blendi BAFTIU	17.02.1998	1	0	2020:	*KF Ballkani Suva Reka*
Bernard BERISHA	21.10.1991	15	0	2019:	*FK Akhmat Grozny (RUS)*
Valon BERISHA	07.02.1993	20	3	2019:	*SS Lazio Roma (ITA)*
Rron BROJA	09.04.1996	1	0	2020:	*FK Partizani Tiranë (ALB)*
Zymer BYTYQI	11.09.1996	2	0	2020:	*Viking FK Stavanger (NOR)*
Bersant CELINA	09.09.1996	20	2	2019/2020:	*Swansea City AFC (WAL)*
Besar HALIMI	12.12.1994	23	1	2019:	*SV Sandhausen (GER)*
Florent HASANI	30.03.1997	3	1	2019:	*Diósgyőri VTK (HUN)*
Ylldren IBRAHIMAJ	24.12.1995	1	0	2019/2020:	*Viking FK Stavanger (NOR)*
Benjamin KOLOLLI	15.05.1992	16	3	2019:	*FC Zürich (SUI)*
Florian LOSHAJ	13.08.1996	1	0	2020:	*FC Politehnica Iaşi (ROU)*
Ismet LUSHAKU	22.09.2000	1	0	2020:	*AFC Eskilstuna (SWE)*
Florent MUSLIJA	06.07.1998	3	0	2019:	*SV Hannover 96 (GER)*
Milot RASHICA	28.06.1996	27	4	2019:	*SV Werder Bremen (GER)*
Anel RASHKAJ	19.08.1989	10	0	2019: / 01.01.2020->	*AFC Eskilstuna (SWE)* / *Unattached*
Herolind SHALA	02.01.1992	17	0	2019/2020:	*Vålerenga Fotball Oslo (NOR)*
Idriz VOCA	15.05.1997	10	0	2019:	*FC Luzern (SUI)*
Valmir VELIU	04.06.2000	1	0	2020:	*KF Llapi Podujevë*
Edon ZHEGROVA	31.03.1999	17	2	2019:	*FC Basel (SUI)*
Forwards					
Arbër HOXHA	06.10.1998	1	0	2020:	*KF Ballkani Suva Reka*
Flamur KASTRATI	14.11.1991	5	0	2020:	*Kristiansund BK (NOR)*
Lirim KASTRATI (II)	02.02.1999	3	0	2020:	*Bologna FC 1909 (ITA)*
Arb MANAJ	01.01.1997	1	0	2020:	*KF Trepça'89 Mitrovicë*
Vedat MURIQI	24.04.1994	23	8	2019:	*Fenerbahèe SK İstanbul (TUR)*
Atdhe NUHIU	29.07.1989	17	4	2019:	*Sheffield Wednesday FC (ENG)*
Elbasan RASHANI	09.05.1993	12	4	2019/2020:	*Odds BK Skien (NOR)*
Jetmir TOPALLI	07.02.1998	1	0	2020:	*KF Ballkani Suva Reka*
National team coach					
Bernard CHALLANDES (Switzerland) [from 02.03.2018]	26.07.1951	20 M; 11 W; 5 D; 4 L; 37-21			

LATVIA

The Country:
Latvijas Republika (Republic of Latvia)
Capital: Rīga
Surface: 64,589 km²
Inhabitants: 1,904,600 [2020]
Time: UTC+2

The FA:
Latvijas Futbola federācija
Olympic Sports Centre, Grostonas Street 6b, 1013 Rīga
Tel: +371 6729 2988
Foundation date: 19.06.1921
Member of FIFA since: 1922
Member of UEFA since: 1992
Website: www.lff.lv

NATIONAL TEAM RECORDS

RECORDS

First international match:	24.09.1922, Rīga:	Latvia – Estonia 1-1
Most international caps:	Vitālijs Astafjevs	- 167 caps (1992-2010)
Most international goals:	Māris Verpakovskis	- 29 goals / 104 caps (1999-2014)

UEFA EUROPEAN CHAMPIONSHIP		FIFA WORLD CUP		OLYMPIC TOURNAMENTS	
1960	-	1930	Did not enter	1908	-
1964	-	1934	Did not enter	1912	-
1968	-	1938	*Entry not accepted by FIFA*	1920	-
1972	-	1950	-	1924	-
1976	-	1954	-	1928	1/8 - Finals
1980	-	1958	-	1936	Did not enter
1984	-	1962	-	1948	-
1988	-	1966	-	1952	-
1992	-	1970	-	1956	-
1996	Qualifiers	1974	-	1960	-
2000	Qualifiers	1978	-	1964	-
2004	Final Tournament (Group Stage)	1982	-	1968	-
2008	Qualifiers	1986	-	1972	-
2012	Qualifiers	1990	-	1976	-
2016	Qualifiers	1994	Qualifiers	1980	-
2020	Qualifiers	1998	Qualifiers	1984	-
		2002	Qualifiers	1988	-
		2006	Qualifiers	1992	-
		2010	Qualifiers	1996	Qualifiers
		2014	Qualifiers	2000	Qualifiers
		2018	Qualifiers	2004	Qualifiers
				2008	Qualifiers
				2012	Qualifiers
				2016	Qualifiers

UEFA NATIONS LEAGUE

2018/2019 – League D

FIFA CONFEDERATIONS CUP 1992-2017

None

LATVIAN CLUB HONOURS IN EUROPEAN CLUB COMPETITIONS:

European Champion Clubs' Cup (1956-1992) / UEFA Champions League (1993-2020)
None

Fairs Cup (1858-1971) / UEFA Cup (1972-2009) / UEFA Europa League (2010-2020)
None

UEFA Super Cup (1972-2019)
None

European Cup Winners' Cup 1961-1999*
None

defunct competition

NATIONAL COMPETITIONS
TABLE OF HONOURS

LATVIAN SSR (SOVIET ERA) CHAMPIONS

1941	*Championship Cancelled*	1959	RER Rīga	1975	VEF Rīga		
1942/1944	*Championship Interrupted*	1960	ASK Rīga	1976	Enerģija Rīga		
1945	FK Dinamo Rīga	1961	ASK Rīga	1977	Enerģija Rīga		
1946	Daugava Liepāja	1962	ASK Rīga	1978	Ķīmiķis Daugavpils		
1947	Daugava Liepāja	1963	ASK Rīga	1979	Elektrons Rīga		
1948	Žmiļova Komanda	1964	ASK Rīga	1980	Ķīmiķis Daugavpils		
1949	Sarkanais Metalurgs Liepāja	1965	ASK Rīga	1981	Elektrons Rīga		
1950	AVN Rīga	1966	ESR Rīga	1982	Elektrons Rīga		
1951	Sarkanais Metalurgs Liepāja	1967	ESR Rīga	1983	VEF Rīga		
1952	AVN Rīga	1968	Starts Brocēni	1984	Torpedo Rīga		
1953	Sarkanais Metalurgs Liepāja	1969	FK Venta Ventspils	1985	FK Alfa		
1954	Sarkanais Metalurgs Liepāja	1970	VEF Rīga	1986	Torpedo Rīga		
1955	Darba Rezerves Rīga	1971	VEF Rīga	1987	Torpedo Rīga		
1956	Sarkanais Metalurgs Liepāja	1972	FK Jūrnieks	1988	RAF Jelgava		
1957	Sarkanais Metalurgs Liepāja	1973	VEF Rīga	1989	RAF Jelgava		
1958	Sarkanais Metalurgs Liepāja	1974	VEF Rīga	1990	Gauja Valmiera		

	CHAMPIONS*	CUP WINNERS	BEST GOALSCORERS	
1910	RV Union Rīga	-	-	
1911	Britannia FC Rīga	-	-	
1912	RV Union Rīga	-	-	
1913	SV Kaiserwald Rīga	-	-	
1914	Britannia FC Rīga	-	-	
1915	Britannia FC Rīga	-	-	
	-------------------------------	-------------------------------	---	
1922	Kaiserwald Rīga	-	-	
1923	Kaiserwald Rīga	-	-	
1924	RFK Rīga	-	-	
1925	RFK Rīga	-	-	
1926	RFK Rīga	-	-	
1927	Olimpia Liepaja	-	-	
1928	Olimpia Liepaja	-	-	
1929	Olimpia Liepaja	-	-	
1930	RFK Rīga	-	-	
1931	RFK Rīga	-	-	
1932	ASK Rīga	-	-	
1933	Olimpia Liepaja	-	-	
1934	RFK Rīga	-	-	
1935	RFK Rīga	-	-	
1936	Olimpia Liepaja	-	-	
1937	*No competition*	RFK Rīga	-	
1938	Olimpia Liepaja	Rīgas Vilki	-	
1939	Olimpia Liepaja	RFK Rīga	-	
1940	RFK Rīga	*No competition*	-	
	-------------------------------	-------------------------------	---	
1991	Skonto FC Rīga	Celtnieks Daugavpils	Vjačeslavs Ževnerovičs (Celtnieks Daugavpils)	27
1992	Skonto FC Rīga	Skonto FC Rīga	Vjačeslavs Ževnerovičs (VEF Riga)	19
1993	Skonto FC Rīga	RAF Jelgava	Aleksandrs Jeļisejevs (Skonto FC Rīga)	20
1994	Skonto FC Rīga	Olimpija Rīga	Vladimirs Babičevs (Skonto FC Rīga)	14
1995	Skonto FC Rīga	Skonto FC Rīga	Vitālijs Astafjevs (Skonto FC Rīga)	19
1996	Skonto FC Rīga	RAF Jelgava	Mihails Miholaps (FK Daugava Rīga)	33
1997	Skonto FC Rīga	Skonto FC Rīga	David Chaladze (GEO, Skonto FC Rīga)	25
1998	Skonto FC Rīga	Skonto FC Rīga	Viktors Dobrecovs (FK Liepājas Metalurgs)	23
1999	Skonto FC Rīga	FK Rīga	Viktors Dobrecovs (FK Liepājas Metalurgs)	22
2000	Skonto FC Rīga	Skonto FC Rīga	Vladimirs Koļesņičenko (Skonto FC Rīga)	17
2001	Skonto FC Rīga	Skonto FC Rīga	Mihails Miholaps (Skonto FC Rīga)	24
2002	Skonto FC Rīga	Skonto FC Rīga	Mihails Miholaps (Skonto FC Rīga)	23
2003	Skonto FC Rīga	FK Ventspils	Viktors Dobrecovs (FK Liepājas Metalurgs)	36
2004	Skonto FC Rīga	FK Ventspils	Aleksandr Katasonov (RUS, FK Liepājas Metalurgs)	21
2005	FK Liepājas Metalurgs	FK Ventspils	Viktors Dobrecovs (FK Liepājas Metalurgs) Igors Sļesarčuks (FK Venta/FK Ventspils)	18
2006	FK Ventspils	FK Liepājas Metalurgs	Mihails Miholaps (Skonto FC Rīga)	15
2007	FK Ventspils	FK Ventspils	Vits Rimkus (FK Ventspils)	20
2008	FK Ventspils	FK Daugava Daugavpils	Vits Rimkus (FK Ventspils)	14
2009	FK Liepājas Metalurgs	*No competition*	Kristaps Grebis (FK Liepājas Metalurgs)	30
2010	Skonto FC Rīga	FK Jelgava	Deniss Rakeļs (FK Liepājas Metalurgs) Nathan Júnior Soares de Carvalho (BRA, Skonto FC Rīga)	18
2011	FK Ventspils	FK Ventspils	Nathan Júnior Soares de Carvalho (BRA, Skonto FC Rīga)	22
2012	FC Daugava Daugavpils	Skonto FC Rīga	Mamuka Ghonghadze	18

Yearbook of European Football-421

			(GEO, FC Daugava Daugavpils)	
2013	FK Ventspils	FK Ventspils	Artūrs Karašausks (Skonto FC Rīga)	16
			Andrejs Kovaļovs (FC Daugava Daugavpils)	
2014	FK Ventspils	FK Jelgava	Vladislavs Gutkovskis (Skonto FC Rīga)	28
2015	FK Liepāja	FK Jelgava	Dāvis Ikaunieks (FK Liepaja)	15
2016	JPFS/FK Spartaks Jūrmala	FK Jelgava	Ģirts Karlsons (FK Ventspils)	17
		FK Ventspils (2016/2017)		
2017	JPFS/FK Spartaks Jūrmala	FK Liepāja	Yevgeniy Kozlov (RUS, JPFS/FK Spartaks Jūrmala)	
			Artūrs Karašausks (FK Liepāja)	12
2018	Rīga FC	Rīga FC	Darko Lemajić (SRB, Rīga FC)	15
2019	Rīga FC	FK Rīgas Futbola Skola	Darko Lemajić	
			(SRB, Rīga FC / FK Rīgas Futbola Skola)	15

*Please note: Champions of the Riga Football League (1910-1915) and Latvian Championship (1922–1940 and since 1991);
RAF Jelgava was called later FK Jelgava.

NATIONAL CHAMPIONSHIP
Virsliga 2019
(09.03.2019 – 09.11.2019)

Results

Round 1 [09-10.03.2019]
FK Jelgava - Rīga FC 0-1(0-1)
Daugavpils - FS Metta/LU 1-0(0-0)
FK Ventspils - Spartaks Jūrmala 2-1(1-0)
FK Rīgas F. S. - FK Liepāja 2-0(0-0)

Round 2 [15-17.03.2019]
FS Metta/LU - Rīga FC 1-2(1-1)
Spartaks Jūrmala - FK Rīgas F. S. 2-3(1-2)
FK Jelgava - FK Ventspils 2-1(1-0)
Valmiera Glass - Daugavpils 2-0(1-0)

Round 3 [30-31.03.2019]
FK Rīgas F. S. - FK Jelgava 2-1(1-0)
FK Liepāja - Spartaks Jūrmala 0-1(0-0)
Rīga FC - Valmiera Glass 0-1(0-1)
FK Ventspils - FS Metta/LU 2-0(1-0)

Round 4 [05-06.04.2019]
FK Jelgava - FK Liepāja 1-2(0-1)
FS Metta/LU - FK Rīgas F. S. 1-2(0-1)
Daugavpils - Rīga FC 0-1(0-1)
Valmiera Glass - FK Ventspils 1-1(1-0)

Round 5 [09-10.04.2019]
Spartaks Jūrmala - FK Jelgava 1-2(0-2)
FK Liepāja - FS Metta/LU 2-1(1-0)
FK Ventspils - Daugavpils 1-1(1-1)
Valmiera Glass - FK Rīgas F. S. 0-2(0-2)

Round 6 [14-15.04.2019]
FS Metta/LU - Spartaks Jūrmala 3-0(2-0)
Rīga FC - FK Ventspils 2-0(1-0)
Valmiera Glass - FK Liepāja 1-0(1-0)
Daugavpils - FK Rīgas F. S. 0-1(0-1)

Round 7 [19-20.04.2019]
Spartaks Jūrmala - Valmiera Glass 2-0(1-0)
FK Liepāja - Daugavpils 2-3(1-0)
FK Jelgava - FS Metta/LU 1-2(0-1)
FK Rīgas F. S. - Rīga FC 3-1(1-0)

Round 8 [23-24.04.2019]
Daugavpils - Spartaks Jūrmala 4-1(4-1)
Valmiera Glass - FK Jelgava 0-0
FK Ventspils - FK Rīgas F. S. 2-0(1-0)
Rīga FC - FK Liepāja 1-0(1-0)

Round 9 [27-28.04.2019]
FS Metta/LU - Valmiera Glass 1-4(0-3)
FK Jelgava - Daugavpils 1-0(0-0)
Spartaks Jūrmala - Rīga FC 0-4(0-3)
FK Ventspils - FK Liepāja 1-1(0-1)

Round 10 [03-04.05.2019]
FS Metta/LU - Daugavpils 0-1(0-0)
Rīga FC - FK Jelgava 1-1(1-1)
Spartaks Jūrmala - FK Ventspils 4-3(1-1)
FK Liepāja - FK Rīgas F. S. 0-0

Round 11 [07-08.05.2019]
Daugavpils - Valmiera Glass 1-0(0-0)
Rīga FC - FS Metta/LU 2-1(0-0)
FK Rīgas F. S. - Spartaks Jūrmala 0-0
FK Ventspils - FK Jelgava 1-1(1-1)

Round 12 [12-13.05.2019]
FK Jelgava - FK Rīgas F. S. 0-0
Spartaks Jūrmala - FK Liepāja 1-0(0-0)
FS Metta/LU - FK Ventspils 2-1(0-0)
Valmiera Glass - Rīga FC 1-0(0-0)

Round 13 [17-18.05.2019]
FK Rīgas F. S. - FS Metta/LU 2-2(0-1)
FK Liepāja - FK Jelgava 1-0(0-0)
Daugavpils - Rīga FC 0-3(0-2)
FK Ventspils - Valmiera Glass 2-2(0-0)

Round 14 [21-22.05.2019]
FK Jelgava - Spartaks Jūrmala 0-3(0-1)
FS Metta/LU - FK Liepāja 1-2(0-2)
Daugavpils - FK Ventspils 0-3(0-1)
FK Rīgas F. S. - Valmiera Glass 0-1(0-1)

Round 15 [25-27.05.2019]
Spartaks Jūrmala - FS Metta/LU 1-0(1-0)
FK Liepāja - Valmiera Glass 1-0(0-0)
FK Ventspils - Rīga FC 1-0(0-0)
FK Rīgas F. S. - Daugavpils 3-2(0-1)

Round 16 [31.05.-01.06.2019]
Valmiera Glass - Spartaks Jūrmala 1-2(0-0)
FS Metta/LU - FK Jelgava 2-1(1-0)
Daugavpils - FK Liepāja 1-0(0-0)
Rīga FC - FK Rīgas F. S. 2-0(0-0)

Round 17 [15-16.06.2019]
FK Jelgava - Valmiera Glass 0-1(0-1)
FK Rīgas F. S. - FK Ventspils 4-1(1-1)
FK Liepāja - Rīga FC 1-2(1-1)
Spartaks Jūrmala - Daugavpils 3-0(0-0)

Round 18 [20-21.06.2019]
FK Liepāja - FK Ventspils 4-0(3-0)
Daugavpils - FK Jelgava 0-2(0-2)
Rīga FC - Spartaks Jūrmala 6-1(3-0)
Valmiera Glass - FS Metta/LU 0-2(0-0)

Round 19 [25-26.06.2019]
FK Ventspils - Spartaks Jūrmala 2-2(2-1)
FK Rīgas F. S. - FK Liepāja 1-2(1-1)
Daugavpils - FS Metta/LU 0-0
Rīga FC - FK Jelgava 0-1(0-0)

Round 20 [29-30.06.2019]
Spartaks Jūrmala - FK Rīgas F. S. 1-0(0-0)
Valmiera Glass - Daugavpils 1-1(0-1)
FS Metta/LU - Rīga FC 0-4(0-1)
FK Jelgava - FK Ventspils 1-2(0-1)

Round 21 [04-06.07.2019]
Rīga FC - Valmiera Glass 0-0
FK Liepāja - Spartaks Jūrmala 2-2(1-2)
FK Ventspils - FS Metta/LU 2-1(1-0)
FK Rīgas F. S. - FK Jelgava 2-0(1-0)

Round 22 [20-21.07.2019]
Daugavpils - Rīga FC 0-4(0-2)
FS Metta/LU - FK Rīgas F. S. 1-1(0-0)
Valmiera Glass - FK Ventspils 2-2(1-1)
FK Jelgava - FK Liepāja 0-0

Round 23 [27-28.07.2019]
Spartaks Jūrmala - FK Jelgava 1-2(0-1)
FS Metta/LU - FK Liepāja 2-3(1-1)
FK Ventspils - Daugavpils 3-0(1-0)
FK Rīgas F. S. - Valmiera Glass 1-0(1-0)

Round 24 [03-05.08.2019]
FS Metta/LU - Spartaks Jūrmala 1-1(0-0)
Valmiera Glass - FK Liepāja 2-1(1-0)
Daugavpils - FK Rīgas F. S. 0-1(0-0)
Rīga FC - FK Ventspils 0-0 [18.09.]

Round 25 [10-11.08.2019]
Spartaks Jūrmala - Valmiera Glass 3-0(1-0)
FK Jelgava - FS Metta/LU 1-0(1-0)
FK Liepāja - Daugavpils 1-2(0-2)
FK Rīgas F. S. - Rīga FC 1-2(1-1)

Round 26 [17-18.08.2019]
Valmiera Glass - FK Jelgava 3-1(1-1)
Daugavpils - Spartaks Jūrmala 2-3(0-2)
FK Ventspils - FK Rīgas F. S. 3-0(1-0)
Rīga FC - FK Liepāja 1-0(0-0)

Round 27 [24-25.08.2019]
FK Liepāja - FK Ventspils 1-2(0-1)
FK Jelgava - Daugavpils 2-2(1-2)
Spartaks Jūrmala - Rīga FC 2-4(1-3)
FS Metta/LU - Valmiera Glass 0-0

Round 28 [30-31.08.2019]
FS Metta/LU - Daugavpils 1-0(0-0)
FK Liepāja - FK Rīgas F. S. 3-3(3-1)
Spartaks Jūrmala - FK Ventspils 0-1(0-0)
FK Jelgava - Rīga FC 0-0 [23.10.]

Round 29 [14-15.09.2019]
FK Ventspils - FK Jelgava 1-1(1-0)
Daugavpils - Valmiera Glass 2-2(1-1)
Rīga FC - FS Metta/LU 5-0(1-0)
FK Rīgas F. S. - Spartaks Jūrmala 6-0(4-0)

Round 30 [21-22.09.2019]
FK Jelgava - FK Rīgas F. S. 1-1(1-0)
Spartaks Jūrmala - FK Liepāja 4-2(1-1)
FS Metta/LU - FK Ventspils 3-3(2-0)
Valmiera Glass - Rīga FC 0-1(0-1)

Round 31 [29-30.09.2019]
FK Ventspils - Valmiera Glass 0-2(0-0)
FK Liepāja - FK Jelgava 3-1(0-0)
Rīga FC - Daugavpils 2-0(0-0)
FK Rīgas F. S. - FS Metta/LU 6-1(4-1)

Round 32 [05.10.2019]
FK Liepāja - FS Metta/LU 2-1(2-0)
FK Jelgava - Spartaks Jūrmala 5-2(2-0)
Daugavpils - FK Ventspils 1-1(1-1)
Valmiera Glass - FK Rīgas F. S. 1-3(0-1)

Round 33 [19-20.10.2019]
FK Ventspils - Rīga FC 2-1(0-1)
FK Rīgas F. S. - Daugavpils 2-0(1-0)
Spartaks Jūrmala - FS Metta/LU 2-2(0-1)
FK Liepāja - Valmiera Glass 2-3(1-1)

Round 34 [27-30.10.2019]
Daugavpils - FK Liepāja 1-0(0-0)
Valmiera Glass - Spartaks Jūrmala 3-0(1-0)
FS Metta/LU - FK Jelgava 0-3(0-3)
Rīga FC - FK Rīgas F. S. 1-1(0-1)

Round 35 [03.11.2019]
FK Liepāja - Rīga FC 2-2(0-0)
FK Jelgava - Valmiera Glass 0-0
FK Rīgas F. S. - FK Ventspils 2-1(1-1)
Spartaks Jūrmala - Daugavpils 2-0(0-0)

Round 36 [09.11.2019]
Daugavpils - FK Jelgava 2-2(1-1)
Rīga FC - Spartaks Jūrmala 4-1(1-0)
Valmiera Glass - FS Metta/LU 3-3(3-2)
FK Ventspils - FK Liepāja 0-1(0-0)

Final Standings

						Total					Home						Away			
1.	**Rīga FC**	32	20	6	6	59	-	21	66	10	4	2	31	-	7	10	2	4	28	-	14
2.	FK Rīgas Futbola Skola	32	17	8	7	55	-	32	59	11	2	3	37	-	14	6	6	4	18	-	18
3.	FK Ventspils	32	12	11	9	47	-	43	47	8	7	1	27	-	14	4	4	8	20	-	29
4.	Valmiera Glass ViA FK	32	12	10	10	37	-	34	46	7	4	5	21	-	17	5	6	5	16	-	17
5.	JPFS/FK Spartaks Jūrmala	32	13	5	14	49	-	64	44	9	1	6	29	-	23	4	4	8	20	-	41
6.	FK Liepāja	32	11	6	15	41	-	43	39	6	4	6	27	-	23	5	2	9	14	-	20
7.	FK Jelgava	32	9	11	12	34	-	37	38	4	6	6	15	-	17	5	5	6	19	-	20
8.	BFC Daugavpils	32	8	7	17	27	-	50	31	5	4	7	15	-	20	3	3	10	12	-	30
9.	FS Metta/Latvijas Universitāte Rīga	32	6	8	18	35	-	60	26	4	4	8	19	-	28	2	4	10	16	-	32
	(Relegation play-offs)																				

Top goalscorers:

15	**Darko Lemajić (SRB)**	*Rīga FC / FK Rīgas Futbola Skola*
11	Oluwatosin Aiyegun (NGA)	*FK Ventspils*
11	Nemanja Belaković (SRB)	*JPFS/FK Spartaks Jūrmala*
10	Tamirlan Dzhamalutdinov (RUS)	*FS Metta/Latvijas Universitāte Rīga*

Relegation Play-offs [13-16.11.2019]

FS Metta/Latvijas Universitāte Rīga - SK Super Nova Olaine   0-0   3-1

NATIONAL CUP
Latvijas Kauss 2019

1/8-Finals [13-17.07.2019]

JDFS Alberts Rīga - FC Caramba Rīga	0-1		SK Super Nova Olaine - Rīga FC	0-6
FK Tukums 2000/TSS - FK Ventspils	4-1		JPFS/FK Spartaks Jūrmala - BFC Daugavpils	0-1
FK Smiltene/BJSS - FK Liepāja	0-4		FK Jelgava - FS Metta/Latvijas Universitāte Rīga	1-0
Valmiera Glass ViA FK - FK Rīgas Futbola Skola	1-2		FK Karosta Liepāja - LDZ Cargo/DFA	4-1

Quarter-Finals [04.08./21.08./01.09.2019]

FC Caramba Rīga - FK Karosta Liepāja	1-2 pen		FK Liepāja - FK Rīgas Futbola Skola	1-2
BFC Daugavpils - FK Jelgava	1-2		Rīga FC - FK Tukums 2000/TSS	4-0

Semi-Finals [25-26.09.2019]

FK Karosta Liepāja - FK Jelgava	0-5		FK Rīgas Futbola Skola - Rīga FC	3-1

Final

26.10.2019; Zemgales Olimpiskā centra, Jelgava; Referee: Aleksandrs Golubevs; Attendance: 1,200
FK Rīgas Futbola Skola - FK Jelgava   **3-2(2-0,2-2)**

FK Rīgas Futbola Skola: Kaspars Ikstens, Vitālijs Jagodinskis, Aleksandrs Solovjovs, Edvinas Girdvainis, Slavko Blagojević, Roberts Savaļnieks (120.Gļebs Kļuškins), Andrejs Cigaņiks, Takayuki Seto (100.Cedric Kouadio), Tomáš Šimkovič (109.Artūrs Zjuzins), Darko Lemajić, Dāvis Ikaunieks (90.Vladislavs Sorokins). Trainer: Valdas Dambrauskas.

FK Jelgava: Vladislavs Kurakins, Ivo Minkevičs, Jeremy Fernandes [*sent off 105*], Stanislav Mikitsey, Viktors Litvinskis, Jakov Biljan, Maksim Marusych (75.Maksim Votinov), Igors Kozlovs, Mate Tsintsadze, Ņikita Ivanovs, Daņiils Hvoiņickis (91.Artjoms Osipovs). Trainer: Oleg Kubarev (Russia).

Goals: 1-0 Ivo Minkevičs (6 own goal), 2-0 Darko Lemajić (45), 2-1 Daņiils Hvoiņickis (52), 2-2 Ivo Minkevičs (53), 3-2 Tomáš Šimkovič (102).

Bērnu Futbola Centrs Daugavpils

Founded: 11.12.2009 (*as BFC Daugava*)
Stadium: Celtnieks Stadions, Daugavpils (4,070)
Trainer: Viktors Morozs 30.07.1980

Goalkeepers:	DOB	M	(s)	G
Ivans Dubodelovs	08.02.2001	1		
Danylo Kucher (UKR)	25.01.1997	31		
Defenders:	**DOB**	**M**	**(s)**	**G**
Daniels Balodis	10.06.1998	27		2
Maksim Grek (MDA)	26.05.1993	13	(2)	
David Idowu (NGA)	23.06.2000	11		1
Aleksandrs Ivanovs	16.11.1985	7	(8)	
Mory Koné (CIV)	21.04.1994	4	(1)	
Chinonso Nnamdi (NGA)	27.05.2000	13	(1)	6
Salvis Petriks	06.01.2002		(1)	
Dmitrijs Rakuls	21.02.2002		(1)	
Elvin Sərkərov (AZE)	24.02.1997	4	(1)	
Əli Şirinov (AZE)	09.08.1998		(1)	
Midfielders:	**DOB**	**M**	**(s)**	**G**
Valerijs Afanasjevs	20.09.1982	12	(3)	
Tural Bayramlı (AZE)	07.01.1998	12		
Dāvis Cucurs	19.03.2000	24		
Obotu Elisha (NGA)	13.04.1999	8		1
Kirils Iļjins	03.05.2001	22	(4)	
Andrejs Kovaļjovs	23.03.1989	10	(2)	1

	DOB	M	(s)	G
Andrei Mironov (RUS)	04.01.1997	1	(2)	
Leonardo Alexis Ossa López (COL)	06.08.1989	7	(3)	
Raivis Skrebels	26.09.1999	18		1
Jurijs Sokolovs	12.09.1983	23		
Vladislavs Timofejevs	25.05.2002		(2)	
Ričards Žaldovskis	05.06.1999	1	(5)	
Forwards:	**DOB**	**M**	**(s)**	**G**
Naisir Carmona Muñoz (COL)	26.09.1998	6	(8)	3
Vüqar Əsgərov (AZE)	14.05.1985	16		7
Kaspars Kokins	26.04.2000	13	(4)	3
Bohdan Kovalenko (UKR)	24.04.1997	3	(6)	
Igors Kovaļkovs	22.02.1999		(4)	
Roberts Magrins	22.01.2001	7	(3)	
Marcio Amaral de Oliveira „Marcinho" (BRA)	24.03.1991	11	(11)	1
Marko Regža	20.01.1999	6	(5)	
Kyosei Satake (JPN)	24.05.1994	1		
Iļja Ševčuks	25.03.1998		(4)	
Maksims Toņiševs	12.05.2000	26		
Yuri Sousa Lima Lellis (BRA)	09.03.1997	1	(1)	
Verners Zalaks	05.04.1997	13	(1)	

Futbola klubs Jelgava

Founded: 2004
Stadium: Zemgales Olimpiskā centra, Jelgava (1,560)
Trainer: Marians Pahars 05.08.1976
[12.06.2019] Oleg Kubarev (RUS) 08.02.1966

Goalkeepers:	DOB	M	(s)	G
Vladislavs Kurakins	09.07.1996	15		
Germans Māliņš	12.10.1987	17		
Defenders:	**DOB**	**M**	**(s)**	**G**
Jeremy Fernandes (CPV)	14.08.1995	29		
Ingus Valters Grinbergs	01.02.2002		(1)	
Viktors Litvinskis	07.02.1996	19	(2)	
Stanislav Mikitsey (UKR)	07.09.1989	14		
Ivo Minkevičs	28.06.1999	14	(4)	
Momčilo Rašo (MNE)	06.02.1997	13		
Valērijs Redjko	10.03.1983	3	(3)	
Renārs Rode	06.04.1989	25		1
Makhmadnaim Sharifi (RUS)	03.06.1992	10	(3)	
Midfielders:	**DOB**	**M**	**(s)**	**G**
Irakli Bidzinashvili (GEO)	27.02.1997	16	(4)	2
Jakov Biljan (CRO)	02.08.1995	21	(1)	
Yaël Eisden (CUW)	11.01.1994	12	(1)	1
Aivars Emsis	01.04.1998	11		4
Eduards Emsis	23.02.1996	3	(3)	
Dāvis Indrāns	06.06.1995	15	(6)	4

	DOB	M	(s)	G
Alyaksandr Kotlyarov (BLR)	30.01.1993	4		
Igors Kozlovs	26.03.1987	11	(3)	3
Andris Krušatins	01.09.1996	2	(5)	
Artis Lazdiņš	03.05.1986	12	(4)	
Guram Lukava (GEO)	14.04.1995	4	(1)	
Vitālijs Rečickis	08.09.1986	3	(2)	
Maksim Marusych (UKR)	17.07.1993	6	(2)	4
Stylianos Panteli (CYP)	07.08.1999		(5)	
Mate Tsintsadze (GEO)	07.01.1995	7	(1)	1
Artjoms Vorobjovs	07.08.1999		(6)	
Ņikita Žarovs	25.03.1999		(1)	
Forwards:	**DOB**	**M**	**(s)**	**G**
Vsevolods Čamkins	20.12.1994	1	(4)	
Daņiils Hvoiņickis	08.04.1998	16	(4)	1
Ņikita Ivanovs	25.03.1996	14	(6)	3
Marks Kurtišs	26.01.1998	2	(1)	1
Artjoms Osipovs	08.01.1989	18		1
Janyro Purperhart (NED)	03.05.1996	6	(2)	2
Leo Salmiņš	24.02.1997	1	(2)	
Maksim Votinov (RUS)	29.08.1988	8	(3)	5

Futbola klubs Liepāja

Founded: 2014
Stadium: Daugava Stadions, Liepāja (5,008)
Trainer: Gordon Young (SCO) 29.04.1964
[23.04.2019] Mareks Zuntners 13.02.1983
[01.05.2019] Aleksandrs Starkovs 26.07.1955
[28.09.2019] Mareks Zuntners 13.02.1983
[06.11.2019] Andrejs Kalinins 26.05.1981

Goalkeepers:	DOB	M	(s)	G
Valentīns Raļkevičs	08.03.1991	23		
Kristaps Zommers	07.01.1997	6		
Krišjānis Zviedris	25.01.1997	3		
Defenders:	**DOB**	**M**	**(s)**	**G**
Deniss Ivanovs	11.01.1984	21	(5)	
Roberts Jaunarājs-Janvāris	23.03.2000	8	(2)	
Antons Jemeļins	19.02.1984	1	(1)	
Clement Boubacar Kanouté (MLI)	01.09.1999	1		
Seydina Keita (SEN)	28.12.1992	22		1
Michael Ofosu-Appiah (GHA)	29.12.1999	1		
Kristers Tobers	13.12.2000	22	(2)	3
Vadims Žuļevs	01.03.1988	23		
Midfielders:	**DOB**	**M**	**(s)**	**G**
Prince Agyemang (GHA)	25.12.1994		(2)	
Michael Ezekiel Apaki (NGA)	22.09.2000		(1)	
Kristers Čudars	03.09.1999	7	(2)	1
Richard Emeka Friday (NGA)	16.02.2000	16	(10)	6
Dmitrijs Hmizs	31.07.1992	1		
Jānis Ikaunieks	16.02.1995	24	(1)	7

	DOB	M	(s)	G
Raivis Jurkovskis	09.12.1996	28		2
Mārtiņš Ķigurs	31.03.1997	19	(2)	1
Igors Kozlovs	26.03.1987	7	(2)	1
Gatis Lūks	18.11.2000	2		
Leonel Strumia (ARG)	29.09.1992	24		1
Cristián Damián Torres	18.06.1985	5	(13)	
Daniils Ulimbaševs	12.03.1992		(1)	
Raivis Viļumsons	14.06.2001		(8)	1
Viktors Ziemelis	27.01.2000	2	(6)	
Forwards:	**DOB**	**M**	**(s)**	**G**
Amâncio José Pinto Fortes (ANG)	18.04.1990	17		5
Vüqar Əsgərov (AZE)	14.05.1985	7	(3)	1
Alexis Lucas Delgado (ARG)	24.03.1995	7	(5)	2
Luiz Paulo Hilario „Dodô" (BRA)	16.10.1987	24		5
Vladislavs Kozlovs	30.11.1987	2	(3)	
Elysee Fabrice Kouadio Kouakou (CIV)	03.10.1990	5		1
Artūrs Smetanovs	20.04.1999	1	(5)	
Danu Spătaru (MDA)	24.05.1994	21	(8)	2
Vladimirs Stepanovs	06.02.2000	1		
Mate Vatsadze (GEO)	17.12.1988	1	(1)	

Futbola klubs Metta / Latvijas Universitāte Rīga

Founded: 02.05.2006
Stadium: Hanzas vidusskolas laukums, Rīga (2,000)
Trainer: Andris Riherts   31.05.1981

Goalkeepers:	DOB	M	(s)	G
Dāvis Ošs	03.12.1994	32		
Defenders:	**DOB**	**M**	**(s)**	**G**
Emīls Birka	25.04.2000	26	(1)	
Daniels Fedorovičs	07.10.2001	1		
Krists Gulbis	15.01.1997	8	(3)	1
Roberts Ķipsts	21.10.1999	1	(2)	
Kabelo Seriba (RSA)	12.05.1997	28		
Kirils Ševeļovs	02.06.1990	23	(3)	
Rendijs Šibass	01.05.1997	24	(4)	
Normunds Uldriķis	29.01.2001	14	(6)	1
Lukman Halilu Zakari (NGA)	23.12.1998	21		2
Midfielders:	**DOB**	**M**	**(s)**	**G**
Tamirlan Dzhamalutdinov (RUS)	28.07.1996	30	(1)	10

	DOB	M	(s)	G
Benson Fazili (CAN)	12.01.2000	18	(4)	
Iļja Korotkovs	24.05.2000	3	(3)	
Jēkabs Lagūns	16.01.2002	11	(18)	2
Kristaps Liepa	14.03.1998	26	(1)	2
Rihards Ozoliņš	31.05.2001	17	(8)	1
Oskars Vientiess	08.10.2002	1	(2)	
Forwards:	**DOB**	**M**	**(s)**	**G**
Ņikita Kovaļonoks	02.07.1995	6	(4)	
Raimonds Krollis	28.10.2001	19	(6)	5
Kgotso Masangane (RSA)	27.05.1998	27	(2)	6
Renārs Varslavāns	23.08.2001	5		1
Vinicius de Oliveira Veneranda (BRA)	11.02.1999		(6)	
Ričards Žaldovskis	05.06.1999	4	(4)	2
Matīss Zēģele	24.09.2000	7	(8)	2

Rīga Football Club

Founded: 2014 (*as merger of FC Caramba Riga and Dinamo Rīga*)
Stadium: Skonto Stadions, Rīga (8,207)
Trainer: Mihails Koņevs   01.07.1963
[28.03.2019]   Oleg Kubarev (BLR)   08.02.1966
[26.04.2019]   Mihails Koņevs   01.07.1963

Goalkeepers:	DOB	M	(s)	G
Roberts Ozols	10.09.1995	19		
Nils Puriņš	01.08.1998	4		
Maksims Uvarenko	17.01.1987	9		
Defenders:	**DOB**	**M**	**(s)**	**G**
Joël Bopesu (FRA)	25.01.1995	14	(7)	2
Antonijs Černomordijs	26.09.1996	24	(1)	1
Vladislavs Gabovs	13.07.1987	5		
Antons Kurakins	01.01.1990	9	(2)	
Herdi Prenga (ALB)	31.08.1994	22	(1)	1
Elvis Stuglis	04.07.1993	15	(4)	3
Georgios Valerianos (GRE)	13.02.1992	2		
Midfielders:	**DOB**	**M**	**(s)**	**G**
Kriss Andersons	14.07.2000	1	(1)	
Felipe Bezerra Brisola (BRA)	06.06.1990	19	(4)	5
Abdisalam Ibrahim (NOR)	01.05.1991	1	(1)	
Vladimir Kamešs	28.10.1988	6	(1)	
Oļegs Laizāns	28.03.1987	16	(8)	5

	DOB	M	(s)	G
Stefan Panić (SRB)	20.09.1992	22	(2)	3
Armands Pētersons	05.12.1990	21	(3)	
Roger Junio Rodrigues Ferreira (BRA)	01.03.1996	5	(3)	2
Ritvars Rugins	17.10.1989	22	(2)	
Tomislav Šarić (SVN)	24.06.1990	20		2
Minori Satō (JPN)	02.03.1991	8	(2)	1
Vyacheslav Sharpar (UKR)	02.06.1987	5	(3)	2
Aleksejs Višņakovs	03.02.1984	17	(8)	4
Forwards:	**DOB**	**M**	**(s)**	**G**
Kamil Biliński (POL)	23.01.1988	8	(12)	5
Roman Debelko (UKR)	08.08.1993	10	(1)	7
Vladislavs Fjodorovs	27.09.1996	17	(8)	2
Artūrs Karašausks	29.01.1992	7	(6)	
Darko Lemajić (SRB)	20.08.1993	8	(2)	5
Ivan Lukjanovs	24.01.1987	2	(3)	2
Deniss Rakels	20.08.1992	9	(3)	3
Davit Skhirtladze (GEO)	16.03.1993	1	(1)	
Myroslav Slavov (UKR)	08.09.1990	4	(5)	3

Futbola klubs Rīgas Futbola Skola

Founded: 2011
Stadium: Stadions Arkādija, Rīga (1,000)
Trainer: Valdas Dambrauskas   07.01.1977

Goalkeepers:	DOB	M	(s)	G
Dmitrijs Grigorjevs	13.05.1992	5		
Kaspars Ikstens	05.06.1988	27		
Defenders:	**DOB**	**M**	**(s)**	**G**
Nauris Bulvītis	15.03.1987	14	(6)	2
Adama Doumbia (CIV)	01.01.2000	1		
Edvinas Girdvainis (LTU)	17.01.1993	14		
Vjačeslavs Isajevs	27.08.1993	9	(3)	1
Vitālijs Jagodinskis	28.02.1992	29		5
Aleksandrs Solovjovs	25.02.1988	18	(3)	4
Vladislavs Sorokins	10.05.1997	23	(4)	
Midfielders:	**DOB**	**M**	**(s)**	**G**
Emeka Michael Basil (NGA)	22.01.2001	1		1
Slavko Blagojević (CRO)	21.03.1987	27		
Andrejs Cigaņiks	12.04.1997	13	(1)	1
Aleksandrs Fertovs	16.06.1987	3	(3)	
Gļebs Kļuškins	01.10.1992	19	(2)	

	DOB	M	(s)	G
Maksim Marusych (UKR)	17.07.1993	3	(4)	1
Olabanjo Alexander Ogunji (NGA)	20.01.2001	1		
Roberts Savaļnieks	04.02.1993	25	(4)	1
Takayuki Seto (JPN)	05.02.1986	20	(4)	1
Tomáš Šimkovič (AUT)	16.04.1987	28	(1)	8
Alans Siņeļņikovs	14.05.1990	4	(8)	
Beka Vachiberadze (GEO)	05.03.1996	6	(4)	
Artūrs Zjuzins	18.06.1991	4	(8)	2
Forwards:	**DOB**	**M**	**(s)**	**G**
Bonfils-Caleb Bimenyimana (BDI)	21.11.1997	1	(2)	
Dāvis Ikaunieks	07.01.1994	7	(5)	6
Andrija Kaluđerović (SRB)	05.07.1987	4	(6)	2
Cedric Kouadio (CIV)	19.05.1996	19	(9)	2
Darko Lemajić (SRB)	20.08.1993	13		10
Maksim Maksimov (RUS)	04.11.1995	2	(2)	
Tomáš Malec (SVK)	05.01.1993	12	(7)	6
Tin Vukmanić (CRO)	17.04.1999		(6)	

Jūrmalas Futbola un Peldēšanas skola/ Futbola klubs Spartaks Jūrmala

	Founded:	2007		
	Stadium:	Slokas Stadions, Jūrmala (2,800)		
	Trainer:	Nunzio Zavettieri (ITA)		10.02.1967

Goalkeepers:	DOB	M	(s)	G
Vitālijs Meļņičenko	11.11.1987	18		
Jevģēnijs Nerugals	26.02.1989	14		
Defenders:	**DOB**	**M**	**(s)**	**G**
Chidiebere Collins Agita (NGA)	08.04.2000	1	(1)	
Ņikita Bērenfelds	07.06.1995	31		
Edgars Fjodorovs	09.07.1995		(1)	
Gints Freimanis	09.05.1985	27	(1)	2
Klāvs Kramēns	07.07.2000	15		1
Ousmane Séyé (SEN)	10.08.1999	4		
Vitālijs Smirnovs	28.06.1986	14	(3)	
Deniss Stradiņš	01.03.2001		(4)	
Igors Tarasovs	16.10.1988	10		3
Midfielders:	**DOB**	**M**	**(s)**	**G**
Samiru Kwari Abdullahi (NGA)	03.01.2001	4	(3)	
Aliyu Yau Adam (NGA)	07.05.2000	6	(4)	2
Aly Barry (SEN)	05.07.1999	8	(5)	
Aivars Emsis	01.04.1998	7	(3)	1
Sergey Eremenko (RUS)	06.01.1999	4	(3)	1

Andrejs Kiriļins	03.11.1995	4	(2)	
Jānis Krautmanis	22.04.1997	6	(1)	
Chikezie Miracle Nwaorisa (NGA)	12.11.2000	8	(11)	2
Alexandre Obambot (CGO)	14.02.1999	6	(5)	
Lucky Onyebuchi Opara (NGA)	09.12.1999	26	(1)	2
Vitālijs Rečickis	08.09.1986	12	(1)	1
Raivis Skrebels	26.09.1999	6	(2)	
Edgars Vardanjans	09.05.1993	9	(6)	
Forwards:	**DOB**	**M**	**(s)**	**G**
Nemanja Belaković (SRB)	08.01.1997	27	(1)	11
Gabriel Charpentier (FRA)	17.05.1999	13	(6)	5
Kingsley Charles Eleje (NGA)	25.05.2000	1	(2)	
Richlord Ennin (CAN)	17.09.1998	19	(3)	5
Edgars Gauračs	10.03.1988	6	(9)	5
Ričards Korzāns	03.05.1997	11	(7)	
Stanley Nnanna Otu (NGA)	30.03.2000	8	(3)	3
Rolands Vagančuks	05.01.1998	2	(1)	
Tin Vukmanić (CRO)	17.04.1999	16		5
Verners Zalaks	05.04.1997	9	(1)	

Valmieras Glass / Vidzemes Augstskola Futbola klubs

	Founded:	1996		
	Stadium:	„Jānis Daliņš" Stadions, Valmiera (2,000)		
	Trainer:	Tamaz Pertia (GEO)		23.12.1974

Goalkeepers:	DOB	M	(s)	G
Vladislavs Lazarevs	25.11.1997	32		
Defenders:	**DOB**	**M**	**(s)**	**G**
Olaide Muhammed Badmus (NGA)	12.04.1999	7	(3)	
Klāvs Kramēns	07.07.2000	6	(5)	
Madis Miķelsons	18.01.1994	22	(6)	
Michael Ofosu-Appiah (GHA)	29.12.1989	16		1
Midfielders:	**DOB**	**M**	**(s)**	**G**
Prince Agyemang (GHA)	25.12.1994	4	(5)	
Toluwalase Emmanuel Arokodare (NGA)	23.11.2000	16		7
Boriss Bogdaškins	21.02.1990	27	(2)	2
Mārcis Ērglis	17.01.1992	25	(5)	3
Pacifique Hector Gbaguidi Djonougbé (BEN)	05.08.1997	13	(5)	1
Aleksejs Grjaznovs	01.10.1997	13	(7)	1
Oleksii Helovani (UKR)	20.02.1998	16	(2)	
Artis Jaudzems	04.04.1995		(3)	

Alvis Jaunzems	16.06.1999	7	(13)	3
Valts Jaunzems	18.09.1995		(3)	
Edgars Jermolaevs	16.06.1992	5	(2)	1
Kriss Kārkliņš	31.01.1996	26		
Jānis Krautmanis	22.04.1997	15		1
Leonardo Silva Lelis „Léo Lelis" (BRA)	15.11.1993	27	(1)	3
Shunsuke Nakamura (JPN)	16.05.1994	25	(5)	2
Vladislavs Soloveičiks	25.05.1999	8	(6)	1
Forwards:	**DOB**	**M**	**(s)**	**G**
Verners Apiņš	14.04.1992		(2)	
Konstantin Cherny (UKR)	17.08.1992	2		
Jorge Duarte Rodrigues Mendes Teixeira(POR)	08.03.199	10	(3)	5
Gatis Kalniņš	12.08.1981	2	(7)	
Kristers Lūsiņš	09.05.2000	1		
Eriks Punculs	18.01.1994	26	(1)	6

Futbola klubs Ventspils

	Founded:	1997		
	Stadium:	Ventspils Olimpiskais Stadions, Ventspils (3,044)		
	Trainer:	Dejan Vukičević (MNE)		27.04.1968
	[15.05.2019]	Igors Klosovs		11.06.1965
	[06.10.2019]	Aleksandrs Kulakovs		14.04.1956

Goalkeepers:	DOB	M	(s)	G
Ivans Baturins	25.06.1997	17		
Vjačeslavs Kudrjavcevs	30.03.1998	4		
Konstantin Machnovskiy (UKR)	01.01.1989	11		
Defenders:	**DOB**	**M**	**(s)**	**G**
Jean Sony Alcénat (HAI)	23.01.1986	11	(4)	
Hélio Monteiro Batista (BRA)	28.01.1990	22	(3)	3
Dmitrijs Klimaševičs	16.04.1995	1		
Ņikita Koļesovs	25.09.1996	9	(1)	
Dmitrijs Litvinskis	17.08.1999	20	(3)	
Artūrs Ļotčikovs	26.01.2000	8	(6)	
Abdoul Mamah (TOG)	24.08.1985	20	(1)	
Giorgi Mchedlishvili (GEO)	18.01.1992	8	(1)	
Medzit Neziri (MKD)	02.09.1990	4	(3)	
Rashid Obuobi (GHA)	18.12.1994	4		
Midfielders:	**DOB**	**M**	**(s)**	**G**
Abdullahi Alfa (NGA)	29.07.1996	9	(1)	
Niks Dusalijevs	17.07.2001	1	(4)	
Jevģēnijs Kazačoks	12.08.1995	23		3

Romāns Mickevičs	29.03.1993	17	(6)	3
Kristers Neilands	09.09.2000		(1)	
Pavel Osipov (RUS)	28.01.1996	8	(8)	1
Guga Palavandishvili (GEO)	14.08.1993	8	(5)	
Ingars Stuglis	12.02.1996	23		2
Raens Tālbergs	14.09.2000	4	(6)	1
Eduards Tīdenbergs	18.12.1994	18	(3)	3
Daniils Ulimbaševs	12.03.1992	10		6
Sename Dové Womé Dobe (TOG)	08.06.1991	1	(6)	
Forwards:	**DOB**	**M**	**(s)**	**G**
Amâncio José Pinto Fortes (ANG)	18.04.1990	4		1
Kirill Burykin (RUS)	06.08.1998		(1)	
Joálisson Santos Oliveira (BRA)	31.03.1991	6	(8)	3
Lucas Villela Rezende (BRA)	24.03.1994	16		2
Anastasijs Mordatenko	24.08.1996	13	(5)	2
Mykhaylo Sergiychuk (UKR)	29.07.1991	3	(6)	1
Kaspars Svārups	28.01.1994	26	(3)	4
Aiyegun Tosin (NGA)	26.06.1998	23		11

1. FK Tukums 2000/TSS (*Promoted*)	27	24	2	1	112	-	14	74
2. SK Super Nova Olaine (*Promotion Play-offs*)	27	19	1	7	95	-	27	58
3. FK Smiltene/BJSS	27	17	2	8	78	-	52	53
4. JDFS Alberts Rīga	27	16	3	8	70	-	47	51
5. FK Auda Rīga	27	14	3	10	62	-	51	45
6. Rēzeknes FA/BJSS	27	13	4	10	72	-	56	43
7. Grobiņas SC	27	10	0	17	56	-	104	30
8. FC New Project Rīga (*Relegated*)	27	6	2	19	35	-	62	20
9. FK Dinamo Rīga/Staiceles (*Relegated*)	27	6	1	20	39	-	78	19
10. Balvu Sporta centrs (*Relegated*)	27	1	0	26	23	-	151	3

NATIONAL TEAM

INTERNATIONAL MATCHES
(16.07.2019 – 15.07.2020)

06.09.2019	Wals-Siezenheim	Austria - Latvia	6-0(2-0)	(ECQ)
09.09.2019	Rīga	Latvia - North Macedonia	0-2(0-2)	(ECQ)
10.10.2019	Rīga	Latvia - Poland	0-3(0-2)	(ECQ)
15.10.2019	Beer Sheba	Israel - Latvia	3-1(3-1)	(ECQ)
16.11.2019	Ljubljana	Slovenia - Latvia	1-0(0-0)	(ECQ)
19.11.2019	Rīga	Latvia - Austria	1-0(0-0)	(ECQ)

06.09.2019 AUSTRIA - LATVIA   **6-0(2-0)**   16th EC. Qualifiers
Wals-Siezenheim Stadion, Wals-Siezenheim; Referee: Robert Hennessy (Republic of Ireland); Attendance: 16,300
LVA: Pāvels Šteinbors, Armands Pētersons, Kaspars Dubra (Cap), Vitālijs Maksimenko, Antonijs Černomordijs, Boriss Bogdaškins, Vladimirs Kamešs, Oļegs Laizāns (82.Roberts Uldriķis), Andrejs Cigaņiks (66.Roberts Savaļnieks), Kristers Tobers (77.Ritvars Rugins), Vladislavs Gutkovskis. Trainer: Slaviša Stojanovič (Slovenia).

09.09.2019 LATVIA - NORTH MACEDONIA   **0-2(0-2)**   16th EC. Qualifiers
Daugava Stadions, Riga; Referee: Espen Eskås (Norway); Attendance: 2,724
LVA: Andris Vaņins (Cap), Armands Pētersons, Vitālijs Maksimenko, Antonijs Černomordijs, Vladimirs Kamešs (84.Valerijs Šabala), Oļegs Laizāns, Ritvars Rugins, Jānis Ikaunieks, Mārtiņš Ķigurs (76.Ēriks Punculs) , Vladislavs Gutkovskis, Roberts Uldriķis (46.Roberts Savaļnieks). Trainer: Slaviša Stojanovič (Slovenia).

10.10.2019 LATVIA - POLAND   **0-3(0-2)**   16th EC. Qualifiers
Daugava Stadions, Riga; Referee: Halis Özkahya (Turkey); Attendance: 7,107
LVA: Andris Vaņins (Cap), Kaspars Dubra, Vitālijs Maksimenko, Vitālijs Jagodinskis, Mārcis Ošs, Oļegs Laizāns (72.Kristers Tobers), Ritvars Rugins, Jānis Ikaunieks, Mārtiņš Ķigurs (86.Andrejs Cigaņiks), Deniss Rakels (72.Artūrs Karašausks), Vladislavs Gutkovskis. Trainer: Slaviša Stojanovič (Slovenia).

15.10.2019 ISRAEL - LATVIA   **3-1(3-1)**   16th EC. Qualifiers
"Yaakov Turner Toto" Stadium, Beersheba; Referee: Arnold Hunter (Northern Ireland); Attendance: 9,150
LVA: Pāvels Šteinbors (Cap), Igors Tarasovs, Vitālijs Jagodinskis, Mārcis Ošs, Antonijs Černomordijs, Vladimirs Kamešs (78.Dāvis Ikaunieks), Roberts Savaļnieks, Jānis Ikaunieks (86.Daniels Ontužāns), Raivis Jurkovskis, Mārtiņš Ķigurs (68.Oļegs Laizāns), Vladislavs Gutkovskis. Trainer: Slaviša Stojanovič (Slovenia).
Goal: Vladimirs Kamešs (40).

16.11.2019 SLOVENIA - LATVIA   **1-0(0-0)**   16th EC. Qualifiers
Stožice Stadium, Ljubljana; Referee: Radu Marian Petrescu (Romania); Attendance: 11,224
LVA: Pāvels Šteinbors (Cap), Igors Tarasovs, Kaspars Dubra, Vitālijs Maksimenko, Mārcis Ošs, Vladimirs Kamešs (88.Ēriks Punculs), Roberts Savaļnieks, Dāvis Ikaunieks (72.Roberts Uldriķis), Vladislavs Fjodorovs, Raivis Jurkovskis, Vladislavs Gutkovskis (85.Oļegs Laizāns). Trainer: Slaviša Stojanovič (Slovenia).

19.11.2019 LATVIA - AUSTRIA   **1-0(0-0)**   16th EC. Qualifiers
Daugava Stadions, Riga; Referee: Alejandro José Hernández Hernández (Spain); Attendance: 2,781
LVA: Pāvels Šteinbors (Cap), Kaspars Dubra, Vitālijs Maksimenko, Mārcis Ošs, Vladimirs Kamešs, Roberts Savaļnieks, Dāvis Ikaunieks (89.Igors Tarasovs), Aleksejs Grjaznovs (90+2.Antonijs Černomordijs), Vladislavs Fjodorovs, Raivis Jurkovskis, Roberts Uldriķis (70.Vladislavs Gutkovskis). Trainer: Slaviša Stojanovič (Slovenia).
Goal: Mārcis Ošs (65).

NATIONAL TEAM PLAYERS
(16.07.2019 – 15.07.2020)

Name	DOB	Caps	Goals	2019/2020:	Club
Goalkeepers					
Pāvels ŠTEINBORS	21.09.1985	12	0	2019:	*MKS Arka Gdynia (POL)*
Andris VAŅINS	30.04.1980	100	0	2019:	*FC Zürich (SUI)*
Defenders					
Antonijs ČERNOMORDIJS	26.09.1996	4	0	2019:	*Rīga FC*
Kaspars DUBRA	20.12.1990	37	2	2019:	*FK Oleksandriya (UKR)*
Vitālijs JAGODINSKIS	28.02.1992	31	0	2019:	*FK Rīgas Futbola Skola*
Raivis JURKOVSKIS	09.12.1996	7	0	2019:	*FK Liepāja*
Vitālijs MAKSIMENKO	08.12.1990	51	1	2019:	*NK Olimpija Ljubljana (SVN)*
Mārcis OŠS	25.07.1991	11	1	2019:	*Neuchâtel Xamax FCS (SUI)*
Armands PĒTERSONS	15.12.1990	2	0	2019:	*Rīga FC*
Igors TARASOVS	16.10.1988	34	1	2019:	*JPFS/FK Spartaks Jūrmala*
Midfielders					
Boriss BOGDAŠKINS	21.02.1990	1	0	2019:	*Valmiera Glass ViA FK*
Andrejs CIGAŅIKS	12.04.1997	8	0	2019:	*FK Rīgas Futbola Skola*
Aleksejs GRJAZNOVS	01.10.1997	1	0	2019:	*Valmiera Glass ViA FK*
Jānis IKAUNIEKS	16.02.1995	26	3	2019:	*FK Liepāja*
Vladimirs KAMEŠS	28.10.1988	24	2	2019:	*Rīga FC*
Mārtiņš ĶIGURS	31.03.1997	3	0	2019:	*FK Liepāja*
Oļegs LAIZĀNS	28.03.1987	54	0	2019:	*Rīga FC*
Daniels ONTUŽĀNS	07.03.2000	2	0	2019:	*FC Bayern München II (GER)*
Ritvars RUGINS	17.10.1989	35	0	2019:	*Rīga FC*
Roberts SAVAĻNIEKS	04.02.1993	20	0	2019:	*FK Rīgas Futbola Skola*
Kristers TOBERS	13.12.2000	6	0	2019:	*FK Liepāja*
Forwards					
Vladislavs FJODOROVS	27.09.1996	5	1	2019:	*Rīga FC*
Vladislavs GUTKOVSKIS	02.04.1995	18	0	2019:	*Bruk-Bet Termalica Nieciecza KS (POL)*
Dāvis IKAUNIEKS	07.01.1994	24	4	2019:	*FK Rīgas Futbola Skola*
Artūrs KARAŠAUSKS	29.01.1992	25	1	2019:	*Rīga FC*
Ēriks PUNCULS	18.01.1994	2	0	2019:	*Valmiera Glass ViA FK*
Deniss RAKEĻS	20.08.1992	32	1	2019:	*Rīga FC*
Valērijs ŠABALA	12.10.1994	53	12	2019:	*MKS Miedź Legnica (POL)*
Roberts ULDRIĶIS	03.04.1998	14	1	2019:	*FC Sion (SUI)*
National team coach					
Slaviša STOJANOVIČ (Slovenia) [since 01.03.2019]	06.12.1969			10 M; 1 W; 0 D; 9 L; 2-28	

LIECHTENSTEIN

The Country:
Fürstentum Liechtenstein (Principality of Liechtenstein)
Capital: Vaduz
Surface: 160 km²
Inhabitants: 38,749 [2020]
Time: UTC+1

The FA:
Liechtensteiner Fussballverband
Landstrasse 149, 9494 Schaan
Tel: +423 237 4747
Foundation date: 1934
Member of FIFA since: 1974
Member of UEFA since: 1974
Website: www.lfv.li

NATIONAL TEAM RECORDS

RECORDS		
First international match:	09.03.1982, Balzers:	Liechtenstein – Switzerland 0-1
Most international caps:	Peter Karl Jehle	- 132 caps (1998-2018)
Most international goals:	Mario Frick	- 16 goals / 125 caps (1993-2015)

UEFA EUROPEAN CHAMPIONSHIP
1960	-
1964	-
1968	-
1972	-
1976	Did not enter
1980	Did not enter
1984	Did not enter
1988	Did not enter
1992	Did not enter
1996	Qualifiers
2000	Qualifiers
2004	Qualifiers
2008	Qualifiers
2012	Qualifiers
2016	Qualifiers
2020	Qualifiers

FIFA WORLD CUP
1930	-
1934	-
1938	-
1950	-
1954	-
1958	-
1962	-
1966	-
1970	-
1974	-
1978	Did not enter
1982	Did not enter
1986	Did not enter
1990	Did not enter
1994	Did not enter
1998	Qualifiers
2002	Qualifiers
2006	Qualifiers
2010	Qualifiers
2014	Qualifiers
2018	Qualifiers

OLYMPIC TOURNAMENTS
1908	-
1912	-
1920	-
1924	-
1928	-
1936	-
1948	-
1952	-
1956	-
1960	-
1964	-
1968	-
1972	-
1976	Did not enter
1980	Did not enter
1984	Did not enter
1988	Qualifiers
1992	Did not enter
1996	Did not enter
2000	Did not enter
2004	Did not enter
2008	Qualifiers
2012	Qualifiers
2016	Qualifiers

UEFA NATIONS LEAGUE
2018/2019 – League D

FIFA CONFEDERATIONS CUP 1992-2017
None

LIECHTENSTEIN CLUB HONOURS IN EUROPEAN CLUB COMPETITIONS:

European Champion Clubs' Cup (1956-1992) / UEFA Champions League (1993-2020)
None

Fairs Cup (1858-1971) / UEFA Cup (1972-2009) / UEFA Europa League (2010-2020)
None

UEFA Super Cup (1972-2019)
None

*European Cup Winners' Cup 1961-1999**
None

*defunct competition

NATIONAL COMPETITIONS
TABLE OF HONOURS

	CHAMPIONS
1932	FC Vaduz (*unofficial*)
1934	FC Triesen
1935	FC Triesen
1936	FC Vaduz
1937	FC Triesen

CUP WINNERS

Season	Winner	Season	Winner	Season	Winner
1945/1946	FC Triesen	1970/1971	FC Vaduz	1995/1996	FC Vaduz
1946/1947	FC Triesen	1971/1972	FC Triesen	1996/1997	FC Balzers
1947/1948	FC Triesen	1972/1973	FC Balzers	1997/1998	FC Vaduz
1948/1949	FC Vaduz	1973/1974	FC Vaduz	1998/1999	FC Vaduz
1949/1950	FC Triesen	1974/1975	FC Triesen	1999/2000	FC Vaduz
1950/1951	FC Triesen	1975/1976	USV Eschen/Mauren	2000/2001	FC Vaduz
1951/1952	FC Vaduz	1976/1977	USV Eschen/Mauren	2001/2002	FC Vaduz
1952/1953	FC Vaduz	1977/1978	USV Eschen/Mauren	2002/2003	FC Vaduz
1953/1954	FC Vaduz	1978/1979	FC Balzers	2003/2004	FC Vaduz
1954/1955	FC Schaan	1979/1980	FC Vaduz	2004/2005	FC Vaduz
1955/1956	FC Vaduz	1980/1981	FC Balzers	2005/2006	FC Vaduz
1956/1957	FC Vaduz	1981/1982	FC Balzers	2006/2007	FC Vaduz
1957/1958	FC Vaduz	1982/1983	FC Balzers	2007/2008	FC Vaduz
1958/1959	FC Vaduz	1983/1984	FC Balzers	2008/2009	FC Vaduz
1959/1960	FC Vaduz	1984/1985	FC Vaduz	2009/2010	FC Vaduz
1960/1961	FC Vaduz	1985/1986	FC Vaduz	2010/2011	FC Vaduz
1961/1962	FC Vaduz	1986/1987	USV Eschen/Mauren	2011/2012	USV Eschen/Mauren
1962/1963	FC Schaan	1987/1988	FC Vaduz	2012/2013	FC Vaduz
1963/1964	FC Balzers	1988/1989	FC Balzers	2013/2014	FC Vaduz
1964/1965	FC Triesen	1989/1990	FC Vaduz	2014/2015	FC Vaduz
1965/1966	FC Vaduz	1990/1991	FC Balzers	2015/2016	FC Vaduz
1966/1967	FC Vaduz	1991/1992	FC Vaduz	2016/2017	FC Vaduz
1967/1968	FC Vaduz	1992/1993	FC Balzers	2017/2018	FC Vaduz
1968/1969	FC Vaduz	1993/1994	FC Schaan	2018/2019	FC Vaduz
1969/1970	FC Vaduz	1994/1995	FC Vaduz	2019/2020	*Competition abandoned*

NATIONAL CUP
Liechtensteiner Cup 2019/2020

First Round [27-28.08.2019]		Seccond Round [17-18.09.2019]	
FC Vaduz III - FC Triesen	0-6	USV Eschen/Mauren III - FC Triesenberg	1-3
FC Triesen II - FC Balzers II	0-1	FC Schaan - USV Eschen/Mauren II	5-3
FC Triesenberg II - FC Schaan II	3-4	FC Schaan II - FC Ruggell II	7-6
		FC Balzers II - FC Triesen	2-4

Quarter-Finals [23/29/30.10.2019]			
FC Triesenberg - FC Ruggell	0-5	FC Schaan II - FC Balzers	0-7
FC Triesen - FC Vaduz	1-3	FC Schaan - USV Eschen/Mauren	0-3

Semi-Finals [11.03.2020]			
FC Balzers - FC Vaduz	1-6	FC Ruggell - USV Eschen/Mauren	*Cancelled*

On 11.05.2020, the competition was abandoned due to the COVID-19 pandemic. The Liechtenstein Football Association selected FC Vaduz (with the highest UEFA club coefficient), to play in the 2020/2021 UEFA Europa League.

INTERNATIONAL MATCHES
(16.07.2019 – 15.07.2020)

05.09.2019	Zenica	Bosnia and Herzegovina - Liechtenstein	5-0(1-0)	(ECQ)
08.09.2019	Athína	Greece - Liechtenstein	1-1(1-0)	(ECQ)
12.10.2019	Vaduz	Liechtenstein - Armenia	1-1(0-1)	(ECQ)
15.10.2019	Vaduz	Liechtenstein - Italy	0-5(0-1)	(ECQ)
15.11.2019	Helsinki	Finland - Liechtenstein	3-0(1-0)	(ECQ)
18.11.2019	Vaduz	Liechtenstein - Bosnia and Herzegovina	0-3(0-0)	(ECQ)

05.09.2019   BOSNIA AND HERZEGOVINA - LIECHTENSTEIN   5-0(1-0)   16th EC. Qualifiers
Stadion Bilino Polje, Zenica; Referee: Glenn Nyberg (Sweden); Attendance: 3,825
LIE: Benjamin Büchel, Martin Rechsteiner, Daniel Kaufmann, Nicolas Hasler, Maximilian Göppel, Andreas Malin, Martin Büchel (Cap), Sandro Wieser (85.Daniel Matthias Brändle), Dennis Salanović, Livio Meier (64.Sandro Wolfinger), Robin Gubser (74.Aron Sele). Trainer: Helgi Kolviðsson (Iceland).

08.09.2019   GREECE - LIECHTENSTEIN   1-1(1-0)   16th EC. Qualifiers
Stádio Olympiako „Spiros Louis", Athína; Referee: Alexander Harkam (Austria); Attendance: 3,445
LIE: Benjamin Büchel, Martin Rechsteiner (82.Jens Hofer), Daniel Kaufmann, Nicolas Hasler, Maximilian Göppel, Andreas Malin, Martin Büchel (Cap), Sandro Wieser, Dennis Salanović, Livio Meier (64.Daniel Matthias Brändle), Robin Gubser (56.Seyhan Yildiz). Trainer: Helgi Kolviðsson (Iceland).
Goal: Dennis Salanović (85).

12.10.2019   LIECHTENSTEIN - ARMENIA   1-1(0-1)   16th EC. Qualifiers
Rheinpark Stadion, Vaduz; Referee: István Kovács (Romania); Attendance: 2,285
LIE: Benjamin Büchel, Martin Rechsteiner, Daniel Kaufmann, Nicolas Hasler, Maximilian Göppel, Andreas Malin, Martin Büchel (Cap), Michele Polverino (83.Aron Sele), Dennis Salanović, Livio Meier (70.Seyhan Yildiz), Robin Gubser (67.Yanik Frick). Trainer: Helgi Kolviðsson (Iceland).
Goal: Yanik Frick (72).

15.10.2019   LIECHTENSTEIN - ITALY   0-5(0-1)   16th EC. Qualifiers
Rheinpark Stadion, Vaduz; Referee: Andris Treimanis (Latvia); Attendance: 5,087
LIE: Benjamin Büchel, Martin Rechsteiner, Daniel Kaufmann, Nicolas Hasler, Seyhan Yildiz (83.Sandro Wolfinger), Maximilian Göppel, Jens Hofer, Martin Büchel, Michele Polverino (Cap) (56.Noah Frick), Dennis Salanović, Robin Gubser (63.Yanik Frick). Trainer: Helgi Kolviðsson (Iceland).

15.11.2019   FINLAND - LIECHTENSTEIN   3-0(1-0)   16th EC. Qualifiers
Telia 5G-areena, Helsinki; Referee: Benoît Bastien (France); Attendance: 9,804
LIE: Benjamin Büchel, Martin Rechsteiner, Nicolas Hasler, Maximilian Göppel, Andreas Malin, Martin Büchel (Cap), Michele Polverino (73.Robin Gubser), Daniel Matthias Brändle, Dennis Salanović, Livio Meier (90+1.Aron Sele), Yanik Frick (84.Ridvan Kardesoglu). Trainer: Helgi Kolviðsson (Iceland).

18.11.2019   LIECHTENSTEIN - BOSNIA AND HERZEGOVINA   0-3(0-0)   16th EC. Qualifiers
Rheinpark Stadion, Vaduz Referee: Halis Özkahya (Turkey); Attendance: 2,993
LIE: Benjamin Büchel, Martin Rechsteiner, Nicolas Hasler, Maximilian Göppel, Andreas Malin, Martin Büchel (Cap), Michele Polverino (67.Noah Frommelt), Daniel Matthias Brändle, Sandro Wolfinger, Dennis Salanović (46.Seyhan Yildiz), Yanik Frick (82.Robin Gubser). Trainer: Helgi Kolviðsson (Iceland).

NATIONAL TEAM PLAYERS
(16.07.2019 – 15.07.2020)

Name	DOB	Caps	Goals	2019/2020:	Club
Goalkeepers					
Benjamin BÜCHEL	04.07.1989	29	0	2019:	*FC Vaduz*
Defenders					
Daniel Matthias BRÄNDLE	23.01.1992	27	0	2019:	*SV Pullach (GER)*
Maximilian GÖPPEL	31.08.1997	30	1	2019:	*FC Vaduz*
Jens HOFER	01.10.1997	6	0	2019:	*FC Vaduz*
Daniel KAUFMANN	22.12.1990	57	1	2019:	*FC Balzers*
Andreas MALIN	31.01.1994	19	0	2019:	*FC Dornbirn (AUT)*
Michele POLVERINO	26.09.1984	79	6	2019:	*FC Balzers*
Martin RECHSTEINER	15.02.1989	47	0	2019:	*FC Balzers*
Seyhan YILDIZ	30.04.1989	36	1	2019:	*FC Balzers*
Midfielders					
Martin BÜCHEL	19.02.1987	82	2	2019:	*FC Red Star Zürich (SUI)*
Noah FROMMELT	18.12.2000	1	0	2019:	*FC Balzers*
Robin GUBSER	17.04.1991	38	1	2019:	*USV Eschen/Mauren*
Nicolas HASLER	04.05.1991	67	3	2019:	*Sporting Kansas City (USA)*
Ridvan KARDESOGLU	12.10.1996	1	0	2019:	*FC Chur 97 (SUI)*
Livio MEIER	10.01.1998	12	0	2019:	*USV Eschen/Mauren*
Aron SELE	02.09.1996	19	0	2019:	*FC Vaduz*
Sandro WIESER	03.02.1993	53	2	2019:	*FC Vaduz*
Sandro WOLFINGER	24.08.1991	33	2	2019:	*USV Eschen/Mauren*
Forwards					
Noah FRICK	26.10.2001	2	0	2019:	*FC Vaduz*
Yanik FRICK	27.05.1998	11	1	2019:	*FC Rapperswil-Jona (SUI)*
Dennis SALANOVIĆ	26.02.1996	41	4	2019:	*FC Thun (SUI)*
National team coach					
Helgi KOLVIÐSSON (Iceland) [since 01.01.2019]	13.09.1971	10 M; 0 W; 2 D; 8 L; 2-31			

LITHUANIA

The Country:
Lietuvos Respublika (Republic of Lithuania)
Capital: Vilnius
Surface: 65,300 km²
Inhabitants: 2,794,329 [2020]
Time: UTC+2

The FA:
Lietuvos futbolo federacija
Stadiono g. 2, 02106 Vilnius
Tel: +370 5263 8741
Foundation date: 1922
Member of FIFA since: 1923
Member of UEFA since: 1992
Website: www.lff.lt

NATIONAL TEAM RECORDS

First international match:	24.06.1923, Kaunas:	Lithuania – Estonia 0-5
Most international caps:	Andrius Skerla	- 84 caps (1998-2012)
Most international goals:	Tomas Danilevičius	- 19 goals / 71 caps (1998-2014)

<table>
<tr><th colspan="2">UEFA EUROPEAN CHAMPIONSHIP</th><th colspan="2">FIFA WORLD CUP</th><th colspan="2">OLYMPIC TOURNAMENTS</th></tr>
<tr><td>1960</td><td>-</td><td>1930</td><td>Did Not Enter</td><td>1908</td><td>-</td></tr>
<tr><td>1964</td><td>-</td><td>1934</td><td>Qualifiers</td><td>1912</td><td>-</td></tr>
<tr><td>1968</td><td>-</td><td>1938</td><td>Qualifiers</td><td>1920</td><td>-</td></tr>
<tr><td>1972</td><td>-</td><td>1950</td><td>-</td><td>1924</td><td>FT/Preliminary Round</td></tr>
<tr><td>1976</td><td>-</td><td>1954</td><td>-</td><td>1928</td><td>-</td></tr>
<tr><td>1980</td><td>-</td><td>1958</td><td>-</td><td>1936</td><td>-</td></tr>
<tr><td>1984</td><td>-</td><td>1962</td><td>-</td><td>1948</td><td>-</td></tr>
<tr><td>1988</td><td>-</td><td>1966</td><td>-</td><td>1952</td><td>-</td></tr>
<tr><td>1992</td><td>-</td><td>1970</td><td>-</td><td>1956</td><td>-</td></tr>
<tr><td>1996</td><td>Qualifiers</td><td>1974</td><td>-</td><td>1960</td><td>-</td></tr>
<tr><td>2000</td><td>Qualifiers</td><td>1978</td><td>-</td><td>1964</td><td>-</td></tr>
<tr><td>2004</td><td>Qualifiers</td><td>1982</td><td>-</td><td>1968</td><td>-</td></tr>
<tr><td>2008</td><td>Qualifiers</td><td>1986</td><td>-</td><td>1972</td><td>-</td></tr>
<tr><td>2012</td><td>Qualifiers</td><td>1990</td><td>-</td><td>1976</td><td>-</td></tr>
<tr><td>2016</td><td>Qualifiers</td><td>1994</td><td>Qualifiers</td><td>1980</td><td>-</td></tr>
<tr><td>2020</td><td>Qualifiers</td><td>1998</td><td>Qualifiers</td><td>1984</td><td>-</td></tr>
<tr><td></td><td></td><td>2002</td><td>Qualifiers</td><td>1988</td><td>-</td></tr>
<tr><td></td><td></td><td>2006</td><td>Qualifiers</td><td>1992</td><td>-</td></tr>
<tr><td></td><td></td><td>2010</td><td>Qualifiers</td><td>1996</td><td>Qualifiers</td></tr>
<tr><td></td><td></td><td>2014</td><td>Qualifiers</td><td>2000</td><td>Qualifiers</td></tr>
<tr><td></td><td></td><td>2018</td><td>Qualifiers</td><td>2004</td><td>Qualifiers</td></tr>
<tr><td></td><td></td><td></td><td></td><td>2008</td><td>Qualifiers</td></tr>
<tr><td></td><td></td><td></td><td></td><td>2012</td><td>Qualifiers</td></tr>
<tr><td></td><td></td><td></td><td></td><td>2016</td><td>Qualifiers</td></tr>
</table>

Please note: *was part of Soviet Union from 1944 to 1990.*

UEFA NATIONS LEAGUE
2018/2019 – League C (relegated to League D)

FIFA CONFEDERATIONS CUP 1992-2017
None

LITHUANIAN CLUB HONOURS IN EUROPEAN CLUB COMPETITIONS:

European Champion Clubs' Cup (1956-1992) / UEFA Champions League (1993-2020)
None

Fairs Cup (1858-1971) / UEFA Cup (1972-2009) / UEFA Europa League (2010-2020)
None

UEFA Super Cup (1972-2019)
None

European Cup Winners' Cup 1961-1999*
None

defunct competition

NATIONAL COMPETITIONS
TABLE OF HONOURS

LITHUANIAN SSR (SOVIET ERA) CHAMPIONS

Year	Champion	Year	Champion	Year	Champion
1945	Spartakas Kaunas	1959/1960	Elnias Šiauliai	1975	Dainava Alytus
1946	Dinamo Kaunas	1960/1961	Elnias Šiauliai	1976	Atmosfera Mažeikiai
1947	Lokomotyvas Kaunas	1961/1962	FK Atletas Kaunas	1977	Statybininkas Šiauliai
1948	Elnias Šiauliai	1962/1963	Statyba Panevėžys	1978	Atlantas Klaipėda
1949	Elnias Šiauliai	1964	Inkaras Kaunas	1979	Atmosfera Mažeikiai
1950	Inkaras Kaunas	1965	Inkaras Kaunas	1980	Atlantas Klaipėda
1951	Inkaras Kaunas	1966	Nevėžis Kėdainiai	1981	Atlantas Klaipėda
1952	Karininkų Namai Vilnius	1967	Saliutas Vilnius	1982	Pažanga Vilnius
1953	Elnias Šiauliai	1968	Statyba Panevėžys	1983	Pažanga Vilnius
1954	Inkaras Kaunas	1969	Statybininkas Šiauliai	1984	Atlantas Klaipėda
1955	Lima Kaunas	1970	FK Atletas Kaunas	1985	Ekranas Panevėžys
1956	Linų Audiniai Plungė	1971	Pažanga Vilnius	1986	Banga Kaunas
1957	Elnias Šiauliai	1972	Nevėžis Kėdainiai	1987	Tauras Tauragė
1958	Elnias Šiauliai	1973	Nevėžis Kėdainiai	1988	SRT Vilnius
1958/1959	Raudonoji Žvaigždė Vilnius	1974	Tauras Šiauliai	1989	Banga Kaunas

Year	CHAMPIONS	CUP WINNERS	BEST GOALSCORERS	
1922	LFLS Kaunas	-	-	
1923	LFLS Kaunas	-	-	
1924	Kovas Kaunas	-	-	
1925	Kovas Kaunas	-	-	
1926	Kovas Kaunas	-	-	
1927	LFLS Kaunas	-	-	
1928	KSS Klaipėda	-	-	
1929	KSS Klaipėda	-	-	
1930	KSS Klaipėda	-	-	
1931	KSS Klaipėda	-	-	
1932	LFLS Kaunas	-	-	
1933	Kovas Kaunas	-	-	
1934	MSK Kaunas	-	-	
1935	Kovas Kaunas	-	-	
1936	Kovas Kaunas	-	-	
1937	KSS Klaipėda	-	-	
1937/1938	KSS Klaipėda	-	-	
1938/1939	LGSF Kaunas	-	-	
1939/1940	*Competition abandoned*	-	-	
1941	*Competition not finished*	-	-	
1942	LFLS Kaunas	-	-	
1942/1943	Tauras Kaunas	-	-	
1943/1944	*Competition not finished*	-	-	
	--	--	--	
1990	FK Sirijus Klaipėda	FK Sirijus Klaipėda	Dalius Bajorūnas (FK Tauras Šiauliai)	22
1991	FK Žalgiris Vilnius	FK Žalgiris Vilnius	Egidijus Meidus (Vilija Kaunas)	13
1991/1992	FK Žalgiris Vilnius	FK Makabi Vilnius	Remigijus Pocius (FK Granitas Klaipėda / FK Sakalas Šiauliai) Vaidotas Šlekys (FK Ekranas Panevėžys)	14
1992/1993	FK Ekranas Panevėžys	FK Žalgiris Vilnius	Vaidotas Šlekys (FK Ekranas Panevėžys)	16
1993/1994	ROMAR Mažeikiai	FK Žalgiris Vilnius	Vaidotas Šlekys (FK Ekranas Panevėžys) Robertas Žalys (FBK Kaunas)	16
1994/1995	FK Inkaras-Grifas Kaunas	FK Inkaras-Grifas Kaunas	Eimantas Poderis (FK Žalgiris Vilnius / FK Inkaras-Grifas Kaunas)	24
1995/1996	FK Inkaras-Grifas Kaunas	FK Kareda-Sakalas Šiauliai	Edgaras Jankauskas (FK Žalgiris Vilnius)	25
1996/1997	FK Kareda Šiauliai	FK Žalgiris Vilnius	Remigijus Pocius (FK Kareda Šiauliai)	14
1997/1998	FK Kareda Šiauliai	FK Ekranas Panevėžys	Vidas Dančenka (FK Kareda Šiauliai)	26
1998/1999	FK Žalgiris Vilnius	FK Kareda Šiauliai	Artūras Fomenka (FK Kareda Šiauliai)	14
1999	FBK Kaunas	*No competition*	Nerijus Vasiliauskas (FK Žalgiris Vilnius)	10
2000	FBK Kaunas	FK Ekranas Panevėžys (1999/2000)	Andrius Velička (FBK Kaunas)	26
2001	FBK Kaunas	FK Atlantas Klaipėda (2000/01)	Remigijus Pocius (FBK Kaunas)	22
2002	FBK Kaunas	FBK Kaunas (2001/02)	Audrius Šlekys (FBK Kaunas)	19
2003	FBK Kaunas	FK Sūduva Marijampolė (2002/03) FK Žalgiris Vilnius (2003)	Ričardas Beniušis (FK Atlantas Klaipėda / FBK Kaunas)	16
2004	FBK Kaunas	FBK Kaunas	Povilas Lukšys (FK Ekranas Panevėžys)	19
2005	FK Ekranas Panevėžys	FBK Kaunas	Mantas Savėnas (FK Ekranas Panevėžys)	27
2006	FBK Kaunas	FK Sūduva Marijampolė	Serhiy Kuznetsov (UKR, FK Vėtra Vilnius)	18
2007	FBK Kaunas	*No competition*	Povilas Lukšys (FK Ekranas Panevėžys)	26
2008	FK Ekranas Panevėžys	FBK Kaunas (2007/08)	Rafael Pompeo Rodrigues Ledesma (BRA, FBK Kaunas)	14
2009	FK Ekranas Panevėžys	FK Sūduva Marijampolė (2008/09)	Valdas Trakys (FK Ekranas Panevėžys)	20
2010	FK Ekranas Panevėžys	FK Ekranas Panevėžys (2009/10)	Povilas Lukšys (FK Sūduva Marijampolė)	16

2011	FK Ekranas Panevėžys	FK Ekranas Panevėžys (2010/11)	Deivydas Matulevičius (FK Žalgiris Vilnius)	19
2012	FK Ekranas Panevėžys	FK Žalgiris Vilnius (2011/12)	Artūras Rimkevičius (FK Šiauliai)	35
2013	FK Žalgiris Vilnius	FK Žalgiris Vilnius (2012/13)	Nerijus Valskis (FK Sūduva Marijampolė)	27
2014	FK Žalgiris Vilnius	FK Žalgiris Vilnius (2013/14)	Niko Tokić (CRO, FK Šiauliai)	19
2015	FK Žalgiris Vilnius	FK Žalgiris Vilnius (2014/15)	Tomas Radzinevičius (FK Sūduva Marijampolė)	28
2016	FK Žalgiris Vilnius	FK Žalgiris Vilnius (2015/16) FK Žalgiris Vilnius (2016)	Andrija Kaluđerović (SRB, FK Žalgiris Vilnius)	20
2017	FK Sūduva Marijampolė	FC Stumbras Kaunas	Darvydas Šernas (FK Žalgiris Vilnius)	18
2018	FK Sūduva Marijampolė	FK Žalgiris Vilnius	Liviu Ion Antal (ROU, FK Žalgiris Vilnius)	23
2019	FK Sūduva Marijampolė	FK Sūduva Marijampolė	Tomislav Kiš (CRO, FK Žalgiris Vilnius)	26

NATIONAL CHAMPIONSHIP
A Lyga 2019
(02.03.2019 – 27.11.2019)

Regular Season - Results

Round 1 [02-03.03.2019]
FK Atlantas - FK Kauno Žalgiris 2-0(1-0)
FC Stumbras - FK Panevėžys 1-0(0-0)
FK Sūduva - FK Riteriai 2-1(0-0)
FK Žalgiris - FK Palanga 5-1(1-1)

Round 2 [09-11.03.2019]
FK Kauno Žalgiris - FK Palanga 6-1(2-0)
FK Panevėžys - FK Žalgiris 0-3(0-1)
FK Atlantas - FK Sūduva 0-5(0-3)
FK Riteriai - FC Stumbras 0-0

Round 3 [15-17.03.2019]
FK Žalgiris - FK Riteriai 1-1(0-0)
FC Stumbras - FK Atlantas 2-0(0-0)
FK Sūduva - FK Kauno Žalgiris 1-0(0-0)
FK Palanga - FK Panevėžys 1-1(1-0)

Round 4 [30.03.-02.04.2019]
FK Kauno Žalgiris - FK Panevėžys 2-0(1-0)
FK Atlantas - FK Žalgiris 0-3(0-1)
FC Stumbras - FK Sūduva 2-0(0-0)
FK Riteriai - FK Palanga 3-1(3-1)

Round 5 [06-07.04.2019]
FK Palanga - FK Atlantas 2-1(0-1)
FC Stumbras - FK Kauno Žalgiris 0-1(0-0)
FK Panevėžys - FK Riteriai 1-2(0-1)
FK Žalgiris - FK Sūduva 1-0(1-0)

Round 6 [13-14.04.2019]
FK Kauno Žalgiris - FK Riteriai 3-1(0-0)
FC Stumbras - FK Žalgiris 1-0(0-0)
FK Atlantas - FK Panevėžys 2-1(1-0)
FK Sūduva - FK Palanga 3-0(1-0)

Round 7 [19-20.04.2019]
FK Panevėžys - FK Sūduva 1-2(1-1)
FK Žalgiris - FK Kauno Žalgiris 3-1(2-1)
FK Palanga - FC Stumbras 2-1(0-0)
FK Riteriai - FK Atlantas 0-0

Round 8 [27.04.2019]
FK Panevėžys - FC Stumbras 1-1(0-1)
FK Palanga - FK Žalgiris 1-4(1-1)
FK Kauno Žalgiris - FK Atlantas 2-1(1-0)
FK Riteriai - FK Sūduva 1-2(0-1)

Round 9 [04-05.05.2019]
FC Stumbras - FK Riteriai 0-3(0-1)
FK Palanga - FK Kauno Žalgiris 0-3(0-2)
FK Sūduva - FK Atlantas 4-0(1-0)
FK Žalgiris - FK Panevėžys 2-1(1-1)

Round 10 [11-12.05.2019]
FK Riteriai - FK Žalgiris 1-0(0-0)
FK Kauno Žalgiris - FK Sūduva 0-3(0-2)
FK Atlantas - FC Stumbras 0-0
FK Panevėžys - FK Palanga 2-1(0-0)

Round 11 [17-18.05.2019]
FK Žalgiris - FK Atlantas 3-0(3-0)
FK Panevėžys - FK Kauno Žalgiris 1-1(1-0)
FK Palanga - FK Riteriai 1-3(1-1)
FK Sūduva - FC Stumbras 2-0(1-0)

Round 12 [21-22.05.2019]
FK Atlantas - FK Palanga 2-1(1-0)
FK Riteriai - FK Panevėžys 1-1(1-1)
FK Kauno Žalgiris - FC Stumbras 4-3(1-3)
FK Sūduva - FK Žalgiris 1-0(0-0)

Round 13 [31.05.-02.06.2019]
FK Žalgiris - FC Stumbras 2-1(0-1)
FK Palanga - FK Sūduva 0-2(0-0)
FK Riteriai - FK Kauno Žalgiris 1-0(0-0)
FK Panevėžys - FK Atlantas 4-1(3-1)

Round 14 [14-15.06.2019]
FK Atlantas - FK Riteriai 2-3(2-0)
FK Kauno Žalgiris - FK Žalgiris 3-4(2-3)
FC Stumbras - FK Palanga 0-3 (awarded)
FK Sūduva - FK Panevėžys 2-1(0-1)

Round 15 [22-23.06.2019]
FC Stumbras - FK Panevėžys 0-3 (awarded)
FK Atlantas - FK Kauno Žalgiris 1-1(0-1)
FK Sūduva - FK Riteriai 1-2(1-1)
FK Žalgiris - FK Palanga 3-2(2-2)

Round 16 [29.06.2019]
FK Riteriai - FC Stumbras 3-0 (awarded)
FK Panevėžys - FK Žalgiris 0-2(0-2)
FK Kauno Žalgiris - FK Palanga 4-0(2-0)
FK Sūduva - FK Atlantas 4-1(0-1)

Round 17 [03-06.07.2019]
FK Sūduva - FK Kauno Žalgiris 3-0(2-0)
FK Palanga - FK Panevėžys 1-2(1-0)
FK Žalgiris - FK Riteriai 2-1(0-1)
FC Stumbras - FK Atlantas 0-3 (awarded)

Round 18 [03-04.08.2019]
FK Sūduva - FC Stumbras 3-0 (awarded)
FK Kauno Žalgiris - FK Panevėžys 2-2(1-1)
FK Riteriai - FK Palanga 1-0(1-0)
FK Atlantas - FK Žalgiris 1-3(1-1)

Round 19 [10-11.08.2019]
FK Riteriai - FK Atlantas 1-1(0-1)
FK Palanga - FC Stumbras 3-0 (awarded)
FK Žalgiris - FK Kauno Žalgiris 3-0(2-0)
FK Panevėžys - FK Sūduva 2-7(1-3) [24.09.]

Round 20 [17-18.08.2019]
FK Kauno Žalgiris - FK Riteriai 1-0(0-0)
FC Stumbras - FK Žalgiris 0-3 (awarded)
FK Atlantas - FK Panevėžys 0-2(0-1)
FK Sūduva - FK Palanga 5-0(1-0) [02.10.]

Round 21 [23-25.08.2019]
FK Panevėžys - FK Riteriai 4-2(1-1)
FC Stumbras - Kauno Žalgiris 0-3 (awarded)
FK Palanga - FK Atlantas 0-2(0-0)
FK Žalgiris - FK Sūduva 1-3(1-2) [20.10.]

Round 22 [31.08.-01.09.2019]
FK Palanga - FK Žalgiris 0-4(0-3)
FK Kauno Žalgiris - FK Atlantas 1-0(0-0)
FK Panevėžys - FC Stumbras 3-0 (awarded)
FK Riteriai - FK Sūduva 1-2(1-0) [15.10.]

Round 23 [13-14.09.2019]
FK Sūduva - FK Atlantas 4-0(3-0)
FK Žalgiris - FK Panevėžys 5-0(1-0)
FK Palanga - FK Kauno Žalgiris 2-3(1-1)
FC Stumbras - FK Riteriai 0-3 (awarded)

Round 24 [21.09.2019]
FK Panevėžys - FK Palanga 3-1(0-1) [12.08.]
FK Riteriai - FK Žalgiris 1-1(1-1)
FK Kauno Žalgiris - FK Sūduva 0-2(0-1)
FK Atlantas - FC Stumbras 3-0 (awarded)

Round 25 [25-28.09.2019]
FK Palanga - FK Riteriai 1-3(1-2)
FC Stumbras - FK Sūduva 0-3 (awarded)
FK Žalgiris - FK Atlantas 4-0(2-0)
FK Panevėžys - FK Kauno Žalgiris 3-3(0-1)

Round 26 [05.10.2019]
FK Kauno Žalgiris - FK Žalgiris 1-2(1-1)
FK Atlantas - FK Riteriai 2-1(0-1)
FC Stumbras - FK Palanga 0-3 (awarded)
FK Sūduva - FK Panevėžys 3-1(2-1)

Round 27 [19.10.2019]
FK Palanga - FK Sūduva 0-4(0-2) [12.10.]
FK Žalgiris - FC Stumbras 3-0 (awarded)
FK Riteriai - FK Kauno Žalgiris 0-0
FK Panevėžys - FK Atlantas 1-1(1-1)

Round 28 [26.10.2019]
Kauno Žalgiris - FC Stumbras 3-0 (awarded)
FK Sūduva - FK Žalgiris 1-0(1-0)
FK Atlantas - FK Palanga 0-1(0-1)
FK Riteriai - FK Panevėžys 4-0(2-0)

Final Standings

		Total						Home						Away				
1. FK Sūduva Marijampolė	28	25	0	3	74	-	15	75	13	0	1	35	-	6	12	0	2	39 - 9
2. FK Žalgiris Vilnius	28	21	2	5	67	-	22	65	12	1	1	38	-	11	9	1	4	29 - 11
3. FK Riteriai Vilnius	28	13	7	8	44	-	29	46	6	6	2	18	-	8	7	1	6	26 - 21
4. FK Kauno Žalgiris Kaunas	28	13	5	10	48	-	39	44	9	1	4	32	-	19	4	4	6	16 - 20
5. FK Panevėžys	28	8	7	13	41	-	53	31	5	4	5	26	-	27	3	3	8	15 - 26
6. FK Atlantas Klaipėda	28	7	5	16	26	-	53	26	5	2	7	15	-	25	2	3	9	11 - 28
7. FK Palanga (*Relegation Play-offs*)	28	6	1	21	29	-	70	19	3	1	10	14	-	33	3	0	11	15 - 37
8. FC Stumbras Kaunas (*Relegated*)	28	4	3	21	12	-	60	15	4	0	10	6	-	28	0	3	11	6 - 32

Please note: FK Trakai changed its name to FK Riteriai and moved to Vilnius.
On 28.06.2019, FC Stumbras Kaunas' license to play at First Level was cancelled, all remaining matches being awarded 0-3 losses.
Teams ranked 1-6 were qualified for the Championship Round.

Championship Round

Results

Round 29 [30-31.10.2019]
FK Sūduva - FK Atlantas 9-1(6-0)
FK Žalgiris - FK Panevėžys 3-1(1-0)
FK Riteriai - FK Kauno Žalgiris 0-1(0-0)

Round 30 [03-04.11.2019]
FK Panevėžys - FK Sūduva 1-5(0-3)
FK Kauno Žalgiris - FK Žalgiris 1-2(1-0)
FK Riteriai - FK Atlantas 5-2(2-2)

Round 31 [08-09.11.2019]
FK Atlantas - FK Panevėžys 1-4(1-1)
FK Žalgiris - FK Riteriai 1-3(1-2)
FK Sūduva - FK Kauno Žalgiris 4-1(1-1)

Round 32 [22-23.11.2019]
FK Žalgiris - FK Atlantas 5-0(3-0)
FK Riteriai - FK Sūduva 5-1(2-1)
FK Kauno Žalgiris - FK Panevėžys 1-0(1-0)

Round 33 [27.11.2019]
FK Sūduva - FK Žalgiris 2-1(1-1)
FK Panevėžys - FK Riteriai 2-0(0-0)
FK Atlantas - FK Kauno Žalgiris 0-2(0-1)

Final Standings

		Total						Home						Away				
1. **FK Sūduva Marijampolė**	33	29	0	4	95	-	24	87	16	0	1	50	-	9	13	0	3	45 - 15
2. FK Žalgiris Vilnius	33	24	2	7	79	-	29	74	14	1	2	47	15		10	1	5	32 - 14
3. FK Riteriai Vilnius	33	16	7	10	57	-	36	55	8	6	3	28	-	12	8	1	7	29 - 24
4. FK Kauno Žalgiris Kaunas	33	16	5	12	54	-	45	53	10	1	5	34	-	21	6	4	7	20 - 24
5. FK Panevėžys	33	10	7	16	49	-	63	37	6	4	6	29	-	32	4	3	10	20 - 31
6. FK Atlantas Klaipėda	33	7	5	21	30	-	78	26	5	2	9	16	-	31	2	3	12	14 - 47

Top goalscorers:	
26 **Tomislav Kiš (CRO,)**	*FK Žalgiris Vilnius*
21 Mihret Topčagić (BIH)	*FK Sūduva Marijampolė*
18 Terem Igoboras Moffi (NGA)	*FK Riteriai Vilnius*
15 Liviu Ion Antal (ROU)	*FK Žalgiris Vilnius*
12 Donatas Kazlauskas	*FK Riteriai Vilnius*
10 João Vitor Brandão Figueiredo (BRA)	*FK Kauno Žalgiris Kaunas*
10 Josip Tadić (CRO)	*FK Sūduva Marijampolė*

Relegation Play-offs [03-09.11.2019]

FK Banga Gargždai - FK Palanga   2-0(1-0)   2-2(1-0)

FK Banga Gargždai promoted to A Lyga 2020.

NATIONAL CUP
Lietuvos futbolo taurė 2019

Third Round [24-29.05.2019]

FC Kupiškis - FK Minija Kretinga	0-3 pen	FK Kauno Žalgiris - FK Riteriai Vilnius	4-3 pen
FC Pakruojis - FK Nevėžis Kėdainiai	1-3	FK Aukštaitija Panevėžys - FK Sūduva Marijampolė	2-3
Marijampolė City FA Suv. - DFK Dainava Alytus	4-3 aet	FK Geležinis Vilkas Vilnius - FK Babrungas Plungė	0-4
Sveikata Kybartai - FK Šilas Kazlų Rūda	1-0	FK Atlantas Klaipėda - FK Žalgiris Vilnius	0-2
FK Kėdainiai - FA Šiauliai	1-2	FK Viltis Vilnius - FC Vilniaus Vytis	2-4
FK TERA Vilnius - FK Banga Gargždai	0-2	FM Ateitis Vilnius - FK Panevėžys	0-1
FK Navigatoriai Vilnius - FC Džiugas Telšiai	0-2	FC Hegelmann Litauen Kaunas - FK Panevėžys	0-4
ŠSPC Radviliškis - FC Stumbras Kaunas	1-2	SC Baltai Kaišiadorys - FKK Spartakas Ukmergė	4-5 aet

1/8-Finals [18/19/25/26.06.2019]

FKK Spartakas Ukmergė - FK Banga Gargždai	0-3	FK Minija Kretinga - FK Kauno Žalgiris	1-2
FK Babrungas Plungė - FK Palanga	0-4	FC Džiugas Telšiai - FC Vilniaus Vytis	2-1
FK Žalgiris Vilnius - FC Stumbras Kaunas	3-0 (awarded)	Sveikata Kybartai - FK Nevėžis Kėdainiai	0-1
Marijampolė City FA Suv. - FK Sūduva Marijampolė	1-4	FA Šiauliai - FK Panevėžys	1-6 aet

Quarter-Finals [27-28.08./08.09.2019]

FK Nevėžis Kėdainiai - FK Žalgiris	1-5	FC Džiugas - FK Palanga	3-5 pen
FK Banga Gargždai - FK Kauno Žalgiris	5-4 pen	FK Sūduva Marijampolė - FK Panevėžys	1-0

Semi-Finals [17-18.09.2019]

FK Sūduva Marijampolė - FK Žalgiris	4-2(2-1,2-2)	FK Banga Gargždai - FK Palanga	2-0

Final

29.09.2019; Utenis stadionas, Utena; Referee: Robertas Šmitas; Attendance: 1,837

FK Sūduva Marijampolė - FK Banga Gargždai   **4-0(1-0)**

FK Sūduva: Ivan Kardum, Karlo Bručić, Semir Kerla, Algis Jankauskas, Povilas Leimonas, Renan Henrique Oliveira Vieira (66.Paulius Golubickas), Andro Švrljuga [*sent off 76*], Giedrius Matulevičius (90.Jovan Čađenović), Ovidijus Verbickas, Eligijus Jankauskas (59.Mihret Topčagić), Josip Tadić. Trainer: Vladimir Cheburin.

FK Banga: Tadas Norbutas, Karolis Urbaitis, Valdas Pocevičius, Deividas Padaigis, Kazimieras Gnedojus, Valdas Antužis (78.Darius Zubauskas), Edvinas Bračkus, Dovydas Norvilas (84.Paulius Lotužys), Jonas Bičkus (55.Gediminas Kruša), Renato Matos da Silva, Deividas Lukošius. Trainer: Aurimas Šlušnys.

Goals: 1-0 Josip Tadić (21), 2-0 Renan Henrique Oliveira Vieira (56), 3-0 Mihret Topčagić (89), 4-0 Mihret Topčagić (90+2).

THE CLUBS 2019

Please note: matches and goals includes statistics of both Regular Season and Championship Round.

Futbolo Klubas Atlantas Klaipėda

Founded:	1962	
Stadium:	Klaipėdos centrinis stadionas, Klaipėda (4,428)	
Trainer:	Viktors Dobrecovs (LVA)	09.01.1977
[02.11.2019]	Donatas Navikas	30.06.1983

Goalkeepers:	DOB	M	(s)	G
Stefano Kunchev (BUL)	20.04.1991	4		
Lukas Paukštė	25.09.1998	21		
Krišjānis Zviedris (LVA)	25.01.1997	6		
Defenders:	**DOB**	**M**	**(s)**	**G**
Andrius Bartkus	21.01.1986	26	(1)	
Jose Antonia Carrion Mayorga (NCA)	20.03.1989	11	(5)	
Marius Činikas	17.05.1986	25	(2)	
Klimas Gusočenko	09.03.1989	6	(3)	
Tomas Gvazdinskas	03.04.2000	4		1
Tomas Snapkauskas	12.06.1992	5		
Tautvydas Špiegis	25.05.2003	4	(1)	
Aurimas Tručinskas	25.10.1994	4		
Pavel Vidanov (BUL)	01.08.1988	1		
Damir Žutić (CRO)	22.07.1993	22	(2)	
Midfielders:	**DOB**	**M**	**(s)**	**G**
Vilius Armanavičius	08.05.1995	29	(1)	1

Marius Vladimir Cocîrlă (ROU)	22.06.1996	11	(2)	
Deivids Dobrecovs (LVA)	26.02.1997	23	(6)	4
Mateo Dunić (CRO)	27.12.1999	2	(3)	
Gustas Gumbaravičius	21.02.2000		(3)	
Akinjide Idowu (NGA)	09.09.1996	26		
Ņikita Juhņevičs (LVA)	28.05.1997	9	(6)	
Jurica Kovačić (CRO)	30.03.1994	7	(5)	
Dimitar Petkov (BUL)	24.08.1987	15		
Titas Vitukynas	23.10.1994	10	(13)	2
Forwards:	**DOB**	**M**	**(s)**	**G**
Bonfils-Caleb Bimenyimana (BDI)	21.11.1997	13		3
Tadas Labukas	10.01.1984	13	(15)	3
Vytautas Lukša	14.08.1984	18	(5)	3
Darvydas Šernas	22.07.1984	23		6
Klaudijus Upstas	30.10.1994	3	(6)	
Martynas Velyvis	23.08.1998		(3)	

Futbolo klubas Kauno Žalgiris Kaunas

Founded:	2004
Stadium:	SM Tauras stadionas, Kaunas (500)
Trainer:	Mindaugas Čepas 06.06.1978

Goalkeepers:	DOB	M	(s)	G
Martynas Matuzas	28.08.1989	7		
Deividas Mikelionis	08.05.1995	24		
Defenders:	**DOB**	**M**	**(s)**	**G**
Martynas Dapkus	16.02.1993	26	(1)	
Arūnas Klimavičius	05.10.1982	13	(4)	1
Tomas Mikuckis	13.01.1983	14		1
Ernestas Mockus	05.08.2000	2		
Rudinilson Gomes Brito Silva „Rudi" (GNB)	20.08.1994	20		
Rimvydas Sadauskas	21.07.1996	12		1
Karolis Šilkaitis	02.06.1996	25	(2)	1
Pijus Širvys	01.04.1998	11	(8)	5
Midfielders:	**DOB**	**M**	**(s)**	**G**
Benas Anisas	29.02.2000	2	(11)	
Yuriy Bushman (UKR)	14.05.1990	26	(1)	4
Dominykas Galkevičius	16.10.1986	13	(7)	2
Edvinas Kloniūnas	28.06.1998	8	(5)	3
Linas Pilibaitis	05.04.1985	28		4
Danielis Romanovskis	19.06.1996	23	(4)	3
Egidijus Vaitkūnas	08.08.1988	15	(2)	1
Forwards:	**DOB**	**M**	**(s)**	**G**
João Vitor Brandão Figueiredo (BRA)	27.05.1996	17		10
Rokas Krušnauskas	04.11.1995	13	(10)	4
Deivydas Matulevičius	08.04.1989	10	(1)	3
Philip Porwei Otele (NGA)	15.04.1999	3	(11)	
Renato Matos da Silva (BRA)	03.05.1996	7	(5)	1
Deividas Šešplaukis	02.02.1998	13	(16)	1
Simonas Urbys	07.11.1995	9	(4)	2

Palangos Futbolo Klubas

Founded:	2011
Stadium:	Palanga stadionas, Palanga (1,212)
Trainer:	Artem Gorlov (RUS) 23.06.1987
[21.07.2019]	Vyacheslav Gerashchenko (BLR) 25.07.1972
[17.09.2019]	Algimantas Briaunys 03.11.1964

Goalkeepers:	DOB	M	(s)	G
Marijan Ćorić (CRO)	06.02.1995	8		
Jackson Allan da Cruz Miguel (BRA)	24.07.1992	3		
Jere Koponen (FIN)	23.05.1992	3	(1)	
Tadas Norbutas	25.02.1994	5		
Marius Paukštė	15.12.1994	6		
Defenders:	**DOB**	**M**	**(s)**	**G**
Laurynas Bauža	18.02.2003		(2)	
Mindaugas Bagužis	11.04.1983	15		
Giorgi Diakvnishvili (GEO)	21.11.1987	5	(3)	1
Matvyi Guiganov (UKR)	28.07.1994	9		
Klimas Gusočenko	09.03.1989	4	(1)	
Christos Intzidis (GRE)	09.01.1993	5		
Aurimas Jurgelevičius	09.01.1997	4	(2)	1
Josip Jurjević (CRO)	10.01.1994	8		
Vladislavs Kuzmins (LVA)	20.01.1996	5	(1)	
Andrew das Neves Lebre (POR)	12.03.1997	7	(1)	
Thomas Mathieu Phibel (GLP)	21.05.1986	16		
Justas Raziūnas	23.01.1995	14	(2)	
Aurimas Skurdelis	06.03.1994	13	(2)	
Alan Facundo Torres (BRA)	29.12.1995		(5)	
Aurimas Tručinskas	25.10.1994	8	(1)	
Midfielders:	**DOB**	**M**	**(s)**	**G**
Ivan Baklanov (RUS)	16.03.1995	6	(4)	1
Josip Balić (CRO)	08.07.1993	9	(2)	
Tomas Dombrauskis	24.09.1996	13	(2)	1
Tadas Eliošius	01.03.1990	1	(1)	
Erikas Jonauskis	18.05.2002	1	(3)	
Gvidas Juška	17.08.1982	2	(8)	
Sergey Karetnik (UKR)	14.02.1995	10		
Andrejs Kiriļins (LVA)	03.11.1995	6	(3)	1
Sergei Mošnikov (EST)	07.01.1988	22	(1)	1
Sergey Rusak (BLR)	03.09.1993	4		
Klaudijus Upstas	30.10.1994	7		
Andriy Yakovlev (MDA)	20.02.1989	8	(1)	
Forwards:	**DOB**	**M**	**(s)**	**G**
Dominykas Jakočiūnas	07.09.2002	1	(3)	
Andrey Myazin (RUS)	27.10.1987	16		4
Kouakou Privat Yao (CIV)	30.06.1991	15	(6)	2
Sam Shaban (ENG)	04.11.1995	2		
Vladimirs Stepanovs (LVA)	06.02.2000		(1)	
Idris Umaev (RUS)	15.01.1999	14		7

Futbolo Klubas Panevėžys

Founded:	2015
Stadium:	Aukštaitija stadionas, Panevėžys (6,600)
Trainer:	Alexandru Curtianu (MDA) 11.02.1974

Goalkeepers:	DOB	M	(s)	G
Rafael Broetto Henrique (BRA)	18.08.1990	15		
Šarūnas Jurevičius	05.03.1989	7		
Marius Suvaizdis	22.02.1995	9		
Defenders:	**DOB**	**M**	**(s)**	**G**
Lukas Čerkauskas	12.03.1994	23	(1)	
Mantas Fridrikas	13.09.1988	24	(1)	
Vytas Gašpuitis	04.03.1994	30		5
Tomas Kačerauskas	26.07.2001	9	(2)	
Andriy Karvatskyi	12.06.1997	12	(3)	
Sigitas Urbys	07.11.1995	20	(2)	
Midfielders:	**DOB**	**M**	**(s)**	**G**
Andrei Ciofu (MDA)	31.05.1994	8		1
Tadas Eliošius	01.03.1990	2	(7)	1
Tautvydas Eliošius	03.11.1991	27	(2)	2
Paulius Janušauskas	28.02.1989	29	(1)	4
Pavel Kruk (BLR)	03.02.1992	24		4
Rafael Pompeu Rodrigues Ledesma (BRA)	31.12.1982	10	(18)	6
Sidimane Sagna (SEN)	04.02.1990	5	(1)	
Tomas Salamanavičius	31.03.1993	1	(12)	1
Jonas Skinderis	04.04.1997	2	(8)	1
Rokas Stanulevičius	02.10.1994	8	(7)	
Ernestas Veliulis	22.08.1992	19	(4)	2
Forwards:	**DOB**	**M**	**(s)**	**G**
Eimantas Abramavicius	13.02.2002	2	(3)	
Patrik Bordon (SVN)	06.04.1988	10	(3)	6
Edvardas Tamulevičius	04.01.1994	1	(5)	
Sebastián Vásquez Gamboa (COL)	24.05.1996	23	(5)	7
Aleksandr Yerkin (RUS)	01.09.1989	21	(2)	2

Futbolo Klubas Riteriai Vilnius

Founded: 2005
Stadium: LFF stadionas, Vilnius (5,067)
Trainer: Auri Skarbalius   12.05.1973
[19.07.2019] Albert Rybak (BLR)   16.05.1973

Goalkeepers:	DOB	M	(s)	G
Tadas Simaitis	29.12.1990	10		
Vincentas Šarkauskas	11.08.1999	6	(1)	
Tomas Švedkauskas	22.06.1994	15		
Defenders:	DOB	M	(s)	G
Dominykas Barauskas	18.04.1997	13	(1)	
Valdemars Borovskis	05.02.1984	31		2
Justinas Januševskis	26.03.1994	18	(2)	1
Rokas Masenzovas	02.08.1994	1	(4)	
Ernestas Stočkūnas	11.05.1998	10	(9)	1
Ricardas Šveikauskas	09.04.1997	27		3
Midfielders:	DOB	M	(s)	G
Elvinas Ališauskas	22.02.1999		(1)	
David Amoah (GHA)	14.03.2000		(1)	
Svajūnas Čyžas	26.01.1998		(3)	
Artūr Dolžnikov	06.06.2000	3		

	DOB	M	(s)	G
Tomas Dombrauskis	24.09.1996	12	(1)	
Rokas Filipavicius	22.12.1999	4	(8)	
Mindaugas Grigaravičius	15.07.1992	16	(13)	8
Valentin Jeriomenko	19.02.1989	25	(2)	1
Donatas Kazlauskas	31.03.1994	29		12
Aleksandr Levšinas	14.08.1999	19	(2)	
Juozas Lubas	22.05.2002		(2)	
Justinas Marazas	23.02.2000	5	(6)	
Matas Ramanauskas	28.06.2000	15	(5)	
Lajo Traoré (CIV)	20.12.1993	16	(2)	1
Dovydas Virkšas	01.07.1997	20	(8)	1
Forwards:	DOB	M	(s)	G
Edvinas Baniulis	03.01.1997	1	(3)	
Artem Gurenko (BLR)	18.06.1994	13	(2)	3
Dominyk Kodz	25.04.2000	3	(6)	
Terem Igoboras Moffi (NGA)	25.05.1999	29		18

Football Club Stumbras Kaunas

Founded: 2013
Stadium: NFA stadionas, Kaunas (500)
Trainer: João Luís Gouveia Martins (POR)   24.04.1967

Goalkeepers:	DOB	M	(s)	G
Rodrigo Martins Josviaki (BRA)	16.02.1995	13		
Defenders:	DOB	M	(s)	G
Juan Gerardo Ramírez Alonso (MEX)	16.05.1998	13		
André Filipe Lopes Almeida (POR)	16.05.1995	3		
Mateus Santos Gama „Mateus Júnior" (BRA)	27.10.1994	7	(5)	
Arnas Paura	29.02.2000		(1)	
Rimvydas Sadauskas	21.07.1996	13		
Midfielders:	DOB	M	(s)	G
Mantas Adomėnas	18.08.1998		(1)	
Domantas Antanavičius	18.11.1998	11	(2)	1
António João Belo Andrade	18.08.1994	13		1
Arnas Borodinas	23.03.1999	1	(3)	

	DOB	M	(s)	G
Andrei Ciofu (MDA)	31.05.1994	12		
Simas Gedžiūnas	02.12.2000		(2)	
Yehor Kondratiuk (UKR)	02.08.2000		(2)	
Matheus Bissi da Silva (BRA)	19.03.1991	10		
Denys Pidruchnyi (UKR)	10.07.2001		(2)	
Gavi Thompson (NGA)	02.02.2000	13		
Forwards:	DOB	M	(s)	G
Alsény Bah (GUI)	26.12.1994	4	(6)	1
Nasro Bouchareb (FRA)	29.01.1994	5	(2)	2
Lukas Kochanauskas	27.02.1990		(1)	
Lucas Villela Rezende (BRA)	24.03.1994	13		4
Levan Matcharashvili (GEO)	24.03.1997	12	(1)	3

Futbolo Klubas Sūduva Marijampolė

Founded: 1921
Stadium: ARVI Football Arena, Marijampolė (6,250)
Trainer: Vladimir Cheburin (KAZ)   07.06.1965

Goalkeepers:	DOB	M	(s)	G
Ivan Kardum (CRO)	18.07.1987	29		
Ignas Plūkas	08.12.1993	2		
Defenders:	DOB	M	(s)	G
Vytautas Andriuškevičius	08.10.1990	4	(1)	
Dominykas Barauskas	18.04.1997	1	(2)	
Michael Blauensteiner (AUT)	11.02.1995	5	(3)	
Karlo Bručić (CRO)	17.04.1992	9		2
Ivan Hladík (SVK)	30.01.1993	15	(4)	
Algis Jankauskas	27.09.1982	26		2
Semir Kerla (BIH)	26.09.1987	22		4
Aleksandar Živanović (SRB)	08.04.1987	31		5
Midfielders:	DOB	M	(s)	G
Jovan Čađenović (MNE)	13.01.1995	11	(3)	
Jeremy de Nooijer (CUW)	15.03.1992	4	(4)	
Povilas Leimonas	16.11.1987	7	(5)	2
Giedrius Matulevičius	05.03.1997	17	(7)	

	DOB	M	(s)	G
Domagoj Pušić (CRO)	24.10.1991	8	(1)	2
Renan Henrique Oliveira Vieira (BRA)	29.12.1989	7	(5)	6
Gratas Sirgėdas	17.12.1994	3	(2)	
Vaidas Slavickas	26.02.1986	13	(3)	1
Karolis Skamarakas	16.07.2001		(1)	
Andro Švrljuga (CRO)	24.10.1985	26		4
Ovidijus Verbickas	04.07.1993	15	(6)	2
Forwards:	DOB	M	(s)	G
Paulius Golubickas	19.08.1990	23	(5)	7
Sandro Gotal (AUT)	09.09.1991	4	(4)	3
Vahid Hambo (FIN)	03.02.1995	1	(3)	
Eligijus Jankauskas	22.06.1998	12	(7)	8
Tosaint Antony Ricketts (CAN)	06.08.1987	13	(2)	7
Josip Tadić (CRO)	22.08.1987	14	(1)	10
Mihret Topčagić (AUT)	21.06.1988	16	(7)	21
Robertas Vėževičius	05.01.1986	3	(16)	3

Futbolo klubas Žalgiris Vilnius

Founded: 1947
Stadium: LFF stadionas, Vilnius (5,067)
Trainer: Marek Zub (POL)   24.08.1964
[15.07.2019] João Luís Gouveia Martins (POR)   24.04.1967

Goalkeepers:	DOB	M	(s)	G
Martin Berkovec	12.02.1989	15		
Laurențiu Brănescu (ROU)	30.03.1994	3		
Armantas Vitkauskas	23.03.1989	13		
Defenders:	DOB	M	(s)	G
Mevlan Adili (MKD)	30.03.1994	9		
Rolandas Baravykas	23.08.1995	14	(10)	4
Andrei Cordoş (ROU)	06.06.1988	9	(1)	1
Venelin Filipov (BUL)	20.08.1990	4	(3)	
Georgas Freidgeimas	10.08.1987		(1)	
Sigitas Olberkis	19.04.1997	6	(2)	
Donovan Carlos Saverio Slijngard (SUR)	28.08.1987	27		2
Midfielders:	DOB	M	(s)	G
Adomas Ankudinovas	28.02.2000		(1)	
Klemen Bolha (SVN)	19.03.1993	16		
Higor Felipe Vidal (BRA)	26.09.1996	4	(4)	
Deividas Linauskas	06.01.1999		(1)	
Pau Morer Vicente (ESP)	10.10.1995	20	(4)	7

	DOB	M	(s)	G
Timur Pukhov (RUS)	17.06.1998		(2)	
Domantas Šimkus	10.02.1996	12	(12)	
Marko Tomić (SRB)	28.10.1991	21		1
Karolis Uzėla	11.03.2000	11		1
Víctor Pérez Alonso (ESP)	12.01.1988	21		2
Modestas Vorobjovas	30.12.1995	28		
Forwards:	DOB	M	(s)	G
Liviu Ion Antal (ROU)	02.06.1989	26	(2)	15
Osvaldas Čipkus	02.08.1999		(1)	
Erton Fejzullahu (SWE)	09.04.1988	6	(1)	2
Gustas Jarusevičius	23.05.2003	1	(4)	2
Tomislav Kiš (CRO)	04.04.1994	31		26
Saulius Mikoliūnas	02.05.1984	28		2
Meinardas Mikulenas	09.07.2002		(2)	
Simonas Urbys	07.11.1995	1	(6)	
Matas Vareika	27.01.2000	6	(17)	4
Hugo Vidémont (FRA)	19.02.1993	9	(3)	3

1.	FC Džiugas Telšiai (*Promoted*)	28	19	4	5	58	-	23	61
2.	FK Banga Gargždai (*Promotion Play-offs*)	28	17	5	6	57	-	24	56
3.	FC Vilniaus Vytis	28	17	4	7	74	-	31	55
4.	DFK Dainava Alytus	28	17	2	9	64	-	32	53
5.	FK Nevėžis Kėdainiai	28	16	4	8	66	-	37	52
6.	FA Šiauliai	28	14	5	9	61	-	37	47
7.	FC Hegelmann Litauen Kaunas	28	12	8	8	57	-	42	44
8.	FK Minija Kretinga	28	12	5	11	54	-	49	41
9.	FK Jonava	28	12	4	12	55	-	46	40
10.	FC Kupiškis	28	10	6	12	49	-	56	36
11.	FK Vilnius	28	10	3	15	56	-	53	33
12.	FK Riteriai Vilnius „B"	28	9	5	14	61	-	49	32
13.	FK Žalgiris Vilnius "B" (*Relegated*)	28	6	4	18	43	-	83	22
14.	FK Atmosfera Mažeikiai (*Relegated*)	28	3	4	21	23	-	96	13
15.	FC Pakruojis (*Relegated*)	28	3	3	22	25	-	145	12
16.	FC Stumbras Kaunas "B" (*Relegated*)	(*withdraw*)							

NATIONAL TEAM

INTERNATIONAL MATCHES
(16.07.2019 – 15.07.2020)

07.09.2019	Vilnius	Lithuania - Ukraine	0-3(0-2)	(ECQ)
10.09.2019	Vilnius	Lithuania - Portugal	1-5(1-1)	(ECQ)
11.10.2019	Kharkiv	Ukraine - Lithuania	2-0(1-0)	(ECQ)
14.10.2019	Vilnius	Lithuania - Serbia	1-2(0-0)	(ECQ)
14.11.2019	Faro/Loulé	Portugal - Lithuania	6-0(2-0)	(ECQ)
17.11.2019	Vilnius	Lithuania - New Zealand	1-0(1-0)	(F)

07.09.2019   **LITHUANIA - UKRAINE**   0-3(0-2)   16th EC. Qualifiers
LFF stadionas, Vilnius; Referee: Irfan Peljto (Bosnia and Herzegovina); Attendance: 5,067
LTU: Emilijus Zubas, Markus Palionis, Edvinas Girdvainis, Saulius Mikoliūnas, Artūras Žulpa, Fedor Černych (Cap) (68.Karolis Laukžemis), Ovidijus Verbickas, Domantas Šimkus, Modestas Vorobjovas, Giedrius Matulevičius (63.Mantas Kuklys), Paulius Golubickas (52.Vykintas Slivka). Trainer: Valdas Urbonas.

10.09.2019   **LITHUANIA - PORTUGAL**   1-5(1-1)   16th EC. Qualifiers
LFF stadionas, Vilnius; Referee: Hendrikus Sebastian "Bas" Nijhuis (Netherlands); Attendance: 5,067
LTU: Ernestas Šetkus (Cap), Markus Palionis, Vytautas Andriuškevičius, Edvinas Girdvainis, Saulius Mikoliūnas, Mantas Kuklys (69.Artūras Žulpa), Vykintas Slivka, Ovidijus Verbickas (77.Donatas Kazlauskas), Domantas Šimkus, Modestas Vorobjovas, Karolis Laukžemis (65.Deimantas Petravičius). Trainer: Valdas Urbonas.
Goal: Vytautas Andriuškevičius (28).

11.10.2019   **UKRAINE - LITHUANIA**   2-0(1-0)   16th EC. Qualifiers
Metalist Stadium, Kharkiv; Referee: Harald Lechner (Austria); Attendance: 32,500
LTU: Vytautas Černiauskas, Linas Klimavičius, Vytautas Andriuškevičius (62.Domantas Šimkus), Edvinas Girdvainis, Saulius Mikoliūnas (Cap), Artūras Žulpa, Arvydas Novikovas, Ovidijus Verbickas, Modestas Vorobjovas, Paulius Golubickas (73.Justas Lasickas), Karolis Laukžemis (77.Deivydas Matulevičius). Trainer: Valdas Urbonas.

14.10.2019   **LITHUANIA - SERBIA**   1-2(0-0)   16th EC. Qualifiers
LFF stadionas, Vilnius; Referee: Paweł Raczkowski (Poland); Attendance: 2,787
LTU: Vytautas Černiauskas, Linas Klimavičius, Edvinas Girdvainis, Rolandas Baravykas, Saulius Mikoliūnas (Cap), Ovidijus Verbickas (56.Artūras Žulpa), Domantas Šimkus, Modestas Vorobjovas, Justas Lasickas, Paulius Golubickas (73.Donatas Kazlauskas), Deivydas Matulevičius (64.Karolis Laukžemis). Trainer: Valdas Urbonas.
Goal: Donatas Kazlauskas (79).

14.11.2019   **PORTUGAL - LITHUANIA**   6-0(2-0)   16th EC. Qualifiers
Estádio Algarve, Faro/Loulé; Referee: Ruddy Buquet (France); Attendance: 18,534
LTU: Ernestas Šetkus, Markus Palionis, Vytautas Andriuškevičius, Edvinas Girdvainis, Saulius Mikoliūnas, Mantas Kuklys (57.Deivydas Matulevičius), Arvydas Novikovas, Fedor Černych (Cap) (80.Donatas Kazlauskas), Vykintas Slivka, Domantas Šimkus, Paulius Golubickas (72.Justas Lasickas). Trainer: Valdas Urbonas.

17.11.2019   **LITHUANIA - NEW ZEALAND**   1-0(1-0)   Friendly International
LFF stadionas, Vilnius; Referee: Trustin Farrugia Cann (Malta); Attendance: 1,832
LTU: Ernestas Šetkus, Markus Palionis (46.Linas Klimavičius), Egidijus Vaitkūnas, Edvinas Girdvainis, Rolandas Baravykas, Saulius Mikoliūnas (Cap) (84.Donatas Kazlauskas), Arvydas Novikovas, Fedor Černych (87.Deivydas Matulevičius), Domantas Šimkus (75.Giedrius Matulevičius), Justas Lasickas, Paulius Golubickas (90+1.Benas Šatkus). Trainer: Valdas Urbonas.
Goal: Arvydas Novikovas (45).

NATIONAL TEAM PLAYERS
(16.07.2019 – 15.07.2020)

Name	DOB	Caps	Goals	2019/2020:	Club
Goalkeepers					
Vytautas ČERNIAUSKAS	12.03.1989	**6**	**0**	2019:	*PFC CSKA Sofia (BUL)*
Ernestas ŠETKUS	25.05.1985	**30**	**0**	2019:	*Hapoel Be'er Sheva FC (ISR)*
Emilijus ZUBAS	10.07.1990	**14**	**0**	2019:	*Bnei Yehuda Tel Aviv FC (ISR)*
Defenders					
Vytautas ANDRIUŠKEVIČIUS	08.10.1990	**34**	**0**	2019:	*FC Tobol Kostanay (KAZ)*
Rolandas BARAVYKAS	23.08.1995	**19**	**1**	2019:	*FK Žalgiris Vilnius*
Edvinas GIRDVAINIS	17.01.1993	**22**	**0**	2019:	*FK Rīgas Futbola Skola (LVA)*
Linas KLIMAVIČIUS	10.04.1989	**27**	**0**	2019:	*FC Dinamo Bucureşti (ROU)*
Saulius MIKOLIŪNAS	02.05.1984	**84**	**5**	2019:	*FK Žalgiris Vilnius*
Markus PALIONIS	12.05.1987	**9**	**0**	2019:	*SSV Jahn Regensburg (GER)*
Benas ŠATKUS	01.04.2001	**1**	**0**	2019:	*1. FC Nürnberg (GER)*
Egidijus VAITKŪNAS	08.08.1988	**44**	**0**	2019:	*FK Kauno Žalgiris Kaunas*
Artūras ŽULPA	10.06.1990	**39**	**1**	2019:	*FC Tobol Kostanay (KAZ)*
Midfielders					
Paulius GOLUBICKAS	19.08.1999	**7**	**0**	2019:	*FK Sūduva Marijampolė*
Donatas KAZLAUSKAS	31.03.1994	**14**	**1**	2019:	*FK Riteriai Vilnius*
Mantas KUKLYS	10.06.1987	**38**	**0**	2019:	*FC Zhetisu Taldiqorghan (KAZ)*
Justas LASICKAS	06.10.1997	**11**	**0**	2019:	*FK Voždovac Beograd (SRB)*
Giedrius MATULEVIČIUS	05.03.1997	**3**	**0**	2019:	*FK Sūduva Marijampolė*
Arvydas NOVIKOVAS	18.12.1990	**58**	**8**	2019:	*Legia Warszawa (POL)*
Deimantas PETRAVIČIUS	02.09.1995	**15**	**1**	2019:	*FC Okzhetpes Kokshetau (KAZ)*
Vykintas SLIVKA	29.04.1995	**39**	**2**	2019:	*Hibernian FC Edinburgh (SCO)*
Domantas ŠIMKUS	10.02.1996	**9**	**0**	2019:	*FK Žalgiris Vilnius*
Ovidijus VERBICKAS	04.07.1993	**16**	**1**	2019:	*FK Sūduva Marijampolė*
Modestas VOROBJOVAS	30.12.1995	**17**	**0**	2019:	*FK Žalgiris Vilnius*
Forwards					
Fedor ČERNYCH	21.05.1991	**55**	**9**	2019:	*FK Orenburg (RUS)*
Karolis LAUKŽEMIS	11.03.1992	**12**	**1**	2019:	*NK Istra 1961 Pula (CRO)*
Deivydas MATULEVIČIUS	08.04.1989	**40**	**5**	2019:	*FK Kauno Žalgiris Kaunas*
National team coach					
Valdas URBONAS [since 02.02.2019]	29.11.1967	10 M;1 W; 2 D; 7 L; 6-25			

LUXEMBOURG

The Country:
Groussherzogtum Lëtzebuerg (Grand Duchy of Luxembourg)
Capital: Lëtzebuerg
Surface: 2,586.4 km²
Inhabitants: 626,108 [2020]
Time: UTC+1

The FA:
Fédération Luxembourgeoise de Football / Lëtzebuerger Foussballfederatioun
BP, 5 Rue de Limpach, 3901 Mondercange
Tel: +352 488 665 1
Foundation date: 1908
Member of FIFA since: 1910
Member of UEFA since: 1954
Website: www.flf.lu

NATIONAL TEAM RECORDS

RECORDS	
First international match:	29.10.1911, Lëtzebuerg: Luxembourg – France 1-4
Most international caps:	Mario Mutsch - 102 caps (2005-2019)
Most international goals:	Léon Mart - 16 goals / 24 caps (1933-1946)

UEFA EUROPEAN CHAMPIONSHIP		FIFA WORLD CUP		OLYMPIC TOURNAMENTS	
1960	Did not enter	1930	Did not enter	1908	-
1964	Qualifiers	1934	Qualifiers	1912	-
1968	Qualifiers	1938	Qualifiers	1920	Round 1
1972	Qualifiers	1950	Qualifiers	1924	1/8 - Finals
1976	Qualifiers	1954	Qualifiers	1928	1/8 - Finals
1980	Qualifiers	1958	Qualifiers	1936	1/8 - Finals
1984	Qualifiers	1962	Qualifiers	1948	1/8 - Finals
1988	Qualifiers	1966	Qualifiers	1952	Round 1
1992	Qualifiers	1970	Qualifiers	1956	-
1996	Qualifiers	1974	Qualifiers	1960	Qualifiers
2000	Qualifiers	1978	Qualifiers	1964	Did not enter
2004	Qualifiers	1982	Qualifiers	1968	Did not enter
2008	Qualifiers	1986	Qualifiers	1972	Qualifiers
2012	Qualifiers	1990	Qualifiers	1976	Qualifiers
2016	Qualifiers	1994	Qualifiers	1980	Did not enter
2020	Qualifiers	1998	Qualifiers	1984	Did not enter
		2002	Qualifiers	1988	Did not enter
		2006	Qualifiers	1992	Qualifiers
		2010	Qualifiers	1996	Qualifiers
		2014	Qualifiers	2000	Qualifiers
		2018	Qualifiers	2004	Qualifiers
				2008	Qualifiers
				2012	Qualifiers
				2016	Qualifiers

UEFA NATIONS LEAGUE

2018/2019 – League D (promoted to League C)

FIFA CONFEDERATIONS CUP 1992-2017

None

LUXEMBOURGIAN CLUB HONOURS IN EUROPEAN CLUB COMPETITIONS:

European Champion Clubs.Cup (1956-1992) / UEFA Champions League (1993-2020)
None
Fairs Cup (1858-1971) / UEFA Cup (1972-2009) / UEFA Europa League (2010-2020)
None
UEFA Super Cup (1972-2019)
None
European Cup Winners.Cup 1961-1999*
None

*defunct competition

NATIONAL COMPETITIONS
TABLE OF HONOURS

	CHAMPIONS	CUP WINNERS	BEST GOALSCORERS
1909/1910	Racing Club Lëtzebuerg	-	-
1910/1911	Sporting Club Lëtzebuerg	-	-
1911/1912	US Hollerich Bonnevoie	-	-
1912/1913	*No competition*	-	-
1913/1914	US Hollerich Bonnevoie	-	-
1914/1915	US Hollerich Bonnevoie	-	-
1915/1916	US Hollerich Bonnevoie	-	-
1916/1917	US Hollerich Bonnevoie	-	-
1917/1918	CS Fola Esch	-	-
1918/1919	Sporting Club Lëtzebuerg	-	-
1919/1920	CS Fola Esch	-	-
1920/1921	AS la Jeunesse d'Esch/Alzette	-	-
1921/1922	CS Fola Esch	Racing Club Lëtzebuerg	-
1922/1923	FA Red Boys Differdange	CS Fola Esch	-
1923/1924	CS Fola Esch	CS Fola Esch	-
1924/1925	CA Spora Lëtzebuerg	FA Red Boys Differdange	-
1925/1926	FA Red Boys Differdange	FA Red Boys Differdange	-
1926/1927	Union Sportive Lëtzebuerg	FA Red Boys Differdange	-
1927/1928	CA Spora Lëtzebuerg	CA Spora Lëtzebuerg	-
1928/1929	CA Spora Lëtzebuerg	FA Red Boys Differdange	-
1929/1930	CS Fola Esch	FA Red Boys Differdange	-
1930/1931	FA Red Boys Differdange	FA Red Boys Differdange	-
1931/1932	FA Red Boys Differdange	CA Spora Lëtzebuerg	-
1932/1933	FA Red Boys Differdange	FC Progrès Niederkorn	-
1933/1934	CA Spora Lëtzebuerg	FA Red Boys Differdange	-
1934/1935	CA Spora Lëtzebuerg	AS la Jeunesse d'Esch/Alzette	-
1935/1936	CA Spora Lëtzebuerg	FA Red Boys Differdange	-
1936/1937	AS la Jeunesse d'Esch/Alzette	AS la Jeunesse d'Esch/Alzette	-
1937/1938	CA Spora Lëtzebuerg	Stade Dudelange	-
1938/1939	Stade Dudelange	Union Sportive Dudelange	-
1939/1940	Stade Dudelange	CA Spora Lëtzebuerg	-
1940-1944	*No competition*	*No competition*	-
1944/1945	Stade Dudelange	FC Progrès Niederkorn	-
1945/1946	Stade Dudelange	AS la Jeunesse d'Esch/Alzette	-
1946/1947	Stade Dudelange	Union Sportive Lëtzebuerg	-
1947/1948	Stade Dudelange	Stade Dudelange	-
1948/1949	CA Spora Lëtzebuerg	Stade Dudelange	-
1949/1950	Stade Dudelange	CA Spora Lëtzebuerg	-
1950/1951	AS la Jeunesse d'Esch/Alzette	SC Tétange	-
1951/1952	National Schifflange	FA Red Boys Differdange	-
1952/1953	FC Progrès Niederkorn	FA Red Boys Differdange	-
1953/1954	AS la Jeunesse d'Esch/Alzette	AS la Jeunesse d'Esch/Alzette	-
1954/1955	Stade Dudelange	CS Fola Esch	-
1955/1956	CA Spora Lëtzebuerg	Stade Dudelange	-
1956/1957	Stade Dudelange	CA Spora Lëtzebuerg	-
1957/1958	AS la Jeunesse d'Esch/Alzette	FA Red Boys Differdange	-
1958/1959	AS la Jeunesse d'Esch/Alzette	Union Sportive Lëtzebuerg	-
1959/1960	AS la Jeunesse d'Esch/Alzette	National Schifflange	-
1960/1961	CA Spora Lëtzebuerg	Alliance Dudelange	-
1961/1962	Union Sportive Lëtzebuerg	Alliance Dudelange	-
1962/1963	AS la Jeunesse d'Esch/Alzette	Union Sportive Lëtzebuerg	-
1963/1964	FC Aris Bonnevoie	Union Sportive Lëtzebuerg	-
1964/1965	Stade Dudelange	CA Spora Lëtzebuerg	-
1965/1966	FC Aris Bonnevoie	CA Spora Lëtzebuerg	-
1966/1967	AS la Jeunesse d'Esch/Alzette	FC Aris Bonnevoie	-
1967/1968	AS la Jeunesse d'Esch/Alzette	Union Sportive Rumelange	-
1968/1969	FC Avenir Beggen	Union Sportive Lëtzebuerg	-
1969/1970	AS la Jeunesse d'Esch/Alzette	Union Sportive Lëtzebuerg	-
1970/1971	Union Sportive Lëtzebuerg	Jeunesse Hautcharage	-
1971/1972	FC Aris Bonnevoie	FA Red Boys Differdange	-
1972/1973	AS la Jeunesse d'Esch/Alzette	AS la Jeunesse d'Esch/Alzette	-
1973/1974	AS la Jeunesse d'Esch/Alzette	AS la Jeunesse d'Esch/Alzette	-
1974/1975	AS la Jeunesse d'Esch/Alzette	Union Sportive Rumelange	-
1975/1976	AS la Jeunesse d'Esch/Alzette	AS la Jeunesse d'Esch/Alzette	-
1976/1977	AS la Jeunesse d'Esch/Alzette	FC Progrès Niederkorn	-
1977/1978	FC Progrès Niederkorn	FC Progrès Niederkorn	-
1978/1979	FA Red Boys Differdange	FA Red Boys Differdange	-
1979/1980	AS la Jeunesse d'Esch/Alzette	CA Spora Lëtzebuerg	-
1980/1981	FC Progrès Niederkorn	AS la Jeunesse d'Esch/Alzette	-
1981/1982	FC Avenir Beggen	FA Red Boys Differdange	-
1982/1983	AS la Jeunesse d'Esch/Alzette	FC Avenir Beggen	-
1983/1984	FC Avenir Beggen	FC Avenir Beggen	-

1984/1985	AS la Jeunesse d'Esch/Alzette	FA Red Boys Differdange	-	
1985/1986	FC Avenir Beggen	Union Sportive Lëtzebuerg	-	
1986/1987	AS la Jeunesse d'Esch/Alzette	FC Avenir Beggen	-	
1987/1988	AS la Jeunesse d'Esch/Alzette	AS la Jeunesse d'Esch/Alzette	Patrick Morocutti (Union Sportive Lëtzebuerg)	26
1988/1989	CA Spora Lëtzebuerg	Union Sportive Lëtzebuerg	Theo Scholten (AS la Jeunesse d'Esch/Alzette) Markus Krahen (GER, FC Avenir Beggen) Armin Krings (FC Avenir Beggen)	21
1989/1990	Union Sportive Lëtzebuerg	FC Swift Hesperange	Markus Krahen (GER, FC Avenir Beggen)	30
1990/1991	Union Sportive Lëtzebuerg	Union Sportive Lëtzebuerg	Patrick Morocutti (Union Sportive Lëtzebuerg)	23
1991/1992	Union Sportive Lëtzebuerg	FC Avenir Beggen	Markus Krahen (GER, FC Avenir Beggen)	19
1992/1993	FC Avenir Beggen	FC Avenir Beggen	Armin Krings (FC Avenir Beggen)	23
1993/1994	FC Avenir Beggen	FC Avenir Beggen	Stefano Fanelli (F91 Dudelange)	19
1994/1995	AS la Jeunesse d'Esch/Alzette	CS Grevenmacher	Yves Heinen (FC Differdange 03)	22
1995/1996	AS la Jeunesse d'Esch/Alzette	Union Sportive Lëtzebuerg	Mikhail Zaritski (FC Avenir Beggen)	18
1996/1997	AS la Jeunesse d'Esch/Alzette	AS la Jeunesse d'Esch/Alzette	Mikhail Zaritski (FC Sporting Mertzig) Franco Iovino (FC Wiltz 71)	19
1997/1998	AS la Jeunesse d'Esch/Alzette	CS Grevenmacher	Mikhail Zaritski (FC Sporting Mertzig)	29
1998/1999	AS la Jeunesse d'Esch/Alzette	AS la Jeunesse d'Esch/Alzette	Frédéric Cicchirillo (FRA, (FC Sporting Mertzig)	25
1999/2000	F91 Dudelange	AS la Jeunesse d'Esch/Alzette	Marcel Christophe (FC Mondercange)	26
2000/2001	F91 Dudelange	FC Etzella Ettelbruck	Mikhail Zaritski (FC Sporting Mertzig)	23
2001/2002	F91 Dudelange	FC Avenir Beggen	Frédéric Cicchirillo (FRA, F91 Dudelange)	24
2002/2003	CS Grevenmacher	CS Grevenmacher	Daniel Huss (CS Grevenmacher)	22
2003/2004	AS la Jeunesse d'Esch/Alzette	F91 Dudelange	José Manuel Gomes de Andrade (POR, CA Spora Lëtzebuerg)	24
2004/2005	F91 Dudelange	CS Pétange	Sergio Pupovac (CS Alliance 01 Lëtzebuerg)	24
2005/2006	F91 Dudelange	F91 Dudelange	Fatih Sözen (TUR, CS Grevenmacher)	23
2006/2007	F91 Dudelange	F91 Dudelange	Daniel da Mota Alves (FC Etzella Ettelbruck)	24
2007/2008	F91 Dudelange	CS Grevenmacher	Emmanuel Coquelet (FRA, F91 Dudelange)	20
2008/2009	F91 Dudelange	F91 Dudelange	Pierre Piskor (FRA, FC Differdange 03)	30
2009/2010	AS la Jeunesse d'Esch/Alzette	FC Differdange 03	Daniel Huss (CS Grevenmacher)	22
2010/2011	F91 Dudelange	FC Differdange 03	Sanel Ibrahimović (BIH, FC Wiltz 71)	18
2011/2012	F91 Dudelange	F91 Dudelange	Omar Er Rafik (MAR, FC Differdange 03)	23
2012/2013	CS Fola Esch	AS la Jeunesse d'Esch/Alzette	Edis Osmanović (BIH, FC Wiltz 71)	21
2013/2014	F91 Dudelange	FC Differdange 03	Sanel Ibrahimović (BIH, AS la Jeunesse d'Esch/Alzette)	22
2014/2015	CS Fola Esch	FC Differdange 03	Sanel Ibrahimović (BIH, AS la Jeunesse d'Esch/Alzette)	21
2015/2016	F91 Dudelange	F91 Dudelange	Julien Jahier (FRA, RFCU Lëtzebuerg)	18
2016/2017	F91 Dudelange	F91 Dudelange	Omar Er Rafik (MAR, FC Differdange 03)	26
2017/2018	F91 Dudelange	Racing FC	David Turpel (F91 Dudelange)	33
2018/2019	F91 Dudelange	F91 Dudelange	Samir Ali Hadji (FRA, CS Fola Esch)	23
2019/2020	*Championship abandoned*	*Competition abandoned*	-	

NATIONAL CHAMPIONSHIP
Division Nationale BGL Ligue 2019/2020
(04.08.2019 – 08.03.2020)

Results

Round 1 [04-05.08.2019]
US Hostert - US Mondorf 0-1
FC Rodange 91 - UNA Strassen 1-2
Victoria Rosport - Etzella Ettelbruck 3-0
F91 Dudelange - Blue Boys Muhlenbach 3-1
Racing FCU - Union Titus Pétange 2-3
Fola Esch - FC Differdange 03 1-2
Progrès Niederkorn - Jeunesse d'Esch 4-0

Round 2 [11.08.2019]
US Hostert - Progrès Niederkorn 3-5
Jeunesse d'Esch - Racing FCU 3-2
Blue Boys Muhlenbach - Victoria Rosport 0-3
Etzella Ettelbruck - FC Rodange 91 5-2
FC Differdange 03 - US Mondorf 1-1
UNA Strassen - Fola Esch 2-4
UT Pétange - F91 Dudelange 2-0 [25.09.]

Round 3 [17-18.08.2019]
F91 Dudelange - Jeunesse d'Esch 1-3
Fola Esch - Etzella Ettelbruck 3-1
FC Rodange 91 - Blue Boys Muhlenbach 1-3
Victoria Rosport - Union Titus Pétange 1-2
Racing FCU - Progrès Niederkorn 1-1
US Mondorf - UNA Strassen 0-0
FC Differdange 03 - US Hostert 3-1

Round 4 [24-26.08.2019]
Union Titus Pétange - FC Rodange 91 4-1
US Hostert - Racing FCU 0-3
Jeunesse d'Esch - Victoria Rosport 2-1
Blue Boys Muhlenbach - Fola Esch 3-2
Etzella Ettelbruck - US Mondorf 1-3
UNA Strassen - FC Differdange 03 1-3
Progrès Niederkorn - F91 Dudelange 2-0

Round 5 [31.08.-01.09.2019]
Victoria Rosport - Progrès Niederkorn 0-3
FC Rodange 91 - Jeunesse d'Esch 3-3
UNA Strassen - US Hostert 4-1
FC Differdange 03 - Etzella Ettelbruck 2-1
US Mondorf - Blue Boys Muhlenbach 3-0
Fola Esch - Union Titus Pétange 2-0
F91 Dudelange - Racing FCU 3-3

Round 6 [14-16.09.2019]
US Hostert - F91 Dudelange 1-0
Etzella Ettelbruck - UNA Strassen 3-2
Racing FCU - Victoria Rosport 2-2
Jeunesse d'Esch - Fola Esch 0-3
Union Titus Pétange - US Mondorf 3-2
Blue Boys Muhlenbach - Differdange 03 0-2
Progrès Niederkorn - FC Rodange 91 1-0

Round 7 [29.09.2019]
Etzella Ettelbruck - US Hostert 0-1
UNA Strassen - Blue Boys Muhlenbach 2-0
US Mondorf - Jeunesse d'Esch 2-3
FC Rodange 91 - Racing FCU 1-1
Victoria Rosport - F91 Dudelange 0-7
FC Differdange 03 - Union Titus Pétange 2-3
Fola Esch - Progrès Niederkorn 2-0

Round 8 [05-06.10.2019]
Jeunesse d'Esch - FC Differdange 03 1-1
US Hostert - Victoria Rosport 2-0
F91 Dudelange - FC Rodange 91 4-0
Racing FCU - Fola Esch 2-2
Progrès Niederkorn - US Mondorf 2-2
Union Titus Pétange - UNA Strassen 2-2
Blue Boys Muhlenb. - Etzella Ettelbruck 1-1

Round 9 [19-20.10.2019]
FC Differdange 03 - Progrès Niederkorn 1-5
US Mondorf - Racing FCU 0-4
Fola Esch - F91 Dudelange 2-1
Etzella Ettelbruck - Union Titus Pétange 1-2
FC Rodange 91 - Victoria Rosport 1-0 [19.11.]
UNA Strassen - Jeunesse d'Esch 1-0 [20.11.]
Blue Boys Muhlenb. - US Hostert 0-1 [08.12.]

Round 10 [26-27.10.2019]
Progrès Niederkorn - UNA Strassen 0-0
US Hostert - FC Rodange 91 2-3
Victoria Rosport - Fola Esch 0-4
F91 Dudelange - US Mondorf 3-1
Racing FCU - FC Differdange 03 3-2
Jeunesse d'Esch - Etzella Ettelbruck 1-1
UT Pétange - Blue Boys Muhlenbach 2-0

Round 11 [03.11.2019]
Fola Esch - FC Rodange 91 5-0
US Mondorf - Victoria Rosport 1-2
Union Titus Pétange - US Hostert 2-0
Blue Boys Muhlenbach - Jeunesse d'Esch 4-2
Etzella Ettelbruck - Progrès Niederkorn 0-4
UNA Strassen - Racing FCU 2-1
FC Differdange 03 - F91 Dudelange 0-3

Round 12 [23-24.11.2019]
Progrès Niederkorn - Blue Boys Muhlenb. 5-2
US Hostert - Fola Esch 1-1
FC Rodange 91 - US Mondorf 1-1
Victoria Rosport - FC Differdange 03 2-3
F91 Dudelange - UNA Strassen 2-2
Racing FCU - Etzella Ettelbruck 0-3
Jeunesse d'Esch - Union Titus Pétange 1-4

Round 13 [30.11.-01.12.2019]
Jeunesse d'Esch - US Hostert 1-2
UNA Strassen - Victoria Rosport 2-2
Etzella Ettelbruck - F91 Dudelange 1-4
FC Differdange 03 - FC Rodange 91 2-1
UT Pétange - Progrès Niederkorn 1-1 [11.12.]
US Mondorf - Fola Esch 2-2 [11.12.]
Blue Boys Müh. - Racing FCU 2-2 [16.02.20]

Round 14 [22-23.02.2020]
Progrès Niederkorn - US Hostert 4-0
F91 Dudelange - Union Titus Pétange 4-2
US Mondorf - FC Differdange 03 1-2
Racing FCU - Jeunesse d'Esch 1-1
Victoria Rosport - Blue Boys Muhlenbach 2-1
FC Rodange 91 - Etzella Ettelbruck 1-2
Fola Esch - UNA Strassen 2-1

Round 15 [29.02.-01.03.2020]
Progrès Niederkorn - Racing FCU 1-2
UNA Strassen - US Mondorf 1-0
Etzella Ettelbruck - Fola Esch 0-1
Union Titus Pétange - Victoria Rosport 2-2
US Hostert - FC Differdange 03 0-3
Blue Boys Muhlenbach - FC Rodange 91 0-3
Jeunesse d'Esch - F91 Dudelange 0-1

Round 16 [04.03.2020]
F91 Dudelange - Progrès Niederkorn 2-3
Fola Esch - Blue Boys Muhlenbach 4-2
FC Rodange 91 - Union Titus Pétange 1-0
Racing FCU - US Hostert 2-1
Victoria Rosport - Jeunesse d'Esch 2-1
US Mondorf - Etzella Ettelbruck 1-2
FC Differdange 03 - UNA Strassen 4-1

Round 17 [08.03.2020]
US Hostert - UNA Strassen 1-5
Etzella Ettelbruck - FC Differdange 03 0-3
Blue Boys Muhlenbach - US Mondorf 1-1
Jeunesse d'Esch - FC Rodange 91 2-1
Progrès Niederkorn - Victoria Rosport 2-1
Racing FCU - F91 Dudelange 1-0
Union Titus Pétange - Fola Esch 0-1

The championship was suspended after 17 Rounds due to Covid-19 pandemic.
On 28.04.2020, the league was abandoned. The title was not awarded, and no teams were relegated, with the league expanded to 16 teams next season for a transitional year.

Final Standings

									Total					Home					Away		
1.	CS Fola Esch	17	12	3	2	41	-	17	39	7	0	1	21	-	7	5	3	1	20	-	10
2.	FC Progrès Niederkorn	17	11	4	2	43	-	17	37	6	2	1	21	-	7	5	2	1	22	-	10
3.	FC Differdange 03	17	11	2	4	36	-	25	35	4	1	3	15	-	16	7	1	1	21	-	9
4.	Union Titus Pétange	17	10	3	4	34	-	23	33	5	3	1	18	-	9	5	0	3	16	-	14
5.	F91 Dudelange	17	8	2	7	38	-	24	26	4	2	2	22	-	15	4	0	5	16	-	9
6.	FC UNA Strassen	17	7	5	5	30	-	26	26	5	1	2	15	-	11	2	4	3	15	-	15
7.	Racing FC Union Lëtzebuerg	17	6	7	4	32	-	27	25	3	4	2	14	-	15	3	3	2	18	-	12
8.	AS La Jeunesse d'Esch/Alzette	17	5	4	8	24	-	34	19	3	2	4	11	-	16	2	2	4	13	-	18
9.	FC Victoria Rosport	17	5	3	9	23	-	35	18	3	0	5	10	-	21	2	3	4	13	-	14
10.	FC Etzella Ettelbrück	17	5	2	10	22	-	34	17	2	0	7	11	-	22	3	2	3	11	-	12
11.	US Hostert	17	5	1	11	17	-	37	16	2	1	6	10	-	21	3	0	5	7	-	16
12.	US Mondorf-les-Bains	17	3	6	8	22	-	28	15	1	2	5	10	-	15	2	4	3	12	-	13
13.	FC Rodange 91	17	4	3	10	21	-	37	15	2	3	3	10	-	12	2	0	7	11	-	25
14.	FC Blue Boys Muhlenbach	17	3	3	11	20	-	39	12	2	3	4	11	-	17	1	0	7	9	-	22

Top goalscorers:		
14	Danel Sinani	F91 Dudelange
13	Moussa Seydi (SEN)	CS Fola Esch
11	Emmanuel Françoise (FRA)	FC Progrès Niederkorn
11	Yann Mabella (FRA)	Racing FC Union Lëtzebuerg
10	Artur Abreu Pereira	Union Titus Pétange

NATIONAL CUP
Coupe du Luxembourg 2019/2020

First Round [05-08.09.2019]

Résidence Walferdange - FC 72 Erpeldange	4-2		US Moutfort - FC Lorentzweiler	0-9
Daring Club Echternach - FC Atert Bissen	1-0		FC Munsbach - FC Brouch	7-2
Vinesca Ehnen - Orania Vianden	2-1		US Folschette - Avenir Beggen	0-1
CeBra 01 - FC Minerva Lintgen	1-2		FC Pratzerthal/Rédange - Young Boys Diekirch	2-1 aet
Jeunesse Useldange - CS Grevenmacher	1-7		FC Green Boys 77 - Sporting Bertrange	3-0
Luna Oberkorn - CS Sanem	0-2		Les Ardoisiers Perlé - FC Stengefort	2-4
Les Aiglons Dalheim - US Sandweiler	0-3		FC Noertzange HF - US Boevange	4-2
ES Clemency - FF Norden 02	2-6		FC Biekerech - Red Star Merl	2-4
AS Luxembourg Porto - Sporting Mertzig	1-0		Tricolore Gasperich - US Reisdorf	3-1
Alliance Aischdall - Union 05 Kayl-Tétange	2-3		Rupensia Lusitanos Larochette - AS Colmar-Berg	6-5 pen
Racing Troisvierges - Berdenia Berburg	1-9		Claravallis Clervaux - US Berdorf	1-5
US Rambrouch - Union Remich/Bous	0-3		Jeunesse Schieren - AS Hosingen	4-0
FC Kehlen - Marisca Mersch	4-1		FC Ehlerange - FC Schengen	1-5
Jeunesse Biwer - The Belval Belvaux	0-2		Kiischpelt Wilwerwiltz - Red Boys Aspelt	2-5
Blo Weiss Itzig - US Feulen	9-1		CS Obercorn - FC Schifflange 95	0-2
FC 47 Bastendorf - FC Koerich/Simmern	5-1		Jeunesse Gilsdorf - Minière Lasauvage	1-2
Olympia Christnach - FC Koeppchen Wormeldange	0-9		Syra Mensdorf - SC Bettembourg	3-4
FC Kopstal - SC Ell	3-5 aet		ES Schouweiler - FC Red-Black/Egalité 07	1-3 aet

Second Round [21-22.09.2019]

FC Schifflange 95 - FC Differdange 03	1-5		SC Ell - FC Mondercange	0-3
FC Pratzerthal/Rédange - Jeunesse Junglinster	1-5		Tricolore Gasperich - FC Rodange 91	0-3
FC Green Boys 77 - US Esch/Alzette	2-4 aet		FC 47 Bastendorf - US Rumelange	0-2
Union Remich/Bous - FC Progrès Niederkorn	0-2		AS Luxembourg Porto - RFC Union Lëtzebuerg	0-7
Berdenia Berburg - FC Wiltz 71	2-3		Résidence Walferdange - FC RM Hamm Benfica	0-7
FF Norden 02 - Alisontia Steinsel	0-4		Jeunesse Schieren - Union Mertert/Wasserbillig	1-2
Daring Club Echternach - F91 Dudelange	1-6		Minière Lasauvage - FC Victoria Rosport	1-6
FC Minerva Lintgen - FC Jeunesse Canach	0-6		Red Boys Aspelt - FC UNA Strassen	1-3
FC Avenir Beggen - FC Etzella Ettelbrück	0-1		FC Red-Black/Egalité 07 - US Hostert	1-4
The Belval Belvaux - FC Swift Hesperange	0-6		Red Star Merl - US Mondorf-les-Bains	0-4
FC Koeppchen Wormeldange - UN Käerjéng 97	1-4		US Sandweiler - FC Mamer 32	0-4
Vinesca Ehnen - Union Titus Pétange	0-7		FC Schengen - FC Blô-Weiss Medernach	4-5 aet
CS Grevenmacher - CS Fola Esch	1-2		FC Kehlen - CS Sanem	2-1 aet
FC Noertzange HF - AS La Jeunesse d'Esch/Alzette	0-4		Rupensia Lusitanos Larochette - Blo Weiss Itzig	2-5
FC Munsbach - FC Blue Boys Muhlenbach	3-6		SC Bettembourg - Union 05 FC de Kayl-Tétange	3-2 pen
FC Stengefort - Yellow Boys Weiler	2-1		US Berdorf - FC Lorentzweiler	2-3

Third Round [09-10.11.2019]

Jeunesse Junglinster - AS La Jeunesse d'Esch/Alzette	1-2		FC Lorentzweiler - FC Progrès Niederkorn	0-5
FC RM Hamm Benfica - FC Swift Hesperange	1-2		Blo Weiss Itzig - FC Differdange 03	2-4
FC Stengefort - FC Victoria Rosport	0-2		FC Rodange 91 - US Mondorf-les-Bains	1-3
SC Bettembourg - FC Blô-Weiss Medernach	6-0		Union Mertert/Wasserbillig - F91 Dudelange	0-2
FC Kehlen - FC Mamer 32	1-0 aet		FC Wiltz 71 - FC Blue Boys Muhlenbach	2-0
US Esch/Alzette - UN Käerjéng 97	4-0		Racing FC Union Lëtzebuerg - US Hostert	5-1
FC Mondercange - Alisontia Steinsel	4-0		Union Titus Pétange - CS Fola Esch	1-2
FC Jeunesse Canach - FC Etzella Ettelbrück	2-0		US Rumelange - FC UNA Strassen	0-4

1/8-Finals [07-08.12.2019]

F91 Dudelange - US Mondorf-les-Bains	4-1		FC Swift Hesperange - FC Jeunesse Canach	5-0
FC Wiltz 71 - AS La Jeunesse d'Esch/Alzette	3-0		US Esch/Alzette - FC Differdange 03	0-1
SC Bettembourg - FC Victoria Rosport	0-3		Racing FC Union Lëtzebuerg - FC UNA Strassen	5-1
FC Mondercange - CS Fola Esch	4-3 pen		FC Kehlen - FC Progrès Niederkorn	0-3

The competition was cancelled due to Covid-19 pandemic. No title was awarded.

Football Club Blue Boys Muhlenbach

Founded:	1932		
Stadium:	Stade „Mathias mamer", Lëtzebuerg (1,100)		
Trainer:	Fangio Buyse (BEL)		27.09.1974
[03.03.2020]	Elvir Pepic		27.05.1977

Goalkeepers:	DOB	M	(s)	G
Boris Olivier Tiotio Bassene (SEN)	16.09.1993	9	(1)	
Vítor Bruno Almeida Gonçalves (POR)	01.03.1984	8	(1)	
Defenders:	**DOB**	**M**	**(s)**	**G**
Mustapha Cheriak (ALG)	09.05.1993	12	(2)	2
Deyingo Deyingo		1		
Rachid Erragui (FRA)	11.10.1992	15	(1)	1
Jasmin Hodžić (MNE)	28.06.1988	13		
Tripy Makonda (FRA)	24.01.1990	11	(1)	1
Malik N'Diaye (FRA)	17.08.1987	12		
William Kevin Rocha Josefa	29.05.1997	14	1	
Midfielders:	**DOB**	**M**	**(s)**	**G**
Chahir Belghazouani (MAR)	06.10.1986	4		1
Denis Dragolovcanin	17.12.1990		(3)	
Mirzet Dragolovcanin	24.06.1997		(4)	

	DOB	M	(s)	G
Munir Dragulovcanin	21.08.1999	3	(9)	
Arnaud Guedj (FRA)	19.07.1997	4	(1)	
Amel Hodžić (SVN)	03.10.1990	1		
Azrack-Yassine Mahamat (CHA)	24.03.1988	14	(1)	1
Ahmed Rani (FRA)	20.08.1987	17		4
Fahir Sabotic	19.10.1998	5	(4)	
Forwards:	**DOB**	**M**	**(s)**	**G**
El Hadji Fine Bop (SEN)	12.10.1994	16	(1)	7
Amel Ćosić	19.11.1989	1	(7)	
Ricardo Dionisio	23.01.1998	6	(5)	
Mike Kenny Ebui (ITA)	01.03.1999	2	(4)	
Šemsudin Džanić (BIH)	12.07.1992	16	(1)	2
Sofiane Rouane (FRA)	14.02.1997	2		
Mamadou Samassa (MLI)	01.05.1986	1		

Foussballclub Déifferdeng 03

Founded:	2003 (*as merger of FA Red Boys Differdange and AS Differdange*)		
Stadium:	Stade Municipal, Differdange (3,000)		
Trainer:	Paolo Amodio		28.05.1973

Goalkeepers:	DOB	M	(s)	G
Andrea Amodio	13.07.1997	17		
Defenders:	**DOB**	**M**	**(s)**	**G**
Théo Brusco	20.11.1999	4	(2)	
Geoffrey Franzoni	18.02.1991	17		1
Mathias Jänisch	27.08.1990	8		
David Kalonji (BEL)	20.06.1989	12		
Dylan Lempereur (FRA)	24.10.1998	4		1
Edin Osmanovic	30.08.2001	11		
David Vandenbroeck (BEL)	12.07.1985	16		5
Midfielders:	**DOB**	**M**	**(s)**	**G**
Gonçalo Almeida da Silva (POR)	26.11.1990	6	(2)	
Gilles Bettmer	31.03.1989	7	(8)	2
Kevin d´Anzico	14.08.2000	3	(1)	

	DOB	M	(s)	G
Younes Denai (FRA)	13.11.1995	5	(1)	
Maxime Deruffe (FRA)	13.05.1988	12	(1)	4
William Ferreira da Cruz	07.12.2000		(4)	1
Marco Aleksandar Ferukoski (MKD)	26.05.1999	2	(2)	
Kilian Gulluni (FRA)	20.04.1999	6	(3)	
Quentin Emile Ange Leite Pereira (FRA)	21.01.1992	12	(1)	3
Ryan Lohei	11.04.2001		(7)	
Cerruti Siya (GER)	17.05.1999	6	(5)	1
Jordan Swistek (FRA)	25.08.1991	8		1
Forwards:	**DOB**	**M**	**(s)**	**G**
Kenan Avdusinovic	03.03.1998	12	(5)	3
Andreas Buch (GER)	25.04.1993	15		8
Valentino Vujinović (GER)	20.02.1999	4	(7)	5

F91 Dudelange

Founded:	1991		
Stadium:	Stade „Jos Nosbaum", Dudelange (2,558)		
Trainer:	Emilio Ferrera Patricio (BEL)		19.06.1977
[17.09.2019]	Bertrand Crasson (BEL)		05.10.1971

Goalkeepers:	DOB	M	(s)	G
Jonathan Joubert	12.09.1979	15		
Tim Kips	01.11.2000	2		
Defenders:	**DOB**	**M**	**(s)**	**G**
Mohamed Bouchouari (BEL)	15.11.2000	11		
Kobe Cools (BEL)	25.07.2000	12	(1)	3
Ricardo Aleixo Delgado	22.02.1994		(1)	
Salif Dramé (SEN)	03.01.1997	3		
Noé Ewert	24.02.1997		(1)	
Mehdi Kirch	27.01.1990	2		
Thibaut Lesquoy (BEL)	07.07.1995	14		
Tom Schnell	08.10.1985	11		
Chris Stumpf	28.08.1994	1		
Midfielders:	**DOB**	**M**	**(s)**	**G**
Sabir Bougrine (BEL)	10.07.1996	9	(1)	1
Mickaël Garos (FRA)	10.05.1988	12		1
Ryan Klapp	10.01.1993	8	(7)	2
Matéo Leveque (FRA)	27.10.1999	3		

	DOB	M	(s)	G
Charles Morren (BEL)	28.02.1992	11	(1)	
Mario Pokar (GER)	18.01.1990	5	(1)	1
Joel Rodrigues da Cruz	18.02.2001		(5)	
Danel Sinani	05.04.1997	12	(5)	14
Delvin Skenderović	23.01.1994	4	(1)	
Dominik Stolz (GER)	04.05.1990	12		5
Forwards:	**DOB**	**M**	**(s)**	**G**
Edis Agović	12.07.1993		(2)	
Antoine Bernier (BEL)	10.09.1997	12	(2)	1
Adel Bettaieb (FRA)	28.01.1997	3	(6)	1
Hearvin Djetou (FRA)	30.03.1995	1		
Sekou Keita Souza (GUI)	12.12.1994	4		3
Corenthyn Lavie (FRA)	06.03.1995	5		
Laurent Mendy (SEN)	18.12.1998	1	(3)	1
Omar Natami (ITA)	15.12.1998	4	(2)	1
Edvin Muratovic	15.02.1997	6	(2)	4
Mehdi Ouamri (FRA)	02.08.1999	3		
Bertino João Cabral Barbosa "Tino" (POR)	06.05.1992	1		

Foussballclub Etzella Ettelbruck

Founded: 21.05.1917
Stadium: Stade Am Deich, Ettelbruck (2,020)
Trainer: Claude Ottelé   01.04.1967
[30.09.2019]   Neil Pattison   13.03.1979

Goalkeepers:	DOB	M	(s)	G
André Leite Barrela	22.01.2001	5		
Sebastian Grub	18.10.1987	12		
Defenders:	**DOB**	**M**	**(s)**	**G**
Losseni Keita (GUI)	01.04.1984	14		1
Lex Nicolay	27.03.1997	14	(2)	1
Kevin Medina dos Santos	10.11.1994		(1)	
Jader Soares	19.08.1996	17		
Pol Schlesser	12.06.1996	13		
Antero Diogo da Silva Ferreira „Vila" (POR)	07.02.1990	17		
Midfielders:	**DOB**	**M**	**(s)**	**G**
Georgy Bella Abega	27.10.2001		(2)	
Bruno Correia Mendes "Bruno Ramírez"(POR)	10.12.1994	8	(6)	2
Adam Bouzid (FRA)	30.11.1987	1	(7)	
Raphael de Sousa	05.03.1993	3	(3)	
Diogo Miguel Zambujo Pimentel (POR)	16.07.1997	7	(1)	
Kevin Holtz	06.03.1993	16		5
João Freitas Morgado (POR)	06.07.1996	1	(3)	
Mefail Kadrija (GER)	22.09.1991	14	(2)	3
Sven Kalisa	14.03.1997	7	(8)	1
A. Martins	21.06.1995	3	(4)	1
Gianni Medina da Mata	22.12.2001		(4)	1
Gonçalo Rodrigues Fernandes (POR)	05.10.2002	2	(1)	
Forwards:	**DOB**	**M**	**(s)**	**G**
Julian Bidon (GER)	22.10.1990	12	(1)	2
Godmer Mabouba (FRA)	23.09.1990	13		1
Kevin N'Cho (FRA)	19.05.1991	4		2
Paulo MiguelMelo Almeida „Tica" (POR)	29.09.1990	4	(1)	2

Cercle sportif Fola Esch

Founded: 1906
Stadium: Stade „Émile Mayrisch", Esch-sur-Alzette (3,826)
Trainer: Jeff Strasser   05.10.1974

Goalkeepers:	DOB	M	(s)	G
Emmanuel Tomas Cabral (POR)	02.08.1996	13		
Thomas Hym (FRA)	29.08.1987	4		
Defenders:	**DOB**	**M**	**(s)**	**G**
Billy Bernard	29.04.1991	6	(2)	1
Rodrigue Dikaba (COD)	28.10.1985	11		1
Julien Klein (FRA)	07.04.1988	15	(1)	
Guillaume Mura (FRA)	09.01.1986	10	(1)	1
Cédric Sacras	28.09.1996	15		1
Midfielders:	**DOB**	**M**	**(s)**	**G**
Lucas Correia	18.04.2002		(3)	1
Achraf Drif (FRA)	22.03.1992	5	(5)	
Bruno Freire	27.03.1999	11	(5)	
Corentin Koçur (BEL)	17.10.1995	6	(3)	2
Gérard Mersch	08.09.1996	3	(9)	
Veldin Muharemović (BIH)	06.12.1984	10	(2)	1
Sylvio Ouassiero (FRA)	07.05.1994	15		
Dejvid Sinani	02.04.1993	15	(2)	4
Forwards:	**DOB**	**M**	**(s)**	**G**
Stefano Bensi	11.08.1988	10	(2)	5
Gauthier Caron (FRA)	27.12.1989	5		1
Ken Corral	08.05.1992	16	(1)	8
Zachary Hadji (FRA)	08.10.1996	1	(13)	2
Moussa Seydi (SEN)	21.08.1996	16	(1)	13

Football Club Union Sportive Hostert

Founded: 1946
Stadium: Stade „Jos Becker", Hostert (1,500)
Trainer: René Peters   15.06.1981

Goalkeepers:	DOB	M	(s)	G
Marc Pleimling	11.06.1989	16		
Valentin Roulez	12.12.1996	1		
Defenders:	**DOB**	**M**	**(s)**	**G**
Gianluca Bei	17.05.1995	14		
Aldin Derviševič	19.08.1989	16		2
Sebastien Do Rosario	12.01.1984	12	(1)	
Amar Duracak (CRO)	17.06.1992	9		
Demir Koljenović (BIH)	09.05.1990	11	(2)	
Alexandre Sacras	14.12.2000	2		
Cedric Steinmetz	27.09.1999	2	(4)	
Midfielders:	**DOB**	**M**	**(s)**	**G**
Kader Bourtal (FRA)	08.10.1991	2	(2)	
Rasheed Eichhorn (GER)	19.09.1997	3	(1)	
Adriano de Sousa Ferraz	20.04.2001		(1)	
Lucas Lamotte (BEL)	06.02.1998	5	(8)	3
Tarek Nouidra (FRA)	09.05.1987	14	(1)	
Léon Schmit	28.09.2001	11	(4)	1
Denis Stumpf	09.09.1997	16	(1)	2
Taiga Tada (JPN)	22.07.1997	13	(3)	
Bigen Yala Lusala (BEL)	20.10.1992	15	(2)	7
Juncai Wang	05.04.1990	12	(3)	2
Forwards:	**DOB**	**M**	**(s)**	**G**
Khaled Ayari (TUN)	17.01.1990	2	(1)	
Admir Desević (MNE)	08.05.1992	2	(9)	
Théo Sully (FRA)	13.02.1996	9	(5)	

Association Sportive la Jeunesse d'Esch/Alzette

Founded: 1907
Stadium: Stade de la Frontière, Esch-sur-Alzette (5,400)
Trainer: Krzysztof Szczesniak (GER)   15.06.1967
[07.11.2019]   Patrick Biergen   11.05.1974

Goalkeepers:	DOB	M	(s)	G
Lucas Fox	02.10.2000	4		
Luca Ivesic	07.04.1995	3		
Kévin Sommer (FRA)	08.11.1989	10		
Defenders:	**DOB**	**M**	**(s)**	**G**
Alessandro Fiorani	19.02.1989	12	(1)	
Emmanuel Lapierre (FRA)	05.08.1993	2		
Halim Medy Meddour (FRA)	11.02.1997	9	(2)	2
Arsène Menèssou (BEN)	03.12.1987	10	(1)	1
David Mendes Merces	08.11.2000	2	(3)	
Clayton de Sousa Moreira	24.02.1988	7	(1)	
Rick Brito Oliveira	25.11.2000	1	(1)	
Vincent Peugnet (FRA)	05.02.1994	4		1
Brandon Soares Rosa	15.08.1998	2	(1)	
Johannes Steinbach (GER)	02.07.1992	17		1
Midfielders:	**DOB**	**M**	**(s)**	**G**
Mehmet Arslan (FRA)	27.01.1998	9	(1)	
Alexis Boury (FRA)	31.10.2001	2	(2)	
David Soares de Sousa	15.07.1995	12	(1)	1
Luca Duriatti	11.02.1998	9	(6)	
Valentine Kouamé (BFA)	16.11.1990	12		
Cedric Soares	19.10.1995	3	(3)	
Miloš Todorović	18.08.1995	17		1
Forwards:	**DOB**	**M**	**(s)**	**G**
Martin Boakye (ITA)	10.02.1995	16		8
Andrea Deidda	15.12.1993	3	(9)	1
Michael Faty (FRA)	11.09.1996	3	(1)	
Almir Klica (MNE)	10.11.1998	8	(7)	3
Frederick Kyereh (GER)	18.10.1993	1	(5)	
Yannick Daniel Jacques Makota Ngalle (CMR)	20.01.1992	9	(3)	5

Union sportive de Mondorf-les-Bains

Founded: 1915
Stadium: Stade "John Grün", Mondorf-les-Bains (3,600)
Trainer: Arno Bonvini 14.10.1975

Goalkeepers:	DOB	M	(s)	G
João Ricardo Silva Machado	09.04.1999	1		
Koray Ozcan (FRA)	01.02.1995	16		
Defenders:	**DOB**	**M**	**(s)**	**G**
Yann Bartholomey	14.11.1998	1	(1)	
Ahmed Benhemine (FRA)	15.01.1987	16		
Christophe de Sousa	16.01.1992	7	(2)	
Fatih Eren (TUR)	17.01.1995	14	(2)	1
Michael Monteiro	11.12.1991	12	(3)	
Bosson Romaric (CIV)	12.04.1988	6		
Midfielders:	**DOB**	**M**	**(s)**	**G**
Tim Bartholomey	01.10.2000		(1)	
Cleidir Paulo Neves Luis (POR)	16.10.1993	7	(7)	
Fabio d'Alessandro	28.06.1996	8	(2)	
David Mendes da Silva	10.11.1986	10	(3)	2
João Carlos Amaral Marques Coimbra (POR)	24.05.1986	15	(2)	

	DOB	M	(s)	G
Rudolf Karl González Vass (DOM)	02.07.1998	3	(5)	
Abel Khaled (ALG)	09.11.1992	3	(1)	
Andy May	02.09.1989	6	(1)	1
Yassine Mohammed (ALG)	07.01.1991	12		4
Amine Nabli (TUN)	27.05.1985	17		2
Rinel Pieume	29.01.1997	1		
Ali Škrijelj	22.06.2000	2	(8)	
Faraji Taarimte (FRA)	17.08.1994	3	(1)	1
Tiago Oliveira		1		1
Forwards:	**DOB**	**M**	**(s)**	**G**
André Oliveira Barros da Silva	26.01.1997	7	(6)	2
Marianel Faladé (FRA)	17.10.1992	3		1
João Pedro Pinto Martins (ANG)	20.06.1982		(1)	
Omar Natami (ITA)	15.12.1998	3		2
Patrick Stumpf (GER)	11.04.1988	10	(4)	4
Alessandro Scanzano	14.03.1996	3		

Football Club Progrès Niederkorn

Founded: 1919
Stadium: Stade „Jos Haupert", Niederkorn (2,800)
Trainer: Roland Vrabec (GER) 06.03.1974

Goalkeepers:	DOB	M	(s)	G
Youn Czekanowicz	08.08.2000	1		
Sebastien Flauss	19.08.1989	16		
Defenders:	**DOB**	**M**	**(s)**	**G**
Filipe Jonni Correia Santos	06.05.1996	2		
Adrien Ferino (FRA)	16.06.1992	14		
Mathias Jänisch	27.08.1990	3	(1)	1
Metin Karayer (FRA)	18.05.1992	15	(2)	2
Yann Matias Marques	12.11.1996	4	(3)	
Aldin Skenderović	28.06.1997	17		
Tom Laterza	09.05.1992	8	(6)	
Ben Vogel	22.12.1994	12	(1)	1

Midfielders:	DOB	M	(s)	G
Yannick Bastos	30.05.1993	12	(2)	1
Yannick Cervellera	04.04.2001		(2)	
Jack Said Mmaee a Nwambeben (BEL)	16.11.1994	7	(7)	4
Belmin Muratović (MNE)	27.03.1998	5	(6)	3
Florik Shala	19.07.1997	2	(14)	4
Christian Silaj	07.04.1992	17		1
Sebastien Thill	29.12.1993	17		1
Forwards:	**DOB**	**M**	**(s)**	**G**
Issa Bah	05.07.2002		(1)	
Mayron de Almeida (BEL)	22.11.1995	13	(2)	6
Emmanuel Françoise (FRA)	08.06.1987	16		11
Kempes Waldemar Tekiela (GER)	15.10.1997	6	(4)	7

Racing Football Club Union Lëtzebuerg

Founded: 12.05.2005 (*as merger of Spora, Union and CS Alliance 01 Lëtzebuerg*)
Stadium: Stade "Achille Hammerel", Lëtzebuerg (5,814)
Trainer: Patrick Grettnich 03.03.1972
[21.08.2019] Régis Brouard (FRA) 17.01.1967

Goalkeepers:	DOB	M	(s)	G
Romain Ruffier (FRA)	04.10.1989	17		
Defenders:	**DOB**	**M**	**(s)**	**G**
Thomas Birk (GER)	05.07.1988	11		1
Jonathan Hennetier (FRA)	06.11.1991	8	(2)	1
Henrique da Silva Gomes (BRA)	20.08.1982	7		
Joscelino Silva Dos Santos (POR)	29.08.1989	8	(3)	
Benoit Nyssen (BEL)	12.09.1997	14		
David Simões	23.09.1997	1		
Pit Simon	17.02.1998	11	(1)	1
Glodi Zingha (ANG)	04.11.1993	1	(2)	
Midfielders:	**DOB**	**M**	**(s)**	**G**
Sota Adachi (JPN)	22.05.1995	1		
Yan Bouché	19.03.1999	5	(7)	2
Dwayn Holter	15.05.1995	10	(3)	2

	DOB	M	(s)	G
Osvaldo Gomes	20.07.1999	1		
Julien Humbert (FRA)	23.06.1984	12	(2)	1
Farid Ikene	15.12.2000	11	(2)	3
Pape Ibra M'Boup (SEN)	19.08.1987	4	(2)	
Kevin Nakache (FRA)	05.04.1989	15		4
Abdelhakim Omrani (ALG)	18.02.1991	4		
Jérôme Simon (FRA)	12.09.1993	5	(1)	
Loris Tinelli	02.02.1999	6	(7)	1
Forwards:	**DOB**	**M**	**(s)**	**G**
Amar Čatić	07.08.1995	1	(5)	
Daniel da Mota Alves	11.09.1985	12		5
Mana Dembélé (MLI)	29.11.1988	5		
Yann Mabella (FRA)	22.02.1996	17		11
Benssad Sulejmani	12.08.1999		(1)	

Football Club Rodange 91

Founded: 1991
Stadium: Stade „Joseph Phillippart", Rodange (3,400)
Trainer: Domenico Micarelli 05.10.1966
[05.08.2019] Vítor José Joaquim Pereira (POR) 27.08.1978
[01.09.2019] Nedžib Selimović (BIH) 10.04.1964

Goalkeepers:	DOB	M	(s)	G
Hugo Filipe Nascimento Magalhães (POR)	29.04.1985	16		
Eldin Latic	20.12.2002		(1)	
Dany Gonçalves Teixeira	20.03.1998	1		
Defenders:	**DOB**	**M**	**(s)**	**G**
David Marques Soares	20.02.1991	14	(1)	
Samuel Dog (FRA)	13.02.1985	11	(1)	
Henid Ramdedović	20.07.1987	15		4
Marco António Freitas Semedo (POR)	08.10.1987	14		
Kenan Korac	18.05.2000	3	(3)	
Irwin Ramdedović	24.09.1999	13		
Midfielders:	**DOB**	**M**	**(s)**	**G**
Dany Albuquerque	14.10.1998	2	(5)	1
Luca Alverdi	17.10.1999	1	(1)	

	DOB	M	(s)	G
Sam Alverdi	23.08.1997	8	(3)	
Valério Barbaro	16.02.1998	8	(7)	
Marco De Sousa	17.08.1986	4	(6)	3
David Fleurival (GLP)	19.02.1984	15		1
Alexis Larrière (FRA)	20.03.1997	4		5
Jean-Paul Makasso (CMR)	05.11.1993	16		
Dzenid Ramdedović	25.02.1992	10	(2)	3
Forwards:	**DOB**	**M**	**(s)**	**G**
Jeffrey da Graça Dias	27.07.1994	4	(4)	
Julien Lacour (FRA)	24.03.1992	2	(1)	
Deniz Muric (BEL)	06.03.1995	11	(3)	2
Momar N`Diaye (SEN)	13.07.1987	13	(3)	2
Arthur Njo-Léa (SUI)	30.11.1995	1	(1)	
Jordan Oukache (FRA)	09.06.1995	1	(3)	

Football Club UNA Strassen

Founded: 1922
Stadium: Complexe Sportif „Jean Wirtz", Strassen (2,000)
Trainer: Manuel Correia (POR) 28.03.1976

Goalkeepers:	DOB	M	(s)	G
Ralph Schon	20.01.1990	17		
Defenders:	**DOB**	**M**	**(s)**	**G**
Gauthier Bernardelli (FRA)	21.08.1992	8	(2)	2
Gilson Delgado (CPV)	19.10.1992	7	(4)	3
Tom Siebenaler	28.09.1990	13		
Alan Stulin (POL)	05.06.1990	6	(5)	
Quentin Zilli (FRA)	16.02.1999	11	(1)	
Midfielders:	**DOB**	**M**	**(s)**	**G**
Alen Agović	28.11.1997	11	(3)	
Denis Agović	13.07.1993	12	(1)	1
Morgan Betorangal	28.08.1988	2	(1)	
Ryunosuke Hayasaka (JPN)	07.06.1994	6	(1)	3
Kevin Lourenço Joaquim	12.05.1992	16		2
Khalid Lahyani (MAR)	24.02.1993	13	(2)	1
Marcel Linn (GER)	10.03.1993	5	(5)	
Tony Mastrangelo	01.09.1994	11	(1)	
Ben Payal	08.09.1988	14	(2)	
Forwards:	**DOB**	**M**	**(s)**	**G**
Adnan Bašić (BIH)	13.12.1996	3	(3)	
Benjamin Runser (FRA)	04.09.1991	11	(3)	8
Kevin Ruppert	16.08.1991	1	(11)	2
Stefan Rocha Lopes	24.09.1998	5	(4)	
Sebastian Szimayer (GER)	15.05.1990	15	(1)	8

Union Titus Pétange

Founded: 2015
Stadium: Stade Municipal de Pétange, Pétange (2,400)
Trainer: Carlos Manuel Fangueiro Soares 19.12.1976

Goalkeepers:	DOB	M	(s)	G
Miguel Ángelo Torres Palha (POR)	26.02.1995	10		
Tom Otellé	20.01.1998	7		
Defenders:	**DOB**	**M**	**(s)**	**G**
Jules Diouf (FRA)	05.03.1992	12		1
Allan Hauguel (FRA)	01.05.1999	16		1
Tun Held	11.01.2001	8		
Kevin Kerger	17.11.1994	3	(1)	
Tiago Miguel Pereira Duque (POR)	25.06.1994	4		
Dylan Martins Teixeira	27.01.2001		(1)	
Midfielders:	**DOB**	**M**	**(s)**	**G**
Artur Abreu Pereira	11.08.1994	16		1x
Emir Bijelić (BIH)	16.01.1998	7	(6)	1
Mathis Fonovich (FRA)	08.02.1997	3	(1)	
Dani Gaspar	16.06.2000		(1)	
Mounir Hamzaoui (MAR)	09.12.1987	17		1
Abdoul Aziz Kaboré (BFA)	01.01.1994	16		
Yannick Kakoko (GER)	26.01.1990	16		
Michel Kettenmeyer	07.02.1989	5	(1)	
Nathan Rodes (BEL)	11.12.1997	4	(2)	
Forwards:	**DOB**	**M**	**(s)**	**G**
Corentin Fatou (FRA)	17.01.1999	1	(9)	2
Eliot Gashi	15.04.1995	11	(3)	3
Joel Kalonji (BEL)	04.01.1998		(4)	
Eddire Mokrani (ALG)	23.01.1991	12	(3)	8
Jonathan Nanizayamo (BDI)	21.02.1992	3	(1)	1
Roberto Gomes	23.08.1998	1		
Patrik Teixeira	10.05.1996	7	(7)	2
Mike Schneider	01.02.1995	5	(3)	
Jordy Soladio (BEL)	12.02.1998	3	(7)	4

Football Club Victoria Rosport

Founded: 01.10.1928
Stadium: VictoriArena, Rosport (1,000)
Trainer: Marc Thomé 04.11.1963

Goalkeepers:	DOB	M	(s)	G
Niklas Bürger (GER)	07.10.1992	17		
Defenders:	**DOB**	**M**	**(s)**	**G**
Daniel Bartsch (GER)	07.05.1987	16	(1)	
Eric Brandenburger	08.09.1998	14	(1)	1
Gilles Feltes	06.12.1990	12	(1)	
Joel Armando da Mata dos Santos (POR)	04.09.1995	3	(4)	
Davis Sprūds (LVA)	28.12.1998	17		3
Philippe Werdel	12.05.1990	9	(3)	
Midfielders:	**DOB**	**M**	**(s)**	**G**
Michel Bechtold	01.07.1995	14	(1)	
Jakob Dallevedove (GER)	21.11.1987	8	(2)	1
Gabriel Gaspar Pereira	20.07.1990	3	(5)	
Timo Heinz (GER)	06.03.1991	1x	(1)	
Kevin Marques	16.01.1998	5	(4)	1
Ramiro Soares Valente	26.01.1989	5	(2)	2
Nelson Rodrigues Afonso	28.05.2002		(1)	
Enis Saiti (MKD)	25.12.1989	4	(3)	
Daito Terauchi (JPN)	14.06.1995	14	(3)	
Florian Weirich (GER)	23.09.1990	13		4
Forwards:	**DOB**	**M**	**(s)**	**G**
Alexander Biedermann (GER)	03.01.1995	8	(8)	8
Patrik Kasel (GER)	04.04.1986	1	(2)	
Jeff Lascak	13.02.1994	9	(3)	3
Mathieu Leroux (FRA)	26.03.1996	4		
Pedro dos Santos (POR)	21.11.1990	1	(4)	

1.	FC Swift Hesperange	15	9	5	1	52	-	17	32
2.	FC Wiltz 71	15	10	2	3	48	-	24	32
3.	US Esch/Alzette	15	9	1	5	32	-	20	28
4.	UN Käerjéng 97	15	8	3	4	41	-	28	27
5.	US Rumelange	15	8	3	4	36	-	23	27
6.	FC RM Hamm Benfica	15	7	5	3	26	-	14	26
7.	FC Mondercange	15	6	4	5	20	-	18	22
8.	FC Jeunesse Canach	15	6	3	6	28	-	32	21
9.	FC Alisontia Steinsel	15	7	0	8	22	-	34	21
10.	FC Mamer 32	15	5	4	6	24	-	33	19
11.	FC Yellow Boys Weiler-la-Tour	15	3	5	7	13	-	24	14
12.	Union Mertert/Wasserbillig	15	2	6	7	21	-	31	12
13.	FC Jeunesse Junglinster	15	2	3	10	14	-	35	9
14.	FC Blô-Weiss Medernach	15	1	0	14	9	-	53	3

The championship was suspended after 15 Rounds due to Covid-19 pandemic.

NATIONAL TEAM

INTERNATIONAL MATCHES
(16.07.2019 – 15.07.2020)

05.09.2019	Belfast	Northern Ireland - Luxembourg	1-0(1-0)	(F)
10.09.2019	Lëtzebuerg	Luxembourg - Serbia	1-3(0-1)	(ECQ)
11.10.2019	Lisboa	Portugal - Luxembourg	3-0(1-0)	(ECQ)
15.10.2019	Aalborg	Denmark - Luxembourg	4-0(2-0)	(F)
14.11.2019	Beograd	Serbia - Luxembourg	3-2(2-0)	(ECQ)
17.11.2019	Lëtzebuerg	Luxembourg - Portugal	0-2(0-1)	(ECQ)

05.09.2019 NORTHERN IRELAND - LUXEMBOURG 1-0(1-0) Friendly International
Windsor Park, Belfast; Referee: Bryn Markham-Jones (Wales); Attendance: 14,108
LUX: Anthony Moris (46.Ralph Schon), Lars Christian Krogh Gerson, Kevin Malget (46.Tim Hall), Laurent Jans (Cap), Dirk Carlson, Olivier Thill (85.Florian Bohnert), Danel Sinani (74.Daniel da Mota Alves), Vincent Thill, Gerson Rodrigues Correia Leal, Leandro Barreiro Martins (73.Chris Philipps), Maurice John Deville (60.David Turpel). Trainer: Luc Holtz.

10.09.2019 LUXEMBOURG - SERBIA 1-3(0-1) 16th EC. Qualifiers
Stade "Josy Barthel", Lëtzebuerg; Referee: Orel Grinfeld (Israel); Attendance: 6,373
LUX: Anthony Moris, Lars Christian Krogh Gerson, Maxime Chanot, Laurent Jans (Cap), Dirk Carlson, Olivier Thill, Danel Sinani (62.Daniel da Mota Alves), Leandro Barreiro Martins, Gerson Rodrigues Correia Leal, Vincent Thill (85.Aurélien Joachim), Maurice John Deville (61.David Turpel). Trainer: Luc Holtz.
Goal: David Turpel (66).

11.10.2019 PORTUGAL - LUXEMBOURG 3-0(1-0) 16th EC. Qualifiers
Estádio "José Alvalade", Lisboa; Referee: Daniel Stefański (Poland); Attendance: 47,305
LUX: Anthony Moris, Lars Christian Krogh Gerson, Maxime Chanot, Laurent Jans (Cap), Dirk Carlson, Leandro Barreiro Martins, Olivier Thill, Vincent Thill (88.Stefano Bensi), Florian Bohnert (46.Danel Sinani), Gerson Rodrigues Correia Leal, David Turpel (59.Daniel da Mota Alves). Trainer: Luc Holtz.

15.10.2019 DENMARK - LUXEMBOURG 4-0(2-0) Friendly International
Portland park, Aalborg; Referee: Bojan Pandžić (Sweden); Attendance: 9,043
LUX: Anthony Moris (46.Ralph Schon), Lars Christian Krogh Gerson, Maxime Chanot, Laurent Jans (Cap), Dirk Carlson, Marvin Martins Santos da Graça (74.Stefano Bensi), Olivier Thill (82.Aldin Skenderovic), Danel Sinani (46.Chris Philipps), Vincent Thill (55.Daniel da Mota Alves), Leandro Barreiro Martins (90.Florian Bohnert), Gerson Rodrigues Correia Leal. Trainer: Luc Holtz.

14.11.2019 SERBIA - LUXEMBOURG 3-2(2-0) 16th EC. Qualifiers
Stadion „Rajko Mitić", Beograd; Referee: Serdar Gözübüyük (Netherlands); Attendance: 1,560
LUX: Anthony Moris, Lars Christian Krogh Gerson, Maxime Chanot, Laurent Jans (Cap), Dirk Carlson, Tim Hall, Chris Philipps (46.Aldin Skenderovic), Olivier Thill (61.David Turpel), Vincent Thill (79.Danel Sinani), Gerson Rodrigues Correia Leal, Maurice John Deville. Trainer: Luc Holtz.
Goals: Gerson Rodrigues Correia Leal (54), David Turpel (75).

17.11.2019 LUXEMBOURG - PORTUGAL 0-2(0-1) 16th EC. Qualifiers
Stade "Josy Barthel", Lëtzebuerg; Referee: Jesús Gil Manzano (Spain); Attendance: 8,000
LUX: Anthony Moris, Lars Christian Krogh Gerson, Maxime Chanot, Laurent Jans (Cap), Dirk Carlson, Aldin Skenderovic, Vincent Thill (82.Aurélien Joachim), Leandro Barreiro Martins (74.Danel Sinani), Gerson Rodrigues Correia Leal, Maurice John Deville, David Turpel (59.Olivier Thill). Trainer: Luc Holtz.

NATIONAL TEAM PLAYERS
(16.07.2019 – 15.07.2020)

Name	DOB	Caps	Goals	2019/2020:	Club
Goalkeepers					
Anthony MORIS	29.04.1990	**28**	**0**	2019:	*Royal Excelsior Virton (BEL)*
Ralph SCHON	20.01.1990	**11**	**0**	2019:	*FC UNA Strassen*
Defenders					
Dirk CARLSON	01.04.1998	**23**	**0**	2019:	*Karlsruher SC (GER)*
Maxime CHANOT	21.11.1989	**39**	**3**	2019:	*New York City FC (USA)*
Marvin Martins Santos DA GRAÇA	17.02.1995	**7**	**1**	2019:	*FK Karpati Lviv (UKR)*
Tim HALL	15.04.1997	**3**	**0**	2019:	*FK Karpati Lviv (UKR)*
Kevin MALGET	15.01.1991	**34**	**2**	2019:	*Royal Excelsior Virton (BEL)*
Chris PHILIPPS	08.03.1994	**55**	**0**	2019:	*Legia Warszawa (POL)*
Aldin SKENDEROVIC	28.06.1997	**13**	**0**	2019:	*FC Progrès Niederkorn*
Midfielders					
Leandro BARREIRO Martins	03.01.2000	**16**	**1**	2019:	*1.FSV Mainz 05 (GER)*
Lars Christian Krogh GERSON	05.02.1990	**75**	**4**	2019:	*IFK Norrköping (SWE)*
Laurent JANS	05.08.1992	**64**	**1**	2019:	*SC Paderborn 07 (GER)*
Gerson RODRIGUES Correia Leal	20.06.1995	**24**	**3**	2019:	*FK Dinamo Kyiv (UKR)*
Danel SINANI	05.04.1997	**21**	**3**	2019:	*F91 Dudelange*
Olivier THILL	17.12.1997	**22**	**2**	2019:	*FK Ufa (RUS)*
Vincent THILL	04.02.2000	**29**	**3**	2019:	*US Orléans Loiret Football (FRA)*
Forwards					
Stefano BENSI	11.08.1988	**50**	**5**	2019:	*CS Fola Esch*
Florian BOHNERT	09.11.1997	**16**	**1**	2019:	*1.FSV Mainz 05 (GER)*
Daniel DA MOTA Alves	11.09.1985	**99**	**7**	2019:	*Racing FC Union Lëtzebuerg*
Maurice John DEVILLE	31.07.1992	**41**	**3**	2019:	*SV Waldhof Mannheim (GER)*
Aurélien JOACHIM	10.08.1986	**80**	**15**	2019:	*Royal Excelsior Virton (BEL)*
David TURPEL	19.10.1992	**52**	**6**	2019:	*Royal Excelsior Virton (BEL)*
National team coach					
Luc HOLTZ [from 03.08.2010]	14.06.1969			83 M; 16 W; 17 D; 50 L; 65-170	

MALTA

The Country:
Republic of Malta (Repubblika ta' Malta)
Capital: Valletta
Surface: 316 km²
Inhabitants: 514,564 [2019]
Time: UTC+1

The FA:
Assoċjazzjoni tal-Futbol ta' Malta
Millennium Stand, Floor 2 National Stadium, Ta'Qali, ATD4000 Malta
Tel: +356 21 232 581
Foundation date: 1900
Member of FIFA since: 1959
Member of UEFA since: 1960
Website: www.mfa.com.mt

NATIONAL TEAM RECORDS

RECORDS		
First international match:	24.02.1957, Gzira:	Malta – Austria 2-3
Most international caps:	Michael Mifsud	- 142 caps (2000-2019)
Most international goals:	Michael Mifsud	- 41 goals / 142 caps (2000-2019)

UEFA EUROPEAN CHAMPIONSHIP

1960	Did not enter
1964	Qualifiers
1968	Did not enter
1972	Qualifiers
1976	Qualifiers
1980	Qualifiers
1984	Qualifiers
1988	Qualifiers
1992	Qualifiers
1996	Qualifiers
2000	Qualifiers
2004	Qualifiers
2008	Qualifiers
2012	Qualifiers
2016	Qualifiers
2020	Qualifiers

FIFA WORLD CUP

1930	Did not enter
1934	Did not enter
1938	Did not enter
1950	Did not enter
1954	Did not enter
1958	Did not enter
1962	Did not enter
1966	Did not enter
1970	Did not enter
1974	Qualifiers
1978	Qualifiers
1982	Qualifiers
1986	Qualifiers
1990	Qualifiers
1994	Qualifiers
1998	Qualifiers
2002	Qualifiers
2006	Qualifiers
2010	Qualifiers
2014	Qualifiers
2018	Qualifiers

OLYMPIC TOURNAMENTS

1908	-
1912	-
1920	-
1924	-
1928	-
1936	-
1948	-
1952	-
1956	-
1960	Did not enter
1964	Did not enter
1968	Did not enter
1972	*Withdrew*
1976	Did not enter
1980	Did not enter
1984	Did not enter
1988	Did not enter
1992	Qualifiers
1996	Qualifiers
2000	Qualifiers
2004	Qualifiers
2008	Qualifiers
2012	Qualifiers
2016	Qualifiers

UEFA NATIONS LEAGUE

2018/2019 – League D

FIFA CONFEDERATIONS CUP 1992-2017

None

MALTESE CLUB HONOURS IN EUROPEAN CLUB COMPETITIONS:

European Champion Clubs' Cup (1956-1992) / UEFA Champions League (1993-2020)
None

Fairs Cup (1858-1971) / UEFA Cup (1972-2009) / UEFA Europa League (2010-2020)
None

UEFA Super Cup (1972-2019)
None

*European Cup Winners' Cup 1961-1999**
None

defunct competition

NATIONAL COMPETITIONS
TABLE OF HONOURS

	CHAMPIONS	CUP WINNERS	BEST GOALSCORERS	
1909/1910	Floriana FC	-	Salvu Samuele (Floriana FC)	4
1910/1911	*No championship*	-	-	
1911/1912	Floriana FC	-	*not known*	
1912/1913	Floriana FC	-	*not known*	
1913/1914	Ħamrun Spartans FC	-	*not known*	
1914/1915	Valletta United FC	-	*not known*	
1915/1916	*No championship*	-	-	
1916/1917	St. George's FC	-	*not known*	
1917/1918	Ħamrun Spartans FC	-	*not known*	
1918/1919	The King's Own Malta Regiment	-	*not known*	
1919/1920	Sliema Wanderers FC	-	*not known*	
1920/1921	Floriana FC	-	*not known*	
1921/1922	Floriana FC	-	*not known*	
1922/1923	Sliema Wanderers FC	-	*not known*	
1923/1924	Sliema Wanderers FC	-	*not known*	
1924/1925	Floriana FC	-	*not known*	
1925/1926	Sliema Wanderers FC	-	*not known*	
1926/1927	Floriana FC	-	*not known*	
1927/1928	Floriana FC	-	*not known*	
1928/1929	Floriana FC	-	P. Friggieri (Floriana FC)	4
1929/1930	Sliema Wanderers FC	-	*not known*	
1930/1931	Floriana FC	-	C. Cauchi (Floriana FC)	4
1931/1932	Valletta United FC	-	not known	
1932/1933	Sliema Wanderers FC	-	not known	
1933/1934	Sliema Wanderers FC	-	A. Brincat (Sliema Wanderers FC)	2
1934/1935	Floriana FC	Sliema Wanderers FC	Tony Nicholl (Sliema Wanderers FC)	11
1935/1936	Sliema Wanderers FC	Sliema Wanderers FC	Anton Mayerhoffer (AUT, Floriana FC)	3
1936/1937	Floriana FC	Sliema Wanderers FC	George Albert Bond (ENG, Floriana FC)	4
1937/1938	Sliema Wanderers FC	Floriana FC	Tony Nicholl (Sliema Wanderers FC) C. Cauchi (Floriana FC)	5
1938/1939	Sliema Wanderers FC	Melita FC St. Julian's	Tony Nicholl (Sliema Wanderers FC)	8
1939/1940	Sliema Wanderers FC	Sliema Wanderers FC	Tony Nicholl (Sliema Wanderers FC)	18
1940-1944	*No championship*	-	-	
1944/1945	Valletta FC	Floriana FC	Tony Nicholl (Sliema Athletics FC)	6
1945/1946	Valletta FC	Sliema Wanderers FC	*not known*	
1946/1947	Ħamrun Spartans FC	Floriana FC	Maurice Decesare (Melita FC St. Julian's) C. Galea (Floriana FC)	11
1947/1948	Valletta FC	Sliema Wanderers FC	Freddie Landolina (Ħamrun Spartans FC)	16
1948/1949	Sliema Wanderers FC	Floriana FC	Salvinu Schembri (Valletta FC) Tony Nicholl (Sliema Wanderers FC)	11
1949/1950	Floriana FC	Floriana FC	Pace (Valletta FC)	16
1950/1951	Floriana FC	Sliema Wanderers FC	Pullu Demanuele (Valletta FC)	14
1951/1952	Floriana FC	Sliema Wanderers FC	Lolly Borg (Floriana FC)	17
1952/1953	Floriana FC	Floriana FC	Pace (Valletta FC)	9
1953/1954	Sliema Wanderers FC	Floriana FC	Tony Nicholl (Sliema Wanderers FC)	12
1954/1955	Floriana FC	Floriana FC	Lolly Borg (Floriana FC) Tony Cauchi (Floriana FC)	13
1955/1956	Sliema Wanderers FC	Sliema Wanderers FC	Sammy Nicholl (Sliema Wanderers FC)	15
1956/1957	Sliema Wanderers FC	Floriana FC	Sammy Nicholl (Sliema Wanderers FC)	14
1957/1958	Floriana FC	Floriana FC	Pullu Demanuele (Floriana FC)	14
1958/1959	Valletta FC	Sliema Wanderers FC	A. Cassar (Ħamrun Spartans FC)	11
1959/1960	Valletta FC	Valletta FC	F. Zammit (Valletta FC) M. Azzopardi (Valletta FC)	12
1960/1961	Hibernians FC Paola	Floriana FC	Tony Cauchi (Floriana FC)	12
1961/1962	Floriana FC	Hibernians FC Paola	Tony Cauchi (Floriana FC)	17
1962/1963	Valletta FC	Sliema Wanderers FC	M. Azzopardi (Valletta FC)	20
1963/1964	Sliema Wanderers FC	Valletta FC	A. Borg (Valletta FC)	11
1964/1965	Sliema Wanderers FC	Sliema Wanderers FC	Joseph Cini (Sliema Wanderers FC)	12
1965/1966	Sliema Wanderers FC	Floriana FC	John Bonnett (Sliema Wanderers FC) Ronald Cocks (Sliema Wanderers FC)	6
1966/1967	Hibernians FC Paola	Floriana FC	A. Delia (Hibernians FC Paola)	8
1967/1968	Floriana FC	Sliema Wanderers FC	Joseph Cini (Sliema Wanderers FC)	10
1968/1969	Hibernians FC Paola	Sliema Wanderers FC	C. Cassar (Hibernians FC Paola)	9
1969/1970	Floriana FC	Hibernians FC Paola	Joseph Cini (Sliema Wanderers FC) Ronald Cocks (Sliema Wanderers FC)	7
1970/1971	Sliema Wanderers FC	Hibernians FC Paola	Raymond Xuereb (Floriana FC)	5
1971/1972	Sliema Wanderers FC	Floriana FC	Tony Giglio (Valletta FC)	9
1972/1973	Floriana FC	Gżira United FC	C. Borg (Ħamrun Spartans FC)	10
1973/1974	Valletta FC	Sliema Wanderers FC	T. Camilleri (Sliema Wanderers FC)	9
1974/1975	Floriana FC	Valletta FC	Raymond Xuereb (Floriana FC)	17

1975/1976	Sliema Wanderers FC	Floriana FC	Richard Aquilina (Sliema Wanderers FC)	9
1976/1977	Floriana FC	Valletta FC	Raymond Xuereb (Floriana FC)	16
1977/1978	Valletta FC	Valletta FC	Leonard Farrugia (Valletta FC)	16
1978/1979	Hibernians FC Paola	Sliema Wanderers FC	C. Brincat (Marsa FC)	11
1979/1980	Valletta FC	Hibernians FC Paola	Emanuel Fabri (Sliema Wanderers FC) Leonard Farrugia (Valletta FC) F. Cristiano (Valletta FC)	15
1980/1981	Hibernians FC Paola	Floriana FC	Ernest Spiteri-Gonzi (Hibernians FC Paola)	13
1981/1982	Hibernians FC Paola	Hibernians FC Paola	Ernest Spiteri-Gonzi (Hibernians FC Paola)	12
1982/1983	Ħamrun Spartans FC	Ħamrun Spartans FC	Leo Refalo (Ħamrun Spartans FC)	7
1983/1984	Valletta FC	Ħamrun Spartans FC	Georgi Ivanov (BUL, Ħamrun Spartans FC) Charles Muscat (Żurrieq FC)	7
1984/1985	Rabat Ajax FC	Żurrieq FC	Leonard Farrugia (Valletta FC)	9
1985/1986	Rabat Ajax FC	Rabat Ajax FC	Gianluca De Ponti (ITA, Żurrieq FC)	8
1986/1987	Ħamrun Spartans FC	Ħamrun Spartans FC	Carmel Busuttil (Rabat Ajax FC)	10
1987/1988	Ħamrun Spartans FC	Ħamrun Spartans FC	Barry Gallagher (ENG, Ħamrun Spartans FC)	7
1988/1989	Sliema Wanderers FC	Ħamrun Spartans FC	Joseph Zarb (Valletta FC)	11
1989/1990	Valletta FC	Sliema Wanderers FC	Joseph Zarb (Valletta FC)	17
1990/1991	Ħamrun Spartans FC	Valletta FC	Joseph Zarb (Valletta FC)	12
1991/1992	Valletta FC	Ħamrun Spartans FC	Stefan Sultana (Ħamrun Spartans FC)	22
1992/1993	Floriana FC	Floriana FC	Carl Zachhau (DEN, Hibernians FC Paola)	22
1993/1994	Hibernians FC Paola	Floriana FC	Carl Zachhau (DEN, Hibernians FC Paola) Joseph Zarb (Valletta FC)	17
1994/1995	Hibernians FC Paola	Valletta FC	Carl Saunders (ENG, Sliema Wanderers FC)	18
1995/1996	Sliema Wanderers FC	Valletta FC	Aldrin Muscat (Sliema Wanderers FC)	18
1996/1997	Valletta FC	Valletta FC	Danilo Dončić (SRB, Valletta FC)	32
1997/1998	Valletta FC	Hibernians FC Paola	Joseph Brincat (Birkirkara FC/Floriana FC)	19
1998/1999	Valletta FC	Valletta FC	Gilbert Agius (Valletta FC)	20
1999/2000	Birkirkara FC	Sliema Wanderers FC	Michael Mifsud (Sliema Wanderers FC)	21
2000/2001	Valletta FC	Valletta FC	Michael Mifsud (Sliema Wanderers FC)	30
2001/2002	Hibernians FC Paola	Birkirkara FC	Danilo Dončić (SRB, Sliema Wanderers FC)	32
2002/2003	Sliema Wanderers FC	Birkirkara FC	Adrian Mifsud (Hibernians FC Paola) Danilo Dončić (SRB, Sliema Wanderers FC) Michael Galea (Birkirkara FC)	18
2003/2004	Sliema Wanderers FC	Sliema Wanderers FC	Danilo Dončić (SRB, Sliema Wanderers FC)	19
2004/2005	Sliema Wanderers FC	Birkirkara FC	Andrew Cohen (Hibernians FC Paola)	21
2005/2006	Birkirkara FC	Hibernians FC Paola	Michael Galea (Birkirkara FC)	19
2006/2007	Marsaxlokk FC	Hibernians FC Paola	Daniel Bogdanović (Marsaxlokk FC)	31
2007/2008	Valletta FC	Birkirkara FC	Omar Sebastián Monesterolo (ARG, Valletta FC)	19
2008/2009	Hibernians FC Paola	Sliema Wanderers FC	Terence Scerri (Hibernians FC Paola)	26
2009/2010	Birkirkara FC	Valletta FC	Camilo Sanvezzo (BRA, Qormi FC)	24
2010/2011	Valletta FC	Floriana FC	Alfred Effiong (NGA, Marsaxlokk FC)	17
2011/2012	Valletta FC	Hibernians FC Paola	Obinna Obiefule (NGA, Marsaxlokk FC/Mosta FC)	34
2012/2013	Birkirkara FC	Hibernians FC Paola	José Luis Negrín (ESP, Melita FC St. Julian's/Rabat Ajax FC)	22
2013/2014	Valletta FC	Valletta FC	Jhonnattann Benites da Conceiçao (BRA, Birkirkara FC) Edison Luiz dos Santos "Tarabai" (BRA, Hibernians FC Paola)	21
2014/2015	Hibernians FC Paola	Birkirkara FC	Jorginho (BRA, Hibernians FC Paola) Edison Luiz dos Santos "Tarabai" (BRA, Hibernians FC Paola)	25
2015/2016	Valletta FC	Sliema Wanderers FC	Mario Fontanella (ITA, Floriana FC)	20
2016/2017	Hibernians FC Paola	Floriana FC	Bojan Kaljević (MNE, Balzan FC)	23
2017/2018	Valletta FC	Valletta FC	Amadou Samb (SEN, Gżira United FC)	21
2018/2019	Valletta FC	Balzan FC	Taylon Nicolas Correa Marcolino (BRA, Hibernians FC Paola)	19
2019/2020	Floriana FC	*Competition abandoned*	Kristian Keqi (ALB, Floriana FC)	14

Results

Round 1 [23-24.08.2019]
Sirens FC - Senglea Athletic 1-1(1-0)
Gżira United - Hamrun Spartans 0-0
Birkirkara FC - Floriana FC 0-1(0-1)
Valletta FC - St. Luċija FC 2-3(1-3)
Tarxien Rainbows - Mosta FC 0-4(0-1)
Gudja United - Hibernians FC 1-1(0-0)
Balzan FC - Sliema Wanderers 2-1(1-0)

Round 2 [28-30.08.2019]
Senglea Athletic - Birkirkara FC 1-0(0-0)
Hibernians FC - Tarxien Rainbows 4-1(2-1)
Floriana FC - Balzan FC 1-0(0-0)
Sliema Wanderers - Valletta FC 1-3(1-1)
St. Luċija FC - Gżira United 0-0
Mosta FC - Sirens FC 3-4(1-2)
Hamrun Spartans - Gudja United 2-2(1-0)

Round 3 [13-15.09.2019]
Tarxien Rainbows - Hamrun Spartans 2-3(1-1)
Gżira United - Sliema Wanderers 1-1(1-0)
Sirens FC - Hibernians FC 2-1(1-0)
Birkirkara FC - Balzan FC 3-3(2-1)
Senglea Athletic - Mosta FC 2-1(1-1)
Gudja United - St. Luċija FC 1-1(0-1)
Valletta FC - Floriana FC 1-1(0-0)

Round 4 [20-22.09.2019]
Mosta FC - Birkirkara FC 1-1(1-0)
Hibernians FC - Senglea Athletic 2-1(2-0)
Hamrun Spartans - Sirens FC 4-0(2-0)
Balzan FC - Valletta FC 0-2(0-1)
Sliema Wanderers - Gudja United 1-1(0-0)
St. Luċija FC - Tarxien Rainbows 2-1(1-1)
Floriana FC - Gżira United 0-0

Round 5 [27-29.09.2019]
Tarxien Rainbows - Sliema Wander. 1-2(0-1)
Gudja United - Floriana FC 0-2(0-2)
Birkirkara FC - Valletta FC 2-2(1-1)
Senglea Athletic - Hamrun Spartans 1-3(1-3)
Sirens FC - St. Luċija FC 3-1(1-1)
Mosta FC - Hibernians FC 1-2(0-1)
Gżira United - Balzan FC 2-0(0-0)

Round 6 [03-06.10.2019]
Valletta FC - Gżira United 1-3(0-1)
Balzan FC - Gudja United 1-0(0-0)
St. Luċija FC - Senglea Athletic 0-0
Hibernians FC - Birkirkara FC 0-1(0-1)
Sliema Wanderers - Sirens FC 0-1(0-0)
Floriana FC - Tarxien Rainbows 2-1(1-1)
Hamrun Spartans - Mosta FC 0-2(0-1)

Round 7 [18-21.10.2019]
Mosta FC - St. Luċija FC 1-0(0-0)
Senglea Athletic - Sliema Wanderers 2-0(0-0)
Sirens FC - Floriana FC 1-4(1-0)
Birkirkara FC - Gżira United 1-3(0-1)
Gudja United - Valletta FC 0-1(0-1)
Tarxien Rainbows - Balzan FC 1-3(0-1)
Hibernians FC - Hamrun Spartans 1-2(1-2)

Round 8 [25-28.10.2019]
Floriana FC - Senglea Athletic 5-0(2-0)
Sliema Wanderers - Mosta FC 0-1(0-0)
Gżira United - Gudja United 6-1(3-1)
Valletta FC - Tarxien Rainbows 3-1(1-0)
Balzan FC - Sirens FC 2-4(1-2)
Hamrun Spartans - Birkirkara FC 0-0
St. Luċija FC - Hibernians FC 0-2(0-1)

Round 9 [01-04.11.2019]
Tarxien Rainbows - Gżira United 0-5(0-2)
Hamrun Spartans - St. Luċija FC 1-1(1-0)
Senglea Athletic - Balzan FC 2-2(0-1)
Mosta FC - Floriana FC 1-3(0-2)
Sirens FC - Valletta FC 0-0
Hibernians FC - Sliema Wanderers 1-0(0-0)
Birkirkara FC - Gudja United 2-3(1-1)

Round 10 [08-10.11.2019]
Balzan FC - Mosta FC 5-0(3-0)
Valletta FC - Senglea Athletic 1-0(1-0)
Sliema Wanderers - Hamrun Spartans 2-0(1-0)
Gudja United - Tarxien Rainbows 3-2(1-1)
St. Luċija FC - Birkirkara FC 0 2(0 1)
Gżira United - Sirens FC 0-1(0-0)
Floriana FC - Hibernians FC 2-2(1-1)

Round 11 [22-25.11.2019]
Hamrun Spartans - Floriana FC 0-0
St. Luċija FC - Sliema Wanderers 0-4(0-1)
Sirens FC - Gudja United 1-1(1-1)
Mosta FC - Valletta FC 0-4(0-2)
Hibernians FC - Balzan FC 2-1(1-1)
Birkirkara FC - Tarxien Rainbows 3-0(1-0)
Senglea Athletic - Gżira United 1-3(1-1)

Round 12 [06-08.12.2019]
Balzan FC - Hamrun Spartans 1-1(1-1)
Gżira United - Mosta FC 3-1(2-0)
Floriana FC - St. Luċija FC 2-1(0-0)
Sliema Wanderers - Birkirkara FC 2-1(1-1)
Gudja United - Senglea Athletic 4-1(1-1)
Tarxien Rainbows - Sirens FC 0-3(0-1)
Valletta FC - Hibernians FC 1-1(1-0)

Round 13 [13-16.12.2019]
Birkirkara FC - Sirens FC 2-0(2-0)
St. Luċija FC - Balzan FC 0-3(0-0)
Hibernians FC - Gżira United 2-0(0-0)
Sliema Wanderers - Floriana FC 1-2(0-1)
Hamrun Spartans - Valletta FC 0-1(0-1)
Senglea Athletic - Tarxien Rainbows 2-2
Mosta FC - Gudja Unit. 1-0(1-0) [08.01.2020]

Round 14 [11-13.01.2020]
St. Luċija FC - Valletta FC 2-2(1-0)
Senglea Athletic - Sirens FC 2-2(1-1)
Sliema Wanderers - Balzan FC 1-2(0-1)
Mosta FC - Tarxien Rainbows 5-2(3-2)
Hibernians FC - Gudja United 2-0(1-0)
Floriana FC - Birkirkara FC 0-1(0-0)
Hamrun Spartans - Gżira United 0-3(0-1)

Round 15 [18-20.01.2020]
Gudja United - Hamrun Spartans 1-1(0-1)
Tarxien Rainbows - Hibernians FC 0-4(0-3)
Balzan FC - Floriana FC 1-3(1-1)
Birkirkara FC - Senglea Athletic 1-1(1-1)
Sirens FC - Mosta FC 2-0(0-0)
Gżira United - St. Luċija FC 1-2(0-2)
Valletta FC - Sliema Wanderers 2-1(0-0)

Round 16 [01-03.02.2020]
Hamrun Spartans - Tarxien Rainbows 2-3(1-1)
Sliema Wanderers - Gżira United 2-0(0-0)
Mosta FC - Senglea Athletic 1-0(0-0)
St. Luċija FC - Gudja United 2-1(2-0)
Floriana FC - Valletta FC 0-1(0-1)
Hibernians FC - Sirens FC 0-2(0-0)
Balzan FC - Birkirkara FC 0-0

Round 17 [08-10.02.2020]
Gudja United - Sliema Wanderers 1-0(0-0)
Valletta FC - Balzan FC 3-1(1-1)
Gżira United - Floriana FC 2-2(0-1)
Birkirkara FC - Mosta FC 2-1(2-0)
Tarxien Rainbows - St. Luċija FC 1-3(1-1)
Senglea Athletic - Hibernians FC 1-1(1-1)
Sirens FC - Hamrun Spartans 1-2(1-1)

Round 18 [15-17.02.2020]
St. Luċija FC - Sirens FC 0-2(0-2)
Sliema Wander. - Tarxien Rainbows 1-0(0-0)
Hibernians FC - Mosta FC 3-1(2-1)
Floriana FC - Gudja United 1-2(1-0)
Balzan FC - Gżira United 1-3(0-0)
Valletta FC - Birkirkara FC 1-4(1-3)
Hamrun Spartans - Senglea Athletic 1-0(0-0)

Round 19 [21-22.02.2020]
Sirens FC - Sliema Wanderers 0-0
Tarxien Rainbows - Floriana FC 0-4(0-3)
Gżira United - Valletta FC 0-1(0-0)
Gudja United - Balzan FC 0-2(0-1)
Mosta FC - Hamrun Spartans 2-1(1-0)
Senglea Athletic - St. Luċija FC 2-5(0-2)
Birkirkara FC - Hibernians FC 2-1(1-1)

Round 20 [06-08.03.2020]
Floriana FC - Sirens FC 3-0(0-0)
Sliema Wanderers - Senglea Athletic 4-1(2-1)
St. Luċija FC - Mosta FC 1-2(1-0)
Hamrun Spartans - Hibernians FC 1-2(0-1)
Valletta FC - Gudja United 0-2(0-0)
Balzan FC - Tarxien Rainbows 3-0(1-0)
Gżira United - Birkirkara FC 0-2(0-1)

Please note: the league was suspended on 12.03.2020 due to Covid-19 pandemic. On 18.05.2020, the MFA Executive Committee decided to terminate the league competition. Floriana FC, topping the league at time of suspension, were declared champions, no teams were relegated.

Final Standings

			Total					Home						Away				
1. **Floriana FC**	20	12	5	3	38 - 15	41	5	2	3	16 - 8		7	3	0	22 - 7
2. Valletta FC	20	11	5	4	32 - 22	38	4	2	4	15 - 17		7	3	0	17 - 5
3. Hibernians FC Paola	20	11	4	5	34 - 20	37	7	0	3	17 - 9		4	4	2	17 - 11
4. Sirens FC San Pawl il-Baħar	20	10	5	5	30 - 26	35	3	4	2	11 - 10		7	1	3	19 - 16
5. Birkirkara FC	20	9	6	5	30 - 20	33	4	3	3	18 - 15		5	3	2	12 - 5
6. Gżira United FC	20	9	5	6	35 - 19	32	3	3	4	15 - 11		6	2	2	20 - 8
7. Balzan FC	20	8	4	8	33 - 29	28	4	2	4	16 - 14		4	2	4	17 - 15
8. Mosta FC	20	9	1	10	29 - 35	28	5	1	4	16 - 17		4	0	6	13 - 18
9. Hamrun Spartans FC	20	6	7	7	24 - 25	25	2	4	5	11 - 14		4	3	2	13 - 11
10. Sliema Wanderers FC	20	7	3	10	24 - 22	24	5	1	5	15 - 12		2	2	5	9 - 10
11. Gudja United FC	20	6	6	8	24 - 30	24	3	3	3	11 - 11		3	3	5	13 - 19
12. Santa Luċija FC	20	6	5	9	24 - 33	23	2	3	6	7 - 19		4	2	3	17 - 14
13. Senglea Athletic FC	20	3	7	10	21 - 39	16	3	4	3	16 - 19		0	3	7	5 - 20
14. Tarxien Rainbows FC	20	1	1	18	18 - 61	4	0	0	9	5 - 31		1	1	9	13 - 30

Top goalscorers:

14	**Kristian Keqi (ALB)**	*Floriana FC*
13	Mario Fontanella (ITA)	*Valletta FC*
11	Andrija Majdevac (SRB)	*Balzan FC*
10	Jefferson Mateus de Assis Estacio (BRA)	*Gżira United FC*
10	Federico Matías Falcone (ARG)	*Birkirkara FC*

NATIONAL CUP
Maltese FA Trophy 2019/2020

Preliminary Round [06-09.2019]

Xagħra United FC - St. Venera Lightnings FC	2-0	Siġġiewi FC - Marsaskala FC	0-0 aet; 4-2 pen
Victoria Hotspurs FC - Mdina Knights FC	7-0	Għaxaq FC - Żebbuġ Rovers FC	4-1
Kirkop United FC - Kerċem Ajax FC	2-3	SK Victoria Wanderers FC - Għajnsielem FC	2-3 aet
Ta' Xbiex - Munxar Falcons FC	1-2	St. Lawrence Spurs FC - Xewkija Tigers FC	0-5

First Round [13-15.09.2019]

Nadur Youngsters FC - Oratory Youths FC	4-0	Qala Saints FC - Dingli Swallows FC	2-3
Kerċem Ajax FC - Munxar Falcons FC	5-0	Għarb Rangers FC - Xewkija Tigers FC	0-2
Sannat Lions FC - Għargħur FC	0-1	Msida St. Joseph FC - Attard FC	1-2
Siġġiewi FC - Victoria Hotspurs FC	0-4	Xagħra United FC - Għajnsielem FC	3-1
Mtarfa FC - Għaxaq FC	0-2		

Second Round [25-28.10.2019]

Qrendi FC - Lija Athletic FC	0-5	Xagħra United FC - Victoria Hotspurs FC	0-3
San Ġwann FC - Marsa FC	2-0	Żejtun Corinthians FC - Naxxar Lions FC	2-1
Żurrieq FC - Melita FC St. Julian's	0-2	Vittoriosa Stars FC - Nadur Youngsters FC	0-3
Marsaxlokk FC - St. Andrews FC	1-3	Birżebbuġa St. Peter's FC - Xewkija Tigers FC	2-7
Rabat Ajax FC - Għargħur FC	4-1	Attard FC - Żabbar St. Patrick FC	0-1
Mġarr United FC - Għaxaq FC	5-1	Żebbuġ Rangers FC – Kalkara FC	3-1
Mellieħa SC - Swieqi United FC	1-4	Qormi FC - Luqa St. Andrew's FC	1-0
Pietà Hotspurs FC - FC St. George's Cospicua	4-1	Dingli Swallows FC - Mqabba FC	1-3
Kerċem Ajax FC - Fgura United FC	2-1	Pembroke Athleta FC - Xgħajra Tornadoes FC	3-0

Third Round [29.11-01.12.2019]

Pembroke Athleta FC - Żabbar St. Patrick FC	6-0	Żejtun Corinthians FC - Hibernians FC Paola	0-3
Balzan FC - San Ġwann FC	3-0	Sliema Wanderers FC - Santa Lucia FC	0-2
Qormi FC - Swieqi United FC	2-2 aet; 4-5 pen	Kerċem Ajax FC - Sirens FC San Pawl il-Baħar	1-4
Tarxien Rainbows FC - Ħamrun Spartans FC	1-2	Floriana FC - Melita FC St. Julian's	6-1
Mqabba FC - Pietà Hotspurs FC	0-3	Rabat Ajax FC - Mosta FC	0-7
Gżira United FC - Senglea Athletic FC	1-2	Birkirkara FC - Nadur Youngsters FC	1-0
St. Andrews FC - Valletta FC	0-4	Żebbuġ Rangers FC - Victoria Hotspurs FC	3-5
Gudja United FC - Lija Athletic FC	3-0	Xewkija Tigers FC - Mġarr United FC	5-2

Fourth Round [24-26.01.2020]

Mosta FC - Birkirkara FC	1-2	Pembroke Athleta FC - Hibernians FC Paola	0-4
Balzan FC - Santa Lucia FC	2-0	Swieqi United FC - Ħamrun Spartans FC	1-3
Pietà Hotspurs FC - Xewkija Tigers FC	2-1	Victoria Hotspurs FC - Gudja United FC	1-3
Floriana FC - Senglea Athletic FC	2-0 aet	Valletta FC - Sirens FC San Pawl il-Baħar	4-1

Quarter-Finals [29.02.-01.03.2020]

Balzan FC - Pietà Hotspurs FC	0-1	Hibernians FC Paola - Ħamrun Spartans FC	2-1 aet
Valletta FC - Gudja United FC	2-0	Floriana FC - Birkirkara FC	1-1 aet; 3-1 pen

The competition was cancelled due to Covid-19 pandemic.

Balzan Football Club

Founded:	1937
Stadium:	St. Aloysius Sports and Recreational Complex, Birkirkara (100)
Trainer:	Jacques Scerri 28.07.1979
[04.03.2020]	Alejandro Pantoja (ESP) 02.05.1984

Goalkeepers:	DOB	M	(s)	G
Sean Mintoff	13.10.1985	4	(1)	
Kristijan Naumovski (MKD)	17.09.1988	16		1
Defenders:	**DOB**	**M**	**(s)**	**G**
Samir Arab	25.03.1994	2	(4)	
Ivan Božović (SRB)	29.05.1990	17		1
Steven Bezzina	05.01.1987	13	(2)	
Gary Camilleri	05.08.1999		(1)	
Zachary Grech	25.08.2000	1	(1)	
Zak Grech	21.07.1999		(1)	
Michael Johnson	11.05.1994	9	(3)	
Aleksandar Kosorić (BIH)	30.01.1987	13		1
Augustine Loof (NED)	01.01.1996	14		1
Midfielders:	**DOB**	**M**	**(s)**	**G**
Arthur Faría Machado (BRA)	10.01.1992	10	(1)	1
Dale Camilleri	17.10.1992	3	(5)	

	DOB	M	(s)	G
Ricardo Calixto Correa Duarte (URU)	20.07.1994	14		5
Paul Fenech	20.12.1986	17	(1)	
Marcus Grima	22.07.2000		(5)	
Stephan Pisani	07.08.1992	16		3
Ryan Scicluna	30.07.1993	4	(5)	
Nenad Šljivić (SRB)	08.06.1985	11		
Forwards:	**DOB**	**M**	**(s)**	**G**
Adeseyi Shinobu Adeyinka Adekoya (USA)	05.12.1995	2	(2)	1
Stefan Dimić (SRB)	01.05.1993	12	(1)	1
Alfred Effiong	29.11.1984	13	(7)	2
Uroš Ljubomirac (SRB)	12.04.1990	15		2
Andrija Majdevac (SRB)	07.08.1997	9	(1)	11
Lydon Micallef	16.05.1992		(4)	
Luke Montebello	13.08.1995	5	(4)	2
Pedro Augusto Mota de Lima (BRA)	13.06.2000		(1)	

Birkirkara Football Club

Founded:	1950
Stadium:	Mġarr Ground, Imgarr (300)
Trainer:	John Buttigieg 05.10.1963
[09.09.2019]	Andréas Gerardus Maria Paus (NED) 09.10.1965

Goalkeepers:	DOB	M	(s)	G
Andrew James Hogg	02.03.1985	20		
Defenders:	**DOB**	**M**	**(s)**	**G**
Glenn Attard	14.01.2001	1		
Claudio Bonanni (ITA)	05.03.1997	5		
Gianluca Bugeja	05.09.1999		(2)	
Óscar Matías Carniello (URU)	18.09.1988	17		1
Jeferson De Sousa Ferreira (BRA)	24.11.1995	3		
Isaac Ntow (GHA)	26.05.1994	17		2
Enrico Pepe	12.11.1989	18		1
Kurt Zammit	26.02.1996	9	(4)	
Midfielders:	**DOB**	**M**	**(s)**	**G**
Cain Attard	10.09.1994	17		
Terence Agius	15.01.1994	1	(1)	
Johan Bezzina	30.05.1994	3	(2)	

	DOB	M	(s)	G
Roderick Briffa	24.08.1981	15	(1)	
Ryan Fenech	20.04.1986	10	(2)	
Matthew Guillaumier	09.04.1998	11	(2)	1
Yannick Yankam	12.12.1997	8	(3)	1
Forwards:	**DOB**	**M**	**(s)**	**G**
Miguel Ángel Alba (ARG)	14.08.1988	8		4
Caio Henrique Rocha De Almeida Prado (BRA)	11.01.1995	17	(1)	4
Diego Ángel Capel Trinidad (ESP)	16.02.1988		(2)	1
Federico Matías Falcone (ARG)	21.02.1990	18	(2)	10
Paul Mbong	02.09.2001	5	(1)	1
Michael Mifsud	17.04.1981	1	(15)	
Luke Montebello	13.08.1995	2		
Edison Luiz dos Santos "Tarabai Santos" (BRA)	09.12.1985	3	(3)	2
Maurizio Vella (ITA)	10.05.1991	12	(1)	

Floriana Football Club

Founded:	1894
Stadium:	Independence Arena, Floriana (3,000)
Trainer:	Vincenzo Potenza (ITA) 03.05.1970

Goalkeepers:	DOB	M	(s)	G
Ini Etim Akpan (NGA)	03.08.1984	20		
Defenders:	**DOB**	**M**	**(s)**	**G**
Moustapha Beye (SEN)	06.08.1995	2	(2)	
Alex Cini	28.10.1991	20		
Marcelo Mariano Dias (BRA)	29.09.1985	2		
Edward Herrera	14.07.1986		(6)	
Jurgen Pisani	03.09.1992	20		1
Enzo Adrián Ruiz (ARG)	20.06.1989	19		
Midfielders:	**DOB**	**M**	**(s)**	**G**
Ulises Jesús Arias (ARG)	05.08.1996	19		
Brandon Diego Paiber	05.06.1995	13	(3)	3

	DOB	M	(s)	G
Clyde Borg	20.03.1992		(14)	
Jan Busuttil	06.03.1999	3	(12)	2
Ryan Camenzuli	08.09.1994	18		1
Stefano D'Agostino (ITA)	03.07.1992	5		1
Francisco Diego Venancio da Silva (BRA)	27.06.1993	19		3
Matías Nicolás García (ARG)	22.07.1996	18		2
Kristian Keqi (ALB)	28.07.1996	20		14
Bradley Sciberras	02.02.2001		(4)	
Forwards:	**DOB**	**M**	**(s)**	**G**
Augusto René Cáseres (ARG)	21.11.1997	5	(6)	1
Tiago Adan Fonseca (BRA)	14.03.1988	16	(2)	9
Terence Vella	20.04.1990	1	(9)	1

Gudja United Football Club

Founded:	1945
Stadium:	„Louis Azzopardi" Stadium, Gudja (1,000)
Trainer:	Josef Mansueto

Goalkeepers:	DOB	M	(s)	G
Timothy Aquilina	12.06.1998	4		
Jonathan Debono	17.07.1985	12	(1)	
Glenn Zammit	05.08.1987	4		
Defenders:	**DOB**	**M**	**(s)**	**G**
Anderson Meyar de Melo (BRA)	02.04.1989		(1)	
Miguel Attard	10.03.1995	2	(2)	
Juan Andrés Bolaños Ramírez (COL)	22.07.1991	19		3
Jonathan Bondin	11.10.1982	17	(1)	
Zachary Cassar	02.11.1998	10	(1)	
Jurgen Farrugia	14.08.1991	6	(4)	
Imanol González Benac (ARG)	06.01.1998	4		
Justin Grioli	20.09.1987	15	(3)	
Allan Ricardo Miranda Albertazzi (CRC)	28.05.1987	9	(1)	1
Hubert Vella	07.02.1994	13	(2)	

Midfielders:	DOB	M	(s)	G
Carlos Alexandre Santana Barroso (BRA)	03.04.1992	5	(2)	1
Tariq Al Mahrooqi (OMA)	02.01.1994		(3)	
Édison David Bilbao Zárate (CHI)	06.03.1987	7		
Anderson Francisco de Barros „Dê" (BRA)	09.04.1986	19		1
Dylan Grima	18.07.1990	2	(3)	
Peter Paul Sammut	28.12.1991	1	(7)	
Forwards:	**DOB**	**M**	**(s)**	**G**
James Brincat	03.12.1996	2	(8)	2
Llywelyn Cremona	07.05.1995	9	(6)	
Aidan Friggieri	28.04.1998	15	(2)	2
Gabriel Mensah (GHA)	05.10.1995	12	(6)	4
Nivaldo Rodrigues Ferreira (BRA)	22.06.1988	4	(2)	1
Miguel Antonio Pérez Jiménez (COL)	22.09.1992	11	(1)	2
Rundell Winchester (TRI)	16.12.1993	16	(3)	5

Gżira United Football Club

Founded: 1947
Stadium: Ta' Qali National Stadium, Attard (17,797)
Trainer: Giovanni Tedesco (ITA) 13.05.1972
[23.01.2020] Paul Zammit 21.09.1969

Goalkeepers:	DOB	M	(s)	G
Justin Haber	09.06.1981	20		
Ryoto Yokokawa (JPN)	11.06.1999		(1)	
Defenders:	**DOB**	**M**	**(s)**	**G**
Arthur Henrique Ricciardi Oyama (BRA)	14.01.1987	11		
Clifford Gatt Baldacchino	09.02.1988	7	(3)	
Sacha Borg	26.04.1993	7	(2)	
Romario Camilleri	13.05.2000		(2)	
Fernando Barbosa Pereira (BRA)	04.12.1992	18		
Karl Pulo	30.07.1989		(2)	
Christian Sammut	25.02.1998		(3)	
Dexter Xuereb	21.09.1997	4	(1)	
Midfielders:	**DOB**	**M**	**(s)**	**G**
Andrew Cohen	13.05.1981	5	(12)	4

	DOB	M	(s)	G
Gianmarco Conti (ITA)	01.02.1992	16		1
Marco Criaco (ITA)	22.05.1989	6		2
Martin George Edward Davis (JAM)	11.10.1996	13	(2)	3
Ben Hamed Koné (CIV)	02.11.1987	17	(1)	5
Nicky Muscat	13.07.1996	18	(2)	
Rodolfo dos Santos Soares (BRA)	20.05.1985	19		2
Zachary Scerri	08.03.1996	17	(1)	1
Forwards:	**DOB**	**M**	**(s)**	**G**
Luca Brincat	04.07.1997		(4)	
Juan Corbalan	03.03.1997	11	(4)	
Ryan Darmanin	12.12.1985		(2)	
Wilfried Domoraud (FRA)	18.08.1988	6		1
Jefferson Mateus de Assis Estácio (BRA)	21.10.1994	12		10
Amadou Samb (SEN)	22.04.1988	13	(3)	6

Ħamrun Spartans Football Club

Founded: 1907
Stadium: "Victor Tedesco" Stadium, Ħamrun (6,000)
Trainer: Manuele Blasi (ITA) 17.08.1980
[04.02.2020] Andrea Ciaramella (ITA) 06.12.1965

Goalkeepers:	DOB	M	(s)	G
Manuel Bartolo	26.08.1983	15		
Jean Claude Debattista	12.08.1995	5		
Defenders:	**DOB**	**M**	**(s)**	**G**
Alessio Capitelli (ITA)	26.02.1997	8	(1)	
Mattia Cinquini (ITA)	11.05.1990	19		
Karl Micallef	08.09.1996	19		
Nikolai Micallef	17.08.2003	1	(1)	
Orestis Nikolopoulos (GRE)	26.08.1991	11		
Rafael Santos Henriques Caetano (BRA)	25.04.1990	1		
Karl Schembri	03.11.1999		(2)	
Andre Scicluna	22.09.1988	2	(3)	1
Valdo Gonçalves Alhinho (POR)	17.12.1988	9		1
Midfielders:	**DOB**	**M**	**(s)**	**G**
Conor Borg	13.05.1997	4	(1)	
Darren Borg	18.06.1999	6	(7)	
Tristan Caruana	15.09.1991	13		

	DOB	M	(s)	G
Marco Criaco (ITA)	22.05.1989	12		2
Cain Cutajar	20.07.2000	2	(1)	
Clayton Failla	08.01.1986	18	(1)	2
Marcello Fava (ITA)	30.01.1995	1	(1)	
Carlos Manuel Flores (MEX)	17.03.1998	3		
Christopher Galea	04.04.2001		(4)	
Matthew Gauci	02.09.1991	3	(2)	
Nicola Leone (ITA)	26.08.1992	19		3
Miguel Tabone	08.01.2002		(1)	
Forwards:	**DOB**	**M**	**(s)**	**G**
Piotr Branicki (POL)	04.01.1983	3		
Ryan Darmanin	12.12.1985	1	(7)	1
Wilfried Domoraud (FRA)	18.08.1988	13		4
Ailton Jorge dos Santos Soares "Dodo" (CPV)	06.12.1990	18		3
Soufiane Lagzir (MAR)	25.10.1994	13	(1)	7
Bradley Schembri	10.08.1998		(5)	

Hibernians Football Club Paola

Founded: 1922
Stadium: Hibernians Ground, Paola (2,968)
Trainer: Stefano Sanderra (ITA) 21.06.1967

Goalkeepers:	DOB	M	(s)	G
Matthew Calleja Cremona	14.09.1994	4	(1)	
Marko Jovičić (SRB)	02.02.1995	16		
Defenders:	**DOB**	**M**	**(s)**	**G**
Andrei Agius	12.08.1986	19		1
Ferdinando Apap	29.07.1992	19		
Myles Beerman	13.03.1999	1	(12)	1
Matthew Ellul	23.05.2002		(1)	
Gabriel Izquier Artiles „Gabri Izquier" (ESP)	29.04.1993	19	(1)	
Márcio Leandro Barbosa de Silveira (BRA)	13.07.1988	10	(5)	
Timothy Tabone Desira	15.07.1995	11	(4)	
Jens Wemmer (GER)	31.10.1985	6	(6)	
Midfielders:	**DOB**	**M**	**(s)**	**G**
Jake Grech	18.11.1997	20		8

	DOB	M	(s)	G
Bjorn Kristensen	05.04.1993	13	(3)	1
Edafe Uzeh (NGA)	22.03.1988	1		
Dunstan Vella	27.04.1996	20		2
Forwards:	**DOB**	**M**	**(s)**	**G**
Charles Atsina (GHA)	24.03.1989	3	(5)	
Ayrton Attard	05.11.2000	1	(2)	
Jurgen Degabriele	10.10.1996	3	(4)	3
Terence Groothusen (ARU)	16.09.1996	7	(5)	3
Imanol Iriberri (ARG)	04.03.1987	13	(3)	8
Jorge Santos Silva (BRA)	23.04.1987	2	(3)	
Simone Mancini (ITA)	07.01.1999		(2)	
Joseph Essien Mbong	15.07.1997	18		2
Leonardi Nanni (ITA)	23.12.1991	12		4
Edison Luiz dos Santos "Tarabai Santos" (BRA)	09.12.1985	2	(1)	

Mosta Football Club

Founded: 1935
Stadium: "Charles Abela" Memorial Stadium, Mosta (600)
Trainer: Mark Miller (ENG) 22.09.1962

Goalkeepers:	DOB	M	(s)	G
Andreas Vella	14.10.1998	18	(1)	
Nicholas Vella	27.08.1989	2		
Defenders:	**DOB**	**M**	**(s)**	**G**
Duane Bonnici	10.10.1995	10	(5)	1
Cláudio José Augusto Sumbane (MOZ)	10.05.1994	2		
Jonas Rodriguez Ekani (CMR)	13.10.1992	2		
Tyron Farrugia	22.02.1989	20		1
Kyle Gatt	12.06.1996	2	(11)	
Christian Grech	20.02.1993	1	(4)	
Pedro Luiz Soares Gusso (BRA)	08.01.1994	5		
Rafael Morisco da Silva (BRA)	04.08.1986	13		2
Mohammed Dahiru Usman (NGA)	28.03.2001		(1)	
Dexter Xuereb	21.09.1997	14		3
Midfielders:	**DOB**	**M**	**(s)**	**G**
Terence Agius	15.01.1994	5		
Gabriel Aquilina	07.12.1995	6	(5)	1
David James Brown	06.09.1996	11		
Jean Diouf (SEN)	06.07.1996	5		
Kyle Frendo	30.06.1995		(1)	

	DOB	M	(s)	G
Dimitri Christian Kassekar (SEN)	28.08.1998	2		
Nikita Kotlov (USA)	20.09.1991	9		6
Santiago Martínez Perlaza (COL)	27.02.1998	2		
Matías Roberto Muchardi (ARG)	09.02.1988	20		1
David Nworah Ifeanyi (NGA)	18.10.1994	1		
Liam Portelli	21.11.2000		(2)	
Ebrima Sohna (GAM)	14.12.1988	4		
Sergio Leonardo Villarreal Ruiz (COL)	29.01.1995	6		
Peter Xuereb	07.05.1992		(2)	
Forwards:	**DOB**	**M**	**(s)**	**G**
Christian Chaney	08.09.1994	7		1
Zachary Brincat	24.06.1998	6	(12)	2
Evo Christ Ememe (NGA)	30.04.2001	2		
Kyle Gatt	18.04.1999	1		
Mamadou Salieu Jallow (GAM)	30.03.1992	7		3
Edin Murga (BIH)	21.12.1994	8		2
Ifeanyi David Onyeanula (NGA)	13.07.2000		(1)	
Akeem Roach (TRI)	10.10.1995	9		
Wéverton Gomes Souza (BRA)	08.03.1992	16		5
Takanori Yokochi (JPN)	27.08.1994	4		1

Santa Luċija Football Club

Founded:	1974		
Stadium:	Grawnd Santa Luċija, Santa Luċija (1,000)		
Trainer:	Oliver Spiteri		04.07.1970

Goalkeepers:	DOB	M	(s)	G
Timothy Aquilina	12.06.1998	6		
Ryan Caruana	25.09.1996	14	(1)	
Defenders:	**DOB**	**M**	**(s)**	**G**
Camilo Del Castillo Escobar (COL)	09.05.1995	10		1
Gabriel Bohrer Mentz (BRA)	11.08.1998	19		
Lee Galea	14.02.1988	4	(7)	
Kevin Pinheiro Correia (BRA)	16.07.1996	10		1
Camilo Andrés Babilonia Navarro (COL)	17.12.1998	2		
Farid Romero Zúñiga (COL)	08.09.1998	12		
Neil Spiteri	03.06.1997		(2)	
Jacob Walker	31.07.1997	14	(3)	1
Midfielders:	**DOB**	**M**	**(s)**	**G**
Nick Borg	25.02.1998	3	(3)	
Jackson David Usuga Mendonza (COL)	20.04.1998	17		2
Neil Micallef	12.01.1999		(5)	

	DOB	M	(s)	G
Adam Magri Overend	03.05.2000	4	(5)	1
Jamie Magrie Overand	07.02.1998	3	(8)	
Luis Carlos Riascos Torres (COL)	17.09.2001	7		
Rei Tachikawa (JPN)	18.01.1998	15		6
Jamie Zerafa	02.03.1998	15	(3)	1
Forwards:	**DOB**	**M**	**(s)**	**G**
Daniel Agius	15.11.1996	11	(6)	
Wilkerson Junnior de Souza Gomes „Batata" (BRA)	09.08.1991	6		2
Omar Elouni	16.03.1999	2	(12)	
Leighton Grech	23.03.1990	5		
Máxuell Maia da Silva „Maxuell Samurai" (BRA)	30.09.1991	5		4
Maycon de Jesús Santana (BRA)	11.07.1992	6		
Diego Luis Mosquera (COL)	05.04.2000	7	(1)	1
Paulo Henrique Santos de Azevedo (BRA)	30.03.1991	4		1
Kevin Duvan Ante Rosero (COL)	03.12.1998	19		2

Senglea Athletic Football Club

Founded:	22.03.1943		
Stadium:	Ta' Qali National Stadium, Attard (17,000)		
Trainer:	Mario Muscat		18.08.1976
[02.01.2020]	Giorgio Roselli (ITA)		01.10.1957
[24.02.2020]	Vladan Tomić (MNE)		23.12.1970

Goalkeepers:	DOB	M	(s)	G
Anthony Curmi	20.11.1982	7		
Matthew Farrugia	17.03.1985	13		
Defenders:	**DOB**	**M**	**(s)**	**G**
Anderson do Nascimento Carneiro (BRA)	04.03.1993	11		
Dejan Debono	20.11.2000	13		
Marcelo Mariano Dias (BRA)	29.09.1985	12		1
Sigitas Olberkis (LTU)	19.04.1997	18		
Karl Pulo	30.07.1989	1		
Mirko Todorović (SRB)	22.08.1985	7		
Connor Zammit	26.09.1998	5	(2)	
Midfielders:	**DOB**	**M**	**(s)**	**G**
Nikola Braunović (MNE)	21.07.1997	4	(1)	
Sean Cipriott	10.09.1997	13	(3)	
Jurgen Debono	13.12.1995	2	(3)	
Daniel Farrugia	02.07.1997		(1)	

	DOB	M	(s)	G
Taisei Marukawa (JPN)	30.01.1997	14	(2)	2
Justin Micallef	28.07.1997	3	(5)	
Manolito Micallef	16.11.1983	16		1
Ricardo Silva de Almeida "Ricardinho" (BRA)	02.06.1989	3	(3)	1
Elvis Sakyi (GHA)	24.11.1996	14		
Gonzalo Nicolas Virano (ARG)	22.07.1999	7	(1)	2
David Xuereb	30.03.1998	8	(2)	
Forwards:	**DOB**	**M**	**(s)**	**G**
Siraj Arab	25.03.1994	4	(1)	
Leighton Grech	23.03.1990	8	(4)	1
Jacinto Júnior Conceição Cabral (BRA)	10.03.1992	5		2
Andrei Spiteri	18.04.2000		(8)	
Jan Tanti	10.04.1998	6	(13)	
Jose Wilkson Teixeira Rocha (BRA)	22.03.1992	16	(3)	7
Wilfried Zamble Bi Koihy (NOR)	08.08.1988	10	(6)	4

Sirens Football Club San Pawl il-Baħar

Founded:	1968	
Stadium:	Sirens Stadium, San Pawl il-Baħar (600)	
Trainer:	Steve D'Amato	

Goalkeepers:	DOB	M	(s)	G
David Cassar	24.11.1987	20		
Defenders:	**DOB**	**M**	**(s)**	**G**
Adrian Borg	20.05.1989	18		
Manuel Ángel Bustos (ARG)	27.06.1995	4	(2)	
Luke Grech	06.01.1994		(1)	
Edward Herrera	14.07.1986	3	(3)	1
Romeu Péricles Romão (BRA)	10.04.1990	15	(1)	
Daniel Sant	14.10.1994	2	(2)	
Sergio Raphael dos Anjos (BRA)	23.10.1992	19		
Thiago Espíndola de Paula „Thiaguinho" (BRA)	14.05.1993	18	(1)	2
Midfielders:	**DOB**	**M**	**(s)**	**G**
Gaston Cesani (ARG)	05.09.1995	2		

	DOB	M	(s)	G
Ryan Grech	03.04.1985	17		
Ricardo da Silva Faria „Ricardinho" (BRA)	09.02.1992	6		3
Luke Sciberras	15.09.1989	1	(9)	
Forwards:	**DOB**	**M**	**(s)**	**G**
Ige Abdullahi Adeshina	01.08.1986	20		3
Siraj Arab	25.03.1994	6	(3)	
Russell Fenech	07.02.1998		(5)	
Flávio dos Santos da Silva Cheveresan (BRA)	11.12.1988	17		5
Emmanuel Ndubuisi Okoye (NGA)	04.04.1991	18		6
Romário Lucas Menezes de Araújo "Romarinho" (BRA)	05.07.1994	13	(2)	5
Wellington Oliveira Vieira „Wellington Petinha" (BRA)	20.01.1993	19		5
Tagro Yves Yao (FRA)	06.08.1988	2		

Sliema Wanderers Football Club

Founded:	1909		
Stadium:	Tigne Sports Complex, Sliema (1,000)		
Trainer:	Alfonso Greco (ITA)		19.05.1969
[13.02.2020]	Andrea Pisanu (ITA)		07.01.1982

Goalkeepers:	DOB	M	(s)	G
Entonjo Elezaj (ALB)	14.07.1996	7		
Jake Galea	15.04.1996	13		
Defenders:	**DOB**	**M**	**(s)**	**G**
Goran Adamović (SRB)	24.04.1987	6	(1)	
Arthur Henrique Ricciardi Oyama (BRA)	14.01.1987	6		1
Robert Johan Carvajal Díaz (COL)	04.05.1991	3		1
Juan Cruz Gill (ARG)	18.07.1983	9	(3)	1
Jonathan Pearson	13.01.1987	7	(2)	
Kurt Shaw	01.04.1999	19		1
Antonio Stelitano	22.10.1987	6	(3)	
Claudio Zappa (ITA)	30.03.1997	12	(2)	4
Midfielders:	**DOB**	**M**	**(s)**	**G**
Edmond Agius	23.02.1987	13	(4)	
Gareth Barone	04.07.2001	2	(4)	
Carlos Calvo Sobrado (ESP)	18.09.1985	2		
José Cleangelo Pereira Dias "Cleo" (BRA)	19.03.1992	5	(3)	1

	DOB	M	(s)	G
Ryan Fenech	20.04.1986	1		
Gilmar da Silva Ribeiro (BRA)	26.03.1990	2	(1)	
Stanimir Milošković (SRB)	21.12.1983	6	(3)	
John Mintoff	23.08.1988	13	(2)	1
Claudio Pani (ITA)	11.03.1986	12	(3)	
Michele Sansone	02.07.1998	11	(2)	1
Mark Scerri	16.01.1990	14	(2)	
Peter Xuereb	07.05.1992	3	(3)	1
Forwards:	**DOB**	**M**	**(s)**	**G**
Kilian Amehi (FRA)	14.11.1997		(2)	
Juri Cisotti (ITA)	05.05.1993	20		5
Jean Paul Farrugia	21.03.1992	10	(3)	3
Gabriel Duarte Lustosa (BRA)	13.01.1997		(1)	
Alexander Satariano	25.10.2001	7	(9)	2
Seydou Sow (SEN)	20.09.1993	6	(2)	1
Federico Vasilchik (ARG)	08.01.1992	5		1

Tarxien Rainbows Football Club

Founded:	1934 (*as Rainbows Tarxien*)		
Stadium:	"Tony Cassar" Sports Ground, Tarxien (1,000)		
Trainer:	Marko Glumac (SRB)		
[02.11.2019]	Demis Paul Scerri		

Goalkeepers:	DOB	M	(s)	G
Rudi Briffa	21.08.1996	19		
Matthew Towns	12.09.1982	1		
Defenders:	**DOB**	**M**	**(s)**	**G**
Keith Attard	01.05.2001		(1)	
Marco Botta (ITA)	20.02.1997	12	(2)	
Gary Camilleri	05.08.1999	13	(1)	
Manuel Farrugia	19.04.2001		(1)	
Prince Loïc Destin Mambouana (FRA)	10.09.1990	17		2
Matthew Tabone	29.04.1992	9		1
Thomas Veronese (ITA)	02.11.1986	20		2
Cedric Zahra	20.10.1999		(4)	
Daniel Zerafa	08.04.1994	13		
Midfielders:	**DOB**	**M**	**(s)**	**G**
Ayrton Azzopardi	12.09.1993	4	(5)	
Miguel Ciantar	17.10.1990	7	(11)	2
Brooke Farrugia	17.07.1993	7	(1)	
Misael Miranda Gómez (MEX)	23.04.1996	12		
Manuel Murillo Torres (COL)	06.10.1996	5		1
Brandon Muscat	03.11.1994	11	(5)	
Kazuki Ohata (JPN)	30.09.1996	1	(1)	
Stiv Shaba (ALB)	19.12.1992	13		1
Matthew Spiteri	06.10.1998	2	(2)	
Marko Stanojević (SRB)	24.05.1997	10	(1)	
Jairo Andrés Tenorio (COL)	02.01.1996	6	(2)	
Daniel Vassallo	03.12.1996		(4)	
Forwards:	**DOB**	**M**	**(s)**	**G**
Aleksa Andrejić (SRB)	24.01.1993	18		9
Luca Brincat	04.07.1997	3	(1)	
Emile Damey (LBR)	01.04.1994	3		
Dhonatan Santos da Hora (BRA)	14.06.1990	2		
Petar Kanzurov (MKD)	29.07.1999	5	(2)	
Mihajlo Jelić	13.10.2000	1	(1)	
Nevin Portelli	16.09.1999	6	(5)	
Dale Tabone	09.05.2001		(3)	

Valletta Football Club

Founded:	1943		
Stadium:	Sirens Stadium, San Pawl il-Baħar (600)		
Trainer:	Darren Abdilla		10.07.1979
[19.02.2020]	Giovanni Tedesco (ITA)		13.05.1972

Goalkeepers:	DOB	M	(s)	G
Henry Bonello	13.10.1988	19		
Yenez Cini	04.01.1994	1	(1)	
Defenders:	**DOB**	**M**	**(s)**	**G**
Jean Borg	08.01.1998	17		
Steve Borg	15.05.1988	18		3
Ryan Camilleri	22.05.1988	11	(2)	
Jonathan Caruana	24.07.1986	8		
Nicolas Pulis	29.01.1998	2	(10)	
Joseph Zerafa	31.05.1988	11	(2)	
Midfielders:	**DOB**	**M**	**(s)**	**G**
Tristan Caruana	15.09.1991	5		
Shaun Dimech	08.08.2001	8	(8)	
Douglas Ricardo Packer (BRA)	13.03.1987	7	(1)	1
Irakli Dzaria (GEO)	01.12.1988	10		2
Rowen Muscat	05.06.1991	17		1
Enmy Manuel Peña Beltré (DOM)	17.09.1992	20		3
Ryan Tonna	27.04.2001		(1)	
Kevin Tulimieri	15.03.1992	6	(7)	1
Forwards:	**DOB**	**M**	**(s)**	**G**
Miguel Ángel Alba (ARG)	14.08.1988	4	(3)	1
Jhony Moisés Cano Barrios (COL)	14.07.1989		(2)	
David Faupala	11.02.1997		(1)	
Mario Fontanella (ITA)	28.06.1989	20		13
Bojan Kaljević	25.01.1986	9	(6)	2
Santiago Malano (ARG)	29.01.1987	3	(2)	
Kyrian Nwoko	04.07.1997	7	(6)	2
Matteo Piciollo (ITA)	15.10.1992	12	(6)	2
Yuri de Jesus Messias (BRA)	11.09.1991	5	(1)	1

SECOND LEVEL
Maltese First Division 2019/2020

1.	Żejtun Corinthians FC (*Promoted*)	19	11	5	3	37	-	23	38
2.	Lija Athletic FC (*Promoted*)	19	11	3	5	47	-	31	36
3.	Qrendi FC	19	11	2	6	38	-	29	35
4.	Naxxar Lions FC	19	8	7	4	32	-	24	31
5.	Pembroke Athleta FC	19	9	3	7	37	-	33	30
6.	St. Andrews FC	19	8	5	6	30	-	18	29
7.	Żebbuġ Rangers FC	19	7	6	6	23	-	20	27
8.	Pietà Hotspurs FC	19	6	6	7	22	-	30	24
9.	Fgura United FC	19	6	4	9	31	-	40	22
10.	Swieqi United FC	19	5	6	8	29	-	29	21
11.	Qormi FC	19	5	6	8	31	-	37	21
12.	Vittoriosa Stars FC Birgu	19	5	4	10	24	-	34	19
13.	Mqabba FC	19	4	4	11	25	-	38	16
14.	FC St. George's Cospicua	19	3	7	9	23	-	43	16

Please note: the league was abandoned on 18.05.2020. No teams were relegated.

INTERNATIONAL MATCHES
(16.07.2019 – 15.07.2020)

05.09.2019	Oslo	Norway - Malta	2-0(2-0)	(ECQ)
08.09.2019	Ploieşti	Romania - Malta	1-0(0-0)	(ECQ)
12.10.2019	Attard	Malta - Sweden	0-4(0-1)	(ECQ)
15.10.2019	Tórshavn	Faroe Islands - Malta	1-0(0-0)	(ECQ)
15.11.2019	Cádiz	Spain - Malta	7-0(2-0)	(ECQ)
18.11.2019	Attard	Malta - Norway	1-2(1-1)	(ECQ)

05.09.2019   NORWAY - MALTA   **2-0(2-0)**   16th EC. Qualifiers

Ullevaal Stadion, Oslo; Referee: Dumitru Muntean (Moldova); Attendance: 11,269
MLT: Henry Bonello, Andrei Agius (Cap), Steve Borg, Zach Muscat, Paul Fenech (64.Jean Paul Farrugia), Rowen Muscat (20.Ferdinando Apap), Dunstan Vella, Juan Carlos Corbalan, Kyrian Nwoko, Jake Grech (77.Alfred Effiong), Joseph Mbong. Trainer: Raymond Farrugia.

08.09.2019   ROMANIA - MALTA   **1-0(0-0)**   16th EC. Qualifiers

Stadionul "Ilie Oană", Ploieşti; Referee: Duje Strukan (Croatia); Attendance: 13,376
MLT: Henry Bonello, Andrei Agius (Cap), Steve Borg, Zach Muscat, Juan Carlos Corbalan, Rowen Muscat, Luke Gambin (81.Joseph Zerafa), Dunstan Vella (86.Jake Grech), Kyrian Nwoko (72.Alfred Effiong), Jean Paul Farrugia, Joseph Mbong. Trainer: Raymond Farrugia.

12.10.2019   MALTA - SWEDEN   **0-4(0-1)**   16th EC. Qualifiers

Ta'Qali National Stadium, Attard; Referee: Sergey Ivanov (Russia); Attendance: 10,702
MLT: Henry Bonello, Joseph Zerafa, Andrei Agius (Cap), Zach Muscat (66.Jonathan Caruana), Rowen Muscat (68.Paul Fenech), Dunstan Vella, Luke Gambin, Kyrian Nwoko, Kurt Shaw, Alfred Effiong (75.Michael Mifsud), Joseph Mbong. Trainer: Raymond Farrugia.

15.10.2019   FAROE ISLANDS - MALTA   **1-0(0-0)**   16th EC. Qualifiers

Tórsvøllur, Tórshavn; Referee: José María Sánchez Martínez (Spain); Attendance: 2,677
MLT: Henry Bonello, Andrei Agius, Steve Borg, Zach Muscat, Paul Fenech (71.Luke Gambin), Rowen Muscat (80.Joseph Zerafa), Dunstan Vella, Kyrian Nwoko, Jake Grech, Michael Mifsud (Cap) (71.Alfred Effiong), Joseph Mbong. Trainer: Raymond Farrugia.

15.11.2019   SPAIN - MALTA   **7-0(2-0)**   16th EC. Qualifiers

Estadio "Ramón de Carranza", Cádiz; Referee: Viktor Kassai (Hungary); Attendance: 19,773
MLT: Henry Bonello, Jonathan Caruana, Andrei Agius (Cap), Zach Muscat, Rowen Muscat (63.Triston Caruana), Jurgen Pisani (75.Jake Grech), Kyrian Nwoko, Juan Carlos Corbalan (33.Karl Micallef), Brandon Paiber, Dunstan Vella, Joseph Mbong. Trainer: Raymond Farrugia.

18.11.2019   MALTA - NORWAY   **1-2(1-1)**   16th EC. Qualifiers

Ta'Qali National Stadium, Attard; Referee: Aliyar Aghayev (Azerbaijan); Attendance: 2,708
MLT: Henry Bonello, Paul Fenech, Joseph Zerafa, Andrei Agius, Steve Borg (74.Ferdinando Apap), Zach Muscat, Rowen Muscat (70.Nikolai Muscat), Dunstan Vella (60.Alfred Effiong), Kyrian Nwoko, Michael Mifsud (Cap), Joseph Mbong. Trainer: Raymond Farrugia.
Goal: Paul Fenech (40).

NATIONAL TEAM PLAYERS
(16.07.2019 – 15.07.2020)

Name	DOB	Caps	Goals	2019/2020:	Club
Goalkeepers					
Henry BONELLO	13.10.1988	17	0	2019:	Valletta FC
Defenders					
Andrei AGIUS	12.08.1986	90	5	2019:	Hibernians FC Paola
Ferdinando APAP	29.07.1992	6	0	2019:	Hibernians FC Paola
Steve BORG	15.05.1988	49	1	2019:	Valletta FC
Jonathan CARUANA	24.07.1986	46	2	2019:	Valletta FC
Karl MICALLEF	08.09.1996	2	0	2019:	Hamrun Spartans FC
Zach MUSCAT	22.08.1993	40	1	2019:	SC Olhanense (POR)
Jurgen PISANI	03.09.1992	1	0	2019:	Floriana FC
Kurt SHAW	01.04.1999	1	0	2019:	Sliema Wanderers FC
Joseph ZERAFA	31.05.1988	36	0	2019:	Valletta FC
Midfielders					
Triston CARUANA	15.09.1991	2	0	2019:	Hamrun Spartans FC
Juan Carlos CORBALAN	13.03.1997	11	1	2019:	Gżira United FC
Paul FENECH	20.12.1986	61	2	2019:	Balzan FC
Luke GAMBIN	16.03.1993	22	0	2019:	Colchester United FC (ENG)
Jake GRECH	18.11.1997	9	0	2019:	Hibernians FC Paola
Nikolai MUSCAT	13.07.1996	1	0	2019:	Gżira United FC
Rowen MUSCAT	05.06.1991	47	1	2019:	Valletta FC
Brandon PAIBER	05.06.1995	1	0	2019:	Floriana FC
Dunstan VELLA	27.04.1996	7	0	2019:	Hibernians FC Paola
Forwards					
Alfred EFFIONG	29.11.1984	37	4	2019:	Balzan FC
Jean Paul FARRUGIA	21.03.1992	16	1	2019:	Sliema Wanderers FC
Joseph MBONG	15.07.1997	18	0	2019:	Hibernians FC Paola
Michael MIFSUD	17.04.1981	142	41	2019:	Birkirkara FC
Kyrian NWOKO	04.07.1997	13	1	2019:	Valletta FC
National team coach					
Raymond FARRUGIA [02.05.2019 – 30.12.2019]	01.10.1955			18 M; 1 W; 4 D; 13 L; 9-43	
Devis MANGIA [from 30.12.2019]	06.06.1974			-	

MOLDOVA

The Country:
Republica Moldova (Republic of Moldova)
Capital: Chişinău
Surface: 33,846 km²
Inhabitants: 2,681,735 [2019]
Time: UTC+2

The FA:
Federaţia Moldovenească de Fotbal
Strada Tricolorului 39, 2012 Chişinău
Tel: +373 22 210 413
Foundation date: 1990
Member of FIFA since: 1994
Member of UEFA since: 1993
Website: www.fmf.md

NATIONAL TEAM RECORDS

RECORDS		
First international match:	02.07.1991, Chişinău:	Moldova – Georgia 2-4
Most international caps:	Alexandru Ion Epureanu	- 91 caps (2006-2018)
Most international goals:	Serghei Cleşcenco	- 11 goals / 69 caps (1991-2006)

UEFA EUROPEAN CHAMPIONSHIP		FIFA WORLD CUP		OLYMPIC TOURNAMENTS	
1960	-	1930	-	1908	-
1964	-	1934	-	1912	-
1968	-	1938	-	1920	-
1972	-	1950	-	1924	-
1976	-	1954	-	1928	-
1980	-	1958	-	1936	-
1984	-	1962	-	1948	-
1988	-	1966	-	1952	-
1992	-	1970	-	1956	-
1996	Qualifiers	1974	-	1960	-
2000	Qualifiers	1978	-	1964	-
2004	Qualifiers	1982	-	1968	-
2008	Qualifiers	1986	-	1972	-
2012	Qualifiers	1990	-	1976	-
2016	Qualifiers	1994	Did Not Enter	1980	-
2020	Qualifiers	1998	Qualifiers	1984	-
		2002	Qualifiers	1988	-
		2006	Qualifiers	1992	Did Not Enter
		2010	Qualifiers	1996	Qualifiers
		2014	Qualifiers	2000	Qualifiers
		2018	Qualifiers	2004	Qualifiers
				2008	Qualifiers
				2012	Qualifiers
				2016	Qualifiers

UEFA NATIONS LEAGUE
2018/2019 – League D (promoted to League C)

FIFA CONFEDERATIONS CUP 1992-2017
None

MOLDOVAN CLUB HONOURS IN EUROPEAN CLUB COMPETITIONS:

European Champion Clubs' Cup (1956-1992) / UEFA Champions League (1993-2020)
None

Fairs Cup (1858-1971) / UEFA Cup (1972-2009) / UEFA Europa League (2010-2020)
None

UEFA Super Cup (1972-2019)
None

*European Cup Winners' Cup 1961-1999**
None

defunct competition

NATIONAL COMPETITIONS
TABLE OF HONOURS

1945	Dinamo Chişinău	1961	KSKhI Chişinău	1977	Stroitel Tiraspol
1946	Dinamo Chişinău	1962	Universitet Chişinău	1978	Nistru Tiraspol
1947	Dinamo Chişinău	1963	Temp Tiraspol	1979	Nistru Ciobruciu
1948	Dinamo Chişinău	1964	Temp Tiraspol'	1980	Nistru Ciobruciu
1949	Burevestnik Bender	1965	Energhia Tiraspol	1981	Grănicerul Glodeni
1950	Krasnoe Znamia Chişinău	1966	Stroindustria Bălţi	1982	Grănicerul Glodeni
1951	Krasnoe Znamia Chişinău	1967	Nistrul Bender	1983	Grănicerul Glodeni
1952	Dinamo Chişinău	1968	Temp Tiraspol	1984	Grănicerul Glodeni
1953	Dinamo Chişinău	1969	Politehnik Chişinău	1985	Iskra-Stal
1954	KSKhI Chişinău	1970	Politehnik Chişinău	1986	Avangard Lazovsk
1955	Burevestnik Bender	1971	Pişcevik Bender	1987	Tekstilshchik Tiraspol
1956	Spartak Tiraspol	1972	Kolhoz im. Lenina Edineţ	1988	Tighina Bender
1957	KSKhI Chişinău	1973	Pişcevik Bender	1989	Tekstilshchik Tiraspol
1958	Moldavkabel' Bender	1974	Dinamo Chişinău	1990	Moldovgidromaş Chişinău
1959	NIISVIV Chişinău	1975	Dinamo Chişinău	1991	Speranţa Nisporeni
1960	Tiraspol	1976	Stroitel Tiraspol		

	CHAMPIONS	CUP WINNERS	BEST GOALSCORERS	
1992	FC Zimbru Chişinău	FC Bugeac Comrat	Serghei Alexandrov (FC Bugeac Comrat)	
			Oleg Flentea (FC Constructorul Chişinău)	13
1992/1993	FC Zimbru Chişinău	FC Tiligul-Tiras Tiraspol	Vladimir Kosse (FC Tiligul-Tiras Tiraspol)	30
1993/1994	FC Zimbru Chişinău	FC Tiligul-Tiras Tiraspol	Vladimir Kosse (FC Tiligul-Tiras Tiraspol)	24
1994/1995	FC Zimbru Chişinău	FC Tiligul-Tiras Tiraspol	Vladislav Gavriliuc	
			(FC Nistru Otaci / FC Zimbru Chişinău)	20
1995/1996	FC Zimbru Chişinău	FC Constructorul Chişinău	Vladislav Gavriliuc (FC Zimbru Chişinău)	34
1996/1997	FC Constructorul Chişinău	FC Zimbru Chişinău	Serghei Rogaciov	
			(FC Constructorul Chişinău / FC Olimpia Bălţi)	35
1997/1998	FC Zimbru Chişinău	FC Zimbru Chişinău	Serghei Clescenco (FC Zimbru Chişinău)	25
1998/1999	FC Zimbru Chişinău	FC Sheriff Tiraspol	Serghei Rogaciov (FC Sheriff Tiraspol)	21
1999/2000	FC Zimbru Chişinău	FC Constructorul Chişinău	Serghei Rogaciov (FC Sheriff Tiraspol)	20
2000/2001	FC Sheriff Tiraspol	FC Sheriff Tiraspol	Ruslan Barburoş (Haiducul Sporting Hânceşti / FC Agro Chişinău / FC Sheriff Tiraspol)	
			David Mujiri (GEO, FC Sheriff Tiraspol)	17
2001/2002	FC Sheriff Tiraspol	FC Sheriff Tiraspol	Ruslan Barburoş (FC Sheriff Tiraspol)	17
2002/2003	FC Sheriff Tiraspol	FC Zimbru Chişinău	Serghei Dadu (FC Tiraspol / FC Sheriff Tiraspol)	19
2003/2004	FC Sheriff Tiraspol	FC Zimbru Chişinău	Vladimir Shishelov (UZB, FC Zimbru Chişinău)	15
2004/2005	FC Sheriff Tiraspol	FC Nistru Otaci	Cătălin Sergiu Lichioiu (ROU, FC Nistru Otaci)	16
2005/2006	FC Sheriff Tiraspol	FC Sheriff Tiraspol	Aliaksei Kuchuk (BLR, FC Sheriff Tiraspol)	13
2006/2007	FC Sheriff Tiraspol	FC Zimbru Chişinău	Aliaksei Kuchuk (BLR, FC Sheriff Tiraspol)	17
2007/2008	FC Sheriff Tiraspol	FC Sheriff Tiraspol	Igor Picuşceac (FC Tiraspol / FC Sheriff Tiraspol)	14
2008/2009	FC Sheriff Tiraspol	FC Sheriff Tiraspol	Oleg Andronic (FC Zimbru Chişinău)	16
2009/2010	FC Sheriff Tiraspol	FC Sheriff Tiraspol	Alexandru Maximov (FC Viitorul Orhei)	
			Jymmy Dougllas França (BRA, FC Sheriff Tiraspol)	13
2010/2011	FC Dacia Chişinău	FC Iskra-Stal Rîbniţa	Gheorghe Boghiu (FC Milsami Orhei)	26
2011/2012	FC Sheriff Tiraspol	FC Milsami Orhei	Wilfried Bendjamin Balima	
			(BFA, FC Sheriff Tiraspol)	18
2012/2013	FC Sheriff Tiraspol	FC Tiraspol	Gheorghe Boghiu (FC Milsami Orhei)	16
2013/2014	FC Sheriff Tiraspol	FC Zimbru Chişinău	Luvannor Henrique de Sousa Silva	
			(BRA, FC Sheriff Tiraspol)	26
2014/2015	FC Milsami Orhei	FC Sheriff Tiraspol	Ricardo Cavalcante Mendes "Ricardinho"	
			(BRA, FC Sheriff Tiraspol)	19
2015/2016	FC Sheriff Tiraspol	FC Zaria Bălţi	Danijel Subotić (SUI, FC Sheriff Tiraspol)	12
2016/2017	FC Sheriff Tiraspol	FC Sheriff Tiraspol	Ricardo Cavalcante Mendes "Ricardinho"	
			(BRA, FC Sheriff Tiraspol)	15
2017	FC Sheriff Tiraspol	FC Milsami Orhei (2017/18)	Vitalie Damaşcan (FC Sheriff Tiraspol)	13
2018	FC Sheriff Tiraspol	FC Sheriff Tiraspol (2018/19)	Vladimir Ambros (CS Petrocub Hînceşti)	12
2019	FC Sheriff Tiraspol	CS Petrocub Hînceşti (2019/20)	Yuri Kendysh (BLR, FC Sheriff Tiraspol)	13

NATIONAL CHAMPIONSHIP
Divizia Naţională 2019
(16.03.2019 – 09.11.2019)

Results

Round 1 [16-17.03.2019]
FC Zimbru - Petrocub Hînceşti 0-1(0-1)
FC Sheriff - Speranţa Nisporeni 1-0(0-0)
Dinamo-Auto - Codru Lozova 3-0(2-0)
Milsami Orhei - FC Sfântul Gheorghe 0-3(0-0)

Round 2 [29-30.03.2019]
Speranţa Nis. – FC Sfântul Gheorghe 2-2(1-0)
FC Sheriff - FC Zimbru 3-0(2-0)
Codru Lozova - Milsami Orhei 0-3(0-1)
Petrocub Hînceşti - Dinamo-Auto 0-1(0-0)

Round 3 [02-03.04.2019]
FC Sfântul Gheorghe - Codru Lozova 2-0(1-0)
FC Zimbru - Speranţa Nisporeni 0-2(0-1)
Dinamo-Auto - FC Sheriff 0-4(0-2)
Milsami Orhei - Petrocub Hînceşti 2-0(0-0)

Round 4 [06-07.04.2019]
FC Zimbru - Dinamo-Auto 1-1(1-0)
Speranţa Nisporeni - Codru Lozova 2-1(1-0)
FC Sheriff - Milsami Orhei 0-1(0-1)
Petrocub Hînceşti - Sfântul Gheorghe 2-2(1-0)

Round 5 [12-13.04.2019]
FC Sfântul Gheorghe - FC Sheriff 0-3(0-2)
Milsami Orhei - FC Zimbru 3-0(0-0)
Dinamo-Auto - Speranţa Nisporeni 0-3(0-2)
Petrocub Hînceşti - Codru Lozova 1-1(0-0)

Round 6 [20-21.04.2019]
Dinamo-Auto - Milsami Orhei 0-0
FC Sheriff - Codru Lozova 2-1(1-1)
FC Zimbru - FC Sfântul Gheorghe 1-2(1-2)
Speranţa Nispor. - Petrocub Hînceşti 1-1(1-1)

Round 7 [26-27.04.2019]
Codru Lozova - FC Zimbru 0-3(0-0)
Petrocub Hînceşti - FC Sheriff 1-0(0-0)
FC Sfântul Gheorghe - Dinamo-Auto 3-1(1-1)
Milsami Orhei - Speranţa Nisporeni 1-1(1-1)

Round 8 [03-04.05.2019]
FC Sfântul Gheorghe - Milsami Orhei 1-1(1-1)
Speranţa Nisporeni - FC Sheriff 0-4(0-1)
Codru Lozova - Dinamo-Auto 2-5(0-1)
Petrocub Hînceşti - FC Zimbru 1-0(0-0)

Round 9 [11-12.05.2019]
Dinamo-Auto - Petrocub Hînceşti 0-1(0-0)
Milsami Orhei - Codru Lozova 0-0
FC Sfântul Gheorghe - Speranţa Nisporeni 0-0
FC Zimbru - FC Sheriff 0-4(0-1)

Round 10 [18-19.05.2019]
Codru Lozova - FC Sfântul Gheorghe 1-2(0-2)
FC Sheriff - Dinamo-Auto 3-0(2-0)
Speranţa Nisporeni - FC Zimbru 1-0(1-0)
Petrocub Hînceşti - Milsami Orhei 1-1(0-0)

Round 11 [25-26.05.2019]
Dinamo-Auto - FC Zimbru 0-0
Codru Lozova - Speranţa Nisporeni 1-3(0-1)
Sfântul Gheorghe - Petrocub Hînceşti 1-0(0-0)
Milsami Orhei - FC Sheriff 1-2(0-1)

Round 12 [30-31.05.2019]
Codru Lozova - Petrocub Hînceşti 0-1(0-0)
Speranţa Nisporeni - Dinamo-Auto 0-1(0-0)
FC Zimbru - Milsami Orhei 0-1(0-0)
FC Sheriff - FC Sfântul Gheorghe 5-0(2-0)

Round 13 [15-16.06.2019]
Codru Lozova - FC Sheriff 0-2(0-1)
Petrocub Hînceşti - Speranţa Nispor. 4-1(2-0)
FC Sfântul Gheorghe - FC Zimbru 2-0(1-0)
Milsami Orhei - Dinamo-Auto 3-1(3-0)

Round 14 [21-22.06.2019]
Speranţa Nisporeni - Milsami Orhei 0-1(0-0)
FC Sheriff - Petrocub Hînceşti 2-0(2-0)
Dinamo-Auto - FC Sfântul Gheorghe 3-0(2-0)
FC Zimbru - Codru Lozova 1-1(0-0)

Round 15 [29-30.06.2019]
Dinamo-Auto - Codru Lozova 4-0(2-0)
FC Sheriff - Speranţa Nisporeni 3-0(2-0)
Milsami Orhei - FC Sfântul Gheorghe 0-2(0-1)
FC Zimbru - Petrocub Hînceşti 0-2(0-1)

Round 16 [03-04.08.2019]
Codru Lozova - Milsami Orhei 0-2(0-2)
Petrocub Hînceşti - Dinamo-Auto 3-0(2-0)
Speranţa Nisp - FC Sfântul Gheorghe 1-2(0-1)
FC Sheriff - FC Zimbru 3-0(0-0)

Round 17 [10-11.08.2019]
FC Sfântul Gheorghe - Codru Lozova 1-0(1-0)
Milsami Orhei - Petrocub Hînceşti 0-3(0-0)
Dinamo-Auto - FC Sheriff 0-3(0-1)
FC Zimbru - Speranţa Nisporeni 2-1(1-1)

Round 18 [17-18.08.2019]
Speranţa Nisporeni - Codru Lozova 1-0(0-0)
FC Zimbru - Dinamo-Auto 2-2(1-1)
Petrocub Hînceşti - Sfântul Gheorghe 0-2(0-0)
FC Sheriff - Milsami Orhei 2-1(2-1)

Round 19 [24-25.08.2019]
Milsami Orhei - FC Zimbru 1-1(0-0)
FC Sheriff - FC Sfântul Gheorghe 2-1(2-0)
Dinamo-Auto - Speranţa Nisporeni 3-4(2-1)
Codru Lozova - Petrocub Hînceşti 0-1(0-1)

Round 20 [31.08.-01.09.2019]
Dinamo-Auto - Milsami Orhei 1-0(1-0)
FC Sheriff - Codru Lozova 2-0(0-0)
FC Zimbru - FC Sfântul Gheorghe 0-1(0-0)
Speranţa Nispor. - Petrocub Hînceşti 1-3(0-2)

Round 21 [14-15.09.2019]
Codru Lozova - FC Zimbru 0-2(0-0)
Petrocub Hînceşti - FC Sheriff 0-0
FC Sfântul Gheorghe - Dinamo-Auto 1-0(0-0)
Milsami Orhei - Speranţa Nisporeni 0-0

Round 22 [20-21.09.2019]
FC Sfântul Gheorghe - Milsami Orhei 3-0(1-0)
Petrocub Hînceşti - FC Zimbru 1-0(0-0)
Codru Lozova - Dinamo-Auto 0-1(0-0)
Speranţa Nisporeni - FC Sheriff 0-0

Round 23 [28-29.09.2019]
Dinamo-Auto - Petrocub Hînceşti 2-0(2-0)
FC Zimbru - FC Sheriff 1-2(0-1)
FC Sfântul Gheorghe - Speranţa Nisporeni 0-0
Milsami Orhei - Codru Lozova 3-0(2-0)

Round 24 [06.10.2019]
Speranţa Nisporeni - FC Zimbru 0-0
Codru Lozova - FC Sfântul Gheorghe 0-4(0-2)
FC Sheriff - Dinamo-Auto 2-0(2-0)
Petrocub Hînceşti - Milsami Orhei 1-1(0-0)

Round 25 [19-20.10.2019]
Dinamo-Auto - FC Zimbru 4-0(1-0)
Milsami Orhei - FC Sheriff 1-1(1-0)
Codru Lozova - Speranţa Nisporeni 0-0
Sfântul Gheorghe - Petrocub Hînceşti 0-2(0-1)

Round 26 [25-26.10.2019]
Speranţa Nisporeni - Dinamo-Auto 1-1(0-0)
Petrocub Hînceşti - Codru Lozova 1-0(1-0)
FC Sfântul Gheorghe - FC Sheriff 0-1(0-0)
FC Zimbru - Milsami Orhei 1-2(0-0)

Round 27 [02.11.2019]
Petrocub Hînceşti - Speranţa Nispor. 2-2(2-1)
Codru Lozova - FC Sheriff 0-3(0-2)
FC Sfântul Gheorghe - FC Zimbru 2-1(2-0)
Milsami Orhei - Dinamo-Auto 0-2(0-1)

Round 28 [09.11.2019]
Speranţa Nisporeni - Milsami Orhei 2-1(0-0)
Dinamo-Auto - FC Sfântul Gheorghe 2-1(0-0)
FC Zimbru - Codru Lozova 0-0
FC Sheriff - Petrocub Hînceşti 1-1(0-1)

Final Standings

		Total								Home						Away			
1. **FC Sheriff Tiraspol**	28	22	4	2	60	-	9	70	12	1	1	31	-	5	10	3	1	29	-	4
2. FC Sfântul Gheorghe Suruceni	28	16	5	7	40	-	28	53	8	3	3	16	-	9	8	2	4	24	-	19
3. CS Petrocub Hîncești	28	14	8	6	34	-	21	50	6	6	2	18	-	11	8	2	4	16	-	10
4. FC Dinamo-Auto Tiraspol	28	12	5	11	38	-	37	41	7	2	5	22	-	16	5	3	6	16	-	21
5. FC Milsami Orhei	28	10	9	9	30	-	28	39	4	5	5	15	-	16	6	4	4	15	-	12
6. CSF Speranța Nisporeni	28	8	11	9	29	-	34	35	4	5	5	12	-	17	4	6	4	17	-	17
7. FC Zimbru Chișinău	28	3	7	18	16	-	43	16	1	4	9	9	-	22	2	3	9	7	-	21
8. FC Codru Lozova (*Relegation Play-off*)	28	0	5	23	8	-	55	5	0	1	13	4	-	32	0	4	10	4	-	23

Please note: FC Zimbru Chișinău withdrew at the end of the season.

Top goalscorers:

13	**Yuri Kendysh (BLR)**	*FC Sheriff Tiraspol*
11	Maxim Iurcu	*CSF Speranța Nisporeni*
10	Maxim Mihailov	*FC Dinamo-Auto Tiraspol*
9	Robert Ndip Tambe (CMR)	*FC Sheriff Tiraspol*

Relegation Play-offs [16.11.2019]

CSF Spartanii Selemet - FC Codru Lozova   0-1(0-0)
FC Codru Lozova remains at first level.

NATIONAL CUP
Cupa Moldovei 2019/2020

Second Round [24-25.05.2019]

CF Ungheni - FC Victoria Bardar	1-4	FC Speranța Drochia - FC Iskra Rîbnița	4-3 pen
FC Sporting Trestieni - FC Sucleia	3-2 aet	FC Tighina Bender - FC Real-Succes Chișinău	5-0
FC Edineț - FC Florești	3-1 pen	FC Slobozia Mare - FC Sireți	1-2
CS Moldova-03 Ungheni - FC Sîngerei	3-1	FC Maiak Chirsova - FC Olimp Comrat	2-0

1/8-Finals [25-26.06./05-07.07.2019]

First Leg		Second Leg	
FC Edineț - FC Milsami Orhei	1-3	FC Milsami Orhei - FC Edineț	6-1
CSF Speranța Nisporeni - FC Speranța Drochia	6-1	FC Speranța Drochia - CSF Speranța Nisporeni	0-3
FC Sheriff Tiraspol - FC Sireți	12-0	FC Sireți - FC Sheriff Tiraspol	0-15
CS Petrocub Hîncești - FC Tighina Bender	7-0	FC Tighina - CS Petrocub Hîncești	0-2
FC Sfântul Gheorghe - CS Moldova-03 Ungheni	1-0	FCM Ungheni - FC Sfântul Gheorghe	0-2
FC Codru Lozova - FC Victoria Bardar	7-1	FC Victoria Bardar - FC Codru Lozova	0-3
FC Sporting Trestieni - FC Zimbru Chișinău	2-4	FC Zimbru Chișinău - Sporting Trestieni	5-1
FC Dinamo-Auto Tiraspol - FC Maiak Chirsova	8-0	FC Maiak Chirsova - FC Dinamo-Auto Tiraspol	0-3

Quarter-Finals [24-25.09./29-30.10.2019]

First Leg		Second Leg	
FC Zimbru Chișinău - CS Petrocub Hîncești	1-2	CS Petrocub Hîncești - FC Zimbru Chișinău	3-1
FC Milsami Orhei - FC Sfântul Gheorghe	0-1	FC Sfântul Gheorghe - FC Milsami Orhei	0-0
FC Codru Lozova - CSF Speranța Nisporeni	2-2	CSF Speranța Nisporeni - FC Codru Lozova	5-0
FC Sheriff Tiraspol - FC Dinamo-Auto Tiraspol	1-0	FC Dinamo-Auto Tiraspol - FC Sheriff Tiraspol	0-5

Semi-Finals [21/25.06.2020]

First Leg		Second Leg	
FC Sfântul Gheorghe - CSF Speranța Nisporeni	5-2	CSF Speranța Nisporeni - FC Sfântul Gheorghe	2-2
CS Petrocub Hîncești - FC Sheriff Tiraspol	1-0	FC Sheriff Tiraspol - CS Petrocub Hîncești	2-1

Final

30.06.2020; Stadionul Zimbru, Chișinău; Referee: Amin Kurgheli (Belarus); Attendance: None
CS Petrocub Hîncești - FC Sfântul Gheorghe Suruceni   **0-0; 5-3 on penalties**

Petrocub Hîncești: Cristian Avram, Petru Racu (58.Vadim Gulceac; 108.Arcadie Rusu), Donalio Melachio Douanla, Ștefan Efros (46.Alexandru Bejan), Ion Jardan, Jacques Onana Ndzomo, Iaser Țurcan, Artiom Rozgoniuc, Alexandru Onica (67.Ilie Damașcan), Vladimir Ambros (Cap) (90+3.Victor Bogaciuc), Sergiu Plătică. Trainer: Lilian Popescu.

FC Sfântul Gheorghe: Nicolae Cebotari, Andrey Novicov, Petru Ojog (114.Igor Bondarenco), Yevhen Smirnov, Serghei Svinarenco, Vitalie Plămădealã (Cap), Alexandru Suvorov (75.Dimitrii Mandrîcenco), Renat Mochulyak (87.Sergiu Istrati), Eugeniu Slivca (75.Sidimane Sagna), Roman Volkov (91.Victor Stînă), Maxim Iurcu (67.Mihail Ghecev). Trainer: Sergiu Cebotari.

Penalties: Ion Jardan 1-0; Victor Stînă 1-1; Ilie Damașcan 2-1; Sidimane Sagna 2-2; Artiom Rozgoniuc 3-2; Serghei Svinarenco 3-3; Iaser Țurcan 4-3; Igor Bondarenco (saved); Arcadie Rusu 5-3.

Football Club Codru Lozova

Founded: 2008
Stadium: Stadionul Zimbru 2, Chişinău (2,000)
Trainer: Valeriu Andronic 21.12.1982

Goalkeepers:	DOB	M	(s)	G
Eugeniu Afanasiev	12.02.1992	6		
Boris Pascarenco	23.06.1997	17		
Nicolae Ţurcan	09.12.1989	5		
Defenders:	**DOB**	**M**	**(s)**	**G**
Alexandru Belevschi	21.03.1995	7		
Vladislav Bobrov (UKR)	10.05.1996	27		
David Cemschi	12.05.1995	11	(1)	
Maxim Cojocaru	29.10.1999	4	(2)	
Petru Costin	08.07.1997	17		
Ion Mamaliga	28.04.1999	21	(3)	1
Ghenadie Ochincă	01.03.1984	2	(1)	
Arcadie Rusu	28.06.1993	11	(2)	2
Valentyn Semenchenko (UKR)	09.04.1998	11	(1)	
Bogdan Stoianov	20.12.1999	1	(4)	
Cristian Ursu	12.02.1998	24	(2)	
Midfielders:	**DOB**	**M**	**(s)**	**G**
Daniel Adam	30.11.1998	10	(8)	
Mihai Apostol	21.01.1997	13		
Andrei Bursuc	23.05.1997	12		3

	DOB	M	(s)	G
Vladislav Chirciu	09.07.1996	10	(1)	
Andrei Drab	21.07.1999		(8)	
Dumitru Garşinschi	25.05.1999	13	(3)	1
Cristian Jalbă	02.02.1997	7	(1)	
Rinat Jalbă	02.02.1997	6	(3)	
Denis Janu	18.05.1995	13		
Valeriu Osipenco	27.07.1996	1	(2)	
Gheorghe Suciu	06.06.1999	13		
Valeriu Tiron	08.04.1993	3	(2)	
Corneliu Ţîbuleac	23.08.1996	5	(1)	
Eduard Zaplitnîi	30.04.1998	4	(2)	
Forwards:	**DOB**	**M**	**(s)**	**G**
Daniel Buhanenco	18.05.1997	6	(4)	
Grigore Coşcodan	26.01.2000	5	(5)	
Ion Donţu	09.09.1999	7	(1)	
Sergiu Nazar	02.07.1997	9	(4)	
Dumitru Rogac	07.11.1998	3	(3)	
Nikita Trifonov (RUS)	06.05.2000	3	(6)	1
Artiom Zabun	23.04.1996	1	(6)	

Football Club Dinamo-Auto Tiraspol

Founded: 24.07.2009
Stadium: Stadionul Dinamo-Auto, Tiraspol (1,300)
Trainer: Igor Dobrovolski (RUS) 27.08.1967

Goalkeepers:	DOB	M	(s)	G
Cristian Avram	27.07.1994	8		
Maxim Bardîş	16.07.1997	2		
Victor Străistari	21.06.1999	11		
Alexandru Zveaghinţev	26.07.1987	7		
Defenders:	**DOB**	**M**	**(s)**	**G**
Vitali Bordian	11.08.1984	9		
Serghei Diulgher	21.03.1991	12	(1)	
Ruslan Gadevici	02.06.1997	3	(1)	
Valerii Macriţchii	13.02.1996	27		4
Oleksandr Masalov (UKR)	22.01.1997	8		
Sandu Mateescu	20.12.1998	4	(2)	
Nurlan Novruzov (AZE)	03.03.1993	5	(2)	
Radu Rogac	07.06.1995	21		
Nicolai Solodovnicov	18.04.2000		(2)	
Ivan Voropai	21.04.1998	16		2

Midfielders:	DOB	M	(s)	G
Artiom Bilinschii	19.11.1996	23	(2)	
Serghei Bobrov	07.09.1991	17	(6)	4
Nichita Ciumacenko	23.01.2000	1	(1)	
Andrei Cobeţ	03.01.1997	13	(8)	2
Magomed-Bashir Gorbakov	08.10.1999	2	(3)	
Vladislav Kraev (UKR)	05.02.1995	7		3
Maxim Mihaliov	22.08.1986	25		9
Vsevolod Nihaev	04.05.1999	10	(9)	
Ņikita Pačko (LVA)	05.04.1997	3		
Andrii Panych (UKR)	27.06.1997	6	(2)	
Forwards:	**DOB**	**M**	**(s)**	**G**
Igor Bugaev	26.06.1984	16	(5)	4
Marin Căruntu	28.11.1997	3	(3)	
Andrei Macriţchii	13.02.1996	18		2
Eugeniu Rebenja	05.03.1995	15	(5)	3
Ivan Urvanţev	02.05.1997	16	(3)	3

Football Club Milsami Orhei

Founded: 2005
Stadium: Complexul Sportiv Raional, Orhei (2,539)
Trainer: Veaceslav Rusnac 27.08.1975

Goalkeepers:	DOB	M	(s)	G
Anatolii Chirinciuc	04.02.1989	9		
Radu Mîţu	04.11.1994	13		
Emil Tîmbur	21.07.1997	6		
Defenders:	**DOB**	**M**	**(s)**	**G**
Fiodor Andriuhin	18.02.1997	10	(2)	1
Guorguy Ba (FRA)	19.03.1998	7	(4)	
Constantin Bogdan	29.12.1993	10	(1)	1
Vadim Bolohan	15.08.1986	19		2
Artur Crăciun	29.06.1998	13		1
Alexandru Cuşnirenco	12.11.2001		(1)	
Dinu Graur	27.12.1994	14	(1)	3
Vasile Jardan	20.07.1993	17	(1)	1
Adrian Rusu	08.09.2000		(1)	
Midfielders:	**DOB**	**M**	**(s)**	**G**
Gheorghe Andronic	25.09.1991	9	(1)	1

	DOB	M	(s)	G
Alexandru Antoniuc	23.05.1989	20	(1)	5
Velantin Frecatel	26.03.2002		(1)	
Oleg Martin	21.10.1999	4	(8)	
Alexandru Onica	25.07.1984	26	(1)	
Artur Pătraş	01.10.1988	7	(5)	
Mihai Plătică	15.03.1990	10		2
Andrei Rusnac	22.09.1996	21	(1)	1
Victor Stînă	20.03.1998	20	(1)	3
Veaceslav Zagaevschii	04.04.1996	16	(8)	3
Forwards:	**DOB**	**M**	**(s)**	**G**
Maxim Antoniuc	15.01.1991	13	(8)	
Daniel Ciobanu	17.07.1998	7	(8)	
Ion Ibrean	21.03.1998	3	(2)	2
Timur Koblov (RUS)	25.01.1997	4	(3)	
Sergiu Nazar	02.07.1997	7	(4)	2
Sergiu Plătică	05.06.1991	23	(1)	1

Club Sportiv Petrocub Hîncești

Founded: 1994
Stadium: Stadionul Municipal, Hîncești (1,500)
Trainer: Lilian Popescu — 15.11.1973

Goalkeepers:	DOB	M	(s)	G
Cristian Avram	27.07.1994	13		
Dorian Răilean	13.10.1993	15		
Defenders:	**DOB**	**M**	**(s)**	**G**
Ion Jardan	10.01.1990	26		1
Maxim Potîrniche	13.06.1989	26		
Arcadie Rusu	28.06.1993	1	(6)	
Vlad Slivca	10.09.1998	7	(7)	
Mihail Tîșcul	25.02.1997	1	(4)	
Iaser Țurcan	07.01.1998	25	(3)	2
Midfielders:	**DOB**	**M**	**(s)**	**G**
Alexandru Ambros	26.04.1999		(5)	
Vladimir Ambros	30.12.1993	19		5
Alexandru Bejan	07.05.1996	14	(4)	2
Vladimir Bogdanović (SRB)	05.10.1986	8	(3)	
Ștefan Burghiu	28.03.1991	2	(2)	
Andrei Cojocari	21.01.1987	11		1
Donalio Melachio Douanla (CMR)	24.09.1997	20	(2)	
Jessie Guera Djou (CMR)	03.05.1997	17		1
Jacques Onana Ndzomo (CMR)	23.08.1993	24		
Vlad Oprea	24.08.1998		(8)	
Christi Taras	26.09.1998	1		
Dan Taras	13.02.1994	22	(2)	6
Alexandru Vlas	24.08.2003		(2)	
Forwards:	**DOB**	**M**	**(s)**	**G**
Grigore Coșcodan	26.01.2000	1	(7)	
Ilie Damașcan	12.10.1996	4	(3)	1
Alexandru Dedov	26.07.1989	3	(4)	2
Vadim Gulceac	06.08.1998	15	(13)	6
Victor Mudrac	03.03.1994	20	(1)	4
Artiom Puntus	31.05.1995	13	(2)	3

Fotbal Club Sfântul Gheorghe Suruceni

Founded: 2003
Stadium: Stadionul Suruceni, Suruceni (1,500)
Trainer: Sergiu Cebotari — 21.02.1981

Goalkeepers:	DOB	M	(s)	G
Dmitrii Burac	20.03.1997	3		
Nicolae Cebotari	24.05.1997	22		
Maxim Railean	27.03.2000	3		
Defenders:	**DOB**	**M**	**(s)**	**G**
Maxim Focșa	21.04.1992	20	(1)	1
Vladimir Ghinaitis	30.03.1995	10	(4)	
Myroslav Mazur (UKR)	11.08.1998	16	(1)	2
Andrey Novicov	24.04.1986	21	(2)	1
Artiom Rozgoniuc	01.10.1995	16	(3)	
Serghei Svinarenco	18.09.1996	23	(1)	
Midfielders:	**DOB**	**M**	**(s)**	**G**
Iurie Cebotari	23.03.1997	3		
Sergiu Istrati	07.08.1988	18	(6)	6
Garegin Kirakosyan (ARM)	26.11.1995	15	(6)	3
Dimitrii Mandrîcenco	13.05.1997	14	(10)	6
Petru Ojog	17.07.1990	24	(1)	
Vadim Paireli	08.11.1995	1	(4)	
Vitalie Plămădeală	21.01.1985	22		2
Dumitru Reniță	02.12.1999		(2)	
Alexandru Vremea	03.11.1991	3	(1)	
Eugeniu Slivca	13.07.1989	17	(5)	1
Alexandru Suvorov	02.02.1987	14	(7)	4
Forwards:	**DOB**	**M**	**(s)**	**G**
Alexandru Boiciuc	21.08.1997	9	(4)	5
Andrei Calac	14.03.1999	7	(9)	2
Artiom Carastoian	10.10.1999	19	(2)	1
Vadim Cemîrtan	21.07.1987	11	(5)	6
Victor Martin	12.03.1997		(2)	

Fotbal Club Sheriff Tiraspol

Founded: 04.04.1997
Stadium: Stadionul Sheriff, Tiraspol (12,746)
Trainer: Goran Sablić (SRB) — 07.06.2018
[30.04.2019] Zoran Zekić (CRO) — 29.04.1974

Goalkeepers:	DOB	M	(s)	G
Dumitru Celeadnic	23.04.1992	24		
Zvonimir Mikulić (CRO)	05.02.1990	4		
Defenders:	**DOB**	**M**	**(s)**	**G**
Evghenii Berco	09.10.1999		(1)	
Cristiano da Silva Leite (BRA)	29.08.1993	23	(1)	
Vadim Dijinari	01.04.1999	2	(2)	1
Jarosław Jach (POL)	17.02.1994	14		
Vladimir Kovačević (SRB)	11.11.1992	4	(3)	2
Liridon Latifi (ALB)	06.02.1994	9	(2)	1
Andrej Lukić (CRO)	02.04.1994	9	(2)	3
Mateo Mužek	29.04.1995	6	(3)	
Ousmane N'Diaye (SEN)	19.08.1991	12	(1)	
Matej Palčič (SVN)	21.06.1993	2		
Veaceslav Posmac	07.11.1990	20	(1)	2
Mateo Sušić (BIH)	18.11.1990	9	(1)	
Midfielders:	**DOB**	**M**	**(s)**	**G**
Gheorghe Anton	27.01.1993	10	(9)	
Wilfried Balima (BFA)	20.03.1985	9	(4)	3
Alexandr Belousov	14.05.1998	21	(1)	1
Ariel Borysiuk (POL)	29.07.1991	9	(1)	1
Maxim Cojocaru	13.01.1998	18	(5)	4
Mihail Ghecev	05.11.1997	5	(2)	2
Artem Gordienko (UKR)	04.03.1991	3	(3)	
Nichita Holodov	28.05.2003	2		
José Ángel Jurado de la Torre (ESP)	21.06.1992	7	(6)	2
Yuri Kendysh (BLR)	10.06.1990	23	(2)	13
Evgheni Oancea	05.01.1996	9	(1)	3
Antun Palić (CRO)	25.06.1988	10	(2)	1
Artiom Rozgoniuc	01.10.1995	1	(1)	
Forwards:	**DOB**	**M**	**(s)**	**G**
Andriy Blyznychenko (UKR)	24.07.1994	3	(2)	3
Gabrijel Boban (CRO)	23.07.1989	8		1
Leandro Joaquim Ribeiro (BRA)	13.01.1995	12	(9)	4
Patrick Pedersen (DEN)	25.11.1991	6	(9)	3
Robert Ndip Tambe (CMR)	22.02.1994	14	(9)	9

Clubul Sportiv de Fotbal Speranța Nisporeni

Founded: 1991
Stadium: Complexul Sportiv Raional, Orhei (2,539)
Trainer: Cristian Efros — 06.01.1992

Goalkeepers:	DOB	M	(s)	G
Daniil Avdyushkin (RUS)	01.10.1993	10		
Denis Macogonenco	20.02.1996	13		
Igor Mostovei	25.09.1999	5		
Defenders:	**DOB**	**M**	**(s)**	**G**
Ion Arabadji	31.07.1984	17	(3)	
Mihail Bolun	16.05.1989	27		1
Bruno Nogueira Barbosa (BRA)	28.04.1994	21	(5)	
Valentin Chișca	14.08.1999		5	
Ștefan Efros	08.05.1990	28		1
Ion Ghimp	11.09.1996	9	1	
Óliver Antonio Fula Perea (COL)	01.03.1988	13		
Ichaka Tiehi (CIV)	01.01.1996	17	(2)	
Midfielders:	**DOB**	**M**	**(s)**	**G**
Ruslan Chelari	27.02.1999	22	(5)	1
Fabrice Eloundou (CMR)	30.08.1994	18	(8)	3
Mihai Gabura	21.07.1998	1		
Alisher Mirzoev (TJK)	01.01.1999	13	(6)	1
Dayron Alexander Mosquera Mendoza (COL)	07.08.1995	22		1
Vlad Oprea	24.08.1998	4	(1)	
Felipe Ponce Ramírez (MEX)	29.03.1988	4	(3)	
Vladimir Titievschii	18.06.1998		(3)	
Serghei Trofan	08.11.1997	2	7	2
Forwards:	**DOB**	**M**	**(s)**	**G**
Yusuf Isah Doma (NGA)	01.11.1998	1	(6)	
Ion Drăgan	14.06.1996	17	(7)	4
Constantin Iavorschi	16.03.1990		(1)	
Maxim Iurcu	01.02.1993	25	(2)	11
Luis Ferney Ríos Misas (COL)	13.08.1989	3	(4)	
Constantin Sandu	15.09.1993	16	(6)	4

Fotbal Club Zimbru Chişinău

Founded:	1947	
Stadium:	Stadionul Zimbru, Chişinău (10,400)	
Trainer:	Sorin Colceag (ROU)	11.03.1972
[01.07.2019]	Vladimir Aga	09.11.1987
[01.11.2019]	Veaceslav Sofroni	30.04.1984

Goalkeepers:	DOB	M	(s)	G
Denis Guţul	15.08.1999	2		
Maksym Kovalov (UKR)	11.07.2000	23		
Mickaël Meira (POR)	25.01.1994	3		
Defenders:	**DOB**	**M**	**(s)**	**G**
Igor Arhirii	17.02.1997	21		
Alexandru Belevschi	21.03.1995	4	(3)	
Victor Bogaciuc	17.10.1999	9	(1)	
Valentin Chişca	14.08.1999	2	(1)	
Alexei Ciopa	27.10.1998	17	(2)	
Serafim Cojocari	07.01.2001	7	(1)	
Mihai Dolghi	08.07.2002	1		
Denis Furtuna	13.10.1999	20	(1)	1
Tudor Iapără	16.05.2000	3		
Sandu Mateescu	20.12.1998	4		
Anatolie Prepeliţă	06.08.1997	21		1
Mihail Tişcul	25.02.1997	4	(2)	
Alexandru Vacarciuc	16.04.2001	8		
Midfielders:	**DOB**	**M**	**(s)**	**G**
Daisuke Araki (JPN)	05.08.2000		(1)	
Artur Barabaş	11.12.2000	4	(6)	
Gheorghe Brînzaniuc	06.05.2001		(4)	

	DOB	M	(s)	G
Andrei Bursuc	23.05.1997	8	(1)	
Vadim Călugher	07.09.1995	10		1
Andrei Cojocari	21.01.1987	13		1
Alexandru Graur	11.02.2001	3	(5)	
Daniel Guştiuc	05.03.1997	6		
Cristian Nagornîi	17.06.1998	11	(1)	
Petru Neagu	13.08.1999	8	(7)	1
Steve Njemane Tanga (FRA)	17.12.1998	5	(2)	
Artur Pătraş	01.10.1988	11		
Daniel Pîslă	14.06.1986	19	(5)	5
Ion Postica	10.01.1999	9	(7)	1
Radu Scoarţă	03.07.1999	11	(2)	1
Pavel Secrier	11.01.1991	7	(3)	
Eugeniu Sidorenco	19.03.1989	7		
Forwards:	**DOB**	**M**	**(s)**	**G**
Oleg Andronic	06.02.1989	2	(5)	
Ion Donţu	09.09.1999	4	(5)	
Nichita Iuraşco	17.05.1999	11	(5)	
Nichita Murovanîi	29.03.2001		(3)	
Maxim Şoimu	17.07.1990	5	(2)	2
Boubacar Traoré (MLI)	24.05.1998	5	(3)	2

SECOND LEVEL
Divizia A 2019

1.	FC Floreşti (*Promoted*)	28	22	3	3	71	-	29	69
2.	FC Dacia Buiucani Chişinău (*Promoted*)	28	22	3	3	68	-	17	69
3.	CSF Spartanii Selemet (*Promotion Play-off*)	28	20	2	6	72	-	28	62
4.	FC Tighina Bender	28	19	3	6	84	-	31	60
5.	FC Cahul-2005	28	14	6	8	60	-	34	48
6.	FC Victoria Bardar	28	14	1	13	58	-	54	43
7.	FC Speranţa Drochia	28	12	5	11	44	-	37	41
8.	FC Grănicerul Glodeni	28	10	4	14	47	-	66	34
9.	FC Sireţi	28	10	3	15	48	-	83	33
10.	FC Zaria Bălţi	28	9	4	15	65	-	60	31
11.	FC Iskra Rîbniţa	28	9	4	15	51	-	62	31
12.	FC Real Succes Chişinău	28	9	4	15	59	-	63	31
13.	FC Ungheni (*Relegated*)	28	9	3	16	55	-	83	30
14.	FC Sîngerei (*Relegated*)	28	6	3	19	38	-	72	21
15.	CSF Sparta Chişinău (*Relegated*)	28	0	2	26	6	-	107	2

Please note: CSF Sparta Chişinău withdrew from the league after round 14. All remaining fixtures are awarded 0–3

INTERNATIONAL MATCHES
(16.07.2019 – 15.07.2020)

07.09.2019	Reykjavík	Iceland - Moldova	3-0(1-0)	(ECQ)
10.09.2019	Chişinău	Moldova - Turkey	0-4(0-1)	(ECQ)
11.10.2019	Andorra la Vella	Andorra - Moldova	1-0(0-0)	(ECQ)
14.10.2019	Chişinău	Moldova - Albania	0-4(0-3)	(ECQ)
14.11.2019	Paris	France - Moldova	2-1(1-1)	(ECQ)
17.11.2019	Chışınău	Moldova - Iceland	1-2(0-1)	(ECQ)
09.01.2020	Doha	Sweden - Moldova	1-0(1-0)	(F)

07.09.2019   ICELAND - MOLDOVA   **3-0(1-0)**   16th EC. Qualifiers
Laugardalsvöllur, Reykjavík; Referee: João Pedro Silva Pinheiro (Portugal); Attendance: 8,338
MDA: Alexei Coşelev, Igor Armaş, Victor Mudrac, Dinu Graur, Oleg Reabciuk, Eugeniu Cebotaru, Alexandru Suvorov, Artur Ioniţă (Cap), Radu Gînsari (80.Constantin Sandu), Cătălin Carp (67.Iaser Ţurcan), Vadim Cemîrtan (65.Maxim Cojocaru). Trainer: Semen Altman (Ukraine).

10.09.2019   MOLDOVA - TURKEY   **0-4(0-1)**   16th EC. Qualifiers
Stadionul Zimbru, Chişinău; Referee: Davide Massa (Italy); Attendance: 8,281
MDA: Alexei Coşelev, Victor Mudrac, Dinu Graur, Iaser Ţurcan, Ştefan Efros, Oleg Reabciuk, Eugeniu Cebotaru, Alexandru Suvorov (75.Artiom Rozgoniuc), Artur Ioniţă (Cap) (81.Mihail Ghecev), Radu Gînsari (68.Vadim Cemîrtan), Constantin Sandu. Trainer: Semen Altman (Ukraine).

11.10.2019   ANDORRA - MOLDOVA   **1-0(0-0)**   16th EC. Qualifiers
Estadi Nacional, Andorra la Vella; Referee: Jonathan Lardot (Belgium); Attendance: 947
MDA: Alexei Coşelev, Veaceslav Posmac, Dinu Graur, Anatolie Prepeliţă, Oleg Reabciuk, Eugeniu Cebotaru, Alexandru Suvorov, Artur Ioniţă (Cap), Maxim Mihaliov (72.Alexandru Dedov), Radu Gînsari [sent off 55], Alexandru Boiciuc. Trainer: Semen Altman (Ukraine).

14.10.2019   MOLDOVA - ALBANIA   **0-4(0-3)**   16th EC. Qualifiers
Stadionul Zimbru, Chişinău; Referee: Chris Kavanagh (England); Attendance: 4,367
MDA: Alexei Coşelev, Veaceslav Posmac, Victor Mudrac (31.Artiom Rozgoniuc), Dinu Graur, Anatolie Prepeliţă, Oleg Reabciuk, Eugeniu Cebotaru, Alexandru Suvorov (60.Alexandru Boiciuc), Artur Ioniţă (Cap), Eugen Sidorenco (80.Constantin Sandu), Gheorghe Anton. Trainer: Semen Altman (Ukraine).

14.11.2019   FRANCE - MOLDOVA   **2-1(1-1)**   16th EC. Qualifiers
Stade de France, Saint-Denis, Paris; Referee: Gediminas Mažeika (Lithuania); Attendance: 64,367
MDA: Alexei Coşelev, Igor Armaş (Cap), Ion Jardan (68.Dinu Graur), Veaceslav Posmac, Artur Crăciun, Artur Ioniţă, Radu Gînsari (74.Nicolae Milinceanu), Vadim Raţă (81.Artur Pătraş), Cătălin Carp, Eugeniu Cociuc, Sergiu Plătică. Trainer: Engin Fırat (Turkey).
Goal: Vadim Raţă (9).

17.11.2019   MOLDOVA - ICELAND   **1-2(0-1)**   16th EC. Qualifiers
Stadionul Zimbru, Chişinău; Referee: Pavel Královec (Czech Republic); Attendance: 6,742
MDA: Alexei Coşelev, Igor Armaş (Cap), Maxim Focşa, Artur Crăciun, Artur Ioniţă, Radu Gînsari (83.Dinu Graur), Vadim Raţă, Cătălin Carp (90.Andrei Cojocari), Eugeniu Cociuc, Sergiu Plătică, Nicolae Milinceanu (60.Vitalie Damaşcan). Trainer: Engin Fırat (Turkey).
Goal: Nicolae Milinceanu (56).

09.01.2020   SWEDEN - MOLDOVA   **1-0(1-0)**   Friendly International
"Hamad bin Khalifa" Stadium, Doha; Referee: Saoud Ali Al Athbah (Qatar); Attendance: 100
MDA: Denis Rusu, Igor Armaş (Cap), Constantin Bogdan, Anatolie Prepeliţă, Alexandru Suvorov (59.Dinu Graur), Vadim Raţă (72.Artur Pătraş), Eugeniu Cociuc (58.Gheorghe Anton), Dan Taras (46.Andrei Cojocari), Vladimir Ambros (46.Alexandru Boiciuc), Cristian Dros, Sergiu Plătică (72.Danu Spătaru). Trainer: Engin Fırat (Turkey).

NATIONAL TEAM PLAYERS
(16.07.2019 – 15.07.2020)

Name	DOB	Caps	Goals	2019/2020:	Club
Goalkeepers					
Alexei COȘELEV	19.11.1993	21	0	2019:	Fortuna Sittard (NED)
Denis RUSU	02.08.1990	1	0	2020:	FC Politehnica Iași (ROU)
Defenders					
Igor ARMAȘ	14.07.1987	58	5	2019/2020:	FC Voluntari (ROU)
Constantin BOGDAN	29.12.1993	2	0	2020:	FC Milsami Orhei
Artur CRĂCIUN	29.06.1998	2	0	2019:	FC Universitatea Cluj-Napoca (ROU)
Ștefan EFROS	08.05.1990	3	0	2019:	CSF Speranța Nisporeni
Maxim FOCȘA	21.04.1992	1	0	2019:	FC Sfântul Gheorghe Suruceni
Dinu GRAUR	27.12.1994	16	0	2019/2020:	AFC Astra Giurgiu (ROU)
Ion JARDAN	10.01.1990	30	0	2019:	CS Petrocub Hîncești
Victor MUDRAC	03.03.1994	3	0	2019:	CS Petrocub Hîncești
Veaceslav POSMAC	07.11.1990	37	2	2019:	FC Sheriff Tiraspol
Anatolie PREPELIȚĂ	06.08.1997	3	0	2019/2020:	JPFS/FK Spartaks Jūrmala (LVA)
Oleg REABCIUK	16.01.1998	16	0	2019:	FC Paços de Ferreira (POR)
Artiom ROZGONIUC	01.10.1995	11	0	2019:	FC Sfântul Gheorghe Suruceni
Midfielders					
Gheorghe ANTON	27.01.1993	8	0	2019:	FC Sheriff Tiraspol
				2020:	Unattached
Cătălin CARP	20.10.1993	29	1	2019:	FK Ufa (RUS)
Eugeniu CEBOTARU	16.10.1984	65	1	2019:	FC Academica Clinceni (ROU)
Eugeniu COCIUC	11.05.1993	19	0	2019/2020:	Səbail FK Bakı (AZE)
Andrei COJOCARI	21.01.1987	40	2	2019/2020:	CS Petrocub Hîncești
Alexandru DEDOV	26.07.1989	55	3	2019:	CS Petrocub Hîncești
Cristian DROS	15.04.1998	1	0	2020:	ASU Politehnica Timișoara (ROU)
Mihail GHECEV	05.11.1997	1	0	2019:	FC Sheriff Tiraspol
Radu GÎNSARI	10.12.1991	39	7	2019:	FK Krylia Sovetov Samara (RUS)
Artur IONIȚĂ	17.08.1990	45	3	2019:	Cagliari Calcio (ITA)
Maxim MIHALIOV	22.08.1986	13	0	2019:	FC Dinamo-Auto Tiraspol
Sergiu PLĂTICĂ	09.06.1991	14	0	2019/2020:	FC Milsami Orhei
Artur PĂTRAȘ	01.10.1988	29	0	2019/2020:	FC Zimbru Chișinău
Vadim RAȚĂ	05.03.1993	7	1	2019/2020:	AFC Chindia Târgoviște (ROU)
Dan SPĂTARU	24.05.1994	9	0	2020:	Unattached
Alexandru SUVOROV	02.02.1987	57	5	2019/2020:	FC Sfântul Gheorghe Suruceni
Dan TARAS	13.02.1994	4	0	2020:	CS Petrocub Hîncești
Iaser ȚURCAN	07.01.1998	4	0	2019:	CS Petrocub Hîncești
Forwards					
Vladimir AMBROS	30.12.1993	12	1	2019/2020:	CS Petrocub Hîncești
Alexandru BOICIUC	21.08.1997	9	0	2019/2020:	FK Karpaty Lviv (UKR)
Vadim CEMÎRTAN	21.07.1987	4	0	2019:	FC Sfântul Gheorghe Suruceni
Maxim COJOCARU	13.01.1998	1	0	2019:	FC Sheriff Tiraspol
Vitalie DAMAȘCAN	24.01.1999	13	1	2019:	Fortuna Sittard (NED)
Nicolae MILINCEANU	01.08.1992	10	1	2019:	FC Vaduz (LIE)
Constantin SANDU	15.09.1993	7	0	2019:	CSF Speranța Nisporeni
Eugen SIDORENCO	19.03.1989	35	7	2019:	FC Zimbru Chișinău
National team coach					
Semen ALTMAN (Ukraine) [19.07. 27.10.2019]	21.04.1946	4 M; 0 W; 0 D; 4 L; 0-12			
Engin FIRAT (Turkey) [from 28.10.2019]	11.06.1970	3 M; 0 W; 0 D; 3 L; 2-5			

MONTENEGRO

The Country:
Crna Gora (Montenegro)
Capital: Podgorica
Surface: 13,812 km²
Inhabitants: 622,359 [2018]
Time: UTC+1

The FA:
Fudbalski savez Crne Gore
Bulevar Veljka Vlahovica bb ME, 81000 Podgorica
Tel: +382 20 445 609
Foundation date: 1931
Member of FIFA since: 2007
Member of UEFA since: 2007
Website: www.fscg.co.me

NATIONAL TEAM RECORDS

RECORDS
First international match:	24.03.2007, Podgorica:	Montenegro – Hungary 2-1
Most international caps:	Fatos Bećiraj	- 69 caps (since 2009)
Most international goals:	Stevan Jovetić	- 24 goals / 51 caps (2007-2018)

UEFA EUROPEAN CHAMPIONSHIP
1960	-
1964	-
1968	-
1972	-
1976	-
1980	-
1984	-
1988	-
1992	-
1996	-
2000	-
2004	-
2008	-
2012	Qualifiers
2016	Qualifiers
2020	Qualifiers

FIFA WORLD CUP
1930	-
1934	-
1938	-
1950	-
1954	-
1958	-
1962	-
1966	-
1970	-
1974	-
1978	-
1982	-
1986	-
1990	-
1994	-
1998	-
2002	-
2006	-
2010	Qualifiers
2014	Qualifiers
2018	Qualifiers

OLYMPIC TOURNAMENTS
1908	-
1912	-
1920	-
1924	-
1928	-
1936	-
1948	-
1952	-
1956	-
1960	-
1964	-
1968	-
1972	-
1976	-
1980	-
1984	-
1988	-
1992	-
1996	-
2000	-
2004	-
2008	-
2012	Qualifiers
2016	Qualifiers

was part of Yugoslavia/Serbia until 2006

UEFA NATIONS LEAGUE
2018/2019 – League C

FIFA CONFEDERATIONS CUP 1992-2017
None

MONTENEGRIN CLUB HONOURS IN EUROPEAN CLUB COMPETITIONS:

European Champion Clubs.Cup (1956-1992) / UEFA Champions League (1993-2020)
None

Fairs Cup (1858-1971) / UEFA Cup (1972-2009) / UEFA Europa League (2010-2020)
None

UEFA Super Cup (1972-2019)
None

European Cup Winners.Cup 1961-1999*
None

defunct competition

NATIONAL COMPETITIONS
TABLE OF HONOURS

	CHAMPIONS	CUP WINNERS	BEST GOALSCORERS	
2006/2007	FK Zeta Golubovci	FK Rudar Pljevlja	Damir Čakar (FK Rudar Pljevlja)	
			Žarko Korać (FK Zeta Golubovci)	16
2007/2008	FK Budućnost Podgorica	FK Mogren Budva	Ivan Jablan (FK Lovćen Cetinje)	13
2008/2009	FK Mogren Budva	OFK Petrovac	Fatos Bećiraj (FK Budućnost Podgorica)	18
2009/2010	FK Rudar Pljevlja	FK Rudar Pljevlja	Ivan Bošković (OFK Grbalj)	28
2010/2011	FK Mogren Budva	FK Rudar Pljevlja	Ivan Vuković (FK Budućnost Podgorica)	20
2011/2012	FK Budućnost Podgorica	FK Čelik Nikšić	Admir Adrović (FK Budućnost Podgorica)	22
2012/2013	FK Sutjeska Nikšić	FK Budućnost Podgorica	Admir Adrović (FK Budućnost Podgorica)	
			Žarko Korać (FK Zeta Golubovci)	15
2013/2014	FK Sutjeska Nikšić	FK Lovćen Cetinje	Stefan Mugoša (OFK Titograd Podgorica)	15
2014/2015	FK Rudar Pljevlja	FK Mladost Podgorica	Goran Vujović (FK Sutjeska Nikšić)	21
2015/2016	FK Mladost Podgorica	FK Rudar Pljevlja	Marko Šćepanović (FK Mladost Podgorica)	19
2016/2017	FK Budućnost Podgorica	FK Sutjeska Nikšić	Zoran Petrović (OFK Titograd Podgorica)	14
2017/2018	FK Sutjeska Nikšić	FK Mladost Podgorica	Igor Ivanović (FK Sutjeska Nikšić)	14
2018/2019	FK Sutjeska Nikšić	FK Budućnost Podgorica	Nikola Krstović (FK Zeta Golubovci)	17
2019/2020	FK Budućnost Podgorica	*Competition cancelled*	Marko Ćetković (FK Sutjeska Nikšić)	10

NATIONAL CHAMPIONSHIP
Prva Crnogorska Fudbal Liga 2019/2020
(03.08.2019 – 25.05.2020)

Results

Please note: OFK Mladost Lješkopolje changed its name to FK Podgorica.

Round 1 [03-05.08.2019]
FK Kom Zlatica - FK Zeta 0-0
OFK Grbalj - Iskra Danilovgrad 2-3(0-1)
OFK Petrovac - FK Podgorica 1-1(1-1)
OFK Titograd - Sutjeska Nikšić 0-1(0-1)
FK Budućnost - Rudar Pljevlja 2-0(1-0)

Round 2 [09-10.08.2019]
FK Zeta - Sutjeska Nikšić 0-0
Iskra Danilovgrad - OFK Titograd 0-0
Rudar Pljevlja - OFK Grbalj 1-3(0-0)
FK Podgorica - FK Budućnost 1-3(0-0)
FK Kom Zlatica - OFK Petrovac 3-2(1-1)

Round 3 [14.08.2019]
OFK Grbalj - FK Podgorica 1-1(0-1)
FK Budućnost - FK Kom Zlatica 3-1(1-0)
OFK Petrovac - FK Zeta 0-2(0-2)
OFK Titograd - Rudar Pljevlja 0-1(0-0)
Sutjeska Nik. - Iskra Danilov. 4-2(1-1)[28.08.]

Round 4 [18.08.2019]
FK Zeta - Iskra Danilovgrad 0-1(0-1)
Rudar Pljevlja - Sutjeska Nikšić 0-4(0-2)
FK Podgorica - OFK Titograd 0-0
FK Kom Zlatica - OFK Grbalj 1-1(0-1)
OFK Petrovac - FK Budućnost 0-3(0-0)

Round 5 [24-25.08.2019]
OFK Grbalj - OFK Petrovac 1-2(0-1)
Iskra Danilovgrad - Rudar Pljevlja 2-0(1-0)
Sutjeska Nikšić - FK Podgorica 1-2(0-1)
OFK Titograd - FK Kom Zlatica 3-1(2-1)
FK Budućnost - FK Zeta 1-1(0-1)

Round 6 [31.08.2019]
FK Zeta - Rudar Pljevlja 2-1(1-1)
FK Podgorica - Iskra Danilovgrad 0-0
FK Kom Zlatica - Sutjeska Nikšić 1-1(0-0)
FK Budućnost - OFK Grbalj 3-2(1-2)
OFK Petrovac - OFK Titograd 0-3(0-2)

Round 7 [14.09.2019]
OFK Grbalj - FK Zeta 0-0
Sutjeska Nikšić - OFK Petrovac 3-0(0-0)
Rudar Pljevlja - FK Podgorica 2-1(2-0)
Iskra Danilovgrad - FK Kom Zlatica 0-2(0-0)
OFK Titograd - FK Budućnost 2-1(1-0)

Round 8 [18.09.2019]
FK Zeta - FK Podgorica 1-0(0-0)
FK Kom Zlatica - Rudar Pljevlja 5-0(3-0)
OFK Petrovac - Iskra Danilovgrad 0-1(0-1)
OFK Grbalj - OFK Titograd 0-2(0-0)
FK Budućnost - Sutjeska Nikšić 1-4(1-3)

Round 9 [22.09.2019]
Sutjeska Nikšić - OFK Grbalj 5-0(2-0)
Iskra Danilovgrad - FK Budućnost 2-2(1-0)
Rudar Pljevlja - OFK Petrovac 4-0(3-0)
FK Podgorica - FK Kom Zlatica 4-2(1-1)
OFK Titograd - FK Zeta 0-1(0-0)

Round 10 [28.09.2019]
FK Zeta - FK Kom Zlatica 0-0
FK Podgorica - OFK Petrovac 1-0(0-0)
Rudar Pljevlja - FK Budućnost 0-3(0-3)
Iskra Danilovgrad - OFK Grbalj 1-0(0-0)
Sutjeska Nikšić - OFK Titograd 1-1(0-0)

Round 11 [05-06.10.2019]
Sutjeska Nikšić - FK Zeta 2-1(1-1)
OFK Grbalj - Rudar Pljevlja 2-2(1-1)
FK Budućnost - FK Podgorica 1-0(1-0)
OFK Petrovac - FK Kom Zlatica 2-1(0-0)
OFK Titograd - Iskra Danilovgrad 0-1(0-1)

Round 12 [19.10.2019]
FK Zeta - OFK Petrovac 1-1(1-0)
FK Kom Zlatica - FK Budućnost 2-3(0-1)
Rudar Pljevlja - OFK Titograd 3-1(2-0)
Iskra Danilovgrad - Sutjeska Nikšić 2-0(0-0)
FK Podgorica - OFK Grbalj 1-1(0-1)

Round 13 [26-27.10.2019]
OFK Grbalj - FK Kom Zlatica 1-1(0-1)
FK Budućnost - OFK Petrovac 3-0(2-0)
Iskra Danilovgrad - FK Zeta 3-1(1-1)
OFK Titograd - FK Podgorica 1-2(0-2)
Sutjeska Nikšić - Rudar Pljevlja 3-0(2-0)

Round 14 [02.11.2019]
FK Zeta - FK Budućnost 2-1(1-1)
OFK Petrovac - OFK Grbalj 2-0(1-0)
FK Kom Zlatica - OFK Titograd 1-2(0-1)
Rudar Pljevlja - Iskra Danilovgrad 1-1(1-0)
FK Podgorica - Sutjeska Nikšić 2-2(0-0)

Round 15 [09-10.11.2019]
Rudar Pljevlja - FK Zeta 1-1(1-1)
Iskra Danilovgrad - FK Podgorica 2-1(1-0)
OFK Titograd - OFK Petrovac 1-2(1-0)
Sutjeska Nikšić - FK Kom Zlatica 2-0(2-0)
OFK Grbalj - FK Budućnost 0-4(0-2) [15.12.]

Round 16 [23.11.2019]
FK Zeta - OFK Grbalj 2-0(1-0)
OFK Petrovac - Sutjeska Nikšić 0-4(0-2)
FK Kom Zlatica - Iskra Danilovgrad 1-1(0-1)
FK Podgorica - Rudar Pljevlja 3-0(1-0)
FK Budućnost - OFK Titograd 2-1(1-0)

Round 17 [01.12.2019]
Rudar Pljevlja - FK Kom Zlatica 3-2(3-1)
Iskra Danilovgrad - OFK Petrovac 1-2(0-0)
Sutjeska Nikšić - FK Budućnost 0-2(0-1)
OFK Titograd - OFK Grbalj 1-0(1-0)
FK Podgorica - FK Zeta 2-0(0-0)

Round 18 [05.12.2019]
FK Zeta - OFK Titograd 1-0(0-0)
OFK Grbalj - Sutjeska Nikšić 1-1(0-0)
OFK Petrovac - Rudar Pljevlja 1-4(0-2)
FK Kom Zlatica - FK Podgorica 1-1(1-0)
FK Budućnost - Iskra Danilovgrad 1-0(0-0)

Round 19 [11.12.2019]
FK Kom Zlatica - FK Zeta 1-0(0-0)
OFK Petrovac - FK Podgorica 1-1(1-1)
OFK Grbalj - Iskra Danilovgrad 3-1(2-0)
OFK Titograd - Sutjeska Nikšić 1-1(1-0)
FK Budućnost - Rudar Pljevlja 2-0(0-0)

Round 20 [17-18.02.2020]
Iskra Danilovgrad - OFK Titograd 3-0(2-0)
FK Kom Zlatica - OFK Petrovac 0-1(0-1)
Rudar Pljevlja - OFK Grbalj 3-1(0-0)
FK Podgorica - FK Budućnost 1-1(0-0)
FK Zeta - Sutjeska Nikšić 1-3(0-1)

Round 21 [22-23.02.2020]
OFK Petrovac - FK Zeta 2-2(2-2)
OFK Grbalj - FK Podgorica 0-0
Sutjeska Nikšić - Iskra Danilovgrad 1-1(1-0)
OFK Titograd - Rudar Pljevlja 1-3(1-0)
FK Budućnost - FK Kom Zlatica 2-0(1-0)

Round 22 [29.02.2020]
FK Kom Zlatica - OFK Grbalj 0-1(0-0)
Rudar Pljevlja - Sutjeska Nikšić 5-1(2-0)
OFK Petrovac - FK Budućnost 0-1(0-0)
FK Podgorica - OFK Titograd 1-1(1-0)
FK Zeta - Iskra Danilovgrad 1-1(0-1)

Round 23 [07.03.2020]
OFK Grbalj - OFK Petrovac 0-0
OFK Titograd - FK Kom Zlatica 2-3(0-1)
Sutjeska Nikšić - FK Podgorica 1-0(1-0)
Iskra Danilovgrad - Rudar Pljevlja 0-2(0-1)
FK Budućnost - FK Zeta 4-1(2-0)

Round 24 [30.05.2020]
FK Zeta - Rudar Pljevlja 2-0(0-0)
FK Kom Zlatica - Sutjeska Nikšić 3-3(2-1)
OFK Petrovac - OFK Titograd 1-0(1-0)
FK Budućnost - OFK Grbalj 1-0(1-0)
FK Podgorica - Iskra Danilovgrad 0-0

Round 25 [03.06.2020]
OFK Grbalj - FK Zeta 0-2(0-1)
Sutjeska Nikšić - OFK Petrovac 0-0
OFK Titograd - FK Budućnost 1-3(1-1)
Iskra Danilovgrad - FK Kom Zlatica 2-0(2-0)
Rudar Pljevlja - FK Podgorica 0-3(0-1)

Round 26 [07.06.2020]
FK Zeta - FK Podgorica 1-1(0-0)
FK Kom Zlatica - Rudar Pljevlja 1-1(0-1)
OFK Petrovac - Iskra Danilovgrad 4-1(3-1)
OFK Grbalj - OFK Titograd 0-0
FK Budućnost - Sutjeska Nikšić 2-0(1-0)

Round 27 [12.06.2020]
Sutjeska Nikšić - OFK Grbalj 4-1(1-1)
Rudar Pljevlja - OFK Petrovac 0-2(0-2)
OFK Titograd - FK Zeta 0-0
FK Podgorica - FK Kom Zlatica 1-1(0-0)
Iskra Danilovgrad - FK Budućnost 4-1(0-0)

Round 28 [16.06.2020]
FK Zeta - FK Kom Zlatica 1-1(1-1)
FK Podgorica - OFK Petrovac 1-1(0-0)
Rudar Pljevlja - FK Budućnost 0-4(0-3)
Iskra Danilovgrad - OFK Grbalj 2-1(1-0)
Sutjeska Nikšić - OFK Titograd 3-1(1-1)

Round 29 [21.06.2020]
Sutjeska Nikšić - FK Zeta 0-0
OFK Grbalj - Rudar Pljevlja 1-0(0-0)
OFK Titograd - Iskra Danilovgrad 2-1(1-0)
OFK Petrovac - FK Kom Zlatica 1-0(0-0)
FK Budućnost - FK Podgorica 1-0(0-0)

Round 30 [25.06.2020]
Rudar Pljevlja - OFK Titograd 1-1(1-1)
FK Zeta - OFK Petrovac 1-1(0-1)
FK Kom Zlatica - FK Budućnost 0-1(0-0)
FK Podgorica - OFK Grbalj 2-0(0-0)
Iskra Danilovgrad - Sutjeska Nikšić 1-0(0-0)

Round 31 [30.06.2020]
Iskra Danilovgrad - FK Zeta 3-1(1-1)
Sutjeska Nikšić - Rudar Pljevlja 2-0(2-0)
OFK Titograd - FK Podgorica 0-0
OFK Grbalj - FK Kom Zlatica 0-1(0-0)
FK Budućnost - OFK Petrovac 1-1(0-0)

Please note: the league was abandoned on 07.07.2020 due to Covid-19 pandemic, table at abandonement being considered final.

Final Standings

									Home					Away				
					Total													
1. **FK Budućnost Podgorica**	31	23	4	4	63	-	26	73	13	2	1	30 - 11	10	2	3	33 - 15
2. FK Sutjeska Nikšić	31	15	10	6	57	-	31	55	10	4	2	32 - 11	5	6	4	25 - 20
3. FK Iskra Danilovgrad	31	15	8	8	43	-	33	53	11	2	3	28 - 13	4	6	5	15 - 20
4. FK Zeta Golubovci	31	9	14	8	29	-	30	41	6	7	2	16 - 11	3	7	6	13 - 19
5. FK Podgorica	31	8	16	7	34	-	27	40	5	9	1	20 - 12	3	7	6	14 - 15
6. OFK Petrovac	31	9	10	12	30	-	46	37	4	4	7	15 - 25	5	6	5	15 - 21
7. FK Rudar Pljevlja	31	10	5	16	38	-	57	35	6	3	6	24 - 28	4	2	10	14 - 29
8. OFK Titograd Podgorica (*Relegation Play-offs*)	31	7	10	14	29	-	38	31	4	3	9	15 - 21	3	7	5	14 - 17
9. FK Kom Zlatica (*Relegation Play-offs*)	31	6	11	14	36	-	45	29	3	7	5	20 - 18	3	4	9	16 - 27
10. OFK Grbalj Radanovići (*Relegated*)	31	4	10	17	23	-	49	22	2	8	6	12 - 20	2	2	11	11 - 29

Top goalscorers:	
10 Marko Ćetković	*FK Sutjeska Nikšić*
9 Draško Božović	*FK Budućnost Podgorica*
9 Igor Ivanović	*FK Budućnost Podgorica*
9 Boban Đorđević	*OFK Grbalj Radanovići*
9 Sava Gardašević	*FK Kom Zlatica*
9 Velizar Janketić	*FK Rudar Pljevlja*
9 Božo Marković	*FK Sutjeska Nikšić*

Promotion / Relegation Play-offs [10-14.07.2020]

FK Kom Zlatica - **FK Jezero Plav**	1-0(0-0)	1-3(0-1)
OFK Titograd Podgorica - FK Bokelj Kotor	0-1(0-1)	1-0 aet; 5-4 pen

FK Jezero Plav promoted to Prva Crnogorska Fudbal Liga 2020/2021.

NATIONAL CUP
Kup Crne Gore 2019/2020

First Round [28.08.-25.09.2019]

FK Rudar Pljevlja - FK Otrant Ulcinj	1-0	OFK Mladost Donja Gorica - FK Drezga	2-4
FK Sloga Radovići - OFK Titograd Podgorica	0-1	FK Bokelj Kotor - FK Jezero Plav	1-0
FK Zeta Golubovci - FK Dečić Tuzi	6-5 pen	FK Gorštak Kolašin - FK Petnjica	0-5
FK Grbalj Radanovići - FK Arsenal Tivat	4-0	Jedinstvo Bijelo Polje - FK KOM Podgorica	1-0
FK Cetinje - FK Podgorica	0-7	FK Mornar Bar - FK Iskra Danilovgrad	0-2
FK Komovi Andrijevica - FK Ibar Rožaje	0-4		

1/8-Finals [02/23.10.2019]

First Leg		Second Leg	
FK Grbalj Radanovići - FK Iskra Danilovgrad	3-1	FK Iskra Danilovgrad - FK Grbalj Radanovići	4-1
FK Ibar Rožaje - FK Zeta Golubovci	0-0	FK Zeta Golubovci - FK Ibar Rožaje	3-0
FK Sutjeska Nikšić - FK Lovćen Cetinje	4-0	FK Lovćen Cetinje - FK Sutjeska Nikšić	0-3
FK Petnjica - FK Podgorica	0-3 *awarded*	FK Podgorica - FK Petnjica	3-0 *awarded*
FK Rudar Pljevlja - FK Budućnost Podgorica	0-0	FK Budućnost Podgorica - FK Rudar Pljevlja	2-1
OFK Petrovac - FK Drezga	2-0	FK Drezga - OFK Petrovac	2-0 aet; 9-10pen
FK Bokelj Kotor - OFK Titograd Podgorica	1-2	OFK Titograd Podgorica - FK Bokelj Kotor	2-1

Quarter-Finals [06/27.11.-15.12.2019]

First Leg		Second Leg	
FK Jedinstvo Bijelo Polje - FK Budućnost Podgorica	0-1	FK Budućnost Podgorica - FK Jedinstvo Bijelo Polje	7-0
FK Zeta Golubovci - FK Sutjeska	0-0	FK Sutjeska Nikšić - FK Zeta Golubovci	1-0
OFK Titograd Podgorica - OFK Petrovac	0-0	OFK Petrovac - OFK Titograd Podgorica	2-0
FK Podgorica - FK Iskra Danilovgrad	0-0	FK Iskra Danilovgrad - FK Podgorica	1-1

Please note: the competition was cancelled before playing the Semi-Finals due to Covid-19 pandemic.

THE CLUBS 2019/2020

Fudbalski Klub Budućnost Podgorica

Founded: 1925
Stadium: Stadion pod Goricom, Podgorica (15,230)
Trainer: Branko Brnović — 08.08.1967
[09.11.2019] Mladen Milinković (SRB) — 14.05.1968

Goalkeepers:	DOB	M	(s)	G
Miloš Dragojević	03.02.1989	31		
Defenders:	**DOB**	**M**	**(s)**	**G**
Vladan Adžić	05.07.1987	11		
Dejan Boljević	30.05.1990	15	(2)	2
Slavko Damjanović	02.11.1992	15		1
Nikola Đurić (SRB)	06.11.1989	8	(2)	
Stefan Milić	06.07.2000	27		1
Periša Pešukić	07.12.1997	10	(1)	
Bojan Roganović	28.09.2000	7	(2)	
Aleksa Vidić (SRB)	29.09.1994	2	(1)	
Velimir Vlahović	20.01.2000		(1)	
Midfielders:	**DOB**	**M**	**(s)**	**G**
Dušan Bakić	23.02.1999	2	(3)	
Draško Božović	30.06.1988	24	(4)	9
Jovan Dašić	29.03.2003	1	(2)	
Petar Grbić	07.08.1988	19	(4)	6
Vasko Kalezić	14.03.1994		(6)	
Mladen Marstjepović	03.03.2003		(1)	

	DOB	M	(s)	G
Miloš Mijić (SRB)	22.11.1989	12	(7)	3
Luka Mirković	01.11.1990	28	(1)	
Marko Mrvaljević	05.06.2001	1	(2)	
Milos Raičković	02.12.1993	17	(4)	2
Vasilije Terzić	12.05.1999	15	(8)	1
Miloš Vučić	26.08.1995	20	(4)	2
Petar Vukčević	02.03.2001	7	(1)	
Forwards:	**DOB**	**M**	**(s)**	**G**
Balša Ćetković	20.12.2003		(1)	
Igor Ivanović	09.09.1990	23	(3)	9
Lazar Mijović	12.03.2003		(2)	
Panagiotis Moraitis (GRE)	01.02.1997	11		8
Damjan Mugoša (MDA)	16.05.2003		(1)	
Mihailo Perović	23.01.1997	7	(7)	4
Dušan Stoiljkovič (SRB)	05.09.1994	15	(12)	7
Vuk Strikovic	10.06.2002		(1)	
Balša Tošković	2003		(1)	
Aleksandar Vujačić	19.03.1990	3	(9)	3
Dejan Zarubica	11.04.1993	10	(9)	5

Omladinski fudbalski klub Grbalj Radanovići

Founded: 1995
Stadium: Stadion Donja Sutvara, Radanovići (1,500)
Trainer: Dušan Vlaisavljević — 05.02.1961
[09.10.2019] Marko Vidojević — 31.01.1975

Goalkeepers:	DOB	M	(s)	G
Mico Perović	04.07.1993	5		
Balša Popović	10.06.2000	26		
Defenders:	**DOB**	**M**	**(s)**	**G**
Anto Babić	25.01.2000	6	(2)	
Nemanja Kartal	17.07.1994	25	(2)	2
Bozidar Popovic	06.01.1995	1		
Bogdan Rašo	06.10.2000	5	(1)	
Eduard Serbul (UKR)	14.04.1993	9	(2)	
Janko Simović	02.04.1987	8		
Đorđije Vučićević	13.03.1999	5	(2)	
Marko Vukčević	07.06.1993	11		
Midfielders:	**DOB**	**M**	**(s)**	**G**
Marko Burzanović	13.01.1998	8	(4)	
Hristijan Denkovski (MKD)	15.04.1994	6	(4)	
Boban Đorđević	20.02.1997	11	(6)	9
Marko Đukanović	22.10.1996	22	(3)	1
Miomir Đuričković	26.07.1997	26	(3)	1
Vladan Kordić	22.06.1998	21	(4)	3

	DOB	M	(s)	G
Dejan Kotorac	31.05.1996	14	(2)	
Lee Joon-soo (KOR)	24.10.1996	2	(3)	
Aleksandar Macanović	16.04.1993	15	(2)	1
Marko Merdović	17.11.1998	24	(2)	
Miloš Milović	22.02.2002	1	(4)	
Aleksa Spaić	25.01.1999		(3)	
Nikola Stanišić	22.03.2000	1	(6)	
Đorđe Štešević	02.06.2002		(7)	
Andrej Vraneš	24.11.1999	7	(2)	
Miloš Vučetić	07.09.2000	2		
Miloš Zečević	28.01.1999	25	(4)	1
Forwards:	**DOB**	**M**	**(s)**	**G**
Radomir Đalović	29.10.1982	7	(4)	1
Benjamin Kacić	28.06.1991	5	(8)	
Yevhenyi Kovalenko (UKR)	11.08.1992	10	(2)	
Dejan Perović	19.08.2002	8	(11)	1
Miloš Perović (BIH)	12.02.1994	1	(5)	
Nemanja Petrov (SRB)	22.08.1995	14		1
Dejan Račić	15.07.1998	11	(5)	2

Fudbalski klub Iskra Danilovgrad

Founded: 1919
Stadium: Stadion „Braće Velašević", Danilovgrad (2,000)
Trainer: Aleksandar Nedović   05.09.1978

Goalkeepers:	DOB	M	(s)	G
Srđan Blažić	26.11.1982	30		
Stefan Spasojević	23.08.1993	1	(1)	
Defenders:	DOB	M	(s)	G
Miloš Drinčić	14.02.1999	27		
Milan Đurišić	11.04.1987	21	(7)	5
Nikola Karaklajić (SRB)	05.02.1995	20	(2)	2
Nikola Kumburović	13.11.1999	17	(2)	1
Miloš Lakić	21.12.1985	5	(2)	
Luka Malešević	01.08.1998	22	(1)	4
Luka Pejović	31.07.1985		(2)	
Midfielders:	DOB	M	(s)	G
Balša Boričić	07.01.1997	23	(3)	2
Goran Burzanović	04.08.1984		(2)	
Driton Camaj	07.03.1997	22	(7)	5
Miroje Jovanović	10.03.1987	18	(3)	1
Kōhei Katō (JPN)	14.06.1989	9	(1)	1
Ognjen Obradović	15.03.2000	20	(1)	3
Vladislav Rogošić	21.09.1994	12	(14)	2
Irfan Šahman	05.10.1993	28		1
Petar Tadić	04.08.2002		(1)	
Milan Vukotić	05.10.2002	20	(2)	2
Forwards:	DOB	M	(s)	G
Bogdan Mandić (MKD)	01.09.1998	3	(10)	1
Bogdan Milič	24.11.1987	16	(12)	3
Zoran Petrović	14.07.1997	7	(5)	2
Ivan Vuković	09.02.1987	16	(11)	5
Sho Yamamoto (JPN)	12.11.1996	4	(4)	

Fudbalski klub Kom Zlatica

Founded: 1958
Stadium: Stadion Zlatica, Podgorica (1,200)
Trainer: Viktor Trenevski (MKD)   08.10.1972
[19.02.2020] Radislav Dragičević (SRB)   13.09.1971

Goalkeepers:	DOB	M	(s)	G
Damir Ljuljanović	23.02.1992	9		
Marko Novović	24.11.1996	6	(1)	
Đorđije Pavličić	03.12.1996	15		
Stojan Vukčević	03.09.2000	1		
Defenders:	DOB	M	(s)	G
Jovica Blagojević (SRB)	26.08.1998	15		
Božidar Đukić	25.09.1997	9	(2)	
Miloš Milović	22.12.1995	25		
Filip Mitrović	17.11.1993	10	(1)	1
Marino Nuculović	28.11.2000	6	(2)	
Mihailo Petrović	12.12.1989	17	(2)	1
Miloš Radulović	06.08.1990	19	(2)	1
Midfielders:	DOB	M	(s)	G
Nikola Đurković	03.01.1994	23	(1)	1
Savo Gazivoda	18.07.1994	1	(4)	
Bojan Golubović	28.11.1986	14	(11)	
Ryosuke Iguchi (JPN)	19.02.2001	2	(2)	
Andrija Kaluđerović	29.10.1993	20	(2)	
Vuk Orlandić	05.01.1997	15	(1)	2
Žarko Popović	11.10.1999	25	(3)	5
Matija Račić	01.09.2001	9	(7)	
Arihiro Sentoku (JPN)	09.12.1998	21	(9)	3
Idriz Toskic	12.10.1995	4		
Nedeljko Vlahović	15.01.1984	10	(13)	2
Forwards:	DOB	M	(s)	G
Aleksandar Dabetić	08.07.1994	3	(1)	
Nikola Dimovski (MKD)	19.07.1999		(2)	
Sava Gardašević	27.01.1993	12	(14)	9
Žarko Grbović	20.06.1995		(4)	
Mirza Hot	06.08.1994	18	(5)	3
Petar Milić (SRB)	12.03.1998	3	(3)	
Goran Vujović	03.05.1987	20	(3)	6
Aleksandr Yarovenko (KAZ)	19.12.1987		(2)	
Nikola Zvrko	07.03.1995	9	(2)	1

Omladinski fudbalski klub Petrovac

Founded: 1969
Stadium: Stadion pod Malim brdom, Petrovac (1,630)
Trainer: Rudolf Marčić   21.08.1974
[23.09.2019] Nenad Vukčević   25.11.1974

Goalkeepers:	DOB	M	(s)	G
Sava Mugoša	10.07.1993	25		
Miroslav Orlic (AUT)	13.01.1993	6		
Defenders:	DOB	M	(s)	G
Zoran Mikijelj	13.12.1991	9	(1)	1
Aleksandar Milić	24.08.1998	23	(1)	
Blažo Rajović	26.03.1986	13		
Andrija Raznatovic	24.12.2000	17	(3)	2
Adrijan Rudović	10.06.1995	3	(2)	
Ryoya Tachibana (JPN)	04.04.1996	10	(6)	1
Nenad Vujović	02.01.1989	16	(2)	
Midfielders:	DOB	M	(s)	G
Zaim Divanović	09.12.2000		(1)	
Mirza Đurđević	06.09.2000	11	(6)	
Nikola Ivanović	20.03.1996	6	(6)	
Demir Kajević	20.04.1989	26	(2)	
Filip Kalačević	12.03.1994	2	(4)	
Miloš Kalezić	09.08.1993	29		7
Marko Marković	05.09.1987	26	(2)	1
Luka Medigović	03.04.1995	19	(1)	
Luka Merdović	06.10.1997	1	(7)	
Halil Muharemović	06.11.1997	19	(4)	3
Stefan Savić (BIH)	09.01.1995	4	(3)	1
Pavle Savković	15.08.1999	7	(6)	
Nikola Savović	30.09.1994	1	(2)	
Petar Vukčević	15.08.1987	30		3
Forwards:	DOB	M	(s)	G
Stefan Đorđević	16.11.1990	4	(10)	
Milovan Ilić	03.12.1997	1	(7)	
Luka Klikovac	01.06.1993	3	(7)	
Boris Kopitović	27.04.1995	14	(2)	8
Pavle Radunović (SRB)	26.05.1996		(3)	
Milivoje Raičević	21.07.1993	8	(1)	2
Igor Vukčević	07.11.1999	8	(1)	1

Fudbalski klub Podgorica

Founded: 1970
Stadium: DG Arena, Podgorica (4,300)
Trainer: Vojo Pejović   27.05.1965

Goalkeepers:	DOB	M	(s)	G
Jasmin Agović	13.02.1991	31		
Defenders:	DOB	M	(s)	G
Bojan Aligrudić	08.02.1995	20	(4)	
Matija Božanović	13.04.1994	22	(2)	2
Nikola Čelebić	04.07.1989	17	(2)	1
Darko Đajić (BIH)	30.08.1992	28		1
Ivan Gazivoda	20.04.1994	3		
Milija Golubović	25.04.1996	15	(3)	1
Stefan Marjanović (SRB)	25.07.1994	4	(3)	
Jasmin Mecinović (MKD)	22.10.1990		(2)	
Jovan Nikolić	21.07.1991	10	(1)	
Radule Živković (SRB)	20.10.1990	7		
Midfielders:	DOB	M	(s)	G
Anđelko Jovanović	18.11.1999	15	(5)	2
Luka Maraš	24.05.1996	12	(5)	1
Jovan Pajović	28.08.1996	25		
Filip Šćekić	28.12.1999	18	(2)	
Balša Sekulić	10.06.1998	13	(16)	5
Petar Sekulović	14.08.1998	1	(1)	
Keita Suzuki (JPN)	20.12.1997	21	(7)	2
Nikola Tripković	26.10.2000	1	(5)	
Jovan Vujović (BIH)	20.01.1996	20	(5)	5
Forwards:	DOB	M	(s)	G
Ivan Bulatović	16.02.1996	6	(8)	
Šaleta Kordić	19.04.1993	16	(11)	6
Lazar Vučićević	05.01.1998	4	(2)	
Nikola Vujnović	11.01.1997	26	(5)	7
Nikola Zvrko	07.03.1995	6	(6)	

Fudbalski klub Rudar Pljevlja

Founded: 1920
Stadium: Stadion pod Golubinjom, Pljevlja (10,000)
Trainer: Edis Mulalić (BIH)   23.10.1975

Goalkeepers:	DOB	M	(s)	G
Ervin Helić	22.07.2002	20		
Amar Kaltak	16.10.1998	5		
Branislav Ružić (BIH)	02.04.1989	6		
Defenders:	**DOB**	**M**	**(s)**	**G**
Igor Ćuković	06.06.1993	30		2
Nemanja Marković (SRB)	03.11.1992	11		
Brajan Matanović			(1)	
Slobodan Perišić	04.10.2000	9	(6)	
Željko Tomašević	05.04.1988	24	(2)	
Midfielders:	**DOB**	**M**	**(s)**	**G**
Jakša Bajčetić	09.07.2002		(1)	
Kristijan Ernec	19.01.2003	2	(7)	
Janko Gogić	22.02.2000	1	(2)	
Aleksa Golubović	19.11.2002	1	(11)	
Velizar Janketić	15.11.1996	25		9

	DOB	M	(s)	G
Marko Krasić (SRB)	01.12.1985	19	(2)	3
Danilo Marković	15.07.1998	28		1
Marko Mujović	03.05.2000		(2)	
Ivan Pupović	11.07.2001	1		
Ivan Racković	13.09.1994	15	(9)	1
Ermin Seratlić	21.08.1990	29		1
Nikola Stijepović	02.11.1993	12		
Berin Tahirović	19.11.1999	7	(9)	
Marko Vuković	20.03.1996	15	(1)	1
Forwards:	**DOB**	**M**	**(s)**	**G**
Predrag Kašćelan	30.06.1990	30		1
Milivoje Mrdak	17.02.1993	2	(21)	
Tiago (BRA)	30.05.1989	25		5
Ivan Vasovic	11.11.1996		(5)	
Vule Vujačić	20.03.1988	24		8

Fudbalski klub Sutjeska Nikšić

Founded: 1927
Stadium: Stadion kraj Bistrice, Nikšić (6,180)
Trainer: Nikola Rakojević   15.01.1958

Goalkeepers:	DOB	M	(s)	G
Vladan Giljen	07.12.1989	21		
Suad Ličina	08.02.1995	10		
Defenders:	**DOB**	**M**	**(s)**	**G**
Darko Bulatović	05.09.1989	23	(1)	1
Stefan Cicmil	16.08.1990	3	(1)	
Bojan Ciger (SRB)	18.06.1994	13	(1)	
Dragan Grivić	12.02.1996	21	(1)	2
Nemanja Nedić	06.04.1995	24	(1)	
Aleksandar Šofranac	21.10.1990	26	(1)	
Marko Vučić	30.12.1996	25	(5)	6
Midfielders:	**DOB**	**M**	**(s)**	**G**
Vladan Bubanja	21.02.1999	18	(6)	1
Marko Ćetković	10.07.1986	29	(2)	10
Novica Erakovic	12.11.1999	16	(4)	1

	DOB	M	(s)	G
Nikola Janjić	14.07.2002	1	(7)	
Branislav Janković	08.02.1992	23	(2)	2
Damir Kojašević	03.06.1987	23	(1)	8
Aleksa Marušić	08.06.1999	10	(7)	3
Milutin Osmajić	25.07.1999	12		1
Milovan Petrovikj (MKD)	23.01.1990	2	(6)	
Miljan Vlaisavljević	16.04.1991	4	(10)	1
Dušan Vuković	27.07.2003		(1)	
Forwards:	**DOB**	**M**	**(s)**	**G**
Marko Bojović	15.06.2002		(2)	
Bojan Božović	02.02.1985	6	(9)	2
Balša Dubljević	02.12.2001	4	(5)	
Božo Marković	26.10.1989	10	(16)	9
Stefan Nikolić	16.04.1990	17	(8)	8
Marko Vuković	20.03.1996		(4)	

Omladinski fudbalski klub Titograd Podgorica

Founded: 1951
Stadium: Stadion FK Mladost, Podgorica (2,000)
Trainer: Dragoljub Đuretić   07.06.1955
[19.11.2019] Zoran Govedarica (SRB)   14.04.1968

Goalkeepers:	DOB	M	(s)	G
Saša Ivanović	26.06.1984	19		
Sergej Joksimović	16.08.2002	12	(1)	
Defenders:	**DOB**	**M**	**(s)**	**G**
Chukwujekwu Ajanah-Chinedu (NGA)	23.10.2000	18	(2)	2
Ermin Alić	23.02.1992	10		1
Balša Banović	26.01.1998	25	(3)	
Amir Muzurović	17.10.2001	9	(1)	
Jovan Nikolić	21.07.1991	16		1
Ivan Novović	26.04.1989	29		3
Bojan Roganović	28.09.2000	8	(1)	
Marko Roganović	21.06.1996	30		
Radule Živković (SRB)	20.10.1990	16	(2)	
Midfielders:	**DOB**	**M**	**(s)**	**G**
Miloš Brnović	26.04.2000	19	(4)	1
Yu Horike (JPN)	02.06.2001	3	(2)	
Petar Mališić	04.09.2001		(1)	

	DOB	M	(s)	G
Marko Matanović	17.07.2000	1	(7)	
Luka Merdović	14.03.1989	13	(12)	4
Marko Miličković	31.03.1998	12	(8)	2
Vojin Pavlović	09.11.1993	10	(6)	
Ognjen Peličić	05.02.1999	9	(1)	
Mirko Raičević	22.03.1982	9	(2)	
Forwards:	**DOB**	**M**	**(s)**	**G**
Admir Adrović	08.05.1988	11	(1)	4
Ivan Bojović	20.02.2001	3	(7)	
Radomir Đalović	29.10.1982	10	(6)	
Ognjen Gašević	02.04.2002	10	(5)	1
Nikola Gluščević	11.06.2001	1	(4)	
Lucas Gomes (BRA)	21.05.1994	5	(5)	
Mendy Mamadou (SEN)	04.10.1998	20	(4)	1
Alden Škrijelj	18.10.2000	6	(9)	1
Igor Vukčević	07.11.1999	7	(3)	3

Fudbalski klub Zeta Golubovci

Founded: 1927
Stadium: Stadion Trešnjica, Golubovci (5,000)
Trainer: Dejan Roganović   28.10.1972

Goalkeepers:	DOB	M	(s)	G
Zoran Aković	26.12.1985	28		
Petar Radulović	10.11.2001	2	(2)	
Danilo Raičević	29.08.1999	1		
Defenders:	**DOB**	**M**	**(s)**	**G**
Jovan Baošić	07.07.1995	27		2
Zvonko Ceklić	11.04.1999	13	(4)	
Ognjen Đinović	12.09.2003	1	(5)	
Nemanja Đurović	18.12.2000		(3)	
Balša Goranović	06.02.1998	15	(6)	1
Stefan Knežević	07.05.1997		(2)	
Stefan Puletić	28.03.2000		(1)	
Nemanja Sekulić	29.03.1994	29		1
Midfielders:	**DOB**	**M**	**(s)**	**G**
Vuk Ajković	10.10.1998	1		

	DOB	M	(s)	G
Davor Kontić	30.10.1999		(4)	
Srdjan Krstović	05.08.2000	22	(8)	6
Lazar Lambulić	12.03.2000	3	(16)	
Matija Lambulić	12.03.2003	9	(18)	
Goran Milojko	05.01.1994	30		2
Elom Nya-Vedji (TOG)	24.11.1997	11		3
Alphonse Soppo (CMR)	15.05.1985	25	(1)	1
Amel Tuzović	31.03.1995	26		
Đorđije Vukčević	18.08.1996	7	(8)	2
Stefan Vukčević	11.04.1997	27	(1)	1
Alex Yamoah (GHA)	10.01.1995	18	(8)	3
Forwards:	**DOB**	**M**	**(s)**	**G**
Armin Bošnjak	20.04.1994	21	(7)	3
Mijat Lambulić	14.11.2001	3	(4)	
Ivan Vukčević	04.12.2001	23	(3)	4

1.	FK Dečić Tuzi (*Promoted*)	30	17	10	3	61	-	33	61
2.	FK Jezero Plav (*Promotion Play-offs*)	30	15	6	9	38	-	28	51
3.	FK Bokelj Kotor (*Promotion Play-offs*)	30	14	7	9	45	-	28	49
4.	FK Jedinstvo Bijelo Polje	30	12	10	8	40	-	32	46
5.	FK Ibar Rožaje	30	11	8	11	41	-	43	41
6.	FK Arsenal Tivat	30	9	9	12	38	-	41	36
7.	FK Mornar Bar	30	8	11	11	36	-	44	35
8.	FK Drezga	30	8	9	13	31	-	47	33
9.	FK Lovćen Cetinje (*Relegated*)	30	6	11	13	31	-	43	29
10.	FK Otrant-Olympic Ulcinj (*Relegated*)	30	7	5	18	30	-	52	26

NATIONAL TEAM

INTERNATIONAL MATCHES
(16.07.2019 – 15.07.2020)

05.09.2019	Podgorica	Montenegro - Hungary	2-1(1-1)	(F)
10.09.2019	Podgorica	Montenegro - Czech Republic	0-3(0-0)	(ECQ)
11.10.2019	Podgorica	Montenegro - Bulgaria	0-0	(ECQ)
14.10.2019	Prishtina	Kosovo - Montenegro	2-0(2-0)	(ECQ)
14.11.2019	London	England - Montenegro	7-0(5-0)	(ECQ)
19.11.2019	Podgorica	Montenegro - Belarus	2-0(2-0)	(F)

05.09.2019   MONTENEGRO - HUNGARY   2-1(1-1)   Friendly International
Stadion pod Goricom, Podgorica; Referee: Dimitar Mečkarovski (North Macedonia); Attendance: 3,370
MNE: Milan Mijatović (46.Danijel Petković), Žarko Tomašević, Risto Radunović, Marko Simić (66.Dušan Lagator), Adam Marušić (55.Stefan Mugoša), Nebojša Kosović (59.Deni Hočko), Nikola Vukčević (77.Branislav Janković), Aleksandar Boljević, Vukan Savićević, Sead Hakšabanović (72.Vladimir Jovović), Fatos Bećiraj (Cap). Trainer: Faruk Hadžibegić.
Goals: Nebojša Kosović (32), Stefan Mugoša (75 penalty).

10.09.2019   MONTENEGRO - CZECH REPUBLIC   0-3(0-0)   16th EC. Qualifiers
Stadion pod Goricom, Podgorica; Referee: Ali Palabıyık (Turkey); Attendance: 5,951
MNE: Danijel Petković, Marko Vešović, Žarko Tomašević, Risto Radunović (73.Fatos Bećiraj), Adam Marušić, Nebojša Kosović (73.Vukan Savićević), Deni Hočko, Nikola Vukčević (Cap) (68.Marko Bakić), Aleksandar Boljević, Dušan Lagator, Stefan Mugoša. Trainer: Faruk Hadžibegić.

11.10.2019   MONTENEGRO - BULGARIA   0-0   16th EC. Qualifiers
Stadion pod Goricom, Podgorica; Referee: Andreas Ekberg (Sweden); Attendance: 2,743
MNE: Danijel Petković, Stefan Savić (Cap) (39.Nebojša Kosović), Marko Simić, Adam Marušić, Nemanja Sekulić, Nikola Vukčević, Aleksandar Boljević, Dušan Lagator, Vladimir Jovović (67.Marko Janković), Sead Hakšabanović (82.Luka Mirković), Fatos Bećiraj. Trainer: Faruk Hadžibegić.

14.10.2019   KOSOVO - MONTENEGRO   2-0(2-0)   16th EC. Qualifiers
Stadiumi „Fadil Vokrri", Prishtina; Referee: Artur Manuel Soares Dias (Portugal); Attendance: 12,494
MNE: Danijel Petković (15.Milan Mijatović), Darko Bulatović, Marko Simić, Adam Marušić, Aleksandar Šćekić, Nebojša Kosović (46.Fatos Bećiraj), Nikola Vukčević (Cap), Aleksandar Boljević, Dušan Lagator, Vladimir Jovović (74.Marko Janković), Stefan Mugoša. Trainer: Faruk Hadžibegić.

14.11.2019   ENGLAND - MONTENEGRO   7-0(5-0)   16th EC. Qualifiers
Wembley Stadium, London; Referee: Antonio Miguel Mateu Lahoz (Spain); Attendance: 77,277
MNE: Milan Mijatović, Marko Vešović, Risto Radunović (46.Momčilo Raspopović), Marko Simić, Aleksandar Šofranac, Deni Hočko, Nikola Vukčević, Dušan Lagator, Vladimir Jovović (65.Marko Janković), Sead Hakšabanović (74.Aleksandar Boljević), Fatos Bećiraj (Cap). Trainer: Faruk Hadžibegić.

19.11.2019   MONTENEGRO - BELARUS   2-0(2-0)   Friendly International
Stadion Pod Goricom, Podgorica; Referee: Trustin Farrugia Cann (Malta); Attendance: 1,000
MNE: Matija Šarkić, Marko Vešović, Marko Simić (63.Boris Kopitović), Momčilo Raspopović, Igor Vujačić, Damir Kojašević (73.Dušan Lagator), Nikola Vukčević (Cap) (63.Deni Hočko; 77.Vladimir Jovović), Aleksandar Boljević, Branislav Janković, Sead Hakšabanović (77.Darko Bulatović), Stefan Mugoša (72.Fatos Bećiraj). Trainer: Faruk Hadžibegić.
Goals: Stefan Mugoša (9), Sead Hakšabanović (14).

NATIONAL TEAM PLAYERS
(16.07.2019 – 15.07.2020)

Name	DOB	Caps	Goals	2019/2020:	Club
Goalkeepers					
Milan MIJATOVIĆ	26.07.1987	9	0	2019:	PFC Levski Sofia (BUL)
Danijel PETKOVIĆ	25.05.1993	21	0	2019:	Angers SCO (FRA)
Matija ŠARKIĆ	23.07.1997	1	0	2019:	Livingston FC (SCO)
Defenders					
Darko BULATOVIĆ	05.09.1989	2	0	2019:	FK Sutjeska Nikšić
Boris KOPITOVIĆ	17.09.1994	7	1	2019:	FC BATE Borisov (BLR)
Adam MARUŠIĆ	17.10.1992	33	0	2019:	SS Lazio Roma (ITA)
Risto RADUNOVIĆ	04.05.1992	5	0	2019:	AFC Astra Giurgiu (ROU)
Momčilo RASPOPOVIĆ	18.03.1994	2	0	2019:	HNK Rijeka (CRO)
Stefan SAVIĆ	08.01.1991	52	5	2019:	Club Atlético de Madrid (ESP)
Marko SIMIĆ	16.06.1987	41	1	2019:	FC Pakhtakor Tashkent (UZB)
Aleksandar ŠOFRANAC	21.10.1990	5	0	2019:	FK Sutjeska Nikšić
Žarko TOMAŠEVIĆ	22.02.1990	38	4	2019:	Astana FC (KAZ)
Igor VUJAČIĆ	08.08.1994	3	0	2019:	FK Partizan Beograd (SRB)
Midfielders					
Marko BAKIĆ	01.11.1993	15	0	2019:	Royal Excel Mouscron (BEL)
Aleksandar BOLJEVIĆ	12.12.1995	17	0	2019:	R Standard Liège (BEL)
Sead HAKŠABANOVIĆ	04.05.1999	8	1	2019:	IFK Norrköping (SWE)
Deni HOČKO	22.04.1994	5	0	2019:	Royal Excel Mouscron (BEL)
Branislav JANKOVIĆ	13.06.1992	5	0	2019:	FK Sutjeska Nikšić
Marko JANKOVIĆ	09.07.1995	21	1	2019:	SPAL Ferrara (ITA)
Vladimir JOVOVIĆ	26.10.1994	32	0	2019:	FK Jablonec (CZE)
Damir KOJAŠEVIĆ	03.06.1987	9	1	2019.	FK Sutjeska Nikšić
Nebojša KOSOVIĆ	24.02.1995	18	1	2019:	FC Kairat Almaty (KAZ)
Dušan LAGATOR	29.03.1994	6	0	2019:	PFK Sochi (RUS)
Luka MIRKOVIĆ	01.11.1990	3	0	2019:	FK Budućnost Podgorica
Vukan SAVIĆEVIĆ	29.01.1994	4	0	2019:	Wisła Kraków (POL)
Nemanja SEKULIĆ	29.03.1994	1	0	2019:	FK Zeta Golubovci
Aleksandar ŠĆEKIĆ	12.12.1991	17	0	2019:	FK Partizan Beograd (SRB)
Marko VEŠOVIĆ	28.08.1991	30	2	2019:	Legia Warszawa (POL)
Nikola VUKČEVIĆ	13.12.1991	40	1	2019:	Levante UD Valencia (ESP)
Forwards					
Fatos BEĆIRAJ	22.05.1988	69	9	2019:	Maccabi Netanya FC (ISR)
Stefan MUGOŠA	23.02.1992	35	10	2019:	Incheon United FC (KOR)
National team coach					
Faruk HADŽIBEGIĆ [from 25.07.2019]		07.10.1957	6 M; 2 W; 1 D; 3 L; 4-13		

NETHERLANDS

The Country:
Nederland (Netherlands)
Capital: Amsterdam
Surface: 41,543 km²
Inhabitants: 17,418,808 [2020]
Time: UTC+1

The FA:
Koninklijke Nederlandse Voetbalbond
Woudenbergseweg 56-58 Postbus 515 3700, Am Zeist
Tel: +31 343 499 201
Foundation date: 1889
Member of FIFA since: 1904
Member of UEFA since: 1954
Website: www.knvb.nl

NATIONAL TEAM RECORDS

RECORDS

First international match:	30.04.1905, Antwerpen: Belgium – Netherlands 1-4
Most international caps:	Wesley Benjamin Sneijder - 134 caps (2003-2018)
Most international goals:	Robin van Persie - 50 goals / 102 caps (2005-2017)

UEFA EUROPEAN CHAMPIONSHIP

1960	Did not enter
1964	Qualifiers
1968	Qualifiers
1972	Qualifiers
1976	Final Tournament (3rd Place)
1980	Final Tournament (Group Stage)
1984	Qualifiers
1988	**Final Tournament (Winners)**
1992	Final Tournament (Semi-Finals)
1996	Final Tournament (Quarter-Finals)
2000	Final Tournament (Semi-Finals)
2004	Final Tournament (Semi-Finals)
2008	Final Tournament (Quarter-Finals)
2012	Final Tournament (Group Stage)
2016	Qualifiers
2020	*Final Tournament (Qualified)*

FIFA WORLD CUP

1930	Did not enter
1934	Final Tournament (1st Round)
1938	Final Tournament (1st Round)
1950	Did not enter
1954	Did not enter
1958	Qualifiers
1962	Qualifiers
1966	Qualifiers
1970	Qualifiers
1974	Final Tournament (Runners-up)
1978	Final Tournament (Runners-up)
1982	Qualifiers
1986	Qualifiers
1990	Final Tournament (2nd Round of 16)
1994	Final Tournament (Quarter-Finals)
1998	Final Tournament (4th Place)
2002	Qualifiers
2006	Final Tournament (2nd Round of 16)
2010	Final Tournament (Runners-up)
2014	Final Tournament (3rd Place)
2018	Qualifiers

OLYMPIC TOURNAMENTS

1908	3rd Place
1912	3rd Place
1920	3rd Place
1924	4th Place
1928	1/8 - Finals
1936	Did not enter
1948	1/8 - Finals
1952	Qualifiers
1956	Did not enter
1960	Qualifiers
1964	Qualifiers
1968	Qualifiers
1972	Qualifiers
1976	Qualifiers
1980	Qualifiers
1984	Qualifiers
1988	Qualifiers
1992	Qualifiers
1996	Qualifiers
2000	Qualifiers
2004	Qualifiers
2008	Quarter-Finals
2012	Qualifiers
2016	Qualifiers

UEFA NATIONS LEAGUE

2018/2019 – League A; Final Tournament – 4th Place

FIFA CONFEDERATIONS CUP 1992-2017

None

NETHERLANDIAN CLUB HONOURS IN EUROPEAN CLUB COMPETITIONS:

European Champion Clubs' Cup (1956-1992) / UEFA Champions League (1993-2020)		
AFC Ajax Amsterdam	4	1970/1971, 1971/1972, 1972/1973, 1994/1995
Feyenoord Rotterdam	1	1969/1970
PSV Eindhoven	1	1987/1988
Fairs Cup (1858-1971) / UEFA Cup (1972-2009) / UEFA Europa League (2010-2020)		
Feyenoord Rotterdam	2	1973/1974, 2001/2002
PSV Eindhoven	1	1977/1978
AFC Ajax Amsterdam	1	1991/1992
UEFA Super Cup (1972-2019)		
AFC Ajax Amsterdam	2	1973, 1995
European Cup Winners' Cup 1961-1999		
AFC Ajax Amsterdam	1	1986/1987

defunct competition

NATIONAL COMPETITIONS
TABLE OF HONOURS

	CHAMPIONS*	CUP WINNERS	BEST GOALSCORERS	
1888/1889	VV Concordia Rotterdam	-	-	
1889/1890	HFC Haarlem	-	-	
1890/1891	HVV Den Haag	-	-	
1891/1892	RAP Amsterdam	-	-	
1892/1893	HFC Haarlem	-	-	
1893/1894	RAP Amsterdam	-	-	
1894/1895	HFC Haarlem	-	-	
1895/1896	HVV Den Haag	-	-	
1896/1897	RAP Amsterdam	-	-	
1897/1898	RAP Amsterdam	-	-	
1898/1899	RAP Amsterdam	RAP Amsterdam	-	
1899/1900	HVV Den Haag	Velocitas Breda	-	
1900/1901	HVV Den Haag	HBS Craeyenhout	-	
1901/1902	HVV Den Haag	Haarlem	-	
1902/1903	HVV Den Haag	HVV Den Haag	-	
1903/1904	HBS Craeyenhout	HFC Haarlem	-	
1904/1905	HVV Den Haag	VOC Rotterdam	-	
1905/1906	HBS Craeyenhout	VV Concordia Rotterdam	-	
1906/1907	HVV Den Haag	VOC Rotterdam	-	
1907/1908	Quick Den Haag	HBS Craeyenhout 2	-	
1908/1909	Sparta Rotterdam	Quick Den Haag 2	-	
1909/1910	HVV Den Haag	Quick Den Haag 2	-	
1910/1911	Sparta Rotterdam	Quick Den Haag	-	
1911/1912	Sparta Rotterdam	HFC Haarlem	-	
1912/1913	Sparta Rotterdam	Koninklijke HFC Haarlem	-	
1913/1914	HVV Den Haag	Dordrechtsche FC	-	
1914/1915	Sparta Rotterdam	Koninklijke HFC Haarlem	-	
1915/1916	Willem II Tilburg	Quick Den Haag	-	
1916/1917	Go Ahead Eagles Deventer	AFC Ajax Amsterdam	-	
1917/1918	AFC Ajax Amsterdam	Racing Club Heemstede	-	
1918/1919	AFC Ajax Amsterdam	*No competition*	-	
1919/1920	Be Quick 1887 Groningen	CVV Rotterdam	-	
1920/1921	NAC Breda	Schoten Harlem	-	
1921/1922	Go Ahead Eagles Deventer	*No competition*	-	
1922/1923	Racing Club Heemstede	*No competition*	-	
1923/1924	SC Feijenoord Rotterdam	*No competition*	-	
1924/1925	HBS Craeyenhout	Zaanlandsche FC	-	
1925/1926	SC Enschede	LONGA Lichtenvoorde	-	
1926/1927	Heracles Almelo	VUC Den Haag	-	
1927/1928	SC Feijenoord Rotterdam	Racing Club Heemstede	-	
1928/1929	PSV Eindhoven	*No competition*	-	
1929/1930	Go Ahead Eagles Deventer	SC Feijenoord Rotterdam	-	
1930/1931	AFC Ajax Amsterdam	*No competition*	-	
1931/1932	AFC Ajax Amsterdam	DFC	-	
1932/1933	Go Ahead Eagles Deventer	*No competition*	-	
1933/1934	AFC Ajax Amsterdam	Velocitas Groningen	-	
1934/1935	PSV Eindhoven	SC Feijenoord Rotterdam	-	
1935/1936	SC Feijenoord Rotterdam	Roermond FC	-	
1936/1937	AFC Ajax Amsterdam	FC Eindhoven	-	
1937/1938	SC Feijenoord Rotterdam	VSV Velsen	-	
1938/1939	AFC Ajax Amsterdam	FC Wageningen	-	
1939/1940	SC Feijenoord Rotterdam	*No competition*	-	
1940/1941	Heracles Almelo	*No competition*	-	
1941/1942	ADO Den Haag	*No competition*	-	
1942/1943	ADO Den Haag	AFC Ajax Amsterdam	-	
1943/1944	AVV De Volewijckers Amsterdam	Willem II Tilburg	-	
1944/1945	*No competition*	*No competition*	-	
1945/1946	HFC Haarlem	*No competition*	-	
1946/1947	AFC Ajax Amsterdam	*No competition*	-	
1947/1948	BVV Den Bosch	FC Wageningen	-	
1948/1949	Schiedamse VV	Quick 1888 Nijmegen	-	
1949/1950	SV Limburgia Brunssum	PSV Eindhoven	-	
1950/1951	PSV Eindhoven	*No competition*	-	
1951/1952	Willem II Tilburg	*No competition*	-	
1952/1953	Racing Club Heemstede	*No competition*	-	
1953/1954	FC Eindhoven	*No competition*	-	
1954/1955	Willem II Tilburg	*No competition*	-	
1955/1956	Rapid JC Kerkrade	*No competition*	-	
1956/1957	AFC Ajax Amsterdam	Fortuna '54 Geleen	Coenraad Henrik Dillen (PSV Eindhoven)	43
1957/1958	VV DOS Utrecht	Sparta Rotterdam	Leonard Canjels (NAC Breda)	32

1958/1959	Sparta Rotterdam	VVV	Leonard Canjels (NAC Breda)	34
1959/1960	AFC Ajax Amsterdam	*No competition*	Hendrik Groot (AFC Ajax Amsterdam)	38
1960/1961	SC Feijenoord Rotterdam	AFC Ajax Amsterdam	Hendrik Groot (AFC Ajax Amsterdam)	41
1961/1962	SC Feijenoord Rotterdam	Sparta Rotterdam	Dick Tol (FC Volendam)	27
1962/1963	PSV Eindhoven	Willem II Tilburg	Pierre Kerkhofs (PSV Eindhoven)	22
1963/1964	DWS Amsterdam	Fortuna '54 Geleen	Frans Geurtsen (DWS Amsterdam)	28
1964/1965	SC Feijenoord Rotterdam	SC Feijenoord Rotterdam	Frans Geurtsen (DWS Amsterdam)	23
1965/1966	AFC Ajax Amsterdam	Sparta Rotterdam	Wilhelmus Martinus Leonardus Johannes van der Kuijlen (PSV Eindhoven) Piet Kruiver (SC Feijenoord Rotterdam)	23
1966/1967	AFC Ajax Amsterdam	AFC Ajax Amsterdam	Hendrik Johannes Cruijff (AFC Ajax Amsterdam)	33
1967/1968	AFC Ajax Amsterdam	ADO Den Haag	Ove Kindvall (SWE, SC Feijenoord Rotterdam)	28
1968/1969	SC Feijenoord Rotterdam	SC Feijenoord Rotterdam	Dirk Wouter Johannes van Dijk (FC Twente Enschede) Bengt Ove Kindvall (SWE, SC Feijenoord Rotterdam)	30
1969/1970	AFC Ajax Amsterdam	AFC Ajax Amsterdam	Wilhelmus Martinus Leonardus Johannes van der Kuijlen (PSV Eindhoven)	26
1970/1971	SC Feijenoord Rotterdam	AFC Ajax Amsterdam	Bengt Ove Kindvall (SWE, SC Feijenoord Rotterdam)	24
1971/1972	AFC Ajax Amsterdam	AFC Ajax Amsterdam	Hendrik Johannes Cruijff (AFC Ajax Amsterdam)	25
1972/1973	AFC Ajax Amsterdam	NAC Breda	Franciscus Janssens (NEC Nijmegen) Willy Brokamp (MVV Maastricht)	18
1973/1974	SC Feyenoord Rotterdam	PSV Eindhoven	Wilhelmus Martinus Leonardus Johannes van der Kuijlen (PSV Eindhoven)	27
1974/1975	PSV Eindhoven	FC Den Haag	Geertruida Maria Geels (AFC Ajax Amsterdam)	30
1975/1976	PSV Eindhoven	PSV Eindhoven	Geertruida Maria Geels (AFC Ajax Amsterdam)	29
1976/1977	AFC Ajax Amsterdam	FC Twente Enschede	Geertruida Maria Geels (AFC Ajax Amsterdam)	34
1977/1978	PSV Eindhoven	AZ'67 Alkmaar	Geertruida Maria Geels (AFC Ajax Amsterdam)	30
1978/1979	AFC Ajax Amsterdam	AFC Ajax Amsterdam	Cornelis Kist (AZ'67 Alkmaar)	34
1979/1980	AFC Ajax Amsterdam	SC Feyenoord Rotterdam	Cornelis Kist (AZ'67 Alkmaar)	27
1980/1981	AZ'67 Alkmaar '67	AZ'67 Alkmaar	Geertruida Maria Geels (Sparta Rotterdam)	22
1981/1982	AFC Ajax Amsterdam	AZ'67 Alkmaar	Willem Cornelis Nicolaas Kieft (AFC Ajax Amsterdam)	32
1982/1983	AFC Ajax Amsterdam	AFC Ajax Amsterdam	Peter Houtman (SC Feyenoord Rotterdam)	30
1983/1984	SC Feyenoord Rotterdam	SC Feyenoord Rotterdam	Marcel van Basten (AFC Ajax Amsterdam)	28
1984/1985	AFC Ajax Amsterdam	FC Utrecht	Marcel van Basten (AFC Ajax Amsterdam)	22
1985/1986	PSV Eindhoven	AFC Ajax Amsterdam	Marcel van Basten (AFC Ajax Amsterdam)	37
1986/1987	PSV Eindhoven	AFC Ajax Amsterdam	Marcel van Basten (AFC Ajax Amsterdam)	31
1987/1988	PSV Eindhoven	PSV Eindhoven	Willem Cornelis Nicolaas Kieft (PSV Eindhoven)	29
1988/1989	PSV Eindhoven	PSV Eindhoven	Romário de Souza Faria (BRA, PSV Eindhoven)	19
1989/1990	AFC Ajax Amsterdam	PSV Eindhoven	Romário de Souza Faria (BRA, PSV Eindhoven)	23
1990/1991	PSV Eindhoven	SC Feyenoord Rotterdam	Romário de Souza Faria (BRA, PSV Eindhoven) Dennis Nicolaas Maria Bergkamp (AFC Ajax Amsterdam)	25
1991/1992	PSV Eindhoven	SC Feyenoord Rotterdam	Dennis Nicolaas Maria Bergkamp (AFC Ajax Amsterdam)	24
1992/1993	SC Feyenoord Rotterdam	AFC Ajax Amsterdam	Dennis Nicolaas Maria Bergkamp (AFC Ajax Amsterdam)	26
1993/1994	AFC Ajax Amsterdam	SC Feyenoord Rotterdam	Jari Olavi Litmanen (FIN, AFC Ajax Amsterdam)	26
1994/1995	AFC Ajax Amsterdam	SC Feyenoord Rotterdam	Ronaldo Luís Nazário de Lima (BRA, PSV Eindhoven)	30
1995/1996	AFC Ajax Amsterdam	PSV Eindhoven	Luc Gilbert Cyrille Nilis (BEL, PSV Eindhoven)	21
1996/1997	PSV Eindhoven	Roda JC Kerkrade	Luc Gilbert Cyrille Nilis (BEL, PSV Eindhoven)	21
1997/1998	AFC Ajax Amsterdam	AFC Ajax Amsterdam	Nikolaos Machlas (GRE, SBV Vitesse Arnhem)	34
1998/1999	SC Feyenoord Rotterdam	AFC Ajax Amsterdam	Rutgerus Johannes Martinus van Nistelrooy (PSV Eindhoven)	31
1999/2000	PSV Eindhoven	Roda JC Kerkrade	Rutgerus Johannes Martinus van Nistelrooy (PSV Eindhoven)	29
2000/2001	PSV Eindhoven	FC Twente Enschede	Mateja Kežman (SRB, PSV Eindhoven)	24
2001/2002	AFC Ajax Amsterdam	AFC Ajax Amsterdam	Petrus Ferdinandus Johannes van Hooijdonk (SC Feyenoord Rotterdam)	24
2002/2003	PSV Eindhoven	FC Utrecht	Mateja Kežman (SRB, PSV Eindhoven)	35
2003/2004	AFC Ajax Amsterdam	FC Utrecht	Mateja Kežman (SRB, PSV Eindhoven)	31
2004/2005	PSV Eindhoven	PSV Eindhoven	Dirk Kuyt (SC Feyenoord Rotterdam)	29
2005/2006	PSV Eindhoven	AFC Ajax Amsterdam	Dirk Jan Klaas Huntelaar (SC Heerenveen/AFC Ajax Amsterdam)	33
2006/2007	PSV Eindhoven	AFC Ajax Amsterdam	Afonso Alves Martins Júnior (BRA, SC Heerenveen)	34
2007/2008	PSV Eindhoven	SC Feyenoord Rotterdam	Dirk Jan Klaas Huntelaar (AFC Ajax Amsterdam)	33
2008/2009	AZ Alkmaar	SC Heerenveen	Mounir El Hamdaoui (MAR, AZ Alkmaar)	23
2009/2010	FC Twente Enschede	AFC Ajax Amsterdam	Luis Alberto Suárez Díaz (URU, AFC Ajax Amsterdam)	35
2010/2011	AFC Ajax Amsterdam	FC Twente Enschede	Björn Vleminckx (BEL, NEC Nijmegen)	23
2011/2012	AFC Ajax Amsterdam	PSV Eindhoven	Bas Dost (SC Heerenveen)	32
2012/2013	AFC Ajax Amsterdam	AZ Alkmaar	Wilfried Guemiand Bony (CIV, SBV Vitesse Arnhem)	31
2013/2014	AFC Ajax Amsterdam	PEC Zwolle	Alfreð Finnbogason (ISL, SC Heerenveen)	29
2014/2015	PSV Eindhoven	FC Groningen	Memphis Depay (PSV Eindhoven)	22
2015/2016	PSV Eindhoven	Feyenoord Rotterdam	Vincent Janssen (AZ Alkmaar)	27
2016/2017	Feyenoord Rotterdam	SBV Vitesse Arnhem	Nicolai Mick Jørgensen (DEN, Feyenoord Rotterdam)	21
2017/2018	PSV Eindhoven	Feyenoord Rotterdam	Alireza Jahanbakhsh (IRN, AZ Alkmaar)	21

2018/2019	AFC Ajax Amsterdam	AFC Ajax Amsterdam	Luuk de Jong (PSV Eindhoven)	
			Dušan Tadić (SRB, AFC Ajax Amsterdam)	28
2019/2020	*Championship cancelled*	*Competition cancelled*	-	

*National Champions (1888–1956), Eredivisie (since 1956)

NATIONAL CHAMPIONSHIP
Eredivisie 2019/2020
(02.08.2019 – 08.03.2020)

Results

Round 1 [02-04.08.2019]
PEC Zwolle - Willem II 1-3(1-1)
Vitesse - AFC Ajax 2-2(1-1)
FC Emmen - FC Groningen 0-1(0-0)
VVV-Venlo - RKC Waalwijk 3-1(0-1)
FC Twente - PSV Eindhoven 1-1(1-0)
Heracles Almelo - SC Heerenveen 0-4(0-3)
Feyenoord - Sparta Rotterdam 2-2(0-0)
ADO Den Haag - FC Utrecht 2-4(2-2)
AZ Alkmaar - Fortuna Sittard 4-0(0-0)

Round 2 [09-11.08.2019]
Sparta Rotterdam - VVV-Venlo 4-1(0-1)
FC Groningen - FC Twente 1-3(0-0)
AFC Ajax - FC Emmen 5-0(1-0)
Willem II - Vitesse 0-2(0-0)
Fortuna Sittard - Heracles Almelo 1-1(0-0)
SC Heerenveen - Feyenoord 1-1(0-1)
RKC Waalwijk - AZ Alkmaar 0-2(0-2)
FC Utrecht - PEC Zwolle 3-1(0-1)
PSV Eindhoven - ADO Den Haag 3-1(1-1)

Round 3 [16-18.08.2019]
Vitesse - PEC Zwolle 3-0(0-0)
ADO Den Haag - Sparta Rotterdam 1-2(0-2)
VVV-Venlo - AFC Ajax 1-4(0-1)
FC Emmen - SC Heerenveen 2-0(2-0)
Fortuna Sittard - Willem II 2-3(1-3)
FC Twente - RKC Waalwijk 3-3(0-1)
Feyenoord - FC Utrecht 1-1(0-1)
AZ Alkmaar - FC Groningen 0-0
Heracles Almelo - PSV Eindhoven 0-2(0-1)

Round 4 [24-26.08.2019]
Willem II - FC Emmen 2-1(1-0)
Heracles Almelo - Vitesse 1-1(0-0)
SC Heerenveen - FC Twente 0-0
RKC Waalwijk - ADO Den Haag 0-3(0-1)
FC Utrecht - VVV-Venlo 1-2(0-2)
PEC Zwolle - Sparta Rotterdam 2-2(1-1)
PSV Eindhoven - FC Groningen 3-1(2-0)
AFC Ajax - Fortuna Sittard 5-0(0-0)
Feyenoord - AZ Alkmaar 0-3(0-1)

Round 5 [30.08.-01.09.2019]
FC Emmen - PEC Zwolle 1-3(1-3)
SC Heerenveen - Fortuna Sittard 1-1(1-1)
FC Groningen - Heracles Almelo 1-2(0-1)
ADO Den Haag - VVV-Venlo 1-0(1-0)
FC Twente - FC Utrecht 3-1(1-0)
Sparta Rotterdam - AFC Ajax 1-4(0-2)
Willem II - Feyenoord 0-1(0-0)
Vitesse - AZ Alkmaar 2-1(1-1)
RKC Waalwijk - PSV Eindhoven 1-3(1-0)

Round 6 [14-15.09.2019]
AZ Alkmaar - Sparta Rotterdam 5-1(4-1)
AFC Ajax - SC Heerenveen 4-1(2-1)
VVV-Venlo - FC Groningen 2-1(1-1)
PSV Eindhoven - Vitesse 5-0(2-0)
FC Utrecht - FC Emmen 3-1(1-0)
PEC Zwolle - RKC Waalwijk 6-2(1-2)
Feyenoord - ADO Den Haag 3-2(3-0)
Heracles Almelo - Willem II 4-1(2-1)
Fortuna Sittard - FC Twente 2-3(0-2)

Round 7 [20-22.09.2019]
FC Twente - Heracles Almelo 2-3(1-2)
Sparta Rotterdam - RKC Waalwijk 4-0(2-0)
FC Groningen - PEC Zwolle 2-0(1-0)
Willem II - VVV-Venlo 1-0(1-0)
Vitesse - Fortuna Sittard 4-2(0-1)
SC Heerenveen - FC Utrecht 1-1(1-1)
FC Emmen - Feyenoord 3-3(2-2)
ADO Den Haag - AZ Alkmaar 0-1(0-0)
PSV Eindhoven - AFC Ajax 1-1(0-0)

Round 8 [27-29.09.2019]
FC Emmen - ADO Den Haag 3-0(1-0)
VVV-Venlo - SC Heerenveen 0-3(0-2)
AFC Ajax - FC Groningen 2-0(0-0)
Fortuna Sittard - Sparta Rotterdam 0-0
RKC Waalwijk - Vitesse 1 2(0 1)
PEC Zwolle - PSV Eindhoven 0-4(0-1)
FC Utrecht - Willem II 2-0(0-0)
AZ Alkmaar - Heracles Almelo 2-0(0-0)
Feyenoord - FC Twente 5-1(2-1)

Round 9 [04-06.10.2019]
FC Groningen - RKC Waalwijk 3-0(2-0)
Heracles Almelo - FC Emmen 2-0(1-0)
Sparta Rotterdam - FC Twente 2-1(0-0)
Vitesse - FC Utrecht 2-1(1-1)
SC Heerenveen - PEC Zwolle 1-0(1-0)
ADO Den Haag - AFC Ajax 0-2(0-1)
Fortuna Sittard - Feyenoord 4-2(3-1)
PSV Eindhoven - VVV-Venlo 4-1(0-0)
Willem II - AZ Alkmaar 1-1(1-1)

Round 10 [19-20.10.2019]
AZ Alkmaar - SC Heerenveen 2-4(1-3)
RKC Waalwijk - AFC Ajax 1-2(0-0)
FC Twente - Willem II 0-1(0-1)
FC Utrecht - PSV Eindhoven 3-0(0-0)
VVV-Venlo - Vitesse 0-4(0-3)
PEC Zwolle - ADO Den Haag 3-1(1-1)
FC Emmen - Fortuna Sittard 2-1(0-1)
FC Groningen - Sparta Rotterdam 2-0(0-0)
Feyenoord - Heracles Almelo 1-1(1-0)

Round 11 [25-27.10.2019]
FC Twente - FC Emmen 4-1(3-0)
Willem II - RKC Waalwijk 2-1(2-1)
Fortuna Sittard - VVV-Venlo 4-1(2-0)
Vitesse - ADO Den Haag 0-2(0-2)
Heracles Almelo - PEC Zwolle 4-0(1-0)
SC Heerenveen - FC Groningen 1-1(1-0)
PSV Eindhoven - AZ Alkmaar 0-4(0-2)
Sparta Rotterdam - FC Utrecht 1-2(1-2)
AFC Ajax - Feyenoord 4-0(4-0)

Round 12 [01-03.11.2019]
PEC Zwolle - AFC Ajax 2-4(1-3)
RKC Waalwijk - Heracles Almelo 2-0(1-0)
Sparta Rotterdam - PSV Eindhoven 2-2(1-0)
AZ Alkmaar - FC Twente 3-0(1-0)
FC Emmen - Vitesse 2-1(2-1)
FC Utrecht - Fortuna Sittard 6-0(3-0)
VVV-Venlo - Feyenoord 0-3(0-2)
FC Groningen - Willem II 2-0(1-0)
ADO Den Haag - SC Heerenveen 1-1(0-0)

Round 13 [08-10.11.2019]
Vitesse - FC Groningen 1-2(0-2)
SC Heerenveen - Sparta Rotterdam 2-1(0-1)
Fortuna Sittard - ADO Den Haag 1-0(1-0)
Heracles Almelo - VVV-Venlo 6-1(2-0)
AFC Ajax - FC Utrecht 4-0(3-0)
Willem II - PSV Eindhoven 2-1(1-0)
FC Twente - PEC Zwolle 2-1(2-0)
Feyenoord - RKC Waalwijk 3-2(2-2)
AZ Alkmaar - FC Emmen 3-0(2-0)

Round 14 [23-24.11.2019]
FC Utrecht - AZ Alkmaar 0-3(0-2)
PEC Zwolle - Fortuna Sittard 3-1(1-0)
AFC Ajax - Heracles Almelo 4-1(1-0)
ADO Den Haag - Willem II 3-3(0-2)
FC Groningen - Feyenoord 1-1(0-1)
PSV Eindhoven - SC Heerenveen 2-1(2-0)
RKC Waalwijk - FC Emmen 1-1(0-1)
VVV-Venlo - FC Twente 2-1(2-1)
Sparta Rotterdam - Vitesse 2-0(1-0)

Round 15 [29.11.-01.12.2019]
SC Heerenveen - Vitesse 3-2(1-2)
Willem II - Sparta Rotterdam 4-0(3-0)
Fortuna Sittard - FC Groningen 1-0(0-0)
Heracles Almelo - ADO Den Haag 4-0(2-0)
FC Twente - AFC Ajax 2-5(2-1)
FC Utrecht - RKC Waalwijk 0-1(0-0)
Feyenoord - PEC Zwolle 1-0(1-0)
AZ Alkmaar - VVV-Venlo 1-0(1-0)
FC Emmen - PSV Eindhoven 1-1(0-1)

Round 16 [06-08.12.2019]
AFC Ajax - Willem II 0-2(0-1)
ADO Den Haag - FC Twente 0-0
PSV Eindhoven - Fortuna Sittard 5-0(3-0)
VVV-Venlo - FC Emmen 2-0(1-0)
PEC Zwolle - AZ Alkmaar 0-3(0-2)
Vitesse - Feyenoord 0-0
FC Groningen - FC Utrecht 0-1(0-0)
RKC Waalwijk - SC Heerenveen 1-3(0-1)
Sparta Rotterdam - Heracles Almelo 0-0

Round 17 [13-15.12.2019]
SC Heerenveen - Willem II 1-2(1-2)
ADO Den Haag - FC Groningen 1-1(1-1)
Fortuna Sittard - RKC Waalwijk 3-2(2-2)
VVV-Venlo - PEC Zwolle 1-2(0-2)
FC Twente - Vitesse 0-3(0-0)
FC Emmen - Sparta Rotterdam 2-0(2-0)
Feyenoord - PSV Eindhoven 3-1(2-0)
AZ Alkmaar - AFC Ajax 1-0(0-0)
Heracles Almelo - FC Utrecht 1-3(1-0)

Round 18 [20-22.12.2019]
RKC Waalwijk - FC Twente 3-0(1-0)
SC Heerenveen - Heracles Almelo 1-1(0-0)
PSV Eindhoven - PEC Zwolle 4-1(2-1)
Sparta Rotterdam - AZ Alkmaar 3-0(2-0)
Willem II - Fortuna Sittard 0-0
AFC Ajax - ADO Den Haag 6-1(4-0)
FC Groningen - FC Emmen 2-0(0-0)
FC Utrecht - Feyenoord 1-2(1-1)
Vitesse - VVV-Venlo 3-0(2-0)

Round 19 [17-19.01.2020]
PEC Zwolle - FC Utrecht 3-3(1-1)
Fortuna Sittard - Vitesse 1-3(0-2)
FC Twente - FC Groningen 0-0
Feyenoord - SC Heerenveen 3-1(3-1)
AZ Alkmaar - Willem II 1-3(1-0)
VVV-Venlo - PSV Eindhoven 1-1(0-0)
AFC Ajax - Sparta Rotterdam 2-1(1-0)
FC Emmen - Heracles Almelo 1-0(1-0)
ADO Den Haag - RKC Waalwijk 2-0(1-0)

Round 20 [24-26.01.2020]
FC Utrecht - ADO Den Haag 4-0(1-0)
SC Heerenveen - AZ Alkmaar 1-2(0-1)
Heracles Almelo - Feyenoord 2-3(1-0)
RKC Waalwijk - VVV-Venlo 1-2(1-0)
Sparta Rotterdam - Fortuna Sittard 1-1(0-1)
Vitesse - FC Emmen 1-1(1-0)
FC Groningen - AFC Ajax 2-1(1-0)
Willem II - PEC Zwolle 0-0
PSV Eindhoven - FC Twente 1-1(0-0)

Round 21 31.01.-02.02.2020 [ ]
AZ Alkmaar - RKC Waalwijk 4-0(2-0)
ADO Den Haag - Vitesse 0-0
Feyenoord - FC Emmen 3-0(1-0)
FC Twente - Sparta Rotterdam 2-0(0-0)
PEC Zwolle - FC Groningen 1-0(1-0)
Willem II - Heracles Almelo 1-0(1-0)
Fortuna Sittard - SC Heerenveen 2-1(1-1)
VVV-Venlo - FC Utrecht 1-1(0-0)
AFC Ajax - PSV Eindhoven 1-0(1-0)

Round 22 [07-11.02.2020]
Heracles Almelo - Fortuna Sittard 2-0(1-0)
FC Groningen - Vitesse 1-0(1-0)
SC Heerenveen - VVV-Venlo 1-1(0-0)
PSV Eindhoven - Willem II 3-0(1-0)
RKC Waalwijk - PEC Zwolle 0-0
FC Emmen - FC Twente 2-0(1-0)
Sparta Rotterdam - ADO Den Haag 4-2(3-1)
AZ Alkmaar - Feyenoord [08.04. not played]
FC Utrecht - AFC Ajax [09.04. not played]

Round 23 [14-16.02.2020]
VVV-Venlo - Heracles Almelo 1-0(1-0)
FC Twente - AZ Alkmaar 2-0(2-0)
ADO Den Haag - PSV Eindhoven 0-3(0-1)
Fortuna Sittard - FC Emmen 0-0
Vitesse - SC Heerenveen 4-2(2-2)
AFC Ajax - RKC Waalwijk 3-0(1-0)
Sparta Rotterdam - FC Groningen 1-2(0-2)
Willem II - FC Utrecht 1-1(0-1)
PEC Zwolle - Feyenoord 3-4(2-1)

Round 24 [21-23.02.2020]
RKC Waalwijk - Sparta Rotterdam 0-1(0-1)
FC Emmen - Willem II 4-2(1-0)
Feyenoord - Fortuna Sittard 2-1(0-0)
SC Heerenveen - ADO Den Haag 2-2(1-2)
FC Groningen - VVV-Venlo 0-1(0-0)
FC Utrecht - FC Twente 2-1(0-0)
AZ Alkmaar - PEC Zwolle 2-0(0-0)
Vitesse - PSV Eindhoven 1-2(0-0)
Heracles Almelo - AFC Ajax 1-0(0-0)

Round 25 [28.02.-01.03.2020]
Willem II - FC Groningen 3-1(2-0)
ADO Den Haag - Heracles Almelo 0-0
VVV-Venlo - Fortuna Sittard 0-0
PEC Zwolle - Vitesse 4-3(1-2)
FC Twente - SC Heerenveen 2-3(0-1)
RKC Waalwijk - FC Utrecht 2-1(0-1)
PSV Eindhoven - Feyenoord 1-1(0-1)
Sparta Rotterdam - FC Emmen 5-1(3-0)
AFC Ajax - AZ Alkmaar 0-2(0-1)

Round 26 [06-08.03.2020]
Fortuna Sittard - PEC Zwolle 1-1(0-0)
AZ Alkmaar - ADO Den Haag 4-0(2-0)
FC Emmen - VVV-Venlo 3-0(0-0)
Vitesse - FC Twente 1-0(0-0)
SC Heerenveen - AFC Ajax 1-3(0-0)
FC Utrecht - Sparta Rotterdam 5-1(1-0)
Feyenoord - Willem II 2-0(2-0)
Heracles Almelo - RKC Waalwijk 4-2(2-2)
FC Groningen - PSV Eindhoven 0-1(0-1)

As effect of the 2020 coronavirus pandemic, on 12.03.2020, all football leagues were suspended until 31.03.2020, as the Dutch government prohibited events due to the Covid-19 pandemic in the Netherlands. A few days later this period was extended until 06.04.2020. Following the decision of the Dutch government to prohibit all gatherings and events until 01.06.2020, this period was further extended.

On 02.04.2020, several clubs indicated they were not willing to play the remainder of the season. The Dutch government announced on 21.04.2020 that all events subject to authorization, would remain prohibited until at least 01.09.2020.

On 24.04.2020 the KNVB announced their final decision:
1) The ranking on 08.03.2020 is the final ranking, but no title will be awarded.
2) There will be no promotion/relegation between the First and Second level.
3) European places will be assigned based on the ranking on 08.03.2020.

Final Standings							Total			Home				Away			
1. AFC Ajax Amsterdam	25	18	2	5	68 - 23	56	11	0	2	40 - 8	7	2	3	28 - 15
2. AZ Alkmaar	25	18	2	5	54 - 17	56	10	1	2	32 - 8	8	1	3	22 - 9
3. Feyenoord Rotterdam	25	14	8	3	50 - 35	50	9	3	1	29 - 15	5	5	2	21 - 20
4. PSV Eindhoven	26	14	7	5	54 - 28	49	8	3	1	32 - 12	6	4	4	22 - 16
5. Willem II Tilburg	26	13	5	8	37 - 34	44	7	4	2	17 - 9	6	1	6	20 - 25
6. FC Utrecht	25	12	5	8	50 - 34	41	8	0	4	30 - 12	4	5	4	20 - 22
7. SBV Vitesse Arnhem	26	12	5	9	45 - 35	41	7	3	3	24 - 15	5	2	6	21 - 20
8. Heracles Almelo	26	10	6	10	40 - 34	36	8	1	4	31 - 17	2	5	6	9 - 17
9. FC Groningen	26	10	5	11	27 - 26	35	7	1	5	17 - 10	3	4	6	10 - 16
10. SC Heerenveen	26	8	9	9	41 - 41	33	3	8	3	17 - 18	5	1	6	24 - 23
11. Sparta Rotterdam	26	9	6	11	41 - 45	33	7	3	3	30 - 16	2	3	8	11 - 29
12. FC Emmen	26	9	5	12	32 - 45	32	9	2	2	26 - 12	0	3	10	6 - 33
13. VVV-Venlo	26	8	4	14	24 - 51	28	5	3	5	14 - 21	3	1	9	10 - 30
14. FC Twente Enschede	26	7	6	13	34 - 46	27	5	3	5	23 - 22	2	3	8	11 - 24
15. PEC Zwolle	26	7	5	14	37 - 55	26	5	2	5	28 - 30	2	3	9	9 - 25
16. Fortuna Sittard	26	6	8	12	29 - 52	26	6	4	3	22 - 17	0	4	9	7 - 35
17. ADO Den Haag	26	4	7	15	25 - 54	19	2	6	5	11 - 17	2	1	10	14 - 37
18. RKC Waalwijk	26	4	3	19	27 - 60	15	3	2	8	13 - 20	1	1	11	14 - 40

Top goalscorers:	
15 Steven Berghuis	*Feyenoord Rotterdam*
15 Cyriel Dessers (NGA)	*Heracles Almelo*
14 Myron Boadu	*AZ Alkmaar*
14 Bryan Linssen	*SBV Vitesse Arnhem*
13 Oussama Idrissi (MAR)	*AZ Alkmaar*
12 Quincy Anton Promes	*AFC Ajax Amsterdam*
12 Tim Matavž (SVN)	*SBV Vitesse Arnhem*

NATIONAL CUP
KNVB Beker 2019/2020

First Round [19-31.10.2019]

FC 's-Gravenzande - SteDoCo Hoornaar	1-3(0-0)	NAC Breda - FC Emmen	3-2(1-1)
SBV Vitesse Arnhem - VBV De Graafschap Doet.	2-0(1-0)	Heracles Almelo - RKC Waalwijk	4-3(2-1)
VV Goes - SC Cambuur Leeuwarden	0-5(0-1)	RKSV Groene Ster - VVV-Venlo	2-2 aet; 4-2 pen
Flevo Boys Emmeloord - VV Katwijk	0-3(0-2)	HV & CV Quick Den Haag - Willem II Tilburg	0-4(0-2)
GVVV Veenendaal - Helmond Sport	2-1(0-0)	VV Excelsior Maassluis - SC Heerenveen	0-3(0-2)
FC Dordrecht - MVV Maastricht	3-1(1-1)	VV Sparta Nijkerk - SV Fortuna Wormerveer	5-2(2-2)
IJsselmeervogels - FC Den Bosch	3-0(1-0)	SV Spakenburg - ASWH Ido-Ambacht	2-0(0-0)
Koninklijke HFC - SC Telstar Velsen	1-2(1-1)	AFC Ajax Zaterdag - OFC Oostzaan	2-2 aet; 2-3 pen
HSV Hoek - PEC Zwolle	0-3(0-0)	Amsterdamsche FC - HSV ODIN '59 Heemskerk	3-3 aet; 2-4 pen
Almere City FC - Go Ahead Eagles Deventer	1-3(1-2)	Harkemase Boys - FC Groningen	1-2(0-1)
Achilles Veen - Roda JC Kerkrade	0-2(0-0)	De Treffers Groesbeek - FC Twente Enschede	0-2(0-2)
SBV Excelsior Rotterdam - NEC Nijmegen	4-2(0-1,2-2)	Sparta Rotterdam - FC Volendam	1-0(1-0)
Rijnsburgse Boys - FC Eindhoven	0-4(0-0)	SV Excelsior '31 Rijssen - FC Utrecht	1-4(0-2)
SV OSS '20 - Tot Ons Plezier Oss	1-2(1-1)	Fortuna Sittard - ADO Den Haag	3-0(0-0)

Second Round [17-19.12.2019]

FC Twente Enschede - Go Ahead Eagles Deventer	2-5(1-2)	Heracles Almelo - FC Dordrecht	3-0(1-0)
IJsselmeervogels - SteDoCo Hoornaar	1-0(1-0)	OFC Oostzaan - SV Spakenburg	0-0 aet; 4-5 pen
SC Heerenveen - Roda JC Kerkrade	2-0(1-0)	AZ Alkmaar - RKSV Groene Ster	3-0(0-0)
SBV Vitesse Arnhem - HSV ODIN '59 Heemskerk	4-0(4-0)	Willem II Tilburg - Sparta Rotterdam	3-0(3-0)
VV Katwijk - Tot Ons Plezier Oss	0-0 aet; 3-4 pen	VV Sparta Nijkerk - NAC Breda	0-1(0-0,0-0)
SBV Excelsior Rotterdam - FC Eindhoven	0-2(0-0)	GVVV Veenendaal - PSV Eindhoven	1-2(0-1,1-1)
Fortuna Sittard - PEC Zwolle	3-0(2-0)	FC Groningen - FC Utrecht	0-1(0-0)
SC Telstar Velsen - AFC Ajax Amsterdam	3-4(1-2)	SC Cambuur Leeuwarden - Feyenoord Rotterdam	1-2(0-0)

1/8-Finals [21-28.01.2020]

Tot Ons Plezier Oss - AZ Alkmaar	0-2(0-1)	SC Heerenveen - Willem II Tilburg	2-2 aet; 4-3 pen
FC Eindhoven - FC Utrecht	1-2(1-0,1-1)	IJsselmeervogels - Go Ahead Eagles Deventer	1-1 aet; 6-7 pen
Heracles Almelo - SBV Vitesse Arnhem	0-2(0-1)	NAC Breda - PSV Eindhoven	2-0(0-0)
AFC Ajax Amsterdam - SV Spakenburg	7-0(3-0)	Fortuna Sittard - Feyenoord Rotterdam	1-2(0-1,1-1)

Quarter-Finals [12-13.02.2020]

AZ Alkmaar - NAC Breda	1-3(0-1)	Go Ahead Eagles Deventer - FC Utrecht	1-4(0-2)
SBV Vitesse Arnhem - AFC Ajax Amsterdam	0-3(0-1)	SC Heerenveen - Feyenoord Rotterdam	0-1(0-1)

Semi-Finals [04-05.03.2020]

FC Utrecht - AFC Ajax Amsterdam	2-0(1-0)	Feyenoord Rotterdam - NAC Breda	7-1(5-0)

Final

19.05.2019; Stadion Feijenoord, Rotterdam
FC Utrecht - Feyenoord Rotterdam   *Not played*

The final game was cancelled due to Covid-19 pandemic. No title was awarded.

THE CLUBS 2019/2020

Alles Door Oefening Den Haag

Founded:	01.02.1905	
Stadium:	Stadion "Cars Jeans", Den Haag (15,000)	
Trainer:	Alfons Groenendijk	17.05.1964
[02.12.2019]	Dirk Heesen	15.09.1969
[24.12.2019]	Alan Scott Pardew (ENG)	18.07.1961

Goalkeepers:	DOB	M	(s)	G
Mike Havekotte	12.09.1995	1		
Luuk Koopmans	18.11.1993	20		
Robert Zwinkels	04.05.1983	5		
Defenders:	**DOB**	**M**	**(s)**	**G**
Tom Beugelsdijk	07.08.1990	18	(1)	1
Aleksandar Bjelica (SRB)	07.01.1994		(2)	
Laurens De Bock (BEL)	07.11.1992	8		
Wilfried Kanon (CIV)	06.07.1993	3	(1)	
Nick Kuipers	08.10.1992		(1)	
Dion Malone	13.02.1989	17	(3)	
Aaron Meijers	28.10.1987	23	(3)	2
Dehninio Muringen	01.02.1999	1		
Shaquille Pinas	19.03.1998	25		3
Robin Polley (GHA)	28.12.1998	1	(1)	
Jordan Spence (ENG)	24.05.1990	3	(1)	
Sam Stubbs (ENG)	20.11.1998	8		
Midfielders:	**DOB**	**M**	**(s)**	**G**
Danny Bakker	16.01.1995	18	(4)	

Cristian Tudor Băluță (ROU)	27.03.1999	4		
Mark Duffy (ENG)	07.10.1985	2	(3)	
John Goossens	25.07.1988	22		2
Thom Haye	09.02.1995	2	(7)	
Lex Immers	08.06.1986	22	(1)	2
Milan van Ewijk	08.09.2000	12		
Lorenzo van Kleef	26.01.2001		(2)	
Forwards:	**DOB**	**M**	**(s)**	**G**
Omar Bogle (ENG)	26.07.1992	4	(1)	1
Paweł Cibicki (SWE)	09.01.1994	1	(2)	
Erik Falkenburg	05.05.1988	10	(6)	1
Thijmen Goppel	16.02.1997	3	(1)	
Elson Quincy Hooi (CUW)	01.10.1991	8	(5)	
Michiel Kramer	03.12.1988	7	(6)	2
Tomáš Necid (CZE)	13.08.1989	14	(7)	6
Bilal Ould-Chikh (MAR)	28.07.1997	3	(10)	
Crysencio Summerville	30.10.2001	17	(4)	2
George Stanley Thomas (ENG)	24.03.1997	3		
Mick van Buren	24.08.1992	1	(3)	

Amsterdamsche Football Club Ajax

Founded: 18.03.1900
Stadium: "Johann Cruijff ArenA", Amsterdam (54,033)
Trainer: Erik ten Hag   02.02.1970

Goalkeepers:	DOB	M	(s)	G
Bruno Miguel Semedo Varela (POR)	04.11.1994	1		
André Onana (CMR)	02.04.1996	24		
Defenders:	**DOB**	**M**	**(s)**	**G**
Edson Omar Álvarez Velázquez (MEX)	24.10.1997	6	(6)	
Daley Blind	09.03.1990	19	(1)	
Sergiño Dest (USA)	03.11.2000	15	(5)	
Noussair Mazraoui (MAR)	14.11.1997	9	(4)	
Perr Schuurs	26.11.1999	7	(3)	1
Nicolás Alejandro Tagliafico (ARG)	31.08.1992	23	(1)	3
Jurriën Timber	17.06.2001	1		
Joël Ivo Veltman	15.01.1992	19		
Midfielders:	**DOB**	**M**	**(s)**	**G**
Siem de Jong	28.01.1989	1	(3)	
Carel Eiting	11.02.1998	3	(3)	
Jurgen Ekkelenkamp	05.04.2000	1	(3)	1
Ryan Gravenberch	15.06.2002	5	(4)	2

	DOB	M	(s)	G
Zakaria Labyad (MAR)	09.03.1993	2		1
Răzvan Gabriel Marin (ROU)	23.05.1996	5	(5)	
Lisandro Martínez (ARG)	18.01.1998	24		2
Donny van de Beek	18.04.1997	22	(1)	8
Hakim Ziyech (MAR)	19.03.1993	21		6
Forwards:	**DOB**	**M**	**(s)**	**G**
Ryan Miguel Guno Babel	19.12.1986	5		
Danilo Pereira Da Silva (BRA)	07.04.1999		(1)	
David Neres Campos (BRA)	03.03.1997	7	(5)	6
Kasper Dolberg (DEN)	06.10.1997	1		
Sontje Hansen	18.05.2002		(1)	
Dirk Jan Klaas Huntelaar	12.08.1983	6	(12)	9
Noa Lang	17.06.1999	2	(3)	3
Quincy Anton Promes	04.01.1992	18	(2)	12
Dušan Tadić (SRB)	20.11.1988	25		11
Lassina Traoré (BFA)	12.01.2001	3	(6)	2

Alkmaar Zaanstreek Alkmaar

Founded: 10.05.1967
Stadium: Stadion AFAS, Alkmaar (17,023)
Trainer: Arnold Martijn Slot   17.09.1978

Goalkeepers:	DOB	M	(s)	G
Marco Bizot	10.03.1991	24		
Rody de Boer	22.08.1997	1	(1)	
Defenders:	**DOB**	**M**	**(s)**	**G**
Pantelis Hatzidiakos (GRE)	18.01.1997	7	(4)	1
Joris Kramer	02.08.1996		(1)	
Ramon Leeuwin	01.09.1987	4	(1)	
Yukinari Sugawara (JPN)	28.06.2000	5	(11)	2
Jonas Svensson (NOR)	06.03.1993	23		1
Ron Vlaar	16.02.1985	10		2
Owen Wijndal	28.11.1999	24		1
Stijn Wuytens (BEL)	08.10.1989	21		
Midfielders:	**DOB**	**M**	**(s)**	**G**
Jordy Clasie	27.06.1991	10	(8)	

	DOB	M	(s)	G
Dani de Wit	28.01.1998	19	(3)	3
Håkon Evjen (NOR)	14.02.2000	1	(2)	
Kenzo Goudmijn	18.12.2001		(1)	
Teun Koopmeiners	28.02.1998	25		11
Fredrik Midtsjø (NOR)	11.08.1993	22	(1)	
Thomas Ouwejan	30.09.1996	4	(6)	
Tijjani Reijnders	29.07.1998		(3)	
Forwards:	**DOB**	**M**	**(s)**	**G**
Zakaria Aboukhlal	18.02.2000		(12)	
Myron Boadu	14.01.2001	24		14
Ferdy Druijf	12.02.1998	1	(11)	1
Albert Guðmundsson (ISL)	15.06.1997	1	(3)	
Oussama Idrissi (MAR)	26.02.1996	25		13
Calvin Stengs	18.12.1998	24	(1)	5

Football Club Emmen

Founded: 21.08.1925
Stadium: De Oude Meerdijk, Emmen (8,600)
Trainer: Dick Lukkien   28.03.1972

Goalkeepers:	DOB	M	(s)	G
Dennis Telgenkamp	09.05.1987	26		
Defenders:	**DOB**	**M**	**(s)**	**G**
Miguel Gianpierre Araujo Blanco (PER)	24.10.1994	12		1
Nick Bakker	21.07.1992	8		1
Jan-Niklas Beste (GER)	04.01.1999	5	(1)	
Glenn Bijl	13.07.1995	24		1
Lorenzo Burnet	11.01.1991	19	(1)	
Ferhat Görgülü	28.03.1991	2	(2)	
Michaël Heylen (BEL)	03.01.1994	19		
Desevio Payne (USA)	30.11.1995		(2)	
Ruben Rooksen	02.03.2000		(3)	
Leon Sopić (CRO)	28.10.2000		(1)	
Keziah Veendorp	17.02.1997	14	(5)	1
Midfielders:	**DOB**	**M**	**(s)**	**G**
Hilal Ben Moussa	22.05.1992	5	(2)	
Henk Bos	12.11.1992	1	(3)	

	DOB	M	(s)	G
Michael Chacón	11.04.1994	24		
Michael de Leeuw	07.10.1986	26		9
Robbert de Vos	26.05.1996	4	(6)	1
Tom Hiariej	25.07.1988	16	(1)	
Wouter Marinus	18.02.1995		(3)	
Sergio Fernando Peña Flores (PER)	28.09.1995	22	(1)	4
Filip Ugrinić (SUI)	05.01.1999	6	(7)	
Forwards:	**DOB**	**M**	**(s)**	**G**
Luka Adžić (SRB)	17.09.1998	1	(2)	1
Jafar Arias (CUW)	16.06.1995	6	(11)	
Kerim Frei (TUR)	19.11.1993	4		1
Anco Jansen	09.03.1989		(7)	1
Marko Kolar (CRO)	31.05.1995	19	(2)	4
Nikolai Laursen (DEN)	19.02.1998	16	(2)	4
Freddy Quispel	23.10.2000		(3)	
Luciano Slagveer	05.10.1993	7	(2)	2

Feyenoord Rotterdam

Founded: 19.07.1908
Stadium: Stadion Feijenoord, Rotterdam (51,177)
Trainer: Jakob "Jaap" Stam   17.07.1972
[30.10.2019] Dirk Nicolaas Advocaat   27.09.1947

Goalkeepers:	DOB	M	(s)	G
Justin Bijlow	22.01.1998	7		
Nick Marsman	01.10.1990	2		
Kenneth Vermeer	10.01.1986	16		
Defenders:	**DOB**	**M**	**(s)**	**G**
Edgar Miguel Ié (POR)	01.05.1994	10	(1)	
Eric Fernando Botteghin (BRA)	31.08.1987	20		2
Lutsharel Geertruida	18.07.2000	11	(6)	
Ridgeciano Haps	12.06.1993	15	(1)	2
Rick Karsdorp	11.02.1995	13	(2)	1
Tyrell Malacia	17.08.1999	12		
Marcos Nicolás Senesi Barón (ARG)	10.05.1997	15	(1)	1
Jerry St. Juste	19.10.1996	1		
Sven van Beek	28.07.1994		(1)	
Jan-Arie van der Heijden	03.03.1988	5		
Midfielders:	**DOB**	**M**	**(s)**	**G**
Yassin Ayoub (MAR)	06.03.1994		(3)	

	DOB	M	(s)	G
Wouter Burger	16.02.2001	2	(4)	
Leroy Fer	05.01.1990	22	(1)	2
Liam Anthony Kelly (IRL)	22.11.1995	1		
Orkun Kökçü (TUR)	29.12.2000	21	(1)	2
Oğuzhan Özyakup (TUR)	23.09.1992	1	(1)	1
Renato Fabrizio Tapia Cortijo (PER)	28.07.1995	7	(8)	
Jens Toornstra	04.04.1989	19	(2)	5
Forwards:	**DOB**	**M**	**(s)**	**G**
Marouan Azarkan	08.12.2001		(1)	
Naoufal Bannis	11.03.2002		(4)	
Steven Berghuis	19.12.1991	24		15
Róbert Boženík (SVK)	18.11.1999	3	(2)	2
Nicolai Jørgensen (DEN)	15.01.1991	11	(2)	5
Sam Larsson (SWE)	10.04.1993	9	(12)	4
Luciano Narsingh	13.09.1990	6	(9)	2
Luis Sinisterra (COL)	17.06.1999	21		5
Dylan Vente	09.05.1999	1		

Fortuna Sittard

Founded: 01.07.1968
Stadium: Fortuna Sittard Stadion, Sittard (10,300)
Trainer: Sjors Ultee — 23.05.1987

Goalkeepers:	DOB	M	(s)	G
Alexei Koşelev (MDA)	19.11.1993	26		
Defenders:	**DOB**	**M**	**(s)**	**G**
Grégoire Amiot (FRA)	10.05.1995	7	(2)	
Martin Angha (SUI)	22.01.1994	15	(1)	1
George Cox (ENG)	14.01.1998	21		1
Wessel Dammers	01.03.1995	9	(2)	
Clint Essers	21.01.1997	12	(6)	
Cian William Thomas Harries (WAL)	01.04.1997	4	(4)	1
Michael Gonçalves Pinto „Mica" (POR)	04.06.1993	7		
Branislav Niňaj (SVK)	17.05.1994	24		
Patrik Raitanen (FIN)	13.06.2001		(2)	
Lazaros Rota (GRE)	23.08.1997	4	(1)	
Agim Zeka (ALB)	06.09.1998		(5)	
Midfielders:	**DOB**	**M**	**(s)**	**G**
Alejandro „Álex" Carbonell Vallés (ESP)	15.09.1997	7	(10)	
Amadou Ciss (SEN)	07.09.1999	22		6
Mark Diemers	11.10.1993	26		7
Nassim el Ablak	07.01.2000		(3)	
Leandro Fernandes	25.12.1999	1	(4)	
Dimitrios Ioannidis (GRE)	13.02.2000		(2)	
Felix Passlack (GER)	29.05.1998	25		2
Jorrit Smeets	25.03.1995	23		
Tesfaldet Tekie (SWE)	04.06.1997	19	(1)	
Adnan Ugur (BEL)	28.06.2001	4	(2)	
Forwards:	**DOB**	**M**	**(s)**	**G**
Vitalie Damaşcan (MDA)	24.01.1999	13	(6)	6
Jacky Donkor (BEL)	12.11.1998		(1)	
Nikolai Frederiksen (DEN)	18.05.2000	1	(1)	
Rasmus Karjalainen (FIN)	04.04.1996	4	(11)	1
Bassala Sambou (ENG)	15.10.1997	12	(10)	2

Football Club Groningen

Founded: 16.06.1971
Stadium: Stadion Noordlease, Groningen (22,550)
Trainer: Danny Buijs — 21.06.1982

Goalkeepers:	DOB	M	(s)	G
Sergio Padt	06.06.1990	26		
Defenders:	**DOB**	**M**	**(s)**	**G**
Amir Absalem	19.06.1997	4	(1)	
Ko Itakura (JPN)	27.01.1997	18	(4)	
Thomas Poll	28.08.2001	1	(1)	
Mike te Wierik	08.06.1992	23		1
Bart van Hintum	16.01.1987	14		
Django Warmerdam	02.09.1995	19	(2)	1
Deyovaisio Zeefuik	11.03.1998	26		
Midfielders:	**DOB**	**M**	**(s)**	**G**
Ritsu Doan (JPN)	16.06.1998	2		1
Ahmed El Messaoudi (MAR)	03.08.1995	15	(5)	1
Gabriel Gudmundsson (SWE)	29.04.1999	4	(7)	2
Ajdin Hrustić (AUS)	05.07.1996	23	(2)	3
Ramon Pascal Lundqvist (SWE)	10.05.1997	17	(3)	5
Azor Matusiwa	28.04.1998	23		
Samir Memišević (BIH)	13.08.1993	6	(5)	1
Sam Schreck (GER)	29.01.1999	6	(7)	
Tomáš Suslov (SVK)	07.06.2002		(1)	
Daniël van Kaam	23.06.2000	9	(2)	
Forwards:	**DOB**	**M**	**(s)**	**G**
Joel Asoro (SWE)	27.04.1999	13	(2)	3
Charlison Benschop (CUW)	21.08.1989	7	(10)	3
Mo el Hankouri (MAR)	01.07.1997	10	(11)	
Romano Postema	07.02.2002	2	(9)	
Daishawn Redan	02.02.2001	4	(1)	
Kaj Sierhuis	27.04.1998	14	(2)	6
Kian Slor	23.03.2002		(2)	

Sportclub Heerenveen

Founded: 20.07.1920
Stadium: Stadion "Abe Lenstra", Heerenveen (26,100)
Trainer: Johnny Jansen — 02.03.1975

Goalkeepers:	DOB	M	(s)	G
Filip Bednarek (POL)	26.09.1992	6		
Warner Hahn	15.06.1992	20		
Defenders:	**DOB**	**M**	**(s)**	**G**
Sven Botman	12.01.2000	26		2
Ibrahim Drešević (KVX)	24.01.1997	26		2
Sherel Floranus	23.08.1998	25		1
Daniel Høegh (DEN)	06.01.1991		(4)	
Ricardo van Rhijn	13.06.1991	16	(3)	
Lucas Woudenberg	25.04.1994	11	(3)	
Midfielders:	**DOB**	**M**	**(s)**	**G**
Hamdi Akujobi	20.01.2000		(3)	
Jordy Bruijn	23.07.1997	8	(9)	1
Hicham Faik	19.03.1993	26		3
Rami Hajal (SWE)	17.09.2001		(5)	
Alen Halilović (CRO)	18.06.1996	4	(13)	1
Rodney Kongolo	09.01.1998	25	(1)	4
Jan Ras	28.01.1999		(3)	
Ben Rienstra	05.06.1990	1		
Joey Veerman	19.11.1998	20	(2)	4
Forwards:	**DOB**	**M**	**(s)**	**G**
Anders Laustrup Dreyer (DEN)	02.05.1998	1	(10)	1
Chidera Ejuke (NGA)	02.01.1998	24	(1)	9
Runar Espejord (NOR)	26.02.1996		(6)	
Jens Odgaard (DEN)	31.03.1999	22	(2)	7
Rein Smit	05.01.2001		(1)	
Mitchell van Bergen	27.08.1999	25		5
Arjen van der Heide	19.11.2001		(5)	

Heracles Almelo

Founded: 1903
Stadium: Stadion Polman, Almelo (12,080)
Trainer: Frank Wormuth (GER) — 13.09.1960

Goalkeepers:	DOB	M	(s)	G
Janis Blaswich (GER)	02.05.1991	26		
Defenders:	**DOB**	**M**	**(s)**	**G**
Navajo Bakboord	29.01.1999	9	(1)	
Tim Breukers	04.11.1987	16	(1)	
Lennart Czyborra (GER)	03.05.1999	19		2
Jeff Hardeveld	27.02.1995	7	(1)	
Mats Knoester	19.11.1998	24	(1)	
Robin Pröpper	23.09.1993	18		
Maximilian Rossmann (GER)	06.05.1995	5	(3)	2
Dario Van Den Buijs (BEL)	12.09.1995	5	(7)	1
Midfielders:	**DOB**	**M**	**(s)**	**G**
Teun Bijleveld	27.05.1998	1	(14)	
Sebastian Jakubiak (GER)	21.06.1993	1	(4)	
Orestis Kiomourtzoglou (GER)	07.05.1998	24		2
Mauro Jaqueson Júnior Ferreira Santos (BRA)	06.05.1999	24	(2)	6
Alexander Merkel (KAZ)	22.02.1992	25		2
Mohammed Osman (SYR)	01.01.1994	10	(3)	
Lucas Schoofs (BEL)	03.01.1997	1		
Adrian Szőke (SRB)	01.07.1998	1	(9)	
Forwards:	**DOB**	**M**	**(s)**	**G**
Delano Burgzorg	07.11.1998	5		1
Jeremy Cijntje (CUW)	08.01.1998	2	(7)	
Cyriel Dessers (NGA)	08.12.1994	26		15
Dabney dos Santos	31.07.1996	9	(9)	
Joey Konings	21.04.1998	8	(7)	1
Silvester van der Water	30.09.1995	20	(3)	7

Prins Hendrik Ende Desespereert Nimmer Combinatie Zwolle

Founded: 12.06.1910
Stadium: Stadion MAC³PARK, Zwolle (12,500)
Trainer: John Stegeman   27.08.1976

Goalkeepers:	DOB	M	(s)	G
Xavier Mous	04.08.1995	13		
Michael Zetterer (GER)	12.07.1995	13		
Defenders:	**DOB**	**M**	**(s)**	**G**
Destan Bajselmani	13.05.1999	1	(2)	
Marc Olivier Doue (FRA)	11.10.2000		(1)	
Sam Kersten	30.01.1998	12	(4)	
Thomas Lam (FIN)	18.12.1993	14		
Yuta Nakayama (JPN)	16.02.1997	13	(1)	2
Kenneth Paal	24.06.1997	19		3
Etiënne Reijnen	05.04.1987	3	(1)	
Bram van Polen	11.10.1985	7	(1)	
Sai van Wermeskerken (JPN)	28.06.1994	14	(4)	
Midfielders:	**DOB**	**M**	**(s)**	**G**
Iliass Bel Hassani	16.09.1992	12	(2)	5
Thomas Bruns	07.01.1992	5	(3)	1
Pelle Clement	19.05.1996	24		2
Rick Dekker	15.03.1995	13	(4)	
Zian Flemming	01.08.1998	2	(2)	
Gustavo Hamer	24.06.1997	25		4
Dean Huiberts	16.05.2000	7	(4)	
Jarni Koorman	15.03.1999	1	(2)	
Darryl Lachman (CUW)	11.11.1989	12	(1)	
Clint Leemans	15.09.1995		(1)	
Mustafa Saymak	11.02.1993	12	(3)	3
Rico Strieder (GER)	06.07.1992	6		
Forwards:	**DOB**	**M**	**(s)**	**G**
Stanley Elbers	14.05.1992	1	(1)	
Reza Ghoochannejhad (IRN)	20.09.1987	7	(6)	7
Dennis Johnsen (NOR)	17.02.1998	10	(13)	1
Lennart Thy (GER)	25.02.1992	19	(5)	6
Vito van Crooy	29.01.1996	11	(5)	
Mike van Duinen	06.11.1991	9	(3)	2
Jarno Westerman	08.06.2002	1	(3)	

Philips Sport Vereniging Eindhoven

Founded: 31.08.1913
Stadium: Stadion Philips, Eindhoven (36,500)
Trainer: Mark Peter Gertruda Andreas van Bommel   22.04.1977
[16.12.2019]   Ernest Anthonius Jacobus Faber   27.08.1971

Goalkeepers:	DOB	M	(s)	G
Robbin Ruiter	25.03.1987	1		
Lars Unnerstall (GER)	20.07.1990	14		
Jeroen Zoet	06.01.1991	11		
Defenders:	**DOB**	**M**	**(s)**	**G**
Timo Baumgartl (GER)	04.03.1996	12	(1)	1
Olivier Boscagli (FRA)	18.11.1997	6	(6)	
Denzel Dumfries	18.04.1996	25		7
Ricardo Rodríguez (SUI)	25.08.1992	5	(1)	
Trent Lucas Sainsbury (AUS)	05.01.1992	1		
Daniel Schwaab (GER)	23.08.1988	17	(1)	1
Jordan Teze	30.09.1999	1	(1)	
Nick Viergever	03.08.1989	23		
Midfielders:	**DOB**	**M**	**(s)**	**G**
Ibrahim Afellay	02.04.1986	1	(2)	
Ritsu Doan (JPN)	16.06.1998	12	(7)	2
Érick Gabriel Gutiérrez Galaviz (MEX)	15.06.1995	9	(6)	1
Jorrit Hendrix	06.02.1995	13	(4)	1
Mohamed Ihattaren	12.02.2002	20	(2)	3
Gastón Rodrigo Pereiro López (URU)	11.06.1995	1	(3)	2
Pablo Rosario	07.01.1997	26		2
Michal Sadílek (CZE)	31.05.1999	13	(1)	1
Ryan Thomas (NZL)	20.12.1994	10	(1)	2
Forwards:	**DOB**	**M**	**(s)**	**G**
Zakaria Aboukhlal	18.02.2000		(1)	
Steven Charles Bergwijn	08.10.1997	16		5
Armindo Tué Na Bangna „Bruma" (POR)	24.10.1994	12	(6)	3
Cody Gakpo	07.05.1999	14	(11)	7
Sam Lammers	30.04.1997	7		2
Hirving Rodrigo Lozano Bahena (MEX)	30.07.1995	1		
Noni Madueke (ENG)	10.03.2002	1	(3)	
Donyell Malen	19.01.1999	14		11
Kostas Mitroglou (GRE)	12.03.1988		(13)	1

Rooms Katholieke Combinatie Waalwijk

Founded: 26.08.1940
Stadium: Mandemakers Stadion, Waalwijk (7,500)
Trainer: Johann Georg Friedrich "Fred" Grim   17.08.1965

Goalkeepers:	DOB	M	(s)	G
Kees Heemskerk	02.05.1991	2	(1)	
Etienne Vaessen	26.07.1995	24		
Defenders:	**DOB**	**M**	**(s)**	**G**
Saïd Bakari (COM)	22.09.1994	13	(5)	1
Hannes Delcroix (BEL)	28.02.1999	23		1
Henrico Drost	21.01.1987	3		
Juriën Gaari (CUW)	23.12.1993	18		
Melle Meulensteen	04.07.1999	11	(3)	3
Hans Mulder	27.04.1987	15	(3)	1
Lars Nieuwpoort	29.10.1994	2	(1)	
Paul Quasten	13.03.1985	11	(2)	1
Fabian Sporkslede	03.08.1993	6		
Ingo van Weert	08.02.1994	2	(6)	1
Midfielders:	**DOB**	**M**	**(s)**	**G**
Clint Leemans	15.09.1995	21		4
Tijjani Reijnders	29.07.1998	5	(3)	
Daan Rienstra	06.10.1992	20	(1)	
Stijn Spierings	12.03.1996	17		3
Anas Tahiri (BEL)	05.05.1995	14	(9)	3
Richard van der Venne	16.05.1992	7		
Stefan Velkov (BUL)	12.12.1996	3		
Kevin Vermeulen	20.11.1990	1	(4)	1
Forwards:	**DOB**	**M**	**(s)**	**G**
Mario Bilate	16.07.1991	14	(3)	
Lennerd Daneels (BEL)	10.04.1998	1	(6)	
Stanley Elbers	14.05.1992	9	(3)	1
Emil Hansson (SWE)	15.06.1998	7		1
Darren Melvin Philip Maatsen	30.01.1991	13	(6)	2
Dylan Seys (BEL)	26.09.1996		(3)	
Sylla Sow	08.08.1996	14	(6)	4
Dylan Vente	09.05.1999	10	(7)	

Sparta Rotterdam

Founded: 01.04.1888
Stadium: Stadion Sparta, Rotterdam (11,000)
Trainer: Hendrikus "Henk" Fraser   07.07.1966

Goalkeepers:	DOB	M	(s)	G
Tim Coremans	10.04.1991	10		
Ariel Harush (ISR)	25.05.1988	16		
Defenders:	**DOB**	**M**	**(s)**	**G**
Dirk Abels	13.06.1997	19	(6)	
Abdallah Aberkane	05.05.2000		(1)	
Lassana Faye	15.06.1998	23		
Jeffry Fortes (CPV)	22.03.1989	5	(1)	
Khalid Karami	29.12.1989	3	(3)	
Jurgen Mattheij	01.04.1993	26		2
Michael Gonçalves Pinto „Mica" (POR)	04.06.1993	2	(1)	
Bart Vriends	09.05.1991	26		2
Midfielders:	**DOB**	**M**	**(s)**	**G**
Adil Auassar	06.10.1986	23		2
Deroy Duarte	04.07.1999	3	(11)	
Laros Duarte	28.02.1997	5	(11)	
Abdou Harroui	13.01.1998	26		4
Mohamed Rayhi	01.07.1994	24	(1)	7
Dante Rigo (BEL)	11.12.1998	10	(6)	
Bryan Smeets	22.11.1992	20	(2)	4
Forwards:	**DOB**	**M**	**(s)**	**G**
Ragnar Ache (GER)	28.07.1998	18	(1)	5
İbrahim Halil Dervişoğlu (TUR)	08.12.1999	15	(2)	5
Youssef el Kachati	30.11.1999		(1)	
Patrick Joosten	14.04.1996	8		3
Joël Piroe	02.08.1999	1	(17)	2
Lars Veldwijk (RSA)	21.08.1991	3	(12)	4

Football Club Twente Enschede

Founded: 01.07.1965
Stadium: Stadion De Groisch Veste, Enschede (30,205)
Trainer: Gonzalo Manuel García García (ESP)   13.10.1983

Goalkeepers:	DOB	M	(s)	G
Jorn Brondeel (BEL)	07.09.1993	1	(1)	
Joël Drommel	16.11.1996	25		
Defenders:	**DOB**	**M**	**(s)**	**G**
Peet Bijen	28.01.1995	18	(2)	1
Julio José Pleguezuelo Selva (ESP)	26.01.1997	16	(3)	
Joel Latibeaudiere (ENG)	06.01.2000	5		1
José Joaquín Matos García (ESP)	06.05.1995	2		
Xandro Schenk	28.04.1993	22		
Giovanni Troupée	20.03.1998	8		
Calvin Verdonk	26.04.1997	22		1
Paul Verhaegh	01.09.1983	5	(2)	
Midfielders:	**DOB**	**M**	**(s)**	**G**
Giorgi Aburjania (GEO)	02.01.1995	5	(12)	2
Jesse Bosch	01.02.2000	3	(1)	

	DOB	M	(s)	G
Wout Brama	21.08.1986	6	(3)	
Javier „Javi" Espinosa González (ESP)	19.09.1992	18	(1)	1
Oriol Busquets Mas (ESP)	20.01.1999	20	(1)	
Godfried Roemeratoe	19.08.1999	12	(3)	
Lindon Selahi (ALB)	26.02.1999	23	(2)	2
Forwards:	**DOB**	**M**	**(s)**	**G**
Aitor Cantalapiedra Fernández (ESP)	10.02.1996	21		7
Emil Berggreen (DEN)	10.05.1993	2	(11)	1
Tom Boere	24.11.1992		(1)	
Noa Noëll Lang	17.06.1999	7		1
Queensy Menig	19.08.1995	4	(7)	1
Keito Nakamura (JPN)	28.07.2000	13	(4)	4
Haris Vučkić (SVN)	21.08.1992	23	(2)	11
Rafik Zekhnini (NOR)	12.01.1998	5	(16)	1

Football Club Utrecht

Founded: 01.07.1970
Stadium: Stadion Galgenwaard, Utrecht (23,750)
Trainer: John van den Brom   04.10.1966

Goalkeepers:	DOB	M	(s)	G
Maarten Paes	14.05.1998	18		
Jeroen Zoet	06.01.1991	7		
Defenders:	**DOB**	**M**	**(s)**	**G**
Emil Bergström (SWE)	19.05.1993	1		
Leon Guwara (GER)	28.06.1996	14	(1)	
Justin Hoogma	11.06.1998	23		1
Willem Janssen	04.07.1986	19		2
Sean Klaiber	13.07.1994	24		4
Lamine Sané (SEN)	22.03.1987		(1)	
Tommy St. Jago	03.01.2000		(1)	
Giovanni Troupée	20.03.1998		(8)	
Mark van der Maarel	12.08.1989	16	(1)	
Midfielders:	**DOB**	**M**	**(s)**	**G**
Urby Emanuelson	16.06.1986	5	(8)	
Simon Gustafson (SWE)	11.01.1995	23		6
Justin Lonwijk	21.12.1999	1		

	DOB	M	(s)	G
Adam Maher	20.07.1993	22	(1)	3
Bart Ramselaar	29.06.1996	12	(4)	5
Rico Strieder (GER)	06.07.1992	2	(3)	
Sander van de Streek	24.03.1993	20	(1)	4
Joris van Overeem	01.06.1994	11	(3)	
Mitchell van Rooijen	22.12.1998	1		
Forwards:	**DOB**	**M**	**(s)**	**G**
Issah Abass (GHA)	26.09.1998	10	(5)	2
Jonas Arweiler (GER)	10.04.1997		(3)	1
Jean-Christophe Bahebeck (FRA)	01.05.1993	6	(9)	3
Vaclav Černý (CZE)	17.10.1997	3	(10)	
Adrián Dalmau Vaquer (ESP)	27.03.1994	4	(3)	4
Patrick Joosten	14.04.1996	3	(4)	
Gyrano Kerk	02.12.1995	24		10
Simon Makienok (DEN)	21.11.1990		(3)	1
Kristoffer Peterson (SWE)	28.11.1994	5	(1)	1
Nick Venema	09.04.1999	1	(2)	1

Stichting Betaald Voetbal Vitesse Arnhem

Founded: 14.05.1892
Stadium: GelreDome, Arnhem (25,500)
Trainer: Leonid Slutski (RUS)   04.05.1971
[03.12.2019] Joseph Oosting   29.01.1972
[30.12.2019] Edward Jeroen Sturing   13.06.1963

Goalkeepers:	DOB	M	(s)	G
Remko Pasveer	08.11.1983	26		
Defenders:	**DOB**	**M**	**(s)**	**G**
Joshua Brenet	20.03.1994	3	(1)	
Max Clark (ENG)	19.01.1996	22	(1)	1
Eli Dasa (ISR)	03.12.1992	9	(1)	
Danilho Doekhi	30.06.1998	26		
Vyacheslav Karavaev (RUS)	20.05.1995	5		1
Julian Lelieveld	09.07.1997	14	(2)	
Armando Obispo	05.03.1999	26		
Midfielders:	**DOB**	**M**	**(s)**	**G**
Riechedly Bazoer	12.10.1996	19	(3)	3
Matúš Bero (SVK)	06.09.1995	22		3
Navarone Foor	04.02.1992	11	(6)	
Keisuke Honda (JPN)	13.06.1986	3	(1)	

	DOB	M	(s)	G
Yassin Oukili	03.01.2001		(3)	
Thulani Caleeb Serero (RSA)	11.04.1990	2	(1)	
Sondre Tronstad (NOR)	26.08.1995	5	(1)	
Patrick Vroegh	29.11.1999	3	(4)	
Forwards:	**DOB**	**M**	**(s)**	**G**
Thomas Buitink	14.01.2000	2	(15)	
Oussama Darfalou (ALG)	29.09.1993		(6)	
Nouha Dicko (MLI)	14.05.1992	14	(5)	4
Hilary Chukwah Gong (NGA)	10.10.1998		(1)	
Jay-Roy Grot	13.03.1998	9	(13)	2
Bryan Linssen	08.10.1990	25		14
Tim Matavž (SVN)	13.01.1989	24	(1)	12
Charly Musonda (BEL)	15.10.1996		(3)	
Oussama Tannane (MAR)	23.03.1994	16	(1)	5

Venlose Voetbal Vereniging Venlo

Founded: 07.02.1903
Stadium: Stadion Seacon, Venlo (8,000)
Trainer: Robert Patrick Maaskant   10.01.1969
[15.11.2019] Jay Driessen   04.08.1969
[19.12.2019] Hans de Koning   05.04.1960

Goalkeepers:	DOB	M	(s)	G
Thorsten Kirschbaum (GER)	20.04.1987	26		
Defenders:	**DOB**	**M**	**(s)**	**G**
Tristan Dekker	27.03.1998		(4)	
Roy Gelmi (SUI)	01.03.1995	1	(2)	
Roel Janssen	16.06.1990	21		
Chris Kum	13.09.1985	19	(1)	
Tobias Pachonik (GER)	04.01.1995	26		1
Nils Röseler (GER)	10.02.1992	25		
Steffen Schäfer (GER)	01.05.1994	8	(1)	
Samuel Benjamin Elias Scheimann (ISR)	03.11.1987	3	(5)	
Damian van Bruggen	18.03.1996	2	(2)	
Stan van Dijck	07.10.2000		(3)	
Midfielders:	**DOB**	**M**	**(s)**	**G**
Aaron Bastiaans	04.04.2002		(1)	1

	DOB	M	(s)	G
Thomas Bruns	07.01.1992	6		
Lee Cattermole (ENG)	21.03.1988	9	(2)	
Simon Janssen	25.09.2000	1	(6)	
Evert Linthorst	03.03.2000	17	(1)	4
Richard Neudecker (GER)	29.10.1996	12	(4)	
Danny Post	07.04.1989	19	(1)	1
Peter van Ooijen	16.02.1992	21	(1)	5
Forwards:	**DOB**	**M**	**(s)**	**G**
Oussama Darfalou (ALG)	29.09.1993	8		3
Johnathan Opoku	18.04.1990	14	(5)	6
Jerome Sinclair (ENG)	20.09.1996	10	(13)	
Elia Soriano (ITA)	26.06.1989	12	(4)	2
Haji Wright (USA)	27.03.1998	16	(6)	
John Yeboah Zamora (GER)	23.06.2000	10	(8)	1

Willem II Tilburg

Founded: 12.08.1896
Stadium: Stadion „Koning Willem II", Tilburg (14,500)
Trainer: Adrianus Cornelis Koster   18.11.1954

Goalkeepers:	DOB	M	(s)	G
Timon Wellenreuther (GER)	03.12.1995	25		
Michael Woud (NZL)	16.01.1999	1		
Defenders:	**DOB**	**M**	**(s)**	**G**
Damil Dankerlui	24.08.1996	7	(9)	1
Freek Heerkens	13.09.1989	22		3
Sebastian Holmén (SWE)	29.04.1992	26		1
Fernando Lewis	31.01.1993	3		
James McGarry (NZL)	09.04.1998		(1)	
Paddy Miquel Nelom (SUR)	22.09.1990	13	(3)	
Justin Ogenia	05.02.1999		(1)	
Jordens Peters	03.05.1987	26		
Midfielders:	**DOB**	**M**	**(s)**	**G**
Mike Ndayishimiye (BEL)	28.05.1999	16	(4)	5

	DOB	M	(s)	G
Bart Nieuwkoop	07.03.1996	11	(6)	
Pol Llonch Puyaltó (ESP)	07.10.1992	24		2
Jhonny Raúl Quiñónez Ruíz (ECU)	11.06.1998		(5)	
Dries Saddiki	09.08.1996	25		
Görkem Sağlam (GER)	11.04.1998	1	(2)	
Marios Vrousai (GRE)	02.07.1998	10	(11)	2
Forwards:	**DOB**	**M**	**(s)**	**G**
Karim Coulibaly (FRA)	03.06.1993		(1)	
Paul Gladon	18.03.1992		(18)	1
Elton Kabangu (BEL)	08.02.1998		(4)	
Mats Köhlert (GER)	02.05.1998	26		6
Ché Nunnely	04.02.1999	25		4
Evangelos Pavlidis (GRE)	21.11.1998	25		11
Rick Zuijderwijk	13.04.2001		(2)	

SECOND LEVEL
Eerste Divisie 2019/2020

1.	SC Cambuur Leeuwarden	29	21	3	5	68 - 25	66
2.	VBV De Graafschap Doetinchem	29	17	11	1	63 - 28	62
3.	FC Volendam	29	16	7	6	57 - 42	55
4.	Jong Ajax Amsterdam	29	16	6	7	72 - 47	54
5.	NAC Breda	29	14	8	7	48 - 30	50
6.	Go Ahead Eagles Deventer	29	12	12	5	49 - 41	48
7.	SBV Excelsior Rotterdam	29	13	8	8	65 - 55	47
8.	NEC Nijmegen	29	12	9	8	51 - 37	45
9.	Almere City FC	29	13	5	11	44 - 42	44
10.	SC Telstar Velsen	29	12	8	9	47 - 48	44
11.	FC Den Bosch	29	10	11	8	56 - 49	38
12.	Jong FC Utrecht	29	10	8	11	48 - 47	38
13.	FC Eindhoven	29	9	7	13	46 - 59	34
14.	Jong AZ Alkmaar	29	7	7	15	45 - 61	28
15.	MVV Maastricht	29	7	6	16	37 - 53	27
16.	Tot Ons Plezier Oss	29	6	7	16	28 - 53	25
17.	SV Roda JC Kerkrade	29	5	10	14	36 - 52	22
18.	Jong PSV Eindhoven	29	5	7	17	34 - 56	22
19.	FC Dordrecht	29	4	8	17	34 - 66	20
20.	Helmond Sport	29	3	8	18	25 - 62	17

As at first level, the saison was cancelled on 24.04.2020. No teams were promoted or relegated.

NATIONAL TEAM

INTERNATIONAL MATCHES
(16.07.2019 – 15.07.2020)

06.09.2019	Hamburg	Germany - Netherlands	2-4(1-0)	(ECQ)
09.09.2019	Tallinn	Estonia - Netherlands	0-4(0-1)	(ECQ)
10.10.2019	Rotterdam	Netherlands - Northern Ireland	3-1(0-0)	(ECQ)
13.10.2019	Minsk	Belarus - Netherlands	1-2(0-2)	(ECQ)
16.11.2019	Belfast	Northern Ireland - Netherlands	0-0	(ECQ)
19.11.2019	Amsterdam	Netherlands - Estonia	5-0(2-0)	(ECQ)

06.09.2019   GERMANY - NETHERLANDS   2-4(1-0)   16th EC. Qualifiers
Volksparkstadion, Hamburg; Referee: Artur Manuel Soares Dias (Portugal); Attendance: 51,299
NED: Jacobus Antonius Peter Cillessen, Denzel Dumfries (58.David Petrus Wenceslaus Henri Pröpper), Virgil van Dijk (Cap), Matthijs de Ligt, Daley Blind, Marten Elco de Roon (58.Donyell Malen), Georginio Gregion Emile Wijnaldum, Frenkie de Jong, Memphis Depay, Quincy Anton Promes, Ryan Miguel Guno Babel (81.Nathan Benjamin Aké). Trainer: Ronald Koeman.
Goals: Frenkie de Jong (59), Jonathan Glao Tah (66 own goal), Donyell Malen (79), Georginio Gregion Emile Wijnaldum (90+1).

09.09.2019   ESTONIA - NETHERLANDS   0-4(0-1)   16th EC. Qualifiers
A. Le Coq Arena, Tallinn; Referee: Serhiy Boyko (Ukraine); Attendance: 11,006
NED: Jacobus Antonius Peter Cillessen, Joël Ivo Veltman, Virgil van Dijk (Cap), Matthijs de Ligt, Daley Blind, David Petrus Wenceslaus Henri Pröpper, Georginio Gregion Emile Wijnaldum, Frenkie de Jong (71.Luuk de Jong), Memphis Depay, Donyell Malen (63.Steven Berghuis), Ryan Miguel Guno Babel (85.Kevin Johannes Willem Strootman). Trainer: Ronald Koeman.
Goals: Ryan Miguel Guno Babel (17, 48), Memphis Depay (76), Georginio Gregion Emile Wijnaldum (84).

10.10.2019   NETHERLANDS - NORTHERN IRELAND   3-1(0-0)   16th EC. Qualifiers
Stadion Feijenoord, Rotterdam; Referee: Benoît Bastien (France); Attendance: 41,348
NED: Jacobus Antonius Peter Cillessen, Denzel Dumfries (78.Luuk de Jong), Virgil van Dijk (Cap), Matthijs de Ligt, Daley Blind, Marten Elco de Roon (66.Donny van de Beek), Georginio Gregion Emile Wijnaldum, Frenkie de Jong, Steven Charles Bergwijn, Memphis Depay, Ryan Miguel Guno Babel (66.Donyell Malen). Trainer: Ronald Koeman.
Goals: Memphis Depay (81), Luuk de Jong (90+1), Memphis Depay (90+4).

13.10.2019   BELARUS - NETHERLANDS   1-2(0-2)   16th EC. Qualifiers
Stadion Dynama, Minsk; Referee: Anastasios Sidiropoulos (Greece); Attendance: 21,639
NED: Jacobus Antonius Peter Cillessen, Joël Ivo Veltman, Virgil van Dijk (Cap), Matthijs de Ligt, Daley Blind, Donny van de Beek (67.Marten Elco de Roon), Georginio Gregion Emile Wijnaldum, Frenkie de Jong, Quincy Anton Promes (67.Luuk de Jong), Steven Charles Bergwijn (89.Ryan Miguel Guno Babel), Donyell Malen. Trainer: Ronald Koeman.
Goals: Georginio Gregion Emile Wijnaldum (32, 41).

16.11.2019   NORTHERN IRELAND - NETHERLANDS   0-0   16th EC. Qualifiers
Windsor Park, Belfast; Referee: Szymon Marciniak (Poland); Attendance: 18,404
NED: Jacobus Antonius Peter Cillessen, Joël Ivo Veltman, Virgil van Dijk (Cap), Matthijs de Ligt, Daley Blind, Marten Elco de Roon (36.David Petrus Wenceslaus Henri Pröpper), Donny van de Beek, Frenkie de Jong, Steven Berghuis (65.Luuk de Jong), Quincy Anton Promes, Ryan Miguel Guno Babel (90.Nathan Benjamin Aké). Trainer: Ronald Koeman.

19.11.2019   NETHERLANDS - ESTONIA   5-0(2-0)   16th EC. Qualifiers
"Johann Cruijff ArenA", Amsterdam; Referee: Davide Massa (Italy); Attendance: 50,386
NED: Jacobus Antonius Peter Cillessen, Nathan Benjamin Aké, Patrick John Miguel van Aanholt, Matthijs de Ligt, David Petrus Wenceslaus Henri Pröpper, Georginio Gregion Emile Wijnaldum (Cap), Frenkie de Jong (75.Kevin Johannes Willem Strootman), Memphis Depay (46.Myron Boadu), Quincy Anton Promes, Luuk de Jong (63.Wout Weghorst), Calvin Stengs. Trainer: Ronald Koeman.
Goals: Georginio Gregion Emile Wijnaldum (6), Nathan Benjamin Aké (19), Georginio Gregion Emile Wijnaldum (66, 79), Myron Boadu (87).

NATIONAL TEAM PLAYERS
(16.07.2019 – 15.07.2020)

Name	DOB	Caps	Goals	2019/2020:	Club
Goalkeepers					
Jacobus Antonius Peter CILLESSEN	22.04.1989	56	0	2019:	*Valencia CF (ESP)*
Defenders					
Nathan Benjamin AKÉ	18.02.1995	13	2	2019:	*AFC Bournemouth (ENG)*
Daley BLIND	09.03.1990	69	2	2019:	*AFC Ajax Amsterdam*
Matthijs DE LIGT	12.08.1999	23	2	2019:	*Juventus FC Torino (ITA)*
Denzel DUMFRIES	18.04.1996	9	0	2019:	*PSV Eindhoven*
Patrick John Miguel VAN AANHOLT	29.08.1990	10	0	2019:	*Crystal Palace FC London (ENG)*
Virgil VAN DIJK	08.07.1991	33	4	2019:	*Liverpool FC (ENG)*
Joël Ivo VELTMAN	15.01.1992	22	2	2019:	*AFC Ajax Amsterdam*
Midfielders					
Frenkie DE JONG	12.05.1997	15	1	2019:	*FC Barcelona (ESP)*
Marten Elco DE ROON	29.03.1991	16	0	2019:	*Atalanta Bergamasca Calcio (ITA)*
David Petrus Wenceslaus Henri PRÖPPER	02.09.1991	19	3	2019:	*Brighton & Hove Albion FC (ENG)*
Kevin Johannes Willem STROOTMAN	13.02.1990	46	3	2019:	*Olympique de Marseille (FRA)*
Donny VAN DE BEEK	18.04.1997	10	0	2019:	*AFC Ajax Amsterdam*
Georginio Gregion Emile WIJNALDUM	11.11.1990	62	18	2019:	*Liverpool FC (ENG)*
Forwards					
Ryan Miguel Guno BABEL	19.12.1986	63	10	2019:	*Galatasaray SK İstanbul (TUR)*
Steven BERGHUIS	19.12.1991	16	0	2019:	*Feyenoord Rotterdam*
Steven Charles BERGWIJN	08.10.1997	9	0	2019:	*PSV Eindhoven*
Myron BOADU	14.01.2001	1	1	2019:	*AZ Alkmaar*
Luuk DE JONG	27.08.1990	24	5	2019:	*Sevilla FC (ESP)*
Memphis DEPAY	13.02.1994	52	19	2019:	*Olympique Lyonnais (FRA)*
Donyell MALEN	19.01.1999	4	1	2019:	*PSV Eindhoven*
Quincy Anton PROMES	04.01.1992	42	7	2019:	*AFC Ajax Amsterdam*
Calvin STENGS	18.12.1998	1	0	2019:	*AZ Alkmaar*
Wout WEGHORST	07.08.1992	4	0	2019:	*VfL Wolfsburg (GER)*
National team coach					
Ronald KOEMAN [from 06.02.2019]	21.03.1963	20 M; 11 W; 5 D; 4 L; 43-18			

NORTH MACEDONIA

The Country:
Република Северна Македонија (Republic of North Macedonia)
Capital: Skopje
Surface: 25,713 km²
Inhabitants: 2,077,132 [2019]
Time: UTC+1

The FA:
Fudbalska Federacija na Severna Makedonija
bul. Asnom bb, 1000 Skopje
Tel: +389 23 129291
Foundation date: 1926
Member of FIFA since: 1926/1994
Member of UEFA since: 1954/1994
Website: www.ffm.com.mk

NATIONAL TEAM RECORDS

RECORDS	
First international match:	13.10.1993, Kranj: Slovenia – Macedonia 1-4
Most international caps:	Goran Pandev – 108 caps (since 2001)
Most international goals:	Goran Pandev – 34 goals / 108 caps (since 2001)

UEFA EUROPEAN CHAMPIONSHIP		FIFA WORLD CUP		OLYMPIC TOURNAMENTS	
1960	-	1930	-	1908	-
1964	-	1934	-	1912	-
1968	-	1938	-	1920	-
1972	-	1950	-	1924	-
1976	-	1954	-	1928	-
1980	-	1958	-	1936	-
1984	-	1962	-	1948	-
1988	-	1966	-	1952	-
1992	-	1970	-	1956	-
1996	Qualifiers	1974	-	1960	-
2000	Qualifiers	1978	-	1964	-
2004	Qualifiers	1982	-	1968	-
2008	Qualifiers	1986	-	1972	-
2012	Qualifiers	1990	-	1976	-
2016	Qualifiers	1994	Did not enter	1980	-
2020	*To be determined*	1998	Qualifiers	1984	-
		2002	Qualifiers	1988	-
		2006	Qualifiers	1992	Did not enter
		2010	Qualifiers	1996	Qualifiers
		2014	Qualifiers	2000	Qualifiers
		2018	Qualifiers	2004	Qualifiers
				2008	Qualifiers
				2012	Qualifiers
				2016	Qualifiers

was part of Yugoslavia until 08.09.1991

UEFA NATIONS LEAGUE
2018/2019 – League D (promoted to League C)

FIFA CONFEDERATIONS CUP 1992-2017
None

MACEDONIAN CLUB HONOURS IN EUROPEAN CLUB COMPETITIONS:

European Champion Clubs' Cup (1956-1992) / UEFA Champions League (1993-2020)
None

Fairs Cup (1858-1971) / UEFA Cup (1972-2009) / UEFA Europa League (2010-2020)
None

UEFA Super Cup (1972-2019)
None

*European Cup Winners' Cup 1961-1999**
None

defunct competition

NATIONAL COMPETITIONS
TABLE OF HONOURS

Royal League
(territory of Vardarska Banovina belonging to the Kingdom of Yugoslavia)

	CHAMPIONS
1929	Pobeda Skopje
1930	Jug Skopje, SSK Skopje, Sparta Skopje*
1931	*Championship not finished*
1932	SSK Skopje
1933	SSK Skopje
1934	SSK Skopje
1935	*Championship not finished*
1936	Gragjanski Skopje
1937	*Championship not finished*
1938	Gragjanski Skopje
1939	Gragjanski Skopje
1940	SSK Skopje
1941	SSK Skopje

*All 3 teams finished with equal number of points

As part of Bulgaria

	CHAMPIONS
1942	Makedonija Skopje
1943	ZhSK Skopje
1944	ZhSK Skopje

Republic League (within F.R. Yugoslavia)

1944/1945	Makedonija Skopje	1960/1961	Pelister Bitola	1976/1977	Rabotnichki Skopje
1945/1946	Pobeda Skopje	1961/1962	Pobeda Prilep	1977/1978	Tikvesh Kavadarci
1946/1947	Makedonija Skopje	1962/1963	Pobeda Prilep	1978/1979	Pobeda Prilep
1947/1948	Dinamo Skopje	1963/1964	Bregalnica Shtip	1979/1980	Rabotnichki Skopje
1948/1949	11 Oktomvri Kumanovo	1964/1965	Teteks Tetovo	1980/1981	Pobeda Prilep
1949/1950	Rabotnik Bitola	1965/1966	Rabotnichki Skopje	1981/1982	Pelister Bitola
1950/1951	Rabotnik Bitola	1966/1967	Bregalnica Shtip	1982/1983	Belasica Strumica
1951/1952	Rabotnichki Skopje	1967/1968	Rabotnichki Skopje	1983/1984	Bregalnica Shtip
1952/1953	Pobeda Prilep	1968/1969	Teteks Tetovo	1984/1985	Teteks Tetovo
1953/1954	Rabotnichki Skopje	1969/1970	MIK Skopje	1985/1986	Pobeda Prilep
1954/1955	Rabotnichki Skopje	1970/1971	Kumanovo	1986/1987	Metalurg Skopje
1955/1956	Vardar Skopje	1971/1972	Tikvesh Kavadarci	1987/1988	Belasica Strumica
1956/1957	Rabotnichki Skopje	1972/1973	Rabotnichki Skopje	1988/1989	Borec-Titov Veles
1957/1958	Rabotnichki Skopje	1973/1974	Teteks Tetovo	1989/1990	Balkan Skopje
1958/1959	Pobeda Prilep	1974/1975	Pelister Bitola	1990/1991	Makedonija Skopje
1959/1960	Pelister Bitola	1975/1976	Bregalnica Shtip	1991/1992	Sasa Makedonska Kamenica

After proclamation of independence - Macedonian First League

	CHAMPIONS	CUP WINNERS	BEST GOALSCORERS	
1992/1993	FK Vardar Skopje	FK Vardar Skopje	Saša Ćirić (FK Vardar Skopje)	36
1993/1994	FK Vardar Skopje	FK Sileks Kratovo	Zoran Boshkovski (FK Sileks Kratovo)	21
1994/1995	FK Vardar Skopje	FK Vardar Skopje	Saša Ćirić (FK Vardar Skopje)	35
1995/1996	FK Sileks Kratovo	FK Sloga Jugomagnat Skopje	Zoran Boshkovski (FK Sileks Kratovo)	20
1996/1997	FK Sileks Kratovo	FK Sileks Kratovo	Vancho Micevski (FK Sileks Kratovo) Miroslav Gjokić (FK Sileks Kratovo)	16
1997/1998	FK Sileks Kratovo	FK Vardar Skopje	Vancho Atanasov (FK Belasica Stremica)	12
1998/1999	FK Sloga Jugomagnat Skopje	FK Vardar Skopje	Rogério Oliveira da Costa (FK Pobeda Prilep)	22
1999/2000	FK Sloga Jugomagnat Skopje	FK Sloga Jugomagnat Skopje	Argjend Beqiri (FK Sloga Jugomagnat Skopje)	19
2000/2001	FK Sloga Jugomagnat Skopje	FK Pelister Bitola	Argjend Beqiri (FK Sloga Jugomagnat Skopje)	27
2001/2002	FK Vardar Skopje	FK Pobeda Prilep	Miroslav Gjokić (FK Pobeda Prilep)	22
2002/2003	FK Vardar Skopje	FK Cementarnica 55 Skopje	Ljubiša Savić (FK Bregalnica Štip / FK Sloga Jugomagnat Skopje)	25
2003/2004	FK Pobeda Prilep	FK Sloga Jugomagnat Skopje	Dragan Dimitrovski (FK Pobeda Prilep)	25
2004/2005	FK Rabotnički Skopje	KF Bashkimi Kumanovo	Aleksandar Stojanovski (FK Belasica Stremica) Stevica Ristić (FK Sileks Kratovo)	26
2005/2006	FK Rabotnički Skopje	FK Makedonija Gjorče Petrov	Stevica Ristić (FK Sileks Kratovo)	27
2006/2007	FK Pobeda Prilep	FK Vardar Skopje	Boban Janchevski (KF Bashkimi Kumanovo / KF Renova Džepčište)	26
2007/2008	FK Rabotnički Skopje	FK Rabotnički Skopje	Ivica Gligorovski (FK Milano Kumanovo)	15
2008/2009	FK Makedonija Gjorče Petrov	FK Rabotnički Skopje	Ivica Gligorovski (FK Milano Kumanovo)	14
2009/2010	KF Renova Džepčište	FK Teteks Tetovo	Bobi Bozhinovski (FK Rabotnički Skopje)	15
2010/2011	KF Shkëndija Tetovo	FK Metalurg Skopje	Hristijan Kirovski (FK Skopje)	20
2011/2012	FK Vardar Skopje	KF Renova Džepčište	Filip Ivanovski (FK Vardar Skopje)	24
2012/2013	FK Vardar Skopje	FK Teteks Tetovo	Jovan Kostovski (FK Vardar Skopje)	22
2013/2014	FK Rabotnički Skopje	FK Rabotnički Skopje	Dejan Blazhevski (FK Horizont Turnovo)	19
2014/2015	FK Vardar Skopje	FK Rabotnički Skopje	Izair Emini (KF Renova Džepčište)	20
2015/2016	FK Vardar Skopje	KF Shkëndija Tetovo	Besart Ibraimi (KF Shkëndija Tetovo)	26
2016/2017	FK Vardar Skopje	FK Pelister Bitola	Besart Ibraimi (KF Shkëndija Tetovo)	20

2017/2018	KF Shkëndija Tetovo	KF Shkëndija Tetovo	Ferhan Hasani (KF Shkëndija Tetovo)	
			Besart Ibraimi (KF Shkëndija Tetovo)	22
2018/2019	KF Shkëndija Tetovo	Fudb. Akademija Pandev Strumica	Vlatko Stojanovski (KF Renova Džepčište)	18
2019/2020	FK Vardar Skopje	*Competition cancelled*	Daniel Avramovski (FK Vardar Skopje)	11

NATIONAL CHAMPIONSHIP
Macedonian First Football League – Prva Liga 2019/2020
(10.08.2019 – 11.03.2020)

Results

Round 1 [10-11.08.2019]
KF Renova - Sileks Kratovo 1-0(1-0)
FC Struga - FK Rabotnički 2-1(1-1)
KF Shkupi - FK Borec 2-0(0-0)
Akademija Pandev - KF Shkëndija 79 1-0(0-0)
Vardar Skopje - FK Makedonija 0-2(0-1)

Round 2 [17-18.08.2019]
FK Rabotnički - KF Shkupi 2-0(1-0)
FK Makedonija - Akademija Pandev 0-0
Sileks Kratovo - KF Shkëndija 79 1-0(0-0)
FK Borec - Vardar Skopje 0-0
KF Renova - FC Struga 2-1(1-0)

Round 3 [24-25.08.2019]
Vardar Skopje - FK Rabotnički 2-0(0-0)
FC Struga - Sileks Kratovo 2-1(1-0)
KF Shkupi - KF Renova 2-2(1-1)
Akademija Pandev - FK Borec 2-0(1-0)
KF Shkëndija 79 - FK Makedonija 1-1(1-1)

Round 4 [31.08.-01.09.2019]
FK Borec - KF Shkëndija 79 1-0(0-0)
FK Rabotnički - Akademija Pandev 1-2(1-1)
Sileks Kratovo - FK Makedonija 3-4(0-2)
FC Struga - KF Shkupi 1-1(0-0)
KF Renova - Vardar Skopje 0-1(0-0)

Round 5 [13-14.09.2019]
Akademija Pandev - KF Renova 2-0(1-0)
KF Shkëndija 79 - FK Rabotnički 3-0(2-0)
Vardar Skopje - FC Struga 3-0(0-0)
FK Makedonija - FK Borec 3-1(1-1)
KF Shkupi - Sileks Kratovo 1-0(0-0)

Round 6 [18.09.2019]
FK Rabotnički - FK Makedonija 1-0(0-0)
Sileks Kratovo - FK Borec 3-0(2-0)
KF Renova - KF Shkëndija 79 0-2(0-0)
FC Struga - Akademija Pandev 0-0
KF Shkupi - Vardar Skopje 1-2(0-1)

Round 7 [21-22.09.2019]
FK Borec - FK Rabotnički 1-1(1-1)
FK Makedonija - KF Renova 0-1(0-0)
Akademija Pandev - KF Shkupi 0-0
Vardar Skopje - Sileks Kratovo 3-0(3-0)
KF Shkëndija 79 - FC Struga 2-0(1-0)

Round 8 [28-29.09.2019]
KF Shkupi - KF Shkëndija 79 2-0(0-0)
KF Renova - FK Borec 2-1(1-0)
FC Struga - FK Makedonija 0-2(0-1)
Sileks Kratovo - FK Rabotnički 1-0(1-0)
Vardar Skopje - Akademija Pandev 1-0(1-0)

Round 9 [04-05.10.2019]
FK Rabotnički - KF Renova 1-0(0-0)
KF Shkëndija 79 - Vardar Skopje 0-0
FK Makedonija - KF Shkupi 0-0
FK Borec - FC Struga 3-2(2-2)
Akademija Pandev - Sileks Kratovo 2-0(1-0)

Round 10 [18-19.10.2019]
KF Shkëndija 79 - Akademija Pandev 0-1(0-1)
Sileks Kratovo - KF Renova 3-0(0-0)
FK Rabotnički - FC Struga 1-2(0-1)
FK Borec - KF Shkupi 2-1(1-1)
FK Makedonija - Vardar Skopje 1-1(0-0)

Round 11 [23.10.2019]
Akademija Pandev - FK Makedonija 4-0(2-0)
KF Shkëndija 79 - Sileks Kratovo 3-0(1-0)
Vardar Skopje - FK Borec 2-0(1-0)
KF Shkupi - FK Rabotnički 2-0(1-0)
FC Struga - KF Renova 1-0(0-0)

Round 12 [26-27.10.2019]
FK Rabotnički - Vardar Skopje 0-2(0-0)
Sileks Kratovo - FC Struga 1-0(0-0)
KF Renova - KF Shkupi 2-2(1-1)
FK Borec - Akademija Pandev 1-0(0-0)
FK Makedonija - KF Shkëndija 79 0-0

Round 13 [02-03.11.2019]
Akademija Pandev - FK Rabotnički 1-1(1-0)
KF Shkëndija 79 - FK Borec 4-0(3-0)
Vardar Skopje - KF Renova 0-1(0-0)
FK Makedonija - Sileks Kratovo 0-1(0-1)
KF Shkupi - FC Struga 0-0

Round 14 [09-10.11.2019]
FC Struga - Vardar Skopje 2-1(2-0)
KF Renova - Akademija Pandev 1-1(0-1)
FK Borec - FK Makedonija 1-1(1-0)
Sileks Kratovo - KF Shkupi 1-0(1-0)
FK Rabotnički - KF Shkëndija 79 1-2(1-1)

Round 15 [23-24.11.2019]
FK Makedonija - FK Rabotnički 2-0(1-0)
FK Borec - Sileks Kratovo 0-0
KF Shkëndija 79 - KF Renova 6-1(1-0)
Akademija Pandev - FC Struga 1-1(0-0)
Vardar Skopje - KF Shkupi 1-1(1-0)

Round 16 [27.11.2019]
KF Shkupi - Akademija Pandev 3-1(0-1)
Sileks Kratovo - Vardar Skopje 2-2(1-0)
FC Struga - KF Shkëndija 79 2-1(0-1)
KF Renova - FK Makedonija 1-1(0-0)
FK Rabotnički - FK Borec 2-1(1-0)

Round 17 [30.11.-01.12.2019]
FK Makedonija - FC Struga 1-1(1-1)
FK Borec - KF Renova 1-0(1-0)
FK Rabotnički - Sileks Kratovo 1-1(1-0)
KF Shkëndija 79 - KF Shkupi 4-0(3-0)
Akademija Pandev - Vardar Skopje 0-3(0-1)

Round 18 [08.12.2019]
Vardar Skopje - KF Shkëndija 79 2-2(1-1)
KF Shkupi - FK Makedonija 2-3(0-2)
FC Struga - FK Borec 1-1(0-0)
Sileks Kratovo - Akademija Pandev 3-1(1-0)
KF Renova - FK Rabotnički 4-3(1-2)

Round 19 [15-16.02.2020]
Vardar Skopje - FK Makedonija 3-1(1-0)
Akademija Pandev - KF Shkëndija 79 1-2(1-1)
KF Renova - Sileks Kratovo 0-1(0-1)
FC Struga - FK Rabotnički 0-1(0-1)
KF Shkupi - FK Borec 2-0(0-0)

Round 20 [22-23.02.2020]
FK Borec - Vardar Skopje 0-1(0-1)
FK Makedonija - Akademija Pandev 1-0(0-0)
Sileks Kratovo - KF Shkëndija 79 0-0
FK Rabotnički - KF Shkupi 2-1(0-1)
KF Renova - FC Struga 2-0(1-0)

Round 21 [29.02.-01.03.2020]
Vardar Skopje - FK Rabotnički 0-0
FC Struga - Sileks Kratovo 0-0
Akademija Pandev - FK Borec 0-0
KF Shkupi - KF Renova 2-3(1-2)
KF Shkëndija 79 - FK Makedonija 4-1(1-0)

Round 22 [07-08.03.2020]
FK Rabotnički - Akademija Pandev 1-0(0-0)
KF Renova - Vardar Skopje 2-0(1-0)
FC Struga - KF Shkupi 1-2(1-2)
Sileks Kratovo - FK Makedonija 1-0(1-0)
FK Borec - KF Shkëndija 79 4-2(2-0)

Round 23 [11.03.2020]
FK Makedonija - FK Borec 0-2(0-2)
KF Shkëndija 79 - FK Rabotnički 0-1(0-0)
Akademija Pandev - KF Renova 0-1(0-1)
Vardar Skopje - FC Struga 1-0(0-0)
KF Shkupi - Sileks Kratovo 1-1(1-0)

Please note: the championship was suspended on 11.03.2020 due to Covid-19 pandemic and abandoned on 04.06.2020. FK Vardar Skopje were declared champions, no teams were relegated.

Final Standings

		Total							Home						Away					
1.	**FK Vardar Skopje**	23	13	7	3	33	-	14	46	8	3	1	20	-	6	5	4	2	13	-	8
2.	FK Sileks Kratovo	23	10	6	7	24	-	21	36	8	2	1	19	-	7	2	4	6	5	-	14
3.	KF Shkëndija Tetovo	23	10	5	8	38	-	20	35	7	2	2	27	-	5	3	3	6	11	-	15
4.	KF Renova Džepčište	23	9	4	10	25	-	33	31	6	3	3	17	-	13	3	1	7	8	-	20
5.	KF Shkupi Čair	23	7	8	8	28	-	28	29	6	3	3	20	-	12	1	5	5	8	-	16
6.	FK Makedonija Gjorče Petrov Skopje	23	7	8	8	24	-	28	29	3	5	3	8	-	7	4	3	5	16	-	21
7.	Fudbalska Akademija Pandev Strumica	23	7	7	9	20	-	20	28	5	4	3	14	-	8	2	3	6	6	-	12
8.	FK Rabotnički Skopje	23	8	4	11	21	-	29	28	6	1	4	13	-	11	2	3	7	8	-	18
9.	FK Borec Veles	23	7	6	10	20	-	31	27	6	4	1	14	-	8	1	2	9	6	-	23
10.	FC Struga Trim-Lum	23	6	7	10	19	-	28	25	5	4	3	12	-	11	1	3	7	7	-	17

Top goalscorers:

11	**Daniel Avramovski**	*FK Vardar Skopje*
9	Armend Alimi	*KF Shkëndija Tetovo*
9	Nikola Prelčec (CRO)	*FK Borec 1919 Veles*
8	Marin Jurina (BIH)	*FC Shkupi Čair*

NATIONAL CUP
Kup na Makedonija 2019/2020

Second Round [19-21/28.08.2019]

FK Novo Crnilishte - FK Bregalnica 2008 Štip	0-22		GFK Osogovo Kočani - FK Pobeda AD Prilep	1-0
FK Ljuboten - GFK Tikveš 1930 Kavadarci	1-5		FK Vëllazërimi 77 Kërçpoë - FK Rabotnički Skopje	0-4
FK Kit-Go Pehčevo - FK Pelister Bitola	4-5 pen		FK Prevalec Veles - FK Borec Veles	0-4
FK Fortuna 1975 Skopje - FK Sileks Kratovo	0-4		FK Lokomotiva Skopje - FC Struga Trim-Lum	1-5
GFK Ohrid - FK Belasica Strumica	5-4 i.E.		FK Kožuf Gevgelija - KF Renova Džepčište	5-6 pen
FK Kravari - FK Labunishta	1-4		FK Teteks Tetovo - KF Shkupi Čair	1-5
KF Gostivari - KF Shkëndija Tetovo	1-4		Kamenica Sasa - FK Vardar Skopje	0-5

1/8-Finals [25.09./30-31.10.2019]

First Leg			Second Leg	
Fud. Akad. Pandev Strumica - GFK Osogovo Kočani	3-0		GFK Osogovo Kočani - Fud. Akad. Pandev Strumica	1-4
FK Bregalnica 2008 Štip - FK Makedonija G. Petrov	1-0		FK Makedonija G. Petrov - FK Bregalnica 2008 Štip	0-0
KF Shkupi Čair - FK Sileks Kratovo	0-0		FK Sileks Kratovo - KF Shkupi Čair	1-1
FK Pelister Bitola - FK Rabotnički Skopje	1-1		FK Rabotnički Skopje - FK Pelister Bitola	4-0
GFK Tikveš 1930 Kavadarci - KF Renova Džepčište	0-2		KF Renova Džepčište - GFK Tikveš 1930 Kavadarci	1-1
FK Labunishta - GFK Ohrid	2-0		GFK Ohrid - FK Labunishta	2-3
FK Borec Veles - FC Struga Trim-Lum	0-0		FC Struga Trim-Lum - FK Borec Veles	1-0
FK Vardar Skopje - KF Shkëndija Tetovo	2-2		KF Shkëndija Tetovo - FK Vardar Skopje	1-0

Quarter-Finals [04.12.2019/04.03.2020]

First Leg			Second Leg	
KF Shkëndija Tetovo - FK Rabotnički Skopje	1-1		FK Rabotnički Skopje - KF Shkëndija Tetovo	2-2
KF Shkupi Čair – Fud. Akademija Pandev Strumica	0-1		Fud. Akademija Pandev Strumica - KF Shkupi Čair	1-1
FC Struga Trim-Lum - KF Renova Džepčište	0-0		KF Renova Džepčište - FC Struga Trim-Lum	1-2
FK Bregalnica 2008 Štip - FK Labunishta	1-0		FK Labunishta - FK Bregalnica 2008 Štip	1-4

The competition was cancelled due to Covid-19 pandemic. No title was awarded.

Fudbalska Akademija Pandev Strumica

Founded:	2010	
Stadium:	Stadion „Blagoj Istatov", Strumica (1,500)	
Trainer:	Jugoslav Trencovski	29.11.1976
[05.03.2020]	Aleksandar Tanevski	24.07.1983

Goalkeepers:	DOB	M	(s)	G
Dušan Čubraković (SRB)	21.07.1995	23		
Defenders:	**DOB**	**M**	**(s)**	**G**
David Atanasovski	21.10.1996	10	(5)	
Mite Cikarski	06.01.1993	5		
Dime Dimov	25.07.1994	17		
Angel Granchov (BUL)	16.10.1992	5		
Tomislav Iliev	02.12.1993	12	(2)	
Vane Jovanov	28.12.1998	16	(2)	
Stefan Kostov	31.10.1996	7	(2)	
Mihail Manevski	25.02.1999	9	(1)	
Mario Maslać (SRB)	09.09.1990	17		1
Midfielders:	**DOB**	**M**	**(s)**	**G**
Bojan Najdenov	27.08.1991		(4)	

	DOB	M	(s)	G
Ivan Nikolov	17.02.2002	4	(3)	
Georgi Stoilov	25.08.1995	18		2
Kristijan Stojkovski	17.09.1991	18	(2)	1
Gjorgji Tanušev	07.01.1991	14	(5)	1
Riste Temelkov	02.10.1997	4	(1)	
Goran Tomovski	21.07.1998	17	(1)	1
Forwards:	**DOB**	**M**	**(s)**	**G**
Ljupco Doriev	13.09.1995	16	(1)	3
Mario Krstovski	03.04.1998	3	(9)	2
Daniel Milovanovikj	10.08.1998	7	(5)	2
Ndue Mujeci (ALB)	24.02.1993	1	(4)	
Saško Pandev	01.05.1987	19	(4)	3
Marko Rajković (SRB)	13.11.1992	5	(9)	4
Kristijan Velinovski	31.05.1999	6	(9)	

Fudbalski klub Borec Veles

Founded:	1919	
Stadium:	Stadion „Zoran Paunov", Veles (2,000)	
Trainer:	Gorazd Mihajlov	21.08.1974

Goalkeepers:	DOB	M	(s)	G
Mikica Gjorgievski	17.05.1994	6		
Burhan Mustafa	22.07.1990	17		
Defenders:	**DOB**	**M**	**(s)**	**G**
Kristijan Eftimov	01.09.1999	20		
Nikola Gavrić (CRO)	17.03.1995	15	(2)	
Nikola Risteski	20.12.1996	5		
Filip Ristovski	03.01.1995	13	(1)	
Oliver Stoimenovski	26.03.1999	8		
Trajce Stojkovski	23.02.1989	21		
Filip Trajanovski	21.03.1999	11		
Midfielders:	**DOB**	**M**	**(s)**	**G**
Aleksandr Anastasov	04.05.1993		(3)	
Martin Blaževski	13.05.1992	5	(3)	
Fernando Silva dos Santos (BRA)	18.05.1991	5		1
Đorđe Ivljanin (SRB)	19.12.1996	1		

	DOB	M	(s)	G
Robert Kocev	14.06.1994	21	(2)	1
Stefan Lazarevikj	18.02.1997	4	(12)	
Kristijan Nikolovski	20.07.1997	12	(8)	
Oliver Peev	08.06.1987	14	(1)	
Trajce Trajkov	29.11.1993	1	(13)	
Jovan Velev (SRB)	12.09.2000		(1)	
Forwards:	**DOB**	**M**	**(s)**	**G**
Emil Abaz	17.01.1998	11	(10)	
Stefan Bogdanovski	15.03.1999	1	(1)	
Dario Desnikj	13.05.1994	4		1
Gjorgi Gjorgiev	18.06.1996	13	(4)	1
Simeon Hristov	04.09.1992	14	(1)	3
Filip Petrov	23.02.1989	4	(5)	
Nikola Prelčec (CRO)	12.11.1989	22		9
Nikola Radović (SRB)	10.07.1992	5		3

Fudbalski klub Makedonija Gjorče Petrov Skopje

Founded:	1932	
Stadium:	Stadion „Gjorče Petrov", Skopje (3,000)	
Trainer:	Aleksandar Tanevski	24.07.1983
[20.11.2019]	Naci Sensoy (KVX)	01.07.1958

Goalkeepers:	DOB	M	(s)	G
Marko Jovanovski	24.07.1988	23		
Defenders:	**DOB**	**M**	**(s)**	**G**
David Atanasovski	21.10.1996	3		
Bianor das Graças Lima da Silva (BRA)	28.06.1994	16		
Fernando Augusto Rodrigues de Araujo (BRA)	25.07.1993	20	(1)	1
Tome Kitanovski	21.05.1992	5		
Martin Kovachev (BUL)	12.03.1982	3		
Esmin Licina	20.03.1998	17		
Filip Misevski	01.11.1991	10	(4)	
Hristijan Pecov	30.04.1994	8		
Midfielders:	**DOB**	**M**	**(s)**	**G**
Ermadin Adem	07.07.1990	15		
Bobi Božinovski	24.02.1981	22	(1)	6
Sefer Emini	15.07.2000	23		1

	DOB	M	(s)	G
Kristijan Filipovski	02.10.1996	5	(10)	
Robson da Silva (BRA)	14.07.1995	15	(5)	1
Blagoja Spirkoski	13.07.1991	1		
Luka Trajkoski	08.02.2000		(5)	
Forwards:	**DOB**	**M**	**(s)**	**G**
Filip Aleksovski	25.03.2000	1	(1)	
Dejan Blaževski	06.12.1985	8	(12)	3
Benjamin Demir	16.05.1996	16	(1)	2
Alen Jasaroski	06.11.1991	9	(11)	3
Paulo Eduardo Carvalho „Padú" (BRA)	31.10.1997	13	(5)	7
Filip Petrov	23.02.1989		(3)	
Alban Sulejmani	14.04.1998		(3)	
Dejan Tanturovski	12.08.1992	3	(2)	
Arbin Vosha	04.08.2001	17	(4)	

Fudbalski klub Rabotnički Skopje

Founded: 04.10.1937
Stadium: "Toše Proeski" National Arena, Skopje (36,460)
Trainer: Aleksandar Vlaho — 18.01.1976
[21.10.2019] Marjanco Andreski — 13.09.1972
[21.12.2019] Ratko Dostanić (SRB) — 25.10.1959

Goalkeepers:	DOB	M	(s)	G
Risto Jankov	05.09.1998		(1)	
Damjan Siskovski	18.03.1995	23		
Defenders:	DOB	M	(s)	G
Sabahudin Alomerović	29.06.1997	2	(1)	
Alexander Borja Córdoba (COL)	25.10.1998	3	(4)	1
Yannick Dao (BFA)	04.12.1998		(3)	
Draško Đorđević (SRB)	01.08.1993	5		
Sebastián Herrera Cardona (COL)	23.01.1995	19		
Marko Klisura (SRB)	15.10.1992	11		
Borjan Panovski	26.07.2000		(4)	
Hristijan Pecov	30.04.1994	3	(1)	
Goran Siljanovski	01.07.1990	13	(3)	
Viktor Velkoski	14.11.1995	17	(2)	2
Midfielders:	DOB	M	(s)	G
Kristijan Ackovski	15.02.1998	9	(3)	
Nemanja Ilić (SRB)	27.08.1992	13		
Stefan Jevtoski	02.09.1997	11	(4)	
Ivan Marković (SRB)	20.06.1994	16	(1)	6
Luka Stankovski	02.09.2002	1		
Filip Stojčevski	04.02.1999	5		
Dragan Stojkov	23.02.1988	20		
Dimitar Todorovski	07.03.2002	10	(3)	1
Miloš Tošeski	24.02.1998		(4)	
Forwards:	DOB	M	(s)	G
Lavdrim Fazliu	06.10.1999	3	(4)	
Meldin Jusufi (BIH)	30.12.1998		(3)	
Mario Kosteski	08.02.2002		(1)	
Strahinja Krstevski	08.06.1997	3	(5)	
Mario Krstovski	03.04.1998	2	(2)	
Boško Papović (SRB)	22.12.1996	1	(5)	
Petar Petkovski	03.01.1997	16	(2)	2
Nikolce Sarkoski	08.03.1994	20	(1)	3
David Tosevski	16.07.2001	16	(5)	4
Yaggo Vitorino Silva Gomes (BRA)	08.06.1993	11	(2)	

Klubi Futbollit Renova Džepčište

Founded: 2003
Stadium: Ecolog Arena, Tetovo (15,000)
Trainer: Bujar Islami — 29.11.1978

Goalkeepers:	DOB	M	(s)	G
Hadis Velii	20.05.1990	23		
Defenders:	DOB	M	(s)	G
Xhelil Abdulla	25.09.1991	5		
Ilber Bekiri	27.12.1999		(4)	
Saimir Fetai	04.04.1989	19	(1)	
Nenad Miškovski	26.12.1986	22		1
Nehar Sadiki	16.03.1998	5	(7)	
Altin Sefo	27.08.2000	4	(2)	
Bashkim Velija	01.08.1993	22	(1)	2
Fisnik Zuka	03.09.1995	22		1
Midfielders:	DOB	M	(s)	G
Armend Aliu	26.04.1996	3	(3)	
Alush Gavazaj (KVX)	24.03.1995	5		
Burim Sadiki	05.08.1989	22		
Meriton Saliji	15.01.1996	5	(1)	
Jasir Selmani	21.01.1991	7	(1)	
Forwards:	DOB	M	(s)	G
Ilirid Ademi	04.03.1995	11	(12)	5
Lutfi Bilali	14.04.1992		(4)	
Argjent Gafuri	30.03.1988	22		4
Florian Kadriu	29.08.1996	21	(2)	3
Bojan Miovski	24.06.1999	17	(1)	2
Remzi Selmani	05.05.1997	16	(1)	7
Shefit Shefiti (ALB)	19.02.1998		(4)	
Lavdrim Skenderi	17.01.1994		(6)	
Alban Taipi	21.03.2003	2	(1)	
Artan Veliu	09.12.1997		(11)	

Klubi Futbollistik Shkëndija Tetovo

Founded: 27.08.1979
Stadium: Ecolog Arena, Tetovo (15,000)
Trainer: Qatip Osmani — 29.06.1969
[03.09.2019] Erhan Selimi — 10.09.1978
[10.10.2019] Ernest Gjoka (ALB) — 25.01.1970

Goalkeepers:	DOB	M	(s)	G
Bekim Redjepi	27.10.1996	1		
Kostadin Zahov	08.11.1987	22		
Defenders:	DOB	M	(s)	G
Egzon Bejtulai	07.01.1994	14	(1)	1
Konstantin Cheshmedijev	29.01.1996	13		
Ardin Dallku (KVX)	01.11.1994	2		
Ján Krivák (SVK)	10.11.1993	5		
Zija Merdjani	22.10.1995	1		
Gledi Mici (ALB)	06.02.1991	20		1
Mevlan Murati	05.03.1994	20		
Medzit Neziri	02.09.1990	13		
Leard Sadriu (KVX)	22.04.2001	4	(1)	
Midfielders:	DOB	M	(s)	G
Valon Ahmedi (ALB)	07.10.1994	3	(1)	
Armend Alimi	11.12.1987	20		9
Zeni Husmani	28.11.1990	6	(3)	
Juan Felipe Alves Ribeiro (BRA)	05.12.1987	8	(2)	1
Ennur Totre	29.10.1996	13	(8)	2
Arbin Zejnullai (ALB)	15.02.1999	8	(1)	1
Forwards:	DOB	M	(s)	G
Aldair Sapalo Amaro Neto (POR)	22.07.1994		(2)	
Samir Fazli	22.04.1991	1	(9)	1
Agim Ibraimi	29.08.1988	17	(4)	4
Besart Ibraimi	17.12.1986	20	(3)	6
Omar Imeri (ALB)	13.12.1999	17	(3)	5
Valmir Nafiu	23.04.1994	3	(5)	
Marjan Radeski	10.02.1995	7	(13)	1
Shefit Shefiti (ALB)	19.02.1998	3	(5)	
Stênio Marcos da Fonseca Salazar Júnior (BRA)	10.06.1991	12	(5)	4

Klubi Futbollistik Shkupi Čair

Founded: 1927
Stadium: Stadion Čair, Skopje (6,000)

	Trainer:		
	Ümit Karan (TUR)		01.10.1976
[01.09.2019]	Bülent Akin (TUR)		28.08.1978
[23.09.2019]	Qatip Osmani		29.06.1969
[02.03.2020]	Muharem Bajrami		29.11.1985

Goalkeepers:	DOB	M	(s)	G
Igor Aleksovski	24.02.1995	13		
Thulio Cler de Freitas (BRA)	29.01.1996	10		
Defenders:	**DOB**	**M**	**(s)**	**G**
Mevlan Adili	30.03.1994	16		
Basilio Ndong Owono Nchama (EQG)	17.01.1999	8	(1)	
Bianor das Graças Lima da Silva (BRA)	28.06.1994	5		
Bojan Gjorgievski	25.01.1992	1	(1)	
Darko Glisić	23.09.1991	5		
Darko Ilieski	14.10.1995	14	(4)	
Ardit Iljazi	16.06.2000	3	(1)	
Fatih Ismaili	29.08.1997	10	(1)	
Besart Krivanjeva	28.02.1996	11	(4)	
Filip Stojanovski	01.12.1996	13		
Midfielders:	**DOB**	**M**	**(s)**	**G**
Muharem Bajrami	29.11.1985	16	(3)	1
Jakup Berisha	20.02.2000	3	(2)	
Sabit Bilalli	15.08.1997	22	(1)	
Dembo Darboe (GAM)	17.08.1998	10	(13)	2
Lamine Diack (SEN)	15.11.2000	18	(4)	1
Besar Iseni	18.01.1997	9	(1)	4
Hamza Ramani	17.09.2002	1	(1)	
Forwards:	**DOB**	**M**	**(s)**	**G**
Benjamin Demir	16.05.1996	2		
Dzemail Esati	05.09.2000	1		
Oumar Goudiaby (SEN)	01.01.1995	5	(13)	2
Marin Jurina (BIH)	26.11.1993	16		8
Fatjon Jusufi	17.12.1995	4	(11)	3
Faouly Keita (GUI)	11.08.1999		(2)	
Musli Lika	28.02.2000	6		
Suhejlj Muharem	25.08.2001	9	(4)	
Sérgio Antonio Da Luiz Junior „Serginho" (BRA)	06.04.1995	22		7

Fudbalski klub Sileks Kratovo

Founded: 1965
Stadium: Stadion Sileks, Kratovo (1,800)
Trainer: Goran Simov (SRB)   31.03.1975

Goalkeepers:	DOB	M	(s)	G
Daniel Božinovski	08.07.1989	19		
Andreja Efremov	02.09.1992	4		
Defenders:	**DOB**	**M**	**(s)**	**G**
Dejan Blagojević (SRB)	18.01.1990	17		2
Srđan Drasković (SRB)	08.01.1991	19	(1)	1
Hristijan Grozdanoski	05.06.1993	14	(1)	
Daniel Karceski	07.03.1992	14	(2)	
Stefan Kocev	23.02.1994	6	(2)	
Filip Kostovski	23.10.2002	3	(1)	
Bozidar Mitrevski	07.01.2001	1	(1)	
Angelce Timovski	13.11.1994	22		1
Midfielders:	**DOB**	**M**	**(s)**	**G**
Filip Duranskl	17.07.1991	16	(1)	1
Alpaj Jusuf	26.03.1998	3	(7)	
Nenad Marinković (SRB)	28.09.1988		(4)	
Slagjan Mitevski	04.05.1991		(2)	
Burhan Mustafov	02.03.1994	4		1
Filip Osman (SRB)	21.12.1991		(4)	
Denis Ristov (SRB)	24.06.1990	8	(2)	1
Metin Rushiti	23.03.2001	1	(1)	
Viktor Serafimovski	24.10.1995	21		2
Miloš Žeravica (SRB)	22.07.1988	18	(3)	2
Forwards:	**DOB**	**M**	**(s)**	**G**
Darko Dodev	16.01.1998	14	(4)	3
Stefan Đurić (SRB)	22.05.1995	4	(16)	1
Darko Grozdanoski	15.04.1999	19	(1)	2
Ivan Ivanovski	27.06.1995	14	(7)	4
Kristijan Kostovski	15.12.1995	12	(7)	3

Football Club Struga Trim-Lum

Founded: 2015
Stadium: Stadion Gradska Plaža, Struga (2,500)

	Trainer:		
	Jeton Bekiri		18.06.1982
[09.03.2020]	Fatmir Veseli		

Goalkeepers:	DOB	M	(s)	G
Uroš Đurić (SRB)	01.12.1993	22		
Nikolche Simonovski	19.11.1993	1		
Defenders:	**DOB**	**M**	**(s)**	**G**
Arlind Aliti	24.11.1999	12	(1)	
Ermin Anrushi	21.08.1995	3	(2)	
Sedat Berisha	03.09.1989	1		
Klisman Cake (ALB)	02.05.1999	16	(1)	1
Fjoralb Deliaj (ALB)	04.04.1997	3		
Hristijan Dragarski	16.04.1992	12	(1)	1
Valentin Kochoski	01.03.1997	16	(2)	1
Blerton Sheji	21.10.2000	10	(3)	
Arben Tafe	06.04.1992	17	(2)	2
Midfielders:	**DOB**	**M**	**(s)**	**G**
Aleksandar Dalčeski	18.04.1991	1	(10)	
Ard Kasami	03.01.1998	22		
Nijaz Lena	25.06.1986	19		3
Burhan Mustafov	02.03.1994	8	(7)	1
Ardit Shaqiri	04.05.1985		(6)	
Flamur Tairi	24.11.1990	21		
Forwards:	**DOB**	**M**	**(s)**	**G**
Dejan Cvetanoski	15.05.1990	13	(8)	2
Abdulhadi Jahja	03.06.1999	7	(7)	1
Hristijan Kirovski	12.10.1985	18	(4)	5
Florent Osmani	28.05.1988	14	(8)	2
Emran Ramadani	29.01.1992	17	(3)	
Alban Sulejmani	14.04.1998		(3)	

Fudbalski Klub Vardar Skopje

Founded: 22.07.1947
Stadium: "Toše Proeski" National Arena, Skopje (36,460)
Trainer: Aleksandar Vasoski   21.11.1979

Goalkeepers:	DOB	M	(s)	G
Filip Gačevski	17.08.1990	22		
Filip Ilikj	26.01.1997	1		
Defenders:	**DOB**	**M**	**(s)**	**G**
Vladica Brdarovski	07.02.1990	23		1
Leovigildo Júnior Reis Rodrigues "Juninho" (BRA)	26.12.1995	20	(1)	5
Mario Mladenovski	16.09.2000	6	(2)	
Stefan Naumceski	07.08.2000		(1)	
Evgen Novak (UKR)	01.02.1989	21		1
Nikola Serafimov	11.08.1999	12		
Kristijan Toševski	06.05.1994	22		1
Midfielders:	**DOB**	**M**	**(s)**	**G**
Ali Adem	01.06.2000	19	(3)	2
Daniel Avramovski	20.02.1995	22		11
Bojan Dimoski	23.11.2001	1	(8)	
Leonid Ignatov	04.01.2002	1	(4)	
Darko Micevski	12.04.1992	20		4
Filip Najdovski	13.09.1992	19	(1)	1
Fitor Redjepi	20.03.2000		(3)	
Forwards:	**DOB**	**M**	**(s)**	**G**
Matej Cvetanoski	18.08.1997	17	(5)	3
Dzemal Ibishi	18.01.2001	6	(7)	2
Bojan Kolevski	20.06.2000	8	(10)	1
Jovan Popzlatanov	06.07.1996	13	(5)	1
David Velkovski	15.12.2000		(8)	

SECOND LEVEL
Vtora Liga 2019/2020

2. MFL Istok (Group East)									
1. FK Belasica Strumica (*Promoted*)	16	13	1	2	36	-	9	40
2. FK Bregalnica 2008 Štip	16	11	4	1	39	-	9	37
3. GFK Tikveš 1930 Kavadarci	16	9	4	3	30	-	12	31
4. FK Kit-Go Pehčevo	16	9	4	3	23	-	13	31
5. FK Kožuf Gevgelija	16	9	3	4	26	-	16	30
6. FK Sasa Makedonska Kamenica	16	7	2	7	26	-	21	23
7. FK Plačkovica Radoviš	16	3	4	9	17	-	30	13
8. FK Pobeda AD Prilep	16	3	3	10	17	-	29	12
9. GFK Osogovo Kočani	16	2	0	14	12	-	44	6
10. FK Pitu Guli Kruševo (*Relegated*)	16	1	1	14	11	-	53	4

2. MFL Zapad (Group West)									
1. FK Pelister Bitola (*Promoted*)	16	10	3	3	32	-	14	33
2. FK Skopje	16	9	2	5	21	-	14	29
3. FK Labunishta	16	8	3	5	25	-	18	27
4. KF Vëllazërimi 77 Kičevo	16	7	4	5	15	-	19	25
5. KF Gostivari	16	6	5	5	21	-	19	23
6. KF Vardari Forinë	16	6	3	7	23	-	21	21
7. KF Korabi Debar	16	6	3	7	24	-	23	21
8. KF Drita Bogovinë	16	6	3	7	19	-	20	21
9. GFK Ohrid	16	4	2	10	15	-	29	14
10. FK Kadino	16	2	4	10	15	-	33	10

NATIONAL TEAM

INTERNATIONAL MATCHES
(16.07.2019 – 15.07.2020)

05.09.2019	Beersheba	Israel - North Macedonia	1-1(0-0)	(ECQ)
09.09.2019	Rīga	Latvia - North Macedonia	0-2(0-2)	(ECQ)
10.10.2019	Skopje	North Macedonia - Slovenia	2-1(0-0)	(ECQ)
13.10.2019	Warszawa	Poland - North Macedonia	2-0(0-0)	(ECQ)
16.11.2019	Wien	Austria - North Macedonia	2-1(1-0)	(ECQ)
19.11.2019	Skopje	North Macedonia - Israel	1-0(1-0)	(ECQ)

05.09.2019   ISRAEL - NORTH MACEDONIA   1-1(0-0)   16th EC. Qualifiers
"Yaakov Turner Toto" Stadium, Beersheba; Referee: Andreas Ekberg (Sweden); Attendance: 15,200
MKD: Stole Dimitrievski, Kire Ristevski, Visar Musliu, Darko Velkovski, Egzon Bejtulai, Arijan Ademi, Boban Nikolov (75.Aleksandar Trajkovski), Enis Bardi (83.Stefan Spirovski), Eljif Elmas, Ilija Nestorovski (Cap) (69.Goran Pandev), Ezgjan Alioski. Trainer: Igor Angelovski.
Goal: Arijan Ademi (64).

09.09.2019   LATVIA - NORTH MACEDONIA   0-2(0-2)   16th EC. Qualifiers
Daugava Stadions, Riga; Referee: Espen Eskås (Norway); Attendance: 2,724
MKD: Stole Dimitrievski, Visar Musliu, Darko Velkovski, Egzon Bejtulai, Arijan Ademi, Ivan Tričkovski, Enis Bardi, Eljif Elmas (88.Marjan Radeski), Goran Pandev (Cap) (75.Boban Nikolov), Aleksandar Trajkovski (65.Ilija Nestorovski), Ezgjan Alioski. Trainer: Igor Angelovski.
Goals: Goran Pandev (14), Enis Bardi (17).

10.10.2019   NORTH MACEDONIA - SLOVENIA   2-1(0-0)   16th EC. Qualifiers
"Toše Proeski" National Arena, Skopje; Referee: Danny Desmond Makkelie (Netherlands); Attendance: 16,500
MKD: Stole Dimitrievski, Stefan Ristovski (81.Gjoko Zajkov), Kire Ristevski, Visar Musliu, Arijan Ademi (77.Kristijan Toševski), Stefan Spirovski, Boban Nikolov, Eljif Elmas, Goran Pandev (Cap) (66.Ivan Tričkovski), Ilija Nestorovski, Ezgjan Alioski. Trainer: Igor Angelovski.
Goals: Eljif Elmas (50, 68).

13.10.2019   POLAND - NORTH MACEDONIA   2-0(0-0)   16th EC. Qualifiers
Stadion PGE Narodowy, Warszawa; Referee: Antonio Miguel Mateu Lahoz (Spain); Attendance: 52,894
MKD: Stole Dimitrievski, Stefan Ristovski (81.Marjan Radeski), Kire Ristevski, Visar Musliu, Egzon Bejtulai, Stefan Spirovski, Boban Nikolov (88.Gjorgji Stoilov), Eljif Elmas, Goran Pandev (Cap), Ilija Nestorovski (74.Aleksandar Trajkovski), Ezgjan Alioski. Trainer: Igor Angelovski.

16.11.2019   AUSTRIA - NORTH MACEDONIA   2-1(1-0)   16th EC. Qualifiers
"Ernst Happel" Stadion, Wien; Referee: Michael Oliver (England); Attendance: 41,100
MKD: Stole Dimitrievski, Stefan Ristovski (Cap), Kire Ristevski, Darko Velkovski, Kristijan Toševski (62.Daniel Avramovski), Mario Mladenovski (46.Gjoko Zajkov), Stefan Spirovski, Tihomir Kostadinov, Enis Bardi, Eljif Elmas, Aleksandar Trajkovski (13.Vlatko Stojanovski). Trainer: Igor Angelovski.
Goal: Vlatko Stojanovski (90+3).

19.11.2019   NORTH MACEDONIA - ISRAEL   1-0(1-0)   16th EC. Qualifiers
"Toše Proeski" Arena, Skopje; Referee: Paolo Valeri (Italy); Attendance: 5,573
MKD: Stole Dimitrievski, Stefan Ristovski, Kire Ristevski, Visar Musliu, Darko Velkovski (72.Gjoko Zajkov), Boban Nikolov, Tihomir Kostadinov, Enis Bardi, Eljif Elmas, Goran Pandev (Cap) (79.Daniel Avramovski), Vlatko Stojanovski (60.Ilija Nestorovski). Trainer: Igor Angelovski.
Goal: Boban Nikolov (45+2).

NATIONAL TEAM PLAYERS
(16.07.2019 – 15.07.2020)

Name	DOB	Caps	Goals	2019/2020:	Club
Goalkeepers					
Stole DIMITRIEVSKI	25.12.1993	**34**	**0**	2019:	*Rayo Vallecano de Madrid (ESP)*
Defenders					
Egzon BEJTULAI	07.01.1994	**11**	**0**	2019:	*KF Shkëndija Tetovo*
Mario MLADENOVSKI	16.09.2000	**1**	**0**	2019:	*FK Vardar Skopje*
Visar MUSLIU	13.11.1994	**20**	**1**	2019:	*Fehérvár FC Székesfehérvár (HUN)*
Kire RISTEVSKI	22.10.1990	**38**	**0**	2019:	*Újpest FC (HUN)*
Stefan RISTOVSKI	12.02.1992	**52**	**1**	2019:	*Sporting Clube de Portugal Lisboa (POR)*
Kristijan TOŠEVSKI	06.05.1994	**8**	**0**	2019:	*FK Vardar Skopje*
Darko VELKOVSKI	21.06.1995	**19**	**0**	2019:	*HNK Rijeka (CRO)*
Gjoko ZAJKOV	10.02.1995	**12**	**0**	2019:	*SC Charleroi (BEL)*
Midfielders					
Arijan ADEMI	29.05.1991	**14**	**3**	2019:	*GNK Dinamo Zagreb (CRO)*
Ezgjan ALIOSKI	12.02.1992	**33**	**6**	2019:	*Leeds United FC (ENG)*
Daniel AVRAMOVSKI	20.02.1995	**4**	**0**	2019:	*FK Vardar Skopje*
Enis BARDI	02.07.1995	**27**	**5**	2019:	*Levante UD Valencia (ESP)*
Eljif ELMAS	27.09.1999	**18**	**4**	2019:	*SSC Napoli (ITA)*
Tihomir KOSTADINOV	04.03.1996	**2**	**0**	2019:	*MFK Ružomberok (SVK)*
Boban NIKOLOV	28.07.1994	**22**	**2**	2019:	*Fehérvár FC Székesfehérvár (HUN)*
Marjan RADESKI	10.02.1995	**16**	**1**	2019:	*KF Shkëndija Tetovo*
Stefan SPIROVSKI	23.08.1990	**31**	**1**	2019: 06.09.2019->	*Ferencvárosi TC (HUN)* *Hapoel Tel Aviv FC (ISR)*
Gjorgji STOILOV	25.08.1995	**1**	**0**	2019:	*Fudbalska Akademija Pandev Strumica*
Forwards					
Ilija NESTOROVSKI	12.03.1990	**36**	**8**	2019:	*Udinese Calcio (ITA)*
Goran PANDEV	27.07.1983	**108**	**34**	2019:	*Genoa C&FC (ITA)*
Vlatko STOJANOVSKI	23.04.1997	**2**	**0**	2019:	*Nîmes Olympique FC (FRA)*
Aleksandar TRAJKOVSKI	05.09.1992	**54**	**15**	2019:	*RCD Mallorca (ESP)*
Ivan TRIČKOVSKI	18.04.1987	**56**	**5**	2019:	*AEK Larnaca FC (CYP)*
National team coach					
Igor ANGELOVSKI [from 16.10.2015]	02.06.1976	37 M; 16 W; 7 D; 14 L; 55-43			

NORTHERN IRELAND

The Country:
Tuaisceart Éireann (Northern Ireland)
Capital: Belfast
Surface: 14,130 km²
Inhabitants: 1,893,700 [2019]
Time: UTC

The FA:
Irish Football Association
National Football Stadium Donegal Avenue BT12 5LW, Belfast
Tel: +44 28 9066 9458
Foundation date: 1880
Member of FIFA since: 1911
Member of UEFA since: 1954
Website: www.irishfa.com

NATIONAL TEAM RECORDS

RECORDS		
First international match:	18.02.1882, Belfast:	Ireland – England 0-13
Most international caps:	Patrick Anthony Jennings	- 119 caps (1964-1986)
Most international goals:	David Jonathan Healy	- 36 goals / 95 caps (2000-2013)

UEFA EUROPEAN CHAMPIONSHIP		FIFA WORLD CUP		OLYMPIC TOURNAMENTS	
1960	Did not enter	1930	Did not enter	1908	-
1964	Qualifiers	1934	Did not enter	1912	-
1968	Qualifiers	1938	Did not enter	1920	-
1972	Qualifiers	1950	Qualifiers	1924	-
1976	Qualifiers	1954	Qualifiers	1928	-
1980	Qualifiers	1958	Final Tournament (Quarter-Finals)	1936	-
1984	Qualifiers	1962	Qualifiers	1948	-
1988	Qualifiers	1966	Qualifiers	1952	-
1992	Qualifiers	1970	Qualifiers	1956	-
1996	Qualifiers	1974	Qualifiers	1960	-
2000	Qualifiers	1978	Qualifiers	1964	-
2004	Qualifiers	1982	Final Tournament (2nd Round)	1968	-
2008	Qualifiers	1986	Final Tournament (Group Stage)	1972	-
2012	Qualifiers	1990	Qualifiers	1976	-
2016	Final Tournament (2nd Round of 16)	1994	Qualifiers	1980	-
2020	*To be determined*	1998	Qualifiers	1984	-
		2002	Qualifiers	1988	-
		2006	Qualifiers	1992	-
		2010	Qualifiers	1996	-
		2014	Qualifiers	2000	-
		2018	Qualifiers	2004	-
				2008	-
				2012	-
				2016	-

UEFA NATIONS LEAGUE

2018/2019 – League B

FIFA CONFEDERATIONS CUP 1992-2017

None

NORTHERN IRISH CLUB HONOURS IN EUROPEAN CLUB COMPETITIONS:

European Champion Clubs.Cup (1956-1992) / UEFA Champions League (1993-2020)
None
Fairs Cup (1858-1971) / UEFA Cup (1972-2009) / UEFA Europa League (2010-2020)
None
UEFA Super Cup (1972-2019)
None
European Cup Winners.Cup 1961-1999*
None

*defunct competition

NATIONAL COMPETITIONS
TABLE OF HONOURS

	CHAMPIONS	CUP WINNERS	BEST GOALSCORERS	
1880/1881	-	Moyola Park AFC	-	
1881/1882	-	Queen's Island FC Belfast	-	
1882/1883	-	Cliftonville FAC	-	
1883/1884	-	Distillery FC Ballyskeagh	-	
1884/1885	-	Distillery FC Ballyskeagh	-	
1885/1886	-	Distillery FC Ballyskeagh	-	
1886/1887	-	Ulster FC Ballynafeigh	-	
1887/1888	-	Cliftonville FAC	-	
1888/1889	-	Distillery FC Ballyskeagh	-	
1889/1890	-	Gordon Highlanders	-	
1890/1891	Linfield FC Belfast	Linfield FC Belfast	Robert Hill (Linfield FC Belfast)	20
1891/1892	Linfield FC Belfast	Linfield FC Belfast	Tim Morrison (Linfield FC Belfast)	21
1892/1893	Linfield FC Belfast	Linfield FC Belfast	Robert Hill (Linfield FC Belfast) James Percy (Cliftonville FAC)	9
1893/1894	Glentoran FC Belfast	Distillery FC Ballyskeagh	Michael McErlean (Linfield FC Belfast)	9
1894/1895	Linfield FC Belfast	Linfield FC Belfast	George Gaukrodger (Linfield FC Belfast) Joe McAllen (Linfield FC Belfast)	4
1895/1896	Distillery FC Ballyskeagh	Distillery FC Ballyskeagh	-	
1896/1897	Glentoran FC Belfast	Cliftonville FAC	Johnny Darling (Linfield FC Belfast) Richard Peden (Linfield FC Belfast)	6
1897/1898	Linfield FC Belfast	Linfield FC Belfast	-	
1898/1899	Distillery FC Ballyskeagh	Linfield FC Belfast	-	
1899/1900	Belfast Celtic FC	Cliftonville FAC	-	
1900/1901	Distillery FC Ballyskeagh	Cliftonville FAC	-	
1901/1902	Linfield FC Belfast	Linfield FC Belfast	-	
1902/1903	Distillery FC Ballyskeagh	Distillery FC Ballyskeagh	-	
1903/1904	Linfield FC Belfast	Linfield FC Belfast	-	
1904/1905	Glentoran FC Belfast	Distillery FC Ballyskeagh	-	
1905/1906	Cliftonville FAC Distillery FC Ballyskeagh (shared)	Shelbourne FC Dublin	-	
1906/1907	Linfield FC Belfast	Cliftonville FAC	-	
1907/1908	Linfield FC Belfast	Bohemians FC Dublin	-	
1908/1909	Linfield FC Belfast	Cliftonville FAC	-	
1909/1910	Cliftonville FAC	Distillery FC Ballyskeagh	-	
1910/1911	Linfield FC Belfast	Shelbourne FC Dublin	-	
1911/1912	Glentoran FC Belfast	Linfield FC Belfast	-	
1912/1913	Glentoran FC Belfast	Linfield FC Belfast	-	
1913/1914	Linfield FC Belfast	Glentoran FC Belfast	-	
1914/1915	Belfast Celtic FC	Linfield FC Belfast	-	
1915/1916	*No competition*	Linfield FC Belfast	-	
1916/1917	*No competition*	Glentoran FC Belfast	-	
1917/1918	*No competition*	Belfast Celtic FC	-	
1918/1919	*No competition*	Linfield FC Belfast	-	
1919/1920	Belfast Celtic FC	Shelbourne FC Dublin	-	
1920/1921	Glentoran FC Belfast	Glentoran FC Belfast	-	
1921/1922	Linfield FC Belfast	Linfield FC Belfast	-	
1922/1923	Linfield FC Belfast	Linfield FC Belfast	-	
1923/1924	Queen's Island FC Belfast	Queen's Island FC Belfast	-	
1924/1925	Glentoran FC Belfast	Distillery FC Ballyskeagh	-	
1925/1926	Belfast Celtic FC	Belfast Celtic FC	-	
1926/1927	Belfast Celtic FC	Ards FC Newtownards	Joseph Gardiner Absolom Bambrick (Glentoran FC Belfast)	28
1927/1928	Belfast Celtic FC	Willowfield FC	-	
1928/1929	Belfast Celtic FC	Ballymena FC	Joseph Gardiner Absolom Bambrick (Linfield FC Belfast)	43
1929/1930	Linfield FC Belfast	Linfield FC Belfast	Joseph Gardiner Absolom Bambrick (Linfield FC Belfast)	50
1930/1931	Glentoran FC Belfast	Linfield FC Belfast	Fred Roberts (Glentoran FC Belfast)	55
1931/1932	Linfield FC Belfast	Glentoran FC Belfast	-	
1932/1933	Belfast Celtic FC	Glentoran FC Belfast	Joseph Gardiner Absolom Bambrick (Linfield FC Belfast)	40
1933/1934	Linfield FC Belfast	Linfield FC Belfast	-	
1934/1935	Linfield FC Belfast	Glentoran FC Belfast	-	
1935/1936	Belfast Celtic FC	Linfield FC Belfast	-	
1936/1937	Belfast Celtic FC	Belfast Celtic FC	-	
1937/1938	Belfast Celtic FC	Belfast Celtic FC	-	
1938/1939	Belfast Celtic FC	Linfield FC Belfast	-	
1939/1940	Belfast Celtic FC	Ballymena United FC	-	
1940/1941	*No competition*	Belfast Celtic FC	-	
1941/1942	*No competition*	Linfield FC Belfast	-	
1942/1943	*No competition*	Belfast Celtic FC	-	

1943/1944	*No competition*	Belfast Celtic FC	-	
1944/1945	*No competition*	Linfield FC Belfast	-	
1945/1946	*No competition*	Linfield FC Belfast	-	
1946/1947	*No competition*	Belfast Celtic FC	-	
1947/1948	Belfast Celtic FC	Linfield FC Belfast	James Jones (Belfast Celtic FC)	28
1948/1949	Linfield FC Belfast	Derry City FC	William Simpson (Linfield FC Belfast)	19
1949/1950	Linfield FC Belfast	Linfield FC Belfast	Sammy Hughes (Glentoran FC Belfast)	23
1950/1951	Glentoran FC Belfast	Glentoran FC Belfast	Sammy Hughes (Glentoran FC Belfast) Walter Allen (Portadown FC)	23
1951/1952	Glenavon FC Lurgan	Ards FC Newtownards	James Jones (Glenavon FC Lurgan)	27
1952/1953	Glentoran FC Belfast	Linfield FC Belfast	Sammy Hughes (Glentoran FC Belfast)	28
1953/1954	Linfield FC Belfast	Derry City FC	James Jones (Glenavon FC Lurgan)	32
1954/1955	Linfield FC Belfast	Dundela FC Belfast	Francis Coyle (Coleraine FC)	20
1955/1956	Linfield FC Belfast	Distillery FC Ballyskeagh	James Jones (Glenavon FC Lurgan)	26
1956/1957	Glenavon FC Lurgan	Glenavon FC Lurgan	James Jones (Glenavon FC Lurgan)	33
1957/1958	Ards FC Newtownards	Ballymena United FC	John Edward Thompson Milburn (Linfield FC Belfast)	29
1958/1959	Linfield FC Belfast	Glenavon FC Lurgan	John Edward Thompson Milburn (Linfield FC Belfast)	26
1959/1960	Glenavon FC Lurgan	Linfield FC Belfast	James Jones (Glenavon FC Lurgan)	29
1960/1961	Linfield FC Belfast	Glenavon FC Lurgan	Trevor Thompson (Glentoran FC Belfast)	22
1961/1962	Linfield FC Belfast	Linfield FC Belfast	Mick Lynch (Ards FC Newtownards)	20
1962/1963	Distillery FC Ballyskeagh	Linfield FC Belfast	Joe Meldrum (Distillery FC Ballyskeagh)	27
1963/1964	Glentoran FC Belfast	Derry City FC	Trevor Thompson (Linfield FC Belfast)	21
1964/1965	Derry City FC	Coleraine FC	Kenny Halliday (Coleraine FC) Dennis Guy (Glenavon FC Lurgan)	19
1965/1966	Linfield FC Belfast	Glentoran FC Belfast	Sammy Pavis (Linfield FC Belfast)	28
1966/1967	Glentoran FC Belfast	Crusaders FC Belfast	Sammy Pavis (Linfield FC Belfast)	25
1967/1968	Glentoran FC Belfast	Crusaders FC Belfast	Sammy Pavis (Linfield FC Belfast)	30
1968/1969	Linfield FC Belfast	Ards FC Newtownards	Danny Hale (Derry City FC)	21
1969/1970	Glentoran FC Belfast	Linfield FC Belfast	Des Dickson (Coleraine FC)	21
1970/1971	Linfield FC Belfast	Distillery FC Ballyskeagh	Bryan Hamilton (Linfield FC Belfast)	18
1971/1972	Glentoran FC Belfast	Coleraine FC	Peter Watson (Distillery FC Ballyskeagh) Des Dickson (Coleraine FC)	15
1972/1973	Crusaders FC Belfast	Glentoran FC Belfast	Des Dickson (Coleraine FC)	23
1973/1974	Coleraine FC	Ards FC Newtownards	Des Dickson (Coleraine FC)	24
1974/1975	Linfield FC Belfast	Coleraine FC	Martin Malone (Portadown FC)	15
1975/1976	Crusaders FC Belfast	Carrick Rangers FC	Des Dickson (Coleraine FC)	23
1976/1977	Glentoran FC Belfast	Coleraine FC	Ronnie McAteer (Crusaders FC Belfast)	20
1977/1978	Linfield FC Belfast	Linfield FC Belfast	Warren Feeney (Glentoran FC Belfast)	17
1978/1979	Linfield FC Belfast	Cliftonville FAC	Tommy Armstrong (Ards FC Newtownards)	21
1979/1980	Linfield FC Belfast	Linfield FC Belfast	James Martin (Glentoran FC Belfast)	17
1980/1981	Glentoran FC Belfast	Ballymena United FC	Des Dickson (Coleraine FC) Paul Malone (Ballymena United FC)	18
1981/1982	Linfield FC Belfast	Linfield FC Belfast	Gary Blackledge (Glentoran FC Belfast)	18
1982/1983	Linfield FC Belfast	Glentoran FC Belfast	James Campbell (Ards FC Newtownards)	15
1983/1984	Linfield FC Belfast	Ballymena United FC	Martin McGaughey (Linfield FC Belfast) Trevor Anderson (Linfield FC Belfast)	15
1984/1985	Linfield FC Belfast	Glentoran FC Belfast	Martin McGaughey (Linfield FC Belfast)	34
1985/1986	Linfield FC Belfast	Glentoran FC Belfast	Trevor Anderson (Linfield FC Belfast)	14
1986/1987	Linfield FC Belfast	Glentoran FC Belfast	Ray McCoy (Coleraine FC) Gary Macartney (Glentoran FC Belfast)	14
1987/1988	Glentoran FC Belfast	Glentoran FC Belfast	Martin McGaughey (Linfield FC Belfast)	18
1988/1989	Linfield FC Belfast	Ballymena United FC	Stephen Baxter (Linfield FC Belfast)	17
1989/1990	Portadown FC	Glentoran FC Belfast	Martin McGaughey (Linfield FC Belfast)	19
1990/1991	Portadown FC	Portadown FC	Stephen Derek McBride (Glenavon FC Lurgan)	22
1991/1992	Glentoran FC Belfast	Glenavon FC Lurgan	Harry McCourt (Omagh Town FAC) Stephen Derek McBride (Glenavon FC Lurgan)	18
1992/1993	Linfield FC Belfast	Bangor FC	Steve Cowan (Portadown FC)	23
1993/1994	Linfield FC Belfast	Linfield FC Belfast	Darren Erskine (Ards FC Newtownards) Stephen Derek McBride (Glenavon FC Lurgan)	22
1994/1995	Crusaders FC Belfast	Linfield FC Belfast	Glenn Ferguson (Glenavon FC Lurgan)	27
1995/1996	Portadown FC	Glentoran FC Belfast	Garry Andrew Haylock (Portadown FC)	19
1996/1997	Crusaders FC Belfast	Glenavon FC Lurgan	Garry Andrew Haylock (Portadown FC)	16
1997/1998	Cliftonville FAC	Glentoran FC Belfast	Vincent Thomas Arkins (Portadown FC)	22
1998/1999	Glentoran FC Belfast	Portadown FC	Vincent Thomas Arkins (Portadown FC)	19
1999/2000	Linfield FC Belfast	Glentoran FC Belfast	Vincent Thomas Arkins (Portadown FC)	29
2000/2001	Linfield FC Belfast	Glentoran FC Belfast	David James Larmour (Linfield FC Belfast)	17
2001/2002	Portadown FC	Linfield FC Belfast	Vincent Thomas Arkins (Portadown FC)	30
2002/2003	Glentoran FC Belfast	Coleraine FC	Vincent Thomas Arkins (Portadown FC)	29
2003/2004	Linfield FC Belfast	Glentoran FC Belfast	Glenn Ferguson (Linfield FC Belfast)	25
2004/2005	Glentoran FC Belfast	Portadown FC	Christopher Morgan (Glentoran FC Belfast)	19
2005/2006	Linfield FC Belfast	Linfield FC Belfast	Peter Thompson (Linfield FC Belfast)	25
2006/2007	Linfield FC Belfast	Linfield FC Belfast	Gary Hamilton (Glentoran FC Belfast)	27
2007/2008	Linfield FC Belfast	Linfield FC Belfast	Peter Thompson (Linfield FC Belfast)	29
2008/2009	Glentoran FC Belfast	Crusaders FC Belfast	Curtis Allen (Lisburn Distillery FC Ballyskeagh)	19
2009/2010	Linfield FC Belfast	Linfield FC Belfast	Rory Christopher Patterson (Coleraine FC)	30
2010/2011	Linfield FC Belfast	Linfield FC Belfast	Peter Thompson (Linfield FC Belfast)	23

2011/2012	Linfield FC Belfast	Linfield FC Belfast	Gary Kyle McCutcheon (Ballymena United FC)	27
2012/2013	Cliftonville FAC	Glentoran FC Belfast	Liam Boyce (Cliftonville FAC)	29
2013/2014	Cliftonville FAC	Glenavon FC Lurgan	Joseph Anthony Gormley (Cliftonville FAC)	27
2014/2015	Crusaders FC Belfast	Glentoran FC Belfast	Joseph Anthony Gormley (Cliftonville FAC)	31
2015/2016	Crusaders FC Belfast	Glenavon FC Lurgan	Paul Heatley (Crusaders FC Belfast) Andrew Waterworth (Linfield FC Belfast)	22
2016/2017	Linfield FC Belfast	Linfield FC Belfast	Andrew Mitchell (Dungannon Swifts)	25
2017/2018	Crusaders FC Belfast	Coleraine FC	Joseph Anthony Gormley (Cliftonville FAC)	22
2018/2019	Linfield FC Belfast	Crusaders FC Belfast	Joseph Anthony Gormley (Cliftonville FAC)	20
2019/2020	Linfield FC Belfast	Glentoran FC Belfast	Joseph Anthony Gormley (Cliftonville FAC)	18

NATIONAL CHAMPIONSHIP
NIFL Premiership 2019/2020
(09.08.2019 – 07.03.2020)

Results

Round 1 [09-10.08.2019]
Glenavon FC - Glentoran FC 1-1(1-1)
Coleraine FC - Cliftonville FAC 1-1(0-0)
Crusaders FC - Carrick Rangers 3-0(2-0)
Dungannon Swifts - Ballymena Unit. 2-2(0-1)
Larne FC - Warrenpoint Town 6-0(2-0)
Linfield FC - Institute FC 3-1(2-1)

Round 2 [13.08.2019]
Carrick Rangers - Larne FC 1-2(1-1)
Cliftonville FAC - Glenavon FC 3-1(3-0)
Glentoran FC - Coleraine FC 2-2(0-0)
Institute FC - Dungannon Swifts 2-3(0-1)
Crusaders FC - Warrenpoint Town 4-0(1-0)
Ballymena Un. - Linfield FC 1-2(1-2) [26.11.]

Round 3 [17.08.2019]
Cliftonville FAC - Crusaders FC 0-2(0-0)
Dungannon Swifts - Glentoran FC 3-1(1-0)
Glenavon FC - Warrenpoint Town 2-0(2-0)
Institute FC - Carrick Rangers 0-2(0-1)
Larne FC - Ballymena United 2-4(1-2)
Linfield FC - Coleraine FC 2-4(0-2)

Round 4 [24.08.2019]
Ballymena United - Glentoran FC 1-2(0-0)
Carrick Rangers - Cliftonville FAC 0-1(0-0)
Coleraine FC - Institute FC 0-0
Crusaders FC - Larne FC 2-2(1-1)
Dungannon Swifts - Glenavon FC 2-1(2-0)
Linfield FC - Warrenpoint T. 7-0(3-0) [22.10.]

Round 5 [30.08.-02.09.2019]
Carrick Rangers - Ballymena United 0-1(0-0)
Glenavon FC - Coleraine FC 0-4(0-1)
Crusaders FC - Dungannon Swifts 3-0(2-0)
Warrenpoint T. - Cliftonville FAC 1-5(0-1)
Glentoran FC - Institute FC 4-0(2-0)
Larne FC - Linfield FC 3-1(2-1) [28.01.2020]

Round 6 [07.09.2019]
Ballymena United - Warrenpoint T. 4-0(1-0)
Cliftonville FAC - Linfield FC 0-1(0-0)
Coleraine FC - Dungannon Swifts 5-0(0-0)
Glentoran FC - Larne FC 2-1(1-1)
Institute FC - Crusaders FC 0-6(0-2)
Glenavon FC - Carrick R. 1-0(1-0) [10.12.]

Round 7 [14.09.2019]
Institute FC - Larne FC 1-4(0-3)
Ballymena United - Coleraine FC 1-1(1-1)
Crusaders FC - Glenavon FC 3-2(1-1)
Dungannon Swifts - Cliftonville FAC 0-4(0-1)
Linfield FC - Glentoran FC 1-0(0-0)
Warrenpoint Town - Carrick Rangers 0-3(0-2)

Round 8 [21-23.09.2019]
Cliftonville FAC - Institute FC 1-0(1-0)
Coleraine FC - Crusaders FC 4-2(2-1)
Glenavon FC - Ballymena United 3-1(1-1)
Glentoran FC - Warrenpoint Town 2-1(1-0)
Larne FC - Dungannon Swifts 0-0
Carrick Rangers - Linfield FC 0-3(0-1)

Round 9 [28.09.2019]
Ballymena United - Cliftonville FAC 2-1(0-1)
Coleraine FC - Larne FC 0-0
Crusaders FC - Glentoran FC 5-2(1-0)
Dungannon Swifts - Carrick Rangers 2-1(2-0)
Linfield FC - Glenavon FC 7-0(4-0)
Warrenpoint Town - Institute FC 1-3(1-3)

Round 10 [04-05.10.2019]
Crusaders FC - Linfield FC 1-0(0-0)
Glentoran FC - Cliftonville FAC 0-1(0-0)
Larne FC - Glenavon FC 6-0(3-0)
Carrick Rangers - Coleraine FC 1-4(1-2)
Institute FC - Ballymena United 1-1(1-0)
Warrenpoint T. - Dungannon Swifts 4-3(0-2)

Round 11 [12.10.2019]
Ballymena United - Crusaders FC 1-1(0-0)
Cliftonville FAC - Larne FC 1-0(0-0)
Coleraine FC - Warrenpoint Town 3-0(2-0)
Dungannon Swifts - Linfield FC 1-4(0-4)
Glentoran FC - Carrick Rangers 3-1(1-1)
Glenavon FC - Institute FC 3-1(3-0) [26.11.]

Round 12 [18-19.10.2019]
Larne FC - Glentoran FC 2-3(1-2)
Carrick Rangers - Dungannon Swifts 1-0(1-0)
Crusaders FC - Coleraine FC 0-2(0-1)
Institute FC - Cliftonville FAC 0-3(0-1)
Linfield FC - Ballymena United 2-1(2-0)
Warrenpoint Town - Glenavon FC 1-3(0-0)

Round 13 [25-26.10.2019]
Glentoran FC - Ballymena United 3-1(0-1)
Carrick Rangers - Warrenpoint Town 1-0(0-0)
Cliftonville FAC - Dungannon Swifts 5-0(0-0)
Coleraine FC - Linfield FC 1-0(0-0)
Larne FC - Institute FC 1-1(1-1)
Glenavon FC - Crusaders FC 2-2(0-1)

Round 14 [02.11.2019]
Ballymena United - Larne FC 0-3(0-1)
Crusaders FC - Institute FC 1-1(1-1)
Dungannon Swifts - Coleraine FC 0-2(0-1)
Glenavon FC - Cliftonville FAC 1-2(1-1)
Linfield FC - Carrick Rangers 2-0(1-0)
Warrenpoint Town - Glentoran FC 0-4(0-4)

Round 15 [09-11.11.2019]
Ballymena United - Carrick Rangers 1-2(1-2)
Cliftonville FAC - Warrenpoint T. 4-0(3-0)
Coleraine FC - Glenavon FC 4-0(2-0)
Institute FC - Glentoran FC 1-1(1-1)
Larne FC - Crusaders FC 0-0
Linfield FC - Dungannon 2-1(1-1) [04.02.20]

Round 16 [15-16.11.2019]
Carrick Rangers - Crusaders FC 1-3(1-0)
Institute FC - Linfield FC 0-3(0-2)
Cliftonville FAC - Ballymena United 1-0(0-0)
Dungannon Swifts - Larne FC 0-1(0-0)
Warrenpoint Town - Coleraine FC 3-1(0-0)
Glentoran - Glenavon 4-0(3-0) [28.01.2020]

Round 17 [22-23.11.2019]
Glenavon FC - Linfield FC 1-0(1-0)
Ballymena United - Institute FC 1-1(0-1)
Coleraine FC - Carrick Rangers 3-2(1-2)
Warrenpoint Town - Crusaders FC 0-1(0-1)
Glentoran FC - Dungannon Swifts 6-1(2-1)
Larne FC - Cliftonville FAC 1-1(1-1)

Round 18 [30.11.2019]
Institute FC - Coleraine FC 2-0(2-0)
Carrick Rangers - Glenavon FC 6-2(2-1)
Cliftonville FAC - Glentoran FC 0-2(0-1)
Dungannon Swifts - Crusaders FC 1-6(1-1)
Linfield FC - Larne FC 1-0(0-0)
Warrenpoint T. - Ballymena United 2-1(2-1)

Round 19 [07.12.2019]
Carrick Rangers - Institute FC 3-0(1-0)
Coleraine FC - Glentoran FC 2-2(0-2)
Crusaders FC - Ballymena United 0-1(0-0)
Dungannon Swifts - Warrenpoint T. 3-1(1-1)
Glenavon FC - Larne FC 1-3(0-2)
Linfield FC - Cliftonville FAC 1-0(0-0)

Round 20 [14.12.2019]
Ballymena United - Dungannon Sw. 3-2(1-1)
Glentoran FC - Crusaders FC 1-1(0-0)
Institute FC - Glenavon FC 1-4(0-3)
Larne FC - Coleraine FC 2-2(1-2)
Warrenpoint Town - Linfield FC 0-2(0-1)
Cliftonville - Carrick Rang 3-1(2-0) [04.02.20]

Round 21 [20-21.12.2019]
Ballymena United - Glenavon FC 2-1(0-0)
Carrick Rangers - Glentoran FC 0-1(0-0)
Cliftonville FAC - Coleraine FC 1-0(0-0)
Dungannon Swifts - Institute FC 2-2(1-2)
Linfield FC - Crusaders FC 1-1(0-1)
Warrenpoint Town - Larne FC 0-2(0-0)

Round 22 [26.12.2019]
Coleraine FC - Ballymena United 2-0(2-0)
Crusaders FC - Cliftonville FAC 1-2(1-1)
Glenavon FC - Dungannon Swifts 5-0(2-0)
Glentoran FC - Linfield FC 3-0(1-0)
Institute FC - Warrenpoint Town 0-1(0-0)
Larne FC - Carrick Rangers 0-0

Round 23 [28.12.2019]
Coleraine FC - Linfield FC 1-1(0-1)
Crusaders FC - Dungannon Swifts 5-0(3-0)
Glenavon FC - Warrenpoint Town 1-1(0-1)
Glentoran FC - Ballymena United 2-0(0-0)
Institute FC - Carrick Rangers 0-3(0-2)
Larne FC - Cliftonville FAC 1-2(1-1)

Round 24 [01.01.2020]
Ballymena United - Larne FC 2-3(0-1)
Carrick Rangers - Coleraine FC 0-2(0-1)
Cliftonville FAC - Glenavon FC 1-0(1-0)
Dungannon Swifts - Glentoran FC 0-2(0-1)
Linfield FC - Institute FC 3-0(2-0)
Warrenpoint Town - Crusaders FC 0-4(0-2)

Round 25 [10-13.01.2020]
Coleraine FC - Crusaders FC 0-1(0-1)
Larne FC - Carrick Rangers 4-0(3-0)
Glenavon FC - Institute FC 2-2(0-1)
Glentoran FC - Warrenpoint Town 2-1(0-0)
Cliftonville FAC - Linfield FC 1-2(1-1)
Dungannon - Ballymena Un. 1-0(1-0) [03.03.]

Round 26 [18.01.2020]
Ballymena United - Glenavon FC 0-3(0-1)
Carrick Rangers - Cliftonville FAC 1-0(0-0)
Crusaders FC - Larne FC 3-0(3-0)
Institute FC - Glentoran FC 0-2(0-2)
Linfield FC - Dungannon Swifts 0-0
Warrenpoint Town - Coleraine FC 0-4(0-1)

Round 27 [25-27.01.2020]
Carrick Rangers - Warrenpoint Town 1-2(1-0)
Crusaders FC - Ballymena United 2-0(0-0)
Dungannon Swifts - Institute FC 2-0(0-0)
Linfield FC - Glenavon FC 8-1(5-1)
Larne FC - Glentoran FC 2-1(0-0)
Coleraine FC - Cliftonville FAC 1-0(0-0)

Round 28 [08.02.2020]
Ballymena United - Carrick Rangers 0-2(0-1)
Cliftonville FAC - Dungannon Swifts 1-1(1-1)
Glenavon FC - Crusaders FC 2-1(0-1)
Glentoran FC - Coleraine FC 0-1(0-0)
Institute FC - Larne FC 0-4(0-0)
Warrenpoint Town - Linfield FC 1-2(0-1)

Round 29 [14.02.2020]
Ballymena United - Linfield FC 1-4(1-2)
Dungannon Swifts - Larne FC 0-2(0-1)
Glentoran FC - Carrick Rangers 0-0
Warrenpoint Town - Institute FC 2-2(1-1)
Coleraine FC - Glenavon FC 2-1(2-0) [03.03.]
Crusaders FC - Cliftonville FAC 0-0 [03.03.]

Round 30 [21-22.02.2020]
Linfield FC - Crusaders FC 4-0(1-0)
Institute FC - Coleraine FC 0-4(0-2)
Carrick Rangers - Dungannon Swifts 1-2(0-1)
Cliftonville FAC - Ballymena United 1-1(0-1)
Glenavon FC - Glentoran FC 2-2(1-1)
Larne FC - Warrenpoint Town 1-0(0-0)

Round 31 [07.03.2020]
Ballymena United - Coleraine FC 0-2(0-1)
Carrick Rangers - Linfield FC 0-2(0-1)
Crusaders FC - Institute FC 2-1(0-1)
Dungannon Swifts - Warrenpoint T. 4-4(1-1)
Glentoran FC - Cliftonville FAC 0-2(0-0)
Larne FC - Glenavon FC 1-0(1-0)

Please note: the season was curtailed on 07.03.2020 due to Covid-19 pandemic. Standings were decided by a points by game average.

Final Standings

									Total					Home					Away				
1.	**Linfield FC Belfast**	(2.23)	31	22	3	6	71	-	24	69	12	2	1	44	-	9	10	1	5	27	-	15
2.	Coleraine FC	(2.10)	31	19	8	4	64	-	24	65	9	5	1	29	-	10	10	3	3	35	-	14
3.	Crusaders FC Belfast	(1.90)	31	17	8	6	66	-	30	59	10	3	3	35	-	13	7	5	3	31	-	17
4.	Cliftonville FAC	(1.90)	31	18	5	8	48	-	22	59	9	2	4	23	-	11	9	3	4	25	-	11
5.	Glentoran FC Belfast	(1.87)	31	17	7	7	60	-	33	58	10	3	3	34	-	13	7	4	4	26	-	20
6.	Larne FC	(1.81)	31	16	8	7	59	-	29	56	7	6	3	32	-	15	9	2	4	27	-	14
7.	Glenavon FC Lurgan	(1.13)	31	10	5	16	46	-	71	35	7	5	3	27	-	20	3	0	13	19	-	51
8.	Carrick Rangers FC	(1.03)	31	10	2	19	34	-	47	32	5	0	11	17	-	25	5	2	8	17	-	22
9.	Dungannon Swifts FC	(0.97)	31	8	6	17	36	-	76	30	6	3	7	23	-	33	2	3	10	13	-	43
10.	Ballymena United FC	(0.87)	31	7	6	18	34	-	54	27	4	3	9	20	-	30	3	3	9	14	-	24
11.	Warrenpoint Town FC	(0.58)	31	5	3	23	26	-	85	18	3	1	11	15	-	40	2	2	12	11	-	45
12.	Institute FC Derry (*Relegated*)	(0.48)	31	2	9	20	23	-	72	15	1	2	12	8	-	41	1	7	8	15	-	31

Top goalscorers:	
18 Joseph Anthony Gormley	*Cliftonville FAC*
15 Robbie McDaid	*Glentoran FC Belfast*
13 Andrew Waterworth	*Linfield FC Belfast*
13 David McDaid	*Larne FC*
12 Jamie McGonigle	*Crusaders FC Belfast*
12 Hrvoje Plum (CRO)	*Glentoran FC Belfast*

NATIONAL CUP
Irish Cup 2019/2020

Fifth Round [04.01.2020]

Queen's University AFC - Linfield FC Belfast	2-1	Larne FC - Belfast Celtic FC	8-0
Knockbreda FC Belfast - Dergview FC	3-2 aet	Ards FC Newtownards - Carrick Rangers FC	1-3
Banbridge Town FC - East Belfast FC	5-4 pen	Cliftonville FC - Hanover FC	6-0
Glenavon FC Lurgan - Coleraine FC	0-2	Glentoran FC Belfast - Portadown FC	5-4 pen
Ballyclare Comrades - Harland & Wolff Welders FC	2-1	Ballymena United FC - Crumlin Star FC Belfast	2-0
Warrenpoint Town FC - Police Service of NI FC	3-1	Loughgall FC - Rathfriland Rangers FC	1-2
Ballinamallard United FC - Dollingstown FC	1-0	Crusaders FC Belfast - Dundela FC Belfast	3-0
Institute FC Derry - Dungannon Swifts FC	2-3	Newry City AFC - Bangor FC	3-1

1/8-Finals [01.02.2020]

Knockbreda FC Belfast - Ballinamallard United FC	2-5	Cliftonville FC - Rathfriland Rangers FC	3-1
Queen's University AFC - Glentoran FC Belfast	2-3	Coleraine FC - Banbridge Town FC	3-0
Ballyclare Comrades FC - Larne FC	0-1 aet	Dungannon Swifts FC - Newry City AFC	4-2 aet
Carrick Rangers FC - Crusaders FC Belfast	1-5	Warrenpoint Town FC - Ballymena United FC	1-2

Quarter-Finals [28-29.02.2020]

Larne FC - Coleraine FC	2-3	Dungannon Swifts FC - Cliftonville FC	1-2
Ballinamallard United FC - Ballymena United FC	0-2	Glentoran FC Belfast - Crusaders FC Belfast	2-1

Semi-Finals [27.07.2020]

Ballymena United FC - Coleraine FC	3-1 pen	Cliftonville FC - Glentoran FC Belfast	6-7 pen

Final

31.07.2020; Windsor Park, Belfast; Referee: Timothy Marshall; Attendance: 500
Glentoran FC Belfast - Ballymena United FC   **2-1(1-0,1-1)**

Glentoran FC: Elliott Morris, Patrick McClean, Joe Crowe (67.Ciarán O'Connor), Keith Cowan, Marcus Kane, Chris Gallagher, Navid Nasseri, Robbie McDaid, Paul O'Neill (83.Jonathan Frazer), Elvio van Overbeek (88.Malachy Smith), Rory Donnelly (118.Gavin Peers). Trainer: Michael McDermott.

Ballymena United: Ross Glendinning, Scot Whiteside, Steven McCullough, Jim Ervin, Jonathan Addis (116.Kofi Balmer), Andy McGrory (37.Tony Kane; 116.Aaron Burns), Jude Winchester (61.James Knowles), Adam Lecky, Leroy Millar, Joshua Kelly, Cathair Friel (106.Kenneth Kane). Trainer: David Jeffrey.

Goals: 1-0 Paul O'Neill (22), 1-1 Cathair Friel (48), 2-1 Robbie McDaid (114).

THE CLUBS 2019/2020

Ballymena United Football Club

Founded:	07.04.1928
Stadium:	The Showgrounds, Ballymena (3,050)
Trainer:	David Jeffrey 28.10.1962

Goalkeepers:	DOB	M	(s)	G
Connor Friel	14.06.2003	2		2
Ross Glendinning	18.05.1993	24		
Jordan Williamson	23.05.1995	6		
Defenders:	**DOB**	**M**	**(s)**	**G**
Kofi Balmer	19.09.2000	14	(2)	
Aaron Burns	29.05.1992	5	(1)	1
Andrew Burns (ENG)	29.05.1992	11	(4)	
Jim Ervin	05.06.1985	25		
Reece Glendinning	09.06.1995	7	(1)	
Tony Kane (IRL)	29.08.1987	12	(4)	1
Steven McCullough	30.08.1994	28	(1)	
Kyle Owens	09.07.1992	2	(1)	
Scot Whiteside	16.06.1997	11	(1)	1
Midfielders:	**DOB**	**M**	**(s)**	**G**
Jonathan Addis	27.09.1992	25		2

	DOB	M	(s)	G
Declan Carville	13.12.1989	14	(2)	
Ryan Harpur (IRL)	01.12.1988	13		2
Joshua Kelly	08.03.1999	14	(5)	1
James Knowles	06.04.1993	7	(4)	1
Adam Lecky	03.05.1991	12	(1)	1
Ryan Mayse	07.12.1993	5	(6)	
Shane McGinty (IRL)	14.04.1994	4	(10)	
Andy McGrory	15.12.1991	27	(1)	7
Leroy Millar	01.09.1995	21		2
Jude Winchester	13.04.1993	17	(1)	2
Forwards:	**DOB**	**M**	**(s)**	**G**
Leo Brown	15.06.2000		(2)	
Cathair Friel	25.05.1993	16	(3)	6
Kenneth Kane	13.08.1999	9	(5)	
Ross Lavery	29.07.1996	5	(9)	2
Joe McCready	24.07.1990	5		1

Please note: Connor Friel (goalkeeper) was used as field player, while Declan Carville (midfielder) played also as goalkeeper.

Carrick Rangers Football Club

Founded: 1939
Stadium: Loughshore Hotel Arena, Carrickfergus (4,500)
Trainer: Niall Currie   12.09.1972

Goalkeepers:	DOB	M	(s)	G
Harry Doherty (IRL)	29.03.1996	8		
Aaron Hogg	14.01.1988	22		
Liam McAuley	06.10.1989	1		
Ben Nicholl	25.12.2002		(1)	
Defenders:	**DOB**	**M**	**(s)**	**G**
Lee Chapman	09.11.1994	25		3
Lee Colligan	11.02.1989		(1)	
James Ferrin	23.09.1989	19		2
Daniel Kelly	06.01.1993	26		4
Caolan Loughran	09.01.1995	17	(2)	4
Reece Neale	14.05.1998	22	(2)	1
Chris Rodgers	03.01.1991	18	(3)	
Mark Surgenor	19.12.1985	30		1
Gerard Thompson	01.12.1995	9	(1)	1
Midfielders:	**DOB**	**M**	**(s)**	**G**
Lloyd Anderson	09.03.1998	21	(8)	4
Mark Carson	09.11.1992	6	(2)	
Kyle Cherry	13.05.1993	19	(5)	1
William Faulkner	18.01.1990	24	(4)	
Adam Gray	04.04.1991		(2)	
Liam Hassin	15.03.2001	5	(13)	
Daniel Magill	24.10.1996	6	(1)	
Ashton McDermott	09.11.1991		(1)	
Darren Murray	24.10.1991	5		
Michael Smith	01.07.1992	14	(14)	3
Forwards:	**DOB**	**M**	**(s)**	**G**
Alex Gawne	22.05.2001	4	(1)	
Guillaume Keke (FRA)	13.03.1991	14	(5)	3
Mark Kelly	23.02.1990	2	(2)	1
Josh McGreevy	19.05.2001		(2)	
Stewart Nixon	08.05.1997	23	(2)	5
Daniel Reynolds	24.03.1999		(5)	
Abby Sanusi (NGA)	20.02.1992		(3)	
Dylan Smiley	30.06.2000		(1)	
Theodore Wilson (SVN)	24.10.1994	1	(2)	1

Cliftonville Football & Athletic Club

Founded: 1879
Stadium: Solitude Stadium, Belfast (2,530)
Trainer: Paddy McLaughlin   10.10.1979

Goalkeepers:	DOB	M	(s)	G
Declan Breen	24.09.2002	1		
Richard Brush (ENG)	26.11.1984	31		
Defenders:	**DOB**	**M**	**(s)**	**G**
Liam Bagnall	17.05.1992	21	(2)	1
Garry Breen (IRL)	17.03.1989	23		1
Odhran Casey	09.04.2002		(1)	
Aaron Donnelly	22.03.2000	24	(1)	
Seanan Foster	29.01.1997	5	(9)	
Joe Gorman (IRL)	01.09.1994	5	(6)	1
Jamie Harney	04.03.1996	24		
Levi Ives	28.07.1997	11	(1)	
Conor McDermott	18.09.1997	29		2
Midfielders:	**DOB**	**M**	**(s)**	**G**
Chris Curran	05.01.1991	25	(4)	2
Ronan Doherty	10.01.1996	30		
Aaron Harkin	03.03.1993	2	(2)	
Mark McKee	01.12.1998	2	(2)	1
Ronan Wilson	01.09.1998	1	(11)	
Forwards:	**DOB**	**M**	**(s)**	**G**
Ryan Curran	13.10.1993	25	(6)	5
Rory Donnelly	18.02.1992	21	(1)	6
Stephen Garrett	13.04.1987		(3)	
Joe Gormley	26.11.1989	30	(1)	17
Thomas Maguire	09.09.1999	2	(18)	1
Michael McCrudden	31.07.1991	6	(2)	
Calvin McCurry	26.12.2001	1	(2)	
Peter McKiernan	06.06.2002		(1)	
Conor McMenamin	24.08.1995	22	(5)	10
Donal Rocks	13.07.2000		(5)	

Please note: Declan Breen (goalkeeper) was used as defender.

Coleraine Football Club

Founded: 1927
Stadium: The Showgrounds, Coleraine (2,496)
Trainer: Oran Kearney   29.07.1978

Goalkeepers:	DOB	M	(s)	G
Christopher Johns	13.05.1995	31		
Defenders:	**DOB**	**M**	**(s)**	**G**
Aaron Burns	29.05.1992		(1)	
Aaron Canning	07.03.1992	28		5
Ben Doherty	24.03.1997	26	(1)	9
Steven Douglas	27.09.1977	4	(2)	
Lyndon Kane	15.02.1997	26		
Gareth McConaghie	05.04.1988	13	(2)	
Adam Mullan	24.10.1995	21		
Lewis Nevin	13.01.2003		(1)	
Stephen O'Donnell	01.09.1992	10	(6)	2
Midfielders:	**DOB**	**M**	**(s)**	**G**
Josh Carson	03.06.1993	27	(1)	3
Jamie Glackin	16.02.1995	25	(5)	7
Aaron Jarvis	10.05.1997	17	(1)	4
Stephen Lowry	14.10.1986	28	(1)	5
Ian Parkhill	07.04.1990	9	(14)	
Dean Shiels	01.02.1985	2	(1)	
Aaron Traynor	24.07.1990	23		2
Andrew Whiteside	08.05.2001		(1)	
Forwards:	**DOB**	**M**	**(s)**	**G**
Curtis Allen	22.02.1988		(3)	
Eoin Bradley	31.12.1983	23	(4)	6
Matthew Fitzpatrick	02.09.1994	2	(2)	1
Alex Gawne	22.05.2001		(10)	3
Nedas Maculaitis (LTU)	06.08.1999	4	(8)	1
Emmett McGuckin	07.03.1991	1	(7)	1
James McLaughlin	06.03.1990	17	(7)	10
Stewart Nixon	08.05.1997	4		1

Crusaders Football Club Belfast

Founded: 1898
Stadium: Seaview Stadium, Belfast (3,383)
Trainer: Stephen Baxter   01.10.1965

Goalkeepers:	DOB	M	(s)	G
Gerard Doherty (IRL)	24.08.1981	21		
Sean O'Neill	11.04.1988	10		
Defenders:	**DOB**	**M**	**(s)**	**G**
Howard Beverland	30.03.1990	12	(2)	1
Rodney Brown	13.08.1995	10		
Billy Joe Burns	28.04.1989	28		2
Colin Coates	26.10.1985	14		
Cameron Dummigan	02.06.1996	2	(1)	
Chris Hegarty	13.08.1992	13	(2)	1
Kyle Owens	09.07.1992	1	(5)	
Michael Ruddy	05.08.1993	9	(2)	
Sean Ward	12.01.1984	5		
Midfielders:	**DOB**	**M**	**(s)**	**G**
Declan Caddell	13.04.1988	17	(7)	2
Ross Clarke	17.05.1993	20	(4)	7
Jordan Forsythe	11.02.1991	23	(1)	3
Rory Hale (IRL)	27.11.1996	17	(2)	2
Philip Lowry	15.07.1989	26	(2)	9
Tom Mathieson	09.01.2000		(1)	
Jamie McGonigle	05.03.1996	20	(7)	12
Jarlath O'Rourke	13.02.1995	19		
Forwards:	**DOB**	**M**	**(s)**	**G**
David Cushley	22.07.1989	7	(14)	3
Paul Heatley	30.06.1987	27	(3)	9
Paul McElroy	07.07.1994	4	(10)	3
Reece McGinley	01.03.2000		(5)	
Jordan Owens	09.07.1989	24	(2)	11
Harry David Robinson	26.09.2000		(1)	
Gary Thompson	26.05.1990	12	(5)	

Dungannon Swifts Football Club

Founded:	1949			
Stadium:	Stangmore Park, Dungannon (5,000)			
Trainer:	Kris Lindsay		05.02.1984	

Goalkeepers:	DOB	M	(s)	G
Stuart Addis	05.07.1979	3		
Conner Byrne	27.03.2003	8	(2)	
Samuel Johnston	26.03.1996	16		
Niall Morgan	17.07.1991	4		
Defenders:	**DOB**	**M**	**(s)**	**G**
Callum Byers	28.07.1997	11		1
Caolin Coyle	23.04.2000	17	(1)	
Adam Harwood	17.01.1995		(2)	
Dylan King	27.08.1998	26	(1)	2
Caomhan McGuinness	14.01.2000	11	(1)	
Ross Redman	23.11.1989	18		
Midfielders:	**DOB**	**M**	**(s)**	**G**
Seanan Clucas	08.11.1992	17		3
Terry Fitzpatrick	23.03.1982	7	(1)	
Ben Gallagher	30.03.2002	10	(5)	1
Kris Lowe	06.01.1996	30		2
Caolan McAleer	19.08.1993	6		
Shane McGinty (IRL)	14.04.1994	6	(1)	
Seán Noble (IRL)	20.03.1996	1	(3)	
Mark Patton	08.07.1990	19	(7)	2
Craig Taylor	01.02.1995		(7)	
Alan Teggart	24.11.1986	25	(1)	
Douglas Wilson	03.03.1994	20	(2)	6
Forwards:	**DOB**	**M**	**(s)**	**G**
Lee Brennan	25.10.1996	1	(4)	
Rhyss Campbell	30.11.1998	11	(13)	2
Michael Carvill	03.04.1988	25	(2)	5
Terry Devlin	06.11.2003		(8)	
Daniel Hughes	03.05.1992	11	(4)	2
Guillaume Keke (FRA)	13.03.1991		(2)	
Oisin Smyth	05.05.2000	23	(4)	4
Ryan Waide	12.02.2000	15	(10)	4

Glenavon Football Club Lurgan

Founded:	1889			
Stadium:	Mourneview Park, Lurgan (4,160)			
Trainer:	Gary Hamilton		06.10.1980	

Goalkeepers:	DOB	M	(s)	G
James Taylor	12.05.1984	4		
Jonny Tuffey	20.01.1987	27		
Defenders:	**DOB**	**M**	**(s)**	**G**
Calum Birney	19.04.1993	4	(1)	
Colin Coates	26.10.1985	2		
Andrew Doyle	28.10.1990	23		1
Caolan Marron	04.07.1998	16	(3)	
Rhys Marshall	16.01.1995	22		4
Seamus Sharkey (ENG)	11.05.1990	5		
James Singleton	22.08.1995	28		1
Midfielders:	**DOB**	**M**	**(s)**	**G**
Patrick Burns	09.01.2001	13	(3)	
Conan Byrne (IRL)	10.07.1985	2	(4)	1
Sammy Clingan	13.01.1984	12	(1)	3
Joshua Daniels	22.02.1996	23	(1)	4
Dylan Davidson	20.03.1999	5	(1)	
Matthew Ferguson	21.11.1995		(1)	
Robert Garrett	05.05.1988	23	(1)	3
Andrew Hall	19.09.1989	10	(1)	2
Aaron Harmon	05.11.1989	20	(4)	2
Conor McCloskey	29.01.1992	12	(14)	4
Stephen Murray	29.12.1988	7	(11)	4
Jack O'Mahony (IRL)	26.02.2000	7	(5)	
Matthew Snoddy	02.06.1993	5	(1)	1
Eoin Wearen (IRL)	02.10.1992	2	(6)	1
Forwards:	**DOB**	**M**	**(s)**	**G**
Oisin Barr	22.07.2002		(1)	
Kyle Beggs (ENG)	06.12.1996	9	(9)	
Gary Hamilton	06.10.1980	5		
Ross Hunter	07.07.2002		(1)	
Jordan Jenkins	28.02.2000	15	(10)	4
Daniel Larmour	03.09.1998	16	(4)	1
Andrew Mitchell	25.01.1994	13	(3)	4
Gregory Moorhouse (IRL)	10.07.1994	3	(3)	1
Daniel Purkis	10.06.1995	8		3

Glentoran Football Club Belfast

Founded:	1882			
Stadium:	The Oval, Belfast (6,054)			
Trainer:	Michael McDermott		07.02.1974	

Goalkeepers:	DOB	M	(s)	G
Marijan Antolović (CRO)	07.05.1989	29		
Elliott Morris	04.05.1981	2		
Defenders:	**DOB**	**M**	**(s)**	**G**
Calum Birney	19.04.1993	2	(2)	
Keith Cowan (IRL)	23.08.1985	2	(1)	1
Joe Crowe	20.04.1998	17	(5)	
William Garrett	31.08.1991	9	(1)	1
Caolan Marron	04.07.1998	5		
Patrick McClean	22.11.1996	27	(1)	2
Gavin Peers (IRL)	10.11.1985	26		1
Ross Redman	23.11.1989	2		
Malachy Smith	08.04.2001	2	(2)	
Cameron Stewart	11.03.1997	4	(10)	1
Midfielders:	**DOB**	**M**	**(s)**	**G**
Seanan Clucas	08.11.1992	2		
Chris Gallagher	30.03.1999	21	(1)	1
Sean Og Gallagher	30.01.2001	1		
Steven Gordon	27.07.1993	2	(3)	
John Herron (SCO)	01.02.1994	16	(3)	1
Marcus Kane	08.12.1991	26		2
Darren Murray	24.10.1991	6	(7)	1
Navid Nasseri (IRN)	26.07.1996	16	(4)	6
Ciarán O'Connor (IRL)	04.07.1996		(3)	
Conor Pepper (IRL)	04.05.1994	23		
Hrvoje Plum (CRO)	28.05.1994	24		12
Forwards:	**DOB**	**M**	**(s)**	**G**
Curtis Allen	22.02.1988	2	(3)	
Thomas Byrne (IRL)	26.01.1999	3		
Rory Donnelly	18.02.1992	3		
Antonio Đurić (CRO)	08.06.1998		(4)	1
Jonathan Frazer	30.05.1996	1	(11)	
Deivydas Matulevičius (LTU)	08.04.1989		(3)	
Robbie McDaid	23.10.1996	29		15
Andrew Mitchell	25.01.1994	4	(1)	
Paul O'Neill	07.01.2000	16	(8)	11
Elvio van Overbeek (NED)	11.01.1994	19	(11)	3

Institute Football Club Derry

Founded: 1905
Stadium: Brandywell Stadium, Derry (7,700)
Trainer: Paul McLaughlin (SCO)   20.02.1984
[16.09.2019]   Sean Connor   12.07.1967

Goalkeepers:	DOB	M	(s)	G
Rory Brown (IRL)	25.05.2000	24		
Martin Gallagher	26.10.1990	2		
Paul Wells	29.08.1992	5		
Defenders:	**DOB**	**M**	**(s)**	**G**
Caoimhin Bonner	15.01.1993	10		
Oran Brogan	23.07.2002	6	(1)	
Graham Crown	02.03.1992	20	(1)	
Dean Curry	11.11.1994	28		
Gianfranco de Carne (ITA)	06.06.1997		(2)	
Peter Doherty (IRL)	29.06.1995	3		
Shaun Leppard	19.07.2000	6	(4)	1
Colm McLaughlin (IRL)	01.08.1993	21	(1)	1
Mark Scoltock	26.03.1985	1		
Matthew Stephenson	06.07.2001		(1)	
Midfielders:	**DOB**	**M**	**(s)**	**G**
Ahu Adebame Obhakhan (ESP)	02.08.1997	4	(2)	1
Jack Bradley	18.09.2001	8	(4)	
Gareth Brown	11.03.1992	20	(6)	1
Cormac Burke	11.08.1993	13	(5)	1
David Carty (ENG)	09.03.1994		(2)	
Raymond Foy (IRL)	10.03.1993	4		
Niall Grace	08.01.1993	14		1
Adam Green	17.05.2002		(2)	
James Henry	20.03.1991	4		
Robbie Hume	02.02.1992		(2)	
Aaron Jarvis	10.05.1997	2		
Thomas McBride	30.05.1992	4		
Aidan McCauley	15.03.1996	24	(2)	1
Aaron McGurk	27.02.2000	6	(5)	1
Shane McNamee	25.08.2000	11	(5)	
Jake Morrow	11.11.1999		(5)	1
Ryan Morrow	12.03.1995	12	(2)	
Alex Pomeroy	08.05.1997	6	(2)	1
Conor Tourish (IRL)	02.03.1995	23	(2)	1
Evan Tweed (IRL)	01.03.1999	14	(6)	1
Forwards:	**DOB**	**M**	**(s)**	**G**
Stephen Curry	05.11.1990	5	(1)	
Jamie Dunne (IRL)	02.07.1997	4	(3)	1
Joe McCready	24.07.1990	23	(1)	8
Jamie McIntyre	01.12.1996	2	(10)	1
Brendan McLaughlin	25.11.1993	9	(7)	
Callum Moorehead	24.07.1998		(2)	
Liam Walsh (IRL)	22.07.1999	3	(1)	

Larne Football Club

Founded: 1889
Stadium: Inver Park, Larne (2,000)
Trainer: Tiernan Lynch   1981

Goalkeepers:	DOB	M	(s)	G
Conor Devlin	23.09.1991	26		
Conor Mitchell	09.05.1996	5		
McKenzie Pauley	09.05.2003		(1)	
Defenders:	**DOB**	**M**	**(s)**	**G**
Shane McEleney	31.01.1991	10	(3)	
Harry Flowers (ENG)	15.04.1996	23	(1)	2
Sean Graham	20.11.2000	5	(4)	2
Dean Jarvis	01.06.1992	8		
Graham Kelly (IRL)	16.10.1997	24	(1)	
Chris Ramsey	24.05.1990	8	(2)	
Ben Tilney (ENG)	28.02.1997	11	(10)	
Albert Watson	08.09.1985	29	(1)	1
Midfielders:	**DOB**	**M**	**(s)**	**G**
Tomas Cosgrove	11.12.1992	24		
Martin Donnelly	28.08.1988	24	(4)	9
Liam Hassin	15.03.2001		(2)	
John Herron (SCO)	01.02.1994	4		
Jeff Hughes	29.05.1985	26	(2)	6
Lee Lynch (IRL)	27.11.1991	17	(11)	3
Conor McKendry	21.10.1998		(8)	1
Andy Mitchell	06.04.1992	1	(3)	1
Mark Randall (ENG)	28.09.1989	21	(7)	7
Fuad Sule (IRL)	20.01.1997	28	(1)	1
Forwards:	**DOB**	**M**	**(s)**	**G**
Cillin Gilmour	12.11.1998		(3)	
David McDaid (IRL)	03.12.1990	24	(3)	13
Jonathan McMurray	19.09.1994	21	(3)	11
Thomas Stewart	12.11.1986		(2)	
Joseph Tully	23.05.1998	2	(2)	

Linfield Football Club Belfast

Founded: 1886
Stadium: Windsor Park, Belfast (18,167)
Trainer: David Jonathan Healy   05.08.1979

Goalkeepers:	DOB	M	(s)	G
Rohan Ferguson	06.12.1997	30		
Alex Moore	27.08.1998	1		
Defenders:	**DOB**	**M**	**(s)**	**G**
Ethan Boyle (IRL)	04.01.1997	4		
Jimmy Callacher	11.06.1991	30		6
Chris Casement	12.01.1988	14	(1)	1
Matthew Clarke	03.03.1994	19	(5)	1
Mark Haughey	23.01.1991	8	(1)	2
Trai Hume	18.03.2002		(2)	
Ross Larkin	10.06.1999	1	(2)	
Ryan McGivern	08.01.1990	9		2
Niall Quinn	02.08.1993	14	(2)	1
Joshua Robinson	30.06.1993	8		1
Mark Stafford	20.08.1987	15	(1)	3
Midfielders:	**DOB**	**M**	**(s)**	**G**
Joel Cooper	29.02.1996	29		11
Stephen Fallon	03.03.1997	26	(3)	4
Bastien Héry (FRA)	23.03.1992	17	(5)	2
Daniel Kearns (IRL)	26.08.1991	4	(4)	
Andy Mitchell	06.04.1992	5	(2)	1
Jamie Mulgrew	05.06.1986	25		
Matthew Shevlin	07.12.1998	1	(10)	
Jordan Stewart	31.03.1995	12	(7)	4
Forwards:	**DOB**	**M**	**(s)**	**G**
Charlie Allen	22.11.2003		(3)	
Rory Currie (SCO)	20.02.1998	1	(4)	
Lorcan Forde	07.11.1999		(1)	
Shayne Lavery	08.12.1998	21	(4)	10
Kyle McClean	03.10.1998	3	(2)	
Kirk Millar	07.08.1992	25	(3)	8
Daniel Reynolds	24.03.1999		(5)	
Andrew Waterworth	11.04.1986	19	(7)	13

<table>
<tr><td colspan="2">

Warrenpoint Town Football Club

</td></tr>
</table>

Founded:	1987	
Stadium:	Milltown Stadium, Warrenpoint (1,280)	
Trainer:	Stephen McDonnell (IRL)	23.03.1992
[24.10.2019]	Barry Gray	11.04.1980

Goalkeepers:	DOB	M	(s)	G
Gareth Buchanan	11.10.1991	2		
Mark Byrne	15.09.2000	12		
Evan Moran (IRL)	22.04.1997	5		
Gabriel Sava (ITA)	15.10.1986	2		
Berat Türker (GER)	04.10.1991	10	(1)	
Defenders:	**DOB**	**M**	**(s)**	**G**
Emmet Bennett (IRL)	08.07.1999	25		1
Colm Deasy (IRL)	04.01.1997	6		1
Dermot McVeigh	24.07.1990	22	(2)	
Ben Mullen (IRL)	22.06.2001	13	(5)	
Lorcan Murnaghan (IRL)	15.03.1999	1	(3)	
Jake O'Connor (IRL)	28.10.1998	2	(2)	
James Prendergast (IRL)		4	(4)	
Anton Reilly (IRL)	09.10.1997	26		
Gavin Smith (IRL)	19.07.1999	7	(5)	
Daniel Wallace	21.10.1994	29		3
Conall Young	19.02.1999	11	(2)	1
Midfielders:	**DOB**	**M**	**(s)**	**G**
Kris Cowan	14.01.2002	10	(1)	
Kealan Dillon (IRL)	21.02.1994	7		

	DOB	M	(s)	G
Philip Donnelly (IRL)	29.04.1992	4		
Lorcan Forde	07.11.1999	12	(4)	1
Stuart Hutchinson	10.05.1991	5	(1)	
Matthew Lynch	07.03.1999	11	(2)	
Francis McCaffrey	22.04.1993	1		
Ciaran McCann	26.03.2000	1	(7)	
Matthew Taylor (ENG)	09.02.2000		(3)	
Dean Watters (IRL)	20.06.1998	22	(2)	
Evan White (IRL)	17.02.1999	7	(1)	
Forwards:	**DOB**	**M**	**(s)**	**G**
Adam Carroll	02.09.2001		(3)	
Ethan Copes	14.07.2001		(1)	
Brandon Doyle	20.08.1998	19	(8)	5
Mark Griffin (AUS)	16.06.1991	2	(2)	
Mark McKee	01.12.1998	2		1
Ciarán O'Connor (IRL)	04.07.1996	11		
Ryan O'Kane	16.08.2003		(3)	
Alan O'Sullivan (IRL)	24.03.1995	29	(1)	10
Eamon Scannell	10.01.1999	15	(4)	1
Ryan Swan (IRL)	13.05.1996	6		2

<table>
<tr><td colspan="2">

SECOND LEVEL
NIFL Championship 2019/2020

</td></tr>
</table>

1.	Portadown FC (*Promoted*)	31	20	6	5	72 - 30	66	(2.13)
2.	Ballinamallard United FC	30	19	3	8	71 - 34	60	(2.00)
3.	Loughgall FC	31	18	4	9	64 - 45	58	(1.87)
4.	Ards FC Newtownards	31	16	6	9	68 - 44	54	(1.74)
5.	Newry City AFC	30	15	6	9	55 - 32	51	(1.70)
6.	Dundela FC Belfast	31	13	7	11	43 - 49	46	(1.48)
7.	Ballyclare Comrades FC	30	11	7	12	53 - 49	40	(1.33)
8.	Harland & Wolff Welders FC Belfast	31	10	5	16	52 - 63	35	(1.13)
9.	Queen's University AFC Belfast	31	11	1	19	59 - 69	34	(1.10)
10.	Dergview FC Castlederg	30	8	5	17	38 - 54	29	(0.97)
11.	Knockbreda FC Belfast	30	7	4	19	36 - 84	25	(0.83)
12.	Police Service of Northern Ireland FC Belfast (*Relegated*)	30	7	2	21	40 - 98	23	(0.77)

<u>Please note</u>: the season was curtailed due to Covid-19 pandemic. Standings were decided by a points by game average.

INTERNATIONAL MATCHES
(16.07.2019 – 15.07.2020)

05.09.2019	Belfast	Northern Ireland - Luxembourg	1-0(1-0)	(F)
09.09.2019	Belfast	Northern Ireland - Germany	0-2(0-0)	(ECQ)
10.10.2019	Rotterdam	Netherlands - Northern Ireland	3-1(0-0)	(ECQ)
14.10.2019	Praha	Czech Republic - Northern Ireland	2-3(0-3)	(F)
16.11.2019	Belfast	Northern Ireland - Netherlands	0-0	(ECQ)
19.11.2019	Frankfurt/Main	Germany - Northern Ireland	6-1(2-1)	(ECQ)

05.09.2019   NORTHERN IRELAND - LUXEMBOURG   1-0(1-0)   Friendly International

Windsor Park, Belfast; Referee: Bryn Markham-Jones (Wales); Attendance: 14,108

NIR: Bailey Peacock-Farrell (67.Michael McGovern), Thomas Michael Flanagan, Shane Kevin Ferguson, Conor McLaughlin, Ciaron Maurice Brown, Corry John Evans (Cap) (67.Liam Francis Peadar Donnelly), George Alan Saville (60.Alfie John McCalmont), Jordan Andrew Thompson (88.Steven Davis), Gavin Whyte (88.Ethan Stuart William Galbraith), Kyle Joseph George Lafferty (59.Shayne Francis Lavery), Joshua Brendan David Magennis. Trainer: Michael Andrew Martin O'Neill.

Goal: Kevin Malget (37 own goal).

09.09.2019   NORTHERN IRELAND - GERMANY   0-2(0-0)   16th EC. Qualifiers

Windsor Park, Belfast; Referee: Daniele Orsato (Italy); Attendance: 18,326

NIR: Bailey Peacock-Farrell, Jonathan Grant Evans, Craig George Cathcart, Stuart Allan Dallas, Jamal Piaras Lewis, Steven Davis (Cap), Niall McGinn (59.Gavin Whyte), Corry John Evans, Patrick James Coleman McNair, George Alan Saville (70.Joshua Brendan David Magennis), Conor James Washington (83.Shayne Francis Lavery). Trainer: Michael Andrew Martin O'Neill.

10.10.2019   NETHERLANDS - NORTHERN IRELAND   3-1(0-0)   16th EC. Qualifiers

Stadion Feijenoord, Rotterdam; Referee: Benoît Bastien (France); Attendance: 41,348

NIR: Bailey Peacock-Farrell, Jonathan Grant Evans, Craig George Cathcart, Michael Smith, Steven Davis (Cap), Corry John Evans (87.Thomas Michael Flanagan), Shane Kevin Ferguson, Stuart Allan Dallas, Patrick James Coleman McNair, George Alan Saville (83.Jordan Andrew Thompson), Kyle Joseph George Lafferty (67.Joshua Brendan David Magennis). Trainer: Michael Andrew Martin O'Neill.

Goal: Joshua Brendan David Magennis (75).

14.10.2019   CZECH REPUBLIC - NORTHERN IRELAND   2-3(0-3)   Friendly International

Stadion Letná, Praha; Referee: Ivan Kružliak (Slovakia); Attendance: 9,139

NIR: Michael McGovern, Jonathan Grant Evans, Craig George Cathcart, Thomas Michael Flanagan, Conor McLaughlin, Steven Davis (Cap) (65.Corry John Evans), Stuart Allan Dallas, Patrick James Coleman McNair, Jordan Andrew Thompson (65.George Alan Saville), Gavin Whyte (87.Niall McGinn), Liam Boyce (71.Joshua Brendan David Magennis). Trainer: Michael Andrew Martin O'Neill.

Goals: Patrick James Coleman McNair (9), Jonathan Grant Evans (23), Patrick James Coleman McNair (40).

16.11.2019   NORTHERN IRELAND - NETHERLANDS   0-0   16th EC. Qualifiers

Windsor Park, Belfast; Referee: Szymon Marciniak (Poland); Attendance: 18,404

NIR: Bailey Peacock-Farrell, Jonathan Grant Evans, Craig George Cathcart, Stuart Allan Dallas, Jamal Piaras Lewis (81.Jordan Andrew Thompson), Steven Davis (Cap), Corry John Evans (70.Niall McGinn), Patrick James Coleman McNair, George Alan Saville (58.Michael Smith), Gavin Whyte, Joshua Brendan David Magennis. Trainer: Michael Andrew Martin O'Neill.

19.11.2019   GERMANY - NORTHERN IRELAND   6-1(2-1)   16th EC. Qualifiers

Commerzbank-Arena, Frankfurt am Main; Referee: Carlos del Cerro Grande (Spain); Attendance: 42,855

NIR: Bailey Peacock-Farrell, Craig George Cathcart, Michael Smith, Thomas Michael Flanagan, Shane Kevin Ferguson, Steven Davis (Cap), Corry John Evans (65.Conor McLaughlin), Patrick James Coleman McNair (77.Liam Boyce), George Alan Saville, Jordan Andrew Thompson, Joshua Brendan David Magennis (83.Shayne Francis Lavery). Trainer: Michael Andrew Martin O'Neill.

Goal: Michael Smith (7).

NATIONAL TEAM PLAYERS
(16.07.2019 – 15.07.2020)

Name	DOB	Caps	Goals	2019/2020:	Club
Goalkeepers					
Michael McGOVERN	12.07.1984	**31**	**0**	2019:	*Norwich City FC (ENG)*
Bailey PEACOCK-FARRELL	29.10.1996	**14**	**0**	2019:	*Burnley FC (ENG)*
Defenders					
Ciaron Maurice BROWN	14.01.1998	**1**	**0**	2019:	*Cardiff City FC (WAL)*
Craig George CATHCART	06.02.1989	**50**	**2**	2019:	*Watford FC (ENG)*
Jonathan Grant EVANS	03.01.1988	**84**	**4**	2019:	*Leicester City FC (ENG)*
Thomas Michael FLANAGAN	21.10.1991	**5**	**0**	2019:	*Sunderland AFC (ENG)*
Jamal Piaras LEWIS	25.01.1998	**12**	**0**	2019:	*Norwich City FC*
Conor Gerard McLAUGHLIN	26.07.1991	**38**	**1**	2019:	*Sunderland AFC (ENG)*
Patrick James Coleman McNAIR	27.04.1995	**34**	**3**	2019:	*Middlesbrough FC (ENG)*
Michael SMITH	04.09.1988	**9**	**1**	2019:	*Heart of Midlothian FC Edinburgh (SCO)*
Midfielders					
Stuart Alan DALLAS	19.04.1991	**44**	**3**	2019:	*Leeds United FC (ENG)*
Steven DAVIS	01.01.1985	**117**	**12**	2019:	*Rangers FC Glasgow (SCO)*
Liam Francis Peadar DONNELLY	07.03.1996	**2**	**0**	2019:	*Motherwell FC (SCO)*
Corry John EVANS	17.07.1990	**59**	**2**	2019:	*Blackburn Rovers FC (ENG)*
Shane Kevin FERGUSON	12.07.1991	**42**	**1**	2019:	*Millwall FC London (ENG)*
Ethan Stuart William GALBRAITH	11.05.2001	**1**	**0**	2019:	*Manchester United FC (ENG)*
Alfie John McCALMONT	25.03.2000	**1**	**0**	2019:	*Leeds United FC (ENG)*
Niall McGINN	20.07.1987	**60**	**4**	2019:	*Aberdeen FC (SCO)*
George Alan SAVILLE	01.06.1993	**21**	**0**	2019:	*Middlesbrough FC (ENG)*
Jordan Andrew THOMPSON	03.01.1997	**7**	**0**	2019:	*Blackpool FC (ENG)*
Gavin WHYTE	31.01.1996	**9**	**1**	2019:	*Cardiff City FC (WAL)*
Forwards					
Liam BOYCE	08.04.1991	**21**	**1**	2019:	*Burton Albion FC (ENG)*
Kyle Joseph George LAFFERTY	16.09.1987	**75**	**20**	2019:	*Sarpsborg 08 FF (NOR)*
Shayne Francis LAVERY	08.12.1998	**4**	**0**	2019:	*Linfield FC Belfast*
Joshua Brendan David MAGENNIS	15.05.1990	**50**	**7**	2019:	*Hull City AFC (ENG)*
Conor James WASHINGTON	18.05.1992	**21**	**4**	2019:	*Heart of Midlothian FC Edinburgh (SCO)*

National team coach		
Michael Andrew Martin O`NEILL [from 18.12.2011]	05.07.1969	72 M; 26 W; 18 D; 28 L; 75-83

NORWAY

The Country:
Kongeriket Norge (Kingdom of Norway)
Capital: Oslo
Surface: 385,203 km²
Inhabitants: 5,367,580 [2020]
Time: UTC+1

The FA:
Norges Fotballforbund
Serviceboks 1 Ullevål Stadium, 0840 Oslo
Tel: +47 2102 9300
Founded: 1902
Member of FIFA since: 1908
Member of UEFA since: 1954
Website: www.fotball.no

NATIONAL TEAM RECORDS

RECORDS

First international match:	12.07.1908, Göteborg: Sweden – Norway 11-3
Most international caps:	John Arne Semundseth Riise - 110 caps (2000-2013)
Most international goals:	Jørgen Juve - 33 goals / 45 caps (1928-1937)

UEFA EUROPEAN CHAMPIONSHIP

1960	Qualifiers
1964	Qualifiers
1968	Qualifiers
1972	Qualifiers
1976	Qualifiers
1980	Qualifiers
1984	Qualifiers
1988	Qualifiers
1992	Qualifiers
1996	Qualifiers
2000	Final Tournament (Group Stage)
2004	Qualifiers
2008	Qualifiers
2012	Qualifiers
2016	Qualifiers
2020	*To be determined*

FIFA WORLD CUP

1930	Did not enter
1934	Did not enter
1938	Final Tournament (1st Round)
1950	Did not enter
1954	Qualifiers
1958	Qualifiers
1962	Qualifiers
1966	Qualifiers
1970	Qualifiers
1974	Qualifiers
1978	Qualifiers
1982	Qualifiers
1986	Qualifiers
1990	Qualifiers
1994	Final Tournament (Group Stage)
1998	Final Tournament (2nd Round of 16)
2002	Qualifiers
2006	Qualifiers
2010	Qualifiers
2014	Qualifiers
2018	Qualifiers

OLYMPIC TOURNAMENTS

1908	-
1912	Final Tournament (Quarter-Finals)
1920	Final Tournament (Quarter-Finals)
1924	Did not enter
1928	Did not enter
1936	Final Tournament (3rd Place)
1948	Did not enter
1952	Final Tournament (Round 1)
1956	Did not enter
1960	Qualifiers
1964	Did not enter
1968	Did not enter
1972	Did not enter
1976	Qualifiers
1980	Qualifiers
1984	Final Tournament (Group Stage)
1988	Qualifiers
1992	Qualifiers
1996	Qualifiers
2000	Qualifiers
2004	Qualifiers
2008	Qualifiers
2012	Qualifiers
2016	Qualifiers

UEFA NATIONS LEAGUE

2018/2019 – League C (promoted to League B)

FIFA CONFEDERATIONS CUP 1992-2017

None

NORWEGIAN CLUB HONOURS IN EUROPEAN CLUB COMPETITIONS:

European Champion Clubs.Cup (1956-1992) / UEFA Champions League (1993-2020)

None

Fairs Cup (1858-1971) / UEFA Cup (1972-2009) / UEFA Europa League (2010-2020)

None

UEFA Super Cup (1972-2019)

None

European Cup Winners.Cup 1961-1999

None

*defunct competition

NATIONAL COMPETITIONS
TABLE OF HONOURS

	CHAMPIONS	CUP WINNERS	BEST GOALSCORERS	
1902	-	Sportsklubben Grane	-	
1903	-	Odds BK Skien	-	
1904	-	Odds BK Skien	-	
1905	-	Odds BK Skien	-	
1906	-	Odds BK Skien	-	
1907	-	Mercantile FK	-	
1908	-	Lyn 1896 FK Oslo	-	
1909	-	Lyn 1896 FK Oslo	-	
1910	-	Lyn 1896 FK Oslo	-	
1911	-	Lyn 1896 FK Oslo	-	
1912	-	Mercantile FK	-	
1913	-	Odds BK Skien	-	
1914	-	Frigg Oslo FK	-	
1915	-	Odds BK Skien	-	
1916	-	Frigg Oslo FK	-	
1917	-	Sarpsborg FK	-	
1918	-	Kvik FK Fredrikshald	-	
1919	-	Odds BK Skien	-	
1920	-	FK Ørn-Horten	-	
1921	-	Frigg Oslo FK Oslo	-	
1922	-	Odds BK Skien	-	
1923	-	SK Brann Bergen	-	
1924	-	Odds BK Skien	-	
1925	-	SK Brann Bergen	-	
1926	-	Odds BK Skien	-	
1927	-	FK Ørn-Horten	-	
1928	-	FK Ørn-Horten	-	
1929	-	Sarpsborg FK	-	
1930	-	FK Ørn-Horten	-	
1931	-	Odds BK Skien	-	
1932	-	Fredrikstad FK	-	
1933	-	Mjøndalen IF	-	
1934	-	Mjøndalen IF	-	
1935	-	Fredrikstad FK	-	
1936	-	Fredrikstad FK	-	
1937	-	Mjøndalen IF	-	
1937/1938	Fredrikstad FK	Fredrikstad FK	-	
1938/1939	Fredrikstad FK	Sarpsborg FK	-	
1939/1940	*Championship abandoned*	Fredrikstad FK	-	
1940/1941	*No competition*	*No competition*	-	
1941/1942	*No competition*	*No competition*	-	
1942/1943	*No competition*	*No competition*	-	
1943/1944	*No competition*	*No competition*	-	
1944/1945	*No competition*	Lyn 1896 FK Oslo	-	
1945/1946	*No competition*	Lyn 1896 FK Oslo	-	
1946/1947	*No competition*	Skeid Fotball Oslo	-	
1947/1948	SK Freidig Trondheim	Sarpsborg FK	-	
1948/1949	Fredrikstad FK	Sarpsborg FK	Arvid Havnås (Sandefjord BK)	12
1949/1950	IF Fram Larvik	Fredrikstad FK	Reidar Dørum (FK Ørn-Horten)	13
1950/1951	Fredrikstad FK	Sarpsborg FK	John Sveinsson (Lyn 1896 FK Oslo)	19
1951/1952	Fredrikstad FK	IL Sparta Sparsborg	Jan Tangen (Strømmen IF)	15
1952/1953	Larvik Turn & Idrettsforening	Viking FK Stavanger	Gunnar Thoresen (Larvik Turn & Idrettsforening) Per Jacobsen (Odds BK Skien)	15
1953/1954	Fredrikstad FK	Skeid Fotball Oslo	Gunnar Thoresen (Larvik Turn & Idrettsforening)	15
1954/1955	Larvik Turn & Idrettsforening	Skeid Fotball Oslo	Harald Hennum (Skeid Fotball Oslo)	13
1955/1956	Larvik Turn & Idrettsforening	Skeid Fotball Oslo	Willy Fossli (Asker Fotball)	17
1956/1957	Fredrikstad FK	Fredrikstad FK	Per Kristoffersen (Fredrikstad FK)	15
1957/1958	Viking FK Stavanger	Skeid Fotball Oslo	Harald Hennum (Skeid Fotball Oslo)	17
1958/1959	Lillestrøm SK	Viking FK Stavanger	Reidar Sundby (Larvik Turn & Idrettsforening)	13
1959/1960	Fredrikstad FK	Rosenborg BK Trondheim	Per Kristoffersen (Fredrikstad FK)	13
1960/1961	Fredrikstad FK	Fredrikstad FK	Per Kristoffersen (Fredrikstad FK)	15
1961/1962	SK Brann Bergen	SK Gjøvik-Lyn	Rolf Birger Pedersen (SK Brann Bergen)	26
1963	SK Brann Bergen	Skeid Fotball Oslo	Leif Eriksen (Vålerenga Fotball Oslo)	16
1964	Lyn 1896 FK Oslo	Rosenborg BK Trondheim	Ole Stavrum (Lyn 1896 FK Oslo)	18
1965	Vålerenga Fotball Oslo	Skeid Fotball Oslo	Harald Berg (Lyn 1896 FK Oslo)	19
1966	Skeid Fotball Oslo	Fredrikstad FK	Per Kristoffersen (Fredrikstad FK)	20
1967	Rosenborg BK Trondheim	Lyn 1896 FK Oslo	Odd Iversen (Rosenborg BK Trondheim)	17
1968	Lyn 1896 FK Oslo	Lyn 1896 FK Oslo	Odd Iversen (Rosenborg BK Trondheim)	30
1969	Rosenborg BK Trondheim	Strømsgodset IF Drammen	Odd Iversen (Rosenborg BK Trondheim)	26
1970	Strømsgodset IF Drammen	Strømsgodset IF Drammen	Steinar Pettersen (Strømsgodset IF Drammen)	16
1971	Rosenborg BK Trondheim	Rosenborg BK Trondheim	Jan Fuglset (Fredrikstad FK)	17

1972	Viking FK Stavanger	SK Brann Bergen	Egil Solberg (Mjøndalen IF)
			Johannes Vold (Viking FK Stavanger) 16
1973	Viking FK Stavanger	Strømsgodset IF Drammen	Stein Karlsen (Hamarkameratene) 17
1974	Viking FK Stavanger	Skeid Fotball Oslo	Odd Berg (Molde FK) 13
1975	Viking FK Stavanger	FK Bodø/Glimt	Arne Dokken (Lillestrøm SK) 18
1976	Lillestrøm SK	SK Brann Bergen	Jan Fuglset (Molde FK) 17
1977	Lillestrøm SK	Lillestrøm SK	Trygve Johannessen (Viking FK Stavanger) 17
1978	IK Start Kristiansand	Lillestrøm SK	Tom Lund (Lillestrøm SK) 17
1979	Viking FK Stavanger	Viking FK Stavanger	Odd Iversen (Vålerenga Fotball Oslo) 16
1980	IK Start Kristiansand	Vålerenga Fotball Oslo	Arne Dokken (Lillestrøm SK) 14
1981	Vålerenga Fotball Oslo	Lillestrøm SK	Pål Jacobsen (Vålerenga Fotball Oslo) 16
1982	Viking FK Stavanger	SK Brann Bergen	Tor Arne Granerud (Hamarkameratene)
			Trygve Johannessen (Viking FK Stavanger) 11
1983	Vålerenga Fotball Oslo	Moss FK	Olav Nysæter (Kongsvinger IL) 14
1984	Vålerenga Fotball Oslo	Fredrikstad FK	Sverre Brandhaug (Rosenborg BK Trondheim) 13
1985	Rosenborg BK Trondheim	Lillestrøm SK	Jørn Andersen (Vålerenga Fotball Oslo) 23
1986	Lillestrøm SK	Tromsø IL	Arve Seland (IK Start Kristiansand) 12
1987	Moss FK	Bryne FK	Jan Kristian Fjærestad (Moss FK) 18
1988	Rosenborg BK Trondheim	Rosenborg BK Trondheim	Jan Åge Fjørtoft (Lillestrøm SK) 14
1989	Lillestrøm SK	Viking FK Stavanger	Jahn Ivar Jakobsen (Rosenborg BK Trondheim) 18
1990	Rosenborg BK Trondheim	Rosenborg BK Trondheim	Tore André Dahlum (IK Start Kristiansand) 20
1991	Viking FK Stavanger	Strømsgodset IF Drammen	Karl Petter Løken (Rosenborg BK Trondheim) 12
1992	Rosenborg BK Trondheim	Rosenborg BK Trondheim	Kjell Roar Kaasa (Kongsvinger IL) 17
1993	Rosenborg BK Trondheim	FK Bodø/Glimt	Mons Ivar Mjelde (Lillestrøm SK) 19
1994	Rosenborg BK Trondheim	Molde FK	Harald Martin Brattbakk (Rosenborg BK Trondheim) 17
1995	Rosenborg BK Trondheim	Rosenborg BK Trondheim	Harald Martin Brattbakk (Rosenborg BK Trondheim) 26
1996	Rosenborg BK Trondheim	Tromsø IL	Harald Martin Brattbakk (Rosenborg BK Trondheim) 28
1997	Rosenborg BK Trondheim	Vålerenga Fotball Oslo	Sigurd Rushfeldt (Rosenborg BK Trondheim) 27
1998	Rosenborg BK Trondheim	Stabæk Fotball Bærum	Sigurd Rushfeldt (Rosenborg BK Trondheim) 25
1999	Rosenborg BK Trondheim	Rosenborg BK Trondheim	Rune Lange (Tromsø IL) 23
2000	Rosenborg BK Trondheim	Odd Grenland Skien	Thorstein Helstad (SK Brann Bergen) 18
2001	Rosenborg BK Trondheim	Viking FK Stavanger	Frode Johnsen (Rosenborg BK Trondheim)
			Thorstein Helstad (SK Brann Bergen)
			Clayton Zane (AUS, Lillestrøm SK) 17
2002	Rosenborg BK Trondheim	Vålerenga Fotball Oslo	Harald Martin Brattbakk (Rosenborg BK Trondheim) 17
2003	Rosenborg BK Trondheim	Rosenborg BK Trondheim	Harald Martin Brattbakk (Rosenborg BK Trondheim) 17
2004	Rosenborg BK Trondheim	SK Brann Bergen	Frode Johnsen (Rosenborg BK Trondheim) 19
2005	Vålerenga Fotball Oslo	Molde FK	Ole Martin Årst (Tromsø IL) 16
2006	Rosenborg BK Trondheim	Fredrikstad FK	Daniel Nannskog (SWE, Stabæk Fotball Bærum) 19
2007	SK Brann Bergen	Lillestrøm SK	Thorstein Helstad (SK Brann Bergen) 22
2008	Stabæk Fotball Bærum	Vålerenga Fotball Oslo	Daniel Nannskog (SWE, Stabæk Fotball Bærum) 16
2009	Rosenborg BK Trondheim	Aalesunds FK	Rade Prica (SWE, Rosenborg BK Trondheim) 17
2010	Rosenborg BK Trondheim	Strømsgodset IF Drammen	Baye Djiby Fall (SEN, Molde FK) 16
2011	Molde FK	Aalesunds FK	Mustafa Abdellaoue (Tromsø IL) 17
2012	Molde FK	IL Hødd Ulsteinvik	Péter Kovács (HUN, Strømsgodset IF Drammen)
			Zdeněk Ondrášek (CZE, Tromsø IL) 14
2013	Strømsgodset IF Drammen	Molde FK	Frode Johnsen (Odds BK Skien) 16
2014	Molde FK	Molde FK	Viðar Örn Kjartansson (ISL, Vålerenga Fotball Oslo) 25
2015	Rosenborg BK Trondheim	Rosenborg BK Trondheim	Alexander Toft Søderlund (Rosenborg BK Trondheim) 22
2016	Rosenborg BK Trondheim	Rosenborg BK Trondheim	Christian Gytkjær (DEN, Rosenborg BK Trondheim) 19
2017	Rosenborg BK Trondheim	Lillestrøm SK	Nicklas Bendtner (DEN, Rosenborg BK Trondheim) 19
2018	Rosenborg BK Trondheim	Rosenborg BK Trondheim	Bi Sylvestre Franck Fortune Boli
			(CIV, Stabæk Fotball Bærum) 17
2019	Molde FK	Viking FK Stavanger	Torgeir Børven (Odds BK Skien) 21

Please note: the Norwegian Championship was called Norgesserien (1937–1948), Hovedserien (1948–1962), 1. divisjon (1963–1989), Tippeligaen (1990–2016) and Eliteserien (since 2017).

NATIONAL CHAMPIONSHIP
Eliteserien 2019
(30.03.2019 – 01.12.2019)

Results

Round 1 [30.03.-01.04.2019]
Odds BK - SK Brann 3-2(1-1)
Vålerenga - Mjøndalen 2-0(1-0)
Ranheim - Tromsø IL 1-2(1-0)
Sarpsborg 08 - Molde FK 1-1(0-0)
Strømsgodset - FK Haugesund 3-2(2-2)
Viking - Kristiansund BK 2-0(1-0)
FK Bodø/Glimt - Rosenborg BK 2-0(1-0)
Stabæk - Lillestrøm SK 1-1(1-1)

Round 2 [06-08.04.2019]
Mjøndalen - FK Bodø/Glimt 4-5(1-2)
Molde FK - Stabæk 3-0(2-0)
FK Haugesund - Sarpsborg 08 1-1(1-0)
Kristiansund BK - Vålerenga 2-0(1-0)
Tromsø IL - Viking 0-2(0-1)
Lillestrøm SK - Ranheim 2-1(1-0)
SK Brann - Strømsgodset 1-1(0-1)
Rosenborg BK - Odds BK 1-1(1-0)

Round 3 [12-14.04.2019]
Strømsgodset - Mjøndalen 2-3(1-3)
Viking - SK Brann 2-1(0-0)
Ranheim - FK Haugesund 0-2(0-0)
Sarpsborg 08 - Lillestrøm SK 1-0(1-0)
Odds BK - Kristiansund BK 2-0(1-0)
FK Bodø/Glimt - Molde FK 3-2(2-0)
Stabæk - Rosenborg BK 3-1(1-1)
Vålerenga - Tromsø IL 4-1(2-0)

Round 4 [22-23.04.2019]
Rosenborg BK - Strømsgodset 0-0
FK Haugesund - Stabæk 3-0(1-0)
Kristiansund BK - Ranheim 0-0
FK Bodø/Glimt - Sarpsborg 08 1-1(1-0)
Lillestrøm SK - Molde FK 0-2(0-0)
Mjøndalen - Tromsø IL 1-1(1-0)
SK Brann - Vålerenga 1-1(1-1)
Odds BK - Viking 1-0(0-0)

Round 5 [27-29.04.2019]
Sarpsborg 08 - Mjøndalen 1-1(0-1)
Tromsø IL - SK Brann 1-2(0-0)
Ranheim - Viking 5-2(1-0)
Strømsgodset - Kristiansund BK 2-3(0-2)
Stabæk - FK Bodø/Glimt 2-0(2-0)
Lillestrøm SK - FK Haugesund 1-0(0-0)
Molde FK - Rosenborg BK 3-0(3-0)
Vålerenga - Odds BK 1-0(0-0)

Round 6 [04-06.05.2019]
Mjøndalen - Stabæk 1-0(0-0)
FK Bodø/Glimt - Lillestrøm SK 4-0(3-0)
Odds BK - Strømsgodset 2-1(1-0)
Kristiansund BK - Tromsø IL 1-0(0-0)
FK Haugesund - Molde FK 1-2(0-1)
SK Brann - Ranheim 0-1(0-0)
Rosenborg BK - Sarpsborg 08 1-0(1-0)
Viking - Vålerenga 1-1(0-0)

Round 7 [11-13.05.2019]
Lillestrøm SK - Rosenborg BK 1-1(1-0)
Tromsø IL - Odds BK 1-2(1-0)
Sarpsborg 08 - Kristiansund BK 0-1(0-0)
Ranheim - Vålerenga 1-5(0-0)
FK Haugesund - FK Bodø/Glimt 1-1(0-0)
Molde FK - Mjøndalen 1-0(0-0)
Stabæk - SK Brann 0-1(0-1)
Strømsgodset - Viking 0-0

Round 8 [16.05.2019]
Viking - Stabæk 3-0(0-0)
Tromsø IL - FK Bodø/Glimt 1-2(1-0)
Odds BK - Ranheim 1-0(0-0)
Kristiansund BK - Molde FK 3-2(2-2)
SK Brann - Sarpsborg 08 2-1(2-0)
Rosenborg BK - FK Haugesund 0-2(0-1)
Mjøndalen - Lillestrøm SK 2-2(2-0)
Vålerenga - Strømsgodset 2-0(1-0)

Round 9 [19-20.05.2019]
Strømsgodset - Tromsø IL 3-1(1-1)
Lillestrøm SK - Odds BK 0-3(0-1)
Sarpsborg 08 - Ranheim 1-3(0-1)
FK Haugesund - Kristiansund BK 0-0
Rosenborg BK - Mjøndalen 3-2(2-1)
FK Bodø/Glimt - SK Brann 1-2(1-2)
Molde FK - Viking 5-1(2-1)
Stabæk - Vålerenga 1-1(0-0) [14.08.]

Round 10 [25-26.05.2019]
Vålerenga - Lillestrøm SK 0-3(0-1)
Ranheim - Strømsgodset 1-0(1-0)
Tromsø IL - Molde FK 2-1(1-0)
Mjøndalen - FK Haugesund 1-4(0-2)
SK Brann - Rosenborg BK 0-1(0-0)
Odds BK - Stabæk 2-1(1-1) [10.07.]
Kristiansund - Bodø/Glimt 1-2(0-1) [14.08.]
Viking - Sarpsborg 08 2-1(0-0) [14.08.]

Round 11 [15-17.06.2019]
FK Haugesund - SK Brann 1-1(0-1)
Mjøndalen - Kristiansund BK 1-1(1-0)
Lillestrøm SK - Viking 0-2(0-1)
FK Bodø/Glimt - Strømsgodset 2-0(0-0)
Sarpsborg 08 - Odds BK 2-0(1-0)
Molde FK - Ranheim 2-0(1-0)
Rosenborg BK - Vålerenga 3-0(1-0)
Stabæk - Tromsø IL 0-1(0-0)

Round 12 [22-23.06.2019]
Strømsgodset - Molde FK 0-4(0-4)
Vålerenga - Sarpsborg 08 1-1(1-1)
Tromsø IL - Rosenborg BK 1-0(0-0)
Ranheim - Mjøndalen 1-1(1-1)
Odds BK - FK Haugesund 3-1(1-0)
Kristiansund BK - Stabæk 0-1(0-0)
Viking - FK Bodø/Glimt 3-4(1-2)
SK Brann - Lillestrøm SK 1-0(0-0)

Round 13 [29.06.-01.07.2019]
Rosenborg BK - Kristiansund BK 1-0(1-0)
Mjøndalen - Viking 1-1(0-1)
Stabæk - Ranheim 0-0
Lillestrøm SK - Tromsø IL 4-0(2-0)
FK Bodø/Glimt - Odds BK 3-0(1-0)
FK Haugesund - Vålerenga 1-4(0-3)
Molde FK - SK Brann 1-1(0-0)
Sarpsborg 08 - Strømsgodset 2-2(0-1)

Round 14 [04-05.07.2019]
Ranheim - Rosenborg BK 2-3(1-1)
SK Brann - Mjøndalen 0-0
Kristiansund BK - Lillestrøm SK 5-2(3-1)
Vålerenga - FK Bodø/Glimt 6-0(4-0)
Odds BK - Molde FK 2-2(0-2)
Tromsø IL - Sarpsborg 08 2-0(1-0)
Strømsgodset - Stabæk 0-2(0-1)
Viking - FK Haugesund 0-0

Round 15 [13-15.07.2019]
SK Brann - Kristiansund BK 2-1(1-0) [10.04.]
Molde FK - Vålerenga 4-1(1-0) [10.04.]
Rosenborg BK - Viking 5-1(2-1)
FK Bodø/Glimt - Ranheim 5-1(1-0)
Mjøndalen - Odds BK 2-0(0-0)
FK Haugesund - Tromsø IL 5-1(3-1)
Lillestrøm SK - Strømsgodset 2-1(2-0)
Stabæk - Sarpsborg 08 3-3(1-2)

Round 16 [03-05.08.2019]
Sarpsborg 08 - Rosenborg BK 1-1(1-1)
Odds BK - Lillestrøm SK 2-1(0-0)
Ranheim - SK Brann 0-3(0-2)
Tromsø IL - Mjøndalen 2-2(1-0)
Stabæk - FK Haugesund 1-1(0-0)
Viking - Molde FK 0-2(0-0)
Vålerenga - Kristiansund BK 1-1(0-1)
Strømsgodset - FK Bodø/Glimt 1-3(0-1)

Round 17 [10-12.08.2019]
SK Brann - Stabæk 2-1(0-0) [21.07.]
Molde FK - Sarpsborg 08 2-1(1-0) [21.07.]
Rosenborg BK - Tromsø IL 5-2(3-1)
FK Haugesund - Ranheim 0-1(0-0)
Kristiansund BK - Odds BK 1-1(0-1)
FK Bodø/Glimt - Viking 2-1(2-0)
Strømsgodset - Vålerenga 3-2(1-0)
Lillestrøm SK - Mjøndalen 3-2(2-1)

Round 18 [17-19.08.2019]
Odds BK - Rosenborg BK 1-1(1-0)
Stabæk - Kristiansund BK 2-0(1-0)
Vålerenga - FK Haugesund 1-2(1-0)
Ranheim - Molde FK 2-3(1-2)
Tromsø IL - Lillestrøm SK 1-1(0-1)
Mjøndalen - SK Brann 2-1(1-1)
Viking - Strømsgodset 4-0(2-0)
Sarpsborg 08 - FK Bodø/Glimt 1-1(0-0)

Round 19 [24-26.08.2019]
Rosenborg BK - Stabæk 3-2(1-1)
Molde FK - Odds BK 2-2(1-1)
SK Brann - Tromsø IL 2-3(1-1)
FK Haugesund - Lillestrøm SK 0-2(0-0)
Kristiansund BK - Mjøndalen 4-0(2-0)
Viking - Ranheim 2-2(0-0)
Strømsgodset - Sarpsborg 08 2-1(0-0)
FK Bodø/Glimt - Vålerenga 4-0(1-0)

Round 20 [30.08.-01.09.2019]
Odds BK - FK Bodø/Glimt 3-1(2-0)
Stabæk - Strømsgodset 2-1(1-0)
Ranheim - Kristiansund BK 1-2(0-0)
Sarpsborg 08 - Viking 2-2(1-0)
Tromsø IL - FK Haugesund 2-2(1-0)
Lillestrøm SK - SK Brann 1-3(1-2)
Mjøndalen - Molde FK 1-3(0-1)
Vålerenga - Rosenborg BK 1-1(0-0)

Round 21 [14-16.09.2019]
Rosenborg BK - Lillestrøm SK 3-1(1-0)
Molde FK - Tromsø IL 3-0(1-0)
FK Haugesund - Mjøndalen 0-0
FK Bodø/Glimt - Stabæk 3-3(1-2)
Strømsgodset - Ranheim 1-0(0-0)
Viking - Odds BK 2-0(1-0)
Kristiansund BK - SK Brann 1-0(1-0)
Sarpsborg 08 - Vålerenga 1-0(1-0)

Round 22 [21-23.09.2019]
SK Brann - FK Haugesund 0-0
Vålerenga - Viking 0-4(0-2)
Ranheim - FK Bodø/Glimt 1-1(1-0)
Odds BK - Sarpsborg 08 3-0(2-0)
Tromsø IL - Strømsgodset 0-1(0-0)
Lillestrøm SK - Kristiansund BK 1-1(1-0)
Mjøndalen - Rosenborg BK 1-2(1-1)
Stabæk - Molde FK 1-2(0-0)

Round 23 [28-30.09.2019]
Rosenborg BK - SK Brann 0-0
Molde FK - Lillestrøm SK 2-1(0-1)
Kristiansund BK - FK Haugesund 2-2(1-0)
Vålerenga - Ranheim 1-1(0-0)
Sarpsborg 08 - Stabæk 0-0
Strømsgodset - Odds BK 2-3(1-2)
FK Bodø/Glimt - Tromsø IL 4-0(2-0)
Viking - Mjøndalen 4-1(1-1)

Round 24 [04-06.10.2019]
Mjøndalen - Strømsgodset 1-1(0-0)
Odds BK - Vålerenga 1-1(0-0)
FK Haugesund - Rosenborg BK 2-1(0-0)
Ranheim - Sarpsborg 08 0-2(0-1)
Tromsø IL - Kristiansund BK 5-0(3-0)
Lillestrøm SK - FK Bodø/Glimt 0-0
Stabæk - Viking 0-0
SK Brann - Molde FK 0-0

Round 25 [19-21.10.2019]
Kristiansund BK - Rosenborg BK 2-2(1-1)
Vålerenga - Stabæk 0-2(0-2)
Molde FK - FK Haugesund 3-1(1-1)
Ranheim - Odds BK 4-1(2-1)
Strømsgodset - Lillestrøm SK 1-1(0-0)
Viking - Tromsø IL 2-1(1-0)
Sarpsborg 08 - SK Brann 1-1(0-1)
FK Bodø/Glimt - Mjøndalen 0-0

Round 26 [26-28.10.2019]
Lillestrøm SK - Vålerenga 0-0
FK Haugesund - Strømsgodset 2-2(1-2)
Kristiansund BK - Viking 4-2(1-0)
Tromsø IL - Ranheim 4-2(2-1)
Stabæk - Odds BK 0-0
Mjøndalen - Sarpsborg 08 0-0
Rosenborg BK - Molde FK 3-1(2-1)
SK Brann - FK Bodø/Glimt 1-1(0-1)

Round 27 [01-04.11.2019]
Strømsgodset - Rosenborg BK 3-3(1-1)
Molde FK - Kristiansund BK 2-0(1-0)
Ranheim - Stabæk 0-2(0-0)
Sarpsborg 08 - Tromsø IL 3-2(1-1)
FK Bodø/Glimt - FK Haugesund 2-2(2-1)
Viking - Lillestrøm SK 3-0(2-0)
Vålerenga - SK Brann 1-0(1-0)
Odds BK - Mjøndalen 3-2(1-1)

Round 28 [08-10.11.2019]
SK Brann - Odds BK 1-0(0-0)
FK Haugesund - Viking 1-0(0-0)
Molde FK - Strømsgodset 4-0(2-0)
Kristiansund BK - Sarpsborg 08 4-0(2-0)
Tromsø IL - Vålerenga 0-0
Lillestrøm SK - Stabæk 1-3(0-2)
Mjøndalen - Ranheim 3-1(1-1)
Rosenborg BK - FK Bodø/Glimt 3-2(1-2)

Round 29 [24.11.2019]
Vålerenga - Molde FK 2-4(1-2)
Ranheim - Lillestrøm SK 2-1(0-0)
Sarpsborg 08 - FK Haugesund 1-1(1-0)
Odds BK - Tromsø IL 2-1(1-0)
FK Bodø/Glimt - Kristiansund BK 3-0(0-0)
Strømsgodset - SK Brann 6-0(4-0)
Stabæk - Mjøndalen 4-2(1-1)
Viking - Rosenborg BK 2-2(2-1)

Round 30 [01.12.2019]
Rosenborg BK - Ranheim 3-2(0-1)
Molde FK - FK Bodø/Glimt 4-2(2-0)
SK Brann - Viking 1-5(1-2)
FK Haugesund - Odds BK 4-1(1-1)
Kristiansund BK - Strømsgodset 1-2(1-1)
Tromsø IL - Stabæk 1-1(0-1)
Lillestrøm SK - Sarpsborg 08 0-0
Mjøndalen - Vålerenga 1-0(0-0)

Final Standings

								Total			Home					Away			
1.	**Molde FK**	30	21	5	4	72 - 31	68	13	2	0	41 - 10	8	3	4	31 - 21
2.	FK Bodø/Glimt	30	15	9	6	64 - 44	54	10	4	1	39 - 12	5	5	5	25 - 32
3.	Rosenborg BK Trondheim	30	14	10	6	53 - 41	52	11	3	1	34 - 16	3	7	5	19 - 25
4.	Odds BK Skien	30	15	7	8	45 - 40	52	12	3	0	31 - 14	3	4	8	14 - 26
5.	Viking FK Stavanger	30	13	8	9	55 - 42	47	9	4	2	32 - 15	4	4	7	23 - 27
6.	Kristiansund BK	30	11	8	11	41 - 41	41	8	4	3	31 - 16	3	4	8	10 - 25
7.	FK Haugesund	30	9	13	8	44 - 37	40	5	6	4	22 - 17	4	7	4	22 - 20
8.	Stabæk Fotball Bærum	30	10	10	10	38 - 36	40	5	7	3	20 - 14	5	3	7	18 - 22
9.	SK Brann Bergen	30	10	10	10	32 - 37	40	5	6	4	14 - 16	5	4	6	18 - 21
10.	Vålerenga Fotball Oslo	30	8	10	12	39 - 44	34	6	4	5	23 - 20	2	6	7	16 - 24
11.	Strømsgodset IF Drammen	30	8	8	14	41 - 54	32	6	3	6	29 - 28	2	5	8	12 - 26
12.	Sarpsborg 08 FF	30	5	15	10	30 - 40	30	4	9	2	18 - 16	1	6	8	12 - 24
13.	Mjøndalen IF	30	6	12	12	38 - 52	30	5	6	4	22 - 22	1	6	8	16 - 30
14.	Lillestrøm SK (*Relegation Play-offs*)	30	7	9	14	32 - 47	30	5	5	5	16 - 19	2	4	9	16 - 28
15.	Tromsø IL (*Relegated*)	30	8	6	16	39 - 58	30	5	5	5	23 - 18	3	1	11	16 - 40
16.	Ranheim IL Trondheim (*Relegated*)	30	7	6	17	36 - 55	27	4	2	9	21 - 30	3	4	8	15 - 25

Top goalscorers:		
21	Torgeir Børven	*Odds BK Skien*
17	Leke James (NGA)	*Molde FK*
15	Ohi Omoijuanfo	*Molde FK*
13	Håkon Evjen	*FK Bodø/Glimt*
11	Magnus Wolff Eikrem	*Molde FK*

Relegation Play-offs [07-11.12.2019]

IK Start Kristiansand - Lillestrøm SK   2-1(0-1)   3-4(0-2)

IK Start Kristiansand promoted for Eliteserien 2020.

NATIONAL CUP
Norgesmesterskapet 2019

Second Round [21-23.05.2019]

Elverum Fotball - Stabæk Fotball Bærum	1-6(0-2)		FK Fyllingsdalen - Nest-Sotra Fotball	0-4(0-2)
Strømmen IF - FK Bodø/Glimt	2-1(1-0,1-1)		Florø SK - Aalesunds FK	0-1(0-0)
Kvik Halden - Lillestrøm SK	1-4(0-2)		IL Hødd - Sogndal Fotball	0-2(0-1)
Moss FK - Kongsvinger IL	1-2(1-1)		Brattvåg IL - Kristiansund BK	1-2(0-0,1-1)
Grorud IL - Hamarkameratene	1-0(0-0,0-0)		Tiller IL - Rosenborg BK Trondheim	0-3(0-0)
Kjelsås Fotball - Skeid Fotball Oslo	3-4(1-0,3-3)		Nardo FK - Ranheim IL Trondheim	0-3(0-1)
Asker SK - KFUM-Kameratene Oslo	2-3(1-1)		Levanger FK - IL Stjørdals-Blink	3-0(0-0)
Bærum SK - Notodden FK	2-1(1-1)		Melbo IL - Tromsø IL	1-2(1-0)
Lørenskog IF - Ullensaker/Kisa IL	1-3(0-3)		Harstad IL - Tromsdalen UIL Tromsø	2-3(0-0)
Fram Larvik - Raufoss IL	1-1 aet; 4-3 pen		IF Fløya - Alta IF	0-3(0-2)
Pors Grenland - Mjøndalen IF	2-4(1-2)		Eidsvold TF - Vålerenga Fotball Oslo	0-5(0-1)
FK Jerv Grimstad - Sandefjord Fotball	1-2(0-0)		Fredrikstad FK - Sarpsborg 08 FF	0-2(0-0)
FK Arendal - Odds BK Skien	0-2(0-1)		Ullern IF - Strømsgodset IF Drammen	0-1(0-1)
Egersunds IK - Bryne FK	2-2 aet; 4-5 pen		Hinna Fotball - Viking FK Stavanger	1-4(0-3)
SK Vard - Sandnes Ulf	0-2(0-0,0-0)		Sunndal Fotball - Molde FK	0-4(0-4)
Sotra SK - FK Haugesund	1-3(0-1)		Åsane Fotball - SK Brann Bergen	0-2(0-0)

Third Round [19-20.06.2019]

Grorud IL - Mjøndalen IF	0-1(0-1)		Nest-Sotra Fotball - KFUM-Kameratene Oslo	0-4(0-4)
Bærum SK - Vålerenga Fotball Oslo	5-3(1-2)		Sogndal Fotball - SK Brann Bergen	1-2(1-2)
Skeid Fotball Oslo - Ranheim IL Trondheim	0-3(0-1)		Levanger FK - Kristiansund BK	1-3(0-0)
Strømmen IF - Lillestrøm SK	1-0(0-0)		Tromsdalen UIL Tromsø - Sarpsborg 08 FF	1-0(0-0)
Ullensaker/Kisa IL - Rosenborg BK Trondheim	1-2(0-0,1-1)		Bryne FK - FK Haugesund	2-6(0-4)
Sandefjord Fotball - Odds BK Skien	1-1 aet; 1-3 pen		Aalesunds FK - Molde FK	4-0(2-0)
Fram Larvik - Strømsgodset IF Drammen	2-1(1-1)		Kongsvinger IL - Tromsø IL	1-0(0-0)
Sandnes Ulf - Viking FK Stavanger	1-2(0-0)		Alta IF - Stabæk Fotball Bærum	1-4(0-1)

1/8-Finals [26.06.2019]

Fram Larvik - Bærum SK	3-1(2-0)		KFUM-Kameratene Oslo - Tromsdalen UIL	2-1(1-1)
Ranheim IL Trondheim - SK Brann Bergen	4-0(1-0)		Kongsvinger IL - Mjøndalen IF	0-3(0-0)
Kristiansund BK - Odds BK Skien	1-2(0-0,1-1)		FK Haugesund - Strømmen IF	2-0(0-0,0-0)
Viking FK Stavanger - Stabæk Fotball Bærum	5-2(3-2)		Rosenborg BK Trondheim - Aalesunds FK	1-1 aet; 4-5 pen

Quarter-Finals [25-26.09.2019]

Ranheim IL Trondheim Fram Larvik	3-0(2-0)		KFUM-Kameratene Oslo - Odds BK Skien	2-5(1-2)
Mjøndalen IF - FK Haugesund	1-3(0-1)		Aalesunds FK - Viking FK Stavanger	1-1 aet; 3-5 pen

Semi-Finals [30-31.10.2019]

Viking FK Stavanger - Ranheim IL Trondheim	3-0(2-0)		Odds BK Skien - FK Haugesund	0-3(0-0)

Final

08.12.2019; Ullevaal Stadion, Oslo; Referee: Espen Eskås; Attendance: 21,895

Viking FK Stavanger - FK Haugesund   1-0(0-0)

Viking: Iven Austbø, Sondre Bjørshol, Runar Hove, Viljar Vevatne, Adrian Pereira, Kristian Thorstvedt, Kristoffer Løkberg (75.Samúel Kári Friðjónsson), Johnny Furdal (67.Fredrik Torsteinbø), Ylldren Ibrahimaj, Benjamin Källman, Zlatko Tripić (Cap) (90.Rolf Daniel Vikstøl). Trainer: Bjarne Berntsen.

FK Haugesund: Helge Sandvik, Mikkel Desler, Doug Bergqvist (77.Pascal Gregor), Benjamin Hansen, Thore Baardsen Pedersen, Christian Grindheim (Cap), Sondre Tronstad, Bruno Miguel Santos Leite (79.Kevin Martin Krygård), Niklas Sandberg, Martin Samuelsen, Kristoffer Velde (90.Ibrahima Koné). Trainer: Jostein Grindhaug.

Goal: 1-0 Zlatko Tripić (51 penalty)

Fotballklubben Bodø/Glimt

Founded: 19.09.2016
Stadium: Aspmyra Stadion, Bodø (7,354)
Trainer: Kjetil Knutsen   02.10.1968

Goalkeepers:	DOB	M	(s)	G
Nikita Khaikin (RUS)	11.07.1995	1		
Ricardo Henrique Schuck Friedrich (BRA)	18.02.1993	29		
Defenders:	**DOB**	**M**	**(s)**	**G**
Vegard Bergan	20.02.1995	17	(4)	1
Fredrik Bjørkan	21.08.1998	29		3
José Isidoro Gómez Torres (ESP)	01.08.1986	1	(2)	
Marius Lode	11.03.1993	26		
Brede Moe	15.12.1991	16		
Erlend Reitan	11.09.1997	29		1
Midfielders:	**DOB**	**M**	**(s)**	**G**
Patrick Berg	24.11.1997	24		
Håkon Evjen	14.02.2000	29		13
Runar Hauge	01.09.2001		(2)	
Morten Konradsen	03.05.1996	13	(10)	2
Vegard Moberg	23.01.1991	13	(7)	2
Felix Myhre	04.03.1999		(2)	
Ulrik Saltnes	10.11.1992	29	(1)	7
Oliver Sigurjónsson (ISL)	03.03.1995		(2)	
Ole Amund Sveen	05.01.1990	6	(4)	1
Forwards:	**DOB**	**M**	**(s)**	**G**
Victor Okoh Boniface (NGA)	23.12.2000	4	(4)	1
Jens Hauge	12.10.1999	8	(21)	7
Geir Herrem	28.01.1988	13	(2)	6
Amadou Konaté (MLI)	01.01.1997		(4)	
Endre Kupen	01.07.1990		(8)	
Amor Layouni (TUN)	03.10.1992	21		10
Philip Zinckernagel (DEN)	16.12.1994	22	(8)	6

Sportsklubben Brann Bergen

Founded: 26.09.1908
Stadium: Brann Stadion, Bergen (17,686)
Trainer: Lars Arne Nilsen   06.04.1964

Goalkeepers:	DOB	M	(s)	G
Eirik Johansen	12.07.1992	3		
Håkon Opdal	11.06.1982	27		
Defenders:	**DOB**	**M**	**(s)**	**G**
Bismar Gilberto Acosta Evans (CRC)	19.12.1986	28		1
Thomas Grøgaard	08.02.1994	7	(6)	
Emil Kalsaas	07.07.2000		(1)	
Ruben Kristiansen	20.02.1988	27	(1)	
Jesper Löfgren (SWE)	03.05.1997		(1)	
Christian Rismark	01.08.1991	14	(6)	1
Taijo Teniste (EST)	31.01.1988	26		1
Vito Wormgoor (NED)	16.11.1988	28		5
Midfielders:	**DOB**	**M**	**(s)**	**G**
Kristoffer Barmen	19.08.1993	21	(4)	1
Fredrik Haugen	13.06.1992	9	(5)	2
Ruben Yttergård Jenssen	04.05.1988	24	(2)	3
Mikael Berg Kvinge	24.06.2003		(2)	
Kristoffer Løkberg	22.01.1992	5	(6)	1
Nicholas Marthinussen	11.04.2000		(1)	
Sander Marthinussen	11.04.2000		(3)	
Andreas Eikeseth Mjøs	08.02.2000		(1)	
Amer Ordagić (BIH)	05.05.1993	13	(1)	
Petter Strand	24.08.1994	19	(2)	3
Forwards:	**DOB**	**M**	**(s)**	**G**
Daouda Karamoko Bamba (CIV)	05.03.1995	17	(4)	7
Veton Berisha	13.04.1994	26		3
Aune Selland Heggebø	29.07.2001	1	(4)	
Henrik Johansen	22.03.1993	1	(4)	
Azar Karadaş	09.08.1981	1	(12)	1
Gilbert Koomson (GHA)	09.09.1994	20	(5)	2
Gilli Rólantsson (FRO)	11.08.1992	13	(11)	1

Fotballklubben Haugesund

Founded: 28.10.1993
Stadium: Haugesund Stadion, Haugesund (8,754)
Trainer: Jostein Grindhaug   20.02.1973

Goalkeepers:	DOB	M	(s)	G
Helge Sandvik	15.02.1990	28		
Oskar Snorre Olsen Frigast (DEN)	26.01.1999	2		
Defenders:	**DOB**	**M**	**(s)**	**G**
Doug Bergqvist (SWE)	29.03.1993	16	(5)	1
Mikkel Desler (DEN)	19.02.1995	29		1
Pascal Gregor (DEN)	18.02.1994	3	(3)	1
Benjamin Hansen (DEN)	07.02.1994	30		1
Fredrik Knudsen	30.08.1996	12	(1)	1
Joakim Nilsen	24.04.1991	5	(8)	
Thore Baardsen Pedersen	11.08.1996	28	(2)	
Stian Lunder Ringstad	29.08.1991	2		
Midfielders:	**DOB**	**M**	**(s)**	**G**
Bruno Miguel Santos Leite (CPV)	26.03.1995	20	(4)	2
Christian Grindheim	17.07.1983	25	(3)	3
Kristoffer Gunnarshaug	05.11.1999	1		
Ikenna Anthony Ikedi (NGA)	19.09.1998		(1)	
Torbjørn Kallevåg	21.08.1993	16	(5)	1
Martin Samuelsen	17.04.1997	15	(13)	6
Niklas Sandberg	18.05.1995	17	(2)	6
Alexander Stølås	30.04.1989	11		4
Sondre Tronstad	26.08.1995	29		1
Kristoffer Velde	09.09.1999	11	(15)	4
Forwards:	**DOB**	**M**	**(s)**	**G**
Shuaibu Lalle Ibrahim (NGA)	19.12.1996		(1)	
Ibrahima Koné (MLI)	16.06.1999	7	(9)	5
Kevin Krygård	17.05.2000	13	(5)	1
Eric Ndayisenga	25.04.2000		(1)	
Ibrahima Wadji (SEN)	05.05.1995	10		4

Kristiansund Ballklubb

Founded: 02.09.2003
Stadium: Kristiansund Stadion, Kristiansund (4,000)
Trainer: Christian Michelsen   14.03.1976

Goalkeepers:	DOB	M	(s)	G
Mor Mbaye (SEN)	03.01.1996	2		
Sean McDermott (IRL)	30.05.1993	28		
Defenders:	**DOB**	**M**	**(s)**	**G**
Christoffer Aasbak	22.07.1993	26	(1)	1
Aliou Coly (SEN)	10.12.1992	20	(3)	
Henrik Gjesdal	19.07.1993	5	(2)	1
Christophe Charles Steven René Psyché (FRA)	28.07.1988	25	(1)	7
Erlend Sivertsen	28.01.1991	4	(4)	
Dan Peter Ulvestad	04.04.1989	24	(1)	
Midfielders:	**DOB**	**M**	**(s)**	**G**
Haris Cirak (SWE)	14.03.1995	6	(3)	
Amidou Diop (SEN)	27.02.1992	26	(1)	1
Andreas Hopmark	06.07.1991	15	(2)	
Jesper Isaksen	13.10.1999	5	(9)	1
Liridon Kalludra (SWE)	05.11.1991	17	(9)	3
Olav Øby	13.10.1994		(3)	
Amahl William Pellegrino	18.06.1990	10		8
Sondre Sørli	30.10.1995	15	(8)	5
Bent Sørmo	22.09.1996	19	(7)	1
Pål Erik Ulvestad	08.09.1990	13	(8)	
Forwards:	**DOB**	**M**	**(s)**	**G**
Thomas Amang (CMR)	09.02.1998	7	(4)	
Bendik Bye	09.03.1990	18	(5)	4
Torgil Gjertsen	12.03.1992	24	(4)	2
Kristoffer Hoven	10.08.1996	2	(4)	1
Flamur Kastrati	14.11.1991	17	(2)	4
Meinhard Olsen (FRO)	10.04.1997	2	(9)	1

Lillestrøm Sportsklubb

Founded: 02.04.1917
Stadium: Åråsen Stadion, Lillestrøm (12,250)
Trainer: Jörgen Lennartsson (SWE) 10.04.1965

Goalkeepers:	DOB	M	(s)	G
Marko Marić (CRO)	03.01.1996	30		
Defenders:	**DOB**	**M**	**(s)**	**G**
Josef Baccay	29.04.2001	4	(2)	
Mats Haakenstad	14.11.1993	13	(6)	1
Frode Kippe	17.01.1978	13	(3)	
Simen Rafn	16.02.1992	29	(1)	1
Tobias Salquist (DEN)	18.05.1995	25		3
Sheriff Sinyan	19.07.1996	10	(9)	
Philip Slørdahl	14.11.2000	1		
Joonas Tamm (EST)	02.02.1992	15		
Midfielders:	**DOB**	**M**	**(s)**	**G**
Raphael Ayagwa (NGA)	13.02.1998		(1)	
Erik Brenden	07.01.1994	3	(15)	
Alex Dyer (MSR)	11.06.1990	8	(3)	
Daniel Gustavsson (SWE)	29.08.1990	23	(2)	2
Matthew Ifeanyi (NGA)	20.01.1997	11		
Magnus Knudsen	15.06.2001		(1)	
Fredrik Krogstad	06.06.1995	21	(6)	1
Aleksander Melgalvis	10.08.1989	18	(8)	3
Simen Mikalsen	04.05.1993	15	(1)	1
Kristoffer Ødemarksbakken	05.12.1995	24	(5)	3
Daniel Pedersen (DEN)	27.07.1992	23	(1)	2
Forwards:	**DOB**	**M**	**(s)**	**G**
Moses Ebiye (NGA)	28.04.1997	3	(9)	1
Thomas Olsen	29.06.1991	25	(1)	8
Arnór Smárason (ISL)	07.09.1988	16	(7)	4

Mjøndalen Idrettsforening Football

Founded: 22.08.1910
Stadium: Consto Arena, Mjøndalen (4,200)
Trainer: Vegard Hansen 08.08.1969

Goalkeepers:	DOB	M	(s)	G
Julian Lund	20.05.1999	25		
Mathias Ranmark	16.10.1995	5		
Defenders:	**DOB**	**M**	**(s)**	**G**
Vetle Dragsnes	06.02.1994	23	(5)	2
Alexander Hansen	01.11.1996	2	(6)	
Quint Jansen (NED)	10.09.1990	28	(1)	1
Sondre Johansen	07.07.1995	29		5
Akeem Latifu (NGA)	16.11.1989	13	(5)	
William Sell	20.12.1998	16	(10)	1
Joackim Solberg	11.04.1989	26	(1)	
Per-Magnus Steiring	07.02.1997	1	(1)	
Midfielders:	**DOB**	**M**	**(s)**	**G**
Stian Aasmundsen	02.11.1989	28	(1)	3
Tonny Brochmann (DEN)	11.08.1989	29		8
Mathias Fredriksen	28.04.1994		(2)	
Christian Gauseth	26.06.1984	24		5
Carl Pontus Silfwer (SWE)	14.08.1991	13	(2)	
Dagur Þórhallsson (ISL)	02.05.2000		(1)	
Forwards:	**DOB**	**M**	**(s)**	**G**
Frank Bamenye	23.10.2001		(2)	
Jacob Bergström (SWE)	26.04.1995	6	(4)	
Jibril Bojang	13.09.1994	1	(12)	
Fredrik Brustad	22.06.1989	21	(9)	2
Vamouti Diomande (CIV)	20.01.1991		(3)	
Sondre Liseth	30.09.1997	21	(3)	3
Olivier Occéan (CAN)	23.10.1981	19	(6)	6
Alfred Scriven	26.01.1998		(9)	2

Molde Fotballklubb

Founded: 19.06.1911
Stadium: Aker Stadion, Molde (11,800)
Trainer: Erling Moe 22.07.1970

Goalkeepers:	DOB	M	(s)	G
Álex Craninx (BEL)	21.10.1995	14		
Andreas Linde (SWE)	24.07.1993	16		
Defenders:	**DOB**	**M**	**(s)**	**G**
Martin Bjørnbak	22.03.1992	25	(1)	
Vegard Forren	16.02.1988	16	(3)	
Ruben Gabrielsen	10.03.1992	25	(1)	2
Kristoffer Haraldseid	17.01.1994	27	(1)	1
Kristoffer Haugen	21.02.1994	20		
Christoffer Remmer (DEN)	16.01.1993	2	(1)	
Christopher Telo (SWE)	04.11.1989	1		
Midfielders:	**DOB**	**M**	**(s)**	**G**
Fredrik Aursnes	10.12.1995	30		1
Tobias Christensen	11.05.2000	2	(4)	1
Magnus Eikrem	08.08.1990	20	(5)	11
Martin Ellingsen	04.05.1995	22	(4)	3
Eirik Hestad	26.06.1995	24	(4)	4
Etzaz Hussain	27.01.1993	11	(5)	4
Fredrik Sjølstad	29.03.1994	7	(9)	1
Henry Wingo (USA)	04.10.1995		(3)	
Forwards:	**DOB**	**M**	**(s)**	**G**
Eirik Andersen	21.09.1992	3	(1)	1
Mathis Bolly (CIV)	14.11.1990	5	(8)	3
Leke Samson James (NGA)	01.11.1992	16	(12)	17
Erling Knudtzon	15.12.1988	13	(7)	4
Mattias Moström (SWE)	25.02.1983	7	(13)	2
Ohi Omoijuanfo	10.01.1994	24	(3)	15

Odds Ballklubb Skien

Founded: 31.03.1894
Stadium: Skagerak Arena, Skien (12,500)
Trainer: Dag-Eilev Fagermo 28.01.1967

Goalkeepers:	DOB	M	(s)	G
Sondre Rossbach	07.02.1996	30		
Defenders:	**DOB**	**M**	**(s)**	**G**
Fredrik Berge	06.02.1990	24	(1)	
Odin Lurås Bjørtuft	19.12.1998	12	(2)	
Steffen Hagen	08.03.1986	28		2
Espen Ruud	26.02.1984	23	(1)	1
Midfielders:	**DOB**	**M**	**(s)**	**G**
Vebjørn Hoff	13.02.1996	29		2
Fredrik Jensen	18.05.1993	23		1
Markus Kaasa	15.07.1997	8	(14)	2
Joshua Kitolano	03.08.2001	10	(11)	1
Fredrik Nordkvelle	13.09.1985	21	(2)	5
Birk Risa	13.02.1998	30		2
Jone Samuelsen	06.07.1984	4	(8)	
André Sødlund	22.12.1996		(6)	
Forwards:	**DOB**	**M**	**(s)**	**G**
Torgeir Børven	03.12.1991	30		21
Filip Delaveris	10.12.2000	6	(9)	3
Marius Larsen	14.05.2000		(2)	
Tobias Lauritsen	30.08.1997	4	(17)	
Bilal Njie	13.06.1998		(6)	
Moussa Njie	02.10.1995	4		
Elbasan Rashani (KVX)	09.05.1993	29		3
Sander Svendsen	06.08.1997	15		

Ranheim Fotball Trondheim

Founded: 17.02.1901
Stadium: EXTRA Arena, Trondheim (3,000)
Trainer: Svein Maalen 25.02.1978

Goalkeepers:	DOB	M	(s)	G
Even Barli	24.07.1991	29		
Magnus Lenes	18.05.1996	1		
Defenders:	DOB	M	(s)	G
Øyvind Alseth	13.08.1994	15	(2)	1
Aleksander Foosnæs	05.06.1994	25	(4)	1
Ivar Furu	07.05.1994	25	(3)	
Torbjørn Heggem	12.01.1999	14	(4)	
Daniel Kvande	08.04.1995	23	(2)	1
Jørgen Øveraas	03.12.1989	15	(1)	1
Midfielders:	DOB	M	(s)	G
Magnus Blakstad	18.01.1994	17	(9)	
Eirik Dønnem	21.07.1990	21	(8)	2
Adrià Mateo López (ESP)	16.03.1995	9	(4)	2
Mads Reginiussen	02.01.1988	29		5
Ivar Rønning	14.02.1993	4	(9)	2
Olaus Skarsem	02.07.1998	16	(4)	1
Sondre Sørløkk	08.05.1997		(6)	
Magnus Stamnestrø	18.04.1992		(1)	
Forwards:	DOB	M	(s)	G
Mushagalusa Bakenga Joar Bahati Namugunga	08.08.1992	10	(2)	2
Vegard Erlien	24.06.1998	7	(3)	2
Michael Karlsen	03.02.1990	17	(9)	7
Ola Solbakken	07.09.1998	20	(6)	4
Erlend Sørhøy	01.08.1994		(3)	
Øyvind Storflor	18.12.1979	14	(7)	1
Erik Tønne	03.07.1991	19	(1)	2

Rosenborg Ballklub Trondheim

Founded: 19.05.1917
Stadium: Lerkendal Stadion, Trondheim (21,405)
Trainer: Eirik Horneland 14.03.1975

Goalkeepers:	DOB	M	(s)	G
André Hansen	17.12.1989	29		
Arild Østbø	19.04.1991	1		
Defenders:	DOB	M	(s)	G
Vegar Hedenstad	26.06.1991	27		2
Even Hovland	14.02.1989	28		5
Birger Solberg Meling	17.12.1994	28		
Tore Reginiussen	10.04.1986	24		3
Gustav Valsvik	26.05.1993	10	(3)	1
Midfielders:	DOB	M	(s)	G
David Babajide Akintola (NGA)	13.01.1996	16	(5)	5
Gjermund Åsen	22.05.1991	14	(9)	1
Đorđe Denić (SRB)	01.04.1996	6	(3)	
Mike Jensen (DEN)	19.02.1988	27		5
Mikael Johnsen	04.07.2000		(2)	
Anders Konradsen	18.07.1990	15	(5)	2
Marius Lundemo	11.04.1994	17	(5)	1
Edvard Sandvik Tagseth	23.01.2001	1		
Anders Trondsen	30.03.1995	14	(8)	
Forwards:	DOB	M	(s)	G
Samuel Adeniyi Adegbenro (NGA)	03.12.1995	18	(2)	5
Nicklas Bendtner (DEN)	16.01.1988	2	(3)	
Erik Botheim	10.01.2000	4	(3)	3
Emil Ceide	03.09.2001	3	(6)	
Yann-Erik de Lanlay	14.05.1992	10	(7)	2
Pål André Helland	04.01.1990	9	(10)	3
Bjørn Maars Johnsen	06.11.1991	4	(7)	5
Alexander Søderlund	03.08.1987	23	(5)	8

Sarpsborg 08 Fotballforening

Founded: 15.01.2008
Stadium: Sarpsborg Stadion, Sarpsborg (4,700)
Trainer: Geir Bakke 23.10.1969

Goalkeepers:	DOB	M	(s)	G
Aslak Falch	25.05.1992	2		
Alexandre Letellier (FRA)	11.12.1990	15		
Aleksandr Vasyutin (RUS)	04.03.1995	13		
Defenders:	DOB	M	(s)	G
Sheldon Michael Louis Bateau (TRI)	29.01.1991	9	(4)	2
Niklas Gunnarsson	27.04.1991	10		
Jørgen Horn	07.06.1987	6		
Nicolai Næss	18.01.1993	20		1
Magnar Ødegaard	11.05.1993	13	(1)	2
Mario Pavelić (AUT)	19.09.1993	7	(1)	
Bart Straalman (NED)	22.08.1996	2		1
Joachim Thomassen	04.05.1988	27		1
Bjørn Utvik	28.02.1996	10		1
Midfielders:	DOB	M	(s)	G
Amin Askar	01.10.1985	10	(3)	
Wilmer Jesús Azofeifa Valverde (CRC)	04.06.1994	2	(3)	
Ole Halvorsen	02.10.1987	23	(4)	2
Sebastian Jarl	11.01.2000		(1)	
Jonathan Lindseth	25.02.1996	26	(2)	3
Mate Maleš (CRO)	11.03.1989		(1)	
Matti Lund Nielsen (DEN)	08.05.1988	23	(3)	
Jon-Helge Tveita	22.10.1992	9		
Gaute Vetti	02.09.1998	11	(3)	
Kristoffer Zachariassen	27.01.1994	29		6
Forwards:	DOB	M	(s)	G
Mustafa Abdellaoue „Mos"	01.08.1988	8	(3)	1
Ismaila Coulibaly (MLI)	25.12.2000	5	(8)	
Anwar Elyounoussi	29.03.1999	1	(5)	
Aboubacar Konté (MLI)	02.03.2001		(1)	
Kyle Lafferty (NIR)	16.09.1987	8	(1)	1
Jørgen Larsen	06.02.2000	16	(7)	4
Kristoffer Larsen	19.01.1992	6	(7)	1
Lars-Jørgen Salvesen	19.02.1996	6	(7)	2
Steffen Skålevik	31.01.1993	11	(10)	1
Alexander Tveter	07.03.1991	2	(2)	1

Stabæk Fotball Bærum

Founded: 16.03.1912
Stadium: Nadderud Stadion, Bærum (7,000)
Trainer: Henning Stille Berg 01.09.1969
[11.06.2019] Jan Jönsson (SWE) 24.05.1960

Goalkeepers:	DOB	M	(s)	G
Marcus Sandberg (SWE)	07.11.1990	30		
Defenders:	DOB	M	(s)	G
Yaw Ihle Amankwah	07.07.1988	15		1
Vadim Demidov	10.10.1986	15		
Andreas Hanche-Olsen	17.01.1997	29		2
Ronald José Hernández Pimentel (VEN)	04.10.1997	24	(3)	
Jeppe Moe	03.08.1995	19		
Steinar Strømnes	19.03.1987	11	(2)	
Madis Vihmann (EST)	05.10.1995	11	(3)	1
Peder Vogt	11.02.2000		(2)	
Midfielders:	DOB	M	(s)	G
Kristoffer Askildsen	09.01.2001	11	(3)	1
Emil Bohinen	12.03.1999	27	(2)	4
Tobias Børkeeiet	18.04.1999	9	(1)	
Daniel Braaten	25.05.1982	10	(8)	2
Ola Brynhildsen	27.04.1999	27	(2)	6
Luc Kassi (CIV)	20.08.1994	18	(5)	4
Nikolaj Kirk (DEN)	19.03.1998	1	(3)	
Tortol Lumanza-Lembi (BEL)	13.04.1994	6	(5)	
Sammy Solitaire Siddharta Skytte (DEN)	20.02.1997	13		1
Youssef Toutouh (DEN)	06.10.1992	6	(1)	
Hugo Vetlesen	29.02.2000	16	(8)	
Forwards:	DOB	M	(s)	G
Oscar Aga	06.01.2001	1	(3)	
Franck Boli (CIV)	07.12.1993	13		6
Oliver Valaker Edvardsen	19.03.1999	3	(5)	2
Herman Geelmuyden	22.01.2002		(5)	
Raymond Gyasi (NED)	05.08.1994		(3)	
Kasper Aalund Junker (DEN)	05.03.1994	11	(1)	6
Kosuke Kinoshita (JPN)	03.10.1994	2	(7)	
Youness Mokhtar (MAR)	29.08.1991	1	(1)	
Matthew Rusike (ZIM)	28.06.1990	1	(2)	

Strømsgodset Toppfotball Drammen

Founded: 10.02.1907
Stadium: Marienlyst Stadion, Drammen (8,935)
Trainer: Björn Petter Ingebretsen 26.05.1967
[15.05.2019] Hakon Wibe-Lund 05.09.1980
[20.06.2019] Henrik Pedersen 02.01.1978

Goalkeepers:	DOB	M	(s)	G
Martin Hansen (DEN)	15.06.1990	13		
Viljar Myhra	21.07.1996	16	(1)	
Morten Sætra	18.06.1997	1		
Defenders:	**DOB**	**M**	**(s)**	**G**
Jacob Glesnes	25.03.1994	30		
Mounir Hamoud	01.02.1985	7	(2)	
Prosper Mendy (FRA)	07.06.1996	14		1
Nicholas Mickelson	24.07.1999		(3)	
Jonathan Parr	21.10.1988	8	(3)	
Stian Ringstad	29.08.1991	10	(3)	
Lars Sætra	24.07.1991	11	(7)	2
Lars-Christopher Vilsvik	18.10.1988	27	(1)	1
Duplexe Tchamba Bangou (CMR)	10.07.1998	15		2
Midfielders:	**DOB**	**M**	**(s)**	**G**
Henning Hauger	17.07.1985	5	(7)	
Johan Hove	07.09.2000	9	(14)	2
Jack Ipalibo (NGA)	06.04.1998	15		
Muhamed Keita	02.09.1990	8	(8)	3
Martin Ovenstad	18.04.1994	4	(6)	1
Amahl Pellegrino	18.06.1990	12	(2)	2
Martin Spelmann (DEN)	21.03.1987	9	(2)	
Halldor Stenevik	02.02.2000		(3)	
Herman Stengel	26.08.1995	28	(2)	1
Yacouba Sylla (MLI)	29.11.1990	10		1
Kristoffer Tokstad	05.07.1991	21		3
Forwards:	**DOB**	**M**	**(s)**	**G**
Mustafa Abdellaoue „Mos"	01.08.1988	13	(3)	3
Mustapha Fofana (SLE)	10.05.2001		(10)	1
Mikkel Maigaard Jakobsen	20.09.1995	15		4
Moses Dramwi Mawa	04.08.1996	14		4
Marcus Pedersen	08.06.1990	2	(2)	1
Sebastian Pedersen	08.06.1999	1	(4)	
Lars-Jørgen Salvesen	19.02.1996	12	(1)	7

Tromsø Idrettslag

Founded: 15.09.1920
Stadium: Alfheim Stadion, Tromsø (6,859)
Trainer: Simo Valakari (FIN) 28.04.1973

Goalkeepers:	DOB	M	(s)	G
Jacob Karlstrøm	09.01.1997	14		
Gudmund Kongshavn	23.01.1991	16		
Defenders:	**DOB**	**M**	**(s)**	**G**
Kent-Are Antonsen	12.02.1995	26	(1)	1
Jostein Gundersen	02.04.1996	11	(4)	1
Anders Jenssen	10.10.1993	19		1
Lasse Nilsen	21.02.1995	19	(4)	1
Marcus Pedersen	16.07.2000	4	(13)	
Juha Pirinen (FIN)	22.10.1991	24	(2)	2
Artem Sokol (RUS)	11.06.1997	4	(5)	
Simen Wangberg	06.05.1991	24		2
Midfielders:	**DOB**	**M**	**(s)**	**G**
Magnus Andersen	28.05.1986	21	(3)	4
Aidan Will Barlow (ENG)	10.01.2000	6	(1)	2
Daniel Berntsen	04.04.1993	17	(4)	
Mikael Ingebrigtsen	21.07.1996	6	(4)	1
Oliver Kjærgaard (DEN)	11.07.1998		(2)	
August Mikkelsen	24.10.2000		(2)	
Morten Gamst Pedersen	08.09.1981	26	(3)	1
Eric Anders Smith (SWE)	08.01.1997	11		
Tomas Stabell	30.01.2002		(1)	
Robert Taylor (FIN)	21.10.1994	27	(1)	4
Onni Valakari (FIN)	18.08.1999	29		7
Forwards:	**DOB**	**M**	**(s)**	**G**
Fitim Azemi	25.06.1992	11	(1)	5
Mushaga Bakenga	08.08.1992	2	(6)	
Runar Espejord	26.02.1996	10	(8)	5
Bryan Solhaug Fiabema	16.02.2003		(1)	
Sigurd Grønli	17.10.2000	1	(4)	
Brayan Andrés Rojas Jiménez (CRC)	30.11.1997	2	(7)	

Viking Fotballklubb Stavanger

Founded: 10.08.1899
Stadium: Viking Stadion, Stavanger (15,900)
Trainer: Bjarne Berntsen 21.12.1956

Goalkeepers:	DOB	M	(s)	G
Iven Austbø	22.02.1985	29		
Amund Wichne	12.05.1997	1	(2)	
Defenders:	**DOB**	**M**	**(s)**	**G**
Axel Andrésson (ISL)	27.01.1998	1		
Sondre Bjørshol	30.04.1994	22		
André Danielsen	20.01.1985	2	(7)	
Runar Hove	08.08.1995	18	(2)	2
Adrian Pereira	31.08.1999	17		2
Viljar Vevatne	07.12.1994	28	(1)	1
Rolf Vikstøl	22.02.1989	15	(1)	1
Midfielders:	**DOB**	**M**	**(s)**	**G**
Zymer Bytyqi	11.09.1996	18	(10)	2
Samúel Kári Friðjónsson (ISL)	22.02.1996	25	(3)	3
Johnny Furdal	04.05.1986	10	(5)	3
Ylldren Ibrahimaj	24.12.1995	27	(1)	4
Lasse Berg Johnsen	18.08.1999		(2)	
Kristoffer Lie Løkberg	22.01.1992	12		
Tord Salte	08.02.1999	14	(4)	
Harald Nilsen Tangen	03.01.2001		(1)	
Kristian Thorstvedt	13.03.1999	21	(5)	10
Fredrik Torsteinbø	13.03.1991	11	(12)	5
Forwards:	**DOB**	**M**	**(s)**	**G**
Jostein Ekeland	24.07.1997	3	(8)	1
Tommy Høiland	11.04.1989	17	(5)	8
Benjamin Källman (FIN)	17.06.1998	9	(2)	3
Even Østensen	02.06.1993	6	(9)	4
Usman Sani Hassan Sale (NGA)	27.08.1995	2	(7)	1
Zlatko Tripić	02.12.1992	22	(2)	5

Vålerenga Fotball Oslo

	Founded:	29.07.1913	
	Stadium:	Intility Arena, Oslo (17,233)	
	Trainer:	Ronny Deila	21.09.1975

Goalkeepers:	DOB	M	(s)	G
Kristoffer Klaesson	27.11.2000	12		
Adambathia Larsen Kwarasey (GHA)	12.12.1987	18		
Defenders:	**DOB**	**M**	**(s)**	**G**
Sam Adekugbe (CAN)	16.01.1995	20	(4)	
Johan Bjørdal	05.05.1986	25	(2)	1
Christian Borchgrevink	11.05.1999	7	(5)	1
Pierre Kanstrup (DEN)	21.02.1989	11		
Markus Nakkim	21.07.1996	3	(4)	1
Amin Mimoun Nouri	10.01.1990	3	(1)	
Ivan Näsberg	22.04.1996	22		
Jonatan Nation	01.07.1990	10		
Midfielders:	**DOB**	**M**	**(s)**	**G**
Mohammed Abu (GHA)	14.11.1991	21	(3)	
Aron Dønnum	20.04.1998	20	(5)	6
Mohammed Fellah	24.05.1989		(6)	

	DOB	M	(s)	G
Magnus Grødem	14.08.1998		(1)	
Erik Israelsson (SWE)	25.02.1989		(6)	
Efraín Juárez (MEX)	22.02.1988	19		
Magnus Lekven	13.01.1988	30		
Felix Myhre	04.03.1999	5	(12)	
Sakarias Opsahl	17.07.1999		(1)	
Herolind Shala (KVX)	01.02.1992	18	(3)	6
Forwards:	**DOB**	**M**	**(s)**	**G**
Fitim Azemi	25.06.1992	4	(7)	
Ousmane Camara (GUI)	28.12.1998	2	(4)	
Chidera Ejuke (NGA)	02.01.1998	14		6
Bård Finne	13.02.1995	21	(8)	8
Mayron Antonio George Clayton (CRC)	23.10.1993	7	(3)	2
Odin Thiago Holm	18.01.2003		(1)	
Deyver Antonio Vega Álvarez (CRC)	19.09.1992	11	(12)	2
Matthías Vilhjálmsson (ISL)	30.01.1987	27	(1)	5

SECOND LEVEL
OBOS-ligaen 2019

1.	Aalesunds FK (*Promoted*)	30	25	4	1	67 - 25	79
2.	Sandefjord Fotball (*Promoted*)	30	19	8	3	53 - 30	65
3.	IK Start Kristiansand (*Promotion Play-offs*)	30	19	5	6	54 - 31	62
4.	KFUM-Kameratene Oslo (*Promotion Play-offs*)	30	13	9	8	58 - 42	48
5.	Kongsvinger IL (*Promotion Play-offs*)	30	14	4	12	38 - 36	46
6.	Sogndal Fotball (*Promotion Play-offs*)	30	13	6	11	51 - 39	45
7.	Nest-Sotra Fotball	30	14	6	10	43 - 31	44
8.	Ullensaker/Kisa IL	30	11	6	13	47 - 47	39
9.	Sandnes Ulf	30	11	5	14	46 - 49	38
10.	Hamarkameratene	30	11	5	14	43 - 47	38
11.	Raufoss IL	30	12	2	16	47 - 59	38
12.	FK Jerv Grimstad	30	8	9	13	34 - 54	33
13.	Strømmen IF	30	7	10	13	32 - 46	30
14.	Notodden Fotballklubb (*Relegation Play-offs*)	30	6	7	17	35 - 53	25
15.	Skeid Fotball Oslo (*Relegated*)	30	4	10	16	38 - 54	22
16.	Tromsdalen UIL Tromsø (*Relegated*)	30	3	4	23	36 - 79	13

Promotion Play-offs

First Round [23.11.2019]	Kongsvinger IL - Sogndal Fotball	1-0(1-0)
Second Round [27.11.2019]	KFUM-Kameratene Oslo - Kongsvinger IL	2-0(1-0)
Third Round [01.12.2019]	IK Start Kristiansand - KFUM-Kameratene Oslo	1-0(1-0)

IK Start Kristiansand qualified for the First Level Relegation/Promotion Play-offs .

Relegation Play-offs (2nd / 3rd Level)

Notodden Fotballklubb – Åsane Fotball	1-3(1-2)	2-2(2-1)

INTERNATIONAL MATCHES
(16.07.2019 – 15.07.2020)

05.09.2019	Oslo	Norway - Malta	2-0(2-0)	(ECQ)
08.09.2019	Stockholm	Sweden - Norway	1-1(0-1)	(ECQ)
12.10.2019	Oslo	Norway - Spain	1-1(0-0)	(ECQ)
15.10.2019	Bucureşti	Romania - Norway	1-1(0-0)	(ECQ)
15.11.2019	Oslo	Norway - Faroe Islands	4-0(2-0)	(ECQ)
18.11.2019	Attard	Malta - Norway	1-2(1-1)	(ECQ)

05.09.2019 NORWAY - MALTA   **2-0(2-0)**   16th EC. Qualifiers
Ullevaal Stadion, Oslo; Referee: Dumitru Muntean (Moldova); Attendance: 11,269
NOR: Rune Almenning Jarstein, Håvard Nordtveit, Even Hovland, Omar Elabdellaoui, Haitam Aleesami, Stefan Marius Johansen (Cap) (76.Mathias Antonsen Normann), Ole Kristian Selnæs, Martin Ødegaard, Sander Gard Bolin Berge, Joshua Christian Kojo King (58.Bjørn Maars Johnsen), Erling Braut Håland (66.Tarik Elyounoussi). Trainer: Lars Edvin Lagerbäck (Sweden).
Goals: Sander Gard Bolin Berge (34), Joshua Christian Kojo King (45+1 penalty).

08.09.2019 SWEDEN - NORWAY   **1-1(0-1)**   16th EC. Qualifiers
Friends Arena, Stockholm; Referee: Slavko Vinčić (Slovenia); Attendance: 38,372
NOR: Rune Almenning Jarstein, Tore Reginiussen, Håvard Nordtveit, Omar Elabdellaoui, Haitam Aleesami, Stefan Marius Johansen (Cap) (76.Erling Braut Håland), Markus Henriksen (64.Tarik Elyounoussi), Ole Kristian Selnæs, Martin Ødegaard, Sander Gard Bolin Berge, Joshua Christian Kojo King. Trainer: Lars Edvin Lagerbäck (Sweden).
Goal: Stefan Marius Johansen (45).

12.10.2019 NORWAY - SPAIN   **1-1(0-0)**   16th EC. Qualifiers
Ullevaal Stadion, Oslo; Referee: Michael Oliver (England); Attendance: 25,200
NOR: Rune Almenning Jarstein, Håvard Nordtveit (30.Even Hovland), Omar Elabdellaoui, Haitam Aleesami, Kristoffer Vassbakk Ajer, Stefan Marius Johansen (Cap) (63.Alexander Sørloth), Markus Henriksen (83.Bjørn Maars Johnsen), Martin Ødegaard, Sander Gard Bolin Berge, Ole Kristian Selnæs, Joshua Christian Kojo King. Trainer: Lars Edvin Lagerbäck (Sweden).
Goal: Joshua Christian Kojo King (90+4 penalty).

15.10.2019 ROMANIA - NORWAY   **1-1(0-0)**   16th EC. Qualifiers
Arena Naţională, Bucureşti; Referee: Bobby Madden (Scotland); Attendance: 29,854
NOR: Rune Almenning Jarstein, Even Hovland, Omar Elabdellaoui, Haitam Aleesami, Kristoffer Vassbakk Ajer, Stefan Marius Johansen (Cap) (46.Alexander Sørloth), Markus Henriksen (81.Mathias Antonsen Normann), Ole Kristian Selnæs (67.Bjørn Maars Johnsen), Martin Ødegaard, Sander Gard Bolin Berge, Joshua Christian Kojo King. Trainer: Lars Edvin Lagerbäck (Sweden).
Goal: Alexander Sørloth (90+2).

15.11.2019 NORWAY - FAROE ISLANDS   **4-0(2-0)**   16th EC. Qualifiers
Ullevaal Stadion, Oslo; Referee: Fran Jović (Croatia); Attendance: 10,400
NOR: Rune Almenning Jarstein, Tore Reginiussen, Omar Elabdellaoui (Cap), Haitam Aleesami, Kristoffer Vassbakk Ajer, Markus Henriksen (71.Mats Møller Dæhli), Ole Kristian Selnæs, Iver Tobias Rørvik Fossum, Sander Gard Bolin Berge (84.Fredrik Stensøe Ulvestad), Joshua Christian Kojo King (78.Tarik Elyounoussi), Alexander Sørloth. Trainer: Lars Edvin Lagerbäck (Sweden).
Goals: Tore Reginiussen (4), Iver Tobias Rørvik Fossum (8), Alexander Sørloth (62, 65).

18.11.2019 MALTA - NORWAY   **1-2(1-1)**   16th EC. Qualifiers
Ta'Qali National Stadium, Attard; Referee: Aliyar Aghayev (Azerbaijan); Attendance: 2,708
NOR: Ørjan Håskjold Nyland, Tore Reginiussen (Cap), Jonas Svensson (65.Tarik Elyounoussi), Birger Solberg Meling, Kristoffer Vassbakk Ajer, Markus Henriksen, Mats Møller Dæhli (46.Omar Elabdellaoui), Iver Tobias Rørvik Fossum, Sander Gard Bolin Berge, Joshua Christian Kojo King (89.Fredrik Stensøe Ulvestad), Alexander Sørloth. Trainer: Lars Edvin Lagerbäck (Sweden).
Goals: Joshua Christian Kojo King (7), Alexander Sørloth (62).

NATIONAL TEAM PLAYERS
(16.07.2019 – 15.07.2020)

Name	DOB	Caps	Goals	2019/2020:	Club
Goalkeepers					
Rune Almenning JARSTEIN	29.09.1984	65	0	2019:	Hertha BSC Berlin (GER)
Ørjan Håskjold NYLAND	10.09.1990	28	0	2019:	Aston Villa FC Birmingham (ENG)
Defenders					
Kristoffer Vassbakk AJER	17.04.1998	14	0	2019:	Celtic FC Glasgow (SCO)
Haitam ALEESAMI	31.07.1991	28	0	2019:	Amiens SC (FRA)
Omar ELABDELLAOUI	05.12.1991	44	0	2019:	Olympiacos SFP Peiraiás (GRE)
Even HOVLAND	14.02.1989	28	0	2019:	Rosenborg BK Trondheim
Birger Solberg MELING	17.12.1994	11	0	2019:	Rosenborg BK Trondheim
Håvard NORDTVEIT	21.06.1990	52	2	2019:	TSG 1899 Hoffenheim (GER)
Tore REGINIUSSEN	10.04.1986	29	4	2019:	Rosenborg BK Trondheim
Jonas SVENSSON	06.03.1993	17	0	2019:	AZ Alkmaar (NED)
Midfielders					
Sander Gard Bolin BERGE	14.02.1998	20	1	2019:	KRC Genk (BEL)
Iver Tobias Rørvik FOSSUM	15.07.1996	14	1	2019:	Aalborg BK (DEN)
Markus HENRIKSEN	25.07.1992	54	3	2019:	Hull City AFC (ENG)
Stefan Marius JOHANSEN	08.01.1991	52	6	2019:	Fulham FC London (ENG)
Mats MØLLER Dæhli	02.03.1995	23	1	2019:	FC St. Pauli Hamburg (GER)
Mathias Antonsen NORMANN	28.05.1996	2	0	2019:	FK Rostov-na-Donu (RUS)
Ole Kristian SELNÆS	07.07.1994	32	2	2019:	Shenzhen FC (CHN)
Fredrik Stensøe ULVESTAD	17.06.1992	3	0	2019:	Djurgårdens IF Stockholm (SWE)
Martin ØDEGAARD	17.12.1998	22	1	2019:	Real Sociedad de Fútbol San Sebastián (ESP)
Forwards					
Tarik ELYOUNOUSSI	23.02.1988	60	10	2019:	AIK Stockholm (SWE)
Erling Braut HÅLAND	21.07.2000	2	0	2019:	FC Red Bull Salzburg (AUT)
Bjørn Maars JOHNSEN	06.11.1991	16	5	2019:	Rosenborg BK Trondheim
Joshua Christian Kojo KING	15.01.1992	46	17	2019:	AFC Bournemouth (ENG)
Alexander SØRLOTH	05.12.1995	22	6	2019:	Trabzonspor Kulübü (TUR)
National team coach					
Lars Edvin LAGERBÄCK (*Sweden*) [from 01.02.2017]	16.07.1948			29 M; 15 W; 8 D; 6 L; 48-29	

POLAND

PZPN

The Country:
Rzeczpospolita Polska (Republic of Poland)
Capital: Warszawa
Surface: 312,679 km²
Inhabitants: 38,383,000 [2019]
Time: UTC+1

The FA:
Polski Związek Piłki Nożnej
Bitwy Warszawskiej 1920 r. 7 02-366, Warszawa
Tel: +48 22 551 2300
Founded: 1919
Member of FIFA since: 1923
Member of UEFA since: 1954
Website: www.pzpn.pl

NATIONAL TEAM RECORDS

RECORDS		
First international match:	18.12.1921, Budapest:	Hungary – Poland 1-0
Most international caps:	Robert Lewandowski	- 112 caps (since 2008)
Most international goals:	Robert Lewandowski	- 61 goals / 112 caps (since 2008)

UEFA EUROPEAN CHAMPIONSHIP	
1960	Qualifiers
1964	Qualifiers
1968	Qualifiers
1972	Qualifiers
1976	Qualifiers
1980	Qualifiers
1984	Qualifiers
1988	Qualifiers
1992	Qualifiers
1996	Qualifiers
2000	Qualifiers
2004	Qualifiers
2008	Final Tournament (Group Stage)
2012	Final Tournament (Group Stage)
2016	Final Tournament (Quarter-Finals)
2020	*Final Tournament (Qualified)*

FIFA WORLD CUP	
1930	Did not enter
1934	Qualifiers
1938	Final Tournament (1st Round)
1950	Did not enter
1954	*Withdrew*
1958	Qualifiers
1962	Qualifiers
1966	Qualifiers
1970	Qualifiers
1974	Final Tournament (3rd Place)
1978	Final Tournament (Round 2)
1982	Final Tournament (3rd Place)
1986	Final Tournament (2nd Round of 16)
1990	Qualifiers
1994	Qualifiers
1998	Qualifiers
2002	Final Tournament (Group Stage)
2006	Final Tournament (Group Stage)
2010	Qualifiers
2014	Qualifiers
2018	Final Tournament (Group Stage)

OLYMPIC TOURNAMENTS	
1908	-
1912	-
1920	-
1924	Preliminary Round
1928	Did not enter
1936	4th Place
1948	Did not enter
1952	Round 1
1956	Did not enter
1960	Group Stage
1964	Qualifiers
1968	Qualifiers
1972	**Winners**
1976	Runners-up
1980	Qualifiers
1984	Qualifiers
1988	Qualifiers
1992	Runners-up
1996	Qualifiers
2000	Qualifiers
2004	Qualifiers
2008	Qualifiers
2012	Qualifiers
2016	Qualifiers

UEFA NATIONS LEAGUE

2018/2019 – League A

FIFA CONFEDERATIONS CUP 1992-2017

None

POLISH CLUB HONOURS IN EUROPEAN CLUB COMPETITIONS:

European Champion Clubs' Cup (1956-1992) / UEFA Champions League (1993-2020)
None

Fairs Cup (1858-1971) / UEFA Cup (1972-2009) / UEFA Europa League (2010-2020)
None

UEFA Super Cup (1972-2019)
None

European Cup Winners' Cup 1961-1999*
None

*defunct competition

NATIONAL COMPETITIONS
TABLE OF HONOURS

	CHAMPIONS	CUP WINNERS	BEST GOALSCORERS	
1920	*Championship abandoned*	-	-	
1921	KS Cracovia Kraków	-	-	
1922	LKS Pogoń Lwów	-	-	
1923	LKS Pogoń Lwów	-	-	
1924	*No competition*	-	-	
1925	LKS Pogoń Lwów	-	-	
1926	LKS Pogoń Lwów	Wisła Kraków	-	
1927	Wisła Kraków	-	Henryk Reyman (Wisła Kraków)	37
1928	Wisła Kraków	-	Ludwik Gintel (KS Cracovia Kraków)	28
1929	KS Warta Poznań	-	Rochus Nastula (Czarni Lwów)	25
1930	KS Cracovia Kraków	-	Karol Kossok (KS Cracovia Kraków)	24
1931	RKS Garbarnia Kraków	-	Walerian Kisieliński (Wisła Kraków)	24
1932	KS Cracovia Kraków	-	Kajetan Kryszkiewicz (KS Warta Poznań)	16
1933	KS Ruch Wielkie Hajduki Chorzów	-	Artur Woźniak (Wisła Kraków)	19
1934	KS Ruch Wielkie Hajduki Chorzów	-	Ernst Wilimowski (KS Ruch Wielkie Hajduki Chorzów)	33
1935	KS Ruch Wielkie Hajduki Chorzów	-	Michał Matyas (LKS Pogoń Lwów)	22
1936	KS Ruch Wielkie Hajduki Chorzów	-	Teodor Peterek (KS Ruch Wielkie Hajduki Chorzów) Ernst Wilimowski (KS Ruch Wielkie Hajduki Chorzów)	18
1937	KS Cracovia Kraków	-	Artur Woźniak (Wisła Kraków)	12
1938	KS Ruch Wielkie Hajduki Chorzów	-	Teodor Peterek (KS Ruch Wielkie Hajduki Chorzów)	21
1939	*Championship abandoned*	-	Ernst Wilimowski (KS Ruch Wielkie Hajduki Chorzów)	12
1940	*No competition*	-	-	
1941	*No competition*	-	-	
1942	*No competition*	-	-	
1943	*No competition*	-	-	
1944	*No competition*	-	-	
1945	*No competition*	-	-	
1946	Polonia Warszawa	-	-	
1947	KS Warta Poznań	-	-	
1948	KS Cracovia Kraków	-	Józef Kohut (Wisła Kraków)	31
1949	Wisła Kraków	-	Teodor Anioła (KKS Lech Poznań)	20
1950	Wisła Kraków	-	Teodor Anioła (KKS Lech Poznań)	21
1951	Unia Chorzów	Unia Chorzów	Teodor Anioła (KKS Lech Poznań)	20
1952	Unia Chorzów	Kolejarz Warszawa	Gerard Cieślik (Unia Chorzów)	11
1953	Unia Chorzów	WKS Gwardia Warszawa (1953/54)	Gerard Cieślik (Unia Chorzów)	24
1954	KS Polonia Bytom	WKS Gwardia Warszawa	Henryk Kempny (KS Polonia Bytom) Ernst Pohl (Legia Warszawa)	13
1955	CWKS Warszawa	CWKS Warszawa	Stanisław Hachorek (WKS Gwardia Warszawa)	16
1956	CWKS Warszawa	CWKS Warszawa	Henryk Kempny (Legia Warszawa)	21
1957	KS Górnik Zabrze	ŁKS Łódź	Lucjan Brychczy (Legia Warszawa)	19
1958	ŁKS Łódź	*No competition*	Władysław Soporek (ŁKS Łódź)	19
1959	KS Górnik Zabrze	*No competition*	Jan Liberda (KS Polonia Bytom) Ernst Pohl (KS Górnik Zabrze)	21
1960	Ruch Chorzów	*No competition*	Marian Norkowski (Polonia Bydgoszcz)	17
1961	KS Górnik Zabrze	*No competition*	Ernst Pohl (KS Górnik Zabrze)	24
1962	KS Polonia Bytom	Zagłębie Sosnowiec	Jan Liberda (KS Polonia Bytom)	16
1962/1963	KS Górnik Zabrze	Zagłębie Sosnowiec	Marian Kielec (MKS Pogoń Szczecin)	18
1963/1964	KS Górnik Zabrze	CWKS Warszawa	Lucjan Brychczy (Legia Warszawa) Józef Gałeczka (Zagłębie Sosnowiec) Jerzy Wilim (TS Szombierki Bytom)	18
1964/1965	KS Górnik Zabrze	KS Górnik Zabrze	Lucjan Brychczy (Legia Warszawa)	18
1965/1966	KS Górnik Zabrze	CWKS Warszawa	Włodzimierz Lubański (KS Górnik Zabrze)	23
1966/1967	KS Górnik Zabrze	Wisła Kraków	Włodzimierz Lubański (KS Górnik Zabrze)	18
1967/1968	Ruch Chorzów	KS Górnik Zabrze	Włodzimierz Lubański (KS Górnik Zabrze)	24
1968/1969	CWKS Legia Warszawa	KS Górnik Zabrze	Włodzimierz Lubański (KS Górnik Zabrze)	22
1969/1970	CWKS Legia Warszawa	KS Górnik Zabrze	Andrzej Jarosik (Zagłębie Sosnowiec)	18
1970/1971	KS Górnik Zabrze	KS Górnik Zabrze	Andrzej Jarosik (Zagłębie Sosnowiec)	13
1971/1972	KS Górnik Zabrze	KS Górnik Zabrze	Ryszard Szymczak (WKS Gwardia Warszawa)	16
1972/1973	FKS Stal Mielec	CWKS Legia Warszawa	Grzegorz Lato (FKS Stal Mielec)	13
1973/1974	Ruch Chorzów	Ruch Chorzów	Zdzisław Kapka (Wisła Kraków)	15
1974/1975	Ruch Chorzów	Stal Rzeszów	Grzegorz Lato (FKS Stal Mielec)	19
1975/1976	FKS Stal Mielec	KS Śląsk Wrocław	Kazimierz Kmiecik (Wisła Kraków)	20
1976/1977	KS Śląsk Wrocław	Zagłębie Sosnowiec	Włodzimierz Mazur (Zagłębie Sosnowiec)	17
1977/1978	Wisła Kraków	Zagłębie Sosnowiec	Kazimierz Kmiecik (Wisła Kraków)	15
1978/1979	Ruch Chorzów	MZKS Arka Gdynia	Kazimierz Kmiecik (Wisła Kraków)	17
1979/1980	TS Szombierki Bytom	CWKS Legia Warszawa	Kazimierz Kmiecik (Wisła Kraków)	24
1980/1981	RTS Widzew Łódź	CWKS Legia Warszawa	Krzysztof Adamczyk (Legia Warszawa)	18
1981/1982	RTS Widzew Łódź	KKS Lech Poznań	Grzegorz Kapica (TS Szombierki Bytom)	15

Season	Champion	Runner-up / Cup Winner	Top Scorer	Goals
1982/1983	KKS Lech Poznań	KS Lechia Gdańsk	Mirosław Okoński (KKS Lech Poznań) Mirosław Tłokiński (RTS Widzew Łódź)	15
1983/1984	KKS Lech Poznań	KKS Lech Poznań	Włodzimierz Ciołek (Górnik Wałbrzych)	14
1984/1985	KS Górnik Zabrze	RTS Widzew Łódź	Leszek Iwanicki (LKP Motor Lublin)	14
1985/1986	KS Górnik Zabrze	GKS Katowice	Andrzej Zgutczyński (KS Górnik Zabrze)	20
1986/1987	KS Górnik Zabrze	KS Śląsk Wrocław	Marek Leśniak (MKS Pogoń Szczecin)	24
1987/1988	KS Górnik Zabrze	KKS Lech Poznań	Dariusz Dziekanowski (Legia Warszawa)	20
1988/1989	Ruch Chorzów	CWKS Legia Warszawa	Krzysztof Warzycha (Ruch Chorzów)	24
1989/1990	KKS Lech Poznań	CWKS Legia Warszawa	Andrzej Juskowiak (KKS Lech Poznań)	18
1990/1991	Zagłębie Lubin	GKS Katowice	Tomasz Dziubiński (Wisła Kraków)	21
1991/1992	KKS Lech Poznań	MKS Miedź Legnica	Jerzy Podbrożny (KKS Lech Poznań) Mirosław Waligóra (KS Hutnik Kraków)	20
1992/1993	KKS Lech Poznań	GKS Katowice	Jerzy Podbrożny (KKS Lech Poznań)	25
1993/1994	Legia Warszawa	Legia Warszawa	Zenon Burzawa (Sokół Pniewy)	21
1994/1995	Legia Warszawa	Legia Warszawa	Bogusław Cygan (FKS Stal Mielec)	16
1995/1996	RTS Widzew Łódź	Ruch Chorzów	Marek Koniarek (RTS Widzew Łódź)	29
1996/1997	RTS Widzew Łódź	Legia Warszawa	Mirosław Trzeciak (ŁKS Łódź)	18
1997/1998	ŁKS Łódź	KS Amica Wronki	Arkadiusz Bąk (Polonia Warszawa) Sylwester Czereszewski (Legia Warszawa) Mariusz Śrutwa (Ruch Chorzów)	14
1998/1999	Wisła Kraków	KS Amica Wronki	Tomasz Frankowski (Wisła Kraków)	21
1999/2000	Polonia Warszawa	KS Amica Wronki	Adam Kompała (KS Górnik Zabrze)	19
2000/2001	Wisła Kraków	Polonia Warszawa	Tomasz Frankowski (Wisła Kraków)	18
2001/2002	Legia Warszawa	Wisła Kraków	Maciej Żurawski (Wisła Kraków)	21
2002/2003	Wisła Kraków	Wisła Kraków	Stanko Svitlica (SRB, Legia Warszawa)	24
2003/2004	Wisła Kraków	KKS Lech Poznań	Maciej Żurawski (Wisła Kraków)	20
2004/2005	Wisła Kraków	KS Dyskobolia Grodzisk Wielkopolski	Tomasz Frankowski (Wisła Kraków)	25
2005/2006	Legia Warszawa	Wisła Płock	Grzegorz Piechna (Korona Kielce)	21
2006/2007	Zagłębie Lubin	KS Dyskobolia Grodzisk Wielkopolski	Piotr Reiss (KKS Lech Poznań)	15
2007/2008	Wisła Kraków	Legia Warszawa	Paweł Brożek (Wisła Kraków)	23
2008/2009	Wisła Kraków	KKS Lech Poznań	Paweł Brożek (Wisła Kraków) Takesure Chinyama (ZIM, Legia Warszawa)	19
2009/2010	KKS Lech Poznań	Jagiellonia Białystok	Robert Lewandowski (KKS Lech Poznań)	18
2010/2011	Wisła Kraków	Legia Warszawa	Tomasz Frankowski (Jagiellonia Białystok)	14
2011/2012	KS Śląsk Wrocław	Legia Warszawa	Artjoms Rudņevs (LVA, KKS Lech Poznań)	22
2012/2013	Legia Warszawa	Legia Warszawa	Róbert Demjan (SVK, TS Podbeskidzie Bielsko-Biała)	14
2013/2014	Legia Warszawa	SP Zawisza Bydgoszcz	Marcin Robak (GKS Piast Gliwice / MKS Pogoń Szczecin)	22
2014/2015	KKS Lech Poznań	Legia Warszawa	Kamil Wilczek (GKS Piast Gliwice)	20
2015/2016	Legia Warszawa	Legia Warszawa	Nemanja Nikolić (HUN, Legia Warszawa)	28
2016/2017	Legia Warszawa	MZKS Arka Gdynia	Marco Filipe Lopes Paixão (POR, KS Lechia Gdańsk) Marcin Robak (KKS Lech Poznań)	18
2017/2018	Legia Warszawa	Legia Warszawa	Carlos Daniel López Huesca "Carlitos" (ESP, Wisła Kraków)	24
2018/2019	GKS Piast Gliwice	KS Lechia Gdańsk	Igor Angulo Alboniga (ESP, KS Górnik Zabrze)	24
2019/2020	Legia Warszawa	KS Cracovia Kraków	Christian Lund Gytkjær (DEN, KKS Lech Poznań)	24

Ruch Chorzów = KS Ruch Wielkie Hajduki Chorzów (1927-1939), Unia Chorzów (1949-1954), Unia-Ruch Chorzów (1955).
Legia Warszawa = CWKS Warszawa (1950-1967), CWKS Legia Warszawa (1967-1990).

NATIONAL CHAMPIONSHIP
Ekstraklasa 2019/2020
(19.07.2019 – 19.07.2020)

Results

Round 1 [19-22.07.2019]
Arka Gdynia - Jagiellonia Białystok 0-3(0-2)
ŁKS Łódź - Lechia Gdańsk 0-0
Raków Częstochowa - Korona Kielce 0-1(0-0)
Wisła Kraków - Śląsk Wrocław 0-1(0-0)
Piast Gliwice - Lech Poznań 1-1(1-0)
Zagłębie Lubin - Cracovia Kraków 1-1(1-1)
Legia Warszawa - Pogoń Szczecin 1-2(0-0)
Wisła Płock - Górnik Zabrze 1-1(0-0)

Round 2 [26-29.07.2019]
Górnik Zabrze - Zagłębie Lubin 1-0(0-0)
Lech Poznań - Wisła Płock 4-0(1-0)
Cracovia Kraków - ŁKS Łódź 1-2(0-1)
Jagiellonia Biał. - Raków Częstoch. 0-1(0-0)
Korona Kielce - Legia Warszawa 1-2(1-1)
Śląsk Wrocław - Piast Gliwice 2-1(0-1)
Lechia Gdańsk - Wisła Kraków 0-0
Pogoń Szczecin - Arka Gdynia 2-0(0-0)

Round 3 [02-05.08.2019]
Arka Gdynia - Korona Kielce 1-1(0-1)
Zagłębie Lubin - Jagiellonia Biał. 2-2(0-1)
Raków Częstoch. - Cracovia Kraków 1-3(1-2)
ŁKS Łódź - Lech Poznań 1-2(1-2)
Wisła Płock - Lechia Gdańsk 1-2(0-1)
Piast Gliwice - Pogoń Szczecin 2-0
Legia Warszawa - Śląsk Wrocław 0-0
Wisła Kraków - Górnik Zabrze 1-0(0-0)

Round 4 [09-12.08.2019]
Lech Poznań - Śląsk Wrocław 1-3(1-3)
Pogoń Szczecin - Wisła Kraków 1-0(0-0)
Zagłębie Lubin - Arka Gdynia 2-0(1-0)
Górnik Zabrze - Raków Częstochowa 1-0(0-0)
ŁKS Łódź - Piast Gliwice 0-1(0-0)
Cracovia Kraków - Korona Kielce 1-0(1-0)
Lechia Gdańsk - Jagiellonia Biał. 1-1(1-0)
Wisła Płock - Legia Warsz. 1-0(1-0) [18.09.]

Round 5 [16-19.08.2019]
Wisła Kraków - ŁKS Łódź 4-0(2-0)
Śląsk Wrocław - Cracovia Kraków 2-1(1-0)
Arka Gdynia - Lech Poznań 0-0
Jagiellonia Białystok - Górnik Zabrze 3-1(2-0)
Piast Gliwice - Wisła Płock 1-0(1-0)
Legia Warszawa - Zagłębie Lubin 1-0(1-0)
Raków Częstoch. - Lechia Gdańsk 2-1(1-0)
Korona Kielce - Pogoń Szczecin 0-1(0-1)

Round 6 [23-26.08.2019]
Jagiellonia Białystok - Wisła Kraków 3-2(2-1)
Cracovia Kraków - Arka Gdynia 3-1(2-0)
Lechia Gdańsk - Śląsk Wrocław 1-1(0-1)
Raków Częstochowa - Lech Poznań 2-3(0-2)
Górnik Zabrze - Korona Kielce 3-0(2-0)
Zagłębie Lubin - Piast Gliwice 0-3(0-1)
ŁKS Łódź - Legia Warszawa 2-3(1-0)
Pogoń Szczecin - Wisła Płock 1-2(1-1)

Round 7 [30.08.-01.09.2019]
Arka Gdynia - Górnik Zabrze 1-0(0-0)
Korona Kielce - Jagiellonia Białystok 0-2(0-1)
Wisła Płock - ŁKS Łódź 2-1(1-1)
Piast Gliwice - Lechia Gdańsk 1-2(0-0)
Wisła Kraków - Zagłębie Lubin 4-2(2-2)
Śląsk Wrocław - Pogoń Szczecin 1-1(1-1)
Lech Poznań - Cracovia Kraków 1-2(0-1)
Legia Warszawa - Raków Częstoch. 3-1(2-0)

Round 8 [13-16.09.2019]
Zagłębie Lubin - Wisła Płock 5-0(3-0)
Jagiellonia Białystok - Legia Warszawa 0-0
Raków Częstochowa - Arka Gdynia 2-0(1-0)
Lechia Gdańsk - Lech Poznań 2-1(2-1)
Korona Kielce - Wisła Kraków 1-1(0-1)
Pogoń Szczecin - ŁKS Łódź 1-0(0-0)
Górnik Zabrze - Śląsk Wrocław 0-0
Cracovia Kraków - Piast Gliwice 2-0(1-0)

Round 9 [20-22.09.2019]
Piast Gliwice - Raków Częstochowa 2-1(0-1)
Lech Poznań - Jagiellonia Białystok 1-1(1-1)
ŁKS Łódź - Arka Gdynia 1-4(0-2)
Lechia Gdańsk - Korona Kielce 2-0(1-0)
Śląsk Wrocław - Zagłębie Lubin 4-4(2-2)
Wisła Płock - Wisła Kraków 2-1(1-1)
Pogoń Szczecin - Górnik Zabrze 1-1(1-0)
Cracovia Kraków - Legia Warszawa 1-2(0-1)

Round 10 [27-30.09.2019]
Korona Kielce - Śląsk Wrocław 1-0(0-0)
Raków Częstochowa - Wisła Płock 1-2(1-0)
Legia Warszawa - Lechia Gdańsk 1-2(1-1)
Górnik Zabrze - Lech Poznań 1-3(1-2)
Arka Gdynia - Piast Gliwice 0-0
Jagiellonia Biał. - Pogoń Szczecin 2-3(1-0)
Wisła Kraków - Cracovia Kraków 0-1(0-0)
Zagłębie Lubin - ŁKS Łódź 3-1(2-0)

Round 11 [04-06.10.2019]
Wisła Płock - Arka Gdynia 4-1(2-0)
Śląsk Wrocław - Jagiellonia Biał. 1-0(0-0)
Pogoń Szczecin - Raków Częstoch. 1-2(1-2)
Lech Poznań - Wisła Kraków 4-0(1-0)
Lechia Gdańsk - Zagłębie Lubin 1-2(0-1)
ŁKS Łódź - Korona Kielce 4-1(2-1)
Cracovia Kraków - Górnik Zabrze 1-1(1-1)
Piast Gliwice - Legia Warszawa 2-0(0-0)

Round 12 [18-21.10.2019]
Zagłębie Lubin - Pogoń Szczecin 0-1(0-1)
Wisła Płock - Piast Gliwice 1-2(0-1)
Korona Kielce - Wisła Płock 0-1(0-1)
Legia Warszawa - Lech Poznań 2-1(0-0)
Jagiellonia Biał. - Cracovia Kraków 3-2(1-1)
Arka Gdynia - Lechia Gdańsk 2-2(0-0)
Górnik Zabrze - ŁKS Łódź 1-1(0-0)
Raków Częstoch. - Śląsk Wrocław 1-0(0-0)

Round 13 [25-27.10.2019]
Cracovia Kraków - Pogoń Szczecin 2-0(0-0)
Lech Poznań - Zagłębie Lubin 1-2(0-1)
ŁKS Łódź - Raków Częstochowa 2-0(2-0)
Piast Gliwice - Korona Kielce 1-0(0-0)
Lechia Gdańsk - Górnik Zabrze 1-1(0-0)
Wisła Płock - Jagiellonia Białystok 3-1(1-0)
Śląsk Wrocław - Arka Gdynia 2-1(1-0)
Legia Warszawa - Wisła Kraków 7-0(3-0)

Round 14 [02-04.11.2019]
Korona Kielce - Zagłębie Lubin 1-0(1-0)
Cracovia Kraków - Lechia Gdańsk 1-0(0-0)
Pogoń Szczecin - Lech Poznań 1-1(1-0)
Jagiellonia Białystok - ŁKS Łódź 2-0(0-0)
Górnik Zabrze - Piast Gliwice 1-1(0-0)
Arka Gdynia - Legia Warszawa 0-1(0-0)
Śląsk Wrocław - Wisła Płock 3-1(2-0)
Raków Częstochowa - Wisła Kraków 1-0(0-0)

Round 15 [08-10.11.2019]
ŁKS Łódź - Śląsk Wrocław 0-1(0-1)
Piast Gliwice - Jagiellonia Białystok 3-1(2-0)
Wisła Płock - Cracovia Kraków 0-0
Legia Warszawa - Górnik Zabrze 5-1(1-0)
Wisła Kraków - Arka Gdynia 0-1(0-0)
Zagłębie Lubin - Raków Częstoch. 2-2(2-1)
Lech Poznań - Korona Kielce 0-0
Lechia Gdańsk - Pogoń Szczecin 0-1(0-1)

Round 16 [22-25.11.2019]
Górnik Zabrze - Wisła Płock 2-2(1-2)
Lech Poznań - Piast Gliwice 3-0(1-0)
Korona Kielce - Raków Częstochowa 3-0(2-0)
Pogoń Szczecin - Legia Warszawa 3-1(1-0)
Lechia Gdańsk - ŁKS Łódź 3-1(2-1)
Jagiellonia Białystok - Arka Gdynia 2-0(0-0)
Śląsk Wrocław - Wisła Kraków 2-1(1-1)
Cracovia Kraków - Zagłębie Lubin 2-0(0-0)

Round 17 [29.11.-01.12.2019]
Zagłębie Lubin - Górnik Zabrze 2-0(1-0)
Wisła Płock - Lech Poznań 0-2(0-1)
Arka Gdynia - Pogoń Szczecin 1-1(1-0)
Piast Gliwice - Śląsk Wrocław 0-3(0-0)
Legia Warszawa - Korona Kielce 4-0(2-0)
Raków Częstoch. - Jagiellonia Biał. 2-1(0-1)
ŁKS Łódź - Cracovia Kraków 1-0(0-0)
Wisła Kraków - Lechia Gdańsk 0-1(0-1)

Round 18 [06-08.12.2019]
Korona Kielce - Arka Gdynia 0-1(0-1)
Górnik Zabrze - Wisła Kraków 4-2(0-1)
Jagiellonia Biał. - Zagłębie Lubin 0-1(0-1)
Lech Poznań - ŁKS Łódź 2-0(0-0)
Lechia Gdańsk - Wisła Płock 2-0(1-0)
Cracovia Kraków - Raków Częstoch. 3-0(0-0)
Pogoń Szczecin - Piast Gliwice 1-0(1-0)
Śląsk Wrocław - Legia Warszawa 0-3(0-1)

Round 19 [13-15.12.2019]
Arka Gdynia - Zagłębie Lubin 2-1(1-1)
Wisła Kraków - Pogoń Szczecin 1-0(1-0)
Raków Częstochowa - Górnik Zabrze 2-1(1-1)
Śląsk Wrocław - Lech Poznań 1-1(1-0)
Legia Warszawa - Wisła Płock 3-1(2-1)
Piast Gliwice - ŁKS Łódź 2-1(0-1)
Korona Kielce - Cracovia Kraków 1-0(1-0)
Jagiellonia Biał. - Lechia Gdańsk 3-0(1-0)

Round 20 [19-21.12.2019]
ŁKS Łódź - Wisła Kraków 2-4(1-3)
Lech Poznań - Arka Gdynia 1-1(0-1)
Cracovia Kraków - Śląsk Wrocław 2-0(0-0)
Pogoń Szczecin - Korona Kielce 0-1(0-0)
Zagłębie Lubin - Legia Warszawa 2-1(0-1)
Lechia Gdańsk - Raków Częstoch. 0-3(0-0)
Wisła Płock - Piast Gliwice 2-1(1-1)
Górnik Zabrze - Jagiellonia Białystok 3-0(1-0)

Round 21 [07-09.02.2020]
Arka Gdynia - Cracovia Kraków 0-1(0-1)
Śląsk Wrocław - Lechia Gdańsk 2-2(0-1)
Korona Kielce - Górnik Zabrze 0-0
Lech Poznań - Raków Częstochowa 3-0(0-0)
Wisła Kraków - Jagiellonia Białystok 3-0(1-0)
Wisła Płock - Pogoń Szczecin 2-3(1-0)
Piast Gliwice - Zagłębie Lubin 2-0(1-0)
Legia Warszawa - ŁKS Łódź 3-1(0-0)

Round 22 [14-16.02.2020]
Górnik Zabrze - Arka Gdynia 2-0(0-0)
Lechia Gdańsk - Piast Gliwice 1-0(0-0)
ŁKS Łódź - Wisła Płock 0-0
Pogoń Szczecin - Śląsk Wrocław 0-0
Raków Częstoch. - Legia Warszawa 2-2(1-0)
Jagiellonia Białystok - Korona Kielce 0-0
Zagłębie Lubin - Wisła Kraków 0-1(0-0)
Cracovia Kraków - Lech Poznań 2-1(0-1)

Round 23 [21-23.02.2020]
ŁKS Łódź - Pogoń Szczecin 0-0
Śląsk Wrocław - Górnik Zabrze 2-1(2-0)
Arka Gdynia - Raków Częstochowa 3-2(0-2)
Legia Warszawa - Jagiellonia Biał. 4-0(2-0)
Piast Gliwice - Cracovia Kraków 1-0(0-0)
Wisła Płock - Zagłębie Lubin 1-1(0-0)
Wisła Kraków - Korona Kielce 2-0(1-0)
Lech Poznań - Lechia Gdańsk 2-0(0-0)

Round 24 [28.02.-01.03.2020]
Raków Częstochowa - Piast Gliwice 2-0(1-0)
Jagiellonia Białystok - Lech Poznań 1-1(1-0)
Wisła Kraków - Wisła Płock 2-2(1-1)
Górnik Zabrze - Pogoń Szczecin 3-1(2-0)
Legia Warszawa - Cracovia Kraków 2-1(2-0)
Korona Kielce - Lechia Gdańsk 1-2(0-1)
Arka Gdynia - ŁKS Łódź 1-1(0-0)
Zagłębie Lubin - Śląsk Wrocław 3-1(0-0)

Round 25 [03-04.03.2020]
Lech Poznań - Górnik Zabrze 4-1(1-1)
Wisła Płock - Raków Częstochowa 0-2(0-1)
Cracovia Kraków - Wisła Kraków 0-2(0-0)
Pogoń Szczecin - Jagiellonia Biał. 1-2(0-1)
ŁKS Łódź - Zagłębie Lubin 3-2(2-1)
Śląsk Wrocław - Korona Kielce 2-1(1-0)
Lechia Gdańsk - Legia Warszawa 0-2(0-0)
Piast Gliwice - Arka Gdynia 1-0(1-0)

Round 26 [06-09.03.2020]
Górnik Zabrze - Cracovia Kraków 3-2(1-1)
Arka Gdynia - Wisła Płock 1-2(0-1)
Zagłębie Lubin - Lechia Gdańsk 4-4(2-3)
Jagiellonia Biał. - Śląsk Wrocław 1-0(0-0)
Raków Częstochowa - Pogoń Szczecin 0-0
Wisła Kraków - Lech Poznań 1-1(1-1)
Legia Warszawa - Piast Gliwice 1-2(1-1)
Korona Kielce - ŁKS Łódź 1-0(0-0)

Round 27 [29-31.05.2020]
Śląsk Wrocław - Raków Częstoch. 1-1(0-0)
Pogoń Szczecin - Zagłębie Lubin 0-3(0-3)
ŁKS Łódź - Górnik Zabrze 0-1(0-1)
Piast Gliwice - Wisła Kraków 4-0(2-0)
Lech Poznań - Legia Warszawa 0-1(0-1)
Wisła Płock - Korona Kielce 1-4(1-2)
Cracovia Kraków - Jagiellonia Biał. 0-1(0-0)
Lechia Gdańsk - Arka Gdynia 4-3(0-0)

Round 28 [05-07.06.2020]
Korona Kielce - Piast Gliwice 1-2(1-0)
Górnik Zabrze - Lechia Gdańsk 2-2(1-0)
Jagiellonia Białystok - Wisła Płock 2-2(0-1)
Zagłębie Lubin - Lech Poznań 3-3(3-1)
Pogoń Szczecin - Cracovia Kraków 1-0(0-0)
Raków Częstochowa - ŁKS Łódź 1-0(1-0)
Arka Gdynia - Śląsk Wrocław 2-1(0-1)
Wisła Kraków - Legia Warszawa 1-3(1-0)

Round 29 [09-10.06.2020]
Lechia Gdańsk - Cracovia Kraków 1-3(0-1)
Piast Gliwice - Górnik Zabrze 0-0
Lech Poznań - Pogoń Szczecin 4-0(2-0)
Zagłębie Lubin - Korona Kielce 1-1(0-1)
Wisła Płock - Śląsk Wrocław 1-2(1-0)
Wisła Kraków - Raków Częstochowa 3-2(1-0)
Legia Warszawa - Arka Gdynia 5-1(1-1)
ŁKS Łódź - Jagiellonia Białystok 0-3(0-2)

Round 30 [14.06.2020]
Arka Gdynia - Wisła Kraków 0-0
Cracovia Kraków - Wisła Płock 1-1(0-0)
Górnik Zabrze - Legia Warszawa 2-0(1-0)
Jagiellonia Białystok - Piast Gliwice 0-2(0-1)
Korona Kielce - Lech Poznań 0-3(0-0)
Pogoń Szczecin - Lechia Gdańsk 1-1(1-0)
Raków Częstoch. - Zagłębie Lubin 2-1(0-0)
Śląsk Wrocław - ŁKS Łódź 4-0(3-0)

Final Standings

1.	Legia Warszawa	30	19	3	8	63	-	30	60
2.	GKS Piast Gliwice	30	16	5	9	36	-	26	53
3.	WKS Śląsk Wrocław	30	13	10	7	42	-	33	49
4.	KKS Lech Poznań	30	13	10	7	55	-	29	49
5.	KS Cracovia Kraków	30	14	4	12	39	-	29	46
6.	MKS Pogoń Szczecin	30	12	9	9	29	-	31	45
7.	Jagiellonia Białystok	30	12	8	10	41	-	39	44
8.	KS Lechia Gdańsk	30	11	10	9	40	-	42	43
9.	KS Górnik Zabrze	30	10	11	9	39	-	38	41
10.	RKS Raków Częstochowa	30	12	5	13	38	-	43	41
11.	Zagłębie Lubin	30	10	8	12	49	-	46	38
12.	Wisła Płock	30	10	8	12	37	-	50	38
13.	Wisła Kraków	30	10	5	15	37	-	47	35
14.	Korona Kielce	30	8	6	16	21	-	37	30
15.	MZKS Arka Gdynia	30	7	8	15	28	-	47	29
16.	ŁKS Łódź	30	5	6	19	26	-	53	21

Teams ranked 1-8 were qualified for the Championship Round, while teams ranked 9-16 were qualified for the Relegation Round.

Relegation Round

Results

Round 31 [19-20.06.2020]
Zagłębie Lubin - ŁKS Łódź 1-0(1-0)
Górnik Zabrze - Korona Kielce 3-2(1-0)
Wisła Płock - Arka Gdynia 0-0
Raków Częstochowa - Wisła Kraków 3-1(1-0)

Round 32 [23.06.2020]
Arka Gdynia - Zagłębie Lubin 3-2(2-1)
Korona Kielce - Raków Częstochowa 0-1(0-1)
ŁKS Łódź - Górnik Zabrze 1-3(0-1)
Wisła Kraków - Wisła Płock 1-0(1-0)

Round 33 [26-27.06.2020]
Raków Częstochowa - Arka Gdynia 3-2(2-0)
Zagłębie Lubin - Korona Kielce 2-1(1-1)
Wisła Płock - ŁKS Łódź 2-0(2-0)
Górnik Zabrze - Wisła Kraków 0-1(0-0)

Round 34 [03-06.07.2020]
ŁKS Łódź - Wisła Kraków 1-2(1-1)
Korona Kielce - Arka Gdynia 1-1(0-1)
Raków Częstochowa - Zagłębie Lub. 1-2(0-2)
Wisła Płock - Górnik Zabrze 1-0(0-0)

Round 35 [10-11.07.2020]
Zagłębie Lubin - Wisła Płock 0-1(0-0)
Górnik Zabrze - Raków Częstochowa 4-1(1-1)
Arka Gdynia - ŁKS Łódź 3-2(3-0)
Wisła Kraków - Korona Kielce 1-1(1-1)

Round 36 [14.07.2020]
Arka Gdynia - Górnik Zabrze 1-2(0-1)
ŁKS Łódź - Raków Częstochowa 3-2(1-2)
Wisła Płock - Korona Kielce 3-1(3-1)
Zagłębie Lubin - Wisła Kraków 3-1(2-1)

Round 37 [18.07.2020]
Górnik Zabrze - Zagłębie Lubin 0-2(0-1)
Korona Kielce - ŁKS Łódź 2-0(0-0)
Raków Częstochowa - Wisła Płock 2-1(0-1)
Wisła Kraków - Arka Gdynia 0-1(0-1)

Final Standings

		Total						Home					Away			
9.	KS Górnik Zabrze	37	14	11	12	51 - 47	53	11	5	3	36 - 20	3	6	9	15 - 27
10.	RKS Raków Częstochowa	37	16	5	16	51 - 56	53	11	3	5	30 - 22	5	2	11	21 - 34
11.	Zagłębie Lubin	37	15	8	14	61 - 53	53	9	6	4	36 - 24	6	2	10	25 - 29
12.	Wisła Płock	37	14	9	14	45 - 54	51	9	4	6	27 - 23	5	5	8	18 - 31
13.	Wisła Kraków	37	13	6	18	44 - 56	45	8	3	7	25 - 18	5	3	11	19 - 38
14.	MZKS Arka Gdynia (Relegated)	37	10	10	17	39 - 57	40	6	7	5	21 - 22	4	3	12	18 - 35
15.	Korona Kielce (Relegated)	37	9	8	20	29 - 48	35	6	3	9	14 - 17	3	5	11	15 - 31
16.	ŁKS Łódź (Relegated)	37	6	6	25	33 - 68	24	5	3	10	21 - 29	1	3	15	12 - 39

Championship Round

Results

Round 31 [20-21.06.2020]
Piast Gliwice - Lech Poznań 0-2(0-0)
Pogoń Szczecin - Lechia Gdańsk 0-1(0-1)
Cracovia Kraków - Jagiellonia Biał. 1-2(0-1)
Legia Warszawa - Śląsk Wrocław 2-0(1-0)

Round 32 [24-25.06.2020]
Lechia Gdańsk - Piast Gliwice 1-0(0-0)
Jagiellonia Białystok - Legia Warszawa 0-0
Lech Poznań - Pogoń Szczecin 0-0
Śląsk Wrocław - Cracovia Kraków 3-2(0-0)

Round 33 [27-29.06.2020]
Legia Warszawa - Piast Gliwice 1-1(0-0)
Jagiellonia Biał. - Lechia Gdańsk 1-2(1-0)
Śląsk Wrocław - Lech Poznań 2-2(0-1)
Cracovia Kraków - Pogoń Szczecin 2-1(1-0)

Round 34 [04-05.07.2020]
Lech Poznań - Legia Warszawa 2-1(2-0)
Lechia Gdańsk - Cracovia Kraków 0-3(0-0)
Pogoń Szczecin - Jagiellonia Biał. 2-2(2-0)
Piast Gliwice - Śląsk Wrocław 1-0(1-0)

Round 35 [11-12.07.2020]
Legia Warszawa - Cracovia Kraków 2-0(1-0)
Śląsk Wrocław - Pogoń Szczecin 2-2(2-1)
Piast Gliwice - Jagiellonia Białystok 2-0(2-0)
Lech Poznań - Lechia Gdańsk 3-2(3-1)

Round 36 [15.07.2020]
Jagiellonia Biał. - Śląsk Wrocław 2-1(1-1)
Cracovia Kraków - Lech Poznań 1-2(0-1)
Lechia Gdańsk - Legia Warszawa 0-0
Pogoń Szczecin - Piast Gliwice 1-0(1-0)

Round 37 [19.07.2020]
Lech Poznań - Jagiellonia Białystok 4-0(4-0)
Legia Warszawa - Pogoń Szczecin 1-2(0-1)
Piast Gliwice - Cracovia Kraków 1-1(0-1)
Śląsk Wrocław - Lechia Gdańsk 1-2(1-1)

Final Standings

		Total						Home					Away			
1.	**Legia Warszawa**	37	21	6	10	70 - 35	69	13	2	4	48 - 16	8	4	6	22 - 19
2.	KKS Lech Poznań	37	18	12	7	70 - 35	66	11	4	4	40 - 14	7	8	3	30 - 21
3.	GKS Piast Gliwice	37	18	7	12	41 - 32	61	12	4	3	25 - 12	6	3	9	16 - 20
4.	KS Lechia Gdańsk	37	15	11	11	48 - 50	56	7	5	6	20 - 22	8	6	5	28 - 28
5.	WKS Śląsk Wrocław	37	14	12	11	51 - 46	54	9	8	2	37 - 28	5	4	9	14 - 18
6.	MKS Pogoń Szczecin	37	14	12	11	37 - 39	54	7	5	6	18 - 17	7	7	5	19 - 22
7.	KS Cracovia Kraków	37	16	5	16	49 - 40	53	10	2	6	26 - 16	6	3	10	23 - 24
8.	Jagiellonia Białystok	37	14	10	13	48 - 51	52	8	5	5	25 - 18	6	5	8	23 - 33

Top goalscorers:

24	**Christian Lund Gytkjær (DEN)**	**KKS Lech Poznań**
16	Igor Angulo Alboniga (ESP)	KS Górnik Zabrze
16	Jorge Félix Muñoz García (ESP)	GKS Piast Gliwice
15	Damjan Bohar (SVN)	Zagłębie Lubin
14	Jarosław Niezgoda	Legia Warszawa
14	Flávio Emanuel Lopes Paixão (POR)	KS Lechia Gdańsk

NATIONAL CUP
Puchar Polski 2019/2020

First Round [24-26.09.2019]				
WKS Gryf Wejherowo - KS Lechia Gdańsk	2-3(2-0)		Rekord Bielsko-Biała - Concordia Elbląg	2-1(0-0)
Stal Brzeg - KS Olimpia Elblag	1-2(0-1)		Elana Toruń - RKS Radomiak Radom	1-2(0-1)
Zagłębie Lubin II - MKS Miedź Legnica	2-2 aet; 1-3 pen		KS Błękitni Stargard Szczeciński - Wisła Kraków	2-1(1-0)
Stilon Gorzow Wielkopolski - KS Olimpia Zambrów	5-1(3-1)		KS Gryf Słupsk - GKS Górnik Łęczna	1-3(1-3)
KS Ruch Chorzów - OKS Stomil Olsztyn	3-3 aet; 3-4 pen		BKS Chemik Bydgoszcz - Wisła Płock	0-1(0-0)
Legia Warszawa II - SKS Wigry Suwałki	2-0(0-0)		KS Cracovia Kraków - Jagiellonia Białystok	4-2(2-1)
MKS Chrobry Głogów - KKS Lech Poznań	0-2(0-0)		GKS Jastrzębie-Zdrój - Bruk-Bet Termalica Nieciecza KS	1-0(0-0)
KSZO Ostrowiec Świętokrzyski - MKS Sandecja Nowy Sącz	1-3(1-2)		MKP Pogoń Siedlce - TS Podbeskidzie Bielsko-Biała	1-0(1-0)
Korona Kielce - Zagłębie Lubin	0-1(0-0)		PGE GKS Bełchatów - GKS Tychy'71	0-2(0-0)
RTS Widzew Łódź - WKS Śląsk Wrocław	2-0(0-0)		GKS Katowice - KS Warta Poznań	0-0 aet; 5-3 pen
ZKS Stal Rzeszow - MKS Pogoń Szczecin	0-1(0-0)		GKS Olimpia Grudziądz - FKS Stal Mielec	0-3(0-1)
KS Garbarnia Kraków - MKS Bytovia Bytów	1-2(0-0)		MKS Chojniczanka Chojnice - RKS Raków Częstochowa	0-1(0-0)
CKS Chełmianka Chełm - MKS Znicz Pruszkow	3-3 aet; 5-4 pen		MKS Puszcza Niepołomice - Legia Warszawa	0-2(0-1)
KS Hutnik Kraków - CWKS Resovia Rzeszów	2-3(1-1,1-1)		Unia Skierniewice - GKS Piast Gliwice	1-5(0-1,1-1)
Polonia Środa Wielkopolska - KS Górnik Zabrze	0-6(0-3)		OKS Odra Opole - MZKS Arka Gdynia	1-0(0-0)
KP Chemik Police - Stal Stalowa Wola	0-4(0-2)		Zagłębie Sosnowiec - ŁKS Łódź	0-3(0-1)

Second Round [29-31.10.2019]				
KS Stilon Gorzow Wielkopolski - Zagłębie Lubin	1-5(0-1)		CKS Chełmianka Chełm - KS Lechia Gdańsk	0-2(0-1)
Rekord Bielsko-Biała - GKS Górnik Łęczna	0-2(0-0)		Stal Stalowa Wola - GKS Katowice	1-1 aet; 4-3 pen
KS Błękitni Stargard Szczeciński - Sandecja Nowy Sącz	3-0(1-0)		FKS Stal Mielec - MKS Pogoń Szczecin	2-0(1-0)
RKS Radomiak Radom - GKS Tychy'71	1-2(0-0)		Legia Warszawa II - OKS Odra Opole	1-0(0-0)
CWKS Resovia Rzeszów - KKS Lech Poznań	0-4(0-2)		KS Olimpia Elbląg - RKS Raków Częstochowa	0-4(0-2)
MKS Bytovia Bytów - KS Cracovia Kraków	2-3(0-0,2-2)		MKP Pogoń Siedlce - GKS Piast Gliwice	0-4(0-2)
MKS Miedź Legnica - GKS Jastrzębie-Zdrój	1-0(0-0,0-0)		RTS Widzew Łódź - Legia Warszawa	2-3(0-0)
ŁKS Łódź - KS Górnik Zabrze	2-0(1-0)		OKS Stomil Olsztyn - Wisła Płock	0-0 aet; 4-1 pen

1/8-Finals [03-05.12.2019]				
Legia Warszawa II - GKS Piast Gliwice	0-2(0-1)		GKS Tychy'71 - ŁKS Łódź	2-0(0-0)
GKS Górnik Łęczna - Legia Warszawa	0-2(0-1)		KS Błękitni Stargard Szczeciński - FKS Stal Mielec	1-2(1-1)
Stal Stalowa Wola - KKS Lech Poznań	0-2(0-1)		MKS Miedź Legnica - OKS Stomil Olsztyn	1-1 aet; 4-3 pen
KS Lechia Gdańsk - Zagłębie Lubin	3-2(0-2)		KS Cracovia Kraków - RKS Raków Częstochowa	0-0 aet; 4-1 pen

Quarter-Finals [10-11.03./26-27.05.2020]				
GKS Tychy'71 - KS Cracovia Kraków	1-2(0-0,1-1)		MKS Miedź Legnica - Legia Warszawa	1-2(0-1)
KS Lechia Gdańsk - GKS Piast Gliwice	2-1(0-0)		FKS Stal Mielec - KKS Lech Poznań	1-3(1-2)

Semi-Finals [07-08.07.2020]				
KS Cracovia Kraków - Legia Warszawa	3-0(2-0)		KKS Lech Poznań - KS Lechia Gdańsk	1-1 aet; 3-4 pen

Final

24.07.2020; Arena Lublin, Lublin; Referee: Referee: Paweł Raczkowski; Attendance: 3,478
KS Cracovia Kraków - KS Lechia Gdańsk   3-2(0-1,2-2)

Cracovia: Lukáš Hroššo, Cornel Emilian Râpă, Michał Helik, David Jablonský, Kamil Pestka, Pelle van Amersfoort, Florian Loshaj (113.Milan Dimun), Mateusz Wdowiak, Ivan Fiolić (120+1.Oleksiy Dytyatev), Sergiu Cătălin Hanca (119.Michal Sipľak), Rafael Guimarães Lopes (Cap) (82.Tomáš Vestenický). Trainer: Michał Probierz.

Lechia: Zlatan Alomerović, Karol Fila, Michał Nalepa, Mario Maloča [*sent off 81*], Rafał Pietrzak (53.Conrado Buchanelli Holz), Jarosław Kubicki, Omran Haydary (83.Patryk Lipski), Maciej Gajos (71.Łukasz Zwoliński), Tomasz Makowski, Žarko Udovičić, Flávio Emanuel Lopes Paixão (Cap) (107.Egzon Kryeziu). Trainer: Piotr Stokowiec.

Goals: 0-1 Omran Haydary (21), 1-1 Pelle van Amersfoort (65), 1-2 Patryk Lipski (85), 2-2 David Jablonský (88), 3-2 Mateusz Wdowiak (117).

Please note: matches and goals includes statistics of both regular season and play-offs (Championship or Relegation).

Morski Klub Sportowy Arka Gdynia

Founded:	1929	
Stadium:	Stadion Miejski, Gdynia (15,139)	
Trainer:	Jacek Zielinski	22.03.1961
[10.10.2019]	Aleksandar Rogić (SRB)	03.08.1981
[10.03.2020]	Krzysztof Sobieraj	25.08.1981
[10.05.2020]	Ireneusz Mamrot	13.12.1970

Goalkeepers:	DOB	M	(s)	G
Kacper Krzepisz	16.12.1999	1		
Marcin Staniszewski	14.01.1997	3		
Pāvels Šteinbors (LVA)	21.09.1985	33		
Defenders:	**DOB**	**M**	**(s)**	**G**
Doug Bergqvist (SWE)	29.03.1993	4	(2)	
Daniel Chmielnicki	05.02.1999	1		
Adam Danch	15.12.1987	21	(7)	2
Frederik Helstrup (DEN)	16.03.1993	14	(2)	
Christian Maghoma (COD)	08.11.1997	19	(1)	
Adam Marciniak	28.09.1988	33	(1)	
Luka Marić (CRO)	25.04.1987	17	(2)	
Michael Olczyk	08.03.1997	2	(1)	
Jakub Wawszczyk	11.01.1998	9	(5)	
Damian Zbozień	25.04.1989	32		
Midfielders:	**DOB**	**M**	**(s)**	**G**
Nabil Aankour (MAR)	09.08.1993	2		
Kamil Antonik	28.11.1998	8	(9)	
Marcin Budziński	06.07.1990	7	(5)	
Azer Bušuladžić (BIH)	12.11.1991	12	(2)	
Goran Cvijanovič (SVN)	09.09.1986	1		

	DOB	M	(s)	G
Adam Deja	24.06.1993	16	(5)	1
Michał Kopczyński	15.06.1992	10	(1)	
Dawid Markiewicz	27.01.2000	3		
Mateusz Młyński	02.01.2001	21	(6)	2
Michał Nalepa	24.03.1995	35	(1)	7
Fernando „Nando" García Puchades (ESP)	13.06.1994	4	(2)	
Santiago "Santi" Samanes Bonito (ESP)	28.07.1995	2	(1)	
Patrick Soboczynski	17.11.2003		(1)	
Mateusz Stepien	12.02.2002		(1)	
Marko Vejinović (NED)	03.02.1990	23	(1)	8
Forwards:	**DOB**	**M**	**(s)**	**G**
Maciej Jankowski	04.01.1990	29	(1)	7
Aleksandar Kolev (BUL)	08.12.1992	1	(1)	
Jan Łoś	20.07.2000	1	(1)	
Marcus Vinícius da Silva de Oliveira (BRA)	29.03.1984	4	(12)	3
Nemanja Mihajlović (SRB)	19.01.1996	3	(5)	1
Fabian Serrarens (NED)	09.02.1991	16	(3)	1
Rafał Siemaszko	11.09.1986	1	(8)	
Davit Skhirtladze (GEO)	16.03.1993	12	(10)	4
Jakub Wilczyński	14.11.2001		(1)	
Oskar Zawada	01.02.1996	7	(5)	1

Miejski Klub Sportowy Cracovia Kraków

Founded:	13.06.1906	
Stadium:	Stadion "Marszałek Józef Piłsudski", Kraków (15,016)	
Trainer:	Michał Probierz	24.09.1972

Goalkeepers:	DOB	M	(s)	G
Lukáš HrOššo (SVK)	19.04.1987	5		
Michal Peškovič (SVK)	08.02.1982	32		
Defenders:	**DOB**	**M**	**(s)**	**G**
Niko Datković (CRO)	21.04.1993	4		
Diego Gustavo Ferraresso Scheda (BRA)	21.05.1992	7	(4)	1
Oleksiy Dytyatev (UKR)	07.11.1988	22	(1)	1
Michał Helik	09.09.1995	22	(1)	1
David Jablonský (CZE)	08.10.1991	26	(2)	1
Kamil Pestka	22.08.1998	19	(7)	1
Cornel Emilian Râpă (ROU)	16.01.1990	35		3
Michal Sipľak (SVK)	02.02.1996	14	(4)	1
Midfielders:	**DOB**	**M**	**(s)**	**G**
Milan Dimun (SVK)	19.09.1996	15	(11)	
Ivan Fiolić (CRO)	29.04.1996	8	(6)	
Janusz Gol	11.11.1985	25	(1)	1
Sergiu Cătălin Hanca (ROU)	04.04.1992	32	(2)	9

	DOB	M	(s)	G
Florian Loshaj (KVX)	13.08.1996	11	(1)	
Sylwester Łusiusz	18.09.1999	22	(4)	
Michał Rakoczy	30.03.2002	4	(5)	1
Mateusz Supryn	04.04.1999		(1)	
Thiago Rodrigues de Souza (BRA)	18.03.1997	6	(6)	
Pelle van Amersfoort (NED)	01.04.1996	32	(2)	8
Forwards:	**DOB**	**M**	**(s)**	**G**
Tomász Bala	08.02.2001		(1)	
Bojan Čečarić (SRB)	10.10.1993	2	(3)	
Daniel Pik	20.07.2000		(4)	
Filip Piszczek	26.05.1995	4	(11)	
Rafael Guimarães Lopes (POR)	28.07.1991	33	(2)	12
Rubén López Huesca „Rubio" (ESP)	24.06.1995		(2)	1
Sebastian Strózik	15.05.1999		(7)	
Tomáš Vestenický (SVK)	06.04.1996	7	(8)	1
Mateusz Wdowiak	28.08.1996	20	(9)	2

Klub Sportowy Górnik Zabrze

Founded:	14.12.1948	
Stadium:	Stadion „Ernest Pohl", Zabrze (24,413)	
Trainer:	Marcin Brosz	11.04.1973

Goalkeepers:	DOB	M	(s)	G
Martin Chudý (SVK)	23.04.1989	37		
Defenders:	**DOB**	**M**	**(s)**	**G**
Paweł Bochniewicz	30.01.1996	33		1
Adrian Gryszkiewicz	13.12.1999	1		
Erik Janža (SVN)	21.06.1993	35	(1)	
Michał Koj	28.07.1993	5	(5)	1
Aleksander Paluszek	09.04.2001	2		
Dariusz Pawłowski	25.02.1999	3	(1)	
Boris Sekulić (SRB)	21.10.1991	21		
Stavros Vasilantonopoulos (GRE)	28.01.1992	11		2
Przemysław Wiśniewski	27.07.1998	35		1
Midfielders:	**DOB**	**M**	**(s)**	**G**
Maciej Ambrosiewicz	24.05.1998		(1)	
Filip Bainović (SRB)	23.06.1996	10	(10)	
Juan Francisco Bauza (ARG)	03.05.1996	3	(3)	
Jesús Jiménez Núñez (ESP)	05.11.1993	36	(1)	12

	DOB	M	(s)	G
Erik Jirka (SVK)	19.09.1997	16	(1)	4
David Kopacz	29.05.1999	12	(11)	
Alasana Manneh (GAM)	08.04.1998	17	(7)	1
Mateusz Matras	23.01.1991	16	(6)	
Szymon Matuszek	07.01.1989	13	(8)	2
Roman Procházka (SVK)	14.03.1989	13	(1)	
Michal Rostkowski	10.08.2000		(1)	
Daniel Ściślak	13.03.2000	12	(10)	
Forwards:	**DOB**	**M**	**(s)**	**G**
Igor Angulo Alboniga (ESP)	26.01.1984	33	(3)	16
Ishmael Baidoo (GHA)	01.12.1998	2	(4)	
Georgios Giakoumakis (GRE)	09.12.1994	9	(3)	3
Piotr Krawczyk	29.12.1994	5	(7)	1
Adam Ryczkowski	30.04.1997	1	(6)	
Łukasz Wolsztyński	08.12.1994	15	(11)	2
Kamil Zapolnik	09.09.1992	11	(6)	1

Jagiellonia Białystok Sportowa Spółka Akcyjna

Founded:	30.05.1920	
Stadium:	Stadion Miejski, Białystok (22,432)	
Trainer:	Ireneusz Mamrot	13.12.1970
[08.12.2019]	Rafał Grzyb	16.01.1983
[01.01.2020]	Ivaylo Petev (BUL)	09.07.1975

Goalkeepers:	DOB	M	(s)	G
Xavier Dziekonski	06.10.2003	2		
Dejan Iliev (MKD)	25.02.1995	4		
Grzegorz Sandomierski	05.09.1989	5		
Damian Węglarz	21.03.1996	26		
Defenders:	**DOB**	**M**	**(s)**	**G**
Zoran Arsenić (CRO)	02.06.1994	27	(3)	
Wojciech Błyszko	05.10.1999	3		
Böðvar Böðvarsson (ISL)	09.04.1995	11		1
Guilherme Haubert Sityá (BRA)	01.04.1990	13		
Andrej Kadlec (SVK)	02.02.1996	16	(2)	
Bartosz Kwiecień	07.05.1994	6	(7)	1
Nemanja Mitrović (SVN)	15.10.1992	3		
Pawel Olszewski	07.06.1999		(1)	
Ivan Runje (CRO)	09.10.1990	27	(1)	3
Dawid Szymonowicz	07.07.1995	4	(3)	
Bogdan Ionuţ Ţiru (ROU)	15.03.1994	11		1
Bartłomiej Wdowik	25.09.2000	3	(5)	
Jakub Wójcicki	09.07.1988	27		
Midfielders:	**DOB**	**M**	**(s)**	**G**
Ariel Borysiuk	29.07.1991	8	(5)	1
Oleg Gorin (UKR)	02.02.2000		(1)	
Martin Košťál (SVK)	23.02.1996	4	(10)	
Przemysław Mystkowski	25.04.1998	6	(9)	1
Marko Poletanović (SRB)	20.07.1993	2	(6)	
Martin Pospíšil (CZE)	26.06.1991	35		2
Taras Romanczuk (UKR)	14.11.1991	35		3
Mile Savković (SRB)	11.03.1992		(3)	
Karol Struski	18.01.2001		(2)	
Forwards:	**DOB**	**M**	**(s)**	**G**
Bartosz Bida	21.02.2001	19	(6)	5
Jesús Imaz Ballesté (ESP)	26.09.1990	31	(4)	11
Juan del Carmen Cámara Mesa (ESP)	13.02.1994	13	(12)	2
Patryk Klimala	05.08.1998	12	(5)	7
Maciej Makuszewski	29.09.1989	12	(1)	1
Ognjen Mudrinski (SRB)	15.11.1991	4	(8)	1
Mikołaj Nawrocki	02.10.2001		(1)	
Tomáš Příkryl (CZE)	04.07.1992	23	(8)	2
Jakov Puljić (CRO)	04.08.1993	15	(1)	5
Aleksander Stawiarz	01.11.2002		(1)	
Krzysztof Toporkiewicz	21.04.2002		(2)	
Mikołaj Wasilewski	19.03.2001		(3)	

Korona Kielce

Founded:	10.07.1973	
Stadium:	Suzuki Arena, Kielce (15,550)	
Trainer:	Gino Lettieri (ITA)	23.12.1966
[31.08.2019]	Sławomir Grzesik	28.04.1970
[16.09.2019]	Miroslaw Smyla	25.07.1969
[06.03.2020]	Maciej Bartoszek	12.04.1977

Goalkeepers:	DOB	M	(s)	G
Marek Kozioł	01.06.1988	29		
Jakub Osobiński	13.04.2000	1	(1)	
Paweł Sokół	02.03.2000	7		
Defenders:	**DOB**	**M**	**(s)**	**G**
Daniel Dziwniel (GER)	19.08.1992	10		
Iván Márquez Álvarez (ESP)	09.06.1994	23	(1)	
Łukasz Kosakiewicz	19.09.1990		(1)	
Adnan Kovačević (BIH)	09.09.1993	34		5
Nemanja Miletić (SRB)	26.07.1991	2		
Piotr Pierzchala	29.06.1999	4	(1)	
Radosław Seweryś	10.01.2004	1		
Grzegorz Szymusik	04.06.1998	17	(2)	1
Themistoklis Tzimopoulos (NZL)	20.11.1985	15	(3)	1
Midfielders:	**DOB**	**M**	**(s)**	**G**
Wiktor Długosz	01.07.2000		(3)	
Michael Gardawski (GER)	25.09.1990	24	(1)	
Ognjen Gnjatić (BIH)	16.10.1991	26		
Ivan Jukić (BIH)	21.06.1996	4	(5)	
Iwo Kaczmarski	16.04.2004	1	(3)	1
Andrés Lioi (ARG)	07.03.1997	9	(4)	
Milán Rádin (SRB)	25.06.1991	18	(9)	1
Oktawian Skrzecz	30.05.1997	1	(1)	
Mateusz Sowiński	31.05.2001		(2)	
Mateusz Spychała	28.01.1998	22	(2)	
Daniel Szelągowski	02.09.2002	3	(2)	3
D'Sean Theobalds (ENG)	21.10.1995	1	(1)	
Rodrigo Zalazar Martínez (URU)	12.08.1999	3	(5)	
Jakub Żubrowski	21.03.1992	27	(1)	1
Forwards:	**DOB**	**M**	**(s)**	**G**
Vato Arveladze (GEO)	04.03.1998	3	(1)	
Marcin Cebula	06.12.1995	24	(2)	2
Bojan Čečarić (SRB)	10.10.1993	6	(1)	
Uroš Đuranović (MNE)	01.02.1994	8	(12)	
Jani Petteri Forsell (FIN)	16.10.1990	14		4
Jakub Górski	16.02.2002		(2)	
Jacek Kiełb	10.01.1988	10	(4)	1
Dawid Lisowski	27.01.2001	2	(5)	
Erik Pačinda (SVK)	09.05.1989	17	(4)	4
Michal Papadopulos (CZE)	14.04.1985	18	(9)	3
Matej Pučko (SVN)	06.10.1993	19	(9)	1
Michał Żyro	20.09.1992	4	(9)	

Kolejowy Klub Sportowy Lech Poznań

Founded:	19.03.1922	
Stadium:	Stadion Miejski, Poznań (43,269)	
Trainer:	Dariusz Zuraw	14.11.1972

Goalkeepers:	DOB	M	(s)	G
Miłosz Mleczko	01.03.1999	1		
Karol Szymanski	25.06.1993	2		
Mickey van der Hart (NED)	13.06.1994	34		
Defenders:	**DOB**	**M**	**(s)**	**G**
Bogdan Butko (UKR)	13.01.1991	10		
Đorđe Crnomarković (SRB)	10.09.1993	23	(3)	
Tomasz Dejewski	22.04.1995	5	(3)	
Robert Gumny	04.06.1998	19	(2)	1
Volodymyr Kostevych (UKR)	23.10.1992	26	(1)	
Tymoteusz Puchacz	23.01.1999	30	(5)	3
Thomas Rogne (NOR)	29.06.1990	19	(1)	1
Ľubomír Šatka (SVK)	02.12.1995	31		1
Midfielders:	**DOB**	**M**	**(s)**	**G**
Daniel „Dani" Ramírez Fernández (ESP)	18.06.1992	16		4
Darko Jevtić (SUI)	08.02.1993	16	(3)	6
Kamil Jóźwiak	22.04.1998	33	(2)	8
Juliusz Letniowski	08.04.1998		(5)	
Jakub Moder	07.04.1999	15	(11)	5
Karlo Muhar (CRO)	17.01.1996	27	(2)	1
Pedro Miguel Amorim Pereira Silva „Pedro Tiba" (POR)	31.08.1988	31	(1)	2
Mateusz Skrzypczak	22.08.2000	1	(1)	
Forwards:	**DOB**	**M**	**(s)**	**G**
Christian Lund Gytkjær (DEN)	06.05.1990	31	(3)	24
João Pedro Reis Amaral (POR)	07.09.1991	10	(5)	3
Jakub Kamiński	05.06.2002	17	(7)	4
Tymoteusz Klupś	26.02.2000	1	(2)	
Maciej Makuszewski	29.09.1989	1	(4)	
Filip Marchwiński	10.01.2002	3	(17)	3
Michał Skóraś	15.02.2000		(5)	
Filip Szymczak	06.05.2002		(4)	
Paweł Tomczyk	04.05.1998	2	(13)	3
Timur Zhamaletdinov (RUS)	21.05.1997	3	(8)	

Klub Sportowy Lechia Gdańsk Spółka Akcyjna

Founded: 07.08.1945
Stadium: Stadion Energa Gdańsk, Gdańsk (43,615)
Trainer: Piotr Stokowiec   25.05.1972

Goalkeepers:	DOB	M	(s)	G
Zlatan Alomerović (GER)	15.06.1991	7		
Dušan Kuciak (SVK)	21.05.1985	30		
Defenders:	**DOB**	**M**	**(s)**	**G**
Błażej Augustyn	26.01.1988	12		1
Conrado Buchanelli Holz (BRA)	03.04.1997	7	(5)	1
Adam Chrzanowski	31.03.1999	1	(1)	
Filip Dymerski	05.04.2002		(1)	
Karol Fila	13.06.1998	30	(1)	
Rafał Kobryń	05.12.1999	7		
Mario Maloča (CRO)	04.05.1989	24	(3)	
Filip Mladenović (SRB)	15.08.1991	24	(1)	
Michał Nalepa	22.01.1993	34		2
Rafał Pietrzak	30.01.1992	10	(1)	
Paweł Żuk	29.01.2001	1	(1)	
Midfielders:	**DOB**	**M**	**(s)**	**G**
Maciej Gajos	19.03.1991	22	(8)	3
Jakub Kałuziński	31.10.2002	3		
Egzon Kryeziu (SVN)	25.04.2000	2		
Jarosław Kubicki	07.08.1995	23	(4)	
Patryk Lipski	12.06.1994	11	(6)	
Daniel Łukasik	28.04.1991	12	(3)	
Tomasz Makowski	19.07.1999	22	(6)	
Jaroslav Mihalík (SVK)	27.07.1994	12	(5)	2
Kenny Saief (USA)	17.12.1993	3	(8)	1
Kristers Tobers (LVA)	13.12.2000	10		
Žarko Udovičić (SRB)	31.08.1987	8	(1)	1
Kacper Urbański	07.09.2004	2	(1)	
Rafał Wolski	10.11.1992	8	(8)	1
Forwards:	**DOB**	**M**	**(s)**	**G**
Jakub Arak	02.04.1995		(7)	
Flávio Emanuel Lopes Paixão (POR)	19.09.1984	20	(11)	14
Omran Haydary (AFG)	13.01.1998	4	(3)	2
Lukáš Haraslín (SVK)	26.05.1996	16	(2)	2
Sławomir Peszko	19.02.1985	13	(5)	3
Artur Sobiech	12.06.1990	15	(3)	6
Egy Maulana Vikri (IDN)	07.07.2000	1		
José Gomes „Zé Gomes" (POR)	08.04.1999	6	(6)	1
Łukasz Zwoliński	24.02.1993	7	(6)	7

Legia Warszawa

Founded: 1916
Stadium: Stadion "Marszałek Józef Piłsudski", Warszawa (31,800)
Trainer: Aleksandar Vuković (SRB)   25.08.1979

Goalkeepers:	DOB	M	(s)	G
Radosław Cierzniak	24.04.1983	3		
Radosław Majecki	16.11.1999	33		
Wojciech Muzyk	07.11.1998	1		
Defenders:	**DOB**	**M**	**(s)**	**G**
Mateusz Grudziński	20.06.2000		(1)	
Iñaki Astiz Ventura (ESP)	05.11.1983	5	(1)	
Artur Jędrzejczyk	04.11.1987	29		
Michał Karbownik	13.03.2001	26	(2)	
Igor Lewczuk	30.05.1985	24	(2)	1
Luís Augusto Martins Rocha (POR)	27.06.1993	9	(4)	
Ariel Mosór	19.02.2003	1	(1)	
William Rémy (FRA)	04.04.1991	1	(4)	
Paweł Stolarski	28.01.1996	12	(1)	
Marko Vešović (MNE)	28.08.1991	21	(1)	2
Mateusz Wieteska	11.02.1997	24	(4)	1
Midfielders:	**DOB**	**M**	**(s)**	**G**
André Renato Soares Martins (POR)	21.01.1990	28	(4)	
Domagoj Antolić (CRO)	30.06.1990	31	(1)	3
Carlos Miguel Ribeiro Dias „Cafú" (POR)	26.02.1993	4	(2)	
Radosław Cielemęcki	19.02.2003	2		
Valeriane Gvilia (GEO)	24.05.1994	24	(11)	8
Tomasz Jodłowiec	08.09.1985	3	(1)	
Mateusz Praszelik	26.09.2000	2	(3)	
Bartosz Slisz	29.03.1999	3	(4)	
Damian Warchoł	19.07.1995		(1)	1
Forwards:	**DOB**	**M**	**(s)**	**G**
Carlos Daniel López Huesca „Carlitos" (ESP)	12.06.1990		(2)	
Mateusz Cholewiak	05.02.1990	5	(9)	2
José Kanté Martínez (GUI)	27.09.1990	14	(9)	10
Kacper Kostorz	21.08.1999		(3)	
Sandro Kulenović (CRO)	04.12.1999	2	(1)	1
Lucas Lima Linhares „Luquinhas" (BRA)	28.09.1996	34	(1)	5
Dominik Adrián Nagy (HUN)	08.05.1995	4	(5)	1
Jarosław Niezgoda	15.03.1995	13	(5)	14
Arvydas Novikovas (LTU)	18.12.1990	13	(4)	4
Tomáš Pekhart (CZE)	26.05.1989	7	(4)	5
Piotr Pyrdoł	27.04.1999	1	(1)	
Maciej Rosołek	02.09.2001	3	(11)	3
Salvador José Milhazes Agra (POR)	11.11.1991	1	(1)	
Vamara Sanogo (FRA)	22.04.1995		(2)	1
Szymon Włodarczyk	05.01.2003	1	(1)	
Paweł Wszołek	30.04.1992	23	(2)	6

Łódzki Klub Sportowy

Founded: 1908
Stadium: Stadion ŁKS, Łódź (5,700)
Trainer: Kazimierz Moskal   09.01.1967
[03.05.2020] Wojciech Stawowy   28.01.1966

Goalkeepers:	DOB	M	(s)	G
Dawid Arndt	22.09.2001	2		
Dominik Budzyński	02.06.1992	1		
Michał Kołba	30.03.1992	7		
Arkadiusz Malarz	19.06.1980	27		
Defenders:	**DOB**	**M**	**(s)**	**G**
Artur Bogusz	18.04.1993	10	(2)	
Carlos Moros Gracia (ESP)	15.04.1993	15	(1)	2
Maciej Dąbrowski	20.04.1987	15		
Jan Grzesik	21.10.1994	29	(1)	1
Kamil Juraszek	26.03.1991	8	(1)	
Adrian Klimczak	26.07.1997	19	(2)	
Kamil Rozmus	13.01.1994	2	(1)	
Maksymilian Rozwandowicz	18.06.1994	17	(1)	1
Jan Sobociński	20.03.1999	25	(2)	2
Tadej Vidmajer (SVN)	10.03.1992	7	(1)	
Midfielders:	**DOB**	**M**	**(s)**	**G**
Antonio Domínguez Sacramento (ESP)	04.04.1993	7	(6)	1
Daniel „Dani" Ramírez Fernández (ESP)	18.06.1992	20		6
Ricardo Martins Guimarães „Guima" (POR)	14.11.1995	21	(4)	2
Bartłomiej Kalinkowski	11.07.1994	10	(3)	
Łukasz Piątek	21.09.1985	17	(5)	1
José Antonio Ruiz López „Pirulo" (ESP)	17.04.1992	21	(11)	1
Przemysław Sajdak	07.02.2000	4	(3)	
Dragoljub Srnić (SRB)	12.01.1992	19	(3)	
Maciej Wolski	29.03.1997	22	(5)	1
Forwards:	**DOB**	**M**	**(s)**	**G**
Patryk Bryła	04.03.1990	5	(4)	
Rafał Kujawa	11.07.1988	7	(8)	4
Wojciech Łuczak	28.07.1989	2	(2)	
Piotr Pyrdoł	27.04.1999	5	(5)	1
Yevhen Radionov (UKR)	06.03.1990		(2)	
Adam Ratajczyk	12.06.2002	12	(6)	1
Samuel "Samu" Corral Valero (ESP)	03.04.1992	7	(5)	3
Łukasz Sekulski	03.11.1990	11	(10)	5
Michał Trąbka	22.04.1997	24	(6)	1
Jakub Wróbel	30.07.1993	9	(5)	

Gliwicki Klub Sportowy Piast Gliwice

Founded: 18.06.1945
Stadium: Stadion Miejski, Gliwice (10,037)
Trainer: Waldemar Fornalik   11.04.1963

Goalkeepers:	DOB	M	(s)	G
František Plach (SVK)	08.03.1992	37		
Defenders:	**DOB**	**M**	**(s)**	**G**
Damian Byrtek	07.03.1991		(1)	
Jakub Czerwiński	06.08.1991	19		1
Jakub Holúbek (SVK)	12.01.1991	3	(2)	
Tomáš Huk (SVK)	22.12.1994	11	(3)	
Mikkel Kirkeskov (DEN)	05.09.1991	36		
Martin Konczkowski	14.09.1993	17	(6)	
Uroš Korun (SVN)	25.05.1987	35		
Piotr Malarczyk	01.08.1991	11		
Tomasz Mokwa	10.02.1993	3	(4)	
Marcin Pietrowski	01.03.1988	3		
Bartosz Rymaniak	13.11.1989	21	(2)	
Midfielders:	**DOB**	**M**	**(s)**	**G**
Remigiusz Borkala	28.02.1999		(1)	

	DOB	M	(s)	G
Patryk Dziczek	25.03.1998	3		
Tom Hateley (ENG)	12.09.1989	32	(1)	1
Tomasz Jodłowiec	08.09.1985	12	(11)	1
Sebastian Milewski	30.04.1998	31	(2)	2
Patryk Sokołowski	25.09.1994	29	(6)	
Forwards:	**DOB**	**M**	**(s)**	**G**
Gerard Badía Cortés (ESP)	18.10.1989	15	(10)	4
Daniel "Dani" Aquino Pintos (ESP)	27.07.1990		(1)	
Jorge Félix Muñoz García (ESP)	22.08.1991	33		16
Tymoteusz Klupś	26.02.2000		(2)	
Piotr Parzyszek	08.09.1993	35	(2)	12
Dominik Steczyk	04.05.1999	3	(15)	
Tiago Alexandre Mendes Alves (POR)	19.06.1996	1	(9)	
Patryk Tuszyński	13.12.1989	6	(25)	1
César Joel Valencia Castillo (ECU)	16.11.1994	1		
Krisztófer Vida (HUN)	23.06.1995	10	(2)	

Morski Klub Sportowy Pogoń Szczecin

Founded: 21.04.1948
Stadium: Stadion „Florian Krygier", Szczecin (18,027)
Trainer: Kosta Runjaić (GER)   04.06.1971

Goalkeepers:	DOB	M	(s)	G
Dante Stipica (CRO)	30.05.1991	37		
Defenders:	**DOB**	**M**	**(s)**	**G**
Jakub Bartkowski	07.11.1991	22	(3)	
Igor Łasicki	26.06.1995	7	(4)	
Mariusz Malec	04.04.1995	7	(1)	
Hubert Matynia	04.11.1995	24	(1)	2
Ricardo Nuno Dos Santos Nunes (RSA)	18.06.1986	14	(1)	1
David Steć (AUT)	10.05.1994	19	(4)	1
Konstantinos Triantafyllopoulos (GRE)	03.04.1993	31	(1)	1
Benedikt Zech (AUT)	03.11.1990	31		
Midfielders:	**DOB**	**M**	**(s)**	**G**
Damian Dąbrowski	27.08.1992	21	(5)	
Kamil Drygas	07.09.1991	8	(5)	2
Kacper Kozłowski	16.10.2003		(3)	
Zvonimir Kožulj (BIH)	15.11.1993	21	(1)	3

	DOB	M	(s)	G
Marcin Listkowski	10.02.1998	23	(9)	2
Kapcer Smoliński	02.07.2001		(3)	1
Srđan Spiridonović (AUT)	13.10.1993	18	(5)	6
Tomáš Podstawski (POR)	30.01.1995	23	(4)	1
Marcel Wędrychowski	13.01.2002		(2)	
Maciej Żurawski	22.12.2000	6	(3)	
Forwards:	**DOB**	**M**	**(s)**	**G**
Soufian Benyamina (GER)	02.03.1990	1	(9)	
Adam Buksa	12.07.1996	18		7
Paweł Cibicki (SWE)	09.01.1994	8	(6)	3
Adam Frączczak	07.08.1987	8	(11)	4
Iker Guarrotxena Vallejo (ESP)	06.12.1992	2	(4)	
Santeri Hostikka (FIN)	30.09.1997	16	(11)	1
Sebastian Kowalczyk	22.08.1998	34	(1)	2
Michalis Manias (GRE)	20.02.1990	7	(7)	
Hubert Turski	31.01.2003	1	(7)	

Robotniczy Klub Sportowy Raków Częstochowa

Founded. 1921
Stadium: GIEKSA Arena, Belchatów (5,264)
Trainer: Marek Papszun   08.08.1974

Goalkeepers:	DOB	M	(s)	G
Michał Gliwa	08.04.1988	13		
Jakub Szumski	06.03.1992	24		
Defenders:	**DOB**	**M**	**(s)**	**G**
Emir Azemović (MNE)	06.01.1997	10	(2)	
Jarosław Jach	17.02.1994	22	(2)	2
Arkadiusz Kasperkiewicz	29.09.1994	5		
Kamil Kościelny	04.08.1991	16	(1)	3
Daniel Mikołajewski	25.08.1999	8		
Andrzej Niewulis	21.04.1989	1		
Tomáš Petrášek	02.03.1992	34		6
Kamil Piątkowski	21.06.2000	18	(6)	1
Dawid Szymonowicz	07.07.1995	8	(5)	
Fran Tudor (CRO)	27.09.1995	14	(2)	1
Midfielders:	**DOB**	**M**	**(s)**	**G**
Jakub Apolinarski	04.05.1999	4	(1)	
Ruslan Babenko (UKR)	08.07.1992	15	(7)	
Daniel Bartl (CZE)	05.07.1989	18	(10)	2
Maciej Domański	05.09.1990	2	(3)	

	DOB	M	(s)	G
Felicio Brown Forbes (CRC)	28.08.1991	21	(6)	10
Ben Lederman (USA)	08.05.2000	1	(5)	
Andrija Luković (SRB)	24.10.1994	4	(3)	
Marko Poletanović (SRB)	20.07.1993	4	(1)	
Igor Sapała	11.10.1995	34		2
Petr Schwarz (CZE)	12.11.1991	34		8
Miłosz Szczepański	22.03.1998	21	(4)	1
David Tijanič (SVN)	16.07.1997	10	(1)	1
Forwards:	**DOB**	**M**	**(s)**	**G**
Jakub Bator	26.10.2000		(1)	
Mateusz Kaczmarek	26.02.2003		(1)	
Aleksandar Kolev (BUL)	08.12.1992	2	(4)	
Patryk Kun	20.04.1995	16	(5)	
Szymon Lewicki	05.04.1988		(1)	
Piotr Malinowski	25.03.1984	9	(11)	2
Sebastian Musiolik	19.05.1996	28	(7)	6
Bryan Nouvier (FRA)	21.06.1995	5	(5)	
Przemysław Oziębała	24.08.1986	1	(5)	
Michał Skóraś	15.02.2000	5	(10)	1

Wrocławski Klub Sportowy Śląsk Wrocław Spółka Akcyjna

Founded: 18.03.1946
Stadium: Stadion Miejski, Wrocław (42,771)
Trainer: Vitezslav Lavicka (CZE)   30.04.1963

Goalkeepers:	DOB	M	(s)	G
Matúš Putnocký (SVK)	01.11.1984	37		
Defenders:	**DOB**	**M**	**(s)**	**G**
Łukasz Broź	17.12.1985	15		3
Piotr Celeban	25.06.1985	6	(1)	
Guillermo Gastón Cotugno Lima (URU)	17.03.1995	3		
Kamil Dankowski	22.07.1996	7	(3)	
Wojciech Golla	12.01.1992	19		1
Mateusz Hołownia	06.05.1998	1	(4)	
Israel Puerto Pineda (ESP)	15.06.1993	32		2
Mariusz Pawelec	14.04.1986	1	(1)	
Dino Štiglec (CRO)	03.10.1990	34		4
Márk Tamás (HUN)	28.10.1993	13		1
Midfielders:	**DOB**	**M**	**(s)**	**G**
Michał Chrapek	03.04.1992	29	(3)	5
Damian Gąska	24.11.1996	2	(16)	
Jakub Łabojko	03.10.1997	26	(7)	2

	DOB	M	(s)	G
Adrian Łyszczarz	22.08.1999	1	(3)	
Krzysztof Mączyński	23.05.1987	29		4
Mateusz Radecki	02.04.1993		(2)	
Marcin Szpakowski	26.09.2001		(1)	
Diego Živulić (CRO)	23.03.1992	15	(4)	
Forwards:	**DOB**	**M**	**(s)**	**G**
Sebastian Bergier	20.12.1999		(11)	
Mateusz Cholewiak	05.02.1990	5	(11)	2
Erik Alexander Expósito Hernández (ESP)	23.06.1996	29	(6)	8
Filip Marković (SRB)	03.03.1992	9	(10)	1
Lubambo Musonda (ZAM)	01.03.1995	22	(3)	
Róbert Pich (SVK)	12.11.1988	32	(4)	7
Przemysław Płacheta	23.03.1998	35		8
Filip Raičević (MNE)	02.07.1993	3	(3)	1
Piotr Samiec-Talar	02.11.2001		(11)	
Daniel Szczepan	05.06.1995	1	(6)	
Mathieu Scalet (FRA)	01.04.1997	1		

Wisła Kraków Spółka Akcyjna

Founded: 1906
Stadium: Stadion „Henryk Reyman", Kraków (33,326)
Trainer: Maciej Stolarczyk   15.01.1972
[14.11.2019] Artur Skowronek   22.05.1982

Goalkeepers:	DOB	M	(s)	G
Michał Buchalik	03.02.1989	31		
Mateusz Lis	27.02.1997	6		
Defenders:	DOB	M	(s)	G
Łukasz Burliga	10.05.1988	10	(3)	1
Marcin Grabowski	21.05.2000	1	(1)	
Hebert Silva Santos (BRA)	23.05.1991	9	(1)	1
Mateusz Hołownia	06.05.1998	7	(2)	
Daniel Hoyo-Kowalski	12.07.2003	1		
Rafał Janicki	05.07.1992	33	(1)	1
Łukasz Klemenz	24.09.1995	33		1
David Niepsuj (GER)	16.08.1995	20	(2)	2
Maciej Sadlok	29.06.1989	32	(3)	1
Dawid Szot	29.04.2001	3	(2)	
Marcin Wasilewski	09.06.1980	7	(8)	
Midfielders:	DOB	M	(s)	G
Vullnet Basha (ALB)	11.07.1990	26	(1)	1
Jakub Błaszczykowski	14.12.1985	19	(3)	7
Víctor Moya Martínez „Chuca" (ESP)	10.06.1997	12	(13)	2

	DOB	M	(s)	G
Jean Carlos Silva Rocha (BRA)	10.05.1996	11	(6)	
Emmanuel Kumah (GHA)	09.02.2000		(1)	
Nikola Kuveljić (SRB)	06.04.1997	7	(5)	
Daniel Morys	26.12.2000		(1)	
Damian Pawłowski	27.01.1999	8	(2)	
Vukan Savićević (MNE)	29.01.1994	20	(2)	4
Kamil Wojtkowski	26.02.1998	20	(2)	2
Georgiy Zhukov (KAZ)	19.11.1994	11	(2)	
Forwards:	DOB	M	(s)	G
Denis Balanyuk (UKR)	16.01.1997	1	(1)	
Jakub Bartosz	13.08.1996		(1)	
Rafał Boguski	09.06.1984	19	(7)	
Paweł Brożek	21.04.1983	17	(2)	8
Aleksander Buksa	15.01.2003	3	(18)	4
Krzysztof Drzazga	20.06.1995	4	(8)	
Michał Mak	14.11.1991	19	(2)	1
Ľubomír Tupta (SVK)	27.03.1998	7	(3)	1
Alon Turgeman (ISR)	09.06.1991	8	(1)	6
Przemysław Zdybowicz	10.01.2000	2	(6)	

Wisła Płock Spółka Akcyjna

Founded: 1947
Stadium: Stadion „Kazimierza Górski", Płock (12,800)
Trainer: Leszek Ojrzyński   31.05.1972
[28.07.2019] Patryk Kniat   01.01.1980
[04.08.2019] Radosław Sobolewski   13.12.1976

Goalkeepers:	DOB	M	(s)	G
Thomas Dähne (GER)	04.01.1994	25		
Krzysztof Kamiński	26.11.1990	9		
Jakub Wrąbel	08.06.1996	1		
Bartłomiej Żynel	09.04.1998	2		
Defenders:	DOB	M	(s)	G
Ángel García Cabezali (ESP)	03.02.1993	20	(4)	1
Jarosław Fojut	17.10.1987	2	(1)	
Michał Marcjanik	15.12.1994	21	(1)	
Damian Michalski	17.05.1998	28	(2)	4
Jakub Rzeźniczak	26.10.1986	15	(1)	2
Bartłomiej Sielewski	09.08.1984	1	(1)	
Cezary Stefańczyk	21.02.1984	22	(3)	
Patryk Stępiński	16.01.1995		(1)	
Piotr Tomasik	31.10.1987	18	(8)	3
Alan Uryga	19.02.1994	37		4
Midfielders:	DOB	M	(s)	G
Hubert Adamczyk	23.02.1998	5	(6)	1
Maciej Ambrosiewicz	24.05.1998	10	(12)	

	DOB	M	(s)	G
Dominik Furman	06.07.1992	36		7
Aleksander Pawlak	14.11.2001	1	(3)	
Damian Rasak	08.02.1996	27	(1)	
Suad Sahiti (KVX)	06.02.1995	7	(11)	
Mateusz Szwoch	19.03.1993	35		4
Jakub Witek	04.12.2002		(1)	
Forwards:	DOB	M	(s)	G
Karol Angielski	20.03.1996	2	(6)	
Torgil Gjertsen (NOR)	12.03.1992	9		2
Dawid Kocyła	23.07.2002	5	(6)	3
Grzegorz Kuświk	23.05.1987	8	(8)	2
Mikołaj Kwietniewski	30.04.1999	3	(9)	1
Giorgi Merebashvili (GEO)	15.08.1986	24	(5)	4
Titas Milašius (LTU)	12.12.2000	1		
Olaf Nowak	24.02.1998		(10)	
Ricardo Cavalcante Mendes „Ricardinho" (BRA)	04.09.1989	15	(2)	4
Cillian Sheridan (IRL)	23.02.1989	13	(2)	2
Alen Stevanović (SRB)	07.01.1991	1		
Oskar Zawada	01.02.1996	4	(3)	

Zagłębie Lubin Spółka Akcyjna

Founded: 10.09.1945
Stadium: Stadion Zagłębia, Lubin (16,068)
Trainer: Ben van Dael (NED)   03.03.1965
[01.09.2019] Pawel Karmelita   28.08.1977
[16.09.2019] Martin Ševela (SVK)   20.11.1975

Goalkeepers:	DOB	M	(s)	G
Kacper Bieszczad	11.09.2002	2		
Konrad Forenc	17.07.1992	17	(1)	
Dominik Hładun	17.09.1995	18		
Defenders:	DOB	M	(s)	G
Saša Balić (MNE)	29.01.1990	31		2
Alan Czerwiński	02.02.1993	35		1
Maciej Dąbrowski	20.04.1987	1	(2)	
Lubomír Guldan (SVK)	30.01.1983	34		1
Dominik Jończy	17.05.1997	4		
Bartosz Kopacz	21.05.1992	35		1
Kamil Kruk	13.03.2000		(2)	
Damian Oko	22.01.1997	11	(2)	
Jakub Tosik	21.05.1987	23	(8)	1
Midfielders:	DOB	M	(s)	G
Evgeniy Bashkirov (RUS)	06.07.1991	12		2
Dawid Pakulski	23.07.1998	1	(8)	1
Łukasz Poręba	13.03.2000	14	(14)	2

	DOB	M	(s)	G
Bartosz Slisz	29.03.1999	19	(2)	2
Filip Starzyński	27.05.1991	35	(2)	8
Jakub Sypek	07.04.2001		(2)	
Mátyás Tajti (HUN)	02.06.1998	1	(2)	
Forwards:	DOB	M	(s)	G
Bartosz Białek	11.11.2001	17	(2)	9
Damjan Bohar (SVN)	18.10.1991	31	(5)	15
Kacper Chodyna	24.05.1999	1		
Dejan Drazič (SRB)	26.09.1995	10		2
Kamil Mazek	22.07.1994		(1)	
Olaf Nowak	24.02.1998		(2)	
Bartłomiej Pawłowski	13.11.1992		(1)	
Rok Sirk (SVN)	10.09.1993	4	(9)	
Asmir Suljić (BIH)	11.09.1991		(5)	
Patryk Szysz	01.04.1998	18	(14)	3
Patryk Tuszyński	13.12.1989	2	(3)	
Saša Živec (SVN)	02.04.1991	31	(2)	9

1.	FKS Stal Mielec (*Promoted*)	34	21	4	9	57	-	31	67
2.	TS Podbeskidzie Bielsko-Biała (*Promoted*)	34	19	8	7	64	-	35	65
3.	KS Warta Poznań (*Promotion Play-offs*)	34	18	6	10	52	-	35	60
4.	RKS Radomiak Radom (*Promotion Play-offs*)	34	16	9	9	52	-	45	57
5.	MKS Miedź Legnica (*Promotion Play-offs*)	34	14	9	11	49	-	44	51
6.	Bruk-Bet Termalica Nieciecza KS (*Promotion Play-offs*)	34	14	8	12	47	-	34	50
7.	MKS Chrobry Głogów	34	14	7	13	41	-	44	49
8.	MKS Puszcza Niepołomice	34	13	9	12	36	-	37	48
9.	GKS Tychy	34	12	11	11	60	-	53	47
10.	OKS Stomil Olsztyn	34	13	7	14	30	-	38	46
11.	Zagłębie Sosnowiec	34	12	8	14	49	-	55	44
12.	MKS Sandecja Nowy Sącz	34	12	8	14	45	-	49	44
13.	OKS Odra Opole	34	11	9	14	33	-	39	42
14.	GKS Jastrzębie-Zdrój	34	9	14	11	41	-	46	41
15.	PGE GKS Bełchatów	34	11	7	16	36	-	45	40
16.	GKS Olimpia Grudziądz (*Relegated*)	34	11	7	16	45	-	56	40
17.	MKS Chojniczanka Chojnice (*Relegated*)	34	8	6	20	46	-	67	30
18.	SKS Wigry Suwałki (*Relegated*)	34	7	5	22	27	-	57	26

Promotion Play-offs (1st / 2nd Level)

Play-offs Semi-Finals (28.07.2020)	RKS Radomiak Radom - MKS Miedź Legnica	3-1(1-0)
	KS Warta Poznań - Bruk-Bet Termalica Nieciecza KS	1-0(0-0)

Play-offs Final (31.07.2020)	KS Warta Poznań - RKS Radomiak Radom	2-0(0-0)

KS Warta Poznań were promoted to the 2020/2021 Ekstraklasa.

NATIONAL TEAM

INTERNATIONAL MATCHES
(16.07.2019 – 15.07.2020)

06.09.2019	Ljubljana	Slovenia - Poland	2-0(1-0)	(ECQ)
09.09.2019	Warszawa	Poland - Austria	0-0	(ECQ)
10.10.2019	Rīga	Latvia - Poland	0-3(0-2)	(ECQ)
13.10.2019	Warszawa	Poland - North Macedonia	2-0(0-0)	(ECQ)
16.11.2019	Jerusalem	Israel - Poland	1-2(0-1)	(ECQ)
19.11.2019	Warszawa	Poland - Slovenia	3-2(1-1)	(ECQ)

06.09.2019   SLOVENIA - POLAND   2-0(1-0)   16th EC. Qualifiers
Stadion Stožice, Ljubljana; Referee: Sergei Karasev (Russia); Attendance: 15,231
POL: Łukasz Fabiański, Michał Pazdan, Bartosz Bereszyński, Tomasz Kędziora, Jan Kacper Bednarek, Mateusz Andrzej Klich (70.Krystian Bielik), Grzegorz Krychowiak, Piotr Zieliński, Kamil Grosicki (70.Jakub Błaszczykowski), Robert Lewandowski (Cap), Krzysztof Piątek (76.Dawid Kownacki). Trainer: Jerzy Józef Brzęczek.

09.09.2019   POLAND - AUSTRIA   0-0   16th EC. Qualifiers
Stadion PGE Narodowy, Warszawa; Referee: Viktor Kassai (Hungary); Attendance: 56,788
POL: Łukasz Fabiański, Kamil Jacek Glik, Bartosz Bereszyński, Tomasz Kędziora, Jan Kacper Bednarek, Grzegorz Krychowiak, Piotr Zieliński, Krystian Bielik, Kamil Grosicki (70.Sebastian Szymański), Robert Lewandowski (Cap), Dawid Kownacki (58.Jakub Błaszczykowski; 77.Mateusz Andrzej Klich). Trainer: Jerzy Józef Brzęczek.

10.10.2019   LATVIA - POLAND   0-3(0-2)   16th EC. Qualifiers
Daugava Stadions, Riga; Referee: Halis Özkahya (Turkey); Attendance: 7,107
POL: Wojciech Tomasz Szczęsny, Kamil Jacek Glik, Tomasz Kędziora, Jan Kacper Bednarek, Maciej Rybus (80.Arkadiusz Reca), Mateusz Andrzej Klich (60.Krzysztof Piątek), Grzegorz Krychowiak, Piotr Zieliński, Sebastian Szymański, Kamil Grosicki (77.Przemysław Frankowski), Robert Lewandowski (Cap). Trainer: Jerzy Józef Brzęczek.
Goals: Robert Lewandowski (9, 13, 76).

13.10.2019   POLAND - NORTH MACEDONIA   2-0(0-0)   16th EC. Qualifiers
Stadion PGE Narodowy, Warszawa; Referee: Antonio Miguel Mateu Lahoz (Spain); Attendance: 52,894
POL: Wojciech Tomasz Szczęsny, Kamil Jacek Glik, Bartosz Bereszyński, Jan Kacper Bednarek, Grzegorz Krychowiak, Piotr Zieliński (90+2.Krzysztof Piątek), Jacek Góralski, Arkadiusz Reca, Sebastian Szymański (68.Arkadiusz Krystian Milik), Kamil Grosicki (74.Przemysław Frankowski), Robert Lewandowski (Cap). Trainer: Jerzy Józef Brzęczek.
Goals: Przemysław Frankowski (74), Arkadiusz Krystian Milik (80).

16.11.2019   ISRAEL - POLAND   1-2(0-1)   16th EC. Qualifiers
Teddy Stadium, Jerusalem; Referee: Mattias Gestranius (Finland); Attendance: 16,700
POL: Wojciech Tomasz Szczęsny, Kamil Jacek Glik (Cap), Tomasz Kędziora, Jan Kacper Bednarek, Grzegorz Krychowiak (84.Dominik Furman), Piotr Zieliński, Arkadiusz Reca, Przemysław Frankowski, Krystian Bielik, Sebastian Szymański (63.Robert Lewandowski), Krzysztof Piątek (70.Mateusz Andrzej Klich). Trainer: Jerzy Józef Brzęczek.
Goals: Grzegorz Krychowiak (4), Krzysztof Piątek (54).

Stadion PGE Narodowy, Warszawa; Referee: Daniel Siebert (Germany); Attendance: 53,946
POL: Wojciech Tomasz Szczęsny, Łukasz Piszczek (45+3.Tomasz Kędziora), Kamil Jacek Glik (7.Artur Jędrzejczyk), Jan Kacper Bednarek, Grzegorz Krychowiak, Piotr Zieliński, Jacek Góralski, Arkadiusz Reca, Sebastian Szymański (86. Kamil Jóźwiak), Kamil Grosicki, Robert Lewandowski (Cap). Trainer: Jerzy Józef Brzęczek.
Goals: Sebastian Szymański (3), Robert Lewandowski (54), Jacek Góralski (81).

NATIONAL TEAM PLAYERS
(16.07.2019 – 15.07.2020)

Name	DOB	Caps	Goals	2019/2020:	Club
Goalkeepers					
Łukasz FABIAŃSKI	18.04.1985	52	0	2019:	West Ham United FC London (ENG)
Wojciech Tomasz SZCZĘSNY	18.04.1990	46	0	2019:	Juventus FC Torino (ITA)
Defenders					
Jan Kacper BEDNAREK	12.04.1996	21	1	2019:	Southampton FC (ENG)
Bartosz BERESZYŃSKI	12.07.1992	22	0	2019:	UC Sampdoria Genova (ITA)
Kamil Jacek GLIK	03.02.1988	73	5	2019:	AS Monaco FC (FRA)
Artur JĘDRZEJCZYK	04.11.1987	40	3	2019:	Legia Warszawa
Tomasz KĘDZIORA	11.06.1994	16	0	2019:	FK Dynamo Kyiv (UKR)
Michał PAZDAN	21.09.1987	38	0	2019:	MKE Ankaragücü SK (TUR)
Łukasz PISZCZEK	03.06.1985	66	3	2019:	BV Borussia Dortmund (GER)
Arkadiusz RECA	17.06.1995	8	0	2019:	SPAL Ferrara (ITA)
Maciej RYBUS	19.08.1989	55	2	2019:	FK Lokomotiv Moscow (RUS)
Midfielders					
Krystian BIELIK	04.01.1998	3	0	2019:	Derby County FC (ENG)
Jakub BŁASZCZYKOWSKI	14.12.1985	108	21	2019:	Wisła Kraków
Przemysław FRANKOWSKI	12.04.1995	10	1	2019:	Chicago Fire SC (USA)
Dominik FURMAN	06.07.1992	3	0	2019:	Wisła Płock
Jacek GÓRALSKI	21.09.1992	13	1	2019:	PFC Ludogorets Razgrad (BUL)
Kamil GROSICKI	08.06.1988	73	13	2019:	Hull City AFC (ENG)
Kamil JÓŹWIAK	22.04.1998	1	0	2019:	KKS Lech Poznań
Mateusz Andrzej KLICH	13.06.1990	23	2	2019:	Leeds United FC (ENG)
Grzegorz KRYCHOWIAK	29.01.1990	69	4	2019:	FK Lokomotiv Moskva (RUS)
Sebastian SZYMAŃSKI	10.05.1999	5	1	2019:	FK Dinamo Moskva (RUS)
Piotr Sebastian ZIELIŃSKI	20.05.1994	51	6	2019:	SSC Napoli (ITA)
Forwards					
Dawid KOWNACKI	14.03.1997	6	1	2019:	TSV Fortuna Düsseldorf (GER)
Robert LEWANDOWSKI	21.08.1988	112	61	2019:	FC Bayern München (GER)
Arkadiusz Krystian MILIK	28.02.1994	49	14	2019:	SSC Napoli (ITA)
Krzysztof PIĄTEK	01.07.1995	10	5	2019:	AC Milan (ITA)

National team coach		
Jerzy Józef BRZĘCZEK [from 12.07.2019]	18.03.1971	16 M; 8 W; 4 D; 4 L; 23-13

PORTUGAL

The Country:
República Portuguesa (Portuguese Republic)
Capital: Lisboa
Surface: 92,212 km²
Inhabitants: 10,295,909 [2019]
Time: UTC

The FA:
Federação Portuguesa de Futebol
Avenida das Seleções 1495-433 Cruz Quebrada - Dafundo
Tel: +351 21 325 2700
Founded: 31.03.1914
Member of FIFA since: 1923
Member of UEFA since: 1954
Website: www.fpf.pt

NATIONAL TEAM RECORDS

RECORDS

First international match:	18.12.1921, Madrid: Spain – Portugal 3-1(2-0)
Most international caps:	Cristiano Ronaldo dos Santos Aveiro - 164 caps (since 2003)
Most international goals:	Cristiano Ronaldo dos Santos Aveiro - 99 goals / 164 caps (since 2003)

UEFA EUROPEAN CHAMPIONSHIP	
1960	Qualifiers
1964	Qualifiers
1968	Qualifiers
1972	Qualifiers
1976	Qualifiers
1980	Qualifiers
1984	Final Tournament (Semi-Finals)
1988	Qualifiers
1992	Qualifiers
1996	Final Tournament (Quarter-Finals)
2000	Final Tournament (Semi-Finals)
2004	Final Tournament (Runners-up)
2008	Final Tournament (Quarter-Finals)
2012	Final Tournament (Semi-Finals)
2016	**Final Tournament (Winners)**
2020	*Final Tournament (Qualified)*

FIFA WORLD CUP	
1930	Did not enter
1934	Qualifiers
1938	Qualifiers
1950	Qualifiers
1954	Qualifiers
1958	Qualifiers
1962	Qualifiers
1966	Final Tournament (3rd Place)
1970	Qualifiers
1974	Qualifiers
1978	Qualifiers
1982	Qualifiers
1986	Final Tournament (Group Stage)
1990	Qualifiers
1994	Qualifiers
1998	Qualifiers
2002	Final Tournament (Group Stage)
2006	Final Tournament (4th Place)
2010	Final Tournament (2nd Round of 16)
2014	Final Tournament (Group Stage)
2018	Final Tournament (2nd Round of 16)

OLYMPIC TOURNAMENTS	
1908	-
1912	-
1920	-
1924	-
1928	Quarter-Finals
1936	Did not enter
1948	Did not enter
1952	Did not enter
1956	Did not enter
1960	Did not enter
1964	Did not enter
1968	Did not enter
1972	Did not enter
1976	Did not enter
1980	Did not enter
1984	Qualifiers
1988	Qualifiers
1992	Qualifiers
1996	4th Place
2000	Qualifiers
2004	Group Stage
2008	Qualifiers
2012	Qualifiers
2016	Quarter-Finals

UEFA NATIONS LEAGUE

2018/2019 – League A; Final Tournament – **Winners**

FIFA CONFEDERATIONS CUP 1992-2017

2017 (3rd Place)

PORTUGUESE CLUB HONOURS IN EUROPEAN CLUB COMPETITIONS:

European Champion Clubs.Cup (1956-1992) / UEFA Champions League (1993-2020)		
Sport Lisboa e Benfica	2	1960/1961, 1961/1962
FC do Porto	2	1986/1987, 2003/2004
Fairs Cup (1858-1971) / UEFA Cup (1972-2009) / UEFA Europa League (2010-2020)		
FC do Porto	2	2002/2003, 2010/2011
UEFA Super Cup (1972-2019)		
FC do Porto	1	1987
European Cup Winners.Cup 1961-1999*		
Sporting Clube de Portugal Lisboa	1	1963/1964

defunct competition

NATIONAL COMPETITIONS
TABLE OF HONOURS

Campeonato de Portugal (1922–1938)*

*created in 1922 and played in cup system, with all the clubs participating in elimination rounds, the winners were named Champions of Portugal. The league sytem started in 1934.

	CHAMPIONS
1922	FC do Porto
1922/1923	Sporting Clube de Portugal Lisboa
1923/1924	SC Olhanense
1924/1925	FC do Porto
1925/1926	CS Marítimo Funchal
1926/1927	CF Os Belenenses Lisboa
1927/1928	Carcavelinhos FC
1928/1929	CF Os Belenenses Lisboa
1929/1930	Sport Lisboa e Benfica
1930/1931	Sport Lisboa e Benfica
1931/1932	FC do Porto
1932/1933	CF Os Belenenses Lisboa
1933/1934	Sporting Clube de Portugal Lisboa
1934/1935	Sport Lisboa e Benfica
1935/1936	Sporting Clube de Portugal Lisboa
1936/1937	FC do Porto
1937/1938	Sporting Clube de Portugal Lisboa

	CHAMPIONS*	CUP WINNERS	BEST GOALSCORERS	
1934/1935	FC do Porto	-	Manuel Esteves Soeiro Vasques (Sporting Clube de Portugal Lisboa)	14
1935/1936	Sport Lisboa e Benfica	-	Artur de Sousa "Pinga" (FC do Porto)	21
1936/1937	Sport Lisboa e Benfica	-	Manuel Esteves Soeiro Vasques (Sporting Clube de Portugal Lisboa)	24
1937/1938	Sport Lisboa e Benfica	-	Fernando Baptista de Seixas Peyroteo de Vasconcelos (Sporting Clube de Portugal Lisboa)	34
1938/1939	FC do Porto	Associação Académica de Coimbra	José Monteiro "Costuras" (FC do Porto)	18
1939/1940	FC do Porto	Sport Lisboa e Benfica	Fernando Baptista de Seixas Peyroteo de Vasconcelos (Sporting Clube de Portugal Lisboa) Slavko Kodrnja (CRO, FC do Porto)	29
1940/1941	Sporting Clube de Portugal Lisboa	Sporting Clube de Portugal Lisboa	Fernando Baptista de Seixas Peyroteo de Vasconcelos (Sporting Clube de Portugal Lisboa)	29
1941/1942	Sport Lisboa e Benfica	CF Os Belenenses Lisboa	Manuel BeloCorreia Dias (FC do Porto)	36
1942/1943	Sport Lisboa e Benfica	Sport Lisboa e Benfica	Júlio Correia da Silva "Julinho" (Sport Lisboa e Benfica)	24
1943/1944	Sporting Clube de Portugal Lisboa	Sport Lisboa e Benfica	Francisco Rodrigues (Vitória FC Setúbal)	28
1944/1945	Sport Lisboa e Benfica	Sporting Clube de Portugal Lisboa	Francisco Rodrigues (Vitória FC Setúbal)	21
1945/1946	CF Os Belenenses Lisboa	Sporting Clube de Portugal Lisboa	Fernando Baptista de Seixas Peyroteo de Vasconcelos (Sporting Clube de Portugal Lisboa)	37
1946/1947	Sporting Clube de Portugal Lisboa	*No competition*	Fernando Baptista de Seixas Peyroteo de Vasconcelos (Sporting Clube de Portugal Lisboa)	43
1947/1948	Sporting Clube de Portugal Lisboa	Sporting Clube de Portugal Lisboa	António Araújo (FC do Porto)	36
1948/1949	Sporting Clube de Portugal Lisboa	Sport Lisboa e Benfica	Fernando Baptista de Seixas Peyroteo de Vasconcelos (Sporting Clube de Portugal Lisboa)	40
1949/1950	Sport Lisboa e Benfica	*No competition*	Júlio Correia da Silva "Julinho" (Sport Lisboa e Benfica)	29
1950/1951	Sporting Clube de Portugal Lisboa	Sport Lisboa e Benfica	Manuel Soeiro Vasques (Sporting Clube de Portugal Lisboa)	29
1951/1952	Sporting Clube de Portugal Lisboa	Sport Lisboa e Benfica	José Pinto de Carvalho Santos Águas (Sport Lisboa e Benfica)	28
1952/1953	Sporting Clube de Portugal Lisboa	Sport Lisboa e Benfica	Sebastião Lucas da Fonseca „Matateu" (CF Os Belenenses Lisboa)	29
1953/1954	Sporting Clube de Portugal Lisboa	Sporting Clube de Portugal Lisboa	João Baptista Martins (Sporting Clube de Portugal Lisboa)	31
1954/1955	Sport Lisboa e Benfica	Sport Lisboa e Benfica	Sebastião Lucas da Fonseca „Matateu" (CF Os Belenenses Lisboa)	32
1955/1956	FC do Porto	FC do Porto	José Pinto de Carvalho Santos Águas (Sport Lisboa e Benfica)	28
1956/1957	Sport Lisboa e Benfica	Sport Lisboa e Benfica	José Pinto de Carvalho Santos Águas (Sport Lisboa e Benfica)	30
1957/1958	Sporting Clube de Portugal Lisboa	FC do Porto	Arsénio Trindade Duarte (GD CUF do Barreiro)	23
1958/1959	FC do Porto	Sport Lisboa e Benfica	José Pinto de Carvalho Santos Águas (Sport Lisboa e Benfica)	26
1959/1960	Sport Lisboa e Benfica	CF Os Belenenses Lisboa	Edmur Pinto Ribeiro (Vitória SC Guimarães)	25

1960/1961	Sport Lisboa e Benfica	Leixões SC Porto	José Pinto de Carvalho Santos Águas (Sport Lisboa e Benfica)	27
1961/1962	Sporting Clube de Portugal Lisboa	Sport Lisboa e Benfica	Azumir Luís Casimiro Veríssimo (BRA, FC do Porto)	23
1962/1963	Sport Lisboa e Benfica	Sporting Clube de Portugal Lisboa	José Augusto Costa Sénica Torres (Sport Lisboa e Benfica)	26
1963/1964	Sport Lisboa e Benfica	Sport Lisboa e Benfica	Eusébio da Silva Ferreira (Sport Lisboa e Benfica)	28
1964/1965	Sport Lisboa e Benfica	Vitória FC Setúbal	Eusébio da Silva Ferreira (Sport Lisboa e Benfica)	28
1965/1966	Sporting Clube de Portugal Lisboa	Sporting Clube de Braga	Eusébio da Silva Ferreira (Sport Lisboa e Benfica) Ernesto de Figueiredo (Sporting Clube de Portugal Lisboa)	25
1966/1967	Sport Lisboa e Benfica	Vitória FC Setúbal	Eusébio da Silva Ferreira (Sport Lisboa e Benfica)	31
1967/1968	Sport Lisboa e Benfica	FC do Porto	Eusébio da Silva Ferreira (Sport Lisboa e Benfica)	43
1968/1969	Sport Lisboa e Benfica	Sport Lisboa e Benfica	Manuel António Leitão da Silva (Associação Académica de Coimbra)	19
1969/1970	Sporting Clube de Portugal Lisboa	Sport Lisboa e Benfica	Eusébio da Silva Ferreira (Sport Lisboa e Benfica)	20
1970/1971	Sport Lisboa e Benfica	Sporting Clube de Portugal Lisboa	Artur Jorge Braga Melo Teixeira (Sport Lisboa e Benfica)	23
1971/1972	Sport Lisboa e Benfica	Sport Lisboa e Benfica	Artur Jorge Braga Melo Teixeira (Sport Lisboa e Benfica)	27
1972/1973	Sport Lisboa e Benfica	Sporting Clube de Portugal Lisboa	Eusébio da Silva Ferreira (Sport Lisboa e Benfica)	40
1973/1974	Sporting Clube de Portugal Lisboa	Sporting Clube de Portugal Lisboa	Héctor Casimiro Yazalde (ARG, Sporting Clube de Portugal Lisboa)	46
1974/1975	Sport Lisboa e Benfica	Boavista FC do Porto	Héctor Casimiro Yazalde (ARG, Sporting Clube de Portugal Lisboa)	30
1975/1976	Sport Lisboa e Benfica	Boavista FC do Porto	Rui Manuel Trindade Jordão (Sport Lisboa e Benfica)	30
1976/1977	Sport Lisboa e Benfica	FC do Porto	Fernando Mendes Soares Gomes (FC do Porto)	26
1977/1978	FC do Porto	Sporting Clube de Portugal Lisboa	Fernando Mendes Soares Gomes (FC do Porto)	25
1978/1979	FC do Porto	Boavista FC do Porto	Fernando Mendes Soares Gomes (FC do Porto)	27
1979/1980	Sporting Clube de Portugal Lisboa	Sport Lisboa e Benfica	Rui Manuel Trindade Jordão (Sporting Clube de Portugal Lisboa)	31
1980/1981	Sport Lisboa e Benfica	Sport Lisboa e Benfica	Tamagnini Manuel Gomes Batista "Nené" (Sport Lisboa e Benfica)	20
1981/1982	Sporting Clube de Portugal Lisboa	Sporting Clube de Portugal Lisboa	Jacques Pereira (FC do Porto)	27
1982/1983	Sport Lisboa e Benfica	Sport Lisboa e Benfica	Fernando Mendes Soares Gomes (FC do Porto)	36
1983/1984	Sport Lisboa e Benfica	FC do Porto	Fernando Mendes Soares Gomes (FC do Porto) Tamagnini Manuel Gomes Batista "Nené" (Sport Lisboa e Benfica)	21
1984/1985	FC do Porto	Sport Lisboa e Benfica	Fernando Mendes Soares Gomes (FC do Porto)	39
1985/1986	FC do Porto	Sport Lisboa e Benfica	Manuel José Tavares Fernandes (Sporting Clube de Portugal Lisboa)	30
1986/1987	Sport Lisboa e Benfica	Sport Lisboa e Benfica	Paulo Roberto Bacinello "Paulinho Cascavel" (BRA, Vitória SC Guimarães)	22
1987/1988	FC do Porto	FC do Porto	Paulo Roberto Bacinello "Paulinho Cascavel" (BRA, Sporting Clube de Portugal Lisboa)	23
1988/1989	Sport Lisboa e Benfica	CF Os Belenenses Lisboa	Vata Matanu Garcia (ANG, Sport Lisboa e Benfica)	16
1989/1990	FC do Porto	CF Estrela da Amadora	Mats Magnusson (SWE, Sport Lisboa e Benfica)	33
1990/1991	Sport Lisboa e Benfica	FC do Porto	José Rui Lopes Águas (Sport Lisboa e Benfica)	25
1991/1992	FC do Porto	Boavista FC do Porto	Richard Daddy Owubokiri (NGA, Boavista FC do Porto)	30
1992/1993	FC do Porto	Sport Lisboa e Benfica	Jorge Paulo Cadete Santos Reis (Sporting Clube de Portugal Lisboa)	18
1993/1994	Sport Lisboa e Benfica	FC do Porto	Rashidi Yekini (NGA, Vitória FC Setúbal)	21
1994/1995	FC do Porto	Sporting Clube de Portugal Lisboa	Hassan Nader (MAR, SC Farense)	21
1995/1996	FC do Porto	Sport Lisboa e Benfica	Domingos José Paciência Oliveira (FC do Porto)	25
1996/1997	FC do Porto	Boavista FC do Porto	Mário Jardel de Almeida Ribeiro (BRA, FC do Porto)	30
1997/1998	FC do Porto	FC do Porto	Mário Jardel de Almeida Ribeiro (BRA, FC do Porto)	26
1998/1999	FC do Porto	SC Beira-Mar Aveiro	Mário Jardel de Almeida Ribeiro (BRA, FC do Porto)	36
1999/2000	Sporting Clube de Portugal Lisboa	FC do Porto	Mário Jardel de Almeida Ribeiro (BRA, FC do Porto)	37
2000/2001	Boavista FC do Porto	FC do Porto	Renivaldo Pereira de Jesus "Pena" (BRA, FC do Porto)	22
2001/2002	Sporting Clube de Portugal Lisboa	Sporting Clube de Portugal Lisboa	Mário Jardel de Almeida Ribeiro (BRA, Sporting Clube de Portugal Lisboa)	42
2002/2003	FC do Porto	FC do Porto	Fary Faye (SEN, SC Beira-Mar Aveiro)	18
2003/2004	FC do Porto	Sport Lisboa e Benfica	Benedict Saul McCarthy (RSA, FC do Porto)	20
2004/2005	Sport Lisboa e Benfica	Vitória FC Setúbal	Liédson da Silva Muniz (BRA, Sporting Clube de Portugal Lisboa)	25
2005/2006	FC do Porto	FC do Porto	Albert Meyong Zé (CMR, CF Os Belenenses Lisboa)	17
2006/2007	FC do Porto	Sporting Clube de Portugal Lisboa	Liédson da Silva Muniz (BRA, Sporting Clube de Portugal Lisboa)	15
2007/2008	FC do Porto	Sporting Clube de Portugal Lisboa	Lisandro López (ARG, FC do Porto)	24
2008/2009	FC do Porto	FC do Porto	Ânderson Miguel da Silva "Nenê" (BRA, CD Nacional Funchal)	20

2009/2010	Sport Lisboa e Benfica	FC do Porto	Óscar René Cardozo Marín (PAR, Sport Lisboa e Benfica) 26
2010/2011	FC do Porto	FC do Porto	Givanildo Vieira de Sousa "Hulk" (BRA, FC do Porto) 23
2011/2012	FC do Porto	Associação Académica de Coimbra	Óscar René Cardozo Marín (PAR, Sport Lisboa e Benfica) 20
2012/2013	FC do Porto	Vitória SC Guimarães	Jackson Arley Martínez Valencia (COL, FC do Porto) 26
2013/2014	Sport Lisboa e Benfica	Sport Lisboa e Benfica	Jackson Arley Martínez Valencia (COL, FC do Porto) 20
2014/2015	Sport Lisboa e Benfica	Sporting Clube de Portugal Lisboa	Jackson Arley Martínez Valencia (COL, FC do Porto) 21
2015/2016	Sport Lisboa e Benfica	Sporting Clube de Braga	Jonas Gonçalves Oliveira (BRA, Sport Lisboa e Benfica) 32
2016/2017	Sport Lisboa e Benfica	Sport Lisboa e Benfica	Bas Dost (NED, Sporting Clube de Portugal Lisboa) 34
2017/2018	FC do Porto	Desportivo das Aves	Jonas Gonçalves Oliveira (BRA, Sport Lisboa e Benfica) 34
2018/2019	Sport Lisboa e Benfica	Sporting Clube de Portugal Lisboa	Haris Seferović (SUI, Sport Lisboa e Benfica) 23
2019/2020	FC do Porto	FC do Porto	Carlos Vinícius Alves Morais (BRA, Sport Lisboa e Benfica) Luis Miguel Afonso Fernandes "Pizzi" (Sport Lisboa e Benfica) Mehdi Taremi (IRN, Rio Ave FC Vila do Conde) 18

*Please note: Campeonato da Liga da Primeira Divisão (1934-1938), Campeonato Nacional da Primeira Divisão (1938-1999), Primeira Liga (since 1999).

NATIONAL CHAMPIONSHIP
Primeira Liga 2019/2020
(09.08.2019 – 26.07.2020)

Please note: Gil Vicente FC Barcelos were promoted directly from the third level by court decision.

Results

Round 1 [09-12.08.2019]
Portimonense SC - Belenenses 0-0
Santa Clara - FC Famalicão 0-2(0-1)
Gil Vicente - FC Porto 2-1(0-0)
Benfica - Paços de Ferreira 5-0(2-0)
Boavista - CD Aves 2-1(1-1)
CS Marítimo - Sporting 1-1(1-1)
Sporting Braga - Moreirense FC 3-1(1-0)
Vitória Setúbal - CD Tondela 0-0
Rio Ave - Vitória Guimarães 1-1(1-1) [08.09.]

Round 2 [16-19.08.2019]
FC Famalicão - Rio Ave 1-0(0-0)
Moreirense FC - Gil Vicente 3-0(2-0)
Belenenses - Benfica 0-2(0-0)
FC Porto - Vitória Setúbal 4-0(2-0)
Paços de Ferreira - Santa Clara 0-1(0-1)
CD Aves - CS Marítimo 3-1(2-1)
Vitória Guimarães - Boavista 1-1(1-0)
Sporting - Sporting Braga 2-1(2-0)
CD Tondela - Portimonense SC 1-2(0-2)

Round 3 [23-25.08.2019]
Vitória Setúbal - Moreirense FC 0-0
Rio Ave - CD Aves 5-1(2-0)
Benfica - FC Porto 0-2(0-1)
Boavista - Paços de Ferreira 1-1(1-1)
CS Marítimo - CD Tondela 2-3(0-1)
Santa Clara - Belenenses 0-0
Portimonense SC - Sporting 1-3(1-2)
Gil Vicente - Sporting Braga 1-1(0-1)
Vitória Guimarães - FC Famalicão 1-1(0-0)

Round 4 [30.08.-01.09.2019]
Moreirense FC - Portimonense SC 1-0(1-0)
Belenenses - Boavista 0-1(0-0)
Paços de Ferreira - CS Marítimo 0-1(0-0)
CD Aves - FC Famalicão 2-3(1-1)
Sporting - Rio Ave 2-3(1-1)
Gil Vicente - Vitória Setúbal 0-0
CD Tondela - Santa Clara 0-0
FC Porto - Vitória Guimarães 3-0(1-0)
Sporting Braga - Benfica 0-4(0-1)

Round 5 [13-15.09.2019]
Vitória Setúbal - Sporting Braga 1-0(0-0)
FC Famalicão - Paços de Ferreira 4-2(1-0)
Benfica - Gil Vicente 2-0(1-0)
Vitória Guimarães - CD Aves 5-1(2-1)
Santa Clara - Moreirense FC 2-0(1-0)
Rio Ave - CD Tondela 2-4(1-2)
CS Marítimo - Belenenses 1-3(0-2)
Portimonense SC - FC Porto 2-3(0-2)
Boavista - Sporting 1-1(1-0)

Round 6 [20-23.09.2019]
Paços de Ferreira - CD Aves 2-1(0-1)
Belenenses - Rio Ave 0-2(0-1)
Moreirense FC - Benfica 1-2(0-0)
Gil Vicente - Boavista 0-0
CD Tondela - Vitória Guimarães 1-3(1-3)
Vitória Setúbal - Portimonense SC 0-0
FC Porto - Santa Clara 2-0(2-0)
Sporting Braga - CS Marítimo 2-2(0-1)
Sporting - FC Famalicão 1-2(1-0)

Round 7 [27-30.09.2019]
Boavista - CD Tondela 0-0
CS Marítimo - Moreirense FC 2-1(0-0)
Benfica - Vitória Setúbal 1-0(0-0)
FC Famalicão - Belenenses 3-1(0-1)
Santa Clara - Gil Vicente 1-0(0-0)
Vitória Guimarães - Paços de Ferreira 1-0(0-0)
Portimonense SC - Sporting Braga 0-1(0-1)
Rio Ave - FC Porto 0-1(0-1)
CD Aves - Sporting 0-1(0-0)

Round 8 [25-28.10.2019]
Paços de Ferreira - Rio Ave 0-0
Gil Vicente - Portimonense SC 1-1(1-1)
Belenenses - CD Aves 3-2(2-2)
Vitória Setúbal - CS Marítimo 0-0
Moreirense FC - Boavista 1-1(1-0)
CD Tondela - Benfica 0-1(0-1)
FC Porto - FC Famalicão 3-0(1-0)
Sporting - Vitória Guimarães 3-1(2-0)
Sporting Braga - Santa Clara 2-0(1-0)

Round 9 [30-31.10.2019]
CD Aves - CD Tondela 0-1(0-0) [05.10.]
Rio Ave - Moreirense FC 1-0(0-1)
CS Marítimo - FC Porto 1-1(1-0)
Vitória Guimarães - Belenenses 5-0(2-0)
Benfica - Portimonense SC 4-0(1-0)
FC Famalicão - Gil Vicente 2-1(1-0)
Paços de Ferreira - Sporting 1-2(0-1)
Boavista - Sporting Braga 2-0(1-0)
Santa Clara - Vitória Setúbal 1-1(1-1)

Round 10 [02-04.11.2019]
Benfica - Rio Ave 2-0(1-0)
Moreirense FC - Vitória Guimarães 1-1(0-0)
Gil Vicente - CS Marítimo 2-0(0-0)
CD Tondela - Sporting 1-0(0-0)
FC Porto - CD Aves 1-0(1-0)
Sporting Braga - FC Famalicão 2-2(0-0)
Belenenses - Paços de Ferreira 1-0(0-0)
Vitória Setúbal - Boavista 1-0(0-0)
Portimonense SC - Santa Clara 1-1(1-0)

Round 11 [08-10.11.2019]
CD Aves - Gil Vicente 1-2(1-2)
Rio Ave - Vitória Setúbal 1-0(1-0)
Santa Clara - Benfica 1-2(1-0)
FC Famalicão - Moreirense FC 3-3(2-0)
Paços de Ferreira - CD Tondela 1-0(1-0)
CS Marítimo - Portimonense SC 1-1(0-1)
Sporting - Belenenses 2-0(0-0)
Vitória Guimarães - Sporting Braga 0-2(0-1)
Boavista - FC Porto 0-1(0-1)

Round 12 [29.11.-02.12.2019]
Santa Clara - Boavista 1-2(0-2)
Moreirense FC - CD Aves 3-2(2-1)
Benfica - CS Marítimo 4-0(3-0)
Portimonense SC - FC Famalicão 2-1(1-0)
CD Tondela - Belenenses 0-1(0-0)
Vitória Setúbal - Vitória Guimarães 1-1(0-0)
Gil Vicente - Sporting 3-1(1-1)
Sporting Braga - Rio Ave 2-0(1-0)
FC Porto - Paços de Ferreira 2-0(1-0)

Round 13 [06-09.12.2019]
Boavista - Benfica 1-4(1-1)
CS Marítimo - Santa Clara 2-2(1-1)
FC Famalicão - CD Tondela 2-3(1-2)
CD Aves - Sporting Braga 1-0(1-0)
Paços de Ferreira - Vitória Setúbal 2-3(0-1)
Vitória Guimarães - Portimonense SC 2-0(1-0)
Sporting - Moreirense FC 1-0(0-0)
Belenenses - FC Porto 1-1(1-1)
Rio Ave - Gil Vicente 1-0(0-0)

Round 14 [13-16.12.2019]
Portimonense SC - Rio Ave 1-1(0-1)
CS Marítimo - Boavista 1-0(1-0)
Benfica - FC Famalicão 4-0(1-0)
Vitória Setúbal - CD Aves 1-0(0-0)
Moreirense FC - Belenenses 2-1(0-0)
Gil Vicente - Vitória Guimarães 2-2(2-0)
Sporting Braga - Paços de Ferreira 0-1(0-1)
Santa Clara - Sporting 0-4(0-1)
FC Porto - CD Tondela 3-0(2-0)

Round 15 [04-05.01.2020]
CD Aves - Santa Clara 0-1(0-0)
Boavista - Portimonense SC 1-1(0-0)
Belenenses - Sporting Braga 1-7(1-4)
Vitória Guimarães - Benfica 0-1(0-1)
Paços de Ferreira - Moreirense FC 1-0(1-0)
CD Tondela - Gil Vicente 1-1(1-1)
Rio Ave - CS Marítimo 0-1(0-0)
Sporting - FC Porto 1-2(1-1)
FC Famalicão - Vitória Setúbal 3-0(1-0)

Round 16 [10-12.01.2020]
Santa Clara - Rio Ave 0-1(0-0)
Benfica - CD Aves 2-1(0-1)
Moreirense FC - FC Porto 2-4(2-2)
Portimonense SC - Paços de Ferreira 0-0
Boavista - FC Famalicão 0-1(0-0)
Vitória Setúbal - Sporting 1-3(0-2)
Gil Vicente - Belenenses 2-0(0-0)
CS Marítimo - Vitória Guimarães 0-0
Sporting Braga - CD Tondela 2-1(0-1)

Round 17 [17-19.01.2020]
FC Porto - Sporting Braga 1-2(0-1)
Sporting - Benfica 0-2(0-0)
CD Aves - Portimonense SC 3-0(0-0)
Vitória Guimarães - Santa Clara 1-0(0-0)
CD Tondela - Moreirense FC 1-1(0-0)
Belenenses - Vitória Setúbal 0-1(0-1)
Paços de Ferreira - Gil Vicente 0-0
FC Famalicão - CS Marítimo 1-1(0-1)
Rio Ave - Boavista 2-0(2-0)

Round 18 [26-29.01.2020]
CD Tondela - Vitória Setúbal 0-3(0-2)
FC Famalicão - Santa Clara 0-1(0-1)
Belenenses - Portimonense SC 2-1(1-0)
Paços de Ferreira - Benfica 0-2(0-1)
CD Aves - Boavista 0-1(0-1)
Vitória Guimarães - Rio Ave 1-2(0-2)
Sporting - CS Marítimo 1-0(0-0)
FC Porto - Gil Vicente 2-1(1-1)
Moreirense FC - Sporting Braga 1-2(0-2)

Round 19 [31.01.-02.02.2020]
Benfica - Belenenses 3-2(2-0)
Rio Ave - FC Famalicão 2-2(0-2)
Portimonense SC - CD Tondela 0-1(0-1)
Vitória Setúbal - FC Porto 0-4(0-2)
CS Marítimo - CD Aves 1-2(1-1)
Gil Vicente - Moreirense FC 1-5(0-2)
Santa Clara - Paços de Ferreira 2-1(0-0)
Sporting Braga - Sporting 1-0(0-0)
Boavista - Vitória Guimarães 2-0(1-0)

Round 20 [07-09.02.2020]
Paços de Ferreira - Boavista 0-1(0-1)
FC Famalicão - Vitória Guimarães 0-7(0-2)
Belenenses - Santa Clara 0-2(0-2)
Sporting Braga - Gil Vicente 2-2(2-0)
FC Porto - Benfica 3-2(3-1)
CD Tondela - CS Marítimo 0-0
Moreirense FC - Vitória Setúbal 1-1(0-1)
Sporting - Portimonense SC 2-1(1-1)
CD Aves - Rio Ave 0-4(0-1)

Round 21 [14-16.02.2020]
Vitória Setúbal - Gil Vicente 1-2(0-1)
Portimonense SC - Moreirense FC 1-1(1-1)
Santa Clara - CD Tondela 1-0(0-0)
Benfica - Sporting Braga 0-1(0-1)
Rio Ave - Sporting 1-1(1-0)
CS Marítimo - Paços de Ferreira 3-0(1-0)
Boavista - Belenenses 1-2(0-1)
Vitória Guimarães - FC Porto 1-2(0-1)
FC Famalicão - CD Aves 1-1(0-0)

Round 22 [21-24.02.2020]
CD Aves - Vitória Guimarães 0-2(0-0)
CD Tondela - Rio Ave 1-2(0-0)
Belenenses - CS Marítimo 1-0(1-0)
Paços de Ferreira - FC Famalicão 2-1(0-0)
Moreirense FC - Santa Clara 2-1(1-1)
Sporting - Boavista 2-0(2-0)
Sporting Braga - Vitória Setúbal 3-1(0-0)
FC Porto - Portimonense SC 1-0(0-0)
Gil Vicente - Benfica 0-1(0-1)

Round 23 [28.02.-03.03.2020]
Portimonense SC - Vitória Setúbal 0-0
Rio Ave - Belenenses 0-0
Boavista - Gil Vicente 0-1(0-0)
CD Aves - Paços de Ferreira 1-3(1-1)
CS Marítimo - Sporting Braga 1-2(0-1)
Vitória Guimarães - CD Tondela 2-0(2-0)
Santa Clara - FC Porto 0-2(0-1)
Benfica - Moreirense FC 1-1(0-0)
FC Famalicão - Sporting 3-1(2-1)

Round 24 [06-08.03.2020]
Sporting Braga - Portimonense SC 3-1(2-0)
CD Tondela - Boavista 1-1(1-1)
Vitória Setúbal - Benfica 1-1(0-0)
FC Porto - Rio Ave 1-1(1-1)
Belenenses - FC Famalicão 0-0
Moreirense FC - CS Marítimo 2-0(1-0)
Gil Vicente - Santa Clara 1-1(0-0)
Sporting - CD Aves 2-0(0-0)
Paços de Ferreira - Vitória Guimarães 1-2(1-0)

Round 25 [03-07.06.2020]
Portimonense SC - Gil Vicente 1-0(0-0)
FC Famalicão - FC Porto 2-1(0-0)
CS Marítimo - Vitória Setúbal 1-1(1-0)
Benfica - CD Tondela 0-0
Vitória Guimarães - Sporting 2-2(1-1)
Santa Clara - Sporting Braga 3-2(1-1)
CD Aves - Belenenses 0-2(0-2)
Boavista - Moreirense FC 0-1(0-0)
Rio Ave - Paços de Ferreira 2-3(1-2)

Round 26 [09-13.06.2020]
Gil Vicente - FC Famalicão 1-3(0-2)
Vitória Setúbal - Santa Clara 2-2(1-1)
Portimonense SC - Benfica 2-2(0-2)
FC Porto - CS Marítimo 1-0(1-0)
Belenenses - Vitória Guimarães 1-1(1-1)
CD Tondela - CD Aves 2-0(1-0)
Moreirense FC - Rio Ave 0-1(0-1)
Sporting - Paços de Ferreira 1-0(0-0)
Sporting Braga - Boavista 0-1(0-0)

Round 27 [15-19.06.2020]
CS Marítimo - Gil Vicente 2-1(2-1)
Santa Clara - Portimonense SC 1-1(0-0)
CD Aves - FC Porto 0-0
Paços de Ferreira - Belenenses 2-1(0-1)
Rio Ave - Benfica 1-2(1-0)
Boavista - Vitória Setúbal 3-1(2-0)
Sporting - CD Tondela 2-0(2-0)
Vitória Guimarães - Moreirense FC 1-1(1-0)
FC Famalicão - Sporting Braga 0-0

Round 28 [21-26.06.2020]
Gil Vicente - CD Aves 3-0(2-0)
Portimonense SC - CS Marítimo 3-2(2-0)
Vitória Setúbal - Rio Ave 1-2(1-1)
Benfica - Santa Clara 3-4(0-1)
FC Porto - Boavista 4-0(0-0)
CD Tondela - Paços de Ferreira 1-3(0-2)
Moreirense FC - FC Famalicão 1-1(0-0)
Sporting Braga - Vitória Guimarães 3-2(2-2)
Belenenses - Sporting 1-3(1-3)

Round 29 [28.06.-01.07.2020]
Boavista - Santa Clara 1-0(1-0)
CD Aves - Moreirense FC 0-1(0-0)
CS Marítimo - Benfica 2-0(0-0)
Paços de Ferreira - FC Porto 0-1(0-1)
FC Famalicão - Portimonense SC 0-1(0-1)
Vitória Guimarães - Vitória Setúbal 2-0(1-0)
Rio Ave - Sporting Braga 4-3(3-2)
Belenenses - CD Tondela 1-1(1-1)
Sporting - Gil Vicente 2-1(1-0)

Round 30 [03-06.07.2020]
Santa Clara - CS Marítimo 0-1(0-0)
Vitória Setúbal - Paços de Ferreira 2-3(2-0)
Portimonense SC - Vitória Guimarães 0-1(0-0)
Benfica - Boavista 3-1(3-0)
Sporting Braga - CD Aves 4-0(0-0)
Gil Vicente - Rio Ave 1-0(1-0)
CD Tondela - FC Famalicão 0-1(0-0)
FC Porto - Belenenses 5-0(1-0)
Moreirense FC - Sporting 0-0

Round 31 [08-11.07.2020]
Boavista - CS Marítimo 0-1(0-1)
CD Aves - Vitória Setúbal 1-0(1-0)
Rio Ave - Portimonense SC 2-1(1-1)
CD Tondela - FC Porto 1-3(0-0)
FC Famalicão - Benfica 1-1(0-1)
Vitória Guimarães - Gil Vicente 1-2(0-0)
Sporting - Santa Clara 1-0(0-0)
Paços de Ferreira - Sporting Braga 1-5(0-3)
Belenenses - Moreirense FC 0-1(0-0)

Round 32 [13-15.07.2020]
CS Marítimo - Rio Ave 0-0
Vitória Setúbal - FC Famalicão 1-2(1-1)
Santa Clara - CD Aves 3-0(2-0)
Portimonense SC - Boavista 2-1(2-0)
Gil Vicente - CD Tondela 3-2(1-0)
Benfica - Vitória Guimarães 2-0(1-0)
Moreirense FC - Paços de Ferreira 1-1(1-0)
Sporting Braga - Belenenses 1-1(1-0)
FC Porto - Sporting 2-0(0-0)

Round 33 [18-21.07.2020]
Rio Ave - Santa Clara 2-2(1-1)
FC Famalicão - Boavista 2-2(2-0)
Belenenses - Gil Vicente 1-0(0-0)
Vitória Guimarães - CS Marítimo 1-0(1-0)
Paços de Ferreira - Portimonense SC 2-1(2-1)
CD Tondela - Sporting Braga 1-0(0-0)
FC Porto - Moreirense FC 6-1(1-1)
Sporting - Vitória Setúbal 0-0
CD Aves - Benfica 0-4(0-1)

Santa Clara - Vitória Guimarães 2-2(2-1)
Gil Vicente - Paços de Ferreira 3-3(2-2)
CS Marítimo - FC Famalicão 3-3(1-1)
Boavista - Rio Ave 0-2(0-1)
Benfica - Sporting 2-1(1-0)
Sporting Braga - FC Porto 2-1(0-1)
Portimonense SC - CD Aves 2-0(0-0)
Vitória Setúbal - Belenenses 2-0(1-0)
Moreirense FC - CD Tondela 1-2(0-1)

Final Standings

			Total					**Home**					**Away**			
1. **FC do Porto**	34	26	4	4	74 - 22	82	15	1	1	44 - 7	11	3	3	30 - 15
2. Sport Lisboa e Benfica	34	24	5	5	71 - 26	77	12	2	3	38 - 13	12	3	2	33 - 13
3. Sporting Clube de Braga	34	18	6	10	61 - 40	60	10	4	3	32 - 20	8	2	7	29 - 20
4. Sporting Clube de Portugal Lisboa	34	18	6	10	49 - 34	60	12	1	4	25 - 13	6	5	6	24 - 21
5. Rio Ave FC Vila do Conde	34	15	10	9	48 - 36	55	6	6	5	27 - 23	9	4	4	21 - 13
6. FC Famalicão	34	14	12	8	53 - 51	54	7	6	4	28 - 26	7	6	4	25 - 25
7. Vitória SC Guimarães	34	13	11	10	53 - 38	50	8	4	5	27 - 15	5	7	5	26 - 23
8. Moreirense FC Moreira de Cónegos	34	10	13	11	42 - 44	43	6	6	5	23 - 20	4	7	6	19 - 24
9. CD Santa Clara Açores	34	11	10	13	36 - 41	43	6	4	7	18 - 21	5	6	6	18 - 20
10. Gil Vicente FC Barcelos	34	11	10	13	40 - 44	43	7	7	3	26 - 21	4	3	10	14 - 23
11. CS Marítimo Funchal	34	9	12	13	34 - 42	39	5	8	4	24 - 21	4	4	9	10 - 21
12. Boavista FC Porto	34	10	9	15	28 - 39	39	5	4	8	15 - 18	5	5	7	13 - 21
13. FC Paços de Ferreira	34	11	6	17	36 - 52	39	6	2	9	15 - 22	5	4	8	21 - 30
14. CD Tondela	34	9	9	16	30 - 44	36	3	5	9	12 - 22	6	4	7	18 - 22
15. Belenenses SAD Lisboa	34	9	8	17	27 - 54	35	5	4	8	13 - 25	4	4	9	14 - 29
16. Vitória FC Setúbal (*Relegated*)	34	7	13	14	27 - 43	34	4	7	6	15 - 20	3	6	8	12 - 23
17. Portimonense SC Portimão	34	7	12	15	30 - 45	33	5	7	5	18 - 18	2	5	10	12 - 27
18. CD das Aves (*Relegated*)	34	5	2	27	24 - 68	17	4	1	12	12 - 26	1	1	15	12 - 42

Please note: Vitória FC Setúbal and CD das Aves failed to produce valid licensing documentation to compete at first level, so both were relegated by the Portuguese Professional Football League to the third level for the next season.

Top goalscorers:

18	**Carlos Vinícius Alves Morais (BRA)**	*Sport Lisboa e Benfica*
18	**Luis Miguel Afonso Fernandes "Pizzi"**	*Sport Lisboa e Benfica*
18	**Mehdi Taremi (IRN)**	*Rio Ave FC Vila do Conde*
17	João Paulo Dias Fernandes "Paulinho"	*Sporting Clube de Braga*
13	Fábio Gonçalves Abreu	*Moreirense FC Moreira de Cónegos*
12	Moussa Marega (MLI)	*FC do Porto*
12	Fábio Santos Martins	*FC Famalicão*
12	Ricardo Jorge Luz Horta	*Sporting Clube de Braga*

NATIONAL CUP
Taça de Portugal 2019/2020

Second Round [28-29.09.2019]

CD Rabo Peixe - Académico de Viseu FC	0-1		SC Beira-Mar - SC Bustelo	2-0
Berço SC - CD Feirense Santa Maria da Feira	1-3		GS Loures - Lusitano Ginásio Clube	3-2
CF União da Madeira - AD Fafe	1-2 aet		CF Esperança de Lagos - Pevidém SC	1-3
CD Carção - UD Vilafranquense	0-2		Eléctrico FC Ponte de Sor - FC de Arouca	1-6
Clube de Condeixa ACD - SC Lusitânia dos Açores	1-0		Lusitânia FC Lourosa - Sporting da Covilhã	4-2
UD Santarém - SC Farense Faro	1-2		SC Mineiro Aljustrelense - Casa Pia AC	0-2
SC Coimbrões - GD Prado	3-1		SC Mirandela - GD Chaves	1-2
GD Coruchense - Club Olímpico Montijo	0-4		SC Vila Pouca de Aguiar - CD Mafra	0-4
AD Portomosense - FC Alverca	0-3		GD Alcochetense - Leixões SC Porto	0-4
Club Sintra Football - Amarante FC	2-0		Mortágua FC - FC de Penafiel	2-3 aet
Amora FC - SC São João Vêr	2-1		Leça FC - UD Oliveirense	1-0
ACD Penedo Gordo - GD Fabril	0-1		Caldas SC - Varzim SC	0-1
Atlético dos Arcos AD - SC Praiense	0-2		Lusitano FC de Vildemoinhos - AA de Coimbra	0-1
AD Oliveirense - FC de Felgueiras 1932	2-1 aet		CD Pinhalnovense - GD Estoril Praia	1-2
CF Canelas 2010 - Ança FC	4-0		UD de Leiria - Real SC Queluz	0-1
Sport Benfica e Castelo Branco - SC Olhanense	3-2		AD Sanjoanense - SC Ideal	1-0
CD Fátima - ACDR Coutada	4-0		CDC de Montalegre - AC Marinhense	0-1
Gondomar SC - Valadares Gaia FC	0-1		FC Vizela - GD Fontinhas	6-1
AR São Martinho - Merelinense FC	0-1		Louletano DG - Ginásio Figueirense	4-2 pen
SC Maria da Fonte - Juventude de Pedras Salgadas	1-5		SC Espinho - CD Nacional Funchal	2-0
CA Pêro Pinheiro - GD Vitória de Sernache	0-1		GD Águias do Moradal - SC União Torreense	1-0
LGC Moncarapachense - Sertanense FC	0-1 aet		Vasco da Gama AC - CD Cova da Piedade	0-4
Sport União Sintrense - Anadia FC	1-2		RD Águeda – Clube Oriental de Lisboa	4-1

Third Round [17-20.10.2019]

FC Alverca - Sporting Clube de Portugal Lisboa	2-0(1-0)	GD Águias do Moradal - Vitória FC Setúbal	0-5(0-4)
CD Cova da Piedade - Sport Lisboa e Benfica	0-4(0-1)	AD Oliveirense - CD Santa Clara Açores	0-3(0-1)
Clube de Condeixa ACD - Rio Ave FC V. do Conde	0-1(0-0)	Lusitânia FC Lourosa - FC Famalicão	1-1 aet; 6-7 pen
Club Sintra Football - Vitória SC Guimarães	1-1 aet; 5-4 pen	Varzim SC - GD Estoril Praia	1-0(0-0)
GD Fabril - Moreirense FC Moreira de Cónegos	1-3(0-1)	CD Mafra - AD Fafe	1-0(0-0,0-0)
Louletano DC - FC Paços de Ferreira	1-2(1-1, 1-1)	AC Marinhense - CD Fátima	1-0(1-0)
Pevidém SC - Belenenses SAD Lisboa	0-2(0-0)	GD Vitória de Sernache - Sertanense FC	4-5 pen
Amora FC - AD Sanjoanense	0-1(0-0)	GS Loures - Sport Benfica e Castelo Branco	4-2(1-1,2-2)
SC Espinho - UD Vilafranquense	2-1(0-1)	Juventude de Pedras Salgadas - RD Águeda	1-0(0-0)
Académico de Viseu FC - Real SC Queluz	3-1(3-0)	Casa Pia AC - FC Vizela	1-3(0-1)
FC de Penafiel - Gil Vicente FC Barcelos	0-2(0-1)	FC de Arouca - Merelinense FC	1-0(0-0)
SC Farense Faro - CD das Aves	5-2(3-0)	Club Olímpico Montijo - Anadia FC	0-1(0-0)
CD Feirense Santa Maria da Feira - CD Tondela	3-0(2-0)	GD Chaves - Boavista FC do Porto	2-1(0-0,0-0)
Ass. Académica de Coimbra - Portimonense SC	2-1(0-0)	Valadares Gaia FC - CF Canelas 2010	10-11 pen
SC Coimbrões - FC do Porto	0-5(0-3)	SC Beira-Mar - CS Marítimo Funchal	2-2 aet; 5-4 pen
Leça FC - Sporting Clube de Braga	1-3(0-2)	Leixões SC Porto - SC Praiense	4-2(1-1)

Fourth Round [22-24.11.2019]

Leixões SC Porto - CD Santa Clara Açores	1-4(0-2)	Juventude de Pedras Salgadas - CF Canelas 2010	0-0 aet; 5-6 pen
Varzim SC - GS Loures	1-0(0-0)	Moreirense FC Moreira de Cónegos - CD Mafra	1-3(0-1)
Sertanense FC - SC Farense Faro	2-1(0-1,1-1)	Anadia FC - SC Beira-Mar	2-1(0-0)
SC Espinho - FC de Arouca	3-2(2-0,2-2)	Club Sintra Football - AC Marinhense	0-2(0-0)
Ac. de Viseu FC - CD Feirense Santa Maria da Feira	1-0(0-0)	FC Paços de Ferreira - AD Sanjoanense	1-0(1-0)
FC Famalicão - Associação Académica de Coimbra	1-0(1-0)	Rio Ave FC Vila do Conde - FC Alverca	1-0(1-0)
Sporting Clube de Braga - Gil Vicente FC Barcelos	1-0(1-0)	FC do Porto - Vitória FC Setúbal	4-0(2-0)
FC Vizela - Sport Lisboa e Benfica	1-2(1-0)	GD Chaves - Belenenses SAD Lisboa	1-0(1-0)

1/8-Finals [17-19.12.2019]

Académico de Viseu FC - GD Chaves	1-0(0-0)	FC Paços de Ferreira - SC Espinho	3-0(1-0)
Varzim SC - Anadia FC	2-1(0-0,1-1)	Sport Lisboa e Benfica - Sporting Clube de Braga	2-1(1-1)
AC Marinhense - Rio Ave FC Vila do Conde	0-2(0-1)	FC do Porto - CD Santa Clara Açores	1-0(1-0)
Sertanense FC - CF Canelas 2010	0-1(0-1)	FC Famalicão - CD Mafra	3-0(0-0)

Quarter-Finals [14-16.01.2020]

FC do Porto - Varzim SC	2-1(2-1)	FC Paços de Ferreira - FC Famalicão	0-1(0-0)
Sport Lisboa e Benfica - Rio Ave FC Vila do Conde	3-2(1-2)	Académico de Viseu FC - CF Canelas 2010	1-0(0-0)

Semi-Finals [04.02./11-12.02.2020]

First Leg		Second Leg	
Sport Lisboa e Benfica - FC Famalicão	3-2(0-0)	FC Famalicão - Sport Lisboa e Benfica	1-1(0-1)
Académico de Viseu FC - FC do Porto	1-1(0-0)	FC do Porto - Académico de Viseu FC	3-0(1-0)

Final

01.08.2020; Estádio Cidade de Coimbra, Coimbra; Referee: Artur Manuel Soares Dias; Attendance: None

FC do Porto - Sport Lisboa e Benfica   **2-1(0-0)**

FC do Porto: Diogo Costa, Wilson Manafá, Chancel Mbemba, Pepe, Alex Telles, Otávio (73.Diogo Leite), Danilo (Cap), Andrés Mateus Uribe Villa (88.Mamadou Loum), Jesús Manuel Corona Ruiz (80.Sérgio Oliveira), Moussa Marega, Luis Fernando Díaz Marulanda [*sent off 38*]. Trainer: Sérgio Paulo Merceiro Da Conceição.

Benfica: Odisseas Vlachodimos, André Almeida, Rúben Dias, Jardel (Cap), Nuno Tavares, Julian Weigl (60.Adel Taarabt), Pizzi (76.Dyego Sousa), Gabriel, Franco Emanuel Cervi (46.Rafa Silva), Chiquinho (60.Carlos Vinícius), Haris Seferović (76.Jota). Trainer: Nélson Alexandre da Silva Veríssimo.

Goals: 1-0 Chancel Mbemba (47), 2-0 Chancel Mbemba (58), 2-1 Carlos Vinícius (84 penalty).

Clube Desportivo das Aves

Founded:	12.11.1930	
Stadium:	Estádio do CD Aves, Aves (5,896)	
Trainer:	Augusto Soares Inácio	01.02.1955
[21.10.2019]	Leandro Garcia Azevedo Pires	16.06.1979
[13.11.2019]	Nuno Miguel Manta Ribeiro dos Santos	25.07.1978

Goalkeepers:	DOB	M	(s)	G
Quentin Beunardeau (FRA)	27.02.1994	21		
Fabio (BRA)	11.05.1990	6		
Raphael Aflalo (BRA)	08.07.1996	5		
Dimitar Sheytanov (BUL)	15.03.1999	2		
Defenders:	**DOB**	**M**	**(s)**	**G**
Afonso Figueiredo	06.01.1993	19	(2)	
Bruninho (BRA)	16.12.1993	1	(3)	
Bruno Jesus (BRA)	22.04.1997		(2)	
Bruno Morais	08.04.1998	14	(1)	
Cláudio Tavares	23.03.1997	1	(2)	
Oumar Diakhité (SEN)	09.12.1993	16		
Adam Dźwigała (POL)	25.09.1995	15	(1)	
Hélder Baldé	03.08.1998	1		
Jaílson (BRA)	21.02.1991	14	(3)	
Adi Mehremić (BIH)	26.04.1992	8		1
Mato Miloš (CRO)	30.06.1993	15		
Ricardo Mangas	19.03.1998	19	(1)	1
Andrej Šimunec (CRO)	02.03.1995	2		
Midfielders:	**DOB**	**M**	**(s)**	**G**
Bruno Lourenço	02.02.1998		(5)	
Bruno Xavier (POL)	27.11.1996		(5)	
Jonathan Buatu Mananga (ANG)	27.09.1993	12		
Claudio Falcão (BRA)	03.07.1994	26		
Valdomiro Tualungo Paulo Lameira „Estrela" (ANG)	22.09.1995	18	(3)	
Luiz Fernando (BRA)	08.04.1995	9	(4)	
Pedro Delgado	07.04.1997	1	(3)	
Reko Silva	21.06.1999	11	(1)	1
Rúben Oliveira	14.12.1994	23	(1)	
Mohamed Touré (CIV)	30.03.1997	1	(3)	
Aaron Tshibola (ENG)	02.01.1995	2	(2)	
Eric Veiga (LUX)	18.02.1997		(2)	
Zidane Banjaqui	15.12.1998	14	(9)	1
Enzo Alan Zidane Fernández (FRA)	24.03.1995	5	(5)	2
Forwards:	**DOB**	**M**	**(s)**	**G**
Kelvin Boateng (GHA)	24.03.2000		(2)	
Abdoulaye Diallo (SEN)	15.01.1996		(3)	
Miguel Tavares	29.08.1998	4	(8)	
Mehrdad Mohammadi (IRN)	29.09.1993	27	(1)	8
José Carlos Moreira Varela (CPV)	15.09.1997	4	(6)	
Marius Mouandilmadji (CHA)	22.01.1998	4	(8)	
Pedro Soares	30.03.1999	6	(3)	
Peu (BRA)	24.04.1993		(2)	
Ricardo Rodrigues	28.06.1995		(3)	
Rúben Macedo	09.03.1996	8	(13)	1
Mahmoud Abdelmonem Abdelhamid Soliman (EGY)	13.04.1994	1	(4)	1
Kevin Yamga (FRA)	07.09.1996	17	(4)	1
Welinton (BRA)	08.06.1993	22	(1)	7

Belenenses Sociedad Anónima Desportiva Lisboa

Founded:	30.06.2018	
Stadium:	Complexo Desportivo do Estádio Nacional, Oeiras (37,593)	
Trainer:	Jorge Manuel Rebelo Fernandes"Silas"	01.09.1976
[05.09.2019]	Pedro Ricardo Torres Ribeiro	26.11.1985
[15.01.2020]	Armando Gonçalves Teixeira Petit	25.09.1976

Goalkeepers:	DOB	M	(s)	G
André Moreira	02.12.1995	14	(1)	
Hervé Koffi (BFA)	16.10.1996	20		
Defenders:	**DOB**	**M**	**(s)**	**G**
Adélcio Varela	22.04.1996		(1)	
Chima Akas (NGA)	03.05.1994	14	(1)	
Diogo Calila	10.10.1998	8	(4)	
Danny Henriques (NED)	29.07.1997	5	(5)	1
Eduardo Kau (BRA)	17.01.1999	2	(1)	
Francisco Miguel Varela Martín (ESP)	26.10.1994	8	(1)	
Gonçalo Silva	04.06.1991	18		
Luís Silva	18.02.1999		(1)	
Nilton Varela	25.05.2001	17	(1)	1
Hakim Ouro-Sama (TOG)	28.12.1997		(4)	
Thibang Sindile Theophilus Phete (RSA)	04.04.1994	12	(2)	
Simón Alonso Ramírez Cuevas (CHI)	03.11.1998		(1)	
Ricardo Ferreira	25.11.1992	4	(1)	
Rúben Lima	03.10.1989	8	(3)	
Manuel Luis da Silva Cafumana „Show" (ANG)	06.03.1999	22	(2)	
Tomás Ribeiro	30.04.1999	13		
Midfielders:	**DOB**	**M**	**(s)**	**G**
André Santos	02.03.1989	25	(2)	2
André Sousa	09.07.1990	11	(2)	1
Benny	04.01.1997	3	(1)	
Chano Boukholda (ALG)	24.05.1996		(3)	
Matija Ljujić (SRB)	28.10.1993	4	(1)	
Jonatan Lucca (BRA)	02.06.1994	4		
Nuno Coelho	23.11.1987	32		
Nuno Henrique	31.03.1999	5	(6)	
Sphephelo S'Miso Sithole (RSA)	03.03.1999		(1)	
Tiago Esgaio	01.08.1995	26	(2)	2
Tomás Castro	13.03.1999	1		
Nicolás Leandro Vélez (ARG)	04.07.1990		(3)	
Forwards:	**DOB**	**M**	**(s)**	**G**
Charles-Andreas Brym (CAN)	08.08.1998		(1)	
Zander Mateo Cassierra Cabezas (COL)	13.04.1997	20	(9)	4
Dieguinho (BRA)	07.06.1992	1	(5)	
Edi Semedo	01.06.1999	1	(9)	
Imad Faraj (FRA)	11.02.1999		(3)	
Alhassane Keita (GUI)	16.04.1992	2	(8)	
Kikas	17.09.1998	6	(6)	1
Licá	08.09.1988	32	(1)	7
Marco Matias	10.05.1989	11	(16)	1
Robinho	31.07.1997	7	(6)	
Salo	18.02.1998		(2)	
Varela	02.02.1985	18	(2)	3

Sport Lisboa e Benfica

Founded:	28.02.1904	
Stadium:	Estádio da Luz, Lisboa (64,642)	
Trainer:	Bruno Miguel Silva do Nascimento	12.05.1976
[30.06.2020]	Nélson Alexandre da Silva Veríssimo	17.04.1977

Goalkeepers:	DOB	M	(s)	G
Mile Svilar (BEL)	27.08.1999	1		
Odisseas Vlachodimos (GRE)	26.04.1994	33		
Defenders:	**DOB**	**M**	**(s)**	**G**
Alejandro "Álex" Grimaldo García (ESP)	20.09.1995	26		
André Almeida	10.09.1990	23		4
Ferro	26.03.1997	25	(1)	1
Jardel (BRA)	29.03.1986	10		
Nuno Tavares	26.01.2000	10	(1)	1
Rúben Dias	14.05.1997	33		2
Tomás Tavares	07.03.2001	9	(3)	
Midfielders:	**DOB**	**M**	**(s)**	**G**
Chiquinho	19.07.1995	17	(8)	2
Ljubomir Fejsa (SRB)	14.08.1988	3		
Florentino Luís	19.08.1999	8	(2)	
Gabriel (BRA)	18.09.1993	19	(3)	2
Gedson Fernandes	09.01.1999	2	(5)	
Gonçalo Ramos	20.06.2001		(1)	2
Andreas Samaris (GRE)	13.06.1989	8	(8)	
Adel Taarabt (MAR)	24.05.1989	19	(5)	1
Julian Weigl (GER)	08.09.1995	17	(1)	1
Andrija Živković (SRB)	11.07.1996		(3)	
Forwards:	**DOB**	**M**	**(s)**	**G**
Caio (BRA)	19.04.1994		(4)	1
Carlos Vinícius (BRA)	22.03.1995	19	(13)	18
Franco Emanuel Cervi (ARG)	26.05.1994	19	(4)	2
Dyego Sousa	14.09.1989	1	(10)	
Jota	30.03.1999	1	(18)	
Pizzi	06.10.1989	33	(1)	18
Rafa Silva	17.05.1993	18	(7)	7
Raúl de Tomás Gómez (ESP)	17.10.1994	6	(1)	
Haris Seferović (SUI)	22.02.1992	14	(16)	5

Boavista Futebol Clube Porto

Founded:	01.08.1903		
Stadium:	Estádio do Bessa, Porto (27,363)		
Trainer:	José Carlos Fernandes „Lito" Vidigal (ANG)	11.07.1969	
[18.12.2019]	Daniel António Lopes Ramos	25.12.1970	

Goalkeepers:	DOB	M	(s)	G
Helton Leite (BRA)	02.11.1990	21		
Rafael Bracalli (BRA)	05.05.1981	13		
Defenders:	**DOB**	**M**	**(s)**	**G**
Carraça	01.03.1993	28	(2)	2
Gustavo Alfonso Dulanto Sanguinetti (PER)	05.09.1995	9	(1)	2
Edu Machado	26.04.1990	1		
Fabiano (BRA)	18.11.1991	26	(1)	
Lucas (BRA)	05.11.1990	8	(4)	2
Marlon (BRA)	20.05.1997	23	(4)	2
Neris (BRA)	17.06.1992	24		1
Ricardo Costa	16.05.1981	30	(1)	1
Midfielders:	**DOB**	**M**	**(s)**	**G**
Yaw Ackah (GHA)	01.06.1990	21	(3)	
Fernando David Cardozo Paniagua (PAR)	08.02.2001	4	(6)	
Idrissa Mandiang (SEN)	27.12.1984	3	(4)	

	DOB	M	(s)	G
Nwankwo Obiora (NGA)	12.07.1991	18	(5)	
Paulinho	08.01.1997	20	(4)	
Rafael Costa (BRA)	19.01.1991	16		2
Reisinho	09.04.1999	2	(4)	
Tomás Reimão	14.07.1998		(1)	
Forwards:	**DOB**	**M**	**(s)**	**G**
Alberto Bueno Calvo (ESP)	20.03.1988	14	(5)	3
Cassiano (BRA)	16.06.1989	13	(14)	2
Gustavo Sauer (BRA)	30.04.1993	23	(5)	1
Heriberto Tavares	19.02.1997	17	(11)	4
Luís Santos	20.01.2000		(3)	
Mateus Galiano da Costa (ANG)	19.06.1984	11	(16)	1
Yusupha Njie (GAM)	03.01.1994	12	(13)	1
Nikola Stojiljković (SRB)	17.08.1992	17	(7)	2
Samuel Pedro	24.04.2001		(1)	

Sporting Clube de Braga

Founded:	19.01.1921		
Stadium:	Estádio Municipal de Braga, Braga (30,287)		
Trainer:	Ricardo Manuel da Silva Sá Pinto	10.10.1972	
[23.12.2019]	Rúben Filipe Marques Amorim	27.01.1985	
[05.03.2020]	Custódio Miguel Dias dc Castro	24.05.1983	
[01.07.2020]	Artur Jorge Araújo Amorim	01.01.1972	

Goalkeepers:	DOB	M	(s)	G
Eduardo	19.09.1982	4		
Matheus Magalhães (BRA)	19.07.1992	29		
Tiago Sá	11.01.1995	1		
Defenders:	**DOB**	**M**	**(s)**	**G**
Bruno Viana (BRA)	05.02.1995	29		
Bruno Wilson	27.12.1996	3	(3)	1
Caju (BRA)	17.07.1995	1		
David Carmo	19.07.1999	16	(2)	
Fabiano (BRA)	14.03.2000		(2)	
Lucas Ferrugem (BRA)	23.01.1997	2		
Nuno Sequeira	19.08.1990	24	(1)	
Pablo Santos (BRA)	18.03.1992	9	(1)	
Pedro Amador	18.12.1998	7	(2)	
Raul Silva (BRA)	04.11.1989	8	(3)	1
Rolando	31.08.1985	1	(2)	
Vítor Tormena (BRA)	04.01.1996	4		
Wallace (BRA)	14.10.1994	8		
Midfielders:	**DOB**	**M**	**(s)**	**G**
Uche Henry Agbo (NGA)	04.12.1995		(1)	

	DOB	M	(s)	G
André Horta	07.11.1996	21	(4)	
Bruno Xadas	02.12.1997		(1)	
Claudemir (BRA)	27.03.1988	4	(1)	
Fransérgio (BRA)	18.10.1990	23	(3)	4
João Novais	10.07.1993	11	(11)	
João Palhinha	09.07.1995	24	(3)	2
Ricardo Esgaio	16.05.1993	28	(2)	1
Samú	27.11.2000		(1)	
Forwards:	**DOB**	**M**	**(s)**	**G**
Ahmed Hassan Mahgoub Abdelmoneim (EGY)	05.03.1993	4	(2)	1
Abel Ruiz Ortega (ESP)	28.01.2000		(6)	1
Diogo Viana	22.02.1990	6		
Galeno (BRA)	22.10.1997	16	(11)	6
Leandro Sanca	04.01.2000		(2)	
Murilo (BRA)	31.10.1994	4	(3)	
Paulinho	09.11.1992	27	(2)	17
Ricardo Horta	15.09.1994	31	(2)	12
Rui Fonte	23.04.1990	6	(19)	4
Trincão	29.12.1999	17	(10)	8
Wilson Eduardo (ANG)	08.07.1990	6	(12)	3

Futebol Clube de Famalicão

Founded:	21.08.1931	
Stadium:	Estádio Municipal 22 de Junho, Vila Nova de Famalicão (5,307)	
Trainer:	João Pedro Ramos Borges de Sousa (ANG)	04.08.1971

Goalkeepers:	DOB	M	(s)	G
Rafael Defendi (BRA)	22.12.1983	18		
Vaná (BRA)	25.04.1991	16	(1)	
Defenders:	**DOB**	**M**	**(s)**	**G**
Alejandro "Álex" Centelles Plaza (ESP)	30.08.1999	19	(8)	
Ibrahim Cissé (CIV)	11.01.1999	1		
Racine Coly (SEN)	08.12.1995	10	(4)	
Ivo Pinto	07.01.1990	14	(1)	
Lionn	29.01.1989	11		
Patrick Willian (BRA)	03.06.1997	16	(5)	1
Patricio Nehuén Pérez (ARG)	24.06.2000	23		1
Thibang Sindile Theophilus Phete (RSA)	04.04.1994		(1)	
Riccieli (BRA)	17.09.1998	17	(8)	1
Roderick Miranda	30.03.1991	22	(2)	2
Joshua Lewis Tymon (ENG)	22.05.1999	4	(1)	

Midfielders:	DOB	M	(s)	G
Guga	18.07.1997	10	(16)	2
Gustavo Enrique (BRA)	30.03.2000	27	(3)	
Lawrence Ofori (GHA)	28.06.1998	1	(2)	
Pedro Gonçalves	28.06.1998	32	(1)	5
Uroš Račić (SRB)	17.03.1998	26	(7)	3
Forwards:	**DOB**	**M**	**(s)**	**G**
Anderson Silva (BRA)	21.11.1997	6	(25)	7
Rubén del Campo (SUI)	22.02.2000	1		
Diogo Gonçalves	06.02.1997	22	(5)	5
Fábio Martins	24.07.1993	29		12
Rúben Lameiras	22.12.1994	18	(4)	2
Nicolás Javier Schiappacasse Oliva (URU)	12.01.1999		(4)	
Antonio Martínez López „Toni Martínez" (ESP)	30.06.1997	27	(5)	10
Walterson (BRA)	28.12.1994	4	(13)	

Gil Vicente Futebol Clube Barcelos

Founded: 1924
Stadium: Estádio Cidade de Barcelos, Barcelos (12,504)
Trainer: Vítor Manuel Oliveira   17.11.1953

Goalkeepers:	DOB	M	(s)	G
Dénis (BRA)	14.04.1987	34		
Defenders:	**DOB**	**M**	**(s)**	**G**
Alex Pinto	08.07.1998	13		
Arthur Henrique (BRA)	17.05.1994	14	(4)	
Edwin Banguera (COL)	12.08.1996	7	(2)	
Fernando Fonseca	14.03.1997	19	(1)	
Henrique Gomes	30.11.1995	21		1
Kellyton (BRA)	08.03.1995	1		
Nogueira (BRA)	27.03.1995	22		
Rodrigão (BRA)	11.09.1995	17		2
Rúben Fernandes	06.05.1986	31		1
Midfielders:	**DOB**	**M**	**(s)**	**G**
Yves Baraye (SEN)	22.06.1992	20	(6)	3
Claude Gonçalves	09.04.1994	22	(2)	1
João Afonso (BRA)	09.02.1995	16	(11)	
Bozhidar Kraev (BUL)	23.06.1997	28	(4)	8
Leonardo Silva (BRA)	27.09.1995		(3)	
Rúben Ribeiro	01.08.1987	11	(2)	4
Samuel Lino (BRA)	23.12.1999	5	(15)	2
Soares (BRA)	30.12.1988	32	(1)	
Juan Felipe Villa Ruiz (COL)	10.10.1999		(1)	
Vítor Carvalho (BRA)	27.05.1997		(10)	2
Forwards:	**DOB**	**M**	**(s)**	**G**
Romário Baldé (GNB)	25.12.1996		(7)	
Erick (BRA)	10.12.1997	3	(5)	
Hugo Vieira	25.07.1988	3	(8)	1
Ahmed Isaiah (NGA)	10.10.1995		(5)	
Lourency (BRA)	02.01.1996	21	(10)	4
Zakaria Naidji (ALG)	19.01.1995	5	(15)	1
Sandro Lima (BRA)	28.10.1990	29	(3)	10

Club Sport Marítimo Funchal

Founded: 20.09.1910
Stadium: Estádio do Marítimo, Funchal (10,566)
Trainer: Nuno Miguel Manta Ribeiro dos Santos   25.07.1978
[14.11.2019] José Manuel Martins Teixeira Gomes   28.08.1970

Goalkeepers:	DOB	M	(s)	G
Amir Abedzadeh (IRN)	26.04.1993	25		
Charles (BRA)	04.02.1994	9		
Defenders:	**DOB**	**M**	**(s)**	**G**
Bebeto (BRA)	01.01.1990	14	(1)	
Fábio China	07.07.1992	14		
Douglas Grolli (BRA)	05.10.1989	5	(1)	
Dejan Kerkez (SRB)	20.01.1996	15	(1)	
Nanu	17.05.1994	32	(1)	2
René (BRA)	21.04.1992	30	(1)	1
Rúben	17.02.1990	19		1
Zainadine Abdula Mulungo Chavango Júnior (MOZ)	24.06.1988	30		2
Midfielders:	**DOB**	**M**	**(s)**	**G**
André Teles	06.04.1997		(1)	
Franck Bambock (FRA)	07.04.1995	22	(5)	2
Bruno Xadas	02.12.1997	9	(3)	1
Jorge Iván Correa (ARG)	04.05.1993	20	(6)	3
Jhon Cley (BRA)	09.03.1994	4	(6)	1
Diego Fernando Moreno Quintero (COL)	27.02.1996	8	(1)	
Pedro Pelágio	21.04.2000	13	(3)	
Josip Vuković (CRO)	02.05.1992	17	(4)	
Forwards:	**DOB**	**M**	**(s)**	**G**
André Mesquita	10.10.1997		(1)	
Leandro Iván Barrera (ARG)	28.02.1991		(3)	
Edgar Costa	14.04.1987	17	(10)	
Erivaldo Jorge Paulo Ferreira (ANG)	08.02.1994	3	(13)	1
Getterson (BRA)	16.05.1991	10	(17)	3
Jefferson (BRA)	13.03.2000		(2)	
Daizen Maeda (JPN)	20.10.1997	18	(5)	3
Marcelinho (BRA)	17.07.1996	7	(7)	1
Felicio Mendes Joao Milson (ANG)	12.10.1999	3	(3)	
Luciano Nequecaur (ARG)	19.07.1992	3	(4)	
Rodrigo Pinho (BRA)	30.05.1991	18	(9)	9
Diederrick Joel Tagueu Tadjo (CMR)	06.12.1993	9	(7)	2

Moreirense Futebol Clube Moreira de Cónegos

Founded: 01.11.1938
Stadium: Parque de Jogos "Comendador Joaquim de Almeida Freitas", Moreira de Cónegos (6,152)
Trainer: Vítor Fernando de Carvalho Campelos   11.05.1975
[18.12.2019] José Ricardo Soares Ribeiro   11.11.1974

Goalkeepers:	DOB	M	(s)	G
Mateus Pasinato (BRA)	28.06.1992	33		
Pedro Trigueira	04.01.1988	1		
Defenders:	**DOB**	**M**	**(s)**	**G**
Abdu Conté	24.03.1998	22	(1)	
Bruno Silva (BRA)	14.09.1992	1		
Anthony D'Alberto (BEL)	13.10.1994	10	(3)	
Djavan (BRA)	31.12.1987	8	(2)	
Rafik Halliche (ALG)	02.09.1986	8	(1)	
Iago Santos (BRA)	22.05.1992	25		1
João Aurélio	17.08.1988	27	(2)	2
Sori Mané	03.04.1996	10	(4)	
Lazar Rosić (SRB)	29.06.1993	18		2
Steven Vitória (CAN)	11.01.1987	16	(3)	5
Midfielders:	**DOB**	**M**	**(s)**	**G**
Alex Soares	01.03.1992	23	(9)	
Ibrahima Camará (GUI)	25.01.1999	2	(6)	
Fábio Pacheco	26.05.1988	24	(1)	1
Filipe Soares	20.05.1999	31	(2)	4
Luiz Henrique (BRA)	19.04.1997		(4)	
Nuno Santos	02.03.1999	9	(5)	1
Pedro Nuno	13.01.1995	15	(13)	2
Forwards:	**DOB**	**M**	**(s)**	**G**
Bilel Aouacheria (FRA)	02.04.1994	21	(8)	1
Fábio Abreu	29.01.1993	27	(7)	13
Gabrielzinho (BRA)	29.09.1996	13	(2)	2
Luís Machado	04.11.1992	10	(11)	1
Nenê (BRA)	28.07.1983	7	(19)	4
Patricio Julián Rodriguez (ARG)	04.05.1990		(1)	
Luther Wesley Singh (RSA)	05.08.1997	13	(8)	3
César David Texeira Torres (URU)	27.02.1991		(2)	

Futebol Clube Paços de Ferreira

Founded: 05.04.1950
Stadium: Estádio Capital do Móvel, Paços de Ferreira (9,076)
Trainer: Filipe André Paula da Rocha „Filó" 19.05.1972
[02.09.2019] Pedro Miguel Marques da Costa Filipe "Pêpa" 14.12.1980

Goalkeepers:	DOB	M	(s)	G
José Oliveira	06.04.2002		(1)	
Marco Sousa	29.01.1995	1		
Ricardo Ribeiro	27.01.1990	31		
Simão Bertelli (BRA)	02.07.1993	2		
Defenders:	**DOB**	**M**	**(s)**	**G**
André Micael	04.02.1989	6	(1)	
Bruno Santos (BRA)	07.02.1993	19	(3)	3
Bruno Teles (BRA)	01.05.1986	17		
Jorge Silva	22.03.1996	15	(1)	
Maracás (BRA)	27.04.1994	25	(1)	2
Marcelo (BRA)	27.07.1989	14	(1)	
Marco Baixinho	11.07.1989	20	(5)	3
Oleg Reabciuk (MDA)	16.01.1998	20	(6)	
Midfielders:	**DOB**	**M**	**(s)**	**G**
Stephen Antunes Eustáquio	21.12.1996	14	(2)	
Bernardo	04.12.1997	1	(4)	
Mohamed Diaby (FRA)	03.09.1996	19	(8)	2
Luíz Carlos (BRA)	05.02.1985	25	(3)	
Matchoi Djaló	10.04.2003	1	(2)	1
Pedrinho	20.12.1992	33		2
Rafael Gava (BRA)	20.05.1993	1	(1)	
Vasco Rocha	29.01.1989	5	(5)	
Forwards:	**DOB**	**M**	**(s)**	**G**
Adriano	07.04.1993	11	(5)	1
Renat Dadashov (GER)	17.05.1999	2	(5)	
Denilson (BRA)	18.07.1995	5	(8)	3
Diogo Almeida	08.09.2000	1	(6)	
Douglas Tanque (BRA)	27.10.1993	23	(6)	11
Hélder Ferreira	05.04.1997	27	(5)	3
João Amaral	07.09.1991	13	(6)	1
Murilo Freitas (BRA)	12.05.1996	12	(6)	
Uilton Silva (BRA)	25.07.1992	5	(21)	2
Welthon (BRA)	21.06.1992	6	(1)	
Yago César (BRA)	26.05.1997		(3)	

Portimonense Sporting Clube Portimão

Founded: 14.08.1914
Stadium: Estádio Municipal, Portimão (5,870)
Trainer: António José dos Santos Folha 21.05.1971
[20.01.2020] Bruno Alexandre Carvalho Lopes 11.04.1984
[10.02.2020] Paulo Sérgio Bento Brito 19.02.1968

Goalkeepers:	DOB	M	(s)	G
Shuichi Gonda (JPN)	03.03.1989	14		
Ricardo Ferreira	03.12.1989	20		
Defenders:	**DOB**	**M**	**(s)**	**G**
Koki Anzai (JPN)	31.05.1995	20	(3)	1
Éverson (BRA)	24.07.1997		(1)	
Emmanuel Hackman (GHA)	14.05.1995	19	(1)	1
Henrique Gelain (BRA)	05.01.1995	19	(4)	
Jadson Morais (BRA)	05.11.1991	28	(3)	3
Júnior Tavares (BRA)	07.08.1996	13	(2)	1
Lucas Possignolo (BRA)	11.05.1994	26		2
Rodrigo Freitas (BRA)	17.06.1998	6	(2)	
Willyan Rocha (BRA)	27.01.1995	16		3
Midfielders:	**DOB**	**M**	**(s)**	**G**
Anderson Oliveira (BRA)	16.07.1998		(9)	
Bruno Tabata (BRA)	30.03.1997	23	(3)	1
José Francisco Cevallos Enríquez (ECU)	18.01.1995	4	(3)	
Dener Clemente (BRA)	13.03.1992	22	(4)	6
Fernando Medeiros (BRA)	10.02.1996	7	(6)	
Lucas Fernandes (BRA)	20.09.1997	23	(4)	2
Luquinha (BRA)	03.10.2000	1		
Paulinho (BRA)	10.07.1994	1	(1)	
Pedro Sá	01.12.1993	24	(1)	
Rômulo (BRA)	10.01.1996	6	(10)	1
Forwards:	**DOB**	**M**	**(s)**	**G**
Mohanad Ali Kadhim Al Shammari (IRQ)	20.06.2000	1	(5)	
Aylton Boa Morte	23.09.1993	29	(4)	4
Beto	31.01.1998		(11)	
Bruno Costa	19.04.1997	8	(9)	
Fali Candé	24.01.1998	8	(1)	
Iury (BRA)	06.09.1995	5	(2)	1
Jackson Arley Martínez Valencia (COL)	03.10.1986	18	(6)	1
Marlos Moreno Durán (COL)	20.09.1996	5	(11)	
Takuma Nishimura (JPN)	22.10.1996	1	(1)	
Ricardo Vaz Tê	01.10.1986	7	(5)	2
José Gomes „Zé Gomes"	08.04.1999		(1)	

Futebol Clube do Porto

Founded: 28.09.1893
Stadium: Estádio do Dragão, Porto (50,034)
Trainer: Sérgio Paulo Merceiro Da Conceição 15.11.1974

Goalkeepers:	DOB	M	(s)	G
Diogo Costa	19.09.1999	3		
Agustín Federico Marchesín (ARG)	16.03.1988	31		
Mouhamed Mbaye (SEN)	13.10.1997		(1)	
Defenders:	**DOB**	**M**	**(s)**	**G**
Alex Telles (BRA)	15.12.1992	28	(3)	11
Diogo Leite	23.01.1999	4	(5)	
Iván Marcano Sierra (ESP)	23.06.1987	23		5
Chancel Mbemba (COD)	08.08.1994	21	(5)	2
Pepe	26.02.1983	24	(1)	1
Tomás Esteves	03.04.2002	2		
Wilson Manafã	23.07.1994	20	(7)	1
Midfielders:	**DOB**	**M**	**(s)**	**G**
Danilo	09.09.1991	23	(3)	2
Fábio Vieira	30.05.2000	2	(6)	2
Mamadou Loum (SEN)	30.12.1996	4	(2)	1
Shoya Nakajima (JPN)	23.08.1994	5	(11)	
Otávio (BRA)	09.02.1995	29	(2)	2
Romário	25.01.2000	4	(5)	
Sérgio Oliveira	02.06.1992	14	(6)	3
Andrés Mateus Uribe Villa (COL)	21.03.1991	22	(4)	1
Vitinha	13.02.2000		(8)	
Forwards:	**DOB**	**M**	**(s)**	**G**
Vincent Aboubakar (CMR)	22.01.1992	1	(4)	
Bruno Costa	19.04.1997	2		
Jesús Manuel Corona Ruiz (MEX)	06.01.1993	33		4
Luis Fernando Díaz Marulanda (COL)	13.01.1997	20	(9)	6
Fábio Silva	19.07.2002	1	(11)	1
João Mário	03.01.2000		(2)	
Moussa Marega (MLI)	14.04.1991	27	(2)	12
Tiquinho Soares (BRA)	17.01.1991	20	(10)	10
José Luís Mendes Andrade „Zé Luís" (CPV)	24.01.1991	11	(8)	7

Rio Ave Futebol Clube Vila do Conde

Founded: 10.05.1939
Stadium: Estádio dos Arcos, Vila do Conde (8,957)
Trainer: Carlos Augusto Soares da Costa Faria Carvalhal   04.12.1965

Goalkeepers:	DOB	M	(s)	G
Paweł Kieszek (POL)	16.04.1984	34		
Defenders:	**DOB**	**M**	**(s)**	**G**
Aderllan (BRA)	09.04.1989	30		
Toni Borevković (CRO)	18.06.1997	31	(1)	
Diogo	01.07.1991	18		
Junio Rocha (BRA)	27.02.1997	2	(5)	
Messias (BRA)	03.11.1994	2	(3)	
Nélson Monte	30.07.1995	19	(1)	
Pedro Amaral	25.08.1997	8	(5)	
Midfielders:	**DOB**	**M**	**(s)**	**G**
Almoatasembellah Ali (LBY)	06.04.1996	11	(1)	
Diego Lopes (BRA)	03.05.1994	29	(1)	6
Filipe Augusto (BRA)	12.08.1993	27	(1)	4
Nikola Jambor (CRO)	25.09.1995	1	(7)	
Joca	30.01.1996		(3)	
Matheus Reis (BRA)	18.02.1995	28	(2)	1
Rúben Gonçalves	23.12.1998	1		
Tarantini	07.10.1983	28	(3)	3
Vitó	18.09.1997	1	(1)	
Forwards:	**DOB**	**M**	**(s)**	**G**
Bruno Moreira	06.09.1987	13	(14)	3
Carlos Mané	11.03.1994	13	(18)	1
Gabrielzinho (BRA)	29.09.1996	2	(6)	
Gelson Dala (ANG)	13.07.1996	5	(9)	6
Leandro Silva (BRA)	16.01.1999		(3)	
Lucas Piazón (BRA)	20.01.1994	15	(4)	2
Nuno Santos	13.02.1995	29	(3)	2
Ronan (BRA)	22.04.1995	1	(11)	1
Schutte	21.05.1998		(1)	
Mehdi Taremi (IRN)	18.07.1992	26	(4)	18

Clube Desportivo Santa Clara Ponta Delgada

Founded: 31.01.1921
Stadium: Estádio de São Miguel, Ponta Delgada (10,000)
Trainer: João Alexandre Oliveira Nunes Henriques   31.10.1972

Goalkeepers:	DOB	M	(s)	G
André Ferreira	29.05.1996	3		
Marco Rocha	12.01.1987	31		
Rodolfo	13.10.1997		(1)	
Defenders:	**DOB**	**M**	**(s)**	**G**
Mamadú Youssuf Candé (GNB)	28.08.1991	15	(2)	
César (BRA)	28.12.1992	11	(3)	1
Fábio Cardoso	19.04.1994	30		2
João Afonso	28.05.1990	32	(1)	2
João Lucas	15.01.1996	4	(1)	
Patrick (BRA)	22.01.1991	12		
Rafael Ramos	09.01.1995	14	(2)	
Pierre Sagna (SEN)	21.08.1990	6	(1)	
Zaidu Sanusi (NGA)	13.06.1997	21	(3)	1
Midfielders:	**DOB**	**M**	**(s)**	**G**
Anderson Carvalho (BRA)	20.05.1990	14	(2)	1
Bruno Lamas (BRA)	13.04.1994	6	(5)	
Chico Ramos	10.04.1995	26	(3)	
Costinha	25.08.1992	14	(2)	
Lincoln (BRA)	07.11.1994	22	(8)	1
Lucas Marques (BRA)	24.05.1995	3		
Nené	10.06.1995	6	(12)	
Denis Omar Pineda Torres (SLV)	10.08.1995	1	(1)	
Osama Rashid (IRQ)	17.01.1992	23	(4)	2
Forwards:	**DOB**	**M**	**(s)**	**G**
Carlos (BRA)	15.08.1995	27	(7)	7
Crysan (BRA)	07.07.1996	2	(11)	3
Diogo Salomão	14.09.1988	1	(9)	
Malick Evouna (GAB)	28.11.1992		(1)	
Guilherme Schettine (BRA)	10.10.1995	6	(9)	3
Thiago Santana (BRA)	04.02.1993	27	(6)	6
Ukra	16.03.1988	7	(8)	1
Zé Manuel	23.10.1990	10	(16)	4

Sporting Clube de Portugal Lisboa

Founded: 01.07.1906
Stadium: Estádio "José Alvalade", Lisboa (50,049)
Trainer: Marcel Keizer (NED)   15.01.1969
[04.09.2019] Leonel Pontes da Encarnação   09.07.1972
[27.09.2019] Jorge Manuel Rebelo Fernandes „Silas"   01.09.1976

Goalkeepers:	DOB	M	(s)	G
Luís Maximiano	05.01.1999	23		
Renan Ribeiro (BRA)	23.03.1990	11		
Defenders:	**DOB**	**M**	**(s)**	**G**
Marcos Javier Acuña (ARG)	28.10.1991	23	(1)	2
Cristian Alexis Borja González (COL)	18.02.1993	15	(8)	1
Sebastián Coates Nion (URU)	07.10.1990	28	(1)	4
Eduardo Quaresma	02.03.2002	9		
Jérémy Mathieu (FRA)	29.10.1983	19		1
Neto	26.05.1988	11	(1)	
Nuno Mendes	19.06.2002	7	(2)	
Stefan Ristovski (MKD)	12.02.1992	19	(2)	
Valentin Rosier (FRA)	19.08.1996	8	(1)	
Thierry Correia	09.03.1999	4		
Tiago Ilori	26.02.1993	6	(2)	
Midfielders:	**DOB**	**M**	**(s)**	**G**
Rodrigo Andrés Battaglia (ARG)	12.07.1991	9	(6)	
Bruno Fernandes	08.09.1994	17		8
Chico Geraldes	18.04.1995	1	(7)	
Idrissa Doumbia (CIV)	14.04.1998	17	(5)	
Eduardo Henrique (BRA)	17.05.1995	8	(7)	
Matheus Nunes (BRA)	27.08.1998	9	(1)	
Miguel Luís	27.02.1999	2		
Rafael Camacho	22.05.2000	9	(10)	
Rodrigo Fernandes	23.03.2001	1	(1)	
Wendel (BRA)	28.08.1997	26	(2)	3
Forwards:	**DOB**	**M**	**(s)**	**G**
Yannick Bolasie Yala (FRA)	24.05.1989	12	(2)	1
Jovane Eduardo Borges Cabral (CPV)	14.06.1998	10	(6)	6
Abdoulay Diaby (MLI)	21.05.1991	1	(1)	
Bas Dost (NED)	31.05.1989		(1)	
Jesé Rodríguez Ruíz (ESP)	26.02.1993	6	(6)	1
Joelson Fernandes	28.02.2003		(4)	
Luiz Phellype (BRA)	27.09.1993	12	(4)	6
Pedro Mendes	01.08.1999		(6)	
Gonzalo Jordy Plata Jimeénez (ECU)	01.11.2000	12	(9)	2
Raphinha (BRA)	14.12.1996	4		2
Andraž Šporar (SVN)	27.02.1994	15	(1)	6
Tiago Tomás	16.06.2002	1	(4)	
Luciano Darío Vietto (ARG)	05.12.1993	19	(5)	4

Clube Desportivo de Tondela

Founded: 06.06.1933
Stadium: Estádio "João Cardoso", Tondela (5,000)
Trainer: José Ignacio „Natxo" González Saénz   29.07.1966

Goalkeepers:	DOB	M	(s)	G
Cláudio Ramos	16.11.1991	29		
Babacar Niasse (SEN)	20.12.1996	5		
Defenders:	**DOB**	**M**	**(s)**	**G**
Bruno Wilson	27.12.1996	15		2
Filipe Ferreira	27.09.1990	28	(1)	
João Vigário	20.11.1995		(1)	
Jota Gonçalves	17.06.2000		(1)	
Fahd Moufi (MAR)	05.05.1996	26		
Marko Petković (SRB)	03.09.1992	6	(1)	
Philipe Sampaio (BRA)	11.11.1994	20	(2)	2
Ricardo Alves	09.05.1991	12	(5)	1
Tiago Almeida	28.08.2001	2	(1)	
Yohan Tavares	02.03.1988	28	(1)	3
Midfielders:	**DOB**	**M**	**(s)**	**G**
Bruno Monteiro	05.10.1984		(1)	
João Pedro	03.04.1993	25	(7)	4
João Reis	24.06.1992	4	(4)	
João Lamine Jaquité (GNB)	22.02.1996	16	(5)	
Pedro Augusto (BRA)	03.03.1997	2	(5)	
José Luis García Vayá „Pepelu" (ESP)	11.08.1998	33		2
Pité	22.08.1994	11	(8)	1
Richard (BRA)	11.10.1999	17	(11)	2
Telmo Arcanjo	21.06.2001	1	(1)	
Forwards:	**DOB**	**M**	**(s)**	**G**
António Xavier	06.07.1992	16	(8)	1
Román Rubilio Castillo Álvarez (HON)	26.11.1991		(1)	
Denilson (BRA)	18.07.1995	10	(2)	3
Jhon Eduard Murillo Romaña (VEN)	04.06.1995	26	(4)	2
Ricardo Valente	03.04.1991	3	(8)	
Ronan (BRA)	22.04.1995	8	(4)	5
Rúben Fonseca	24.02.2000	3	(7)	
Tomislav Štrkalj (CRO)	02.08.1996	10	(9)	
Jonathan Josué Rubio Toro (HON)	21.10.1996	18	(14)	1

Vitória Sport Clube de Guimarães

Founded: 22.09.1922
Stadium: Estádio "D. Afonso Henriques", Guimarães (30,007)
Trainer: Ivo Ricardo Abreu Vieira   10.01.1976

Goalkeepers:	DOB	M	(s)	G
Douglas Jesus (BRA)	09.03.1983	29		
Miguel Silva	07.04.1995	5		
Defenders:	**DOB**	**M**	**(s)**	**G**
Valeriy Bondarenko (UKR)	03.02.1994	8		
Frederico Venâncio	04.02.1993	20		
Víctor Hugo García Hernández (VEN)	11.06.1994	10		
Florent Hanin (FRA)	04.02.1990	26	(2)	1
Pedro Henrique (BRA)	18.12.1992	20	(4)	
Rafa Soares	09.05.1995	8	(2)	
Falaye Sacko (MLI)	01.05.1995	23		
Easah Suliman (ENG)	26.01.1998	5	(1)	
Edmond Fayçal Tapsoba (BFA)	02.02.1999	16		4
Midfielders:	**DOB**	**M**	**(s)**	**G**
Elias Abouchabaka (GER)	31.03.2000		(1)	
Ndubusi Mikel Agu (NGA)	27.05.1993	14	(2)	1
Almoatasembellah Ali Mohamed Al Musrati (LBY)	06.04.1996	4	(1)	
Joseph Amoah (GHA)	26.06.1994	2	(2)	
André Almeida	30.05.2000	3	(5)	1
André André	26.08.1989	14	(2)	4
João Carlos Teixeira	18.01.1993	14	(7)	8
Lucas Evangelista (BRA)	06.05.1995	17	(2)	1
Pêpê	20.05.1997	22	(9)	3
Denis Poha (FRA)	28.05.1997	14	(6)	
Rochinha	03.05.1995	9	(12)	1
Forwards:	**DOB**	**M**	**(s)**	**G**
Alexandre Guedes	11.02.1994	1	(1)	1
André Pereira	05.05.1995	7	(2)	2
Bruno Duarte (BRA)	24.03.1996	18	(6)	8
Davidson (BRA)	05.03.1991	16	(10)	5
Marcus Edwards (ENG)	03.12.1998	23	(3)	7
Jefferson Anilson Silva Encada (GNB)	17.04.1998		(1)	
João Pedro	13.11.1996	1	(9)	2
Ola John (NED)	19.05.1992	13	(3)	
Léo Bonatini (BRA)	28.03.1994	10	(9)	3
Abou Ouattara (BFA)	26.12.1999	2	(8)	1

Vitória Futebol Clube de Setúbal

Founded: 20.11.1910
Stadium: Estádio do Bonfim, Setúbal (14,274)
Trainer: Sandro Miguel Laranjeira Mendes   04.02.1977
[28.10.2019]   Albert Meyong Zé (CMR)   19.10.1980
[11.11.2019]   Julio Velázquez Santiago (ESP)   05.10.1981
[02.07.2019]   Albert Meyong Zé (CMR)   19.10.1980
[06.07.2020]   José Carlos Fernandes „Lito Vidigal" (ANG)   11.07.1969

Goalkeepers:	DOB	M	(s)	G
Lucas Paes (BRA)	07.12.1997	1	(1)	
Giorgi Makaridze (GEO)	31.03.1990	32		
Milton Raphael (BRA)	11.05.1991	1		
Defenders:	**DOB**	**M**	**(s)**	**G**
André Sousa	26.02.1998	16	(2)	
Artur Jorge	14.08.1994	29	(1)	
Bruno Pires (BRA)	12.05.1992	18	(2)	3
João Meira	30.04.1987	6	(2)	
Jubal Júnior (BRA)	29.08.1993	20	(4)	2
Mano	09.04.1987	6	(1)	
Sílvio	28.09.1987	31		
Vasco Fernandes	12.11.1986	1		
Midfielders:	**DOB**	**M**	**(s)**	**G**
Carlinhos (BRA)	22.06.1994	28	(2)	4
Éber Bessa (BRA)	21.03.1992	25	(6)	2
Leandrinho (BRA)	25.09.1993	6	(9)	
Leandro Vilela (BRA)	29.06.1995	5	(6)	
Nuno Pinto	06.08.1986	8	(2)	
Nuno Valente	22.11.1991	13	(5)	
Rodrigo Mathiola (BRA)	14.08.1997	2	(6)	1
Semedo	11.01.1985	29		1
Tiago Castro	31.01.1996	1		
Cristóbal Montiel Rodríguez „Tòfol" (ESP)	11.04.2000	2	(4)	
Forwards:	**DOB**	**M**	**(s)**	**G**
Alex	27.08.1991	1	(3)	
Mirko Antonucci (ITA)	11.03.1999	1	(5)	1
Nabil Ghilas (ALG)	20.04.1990	10	(5)	2
Guedes	07.05.1987	13	(6)	4
Khalid Hachadi (MAR)	03.05.1998	9	(9)	1
Hildeberto	02.03.1996	17	(8)	3
Leonardo Chão	01.08.1999		(1)	
Brian Ezequiel Mansilla (ARG)	16.04.1997	22	(7)	
Kgaogelo Rathete Sekgota (RSA)	22.06.1997		(1)	
Zéquinha	07.01.1987	21	(9)	2

SECOND LEVEL
LigaPro 2019/2020

1.	CD Nacional Funchal (*Promoted*)	24	14	8	2	36	-	16	50
2.	SC Farense Faro (*Promoted*)	24	15	3	6	35	-	22	48
3.	CD Feirense Santa Maria da Feira	24	11	9	4	27	-	18	42
4.	CD Mafra	24	10	9	5	33	-	24	39
5.	GD Estoril Praia	24	12	3	9	35	-	26	39
6.	Varzim SC	24	10	7	7	32	-	31	37
7.	Associação Académica de Coimbra	24	10	5	9	34	-	26	35
8.	Académico de Viseu FC	24	9	7	8	21	-	24	34
9.	Leixões SC Porto	24	8	9	7	23	-	22	33
10.	Sporting da Covilhã	24	9	5	10	29	-	27	32
11.	UD Oliveirense	24	9	5	10	36	-	31	32
12.	GD Chaves	24	9	5	10	26	-	26	32
13.	FC do Porto "B"	24	7	8	9	35	-	36	29
14.	Sport Lisboa e Benfica "B"	24	7	7	10	31	-	35	28
15.	FC de Penafiel	24	6	10	8	23	-	24	28
16.	UD Vilafranquense	24	6	6	12	27	-	45	24
17.	CD Cova da Piedade	24	4	5	15	20	-	42	17
18.	Casa Pia Atlético Clube	24	2	5	17	19	-	47	11

Please note: the league was suspended on 12.03.2020 due to Covid-19 pandemic, being abandoned on 05.05.2020. No teams were relegated, as a result of punishing two clubs at first level (Vitória FC Setúbal and CD das Aves) with direct relegation to the third level.

NATIONAL TEAM

INTERNATIONAL MATCHES
(16.07.2019 – 15.07.2020)

07.09.2019	Beograd	Serbia - Portugal	2-4(0-1)	(ECQ)
10.09.2019	Vilnius	Lithuania - Portugal	1-5(1-1)	(ECQ)
11.10.2019	Lisboa	Portugal - Luxembourg	3-0(1-0)	(ECQ)
14.10.2019	Kyiv	Ukraine - Portugal	2-1(2-0)	(ECQ)
14.11.2019	Faro/Loulé	Portugal - Lithuania	6-0(2-0)	(ECQ)
17.11.2019	Lëtzebuerg	Luxembourg - Portugal	0-2(0-1)	(ECQ)

07.09.2019   **SERBIA - PORTUGAL**   **2-4(0-1)**   16th EC. Qualifiers
Stadion "Rajko Mitić", Beograd; Referee: Cüneyt Çakır (Turkey); Attendance: 39,839
POR: Rui Patrício, Nélson Semedo (65.João Cancelo), José Fonte, Rúben Dias, Raphaël Guerreiro, Danilo Pereira, William Carvalho, Gonçalo Guedes (70.João Félix), Bruno Fernandes (85.João Moutinho), Bernardo Silva, Cristiano Ronaldo (Cap). Trainer: Fernando Manuel Fernandes da Costa Santos.
Goals: William Carvalho (42), Gonçalo Guedes (58), Cristiano Ronaldo (80), Bernardo Silva (86).

10.09.2019   **LITHUANIA - PORTUGAL**   **1-5(1-1)**   16th EC. Qualifiers
LFF stadionas, Vilnius; Referee: Hendrikus Sebastian "Bas" Nijhuis (Netherlands); Attendance: 5,067
POR: Rui Patrício, José Fonte, João Cancelo, Rúben Dias, Raphaël Guerreiro, William Carvalho, Rúben Neves, Bruno Fernandes (56.Rafa Silva), Cristiano Ronaldo (Cap) (79.Gonçalo Guedes), João Félix, Bernardo Silva (89.Pizzi). Trainer: Fernando Manuel Fernandes da Costa Santos.
Goals: Cristiano Ronaldo (7 penalty, 62, 65, 76), William Carvalho (90+2).

11.10.2019   **PORTUGAL - LUXEMBOURG**   **3-0(1-0)**   16th EC. Qualifiers
Estádio "José Alvalade", Lisboa; Referee: Daniel Stefański (Poland); Attendance: 47,305
POR: Rui Patrício, Nélson Semedo, Pepe, Rúben Dias, Raphaël Guerreiro, Danilo Pereira, João Moutinho (89.Rúben Neves), Bruno Fernandes, Bernardo Silva (77.Gonçalo Guedes), Cristiano Ronaldo (Cap), João Félix (88.João Mário). Trainer: Fernando Manuel Fernandes da Costa Santos.
Goals: Bernardo Silva (16), Cristiano Ronaldo (65), Gonçalo Guedes (89).

14.10.2019   **UKRAINE - PORTUGAL**   **2-1(2-0)**   16th EC. Qualifiers
Olympiyskiy Stadium, Kyiv; Referee: Anthony Taylor (England); Attendance: 65,883
POR: Rui Patrício, Nélson Semedo, Pepe, Rúben Dias, Raphaël Guerreiro, Danilo Pereira, João Moutinho (56.Bruno Fernandes), João Mário (68.Bruma), Gonçalo Guedes (46.João Félix), Bernardo Silva, Cristiano Ronaldo (Cap). Trainer: Fernando Manuel Fernandes da Costa Santos.
Goal: Cristiano Ronaldo (72 penalty).

14.11.2019   **PORTUGAL - LITHUANIA**   **6-0(2-0)**   16th EC. Qualifiers
Estádio Algarve, Faro/Loulé; Referee: Ruddy Buquet (France); Attendance: 18,534
POR: Rui Patrício, José Fonte, Rúben Dias, Mário Rui, Ricardo Pereira, Rúben Neves, Pizzi, Bruno Fernandes (72.João Moutinho), Bernardo Silva (66.Bruma), Cristiano Ronaldo (Cap) (83.Diogo Jota), Gonçalo Paciência. Trainer: Fernando Manuel Fernandes da Costa Santos.
Goals: Cristiano Ronaldo (7 penalty, 22), Pizzi (52), Gonçalo Paciência (56), Bernardo Silva (63), Cristiano Ronaldo (65).

17.11.2019   **LUXEMBOURG - PORTUGAL**   **0-2(0-1)**   16th EC. Qualifiers
Stade "Josy Barthel", Lëtzebuerg; Referee: Jesús Gil Manzano (Spain); Attendance: 8,000
POR: Rui Patrício, José Fonte, Rúben Dias, Raphaël Guerreiro, Ricardo Pereira, Pizzi (62.João Moutinho), Danilo Pereira, Bruno Fernandes (90.Rúben Neves), Cristiano Ronaldo (Cap), Bernardo Silva, André Silva (71.Diogo Jota). Trainer: Fernando Manuel Fernandes da Costa Santos.
Goals: Bruno Fernandes (39), Cristiano Ronaldo (86).

NATIONAL TEAM PLAYERS
(16.07.2019 – 15.07.2020)

Name	DOB	Caps	Goals	2019/2020:	Club
Goalkeepers					
RUI Pedro dos Santos PATRÍCIO	15.02.1988	**87**	**0**	2019:	*Wolverhampton Wanderers FC (ENG)*
Defenders					
JOÃO Pedro Cavaco CANCELO	27.05.1994	**16**	**3**	2019:	*Manchester City FC (ENG)*
JOSÉ Miguel da Rocha FONTE	22.12.1983	**42**	**0**	2019:	*Lille OSC (FRA)*
MÁRIO RUI Silva Duarte	27.05.1991	**9**	**0**	2019:	*SSC Napoli (ITA)*
NÉLSON Cabral SEMEDO "Nelsinho"	16.11.1993	**13**	**0**	2019:	*FC Barcelona (ESP)*
Képler Laveran Lima Ferreira "PEPE"	26.02.1983	**108**	**7**	2019:	*FC do Porto*
RAPHAËL Adelino José GUERREIRO	22.12.1993	**39**	**2**	2019:	*BV Borussia Dortmund (GER)*
RICARDO Domingos Barbosa PEREIRA	06.10.1993	**7**	**0**	2019:	*Leicester City FC (ENG)*
RÚBEN Santos Gato Alves DIAS	14.05.1997	**17**	**0**	2019:	*Sport Lisboa e Benfica*
Midfielders					
BRUNO Miguel Borges FERNANDES	08.09.1994	**19**	**2**	2019:	*Sporting Clube de Portugal Lisboa*
DANILO Luís Hélio PEREIRA	09.09.1991	**37**	**2**	2019:	*FC do Porto*
JOÃO MÁRIO Naval da Costa Eduardo	19.01.1993	**45**	**2**	2019:	*FK Lokomotiv Moskva (RUS)*
JOÃO Filipe Iria Santos MOUTINHO	08.09.1986	**121**	**7**	2019:	*Wolverhampton Wanderers FC (ENG)*
Luís Miguel Afonso Fernandes "PIZZI"	06.10.1989	**17**	**3**	2019:	*Sport Lisboa e Benfica*
Rafael Alexandre "RAFA" Fernandes Ferreira da SILVA	17.05.1993	**17**	**0**	2019:	*Sport Lisboa e Benfica*
RÚBEN Diogo da Silva NEVES	13.03.1997	**16**	**0**	2019:	*Wolverhampton Wanderers FC (ENG)*
WILLIAM Silva de CARVALHO	07.04.1992	**59**	**2**	2019:	*Real Betis Balompié Sevilla (ESP)*
Forwards					
ANDRÉ Miguel Valente SILVA	06.11.1995	**34**	**15**	2019:	*Eintracht Frankfurt (GER)*
BERNARDO Mota Veiga de Carvalho e SILVA	10.08.1994	**43**	**6**	2019:	*Manchester City FC (ENG)*
Armindo Tué Na Bangna "BRUMA"	24.10.1994	**9**	**1**	2019:	*PSV Eindhoven (NED)*
CRISTIANO RONALDO dos Santos Aveiro	05.02.1985	**164**	**99**	2019:	*Juventus FC Torino (ITA)*
Diogo José Teixeira da Silva "DIOGO JOTA"	04.12.1996	**2**	**0**	2019:	*Wolverhampton Wanderers FC (ENG)*
GONÇALO Manuel Ganchinho GUEDES	29.11.1996	**21**	**6**	2019:	*Valencia CF (ESP)*
GONÇALO Mendes PACIÊNCIA	01.08.1994	**2**	**1**	2019:	*Eintracht Frankfurt (GER)*
JOÃO FÉLIX Sequeira	10.11.1999	**5**	**0**	2019:	*Club Atlético de Madrid (ESP)*
National team coach					
FERNANDO Manuel Fernandes da Costa SANTOS [from 23.09.2014]	10.10.1954	71 M; 44 W; 16 D; 11 L; 141-53			

REPUBLIC OF IRELAND

The Country:
Éire (Republic of Ireland)
Capital: Dublin
Surface: 70,273 km²
Inhabitants: 4,921,500 [2019]
Time: UTC

The FA:
Football Association of Ireland
National Sports Campus Abbotstown, Dublin 15
Tel: +353 1 8999 500
Founded: 1921
Member of FIFA since: 1923
Member of UEFA since: 1954
Website: www.fai.ie

NATIONAL TEAM RECORDS

RECORDS
First international match:	21.03.1926, Torino:	Italy – Republic of Ireland 3-0
Most international caps:	Robert David Keane	- 146 caps (1998-2016)
Most international goals:	Robert David Keane	- 68 goals / 146 caps (1998-2016)

UEFA EUROPEAN CHAMPIONSHIP		FIFA WORLD CUP		OLYMPIC TOURNAMENTS	
1960	Qualifiers	1930	Did not enter	1908	-
1964	Qualifiers	1934	Qualifiers	1912	-
1968	Qualifiers	1938	Qualifiers	1920	-
1972	Qualifiers	1950	Qualifiers	1924	Quarter-Finals
1976	Qualifiers	1954	Qualifiers	1928	-
1980	Qualifiers	1958	Qualifiers	1936	-
1984	Qualifiers	1962	Qualifiers	1948	Preliminary Round
1988	Final Tournament (Group Stage)	1966	Qualifiers	1952	Did not enter
1992	Qualifiers	1970	Qualifiers	1956	Did not enter
1996	Qualifiers	1974	Qualifiers	1960	Qualifiers
2000	Qualifiers	1978	Qualifiers	1964	Did not enter
2004	Qualifiers	1982	Qualifiers	1968	Did not enter
2008	Qualifiers	1986	Qualifiers	1972	Qualifiers
2012	Final Tournament (Group Stage)	1990	Final Tournament (Quarter-Finals)	1976	Qualifiers
2016	Final Tournament (2nd Round of 16)	1994	Final Tournament (2nd Round of 16)	1980	Qualifiers
2020	*To be determined*	1998	Qualifiers	1984	Did not enter
		2002	Final Tournament (2nd Round of 16)	1988	Qualifiers
		2006	Qualifiers	1992	Qualifiers
		2010	Qualifiers	1996	Qualifiers
		2014	Qualifiers	2000	Qualifiers
		2018	Qualifiers	2004	Qualifiers
				2008	Qualifiers
				2012	Qualifiers
				2016	Qualifiers

UEFA NATIONS LEAGUE
2018/2019 – League B

FIFA CONFEDERATIONS CUP 1992-2017
None

IRISH CLUB HONOURS IN EUROPEAN CLUB COMPETITIONS:

European Champion Clubs.Cup (1956-1992) / UEFA Champions League (1993-2020)
None
Fairs Cup (1858-1971) / UEFA Cup (1972-2009) / UEFA Europa League (2010-2020)
None
UEFA Super Cup (1972-2019)
None
European Cup Winners.Cup 1961-1999*
None

defunct competition

NATIONAL COMPETITIONS
TABLE OF HONOURS

	CHAMPIONS	CUP WINNERS	BEST GOALSCORERS	
1921/1922	St. James' Gate	St. James' Gate FC Dublin	Jack Kelly (St. James' Gate FC Dublin)	11
1922/1923	Shamrock Rovers FC Dublin	Alton United	Bob Fullam (Shamrock Rovers FC Dublin)	27
1923/1924	Bohemian FC Dublin	Athlone Town FC	Dave Roberts (Bohemian FC Dublin)	20
1924/1925	Shamrock Rovers FC Dublin	Shamrock Rovers FC Dublin	Billy Farrell (Shamrock Rovers FC Dublin)	25
1925/1926	Shelbourne FC Dublin	Fordsons FC Cork	Billy Farrell (Shamrock Rovers FC Dublin)	24
1926/1927	Shamrock Rovers FC Dublin	Drumcondra	David Byrne (Shamrock Rovers FC Dublin) John McMillan (Shelbourne FC Dublin)	17
1927/1928	Bohemian FC Dublin	Bohemian FC Dublin	Charlie Heinemann (Fordsons FC Cork)	24
1928/1929	Shelbourne FC Dublin	Shamrock Rovers FC Dublin	Eddie Carroll (Dundalk FC)	17
1929/1930	Bohemian FC Dublin	Shamrock Rovers FC Dublin	Johnny Ledwidge (Shelbourne FC Dublin)	16
1930/1931	Shelbourne FC Dublin	Shamrock Rovers FC Dublin	Alec Hair (Shelbourne FC Dublin)	29
1931/1932	Shamrock Rovers FC Dublin	Shamrock Rovers FC Dublin	Pearson Ferguson (Cork FC) Jack Forster (Waterford FC)	21
1932/1933	Dundalk FC	Shamrock Rovers FC Dublin	George Ebbs (St. James' Gate FC Dublin)	20
1933/1934	Bohemian FC Dublin	Cork FC	Alf Rigby (St. James' Gate FC Dublin)	13
1934/1935	Dolphin	Bohemian FC Dublin	Alf Rigby (St. James' Gate FC Dublin)	17
1935/1936	Bohemian FC Dublin	Shamrock Rovers FC Dublin	Jimmy Turnbull (Cork FC)	37
1936/1937	Sligo Rovers FC	Waterford FC	Bob Slater (Shelbourne FC Dublin, Waterford FC)	20
1937/1938	Shamrock Rovers FC Dublin	St. James' Gate FC Dublin	Willie Byrne (St. James' Gate FC Dublin)	25
1938/1939	Shamrock Rovers FC Dublin	Shelbourne FC Dublin	Paddy Bradshaw (St. James' Gate FC Dublin)	22
1939/1940	St. James' Gate	Shamrock Rovers FC Dublin	Paddy Bradshaw (St. James' Gate FC Dublin)	29
1940/1941	Cork United FC	Cork United FC	Mick O'Flanagan (Bohemian FC Dublin)	19
1941/1942	Cork United FC	Dundalk FC	Tommy Byrne (Limerick FC)	20
1942/1943	Cork United FC	Drumcondra	Sean McCarthy (Cork United FC)	16
1943/1944	Shelbourne FC Dublin	Shamrock Rovers FC Dublin	Sean McCarthy (Cork United FC)	16
1944/1945	Cork United FC	Shamrock Rovers FC Dublin	Sean McCarthy (Cork United FC)	26
1945/1946	Cork United FC	Drumcondra FC Dublin	Paddy O'Leary (Cork United FC)	15
1946/1947	Shelbourne FC Dublin	Cork United FC	Paddy Coad (Shamrock Rovers FC Dublin) Alf Hanson (Shelbourne FC Dublin)	11
1947/1948	Drumcondra FC Dublin	Shamrock Rovers FC Dublin	Sean McCarthy (Cork United FC)	13
1948/1949	Drumcondra FC Dublin	Dundalk FC	Bernard Lester (Transport FC Dublin) Eugene Noonan (Waterford FC) Paddy O'Leary (Cork Athletic FC)	12
1949/1950	Cork Athletic FC	Transport FC Dublin	Dave McCulloch (Waterford FC)	19
1950/1951	Cork Athletic FC	Cork Athletic FC	Dessie Glynn (Drumcondra FC Dublin)	20
1951/1952	St. Patrick's Athletic FC Dublin	Dundalk FC	Shay Gibbons (St. Patrick's Athletic FC Dublin)	26
1952/1953	Shelbourne FC Dublin	Cork Athletic FC	Shay Gibbons (St. Patrick's Athletic FC Dublin)	22
1953/1954	Shamrock Rovers FC Dublin	Drumcondra FC Dublin	Danny Jordan (Bohemian FC Dublin)	14
1954/1955	St. Patrick's Athletic FC Dublin	Shamrock Rovers FC Dublin	Jimmy Gauld (Waterford FC)	30
1955/1956	St. Patrick's Athletic FC Dublin	Shamrock Rovers FC Dublin	Shay Gibbons (St. Patrick's Athletic FC Dublin)	21
1956/1957	Shamrock Rovers FC Dublin	Drumcondra FC Dublin	Tommy Hamilton (Shamrock Rovers FC Dublin) Donal Leahy (Evergreen United FC Cork)	15
1957/1958	Drumcondra FC Dublin	Dundalk FC	Donal Leahy (Evergreen United FC Cork)	16
1958/1959	Shamrock Rovers FC Dublin	St. Patrick's Athletic FC Dublin	Donal Leahy (Evergreen United FC Cork)	22
1959/1960	Limerick FC	Shelbourne FC Dublin	Austin Noonan (Cork Celtic FC)	27
1960/1961	Drumcondra FC Dublin	St. Patrick's Athletic FC Dublin	Dan McCaffrey (Drumcondra FC Dublin)	29
1961/1962	Shelbourne FC Dublin	Shamrock Rovers FC Dublin	Eddie Bailham (Shamrock Rovers FC Dublin)	21
1962/1963	Dundalk FC	Shelbourne FC Dublin	Mick Lynch (Waterford FC)	12
1963/1964	Shamrock Rovers FC Dublin	Shamrock Rovers FC Dublin	Eddie Bailham (Shamrock Rovers FC Dublin) Jimmy Hasty (Dundalk FC) Johnny Kingston (Cork Hibernians FC)	18
1964/1965	Drumcondra FC Dublin	Shamrock Rovers FC Dublin	Jackie Mooney (Shamrock Rovers FC Dublin)	16
1965/1966	Waterford FC	Shamrock Rovers FC Dublin	Mick Lynch (Waterford FC)	17
1966/1967	Dundalk FC	Shamrock Rovers FC Dublin	Johnny Brooks (Sligo Rovers FC) Danny Hale (Dundalk FC)	15
1967/1968	Waterford FC	Shamrock Rovers FC Dublin	Carl Davenport (Cork Celtic FC) Ben Hannigan (Dundalk FC)	15
1968/1969	Waterford FC	Shamrock Rovers FC Dublin	Mick Leech (Shamrock Rovers FC Dublin)	19
1969/1970	Waterford FC	Bohemian FC Dublin	Brendan Bradley (Finn Harps FC Ballybofey)	18
1970/1971	Cork Hibernians FC	Limerick FC	Brendan Bradley (Finn Harps FC Ballybofey)	20
1971/1972	Waterford FC	Cork Hibernians FC	Alfie Hale (Waterford FC) Tony Marsden (Cork Hibernians FC)	22
1972/1973	Waterford FC	Cork Hibernians FC	Alfie Hale (Waterford FC) Terry Harkin (Finn Harps FC Ballybofey)	20
1973/1974	Cork Celtic FC	Finn Harps FC Ballybofey	Terry Flanagan (Bohemian FC Dublin) Turlough O'Connor (Bohemian FC Dublin)	18
1974/1975	Bohemian FC Dublin	Home Farm FC Dublin	Brendan Bradley (Finn Harps FC Ballybofey)	21
1975/1976	Dundalk FC	Bohemian FC Dublin	Brendan Bradley (Finn Harps FC Ballybofey)	29
1976/1977	Sligo Rovers FC	Dundalk FC	Syd Wallace (Waterford FC)	16
1977/1978	Bohemian FC Dublin	Shamrock Rovers FC Dublin	Turlough O'Connor (Bohemian FC Dublin)	24
1978/1979	Dundalk FC	Dundalk FC	John Delamere (Sligo Rovers FC, Shelbourne FC Dublin)	17

1979/1980	Limerick United FC	Waterford FC	Alan Campbell (Shamrock Rovers FC Dublin)	22
1980/1981	Athlone Town FC	Dundalk FC	Eugene Davis (Athlone Town FC)	23
1981/1982	Dundalk FC	Limerick United FC	Michael O'Connor (Athlone Town FC)	22
1982/1983	Athlone Town FC	Sligo Rovers FC	Noel Larkin (Athlone Town FC)	18
1983/1984	Shamrock Rovers FC Dublin	UCD	Alan Campbell (Shamrock Rovers FC Dublin)	24
1984/1985	Shamrock Rovers FC Dublin	Shamrock Rovers FC Dublin	Thomas Gaynor (Limerick City FC) Michael O'Connor (Athlone Town FC)	17
1985/1986	Shamrock Rovers FC Dublin	Shamrock Rovers FC Dublin	Tommy Gaynor (Limerick City FC)	15
1986/1987	Shamrock Rovers FC Dublin	Shamrock Rovers FC Dublin	Michael Byrne (Shamrock Rovers FC Dublin)	12
1987/1988	Dundalk FC	Dundalk FC	Jonathan Speak (Derry City FC)	24
1988/1989	Derry City FC	Derry City FC	William Robert Hamilton (NIR, Limerick City FC)	21
1989/1990	St. Patrick's Athletic FC Dublin	Bray Wanderers FC	Mark Ennis (St. Patrick's Athletic FC Dublin)	19
1990/1991	Dundalk FC	Galway United FC	Peter Hanrahan (Dundalk FC)	18
1991/1992	Shelbourne FC Dublin	Bohemian FC Dublin	John Caulfield (Cork City FC)	16
1992/1993	Cork City FC	Shelbourne FC Dublin	Pat Morley (Cork City FC)	20
1993/1994	Shamrock Rovers FC Dublin	Sligo Rovers FC	Stephen Geoghegan (Shamrock Rovers FC Dublin)	23
1994/1995	Dundalk FC	Derry City FC	John Caulfield (Cork City FC)	16
1995/1996	St. Patrick's Athletic FC Dublin	Shelbourne FC Dublin	Stephen Geoghegan (Shelbourne FC Dublin)	19
1996/1997	Derry City FC	Shelbourne FC Dublin	Anthony Cousins (Shamrock Rovers FC Dublin) Stephen Geoghegan (Shelbourne FC Dublin)	16
1997/1998	St. Patrick's Athletic FC Dublin	Cork City FC	Stephen Geoghegan (Shelbourne FC Dublin)	17
1998/1999	St. Patrick's Athletic FC Dublin	Bray Wanderers FC	Trevor Molloy (St. Patrick's Athletic FC Dublin)	15
1999/2000	Shelbourne FC Dublin	Shelbourne FC Dublin	Patrick Morley (Cork City FC)	20
2000/2001	Bohemian FC Dublin	Bohemian FC Dublin	Glen Crowe (Bohemian FC Dublin)	25
2001/2002	Shelbourne FC Dublin	Dundalk FC	Glen Crowe (Bohemian FC Dublin)	21
2002/2003	Bohemian FC Dublin	Derry City FC (2000)	Glen Crowe (Bohemian FC Dublin)	18
2003	Shelbourne FC Dublin	Longford Town FC	Jason Byrne (Shelbourne FC Dublin)	21
2004	Shelbourne FC Dublin	Longford Town FC	Jason Byrne (Shelbourne FC Dublin)	25
2005	Cork City FC	Drogheda United FC	Jason Byrne (Shelbourne FC Dublin)	22
2006	Shelbourne FC Dublin	Derry City FC	Jason Byrne (Shelbourne FC Dublin)	15
2007	Drogheda United FC	Cork City FC	Dave Mooney (Longford Town FC)	19
2008	Bohemian FC Dublin	Bohemian FC Dublin	Dave Mooney (Cork City FC) Mark Quigley (St. Patrick's Athletic FC Dublin) Mark Farren (Derry City FC)	15
2009	Bohemian FC Dublin	Sporting Fingal	Gary Michael Nolan Twigg (SCO, Shamrock Rovers FC Dublin)	24
2010	Shamrock Rovers FC Dublin	Sligo Rovers FC	Gary Michael Nolan Twigg (SCO, Shamrock Rovers FC Dublin)	20
2011	Shamrock Rovers FC Dublin	Sligo Rovers FC	Eamon Zayed (LBY, Derry City FC)	22
2012	Sligo Rovers FC	Derry City FC	Gary Michael Nolan Twigg (SCO, Shamrock Rovers FC Dublin)	22
2013	St. Patrick's Athletic FC Dublin	Sligo Rovers FC	Rory Christopher Patterson (NIR, Derry City FC)	18
2014	Dundalk FC	St. Patrick's Athletic FC Dublin	Patrick James Hoban (Dundalk FC) Christopher Joseph Fagan (St. Patrick's Athletic FC Dublin)	20
2015	Dundalk FC	Dundalk FC	Richard Patrick Towell (Dundalk FC)	25
2016	Dundalk FC	Cork City FC	Seán Patrick Maguire (Cork City FC)	18
2017	Cork City FC	Cork City FC	Seán Patrick Maguire (Cork City FC)	20
2018	Dundalk FC	Dundalk FC	Patrick James Hoban (Dundalk FC)	29
2019	Dundalk FC	Shamrock Rovers FC	Joseph Ogedi Junior Chukwuemka Ogedi-Uzokwe (ENG, Derry City FC)	14

NATIONAL CHAMPIONSHIP
League of Ireland Premier Division 2019
(15.02.2019 – 25.10.2019)

Results

Round 1 [15.02.2019]
Bohemian FC - Finn Harps 1-0(1-0)
Derry City - UC Dublin 3-0(1-0)
Dundalk FC - Sligo Rovers 1-1(0-1)
St Patrick's Athletic - Cork City 1-0(1-0)
Waterford FC - Shamrock Rovers 1-2(1-0)

Round 2 [22.02.2019]
Cork City - Waterford FC 0-2(0-1)
Sligo Rovers - St Patrick's Athletic 0-1(0-0)
UC Dublin - Bohemian FC 0-2(0-2)
Finn Harps - Dundalk FC 1-1(1-0)
Shamrock Rovers - Derry City 2-0(1-0)

Round 3 [25.02.2019]
Bohemian FC - Shamrock Rovers 1-0(0-0)
Derry City - Waterford FC 3-2(1-0)
Dundalk FC - UC Dublin 2-1(0-1)
St Patrick's Athletic - Finn Harps 0-0
Sligo Rovers - Cork City 1-2(0-1)

Round 4 [01.03.2019]
Cork City - Derry City 0-0
UC Dublin - St Patrick's Athletic 1-1(0-1)
Waterford FC - Bohemian FC 0-0
Finn Harps - Sligo Rovers 1-2(0-1)
Shamrock Rovers - Dundalk FC 0-0

Round 5 [08-09.03.2019]
Bohemian FC - Derry City 1-1(0-0)
Dundalk FC - Waterford FC 4-0(2-0)
St Patrick's Athletic - Shamrock Rov. 0-1(0-1)
Finn Harps - Cork City 3-4(2-2)
Sligo Rovers - UC Dublin 1-0(1-0)

Round 6 [15.03.2019]
Cork City - Bohemian FC 2-0(1-0)
Derry City - Dundalk FC 0-2(0-1)
UC Dublin - Finn Harps 3-0(0-0)
Waterford FC - St Patrick's Athletic 2-0(1-0)
Shamrock Rovers - Sligo Rovers 3-0(1-0)

Round 7 [22.03.2019]
Finn Harps - Shamrock Rovers 0-1(0-0)
Dundalk FC - Bohemian FC 1-0(0-0) [15.04.]
St Patrick's Athl - Derry City 1-3(1-3) [15.04.]
UC Dublin - Cork City 2-1(0-1) [15.04.]
Sligo Rovers - Waterford FC 0-0 [15.04.]

Round 8 [29.03.2019]
Bohemian FC - St Patrick's Athletic 1-0(1-0)
Derry City - Sligo Rovers 2-0(0-0)
Dundalk FC - Cork City 1-0(1-0)
Waterford FC - Finn Harps 4-0(1-0)
Shamrock Rovers - UC Dublin 3-1(1-1)

Round 9 [05-06.04.2019]
Cork City - Shamrock Rovers 1-3(1-2)
St Patrick's Athletic - Dundalk FC 1-0(1-0)
UC Dublin - Waterford FC 4-1(2-1)
Finn Harps - Derry City 2-3(0-0)
Sligo Rovers - Bohemian FC 0-2(0-0)

Round 10 [12.04.2019]
Cork City - St Patrick's Athletic 1-1(1-0)
UC Dublin - Derry City 0-2(0-1)
Sligo Rovers - Dundalk FC 2-1(2-1)
Finn Harps - Bohemian FC 0-1(0-1)
Shamrock Rovers - Waterford FC 2-1(1-0)

Round 11 [19.04.2019]
Bohemian FC - UC Dublin 3-0(1-0)
Derry City - Shamrock Rovers 0-1(0-1)
Dundalk FC - Finn Harps 3-0(1-0)
St Patrick's Athletic - Sligo Rovers 2-1(2-0)
Waterford FC - Cork City 2-0(0-0)

Round 12 [22-23.04.2019]
UC Dublin - Dundalk FC 1-3(1-1)
Waterford FC - Derry City 2-2(0-1)
Cork City - Sligo Rovers 0-0
Finn Harps - St Patrick's Athletic 0-2(0-1)
Shamrock Rovers - Bohemian FC 0-1(0-1)

Round 13 [26.04.2019]
Bohemian FC - Waterford FC 0-0
Derry City - Cork City 2-0(1-0)
St Patrick's Athletic - UC Dublin 2-0(0-0)
Sligo Rovers - Finn Harps 1-1(0-1)
Dundalk FC - Shamrock Rovers 2-1(1-0)

Round 14 [29.04.2019]
Cork City - Finn Harps 1-1(0-0)
Derry City - Bohemian FC 0-2(0-0)
UC Dublin - Sligo Rovers 0-2(0-0)
Waterford FC - Dundalk FC 0-3(0-1)
Shamrock Rovers - St Patrick's Athl. 1-0(1-0)

Round 15 [03-04.05.2019]
Bohemian FC - Cork City 0-1(0-1)
Dundalk FC - Derry City 2-2(0-0)
St Patrick's Athletic - Waterford FC 0-3(0-0)
Finn Harps - UC Dublin 3-0(1-0)
Sligo Rovers - Shamrock Rovers 2-1(0-0)

Round 16 [10-11.05.2019]
Shamrock Rov. - Finn Harps 3-0(3-0) 04.03.]
Bohemian FC - Dundalk FC 0-2(0-1)
Cork City - UC Dublin 2-0(1-0)
Derry City - St Patrick's Athletic 1-1(1-1)
Waterford FC - Sligo Rovers 3-3(2-1)

Round 17 [17-18.05.2019]
Cork City - Dundalk FC 0-2(0-1)
St Patrick's Athletic - Bohemian FC 1-1(1-0)
UC Dublin - Shamrock Rovers 0-1(0-1)
Finn Harps - Waterford FC 3-2(2-1)
Sligo Rovers - Derry City 0-0

Round 18 [24.05.2019]
Bohemian FC - Sligo Rovers 1-2(0-0)
Derry City - Finn Harps 4-0(2-0)
Dundalk FC - St Patrick's Athletic 1-0(0-0)
Waterford FC - UC Dublin 1-0(1-0)
Shamrock Rovers - Cork City 2-0(0-0)

Round 19 [31.05.2019]
Bohemian FC - Finn Harps 5-3(2-1)
Dundalk FC - Sligo Rovers 4-0(1-0)
St Patrick's Athletic - Cork City 1-1(0-0)
Derry City - UC Dublin 0-0 [12.07.]
Waterford FC - Shamrock R. 1-5(0-2) [19.08.]

Round 20 [08.06.2019]
Shamrock Rovers - Derry City 2-2(0-0)
Sligo Rovers - St Patrick's Athletic 1-1(0-0)
Finn Harps - Dundalk FC 0-3(0-2)
UC Dublin - Bohemian FC 3-0 *awarded*
Cork City - Waterford FC 1-2(1-0) [02.09.]

Round 21 [14.06.2019]
St Patrick's Athletic - Finn Harps 1-0(0-0)
Sligo Rovers - Cork City 1-1(1-1)
Bohemian FC - Shamrock Rovers 2-1(1-0)
Derry City - Waterford FC 2-0(2-0) [29.07.]
Dundalk FC - UC Dublin 3-0(3-0) [26.08.]

Round 22 [28.06.2019]
Cork City - Derry City 1-4(0-3)
UC Dublin - St Patrick's Athletic 0-1(0-1)
Waterford FC - Bohemian FC 1-2(1-1)
Finn Harps - Sligo Rovers 2-0(1-0)
Shamrock Rovers - Dundalk FC 0-1(0-0)

Round 23 [01.07.2019]
Dundalk FC - Waterford FC 3-0(2-0)
St Patrick's Athletic - Shamrock Rov. 0-2(0-1)
Sligo Rovers - UC Dublin 5-1(3-1)
Bohemian FC - Derry City 0-0
Finn Harps - Cork City 0-0

Round 24 [05.07.2019]
Derry City - Dundalk FC 2-2(1-0)
UC Dublin - Finn Harps 1-0(1-0)
Waterford FC - St Patrick's Athletic 1-2(1-1)
Cork City - Bohemian FC 0-0
Shamrock Rovers - Sligo Rovers 0-0

Round 25 [13.07.2019]
Dundalk FC - Bohemian FC 2-1(0-1) [20.05.]
UC Dublin - Cork City 0-1(0-0) [20.05.]
Finn Harps - Shamrock Rov. 0-3(0-2) [20.05.]
St Patrick's Athl - Derry City 1-0(1-0) [21.05.]
Sligo Rovers - Waterford FC 0-0 [21.05.]

Round 26 [19-21.07.2019]
Derry City - Sligo Rovers 3-0(1-0)
Waterford FC - Finn Harps 0-1(0-0)
Bohemian FC - St Patrick's Athletic 3-0(1-0)
Shamrock Rovers - UC Dublin 7-0(4-0)
Dundalk FC - Cork City 1-0(0-0) [06.09.]

Round 27 [26-28.07.2019]
UC Dublin - Waterford FC 1-2(0-1)
Finn Harps - Derry City 1-0(0-0)
St Patrick's Athletic - Dundalk FC 0-1(0-0)
Sligo Rovers - Bohemian FC 1-1(1-1)
Cork City - Shamrock Rovers 1-1(1-0)

Round 28 [02.08.2019]
UC Dublin - Derry City 1-3(1-1)
Cork City - St Patrick's Athletic 0-1(0-0)
Finn Harps - Bohemian FC 1-0(1-0)
Shamrock R. - Waterford FC 2-1(1-1) [27.08.]
Sligo Rovers - Dundalk FC 0-2(0-1) [02.09.]

Round 29 [16.08.2019]
Bohemian FC - UC Dublin 10-1(2-0)
Derry City - Shamrock Rovers 0-2(0-0)
St Patrick's Athletic - Sligo Rovers 2-1(0-1)
Waterford FC - Cork City 1-2(0-0)
Dundalk FC - Finn Harps 5-0(1-0)

Round 30 [30.08.2019]
Cork City - Sligo Rovers 2-4(1-2)
UC Dublin - Dundalk FC 0-5(0-2)
Waterford FC - Derry City 1-1(1-1)
Shamrock Rovers - Bohemian FC 1-0(1-0)
Finn Harps - St Patrick's Athl 1-2(1-0) [06.09.]

Round 31 [13.09.2019]	
Bohemian FC - Waterford FC	1-2(0-1)
St Patrick's Athletic - UC Dublin	0-0
Sligo Rovers - Finn Harps	3-1(3-0)
Dundalk FC - Shamrock Rov	3-2(2-0) [23.09.]
Derry City - Cork City	4-0(2-0) [27.09.]

Round 32 [20.09.2019]	
Cork City - Finn Harps	0-0
Derry City - Bohemian FC	0-0
UC Dublin - Sligo Rovers	0-2(0-2)
Waterford FC - Dundalk FC	0-1(0-1)
Shamrock Rovers - St Patrick's Athletic	0-0

Round 33 [04-05.10.2019]	
Bohemian FC - Cork City	1-0(0-0)
Dundalk FC - Derry City	1-0(0-0)
St Patrick's Athletic - Waterford FC	0-2(0-1)
Finn Harps - UC Dublin	0-0
Sligo Rovers - Shamrock Rovers	0-0

Round 34 [08-11.10.2019]	
Waterford FC - Sligo Rovers	2-0(1-0)
Bohemian FC - Dundalk FC	2-1(1-0)
Cork City - UC Dublin	3-2(1-0)
Shamrock Rovers - Finn Harps	1-0(0-0)
Derry City - St Patrick's Athl	1-3(0-0) [22.10.]

Round 35 [18-19.10.2019]	
Cork City - Dundalk FC	1-0(1-0)
St Patrick's Athletic - Bohemian FC	0-0
UC Dublin - Shamrock Rovers	0-3(0-2)
Finn Harps - Waterford FC	1-0(1-0)
Sligo Rovers - Derry City	1-2(1-2)

Round 36 [25.10.2019]	
Bohemian FC - Sligo Rovers	2-1(0-1)
Derry City - Finn Harps	4-0(2-0)
Dundalk FC - St Patrick's Athletic	4-0(2-0)
Shamrock Rovers - Cork City	3-0(2-0)
Waterford FC - UC Dublin	4-2(2-1)

Final Standings

									Total				Home				Away		
1.	**Dundalk FC**	36	27	5	4	73 - 18	86	16	2	0	43 - 8	11	3	4	30 - 10
2.	Shamrock Rovers FC	36	23	6	7	62 - 21	75	12	4	2	32 - 7	11	2	5	30 - 14
3.	Bohemian FC Dublin	36	17	9	10	47 - 28	60	11	3	4	34 - 15	6	6	6	13 - 13
4.	Derry City FC	36	15	12	9	56 - 34	57	9	4	5	31 - 15	6	8	4	25 - 19
5.	St. Patrick's Athletic FC Dublin	36	14	10	12	29 - 35	52	7	5	6	13 - 16	7	5	6	16 - 19
6.	Waterford FC	36	12	7	17	46 - 53	43	6	4	8	26 - 26	6	3	9	20 - 27
7.	Sligo Rovers FC	36	10	12	14	38 - 47	42	5	8	5	19 - 17	5	4	9	19 - 30
8.	Cork City FC	36	9	10	17	29 - 49	37	4	7	7	16 - 23	5	3	10	13 - 26
9.	Finn Harps FC Ballybofey *(Relegation Play-offs)*	36	7	7	22	26 - 64	28	6	3	9	19 - 24	1	4	13	7 - 40
10.	University College Dublin AFC *(Relegated)*	36	5	4	27	25 - 82	19	5	1	12	17 - 30	0	3	15	8 - 52

Top goalscorers:

14	**Joseph Ogedi Junior Chukwuemka Ogedi-Uzokwe (ENG)**	*Derry City FC*
13	Patrick James Hoban	*Dundalk FC*
12	Michael Duffy	*Dundalk FC*
11	Daniel Mandroiu	*Bohemian FC Dublin*
11	David Parkhouse (NIR)	*Derry City FC*
11	Aaron Greene	*Shamrock Rovers FC*
11	Romeo Ovando Parkes (JAM)	*Sligo Rovers FC*

Relegation Play-offs [28.10.-01.11.2019]

Drogheda United FC - Finn Harps FC Ballybofey 1-0(0-0) 0-2(0-1,0-1)

Finn Harps FC Ballybofey remains at First Level.

NATIONAL CUP
FAI Cup 2019

Second Round [09-13.08.2019]

Cobh Wanderers FC - Limerick FC	0-1(0-0)	St. Michaels AFC Tipperary Town - Glengad United	0-0 aet; 7-8 pen
St. Patrick's Athletic FC Dublin - Bray Wanderers FC	2-1(0-1)	Crumlin United FC - Malahide United FC	3-1(3-1)
Bohemian FC Dublin - Shelbourne FC Dublin	3-2(0-0)	Cobh Ramblers FC - Dundalk FC	0-1(0-0)
Cabinteely FC - Cork City FC	2-2 aet; 4-5 pen	Lucan United FC - Killester Donnycarney FC	2-1(1-0)
Glebe North - Sligo Rovers FC	0-8(0-2)	University College Dublin AFC - Letterkenny Rovers	5-2(0-1)
Derry City FC - Wexford FC Crossabeg	1-0(0-0)	Collinstown FC - Galway United FC	1-2(1-2)
Drogheda United FC - Avondale United FC	2-1(1-0)	Maynooth University Town - Waterford FC	0-2(0-1)
Shamrock Rovers FC - Finn Harps FC Ballybofey	1-0(1-0)	Longford Town FC - Athlone Town FC	3-1(0-1)

1/8-Finals [23-25.08.2019]

UC Dublin AFC - St Patrick's Athletic FC Dublin	3-1(2-0)	Shamrock Rovers FC - Drogheda United FC	4-0(0-0)
Derry City FC - Dundalk FC	2-3(0-1,2-2)	Glengad United FC - Waterford FC	0-2(0-0)
Galway United FC - Cork City FC	1-0(1-0)	Sligo Rovers FC - Limerick FC	6-2(3-2)
Bohemian FC Dublin - Longford Town FC	1-1 aet; 5-4 pen	Crumlin United FC - Lucan United FC	3-1(3-0)

Quarter-Finals [06/07/09/16.09.2019]

Galway United - Shamrock Rovers FC	1-2(1-0)	Waterford FC - Dundalk FC	1-3(0-3)
Sligo Rovers FC - University College Dublin AFC	4-0(2-0)	Crumlin United FC - Bohemian FC Dublin	0-2(0-1)

Semi-Finals [27-29.09.2019]

Bohemian FC Dublin - Shamrock Rovers FC	0-2(0-1)	Sligo Rovers FC - Dundalk FC	0-1(0-0)

03.11.2019; Aviva Stadium, Dublin; Referee: Derek Tomney; Attendance: 33,111
Shamrock Rovers FC - Dundalk FC   **1-1(0-0,1-1,1-1); 4-2 on penalties**

Shamrock Rovers: Alan Mannus, Roberto Lopes, Lee Grace, Ronan Finn, Joey O'Brien, Sean Kavanagh (68.Neil Farrugia), Aaron McEneff, Jack Byrne, Gary O'Neill, Aaron Greene (111.Daniel Lafferty), Graham Dylan Burke (90+1.Greg Bolger). Trainer: Stephen Bradley.

Dundalk FC: Gary Rogers, Brian Gartland, Dane Massey, Sean Gannon, Sean Hoare (90+1.Georgie Kelly), Daniel Cleary, Sean Murray (61.Daniel Kelly), Jamie McGrath, Patrick Hoban (99.Jordan Flores), Robbie Benson (112.John Mountney), Michael Duffy. Trainer: Vinny Perth.

Goals: 1-0 Aaron McEneff (89 penalty), 1-1 Michael Duffy (90+3).

Penalties: Jamie McGrath 0-1; Jack Byrne 1-1; Michael Duffy (missed); Joey O'Brien 2-1; Daniel Cleary (saved); Greg Bolger 3-1; Jordan Flores 3-2; Gary O'Neill 4-2.

THE CLUBS 2019

Bohemian Football Club Dublin

Founded: 06.09.1890
Stadium: Dalymount Park, Dublin (7,955)
Trainer: Keith Long   14.11.1973

Goalkeepers:	DOB	M	(s)	G
James Talbot	24.04.1997	36		
Defenders:	**DOB**	**M**	**(s)**	**G**
Michael Barker	16.08.1993	10	(2)	1
Aaron Barry	24.11.1992	14	(5)	
Robert Cornwall	16.10.1994	17		
James Finnerty	01.02.1999	31		2
Patrick Kirk	02.06.1998	13	(2)	
Darragh Leahy	15.04.1998	24	(1)	
Derek Pender	02.10.1983	24		1
Luke Wade-Slater	02.03.1998	22	(6)	1
Midfielders:	**DOB**	**M**	**(s)**	**G**
Scott Allardice (SCO)	31.03.1998	10	(8)	
Keith Buckley	17.06.1992	23	(1)	1
Kevin Devaney	26.09.1990	15		1
Conor Levingston	21.01.1998	28	(2)	4

	DOB	M	(s)	G
Andy Lyons	02.08.2000	11	(3)	
Daniel Mandriou	20.10.1998	25	(3)	11
Robert McCourt	06.04.1998	6	(8)	
Keith Ward	12.10.1990	22	(7)	1
Forwards:	**DOB**	**M**	**(s)**	**G**
Sam Byrne	23.07.1995		(5)	
Dinny Corcoran	13.02.1989	15	(1)	7
Dawson Devoy	20.11.2001	1	(5)	
Daniel Grant	23.10.2000	18	(6)	4
Evan Ferguson	19.10.2004		(1)	
Ryan Graydon	11.04.1999	3	(9)	
Ali Reghba	14.01.2000	3	(8)	
Ryan Swan	13.05.1996	9	(11)	4
Ross Tierney	06.03.2001	6	(2)	2
Andre Wright (ENG)	07.12.1996	10		5

Cork City Football Club

Founded: 1984
Stadium: Turners Cross, Cork (7,485)
Trainer: Johnathan Caulfield (USA)   11.10.1964
[02.05.2019] John Cotter   05.08.1977
[30.06.2019] Frank Kelleher
[26.08.2019] Neale Fenn   18.01.1977

Goalkeepers:	DOB	M	(s)	G
Mark McNulty	13.10.1980	28		
Tadhg Ryan	01.03.1997	8		
Defenders:	**DOB**	**M**	**(s)**	**G**
Alan Bennett	04.10.1981	3	(4)	
Gary Boylan	24.04.1996	4		
Dan Casey	29.10.1997	28	(1)	3
Shane Griffin	08.09.1994	19	(3)	1
Joshua Honohan	28.03.2001	1	(1)	
Colm Horgan	02.07.1994	18	(2)	
Ronan Hurley	11.09.1999	9	(2)	
Conor McCarthy	11.04.1998	35		4
Sean McLoughlin	13.11.1996	20		2
Jake O'Brien	15.05.2001	1		
Pierce Phillips	28.09.1998	1	(3)	
Midfielders:	**DOB**	**M**	**(s)**	**G**
Garry Buckley	19.08.1993	27	(2)	
Alec Byrne	21.06.1999	6	(2)	
Garry Comerford	29.10.1993	8	(6)	
Joel Coustrain	22.01.1996	7	(2)	
Rory Doyle	30.06.2000		(1)	

	DOB	M	(s)	G
Dale Holland	07.01.2000		(2)	
Conor McCormack	18.05.1990	31		1
Gearóid Morrissey	17.11.1991	23		3
Kevin O'Connor		17	(1)	1
Mark O'Sullivan	01.02.1983	6	(3)	1
Dan Smith (ENG)	05.09.1999	1	(7)	
James Tilley (ENG)	13.06.1998	16	(3)	
Forwards:	**DOB**	**M**	**(s)**	**G**
Cian Bargary	22.11.2000		(2)	1
Darragh Crowley	20.02.2000	1	(9)	
Graham Cummins	29.12.1987	13	(5)	5
Ricardo Dinanga	06.12.2001		(1)	
Matthew Gillam (ENG)	18.07.1998		(3)	
Cian Murphy	08.06.2000	1		
Liam Nash (ENG)	10.01.1996	2	(3)	
Daire O'Connor	15.04.1997	23	(6)	4
Darragh Rainsford	15.11.1994	3	(7)	
Karl Sheppard	14.02.1991	26	(1)	3
Eoghan Stokes	17.05.1996	7	(4)	
Beineon Whitmarsh	11.01.2000	3	(4)	

Derry City Football Club

Founded: 1928
Stadium: "Ryan McBride" Brandywell Stadium, Derry (3,700)
Trainer: Declan Devine (NIR) 15.09.1973

Goalkeepers:	DOB	M	(s)	G
Peter Cherrie (SCO)	01.10.1983	34		
Nathan Gartside (NIR)	08.03.1998	2	(1)	
Defenders:	**DOB**	**M**	**(s)**	**G**
Ronan Boyce	02.12.2002		(1)	
Darren Cole (SCO)	03.01.1992	22	(3)	3
Ciaran Coll	19.08.1991	31	(1)	1
Ally Gilchrist (SCO)	03.03.1995	28	(1)	
Joshua Kerr (SCO)	24.02.1998	6	(3)	
Patrick McClean (NIR)	22.11.1996	7	(3)	1
Conor McDermott (NIR)	18.09.1997	4	(2)	
Mark McChrystal (NIR)	26.06.1984		(1)	
Eoin Toal (NIR)	15.02.1999	34	(1)	2
Midfielders:	**DOB**	**M**	**(s)**	**G**
Gerardo Alfredo Bruna Blanco (ARG)	29.01.1991	14	(11)	1
Adrian Delap	30.11.1998	2	(16)	1
Grant Gillespie (SCO)	02.07.1991	5	(3)	1
Ciaron Harkin (NIR)	15.01.1996	32	(2)	5
Jack Malone (NIR)	05.04.2000	2	(5)	1
Darren McCauley (NIR)	21.02.1991	3	(6)	
Jamie McDonagh (NIR)	08.05.1996	24	(3)	4
Barry McNamee (NIR)	17.02.1992	30	(3)	2
Gianni Seraf (ALG)	05.07.1994		(4)	
Gregory Sloggett	03.07.1996	34		1
Evan Tweed	01.03.1999		(2)	
Forwards:	**DOB**	**M**	**(s)**	**G**
Conor Davis	03.06.1998	2	(5)	1
Michael McCrudden (NIR)	31.07.1991	5	(10)	
Shane McNamee	01.06.1999		(2)	
Junior Ogedi-Uzokwe (ENG)	03.03.1994	32		14
David Parkhouse (NIR)	24.10.1999	34		11
Eoghan Stokes	17.05.1996	9	(11)	3

Dundalk Football Club

Founded: 1903
Stadium: Oriel Park, Dundalk (4,500)
Trainer: Vinny Perth 02.08.1976

Goalkeepers:	DOB	M	(s)	G
Aaron McCarey	14.01.1992	1		
Gary Rogers	25.09.1981	35		
Defenders:	**DOB**	**M**	**(s)**	**G**
Andrew Boyle	07.03.1991	8		1
Daniel Cleary	09.03.1996	22	(1)	2
Cameron Dummigan (NIR)	02.06.1996	5	(9)	1
Sean Gannon	11.07.1991	32	(1)	1
Brian Gartland	04.11.1986	21	(1)	2
Dylan Hand	15.03.1999		(1)	
Sean Hoare	15.03.1994	28		4
Dean Jarvis (NIR)	01.06.1992	15	(4)	1
Dane Massey	17.04.1988	21	(2)	2
Midfielders:	**DOB**	**M**	**(s)**	**G**
Jordan Flores (ENG)	04.10.1995	7	(9)	1
Jamie McGrath	30.09.1996	20	(6)	2
Joe McKee (SCO)	30.10.1992	1	(4)	
John Mountney	22.02.1993	12	(11)	6
Sean Murray	11.10.1993	18	(7)	3
Chris Shields	27.12.1990	28	(1)	
Forwards:	**DOB**	**M**	**(s)**	**G**
Robbie Benson	07.05.1992	9	(4)	1
Michael Duffy (NIR)	28.07.1994	31	(3)	12
Mark Hanratty	18.07.2002		(1)	
Patrick Hoban	28.07.1991	30	(4)	13
Daniel Kelly	21.05.1996	24	(9)	9
Georgie Kelly (NIR)	12.11.1996	6	(23)	8
Lido Lotefa (CGO)	18.04.2000		(3)	
Patrick McEleney (NIR)	26.09.1992	22	(2)	2

Finn Harps Football Club Ballybofey

Founded: 1954
Stadium: Finn Park, Ballybofey (6,000)
Trainer: Oliver Horgan 17.02.1968

Goalkeepers:	DOB	M	(s)	G
Jamie Bell	11.01.1999	1		
Peter Burke	03.03.1996	13	(1)	
Ciarán Gallagher	01.04.1992	7		
Mark McGinley	26.03.1990	15		
Defenders:	**DOB**	**M**	**(s)**	**G**
Harry Ascroft (AUS)	01.07.1995	13	(3)	2
Keith Cowan	23.08.1985	28	(2)	2
Colm Deasy	04.01.1997	9	(2)	
Kieran Farren	21.11.2000	1		
John Kavanagh	19.07.1994	15		
Niall Logue (NIR)	07.08.1995	13	(4)	1
Daniel O'Reilly	11.04.1995	31	(2)	2
Mark Russell (SCO)	22.03.1996	23	(2)	
Joshua Smith (USA)	10.03.1992	3	(2)	1
Sam Todd (NIR)	28.04.1998	32		
Midfielders:	**DOB**	**M**	**(s)**	**G**
Jacob Borg (MLT)	22.05.1991	27	(4)	
Mark Coyle	13.02.1997	21	(3)	1
Raffaele Cretaro	15.10.1981	20	(7)	2
Jack Doherty	14.06.2001		(1)	
Shaun Doherty	25.11.1993	1	(2)	
Michael Gallagher	09.07.2000	2	(2)	
Gareth Harkin (NIR)	19.12.1987	17	(4)	
Ruairí Harkin (NIR)	11.10.1989	6	(1)	
Caolan McAleer (NIR)	19.08.1993	19	(5)	3
Niall McGinley	17.09.2000	2	(2)	
Anthony McNamee	16.08.1993	14	(15)	1
Mikey Place	09.04.1998	12	(17)	4
Forwards:	**DOB**	**M**	**(s)**	**G**
Sean Boyd	20.06.1998	12	(2)	2
Nathan Boyle (NIR)	14.04.1994	24	(7)	5
Stephen Doherty	22.06.2000	2	(4)	
Mark Timlin	07.11.1994	9	(5)	
Sam Verdon	03.09.1995	1		
Liam Walsh	22.07.1999	3	(2)	

Shamrock Rovers Football Club Dublin

Founded: 1899
Stadium: Tallaght Stadium, Dublin (6,000)
Trainer: Stephen Bradley 19.11.1984

Goalkeepers:	DOB	M	(s)	G
Alan Mannus (NIR)	19.05.1982	36		
Defenders:	**DOB**	**M**	**(s)**	**G**
Eric Abulu (GER)	27.04.2000		(2)	
Sam Bone (ENG)	06.02.1998	3	(2)	
Ethan Boyle	04.01.1997	12	(4)	1
Sean Callan	14.12.1999	1		
James Furlong	07.06.2002	1		
Lee Grace	01.12.1992	34		1
Daniel Lafferty (NIR)	18.05.1989	6	(1)	
Roberto Lopes	17.06.1992	33	(2)	3
Midfielders:	**DOB**	**M**	**(s)**	**G**
Greg Bolger	09.09.1988	24	(4)	3
Jack Byrne	24.04.1996	31	(1)	8
Trevor Clarke	26.03.1998	18	(3)	1
Joel Coustrain	22.01.1996	2	(9)	
Dean Dillon	08.06.1999		(2)	
Ronan Finn	21.12.1987	28	(2)	3
Brandon Kavanagh	21.09.2000	6	(16)	1
Sean Kavanagh	20.01.1994	21	(6)	3
Aaron McEneff	09.07.1995	23	(4)	10
Joey O'Brien	17.02.1986	23	(1)	2
Gary O'Neill	27.01.1995	7	(4)	
Dylan Watts	11.04.1997	25	(7)	3
Forwards:	**DOB**	**M**	**(s)**	**G**
Graham Dylan Burke	21.09.1993	7	(3)	3
Daniel Carr (TRI)	29.05.1994	15	(8)	4
Graham Cummins	29.12.1987	7	(1)	3
Neil Farrugia	19.05.1999	2	(1)	
Aaron Greene	02.01.1990	30	(4)	11
Thomas Oluwa	08.02.2001		(4)	1
Orhan Vojic (AUT)	20.01.1997	1	(11)	1

Sligo Rovers Football Club

Founded: 1928
Stadium: The Showgrounds, Sligo (5,500)
Trainer: Liam Buckley — 14.04.1960

Goalkeepers:	DOB	M	(s)	G
Mitchell Beeney (ENG)	03.10.1995	13		
Edward McGinty (SCO)	05.08.1999	21		
Luke McNicholas	01.01.2000	2		
Defenders:	DOB	M	(s)	G
Lewis Banks (ENG)	14.04.1997	30	(2)	1
Kyle Callan-McFadden	20.04.1995	24	(1)	1
Regan Donelon	17.04.1996	18	(3)	
John Dunleavy	03.07.1991	23	(2)	1
Danny Kane	23.04.1997	9		
Dante Leverock (BER)	11.04.1992	21	(1)	2
Scott Lynch			(1)	
John Mahon	26.11.1999	31	(3)	
Niall Morahan	30.05.2000	14	(11)	
Niall Robert Watson (ENG)	15.06.2000	1	(4)	1

Midfielders:	DOB	M	(s)	G
David Cawley	19.09.1991	26	(3)	2
Jack Keaney	18.01.1999	16	(2)	3
Liam Kerrigan	09.05.2000	7	(5)	
James McGrath	06.01.2000		(1)	
John Russell	18.05.1985	3	(7)	
Kris Twardek (CAN)	08.03.1997	27	(9)	2
Sam Warde	13.03.1998	14	(9)	1
Forwards:	DOB	M	(s)	G
Darren Collins	29.09.2000		(1)	
Ronan Coughlan	02.10.1995	25	(2)	8
Daryl Fordyce (NIR)	02.01.1987	25	(4)	2
Brian Morley	14.05.1998	1	(6)	
Ronan Murray	12.09.1991	17	(4)	1
Romeo Ovando Parkes (JAM)	11.11.1990	28	(2)	11

St. Patrick's Athletic Football Club Dublin

Founded: 1929
Stadium: Richmond Park, Dublin (2,800)
Trainer: Harry Kenny — 13.04.1962
[31.08.2019] Stephen O'Donnell — 15.01.1986

Goalkeepers:	DOB	M	(s)	G
Brendan Clarke	17.09.1985	34		
Barry Murphy	08.06.1985	2		
Defenders:	DOB	M	(s)	G
Ian Bermingham	08.01.1989	35		
Lee Desmond	22.01.1995	31		1
Ciaran Kelly	04.07.1998	24	(1)	1
Simon Madden	01.05.1988	28		1
Kevin Toner	18.07.1996	26		3
David Webster	07.04.1990	23	(1)	1
Midfielders:	DOB	M	(s)	G
Connor Clifford	01.10.1991	22	(3)	2
Cian Coleman	01.01.1997	13	(7)	

	DOB	M	(s)	G
James Doona	15.01.1998	1	(14)	2
Chris Forrester	17.12.1992	20	(10)	2
Jamie Lennon	09.05.1998	23	(5)	
Darragh Markey	23.05.1997	20	(5)	2
Rhys McCabe (SCO)	24.07.1992	21	(4)	1
Brandon Miele	28.08.1994	4	(3)	
Forwards:	DOB	M	(s)	G
Dean Clarke	29.03.1993	14	(7)	2
Michael Drennan (NIR)	02.02.1994	25	(1)	6
Ronan Hale	08.09.1998	3	(4)	1
Glen McAuley	24.02.2000	3	(5)	1
Gary Shaw	10.05.1992	20	(9)	1
Jake Walker	19.08.2000	4	(18)	1

University College Dublin Association Football Club

Founded: 1895
Stadium: UCSD Bowl, Dublin (3,000)
Trainer: Colin O'Neill — 28.06.1976

Goalkeepers:	DOB	M	(s)	G
Conor Kearns	06.05.1998	30		
Tom Murphy	26.08.2000	2		
Gavin Sheridan	03.01.1996	4		
Defenders:	DOB	M	(s)	G
Isaac Akinsete	02.01.2002	1	(1)	
Ciaran Behan			(5)	
Luke Boore	28.03.1999	5	(2)	
Kevin Coffey	06.05.1998	4	(5)	
Joshua Collins	27.06.1997	20		
Darragh Corcoran	17.05.1998		(1)	
Mark Dignam	17.04.1999	29		
Evan Farrell	05.03.1999	21	(1)	
Jason McClelland	03.05.1997	33	(2)	2
Aaron McGrath	30.03.2001	1	(2)	
Daniel Mullen	13.04.2000		(2)	
Liam Scales	08.08.1998	30		1
Hugh Torfeldt	24.05.2001		(1)	

Midfielders:	DOB	M	(s)	G
Paul Doyle	10.04.1998	25	(3)	
Dara Keane	24.12.1998	10	(3)	1
Jack Keaney	18.01.1999	11		3
Liam Kerrigan	09.05.2000	8		1
Harry McEvoy	16.08.2001	13	(1)	
Timmy Molloy	07.04.1994	13	(1)	1
Richie O'Farrell	18.09.2000	26	(8)	3
Gary O'Neill	27.01.1995	18	(1)	2
Jack Ryan	07.02.2000		(3)	
Daniel Tobin	27.02.1997	24		
Forwards:	DOB	M	(s)	G
Danu Kinsella Bishop	22.12.2001	4	(9)	
Sam John Byrne	23.07.1995	4	(6)	1
Conor Davis	03.06.1998	13	(2)	1
Neil Farrugia	19.05.1999	16	(2)	1
Yousef Mahdy	20.01.1998	25	(10)	5
Sean McDonald	26.01.1998	6	(12)	1

Waterford Football Club Dublin

Founded: 1930
Stadium: Waterford Regional Sports Centre, Waterford (5,500)
Trainer: Alan Reynolds — 12.06.1974

Goalkeepers:	DOB	M	(s)	G
Matthew Connor	08.04.1997	34		
Hugo Keto (FIN)	09.02.1998	2		
Defenders:	DOB	M	(s)	G
Sam Bone (ENG)	06.02.1998	7	(3)	
Kenny Browne	07.08.1986	14		
Damien Delaney	20.07.1981	20		1
Rory Feely	03.01.1997	31	(1)	1
John Kavanagh	19.07.1994	5		
Maxim Kouogun	14.03.1997	21	(3)	1
Jonathan Lunney	02.02.1998	31	(2)	1
Kevin Lynch	21.03.1992	24		
Darragh Power	29.12.2000		(1)	
Aaron Simpson (ENG)	04.07.1997	7	(1)	
Rob Slevin	14.07.1998	11	(1)	
Midfielders:	DOB	M	(s)	G
Karolis Chvedukas (LTU)	21.04.1991	13	(6)	

	DOB	M	(s)	G
Shane Duggan	03.01.1989	30	(3)	5
William Fitzgerald	19.05.1999	2	(4)	
Cory Galvin	10.01.1996	11	(12)	4
Shane Griffin	31.12.1999		(2)	
Bastien Héry (FRA)	23.03.1992	17	(3)	1
Tom Holland	22.04.1997	12	(1)	1
John Martin	05.01.1999	4	(3)	
Dean O'Halloran	02.01.1996	5	(6)	1
Georgie Poynton	28.08.1997	16	(11)	1
Forwards:	DOB	M	(s)	G
Ismahil Akinade (NGA)	11.02.1994	10	(7)	3
Aaron Drinan	06.05.1998	15	(3)	7
Zachary Elbouzedi	05.04.1998	24	(3)	6
Walter Figueira (ENG)	17.03.1995	9	(2)	2
Michael O'Connor	31.07.1998	10	(3)	4
Scott Twine (ENG)	14.07.1999	7	(7)	1
Dean Walsh	23.04.1997	4	(9)	2

SECOND LEVEL
League of Ireland First Division 2019

1.	Shelbourne FC Dublin (*Promoted*)	27	19	3	5	50 - 19	60
2.	Drogheda United FC (*Promotion Play-offs*)	27	16	3	8	59 - 36	51
3.	Longford Town FC (*Promotion Play-offs*)	27	16	3	8	41 - 23	51
4.	Cabinteely FC (*Promotion Play-offs*)	27	14	8	5	39 - 28	53
5.	Bray Wanderers FC	27	14	4	9	44 - 26	46
6.	Cobh Ramblers FC	27	8	7	12	38 - 51	31
7.	Galway United FC	27	7	5	15	36 - 42	26
8.	Athlone Town FC	27	4	6	17	30 - 61	18
9.	Wexford FC Crossabeg	27	2	5	20	22 - 65	11
10.	Limerick FC	27	10	6	11	33 - 41	10

Promotion Play-offs (1st / 2nd Level)

Semi-Finals [05-08.10.2019]	Cabinteely FC - Longford Town FC	0-0	1-1
Finals [05-08.10.2019]	Cabinteely FC - **Drogheda United FC**	1-1	1-5

NATIONAL TEAM

INTERNATIONAL MATCHES
(16.07.2019 – 15.07.2020)

05.09.2019	Dublin	Republic of Ireland - Switzerland	1-1(0-0)	(ECQ)
10.09.2019	Dublin	Republic of Ireland - Bulgaria	3-1(0-0)	(F)
12.10.2019	Tbilisi	Georgia - Republic of Ireland	0-0	(ECQ)
15.10.2019	Lancy	Switzerland - Republic of Ireland	2-0(1-0)	(ECQ)
14.11.2019	Dublin	Republic of Ireland - New Zealand	3-1(1-1)	(F)
18.11.2019	Dublin	Republic of Ireland - Denmark	1-1(0-0)	(ECQ)

05.09.2019 REPUBLIC OF IRELAND - SWITZERLAND 1-1(0-0) 16th EC. Qualifiers
Aviva Stadium, Dublin; Referee: Carlos del Cerro Grande (Spain); Attendance: 44,111
IRL: Darren Edward Andrew Randolph, Séamus Coleman (Cap), Richard John Keogh, Enda John Stevens, Shane Patrick Michael Duffy, Glenn David Whelan, Conor Hourihane (82.Scott Andrew Hogan), James Joseph McClean, Jeffrey Patrick Hendrick, David James McGoldrick (90+2.Alan James Browne), Callum Jack Robinson (58.Alan Christopher Judge). Trainer: Michael Joseph McCarthy.
Goal: David James McGoldrick (85).

10.09.2019 REPUBLIC OF IRELAND - BULGARIA 3-1(0-0) Friendly International
Aviva Stadium, Dublin; Referee: Tobias Welz (Germany); Attendance: 18,259
IRL: Mark Travers (76.Kieran Michael O'Hara), Kevin Finbarr Long, John Egan (Cap), Cyrus Sylvester Frederick Christie, Alan Christopher Judge (59.Jack Byrne), Conor Hourihane (69.James Joseph McClean), Callum Joshua Ryan O'Dowda (76.Enda John Stevens), Alan James Browne, Ronan Curtis (84.Jeffrey Patrick Hendrick), Joshua Jon Cullen, Scott Andrew Hogan (60.James Collins). Trainer: Michael Joseph McCarthy.
Goals: Alan James Browne (56), Kevin Finbarr Long (83), James Collins (86).

12.10.2019 GEORGIA - REPUBLIC OF IRELAND 0-0 16th EC. Qualifiers
„Boris Paichadze“ Dinamo Arena, Tbilisi; Referee: Marco Guida (Italy); Attendance: 24,835
IRL: Darren Edward Andrew Randolph, Séamus Coleman (Cap), Shane Patrick Michael Duffy, John Egan, Matthew James Doherty, Glenn David Whelan, Conor Hourihane (90+3.Derrick Williams), James Joseph McClean, Jeffrey Patrick Hendrick, James Collins (79.Aaron Anthony Connolly), Callum Jack Robinson (73.Alan James Browne). Trainer: Michael Joseph McCarthy.

15.10.2019 SWITZERLAND - REPUBLIC OF IRELAND 2-0(1-0) 16th EC. Qualifiers
Stade de Genève, Lancy; Referee: Szymon Marciniak (Poland); Attendance: 24,766
IRL: Darren Edward Andrew Randolph, Séamus Coleman (Cap) [*sent off 76*], Enda John Stevens, Shane Patrick Michael Duffy, John Egan, Glenn David Whelan, James Joseph McClean, Jeffrey Patrick Hendrick, Alan James Browne, James Collins (46.Callum Joshua Ryan O'Dowda), Aaron Anthony Connolly (70.Scott Andrew Hogan). Trainer: Michael Joseph McCarthy.

14.11.2019 REPUBLIC OF IRELAND - NEW ZEALAND 3-1(1-1) Friendly International
Aviva Stadium, Dublin; Referee: Robert Ian Jenkins (Wales); Attendance: 18,728
IRL: Kieran Michael O'Hara (66.Mark Travers), Kevin Finbarr Long, Ciaran Clark, Derrick Williams (56.Callum Joshua Ryan O'Dowda), Lee Patrick O'Connor, Robert Brady (Cap), Jack Byrne (63.Alan Christopher Judge), Alan James Browne (66.Conor Hourihane), Joshua Jon Cullen, Seán Patrick Maguire (73.James Collins), Troy Daniel Parrott (63.Callum Jack Robinson). Trainer: Michael Joseph McCarthy.
Goals: Derrick Williams (45), Seán Patrick Maguire (52), Callum Jack Robinson (75).

18.11.2019 REPUBLIC OF IRELAND - DENMARK 1-1(0-0) 16th EC. Qualifiers
Aviva Stadium, Dublin; Referee: Dr. Felix Brych (Germany); Attendance: 51,700
IRL: Darren Edward Andrew Randolph, Enda John Stevens, Shane Patrick Michael Duffy (Cap), John Egan (46.Ciaran Clark), Matthew James Doherty, Glenn David Whelan (82.Seán Patrick Maguire), Conor Hourihane (68.Callum Jack Robinson), James Joseph McClean, Jeffrey Patrick Hendrick, Alan James Browne, David James McGoldrick. Trainer: Michael Joseph McCarthy.
Goal: Matthew James Doherty (85).

NATIONAL TEAM PLAYERS
(16.07.2019 – 15.07.2020)

Name	DOB	Caps	Goals	2019/2020:	Club
Goalkeepers					
Kieran Michael O'HARA	22.04.1996	2	0	2019:	*Burton Albion FC (ENG)*
Darren Edward Andrew RANDOLPH	12.05.1987	42	0	2019:	*Middlesbrough FC (ENG)*
Mark TRAVERS	18.05.1999	2	0	2019:	*AFC Bournemouth (ENG)*
Defenders					
Cyrus Sylvester Frederick CHRISTIE	30.09.1992	24	2	2019:	*Fulham FC London (ENG)*
Ciaran CLARK	26.09.1989	34	2	2019:	*Newcastle United FC (ENG)*
Séamus COLEMAN	11.10.1988	56	1	2019:	*Everton FC Liverpool (ENG)*
Matthew James DOHERTY	16.01.1992	9	1	2019:	*Wolverhampton Wanderers FC (ENG)*
Shane Patrick Michael DUFFY	01.01.1992	33	3	2019:	*Brighton & Hove Albion FC (ENG)*
John EGAN	20.10.1992	8	0	2019:	*Sheffield United FC (ENG)*
Richard John KEOGH	11.08.1986	26	1	2019:	*Derby County FC (ENG)*
Kevin Finbarr LONG	18.08.1990	13	1	2019:	*Burnley FC (ENG)*
Lee Patrick O'CONNOR	28.07.2000	1	0	2019:	*Celtic FC Glasgow (SCO)*
Enda John STEVENS	09.07.1990	14	0	2019:	*Sheffield United FC (ENG)*
Derrick Shaun WILLIAMS	17.01.1993	3	1	2019:	*Blackburn Rovers FC (ENG)*
Midfielders					
Robert BRADY	14.01.1992	46	8	2019:	*Burnley FC (ENG)*
Alan James BROWNE	15.04.1995	9	1	2019:	*Preston North End FC (ENG)*
Jack BYRNE	24.04.1996	2	0	2019:	*Shamrock Rovers FC Dublin*
Ronan CURTIS	29.03.1996	3	0	2019:	*Portsmouth FC (ENG)*
Jeffrey Patrick HENDRICK	31.01.1992	54	2	2019:	*Burnley FC (ENG)*
Conor HOURIHANE	02.02.1991	17	1	2019:	*Aston Villa FC Birmingham (ENG)*
Alan Christopher JUDGE	11.11.1988	9	1	2019:	*Ipswich Town FC (ENG)*
James Joseph McCLEAN	22.04.1989	72	10	2019:	*Stoke City FC (ENG)*
Callum Joshua Ryan O'DOWDA	23.04.1995	18	0	2019:	*Bristol City FC (ENG)*
Glenn David WHELAN	13.01.1984	91	2	2019:	*Heart of Midlothian FC Edinburgh (SCO)*
Forwards					
James COLLINS	01.12.1990	4	1	2019:	*Luton Town FC (ENG)*
Aaron Anthony CONNOLLY	28.01.2000	2	0	2019:	*Brighton & Hove Albion FC (ENG)*
Joshua Jon CULLEN	07.04.1996	2	0	2019:	*Charlton Athletic FC London (ENG)*
Scott Andrew HOGAN	13.04.1992	8	0	2019:	*Stoke City FC (ENG)*
Seán Patrick MAGUIRE	01.05.1994	8	1	2019:	*Preston North End FC (ENG)*
David James McGOLDRICK	29.11.1987	12	1	2019:	*Sheffield United FC (ENG)*
Troy Daniel PARROTT	04.02.2002	1	0	2019:	*Tottenham Hotspur FC London (ENG)*
Callum Jack ROBINSON	02.02.1995	12	1	2019:	*Sheffield United FC (ENG)*

National team coach

Michael Joseph "Mick" McCARTHY [25.11.2019 – 04.04.2020]	07.02.1959	10 M; 5 W; 4 D; 1 L; 13-7
		Complete record as trainer of Republic of Ireland:
		78 M; 34 W; 24 D; 20 L; 125-74
		(27.03.1996 – 16.10.2002) & (25.11.2019 – 04.04.2020)

ROMANIA

The Country:
Românâ (Romania)
Capital: Bucureşti
Surface: 238,397 km²
Inhabitants: 19,317,984 [2020]
Time: UTC+2

The FA:
Federaţia Română de Fotbal
Casa Fotbalului, Str. Serg. Şerbanică Vasile 12, 22186 Bucureşti
Tel: +40 21 325 0678
Founded: 00.00.1909
Member of FIFA since: 1923
Member of UEFA since: 1954
Website: www.frf.ro

NATIONAL TEAM RECORDS

RECORDS		
First international match:	08.06.1922, Beograd:	Yugoslavia – Romania 1-2
Most international caps:	Dorinel Ionel Munteanu	- 134 caps (1991-2007)
Most international goals:	Gheorghe Hagi	- 35 goals / 125 caps (1983-2000)
	Adrian Mutu	- 35 goals / 77 caps (2000-2013)

UEFA EUROPEAN CHAMPIONSHIP	
1960	Qualifiers
1964	Qualifiers
1968	Qualifiers
1972	Qualifiers
1976	Qualifiers
1980	Qualifiers
1984	Final Tournament (Group Stage)
1988	Qualifiers
1992	Qualifiers
1996	Final Tournament (Group Stage)
2000	Final Tournament (Quarter-Finals)
2004	Qualifiers
2008	Final Tournament (Group Stage)
2012	Qualifiers
2016	Final Tournament (Group Stage)
2020	*To be determined*

FIFA WORLD CUP	
1930	Final Tournament (Group Stage)
1934	Final Tournament (1st Round)
1938	Final Tournament (1st Round)
1950	Did not enter
1954	Qualifiers
1958	Qualifiers
1962	*Withdrew*
1966	Qualifiers
1970	Final Tournament (Group Stage)
1974	Qualifiers
1978	Qualifiers
1982	Qualifiers
1986	Qualifiers
1990	Final Tournament (2nd Round of 16)
1994	Final Tournament (Quarter-Finals)
1998	Final Tournament (2nd Round of 16)
2002	Qualifiers
2006	Qualifiers
2010	Qualifiers
2014	Qualifiers
2018	Qualifiers

OLYMPIC TOURNAMENTS	
1908	-
1912	-
1920	-
1924	-
1928	1/8 - Finals
1936	Did not enter
1948	Did not enter
1952	Preliminary Round
1956	Did not enter
1960	Qualifiers
1964	Quarter-Finals
1968	Qualifiers
1972	Qualifiers
1976	Qualifiers
1980	Qualifiers
1984	Qualifiers
1988	Qualifiers
1992	Qualifiers
1996	Qualifiers
2000	Qualifiers
2004	Qualifiers
2008	Qualifiers
2012	Qualifiers
2016	Qualifiers

UEFA NATIONS LEAGUE
2018/2019 – League C (promoted to League B)

FIFA CONFEDERATIONS CUP 1992-2017
None

ROMANIAN CLUB HONOURS IN EUROPEAN CLUB COMPETITIONS:

European Champion Clubs.Cup (1956-1992) / UEFA Champions League (1993-2020)		
FC Steaua Bucureşti	1	1985/1986

Fairs Cup (1858-1971) / UEFA Cup (1972-2009) / UEFA Europa League (2010-2020)		
None		

UEFA Super Cup (1972-2019)		
FC Steaua Bucureşti	1	1986

European Cup Winners.Cup 1961-1999*		
None		

*defunct competition

NATIONAL COMPETITIONS
TABLE OF HONOURS

	CHAMPIONS*	CUP WINNERS	BEST GOALSCORERS	
1909/1910	Olympia Bucureşti	-	-	
1910/1911	Olympia Bucureşti	-	-	
1911/1912	United Ploieşti	-	-	
1912/1913	Colentina AC Bucureşti	-	-	
1913/1914	Colentina AC Bucureşti	-	-	
1914/1915	Româno-Americană Bucureşti	-	-	
1915/1916	Prahova Ploieşti	-	-	
1916/1917	*No competition*	-	-	
1917/1918	*No competition*	-	-	
1918/1919	*No competition*	-	-	
1919/1920	AS Venus Bucureşti	-	-	
1920/1921	AS Venus Bucureşti	-	-	
1921/1922	Chinezul Timişoara	-	-	
1922/1923	Chinezul Timişoara	-	-	
1923/1924	Chinezul Timişoara	-	-	
1924/1925	Chinezul Timişoara	-	-	
1925/1926	Chinezul Timişoara	-	-	
1926/1927	Chinezul Timişoara	-	-	
1927/1928	CS Colţea Braşov	-	-	
1928/1929	AS Venus Bucureşti	-	-	
1929/1930	FC Juventus Bucureşti	-	-	
1930/1931	UD Reşiţa	-	-	
1931/1932	AS Venus Bucureşti	-	-	
1932/1933	FC Ripensia Timişoara	-	-	
1933/1934	AS Venus Bucureşti	FC Ripensia Timişoara	Ştefan Dobay (FC Ripensia Timişoara)	25
1934/1935	FC Ripensia Timişoara	ACS CFR Bucureşti	Ştefan Dobay (FC Ripensia Timişoara)	24
1935/1936	FC Ripensia Timişoara	FC Ripensia Timişoara	Ştefan Barbu (ACS CFR Bucureşti)	23
1936/1937	AS Venus Bucureşti	FC Rapid Bucureşti	Ştefan Dobay (FC Ripensia Timişoara) Traian Iordache (Unirea Tricolor Bucureşti)	21
1937/1938	FC Ripensia Timişoara	FC Rapid Bucureşti	Árpád Thierjung (Chinezul Timişoara)	22
1938/1939	AS Venus Bucureşti	FC Rapid Bucureşti	Adalbert Marksteiner [Béla Marosvári] (FC Ripensia Timişoara)	21
1939/1940	AS Venus Bucureşti	FC Rapid Bucureşti	Ştefan Auer II [István Avar] (FC Rapid Bucureşti)	21
1940/1941	Unirea Tricolor Bucureşti	FC Rapid Bucureşti	Ion Bogdan (FC Rapid Bucureşti) Valeriu Niculescu (Unirea Tricolor Bucureşti)	21
1941/1942	*No competition*	FC Rapid Bucureşti	-	
1942/1943	*No competition*	CFR Turnu Severin	-	
1943/1944	*No competition*	*No competition*	-	
1944/1945	*No competition*	*No competition*	-	
1945/1946	*No competition*	*No competition*	-	
1946/1947	IT Arad	*No competition*	Ladislau Bonyhádi (IT Arad)	26
1947/1948	IT Arad	IT Arad	Ladislau Bonyhádi (IT Arad)	49
1948/1949	IC Oradea	CSCA Bucureşti	Gheorghe Váczi (IC Oradea)	24
1950	Flamura Roşie Arad	CCA Bucureşti	Andrei Rădulescu (Locomotiva Bucureşti)	18
1951	CCA Bucureşti	CCA Bucureşti	Gheorghe Váczi (Progresul Oradea)	23
1952	CCA Bucureşti	CCA Bucureşti	Titus Ozon (CS Dinamo Bucureşti)	17
1953	CCA Bucureşti	Flamura Roşie Arad	Titus Ozon (CS Dinamo Bucureşti)	12
1954	Flamura Roşie Arad	Metalul Reşiţa	Alexandru Ene I (CS Dinamo Bucureşti)	20
1955	CS Dinamo Bucureşti	CCA Bucureşti	Ion Ciosescu (Ştiinţa Timişoara)	18
1956	CCA Bucureşti	Progresul Oradea	Ion Alecsandrescu (CCA Bucureşti)	18
1957/1958	FC Petrolul Ploieşti	CS Ştiinţa Timişoara	Ion Ciosescu (CS Ştiinţa Timişoara)	21
1958/1959	FC Petrolul Ploieşti	CS Dinamo Bucureşti	Gheorghe Ene (CS Rapid Bucureşti)	17
1959/1960	CCA Bucureşti	Progresul Bucureşti	Gheorghe Constantin (CCA Bucureşti)	20
1960/1961	CCA Bucureşti	Arieşul Turda	Gheorghe Constantin (CCA Bucureşti)	22
1961/1962	CS Dinamo Bucureşti	CSA Steaua Bucureşti	Gheorghe Constantin (CSA Steaua Bucureşti)	24
1962/1963	CS Dinamo Bucureşti	FC Petrolul Ploieşti	Ion Gheorghe Ionescu (CS Rapid Bucureşti)	20
1963/1964	CS Dinamo Bucureşti	CS Dinamo Bucureşti	Constantin Frăţilă (CS Dinamo Bucureşti) Cornel Pavlovici (CSA Steaua Bucureşti)	19
1964/1965	CS Dinamo Bucureşti	Ştiinţa Cluj	Mihai Adam (Ştiinţa Cluj)	18
1965/1966	FC Petrolul Ploieşti	CSA Steaua Bucureşti	Ion Gheorghe Ionescu (CS Rapid Bucureşti)	24
1966/1967	CS Rapid Bucureşti	CSA Steaua Bucureşti	Ion Oblemenco (Universitatea Craiova)	17
1967/1968	CSA Steaua Bucureşti	CS Dinamo Bucureşti	Mihai Adam (CS Universitatea Cluj)	15
1968/1969	UT Arad	CSA Steaua Bucureşti	Florea Dumitrache (CS Dinamo Bucureşti)	22
1969/1970	UT Arad	CSA Steaua Bucureşti	Ion Oblemenco (CS Universitatea Craiova)	19
1970/1971	CS Dinamo Bucureşti	CSA Steaua Bucureşti	Constantin Moldoveanu (Politehnica Iaşi) Florea Dumitrache (CS Dinamo Bucureşti) Gheorghe Tătaru (CSA Steaua Bucureşti)	15
1971/1972	FC Argeş Piteşti	CS Rapid Bucureşti	Ion Oblemenco (CS Universitatea Craiova)	20
1972/1973	CS Dinamo Bucureşti	CS Chimia Râmnicu Vâlcea	Ion Oblemenco (CS Universitatea Craiova)	21
1973/1974	CS Universitatea Craiova	CSM Jiul Petroşani	Mihai Adam (CFR Cluj-Napoca)	23
1974/1975	CS Dinamo Bucureşti	CS Rapid Bucureşti	Dudu Georgescu (CS Dinamo Bucureşti)	33

1975/1976	CSA Steaua București	CSA Steaua București	Dudu Georgescu (CS Dinamo București)	31
1976/1977	CS Dinamo București	CS Universitatea Craiova	Dudu Georgescu (CS Dinamo București)	47
1977/1978	CSA Steaua București	CS Universitatea Craiova	Dudu Georgescu (CS Dinamo București)	24
1978/1979	FC Argeș Pitești	CSA Steaua București	Marin Radu II (FC Argeș Pitești)	22
1979/1980	CS Universitatea Craiova	CS Politehnica Timișoara	Septimiu Câmpeanu II (CS Universitatea Cluj)	24
1980/1981	CS Universitatea Craiova	CS Universitatea Craiova	Marin Radu II (FC Argeș Pitești)	28
1981/1982	CS Dinamo București	CS Dinamo București	Anghel Iordănescu (CSA Steaua București)	20
1982/1983	CS Dinamo București	CS Universitatea Craiova	Petre Grosu (FC Bihor Oradea)	20
1983/1984	CS Dinamo București	CS Dinamo București	Marcel Coraș (CF Sportul Studențesc București)	20
1984/1985	CSA Steaua București	CSA Steaua București	Gheorghe Hagi (CF Sportul Studențesc București)	20
1985/1986	CSA Steaua București	CS Dinamo București	Gheorghe Hagi (CF Sportul Studențesc București)	31
1986/1987	CSA Steaua București	CSA Steaua București	Rodion Gorun Cămătaru (CS Dinamo București)	44
1987/1988	CSA Steaua București	CSA Steaua București	Victor Pițurcă (CSA Steaua București)	34
1988/1989	CSA Steaua București	CSA Steaua București	Dorin Mateuț (CS Dinamo București)	43
1989/1990	CS Dinamo București	CS Dinamo București	Gavril Balint (CSA Steaua București)	19
1990/1991	CS Universitatea Craiova	CS Universitatea Craiova	Ovidiu Cornel Hanganu (FC Corvinul Hunedoara)	24
1991/1992	CS Dinamo București	CSA Steaua București	Gábor Gerstenmájer (CS Dinamo București)	21
1992/1993	CSA Steaua București	FC Universitatea Craiova	Ilie Dumitrescu (CSA Steaua București)	24
1993/1994	CSA Steaua București	ACF Gloria Bistrița	Gheorghe Craioveanu (FC Universitatea Craiova)	21
1994/1995	CSA Steaua București	FC Petrolul Ploiești	Gheorghe Craioveanu (FC Universitatea Craiova)	27
1995/1996	CSA Steaua București	CSA Steaua București	Ion Vlădoiu (CSA Steaua București)	25
1996/1997	CSA Steaua București	CSA Steaua București	Sabin Ilie (CSA Steaua București)	31
1997/1998	CSA Steaua București	UFC Rapid București	Constantin Barbu (FC Argeș Pitești) Ion Vasile Oană (ACF Gloria Bistrița)	22
1998/1999	UFC Rapid București	FC Steaua București	Ioan Viorel Ganea (ACF Gloria Bistrița)	28
1999/2000	FC Dinamo București	FC Dinamo București	Marian Savu (FC Național București)	20
2000/2001	FC Steaua București	FC Dinamo București	Marius Constantin Niculae (FC Dinamo București)	20
2001/2002	FC Dinamo București	UFC Rapid București	Cătălin Cursaru (FCM Bacău)	17
2002/2003	UFC Rapid București	FC Dinamo București	Claudiu Nicu Răducanu (FC Steaua București)	21
2003/2004	FC Dinamo București	FC Dinamo București	Ionel Daniel Dănciulescu (FC Dinamo București)	21
2004/2005	FC Steaua București	FC Dinamo București	Gheorghe Bucur (CF Sportul Studențesc București) Claudiu Iulian Niculescu (FC Dinamo București)	21
2005/2006	FC Steaua București	UFC Rapid București	Ionuț Costinel Mazilu (CF Sportul Studențesc București)	22
2006/2007	FC Dinamo București	UFC Rapid București	Claudiu Iulian Niculescu (FC Dinamo București)	18
2007/2008	FC CFR 1907 Cluj-Napoca	FC CFR 1907 Cluj-Napoca	Ionel Daniel Dănciulescu (FC Dinamo București)	21
2008/2009	FC Unirea Urziceni	FC CFR 1907 Cluj-Napoca	Gheorghe Bucur (FC Timișoara) Florin Constantin Costea (FC Universitatea Craiova)	17
2009/2010	FC CFR 1907 Cluj-Napoca	FC CFR 1907 Cluj-Napoca	Andrei Cristea (FC Dinamo București)	16
2010/2011	ASC Oțelul Galați	FC Steaua București	Ianis Alin Zicu (FC Timișoara)	18
2011/2012	FC CFR 1907 Cluj-Napoca	FC Dinamo București	Wesley Lopes da Silva (BRA, FC Vaslui)	27
2012/2013	FC Steaua București	FC Petrolul Ploiești	Raul Andrei Rusescu (FC Steaua București)	21
2013/2014	FC Steaua București	AFC Astra Giurgiu	Liviu Ion Antal (FC Vaslui)	14
2014/2015	FC Steaua București	FC Steaua București	Grégory Tadé (FRA, FC CFR 1907 Cluj-Napoca)	18
2015/2016	AFC Astra Giurgiu	FC CFR 1907 Cluj-Napoca	Adrian Ioan Hora (CS Pandurii Târgu Jiu)	19
2016/2017	FC Viitorul Constanța	FC Voluntari	Azdren Llullaku (ALB, CS Gaz Metan Mediaș)	16
2017/2018	FC CFR 1907 Cluj-Napoca	CS Universitatea Craiova	Marius George Țucudean (FC Viitorul Constanța, FC CFR 1907 Cluj-Napoca) Harlem-Eddy Gnohéré (FRA, FCSB București)	15
2018/2019	FC CFR 1907 Cluj-Napoca	FC Viitorul Constanța	Marius George Țucudean (FC CFR 1907 Cluj-Napoca)	18
2019/2020	FC CFR 1907 Cluj-Napoca	SC FCSB București	Gabriel Cristian Iancu (FC Viitorul Constanța)	18

* Romanian Football Championship (1909–1921), Divizia A (1921–2006), Liga I (since 2006).

Club name changements:

FC Rapid București = ACS CFR București (1923-1936), FC Rapid București (1936-1945), CFR București (1945-1949), Locomotiva București (1949-1958), CS Rapid București (1958-1992), UFC Rapid București (1992-2016), Academia Rapid București (2017), FC Rapid București (since 2018).

UT Arad = IT Arad (1945–1949), Flamura Roșie Arad (1950–1957), UT Arad (1958–2014), UTA Bătrâna Doamnă Arad (2014–2017), UT Arad (since 2017).

ACS CAO Oradea = CA Oradea (1919-1940), Nagyváradi AC (1940-1944), Libertatea Oradea (1945-1948), IC Oradea (1948-1951), Progresul Oradea (1951-1958), CS Oradea (1958-1961), Crișana Oradea (1961-1963).

FCSB București = ASA București (1947-1948), CSCA București (1948-1950), CCA București (1950-1961), CSA Steaua București (1961-1998), FC Steaua București (1998-2017), FCSB București (since 2017).

FC Dinamo București = CS Dinamo București (1945-1992), FC Dinamo București (since 1992).

ACS Poli Timișoara = SS Politehnica Timișoara (1921-1948), CSU Timișoara (1948-1950), CS Știința Timișoara (1950-1966), CS Politehnica Timișoara (1966-1969), FC Ripensia Timișoata (1969), CS Politehnica Timișoara (1969-1992), FC Politehnica Timișoara (1992-2012), ACS Poli Timișoara (since 2012).

FC Universitatea Cluj-Napoca = Universitatea Cluj (1919-1948), CSU Cluj (1948-1949), Știința Cluj (1949-1966), CS Universitatea Cluj (1966-1974), CS Universitatea Cluj-Napoca (1974-1992), FC Universitatea Cluj-Napoca (since 1992).

CS Universitatea Craiova = CSU Craiova (1948-1950), Știința Craiova (1950-1966), CS Universitatea Craiova (1966-1992), FC Universitatea Craiova (1992-2011), CS Universitatea Craiova (since 2013).

Regular Season - Results

Round 1 [12-15.07.2019]
FC Voluntari - Sepsi OSK 0-0
Astra Giurgiu - FC Botoşani 2-2(1-2)
CFR Cluj - Politehnica Iaşi 1-1(1-0)
Univ. Craiova - FC Academica 3-2(2-1)
FCSB Bucureşti - FC Hermannstadt 4-3(2-1)
Gaz Metan - Chindia Târgovişte 2-2(2-0)
Viitorul Const. - Dinamo Bucureşti 5-0(1-0)

Round 2 [19-22.07.2019]
FC Hermannstadt - Gaz Metan 0-2(0-0)
Chindia Târgovişte - Viitorul Const. 0-1(0-0)
FC Botoşani - FC Voluntari 4-1(2-1)
FC Academica - CFR Cluj 1-4(0-3)
Politehnica Iaşi - Astra Giurgiu 1-0(1-0)
Dinamo Bucureşti - Univ. Craiova 0-2(0-1)
Sepsi OSK - FCSB Bucureşti 0-0

Round 3 [26-29.07.2019]
Politehnica Iaşi - FC Academica 2-0(0-0)
FC Voluntari - Astra Giurgiu 1-2(1-1)
Gaz Metan Mediaş - Sepsi OSK 1-1(1-0)
CFR Cluj - Dinamo Bucureşti 1-0(0-0)
Univ. Craiova - Chindia Târgovişte 1-0(0-0)
Viitorul Const. - FC Hermannstadt 3-2(0-1)
FCSB Bucureşti - FC Botoşani 0-2(0-2)

Round 4 [02-05.08.2019]
Dinamo Bucureşti - FC Academica 4-2(0-0)
FC Botoşani - Gaz Metan Mediaş 1-1(0-1)
Chindia Târgovişte - CFR Cluj 1-4(1-0)
FC Hermannstadt - Univ. Craiova 2-1(0-1)
Sepsi OSK - Viitorul Constanţa 2-2(1-0)
FC Voluntari - Politehnica Iaşi 0-0
Astra Giurgiu - FCSB Bucureşti 2-1(1-1)

Round 5 [09-12.08.2019]
FC Academica - Chindia Târgovişte 3-1(2-1)
Politehnica Iaşi - Dinamo Bucureşti 2-0(2-0)
Gaz Metan Mediaş - Astra Giurgiu 1-0(0-0)
CFR Cluj - FC Hermannstadt 3-0(1-0)
Universitatea Craiova - Sepsi OSK 0-1(0-0)
FCSB Bucureşti - FC Voluntari 1-3(0-1)
Viitorul Constanţa - FC Botoşani 2-2(1-1)

Round 6 [16-19.08.2019]
FC Hermannstadt - FC Academica 2-1(1-0)
Chindia Târgovişte - Dinamo Buc. 3-2(2-0)
Sepsi OSK - CFR Cluj 1-1(1-1)
FC Botoşani - Universitatea Craiova 1-1(1-1)
FCSB Bucureşti - Politehnica Iaşi 1-2(0-1)
FC Voluntari - Gaz Metan Mediaş 0-3(0-2)
Astra Giurgiu - Viitorul Constanţa 1-1(1-1)

Round 7 [23-26.08.2019]
Politehnica Iaşi - Chindia Târgovişte 2-2(2-1)
Universitatea Craiova - Astra Giurgiu 1-0(0-0)
FC Academica - Sepsi OSK 1-1(1-1)
CFR Cluj - FC Botoşani 4-1(3-0)
Viitorul Constanţa - FC Voluntari 4-0(1-0)
Gaz Metan Mediaş - FCSB Bucureşti 4-0(1-0)
Dinamo Bucureşti - FC Hermannstadt 3-0(1-0)

Round 8 [30.08.-02.09.2019]
FC Botoşani - FC Academica 2-2(2-2)
FC Voluntari - Universitatea Craiova 1-2(1-0)
Gaz Metan Mediaş - Politehnica Iaşi 3-2(0-0)
Astra Giurgiu - CFR Cluj 3-2(1-1)
FC Hermannstadt - Chindia Târgov. 2-1(1-0)
FCSB Bucureşti - Viitorul Constanţa 2-1(1-1)
Sepsi OSK - Dinamo Bucureşti 0-1(0-0)

Round 9 [13-16.09.2019]
FC Academica - Astra Giurgiu 1-1(1-1)
CFR Cluj - FC Voluntari 5-0(3-0)
Chindia Târgovişte - Sepsi OSK 0-0
Dinamo Bucureşti - FC Botoşani 1-0(0-0)
Politehnica Iaşi - FC Hermannstadt 0-0
Univ. Craiova - FCSB Bucureşti 0-1(0-0)
Viitorul Constanţa - Gaz Metan 4-1(1-0)

Round 10 [20-23.09.2019]
Gaz Metan Mediaş - Univ. Craiova 2-3(1-2)
FC Voluntari - FC Academica 1-2(0-1)
Sepsi OSK - FC Hermannstadt 3-0(2-0)
Astra Giurgiu - Dinamo Bucureşti 3-2(0-1)
FC Botoşani - Chindia Târgovişte 0-3(0-2)
FCSB Bucureşti - CFR Cluj 0-0
Viitorul Constanţa - Politehnica Iaşi 2-1(0-1)

Round 11 [27-30.09.2019]
Dinamo Bucureşti - FC Voluntari 2-1(0-0)
FC Hermannstadt - FC Botoşani 0-1(0-0)
Chindia Târgovişte - Astra Giurgiu 1-0(0-0)
FC Academica - FCSB Bucureşti 0-3(0-1)
CFR Cluj - Gaz Metan Mediaş 3-0(2-0)
Politehnica Iaşi - Sepsi OSK 1-1(0-0)
Univ. Craiova - Viitorul Constanţa 3-1(2-1)

Round 12 [04-07.10.2019]
FC Botoşani - Sepsi OSK 1-1(0-0)
Univ. Craiova - Politehnica Iaşi 1-1(0-0)
Gaz Metan Mediaş - FC Academica 2-1(0-0)
FCSB Bucureşti - Dinamo Bucureşti 1-1(1-1)
Viitorul Constanţa - CFR Cluj 3-1(2-0)
FC Voluntari - Chindia Târgovişte 0-1(0-1)
Astra Giurgiu - FC Hermannstadt 0-0

Round 13 [18-21.10.2019]
FC Hermannstadt - FC Voluntari 0-0
Dinamo Bucureşti - Gaz Metan 2-0(1-0)
CFR Cluj - Universitatea Craiova 2-0(0-0)
FC Academica - Viitorul Constanţa 0-0
Sepsi OSK - Astra Giurgiu 2-3(1-2)
Chindia Târgovişte - FCSB Bucureşti 1-2(1-1)
Politehnica Iaşi - FC Botoşani 0-3(0-1)

Round 14 [25-28.10.2019]
Sepsi OSK - FC Voluntari 0-0
Chindia Târgovişte - Gaz Metan 1-1(0-0)
FC Hermannstadt - FCSB Bucureşti 0-4(0-2)
FC Academica - Universitatea Craiova 0-0
FC Botoşani - Astra Giurgiu 1-2(0-0)
Dinamo Bucureşti - Viitorul Const. 3-2(2-0)
Politehnica Iaşi - CFR Cluj 2-1(1-1)

Round 15 [01-04.11.2019]
Viitorul Const. - Chindia Târgovişte 3-0(2-0)
Gaz Metan - FC Hermannstadt 1-1(0-0)
CFR Cluj - FC Academica 3-0(0-0)
FC Voluntari - FC Botoşani 1-2(1-0)
FCSB Bucureşti - Sepsi OSK 2-1(0-1)
Astra Giurgiu - Politehnica Iaşi 4-0(1-0)
Univ. Craiova - Dinamo Bucureşti 4-1(3-0)

Round 16 [08-10.11.2019]
Astra Giurgiu - FC Voluntari 1-0(1-0)
FC Hermannstadt - Viitorul Const. 1-1(1-1)
FC Academica - Politehnica Iaşi 1-0(0-0)
Chindia Târgovişte - Univ. Craiova 1-1(0-0)
FC Botoşani - FCSB Bucureşti 0-2(0-1)
Sepsi OSK - Gaz Metan Mediaş 0-1(0-0)
Dinamo Bucureşti - CFR Cluj 0-0

Round 17 [22-25.11.2019]
CFR Cluj - Chindia Târgovişte 4-0(1-0)
Politehnica Iaşi - FC Voluntari 2-2(0-1)
FCSB Bucureşti - Astra Giurgiu 1-3(1-1)
FC Academica - Dinamo Bucureşti 2-2(2-2)
Gaz Metan Mediaş - FC Botoşani 0-0
Univ. Craiova - FC Hermannstadt 3-0(1-0)
Viitorul Constanţa - Sepsi OSK 4-1(1-1)

Round 18 [29.11.-02.12.2019]
Astra Giurgiu - Gaz Metan Mediaş 1-0(1-0)
Dinamo Bucureşti - Politehnica Iaşi 1-0(0-0)
Sepsi OSK - Universitatea Craiova 1-0(1-0)
Chindia Târgovişte - FC Academica 2-5(2-3)
FC Hermannstadt - CFR Cluj 1-0(0-0)
FC Botoşani - Viitorul Constanţa 1-0(1-0)
Voluntari - FCSB Buc. 1-2(1-2) [06.02.2020]

Round 19 [03-05.12.2019]
Gaz Metan Mediaş - FC Voluntari 1-0(0-0)
Politehnica Iaşi - FCSB Bucureşti 1-2(1-1)
FC Academica - FC Hermannstadt 1-1(0-0)
CFR Cluj - Sepsi OSK 1-0(0-0)
Dinamo Bucureşti - Chindia Târgov. 4-1(1-1)
Universitatea Craiova - FC Botoşani 3-1(2-1)
Viitorul Constanţa - Astra Giurgiu 0-1(0-0)

Round 20 [06-10.12.2019]
FCSB Bucureşti - Gaz Metan Mediaş 2-0(0-0)
Chindia Târgovişte - Politehnica Iaşi 2-1(0-0)
FC Hermannstadt - Dinamo Bucureşti 4-2(1-0)
FC Botoşani - CFR Cluj 2-1(1-1)
Astra Giurgiu - Universitatea Craiova 1-0(0-0)
FC Voluntari - Viitorul Constanţa 1-2(0-0)
Sepsi OSK - FC Academica 4-0(0-0)

Round 21 [13-16.12.2019]
Dinamo Bucureşti - Sepsi OSK 1-2(0-0)
FC Academica - FC Botoşani 1-1(0-0)
Politehnica Iaşi - Gaz Metan Mediaş 1-2(0-0)
Universitatea Craiova - FC Voluntari 2-1(0-0)
Chindia Târgov. - FC Hermannstadt 1-1(0-1)
Viitorul Constanţa - FCSB Bucureşti 0-2(0-2)
CFR Cluj - Astra Giurgiu 2-0(1-0)

Round 22 [19-22.12.2019]
FC Botoşani - Dinamo Bucureşti 1-0(0-0)
Astra Giurgiu - FC Academica 3-1(2-0)
Gaz Metan - Viitorul Constanţa 1-0(0-0)
FC Hermannstadt - Politehnica Iaşi 1-0(1-0)
FC Voluntari - CFR Cluj 0-4(0-3)
Sepsi OSK - Chindia Târgovişte 3-1(1-1)
FCSB Bucureşti - Univ. Craiova 2-0(2-0)

Round 23 [31.01.-03.02.2020]
Univ. Craiova - Gaz Metan Mediaş 3-1(2-1)
FC Academica - FC Voluntari 1-2(1-1)
FC Hermannstadt - Sepsi OSK 2-2(0-1)
Dinamo Bucureşti - Astra Giurgiu 2-0(0-0)
Chindia Târgovişte - FC Botoşani 0-1(0-0)
CFR Cluj - FCSB Bucureşti 1-0(0-0)
Politehnica Iaşi - Viitorul Constanţa 1-2(1-0)

Round 24 [07-10.02.2020]
Astra Giurgiu - Chindia Târgovişte 1-2(0-0)
Gaz Metan Mediaş - CFR Cluj 0-0
Sepsi OSK - Politehnica Iaşi 1-0(0-0)
FC Voluntari - Dinamo Bucureşti 2-1(0-1)
Viitorul Constanţa - Univ. Craiova 1-2(1-1)
FC Botoşani - FC Hermannstadt 2-1(1-1)
FCSB Bucureşti - FC Academica 0-0

Round 25 [14-17.02.2020]	Round 26 [22-24.02.2020]
Chindia Târgovişte - FC Voluntari 1-2(0-1)	FC Voluntari - FC Hermannstadt 2-0(1-0)
CFR Cluj - Viitorul Constanţa 0-0	FCSB Bucureşti - Chindia Târgovişte 1-1(1-0)
FC Academica - Gaz Metan Mediaş 2-3(1-2)	Viitorul Constanţa - FC Academica 0-0
Politehnica Iaşi - Univ. Craiova 2-5(0-3)	Gaz Metan - Dinamo Bucureşti 1-0(1-0)
Sepsi OSK - FC Botoşani 0-1(0-0)	Astra Giurgiu - Sepsi OSK 2-2(0-2)
Dinamo Bucureşti - FCSB Bucureşti 2-1(1-1)	Universitatea Craiova - CFR Cluj 0-2(0-1)
FC Hermannstadt - Astra Giurgiu 2-2(0-0)	FC Botoşani - Politehnica Iaşi 2-1(0-1)

Final Standings

		Total							Home					Away				
1.	FC CFR 1907 Cluj-Napoca	26	15	7	4	51	-	16	52	11	2	0	30	- 2	4	5	4	21	- 14
2.	CS Universitatea Craiova	26	14	4	8	41	-	28	46	9	1	3	24	- 12	5	3	5	17	- 16
3.	FC Botoşani	26	12	9	5	36	-	30	45	6	4	3	18	- 16	6	5	2	18	- 14
4.	SC FCSB Bucureşti	26	13	5	8	37	-	29	44	5	4	4	17	- 17	8	1	4	20	- 12
5.	CS Gaz Metan Mediaş	26	12	7	7	34	-	30	43	7	5	1	19	- 10	5	2	6	15	- 20
6.	AFC Astra Giurgiu	26	13	6	7	38	-	29	42	8	4	1	24	- 13	5	2	6	14	- 16
7.	FC Viitorul Constanţa	26	11	7	8	44	-	29	40	8	2	3	31	- 13	3	5	5	13	- 16
8.	FC Dinamo Bucureşti	26	10	4	12	37	-	41	34	9	2	2	25	- 12	1	2	10	12	- 29
9.	ACS Sepsi OSK Sfântu Gheorghe	26	7	12	7	30	-	26	33	5	4	4	17	- 10	2	8	3	13	- 16
10.	AFC Chindia Târgovişte	26	6	7	13	29	-	47	25	3	4	6	14	- 21	3	3	7	15	- 26
11.	AFC Hermannstadt Sibiu	26	5	10	11	26	-	44	25	5	5	3	17	- 18	0	5	8	9	- 26
12.	FC Politehnica Iaşi	26	5	7	14	26	-	40	22	4	4	5	17	- 20	1	3	9	9	- 20
13.	FC Academica Clinceni	26	4	10	12	30	-	47	22	2	7	4	14	- 19	2	3	8	16	- 28
14.	FC Voluntari	26	5	5	16	22	-	45	20	2	2	9	10	- 21	3	3	7	12	- 24

Teams ranked 1-6 were qualified for the Championship Round, while teams ranked 7-14 were qualified for the Relegation Round. In both rounds, points from Regular Season were halved and rounded upwards.

Relegation Round

Results

Round 1 [28.02.-02.03.2020]	Round 2 [07-09.03.2020]	Round 3 [13-14.06.2020]
Sepsi OSK - Politehnica Iaşi 1-1(0-1)	FC Academica - Viitorul Constanţa 2-3(1-1)	FC Voluntari - FC Academica 3-0(2-0)
Dinamo Bucureşti - FC Academica 0-1(0-0)	Politehnica Iaşi - Dinamo Bucureşti 1-0(0-0)	Sepsi OSK - FC Hermannstadt 1-1(1-0)
Viitorul Constanţa - FC Voluntari 0-0	Chindia Târgovişte - Sepsi OSK 1-1(1-0)	Viitorul Constanţa - Politehnica Iaşi 2-1(1-1)
FC Hermannstadt - Chindia Târgov. 1-0(1-0)	FC Voluntari - FC Hermannstadt 1-1(0-0)	Dinamo Buc. - Chindia Târgov. *not played*

Round 4 [16-18.06.2020]	Round 5 [21-22.06.2020]	Round 6 [26-28.06.2020]
Sepsi OSK - FC Voluntari 1-2(1-0)	FC Voluntari - Politehnica Iaşi 1-0(1-0)	FC Hermannstadt - FC Academica 0-1(0-0)
Chindia Târgovişte - Viitorul Const. 2-1(1-0)	Dinamo Bucureşti - Sepsi OSK 1-3(0-1)	Chindia Târgovişte - Politehnica Iaşi 0-2(0-1)
Politehnica Iaşi - FC Academica 0-1(0-0)	FC Academica - Chindia Târgovişte 1-0(0-0)	Sepsi OSK - Viitorul Constanţa 3-3(1-2)
FC Hermannstadt - Dinamo Buc. *not played*	Viitorul Const. - FC Hermannstadt 4-1(1-0)	Dinamo Bucureşti - FC Voluntari 0-1(0-0)

Round 7 [30.06.-02.07.2020]	Round 8 [05-06.07.2020]	Round 9 [11-13.07.2020]
Politehnica Iaşi - FC Hermannstadt 2-3(2-1)	Politehnica Iaşi - Sepsi OSK 3-1(1-1)	Viitorul Constanţa - FC Academica 5-0(1-0)
FC Academica - Sepsi OSK 1-0(0-0)	FC Academica - Dinamo Bucureşti 1-3(0-1)	FC Hermannstadt - FC Voluntari 2-1(1-0)
FC Voluntari - Chindia Târgovişte 2-0(1-0)	Chindia Târgov. - FC Hermannstadt 0-1(0-0)	Dinamo Bucureşti - Politehnica Iaşi 1-1(1-0)
Viitorul Const. - Dinamo Bucureşti 1-0(1-0)	FC Voluntari - Viitorul Constanţa 0-0	Sepsi OSK - Chindia Târgovişte 2-0(1-0)

Round 10 [17-20.07.2020]	Round 11 [25-26.07.2020]	Round 12 [29-30.07.2020]
FC Academica - FC Voluntari 2-1(1-0)	FC Academica - Politehnica Iaşi 3-0(1-0)	Chindia Târgovişte - FC Academica 3-1(1-0)
FC Hermannstadt - Sepsi OSK 2-2(1-1)	Viitorul Constanţa - Chindia Târgov. 4-1(1-0)	FC Hermannstadt - Viitorul Const. 2-0(0-0)
Politehnica Iaşi - Viitorul Constanţa 1-1(1-0)	FC Voluntari - Sepsi OSK 2-0(0-0)	Politehnica Iaşi - FC Voluntari 2-1(1-1)
Chindia Târgov. - Dinamo Buc. *not played*	Dinamo Buc. - FC Hermannstadt *not played*	Sepsi OSK - Dinamo Bucureşti *not played*

Round 13 [01-02.08.2020]	Round 14 [05.08.2020]
FC Academica - FC Hermannstadt 0-2(0-1)	Dinamo Bucureşti - Viitorul Const. 1-1(1-1)
Viitorul Constanţa - Sepsi OSK 0-3(0-3)	Sepsi OSK - FC Academica 1-0(1-0)
Politehnica Iaşi - Chindia Târgovişte 1-0(0-0)	FC Hermannstadt - Politehnica Iaşi 2-2(1-1)
FC Voluntari - Dinamo Bucureşti 1-2(0-1)	Chindia Târgovişte - FC Voluntari 2-0(2-0)

Final Standings

		Total							Home					Away				
7.	FC Viitorul Constanţa	14	6	5	3	25	-	17	43	5	1	1	16	- 6	1	4	2	9	- 11
8.	AFC Hermannstadt Sibiu	12	6	4	2	18	-	14	35	3	2	1	9	- 6	3	2	1	9	- 8
9.	ACS Sepsi OSK Sfântu Gheorghe	13	4	5	4	19	-	17	34	2	3	1	9	- 7	2	2	3	10	- 10
10.	FC Academica Clinceni	14	7	0	7	14	-	21	32	4	0	3	10	- 9	3	0	4	4	- 12
11.	FC Voluntari	14	6	3	5	16	-	12	31	4	2	1	10	- 3	2	1	4	6	- 9
12.	FC Politehnica Iaşi	14	5	4	5	17	-	17	30	4	1	2	10	- 7	1	3	3	7	- 10
13.	FC Dinamo Bucureşti	9	2	2	5	8	-	11	25	0	2	3	3	- 7	2	0	2	5	- 4
14.	AFC Chindia Târgovişte	12	3	1	8	9	-	17	23	3	1	2	8	- 6	0	0	6	1	- 11
	(*Liga I Play-offs*)																		

Championship Round

Results

Round 1 [29.02.-02.03.2020]
FC Botoşani - FCSB Bucureşti 2-2(1-2)
Univ. Craiova - Gaz Metan Mediaş 2-1(2-1)
CFR Cluj - Astra Giurgiu 2-1(1-0)

Round 2 [06-09.03.2020]
Astra Giurgiu - FC Botoşani 1-0(0-0)
FCSB Bucureşti - Univ. Craiova 4-1(1-1)
Gaz Metan Mediaş - CFR Cluj 0-0

Round 3 [14-15.06.2020]
CFR Cluj - FCSB Bucureşti 1-0(1-0)
Astra Giurgiu - Gaz Metan Mediaş 0-0
Univ. Craiova - FC Botoşani 2-1(1-0) [23.06.]

Round 4 [19-21.06.2020]
Universitatea Craiova - Astra Giurgiu 2-1(0-0)
FC Botoşani - CFR Cluj 0-2(0-2)
FCSB Bucureşti - Gaz Metan Mediaş 2-2(1-0)

Round 5 [26-29.06.2020]
Gaz Metan Mediaş - FC Botoşani 0-2(0-2)
CFR Cluj - Universitatea Craiova 2-3(0-1)
Astra Giurgiu - FCSB Bucureşti 3-2(1-2)

Round 6 [03-05.07.2020]
Gaz Metan Mediaş - Univ. Craiova 1-2(1-1)
FCSB Bucureşti - FC Botoşani 1-1(1-1)
Astra Giurgiu - CFR Cluj 2-2(1-2)

Round 7 [10-13.07.2020]
FC Botoşani - Astra Giurgiu 0-0
Univ. Craiova - FCSB Bucureşti 2-1(1-1)
CFR Cluj - Gaz Metan Mediaş 2-0(1-0)

Round 8 [17-19.07.2020]
Gaz Metan Mediaş - Astra Giurgiu 0-4(0-1)
FC Botoşani - Universitatea Craiova 0-2(0-0)
FCSB Bucureşti - CFR Cluj 0-2(0-0) [31.07.]

Round 9 [25-28.07.2020]
Gaz Metan Mediaş - FCSB Bucureşti 0-1(0-1)
CFR Cluj - FC Botoşani 1-0(1-0)
Astra Giurgiu - Univ. Craiova *not played*

Round 10 [01-03.08.2020]
FC Botoşani - Gaz Metan Mediaş 4-1(3-1)
Astra Giurgiu - FCSB Bucureşti *not played*
Universitatea Craiova - CFR Cluj 1-3(1-1)

Final Standings

								Home					Away				
					Total												
1. **FC CFR 1907 Cluj-Napoca**	10	7	2	1	17	-	7	49	4	0	1	8 - 4	3	2	0	9 - 3
2. CS Universitatea Craiova	9	7	0	2	17	-	14	44	4	0	1	9 - 7	3	0	1	8 - 7
3. AFC Astra Giurgiu	8	3	3	2	12	-	8	33	2	2	0	6 - 4	1	1	2	6 - 4
4. FC Botoşani	10	2	3	5	10	-	12	32	1	2	2	6 - 7	1	1	3	4 - 5
5. SC FCSB Bucureşti	9	2	3	4	13	-	14	31	1	2	1	7 - 6	1	1	3	6 - 8
6. CS Gaz Metan Mediaş	10	0	3	7	5	-	19	25	0	1	4	1 - 9	0	2	3	4 - 10

Top goalscorers:	
18 **Gabriel Cristian Iancu**	*FC Viitorul Constanţa*
14 Denis Alibec	*AFC Astra Giurgiu*
14 Alexandru Cicâldău	*CS Universitatea Craiova*
13 Ciprian Ioan Deac	*FC CFR 1907 Cluj-Napoca*
12 Gabriel Debeljuh (CRO)	*AFC Hermannstadt Sibiu*
12 Florinel Teodor Coman	*SC FCSB Bucureşti*

Liga I (Relegation) Play-offs [09-12.08.2020]

AFC Chindia Târgovişte - CS Mioveni   2-0(2-0)   1-1(1-1)

AFC Chindia Târgovişte remains at first level.

NATIONAL CUP
Cupa României 2019/2020

Fifth Round [24-26.09.2019]

ACS Flacăra Horezu - AFC Astra Giurgiu	0-2(0-1)		CS Făurei - CS Mioveni	1-5(0-0)
ACS Foresta Suceava - CS Gaz Metan Mediaş	2-1(2-1)		ACS Industria Galda - FC Petrolul Ploieşti	0-1(0-1)
FC UTA Arad - FC Dinamo Bucureşti	1-3(1-1)		CSM Reşiţa - CS Universitatea Craiova	0-1(0-1)
AFC Metalul Buzău - FK Miercurea Ciuc	1-0(1-0)		FC Botoşani - FC CFR 1907 Cluj-Napoca	2-2 aet; 4-2 pen
AFC Turris-Oltul T. Măg. - FC Academica Clinceni	2-3(0-1)		CS Sănătatea Cluj - FC Viitorul Constanţa	1-0(1-0)
CS Concordia Chiajna - FC Voluntari	2-3(1-2)		FC Ripensia Timişoara - Sepsi OSK Sf. Gheorghe	1-4(1-3)
FC Universitatea Craiova - FC Universitatea Cluj	2-3(2-1,2-2)		FC Rapid Bucureşti - FC Politehnica Iaşi	0-1(0-0)
AFC Chindia Târgovişte - AFC Hermannstadt Sibiu	0-1(0-0)		FC Metaloglobus Bucureşti – SC FCSB Bucureşti	0-2(0-2)

1/8-Finals [29-31.10.2019]

CS Mioveni - AFC Hermannstadt Sibiu	0-2(0-0)		ACS Foresta Suceava - FC Dinamo Bucureşti	0-4(0-1)
FC Universitatea Cluj - SC FCSB Bucureşti	0-1(0-1)		AFC Metalul Buzău - FC Politehnica Iaşi	0-3(0-1)
FC Academica Clinceni - FC Botoşani	2-0(1-0)		ACS Sepsi OSK Sf. Gheorghe - AFC Astra Giurgiu	4-2(2-1)
CS Sănătatea Cluj - FC Petrolul Ploieşti	0-7(0-3)		FC Voluntari - CS Universitatea Craiova	1-4(1-2)

Quarter-Finals [03-05.03.2020]

FC Academica Clinceni - FC Dinamo Bucureşti	0-1(0-0)		FC Politehnica Iaşi - CS Universitatea Craiova	3-2(2-0)
FC Petrolul Ploieşti - ACS Sepsi OSK Sf. Gheorghe	0-1(0-1)		AFC Hermannstadt Sibiu - SC FCSB Bucureşti	1-2(0-0)

Semi-Finals [24-25.06./08-09.07.2020]

First Leg			Second Leg	
ACS Sepsi OSK Sf. Gheorghe - FC Politehnica Iaşi	5-1(1-1)		FC Politehnica Iaşi - ACS Sepsi OSK Sf. Gheorghe	0-3(0-1)
FC Dinamo Bucureşti - SC FCSB Bucureşti	0-3(0-1)		SC FCSB Bucureşti - FC Dinamo Bucureşti	1-0(1-0)

Final

22.07.2020; Stadionul "Ilie Oană", Ploieşti; Referee: Sebastian Colţescu; Attendance: None
SC FCSB Bucureşti - ACS Sepsi OSK Sfântu Gheorghe   **1-0(0-0)**

FCSB Bucureşti: Andrei Vlad, Valentin Creţu, George Miron, Iulian Cristea, Ionuţ Panţîru (89.Alexandru Pantea), Ionuţ Vînă (46.Adrian Petre), Darius Olaru (46.Olimpiu Moruţan), Ovidiu Popescu, Dennis Man, Florinel Teodor Coman (90+3.Ovidiu Perianu), Florin Lucian Tănase (Cap). Trainer: Anton Petrea.

Sepsi OSK: Roland Niczuly, Radoslav Dimitrov (75.Tomás Díaz Grassano), Rachid Bouhenna (Cap) [*sent off 80*], Răzvan Tincu, Florin Ştefan, Gabriel Vaşvari, Ronaldo Deaconu, Anass Achahbar (83.Daniel Celea), Nicolae Cârnaţ, (46.Lóránd Fülöp), Goran Karanović (46.Pavol Šafranko), Marius Ştefănescu (75.Balázs Csiszér). Trainer: Leontin Florian Grozavu.

Goal: 1-0 Dennis Man (65).

THE CLUBS 2019/2020

Please <u>note</u>: matches and goals includes statistics of both regular season and play-offs (Championship or Relegation).

Football Club Academica Clinceni

Founded:	2005 (*as CS Buftea*)
Stadium:	Stadionul Clinceni, Clinceni (4,500)
Trainer:	Ilie Poenaru 11.11.1976

Goalkeepers:	DOB	M	(s)	G
Nicolae Calancea (MDA)	29.08.1986	2		
Miguel José Oliveira Silva Santos (POR)	21.10.1994	8		
Andrei Ureche	27.07.1998	2		
Octavian Vâlceanu	13.10.1996	28		
Defenders:	**DOB**	**M**	**(s)**	**G**
Florin Achim	16.07.1991	21	(12)	2
Cristian Albu	17.08.1993	16		2
Florin Bejan	28.03.1991	10	(2)	
Okan Chatziterzoglu (GRE)	05.03.1996	14	(1)	
Mihai Dobrescu	12.09.1992	29	(5)	2
David Humanes Muñoz (ESP)	13.11.1996	11		
Giannis Kontoes (GRE)	24.05.1986	7	(6)	
Gabriel Matei	26.02.1990	28	(1)	
Alon Netzer (ISR)	02.06.1993	1		
Paul Pârvulescu	11.08.1988	13	(5)	
Răzvan Patrichi	29.04.1986	30	(2)	1
Andreï Răuţă	04.07.1995	10	(4)	
Andrei Şuşu	22.01.2001	3	(1)	
Midfielders:	**DOB**	**M**	**(s)**	**G**
Bogdan Barbu	13.04.1992	5	(4)	1
Laurenţiu Buş	27.08.1987	3	(3)	

	DOB	M	(s)	G
Eugen Cebotaru (MDA)	16.10.1984	31	(4)	4
Marius Florian Ciobanu Vanghene	31.03.2003		(4)	
Bogdan Ilie	30.10.1999	3	(6)	
Robert Ion	05.09.2000	16	(16)	2
Jean Alexandre Deretti (BRA)	01.05.1993	5	(5)	1
George Merloi	15.10.1999	21	(7)	4
Vasile Olariu	06.07.1987	2		
Imran Oulad Omar (MAR)	11.12.1997		(2)	
Paul Paţurcă	20.03.1996	1	(2)	
Adrian Şut	30.04.1999	29	(1)	6
Denis Ventúra (SVK)	01.08.1995	6	(8)	
Forwards:	**DOB**	**M**	**(s)**	**G**
Alexandru Buziuc	15.03.1994	34	(4)	5
Cristian Cosmin Dumitru	13.12.2001	2	(8)	
Danny Esteves (POR)	29.07.1994		(1)	
Jovan Marković	23.03.2001	5	(8)	1
Sofiane Moussa (TUN)	06.02.1988	4	(1)	
Aristote N'Dongala (COD)	19.01.1994		(1)	
Philippe Nsiah (FRA)	24.10.1994	5	(6)	1
Alexandru Popescu	06.01.1998	5	(2)	
Jakub Vojtuš (SVK)	22.10.1993	30	(3)	9

Asociaţia Fotbal Club Astra Giurgiu

Founded: 18.09.1921 (*as Clubul Sportiv Astra-Română Giurgiu*)
Stadium: Stadionul "Marin Anastasovici", Giurgiu (8,500)
Trainer: Dan Alexa   28.10.1979
[09.10.2019]   Bogdan Andone   07.01.1975

Goalkeepers:	DOB	M	(s)	G
Georgi Kitanov (BUL)	06.03.1995	12		
David Lazăr	08.08.1991	22		
Defenders:	**DOB**	**M**	**(s)**	**G**
Alexandru Dandea	23.01.1988	5	(9)	
David Carneiro Dias Resende Bruno (POR)	14.02.1992	16	(5)	
Constantin Dima	21.07.1999	23	(2)	
Daniel Graovac (BIH)	08.08.1993	32		
Dinu Graur (MDA)	27.12.1994	5	(1)	
Risto Radunović (MNE)	04.05.1992	32		2
Gabriel Simion	22.05.1998	27	(2)	
Gabriel Tamaş	09.11.1983	22		1
David Tiram (ISR)	16.09.1993	1		1
Andrei Truşescu	27.05.1999	1		
Midfielders:	**DOB**	**M**	**(s)**	**G**
Ionuţ Biceanu	26.02.1994	3	(8)	
Constantin Budescu	19.02.1989	18	(1)	6
Ljuban Crepulja (CRO)	02.09.1993	32	(1)	1
Gabriel Nicolae Enache	18.08.1990	3	(4)	1
Dragoş Gheorghe	10.01.1999	1	(2)	

	DOB	M	(s)	G
Valentin Gheorghe	14.02.1997	22	(8)	10
Alexandru Ioniţă	14.12.1994	3	(3)	1
Florentin Matei	15.04.1993	7	(6)	
Romario Moise	21.09.1996	1	(2)	
Marius Cătălin Pahonţu	22.08.1999	1		
Mihai Răduţ	18.03.1990	21	(7)	3
Gabriel Serban	11.02.2000	4		
Takayuki Seto (JPN)	05.02.1986	5	(2)	1
Toni Brita Silva Sá (GNB)	15.09.1993		(1)	
Albert Stahl	11.01.1999	10	(3)	
Forwards:	**DOB**	**M**	**(s)**	**G**
Goodness Ajayi (NGA)	06.10.1994		(3)	
Denis Alibec	05.01.1991	23	(2)	14
Raoul Baicu	05.04.2000	1	(2)	1
Silviu Balaure	06.02.1996		(6)	1
Julien Bègue (FRA)	08.08.1993	7	(16)	1
Kehinde Fatai (NGA)	19.02.1990	6	(4)	2
Robert Grecu	02.06.1998	2		
Vahid Hambo (FIN)	03.02.1995		(1)	
Oumare Tounkara (FRA)	25.05.1990	6	(8)	

Fotbal Club Botoşani

Founded: 2001
Stadium: Stadionul Municipal, Botoşani (7,782)
Trainer: Marius Croitoru   02.10.1980

Goalkeepers:	DOB	M	(s)	G
Hidajet Hankič (AUT)	29.06.1994	10	(1)	
Eduard Pap	01.07.1994	26		
Defenders:	**DOB**	**M**	**(s)**	**G**
Nikos Baxevanos (GRE)	16.07.1999		(1)	
Andrei Chindriş	12.01.1999	33		
Denis Hăruţ	25.02.1999	34		
Marcel Holzmann (AUT)	03.09.1990	3	(8)	
Nikita Koļesovs (LVA)	25.09.1996	2		
George Miron	28.05.1994	21		2
Adrian Moescu	31.05.2001	1		
Andrei Patache	29.10.1987	5	(8)	
Andrei Piţian	16.11.1995		(5)	
Aristides Soiledis (GRE)	08.02.1991	3		
Alin Şeroni	26.03.1987	12		
Midfielders:	**DOB**	**M**	**(s)**	**G**
Răzvan Andronic	07.01.2000	5	(3)	1
David Babunski (MKD)	01.03.1994	2	(5)	
Batista Cascini (ARG)	04.06.1997	4	(5)	
George Cimpanu	08.10.2000	3	(14)	2
Alexandru Corban	29.01.1998	1	(1)	

	DOB	M	(s)	G
Marian Croitoru	09.08.2003		(1)	
Mario Ebenhofer (AUT)	29.07.1992	7	(6)	
Eduard Florescu	27.06.1997	9	(6)	2
Bryan Mendoza (ARG)	14.03.1993	1	(4)	
Hervin Ongenda (FRA)	24.06.1995	16	(1)	3
Enriko Papa (ALB)	12.03.1993	31		2
Michael Leonel Pierce (ARG)	28.07.1993	1	(5)	
Jonathan Yoni Emanuel Rodríguez (ARG)	07.06.1990	29		2
Alexandru Ţigănaşu	12.06.1990	30		2
Forwards:	**DOB**	**M**	**(s)**	**G**
Stefan Aškovski (MKD)	24.02.1992	29	(5)	4
Alexandru Caia	10.04.2003		(1)	
Alessio Carlone (BEL)	20.01.1996	4	(4)	
Minas Chalkiadakis (GRE)	05.02.1995	1	(3)	
Marko Dugandžić (CRO)	07.04.1994	13		8
Realdo Fili (ALB)	14.05.1996		(4)	
Cătălin Golofca	21.04.1990	5	(1)	1
Hamidou Keyta (FRA)	17.12.1994	11	(12)	3
Sofiane Moussa (TUN)	06.02.1988	4	(7)	1
Reagy Ofosu (GER)	20.09.1991	30	(4)	6
Mihai Roman I	16.10.1984	10	(4)	4

Fotbal Club Căile Ferate Române 1907 Cluj-Napoca

Founded: 1907 (*as Kolozsvári Vasutas Sport Club*)
Stadium: Stadionul "Dr. Constantin Rădulescu", Cluj-Napoca (23,500)
Trainer: Dan Vasile Petrescu   22.12.1967

Goalkeepers:	DOB	M	(s)	G
Giedrius Arlauskis (LTU)	01.12.1987	28		
Otto Hindrich	05.08.2002	1		
Jesús Fernández Collado (ESP)	11.06.1988	2		
Adrian Vasile Rus	12.02.1994		(1)	
Grzegorz Sandomierski (POL)	05.09.1989	1		
Cosmin Vâtcă	12.05.1982	4		
Defenders:	**DOB**	**M**	**(s)**	**G**
Andrei Burcă	15.04.1993	19	(2)	2
Mihai Butean	14.09.1996	4		
Mário Jorge Melico Paulino "Camora" (POR)	21.09.1986	29		2
Mike Botuli Cestor (COD)	30.04.1992	10	(1)	1
Denis Ciobotariu	10.06.1998		(1)	
Andrei Joca	22.06.2000	4	(1)	
Cristian Marian Manea	09.08.1997	5		
Andrei Mureşan	01.08.1985	7		
Alexandru Paşcanu	28.09.1998	2	(2)	
Paulo Vinícius de Souza Nascimento (BRA)	12.08.1984	25		5
Andrei Peteleu	20.08.1992	13		
Mateo Sušić (BIH)	18.11.1990	15	(1)	2
Midfielders:	**DOB**	**M**	**(s)**	**G**
Kévin Boli (CIV)	21.06.1991	15		2

	DOB	M	(s)	G
Mihai Bordeianu	18.11.1991	13	(8)	2
Valentin Costache	02.08.1998	31	(3)	4
Juan Emmanuel Culio (ARG)	30.08.1983	8	(1)	4
Ciprian Ioan Deac	16.02.1986	23	(2)	13
Damjan Đoković (CRO)	18.04.1990	15	(3)	1
Alin Fica	14.06.2001	2		
Ovidiu Hoban	27.12.1982	21	(5)	1
Cătălin Itu	26.10.1999	31	(2)	4
Luís Miguel Coimbra Aurélio (POR)	17.08.1988	3	(8)	1
Mickaël Pereira (FRA)	08.12.1987	10	(6)	2
Claudiu Petrila	07.11.2000	1	(14)	
Yacouba Sylla (MLI)	29.11.1990	2	(2)	
Forwards:	**DOB**	**M**	**(s)**	**G**
Alexandru Mihăiţă Chipciu	18.05.1989	3	(6)	
Cătălin Golofca	21.04.1990	1	(6)	
Sebastian Mailat	01.01.1997		(1)	
Billel Omrani (FRA)	02.06.1993	12	(16)	7
Alexandru Păun	01.04.1995	13	(11)	7
Mário Júnior Rondon Fernández (VEN)	26.03.1986	15	(9)	2
Lacina Traoré (CIV)	20.05.1990	6	(5)	2
Marius George Ţucudean	30.04.1991	2	(4)	1

Asociaţia Fotbal Club Chindia Târgovişte

Founded: 11.08.2010
Stadium: Stadionul „Ilie Oană", Ploieşti (15,073)
Trainer: Dinu Viorel Moldovan — 08.07.1972

Goalkeepers:	DOB	M	(s)	G
Mihai Aioani	07.11.1999	30		
Dinu Moldovan	03.05.1990	8		
Defenders:	DOB	M	(s)	G
Alexandru Benga	15.06.1989	30		1
Laurenţiu Corbu	10.05.1994	11	(1)	
Bradley Diallo (FRA)	20.07.1990	9	(1)	1
Cornel Dinu	09.06.1989	5	(4)	
Alin Dudea	06.06.1997	2	(3)	
Denis Dumitraşcu	27.04.1995	13	(14)	
Adrian Ionita	11.03.2000	3	(1)	1
Mihai Leca	14.04.1992	18	(1)	1
Marius Martac	05.07.1991	34	(1)	
Robert Neciu	10.01.1999	11	(2)	
Andrei Piţian	16.11.1995	17	(1)	1
Midfielders:	DOB	M	(s)	G
Cosmin Atanase	03.01.2001		(1)	
Ovidiu Bic	23.02.1994	34	(1)	3
Cristian Cherchez	01.02.1991	8	(5)	3

	DOB	M	(s)	G
Liviu Mihai	12.03.1988	12	(8)	2
Alex Negrea	01.10.1998	4	(1)	
Daniel Novac	26.09.1987	12	(4)	
Alexandru Piftor	09.05.1999	5		
Vadim Raţă (MDA)	05.05.1993	26	(6)	2
Andrei Şerban	30.06.1995	10	(1)	
Forwards:	DOB	M	(s)	G
Valentin Alexandru	17.09.1991	1		
Cătălin Barbu	05.08.1999	5	(1)	
Valmir Berisha (SWE)	06.06.1996	10	(5)	2
Andrei Burlacu	12.01.1997	4	(10)	1
Filip Dangubić (CRO)	05.05.1995	5	(9)	1
Ioan Andrei Vasile Dumiter	10.04.1999	11	(1)	1
Daniel Florea	17.04.1988	13	(11)	4
Josip Ivančić (CRO)	29.03.1991	12	(8)	2
Mihai Neicuţescu	29.09.1998	4		2
Cristian Neguţ	09.12.1995	27	(8)	5
Mihai Voduţ	28.07.1994	8	(4)	2
Blaise Yaméogo (BFA)	28.12.1993	16	(11)	2

Fotbal Club Dinamo Bucureşti

Founded: 14.05.1948
Stadium: Stadionul Dinamo, Bucureşti (15,032)
Trainer: Eugen Neagoe — 22.08.1967
[13.08.2019] Dušan Uhrin (CZE) — 11.10.1967
[11.03.2020] Adrian Mihalcea — 24.05.1976
[14.07.2020] Gheorghe Mulţescu — 13.11.1951

Goalkeepers:	DOB	M	(s)	G
Riccardo Piscitelli (ITA)	10.10.1993	26		
Cătălin Straton	09.10.1989	9		
Defenders:	DOB	M	(s)	G
Florin Bejan	28.03.1991	4		
Denis Ciobotariu	10.06.1998	18		2
Laurenţiu Corbu	10.05.1994	14	(2)	
Marco Ehmann (GER)	03.08.2000	2		
Gabriel Rodrigues de Moura (BRA)	18.06.1988	9	(3)	
Ricardo Grigore	07.04.1999	12	(6)	2
Szabolcs Kilyen	19.03.1998	3	(2)	
Linas Klimavičius (LTU)	10.04.1989	10		1
Kristián Koštrna (SVK)	15.12.1993	7	(1)	
Mihai Popescu	07.05.1993	24		1
Ante Puljić (CRO)	05.11.1987	21	(1)	1
Lukáš Skovajsa (SVK)	27.03.1994	10	(1)	
Deian Sorescu	29.08.1997	30	(2)	10
Midfielders:	DOB	M	(s)	G
Ahmed Bani	22.08.2002	3	(3)	1

	DOB	M	(s)	G
Ioan Borcea	06.07.2002	1		
Kévin Bru (MRI)	12.12.1988	5	(3)	
Geani Creţu	12.01.2000	1	(1)	
Diego Fabbrini (ITA)	31.07.1990	14	(3)	1
Ioan Filip	20.05.1989	24	(1)	1
Andreas Mihaiu	19.08.1998	9	(7)	
Filip Mrzljak (CRO)	16.04.1993	23	(1)	2
Dan Nicolae Nistor	05.06.1988	15	(1)	4
Alexandru Răuţă	17.06.1992	15	(10)	
Ionuţ Şerban	07.08.1995	1	(3)	
Forwards:	DOB	M	(s)	G
Armindo Rodrigues Mendes Furtado „Brito"(CPV)	16.11.1987	1	(3)	
Valentin Lazăr	21.08.1989	6	(6)	1
Robert Moldoveanu	08.03.1999	17	(11)	2
Mattia Montini (ITA)	28.02.1992	15	(7)	4
Mihai Neicutescu	29.09.1998	8		
Slavko Perović (SRB)	09.06.1989	14	(3)	6
Daniel Popa	14.07.1994	6	(27)	4
Andrei Sin	26.10.1991	8	(6)	1

Sport Club Fotbal Club FCSB Bucureşti

Founded: 07.06.1947 (*as AS Armata Bucureşti*)
Stadium: Arena Naţională, Bucureşti (55,634)
Trainer: Bogdan Andone — 07.01.1975
[01.08.2019] Vergil Andronache — 16.09.1970
[23.08.2019] Bogdan Vintilă — 27.02.1972

Goalkeepers:	DOB	M	(s)	G
Cristian Bălgrădean	21.03.1988	19	(1)	
Andrei Vlad	15.04.1999	16		
Defenders:	DOB	M	(s)	G
Mihai Alexandru Bălaşa	14.01.1995	3	(1)	
Claudiu Belu-Iordache	07.11.1993	4	(1)	
Marian Botezatu	26.12.2000	1		
Bozhidar Chorbadzhiyski (BUL)	08.08.1995	3		
Valentin Creţu	02.01.1989	26		
Lucian Filip	25.09.1990	7	(4)	
Cristian Marian Manea	09.08.1997	2		
Andrei Ovidiu Marc	29.04.1993	2		
George Miron	28.05.1994	8	(1)	1
Marko Momčilović (SRB)	11.06.1987	1		
Alexandru Pantea	11.09.2003	2	(2)	
Ionuţ Panţîru	22.03.1996	23		
Bogdan Planić (SRB)	19.01.1992	21		
Aristides Soiledis (GRE)	08.02.1991	11	(4)	1
Midfielders:	DOB	M	(s)	G
Laurenţiu Ardelean	08.02.2001	1		
Iulian Cristea	17.07.1994	27	(1)	1
Olimpiu Moruţan	25.04.1999	11	(14)	1
Thierry Rua Moutinho (SUI)	26.02.1991	5	(2)	
Dragoş Nedelcu	16.02.1997	8	(3)	1

	DOB	M	(s)	G
Răzvan Oaidă	02.03.1998	19	(3)	3
Darius Olaru	03.03.1998	10	(2)	2
Vlăduţ Pandele	09.07.2003		(2)	
Ovidiu Perianu	16.04.2002	4		
Mihai Doru Pintilii	09.11.1984	5		
Ovidiu Popescu	27.02.1994	23	(4)	1
Sorin Şerban	17.03.2000	1		
Florin Lucian Tănase	30.12.1994	27	(3)	7
Forwards:	DOB	M	(s)	G
Florinel Teodor Coman	10.04.1998	25	(3)	12
Diogo Ferreira Salomão (POR)	14.09.1988	2	(1)	
Cristián Dumitru	13.12.2001	2	(3)	
Łukasz Gikiewicz (POL)	26.10.1987	3		
Harlem-Eddy Gnohéré (FRA)	21.02.1988	5	(13)	6
Adrian Ioan Hora	21.08.1988	6	(5)	1
Andrei Istrate	15.03.2002	1	(1)	
Dennis Man	26.08.1998	21	(2)	7
Adrian Niţă	08.03.2003	2	(2)	
Adrian Petre	11.02.1998	6	(2)	1
Adrian Dumitru Popa	24.07.1988	6	(11)	2
Mihai Roman I	16.10.1984	3	(1)	
Hava Juvhel Tsoumou (GER)	27.12.1990	1	(1)	1
Ionuţ Vînă	20.02.1995	12	(11)	1

Clubul Sportiv Gaz Metan Mediaş

Founded: 1945 (*as Karres Mediaş*)
Stadium: Stadionul Gaz Metan, Mediaş (7,814)
Trainer: Edward Iordănescu   16.06.1978
[08.06.2020]   Dušan Uhrin (CZE)   11.10.1967

Goalkeepers:	DOB	M	(s)	G			DOB	M	(s)	G
Răzvan Pleşca	25.11.1982	34			Paul Costea	02.03.1999		(3)	
Albert Popa	05.04.1999	1			Mickaël Diakota (FRA)	06.10.1990	5	(10)	
Ricardo Jorge Cecília Batista (POR)	19.11.1986	1			Lukáš Droppa (CZE)	22.04.1989	29	(2)	
Defenders:	**DOB**	**M**	**(s)**	**G**	Boubacar Fofana (GUI)	06.11.1989	24		
Eduard Avram	11.03.2003		(5)		Ionuţ Larie	16.01.1987	34		
Nasser Chamed (COM)	04.10.1993	17	(15)	5	Daniel Nicula	20.03.2003		(3)	
Mite Cikarski (MKD)	06.01.1993	1			Darius Olaru	03.03.1998	21		3
Marius Constantin	25.10.1984	30		8	Roberto Romeo (ITA)	27.04.1990	12	(10)	2
Valentin Creţu	02.01.1989	3			Neluţ Roşu	05.07.1993	9	(14)	1
Gabriel Rodrigues de Moura (BRA)	18.06.1988	10	(2)		Răzvan Trif	09.10.1997	4	(3)	
Thomas Juel-Nielsen (DEN)	18.06.1990	3	(2)	1	**Forwards:**	**DOB**	**M**	**(s)**	**G**
Marian Pleaşcă	06.02.1990	10	(3)		Sergiu Buş	02.11.1992	30		10
Răzvan Popa	04.01.1997	10	(9)		Rareş Dogaru	11.12.2003		(4)	
Mihai Velisar	30.08.1998	35		2	Stephan Drăghici	30.01.1998	5	(10)	
Midfielders:	**DOB**	**M**	**(s)**	**G**	Nicolao Dumitru (ITA)	12.10.1991	26	(3)	5
Mihai Butean	14.09.1996	10	(1)		Ely Ernesto Lopes Fernandes (CPV)	04.11.1990	14	(12)	1
Sergiu Ciocan	22.09.1998	12	(1)		Adrian Hora	21.08.1988	5		1
					Moussa Sanoh (NED)	20.07.1995	1	(5)	

Asociaţia Fotbal Club Hermannstadt Sibiu

Founded: 29.07.2015
Stadium: Stadionul Municipal, Sibiu (5,000)
Trainer: Constantin Enache   11.03.1973
[20.08.2019]   Dănuţ Perja   14.11.1974
[02.10.2019]   Eugen Neagoe   22.08.1967
[07.01.2020]   Vasile Miriuţă (HUN)   19.09.1968
[19.06.2020]   Rubén Albés Yáñez (ESP)   24.02.1985

Goalkeepers:	DOB	M	(s)	G			DOB	M	(s)	G
Cristiano Pereira Figueiredo (POR)	29.11.1990	31			Răzvan Dâlbea	08.10.1981	20	(6)	3
Emanuel Rodrigues Novo (POR)	26.08.1992	6			Lucian Dumitriu	21.09.1992	9	(15)	1
Ionuţ Pop	01.08.1997	1			Daniel Offenbacher (AUT)	18.02.1992	6	(1)	
Defenders:	**DOB**	**M**	**(s)**	**G**	Petrişor Petrescu	29.06.1993	24	(11)	5
Sorin Buşu	08.07.1989	9	(16)		Sergiu Popovici	23.03.1993	1		
Lucian Buzan	09.03.1999	9	(1)		Romário Santos Pires (BRA)	16.01.1989	29	(1)	3
Alexandru Dandea	23.01.1988	3	(1)	1	Daniel Tătar	21.10.1987	6	(3)	
Alin Dobrosavlevici	21.10.1994	3	(1)		**Forwards:**	**DOB**	**M**	**(s)**	**G**
Srdjan Luchin	04.03.1986	20	(3)		Adrian Bălan	14.03.1990	5	(4)	2
Alexandru Măţel	17.10.1989	8			Ştefan Blănaru	20.02.1989		(3)	
Raul Opruţ	04.01.1998	33			David Caiado Dias (POR)	02.05.1987	22	(2)	
Kévin Rimane (GYF)	23.02.1991	12	(7)		Gabriel Debeljuh (CRO)	28.09.1996	23	(7)	12
Ionuţ Stoica	06.01.1988	25	(1)	3	Joálisson Santos Oliveira (BRA)	31.03.1991	15	(8)	1
Tiago Miguel Monteiro de Almeida (CPV)	13.09.1990	6	(8)	1	Mattia Persano (ITA)	21.09.1996		(2)	
Ousmane Viera (CIV)	21.12.1986	30		3	Stjepan Plazonja (CRO)	02.01.1998		(1)	
Midfielders:	**DOB**	**M**	**(s)**	**G**	Andrei Sîntean	16.06.1999	4	(2)	
Afonso Miguel Castro Vilhena Taira (POR)	17.06.1992	6	(4)		Juvhel Tsoumou (CGO)	27.12.1990	2	(2)	1
Andrei Cordea	24.06.1999	16	(2)		Alexandru Vodă	22.07.1998	15		1
					Yazalde Gomes Pinto (POR)	21.09.1988	19	(15)	6

Fotbal Club Politehnica Iaşi

Founded: 16.08.2010 (*as ACSMU Politehnica Iaşi*)
Stadium: Stadionul "Emil Alexandrescu", Iaşi (12,500)
Trainer: Mihai Teja   22.09.1978
[08.01.2020]   Mircea Rednic   09.04.1962

Goalkeepers:	DOB	M	(s)	G			DOB	M	(s)	G
Teodor Axinte	02.02.2000	7			Răzvan Grădinaru	23.08.1995	16	(1)	
Denis Rusu (MDA)	02.08.1990	20			Ovidiu Horşia	30.10.2000	31	(3)	5
Ştefan Târnovanu	09.05.2000	13			Florian Loshaj (KVX)	13.08.1996	19		3
Defenders:	**DOB**	**M**	**(s)**	**G**	Ionuţ Panţîru	22.03.1996	3		
Adrià Gallego Arias (ESP)	24.02.1990	14	(1)	1	Juan Pablo Passaglia (ARG)	24.05.1989	33	(4)	5
Bradley Diallo (FRA)	20.07.1990	17			Luís Carlos Almada Soares „Platini" (CPV)	16.04.1986	16	(13)	1
Bourama Fomba (MLI)	10.07.1999	1	(3)		Doru Popadiuc	18.02.1995	9	(9)	
Cosmin Frăsinescu	10.02.1985	35		3	João Tiago Almeida Teixeira (POR)	07.05.1996	2	(1)	
Linas Klimavičius (LTU)	10.04.1989	13			Sorin Şerban	17.03.2000	12	(1)	
Rodny Lopes Cabral (NED)	28.01.1995	16	(6)	1	**Forwards:**	**DOB**	**M**	**(s)**	**G**
Marius Mihalache	14.12.1984	18	(3)		Gai Assulin (ISR)	09.04.1991		(4)	
Razvan Onea	19.05.1998	7	(3)		Adrian Ionuţ Bălan	14.03.1990	11	(8)	5
Andrei Radu	21.06.1996	17			Alessio Carlone (BEL)	20.01.1996	1	(5)	
Midfielders:	**DOB**	**M**	**(s)**	**G**	Lucas Nicolás Chacana (ARG)	16.06.1993	5	(11)	1
Narcis Bădic	15.07.1991	4			Andrei Cristea	15.05.1984	21	(11)	6
Cosmin Bîrnoi	17.08.1997	3	(3)		Vlad Danale	28.01.1998	2	(1)	
Nicandro Breeveld (SUR)	07.10.1986	20	(4)	1	Mahamadou Habibou (CTA)	16.04.1987	1	(4)	
Marius Chelaru	02.03.1997	2	(2)		Andrei Haţiegan	04.04.1998	5	(3)	
Francisc Cristea	15.01.2001	7	(4)		Aleksandru Longher	08.06.2000	1	(1)	
Manuel Ignacio De Iriondo (ARG)	06.05.1993	9	(9)	1	Kevin Luckassen (NED)	27.07.1993	12	(3)	5
Dídac Ángel Devesa Albis (ESP)	30.12.1990	3	(3)		Michael Omoh (NGA)	29.08.1991	14	(4)	4
					Alexandru Zaharia	09.09.2000		(4)	

Asociația Club Sportiv Sepsi Oltul Sport Klub Sfântu Gheorghe

Founded: 2011
Stadium: Stadionul Municipal, Sfântu Gheorghe (5,200)
Trainer: Csaba László (HUN) — 13.02.1964
[13.11.2019] Leontin Florian Grozavu — 19.08.1967

	DOB	M	(s)	G
Goalkeepers:				
Csongor Fejér	11.10.1995	9		
Roland Niczuly	21.09.1995	30		
Defenders:				
Rachid Bouhenna (ALG)	29.06.1991	26	(4)	1
Daniel Celea	06.07.1995	4	(4)	
Balázs Csiszér	03.03.1999	7	(5)	
Oumar Diakhité (SEN)	09.12.1993	2	(1)	
Radoslav Dimitrov (BUL)	12.08.1988	24	(3)	
Szabolcs István Kilyen	19.03.1998	10		
Hugo Konongo (CGO)	14.02.1992	6	(1)	
Florin Ștefan	09.05.1996	33		2
Răzvan Tincu	15.07.1987	35		1
Midfielders:				
Anass Achahbar (NED)	13.01.1994	9	(5)	
Jacob Adebanjo (NGA)	05.09.1993		(2)	
Hrvoje Barišić (CRO)	03.02.1991	15		
Hilal Ben Moussa (NED)	22.05.1992	1		
Ronaldo Deaconu	13.05.1997	12	(10)	1
Dylan Armando Flores Knowles (CRC)	30.05.1993	10	(5)	2
István Fülöp	18.05.1990	22	(8)	4
Lóránd Fülöp	24.07.1997	3	(8)	3
Peter Gál-Andrezly (SVK)	03.05.1990	16	(6)	2
Lóránt Kovács	06.06.1993	7	(1)	
Călin Popescu	15.11.2001	1	(1)	
Gabriel Vașvari	13.11.1986	35	(1)	7
Stefan Velev (BUL)	02.05.1989	16	(6)	
Forwards:				
Nicolae Cârnaț	08.04.1998	30	(3)	6
Tomás Díaz Grassano (ARG)	24.04.1997	1	(10)	
Ioan Dumiter	10.04.1999	4	(1)	
Yasin Khalid Abdelrahman Hamed	09.12.1999	4		
Goran Karanović (SUI)	13.10.1987	10	(19)	8
Pavol Šafranko (SVK)	16.11.1994	26	(8)	9
Edgar Nicaise Constant Salli (CMR)	17.08.1992		(12)	
Marko Simonovski (MKD)	02.01.1992		(2)	
Marius Ștefănescu	14.08.1998	21	(6)	3

Universitatea Craiova 1948 Club Sportiv

Founded: 1948; re-founded 2013
Stadium: Stadionul "Ion Oblemenco", Craiova (30,929)
Trainer: Corneliu Papură — 05.09.1973
[03.09.2019] Victor Pițurcă — 08.05.1956
[05.01.2020] Corneliu Papură — 05.09.1973
[07.05.2020] Cristiano Bergodi (ITA) — 14.10.1964

	DOB	M	(s)	G
Goalkeepers:				
Mirko Pigliacelli (ITA)	30.06.1993	29		
Laurențiu Popescu	18.01.1997	6		
Defenders:				
Stephane Acka (CIV)	11.10.1990	25	(2)	
Mihai Bălașa	14.01.1995	20	(2)	3
Florin Borta	21.06.1999	2		
Uroš Ćosić (SRB)	24.10.1992	15	(2)	1
Claude Dielna (FRA)	14.12.1987		(1)	
Antoni Ivanov (BUL)	11.09.1995	15	(11)	1
Ivan Martić (CRO)	02.10.1990	12	(3)	1
Alexandru Mățel	17.10.1989	4	(1)	
Tiago Emanuel Canelas Almeida Ferreira (POR)	10.07.1993	8	(1)	
Bogdan Vătăjelu	24.04.1993	10	(12)	2
Ștefan Vlădoiu	28.12.1998	19	(1)	
Midfielders:				
Nicușor Bancu	18.09.1992	30	(1)	4
Alexandru Cicâldău	08.07.1997	31	(1)	14
Vasile Constantin	18.01.1998	3	(1)	2
Cornel Alexandru Ioniță	14.12.1994	2	(4)	
Renato Kelić (CRO)	31.03.1991	7	(1)	
Alexandru Mateiu	10.12.1989	21	(6)	
Dan Nistor	05.06.1988	13		3
Kamer Qaka (ALB)	11.04.1995	8	(4)	
Marian Șerban	07.07.2000	1		
Goran Zakarić (BIH)	07.11.1992	7	(3)	
Forwards:				
Ștefan Baiaram	31.12.2002	6	(5)	
Raoul Baicu	05.04.2000		(1)	
Cristian Bărbuț	22.04.1995	17	(10)	2
Carlos Manuel dos Santos Fortes (POR)	09.11.1994	2	(6)	1
Gustavo Di Mauro Vagenin (BRA)	14.11.1991		(6)	1
Andrei Ivan	04.01.1997	19	(5)	2
Elvir Koljič (BIH)	08.07.1995	8	(7)	6
Jovan Marković	23.03.2001	3		
Valentin Mihăilă	02.02.2000	25	(2)	7
Luis Emanuel Nițu	30.05.2001	11		3
Mihai Roman II	31.05.1992	6	(9)	3

Fotbal Club Viitorul Constanța

Founded: 2009
Stadium: Stadionul Viitorul, Constanța (4,554)
Trainer: Gheorghe Hagi — 05.02.1965

	DOB	M	(s)	G
Goalkeepers:				
Cătălin Căbuz	18.06.1996	29		
Árpád Tordai	11.03.1997	11		
Defenders:				
Radu Boboc	24.04.1999	30	(3)	2
Tiberiu Căpușă	06.04.1998	3	(1)	
Bradley de Nooijer (NED)	07.11.1997	27	(5)	
Damien Dussaut (FRA)	08.11.1994	8	(6)	1
Cristian Ganea	24.05.1992	9	(1)	1
Virgil Ghiță	04.06.1998	26	(1)	4
Alexandru Gabriel Georgescu	10.07.2001		(1)	
Darius Grosu	07.06.2002		(2)	
Paul Iacob	21.06.1996	11	(13)	
Bas Kuipers (NED)	17.08.1994	1		
Bogdan Gheorghe Lazăr	26.06.2003		(2)	
Sebastian Mladen	11.12.1991	31	(1)	
Bogdan Țîru	15.03.1994	19		3
Midfielders:				
Vlad Achim	07.04.1989	22	(6)	5
Luca Cristian Andronache	26.07.2003		(1)	
Andrei Artean	14.08.1993	35	(2)	
Cosmin Bîrnoi	17.08.1997	1		
Stefan Bodișteanu	01.02.2003		(3)	
Carlos Casap	29.12.1998	6	(6)	
Andrei Ciobanu	18.01.1998	26	(6)	3
Marco Dulca	11.05.1999	3	(11)	
Malcom Edjouma (FRA)	08.10.1996	1	(2)	
Eric de Oliveira Pereira (BRA)	05.12.1985	4	(2)	5
Steliano Filip	15.05.1994	2	(10)	
Lyes Houri (FRA)	19.01.1996	18	(3)	1
Cosmin Matei	30.09.1991	17	(6)	4
Alexandru Mățan	29.08.1999	3		
Andrei Tîrcoveanu	22.05.1997	2		
Forwards:				
Abdelmajid Najib Ammari (ALG)	10.04.1992		(1)	
Andreiaș Calcan	09.04.1994	5	(4)	1
Aurelian Chițu	25.03.1991	9	(6)	
Denis Mihai Drăguș	06.07.1999		(1)	
George Ganea	26.05.1999	21	(8)	4
Gabriel Cristian Iancu	15.04.1994	26	(2)	18
Louis Munteanu	16.06.2002	4	(15)	3
Alexi Pitu	05.06.2002	2	(7)	
Rivaldo Vitor Borba Ferreira Júnior "Rivaldinho" (BRA)	29.04.1995	26	(2)	11
Jacques Zoua Daogari (CMR)	06.09.1991	2	(4)	1

Fotbal Club Voluntari

Founded:	2010 (*as Inter Voluntari*)	
Stadium:	Stadionul „Anghel Iordănescu", Voluntari (4,600)	
Trainer:	Cristiano Bergodi (ITA)	14.10.1964
[09.01.2020]	Mihai Teja	22.09.1978

Goalkeepers:	DOB	M	(s)	G
Valentin Cojocaru	01.10.1995	19		
Bozhidar Mitrev (BUL)	31.03.1987	8		
Victor Râmniceanu	30.11.1989	13		
Defenders:	**DOB**	**M**	**(s)**	**G**
Cosmin Achim	19.09.1995	21	(2)	
Igor Armaş (MDA)	14.07.1987	19	(2)	
Ionuţ Balaur	06.06.1989	16	(4)	1
Claudiu Belu-Iordache	07.11.1993	9	(5)	1
Julio César Rodríguez López (ESP)	07.12.1995	6	(1)	
Milan Kocič (SVN)	16.02.1990	13	(2)	
Aïssa Laïdouni (FRA)	13.12.1996	18	(5)	1
Constantin Nica	18.03.1993	2		
Alexandru Paşcanu	28.09.1998	19		1
Andraž Struna (SVN)	23.04.1989	19	(3)	1
Alexandru Vlad	06.12.1989	27	(4)	
Midfielders:	**DOB**	**M**	**(s)**	**G**
Claudiu Borţoneanu	04.10.1999		(2)	
Mihai Căpăţînă	16.12.1995	37	(2)	8
Cristian Costin	17.06.1998	15	(8)	
Gabriel Deac	26.04.1995	4	(3)	

	DOB	M	(s)	G
Pablo de Lucas Torres (ESP)	20.09.1986	19		
Eric de Oliveira Pereira (BRA)	05.12.1985	4	(6)	2
Ion Gheorghe	08.10.1999	36	(2)	4
Nicolás Martín Gorobsov (ARG)	25.11.1989	26	(5)	
Alexandru Măţan	29.08.1999	21	(4)	1
Vlad Mihalcea	28.10.1998		(2)	
Doru Popadiuc	18.02.1995	3	(5)	
Ricardo José Veiga Varzim Miranda (POR)	24.03.1994	8	(2)	1
Franco Signorelli (VEN)	01.01.1991	2	(3)	
Forwards:	**DOB**	**M**	**(s)**	**G**
Abdelhak Belahmeur (FRA)	26.07.1991		(1)	
Daniel Benzar	30.12.1997		(12)	
Avtandil Ebralidze (GEO)	03.10.1991	8	(6)	1
Martin Harrer (AUT)	19.05.1992		(4)	
Vlad Morar	01.08.1993	1	(7)	
Athanasios Papazoglou (GRE)	30.03.1988	8	(3)	1
Moussa Sanoh (NED)	20.07.1995	10	(6)	1
Marko Simonovski (MKD)	02.01.1992	12	(7)	4
Alexandru Ionuţ Stoica	23.01.2000		(2)	
Cătălin Ţîră	18.06.1994	13	(12)	5
Alexandru Tudorie	19.03.1996	4	(5)	3

SECOND LEVEL
Liga II 2019/2020

1.	FC UT Arad	23	15	5	3	49	-	13	50
2.	CS Mioveni	23	10	9	4	36	-	22	39
3.	AFC Turris-Oltul Turnu Măgurele	22	11	6	5	36	-	25	39
4.	FC Argeş Piteşti	23	10	8	5	34	-	25	38
5.	FC Petrolul Ploieşti	23	10	8	5	23	-	20	38
6.	FC Rapid 1923 Bucureşti	23	10	7	6	32	-	20	37
7.	FC Metaloglobus Bucureşti	23	10	7	6	28	-	20	37
8.	SCM Gloria Buzău	23	9	6	8	35	-	27	33
9.	FC Farul Constanţa 1920	23	9	6	8	27	-	20	33
10.	ACS Viitorul Pandurii Târgu Jiu	22	9	6	7	30	-	25	33
11.	ASU Politehnica Timişoara	22	8	8	6	20	-	12	32
12.	AFC Dunărea Călăraşi	23	8	7	8	29	-	30	31
13.	FC Ripensia Timişoara	23	6	10	7	28	-	34	28
14.	FC Universitatea Cluj	23	5	12	6	29	-	26	27
15.	CSM Reşiţa	22	6	6	10	30	-	35	24
16.	CS Concordia Chiajna	22	6	6	10	20	-	30	24
17.	FK Miercurea Ciuc	23	5	7	11	17	-	33	22
18.	CS Sportul Snagov (*Relegated*)*	23	2	3	18	16	-	59	9
19.	CS Pandurii Lignitul Târgu Jiu	23	1	5	17	10	-	53	8
20.	ASC Daco-Getica Bucureşti (*Relegated*)**	0	0	0	0	0	-	0	0

The season was interrupted on 09.03.2020 and cancelled on 14.05.2020 due to Covid-19 pandemic. No teams were relegated, excepting both teams already dissolved or excluded (see below).
Teams ranked 1-6 were qualified for the Promotion Play-offs.

*CS Sportul Snagov (dissolved) withdrew during the winter break and lost all following matches by forfeit.
**ASC Daco-Getica Bucureşti withdrew after 13 Rounds and were excluded, all its results being cancelled.

	Promotion Play-off								
1.	FC UT Arad (*Promoted*)	5	1	2	2	8	-	8	30
2.	FC Argeş Piteşti (*Promoted*)	5	2	2	1	7	-	6	27
3.	CS Mioveni (*Liga I Play-offs*)	5	2	1	2	5	-	6	27
4.	AFC Turris-Oltul Turnu Măgurele	5	1	3	1	5	-	5	26
5.	FC Petrolul Ploieşti	5	1	3	1	4	-	4	25
6.	FC Rapid 1923 Bucureşti	5	1	3	1	4	-	4	25

INTERNATIONAL MATCHES
(16.07.2019 – 15.07.2020)

05.09.2019	Bucureşti	Romania - Spain	1-2(0-1)	(ECQ)
08.09.2019	Ploieşti	Romania - Malta	1-0(0-0)	(ECQ)
12.10.2019	Tórshavn	Faroe Islands - Romania	0-3(0-0)	(ECQ)
15.10.2019	Bucureşti	Romania - Norway	1-1(0-0)	(ECQ)
15.11.2019	Bucureşti	Romania - Sweden	0-2(0-2)	(ECQ)
18.11.2019	Madrid	Spain - Romania	5-0(4-0)	(ECQ)

05.09.2019   ROMANIA - SPAIN   1-2(0-1)   16th EC. Qualifiers
Arena Naţională, Bucureşti; Referee: Deniz Aytekin (Germany); Attendance: 50,024
ROU: Ciprian Tătăruşanu, Romario Sandu Benzar, Vlad Chircheş (Cap), Dragoş Grigore, Alin Dorinel Toşca, Ionuţ Nedelcearu, Ciprian Ioan Deac (72.Alexandru Iulian Maxim), Nicolae Claudiu Stanciu (63.Ianis Hagi), Răzvan Gabriel Marin, Claudiu Andrei Keşerü (56.Florin Andone), George Alexandru Puşcaş. Trainer: Cosmin Marius Contra.
Goal: Florin Andone (59).

08.09.2019   ROMANIA - MALTA   1-0(0-0)   16th EC. Qualifiers
Stadionul "Ilie Oană", Ploieşti; Referee: Duje Strukan (Croatia); Attendance: 13,376
ROU: Ciprian Tătăruşanu, Vlad Chircheş (Cap), Adrián Rus, Florin Bogdan Ştefan, Alexandru Mihăiţă Chipciu, Mihai Cătălin Bordeianu, Răzvan Gabriel Marin (59.Nicolae Claudiu Stanciu), Alexandru Cicâldău, Ianis Hagi (72.Gheorghe Teodor Grozav), Florin Andone, George Alexandru Puşcaş (76.Claudiu Andrei Keşerü). Trainer: Cosmin Marius Contra.
Goal: George Alexandru Puşcaş (47).

12.10.2019   FAROE ISLANDS - ROMANIA   0-3(0-0)   16th EC. Qualifiers
Tórsvøllur, Tórshavn; Referee: Əliyar Ağayev (Azerbaijan); Attendance: 2,381
ROU: Ciprian Tătăruşanu, Romario Sandu Benzar, Vlad Chircheş (Cap) (39.Adrián Rus), Ionuţ Nedelcearu, Nicuşor Silviu Bancu, Paul Viorel Anton, Nicolae Claudiu Stanciu, Ianis Hagi, Florin Andone (65.Claudiu Andrei Keşerü), George Alexandru Puşcaş, Florinel Teodor Coman (69.Alexandru Ionuţ Mitriţă). Trainer: Cosmin Marius Contra.
Goals: George Alexandru Puşcaş (74), Alexandru Ionuţ Mitriţă (83), Claudiu Andrei Keşerü (90+4).

15.10.2019   ROMANIA - NORWAY   1-1(0-0)   16th EC. Qualifiers
Arena Naţională, Bucureşti; Referee: Bobby Madden (Scotland); Attendance: 29,854
ROU: Ciprian Tătăruşanu, Romario Sandu Benzar (Cap), Ionuţ Nedelcearu, Adrián Rus, Nicuşor Silviu Bancu, Ciprian Ioan Deac, Paul Viorel Anton (84.Mihai Cătălin Bordeianu), Nicolae Claudiu Stanciu, Răzvan Gabriel Marin, Alexandru Ionuţ Mitriţă (78.Dan Nicolae Nistor), George Alexandru Puşcaş (63.Florin Andone). Trainer: Cosmin Marius Contra.
Goal: Alexandru Ionuţ Mitriţă (62).

15.11.2019   ROMANIA - SWEDEN   0-2(0-2)   16th EC. Qualifiers
Arena Naţională, Bucureşti; Referee: Daniele Orsato (Italy); Attendance: 49,678
ROU: Ciprian Tătăruşanu (Cap), Vasile Mogoş, Ionuţ Nedelcearu, Adrián Rus, Nicuşor Silviu Bancu, Tudor Cristian Băluţă, Ciprian Ioan Deac (46.Ianis Hagi), Nicolae Claudiu Stanciu (72.Denis Alibec), Claudiu Andrei Keşerü (57.Florinel Teodor Coman), Alexandru Ionuţ Mitriţă, George Alexandru Puşcaş. Trainer: Cosmin Marius Contra.

18.11.2019   SPAIN - ROMANIA   5-0(4-0)   16th EC. Qualifiers
Metropolitano Stadium, Madrid; Referee: Aleksei Kulbakov (Belarus); Attendance: 36,198
ROU: Ciprian Tătăruşanu (Cap), Romario Sandu Benzar, Alin Dorinel Toşca, Adrián Rus, Ionuţ Nedelcearu, Tudor Cristian Băluţă, Nicolae Claudiu Stanciu, Răzvan Gabriel Marin (65.Alexandru Cicâldău), Ianis Hagi (73.Dan Nicolae Nistor), George Alexandru Puşcaş, Florinel Teodor Coman (56.Alexandru Ionuţ Mitriţă). Trainer: Cosmin Marius Contra.

NATIONAL TEAM PLAYERS
(16.07.2019 – 15.07.2020)

Name	DOB	Caps	Goals	2019/2020:	Club
Goalkeepers					
Anton Ciprian TĂTĂRUŞAN	09.02.1986	**68**	**0**	2019:	*Olympique Lyonnais (FRA)*
Defenders					
Nicuşor Silviu BANCU	18.09.1992	**13**	**0**	2019:	*CS Universitatea Craiova*
Romario Sandu BENZAR	26.03.1992	**19**	**0**	2019:	*US Lecce (ITA)*
Vlad Iulian CHIRICHEŞ	14.11.1989	**58**	**0**	2019:	*US Sassuolo Calcio (ITA)*
Dragoş GRIGORE	07.09.1986	**37**	**0**	2019:	*PFC Ludogorets Razgrad (BUL)*
Vasile MOGOŞ	31.10.1992	**1**	**0**	2019:	*US Cremonese (ITA)*
Ionuţ NEDELCEARU	25.04.1996	**9**	**0**	2019:	*FK Ufa (RUS)*
Adrián RUS	18.03.1996	**5**	**0**	2019:	*Fehérvár FC Székesfehérvár (HUN)*
Florin Bogdan ŞTEFAN	09.05.1996	**1**	**0**	2019:	*ACS Sepsi OSK Sfântu Gheorghe*
Alin Dorinel TOŞCA	14.03.1992	**18**	**0**	2019:	*Gazişehir Gaziantep FK (TUR)*
Midfielders					
Paul Viorel ANTON	10.05.1991	**11**	**0**	2019:	*FK Krylia Sovetov Samara (RUS)*
Tudor Cristian BĂLUŢĂ	27.03.1999	**7**	**0**	2019:	*Brighton & Hove Albion FC (ENG)*
Mihai Cătălin BORDEIANU	18.11.1991	**2**	**0**	2019:	*FC CFR 1907 Cluj-Napoca*
Alexandru Mihăiţă CHIPCIU	18.05.1989	**47**	**6**	2019:	*RSC Anderlecht Bruxelles (BEL)*
Alexandru CICÂLDĂU	08.07.1997	**6**	**0**	2019:	*CS Universitatea Craiova*
Ciprian Ioan DEAC	16.02.1986	**23**	**4**	2019:	*FC CFR 1907 Cluj-Napoca*
Gheorghe Teodor GROZAV	29.09.1990	**30**	**5**	2019:	*Kisvárda FC (HUN)*
Ianis HAGI	22.10.1998	**10**	**0**	2019:	*KRC Genk (BEL)*
Răzvan Gabriel MARIN	23.05.1996	**21**	**1**	2019:	*AFC Ajax Amsterdam (NED)*
Alexandru Iulian MAXIM	08.07.1990	**38**	**5**	2019:	*1.FSV Mainz 05 (GER)*
Alexandru Ionuţ MITRIŢĂ	08.02.1995	**11**	**2**	2019:	*New York City FC (USA)*
Dan Nicolae NISTOR	06.05.1988	**4**	**0**	2019:	*FC Dinamo Bucureşti*
Nicolae Claudiu STANCIU	07.05.1993	**37**	**10**	2019:	*SK Slavia Praha (CZE)*
Forwards					
Denis ALIBEC	05.01.1991	**10**	**0**	2019:	*AFC Astra Giurgiu*
Florin ANDONE	11.04.1993	**25**	**2**	2019:	*Galatasaray SK İstanbul (TUR)*
Florinel Teodor COMAN	10.04.1998	**3**	**0**	2019:	*SC FCSB Bucureşti*
Claudiu Andrei KEŞERÜ	02.12.1986	**37**	**13**	2019:	*PFC Ludogorets Razgrad (BUL)*
George Alexandru PUŞCAŞ	08.04.1996	**14**	**6**	2019:	*Reading FC (ENG)*
National team coach					
Cosmin Marius CONTRA [from 22.09.2017]	15.12.1975		24 M; 13 W; 6 D; 5 L; 39-26		

RUSSIA

The Country:
Российская Федерация (Russian Federation)
Capital: Moskva
Surface: 17,098,246 km²
Inhabitants: 146,748,590 [2020]
Time: UTC+2 to +12

The FA:
Российский Футбольный Союз (Russian Football Union)
Ulitsa Narodnaya 7, 115 172 Moskva
Tel: +7 495 926 1300
Founded: 19.01.1912
Member of FIFA since: 1912-1917 and since 1992
Member of UEFA since: 1954
Website: www.rfs.ru

NATIONAL TEAM RECORDS

RECORDS

First international match:	30.06.1912, Stockholm:	Finland – Russia 2-1
Most international caps:	Sergey Ignashevich	- 127 caps (2002-2018)
Most international goals:	Aleksandr Kerzhakov	- 30 goals / 91 caps (2002-2016)

UEFA EUROPEAN CHAMPIONSHIP*

1960	**Final Tournament (Winners)**
1964	Final Tournament (Runners-up)
1968	Final Tournament (4th Place)
1972	Final Tournament (Runners-up)
1976	Qualifiers
1980	Qualifiers
1984	Qualifiers
1988	Final Tournament (Runners-up)
1992	Final Tournament (Group Stage)
1996	Final Tournament (Group Stage)
2000	Qualifiers
2004	Final Tournament (Group Stage)
2008	Final Tournament (Semi-Finals)
2012	Final Tournament (Group Stage)
2016	Final Tournament (Group Stage)
2020	*Final Tournament (Qualified)*

*from 1960 to 1992 as Soviet Union/C.I.S.

FIFA WORLD CUP**

1930	**Final Tournament (Winners)**
1934	Final Tournament (Runners-up)
1938	Final Tournament (4th Place)
1950	Final Tournament (Runners-up)
1954	Qualifiers
1958	Qualifiers
1962	Qualifiers
1966	Final Tournament (Runners-up)
1970	Final Tournament (Group Stage)
1974	Did not enter
1978	Did not enter
1982	Did not enter
1986	Did not enter
1990	Did not enter
1994	Final Tournament (Group Stage)
1998	Qualifiers
2002	Final Tournament (Group Stage)
2006	Qualifiers
2010	Qualifiers
2014	Final Tournament (Group Stage)
2018	Final Tournament (Quarter-Finals)

**from 1930 to 1990 as Soviet Union

OLYMPIC TOURNAMENTS

1908	-
1912	Quarter-Finals
1920	-
1924	-
1928	-
1936	-
1948	-
1952	-
1956	-
1960	-
1964	-
1968	-
1972	-
1976	-
1980	-
1984	-
1988	-
1992	-
1996	Qualifiers
2000	Qualifiers
2004	Qualifiers
2008	Qualifiers
2012	Qualifiers
2016	Qualifiers

UEFA NATIONS LEAGUE

2018/2019 – League B

FIFA CONFEDERATIONS CUP 1992-2017

2017 (Group Stage)

RUSSIAN CLUB HONOURS IN EUROPEAN CLUB COMPETITIONS:

European Champion Clubs.Cup (1956-1992) / UEFA Champions League (1993-2020)		
None		
Fairs Cup (1858-1971) / UEFA Cup (1972-2009) / UEFA Europa League (2010-2020)		
FK CSKA Moskva	1	2004/2005
FK Zenit Saint Petersburg	1	2007/2008
UEFA Super Cup (1972-2019)		
FK Zenit Saint Petersburg	1	2008
European Cup Winners.Cup 1961-1999*		
None		

*defunct competition

NATIONAL COMPETITIONS
TABLE OF HONOURS

Football championship of Russian Empire

	CHAMPIONS
1912	Saint Petersburg
1913	Odessa
1914	*Championship cancelled*

Football championship of Russian SFSR among city teams

	CHAMPIONS
1920	Moskva
1921	*No competition*
1922	Moskva
1923	*No competition*
1924	Leningrad
1925	*No competition*
1926	*No competition*
1927	Moskva
1928	Moskva
1929	*No competition*
1930	*No competition*
1931	Moskva
1932	Leningrad
1933	*No competition*
1934	Voronezh
1935	*No competition*

Soviet League (1936–1991)

	CHAMPIONS	CUP WINNERS	BEST GOALSCORERS	
1936 (spring)	Dinamo Moskva	-	Mikhail Semichastny (Dinamo Moskva)	6
1936 (autumn)	Spartak Moskva	Lokomotiv Moskva	Georgy Glazkov (Spartak Moskva)	7
1937	Dinamo Moskva	Dinamo Moskva	Boris Paichadze (Dinamo Tbilisi) Leonid Rumyantsev (Spartak Moskva) Vasily Smirnov (Dinamo Moskva)	8
1938	Spartak Moskva	Spartak Moskva	Makar Goncharenko (Dinamo Kiev)	19
1939	Spartak Moskva	Spartak Moskva	Grigory Fedotov (CDKA Moskva)	21
1940	Dinamo Moskva	*No competition*	Grigory Fedotov (CDKA Moskva) Sergey Solovyov (Dinamo Moskva)	21
1941	*No competition*	*No competition*	-	
1942	*No competition*	*No competition*	-	
1943	*No competition*	*No competition*	-	
1944	*No competition*	Zenit Leningrad	-	
1945	Dinamo Moskva	CDKA Moskva	Vsevolod Bobrov (CDKA Moskva)	24
1946	CDKA Moskva	Spartak Moskva	Aleksandr Ponomaryov (Torpedo Moskva)	18
1947	CDKA Moskva	Spartak Moskva	Vsevolod Bobrov (CDKA Moskva) Valentin Nikolayev (CDKA Moskva) Sergey Solovyov (Dinamo Moskva)	14
1948	CDKA Moskva	CDKA Moskva	Sergey Solovyov (Dinamo Moskva)	25
1949	Dinamo Moskva	Torpedo Moskva	Nikita Simonyan (Spartak Moskva)	26
1950	CDKA Moskva	Spartak Moskva	Nikita Simonyan (Spartak Moskva)	34
1951	CDSA Moskva	CDSA Moskva	Avtandil Gogoberidze (Dinamo Tbilisi)	16
1952	Spartak Moskva	Torpedo Moskva	Andrey Zazroyev (Dinamo Kiev)	11
1953	Spartak Moskva	Dinamo Moskva	Nikita Simonyan (Spartak Moskva)	14
1954	Dinamo Moskva	Dynamo Kiev	Anatoli Ilyin (Spartak Moskva) Vladimir Ilyin (Dinamo Moskva) Antonin Sochnev (Trudovye Reserve Leningrad)	11
1955	Dinamo Moskva	CDSA Moskva	Eduard Streltsov (Torpedo Moskva)	15
1956	Spartak Moskva	*No competition*	Vasily Buzunov (ODO Sverdlovsk)	17
1957	Dinamo Moskva	Lokomotiv Moskva	Vasily Buzunov (CSK MO Moskva)	16
1958	Spartak Moskva	Spartak Moskva	Anatoli Ilyin (Spartak Moskva)	19
1959	Dinamo Moskva	-	Zaur Kaloyev (Dinamo Tbilisi)	16
1960	Torpedo Moskva	Torpedo Moskva (1959/60)	Zaur Kaloyev (Dinamo Tbilisi) Gennady Gusarov (Torpedo Moskva)	20
1961	Dinamo Kiev	Shakhtyor Stalino	Gennady Gusarov (Torpedo Moskva)	22
1962	Spartak Moskva	Shakhtyor Stalino	Mikhail Mustygin (Belarus Minsk)	17
1963	Dinamo Moskva	Spartak Moskva	Oleg Kopaev (SKA Rostov-na-Donu)	27
1964	Dinamo Tbilisi	Dynamo Kiev	Vladimir Fedotov (CSKA Moskva)	16

1965	Torpedo Moskva	Spartak Moskva	Oleg Kopaev (SKA Rostov-na-Donu)	18
1966	Dinamo Kiev	Dynamo Kiev (1965/66)	Ilya Datunashvili (Dinamo Tbilisi)	20
1967	Dinamo Kiev	Dinamo Moskva (1966/67)	Mikhail Mustygin (Dinamo Minsk)	19
1968	Dinamo Kiev	Torpedo Moskva (1967/68)	Georgi Gavasheli (Dinamo Tbilisi) Berador Abduraimov (Pakhtakor Tashkent)	22
1969	Spartak Moskva	Karpaty Lviv	Nikolai Osyanin (Spartak Moskva) Vladimir Proskurin (SKA Rostov-na-Donu) Dzhemal Kherhadze (Torpedo Kutaisi)	16
1970	CSKA Moskva	Dinamo Moskva	Givi Nodia (Dinamo Tbilisi)	17
1971	Dinamo Kiev	Spartak Moskva	Eduard Malofeev (Dinamo Minsk)	16
1972	Zarya Voroshilovgrad	Torpedo Moskva	Oleg Blokhin (Dinamo Kiev)	14
1973	Ararat Yerevan	Ararat Yerevan	Oleg Blokhin (Dinamo Kiev)	18
1974	Dinamo Kiev	Dynamo Kiev	Oleg Blokhin (Dinamo Kiev)	20
1975	Dinamo Kiev	Ararat Yerevan	Oleg Blokhin (Dinamo Kiev)	18
1976 (spring)	Dinamo Moskva	-	Arkady Andreasian (Ararat Yerevan)	8
1976 (autumn)	Torpedo Moskva	Dinamo Tbilisi	Aleksandr Markin (Zenit Leningrad)	13
1977	Dinamo Kiev	Dinamo Moskva	Oleg Blokhin (Dinamo Kiev)	17
1978	Dinamo Tbilisi	Dynamo Kiev	Georgi Yartsev (Spartak Moskva)	19
1979	Spartak Moskva	Dinamo Tbilisi	Vitali Starukhin (Shakhtar Donetsk)	26
1980	Dinamo Kiev	Shakhtar Donetsk	Sergey Andreev (SKA Rostov-na-Donu)	20
1981	Dinamo Kiev	SKA Rostov-on-Don	Ramaz Shengelia (Dinamo Tbilisi)	23
1982	Dinamo Minsk	Dynamo Kiev	Andrei Yakubik (Pakhtakor Tashkent)	23
1983	Dnipro Dnipropetrovsk	Shakhtar Donetsk	Yuriy Gavrilov (Spartak Moskva)	18
1984	Zenit Leningrad	Dinamo Moskva	Sergey Andreev (SKA Rostov-na-Donu)	20
1985	Dinamo Kiev	Dynamo Kiev	Oleg Protasov (Dnipro Dnipropetrovsk)	35
1986	Dinamo Kiev	Torpedo Moskva	Aleksandr Borodyuk (Dinamo Moskva)	21
1987	Spartak Moskva	Dynamo Kiev	Oleg Protasov (Dnipro Dnipropetrovsk)	18
1988	Dnipro Dnipropetrovsk	Metalist Kharkiv	Yevhen Shakhov (Dnipro Dnipropetrovsk) Aleksandr Borodyuk (Dinamo Moskva)	16
1989	Spartak Moskva	Dnipro Dnipropetrovsk	Sergey Rodionov (Spartak Moskva)	16
1990	Dinamo Kiev	Dynamo Kiev	Oleg Protasov (Dinamo Kiev) Valery Shmarov (Spartak Moskva)	12
1991	CSKA Moskva	CSKA Moskva	Igor Kolyvanov (Dinamo Moskva)	18

Russian League (1992–present)

	CHAMPIONS	CUP WINNERS	BEST GOALSCORERS	
1992	FK Spartak Moskva	FK Spartak Moskva	Vali Gasimov (AZE, FK Dinamo Moskva)	16
1993	FK Spartak Moskva	FK Torpedo Moskva	Viktor Panchenko (FK KamAZ Naberezhnye Chelny)	21
1994	FK Spartak Moskva	FK Spartak Moskva	Igor Simutenkov (FK Dinamo Moskva)	21
1995	FK Alania Vladikavkaz	FK Dinamo Moskva	Oleg Veretennikov (Rotor Volgograd)	25
1996	FK Spartak Moskva	FK Lokomotiv Moskva	Aleksandr Maslov (FK Rostselmash Rostov-na-Donu)	23
1997	FK Spartak Moskva	FK Lokomotiv Moskva	Oleg Veretennikov (FK Rotor Volgograd)	22
1998	FK Spartak Moskva	FK Spartak Moskva	Oleg Veretennikov (FK Rotor Volgograd)	22
1999	FK Spartak Moskva	FK Zenit Saint Petersburg	Georgi Demetradze (GEO, FK Alania Vladikavkaz)	21
2000	FK Spartak Moskva	FK Lokomotiv Moskva	Dmitriy Loskov (FK Lokomotiv Moskva)	18
2001	FK Spartak Moskva	FK Lokomotiv Moskva	Dmitriy Vyazmikin (FK Torpedo Moskva)	18
2002	FK Lokomotiv Moskva	FK CSKA Moskva	Rolan Gusev (FK CSKA Moskva) Dmitriy Kirichenko (FK CSKA Moskva)	15
2003	FK CSKA Moskva	FK Spartak Moskva	Dmitriy Loskov (FK Lokomotiv Moskva)	14
2004	FK Lokomotiv Moskva	FK Terek Grozny	Aleksandr Kerzhakov (FK Zenit Saint Petersburg)	18
2005	FK CSKA Moskva	FK CSKA Moskva	Dmitriy Kirichenko (FK Moskva)	14
2006	FK CSKA Moskva	FK CSKA Moskva	Roman Pavlyuchenko (FK Spartak Moskva)	18
2007	FK Zenit Saint Petersburg	FK Lokomotiv Moskva	Roman Pavlyuchenko (FK Spartak Moskva) Roman Adamov (FK Moskva)	14
2008	FK Rubin Kazan	FK CSKA Moskva	Vágner Silva de Souza "Vágner Love" (BRA, FK CSKA Moskva)	20
2009	FK Rubin Kazan	FK CSKA Moskva	Welliton Soares de Morais (BRA, FK Spartak Moskva)	21
2010	FK Zenit Saint Petersburg	FK Zenit Saint Petersburg	Welliton Soares de Morais (BRA, FK Spartak Moskva)	19
2010/2011	-	FK CSKA Moskva	-	
2011/2012	FK Zenit Saint Petersburg	FK Rubin Kazan	Seydou Doumbia (CIV, FK CSKA Moskva)	28
2012/2013	FK CSKA Moskva	FK CSKA Moskva	Yura Movsisyan (ARM, FK Spartak Moskva) Francisco Wánderson do Carmo Carneiro (BRA, FK Krasnodar)	13
2013/2014	FK CSKA Moskva	FK Rostov	Seydou Doumbia (CIV, FK CSKA Moskva)	18
2014/2015	FK Zenit Saint Petersburg	FK Lokomotiv Moskva	Givanildo Vieira de Sousa "Hulk" (BRA, FK Zenit Saint Petersburg)	15
2015/2016	FK CSKA Moskva	FK Zenit Saint Petersburg	Fyodor Smolov (FK Krasnodar)	20
2016/2017	FK Spartak Moskva	FK Lokomotiv Moskva	Fyodor Smolov (FK Krasnodar)	18
2017/2018	FK Lokomotiv Moskva	FK Tosno	Quincy Anton Promes (NED, FK Spartak Moskva)	15
2018/2019	FK Zenit Saint Petersburg	FK Lokomotiv Moskva	Fedor Chalov (FK CSKA Moskva)	15

| 2019/2020 | FK Zenit Saint Petersburg | FK Zenit Saint Petersburg | Sardar Azmoun (IRN, FK Zenit Saint Petersburg) Artyom Dzyuba (FK Zenit Saint Petersburg) 17 |

Club name changements: **FK CSKA Moskva** = OPPW Moskva (1924-1928), CDKA Moskva (1928-1951), CDSA Moskva (1951-1953), WWS Moskva (1953-1957), CSKMO Moskva (1957-1960), CSKA Moskva (1960-1988), FK CSKA Moskva (since 1988).

NATIONAL CHAMPIONSHIP
Premier League 2019/2020
(12.07.2019 – 22.07.2020)

Results

Round 1 [12-15.07.2019]
Arsenal Tula - Dinamo Moskva 1-1(0-1)
FK Ural - FK Ufa 3-2(1-0)
Spartak Moskva - PFK Sochi 1-0(0-0)
FK Rostov - FK Orenburg 2-1(2-0)
Krylia Sovetov - CSKA Moskva 2-0(0-0)
FK Zenit - FK Tambov 2-1(0-0)
Akhmat Grozny - FK Krasnodar 1-0(1-0)
Lokomotiv Moskva - Rubin Kazan 1-1(0-0)

Round 2 [20-21.07.2019]
FK Ufa - FK Krasnodar 2-3(2-0)
Krylia Sovetov - Arsenal Tula 2-3(1-2)
CSKA Moskva - FK Orenburg 2-1(2-1)
FK Rostov - Spartak Moskva 2-2(1-1)
FK Ural - Akhmat Grozny 3-0(1-0)
Lokomotiv Moskva - FK Tambov 2-1(2-1)
Dinamo Moskva - Rubin Kazan 0-1(0-0)
PFK Sochi - FK Zenit 0-2(0-1)

Round 3 [26-29.07.2019]
Dinamo Moskva - FK Ural 2-0(2-0)
FK Ufa - Krylia Sovetov 2-1(2-1)
FK Tambov - Spartak Moskva 2-0(1-0)
FK Krasnodar - PFK Sochi 3-0(2-0)
FK Orenburg - FK Zenit 0-2(0-1)
Arsenal Tula - FK Rostov 2-3(0-1)
CSKA Moskva - Lokomotiv Moskva 1-0(1-0)
Rubin Kazan - Akhmat Grozny 1-0(0-0)

Round 4 [03-05.08.2019]
FK Ural - FK Rostov 2-2(1-0)
Krylia Sovetov - Lokomotiv Moskva 1-2(0-1)
Spartak Moskva - Dinamo Moskva 0-0
FK Zenit - FK Krasnodar 1-1(0-0)
FK Tambov - Arsenal Tula 0-1(0-1)
Rubin Kazan - CSKA Moskva 0-1(0-1)
PFK Sochi - FK Ufa 0-0
Akhmat Grozny - FK Orenburg 2-1(0-0)

Round 5 [10-12.08.2019]
FK Orenburg - FK Tambov 2-2(0-1)
FK Krasnodar - Rubin Kazan 1-0(1-0)
Dinamo Moskva - FK Zenit 0-2(0-1)
Arsenal Tula - FK Ufa 1-0(1-0)
Lokomotiv Moskva - FK Ural 4-0(2-0)
CSKA Moskva - PFK Sochi 0-0
Akhmat Grozny - Spartak Moskva 1-3(0-2)
FK Rostov - Krylia Sovetov 1-0(1-0)

Round 6 [16-19.08.2019]
FK Orenburg - PFK Sochi 1-1(0-0)
FK Ural - Krylia Sovetov 1-3(0-1)
FK Tambov - FK Krasnodar 0-2(0-1)
FK Zenit - Akhmat Grozny 0-0
Rubin Kazan - Arsenal Tula 1-0(0-0)
FK Ufa - FK Rostov 2-0(1-0)
Dinamo Moskva - Lokomotiv M. 1-2(1-1)
Spartak Moskva - CSKA Moskva 2-1(0-0)

Round 7 [24-26.08.2019]
FK Tambov - Dinamo Moskva 0-2(0-1)
FK Ufa - FK Zenit 1-0(0-0)
FK Krasnodar - Lokomotiv Moskva 1-1(1-1)
CSKA Moskva - Akhmat Grozny 3-0(1-0)
FK Rostov - Rubin Kazan 2-1(1-1)
Krylia Sovetov - Spartak Moskva 1-2(1-0)
Arsenal Tula - FK Orenburg 2-1(1-0)
FK Ural - PFK Sochi 3-1(1-1)

Round 8 [30.08.-01.09.2019]
Krylia Sovetov - Dinamo Moskva 0-0
FK Ufa - FK Orenburg 1-2(0-1)
Rubin Kazan - PFK Sochi 0-3(0-1)
Lokomotiv Moskva - FK Rostov 1-2(0-1)
Akhmat Grozny - FK Tambov 1-1(0-1)
FK Ural - FK Krasnodar 2-4(1-2)
Arsenal Tula - CSKA Moskva 1-2(1-1)
Spartak Moskva - FK Zenit 0-1(0-1)

Round 9 [13-16.09.2019]
FK Zenit - Arsenal Tula 3-1(1-0)
Spartak Moskva - FK Ural 1-2(1-0)
PFK Sochi - Lokomotiv Moskva 0-1(0-1)
FK Orenburg - Rubin Kazan 2-1(0-0)
FK Tambov - CSKA Moskva 0-2(0-0)
FK Krasnodar - Krylia Sovetov 4-2(1-1)
Dinamo Moskva - FK Ufa 0-0
FK Rostov - Akhmat Grozny 2-1(0-1)

Round 10 [20-22.09.2019]
FK Ufa - Spartak Moskva 1-0(1-0)
Akhmat Grozny - Krylia Sovetov 1-1(1-0)
FK Zenit - Rubin Kazan 5-0(0-0)
FK Tambov - FK Rostov 2-1(1-1)
FK Orenburg - Lokomotiv Moskva 2-3(0-1)
Dinamo Moskva - PFK Sochi 2-3(0-1)
Arsenal Tula - FK Ural 1-1(1-0)
CSKA Moskva - FK Krasnodar 3-2(3-0)

Round 11 [28-30.09.2019]
Krylia Sovetov - FK Tambov 2-0(0-0)
FK Rostov - Dinamo Moskva 3-0(2-0)
Lokomotiv Moskva - FK Zenit 1-0(0-0)
FK Ural - CSKA Moskva 0-3(0-1)
Rubin Kazan - FK Ufa 0-0
Spartak Moskva - FK Orenburg 1-2(0-1)
FK Krasnodar - Arsenal Tula 2-0(1-0)
PFK Sochi - Akhmat Grozny 2-0(1-0)

Round 12 [05-06.10.2019]
FK Ufa - Akhmat Grozny 0-1(0-1)
FK Orenburg - Dinamo Moskva 2-0(0-0)
Rubin Kazan - FK Tambov 2-1(2-0)
PFK Sochi - Krylia Sovetov 0-2(0-1)
FK Ural - FK Zenit 1-3(0-2)
Lokomotiv Moskva - Arsenal Tula 2-1(2-1)
CSKA Moskva - FK Rostov 1-3(0-2)
FK Krasnodar - Spartak Moskva 2-1(2-1)

Round 13 [18-20.10.2019]
Akhmat Grozny - Lokomotiv Moskva 0-2(0-1)
FK Tambov - FK Ural 1-2(0-0)
Spartak Moskva - Rubin Kazan 0-0
FK Zenit - FK Rostov 6-1(3-0)
FK Orenburg - Krylia Sovetov 0-1(0-1)
FK Ufa - CSKA Moskva 1-1(0-1)
Arsenal Tula - PFK Sochi 1-1(1-1)
Dinamo Moskva - FK Krasnodar 1-1(1-1)

Round 14 [25-27.10.2019]
Rubin Kazan - FK Ural 0-0
FK Tambov - FK Ufa 3-0(1-0)
Akhmat Grozny - Arsenal Tula 1-1(1-0)
FK Rostov - PFK Sochi 2-0(1-0)
Krylia Sovetov - FK Zenit 0-2(0-1)
CSKA Moskva - Dinamo Moskva 0-1(0-0)
Lokomotiv M. - Spartak Moskva 0-3(0-0)
FK Krasnodar - FK Orenburg 1-1(1-1)

Round 15 [02-04.11.2019]
Dinamo Moskva - Akhmat Grozny 1-1(0-1)
FK Ufa - Lokomotiv Moskva 1-1(0-0)
PFK Sochi - FK Tambov 1-2(1-1)
FK Zenit - CSKA Moskva 1-0(0-1)
FK Krasnodar - FK Rostov 2-2(0-2)
FK Ural - FK Orenburg 1-2(0-2)
Krylia Sovetov - Rubin Kazan 0-0
Spartak Moskva - Arsenal Tula 0-1(0-1)

Round 16 [08-10.11.2019]
Akhmat Grozny - FK Ural 0-0
Rubin Kazan - Dinamo Moskva 0-1(0-1)
FK Rostov - FK Tambov 1-2(1-0)
Spartak Moskva - Krylia Sovetov 2-0(1-0)
FK Orenburg - FK Ufa 0-0
Arsenal Tula - FK Zenit 0-1(0-0)
PFK Sochi - CSKA Moskva 2-3(2-1)
Lokomotiv Moskva - FK Krasnodar 1-1(1-1)

Round 17 [22-24.11.2019]
FK Tambov - Lokomotiv Moskva 2-3(1-2)
FK Orenburg - Akhmat Grozny 1-2(0-1)
Rubin Kazan - FK Zenit 2-0(1-0)
Dinamo Moskva - FK Rostov 2-1(1-1)
FK Ufa - PFK Sochi 1-1(0-1)
FK Ural - Spartak Moskva 0-0
Arsenal Tula - FK Krasnodar 1-2(1-2)
CSKA Moskva - Krylia Sovetov 1-0(0-0)

Round 18 [30.11.-02.12.2019]
Krylia Sovetov - FK Ufa 0-1(0-1)
FK Rostov - FK Ural 0-0
Akhmat Grozny - Rubin Kazan 1-1(1-0)
Lokomotiv M. - Dinamo Moskva 1-2(1-1)
FK Zenit - Spartak Moskva 1-0(1-0)
FK Krasnodar - FK Tambov 0-0
CSKA Moskva - Arsenal Tula 0-1(0-0)
PFK Sochi - FK Orenburg 5-1(2-0) [11.03.]

Round 19 [06-08.12.2019]
FK Zenit - Dinamo Moskva 3-0(3-0)
Arsenal Tula - Lokomotiv Moskva 4-0(0-0)
FK Tambov - FK Orenburg 3-0(0-0)
FK Krasnodar - CSKA Moskva 1-1(0-1)
Akhmat Grozny - FK Ufa 0-1(0-1)
Krylia Sovetov - FK Ural 1-1(0-0)
PFK Sochi - Rubin Kazan 1-1(0-0)
Spartak Moskva - FK Rostov 1-4(0-1)

Round 20 [28.02.-01.03.2020]
Krylia Sovetov - FK Orenburg 1-1(1-0)
CSKA Moskva - FK Ural 1-1(0-0)
Dinamo Moskva - Spartak Moskva 0-2(0-1)
FK Zenit - Lokomotiv Moskva 0-0
Akhmat Grozny - FK Rostov 1-1(0-1)
FK Tambov - Rubin Kazan 0-0
FK Krasnodar - FK Ufa 2-0(0-0)
PFK Sochi - Arsenal Tula 1-2(0-1)

Round 21 [07-09.03.2020]
FK Orenburg - Arsenal Tula 2-0(1-0)
Dinamo Moskva - FK Tambov 1-0(1-0)
Rubin Kazan - Krylia Sovetov 0-1(0-1)
PFK Sochi - FK Ural 2-0(1-0)
Lokomotiv Moskva - Akhmat Grozny 1-0(1-0)
FK Rostov - CSKA Moskva 3-2(1-1)
Spartak Moskva - FK Krasnodar 0-1(0-0)
FK Zenit - FK Ufa 0-0

Round 22 [13-16.03.2020]
Akhmat Grozny - Dinamo Moskva 2-3(1-1)
FK Orenburg - Spartak Moskva 1-3(1-1)
FK Zenit - FK Ural 7-1(4-0)
Arsenal Tula - Rubin Kazan 0-1(0-1)
PFK Sochi - FK Krasnodar 2-0(0-0)
CSKA Moskva - FK Ufa 0-0
FK Rostov - Lokomotiv Moskva 1-3(0-3)
FK Tambov - Krylia Sovetov 3-0(1-0)

Round 23 [19-21.06.2020]
Krylia Sovetov - Akhmat Grozny 2-4(1-0)
PFK Sochi - FK Rostov 10-1(4-1)
FK Ural - Rubin Kazan 1-2(1-1)
Arsenal Tula - Spartak Moskva 2-3(0-1)
CSKA Moskva - FK Zenit 0-4(0-3)
FK Ufa - FK Tambov 2-1(1-0)
Lokomotiv Moskva - FK Orenburg 1-0(1-0)
FK Krasnodar - Dinamo M. 0-2(0-1) [19.07.]

Round 24 [26-28.06.2020]
Akhmat Grozny - PFK Sochi 1-1(1-1)
FK Zenit - Krylia Sovetov 2-1(0-1)
FK Orenburg - FK Krasnodar 0-3 *awarded*
Spartak Moskva - FK Ufa 0-0
Rubin Kazan - Lokomotiv Moskva 0-2(0-2)
Dinamo Moskva - CSKA Moskva 0-0
FK Rostov - Arsenal Tula 2-1(2-0)
FK Ural - FK Tambov 2-1(1-0)

Round 25 [30.06.-01.07.2020]
Lokomotiv Moskva - Krylia Sovetov 1-1(0-1)
CSKA Moskva - Spartak Moskva 2-0(1-0)
FK Ufa - Rubin Kazan 0-0
FK Orenburg - FK Ural 0-3 Wert.
FK Tambov - FK Zenit 1-2(0-1)
Arsenal Tula - Akhmat Grozny 1-3(0-2)
FK Rostov - FK Krasnodar 1-1(0-1)
PFK Sochi - Dinamo Moskva 1-1(0-0)

Round 26 [04-05.07.2020]
Dinamo Moskva - Arsenal Tula 0-1(0-1)
Spartak Moskva - FK Tambov 2-3(1-0)
Krylia Sovetov - FK Rostov 0-0
Lokomotiv Moskva - PFK Sochi 0-0
Akhmat Grozny - CSKA Moskva 0-4(0-0)
FK Ufa - FK Ural 1-1(0-0)
Rubin Kazan - FK Orenburg 1-0(0-0)
FK Krasnodar - FK Zenit 2-4(1-2)

Round 27 [07-09.07.2020]
FK Tambov - Akhmat Grozny 1-2(1-1)
Arsenal Tula - Krylia Sovetov 2-4(1-1)
FK Zenit - PFK Sochi 2-1(1-1)
FK Orenburg - CSKA Moskva 0-4(0-1)
Spartak Moskva - Lokomotiv M. 1-1(1-1)
FK Rostov - FK Ufa 1-2(1-0)
FK Ural - Dinamo Moskva 2-1(1-1)
Rubin Kazan - FK Krasnodar 1-0(0-0)

Round 28 [11-12.07.2020]
Arsenal Tula - FK Tambov 2-1(1-0)
Akhmat Grozny - FK Zenit 1-1(1-1)
PFK Sochi - Spartak Moskva 1-0(1-0)
Lokomotiv Moskva - FK Ufa 1-1(0-1)
CSKA Moskva - Rubin Kazan 1-1(0-0)
Dinamo Moskva - Krylia Sovetov 2-0(2-0)
FK Orenburg - FK Rostov 0-0
FK Krasnodar - FK Ural 3-0(1-0)

Round 29 [15-16.07.2020]
FK Ural - Arsenal Tula 1-3(1-1)
Spartak Moskva - Akhmat Grozny 3-0(0-0)
Krylia Sovetov - FK Krasnodar 0-0
FK Zenit - FK Orenburg 4-1(1-1)
FK Tambov - PFK Sochi 3-0 *awarded*
Rubin Kazan - FK Rostov 0-0
FK Ufa - Dinamo Moskva 0-1(0-0)
Lokomotiv Moskva - CSKA Moskva 2-1(1-0)

Round 30 [22.07.2020]
FK Rostov - FK Zenit 1-2(1-0)
FK Krasnodar - Akhmat Grozny 4-0(1-0)
CSKA Moskva - FK Tambov 2-0(1-0)
Dinamo Moskva - FK Orenburg 0-1(0-1)
Rubin Kazan - Spartak Moskva 1-2(1-1)
Krylia Sovetov - PFK Sochi 3-0 *awarded*
FK Ufa - Arsenal Tula 0-0
FK Ural - Lokomotiv Moskva 0-1(0-1)

Final Standings

									Home					Away				
1.	**FK Zenit Saint Petersburg**	30	22	6	2	65 - 18	72	10	5	0	37 - 9	12	1	2	28 - 9
2.	FK Lokomotiv Moskva	30	16	9	5	41 - 29	57	7	5	3	19 - 14	9	4	2	22 - 15
3.	FK Krasnodar	30	14	10	6	49 - 30	52	8	5	2	28 - 14	6	5	4	21 - 16
4.	FK CSKA Moskva	30	14	8	8	43 - 29	50	7	4	4	17 - 14	7	4	4	26 - 15
5.	FK Rostov	30	12	9	9	45 - 50	45	8	3	4	24 - 18	4	6	5	21 - 32
6.	FK Dinamo Moskva	30	11	8	11	27 - 30	41	4	4	7	12 - 15	7	4	4	15 - 15
7.	FK Spartak Moskva	30	11	6	13	35 - 33	39	4	4	7	14 - 16	7	2	6	21 - 17
8.	FK Arsenal Tula	30	11	5	14	37 - 41	38	4	3	8	21 - 24	7	2	6	16 - 17
9.	FK Ufa	30	8	14	8	22 - 24	38	5	6	4	15 - 13	3	8	4	7 - 11
10.	FK Rubin Kazan	30	8	11	11	18 - 28	35	5	3	7	8 - 13	3	8	4	10 - 15
11.	FK Ural Yekaterinburg	30	9	8	13	36 - 53	35	5	2	8	22 - 28	4	6	5	14 - 25
12.	PFK Sochi	30	8	9	13	40 - 39	33	6	3	6	28 - 16	2	6	7	12 - 23
13.	RFK Akhmat Grozny	30	7	10	13	27 - 46	31	2	8	5	13 - 21	5	2	8	14 - 25
14.	FK Tambov	30	9	4	17	37 - 41	31	6	1	8	21 - 17	3	3	9	16 - 24
15.	PFK Krylia Sovetov Samara *(Relegated)*	30	8	7	15	33 - 40	31	3	5	7	16 - 18	5	2	8	17 - 22
16.	FK Orenburg *(Relegated)*	30	7	6	17	28 - 52	27	3	4	8	13 - 25	4	2	9	15 - 27

Top goalscorers:

17	**Sardar Azmoun (IRN)**	*FK Zenit St Petersburg*
17	**Artyom Dzyuba**	*FK Zenit St Petersburg*
15	Evgeniy Lutsenko	*FK Arsenal Tula*
12	Aleksey Miranchuk	*FK Lokomotiv Moskva*
12	Aleksandr Sobolev	*PFK Krylia Sovetov Samara / FK Spartak Moskva*
12	Nikola Vlašić (CRO)	*FK CSKA Moskva*

NATIONAL CUP
Kubok Rossii (Кубок России) 2019/2020

Fourth Round [21.08./03.09.2019]

FK Chita - FK Luch Vladivostok	0-1(0-1)	FK Ryazan - FK Chertanovo Moskva	1-4(0-2)
FK Alania Vladikavkaz - FK Rotor Volgograd	2-1(1-1)	FK Shinnik Yaroslavl - FK Tekstilshchik Ivanovo	1-0(1-0)
FK Ararat Moskva - FK Nizhny Novgorod	0-3(0-2)	FK Salyut Belgorod - FK Fakel Voronezh	1-3(1-1)
FK Veles Moskva - FK Torpedo Moskva	3-3 aet; 5-6 pen	FK Kamaz N. Chely - FK Neftekhimik Nizhnekamsk	2-0(0-0)
FK Chernomorets Novorossisk - FK Armavir	3-0(1-0)	FK Khimki - FK Avangard Kursk	4-1(3-1)
FK Inter Cherkessk - FK Chayka Peschanokopskoye	2-5(1-3)	FK Sakhalin Yuzhno-Sakhal. - FK SKA-Khabarovsk	0-2(0-1)
FK Akron Tolyatti - FK Mordovia Saransk	1-1 aet; 3-5 pen	FK Irtysh Omsk - FK Tom Tomsk	0-2(0-1)
FK Leningradets St. Petersburg- FK Baltika Kalining.	1-2(0-1)	FK Tyumen - FK Yenisey Krasnoyarsk	0-1(0-0)

Fifth Round [25.09.2019]

FK SKA-Khabarovsk - RFK Akhmat Grozny	2-2 aet; 2-4 pen	FK Mordovia Saransk - FK Rostov	0-2(0-0)
FK Luch Vladivostok - RFK Akhmat Grozny	1-0(1-0)	FK Chertanovo Moskva - FK Orenburg	0-2(0-0,0-0)
FK Tom Tomsk - FK Tambov	4-0(2-0)	FK Khimki - FK Rubin Kazan	3-0(1-0)
FK Yenisey Krasnoyarsk - FK Zenit Saint Petersburg	1-2(1-0)	FK Nizhny Novgorod - FK Krasnodar	1-0(0-0)
FK Chayka Peschanokopskoye - FK Ufa	0-1(0-1)	FK Fakel Voronezh - FK Arsenal Tula	1-2(1-1)
FK Alania Vladikavkaz - FK CSKA Moskva	1-3(1-2)	FK Chernomorets Novoros. - FK Ural Yekaterinburg	0-2(0-0)
FK Shinnik Yaroslavl - FK Sochi	0-0 aet; 5-4 pen	FK Torpedo Moskva - PFK Krylia Sovetov Samara	2-0(2-0)
FK Kamaz Naberezhnye Chely - FK Spartak Moskva	1-2(1-1)	FK Baltika Kaliningrad - FK Lokomotiv Moskva	1-1 aet; 4-1 pen

1/8-Finals [30-31.10.2019]

FK Ural Yekaterinburg - FK Arsenal Tula	2-2 aet; 5-4 pen	FK Zenit Saint Petersburg - FK Tom Tomsk	4-0(1-0)
RFK Akhmat Grozny - FK Luch Vladivostok	5-1(2-0)	FK Orenburg - FK Khimki	1-2(0-2)
FK Nizhny Novgorod - FK Shinnik Yaroslavl	2-2 aet; 0-3 pen	FK Torpedo Moskva - Baltika Kaliningrad	1-0(0-0)
FK CSKA Moskva - FK Ufa	1-0(0-0)	FK Spartak Moskva - FK Rostov	2-1(1-0)

Quarter-Finals [04-05.03./24.06.2020]

RFK Akhmat Grozny - FK Zenit Saint Petersburg	1-2(0-0,1-1)	FK Khimki - FK Torpedo Moskva	5-1(1-0)
FK Spartak Moskva - FK CSKA Moskva	3-2(2-2,2-2)	FK Shinnik Yaroslavl - FK Ural Yekaterinburg	0-2(0-1)

Semi-Finals [19.07.2020]

FK Khimki - FK Ural Yekaterinburg	3-1(3-0)	FK Zenit Saint Petersburg - FK Spartak Moskva	2-1(2-1)

Final

25.07.2020; Central Stadium, Yekaterinburg; Referee: Vladimir Moskalyov; Attendance: 3,408
FK Zenit Saint Petersburg - FK Khimki   **1-0(0-0)**

FK Zenit: Mikhail Kerzhakov, Douglas dos Santos Justino de Melo (76.Sebastián Driussi), Branislav Ivanović, Vyacheslav Karavayev (90.Igor Smolnikov), Yaroslav Rakitskiy, Wilmar Enrique Barrios Teherán, Daler Kuzyaev, Magomed Ozdoev (75.Yuriy Zhirkov), Sardar Azmoun (88.Oleg Shatov), Malcom Filipe Silva de Oliveira (88.Aleksey Sutormin), Artyom Dzyuba. Trainer: Sergey Semak.

FK Khimki: Ilya Lantratov, Dmitry Tikhiy, Egor Danilkin, Evgeniy Gapon, Aleksandr Smirnov (65.Ilya Kukharchuk), Alexander Troshechkin, Maksim Martusevich, Artyom Polyarus (88.Mohamed Konaté), Arshak Koryan (81.Kamran Aliev), Kirill Bozhenov, Vladimir Dyadyun (64.Dmitriy Barkov). Trainer: Sergey Yuran.

Goal: 1-0 Artyom Dzyuba (84 penalty).

THE CLUBS 2019/2020

Respublikanskiy Fudbolnij Klub Akhmat Grozny

Founded:	1958	
Stadium:	Akhmat-Arena, Grozny (30,597)	
Trainer:	Rashid Rakhimov	18.03.1965
[01.10.2019]	Igor Shalimov	02.02.1969

Goalkeepers:	DOB	M	(s)	G
Evgeniy Gorodov	13.12.1985	25		
Vitaliy Gudiev	22.04.1995	4		
Aleksandr Melikhov	23.03.1998	1		
Defenders:	**DOB**	**M**	**(s)**	**G**
Arsen Adamov	20.10.1999	1		
Wilker José Ángel Romero (VEN)	18.03.1993	18	(1)	1
Miroslav Bogosavac (SRB)	14.10.1996	9	(1)	
Konrad Michalak (POL)	19.09.1997	2	(4)	
Magomed Musalov	09.02.1994	9		
Maksim Nenakhov	13.12.1998	9		
Zoran Nižić (CRO)	11.10.1989	18	(3)	
Andrei Semyonov	24.03.1989	30		1
Rizvan Utsiev	07.02.1988	14		
Midfielders:	**DOB**	**M**	**(s)**	**G**
Bernard Berisha (KVX)	24.10.1991	17	(5)	3
Mikhail Gashchenkov	19.06.1992	3	(3)	

Roland Gigolayev	04.01.1990	8		
Denis Glushakov	27.01.1987	22	(2)	4
Vladimir Ilyin	20.05.1992	5	(3)	2
Ismael Silva Lima (BRA)	01.12.1994	28	(1)	1
Oleg Ivanov	04.08.1986	25	(2)	1
Khalid Kadyrov	19.04.1994		(1)	
Evgeny Kharin	11.06.1995	17	(5)	2
Ravanelli Ferreira dos Santos (BRA)	29.08.1997	3	(2)	
Odise Roshi (ALB)	22.05.1991	19	(7)	7
Lechi Sadulayev	08.01.2000	2	(4)	
Anton Shvets	26.04.1993	15	(4)	
Damian Szymański (POL)	16.06.1995	2	(2)	
Forwards:	**DOB**	**M**	**(s)**	**G**
Felipe dos Reis Pereira Vizeu do Carmo (BRA)	12.03.1997	3	(4)	1
Ablaye Mbengue (SEN)	15.05.1992	5	(11)	1
Magomed Mitrishev	10.09.1992	2	(7)	
Andrés Fabián Ponce Núñez (VEN)	11.11.1996	14	(6)	3

Fudbolnij Klub Arsenal Tula

Founded: 1946
Stadium: Arsenal Stadium, Tula (20,048)
Trainer: Igor Cherevchenko   21.08.1974
[02.07.2020]   Sergey Podpaly   13.09.1963

Goalkeepers:	DOB	M	(s)	G
Mikhail Levashov	04.10.1991	18		
Yuriy Lodygin	26.05.1990	2		
Artur Nigmatullin	17.05.1991	1		
Egor Shamov	02.06.1994	9		
Defenders:	**DOB**	**M**	**(s)**	**G**
Robert Bauer (GER)	09.04.1995	12	(2)	1
Maksim Belyaev	30.09.1991	29		
Aleksandr Denisov	23.02.1989	12	(1)	1
Aleksandr Dovbnya	14.02.1996	4	(1)	
Gia Grigalava (GEO)	05.08.1989	22		1
Anri Khagush	23.09.1986	4	(3)	
Kirill Kombarov	22.01.1987	16	(3)	
Artyom Sokol	11.06.1997	1	(2)	
Víctor Guillermo Álvarez Delgado (ESP)	14.03.1993	24		1
Maksim Volodko (BLR)	10.11.1992		(4)	
Midfielders:	**DOB**	**M**	**(s)**	**G**
Lameck Banda (ZAM)	29.01.2001	1	(8)	
Kantemir Berkhamov	07.08.1988	1		1
Goran Čaušić (SRB)	05.05.1992	20	(1)	2
Igor Gorbatenko	13.02.1989	20	(4)	1
Valeriy Gromyko (BLR)	23.01.1997		(3)	
Evans Kangwa (ZAM)	21.06.1992	14	(8)	3
Kings Kangwa (ZAM)	04.06.1999	4	(4)	
Daniil Khlusevich	26.02.2001	4	(1)	1
Georgi Kostadinov (BUL)	07.09.1990	23	(1)	
Yuriy Kovalev (BLR)	27.01.1993	1	(4)	
Vladislav Panteleyev	15.08.1996	3	(3)	2
Sergey Tkachev	19.05.1989	22	(5)	2
Forwards:	**DOB**	**M**	**(s)**	**G**
Guram Adzhoev	27.02.1995		(1)	
Daniil Lesovoy	12.01.1998	22	(5)	3
Aleksandr Lomovitskiy	27.01.1998	14	(10)	2
Evgeniy Lutsenko	25.02.1987	25	(3)	15
Roman Minaev	24.12.1997		(3)	
Alexandru Tudorie (ROU)	19.03.1996	2	(5)	1

Profesionalniy Fudbolnij Klub CSKA [Central Sport Club of the Army] Moskva

Founded: 27.08.1911
Stadium: VEB Arena, Moskva (30,000)
Trainer: Viktor Goncharenko   10.09.1977

Goalkeepers:	DOB	M	(s)	G
Igor Akinfeyev	08.04.1986	30		
Defenders:	**DOB**	**M**	**(s)**	**G**
Igor Diveyev	27.09.1999	26		
Cèdric Gogoua (CIV)	10.07.1994	3	(1)	1
Vadim Karpov	14.07.2002	12	(1)	
Hörður Magnússon (ISL)	11.02.1993	26	(1)	2
Mário Figueira Fernandes	19.09.1990	29		3
Georgiy Shchennikov	27.04.1991	9		2
Zvonimir Šarlija (CRO)	29.08.1996	6	(5)	
Viktor Vasin	06.10.1988	9	(2)	
Midfielders:	**DOB**	**M**	**(s)**	**G**
Ilzat Akhmetov	31.12.1997	17	(4)	2
Jaka Bijol (SVN)	05.02.1999	4	(21)	1
Kristijan Bistrović (CRO)	09.04.1998	15	(13)	1
Alan Dzagoev	17.06.1990	6	(4)	
Dmitriy Efremov	01.04.1995	1	(1)	
Konstantin Kuchaev	18.03.1998	14	(11)	
Lucas Santos da Silva (BRA)	07.03.1999		(2)	
Konstantin Maradishvili	07.02.2000	7	(4)	
Kirill Nababkin	08.09.1986	9	(4)	
Ivan Oblyakov	05.07.1998	28		4
Arnór Sigurðsson (ISL)	15.05.1999	19	(3)	4
Nayair Tiknizyan	12.05.1999		(5)	
Nikola Vlašić (CRO)	04.10.1997	30		12
Forwards:	**DOB**	**M**	**(s)**	**G**
Fedor Chalov	10.04.1998	29	(1)	8
Takuma Nishimura (JPN)	22.10.1996	1	(4)	
Ilya Shkurin (BLR)	17.08.1999		(4)	

Fudbolnij Klub Dinamo Moskva

Founded: 18.04.1923
Stadium: VTB Arena, Moskva (26,319)
Trainer: Dmitriy Khokhlov   22.12.1975
[08.10.2019]   Kirill Novikov   14.01.1981

Goalkeepers:	DOB	M	(s)	G
Igor Leshchuk	20.02.1996	7	(1)	
Anton Shunin	27.01.1987	23		
Defenders:	**DOB**	**M**	**(s)**	**G**
Roman Evgenyev	23.02.1999	11	(3)	
Grigori Morozov	06.06.1994	17	(4)	1
Ivan Ordets (UKR)	08.07.1992	16	(1)	1
Sergey Parshivlyuk	18.03.1989	15	(2)	
Zaurbek Pliev	27.09.1991	10	(4)	
Konstantin Rausch	15.03.1990	16	(2)	1
Vladimir Rykov	13.11.1987	18	(1)	
Dmitriy Skopintsev	02.03.1997	10		1
Toni Šunjić (BIH)	15.12.1988	17	(2)	
Midfielders:	**DOB**	**M**	**(s)**	**G**
Oscar Hiljemark (SWE)	28.06.1992	5	(9)	
Charles Kaboré (BFA)	09.02.1988	15	(5)	
Roman Neustädter	18.02.1988	19	(1)	
Maximilian Philipp (GER)	01.03.1994	15	(5)	8
Igor Shkolik	09.01.2001	1	(2)	
Anton Sosnin	27.01.1990	1	(3)	
Samba Sow (MLI)	29.04.1989		(1)	
Abdul-Aziz Tetteh (GHA)	25.05.1990	1	(2)	
Artur Yusupov	01.09.1989	19	(2)	1
Forwards:	**DOB**	**M**	**(s)**	**G**
Maksim Danilin	26.05.2001	1	(1)	
Vyacheslav Grulev	23.03.1999	4	(9)	1
Sylvester Emeka Igboun (NGA)	08.09.1990	17	(3)	2
João Natailton Ramos dos Santos „Joãozinho" (BRA)	25.12.1988	18	(1)	2
Vladsilav Karapuzov	06.01.2000	2	(3)	
Nikolay Komlichenko	29.06.1995	7	(4)	3
Miguel Felipe Nunes Cardoso (POR)	19.06.1994	3	(3)	1
Clinton Mua N'Jie (CMR)	15.08.1993	7	(12)	1
Kirill Panchenko	16.10.1989	12	(10)	2
Ramil Sheydaev (AZE)	15.03.1996	5	(3)	
Sebastian Szymański (POL)	10.05.1999	18	(4)	1

Fudbolnij Klub Krasnodar

Founded:	22.02.2008		
Stadium:	Krasnodar Stadium, Krasnodar (34,291)		
Trainer:	Murad Musaev		10.11.1983

Goalkeepers:	DOB	M	(s)	G
Denis Adamov	20.02.1998	1	(1)	
Stanislav Kritsyuk	01.12.1990	1		
Matvey Safonov	25.02.1999	27		
Defenders:	**DOB**	**M**	**(s)**	**G**
Jón Fjóluson (ISL)	10.04.1989	8	(2)	
Yuriy Gazinskiy	20.07.1989	10	(1)	
Aleksandr Martinovich (BLR)	26.08.1987	21	(1)	1
Sergey Petrov	02.01.1991	27		2
Cristian Leonel Ramírez Zambrano (ECU)	12.08.1994	24	(2)	
Egor Sorokin	04.11.1995	6	(2)	
Uroš Spajić (SRB)	13.02.1993	15		1
Midfielders:	**DOB**	**M**	**(s)**	**G**
Rémy Cabella (FRA)	08.03.1990	5	(4)	2
Aleksandr Chernikov	01.02.2000	3	(3)	
Kaio Pantaleão (BRA)	18.09.1995	10	(1)	
Ruslan Kambolov	01.01.1990	10	(6)	
Manuel Henriques Tavares Fernandes (POR)	05.02.1986	10	(6)	2

	DOB	M	(s)	G
Aleks Matsukatov	11.01.1999		(2)	
Younes Namli (DEN)	20.06.1994	6	(4)	1
Mats Kristoffer Olsson (SWE)	30.06.1995	23	(4)	1
Dmitriy Skopintsev	02.03.1997	2	(3)	1
Dmitriy Stotskiy	01.12.1989	8	(4)	
Daniil Utkin	12.10.1999	12	(10)	4
Tonny Vilhena (NED)	03.01.1995	20		2
Forwards:	**DOB**	**M**	**(s)**	**G**
Ariclenes da Silva Ferreira „Ari"	11.12.1985	18		6
Bengt Erik Marcus Berg (SWE)	17.08.1986	15	(8)	9
Ivan Ignatyev	06.01.1999	5	(8)	4
Maksim Kutovoi	01.07.2001		(3)	
German Onugkha	06.07.1996		(2)	
Nikita Sergeyev	17.10.1999		(4)	
Magomed Suleymanov	16.12.1999	12	(15)	4
Ilya Vorotnikov	11.02.2001		(1)	
Wanderson Maciel Sousa Campos (BRA)	07.10.1994	20	(1)	3

Professionalnij Fudbolnij Klub Krylia Sovetov Samara

Founded:	1942		
Stadium:	Samara Arena, Samara (44,918)		
Trainer:	Miodrag Božović (MNE)		22.06.1968
[29.06.2020]	Andrey Talalaev		05.10.1972

Goalkeepers:	DOB	M	(s)	G
Evgeni Frolov	05.02.1988	10		
Sergey Ryzhikov	19.09.1980	19		
Defenders:	**DOB**	**M**	**(s)**	**G**
Aleksandr Anyukov	28.09.1982	18		
Taras Burlak	22.02.1990	8		2
Nikita Chernov	14.01.1996	23		1
Nikita Chicherin	18.08.1990	4	(2)	
Maksim Karpov	17.03.1995	21		1
Dmitriy Kombarov	22.01.1987	20	(2)	
Vitaliy Lystsov	11.07.1995	7	(1)	1
Vladimir Poluyakhtov	11.07.1989	11	(1)	
Mehdi Zeffane (FRA)	19.05.1992	6		
Midfielders:	**DOB**	**M**	**(s)**	**G**
Safaa Hadi Abdullah Al Fujairi (IRQ)	14.10.1998		(4)	
Paul Viorel Anton (ROU)	10.05.1991	14	(3)	2
Alexandru Gaţcan (MDA)	27.03.1984	21	(1)	

	DOB	M	(s)	G
Gennady Kiselev	03.01.1999		(2)	
Srđan Mijailović (SRB)	10.11.1993	12	(3)	1
Danila Smirnov	07.06.2001		(3)	
Artiom Timofeyev	12.01.1994	18	(3)	
Vladislav Tyuriyn	18.04.2000		(1)	
Forwards:	**DOB**	**M**	**(s)**	**G**
Radu Gînsari (MDA)	10.12.1991	7	(3)	1
Maksim Glushenkov	28.07.1999	8	(2)	3
Egor Golenkov	07.07.1999		(9)	
Dmitry Kabutov	26.03.1992	24	(4)	
Maksim Kanunnikov	14.07.1991	12	(3)	1
Dmitriy Molchanov	01.10.2000		(2)	
Denis Popovič (SVN)	15.10.1989	8	(2)	3
Dejan Radonjić (CRO)	23.07.1990	8	(19)	4
Aleksandr Sobolev	07.03.1997	18		10
Anton Terekhov	30.01.1998	1	(11)	
Anton Zinkovskiy	14.04.1996	21	(6)	

Fudbolnij Klub Lokomotiv Moskva

Founded:	23.07.1922		
Stadium:	RZD (Lokomotiv) Stadium, Moskva (27,320)		
Trainer:	Yuriy Semin		11.05.1947
[01.06.2020]	Marko Nikolić (SRB)		20.07.1979

Goalkeepers:	DOB	M	(s)	G
Guilherme Alvin Marinato	12.12.1985	24		
Anton Kochenkov	02.04.1987	6	(1)	
Defenders:	**DOB**	**M**	**(s)**	**G**
Artur Cherny	11.12.2000		(1)	
Vedran Ćorluka (CRO)	05.02.1986	27		
Benedikt Höwedes (GER)	29.02.1988	18		
Brian Oladapo Idowu (NGA)	18.05.1992	5	(7)	
Vladislav Ignatiev	20.01.1987	23		1
Solomon Kverkvelia (GEO)	06.02.1992	5	(4)	
Mikhail Lysov	29.01.1998		(1)	
Murilo Cerqueira Paim (BRA)	27.03.1997	21	(4)	
Maciej Rybus (POL)	19.08.1989	18	(1)	
Dmitriy Zhivoglyadov	29.05.1994	12	(2)	
Midfielders:	**DOB**	**M**	**(s)**	**G**
Dmitry Barinov	11.09.1996	23		1

	DOB	M	(s)	G
João Mário Naval da Costa Eduardo (POR)	19.01.1993	16	(2)	1
Aleksandr Kolomeytsev	21.02.1989	5	(5)	1
Grzegorz Krychowiak (POL)	29.01.1990	26		9
Daniil Kulikov	24.06.1998	3	(3)	
Stanislav Magkeyev	27.03.1999	7	(3)	
Aleksey Miranchuk	17.10.1995	25	(2)	12
Anton Miranchuk	17.10.1995	13	(4)	3
Dmitry Rybchinsky	19.08.1998	2	(5)	
Rifat Zhemaletdinov	20.09.1996	18	(5)	2
Forwards:	**DOB**	**M**	**(s)**	**G**
Luka Đorđević (MNE)	09.07.1994	1	(3)	
Éderzito António Macedo Lopes „Éder" (POR)	22.12.1987	20	(3)	5
Jefferson Agustin Farfán Guadalupe (PER)	26.10.1984		(3)	1
Fedor Smolov	09.02.1990	10	(4)	3
Timur Suleymanov	17.03.2000	1	(3)	
Roman Tugarev	22.07.1998	1	(4)	

Fudbolnij Klub Orenburg

Founded: 1976
Stadium: Gazovik Stadium, Orenburg (7,520)
Trainer: Vladimir Fedotov — 12.08.1966
[08.12.2019] Konstantin Emeljanov — 28.03.1970
[19.06.2020] Konstantin Paramonov — 26.11.1973

Goalkeepers:	DOB	M	(s)	G
Aleksandr Dovbnya	10.04.1987	5		
Andrey Klimovich (BLR)	27.08.1988	20		
Aleksandr Rudenko	04.03.1993	3		
Defenders:	**DOB**	**M**	**(s)**	**G**
Adi Gotlieb (ISR)	16.08.1992	4	(1)	
Danil Khoroshkov	24.12.2001		(1)	
Saveliy Kozlov	19.01.1997	5	(4)	
Daniil Krivoruchko	24.03.1998		(2)	
Ivan Lapshov	01.05.1999		(1)	
Andrey Malykh	24.08.1988	23		1
Uroš Radaković (SRB)	31.03.1994	15		1
Vitaliy Shakov	09.01.1991	18		
Mikhail Sivakov (BLR)	16.01.1988	17	(2)	
Sergey Terekhov	27.06.1990	27		
Georgiy Zotov	12.01.1990	18	(2)	1
Midfielders:	**DOB**	**M**	**(s)**	**G**
Vadim Afonin (UZB)	29.09.1987	5	(5)	
Timur Ayupov	26.07.1993	20	(2)	
David Bidlovskiy	22.01.1999		(2)	
Kirill Kaplenko	15.06.1999		(1)	
Islambek Kuat (KAZ)	12.01.1993	3		
Artyom Kulishev	26.08.1993	10	(8)	3
Danil Lipovoy	22.09.1999	4	(1)	
Nikita Malyarov	23.10.1989	3		1
Danijel Miškić (CRO)	11.10.1993	22		
Ricardo Alves Coelho da Silva (POR)	25.03.1993	21		3
Filip Rogić (SWE)	14.06.1993	10	(1)	1
Žiga Škoflek (SVN)	22.07.1994	7	(4)	1
Forwards:	**DOB**	**M**	**(s)**	**G**
Fiodor Černych (LTU)	21.05.1991	5	(6)	
Andrea Chukanov	18.12.1995	9	(8)	
Đorđe Despotović (SRB)	04.03.1992	20		8
Joel Fameyeh (GHA)	14.05.1997	11	(12)	7
Artyom Galadzhan	22.05.1998		(4)	
Mamadou Sylla (SEN)	20.03.1994	3	(2)	

Fudbolnij Klub Rostov

Founded: 1930
Stadium: Rostov Arena, Rostov-na-Donu (45,000)
Trainer: Valeriy Karpin — 02.02.1969

Goalkeepers:	DOB	M	(s)	G
Egor Baburin	09.08.1993	12		
Sergey Pesyakov	16.12.1988	17		
Denis Popov	29.08.2002	1		
Defenders:	**DOB**	**M**	**(s)**	**G**
Vladimir Abramov	05.04.2002	1		
Evgeniy Chernov	23.10.1992	29		
Dmitriy Chistyakov	13.01.1994	22		1
Dennis Hadžikadunić (SWE)	09.07.1998	15	(2)	1
Timofey Kalistratov	18.02.2003	1		
Aleksey Kozlov	25.12.1986	24		
Arseniy Logashov	20.08.1991	2	(8)	
Maksim Osipenko	16.05.1994	9		
Ragnar Sigurðsson	19.06.1986	12	(1)	
Danila Vedernikov	06.06.2001		(5)	
Midfielders:	**DOB**	**M**	**(s)**	**G**
Khoren Bairamyan (ARM)	07.01.1992	24	(2)	4
Evgeniy Cherkes	23.06.2001		(1)	
Roman Eremenko (FIN)	19.03.1987	16	(3)	5
Alexandru Gațcan (MDA)	27.03.1984		(1)	
Kirill Girnyk	31.03.2003	1		
Danil Glebov	03.11.1999	13	(6)	
Pavel Gorelov	22.01.2003	1		
Aleksey Ionov	18.02.1989	25		6
Nikita Kashtan	01.09.2003		(1)	
Sergey Kochkanyan	05.05.2003		(1)	
Nikita Kolotievsky	04.03.2001	1		
Ivan Komarov	15.04.2003		(1)	
Aleksey Kornienko	15.01.2003		(1)	
Nikita Kupriyanov	23.04.2002	1		
Pavel Mamaev	17.09.1988	6	(1)	2
Mathias Normann (NOR)	28.05.1996	22	(1)	1
Ivelin Popov (BUL)	26.10.1987	23	(2)	5
Wiliam Rogava	25.01.2003	1		
Roman Romanov	28.03.2003	1		1
Aleksandr Saplinov	12.08.1997	6	(15)	1
Maksim Stavtsev	29.01.2004		(1)	
Baktiyor Zaynutdinov (KAZ)	02.04.1998	10	(7)	4
Aleksandr Zuev	26.06.1996	1	(6)	1
Forwards:	**DOB**	**M**	**(s)**	**G**
Aleksandr Dolgov	24.09.1998	1	(14)	
Danil Khromov	25.12.2002	1		
Danila Proshliakov	08.03.2000	1	(6)	
Eldor Shomurodov (UZB)	29.06.1995	28		11
Björn Sigurðarson (ISL)	26.02.1991	1	(5)	2
Tamaz Topuriya	29.01.2002	1		

Fudbolnij Klub Rubin Kazan

Founded: 20.04.1958
Stadium: Kazan Arena, Kazan (45,093)
Trainer: Roman Sharonov — 08.09.1976
[19.12.2019] Leonid Slutski — 04.05.1971

Goalkeepers:	DOB	M	(s)	G
Yury Dyupin	17.03.1988	30		
Defenders:	**DOB**	**M**	**(s)**	**G**
Oleg Danchenko (UKR)	01.08.1994	19		
Vitaliy Denisov (UZB)	23.02.1987	7	(1)	
Pablo Renan dos Santos (BRA)	18.03.1992	9		
Konstantin Pliev	26.10.1996	11	(1)	
Nikolay Poyarkov	16.10.1999	6	(1)	
Egor Sorokin	04.11.1995	13	(1)	
Carl Starfelt (SWE)	01.06.1995	10		
Danil Stepanov	25.01.2000	7	(2)	
Filip Uremović (CRO)	11.02.1997	25		
Midfielders:	**DOB**	**M**	**(s)**	**G**
Oliver Abildgaard (DEN)	10.06.1996	10	(1)	
Roman Akbashev	01.11.1991		(1)	
Soltmurad Bakaev	05.08.1999	3	(7)	1
Evgeniy Bashkirov	06.07.1991	8	(3)	1
Zuriko Davitashvili (GEO)	15.02.2001	19	(7)	2
Darko Jevtić (SUI)	08.02.1993	8	(2)	
Nikolai Kipiani	25.01.1997		(3)	
Igor Konovalov	08.07.1996	27	(2)	1
Khvicha Kvaratskhelia (GEO)	12.02.2001	14	(13)	3
Denis Makarov	18.02.1998	4	(3)	
Nikita Makarov	02.01.2001	2	(3)	2
Pavel Mogilevets	25.01.1993	16	(4)	
Vyacheslav Podberezkin	21.06.1992	19	(2)	
Ilya Samoshnikov	14.11.1997	5	(1)	
Dmitriy Tarasov	18.03.1987		(4)	
Aleksandr Tashaev	23.06.1994	7		
Kamil Zakirov	15.11.1998	1	(2)	
Aleksandr Zuev	26.06.1996	17		
Forwards:	**DOB**	**M**	**(s)**	**G**
Ivan Ignatyev	06.01.1999	11		
Viðar Örn Kjartansson (ISL)	11.03.1990	10	(6)	
Evgeniy Markov	07.07.1994	9	(13)	5
Beka Mikeltadze (GEO)	26.11.1997	3	(8)	1

Professionalnij Fudbolnij Klub Sochi

Founded:	06.06.2018		
Stadium:	Fisht Olympic Stadium, Sochi (47,659)		
Trainer:	Aleksandr Tochilin		27.04.1974
[20.11.2019]	Roman Berezovskiy (ARM)		05.08.1974
[01.01.2020]	Vladimir Fedotov		12.08.1966

Goalkeepers:	DOB	M	(s)	G
Soslan Dzhanaev	13.03.1987	22		
Evgeni Frolov	05.02.1988	1		
Nikolay Zabolotniy	16.04.1990	5		
Defenders:	**DOB**	**M**	**(s)**	**G**
Nikita Kalugin	12.03.1998	13	(3)	
Fedor Kudryashov	05.04.1987	15	(1)	1
Timofey Margasov	12.06.1992	12	(3)	
Miha Mevlja (SVN)	12.06.1990	19		1
Ivan Miladinović (SRB)	14.08.1994	22		
Vadim Milyutin	08.04.2002		(1)	
Elmir Nabiullin	08.03.1995	13	(7)	
Ivan Novoseltsev	25.08.1991	18		1
Pavel Shakuro	25.07.1997	1	(1)	
Kirill Zaika	07.10.1992	10		1
Igor Yurganov	10.12.1993	6	(3)	
Midfielders:	**DOB**	**M**	**(s)**	**G**
Akmal Bakhtiyarov (KAZ)	02.06.1998		(2)	

	DOB	M	(s)	G
Andrey Bokovoy	04.03.2000		(2)	
Nikita Burmistrov	06.07.1989	19	(4)	1
Giannelli Imbula (FRA)	12.09.1992		(1)	
Yan Kazaev	26.11.1991	3	(1)	
Nikita Koldunov	19.04.2000		(2)	1
Dušan Lagator (MNE)	29.03.1994	6	(7)	1
Andrey Mostovoy	05.11.1997	24	(1)	6
Evgeniy Pesegov	21.02.1989	4		
Aleksey Pomerko	03.05.1990	8	(2)	
Ibrahim Tsallagov	12.12.1990	25	(1)	1
Forwards:	**DOB**	**M**	**(s)**	**G**
Alexander Karapetyan (ARM)	23.12.1987	3	(18)	2
Aleksandr Kokorin	19.03.1991	10		7
Christian Noboa (ECU)	09.04.1985	18	(1)	4
Vladimir Obukhov	08.02.1992	1	(2)	
Dmitriy Poloz	12.07.1991	14	(10)	5
Anton Zabolotny	13.06.1991	16	(5)	5

Fudbolnij Klub Spartak Moskva

Founded:	18.04.1922		
Stadium:	Otkrytiye Arena, Moskva (45,360)		
Trainer:	Oleg Kononov		23.03.1966
[29.09.2019]	Sergey Kuznetsov		31.08.1982
[14.10.2019]	Domenico Tedesco (GER)		12.09.1985

Goalkeepers:	DOB	M	(s)	G
Aleksandr Maksimenko	19.03.1998	29		
Artyom Rebrov	04.03.1984	1		
Defenders:	**DOB**	**M**	**(s)**	**G**
Ayrton Lucas Dantas de Medeiros (BRA)	19.06.1997	27		
Georgi Dzhikiya	21.11.1993	27		1
Andrey Eshchenko	09.02.1984	8	(6)	
Ilya Gaponov	25.10.1997	4		
Samuel Gigot (FRA)	12.10.1993	26		4
Ilya Golosov	09.08.2001		(2)	
Ilya Kutepov	29.07.1993	10	(1)	
Pavel Maslov	14.04.2000	9		
Nikolai Rasskazov	04.01.1998	17	(3)	1
Midfielders:	**DOB**	**M**	**(s)**	**G**
Jano Ananidze (GEO)	10.10.1992	4	(2)	
Zelimkhan Bakayev	01.07.1996	26	(1)	6
Nikita Bakalyuk	03.04.2001		(1)	
Fernando Lucas Martins (BRA)	03.03.1992	3		
Ayaz Guliev	27.11.1996	8	(3)	

	DOB	M	(s)	G
Mikhail Ignatov	04.05.2000		(1)	
Alex Král (CZE)	19.05.1998	18	(1)	
Aleksandr Lomovitskiy	27.01.1998	1		
Dmitry Markitesov	22.03.2001		(2)	
Lorenzo Antonio Melgarejo Sanabria (PAR)	10.08.1990	6	(6)	1
Georgi Melkadze	04.04.1997		(2)	
Aleksandr Tashaev	23.06.1994	1	(2)	
Guus Til (NED)	22.12.1997	10	(8)	2
Nail Umyarov	27.06.2000	12	(5)	
Roman Zobnin	11.02.1994	24	(1)	2
Forwards:	**DOB**	**M**	**(s)**	**G**
Soltmurad Bakaev	05.08.1999		(2)	
Maksim Glushenkov	28.07.1999		(1)	
Jordan Larsson (SWE)	20.06.1997	19	(7)	7
Luiz Adriano de Souza da Silva (BRA)	12.04.1987	3		1
Reziuan Mirzov	22.06.1993	4	(17)	1
Ezequiel Ponce Martínez (ARG)	29.03.1997	18	(9)	6
André Horst Schürrle (GER)	06.11.1990	9	(4)	1
Aleksandr Sobolev	07.03.1997	6	(5)	2

Fudbolnij Klub Tambov

Founded:	2013		
Stadium:	Mordovia Arena, Tambov (44,442)		
Trainer:	Aleksandr Grigoryan		28.09.1966
[21.10.2019]	Sergey Pervushin		19.03.1970

Goalkeepers:	DOB	M	(s)	G
Georgi Sheliya (GEO)	11.12.1988	29		
Defenders:	**DOB**	**M**	**(s)**	**G**
Oleksandr Filin (UKR)	25.06.1996	8	(1)	
Aboussy Cèdric Gogoua Kouame (CIV)	10.07.1994	5		2
Aleksey Gritsaenko	25.05.1995	19		1
Oleksandr Kaplienko (UKR)	07.03.1996	4	(5)	
Maksim Osipenko	16.05.1994	17		1
Adessoye Oyewole	18.09.1982	26		1
Aleksey Rybin	26.01.1988	19		
Evgeniy Shlyakov	30.08.1991	5	(2)	
Soslan Takazov	28.02.1993	15	(3)	1
Igor Yurganov	10.12.1993	3	(4)	
Midfielders:	**DOB**	**M**	**(s)**	**G**
Valeriu Ciupercă (MDA)	12.06.1992	20	(3)	2
Usman Muhammed Edu (NGA)	02.03.1994	1		
Vladimir Kabakhidze	09.09.1999		(5)	
Pavel Karasev	10.07.1992	22	(5)	
Khetag Khosonov	18.06.1998		(8)	

	DOB	M	(s)	G
Anton Kilin	14.11.1990	22	(3)	2
Danil Klenkin	14.07.1990		(3)	
Vladislav Kulik	27.02.1985	2	(3)	
Georgi Melkadze	04.04.1997	18		7
Nikita Salamatov	23.02.1994		(1)	
Guram Tetrashvili	02.08.1988	24	(1)	
Forwards:	**DOB**	**M**	**(s)**	**G**
Khyzyr Appaev	27.01.1990	7	(6)	
Andrey Chasovskikh	31.05.1991		(3)	
Oleg Chernyshov	23.12.1986	2	(6)	
Artyom Fedchuk	20.12.1994	1	(6)	
Amur Kalmykov	29.05.1994	1	(2)	
Mohamed Konaté (CIV)	12.12.1997	1	(1)	
Mikhail Kostyukov	09.08.1991	25	(2)	7
Khasan Mamtov	28.04.1984	3	(14)	1
Ivan Markelov	17.04.1988	3	(2)	
Miguel Felipe Nunes Cardoso (POR)	19.06.1994		(1)	
Olabiran Blessing Muyiwa (NGA)	07.09.1998		(8)	1
Vladimir Obukhov	08.02.1992	17		7

Fudbolnij Klub Ufa

Founded: 2009
Stadium: Neftyanik Stadium, Ufa (15,132)
Trainer: Vadim Evseyev   08.01.1976

Goalkeepers:	DOB	M	(s)	G
Aleksandr Belenov	13.09.1986	26		
Aleksey Chernov	03.06.1998	4		
Defenders:	**DOB**	**M**	**(s)**	**G**
Pavel Alikin	06.03.1984	7	(2)	
Bojan Jokić (SVN)	17.05.1986	14	(1)	
Danil Krugovoy	28.05.1998	8	(4)	
Ionuţ Nedelcearu (ROU)	25.04.1996	20		
Aleksey Nikitin	27.01.1992	8		
Aleksandr Putsko	24.02.1993	19	(1)	
Aleksandr Sukhov	03.01.1986	28		
Jemal Tabidze (GEO)	18.03.1996	25		1
Denis Terentyev	13.08.1992	3	(7)	1
Midfielders:	**DOB**	**M**	**(s)**	**G**
Azer Aliev	12.05.1994	16	(3)	1
Nikita Belousov	26.02.2002	1		
Igor Bezdenezhnykh	08.08.1996	2		
Cătălin Carp (MDA)	20.10.1993	24		1
Danila Emelyanov	23.01.2000	7	(5)	
Daniil Fomin	02.03.1997	27		6
Artyom Golubev	21.01.1999	9	(10)	
Oliver Thill (LUX)	17.12.1996	17	(5)	
Oston Urunov (UZB)	19.12.2000	9	(1)	
Azamat Zaseyev	29.04.1988		(1)	
Forwards:	**DOB**	**M**	**(s)**	**G**
Gamid Agalarov	16.07.2000	3	(2)	
Lovro Bizjak (SVN)	12.11.1993	14	(11)	2
Nikolay Giorgobiani	16.07.1997	5	(9)	1
Sylvester Emeka Igboun (NGA)	08.09.1990	6		2
Andrey Kozlov	23.02.1989	9	(7)	1
Vyacheslav Krotov	14.02.1993	15	(6)	3
Magomed Rabadanov	05.02.2002		(1)	
Dmitry Sysuyev	13.01.1988	1	(1)	
Andrés Vombergar (SVN)	20.11.1994	3	(11)	1

Fudbolnij Klub Ural Yekaterinburg

Founded: 1930
Stadium: Central Stadium, Yekaterinburg (35,696)
Trainer: Dmitriy Parfenov   11.09.1974
[20.07.2020]   Yuri Matveyev   08.06.1977

Goalkeepers:	DOB	M	(s)	G
Oleg Baklov	20.10.1994	3		
Yaroslav Godzyur (UKR)	06.03.1985	25		
Vladislav Poletaev	05.01.2000	1		
Defenders:	**DOB**	**M**	**(s)**	**G**
Aleksei Gerasimov	15.04.1993	4		
Varazdat Haroyan (ARM)	24.08.1992	17	(1)	1
Igor Kalinin	11.11.1995	6		
Denis Kulakov (UKR)	01.05.1986	28		
Artyom Mamin	25.07.1997	1		
Mikhail Merkulov	26.01.1994	18		
Islamzhan Nasyrov	08.04.1998	1	(6)	
Denis Polyakov (BLR)	17.04.1991	15	(2)	
Maciej Wilusz (POL)	25.09.1988	8		
Nikolai Zolotov (BLR)	11.11.1994	4	(3)	
Midfielders:	**DOB**	**M**	**(s)**	**G**
Rafał Augustyniak (POL)	14.10.1993	24	(5)	1
Yuriy Bavin	05.02.1994	8	(13)	3
Eric Cosmin Bicfalvi (ROU)	05.02.1988	24	(2)	8
Petrus Boumal (CMR)	20.04.1993	14	(2)	
Dmitriy Efremov	01.04.1995	2	(6)	
Andrey Egorychev	14.02.1993	17	(9)	
Othman El Kabir (NED)	17.07.1991	20	(2)	6
Roman Emelyanov	08.05.1992	14		
Artyom Fiedler	14.07.1983	6	(1)	
Chingiz Magomadov	01.08.1998	1		
Artyom Shabolin	19.07.2000		(1)	
Forwards:	**DOB**	**M**	**(s)**	**G**
Nikolai Dimitrov (BUL)	15.10.1987	15	(3)	1
Vladimir Ilyin	20.05.1992	11	(7)	4
Michał Kucharczyk (POL)	20.03.1991	11	(5)	
Andrey Panyukov	25.09.1994	15	(9)	4
Pavel Pogrebnyak	08.11.1983	6	(10)	3
Artyom Yusupov	29.04.1997		(3)	

Fudbolnij Klub Zenit Saint Petersburg

Founded: 25.05.1925
Stadium: Gazprom Arena, Saint Petersburg (67,800)
Trainer: Sergei Semak   27.02.1976

Goalkeepers:	DOB	M	(s)	G
Mikhail Kerzhakov	28.01.1987	9	(1)	
Andrey Lunev	13.11.1991	19		
Aleksandr Vasyutin	04.03.1995	2		
Defenders:	**DOB**	**M**	**(s)**	**G**
Douglas dos Santos Justino de Melo (BRA)	22.03.1994	27	(1)	
Branislav Ivanović (SRB)	22.02.1984	25		4
Vyacheslav Karavayev	20.05.1995	17	(3)	1
Emanuel Hernán Mammana (ARG)	10.02.1996	2	(1)	
Yordan Hernando Osorio Paredes (VEN)	10.05.1994	4	(3)	
Danila Prokhin	24.05.2001	3		
Yaroslav Rakitskiy (UKR)	03.08.1989	27		
Igor Smolnikov	08.08.1988	11	(1)	
Denis Terentyev	13.08.1992	1	(1)	
Midfielders:	**DOB**	**M**	**(s)**	**G**
Wilmar Enrique Barrios Teherán (COL)	17.10.1993	25	(1)	1
Aleksandr Erokhin	13.10.1989	9	(14)	2
Claudio Matías Kranevitter (ARG)	21.05.1993		(2)	
Daler Kuzyaev	15.01.1993	9	(11)	
Leon Musaev	25.01.1999	3	(6)	
Magomed Ozdoev	05.11.1992	26		3
Oleg Shatov	29.07.1990	5	(7)	2
Aleksey Sutormin	10.01.1994	8	(16)	3
Yuriy Zhirkov	20.08.1983	13	(8)	2
Forwards:	**DOB**	**M**	**(s)**	**G**
Sardar Azmoun (IRN)	01.01.1995	24	(4)	17
Sebastián Driussi (ARG)	09.02.1996	20	(5)	4
Artyom Dzyuba	22.08.1988	25	(3)	17
Róbert Mak (SVK)	08.03.1991		(5)	1
Malcom Filipe Silva de Oliveira (BRA)	26.02.1997	9	(3)	4
Emiliano Ariel Rigoni (ARG)	04.02.1993	6	(6)	2
Daniil Shamkin	22.06.2002	1	(3)	

1.	FK Rotor Volgograd (*Promoted*)	27	17	5	5	41	-	21	56
2.	FK Khimki (*Promoted*)	27	16	6	5	50	-	19	54
3.	FK Chertanovo Moskva	27	15	9	3	37	-	19	54
4.	FK Torpedo Moskva	27	16	5	6	39	-	25	53
5.	FK Neftekhimik Nizhnekamsk	27	13	9	5	38	-	25	48
6.	FK SKA-Khabarovsk	27	12	7	8	42	-	30	43
7.	FK Baltika Kaliningrad	27	12	7	8	34	-	23	43
8.	FK Shinnik Yaroslavl	27	12	7	8	43	-	35	43
9.	FK Tom Tomsk	27	10	9	8	32	-	26	39
10.	FK Chayka Peschanokopskoye	27	10	8	9	31	-	29	38
11.	FK Nizhny Novgorod	27	9	9	9	28	-	29	36
12.	FK Armavir (*Relegated*)	27	7	9	11	23	-	29	30
13.	FK Avangard Kursk (*Relegated*)	27	5	14	8	29	-	39	29
14.	FK Yenisey Krasnoyarsk	27	7	7	13	23	-	40	28
15.	FK Krasnodar-2	27	6	10	11	32	-	34	28
16.	FK Luch Vladivostok (*Relegated*)	27	6	9	12	28	-	40	27
17.	FK Spartak-2 Moskva	27	6	8	13	38	-	45	26
18.	FK Tekstilshchik Ivanovo	27	5	4	18	25	-	52	19
19.	FK Fakel Voronezh	27	4	7	16	14	-	44	19
20.	FK Mordovia Saransk (*Relegated*)	27	4	7	16	21	-	44	19

Please note: the league was abandoned on 15.05.2020 and the top-2 teams were promoted to the Premier League 2020-2021. No teams were relegated, but four teams could not acquire the license for the next season being nevertheless relegated in lower divisions.

NATIONAL TEAM

INTERNATIONAL MATCHES
(16.07.2019 – 15.07.2020)

06.09.2019	Glasgow	Scotland - Russia	1-2(1-1)	(ECQ)
09.09.2019	Kaliningrad	Russia - Kazakhstan	1-0(0-0)	(ECQ)
10.10.2019	Moskva	Russia - Scotland	4-0(0-0)	(ECQ)
13.10.2019	Nicosia	Cyprus - Russia	0-5(0-2)	(ECQ)
16.11.2019	Saint Petersburg	Russia - Belgium	1-4(0-3)	(ECQ)
19.11.2019	Serravalle	San Marino - Russia	0-5(0-2)	(ECQ)

06.09.2019 SCOTLAND - RUSSIA 1-2(1-1) 16th EC. Qualifiers
Hampden Park, Glasgow; Referee: Anastasios Sidiropoulos (Greece); Attendance: 32,432
RUS: Guilherme Alvim Marinato, Mário Figueira Fernandes, Andrey Semyonov, Georgiy Dzhikiya, Fyodor Kudryashov, Aleksey Ionov (80.Aleksandr Yerokhin), Magomed Ozdoyev, Roman Zobnin (66.Dmitriy Barinov), Yuriy Zhirkov, Aleksandr Golovin (89.Ilzat Akhmetov), Artyom Dzyuba (Cap). Trainer: Stanislav Cherchesov.
Goals: Artyom Dzyuba (40), Stephen Gerard O'Donnell (59 own goal).

09.09.2019 RUSSIA - KAZAKHSTAN 1-0(0-0) 16th EC. Qualifiers
Kaliningrad Stadium, Kaliningrad; Referee: Nikola Dabanović (Montenegro); Attendance: 31,818
RUS: Guilherme Alvim Marinato, Mário Figueira Fernandes, Andrey Semyonov, Georgiy Dzhikiya, Yuriy Zhirkov, Magomed Ozdoyev, Denis Cheryshev (55.Fyodor Kudryashov), Aleksandr Golovin, Anton Miranchuk (57.Aleksey Ionov), Ilzat Akhmetov (63.Roman Zobnin), Artyom Dzyuba (Cap). Trainer: Stanislav Cherchesov.
Goal: Mário Figueira Fernandes (89).

10.10.2019 RUSSIA - SCOTLAND 4-0(0-0) 16th EC. Qualifiers
Luzhniki Stadium, Moskva; Referee: Jakob Kehlet (Denmark); Attendance: 65,703
RUS: Guilherme Alvim Marinato, Mário Figueira Fernandes, Andrey Semyonov, Georgiy Dzhikiya, Fyodor Kudryashov, Aleksey Ionov (79.Ilzat Akhmetov), Dmitriy Barinov, Aleksandr Golovin, Yuriy Zhirkov (66.Denis Cheryshev), Magomed Ozdoyev, Artyom Dzyuba (Cap) (86.Nikolay Komlichenko). Trainer: Stanislav Cherchesov.
Goals: Artyom Dzyuba (57), Magomed Ozdoyev (60), Artyom Dzyuba (70), Aleksandr Golovin (84).

13.10.2019 CYPRUS - RUSSIA 0-5(0-2) 16th EC. Qualifiers
Stádio GSP, Nicosia; Referee: Srđan Jovanović (Serbia); Attendance: 9,439
RUS: Guilherme Alvim Marinato, Andrey Semyonov, Sergey Petrov (37.Vyacheslav Karavayev), Georgiy Dzhikiya, Fyodor Kudryashov, Aleksey Ionov (77.Zelimkhan Bakayev), Magomed Ozdoyev, Denis Cheryshev, Aleksandr Golovin, Ilzat Akhmetov (61.Daler Kuzyayev), Artyom Dzyuba (Cap). Trainer: Stanislav Cherchesov.
Goals: Denis Cheryshev (9), Magomed Ozdoyev (23), Artyom Dzyuba (79), Aleksandr Golovin (89), Denis Cheryshev (90+2).

16.11.2019 RUSSIA - BELGIUM 1-4(0-3) 16th EC. Qualifiers
Krestovsky Stadium, Saint Petersburg; Referee: Artur Manuel Soares Dias (Portugal); Attendance: 53,317
RUS: Guilherme Alvim Marinato, Mário Figueira Fernandes, Andrey Semyonov, Sergey Petrov, Georgiy Dzhikiya, Yuriy Zhirkov (50.Zelimkhan Bakayev), Aleksey Ionov, Magomed Ozdoyev, Roman Zobnin (62.Daler Kuzyayev), Aleksey Miranchuk, Artyom Dzyuba (Cap) (80.Nikolay Komlichenko). Trainer: Stanislav Cherchesov.
Goal: Georgiy Dzhikiya (79).

19.11.2019   **SAN MARINO - RUSSIA**   **0-5(0-2)**   16th EC. Qualifiers

San Marino Stadium, Serravalle; Referee: Thorvaldur Árnason (Iceland); Attendance: 1,604
RUS: Anton Shunin, Maksim Belyayev, Sergey Petrov, Georgiy Dzhikiya, Fyodor Kudryashov, Aleksey Ionov (58.Aleksandr Golovin), Magomed Ozdoyev (59.Roman Zobnin), Daler Kuzyayev, Aleksey Miranchuk (65.Nikolay Komlichenko, Zelimkhan Bakayev, Artyom Dzyuba (Cap). Trainer: Stanislav Cherchesov.
Goals: Daler Kuzyayev (3), Sergey Petrov (19), Aleksey Miranchuk (49), Aleksey Ionov (56), Nikolay Komlichenko (78).

NATIONAL TEAM PLAYERS
(16.07.2019 – 15.07.2020)

Name	DOB	Caps	Goals	2019:	Club
Goalkeepers					
GUILHERME Alvim Marinato	12.12.1985	13	0	2019:	FK Lokomotiv Moskva
Anton SHUNIN	27.01.1987	3	0	2019:	FK Dinamo Moskva
Defenders					
Maksim BELYAYEV	30.09.1991	1	0	2019:	FK Arsenal Tula
Georgiy DZHIKIYA	21.11.1993	23	1	2019:	FK Spartak Moskva
Mário Figueira FERNANDES	19.09.1990	22	2	2019:	FK CSKA Moskva
Vyacheslav KARAVAYEV	20.05.1995	1	0	2019:	FK Zenit Saint Petersburg
Fyodor KUDRYASHOV	05.04.1987	35	1	2019:	PFK Sochi
Sergey PETROV	02.01.1991	5	1	2019:	FK Krasnodar
Andrey SEMYONOV	24.03.1989	16	0	2019:	RFK Akhmat Grozny
Midfielders					
Ilzat AKHMETOV	31.12.1997	7	0	2019:	FK CSKA Moskva
Zelimkhan BAKAYEV	01.07.1996	3	0	2019:	FK Spartak Moskva
Dmitriy BARINOV	11.09.1996	4	0	2019:	FK Lokomotiv Moskva
Denis CHERYSHEV	26.12.1990	25	11	2019:	Valencia CF (ESP)
Yuriy GAZINSKIY	20.07.1989	18	1	2019:	FK Krasnodar
Aleksandr GOLOVIN	30.05.1996	33	5	2019:	AS Monaco FC (FRA)
Aleksey IONOV	18.02.1989	26	4	2019:	FK Rostov
Daler KUZYAYEV	15.01.1993	21	1	2019:	FK Zenit Saint Petersburg
Aleksey MIRANCHUK	17.10.1995	25	5	2019:	FK Lokomotiv Moskva
Anton MIRANCHUK	17.10. 1995	11	1	2019:	FK Lokomotiv Moskva
Magomed OZDOYEV	05.11.1992	21	3	2019:	FK Zenit Saint Petersburg
Aleksandr YEROKHIN	13.10.1989	24	1	2019:	FK Zenit Saint Petersburg
Yuriy ZHIRKOV	20.08.1983	92	2	2019:	FK Zenit Saint Petersburg
Roman ZOBNIN	11.02.1994	27	0	2019:	FK Spartak Moskva
Forwards					
Artyom DZYUBA	22.08.1988	42	24	2019:	FK Zenit Saint Petersburg
Nikolay KOMLICHENKO	29.06.1995	3	0	2019:	FK Mladá Boleslav (CZE)

National team coach

Stanislav Salamovich CHERCHESOV [from 11.08.2016]	02.09.1963	41 M; 18 W; 9 D; 14 L; 79-52

SAN MARINO

The Country:
Repubblica di San Marino (Republic of San Marino)
Capital: San Marino
Surface: 61,2 km²
Inhabitants: 34,232 [2020]
Time: UTC+1

The FA:
Federazione Sammarinese Giuoco Calcio
Strada di Montecchio, 17 47890 San Marino
Tel: +378 0549 990 515
Founded: 1931
Member of FIFA since: 1988
Member of UEFA since: 1988
Website: www.fsgc.sm

NATIONAL TEAM RECORDS

RECORDS

First international match:	23.08.1986, Serravalle: San Marino – Canada Olympic Team 0-1
Most international caps:	Andy Selva - 73 caps (1998-2016)
Most international goals:	Andy Selva - 8 goals / 73 caps (1998-2016)

UEFA EUROPEAN CHAMPIONSHIP		FIFA WORLD CUP		OLYMPIC TOURNAMENTS	
1960	Did not enter	1930	Did not enter	1908	-
1964	Did not enter	1934	Did not enter	1912	-
1968	Did not enter	1938	Did not enter	1920	-
1972	Did not enter	1950	Did not enter	1924	-
1976	Did not enter	1954	Did not enter	1928	-
1980	Did not enter	1958	Did not enter	1936	Did not enter
1984	Did not enter	1962	Did not enter	1948	Did not enter
1988	Did not enter	1966	Did not enter	1952	Did not enter
1992	Qualifiers	1970	Did not enter	1956	Did not enter
1996	Qualifiers	1974	Did not enter	1960	Did not enter
2000	Qualifiers	1978	Did not enter	1964	Did not enter
2004	Qualifiers	1982	Did not enter	1968	Did not enter
2008	Qualifiers	1986	Did not enter	1972	Did not enter
2012	Qualifiers	1990	Did not enter	1976	Did not enter
2016	Qualifiers	1994	Qualifiers	1980	Did not enter
2020	Qualifiers	1998	Qualifiers	1984	Did not enter
		2002	Qualifiers	1988	Did not enter
		2006	Qualifiers	1992	Did not enter
		2010	Qualifiers	1996	Qualifiers
		2014	Qualifiers	2000	Did not enter
		2018	Qualifiers	2004	Qualifiers
				2008	Qualifiers
				2012	Qualifiers
				2016	Qualifiers

UEFA NATIONS LEAGUE

2018/2019 – League D

FIFA CONFEDERATIONS CUP 1992-2017

None

SAN MARINESE CLUB HONOURS IN EUROPEAN CLUB COMPETITIONS:

European Champion Clubs' Cup (1956-1992) / UEFA Champions League (1993-2020)
None

Fairs Cup (1858-1971) / UEFA Cup (1972-2009) / UEFA Europa League (2010-2020)
None

UEFA Super Cup (1972-2019)
None

*European Cup Winners' Cup 1961-1999**
None

*defunct competition

NATIONAL COMPETITIONS
TABLE OF HONOURS

Please note: until the introduction of a regular championship in 1985/86, the Coppa Titano was the only annual tournament for San Marinese clubs.

CUP WINNERS 1937-1985

1937	AC Libertas Borgo Maggiore	1970	SP Tre Penne Città di San Marino
1938-1949	*No competition*	1971	SP Tre Fiori Fiorentino
1950	AC Libertas Borgo Maggiore	1972	FC Domagnano
1951-1953	*No competition*	1973	*Competition abandoned*
1954	AC Libertas Borgo Maggiore	1974	SP Tre Fiori Fiorentino
1955-1957	*No competition*	1975	SP Tre Fiori Fiorentino
1958	AC Libertas Borgo Maggiore	1976	SS Juvenes Serravalle
1959	AC Libertas Borgo Maggiore	1977	SS Juvenes Serravalle
1960	*No competition*	1978	SS Juvenes Serravalle
1961	AC Libertas Borgo Maggiore	1979	SS Juvenes Serravalle
1962-1964	*No competition*	1980	SS Cosmos Serravalle
1965	SS Juvenes Serravalle	1981	SS Cosmos Serravalle
1966	SP Tre Fiori Fiorentino	1982	SP Tre Penne Città di San Marino
1967	SP Tre Penne Città di San Marino	1983	SP Tre Penne Città di San Marino
1968	SS Juvenes Serravalle	1984	SS Juvenes Serravalle
1969	*Competition abandoned*	1985	SP Tre Fiori Fiorentino

	CHAMPIONS	CUP WINNERS	BEST GOALSCORERS	
1985/1986	SC Faetano	SP La Fiorita Montegiardino	-	
1986/1987	SP La Fiorita Montegiardino	AC Libertas Borgo Maggiore	-	
1987/1988	SP Tre Fiori Fiorentino	FC Domagnano	-	
1988/1989	FC Domagnano	AC Libertas Borgo Maggiore	-	
1989/1990	SP La Fiorita Montegiardino	FC Domagnano	-	
1990/1991	SC Faetano	AC Libertas Borgo Maggiore	-	
1991/1992	SS Montevito Fiorentino	FC Domagnano	-	
1992/1993	SP Tre Fiori Fiorentino	SC Faetano	-	
1993/1994	SP Tre Fiori Fiorentino	SC Faetano	-	
1994/1995	SP Tre Fiori Fiorentino	SS Cosmos Serravalle	-	
1995/1996	AC Libertas Borgo Maggiore	FC Domagnano	-	
1996/1997	SS Folgore/Falciano Serravalle	SS Murata	-	
1997/1998	SS Folgore/Falciano Serravalle	SC Faetano	Damiano Vannucci (SS Virtus Acquaviva)	21
1998/1999	SC Faetano	SS Cosmos Serravalle	-	
1999/2000	SS Folgore/Falciano Serravalle	SP Tre Penne Città di San Marino	-	
2000/2001	SS Cosmos Serravalle	FC Domagnano	-	
2001/2002	FC Domagnano	FC Domagnano	-	
2002/2003	FC Domagnano	FC Domagnano	-	
2003/2004	SS Pennarossa Chiesanuova	SS Pennarossa Chiesanuova	Damiano Vannucci (SS Virtus Acquaviva)	15
2004/2005	FC Domagnano	SS Pennarossa Chiesanuova	Matteo Pazzaglia (SS Montevito Fiorentino)	19
2005/2006	SS Murata	AC Libertas Borgo Maggiore	-	
2006/2007	SS Murata	SS Murata	-	
2007/2008	SS Murata	SS Murata	-	
2008/2009	SP Tre Fiori Fiorentino	AC Juvenes/Dogana	-	
2009/2010	SP Tre Fiori Fiorentino	SP Tre Fiori Fiorentino	Simon Parma (SS Virtus Acquaviva)	13
2010/2011	SP Tre Fiori Fiorentino	AC Juvenes/Dogana	Jose Hirsch (SS Virtus Acquaviva) Marco Fantini (AC Juvenes/Dogana) Roberto Gatti (ITA, SS Murata) Alessandro Giunta (ITA, SP Tre Fiori Fiorentino) Francesco Viroli (ITA, SC Faetano)	13
2011/2012	SP Tre Penne Città di San Marino	SP La Fiorita Montegiardino	Cristian Rubén Menin (SS SS Cosmos Serravalle) Simon Parma (SP La Fiorita Montegiardino)	11
2012/2013	SP Tre Penne Città di San Marino	SP La Fiorita Montegiardino	Alberto Cannini (SP Tre Fiori Fiorentino) Denis Iencinella (FC Fiorentino)	17
2013/2014	SP La Fiorita Montegiardino	AC Libertas Borgo Maggiore	Valentin Grigore (ROU, SS Cosmos Serravalle) Giacomo Gualtieri (SP La Fiorita Montegiardino)	18
2014/2015	SS Folgore/Falciano Serravalle	SS Folgore/Falciano Serravalle	Daniele Friguglietti (ITA, San Giovanni)	16
2015/2016	SP Tre Penne Città di San Marino	SP La Fiorita Montegiardino	Marco Martini (ITA, SP La Fiorita Montegiardino)	20
2016/2017	SP La Fiorita Montegiardino	SP Tre Penne Città di San Marino	Marco Martini (ITA, SP La Fiorita Montegiardino)	27
2017/2018	SP La Fiorita Montegiardino	SP La Fiorita Montegiardino	Imre Badalassi (ITA, SP Tre Fiori Fiorentino)	18
2018/2019	SP Tre Penne Città di San Marino	SP Tre Fiori Fiorentino	Andrea Compagno (ITA, SP Tre Fiori Fiorentino)	22
2019/2020	SP Tre Fiori Fiorentino	*Competition cancelled*	Eric Fedeli (ITA, SS Murata Città di San Marino)	16

First Phase (Regular Season)

Round 1 [20-22.09.2019]
SP Cailungo - FC Fiorentino 1-0
SS Folgore/Falciano - SP La Fiorita 0-0
FC Domagnano - SS Murata 1-2
SS Pennarossa - AC Juvenes/Dogana 3-2
SP Tre Fiori - SC Faetano 3-2
AC Libertas - SS San Giovanni 2-0
SP Tre Penne - SS Virtus 1-0

Round 2 [27-29.09.2019]
AC Juvenes/Dogana - SC Faetano 0-2
SS Cosmos - SS Virtus 1-2
SS Murata - SS Folgore/Falciano 1-1
SP La Fiorita - SS Pennarossa 2-0
FC Fiorentino - SS San Giovanni 0-1
FC Domagnano - SP Tre Fiori 0-4
SP Tre Penne - AC Libertas 1-0

Round 3 [04-06.10.2019]
AC Libertas - SS Cosmos 3-2
SS San Giovanni - SP Tre Penne 2-7
SS Folgore/Falciano - FC Domagnano 2-2
SP Tre Fiori - SP La Fiorita 1-2
SS Virtus - SP Cailungo 0-1
SC Faetano - SS Pennarossa 3-5
AC Juvenes/Dogana - SS Murata 0-3

Round 4 [19-20.10.2019]
SS Virtus - AC Libertas 2-4
SP Tre Penne - FC Fiorentino 4-2
SP Cailungo - SS Cosmos 2-1
SP La Fiorita - SC Faetano 2-1
SP Tre Fiori - SS Folgore/Falciano 1-0
SS Murata - SS Pennarossa 2-1
FC Domagnano - AC Juvenes/Dogana 2-1

Round 5 [02-03.11.2019]
SS Pennarossa - SP Tre Fiori 2-0
SP La Fiorita - FC Domagnano 1-0
SC Faetano - SS Murata 0-2
AC Juvenes/Dogana - SS Folgore/Falciano 1-5
FC Fiorentino - SS Cosmos 3-0
SS San Giovanni - SS Virtus 1-3
AC Libertas - SP Cailungo 3-1

Round 6 [23-24.11.2019]
SS Murata - SP Tre Fiori 2-2
FC Domagnano - SC Faetano 2-0
SS Folgore/Falciano - SS Pennarossa 4-1
AC Juvenes/Dogana - SP La Fiorita 1-3
SS San Giovanni - SP Cailungo 0-1
FC Fiorentino - AC Libertas 0-4
SS Cosmos - SP Tre Penne 0-4

Round 7 [30.11.-01.12.2019]
SS Cosmos - SS San Giovanni 0-2
SP Cailungo - SP Tre Penne 1-3
SS Virtus - FC Fiorentino 3-3
SP Tre Fiori - AC Juvenes/Dogana 4-0
SC Faetano - SS Folgore/Falciano 1-1
SS Murata - SP La Fiorita 0-1
SS Pennarossa - FC Domagnano 3-1

Gruppo A - Final Standings

							Total				Home				Away	
1.	SP La Fiorita Montegiardino	7	5	2	0	10 - 3	17	3	0	0	5 - 1	2	2	0	5 - 2
2.	SP Tre Fiori Fiorentino	7	4	2	1	15 - 7	14	3	1	0	9 - 3	1	1	1	6 - 4
3.	SS Murata Città di San Marino	7	4	1	2	11 - 8	13	1	1	2	4 - 7	3	0	0	7 - 1
4.	SS Folgore Falciano Calcio Serravalle	7	3	3	1	15 - 6	12	1	2	0	6 - 3	2	1	1	9 - 3
5.	SS Pennarossa Chiesanuova	7	4	0	3	11 - 11	12	3	0	0	8 - 3	1	0	3	3 - 8
6.	FC Domagnano	7	2	1	4	8 - 13	7	2	0	2	5 - 7	0	1	2	3 - 6
7.	SC Faetano	7	1	1	5	6 - 11	4	0	1	2	1 - 4	1	0	3	5 - 7
8.	AC Juvenes/Dogana Serravalle	7	0	0	7	5 - 22	0	0	0	4	2 - 13	0	0	3	3 - 9

Gruppo B - Final Standings

							Total				Home				Away	
1.	SP Tre Penne Città di San Marino	6	6	0	0	20 - 5	18	3	0	0	6 - 2	3	0	0	14 - 3
2.	AC Libertas Borgo Maggiore	6	5	0	1	16 - 6	15	3	0	0	8 - 3	2	0	1	8 - 3
3.	SP Cailungo Borgo Maggiore	6	4	0	2	7 - 7	12	2	0	1	4 - 4	2	0	1	3 - 3
4.	SS Virtus Acquaviva	6	2	1	3	10 - 11	7	0	1	2	5 - 8	2	0	1	5 - 3
5.	SS San Giovanni Borgo Maggiore	6	2	0	4	6 - 13	6	0	0	3	3 - 11	2	0	1	3 - 2
6.	FC Fiorentino	6	1	1	4	8 - 13	4	1	0	2	3 - 5	0	1	2	5 - 8
7.	SS Cosmos Serravalle	6	0	0	6	4 - 16	0	0	0	3	1 - 8	0	0	3	3 - 8

Please note: the top four clubs from each group advanced to group 1 of the second stage, while the other teams advanced to group 2 of the second stage.

Second Stage

Results

Round 1 [07-08.12.2019]
SP Tre Fiori - SP Tre Penne 3-3
SS Virtus - SP Cailungo 1-3
SS Murata - SP La Fiorita 1-2
AC Libertas - SS Folgore/Falciano 1-1
FC Fiorentino - SS Pennarossa 1-4
SS San Giovanni - FC Domagnano 1-1
AC Juvenes/Dogana - SC Faetano 1-2

Round 2 [14-15.12.2019]
SS Cosmos - SS San Giovanni 3-3
FC Domagnano - AC Juvenes/Dogana 2-1
SS Pennarossa - SC Faetano 3-3
SS Folgore/Falciano - SP Cailungo 3-0
SP Tre Fiori - SS Virtus 3-1
SP La Fiorita - AC Libertas 5-0
SP Tre Penne - SS Murata 2-1

Round 3 [18-19.01.2020]
SS Virtus - SP La Fiorita 0-0
SS Folgore/Falciano - SP Tre Penne 0-0
SS Murata - SP Tre Fiori 1-2
SP Cailungo - AC Libertas 0-1
AC Juvenes/Dogana - SS Cosmos 0-3
SS San Giovanni - FC Fiorentino 1-2
SC Faetano - FC Domagnano 1-0

Round 4 [25-28.01.2020]
SP Tre Fiori - SS Folgore/Falciano 1-1
SP Tre Penne - AC Libertas 3-0
FC Fiorentino - SS Cosmos 1-1
FC Domagnano - SS Pennarossa 4-0
SS San Giovanni - AC Juvenes/Dogana 0-0
SS Virtus - SS Murata 3-4
SP La Fiorita - SP Cailungo 2-1

Round 5 [01-02.02.2020]
SP La Fiorita - SP Tre Fiori 1-2
AC Libertas - SS Virtus 2-3
SS Folgore/Falciano - SS Murata 5-0
SP Cailungo - SP Tre Penne 0-1
AC Juvenes/Dogana - FC Fiorentino 1-1
SC Faetano - SS San Giovanni 1-0
SS Pennarossa - SS Cosmos 5-1

Round 6 [08-09.02.2020]
SC Faetano - FC Fiorentino 4-0
SS Cosmos - FC Domagnano 1-0
AC Juvenes/Dogana - SS Pennarossa 0-0
SS Folgore/Falciano - SP La Fiorita 2-0
SS Murata - AC Libertas 1-0
SP Tre Fiori - SP Cailungo 6-3
SP Tre Penne - SS Virtus 3-1

Round 7 [15-16.02.2020]
SS San Giovanni - SS Pennarossa 0-3
FC Fiorentino - FC Domagnano 1-3
SS Cosmos - SC Faetano 1-3
AC Libertas - SP Tre Fiori 1-4
SP Tre Penne - SP La Fiorita 1-1
SP Cailungo - SS Murata 1-1
SS Virtus - SS Folgore/Falciano 1-2

Round 8 [22-23.02.2020]
SP Tre Penne - SP Tre Fiori 0-2
SP Cailungo - SS Virtus 1-4
SP La Fiorita - SS Murata 2-1
SS Folgore/Falciano - AC Libertas 0-0
SS Pennarossa - FC Fiorentino 7-3
FC Domagnano - SS San Giovanni 2-1
SC Faetano - AC Juvenes/Dogana 3-1

The competition was abandoned due to Covid-19 pandemic, table at abandonement being considered final.

Gruppo A - Final Standings

					Total			Home					Away			
1.	**SP Tre Fiori Fiorentino**	8	6	2	0	23 - 11	20	1	2	0	7 - 5	5	0	0	16 - 6
2.	SS Folgore Falciano Calcio Serravalle	8	4	4	0	14 - 3	16	2	2	0	8 - 0	2	2	0	6 - 3
3.	SP Tre Penne Città di San Marino	8	4	3	1	13 - 8	15	2	1	1	6 - 4	2	2	0	7 - 4
4.	SP La Fiorita Montegiardino	8	4	2	2	13 - 8	14	3	0	2	10 - 6	1	2	0	3 - 2
5.	SS Virtus Acquaviva	8	2	1	5	14 - 18	7	0	1	4	6 - 12	2	0	1	8 - 6
6.	SS Murata Città di San Marino	8	2	1	5	10 - 17	7	0	0	2	2 - 4	2	1	3	8 - 13
7.	AC Libertas Borgo Maggiore	8	1	2	5	5 - 17	5	0	1	3	4 - 9	1	1	2	1 - 8
8.	SP Cailungo Borgo Maggiore	8	1	1	6	9 - 19	4	0	1	4	5 - 13	1	0	2	4 - 6

Gruppo B - Final Standings

					Total			Home					Away			
1.	SC Faetano	7	6	1	0	17 - 6	19	4	0	0	9 - 1	2	1	0	8 - 5
2.	SS Pennarossa Chiesanuova	7	4	2	1	22 - 12	14	2	1	0	15 - 7	2	1	1	7 - 5
3.	FC Domagnano	7	4	1	2	12 - 6	13	3	0	0	8 - 2	1	1	2	4 - 4
4.	SS Cosmos Serravalle	6	2	2	2	10 - 12	8	1	1	1	5 - 6	1	1	1	5 - 6
5.	FC Fiorentino	7	1	2	4	9 - 21	5	0	1	2	3 - 8	1	1	2	6 - 13
6.	SS San Giovanni Borgo Maggiore	7	0	3	4	6 - 12	3	0	2	2	2 - 6	0	1	2	4 - 6
7.	AC Juvenes/Dogana Serravalle	7	0	3	4	4 - 11	3	0	2	2	2 - 6	0	1	2	2 - 5

Top goalscorer: Eric Fedeli (ITA, SS Murata Città di San Marino) – 16 goals

NATIONAL CUP
Coppa Titano Final 2019/2020

1/8-Finals [26-27.10./09-10.11.2019]					
First Leg			**Second Leg**		
SS Folgore Falciano Calcio Serravalle - SC Faetano	2-1		SC Faetano - SS Folgore Falciano Calcio Serravalle	0-2	
AC Juvenes/Dogana Serravalle - AC Libertas Borgo Maggiore	2-1		AC Libertas Bor. Maggiore - AC Juvenes/Dogana Serravalle	2-0	
SS San Giovanni Borgo Maggiore - SS Cosmos Serravalle	1-4		SS Cosmos Serravalle - SS San Giovanni Borgo Maggiore	1-0	
SS Pennarossa Chiesanuova - SP La Fiorita Montegiardino	2-3		SP La Fiorita Montegiardino - SS Pennarossa Chiesanuova	2-2	
FC Domagnano - FC Fiorentino	2-1		FC Fiorentino - FC Domagnano	0-0	
SS Virtus Acquaviva - SP Cailungo Borgo Maggiore	1-2		SP Cailungo Borgo Maggiore - SS Virtus Acquaviva	3-0	
SS Murata Città di San Marino - SP Tre Penne C.di S. Marino	0-2		SP Tre Penne C.di S. Marino - SS Murata Città di San Marino	2-2	

Quarter-Finals [26-27.11./10-11.12.2019]					
First Leg			**Second Leg**		
SP Tre Fiori - FC Domagnano	4-1		FC Domagnano - SP Tre Fiori	1-4	
SS Cosmos Serravalle - SP La Fiorita Montegiardino	1-3		SP La Fiorita Montegiardino - SS Cosmos Serravalle	5-0	
SS Folgore Falciano Calcio - AC Libertas Borgo Maggiore	2-1		AC Libertas Borgo Maggiore - SS Folgore Falciano Calcio	1-2	
SP Cailungo Borgo Maggiore - SP Tre Penne	0-5		SP Tre Penne - SP Cailungo Borgo Maggiore	6-0	

The competition was cancelled due to Covid-19 pandemic.

THE CLUBS 2019/2020

Please note: matches and goals includes statistics of both first season and second stage.

Società Polisportiva Cailungo Borgo Maggiore

Founded:	1974	
Stadium:	Stadio Fonte Dell'Ovo, Città di San Marino (500)	
Trainer:	Claudio Bartoletti	09.06.1958

Goalkeepers:	DOB	M	(s)	G
Massimo Francioni	17.06.1993	3		
Alberto Gallinetta (ITA)	16.04.1992	11		
Defenders:	**DOB**	**M**	**(s)**	**G**
Maicol Acquarelli (ITA)	21.09.1993	9	(1)	1
Xhulio Gega (ALB)	17.02.1995	5		
Mattia Gualandi	08.04.1994	7	(3)	
Filippo Ioli	30.03.2001	3	(1)	
Manuel Iuzzolino (ITA)	05.05.1990	11		
Nicolò Poli (ITA)	10.10.1989	1	(1)	
Luca Ricci	25.03.1993	10		
Michele Rossi	26.01.1995	5	(3)	1
Midfielders:	**DOB**	**M**	**(s)**	**G**
Luca Baravelli	26.03.2000	4	(1)	

	DOB	M	(s)	G
Valentino Chiaravallotti (ITA)	14.02.1989	4		
Simone Ciavatta	18.09.1991	7	(4)	
Michele Conti (ITA)	26.04.1991	6	(4)	1
Aziz Diallo (SEN)	11.05.1997	5	(3)	
Marco Oliva (ITA)	25.06.1989	8	(1)	
Andrea Tamagnini	27.09.1997	6	(5)	2
Denis Veronesi	17.07.1988	1	(4)	
Mattia Vitali	26.05.2000	11	(2)	2
Forwards:	**DOB**	**M**	**(s)**	**G**
Viktor Ndoka (ALB)	24.03.1991	6		1
Enrico Pellino (ITA)	24.05.1997	7	(2)	4
Jacopo Raschi	28.04.1998	8	(1)	1
Raul Ura	10.09.1998	10		3
Giacomo Zaghini	06.06.1989	6	(3)	

Società Sportiva Cosmos Serravalle

Founded:	1979	
Stadium:	San Marino Stadium, Serravalle (7,000)	
Trainer:	Cristian Protti	17.04.1973

Goalkeepers:	DOB	M	(s)	G
Lorenzo Batori (ITA)	07.11.1993	2		
Andrea Gregori	30.12.1987	10		
Defenders:	**DOB**	**M**	**(s)**	**G**
Francesco Baschetti (ITA)	08.01.1986	5	(1)	1
Alex Cavalli	26.02.1992	5		
Matteo Ferrari	20.10.1994	6		
Daniel Giulianelli	12.01.1995	3	(5)	
Fabiano Grassi (ITA)	06.05.1988	5	(1)	
Stefano Sartini	02.05.2000	10	(1)	3
Daniele Villa (ITA)	24.05.1982	4		
Nicola Zafferani	06.11.1991	6	(2)	
Midfielders:	**DOB**	**M**	**(s)**	**G**
Nicola Canini	14.08.1988	3	(2)	

	DOB	M	(s)	G
Michele Cervellini	14.04.1988	10		
Fabio Giovagnoli (ITA)	10.06.1992	6	(3)	2
Lorenzo Marcattili	20.09.1993	2		
Manuel Muccioli (ITA)	12.12.1996	9	(1)	
Riccardo Santini	13.10.1986	8		
Kevin Zonzini	11.08.1997	7	(1)	2
Forwards:	**DOB**	**M**	**(s)**	**G**
Mario Antonio Salvemini (ITA)	08.02.1992	5	(2)	2
Antonio Azzurro (ITA)	10.01.1999	2	(4)	
Riccardo Bonfigli (ITA)	13.12.1997	9	(3)	1
Manuel Canini (ITA)	22.08.1991	7	(1)	2
Achille Della Valle	31.01.1989	4	(5)	1
Jacopo Gualandi (ITA)	11.01.1996	2	(1)	
Marseljan Mema (ALB)	13.02.1997	3	(1)	

Football Club Domagnano

Founded:	1966	
Stadium:	Campo sportivo, Domagnano (500)	
Trainer:	Oscar Lasagni (ITA)	04.10.1971
[02.12.2019]	Paolo Cangini	26.07.1967

Goalkeepers:	DOB	M	(s)	G
Gabriele Giulianelli	09.09.1998	1		
Simone Venturini	27.05.1998	13		
Defenders:	**DOB**	**M**	**(s)**	**G**
Andrea Battistini (ITA)	26.05.1991	12	(1)	
Elia Bollini	13.10.1997		(3)	
Angelo Faetanini	17.01.1993	9	(4)	
Guido Ghetti (ITA)	25.06.1978	14		1
Simone Nanni	03.08.2000	1	(2)	
Giovanni Rossi (ITA)	15.02.1989	10	(1)	
Luca Rossi	14.04.1993	7	(1)	
Mattia Valentini	10.12.1998	7		
Midfielders:	**DOB**	**M**	**(s)**	**G**
Mattia Ceccaroli	03.02.1999	7	(3)	

	DOB	M	(s)	G
Paolo Rossi (ITA)	06.09.1983	13		3
Stefano Sacco (ITA)	10.02.1991	11		1
Pape Sow (SEN)	10.08.1996		(3)	
Andrea Venerucci	21.11.1989	11		1
Davide Venerucci	08.06.1997	3	(7)	1
Forwards:	**DOB**	**M**	**(s)**	**G**
Alessio Ambrogetti (ITA)	14.01.1989	13	(1)	4
Nicolò Angelini	15.03.1992	3	(2)	1
Marco Bernardi	02.01.1994	7		
Davide Capelli (ITA)	05.06.1999		(3)	
Riccardo Paganelli (ITA)	09.06.1987	4		2
Pietro Semprini	27.01.1993	7	(2)	5
Luca Simoncelli (ITA)	07.07.1997	1	(3)	1

Società Calcio Faetano

Founded: 1962
Stadium: San Marino Stadium, Serravalle (7,000)
Trainer: Massimo Gorı 29.05.1961
[02.12.2019] Renato Cioffi 16.10.1971

Goalkeepers:	DOB	M	(s)	G
Manuel Ermeti (ITA)	11.08.1981	12		
Sîmone Guidi	14.06.2000	2		
Defenders:	**DOB**	**M**	**(s)**	**G**
Nicola Aldrovandi (ITA)	06.10.1999	5		1
Jacopo Avantaggiati	15.09.1995	5		
Mirko Bartolucci (ITA)	15.10.1999	3	(3)	
Francesco De Rosa (ITA)	10.10.1983	6	(1)	
Alex Della Valle	13.06.1990	11		
Luca Filippi (ITA)	27.09.1988	7		
Giacomo Guerra	10.03.1994		(1)	
Roberto Peluso (ITA)	06.04.1989		(3)	
Filippo Quaranta	11.09.1998	5	(6)	
Giacomo Rinaldi	23.03.1990	8	(5)	
Francesco Zaghini (ITA)	18.10.1999	5		

Midfielders:	DOB	M	(s)	G
Manuel Cocco (ITA)	01.05.2000	11	(3)	
German Dominella	20.07.2000		(5)	
Assane Fall (SEN)	26.02.1994	11	(2)	1
Kevin Marigliano (ITA)	10.05.1993	9		3
Jacopo Muggeo (ITA)	19.08.1990	10	(2)	
Cristiano Paci (ITA)	23.11.1985		(1)	
Raffaele Seccia (ITA)	03.02.1993	6	(1)	
Tommaso Saccavino (ITA)	31.12.1999	5		
Luca Tomassoni (ITA)	21.11.1994		(3)	
Forwards:	**DOB**	**M**	**(s)**	**G**
Paolo Basile (ITA)	08.06.1992	3		1
Alessio Indelicato (ITA)	26.09.1995	5		4
Marseljan Mema (ALB)	13.02.1997	7	(2)	
Massimo Moroni	17.02.1990	4	(1)	1
Michele Pieri (ITA)	16.06.1992	14		11

Football Club Fiorentino

Founded: 1974
Stadium: Campo Sportivo, Fiorentino (700)
Trainer: Massimo Campo (ITA) 15.04.1975
[28.12.2019] Manuel Amati (ITA) 01.01.1980

Goalkeepers:	DOB	M	(s)	G
Michele Berardi	30.11.1991	4	(1)	
Luca Bianchi (ITA)	07.01.1990	9		
Defenders:	**DOB**	**M**	**(s)**	**G**
Juri Biordi	01.01.1995	7		
Matteo Camillini (ITA)	10.01.1984	3		1
Andrea Ceccolli	22.09.1993	9	(4)	
Nicolò Ferrari (ITA)	03.02.1991	11		
Luca Filippi (ITA)	27.09.1988	3	(1)	
Marco Giovanni Manolio (ITA)	10.04.2000	3	(3)	
Mirko Paglialonga (ITA)	19.09.1983	8	(3)	
Alessandro Terenzi	23.05.2000		(3)	
Simone Zingone (ITA)	07.10.2000	8		1
Midfielders:	**DOB**	**M**	**(s)**	**G**
Maximiliano Baizan	23.03.1993	2	(1)	

	DOB	M	(s)	G
Pietro Calzolari	28.10.1991	8	(1)	1
Marco Cecchetti	03.02.1997	2	(2)	
Alessandro Giangrandi (ITA)	09.12.1996	13		1
Nicola Generali (ITA)	28.05.1999	1		
Cristian Mihail Ibănescu (ROU)	03.10.1998		(3)	
Lorenzo Liverani	13.05.1993	6	(4)	
Alessandro Molinari	14.05.1989	9		
Francesco Pari (ITA)	21.09.1999	1	(1)	
Forwards:	**DOB**	**M**	**(s)**	**G**
Aldon Jose Aragao Neto (BRA)	04.10.1991	3	(1)	1
Matteo Baldini (ITA)	02.10.1998	7	(2)	3
Tommaso Guidi	21.10.1998	6	(2)	1
Pietro Protino (ITA)	26.05.1991	11	(1)	6
Simone Rossi (ITA)	13.06.1987	5	(1)	1
Fabrizio Zingone (ITA)	07.10.2000	3	(5)	

Società Sportiva Folgore Falciano Calcio Serravalle

Founded: 1972
Stadium: San Marino Stadium, Serravalle (7,000)
Trainer: Omar Lepri (ITA) 10.05.1977

Goalkeepers:	DOB	M	(s)	G
Davide Bicchiarelli	19.05.1985	15		
Defenders:	**DOB**	**M**	**(s)**	**G**
Cristian Brolli	28.02.1992	14		
Giacomo Francioni	25.10.2000	3	(2)	
Luca Nanni	30.01.1995	4	(4)	
Daniel Piscaglia (ITA)	06.12.1992	12		2
Roberto Rosini (ITA)	27.09.1991	14		
Andrea Sabbadini (ITA)	21.05.1985		(3)	
Francesco Sartori (ITA)	07.03.1993	15		3
Fabio Sottile (ITA)	05.02.1993	11	(1)	1
Midfielders:	**DOB**	**M**	**(s)**	**G**
Diego Acunzo (ITA)	19.03.1998	1	(2)	

	DOB	M	(s)	G
Riccardo Aluigi	29.03.1994	7	(4)	
Luca Bezzi (ITA)	05.06.1989	9	(1)	
Marco Domeniconi	29.01.1984	5		
Lorenzo Dormi (ITA)	11.02.1995	14	(1)	7
Mattia Giardi	15.12.1991	6		
Mattia Lualdi (ITA)	26.07.1992	1		
Andrea Nucci (ITA)	06.09.1986	14		1
Forwards:	**DOB**	**M**	**(s)**	**G**
Imre Badalassi (ITA)	08.02.1995	14		11
Marco Bernardi	02.01.1994	1	(3)	
Matteo Giardi	14.04.1997	1	(4)	
Riccardo Paganelli (ITA)	09.06.1987	4	(4)	1
Andrea Zanigni (ITA)	12.09.1988		(2)	

Associazione Calcio Juvenes/Dogana Serravalle

Founded: 2000 (*as merger of SS Juvenes Serravalle and GS Dogana*)
Stadium: San Marino Stadium, Serravalle (7,000)
Trainer: Massimo Mancini (ITA)
[18.11.2019] Ignazio Damato (ITA) 23.02.1972

Goalkeepers:	DOB	M	(s)	G
Mattia Manzaroli	03.10.1991	14		
Defenders:	**DOB**	**M**	**(s)**	**G**
Gianni Abbondanza (ITA)	27.01.1991	6		
Enrico Casadei	18.02.1996	2		1
Davide Ceccarini (ITA)	18.06.1992	3	(2)	
Paolo Ceresara (ITA)	01.10.1999	2	(1)	
Alex Gattei Colonna (ITA)	16.07.1988	5		
Antonio Ferraro (ITA)	10.08.1995	11	(2)	
Cristian Gatti	06.05.1999	4	(1)	
Mattia Merlini	23.12.1993	8	(2)	
Michael Parma (ITA)	28.03.1998	11		
Luca Pelliccioni	10.01.1996		(1)	
Federico Salvi (ITA)	23.05.1995	10	(3)	

Midfielders:	DOB	M	(s)	G
Mattia Ancora (ITA)	11.03.1999		(5)	
Thomas Brighi (ITA)	09.01.1996	11	(3)	
Amdy Dieng (SEN)	09.05.1991	8	(1)	
Lorenzo Gasperoni	03.01.1990	10		
Giacomo Leardini (ITA)	24.07.1991	3	(1)	
Manuele Lombardini (ITA)	08.05.1982	6		
Thomas Raschi	11.07.1996	7	(5)	1
Forwards:	**DOB**	**M**	**(s)**	**G**
Fabio Della Marchina (ITA)	05.02.1989	3	(5)	
Davide Merli (ITA)	08.02.2000	6	(5)	
Flamur Vucaj (ALB)	12.11.1993	11	(3)	4
Luca Zavattini (ITA)	26.06.1989	8	(1)	3
Eugenio Zucchi	26.02.1999	5	(3)	

Società Polisportiva La Fiorita Montegiardino

Founded: 1967
Stadium: Stadio "Igor Crescentini", Montegiardino (700)
Trainer: Juri Tamburini (ITA)   07.07.1977

Goalkeepers:	DOB	M	(s)	G
Alex Stimac (ITA)	22.06.1996	6		
Gianluca Vivan (ITA)	27.12.1983	9		
Defenders:	**DOB**	**M**	**(s)**	**G**
Mattia Alberighi (ITA)	08.01.1998	4	(2)	
Giovanni Casolla (ITA)	18.08.1987	11	(2)	
Roberto Di Maio (ITA)	21.09.1982	12		
Marco Gasperoni (ITA)	18.02.1992	13		1
Manuel Miori (ITA)	28.04.2000	3		
Samuele Olivi (ITA)	01.08.1980	13		
Filippo Santi	23.01.2001	3	(1)	
Carlo Valentini	15.03.1982	5	(2)	
Michele Zanotti	25.11.1988		(2)	
Midfielders:	**DOB**	**M**	**(s)**	**G**
Armando Amati (ITA)	15.01.1995	12		1
Simone Loiodice (ITA)	16.03.1989	13		
Riccardo Michelotti	13.09.1999	1		
Cristian Pitti (ITA)	15.04.1981		(1)	
Luca Righini (ITA)	25.12.1990	12	(1)	5
Danilo Rinaldi	18.04.1986	4	(2)	2
Tommaso Zafferani	19.02.1996	7	(5)	1
Forwards:	**DOB**	**M**	**(s)**	**G**
Fabrizio Castellazzi (ITA)	29.07.1984	4		1
Simone Chezzi (ITA)	13.01.2000	1	(3)	1
Tommaso Guidi	21.10.1998	2	(3)	
Samuel Pancotti	31.10.2000	13	(1)	3
Danilo Ezequiel Rinaldi	18.04.1986	1	(1)	
Antonio Manuel Rodriguez de Miguel "Toni" (ESP)	01.01.1987	3	(6)	1
Mirco Vassallo (ITA)	28.02.1993	10	(4)	5
Petrişor Voinea (ROU)	28.05.1990	3	(1)	1
Alessandro Guidi	14.12.1986		(2)	

Associazione Calcio Libertas Borgo Maggiore

Founded: 1928
Stadium: Campo sportivo, Borgo Maggiore (1,000)
Trainer: Marco Tognacci   15.10.1970

Goalkeepers:	DOB	M	(s)	G
Fabio Gentilini (ITA)	09.09.1984	10		
Matteo Zavoli	06.07.1996	4		
Defenders:	**DOB**	**M**	**(s)**	**G**
Samuele Buda (ITA)	04.07.1986	14		2
Riccardo Mezzadri (ITA)	14.04.1986	11		1
Diego Moretti	07.02.2000	2	(2)	
Federico Pesaresi (ITA)	09.08.1996	7	(3)	1
Luca Righi (ITA)	10.02.1981	12		
Davide Simoncini	03.08.1986	10	(1)	1
Midfielders:	**DOB**	**M**	**(s)**	**G**
Maicol Berretti	01.05.1989	9	(2)	
Nicola Cavalli	15.12.1986		(4)	
Fabio Dall'Ara (ITA)	18.06.1984	7		
Riccardo Ercolani	17.07.1985		(3)	
Matteo Gaiani (ITA)	02.01.1995	12	(1)	1
Enrico Golinucci	16.07.1991	9	(3)	3
Tiziano Mottola (ITA)	06.07.1986	5	(2)	1
Marco Narducci (ITA)	16.09.1989	6		
Francesco Stacchini	18.01.1997		(1)	
Andrea Ulizio (ITA)	06.03.1994	2	(1)	
Forwards:	**DOB**	**M**	**(s)**	**G**
Christopher Brandino (ITA)	20.09.1987	9	(3)	4
Ivan Graziani (ITA)	09.01.1982	7	(1)	2
Giorgio Mariotti	06.05.1986	1	(6)	1
Gian Luca Morelli (ITA)	13.02.1985	13	(1)	4
Simone Rossi (ITA)	13.06.1987	4	(1)	

Società Sportiva Murata Città di San Marino

Founded: 1966
Stadium: Campo sportivo, Montegiardino (1,000)
Trainer: Achille Fabbri (ITA)   24.02.1966

Goalkeepers:	DOB	M	(s)	G
Simone Benedettini	21.01.1997	5		
Denis Broccoli (ITA)	10.08.1988	2		
Matteo Renzetti (ITA)	15.11.1997	8		
Defenders:	**DOB**	**M**	**(s)**	**G**
Nicola Albani	15.04.1981	9		
Nicholas Arrigoni (ITA)	09.01.1995	12		
Michele Carlini	25.11.1997		(2)	
Hervé Diedhiou (SEN)	05.01.1994	6		1
Luca Ortibaldi	29.04.1988	8	(1)	
Nabila Samba (SEN)	15.09.1992	9	(2)	
Tommaso Spagnoli (ITA)	05.01.1999	3	(4)	
Midfielders:	**DOB**	**M**	**(s)**	**G**
Michele Bozzetto (ITA)	08.05.1996	13		
Marco Cecchetti	03.02.1997	7		
Fabrizio Cupi (ITA)	09.12.1984	15		1
Matteo Nanni	07.03.1993	6	(6)	
Stefano Pari	13.12.1993		(3)	
Davide Pasolini (ITA)	13.10.1989	6		
Ivan Tani (ITA)	19.05.1993	14	(1)	1
Nicolò Valli (ITA)	16.01.1999	2	(4)	
Souhail Zouhri (MAR)	03.02.1994	1	(3)	
Forwards:	**DOB**	**M**	**(s)**	**G**
Daniele Babboni	09.01.2000	1	(1)	
Gianmarco Baschetti	29.04.1991	9	(2)	1
Marco Casadei	20.09.1985	1	(4)	
Eric Fedeli (ITA)	13.01.1992	15		16
Patrik Giulianelli (ITA)	18.04.1998	6	(4)	2
Espedito Marinaro (ITA)	10.09.1992	2	(2)	
David Tomassini	14.03.2000	5		

Società Sportiva Pennarossa Chiesanuova

Founded: 1968
Stadium: Campo sportivo, Chiesanuova (300)
Trainer: Daniele Abbondanza (GER)   30.08.1962
[13.02.2020] Andy Selva   23.05.1976

Goalkeepers:	DOB	M	(s)	G
Andrea Manzaroli	12.02.1995	9		
Matteo Ugolini	27.01.1986	5		
Defenders:	**DOB**	**M**	**(s)**	**G**
Adam Adami Martins (BRA)	24.06.1992	12		1
Marco Baldani	05.12.1997	2	(1)	
Michele Cevoli	22.07.1998	4		
Kevin Martin (ITA)	24.03.1995	13		1
Gabriele Raffaelli (ITA)	28.05.1994	8	(1)	
Luca Righi	01.04.1995	10		
Dante Rossi	12.07.1987	1		
Midfielders:	**DOB**	**M**	**(s)**	**G**
Maximiliano Baizan	23.03.1993	2	(4)	1
Matias Colagiovanni (ARG)	16.01.1993	8	(5)	4
Alessandro Conti (ITA)	07.01.1998	10	(3)	3
Daniele Conti (ITA)	06.06.1990	7	(1)	1
Amrane Kabah (MAR)	02.08.1999		(1)	
Matteo Sebastiani (ITA)	12.12.1990	10	(3)	
Enzo Zago (ITA)	27.06.2000	11	(1)	1
Forwards:	**DOB**	**M**	**(s)**	**G**
Nicola Ciacci	07.07.1982	8	(5)	2
Luca De Bonis (ITA)	23.12.1999	4		1
Francesko Halilaj (ITA)	09.05.1992	9	(3)	3
Adolfo José Hirsch	31.01.1986	11		3
Francesco Ottaviani (ITA)	17.09.2000		(1)	
Mattia Stefanelli	12.03.1993	10	(3)	12

Società Sportiva San Giovanni Borgo Maggiore

Founded: 1948
Stadium: Stadio Borgo Maggiore, Borgo Maggiore (1,000)
Trainer: Paolo Baffoni (ITA) 05.01.1964

Goalkeepers:	DOB	M	(s)	G
Santino Arena (ITA)	11.02.1987	9		
Marco Baschetti (ITA)	10.01.1997	4	(2)	
Defenders:	**DOB**	**M**	**(s)**	**G**
Nicola Conti (ITA)	04.01.1997	10		
Samuele Paoloni	18.01.1997	12		
Enea Senja (ALB)	10.01.1999	11		
Nicolo Tamagnini	07.02.1988	7	(1)	
Michele Tasini (ITA)	01.11.1995	12		1
Federico Urbinati (ITA)	16.01.1997	3		
Midfielders:	**DOB**	**M**	**(s)**	**G**
Daniel Alberelli (ITA)	25.05.1995	6	(3)	
Andrea Bernardi	08.11.1988	2	(1)	
Andrea Borgagni	21.10.1996	6	(3)	
Edoardo Cecchetti	14.07.1993	1	(1)	
Marco Giannessi (ITA)	04.06.1996	3	(4)	1
Alessandro Grilli	04.06.1989		(4)	1
Leonardo Magnani (ITA)	08.10.1998	12		1
Simone Matteoni	26.04.1992	1	(1)	
Armando Senja (ALB)	26.07.1997	9		
Giulio Strologo (ITA)	01.08.1991	10		1
Andrea Zanotti	05.05.1992		(3)	
Forwards:	**DOB**	**M**	**(s)**	**G**
Lorenzo Fortunato (ITA)	13.12.1998	3	(2)	1
Andrea Moroni	10.10.1985	7	(4)	
Alberto Righini (ITA)	12.05.1998	2	(1)	
Filippo Righini (ITA)	14.09.1992	1	(6)	
Marco Ugolini (ITA)	23.12.1986	12		6

Società Polisportiva Tre Fiori Fiorentino

Founded: 1949
Stadium: Stadio di Fiorentino, Fiorentino (1,000)
Trainer: Matteo Cecchetti (ITA) 01.01.1979

Goalkeepers:	DOB	M	(s)	G
Aldo Simoncini	30.08.1986	15		
Defenders:	**DOB**	**M**	**(s)**	**G**
Luca Angelini (ITA)	17.09.1989	10	(1)	1
Juri Biordi	01.01.1995	6		
Claudio Cuzzilla (ITA)	18.02.1998	9	(2)	
Alessandro D'Addario	09.09.1997	12	(1)	2
Nicola Della Valle	19.05.1997	8	(4)	1
Stefano Ferrario (ITA)	28.03.1985	2		1
Daniele Lusini (ITA)	10.03.1982	10	(1)	
Andrea Muccioli	13.02.2000	2		
Enea Righetti (ITA)	08.10.1986	11	(2)	
Midfielders:	**DOB**	**M**	**(s)**	**G**
Giovanni Bonini	05.09.1986	8	(1)	
Daniele Compagno (ITA)	16.08.1994	7	(2)	
Federico Dolcini	22.03.2000	4	(9)	2
Giuliano Matias Foglia	21.08.1993		(2)	
Lounseny Kalissa (GUI)	07.02.1999	4		1
Francesco Lunardini (ITA)	03.11.1984	12		
Simone Matteoni	26.04.1992		(3)	
David Pop (ROU)	16.09.1999	2		
Giacomo Pracucci (ITA)	21.01.1997	9	(3)	
Andrea Raimondi (ITA)	18.06.1999		(2)	
Marco Zannoni (ITA)	14.08.1982		(3)	
Forwards:	**DOB**	**M**	**(s)**	**G**
Joel Apezteguía Hijuelos (CUB)	17.12.1983	10	(4)	9
Andrea Compagno (ITA)	22.04.1996	12	(1)	11
Eric D'Angeli (ITA)	04.05.2000	1	(2)	
Bojan Gjurchinoski (CRO)	13.04.1994	13	(2)	10

Società Polisportiva Tre Penne Città di San Marino

Founded: 1956
Stadium: Stadio Fonte Dell'Ovo, Città di San Marino (500)
Trainer: Stefano Ceci 16.10.1969

Goalkeepers:	DOB	M	(s)	G
Mattia Migani (ITA)	10.03.1992	12		
Mauro Lanzoni (ITA)	20.09.1987	2	(1)	
Defenders:	**DOB**	**M**	**(s)**	**G**
Stefano Fraternali (ITA)	13.04.1986	13	(1)	2
Christofer Genestreti (ITA)	30.05.1984	8		
Dario Merendino (ITA)	14.11.1983	7	(2)	
Simone Nanni	03.08.2000	2	(2)	
Mirko Palazzi	21.03.1987	4		
Andrea Rossi	20.07.1987	8	(1)	1
Midfielders:	**DOB**	**M**	**(s)**	**G**
Michael Battistini	08.10.1996	9		1
Luca Ceccaroli	05.07.1995	9	(4)	4
Nicola Chiaruzzi	25.12.1987	1	(4)	1
Enrico Cibelli	14.07.1987	9	(2)	2
Nicola Gai (ITA)	06.12.1987	14		6
Alex Gasperoni	30.06.1984	5		
Luca Nacci	27.05.2002		(1)	
Luca Patregnani (ITA)	08.04.1985	12	(1)	2
Francesco Perrotta (ITA)	27.08.1981	8	(2)	2
Matteo Semprini (ITA)	30.03.1995	9	(2)	
Giacomo Zafferani	16.07.1996	1	(2)	
Forwards:	**DOB**	**M**	**(s)**	**G**
Michael Angelini (ITA)	25.11.1983	5	(1)	1
Alessandro Chiurato (ITA)	16.01.1983	7	(1)	7
Luca Sorrentino (ITA)	08.05.1994	9	(3)	4

Società Sportiva Virtus Acquaviva

Founded: 1964
Stadium: Stadio di Acquaviva, Acquaviva (2,000)
Trainer: Luigi Bizzotto (ITA) 08.03.1960

Goalkeepers:	DOB	M	(s)	G
Simone Guerra (ITA)	31.10.1982	12		
Thomas Paolini	21.06.2002	2		
Defenders:	**DOB**	**M**	**(s)**	**G**
Christian Babbini (ITA)	01.02.1986	12		2
Manuel Battistini	22.07.1994	6		1
Francesco Bonfè	27.05.1994	1	(7)	
Patrik D'Altri (ITA)	25.12.1992	2		
Alex De Biagi	02.01.2000	2	(3)	
Xhulio Gega (ALB)	17.02.1995	8		
Nicola Gori (ITA)	08.05.1997	13		
Mirko Mantovani	14.11.1986	10	(1)	
Andrea Righi	16.09.1997	3	(2)	
Midfielders:	**DOB**	**M**	**(s)**	**G**
Mariano Alvarez	05.02.1996	7	(5)	2
Roberto Baiardi (ITA)	18.09.1987	14		2
Ismael Bangoura (GUI)	08.11.1994	5		
Lorenzo Battafarano	10.07.1998		(3)	
Nicholas Brilli (ITA)	05.02.1990	3	(1)	
Pedro Joel Cruz Saravia (PER)	26.07.1998	4	(3)	
Alessandro Liverani	12.10.2000	5	(1)	
Kevin Marigliano (ITA)	10.05.1993	3	(2)	
Luca Tosi	23.07.1994	6	(4)	
Forwards:	**DOB**	**M**	**(s)**	**G**
Nicola Angeli (ITA)	28.05.1989	6		4
Simone Brigliadori (ITA)	28.04.1995	13	(1)	5
Ramiro Lago (ARG)	14.10.1987	13	(1)	6
Andrea Nicolas Montanari (ITA)	04.04.1995		(4)	1
Adrián Ricchiuti (ARG)	30.06.1978	4		1

INTERNATIONAL MATCHES
(16.07.2019 – 15.07.2020)

06.09.2019	Serravalle	San Marino - Belgium	0-4(0-1)	(ECQ)
09.09.2019	Serravalle	San Marino - Cyprus	0-4(0-2)	(ECQ)
10.10.2019	Bruxelles	Belgium - San Marino	9-0(6-0)	(ECQ)
13.10.2019	Glasgow	Scotland - San Marino	6-0(3-0)	(ECQ)
16.11.2019	Serravalle	San Marino - Kazakhstan	1-3(0-3)	(ECQ)
19.11.2019	Serravalle	San Marino - Russia	0-5(0-2)	(ECQ)

06.09.2019   **SAN MARINO - BELGIUM**   **0-4(0-1)**   16th EC. Qualifiers
San Marino Stadium, Serravalle; Referee: Horaţiu Feşnic (Romania); Attendance: 2,523
SMR: Simone Benedettini, Davide Simoncini (Cap), Mirko Palazzi, Cristian Brolli, Manuel Battistini, Andrea Grandoni, Mattia Giardi (67.Alex Gasperoni), Enrico Golinucci (66.Alessandro Golinucci), Marcello Mularoni, Filippo Berardi (74.Matteo Giampaolo Vitaioli), Nicola Nanni. Trainer: Franco Varrella.

09.09.2019   **SAN MARINO - CYPRUS**   **0-4(0-2)**   16th EC. Qualifiers
San Marino Stadium, Serravalle; Referee: Iwan Arwel Griffith (Wales); Attendance: 662
SMR: Simone Benedettini, Fabio Vitaioli, Davide Simoncini (Cap), Andrea Grandoni, Alessandro D'Addario, Alex Gasperoni (61.Adolfo José Hirsch), Alessandro Golinucci, Filippo Berardi, Lorenzo Lunadei, Matteo Giampaolo Vitaioli (61.Michele Cevoli), Fabio Tomassini (62.Nicola Nanni). Trainer: Franco Varrella.

10.10.2019   **BELGIUM - SAN MARINO**   **9-0(6-0)**   16th EC. Qualifiers
Stade "Roi Baudouin", Bruxelles; Referee: Anastasios Papapetrou (Greece); Attendance: 34,504
SMR: Simone Benedettini, Davide Simoncini (Cap), Mirko Palazzi, Cristian Brolli, Manuel Battistini, Andrea Grandoni (78.Lorenzo Lunadei), Mattia Giardi (46.Adolfo José Hirsch), Enrico Golinucci, Marcello Mularoni, Filippo Berardi (46.Alessandro Golinucci), Nicola Nanni. Trainer: Franco Varrella.

13.10.2019   **SCOTLAND - SAN MARINO**   **6-0(3-0)**   16th EC. Qualifiers
Hampden Park, Glasgow; Referee: Jérôme Brisard (France); Attendance: 20,699
SMR: Aldo Simoncini, Cristian Brolli, Manuel Battistini, Alessandro D'Addario (46.Andrea Grandoni), Alex Gasperoni (Cap), Mattia Giardi (46.Adolfo José Hirsch), Alessandro Golinucci, Luca Censoni, Marcello Mularoni, Filippo Berardi (80.Luca Ceccaroli), Nicola Nanni. Trainer: Franco Varrella.

16.11.2019   **SAN MARINO - KAZAKHSTAN**   **1-3(0-3)**   16th EC. Qualifiers
San Marino Stadium, Serravalle; Referee: Ali Palabıyık (Turkey); Attendance: 643
SMR: Simone Benedettini, Davide Simoncini (Cap), Mirko Palazzi, Cristian Brolli, Manuel Battistini, Andrea Grandoni (80.Luca Ceccaroli), Alessandro Golinucci (60.Lorenzo Lunadei), Marcello Mularoni, Filippo Berardi, Enrico Golinucci, Nicola Nanni (64.Adolfo José Hirsch). Trainer: Franco Varrella.
Goal: Filippo Berardi (77).

19.11.2019   **SAN MARINO - RUSSIA**   **0-5(0-2)**   16th EC. Qualifiers
San Marino Stadium, Serravalle; Referee: Thorvaldur Árnason (Iceland); Attendance: 1,604
SMR: Aldo Simoncini, Fabio Vitaioli, Davide Simoncini (Cap), Mirko Palazzi, Alessandro D'Addario (64.Fabio Tomassini), Alex Gasperoni (46.Manuel Battistini), Mattia Giardi, Luca Censoni, Filippo Berardi, Lorenzo Lunadei, Marco Bernardi (61.Adolfo José Hirsch). Trainer: Franco Varrella.

NATIONAL TEAM PLAYERS
(16.07.2019 – 15.07.2020)

Name	DOB	Caps	Goals	2019/2020:	Club
Goalkeepers					
Simone BENEDETTINI	21.01.1997	4	0	2019:	*AC Cattolica Calcio (ITA)*
Aldo SIMONCINI	30.08.1986	62	0	2019:	*AC Libertas Borgo Maggiore*
Defenders					
Manuel BATTISTINI	11.07.1994	29	0	2019:	*AC Libertas Borgo Maggiore*
Cristian BROLLI	28.02.1992	29	0	2019:	*SS Folgore Falciano Calcio Serravalle*
Michele CEVOLI	22.07.1998	7	0	2019:	*AC Cattolica Calcio (ITA)*
Alessandro D'ADDARIO	09.09.1997	4	0	2019:	*SP Tre Fiori Fiorentino*
Andrea GRANDONI	23.03.1997	16	0	2019:	*ACD Marignanese Calcio (ITA)*
Mirko PALAZZI	21.03.1987	50	1	2019:	*SP Tre Penne Città di San Marino*
Davide SIMONCINI	30.08.1986	62	0	2019:	*AC Libertas Borgo Maggiore*
Fabio VITAIOLI	05.04.1984	55	0	2019:	*ASD Tropical Coriano (ITA)*
Midfielders					
Luca CECCAROLI	05.07.1995	2	0	2019:	*SP Tre Penne Città di San Marino*
Luca CENSONI	18.07.1996	4	0	2019:	*SSD Fya Riccione (ITA)*
Alex GASPERONI	30.06.1984	48	1	2019:	*SP Tre Penne Città di San Marino*
Mattia GIARDI	15.12.1991	10	0	2019:	*SP Tre Fiori Fiorentino*
Alessandro GOLINUCCI	10.10.1994	18	0	2019:	*ASD Tropical Coriano (ITA)*
Enrico GOLINUCCI	16.07.1991	18	0	2019:	*AC Libertas Borgo Maggiore*
Lorenzo LUNADEI	12.07.1997	13	0	2019:	*SSD Fya Riccione (ITA)*
Marcello MULARONI	08.09.1998	11	0	2019:	*US Pietracuta San Leo (ITA)*
Forwards					
Filippo BERARDI	18.05.1997	14	1	2019:	*US Vibonese Calcio (ITA)*
Marco BERNARDI	02.01.1994	7	0	2019:	*FC Domagnano*
Adolfo José HIRSCH	31.01.1986	33	0	2019:	*SP La Fiorita Montegiardino*
Nicola NANNI	02.05.2000	10	0	2019:	*SS Monopoli 1966 (ITA)*
Fabio TOMASSINI	05.02.1996	15	0	2019:	*US Pietracuta San Leo (ITA)*
Matteo Giampaolo VITAIOLI	27.10.1989	59	1	2019:	*ASD Tropical Coriano (ITA)*

National team coach		
Franco VARRELLA [from 15.01.2019]	25.01.1953	16 M; 0 W; 0 D; 16 L; 1-67

SCOTLAND

The Country:
Scotland
Capital: Edinburgh
Surface: 77,933 km²
Inhabitants: 5,463,300 [2019]
Time: UTC

The FA:
Scottish Football Association
Hampden Park G42 9AY Glasgow
Tel: +44 141 616 6000
Founded: 1873
Member of FIFA since: 1910
Member of UEFA since: 1954
Website: www.scottishfa.co.uk

NATIONAL TEAM RECORDS

RECORDS		
First international match:	30.11.1872, Glasgow:	Scotland – England 0-0
Most international caps:	Kenneth Mathieson Dalglish	- 102 caps (1971-1986)
Most international goals:	Denis Law	- 30 goals / 55 caps (1958-1974)
	Kenneth Mathieson Dalglish	- 30 goals / 102 caps (1971-1986)

UEFA EUROPEAN CHAMPIONSHIP		FIFA WORLD CUP		OLYMPIC TOURNAMENTS	
1960	Did not enter	1930	Did not enter	1908	-
1964	Did not enter	1934	Did not enter	1912	-
1968	Qualifiers	1938	Did not enter	1920	-
1972	Qualifiers	1950	Withdrew after being qualified	1924	-
1976	Qualifiers	1954	Final Tournament (Group Stage)	1928	-
1980	Qualifiers	1958	Final Tournament (Group Stage)	1936	-
1984	Qualifiers	1962	Qualifiers	1948	-
1988	Qualifiers	1966	Qualifiers	1952	-
1992	Final Tournament (Group Stage)	1970	Qualifiers	1956	-
1996	Final Tournament (Group Stage)	1974	Final Tournament (Group Stage)	1960	-
2000	Qualifiers	1978	Final Tournament (Group Stage)	1964	-
2004	Qualifiers	1982	Final Tournament (Group Stage)	1968	-
2008	Qualifiers	1986	Final Tournament (Group Stage)	1972	-
2012	Qualifiers	1990	Final Tournament (Group Stage)	1976	-
2016	Qualifiers	1994	Qualifiers	1980	-
2020	To be determined	1998	Final Tournament (Group Stage)	1984	-
		2002	Qualifiers	1988	-
		2006	Qualifiers	1992	-
		2010	Qualifiers	1996	-
		2014	Qualifiers	2000	-
		2018	Qualifiers	2004	-
				2008	-
				2012	-
				2016	-

UEFA NATIONS LEAGUE

2018/2019 – League C (promoted to League B)

FIFA CONFEDERATIONS CUP 1992-2017

None

SCOTTISH CLUB HONOURS IN EUROPEAN CLUB COMPETITIONS:

European Champion Clubs.Cup (1956-1992) / UEFA Champions League (1993-2020)		
Celtic FC Glasgow	1	1966/1967
Fairs Cup (1858-1971) / UEFA Cup (1972-2009) / UEFA Europa League (2010-2020)		
None		
UEFA Super Cup (1972-2019)		
Aberdeen FC	1	1983
*European Cup Winners.Cup 1961-1999**		
Rangers FC Glasgow	1	1971/1972
Aberdeen FC	1	1982/1983

*defunct competition

NATIONAL COMPETITIONS
TABLE OF HONOURS

	CHAMPIONS	CUP WINNERS	BEST GOALSCORERS	
1873/1874	-	Queen's Park FC Glasgow	-	
1874/1875	-	Queen's Park FC Glasgow	-	
1875/1876	-	Queen's Park FC Glasgow	-	
1876/1877	-	Vale of Leven FC Alexandria	-	
1877/1878	-	Vale of Leven FC Alexandria	-	
1878/1879	-	Vale of Leven FC Alexandria	-	
1879/1880	-	Queen's Park FC Glasgow	-	
1880/1881	-	Queen's Park FC Glasgow	-	
1881/1882	-	Queen's Park FC Glasgow	-	
1882/1883	-	Dumbarton FC	-	
1883/1884	-	Queen's Park FC Glasgow	-	
1884/1885	-	Renton FC	-	
1885/1886	-	Queen's Park FC Glasgow	-	
1886/1887	-	Hibernian FC Edinburgh	-	
1887/1888	-	Renton FC	-	
1888/1889	-	Third Lanark AC Glasgow	-	
1889/1890	-	Queen's Park FC Glasgow	-	
1890/1891	Dumbarton FC Rangers FC Glasgow [joint winners]	Heart of Midlothian FC Edinburgh	Jack Bell (Dumbarton FC)	20
1891/1892	Dumbarton FC	Celtic FC Glasgow	Jack Bell (Dumbarton FC)	23
1892/1893	Celtic FC Glasgow	Queen's Park FC Glasgow	Sandy McMahon (Celtic FC Glasgow) John Campbell (Celtic FC Glasgow)	11
1893/1894	Celtic FC Glasgow	Rangers FC Glasgow	Sandy McMahon (Celtic FC Glasgow)	16
1894/1895	Heart of Midlothian FC Edinburgh	St. Bernard's FC Edinburgh	James Miller (Clyde FC Cumbernauld)	12
1895/1896	Celtic FC Glasgow	Heart of Midlothian FC Edinburgh	Allan Martin (Celtic FC Glasgow)	19
1896/1897	Heart of Midlothian FC Edinburgh	Rangers FC Glasgow	Willie Taylor (Heart of Midlothian FC Edinburgh)	12
1897/1898	Celtic FC Glasgow	Rangers FC Glasgow	Robert Hamilton (Rangers FC Glasgow)	18
1898/1899	Rangers FC Glasgow	Celtic FC Glasgow	Robert Hamilton (Rangers FC Glasgow)	25
1899/1900	Rangers FC Glasgow	Celtic FC Glasgow	Robert Hamilton (Rangers FC Glasgow) William Michael (Heart of Midlothian FC Edinburgh)	15
1900/1901	Rangers FC Glasgow	Heart of Midlothian FC Edinburgh	Robert Hamilton (Rangers FC Glasgow)	20
1901/1902	Rangers FC Glasgow	Hibernian FC Edinburgh	William Maxwell (Third Lanark AC Glasgow)	10
1902/1903	Hibernian FC Edinburgh	Rangers FC Glasgow	David Reid (Hibernian FC Edinburgh)	14
1903/1904	Third Lanark AC Glasgow	Celtic FC Glasgow	Robert Hamilton (Rangers FC Glasgow)	28
1904/1905	Celtic FC Glasgow	Third Lanark AC Glasgow	Robert Hamilton (Rangers FC Glasgow) James Quinn (Celtic FC Glasgow)	19
1905/1906	Celtic FC Glasgow	Heart of Midlothian FC Edinburgh	James Quinn (Celtic FC Glasgow)	20
1906/1907	Celtic FC Glasgow	Celtic FC Glasgow	James Quinn (Celtic FC Glasgow)	29
1907/1908	Celtic FC Glasgow	Celtic FC Glasgow	Jock Simpson (Falkirk FC)	32
1908/1909	Celtic FC Glasgow	*No competition*	John Hunter (Dundee FC)	29
1909/1910	Celtic FC Glasgow	Dundee FC	James Quinn (Celtic FC Glasgow) Jock Simpson (Falkirk FC)	24
1910/1911	Rangers FC Glasgow	Celtic FC Glasgow	William Reid (Rangers FC Glasgow)	38
1911/1912	Rangers FC Glasgow	Celtic FC Glasgow	William Reid (Rangers FC Glasgow)	33
1912/1913	Rangers FC Glasgow	Falkirk FC	James Reid (Airdrieonians FC)	30
1913/1914	Celtic FC Glasgow	Celtic FC Glasgow	James Reid (Airdrieonians FC)	27
1914/1915	Celtic FC Glasgow	*No competition*	Tom Gracie (Heart of Midlothian FC Edinburgh) James Richardson (Ayr United FC)	29
1915/1916	Celtic FC Glasgow	*No competition*	James McColl (Celtic FC Glasgow)	34
1916/1917	Celtic FC Glasgow	*No competition*	Herbert George Yarnall (ENG, Airdrieonians FC)	39
1917/1918	Rangers FC Glasgow	*No competition*	Hugh Ferguson (Motherwell FC)	35
1918/1919	Celtic FC Glasgow	*No competition*	David McLean (Rangers FC Glasgow)	29
1919/1920	Rangers FC Glasgow	Kilmarnock FC	Hugh Ferguson (Motherwell FC)	33
1920/1921	Rangers FC Glasgow	Partick Thistle FC Glasgow	Hugh Ferguson (Motherwell FC)	43
1921/1922	Celtic FC Glasgow	Greenock Morton FC	Duncan Walker (St. Mirren FC Paisley)	45
1922/1923	Rangers FC Glasgow	Celtic FC Glasgow	John White (Heart of Midlothian FC Edinburgh)	30
1923/1924	Rangers FC Glasgow	Airdrieonians FC	David Halliday (Dundee FC)	38
1924/1925	Rangers FC Glasgow	Celtic FC Glasgow	William Alexander Devlin (Cowdenbeath FC)	33
1925/1926	Celtic FC Glasgow	St. Mirren FC Paisley	William Alexander Devlin (Cowdenbeath FC)	40
1926/1927	Rangers FC Glasgow	Celtic FC Glasgow	James Edward McGrory (Celtic FC Glasgow)	49
1927/1928	Rangers FC Glasgow	Rangers FC Glasgow	James Edward McGrory (Celtic FC Glasgow)	47
1928/1929	Rangers FC Glasgow	Kilmarnock FC	Evelyn Morrison (Falkirk FC)	43
1929/1930	Rangers FC Glasgow	Rangers FC Glasgow	Benjamin Collard Yorston (Aberdeen FC)	38
1930/1931	Rangers FC Glasgow	Celtic FC Glasgow	Bernard Joseph Battles Jr. (Heart of Midlothian FC Edinburgh)	44
1931/1932	Motherwell FC	Rangers FC Glasgow	William MacFadyen (Motherwell FC)	52
1932/1933	Rangers FC Glasgow	Celtic FC Glasgow	William MacFadyen (Motherwell FC)	45
1933/1934	Rangers FC Glasgow	Rangers FC Glasgow	James Smith (Rangers FC Glasgow)	41
1934/1935	Rangers FC Glasgow	Rangers FC Glasgow	James Smith (Rangers FC Glasgow)	36
1935/1936	Celtic FC Glasgow	Rangers FC Glasgow	James Edward McGrory (Celtic FC Glasgow)	50

1936/1937	Rangers FC Glasgow	Celtic FC Glasgow	David Wilson (Hamilton Academical)	34
1937/1938	Celtic FC Glasgow	East Fife FC Methil	Andrew Black (Heart of Midlothian FC Edinburgh)	40
1938/1939	Rangers FC Glasgow	Clyde FC Cumbernauld	Alexander Venters (Rangers FC Glasgow)	35
1939/1940	*No competition*	*No competition*	-	
1940/1941	*No competition*	*No competition*	-	
1941/1942	*No competition*	*No competition*	-	
1942/1943	*No competition*	*No competition*	-	
1943/1944	*No competition*	*No competition*	-	
1944/1945	*No competition*	*No competition*	-	
1945/1946	*No competition*	*No competition*	-	
1946/1947	Rangers FC Glasgow	Aberdeen FC	Robert Carmichael Mitchell (Third Lanark AC Glasgow)	22
1947/1948	Hibernian FC Edinburgh	Rangers FC Glasgow	Archie Aikman (Falkirk FC)	20
1948/1949	Rangers FC Glasgow	Rangers FC Glasgow	Alexander Gair Stott (Dundee FC)	30
1949/1950	Rangers FC Glasgow	Rangers FC Glasgow	Willie Bauld (Heart of Midlothian FC Edinburgh)	30
1950/1951	Hibernian FC Edinburgh	Celtic FC Glasgow	Lawrance Reilly (Hibernian FC Edinburgh)	22
1951/1952	Hibernian FC Edinburgh	Motherwell FC	Lawrance Reilly (Hibernian FC Edinburgh)	27
1952/1953	Rangers FC Glasgow	Rangers FC Glasgow	Lawrance Reilly (Hibernian FC Edinburgh) Charlie Fleming (East Fife FC Methil)	30
1953/1954	Celtic FC Glasgow	Celtic FC Glasgow	James Wardhaugh (Heart of Midlothian FC Edinburgh)	27
1954/1955	Aberdeen FC	Clyde FC Cumbernauld	Willie Bauld (Heart of Midlothian FC Edinburgh)	21
1955/1956	Rangers FC Glasgow	Heart of Midlothian FC Edinburgh	James Wardhaugh (Heart of Midlothian FC Edinburgh)	28
1956/1957	Rangers FC Glasgow	Falkirk FC	Hugh Baird (Airdrieonians FC)	33
1957/1958	Heart of Midlothian FC Edinburgh	Clyde FC Cumbernauld	James Wardhaugh (Heart of Midlothian FC Edinburgh) James Murray (Heart of Midlothian FC Edinburgh)	28
1958/1959	Rangers FC Glasgow	St. Mirren FC Paisley	Joseph Henry Baker (Hibernian FC Edinburgh)	25
1959/1960	Heart of Midlothian FC Edinburgh	Rangers FC Glasgow	Joseph Henry Baker (Hibernian FC Edinburgh)	42
1960/1961	Rangers FC Glasgow	Dunfermline Athletic FC	Alexander Harley (Third Lanark AC Glasgow)	42
1961/1962	Dundee FC	Rangers FC Glasgow	Alan John Gilzean (Dundee FC)	24
1962/1963	Rangers FC Glasgow	Rangers FC Glasgow	James Millar (Rangers FC Glasgow)	27
1963/1964	Rangers FC Glasgow	Rangers FC Glasgow	Alan John Gilzean (Dundee FC)	32
1964/1965	Kilmarnock FC	Celtic FC Glasgow	Jim Forrest (Rangers FC Glasgow)	30
1965/1966	Celtic FC Glasgow	Rangers FC Glasgow	James McBride (Celtic FC Glasgow) Alexander Chapman Ferguson (Dunfermline Athletic FC)	31
1966/1967	Celtic FC Glasgow	Celtic FC Glasgow	Thomas Stephen Chalmers (Celtic FC Glasgow)	21
1967/1968	Celtic FC Glasgow	Dunfermline Athletic FC	Robert Lennox (Celtic FC Glasgow)	32
1968/1969	Celtic FC Glasgow	Celtic FC Glasgow	Kenneth Cameron (Dundee United FC)	26
1969/1970	Celtic FC Glasgow	Aberdeen FC	Colin Anderson Stein (Rangers FC Glasgow)	24
1970/1971	Celtic FC Glasgow	Celtic FC Glasgow	Henry Anthony Hood (Celtic FC Glasgow)	22
1971/1972	Celtic FC Glasgow	Celtic FC Glasgow	Joseph Montgomery Harper (Aberdeen FC)	33
1972/1973	Celtic FC Glasgow	Rangers FC Glasgow	Alan Fordyce Gordon (Hibernian FC Edinburgh)	27
1973/1974	Celtic FC Glasgow	Celtic FC Glasgow	John Kelly Deans (Celtic FC Glasgow)	26
1974/1975	Rangers FC Glasgow	Celtic FC Glasgow	Andrew Mullen Gray (Dundee United FC) William Pettigrew (Motherwell FC)	20
1975/1976	Rangers FC Glasgow	Rangers FC Glasgow	Kenneth Mathieson Dalglish (Celtic FC Glasgow)	24
1976/1977	Celtic FC Glasgow	Celtic FC Glasgow	William Pettigrew (Motherwell FC)	21
1977/1978	Rangers FC Glasgow	Rangers FC Glasgow	Derek Joseph Johnstone (Rangers FC Glasgow)	25
1978/1979	Celtic FC Glasgow	Rangers FC Glasgow	Andrew Ritchie (Greenock Morton FC)	22
1979/1980	Aberdeen FC	Celtic FC Glasgow	Douglas McKenzie Somner (St. Mirren FC Paisley)	25
1980/1981	Celtic FC Glasgow	Rangers FC Glasgow	Francis Peter McGarvey (Celtic FC Glasgow)	23
1981/1982	Celtic FC Glasgow	Aberdeen FC	George McKinley Cassidy McCluskey (Celtic FC Glasgow)	21
1982/1983	Dundee United FC	Aberdeen FC	Charles Nicholas (Celtic FC Glasgow)	29
1983/1984	Aberdeen FC	Aberdeen FC	Brian John McClair (Celtic FC Glasgow)	23
1984/1985	Aberdeen FC	Celtic FC Glasgow	Douglas Francis McDougall (Aberdeen FC)	22
1985/1986	Celtic FC Glasgow	Aberdeen FC	Alistair Murdoch McCoist (Rangers FC Glasgow)	24
1986/1987	Rangers FC Glasgow	St. Mirren FC Paisley	Brian John McClair (Celtic FC Glasgow)	35
1987/1988	Celtic FC Glasgow	Celtic FC Glasgow	Tommy Coyne (Dundee FC)	33
1988/1989	Rangers FC Glasgow	Celtic FC Glasgow	Mark Edward McGhee (Celtic FC Glasgow) Charles Nicholas (Aberdeen FC)	16
1989/1990	Rangers FC Glasgow	Aberdeen FC	John Grant Robertson (Heart of Midlothian FC Edinburgh)	17
1990/1991	Rangers FC Glasgow	Motherwell FC	Tommy Coyne (Celtic FC Glasgow)	18
1991/1992	Rangers FC Glasgow	Rangers FC Glasgow	Alistair Murdoch McCoist (Rangers FC Glasgow)	34
1992/1993	Rangers FC Glasgow	Rangers FC Glasgow	Alistair Murdoch McCoist (Rangers FC Glasgow)	34
1993/1994	Rangers FC Glasgow	Dundee United FC	Mark Wayne Hateley (ENG, Rangers FC Glasgow)	22
1994/1995	Rangers FC Glasgow	Celtic FC Glasgow	Tommy Coyne (Motherwell FC)	16
1995/1996	Rangers FC Glasgow	Rangers FC Glasgow	Petrus Ferdinandus Johannes van Hooijdonk (NED, Celtic FC Glasgow)	26
1996/1997	Rangers FC Glasgow	Kilmarnock FC	Jorge Paulo Cadete Santos Reis (POR, Celtic FC Glasgow)	25
1997/1998	Celtic FC Glasgow	Heart of Midlothian FC Edinburgh	Marco Negri (ITA, Rangers FC Glasgow)	32
1998/1999	Rangers FC Glasgow	Rangers FC Glasgow	Henrik Edward Larsson (SWE, Celtic FC Glasgow)	29

1999/2000	Rangers FC Glasgow	Rangers FC Glasgow	Mark Anthony Viduka (AUS, Celtic FC Glasgow)	25
2000/2001	Celtic FC Glasgow	Celtic FC Glasgow	Henrik Edward Larsson (SWE, Celtic FC Glasgow)	35
2001/2002	Celtic FC Glasgow	Rangers FC Glasgow	Henrik Edward Larsson (SWE, Celtic FC Glasgow)	29
2002/2003	Rangers FC Glasgow	Rangers FC Glasgow	Henrik Edward Larsson (SWE, Celtic FC Glasgow)	28
2003/2004	Celtic FC Glasgow	Celtic FC Glasgow	Henrik Edward Larsson (SWE, Celtic FC Glasgow)	30
2004/2005	Rangers FC Glasgow	Celtic FC Glasgow	John Hartson (WAL, Celtic FC Glasgow)	25
2005/2006	Celtic FC Glasgow	Heart of Midlothian FC Edinburgh	Kris Boyd (Kilmarnock FC / Rangers FC Glasgow)	32
2006/2007	Celtic FC Glasgow	Celtic FC Glasgow	Kris Boyd (Rangers FC Glasgow)	20
2007/2008	Celtic FC Glasgow	Rangers FC Glasgow	Scott Douglas McDonald (AUS, Celtic FC Glasgow)	25
2008/2009	Rangers FC Glasgow	Rangers FC Glasgow	Kris Boyd (Rangers FC Glasgow)	27
2009/2010	Rangers FC Glasgow	Dundee United FC	Kris Boyd (Rangers FC Glasgow)	23
2010/2011	Rangers FC Glasgow	Celtic FC Glasgow	Kenneth Miller (Rangers FC Glasgow)	21
2011/2012	Celtic FC Glasgow	Heart of Midlothian FC Edinburgh	Gary Hooper (ENG, Celtic FC Glasgow)	24
2012/2013	Celtic FC Glasgow	Celtic FC Glasgow	Michael Higdon (ENG, Motherwell FC)	26
2013/2014	Celtic FC Glasgow	St. Johnstone FC Perth	Kristian Arran Commons (Celtic FC Glasgow)	27
2014/2015	Celtic FC Glasgow	Inverness Caledonian Thistle FC	Adam Christopher Rooney (IRL, Aberdeen FC)	18
2015/2016	Celtic FC Glasgow	Hibernian FC Edinburgh	Leigh Griffiths (Celtic FC Glasgow)	31
2016/2017	Celtic FC Glasgow	Celtic FC Glasgow	Liam Boyce (NIR, Ross County FC Dingwall)	23
2017/2018	Celtic FC Glasgow	Celtic FC Glasgow	Kris Boyd (Kilmarnock FC)	18
2018/2019	Celtic FC Glasgow	Celtic FC Glasgow	Alfredo José Morelos Aviléz (COL, Rangers FC Glasgow)	18
2019/2020	Celtic FC Glasgow	*Not yet finished*	Odsonne Édouard (FRA, Celtic FC Glasgow)	22

NATIONAL CHAMPIONSHIP
Scottish Premiership 2019/2020
(03.08.2019 – 08.03.2020)

Results

Round 1 [03-04.08.2019]
Celtic FC - St. Johnstone FC 7-0(3-0)
Hibernian FC - St. Mirren FC 1-0(0-0)
Livingston FC - Motherwell FC 0-0
Ross County FC - Hamilton 3-0(2-0)
Kilmarnock FC - Rangers FC 1-2(0-1)
Aberdeen FC - Heart of Midlothian 3-2(1-0)

Round 2 [10-11.08.2019]
Motherwell FC - Celtic FC 2-5(1-2)
St. Johnstone FC - Livingston FC 2-2(0-2)
Hamilton - Kilmarnock FC 2-0(1-0)
Heart of Midlothian - Ross County FC 0-0
Rangers FC - Hibernian FC 6-1(2-1)
St. Mirren FC - Aberdeen FC 1-0(1-0)

Round 3 [24-25.08.2019]
Hamilton - Motherwell FC 1-3(1-2)
Hibernian FC - St. Johnstone FC 2-2(1-0)
Kilmarnock FC - Aberdeen FC 0-0
Ross County FC - Livingston FC 1-4(1-3)
St. Mirren FC - Rangers FC 0-1(0-0)
Celtic FC - Heart of Midlothian 3-1(1-0)

Round 4 [31.08.-01.09.2019]
Aberdeen FC - Ross County FC 3-0(2-0)
Heart of Midlothian - Hamilton 2-2(1-0)
Livingston FC - St. Mirren FC 2-1(1-0)
Motherwell FC - Hibernian FC 3-0(1-0)
St. Johnstone FC - Kilmarnock FC 0-1(0-1)
Rangers FC - Celtic FC 0-2(0-1)

Round 5 [14.09.2019]
Hamilton - Celtic FC 0-1(0-1)
Aberdeen FC - St. Johnstone FC 1-1(1-1)
Heart of Midlothian - Motherwell FC 2-3(0-1)
Kilmarnock FC - Hibernian FC 2-0(0-0)
Rangers FC - Livingston FC 3-1(0-0)
Ross County FC - St. Mirren FC 2-1(0-0)

Round 6 [21-22.09.2019]
Livingston FC - Aberdeen FC 0-2(0-1)
Motherwell FC - Ross County FC 1-2(0-0)
St. Mirren FC - Hamilton 0-0
St. Johnstone FC - Rangers FC 0-4(0-0)
Celtic FC - Kilmarnock FC 3-1(1-1)
Hibernian FC - Heart of Midlothian 1-2(0-0)

Round 7 [28.09.2019]
Hibernian FC - Celtic FC 1-1(1-1)
Hamilton - Livingston FC 2-1(1-1)
Kilmarnock FC - Ross County FC 0-0
Rangers FC - Aberdeen FC 5-0(2-0)
St. Johnstone FC - Motherwell FC 0-1(0-1)
St. Mirren FC - Heart of Midlothian 0-0

Round 8 [05-06.10.2019]
Aberdeen FC - Hibernian FC 1-1(0-0)
Heart of Midlothian - Kilmarnock FC 0-1(0-1)
Motherwell FC - St. Mirren FC 2-0(1-0)
Ross County FC - St. Johnstone FC 2-2(1-1)
Livingston FC - Celtic FC 2-0(0-0)
Rangers FC - Hamilton 5-0(2-0)

Round 9 [19-20.10.2019]
Celtic FC - Ross County FC 6-0(1-0)
Hamilton - Hibernian FC 1-1(0-1)
Kilmarnock FC - Livingston FC 2-1(1-0)
Motherwell FC - Aberdeen FC 0-3(0-1)
St. Mirren FC - St. Johnstone FC 2-0(1-0)
Heart of Midlothian - Rangers FC 1-1(1-1)

Round 10 [26-27.10.2019]
Hibernian FC - Ross County FC 2-2(0-0)
Kilmarnock FC - St. Mirren FC 1-0(0-0)
Livingston FC - Heart of Midlothian 0-0
St. Johnstone FC - Hamilton 3-2(1-1)
Aberdeen FC - Celtic FC 0-4(0-4)
Rangers FC - Motherwell FC 2-1(1-1)

Round 11 [30.10.2019]
Celtic FC - St. Mirren FC 2-0(0-0)
Hamilton - Aberdeen FC 0-1(0-1)
Hibernian FC - Livingston FC 2-2(0-2)
Motherwell FC - Kilmarnock FC 2-1(1-1)
Ross County FC - Rangers FC 0-4(0-3)
St. Johnstone - Heart of Midlothian 1-0(0-0)

Round 12 [02.11.2019]
Rangers FC - St. Johnstone FC *not played*
Aberdeen FC - Kilmarnock FC 3-0(2-0)
Hamilton - Ross County FC 2-2(0-1)
Motherwell FC - Livingston FC 2-1(0-0)
St. Mirren - Hibernian FC 1-2(0-1) [26.11.]
Heart of Midlothian - Celtic 0-2(0-2) [18.12.]

Round 13 [09-10.11.2019]
Heart of Midlothian - St. Mirren FC 5-2(3-2)
Kilmarnock FC - Hamilton 2-2(1-2)
Ross County FC - Aberdeen FC 1-3(1-1)
St. Johnstone FC - Hibernian FC 1-4(0-2)
Celtic FC - Motherwell FC 2-0(1-0)
Livingston FC - Rangers FC 0-2(0-1)

Round 14 [23-24.11.2019]
Celtic FC - Livingston FC 4-0(1-0)
Hibernian FC - Motherwell FC 3-1(2-1)
Kilmarnock FC - Heart of Midlothian 3-0(3-0)
St. Mirren FC - Ross County FC 2-1(1-1)
Hamilton - Rangers FC 1-3(1-2)
St. Johnstone FC - Aberdeen FC 1-1(0-1)

Round 15 [30.11.-01.12.2019]
Aberdeen FC - St. Mirren FC 2-1(1-1)
Hibernian FC - Kilmarnock FC 2-2(1-0)
Livingston FC - Hamilton 0-0
Motherwell FC - St. Johnstone FC 4-0(1-0)
Ross County FC - Celtic FC 1-4(1-2)
Rangers FC - Heart of Midlothian 5-0(2-0)

Round 16 [04.12.2019]
Aberdeen FC - Rangers FC 2-2(1-2)
Celtic FC - Hamilton 2-1(1-0)
Heart of Midlothian - Livingston FC 1-1(0-1)
Kilmarnock FC - St. Johnstone FC 0-0
Ross County FC - Hibernian FC 2-1(0-1)
St. Mirren FC - Motherwell FC 0-3(0-2)

Round 17 [07.12.2019]
Hamilton - St. Mirren FC 0-1(0-0)
Hibernian FC - Aberdeen FC 3-0(0-0)
Livingston FC - Kilmarnock FC 3-0(0-0)
Motherwell FC - Heart of Midlothian 1-0(1-0)
Rangers - Ross County 2-0(1-0) [29.01.2020]
St. Johnstone - Celtic 0-3(0-3) [29.01.2020]

Round 18 14-15.12.2019 [ ]
Aberdeen FC - Hamilton 1-0(0-0)
Heart of Midlothian - St. Johnstone 0-1(0-0)
Ross County FC - Kilmarnock FC 1-0(0-0)
St. Mirren FC - Livingston FC 3-3(1-2)
Motherwell FC - Rangers FC 0-2(0-1)
Celtic FC - Hibernian FC 2-0(1-0)

Round 19 [20-21.12.2019]
Hibernian FC - Rangers FC 0-3(0-2)
Celtic FC - Aberdeen FC 2-1(1-1)
Hamilton - Heart of Midlothian 2-1(0-0)
Kilmarnock FC - Motherwell FC 0-1(0-0)
Livingston FC - Ross County FC 4-0(2-0)
St. Johnstone FC - St. Mirren FC 0-0

Round 20 [26.12.2019]
Heart of Midlothian - Hibernian FC 0-2(0-2)
Aberdeen FC - Livingston FC 2-1(1-0)
Hamilton - St. Johnstone FC 0-1(0-0)
Rangers FC - Kilmarnock FC 1-0(0-0)
Ross County FC - Motherwell FC 1-2(1-0)
St. Mirren FC - Celtic FC 1-2(0-2)

Round 21 [29.12.2019]
Celtic FC - Rangers FC 1-2(1-1)
Heart of Midlothian - Aberdeen FC 1-1(0-0)
Livingston FC - Hibernian FC 2-0(0-0)
Motherwell FC - Hamilton 1-2(1-0)
St. Johnstone FC - Ross County FC 1-1(0-0)
St. Mirren FC - Kilmarnock FC 1-0(1-0)

Round 22 [22.01.2020]
Aberdeen FC - Motherwell FC 0-1(0-1)
Hibernian FC - Hamilton 2-1(0-1)
Kilmarnock FC - Celtic FC 1-3(0-1)
Livingston FC - St. Johnstone FC 1-0(0-0)
Rangers FC - St. Mirren FC 1-0(1-0)
Ross County FC - Heart of Midlothian 0-0

Round 23 [25-26.01.2020]
Celtic FC - Ross County FC 3-0(1-0)
Hamilton - Livingston FC 2-4(1-2)
Motherwell FC - Hibernian FC 0-0
St. Johnstone FC - Kilmarnock FC 2-1(1-1)
St. Mirren FC - Aberdeen FC 0-0
Heart of Midlothian - Rangers FC 2-1(0-0)

Round 24 [01-02.02.2020]
Hibernian FC - St. Mirren FC 2-2(2-2)
Kilmarnock FC - Ross County FC 3-1(0-1)
Livingston FC - Motherwell FC 1-0(0-0)
Rangers FC - Aberdeen FC 0-0
St. Johnstone - Heart of Midlothian 3-3(1-2)
Hamilton - Celtic FC 1-4(1-1)

Round 25 [05.02.2020]
Aberdeen FC - St. Johnstone FC 0-1(0-1)
Heart of Midlothian - Kilmarnock FC 2-3(0-2)
Motherwell FC - Celtic FC 0-4(0-1)
Rangers FC - Hibernian FC 2-1(1-1)
Ross County FC - Livingston FC 2-0(1-0)
St. Mirren FC - Hamilton 1-1(0-1)

Round 26 [11-12.02.2020]
Hamilton - Aberdeen FC 1-3(0-3)
Celtic FC - Heart of Midlothian 5-0(1-0)
Hibernian FC - Ross County FC 3-0(2-0)
Kilmarnock FC - Rangers FC 2-1(0-1)
Livingston FC - St. Mirren FC 2-1(1-0)
St. Johnstone FC - Motherwell FC 2-1(1-1)

Round 27 [15-16.02.2020]
Heart of Midlothian - Hamilton 2-2(0-2)
Ross County FC - St. Johnstone FC 1-1(0-1)
Aberdeen FC - Celtic FC 1-2(1-1)
Rangers FC - Livingston FC 1-0(0-0)
Kilmarnock FC - Hibernian FC 1-2(1-2)
Motherwell - St. Mirren FC 1-2(1-0) [25.02.]

Round 28 [22-23.02.2020]
Aberdeen FC - Ross County FC 1-2(1-1)
Hamilton - Motherwell FC 0-0
Hibernian FC - Livingston FC 1-1(0-0)
St. Johnstone FC - Rangers FC 2-2(1-0)
Celtic FC - Kilmarnock FC 3-1(2-1)
St. Mirren - Heart of Midloth 1-0(0-0) [11.03.]

Round 29 [03-04.03.2020]
Hibernian FC - Heart of Midlothian 1-3(0-0)
Kilmarnock FC - Aberdeen FC 2-2(2-1)
Livingston FC - Celtic FC 2-2(1-1)
Motherwell FC - Ross County FC 4-1(2-1)
Rangers FC - Hamilton 0-1(0-0)
St. Mirren FC - St. Johnstone FC 0-0

Round 30 [07-08.03.2020]
Aberdeen FC - Hibernian FC 3-1(0-1)
Celtic FC - St. Mirren FC 5-0(2-0)
Hamilton - Kilmarnock FC 1-0(0-0)
Heart of Midlothian - Motherwell FC 1-1(0-1)
St. Johnstone FC - Livingston FC 1-0(0-0)
Ross County FC - Rangers FC 0-1(0-0)

Please note: The season was suspended on 13.03.2020 due to Covid-19 pandemic. Later, on 18.05.2020, the Scottish Premiership was curtailed and standings were decided by a points by game average.

		Total						Home						Away				
1. **Celtic FC Glasgow**	(2.67)	30	26	2	2	89	-	19	80	14	0	1	50 - 7		12	2	1	39 - 12
2. Rangers FC Glasgow	(2.31)	29	21	4	4	64	-	19	67	11	1	2	33 - 7		10	3	2	31 - 12
3. Motherwell FC	(1.53)	30	14	4	12	41	-	38	46	7	1	7	23 - 23		7	3	5	18 - 15
4. Aberdeen FC	(1.50)	30	12	9	9	40	-	36	45	7	3	5	23 - 19		5	6	4	17 - 17
5. Livingston FC	(1.30)	30	10	9	11	41	-	39	39	8	4	2	19 - 8		2	5	9	22 - 31
6. St. Johnstone FC Perth	(1.24)	29	8	12	9	28	-	46	36	5	6	5	19 - 26		3	6	4	9 - 20
7. Hibernian FC Edinburgh	(1.23)	30	9	10	11	42	-	49	37	5	7	3	26 - 22		4	3	8	16 - 27
8. Kilmarnock FC	(1.10)	30	9	6	15	31	-	41	33	6	5	4	20 - 15		3	1	11	11 - 26
9. St. Mirren FC Paisley	(0.97)	30	7	8	15	24	-	41	29	5	6	4	13 - 13		2	2	11	11 - 28
10. Ross County FC Dingwall	(0.97)	30	7	8	15	29	-	60	29	5	3	6	17 - 23		2	5	9	12 - 37
11. Hamilton Academical FC	(0.90)	30	6	9	15	30	-	50	27	4	3	9	16 - 26		2	6	6	14 - 24
12. Heart of Midlothian FC Edinburgh (*Relegated*)	(0.77)	30	4	11	15	31	-	52	23	2	7	6	19 - 23		2	4	9	12 - 29

Final Standings

Top goalscorers:	
22 **Odsonne Édouard (FRA)**	*Celtic FC Glasgow*
13 Jermain Colin Defoe (ENG)	*Rangers FC Glasgow*
12 Christian Rhys Doidge (WAL)	*Hibernian FC Edinburgh*
12 Alfredo José Morelos Aviléz (COL)	*Rangers FC Glasgow*
11 Sam Cosgrove (ENG)	*Aberdeen FC*
11 Ryan Christie	*Celtic FC Glasgow*

NATIONAL CUP
Scottish Cup 2019/2020

First Round [20-21/28/30.09.2019]

Kelty Hearts FC - Auchinleck Talbot FC	0-3(0-2)		Inverurie Loco Works FC - Wick Academy FC	3-2(0-2)
Broxburn Athletic FC - East Stirlingshire FC Falkirk	3-2(2-1)		Linlithgow Rose FC - Huntly FC	1-0(0-0)
Buckie Thistle FC - Civil Service Strollers FC	4-1(3-0)		Keith FC - University of Stirling FC	2-3(0-1)
Caledonian Braves FC - Rothes FC	3-4(0-2)		Nairn County FC - Clachnacuddin FC Inverness	0-0
Cumbernauld Colts FC - Penicuik Athletic FC	1-5(0-3)		Spartans FC Edinburgh - Deveronvale FC	1-1(1-1)
Dalbeattie Star FC - Gala Fairydean Rovers FC	1-3(0-2)		Strathspey Thistle FC - Lossiemouth FC	2-1(1-0)
Edinburgh University AFC - Lochee United FC	1-3(0-0)		Turriff United FC - Formartine United FC Pitmedden	1-5(0-3)
Forres Mechanics FC - Banks O' Dee FC Aberdeen	1-4(0-0)		*Replay:*	
Fort William FC - Vale of Leithen FC	5-0(1-0)		Clachnacuddin FC Inverness - Nairn County FC	2-1(1-0)
Fraserburgh FC - Bonnyrigg Rose AFC	0-1(0-0)		Deveronvale FC - Spartans FC Edinburgh	1-2(1-1)
Gretna FC 2008 - Hill of Beath Hawthorn FC	1-0(0-0)			

Second Round [18-20./26-27.10.2019]

Bonnyrigg Rose AFC - Buckie Thistle FC	2-0(0-0)		Albion Rovers FC Coatbridge - Fort William FC	1-1(1-0)
Edinburgh City FC - Banks O' Dee FC Aberdeen	3-1(2-1)		Spartans FC Edinburgh - Queen's Park FC Glasgow	0-2(0-2)
Auchinleck Talbot FC - Cove Rangers FC	1-0(0-0)		Clachnacuddin FC Inverness - Brora Rangers FC	0-7(0-4)
Stirling Albion FC - Strathspey Thistle FC	2-0(0-0)		University of Stirling FC - Linlithgow Rose FC	0-2(0-0)
Lochee United FC - BSC Glasgow FC	1-1(1-0)		Penicuik Athletic FC - Stenhousemuir FC Falkirk	3-0(0-0)
Annan Athletic FC - Brechin City FC	2-2(2-0)		*Replay:*	
Formartine United FC - Gala Fairydean Rovers FC	2-2(0-1)		Brechin City FC - Annan Athletic FC	0-2(0-0)
Elgin City FC - Berwick Rangers FC	3-1(1-1)		Gala Fairydean Rovers FC - Formartine United FC	1-2(0-0)
Rothes FC - Inverurie Loco Works FC	1-3(0-2)		Broxburn Athletic FC - Cowdenbeath FC	3-0(1-0)
Cowdenbeath FC - Broxburn Athletic FC	1-1(0-0)		Fort William FC - Albion Rovers FC Coatbridge	0-5(0-4)
East Kilbride FC - Gretna FC 2008	3-1(2-1)		BSC Glasgow FC - Lochee United FC	2-1(1-0)

Third Round [22-23./27.11./03.12.2019]

Linlithgow Rose FC - Falkirk FC	1-4(1-2)		Inverurie Loco Works FC - Broxburn Athletic FC	0-1(0-0)
Auchinleck Talbot FC - Arbroath FC	1-1(1-0)		Partick Thistle FC Glasgow - Penicuik Athletic FC	1-0(1-0)
Albion Rovers FC Coatbridge - Airdrieonians FC	1-4(0-1)		Queen of the South FC - Queen's Park FC Glasgow	1-2(0-2)
Bonnyrigg Rose AFC - Montrose FC	2-1(2-1)		Raith Rovers - Peterhead FC	1-0(1-0)
Dumbarton FC - Forfar Athletic FC	3-1(1-1)		Stirling Albion FC - Clyde FC	0-2(0-1)
East Fife FC Methil - BSC Glasgow FC	3-4(2-1)		Stranraer FC - Dunfermline Athletic	1-0(0-0)
Edinburgh City FC - Annan Athletic FC	4-3(3-0)		*Replay:*	
Elgin City FC - Alloa Athletic FC	1-3(1-0)		Arbroath FC - Auchinleck Talbot FC	3-0(1-0)
Formartine United FC Pitmedden - East Kilbride FC	0-4(0-1)		Brora Rangers FC - Greenock Morton FC	1-3(0-1)
Greenock Morton FC - Brora Rangers FC	1-1(1-1)			

Fourth Round [17-19./28.01.2020]

Rangers FC Glasgow - Stranraer FC	2-0(1-0)		St. Johnstone FC - Greenock Morton FC	3-0(1-0)
St. Mirren FC Paisley - Broxburn Athletic FC	3-0(0-0)		Hamilton Academical FC - Edinburgh City FC	5-0(3-0)
Kilmarnock FC - Queen's Park FC Glasgow	6-0(3-0)		East Kilbride FC - BSC Glasgow FC	1-3(0-3)
Heart of Midlothian FC Edinb. - Airdrieonians FC	5-0(1-0)		Partick Thistle FC Glasgow - Celtic FC Glasgow	1-2(0-1)
Alloa Athletic FC - Inverness Caledonian Thistle FC	2-3(1-1)		Dundee FC - Motherwell FC	0-3(0-2)
Livingston FC - Raith Rovers FC Kirkcaldy	3-1(0-1)		Dundee United FC - Hibernian FC Edinburgh	2-2(1-1)
Arbroath FC - Falkirk FC	0-0		*Replay:*	
Ayr United FC - Ross County FC Dingwall	1-0(1-0)		Falkirk FC - Arbroath FC	2-0(0-0)
Aberdeen FC - Dumbarton FC	1-0(0-0)		Hibernian FC Edinburgh - Dundee United FC	4-2(1-1)
Bonnyrigg Rose AFC - Clyde FC Cumbernauld	0-1(0-0)			

1/8-Finals [08-09./18-19.02.2020]

Hamilton Academical FC - Rangers FC Glasgow	1-4(1-1)		BSC Glasgow FC - Hibernian FC Edinburgh	1-4(1-2)
Aberdeen FC - Kilmarnock FC	0-0		Clyde FC Cumbernauld - Celtic FC Glasgow	0-3(0-2)
Ayr United FC - St. Johnstone FC	1-2(1-2)		*Replay:*	
Inverness Caledonian Thistle FC - Livingston FC	1-0(0-0)		Motherwell FC - St. Mirren FC Paisley	4-4 aet; 2-3 pen
St. Mirren FC Paisley - Motherwell FC	1-1(0-1)		Kilmarnock FC - Aberdeen FC	3-4(1-0,1-1)
Falkirk FC - Heart of Midlothian FC Edinburgh	0-1(0-0)			

Quarter-Finals [28.02.-01.03.2020]

Hibernian FC Edinburgh - Inverness Cal. Thistle FC	5-2(1-0)		St. Mirren FC Paisley - Aberdeen FC	0-2(0-1)
Heart of Midlothian FC - Rangers FC Glasgow	1-0(0-0)		St. Johnstone FC - Celtic FC Glasgow	0-1(0-0)

Semi-Finals [*scheduled on 31.10.-01.11.2020*]

Heart of Midlothian FC - Hibernian FC Edinburgh	Celtic FC Glasgow - Aberdeen FC

The competition was suspended on 13.03.2020 due to Covid-19 pandemic.
The Semi-Finals and Final were postponed (the competition will be continued in autumn 2020).

Missing results will be presented in next year's yearbook.

THE CLUBS 2019/2020

Aberdeen Football Club

Founded: 14.04.1903
Stadium: Pittodrie Stadium, Aberdeen (20,866)
Trainer: Derek-John McInnes   05.07.1971

Goalkeepers:	DOB	M	(s)	G
Joe Lewis (ENG)	06.10.1987	30		
Defenders:	**DOB**	**M**	**(s)**	**G**
Andrew Considine	01.04.1987	25	(2)	4
Michael Devlin	03.10.1993	11	(3)	
Ronald José Hernández Pimentel (VEN)	04.10.1997	1	(1)	
Greg Leigh (ENG)	30.09.1994	18		1
Shay Logan (ENG)	29.01.1988	23	(3)	
Scott McKenna	12.11.1996	24		1
Ash Taylor (WAL)	02.09.1990	14		1
Zak Vyner (ENG)	14.05.1997	15	(1)	1
Midfielders:	**DOB**	**M**	**(s)**	**G**
Craig Bryson	06.11.1986	5	(3)	
Dean Campbell	19.03.2001	6	(9)	
Lewis Ferguson	24.08.1999	28		1
Stephen Gleeson (IRL)	03.08.1988		(1)	
Ryan Hedges (WAL)	08.07.1995	14	(8)	4
Dylan McGeouch	15.01.1993	6	(1)	
Funso Ojo (BEL)	28.08.1991	16		
Ethan Ross	15.08.2001	1	(1)	
Forwards:	**DOB**	**M**	**(s)**	**G**
Bruce Anderson	23.09.1998	1	(10)	1
Sam Cosgrove (ENG)	02.12.1996	22	(3)	11
Jon Gallagher (IRL)	23.02.1996	11	(11)	1
Matthew Kennedy (NIR)	01.11.1994	7	(1)	
Curtis Main (ENG)	20.06.1992	12	(6)	4
Niall McGinn (NIR)	20.07.1987	22	(6)	6
Connor McLennan	05.10.1999	9	(9)	3
James Wilson (ENG)	01.12.1995	7	(4)	
Scott Wright	08.08.1997	2	(1)	

Celtic Football Club Glasgow

Founded: 06.11.1887
Stadium: Celtic Park, Glasgow (60,411)
Trainer: Neil Francis Lennon (NIR)   25.06.1971

Goalkeepers:	DOB	M	(s)	G
Scott Bain	22.11.1991	2		
Fraser Forster (ENG)	17.03.1988	28		
Defenders:	**DOB**	**M**	**(s)**	**G**
Hatem Abd Elhamed (ISR)	18.03.1991	3	(2)	
Kristoffer Ajer (NOR)	17.04.1998	28		3
Moritz Bauer (AUT)	25.01.1992	6	(3)	
Boli Bolingoli-Mbombo (BEL)	01.07.1995	14		
Jeremie Frimpong (NED)	10.12.2000	12	(2)	2
Christopher Jullien (FRA)	22.03.1993	28		4
Tony Ralston	16.11.1998		(2)	
Jozo Šimunović (CRO)	04.08.1994	6		1
Stephen Welsh	19.01.2000	1		
Midfielders:	**DOB**	**M**	**(s)**	**G**
Nir Bitton (ISR)	30.10.1991	9	(6)	
Scott Brown	25.06.1985	29		2
Ryan Christie	22.02.1995	17	(7)	11
James Forrest	07.07.1991	28		10
Jonny Hayes (IRL)	09.07.1987	5	(9)	1
Callum McGregor	14.06.1993	30		9
Lewis Morgan	30.09.1996	3	(2)	
Olivier Ntcham (FRA)	09.02.1996	17	(6)	4
Tom Rogić (AUS)	16.12.1992	6	(10)	2
Scott Sinclair (ENG)	25.03.1989		(2)	
Greg Taylor	05.11.1997	11	(1)	
Forwards:	**DOB**	**M**	**(s)**	**G**
Vakoun Bayo (CIV)	10.01.1997	1	(7)	2
Karamoko Dembélé (ENG)	22.02.2003		(1)	
Odsonne Édouard (FRA)	16.01.1998	25	(2)	22
Mohamed Elyounoussi (NOR)	04.08.1994	7	(3)	4
Leigh Griffiths	20.08.1990	10	(11)	9
Mikey Johnston	19.04.1999	4	(7)	2
Patryk Klimala (POL)	05.08.1998		(2)	
Marian Shved (UKR)	16.07.1997		(1)	

Hamilton Academical Football Club

Founded: 1874
Stadium: New Douglas Park, Hamilton (6,018)
Trainer: Brian Rice   11.10.1963

Goalkeepers:	DOB	M	(s)	G
Luke Southwood (ENG)	06.12.1997	15		
Owain Fôn Williams (WAL)	17.03.1987	15		
Defenders:	**DOB**	**M**	**(s)**	**G**
Brian Easton	05.03.1988	17	(1)	
Markus Fjørtoft (NOR)	12.01.1994	5	(2)	
Alexandros Gogić (CYP)	13.04.1994	29		1
Jamie Hamilton	01.03.2002	11	(1)	
Johnny Hunt (ENG)	23.08.1990	10	(6)	
Aaron McGowan (ENG)	24.07.1996	22		1
Scott McMann	09.07.1996	27		
George William Stanger	15.08.2000	1		
Sam Alan Stubbs (ENG)	20.11.1998	19		
Shaun Want	09.02.1997	9	(2)	1
Samuel John Woods (ENG)	11.09.1998	3		1
Midfielders:	**DOB**	**M**	**(s)**	**G**
Blair Alston	23.03.1992	14	(5)	1
Adrian Beck (GER)	09.06.1997	2	(4)	
Will Collar (ENG)	03.02.1997	14	(2)	1
Ronan Hughes	15.12.1998	5	(3)	
Scott Martin	01.04.1997	18	(2)	
Ciaran McKenna	25.03.1998	2	(1)	
Reegan Mimnaugh	18.12.2001		(1)	
Lewis Smith	16.03.2000	17	(6)	3
David Templeton	07.01.1989	3	(3)	1
Forwards:	**DOB**	**M**	**(s)**	**G**
Ross Cunningham	23.05.1998	6	(3)	3
Andy Dales (ENG)	13.11.1994	1	(1)	
Steve Davies (ENG)	29.12.1987	5	(8)	2
Darian MacKinnon	09.10.1986	3	(3)	
Mickel Miller (ENG)	02.12.1995	16	(5)	3
David Moyo (ZIM)	17.12.1994	8	(12)	2
George Oakley (ENG)	18.11.1995	17	(4)	4
Marios Ogboe (GRE)	10.10.1994	16	(7)	6
Andrew Winter	10.03.2002		(3)	

Heart of Midlothian Football Club Edinburgh

Founded:	1874		
Stadium:	Tynecastle Park, Edinburgh (20,099)		
Trainer:	Craig Levein		22.10.1964
[07.12.2019]	Daniel Stendel (GER)		04.04.1974

Goalkeepers:	DOB	M	(s)	G
Colin Doyle (IRL)	12.08.1985	2		
Joel Castro Dinis Pereira (POR)	28.06.1996	20		
Zdeněk Zlámal (CZE)	05.11.1985	8		
Defenders:	**DOB**	**M**	**(s)**	**G**
Christophe Didier Berra	31.01.1985	18	(1)	1
Clevid Dikamona (FRA)	23.06.1990	8	(3)	
Craig Halkett	29.05.1995	24		2
Aaron Hickey	10.06.2002	23		1
Toby Peter Sibbick (ENG)	23.05.1999	2		
Michael Smith (NIR)	04.09.1988	23		
John Souttar	25.09.1996	7		
Midfielders:	**DOB**	**M**	**(s)**	**G**
Oliver Bozanić (AUS)	08.01.1989	13	(5)	3
Jamie Brandon	05.02.1998	5	(3)	
Sean Clare (ENG)	18.09.1996	24	(2)	4
Loïc Damour (FRA)	08.01.1991	13	(5)	
Ben Garuccio (AUS)	15.06.1995	2	(2)	
Andy Irving	13.05.2000	14	(4)	
Marcel Langer (GER)	16.02.1997	1	(1)	
Ryotaro Meshino (JPN)	18.06.1998	9	(10)	3
Lewis Moore	04.06.1998	6	(1)	
Callumn Morrison	05.07.1999	2	(2)	
Jake David Mulraney (IRL)	05.04.1996	12	(5)	1
Glenn David Whelan (IRL)	13.01.1984	13	(2)	
Aidy White (IRL)	10.10.1991	12	(2)	
Forwards:	**DOB**	**M**	**(s)**	**G**
Donis Avdijaj (KVX)	25.08.1996	1	(2)	
Liam Boyce (NIR)	08.04.1991	6	(2)	2
Euan Henderson	26.06.2000	5	(6)	
Uche Ikpeazu (UGA)	28.02.1995	15	(8)	2
Aidan Keena (IRL)	25.04.1999	1	(4)	
Steven MacLean	23.08.1982	8	(3)	1
Anthony McDonald	17.03.2001	1		
Steven Naismith	14.09.1986	14	(3)	4
Jamie Walker	25.06.1993	10	(5)	3
Conor Washington (NIR)	18.05.1992	7	(8)	3
Craig Wighton	27.07.1997	1	(1)	

Hibernian Football Club Edinburgh

Founded:	06.08.1875		
Stadium:	Easter Road Stadium, Edinburgh (20,421)		
Trainer:	Paul Heckingbottom (ENG)		17.07.1977
[04.11.2019]	Eddie May		30.08.1967
[18.11.2019]	Jack Ross		05.06.1976

Goalkeepers:	DOB	M	(s)	G
Ofir Marciano (ISR)	07.10.1989	19		
Christopher Ethan Maxwell (WAL)	30.07.1990	11	(1)	
Defenders:	**DOB**	**M**	**(s)**	**G**
David Gray	04.05.1988	3	(1)	
Paul Hanlon	20.01.1990	30		2
Adam Jackson (ENG)	18.05.1994	12	(2)	3
Thomas James (WAL)	15.04.1996	6		
Sean Mackie	04.11.1998	1	(1)	
Paul McGinn	22.10.1990	6	(1)	
Darren McGregor	07.08.1985	4	(2)	
Jason Naismith	25.06.1994	13		1
Ryan Porteous	25.03.1999	14		1
Steven Whittaker	16.06.1984	5	(2)	
Midfielders:	**DOB**	**M**	**(s)**	**G**
Greg Docherty	10.09.1996	5	(1)	1
Jamie Gullan	02.07.1999	1	(4)	
Melker Hallberg (SWE)	20.10.1995	18	(2)	1
Daryl Horgan (IRL)	10.08.1992	12	(16)	3
Stephen Mallan	25.03.1996	14	(6)	3
Glenn Middleton	01.01.2000	4	(2)	
Fraser Murray	07.05.1999		(7)	
Joe Newell (ENG)	15.03.1993	13	(6)	
Stéphane Oméonga (BEL)	27.03.1996	4	(4)	
Vykintas Slivka (LTU)	29.04.1995	12	(4)	
Lewis Stevenson	05.01.1988	26	(1)	
Joshua Vela (ENG)	14.12.1993	9		
Forwards:	**DOB**	**M**	**(s)**	**G**
Scott Allan	28.11.1991	28	(2)	5
Martin Boyle (AUS)	25.04.1993	15	(5)	5
Christian Doidge (WAL)	25.08.1992	25	(3)	12
Florian Kamberi (SUI)	08.03.1995	16	(4)	3
Marc McNulty	14.09.1992	4	(2)	1
Oliver Shaw	12.09.1998		(4)	

Kilmarnock Football Club

Founded:	05.01.1869		
Stadium:	Rugby Park, Kilmarnock (17,889)		
Trainer:	Angelo Alessio (ITA)		29.04.1965
[30.12.2019]	Alex Dyer (GER)		14.11.1965

Goalkeepers:	DOB	M	(s)	G
Laurenţiu Constantin Brănescu (ROU)	30.03.1994	26		
Jan Koprivec (SVN)	15.07.1988	4	(1)	
Defenders:	**DOB**	**M**	**(s)**	**G**
Kirk Broadfoot	08.08.1984	6	(3)	
Alex Bruce (NIR)	28.09.1984	11	(5)	1
Dario Del Fabro (ITA)	24.03.1995	21	(1)	1
Stuart Findlay	14.09.1995	18		1
Niko Hämäläinen (FIN)	05.03.1997	27	(1)	
Stephen Hendrie	08.01.1995	1	(1)	
Connor Johnson (ENG)	10.03.1998	3	(1)	
Ross Millen	28.09.1994	2	(2)	
Stephen Gerard O'Donnell	11.05.1992	28		3
Ally Taylor	12.09.2001		(1)	
Midfielders:	**DOB**	**M**	**(s)**	**G**
Eamonn Brophy	10.03.1996	24	(4)	9
Chris Burke	02.12.1983	20	(6)	6
Gary Dicker (IRL)	31.07.1986	30		2
Mohamed el Makrini (NED)	06.07.1987	19	(2)	2
Alan Power (IRL)	23.01.1988	28		
Greg Taylor	05.11.1997	2		
Dominic Thomas	14.02.1996	3	(17)	1
Iain Wilson	15.12.1998	3	(1)	
Forwards:	**DOB**	**M**	**(s)**	**G**
Harry Bunn (ENG)	21.11.1992	2	(1)	
Innes Cameron	22.08.2000		(1)	
Kyle Connell (ENG)	02.08.2001		(1)	
Simeon Alexander Jackson (CAN)	28.03.1987	1	(3)	
Nicke Kabamba (ENG)	01.02.1993	9		2
Greg Kiltie	18.01.1997	2	(8)	1
Rory McKenzie	07.10.1993	24	(3)	1
Liam Millar (CAN)	27.09.1999	14	(6)	1
Serigne Osman Petter Sow (SWE)	22.04.1990	2	(6)	
Harvey St. Clair	13.11.1998		(2)	

Livingston Football Club

Founded: 1943
Stadium: Almondvale Stadium, Livingston (9,512)
Trainer: Gary Holt   09.03.1973

Goalkeepers:	DOB	M	(s)	G
Robbie McCrorie	18.03.1998	8		
Ryan James Schofield (ENG)	11.12.1999	1		
Ross Stewart	16.04.1995	7		
Matija Šarkić (MNE)	23.07.1997	14		
Defenders:	**DOB**	**M**	**(s)**	**G**
Efe Eric Ambrose Emoubo (NGA)	18.10.1988	3		
Ciaron Brown (ENG)	14.01.1998	9		
Nicky Devlin	17.10.1993	11		
Jon Guthrie (ENG)	29.07.1992	28		6
Ricki Lamie	20.06.1993	19	(3)	1
Steve Lawson (FRA)	08.08.1994	13	(6)	
Alan Lithgow	12.03.1988	9	(3)	2
Jack McMillan	18.12.1997	19	(2)	
Hakeem Odofin (ENG)	13.04.1998	3	(4)	
Cécé Franck Pepe (FRA)	09.07.1996		(2)	
Ibrahima Savane (FRA)	10.09.1993		(1)	
Aaron Taylor-Sinclair	08.04.1991	12	(2)	3
Midfielders:	**DOB**	**M**	**(s)**	**G**
Marvin Bartley (ENG)	04.07.1986	27	(1)	1
Robbie Crawford	22.06.1994	13	(7)	
Chris Erskine	08.02.1987	3	(7)	
Keaghan Jacobs (RSA)	09.09.1989	14	(10)	
Steven Lawless	12.04.1991	29	(1)	8
Scott Robinson	12.03.1992	13	(9)	2
Craig Sibbald	18.05.1995	14	(4)	2
Jack Thomas Stobbs (ENG)	27.02.1997	1	(3)	1
Forwards:	**DOB**	**M**	**(s)**	**G**
Lyndon Dykes	07.10.1995	25		9
Dolly Doningos Menga (ANG)	02.05.1993		(3)	
Lee Miller	18.03.1983		(3)	1
Scott Pittman	09.07.1992	23		3
Aymen Souda (FRA)	28.02.1993	11	(6)	2
Scott Tiffoney	26.08.1998	1	(7)	

Motherwell Football Club

Founded: 17.05.1886
Stadium: Fir Park, Motherwell (13,677)
Trainer: Stephen Robinson (NIR)   10.12.1974

Goalkeepers:	DOB	M	(s)	G
Mark Gillespie (ENG)	27.03.1992	30		
Defenders:	**DOB**	**M**	**(s)**	**G**
Jake Carroll (IRL)	11.08.1991	21		2
Liam Donnelly (NIR)	07.03.1996	22		7
Charles Dunne (IRL)	13.02.1993	3		
Declan Gallagher	13.02.1991	30		2
Peter Hartley (ENG)	03.04.1988	23	(2)	2
Barry Maguire	27.04.1998	4	(3)	
Bevis Mugabi (ENG)	01.05.1995	6	(4)	
Richard Tait	02.12.1989	12	(2)	
Midfielders:	**DOB**	**M**	**(s)**	**G**
Rolando Aarons (ENG)	16.11.1995	6		
Allan Campbell	04.07.1998	30		5
Liam Grimshaw (ENG)	02.02.1995	25		
Christian Ilić (CRO)	22.07.1996	3	(5)	
Mark O'Hara	12.12.1995	9	(8)	1
Liam Polworth	12.10.1994	28	(2)	1
David Turnbull	10.07.1999		(2)	
Forwards:	**DOB**	**M**	**(s)**	**G**
Devante Dewar Cole (ENG)	10.05.1995	12	(7)	4
Jermaine Hylton (ENG)	28.06.1993	18	(10)	2
Chris Long (ENG)	25.02.1995	21	(4)	7
Ross MacIver	28.02.1999	1	(6)	1
Christy Manzinga (FRA)	31.01.1995		(6)	1
Mikael Ndjoli (ENG)	16.12.1998		(1)	
James Scott	30.08.2000	15	(7)	3
Sherwin Seedorf (NED)	17.03.1998	9	(13)	2
Tony Watt	29.12.1993	2	(2)	1

Rangers Football Club Glasgow

Founded: 1872
Stadium: Ibrox Park Stadium, Glasgow (50,817)
Trainer: Steven George Gerrard (ENG)   30.05.1980

Goalkeepers:	DOB	M	(s)	G
Wesley Foderingham (ENG)	14.01.1991	2		
Allan McGregor	31.01.1982	27		
Defenders:	**DOB**	**M**	**(s)**	**G**
Borna Barišić (CRO)	10.11.1992	22		2
George Edmundson (ENG)	31.08.1997	4	(3)	1
Jon Flanagan (ENG)	01.01.1993	5		
Connor Goldson (ENG)	18.12.1992	29		3
Filip Helander (SWE)	22.04.1993	8		1
Nikola Katić (CRO)	10.10.1996	17	(2)	2
Matt Polster (USA)	08.06.1993	3	(3)	
James Tavernier (ENG)	31.10.1991	24		3
Midfielders:	**DOB**	**M**	**(s)**	**G**
Scott Arfield (CAN)	01.11.1988	22	(4)	5
Joseph Oluwaseyi Ayodele-Aribo (NGA)	21.07.1996	25	(2)	3
Steven Davis (NIR)	01.01.1985	20	(4)	
Ianis Hagi (ROU)	22.10.1998	6	(1)	1
Andy Halliday	11.10.1991	4	(2)	
Ryan Jack	27.02.1992	19		4
Jordan Jones (NIR)	24.10.1994	2	(5)	
Glen Kamara (FIN)	28.10.1995	18	(1)	
Ryan Kent (ENG)	11.11.1996	18	(3)	7
Andrew Philip King (WAL)	29.10.1988		(2)	
Forwards:	**DOB**	**M**	**(s)**	**G**
Brandon Barker (ENG)	04.10.1996	2	(4)	1
Jermain Colin Defoe (ENG)	07.10.1982	11	(9)	13
Florian Kamberi (ALB)	08.03.1995	1	(5)	1
Alfredo José Morelos Aviléz (COL)	21.06.1996	18	(8)	12
Jamie Murphy	28.08.1989		(2)	
Oluwaseyi Babajide Ojo (NGA)	19.06.1997	9	(10)	1
Greg Stewart	17.03.1990	3	(13)	3

Ross County Football Club Dingwall

Founded: 1929
Stadium: Victoria Park, Dingwall (6,541)
Trainer: Stuart Kettlewell &   04.06.1984
     Steven Ferguson   18.05.1977

Goalkeepers:	DOB	M	(s)	G
Nathan Joseph Baxter (ENG)	08.11.1998	13		
Ross Laidlaw	12.07.1992	17		
Defenders:	**DOB**	**M**	**(s)**	**G**
Joe Chalmers	03.01.1994	6	(8)	3
Coll Donaldson	09.04.1995	7		
Liam Fontaine (ENG)	07.01.1986	22		1
Ricky Foster	31.07.1985	20	(1)	
Marcus Fraser	23.06.1994	25	(1)	1
Tom Grivosti (ENG)	15.06.1999	5	(1)	
Sean Kelly	01.11.1993	18		
Callum Morris (NIR)	03.02.1990	17		
Josh Mullin	23.09.1992	21	(6)	1
Jordan Tillson (ENG)	05.03.1993	5	(2)	
Keith Watson	14.11.1989	14	(3)	
Midfielders:	**DOB**	**M**	**(s)**	**G**
Don Cowie	15.02.1983	7	(2)	
Ross Draper (ENG)	20.10.1988	8	(3)	
Michael Gardyne	23.01.1986	13	(1)	
Ewan Henderson	27.03.2000	6	(3)	
Harrison Paton (CAN)	23.05.1998	11	(8)	
Simon Power (IRL)	13.05.1998		(1)	
Lewis Spence	28.01.1996	10	(5)	
Blair Spittal	19.12.1995	10	(10)	2
Forwards:	**DOB**	**M**	**(s)**	**G**
Lee Erwin	19.03.1994	11	(6)	1
Brian Graham	23.11.1987	5	(13)	4
Billy McKay (NIR)	22.10.1988	22	(5)	7
Oliver Shaw	12.09.1998	2	(5)	
Ross Stewart	01.09.1996	19	(2)	7
Iain Vigurs	07.05.1988	16		2

St. Johnstone Football Club Perth

Founded:	1884		
Stadium:	McDiarmid Park, Perth (10,696)		
Trainer:	Thomas James Wright (NIR)		29.08.1963

Goalkeepers:	DOB	M	(s)	G
Zander Clark	26.06.1992	29		
Defenders:	**DOB**	**M**	**(s)**	**G**
Callum Booth	30.05.1991	12	(1)	
Wallace Duffy	12.04.1999	11		
Ricky Foster	31.07.1985	2		
Liam Gordon	26.01.1996	16		
Jason Kerr	06.02.1997	29		1
Jamie McCart	20.06.1997	7	(1)	
Anthony Ralston	16.11.1998	21	(1)	
Scott Tanser (ENG)	23.10.1994	19	(2)	
Madis Vihmann (EST)	05.10.1995	2	(2)	
Midfielders:	**DOB**	**M**	**(s)**	**G**
Matt Butcher (ENG)	14.05.1997	3	(3)	
Ross Callachan	04.09.1993	1	(1)	
Liam Craig	27.12.1986	9	(6)	
Murray Davidson	07.03.1988	17		
Jason Holt	19.02.1993	15	(2)	
Ali McCann (NIR)	04.12.1999	26	(3)	4
Danny Swanson	28.12.1986	3	(4)	
David Wotherspoon (CAN)	16.01.1990	15	(6)	3
Drey Wright (ENG)	30.04.1994	16	(6)	
Forwards:	**DOB**	**M**	**(s)**	**G**
Callum Hendry	08.12.1997	5	(15)	7
Chris Kane	05.09.1994	11	(12)	1
Matthew Kennedy (NIR)	01.11.1994	16	(2)	3
Stevie May	03.11.1992	20	(4)	6
Michael O'Halloran	06.01.1991	14	(10)	2

St. Mirren Football Club Paisley

Founded:	1877		
Stadium:	St. Mirren Park, St. Mirren (7,937)		
Trainer:	James Michael Goodwin (IRL)		20.11.1981

Goalkeepers:	DOB	M	(s)	G
Václav Hladký (CZE)	14.11.1990	30		
Defenders:	**DOB**	**M**	**(s)**	**G**
Kirk John Broadfoot	08.08.1984	7	(1)	
Akinlolu Richard Olamide Famewo (ENG)	09.11.1998	9		
Lee James Stephen Hodson (NIR)	02.10.1991	5	(2)	
Gary MacKenzie	15.10.1985	9	(1)	
Conor McCarthy (IRL)	11.04.1998	9		1
Sean McLoughlin (IRL)	13.11.1996	21		1
Calum Waters	10.03.1996	27		
Midfielders:	**DOB**	**M**	**(s)**	**G**
Tony Andreu (FRA)	22.05.1988	16	(12)	2
Oan Djorkaeff (ARM)	30.04.1997		(2)	
İlkay Durmuş (GER)	01.05.1994	21	(7)	4
Ryan Flynn	04.09.1988	22		
Sam Foley (IRL)	17.10.1986	27		1
Scott Glover	16.11.2000	1		
Cameron MacPherson	29.12.1998	15	(1)	2
Kyle Magennis	26.08.1998	22		1
Paul McGinn	22.10.1990	21	(1)	
Stephen McGinn	02.12.1988	7	(2)	
Jamie McGrath (IRL)	30.09.1996	4	(3)	
Ross Wallace	23.05.1985	2	(1)	
Forwards:	**DOB**	**M**	**(s)**	**G**
Cameron Breadner	13.10.2000		(2)	
Seifedin Chabbi (AUT)	04.07.1993		(2)	
Cody Cooke (ENG)	02.03.1993		(6)	
Alex Jakubiak	27.08.1996	4	(3)	
Kyle McAllister	21.01.1999	4	(11)	
Junior Morias (ENG)	04.07.1995	14	(12)	2
Danny Mullen	01.03.1995	7	(10)	2
Jonathan Obika (ENG)	12.09.1990	26	(4)	8

SECOND LEVEL
Scottish Championship 2019/2020

1.	Dundee United FC (*Promoted*)	28	18	5	5	52 - 22	59	(2.11)
2.	Inverness Caledonian Thistle FC	27	14	3	10	39 - 32	45	(1.67)
3.	Dundee FC	27	11	8	8	32 - 31	41	(1.52)
4.	Ayr United FC	27	12	4	11	38 - 35	40	(1.48)
5.	Arbroath FC	26	10	6	10	24 - 26	36	(1.38)
6.	Dunfermline Athletic FC	28	10	7	11	41 - 36	37	(1.32)
7.	Greenock Morton FC	28	10	6	12	45 - 52	36	(1.29)
8.	Alloa Athletic FC	28	7	10	11	33 - 43	31	(1.11)
9.	Queen of the South FC Dumfries	28	7	7	14	28 - 40	28	(1.00)
10.	Partick Thistle FC Glasgow (*Relegated*)	27	6	8	13	32 - 47	26	(0.96)

Please note: the season was curtailed due to Covid-19 pandemic. Standings were decided by a points by game average.

INTERNATIONAL MATCHES
(16.07.2019 – 15.07.2020)

06.09.2019	Glasgow	Scotland - Russia	1-2(1-1)	(ECQ)
09.09.2019	Glasgow	Scotland - Belgium	0-4(0-3)	(ECQ)
10.10.2019	Moskva	Russia - Scotland	4-0(0-0)	(ECQ)
13.10.2019	Glasgow	Scotland - San Marino	6-0(3-0)	(ECQ)
16.11.2019	Nicosia	Cyprus - Scotland	1-2(0-1)	(ECQ)
19.11.2019	Glasgow	Scotland - Kazakhstan	3-1(0-1)	(ECQ)

06.09.2019   SCOTLAND - RUSSIA   1-2(1-1)   16th EC. Qualifiers
Hampden Park, Glasgow; Referee: Anastasios Sidiropoulos (Greece); Attendance: 32,432
SCO: David James Marshall, Charles Patrick Mulgrew, Liam David Ian Cooper, Stephen Gerard O'Donnell, Andrew Henry Robertson (Cap), James Forrest (62.Kenneth McLean), Callum William McGregor, Ryan Fraser, John McGinn (62.Ryan Christie), Scott Francis McTominay (78.Matthew Phillips), Oliver Robert McBurnie. Trainer: Stephen Clarke.
Goal: John McGinn (11).

09.09.2019   SCOTLAND - BELGIUM   0-4(0-3)   16th EC. Qualifiers
Hampden Park, Glasgow; Referee: Paweł Gil (Poland); Attendance: 25,524
SCO: David James Marshall, Charles Patrick Mulgrew, Liam David Ian Cooper, Stephen Gerard O'Donnell, Andrew Henry Robertson (Cap), Robert Snodgrass, Matthew Phillips (77.Johnathon Simpson Snedden Russell), Kenneth McLean, Callum William McGregor (68.Stuart Armstrong), Ryan Christie (86.John McGinn), Scott Francis McTominay. Trainer: Stephen Clarke.

10.10.2019   RUSSIA - SCOTLAND   4-0(0-0)   16th EC. Qualifiers
Luzhniki Stadium, Moskva; Referee: Jakob Kehlet (Denmark); Attendance: 65,703
SCO: David James Marshall, Charles Patrick Mulgrew, Michael James Devlin, Andrew Henry Robertson (Cap), John Alexander Fleck (81.Stuart Armstrong), Robert Snodgrass, Liam Jordan Palmer, Callum William McGregor, Ryan Fraser (68.Ryan Christie), John McGinn, Oliver Jasen Burke (46.Lawrence Shankland). Trainer: Stephen Clarke.

13.10.2019   SCOTLAND - SAN MARINO   6-0(3-0)   16th EC. Qualifiers
Hampden Park, Glasgow; Referee: Jérôme Brisard (France); Attendance: 20,699
SCO: Jonathan Peter McLaughlin, Michael James Devlin, Stuart John Findlay, Andrew Henry Robertson (Cap), James Forrest, Liam Jordan Palmer, Callum William McGregor (70.Johnathon Simpson Snedden Russell), John McGinn (70.Stuart Armstrong), Ryan Christie, Scott Francis McTominay, Lawrence Shankland. Trainer: Stephen Clarke.
Goals: John McGinn (12, 27, 45+1), Lawrence Shankland (65), Stuart Findlay (67), Stuart Armstrong (87).

16.11.2019   CYPRUS - SCOTLAND   1-2(0-1)   16th EC. Qualifiers
Stádio GSP, Nicosia; Referee: Harald Lechner (Austria); Attendance: 7,595
SCO: David James Marshall, Declan Patrick Gallagher, Scott Fraser McKenna, Greg John Taylor, Ryan Jack, James Forrest (72.Oliver Jasen Burke), Liam Jordan Palmer, Callum William McGregor, John McGinn, Ryan Christie (90+2.Michael James Devlin), Steven John Naismith (Cap) (62.Oliver Robert McBurnie). Trainer: Stephen Clarke.
Goals: Ryan Christie (12), John McGinn (53).

19.11.2019   SCOTLAND - KAZAKHSTAN   3-1(0-1)   16th EC. Qualifiers
Hampden Park, Glasgow; Referee: Hendrikus Sebastian "Bas" Nijhuis (Netherlands); Attendance: 19,515
SCO: David James Marshall, Declan Patrick Gallagher, Scott Fraser McKenna, Greg John Taylor, Ryan Jack, James Forrest, Liam Jordan Palmer, Callum William McGregor, John McGinn (90+2.Stuart Armstrong), Ryan Christie (83.John Alexander Fleck), Steven John Naismith (Cap) (77.Oliver Jasen Burke). Trainer: Stephen Clarke.
Goals: John McGinn (48), Steven John Naismith (64), John McGinn (90+1).

NATIONAL TEAM PLAYERS
(16.07.2019 – 15.07.2020)

Name	DOB	Caps	Goals	2019/2020:	Club

Goalkeepers

Name	DOB	Caps	Goals	2019/2020:	Club
David James MARSHALL	05.03.1985	34	0	2019:	Wigan Athletic FC (ENG)
Jonathan Peter McLAUGHLIN	09.09.1987	2	0	2019:	Sunderland AFC (ENG)

Defenders

Name	DOB	Caps	Goals	2019/2020:	Club
Liam David Ian COOPER	30.08.1991	2	0	2019:	Leeds United FC (ENG)
Michael James DEVLIN	03.10.1993	3	0	2019:	Aberdeen FC
Stuart John FINDLAY	14.09.1995	1	0	2019:	Kilmarnock FC
Declan Patrick GALLAGHER	13.02.1991	2	0	2019:	Motherwell FC
Scott Fraser McKENNA	12.11.1996	14	0	2019:	Aberdeen FC
Charles Patrick MULGREW	06.03.1986	44	3	2019:	Wigan Athletic FC (ENG)
Stephen Gerard O'DONNELL	11.05.1992	11	0	2019:	Kilmarnock FC
Liam Jordan PALMER	19.09.1991	5	0	2019:	Sheffield Wednesday FC (ENG)
Andrew Henry ROBERTSON	11.03.1994	34	3	2019:	Liverpool FC (ENG)
Greg John TAYLOR	05.11.1997	3	0	2019:	Celtic FC Glasgow

Midfielders

Name	DOB	Caps	Goals	2019/2020:	Club
Stuart ARMSTRONG	30.03.1992	19	2	2019:	Southampton FC (ENG)
John Alexander FLECK	24.08.1991	2	0	2019:	Sheffield United FC (ENG)
James FORREST	07.07.1991	34	5	2019:	Celtic FC Glasgow
Ryan JACK	27.02.1992	4	0	2019:	Rangers FC Glasgow
John McGINN	18.10.1994	21	7	2019:	Aston Villa FC Birmingham (ENG)
Callum William McGREGOR	14.06.1993	19	0	2019:	Celtic FC Glasgow
Kenneth McLEAN	08.01.1992	9	1	2019:	Norwich City FC (ENG)
Scott Francis McTOMINAY	08.12.1996	12	0	2019:	Manchester United FC (ENG)
Robert SNODGRASS	07.09.1987	28	7	2019:	West Ham United FC London (ENG)

Forwards

Name	DOB	Caps	Goals	2019/2020:	Club
Oliver Jasen BURKE	07.04.1997	11	1	2019:	Deportivo Alavés Vitoria-Gasteiz (ESP)
Ryan CHRISTIE	22.02.1995	11	1	2019:	Celtic FC Glasgow
Ryan FRASER	24.02.1994	11	1	2019:	AFC Bournemouth (ENG)
Oliver Robert McBURNIE	04.06.1996	9	0	2019:	Sheffield United FC (ENG)
Steven John NAISMITH	14.09.1986	51	10	2019:	Heart of Midlothian FC Edinburgh
Matthew PHILLIPS	13.03.1991	16	1	2019:	West Bromwich Albion FC (ENG)
Johnathon Simpson Snedden RUSSELL	08.04.1990	14	1	2019:	Sporting Kansas City (USA)
Lawrence SHANKLAND	10.08.1995	2	1	2019:	Dundee United FC

National team coach

Stephen "Steve" CLARKE [from 20.05.2019]	29.08.1963	8 M; 4 W; 0 D; 4 L; 14-16			

SERBIA

The Country:
Република Србија (Republic of Serbia)
Capital: Beograd
Surface: 77,474 km²
Inhabitants: 6,963,764 [2019]
Time: UTC+1

The FA:
Fudbalski savez Srbije
35, Terazije CP 263, 11000 Beograd
Tel: +381 11 323 4253
Founded: 1919
Member of FIFA since: 1921
Member of UEFA since: 1954
Website: www.fss.org.rs

NATIONAL TEAM RECORDS

RECORDS
First international match:	28.08.1920, Antwerpen: Czechoslovakia – Yugoslavia 7-0
Most international caps:	Branislav Ivanović - 105 caps (2005-2018)
Most international goals:	Stjepan Bobek - 38 goals / 63 caps (1946-1956)

UEFA EUROPEAN CHAMPIONSHIP*
1960	Final Tournament (Runners-up)
1964	Qualifiers
1968	Final Tournament (Runners-up)
1972	Qualifiers
1976	Final Tournament (4th Place)
1980	Qualifiers
1984	Final Tournament (Group Stage)
1988	Qualifiers
1992	Qualified / Suspended
1996	Suspended
2000	Final Tournament (Quarter-Finals)
2004	Qualifiers
2008	Qualifiers
2012	Qualifiers
2016	Qualifiers
2020	To be determined

FIFA WORLD CUP*
1930	Final Tournament (4th Place)
1934	Qualifiers
1938	Qualifiers
1950	Final Tournament (Group Stage)
1954	Final Tournament (Quarter-Finals)
1958	Final Tournament (Quarter-Finals)
1962	Final Tournament (4th Place)
1966	Qualifiers
1970	Qualifiers
1974	Final Tournament (2nd Round)
1978	Qualifiers
1982	Final Tournament (Group Stage)
1986	Qualifiers
1990	Final Tournament (Quarter-Finals)
1994	Suspended
1998	Final Tournament (2nd Round of 16)
2002	Qualifiers
2006	Final Tournament (Group Stage)
2010	Final Tournament (Group Stage)
2014	Qualifiers
2018	Final Tournament (Group Stage)

OLYMPIC TOURNAMENTS*
Year	Result
1908	-
1912	-
1920	Round 1
1924	Qualifiers
1928	1/8 - Finals
1936	Did not enter
1948	Runners-up
1952	Runners-up
1956	Runners-up
1960	**Winners**
1964	Quarter-Finals
1968	Did not enter
1972	Qualifiers
1976	Qualifiers
1980	4th Place
1984	3rd Place
1988	Group Stage
1992	Qualifiers
1996	Suspended
2000	Qualifiers
2004	Group Stage
2008	Group Stage
2012	Qualifiers
2016	Qualifiers

*as Yugoslavia (1930-2002), Serbia and Montenegro (2002-2006).

UEFA NATIONS LEAGUE
2018/2019 – League C (promoted to League B)

FIFA CONFEDERATIONS CUP 1992-2017
None

SERBIAN CLUB HONOURS IN EUROPEAN CLUB COMPETITIONS:

European Champion Clubs.Cup (1956-1992) / UEFA Champions League (1993-2020)		
FK Crvena Zvezda Beograd	1	1990/1991

Fairs Cup (1858-1971) / UEFA Cup (1972-2009) / UEFA Europa League (2010-2020)
None

UEFA Super Cup (1972-2019)
None

European Cup Winners.Cup 1961-1999*
None

*defunct competition

NATIONAL COMPETITIONS
TABLE OF HONOURS

Kingdom of Yugoslavia (1923–1940)

	CHAMPIONS	CUP WINNERS	BEST GOALSCORERS	
1923	HŠK Građanski Zagreb	HAŠK Zagreb	Dragan Jovanović (SK Jugoslavija Beograd)	4
1924	SK Jugoslavija Beograd	Zagreb XI	Dragan Jovanović (SK Jugoslavija Beograd)	6
1925	SK Jugoslavija Beograd	Zagreb XI	Dragan Jovanović (SK Jugoslavija Beograd)	4
1926	HŠK Građanski Zagreb	Zagreb XI	Dušan Petković (SK Jugoslavija Beograd)	4
1927	NK Hajduk Split	Beograd XI	Kuzman Sotirović (BSK Beograd)	6
1928	HŠK Građanski Zagreb	*No competition*	Ljubo Benčić (NK Hajduk Split)	8
1929	NK Hajduk Split	*No competition*	Đorđe Vujadinović (BSK Beograd)	10
1930	HŠK Concordia Zagreb	*No competition*	Blagoje Marjanović (BSK Beograd)	10
1930/1931	BSK Beograd	*No competition*	Đorđe Vujadinović (BSK Beograd)	12
1931/1932	HŠK Concordia Zagreb	*No competition*	Svetislav Valjarević (HŠK Concordia Zagreb)	10
1932/1933	BSK Beograd	*No competition*	Vladimir Kragić (NK Hajduk Split)	21
1933/1934	*No competition*	BSK Beograd	-	
1934/1935	BSK Beograd	*No competition*	Leo Lemešić (NK Hajduk Split)	18
1935/1936	BSK Beograd	SK Jugoslavija	Blagoje Marjanović (BSK Beograd)	5
1936/1937	HŠK Građanski Zagreb	*No competition*	Blagoje Marjanović (BSK Beograd)	21
1937/1938	HAŠK Zagreb	*No competition*	August Lešnik (HŠK Građanski Zagreb)	17
1938/1939	BSK Beograd	*No competition*	August Lešnik (HŠK Građanski Zagreb)	22
1939/1940	HŠK Građanski Zagreb	HŠK Građanski Zagreb	Svetislav Glišović (BSK Beograd)	10

SFR Yugoslavia (1945–1992)

	CHAMPIONS	CUP WINNERS	BEST GOALSCORERS	
1945	S.R. Serbia	*No competition*	Stjepan Bobek (JNA)	8
1946/1947	FK Partizan Beograd	FK Partizan Beograd	Franjo Wölfl (NK Dinamo Zagreb)	28
1947/1948	NK Dinamo Zagreb	FK Crvena Zvezda Beograd	Franjo Wölfl (NK Dinamo Zagreb)	22
1948/1949	FK Partizan Beograd	FK Crvena Zvezda Beograd	Frane Matošić (NK Hajduk Split)	17
1950	NK Hajduk Split	FK Crvena Zvezda Beograd	Marko Valok (FK Partizan Beograd)	17
1951	FK Crvena Zvezda Beograd	NK Dinamo Zagreb	Kosta Tomašević (FK Crvena Zvezda Beograd)	16
1952	NK Hajduk Split	FK Partizan Beograd	Stanoje Jocić (BSK Beograd)	13
1952/1953	FK Crvena Zvezda Beograd	BSK Beograd	Todor Živanović (FK Crvena Zvezda Beograd)	17
1953/1954	NK Dinamo Zagreb	FK Partizan Beograd	Stjepan Bobek (FK Partizan Beograd)	21
1954/1955	NK Hajduk Split	BSK Beograd	Predrag Marković (BSK Beograd) Kosta Tomašević (FK Spartak Subotica) Bernard Vukas (NK Hajduk Split)	20
1955/1956	FK Crvena Zvezda Beograd	*No competition*	Muhamed Mujić (FK Velež Mostar) Tihomir Ognjanov (FK Spartak Subotica) Todor Veselinović (FK Vojvodina Novi Sad)	21
1956/1957	FK Crvena Zvezda Beograd	FK Partizan Beograd	Todor Veselinović (FK Vojvodina Novi Sad)	28
1957/1958	NK Dinamo Zagreb	FK Crvena Zvezda Beograd	Todor Veselinović (FK Vojvodina Novi Sad)	19
1958/1959	FK Crvena Zvezda Beograd	FK Crvena Zvezda Beograd	Bora Kostić (FK Crvena Zvezda Beograd)	25
1959/1960	FK Crvena Zvezda Beograd	NK Dinamo Zagreb	Bora Kostić (FK Crvena Zvezda Beograd)	19
1960/1961	FK Partizan Beograd	FK Vardar Skoplje	Zoran Prljinčević (FK Radnički Beograd) Todor Veselinović (FK Vojvodina Novi Sad)	16
1961/1962	FK Partizan Beograd	OFK Beograd	Dražan Jerković (NK Dinamo Zagreb)	16
1962/1963	FK Partizan Beograd	NK Dinamo Zagreb	Mišo Smajlović (FK Željezničar Sarajevo)	18
1963/1964	FK Crvena Zvezda Beograd	FK Crvena Zvezda Beograd	Asim Ferhatović (FK Sarajevo)	19
1964/1965	FK Partizan Beograd	NK Dinamo Zagreb	Zlatko Dračić (NK Zagreb)	23
1965/1966	FK Vojvodina Novi Sad	OFK Beograd	Petar Nadoveza (NK Hajduk Split)	21
1966/1967	FK Sarajevo	NK Hajduk Split	Mustafa Hasanagić (FK Partizan Beograd)	18
1967/1968	FK Crvena Zvezda Beograd	FK Crvena Zvezda Beograd	Slobodan Santrač (OFK Beograd)	22
1968/1969	FK Crvena Zvezda Beograd	NK Dinamo Zagreb	Vojin Lazarević (FK Crvena Zvezda Beograd)	22
1969/1970	FK Crvena Zvezda Beograd	FK Crvena Zvezda Beograd	Slobodan Santrač (OFK Beograd) Dušan Bajević (FK Velež Mostar)	20
1970/1971	NK Hajduk Split	FK Crvena Zvezda Beograd	Petar Nadoveza (NK Hajduk Split) Božo Janković (FK Željezničar Sarajevo)	20
1971/1972	FK Željezničar Sarajevo	NK Hajduk Split	Slobodan Santrač (OFK Beograd)	33
1972/1973	FK Crvena Zvezda Beograd	NK Hajduk Split	Slobodan Santrač (OFK Beograd) Vojin Lazarević (FK Crvena Zvezda Beograd)	25
1973/1974	NK Hajduk Split	NK Hajduk Split	Danilo Popivoda (Olimpija Ljubljana)	17
1974/1975	NK Hajduk Split	NK Hajduk Split	Dušan Savić (FK Crvena Zvezda Beograd) Boško Đorđević (FK Partizan Beograd)	20
1975/1976	FK Partizan Beograd	NK Hajduk Split	Nenad Bjeković (FK Partizan Beograd)	24
1976/1977	FK Crvena Zvezda Beograd	NK Rijeka	Zoran Filipović (FK Crvena Zvezda Beograd)	21
1977/1978	FK Partizan Beograd	NK Rijeka	Radomir Savić (FK Sarajevo)	21
1978/1979	NK Hajduk Split	NK Dinamo Zagreb	Dušan Savić (FK Crvena Zvezda Beograd)	24
1979/1980	FK Crvena Zvezda Beograd	FK Crvena Zvezda Beograd	Safet Sušić (FK Sarajevo) Dragoljub Kostić (FK Napredak Kruševac)	17
1980/1981	FK Crvena Zvezda Beograd	FK Velež Mostar	Milan Radović (NK Rijeka)	26
1981/1982	NK Dinamo Zagreb	FK Crvena Zvezda Beograd	Snješko Cerin (NK Dinamo Zagreb)	19

1982/1983	FK Partizan Beograd	NK Dinamo Zagreb	Sulejman Halilović (NK Dinamo Vinkovci)	18
1983/1984	FK Crvena Zvezda Beograd	NK Hajduk Split	Darko Pančev (FK Vardar Skoplje)	19
1984/1985	FK Sarajevo	FK Crvena Zvezda Beograd	Zlatko Vujović (NK Hajduk Split)	25
1985/1986	FK Partizan Beograd	FK Velež Mostar	Davor Čop (NK Dinamo Vinkovci)	20
1986/1987	FK Vardar Skoplje	NK Hajduk Split	Radmilo Mihajlović (FK Željezničar Sarajevo)	23
1987/1988	FK Crvena Zvezda Beograd	FK Borac Banja Luka	Duško Milinković (FK Rad Beograd)	16
1988/1989	FK Vojvodina Novi Sad	FK Partizan Beograd	Davor Šuker (NK Osijek)	18
1989/1990	FK Crvena Zvezda Beograd	FK Crvena Zvezda Beograd	Darko Pančev (FK Crvena Zvezda Beograd)	25
1990/1991	FK Crvena Zvezda Beograd	NK Hajduk Split	Darko Pančev (FK Crvena Zvezda Beograd)	34
1991/1992	FK Crvena Zvezda Beograd	*No competition*	Darko Pančev (FK Crvena Zvezda Beograd)	25

First League of Serbia and Montenegro (1992–2006)

	CHAMPIONS	CUP WINNERS	BEST GOALSCORERS	
1992/1993	FK Partizan Beograd	FK Crvena Zvezda Beograd	Anto Drobnjak (FK Crvena Zvezda Beograd) Vesko Mihajlović (FK Vojvodina Novi Sad)	22
1993/1994	FK Partizan Beograd	FK Partizan Beograd	Savo Milošević (FK Partizan Beograd)	21
1994/1995	FK Crvena Zvezda Beograd	FK Crvena Zvezda Beograd	Savo Milošević (FK Partizan Beograd)	30
1995/1996	FK Partizan Beograd	FK Crvena Zvezda Beograd	Vojislav Budimirović (FK Čukarički)	23
1996/1997	FK Partizan Beograd	FK Crvena Zvezda Beograd	Zoran Jovičić (FK Crvena Zvezda Beograd)	21
1997/1998	FK Obilić Beograd	FK Partizan Beograd	Saša Marković (FK Železnik Beograd/ FK Crvena Zvezda Beograd)	27
1998/1999	FK Partizan Beograd	FK Crvena Zvezda Beograd	Dejan Osmanović (FK Hajduk Kula)	16
1999/2000	FK Crvena Zvezda Beograd	FK Crvena Zvezda Beograd	Mateja Kežman (FK Partizan Beograd)	27
2000/2001	FK Crvena Zvezda Beograd	FK Partizan Beograd	Petar Divić (OFK Beograd)	27
2001/2002	FK Partizan Beograd	FK Crvena Zvezda Beograd	Zoran Đurašković (FK Mladost Lučani)	27
2002/2003	FK Partizan Beograd	FK Sartid Smederevo	Zvonimir Vukić (FK Partizan Beograd)	22
2003/2004	FK Crvena Zvezda Beograd	FK Crvena Zvezda Beograd	Nikola Žigić (FK Crvena Zvezda Beograd)	19
2004/2005	FK Partizan Beograd	FK Železnik Beograd	Marko Pantelić (FK Crvena Zvezda Beograd)	21
2005/2006	FK Crvena Zvezda Beograd	FK Crvena Zvezda Beograd	Srđan Radonjić (FK Partizan Beograd)	20

Serbian Superliga (since 2006)

	CHAMPIONS	CUP WINNERS	BEST GOALSCORERS	
2006/2007	FK Crvena Zvezda Beograd	FK Crvena Zvezda Beograd	Srđan Baljak (FK Banat Zrenjanin)	18
2007/2008	FK Partizan Beograd	FK Partizan Beograd	Nenad Jestrović (FK Crvena Zvezda Beograd)	13
2008/2009	FK Partizan Beograd	FK Partizan Beograd	Lamine Diarra (SEN, FK Partizan Beograd)	19
2009/2010	FK Partizan Beograd	FK Crvena Zvezda Beograd	Dragan Mrđa (FK Vojvodina Novi Sad)	22
2010/2011	FK Partizan Beograd	FK Partizan Beograd	Ivica Iliev (FK Partizan Beograd) Andrija Kaluđerović (FK Crvena Zvezda Beograd)	13
2011/2012	FK Partizan Beograd	FK Crvena Zvezda Beograd	Darko Spalević (FK Radnički Kragujevac)	19
2012/2013	FK Partizan Beograd	FK Jagodina	Miloš Stojanović (FK Jagodina)	19
2013/2014	FK Crvena Zvezda Beograd	FK Vojvodina Novi Sad	Dragan Mrđa (FK Crvena Zvezda Beograd)	19
2014/2015	FK Partizan Beograd	FK Čukarički	Patrick Friday Eze (NGA, FK Mladost Lučani)	15
2015/2016	FK Crvena Zvezda Beograd	FK Partizan Beograd	Aleksandar Katai (FK Crvena Zvezda Beograd)	21
2016/2017	FK Partizan Beograd	FK Partizan Beograd	Uroš Đurđević (FK Partizan Beograd) Leonardo da Silva Souza (BRA, FK Partizan Beograd)	24
2017/2018	FK Crvena Zvezda Beograd	FK Partizan Beograd	Aleksandar Pešić (FK Crvena Zvezda Beograd)	25
2018/2019	FK Crvena Zvezda Beograd	FK Partizan Beograd	Nermin Haskić (BIH, FK Radnički Niš)	24
2019/2020	FK Crvena Zvezda Beograd	FK Vojvodina Novi Sad	Nenad Lukić (TSC Bačka Topola) Vladimir Silađi (TSC Bačka Topola) Nikola Petković (FK Javor Ivanjica)	16

NATIONAL CHAMPIONSHIP
Serbian SuperLiga 2019/2020
(19.07.2019 – 20.06.2020)

Results

Round 1 [19-21.07.2019]
FK Voždovac - Bačka Topola 1-2(0-0)
Spartak Subotica - Rad Beograd 2-1(0-1)
FK Čukarički - FK Napredak 1-0(1-0)
Crvena Zvezda - FK Javor 2-0(2-0)
Mladost Lučani - Radnik Surdulica 2-1(0-1)
Vojvodina - FK Mačva 3-1(0-0)
FK Inđija - Partizan 0-1(0-1)
Radnički Niš - Proleter Novi Sad 3-0(2-0)

Round 2 [27-28.07.2019]
Bačka Topola - Mladost Lučani 5-1(3-0)
Crvena Zvezda - Radnički Niš 2-0(1-0)
FK Mačva - FK Inđija 2-2(0-1)
Proleter Novi Sad - FK Voždovac 2-2(0-0)
Radnik Surdulica - Spartak Subotica 4-0(2-0)
FK Napredak - Vojvodina 0-2(0-0)
Rad Beograd - FK Čukarički 2-3(2-1) [28.08.]
FK Javor - Partizan 0-2(0-1) [25.09.]

Round 3 [02-04.08.2019]
Mladost Lučani - Proleter Novi Sad 1-1(0-1)
FK Inđija - FK Napredak 1-0(0-0)
Radnički Niš - FK Javor 2-1(2-1)
Vojvodina - Rad Beograd 5-0(3-0)
FK Čukarički - Radnik Surdulica 1-0(1-0)
Partizan - FK Mačva 4-0(2-0)
Spartak Subotica - Bačka Topola 1-2(1-1)
Voždovac - Crvena Zvezda 1-3(1-2) [25.09.]

Round 4 [09-11.08.2019]
Crvena Zvezda - Mladost Lučani 2-0(2-0)
Bačka Topola - FK Čukarički 1-0(0-0)
FK Javor - FK Mačva 3-1(1-0)
Rad Beograd - FK Inđija 1-0(0-0)
Radnički Niš - FK Voždovac 2-1(1-0)
FK Napredak - Partizan 2-2(2-1)
Proleter Novi Sad - Spartak Subotica 0-1(0-1)
Radnik Surdulica - Vojvodina 0-4(0-3)

Round 5 [16-18.08.2019]
FK Voždovac - FK Javor 2-1(2-1)
FK Inđija - Radnik Surdulica 2-1(1-1)
FK Čukarički - Proleter Novi Sad 2-1(1-0)
Mladost Lučani - Radnički Niš 1-1(1-1)
Spartak Subotica - Crvena Zvezda 2-3(1-1)
Partizan - Rad Beograd 3-0(1-0)
FK Mačva - FK Napredak 0-1(0-0)
Vojvodina - Bačka Topola 2-2(0-0)

Round 6 [24-25.08.2019]
FK Voždovac - Mladost Lučani 2-0(1-0)
FK Javor - FK Napredak 2-2(1-0)
Proleter Novi Sad - Vojvodina 0-1(0-1)
Rad Beograd - FK Mačva 2-0(1-0)
Radnički Niš - Spartak Subotica 2-1(0-0)
Bačka Topola - FK Inđija 2-0(2-0)
Radnik Surdulica - Partizan 1-2(0-1) [15.12.]
Crvena Zvezda - Čukarički 3-1(1-1) [15.12.]

Round 7 [31.08.-01.09.2019]
Vojvodina - Crvena Zvezda 1-2(1-1)
FK Mačva - Radnik Surdulica 1-1(1-0)
Spartak Subotica - FK Voždovac 2-1(1-1)
FK Inđija - Proleter Novi Sad 1-2(1-1)
FK Čukarički - Radnički Niš 1-0(0-0)
Mladost Lučani - FK Javor 3-3(1-1)
FK Napredak - Rad Beograd 4-0(1-0)
Partizan - Bačka Topola 1-1(1-1)

Round 8 [13-15.09.2019]
Radnički Niš - Vojvodina 1-2(1-1)
Crvena Zvezda - FK Inđija 2-1(0-1)
FK Javor - Rad Beograd 1-1(0-0)
Radnik Surdulica - FK Napredak 1-4(1-2)
FK Voždovac - FK Čukarički 2-2(0-1)
Proleter Novi Sad - Partizan 0-3(0-0)
Bačka Topola - FK Mačva 0-0
Mladost Lučani - Spartak Subotica 2-0(1-0)

Round 9 [21-22.09.2019]
FK Inđija - Radnički Niš 0-1(0-1)
FK Čukarički - Mladost Lučani 1-0(0-0)
FK Napredak - Bačka Topola 1-3(0-2)
Rad Beograd - Radnik Surdulica 0-1(0-0)
Spartak Subotica - FK Javor 1-0(1-0)
FK Mačva - Proleter Novi Sad 0-1(0-0)
Vojvodina - FK Voždovac 1-2(0-0)
Partizan - Crvena Zvezda 2-0(0-0)

Round 10 [28-30.09.2019]
Radnički Niš - Partizan 1-4(1-2)
Crvena Zvezda - FK Mačva 3-1(3-0)
Bačka Topola - Rad Beograd 2-0(1-0)
Mladost Lučani - Vojvodina 1-2(1-1)
Proleter Novi Sad - FK Napredak 2-0(1-0)
FK Voždovac - FK Inđija 4-1(1-0)
Spartak Subotica - FK Čukarički 0-1(0-0)
FK Javor - Radnik Surdulica 0-0

Round 11 [04-06.10.2019]
Vojvodina - Spartak Subotica 2-0(2-0)
FK Čukarički - FK Javor 2-0(1-0)
FK Mačva - Radnički Niš 0-1(0-0)
Rad Beograd - Proleter Novi Sad 1-1(0-1)
Radnik Surdulica - Bačka Topola 1-0(0-0)
FK Inđija - Mladost Lučani 0-2(0-1)
FK Napredak - Crvena Zvezda 0-1(0-0)
Partizan - FK Voždovac 1-2(0-1)

Round 12 [18-19.10.2019]
FK Čukarički - Vojvodina 0-0
Crvena Zvezda - Rad Beograd 3-1(2-0)
Mladost Lučani - Partizan 1-0(0-0)
FK Voždovac - FK Mačva 2-0(1-0)
FK Javor - Bačka Topola 3-2(1-2)
Proleter Novi Sad - Radnik Surdulica 2-1(2-1)
Radnički Niš - FK Napredak 4-1(3-0)
Spartak Subotica - FK Inđija 3-0(2-0)

Round 13 [25-27.10.2019]
FK Napredak - FK Voždovac 1-1(0-0)
Radnik Surdulica - Crvena Zvezda 0-5(0-3)
FK Mačva - Mladost Lučani 0-1(0-1)
Rad Beograd - Radnički Niš 1-2(0-0)
Vojvodina - FK Javor 2-2(2-1)
FK Inđija - FK Čukarički 1-3(0-0)
Partizan - Spartak Subotica 4-0(3-0)
Bačka Topola - Proleter Novi Sad 1-1(1-1)

Round 14 [30.10.2019]
FK Čukarički - Partizan 2-1(1-0)
Radnički Niš - Radnik Surdulica 0-2(0-1)
Crvena Zvezda - Bačka Topola 3-1(2-0)
FK Voždovac - Rad Beograd 2-1(0-0)
FK Javor - Proleter Novi Sad 1-0(1-0)
Mladost Lučani - FK Napredak 0-1(0-0)
Spartak Subotica - FK Mačva 3-1(2-1)
Vojvodina - FK Inđija 1-0(1-0)

Round 15 [02-03.11.2019]
Partizan - Vojvodina 4-0(2-0)
Proleter Novi Sad - Crvena Zvezda 0-2(0-0)
FK Inđija - FK Javor 2-3(0-1)
Bačka Topola - Radnički Niš 2-0(0-0)
FK Mačva - FK Čukarički 0-0
FK Napredak - Spartak Subotica 0-1(0-1)
Rad Beograd - Mladost Lučani 0-0
Radnik Surdulica - FK Voždovac 2-2(0-0)

Round 16 [09-10.11.2019]
FK Napredak - FK Čukarički 3-1(0-0)
Rad Beograd - Spartak Subotica 2-0(2-0)
Radnik Surdulica - Mladost Lučani 0-1(0-1)
FK Mačva - Vojvodina 0-1(0-1)
Bačka Topola - FK Voždovac 2-2(1-1)
FK Javor - Crvena Zvezda 1-1(1-0)
Partizan - FK Inđija 3-0(1-0)
Proleter N. S. - Radnički Niš 1-1(0-1) [14.12.]

Round 17 [22-24.11.2019]
Partizan - FK Javor 6-2(4-2)
FK Čukarički - Rad Beograd 2-0(1-0)
FK Voždovac - Proleter Novi Sad 2-0(0-0)
Mladost Lučani - Bačka Topola 0-3(0-2)
Radnički Niš - Crvena Zvezda 0-2(0-1)
Vojvodina - FK Napredak 2-1(1-1)
FK Inđija - FK Mačva 0-0
Spartak Subotica - Radnik Surdulica 3-1(1-0)

Round 18 [29.11.-01.12.2019]
Proleter Novi Sad - Mladost Lučani 0-1(0-0)
Bačka Topola - Spartak Subotica 2-2(1-1)
FK Javor - Radnički Niš 0-7(0-2)
FK Napredak - FK Inđija 1-3(1-0)
Rad Beograd - Vojvodina 1-2(1-2)
Radnik Surdulica - FK Čukarički 3-3(2-3)
Crvena Zvezda - FK Voždovac 2-0(0-0)
FK Mačva - Partizan 0-2(0-1)

Round 19 [04.12.2019]
FK Inđija - Rad Beograd 1-0(1-0)
FK Čukarički - Bačka Topola 2-1(0-1)
FK Voždovac - Radnički Niš 1-0(0-0)
Mladost Lučani - Crvena Zvezda 0-1(0-0)
FK Mačva - FK Javor 2-1(2-1)
Partizan - FK Napredak 2-3(2-1)
Spartak Subotica - Proleter Novi Sad 4-1(1-1)
Vojvodina - Radnik Surdulica 1-0(0-0)

Round 20 [07-08.12.2019]
Crvena Zvezda - Spartak Subotica 3-1(2-1)
Rad Beograd - Partizan 1-2(1-1)
Bačka Topola - Vojvodina 2-0(1-0)
FK Javor - FK Voždovac 1-2(1-1)
FK Napredak - FK Mačva 2-1(1-0)
Proleter Novi Sad - FK Čukarički 2-1(1-0)
Radnički Niš - Mladost Lučani 3-0(1-0)
Radnik Surdulica - FK Inđija 2-0(0-0)

Round 21 [15-16.02.2020]
FK Inđija - Bačka Topola 1-1(0-0)
FK Čukarički - Crvena Zvezda 0-2(0-2)
Mladost Lučani - FK Voždovac 2-1(1-0)
FK Napredak - FK Javor 1-1(0-0)
FK Mačva - Rad Beograd 1-0(1-0)
Vojvodina - Proleter Novi Sad 1-0(0-0)
Partizan - Radnik Surdulica 3-0(1-0)
Spartak Subotica - Radnički Niš 1-1(1-1)

Round 22 [21-22.02.2020]
FK Voždovac - Spartak Subotica 2-3(2-0)
FK Javor - Mladost Lučani 1-2(0-1)
Bačka Topola - Partizan 1-1(0-0)
Proleter Novi Sad - FK Inđija 1-0(0-0)
Rad Beograd - FK Napredak 2-0(2-0)
Radnički Niš - FK Čukarički 2-0(0-0)
Radnik Surdulica - FK Mačva 2-2(0-0)
Crvena Zvezda - Vojvodina 2-0(1-0)

Round 23 [26.02.2020]
Spartak Subotica - Mladost Lučani 3-1(1-0)
FK Inđija - Crvena Zvezda 1-1(1-0)
FK Čukarički - FK Voždovac 2-1(2-0)
FK Mačva - Bačka Topola 0-1(0-1)
FK Napredak - Radnik Surdulica 0-1(0-0)
Partizan - Proleter Novi Sad 3-1(2-0)
Rad Beograd - FK Javor 1-1(0-0)
Vojvodina - Radnički Niš 3-0(1-0)

Round 24 [01.03.2020]
FK Voždovac - Vojvodina 1-2(1-1)
Bačka Topola - FK Napredak 2-1(1-0)
FK Javor - Spartak Subotica 2-2(1-1)
Mladost Lučani - FK Čukarički 1-0(0-0)
Proleter Novi Sad - FK Mačva 1-1(0-0)
Radnički Niš - FK Inđija 2-1(0-0)
Radnik Surdulica - Rad Beograd 1-0(1-0)
Crvena Zvezda - Partizan 0-0

Round 25 [06-08.03.2020]
FK Čukarički - Spartak Subotica 4-1(3-0)
FK Mačva - Crvena Zvezda 0-3(0-3)
FK Napredak - Proleter Novi Sad 0-0
Rad Beograd - Bačka Topola 3-4(1-3)
Radnik Surdulica - FK Javor 2-0(1-0)
Vojvodina - Mladost Lučani 2-1(0-0)
Partizan - Radnički Niš 1-0(0-0)
FK Inđija - FK Voždovac 3-0(1-0)

Round 26 [14.03.2020]
Bačka Topola - Radnik Surdulica 2-1(1-1)
FK Voždovac - Partizan 1-2(0-0)
FK Javor - FK Čukarički 2-2(1-1)
Mladost Lučani - FK Inđija 2-1(1-1)
Radnički Niš - FK Mačva 3-1(1-1)
Spartak Subotica - Vojvodina 0-0
Crvena Zvezda - FK Napredak 3-0(1-0)
Proleter Novi Sad - Rad Beograd 5-0(1-0)

Round 27 [29-31.05.2020]
FK Inđija - Spartak Subotica 1-2(1-1)
Vojvodina - FK Čukarički 1-1(1-0)
Rad Beograd - Crvena Zvezda 0-5(0-3)
Radnik Surdulica - Proleter Novi Sad 1-1(0-1)
Partizan - Mladost Lučani 4-1(2-1)
FK Napredak - Radnik Surdulica 1-0(1-0)
Bačka Topola - FK Javor 6-1(2-0)
FK Mačva - FK Voždovac 0-1(0-0)

Round 28 [05-07.06.2020]
Proleter Novi Sad - Bačka Topola 1-3(0-1)
FK Voždovac - FK Napredak 1-0(0-0)
FK Javor - Vojvodina 1-3(0-0)
Spartak Subotica - Partizan 3-2(1-2)
Crvena Zvezda - Radnik Surdulica 4-1(2-1)
FK Čukarički - FK Inđija 0-1(0-0)
Radnički Niš - Rad Beograd 4-3(2-2)
Mladost Lučani - FK Mačva 2-1(1-1)

Round 29 [12-14.06.2020]
Proleter Novi Sad - FK Javor 2-2(1-1)
Rad Beograd - FK Voždovac 0-2(0-0)
FK Mačva - Spartak Subotica 1-4(0-2)
FK Napredak - Mladost Lučani 1-0(1-0)
Radnik Surdulica - Radnički Niš 2-4(1-1)
FK Inđija - Vojvodina 2-0(1-0)
Bačka Topola - Crvena Zvezda 2-1(2-0)
Partizan - FK Čukarički 4-1(3-0)

Round 30 [18-20.06.2020]
Mladost Lučani - Rad Beograd 2-0(0-0)
FK Voždovac - Radnik Surdulica 1-1(1-0)
Spartak Subotica - FK Napredak 0-2(0-1)
Vojvodina - Partizan 1-0(1-0)
Radnički Niš - Bačka Topola 3-1(3-1)
FK Javor - FK Inđija 5-0(2-0)
FK Čukarički - FK Mačva 3-1(1-1)
Crvena Zvezda - Proleter Novi Sad 2-1(2-1)

The Play-off stage was cancelled due to Covid-19 pandemic. No teams were relegated.

					Final Standings										
					Total			**Home**				**Away**			
1. **FK Crvena Zvezda Beograd**	30	25	3	2	68 - 18	78	14	1	0	36 - 8	11	2	2	32 - 10
2. FK Partizan Beograd	30	20	4	6	69 - 25	64	12	1	2	45 - 11	8	3	4	24 - 14
3. FK Vojvodina Novi Sad	30	19	5	6	47 - 27	62	10	3	2	28 - 12	9	2	4	19 - 15
4. FK TSC Bačka Topola	30	17	8	5	59 - 34	59	10	5	0	32 - 11	7	3	5	27 - 23
5. FK Radnički Niš	30	16	4	10	51 - 37	52	11	0	4	32 - 20	5	4	6	19 - 17
6. FK Čukarički Beograd	30	15	6	9	42 - 36	51	12	1	2	23 - 9	3	5	7	19 - 27
7. FK Spartak Subotica	30	14	4	12	46 - 48	46	9	2	4	28 - 17	5	2	8	18 - 31
8. FK Voždovac Beograd	30	13	6	11	45 - 41	45	8	2	5	25 - 18	5	4	6	20 - 23
9. FK Mladost Lučani	30	13	4	13	31 - 40	43	8	3	4	20 - 16	5	1	9	11 - 24
10. FK Napredak Kruševac	30	9	6	15	33 - 41	33	4	5	6	17 - 18	5	1	9	16 - 23
11. FK Radnik Surdulica	30	8	7	15	34 - 50	31	5	4	6	22 - 28	3	3	9	12 - 22
12. FK Proleter Novi Sad	30	7	9	14	30 - 42	30	5	4	6	19 - 19	2	5	8	11 - 23
13. FK Javor Ivanjica	30	6	10	14	43 - 62	28	5	5	5	25 - 26	1	5	9	18 - 36
14. FK Inđija	30	7	4	19	26 - 48	25	5	3	7	16 - 17	2	1	12	10 - 31
15. FK Rad Beograd	30	4	3	23	23 - 63	15	4	3	8	17 - 23	0	0	15	6 - 40
16. FK Mačva Šabac	30	2	7	21	18 - 53	13	2	3	10	7 - 20	0	4	11	11 - 33

Top goalscorers:	
16 **Nenad Lukić**	***TSC Bačka Topola***
16 **Vladimir Silađi**	***TSC Bačka Topola***
16 **Nikola Petković**	***FK Javor Ivanjica***
15 Stefan Mihajlović	*FK Radnički Niš*
13 El Fardou Mohamed Ben Nabouhane (COM)	*FK Crvena Zvezda Beograd*

NATIONAL CUP
Kup Srbije 2019/2020

First Round [25-26.09./09-10.10.2019]

FK Sinđelić Beograd - FK Zemun Beograd	0-0; 4-2 pen		FK Mačva Šabac - FK Metalac Gornji Milanovac	1-0(1-0)
FK Budućnost Dobanovci - FK Radnički Niš	1-4(1-3)		FK Čukarički Beograd - OFK Žarkovo	3-1(3-0)
FK Napredak - FK TSC Bačka Topola	1-1; 3-4 pen		FK Spartak Subotica - FK Novi Pazar	2-0(1-0)
FK Zlatibor Čajetina - FK Vojvodina Novi Sad	1-4(0-2)		FK Trayal Kruševac - FK Radnik Surdulica	2-3(1-2)
FK Inđija - FK Dinamo Vranje	2-0(2-0)		FK Vodojaža - FK Partizan Beograd	0-6(0-1)
OFK Beograd - FK Rad Beograd	3-2(2-1)		FK Proleter Novi Sad - FK Javor Ivanjica	2-1(0-1)
FK Bratstvo 1946 - FK Mladost Lučani	1-3(0-2)		FK Voždovac Beograd - FK Teleoptik Zemun	2-2; 7-8 pen
OFK Bačka Palanka - FK Radnički 1923 Kragujevac	1-0(0-0)		FK Trepča - FK Crvena Zvezda Beograd	0-8(0-2)

1/8-Finals [23.10/20.11.2019/10.03.2020]

FK Radnički Niš - OFK Bačka Bačka Palanka	2-0(0-0)		FK Mladost Lučani - FK TSC Bačka Topola	1-1; 5-4 pen
FK Teleoptik Zemun - FK Čukarički Beograd	0-1(0-1)		FK Vojvodina Novi Sad - FK Sinđelić Beograd	4-0(2-0)
FK Inđija - FK Proleter Novi Sad	2-1(2-0)		FK Crvena Zvezda Beograd - FK Mačva Šabac	1-0(0-0)
OFK Beograd - FK Radnik Surdulica	1-2(1-1)		FK Partizan Beograd - FK Spartak Subotica	4-0(1-0)

Quarter-Finals [02-03.06.2020]

FK Inđija - FK Crvena Zvezda Beograd	1-2(0-2)		FK Radnik Surdulica - FK Partizan Beograd	1-2(1-2)
FK Čukarički Beograd - FK Radnički Niš	3-2(1-2)		FK Vojvodina Novi Sad - Mladost Lučani	0-0; 5-4 pen

Semi-Finals [10.06.2020]

FK Čukarički Beograd - FK Vojvodina Novi Sad	0-1(0-1)		FK Partizan Beograd - FK Crvena Zvezda Beograd	1-0(0-0)

Final

24.06.2020; Stadion Čair, Niš; Referee: Danilo Grujić; Attendance: 5,000

FK Vojvodina Novi Sad - FK Partizan Beograd   **2-2(1-0,2-2,2-2); 4-2 on penalties**

Vojvodina: Emil Rockov, Siniša Saničanin, Stefan Đorđević, Nikola Andrić, Slavko Bralić, Aranđel Stojković, Nikola Drinčić, Petar Bojić (81.Lazar Stojsavljević), Miljan Vukadinović (66.Miodrag Gemović), Nemanja Čović (81.Dejan Zukić), Momčilo Mrkaić (55.Mladen Devetak). Trainer: Nenad Lalatović.
Please note: Nikola Simić was sent off on the bench (120).

Partizan: Strahinja Pavlović, Bojan Ostojić (46.Uroš Vitas), Slobodan Urošević, Nemanja Miletić, Bibras Natcho, Saša Zdjelar, Aleksandar Šćekić (46.Seydouba Soumah; 76.Lazar Pavlović), Slobodan Stanojlović, Umar Sadiq, Takuma Asano (72.Bojan Matić), Lazar Marković (32.Filip Stevanović). Trainer: Savo Milošević.
Please note: Nemanja Stevanović was sent off on the bench (120).

Goals: 1-0 Miljan Vukadinović (38), 2-0 Petar Bojić (56), 2-1 Filip Stevanović (80), 2-2 Strahinja Pavlović (90+6).

Penalties: Bibras Natcho 0-1; Aranđel Stojković 1-1; Uroš Vitas (missed); Miodrag Gemović 2-1; Filip Stevanović 2-2; Mladen Devetak 3-2; Saša Zdjelar (missed); Stefan Đorđević 4-2.

THE CLUBS 2019/2020

Fudbalski Klub Crvena Zvezda Beograd

Founded:	04.03.1945		
Stadium:	Stadion „Rajko Mitić", Beograd (55,538)		
Trainer:	Vladan Milojević		09.03.1970
[21.12.2019]	Dejan Stanković		11.09.1978

Goalkeepers:	DOB	M	(s)	G
Milan Borjan (CAN)	23.10.1987	26		
Zoran Popović	28.05.1988	4		
Defenders:	**DOB**	**M**	**(s)**	**G**
Srđan Babić	22.04.1996	10	(1)	3
Miloš Degenek (AUS)	28.04.1994	20	(3)	2
Milan Gajić	28.01.1996	14	(1)	1
Marko Gobeljić	13.09.1992	16	(1)	2
Jander Ribeiro Santana (BRA)	08.07.1988	7	(1)	1
Marko Konatar	25.03.2000	1		
Nemanja Milunović	31.05.1989	18	(2)	2
Radovan Pankov	05.08.1995	18	(5)	1
Milan Rodić	02.04.1991	17	(1)	
Filip Stojković (MNE)	22.01.1993	1		
Midfielders:	**DOB**	**M**	**(s)**	**G**
José Alberto Cañas Ruiz Herrera (ESP)	27.05.1987	9		1
Mateo Ezequiel García (ARG)	10.09.1996	11	(4)	4
Željko Gavrić	05.12.2000	8	(1)	1
Mirko Ivanić (MNE)	13.09.1993	10	(9)	2

	DOB	M	(s)	G
Dušan Jovančić	19.10.1990	10	(4)	
Branko Jovičić	18.03.1993	4	(3)	1
Marko Marin (GER)	13.03.1989	12		3
Veljko Nikolić	29.08.1999	10	(1)	1
Njegoš Petrović	18.07.1999	15	(2)	1
Sékou Sanogo (CIV)	05.05.1989		(1)	
Veljko Simić	17.02.1995	5	(12)	3
Miloš Vulić	19.08.1996	12	(9)	2
Forwards:	**DOB**	**M**	**(s)**	**G**
Richmond Boakye (GHA)	28.01.1993	8	(2)	1
El Fardou Mohamed Ben Nabouhane (COM)	10.06.1989	21		13
Milan Jevtović	13.06.1993	4	(2)	2
Nikola Krstović (MNE)	05.04.2000	1	(5)	
Milan Pavkov	09.02.1994	11	(9)	7
Andrija Radulović	03.07.2002		(3)	1
António Manuel Fernandes Mendes „Tomané" (POR)	23.10.1992	14	(4)	5
Rajiv van La Parra (NED)	04.06.1991	3	(1)	
Aleksa Vukanović	18.06.1992	10	(10)	6

Fudbalski Klub Čukarički Beograd

Founded: 04.07.1926 (*as Čukarički SK*)
Stadium: Stadion Čukarički, Beograd (4,070)
Trainer: Aleksandar Veselinović   23.05.1970

Goalkeepers:	DOB	M	(s)	G
Nemanja Belić	24.04.1987	9		
Đorđe Petrović	08.10.1999	21		
Defenders:	**DOB**	**M**	**(s)**	**G**
Miroslav Bogosavac	14.10.1996	12		1
Nikola Ćirković	04.12.1991	24		
Dimitrije Kamenović	16.07.2000	13	(4)	
Boris Kopitović (MNE)	17.09.1994	1		
Miloš Ostojić	03.08.1991	17		
Darko Puškarić	13.07.1985	9	(1)	
Stefan Radojičić	30.05.2001	1	(1)	
Miladin Stevanović	11.02.1996	4	(1)	
Stefan Šapić	26.02.1997	29		4
Stefan Veličković	17.01.1999	10		
Midfielders:	**DOB**	**M**	**(s)**	**G**
Kosta Aleksić	09.03.1998		(9)	
Marko Docić	21.04.1993	19	(2)	7
Uros Drezgić	04.10.2002	1	(1)	
Aleksandar Đorđević	20.12.1999	7	(5)	
Mitar Ergelaš	20.08.2002		(3)	
Uroš Ignjatović	18.02.2001		(1)	
Asmir Kajević (MNE)	15.02.1990	14	(11)	2
Stefan Kovač	14.01.1999	29		1
Jovan Lukić	20.01.2002		(2)	
Viktor Lukić	06.10.2000		(1)	
Luka Luković	16.10.1996	1	(3)	
Samuel Owusu (GHA)	28.03.1996	2		
Luka Stojanović	04.01.1994	16	(3)	9
Luka Zorić	02.03.1998	5	(3)	
Forwards:	**DOB**	**M**	**(s)**	**G**
Veljko Birmančević	05.03.1998	19	(7)	2
Stefan Cvetković	12.01.1998		(1)	
Petar Mićin	29.09.1998	4	(7)	
Ibrahima N'Diaye (SEN)	01.02.1994	19	(5)	2
Bojica Nikčević (MNE)	04.02.2000		(4)	
Eze Vincent Okeuhie (NGA)	06.06.1993	3	(1)	
Dilan Andrés Ortíz Aragón (COL)	15.03.2000	1	(5)	1
Milan Savić (BIH)	19.05.2000	1	(2)	
Slobodan Tedić	13.04.2000	26	(1)	9
Milutin Vidosavljević	21.02.2001	13	(11)	3

Fudbalski klub Inđija

Founded: 1933
Stadium: Stadion Inđija, Inđija (4,500)
Trainer: Srđan Blagojević   06.06.1973
[23.10.2019]   Aleksandar Janjić   28.02.1969

Goalkeepers:	DOB	M	(s)	G
Marko Knežević	29.03.1989	1		
Miloje Preković	07.06.1991	27		
Dejan Stanivuković	19.06.1994	2		
Defenders:	**DOB**	**M**	**(s)**	**G**
Nikola Anđelković	18.12.1992	3		
Luka Cucin	24.11.1998	10		
Luka Čermelj	29.07.1995	11	(3)	1
Nikola Dimitrijević	10.05.1991	16	(5)	
Miljan Ilić	23.05.1993	19	(4)	
Nikola Janković	07.06.1993	3	(1)	
Mihailo Jovanović	15.02.1989	6	(1)	1
Ivan Josović	27.12.1989	9	(2)	
Žarko Marković	28.01.1987		(1)	
Miloš Mihajlov	15.12.1982	9		
Ivan Rogač	18.06.1992	20		1
Nemanja Vidić (SVN)	06.08.1989	27		1
Midfielders:	**DOB**	**M**	**(s)**	**G**
Mihajlo Banjac	10.11.1999	8	(12)	1
Ognjen Bjeličić	29.07.1997	17		
Nemanja Bosančić	01.03.1995	17	(6)	1
Srđan Dimitrov	28.07.1992	13	(6)	2
Milan Janjić	02.09.1992	14	(7)	
Aleksa Jovanović	27.05.1999	3	(1)	
Ognjen Krasić	09.04.1988	4	(2)	1
Vladan Milosavljev	01.02.1987	16	(8)	2
Vojin Pavlović (MNE)	09.11.1993	2		
Stefan Purtić	06.08.1998	5	(5)	2
Branislav Tomić	12.02.1995	14	(2)	3
Boško Vrastanović	22.04.1995		(3)	
Forwards:	**DOB**	**M**	**(s)**	**G**
Aleksa Andrejić	24.01.1993		(1)	
Nebojša Bastajić	20.08.1990	20	(5)	3
Brana Ilić	16.02.1985	19	(7)	3
Vasilije Janjić	25.01.1995	6	(7)	1
Saša Jovanović	30.08.1993	4	(3)	
Miroslav Marković	04.11.1989	4	(2)	1
Filip Rajevac	21.06.1992	1	(4)	1

Fudbalski klub Javor Ivanjica

Founded: 1912
Stadium: Stadion Ivanjica, Ivanjica (3,000)
Trainer: Igor Bondžulić   05.10.1980

Goalkeepers:	DOB	M	(s)	G
Nemanja Jevrić	30.05.1997	5		
Đorđe Lazović	16.11.1992	24		
Rastko Šuljagić	27.01.1995	1		
Defenders:	**DOB**	**M**	**(s)**	**G**
Aleksa Amanović (MKD)	24.10.1996	19		
Boban Đerić (BIH)	20.08.1993	11	(3)	
Veljko Filipović	11.10.1999		(1)	
Marko Jevremović	23.02.1996	29		1
Marko Kolaković	09.02.1993	19		1
Filip Pavišić	15.01.1994	16	(3)	2
Luka Radivojević	09.11.1999	9	(1)	1
Ivan Rogač	18.06.1992	5	(2)	2
Nenad Sević	25.04.1996	11	(10)	2
Midfielders:	**DOB**	**M**	**(s)**	**G**
Zeljko Basarić	08.03.2001		(2)	
Nikola Cuckić	11.04.1997	5	(4)	
Ivan Cvetković	12.02.1981	1	(15)	
Dino Dolmagić	26.02.1994	21		2
Nikola Kuveljić	06.04.1997	18		3
Luka Luković	16.10.1996	7	(1)	1
Miroslav Maričić	01.08.1998	20	(6)	2
Nikola Petković	23.09.1996	30		16
Nedeljko Piščević	20.04.1995	28		1
Zoran Švonja	04.10.1996		(3)	
Vanja Zvekanov	25.05.2000	4	(6)	2
Forwards:	**DOB**	**M**	**(s)**	**G**
Vladimir Jovanović	06.03.2001		(7)	
Alija Krnić (MNE)	02.01.1998	11	(8)	2
Ivan Marković	23.12.1991	1	(2)	
Nikola Milošević	08.12.1996		(8)	
Nemanja Mladenović	03.03.1993	4	(3)	
Momčilo Mrkaić (BIH)	21.09.1990	19		2
Lazar Nikolić	01.08.1999	9	(4)	
Saša Varga	19.02.1993	3	(3)	1

Fudbalski Klub Mačva Šabac

Founded:	1919	
Stadium:	Stadion Gradski, Šabac (8,000)	
Trainer:	Darko Tešović	03.08.1970
[27.08.2019]	Marko Mićović	13.10.1974
[09.09.2019]	Dragan Aničić	04.11.1970

Goalkeepers:	DOB	M	(s)	G
Miloš Gordić	05.03.2000	3		
Dušan Puletić	05.01.1989	20		
Mladen Živković	26.08.1989	7		
Defenders:	**DOB**	**M**	**(s)**	**G**
Nikola Dukić	10.01.1998	9	(3)	
Marko Jevtić	17.02.1996	13	(1)	
Slavko Marić	07.03.1984	11	(2)	
Marko Mijailović	14.08.1997	26	(1)	1
Filip Pejović	26.06.1982	26		
Igor Ristivojević	08.08.1988	12	(2)	
Nemanja Tošić	23.01.1997	18		
Midfielders:	**DOB**	**M**	**(s)**	**G**
Miloš Adamović	19.06.1988	22	(1)	5
Filip Božić (BIH)	09.03.1999	11	(6)	2
Filip Čermelj	28.09.1998		(2)	
Stefan Ilić	27.07.1998	2	(4)	
Lazar Ivić	24.10.1992	18	(1)	
Predrag Jeremić	22.11.1987	2		
Nenad Jovanović	12.05.1988	26	(1)	1

	DOB	M	(s)	G
Branislav Knežević	21.07.2002		(4)	
Nikola Kovačević	14.04.1994	3	(6)	
Nenad Marinković	28.09.1988	9	(1)	
Branislav Marković	17.03.1997	17	(4)	2
Ognjen Mijailović	30.04.2003		(3)	
Stefan Milosavljević	09.05.1992	15	(4)	
Nikola Milinković	18.02.1991	7	(4)	
Ivan Obrovac	08.12.1986	4	(4)	
Aleksandar Stevanović	14.07.1996	4	(7)	1
Mile Vujasin	10.10.1993	4	(5)	
Forwards:	**DOB**	**M**	**(s)**	**G**
Nikola Aščerić	19.04.1991	10	(6)	1
Aleksandar Đoković	16.12.1991	4	(1)	
Petar Gigić	07.03.1997	7	(1)	2
Marko Jeremić	16.07.1993		(3)	
Branko Mihajlović	20.02.1991	3	(4)	1
Igor Stanojević	24.10.1991	1	(5)	
Đorđe Šušnjar	18.02.1992	11	(6)	
Stefan Trimanović	23.01.2001		(1)	
Miloš Zukanović	08.02.1996	5	(4)	1

Fudbalski Klub Mladost Lučani

Founded:	1952	
Stadium:	Stadion Mladost, Lučani (8,000)	
Trainer:	Goran Stanić (MKD)	18.09.1972

Goalkeepers:	DOB	M	(s)	G
Damjan Knežević	08.01.2000	4		
Dragan Rosić	22.09.1996	4		
Zlatko Zečević	10.08.1983	18		
Mladen Živković	26.08.1989	4		
Defenders:	**DOB**	**M**	**(s)**	**G**
Nikola Andrić	23.05.1992	19		
Petar Jovanović (BIH)	12.07.1982	7		
Nikola Leković	19.12.1989	19		
Nemanja Mićević	28.01.1999	13	(1)	
Ivan Milošević	03.11.1984	13		
Ivan Pešić	07.07.1989	2	(12)	
Nikola Radović	05.01.2000	2	(1)	
Uroš Sindić	19.01.1986	7	(9)	
Miloš Šatara (BIH)	28.10.1995	26		3
Mihailo Vesnić	05.01.2001		(1)	
Midfielders:	**DOB**	**M**	**(s)**	**G**
Lazar Jovanović	13.07.1993	23	(1)	3
Veljko Kijevcanin	03.08.1999	2	(2)	
Damjan Krajisnik (BIH)	24.04.1997	9		1
Vukasin Marković	13.06.2001		(3)	
Bogdan Milošević	17.02.1989	27	(1)	

	DOB	M	(s)	G
Ivan Obrovac	08.12.1986		(5)	
Predrag Pavlović	19.08.1986	19	(2)	5
Miloš Ristić	06.04.1994	1	(2)	
Danilo Sekulić	18.04.1990	7	(2)	
Lazar Selenić	21.08.1999	4	(2)	
Marko Stanić	04.06.2001		(2)	
Filip Stojanović	19.05.1988	7	(7)	
Filip Žunić	16.05.2002		(1)	
Forwards:	**DOB**	**M**	**(s)**	**G**
Viktor Amos (NGA)	05.03.1999		(1)	
Đorđe Babić	04.08.2000	3	(2)	2
Milan Bojović	13.04.1987	16	(2)	7
Eliomar (BRA)	16.03.1988	16	(6)	4
Aleksandar Ješić	13.09.1994	8	(1)	
Nemanja Kos	30.11.2002		(1)	
Ognjen Milanović	04.10.2001		(1)	
Obiora Odita (NGA)	14.05.1983	18	(6)	1
Nenad Perović	20.06.2002	2		
Vladimir Radivojević	04.02.1986	26		5
Zakaria Isa Suraka (GHA)	17.01.1996	3	(4)	
Ibrahim Tanko (GHA)	30.04.1999	1	(9)	

Fudbalski Klub Napredak Kruševac

Founded:	08.12.1946	
Stadium:	Stadion Mladost, Kruševac (10,331)	
Trainer:	Predrag Rogan	02.08.1974
[11.12.2019]	Ivan Stefanović	09.08.1975
[12.03.2020]	Dragan Ivanović	02.12.1969

Goalkeepers:	DOB	M	(s)	G
Marko Kordić (MNE)	22.02.1995	9		
Marko Milošević	07.02.1991	20		
Aleksandar Stanković	17.02.1998	1		
Defenders:	**DOB**	**M**	**(s)**	**G**
Nikola Aksentijević	09.03.1993	22	(1)	
Mitar Ćuković (MNE)	06.04.1995	14	(3)	
Filip Kovačević	26.03.2000		(1)	
Nemanja Lakić-Pešić	22.09.1991	4	(1)	
Miloš Milovanović	09.12.1987	27		
Milan Obradović	27.12.1999	13	(6)	
Tomislav Pajović	15.03.1986	15	(1)	
Uroš Rasković	02.09.2000	1		
Dušan Stević	25.07.1995	5		
Midfielders:	**DOB**	**M**	**(s)**	**G**
Kosta Aleksić	09.03.1998	2	(3)	
Regis Baha (CMR)	21.10.1996	7	(4)	
Miroslav Bjeloš	29.10.1990	20	(3)	6
Aleksandar Desančić	20.02.1996	7	(7)	
Ivan Đorić	07.07.1995	11	(7)	

	DOB	M	(s)	G
Nikola Eskić (BIH)	19.12.1997	15	(5)	1
Igor Ivanović	28.07.1997	18		6
Nemanja Kojić	03.02.1990	7	(2)	1
Jovan Markoski	23.06.1980	6	(9)	
Aleksandar Mesarović	27.09.1998		(1)	
Miloš Mijić	22.11.1989	8	(1)	1
Miloš Ožegović	11.05.1992	21	(1)	1
Milan Spremo	27.04.1995	22	(3)	1
Miljan Vukadinović (CZE)	27.12.1992	5	(8)	4
Milan Vušurović (MNE)	18.04.1995	4	(1)	
Đuro Zec	06.03.1990	19		4
Forwards:	**DOB**	**M**	**(s)**	**G**
Aleksandar Deljanin	05.10.2002		(1)	
Nenad Gavrić	12.12.1991	13	(5)	4
Andrej Ilić	03.04.2000	3	(13)	
Marko Mrkić	20.08.1996	2	(1)	1
Ibrahima N'Diaye (SEN)	01.02.1994	1		
Aboubakar Oumarou (CMR)	04.01.1987	1		
Marko Pavićević	03.09.1986	5	(2)	1
Dejan Vidić	10.08.1993	2	(2)	

Fudbalski Klub Partizan Beograd

Founded: 04.10.1945
Stadium: Stadion Partizan, Beograd (32,710)
Trainer: Savo Milošević   01.09.1973

Goalkeepers:	DOB	M	(s)	G
Filip Kljajić	16.08.1990	2		
Aleksandar Popović	27.09.1999	1		
Nemanja Stevanović	08.05.1992	2		
Vladimir Stojković	28.07.1983	25		
Defenders:	**DOB**	**M**	**(s)**	**G**
Rajko Brežančić	21.08.1989	10	(2)	1
Dominik Dinga	07.04.1998		(1)	
Nemanja Miletić	16.01.1991	23		2
Bojan Ostojić	12.02.1984	24		1
Strahinja Pavlović	24.05.2001	26		1
Periša Pešukić (MNE)	07.12.1997	1		
Zlatan Šehović	08.08.2000		(1)	
Slobodan Urošević	15.04.1994	22		1
Uroš Vitas	06.07.1992	4	(1)	1
Igor Vujačić (MNE)	08.08.1994	6	(2)	
Midfielders:	**DOB**	**M**	**(s)**	**G**
Bibras Natcho (ISR)	18.02.1988	20	(2)	8
Lazar Pavlović	02.11.2001	3	(13)	
Milan Smiljanić	19.11.1986	2	(5)	
Seydouba Soumah (GUI)	11.06.1991	17	(8)	10
Slobodan Stanojlović	28.12.2001		(1)	
Aleksandar Šćekić (MNE)	12.12.1991	18	(5)	2
Zoran Tošić	28.04.1987	13	(4)	5
Saša Zdjelar	20.03.1995	28		1
Forwards:	**DOB**	**M**	**(s)**	**G**
Takuma Asano (JPN)	10.11.1994	21	(2)	4
Petar Gigić	07.03.1997		(1)	
Đorđe Ivanović (CRO)	20.11.1995	3	(12)	3
Strahinja Jovanović	01.06.1999		(1)	
Nikola Lakčević	28.10.1999		(9)	
Aleksandar Lutovac	28.06.1997	6	(2)	
Lazar Marković	02.03.1994	7	(3)	5
Bojan Matić	22.12.1991	4	(6)	3
Ognjen Ožegović	09.06.1994	3	(2)	2
Umar Sadiq (NGA)	02.02.1997	22	(2)	12
Filip Stevanović	25.09.2002	17	(8)	7
Nikola Štulić	08.09.2001		(2)	

Fudbalski Klub Proleter Novi Sad

Founded: 1951
Stadium: Stadion Karađorđe, Novi Sad (14,458)
Trainer: Milic Čurčić   26.01.1981
[17.09.2019] Branko Žigić   30.12.1981

Goalkeepers:	DOB	M	(s)	G
Nikola Petrić	11.05.1991	30		
Defenders:	**DOB**	**M**	**(s)**	**G**
Aleksandar Andrejević	28.03.1992	27		1
Miljan Jablan	30.01.1985	1	(1)	
Dušan Joković	04.07.1999	6	(1)	2
Branislav Jovanović	21.09.1985	19	(1)	3
Stefan Jovanović	07.04.1994	7	(1)	
Bojan Kovačević	28.04.1996	15		
Leandro Climaco Pinto (BRA)	24.01.1994	24		1
Illia Lukashevich (BLR)	01.08.1998	2	(1)	
Ognjen Mitrović	30.06.1999	12		
Aleksandar Tanasin	15.11.1991	24		
Artur Yedigaryan (ARM)	26.06.1987	2	(1)	
Midfielders:	**DOB**	**M**	**(s)**	**G**
Siniša Babić	13.02.1991	19	(2)	5
Milorad Balabanović	18.01.1990	15	(6)	1
Petar Karaklajić	01.02.2000	8	(1)	
Slobodan Novaković	15.10.1986	4	(12)	1
Marko Pantić	18.06.1998	1	(5)	
Aleksa Pejić	09.07.1999	17	(9)	2
Uglješa Radinović	25.08.1993	11	(8)	2
Goran Smiljanić	31.01.1990	2	(3)	
Srđan Šćepanović	23.10.1998	9	(10)	1
Forwards:	**DOB**	**M**	**(s)**	**G**
Stefan Čolović	16.04.1994	19		1
Lazar Marjanović	08.09.1989	22	(7)	1
Milan Mirosavljev	24.04.1995	26	(1)	6
Andrija Ratković	14.11.1997		(4)	
Anes Rušević	02.12.1996	3	(17)	2
Uroš Stamenić	14.10.1996	2	(2)	1
Uroš Vesić	28.06.1998	3		

Fudbalski Klub Rad Beograd

Founded: 10.03.1958
Stadium: Stadion „Kralj Petar Prvi", Beograd (6,000)
Trainer: Bogdan Korak   02.11.1959
[16.08.2019] Srđan Stojčevski   15.08.1985
[23.08.2019] Dragan Radojičić   03.06.1970
[15.12.2019] Marko Mićović   13.10.1974
[09.06.2020] Branko Mirjačić   14.03.1983

Goalkeepers:	DOB	M	(s)	G
Dušan Marković	03.04.1998	30		
Defenders:	**DOB**	**M**	**(s)**	**G**
Đorđe Bašanović	31.07.1996	5	(1)	
Marko Dobrijević	19.03.2002	4		
Milan Jagodić	11.03.1991	8	(3)	1
Branislav Jovanović	21.09.1985	3		
Milan Lazarević	10.01.1997	9	(1)	
Branislav Milošević	13.05.1988	25		
Marko Nikolić	31.03.1998	14	(3)	1
Milan Perendija	05.01.1986	19		3
Nemanja Petrović	17.04.1992	19		
Goran Smiljanić	31.01.1990	10	(3)	1
Dušan Stević	25.07.1995	5	(1)	
Petar Stojanović	23.03.2001		(5)	
Nikola Šipčić	17.05.1995	1		
Strahinja Tanasijević	12.06.1997	8		
Miloš Tanović	19.05.1996		(2)	
Nikola Tričković	15.11.1999	5		
Midfielders:	**DOB**	**M**	**(s)**	**G**
Miloš Bosančić	22.05.1988	5	(1)	
Aleksandar Busnić	04.12.1997	18	(4)	1
Uroš Damnjanović	08.02.1995	1	(4)	
Bogdan Mladenović	04.04.1996	1		
Njegoš Petrović	18.07.1999	2		
Branko Riznić	04.10.1999	7	(5)	1
Ostoja Stjepanović (MKD)	17.02.1985	14	(1)	
Miloš Šaka	12.04.1994	7	(4)	1
Aleksandar Trninić	27.03.1987	9	(3)	
Dušan Zivković	31.07.1996	12	(11)	
Forwards:	**DOB**	**M**	**(s)**	**G**
Darko Bjedov	28.03.1989	9	(5)	1
Marko Dedijer	08.05.2001		(2)	
Vanja Ilić	03.01.1999	13	(7)	
Saša Jovanović	30.08.1993	5	(3)	
Andrija Kaluđerović	05.07.1987	9		7
Filip Kasalica (MNE)	17.12.1988	22	(3)	2
Ljubomir Kovacević (MNE)	23.02.2000		(8)	
Yevheniy Kovalenko (UKR)	11.08.1992	4	(3)	
Matija Stojković	21.07.2001		(1)	
Miloš Trifunović	15.10.1984	14	(5)	2
Veljko Trifunović	04.08.1998	9	(7)	2
Jovan Zogović	11.02.2001	4	(1)	

Fudbalski Klub Radnički Niš

Founded:	24.04.1923		
Stadium:	Stadion Čair, Niš (18,151)		
Trainer:	Simo Krunić (BIH)		13.01.1967
[20.08.2019]	Milorad Kosanović		04.01.1951
[25.02.2020]	Radoslav Batak (MNE)		15.08.1977

Goalkeepers:	DOB	M	(s)	G
Stefan Ilić	25.02.2001		(1)	
Marko Knežević	29.03.1989	1		
Nikola Petrović	10.04.1988	20		
Borivoje Ristić	19.09.1983	9	(1)	
Defenders:	**DOB**	**M**	**(s)**	**G**
Taras Bondarenko (UKR)	23.09.1992	11	(1)	
Petar Ćirković	19.11.1999		(2)	
Lazar Đorđević	14.07.1992	20		3
Stefan Đorđević	13.03.1991	14	(1)	
Hao Runze (CHN)	03.05.1997		(1)	1
Bojan Letić (BIH)	21.12.1992	8	(1)	
Mario Maslać	09.09.1990	5		
Dragan Nedeljkovic	06.02.2001		(1)	
Nemanja Nikolić (BIH)	21.02.2001		(1)	
Ivan Ostojić	26.06.1989	18	(1)	1
Nikola Stevanović	13.09.1998	16	(4)	1
Aleksandar Todorovski (MKD)	26.02.1984	27		
Midfielders:	**DOB**	**M**	**(s)**	**G**
Veljko Batrović (MNE)	05.03.1994	4	(3)	1
Ognjen Bjeličić	29.07.1997	3	(4)	
Erik Jirka (SVK)	19.09.1997	14	(2)	4

	DOB	M	(s)	G
Aleksa Jovanović	27.05.1999	2	(2)	
Dejan Meleg	01.10.1994	12	(9)	
Uroš Miloradović	14.10.2000	1	(6)	
Stefan Milosavljević	09.05.1992		(2)	
Stefan Mitrović	15.08.2002	2	(5)	1
Ryota Noma (JPN)	15.11.1991	10		2
Dušan Pantelić	15.04.1993	19		1
Aleksandr Pejović	28.12.1990	10		
Andrija Sekulić	11.04.2002		(1)	
Rebin Ghareeb Solaka Adhamat (IRQ)	12.04.1992	13		
Saša Stojanović	21.01.1983	3	(10)	
Nemanja Subotić	23.01.1992	10		
Nemanja Tomić	21.01.1988	4	(1)	
Forwards:	**DOB**	**M**	**(s)**	**G**
Milan Bojović	13.04.1987		(1)	
Nikola Čumić	20.11.1998	22	(1)	12
Vladimir Đilas	03.03.1983		(3)	
Nermin Haskić (BIH)	27.06.1989	14	(4)	7
Filip Knežević	08.11.1991	11	(14)	
Nemanja Kojić	03.02.1990	3	(4)	
Stefan Mihajlović	24.06.1994	23	(6)	15
Milosav Sićović	12.11.1999	1	(1)	

Fudbalski Klub Radnik Surdulica

Founded:	1926		
Stadium:	Stadion Surdulica, Surdulica (3,312)		
Trainer:	Slaviša Božičić		08.01.1966
[20.08.2019]	Nenad Vanić		30.08.1970
[30.10.2019]	Simo Krunić (BIH)		13.01.1967

Goalkeepers:	DOB	M	(s)	G
Ivan Kostić	24.10.1995	19		
Nemanja Kostić	23.04.2004		(1)	
Nikola Vasiljević	24.06.1996	8		
Nikola Vujanac	22.06.1991	3		
Defenders:	**DOB**	**M**	**(s)**	**G**
Ronaldo Demić	25.04.2000		(1)	
Predrag Đorđević	30.06.1990	18	(4)	1
Ranko Jokić	22.04.1999	11	(1)	
Ivan Kričak	19.07.1996	25		
Žarko Marković	28.01.1987	15		
Vladan Pavlović	24.02.1984	1	(11)	
Nenad Stanković	16.09.1992	8	(1)	
Dušan Stevanović	22.06.1996	21		
Uroš Stojanović	23.08.1995	20		
Midfielders:	**DOB**	**M**	**(s)**	**G**
Uroš Damnjanović	08.02.1995	6	(5)	
Ognjen Dimitrić	04.06.1998	7	(6)	
Filip Jović	06.08.1997	6		1
Lazar Kojić	11.12.1999		(2)	

	DOB	M	(s)	G
Miroljub Kostić	05.06.1988	22	(1)	
Vuk Mitošević	12.02.1991	19	(2)	1
Bratislav Pejčić	17.01.1983	6	(5)	
Risto Ristović	05.05.1988	4	(3)	
Filip Stanisavljević	20.05.1987	18	(4)	1
Bogdan Stojković	14.10.2002		(3)	
Nemanja Tomić	21.01.1988	12	(3)	2
Forwards:	**DOB**	**M**	**(s)**	**G**
Bojan Bojić	03.03.2000	9	(5)	2
Zoran Danoski (MKD)	20.10.1990	21	(4)	3
Osi Demirović	21.01.2001		(1)	
Boban Georgiev (MKD)	26.01.1997	9	(8)	3
Sead Islamović	24.09.1999	2	(3)	
Milan Makarić	04.10.1995	19	(5)	8
Luka Mićić	28.02.1995	2	(5)	1
Evgeniy Pavlov (UKR)	12.03.1991	10	(6)	7
Bogdan Stamenković	19.01.1998	6	(6)	2
Witan Sulaeman (IDN)	08.10.2001	1	(1)	
Igor Zlatanović	10.02.1998	2		1

Fudbalski Klub Spartak Subotica

Founded:	21.04.1945		
Stadium:	Stadion Subotica, Subotica (13,000)		
Trainer:	Vladimir Gaćinović (BIH)		03.01.1966

Goalkeepers:	DOB	M	(s)	G
Ivan Dokić	25.03.2000	11		
Mišo Dubljanić (MNE)	20.12.1999	8	(1)	
Filip Dujmović (BIH)	12.03.1999	4		
Miloš Ostojić	21.04.1996	7		
Defenders:	**DOB**	**M**	**(s)**	**G**
Luka Cucin	24.11.1998	4	(1)	
David Dunđerski	28.10.1999	23	(2)	2
Mihajlo Ivančević	07.04.1999	6	(3)	
Filip Jović	27.02.2000		(1)	
Ognjen Mažić	20.06.2002		(1)	
Stefan Milošević	07.04.1995	24		
Mihailo Milutinović	14.02.1995	2	(1)	
Vladimir Otašević	08.06.1986	25		2
Nemanja Tekijaški	02.03.1997	28		1
Aleksa Urošević	09.05.2000	4	(3)	
Aleksandar Vidović	12.05.2001	4	(1)	
Midfielders:	**DOB**	**M**	**(s)**	**G**
André Filipe Carneiro Leal „Andrezinho" (POR)	16.08.1995	1	(9)	
Aleksa Đurasović	23.12.2002	1	(1)	
Branimir Jočić	10.07.1994	20	(1)	1

	DOB	M	(s)	G
Milan Marčić	14.03.1996	27		4
Andrija Milić	15.07.2001		(2)	
Viktor Molnar	23.06.1905		(1)	
Nikola Srećković	26.04.1996	20	(5)	5
Lazar Tufegdžić	22.02.1997	23	(1)	6
Vladan Vidaković	14.03.1999	16	(8)	2
Forwards:	**DOB**	**M**	**(s)**	**G**
Mihajlo Baic	21.11.2002	1	(6)	
Luka Bijelović	11.04.2001	1	(2)	1
Stefan Denković (MNE)	16.06.1991	20	(5)	8
Damjan Gojkov	02.01.1998	2	(13)	1
Srđan Hrstić	18.07.2003		(1)	
Strahinja Jovanović	01.06.1999	1	(4)	
Uroš Kilibarda	24.06.1905		(1)	
Nemanja Mladenović	03.03.1993	6	(2)	
Nemanja Nikolić	19.10.1992	8		6
Nemanja Obradović	29.05.1989	16		5
Stefan Šormaz	10.08.1999	15	(9)	2
Nikola Tripković	28.01.1998		(1)	
Nikša Vujanović (MNE)	03.03.2001	1	(2)	
Sho Yamamoto (JPN)	12.11.1996	1	(1)	

Fudbalski Klub Vojvodina Novi Sad

Founded: 06.03.1914
Stadium: Stadion Karađorđe, Novi Sad (14,458)
Trainer: Nenad Lalatović   22.12.1977

Goalkeepers:	DOB	M	(s)	G
Emil Rockov	27.01.1995	27		
Nikola Simić	21.12.1996	3		
Defenders:	**DOB**	**M**	**(s)**	**G**
Nikola Andrić	23.05.1992	6	(1)	
Slavko Bralić (CRO)	15.12.1992	7		
Mladen Devetak	12.03.1999	20	(1)	1
Stefan Đorđević	13.03.1991	7		
Đorđe Đurić	10.08.1991	7	(2)	
Nikola Petković	28.03.1986	3		
Siniša Saničanin (BIH)	24.04.1995	28		
Aranđel Stojković	02.03.1995	25	(2)	2
Ranko Veselinović	24.03.1999	19		1
Nemanja Vučić	11.06.1996	2		
Midfielders:	**DOB**	**M**	**(s)**	**G**
Petar Bojić	04.09.1991	27	(1)	5
Nikola Drinčić (MNE)	07.09.1984	30		2
Marko Đurišić	17.07.1997	11	(4)	
Željko Filipović (SVN)	03.10.1988	1		
Jovan Kokir	25.04.2000		(9)	
Bogdan Mladenović	04.04.1996	4	(1)	
Mihajlo Nešković	09.02.2000	4	(10)	2
Eze Okeuhie (NGA)	06.06.1993	17		3
Mirko Topić	05.02.2001	13	(4)	1
Miljan Vukadinović	27.12.1992	8		2
Dejan Zukić	07.05.2001	2	(25)	4
Forwards:	**DOB**	**M**	**(s)**	**G**
Vukasin Bogdanović	04.10.2002		(1)	
Nemanja Čović	18.06.1991	3	(6)	2
Ognjen Đuričin	03.09.1995	15	(9)	3
Miodrag Gemović	25.12.1994	12	(11)	3
Bojan Matić	22.12.1991	17	(1)	9
Momčilo Mrkaić (BIH)	21.09.1990	9		2
Nemanja Nikolić	19.10.1992	3	(6)	3

Fudbalski Klub Voždovac Beograd

Founded: 1912
Stadium: Stadion Shopping Center, Beograd (5,175)
Trainer: Radomir Koković   06.01.1984
[12.03.2020] Jovan Damjanović   04.10.1982

Goalkeepers:	DOB	M	(s)	G
Marko Ilić	03.02.1998	26		
Marko Trkulja	21.06.1990	4		
Defenders:	**DOB**	**M**	**(s)**	**G**
Vasilije Bakić	24.05.2000	2	(1)	
Strahinja Bošnjak	18.02.1999	5		
Nenad Cvetković	06.01.1996	20	(1)	
Damjan Daničić	24.01.2000	4	(2)	
Stefan Hajdin	15.04.1994	25	(1)	2
Luka Jakovljević	18.04.2000		(4)	
Bojan Kovačević	28.04.1996	1		
Justas Lasickas (LTU)	06.10.1997	23		1
Miloš Mihajlov	15.12.1982	2	(3)	
Nikola Mikić	13.09.1985	27		
Nemanja Pejčinović	04.11.1987	5	(1)	
Nemanja Vučić	11.06.1996		(2)	1
Marko Živković	17.05.1994	13		
Midfielders:	**DOB**	**M**	**(s)**	**G**
Edin Ajdinović	07.06.2001	4		
Miloš Bosančić	22.05.1988	1	(1)	
Strahinja Karišić	03.07.1997	1		
Ognjen Krasić	09.04.1988	5	(10)	1
Ivan Milosavljević	19.03.2000	4		1
Nemanja Nikolić (MNE)	01.01.1988	25		7
Jovan Nišić	03.03.1998	22	(2)	3
Stefan Purtić	06.08.1998	9	(7)	1
Pavle Radulović (MNE)	22.03.2001		(2)	
Miloš Stojčev (MNE)	19.01.1987	18	(2)	5
Lazar Zlićić	07.02.1997	15	(2)	3
Forwards:	**DOB**	**M**	**(s)**	**G**
Luka Cvetićanin	11.02.2003	4	(9)	
Marko Dević (UKR)	27.10.1983	4	(8)	4
Marko Gjorgjievski (MKD)	18.04.2000	7	(8)	3
Aleksa Janković	12.04.2000	6	(2)	1
Aleksandar Jevtić	30.03.1985	7		3
Alen Mašović	07.08.1994	14	(5)	5
Aleksandar Stanisavljević	11.06.1989	12	(2)	2
Dragan Stoisavljević	25.11.2003	3	(7)	1
Filip Stuparević	30.08.2000	9		
Viktor Živojinović	15.03.1999	3	(7)	

Fudbalski Klub Topolyai Sport Club Bačka Topola

Founded: 1913 (*as Topolyai Sport Club*)
Stadium: Stadion Senta, Senta (5,000)
Trainer: Zoltán Sabo   26.05.1972

Goalkeepers:	DOB	M	(s)	G
Nenad Filipović	24.04.1987	28		
Nemanja Jorgić	07.04.1988	2	(1)	
Defenders:	**DOB**	**M**	**(s)**	**G**
Goran Antonić	03.11.1990	24	(4)	1
Filip Babić	27.05.1995	16	(4)	
Bojan Balaž	05.01.2001	5	(4)	
Srđan Grabež	02.04.1991	18	(3)	2
Igor Kudrić	27.05.2001		(1)	
Luka Pantović	27.06.2001		(1)	
Dajan Ponjević	10.02.1989	18	(2)	
Nebojša Skopljak	12.05.1987	18	(5)	
Dragan Svitić	17.03.1992	1		
Boris Varga	14.08.1993	26		1
Midfielders:	**DOB**	**M**	**(s)**	**G**
Filip Arsenijević	02.09.1983	12	(5)	
Vasilije Đurić	10.07.1998	2	(8)	
Dejan Matićević	10.03.1992	25	(1)	6
David Šinković	07.05.1998		(14)	1
Saša Tomanović	20.09.1989	26	(1)	3
Janko Tumbasević (MNE)	14.01.1985	25		6
Forwards:	**DOB**	**M**	**(s)**	**G**
Borko Duronjić	24.09.1997	15	(12)	1
Mladen Galić (BIH)	09.10.1987		(18)	
Nenad Lukić	02.09.1992	30		16
Ersan Rovčanin	24.03.1993		(12)	
Vladimir Siladi	23.04.1993	29		16
Đuro Zec	06.03.1990	10		5

The Play-off stage was cancelled due to Covid-19 pandemic.

1.	FK Zlatibor Čajetina (*Promoted*)	30	14	12	4	33	-	18	54
2.	FK Grafičar Beograd	30	16	6	8	49	-	27	54
3.	FK Metalac Gornji Milanovac (*Promoted*)	30	16	5	9	41	-	34	53
4.	OFK Bačka Bačka Palanka (*Promoted*)	30	16	5	9	40	-	26	53
5.	FK Kolubara Lazarevac	30	13	8	9	35	-	25	47
6.	FK Kabel Novi Sad[(1)]	30	14	10	6	31	-	20	42
7.	FK Radnički 1923 Kragujevac	30	11	9	10	31	-	26	42
8.	FK Radnički Pirot	30	11	8	11	34	-	34	41
9.	OFK Žarkovo	30	10	10	10	35	-	36	40
10.	FK Novi Pazar (*Promoted*)	30	11	7	12	32	-	31	40
11.	FK Dinamo Vranje	30	10	8	12	35	-	38	38
12.	FK Zemun Beograd	30	8	9	13	25	-	29	33
13.	FK Trayal Kruševac	30	7	10	13	21	-	30	31
14.	FK Sinđelić Beograd (*Relegated*)	30	6	7	17	27	-	55	25
15.	FK Budućnost Dobanovci	30	5	7	18	21	-	41	22
16.	FK Smederevo 1924[(1)] (*Relegated*)	30	9	5	16	27	-	47	22

[(1)] *10 points deducted due to match fixing.*
Please note: FK Grafičar Beograd rejected promotion to SuperLiga 2020/2021.
FK Sinđelić Beograd was relegated due to financial problems, while FK Smederevo 1924 was relegated due to match fixing.

NATIONAL TEAM

INTERNATIONAL MATCHES
(16.07.2019 – 15.07.2020)

07.09.2019	Beograd	Serbia - Portugal	2-4(0-1)	(ECQ)
10.09.2019	Lëtzebuerg	Luxembourg - Serbia	1-3(0-1)	(ECQ)
10.10.2019	Kruševac	Serbia - Paraguay	1-0(0-0)	(F)
14.10.2019	Vilnius	Lithuania - Serbia	1-2(0-0)	(ECQ)
14.11.2019	Beograd	Serbia - Luxembourg	3-2(2-0)	(ECQ)
17.11.2019	Beograd	Serbia - Ukraine	2-2(1-1)	(ECQ)

07.09.2019   SERBIA - PORTUGAL   2-4(0-1)   16th EC. Qualifiers
Stadion "Rajko Mitić", Beograd; Referee: Cüneyt Çakır (Turkey); Attendance: 39,839
SRB: Marko Dmitrović, Aleksandar Kolarov (Cap), Nikola Maksimović, Matija Nastasić, Nikola Milenković, Nemanja Matić, Darko Lazović (59.Adem Ljajić), Luka Milivojević (87.Luka Jović), Filip Kostić (83.Aleksandar Katai), Dušan Tadić, Aleksandar Mitrović. Trainer: Ljubiša Tumbaković.
Goals: Nikola Milenković (68), Aleksandar Mitrović (85).

10.09.2019   LUXEMBOURG - SERBIA   1-3(0-1)   16th EC. Qualifiers
Stade "Josy Barthel", Lëtzebuerg; Referee: Orel Grinfeld (Israel); Attendance: 6,373
SRB: Marko Dmitrović, Antonio Rukavina, Aleksandar Kolarov (Cap), Nikola Maksimović, Uroš Spajić, Adem Ljajić, Luka Milivojević, Aleksandar Katai (46.Nemanja Radonjić), Saša Lukić (61.Mijat Gaćinović), Sergej Milinković-Savić (79.Nemanja Matić), Aleksandar Mitrović. Trainer: Ljubiša Tumbaković.
Goals: Aleksandar Mitrović (36), Nemanja Radonjić (55), Aleksandar Mitrović (78).

10.10.2019   SERBIA - PARAGUAY   1-0(0-0)   Friendly International
Stadion Mladost, Kruševac; Referee: Nejc Kajtazović (Slovenia); Attendance: 5,000
SRB: Predrag Rajković (89.Emil Rockov), Aleksandar Kolarov (Cap) (67.Nemanja Milunović), Filip Mladenović (66.Milan Rodić), Nemanja Miletić (46.Marko Gobeljić), Adem Ljajić, Luka Milivojević (46.Saša Lukić), Mijat Gaćinović, Nemanja Radonjić, Stefan Mitrović, Nemanja Maksimović (66.Nemanja Gudelj), Aleksandar Mitrović. Trainer: Ljubiša Tumbaković.
Goal: Aleksandar Mitrović (90).

14.10.2019   LITHUANIA - SERBIA   1-2(0-0)   16th EC. Qualifiers
LFF stadionas, Vilnius; Referee: Paweł Raczkowski (Poland); Attendance: 2,787
SRB: Marko Dmitrović, Filip Mladenović, Aleksandar Kolarov (Cap), Nikola Milenković, Nemanja Miletić, Adem Ljajić (85.Nemanja Gudelj), Luka Milivojević (72.Saša Lukić), Filip Kostić (46.Mijat Gaćinović), Nemanja Radonjić, Nemanja Maksimović, Aleksandar Mitrović. Trainer: Ljubiša Tumbaković.
Goals: Aleksandar Mitrović (49, 53).

14.11.2019   SERBIA - LUXEMBOURG   3-2(2-0)   16th EC. Qualifiers
Stadion „Rajko Mitić", Beograd; Referee: Serdar Gözübüyük (Netherlands); Attendance: 1,560
SRB: Marko Dmitrović, Aleksandar Kolarov (Cap), Nikola Maksimović, Filip Mladenović, Luka Milivojević, Nikola Milenković, Adem Ljajić (79.Filip Đuričić), Sergej Milinković-Savić (62.Nemanja Radonjić), Nemanja Maksimović, Dušan Tadić (90+1.Saša Lukić), Aleksandar Mitrović. Trainer: Ljubiša Tumbaković.
Goals: Aleksandar Mitrović (11, 43), Nemanja Radonjić (70).

17.11.2019   SERBIA - UKRAINE   2-2(1-1)   16th EC. Qualifiers
Stadion "Rajko Mitić", Beograd; Referee: Robert Madden (Scotland); Attendance: 4,457
SRB: Predrag Rajković, Aleksandar Kolarov (Cap), Nikola Maksimović, Milan Rodić, Nikola Milenković, Adem Ljajić (69.Mijat Gaćinović), Nemanja Gudelj, Nemanja Maksimović (76.Luka Milivojević), Dušan Tadić, Nemanja Radonjić (82.Sergej Milinković-Savić), Aleksandar Mitrović. Trainer: Ljubiša Tumbaković.
Goals: Dušan Tadić (9 penalty), Aleksandar Mitrović (56).

NATIONAL TEAM PLAYERS
(16.07.2019 – 15.07.2020)

Name	DOB	Caps	Goals	2019/2020:	Club
Goalkeepers					
Marko DMITROVIĆ	24.01.1992	13	0	2019:	*SD Eibar (ESP)*
Predrag RAJKOVIĆ	31.10.1995	13	0	2019:	*Stade de Reims (FRA)*
Emil ROCKOV	27.01.1995	1	0	2019:	*FK Vojvodina Novi Sad*
Defenders					
Marko GOBELJIĆ	13.09.1992	3	0	2019:	*FK Crvena Zvezda Beograd*
Aleksandar KOLAROV	10.11.1985	90	11	2019:	*AS Roma (ITA)*
Nikola MAKSIMOVIĆ	25.11.1991	24	0	2019:	*SSC Napoli (ITA)*
Nikola MILENKOVIĆ	12.10.1997	19	1	2019:	*ACF Fiorentina (ITA)*
Nemanja MILETIĆ	16.01.1991	3	0	2019:	*FK Partizan Beograd*
Nemanja MILUNOVIĆ	31.05.1989	4	1	2019:	*FK Crvena Zvezda Beograd*
Stefan MITROVIĆ	22.05.1990	15	0	2019:	*Racing Club Strasbourg (FRA)*
Filip MLADENOVIĆ	15.08.1991	10	0	2019:	*KS Lechia Gdańsk (POL)*
Matija NASTASIĆ	28.03.1993	29	0	2019:	*FC Schalke 04 Gelsenkirchen (GER)*
Milan RODIĆ	02.04.1991	7	0	2019:	*FK Crvena Zvezda Beograd*
Antonio RUKAVINA	26.01.1984	59	0	2019:	*Astana FC (KAZ)*
Uroš SPAJIĆ	13.02.1993	11	0	2019:	*FK Krasnodar (RUS)*
Midfielders					
Filip ĐURIČIĆ	30.01.1992	25	4	2019:	*US Sassuolo Calcio (ITA)*
Mijat GAĆINOVIĆ	08.02.1995	18	2	2019:	*Eintracht Frankfurt (GER)*
Nemanja GUDELJ	16.11.1991	25	1	2019:	*Sevilla FC (ESP)*
Aleksandar KATAI	06.02.1991	9	0	2019:	*Chicago Fire SC (USA)*
Filip KOSTIĆ	01.11.1992	32	2	2019:	*Eintracht Frankfurt (GER)*
Darko LAZOVIĆ	15.09.1990	9	0	2019:	*Hellas Verona FC (ITA)*
Adem LJAJIĆ	29.09.1991	45	9	2019:	*Beşiktaş JK İstanbul (TUR)*
Saša LUKIĆ	13.08.1996	12	0	2019:	*Torino FC (ITA)*
Nemanja MAKSIMOVIĆ	26.01.1995	19	0	2019:	*Getafe CF (ESP)*
Nemanja MATIĆ	01.08.1988	48	2	2019:	*Manchester United FC (ENG)*
Sergej MILINKOVIĆ-SAVIĆ	27.02.1995	15	0	2019:	*SS Lazio Roma (ITA)*
Luka MILIVOJEVIĆ	07.04.1991	36	1	2019:	*Crystal Palace FC London (ENG)*
Nemanja RADONJIĆ	15.02.1996	16	2	2019:	*Olympique de Marseille (ITA)*
Dušan TADIĆ	20.11.1988	67	16	2019:	*AFC Ajax Amsterdam (NED)*
Forwards					
Luka JOVIĆ	23.12.1997	7	2	2019:	*Real Madrid CF (ESP)*
Aleksandar MITROVIĆ	16.09.1994	55	34	2019:	*Fulham FC London (ENG)*
National team coach					
Ljubiša TUMBAKOVIĆ [from 01.07.2019]		02.09.1952	6 M; 4 W; 1 D; 1 L; 13-10		

SLOVAKIA

The Country:
Slovenská republika (Slovak Republic)
Capital: Bratislava
Surface: 49,035 km²
Inhabitants: 5,457,926 [2020]
Time: UTC+1

The FA:
Slovenský futbalový zväz
Tomášikova 30C, 821 01 Bratislava
Tel: +421 2 4820 6000
Founded: 04.11.1938
Member of FIFA since: 1994
Member of UEFA since: 1993
Website: www.futbalsfz.sk

NATIONAL TEAM RECORDS

RECORDS		
First international match:	27.08.1939, Bratislava:	Slovakia – Germany 2-0
Most international caps:	Marek Hamšik	- 120 caps (since 2007)
Most international goals:	Marek Hamšik	- 25 goals / 120 caps (since 2007)

UEFA EUROPEAN CHAMPIONSHIP		FIFA WORLD CUP		OLYMPIC TOURNAMENTS	
1960	-	1930	-	1908	-
1964	-	1934	-	1912	-
1968	-	1938	-	1920	-
1972	-	1950	-	1924	-
1976	-	1954	-	1928	-
1980	-	1958	-	1936	-
1984	-	1962	-	1948	-
1988	-	1966	-	1952	-
1992	-	1970	-	1956	-
1996	Qualifiers	1974	-	1960	-
2000	Qualifiers	1978	-	1964	-
2004	Qualifiers	1982	-	1968	-
2008	Qualifiers	1986	-	1972	-
2012	Qualifiers	1990	-	1976	-
2016	Final Tournament (2nd Round of 16)	1994	-	1980	-
2020	*To be determined*	1998	Qualifiers	1984	-
		2002	Qualifiers	1988	-
		2006	Qualifiers	1992	-
		2010	Final Tournament (2nd Round of 16)	1996	Qualifiers
		2014	Qualifiers	2000	Group Stage
		2018	Qualifiers	2004	Qualifiers
				2008	Qualifiers
				2012	Qualifiers
				2016	Qualifiers

Please note: was part of Czechoslovakia 1918-1939 and 1945-1992.

UEFA NATIONS LEAGUE

2018/2019 – League B

FIFA CONFEDERATIONS CUP 1992-2017

None

SLOVAK CLUB HONOURS IN EUROPEAN CLUB COMPETITIONS:

European Champion Clubs.Cup (1956-1992) / UEFA Champions League (1993-2020)		
None		

Fairs Cup (1858-1971) / UEFA Cup (1972-2009) / UEFA Europa League (2010-2020)		
None		

UEFA Super Cup (1972-2019)		
None		

*European Cup Winners.Cup 1961-1999**		
ŠK Slovan Bratislava*	1	1968/1969
represented Czechoslovakia		

defunct competition

Please note: Slovakia was part of Czechoslovakia (1918–1993). First Slovak championship [Zväzové Majstrovstvá Slovenska] was played between Slovak teams (1925–1933).

Zväzové Majstrovstvá Slovenska (1925-1933)

	CHAMPIONS
1925	1. ČsŠK Bratislava
1925/1926	1. ČsŠK Bratislava
1926/1927	1. ČsŠK Bratislava
1927/1928	SK Žilina
1928/1929	SK Žilina
1929/1930	1. ČsŠK Bratislava
1930/1931	Ligeti SC Bratislava
1931/1932	1. ČsŠK Bratislava
1932/1933	SC Rusj Uzhorod

Slovenská liga (1939–1945)

	CHAMPIONS
1938/1939	Sparta Považská Bystrica
1939/1940	ŠK Bratislava
1940/1941	ŠK Bratislava
1941/1942	ŠK Bratislava
1942/1943	OAP Bratislava
1943/1944	ŠK Bratislava

	CHAMPIONS	CUP WINNERS	BEST GOALSCORERS	
1993/1994	ŠK Slovan Bratislava	ŠK Slovan Bratislava	Pavol Diňa (DAC Dunajska Streda)	19
1994/1995	ŠK Slovan Bratislava	FK Inter Bratislava	Robert Semenik (MFK Dukla Banská Bystrica)	18
1995/1996	ŠK Slovan Bratislava	FC Chemlon Humenné	Robert Semenik (1. FC Košice)	29
1996/1997	1. FC Košice	ŠK Slovan Bratislava	Jozef Kožlej (1. FC Košice)	22
1997/1998	1. FC Košice	FC Spartak Trnava	Ľubomír Luhový (FC Spartak Trnava)	17
1998/1999	ŠK Slovan Bratislava	ŠK Slovan Bratislava	Martin Fabuš (TJ Ozeta Dukla Trenčín)	19
1999/2000	FK Inter Bratislava	FK Inter Bratislava	Szilárd Németh (FK Inter Bratislava)	16
2000/2001	FK Inter Bratislava	FK Inter Bratislava	Szilárd Németh (FK Inter Bratislava)	23
2001/2002	MŠK Žilina	FK VTJ Koba Senec	Marek Mintál (MŠK Žilina)	21
2002/2003	MŠK Žilina	FK Matador Púchov	Marek Mintál (MŠK Žilina) Martin Fabuš (Laugaricio Trenčín / MŠK Žilina)	20
2003/2004	MŠK Žilina	FC Artmedia Petržalka	Roland Števko (MFK Ružomberok)	17
2004/2005	Artmedia Bratislava	MFK Dukla Banská Bystrica	Filip Šebo (FC Artmedia Petržalka)	22
2005/2006	MFK Ružomberok	MFK Ružomberok	Róbert Rák (FC Nitra) Erik Jendrišek (MFK Ružomberok)	21
2006/2007	MŠK Žilina	FC ViOn Zlaté Moravce	Tomáš Oravec (FC Artmedia Petržalka)	16
2007/2008	FC Artmedia Petržalka	FC Artmedia Petržalka	Ján Novák (MFK Košice)	17
2008/2009	ŠK Slovan Bratislava	MFK Košice	Pavol Masaryk (ŠK Slovan Bratislava)	15
2009/2010	MŠK Žilina	ŠK Slovan Bratislava	Róbert Rák (FC Nitra)	18
2010/2011	ŠK Slovan Bratislava	ŠK Slovan Bratislava	Filip Šebo (ŠK Slovan Bratislava)	22
2011/2012	MŠK Žilina	MŠK Žilina	Pavol Masaryk (MFK Ružomberok)	18
2012/2013	ŠK Slovan Bratislava	ŠK Slovan Bratislava	David Depetris (AS Trenčín)	16
2013/2014	ŠK Slovan Bratislava	MFK Košice	Tomáš Malec (AS Trenčín)	14
2014/2015	AS Trenčín	AS Trenčín	Matej Jelić (CRO, MŠK Žilina) Jan Kalabiška (CZE, FK Senica)	19
2015/2016	AS Trenčín	AS Trenčín	Gino Ronald van Kessel (CUW, AS Trenčín)	17
2016/2017	MŠK Žilina	ŠK Slovan Bratislava	Filip Hlohovský (MŠK Žilina) Seydouba Soumah (GUI, ŠK Slovan Bratislava)	20
2017/2018	FC Spartak Trnava	ŠK Slovan Bratislava	Samuel Mráz (MŠK Žilina)	21
2018/2019	ŠK Slovan Bratislava	FC Spartak Trnava	Andraž Šporar (SVN, ŠK Slovan Bratislava)	29
2019/2020	ŠK Slovan Bratislava	ŠK Slovan Bratislava	Andraž Šporar (SVN, ŠK Slovan Bratislava)	12

NATIONAL CHAMPIONSHIP
Slovak Fortuna Liga 2019/2020
(20.07.2019 – 11.07.2020)

Regular Season - Results

Round 1 [20-21.07.2019]
MFK Zemplín - MŠK Žilina 0-3(0-3)
FK Senica - AS Trenčín 3-1(0-1)
FK Pohronie - Slovan Bratislava 1-3(0-1)
MFK Ružomberok - FC Nitra 1-0(0-0)
Spartak Trnava - ŠKF Sereď 2-0(1-0)
Zlaté Moravce - Dunajská Streda 1-2(1-0)

Round 2 [27-28.07.2019]
FC Nitra - Zlaté Moravce 0-1(0-1)
ŠKF Sereď - FK Senica 2-1(0-0)
AS Trenčín - MFK Ružomberok 1-1(1-1)
Slovan Bratislava - MFK Zemplín 3-0(2-0)
Dunajská Streda - FK Pohronie 5-1(2-0)
MŠK Žilina - Spartak Trnava 4-2(2-0)

Round 3 [03-04.08.2019]
FK Senica - Slovan Bratislava 0-3(0-2)
MFK Ružomberok - FK Pohronie 0-1(0-0)
Zlaté Moravce - MFK Zemplín 1-0(1-0)
MŠK Žilina - AS Trenčín 2-1(1-0)
Spartak Trnava - FC Nitra 2-0(1-0)
ŠKF Sereď - Dunajská Streda 3-1(0-0)

Round 4 [10-11.08.2019]
MFK Ružomberok - MŠK Žilina 2-3(0-3)
MFK Zemplín - FK Senica 3-0(3-0)
FC Nitra - ŠKF Sereď 3-2(1-0)
Slovan Bratislava - Zlaté Moravce 4-0(1-0)
AS Trenčín - Dunajská Streda 2-1(0-1)
FK Pohronie - Spartak Trnava 2-2(0-1)

Round 5 [17-18.08.2019]
Spartak Trnava - AS Trenčín 1-2(1-1)
FK Senica - MFK Ružomberok 2-2(2-1)
ŠKF Sereď - Slovan Bratislava 0-4(0-2)
Zlaté Moravce - FK Pohronie 0-0
MŠK Žilina - FC Nitra 3-0(2-0)
Dunajská Streda - MFK Zemplín 1-1(0-1)

Round 6 [23-25.08.2019]
FK Senica - Zlaté Moravce 1-3(1-1)
MFK Zemplín - ŠKF Sereď 1-1(1-1)
FK Pohronie - AS Trenčín 0-4(0-2)
MFK Ružomberok - Spartak Trnava 0-1(0-1)
Slovan Bratislava - MŠK Žilina 1-1(1-0)
FC Nitra - Dunajská Streda 1-2(1-1)

Round 7 [31.08.-01.09.2019]
Spartak Trnava - MFK Zemplín 2-1(0-1)
ŠKF Sereď - FK Pohronie 3-3(1-2)
Zlaté Moravce - MFK Ružomberok 4-2(3-0)
MŠK Žilina - FK Senica 5-0(1-0)
Dunajská Streda - Slovan Bratislava 5-2(2-1)
AS Trenčín - FC Nitra 2-2(2-0)

Round 8 [14-15.09.2019]
FK Pohronie - FC Nitra 0-3(0-2)
MFK Zemplín - AS Trenčín 2-1(2-0)
MFK Ružomberok - ŠKF Sereď 1-1(1-0)
FK Senica - Dunajská Streda 0-1(0-0)
Zlaté Moravce - MŠK Žilina 0-0
Slovan Bratislava - Spartak Trnava 2-0(1-0)

Round 9 [18-22.09.2019]
Spartak Trnava - FK Senica 0-0
Dunajská Streda - MFK Ružomberok 0-1(0-1)
FC Nitra - MFK Zemplín 0-2(0-0)
ŠKF Sereď - Zlaté Moravce 0-0
MŠK Žilina - FK Pohronie 2-1(1-0)
AS Trenčín - Slovan Bratislava 2-4(1-2)

Round 10 [28-29.09.2019]
ŠKF Sereď - AS Trenčín 1-1(0-1)
MFK Zemplín - MFK Ružomberok 0-1(0-0)
FK Senica - FK Pohronie 1-0(0-0)
Slovan Bratislava - FC Nitra 5-0(2-0)
Dunajská Streda - MŠK Žilina 1-0(1-0)
Zlaté Moravce - Spartak Trnava 1-3(0-3)

Round 11 [05-06.10.2019]
Spartak Trnava - Dunajská Streda 1-2(0-1)
FC Nitra - FK Senica 1-4(0-2)
FK Pohronie - MFK Zemplín 2-2(1-1)
MŠK Žilina - ŠKF Sereď 1-0(1-0)
AS Trenčín - Zlaté Moravce 2-2(1-1)
Ružomberok - Slovan Bratislava 1-1(1-0)

Round 12 [19-20.10.2019]
FC Nitra - MFK Ružomberok 1-2(0-1)
ŠKF Sereď - Spartak Trnava 2-1(1-0)
Slovan Bratislava - FK Pohronie 2-1(1-0)
MŠK Žilina - MFK Zemplín 1-1(1-1)
AS Trenčín - FK Senica 2-3(1-1)
Dunajská Streda - Zlaté Moravce 2-1(1-0)

Round 13 [26-27.10.2019]
MFK Ružomberok - AS Trenčín 2-2(1-1)
FK Pohronie - Dunajská Streda 0-2(0-0)
FK Senica - ŠKF Sereď 0-1(0-0)
Zlaté Moravce - FC Nitra 1-0(0-0)
MFK Zemplín - Slovan Bratislava 0-1(0-1)
Spartak Trnava - MŠK Žilina 0-1(0-1)

Round 14 [02-03.11.2019]
FC Nitra - Spartak Trnava 1-0(1-0)
Dunajská Streda - ŠKF Sereď 0-0
MFK Zemplín - Zlaté Moravce 2-2(1-1)
FK Pohronie - MFK Ružomberok 1-2(0-2)
Slovan Bratislava - FK Senica 2-0(1-0)
AS Trenčín - MŠK Žilina 3-0(0-0)

Round 15 [09-10.11.2019]
MŠK Žilina - MFK Ružomberok 1-2(0-1)
Dunajská Streda - AS Trenčín 3-1(1-1)
FK Senica - MFK Zemplín 4-0(0-0)
ŠKF Sereď - FC Nitra 0-1(0-0)
Spartak Trnava - FK Pohronie 3-2(0-2)
Zlaté Moravce - Slovan Bratislava 0-1(0-0)

Round 16 [23.11.2019]
MFK Zemplín - Dunajská Streda 5-0(5-0)
FC Nitra - MŠK Žilina 0-0
FK Pohronie - Zlaté Moravce 1-1(0-1)
AS Trenčín - Spartak Trnava 1-0(1-0)
MFK Ružomberok - FK Senica 2-2(0-2)
Slovan Bratislava - ŠKF Sereď 2-0(0-0)

Round 17 [29.11.-01.12.2019]
Spartak Trnava - MFK Ružomberok 2-0(1-0)
Dunajská Streda - FC Nitra 1-0(0-0)
ŠKF Sereď - MFK Zemplín 0-2(0-0)
AS Trenčín - FK Pohronie 0-1(0-1)
Zlaté Moravce - FK Senica 0-0
MŠK Žilina - Slovan Bratislava 0-0

Round 18 [07-08.12.2019]
MFK Zemplín - Spartak Trnava 2-0(1-0)
FC Nitra - AS Trenčín 1-1(0-0)
FK Pohronie - ŠKF Sereď 2-1(1-0)
MFK Ružomberok - Zlaté Moravce 0-0
Slovan Bratislava - Dunajská Streda 2-0(1-0)
FK Senica - MŠK Žilina 1-2(1-1)

Round 19 [15-16.02.2020]
FC Nitra - FK Pohronie 0-0
ŠKF Sereď - MFK Ružomberok 2-2(0-1)
AS Trenčín - MFK Zemplín 8-1(2-1)
MŠK Žilina - Zlaté Moravce 3-0(1-0)
Dunajská Streda - FK Senica 0-0
Spartak Trnava - Slovan Bratislava 0-0

Round 20 [22-23.02.2020]
MFK Zemplín - FC Nitra 1-0(1-0)
FK Pohronie - MŠK Žilina 0-1(0-0)
MFK Ružomberok - Dunajská Streda 0-0
Slovan Bratislava - AS Trenčín 2-0(1-0)
Zlaté Moravce - ŠKF Sereď 1-3(1-1)
FK Senica - Spartak Trnava 2-0(2-0)

Round 21 [01.03.2020]
FC Nitra - Slovan Bratislava 0-1(0-0)
FK Pohronie - FK Senica 0-0
MFK Ružomberok - MFK Zemplín 1-1(0-0)
AS Trenčín - ŠKF Sereď 2-1(1-1)
Spartak Trnava - Zlaté Moravce 2-1(0-0)
MŠK Žilina - Dunajská Streda 2-2(0-2)

Round 22 [07.03.2020]
Dunajská Streda - Spartak Trnava 0-1(0-1)
MFK Zemplín - FK Pohronie 1-0(0-0)
FK Senica - FC Nitra 0-3(0-0)
ŠKF Sereď - MŠK Žilina 0-3(0-2)
Slovan Bratislava - Ružomberok 1-0(0-0)
Zlaté Moravce - AS Trenčín 2-0(1-0)

Final Standings

1.	ŠK Slovan Bratislava	22	17	4	1	46 - 11	55
2.	MŠK Žilina	22	13	6	3	38 - 17	45
3.	FK DAC Dunajská Streda	22	11	5	6	31 - 25	38
4.	MFK Zemplín Michalovce	22	8	6	8	28 - 32	30
5.	FC Spartak Trnava	22	9	3	10	25 - 26	30
6.	MFK Ružomberok	22	6	10	6	25 - 27	28
7.	AS Trenčín	22	7	6	9	39 - 35	27
8.	FC ViOn Zlaté Moravce	22	6	8	8	22 - 28	26
9.	FK Senica	22	6	6	10	24 - 33	24
10.	ŠKF Sereď	22	5	7	10	23 - 34	22
11.	FC Nitra	22	5	4	13	17 - 31	19
12.	FK Pohronie Žiar nad Hronom	22	3	7	12	19 - 38	16

Teams ranked 1-6 were qualified for the Championship Round, while teams ranked 7-12 were qualified for the Relegation Round.

Relegation Round

Round 23 [13.06.2020]
AS Trenčín - FK Pohronie 4-0(2-0)
Zlaté Moravce - FC Nitra 2-1(1-1)
FK Senica - ŠKF Sereď 1-1(1-1)

Round 24 [20-21.06.2020]
FC Nitra - FK Senica 2-0(0-0)
Zlaté Moravce - AS Trenčín 2-3(0-2)
ŠKF Sereď - FK Pohronie 2-2(0-2)

Round 25 [27.06.2020]
FK Pohronie - Zlaté Moravce 1-0(0-0)
ŠKF Sereď - FC Nitra 1-0(0-0)
FK Senica - AS Trenčín 1-3(0-3)

Round 26 [04.07.2020]
AS Trenčín - ŠKF Sereď 3-2(2-2)
FC Nitra - FK Pohronie 0-2(0-0)
FK Senica - Zlaté Moravce 0-0

Round 27 [11.07.2020]
AS Trenčín - FC Nitra 0-3(0-0)
Zlaté Moravce - ŠKF Sereď 1-0(1-0)
FK Pohronie - FK Senica 1-0(1-0)

Final Standings

		Total					Home					Away				
7. AS Trenčín	27	11	6	10	52 - 43	39	7	3	4	32 - 21		4	3	6	20 - 22
8. FC ViOn Zlaté Moravce	27	8	9	10	27 - 33	33	6	3	5	16 - 15		2	6	5	11 - 18
9. ŠKF Sereď	27	6	9	12	29 - 41	27	4	5	4	16 - 21		2	4	8	13 - 20
10. FK Senica	27	6	8	13	26 - 40	26	4	3	7	16 - 20		2	5	6	10 - 20
11. FK Pohronie Žiar nad Hronom	27	6	8	13	25 - 44	26	3	4	6	11 - 21		3	4	7	14 - 23
12. FC Nitra (*Relegation Play-offs*)	27	7	4	16	23 - 36	25	3	3	7	10 - 17		4	1	9	13 - 19

Please note: AS Trenčín were qualified for the Europa League play-offs.

Championship Round

Round 23 [13-14.06.2020]
Slovan Bratislava - Ružomberok 1-0(0-0)
Dunajská Streda - MFK Zemplín 5-0(1-0)
MŠK Žilina - Spartak Trnava 2-1(1-0)

Round 24 [20-21.06.2020]
MŠK Žilina - Slovan Bratislava 2-3(1-2)
MFK Zemplín - MFK Ružomberok 1-1(0-0)
Spartak Trnava - Dunajská Streda 0-2(0-0)

Round 25 [27.06.-01.07.2020]
MFK Zemplín - Spartak Trnava 2-2(0-2)
MFK Ružomberok - MŠK Žilina 2-1(1-0)
Dunajská Streda - Slovan Bratislava 1-3(1-1)

Round 26 [04.07.2020]
Spartak Trnava - MFK Ružomberok 2-0(1-0)
Dunajská Streda - MŠK Žilina 2-0(0-0)
Slovan Bratislava - MFK Zemplín 4-0(2-0)

Round 27 [11.07.2020]
Slovan Bratislava - Spartak Trnava 0-0
MFK Ružomberok - Dunajská Streda 0-1(0-0)
MŠK Žilina - MFK Zemplín 5-0(2-0)

Final Standings

		Total					Home					Away				
1. **ŠK Slovan Bratislava**	27	21	5	1	57 - 14	68	12	2	0	31 - 2		9	3	1	26 - 12
2. MŠK Žilina	27	15	6	6	48 - 25	51	9	3	2	33 - 13		6	3	4	15 - 12
3. FK DAC Dunajská Streda	27	15	5	7	42 - 28	50	8	3	3	26 - 11		7	2	4	16 - 17
4. FC Spartak Trnava	27	10	5	12	30 - 32	35	7	2	4	17 - 11		3	3	8	13 - 21
5. MFK Ružomberok	27	7	11	9	28 - 33	32	2	7	4	12 - 14		5	4	5	16 - 19
6. MFK Zemplín Michalovce	27	8	8	11	31 - 49	32	6	4	3	20 - 12		2	4	8	11 - 37

Please note: teams ranked 4-6 were qualified for the Europa League play-offs.

Top goalscorers:

12	**Andraž Šporar (SVN)**	*ŠK Slovan Bratislava*
11	Milan Ristovski (MKD)	*FC Nitra*
10	Osman Bukari (GHA)	*AS Trenčín*
9	Ján Bernát	*MŠK Žilina*
9	Zsolt Kalmár (HUN)	*FK DAC Dunajská Streda*
9	Rafael Rogério da Silva „Rafael Ratão" (BRA)	*ŠK Slovan Bratislava*

Europa League Play-offs [14-17.07.2020]

Semi-Finals
MFK Ružomberok - MFK Zemplín Michalovce — 1-0(0-0)
FC Spartak Trnava - AS Trenčín — 3-0(1-0)

Europa League Play-off Final
FC Spartak Trnava - **MFK Ružomberok** — 0-2(0-0)

Relegation Play-offs [14-17.07.2020]

FK Dubnica nad Váhom - FC Nitra — 0-0 — 0-3(0-2)

FC Nitra remains at first level.

NATIONAL CUP
Slovenský Pohár 2019/2020

Third Round [04/10-11/17-18/24-25.09./12.10.2019]

ŠK Vegum Dol. Vestenice - FC ViOn Zlaté Moravce	0-6	OFK AGRIFOP Stakčín - MŠK Spartak Medzilaborce	2-5
TJ Prameň Kováčová - FK Slavoj Trebišov	0-3	MFK Vranov nad Topľou - ŠK Partizán Bardejov	1-1 aet; 4-5 pen
PŠC Pezinok - FK Senica	0-6	FK Kechnec - TJ Mladosť Kalša	1-1aet; 1-3 pen
TJ Veľké Lovce - FC Nitra	0-7	MŠK Spišské Podhradie - FK Železiarne Podbrezová	1-0
FK Predmier - MFK Tatran Liptovský Mikuláš	1-2	1. FC Tatran Prešov - FK Poprad	0-2
MŠK Fomat Martin - MFK Ružomberok	0-2	OFK Šarišské Michaľany - FK Košice	0-2
Slávia TU Košice - MFK Zemplín	1-1 aet; 4-3 pen	FC Pata - FC Petržalka Bratislava	1-2
FK Šalková - AS Trenčín	1-5	FK Bestrent Horná Krupá - MFK Skalica	2-4
OFK Dunajská Lužná - Lokomotíva DNV	7-0	FK Strečno - MFK Dukla Banská Bystrica	1-10
TJ Družstevník Bešeňov - FK Slovan Levice	2-0	FTC Fiľakovo - FK DAC Dunajská Streda	0-0 aet; 5-6 pen
FK Kolárovo - FK Marcelová	0-1	OŠK Trenčianske Stankovce - AFC Nové Mesto	0-2
TJ Družstevník Jacovce - MFK Alekšince	2-0	MSK Novohrad Lučenec - KFC Komárno	0-1
TJ Družstevník Radimov - TJ Slavoj Boleráz	1-0	MFK Stará Ľubovňa - MŠK Žilina	2-3
TJ Tatran Krásno - FC Spartak Trnava	0-4	FK Rakytovce 85 - FK Pohronie Žiar nad Hronom	1-5
TJ Spartak Vysoká nad Kysucou - MŠK Púchov	0-0 aet; 9-8 pen	Partizán Domaniža - OFK Malženice	3-6
ŠK Belá - ŠKF Sereď	0-10	TJ Družstevník Oravská Poruba - Slovan Bratislava	0-7

Fourth Round [24-25.09./02.10./09.10/16.11.2019]

TJ Družstevník Jacovce - FC Spartak Trnava	0-8	TJ Mladosť Kalša - MFK Ružomberok	2-6
KFC Komárno - FC Nitra	0-2	AFC Nové Mesto - MŠK Žilina	0-4
OFK Dunajská Lužná - FC Petržalka Bratislava	0-3	FK Marcelová - MFK Skalica	0-3
FK Košice - AS Trenčín	2-2 aet; 1-4 pen	TJ Družstevník Radimov - FK DAC Dunajská Streda	0-2
FK Slavoj Trebišov - FC ViOn Zlaté Moravce	1-2	OFK Malženice - FK Senica	0-0 aet; 1-4 pen
Spartak Medzilaborce - MFK Dukla Banská Bystrica	1-2	Slávia TU Košice - FK Pohronie Žiar nad Hronom	0-3
TJ Družstevník Bešeňov - MFK Tatran Lipt. Mikuláš	1-7	ŠK Partizán Bardejov - ŠK Slovan Bratislava	2-5
TJ Spartak Vysoká nad Kysucou - ŠKF Sereď	0-4	MŠK Spišské Podhradie - FK Poprad	0-3

1/8-Finals [30.10./14.11./04.12.2019]

AS Trenčín - MFK Skalica	4-0(1-0)	FK Senica - MFK Ružomberok	1-1 aet; 3-4 pen
ŠKF Sereď - FC Petržalka	3-0(1-0)	FK DAC Dunajská Streda - FC Spartak Trnava	0-0 aet; 4-3 pen
FK Poprad - MFK Dukla Banská Bystrica	3-0(0-0)	FK Pohronie Žiar nad Hronom - FC ViOn Zlaté Mor.	0-1(0-0)
FC Nitra - MFK Tatran Liptovský Mikuláš	3-2(1-1)	ŠK Slovan Bratislava - MŠK Žilina	2-0(2-0)

Quarter-Finals [04.03.2020]

ŠKF Sereď - MFK Ružomberok	0-2(0-2)	FC Nitra - FC ViOn Zlaté Moravce	1-1 aet; 4-5 pen
AS Trenčín - ŠK Slovan Bratislava	2-2 aet; 5-6 pen	FK DAC Dunajská Streda - FK Poprad	2-0(1-0)

Semi-Finals [16-17/23-24.06.2020]

First Leg		Second Leg	
ŠK Slovan Bratislava - FC ViOn Zlaté Moravce	4-1(2-1)	FC ViOn Zlaté Moravce - ŠK Slovan Bratislava	0-2(0-1)
FK DAC Dunajská Streda - MFK Ružomberok	1-1(1-0)	MFK Ružomberok - FK DAC Dunajská Streda	3-0(1-0)

Final

08.07.2020; Stadion Tehelné pole, Bratislava; Referee: Filip Glova; Attendance: 3,624
ŠK Slovan Bratislava - MFK Ružomberok   1-0(0-0)

Slovan Bratislava: Michal Šulla, Myenty Abena (46.Vernon De Marco Morlacchi), Jurij Medveděv (83.Vladimír Weiss), Vasil Bozhikov, Kenan Bajrič, Joeri de Kamps, Ibrahim Rabiu, Mohammed Rharsalla Khadfi (83.Erik Daniel), Alen Ožbolt (74.José Antonio Delgado Villar „Nono"), Dávid Strelec (64.Rafael Rogério da Silva „Rafael Ratão"), Žan Medved. Trainer: Ján Kozák.

MFK Ružomberok: Matúš Macík, Alexander Mojžiš, Ján Maslo, Filip Twardzik, Matej Čurma, David Filinsky (72.Dalibor Takáč), Timotej Múdry (80.Matúš Kmeť), Adam Brenkus (61.Matej Madlenak), Lukáš Kojnok (72.Peter Ďungel), Martin Regáli, Štefan Gerec (80.Tihomir Kostadinov). Trainer: Ján Haspra.

Goal: 1-0 Alen Ožbolt (48).

THE CLUBS 2019/2020

Please note: matches and goals includes statistics of both regular season and play-offs (Championship or Relegation Round).

Futbalový klub DAC 1904 Dunajská Streda

Founded:	1904 (*as Dunaszerdahelyi Atlétikai Club*)	
Stadium:	MOL Aréna, Dunajská Streda (9,901)	
Trainer:	Peter Hyballa (GER)	05.12.1975
[06.01.2020]	Marino Rodrigues Cristovão Hélder (POR)	21.03.1971
[01.06.2020]	Bernd Storck (GER)	25.01.1963

Goalkeepers:	DOB	M	(s)	G
Martin Jedlička (CZE)	24.01.1998	24		
Benjamín Szaráz	09.03.1998	3		
Defenders:	**DOB**	**M**	**(s)**	**G**
Danilo Beskorovayniy (UKR)	07.02.1999	19		
Éric Javier Davis Grajales (PAN)	31.03.1991	22	(2)	2
Kristián Koštrna	15.12.1993	11	(1)	1
Dominik Kružliak	10.07.1996	25		1
Dušan Lalatović (SRB)	29.11.1998	1	(1)	
Matúš Malý	11.07.2001	2	(1)	
Milan Šimčák	23.08.1995	2	(4)	
Lorenco Šimić (CRO)	15.07.1996	4		
Timotej Zahumenský	17.07.1995		(1)	
Midfielders:	**DOB**	**M**	**(s)**	**G**
Andrija Balić (CRO)	11.08.1997	6		1
Martin Bednár	22.04.1999	2	(2)	
César Rodolfo Blackman Camarena (PAN)	02.04.1998	22	(4)	1
Andrej Fábry	01.03.1997	17	(7)	3

	DOB	M	(s)	G
Zsolt Kalmár (HUN)	09.06.1995	12	(4)	9
Sainey Njie (GAM)	30.08.2001	3	(1)	
Matej Oravec	30.03.1998	16	(1)	
Connor Ronan (IRL)	06.03.1998	13	(1)	
András Schäfer (HUN)	13.04.1999	7	(1)	
Dominik Veselovský	19.07.2002		(5)	
Krisztófer Vida (HUN)	23.06.1995	18	(1)	7
Máté Vida (HUN)	08.03.1996	23	(1)	2
Forwards:	**DOB**	**M**	**(s)**	**G**
Ernest Boateng (GHA)	06.06.2001	1	(1)	
Lukáš Čmelík	13.04.1996	1	(6)	
Marko Divković (CRO)	11.06.1999	18	(6)	5
Krisztián Németh (HUN)	05.01.1989		(1)	
Ricardo Antonio Phillips Hinds (PAN)	06.05.2001	1	(2)	
Eric Kleybel Ramírez Matheus (VEN)	20.11.1994	19	(4)	7
Zuberu Sharani (GHA)	07.01.2000		(5)	1
Jakub Švec	03.12.2000		(1)	
Abdulrahman Taiwo (NGA)	05.08.1998	5	(4)	2

Football Club Nitra

Founded:	1909 (*as as Nyitrai ÖTTSO*)	
Stadium:	Štadión pod Zoborom, Nitra (5,500)	
Trainer:	Marián Süttö	23.12.1965
[27.10.2019]	Gergely Geri	19.01.1977
[06.01.2020]	Anatoliy Demyanenko (UKR)	19.02.1959

Goalkeepers:	DOB	M	(s)	G
Martin Kuciak	15.03.1982	1		
Dávid Šipoš	14.08.1998	26		
Defenders:	**DOB**	**M**	**(s)**	**G**
Marek Dubeň	11.07.1994	4	(3)	
Ondrej Elexa	07.10.2000	1	(2)	
Lukáš Fabiš	05.05.1998	10	(8)	
Pavol Farkaš	27.03.1985	19		
Midat Galbaev (KAZ)	14.03.1997	1		
João Augusto Carpes da Silva (BRA)	25.02.1999	2		
Matúš Kuník	14.05.1997	20	(1)	
Daniel Magda	25.11.1997	24	(2)	
Isaac Muleme (UGA)	10.10.1992	4	(2)	
Dmitriy Nemchaninov (UKR)	27.01.1990	5		
Oliver Podhorín	06.07.1992	24		1
Midfielders:	**DOB**	**M**	**(s)**	**G**
Frederik Bilovský	03.03.1992	9	(3)	
Daniel Junio de Jesus Nascimento (BRA)	22.05.1998	8		
Michal Faško	24.08.1994	22	(1)	1

	DOB	M	(s)	G
Duje Javorčić (CRO)	25.11.1999	3	(1)	
Sebastián Kóša	13.09.2003	3		
Ante Kulis (CRO)	17.11.2000		(2)	
Milan Ristovski (MKD)	08.04.1998	26	(1)	11
Samuel Šefčík	04.11.1996	16	(2)	3
Miloš Šimončič	27.05.1987	2	(3)	
Šimon Štefanec	05.09.1998	1	(6)	
Patrik Šurnovský	13.11.1997	7	(2)	
Ondrej Vrábel	23.04.1999	14	(3)	2
Forwards:	**DOB**	**M**	**(s)**	**G**
Marián Chobot	31.08.1994	23	(1)	4
Patrik Danek	02.10.2001		(5)	
Marek Fábry	07.08.1998		(10)	
Nikola Gatarić (CRO)	09.03.1992	20	(4)	
Dominik Guláš	28.06.1999		(6)	
Tomas Hambalek	21.06.2001		(3)	
Matúš Mikuš	08.07.1991		(2)	
Jakub Tancík	04.01.2000	2	(1)	

Futbalový klub Pohronie Žiar nad Hronom Dolná Ždaňa

Founded:	2012	
Stadium:	Štadión Mestský, Žiar nad Hronom (2,309)	
Trainer:	Milan Němec	14.02.1959
[01.08.2019]	Rastislav Urgela	29.03.1976
[20.08.2019]	Jan Rosinsky	23.05.1952
[14.10.2019]	Mikuláš Radványi	22.11.1968

Goalkeepers:	DOB	M	(s)	G
Tomáš Jenčo	29.09.1988	16		
Martin Vantruba	07.02.1998	11		
Defenders:	**DOB**	**M**	**(s)**	**G**
Patrik Abrahám	10.12.1991	21	(3)	5
Marek Kristián Bartoš	13.10.1996	12		
Peter Chribik	02.02.1999	8	(1)	
Ján Hatok	11.07.1990	13	(1)	
Patrik Jacko	26.09.1992	17		1
Yusuf Nasri Mainge (KEN)	26.12.1999	3		
Michel Abomo Meda (CMR)	24.12.2000	2	(2)	
Ján Nosko	25.05.1988	14		
Petr Pavlík (CZE)	22.07.1987	8		2
Lukáš Tesák	08.03.1985	11	(1)	
Richard Župa	27.04.1998	18	(3)	
Midfielders:	**DOB**	**M**	**(s)**	**G**
Cédric Badolo (BFA)	04.11.1998	6	(8)	1
Ján Dzúrik	18.07.1993	12	(2)	

	DOB	M	(s)	G
Alieu Fadera (GAM)	03.11.2001	1	(2)	1
Michal Klec	05.12.1995	11	(7)	3
Michal Obročník	04.06.1991	4		
Lukáš Pelegríni	10.05.1988	20	(5)	3
Jan Sojka	07.10.1990	1	(1)	
James Michael Weir (ENG)	04.08.1995	5		1
Forwards:	**DOB**	**M**	**(s)**	**G**
Patrick Blahut	07.10.1997	18	(8)	
Roland Gerebenits	07.05.2000	3	(2)	
Dávid Hrnčár	10.12.1997	13	(4)	1
Dávid Kondrlík	31.05.1997	1	(2)	
Kojo Matić (SRB)	07.11.1995	5		
Peter Mazán	13.05.1990	14	(6)	1
András Mészáros	29.03.1996	7	(8)	2
Matúš Mikuš	08.07.1991		(3)	
Jakub Sedláček	09.03.1998	10	(3)	
Ismar Tandir (BIH)	19.08.1995	4	(1)	
Mateusz Zachara (POL)	27.03.1990	8	(6)	2

Mestský futbalový klub Ružomberok

Founded: 1906 (*as Rózsahegyi Sport Club*)
Stadium: Štadión pod Čebraťom, Ružomberok (4,817)
Trainer: Ján Haspra 29.05.1969

Goalkeepers:	DOB	M	(s)	G
Ivan Krajčírik	15.06.2000	13		
Matúš Macík	19.05.1993	14		
Defenders:	**DOB**	**M**	**(s)**	**G**
Matej Čurma	27.03.1996	24		
David Filinsky	18.01.1999	3	(1)	
Alex Holub	15.03.2000	2	(1)	
Michal Jonec	30.07.1996	5	(2)	
Ján Maslo	05.02.1986	20		1
Alexander Mojžiš	02.01.1999	22		2
Mário Mrva	16.02.1999	8		
Filip Twardzik (CZE)	10.02.1993	22		6
Midfielders:	**DOB**	**M**	**(s)**	**G**
Mário Almaský	25.06.1991		(3)	
Miroslav Almaský	08.07.1994	2	(1)	
Adam Brenkus	08.01.1999	7	(3)	
Peter Ďungel	06.09.1993	4	(3)	
Filip Hašek (CZE)	20.03.1997	2	(1)	

	DOB	M	(s)	G
Viktor Jedinák	08.02.1998		(4)	
Matúš Kmeť	27.06.2000	3	(4)	1
Matej Kochan	21.11.1992		(2)	
Lukáš Kojnok	30.05.1997	17	(1)	1
Tihomir Kostadinov (MKD)	04.03.1996	22		1
Timotej Múdry	04.04.2000	2	(5)	
Kristi Qose (ALB)	10.06.1995	13	(2)	2
Dalibor Takáč	11.10.1997	20	(5)	3
Marek Zsigmund	20.04.1997	16	(1)	
Forwards:	**DOB**	**M**	**(s)**	**G**
Ladislav Almási	06.03.1999	4	(3)	2
Tomáš Bobček	08.09.2001	10	(8)	1
Štefan Gerec	10.11.1992	13	(8)	4
Rastislav Kružliak	11.07.1999	1	(3)	
Matej Madlenak	07.02.1999	4		
Ondřej Novotný (CZE)	05.02.1998	6	(9)	1
Martin Regáli	12.10.1993	18	(5)	2

Futbalový klub Senica

Founded: 1921
Stadium: OMS Arena, Senica (5,070)
Trainer: Michal Ščasný 19.08.1978
[14.02.2020] Jozef Olejnik 20.03.1974
[16.02.2020] Eduard Pagac 01.05.1978
[18.02.2020] Patrik Durkáč 14.03.1979
[07.03.2020] Ján Bíreš 02.06.1970
[01.07.2020] Patrik Durkáč 14.03.1979

Goalkeepers:	DOB	M	(s)	G
Federico Taborda (ARG)	01.11.1988	7		
Vojtěch Vorel (CZE)	18.06.1996	20		
Defenders:	**DOB**	**M**	**(s)**	**G**
Denis Baumgartner	02.02.1998	11	(7)	
Gustavo Cascardo de Assis (BRA)	24.03.1997	15	(1)	
João Francisco Favaro Amaral (BRA)	22.04.1992	9		
Simon Horniak	01.03.2001		(1)	
Tomáš Košút	13.01.1990	3	(1)	
Lukáš Kučera	18.04.2000	2	(1)	
Mario Mihal	27.02.2001	7	(1)	
Erik Otrísal	28.06.1996	3		
Midfielders:	**DOB**	**M**	**(s)**	**G**
Jakub Buchel	16.09.2002		(2)	
Frank Andersson Castañeda Vélez (COL)	17.07.1994	17		8
Filip Cernak	07.06.2001	1	(6)	
Lovro Cvek (CRO)	06.07.1995	13		
Filip Deket	01.05.1993	1		
Joss Didiba Moudoumbou (CMR)	07.11.1997	23	(2)	2

	DOB	M	(s)	G
Dominik Duda (CZE)	03.03.1995	5		
Sofian El Moudane (FRA)	16.03.1994	15		2
Mihovil Klapan (CRO)	27.03.1995	18		
Jakub Krč	02.09.1997	6	(1)	
Kristián Lukáčik	29.03.1998	6	(1)	
Luis Alejandro Ramírez López (VEN)	22.04.1996	3	(10)	
Roberto Dias Correia Filho (BRA)	08.08.1988	16		1
Julián Caro Sepulveda (COL)	07.02.2000		(1)	
Marko Totka	12.09.2000	14	(7)	
Tenton Yenne (NGA)	07.07.2000	22		1
Forwards:	**DOB**	**M**	**(s)**	**G**
Edmund Addo (GHA)	17.05.2000	15	(2)	
Samson Olanrewaju Akinyoola (NGA)	03.03.2000	10	(8)	4
Filip Buchel	16.09.2002	3	(3)	
Peter Eneji Moses (NGA)	08.04.1999	10	(2)	4
Jamarl Anthony Joseph (ENG)	12.07.1995		(1)	
David Melis	18.09.2001	8		
Kwaku Bonsu Osei (GHA)	17.08.2000	1		1
Sadam Sulley (GHA)	16.10.1996	13	(5)	2

Športový Klub Futbalu Sereď

Founded: 28.06.1914 (*as Sereďský športový klub*)
Stadium: Štadión Myjava, Myjava (2,709)
Trainer: Slavche Vojnski (MKD) 28.04.1974
[19.12.2019] Róland Praj 06.10.1967
[09.02.2020] Peter Lérant 30.01.1977

Goalkeepers:	DOB	M	(s)	G
Dejan Iliev (MKD)	25.02.1995	18		
Adnan Kanurić (BIH)	08.08.2000	8		
Mathew Yakubu	03.09.1999	1		
Defenders:	**DOB**	**M**	**(s)**	**G**
Djiby Ba (SEN)	21.03.1993	25		3
Bruno Dip Rapanelli (BRA)	17.02.1998		(1)	
Tomáš Hučko	03.10.1985	24	(1)	3
Martin Mečiar	23.07.1993	2	(2)	1
Ľubomir Michalík	13.08.1983	12		
Tomás Soares Dábo (GNB)	20.10.1993	16		
Martin Sus (CZE)	15.03.1990	5		
Nikola Unković (SRB)	19.12.1999		(1)	
Midfielders:	**DOB**	**M**	**(s)**	**G**
Banjole Olawale Adekuoroye (NGA)	16.02.1996	9	(6)	
Aldo Omar Baéz (ARG)	05.09.1988	1		
Cléber Nascimento do Silva (BRA)	03.06.1986	11	(6)	1
Filip Duranski (MKD)	17.07.1991	7		
Alex Iván	11.10.1997	26		1

	DOB	M	(s)	G
Roko Jureškin (CRO)	29.09.2000	1	(5)	1
Kristián Lukáčik	29.03.1998	7	(1)	
Matheus do Amaro Olavo (BRA)	30.11.1994	2	(5)	
Abdelaziz Metalsi (BIH)	19.04.1994	5		
Adam Morong	16.06.1993	19	(3)	3
Filip Pankarićan (SRB)	28.03.1993	14	(9)	3
Denis Potoma	15.02.2000	4	(4)	1
Maj Rorić (SVN)	07.02.2000	11	(6)	
Martin Slaninka	26.03.1996	15	(3)	
Nicolas Šumský (CZE)	13.11.1993	3		
Denis Ventúra	01.08.1995	15		1
Forwards:	**DOB**	**M**	**(s)**	**G**
Senad Jarović (GER)	20.01.1998	4	(4)	
Panagiotis Louka (CYP)	08.09.2000	2	(10)	
Dino Špehar (CRO)	08.02.1994	19	(4)	5
Ľubomír Ulrich	01.02.1989	1		
Aleksandar Vucenovic (AUT)	10.10.1997	3	(3)	
Matej Vuk (CRO)	10.06.2000	7	(2)	4

Športový klub Slovan Bratislava

Founded: 03.05.1919 (*as 1. ČsŠK Bratislava*)
Stadium: Štadión Tehelné pole, Bratislava (22,500)
Trainer: Martin Ševela   20.11.1975
[23.07.2019]   Ján Kozák   22.04.1980

Goalkeepers:	DOB	M	(s)	G
Dominik Greif	06.04.1997	20		
Michal Šulla	15.07.1991	6		
Martin Trnovský	07.06.2000	1		
Defenders:	**DOB**	**M**	**(s)**	**G**
Myenty Abena (NED)	12.12.1994	17	(1)	2
Mitch Apau (NED)	27.04.1990	11		
Kenan Bajrič (SVN)	20.12.1994	17		3
Vasil Bozhikov (BUL)	02.06.1988	17		
Vernon De Marco Morlacchi (ARG)	18.11.1992	13	(4)	1
Richárd Guzmics (HUN)	16.04.1987	2	(2)	
Marin Ljubičić (CRO)	15.06.1988	13	(3)	
Lucas Lovat (BRA)	15.01.1997	5		
Jurij Medveděv (CZE)	18.06.1996	8	(3)	
Lukáš Pauschek	09.12.1992	7	(2)	
Artem Sukhotsky (UKR)	06.12.1992	12		2
Midfielders:	**DOB**	**M**	**(s)**	**G**
Erik Daniel (CZE)	04.02.1992	17	(7)	1
Joeri de Kamps (NED)	10.02.1992	11	(8)	
Dávid Holman (HUN)	17.03.1993	11	(7)	5
Filip Lichý	25.01.2001	2	(1)	
Alen Mustafić (BIH)	05.07.1999	2		
José Antonio Delgado Villar „Nono" (ESP)	30.03.1993	16	(5)	4
Ibrahim Rabiu (NGA)	15.03.1991	16	(2)	1
Vladimír Weiss	30.11.1989	1	(2)	
Forwards:	**DOB**	**M**	**(s)**	**G**
Aleksandar Čavrić (SRB)	18.05.1994	5	(2)	2
Dejan Drazič (SRB)	26.09.1995	12	(4)	1
Ezekiel Henty (NGA)	13.05.1993	4	(1)	
Žan Medved (SVN)	14.06.1999	2	(3)	2
Mohammed Rharsalla Khadfi (MAR)	15.09.1993	14	(9)	6
Alen Ožbolt (SVN)	24.06.1996	4	(2)	1
Rafael Rogério da Silva „Rafael Ratão" (BRA)	30.11.1995	14	(6)	9
Andraž Šporar (SVN)	27.02.1994	9	(2)	12
Dávid Strelec	04.04.2001	8	(4)	4

Asociácia športov Trenčín

Founded: 1992 (*as TJ Ozeta Dukla Trenčín*)
Stadium: Štadión pod Dubňom, Žilina (11,258)
Trainer: Matthias Kohler (GER)   09.06.1991
[22.10.2019]   Norbert Hrnčár   09.06.1970
[29.06.2020]   Juraj Ančic   12.07.1981

Goalkeepers:	DOB	M	(s)	G
Menno Bergsen (NED)	26.08.1999	4		
Denis Chudý	01.02.2000	5		
Igor Šemrinec	22.11.1987	18		
Defenders:	**DOB**	**M**	**(s)**	**G**
Keston Julien (TRI)	26.10.1998	17		3
Steve Kapuadi (FRA)	30.04.1998	7		
Peter Kleščík	18.09.1988	13	(2)	
Cole Kpekawa (ENG)	20.05.1996	1		
Richard Križan	23.09.1997	10	(2)	
Adam Laczkó	02.04.1997	1		
Ruben Ligeon (NED)	24.05.1992	15	(2)	1
Urban Mazanovský	17.12.2003	1		
John Andrew Neeskens Ramírez (USA)	17.11.1993	1	(1)	1
Erik Nielsen Duarte Boaventura (CPV)	31.10.1996	1		
Adrián Slávik	12.04.1999	5	(2)	
Lukáš Skovajsa	27.03.1994	11		
Martin Šulek	15.01.1998	22		1
Midfielders:	**DOB**	**M**	**(s)**	**G**
Hamza Ćataković (BIH)	15.01.1997	18	(7)	7
Milan Corryn (BEL)	04.04.1999	4	(11)	1
Aschraf el Mahdioui (NED)	24.05.1996	11	(2)	1
Jakub Kadák	14.12.2000	4	(12)	4
Ryan Koolwijk (NED)	08.08.1985	18	(2)	2
Mohammed Lamine (GHA)	02.02.2002	1	(2)	
Paulo Junior Dos Gomes Santos (CPV)	25.10.2000		(1)	
Ante Roguljić (CRO)	11.03.1996	25		8
Desley Ubbink (NED)	15.06.1993		(1)	
Abdul Zubairu (NGA)	03.10.1998	21	(3)	2
Forwards:	**DOB**	**M**	**(s)**	**G**
Osman Bukari (GHA)	13.12.1998	25		10
Ivenzo Comvalius (SUR)	24.06.1997	10	(4)	1
David Alberto Depetris (ARG)	11.11.1988	5	(16)	2
Ahmad Abubakar Ghali (NGA)	23.06.2000	4	(1)	1
Lukáš Letenay	19.04.2001	1	(1)	
Adam Tučný	21.05.2002		(1)	
Gino Ronald van Kessel (CUW)	09.03.1993	18	(4)	6

Football Club Spartak Trnava

Founded: 30.05.1923 (*as TŠS Trnava*)
Stadium: Štadión "Antona Malatinského", Trnava (19,200)
Trainer: Ricardo José Moutinho Chéu (POR)   14.05.1981
[05.06.2020]   Marián Šarmír   01.05.1976

Goalkeepers:	DOB	M	(s)	G
Petr Bolek (CZE)	13.06.1984	1		
Ľuboš Kamenár	17.06.1987	1		
Dobrivoj Rusov	13.01.1993	24		
Dominik Takáč	12.01.1999	1	(1)	
Defenders:	**DOB**	**M**	**(s)**	**G**
Oliver Burian	18.05.2001		(1)	
João Diogo Gomes de Freitas (POR)	28.02.1988	16		
Lucas Lovat (BRA)	15.01.1997	14		1
Marko Marinković (SRB)	06.01.1994	1	(2)	
Jozef Menich	15.09.1994	3	(3)	
Bogdan Alexandru Mitrea (ROU)	29.09.1987	20		6
Malkolm Moënza (SWE)	15.11.1993	9		
Milan Sekera	14.02.2002		(3)	
Matúš Turňa	11.05.1986	17	(1)	
Timotej Zahumenský	17.07.1995	5		
Midfielders:	**DOB**	**M**	**(s)**	**G**
Izuchukwu Jude Anthony (NGA)	03.11.1997	9		
Yusuf Bamidele (NGA)	22.02.2001	4	(3)	1
Samuel Benovič	03.01.2001	1	(1)	
Martin Gamboš	23.01.1998	12	(7)	1
Erik Grendel	13.10.1988	7	(4)	
Emir Halilović (BIH)	04.11.1989	15	(1)	2
Alexander Horvat	25.09.2000		(3)	
Matej Jakúbek	19.01.1995	2	(1)	
Joel Vieira Pereira (POR)	28.09.1996	2	(1)	
Nsumoh Johnson Kalu (NGA)	23.06.1905		(2)	
Jakub Krč	02.09.1997	2		
Ivan Mesík	01.06.2001	16		1
Marko Tešija (CRO)	14.01.1992	24		2
Theofanis Tzandaris (GRE)	13.06.1993	8		1
Dijan Vukojević (SWE)	12.09.1995	3	(3)	
Yann Michael Yao (CIV)	20.06.1997	8	(1)	
Forwards:	**DOB**	**M**	**(s)**	**G**
Allecks Alves (BRA)	11.03.2001		(1)	
Filip Dangubić (CRO)	05.05.1995	13	(4)	
Marko Kelemen	29.04.2000		(7)	
Thomas Kotlár	05.08.2003		(1)	
Kristián Mihálek	10.03.2000		(6)	
Štefan Molnár	04.11.1994			
Petar Orlandić (MNE)	06.08.1990	3	(1)	1
Filip Oršula	25.02.1993	5	(8)	1
Rafael Tavares (BRA)	26.06.2000	18	(4)	2
Saymon De Barros Cabral (BRA)	09.07.2001	5		
Alex Sobczyk (AUT)	20.05.1997	24	(1)	7
Gino Ronald van Kessel (CUW)	09.03.1993		(2)	
Kubilay Yilmaz (AUT)	09.07.1996	4	(6)	3

Mestský Futbalový klub Zemplín Michalovce

Founded: 1912 (*as NAC Michalovce*)
Stadium: Mestský futbalový štadión, Michalovce (4,440)
Trainer: Anton Šoltís   05.02.1976
[12.11.2019]   Jozef Majoroš   21.03.1978

Goalkeepers:	DOB	M	(s)	G
Rostyslav Dehtiar (UKR)	30.03.1999	1		
Tomáš Dráb	01.06.1999	2		
Matús Kira	10.10.1994	24		
Defenders:	**DOB**	**M**	**(s)**	**G**
José Carrillo Mancilla (ESP)	04.03.1995	23		1
Vadim Chervak (UKR)	27.05.1999	5		
Martin Kolesár	10.12.1997	11	(3)	
Dimitrios Konstantinidis (GRE)	02.06.1994	8		2
Alejandro Méndez García	28.07.2001	3	(1)	
Denis Petro	18.06.1999	1	(1)	
Ían Pino Soler (ESP)	23.01.1996	14		1
Matúš Vojtko	05.10.2000	18	(2)	1
Midfielders:	**DOB**	**M**	**(s)**	**G**
Matúš Begala	07.04.2001	5	(1)	
Stanislav Danko	17.03.1994	11	(6)	1
Jakub Grič	05.07.1996	16	(4)	1
Peter Kolesár	09.07.1998	12	(7)	2
Lukas Lukco	27.07.2001		(1)	
Til Mavretic (SVN)	19.11.1997	3	(3)	
Giorgos Neofytidis (GRE)	28.07.2000	4	(4)	
Marian Pasztor	12.01.2001		(1)	
Pedro Martínez García (ESP)	09.02.1996	9	(2)	2
Lazaros Rota (GRE)	23.08.1997	14		1
Kyriakos Savvidis (GRE)	20.06.1995	22		
Matej Trusa	29.11.2000	6		2
Jozef-Šimon Turík	19.07.1995	11	(2)	1
Igor Žofčák	10.04.1983	19	(2)	2
Forwards:	**DOB**	**M**	**(s)**	**G**
Cheick Alan Diarra (FRA)	23.06.1993	3	(4)	
Armen Hovhannisyan (ARM)	07.03.2000	2	(9)	2
Christos Kountouriotis (GRE)	02.01.1998	8	(13)	1
Milan Kvocera	01.01.1998	11	(4)	2
Emmanuel Mensah (GHA)	30.06.1994	1	(3)	
Dimitrios Popovits (GRE)	11.02.1995	14	(3)	
Modibo Issa Sidibé (NIG)	05.12.1985	16	(4)	8

Football Club Viliam Ondrejka Zlaté Moravce

Founded: 1995
Stadium: Štadión FC ViOn, Zlaté Moravce (4,000)
Trainer: Karol Praženica   15.11.1970
[01.07.2020]   Ľuboš Benkovský   22.02.1989

Goalkeepers:	DOB	M	(s)	G
Adrián Chovan	08.10.1995	2		
Branislav Pindroch	30.10.1991	25		
Defenders:	**DOB**	**M**	**(s)**	**G**
Antonio Asanović (CRO)	30.11.1991	24		
Martin Chren	02.01.1984	7	(1)	
Peter Čögley	11.08.1988	14		
Jacy Maranhão Oliveira (BRA)	11.07.1997	2	(4)	
Michal Pintér	04.02.1994	18	(1)	
Martin Tóth	13.10.1986	16		
Midfielders:	**DOB**	**M**	**(s)**	**G**
Jakub Brašeň	02.05.1989	25		1
Tomáš Ďubek	22.01.1987	25	(1)	8
Denis Duga	05.09.1994	17	(3)	1
Tomce Grozdanovski (MKD)	14.03.2000	8	(8)	
David Haspra	06.11.2000	3		
Adam Mihálik	24.07.2000		(3)	
Peter Orávik	18.12.1988	3	(8)	
Dávid Richtárech	22.04.1996	8	(12)	1
Sílvio Rodrigues Pereira Júnior (BRA)	04.05.1994	1	(11)	1
Anton Sloboda	10.07.1987	19		3
Forwards:	**DOB**	**M**	**(s)**	**G**
Boris Cmiljanić (MNE)	17.03.1996	3	(3)	1
Gustavo Henrique Cabral De Souza (BRA)	20.12.1999	1	(10)	
Dávid Hrnčár	10.12.1997	8		
Senad Jarović (GER)	20.01.1998	12	(1)	4
Marko Kelemen	29.04.2000	1	(1)	
Martin Kovaľ	10.02.1999	27		2
András Mészáros	29.03.1996	5	(2)	1
Murilo Henrique Calvacante (BRA)	15.03.1999	1		
Jakub Švec	03.12.2000	11	(10)	2
Vladimír Tkáč	09.01.1998	4		
Martin Válovčan	14.05.1993	7	(1)	

Mestský Športový klub Žilina

Founded: 20.06.1908 (*as Zsolnai Testgyakorlók Köre*)
Stadium: Štadión pod Dubňom, Žilina (11,258)
Trainer: Jaroslav Kentoš   14.05.1974
[02.01.2020]   Pavol Staňo   29.09.1977

Goalkeepers:	DOB	M	(s)	G
Dominik Holec	28.07.1994	22		
Samuel Petráš	10.04.1999	5		
Defenders:	**DOB**	**M**	**(s)**	**G**
Benson Anang (GHA)	01.05.2000	6	(2)	
Besir Demiri (ALB)	01.08.1994	21		2
Filip Kaša (CZE)	01.01.1994	20		1
Jakub Kiwior (POL)	15.02.2000	9	(4)	
Adam Kopas	16.08.1999	4		
Martin Králik	03.04.1995	22		3
Jan Minarik	25.07.1997	11	(3)	
Branislav Sluka	23.01.1999	17	(1)	3
Midfielders:	**DOB**	**M**	**(s)**	**G**
Ján Bernát	10.01.2001	18	(4)	9
Iván Santiago Díaz (ARG)	23.01.1993	9	(2)	
Dávid Ďuriš	18.03.1999	15	(8)	6
Enis Fazlagić (MKD)	27.03.2000	10	(3)	
Miroslav Gono	01.11.2000	4	(2)	
Miroslav Káčer	02.02.1996	22		4
Patrik Myslovič	28.05.2001	4	(6)	1
Jakub Paur	04.07.1992	7	(3)	1
Viktor Pečovský	24.05.1983	5	(2)	
Michal Tomič	30.03.1999	10	(2)	1
Kristián Vallo	02.06.1998	12	(6)	2
Forwards:	**DOB**	**M**	**(s)**	**G**
Filip Balaj	02.08.1997	6	(11)	3
Vahan Bichakhchyan (ARM)	09.07.1999	1	(7)	1
Róbert Boženík	18.11.1999	16		3
Patrik Iľko	16.02.2001	4	(3)	1
Lukáš Jánošík	05.03.1994	13	(2)	3
Adrián Kaprálik	10.06.2002		(2)	
Dawid Kurminowski (POL)	24.02.1999	4	(8)	4

Please note: the league was suspended on 08.03.2020 due to Covid-19 pandemic. Top-6 teams (at the time of abandonment) formed a promotion group, playing an additional single round robin among each other, with the exception of four matches already played between this teams in rounds 16-17-18.

1.	MFK Dukla Banská Bystrica	18	13	2	3	41	-	20	41
2.	FK Dubnica nad Váhom	18	12	2	4	39	-	24	38
3.	MFK Skalica	18	11	2	5	33	-	19	35
4.	FK Poprad	17	10	1	6	26	-	16	31
5.	MŠK Žilina „B“	18	10	1	7	38	-	29	31
6.	FK Železiarne Podbrezová	18	9	1	8	26	-	26	28
7.	MFK Tatran Liptovský Mikuláš	18	8	2	8	28	-	30	26
8.	MŠK Púchov	18	7	3	8	22	-	24	24
9.	MFK Ružomberok „B“*	18	7	1	10	23	-	36	22
10.	FC Košice	17	5	6	6	22	-	18	21
11.	ŠK Partizán Bardejov	18	6	3	9	19	-	23	21
12.	FC ŠTK 1914 Šamorín	18	6	3	9	24	-	31	21
13.	KFC Komárno	18	5	5	8	19	-	28	20
14.	FC Petržalka Bratislava	18	5	2	11	24	-	34	17
15.	ŠK Slovan Bratislava "B"	18	5	2	11	16	-	31	17
16.	FK Slavoj Trebišov	18	3	6	9	23	-	34	15

*withdrew due to financial reasons.

	Promotion Group								
1.	FK Dubnica nad Váhom (*Promotion Play-offs*)	20	14	4	2	45	-	22	46
2.	MFK Dukla Banská Bystrica	20	14	3	3	52	-	23	45
3.	MFK Skalica	20	12	3	5	32	-	19	39
4.	FK Železiarne Podbrezová	20	10	2	8	31	-	28	32
5.	MŠK Žilina „B“	20	10	1	9	41	-	33	31
6.	FK Poprad	20	10	0	10	26	-	29	30

NATIONAL TEAM

INTERNATIONAL MATCHES
(16.07.2019 – 15.07.2020)

06.09.2019	Trnava	Slovakia - Croatia	0-4(0-1)	(ECQ)
09.09.2019	Budapest	Hungary - Slovakia	1-2(0-1)	(ECQ)
10.10.2019	Trnava	Slovakia - Wales	1-1(0-1)	(ECQ)
13.10.2019	Bratislava	Slovakia - Paraguay	1-1(0-0)	(F)
16.11.2019	Rijeka	Croatia - Slovakia	3-1(0-1)	(ECQ)
19.11.2019	Trnava	Slovakia - Azerbaijan	2-0(1-0)	(ECQ)

06.09.2019   SLOVAKIA - CROATIA   **0-4(0-1)**   16th EC. Qualifiers
Štadión „Antona Malatinského", Trnava; Referee: Dr. Felix Brych (Germany); Attendance: 18,098
SVK: Martin Dúbravka, Milan Škriniar, Denis Vavro, Martin Valjent, Dávid Hancko, Marek Hamšík (Cap), Juraj Kucka (63.Lukáš Haraslín), Róbert Mak (79.Michal Ďuriš), Albert Rusnák (46.Róbert Boženík), Ondrej Duda, Stanislav Lobotka. Trainer: Pavel Hapal (Czech Republic).

09.09.2019   HUNGARY - SLOVAKIA   **1-2(0-1)**   16th EC. Qualifiers
Groupama Arena, Budapest; Referee: Antonio Miguel Mateu Lahoz (Spain); Attendance: 21,700
SVK: Martin Dúbravka, Ľubomír Šatka, Milan Škriniar, Denis Vavro, Dávid Hancko, Marek Hamšík (Cap), Juraj Kucka (85.Ján Greguš), Róbert Mak (86.Lukáš Haraslín), Albert Rusnák, Stanislav Lobotka, Róbert Boženík (77.Michal Ďuriš). Trainer: Pavel Hapal (Czech Republic).
Goals: Róbert Mak (40), Róbert Boženík (56).

10.10.2019   SLOVAKIA - WALES   **1-1(0-1)**   16th EC. Qualifiers
Štadión "Antona Malatinského", Trnava; Referee: Carlos del Cerro Grande (Spain); Attendance: 18,071
SVK: Martin Dúbravka, Peter Pekarík, Norbert Gyömbér [*sent off 88*], Milan Škriniar, Dávid Hancko, Marek Hamšík (Cap), Juraj Kucka, Róbert Mak (79.Lukáš Haraslín), Albert Rusnák, Stanislav Lobotka, Róbert Boženík (86.Pavol Šafranko). Trainer: Pavel Hapal (Czech Republic).
Goal: Juraj Kucka (53).

13.10.2019   SLOVAKIA - PARAGUAY   **1-1(0-0)**   Friendly International
Štadión Tehelné pole, Bratislava; Referee: Slavko Vinčić (Slovenia); Attendance: 6,669
SVK: Dominik Greif, Martin Škrtel (Cap) (32.Denis Vavro), Róbert Mazáň (87.Tomáš Hubočan), Ľubomír Šatka, Martin Valjent, Ján Greguš (46.Róbert Boženík), Patrik Hrošovský (71.Marek Hamšík), Ondrej Duda (46.László Bénes), Adam Nemec (31.Matúš Bero), Michal Ďuriš, Lukáš Haraslín. Trainer: Pavel Hapal (Czech Republic).
Goal: Róbert Boženík (59).

16.11.2019   CROATIA - SLOVAKIA   **3-1(0-1)**   16th EC. Qualifiers
Stadion Rujevica, Rijeka; Referee: Clément Turpin (France); Attendance: 8,212
SVK: Martin Dúbravka, Peter Pekarík, Milan Škriniar, Denis Vavro, Dávid Hancko, Marek Hamšík (Cap), Juraj Kucka (79.Patrik Hrošovský), Róbert Mak [*sent off 66*], Albert Rusnák (63.Lukáš Haraslín), Stanislav Lobotka, Róbert Boženík (72.Michal Ďuriš). Trainer: Pavel Hapal (Czech Republic).
Goal: Róbert Boženík (32).

19.11.2019 **SLOVAKIA - AZERBAIJAN** **2-0(1-0)** 16th EC. Qualifiers

Štadión "Antona Malatinského", Trnava; Referee: Serhiy Boyko (Ukraine); Attendance: 7,825
SVK: Martin Dúbravka, Peter Pekarik, Norbert Gyömbér, Milan Škriniar, Dávid Hancko, Marek Hamšík (Cap), Juraj Kucka (85.Ondrej Duda), Matúš Bero, Stanislav Lobotka, Lukáš Haraslín (71.Michal Ďuriš), Róbert Boženík (77.Samuel Mráz). Trainer: Pavel Hapal (Czech Republic).
Goals: Róbert Boženík (19), Marek Hamšík (86).

NATIONAL TEAM PLAYERS
(16.07.2019 – 15.07.2020)

Name	DOB	Caps	Goals	2019/2020:	Club
Goalkeepers					
Martin DÚBRAVKA	15.01.1989	23	0	2019:	*Newcastle United FC (ENG)*
Dominik GREIF	06.04.1997	2	0	2019:	*ŠK Slovan Bratislava*
Defenders					
Norbert GYÖMBÉR	03.07.1992	23	0	2019:	*AC Perugia Calcio (ITA)*
Dávid HANCKO	13.12.1997	12	1	2019:	*AC Sparta Praha (CZE)*
Tomáš HUBOČAN	17.09.1985	65	0	2019:	*AC Omonia Nicosia (CYP)*
Róbert MAZÁŇ	09.02.1994	8	0	2019:	*CD Tenerife (ESP)*
Peter PEKARÍK	30.10.1986	91	2	2019:	*Hertha BSC Berlin (GER)*
Ľubomír ŠATKA	02.12.1995	9	0	2019:	*KKS Lech Poznań (POL)*
Milan ŠKRINIAR	11.02.1995	31	0	2019:	*FC Internazionale Milano (ITA)*
Martin ŠKRTEL	15.12.1984	104	6	2019:	*İstanbul Başakşehir FK (TUR)*
Martin VALJENT	11.12.1995	3	0	2019:	*RCD Mallorca (ESP)*
Denis VAVRO	10.04.1996	7	0	2019:	*SS Lazio Roma (ITA)*
Midfielders					
Matúš BERO	06.09.1995	11	0	2019:	*SBV Vitesse Arnhem (NED)*
László BÉNES	09.09.1997	3	0	2019:	*Borussia VfL Mönchengladbach (GER)*
Ondrej DUDA	05.12.1994	36	5	2019:	*Hertha BSC Berlin (GER)*
Ján GREGUŠ	29.01.1991	26	3	2019:	*Minnesota United FC (USA)*
Marek HAMŠÍK	27.07.1987	120	25	2019:	*Dalian Yifamg FC (CHN)*
Lukáš HARASLÍN	26.05.1996	8	1	2019:	*KS Lechia Gdańsk (POL)*
Patrik HROŠOVSKÝ	22.04.1992	25	0	2019:	*KRC Genk (BEL)*
Juraj KUCKA	26.02.1987	72	9	2019:	*Parma Calcio 1913 (ITA)*
Stanislav LOBOTKA	25.11.1994	22	3	2019:	*RC Celta de Vigo (ESP)*
Róbert MAK	08.03.1991	58	12	2019:	*FK Zenit Saint Petersburg (RUS)*
Albert RUSNÁK	07.07.1994	24	5	2019:	*Real Salt Lake (USA)*
Forwards					
Róbert BOŽENÍK	18.11.1999	8	4	2019:	*MŠK Žilina*
Michal ĎURIŠ	01.06.1988	47	5	2019:	*Anorthosis Famagusta FC (CYP)*
Samuel MRÁZ	13.05.1997	3	1	2019:	*Brøndby IF (DEN)*
Adam NEMEC	02.09.1985	43	13	2019:	*Pafos FC Paphos (CYP)*
Pavol ŠAFRANKO	16.11.1994	4	0	2019:	*ACS Sepsi OSK Sfântu Gheorghe (ROU)*
National team coach					
Pavel HAPAL (Czech Republic) [from 22.10.2019]	27.07.1969	12 M; 6 W; 2 D; 4 L; 23-14			

SLOVENIA

The Country:
Republika Slovenija (Republic of Slovenia)
Capital: Ljubljana
Surface: 20,273 km²
Inhabitants: 2,095,861 [2020]
Time: UTC+1

The FA:
Nogometna zveza Slovenije
Predoslje 40 a, p.p. 130, 4000 Kranj
Tel: +386 4 27 59 400
Founded: 23.04.1920
Member of FIFA since: 1992
Member of UEFA since: 1992
Website: www.nzs.si

NATIONAL TEAM RECORDS

RECORDS

First international match:	03.06.1992, Tallinn:	Estonia – Slovenia 1-1
Most international caps:	Boštjan Cesar	- 101 caps (2003-2018)
Most international goals:	Zlatko Zahovič	- 35 goals / 80 caps (1992-2004)

UEFA EUROPEAN CHAMPIONSHIP

Year	Result
1960	-
1964	-
1968	-
1972	-
1976	-
1980	-
1984	-
1988	-
1992	-
1996	Qualifiers
2000	Final Tournament (Group Stage)
2004	Qualifiers
2008	Qualifiers
2012	Qualifiers
2016	Qualifiers
2020	Qualifiers

FIFA WORLD CUP

Year	Result
1930	-
1934	-
1938	-
1950	-
1954	-
1958	-
1962	-
1966	-
1970	-
1974	-
1978	-
1982	-
1986	-
1990	-
1994	Did not enter
1998	Qualifiers
2002	Final Tournament (Group Stage)
2006	Qualifiers
2010	Final Tournament (Group Stage)
2014	Qualifiers
2018	Qualifiers

OLYMPIC TOURNAMENTS

Year	Result
1908	-
1912	-
1920	-
1924	-
1928	-
1936	-
1948	-
1952	-
1956	-
1960	-
1964	-
1968	-
1972	-
1976	-
1980	-
1984	-
1988	-
1992	-
1996	Qualifiers
2000	Qualifiers
2004	Qualifiers
2008	Qualifiers
2012	Qualifiers
2016	Qualifiers

Please note: was part of Yugoslavia between 1930-1990.

UEFA NATIONS LEAGUE

2018/2019 – League C

FIFA CONFEDERATIONS CUP 1992-2017

None

SLOVENIAN CLUB HONOURS IN EUROPEAN CLUB COMPETITIONS:

European Champion Clubs.Cup (1956-1992) / UEFA Champions League (1993-2020)
None

Fairs Cup (1858-1971) / UEFA Cup (1972-2009) / UEFA Europa League (2010-2020)
None

UEFA Super Cup (1972-2019)
None

European Cup Winners.Cup 1961-1999*
None

*defunct competition

	CHAMPIONS	CUP WINNERS	BEST GOALSCORERS	
1991/1992	NK Olimpija Ljubljana	NK Maribor	Zoran Ubavič (NK Olimpija Ljubljana)	29
1992/1993	NK Olimpija Ljubljana	NK Olimpija Ljubljana	Sašo Udovič (ND Slovan Ljubljana)	25
1993/1994	NK Olimpija Ljubljana	NK Maribor	Štefan Škaper (NK Beltinci)	23
1994/1995	NK Olimpija Ljubljana	NK Mura Murska Sobota	Štefan Škaper (NK Beltinci)	25
1995/1996	ND Gorica	NK Olimpija Ljubljana	Ermin Šiljak (NK Olimpija Ljubljana)	28
1996/1997	NK Maribor	NK Maribor	Faik Kamberović (BIH, NK Celje)	21
1997/1998	NK Maribor	NK Rudar Velenje	Ismet Ekmečić (NK Olimpija Ljubljana)	21
1998/1999	NK Maribor	NK Maribor	Novica Nikčević (SRB, ND Gorica)	17
1999/2000	NK Maribor	NK Olimpija Ljubljana	Kliton Bozgo (ALB, NK Maribor)	24
2000/2001	NK Maribor	ND Gorica	Damir Pekič (NK Celje)	23
2001/2002	NK Maribor	ND Gorica	Romano Obilinović (CRO, NK Primorje Ajdovščina)	16
2002/2003	NK Maribor	NK Olimpija Ljubljana	Marko Kmetec (NK Ljubljana / NK Olimpija Ljubljana)	21
2003/2004	ND Gorica	NK Maribor	Dražen Žeželj (NK Ljubljana / NK Primorje Ajdovščina)	19
2004/2005	ND Gorica	NK Celje	Kliton Bozgo (ALB, NK Maribor)	18
2005/2006	ND Gorica	FC Koper	Miran Burgič (ND Gorica)	24
2006/2007	NK Domžale	FC Koper	Nikola Nikezić (MNE, NK Domžale / ND Gorica)	22
2007/2008	NK Domžale	NK Interblock Ljubljana	Dario Zahora (CRO, NK Domžale)	22
2008/2009	NK Maribor	NK Interblock Ljubljana	Etien Velikonja (ND Gorica)	17
2009/2010	FC Koper	NK Maribor	Milan Osterc (FC Koper)	23
2010/2011	NK Maribor	NK Domžale	Marcos Magno Morales Tavares (BRA, NK Maribor)	16
2011/2012	NK Maribor	NK Maribor	Dare Vršič (NK Olimpija Ljubljana)	22
2012/2013	NK Maribor	NK Maribor	Marcos Magno Morales Tavares (BRA, NK Maribor)	17
2013/2014	NK Maribor	ND Gorica	Mate Eterović (CRO, NK Rudar Velenje)	19
2014/2015	NK Maribor	FC Koper	Marcos Magno Morales Tavares (BRA, NK Maribor)	17
2015/2016	NK Olimpija Ljubljana	NK Maribor	Rok Kronaveter (NK Olimpija Ljubljana) / Jean-Philippe Mendy (FRA, NK Maribor) / Andraž Šporar (NK Olimpija Ljubljana)	17
2016/2017	NK Maribor	NK Domžale	John Mary Honi Uzuegbunam (CMR, NK Rudar Velenje)	17
2017/2018	NK Olimpija Ljubljana	NK Olimpija Ljubljana	Luka Zahović (NK Maribor)	18
2018/2019	NK Maribor	NK Olimpija Ljubljana	Luka Zahović (NK Maribor)	18
2019/2020	NK Celje	NŠ Mura Murska Sobota	Ante Vukušic (CRO, NK Olimpija Ljubljana)	26

NATIONAL CHAMPIONSHIP
Prva liga Telekom Slovenije 2019/2020
(13.07.2019 – 22.07.2020)

Results

Round 1 [13-14.07.2019]
NK Tabor - NK Aluminij 0-2(0-2)
NK Maribor - NK Triglav 1-2(0-1)
NK Bravo - Olimpija Ljubljana 0-2(0-1)
NK Celje - NŠ Mura 2-2(0-2)
NK Domžale - Rudar Velenje 2-2(1-1)

Round 2 [19-21.07.2019]
NK Aluminij - NK Triglav 2-1(0-1)
NK Tabor - NK Celje 1-0(1-0)
Rudar Velenje - NK Maribor 1-1(0-1)
NŠ Mura - NK Bravo 4-3(2-1)
Olimpija Ljubljana - NK Domžale 4-2(2-2)

Round 3 [26-28.07.2019]
NK Celje - NK Aluminij 0-0
NK Triglav - Rudar Velenje 3-2(2-1)
NK Bravo - NK Tabor 1-0(0-0)
NK Maribor - Olimpija Ljubljana 0-0
NK Domžale - NŠ Mura 0-0 [12.09.]

Round 4 [02-04.08.2019]
NK Celje - NK Bravo 2-2(1-2)
NK Aluminij - Rudar Velenje 1-1(1-0)
NŠ Mura - NK Maribor 1-1(1-0)
NK Tabor - NK Domžale 2-1(2-0)
Olimpija Ljubljana - NK Triglav 4-2(3-1)

Round 5 [09-11.08.2019]
NK Bravo - NK Aluminij 0-1(0-0)
NK Triglav - NŠ Mura 1-3(0-2)
NK Maribor - NK Tabor 4-2(1-1)
NK Domžale - NK Celje 3-5(0-3)
Rudar Velenje - Olimpija Ljubljana 0-3(0-2)

Round 6 [17-18.08.2019]
NK Tabor - NK Triglav 2-0(1-0)
NK Celje - NK Maribor 2-1(1-0)
NK Bravo - NK Domžale 0-0
NŠ Mura - Rudar Velenje 2-0(0-0)
NK Aluminij - Olimpija Ljubljana 1-0(0-0)

Round 7 [24-26.08.2019]
Olimpija Ljubljana - NŠ Mura 1-1(0-0)
NK Triglav - NK Celje 0-6(0-3)
Rudar Velenje - NK Tabor 2-2(1-1)
NK Maribor - NK Bravo 4-0(1-0)
NK Domžale - NK Aluminij 1-1(0-1)

Round 8 [30.08.-01.09.2019]
NK Bravo - NK Triglav 1-0(0-0)
NK Tabor - Olimpija Ljubljana 1-2(1-1)
NK Aluminij - NŠ Mura 2-0(1-0)
NK Celje - Rudar Velenje 3-0(2-0)
NK Domžale - NK Maribor 0-1(0-1)

Round 9 [13-15.09.2019]
Rudar Velenje - NK Bravo 1-4(0-2)
NK Maribor - NK Aluminij 2-1(0-0)
NK Triglav - NK Domžale 2-3(1-1)
Olimpija Ljubljana - NK Celje 2-2(1-0)
NŠ Mura - NK Tabor 1-0(0-0)

Round 10 [21-22.09.2019]
NK Aluminij - NK Tabor 3-0(2-0)
Rudar Velenje - NK Domžale 2-3(0-3)
NK Triglav - NK Maribor 1-3(0-1)
NŠ Mura - NK Celje 1-0(0-0)
Olimpija Ljubljana - NK Bravo 3-1(3-0)

Round 11 [25-26.09.2019]
NK Bravo - NŠ Mura 3-3(1-1)
NK Domžale - Olimpija Ljubljana 1-4(1-2)
NK Maribor - Rudar Velenje 5-0(3-0)
NK Triglav - NK Aluminij 1-0(0-0)
NK Celje - NK Tabor 2-0(1-0)

Round 12 [28-30.09.2019]
Olimpija Ljubljana - NK Maribor 2-4(1-2)
NŠ Mura - NK Domžale 3-0(1-0)
NK Tabor - NK Bravo 3-1(0-0)
Rudar Velenje - NK Triglav 1-1(1-0)
NK Aluminij - NK Celje 0-0

Round 13 [05-06.10.2019]
NK Bravo - NK Celje 2-2(1-0)
NK Domžale - NK Tabor 1-0(1-0)
NK Maribor - NŠ Mura 0-0
NK Triglav - Olimpija Ljubljana 2-3(1-0)
Rudar Velenje - NK Aluminij 1-2(1-0)

Round 14 [19-20.10.2019]
NŠ Mura - NK Triglav 2-2(0-1)
Olimpija Ljubljana - Rudar Velenje 6-0(4-0)
NK Celje - NK Domžale 2-1(1-1)
NK Tabor - NK Maribor 4-1(1-1)
NK Aluminij - NK Bravo 5-1(2-0)

Round 15 [26-27.10.2019]
NK Triglav - NK Tabor 3-2(2-2)
Olimpija Ljubljana - NK Aluminij 3-1(1-0)
NK Maribor - NK Celje 1-0(0-0)
Rudar Velenje - NŠ Mura 1-2(1-0)
NK Domžale - NK Bravo 2-0(2-0)

Round 16 [02-03.11.2019]
NK Bravo - NK Maribor 0-1(0-1)
NK Celje - NK Triglav 4-0(2-0)
NK Tabor - Rudar Velenje 1-1(0-0)
NŠ Mura - Olimpija Ljubljana 3-1(0-0)
NK Aluminij - NK Domžale 4-2(1-1)

Round 17 [09-10.11.2019]
Rudar Velenje - NK Celje 3-3(3-2)
NK Maribor - NK Domžale 4-1(2-0)
NK Triglav - NK Bravo 1-0(0-0)
Olimpija Ljubljana - NK Tabor 2-0(1-0)
NŠ Mura - NK Aluminij 2-4(2-2)

Round 18 [23-24.11.2019]
NK Bravo - Rudar Velenje 2-1(1-1)
NK Domžale - NK Triglav 3-0(2-0)
NK Celje - Olimpija Ljubljana 1-3(1-2)
NK Tabor - NŠ Mura 1-1(0-0)
NK Aluminij - NK Maribor 0-2(0-1)

Round 19 [30.11.-01.12.2019]
NK Tabor - NK Aluminij 1-1(1-0)
NK Celje - NŠ Mura 1-0(1-0)
NK Maribor - NK Triglav 0-2(0-2)
NK Bravo - Olimpija Ljubljana 1-2(0-0)
NK Domžale - Rudar Velenje 2-1(1-0)

Round 20 [04-05.12.2019]
NK Tabor - NK Celje 0-4(0-2)
NK Aluminij - NK Triglav 8-1(4-0)
Rudar Velenje - NK Maribor 1-1(1-1)
Olimpija Ljubljana - NK Domžale 0-1(0-0)
NŠ Mura - NK Bravo 1-1(1-1)

Round 21 [22-23.02.2020]
NK Triglav - Rudar Velenje 3-0(1-0)
NK Celje - NK Aluminij 2-0(1-0)
NK Maribor - Olimpija Ljubljana 1-1(0-1)
NK Bravo - NK Tabor 2-1(1-1)
NK Domžale - NŠ Mura 1-2(0-1)

Round 22 [25-26.02.2020]
Olimpija Ljubljana - NK Triglav 0-2(0-1)
NK Aluminij - Rudar Velenje 1-0(0-0)
NK Tabor - NK Domžale 2-1(1-1)
NŠ Mura - NK Maribor 1-2(0-1)
NK Celje - NK Bravo 2-2(1-1)

Round 23 [29.02.-01.03.2020]
Rudar Velenje - Olimpija Ljubljana 1-1(0-1)
NK Bravo - NK Aluminij 0-0
NK Maribor - NK Tabor 0-0
NK Triglav - NŠ Mura 1-1(1-1)
NK Domžale - NK Celje 1-1(0-1)

Round 24 [03-05.03.2020]
NK Aluminij - Olimpija Ljubljana 1-2(0-2)
NK Bravo - NK Domžale 2-1(0-0)
NK Celje - NK Maribor 2-0(0-0)
NŠ Mura - Rudar Velenje 1-1(1-0)
NK Tabor - NK Triglav 3-1(1-1)

Round 25 [07-08.03.2020]
NK Domžale - NK Aluminij 1-3(0-1)
NK Maribor - NK Bravo 1-2(0-2)
NK Triglav - NK Celje 0-5(0-2)
Rudar Velenje - NK Tabor 0-1(0-0)
Olimpija Ljubljana - NŠ Mura 1-0(0-0)

Round 26 [05-07.06.2020]
NK Aluminij - NŠ Mura 1-3(0-1)
NK Celje - Rudar Velenje 2-0(0-0)
NK Tabor - Olimpija Ljubljana 0-3(0-1)
NK Bravo - NK Triglav 1-0(0-0)
NK Domžale - NK Maribor 1-2(0-0)

Round 27 [12-14.06.2020]
NK Triglav - NK Domžale 1-1(0-0)
Rudar Velenje - NK Bravo 1-3(0-3)
Olimpija Ljubljana - NK Celje 0-1(0-1)
NŠ Mura - NK Tabor 3-2(2-0)
NK Maribor - NK Aluminij 3-0(1-0)

Round 28 [16-18.06.2020]
NŠ Mura - NK Celje 3-1(2-1)
NK Aluminij - NK Tabor 0-2(0-0)
Rudar Velenje - NK Domžale 2-3(0-1)
Olimpija Ljubljana - NK Bravo 0-5(0-4)
NK Triglav - NK Maribor 1-3(0-0)

Round 29 [20-21.06.2020]
NK Bravo - NŠ Mura 1-0(0-0)
NK Celje - NK Tabor 1-1(0-0)
NK Triglav - NK Aluminij 1-4(0-1)
NK Domžale - Olimpija Ljubljana 0-1(0-0)
NK Maribor - Rudar Velenje 3-0(1-0)

Round 30 [26-28.06.2020]
Rudar Velenje - NK Triglav 0-1(0-1)
NK Tabor - NK Bravo 0-0
NK Aluminij - NK Celje 0-2(0-2)
NŠ Mura - NK Domžale 0-1(0-0)
Olimpija Ljubljana - NK Maribor 1-0(0-0)

Round 31 [03-05.07.2020]
NK Bravo - NK Celje 1-2(1-0)
NK Domžale - NK Tabor 2-1(0-0)
Rudar Velenje - NK Aluminij 1-3(1-2)
NK Triglav - Olimpija Ljubljana 3-7(2-3)
NK Maribor - NŠ Mura 3-2(2-0)

Round 32 [07-09.07.2020]
NK Celje - NK Domžale 4-1(1-1)
NK Aluminij - NK Bravo 1-2(1-0)
NŠ Mura - NK Triglav 2-0(2-0)
NK Tabor - NK Maribor 4-1(3-1)
Olimpija Ljubljana - Rudar Velenje 5-0(4-0)

Round 33 [11-13.07.2020]
NK Domžale - NK Bravo 1-1(0-0)
NK Triglav - NK Tabor 1-2(0-1)
NK Maribor - NK Celje 1-2(0-2)
Olimpija Ljubljana - NK Aluminij 0-1(0-1)
Rudar Velenje - NŠ Mura 0-0

Round 34 [15-16.07.2020]
NK Bravo - NK Maribor 0-3(0-0)
NK Celje - NK Triglav 2-2(0-1)
NK Tabor - Rudar Velenje 1-0(1-0)
NK Aluminij - NK Domžale 2-5(2-0)
NŠ Mura - Olimpija Ljubljana 1-1(1-1)

Round 35 [19.07.2020]
NŠ Mura - NK Aluminij 1-1(0-0)
NK Triglav - NK Bravo 1-4(0-0)
Olimpija Ljubljana - NK Tabor 1-2(0-1)
Rudar Velenje - NK Celje 0-2(0-2)
NK Maribor - NK Domžale 2-1(1-0)

Round 36 [22.07.2020]
NK Aluminij - NK Maribor 1-4(0-0)
NK Bravo - Rudar Velenje 1-1(0-1)
NK Tabor - NŠ Mura 1-2(1-0)
NK Domžale - NK Triglav 2-1(1-0)
NK Celje - Olimpija Ljubljana 2-2(1-0)

Final Standings

								Home				Away			
1. **NK Celje**	36	19	12	5	74 - 36	69	10	7	1	36 - 17	9	5	4	38 - 19
2. NK Maribor	36	20	7	9	66 - 39	67	10	4	4	35 - 16	10	3	5	31 - 23
3. NK Olimpija Ljubljana	36	20	7	9	73 - 44	67	9	2	7	35 - 25	11	5	2	38 - 19
4. NŠ Mura Murska Sobota	36	14	14	8	54 - 42	56	9	6	3	32 - 21	5	8	5	22 - 21
5. NK Aluminij Kidričevo	36	16	7	13	58 - 48	55	8	2	8	33 - 28	8	5	5	25 - 20
6. NK Bravo Ljubljana	36	13	10	13	50 - 53	49	7	5	6	18 - 20	6	5	7	32 - 33
7. NK Tabor Sežana	36	13	7	16	45 - 51	46	9	4	5	27 - 22	4	3	11	18 - 29
8. NK Domžale	36	12	7	17	52 - 64	43	6	5	7	24 - 26	6	2	10	28 - 38
9. NK Triglav Kranj (*Relegation Play-offs*)	36	9	5	22	44 - 87	32	5	2	11	26 - 49	4	3	11	18 - 38
10. NK Rudar Velenje (*Relegated*)	36	0	12	24	28 - 80	12	0	7	11	18 - 36	0	5	13	10 - 44

Top goalscorers:	
26 Ante Vukušic (CRO)	*NK Olimpija Ljubljana*
23 Dario Vizinger (CRO)	*NK Celje*
18 Mitja Lotrič	*NK Celje*
15 Aljoša Matko	*AŠK Bravo Ljubljana*
15 Ante Živković (CRO)	*NK Aluminij Kidričevo*

Relegation Play-offs [26-30.07.2020]

ND Gorica - NK Triglav Kranj   1-1(1-1)   5-0(2-0)

ND Gorica promoted to the 2020/2021 Prva liga Slovenije.

NATIONAL CUP
Pokal Nogometne zveze Slovenije 2019/2020

First Round [14-15.08.2019]

ŠD Videm - NK Tabor Sežana	1-4		NK Odranci - NK Aluminij Kidričevo	1-3
NK Bistrica - NK Brda Dobrovo	2-2 aet; 3-4 pen		NK Tolmin - NK Šampion Celje	3-2
NK Bled Hirter - NK Celje	1-3		ŠD Šenčur - NK Nafta Lendava 1903	0-1
NK Brežice 1919 - NK Triglav Kranj	1-2		NK Dobrovce - NK Radomlje	0-10
NK Grad - NK Krško	1-4		FC Koper - ND Beltinci	6-0
ŠD Partizan Pesnica - ND Gorica	1-5		NK Bravo Ljubljana - NK Rudar Velenje	1-4 aet

1/8-Finals [11.09./18-19.09.2019]

NK Tolmin - NK Celje	0-6(0-2)		NK Brda Dobrovo - NK Domžale	0-3(0-1)
NK Radomlje - ND Gorica	3-2(2-2,2-2)		FC Koper - NK Maribor	3-2(1-1)
NK Nafta Lendava 1903 - NK Krško	2-0(1-0)		NK Aluminij Kidričevo - NK Tabor Sežana	1-0(0-0)
NK Triglav Kranj - NŠ Mura Murska Sobota	1-3(0-3)		NK Olimpija Ljubljana - NK Rudar Velenje	0-1(0-0)

Quarter-Finals [16.10./22.10./24.10.-29-30.10.2019]

First Leg			Second Leg	
NK Aluminij Kidričevo - FC Koper	1-0(0-0)		FC Koper - NK Aluminij Kidričevo	3-2(2-1)
NK Nafta Lendava 1903 - NK Rudar Velenje	2-1(0-0)		NK Rudar Velenje - NK Nafta Lendava 1903	0-2(0-1)
NK Celje - NK Radomlje	1-1(1-0)		NK Radomlje - NK Celje	0-0
NK Domžale - NŠ Mura Murska Sobota	3-2(1-1)		NŠ Mura - NK Domžale	3-2 aet; 5-4 pen

Semi-Finals [09-10.06.2020]

NK Aluminij Kidričevo - NŠ Mura Murska Sobota	0-4(0-1)		NK Radomlje - NK Nafta Lendava 1903	1-1 aet; 2-4 pen

Final

24.06.2020; Nacionalni Nogometni Center Brdo, Kranj; Referee: Rade Obrenović; Attendance: 200
NŠ Mura Murska Sobota - NK Nafta Lendava 1903   **2-0(0-0)**

Mura Murska: Matko Obradović, Žiga Kous, Klemen Šturm, Jan Gorenc, Matic Maruško, Nino Kouter, Tomi Horvat (87.Jon Šporn), Luka Šušnjara (72.Staniša Mandić), Kai Cipot (65.Žan Karničnik), Luka Bobičanec, Amadej Maroša (87.Kevin Žižek). Trainer: Ante Šimundža.

Nafta Lendava: Florijan Raduha, Leon Leuštek, Bence Gergényi, Žiga Živko, Mihael Rebernik, Tadej Pirtovšek, Rok Pirtovšek, Ernő Roland Paku, Gábor Végh (58.Dominik Drk), Meshack Izuchukwu Ubochioma, Alen Ploj (85.Lucian Pozsgai). Trainer: Dejan Dončić.

Goals: 1-0 Amadej Maroša (48), 2-0 Žan Karničnik (73).

Nogometni klub Aluminij Kidričevo

Founded: 1946
Stadium: Aluminij Sports Park, Kidričevo (532)
Trainer: Slobodan Grubor (AUT)　　　09.09.1968

Goalkeepers:	DOB	M	(s)	G
Luka Janžekovič	14.03.1997	19		
Matija Kovačić (CRO)	25.02.1994	17		
Defenders:	**DOB**	**M**	**(s)**	**G**
Stanley Amuzie (NGA)	28.02.1996	10	(3)	
Nemanja Jakšić (SRB)	11.07.1995	27	(3)	2
Ivan Kontek (CRO)	29.01.1997	26	(2)	
Ilija Martinović (MNE)	31.01.1994	18		
Sanin Muminović (BIH)	02.11.1990	8	(1)	
Renato Pantalon (CRO)	27.10.1997	19	(4)	
Gašper Pečnik	18.05.2003	3	(2)	
Luka Petek	13.10.1997	8	(1)	
Aljaž Ploj	30.08.1998	20	(2)	
Stipe Vrdoljak (CRO)	02.08.1993	6	(3)	1
Midfielders:	**DOB**	**M**	**(s)**	**G**
Marcel Čermák (CZE)	25.11.1998	12	(10)	
Lovro Grajfoner	25.01.2000	5	(2)	
Lucas Horvat	13.10.1985	13	(6)	
Alen Krajnc	01.07.1995	13	(1)	2
Nikola Leko (BIH)	30.09.1996	22	(2)	9
Jure Matjašič	31.05.1992	23	(8)	2
Dejan Petrovič	12.01.1998	20		
Miloš Šaka (SRB)	12.04.1994	10	(3)	
Matic Vrbanec	28.10.1996	25	(3)	5
Forwards:	**DOB**	**M**	**(s)**	**G**
David Bosilj	01.02.2002	6	(10)	3
Mihael Klepač (CRO)	19.09.1997	18	(9)	9
Nik Marinšek	16.02.1999	4	(15)	
Tilen Pečnik	16.05.1998	9	(11)	4
Luka Štor	05.07.1998	6	(5)	4
Ante Živković (CRO)	21.05.1993	29	(4)	15

Nogometni klub Bravo Ljubljana

Founded: 2006
Stadium: Ljubljana Sports Park, Ljubljana (2,308)
Trainer: Dejan Grabić　　　21.09.1980

Goalkeepers:	DOB	M	(s)	G
Domen Gril	10.06.2001	10		
Igor Vekič	06.05.1998	26		
Defenders:	**DOB**	**M**	**(s)**	**G**
David Brekalo	03.12.1998	21	(2)	3
Vanja Drkušič	30.10.1999	15		1
Marko Klemenčič	09.03.1997	1		
Almin Kurtović	16.03.2000	20	(1)	
Matevž Matko	09.10.2001	17	(3)	
Jurij Španja	13.08.1999		(2)	
Mark Španring	13.06.2001	3	(2)	
Žan Trontelj	21.01.2000	18		
Ante Vrljičak	26.04.1997	13	(1)	
David Zec	05.01.2000	11		
Midfielders:	**DOB**	**M**	**(s)**	**G**
Ovbokha Agboyi (NGA)	14.12.1994	33		2
Nejc Gradišar	06.08.2002	1		
Andraž Kirm	06.09.1984	11	(3)	
Alen Krcič	19.11.1988	7	(4)	
Sandi Ogrinec	05.06.1998	12	(3)	2
Michael Olusoji Ogungbaro (NGA)	10.07.1996	3		
Lan Piskule	22.01.1999	1	(2)	
Gal Primc	15.09.1996	10	(9)	1
Luka Žinko	23.03.1983	29	(2)	3
Forwards:	**DOB**	**M**	**(s)**	**G**
Besart Abdurahimi (MKD)	31.07.1990	11	(7)	1
Roko Baturina (CRO)	20.06.2000	13	(3)	8
Marko Dabro (CRO)	28.03.1997		(1)	
Milan Đajić	26.09.1992	3	(7)	2
Jaka Ihbeisheh (PLE)	29.08.1986	18	(3)	
Miha Kancilija	04.04.2001	2	(15)	1
Martin Kramarič	14.11.1997	13	(2)	1
Mitja Križan	05.06.1997	6	(2)	1
Aljoša Matko	29.03.2000	28	(4)	15
Ibrahim Mensah (GHA)	11.01.1995	12	(8)	5
Mustafa Nukić	03.12.1990	28	(6)	3

Nogometni klub Celje

Founded: 28.12.1919 (*as SK Celje*)
Stadium: Stadion Z'dežele, Celje (13,059)
Trainer: Dušan Kosič　　　23.04.1971

Goalkeepers:	DOB	M	(s)	G
Metod Jurhar	07.12.1997	3		
Matjaž Rozman	03.01.1987	33		
Defenders:	**DOB**	**M**	**(s)**	**G**
Amadej Brecl	06.04.1997	3	(9)	
Josip Ćalušić (CRO)	11.10.1993	23	(5)	
Advan Kadušić (BIH)	14.10.1997	16		2
Denis Marandici (MDA)	18.09.1996	16		
Dušan Stojinović	26.08.2000	29		1
Deni Štraus	20.04.1996	9		
Lan Štravs	03.03.2000	7	(11)	
Jure Travner	28.09.1985	9	(6)	
Tadej Vidmajer	10.03.1992	16		2
Žan Zaletel	16.09.1999	34		
Midfielders:	**DOB**	**M**	**(s)**	**G**
Domantas Antanavičius (LTU)	18.11.1998	1	(8)	
Žan Benedičič	03.10.1995	20	(3)	3
Jakob Novak	04.03.1998	22	(1)	1
Janez Pišek	04.05.1998	4		
Karlo Plantak (CRO)	11.11.1997	12	(12)	
Nino Pungaršek	01.11.1995	9	(6)	
Rok Štraus	03.03.1987	4	(14)	
Juš Štusej	20.04.2000		(5)	
Valentin Zekhov (RUS)	29.04.2001		(1)	
Forwards:	**DOB**	**M**	**(s)**	**G**
Ivan Božić (CRO)	08.06.1997	30	(4)	10
Stian Džumhur	21.08.2000		(3)	
Luka Kerin	23.03.1999	27	(3)	9
Tom Kljun	29.01.2004		(2)	
Gašper Koritnik	06.01.2001		(14)	3
Mitja Lotrič	03.09.1994	34		18
Dario Vizinger (CRO)	06.06.1998	35		23

Nogometni klub Domžale

Founded: 07.11.1920 (*as SK Disk Domžale*)
Stadium: Športni park Domžale (3,100)
Trainer: Simon Rožman — 06.04.1983
[05.09.2019] Andrej Razdrh — 28.11.1976
[15.06.2020] Dejan Djuranović — 05.05.1968

Goalkeepers:	DOB	M	(s)	G
Ajdin Mulalič	13.09.1994	29		
Grega Sorčan	05.03.1996	7		
Defenders:	**DOB**	**M**	**(s)**	**G**
Josip Čorluka (CRO)	03.03.1995	11	(3)	
Gaber Dobrovoljc	27.01.1993	2	(2)	
Matic Fink	27.02.1990	12	(2)	1
Branko Ilič	06.02.1983	16		
Sven Karič	07.03.1998	20	(3)	2
Tilen Klemenčič	21.08.1995	20		2
Ivan Makovec	27.03.2001	6	(2)	
Benjamin Markuš	30.01.2001	2	(1)	
Gregor Sikošek	13.02.1994	19	(3)	1
Nikola Vujadinović (MNE)	31.07.1986	14		2
Damjan Vukliševič	28.06.1995	12	(3)	1
Andraž Žinič	12.02.1999	11	(4)	
Midfielders:	**DOB**	**M**	**(s)**	**G**
Adam Gnezda Čerin	16.07.1999	7		
Marco da Silva (FRA)	10.04.1992		(2)	
Zeni Husmani (MKD)	28.11.1990	14		1
Senijad Ibričić (BIH)	26.09.1985	30		10
Mattias Käit (EST)	29.06.1998	10	(5)	1
Kim Do-hyun (KOR)	09.04.1994	3	(7)	
Til Mavretic	19.11.1997	3	(9)	
Kaheem Anthony Parris (JAM)	06.01.2000		(1)	
Nick Perc	27.05.2003		(1)	
Janez Pišek	04.05.1998	19	(3)	
Jošt Pišek	10.03.2002		(1)	
Žiga Repas	29.05.2001	1	(2)	
Tamar Svetlin	30.07.2001	15	(6)	1
Jošt Urbančič	12.04.2001	2	(2)	
Forwards:	**DOB**	**M**	**(s)**	**G**
Arnel Jakupović (AUT)	29.05.1998	23	(7)	11
Dario Kolobarić	06.02.2000		(3)	
Dejan Lazarevič	15.02.1990	9	(13)	
Tonći Mujan (CRO)	19.07.1995	14	(3)	
Shamar Nicholson (JAM)	16.03.1997	3		
Tian Pantelić	31.05.2001		(1)	
Tilen Pečnik	16.05.1998		(1)	
Matej Podlogar	23.02.1991	26	(9)	5
Matija Rom	01.11.1998	4	(2)	
Rauno Sappinen (EST)	23.01.1996	4	(6)	2
Emir Saitoski (MKD)	08.05.2003		(1)	
Predrag Sikimić (SRB)	29.08.1982	10	(4)	2
Slobodan Vuk	15.09.1989	18	(9)	8

Nogometni klub Maribor

Founded: 12.12.1960
Stadium: Stadion Ljudski vrt, Maribor (12,702)
Trainer: Darko Milanič — 18.12.1967
[23.04.2020] Sergej Jakirović (BIH) — 23.12.1976

Goalkeepers:	DOB	M	(s)	G
Jasmin Handanovič	28.01.1978	10	(1)	
Kenan Pirić (BIH)	07.07.1994	26		
Defenders:	**DOB**	**M**	**(s)**	**G**
Saša Ivković (SRB)	13.05.1993	6		
Denis Klinar	21.02.1992	14	(3)	
Luka Koblar	08.08.1999	5	(5)	
Žan Kolmanič	03.03.2000	5	(1)	
Rok Maher	20.07.2001		(1)	
Nemanja Mitrovič	15.10.1992	27		1
Špiro Peričić (CRO)	08.10.1993	27		2
Aleksander Rajčevič	17.11.1986	9		
Luka Uskoković (MNE)	10.04.1996	1		
Mitja Viler	01.09.1986	28		1
Midfielders:	**DOB**	**M**	**(s)**	**G**
Alexandru Crețu (ROU)	24.04.1992	24	(3)	1
Amir Derviševič	04.07.1992	13	(7)	6
Dino Hotič (BIH)	26.07.1995	15	(4)	4
Andrej Kotnik	04.08.1995	7	(15)	1
Rok Kronaveter	07.12.1986	27	(1)	14
Rene Mihelič	05.07.1988		(3)	
Martin Milec	20.09.1991	20	(2)	1
Sandi Ogrinec	05.06.1998	2	(1)	
Aleks Pihler	15.01.1994	20	(7)	2
Rudi Vancaš	15.03.1994	31	(2)	7
Blaž Vrhovec	20.02.1992	19	(6)	
Forwards:	**DOB**	**M**	**(s)**	**G**
Gregor Bajde	29.04.1994	5	(5)	4
Felipe Silva Correa dos Santos (BRA)	03.01.1997	2	(10)	1
Martin Kramarič	14.11.1997	4	(3)	
Marcos Magno Morales Tavares (BRA)	30.03.1984	2	(29)	6
Jasmin Mešanović (BIH)	06.01.1992	20	(10)	2
Nardin Mulahusejnović (BIH)	09.02.1998	2	(3)	1
Luka Zahovič	15.11.1995	25	(3)	10

Nogometna šola Mura Murska Sobota

Founded: 14.05.2012
Stadium: Mestni stadion Fazanerija, Murska Sobota (3,782)
Trainer: Ante Šimundža — 28.09.1971

Goalkeepers:	DOB	M	(s)	G
Matko Obradović (CRO)	11.05.1991	30		
Dean Šafarić (CRO)	02.01.1993	2		
Marko Zalokar	18.06.1990	4		
Defenders:	**DOB**	**M**	**(s)**	**G**
Jan Gorenc	26.07.1999	11	(1)	1
Marin Karamarko (CRO)	14.04.1998	26	(1)	1
Žan Karničnik	18.09.1994	19	(14)	3
Alan Kaučič	12.08.2001	4		
Žiga Kous	27.10.1992	21	(3)	
Žiga Laci	20.07.2002	1	(1)	1
Klemen Pucko	27.01.1996	15	(4)	
Klemen Šturm	27.06.1994	22	(1)	1
Midfielders:	**DOB**	**M**	**(s)**	**G**
Marko Brkić (BIH)	11.04.2000	10	(10)	
Tio Cipot	20.04.2003		(2)	
Tomi Horvat	24.03.1999	22	(8)	1
Nino Kouter	19.12.1993	25	(5)	2
Alen Kozar	07.04.1995	10		
Matic Maruško	30.11.1990	32	(1)	3
Jon Šporn	22.05.1997	21	(3)	
Luka Šušnjara	04.04.1997	27	(8)	8
Forwards:	**DOB**	**M**	**(s)**	**G**
Luka Bobičanec (CRO)	23.05.1993	28	(3)	12
Andrija Bubnjar (CRO)	29.06.1997	12	(6)	1
Kai Cipot	28.04.2001	8	(8)	2
Armin Ćerimagić (BIH)	14.01.1994		(3)	
Andrija Filipović (CRO)	18.04.1997	3	(5)	
Staniša Mandić (MNE)	27.01.1995	7	(2)	1
Amadej Maroša	07.02.1994	27	(9)	13
Fejsal Mulić (SRB)	03.10.1994	5	(9)	2
Kevin Žižek	21.06.1998	4	(10)	1

Nogometni klub Olimpija Ljubljana

Founded:	02.03.2005 (*as NK Bežigrad Ljubljana*)	
Stadium:	Stadion Stožice, Ljubljana (16,038)	
Trainer:	Safet Hadžič	08.11.1968
[19.06.2020]	Dino Skender (CRO)	10.12.1983

Goalkeepers:	DOB	M	(s)	G
Nejc Vidmar	31.03.1989	36		
Defenders:	**DOB**	**M**	**(s)**	**G**
Jan Andrejašič	16.09.1995	12	(4)	
Macky Frank Bagnack Mouegni (CMR)	07.06.1995	24	(1)	1
Eric Boakye (GHA)	19.11.1999	20	(1)	1
Goran Brkić (SRB)	28.04.1991	3		
Ben Gasser	21.03.1995		(1)	
Jan Gorenc	26.07.1999		(2)	
Mario Jurčevič	01.06.1995	27	(3)	1
Daniel Kamy Ntankeu Yves (CMR)	08.03.1996	5	(3)	1
Vitālijs Maksimenko (LVA)	08.12.1990	9	(4)	
Miral Samardžič	17.02.1987	32		
Denis Šme	22.03.1994	10	(3)	
Midfielders:	**DOB**	**M**	**(s)**	**G**
Timi Elšnik	29.04.1998	3	(8)	3
Nik Kapun	09.01.1994		(1)	
Rok Kidrič	27.04.1995		(7)	
Bojan Knežević (CRO)	28.01.1997	4	(7)	1
Oliver Kregar	22.06.2000		(6)	
Enrik Ostrc	21.06.2002	11		1
Michael Pavlović	23.06.1905	5	(4)	
Stefan Petrović	30.04.2001		(1)	
Marko Putinčanin (SRB)	16.12.1987	11		
Asmir Suljić (BIH)	11.09.1991	3	(1)	2
Tomislav Tomić (BIH)	16.11.1990	32	(2)	1
Vitja Valenčič	12.03.1999	12	(8)	1
Forwards:	**DOB**	**M**	**(s)**	**G**
Roman Bezjak	21.02.1989	7	(9)	2
Joaquim Manuel Welo Lupeta „Jucie Lupeta" (POR)	24.03.1993	2	(10)	4
Haris Kadrić	16.03.2000	1	(7)	1
Luka Menalo (BIH)	22.07.1996	29	(4)	10
Stefan Savić (AUT)	09.01.1994	33	(2)	6
Ante Vukušic (CRO)	04.06.1991	34	(1)	26
Endri Çekiçi (ALB)	23.11.1996	31		10

Nogometni klub Rudar Velenje

Founded:	1948	
Stadium:	Mestni stadion ob jezeru, Velenje (2,341)	
Trainer:	Almir Sulejmanović	26.01.1978
[29.07.2019]	Janez Žilnik	30.04.1964
[07.09.2019]	Nikola Jaroš (CRO)	13.02.1978
[28.10.2019]	Andrej Panadić (CRO)	09.03.1969
[01.04.2020]	Dominik Beršnjak	15.07.1981

Goalkeepers:	DOB	M	(s)	G
Matej Radan	13.05.1990	19		
Tomaž Stopajnik	14.01.2001	17	(1)	
Defenders:	**DOB**	**M**	**(s)**	**G**
Marko Ćosić (CRO)	02.03.1994	10	(1)	1
Elvedin Džinić	25.08.1985	18	(2)	
Leo Ejup	09.09.1994	2	(2)	1
Josip Filipović (CRO)	08.05.1996	31	(2)	
David Hrubik (SRB)	19.06.1997	15	(1)	
Gašper Jovan	25.02.2001	6	(4)	
David Kašnik	16.01.1987	17		
Jovan Pavlović (SRB)	11.02.2000	9		
Robert Pušaver	09.05.1995	24	(2)	
Tim Turinek	15.07.2001		(2)	
Midfielders:	**DOB**	**M**	**(s)**	**G**
Mislav Anđelković (CRO)	22.04.1988	11		
Cene Kitek	09.04.2000	6	(6)	
Rijad Kobiljar (BIH)	08.04.1996	13	(4)	2
Aljaž Krefl	20.02.1994	27	(3)	
Sanjin Lelić (BIH)	11.01.1997	8	(5)	1
Luka Lovenjak	20.09.2001	3	(11)	
Vid Plešnik	23.06.1905		(1)	
Nejc Pušnik	06.08.1998	2		
Žiga Škoflek	22.07.1994	4		2
Damjan Trifkovič	22.07.1987	18	(4)	2
Pavel Vižintin	24.06.1905	1	(4)	
Adam Vošnjak	26.07.2000	18	(8)	1
Forwards:	**DOB**	**M**	**(s)**	**G**
Leon Črnčič	02.03.1990	29	(2)	1
Sandro Jovanović	23.04.2002	6	(4)	1
Haris Kadrić	16.03.2000	1	(6)	
Nace Koprivnik	27.06.1999	4	(9)	
Mićo Kuzmanović (BIH)	18.03.1996	23	(4)	4
Mateo Panadić (CRO)	06.10.1994	5	(6)	2
Borna Petrović (CRO)	16.10.1997	12	(4)	3
Dem Pljava	19.06.1999	1	(6)	
Dominik Radić (CRO)	26.07.1996	29		5
Nemanja Tomašević (SRB)	09.08.1999	2	(3)	
Milan Tučić	15.08.1996	5	(1)	1

Nogometni klub Tabor Sežana

Founded:	1923	
Stadium:	Stadion „Rajko Štolfa", Sežana (1,200)	
Trainer:	Andrej Razdrh	28.11.1976
[08.09.2019]	Almir Sulejmanović	26.01.1978
[03.01.2020]	Mauro Camoranesi (ITA)	04.10.1976

Goalkeepers:	DOB	M	(s)	G
David Adam	15.11.1993	7		
Arian Rener	06.03.1999	20	(1)	
David Šugić (CRO)	07.02.2000	9		
Defenders:	**DOB**	**M**	**(s)**	**G**
Toni Aliaj (CRO)	06.01.1999		(2)	
Antonio Azinović (CRO)	17.01.1992	31	(1)	1
Ivor Horvat (CRO)	19.08.1991	11	(7)	
Žan Humar	20.06.1997		(1)	
Denis Kouao (CIV)	23.11.1996	13		1
Damir Mehmedović (AUT)	11.12.1997	2		
Klemen Nemanič	07.11.1996	18	(2)	
Jurij Požrl	02.04.1997	3	(1)	
Marko Ristić (SRB)	09.03.1987	29		1
Erik Salkič	14.10.1997	19	(4)	2
Guy Yaméogo (CIV)	30.12.2000	12		
Mario Zebić (CRO)	17.12.1995	23	(3)	1
Midfielders:	**DOB**	**M**	**(s)**	**G**
Mario Babić (CRO)	03.07.1992	20	(5)	5
Stjepan Babić (CRO)	04.12.1988	15	(1)	
Kevin Doukouré (CIV)	30.03.1999	7	(2)	1
Miha Hlad	24.06.1905		(2)	
Marko Krivičič	01.02.1996	21	(3)	3
Dominik Mihaljević (CRO)	27.08.1994	24	(9)	1
Lucas Abel Pittinari (ARG)	30.11.1991		(4)	
Leon Sever	09.04.1998	25	(9)	5
Mattia Specogna (ITA)	19.03.2002	1	(2)	
Stefan Stevanović (SRB)	23.11.1990	13	(11)	4
Marko Vukelić	19.01.1992	3	(10)	
Forwards:	**DOB**	**M**	**(s)**	**G**
Andrew Agnoletti (ITA)	17.06.2002		(2)	
Louis Marie Rodrigue Bongongui Assougou (CMR)	07.02.1993	26	(3)	4
Karolis Laukžemis (LTU)	11.03.1992	2	(9)	2
Lazar Milošev (SRB)	20.06.1996	10	(7)	
Fahd Ndzengue (GAB)	07.07.2000	2	(2)	1
Predrag Sikimić (SRB)	29.08.1982	20		12
Dino Stančič	25.01.1992	10	(9)	1
Marsel Stare	28.08.2000		(1)	

Nogometni klub Triglav Kranj

Founded: 1920 (*as SK Korotan*); re-founded 1997
Stadium: Stadion Stanka Mlakarja, Kranj (2,060)
Trainer: Dejan Dončić   21.10.1972
[24.09.2019] Vlado Šmit   06.04.1980

Goalkeepers:	DOB	M	(s)	G
Jalen Arko	09.09.1999	23		
Luka Čadež	01.03.2000	13		
Defenders:	**DOB**	**M**	**(s)**	**G**
Momir Bojić	15.10.1993	2	(1)	
Luka Brkić	23.07.2002	1	(2)	
Kristjan Česen	17.07.1997	13	(7)	1
Erik Gliha	13.02.1997	13		
Tin Karamatić (CRO)	01.03.1993	1		
Žan Kocjančič	19.02.2000	3		1
Ožbej Kuhar	21.04.1997	8	(3)	
Žan Kumer	16.05.1996	19	(2)	1
Milan Milanović (SRB)	31.03.1991	23		7
Veron Salja	29.05.1998	10	(7)	
Jan Jure Stojanovič	13.01.2002		(2)	
Midfielders:	**DOB**	**M**	**(s)**	**G**
Berat Beqiri (ALB)	03.06.1996	9	(4)	2
Goran Brkić (SRB)	28.04.1991	9	(1)	1
Marko Gajić	10.04.1997	11	(9)	1
Ernest Grvala	11.10.1996		(1)	
Elvedin Herić (BIH)	09.02.1997	4	(3)	
Filip Janković (SRB)	17.01.1995	12	(7)	3

	DOB	M	(s)	G
Egzon Kryeziu	25.04.2000	15	(5)	2
Luka Lipovek	13.09.2000	1		
Aleš Mertelj	22.03.1987	23		
Tilen Mlakar	26.04.1995	28	(2)	2
Žan Rogelj	25.11.1999	28		1
Pokorn Tevž	16.06.2000	2		
David Tijanič	16.07.1997	20		5
Gašper Udovič	22.05.1995	20	(11)	
Marten Wilmots (BEL)	29.01.1999	11	(1)	
Reno Wilmots (BEL)	16.03.1997	7	(4)	
Aleks Zlatkov	19.03.2002	1	(1)	
Forwards:	**DOB**	**M**	**(s)**	**G**
Ahmetaj Albin	18.08.2002	1	(3)	
Armin Čerimagić (BIH)	14.01.1994	12		1
Qendrim Hasanaj	03.05.1999	5	(9)	1
Janko Ivetić	23.02.2001	1	(1)	
Anis Jašaragič	09.08.1999	3	(2)	
Luka Majcen	25.07.1989	25	(3)	9
Gaber Petrič	11.05.1998	11	(11)	5
Victor Aliaga (ESP)	24.09.1997	6	(4)	1
Luka Vukovič	03.01.2002	1	(4)	
Tom Žurga	17.01.1998	1	(7)	

SECOND LEVEL
Slovenian Second League 2019/2020

Please note: the league was abandoned after 20 Rounds, table at abandonment being considered as final table.

1.	FC Koper (*Promoted*)	20	13	5	2	42	-	13	44
2.	ND Gorica (*Promotion Play-offs*)	20	13	2	5	40	-	22	41
3.	NK Radomlje	20	12	4	4	48	-	23	40
4.	NK Nafta Lendava 1903	20	11	4	5	45	-	24	37
5.	NK Fužinar Ravne na Koroškem	20	11	4	5	35	-	22	37
6.	NK Krško	20	9	4	7	37	-	25	31
7.	NK Krka Novo Mesto	20	8	7	5	31	-	32	31
8.	NK Vitanest Bilje	20	8	5	7	28	-	25	29
9.	NK Dob	20	7	8	5	37	-	35	29
10.	NK Jadran Dekani	20	7	3	10	29	-	40	24
11.	NK Drava Ptuj	20	6	3	11	28	-	34	21
12.	ND Beltinci	20	5	5	10	20	-	36	20
13.	NK Brda Dobrovo	20	4	7	9	22	-	38	19
14.	NK Brežice 1919	20	3	7	10	13	-	29	16
15.	NK Rogaška Slatina (*Relegated*)	20	4	2	14	16	-	47	14
16.	NK Koroška Dravograd (*Relegated*)	20	2	4	14	23	-	49	10

NATIONAL TEAM

INTERNATIONAL MATCHES
(16.07.2019 – 15.07.2020)

06.09.2019	Ljubljana	Slovenia - Poland	2-0(1-0)	(ECQ)
09.09.2019	Ljubljana	Slovenia - Israel	3-2(1-0)	(ECQ)
10.10.2019	Skopje	North Macedonia - Slovenia	2-1(0-0)	(ECQ)
13.10.2019	Ljubljana	Slovenia - Austria	0-1(0-1)	(ECQ)
16.11.2019	Ljubljana	Slovenia - Latvia	1-0(0-0)	(ECQ)
19.11.2019	Warszawa	Poland - Slovenia	3-2(1-1)	(ECQ)

06.09.2019   SLOVENIA - POLAND   **2-0(1-0)**   16th EC. Qualifiers

Stadion Stožice, Ljubljana; Referee: Sergei Karasev (Russia); Attendance: 15,231
SVN: Jan Oblak (Cap), Aljaž Struna, Miha Mevlja, Jure Balkovec, Petar Stojanović, Josip Iličić, Rene Krhin, Jasmin Kurtič, Benjamin Verbič (62.Domen Črnigoj; 90+1.Robert Berić), Roman Bezjak, Andraž Šporar (85.Denis Popović). Trainer: Matjaž Kek.
Goals: Aljaž Struna (35), Andraž Šporar (65).

09.09.2019   SLOVENIA - ISRAEL   **3-2(1-0)**   16th EC. Qualifiers

Stadion Stožice, Ljubljana; Referee: Anthony Taylor (England); Attendance: 10,669
SVN: Jan Oblak, Miha Mevlja, Bojan Jokić (Cap) (46.Jure Balkovec), Aljaž Struna (54.Miha Blažič), Petar Stojanović, Josip Iličić, Rene Krhin (81.Denis Popović), Jasmin Kurtič, Benjamin Verbič, Roman Bezjak, Andraž Šporar. Trainer: Matjaž Kek.
Goals: Benjamin Verbič (43), Roman Bezjak (66), Benjamin Verbič (90).

10.10.2019   NORTH MACEDONIA - SLOVENIA   **2-1(0-0)**   16th EC. Qualifiers

"Toše Proeski" National Arena, Skopje; Referee: Danny Desmond Makkelie (Netherlands); Attendance: 16,500
SVN: Jan Oblak (Cap), Aljaž Struna, Miha Mevlja, Jure Balkovec, Petar Stojanović, Josip Iličić, Rene Krhin (48.Denis Popović), Jasmin Kurtič, Benjamin Verbič (65.Miha Zajc), Roman Bezjak (79.Robert Berić), Andraž Šporar. Trainer: Matjaž Kek.
Goal: Josip Iličić (90+5 penalty).

13.10.2019   SLOVENIA - AUSTRIA   **0-1(0-1)**   16th EC. Qualifiers

Stadion Stožice, Ljubljana; Referee: Cüneyt Çakır (Turkey); Attendance: 15,108
SVN: Jan Oblak (Cap), Aljaž Struna, Miha Mevlja, Jure Balkovec, Jasmin Kurtič, Petar Stojanović, Josip Iličić, Rene Krhin (79.Denis Popović [*sent off* 89]), Benjamin Verbič (69.Robert Berić), Roman Bezjak (61.Miha Zajc), Andraž Šporar. Trainer: Matjaž Kek.

16.11.2019   SLOVENIA - LATVIA   **1-0(0-0)**   16th EC. Qualifiers

Stožice Stadium, Ljubljana; Referee: Radu Marian Petrescu (Romania); Attendance: 11,224
SVN: Jan Oblak, Bojan Jokić (Cap), Aljaž Struna, Miha Mevlja, Josip Iličić, Petar Stojanović, Rene Krhin (74.Jaka Bijol), Haris Vučkič (62.Miha Zajc), Jasmin Kurtič, Benjamin Verbič (90+1.Roman Bezjak), Andraž Šporar. Trainer: Matjaž Kek.
Goal: Igors Tarasovs (53 own goal).

19.11.2019   POLAND - SLOVENIA   **3-2(1-1)**   16th EC. Qualifiers

Stadion PGE Narodowy, Warszawa; Referee: Daniel Siebert (Germany); Attendance: 53,946
SVN: Jan Oblak (Cap), Miha Mevlja, Miha Blažič, Jure Balkovec, Petar Stojanović, Josip Iličić, Rene Krhin, Jasmin Kurtič [*sent off* 86], Benjamin Verbič (86.Rajko Rep), Jaka Bijol (72.Miha Zajc), Tim Matavž (89.Haris Vučkič). Trainer: Matjaž Kek.
Goals: Tim Matavž (14), Josip Iličić (61).

NATIONAL TEAM PLAYERS
(16.07.2019 – 15.07.2020)

Name	DOB	Caps	Goals	2019/2020:	Club
Goalkeepers					
Jan OBLAK	07.01.1993	**28**	**0**	2019:	*Club Atlético de Madrid (ESP)*
Defenders					
Jure BALKOVEC	09.09.1994	**6**	**0**	2019:	*Empoli FC (ITA)*
Miha BLAŽIČ	08.05.1993	**5**	**0**	2019:	*Ferencvárosi TC (HUN)*
Bojan JOKIĆ	17.05.1986	**100**	**1**	2019:	*FK Ufa (RUS)*
Miha MEVLJA	12.06.1990	**27**	**1**	2019:	*PFK Sochi (RUS)*
Petar STOJANOVIĆ	07.10.1995	**16**	**0**	2019:	*GNK Dinamo Zagreb (CRO)*
Aljaž STRUNA	04.08.1990	**21**	**1**	2019:	*Houston Dynamo (USA)*
Midfielders					
Jaka BIJOL	05.02.1999	**8**	**0**	2019:	*FK CSKA Moskva (RUS)*
Domen ČRNIGOJ	18.11.1995	**12**	**2**	2019:	*FC Lugano (SUI)*
Josip ILIČIĆ	29.01.1988	**65**	**9**	2019:	*Atalanta Bergamasca Calcio (ITA)*
Rene KRHIN	21.05.1990	**48**	**2**	2019:	*FC Nantes (FRA)*
Jasmin KURTIĆ	10.01.1989	**58**	**1**	2019:	*SPAL Ferrara (ITA)*
Denis POPOVIČ	15.10.1989	**6**	**0**	2019:	*FC Zürich (SUI)*
Benjamin VERBIČ	27.11.1993	**29**	**5**	2019:	*FK Dinamo Kyiv (UKR)*
Haris VUČKIĆ	21.08.1992	**3**	**0**	2019:	*FC Twente Enschede (NED)*
Miha ZAJC	01.07.1994	**19**	**5**	2019:	*Fenerbahçe SK İstanbul (TUR)*
Forwards					
Robert BERIĆ	17.06.1991	**25**	**2**	2019:	*AS Saint-Étienne (FRA)*
Roman BEZJAK	21.02.1989	**33**	**5**	2019:	*APOEL FC Nicosia (CYP)*
Tim MATAVŽ	13.01.1989	**38**	**11**	2019:	*SBV Vitesse Arnhem (NED)*
Rajko REP	20.06.1990	**1**	**0**	2019:	*TSV Hartberg (AUT)*
Andraž ŠPORAR	27.02.1994	**19**	**2**	2019:	*ŠK Slovan Bratislava (SVK)*

National team coach				
Matjaž KEK [from 27.11.2019]	09.09.1961	10 M; 4 W; 2 D; 4 L; 16-11		
		Complete record as trainer of Slovenia:		
		59 M; 25 W; 10 D; 24 L; 77-52		
		(07.02.2007 – 11.10.2011) & (from 27.11.2019)		

SPAIN

The Country:
Reino de España (Kingdom of Spain)
Capital: Madrid
Surface: 505,990 km²
Inhabitants: 47,431,256 [2020]
Time: UTC

The FA:
Real Federación Española de Fútbol
Ramón y Cajal, s/n Apartado postal 385, 28230 Las Rozas (Madrid)
Tel: +34 91 495 9800
Founded: 14.10.1909
Member of FIFA since: 1913
Member of UEFA since: 1954
Website: www.rfef.es

NATIONAL TEAM RECORDS

RECORDS

First international match:	28.08.1920, Bruxelles:	Spain – Denmark 1-0
Most international caps:	Sergio Ramos García	- 170 caps (since 2005)
Most international goals:	David Villa Sánchez	- 59 goals / 98 caps (2005-2017)

UEFA EUROPEAN CHAMPIONSHIP		FIFA WORLD CUP		OLYMPIC TOURNAMENTS	
1960	Qualifiers	1930	Did not enter	1908	-
1964	**Final Tournament (Winners)**	1934	Final Tournament (Quarter-Finals)	1912	-
1968	Qualifiers	1938	*Withdrew*	1920	Quarter-Finals
1972	Qualifiers	1950	Final Tournament (4th Place)	1924	Preliminary Round
1976	Qualifiers	1954	Qualifiers	1928	Quarter-Finals
1980	Final Tournament (Group Stage)	1958	Qualifiers	1936	Did not enter
1984	Final Tournament (Runners-up)	1962	Final Tournament (Group Stage)	1948	Did not enter
1988	Final Tournament (Group Stage)	1966	Final Tournament (Group Stage)	1952	Did not enter
1992	Qualifiers	1970	Qualifiers	1956	Did not enter
1996	Final Tournament (Quarter-Finals)	1974	Qualifiers	1960	Did not enter
2000	Final Tournament (Quarter-Finals)	1978	Final Tournament (Group Stage)	1964	Qualifiers
2004	Final Tournament (Group Stage)	1982	Final Tournament (2nd Round)	1968	Quarter-Finals
2008	**Final Tournament (Winners)**	1986	Final Tournament (Quarter-Finals)	1972	Qualifiers
2012	**Final Tournament (Winners)**	1990	Final Tournament (2nd Round of 16)	1976	Group Stage
2016	Final Tournament (2nd Round of 16)	1994	Final Tournament (Quarter-Finals)	1980	Group Stage
2020	*Final Tournament (Qualified)*	1998	Final Tournament (Group Stage)	1984	Qualifiers
		2002	Final Tournament (Quarter-Finals)	1988	Qualifiers
		2006	Final Tournament (2nd Round of 16)	1992	**Winners**
		2010	**Final Tournament (Winners)**	1996	Quarter-Finals
		2014	Final Tournament (Group Stage)	2000	Runners-up
		2018	Final Tournament (2nd Round of 16)	2004	Qualifiers
				2008	Qualifiers
				2012	Group Stage
				2016	Qualifiers

UEFA NATIONS LEAGUE

2018/2019 – League A

FIFA CONFEDERATIONS CUP 1992-2017

2009 (3rd Place), 2013 (Runners-up)

SPANISH CLUB HONOURS IN EUROPEAN CLUB COMPETITIONS:

European Champion Clubs.Cup (1956-1992) / UEFA Champions League (1993-2020)		
Real Madrid CF	13	1955/1956, 1956/1957, 1957/1958, 1958/1959, 1959/1960, 1965/1966, 1997/1998, 1999/2000, 2001/2002, 2013/2014, 2015/2016, 2016/2017, 2017/2018
FC Barcelona	5	1991/1992, 2005/2006, 2008/2009, 2010/2011, 2014/2015
Fairs Cup (1858-1971) / UEFA Cup (1972-2009) / UEFA Europa League (2010-2020)		
Sevilla FC	6	2005/2006, 2006/2007, 2013/2014, 2014/2015, 2015/2016, 2019-2020
FC Barcelona	3	1955-1958, 1958-1960, 1965/1966
Club Atlético de Madrid	3	2009/2010, 2011/2012, 2017/2018
Valencia CF	3	1961/1962, 1962/1963, 2003/2004

Real Madrid CF	2	1984/1985, 1985/1986
Real Zaragoza	1	1963/1964
UEFA Super Cup (1972-2019)		
FC Barcelona	5	1992, 1997, 2009, 2011, 2015
Real Madrid CF	4	2002, 2014, 2016, 2017
Club Atlético de Madrid	3	2010, 2012, 2018
Valencia CF	2	1980, 2004
Sevilla FC	1	2006
European Cup Winners.Cup 1961-1999*		
FC Barcelona	4	1978/1979, 1981/1982, 1988/1989, 1996/1997
Club Atlético de Madrid	1	1961/1962
Valencia CF	1	1979/1980
Real Zaragoza	1	1994/1995

*defunct competition

NATIONAL COMPETITIONS
TABLE OF HONOURS

	CHAMPIONS	CUP WINNERS	BEST GOALSCORERS	
1903	-	Athletic Club Bilbao	-	
1904	-	Athletic Club Bilbao	-	
1905	-	Madrid FC	-	
1906	-	Madrid FC	-	
1907	-	Madrid FC	-	
1908	-	Madrid FC	-	
1909	-	Real Sociedad de Fútbol San Sebastián	-	
1910	-	FC Barcelona (FEF)* Athletic Club Bilbao (UECF)**	-	
1911	-	Athletic Club Bilbao	-	
1912	-	FC Barcelona	-	
1913	-	Racing Club de Irún (FEF) FC Barcelona (UECF)	-	
1914	-	Athletic Club Bilbao	-	
1915	-	Athletic Club Bilbao	-	
1916	-	Athletic Club Bilbao	-	
1917	-	Madrid FC	-	
1918	-	Real Unión Club de Irún	-	
1919	-	Arenas Club de Getxo	-	
1920	-	FC Barcelona	-	
1921	-	Athletic Club Bilbao	-	
1922	-	FC Barcelona	-	
1923	-	Athletic Club Bilbao	-	
1924	-	Real Unión Club de Irún	-	
1925	-	FC Barcelona	-	
1926	-	FC Barcelona	-	
1927	-	Real Unión Club de Irún	-	
1928	-	FC Barcelona	-	
1929	FC Barcelona	RCD Español Barcelona	Francisco "Paco" Bienzobas Ocáriz (Real Sociedad de Fútbol San Sebastián)	14
1929/1930	Athletic Club Bilbao	Athletic Club Bilbao	Guillermo Gorostiza Paredes (Athletic Club Bilbao)	19
1930/1931	Athletic Club Bilbao	Athletic Club Bilbao	Agustín Sauto Arana "Bata" (Athletic Club Bilbao)	27
1931/1932	Real Madrid FC	Athletic Club Bilbao	Guillermo Gorostiza Paredes (Athletic Club Bilbao)	12
1932/1933	Real Madrid FC	Athletic Club Bilbao	Manuel Olivares Lapeña (Real Madrid FC)	16
1933/1934	Athletic Club Bilbao	Real Madrid FC	Isidro Lángara Galarraga (Real Oviedo CF)	27
1934/1935	Real Betis Balompié Sevilla	Sevilla FC	Isidro Lángara Galarraga (Real Oviedo CF)	26
1935/1936	Athletic Club Bilbao	Real Madrid FC	Isidro Lángara Galarraga (Real Oviedo CF)	27
1936/1937	*League Cancelled*	*No competition*	-	
1937/1938	*League Cancelled*	*No competition*	-	
1938/1939	*League Cancelled*	Sevilla FC	-	
1939/1940	Atlético Aviación Madrid	RCD Español Barcelona	Víctor Unamuno Ibarzabal (Athletic Club Bilbao)	22
1940/1941	Atlético Aviación Madrid	Valencia CF	Prudencio Sánchez Fernández "Pruden" (Atlético Aviación Madrid)	30
1941/1942	Valencia CF	CF Barcelona	Edmundo Suárez Trabanco "Mundo" (Valencia CF)	27
1942/1943	Atlético Club de Bilbao	Atlético Club de Bilbao	Mariano Martín Alonso (CF Barcelona)	32
1943/1944	Valencia CF	Atlético Club de Bilbao	Edmundo Suárez Trabanco "Mundo" (Valencia CF)	27
1944/1945	CF Barcelona	Atlético Club de Bilbao	Pedro Telmo Zarraonandía Montoya (Atlético Club de Bilbao)	19
1945/1946	Sevilla FC	Real Madrid CF	Pedro Telmo Zarraonandía Montoya (Atlético Club de Bilbao)	24
1946/1947	Valencia CF	Real Madrid CF	Pedro Telmo Zarraonandía Montoya (Atlético Club de Bilbao)	34
1947/1948	CF Barcelona	Sevilla FC	Manuel Fernández Fernández "Pahiño" (RC Celta de Vigo)	23
1948/1949	CF Barcelona	Valencia CF	César Rodríguez Álvarez (CF Barcelona)	28
1949/1950	Club Atlético de Madrid	Atlético Club de Bilbao	Pedro Telmo Zarraonandía Montoya (Atlético Club de Bilbao)	25

1950/1951	Club Atlético de Madrid	CF Barcelona	Pedro Telmo Zarraonandía Montoya (Atlético Club de Bilbao)	38
1951/1952	CF Barcelona	CF Barcelona	Manuel Fernández Fernández "Pahiño" (Real Madrid CF)	28
1952/1953	CF Barcelona	CF Barcelona	Pedro Telmo Zarraonandía Montoya (Atlético Club de Bilbao)	24
1953/1954	Real Madrid CF	Valencia CF	Alfredo Stéfano Di Stéfano Laulhé (Real Madrid CF)	27
1954/1955	Real Madrid CF	Atlético Club de Bilbao	Juan Arza Iñigo (Sevilla FC)	28
1955/1956	Atlético Club de Bilbao	Atlético Club de Bilbao	Alfredo Stéfano Di Stéfano Laulhé (Real Madrid CF)	24
1956/1957	Real Madrid CF	CF Barcelona	Alfredo Stéfano Di Stéfano Laulhé (Real Madrid CF)	31
1957/1958	Real Madrid CF	Atlético Club de Bilbao	Manuel Badenes Calduch (Real Valladolid CF) Alfredo Stéfano Di Stéfano Laulhé (Real Madrid CF) Ricardo de la Virgen (Valencia CF)	19
1958/1959	CF Barcelona	CF Barcelona	Alfredo Stéfano Di Stéfano Laulhé (Real Madrid CF	23
1959/1960	CF Barcelona	Club Atlético de Madrid	Ferenc Puskás (HUN, Real Madrid CF)	26
1960/1961	Real Madrid CF	Club Atlético de Madrid	Ferenc Puskás (HUN, Real Madrid CF)	27
1961/1962	Real Madrid CF	Real Madrid CF	Juan Roberto Seminario Rodríguez (PER, Real Zaragoza)	25
1962/1963	Real Madrid CF	CF Barcelona	Ferenc Puskás (HUN, Real Madrid CF)	26
1963/1964	Real Madrid CF	Real Zaragoza	Ferenc Puskás (HUN, Real Madrid CF)	20
1964/1965	Real Madrid CF	Club Atlético de Madrid	Cayetano Ré Ramírez (PAR, CF Barcelona)	25
1965/1966	Club Atlético de Madrid	Real Zaragoza	Luciano Sánchez Rodríguez "Vavá" (Elche CF)	19
1966/1967	Real Madrid CF	Valencia CF	Waldo Machado da Silva (BRA, Valencia CF)	24
1967/1968	Real Madrid CF	CF Barcelona	Fidel Uriarte Macho (Atlético Club de Bilbao)	22
1968/1969	Real Madrid CF	Atlético Club de Bilbao	Amancio Amaro Varela (Club Atlético de Madrid) José Eulogio Gárate Ormaechea (Real Madrid CF)	14
1969/1970	Club Atlético de Madrid	Real Madrid CF	Amancio Amaro Varela (Real Madrid CF) José Luis Aragonés Suárez (Club Atlético de Madrid) José Eulogio Gárate Ormaechea (Club Atlético de Madrid)	16
1970/1971	Valencia CF	CF Barcelona	José Eulogio Gárate Ormaechea (Club Atlético de Madrid) Carles Rexach i Cerdà (CF Barcelona)	17
1971/1972	Real Madrid CF	Club Atlético de Madrid	Enrique Porta Guíu (Granada CF)	20
1972/1973	Club Atlético de Madrid	Athletic Club Bilbao	Mariano Arias Chamorro "Marianín" (Real Oviedo CF)	19
1973/1974	CF Barcelona	Real Madrid CF	Enrique Castro González "Quini" (Real Sporting de Gijón)	20
1974/1975	Real Madrid CF	Real Madrid CF	Carlos Ruiz Herrero (Athletic Club Bilbao)	19
1975/1976	Real Madrid CF	Club Atlético de Madrid	Enrique Castro González "Quini" (Real Sporting de Gijón)	21
1976/1977	Club Atlético de Madrid	Real Betis Balompié Sevilla	Mario Alberto Kempes Chiodi (ARG, Valencia CF)	24
1977/1978	Real Madrid CF	FC Barcelona	Mario Alberto Kempes Chiodi (ARG, Valencia CF)	28
1978/1979	Real Madrid CF	Valencia CF	Johann Krankl (AUT, FC Barcelona)	29
1979/1980	Real Madrid CF	Real Madrid CF	Enrique Castro González "Quini" (Real Sporting de Gijón)	24
1980/1981	Real Sociedad de Fútbol San Sebastián	FC Barcelona	Enrique Castro González "Quini" (FC Barcelona)	20
1981/1982	Real Sociedad de Fútbol San Sebastián	Real Madrid CF	Enrique Castro González "Quini" (FC Barcelona)	26
1982/1983	Athletic Club Bilbao	FC Barcelona	Hipólito Rincón Povedano (Real Betis Balompié Sevilla)	20
1983/1984	Athletic Club Bilbao	Athletic Club Bilbao	Jorge Orosmán da Silva Echeverrito (URU, Real Valladolid CF) Juan Gómez González "Juanito" (Real Madrid CF)	17
1984/1985	FC Barcelona	Club Atlético de Madrid	Hugo Sánchez Márquez (MEX, Club Atlético de Madrid)	19
1985/1986	Real Madrid CF	Real Zaragoza	Hugo Sánchez Márquez (MEX, Real Madrid CF)	22
1986/1987	Real Madrid CF	Real Sociedad de Fútbol San Sebastián	Hugo Sánchez Márquez (MEX, Real Madrid CF)	34
1987/1988	Real Madrid CF	FC Barcelona	Hugo Sánchez Márquez (MEX, Real Madrid CF)	29
1988/1989	Real Madrid CF	Real Madrid CF	Baltazar Maria de Morais Júnior (BRA, Club Atlético de Madrid)	35
1989/1990	Real Madrid CF	FC Barcelona	Hugo Sánchez Márquez (MEX, Real Madrid CF)	38
1990/1991	FC Barcelona	Club Atlético de Madrid	Emilio Butragueño Santos (Real Madrid CF)	19
1991/1992	FC Barcelona	Club Atlético de Madrid	Manuel Sánchez Delgado "Manolo" (Club Atlético de Madrid)	27
1992/1993	FC Barcelona	Real Madrid CF	José Roberto Gama de Oliveira "Bebeto" (RC Deportivo La Coruña)	29
1993/1994	FC Barcelona	Real Zaragoza	Romário de Souza Faria (BRA, FC Barcelona)	30
1994/1995	Real Madrid CF	RC Deportivo La Coruña	Iván Luis Zamorano Zamora (CHI, Real Madrid CF)	28
1995/1996	Club Atlético de Madrid	Club Atlético de Madrid	Juan Antonio Pizzi Torroja (CD Tenerife)	31
1996/1997	Real Madrid CF	FC Barcelona	Ronaldo Luís Nazário de Lima (BRA, FC Barcelona)	34
1997/1998	FC Barcelona	FC Barcelona	Christian Vieri (Club Atlético de Madrid)	24
1998/1999	FC Barcelona	Valencia CF	Raúl González Blanco (Real Madrid CF)	25
1999/2000	RC Deportivo La Coruña	RCD Espanyol Barcelona	Salvador Ballesta Vialcho "Salva" (Real Racing Club de Santander)	27
2000/2001	Real Madrid CF	Real Zaragoza	Raúl González Blanco (Real Madrid CF)	24
2001/2002	Valencia CF	RC Deportivo La Coruña	Diego Tristán Herrera (RC Deportivo La Coruña)	21

2002/2003	Real Madrid CF	RCD Mallorca	Rudolphus Antonius "Roy" Makaay (NED, RC Deportivo La Coruña)	29
2003/2004	Valencia CF	Real Zaragoza	Ronaldo Luís Nazário de Lima (BRA, Real Madrid CF)	25
2004/2005	FC Barcelona	Real Betis Balompié Sevilla	Diego Forlán Corazzo (URU, Villarreal CF)	25
2005/2006	FC Barcelona	RCD Espanyol Barcelona	Samuel Eto'o Fils (CMR, FC Barcelona)	26
2006/2007	Real Madrid CF	Sevilla FC	Rutgerus Johannes Martinus "Ruud" van Nistelrooy (NED, Real Madrid CF)	25
2007/2008	Real Madrid CF	Valencia CF	Daniel González Güiza (RCD Mallorca)	27
2008/2009	FC Barcelona	FC Barcelona	Diego Forlán Corazzo (URU, Club Atlético de Madrid)	32
2009/2010	FC Barcelona	Sevilla FC	Lionel Andrés Messi Cuccittini (ARG, FC Barcelona)	34
2010/2011	FC Barcelona	Real Madrid CF	Cristiano Ronaldo dos Santos Aveiro (POR, Real Madrid CF)	40
2011/2012	Real Madrid CF	FC Barcelona	Lionel Andrés Messi Cuccittini (ARG, FC Barcelona)	50
2012/2013	FC Barcelona	Club Atlético de Madrid	Lionel Andrés Messi Cuccittini (ARG, FC Barcelona)	46
2013/2014	Club Atlético de Madrid	Real Madrid CF	Cristiano Ronaldo dos Santos Aveiro (POR, Real Madrid CF)	31
2014/2015	FC Barcelona	FC Barcelona	Cristiano Ronaldo dos Santos Aveiro (POR, Real Madrid CF)	48
2015/2016	FC Barcelona	FC Barcelona	Luis Alberto Suárez Díaz (URU, FC Barcelona)	40
2016/2017	Real Madrid CF	FC Barcelona	Lionel Andrés Messi Cuccittini (ARG, FC Barcelona)	37
2017/2018	FC Barcelona	FC Barcelona	Lionel Andrés Messi Cuccittini (ARG, FC Barcelona)	34
2018/2019	FC Barcelona	Valencia CF	Lionel Andrés Messi Cuccittini (ARG, FC Barcelona)	36
2019/2020	Real Madrid CF	*Final postponed*	Lionel Andrés Messi Cuccittini (ARG, FC Barcelona)	25

*FEF = Federación Española de Fútbol
**UECF = Unión Española de Clubes de Fútbol
Name changements:
Real Madrid CF = Madrid FC (1902-1920); Real Madrid FC (1920-1938), Real Madrid CF (since 1938).
Athletic Club Bilbao = Atlético Club de Bilbao (1940-1972)
FC FC Barcelona = CF FC Barcelona (1941-1974)
Real Unión Club de Irún = Racing Club de Irún (1901-1915)
RCD Espayol Barcelona = RCD Español Barcelona Barcelona (1910-1995)
Sevilla FC = Sevilla CF (1938-1986)
Club Atlético de Madrid = Athletic Club Madrid (1903-1926); Club Club Atlético de Madrid (1926-1939); Atlético Aviación Madrid (1939-1947); Club Atlético de Madrid (since 1947)
Valencia CF = Valencia FC (1919-1940)

NATIONAL CHAMPIONSHIP
La Liga 2019/2020
(16.08.2019 – 19.07.2020)

Results

Round 1 [16-18.08.2019]
Athletic Bilbao - FC Barcelona 1-0(0-0)
Celta Vigo - Real Madrid 1-3(0-1)
Valencia CF - Real Sociedad 1-1(0-0)
RCD Mallorca - SD Eibar 2-1(1-0)
CD Leganés - CA Osasuna 0-1(0-0)
Villarreal CF - Granada CF 4-4(1-1)
CD Alavés - Levante UD 1-0(0-0)
Espanyol Barcelona - Sevilla FC 0-2(0-1)
Real Betis - Real Valladolid 1-2(0-0)
Atlético Madrid - Getafe CF 1-0(1-0)

Round 2 [23-25.08.2019]
Granada CF - Sevilla FC 0-1(0-0)
Levante UD - Villarreal CF 2-1(0-1)
CA Osasuna - SD Eibar 0-0
Real Madrid - Real Valladolid 1-1(0-0)
Celta Vigo - Valencia CF 1-0(1-0)
Getafe CF - Athletic Bilbao 1-1(1-1)
CD Alavés - Espanyol Barcelona 0-0
RCD Mallorca - Real Sociedad 0-1(0-0)
CD Leganés - Atlético Madrid 0-1(0-0)
FC Barcelona - Real Betis 5-2(1-1)

Round 3 [30.08.-01.09.2019]
Sevilla FC - Celta Vigo 1-1(0-0)
Athletic Bilbao - Real Sociedad 2-0(2-0)
CA Osasuna - FC Barcelona 2-2(1-0)
Getafe CF - CD Alavés 1-1(1-1)
Levante UD - Real Valladolid 2-0(0-0)
Real Betis - CD Leganés 2-1(0-0)
Valencia CF - RCD Mallorca 2-0(1-0)
Atlético Madrid - SD Eibar 3-2(1-2)
Espanyol Barcelona - Granada CF 0-3(0-1)
Villarreal CF - Real Madrid 2-2(1-1)

Round 4 [13-15.09.2019]
RCD Mallorca - Athletic Bilbao 0-0
Real Madrid - Levante UD 3-2(3-0)
CD Leganés - Villarreal CF 0-3(0-2)
Real Sociedad - Atlético Madrid 2-0(0-0)
FC Barcelona - Valencia CF 5-2(2-1)
SD Eibar - Espanyol Barcelona 1-2(0-0)
CD Alavés - Sevilla FC 0-1(0-1)
Celta Vigo - Granada CF 0-2(0-1)
Real Valladolid - CA Osasuna 1-1(0-0)
Real Betis - Getafe CF 1-1(0-1)

Round 5 [20-22.09.2019]
CA Osasuna - Real Betis 0-0
Villarreal CF - Real Valladolid 2-0(0-0)
Levante UD - SD Eibar 0-0
Atlético Madrid - Celta Vigo 0-0
Granada CF - FC Barcelona 2-0(1-0)
Getafe CF - RCD Mallorca 4-2(2-0)
Espanyol Barcelona - Real Sociedad 1-3(0-2)
Valencia CF - CD Leganés 1-1(1-1)
Athletic Bilbao - CD Alavés 2-0(1-0)
Sevilla FC - Real Madrid 0-1(0-0)

Round 6 [24-26.09.2019]
Real Valladolid - Granada CF 1-1(1-1)
Real Betis - Levante UD 3-1(1-1)
FC Barcelona - Villarreal CF 2-1(2-1)
CD Leganés - Athletic Bilbao 1-1(0-0)
RCD Mallorca - Atlético Madrid 0-2(0-1)
Valencia CF - Getafe CF 3-3(3-1)
Real Madrid - CA Osasuna 2-0(1-0)
SD Eibar - Sevilla FC 3-2(0-2)
Celta Vigo - Espanyol Barcelona 1-1(0-0)
Real Sociedad - CD Alavés 3-0(3-0)

Round 7 [27-29.09.2019]
Villarreal CF - Real Betis 5-1(1-0)
Athletic Bilbao - Valencia CF 0-1(0-1)
Getafe CF - FC Barcelona 0-2(0-1)
Granada CF - CD Leganés 1-0(1-0)
Atlético Madrid - Real Madrid 0-0
Espanyol Barcelona - Real Valladolid 0-2(0-1)
SD Eibar - Celta Vigo 2-0(0-0)
CD Alavés - RCD Mallorca 2-0(0-0)
Levante UD - CA Osasuna 1-1(1-0)
Sevilla FC - Real Sociedad 3-2(1-1)

Round 8 [04-06.10.2019]
Real Betis - SD Eibar 1-1(0-1)
CD Leganés - Levante UD 1-2(0-1)
Real Madrid - Granada CF 4-2(2-0)
Valencia CF - CD Alavés 2-1(1-0)
CA Osasuna - Villarreal CF 2-1(0-1)
RCD Mallorca - Espanyol Barcelona 2-0(1-0)
Celta Vigo - Athletic Bilbao 1-0(0-0)
Real Valladolid - Atlético Madrid 0-0
Real Sociedad - Getafe CF 1-2(1-0)
FC Barcelona - Sevilla FC 4-0(3-0)

Round 9 [18-20.10.2019]
Granada CF - CA Osasuna 1-0(1-0)
SD Eibar - FC Barcelona 0-3(0-1)
Atlético Madrid - Valencia CF 1-1(1-0)
Getafe CF - CD Leganés 2-0(0-0)
RCD Mallorca - Real Madrid 1-0(1-0)
CD Alavés - Celta Vigo 2-0(0-0)
Real Sociedad - Real Betis 3-1(2-1)
Espanyol Barcelona - Villarreal CF 0-1(0-1)
Athletic Bilbao - Real Valladolid 1-1(1-0)
Sevilla FC - Levante UD 1-0(0-0)

Round 10 [25-27.10.2019]
Villarreal CF - CD Alavés 4-1(1-0)
CD Leganés - RCD Mallorca 1-0(1-0)
Real Valladolid - SD Eibar 2-0(2-0)
Atlético Madrid - Athletic Bilbao 2-0(1-0)
Celta Vigo - Real Sociedad 0-1(0-0)
Granada CF - Real Betis 1-0(0-0)
Levante UD - Espanyol Barcelona 0-1(0-1)
Sevilla FC - Getafe CF 2-0(0-0)
CA Osasuna - Valencia CF 3-1(1-1)
FC Barcelona - Real Madrid 0-0 [18.12.]

Round 11 [29-31.10.2019]
CD Alavés - Atlético Madrid 1-1(0-0)
FC Barcelona - Real Valladolid 5-1(3-1)
Real Sociedad - Levante UD 1-2(0-2)
Valencia CF - Sevilla FC 1-1(0-1)
Athletic Bilbao - Espanyol Barcelona 3-0(2-0)
Real Betis - Celta Vigo 2-1(1-0)
Real Madrid - CD Leganés 5-0(3-0)
SD Eibar - Villarreal CF 2-1(0-0)
RCD Mallorca - CA Osasuna 2-2(1-0)
Getafe CF - Granada CF 3-1(2-0)

Round 12 [02-03.11.2019]
Espanyol Barcelona - Valencia CF 1-2(1-0)
Levante UD - FC Barcelona 3-1(0-1)
Sevilla FC - Atlético Madrid 1-1(1-0)
Real Madrid - Real Betis 0-0
Real Valladolid - RCD Mallorca 3-0(1-0)
Villarreal CF - Athletic Bilbao 0-0
CA Osasuna - CD Alavés 4-2(3-1)
Celta Vigo - Getafe CF 0-1(0-1)
CD Leganés - SD Eibar 1-2(1-1)
Granada CF - Real Sociedad 1-2(1-1)

Round 13 [08-10.11.2019]
Real Sociedad - CD Leganés 1-1(0-0)
CD Alavés - Real Valladolid 3-0(2-0)
Valencia CF - Granada CF 2-0(0-0)
SD Eibar - Real Madrid 0-4(0-3)
FC Barcelona - Celta Vigo 4-1(2-1)
RCD Mallorca - Villarreal CF 3-1(2-0)
Athletic Bilbao - Levante UD 2-1(0-1)
Atlético Madrid - Espanyol Barcel. 3-1(1-1)
Getafe CF - CA Osasuna 0-0
Real Betis - Sevilla FC 1-2(1-1)

Round 14 [22-24.11.2019]
Levante UD - RCD Mallorca 2-1(0-0)
CD Leganés - FC Barcelona 1-2(1-0)
Real Betis - Valencia CF 2-1(1-1)
Granada CF - Atlético Madrid 1-1(0-0)
Real Madrid - Real Sociedad 3-1(1-1)
Espanyol Barcelona - Getafe CF 1-1(1-1)
CA Osasuna - Athletic Bilbao 1-2(0-1)
SD Eibar - CD Alavés 0-2(0-0)
Villarreal CF - Celta Vigo 1-3(0-0)
Real Valladolid - Sevilla FC 0-1(0-1)

Round 15 [29.11.-01.12.2019]
Celta Vigo - Real Valladolid 0-0
CD Alavés - Real Madrid 1-2(0-0)
Real Sociedad - SD Eibar 4-1(1-1)
RCD Mallorca - Real Betis 1-2(0-2)
Valencia CF - Villarreal CF 2-1(0-0)
Sevilla FC - CD Leganés 1-0(0-0)
Athletic Bilbao - Granada CF 2-0(1-0)
Espanyol Barcelona - CA Osasuna 2-4(1-0)
Getafe CF - Levante UD 4-0(0-0)
Atlético Madrid - FC Barcelona 0-1(0-0)

Round 16 [06-08.12.2019]
Villarreal CF - Atlético Madrid 0-0
Real Madrid - Espanyol Barcelona 2-0(1-0)
Granada CF - CD Alavés 3-0(0-0)
Levante UD - Valencia CF 2-4(2-1)
FC Barcelona - RCD Mallorca 5-2(4-1)
SD Eibar - Getafe CF 0-1(0-0)
Real Betis - Athletic Bilbao 3-2(3-1)
Real Valladolid - Real Sociedad 0-0
CD Leganés - Celta Vigo 3-2(2-0)
CA Osasuna - Sevilla FC 1-1(1-1)

Round 17 [13-15.12.2019]
CD Alavés - CD Leganés 1-1(0-1)
Granada CF - Levante UD 1-2(0-0)
Real Sociedad - FC Barcelona 2-2(1-1)
Athletic Bilbao - SD Eibar 0-0
Atlético Madrid - CA Osasuna 2-0(0-0)
Getafe CF - Real Valladolid 2-0(1-0)
Celta Vigo - RCD Mallorca 2-2(1-1)
Espanyol Barcelona - Real Betis 2-2(2-1)
Sevilla FC - Villarreal CF 1-2(0-1)
Valencia CF - Real Madrid 1-1(0-0)

Round 18 [20-22.12.2019]
SD Eibar - Granada CF 3-0(2-0)
RCD Mallorca - Sevilla FC 0-2(0-1)
FC Barcelona - CD Alavés 4-1(2-0)
Villarreal CF - Getafe CF 1-0(0-0)
Real Valladolid - Valencia CF 1-1(0-0)
CD Leganés - Espanyol Barcelona 2-0(1-0)
CA Osasuna - Real Sociedad 3-4(1-3)
Real Betis - Atlético Madrid 1-2(0-0)
Levante UD - Celta Vigo 3-1(0-1)
Real Madrid - Athletic Bilbao 0-0

Round 19 [03-05.01.2020]
Real Valladolid - CD Leganés 2-2(1-2)
Sevilla FC - Athletic Bilbao 1-1(0-1)
Valencia CF - SD Eibar 1-0(1-0)
Getafe CF - Real Madrid 0-3(0-1)
Atlético Madrid - Levante UD 2-1(2-1)
Espanyol Barcelona - FC Barcelona 2-2(1-0)
Granada CF - RCD Mallorca 1-0(1-0)
Real Sociedad - Villarreal CF 1-2(1-0)
CD Alavés - Real Betis 1-1(1-0)
Celta Vigo - CA Osasuna 1-1(0-0)

Round 20 [17-19.01.2020]
CD Leganés - Getafe CF 0-3(0-3)
Levante UD - CD Alavés 0-1(0-0)
Real Madrid - Sevilla FC 2-1(0-0)
CA Osasuna - Real Valladolid 0-0
SD Eibar - Atlético Madrid 2-0(1-0)
RCD Mallorca - Valencia CF 4-1(3-0)
Real Betis - Real Sociedad 3-0(2-0)
Villarreal CF - Espanyol Barcelona 1-2(0-1)
Athletic Bilbao - Celta Vigo 1-1(0-0)
FC Barcelona - Granada CF 1-0(0-0)

Round 21 [24-26.01.2020]
CA Osasuna - Levante UD 2-0(0-0)
Espanyol Barcelona - Athletic Bilbao 1-1(0-1)
Valencia CF - FC Barcelona 2-0(0-0)
CD Alavés - Villarreal CF 1-2(0-1)
Sevilla FC - Granada CF 2-0(2-0)
Atlético Madrid - CD Leganés 0-0
Celta Vigo - SD Eibar 0-0
Getafe CF - Real Betis 1-0(0-0)
Real Sociedad - RCD Mallorca 3-0(0-0)
Real Valladolid - Real Madrid 0-1(0-0)

Round 22 [01-02.02.2020]
Granada CF - Espanyol Barcelona 2-1(1-1)
Real Madrid - Atlético Madrid 1-0(0-0)
RCD Mallorca - Real Valladolid 0-1(0-0)
Valencia CF - Celta Vigo 1-0(0-0)
CD Leganés - Real Sociedad 2-1(0-1)
SD Eibar - Real Betis 1-1(1-1)
Athletic Bilbao - Getafe CF 0-2(0-1)
Sevilla FC - CD Alavés 1-1(0-0)
Villarreal CF - CA Osasuna 3-1(1-0)
FC Barcelona - Levante UD 2-1(2-0)

Round 23 [07-09.02.2020]
CD Alavés - SD Eibar 2-1(0-0)
Levante UD - CD Leganés 2-0(2-0)
Getafe CF - Valencia CF 3-0(0-0)
Real Valladolid - Villarreal CF 1-1(1-0)
Atlético Madrid - Granada CF 1-0(1-0)
Espanyol Barcelona - RCD Mallorca 1-0(0-0)
Real Sociedad - Athletic Bilbao 2-1(0-0)
CA Osasuna - Real Madrid 1-4(1-2)
Celta Vigo - Sevilla FC 2-1(0-1)
Real Betis - FC Barcelona 2-3(2-2)

Round 24 [14-16.02.2020]
Valencia CF - Atlético Madrid 2-2(1-2)
RCD Mallorca - CD Alavés 1-0(0-0)
FC Barcelona - Getafe CF 2-1(2-0)
Villarreal CF - Levante UD 2-1(1-0)
Granada CF - Real Valladolid 2-1(0-0)
Sevilla FC - Espanyol Barcelona 2-2(1-1)
CD Leganés - Real Betis 0-0
Athletic Bilbao - CA Osasuna 0-1(0-1)
Real Madrid - Celta Vigo 2-2(0-1)
SD Eibar - Real Sociedad 1-2(0-1) [10.03.]

Round 25 [21-23.02.2020]
Real Betis - RCD Mallorca 3-3(2-2)
Celta Vigo - CD Leganés 1-0(0-0)
FC Barcelona - SD Eibar 5-0(3-0)
Real Sociedad - Valencia CF 3-0(2-0)
Levante UD - Real Madrid 1-0(0-0)
CA Osasuna - Granada CF 0-3(0-3)
CD Alavés - Athletic Bilbao 2-1(1-1)
Real Valladolid - Espanyol Barcelona 2-1(0-0)
Getafe CF - Sevilla FC 0-3(0-1)
Atlético Madrid - Villarreal CF 3-1(1-1)

Round 26 [28.02.-01.03.2020]
Real Sociedad - Real Valladolid 1-0(0-0)
SD Eibar - Levante UD 3-0(1-0)
Valencia CF - Real Betis 2-1(0-0)
CD Leganés - CD Alavés 1-1(0-0)
Granada CF - Celta Vigo 0-0
Sevilla FC - CA Osasuna 3-2(2-0)
Athletic Bilbao - Villarreal CF 1-0(0-0)
Espanyol Barcel. - Atlético Madrid 1-1(1-0)
RCD Mallorca - Getafe CF 0-1(0-0)
Real Madrid - FC Barcelona 2-0(0-0)

Round 27 [06-08.03.2020]
CD Alavés - Valencia CF 1-1(0-1)
SD Eibar - RCD Mallorca 1-2(0-1)
Atlético Madrid - Sevilla FC 2-2(2-2)
FC Barcelona - Real Sociedad 1-0(0-0)
Getafe CF - Celta Vigo 0-0
CA Osasuna - Espanyol Barcelona 1-0(0-0)
Real Valladolid - Athletic Bilbao 1-4(0-2)
Levante UD - Granada CF 1-1(1-0)
Villarreal CF - CD Leganés 1-2(1-0)
Real Betis - Real Madrid 2-1(1-1)

Round 28 [11-14.06.2020]
Sevilla FC - Real Betis 2-0(0-0)
Granada CF - Getafe CF 2-1(0-1)
Valencia CF - Levante UD 1-1(0-0)
Espanyol Barcelona - CD Alavés 2-0(1-0)
Celta Vigo - Villarreal CF 0-1(0-0)
CD Leganés - Real Valladolid 1-2(0-1)
RCD Mallorca - FC Barcelona 0-4(0-2)
Athletic Bilbao - Atlético Madrid 1-1(1-1)
Real Madrid - SD Eibar 3-1(3-0)
Real Sociedad - CA Osasuna 1-1(0-1)

Round 29 [15-18.06.2020]
Levante UD - Sevilla FC 1-1(0-0)
Real Betis - Granada CF 2-2(0-1)
Getafe CF - Espanyol Barcelona 0-0
Villarreal CF - RCD Mallorca 1-0(1-0)
FC Barcelona - CD Leganés 2-0(1-0)
SD Eibar - Athletic Bilbao 2-2(1-1)
Real Valladolid - Celta Vigo 1-1(0-0)
CA Osasuna - Atlético Madrid 0-5(0-1)
CD Alavés - Real Sociedad 2-0(0-0)
Real Madrid - Valencia CF 3-0(0-0)

Round 30 [19-21.06.2020]
Granada CF - Villarreal CF 0-1(0-1)
RCD Mallorca - CD Leganés 1-1(1-0)
Sevilla FC - FC Barcelona 0-0
Espanyol Barcelona - Levante UD 1-3(1-1)
Athletic Bilbao - Real Betis 1-0(1-0)
Getafe CF - SD Eibar 1-1(1-1)
Atlético Madrid - Real Valladolid 1-0(0-0)
Celta Vigo - CD Alavés 6-0(4-0)
Valencia CF - CA Osasuna 2-0(2-0)
Real Sociedad - Real Madrid 1-2(0-0)

Round 31 [22-25.06.2020]
Villarreal CF - Sevilla FC 2-2(2-1)
CD Leganés - Granada CF 0-0
Levante UD - Atlético Madrid 0-1(0-1)
Real Valladolid - Getafe CF 1-1(1-1)
FC Barcelona - Athletic Bilbao 1-0(0-0)
CD Alavés - CA Osasuna 0-1(0-0)
Real Sociedad - Celta Vigo 0-1(0-1)
Real Madrid - RCD Mallorca 2-0(1-0)
SD Eibar - Valencia CF 1-0(1-0)
Real Betis - Espanyol Barcelona 1-0(0-0)

Round 32 [26-29.06.2020]
Sevilla FC - Real Valladolid 1-1(0-1)
Athletic Bilbao - RCD Mallorca 3-1(2-0)
Celta Vigo - FC Barcelona 2-2(0-1)
CA Osasuna - CD Leganés 1-1(1-0)
Atlético Madrid - CD Alavés 2-1(0-0)
Levante UD - Real Betis 4-2(2-0)
Villarreal CF - Valencia CF 2-0(2-0)
Granada CF - SD Eibar 1-2(0-1)
Espanyol Barcelona - Real Madrid 0-1(0-1)
Getafe CF - Real Sociedad 2-1(1-0)

Round 33 [30.06.-02.07.2020]
RCD Mallorca - Celta Vigo 5-1(3-0)
CD Leganés - Sevilla FC 0-3(0-2)
FC Barcelona - Atlético Madrid 2-2(1-1)
CD Alavés - Granada CF 0-2(0-1)
Valencia CF - Athletic Bilbao 0-2(0-1)
Real Betis - Villarreal CF 0-2(0-2)
Real Valladolid - Levante UD 0-0
SD Eibar - CA Osasuna 0-2(0-1)
Real Sociedad - Espanyol Barcelona 2-1(0-1)
Real Madrid - Getafe CF 1-0(0-0)

Round 34 [03-06.07.2020]
Atlético Madrid - RCD Mallorca 3-0(2-0)
Celta Vigo - Real Betis 1-1(1-0)
Real Valladolid - CD Alavés 1-0(0-0)
Granada CF - Valencia CF 2-2(0-0)
Athletic Bilbao - Real Madrid 0-1(0-0)
Espanyol Barcelona - CD Leganés 0-1(0-0)
CA Osasuna - Getafe CF 0-0
Villarreal CF - FC Barcelona 1-4(1-3)
Levante UD - Real Sociedad 1-1(1-1)
Sevilla FC - SD Eibar 1-0(0-0)

Round 35 [07-10.07.2020]
Valencia CF - Real Valladolid 2-1(1-0)
Celta Vigo - Atlético Madrid 1-1(0-1)
Real Betis - CA Osasuna 3-0(2-0)
Getafe CF - Villarreal CF 1-3(0-0)
FC Barcelona - Espanyol Barcelona 1-0(0-0)
SD Eibar - CD Leganés 0-0
RCD Mallorca - Levante UD 2-0(1-0)
Athletic Bilbao - Sevilla FC 1-2(1-0)
Real Sociedad - Granada CF 2-3(0-2)
Real Madrid - CD Alavés 2-0(1-0)

Round 36 [11-13.07.2020]
CA Osasuna - Celta Vigo 2-1(1-1)
Real Valladolid - FC Barcelona 0-1(0-1)
Atlético Madrid - Real Betis 1-0(0-0)
Espanyol Barcelona - SD Eibar 0-2(0-2)
Levante UD - Athletic Bilbao 1-2(0-2)
CD Leganés - Valencia CF 1-0(1-0)
Sevilla FC - RCD Mallorca 2-0(1-0)
CD Alavés - Getafe CF 0-0
Villarreal CF - Real Sociedad 1-2(0-0)
Granada CF - Real Madrid 1-2(0-2)

Round 37 [16.07.2020]
SD Eibar - Real Valladolid 3-1(2-0)
Athletic Bilbao - CD Leganés 0-2(0-0)
FC Barcelona - CA Osasuna 1-2(0-1)
Real Betis - CD Alavés 1-2(0-0)
Celta Vigo - Levante UD 2-3(2-2)
Getafe CF - Atlético Madrid 0-2(0-0)
RCD Mallorca - Granada CF 1-2(1-1)
Real Madrid - Villarreal CF 2-1(1-0)
Real Sociedad - Sevilla FC 0-0
Valencia CF - Espanyol Barcelona 1-0(1-0)

Round 38 [19.07.2020]
CD Alavés - FC Barcelona 0-5(0-3)
Villarreal CF - SD Eibar 4-0(0-0)
Real Valladolid - Real Betis 2-0(1-0)
Atlético Madrid - Real Sociedad 1-1(1-0)
Espanyol Barcelona - Celta Vigo 0-0
Granada CF - Athletic Bilbao 4-0(1-0)
CD Leganés - Real Madrid 2-2(1-1)
Levante UD - Getafe CF 1-0(0-0)
CA Osasuna - RCD Mallorca 2-2(1-1)
Sevilla FC - Valencia CF 1-0(0-0)

Final Standings

						Total			Home					Away				
1.	**Real Madrid CF**	38	26	9	3	70 - 25	87	15	4	0	40 - 11	11	5	3	30 - 14
2.	FC Barcelona	38	25	7	6	86 - 38	82	16	2	1	52 - 16	9	5	5	34 - 22
3.	Club Atlético de Madrid	38	18	16	4	51 - 27	70	12	6	1	28 - 11	6	10	3	23 - 16
4.	Sevilla FC	38	19	13	6	54 - 34	70	10	7	2	26 - 14	9	6	4	28 - 20
5.	Villarreal CF	38	18	6	14	63 - 49	60	9	5	5	37 - 25	9	1	9	26 - 24
6.	Real Sociedad de Fútbol San Sebastián	38	16	8	14	56 - 48	56	9	4	6	33 - 20	7	4	8	23 - 28
7.	Granada CF	38	16	8	14	52 - 45	56	10	3	6	26 - 16	6	5	8	26 - 29
8.	Getafe CF	38	14	12	12	43 - 37	54	8	6	5	25 - 20	6	6	7	18 - 17
9.	Valencia CF	38	14	11	13	46 - 53	53	11	7	1	29 - 16	3	4	12	17 - 37
10.	CA Osasuna Pamplona	38	13	13	12	46 - 54	52	7	7	5	26 - 29	6	6	7	20 - 25
11.	Athletic Club Bilbao	38	13	12	13	41 - 38	51	9	4	6	21 - 14	4	8	7	20 - 24
12.	Levante UD Valencia	38	14	7	17	47 - 53	49	9	5	5	27 - 19	5	2	12	20 - 34
13.	Real Valladolid CF	38	9	15	14	32 - 43	42	5	10	4	18 - 15	4	5	10	14 - 28
14.	SD Eibar	38	11	9	18	39 - 56	42	8	3	8	25 - 25	3	6	10	14 - 31
15.	Real Betis Balompié Sevilla	38	10	11	17	48 - 60	41	9	4	6	34 - 27	1	7	11	14 - 33
16.	Deportivo Alavés Vitoria-Gasteiz	38	10	9	19	34 - 59	39	7	6	6	20 - 19	3	3	13	14 - 40
17.	RC Celta de Vigo	38	7	16	15	37 - 49	37	5	8	6	22 - 20	2	8	9	15 - 29
18.	CD Leganés (Relegated)	38	8	12	18	30 - 51	36	5	5	9	17 - 26	3	7	9	13 - 25
19.	RCD Mallorca (Relegated)	38	9	6	23	40 - 65	33	8	3	8	25 - 22	1	3	15	15 - 43
20.	RCD Espanyol Barcelona (Relegated)	38	5	10	23	27 - 58	25	2	6	11	15 - 31	3	4	12	12 - 27

NATIONAL CUP
Copa del Rey 2019/2020

First Round [11/17-19.12.2019/08.01.2020]

UD Logroñés - Club Marino de Luanco	2-1(1-0)	Comillas CF - Villarreal CF	0-5(0-2)
CD Lealtad de Villaviciosa - Cádiz CF	0-1(0-0)	Tolosa CF - Real Valladolid CF	0-3(0-1)
Coruxo FC - CD Mirandés	4-5(2-2,4-4)	CD El Álamo - RCD Mallorca	0-1(0-0)
Real Jaén CF - Deportivo Alavés Vitoria-Gasteiz	3-1(1-0)	CD Tudelano - Albacete Balompié	0-1(0-1)
SD Logroñés - SD Eibar	0-5(0-0)	Bergantiños FC - Sevilla FC	0-1(0-1)
CE L'Hospitalet - Granada CF	2-3(2-0,2-2)	CF Badalona - Real Oviedo CF	3-1(1-0)
CF Illueca - RC Deportivo La Coruña	0-2(0-0)	UD Melilla - UCAM Murcia CF	1-2(0-2)
UP Langreo - CD Ebro	2-3(0-1)	Sestao River Club - CD Lugo	1-1 aet; 6-5 pen
Marbella FC - CD Guijuelo	2-1(0-1)	Barakaldo CF - Villarrubia CF	0-0 aet; 5-3 pen
CD Castellón - UD Las Palmas	0-2(0-0)	Melilla CD - Levante UD Valencia	0-5(0-3)
CP Cacereño - AD Alcorcón	1-0(0-0)	CD Peña Azagresa - RC Celta de Vigo	0-2(0-1)
UD Socuéllamos - Real Zaragoza	0-1(0-1)	CA Antoniano - Real Betis Balompié Sevilla	0-4(0-2)
Club Portugalete - Extremadura UD Almendralejo	1-0(0-0)	Club Lleida Esportiu - RCD Espanyol Barcelona	0-2(0-0)
Peña Sport FC - CF Fuenlabrada	0-1(0-0,0-0)	SCR Peña Deportiva - SD Ponferradina	0-1(0-0,0-0)
SD Tarazona - Rayo Vallecano de Madrid	0-1(0-0,0-0)	CD Leonesa - Las Rozas CF	3-0(1-0)
Gimnástica Segoviana CF - Elche CF	0-2(0-1)	SD Amorebieta - CD Badajoz	0-1(0-0)
Zamora CF - Real Sporting de Gijón	2-1(1-0)	UE Llagostera - Club Haro Deportivo	0-1(0-0,0-0)
UM Escobedo - Málaga CF	2-0(0-0)	CF Rayo Majadahonda - Racing Club de Ferrol	1-0(0-0)
Unionistas de Salamanca CF - CD Atlético Baleares	1-0(1-0)	CD Laredo - SD Huesca	0-1(0-0)
Hércules Alicante CF - RC Recreativo de Huelva	0-1(0-1)	UD Tamaraceite - UD Almería	3-2(0-1,2-2)
CF Intercity S. Joan d'Alacant - Athletic Club Bilbao	0-3(0-1)	Club Gimnàstic de Tarragona - UE Olot	3-1(1-1,1-1)
FC Andorra - CD Leganés	1-1 aet; 5-6 pen	UE Cornellà - Orihuela CF	0-0 aet; 4-5 pen
AD Ceuta - CD Numancia	1-1 aet; 3-2 pen	CD Becerril - Real Sociedad de Fútbol San Sebastián	0-8(0-2)
Real Murcia CF - Real Racing Club de Santander	1-0(1-0)	CF Lorca Deportiva - CA Osasuna Pamplona	0-3(0-1)
FC Cartagena - SD Leioa	4-1(3-0)	Linares Deportivo - Girona FC	1-2(1-0)
CD Mensajero - CD Tenerife	0-3(0-2)	Mérida AD - CF La Nucía	2-2 aet; 3-2 pen
UD San Sebastiánde los Reyes - Córdoba CF	2-0(1-0)	Pontevedra CF - UD Ibiza	0-2(0-1)
El Palmar CF - Getafe CF	1-2(1-0)		

Second Round [11-12.01.2020]

Zamora CF - RCD Mallorca	0-1(0-1)	Real Club Recreativo de Huelva - CF Fuenlabrada	0-0 aet; 5-4 pen
Club Haro Deportivo - CA Osasuna Pamplona	1-2(0-0)	FC Cartagena - Girona FC	2-4(0-1,2-2)
Club Gimnàstic de Tarragona - Real Zaragoza	1-3(0-2)	UD Logroñés - Cádiz CF	1-1 aet; 4-2 pen
UCAM Murcia CF - CD Mirandés	2-3(1-0,2-2)	UD Tamaraceite - Granada CF	0-1(0-1)
Real Murcia CF - CD Leganés	0-4(0-1)	Marbella FC - Real Valladolid CF	0-0 aet; 1-4 pen
Club Portugalete - Real Betis Balompié Sevilla	0-3(0-1)	Orihuela CF - Villarreal CF	1-2(0-0,1-1)
CD Ebro - SD Ponferradina	1-0(0-0,0-0)	UM Escobedo - Sevilla FC	0-5(0-2)
CF Rayo Majadahonda - CD Tenerife	1-1 aet; 2-4 pen	CP Cacereño - SD Eibar	1-2(0-0)
UD Ibiza - Albacete Balompié	1-1 aet; 5-3 pen	UD SS Reyes - RCD Espanyol Barcelona	0-2(0-1)
Yeclano Deportivo - Elche CF	1-2(0-1)	Unionistas CF - RC Deportivo La Coruña	1-1 aet; 8-7 pen
CD Badajoz - UD Las Palmas	2-1(2-0)	Real Jaén CF - Levante UD Valencia	1-1 aet; 4-5 pen
Sestao River Club - Athletic Club Bilbao	0-4(0-2)	AD Ceuta - Real Sociedad de Fútbol San Sebastián	0-4(0-0)
CF Badalona - Getafe CF	2-0(0-0)	Mérida AD - RC Celta de Vigo	1-4(1-2)
CD Leonesa - SD Huesca	2-1(0-1)	Barakaldo CF - Rayo Vallecano de Madrid	0-2(0-1)

Third Round [21-23.01.2020]

Real Zaragoza - RCD Mallorca	3-1(0-0)	Girona FC - Villarreal CF	0-3(0-0)
RC Recreativo de Huelva - CA Osasuna Pamplona	2-3(2-0,2-2)	Real Sociedad de Fútbol San Sebastián - RCD Espanyol Barcelona	2-0(1-0)
Sevilla FC - Levante UD Valencia	3-1(1-1)	CF Badalona - Granada CF	1-3(0-1,1-1)
UD Ibiza - FC Barcelona	1-2(1-0)	CD Mirandés - RC Celta de Vigo	2-1(1-0,1-1)
Elche CF - Athletic Club Bilbao	1-1 aet; 4-5 pen	CD Ebro - CD Leganés	0-1(0-1)
UD Logroñés - Valencia CF	0-1(0-1)	CD Leonesa - Atlético Madrid	2-1(0-0,1-1)
Unionistas CF - Real Madrid CF	1-3(0-1)	Rayo Vallecano - Real Betis Balompié Sevilla	2-2 aet; 4-2 pen
CD Tenerife - Real Valladolid CF	2-1(0-0)	CD Badajoz - SD Eibar	3-1(2-1)

1/8-Finals [28-30.01.2020]

CD Tenerife - Athletic Club Bilbao	3-3 aet; 2-4 pen	Real Zaragoza - Real Madrid CF	0-4(0-2)
CD Leonesa - Valencia CF	0-0 aet; 2-4 pen	Real Socied. San Sebastián - CA Osasuna Pamplona	3-1(1-1)
Rayo Vallecano de Madrid - Villarreal CF	0-2(0-0)	FC Barcelona - CD Leganés	5-0(2-0)
CD Badajoz - Granada CF	2-3(1-1,2-2)	CD Mirandés - Sevilla FC	3-1(2-0)

Quarter-Finals [04-06.02.2020]			
Granada CF - Valencia CF	2-1(1-1)	Real Madrid CF - Real Sociedad San Sebastián	3-4(0-1)
CD Mirandés - Villarreal CF	4-2(2-1)	Athletic Club Bilbao - FC Barcelona	1-0(0-0)

Semi-Finals [12-13.02./04-05.03.2020]			
First Leg		**Second Leg**	
Athletic Club Bilbao - Granada CF	1-0(1-0)	Granada CF - Athletic Club Bilbao	2-1(0-0)
Real Sociedad San Sebastián - CD Mirandés	2-1(2-1)	CD Mirandés - Real Sociedad San Sebastián	0-1(0-1)

Final

The final between Athletic Club Bilbao and Real Sociedad de Fútbol San Sebastián was postponed due to Covid-19 pandemic.

THE CLUBS 2019/2020

Deportivo Alavés Vitoria-Gasteiz

Founded:	23.01.1921	
Stadium:	Estadio Mendizorrotza, Vitoria-Gasteiz (19,840)	
Trainer:	Asier Garitano Aguirrezábal	06.12.1969
[06.07.2020]	Juan Ramón López Muñiz	02.11.1968

Goalkeepers:	DOB	M	(s)	G
Fernando Pacheco Flores	18.05.1992	27		
Roberto Jiménez Gago	10.02.1986	8	(1)	
Antonio Sivera Salvá	11.08.1996	3		
Defenders:	**DOB**	**M**	**(s)**	**G**
Adrián Marín Gómez	09.01.1997	9	(3)	
Rubén Duarte Sánchez	18.10.1995	30	(1)	
Rodrigo Ely (ITA)	03.11.1993	24	(1)	2
Javier López Carballo	25.03.2002	1		
Víctor Laguardia Cisneros	05.11.1989	31		1
Lisandro Magallán Orueta (ARG)	27.09.1993	13	(4)	1
Guillermo Alfonso Maripán Loayza (CHI)	06.05.1994	1		
Martín Aguirregabiria Padilla	10.05.1996	23	(8)	1
Alberto Rodríguez Baro „Tachi"	10.09.1997	2	(4)	
Joaquín „Ximo" Navarro Jiménez	23.01.1990	22	(1)	
Midfielders:	**DOB**	**M**	**(s)**	**G**
Mohamed Abdallahi Mahmoud (MTN)	04.05.2000	1	(2)	
Víctor Camarasa Ferrando	28.05.1994	15	(2)	

	DOB	M	(s)	G
Paulino de la Fuente Gómez	27.06.1997		(3)	
Ljubomir Fejsa (SRB)	14.08.1988	11	(2)	
Javier „Javi" Muñoz Jiménez	28.02.1995	1		
Luis Jesús Rioja González „Luisito"	16.10.1993	19	(9)	
Manuel „Manu„ Alejandro García Sánchez	26.04.1986	22	(8)	
Pere Pons Riera	20.02.1993	7	(23)	1
Tomás Pina Isla	14.10.1987	17	(3)	1
Aleix Vidal Parreu	21.08.1989	26	(3)	2
Mubarak Wakaso (GHA)	25.07.1990	15	(1)	
Forwards:	**DOB**	**M**	**(s)**	**G**
Borja Sainz Eguskiza	01.02.2001	5	(14)	1
Jorge Franco Alviz „Burgui"	29.10.1993		(2)	
Oliver Jasen Burke (SCO)	07.04.1997	14	(17)	1
John Alberto Guidetti (SWE)	15.04.1992	1	(4)	
Édgar Antonio Méndez Ortega	02.01.1990	10	(6)	1
José Luis Mato Sanmartín „Joselu"	27.03.1990	31	(5)	11
Lucas Pérez Martínez	10.09.1988	29	(5)	11
José Luis Rodríguez Francis (PAN)	19.06.1998		(1)	

Athletic Club Bilbao

Founded:	1898	
Stadium:	Estadio San Mamés, Bilbao (53,289)	
Trainer:	Gaizka Garitano Agirre	09.07.1975

Goalkeepers:	DOB	M	(s)	G
Iago Herrerín Buisán	25.01.1988	4	(1)	
Unai Simón Mendibil	11.06.1997	34		
Defenders:	**DOB**	**M**	**(s)**	**G**
Mikel Balenziaga Oruesagasti	29.02.1988	6	(3)	
Ander Capa Rodríguez	08.02.1992	32	(3)	3
Óscar de Marcos Arana	14.04.1989	6	(7)	
Iñigo Lekue Martínez	04.05.1993	6	(8)	
Iñigo Martínez Berridi	17.05.1991	33		1
Unai Núñez Gestoso	30.01.1997	16	(4)	
Yeray Álvarez López	24.01.1995	32		
Yuri Berchiche Izeta	10.02.1990	32	(1)	2
Midfielders:	**DOB**	**M**	**(s)**	**G**
Beñat Etxebarria Urkiaga	19.02.1987	3	(8)	
Iñigo Córdoba Querejeta	13.03.1997	21	(3)	1

	DOB	M	(s)	G
Daniel „Dani" García Carrillo	24.05.1990	33	(3)	
Oihan Sancet Tirapu	25.04.2000	9	(8)	1
Raúl García Escudero	11.07.1986	33	(2)	15
Mikel San José Domínguez	30.05.1989	3	(6)	
Unai López Cabrera	30.10.1995	24	(2)	1
Unai Vencedor París	15.11.2000	1		
Mikel Vesga Arruti	08.04.1993	13	(7)	
Forwards:	**DOB**	**M**	**(s)**	**G**
Aritz Aduriz Zubeldia	11.02.1981		(14)	1
Ibai Gómez Pérez	11.11.1989	6	(11)	
Kenan Kodro (BIH)	19.08.1993	4	(8)	1
Gaizka Larrazabal Goikoetxea „Larra"	17.12.1997	2	(8)	
Iker Muniain Goñi	19.12.1992	26	(5)	5
Asier Villalibre Molina	30.09.1997	5	(14)	3
Iñaki Williams Dannis	15.06.1994	34	(4)	6

Club Atlético de Madrid

Founded:	26.04.1903 (*as Athletic Club de Madrid*)	
Stadium:	Estadio Metropolitano, Madrid (67,703)	
Trainer:	Diego Pablo Simeone (ARG)	28.04.1970

Goalkeepers:	DOB	M	(s)	G
Antonio Adán Garrido	13.05.1987		(1)	
Jan Oblak (SVN)	07.01.1993	38		
Defenders:	**DOB**	**M**	**(s)**	**G**
Santiago Arias Naranjo (COL)	13.01.1992	11	(3)	
Felipe Augusto de Almeida Monteiro (BRA)	16.05.1989	23	(2)	1
José María Giménez de Vargas (URU)	20.01.1995	19	(2)	
Manuel "Manu" Sánchez de la Peña	24.08.2000	4	(1)	
Mario Hermoso Canseco	18.06.1995	15	(2)	
Renan Augusto Lodi dos Santos (BRA)	08.04.1998	28	(4)	1
Stefan Savić (MNE)	08.01.1991	22		
Kieran John Trippier (ENG)	19.09.1990	23	(2)	
Šime Vrsaljko (CRO)	10.01.1992	4	(1)	
Midfielders:	**DOB**	**M**	**(s)**	**G**
Yannick Ferreira-Carrasco (BEL)	04.09.1993	6	(9)	1
Héctor Miguel Herrera López (MEX)	19.04.1990	12	(9)	
Jorge Resurrección Merodio „Koke"	08.01.1992	30	(2)	4

	DOB	M	(s)	G
Thomas Benoît Lemar (FRA)	12.11.1995	10	(12)	
Marcos Llorente Moreno	30.01.1995	16	(13)	3
Óscar Clemente Mues	26.03.1999		(1)	
Thomas Partey (GHA)	13.06.1993	29	(6)	3
Saúl Ñíguez Esclapez	21.11.1994	35		6
Antonio Moya Vega „Toni Moya"	20.03.1998		(1)	
Forwards:	**DOB**	**M**	**(s)**	**G**
Ángel Martín Correa Martínez (ARG)	09.03.1995	22	(11)	5
Darío Poveda Romera	13.03.1997		(1)	
Diego da Silva Costa	07.10.1988	14	(9)	5
German Valera Karabinaite	16.03.2002		(1)	
João Félix Sequeira (POR)	10.11.1999	21	(6)	6
Álvaro Borja Morata Martín	23.10.1992	25	(9)	12
Rodrigo Riquelme Reche	02.04.2000		(1)	
Ivan Šaponjić (SRB)	02.08.1997		(2)	
Sergio Camello Pérez	10.02.2001		(2)	
Víctor Machín Pérez „Vitolo"	02.11.1989	11	(17)	3

Futbol Club Barcelona

Founded: 29.11.1899 (*as Foot-Ball Club Barcelona*)
Stadium: Estadio Camp Nou, Barcelona (99,354)
Trainer: Ernesto Valverde Tejedor   09.02.1964
[13.01.2020] Enrique Setién Solar   27.09.1958

Goalkeepers:	DOB	M	(s)	G
Norberto Murara Neto (BRA)	19.07.1989	2		
Marc-André ter Stegen (GER)	30.04.1992	36		

Defenders:	DOB	M	(s)	G
Ronald Federico Araújo da Silva (URU)	07.03.1999	2	(4)	
Héctor Junior Firpo Adamés	22.08.1996	11	(6)	1
Jordi Alba Ramos	21.03.1989	25	(2)	2
Clément Nicolas Laurent Lenglet (FRA)	17.06.1995	28		2
Nélson Cabral Semedo (POR)	16.11.1993	24	(8)	1
Gerard Piqué i Bernabéu	02.02.1987	35		1
Sergi Roberto Carnicer	07.02.1992	27	(3)	1
Jean-Clair Todibo (FRA)	30.12.1999	1	(1)	
Samuel Yves Umtiti (FRA)	14.11.1993	10	(3)	
Moussa Wagué (SEN)	04.10.1998	1		

Midfielders:	DOB	M	(s)	G
Arthur Henrique Ramos de Oliveira Melo (BRA)	12.08.1996	14	(7)	3
Sergio Busquets Burgos	16.07.1988	29	(4)	2
Carles Aleñá Castillo	05.01.1998	2	(2)	
Frenkie de Jong (NED)	12.05.1997	24	(5)	2
Rafael Alcântara do Nascimento „Rafinha" (BRA)	12.02.1993	2	(1)	
Ivan Rakitić (CRO)	10.03.1988	16	(15)	1
Ricard "Riqui" Puig Martí	13.08.1999	5	(6)	
Arturo Erasmo Vidal Pardo (CHI)	22.05.1987	16	(17)	8

Forwards:	DOB	M	(s)	G
Álex Collado Gutiérrez	22.04.1999		(1)	
Martin Braithwaite Christensen (DEN)	05.06.1991	4	(7)	1
Carles Pérez Sayol	16.02.1998	5	(5)	1
Ousmane Dembélé (FRA)	15.05.1997	3	(2)	1
Anssumane „Ansu" Fati	31.10.2002	11	(13)	7
Antoine Griezmann (FRA)	21.03.1991	31	(4)	9
Lionel Andrés Messi Cuccitini (ARG)	24.06.1987	32	(1)	25
Luis Alberto Suárez Díaz (URU)	24.01.1987	22	(6)	16

Real Club Celta de Vigo

Founded: 23.08.1923
Stadium: Estadio Balaídos, Vigo (29,000)
Trainer: Francisco "Fran" Escribá Segura   03.05.1965
[04.11.2019] Óscar García Junyent   26.04.1973

Goalkeepers:	DOB	M	(s)	G
Iván Villar Martínez	09.07.1997	3	(1)	
Rubén Blanco Veiga	25.07.1995	33		
Sergio Álvarez Conde	03.08.1986	2		

Defenders:	DOB	M	(s)	G
Joseph Aidoo (GHA)	29.09.1995	27	(5)	
Néstor Alejandro Araujo Razo (MEX)	29.08.1991	32	(2)	1
David Costas Cordal	26.03.1995	3	(3)	
Hugo Mallo Novegil	22.06.1991	22	(5)	
Jorge Sáenz de Mera Colmeiro	17.11.1996	5	(2)	
David Juncà Reñe	16.11.1993	3		
Kevin Vázquez Comesaña	23.03.1993	16	(1)	
Jeison Fabián Murillo Cerón (COL)	27.05.1992	17	(1)	1
Lucas René Olaza Catrofe (URU)	21.07.1994	35		1

Midfielders:	DOB	M	(s)	G
Filip Bradarić (CRO)	11.01.1992	7	(7)	
Brais Méndez Portela	07.01.1997	15	(16)	
Denis Suárez Fernández	06.01.1994	20	(6)	1
Pape Cheikh Diop Gueye	08.08.1997	6	(10)	
Francisco José "Fran" Beltrán Peinado	03.02.1999	22	(6)	1
Iker Losada Aragunde	01.08.2001		(2)	1
Jacobo González Rodrígañez	25.03.1997	1	(1)	
Stanislav Lobotka (SVK)	25.11.1994	17		
Rafael Alcântara do Nascimento „Rafinha" (BRA)	12.02.1993	25	(4)	4
Sergio Bermejo Lillo	17.08.1997		(1)	
Okay Yokuşlu (TUR)	09.03.1994	24	(2)	

Forwards:	DOB	M	(s)	G
Gabriel Matías Fernández Leites (URU)	13.05.1994	5	(15)	1
Iago Aspas Juncal	01.08.1987	37		14
Juan Hernández García	06.12.1994	1	(4)	
Manuel Agudo Durán „Nolito"	15.10.1986	1	(6)	2
Santiago „Santi" Mina Lorenzo	07.12.1995	21	(13)	6
Pione Sisto Ifolo Emirmija (DEN)	04.02.1995	8	(13)	2
Fedor Smolov (RUS)	09.02.1990	10	(4)	2

Sociedad Deportiva Eibar

Founded: 30.11.1940
Stadium: Estadio Ipurua, Eibar (7,083)
Trainer: José Luis Mendilibar Etxebarria   14.03.1961

Goalkeepers:	DOB	M	(s)	G
Marko Dmitrović (SRB)	24.01.1992	35		
Yoel Rodríguez Oterino	28.08.1988	3		

Defenders:	DOB	M	(s)	G
Álvaro Tejero Sacristán	20.07.1996	16	(2)	
Anaitz Arbilla Zabala	15.05.1987	22	(2)	1
Pedro Bigas Rigo	15.05.1990	21	(2)	3
Esteban Rodrigo Burgos (ARG)	09.01.1992	11	(4)	1
José Ángel Valdés Díaz „Cote"	05.09.1989	27	(1)	1
Iván Andrés Ramis Barrios	25.10.1984	6	(1)	1
Paulo André Rodrigues de Oliveira (POR)	08.01.1992	23	(3)	1
Luís Rafael Soares Alves „Rafa Soares" (POR)	09.05.1995	6		
Roberto „Rober" Antonio Correa Silva	20.09.1992	11	(1)	

Midfielders:	DOB	M	(s)	G
Miguel Ángel Atienza Villa	27.05.1999		(3)	
Sebastián Carlos Cristóforo Pepe (URU)	23.08.1993	9	(9)	
Pape Diop (SEN)	19.03.1986	25	(5)	1
Eduardo „Edu" Expósito Jaén	01.08.1996	24	(11)	4
Gonzalo Escalante (ARG)	27.03.1993	18	(5)	
Takashi Inui (JPN)	02.06.1988	23	(6)	2
Pedro León Sánchez Gil	24.11.1986	23	(8)	1
Sergio Álvarez Díaz	23.01.1992	14	(4)	

Forwards:	DOB	M	(s)	G
Charles Días de Oliveira (BRA)	04.04.1984	13	(17)	6
Pablo Ezequiel de Blasis (ARG)	04.02.1988	15	(15)	2
Enrique García Martínez „Kike García"	25.11.1989	20	(7)	5
Miguel Mari Sánchez	30.06.1997		(1)	
Fabián Ariel Orellana Valenzuela (CHI)	27.01.1986	28	(1)	8
Enrique González Casín „Quique"	16.05.1990	4	(11)	
Sergi Enrich Ametller	26.02.1990	21	(9)	1

Reial Club Deportiu Espanyol de Barcelona

Founded:	28.10.1900 (*as Sociedad Española de Football*)	
Stadium:	RCDE Stadium [Estadi Cornellà-El Prat], Barcelona (40,500)	
Trainer:	David Gallego Rodríguez	26.01.1972
[07.10.2019]	Pablo Javier Machín Díez	07.04.1975
[27.12.2019]	Abelardo Fernández Artuña	19.04.1970
[28.06.2020]	Francisco Joaquín Pérez Rufete	20.11.1976

Goalkeepers:	DOB	M	(s)	G
Diego López Rodríguez	03.11.1981	36		
Oier Olazábal Paredes	14.09.1989	2		
Defenders:	**DOB**	**M**	**(s)**	**G**
Adrià Giner Pedrosa	13.05.1998	11	(9)	1
Leandro Daniel Cabrera Sasía (URU)	17.06.1991	17		
Sébastien Corchia (FRA)	01.11.1990	3		
Dídac Vilà Rosselló	09.06.1989	28	(2)	
Bernardo José Espinosa Zúñiga (COL)	11.07.1989	26		3
Fernando Calero Villa	14.09.1995	12	(3)	
Javier López Rodriguez „Javi López"	21.01.1986	16	(1)	
Lluís López Mármol	05.03.1997	3	(1)	
Edinaldo Gomes Pereira „Naldo" (BRA)	25.08.1988	15	(3)	
Gonzalo Ávila Gordón „Pipa"	26.01.1998	5	(2)	
Víctor Gómez Perea	01.04.2000	14	(4)	
Midfielders:	**DOB**	**M**	**(s)**	**G**
David López Silva	09.10.1989	29	(3)	4
Esteban Félix Granero Molina	02.07.1987	5	(6)	1

Ander Iturraspe Derteano	08.03.1989	3	(5)	
Marc Roca Junqué	26.11.1996	35		2
Óscar Melendo Jiménez	23.08.1997	12	(12)	
Nicolás „Nico" Melamed Ribaudo	11.04.2001	2	(4)	
Pol Lozano Vizuete	06.10.1999	2	(3)	
Sergi Darder Moll	22.12.1993	29	(7)	2
Matías Ezequiel Vargas Martin (ARG)	08.05.1997	10	(11)	
Víctor Sánchez Mata	08.09.1987	20	(5)	
Forwards:	**DOB**	**M**	**(s)**	**G**
Jonathan Calleri (ARG)	23.09.1993	20	(7)	1
Víctor Campuzano Bonilla	31.05.1997	9	(11)	
Adrián Embarba Blázquez	05.07.1992	17	(1)	2
Facundo Ferreyra (ARG)	14.03.1991	5	(11)	1
Raúl de Tomás Gómez	17.10.1994	11	(3)	4
Kévin Soni (CMR)	17.04.1998		(1)	
Pablo Daniel Piatti (ARG)	31.03.1989		(3)	
Wu Lei (CHN)	19.11.1991	21	(12)	4

Getafe Club de Fútbol

Founded:	08.07.1983	
Stadium:	Estadio Coliseum „Alfonso Pérez", Getafe (17,000)	
Trainer:	José „Pepe" Bordalás Jiménez	05.03.1964

Goalkeepers:	DOB	M	(s)	G
David Soria Solís	04.04.1993	38		
Defenders:	**DOB**	**M**	**(s)**	**G**
Vitorino Gabriel Pacheco Antunes (POR)	01.04.1987		(1)	
Bruno González Cabrera		2		
Erick Cathriel Cabaco Almada (URU)	19.04.1995	3	(1)	
Leandro Daniel Cabrera Sasía (URU)	17.06.1991	18		2
José Manuel Rodríguez Benito „Chema"	03.03.1992	3	(1)	
Dakonam Djené (TOG)	31.12.1991	34		
Xabier Etxeita Gorritxategi	31.10.1987	16	(1)	
Allan-Roméo Nyom (CMR)	10.05.1988	31	(3)	2
Mathías Olivera Miramontes (URU)	31.10.1997	21	(3)	
Raúl García Carnero	30.04.1989	3	(1)	
Damián Nicolás Suárez Suárez (URU)	27.04.1988	30		1
Midfielders:	**DOB**	**M**	**(s)**	**G**
Mauro Wilney Arambarri Rosa (URU)	30.09.1995	34	(1)	1
David Timor Copoví	17.10.1989	10	(12)	3

Marc Cucurella Saseta	22.07.1998	37		1
Peter Etebo Oghenekaro (NGA)	09.11.1995	6	(4)	1
Fayçal Fajr (MAR)	01.08.1988	5	(5)	
David Remeseiro Salgueiro „Jason"	06.07.1994	14	(6)	1
Robert Kenedy Nunes do Nascimento (BRA)	08.02.1996	3	(16)	1
Nemanja Maksimović (SRB)	26.01.1995	33	(2)	2
Markel Bergara Larrañaga	05.05.1986		(2)	
Francisco Portillo Soler	13.06.1990	3	(13)	
Florent Gregoire Poulolo (MTQ)	02.01.1997		(1)	
Forwards:	**DOB**	**M**	**(s)**	**G**
Ángel Luís Rodríguez Díaz	26.04.1987	9	(23)	10
Deyverson Brum Silva Acosta (BRA)	08.05.1991	3	(2)	
Amath Diedhiou (SEN)	16.07.1996		(7)	
Enric Gallego Puigsech	12.09.1986	2	(3)	
Hugo Duro Perales	10.11.1999	4	(8)	1
Jaime Mata Arnaiz	24.10.1988	33	(1)	11
Jorge Molina Vidal	22.04.1982	23	(11)	5

Granada Club de Fútbol

Founded:	14.04.1931 (*as Club Recreativo Granada*)	
Stadium:	Nuevo Estadio de los Cármenes, Granada (19,336)	
Trainer:	Diego Martínez Penas	16.12.1980

Goalkeepers:	DOB	M	(s)	G
Aarón Escandell Banacloche	27.09.1995	3		
Rui Tiago Dantas da Silva (POR)	07.02.1994	35		
Defenders:	**DOB**	**M**	**(s)**	**G**
Alejandro „Alex" Martínez Sánchez	12.08.1990		(1)	
Domingos Sousa Coutinho Meneses Duarte (POR)	10.03.1995	34	(2)	3
Dimitri Foulquier (GPE)	23.03.1993	12	(5)	1
Germán Sánchez Barahona	12.12.1986	26	(2)	2
Jesús Vallejo Lázaro	05.01.1997	7	(4)	
José Antonio Martínez Gil	12.02.1993	13	(7)	
Ismail Köybaşı (TUR)	10.07.1989	3	(1)	
Carlos Neva Tey	12.06.1996	25	(1)	
Joaquín José Marín Ruiz „Quini"	24.09.1989	8	(2)	
Víctor David Díaz Miguel	12.06.1988	33	(3)	1
Midfielders:	**DOB**	**M**	**(s)**	**G**
Ramon Olamilekan Azeez (NGA)	12.12.1992	14	(11)	2

Yan Brice Eteki (CMR)	26.08.1997	18	(10)	
Federico „Fede" Vico Villegas	04.07.1994	11	(7)	2
Gil Bastião Dias (POR)	28.09.1996	3	(9)	
Maxime Gonalons (FRA)	10.03.1989	17	(2)	
Yangel Clemente Herrera Ravelo (VEN)	07.01.1998	28	(2)	2
Ángel Montoro Sánchez	25.06.1988	11	(4)	2
Forwards:	**DOB**	**M**	**(s)**	**G**
Gustavo Adrián Ramos Vásquez (COL)	22.01.1986	2	(5)	
Álvaro Vadillo Cifuentes	12.09.1994	15	(7)	3
Antonio Cortés Heredia „Antoñín"	16.04.2000	2	(6)	1
Carlos Fernández Luna	22.05.1996	21	(13)	10
Darwin Daniel Machís Marcano (VEN)	07.02.1993	20	(16)	7
Mario Rodríguez Ruiz	03.03.1997		(1)	
José Antonio Rodríguez Díaz „Puertas"	21.02.1992	27	(9)	7
Roberto Soldado Rillo	27.05.1985	30	(3)	7

Club Deportivo Leganés

Founded: 26.06.1928
Stadium: Estadio Butarque, Leganés (11,454)
Trainer: Mauricio Andrés Pellegrino Luna (ARG) 05.10.1971
[22.10.2019] Luis Cembranos Martínez 06.06.1972
[04.11.2019] Javier Aguirre Onandía (MEX) 01.12.1958

Goalkeepers:	DOB	M	(s)	G
Iván Cuéllar Sacristán	27.05.1984	27		
Juan Soriano Oropesa	23.08.1997	11		
Defenders:	**DOB**	**M**	**(s)**	**G**
Chidozie Collins Awaziem (NGA)	01.01.1997	21	(5)	
Unai Bustinza Martínez	02.02.1992	31	(2)	
Marc Navarro Ceciliano	02.07.1995	3	(1)	
Kenneth Josiah Omeruo (NGA)	17.10.1993	22	(1)	1
Rodrigo Tarín Higón	05.07.1996	12	(2)	
Kévin Manuel Rodrigues (POR)	05.03.1994	22	(4)	1
Roberto José Rosales Altuve (VEN)	20.11.1988	21	(4)	
Jonathan Cristian Silva (ARG)	29.06.1994	32	(1)	1
Dimitrios Siovas (GRE)	16.09.1988	23	(1)	
Midfielders:	**DOB**	**M**	**(s)**	**G**
Aitor Ruibal García	22.03.1996	13	(12)	
Ibrahim Amadou (FRA)	06.04.1993	9	(1)	
Javier Eraso Goñi	22.03.1990	11	(9)	

	DOB	M	(s)	G
José Manuel Arnaiz Díaz	15.04.1995	2	(10)	
Óscar Rodríguez Arnaiz	28.06.1998	22	(8)	9
José Luis García del Pozo „Recio"	11.01.1991	18	(7)	
Christian Rivera Hernández	09.07.1997	3	(2)	
Roque Mesa Quevedo	07.06.1989	22	(7)	1
Rubén Pérez del Mármol	26.04.1989	25	(1)	1
Forwards:	**DOB**	**M**	**(s)**	**G**
Roger Claver Djapone Assalé (CIV)	13.11.1993	2	(12)	2
Martin Braithwaite Christensen (DEN)	05.06.1991	21	(3)	6
Bryan Gil Salvatierra	11.02.2001	4	(8)	1
Guido Marcelo Carrillo (ARG)	25.05.1991	13	(11)	1
Youssef En-Nesyri (MAR)	01.06.1997	15	(3)	4
Miguel Ángel Guerrero Martín	12.07.1990	9	(4)	1
Javier Avilés Cortés	17.08.1997	1	(8)	1
Manuel „Manu" Garrido Álvarez	10.06.2000	2	(2)	
Sabin Merino Zuloaga	04.01.1992	1	(1)	

Levante Unión Deportiva Valencia

Founded: 09.09.1909
Stadium: Estadio Ciutat de València, Valencia (26,354)
Trainer: Francisco José López Fernández 19.09.1967

Goalkeepers:	DOB	M	(s)	G
Aitor Fernández Abarisketa	03.05.1991	36		
Jorge Ruiz Ojeada „Koke Vegas"	27.09.1995	2		
Defenders:	**DOB**	**M**	**(s)**	**G**
Bruno González Cabrera	24.05.1990	5	(1)	
Erick Cathriel Cabaco Almada (URU)	19.04.1995	9	(2)	
Carlos Clerc Martínez	21.02.1992	20	(3)	
Jorge Andújar Moreno „Coke"	26.04.1987	11	(6)	1
Óscar Esau Duarte Gaitan (CRC)	03.06.1989	5	(3)	
Eliseo Falcón Falcón „Eli"	11.02.1997	1		
Gonzalo Pereira Cejudo	14.02.1997		(1)	
Jorge Miramón Santagertrudis	02.06.1989	27	(5)	
Roberto Suárez Pier „Róber"	16.02.1995	2	(2)	
Rúben Miguel Nunes Vezo (POR)	25.04.1994	29		
Sergio Postigo Redondo	04.11.1988	27	(1)	1
Antonio García Aranda „Toño García"	07.11.1989	18	(2)	

Midfielders:	DOB	M	(s)	G
Alejandro „Álex" Blesa Pina	15.01.2002		(1)	
Enis Bardhi (MKD)	02.07.1995	23	(7)	7
José Ángel Gómez Campaña	31.05.1993	35	(2)	2
Giorgi Kochorashvili (GEO)	29.06.1999		(1)	
Gonzalo Julián Melero Manzanares	02.01.1994	14	(11)	2
Pablo Martínez Andrés	22.02.1998		(5)	
Nemanja Radoja (SRB)	06.02.1993	22	(4)	1
Rubén Rochina Naixes	23.03.1991	22	(6)	5
Nikola Vukčević (MNE)	13.12.1991	20	(10)	
Forwards:	**DOB**	**M**	**(s)**	**G**
Borja Mayoral Moya	05.04.1997	24	(10)	8
Hernâni Jorge Santos Fortes (POR)	20.08.1991	5	(15)	2
Joan Monterde	18.12.1997		(1)	
José Luis Morales Nogales	23.07.1987	29	(9)	4
Roger Martí Salvador	03.01.1991	26	(10)	11
Sergio León Limones	06.01.1989	6	(16)	1

Racing Club Deportivo Mallorca

Founded: 05.03.1916 (as Alfonso XIII Foot-Ball Club)
Stadium: Visit Mallorca Estadi, Palma de Mallorca (24,262)
Trainer: Vicente Moreno Peris 26.10.1974

Goalkeepers:	DOB	M	(s)	G
Fabricio Agosto Ramírez	31.12.1987	1		
Manuel Reina Rodríguez „Manolo Reina"	01.04.1985	36		
Miquel Parera Pizá	18.05.1996	1		
Defenders:	**DOB**	**M**	**(s)**	**G**
Lumor Agbenyenu (GHA)	15.08.1996	20	(3)	1
Abdul Rahman Baba (GHA)	02.07.1994	2		
Francisco Gámez López	27.07.1991	18	(5)	
Joan Sastre"Fran"	30.04.1997	16	(3)	
Leonardo Koutris (GRE)	23.07.1995	1	(1)	
Antonio José Raíllo Arenas	08.10.1991	32		1
Aleksandar Sedlar (SRB)	13.12.1991	9	(3)	
Martin Valjent (SVK)	11.12.1995	36		
Francisco Javier Campos Coll „Xisco Campos"	10.03.1982	4	(5)	
Midfielders:	**DOB**	**M**	**(s)**	**G**
Iddrisu Baba Mohammed (GHA)	22.01.1996	35	(1)	
Daniel „Dani" Rodríguez Vázquez	06.06.1988	36	(1)	5
Aleix Febas Pérez	02.02.1996	22	(7)	

	DOB	M	(s)	G
Ki Sung-yueng (KOR)	24.01.1989		(1)	
Marc Pedraza Sarto	06.02.1987	2	(1)	
Rafael Obrador Burguera	24.02.2004		(1)	
Luka Romero Bezzana (ARG)	18.11.2004		(1)	
Salvador „Salva" Sevilla López	18.03.1984	31	(4)	5
Josep Señé Escudero	12.10.1991	1	(5)	
Forwards:	**DOB**	**M**	**(s)**	**G**
Abdón Prats Bastidas	07.12.1992		(20)	
Alejandro Pozo Pozo	22.02.1999	16	(3)	1
Alexander „Álex" Alegría Moreno	14.10.1992		(6)	
Aridai Cabrera Suárez	26.09.1988		(2)	
Ante Budimir (CRO)	22.07.1991	33	(2)	13
Pablo Chavarría (ARG)	02.01.1988	1	(12)	
Juan Camilo Hernández Suárez (COL)	22.04.1999	17	(5)	5
Takefusa Kubo (JPN)	04.06.2001	23	(12)	4
Yannis Salibur-Ilongo (FRA)	24.01.1991		(4)	
Aleksandar Trajkovski (MKD)	05.09.1992	1	(13)	
Lago Junior Wakalible (CIV)	31.12.1990	24	(11)	4

Club Atlético Osasuna Pamplona

Founded: 24.10.1920
Stadium: Estadio El Sadar, Pamplona (18,570)
Trainer: Jagoba Arrasate Elustondo   22.04.1978

Goalkeepers:	DOB	M	(s)	G
Sergio Herrera Pirón	05.06.1993	18	(1)	
Juan Manuel Pérez Ruiz	15.07.1996	2		
Rubén Iván Martínez Andrade	22.06.1984	18	(1)	
Defenders:	**DOB**	**M**	**(s)**	**G**
Aridane Hernández Umpiérrez	23.03.1989	29		3
David García Zubiria	14.02.1994	31	(1)	
Pervis Josué Estupiñán Tenorio (ECU)	21.01.1998	32	(4)	1
Manuel Castellano Castro „Lillo"	27.03.1989	2	(2)	
Ignacio „Nacho" Vidal Miralles	24.01.1995	26	(4)	
Raúl Rodríguez Navas	11.05.1988	8	(1)	
Facundo Sebastián Roncaglia (ARG)	10.02.1987	15	(1)	1
Antonio Latorre Grueso „Toni Lato"	21.11.1997	6	(2)	1
Unai García Lugea	03.02.1992	6	(2)	1
Midfielders:	**DOB**	**M**	**(s)**	**G**
Aimar Oroz Huarte	27.11.2001		(1)	
Darko Brašanac (SRB)	12.02.1992	27	(4)	
Francisco "Fran" Mérida Pérez	04.03.1990	12	(11)	

	DOB	M	(s)	G
Iñigo Pérez Soto	18.01.1988	11	(11)	2
José Manuel Arnáiz Díaz	15.04.1995	8	(6)	2
Luis Perea Hernández	25.08.1997		(2)	
Jon Moncayola Tollar	13.05.1998	15	(12)	1
Oier Sanjurjo Maté	25.05.1986	27	(2)	2
Robert Ibáñez Castro	22.03.1993	5	(9)	1
Roberto Torres Morales	07.03.1989	31	(5)	7
Rubén García Santos	14.07.1993	25	(5)	8
Forwards:	**DOB**	**M**	**(s)**	**G**
Adrián López Álvarez	08.01.1988	17	(9)	2
Luis Ezequiel Ávila (ARG)	06.02.1994	18	(2)	9
Brandon Thomas Llamas	04.02.1995	5	(3)	
Enric Gallego Puigsech	12.09.1986	9	(5)	3
Javier Martínez Calvo „Javi"	22.12.1999		(1)	
Juan Villar Vázquez	19.05.1988	2	(8)	1
Enrique Barja Afonso „Kike Barja"	01.04.1997	4	(4)	
Marc Cardona Rovira	08.07.1995	9	(10)	1

Real Betis Balompié Sevilla

Founded: 12.09.1907
Stadium: Estadio "Benito Villamarín", Sevilla (60,721)
Trainer: Joan Francesc Ferrer Sicilia "Rubi"   05.02.1970
[21.06.2020]   Humberto Alexis Trujillo Oramas   30.07.1965

Goalkeepers:	DOB	M	(s)	G
Daniel „Dani" Martín Fernández	08.07.1998	5	(1)	
Joel Robles Blázquez	17.06.1990	33		
Defenders:	**DOB**	**M**	**(s)**	**G**
Antonio Barragán Fernández	12.06.1987	7	(5)	
Marc Bartra Aragall	15.01.1991	29	(1)	3
Emerson Aparecido Leite de Souza Junior (BRA)	14.01.1999	32	(1)	3
Zouhair Feddal (MAR)	23.12.1989	16	(1)	1
Aïssa Mandi (ALG)	22.10.1991	29		
Alfonso Pedraza Sag	09.04.1996	15	(6)	1
Sidnei Rechel da Silva Júnior (BRA)	23.08.1989	14		1
Midfielders:	**DOB**	**M**	**(s)**	**G**
Alexandre "Álex" Moreno Lopera	08.06.1993	25	(6)	
Sergio Canales Madrazo	16.02.1991	36		6
Carles Aleñá Castillo	05.01.1998	7	(10)	1
Édgar González Estrada	01.04.1997	9	(1)	

	DOB	M	(s)	G
Nabil Fekir (FRA)	18.07.1993	31	(1)	7
José Andrés Guardado Hernández (MEX)	28.09.1986	25	(3)	
Ismael Gutiérrez Montilla	07.08.2000	1	(2)	
Francisco Javier „Javi" García Fernández	08.02.1987	4	(4)	
Wilfrid Jaures Kaptoum (CMR)	07.07.1996	2	(3)	
Guido Rodríguez (ARG)	12.04.1994	11	(3)	1
William Silva de Carvalho (POR)	07.04.1992	11	(2)	
Forwards:	**DOB**	**M**	**(s)**	**G**
Borja Iglesias Quintas	17.01.1993	21	(14)	3
Cristian Tello Herrera	11.08.1991	5	(22)	2
Joaquín Sánchez Rodríguez	21.07.1981	25	(9)	8
Juan Miguel Jiménez López „Juanmi"	20.05.1993	2	(6)	1
Diego Lainez Leyva (MEX)	09.06.2000	2	(13)	
Lorenzo Morón García „Loren"	30.12.1993	21	(15)	10
Raúl Garcia de Haro	03.11.2000		(3)	

Real Madrid Club de Fútbol

Founded: 06.03.1902 (*as Madrid Football Club*)
Stadium: Estadio "Santiago Bernabéu", Madrid (81,044)
Trainer: Zinédine Zidane (FRA)   23.06.1972

Goalkeepers:	DOB	M	(s)	G
Alphonse Aréola (FRA)	27.02.1993	4		
Thibaut Courtois (BEL)	11.05.1992	34		
Defenders:	**DOB**	**M**	**(s)**	**G**
Daniel „Dani" Carvajal Ramos	11.01.1992	31		1
Eder Gabriel Militão (BRA)	18.01.1998	10	(5)	
Marcelo Vieira da Silva Júnior (BRA)	12.05.1988	15		1
Ferland Mendy (FRA)	08.06.1995	19	(6)	1
José Ignacio Fernández Iglesias „Nacho"	18.01.1990	4	(2)	1
Álvaro Odriozola Arzalluz		4		
Sergio Ramos García	30.03.1986	35		11
Raphaël Varane (FRA)	25.04.1993	32		2
Midfielders:	**DOB**	**M**	**(s)**	**G**
Brahim Abdelkader Díaz	03.08.1999		(6)	
Carlos Henrique Casemiro (BRA)	23.02.1992	35		4

	DOB	M	(s)	G
Francisco Román Alarcón Suárez „Isco"	21.04.1992	15	(8)	1
Toni Kroos (GER)	04.01.1990	31	(4)	4
Marco Asensio Willemsen	21.01.1996	3	(6)	3
Luka Modrić (CRO)	09.09.1985	22	(9)	3
James David Rodríguez Rubio (COL)	12.07.1991	5	(3)	1
Federico Santiago Valverde Dipetta (URU)	22.07.1998	21	(12)	2
Forwards:	**DOB**	**M**	**(s)**	**G**
Gareth Frank Bale (WAL)	16.07.1989	12	(4)	2
Karim Mostafa Benzema (FRA)	19.12.1987	36	(1)	21
Eden Michael Hazard (BEL)	07.01.1991	14	(2)	1
Luka Jović (SRB)	23.12.1997	4	(13)	2
Lucas Vázquez Iglesias	01.07.1991	8	(10)	2
Mariano Díaz Mejía (DOM)	01.08.1993		(5)	1
Rodrygo Silva de Goes (BRA)	09.01.2001	12	(7)	2
Vinícius José Paixão de Oliveira Júnior (BRA)	12.07.2000	12	(17)	3

Real Sociedad de Fútbol San Sebastián

Founded: 07.09.1909
Stadium: Estadio Anoeta [Reale Arena], San Sebastián (32,000)
Trainer: Imanol Alguacil Barrenetxea   04.07.1971

Goalkeepers:	DOB	M	(s)	G
Miguel Ángel Moyá Rumbo	02.04.1984	13		
Alejandro Remiro Gargallo	24.03.1995	25		
Defenders:	**DOB**	**M**	**(s)**	**G**
Aihen Muñoz Capellán	16.08.1997	11	(4)	
Andoni Gorosabel Espinosa	04.08.1996	8	(6)	
Aritz Elustondo Irribaría	28.03.1994	17	(5)	
Jon Pacheco Dozagarat	08.01.2001	1		
Joseba Zaldúa Bengoetxea	24.06.1992	29	(1)	
Kévin Manuel Rodrigues (POR)	05.03.1994		(1)	
Robin Le Normand (FRA)	11.11.1996	25	(6)	1
Diego Javier Llorente Ríos	16.08.1993	27	(2)	1
Ignacio „Nacho" Monreal Eraso	26.02.1986	27	(2)	2
Midfielders:	**DOB**	**M**	**(s)**	**G**
Ander Guevara Lajo	07.07.1997	11	(3)	
Asier Illarramendi Andonegu „Illarra"	08.03.1990	3		

	DOB	M	(s)	G
Adnan Januzaj (BEL)	05.02.1995	13	(11)	3
Luca Sangalli Fuentes	10.02.1995	5	(6)	
Martín Zubimendi Ibáñez	02.02.1999	6	(3)	
Mikel Merino Zazón	22.06.1996	35	(1)	5
Martin Ødegaard (NOR)	17.12.1998	29	(2)	4
Cristián Portugués Manzanera „Portu"	21.05.1992	25	(10)	7
Igor Zubeldía Elorza	30.03.1997	29	(4)	
David Zurutuza Veillet	19.07.1986	2	(3)	
Forwards:	**DOB**	**M**	**(s)**	**G**
Ander Barrenetxea Muguruza	27.12.2001	3	(14)	1
Naïs Djouahra (FRA)	23.11.1999		(2)	
Alexander Isak (SWE)	21.09.1999	14	(23)	9
Mikel Oyarzabal Ugarte	21.04.1997	36	(1)	10
Roberto López Alcaide	24.04.2000		(3)	
Willian José da Silva (BRA)	23.11.1991	24	(13)	11

Sevilla Fútbol Club

Founded: 25.01.1890
Stadium: Estadio "Ramón Sánchez Pizjuán", Sevilla (42,714)
Trainer: Julen Lopetegui Agote 28.09.1966

Goalkeepers:	DOB	M	(s)	G
Yassine Bounou (MAR)	05.04.1991	5	(1)	
Tomáš Vaclík (CZE)	29.03.1989	33		
Defenders:	**DOB**	**M**	**(s)**	**G**
Alejandro Pozo Pozo	22.02.1999		(3)	
Daniel Filipe Martins Carriço (POR)	04.08.1988	10	(1)	
Diego Carlos Santos Silva (BRA)	15.03.1993	35		2
Sergio Escudero Palomo	02.09.1989	8	(3)	1
Jesús Navas González	21.11.1985	37	(1)	
Jules Koundé (FRA)	12.11.1998	25	(4)	1
Sergio Reguilón Rodríguez	16.12.1996	29	(2)	2
Sergi Gómez Solà	28.03.1992	8	(5)	
Midfielders:	**DOB**	**M**	**(s)**	**G**
Éver Maximiliano David Banega (ARG)	29.06.1988	28	(5)	3
Fernando Francisco Reges (BRA)	25.07.1987	30	(4)	2
Nemanja Gudelj (SRB)	16.11.1991	9	(15)	
Joan Jordán Moreno	06.07.1994	27	(7)	2
Lucas Ariel Ocampos (ARG)	11.07.1994	31	(2)	14
Óliver Torres Muñoz	10.11.1994	21	(7)	3
Marcos Paulo Mesquita Lopes „Rony Lopes" (POR)	28.12.1995	2	(3)	
Franco Damian Vázquez (ITA)	22.02.1989	11	(20)	3
Forwards:	**DOB**	**M**	**(s)**	**G**
Bryan Gil Salvatierra	11.02.2001		(2)	
Munas Dabbur (ISR)	14.05.1992		(2)	
Luuk de Jong (NED)	27.08.1990	24	(11)	6
Youssef En-Nesyri (MAR)	01.06.1997	7	(11)	4
Javier Hernández Balcazar (MEX)	01.06.1988	4	(5)	1
Munir El Haddadi Mohamed	01.09.1995	14	(7)	5
Manuel Agudo Durán „Nolito"	15.10.1986	12	(3)	3
Jesús Joaquín Fernández Sáez de la Torre „Suso"	19.11.1993	8	(9)	1

Valencia Club de Fútbol

Founded: 18.03.1909
Stadium: Estadio Mestalla, Valencia (55,000)
Trainer: Marcelino García Toral 14.08.1965
[11.09.2019] Albert Celades López 29.09.1975
[29.06.2020] Salvador González Marco „Voro" 09.10.1963

Goalkeepers:	DOB	M	(s)	G
Jacobus Antonius Peter Cillessen (NED)	22.04.1989	24		
Jaume Doménech Sánchez	05.11.1990	14	(1)	
Defenders:	**DOB**	**M**	**(s)**	**G**
Adrià Guerrero Aguilar	28.01.1998	1	(1)	
Mouctar Diakhaby (FRA)	19.12.1996	15	(6)	
Alessandro Florenzi (ITA)	11.03.1991	9	(3)	
Gabriel Armando de Abreu „Gabriel Paulista" (BRA)	26.11.1990	31	(2)	1
Ezequiel Marcelo Garay (ARG)	10.10.1986	17		
José Luis Gayà Peña	25.05.1995	23	(1)	
Hugo Guillamón Sammartín	31.01.2000	5	(1)	
Jaume Vincent Costa Jordá	18.03.1988	15	(4)	
Eliaquim Mangala (FRA)	13.02.1991	8		
Cristiano Piccini (ITA)	26.09.1992	1	(1)	
Thierry Rendall Correia (POR)	09.03.1999	3	(1)	
Daniel Wass (DEN)	31.05.1989	30	(5)	1
Midfielders:	**DOB**	**M**	**(s)**	**G**
Carlos Soler Barragán	02.01.1997	24	(4)	2
Francis Coquelin (FRA)	13.05.1991	21	(5)	
Geoffrey Kondogbia (CTA)	15.02.1993	21	(6)	1
Lee Kang-in (KOR)	19.02.2001	3	(14)	2
Daniel Parejo Muñoz	16.04.1989	35		8
Vicente Esquerdo Santas	02.01.1999		(3)	
Forwards:	**DOB**	**M**	**(s)**	**G**
Denis Cheryshev (RUS)	26.12.1990	9	(15)	1
Ferrán Torres García	29.02.2000	26	(8)	4
Kevin Dominique Gameiro (FRA)	09.05.1987	17	(12)	6
Maximiliano Gómez González (URU)	14.08.1996	25	(8)	10
Gonçalo Manuel Ganchinho Guedes (POR)	29.11.1996	14	(7)	2
Manuel „Manu" Javier Vallejo Galván	14.02.1997	3	(8)	2
Rodrigo Moreno Machado	06.03.1991	23	(4)	4
Rubén Sobrino Pozuelo	01.06.1992	1	(12)	1

Real Valladolid Club de Fútbol

Founded: 20.06.1928
Stadium: Estadio "José Zorrilla", Valladolid (26,512)
Trainer: Sergio González Soriano 10.11.1976

Goalkeepers:	DOB	M	(s)	G
Jordi Masip López	03.01.1989	35		
José Antonio Caro Díaz	03.05.1994	3		
Samuel Pérez Fariña	26.04.1997		(1)	
Defenders:	**DOB**	**M**	**(s)**	**G**
Federico Barba (ITA)	01.09.1993	5		
Javier „Javi" Moyano Lujano	23.02.1986	26		
Javier „Javi" Sánchez de Felipe	14.03.1997	6	(2)	
Joaquín Fernández Moreno	31.05.1996	19	(1)	2
Francisco José „Kiko" Olivas Alba	21.08.1988	33	(2)	2
José Ignacio Martínez García „Nacho"	07.03.1989	21	(2)	
Pedro Antonio Porro Sauceda	13.09.1999	7	(6)	
Raúl García Carnero	30.04.1989	12		
Karim Salisú (GHA)	17.04.1999	30	(1)	1
Midfielders:	**DOB**	**M**	**(s)**	**G**
Rubén Alcaraz Jiménez	01.05.1991	20	(7)	2
Antonio Jesús Regal Angulo „Antoñito"	24.12.1987	11	(4)	
Hatem Ben Arfa (FRA)	07.03.1987	2	(3)	
Federico San Emeterio Díaz „Fede"	16.03.1997	20	(5)	
Enrique „Kike" Pérez Muñoz	14.02.1997	2	(4)	
Matheus Fernandes Siqueira (BRA)	30.06.1998	2	(1)	
Miguel Alfonso Herrero Javaloyas „Míchel"	29.07.1988	27	(2)	1
Laureano Antonio „Toni" Villa Suárez	07.01.1995	18	(5)	
Anuar Tuhami (MAR)	15.01.1995	1	(10)	
Forwards:	**DOB**	**M**	**(s)**	**G**
Jorge De Frutos Sebastián	20.02.1997		(3)	
Miguel de la Fuente Escudero	03.09.1999	2	(5)	
Óscar Plano Pedreño	11.02.1991	28	(8)	4
Pablo Hervías Ruiz	08.03.1993	9	(16)	1
Sandro Ramírez Castillo	09.07.1995	15	(9)	3
Sergi Guardiola Navarro	29.05.1991	31	(4)	8
Enes Ünal (TUR)	10.05.1997	23	(12)	6
Víctor García Raja	01.01.1997	1	(1)	1
Waldo Rubio Marín	17.08.1995	9	(12)	

Villarreal Club de Fútbol

Founded: 10.03.1923
Stadium: Estadio de la Cerámica, Villarreal (24,890)
Trainer: Javier Calleja Revilla 12.05.1978

Goalkeepers:	DOB	M	(s)	G
Andrés Fernández Moreno	17.12.1986	4		
Sergio Asenjo Andrés	28.06.1989	34		
Defenders:	**DOB**	**M**	**(s)**	**G**
Alberto Moreno Pérez	05.07.1992	17	(1)	
Sofian Chakla (MAR)	02.09.1993	2		
José Ramiro Funes Mori (ARG)	05.03.1991	5	(2)	
Mario Gaspar Pérez Martínez	24.11.1990	22	(3)	
Pau Francisco Torres	16.01.1997	33	(1)	2
Raúl Albiol Tortajada	04.09.1985	36		1
Rubén Peña Jiménez	18.07.1991	21	(5)	2
Xavier "Xavi" Quintillà Guasch	23.08.1996	17	(2)	
Midfielders:	**DOB**	**M**	**(s)**	**G**
Alejandro „Álex" Baena Rodríguez	20.07.2001		(1)	
André-Frank Zambo Anguissa (CMR)	16.11.1995	28	(8)	2
Bruno Soriano Llido	12.06.1984	1	(6)	
Vicente Iborra de la Fuente	16.01.1988	33	(1)	1
Javier „Javi" Ontiveros Parra	09.09.1997	7	(23)	2
Manuel „Manu" Morlanes Ariño	12.01.1999	3	(6)	
Moisés Gómez Bordonado „Moi Gómez"	23.06.1994	26	(11)	5
Santiago "Santi" Cazorla González	13.12.1984	29	(6)	11
Manuel Trigueros Muñoz	17.10.1991	17	(12)	2
Forwards:	**DOB**	**M**	**(s)**	**G**
Carlos Arturo Bacca Ahumada (COL)	08.09.1986	7	(12)	2
Samuel Chukwueze (NGA)	22.05.1999	20	(17)	3
Fernando Niño Rodríguez „Fer Niño"	24.10.2000	1	(4)	1
Gerard Moreno Balagueró	07.04.1992	33	(2)	18
Francisco Alcácer García „Paco Alcácer"	30.08.1993	11	(2)	4
Karl Toko Ekambi (CMR)	14.09.1992	11	(7)	6

SECOND LEVEL
Segunda División 2019/2020

1.	SD Huesca (*Promoted*)	42	21	7	14	55	-	42	70
2.	Cádiz CF (*Promoted*)	42	19	12	11	50	-	39	69
3.	Real Zaragoza (*Promotion Play-offs*)	42	18	11	13	59	-	53	65
4.	Unión Deportiva Almería (*Promotion Play-offs*)	42	17	13	12	62	-	43	64
5.	Girona FC (*Promotion Play-offs*)	42	17	12	13	48	-	43	63
6.	Elche CF (*Promotion Play-offs*)	42	16	13	13	52	-	44	61
7.	Rayo Vallecano de Madrid	42	13	21	8	60	-	50	60
8.	CF Fuenlabrada	42	15	15	12	47	-	40	60
9.	UD Las Palmas	42	14	15	13	49	-	46	57
10.	Agrupación Deportiva Alcorcón	42	13	18	11	52	-	50	57
11.	CD Mirandés	42	13	17	12	55	-	59	56
12.	CD Tenerife	42	14	13	15	50	-	46	55
13.	Real Sporting de Gijón	42	14	12	16	40	-	38	54
14.	Málaga CF	42	11	20	11	35	-	33	53
15.	Real Oviedo CF	42	13	14	15	49	-	53	53
16.	CD Lugo	42	12	16	14	43	-	54	52
17.	Albacete Balompié	42	13	13	16	36	-	46	52
18.	SD Ponferradina	42	12	15	15	45	-	50	51
19.	RC Deportivo La Coruña (*Relegated*)	42	12	15	15	43	-	60	51
20.	CD Numancia de Soria (*Relegated*)	42	13	11	18	45	-	53	50
21.	Extremadura UD Almendralejo (*Relegated*)	42	10	13	19	43	-	59	43
22.	Real Racing Club de Santander (*Relegated*)	42	5	18	19	39	-	56	33

Promotion Play-offs [13-23.08.2020]

Semi-Finals			
Girona FC - Unión Deportiva Almería	1-0(0-0)	2-1(1-1)
Elche CF -	0-0	1-0(0-0)

Play-off Finals			
Elche CF - Girona FC	0-0	1-0(0-0)

Elche CF promoted to La Liga 2020/2021.

NATIONAL TEAM

INTERNATIONAL MATCHES
(16.07.2019 – 15.07.2020)

05.09.2019	Bucureşti	Romania - Spain	1-2(0-1)	(ECQ)
08.09.2019	Gijón	Spain - Faroe Islands	4-0(1-0)	(ECQ)
12.10.2019	Oslo	Norway - Spain	1-1(0-0)	(ECQ)
15.10.2019	Stockholm	Sweden - Spain	1-1(0-0)	(ECQ)
15.11.2019	Cádiz	Spain - Malta	7-0(2-0)	(ECQ)
18.11.2019	Madrid	Spain - Romania	5-0(4-0)	(ECQ)

05.09.2019 ROMANIA - SPAIN   **1-2(0-1)**   16th EC. Qualifiers
Arena Naţională, Bucureşti; Referee: Deniz Aytekin (Germany); Attendance: 50,024
ESP: Kepa, Jordi Alba, Sergio Ramos (Cap), Diego Llorente, Jesús Navas, Sergio Busquets, Saúl, Dani Ceballos (77.Pablo Sarabia), Fabián Ruiz, Rodrigo (71.Mikel Oyarzabal), Paco Alcácer (85.Mario Hermoso). Trainer: Luis Enrique Martínez García.
Goals: Sergio Ramos (29 penalty), Paco Alcácer (47).

08.09.2019 SPAIN - FAROE ISLANDS   **4-0(1-0)**   16th EC. Qualifiers
Estadio Municipal El Molinón, Gijón; Referee: Krzysztof Jakubik (Poland); Attendance: 23,644
ESP: David de Gea, Dani Carvajal, Sergio Ramos (Cap) (84.Unai Núñez), José Gayá, Mario Hermoso, Dani Parejo, Thiago Alcântara, Rodri Hernández, Rodrigo, Suso (68.Pablo Sarabia), Mikel Oyarzabal (60.Paco Alcácer). Trainer: Luis Enrique Martínez García.
Goals: Rodrigo (13, 50), Paco Alcácer (90, 90+3).

12.10.2019 NORWAY - SPAIN   **1-1(0-0)**   16th EC. Qualifiers
Ullevaal Stadion, Oslo; Referee: Michael Oliver (England); Attendance: 25,200
ESP: Kepa, Raúl Albiol, Sergio Ramos (Cap), Juan Bernat (88.Iñigo Martínez), Jesús Navas, Sergio Busquets, Saúl, Dani Ceballos (64.Santi Cazorla), Fabián Ruiz, Rodrigo, Mikel Oyarzabal (78.Rodri Hernández). Trainer: Luis Enrique Martínez García.
Goal: Saúl (47).

15.10.2019 SWEDEN - SPAIN   **1-1(0-0)**   16th EC. Qualifiers
Friends Arena, Stockholm; Referee: Clément Turpin (France); Attendance: 49,712
ESP: David de Gea (60.Kepa), Dani Carvajal (81.Jesús Navas), Raúl Albiol (Cap), Iñigo Martínez, Juan Bernat, Thiago Alcântara (66.Rodrigo), Dani Ceballos, Fabián Ruiz, Rodri Hernández, Gerard, Mikel Oyarzabal. Trainer: Luis Enrique Martínez García.
Goal: Rodrigo (90+2).

15.11.2019   SPAIN - MALTA   7-0(2-0)   16th EC. Qualifiers

Estadio "Ramón de Carranza", Cádiz; Referee: Viktor Kassai (Hungary); Attendance: 19,773
ESP: Pau López, Raúl Albiol, Sergio Ramos (Cap) (60.Pau Torres), Juan Bernat, Jesús Navas, Santi Cazorla (53.Paco Alcácer), Thiago Alcântara, Pablo Sarabia, Rodri Hernández, Álvaro Morata (66.Dani Olmo), Gerard. Trainer: Luis Enrique Martínez García.
Goals: Álvaro Morata (23), Santi Cazorla (41), Pau Torres (62), Pablo Sarabia (63), Dani Olmo (69), Gerard (71), Jesús Navas (85).

18.11.2019   SPAIN - ROMANIA   5-0(4-0)   16th EC. Qualifiers

Metropolitano Stadium, Madrid; Referee: Aleksei Kulbakov (Belarus); Attendance: 36,198
ESP: Kepa, Dani Carvajal, Sergio Ramos (Cap) (62.Raúl Albiol), Iñigo Martínez, José Gayá, Santi Cazorla (67.Paco Alcácer), Sergio Busquets, Saúl, Fabián Ruiz, Álvaro Morata, Gerard (56.Mikel Oyarzabal). Trainer: Luis Enrique Martínez García.
Goals: Fabián Ruiz (8), Gerard (33, 43), Adrián Rus (45+1 own goal), Mikel Oyarzabal (90+2).

NATIONAL TEAM PLAYERS
(16.07.2019 – 15.07.2020)

Name	DOB	Caps	Goals	2019/2020:	Club
Goalkeepers					
DAVID DE GEA Quintana	07.11.1990	41	0	2019:	*Manchester United FC (ENG)*
KEPA Arrizabalaga Revuelta	03.10.1994	11	0	2019:	*Chelsea FC London (ENG)*
PAU LÓPEZ Sabata	13.12.1994	2	0	2019:	*AS Roma (ITA)*
Defenders					
Daniel "DANI" CARVAJAL Ramos	11.01.1992	24	0	2019:	*Real Madrid CF*
DIEGO Javier LLORENTE Ríos	16.08.1993	5	0	2019:	*Real Sociedad de Fútbol San Sebastián*
IÑIGO MARTÍNEZ Berridi	17.05.1991	11	0	2019:	*Athletic Club Bilbao*
JESÚS NAVAS González	21.11.1985	42	5	2019:	*Sevilla FC*
JORDI ALBA Ramos	21.03.1989	70	8	2019:	*FC Barcelona*
JOSÉ Luis GAYÀ Peña	25.03.1995	7	1	2019:	*Valencia CF*
JUAN BERNAT Velasco	01.03.1993	11	1	2019:	*Paris Saint-Germain FC (FRA)*
MARIO HERMOSO Canseco	18.06.1995	5	0	2019:	*Club Atlético de Madrid*
PAU Francisco TORRES	16.01.1997	1	1	2019:	*Villarreal CF*
RAÚL ALBIOL Tortajada	04.09.1985	56	0	2019:	*Villarreal CF*
SERGIO RAMOS García	30.03.1986	170	21	2019:	*Real Madrid CF*
UNAI NÚÑEZ Gestoso	30.01.1997	1	0	2019:	*Athletic Club Bilbao*
Midfielders					
Daniel "DANI" CEBALLOS Fernández	07.08.1996	9	1	2019:	*Arsenal FC London (ENG)*
Daniel "DANI" PAREJO Muñoz	16.04.1989	4	0	2019:	*Valencia CF*
Daniel "DANI" OLMO Carvajal	07.05.1998	1	1	2019:	*GNK Dinamo Zagreb (CRO)*
FABIÁN RUIZ Peña	03.04.1996	6	1	2019:	*SSC Napoli (ITA)*
PABLO SARABIA García	11.05.1992	3	1	2019:	*Paris Saint-Germain FC (FRA)*
Rodrigo "RODRI" HERNÁNDEZ Cascante	22.06.1996	11	0	2019:	*Manchester City FC (ENG)*
Santiago "SANTI" CAZORLA González	13.12.1984	81	15	2019:	*Villarreal CF*
SAÚL Ñíguez Esclápez	21.11.1994	19	3	2019:	*Club Atlético de Madrid*
SERGI ROBERTO Carnicer	07.02.1992	8	1	2019:	*FC Barcelona*
SERGIO BUSQUETS Burgos	16.07.1988	116	2	2019:	*FC Barcelona*
SERGIO CANALES Madrazo	16.02.1991	5	0	2019:	*Real Betis Balompié Sevilla*
Jesús Joaquín Fernández Sáez de la Torre "SUSO"	19.11.1993	5	0	2019:	*AC Milan (ITA)*
THIAGO ALCÂNTARA do Nascimento	11.04.1991	37	2	2019:	*FC Bayern München (GER)*
Forwards					
ÁLVARO Borja MORATA Martín	23.10.1992	33	17	2019:	*Club Atlético de Madrid*
GERARD Moreno Balaguero	07.04.1992	3	3	2019:	*Villarreal CF*
MIKEL OYARZABAL Ugarte	21.04.1997	7	2	2019:	*Real Sociedad de Fútbol San Sebastián*
Francisco "PACO" ALCÁCER García	30.08.1993	19	12	2019:	*BV Borussia Dortmund (GER)*
RODRIGO Moreno Machado	06.03.1991	22	8	2019:	*Valencia CF*

National team coach

LUIS ENRIQUE Martínez García [09.07.2019 – 19.06.2019]	08.05.1970	10 M; 8 W; 0 D; 2 L; 28-10	

SWEDEN

The Country:
Konungariket Sverige (Kingdom of Sweden)
Capital: Stockholm
Surface: 450,295 km²
Inhabitants: 10,343,403 [2020]
Time: UTC+1

The FA:
Svenska Fotbollsförbundet
Evenemangsgatan 31, 171 23 Solna
Tel: +46 8 735 0900
Founded: 1904
Member of FIFA since: 1904
Member of UEFA since: 1954
Website: www.svenskfotboll.se

NATIONAL TEAM RECORDS

RECORDS
First international match:	12.07.1908, Göteborg:	Sweden – Norway 11-3
Most international caps:	Anders Gunnar Svensson	- 148 caps (1999-2013)
Most international goals:	Zlatan Ibrahimović	- 62 goals / 116 caps (2001-2016)

UEFA EUROPEAN CHAMPIONSHIP
1960	Did not enter
1964	Qualifiers
1968	Qualifiers
1972	Qualifiers
1976	Qualifiers
1980	Qualifiers
1984	Qualifiers
1988	Qualifiers
1992	Final Tournament (Semi-Finals)
1996	Qualifiers
2000	Final Tournament (Group Stage)
2004	Final Tournament (Quarter-Finals)
2008	Final Tournament (Group Stage)
2012	Final Tournament (Group Stage)
2016	Final Tournament (Group Stage)
2020	*Final Tournament (Qualified)*

FIFA WORLD CUP
1930	Did not enter
1934	Final Tournament (Quarter-Finals)
1938	Final Tournament (4th Place)
1950	Final Tournament (3rd Place)
1954	Qualifiers
1958	Final Tournament (Runners-up)
1962	Qualifiers
1966	Qualifiers
1970	Final Tournament (Group Stage)
1974	Final Tournament (2nd Round)
1978	Final Tournament (Group Stage)
1982	Qualifiers
1986	Qualifiers
1990	Final Tournament (Group Stage)
1994	Final Tournament (3rd Place)
1998	Qualifiers
2002	Final Tournament (2nd Round of 16)
2006	Final Tournament (2nd Round of 16)
2010	Qualifiers
2014	Qualifiers
2018	Final Tournament (Quarter-Finals)

OLYMPIC TOURNAMENTS
1908	4th Place
1912	Round 1
1920	Quarter-Finals
1924	3rd Place
1928	Did not enter
1936	1/8 - Finals
1948	**Winners**
1952	3rd Place
1956	Did not enter
1960	Did not enter
1964	Qualifiers
1968	Did not enter
1972	Did not enter
1976	Did not enter
1980	Did not enter
1984	Did not enter
1988	Quarter-Finals
1992	Quarter-Finals
1996	Qualifiers
2000	Qualifiers
2004	Qualifiers
2008	Qualifiers
2012	Qualifiers
2016	Group Stage

UEFA NATIONS LEAGUE
2018/2019 – League B (promoted to League A)

FIFA CONFEDERATIONS CUP 1992-2017
None

SWEDISH CLUB HONOURS IN EUROPEAN CLUB COMPETITIONS:

European Champion Clubs.Cup (1956-1992) / UEFA Champions League (1993-2020)		
None		
Fairs Cup (1858-1971) / UEFA Cup (1972-2009) / UEFA Europa League (2010-2020)		
IFK Göteborg	2	10981/1982, 1986/1987
UEFA Super Cup (1972-2019)		
None		
European Cup Winners.Cup 1961-1999*		
None		

defunct competition

NATIONAL COMPETITIONS
TABLE OF HONOURS

	CHAMPIONS*	CUP WINNERS	BEST GOALSCORERS	
1896	Örgryte IS Göteborg	-	-	
1897	Örgryte IS Göteborg	-	-	
1898	Örgryte IS Göteborg	-	-	
1899	Örgryte IS Göteborg	-	-	
1900	AIK Stockholm	-	-	
1901	AIK Stockholm	-	-	
1902	Örgryte IS Göteborg	-	-	
1903	Göteborgs IF	-	-	
1904	Örgryte IS Göteborg	-	-	
1905	Örgryte IS Göteborg	-	-	
1906	Örgryte IS Göteborg	-	-	
1907	Örgryte IS Göteborg	-	-	
1908	IFK Göteborg	-	-	
1909	Örgryte IS Göteborg	-	-	
1910	IFK Göteborg	-	-	
1911	AIK Stockholm	-	-	
1912	Djurgårdens IF Stockholm	-	-	
1913	Örgryte IS Göteborg	-	-	
1914	AIK Stockholm	-	-	
1915	Djurgårdens IF Stockholm	-	-	
1916	AIK Stockholm	-	-	
1917	Djurgårdens IF Stockholm	-	-	
1918	IFK Göteborg	-	-	
1919	GAIS Göteborg	-	-	
1920	Djurgårdens IF Stockholm	-	-	
1921	IFK Eskilstuna	-	-	
1922	GAIS Göteborg	-	-	
1923	AIK Stockholm	-	-	
1924	Fässbergs IF Mölndal	-	-	
1925	Brynäs IF Gävle	-	-	
	-------------------------------	-------------------------------	--	
1930/1931	GAIS Göteborg	-	John Nilsson (GAIS Göteborg)	26
1931/1932	AIK Stockholm	-	Carl-Erik Holmberg (Örgryte IS Göteborg)	29
1932/1933	Helsingborgs IF	-	Torsten Bunke (Helsingborgs IF)	21
1933/1934	Helsingborgs IF	-	Sven Jonasson (IF Elfsborg Borås)	20
1934/1935	IFK Göteborg	-	Harry Andersson (IK Sleipner Norrköping)	23
1935/1936	IF Elfsborg Borås	-	Sven Jonasson (IF Elfsborg Borås)	24
1936/1937	AIK Stockholm	-	Olle Zethlerlund (AIK Stockholm)	23
1937/1938	IK Sleipner Norrköping	-	Curt Hjelm (IK Sleipner Norrköping)	13
1938/1939	IF Elfsborg Borås	-	Erik Persson (AIK Stockholm) Ove Andersson (Malmö FF) Yngve Lindgren (Örgryte IS Göteborg)	16
1939/1940	IF Elfsborg Borås	-	Anders Pålsson (Helsingborgs IF)	17
1940/1941	Helsingborgs IF	Helsingborgs IF	Stig Nyström (IK Brage Borlänge)	17
1941/1942	IFK Göteborg	GAIS Göteborg	Sven Jacobsson (GAIS Göteborg)	20
1942/1943	IFK Norrköping	IFK Norrköping	Gunnar Nordahl (Degerfors IF)	16
1943/1944	Malmö FF	Malmö FF	Leif Larsson (IFK Göteborg)	19
1944/1945	IFK Norrköping	IFK Norrköping	Gunnar Nordahl (IFK Norrköping)	27
1945/1946	IFK Norrköping	Malmö FF	Gunnar Nordahl (IFK Norrköping)	25
1946/1947	IFK Norrköping	Malmö FF	Gunnar Gren (IFK Göteborg)	18
1947/1948	IFK Norrköping	Råå IF	Gunnar Nordahl (IFK Norrköping)	18
1948/1949	Malmö FF	AIK Stockholm	Carl-Johan Franck (Helsingborgs IF)	19
1949/1950	Malmö FF	AIK Stockholm	Ingvar Rydell (Malmö FF)	22
1950/1951	Malmö FF	Malmö FF	Hasse Jeppson (Djurgårdens IF Stockholm)	17
1951/1952	IFK Norrköping	*No competition*	Karl-Alfred Jacobsson (GAIS Göteborg)	17
1952/1953	Malmö FF	Malmö FF	Karl-Alfred Jacobsson (GAIS Göteborg)	24
1953/1954	GAIS Göteborg	*No competition*	Karl-Alfred Jacobsson (GAIS Göteborg)	21
1954/1955	Djurgårdens IF Stockholm	*No competition*	Kurt Hamrin (AIK Stockholm)	22
1955/1956	IFK Norrköping	*No competition*	Sylve Bengtsson (Halmstads BK)	22
1956/1957	IFK Norrköping	*No competition*	Harry Bild (IFK Norrköping)	19
1957/1958	IFK Göteborg	*No competition*	Bertil Johansson (IFK Göteborg) Henry Källgren (IFK Norrköping)	27
1959	Djurgårdens IF Stockholm	*No competition*	Rune Börjesson (Örgryte IS Göteborg)	21
1960	IFK Norrköping	*No competition*	Rune Börjesson (Örgryte IS Göteborg)	24
1961	IF Elfsborg Borås	*No competition*	Bertil Johansson (IFK Göteborg)	20
1962	IFK Norrköping	*No competition*	Leif Skiöld (Djurgårdens IF Stockholm)	21
1963	IFK Norrköping	*No competition*	Lars Heinermann (Degerfors IF) Bo Larsson (Malmö FF)	17
1964	Djurgårdens IF Stockholm	*No competition*	Krister Granbom (Helsingborgs IF)	22
1965	Malmö FF	*No competition*	Bo Larsson (Malmö FF)	28
1966	Djurgårdens IF Stockholm	*No competition*	Ove Kindvall (IFK Norrköping)	20

1967	Malmö FF	Malmö FF	Dag Szepanski (Malmö FF)	22
1968	Östers IF Växjö	No competition	Ove Eklund (Åtvidabergs FF)	16
1969	IFK Göteborg	IFK Norrköping (1968/69)	Reine Almqvist (IFK Göteborg)	16
1970	Malmö FF	Åtvidabergs FF (1969/70)	Bo Larsson (Malmö FF)	16
1971	Malmö FF	Åtvidabergs FF (1970/71)	Roland Sandberg (Åtvidabergs FF)	17
1972	Åtvidabergs FF	Landskrona BoIS (1971/72)	Ralf Edström (Åtvidabergs FF) Roland Sandberg (Åtvidabergs FF)	16
1973	Åtvidabergs FF	Malmö FF (1972/73)	Jan Mattsson (Östers IF Växjö)	20
1974	Malmö FF	Malmö FF (1973/74)	Jan Mattsson (Östers IF Växjö)	22
1975	Malmö FF	Malmö FF (1974/75)	Jan Mattsson (Östers IF Växjö)	31
1976	Halmstads BK	AIK Stockholm (1975/76)	Rutger Backe (Halmstads BK)	21
1977	Malmö FF	Östers IF Växjö (1976/77)	Reine Almqvist (IFK Göteborg) Mats Aronsson (Landskrona BoIS)	15
1978	Östers IF Växjö	Malmö FF (1977/78)	Tommy Berggren (Djurgårdens IF Stockholm)	19
1979	Halmstads BK	IFK Göteborg (1978/79)	Mats Werner (Hammarby IF)	14
1980	Östers IF Växjö	Malmö FF (1979/80)	Billy Ohlsson (Hammarby IF)	19
1981	Östers IF Växjö	Kalmar FF (1980/81)	Torbjörn Nilsson (IFK Göteborg)	20
1982	IFK Göteborg	IFK Göteborg (1981/82)	Dan Corneliusson (IFK Göteborg)	12
1983	IFK Göteborg	IFK Göteborg (1982/83)	Thomas Ahlström (IF Elfsborg Borås)	16
1984	IFK Göteborg	Malmö FF (1983/84)	Billy Ohlsson (Hammarby IF)	14
1985	Örgryte IS Göteborg	AIK Stockholm (1984/85)	Sören Börjesson (Örgryte IS Göteborg) Peter Karlsson (Kalmar FF) William Lansdowne (ENG, Kalmar FF)	10
1986	Malmö FF	Malmö FF (1985/86)	Johnny Ekström (IFK Göteborg)	13
1987	IFK Göteborg	Kalmar FF (1986/87)	Lasse Larsson (Malmö FF)	19
1988	Malmö FF	IFK Norrköping (1987/88)	Dan Martin Nataniel Dahlin (Malmö FF)	17
1989	IFK Norrköping	Malmö FF (1988/89)	Jan Hellström (IFK Norrköping)	16
1990	IFK Göteborg	Djurgårdens IF Stockholm (1989/90)	Kaj Eskelinen (IFK Göteborg)	10
1991	IFK Göteborg	IFK Norrköping (1990/91) IFK Göteborg (1991)	Bernt Kennet Andersson (IFK Göteborg)	13
1992	AIK Stockholm	No competition	Hans Eklund (Östers IF Växjö)	16
1993	IFK Göteborg	Degerfors IF (1992/93)	Henrik Bertilsson (Halmstads BK) Mats Lilienberg (Trelleborgs FF)	18
1994	IFK Göteborg	IFK Norrköping (1993/94)	Niclas Kindvall (IFK Norrköping)	23
1995	IFK Göteborg	Halmstads BK (1994/95)	Niklas Skoog (Västra Frölunda IF)	17
1996	IFK Göteborg	AIK Stockholm (1995/96)	Andreas Andersson (IFK Göteborg)	19
1997	Halmstads BK	AIK Stockholm (1996/97)	Mats Lilienberg (Halmstads BK) Christer Mattiasson (IF Elfsborg Borås) Dan Sahlin (Örebro SK)	14
1998	AIK Stockholm	Helsingborgs IF (1997/98)	Arild Stavrum (Helsingborgs IF)	18
1999	Helsingborgs IF	AIK Stockholm (1998/99)	Marcus Allbäck (Örgryte IS Göteborg)	15
2000	Halmstads BK	Örgryte IS Göteborg (1999/2000)	Fredrik Berglund (IF Elfsborg Borås)	18
2001	Hammarby IF	IF Elfsborg Borås (2000/01)	Stefan Selaković (Halmstads BK)	15
2002	Djurgårdens IF Stockholm	Djurgårdens IF Stockholm	Peter Emeka Ijeh (NGA, Malmö FF)	24
2003	Djurgårdens IF Stockholm	IF Elfsborg Borås	Niklas Skoog (Malmö FF)	22
2004	Malmö FF	Djurgårdens IF Stockholm	Markus Rosenberg (Halmstads BK)	14
2005	Djurgårdens IF Stockholm	Djurgårdens IF Stockholm	Gunnar Heiðar Þorvaldsson (ISL, Halmstads BK)	16
2006	IF Elfsborg Borås	Helsingborgs IF	Ariclenes da Silva Ferreira "Ari" (BRA, Kalmar FF)	15
2007	IFK Göteborg	Kalmar FF	Bengt Eric Marcus Berg (IFK Göteborg) Razak Omotoyossi (BEN, Helsingborgs IF)	14
2008	Kalmar FF	IFK Göteborg	Patrik Ingelsten (Kalmar FF)	19
2009	AIK Stockholm	AIK Stockholm	Tobias Hysén (IFK Göteborg) Francisco Wánderson do Carmo Carneiro (BRA, GAIS Göteborg)	18
2010	Malmö FF	Helsingborgs IF	Alexander Gerndt (Gefle IF / Helsingborgs IF)	20
2011	Helsingborgs IF	Helsingborgs IF	Mathias Ranégie (BK Häcken Göteborg / Malmö FF)	21
2012	IF Elfsborg Borås	No competition	Abdul Majeed Waris (GHA, BK Häcken Göteborg)	23
2013	Malmö FF	IFK Göteborg (2012/13)	Imad Khalili (IFK Norrköping / Helsingborgs IF)	15
2014	Malmö FF	IF Elfsborg Borås (2013/14)	Lasse Vibe (IFK Göteborg)	23
2015	IFK Norrköping	IFK Göteborg (2014/15)	Emir Kujović (IFK Norrköping)	21
2016	Malmö FF	BK Häcken Göteborg (2015/16)	John Owoeri (NGA, BK Häcken Göteborg)	17
2017	Malmö FF	Östersunds FK (2016/17)	Karl Albin Elis Holmberg (IFK Norrköping) Magnus Eriksson (Djurgårdens IF Stockholm)	14
2018	AIK Stockholm	Djurgårdens IF Stockholm (2017/18)	Paulo José de Oliveira „Paulinho" (BRA, BK Häcken Göteborg)	20
2019	Djurgårdens IF Stockholm	BK Häcken Göteborg (2018/2019)	Mohamed Buya Turay (SLE, Djurgårdens IF Stockholm)	15

*Svenska Mästerskapet (1896–1925), Allsvenskan (1931–1981), Allsvenskan Play-offs (1982–1990), Mästerskapsserien (1991–1992), Allsvenskan (since 1993).

NATIONAL CHAMPIONSHIP
Allsvenskan 2019
(31.03.2019 – 02.11.2019)

Results

Round 1 [31.03.-01.04.2019]
AIK Stockholm - Östersunds FK 0-0
Falkenbergs FF - Örebro SK 1-0(0-0)
Kalmar FF - IK Sirius 0-2(0-1)
AFC Eskilstuna - IFK Göteborg 3-1(1-0)
Helsingborgs IF - IFK Norrköping 3-1(2-1)
Djurgårdens IF - GIF Sundsvall 2-2(2-1)
IF Elfsborg - Hammarby IF 1-1(1-1)
Malmö FF - BK Häcken 1-1(0-0)

Round 2 [06-08.04.2019]
BK Häcken - Helsingborgs IF 2-1(1-0)
GIF Sundsvall - Malmö FF 3-1(0-0)
IFK Göteborg - IF Elfsborg 3-0(2-0)
Östersunds FK - Falkenbergs FF 3-2(1-1)
Hammarby IF - Kalmar FF 1-1(0-0)
IFK Norrköping - AIK Stockholm 0-0
Örebro SK - Djurgårdens IF 0-3(0-1)
IK Sirius - AFC Eskilstuna 3-2(3-1)

Round 3 [12-15.04.2019]
AFC Eskilstuna - Örebro SK 1-1(0-0)
Falkenbergs FF - BK Häcken 0-3(0-0)
Kalmar FF - IFK Norrköping 2-2(0-0)
AIK Stockholm - IK Sirius 2-1(0-1)
IF Elfsborg - GIF Sundsvall 3-1(1-1)
Malmö FF - Östersunds FK 2-0(1-0)
Djurgårdens IF - IFK Göteborg 2-1(0-0)
Helsingborgs IF - Hammarby IF 2-1(1-1)

Round 4 [19-22.04.2019]
Östersunds FK - IF Elfsborg 1-1(0-1)
IFK Norrköping - Falkenbergs FF 4-3(2-1)
Örebro SK - AIK Stockholm 2-1(0-0)
GIF Sundsvall - Kalmar FF 1-2(1-2)
IK Sirius - Malmö FF 0-1(0-0)
BK Häcken - Djurgårdens IF 0-1(0-0)
Hammarby IF - AFC Eskilstuna 3-1(2-0)
IFK Göteborg - Helsingborgs IF 3-1(2-0)

Round 5 [24-25.04.2019]
AFC Eskilstuna - Östersunds FK 0-1(0-1)
AIK Stockholm - BK Häcken 1-0(0-0)
IF Elfsborg - Örebro SK 4-2(3-0)
Falkenbergs FF - IK Sirius 0-0
Malmö FF - Hammarby IF 4-1(0-1)
Djurgårdens IF - IFK Norrköping 1-1(0-1)
Helsingborgs IF - GIF Sundsvall 1-1(0-0)
Kalmar FF - IFK Göteborg 1-1(0-0)

Round 6 [27-29.04.2019]
IK Sirius - IF Elfsborg 2-4(1-4)
BK Häcken - AFC Eskilstuna 3-0(0-0)
Hammarby IF - Djurgårdens IF 2-1(2-1)
IFK Norrköping - Malmö FF 1-1(1-1)
IFK Göteborg - AIK Stockholm 3-0(1-0)
Örebro SK - Kalmar FF 1-1(0-0)
Östersunds FK - Helsingborgs IF 3-0(2-0)
GIF Sundsvall - Falkenbergs FF 3-1(1-0)

Round 7 [04-06.05.2019]
AIK Stockholm - AFC Eskilstuna 2-1(1-0)
IK Sirius - IFK Göteborg 2-4(2-1)
Falkenbergs FF - Malmö FF 1-2(1-2)
BK Häcken - GIF Sundsvall 0-0(0-0)
Kalmar FF - Östersunds FK 1-1(0-1)
Örebro SK - Hammarby IF 2-3(0-1)
IF Elfsborg - IFK Norrköping 0-0
Helsingborgs IF - Djurgårdens IF 1-1(0-1)

Round 8 [10-13.05.2019]
Hammarby IF - IK Sirius 2-0(2-0)
Östersunds FK - BK Häcken 1-1(1-1)
AFC Eskilstuna - Falkenbergs FF 0-0
Kalmar FF - Helsingborgs IF 1-0(0-0)
GIF Sundsvall - Örebro SK 1-2(0-0)
Djurgårdens IF - AIK Stockholm 0-2(0-0)
Malmö FF - IF Elfsborg 4-1(1-0)
IFK Norrköping - IFK Göteborg 1-2(1-1)

Round 9 [14-16.05.2019]
Hammarby IF - Östersunds FK 4-0(3-0)
IF Elfsborg - AFC Eskilstuna 1-0(0-0)
Falkenbergs FF - Djurgårdens IF 0-3(0-3)
BK Häcken - Kalmar FF 1-0(0-0)
Helsingborgs IF - AIK Stockholm 1-3(1-2)
IK Sirius - GIF Sundsvall 1-0(1-0)
IFK Göteborg - Malmö FF 0-0
Örebro SK - IFK Norrköping 1-2(0-1)

Round 10 [18-20.05.2019]
AFC Eskilstuna - Helsingborgs IF 1-1(0-0)
Malmö FF - Kalmar FF 1-0(0-0)
IK Sirius - BK Häcken 3-4(1-2)
Djurgårdens IF - IF Elfsborg 2-0(2-0)
AIK Stockholm - Falkenbergs FF 2-0(0-0)
IFK Göteborg - Hammarby IF 0-0
IFK Norrköping - GIF Sundsvall 2-0(2-0)
Östersunds FK - Örebro SK 1-3(0-2)

Round 11 [24-27.05.2019]
GIF Sundsvall - AIK Stockholm 1-1(1-1)
BK Häcken - IFK Göteborg 1-2(0-1)
Malmö FF - AFC Eskilstuna 5-0(1-0)
Helsingborgs IF - Falkenbergs FF 1-1(0-1)
Djurgårdens IF - Östersunds FK 3-1(2-1)
Kalmar FF - IF Elfsborg 1-1(0-0)
Hammarby IF - IFK Norrköping 2-2(1-2)
Örebro SK - IK Sirius 0-2(0-1)

Round 12 [01-02.06.2019]
IFK Göteborg - Örebro SK 0-1(0-1)
IK Sirius - Djurgårdens IF 0-2(0-1)
Falkenbergs FF - Kalmar FF 0-0
Östersunds FK - GIF Sundsvall 1-1(0-1)
AFC Eskilstuna - IFK Norrköping 0-2(0-1)
AIK Stockholm - Hammarby IF 2-0(2-0)
IF Elfsborg - BK Häcken 0-0
Helsingborgs IF - Malmö FF 0-1(0-1)

Round 13 [28.06.-01.07.2019]
Örebro SK - Helsingborgs IF 0-1(0-1)
Östersunds FK - IFK Göteborg 0-0
Falkenbergs FF - IF Elfsborg 2-1(1-1)
GIF Sundsvall - AFC Eskilstuna 0-0
AIK Stockholm - Malmö FF 0-0
IFK Norrköping - IK Sirius 0-1(0-0)
Djurgårdens IF - Kalmar FF 2-0(0-0)
BK Häcken - Hammarby IF 2-0(1-0)

Round 14 [06-08.07.2019]
Kalmar FF - AIK Stockholm 0-1(0-0)
IK Sirius - Östersunds FK 1-1(0-0)
IFK Göteborg - GIF Sundsvall 2-1(2-0)
Malmö FF - Örebro SK 2-1(1-1)
Hammarby IF - Falkenbergs FF 6-2(3-0)
IFK Norrköping - BK Häcken 2-1(1-0)
AFC Eskilstuna - Djurgårdens IF 1-1(0-0)
IF Elfsborg - Helsingborgs IF 1-1(0-0)

Round 15 [13-15.07.2019]
AIK Stockholm - IF Elfsborg 3-0(2-0)
Falkenbergs FF - IFK Göteborg 1-1(0-0)
AFC Eskilstuna - Kalmar FF 3-1(2-0)
BK Häcken - Örebro SK 3-0(0-0)
Östersunds FK - IFK Norrköping 2-1(0-0)
Djurgårdens IF - Malmö FF 1-1(0-0)
Helsingborgs IF - IK Sirius 1-0(0-0)
GIF Sundsvall - Hammarby IF 2-3(1-2)

Round 16 [20-22.07.2019]
AIK Stockholm - Helsingborgs IF 2-0(1-0)
Örebro SK - Falkenbergs FF 4-0(3-0)
GIF Sundsvall - BK Häcken 0-1(0-0)
IFK Göteborg - AFC Eskilstuna 1-0(1-0)
Malmö FF - IK Sirius 1-1(1-1)
IFK Norrköping - Östersunds FK 3-0(2-0)
Hammarby IF - IF Elfsborg 5-2(4-1)
Kalmar FF - Djurgårdens IF 0-1(0-0)

Round 17 [27-29.07.2019]
Falkenbergs FF - GIF Sundsvall 2-0(2-0)
IK Sirius - AIK Stockholm 0-2(0-0)
AFC Eskilstuna - Hammarby IF 1-6(1-3)
Djurgårdens IF - BK Häcken 2-0(0-0)
Östersunds FK - Malmö FF 0-0
IFK Göteborg - IFK Norrköping 0-0
IF Elfsborg - Kalmar FF 2-1(0-1)
Helsingborgs IF - Örebro SK 1-4(1-3)

Round 18 [03-05.08.2019]
Malmö FF - GIF Sundsvall 2-1(1-1) [28.05.]
AIK Stockh. - Norrköping 0-2(0-1) [25.06.]
Östersunds FK - AFC Eskilstuna 1-2(1-1)
Falkenbergs FF - Helsingborgs IF 1-1(1-0)
Kalmar FF - Hammarby IF 2-2(0-1)
BK Häcken - IK Sirius 4-1(3-1)
IF Elfsborg - Djurgårdens IF 0-1(0-0)
Örebro SK - IFK Göteborg 2-2(0-1)

Round 19 [10-12.08.2019]
Djurgårdens IF - IK Sirius 4-0(3-0)
GIF Sundsvall - Östersunds FK 1-1(1-0)
AFC Eskilstuna - AIK Stockholm 2-4(1-1)
BK Häcken - Malmö FF 1-1(0-0)
Hammarby IF - Helsingborgs IF 2-1(2-0)
IFK Norrköping - IF Elfsborg 2-0(2-0)
IFK Göteborg - Falkenbergs FF 1-1(0-1)
Kalmar FF - Örebro SK 1-1(0-0)

Round 20 [17-19.08.2019]
Hammarby IF - GIF Sundsvall 3-0(2-0)
AIK Stockholm - Kalmar FF 1-2(0-2)
Örebro SK - BK Häcken 1-2(0-1)
IK Sirius - IFK Norrköping 0-2(0-0)
Malmö FF - Falkenbergs FF 5-0(2-0)
Djurgårdens IF - AFC Eskilstuna 3-0(2-0)
IF Elfsborg - Östersunds FK 4-1(3-0)
Helsingborgs IF - IFK Göteborg 1-2(1-0)

Round 21 [24-26.08.2019]
IK Sirius - Örebro SK 3-4(0-3)
AFC Eskilstuna - BK Häcken 0-2(0-0)
IFK Norrköping - Helsingborgs IF 5-0(2-0)
Östersunds FK - AIK Stockholm 1-3(0-0)
Malmö FF - Djurgårdens IF 0-1(0-0)
Falkenbergs FF - Hammarby IF 0-2(0-2)
IFK Göteborg - Kalmar FF 4-0(1-0)
GIF Sundsvall - IF Elfsborg 1-2(1-1)

Round 22 [30.08.-01.09.2019]
Helsingborgs IF - Östersunds FK 2-0(2-0)
IF Elfsborg - IK Sirius 1-1(1-0)
Örebro SK - AFC Eskilstuna 3-1(2-1)
AIK Stockholm - Djurgårdens IF 1-0(1-0)
Kalmar FF - Malmö FF 0-5(0-2)
GIF Sundsvall - IFK Göteborg 0-2(0-1)
BK Häcken - Falkenbergs FF 4-1(2-1)
IFK Norrköping - Hammarby IF 2-0(1-0)

Round 23 [13-16.09.2019]
IK Sirius - Falkenbergs FF 2-0(1-0)
Örebro SK - GIF Sundsvall 0-0
Östersunds FK - Kalmar FF 1-2(1-0)
BK Häcken - AIK Stockholm 1-2(0-1)
Hammarby IF - IFK Göteborg 6-2(3-1)
Malmö FF - IFK Norrköping 1-0(0-0)
AFC Eskilstuna - IF Elfsborg 2-2(1-0)
Djurgårdens IF - Helsingborgs IF 2-0(0-0)

Round 24 [20-22.09.2019]
GIF Sundsvall - Djurgårdens IF 1-4(1-3)
Falkenbergs FF - Östersunds FK 1-0(1-0)
Kalmar FF - BK Häcken 1-1(1-0)
IFK Norrköping - Örebro SK 3-0(2-0)
IFK Göteborg - IK Sirius 2-1(2-0)
Hammarby IF - AIK Stockholm 2-1(1-0)
IF Elfsborg - Malmö FF 0-3(0-0)
Helsingborgs IF - AFC Eskilstuna 2-1(1-0)

Round 25 [24-26.09.2019]
Djurgårdens IF - Falkenbergs FF 1-0(0-0)
Kalmar FF - GIF Sundsvall 0-2(0-1)
AIK Stockholm - IFK Göteborg 1-0(1-0)
BK Häcken - IF Elfsborg 1-2(1-1)
Örebro SK - Östersunds FK 2-0(0-0)
IK Sirius - Hammarby IF 1-3(0-0)
Malmö FF - Helsingborgs IF 3-0(3-0)
IFK Norrköping - AFC Eskilstuna 4-0(3-0)

Round 26 [29-30.09.2019]
IF Elfsborg - AIK Stockholm 1-1(0-0)
IFK Göteborg - BK Häcken 0-0
GIF Sundsvall - IK Sirius 2-1(0-0)
AFC Eskilstuna - Malmö FF 0-1(0-0)
Falkenbergs FF - IFK Norrköping 0-2(0-1)
Hammarby IF - Örebro SK 5-1(1-1)
Helsingborgs IF - Kalmar FF 2-0(0-0)
Östersunds FK - Djurgårdens IF 1-2(1-1)

Round 27 [05-06.10.2019]
GIF Sundsvall - IFK Norrköping 4-4(3-0)
AIK Stockholm - Örebro SK 2-0(0-0)
IK Sirius - Helsingborgs IF 2-1(1-0)
Djurgårdens IF - Hammarby IF 1-2(0-0)
BK Häcken - Östersunds FK 1-1(1-0)
Kalmar FF - AFC Eskilstuna 0-0
IF Elfsborg - Falkenbergs FF 4-0(1-0)
Malmö FF - IFK Göteborg 1-0(0-0)

Round 28 [18-21.10.2019]
AFC Eskilstuna - GIF Sundsvall 1-0(0-0)
Helsingborgs IF - BK Häcken 0-2(0-1)
Östersunds FK - IK Sirius 2-0(0-0)
Falkenbergs FF - AIK Stockholm 1-5(0-2)
Hammarby IF - Malmö FF 2-0(1-0)
IFK Norrköping - Kalmar FF 1-0(0-0)
IFK Göteborg - Djurgårdens IF 0-1(0-0)
Örebro SK - IF Elfsborg 2-2(1-1)

Round 29 [26-28.10.2019]
GIF Sundsvall - Helsingborgs IF 1-2(0-0)
Kalmar FF - Falkenbergs FF 2-3(0-0)
AFC Eskilstuna - IK Sirius 0-0
BK Häcken - IFK Norrköping 0-1(0-0)
Östersunds FK - Hammarby IF 1-2(0-0)
Djurgårdens IF - Örebro SK 3-0(1-0)
IF Elfsborg - IFK Göteborg 2-0(1-0)
Malmö FF - AIK Stockholm 2-0(0-0)

Round 30 [02.11.2019]
AIK Stockholm - GIF Sundsvall 2-1(0-0)
Falkenbergs FF - AFC Eskilstuna 1-0(0-0)
IFK Göteborg - Östersunds FK 7-1(2-1)
Hammarby IF - BK Häcken 4-1(1-0)
Helsingborgs IF - IF Elfsborg 1-2(0-1)
IFK Norrköping - Djurgårdens IF 2-2(2-0)
Örebro SK - Malmö FF 0-5(0-2)
IK Sirius - Kalmar FF 3-0(0-0)

Final Standings

										Home						Away				
1.	**Djurgårdens IF Stockholm**	30	20	6	4	53	-	19	66	10	3	2	29 - 10	10	3	2	24 - 9
2.	Malmö FF	30	19	8	3	56	-	16	65	12	2	1	34 - 7	7	6	2	22 - 9
3.	Hammarby IF Stockholm	30	20	5	5	75	-	38	65	13	2	0	49 - 15	7	3	5	26 - 23
4.	AIK Stockholm	30	19	5	6	47	-	24	62	11	2	2	21 - 7	8	3	4	26 - 17
5.	IFK Norrköping	30	16	9	5	54	-	26	57	10	3	2	32 - 10	6	6	3	22 - 16
6.	BK Häcken Göteborg	30	14	7	9	44	-	29	49	8	2	5	25 - 13	6	5	4	19 - 16
7.	IFK Göteborg	30	13	9	8	46	-	31	48	8	5	2	26 - 7	5	4	6	20 - 24
8.	IF Elfsborg Borås	30	11	10	9	44	-	45	43	7	6	2	24 - 13	4	4	7	20 - 32
9.	Örebro SK	30	9	6	15	40	-	56	33	4	4	7	20 - 25	5	2	8	20 - 31
10.	Helsingborgs IF	30	8	6	16	29	-	49	30	6	3	6	19 - 20	2	3	10	10 - 29
11.	IK Sirius Uppsala	30	8	5	17	34	-	51	29	5	1	9	23 - 30	3	4	8	11 - 21
12.	Östersunds FK	30	5	10	15	27	-	52	25	4	5	6	19 - 20	1	5	9	8 - 32
13.	Falkenbergs FF	30	6	7	17	25	-	62	25	5	4	6	11 - 20	1	3	11	14 - 42
14.	Kalmar FF (*Relegation Play-offs*)	30	4	11	15	22	-	47	23	1	8	6	12 - 23	3	3	9	10 - 24
15.	GIF Sundsvall (*Relegated*)	30	4	8	18	31	-	50	20	3	4	8	21 - 27	1	4	10	10 - 23
16.	AFC Eskilstuna (*Relegated*)	30	4	8	18	23	-	55	20	3	6	6	15 - 23	1	2	12	8 - 32

Top goalscorers:	
15 **Mohamed Buya Turay (SLE)**	*Djurgårdens IF Stockholm*
14 Robin Söder	*IFK Göteborg*
14 Muamer Tanković	*Hammarby IF Stockholm*
13 Nikola Đurđić (SRB)	*Hammarby IF Stockholm*
13 Nils Markus Rosenberg	*Malmö FF*

Relegation Play-offs [06-10.11.2019]

IK Brage Borlänge - Kalmar FF   0-2(0-1)   2-2(0-0)

Kalmar FF remains at First Level for the Allsvenskan 2020.

NATIONAL CUP
Svenska Cupen 2019/2020

Second Round [14/21/22.08./09-10.11.2019]

Carlstad United BK - AFC Eskilstuna	2-3(2-1)		Nyköpings BIS - Örebro SK	0-1(0-1)
IFK Stocksund - Östersunds FK	0-1(0-1)		Forssa BK - Syrianska FC Söldertälje	2-4(2-2)
Lunds BK - Varbergs BoIS	0-1(0-0)		IFK Luleå - Hammarby IF Stockholm	1-3(1-2)
Tvååkers IF - Trelleborgs FF	2-0(1-0)		Sandvikens IF - IK Frej	2-1(0-0)
Qviding FIF - BK Häcken Göteborg	1-3(0-1)		FC Gute - Dalkurd FF	2-4(1-2)
Gottne IF - IF Brommapojkarna	2-4(0-1,2-2)		IFK Timra - IFK Norrköping	1-6(0-3)
Karlstad BK - IK Sirius Uppsala	1-1 aet; 3-5 pen		Eskilsminne IF - Norrby IF Borås	1-0(0-0)
Gamla Upsala SK - Västerås SK	1-3(0-2)		FK Karlskrona - Östers IF Växjö	2-1(2-0)
Sollentuna FK - Degerfors IF	4-3(1-1)		Vårgårda IK - Falkenbergs FF	0-4(0-1)
IFK Lidingö FK - GIF Sundsvall	1-3(0-0,1-1)		IK Gauthiod - IF Elfsborg Borås	1-3(0-0,1-1)
Torns IF - Jönköpings Södra IF	1-2(0-0,1-1)		BK Astrio Halmstad - IFK Göteborg	0-4(0-1)
FC Rosengård 1917 - Kalmar FF	1-2(0-2)		Dagsbergs IF - IK Brage Borlänge	0-12(0-5)
Husqvarna FF - Mjällby AIF Hällevik	0-4(0-0)		Akropolis IF Spånga - Djurgårdens IF Stockholm	1-2(0-2)
Utsiktens BK - Örgryte IS Göteborg	0-1(0-1)		Oskarshamns AIK - Helsingborgs IF	2-1(0-1)
Raslätts SK - GAIS Göteborg	0-1(0-1)		Enskede IK - AIK Stockholm	0-7(0-4)
FC Trollhättan - Halmstads BK	1-2(1-0)		IFK Värnamo - Malmö FF	0-2(0-0)

Third Round [15.02.2020-09.03.2020]

Group 1			Group 2	
Djurgårdens IF Stockholm - Dalkurd FF	3-2(3-1)		Malmö FF - Syrianska FC Söldertälje	8-0(3-0)
Sandvikens IF - Mjällby AIF Hällevik	1-3(1-0)		FK Karlskrona - AFC Eskilstuna	1-1(0-1)
Mjällby AIF Hällevik - Dalkurd FF	5-0(4-0)		FK Karlskrona - Malmö FF	1-2(1-0)
Sandvikens IF - Djurgårdens IF Stockholm	2-2(0-2)		AFC Eskilstuna - Syrianska FC Söldertälje	6-1(3-0)
Dalkurd FF - Sandvikens IF	3-1(2-0)		Syrianska FC Söldertälje - FK Karlskrona	5-1(1-1)
Djurgårdens IF Stockholm - Mjällby AIF Hällevik	1-2(1-1)		Malmö FF - AFC Eskilstuna	3-0(0-0)
Qualified: Mjällby AIF Hällevik			*Qualified*: Malmö FF	

Group 3			Group 4	
Hammarby IF Stockholm - Varbergs BoIS	5-1(2-0)		AIK Stockholm - Jönköpings Södra IF	2-2(0-0)
GIF Sundsvall - IF Brommapojkarna	2-2(2-1)		Kalmar FF - Örgryte IS Göteborg	3-0(2-0)
IF Brommapojkarna - Hammarby IF Stockholm	0-2(0-1)		Örgryte IS Göteborg - AIK Stockholm	0-1(0-1)
GIF Sundsvall - Varbergs BoIS	1-4(1-2)		Kalmar FF - Jönköpings Södra IF	5-0(4-0)
Varbergs BoIS - IF Brommapojkarna	1-1(1-0)		Jönköpings Södra IF - Örgryte IS Göteborg	2-0(2-0)
Hammarby IF Stockholm - GIF Sundsvall	4-0(0-0)		AIK Stockholm - Kalmar FF	3-1(1-0)
Qualified: Hammarby IF Stockholm			*Qualified*: AIK Stockholm	

Group 5			Group 6	
IFK Norrköping - Halmstads BK	1-0(1-0)		BK Häcken Göteborg - GAIS Göteborg	3-0(2-0)
Tvååkers IF - Falkenbergs FF	1-3(0-1)		Eskilsminne IF - Östersunds FK	0-5(0-2)
Tvååkers IF - IFK Norrköping	2-1(0-1)		Eskilsminne IF - BK Häcken Göteborg	0-4(0-1)
Falkenbergs FF - Halmstads BK	1-0(0-0)		Östersunds FK - GAIS Göteborg	4-0(3-0)
Halmstads BK - Tvååkers IF	2-1(0-0)		GAIS Göteborg - Eskilsminne IF	4-1(1-1)
IFK Norrköping - Falkenbergs FF	1-0(0-0)		BK Häcken Göteborg - Östersunds FK	2-0(2-0)
Qualified: Falkenbergs FF			*Qualified*: BK Häcken Göteborg	

Group 7			Group 8	
IFK Göteborg - Västerås SK	2-0(2-0)		IF Elfsborg Borås - IK Brage Borlänge	3-0(1-0)
Sollentuna FK - IK Sirius Uppsala	1-8(1-6)		Oskarshamns AIK - Örebro SK	1-4(0-1)
Sollentuna FK - IFK Göteborg	0-2(0-1)		Oskarshamns AIK - IF Elfsborg Borås	2-1(1-1)
IK Sirius Uppsala - Västerås SK	0-3(0-2)		Örebro SK - IK Brage Borlänge	3-3(1-2)
Västerås SK - Sollentuna FK	4-0(2-0)		IK Brage Borlänge - Oskarshamns AIK	3-1(1-1)
IFK Göteborg - IK Sirius Uppsala	1-1(1-1)		IF Elfsborg Borås - Örebro SK	1-0(0-0)
Qualified: IFK Göteborg			*Qualified*: IF Elfsborg Borås	

Quarter-Finals [25.06.2020]

BK Häcken Göteborg - IF Elfsborg Borås	1-2(0-0)		Mjällby AIF Hällevik - Falkenbergs FF	1-0(0-0)
Hammarby IF Stockholm - IFK Göteborg	1-3(1-0,1-1)		Malmö FF - AIK Stockholm	4-1(1-1)

Semi-Finals [09.07.2020]

IF Elfsborg Borås - IFK Göteborg	0-1(0-0,0-0)		Mjällby AIF Hällevik - Malmö FF	0-0 aet; 2-4 pen

30.07.2020; Ullevi Stadion, Göteborg; Referee: Glen Nyberg; Attendance: None
IFK Göteborg - Malmö FF   **2-1(1-0,1-1)**

IFK Göteborg: Giannis Anestis, Alexander Jallow, Mattias Bjärsmyr, Victor Wernersson, August Erlingmark (Cap) (68.Alexander Farnerud), Alhassan Yusuf, Hosam Aiesh, Tobias Sana (117.Adil Titi), Patrik Karlsson-Lagemyr (106.André Calisir), Sargon Abraham (82.Emil Holm). Trainer: Poya Asbaghi.

Malmö FF: Johan Dahlin, Eric Larsson, Jonas Knudsen, Anel Ahmedhodžić, Søren Rieks (14.Carl Marcus Christer Antonsson; 105.Guillermo Federico Molins Palmeiro), Oscar Lewicki (24.Behrang Safari), Anders Christiansen, Bonke Innocent (85.Erdal Rakip), Isaac Kiese Thelin, Nils Ola Toivonen, Jo Inge Berget. Trainer: Jon Dahl Tomasson (Denmark).

Goals: 0-1 Nils Ola Toivonen (40), 1-1 Patrik Karlsson-Lagemyr (86), 2-1 Alexander Farnerud (94).

THE CLUBS 2019

Athletic Football Club Eskilstuna

Founded: 10.12.2004 (*FC Väsby United*)
Stadium: Tunavallen, Eskilstuna (7,500)
Trainer: Nemanja Miljanovic — 04.08.1971
[06.09.2019] Saulius Sirmelis — 31.05.1956

Goalkeepers:	DOB	M	(s)	G
Mihail Ivanov (BUL)	07.08.1989	2	(1)	
Igor Levchenko (UKR)	23.02.1991	16		
Ole Söderberg	20.07.1990	12		
Defenders:	DOB	M	(s)	G
Jesper Björkman	29.04.1993	26		
Adnan Ćatić	15.01.2000	5		
Mehmed Drešević	06.06.1992	4	(2)	
Kadir Hodžić	05.08.1994	27		2
Gustav Jarl	28.05.1995	16	(2)	1
Adnan Kojić	28.10.1995	27		
José León Bernal (ESP)	03.02.1995	13		
Wilhelm Loeper	30.03.1998	18	(9)	1
George Felix Michel Melki (LIB)	23.07.1994	8		
Artem Rakhmanov (BLR)	10.07.1990		(5)	1
Pontus Rödin	16.08.2000	2	(1)	
Soya Takahashi (JPN)	29.02.1996	6	(2)	
Midfielders:	DOB	M	(s)	G
Michael Anaba (GHA)	05.12.1993	8	(1)	
Ivan Bobko (UKR)	10.12.1990	3	(4)	1
Mamadou Kouyaté (MLI)	13.09.1997		(1)	
Jacob Lackell	05.07.2001		(4)	
Ismet Lushaku	22.09.2000	10	(3)	
Daniel Miljanović	11.04.2001	3	(7)	
Adi Nalić	01.12.1997	20		5
Samuel Onyekachukwu Nnamani (NGA)	03.06.1995	25	(3)	7
Anel Raskaj	19.08.1989	27		
Sandro Tsveiba (RUS)	05.09.1993	11	(1)	
Pavle Vagić	24.01.2000	2	(3)	1
Forwards:	DOB	M	(s)	G
Ferid Ali	07.04.1992	5	(3)	
Denni Avdić	05.09.1988	10	(6)	1
Vladislav Bragin (RUS)	25.01.1998		(1)	
Ousmane Camara (GUI)	28.12.1998	10	(5)	2
Dženis Kozica	28.04.1993	13	(2)	1
Luka Mijaljević	09.03.1991		(3)	
Kristijan Miljević (SRB)	15.07.1992	1	(5)	

Allmänna Idrottsklubben Stockholm

Founded: 15.02.1891
Stadium: Friends Arena, Stockholm (50,000)
Trainer: Rikard Norling — 04.06.1971

Goalkeepers:	DOB	M	(s)	G
Budimir Janošević (SRB)	21.10.1989	3		
Oscar Linnér	23.02.1997	27		
Defenders:	DOB	M	(s)	G
Panajotis Dimitriadis	12.08.1986	23	(2)	
Per Karlsson	02.01.1986	28		
Robert Lundström	01.11.1989	8	(5)	
George Felix Michel Melki (LIB)	23.07.1994	3	(5)	
Karol Mets (EST)	16.05.1993	25	(1)	1
Midfielders:	DOB	M	(s)	G
Enoch Adu (GHA)	14.09.1990	27		
Daniel Granli (NOR)	01.05.1994	9	(2)	
Bilal Hussein	22.04.2000	10	(6)	
Sebastian Bengt Ulf Larsson	06.06.1985	25	(3)	6
Rasmus Lindkvist	16.05.1990	15	(3)	1
Heradi Rashidi	24.07.1994	10	(10)	1
Anton Salétros	12.04.1996	18	(8)	2
Daniel Sundgren	22.11.1990	15		3
Saku Ylätupa (FIN)	04.08.1999	2	(4)	
Forwards:	DOB	M	(s)	G
Nabil Bahoui	05.02.1991	2	(6)	2
Tarik Elyounoussi (NOR)	23.02.1988	24	(4)	11
Henok Goitom (ERI)	22.09.1984	23	(7)	11
Jack Lahne	24.10.2001	5	(4)	1
Chinedu Obasi Ogbuke (NGA)	01.06.1986	15	(3)	5
Kolbeinn Sigþórsson (ISL)	14.03.1990	12	(5)	3
Stefan Silva	11.03.1990	1	(3)	

Bollklubben Häcken Göteborg

Founded: 02.08.1940
Stadium: Bravida Arena, Göteborg (6,500)
Trainer: Andreas Alm — 19.06.1973

Goalkeepers:	DOB	M	(s)	G
Peter Abrahamsson	18.07.1988	29		
Christoffer Källqvist	26.08.1983	1		
Defenders:	DOB	M	(s)	G
Kari Arkivuo (FIN)	23.06.1983	7	(1)	
Elohor Godswill Ekpolo (NGA)	14.05.1995	26		1
Johan Hammar	22.02.1994	5	(7)	1
Rasmus Lindgren	29.11.1984	26		
Juhani Ojala (FIN)	19.06.1989	2	(1)	1
Óskar Sverrisson	26.11.1992	2	(4)	
Joona Toivio (FIN)	10.03.1988	28		2
Midfielders:	DOB	M	(s)	G
Adam Andersson	11.11.1996	25	(3)	2
Gustav Berggren	07.09.1997	17	(8)	2
Mervan Çelik	26.05.1990	3	(8)	1
Alexander Faltsetas	04.07.1987	19	(2)	
Erik Friberg	10.02.1986	23	(1)	2
Daleho Irandust	04.06.1998	26	(1)	4
Imam Seedy Jagne	01.10.2003		(1)	
Ahmed Yasin Ghani Mousa (IRQ)	22.04.1991	25	(2)	2
Ali Youssef	05.08.2000	2	(5)	
Forwards:	DOB	M	(s)	G
Alexander Jeremejeff	12.10.1993	19		8
Kwame Kizito (GHA)	21.07.1996	7	(6)	3
Viktor Lundberg	04.03.1991	10	(16)	1
Mohammed Nasiru (GHA)	06.06.1994	8	(4)	1
Gustaf Nilsson	23.05.1997	4	(7)	1
Paulo José de Oliveira „Paulinho" (BRA)	09.04.1986	16	(5)	11

Djurgårdens Idrottsförening Stockholm

Founded: 12.03.1891
Stadium: Tele2 Arena, Stockholm (30,000)
Trainer: Thomas Lagerlöf & — 15.11.1971
Kim Bergstrand — 18.04.1968

Goalkeepers:	DOB	M	(s)	G
Per Bråtveit (NOR)	15.02.1996	10		
Tommi Vaiho	13.09.1988	20		
Defenders:	**DOB**	**M**	**(s)**	**G**
Johan Andersson	15.06.1995	1		
Jonathan Augustinsson	30.03.1996	9	(7)	
Erik Berg	30.12.1988	10	(1)	2
Marcus Danielsson	08.04.1989	27		4
Elliot Käck	18.09.1989	27		
Jacob Larsson	08.04.1994	25		2
Aslak Witry (NOR)	10.03.1996	24	(1)	3
Midfielders:	**DOB**	**M**	**(s)**	**G**
Astrit Ajdarević (ALB)	17.04.1990	16	(10)	
Curtis Edwards (ENG)	12.01.1994	11	(1)	1
Hampus Finndell	06.06.2000		(3)	
Jesper Karlström	21.06.1995	28		2
Oscar Pettersson	01.02.2000		(2)	
Haris Radetinac (SRB)	28.10.1985	15	(9)	1
Jonathan Ring	05.12.1991	28	(1)	7
Besard Šabović	05.01.1998		(1)	
Fredrik Ulvestad (NOR)	17.06.1992	30		5
Kevin Walker	03.08.1989	8	(13)	2
Forwards:	**DOB**	**M**	**(s)**	**G**
Nicklas Bärkroth	19.01.1992	8	(11)	3
Adam Bergmark Wiberg	07.05.1997		(5)	
Mohamed Buya (SLE)	10.01.1995	28	(1)	15
Edward Chilufya (ZAM)	17.09.1999	3	(6)	1
Dženis Kozica	28.04.1993		(8)	
Emir Kujović	22.06.1988	2	(7)	4

Falkenbergs Fotbollsförening

Founded: 03.01.1928
Stadium: Falcon Alkoholfri Arena, Falkenberg (5,565)
Trainer: Hans Eklund — 16.04.1979

Goalkeepers:	DOB	M	(s)	G
Johan Brattberg	28.12.1996	9	(1)	
Hampus Nilsson	17.07.1990	21		
Defenders:	**DOB**	**M**	**(s)**	**G**
Jacob Ericsson	17.09.1993	30		
Carl Johansson	23.05.1994	24		1
Ludvig Johansson	14.05.1998		(1)	
Tibor Joza	10.08.1986	14	(4)	1
Per Karlsson	20.04.1989	17	(4)	
Tobias Karlsson	14.01.1989	26		
Mahmut Özen	01.09.1988	9	(1)	
Midfielders:	**DOB**	**M**	**(s)**	**G**
John Björkengren	09.12.1998	28		2
Christoffer Carlsson	15.01.1989	24	(2)	2
Dominic Chatto Bashir Jamilu (NGA)	07.12.1985		(1)	
John Chibuike (NGA)	10.10.1988	14	(6)	4
Tobias Englund	06.02.1989	11	(7)	
Mergim Laci	02.04.1998		(1)	
Johan Lassagård	22.06.1994		(1)	
Marcus Mathisen (DEN)	27.02.1996	17	(1)	1
Robin Östlind	14.03.1990	13	(7)	3
Anton Wede	20.04.1990	12	(15)	1
Forwards:	**DOB**	**M**	**(s)**	**G**
Nsima Peter (NGA)	28.12.1988	14	(9)	4
Kirill Pogrebnyak (RUS)	27.06.1992	14	(5)	2
Karl Söderström	26.10.1985	28	(1)	1
Edi Sylisufaj	08.03.1999	5	(14)	1

Gymnastik- och Idrottsföreningen Sundsvall

Founded: 25.08.1903
Stadium: Idrottsparken, Sundsvall (7,700)
Trainer: Joel Cedergren — 22.07.1974
[02.09.2019] Tony Gustavsson — 14.08.1973

Goalkeepers:	DOB	M	(s)	G
William Eskelinen	03.09.1996	15		
David Mitov Nilsson	12.01.1991	11		
Lloyd Saxton (ENG)	18.04.1990	4		
Defenders:	**DOB**	**M**	**(s)**	**G**
Eric Björkander	11.06.1996	16	(3)	1
Alexander Blomqvist	03.08.1994	20	(2)	
Carlos Moros Gracia (ESP)	15.04.1993	28		2
Pa Konaté	25.04.1994	22	(3)	1
David Myrestam	04.04.1987	10	(2)	
Pol Moreno Sánchez (ESP)	09.05.1994	13	(11)	
Dennis Oscar Olsson	03.10.1994	4	(3)	
Jonathan Tamimi-Syberg (JOR)	12.10.1994	29		
Midfielders:	**DOB**	**M**	**(s)**	**G**
Oliver Berg (NOR)	28.08.1993	17	(6)	1
Johan Lars Blomberg	14.06.1987	11		3
Jesper Carström	18.05.2002		(1)	
Juan José Ciércoles Sagra (ESP)	27.05.1988	26		
Pol Roigé Rodríguez (ESP)	28.01.1994	7	(5)	1
David Batanero Puigbó (ESP)	27.09.1988	26	(2)	2
Tobias Eriksson	19.03.1985	10	(8)	4
Albin Palmlöv	17.12.2001	1	(1)	
Maic Sema	02.12.1988	16		2
Forwards:	**DOB**	**M**	**(s)**	**G**
Omar Eddahri	30.08.1990	6	(7)	3
Linus Hallenius	01.04.1989	13		6
David Haro Iniesta (ESP)	17.07.1990		(7)	1
Marc Mas Costa (ESP)	01.06.1990	6	(3)	
Chidi Dauda Omeje (NGA)	05.05.1990		(4)	
Peter Wilson	09.10.1996	19	(8)	4

Hammarby Idrottsförening Fotbollförening Stockholm

Founded: 07.03.1897
Stadium: Tele2 Arena, Stockholm (30,000)
Trainer: Stefan Billborn — 15.11.1972

Goalkeepers:	DOB	M	(s)	G
Davor Blažević	07.02.1993	12	(1)	
Gianluca Curci (ITA)	12.07.1985	12		
Johan Sellberg-Wiland	24.01.1981	6	(1)	
Defenders:	**DOB**	**M**	**(s)**	**G**
Marcus Degerlund	16.03.1998		(1)	
David Fällman	02.04.1990	17	(1)	1
Mads Fenger (DEN)	10.09.1990	23		1
Jean Carlos de Brito (BRA)	09.06.1995	1	(2)	
Odilon Kossounou (CIV)	04.01.2001	4	(5)	
Richard Göran Emil Magyar	03.05.1991	12	(2)	2
Simon Sandberg	25.03.1994	27	(1)	
Mats Solheim (NOR)	03.12.1987	14	(13)	3
Midfielders:	**DOB**	**M**	**(s)**	**G**
Jeppe Andersen (DEN)	06.12.1992	26		2
Leo Bengtsson	26.05.1998		(6)	
Darijan Bojanić	28.12.1994	27	(2)	4
Alexander Kačaniklić	13.08.1991	21	(4)	10
Serge-Junior Martinsson Ngouali (GAB)	23.01.1992	3	(4)	1
Vladimir Rodić (MNE)	07.09.1993	6	(15)	6
Aimar Sher	20.12.2002		(1)	
Dennis Widgren	28.03.1994	25		
Forwards:	**DOB**	**M**	**(s)**	**G**
Loue Bayere Junior (CIV)	14.01.2001		(1)	
Nikola Đurđić (SRB)	01.04.1986	27		13
Aron Jóhannsson (USA)	10.11.1990	4	(6)	
Imad Khalili (PLE)	03.04.1987	17	(6)	8
Viðar Kjartansson (ISL)	11.03.1990	15		7
Tim Söderström	04.01.1994	3	(15)	
Muamer Tanković	22.02.1995	28		14

Helsingborgs Idrottsförening

Founded: 04.06.1907
Stadium: Olympiastadion, Helsingborg (16,500)
Trainer: Per-Ola Ljung — 07.11.1967
[30.08.2019] Henrik Edward Larsson — 20.09.1971
[02.09.2019] Alexander Tengryd — 29.01.1986
[03.09.2019] Olof Mellberg — 03.09.1977

Goalkeepers:	DOB	M	(s)	G
Kalle Joelsson	21.03.1998	15		
Anders Rosenkrantz Lindegaard (DEN)	13.04.1984	15		
Defenders:	DOB	M	(s)	G
Adam Eriksson	13.07.1990	28		
Andreas Granqvist	16.04.1985	22		
Markus Holgersson	12.04.1985	30		1
Fredrik Liverstam	04.03.1988	16	(1)	1
Anders Randrup (DEN)	16.07.1988	18	(4)	
Carl Thulin	05.07.1999	1	(1)	
Charlie Weberg	22.05.1998	10		
Midfielders:	DOB	M	(s)	G
Mohammed Abubakari (GHA)	15.02.1986	25		1
Ibrahim Bancé (BFA)	15.01.2001	1	(5)	
Kundai Benyu (ENG)	12.12.1997	2	(8)	1
Alexander Farnerud	01.05.1984	16	(3)	2
Armin Gigović	06.04.2002	10	(4)	
Daníel Hafsteinsson (ISL)	12.11.1999	1	(5)	
Andreas Landgren	17.03.1989	14	(1)	1
Tobias Pilegaard Mikkelsen (DEN)	18.09.1986	3	(5)	2
Johan Persson	20.06.1984	3	(11)	
Ian Pettersson	21.07.2002		(1)	
Filip Sjöberg	12.04.2000	2	(8)	
Forwards:	DOB	M	(s)	G
Andri Bjarnason (ISL)	12.11.1990	6	(2)	3
David Boysen (DEN)	30.04.1991	3	(7)	1
Salisu Abdullahi Gero (NGA)	10.10.1993	11	(2)	3
Rasmus Jönsson	27.01.1990	13		4
Tashreeq Matthews (RSA)	12.09.2000		(2)	
Noel Mbo (ENG)	14.03.1999		(1)	
Mamudo Moro (GHA)	07.03.1995	23	(1)	1
Max Svensson	19.06.1998	26	(4)	7
Francisco Wanderson do Carmo Carneiro (BRA)	18.02.1986	16	(4)	

Idrottsföreningen Elfsborg Borås

Founded: 26.06.1904 (*as Borås Fotbollslag*)
Stadium: Borås Arena, Borås (16,899)
Trainer: Bo Jimmy Thelin — 14.03.1978

Goalkeepers:	DOB	M	(s)	G
Tim Rönning	15.02.1999	8		
Kevin Stuhr-Ellegaard (DEN)	23.05.1983	22		
Defenders:	DOB	M	(s)	G
Alejandro Fernández Portillo (ESP)	06.11.1992	9		1
Stian Gregersen (NOR)	17.05.1995	26		1
Gustav Henriksson	03.02.1998	10	(3)	
Frederik Holst (DEN)	24.09.1994	26		1
Jon Jönsson	08.07.1983	2	(4)	
Rami Kaib	08.05.1997	8	(1)	1
Jesper Manns	05.08.1995	1		
Joakim Nilsson	06.02.1994	10		
Joseph Stanley Okumu (KEN)	26.05.1997	3		
Simon Strand	25.05.1993	25		1
Midfielders:	DOB	M	(s)	G
Rasmus Alm	17.08.1995	7	(2)	2
Alex James Dyer (MSR)	11.06.1990		(2)	
Robert Gojani	19.10.1992	22		
Samuel Holmén	28.06.1984	20	(5)	2
Stefan Ishizaki	15.05.1982	9	(12)	2
Jesper Karlsson	25.07.1998	15	(10)	8
Jonathan Levi	23.01.1996	17	(4)	5
Simon Lundevall	23.09.1988	6	(15)	1
Sivert Heltne Nilsen (NOR)	02.10.1991	10		1
Simon Olsson	14.09.1997	26		2
Forwards:	DOB	M	(s)	G
Paweł Cibicki	09.01.1994	14		5
Per Frick	14.04.1992	16	(4)	6
Deniz Hümmet	13.09.1996	9	(15)	3
Kevin Kabran	22.11.1993	7	(4)	
Marokhy Ndione	04.11.1999	2	(6)	1

Idrottsföreningen Kamraterna Göteborg

Founded: 04.10.1904
Stadium: Gamla Ullevi Stadion, Göteborg (18,600)
Trainer: Poya Asbaghi — 17.07.1985

Goalkeepers:	DOB	M	(s)	G
Tom Amos	06.02.1998		(1)	
Giannis Anestis (GRE)	09.03.1991	30		
Defenders:	DOB	M	(s)	G
André Calisir (ARM)	13.06.1990	27		2
Kristopher Da Graca	16.01.1998	16	(6)	
Edvin Dahlqvist	14.06.1999		(1)	
Emil Holm	13.05.2000	2	(9)	
Samuel Ohlsson	13.05.2001		(1)	
Sebastian Ohlsson	26.05.1993	14	(2)	1
Carl Starfelt	01.06.1995	14		1
Victor Wernersson	06.07.1995	29		
Rasmus Wikström	18.03.2001	1	(1)	
Midfielders:	DOB	M	(s)	G
Sargon Abraham	07.02.1991	7	(11)	1
Amin Affane	21.01.1994	1	(7)	
Noah Alexandersson	30.09.2001	1	(2)	
Sebastian Eriksson	31.01.1989	15	(1)	2
August Erlingmark	22.04.1998	25	(2)	
Giorgi Kharaishvili (GEO)	29.07.1996	28		7
Tobias Sana	11.07.1989	11	(1)	
Adil Titi	20.08.1999		(8)	
Nzuzi Bundebele Toko (COD)	20.12.1990	13	(4)	
Lasse Vibe (DEN)	22.02.1987	10	(10)	5
Alhassan Yusuf (NGA)	18.07.2000	24	(2)	2
Forwards:	DOB	M	(s)	G
Hosam Aiesh	14.04.1995	9	(1)	1
Junes Barny	04.11.1989	5	(4)	
Patrik Karlsson-Lagemyr	18.12.1996	13		4
Benjamin Nygren	08.07.2001	12		4
Måns Saebbö	21.08.2000		(1)	1
Robin Söder	01.04.1991	23	(4)	14

Idrottsföreningen Kamraterna Norrköping

Founded: 29.05.1897
Stadium: Nya Parken, Norrköping (15,734)
Trainer: Jens Gustafsson — 15.10.1978

Goalkeepers:	DOB	M	(s)	G
Isak Pettersson	06.06.1997	30		
Defenders:	DOB	M	(s)	G
Kevin Javier Álvarez Hernández (HON)	03.08.1996		(1)	
Egzon Binaku	27.08.1995	3	(3)	
Henrik Castegren	28.03.1996	9	(5)	
Filip Dagerstål	01.02.1997	27		1
Manasse Kusu	22.12.2001		(2)	
Kasper Larsen (DEN)	25.01.1993	21	(1)	1
Rasmus Lauritsen (DEN)	27.02.1996	25	(1)	5
Ian Rey Smith Quirós (CRC)	06.03.1998	14	(3)	
Christopher Rasmus Nilsson Telo	04.11.1989		(1)	
Midfielders:	DOB	M	(s)	G
Pontus Almqvist	10.07.1999		(7)	
Andreas Blomqvist	05.05.1992	8	(5)	1
Alexander Fransson	02.04.1994	28		5
Lars Gerson (LUX)	05.02.1990	26	(2)	4
Sead Hakšabanović	04.05.1999	19	(10)	6
Alexander Jakobsen (EGY)	18.03.1994		(7)	
Ísak Jóhannesson (ISL)	23.03.2003		(1)	
Maic Ndongala Namputu Sema	02.12.1988	1	(4)	
Simon Thern	18.09.1992	18	(4)	2
Guðmundur Þórarinsson (ISL)	15.04.1992	27	(1)	
Forwards:	DOB	M	(s)	G
Karl Holmberg	03.03.1993	10	(15)	4
Jordan Larsson	20.06.1997	15	(1)	11
Christoffer Nyman	05.10.1992	26	(3)	10
Simon Skrabb (FIN)	19.01.1995	23	(5)	4
Johannes Vall	19.10.1992		(3)	

Idrottsklubben Sirius Uppsala

Founded: 1907
Stadium: Studenternas IP, Uppsala (6,300)
Trainer: Henrik Rydström 16.02.1976

Goalkeepers:	DOB	M	(s)	G
John Alvbåge	10.08.1982	7		
Lukas Jonsson	21.10.1992	23		
Defenders:	**DOB**	**M**	**(s)**	**G**
Jesper Arvidsson	01.01.1985	8	(1)	
Tim Björkström	08.01.1991	29		1
Axel Björnström	10.09.1995	17	(8)	1
Kebba Ceesay	14.11.1987	23	(3)	1
Daniel Jarl	13.04.1992	8	(3)	
Karl Larson	28.10.1991	28	(1)	2
André Österholm	17.06.1996		(1)	
Midfielders:	**DOB**	**M**	**(s)**	**G**
Robert Åhman-Persson	26.03.1987	3		
Elias Andersson	31.01.1996	22	(3)	1
Isak Bråholm	24.09.2000	1	(6)	

	DOB	M	(s)	G
Sherko Faiqi	18.07.1999		(2)	
Christer Gustafsson	31.12.1987	15	(6)	4
Philip Haglund	22.03.1987	27	(2)	7
Jonas Lindberg	24.03.1989	12	(7)	2
Okechukwu Henry Offia (NGA)	26.12.1999	7	(1)	
Abdul Razak (CIV)	11.11.1992	2	(7)	1
Mohammed Saeid	24.12.1990	20	(4)	4
Adam Ståhl	08.10.1994	14	(4)	1
Niklas Thor	21.02.1986	26	(2)	1
Stefano Vecchia	23.01.1995		(9)	
Forwards:	**DOB**	**M**	**(s)**	**G**
John Junior Igbarumah (NIG)	13.02.1992	4	(7)	1
Sam Lundholm	01.07.1994	22	(4)	5
Joakim Persson	03.04.2002		(2)	
Ian Sirelius	28.10.1987	12	(5)	

Kalmar Fotbollsförening

Founded: 15.06.1910 (as IF Göta)
Stadium: Guldfågeln Arena, Kalmar (12,000)
Trainer: Magnus Pehrsson 25.05.1976
[01.11.2019] Jens Nilsson 30.07.1972

Goalkeepers:	DOB	M	(s)	G
Lucas Johansson	11.07.1994	30		
Defenders:	**DOB**	**M**	**(s)**	**G**
Viktor Agardius	23.10.1989	26	(1)	1
Chima Akas Uche (NGA)	03.05.1994	6		
Fidan Aliti (KVX)	03.10.1993	27		2
Henrik Löfkvist	05.05.1995	16		1
Jesper Per Manns	05.08.1995	8	(2)	
Emin Nouri (AZE)	22.07.1985	13	(3)	
Midfielders:	**DOB**	**M**	**(s)**	**G**
Samuel Adrian	02.03.1998	4		
Rasmus Elm	17.03.1988	16	(4)	
Viktor Elm	13.11.1985	25		3
Carl Gustafsson	18.03.2000	4	(3)	
Herman Hallberg	22.05.1997	11	(5)	
Alexander Amir Adel Jakobsen (EGY)	18.03.1994	7	(2)	1
Isak Jansson	31.01.2002		(1)	

	DOB	M	(s)	G
Piotr Johansson	28.02.1995	18	(1)	
Rafinha Gimenes da Silva (BRA)	05.08.1993	10	(6)	
Romario Pereira Sipião (BRA)	10.08.1985	27		4
Filip Sachpekidis	03.07.1997	2	(3)	
Forwards:	**DOB**	**M**	**(s)**	**G**
Papa Diouf (SEN)	22.06.1989	8	(4)	2
Adrian Edqvist	20.05.1999		(2)	
Mahmoud Khair Mohammed Dahadha (PLE)	26.06.1993	5	(5)	1
Mostafa El Kabir (MAR)	05.10.1988	5	(3)	
Nils Fröling	20.04.2000	21	(7)	5
Geir André Herrem (NOR)	28.01.1988	5	(2)	
Alexander Ahl Holmström	04.04.1999	5	(7)	
Isak Magnusson	16.06.1998	9	(8)	
Emaxwell Souza de Lima „Maxwell" (BRA)	11.02.1995	7	(7)	
York Rafael	17.03.1999	4	(6)	
Måns Söderqvist	08.02.1993	11	(6)	1

Malmö Fotbollförening

Founded: 24.02.1910
Stadium: Eleda Stadion, Malmö (22,500)
Trainer: Uwe Rösler (GER) 15.11.1968

Goalkeepers:	DOB	M	(s)	G
Johan Dahlin	08.09.1986	29		
Dušan Melichárek (CZE)	29.11.1983	1	(1)	
Defenders:	**DOB**	**M**	**(s)**	**G**
Anel Ahmedhodžić	26.03.1999		(1)	
Felix Olof Allan Nelson Beijmo	31.01.1998	8		1
Rasmus Bengtsson	26.06.1986	21	(2)	1
Franz Brorsson	30.01.1996	5	(4)	
Jonas Hjort Knudsen (DEN)	16.09.1992	9	(2)	
Eric Larsson	15.07.1991	25		
Lasse Nielsen (DEN)	08.01.1988	6	(4)	
Behrang Safari	09.02.1985	13	(3)	
Andreas Vindheim (NOR)	04.08.1995	8	(2)	
Midfielders:	**DOB**	**M**	**(s)**	**G**
Fouad Bachirou (COM)	15.04.1990	20	(4)	

	DOB	M	(s)	G
Anders Christiansen (DEN)	08.06.1990	22	(2)	9
Romain Gall (USA)	31.01.1995	3	(13)	1
Bonke Innocent (NGA)	20.01.1996	11		
Oscar Lewicki	14.07.1992	25	(2)	
Erdal Rakip	13.02.1996	5	(9)	
Søren Rieks (DEN)	07.04.1987	24	(3)	9
Arnór Ingvi Traustason (ISL)	30.04.1993	25	(2)	7
Forwards:	**DOB**	**M**	**(s)**	**G**
Carl Marcus Christer Antonsson	08.05.1991	21	(5)	6
Jo Inge Berget (NOR)	11.09.1990	16	(8)	2
Guillermo Federico Molins Palmeiro	26.09.1988	11	(15)	6
Tim Prica	23.04.2002		(1)	
Nils Markus Rosenberg	27.09.1982	22	(5)	13
Carlos Strandberg	14.04.1996		(1)	

Örebro Sportklubb

Founded: 28.10.1908
Stadium: Behrn Arena, Örebro (12,300)
Trainer: Axel Kjäll 01.06.1981

Goalkeepers:	DOB	M	(s)	G
Oscar Jansson	23.12.1990	30		
Defenders:	**DOB**	**M**	**(s)**	**G**
Hussein Ali	01.03.2002	1	(2)	
Michael Almebäck	04.04.1988	26		
Helmer Andersson	08.09.2001	3	(2)	
Niclas Bergmark	07.01.2002	4	(3)	
Daniel Björkman	21.02.1993	4	(6)	
Daniel Björnkvist	08.01.1989	19	(1)	
Arvid Brorsson	08.05.1999	11	(4)	
Albin Granlund (FIN)	01.09.1989	20	(3)	
Martin Lorentzson	21.07.1984	23	(2)	
Kevin Wright (ENG)	28.12.1995	25	(1)	1
Midfielders:	**DOB**	**M**	**(s)**	**G**
Yaser Safa Qasim Al Qadefaje (IRQ)	10.05.1991	6	(6)	

	DOB	M	(s)	G
Simon Amin	13.11.1997	8	(5)	
Johan Bertilsson	15.02.1988	21	(7)	4
Martin Broberg	24.09.1990	12	(6)	2
Nordin Gerzić	09.11.1983	29		
Johan Mårtensson	16.02.1989	3	(1)	
Filip Rogić	14.06.1993	19	(1)	8
Forwards:	**DOB**	**M**	**(s)**	**G**
Adam Bark	15.02.2000		(1)	
Rodin Deprem	23.05.1998	2	(3)	
Jake Larsson	09.01.1994	25	(2)	8
Agon Mehmeti (ALB)	20.11.1989		(15)	2
Michael Junior Omoh (NGA)	29.08.1991	2	(8)	
Viktor Prodell	29.02.1988	19	(2)	2
Carlos Strandberg	14.04.1996	18	(1)	11

Östersunds Fotbollsklubb

Founded: 31.10.1996
Stadium: Jämtkraft Arena, Östersund (8,466)
Trainer: Ian Burchnall (ENG)   11.02.1983

Goalkeepers:	DOB	M	(s)	G
Aly Keita	08.12.1986	23		
Sixten Mohlin	17.01.1996	7		
Defenders:	**DOB**	**M**	**(s)**	**G**
Eirik Haugan (NOR)	27.08.1997	12		
Thomas Isherwood	28.01.1998	15	(3)	2
Ronald Mukiibi	16.09.1991	8	(3)	
Kalpi Wilfried Ouattara (CIV)	29.12.1998	7		
Tom Pettersson	25.03.1990	22	(1)	1
Noah Sonko Sundberg	06.06.1996	28		1
Isak Ssewankambo	27.02.1996	21	(3)	2
Midfielders:	**DOB**	**M**	**(s)**	**G**
Rewan Amin (IRQ)	08.01.1996	17	(6)	
Henrik Bellman	24.03.1999		(2)	
Charlie Colkett (ENG)	04.09.1996	23	(2)	1
Curtis Edwards (ENG)	12.01.1994	13	(1)	1
Ludvig Fritzson	25.08.1995	4	(10)	

	DOB	M	(s)	G
Jamie Hopcutt (ENG)	23.06.1992	10	(9)	1
Felix Hörberg	19.05.1999	10	(1)	
Simon Kroon	16.06.1993	7	(4)	2
Samuel Laryeal Mensah (GHA)	19.05.1989	16	(3)	
Ravel Ryan Morrison (JAM)	02.02.1993	5	(1)	
Alex Purver (ENG)	01.12.1995	3		
Jerell Sellars (ENG)	28.04.1995	4	(1)	
Tesfaldet Simon Tekie	04.06.1997	10	(2)	1
Marco Weymans (BEL)	09.07.1997	7	(7)	
Forwards:	**DOB**	**M**	**(s)**	**G**
Hosam Aiesh	14.04.1995	13	(1)	3
Alhaji Gero (NGA)	10.10.1993	5	(8)	1
Dino Islamović	17.01.1994	23	(5)	7
Francis Jno-Baptiste (ENG)	08.11.1999	2	(1)	
Jordan Attah Kadiri (NGA)	11.03.2000	6	(4)	3
Nebiyou Sundance Perry (USA)	02.10.1999	2	(4)	
Blair Sebastian Turgott (ENG)	22.05.1994	7	(5)	1

SECOND LEVEL
Superettan 2019

1.	Mjällby AIF Hällevik (*Promoted*)	30	17	6	7	44	-	31	57
2.	Varbergs BoIS (*Promoted*)	30	15	10	5	49	-	27	55
3.	IK Brage Borlänge (*Promotion Play-offs*)	30	16	6	8	54	-	33	54
4.	Jönköpings Södra IF	30	15	7	8	52	-	31	52
5.	Degerfors IF	30	15	6	9	46	-	34	51
6.	Halmstads BK	30	14	4	12	45	-	34	46
7.	Örgryte IS Göteborg	30	12	10	8	43	-	37	46
8.	Dalkurd FF Uppsala	30	13	5	12	43	-	47	44
9.	Norrby IF Borås	30	11	9	10	43	-	43	42
10.	Västerås SK Fotboll	30	8	10	12	41	-	40	34
11.	Trelleborgs FF	30	7	11	12	34	-	47	32
12.	GAIS Göteborg	30	8	8	14	23	-	40	32
13.	Östers IF Växjö (*Relegation Play-offs*)	30	6	11	13	32	-	43	29
14.	IK Frej (*Relegation Play-offs*)	30	7	8	15	35	-	55	29
15.	IF Brommapojkarna (*Relegated*)	30	6	10	14	38	-	49	28
16.	Syrianska FC Söldertälje (*Relegated*)	30	6	7	17	29	-	60	25

Relegation Play-offs (2nd / 3rd Level)

Landskrona BoIS - **Östers IF Växjö**	1-1(1-1)	0-1(0-0)
Umeå FC - IK Frej	1-1(0-0)	2-2(2-2)

INTERNATIONAL MATCHES
(16.07.2019 – 15.07.2020)

05.09.2019	Tórshavn	Faroe Islands - Sweden	0-4(0-4)	(ECQ)
08.09.2019	Stockholm	Sweden - Norway	1-1(0-1)	(ECQ)
12.10.2019	Attard	Malta - Sweden	0-4(0-1)	(ECQ)
15.10.2019	Stockholm	Sweden - Spain	1-1(0-0)	(ECQ)
15.11.2019	Bucureşti	Romania - Sweden	0-2(0-2)	(ECQ)
18.11.2019	Stockholm	Sweden - Faroe Islands	3-0(1-0)	(ECQ)
09.01.2020	Doha	Sweden - Moldova	1-0(1-0)	(F)
12.01.2020	Doha	Sweden - Kosovo	1-0(0-0)	(F)

05.09.2019 FAROE ISLANDS - SWEDEN 0-4(0-4) 16th EC. Qualifiers
Tórsvøllur, Tórshavn; Referee: Tiago Bruno Lopes Martins (Portugal); Attendance: 3,108
SWE: Robin Patrick Olsen, Carl Mikael Lustig (46.Emil Henry Kristoffer Krafth), Victor Jörgen Nilsson Lindelöf, Andreas Granqvist (Cap), Pierre Bengtsson, Mats Kristoffer Olsson, Albin Ekdal (63.Karl Gustav Johan Svensson), Sebastian Bengt Ulf Larsson (73.Jakup Jimmy Durmaz), Robin Kwamina Quaison, Bengt Eric Marcus Berg, Alexander Isak. Trainer: Jan Olof Andersson.
Goals: Alexander Isak (12, 15), Victor Jörgen Nilsson Lindelöf (23), Robin Kwamina Quaison (41).

08.09.2019 SWEDEN - NORWAY 1-1(0-1) 16th EC. Qualifiers
Friends Arena, Stockholm; Referee: Slavko Vinčić (Slovenia); Attendance: 38,372
SWE: Robin Patrick Olsen, Carl Mikael Lustig, Victor Jörgen Nilsson Lindelöf, Andreas Granqvist (Cap), Pierre Bengtsson, Mats Kristoffer Olsson, Albin Ekdal (84.Karl Gustav Johan Svensson), Sebastian Bengt Ulf Larsson, Emil Peter Forsberg, Robin Kwamina Quaison (77.Martin Sebastian Andersson), Alexander Isak (77.Bengt Eric Marcus Berg). Trainer: Jan Olof Andersson.
Goal: Emil Peter Forsberg (60).

12.10.2019 MALTA - SWEDEN 0-4(0-1) 16th EC. Qualifiers
Ta'Qali National Stadium, Attard; Referee: Sergey Ivanov (Russia); Attendance: 10,702
SWE: Robin Patrick Olsen, Carl Mikael Lustig, Marcus Danielsson, Andreas Granqvist (Cap), Pierre Bengtsson, Mats Kristoffer Olsson, Albin Ekdal (63.Karl Gustav Johan Svensson), Sebastian Bengt Ulf Larsson, Emil Peter Forsberg, Robin Kwamina Quaison (71.Alexander Isak), Bengt Eric Marcus Berg (79.Martin Sebastian Andersson). Trainer: Jan Olof Andersson.
Goals: Marcus Danielsson (11), Sebastian Bengt Ulf Larsson (58 penalty), Andrei Agius (66 own goal), Sebastian Bengt Ulf Larsson (71 penalty).

15.10.2019 SWEDEN - SPAIN 1-1(0-0) 16th EC. Qualifiers
Friends Arena, Stockholm; Referee: Clément Turpin (France); Attendance: 49,712
SWE: Robin Patrick Olsen, Carl Mikael Lustig, Victor Jörgen Nilsson Lindelöf, Andreas Granqvist (Cap), Pierre Bengtsson, Mats Kristoffer Olsson, Albin Ekdal (83.Karl Gustav Johan Svensson), Sebastian Bengt Ulf Larsson, Emil Peter Forsberg, Robin Kwamina Quaison (77.Alexander Isak), Bengt Eric Marcus Berg (90+3.Martin Sebastian Andersson). Trainer: Jan Olof Andersson.
Goal: Bengt Eric Marcus Berg (50).

15.11.2019 ROMANIA - SWEDEN 0-2(0-2) 16th EC. Qualifiers
Arena Naţională, Bucureşti; Referee: Daniele Orsato (Italy); Attendance: 49,678
SWE: Robin Patrick Olsen, Carl Mikael Lustig, Victor Jörgen Nilsson Lindelöf, Andreas Granqvist (Cap), Pierre Bengtsson, Mats Kristoffer Olsson, Albin Ekdal, Sebastian Bengt Ulf Larsson (69.Karl Gustav Johan Svensson), Emil Peter Forsberg, Robin Kwamina Quaison, Bengt Eric Marcus Berg (78.Alexander Isak). Trainer: Jan Olof Andersson.
Goals: Bengt Eric Marcus Berg (18), Robin Kwamina Quaison (34).

18.11.2019 SWEDEN - FAROE ISLANDS 3-0(1-0) 16th EC. Qualifiers
Friends Arena, Stockholm; Referee: Matej Jug (Slovenia); Attendance: 19,500
SWE: Kristoffer Nordfeldt, Marcus Danielsson, Pontus Sven Gustav Jansson (Cap), Filip Viktor Helander, Riccardo Gagliolo, Mats Kristoffer Olsson, Mattias Olof Svanberg, Ken Nlata Sema (65.Dejan Kuluševski), Muamer Tanković, Martin Sebastian Andersson (65.John Olof Alberto Guidetti), Alexander Isak. Trainer: Jan Olof Andersson.
Goals: Martin Sebastian Andersson (29), Mattias Olof Svanberg (72), John Guidetti (80).

09.01.2020 SWEDEN - MOLDOVA 1-0(1-0) Friendly International
"Hamad bin Khalifa" Stadium, Doha; Referee: Saoud Ali Al Athbah (Qatar); Attendance: 100
SWE: Pontus Jacob Ragne Dahlberg, Eric Joel Andersson, Marcus Danielsson (Cap), Anel Ahmedhodžić, Carl Adam Andersson, Karl Gustav Vilhelm Berggren, Darijan Bojanić, Daleho Irandust (78.Alexander Kačaniklić), Dino Islamović, Karl Jesper Karlsson (78.Muamer Tanković), Jordan Larsson (75.Simon Fredrik Hedlund). Trainer: Jan Olof Andersson.
Goal: Jordan Larsson (32).

12.01.2020 SWEDEN - KOSOVO 1-0(0-0) Friendly International
"Hamad bin Khalifa" Stadium, Doha; Referee: Mohammad Ahmed Al Shammari (Qatar); Attendance: 75
SWE: Peter Anders Abrahamsson (46.Carl Isak Emanuel Pettersson), Simon Christer Sandberg, Jacob Hugo Une Larsson, Kristopher Santos Da Graca (65.Marcus Danielsson), Carl Adam Andersson (46.Eric Joel Andersson), Jan August Erlingmark (64.Darijan Bojanić), Anton Janos Jönsson Salétros, Alexander Kačaniklić, Muamer Tanković (73.Karl Jesper Karlsson), Simon Fredrik Hedlund, Robin Mikael Söder (Cap). Trainer: Jan Olof Andersson.
Goal: Simon Fredrik Hedlund (75).

NATIONAL TEAM PLAYERS
(16.07.2019 – 15.07.2020)

Name	DOB	Caps	Goals	2019/2020:	Club
Goalkeepers					
Peter Anders ABRAHAMSSON	18.07.1988	2	0	2020:	BK Häcken Göteborg
Pontus Jacob Ragne DAHLBERG	21.01.1999	2	0	2020:	Watford FC (ENG)
Kristoffer NORDFELDT	23.06.1989	11	0	2019:	Swansea City AFC (WAL)
Robin Patrick OLSEN	08.01.1990	36	0	2019:	Cagliari Calcio (ITA)
Carl Isak Emanuel PETTERSSON	06.06.1997	2	0	2020:	IFK Norrköping
Defenders					
Anel AHMEDHODŽIĆ	26.03.1999	1	0	2020:	Malmö FF
Carl Adam ANDERSSON	11.11.1996	4	0	2020:	BK Häcken Göteborg
Eric Joel ANDERSSON	11.11.1996	5	0	2020:	FC Midtjylland Herning (DEN)
Pierre BENGTSSON	12.04.1988	29	0	2019:	FC København (DEN)
Kristopher Santos DA GRACA	16.01.1998	1	0	2020:	IFK Göteborg
Marcus DANIELSSON	08.04.1989	4	1	2019/2020:	Djurgårdens IF Stockholm
Riccardo GAGLIOLO	28.04.1990	1	0	2019:	Parma Calcio 1913 (ITA)
Andreas GRANQVIST	16.04.1985	88	9	2019:	Helsingborgs IF
Filip Viktor HELANDER	22.04.1993	11	0	2019:	Rangers FC Glasgow (SCO)
Pontus Sven Gustav JANSSON	13.02.1991	23	0	2018/2019:	Brentford FC London (ENG)
Emil Henry Kristoffer KRAFTH	02.08.1994	21	0	2018/2019:	Newcastle United FC (ENG)
Sebastian Bengt Ulf LARSSON	06.06.1985	118	8	2019:	AIK Stockholm
Victor Jörgen Nilsson LINDELÖF	17.07.1994	33	3	2019:	Manchester United FC (ENG)
Carl Mikael LUSTIG	13.12.1986	82	6	2019:	KAA Gent (BEL)
Simon Christer SANDBERG	25.03.1994	1	0	2020:	Hammarby IF Stockholm
Ken Nlata SEMA	30.09.1993	7	0	2018:	Udinese Calcio (ITA)
Jacob Hugo UNE LARSSON	08.04.1994	3	0	2020:	Djurgårdens IF Stockholm
Midfielders					
Karl Gustav Vilhelm BERGGREN	07.09.1997	1	0	2020:	BK Häcken Göteborg
Darijan BOJANIĆ	28.12.1994	2	0	2020:	Hammarby IF Stockholm
Jakup Jimmy DURMAZ	22.03.1989	49	3	2018:	Galatasaray SK İstanbul (TUR)
Albin EKDAL	28.07.1989	50	0	2019:	UC Sampdoria Genova (ITA)
Jan August ERLINGMARK	22.04.1998	1	0	2020:	IFK Göteborg
Emil Peter FORSBERG	23.10.1991	49	8	2019:	RasenBallsport Leipzig (GER)
Daleho IRANDUST	04.06.1998	3	0	2020:	BK Häcken Göteborg
Alexander ISAK	21.09.1999	12	2	2019:	Real Sociedad de Fútbol San Sebastián (ESP)
Alexander KAČANIKLIĆ	13.08.1991	21	3	2020:	Hammarby IF Stockholm
Karl Jesper KARLSSON	25.07.1998	2	0	2020:	IF Elfsborg Borås
Dejan KULUŠEVSKI	25.04.2000	1	0	2019:	Parma Calcio 1913 (ITA)
Mats Kristoffer OLSSON	30.06.1995	15	0	2019:	FK Krasnodar (RUS)
Anton Janos Jönsson SALÉTROS	12.04.1996	1	0	2020:	FK Rostov (RUS)
Mattias Olof SVANBERG	05.01.1999	1	1	2019:	Bologna FC 1909 (ITA)
Karl Gustav Johan SVENSSON	07.02.1987	27	0	2019:	Seattle Sounders (USA)
Muamer TANKOVIĆ	22.02.1995	5	0	2019/2020:	Hammarby IF Stockholm
Forwards					
Martin Sebastian ANDERSSON	15.07.1991	9	3	2019:	1. FC Union Berlin (GER)
Bengt Eric Marcus BERG	17.08.1986	76	21	2019:	FK Krasnodar (RUS)
John Olof Alberto GUIDETTI	15.04.1992	28	3	2019:	Deportivo Alavés Vitoria-Gasteiz (ESP)
Simon Fredrik HEDLUND	11.03.1993	2	1	2020:	Brøndby IF (DEN)
Dino ISLAMOVIĆ	17.01.1994	1	0	2020:	Rosenborg BK Trondheim (NOR)
Carl Henrik Jordan LARSSON	20.06.1997	3	1	2020:	FK Spartak Moskva (RUS)
Robin Kwamina QUAISON	09.10.1993	15	7	2019:	1. FSV Mainz 05 (GER)
Robin Mikael SÖDER	01.04.1991	1	0	2020:	IFK Göteborg
National team coach					
Jan Olof "Janne" ANDERSSON [from 23.06.2016]	29.09.1962				48 M; 24 W; 12 D; 12 L; 82-40

SWITZERLAND

The Country:
Schweizerische Eidgenossenschaft (Swiss Confederation)
Capital: Bern
Surface: 41,285 km²
Inhabitants: 8,570,146 [2019]
Time: UTC+1

The FA:
Schweizerischer Fussballverband
Worbstrasse 48, Postfach 3000, Bern 15
Tel: +41 31 950 8111
Founded: 07.04.1895
Member of FIFA since: 1904
Member of UEFA since: 1954
Website: www.football.ch

NATIONAL TEAM RECORDS

RECORDS

First international match:	12.02.1905, Paris:	France – Switzerland 1-0
Most international caps:	Heinz Hermann	- 118 caps (1978-1991)
Most international goals:	Alexander Frei	- 42 goals / 84 caps (2001-2011)

UEFA EUROPEAN CHAMPIONSHIP

1960	Did not enter
1964	Qualifiers
1968	Qualifiers
1972	Qualifiers
1976	Qualifiers
1980	Qualifiers
1984	Qualifiers
1988	Qualifiers
1992	Qualifiers
1996	Final Tournament (Group Stage)
2000	Qualifiers
2004	Final Tournament (Group Stage)
2008	Final Tournament (Group Stage)
2012	Qualifiers
2016	Final Tournament (2nd Round of 16)
2020	*Final Tournament (Qualified)*

FIFA WORLD CUP

1930	Did not enter
1934	Final Tournament (Quarter-Finals)
1938	Final Tournament (Quarter-Finals)
1950	Final Tournament (Group Stage)
1954	Final Tournament (Quarter-Finals)
1958	Qualifiers
1962	Final Tournament (Group Stage)
1966	Final Tournament (Group Stage)
1970	Qualifiers
1974	Qualifiers
1978	Qualifiers
1982	Qualifiers
1986	Qualifiers
1990	Qualifiers
1994	Final Tournament (2nd Round of 16)
1998	Qualifiers
2002	Qualifiers
2006	Final Tournament (2nd Round of 16)
2010	Final Tournament (Group Stage)
2014	Final Tournament (2nd Round of 16)
2018	Final Tournament (2nd Round of 16)

OLYMPIC TOURNAMENTS

1908	-
1912	-
1920	-
1924	Runners-up
1928	1/8 - Finals
1936	Did not enter
1948	Did not enter
1952	Did not enter
1956	Did not enter
1960	Qualifiers
1964	Qualifiers
1968	Qualifiers
1972	Qualifiers
1976	Did not enter
1980	Did not enter
1984	Did not enter
1988	Qualifiers
1992	Qualifiers
1996	Qualifiers
2000	Qualifiers
2004	Qualifiers
2008	Qualifiers
2012	Group Stage
2016	Qualifiers

UEFA NATIONS LEAGUE

2018/2019 – League A; Final Tournament – 4th Place

FIFA CONFEDERATIONS CUP 1992-2017

None

SWISS CLUB HONOURS IN EUROPEAN CLUB COMPETITIONS:

European Champion Clubs' Cup (1956-1992) / UEFA Champions League (1993-2020)
None

Fairs Cup (1858-1971) / UEFA Cup (1972-2009) / UEFA Europa League (2010-2020)
None

UEFA Super Cup (1972-2019)
None

*European Cup Winners' Cup 1961-1999**
None

*defunct competition

NATIONAL COMPETITIONS
TABLE OF HONOURS

	CHAMPIONS	CUP WINNERS	BEST GOALSCORERS	
1898/1899	Anglo-American Club FC Zürich	-	-	
1899/1900	Grasshopper Club Zürich	-	-	
1900/1901	Grasshopper Club Zürich	-	-	
1901/1902	FC Zürich	-	-	
1902/1903	BSC Young Boys Bern	-	-	
1903/1904	FC St. Gallen	-	-	
1904/1905	Grasshopper Club Zürich	-	-	
1905/1906	FC Winterthur	-	-	
1906/1907	Servette FC Genève	-	-	
1907/1908	FC Winterthur	-	-	
1908/1909	BSC Young Boys Bern	-	-	
1909/1910	BSC Young Boys Bern	-	-	
1910/1911	BSC Young Boys Bern	-	-	
1911/1912	FC Aarau	-	-	
1912/1913	Montriond Lausanne	-	-	
1913/1914	FC Aarau	-	-	
1914/1915	SC Brühl St. Gallen	-	-	
1915/1916	Cantonal Neuchâtel	-	-	
1916/1917	FC Winterthur	-	-	
1917/1918	Servette FC Genève	-	-	
1918/1919	Étoile La Chaux-de-Fonds	-	-	
1919/1920	BSC Young Boys Bern	-	-	
1920/1921	Grasshopper Club Zürich	-	-	
1921/1922	Servette FC Genève	-	-	
1922/1923	*Title not awarded*	-	-	
1923/1924	FC Zürich	-	-	
1924/1925	Servette FC Genève	-	-	
1925/1926	Servette FC Genève	Grasshopper Club Zürich	-	
1926/1927	Grasshopper Club Zürich	Grasshopper Club Zürich	-	
1927/1928	Grasshopper Club Zürich	Servette FC Genève FC	-	
1928/1929	BSC Young Boys Bern	Urania Genève Sport	-	
1929/1930	Servette FC Genève	BSC Young Boys Bern	-	
1930/1931	Grasshopper Club Zürich	FC Lugano	-	
1931/1932	FC Lausanne-Sport	Grasshopper Club Zürich	-	
1932/1933	Servette FC Genève	FC Basel	-	
1933/1934	Servette FC Genève	Grasshopper Club Zürich	Leopold Kielholz (Servette FC Genève)	40
1934/1935	FC Lausanne-Sport	FC Lausanne-Sport	Engelbert Bösch (AUT, FC Bern)	27
1935/1936	FC Lausanne-Sport	Young Fellows FC Zürich	Willy Jäggi (FC Lausanne-Sport)	27
1936/1937	Grasshopper Club Zürich	Grasshopper Club Zürich	Alessandro Frigerio Payán (Young Fellows FC Zürich)	23
1937/1938	FC Lugano	Grasshopper Club Zürich	Numa Monnard (FC Basel)	20
1938/1939	Grasshopper Club Zürich	FC Lausanne-Sport	Josef Artimovics (AUT, FC Grenchen)	15
1939/1940	Servette FC Genève	Grasshopper Club Zürich	Georges Aeby (Servette FC Genève)	22
1940/1941	FC Lugano	Grasshopper Club Zürich	Alessandro Frigerio Payán (FC Lugano)	26
1941/1942	Grasshopper Club Zürich	Grasshopper Club Zürich	Alessandro Frigerio Payán (FC Lugano)	23
1942/1943	Grasshopper Club Zürich	Grasshopper Club Zürich	Lauro Amadò (Grasshopper Club Zürich)	31
1943/1944	FC Lausanne-Sport	FC Lausanne-Sport	Erich Andres (Young Fellows FC Zürich)	23
1944/1945	Grasshopper Club Zürich	BSC Young Boys Bern	Hans-Peter Friedländer (Grasshopper Club Zürich)	26
1945/1946	Servette FC Genève	Grasshopper Club Zürich	Hans-Peter Friedländer (Grasshopper Club Zürich)	25
1946/1947	FC Biel-Bienne	FC Basel	Lauro Amadò (Grasshopper Club Zürich) Hans Blaser (BSC Young Boys Bern)	19
1947/1948	AC Bellinzona	FC La Chaux-de-Fonds	Josef Righetti (FC Grenchen)	26
1948/1949	FC Lugano	Servette FC Genève FC	Jacques Fatton (Servette FC Genève)	21
1949/1950	Servette FC Genève	FC Lausanne-Sport	Jacques Fatton (Servette FC Genève)	32
1950/1951	FC Lausanne-Sport	FC La Chaux-de-Fonds	Hans-Peter Friedländer (FC Lausanne-Sport)	23
1951/1952	Grasshopper Club Zürich	Grasshopper Club Zürich	Josef Hügi (FC Basel)	24
1952/1953	FC Basel	BSC Young Boys Bern	Josef Hügi (FC Basel) Eugen Meier (BSC Young Boys Bern)	32
1953/1954	FC La Chaux-de-Fonds	FC La Chaux-de-Fonds	Josef Hügi (FC Basel)	29
1954/1955	FC La Chaux-de-Fonds	FC La Chaux-de-Fonds	Marcel Mauron (FC La Chaux-de-Fonds)	30
1955/1956	Grasshopper Club Zürich	Grasshopper Club Zürich	Branislav Vukosavljević (YUG, Grasshopper Club Zürich)	33
1956/1957	BSC Young Boys Bern	FC La Chaux-de-Fonds	Adrien Kauer (FC La Chaux-de-Fonds)	29
1957/1958	BSC Young Boys Bern	BSC Young Boys Bern	Ernst Wechselberger (GER, BSC Young Boys Bern)	22
1958/1959	BSC Young Boys Bern	FC Grenchen	Eugen Meier (BSC Young Boys Bern)	24
1959/1960	BSC Young Boys Bern	FC Luzern	Willy Schneider (BSC Young Boys Bern)	25
1960/1961	Servette FC Genève	FC La Chaux-de-Fonds	Giuliano Robbiani (Grasshopper Club Zürich)	27
1961/1962	Servette FC Genève	FC Lausanne-Sport	Jacques Fatton (Servette FC Genève)	25
1962/1963	FC Zürich	FC Basel	Peter von Burg (FC Zürich)	24
1963/1964	FC La Chaux-de-Fonds	FC Lausanne-Sport	Michel Desbiolles (Servette FC Genève)	23

1964/1965	FC Lausanne-Sport	FC Sion	Rolf Blättler (Grasshopper Club Zürich)	
			Pierre Kerkhoffs (NED, FC Lausanne-Sport)	19
1965/1966	FC Zürich	FC Zürich	Rolf Blättler (Grasshopper Club Zürich)	28
1966/1967	FC Basel	FC Basel	Rolf Blättler (Grasshopper Club Zürich)	24
1967/1968	FC Zürich	FC Lugano	Friedrich Künzli (FC Zürich)	28
1968/1969	FC Basel	FC St. Gallen	Hans-Otto Peters (GER, FC Biel-Bienne)	24
1969/1970	FC Basel	FC Zürich	Friedrich Künzli (FC Zürich)	19
1970/1971	Grasshopper Club Zürich	Servette FC Genève FC	Walter Müller (BSC Young Boys Bern)	19
1971/1972	FC Basel	FC Zürich	Herbert Dimmeler (FC Winterthur)	
			Bernd Dörfel (GER, Servette FC Genève)	17
1972/1973	FC Basel	FC Zürich	Ottmar Hitzfeld (FC Basel)	
			Jan-Olof Grahn (FC Lausanne-Sport)	18
1973/1974	FC Zürich	FC Sion	Daniel Jeandupeux (FC Zürich)	22
1974/1975	FC Zürich	FC Basel	Ilija Katić (FC Zürich)	23
1975/1976	FC Zürich	FC Zürich	Peter Risi (FC Zürich)	33
1976/1977	FC Basel	BSC Young Boys Bern	Franco Cucinotta (ITA, FC Zürich)	28
1977/1978	Grasshopper Club Zürich	Servette FC Genève FC	Friedrich Künzli (FC Lausanne-Sport)	21
1978/1979	Servette FC Genève	Servette FC Genève FC	Peter Risi (FC Zürich)	16
1979/1980	FC Basel	FC Sion	Claudio Sulser (Grasshopper Club Zürich)	25
1980/1981	FC Zürich	FC Lausanne-Sport	Peter Risi (FC Luzern)	18
1981/1982	Grasshopper Club Zürich	FC Sion	Claudio Sulser (Grasshopper Club Zürich)	23
1982/1983	Grasshopper Club Zürich	Grasshopper Club Zürich	Jean-Paul Brigger (Servette FC Genève)	23
1983/1984	Grasshopper Club Zürich	Servette FC Genève FC	Georges Bregy (FC Sion)	21
1984/1985	Servette FC Genève	FC Aarau	Dominique Cina (FC Sion)	24
1985/1986	BSC Young Boys Bern	FC Sion	Steen Thychosen (DEN, FC Lausanne-Sport)	21
1986/1987	Neuchâtel Xamax FCS	BSC Young Boys Bern	John Hartmann Eriksen (DEN, Servette FC Genève)	28
1987/1988	Neuchâtel Xamax FCS	Grasshopper Club Zürich	John Hartmann Eriksen (DEN, Servette FC Genève)	36
1988/1989	FC Luzern	Grasshopper Club Zürich	Karl-Heinz Rummenigge	
			(GER, Servette FC Genève)	24
1989/1990	Grasshopper Club Zürich	Grasshopper Club Zürich	Iván Luis Zamorano Zamora (CHI, FC St. Gallen)	23
1990/1991	Grasshopper Club Zürich	FC Sion	Dario Zuffi (BSC Young Boys Bern)	17
1991/1992	FC Sion	FC Luzern	Miklos Jon Molnar (DEN, Servette FC Genève)	18
1992/1993	FC Aarau	FC Lugano	„Sonny" Anderson da Silva	
			(BRA, Servette FC Genève)	20
1993/1994	Servette FC Genève	Grasshopper Club Zürich	Élber de Souza (BRA, Grasshopper Club Zürich)	21
1994/1995	Grasshopper Club Zürich	FC Sion	Petar Aleksandrov (BUL, Neuchâtel Xamax FCS)	24
1995/1996	Grasshopper Club Zürich	FC Sion	Petar Aleksandrov (BUL, FC Luzern)	
			Viorel Dinu Moldovan	
			(ROU, Neuchâtel Xamax FCS)	19
1996/1997	FC Sion	FC Sion	Viorel Dinu Moldovan (ROU, Grasshopper Club Zürich)	27
1997/1998	Grasshopper Club Zürich	FC Lausanne-Sport	Shabani Christophe Nonda (COD, FC Zürich)	24
1998/1999	Servette FC Genève	FC Lausanne-Sport	Alexandre Rey (Servette FC Genève)	19
1999/2000	FC St. Gallen	FC Zürich	Charles Amoah (GHA, FC St. Gallen)	25
2000/2001	Grasshopper Club Zürich	Servette FC Genève FC	Stéphane Chapuisat (Grasshopper Club Zürich)	
			Christian Eduardo Giménez (ARG, FC Lugano)	21
2001/2002	FC Basel	FC Basel	Christian Eduardo Giménez (ARG, FC Lugano)	
			Richard Darío Núñez Pereyra	
			(URU, Grasshopper Club Zürich)	28
2002/2003	Grasshopper Club Zürich	FC Basel	Richard Darío Núñez Pereyra	
			(URU, Grasshopper Club Zürich)	27
2003/2004	FC Basel	FC Will 1900	Stéphane Chapuisat (BSC Young Boys Bern)	23
2004/2005	FC Basel	FC Zürich	Christian Eduardo Giménez (ARG, FC Basel)	27
2005/2006	FC Zürich	FC Sion	Alhassane Keita Otchico (GUI, FC Zürich)	20
2006/2007	FC Zürich	FC Basel	Mladen Petrić (CRO, FC Basel)	19
2007/2008	FC Basel	FC Basel	Hakan Yakin (BSC Young Boys Bern)	24
2008/2009	FC Zürich	FC Sion	Seydou Doumbia (CIV, BSC Young Boys Bern)	20
2009/2010	FC Basel	FC Basel	Seydou Doumbia (CIV, BSC Young Boys Bern)	30
2010/2011	FC Basel	FC Sion	Alexander Frei (FC Basel)	27
2011/2012	FC Basel	FC Basel	Alexander Frei (FC Basel)	24
2012/2013	FC Basel	Grasshopper Club Zürich	Ezequiel Óscar Scarione (ARG, FC St. Gallen)	21
2013/2014	FC Basel	FC Zürich	Shkëlzen Taib Gashi	
			(ALB, Grasshopper Club Zürich)	19
2014/2015	FC Basel	FC Sion	Shkëlzen Taib Gashi (ALB, FC Basel)	21
2015/2016	FC Basel	FC Zürich	Moanes Daobur (ISR, Grasshopper Club Zürich)	19
2016/2017	FC Basel	FC Basel	Seydou Doumbia (CIV, FC Basel)	20
2017/2018	BSC Young Boys Bern	FC Zürich	Albian Afrim Ajeti (FC Basel)	17
2018/2019	BSC Young Boys Bern	FC Basel	Guillaume Hoarau (FRA, BSC Young Boys Bern)	24
2019/2020	BSC Young Boys Bern	BSC Young Boys Bern	Jean-Pierre Nsamé (CMR, BSC Young Boys Bern)	32

Name changements of first level: Serie A (1898–1931), National League (1931–1944), National League A (1944–2003), Super League (since 2003).

NATIONAL CHAMPIONSHIP
Swiss Super League 2019/2020
(19.07.2019 – 03.08.2020)

Results

Round 1 [19-21.07.2019]
FC Sion - FC Basel 1-4(1-1)
FC Thun - Neuchâtel Xamax 2-2(0-1)
FC St.Gallen - FC Luzern 0-2(0-0)
Young Boys - Servette Genève 1-1(1-1)
FC Zürich - FC Lugano 0-4(0-3)

Round 2 [27-28.07.2019]
FC Basel - FC St.Gallen 1-2(0-1)
Servette Genève - FC Sion 0-0
FC Lugano - FC Thun 0-0
FC Luzern - FC Zürich 0-0
Neuchâtel Xamax - Young Boys 0-1(0-0)

Round 3 [03-04.08.2019]
FC Sion - FC Zürich 3-1(1-1)
FC Thun - FC Basel 2-3(1-1)
Neuchâtel Xamax - FC St.Gallen 1-1(0-1)
Servette Genève - FC Luzern 1-0(0-0)
Young Boys - FC Lugano 2-0(1-0)

Round 4 [10-11.08.2019]
FC Basel - Servette Genève 3-1(2-1)
FC St.Gallen - Young Boys 2-3(1-2)
FC Lugano - FC Sion 0-1(0-0)
FC Luzern - FC Thun 0-2(0-1)
FC Zürich - Neuchâtel Xamax 2-2(1-0)

Round 5 [24-25.08.2019]
Neuchâtel Xamax - FC Basel 0-3(0-0)
Young Boys - FC Zürich 4-0(1-0)
FC Sion - FC Luzern 2-1(1-0)
FC St.Gallen - FC Lugano 3-2(0-1)
FC Thun - Servette Genève 0-4(0-2)

Round 6 [31.08.-01.09.2019]
FC Zürich - FC St.Gallen 2-1(1-1) [14.08.]
Servette Genève - Neuchâtel Xamax 2-2(0-2)
FC Basel - FC Lugano 2-1(1-0)
FC Luzern - Young Boys 2-2(1-2)
FC Thun - FC Sion 0-1(0-1)

Round 7 [21-22.09.2019]
Neuchâtel Xamax - FC Sion 1-3(1-1)
FC St.Gallen - Servette Genève 3-1(2-0)
FC Lugano - FC Luzern 1-1(1-1)
Young Boys - FC Basel 1-1(0-1)
FC Zürich - FC Thun 2-0(1-0)

Round 8 [25-26.09.2019]
FC Basel - FC Zürich 4-0(1-0)
FC Sion - FC St.Gallen 1-2(0-1)
FC Thun - Young Boys 1-1(0-0)
FC Luzern - Neuchâtel Xamax 1-0(0-0)
Servette Genève - FC Lugano 0-0

Round 9 [28-29.09.2019]
FC St.Gallen - FC Thun 4-0(2-0)
Young Boys - FC Sion 3-2(2-1)
FC Basel - FC Luzern 3-0(1-0)
FC Lugano - Neuchâtel Xamax 0-1(0-1)
Servette Genève - FC Zürich 0-1(0-1)

Round 10 [05-06.10.2019]
Neuchâtel Xamax - Servette Genève 2-2(0-2)
FC Thun - FC Luzern 0-2(0-0)
FC Sion - FC Lugano 1-2(0-0)
FC St.Gallen - FC Basel 0-0
FC Zürich - Young Boys 0-4(0-1)

Round 11 [19-20.10.2019]
FC Basel - FC Thun 3-1(0-0)
Young Boys - Neuchâtel Xamax 4-1(1-0)
FC Lugano - FC Zürich 0-0
FC Luzern - FC Sion 3-1(0-1)
Servette Genève - FC St.Gallen 1-2(0-1)

Round 12 [26-27.10.2019]
Neuchâtel Xamax - FC Luzern 2-0(1-0)
FC Sion - Servette Genève 1-1(1-1)
FC Lugano - FC St.Gallen 3-0(2-0)
Young Boys - FC Thun 4-2(2-0)
FC Zürich - FC Basel 3-2(2-1)

Round 13 [02-03.11.2019]
FC St.Gallen - FC Sion 3-0(0-0)
FC Thun - FC Zürich 0-1(0-1)
FC Basel - Neuchâtel Xamax 1-1(0-1)
FC Luzern - FC Lugano 1-2(0-0)
Servette Genève - Young Boys 3-0(0-0)

Round 14 [09-10.11.2019]
FC Luzern - Servette Genève 1-2(0-2)
Neuchâtel Xamax - FC Thun 2-3(0-0)
FC Lugano - FC Basel 0-3(0-2)
Young Boys - FC St.Gallen 4-3(2-2)
FC Zürich - FC Sion 4-2(2-2)

Round 15 [23-24.11.2019]
Servette Genève - FC Basel 2-0(1-0)
FC Zürich - FC Luzern 3-0(1-0)
FC Sion - Young Boys 3-4(2-3)
FC St.Gallen - Neuchâtel Xamax 4-1(2-0)
FC Thun - FC Lugano 0-3(0-2)

Round 16 [30.11.-01.12.2019]
Neuchâtel Xamax - FC Zürich 0-1(0-0)
FC Sion - FC Thun 2-1(0-1)
FC Basel - Young Boys 3-0(2-0)
FC Lugano - Servette Genève 1-0(0-0)
FC Luzern - FC St.Gallen 1-4(1-1)

Round 17 [07-08.12.2019]
Neuchâtel Xamax - FC Lugano 1-1(1-0)
Young Boys - FC Luzern 1-0(0-0)
FC Basel - FC Sion 4-0(2-0)
FC Thun - FC St.Gallen 1-4(0-2)
FC Zürich - Servette Genève 0-5(0-2)

Round 18 [14-15.12.2019]
Servette Genève - FC Thun 2-1(0-0)
FC St.Gallen - FC Zürich 1-3(1-2)
FC Lugano - Young Boys 0-0
FC Luzern - FC Basel 2-1(1-0)
FC Sion - Neuchâtel Xamax 1-1(1-0)

Round 19 [25-26.01.2020]
Neuchâtel Xamax - Servette Genève 1-2(0-2)
FC Zürich - FC Luzern 2-3(1-3)
FC St.Gallen - FC Lugano 3-1(0-1)
FC Thun - FC Sion 2-1(2-0)
Young Boys - FC Basel 2-0(1-0)

Round 20 [01-02.02.2020]
FC Lugano - Neuchâtel Xamax 1-1(1-1)
FC Luzern - Young Boys 2-0(0-0)
FC Basel - FC St.Gallen 1-2(1-1)
Servette Genève - FC Thun 2-0(0-0)
FC Sion - FC Zürich 1-1(1-1)

Round 21 [08-09.02.2020]
Young Boys - FC Sion 1-0(1-0)
FC Zürich - FC Basel 0-4(0-2)
Neuchâtel Xamax - FC Luzern 0-1(0-1)
FC St.Gallen - Servette Genève 1-0(1-0)
FC Thun - FC Lugano 3-2(2-1)

Round 22 [15-16.02.2020]
FC Basel - FC Thun 0-1(0-0)
FC Sion - Neuchâtel Xamax 1-2(0-1)
FC Lugano - Young Boys 2-1(1-0)
FC Luzern - FC St.Gallen 1-0(1-0)
Servette Genève - FC Zürich 4-1(1-0)

Round 23 [22-23.02.2020]
FC Thun - FC Luzern 1-1(1-1)
FC Zürich - Neuchâtel Xamax 1-1(1-1)
FC Basel - Servette Genève 2-2(2-0)
FC Lugano - FC Sion 0-0
FC St.Gallen - Young Boys 3-3(1-2)

Round 24 [19-21.06.2020]
Young Boys - FC Zürich 3-2(1-2)
Neuchâtel Xamax - FC Thun 2-1(1-0)
FC Sion - FC St.Gallen 1-2(0-1)
FC Luzern - FC Basel 2-1(1-0)
Servette Genève - FC Lugano 1-1(0-1)

Round 25 [23-25.06.2020]
FC Thun - Young Boys 1-0(0-0)
Neuchâtel Xamax - FC Basel 1-2(1-1)
FC Lugano - FC Luzern 2-0(0-0)
FC Sion - Servette Genève 1-1(1-1)
FC St.Gallen - FC Zürich 0-4(0-1)

Round 26 [27-28.06.2020]
FC Luzern - Servette Genève 2-2(0-2)
Young Boys - Neuchâtel Xamax 6-0(4-0)
FC Basel - FC Sion 2-0(0-0)
FC St.Gallen - FC Thun 3-2(3-0)
FC Zürich - FC Lugano 1-0(0-0)

Round 27 [30.06.-02.07.2020]
Servette Genève - Young Boys 1-1(0-0)
FC Lugano - FC Basel 2-1(0-0)
Neuchâtel Xamax - FC St.Gallen 1-2(1-1)
FC Thun - FC Zürich 3-2(3-2)
FC Sion - FC Luzern 0-2(0-1)

Round 28 [04-05.07.2020]
FC Basel - Neuchâtel Xamax 2-0(1-0)
FC Zürich - Servette Genève 2-0(1-0)
FC Luzern - FC Thun 3-0(2-0)
FC St.Gallen - FC Sion 2-1(2-1)
Young Boys - FC Lugano 3-0(1-0)

Round 29 [07-09.07.2020]
Neuchâtel Xamax - FC Zürich 1-1(1-1)
Young Boys - FC Thun 4-0(1-0)
Servette Genève - FC Luzern 2-0(2-0)
FC Sion - FC Basel 1-0(1-0)
FC Lugano - FC St.Gallen 3-3(1-2)

Round 30 [11-12.07.2020]
FC Basel - Young Boys 3-2(1-0)
FC Luzern - FC Lugano 3-3(0-2)
Servette Genève - FC St.Gallen 1-1(0-1)
FC Thun - Neuchâtel Xamax 3-0(2-0)
FC Zürich - FC Sion 0-2(0-1) [28.07.]

Round 31 [14-16.07.2020]	
FC Basel - FC Zürich	4-0(2-0)
FC Lugano - FC Thun	1-1(0-0)
Young Boys - Servette Genève	4-2(1-1)
Neuchâtel Xamax - FC Sion	0-0
FC St.Gallen - FC Luzern	4-1(3-0)

Round 32 [18-19.07.2020]	
FC Zürich - Young Boys	0-5(0-2)
FC Luzern - Neuchâtel Xamax	1-2(0-1)
Servette Genève - FC Basel	2-2(1-1)
FC Sion - FC Lugano	1-1(0-1)
FC Thun - FC St.Gallen	2-1(0-0)

Round 33 22-23.07.2020 [ ]	
FC Thun - Servette Genève	5-1(2-0)
FC Lugano - FC Zürich	1-0(1-0)
FC Luzern - FC Sion	1-2(0-2)
FC St.Gallen - FC Basel	0-5(0-2)
Neuchâtel Xamax - Young Boys	0-1(0-1)

Round 34 [25-26.07.2020]	
FC Sion - FC Thun	1-1(0-0)
FC Zürich - FC St.Gallen	1-3(1-1)
FC Basel - FC Lugano	4-4(2-3)
Servette Genève - Neuchâtel Xamax	4-1(1-1)
Young Boys - FC Luzern	1-0(0-0)

Round 35 [31.07.2020]	
FC Lugano - Servette Genève	3-1(1-1)
FC Luzern - FC Zürich	2-1(1-1)
FC Sion - Young Boys	0-1(0-1)
FC St.Gallen - Neuchâtel Xamax	6-0(4-0)
FC Thun - FC Basel	0-0

Round 36 [03.08.2020]	
FC Basel - FC Luzern	0-0
Neuchâtel Xamax - FC Lugano	0-1(0-0)
Servette Genève - FC Sion	1-2(1-1)
Young Boys - FC St.Gallen	3-1(2-1)
FC Zürich - FC Thun	3-3(2-0)

Final Standings

						Total					Home					Away	
1.	**BSC Young Boys Bern**	36	23	7	6	80 - 41	76	16	2	0	51 - 15	7	5	6	29 - 26
2.	FC St. Gallen	36	21	5	10	79 - 56	68	11	2	5	42 - 29	10	3	5	37 - 27
3.	FC Basel	36	18	8	10	74 - 38	62	11	4	3	42 - 17	7	4	7	32 - 21
4.	Servette FC Genève	36	12	13	11	57 - 48	49	8	7	3	29 - 15	4	6	8	28 - 33
5.	FC Lugano	36	11	14	11	46 - 46	47	6	8	4	18 - 17	5	6	7	28 - 29
6.	FC Luzern	36	13	7	16	42 - 50	46	8	4	6	28 - 25	5	3	10	14 - 25
7.	FC Zürich	36	12	7	17	45 - 72	43	7	3	8	26 - 41	5	4	9	19 - 31
8.	FC Sion	36	10	9	17	40 - 55	39	4	6	8	22 - 28	6	3	9	18 - 27
9.	FC Thun (*Relegation Play-offs*)	36	10	8	18	45 - 67	38	7	4	7	26 - 29	3	4	11	19 - 38
10.	Neuchâtel Xamax FCS (*Relegated*)	36	5	12	19	33 - 68	27	2	5	11	15 - 26	3	7	8	18 - 42

Top goalscorers:

32	**Jean-Pierre Nsamé (CMR)**	*BSC Young Boys Bern*
19	Cedric Jan Itten	*FC St. Gallen*
14	Arthur Mendonça Cabral (BRA)	*FC Basel*
14	Ermedin Demirović (BIH)	*FC St. Gallen*
13	Kenal Ademi (GER)	*FC Basel*
13	Raphaël Nuzzolo	*Neuchâtel Xamax FCS*
13	Jordi Quintillà Guasch (ESP)	*FC St. Gallen*

Relegation Play-offs [07-10.08.2020]

FC Vaduz - FC Thun	2-0(1-0)	3-4(1-1)

FC Vaduz promoted to the Swiss Super League 2020/2021.

NATIONAL CUP
Schweizer Cup 2019/2020

First Round [16-18.08.2019]

FC Concordia Basel - FC Lugano	0-5(0-2)	FC Bulle - FC Chiasso	2-1 aet
Étoile Carouge FC - BSC Young Boys Bern	0-1(0-0)	FC Allschwil - FC Sion	1-10(0-6)
FC Wohlen - FC Wettswil-Bonstetten	2-1(1-0)	Iliria Solothurn - FC Lausanne-Sport	1-6(1-3)
FC Wetzikon - FC Meyrin	1-3(0-1)	AC Taverne - SC Kriens	1-4(0-1)
SC Young Fellows/Juventus Zürich - FC Winterthur	0-3(0-2)	FC Gambarogno-Contone - AC Bellinzona	0-5(0-4)
FC Red Star Zürich - FC Wil 1900	1-3(1-0)	FC Mutschellen - FC Stade Nyonnais	0-3(0-1)
FC Rothorn - FC Sursee	1-3(0-0,1-1)	FC Monthey - FC St.Gallen	1-4(1-2)
FC Altstätten - FC Bassecourt	1-3(0-2)	FC Béroche-Gorgier - FC Olten	1-1 aet; 6-5 pen
FC Black Stars Basel - FC Zürich	1-2(1-1)	SC Cham - FC Aarau	2-2 aet; 3-5 pen
FC Echallens - Servette FC Genève	0-6(0-1)	FC Linth 04 - FC Schaffhausen	3-1(1-1)
Pully Football - FC Basel	1-4(1-1)	FC Uster - FC Lancy	1-3(0-1)
FC Seefeld Zürich - Grasshopper Club Zürich	1-9(1-2)	FC Schönberg - Olympique de Genève FC	1-5(1-2)
FC Muri - FC Rapperswil-Jona	2-3(0-1)	FC Escholzmatt-Marbach - FC Bavois	0-14(0-6)
FC Rotkreuz - FC Freienbach	0-2(0-0)	FC Signal - FC Thun	0-2(0-0)
FC Saxon Sports - FC Spiez	2-4(1-1)	AS Calcio Kreuzlingen - FC Luzern	0-2(0-1)
FC Perly-Certoux - FC Stade Lausanne Ouchy	0-5(0-1)	Yverdon-Sport FC - Neuchâtel Xamax FCS	1-2(0-0)

Second Round [13-15.09.2019]

Grasshopper Club Zürich - Servette FC Genève	1-0(0-0,0-0)	FC Lausanne-Sport - FC Lugano	3-0(0-0)
FC Winterthur - FC St.Gallen	2-0(0-0)	FC Wil 1900 - FC Zürich	1-2(1-1)
FC Spiez - FC Linth 04	0-4(0-0,0-0)	FC Meyrin - FC Basel	0-3(0-0)
FC Sursee - FC Bulle	1-2(0-1)	FC Stade Nyonnais - FC Thun	0-1(0-1)
Olympique de Genève FC - FC Bavois	1-2(0-0)	AC Bellinzona - Neuchâtel Xamax FCS	1-2(0-1)
FC Freienbach - BSC Young Boys Bern	2-11(0-5)	FC Bassecourt - FC Rapperswil-Jona	0-3(0-1)
SC Kriens - FC Stade Lausanne Ouchy	2-4(2-1)	FC Aarau - FC Sion	1-2(1-1)
FC Béroche-Gorgier - FC Lancy	2-1(0-1)	FC Wohlen - FC Luzern	0-4(0-0)

1/8-Finals [29-31.10.2019]			
FC Béroche-Gorgier - FC Bavois	1-7(0-4)	BSC Young Boys Bern - FC Zürich	4-0(2-0)
Grasshopper Club Zürich - FC Luzern	0-1(0-0)	FC Stade Lausanne Ouchy - FC Basel	1-2(0-0)
FC Winterthur - FC Thun	1-0(1-0)	FC Bulle - FC Rapperswil-Jona	2-3(0-2)
FC Linth 04 - FC Sion	0-2(0-1)	FC Lausanne-Sport - Neuchâtel Xamax FCS	6-0(4-0)

Quarter-Finals [14.06./05-06.08.2020]			
FC Lausanne-Sport - FC Basel	2-3(0-0,2-2)	FC Rapperswil-Jona - FC Sion	1-2(0-2)
FC Winterthur - FC Bavois	4-0(2-0)	FC Luzern - BSC Young Boys Bern	1-2(1-1,1-1)

Semi-Finals [09/25.08.2020]			
BSC Young Boys Bern - FC Sion	3-1(0-0)	FC Basel - FC Winterthur	6-1(3-1)

Final

30.08.2020; Wankdorf Stadion, Bern; Referee: Sandro Schärer; Attendance: 1,000
BSC Young Boys Bern - FC Basel   **2-1(0-1)**

Young Boys: David von Ballmoos, Mohamed Camara, Ulisses Garcia (82.Marvin Spielmann), Jordan Lefort, Miralem Sulejmani (66.Vincent Sierro), Michel Aebischer, Fabian Lustenberger (49.Cédric Zesiger), Christopher Pereira (66.Gianluca Gaudino), Nicolas Ngamaleu (82.Guillaume Hoarau), Christian Fassnacht, Jean-Pierre Nsamé. Trainer: Gerardo Seoane.

FC Basel: Đorđe Nikolić, Silvan Widmer, Omar Federico Alderete Fernández, Jasper van der Werff, Raoul Petretta, Valentin Stocker (86.Samuele Campo), Fabian Frei, Yannick Marchand (80.Eray Cömert), Ricky van Wolfswinkel, Afimico Pululu, Kemal Ademi. Trainer: Marcel Koller.

Goals: 0-1 Omar Federico Alderete Fernández (42), 1-1 Jean-Pierre Nsamé (50), 2-1 Marvin Spielmann (89).

THE CLUBS 2019/2020

Fussball Club Basel 1893

Founded:	15.11.1893	
Stadium:	St. Jakob-Park, Basel (37,994)	
Trainer:	Marcel Koller	11.11.1960

Goalkeepers:	DOB	M	(s)	G
Đorđe Nikolić (SRB)	13.04.1997	4	(1)	
Jonas Omlin	10.01.1994	32		
Defenders:	**DOB**	**M**	**(s)**	**G**
Omar Federico Alderete Fernández (PAR)	26.12.1996	28		2
Éder Fabián Álvarez Balanta (COL)	28.02.1993	3	(1)	
Emil Bergström (SWE)	19.05.1993	5	(3)	
Eray Cömert	04.02.1998	32	(1)	2
Konstantinos Dimitriou (GRE)	30.06.1999	1		
Elis Isufi	21.05.2000	4	(2)	
Louis Lurvink	24.01.2002		(1)	
Raoul Petretta (ITA)	24.03.1997	26	(2)	1
Blas Miguel Riveros Galeano (PAR)	03.02.1998	10	(7)	
Jasper van der Werff	09.12.1998	10	(4)	
Silvan Widmer	05.03.1993	32		2
Midfielders:	**DOB**	**M**	**(s)**	**G**
Kevin Bua	11.08.1993	14	(5)	4
Orges Bunjaku	05.07.2001	3	(2)	
Samuele Campo	06.07.1995	20	(5)	6
Fabian Frei	08.01.1989	31	(2)	10
Zdravko Kuzmanović (SRB)	22.09.1987		(3)	
Yannick Marchand	09.02.2000	1	(6)	
Eric Dos Santos Rodrigues „Ramires" (BRA)	10.08.2000	2	(7)	
Mihailo Stevanovic	04.01.2002		(1)	
Valentin Stocker	12.04.1989	26	(3)	8
Taulant Xhaka (ALB)	28.03.1991	29	(3)	
Luca Zuffi	27.03.1990	14	(5)	3
Forwards:	**DOB**	**M**	**(s)**	**G**
Kemal Ademi	23.01.1996	15	(11)	13
Albian Afrim Ajeti	26.02.1997	1		1
Arthur Mendonça Cabral (BRA)	25.04.1998	20	(6)	14
Dimitri Joseph Oberlin Mfomo	27.09.1997	1	(5)	
Noah Okafor	24.05.2000	7	(7)	
Afimico Pululu (FRA)	23.03.1999	12	(9)	1
Tician Tushi	02.04.2001	2	(5)	
Ricky van Wolfswinkel (NED)	27.01.1989	3	(7)	2
Lirik Vishi	13.06.2001	1	(2)	
Julian Von Moos	01.04.2001		(1)	
Edon Zhegrova (KVX)	31.03.1999	7	(7)	2

Football Club Lugano

Founded:	1908; re-founded 2004 (*as AC Lugano*)	
Stadium:	Stadio Cornaredo, Lugano (6,390)	
Trainer:	Fabio Celestini	31.10.1975
[28.10.2019]	Maurizio Jacobacci	11.01.1963

Goalkeepers:	DOB	M	(s)	G
Noam Baumann	10.04.1996	35		
David Da Costa	19.04.1986	1	(1)	
Defenders:	**DOB**	**M**	**(s)**	**G**
Fabio Daprelà	19.02.1991	29	(1)	1
Jefferson Nascimento (BRA)	05.07.1988	4	(4)	1
Ákos Kecskés (HUN)	04.01.1996	25	(1)	2
Numa Lavanchy	25.08.1993	32	(1)	2
Mijat Marić	30.04.1984	28		6
Linus Obexer	05.06.1997	8	(3)	
Daniel Pavlović (BIH)	22.04.1988	1	(3)	
Fulvio Sulmoni	04.01.1986	6		
Joel Untersee	11.02.1994	1		
Eloge Yao (CIV)	20.01.1996	22	(3)	
Midfielders:	**DOB**	**M**	**(s)**	**G**
Marco Aratore	04.06.1991	18	(4)	3
Mattia Bottani	24.05.1991	11	(7)	2
Olivier Custodio	10.02.1995	27	(1)	2
Miroslav Čovilo (SRB)	06.05.1986	12	(11)	
Domen Črnigoj (SVN)	18.11.1995		(3)	
Stefano Guidotti (ITA)	16.06.1999	6	(6)	1
Sandi Lovrič (AUT)	28.03.1998	17	(10)	3
Christophe Lungoyi	04.07.2000	4	(8)	2
Roman Macek (CZE)	18.04.1997	1	(4)	
Francisco José Rodríguez Araya	14.09.1995	6	(4)	1
Jonathan Maximiliano Sabbatini Perfecto (URU)	31.03.1988	26		1
Ransford Selasi (GHA)	19.08.1996	4	(3)	
Bálint Vécsei (HUN)	13.07.1993	12	(2)	3
Forwards:	**DOB**	**M**	**(s)**	**G**
Carlos Alberto de Souza Júnior „Carlinhos" (BRA)	08.08.1994	13	(1)	2
Nicola Dalmonte (ITA)	13.09.1997	4	(6)	1
Alexander Gerndt (SWE)	14.07.1986	17	(8)	6
Filip Holender (HUN)	27.07.1994	15	(12)	5
Rangelo Janga (CUW)	16.04.1992	10	(3)	
David Jovanovic	13.03.2001		(1)	
Franklin Sasere (NGA)	27.06.1998	1	(4)	

Fussball-Club Luzern

Founded: 12.08.1901
Stadium: Swissporarena, Luzern (16,490)
Trainer: Thomas Häberli   11.04.1974
[02.01.2020] Fabio Celestini   31.10.1975

Goalkeepers:	DOB	M	(s)	G
Simon Enzler	16.10.1997	1		
Marius Müller (GER)	12.07.1993	35		
Defenders:	**DOB**	**M**	**(s)**	**G**
Remo Arnold	17.01.1997	1		
Ashvin Balaruban	08.08.2001	1	(1)	
Marco Burch	19.10.2000	7		
Marco Bürki	10.07.1993	8	(2)	
Lazar Ćirković (SRB)	22.08.1992	6	(4)	
Simon Grether	20.05.1992	20	(3)	
Otar Kakabadze (GEO)	27.06.1995	15	(5)	
Stefan Knežević	30.10.1996	28	(1)	
Lucas Alves de Araujo „Lucão"(BRA)	22.07.1992	32		2
Marvin Schulz (GER)	15.01.1995	22	(2)	
Christian Schwegler	06.06.1984	7	(2)	
Silvan Sidler	07.07.1998	25	(7)	
Midfielders:	**DOB**	**M**	**(s)**	**G**
Lorik Emini	29.08.1999	10	(2)	1
Julian Hermann	26.05.2001		(1)	
Ardon Jashari	30.07.2002		(2)	
David Mistrafović	25.05.2001	12	(4)	
Tsiy William Ndenge (GER)	13.06.1997	10	(1)	
Tyrone Owusu	08.06.2003		(1)	
Christian Schneuwly	07.02.1988		(2)	1
Pascal Schürpf	15.07.1989	26	(7)	8
Idriz Voca (KVX)	15.05.1997	29	(1)	2
Forwards:	**DOB**	**M**	**(s)**	**G**
Salah Binous	04.08.2000		(5)	1
Shkelqim Demhasaj	19.04.1996	5	(10)	
Blessing Chibukie Eleke (NGA)	05.03.1996	13	(13)	4
Lino Lang	23.05.2000	1	(2)	1
Darian Males	03.05.2001	10	(9)	1
Francesco Margiotta (ITA)	15.07.1993	31	(4)	11
Mark Marleku (KVX)	27.04.2000	1	(6)	1
Ryder Matos Santos Pinto (BRA)	27.02.1993	17	(6)	1
Ibrahima N'Diaye (SEN)	06.07.1998	23	(1)	6
Eric Tia (CIV)	28.11.1996		(2)	
Nenad Zivkovic	19.03.2002		(2)	

Neuchâtel Xamax FCS

Founded: 1916 / 2013 merger with FC Serrières)
Stadium: Stade de la Maladière, Neuchâtel (11,997)
Trainer: Joël Magnin   31.05.1971
[05.07.2020] Stéphane Henchoz   07.09.1974

Goalkeepers:	DOB	M	(s)	G
Matthias Minder	03.02.1993	3	(1)	
Basil Sinzig	21.12.1999	1		
Laurent Walthert	30.03.1984	32		
Defenders:	**DOB**	**M**	**(s)**	**G**
Leroy Abanda Mfomo (FRA)	07.06.2000	7	(2)	
André Luis Neitzke (BRA)	24.11.1986	28	(4)	1
Johan Danon Djourou-Gbadjere	18.01.1987	5		
Igor Đurić	30.08.1988	26	(2)	
Yoan Epitaux	06.03.2001		(1)	
Léo Farine	11.07.1996	1		
Mike Gomes	19.09.1988	25	(1)	
Mārcis Ošs (LVA)	25.07.1991	22	(1)	4
Fabio Saiz Pennarossa	01.03.2001		(1)	
Léo Seydoux	16.03.1998	28	(7)	
Arbenit Xhemajli	23.04.1998	19	(4)	2
Midfielders:	**DOB**	**M**	**(s)**	**G**
Safet Alić (BIH)	04.02.1999		(4)	
Musa Araz	17.01.1994	13	(1)	1
Thibault Corbaz	07.01.1994	18	(11)	
Serey Dié (CIV)	07.11.1984	5		1
Pietro Di Nardo	08.02.1990	5	(3)	
Charles-André Doudin	12.09.1986	9	(8)	
Maren Haile-Selassie	13.03.1999	9	(15)	1
Janick Kamber	26.02.1992	14	(6)	1
Xavier Kouassi (CIV)	28.12.1989	9	(1)	
Liridon Mulaj	04.01.1999	3	(7)	
Freddy Mveng Mbezele (CMR)	29.05.1992	16	(5)	
Noha Sylvestre	29.12.1997	2		
Forwards:	**DOB**	**M**	**(s)**	**G**
Dylan Dugourd	01.12.1995	1	(1)	
Gaëtan Karlen	07.06.1993	16	(3)	7
Raphaël Nuzzolo	05.07.1983	35		13
Samir Ramizi (KVX)	24.07.1991	24	(8)	1
Diafra Sakho (SEN)	24.12.1989	3	(5)	
Taulant Seferi (MKD)	15.11.1996	14	(15)	1
Yannis Tafer (FRA)	11.02.1991	3	(5)	

Servette Football Club Genève 1890

Founded: 20.03.1890
Stadium: Stade de Genève, Genève (30,084)
Trainer: Alain Geiger   05.11.1960

Goalkeepers:	DOB	M	(s)	G
Jérémy Frick	08.03.1993	34		
Joël Kiassumbua (COD)	06.04.1992	2	(2)	
Defenders:	**DOB**	**M**	**(s)**	**G**
Michael Gonçalves	10.03.1995	8	(6)	
Noah Henchoz	22.02.2002	1	(1)	
Dennis Iapichino	27.07.1990	22		
Kastriot Imeri	27.06.2000	7	(17)	1
Lucas Monteiro Fernandes	25.05.2001		(2)	
Steve Rouiller	10.07.1990	33		2
Christopher Routis	03.03.1990	10	(9)	
Vincent Sasso (FRA)	16.02.1991	31	(1)	1
Anthony Sauthier	05.02.1991	30		
Yoan Severin (FRA)	24.01.1997	4		
Nicolas Vouilloz	11.05.2001	4	(5)	
Midfielders:	**DOB**	**M**	**(s)**	**G**
Ricardo Azevedo	02.12.2001		(14)	
Boris Cespedes	19.06.1995	15	(13)	3
Timothé Cognat (FRA)	25.01.1998	31	(1)	2
Alexis Guérin (FRA)	05.08.2000		(1)	
Mathis Jan Holcbecher	21.01.2001		(2)	
Andrea Maccoppi (ITA)	22.01.1987	5	(5)	
Alexis Martial (FRA)	15.06.2001	1	(1)	
Matteo Mazzolini (FRA)	09.01.2001	1	(1)	
Gaël Bella Ondoua (CMR)	04.11.1995	29	(1)	2
Park Jung-bin (KOR)	22.02.1994	5	(1)	4
Rayan Souici (FRA)	28.02.1998	2	(4)	
Miroslav Stevanović (BIH)	29.07.1990	33	(1)	8
Sébastien Wüthrich	29.05.1990	16		4
Forwards:	**DOB**	**M**	**(s)**	**G**
Alban Ajdini (ALB)	09.07.1999	1	(3)	
Koro Issa Ahmed Koné (CIV)	05.07.1989	22	(7)	11
Grejohn Kyei (FRA)	12.08.1995	14	(9)	4
Mychell Ruan da Silva Chagas (BRA)	06.06.1991	1	(7)	
Matteo Regillo	24.04.2002		(1)	
Alex Schalk (NED)	07.08.1992	10	(11)	7
Varol Tasar (TUR)	04.10.1996	24	(2)	6

Football Club de Sion

Founded: 1909
Stadium: Stade Tourbillon, Sion (14,283)
Trainer: Stéphane Henchoz 07.09.1974
[05.11.2019] Christian Zermatten 21.06.1966
[01.01.2020] Ricardo Nuno Pereira Dionísio (POR) 04.12.1982
[03.06.2020] Paolo Tramezzani (ITA) 30.07.1970

Goalkeepers:	DOB	M	(s)	G
Timothy Fayulu	24.07.1999	1		
Kevin Fickentscher	06.07.1988	28		
Anton Mitryushkin (RUS)	08.02.1996	7	(1)	
Defenders:	DOB	M	(s)	G
Ayoub Abdellaoui (ALG)	16.02.1993	23	(2)	
Mattias Andersson (SWE)	13.03.1998	3		
Jan Bamert	09.03.1998	18	(2)	
Dimitri Cavaré (FRA)	05.02.1995	1	(2)	
Johan Danon Djourou-Gbadjere	18.01.1987	1	(1)	
Mickaël Facchinetti	15.02.1991	20	(3)	
Arian Kabashi (KVX)	26.09.1996		(4)	
Ermir Lenjani (ALB)	05.08.1989	31	(1)	6
Quentin Maceiras	10.10.1995	30		
Jean Ruiz (FRA)	06.04.1998	14	(4)	
Midfielders:	DOB	M	(s)	G
José Aguilar Martínez (ESP)	05.02.2001	1		
Edgar André	28.06.1999	2	(2)	
Baltazar Costa Rodrigues de Oliveira (BRA)	06.05.2000	11	(1)	1
Valon Behrami	19.04.1985	4		
Anto Grgic	28.11.1996	30	(4)	2
Pajtim Kasami	02.06.1992	32	(3)	11
Xavier Kouassi (CIV)	28.12.1989	17		
Berkan Kutlu (TUR)	25.01.1998		(2)	
Birama N'Doye (SEN)	27.03.1994	21	(2)	2
Alexandre Dimitri Song Billong (CMR)	09.09.1987	5	(6)	
Sandro Theler	15.12.2000	2	(3)	1
Bastien Toma	24.06.1999	22	(5)	2
Guy Christian Zock A Bep (CMR)	06.05.1994	17	(2)	
Forwards:	DOB	M	(s)	G
Yannick Cotter	03.01.2002		(2)	
Seydou Doumbia (CIV)	31.12.1987	6	(9)	5
Yassin Fortune (FRA)	30.01.1999	6	(5)	
Cleilton Monteiro da Costa „Itaitinga" (BRA)	04.10.1998	10	(15)	3
Jared Khasa	04.11.1997	2	(11)	
Patrick Luan dos Santos (BRA)	31.10.1998	15	(5)	2
Filip Stojilković	04.01.2000	4	(7)	1
Roberts Uldriķis (LVA)	03.04.1998	12	(12)	4
Yamato Wakatsuki (JPN)	18.01.2002		(1)	

Fussballclub St. Gallen 1879

Founded: 19.04.1879
Stadium: kybunpark, St. Gallen (19,456)
Trainer: Peter Zeidler (GER) 08.08.1962

Goalkeepers:	DOB	M	(s)	G
Lawrence Ati-Zigi (GHA)	29.11.1996	18		
Dejan Stojanović (AUT)	19.07.1993	18		
Defenders:	DOB	M	(s)	G
Fabiano Donato Alves (BRA)	01.12.1994		(6)	1
Silvan Hefti	25.10.1997	34		3
Yannis Letard (FRA)	18.08.1998	25	(1)	1
Musah Nuhu (GHA)	17.01.1997		(4)	
Vincent Rüfli	22.01.1988	4	(12)	1
Leonidas Stergiou	03.03.2002	34		1
Alain Wiss	21.08.1990	1	(7)	
Midfielders:	DOB	M	(s)	G
Axel Bakayoko (FRA)	06.01.1998	4	(19)	
Moreno Costanzo	20.02.1988		(7)	
Betim Fazliji (SRB)	25.04.1999	20	(6)	2
Lukas Görtler (GER)	15.06.1994	34		3
Jordi Quintillà Guasch (ESP)	25.10.1993	33		13
Alessandro Kräuchi	03.06.1998	2	(6)	
Dereck Kutesa	06.12.1997	4		
Miro Muheim	24.03.1998	32	(1)	
Tim Staubli	16.04.2000	2	(11)	
Forwards:	DOB	M	(s)	G
André David de Oliveira Ribeiro (POR)	09.06.1997	4	(14)	2
Boris Babic	10.11.1997	16	(3)	7
Angelo Campos Oliveira (POR)	30.03.2000		(8)	
Ermedin Demirović (BIH)	25.03.1998	26	(2)	14
Jérémy Guillemenot	06.01.1998	23	(9)	6
Cedric Jan Itten	27.12.1996	30	(4)	19
Víctor Ruiz Abril (ESP)	02.11.1993	32	(1)	5

Fussballclub Thun 1898

Founded: 1898
Stadium: Stockhorn Arena, Thun (10,014)
Trainer: Marc Schneider 23.07.1980

Goalkeepers:	DOB	M	(s)	G
Guillaume Faivre	20.02.1987	31		
Andreas Hirzel	25.03.1993	5		
Defenders:	DOB	M	(s)	G
Kevin Bigler	05.10.1992	2	(1)	
Roy Gelmi	01.03.1995	15		
Stefan Glarner	21.11.1987	29	(3)	
Nikki Havenaar (JPN)	16.02.1995	22	(3)	4
Nias Hefti	18.09.1999	24	(5)	1
Sven Joss	18.07.1994	8	(2)	
Chris Kablan	30.11.1994	24	(3)	5
Miguel Rodrigues	07.12.1996	6	(1)	
Midfielders:	DOB	M	(s)	G
Hiran Ahmed (GER)	06.04.2000	3	(8)	
Leonardo Bertone	14.03.1994	16		1
Magnus Breitenmoser	06.08.1998		(2)	
Miguel Castroman	17.03.1995	26	(4)	4
Kenan Fatkić (SVN)	20.08.1997	14	(12)	
Nicolas Hasler (LIE)	04.05.1991	17	(1)	
Gregory Karlen	30.01.1995	13	(2)	3
Justin Roth	29.10.2000	7	(1)	
Dennis Salanović (LIE)	26.02.1996	8	(11)	1
Dejan Sorgić (SRB)	15.09.1989	1		1
Basil Stillhart	24.03.1994	33		2
Nicola Sutter	08.05.1995	21	(2)	
Matteo Tosetti	15.02.1992	15	(13)	3
Forwards:	DOB	M	(s)	G
Hassane Bandé (BFA)	30.10.1998	6	(5)	
Saleh Chihadeh	25.08.1994	3	(11)	2
Ridge Munsy (COD)	09.07.1989	16	(10)	12
Simone Rapp	01.10.1992	23	(9)	6
Uroš Vašić	25.10.2001	8	(4)	

Berner Sport Club Young Boys

Founded: 14.03.1898
Stadium: Wankdorf Stadion, Bern (31,789)
Trainer: Gerardo Seoane   30.10.1978

Goalkeepers:	DOB	M	(s)	G
Dario Marzino	19.09.1996		(1)	
David von Ballmoos	30.12.1994	34		
Marco Wölfli	22.08.1982	2	(1)	
Defenders:	**DOB**	**M**	**(s)**	**G**
Nicolas Bürgy	07.08.1995	9	(10)	1
Mohamed Camara (GUI)	28.08.1997	9		1
Ulisses Garcia	11.01.1996	20	(6)	1
Saidy Janko	22.10.1995	28	(5)	
Jordan Lefort (FRA)	09.08.1993	13	(2)	
Jordan Lotomba	29.09.1998	19	(8)	
Esteban Petignat	17.05.2000	1	(2)	
Pascal Schüpbach	11.04.2000		(1)	
Frederik Sørensen (DEN)	14.04.1992	12	(4)	
Gregory Wüthrich	04.12.1994		(1)	
Cédric Zesiger	24.06.1998	19	(4)	2

Midfielders:	DOB	M	(s)	G
Michel Aebischer	06.01.1997	30	(2)	3
Gianluca Gaudino (GER)	11.11.1996	11	(14)	4
Fabian Lustenberger	02.05.1988	30		
Christopher Pereira (LUX)	19.02.1997	18	(4)	2
Vincent Sierro	08.10.1995	12	(5)	1
Marvin Spielmann	23.02.1996	9	(13)	1
Miralem Sulejmani (SRB)	05.12.1988	6	(9)	4
Forwards:	**DOB**	**M**	**(s)**	**G**
Roger Assalé (CIV)	13.11.1993	10	(4)	4
Samuel Ballet	12.03.2001		(1)	1
Meschack Elia (COD)	06.08.1997	5	(7)	2
Christian Fassnacht	11.11.1993	30		7
Guillaume Hoarau (FRA)	05.03.1984	9	(8)	2
Felix Mambimbi	18.01.2001	6	(11)	1
Nicolas Ngamaleu (CMR)	09.07.1994	24	(9)	7
Jean-Pierre Nsamé (CMR)	01.05.1993	30	(2)	32

Fussballclub Zürich

Founded: 01.08.1896
Stadium: Letzigrund Stadion, Zürich (26,104)
Trainer: Ludovic Magnin   20.04.1979

Goalkeepers:	DOB	M	(s)	G
Novem Baumann	04.12.1995	1		
Yanick Brecher	25.05.1993	33		
Andris Vaņins (LVA)	30.04.1980	2		
Defenders:	**DOB**	**M**	**(s)**	**G**
Umaru Bangura (SLE)	07.10.1987	12	(2)	
Dagou Willie Anderson Britto (CIV)	15.12.1996	10	(9)	
Basil Erne	02.06.2000		(1)	
Pa Modou Jagne (GAM)	26.12.1989	13	(5)	
Lenny Janko	05.02.2002		(1)	
José Júlio Gomes Gonçalves (POR)	17.09.1985	1		
Michael Kempter	12.01.1995	12	(1)	
Levan Kharabadze (GEO)	26.01.2000	7	(1)	
Mirlind Kryeziu	26.01.1997	14	(7)	1
Nathan Raphael Pelae Cardoso (BRA)	13.05.1995	26	(2)	2
Becir Omeragic	20.01.2002	19		
Mads Pedersen (DEN)	01.09.1996	2		
Kevin Rüegg	05.08.1998	25	(3)	1
Enit Sadıku	14.07.1998		(1)	
Ilan Sauter	06.02.2001	2	(1)	
Silvan Jeremy Wallner	15.01.2002	1		
Midfielders:	**DOB**	**M**	**(s)**	**G**
Izer Aliu	15.11.1999		(2)	
Soheil Arghandewall (GER)	19.08.2001	1		

	DOB	M	(s)	G
Diego Miguel Corvalan Couceiro	17.02.2002		(1)	
Toni Domgjoni (CRO)	04.09.1998	27	(4)	1
Vasilije Janjičić	02.11.1998	5	(7)	
Salim Khelifi	26.01.1994	1	(1)	
Benjamin Kololli (KVX)	15.05.1992	18	(9)	6
Hekuran Kryeziu (KVX)	12.02.1993	10	(3)	
Antonio Marchesano	18.01.1991	29	(2)	5
Nils Ramiro Reichmuth	22.02.2002	1	(1)	
Marco Schönbächler	11.01.1990	27	(2)	7
Stephan Vinicius Seiler (BRA)	16.09.2000	2	(6)	
Simon Sohm	11.04.2001	22	(9)	1
Adrian Winter	08.07.1986	3	(9)	
Lavdim Zumberi	27.11.1999	1		
Forwards:	**DOB**	**M**	**(s)**	**G**
Assan Ceesay (GAM)	17.03.1994	8	(4)	1
Matteo di Giusto	18.08.2000		(1)	
Henri Koide	06.04.2001	3	(6)	
Blaž Kramer (SVN)	01.06.1996	21	(10)	10
Mimoun Mahi (MAR)	13.03.1994	12	(6)	2
Nedim Omeragic	01.02.1999		(1)	
Denis Popovič (SVN)	15.10.1989	8	(1)	
Lavdrim Rexhepi (KVX)	12.02.1998	1		
Shpetim Sulejmani	02.06.1995	1		
Aiyegun Tosin (NGA)	26.06.1998	15	(3)	7

SECOND LEVEL
Swiss Challenge League 2019/2020

1.	FC Lausanne-Sport (*Promoted*)	36	22	7	7	84 - 36	73
2.	FC Vaduz (*Promotion Play-offs*)	36	18	10	8	78 - 53	64
3.	Grasshopper Club Zürich	36	17	10	9	69 - 52	61
4.	FC Winterthur	36	15	10	11	56 - 58	55
5.	SC Kriens	36	16	6	14	58 - 59	54
6.	FC Wil 1900	36	14	7	15	60 - 61	49
7.	FC Stade Lausanne Ouchy	36	11	9	16	47 - 64	42
8.	FC Aarau	36	10	11	15	65 - 80	41
9.	FC Schaffhausen	36	6	14	16	34 - 62	32
10.	FC Chiasso	36	5	8	23	44 - 70	23

No teams were relagated.

INTERNATIONAL MATCHES
(16.07.2019 – 15.07.2020)

05.09.2019	Dublin	Republic of Ireland - Switzerland	1-1(0-0)	(ECQ)
08.09.2019	Sion	Switzerland - Gibraltar	4-0(3-0)	(ECQ)
12.10.2019	København	Denmark - Switzerland	1-0(0-0)	(ECQ)
15.10.2019	Lancy	Switzerland - Republic of Ireland	2-0(1-0)	(ECQ)
15.11.2019	St. Gallen	Switzerland - Georgia	1-0(0-0)	(ECQ)
18.11.2019	Gibraltar	Gibraltar - Switzerland	1-6(0-1)	(ECQ)

05.09.2019 REPUBLIC OF IRELAND - SWITZERLAND 1-1(0-0) 16th EC. Qualifiers
Aviva Stadium, Dublin; Referee: Carlos del Cerro Grande (Spain); Attendance: 44,111
SUI: Yann Sommer, Fabian Lukas Schär, Melingo Kevin Mbabu (90+4.Edimilson Fernandes Ribeiro), Nico Elvedi, Manuel Obafemi Akanji, Ricardo Iván Rodríguez Araya, Denis Lemi Zakaria Lako Lado, Granit Xhaka (Cap), Remo Marco Freuler (90.Admir Mehmedi), Haris Seferović, Breel Donald Embolo (86.Albian Afrim Ajeti). Trainer: Vladimir Petković (Bosnia and Herzegovina).
Goal: Fabian Lukas Schär (74).

08.09.2019 SWITZERLAND - GIBRALTAR 4-0(3-0) 16th EC. Qualifiers
Stade Tourbillon, Sion; Referee: Pavel Orel (Czech Republic); Attendance: 8,318
SUI: Yann Sommer, Fabian Lukas Schär, Loris Benito Souto (65.Renato Steffen), Nico Elvedi, Ricardo Iván Rodríguez Araya, Denis Lemi Zakaria Lako Lado, Granit Xhaka (Cap) (74.Rubén Estephan Vargas Martínez), Edimilson Fernandes Ribeiro, Admir Mehmedi, Albian Afrim Ajeti, Breel Donald Embolo (55.Mario Gavranović). Trainer: Vladimir Petković (Bosnia and Herzegovina).
Goals: Denis Lemi Zakaria Lako Lado (37), Admir Mehmedi (43), Ricardo Iván Rodríguez Araya (45+4), Mario Gavranović (87).

12.10.2019 DENMARK - SWITZERLAND 1-0(0-0) 16th EC. Qualifiers
Parken Stadium, København; Referee: Aleksei Kulbakov (Belarus); Attendance: 35,964
SUI: Yann Sommer, Stephan Lichtsteiner (Cap) (68.Melingo Kevin Mbabu), Nico Elvedi, Fabian Lukas Schär, Manuel Obafemi Akanji, Ricardo Iván Rodríguez Araya (87.Josip Drmić), Denis Lemi Zakaria Lako Lado, Admir Mehmedi (83.Remo Marco Freuler), Granit Xhaka, Haris Seferović, Breel Donald Embolo. Trainer: Vladimir Petković (Bosnia and Herzegovina).

15.10.2019 SWITZERLAND - REPUBLIC OF IRELAND 2-0(1-0) 16th EC. Qualifiers
Stade de Genève, Lancy; Referee: Szymon Marciniak (Poland); Attendance: 24,766
SUI: Yann Sommer, Stephan Lichtsteiner (Cap) (70.Remo Marco Freuler), Fabian Lukas Schär, Nico Elvedi, Manuel Obafemi Akanji, Ricardo Iván Rodríguez Araya, Denis Lemi Zakaria Lako Lado, Granit Xhaka, Admir Mehmedi (28.Edimilson Fernandes Ribeiro), Haris Seferović, Breel Donald Embolo (88.Renato Steffen). Trainer: Vladimir Petković (Bosnia and Herzegovina).
Goals: Haris Seferović (16), Edimilson Fernandes Ribeiro (90+3).

15.11.2019 SWITZERLAND - GEORGIA 1-0(0-0) 16th EC. Qualifiers
kybunpark Stadion, St. Gallen; Referee: Danny Desmond Makkelie (Netherlands); Attendance: 16,400
SUI: Yann Sommer, Stephan Lichtsteiner (Cap), Nico Elvedi, Manuel Obafemi Akanji, Ricardo Iván Rodríguez Araya, Denis Lemi Zakaria Lako Lado, Granit Xhaka, Renato Steffen, Edimilson Fernandes Ribeiro (84.Djibril Sow), Rubén Estephan Vargas Martínez (78.Christian Fassnacht), Albian Afrim Ajeti (71.Cedric Jan Itten). Trainer: Vladimir Petković (Bosnia and Herzegovina).
Goal: Cedric Jan Itten (77).

18.11.2019 GIBRALTAR - SWITZERLAND 1-6(0-1) 16th EC. Qualifiers
Victoria Stadium, Gibraltar; Referee: Benoît Millot (France); Attendance: 2,079
SUI: Yann Sommer, Michael Rico Lang, Loris Benito Souto, Nico Elvedi, Manuel Obafemi Akanji (65.Eray Ervin Cömert), Ricardo Iván Rodríguez Araya, Denis Lemi Zakaria Lako Lado (60.Djibril Sow), Granit Xhaka (Cap), Christian Fassnacht, Cedric Jan Itten, Rubén Estephan Vargas Martínez (85.Michel Aebischer). Trainer: Vladimir Petković (Bosnia and Herzegovina).
Goals: Cedric Jan Itten (10), Rubén Estephan Vargas Martínez (50), Christian Fassnacht (57), Loris Benito Souto (75), Cedric Jan Itten (84), Granit Xhaka (86).

NATIONAL TEAM PLAYERS
(16.07.2019 – 15.07.2020)

Name	DOB	Caps	Goals	2019/2020:	Club
Goalkeepers					
Yann SOMMER	17.12.1988	53	0	2019:	Borussia VfL Mönchengladbach (GER)
Defenders					
Manuel Obafemi AKANJI	19.07.1995	22	0	2019:	BV Borussia 09 Dortmund (GER)
Loris BENITO Souto	07.01.1992	5	1	2019:	FC Girondins de Bordeaux (FRA)
Eray Ervin CÖMERT	04.02.1998	1	0	2019:	FC Basel
Nico ELVEDI	30.09.1996	17	1	2019:	Borussia VfL Mönchengladbach (GER)
Michael Rico LANG	08.02.1991	31	3	2019:	SV Werder Bremen (GER)
Stephan LICHTSTEINER	16.01.1984	108	8	2019:	FC Augsburg (GER)
Melingo Kevin MBABU	19.04.1995	8	0	2019:	VfL Wolfsburg (GER)
Ricardo Iván RODRÍGUEZ Araya	25.08.1992	71	8	2019:	AC Milan (ITA)
Fabian Lukas SCHÄR	20.12.1991	54	8	2019:	Newcastle United FC (ENG)
Midfielders					
Michel AEBISCHER	06.01.1997	1	0	2019:	BSC Young Boys Bern
Christian FASSNACHT	11.11.1993	5	1	2019:	BSC Young Boys Bern
Edimilson FERNANDES Ribeiro	15.04.1996	14	0	2019:	1.FSV Mainz 05 (GER)
Remo Marco FREULER	15.04.1992	21	1	2019:	Atalanta Bergamasca Calcio (ITA)
Djibril SOW	06.02.1997	6	0	2019:	Eintracht Frankfurt (GER)
Renato STEFFEN	03.11.1991	10	0	2019:	VfL Wolfsburg (GER)
Granit XHAKA	27.09.1992	82	12	2019:	Arsenal FC London (ENG)
Denis Lemi ZAKARIA Lako Lado	20.11.1996	28	2	2019:	Borussia VfL Mönchengladbach (GER)
Forwards					
Albian Afrim AJETI	26.02.1997	10	1	2019:	West Ham United FC London (ENG)
Josip DRMIĆ	08.08.1992	35	10	2019:	Norwich City FC (ENG)
Breel Donald EMBOLO	14.02.1997	36	4	2019:	Borussia VfL Mönchengladbach (GER)
Mario GAVRANOVIĆ	24.11.1989	22	7	2019:	GNK Dinamo Zagreb (CRO)
Cedric Jan ITTEN	27.12.1996	2	3	2019:	FC St. Gallen
Admir MEHMEDI	16.03.1991	65	9	2019:	VfL Wolfsburg (GER)
Haris SEFEROVIĆ	22.02.1992	64	18	2019:	Sport Lisboa e Benfica (POR)
Rubén Estephan VARGAS Martínez	05.08.1998	3	1	2019:	FC Augsburg (GER)

National team coach

Vladimir PETKOVIĆ (Bosnia and Herzegovina) [from 01.08.2014]	15.08.1963	60 M; 35 W; 11 D; 14 L; 114-50

TURKEY

The Country:
Türkiye Cumhuriyeti (Republic of Turkey)
Capital: Ankara
Surface: 783,356 km²
Inhabitants: 83,154,997 [2019]
Time: UTC+3

The FA:
Türkiye Futbol Federasyonu
Hasan Dogan Milli Takimlar Kamp ve Egitim Tesisleri Riva Beykoz, İstanbul
Tel: +90 216 554 51 00
Founded: 1923
Member of FIFA since: 1923
Member of UEFA since: 1962
Website: www.tff.org

NATIONAL TEAM RECORDS

RECORDS

First international match:	26.10.1923, İstanbul:	Turkey – Romania 2-2
Most international caps:	Rüştü Reçber	- 120 caps (1994-2012)
Most international goals:	Hakan Şükür	- 51 goals / 112 caps (1992-2007)

UEFA EUROPEAN CHAMPIONSHIP

1960	Qualifiers
1964	Qualifiers
1968	Qualifiers
1972	Qualifiers
1976	Qualifiers
1980	Qualifiers
1984	Qualifiers
1988	Qualifiers
1992	Qualifiers
1996	Final Tournament (Group Stage)
2000	Final Tournament (Quarter-Finals)
2004	Qualifiers
2008	Final Tournament (Semi-Finals)
2012	Qualifiers
2016	Final Tournament (Group Stage)
2020	*Final Tournament (Qualified)*

FIFA WORLD CUP

1930	Did not enter
1934	*Withdrew*
1938	Did not enter
1950	*Qualified but withdrew*
1954	Final Tournament (Group Stage)
1958	*Withdrew*
1962	Qualifiers
1966	Qualifiers
1970	Qualifiers
1974	Qualifiers
1978	Qualifiers
1982	Qualifiers
1986	Qualifiers
1990	Qualifiers
1994	Qualifiers
1998	Qualifiers
2002	Final Tournament (3rd Place)
2006	Qualifiers
2010	Qualifiers
2014	Qualifiers
2018	Qualifiers

OLYMPIC TOURNAMENTS

1908	-
1912	-
1920	-
1924	Preliminary Round
1928	1/8 - Finals
1936	1/8 - Finals
1948	Quarter-Finals
1952	Quarter-Finals
1956	*Withdrew*
1960	Group Stage
1964	Qualifiers
1968	Qualifiers
1972	Qualifiers
1976	Qualifiers
1980	Group Stage
1984	*Withdrew*
1988	Qualifiers
1992	Qualifiers
1996	Qualifiers
2000	Qualifiers
2004	Qualifiers
2008	Qualifiers
2012	Qualifiers
2016	Qualifiers

UEFA NATIONS LEAGUE

2018/2019	League B

FIFA CONFEDERATIONS CUP 1992-2017

2003 (3rd Place)

TURKISH CLUB HONOURS IN EUROPEAN CLUB COMPETITIONS:

European Champion Clubs.Cup (1956-1992) / UEFA Champions League (1993-2020)		
None		
Fairs Cup (1858-1971) / UEFA Cup (1972-2009) / UEFA Europa League (2010-2020)		
Galatasaray SK İstanbul	1	1999/2000
UEFA Super Cup (1972-2019)		
Galatasaray SK İstanbul	1	2000
European Cup Winners.Cup 1961-1999*		
None		

*defunct competition

NATIONAL COMPETITIONS
TABLE OF HONOURS

Turkish Football Championship (1924–1951)*

	CHAMPIONS
1924	Harbiye Ankara
1925-1926	*No competition*
1927	Muhafızgücü SK Ankara
1928 - 1931	*No competition*
1932	İstanbulspor
1933	Fenerbahçe SK İstanbul
1934	Beşiktaş JK İstanbul
1935	Fenerbahçe SK İstanbul
1936 - 1939	*No competition*
1940	Eskişehir Demirspor
1941	Gençlerbirliği Ankara SK Ankara
1942	Harp Okulu SK Ankara
1943	*No competition*
1944	Fenerbahçe SK İstanbul
1945	Harp Okulu SK Ankara
1946	Gençlerbirliği Ankara SK Ankara
1947	Ankara Demirspor
1948	*No competition*
1949	MKE Ankaragücü
1950	Göztepe SK İzmir
1951	Beşiktaş JK İstanbul

*Not recognized by Turkish FA.

National Division (1937–1950)*

	CHAMPIONS
1937	Fenerbahçe SK İstanbul
1938	Güneş SK İstanbul
1939	Galatasaray SK İstanbul
1940	Fenerbahçe SK İstanbul
1941	Beşiktaş JK İstanbul
1942	*No competition*
1943	Fenerbahçe SK İstanbul
1944	Beşiktaş JK İstanbul
1945	Fenerbahçe SK İstanbul
1946	Fenerbahçe SK İstanbul
1947	Beşiktaş JK İstanbul
1948	*No competition*
1949	*No competition*
1950	Fenerbahçe SK İstanbul

	CHAMPIONS	CUP WINNERS	BEST GOALSCORERS	
1956/1957**	Beşiktaş JK İstanbul	-	Nazmi Bilge (Beşiktaş JK İstanbul)	8
1957/1958**	Beşiktaş JK İstanbul	-	Lefter Küçükandonyadis (Fenerbahçe SK İstanbul) Metin Oktay (Galatasaray SK İstanbul)	10
1958/1959	Fenerbahçe SK İstanbul	-	Metin Oktay (Galatasaray SK İstanbul)	11
1959/1960	Beşiktaş JK İstanbul	-	Metin Oktay (Galatasaray SK İstanbul)	33
1960/1961	Fenerbahçe SK İstanbul	-	Metin Oktay (Galatasaray SK İstanbul)	36
1961/1962	Galatasaray SK İstanbul	-	Fikri Elma (Ankara Demirspor)	21
1962/1963	Galatasaray SK İstanbul	Galatasaray SK İstanbul	Metin Oktay (Galatasaray SK İstanbul)	38
1963/1964	Fenerbahçe SK İstanbul	Galatasaray SK İstanbul	Güven Önüt (Beşiktaş JK İstanbul)	19
1964/1965	Fenerbahçe SK İstanbul	Galatasaray SK İstanbul	Metin Oktay (Galatasaray SK İstanbul)	17
1965/1966	Beşiktaş JK İstanbul	Galatasaray SK İstanbul	Ertan Adatepe (MKE Ankaragücü)	20
1966/1967	Beşiktaş JK İstanbul	Altay SK İzmir	Ertan Adatepe (MKE Ankaragücü)	18
1967/1968	Fenerbahçe SK İstanbul	Fenerbahçe SK İstanbul	Fevzi Zemzem (Göztepe SK İzmir)	19
1968/1969	Galatasaray SK İstanbul	Göztepe SK İzmir	Metin Oktay (Galatasaray SK İstanbul)	17
1969/1970	Fenerbahçe SK İstanbul	Göztepe SK İzmir	Fethi Heper (Eskişehirspor Kulübü)	13
1970/1971	Galatasaray SK İstanbul	Eskişehirspor Kulübü	Ogün Altıparmak (Fenerbahçe SK İstanbul)	16
1971/1972	Galatasaray SK İstanbul	MKE Ankaragücü	Fethi Heper (Eskişehirspor Kulübü)	20
1972/1973	Galatasaray SK İstanbul	Galatasaray SK İstanbul	Osman Arpacıoğlu (Fenerbahçe SK İstanbul)	16
1973/1974	Fenerbahçe SK İstanbul	Fenerbahçe SK İstanbul	Cemil Turan (Fenerbahçe SK İstanbul)	14
1974/1975	Fenerbahçe SK İstanbul	Beşiktaş JK İstanbul	Ömer Kaner (Eskişehirspor Kulübü)	14
1975/1976	Trabzonspor Kulübü	Galatasaray SK İstanbul	Cemil Turan (Fenerbahçe SK İstanbul) Ali Osman Renklibay (MKE Ankaragücü)	17
1976/1977	Trabzonspor Kulübü	Trabzonspor Kulübü	Necmi Perekli (Trabzonspor Kulübü)	18
1977/1978	Fenerbahçe SK İstanbul	Trabzonspor Kulübü	Cemil Turan (Fenerbahçe SK İstanbul)	17
1978/1979	Trabzonspor Kulübü	Fenerbahçe SK İstanbul	Özer Umdu (Adanaspor AŞ)	15
1979/1980	Trabzonspor Kulübü	Altay SK İzmir	Mustafa Denizli (Altay SK İzmir) Bahtiyar Yorulmaz (Bursaspor Kulübü)	12
1980/1981	Trabzonspor Kulübü	MKE Ankaragücü	Bora Öztürk (Adanaspor AŞ)	15
1981/1982	Beşiktaş JK İstanbul	Galatasaray SK İstanbul	Selçuk Yula (Fenerbahçe SK İstanbul)	16
1982/1983	Fenerbahçe SK İstanbul	Fenerbahçe SK İstanbul	Selçuk Yula (Fenerbahçe SK İstanbul)	19
1983/1984	Trabzonspor Kulübü	Trabzonspor Kulübü	Tarik Hodžić (YUG, Galatasaray SK İstanbul)	16
1984/1985	Fenerbahçe SK İstanbul	Galatasaray SK İstanbul	Aykut Yiğit (Sakaryaspor Kulübü)	20
1985/1986	Beşiktaş JK İstanbul	Bursaspor Kulübü	Tanju Çolak (Samsunspor Kulübü)	33
1986/1987	Galatasaray SK İstanbul	Gençlerbirliği Ankara	Tanju Çolak (Samsunspor Kulübü)	25
1987/1988	Galatasaray SK İstanbul	Sakaryaspor Kulübü	Tanju Çolak (Galatasaray SK İstanbul)	39
1988/1989	Fenerbahçe SK İstanbul	Beşiktaş JK İstanbul	Aykut Kocaman (Fenerbahçe SK İstanbul)	29
1989/1990	Beşiktaş JK İstanbul	Beşiktaş JK İstanbul	Feyyaz Uçar (Beşiktaş JK İstanbul)	28
1990/1991	Beşiktaş JK İstanbul	Galatasaray SK İstanbul	Tanju Çolak (Galatasaray SK İstanbul)	31
1991/1992	Beşiktaş JK İstanbul	Trabzonspor Kulübü	Aykut Kocaman (Fenerbahçe SK İstanbul)	25
1992/1993	Galatasaray SK İstanbul	Galatasaray SK İstanbul	Tanju Çolak (Fenerbahçe SK İstanbul)	27
1993/1994	Galatasaray SK İstanbul	Beşiktaş JK İstanbul	Bülent Uygun (Fenerbahçe SK İstanbul)	22
1994/1995	Beşiktaş JK İstanbul	Trabzonspor Kulübü	Aykut Kocaman (Fenerbahçe SK İstanbul)	27
1995/1996	Fenerbahçe SK İstanbul	Galatasaray SK İstanbul	Shota Arveladze (GEO, Trabzonspor Kulübü)	25
1996/1997	Galatasaray SK İstanbul	Kocaelispor Kulübü	Hakan Şükür (Galatasaray SK İstanbul)	38

1997/1998	Galatasaray SK İstanbul	Beşiktaş JK İstanbul	Hakan Şükür (Galatasaray SK İstanbul)	33
1998/1999	Galatasaray SK İstanbul	Galatasaray SK İstanbul	Hakan Şükür (Galatasaray SK İstanbul)	19
1999/2000	Galatasaray SK İstanbul	Galatasaray SK İstanbul	Serkan Aykut (Samsunspor Kulübü)	30
2000/2001	Fenerbahçe SK İstanbul	Gençlerbirliği Ankara	Okan Yılmaz (Bursaspor Kulübü)	23
2001/2002	Galatasaray SK İstanbul	Kocaelispor Kulübü	Arif Erdem (Galatasaray SK İstanbul) İlhan Mansız (Beşiktaş JK İstanbul)	21
2002/2003	Beşiktaş JK İstanbul	Trabzonspor Kulübü	Okan Yılmaz (Bursaspor Kulübü)	24
2003/2004	Fenerbahçe SK İstanbul	Trabzonspor Kulübü	Zafer Biryol (Atiker Konyaspor Kulübü)	25
2004/2005	Fenerbahçe SK İstanbul	Galatasaray SK İstanbul	Fatih Tekke (Trabzonspor Kulübü)	31
2005/2006	Galatasaray SK İstanbul	Beşiktaş JK İstanbul	Gökhan Ünal (Kayseri Erciyesspor Kulübü)	25
2006/2007	Fenerbahçe SK İstanbul	Beşiktaş JK İstanbul	Alexsandro de Souza "Alex" (BRA, Fenerbahçe SK İstanbul)	19
2007/2008	Galatasaray SK İstanbul	Kayseri Erciyesspor Kulübü	Semih Şentürk (Fenerbahçe SK İstanbul)	17
2008/2009	Beşiktaş JK İstanbul	Beşiktaş JK İstanbul	Milan Baroš (CZE, Galatasaray SK İstanbul)	20
2009/2010	Bursaspor Kulübü	Trabzonspor Kulübü	Ariza Makukula (POR, Kayseri Erciyesspor Kulübü)	21
2010/2011	Fenerbahçe SK İstanbul	Beşiktaş JK İstanbul	Alexsandro de Souza "Alex" (BRA, Fenerbahçe SK İstanbul)	28
2011/2012	Galatasaray SK İstanbul	Fenerbahçe SK İstanbul	Burak Yılmaz (Trabzonspor Kulübü)	33
2012/2013	Galatasaray SK İstanbul	Fenerbahçe SK İstanbul	Burak Yılmaz (Galatasaray SK İstanbul)	24
2013/2014	Fenerbahçe SK İstanbul	Galatasaray SK İstanbul	Aatif Chahechouhe (MAR, Sivasspor Kulübü)	17
2014/2015	Galatasaray SK İstanbul	Galatasaray SK İstanbul	José Fernando Viana de Santana "Fernandão" (BRA, Bursaspor Kulübü)	22
2015/2016	Beşiktaş JK İstanbul	Galatasaray SK İstanbul	Mario Gómez García (Beşiktaş JK İstanbul)	26
2016/2017	Beşiktaş JK İstanbul	Atiker Konyaspor Kulübü	Vágner Silva de Souza (BRA, Alanyaspor)	23
2017/2018	Galatasaray SK İstanbul	Akhisar Belediyespor Gençlik SK	Bafétimbi Gomis (FRA, Galatasaray SK İstanbul)	29
2018/2019	Galatasaray SK İstanbul	Galatasaray SK İstanbul	Mbaye Diagne (SEN, Kasımpaşa Spor Kulübü / Galatasaray SK İstanbul)	30
2019/2020	İstanbul Başakşehir FK	Trabzonspor Kulübü	Alexander Sørloth (NOR, Trabzonspor Kulübü)	24

**recognized by Turkish FA only since 2002.

NATIONAL CHAMPIONSHIP
Süper Lig 2019/2020
(16.08.2019 – 26.07.2020)

Results

Round 1 [16-19.08.2019]
Denizlispor - Galatasaray 2-0(0-0)
Gençlerbirliği - Çaykur Rizespor 0-1(0-0)
Kayserispor - Alanyaspor 0-1(0-0)
Sivasspor - Beşiktaş 3-0(1-0)
Konyaspor - MKE Ankaragücü 0-0
Göztepe - Antalyaspor 0-1(0-1)
Kasımpaşa - Trabzonspor 1-1(1-1)
Malatyaspor - İstanbul Başakşehir 3-0(0-0)
Fenerbahçe - Gazişehir 5-0(3-0)

Round 2 [23-26.08.2019]
Beşiktaş - Göztepe 3-0(1-0)
MKE Ankaragücü - Kayserispor 1-1(0-0)
Alanyaspor - Kasımpaşa 4-1(1-1)
İstanbul Başakşehir - Fenerbahçe 1-2(1-0)
Çaykur Rizespor - Sivasspor 2-1(0-0)
Trabzonspor - Malatyaspor 2-1(1-0)
Antalyaspor - Denizlispor 0-2(0-1)
Galatasaray - Konyaspor 1-1(0-0)
Gazişehir - Gençlerbirliği 4-1(2-0)

Round 3 [30.08.-01.09.2019]
Kasımpaşa - MKE Ankaragücü 0-1(0-1)
Kayserispor - Galatasaray 2-3(1-0)
Konyaspor - Antalyaspor 2-2(0-1)
Beşiktaş - Çaykur Rizespor 1-1(0-1)
Göztepe - Denizlispor 0-0
Gençlerbirliği - İstanbul Başakşehir 1-2(1-0)
Sivasspor - Gazişehir 1-1(0-1)
Fenerbahçe - Trabzonspor 1-1(1-1)
Malatyaspor - Alanyaspor 2-3(0-3)

Round 4 [13-16.09.2019]
Galatasaray - Kasımpaşa 1-0(1-0)
İstanbul Başakşehir - Sivasspor 1-1(0-1)
Antalyaspor - Kayserispor 2-2(1-1)
Gazişehir - Beşiktaş 3-2(1-0)
MKE Ankaragücü - Malatyaspor 0-4(0-3)
Çaykur Rizespor - Göztepe 0-0
Denizlispor - Konyaspor 0-1(0-0)
Trabzonspor - Gençlerbirliği 2-2(1-1)
Alanyaspor - Fenerbahçe 3-1(1-1)

Round 5 [20-23.09.2019]
Göztepe - Konyaspor 1-0(0-0)
Kasımpaşa - Antalyaspor 3-0(0-0)
Kayserispor - Denizlispor 1-1(1-0)
Fenerbahçe - MKE Ankaragücü 2-1(1-1)
Çaykur Rizespor - Gazişehir 1-2(0-2)
Gençlerbirliği - Alanyaspor 1-1(1-0)
Malatyaspor - Galatasaray 1-1(0-1)
Beşiktaş - İstanbul Başakşehir 1-1(0-0)
Sivasspor - Trabzonspor 2-1(1-1)

Round 6 [27-30.09.2019]
İstanbul Başakşehir - Çaykur Rizes. 5-0(2-0)
Denizlispor - Kasımpaşa 0-1(0-0)
Alanyaspor - Sivasspor 1-1(0-1)
Galatasaray - Fenerbahçe 0-0
Konyaspor - Kayserispor 2-1(1-1)
MKE Ankaragücü - Gençlerbirliği 2-1(0-0)
Antalyaspor - Malatyaspor 3-0(1-0)
Trabzonspor - Beşiktaş 4-1(2-0)
Gazişehir - Göztepe 1-1(0-0)

Round 7 [04-06.10.2019]
Fenerbahçe - Antalyaspor 0-1(0-1)
Malatyaspor - Denizlispor 5-1(2-0)
Kasımpaşa - Konyaspor 1-4(1-3)
Göztepe - Kayserispor 4-0(3-0)
Gençlerbirliği - Galatasaray 0-0
Sivasspor - MKE Ankaragücü 3-1(1-1)
Beşiktaş - Alanyaspor 2-0(0-0)
Gaziantep FK - İstanbul Başakşehir 1-2(1-1)
Çaykur Rizespor - Trabzonspor 1-2(1-0)

Round 8 [18-21.10.2019]
Galatasaray - Sivasspor 3-2(2-0)
Antalyaspor - Gençlerbirliği 0-6(0-5)
İstanbul Başakşehir - Göztepe 2-1(1-0)
Trabzonspor - Gaziantep FK 4-1(2-0)
MKE Ankaragücü - Beşiktaş 0-0
Kayserispor - Kasımpaşa 1-0(1-0)
Alanyaspor - Çaykur Rizespor 5-2(2-0)
Denizlispor - Fenerbahçe 1-2(0-1)
Konyaspor - Malatyaspor 0-2(0-1)

Round 9 [25-28.10.2019]
Çaykur Rizespor - MKE Ankaragücü 2-0(1-0)
Sivasspor - Antalyaspor 2-1(0-0)
Gaziantep FK - Alanyaspor 1-1(0-1)
Fenerbahçe - Konyaspor 5-1(3-1)
Malatyaspor - Kayserispor 4-0(1-0)
Gençlerbirliği - Denizlispor 2-0(1-1)
Göztepe - Kasımpaşa 1-4(1-1)
Beşiktaş - Galatasaray 1-0(0-0)
İstanbul Başakşehir - Trabzonspor 2-2(0-0)

Round 10 [01-04.11.2019]
Galatasaray - Çaykur Rizespor 2-0(2-0)
Konyaspor - Gençlerbirliği 1-1(1-0)
Alanyaspor - İstanbul Başakşehir 0-0
Trabzonspor - Göztepe 0-1(0-1)
Antalyaspor - Beşiktaş 1-2(0-2)
Denizlispor - Sivasspor 0-2(0-1)
Kasımpaşa - Malatyaspor 2-2(1-0)
Kayserispor - Fenerbahçe 1-0(0-0)
MKE Ankaragücü - Gaziantep FK 1-2(0-1)

Round 11 [08-10.11.2019]
Fenerbahçe - Kasımpaşa 3-2(2-1)
Gençlerbirliği - Kayserispor 2-1(1-0)
Çaykur Rizespor - Antalyaspor 1-0(1-0)
Sivasspor - Konyaspor 2-0(0-0)
Gaziantep FK - Galatasaray 0-2(0-2)
Göztepe - Malatyaspor 1-1(1-0)
Trabzonspor - Alanyaspor 1-0(0-0)
İstanbul Başakşehir - Ankaragücü 2-1(1-0)
Beşiktaş - Denizlispor 1-0(0-0)

Round 12 [22-25.11.2019]
Galatasaray - İstanbul Başakşehir 0-1(0-0)
Denizlispor - Çaykur Rizespor 2-0(0-0)
MKE Ankaragücü - Trabzonspor 0-3(0-1)
Konyaspor - Beşiktaş 1-0(0-0)
Kayserispor - Sivasspor 1-4(1-1)
Alanyaspor - Göztepe 0-1(0-0)
Kasımpaşa - Gençlerbirliği 1-2(0-0)
Malatyaspor - Fenerbahçe 0-0
Antalyaspor - Gaziantep FK 1-1(0-1)

Round 13 [29.11.-02.12.2019]
Gençlerbirliği - Malatyaspor 3-3(0-1)
Çaykur Rizespor - Konyaspor 3-1(2-1)
Sivasspor - Kasımpaşa 2-0(2-0)
Alanyaspor - MKE Ankaragücü 5-0(2-0)
Göztepe - Fenerbahçe 2-2(1-1)
Gaziantep FK - Denizlispor 1-2(0-0)
İstanbul Başakşehir - Antalyaspor 2-0(0-0)
Trabzonspor - Galatasaray 1-1(0-0)
Beşiktaş - Kayserispor 4-1(3-0)

Round 14 [06-09.12.2019]
Fenerbahçe - Gençlerbirliği 5-2(3-1)
Malatyaspor - Sivasspor 1-3(1-2)
MKE Ankaragücü - Göztepe 1-3(1-1)
Galatasaray - Alanyaspor 1-0(1-0)
Konyaspor - Gaziantep FK 0-0
Antalyaspor - Trabzonspor 1-3(1-3)
Denizlispor - İstanbul Başakşehir 1-1(0-0)
Kasımpaşa - Beşiktaş 2-3(1-1)
Kayserispor - Çaykur Rizespor 1-0(1-0)

Round 15 [13-16.12.2019]
Alanyaspor - Antalyaspor 0-0
Çaykur Rizespor - Kasımpaşa 0-3(0-2)
Gençlerbirliği - Göztepe 3-1(2-1)
Galatasaray - MKE Ankaragücü 2-2(0-0)
Gaziantep FK - Kayserispor 3-0(0-0)
Sivasspor - Fenerbahçe 3-1(1-0)
Beşiktaş - Malatyaspor 0-2(0-0)
İstanbul Başakşehir - Konyaspor 1-1(1-0)
Trabzonspor - Denizlispor 1-2(1-0)

Round 16 [20-23.12.2019]
Antalyaspor - MKE Ankaragücü 2-2(1-0)
Malatyaspor - Çaykur Rizespor 0-2(0-1)
Kasımpaşa - Gaziantep FK 3-4(1-4)
Göztepe - Galatasaray 2-1(1-1)
Gençlerbirliği - Sivasspor 2-2(0-1)
Kayserispor - İstanbul Başakşehir 1-4(1-2)
Fenerbahçe - Beşiktaş 3-1(2-1)
Denizlispor - Alanyaspor 1-5(0-3)
Konyaspor - Trabzonspor 0-1(0-1)

Round 17 [27-29.12.2019]
Beşiktaş - Gençlerbirliği 4-1(0-1)
MKE Ankaragücü - Denizlispor 2-2(0-2)
İstanbul Başakşehir - Kasımpaşa 5-1(4-0)
Trabzonspor - Kayserispor 6-2(2-1)
Galatasaray - Antalyaspor 5-0(3-0)
Sivasspor - Göztepe 1-0(0-0)
Alanyaspor - Konyaspor 2-1(1-1)
Gaziantep FK - Malatyaspor 1-1(1-0)
Çaykur Rizespor - Fenerbahçe 1-2(1-1)

Round 18 [17-20.01.2020]
MKE Ankaragücü - Konyaspor 0-1(0-0)
Alanyaspor - Kayserispor 5-1(1-0)
İstanbul Başakşehir - Malatyaspor 4-1(4-0)
Gaziantep FK - Fenerbahçe 0-2(0-0)
Antalyaspor - Göztepe 0-3(0-3)
Galatasaray - Denizlispor 2-1(1-0)
Trabzonspor - Kasımpaşa 6-0(3-0)
Beşiktaş - Sivasspor 1-2(1-2)
Çaykur Rizespor - Gençlerbirliği 2-0(0-0)

Round 19 [24-27.01.2020]
Gençlerbirliği - Gaziantep FK 1-0(0-0)
Kayserispor - MKE Ankaragücü 1-1(1-0)
Kasımpaşa - Alanyaspor 1-2(0-1)
Fenerbahçe - İstanbul Başakşehir 2-0(0-0)
Denizlispor - Antalyaspor 0-3(0-2)
Göztepe - Beşiktaş 2-1(2-1)
Konyaspor - Galatasaray 0-3(0-2)
Sivasspor - Çaykur Rizespor 1-1(0-0)
Malatyaspor - Trabzonspor 1-3(1-2)[11.03.]

Round 20 [31.01.-03.02.2020]
İstanbul Başakşehir - Gençlerbirliği 3-1(1-1)
Antalyaspor - Konyaspor 0-0
Çaykur Rizespor - Beşiktaş 1-2(1-1)
Trabzonspor - Fenerbahçe 2-1(2-1)
MKE Ankaragücü - Kasımpaşa 1-1(0-1)
Alanyaspor - Malatyaspor 2-1(1-0)
Gaziantep FK - Sivasspor 5-1(3-1)
Galatasaray - Kayserispor 4-1(2-0)
Denizlispor - Göztepe 1-1(0-1)

Round 21 [07-09.02.2020]
Malatyaspor - MKE Ankaragücü 0-1(0-0)
Konyaspor - Denizlispor 0-0
Beşiktaş - Gaziantep FK 3-0(0-0)
Gençlerbirliği - Trabzonspor 0-2(0-0)
Fenerbahçe - Alanyaspor 1-1(0-1)
Kayserispor - Antalyaspor 2-2(1-1)
Sivasspor - İstanbul Başakşehir 1-1(0-0)
Kasımpaşa - Galatasaray 0-3(0-3)
Göztepe - Çaykur Rizespor 2-0(0-0)[17.03.]

Round 22 [14-17.02.2020]
İstanbul Başakşehir - Beşiktaş 1-0(0-0)
Denizlispor - Kayserispor 0-1(0-0)
Konyaspor - Göztepe 1-3(1-1)
MKE Ankaragücü - Fenerbahçe 2-1(1-0)
Alanyaspor - Gençlerbirliği 0-1(0-0)
Trabzonspor - Sivasspor 2-1(2-0)
Galatasaray - Malatyaspor 1-0(1-0)
Antalyaspor - Kasımpaşa 3-1(0-0)
Gaziantep FK - Çaykur Rizespor 2-0(0-0)

Round 23 [21-24.02.2020]
Sivasspor - Alanyaspor 1-0(1-0)
Kayserispor - Konyaspor 2-2(1-2)
Göztepe - Gaziantep FK 1-0(0-0)
Beşiktaş - Trabzonspor 2-2(0-1)
Malatyaspor - Antalyaspor 1-2(1-1)
Gençlerbirliği - MKE Ankaragücü 1-0(0-0)
Fenerbahçe - Galatasaray 1-3(1-1)
Kasımpaşa - Denizlispor 2-0(1-0)
Çaykur Rizes. - İstanbul Başakşehir 1-2(0-1)

Round 24 [28.02.-02.03.2020]
Alanyaspor - Beşiktaş 1-2(1-0)
Konyaspor - Kasımpaşa 0-0
Trabzonspor - Çaykur Rizespor 5-2(0-1)
Antalyaspor - Fenerbahçe 2-2(0-1)
Denizlispor - Malatyaspor 2-0(1-0)
MKE Ankaragücü - Sivasspor 0-3(0-0)
Galatasaray - Gençlerbirliği 3-0(2-0)
İstanbul Başakşehir - Gaziantep FK 3-1(0-0)
Kayserispor - Göztepe 1-0(0-0)

Round 25 [06-09.03.2020]
Beşiktaş - MKE Ankaragücü 2-1(1-0)
Malatyaspor - Konyaspor 1-1(0-1)
Gaziantep FK - Trabzonspor 1-1(0-1)
Göztepe - İstanbul Başakşehir 0-3(0-1)
Fenerbahçe - Denizlispor 2-2(1-1)
Kasımpaşa - Kayserispor 5-1(3-0)
Çaykur Rizespor - Alanyaspor 1-1(0-1)
Sivasspor - Galatasaray 2-2(1-2)
Gençlerbirliği - Antalyaspor 1-1(0-0)

Round 26 [13-16.03.2020]
MKE Ankaragücü - Çaykur Rizespor 2-1(2-1)
Kasımpaşa - Göztepe 2-0(1-0)
Denizlispor - Gençlerbirliği 1-0(0-0)
Alanyaspor - Gaziantep FK 1-0(1-0)
Konyaspor - Fenerbahçe 1-0(1-0)
Kayserispor - Malatyaspor 2-1(2-0)
Trabzonspor - İstanbul Başakşehir 1-1(0-0)
Galatasaray - Beşiktaş 0-0
Antalyaspor - Sivasspor 1-0(0-0)

Round 27 [12-15.06.2020]
Fenerbahçe - Kayserispor 2-1(0-0)
Göztepe - Trabzonspor 1-3(0-1)
İstanbul Başakşehir - Alanyaspor 2-0(0-0)
Beşiktaş - Antalyaspor 1-2(0-2)
Malatyaspor - Kasımpaşa 1-2(1-0)
Gençlerbirliği - Konyaspor 2-1(0-0)
Gaziantep FK - MKE Ankaragücü 1-1(1-0)
Çaykur Rizespor - Galatasaray 2-0(1-0)
Sivasspor - Denizlispor 1-0(1-0)

Round 28 [19-22.06.2020]
Ankaragücü - İstanbul Başakşehir 1-2(1-0)
Kayserispor - Gençlerbirliği 2-0(1-0)
Denizlispor - Beşiktaş 1-5(0-1)
Malatyaspor - Göztepe 2-1(1-0)
Kasımpaşa - Fenerbahçe 2-0(0-0)
Galatasaray - Gaziantep FK 3-3(2-1)
Konyaspor - Sivasspor 2-2(2-1)
Alanyaspor - Trabzonspor 2-2(1-1)
Antalyaspor - Çaykur Rizespor 3-1(1-0)

Round 29 [26-29.06.2020]
Beşiktaş - Konyaspor 3-0(2-0)
Fenerbahçe - Malatyaspor 3-2(0-0)
Göztepe - Alanyaspor 3-3(1-2)
Trabzonspor - MKE Ankaragücü 1-1(1-0)
Çaykur Rizespor - Denizlispor 2-2(1-2)
Sivasspor - Kayserispor 0-2(0-1)
İstanbul Başakşehir - Galatasaray 1-0(0-0)
Gaziantep FK - Antalyaspor 1-1(0-0)
Gençlerbirliği - Kasımpaşa 0-2(0-1)

Round 30 [03-06.07.2020]
Denizlispor - Gaziantep FK 0-1(0-1)
MKE Ankaragücü - Alanyaspor 1-4(0-0)
Malatyaspor - Gençlerbirliği 0-0
Antalyaspor - İstanbul Başakşehir 0-2(0-0)
Fenerbahçe - Göztepe 2-1(2-0)
Kasımpaşa - Sivasspor 0-0
Galatasaray - Trabzonspor 1-3(0-1)
Konyaspor - Çaykur Rizespor 1-0(0-0)
Kayserispor - Beşiktaş 3-1(0-0)

Round 31 [07-09.07.2020]
Gençlerbirliği - Fenerbahçe 1-1(0-0)
İstanbul Başakşehir - Denizlispor 2-0(0-0)
Sivasspor - Malatyaspor 0-1(0-0)
Trabzonspor - Antalyaspor 2-2(2-1)
Alanyaspor - Galatasaray 4-1(2-1)
Göztepe - MKE Ankaragücü 2-2(2-1)
Çaykur Rizespor - Kayserispor 3-2(1-1)
Beşiktaş - Kasımpaşa 3-2(1-2)
Gaziantep FK - Konyaspor 3-1(0-1)

Round 32 [11-13.07.2020]
Göztepe - Gençlerbirliği 1-3(0-2)
MKE Ankaragücü - Galatasaray 1-0(0-0)
Antalyaspor - Alanyaspor 1-0(1-0)
Fenerbahçe - Sivasspor 1-2(1-2)
Kasımpaşa - Çaykur Rizespor 2-0(0-0)
Kayserispor - Gaziantep FK 1-1(0-0)
Denizlispor - Trabzonspor 2-1(0-1)
Konyaspor - İstanbul Başakşehir 4-3(3-1)
Malatyaspor - Beşiktaş 0-1(0-0)

Round 33 [18-19.07.2020]
Galatasaray - Göztepe 3-1(0-0)
Gaziantep FK - Kasımpaşa 2-2(1-2)
Alanyaspor - Denizlispor 1-0(0-0)
MKE Ankaragücü - Antalyaspor 0-1(0-0)
İstanbul Başakşehir - Kayserispor 1-0(1-0)
Beşiktaş - Fenerbahçe 2-0(0-0)
Çaykur Rizespor - Malatyaspor 3-0(3-0)
Sivasspor - Gençlerbirliği 2-0(1-0)
Trabzonspor - Konyaspor 3-4(1-1)

Antalyaspor - Galatasaray 2-2(1-0)
Denizlispor - MKE Ankaragücü 0-1(0-0)
Fenerbahçe - Çaykur Rizespor 3-1(1-0)
Gençlerbirliği - Beşiktaş 0-3(0-0)
Göztepe - Sivasspor 3-1(1-0)
Kayserispor - Trabzonspor 1-2(0-0)
Konyaspor - Alanyaspor 2-3(2-0)
Malatyaspor - Gaziantep FK 0-1(0-0)
Kasımpaşa - İstanbul Başakşehir 3-2(2-0)

Final Standings

										Total					Home					Away		
1.	İstanbul Başakşehir FK	34	20	9	5	65	-	34	69	12	4	1	38	-	13	8	5	4	27	-	21
2.	Trabzonspor Kulübü	34	18	11	5	76	-	42	65	9	5	3	43	-	23	9	6	2	33	-	19
3.	Beşiktaş JK İstanbul	34	19	5	10	59	-	40	62	11	3	3	34	-	15	8	2	7	25	-	25
4.	Sivasspor Kulübü	34	17	9	8	55	-	38	60	11	4	2	27	-	12	6	5	6	28	-	26
5.	Alanyaspor	34	16	9	9	61	-	37	57	10	4	3	36	-	15	6	5	6	25	-	22
6.	Galatasaray SK İstanbul	34	15	11	8	55	-	37	56	10	5	2	32	-	15	5	6	6	23	-	22
7.	Fenerbahçe SK İstanbul	34	15	8	11	58	-	46	53	11	3	3	41	-	22	4	5	8	17	-	24
8.	Gaziantep FK	34	11	13	10	49	-	50	46	6	7	4	30	-	21	5	6	6	19	-	29
9.	Antalyaspor Kulübü	34	11	12	11	41	-	52	45	5	6	6	22	-	29	6	6	5	19	-	23
10.	Kasımpaşa Spor Kulübü İstanbul	34	12	7	15	53	-	58	43	7	3	7	30	-	25	5	4	8	23	-	33
11.	Göztepe SK İzmir	34	11	9	14	44	-	49	42	6	6	5	26	-	26	5	3	9	18	-	23
12.	Gençlerbirliği SK Ankara	34	9	9	16	39	-	56	36	5	6	6	18	-	23	4	3	10	21	-	33
13.	Konyaspor Kulübü	34	8	12	14	36	-	52	36	4	7	6	16	-	22	4	5	8	20	-	30
14.	Denizlispor Kulübü	34	9	8	17	31	-	48	35	5	2	10	14	-	25	4	6	7	17	-	23
15.	Çaykur Rizespor Kulübü	34	10	5	19	38	-	57	35	8	3	6	26	-	20	2	2	13	12	-	37
16.	Yeni Malatya Spor Kulübü	34	8	8	18	44	-	51	32	4	4	9	22	-	22	4	4	9	22	-	29
17.	Kayserispor Kulübü	34	8	8	18	40	-	72	32	6	6	5	23	-	24	2	2	13	17	-	48
18.	MKE Ankaragücü	34	7	11	16	31	-	56	32	4	4	9	15	-	30	3	7	7	16	-	26

No teams were relegated.

Top goalscorers:

24	**Alexander Sørloth (NOR)**	*Trabzonspor Kulübü*
22	Papiss Demba Rodney Cissé (SEN)	*Alanyaspor*
17	Adis Jahović (MKD)	*Yeni Malatya Spor Kulübü / Antalyaspor Kulübü*
15	Vedat Muriqi (KVX)	*Fenerbahçe SK İstanbul*
14	Sorin Bogdan Stancu (ROU)	*Gençlerbirliği SK Ankara*

NATIONAL CUP
Türkiye Kupasi 2019/2020

Fourth Round [29-31.10.2019]

Altınordu FK İzmir - Amed SK	3-1(2-0)	Fatih Karagümrük SK - Bandırmaspor	4-1(2-1)
1074 Çankırıspor - Çaykur Rizespor Kulübü	1-3(0-2)	İstanbulspor - Büyükçekmece Tepecikspor AŞ	5-2(1-1,2-2)
Hekimoğlu Trabzon - Menemenspor Kulübü İzmir	3-0(1-0)	Karacabey Belediyespor AŞ - Tuzlaspor	1-3(0-1)
Niğde Anadolu FK - Antalyaspor Kulübü	0-0 aet; 2-3 pen	Büyükşehir Belediye - Bodrum Belediye	3-1(2-0)
Eyüpspor SK İstanbul - Konyaspor Kulübü	1-0(0-0,0-0)	Gençlerbirliği SK Ankara - Esenler Erokspor	0-2(0-1)
Altay SK İzmir - Görelespor	1-0(0-0)	Göztepe SK İzmir - Sivas Belediyespor	3-0(2-0)
Adanaspor AŞ - Diyarbekirspor	3-0(1-0)	Tarsus İdman Yurdu - Fenerbahçe SK İstanbul	1-3(0-2)
Alanyaspor - İnegölspor	3-0(3-0)	Bayburt İl Özel İdare - Bursaspor Kulübü	1-2(1-1)
Vanspor FK - Sancaktepe Belediye	1-0(1-0)	Başkent Akademi - Sivasspor Kulübü	0-6(0-3)
Kastamonuspor 1966 - 24 Erzincanspor	1-1 aet; 4-5 pen	Kırklarelispor Kulübü - MKE Ankaragücü	1-0(1-0)
Gümüşhanespor Kulübü - Samsunspor Kulübü	0-3(0-0)	Kayserispor Kulübü - Bayrampaşaspor Kulübü	2-0(0-0,0-0)
Ankara Keçiörengücü SK - Siirt İl Özel İdaresi Spor	3-1(1-1)	Gaziantep FK - Turgutluspor	3-0(1-0)
Payasspor Kulübü - Manisa FK	2-3(1-1)	Denizlispor Kulübü – İçel İdmanyurdu	4-1(2-1)
Kemerspor 2003 Kulübü Derneği - Kasımpaşa SK	2-3(1-2)		

Fifth Round [03-05./17-19.12.2019]

First Leg		Second Leg	
Fatih Karagümrük SK - Göztepe SK İzmir	1-2(0-1)	Göztepe SK İzmir - Fatih Karagümrük SK	2-1(1-1)
Yeni Malatya Spor - Ankara Keçiörengücü SK	3-1(2-0)	Ankara Keçiörengücü SK - Yeni Malatya Spor	2-2(0-0)
Alanyaspor - Adanaspor AŞ	5-1(1-0)	Adanaspor AŞ - Alanyaspor	1-7(0-4)
Esenler Erokspor - Sivasspor Kulübü	0-2(0-1)	Sivasspor Kulübü - Esenler Erokspor	0-1(0-0)
Fenerbahçe SK İstanbul - İstanbulspor	4-0(2-0)	İstanbulspor - Fenerbahçe SK İstanbul	0-2(0-0)
Hekimoğlu Trabzon - İstanbul Başakşehir FK	0-1(0-1)	İstanbul Başakşehir FK - Hekimoğlu Trabzon	2-0(0-0)
Eyüpspor SK İstanbul - Antalyaspor Kulübü	0-3(0-2)	Antalyaspor Kulübü - Eyüpspor SK İstanbul	2-2(1-1)
Kasımpaşa Spor Kulübü - Vanspor FK	2-1(2-1)	Vanspor FK - Kasımpaşa Spor Kulübü	2-2(1-1,2-1)
Büyükşehir Belediye Erzurumspor - Bursaspor Kul.	4-2(1-1)	Bursaspor Kul. - Büyükşehir Belediye Erzurumspor	2-1(0-1)
Altay SK İzmir - Trabzonspor Kulübü	1-2(0-1)	Trabzonspor Kulübü - Altay SK İzmir	4-1(0-0)
Galatasaray SK İstanbul - Tuzlaspor	0-2(0-0)	Tuzlaspor - Galatasaray SK İstanbul	0-4(0-3)
Kırklarelispor Kulübü - Gaziantep FK	2-1(1-0)	Gaziantep FK - Kırklarelispor Kulübü	3-2(1-1)
Kayserispor Kulübü - Manisa FK	3-2(1-0)	Manisa FK - Kayserispor Kulübü	3-3(1-0)
Altınordu FK İzmir - Denizlispor Kulübü	3-5(1-1)	Denizlispor Kulübü - Altınordu FK İzmir	2-2(2-0)
Çaykur Rizespor - Samsunspor Kulübü Derneği	3-2(3-1)	Samsunspor Kulübü Derneği - Çaykur Rizespor	1-1(0-0)
Beşiktaş JK İstanbul - 24 Erzincanspor	3-0(2-0)	24 Erzincanspor - Beşiktaş JK İstanbul	2-0(1-0)

1/8-Finals [14-16./21-23.01.2020]

First Leg		Second Leg	
İstanbul Başakşehir FK - Kırklarelispor Kulübü	1-1(0-0)	Kırklarelispor Kulübü - İstanbul Başakşehir FK	0-0
Sivasspor Kulübü - Yeni Malatya Spor Kulübü	4-0(3-0)	Yeni Malatya Spor Kulübü - Sıvasspor Kulübü	2-1(0-1)
Kayserispor Kulübü - Fenerbahçe SK İstanbul	0-0	Fenerbahçe SK İstanbul - Kayserispor Kulübü	2-0(2-0)
Alanyaspor - Kasımpaşa Spor Kulübü	3-1(3-1)	Kasımpaşa Spor Kulübü - Alanyaspor	3-2(2-1)
Büyükşehir Belediye Erzurum. - Beşiktaş JK İstanbul	3-2(1-1)	Beşiktaş JK İstanbul - Büyükşehir Belediye Erzurum.	2-3(1-1)
Çaykur Rizespor Kulübü - Galatasaray SK İstanbul	1-1(1-1)	Galatasaray SK İstanbul - Çaykur Rizespor Kulübü	2-1(0-0)
Antalyaspor Kulübü - Göztepe SK İzmir	4-3(2-2)	Göztepe SK İzmir - Antalyaspor Kulübü	2-2(1-2)
Trabzonspor Kulübü - Denizlispor Kulübü	2-0(1-0)	Denizlispor Kulübü - Trabzonspor Kulübü	2-0 aet; 2-4 pen

Quarter-Finals [04-06./11-13.02.2020]

First Leg		Second Leg	
Trabzonspor Kulübü - Büyükşehir Belediye Erzurum.	5-0(3-0)	Büyükşehir Belediye Erzur. - Trabzonspor Kulübü	1-4(1-1)
Kırklarelispor Kulübü - Fenerbahçe SK İstanbul	0-3(0-1)	Fenerbahçe SK İstanbul - Kırklarelispor Kulübü	1-0(0-0)
Alanyaspor - Galatasaray SK İstanbul	2-0(1-0)	Galatasaray SK İstanbul - Alanyaspor	3-1(1-1)
Antalyaspor Kulübü - Sivasspor Kulübü	0-0	Sivasspor Kulübü - Antalyaspor Kulübü	1-1(1-0)

Semi-Finals [03-04./16.18.06.03.2020]

First Leg		Second Leg	
Trabzonspor Kulübü - Fenerbahçe SK İstanbul	2-1(0-0)	Fenerbahçe SK İstanbul - Trabzonspor Kulübü	1-3(1-1)
Antalyaspor Kulübü - Alanyaspor	0-1(0-0)	Alanyaspor - Antalyaspor Kulübü	4-0(2-0)

Final

29.07.2020; Atatürk Olimpiyat Stadı, İstanbul; Referee: Ali Palabıyık; Attendance: None

Trabzonspor Kulübü - Alanyaspor   **2-0(1-0)**

Trabzonspor: Uğurcan Çakir, Hüseyin Türkmen, Gastón Campi, João Pedro da Silva Pereira (90.Manuel Marouane Da Costa Trindade Senoussi), Filip Novák (79.Kâmil Çörekçi), Guilherme Costa Marques, José Ernesto Sosa, Abdülkadir Ömür, Abdülkadir Parmak (90.Papa N'Diaye), Alexander Sørloth, Caleb Ekuban (41.Bilal Başaçıkoğlu). Trainer: Edward Ikem Newton (England).

Alanyaspor: José Carlos Coentrão Marafona, Fabrice N'Sakala, José Carlos Coentrão Marafona „Juanfran", Giorgos Tzavellas, Steven Caulker, Ceyhun Gülselam (74.Mustafa Pektemek), Efecan Karaca (63.Onur Bulut), Manolis Siopis (54.Salih Uçan), Papiss Demba Cissé, Antenor Junior Fernandes da Silva Vitoria, Anastasios Bakasetas. Trainer: Erol Bulut.

Goals: 1-0 Abdülkadir Ömür (25), 2-0 Alexander Sørloth (90+10).

THE CLUBS 2019/2020

Alanyaspor

Founded: 1948
Stadium: Bahçeşehir Okulları Stadyumu, Alanya (10,130)
Trainer: Erol Bulut — 30.01.1975

Goalkeepers:	DOB	M	(s)	G
Cenk Gönen	21.02.1988	1		
José Carlos Coentrão Marafona (POR)	28.05.1987	33		
Defenders:	**DOB**	**M**	**(s)**	**G**
Wanderson Sousa Carneiro "Baiano" (BRA)	23.02.1987	11		
Steven Caulker (ENG)	29.12.1991	28	(1)	1
José Carlos Coentrão Marafona „Juanfran" (ESP)	11.09.1988	12	(1)	
Lokman Gör	15.12.1990	1		
Fabrice N'Sakala (COD)	21.07.1990	29		
Giorgos Tzavellas (GRE)	26.11.1987	16	(2)	1
Welinton Souza Silva (BRA)	10.04.1989	23		2
Midfielders:	**DOB**	**M**	**(s)**	**G**
Yacine Bammou (MAR)	11.09.1991	6	(12)	2
Ceyhun Gülselam	25.12.1987	25	(6)	3
Efecan Karaca	16.11.1989	30	(3)	2

	DOB	M	(s)	G
Emircan Altıntaş	15.07.1995	2	(6)	
Kaan Kanak	06.10.1990	5		
Musa Çağıran	17.11.1992	5	(12)	
Salih Uçan	06.01.1994	16	(10)	1
Manolis Siopis (GRE)	14.05.1994	22	(5)	
Tayfur Bingöl	11.01.1993		(1)	
Umut Güneş	16.03.2000		(3)	
Forwards:	**DOB**	**M**	**(s)**	**G**
Anastasios Bakasetas (GRE)	28.06.1993	33	(1)	10
Papiss Demba Cissé (SEN)	03.06.1985	30	(2)	22
Djalma Braume Manuel Abel Campos (ANG)	30.05.1987	9	(13)	4
Antenor Junior Fernandes da Silva Vitoria (CHI)	10.04.1988	22	(8)	9
Mustafa Pektemek	11.08.1988	1	(11)	1
Onur Bulut	16.04.1994	14	(9)	3

Makina ve Kimya Endüstrisi Ankaragücü

Founded: 31.08.1910
Stadium: Eryaman Stadyumu, Ankara (20,071)

Trainer:	Aykan Atik	28.12.1971
[03.09.2019]	Metin Diyadin	16.02.1968
[13.11.2019]	Mustafa Kaplan	02.09.1967
[22.01.2020]	Aykan Atik	28.12.1971
[30.01.2020]	Mustafa Reşit Akçay	28.12.1971
[24.06.2020]	Ibrahim Üzülmez	10.03.1974

Goalkeepers:	DOB	M	(s)	G
Korcan Çelikay	31.12.1987	21		
Ricardo Henrique Schuck Friedrich (BRA)	18.02.1993	13		
Defenders:	**DOB**	**M**	**(s)**	**G**
Alihan Kubalas	26.10.1991	7	(2)	1
Atila Turan	10.04.1992	6	(5)	
Cebrail Karayel	15.08.1994	9	(8)	
Fatih Tultak	28.02.2001	1		
Stelios Kitsiou (GRE)	28.09.1993	31		2
Ante Kulušić (CRO)	06.06.1986	31		
Michał Pazdan (POL)	21.09.1987	30	(1)	
Tiago Miguel Baía Pinto (POR)	01.02.1988	27	(1)	
Yalçın Ayhan	01.05.1982	1	(3)	
Midfielders:	**DOB**	**M**	**(s)**	**G**
Ahmet Can Arik	22.08.1997		(1)	
Aydın Karabulut	25.01.1988	8	(10)	1
Ender Aygören	16.06.2000		(2)	
Héctor Miguel Canteros (ARG)	15.03.1989	12	(2)	1
Ricardo Faty (SEN)	04.08.1986	23	(6)	
Daniel Łukasik (POL)	28.04.1991	14		

	DOB	M	(s)	G
Mahmut Akan	14.07.1994		(1)	
Mehmet Sak	04.04.1990	5	(4)	
Wilfred Moke (COD)	12.02.1988	13	(4)	
Orkan Çınar	29.01.1996		(3)	
Ezequiel Óscar Scarione (ARG)	14.07.1985	9	(5)	4
Sedat Ağçay	22.09.1981	23	(4)	
Miloš Stanojević (SRB)	20.11.1993	2	(1)	
Forwards:	**DOB**	**M**	**(s)**	**G**
Alper Önal	06.06.1996		(6)	
Berke Gürbüz	27.01.2003		(1)	
Hasan Kaya	10.11.1995	5	(6)	
İlhan Parlak	18.01.1987	21	(12)	7
Saba Lobzhanidze (GEO)	18.12.1994	12	(3)	1
Konrad Michalak (POL)	19.09.1997	10	(4)	
Dever Akeem Orgill (JAM)	08.03.1990	28	(1)	5
Gelmin Javier Rivas Boada (VEN)	23.03.1989	1	(6)	1
Gerson Rodrigues (LUX)	20.06.1995	11		6
Zaur Sadaev (RUS)	06.11.1989		(5)	
Sitki Imdat	05.10.2001		(1)	

Antalyaspor Kulübü

Founded: 02.07.1966
Stadium: Antalya Stadyumu, Antalya (32,537)

Trainer:	Bülent Korkmaz	24.11.1968
[15.11.2019]	Stjepan Tomas (CRO)	06.03.1976
[04.01.2020]	Tamer Tuna	01.07.1976

Goalkeepers:	DOB	M	(s)	G
Ruud Boffin (BEL)	05.11.1987	23		
Ferhat Kaplan	07.01.1989	11		
Defenders:	**DOB**	**M**	**(s)**	**G**
Bahadir Öztürk	10.01.1995	11		
Ondřej Čelůstka (CZE)	18.06.1989	23	(1)	1
Luis Francisco Grando „Chico"(BRA)	02.02.1987	11	(11)	1
Diego Ângelo de Oliveira (BRA)	12.02.1986	15		1
Eren Albayrak	23.04.1991	11	(3)	
Ersan Gülüm	17.05.1987	3		1
Fedor Kudryashov (RUS)	05.04.1987	17		
Salih Dursun	12.07.1991	1	(4)	
Nazim Sangaré	30.05.1994	23		1
Tarık Çamdal	24.03.1991	3	(1)	
Midfielders:	**DOB**	**M**	**(s)**	**G**
Harun Alpsoy (SUI)	03.03.1997		(3)	
Bünyamin Balcı	31.05.2000	14	(2)	
Aatif Chahechouhe (FRA)	02.07.1986	13	(4)	1

	DOB	M	(s)	G
Charles Fernando Basílio da Silva (BRA)	14.02.1985	14	(3)	
Delvin N'Dinga (CGO)	14.03.1988	5	(1)	
Doğukan Sinik	21.01.1999	13	(8)	
Hakan Özmert	03.06.1985	21	(4)	2
Mevlut Ekelik	16.12.2004		(1)	
Serdar Özkan	01.01.1987	7	(5)	3
Ufuk Akyol (GER)	27.08.1997	22	(6)	3
Veysel Sarı	25.07.1988	15		
Yekta Kurtuluş	11.12.1985	4	(3)	1
Forwards:	**DOB**	**M**	**(s)**	**G**
Amilton Minervino da Silva (BRA)	12.08.1989	24	(4)	2
Gustavo Blanco Leschuk (ARG)	05.11.1991	12	(13)	4
Alfredo Gomes Ribeiro „Fredy"(ANG)	27.03.1990	14	(10)	3
Jacinto Muondo Dala „Gelson Dala" (ANG)	13.07.1996	2	(4)	
Adis Jahović (MKD)	18.03.1987	13		6
Paul Omo Mukairu (NGA)	18.01.2000	14	(10)	3
Lukas Josef Podolski (GER)	04.06.1985	6	(3)	2
Sinan Gümüş (GER)	15.01.1994	9	(1)	5

Beşiktaş Jimnastik Kulübü İstanbul

Founded: 04.03.1903
Stadium: Vodafone Park, İstanbul (41,188)
Trainer: Abdullah Avcı   31.07.1963
[26.01.2020] Recep Ucar   22.09.1975
[29.01.2020] Sergen Yalçın   05.10.1972

Goalkeepers:	DOB	M	(s)	G
Ersin Destanoğlu	01.01.2001	8		
Loris Karius (GER)	22.06.1993	25		
Utku Yuvakuran	02.11.1997	1		
Defenders:	**DOB**	**M**	**(s)**	**G**
Caner Erkin	04.10.1988	27	(3)	3
Douglas (BRA)	06.08.1990	3	(2)	
Erdoğan Kaya	27.03.2001		(1)	
Gökhan Gönül	04.01.1985	29	(1)	4
Pedro Miguel Braga Rebocho (POR)	23.01.1995	8	(1)	
Rıdvan Yılmaz	21.05.2001	6		
Enzo Pablo Roco Roco (CHI)	16.08.1992	10	(1)	
Víctor Ruiz Torre (ESP)	25.01.1989	23		
Domagoj Vida (CRO)	29.04.1989	31		5
Midfielders:	**DOB**	**M**	**(s)**	**G**
Kevin-Prince Boateng (GHA)	06.03.1987	6	(5)	3
Dorukhan Toköz	21.05.1996	6	(1)	
Mohamed Naser Elsayed Elneny (EGY)	11.07.1992	27		1

	DOB	M	(s)	G
Atiba Hutchinson (CAN)	08.02.1983	29	(1)	6
Kartal Yılmaz	04.11.2000		(5)	
Gary Alexis Medel Soto (CHI)	03.08.1987	2		
Muhayer Oktay	28.04.1999		(1)	
Necip Uysal	24.01.1991	6	(9)	
Oğuzhan Özyakup	23.09.1992	4	(8)	1
Orkan Çınar	29.01.1996		(3)	
Forwards:	**DOB**	**M**	**(s)**	**G**
Tyler Boyd (NZL)	30.12.1994	13	(8)	1
Burak Yılmaz	15.07.1985	24	(1)	13
Abdoulay Diaby (MLI)	21.05.1991	22	(9)	5
Güven Yalçın	18.01.1999	7	(13)	3
Jeremain Marciano Lens (NED)	24.11.1987	17	(6)	2
Adem Ljajić (SRB)	29.09.1991	17	(7)	5
Mehmet Nayir	28.06.1993	3	(14)	4
Georges-Kévin N'Koudou (FRA)	13.02.1995	19	(7)	3
Ricardo Andrade Quaresma Bernardo (POR)	26.09.1983	1		

Çaykur Rizespor Kulübü

Founded: 19.05.1953
Stadium: "Rize Şehir" Stadyumu, Rize (15,332)
Trainer: İsmail Kartal   15.06.1961
[03.03.2020] Ünal Karaman   29.06.1966
[16.07.2020] Mehmet Karaca   14.04.1962

Goalkeepers:	DOB	M	(s)	G
Gökhan Akkan	01.01.1995	25		
Tarik Çetin	08.01.1997	7	(2)	
Zafer Görgen	21.06.2000	2	(1)	
Defenders:	**DOB**	**M**	**(s)**	**G**
Mohamed Aberhoune (MAR)	03.05.1989	19	(1)	2
Alberk Koç	15.02.1997	1	(2)	
Burak Albayrak	12.01.1998	5	(2)	
Dimitrios Chatziisaias (GRE)	21.09.1992	8	(1)	
Ivanildo Jorge Mendes Fernandes (POR)	26.03.1996	11		1
Dario Melnjak (CRO)	31.10.1992	33	(1)	3
Orhan Ovacıklı	23.11.1988	8	(6)	
Montassar Talbi (TUN)	26.05.1998	27		
Midfielders:	**DOB**	**M**	**(s)**	**G**
Abdullah Durak	01.04.1987	18	(7)	
Joseph Larweh Attamah (GHA)	22.05.1994	11	(3)	
Atakan Akkaynak (GER)	05.01.1999		(4)	
Barış Alıcı	24.06.1997		(7)	

	DOB	M	(s)	G
Nill De Pauw (BEL)	06.01.1990	6	(1)	
Ismaël Diomandé (CIV)	28.08.1992	20	(4)	
Denys Garmash (UKR)	19.04.1990	9	(5)	3
Mikola Morozyuk (UKR)	17.01.1988	23	(2)	
Oğuz Güçtekin	06.04.1999	7	(7)	
Fernando Henrique Boldrin „Rick" (BRA)	23.02.1989	29	(1)	6
Aminu Umar (NGA)	06.03.1995	15	(3)	3
Amedej Vetrih (SVN)	16.09.1990	22	(2)	
Yan Medeiros Sasse (BRA)	24.06.1997	4	(12)	1
Forwards:	**DOB**	**M**	**(s)**	**G**
Andriy Boryachuk (UKR)	23.04.1996		(5)	
Mostafa El Kabir (MAR)	05.10.1988	2		
Oğulcan Cağlayan	22.03.1996	14	(8)	3
Braian José Samudio Segovia (PAR)	23.12.1995	23	(8)	5
Marko Šćepović (SRB)	23.05.1991	3	(7)	
Milan Škoda (CZE)	16.01.1986	17		10
Tunay Torun	21.04.1990	5	(4)	1

Denizlispor Kulübü

Founded: 26.05.1966
Stadium: Denizli Atatürk Stadyumu, Denizli (18,745)
Trainer: Yücel İldiz   04.06.1953
[11.10.2019] Mehmet Özdilek   01.04.1966
[24.02.2020] Bülent Uygun   01.08.1971
[04.07.2020] Levent Kartop   21.08.1979

Goalkeepers:	DOB	M	(s)	G
Hüseyin Altıntaş	11.09.1994	3		
Adam Stachowiak (POL)	18.12.1986	26		
Tolgahan Acar	04.06.1986	5		
Defenders:	**DOB**	**M**	**(s)**	**G**
Syam Ben Youssef (TUN)	31.03.1989	3	(1)	
Muhammet Özkal	26.11.1999		(3)	1
Mustafa Yumlu	25.09.1987	25	(3)	3
Oğuz Yilmaz	01.01.1993	26	(1)	
Özgür Çek	03.01.1991	5	(9)	
Cristian Ionuţ Săpunaru (ROU)	05.04.1984	13	(1)	
Tiago Jorge Oliveira Lopes (POR)	04.01.1989	18	(5)	
Zeki Yavru	05.09.1991	27	(2)	
Midfielders:	**DOB**	**M**	**(s)**	**G**
Ismaïl Aissati (MAR)	16.08.1988	29	(4)	

	DOB	M	(s)	G
Zakarya Bergdich (MAR)	07.01.1989	22		
Marc Kibong Mbamba (CMR)	15.10.1988	4	(8)	
Radosław Murawski (POL)	22.04.1994	32		4
Olcay Şahan	26.05.1987	16	(10)	1
Ogenyi Eddy Onazi (NGA)	25.12.1992	4	(5)	
Recep Nıyaz	02.08.1995	14	(6)	1
Isaac Sackey (GHA)	04.04.1994	17	(3)	
Sedat Şahintürk	07.02.1996	1	(9)	
Forwards:	**DOB**	**M**	**(s)**	**G**
Modou Barrow (GAM)	13.10.1992	23	(1)	3
Burak Çalık	05.02.1989	1	(2)	
Oscar Eduardo Estupiñán Vallesilla (COL)	29.12.1996	10	(18)	7
Hugo Rodallega Martínez (COL)	25.07.1985	30	(1)	6
Mehmet Akyüz	02.01.1986	1	(6)	
Hadi Sacko (FRA)	24.03.1994	19	(9)	3

Fenerbahçe Spor Kulübü İstanbul

Founded: 03.05.1907 (as *Fenerbahçe Futbol Kulübü*)
Stadium: Ülker („Şükrü Saracoğlu") Stadyumu, Istanbul (47,834)
Trainer: Ersun Yanal 17.12.1961
[04.03.2020] Zeki Göle 26.09.1979
[09.06.2020] Tahir Karapınar 20.04.1967

Goalkeepers:	DOB	M	(s)	G
Altay Bayındır	14.04.1998	32		
Harun Tekin	17.06.1989	2		
Defenders:	DOB	M	(s)	G
Nabil Dirar (MAR)	25.02.1986	27	(1)	2
Emre Miray Köksal	18.10.2001		(1)	
Simon Falette (GUI)	19.02.1992	8		
Hasan-Ali Kaldırım	09.12.1989	17	(1)	
Mathias Jattah-Njie Jørgensen (DEN)	23.04.1990	14	(2)	2
Adil Rami (FRA)	27.12.1985	1		
Sadık Çiftpinar	01.01.1993	2	(2)	
Serdar Aziz	23.10.1990	22		4
Midfielders:	DOB	M	(s)	G
Alper Potuk	08.04.1991	1	(4)	
Deniz Türüç	29.01.1993	15	(11)	3
Emre Belözoğlu	07.09.1980	16	(10)	3
Emre Nasuh	01.01.2001		(1)	
Ferdi Kadıoğlu (NED)	07.10.1999	8	(15)	4
Garry Mendes Rodrigues (CPV)	27.11.1990	20	(6)	4
Mauricio Anibal Isla Isla (CHI)	12.06.1988	19		
Jailson Marques Siqueira (BRA)	07.09.1995	18	(9)	1
Luiz Gustavo Dias (BRA)	23.07.1987	28		3
Mehmet Ekici	25.03.1990	5	(3)	
Murat Sağlam (GER)	10.04.1998		(1)	
Ömer Beyaz	29.08.2003	2	(2)	
Ozan Tufan	23.03.1995	33		6
Tolga Ciğerci	23.03.1992	20	(6)	2
Tolgay Arslan (GER)	16.08.1990	5	(8)	
Miha Zajc (SVN)	01.07.1994	1	(9)	1
Forwards:	DOB	M	(s)	G
Max Bennet Kruse (GER)	19.03.1988	20		7
Mevlüt Erdinç	25.02.1987	1	(11)	
Muhammed Gümüşkaya	01.01.2001		(1)	
Victor Moses (NGA)	12.12.1990	6		1
Vedat Muriqi (KVX)	24.04.1994	30	(2)	15
Allahyar Sayyadmanesh (IRN)	29.06.2001	1	(1)	

Galatasaray Spor Kulübü İstanbul

Founded: 30.10.1905 (as *Galata-Serai Football Club*)
Stadium: Türk Telekom Stadyumu, Istanbul (52,223)
Trainer: Fatih Terim 04.09.1953

Goalkeepers:	DOB	M	(s)	G
Néstor Fernando Muslera Micol (URU)	16.06.1986	26		
Okan Koçuk	27.07.1995	8	(1)	
Defenders:	DOB	M	(s)	G
Ahmet Çalık	26.02.1994	6	(5)	
Emin Bayram	02.04.2003	1	(3)	
Emre Taşdemir	08.08.1995	3	(3)	
Martin Linnes (NOR)	20.09.1991	6	(6)	
Christian Luyindama Nekadio (COD)	08.01.1994	10		
Marcos do Nascimento Teixeira "Marcão" (BRA)	05.06.1996	28		
Mariano Ferreira Filho (BRA)	23.06.1986	26	(2)	
Yuto Nagatomo (JPN)	12.09.1986	14	(1)	1
Ömer Bayram	27.07.1991	25	(4)	1
Marcelo Josemir Saracchi Pintos (URU)	23.04.1998	14		2
Şener Özbayraklı	23.01.1990	4	(4)	
Midfielders:	DOB	M	(s)	G
Younès Belhanda (MAR)	25.02.1990	21	(2)	5
Ryan Donk (SUR)	30.03.1986	23	(3)	3
Emre Akbaba	04.10.1992	12	(5)	4
Sofiane Féghouli (ALG)	26.12.1989	27		6
Mario Lemina (GAB)	01.09.1993	19	(1)	
Steven N'Kemboanza Mike Christopher N'Zonzi(FRA)	15.12.1988	10		
Jesse Tamunobaraboye Sekidika (NGA)	14.07.1996		(6)	
Selçuk İnan	10.02.1985	3	(5)	
Jean Michaël Seri (CIV)	19.07.1991	23	(4)	2
Taylan Antalyalı	08.01.1995	6	(9)	1
Forwards:	DOB	M	(s)	G
Adem Büyük	30.08.1987	12	(14)	7
Florin Andone (ROU)	11.04.1993	6	(3)	2
Ryan Guno Babel (NED)	19.12.1986	13	(2)	5
Mbaye Diagne (SEN)	28.10.1991	3		
Jakup Jimmy Durmaz (SWE)	22.03.1989	1	(10)	
Emre Mor	24.07.1997	3	(7)	
Radamel Falcao García Zárate (COL)	10.02.1986	13	(3)	10
Henry Chukwuemeka Onyekuru (NGA)	05.06.1997	8	(2)	1
Yunus Akgün	07.07.2000		(5)	1

Gaziantep Futbol Kulübü

Founded: 1988 (as *Sankospor*)
Stadium: Gaziantep Arena, Gaziantep (33,502)
Trainer: Marius Ninel Şumudică (ROU) 04.03.1971

Goalkeepers:	DOB	M	(s)	G
Günay Güvenc (GER)	25.07.1991	31		
Haydar Yilmaz	19.01.1984	1		
Yuriy Lodygin (RUS)	26.05.1990	2		
Defenders:	DOB	M	(s)	G
Papy Djilobodji (SEN)	01.12.1988	33		6
Iraneuton Sousa Morais Junior (BRA)	22.07.1986	29		
Jean-Armel Kana-Biyik (CMR)	03.07.1989	33		1
Oğuz Ceylan	15.12.1990	30		1
Paweł Olkowski (POL)	13.02.1990	6	(3)	
Alin Dorinel Toşca (ROU)	14.03.1992	34		
Midfielders:	DOB	M	(s)	G
André Alexandre Carreira Sousa (POR)	09.07.1990	12	(1)	1
Raman Chibsah (GHA)	10.03.1993	10	(14)	1
Souleymane Diarra (MLI)	30.01.1995	12	(12)	2
Furkan Soyalp	12.06.1995	4	(11)	1
Gökhan Alsan	01.04.1990		(1)	
Güray Vural	11.06.1988	27	(2)	5
Jefferson Nogueira Junior (BRA)	22.01.1994	14	(6)	1
Kenan Özer	16.08.1987	12	(17)	3
Kubilay Aktaş	29.01.1995	2	(2)	
Alexandru Iulian Maxim (ROU)	08.07.1990	15		7
Mehmet Uğurlu	09.07.1988	2	(2)	
Abdul-Aziz Tetteh (GHA)	25.05.1990	6		
Forwards:	DOB	M	(s)	G
Tobi Olarenwaju Ayobami Kayode (NGA)	08.05.1993	27		10
Muğdat Çelik	03.01.1990		(5)	
Muhammed Demir	10.01.1992	13	(9)	3
Bartłomiej Pawłowski (POL)	13.11.1992	2	(16)	1
Patrick Twumasi (GHA)	09.05.1994	17	(9)	6

Gençlerbirliği Spor Kulübü Ankara

Founded: 14.03.1923
Stadium: Eryaman Stadyumu, Ankara (20,071)
Trainer: Mustafa Kaplan — 02.09.1967
[01.11.2019] Hamza Hamzaoğlu — 15.01.1970

Goalkeepers:	DOB	M	(s)	G
Burak Capkinoglu	25.02.1994		(1)	
Abdoulaye Diallo (SEN)	30.03.1992	4		
Ertaç Özbir	25.10.1989	15		
Kristoffer Nordfeldt (SWE)	23.06.1989	15		
Defenders:	DOB	M	(s)	G
Arda Kizildag	15.10.1998	3		
Nils Erik Mattias Bjärsmyr (SWE)	03.01.1986	7	(1)	
Erdem Özgenç	22.08.1984	19	(2)	
Flávio da Silva Ramos (BRA)	12.05.1994	26		
Halil Pehlivan	21.08.1993	20	(2)	
Pierre-Yves Polomat (MTQ)	27.12.1993	17	(2)	
Zargo Touré (SEN)	11.11.1989	32		
Mike van Beijnen (NED)	07.03.1999		(1)	
Midfielders:	DOB	M	(s)	G
Ahmet Oğuz	16.01.1993	12	(6)	
Berat Ayberk Özdemir	23.05.1998	22	(9)	2
Sadio Diallo (GUI)	28.12.1990	1	(5)	
Fabricio Santos de Jesus (BRA)	13.06.1992	24	(1)	
Rahmetullah Berişbek	22.03.1999	1	(20)	1
Sami Altiparmak	20.04.2001	1	(3)	
Sefa Yilmaz	14.02.1990	10	(7)	
Stéphane Sessègnon (BEN)	01.06.1984	28	(2)	3
Soner Dikmen	01.09.1993	4	(4)	
Yasin Pehlivan (AUT)	05.01.1989	12	(4)	1
Forwards:	DOB	M	(s)	G
Floyd Ama Nino Ayité (TOG)	15.12.1988	11	(8)	3
Daniel João Santos Candeias (POR)	25.02.1988	32		3
İlker Karakaş	11.01.1999	1	(9)	
Nadir Çiftçi	12.02.1992	5	(8)	
Mats Seuntjens (NED)	17.04.1992	6	(12)	
Giovanni-Guy Yann Sio (CIV)	31.03.1989	25	(3)	10
Sorin Bogdan Stancu (ROU)	28.06.1987	21	(3)	14

Göztepe Spor Kulübü İzmir

Founded: 14.06.1925 (*as Göztepe Gençlik Kulübü*)
Stadium: „Gürsel Aksel" Stadyumu, İzmir (25,035)
Trainer: Tamer Tuna — 01.07.1976
[04.11.2019] Ilhan Palut — 12.11.1976

Goalkeepers:	DOB	M	(s)	G
António Alberto Bastos Pimparel "Beto" (POR)	01.05.1982	30		
Mehmet Bakırbaş	01.06.1996	4	(3)	
Defenders:	DOB	M	(s)	G
Alpaslan Öztürk	16.07.1993	21	(3)	7
Atınç Nukan	20.07.1993	4	(2)	
Berkan Emir	06.02.1988	30		3
Lamine Gassama (SEN)	20.10.1989	26	(2)	
Murat Paluli	09.08.1994	8	(2)	
Bubacarr Sanneh (GAM)	14.11.1994	2		
Léo Schwechlen (FRA)	05.06.1989	6		
Cristian Chagas Tarouco "Titi" (BRA)	12.03.1988	29	(1)	
Wallace Reis da Silva (BRA)	26.12.1987	5	(3)	1
Midfielders:	DOB	M	(s)	G
André Castro Pereira (POR)	02.04.1988	22	(10)	3
Celso Borges Mora (CRC)	27.05.1988	17	(9)	1
Halil Akbunar	09.10.1993	24	(7)	5
Kerem Kesgin	05.11.2000		(3)	
José Márcio da Costa „Márcio Mossoró"(BRA)	04.07.1983	16	(9)	1
André Biyogo Poko (GAB)	07.03.1993	12	(2)	
Serdar Gürler	14.09.1991	26		7
Soner Aydoğdu	05.01.1991	30		5
Yalçın Kayan	30.01.1999	2	(10)	
Yasin Öztekin	19.03.1987	1	(7)	
Forwards:	DOB	M	(s)	G
Batuhan Kırdaroğlu	10.09.2000		(1)	
Deniz Kadah	02.03.1986	4	(12)	
Ege Özkayımoğlu	18.07.2001		(3)	
Eren Derdiyok (SUI)	12.06.1988	3	(2)	
Cameron Jerome (ENG)	14.08.1986	19	(3)	3
Stefano Napoleoni (ITA)	26.06.1986	23	(6)	6
Zlatko Tripić (NOR)	02.12.1992	7	(4)	
Kamil Wilczek (POL)	14.01.1988	8	(6)	1

İstanbul Başakşehir Futbol Kulübü

Founded: 1990 (*as İstanbul Büyükşehir Belediyespor*); re-founded 2004
Stadium: Başakşehir „Fatih Terim" Stadyumu, Istanbul (17,801)
Trainer: Okan Buruk — 19.10.1973

Goalkeepers:	DOB	M	(s)	G
Mert Günok	01.03.1989	33		
Volkan Babacan	11.08.1988	1		
Defenders:	DOB	M	(s)	G
Aziz Eraltay Behich (AUS)	16.12.1990	5		
Aurélien Bayard Chedjou Fongang (CMR)	20.06.1985	2		
Gaël Clichy (FRA)	26.07.1985	30	(1)	2
Alexandru Epureanu (MDA)	27.09.1986	28	(1)	
Uilson de Souza Paula Junior "Junior Caiçara" (BRA)	27.04.1989	33		
Luís Miguel Vieira Silva	08.10.1990	1		
Carlos dos Santos Rodrigues „Ponck" (CPV)	13.01.1995	17	(5)	1
Martin Škrtel (SVK)	15.12.1984	18	(2)	3
Midfielders:	DOB	M	(s)	G
Arda Turan	30.01.1987	2	(7)	
Okechukwu Godson Azubuike (NGA)	19.04.1997	9	(8)	
Berkay Özcan	15.02.1998	4	(15)	
Furkan Soyalp	12.06.1995		(1)	
Gökhan Inler (SUI)	27.06.1984	2	(8)	
İrfan Kahveci	15.07.1995	29		4
Mahmut Tekdemir	20.01.1988	21	(3)	3
José Márcio da Costa „Márcio Mossoró"(BRA)	04.07.1983	1		
Mehmet Topal	03.03.1986	14	(11)	
Soner Aydoğdu	05.01.1991	1		
Edin Višća (BIH)	17.02.1990	33		13
Forwards:	DOB	M	(s)	G
Danijel Aleksić (SRB)	30.04.1991	15	(9)	6
Demba Ba (SEN)	25.05.1985	17	(11)	13
Enzo Crivelli (FRA)	06.02.1995	29	(1)	11
Eljero George Rinaldo Elia (NED)	13.02.1987	17	(6)	3
Fredrik Gulbrandsen (NOR)	10.09.1992	9	(11)	3
Kerim Frei Koyunlu	19.11.1993		(3)	
Muhammet Arslantaş	27.01.2001		(1)	
Róbson de Souza „Robinho" (BRA)	25.01.1984	3	(12)	

Kasımpaşa Spor Kulübü İstanbul

Founded: 15.01.1921
Stadium: „Recep Tayyip Erdoğan" Stadyumu, Istanbul (14,234)
Trainer: Kemal Özdeş — 10.05.1970
[04.12.2019] Tayfur Havutçu — 23.04.1970
[19.01.2020] Erkan Coker — 10.09.1969
[06.02.2020] Fuat Çapa — 15.08.1968

Goalkeepers:	DOB	M	(s)	G
Fatih Öztürk (FRA)	22.12.1986	20		
Ramazan Köse	12.05.1988	14		
Defenders:	**DOB**	**M**	**(s)**	**G**
Syam Habib Ben Youssef (TUN)	31.03.1989	15		1
Tomáš Břečka (CZE)	12.05.1994	10	(1)	1
Oussema Haddadi (TUN)	28.01.1992	16		
Florent Hadergjonaj (KVX)	31.07.1994	13		
Karim Hafez Ramadan Seif Eldin (EGY)	12.03.1996	13		
Jorge Filipe Oliveira Fernandes (POR)	02.04.1997	12	(6)	
Yassine Meriah (TUN)	02.07.1993	15		
Özgür Çek	03.01.1991	3	(1)	
Loret Sadiku (ALB)	28.07.1991	7	(2)	
Zvonimir Šarlija (CRO)	29.08.1996	5	(1)	1
Mickaël Tirpan (BEL)	23.10.1993	13		
Olivier Veigneau (FRA)	16.07.1985	3	(2)	
Midfielders:	**DOB**	**M**	**(s)**	**G**
Aytaç Kara	23.03.1993	32		5
Doğucan Haspolat (NED)	11.02.2000	1	(3)	

	DOB	M	(s)	G
Haris Hajradinović (BIH)	18.02.1994	29	(1)	4
Tobias Heintz (NOR)	13.07.1998	2	(6)	
İlhan Depe	10.09.1992	7	(17)	
Abdul Khalili (SWE)	07.06.1992	12	(4)	2
David Pavelka (CZE)	18.05.1991	6	(4)	
Strahil Popov (BUL)	31.08.1990	14		
Tarkan Serbest	02.05.1994	6	(7)	
Uğurcan Yazğılı	09.04.1999		(1)	
Veysel Sarı	25.07.1988	11	(2)	2
Yusuf Erdoğan	07.08.1992	8	(13)	4
Forwards:	**DOB**	**M**	**(s)**	**G**
Ahmet Demirli	07.08.2000		(2)	
Anıl Koç	29.01.1995		(7)	1
Gerard Gohou (CIV)	29.12.1988	2	(6)	
Bengali-Fodé Koita (FRA)	21.10.1990	23	(1)	12
Mustafa Pektemek	11.08.1988	11	(5)	3
Dieumerci Ndongala (COD)	14.06.1991	8	(6)	2
Ricardo Andrade Quaresma Bernardo (POR)	26.09.1983	19	(7)	4
Mame Thiam (SEN)	09.10.1992	24	(1)	11

Kayseri Spor Kulübü

Founded: 1966
Stadium: „Kadir Has" Stadyumu, Kayseri (32,864)
Trainer: Hikmet Karaman — 09.03.1960
[10.10.2019] Samet Aybaba — 02.09.1955
[31.10.2019] Bülent Uygun — 01.08.1971
[27.12.2019] Omer Mahir — 01.04.1987
[30.12.2019] Robert Prosinečki (CRO) — 12.01.1969

Goalkeepers:	DOB	M	(s)	G
İsmail Çipe	05.01.1995	5		
Silviu Lung jr. (ROU)	04.06.1989	29		
Defenders:	**DOB**	**M**	**(s)**	**G**
Aymen Abdennour (TUN)	06.08.1989	11	(1)	
Alpay Çelebi	04.04.1999	1		
Diego Ângelo de Oliveira (BRA)	12.02.1986	14		1
Brice Florentin Dja Djedjé (CIV)	23.12.1990	29	(2)	
Emre Taşdemir	08.08.1995	9	(1)	
Karahan Subaşı	01.01.1996	18	(3)	
Levent Gülen (SUI)	24.02.1994	1	(1)	
Mert Kula	01.01.1995	5	(2)	
Hugo Miguel de Almeida Costa Lopes (POR)	19.12.1986	23	(3)	
Oğuzhan Çapar	08.10.1996	1		
Osman Cötür	13.09.2001	1		
Benoît Poulain (FRA)	27.07.1987	14		1
Ramazan Civelek	05.01.2000	1		
Cristian Ionuţ Săpunaru (ROU)	05.04.1984	13		1
Midfielders:	**DOB**	**M**	**(s)**	**G**
Adryan Oliveira Tavares (BRA)	10.08.1994		(3)	
Aksel Aktas	15.07.1999	2	(13)	
Atila Turan (FRA)	10.04.1992	4	(1)	
Cenk Şahin	22.09.1994	4	(7)	

	DOB	M	(s)	G
Emre Demir	15.01.2004	5	(6)	1
Furkan Polat	20.04.1998		(4)	
Gustavo Campanharo (BRA)	04.04.1992	14	(1)	
Hasan Acar	16.12.1994	21		3
Bernard Mensah (GHA)	17.10.1994	25		5
Paul-Georges Ntep De Madiba (CMR)	29.07.1992	2	(3)	
Nurettin Korkmaz	27.06.2002	1	(3)	
Ben Rienstra (NED)	05.06.1990	17	(9)	
Samil Çinaz (GER)	08.03.1986	5		
Anthony Chigaemezu Uzodimma (NGA)	17.04.1999	1		
Forwards:	**DOB**	**M**	**(s)**	**G**
Emmanuel Sheyi Adebayor (TOG)	26.02.1984	8		2
Bilal Başaçıkoğlu	26.03.1995	5	(6)	
Artem Kravets (UKR)	03.06.1989	15	(4)	8
Zoran Kvržić (BIH)	07.08.1988	10		
Muris Mešanović (BIH)	06.07.1990	13	(1)	3
Ömer Uzun (GER)	23.02.2000	1	(2)	1
Pedro Henrique Konzen Medina da Silva (BRA)	16.06.1990	24	(2)	10
Selahattin Seyhun	28.06.1999		(1)	
Mario Šitum (CRO)	04.04.1992	5	(12)	
Umut Bulut	15.03.1983	11		3
Ümran Zambak	27.11.2000		(1)	
Ziya Alkurt	26.09.1990	6	(5)	

Konyaspor Kulübü

Founded: 22.06.1922
Stadium: Konya Büyükşehir Stadyumu, Konya (42,000)
Trainer: Aykut Kocaman — 05.04.1965
[13.02.2020] Bülent Korkmaz — 24.11.1968

Goalkeepers:	DOB	M	(s)	G
Ertuğrul Taşkıran	05.11.1989	8	(2)	
Serkan Kırıntılı	15.02.1985	26		
Defenders:	**DOB**	**M**	**(s)**	**G**
Ali Yaşar (BEL)	08.03.1995		(3)	
Marin Aničić (BIH)	17.08.1989	27	(1)	1
Ali Turan	06.09.1983	15	(2)	
Fallou Diagné (SEN)	14.08.1989	3	(1)	
Ferhat Öztorun	08.05.1987	9	(1)	
Guilherme Haubert Sityá (BRA)	01.04.1990	9		
Jens Jønsson (DEN)	10.01.1993	32		1
Selim Ay	31.07.1991	14	(2)	
Nejc Skubić (SVN)	13.06.1989	30		3
Uğur Demirok	08.07.1988	12	(1)	
Volkan Fındıklı	13.10.1990	7	(7)	

Midfielders:	DOB	M	(s)	G
Ali Çamdalı	22.02.1984		(2)	
Alper Uludağ	11.12.1990	17	(3)	1
Amir Hadžiahmetović (BIH)	08.03.1997	16	(7)	1
Marko Jevtović (SRB)	24.07.1993	20	(4)	3
Deni Milošević (BIH)	09.03.1995	31	(1)	5
Farouk Miya (UGA)	26.11.1997	15	(10)	8
Ömer Şahiner	02.01.1992	30		4
Levan Shengelia (GEO)	27.10.1995	16	(7)	2
Forwards:	**DOB**	**M**	**(s)**	**G**
Rijad Bajić (BIH)	06.05.1994	20	(7)	4
Erdon Daci (MKD)	04.07.1998	7	(15)	1
Cristopher Paolo César Hurtado Huertas (PER)	27.07.1992	2	(10)	
Róbert Mak (SVK)	08.03.1991	2	(2)	
Mücahit Can Akçay	13.04.1998	1	(6)	
Rogerio Conceicão do Rosario „Thuram" (BRA)	01.02.1991	5	(10)	1

Sivasspor Kulübü

Founded: 09.05.1967
Stadium: Sivas Arena, Sivas (27,532)
Trainer: Rıza Çalımbay   02.02.1963

Goalkeepers:	DOB	M	(s)	G
Ali Vural	10.07.1990	1		
Muammer Yıldırım	14.09.1990		(1)	
Mamadou Samassa (MLI)	16.02.1990	33		
Defenders:	**DOB**	**M**	**(s)**	**G**
Aaron Appindangoyé (GAB)	20.02.1992	34		
Barış Yardımcı	14.08.1992	3	(2)	
Samba Camara (FRA)	14.11.1992	2	(3)	
Caner Osmanpaşa	15.01.1988	32		
Fatih Aksoy	06.11.1997	22	(1)	
Marcelo Augusto Ferreira Teixeira (BRA)	13.10.1987	29		
Paul Papp (ROU)	11.11.1989	1	(2)	
Uğur Çiftçi	04.05.1992	28		1
Ziya Erdal	05.01.1988	12	(7)	1
Midfielders:	**DOB**	**M**	**(s)**	**G**
Claudemir Domingues de Souza (BRA)	27.03.1988	4	(7)	

	DOB	M	(s)	G
Isaac Cofie (GHA)	20.09.1991	11	(6)	
Armin Đerlek (SRB)	15.07.2000		(9)	
Emre Kılınç	23.08.1994	26	(2)	8
Erdoğan Yeşilyurt	06.11.1993	15	(14)	4
Hakan Arslan	18.07.1988	26	(2)	7
Mert Hakan Yandaş	19.08.1994	32		6
Serhiy Rybalka (UKR)	01.04.1990		(3)	
Yasin Öztekin	19.03.1987	4	(9)	1
Forwards:	**DOB**	**M**	**(s)**	**G**
Fernando Andrade dos Santos (BRA)	08.01.1993	17	(10)	6
Arouna Koné (CIV)	11.11.1983	8	(21)	7
Petar Škuletić (SRB)	29.06.1990		(7)	1
Abdou Razak Traoré (BFA)	28.12.1988	3	(6)	
Volkan Egri	02.04.1998		(1)	
Mustapha Yatabaré (MLI)	26.01.1986	31		13

Trabzonspor Kulübü

Founded: 02.08.1967
Stadium: „Şenol Güneş" Stadyumu, Trabzon (41,513)
Trainer: Ünal Karaman   29.06.1966
[02.01.2020] Hüseyin Çimşir   26.05.1979
[20.07.2020] Edward Ikem Newton (ENG)   13.12.1971

Goalkeepers:	DOB	M	(s)	G
Erce Kardeşler	14.03.1994	1	(2)	
Uğurcan Çakır	05.04.1996	33		
Defenders:	**DOB**	**M**	**(s)**	**G**
Abdurahim Dursun	01.12.1998		(1)	
Gastón Matías Campi (ARG)	06.04.1991	23	(1)	
Manuel Marouane Da Costa Trindade Senoussi (MAR)	06.05.1986	9	(2)	1
Ivanildo Jorge Mendes Fernandes (POR)	26.03.1996	3		
Majid Hosseini (IRN)	20.06.1996	13	(3)	1
Hüseyin Türkmen	01.01.1998	23	(4)	
João Pedro da Silva Pereira (POR)	25.02.1984	28		1
Filip Novák (CZE)	26.06.1990	30		7
Midfielders:	**DOB**	**M**	**(s)**	**G**
Abdülkadir Ömür	25.06.1999	12	(2)	2
Abdülkadir Parmak	28.12.1994	21	(6)	1
Ahmet Canbaz	27.04.1998	1	(3)	
Cafer Tosun	20.11.1999		(2)	

	DOB	M	(s)	G
Doğan Erdoğan	22.08.1996	3	(17)	
Firatcan Üzüm	04.06.1999		(3)	
Guilherme Costa Marques (BRA)	21.05.1991	7	(7)	
Kâmil Çörekçi	01.02.1992	13	(4)	
Papa N'Diaye (SEN)	27.10.1990	13	(4)	1
John Michael Nchekubu Obinna (NGA)	22.04.1987	17	(2)	
Serkan Asan	28.04.1999	2	(5)	
José Ernesto Sosa (ARG)	19.06.1985	29		9
Forwards:	**DOB**	**M**	**(s)**	**G**
Donis Avdijaj (KVX)	25.08.1996	3	(5)	1
Bilal Başaçıkoğlu	26.03.1995		(7)	
Caleb Ekuban (GHA)	23.03.1994	15	(7)	5
Koray Kılınç	04.03.2000		(5)	
Anthony Nnaduzor Nwakaeme (NGA)	21.03.1989	26	(3)	11
Yusuf Sari	20.11.1998	8	(6)	3
Alexander Sørloth (NOR)	05.12.1995	34		24
Daniel Andre Sturridge (ENG)	01.09.1989	7	(4)	4

Yeni Malatya Spor Kulübü

Founded: 1986
Stadium: Malatya Arena, Malatya (27,044)
Trainer: Sergen Yalçın   05.10.1972
[16.01.2020] Ali Ravcı   01.01.1973
[23.01.2020] Kemal Özdeş   10.05.1970
[04.03.2020] Hikmet Karaman   09.03.1960

Goalkeepers:	DOB	M	(s)	G
Fabien Farnolle (BEN)	21.09.1984	34		
Defenders:	**DOB**	**M**	**(s)**	**G**
Buğra Çağıran	01.01.1995	1	(4)	
Issam Chebake (MAR)	12.10.1989	26		1
Teenage Hadebe (ZIM)	17.09.1995	23		
Karim Hafez (EGY)	12.03.1996	11	(2)	
Arturo Rafael Mina Meza (ECU)	08.10.1990	21	(2)	
Mustafa Akbaş	30.05.1990	15	(2)	
Özer Özdemir	05.02.1998	5	(3)	
Sakıb Aytaç	24.11.1991	22		
Yiğithan Güveli	16.05.1998		(2)	
Midfielders:	**DOB**	**M**	**(s)**	**G**
Afriyie Acquah (GHA)	05.01.1992	25	(2)	1
Ghaylène Chaalali (TUN)	28.02.1994	6	(5)	
Mitchell Donald (SUR)	10.12.1988	23	(8)	5

	DOB	M	(s)	G
Ahmed Ildız	29.11.1996	2	(12)	
Erkan Kaş	10.09.1991	3	(7)	
Gökhan Töre	20.01.1992	18	(5)	1
Guilherme Costa Marques (BRA)	21.05.1991	16	(2)	5
Murat Yıldırım	18.05.1987	18	(7)	1
Youssouf Nyange Ndayishimiye (BDI)	27.10.1998	2	(6)	1
Rémi Walter (FRA)	26.04.1995	3	(6)	
Robin Yalcin (GER)	25.01.1994	30	(1)	3
Forwards:	**DOB**	**M**	**(s)**	**G**
Thievy Bifouma (CGO)	13.05.1992	16	(5)	6
Eren Tozlu	27.12.1990		(6)	1
Moryké Fofana (CIV)	23.11.1991	18	(11)	1
Adis Jahović (MKD)	18.03.1987	18		11
Viðar Örn Kjartansson (ISL)	11.03.1990	3	(12)	2
Umut Bulut	15.03.1983	15	(2)	3

SECOND LEVEL
TFF First League 2019/2020

1.	Hatayspor Antakya (*Promoted*)	34	19	9	6	48	-	28	66
2.	Büyükşehir Belediye Erzurumspor (*Promoted*)	34	18	8	8	41	-	25	62
3.	Adana Demirspor Kulübü (*Promotion Play-offs*)	34	17	10	7	68	-	44	61
4.	Akhisar Belediye Gençlik ve SK (*Promotion Play-offs*)	34	16	9	9	46	-	39	57
5.	Fatih Karagümrük SK (*Promotion Play-offs*)	34	15	11	8	53	-	39	56
6.	Bursaspor Kulübü[1] (*Promotion Play-offs*)	34	17	8	9	49	-	41	56
7.	Altay SK İzmir	34	14	12	8	45	-	37	54
8.	Ankara Keçiörengücü SK	34	13	11	10	33	-	28	50
9.	Menemenspor Kulübü İzmir	34	11	11	12	42	-	46	44
10.	Giresunspor Kulübü	34	12	8	14	40	-	47	44
11.	Ümraniyespor Kulübü	34	12	8	14	48	-	51	44
12.	İstanbulspor	34	9	13	12	45	-	43	40
13.	Balıkesirspor Kulübü Derneği	34	9	11	14	36	-	48	38
14.	Altınordu FK İzmir	34	8	13	13	37	-	44	37
15.	Boluspor Kulübü	34	6	15	13	30	-	41	33
16.	Osmanlıspor FK Ankara[1]	34	8	9	17	41	-	53	30
17.	Adanaspor AŞ	34	3	12	19	31	-	53	21
18.	Eskişehirspor Kulübü[2]	34	7	6	21	34	-	60	12

[1] *3 points deducted*
[2] *15 points deducted*

Relegation Play-offs

Bursaspor Kulübü - Adana Demirspor Kulübü	0-0	1-4
Fatih Karagümrük SK - Akhisar Belediye Gençlik ve SK	3-3	1-0
Adana Demirspor Kulübü - Fatih Karagümrük SK	1-1; 5-6 pen	

Fatih Karagümrük SK promoted to the 2020/2021 Süper Lig.

NATIONAL TEAM

INTERNATIONAL MATCHES
(16.07.2019 – 15.07.2020)

07.09.2019	İstanbul	Turkey - Andorra	1-0(0-0)	(ECQ)
10.09.2019	Chişinău	Moldova - Turkey	0-4(0-1)	(ECQ)
11.10.2019	Istanbul	Turkey - Albania	1-0(0-0)	(ECQ)
14.10.2019	Paris	France - Turkey	1-1(0-0)	(ECQ)
14.11.2019	İstanbul	Turkey - Iceland	0-0	(ECQ)
17.11.2019	Andorra la Vella	Andorra - Turkey	0-2(0-2)	(ECQ)

07.09.2019 TURKEY - ANDORRA **1-0(0-0)** 16th EC. Qualifiers
Vodafone Park, Istanbul; Referee: Donald Robertson (Scotland); Attendance: 42,600
TUR: Fehmi Mert Günok, Zeki Çelik, Çağlar Söyüncü, Merih Demiral, Cengiz Umut Meraş (61.Ozan Tufan), Emre Belözoğlu (Cap), Hakan Çalhanoğlu (80.Emre Kılınç), İrfan Can Kahveci, Yusuf Yazıcı, Cenk Tosun, Güven Yalçın (46.Kenan Karaman). Trainer: Şenol Güneş.
Goal: Ozan Tufan (89).

10.09.2019 MOLDOVA - TURKEY **0-4(0-1)** 16th EC. Qualifiers
Stadionul Zimbru, Chişinău; Referee: Davide Massa (Italy); Attendance: 8,281
TUR: Fehmi Mert Günok, Kaan Ayhan, Zeki Çelik, Merih Demiral, Cengiz Umut Meraş, İrfan Can Kahveci (80.Yusuf Yazıcı), Deniz Türüç, Ozan Tufan, Dorukhan Toköz (87.Abdulkadir Parmak), Cenk Tosun (Cap), Kenan Karaman (70.Hakan Çalhanoğlu). Trainer: Şenol Güneş.
Goals: Cenk Tosun (37), Deniz Türüç (57), Cenk Tosun (79), Yazıcı (88).

11.10.2019 TURKEY - ALBANIA **1-0(0-0)** 16th EC. Qualifiers
„Şükrü Saracoğlu" Stadyumu, İstanbul; Referee: Ovidiu Alin Haţegan (Romania); Attendance: 41,438
TUR: Fehmi Mert Günok, Kaan Ayhan (46.Çağlar Söyüncü), Zeki Çelik, Merih Demiral, Cengiz Umut Meraş, Emre Belözoğlu (Cap) (66.İrfan Can Kahveci), Mahmut Tekdemir, Hakan Çalhanoğlu, Ozan Tufan (80.Yusuf Yazıcı), Burak Yılmaz, Cenk Tosun. Trainer: Şenol Güneş.
Goal: Cenk Tosun (90).

14.10.2019 FRANCE - TURKEY **1-1(0-0)** 16th EC. Qualifiers
Stade de France, Saint-Denis, Paris; Referee: Dr. Felix Brych (Germany); Attendance: 72,154
TUR: Fehmi Mert Günok, Zeki Çelik (53.Kaan Ayhan), Merih Demiral, Çağlar Söyüncü, Cengiz Umut Meraş, Mahmut Tekdemir, Okay Yokuşlu (46.Hakan Çalhanoğlu), İrfan Can Kahveci, Ozan Tufan (81.Cenk Tosun), Burak Yılmaz (Cap), Kenan Karaman. Trainer: Şenol Güneş.
Goal: Kaan Ayhan (81).

14.11.2019 TURKEY - ICELAND **0-0** 16th EC. Qualifiers
Türk Telekom Arena, İstanbul; Referee: Anthony Taylor (England); Attendance: 48,329
TUR: Fehmi Mert Günok, Zeki Çelik (90+4.Ömer Bayram), Çağlar Söyüncü, Merih Demiral, Cengiz Umut Meraş, Mahmut Tekdemir, Okay Yokuşlu, Hakan Çalhanoğlu (87.Kaan Ayhan), Ozan Tufan, Cengiz Ünder (81.Yusuf Yazıcı), Burak Yılmaz (Cap). Trainer: Şenol Güneş.

17.11.2019 ANDORRA - TURKEY **0-2(0-2)** 16th EC. Qualifiers
Estadi Nacional, Andorra la Vella; Referee: Ivan Kružliak (Slovakia); Attendance: 2,357
TUR: Uğurcan Çakır, Ömer Bayram, Kaan Ayhan, Nazim Sangaré, Merih Demiral (80.Yıldırım Mert Çetin), Ozan Muhammed Kabak, Hakan Çalhanoğlu (Cap) (60.Berkay Özcan), Ozan Tufan, Yusuf Yazıcı, Enes Ünal, Ahmed Kutucu (85.Emre Kılınç). Trainer: Şenol Güneş.
Goals: Enes Ünal (17, 21 penalty).

NATIONAL TEAM PLAYERS
(16.07.2019 – 15.07.2020)

Name	DOB	Caps	Goals	2019/2020:	Club
Goalkeepers					
FEHMI Mert Günok	01.03.1989	15	0	2019:	*İstanbul Başakşehir FK*
UĞURCAN Çakır	05.04.1996	2	0	2019:	*Trabzonspor Kulübü*
Defenders					
ÇAĞLAR Söyüncü	23.05.1996	28	1	2019:	*Leicester City FC (ENG)*
KAAN Ayhan	10.11.1994	28	3	2019:	*TSV Fortuna Düsseldorf (GER)*
MERIH Demiral	05.03.1998	12	0	2019:	*Juventus FC Torino (ITA)*
Yildırım MERT Çetin	01.01.1997	1	0	2019:	*AS Roma (ITA)*
OZAN Muhammed Kabak	25.03.2000	1	0	2019:	*FC Schalke 04 Gelsenkirchen (GER)*
ÖMER Bayram	27.07.1991	9	0	2019:	*Galatasaray SK İstanbul*
Nazim SANGARÉ	30.05.1994	2	0	2019:	*Antalyaspor Kulübü*
Cengiz UMUT Meraş	20.12.1995	6	0	2019:	*Le Havre AC (FRA)*
ZEKI Çelik	17.02.1997	14	2	2019:	*Lille OSC (FRA)*
Midfielders					
ABDULKADIR Parmak	28.12.1994	1	0	2019:	*Trabzonspor Kulübü*
BERKAY Özcan	15.02.1998	4	0	2019:	*İstanbul Başakşehir FK*
CENGIZ Ünder	14.07.1997	20	6	2019:	*AS Roma (ITA)*
DENIZ Türüç	29.01.1993	6	1	2019:	*Fenerbahçe SK İstanbul*
DORUKHAN Toköz	21.05.1996	6	1	2019:	*Beşiktaş JK İstanbul*
EMRE Belözoğlu	07.09.1980	101	9	2019:	*Fenerbahçe SK İstanbul*
EMRE Kılınç	23.08.1994	2	0	2019:	*Sivasspor Kulübü*
HAKAN Çalhanoğlu	08.02.1994	47	10	2019:	*AC Milan (ITA)*
İRFAN Can Kahveci	15.06.1995	14	0	2019:	*İstanbul Başakşehir FK*
KENAN Karaman	05.03.1994	10	1	2019:	*TSV Fortuna Düsseldorf (GER)*
MAHMUT Tekdemir	20.01.1988	15	0	2019:	*İstanbul Başakşehir FK*
OKAY Yokuşlu	09.03.1994	24	1	2019:	*RC Celta de Vigo (ESP)*
OZAN Tufan	23.03.1995	49	5	2019:	*Fenerbahçe SK İstanbul*
YUSUF Yazıcı	29.01.1997	19	1	2019:	*Lille OSC (FRA)*
Forwards					
AHMED Kutucu	01.03.2000	1	0	2019:	*FC Schalke 04 Gelsenkirchen (GER)*
BURAK Yılmaz	15.07.1985	59	24	2019:	*Beşiktaş JK İstanbul*
CENK Tosun	07.06.1991	42	16	2019:	*Everton FC Liverpool (ENG)*
ENES Ünal	10.05.1997	13	2	2019:	*Real Valladolid CF (ESP)*
GÜVEN Yalçın	18.01.1999	3	0	2019:	*Beşiktaş JK İstanbul*

National team coach		
ŞENOL Güneş [from 18.03.2019]	01.06.1952	12 M; 9 W; 2 D; 1 L; 22-4
		Complete record as trainer of Turkey:
		62 M; 32 W; 15 D; 15 L; 93-54
		(16.08.2000 – 19.11.2003) & (from 18.03.2019)

UKRAINE

UKRAINE

The Country:
Україна (Ukraine)
Capital: Kyiv
Surface: 603,628 km²
Inhabitants: 41,660,982 [2020]
Time: UTC+2

The FA:
Федерація Футболу України [Football Federation of Ukraine]
Provulok Laboratornyi, 7-A P.O. Box 55, 01133 Kyiv
Tel: +380 44 521 0535
Founded: 1991
Member of FIFA since: 1992
Member of UEFA since: 1992
Website: ffu.ua

NATIONAL TEAM RECORDS

RECORDS		
First international match:	29.04.1992, Uzhgorod:	Ukraine – Hungary 1-3
Most international caps:	Anatoliy Tymoshchuk	- 144 caps (2000-2016)
Most international goals:	Andriy Shevchenko	- 48 goals / 111 caps (1995-2012)

UEFA EUROPEAN CHAMPIONSHIP	
1960	-
1964	-
1968	-
1972	-
1976	-
1980	-
1984	-
1988	-
1992	-
1996	Qualifiers
2000	Qualifiers
2004	Qualifiers
2008	Qualifiers
2012	Final Tournament (Group Stage)
2016	Final Tournament (Group Stage)
2020	*Final Tournament (Qualified)*

FIFA WORLD CUP	
1930	-
1934	-
1938	-
1950	-
1954	-
1958	-
1962	-
1966	-
1970	-
1974	-
1978	-
1982	-
1986	-
1990	-
1994	Did not enter
1998	Qualifiers
2002	Qualifiers
2006	Final Tournament (Quarter-Finals)
2010	Qualifiers
2014	Qualifiers
2018	Qualifiers

OLYMPIC TOURNAMENTS	
1908	-
1912	-
1920	-
1924	-
1928	-
1936	-
1948	-
1952	-
1956	-
1960	-
1964	-
1968	-
1972	-
1976	-
1980	-
1984	-
1988	-
1992	-
1996	Qualifiers
2000	Qualifiers
2004	Qualifiers
2008	Qualifiers
2012	Qualifiers
2016	Qualifiers

was part of Soviet Union between 1930-1990

UEFA NATIONS LEAGUE

2018/2019 – League B (promoted to League A)

FIFA CONFEDERATIONS CUP 1992-2017

None

UKRAINIAN CLUB HONOURS IN EUROPEAN CLUB COMPETITIONS:

European Champion Clubs' Cup (1956-1992) / UEFA Champions League (1993-2020)		
None		

Fairs Cup (1858-1971) / UEFA Cup (1972-2009) / UEFA Europa League (2010-2020)		
FK Shakhtar Donetsk	1	2008/2009

UEFA Super Cup (1972-2019)		
FK Dinamo Kyiv*	1	1975

*European Cup Winners' Cup 1961-1999**		
FK Dinamo Kyiv*	2	1974/1975, 1985/1986

represented the Soviet Union

defunct competition

Championship of cities

	CHAMPIONS
1921	Kharkiv
1922	Kharkiv
1923	Kharkiv
1924	Kharkiv
1925	No competition
1926	No competition
1927	Kharkiv
1928	Kharkiv
1929	No competition
1930	No competition
1931	Kyiv
1932	Kharkiv
1933	No competition
1934	Kharkiv
1935	Dnipropetrovsk

Championship of the Proletarian Sports Society Dinamo

	CHAMPIONS
1929	Dinamo Kharkiv
1931	Dinamo Kyiv
1932	Dinamo Kharkiv
1933	Dinamo Kyiv
1934	Dinamo Kharkiv
1935	Dinamo Kyiv

UKRAINIAN SSR (SOVIET ERA) CHAMPIONS

Year	Champion	Year	Champion	Year	Champion
1936	Zavod Ordzhonikidze Kramators'k	1958	Arsenal Kyiv	1975	Krivbas Kryvyi Rih
1937	Spartak Dnipropetrovs'k	1959	Avangard Zhovti Vody	1976	Krivbas Kryvyi Rih
1938	Dzerzhynec Voroshylovgrad	1960	Metalurg Zaporizhzhya	1977	SKA Odesa
1939	Lokomotyv Zaporizhzhya	1961	Chornomorets Odesa	1978	Metalist Kharkiv
1940	Lokomotyv Zaporizhzhya	1962	Trudovi Rezervy Voroshylovgrad	1979	Kolos Nikopil
1941-1945	No competition	1963	SKA Odesa	1980	SKA Kyiv
1946	Spartak Uzhgorod	1964	Lokomotyv Vinnytsa	1981	Krivbas Kryvyi Rih
1947	Bil'shovyk Mukacheve	1965	SKA L'viv	1982	Bukovyna Chernivtsi
1948	Torpedo Odesa	1966	Avangard Zhovti Vody	1983	SKA Kyiv
1949	Pishevik Odesa	1967	Avtomobilist Zhytomyr	1984	Nyva Vinnytsa
1950	Spartak Uzhgorod	1968	Avangard Ternopil	1985	Tavrya Simferopil
1951	Budinok ofitseriv Kyiv	1969	Spartak Ivano-Frankivs'k	1986	Zarya Voroshylovgrad
1952	Metalurg Zaporizhzhya	1970	Metalurg Zaporizhzhya	1987	Tavrya Simferopil
1953	Spartak Uzhgorod	1971	Krivbas Kryvyi Rih	1988	Bukovyna Chernivtsi
1954	Mashinobudivnik Kyiv	1972	Spartak Ivano-Frankivs'k	1989	Volyn Lutsk
1955	Spartak Stanislav	1973	Tavria Simferopil	1990	Bukovyna Chernivtsi
1956	Shakhtar Stakhanov	1974	Sudostroitel Nikolaev	1991	Karpaty Lviv
1957	SKVO Odesa				

	CHAMPIONS	CUP WINNERS	BEST GOALSCORERS	
1992	SC Tavriya Simferopol	FK Chornomorets Odesa	Yuriy Hudymenko (SC Tavriya Simferopol)	12
1992/1993	FK Dinamo Kyiv	FK Dinamo Kyiv	Serhiy Husyev (FK Chornomorets Odesa)	17
1993/1994	FK Dinamo Kyiv	FK Chornomorets Odesa	Tymerlan Huseinov (FK Chornomorets Odesa)	18
1994/1995	FK Dinamo Kyiv	FK Shakhtar Donetsk	Arsen Avakov (TJK, FK Metalurh Zaporizhya)	21
1995/1996	FK Dinamo Kyiv	FK Dinamo Kyiv	Tymerlan Huseinov (FK Chornomorets Odesa)	20
1996/1997	FK Dinamo Kyiv	FK Shakhtar Donetsk	Oleh Matveyev (FK Shakhtar Donetsk)	21
1997/1998	FK Dinamo Kyiv	FK Dinamo Kyiv	Serhiy Rebrov (FK Dinamo Kyiv)	22
1998/1999	FK Dinamo Kyiv	FK Dinamo Kyiv	Andriy Shevchenko (FK Dinamo Kyiv)	18
1999/2000	FK Dinamo Kyiv	FK Dinamo Kyiv	Maksim Shatskikh (UZB, FK Dinamo Kyiv)	20
2000/2001	FK Dinamo Kyiv	FK Shakhtar Donetsk	Andrij Vorobej (FK Shakhtar Donetsk)	21
2001/2002	FK Shakhtar Donetsk	FK Shakhtar Donetsk	Serhiy Shyshchenko (FK Metalurh Donetsk)	12
2002/2003	FK Dinamo Kyiv	FK Dinamo Kyiv	Maksim Shatskikh (UZB, FK Dinamo Kyiv)	22
2003/2004	FK Dinamo Kyiv	FK Shakhtar Donetsk	Giorgi Demetradze (GEO, FK Metalurh Donetsk)	18
2004/2005	FK Shakhtar Donetsk	FK Dinamo Kyiv	Olexandr Kosyrin (FK Chornomorets Odesa)	14
2005/2006	FK Shakhtar Donetsk	FK Dinamo Kyiv	Evaeverson Lemos da Silva "Brandão" (FK Shakhtar Donetsk) Emmanuel Osei Okoduwa (NGA, FK Arsenal Kyiv)	15
2006/2007	FK Dinamo Kyiv	FK Dinamo Kyiv	Oleksandr Hladkyi (FK Kharkhiv)	13
2007/2008	FK Shakhtar Donetsk	FK Shakhtar Donetsk	Marko Dević (FK Metalist Kharkhiv)	19
2008/2009	FK Dinamo Kyiv	FK Vorskla Poltava	Olexander Kowpak (SC Tavriya Simferopol)	17
2009/2010	FK Shakhtar Donetsk	SC Tavriya Simferopol	Artem Milevsky (FK Dinamo Kyiv)	17
2010/2011	FK Shakhtar Donetsk	FK Shakhtar Donetsk	Yevhen Seleznyov (FC Dnipro Dnipropetrovsk)	17
2011/2012	FK Shakhtar Donetsk	FK Shakhtar Donetsk	Yevhen Seleznyov (FK Shakhtar Donetsk) Maicon Pereira de Oliveira (VRA, FK Volyn Lutsk)	14
2012/2013	FK Shakhtar Donetsk	FK Shakhtar Donetsk	Henrikh Mkhitaryan (ARM, FK Shakhtar Donetsk)	25
2013/2014	FK Shakhtar Donetsk	FK Dinamo Kyiv	Luiz Adriano de Souza da Silva (FK Shakhtar Donetsk)	20
2014/2015	FK Dinamo Kyiv	FK Dinamo Kyiv	Alex Teixeira Santos (BRA, FK Shakhtar Donetsk) Eric Cosmin Bicfalvi (ROU, FK Volyn Lutsk)	17
2015/2016	FK Dinamo Kyiv	FK Shakhtar Donetsk	Alex Teixeira Santos (BRA, FK Shakhtar Donetsk)	22

2016/2017	FK Shakhtar Donetsk	FK Shakhtar Donetsk	Andriy Yarmolenko (FK Dinamo Kyiv)	15
2017/2018	FK Shakhtar Donetsk	FK Shakhtar Donetsk	Facundo Ferreyra (ARG, FK Shakhtar Donetsk)	21
2018/2019	FK Shakhtar Donetsk	FK Shakhtar Donetsk	Aluísio Chaves Ribeiro Moraes Júnior (FK Shakhtar Donetsk)	19
2019/2020	FK Shakhtar Donetsk	FK Dinamo Kyiv	Aluísio Chaves Ribeiro Moraes Júnior (FK Shakhtar Donetsk)	20

NATIONAL CHAMPIONSHIP
Ukrainian Premier League 2019/2020
(28.07.2019 – 19.07.2020)

Regular Season - Results

Round 1 [28-31.07.2019]
Vorskla Poltava - Zorya Luhansk 0-1(0-1)
Desna Chernihiv - FK Lviv 1-2(1-0)
Kolos Kovalivka - FK Mariupol 2-1(1-1)
SC Dnipro-1 - Olimpik Donetsk 2-0(2-0)
FK Oleksandriya - Shakhtar Donetsk 1-3(1-0)
Karpaty Lviv - Dinamo Kyiv 0-2(0-2)

Round 2 [03-04.08.2019]
FK Mariupol - FK Oleksandriya 2-1(0-0)
Desna Chernihiv - Vorskla Poltava 2-0(1-0)
FK Lviv - Dinamo Kyiv 0-3(0-2)
Olimpik Donetsk - Kolos Kovalivka 0-1(0-0)
Zorya Luhansk - SC Dnipro-1 1-1(0-1)
Shakhtar Donetsk - Karpaty Lviv 3-0(2-0)

Round 3 [10-11.08.2019]
Dinamo Kyiv - Shakhtar Donetsk 1-2(1-1)
FK Oleksandriya - Olimpik Donetsk 2-1(1-0)
Vorskla Poltava - FK Lviv 3-2(2-1)
SC Dnipro-1 - Desna Chernihiv 0-1(0-0)
Kolos Kovalivka - Zorya Luhansk 1-3(1-2)
Karpaty Lviv - FK Mariupol 1-1(1-1)

Round 4 [17-18.08.2019]
Vorskla Poltava - SC Dnipro-1 1-1(0-0)
Desna Chernihiv - Kolos Kovalivka 0-0
Olimpik Donetsk - Karpaty Lviv 1-3(0-2)
Zorya Luhansk - FK Oleksandriya 1-2(0-0)
FK Lviv - Shakhtar Donetsk 0-2(0-2)
FK Mariupol - Dinamo Kyiv 0-1(0-0) [25.09.]

Round 5 [24-26.08.2019]
Kolos Kovalivka - Vorskla Poltava 0-3(0-1)
FK Oleksandriya - Desna Chernihiv 0-3(0-0)
Dinamo Kyiv - Olimpik Donetsk 1-1(0-0)
Karpaty Lviv - Zorya Luhansk 0-1(0-0)
Shakhtar Donetsk - FK Mariupol 5-1(3-0)
SC Dnipro-1 - FK Lviv 2-3(0-1)

Round 6 [30.08.-01.09.2019]
Desna Chernihiv - Karpaty Lviv 0-0
SC Dnipro-1 - Kolos Kovalivka 2-1(0-1)
Vorskla Poltava - FK Oleksandriya 0-1(0-1)
FK Lviv - FK Mariupol 0-1(0-0)
Olimpik Donetsk - Shakhtar Donetsk 0-4(0-2)
Zorya Luhansk - Dinamo Kyiv 2-2(1-2)

Round 7 [14-15.09.2019]
FK Oleksandriya - SC Dnipro-1 2-0(0-0)
Karpaty Lviv - Vorskla Poltava 2-1(0-1)
Shakhtar Donetsk - Zorya Luhansk 4-3(1-2)
FK Mariupol - Olimpik Donetsk 1-1(1-0)
Dinamo Kyiv - Desna Chernihiv 1-2(0-1)
Kolos Kovalivka - FK Lviv 1-0(0-0)

Round 8 [20-22.09.2019]
SC Dnipro-1 - Karpaty Lviv 2-0(1-0)
FK Lviv - Olimpik Donetsk 0-1(0-0)
Zorya Luhansk - FK Mariupol 0-0
Desna Chernihiv - Shakhtar Donetsk 0-1(0-1)
Vorskla Poltava - Dinamo Kyiv 0-5(0-3)
Kolos Kovalivka - FK Oleksandriya 1-1(1-0)

Round 9 [27-29.09.2019]
Shakhtar Donetsk - Vorskla Poltava 4-0(1-0)
Karpaty Lviv - Kolos Kovalivka 1-2(1-2)
FK Oleksandriya - FK Lviv 2-0(1-0)
FK Mariupol - Desna Chernihiv 0-4(0-2)
Dinamo Kyiv - SC Dnipro-1 2-0(1-0)
Olimpik Donetsk - Zorya Luhansk 0-5(0-1)

Round 10 [05-06.10.2019]
Vorskla Poltava - FK Mariupol 1-1(0-0)
Desna Chernihiv - Olimpik Donetsk 1-0(0-0)
FK Lviv - Zorya Luhansk 0-0
SC Dnipro-1 - Shakhtar Donetsk 0-2(0-1)
Kolos Kovalivka - Dinamo Kyiv 0-4(0-0)
FK Oleksandriya - Karpaty Lviv 2-1(0-0)

Round 11 [18-20.10.2019]
Shakhtar Donetsk - Kolos Kovalivka 6-0(5-0)
Karpaty Lviv - FK Lviv 0-0
Zorya Luhansk - Desna Chernihiv 2-1(0-1)
FK Mariupol - SC Dnipro-1 1-0(0-0)
Dinamo Kyiv - FK Oleksandriya 1-0(1-0)
Olimpik Donetsk - Vorskla Poltava 2-0(0-0)

Round 12 [26-27.10.2019]
FK Mariupol - Kolos Kovalivka 2-0(1-0)
Zorya Luhansk - Vorskla Poltava 4-0(2-0)
Olimpik Donetsk - SC Dnipro-1 3-2(1-1)
FK Lviv - Desna Chernihiv 1-4(0-3)
Dinamo Kyiv - Karpaty Lviv 1-1(0-0)
Shakhtar Donetsk - FK Oleksandriya 0-0

Round 13 [02-03.11.2019]
Karpaty Lviv - Shakhtar Donetsk 0-3(0-1)
Vorskla Poltava - Desna Chernihiv 0-1(0-0)
SC Dnipro-1 - Zorya Luhansk 1-4(0-2)
FK Oleksandriya - FK Mariupol 3-1(0-0)
Dinamo Kyiv - FK Lviv 4-0(2-0)
Kolos Kovalivka - Olimpik Donetsk 1-2(0-0)

Round 14 [09-10.11.2019]
Desna Chernihiv - SC Dnipro-1 1-1(0-1)
FK Mariupol - Karpaty Lviv 2-2(1-0)
FK Lviv - Vorskla Poltava 2-0(2-0)
Zorya Luhansk - Kolos Kovalivka 2-0(1-0)
Shakhtar Donetsk - Dinamo Kyiv 1-0(1-0)
Olimpik Donetsk - FK Oleksandriya 0-0

Round 15 [22-24.11.2019]
Shakhtar Donetsk - FK Lviv 4-1(1-1)
FK Oleksandriya - Zorya Luhansk 1-0(0-0)
SC Dnipro-1 - Vorskla Poltava 1-0(0-0)
Karpaty Lviv - Olimpik Donetsk 1-2(1-2)
Kolos Kovalivka - Desna Chernihiv 2-0(1-0)
Dinamo Kyiv - FK Mariupol 3-0(1-0)

Round 16 [30.11.-01.12.2019]
Zorya Luhansk - Karpaty Lviv 2-0(0-0)
FK Lviv - SC Dnipro-1 0-2(0-1)
Vorskla Poltava - Kolos Kovalivka 1-0(1-0)
Desna Chernihiv - FK Oleksandriya 2-0(0-0)
FK Mariupol - Shakhtar Donetsk 1-1(0-1)
Olimpik Donetsk - Dinamo Kyiv 1-3(1-1)

Round 17 [06-08.12.2019]
Shakhtar Donetsk - Olimpik Donetsk 3-0(1-0)
FK Oleksandriya - Vorskla Poltava 3-0(0-0)
Kolos Kovalivka - SC Dnipro-1 4-0(1-0)
Karpaty Lviv - Desna Chernihiv 2-6(1-2)
FK Mariupol - FK Lviv 0-0
Dinamo Kyiv - Zorya Luhansk 1-2(1-1)

Round 18 [14-15.12.2019]
FK Lviv - Kolos Kovalivka 3-2(2-1)
Zorya Luhansk - Shakhtar Donetsk 1-2(0-0)
Olimpik Donetsk - FK Mariupol 1-2(0-0)
Desna Chernihiv - Dinamo Kyiv 0-1(0-1)
Vorskla Poltava - Karpaty Lviv 2-1(2-1)
SC Dnipro-1 - FK Oleksandriya 1-2(0-0)

Round 19 [22-23.02.2020]
FK Mariupol - Zorya Luhansk 1-2(0-0)
Dinamo Kyiv - Vorskla Poltava 2-1(0-0)
Karpaty Lviv - SC Dnipro-1 1-1(1-1)
FK Oleksandriya - Kolos Kovalivka 1-2(0-0)
Shakhtar Donetsk - Desna Chernihiv 1-0(0-0)
Olimpik Donetsk - FK Lviv 0-1(0-0)

Round 20 [28.02.-01.03.2020]
SC Dnipro-1 - Dinamo Kyiv 3-1(0-1)
Desna Chernihiv - FK Mariupol 4-0(2-0)
FK Lviv - FK Oleksandriya 1-1(0-1)
Kolos Kovalivka - Karpaty Lviv 2-1(2-0)
Zorya Luhansk - Olimpik Donetsk 1-0(0-0)
Vorskla Poltava - Shakhtar Donetsk 1-0(1-0)

Round 21 [03-04.03.2020]
Dinamo Kyiv - Kolos Kovalivka 2-0(1-0)
FK Mariupol - Vorskla Poltava 3-0(1-0)
Zorya Luhansk - FK Lviv 2-0(0-0)
Olimpik Donetsk - Desna Chernihiv 1-2(1-1)
Shakhtar Donetsk - SC Dnipro-1 4-1(4-0)
Karpaty Lviv - FK Oleksandriya 0-4(0-1)

Round 22 [07-08.03.2020]
Desna Chernihiv - Zorya Luhansk 1-0(1-0)
Vorskla Poltava - Olimpik Donetsk 1-0(0-0)
FK Oleksandriya - Dinamo Kyiv 1-3(0-1)
FK Lviv - Karpaty Lviv 0-0
SC Dnipro-1 - FK Mariupol 3-0(0-0)
Kolos Kovalivka - Shakhtar Donetsk 3-4(1-2)

Final Standings

1.	FK Shakhtar Donetsk	22	19	2	1	59	-	14	59
2.	FK Dinamo Kyiv	22	14	3	5	44	-	17	45
3.	FK Zorya Luhansk	22	13	4	5	39	-	18	43
4.	FK Desna Chernihiv	22	13	3	6	36	-	15	42
5.	FK Oleksandriya	22	11	4	7	30	-	23	37
6.	FK Kolos Kovalivka	22	8	2	12	25	-	39	26
7.	SC Dnipro-1	22	7	4	11	26	-	34	25
8.	FK Mariupol	22	6	7	9	21	-	35	25
9.	FK Lviv	22	5	5	12	16	-	35	20
10.	FK Vorskla Poltava	22	6	2	14	15	-	38	20
11.	FK Olimpik Donetsk	22	5	3	14	17	-	37	18
12.	FK Karpaty Lviv	22	2	7	13	17	-	40	13

Teams ranked 1-6 were qualified for the Championship Round, while teams ranked 7-12 were qualified for the Relegation Round.

Championship Round

Round 23 [14-15.03.2020]
FK Oleksandriya - Kolos Kovalivka 4-2(1-1)
Zorya Luhansk - Shakhtar Donetsk 1-0(0-0)
Dinamo Kyiv - Desna Chernihiv 1-1(0-0)

Round 24 [30-31.05.2020]
Kolos Kovalivka - Desna Chernihiv 0-2(0-0)
FK Oleksandriya - Zorya Luhansk 1-0(0-0)
Shakhtar Donetsk - Dinamo Kyiv 3-1(1-1)

Round 25 [06-07.06.2020]
Shakhtar Donetsk - Desna Chernihiv 3-2(2-1)
Zorya Luhansk - Kolos Kovalivka 1-0(1-0)
Dinamo Kyiv - FK Oleksandriya 5-1(2-1)

Round 26 [13-14.06.2020]
Zorya Luhansk - Dinamo Kyiv 1-3(0-0)
Kolos Kovalivka - Shakhtar Donetsk 0-1(0-0)
FK Oleksandriya - Desna Chernihiv 1-5(0-2)

Round 27 [20-22.06.2020]
Shakhtar Donetsk - FK Oleksandriya 3-2(1-0)
Desna Chernihiv - Zorya Luhansk 1-2(0-1)
Dinamo Kyiv - Kolos Kovalivka 2-1(0-0)

Round 28 [27-28.06.2020]
Kolos Kovalivka - FK Oleksandriya 2-1(2-0)
Shakhtar Donetsk - Zorya Luhansk 0-0
Desna Chernihiv - Dinamo Kyiv 3-2(2-1)

Round 29 [04-05.07.2020]
Dinamo Kyiv - Shakhtar Donetsk 2-3(0-2)
Desna Chernihiv - Kolos Kovalivka 5-1(2-0)
Zorya Luhansk - FK Oleksandriya 2-2(1-1)

Round 30 [11-12.07.2020]
Kolos Kovalivka - Zorya Luhansk 0-2(0-2)
Desna Chernihiv - Shakhtar Donetsk 2-4(1-2)
FK Oleksandriya - Dinamo Kyiv 2-2(1-0)

Round 31 [15-16.07.2020]
Shakhtar Donetsk - Kolos Kovalivka 2-0(0-0)
Dinamo Kyiv - Zorya Luhansk 3-1(3-1)
Desna Chernihiv - FK Oleksandriya 1-3(1-1)

Round 32 [19.07.2020]
Kolos Kovalivka - Dinamo Kyiv 2-0(0-0)
Zorya Luhansk - Desna Chernihiv 1-1(0-1)
FK Oleksandriya - Shakhtar Donetsk 2-2(0-2)

Final Standings

				Total				Home					Away				
1.	**FK Shakhtar Donetsk**	32	26	4	2	80 - 26	82	14	2	0	46 - 11	12	2	2	34 - 15
2.	FK Dinamo Kyiv	32	18	5	9	65 - 35	59	9	3	4	32 - 16	9	2	5	33 - 19
3.	FK Zorya Luhansk	32	17	7	8	50 - 29	58	8	5	3	24 - 14	9	2	5	26 - 15
4.	FK Desna Chernihiv	32	17	5	10	59 - 33	56	7	3	6	24 - 17	10	2	4	35 - 16
5.	FK Oleksandriya	32	14	7	11	49 - 47	49	9	2	5	28 - 25	5	5	6	21 - 22
6.	FK Kolos Kovalivka	32	10	2	20	33 - 59	32	7	1	8	21 - 25	3	1	12	12 - 34

Relegation Round

Round 23 [14-15.03.2020]
FK Lviv - Karpaty Lviv 1-1(0-1)
SC Dnipro-1 - FK Mariupol 2-0(0-0)
Olimpik Donetsk - Vorskla Poltava 1-1(1-1)

Round 24 [30-31.05.2020]
SC Dnipro-1 - Olimpik Donetsk 3-1(1-0)
Karpaty Lviv - FK Mariupol 0-3 *awarded*
Vorskla Poltava - FK Lviv 1-1(1-0)

Round 25 [07.06.2020]
Vorskla Poltava - Karpaty Lviv *not played*
Olimpik Donetsk - FK Mariupol 2-2(1-1)
FK Lviv - SC Dnipro-1 1-2(1-1)

Round 26 [13.06.2020]
FK Mariupol - Vorskla Poltava 1-1(0-0)
Olimpik Donetsk - FK Lviv 2-0(0-0)
Karpaty Lviv - SC Dnipro-1 *not played*

Round 27 [19-21.06.2020]
FK Mariupol - FK Lviv 3-0(2-0)
Vorskla Poltava - SC Dnipro-1 2-0(1-0)
Karpaty Lviv - Olimpik Donetsk *not played*

Round 28 [27-28.06.2020]
Karpaty Lviv - FK Lviv 1-1(0-1)
FK Mariupol - SC Dnipro-1 2-1(2-0)
Vorskla Poltava - Olimpik Donetsk 0-0

Round 29 [03-05.07.2020]
FK Lviv - Vorskla Poltava 2-2(0-1)
FK Mariupol - Karpaty Lviv 3-0 *awarded*
Olimpik Donetsk - SC Dnipro-1 0-2(0-1)

Round 30 [11-12.07.2020]
SC Dnipro-1 - FK Lviv 3-2(1-2)
Karpaty Lviv - Vorskla Poltava *not played*
FK Mariupol - Olimpik Donetsk 1-4(0-3)

Round 31 [15-16.07.2020]
SC Dnipro-1 - Karpaty Lviv *not played*
FK Lviv - Olimpik Donetsk 1-5(1-3)
Vorskla Poltava - FK Mariupol 1-2(0-0)

Round 32 [19.07.2020]
Olimpik Donetsk - Karpaty Lviv *not played*
FK Lviv - FK Mariupol 0-2(0-1)
SC Dnipro-1 - Vorskla Poltava 3-0(2-0)

Final Standings

		Total						Home				Away			
7.	SC Dnipro-1	30	13	4	13	42 - 42	43	10	0	5	28 - 17	3	4	8	14 - 25
8.	FK Mariupol	30	10	9	11	34 - 46	39	6	5	4	20 - 18	4	4	7	14 - 28
9.	FK Olimpik Donetsk	30	8	6	16	32 - 47	30	3	3	9	14 - 28	5	3	7	18 - 19
10.	FK Vorskla Poltava	30	7	7	16	23 - 48	28	6	4	5	14 - 16	1	3	11	9 - 32
11.	FK Lviv	32	5	9	18	25 - 57	24	2	5	9	12 - 28	3	4	9	13 - 29
12.	FK Karpaty Lviv (*expelled*)*	24	2	9	13	19 - 42	15	1	4	7	9 - 24	1	5	6	10 - 18

*Please note: FK Karpaty Lviv was expelled from the league for failing to appear to two games (Round 24 & 29).

Top goalscorers:

20	**Aluísio Chaves Ribeiro Moraes Júnior**	***FK Shakhtar Donetsk***
16	Oleksandr Filippov	*FK Desna Chernihiv*
14	Vladyslav Supriaha	*SC Dnipro-1*
14	Viktor Tsyhankov	*FK Dinamo Kyiv*
13	Marlos Romero Bonfim	*FK Shakhtar Donetsk*

NATIONAL CUP
Ukrainian Cup 2019/2020

First Round [20.08.2019]

SC Tavriya Simferopol – FK Real Pharma Odessa	5-0	FK Nyva Vinnytsa - FC Nikopol	5-1
FK Enerhiya Nova Kakhovka - FK Bukovina	1-4	FC Kalush - FK VPK-Ahro Shevchenkivka	1-0
FK Hirnik Kriviy Rih - SC Chaika Petropavlivska	0-1	FK Kristal Kherson - FC Dinaz Vyshhorod	2-4 pen
NK Veres Rivne - PFK Niva Ternopil	2-1	FK Alians Lypova Dolyna - FC Uzhhorod	2-0
FK Podillya-Khmelnitskiy – FK Polissya Zhitomir	1-0	FK Avanhard Bziv - FK Vovchansk	0-2 aet

Second Round [27.08.2019]

SC Tavriya Simferopol - FK Bukovina	2-3	Inhulets Petrove - FC Metalist 1925 Kharkiv	2-0
MFK Mikolaiv - FK Prykarpattia Ivano-Frankivsk	5-1	FC Kalush - FC Mynai	1-2
FC Dinaz Vyshhorod - FK Nyva Vinnytsa	1-0	FC Cherkaskyi Dnipro - MFK Kremin Kremenchuk	1-2
FK Podillya-Khmelnitskiy - FK Volyn Lutsk	4-5 pen	FK Vovchansk - FK Obolon-Brovar Kyiv	0-1 aet
NK Veres Rivne - FK Rukh Lviv	1-2	FK Avanhard Kramatorsk - FK Balkany Zorya	3-4 pen
FK Hirnyk-Sport Hor. Pl. – FK Metalurg Zaporizhya	6-5 pen	FK Alians Lypova Dolyna - SC Chaika Petrop. Bor.	4-1

Third Round [25.09./02.10.2019]

MFK Kremin Kremenchuk - FK Olimpik Donetsk	2-3(1-2)	Ahrobiznes Volochysk - SC Dnipro-1	1-3(0-2)
MFK Mykolaiv - FK Chornomorets Odesa	1-0(0-0)	FK Inhulets Petrove - FK Karpaty Lviv	0-0 aet; 7-6 pen
FC Dinaz Vyshhorod - FK Oleksandriya	0-1(0-0,0-0)	FK Alians Lypova Dolyna - FK Balkany Zorya	1-0(1-0)
FSK Bukovina Chernivtsi - FK Lviv	0-2(0-1)	FK Obolon-Brovar Kyiv - FK Hirnyk-Sport Hor.Pl.	0-2(0-0,0-0)
FC Mynai - FK Volyn Lutsk	1-0(0-0)	FK Rukh Lviv - FK Mariupol	0-1(0-0)

1/8-Finals [30.10.2019]

FC Mynai - FK Lviv	2-0(0-0)	FK Kolos Kovalivka - FK Vorskla Poltava	0-1(0-0)
MFK Mykolaiv - FK Desna Chernihiv	2-4(1-2)	FK Alians Lypova Dolyna - FK Hirnyk-Sport Hor. Pl	5-3(2-1)
FK Mariupol - FK Olimpik Donetsk	1-0(0-0)	FK Oleksandriya - FK Zorya Luhansk	1-1 aet; 5-4 pen
FK Inhulets Petrove - SC Dnipro-1	2-1(1-1)	FK Dinamo Kyiv - FK Shakhtar Donetsk	2-1(1-0,1-1)

Quarter-Finals [11-12.03.2020]

FC Mynai - FK Inhulets Petrove	1-1 aet; 6-5 pen	FK Dinamo Kyiv - FK Oleksandriya	1-0(0-0,0-0)
FK Alians Lypova Dolyna - FK Mariupol	2-4(2-2)	FK Desna Chernihiv - FK Vorskla Poltava	0-1(0-0)

Semi-Finals [17-24.06.2020]

FC Mynai - FK Dinamo Kyiv	0-2(0-2)	FK Mariupol - FK Vorskla Poltava	1-1 aet; 2-3 pen

Final

08.07.2020; Metalist Stadium, Kharkiv; Referee: Kateryna Monzul; Attendance: None

FK Dinamo Kyiv - FK Vorskla Poltava **1-1(1-1,1-1,1-1); 8-7 on penalties**

Dinamo Kyiv: Georgiy Bushchan, Artem Shabanov, Oleksandr Syrota, Tomasz Kędziora, Serhiy Sydorchuk (Cap), Benjamin Verbič, Volodymyr Shepeliev (117.Oleksandr Andrievsky), Vitaliy Buyalskiy (99.Mykola Shaparenko), Carlos María de Pena Bonino, Vitali Mykolenko, Heorhiy Tsitaishvili (60.Viktor Tsyhankov). Trainer: Oleksiy Mykhaylychenko.

Vorskla Poltava: Dmytro Riznyk, Najeeb Yakubu (73.Evgeniy Opanasenko), Volodimir Chesnakov (Cap), Vadim Sapay, Ibrahim Kane, Ihor Perduta, Oleksandr Sklyar (95.Edin Šehić), David Puclin, Pape-Alioune Ndiaye, Vladyslav Kulach (76.Luiz Gustavo Novaes Palhares „Luizão“), Ruslan Stepanyuk (115.Volodymyr Baenko). Trainer: Yuriy Maksimov.

Goals: 0-1 Ruslan Stepanyuk (11), 1-1 Benjamin Verbič (28).

Penalties: David Puclin 0-1; Benjamin Verbič 1-1; Ibrahim Kane 1-2; Viktor Tsyhankov 2-2; Luiz Gustavo Novaes Palhares „Luizão“ 2-3; Tomasz Kędziora 3-3; Evgeniy Opanasenko 3-4; Carlos María de Pena Bonino 4-4; Pape-Alioune Ndiaye 4-5; Oleksandr Andrievsky 5-5; Volodimir Chesnakov 5-6; Serhiy Sydorchuk 6-6; Ihor Perduta 6-7; Mykola Shaparenko 7-7; Vadim Sapay (saved); Vitali Mykolenko (saved); Volodymyr Baenko (missed); Artem Shabanov 8-7.

Please <u>note</u>: matches and goals includes statistics of both regular season and play-offs (Championship or Relegation).

Futbolnij Klub Desna Chernihiv

			Founded:	1960		
			Stadium:	Chernihiv Stadium, Chernihiv (12,060)		
			Trainer:	Oleksandr Riabokon		21.02.1964

Goalkeepers:	DOB	M	(s)	G		Andriy Dombrovskiy	12.08.1995	12	(5)	
Ihor Litovka	05.06.1988	2				Artem Favorov	19.03.1994	15	(1)	1
Evgen Past	16.03.1988	30				Vladislav Kalitvintsev	04.01.1993	21	(5)	6
Defenders:	DOB	M	(s)	G		Egor Kartushov	05.01.1991	15	(16)	2
Vitaliy Ermakov	07.06.1992	1	(9)			Orest Kuzyk	17.05.1995	15	(5)	1
Denis Favorov	01.04.1991	31		8		Andriy Mostoviy	24.01.1988	23	(6)	
Andriy Gitchenko	02.10.1984	29	(2)	3		Vladislav Ohirya	03.04.1990	27	(1)	
Maksym Imerekov	23.01.1991	25		2		Sergey Starenkiy	20.09.1984	1	(7)	1
Yukhym Konoplia	26.08.1999	12	(10)			Andriy Totovytskyy	20.01.1993	6	(6)	4
Vitali Pryndeta	02.02.1993		(1)			**Forwards:**	DOB	M	(s)	G
Joonas Tamm (EST)	02.02.1992	12	(1)	1		Pylyp Budkovsky	10.03.1992	5	(8)	3
Artur Zapadnya	04.06.1990	6	(1)			Maksym Degtyarev	30.05.1993	6	(9)	2
Midfielders:	DOB	M	(s)	G		Oleksandr Filipov	23.10.1992	26	(4)	16
Levan Arveladze	06.04.1993	8	(3)	1		Oleksiy Gutsulyak	25.12.1997	3	(1)	
Andriy Bogdanov	21.01.1990	11				Dmytro Khlyobas	09.05.1994	10	(10)	7

Sport Club Dnipro-1

			Founded:	10.03.2017		
			Stadium:	Dnipro Arena, Dnipro (31,003)		
			Trainer:	Dmytro Mikhaylenko		13.07.1973

Goalkeepers:	DOB	M	(s)	G		Aleksandr Kobakhidze (GEO)	11.02.1987		(2)	
Andriy Klishchuk	03.07.1992	9				Ihor Kogut	07.03.1996	21	(3)	4
Valeri Yurchuk	12.04.1990	21				Serhiy Kravchenko	24.04.1983	20	(3)	
Defenders:	DOB	M	(s)	G		Oleksandr Nazarenko	01.02.2000	16	(10)	2
Volodymyr Adamyuk	17.07.1991	12		1		Griffin Sabatini (SUI)	23.09.1998		(1)	
Papa Gueye (SEN)	07.06.1984	11	(2)			Vladyslav Shapoval	08.05.1995	11	(3)	1
Serhiy Loginov	24.08.1990	29				Oleksandr Snyzhko	20.08.1996	4	(8)	
Maksim Lopyrenok	13.04.1995	20	(4)			Yury Vakulko	10.11.1997	16	(6)	
Lucas Taylor Maia Reis (BRA)	10.04.1995	4	(1)	1		Yegor Yarmolyuk	01.03.2004	1	(1)	
Volodimir Poloviy	28.07.1985	15	(3)	1		Ihor Zagalskiy	19.05.1991	2	(1)	
Yuri Romaniuk	06.05.1997	2	(1)			**Forwards:**	DOB	M	(s)	G
Oleksandr Safronov	11.06.1999	10	(2)			Oleksiy Chichikov	30.09.1987	13	(10)	3
Oleksandr Svatok	27.09.1994	5	(1)			Francisco Di Franco (ARG)	28.01.1995	10	(1)	
Andriy Tsurikov	05.10.1992	6		1		Oleksiy Khoblenko	04.04.1994	10	(1)	5
Midfielders:	DOB	M	(s)	G		Dmytro Korkishko	04.05.1990	11	(11)	3
Arseniy Batahov	05.03.2002	10	(4)			Stanislav Kulish	08.02.1989	8	(5)	2
Oleksandr Belyaev	04.10.1999		(1)			Vladyslav Supriaha	15.02.2000	16	(8)	14
Serhiy Buletsa	16.02.1999	17	(9)	4						

Futbolnij Klub Dinamo Kyiv

			Founded:	13.05.1927		
			Stadium:	NSC Olimpiyskiy, Kyiv (70,050) /		
				"Lobanovsky" Dinamo Stadium, Kyiv (16,873)		
			Trainer:	Alyaksandr Khatskevich (BLR)		19.10.1973
			[15.08.2019]	Oleksiy Mykhaylychenko		30.03.1963

Goalkeepers:	DOB	M	(s)	G		Denys Garmash	19.04.1990	10	(3)	
Denis Boyko	29.01.1988	12				Oleksandr Karavayev	02.06.1992	20	(8)	
Georgiy Bushchan	31.05.1994	20				Mykola Shaparenko	04.10.1998	8	(7)	1
Defenders:	DOB	M	(s)	G		Volodymyr Shepeliev	01.06.1997	20	(6)	
Mykyta Burda	24.03.1995	8	(1)			Serhiy Sydorchuk	02.05.1991	22	(3)	1
Tamás Kádár (HUN)	14.03.1990	12	(1)			Viktor Tsyhankov	15.11.1997	21	(6)	14
Abdul Kadiri Mohammed (GHA)	07.03.1996	9	(6)			**Forwards:**	DOB	M	(s)	G
Tomasz Kędziora (POL)	11.06.1994	24	(3)			Olabiran Blessing Muyiwa (NGA)	07.09.1998		(1)	
Vitali Mykolenko	29.05.1999	23		3		Artem Besedin	31.03.1996	9	(4)	8
Josip Pivarić (CRO)	30.01.1989	1	(1)			Carlos María de Pena Bonino (URU)	11.03.1992	15	(13)	9
Denys Popov	17.02.1999	15	(1)	1		Francisco Sol Ortíz (ESP)	13.03.1992	6	(7)	1
Artem Shabanov	07.03.1992	25	(1)	2		Ibrahim Kargbo (BEL)	03.01.2000	1	(1)	
Oleksandr Syrota	11.06.2000	2				Gerson Leal Rodrigues Gouveia (LUX)	20.06.1995	6	(2)	2
Midfielders:	DOB	M	(s)	G		Nazariy Rusyn	25.10.1998	11	(1)	2
Oleksandr Andrievsky	25.06.1994	5	(2)			Heorhiy Tsitaishvili	18.11.2000	6	(4)	
Vitaliy Buyalskiy	06.01.1993	23	(4)	9		Benjamin Verbič (SVN)	27.11.1993	16	(9)	11
Mikkel Duelund (DEN)	29.06.1997	2	(6)							

Futbolnij Klub Karpaty Lviv

Founded: 18.01.1963
Stadium: Ukraina Stadium, Lviv (28,051)
Trainer: Oleksandr Chyzhevskiy — 27.05.1971
[03.09.2019] Roman Shanzar — 28.05.1979

Goalkeepers:	DOB	M	(s)	G
Andriy Artym	21.02.2000	2	(1)	
Anton Kanibolotskiy	16.05.1988	1		
Oleh Kudryk	17.10.1996	11		
Roman Pidkivka	09.05.1995	10		
Defenders:	**DOB**	**M**	**(s)**	**G**
Vladyslav Dubinchak	01.07.1998	19		
Andro Giorgadze (GEO)	03.05.1996	6		
Tim Hall (LUX)	15.04.1997	18		1
Oleksiy Kovtun	05.02.1995	6		
Oleksandr Kucher	22.10.1982	4		
Marvin Martins (LUX)	17.02.1995	22		1
Vasyl Pryima	10.06.1991		(2)	
Denys Sliusar	27.05.2002	1		
Roman Slyva	23.09.2000	1		
Oleh Veremiyenko	13.02.1999	6		
Midfielders:	**DOB**	**M**	**(s)**	**G**
Mohamed Abukar (FIN)	01.01.1999		(1)	
Oleksiy Khakhlov	06.02.1999	2	(1)	
Maksym Khlan	27.01.2003		(1)	
Dmytro Klyots	15.04.1996	21	(1)	
Artem Kozak	28.05.1998	4	(6)	1
Egor Nazaryna	10.07.1997	15		5
Gennady Pasich	13.07.1993	4		
Ostap Prytula	24.06.2000	5	(1)	
Vasyl Runich	31.01.2000		(1)	
Oleksiy Sych	01.04.2001	2		
Volodymyr Tanchyk	17.10.1991	2		
Yuri Tlumak	24.06.1905		(1)	
Roman Tolochko	25.10.1998	1		
Serhiy Vakulenko	07.09.1993	16		
Nazar Verbniy	26.07.1997	8		
Volodymyr Yakimets	03.03.1998	4	(5)	
Forwards:	**DOB**	**M**	**(s)**	**G**
Alexandru Boiciuc (MDA)	21.08.1997	9	(7)	2
Yaroslav Deda	28.05.1999	2	(6)	1
Matar Dièye (SEN)	10.01.1998	3		1
Francisco Di Franco (ARG)	28.01.1995	14	(1)	1
Oleksiy Gutsulyak	25.12.1997	9	(3)	2
João Diogo Jennings (BRA)	13.01.1999	9	(3)	
Ihor Karpenko	24.09.1997	2	(1)	
Kirill Kirilenko (BLR)	08.10.2000	2	(2)	
Hisham Layous (ISR)	13.11.2000		(8)	
Rostyslav Liakh	12.10.2000	9	(2)	
Melvyn Lorenzen (UGA)	26.11.1994	2	(2)	
Cristian Ioan Ponde (POR)	26.01.1995	9	(2)	1
Andriy Remeniuk	03.02.1999		(1)	
Frane Vojković (CRO)	20.12.1996	3	(9)	1

Futbolnij Klub Kolos Kovalivka

Founded: 2012
Stadium: NSC Olimpiyskiy, Kyiv (70,050)
Trainer: Ruslan Kostyshyn — 08.01.1977

Goalkeepers:	DOB	M	(s)	G
Yevheniy Kucherenko	27.08.1999	1		
Evgen Volinets	26.08.1993	23		
Anton Yashkov	30.01.1992	8		
Defenders:	**DOB**	**M**	**(s)**	**G**
Oleksandr Chornomorets	05.04.1993	16	(3)	
Evgen Efremov	17.01.1994	10		
Vladislav Emets	09.09.1997	10		
Maksym Maksymenko	28.05.1990	17	(1)	
Oleksandr Mihunov	13.04.1994	6		
Vadym Paramonov	18.03.1991	17	(4)	1
Kyrylo Petrov	22.06.1990	9		1
Andriy Sakhnevych	17.04.1989	5		
Oleksy Zozulya	15.04.1992	17	(1)	
Midfielders:	**DOB**	**M**	**(s)**	**G**
Andriy Bogdanov	21.01.1990	13	(1)	
Yehor Demchenko	25.07.1997		(2)	
Vitaly Gavrish	18.03.1986	18		3
Oleg Ilin	08.06.1997	20	(3)	2
Dzhemal Kyzylatesh	14.09.1994	1	(5)	
Vadim Milko	22.08.1986	25	(2)	2
Yevgeniy Morozko	15.02.1993	16	(10)	1
Vladyslav Nekhtiy	19.12.1991	11	(3)	
Pavel Orekhovskiy	13.05.1996	15	(4)	1
Oleksandr Pozdeiev	14.06.1986	1		
Vyacheslav Ryabov	21.06.1989	2	(4)	
Yevheniy Smyrniy	18.08.1998	19	(4)	5
Stanislav Sorokin	03.05.2000	1	(2)	1
Oleksandr Volkov	07.02.1989	8	(2)	1
Evgeniy Zadoya	05.01.1991	13	(5)	
Forwards:	**DOB**	**M**	**(s)**	**G**
Denis Antyukh	30.07.1997	2	(5)	
Oleksandr Bondarenko	28.07.1989	4	(8)	
Mamadou Danfa (SEN)	06.03.2001		(1)	
Denys Kostyshyn	31.08.1997	11	(10)	3
Oleg Kozhushko	17.02.1998	3	(19)	1
Vladimir Lisenko	20.04.1988	19	(6)	6
Árni Vilhjálmsson (ISL)	09.05.1994	11	(4)	5

Futbolnij Klub Lviv

Founded: 2006
Stadium: Arena Lviv, Lviv (34,915)
Trainer: Bohdan Blavatskiy — 07.06.1963
[10.09.2019] Volodymyr Mazyar — 28.09.1977
[01.11.2019] Yeghishe Melikyan (ARM) — 13.08.1979
[22.06.2020] Giorgi Tsetsadze (GEO) — 03.09.1974

Goalkeepers:	DOB	M	(s)	G
Oleksandr Bandura	30.05.1986	5	(1)	
German Penkov	26.05.1994	2		
Bogdan Sarnavskiy	29.01.1995	25		
Defenders:	**DOB**	**M**	**(s)**	**G**
Volodymyr Adamyuk	17.07.1991	3		
Joël Bopesu (FRA)	25.01.1995	12	(1)	
Serhiy Borzenko	22.06.1986	31		1
Anton Bratkov	14.05.1993	29	(1)	
Ihor Gonchar	10.01.1993	21	(2)	
Yegor Klymenchuk	11.11.1997	2	(5)	
Yury Kravchuk	06.04.1994	2	(2)	
Serhiy Lyulka	22.02.1990	17	(2)	
Oleksandr Nasonov	28.04.1992	1	(1)	
Vladyslav Pryimak	30.08.1996	16	(7)	
Ruslan Zubkov	24.11.1991		(7)	
Vicente de Paula Mercedes	02.03.1996	1	(2)	
Midfielders:	**DOB**	**M**	**(s)**	**G**
Jonatan da Silva Lima (BRA)	04.01.1992	5	(1)	
Nikita Khodakovsky	18.10.1996		(2)	
Mykola Kvasniy	04.01.1995	8	(3)	
Luiz Felipe Veloso Santos (BRA)	07.04.1997		(3)	
Martan Fernando Gonsalves Pimenta „Marthã" (BRA)	20.06.1997	15		
Artem Nedolia	20.10.1993	1	(2)	
Rafael Sabino dos Santos (BRA)	17.06.1996	20	(2)	1
Mykyta Tatarkov	04.01.1995	19		2
Welves Santos Damacena (BRA)	24.11.2000	3	(13)	
Forwards:	**DOB**	**M**	**(s)**	**G**
Alvaro Luis Tavares Vieira (BRA)	10.03.1995	18	(6)	3
Yaroslav Bogunov	04.09.1993	15	(12)	1
Bruno Duarte da Silva (BRA)	24.03.1996	3		1
Filipe Pachtmann (BRA)	11.04.2000		(3)	
Matheus Felipe Camargo Iacovelli (BRA)	13.03.1998	8	(5)	2
Nazariy Nych	19.02.1999	2	(6)	
Pedro Vitor Ferreira da Silva (BRA)	20.03.1998	11	(2)	1
José Vitor Rodrigues da Silva dos Santos (BRA)	28.04.1998	14	(4)	3
Renan Abner do Carmo de Oliveira (BRA)	08.05.1997	20	(7)	6
Rogerio Alves dos Santos „Shina" (BRA)	02.08.1996	22	(3)	4

Futbolnij Klub Mariupol

Founded: 1963
Stadium: "Volodymir Boiko" Stadium, Mariupol (12,680)
Trainer: Oleksandr Babich   15.02.1979

Goalkeepers:	DOB	M	(s)	G
Evgen Galchuk	05.03.1992	23		
Rustam Khudzhamov	05.10.1982	6		
Artem Pospelov	11.01.1998	1		
Defenders:	**DOB**	**M**	**(s)**	**G**
Oleksiy Bykov	29.03.1998	18		
Serhiy Chobotenko	16.01.1997	24	(1)	3
Joyskim Dawa (CMR)	09.04.1996	15	(6)	
Ihor Kiryukhantsev	29.01.1996	20	(3)	3
Viktor Korniyenko	14.02.1999	13	(4)	1
Nazariy Muravskiy	03.02.2000	5	(2)	
Mikita Peterman	12.06.1999	2	(3)	
Kyrylo Romaniuk	21.03.2001		(1)	
Danylo Sagutkin	19.04.1996	1		
Ihor Tishchenko	11.05.1989	8	(10)	
Serhiy Yavorskiy	05.07.1989	18	(2)	
Midfielders:	**DOB**	**M**	**(s)**	**G**
Anton Baydal	08.02.2000		(2)	

	DOB	M	(s)	G
Vladyslav Bondar	24.03.2000		(1)	
Maksym Chekh	03.01.1999	13	(6)	1
Valeriy Fedorchuk	05.10.1988	24	(1)	1
Serhiy Gorbunov	14.03.1994	15	(5)	
Danylo Ignatenko	13.03.1997	8	(1)	
Dmytro Myshnov	26.01.1994	27	(1)	4
Pavel Polegenko	06.01.1995	10	(5)	
Illia Putria	15.05.1998	2	(6)	1
Vyacheslav Tankovski	16.08.1995	7	(2)	
Dmytro Topalov	12.03.1998	14	(12)	4
Andriy Vyskrebentsevys	27.10.2000		(1)	
Forwards:	**DOB**	**M**	**(s)**	**G**
Vyacheslav Churko	10.05.1993	21	(5)	5
Artem Dudik	02.01.1997		(1)	
Ruslan Fomin	02.03.1986	7	(6)	4
Oleksiy Kashchuk	29.06.2000	5	(11)	3
Andriy Kulakov	28.04.1999	8	(4)	
Vladislav Vakula	29.04.1999	15		3

Futbolnij Klub Oleksandriya

Founded: 1948
Stadium: CSC Nika Stadium, Oleksandriya (7,000)
Trainer: Volodymyr Sharan   18.09.1971

Goalkeepers:	DOB	M	(s)	G
Oleg Bilyk	11.01.1998	6	(1)	
Yuri Pankiv	03.11.1984	26		
Defenders:	**DOB**	**M**	**(s)**	**G**
Vladislav Baboglo	14.11.1998	16	(2)	2
Glib Bukhal	12.11.1995	16	(5)	
Oleksiy Dovgiy	02.11.1989	11	(5)	2
Kaspars Dubra (LVA)	20.12.1990	26		
Oleksandr Melnyk	10.02.2000	1		
Denis Miroshnichenko	11.10.1994	24	(2)	
Pavlo Pashaev (AZE)	04.01.1988	16	(4)	
Kyrylo Prokopchuk	14.02.1998		(1)	
Anton Shendrik	26.05.1986	8	(4)	1
Timur Stetskov	27.01.1998	8	(4)	
Midfielders:	**DOB**	**M**	**(s)**	**G**
Yevhen Banada	29.02.1992	21	(5)	5
Artem Gordienko	04.03.1991	4	(5)	

	DOB	M	(s)	G
Dmytro Grechyshkin	22.09.1991	28	(1)	5
Vasili Gritsuk	21.11.1987	5	(10)	1
João Tiago Silva Teixeira (POR)	07.05.1996		(2)	
Kirilo Kovalets	02.07.1993	17	(5)	7
Valeri Luchkevych	11.01.1996	28	(1)	1
Bogdan Myshenko	29.12.1994	4	(2)	2
Yevhen Protasov	23.07.1997	2	(3)	
Maksym Tretyakov	06.03.1996	26	(3)	10
Roman Vantukh	04.07.1998	5	(2)	
Maksym Zaderaka	07.09.1994	11	(14)	2
Andriy Zaporozhan	21.03.1983	7	(2)	1
Forwards:	**DOB**	**M**	**(s)**	**G**
Denys Bezborodko	31.05.1994	15	(8)	3
Dmytro Shastal	30.12.1995	7	(11)	2
Artem Sitalo	01.08.1989	14	(8)	4
Denys Ustymenko	12.04.1999		(2)	

Futbolnij Klub Olimpik Donetsk

Founded: 2001
Stadium: "Lobanovsky" Dinamo Stadium, Kyiv (16,873)
Trainer: Júlio César Santos Correa (BRA)   18.11.1978
[19.08.2019] Ihor Klimovskiy   17.02.1972
[02.09.2019] Vicente Gómez Fernández (ESP)   08.09.1971
[13.03.2020] Ihor Klimovskiy   17.02.1972

Goalkeepers:	DOB	M	(s)	G
Andriy Chekotun	02.09.2002	1		
Betim Halimi (KVX)	28.02.1996	5	(1)	
Vladimir Krynsky	14.01.1997	15		
Artem Kychak	16.05.1989	5		
German Penkov	26.05.1994	4		
Defenders:	**DOB**	**M**	**(s)**	**G**
Aliyu Audu Abubakar (NGA)	15.06.1996	2		
Vitali Goshkoderia	08.01.1988		(2)	
Dmitro Grishko	02.12.1985	26		
Yegor Klymenchuk	11.11.1997	2	(2)	
Orest Lebedenko	23.09.1998	10		
Pavlo Lukyanchuk	19.05.1996	8	(3)	1
Dmytro Lytvyn	21.11.1996	4	(1)	
Ihor Snurnitsyn	07.03.2000	10		
Ivan Trubochkin	17.03.1993	1	(2)	
Evgeniy Tsymbalyuk	19.06.1996	24		1
Ivan Zotko	09.07.1996	16		
Midfielders:	**DOB**	**M**	**(s)**	**G**
Fabio Alexander Freitas de Almeida „Fabinho" (BRA)	07.07.1996	7	(6)	
Mykyta Kravchenko	14.06.1997	12		

	DOB	M	(s)	G
Andriy Kravchuk	26.02.1999	12	(4)	2
Pavlo Ksonz	02.01.1987	18	(5)	
Evgeny Pasich	13.07.1993	11	(8)	1
Gennady Pasich	13.07.1993	2	(7)	
Serhiy Politylo	09.01.1989	26	(2)	4
Danielis Romanovskis (LTU)	19.06.1996	6	(2)	
Dramane Salou (BFA)	22.05.1998	5	(2)	
Roman Vantukh	04.07.1998	9	(1)	1
Nazar Verbniy	26.07.1997	3	(2)	
Taras Zaviyskiy	12.04.1995	14	(6)	2
Forwards:	**DOB**	**M**	**(s)**	**G**
Denis Balanyuk	16.01.1997	2	(5)	1
Vitaliy Balashov	15.01.1991	9	(10)	2
Geoffrey Charles Chinedu (NGA)	01.10.1997	1	(10)	
Temur Chogadze (GEO)	05.05.1998	2	(3)	
Maksym Degtyarev	30.05.1993	5	(2)	5
Matar Dièye (SEN)	10.01.1998	10		1
Maxime Do Couto Teixeira (FRA)	13.12.1996	21	(6)	4
Demir Imeri (MKD)	27.10.1995	5	(3)	1
Shahab Zahedi Tabar (IRN)	18.08.1995	17	(6)	6

Futbolnij Klub Shakhtar Donetsk

Founded: 24.05.1936
Stadium: OSC Metalist Stadium, Kharkiv (40,003)
Trainer: Luís Manuel Ribeiro de Castro (POR)   03.09.1961

Goalkeepers:	DOB	M	(s)	G
Andriy Pyatov	28.06.1984	23		
Oleksiy Shevchenko	24.02.1992	2		
Anatoliy Trubin	01.08.2001	7		
Defenders:	DOB	M	(s)	G
Valeriy Bondar	27.02.1999	7	(4)	1
Domilson Cordeiro dos Santos „Dodô" (BRA)	17.11.1998	20	(3)	1
Ismaily Gonçalves dos Santos(BRA)	11.01.1990	20	(1)	2
Davit Khotcholava (GEO)	08.02.1993	8	(2)	
Serhiy Krivtsov	15.03.1991	23		2
Mykola Matvienko	02.05.1996	24	(2)	1
Vitor Eduardo da Silva Matos „Vitão" (BRA)	02.02.2000	3	(1)	
Midfielders:	DOB	M	(s)	G
Alan Patrick Lourenço (BRA)	13.05.1991	22	(3)	4
Serhiy Bolbat	13.06.1993	13	(4)	
Artem Bondarenko	21.08.2000	1	(4)	
Yevhen Konoplyanka	29.09.1989	14	(6)	4
Viktor Kovalenko	14.02.1996	7	(10)	1

	DOB	M	(s)	G
Marcos Antônio Silva Santos (BRA)	13.06.2000	14	(7)	2
Marlos Romero Bonfim	07.06.1988	17	(7)	13
Maycon de Andrade Barberan(BRA)	15.07.1997	6	(4)	1
Oleksandr Pikhalonok	07.05.1997	2	(3)	
Taras Stepanenko	08.08.1989	24		1
Forwards:	DOB	M	(s)	G
Gustavo Ezequiel Blanco Leschuk (ARG)	05.11.1991		(2)	
Andriy Boryachuk	23.04.1996	1	(2)	1
Bruno Ferreira Bonfim „Dentinho" (BRA)	19.01.1989	4	(7)	2
Fernando dos Santos Pedro (BRA)	01.03.1999	3	(6)	1
Aluísio Chaves Ribeiro Moraes Júnior	04.04.1987	23	(4)	20
Marcos Robson Cipriano (BRA)	27.02.1999	9	(3)	1
Danylo Sikan	16.04.2001	3	(4)	
Manor Solomon (ISR)	24.07.1999	10	(10)	3
Taison Barcellos Freda (BRA)	13.01.1988	21	(4)	10
Mateus Cardoso Lemos Martins „Tetê" (BRA)	15.02.2000	19	(7)	8
Vladislav Vakula	29.04.1999	1	(1)	

Futbolnij Klub Vorskla Poltava

Founded: 1955
Stadium: Vorskla Stadium, Poltava (24,795)
Trainer: Vitaliy Kosovskiy   11.08.1973
[15.11.2019]   Yuriy Maksimov   08.12.1968

Goalkeepers:	DOB	M	(s)	G
Pavlo Isenko	21.07.2003	2		
Danylo Kanevtsev	26.07.1996	1		
Dmytro Riznyk	30.01.1999	14		
Oleksandr Tkachenko	19.02.1993	13	(1)	
Defenders:	DOB	M	(s)	G
Artur Sergio Batista de Souza (BRA)	05.08.1994	11	(3)	
Volodymyr Baenko	09.02.1990	13	(2)	1
Artem Biliy	03.10.1999	2	(1)	
Volodimir Chesnakov	12.02.1988	25		
Valeriy Dubko	22.03.2001	2	(2)	
Ibrahim Kane (MLI)	23.06.2000	17	(2)	1
Evgeny Martynenko	25.06.1993	10	(1)	
Zurab Ochihava	18.05.1995		(3)	
Evgeniy Opanasenko	25.08.1990	1	(1)	
Yevhen Pavlyuk	18.08.2002	3	(1)	1
Ihor Perduta	15.11.1990	24		2
Taras Sakiv	19.11.1997	2	(1)	
Vadim Sapay	07.02.1986	13		
Najeeb Yakubu (GHA)	01.05.2000	4	(9)	1
Midfielders:	DOB	M	(s)	G
Artem Cheliadin	29.12.1999	4	(3)	1

	DOB	M	(s)	G
Artem Gabelyuk	02.01.1995	11	(2)	
Ilya Gadzhuk	02.08.2002	3	(1)	
Dmitro Kravchenko	25.02.1995	2	(3)	
Danilo Kravchuk	02.07.2001	3	(4)	1
Luiz Gustavo Novaes Palhares „Luizão"(BRA)	20.02.1998	18	(2)	1
Maksym Melnychuk	18.09.1999	7		
Pape-Alioune Ndiaye (FRA)	04.02.1998	12	(2)	
Todor Petrović (SRB)	18.08.1994	11	(2)	
David Puclin (CRO)	17.06.1992	9		
Pavlo Rebenok	23.07.1985	10	(10)	
Oleksandr Sklyar	26.02.1991	14	(3)	
Ruslan Stepanyuk	16.01.1992	9		4
Andriy Stryzhak	22.10.1999	3	(2)	
Oleg Vlasov	25.10.2002	3	(1)	
Forwards:	DOB	M	(s)	G
Denys Halata	04.09.2000		(4)	
Rubin Hebaj (ALB)	30.07.1998	1	(4)	
Yuriy Kolomoyets	22.03.1990	12	(1)	2
Yuriy Kozyrenko	27.11.1999	6	(3)	
Vladyslav Kulach	07.05.1993	8	(1)	2
Edin Šehić (BIH)	03.02.1995	9	(2)	2
Denis Vasin	04.03.1989	14	(8)	4

Futbolnij Klub Zorya Luhansk

Founded: 1923
Stadium: Slavutych-Arena, Zaporizhia (12,000)
Trainer: Viktor Skrypnyk   19.11.1969

Goalkeepers:	DOB	M	(s)	G
Zauri Makharadze (GEO)	24.03.1993	8		
Dmytro Matsapura	10.03.2000	3		
Nikita Shevchenko	26.01.1993	18		
Nikola Vasilj (BIH)	02.12.1995	3	(1)	
Defenders:	DOB	M	(s)	G
Joel Abu Hanna (GER)	22.01.1998	18	(4)	1
Maksym Biliy	21.06.1990	1	(1)	
Nikita Kamenyuka	03.06.1985	3	(6)	
Bogdan Mykhaylychenko	21.03.1997	29		3
Oleksandr Tymchyk	20.01.1997	27	(3)	
Vitaliy Vernidub	17.10.1987	21	(3)	1
Midfielders:	DOB	M	(s)	G
Levan Arveladze	06.04.1993	1	(6)	
Vladimir Belotserkovets	22.01.2000		(1)	
Ihor Chaykovskiy	07.10.1991		(3)	

	DOB	M	(s)	G
Yevgen Cheberko	23.01.1998	24	(3)	
Andrejs Cigaņiks (LVA)	12.04.1997	2	(2)	
Lovro Cvek (CRO)	06.07.1995	6	(5)	
Dmitriy Ivanisenya	11.01.1994	26	(3)	1
Vladyslav Kabayev	01.09.1995	26	(3)	7
Dmytro Khomchenovsky	16.04.1990	17	(8)	3
Vladyslav Kochergin	30.04.1996	32		7
Bohdan Liedniev	07.04.1998	21	(6)	11
Vladlen Yurchenko	22.01.1994	29		7
Forwards:	DOB	M	(s)	G
Pylyp Budkovsky	10.03.1992	5	(6)	1
Artem Gromov	14.01.1990	15	(7)	2
Maksym Lunyov	22.05.1998	3	(18)	
Mihailo Perović (MNE)	23.01.1997	5	(6)	1
Nazariy Rusyn	25.10.1998	9	(5)	5

SECOND LEVEL
Ukrainian First League 2019/2020

1.	FK Mynai Uzhgorod (*Promoted*)	30	19	5	6	51	-	28	62
2.	FK Rukh Vynnyky (*Promoted*)	30	18	7	5	51	-	21	61
3.	FK Inhulets Petrove (*Promoted*)	30	17	9	4	47	-	22	60
4.	FK Ahrobiznes Volochysk	30	19	3	8	52	-	30	60
5.	FK Volyn Lutsk	30	17	6	7	57	-	36	57
6.	FK Obolon-Brovar Kyiv	30	14	9	7	40	-	31	51
7.	FC Metalist 1925 Kharkiv	30	15	6	9	44	-	34	51
8.	FK Avanhard Kramatorsk	30	13	6	11	37	-	40	45
9.	FK Hirnyk-Sport Horishni Plavni	30	12	3	15	42	-	48	39
10.	FK Chornomorets Odesa	30	10	9	11	40	-	37	39
11.	MFK Mykolaiv	30	8	10	12	45	-	45	34
12.	FK Prykarpattia Ivano-Frankivsk	30	9	3	18	44	-	51	30
13.	MFK Kremin Kremenchuk	30	7	6	17	35	-	57	27
14.	FK Balkany Zorya (*Relegated*)	30	5	10	15	27	-	51	25
15.	MFK Metalurh Zaporizhya (*Relegation Play-offs*)	30	6	4	20	28	-	58	22
16.	FK Cherkashchyna Cherkasy (*Relegation Play-offs*)	30	1	4	25	23		74	7

<u>Please note</u>: FK Balkany Zorya were relegated on own initiative.

Relegation Play-offs [16-20.08.2020]

NK Veres Rivne - FK Cherkashchyna Cherkasy	2-0(0-0)	1-1(1-0)
MFK Metalurh Zaporizhya - FK Alians Lypova Dolyna	0-2(0-1)	0-1(0-0)

NK Veres Rivne and FK Alians Lypova Dolyna were promoted for the Ukrainian First League 2020/2021.

NATIONAL TEAM

INTERNATIONAL MATCHES
(16.07.2019 – 15.07.2020)

07.09.2019	Vilnius	Lithuania - Ukraine	0-3(0-2)	(ECQ)
10.09.2019	Dnipro	Ukraine - Nigeria	2-2(0-2)	(F)
11.10.2019	Kharkiv	Ukraine - Lithuania	2-0(1-0)	(ECQ)
14.10.2019	Kyiv	Ukraine - Portugal	2-1(2-0)	(ECQ)
14.11.2019	Zaporizhia	Ukraine - Estonia	1-0(0-0)	(F)
17.11.2019	Beograd	Serbia - Ukraine	2-2(1-1)	(ECQ)

07.09.2019   LITHUANIA - UKRAINE   **0-3(0-2)**   16th EC. Qualifiers
LFF stadionas, Vilnius; Referee: Irfan Peljto (Bosnia and Herzegovina); Attendance: 5,067
UKR: Andriy Pyatov (Cap), Serhiy Kryvtsov, Oleksandr Zinchenko, Mykola Matviyenko, Vitaliy Mykolenko, Marlos Romero Bonfim, Taras Stepanenko, Ruslan Malinovskiy (80.Roman Bezus), Serhiy Bolbat, Andriy Yarmolenko (60.Viktor Tsyhankov), Roman Yaremchuk (65.Aluísio Chaves Ribeiro Moraes Júnior). Trainer: Andriy Shevchenko.
Goals: Oleksandr Zinchenko (7), Marlos Romero Bonfim (27), Ruslan Malinovskiy (62).

10.09.2019   UKRAINE - NIGERIA   **2-2(0-2)**   Friendly International
Dnipro-Arena, Dnipro; Referee: Paolo Valeri (Italy); Attendance: 27,320
UKR: Andriy Lunin, Mykyta Burda, Eduard Sobol, Oleksandr Zinchenko, Mykola Matviyenko, Ruslan Malinovskiy (73.Volodymyr Shepelev), Oleksandr Karavayev, Viktor Kovalenko (67.Vitaliy Buyalskiy), Viktor Tsyhankov (73.Yevhen Konoplyanka), Aluísio Chaves Ribeiro Moraes Júnior (37.Roman Yaremchuk), Andriy Yarmolenko (Cap) (58.Marlos Romero Bonfim). Trainer: Andriy Shevchenko.
Goals: Oleksandr Zinchenko (78), Roman Yaremchuk (79).

11.10.2019   UKRAINE - LITHUANIA   **2-0(1-0)**   16th EC. Qualifiers
Metalist Stadium, Kharkiv; Referee: Harald Lechner (Austria); Attendance: 32,500
UKR: Andriy Pyatov (Cap), Serhiy Kryvtsov, Eduard Sobol, Oleksandr Zinchenko, Mykola Matviyenko, Marlos Romero Bonfim (59.Yevhen Konoplyanka), Taras Stepanenko (73.Serhiy Sydorchuk), Ruslan Malinovskiy, Serhiy Bolbat, Aluísio Chaves Ribeiro Moraes Júnior, Andriy Yarmolenko (64.Viktor Tsyhankov). Trainer: Andriy Shevchenko.
Goals: Ruslan Malinovskiy (29, 58).

14.10.2019   UKRAINE - PORTUGAL   **2-1(2-0)**   16th EC. Qualifiers
Olympiyskiy Stadium, Kyiv; Referee: Anthony Taylor (England); Attendance: 65,883
UKR: Andriy Pyatov (Cap), Serhiy Kryvtsov, Oleksandr Zinchenko, Mykola Matviyenko, Vitaliy Mykolenko (90+4.Ihor Plastun), Marlos Romero Bonfim (63.Yevhen Konoplyanka), Taras Stepanenko [*sent off 72*], Ruslan Malinovskiy, Oleksandr Karavayev, Andriy Yarmolenko, Roman Yaremchuk (73.Viktor Kovalenko). Trainer: Andriy Shevchenko.
Goals: Roman Yaremchuk (6), Andriy Yarmolenko (27).

14.11.2019   UKRAINE - ESTONIA   **1-0(0-0)**   Friendly International
Slavutych Arena, Zaporizhya; Referee: Juan Martínez Munuera (Spain); Attendance: 11,756
UKR: Andriy Lunin, Ihor Plastun, Eduard Sobol, Mykola Matviyenko (46.Artem Shabanov), Yevhen Shakhov (75.Volodymyr Shepelev), Serhiy Sydorchuk (46.Dmytro Ivanisenya), Serhiy Bolbat, Viktor Kovalenko (46.Vitaliy Buyalskiy), Viktor Tsyhankov (46.Roman Bezus), Andriy Yarmolenko (Cap) (66.Maryan Shved), Artem Besyedin. Trainer: Andriy Shevchenko.
Goal: Roman Bezus (90+2).

17.11.2019 **SERBIA - UKRAINE** 2-2(1-1) 16th EC. Qualifiers

Stadion "Rajko Mitić", Beograd; Referee: Robert Madden (Scotland); Attendance: 4,457

UKR: Andriy Pyatov (Cap), Serhiy Kryvtsov, Mykola Matviyenko, Vitaliy Mykolenko, Serhiy Sydorchuk, Ruslan Malinovskiy (88.Yevhen Shakhov), Oleksandr Karavayev, Viktor Kovalenko (77.Volodymyr Shepelev), Viktor Tsyhankov (77.Artem Besyedin), Andriy Yarmolenko, Roman Yaremchuk. Trainer: Andriy Shevchenko.

Goals: Roman Yaremchuk (33), Artem Besyedin (90+3).

NATIONAL TEAM PLAYERS
(16.07.2019 – 15.07.2020)

Name	DOB	Caps	Goals	2019/2020:	Club
Goalkeepers					
Andriy LUNIN	11.02.1999	5	0	2019:	*Real Valladolid CF (ESP)*
Andriy PYATOV	28.06.1984	93	0	2019:	*FK Shakhtar Donetsk*
Defenders					
Serhiy BOLBAT	13.06.1993	5	0	2019:	*FK Shakhtar Donetsk*
Mykyta BURDA	24.04.1995	8	0	2019:	*FK Dinamo Kyiv*
Oleksandr KARAVAYEV	02.06.1992	25	1	2019:	*FK Dinamo Kyiv*
Serhiy KRYVTSOV	15.03.1991	16	0	2019:	*FK Shakhtar Donetsk*
Mykola MATVIYENKO	02.05.1996	25	0	2019:	*FK Shakhtar Donetsk*
Vitaliy MYKOLENKO	29.05.1999	8	0	2019:	*FK Dinamo Kyiv*
Ihor PLASTUN	20.08.1990	4	0	2019:	*KAA Gent (BEL)*
Artem SHABANOV	07.03.1992	2	0	2019:	*FK Dinamo Kyiv*
Eduard SOBOL	20.04.1995	11	0	2019:	*Club Brugge KV (BEL)*
Oleksandr ZINCHENKO	15.12.1996	31	4	2019:	*Manchester City FC (ENG)*
Midfielders					
Roman BEZUS	26.09.1990	22	5	2019:	*KAA Gent (BEL)*
Vitaliy BUYALSKIY	06.01.1993	8	0	2019:	*FK Dinamo Kyiv*
Dmytro IVANISENYA	11.01.1994	1	0	2019:	*FK Zorya Luhansk*
Yevhen KONOPLYANKA	29.09.1989	85	21	2019:	*FK Shakhtar Donetsk*
Viktor KOVALENKO	14.02.1996	26	0	2019:	*FK Shakhtar Donetsk*
Ruslan MALINOVSKIY	04.05.1993	27	5	2019:	*Atalanta Bergamasca Calcio (ITA)*
MARLOS Romero Bonfim	07.06.1988	16	1	2019:	*FK Shakhtar Donetsk*
Yevhen SHAKHOV	30.11.1990	7	1	2019:	*US Lecce (ITA)*
Volodymyr SHEPELEV	01.06.1997	6	0	2019:	*FK Dinamo Kyiv*
Maryan SHVED	16.07.1997	2	0	2019:	*Celtic FC Glasgow (SCO)*
Taras STEPANENKO	08.08.1989	57	3	2019:	*FK Shakhtar Donetsk*
Serhiy SYDORCHUK	02.05.1991	28	2	2019:	*FK Dinamo Kyiv*
Viktor TSYHANKOV	15.11.1997	20	3	2019:	*FK Dinamo Kyiv*
Andriy YARMOLENKO	23.10.1989	86	37	2019:	*West Ham United FC London (ENG)*
Forwards					
Artem BESYEDIN	31.03.1996	13	2	2019:	*FK Dinamo Kyiv*
Aluísio Chaves Ribeiro Moraes JÚNIOR	04.04.1987	5	0	2019:	*FK Shakhtar Donetsk*
Roman YAREMCHUK	27.11.1995	12	5	2019:	*KAA Gent (BEL)*

National team coach		
Andriy SHEVCHENKO [from 15.07.2016]	29.09.1976	33 M; 19 W; 9 D; 5 L; 50-26

WALES

The Country:
Cymru (Wales)
Capital: Cardiff
Surface: 20,779 km²
Inhabitants: 3,153,000 [2019]
Time: UTC

The FA:
Football Association of Wales
11/12 Neptune Court Vanguard Way, CF24 5PJ Cardiff
Tel: +44 29 2043 5830
Founded: 1876
Member of FIFA: 1910-1920; 1924-1928; since 1946
Member of UEFA since: 1954
Website: www.faw.org.uk

NATIONAL TEAM RECORDS

RECORDS

First international match:	25.03.1876, Glasgow: Scotland – Wales 4-0
Most international caps:	Christopher Ross Gunter - 96 caps (since 2007)
Most international goals:	Gareth Frank Bale - 33 goals / 83 caps (since 2006)

UEFA EUROPEAN CHAMPIONSHIP

1960	Did not enter
1964	Qualifiers
1968	Qualifiers
1972	Qualifiers
1976	Qualifiers
1980	Qualifiers
1984	Qualifiers
1988	Qualifiers
1992	Qualifiers
1996	Qualifiers
2000	Qualifiers
2004	Qualifiers
2008	Qualifiers
2012	Qualifiers
2016	Final Tournament (Semi-Finals)
2020	*Final Tournament (Qualified)*

FIFA WORLD CUP

1930	*Not a FIFA member*
1934	*Not a FIFA member*
1938	*Not a FIFA member*
1950	Qualifiers
1954	Qualifiers
1958	Final Tournament (Quarter-Finals)
1962	Qualifiers
1966	Qualifiers
1970	Qualifiers
1974	Qualifiers
1978	Qualifiers
1982	Qualifiers
1986	Qualifiers
1990	Qualifiers
1994	Qualifiers
1998	Qualifiers
2002	Qualifiers
2006	Qualifiers
2010	Qualifiers
2014	Qualifiers
2018	Qualifiers

OLYMPIC TOURNAMENTS

1908	-
1912	-
1920	-
1924	-
1928	-
1936	-
1948	-
1952	-
1956	-
1960	-
1964	-
1968	-
1972	-
1976	-
1980	-
1984	-
1988	-
1992	-
1996	-
2000	-
2004	-
2008	-
2012	-
2016	-

UEFA NATIONS LEAGUE

2018/2019 – League B

FIFA CONFEDERATIONS CUP 1992-2017

None

WELSH CLUB HONOURS IN EUROPEAN CLUB COMPETITIONS:

European Champion Clubs.Cup (1956-1992) / UEFA Champions League (1993-2020)
None

Fairs Cup (1858-1971) / UEFA Cup (1972-2009) / UEFA Europa League (2010-2020)
None

UEFA Super Cup (1972-2019)
None

*European Cup Winners.Cup 1961-1999**
None

*defunct competition

NATIONAL COMPETITIONS
TABLE OF HONOURS

	CHAMPIONS*	CUP WINNERS	BEST GOALSCORERS
1877/1878	-	Wrexham AFC	-
1878/1879	-	Newtown White Stars FC	-
1879/1880	-	Ruabon Druids FC	-
1880/1881	-	Ruabon Druids FC	-
1881/1882	-	Ruabon Druids FC	-
1882/1883	-	Wrexham AFC	-
1883/1884	-	Oswestry Town FC Shropshire(ENG)	-
1884/1885	-	Ruabon Druids FC	-
1885/1886	-	Ruabon Druids FC	-
1886/1887	-	Chirk AAA FC	-
1887/1888	-	Chirk AAA FC	-
1888/1889	-	Bangor City FC	-
1889/1890	-	Chirk AAA FC	-
1890/1891	-	Shrewsbury Town FC (ENG)	-
1891/1892	-	Chirk AAA FC	-
1892/1893	-	Wrexham AFC	-
1893/1894	-	Chirk AAA FC	-
1894/1895	-	Newtown AFC	-
1895/1896	-	Bangor City FC	-
1896/1897	-	Wrexham AFC	-
1897/1898	-	Ruabon Druids FC	-
1898/1899	-	Ruabon Druids FC	-
1899/1900	-	Aberystwyth Town FC	-
1900/1901	-	Oswestry Town FC Shropshire(ENG)	-
1901/1902	-	Wellington Town FC (ENG)	-
1902/1903	-	Wrexham AFC	-
1903/1904	-	Ruabon Druids FC	-
1904/1905	-	Wrexham AFC	-
1905/1906	-	Wellington Town FC (ENG)	-
1906/1907	-	Oswestry Town FC Shropshire(ENG)	-
1907/1908	-	Chester City FC (ENG)	-
1908/1909	-	Wrexham AFC	-
1909/1910	-	Wrexham AFC	-
1910/1911	-	Wrexham AFC	-
1911/1912	-	Cardiff City	-
1912/1913	-	Swansea Town AFC	-
1913/1914	-	Wrexham AFC	-
1914/1915	-	Wrexham AFC	-
1915/1916	-	*No competition*	-
1916/1917	-	*No competition*	-
1917/1918	-	*No competition*	-
1918/1919	-	*No competition*	-
1919/1920	-	Cardiff City FC	-
1920/1921	-	Wrexham AFC	-
1921/1922	-	Cardiff City FC	-
1922/1923	-	Cardiff City FC	-
1923/1924	-	Wrexham AFC	-
1924/1925	-	Wrexham AFC	-
1925/1926	-	Ebbw Vale FC	-
1926/1927	-	Cardiff City FC	-
1927/1928	-	Cardiff City FC	-
1928/1929	-	Connah's Quay & Shotton FC	-
1929/1930	-	Cardiff City FC	-
1930/1931	-	Wrexham AFC	-
1931/1932	-	Swansea Town AFC	-
1932/1933	-	Chester City FC (ENG)	-
1933/1934	-	Bristol City FC (ENG)	-
1934/1935	-	Tranmere Rovers FC (ENG)	-
1935/1936	-	Crewe Alexandra FC (ENG)	-
1936/1937	-	Crewe Alexandra FC (ENG)	-
1937/1938	-	Shrewsbury Town FC (ENG)	-
1938/1939	-	South Liverpool FC (ENG)	-
1939/1940	-	Wellington Town FC (ENG)	-
1940/1941	-	*No competition*	-
1941/1942	-	*No competition*	-
1942/1943	-	*No competition*	-
1943/1944	-	*No competition*	-
1944/1945	-	*No competition*	-
1945/1946	-	*No competition*	-
1946/1947	-	Chester City FC (ENG)	-
1947/1948	-	Lovell's Athletic FC	-
1948/1949	-	Merthyr Tydfil FC	-

Season		Champion	Top scorer	
1949/1950	-	Swansea Town AFC	-	
1950/1951	-	Merthyr Tydfil FC	-	
1951/1952	-	Rhyl FC	-	
1952/1953	-	Rhyl FC	-	
1953/1954	-	Flint Town United FC	-	
1954/1955	-	Barry Town United FC	-	
1955/1956	-	Cardiff City FC	-	
1956/1957	-	Wrexham AFC	-	
1957/1958	-	Wrexham AFC	-	
1958/1959	-	Cardiff City FC	-	
1959/1960	-	Wrexham AFC	-	
1960/1961	-	Swansea Town AFC	-	
1961/1962	-	Bangor City FC	-	
1962/1963	-	Borough United FC	-	
1963/1964	-	Cardiff City FC	-	
1964/1965	-	Cardiff City FC	-	
1965/1966	-	Swansea Town AFC	-	
1966/1967	-	Cardiff City FC	-	
1967/1968	-	Cardiff City FC	-	
1968/1969	-	Cardiff City FC	-	
1969/1970	-	Cardiff City FC	-	
1970/1971	-	Cardiff City FC	-	
1971/1972	-	Wrexham AFC	-	
1972/1973	-	Cardiff City FC	-	
1973/1974	-	Cardiff City FC	-	
1974/1975	-	Wrexham AFC	-	
1975/1976	-	Cardiff City FC	-	
1976/1977	-	Shrewsbury Town FC (ENG)	-	
1977/1978	-	Wrexham AFC	-	
1978/1979	-	Shrewsbury Town FC (ENG)	-	
1979/1980	-	Newport County AFC	-	
1980/1981	-	Swansea City FC	-	
1981/1982	-	Swansea City FC	-	
1982/1983	-	Swansea City FC	-	
1983/1984	-	Shrewsbury Town FC (ENG)	-	
1984/1985	-	Shrewsbury Town FC (ENG)	-	
1985/1986	-	Wrexham AFC	-	
1986/1987	-	Merthyr Tydfil FC	-	
1987/1988	-	Cardiff City FC	-	
1988/1989	-	Swansea City FC	-	
1989/1990	-	Hereford United FC (ENG)	-	
1990/1991	-	Swansea City FC	-	
1991/1992	-	Cardiff City FC	-	
1992/1993	Cwmbrân Town AFC	Cardiff City FC	Steve Woods (Ebbw Vale FC)	29
1993/1994	Bangor City FC	Barry Town United FC	Dave Taylor (Porthmadog FC)	43
1994/1995	Bangor City FC	Wrexham AFC	Frank Mottram (Bangor City FC)	31
1995/1996	Barry Town United FC	Llansantffraid FC	Ken McKenna (Conwy United FC)	38
1996/1997	Barry Town United FC	Barry Town United FC	Anthony Bird (Barry Town United FC)	42
1997/1998	Barry Town United FC	Bangor City FC	Eifion Wyn Williams (Barry Town United FC)	40
1998/1999	Barry Town United FC	Inter CableTel Cardiff	Eifion Wyn Williams (Barry Town United FC)	28
1999/2000	Total Network Solutions	Bangor City FC	Chris Summers (Cwmbrân Town AFC)	28
2000/2001	Barry Town United FC	Barry Town United FC	Graham Evans (Caersws FC)	25
2001/2002	Barry Town United FC	Barry Town United FC	Marc Lloyd-Williams (Bangor City FC)	47
2002/2003	Barry Town United FC	Barry Town United FC	Graham Evans (Caersws FC)	24
2003/2004	Rhyl FC	Rhyl FC	Graham Evans (Caersws FC)	24
2004/2005	Total Network Solutions	Total Network Solutions	Marc Lloyd-Williams (Total Network Solutions)	31
2005/2006	Total Network Solutions	Rhyl FC	Rhys Griffiths (Port Talbot Town FC)	28
2006/2007	The New Saints FC	Carmarthen Town FC	Rhys Griffiths (Llanelli Town AFC)	30
2007/2008	Llanelli Town AFC	Bangor City FC	Rhys Griffiths (Llanelli Town AFC)	40
2008/2009	Rhyl FC	Bangor City FC	Rhys Griffiths (Llanelli Town AFC)	31
2009/2010	The New Saints FC	Bangor City FC	Rhys Griffiths (Llanelli Town AFC)	30
2010/2011	Bangor City FC	Llanelli Town AFC	Rhys Griffiths (Llanelli Town AFC)	25
2011/2012	The New Saints FC	The New Saints FC	Rhys Griffiths (Llanelli Town AFC)	24
2012/2013	The New Saints FC	Prestatyn Town FC	Michael Wilde (The New Saints FC)	25
2013/2014	The New Saints FC	The New Saints FC	Chris Venables (Aberystwyth Town FC)	20
2014/2015	The New Saints FC	The New Saints FC	Chris Venables (Aberystwyth Town FC)	28
2015/2016	The New Saints FC	The New Saints FC	Chris Venables (Bala Town FC)	20
2016/2017	The New Saints FC	Bala Town FC	Jason Oswell (ENG, Newtown AFC)	22
2017/2018	The New Saints FC	Connah's Quay Nomads FC	Gregory Alexander Draper (NZL, The New Saints FC)	11
2018/2019	The New Saints FC	The New Saints FC	Steven Anthony Tames (ENG, Bala Town FC)	17
2019/2020	Connah's Quay Nomads FC	*Competition cancelled*	Chris Venables (Bala Town FC)	22

Please note: Championship called League of Wales (1992–2002) and Welsh Premier League (since 2002)

NATIONAL CHAMPIONSHIP
Cymru Premier League 2019/2020
(16.08.2019 – 07.03.2020)

Regular Season - Results

Round 1 [16-18.08.2019]
Aberystwyth Town - Carmarthen T. 3-2(1-1)
Airbus UK - Bala Town 1-2(0-2)
Newtown AFC - Cefn Druids 0-0
Pen-y-bont FC - Barry Town 1-2(0-0)
Connah's Quay - Metropolitan 1-1(0-0)
The New Saints - Caernarfon Town 1-0(1-0)

Round 2 [23.08.2019]
Bala Town - The New Saints 3-1(0-1)
Barry Town - Aberystwyth Town 3-1(2-0)
Caernarfon Town - Connah's Quay 0-0
Cefn Druids - Airbus UK 3-1(2-1)
Pen-y-bont FC - Metropolitan 1-3(0-1)
Carmarthen Town - Newtown AFC 1-2(1-1)

Round 3 [26.08.2019]
Aberystwyth T. - The New Saints 1-10(0-5)
Barry Town - Bala Town 2-2(1-0)
Caernarfon Town - Cefn Druids 1-1(1-0)
Metropolitan - Airbus UK 1-0(1-0)
Connah's Quay - Carmarthen Town 1-1(0-0)
Newtown AFC - Pen-y-bont FC 1-1(0-0)

Round 4 [30-31.08.2019]
Bala Town - Connah's Quay 0-1(0-0)
Metropolitan - Newtown AFC 1-0(0-0)
Carmarthen Town - Barry Town 0-1(0-0)
Cefn Druids - Aberystwyth Town 1-2(1-1)
Airbus UK - Caernarfon Town 2-3(1-0)
The New Saints - Pen-y-bont FC 2-1(0-1)

Round 5 [07-10.09.2019]
Aberystwyth Town - Airbus UK 1-2(0-1)
Barry Town - Caernarfon Town 0-0
Carmarthen Town - Metropolitan 2-2(1-1)
Pen-y-bont FC - Bala Town 1-6(1-5)
Connah's Quay - Cefn Druids 1-0(1-0)
The New Saints - Newtown AFC 2-1(2-0)

Round 6 [13-16.09.2019]
Connah's Quay - Aberystwyth Town 4-1(2-0)
Airbus UK - Barry Town 0-1(0-1)
Caernarfon Town - Pen-y-bont FC 3-2(2-2)
Cefn Druids - Carmarthen Town 3-3(1-2)
Newtown AFC - Bala Town 1-0(0-0)
Metropolitan - The New Saints 1-1(1-0)

Round 7 [20-22.09.2019]
Aberystwyth Town - Caernarfon T. 2-3(1-2)
Newtown AFC - Connah's Quay 1-1(1-0)
Bala Town - Metropolitan 1-2(0-0)
Carmarthen Town - The New Saints 2-6(2-2)
Pen-y-bont FC - Airbus UK 3-1(1-0)
Barry Town - Cefn Druids 1-0(1-0)

Round 8 [27-29.09.2019]
Bala Town - Aberystwyth Town 2-0(1-0)
Caernarfon Town - Newtown AFC 1-0(0-0)
Airbus UK - Carmarthen Town 1-0(1-0)
The New Saints - Barry Town 0-1(0-1)
Connah's Quay - Pen-y-bont FC 3-1(1-0)
Metropolitan - Cefn Druids 2-1(1-1) [23.11.]

Round 9 [04-05.10.2019]
Caernarfon Town - The New Saints 1-0(0-0)
Pen-y-bont FC - Aberystwyth Town 1-1(0-0)
Cefn Druids - Bala Town 0-3(0-3)
Airbus UK - Metropolitan 1-1(0-1)
Carmarthen Town - Connah's Quay 1-2(1-1)
Newtown AFC - Barry Town 2-3(1-3)

Round 10 [11-15.10.2019]
Cefn Druids - Newtown AFC 1-2(0-2)
Aberystwyth Town - Metropolitan 2-1(1-0)
Bala Town - Carmarthen Town 2-1(2-1)
The New Saints - Airbus UK 6-2(4-0)
Connah's Quay - Caernarfon Town 4-2(1-1)
Barry Town - Pen-y-bont FC 3-0(1-0) [22.11.]

Round 11 [18-19.10.2019]
Cefn Druids - Caernarfon Town 3-1(0-1)
Carmarthen Town - Aberystwyth Town 0-0
Airbus UK - Newtown AFC 2-0(1-0)
Bala Town - Barry Town 1-1(1-1)
Metropolitan - Connah's Quay 0-1(0-0)
Pen-y-bont FC - The New Saints 2-3(1-2)

Round 12 [25-27.10.2019]
Aberystwyth Town - Connah's Quay 1-1(0-1)
Newtown AFC - Metropolitan 1-0(0-0)
The New Saints - Bala Town 1-0(0-0)
Barry Town - Airbus UK 2-0(0-0)
Caernarfon Town - Carmarthen Town 2-0(1-0)
Pen-y-bont FC - Cefn Druids 2-3(2-0)

Round 13 [01-02.11.2019]
Bala Town - Newtown AFC 4-0(2-0)
Metropolitan - Pen-y-bont FC 1-1(1-0)
Connah's Quay - The New Saints 1-1(0-0)
Airbus UK - Aberystwyth Town 1-5(1-2)
Caernarfon Town - Barry Town 4-1(1-1)
Carmarthen Town - Cefn Druids 1-2(1-2)

Round 14 [08-09.11.2019]
Newtown AFC - Caernarfon Town 3-1(2-0)
Aberystwyth Town - Bala Town 0-5(0-2)
Barry Town - Connah's Quay 0-4(0-3)
Airbus UK - Pen-y-bont FC 1-2(1-1)
Cefn Druids - Metropolitan 2-1(2-1) [03.12.]
The New Saints - Carmarthen 1-0(0-0)[03.12.]

Round 15 [15-16.11.2019]
Connah's Quay - Newtown AFC 3-1(2-1)
The New Saints - Aberystwyth Town 2-0(2-0)
Bala Town - Airbus UK 1-0(0-0)
Metropolitan - Carmarthen Town 0-3(0-2)
Cefn Druids - Barry Town 1-0(1-0)
Pen-y-bont FC - Caernarfon 0-0 [04.01.2020]

Round 16 [29-30.11.2019]
Aberystwyth Town - Cefn Druids 1-3(1-1)
Caernarfon Town - Metropolitan 2-1(1-0)
Airbus UK - The New Saints 0-12(0-5)
Barry Town - Newtown AFC 0-1(0-0)
Carmarthen Town - Bala Town 0-3(0-1)
Pen-y-bont FC - Connah's Quay 0-0

Round 17 [13-17.12.2019]
Caernarfon Town - Airbus UK 5-0(0-0)
Cefn Druids - Connah's Quay 2-0(1-0)
Barry Town - The New Saints 1-4(1-2)
Metropolitan - Aberystwyth Town 1-2(0-0)
Newtown AFC - Carmarthen Town 1-0(1-0)
Bala Town - Pen-y-bont FC 4-0(1-0)

Round 18 [20-21.12.2019]
Aberystwyth Town - Barry Town 0-1(0-0)
Connah's Quay - Bala Town 2-1(0-1)
The New Saints - Metropolitan 1-2(1-2)
Airbus UK - Cefn Druids 1-1(1-0)
Carmarthen Town - Caernarfon Town 0-1(0-0)
Pen-y-bont FC - Newtown AFC 0-2(0-0)

Round 19 [26.12.2019]
Barry Town - Metropolitan 1-1(1-1)
Carmarthen Town - Pen-y-bont FC 3-2(3-1)
Cefn Druids - The New Saints 0-5(0-2)
Connah's Quay - Airbus UK 2-1(2-0)
Newtown AFC - Aberystwyth Town 0-0
Caernarfon Town - Bala Town 1-2(0-0)

Round 20 [30.12.2019-01.01.2020]
Bala Town - Caernarfon Town 3-0(1-0)
Metropolitan - Barry Town 0-1(0-0)
The New Saints - Cefn Druids 2-1(0-0)
Aberystwyth Town - Newtown AFC 1-2(0-1)
Airbus UK - Connah's Quay 0-4(0-0)
Pen-y-bont FC - Carmarthen Town 1-1(1-0)

Round 21 [10-11.01.2020]
Caernarfon Town - Aberystwyth T. 0-3(0-1)
Newtown AFC - The New Saints 0-2(0-0)
Carmarthen Town - Airbus UK 2-2(2-1)
Cefn Druids - Pen-y-bont FC 2-3(1-1)
Connah's Quay - Barry Town 2-0(0-0)
Metropolitan - Bala Town 1-0(0-0)

Round 22 [18.01.2020]
Aberystwyth Town - Pen-y-bont FC 1-0(1-0)
Bala Town - Cefn Druids 1-2(0-0)
Barry Town - Carmarthen Town 7-1(5-1)
Metropolitan - Caernarfon Town 2-0(1-0)
Newtown AFC - Airbus UK 0-0
The New Saints - Connah's Quay 2-1(1-1)

1.	The New Saints FC	22	16	2	4	65	-	21	50
2.	Connah's Quay Nomads FC	22	13	7	2	39	-	17	46
3.	Bala Town FC	22	13	2	7	46	-	18	41
4.	Barry Town United FC	22	12	4	6	32	-	25	40
5.	Caernarfon Town FC	22	10	4	8	31	-	30	34
6.	Newtown AFC	22	9	5	8	21	-	24	32
7.	Cardiff Metropolitan University FC	22	8	7	7	26	-	25	31
8.	Cefn Druids AFC	22	9	4	9	32	-	34	31
9.	Aberystwyth Town FC	22	6	5	11	28	-	46	23
10.	Pen-y-Bont FC Bridgent	22	3	6	13	25	-	46	15
11.	Airbus UK Broughton FC	22	3	4	15	19	-	57	13
12.	Carmarthen Town AFC	22	2	6	14	24	-	45	12

Teams ranked 1-6 were qualified for the Championship Round, while teams ranked 7-12 were qualified for the Relegation Round.

Championship Round

Round 23 [07-08.02.2020]
The New Saints - Newtown AFC 1-2(1-2)
Caernarfon Town - Bala Town 1-2(1-0)
Barry Town - Connah's Quay 0-1(0-1)

Round 24 [14-15.02.2020]
Connah's Quay - Caernarfon Town 4-0(2-0)
Bala Town - The New Saints 1-1(1-0)
Newtown AFC - Barry Town *not played*

Round 25 [21-22.02.2020]
Connah's Quay - The New Saints 1-0(1-0)
Barry Town - Caernarfon Town 1-1(0-0)
Newtown AFC - Bala Town 1-2(0-2)

Round 26 [06.03.2020]
Caernarfon Town - Newtown AFC 3-1(0-1)
Bala Town - Connah's Quay 2-2(1-2)
The New Saints - Barry Town 2-2(2-0)

Relegation Round

Round 23 [07-08.02.2020]
Airbus UK - Cefn Druids 2-3(1-2)
Pen-y-bont FC - Carmarthen Town 1-2(1-0)
Metropolitan - Aberystwyth Town 3-1(1-1)

Round 24 [14.02.2020]
Aberystwyth Town - Airbus UK 5-3(2-1)
Carmarthen Town - Metropolitan *not played*
Cefn Druids - Pen-y-bont FC *not played*

Round 25 [21-22.02.2020]
Aberystwyth Town - Pen-y-bont FC 0-1(0-0)
Metropolitan - Airbus UK 1-1(0-1)
Carmarthen Town - Cefn Druids 1-0(0-0)

Round 26 [06-07.03.2020]
Cefn Druids - Aberystwyth Town 2-2(1-1)
Pen-y-bont FC - Metropolitan 2-0(1-0)
Carmarthen Town - Airbus UK 1-3

On 13.03.2020, all matches were suspended due to the Covid-19 pandemic. On 19.05.2020, the league was cancelled and Connah's Quay Nomads FC were declared 2019/2020 champions.

Final Standings

										Total						Home					Away	
1.	**Connah's Quay Nomads FC**	(2.15)	26	16	8	2	47	-	19	56	10	3	0	29	-	10	6	5	2	18	-	9
2.	The New Saints FC	(2.00)	26	16	4	6	69	-	27	52	9	1	3	23	-	13	7	3	3	46	-	14
3.	Bala Town FC	(1.88)	26	15	4	7	53	-	23	49	7	3	3	25	-	11	8	1	4	28	-	12
4.	Barry Town United FC	(1.68)	25	12	6	7	35	-	29	42	5	4	4	21	-	16	7	2	3	14	-	13
5.	Caernarfon Town FC	(1.46)	26	11	5	10	36	-	38	38	8	2	3	24	-	13	3	3	7	12	-	25
6.	Newtown AFC	(1.40)	25	10	5	10	25	-	30	35	4	5	3	11	-	10	6	0	7	14	-	20
7.	Cardiff Metropolitan University	(1.40)	25	9	8	8	30	-	29	35	6	3	4	14	-	12	3	5	4	16	-	17
8.	Cefn Druids AFC	(1.40)	25	10	5	10	37	-	39	35	5	2	5	20	-	23	5	3	5	17	-	16
9.	Aberystwyth Town FC	(1.04)	26	7	6	13	36	-	55	27	3	2	8	18	-	35	4	4	5	18	-	20
10.	Pen-y-Bont FC Bridgent	(0.84)	25	5	6	14	29	-	48	21	2	4	7	15	-	24	3	2	7	14	-	24
11.	Carmarthen Town AFC (*Relegated*)	(0.72)	25	4	6	15	28	-	49	18	2	3	8	14	-	26	2	3	7	14	-	23
12.	Airbus UK Broughton FC (*Relegated*)	(0.65)	26	4	5	17	28	-	67	17	2	2	8	12	-	34	2	3	9	16	-	33

Top goalscorers:

22	**Chris Venables**	***Bala Town FC***
18	Gregory Alexander Draper (NZL)	*The New Saints FC*
14	James Insall (ENG)	*Connah's Quay Nomads FC*
13	Kayne McLaggon	*Barry Town United FC*
12	Luke Bowen	*Carmarthen Town AFC*
11	Louis Robles (ENG)	*Bala Town FC*
11	Dean Ebbe (IRL)	*The New Saints FC*
10	Henry Jones	*Bala Town FC*

NATIONAL CUP
Welsh Cup 2019/2020

First Round [18/19/23/29.10.-02.11.2019]

Cambrian & Clydach - Ynyshir Albions FC	7-3		Cefn Cribwr Athletic Club - Tredegar Town FC	2-1 aet
Greenfield FC - Caersws FC	3-1		Pontypridd Town AFC - Caerau Ely AFC	3-1
Guilsfield FC - Brymbo FC	2-1		Cwmbran Celtic FC - Pontardawe Town FC	2-3 aet
Coedpoeth United - Gresford Athletic FC	0-5		Ammanford AFC - Cardiff Draconians FC	4-1
Holywell Town FC - Llandudno FC	2-3		Builth Wells FC - Ton Pentre FC	3-2
Prestatyn Sports - FC Queens Park Caia Park	2-3		Haverfordwest County AFC - Penlan Club FC	5-0
Conwy Borough FC - Ruthin Town FC	1-2		Aberbargoed Buds FC - Aberaeron FC	3-1
Waterloo Rovers FC - Mold Alexandra FC	1-8		Afan Lido FC Port Talbot - Monmouth Town FC	3-1
Bangor 1876 FC - Penycae FC	3-2 pen		Chepstow Town FC - Taff's Well AFC	3-2
Blaenau Ffestiniog Amateur FC - Buckley Town FC	0-2		Penrhyncoch FC - Cardiff Corinthians FC	2-1 aet
Nefyn United - Bangor City FC	0-2		Swansea University FC - Caerleon AFC	4-1
Flint Town United FC - Four Crosses FC	9-0		Abertillery Bluebirds - Penparcau FC	3-1
Corwen FC - Colwyn Bay FC	2-3		Llantwit Major FC - Llandrindod Wells FC	0-1
Nantlle Vale FC Penygroes - Rhydymwyn FC	2-0		Chirk AAA - Llannefydd FC	0-3
Rhyl FC - Llangefni Town FC	2-0		Croesyceiliog AFC - Abergavenny Town FC	2-1
Holyhead Hotspur FC - Montgomery Town FC	4-2		FC Cwmaman - STM Sports AFC Cardiff	2-6
Llanrhaeadr FC - Prestatyn Town FC	1-4		Llanelli Town AFC - Cwmamman United FC	2-1
Briton Ferry Llansawel AFC - Undy Athletic FC	3-4 pen		Porthmadog FC - Llanberis FC	7-0
Trefelin BGC - Llanidloes Town FC	3-4 pen		Aberffraw FC - Llanrug United FC	0-1
Garden Village AFC Swansea - Goytre United FC	1-3		Llanfair United - Mynydd Isa FC	5-3

Second Round [09-16.11.2019]

Llannefydd FC - Guilsfield FC	1-5		Bangor 1876 FC - Ruthin Town FC	0-2
Greenfield FC - Flint Town United FC	1-3		Ammanford AFC - Ton Pentre FC	3-1
Abertillery Bluebirds - Llanidloes Town FC	4-3		Undy Athletic FC - Swansea University FC	5-6
Porthmadog FC - Gresford Athletic FC	4-1		Pontypridd Town AFC - Llandrindod Wells FC	1-0
Holyhead Hotspur FC - Buckley Town FC	0-3		Afan Lido FC Port Talbot - Aberbargoed Buds FC	2-1
Nantlle Vale FC Penygroes - Colwyn Bay FC	0-1		Llanelli Town AFC - Penrhyncoch FC	0-1
Mold Alexandra FC - Llanrug United FC	8-1		Haverfordwest County AFC - Cambrian & Clydach	1-2
Rhyl FC - FC Queens Park Caia Park	3-0		Goytre United FC - Cefn Cribwr Athletic Club	6-4
Llandudno FC - Llanfair United	4-1		Chepstow Town FC - STM Sports AFC Cardiff	0-5
Bangor City FC - Prestatyn Town FC	0-3		Pontardawe Town FC - Croesyceiliog AFC	6-1

Third Round [06-14.12.2019]

Colwyn Bay FC - Airbus UK Broughton FC	1-0 aet		Aberystwyth Town FC - Ruthin Town FC	2-1
Carmarthen Town AFC - Ammanford AFC	0-4		Cefn Druids AFC - Guilsfield FC	2-0
Pontardawe Town FC - Buckley Town FC	3-1		Abertillery Bluebirds - Connah's Quay Nomads FC	0-3
Rhyl FC - STM Sports AFC Cardiff	2-0		Penrhyncoch FC - Prestatyn Town FC	1-2
Swansea University FC - Cambrian & Clydach	3-0		Goytre United FC - Caernarfon Town FC	0-4
The New Saints FC - Mold Alexandra FC	9-0		Flint Town United FC - Bala Town FC	2-0
Barry Town United FC - Newtown AFC	0-1		Afan Lido FC Port Talbot - Llandudno FC	5-1
Cardiff Metropolitan University - Pontypridd Town	1-0		Penybont FC - Porthmadog FC	6-1

1/8-Finals [24-25.01.2020]

Flint Town United FC - Colwyn Bay FC	3-2		The New Saints FC - Aberystwyth Town FC	4-0
Penybont FC - Cardiff Metropolitan University FC	1-2		Cefn Druids AFC - Pontardawe Town FC	2-0
Ammanford AFC - Caernarfon Town FC	0-4		Connah's Quay Nomads - Afan Lido FC Port Talbot	8-0
Swansea University FC - Prestatyn Town FC	0-1		Newtown AFC - Rhyl FC	4-1

Quarter-Finals [28.02.-03.03.2020]

Caernarfon Town FC - Cefn Druids AFC	4-0		The New Saints FC - Newtown AFC	6-1
Connah's Quay Nomads - Cardiff Metropolitan Univ.	1-2		Flint Town United FC - Prestatyn Town FC	0-1

Semi-Finals [scheduled 04-05.04.2020]

Caernarfon Town FC - Cardiff Metropolitan Univ.	*postponed*		Prestatyn Town FC - The New Saints FC	*postponed*

Semi-Finals and Final were postponed due to Covid-19 pandemic.
On 30.07.2020, the remainder of the competition was cancelled.

Please note: matches and goals includes statistics of both regular season and play-offs (Championship and Relegation).

Aberystwyth Town Football Club

Founded:	1884	
Stadium:	Park Avenue, Aberystwyth (5,000)	
Trainer:	Matthew Bishop	15.09.1973

Goalkeepers:	DOB	M	(s)	G
Terry McCormick (ENG)	25.09.1983	1		
Alexander Anthony Pennock		5	(1)	
Connor Roberts	08.12.1992	20		
Defenders:	**DOB**	**M**	**(s)**	**G**
Wes Baynes (ENG)	12.10.1988	23		1
Ben Birch (ENG)	01.07.1995	1		
Adam Davies	19.11.1993	3	(1)	
Adam Hughes (ENG)	29.11.1996	11	(2)	1
Stuart Jones	14.03.1984	18		
David Thompson (ENG)	27.02.1991	3	(1)	
Ryan Wollacott (ENG)	01.12.1994	10		1
Midfielders:	**DOB**	**M**	**(s)**	**G**
Edmilson Pedro Vaz (GNB)	01.04.1996	12	(4)	
Ryan Edwards	22.06.1988	1	(2)	
Ryan Edwards	25.05.1994	15	(3)	1
Steffan Edwards	10.10.1989	2	(3)	

	DOB	M	(s)	G
Ilan Hughes	22.04.1993	4	(1)	
Lee Jenkins	28.06.1979	21	(1)	
Matthew Jones	14.07.1999	21	(2)	3
Geoff Kellaway (ENG)	07.04.1986	10	(9)	3
Pavel Pinto Vieira (GNB)	15.02.1992	4	(1)	
Joe Phillips (ENG)	20.10.1994	12	(6)	2
Tom Price	26.11.1999	13	(1)	
Richard Ricketts		6	(4)	
James Rowland (ENG)	03.12.2001	2	(1)	
Forwards:	**DOB**	**M**	**(s)**	**G**
Porya Ahmadi (IRN)	08.01.1993		(2)	
Alex Boss	09.10.1998	2	(15)	
Luke Boundford	30.01.1988	13	(5)	2
Aaron Dotse-Pomeyie			(3)	
Paulo Mendes	08.07.1993	25	(1)	6
Alhagi Touray Sisay (ESP)		5		4
Marc Williams	27.07.1988	24	(1)	9

Airbus UK Broughton Football Club

Founded:	1946 (*as Vickers-Armstrong FC*)	
Stadium:	Hollingsworth Group International Airfield, Broughton (1,600)	
Trainer:	Stephen O'Shaughnessy	13.10.1967

Goalkeepers:	DOB	M	(s)	G
Ollie Byrne (ENG)	31.12.1997	3		
Lewis Hall		7		
Dave Roberts (ENG)	10.12.1988	15		
Defenders:	**DOB**	**M**	**(s)**	**G**
Danny Edwards			(3)	
Jordan Evans	23.09.1995	11	(6)	1
Walid Gharbaoui (FRA)	21.05.1995	2	(1)	
Sam Hart (ENG)	29.11.1991	23	(1)	
Joe Palmer	13.08.1999	22	(2)	1
Jake Phillips	31.01.1997	22	(1)	
Kristian Platt (ENG)	15.12.1991	17	(1)	3
Craig Rogers	21.02.1990	3		
Curtis Strong	26.09.1995	17	(1)	1
Steve Tomassen (ENG)	03.09.1993	22		
Liam Williams (ENG)		9		1
Midfielders:	**DOB**	**M**	**(s)**	**G**
Ryan Edwards	22.06.1988	15		1

	DOB	M	(s)	G
Harvey Ellis			(2)	
Ellis Hickey			(2)	
George Hughes (ENG)	23.03.1999	23		
Ollie Lanceley		2	(8)	3
Sam McCormick			(1)	
Brady McGilloway	13.06.1999	8	(5)	
Owen Lee Payne		2	(6)	
George Peers		6	(6)	3
Toby Vickery			(1)	
Niall Watson (ENG)	15.06.2000	3		3
Forwards:	**DOB**	**M**	**(s)**	**G**
Alex Darlington	26.12.1988	10	(4)	2
James Hooper	14.10.1993	1	(13)	
Iwan Jones			(1)	
Andy Owens (ENG)	15.10.1989	23		8
Matthew Sargent	24.07.2001	16	(1)	
Nathan Woolfe (ENG)	06.10.1988	4		

Please note: Sam Hart played one match as goalkeeper (Round 14, Airbus UK - Pen-y-bont FC 1-2).

Bala Town Football Club

Founded:	1880	
Stadium:	Maes Tegid Stadium, Bala (3,000)	
Trainer:	Colin Caton	22.08.1970

Goalkeepers:	DOB	M	(s)	G
Ashley Morris	31.07.1984	9	(1)	
Josh Tibbetts (ENG)	05.07.1998	17		
Defenders:	**DOB**	**M**	**(s)**	**G**
Andrew Burns (IRL)	02.07.1993	26		
Evan Horwood (ENG)	10.03.1986		(6)	
Stuart Jones (ENG)	28.08.1986	7	(1)	2
Shaun Kelly (ENG)	11.12.1988	9		
Sean Smith (ENG)	12.12.1994	26		
Jonny Spittle (ENG)	13.08.1994	10	(1)	2
Anthony Stephens	21.01.1994	25		
Thomas Stephens (ENG)	20.11.1997		(1)	

Midfielders:	DOB	M	(s)	G
Nathan Burke (ENG)	15.09.1995	26		
Henry Jones	18.09.1993	20	(3)	10
Steven Leslie (SCO)	05.11.1987	13	(12)	
Lassana Nalatche Mendes (GNB)	26.12.1996	24	(1)	3
Lee Molyneux (ENG)	24.02.1989	4	(13)	
Oliver Shannon (ENG)	12.09.1995	3	(2)	
Forwards:	**DOB**	**M**	**(s)**	**G**
Mike Hayes (ENG)	21.11.1987	1	(11)	1
Louis Robles (ENG)	11.09.1996	24		11
Kieran Smith (ENG)	03.06.1992	17	(6)	1
Chris Venables	23.07.1985	25		22

Barry Town United Football Club

Founded: 1912 (*as Barry AFC*)
Stadium: Jenner Park, Barry (3,500)
Trainer: Gavin Chesterfield

Goalkeepers:	DOB	M	(s)	G
Mike Lewis	04.04.1989	13		
George Ratcliffe	12.09.2000	12		
Defenders:	**DOB**	**M**	**(s)**	**G**
Rhys Abbruzzese	23.03.1998	6	(1)	
Luke Cooper	02.04.1993	24		2
Luke Cummings	25.10.1991	25		2
Chris Hugh	22.01.1992	22		1
Paul Morgan	28.06.1994	3	(3)	
Curtis Watkins	11.09.1995	12	(3)	
Midfielders:	**DOB**	**M**	**(s)**	**G**
Alexander Brookes-Bent	09.07.2001		(1)	
David Cotterill	04.12.1987	1	(1)	
Tom Fry	31.05.1997	2		
Lathan Garrett			(1)	
Clayton Green	27.02.1994	21	(1)	4
Troy Greening (ENG)	17.04.1993	1		
Jonathan Hood	07.02.1991	9	(1)	1
Jack Pascoe			(1)	
Kyle Patten	21.07.1994	3		
Robbie Patten	29.11.1996	5	(1)	
Evan Press	26.06.2000	18	(4)	2
Keyon Reffell	06.10.1990	11	(4)	2
Callum Sainty	12.05.1996	5	(4)	
Theo Wharton (SKN)	15.11.1994	4		
Forwards:	**DOB**	**M**	**(s)**	**G**
Jack Compton	02.09.1988	6	(9)	1
Jordan Cotterill	20.10.1988	6	(4)	1
Drew Fahiya	17.04.1988	13	(6)	2
Kayne McLaggon	21.09.1990	23		13
Eli Phipps	29.07.1997	2	(12)	
Sion Spence	02.10.2000	13		1
Momodou Touray	30.07.1999	15	(5)	3

Caernarfon Town Football Club

Founded: 1937
Stadium: The Oval, Caernarfon (3,000)
Trainer: Sean Eardley

Goalkeepers:	DOB	M	(s)	G
Alex Ramsay	15.07.1993	26		
Defenders:	**DOB**	**M**	**(s)**	**G**
Gareth Edwards	20.07.1983	14	(3)	
Noah Edwards	30.05.1996	15	(2)	2
Mike Pearson	19.01.1988	5	(1)	
Aled Williams		1		
Gruff John Williams	22.06.1994	15	(4)	1
Joe Williams	17.02.1989	13	(1)	
Midfielders:	**DOB**	**M**	**(s)**	**G**
Sion Bradley	20.02.1998	19	(4)	3
Ben Clark	14.10.2000	11		
Jamie Crowther	10.02.1992	15	(1)	1
Gareth Evans	29.04.1987	13	(4)	2
Sam Jones	09.11.1999	6	(13)	1
Leo Smith	15.05.1998	20	(1)	4
Ryan Williams	10.05.1998	26		
Telor Williams			(2)	
Forwards:	**DOB**	**M**	**(s)**	**G**
Jamie Breeze	10.01.1992	19	(5)	6
Danny Brookwell	09.03.1993	15	(8)	1
Shaun Cavanagh	18.12.1997	4	(6)	
Nathan Craig	25.10.1991	16	(2)	4
Mohammed El-Arab			(1)	
Cai Jones	03.10.1992	9	(10)	2
Darren Thomas	20.01.1987	24	(1)	7

Cardiff Metropolitan University Football Club

Founded: 2000 (*as UWIC Inter Cardiff*)
Stadium: Cyncoed Campus, Cardiff (1,620)
Trainer: Christian Edwards 25.11.1975

Goalkeepers:	DOB	M	(s)	G
Will Fuller	07.07.1993	17		
Alex Lang	10.10.1999	8	(1)	1
Defenders:	**DOB**	**M**	**(s)**	**G**
Matthew Clubb		2		
Mael Davies	10.10.1998	22	(1)	5
Emlyn Lewis	14.06.1996	25		
Kyle McCarthy	12.04.1993	15	(3)	
Dylan Rees	17.09.1996	14	(3)	1
Guto Williams	10.05.2000	6	(2)	
Bradley Woolridge	16.12.1992	19	(1)	
Midfielders:	**DOB**	**M**	**(s)**	**G**
Chris Baker	29.11.1993	17	(4)	2
Charlie Corsby	14.10.1991	23	(1)	
Joel Edwards (ENG)	18.08.1991	21	(1)	1
Ioan Evans	30.05.1997	1		
Joe Evans		16	(3)	
Will Evans	01.07.1997	23		7
Rhydian Morgan	19.06.1999	1	(1)	
Dion Phillips	12.09.1998	1	(14)	1
Dave Thomas	01.02.1999	1	(3)	
Forwards:	**DOB**	**M**	**(s)**	**G**
Eliot Evans	26.11.1991	21	(1)	8
Jordan Lam	16.08.1994	19		4
Dan Spencer	19.05.1993	3	(9)	
Liam Warman	01.05.1999		(7)	

Carmarthen Town Association Football Club

Founded: 1950
Stadium: Richmond Park, Carmarthen (3,000)
Trainer: Neil Smothers 08.12.1977

Goalkeepers:	DOB	M	(s)	G
Lee Idzi	08.02.1988	23		
Thomas Alan Windsor		2		
Defenders:	**DOB**	**M**	**(s)**	**G**
Declan Carroll	04.07.1993	14	(6)	1
Craig Hanford	08.07.1984		(1)	
Alaric Jones		4	(1)	
Jordan Knott	13.09.1993	21		1
James Parry	27.05.1995	2		
Lewis Rocke	09.06.2001	2	(3)	
Cai Smith	03.09.1998	4	(1)	
Lee Surman	03.04.1986	25		
Dave Vincent	17.06.1990	17	(1)	1
Midfielders:	**DOB**	**M**	**(s)**	**G**
Cameron Berry	25.06.2000	2	(1)	
Kalilo Djalo-Embaló (SEN)	07.10.1996	3		1
Mabon Evans		1	(3)	
Lewis Harling	11.06.1992	19		
Ceri Morgan	22.01.1991	11	(4)	
Adam Robbins		5		
Callum Saunders	26.09.1995	1		1
Elliot Scotcher	03.03.1994	13	(1)	3
Liam Thomas	06.11.1991	19	(4)	6
Jordan Vickers		19	(3)	
Greg Walters	10.01.1995	21	(2)	
Jay Woodford		7	(3)	
Forwards:	**DOB**	**M**	**(s)**	**G**
Luke Bowen	07.03.1988	22		12
Josh Bull	15.04.1993	7	(9)	1
Noah Daley	2001	2	(3)	
Gwion Howell	12.02.1997	1	(3)	
Chris Jones	14.02.1990	9	(9)	

Cefn Druids Association Football Club Cefn Mawr

Founded: 1872
Stadium: The Rock Stadium, Wrexham (3,000)
Trainer: Huw Griffiths — 09.02.1977
[05.02.2020] Stuart Gelling (ENG) — 08.09.1973

Goalkeepers:	DOB	M	(s)	G
Michael Jones (ENG)	03.12.1987	25		
Defenders:	**DOB**	**M**	**(s)**	**G**
Naim Arsan	14.12.1993	21	(1)	
Neil Ashton (ENG)	15.01.1985	21		1
Phil Mooney (ENG)	19.01.1991	14		
Alec Mudimu (ZIM)	08.04.1995	12		3
Joash Nembhard (ENG)	13.03.1998	2		
Nathan Peate	02.05.1991	25		2
Aaron Simpson	19.10.1995	11	(1)	
Midfielders:	**DOB**	**M**	**(s)**	**G**
Harry Brazel (ENG)		2		
Iwan Cartwright	09.08.1996	16	(4)	
Ben Davis			(1)	
Morgan Daykin		1	(1)	
Charley Edge	14.05.1997	7	(7)	1
Steffan Edwards	10.10.1989	4	(1)	
Joe Faux (AUS)	08.07.1999	15	(2)	1
Jaden Jones			(1)	
Ryan Kershaw	21.09.1995	9	(3)	1
Matty Owen	23.07.1994	2	(4)	
Arkadiusz Piskorski (POL)	24.04.1990		(2)	
Tom Reilly (ENG)	07.02.2000	5	(1)	
Forwards:	**DOB**	**M**	**(s)**	**G**
James Davies	02.10.1993	19	(2)	9
Papé Ibrahima Diakhité (FRA)	30.08.1995	1	(4)	
Remy Howarth (ENG)	14.09.1997	18	(3)	3
Tyrone Ofori (ENG)	26.07.2000	11	(6)	2
Michael Pritchard	10.12.1991	11	(1)	1
Jamie Reed	13.08.1987	4		4
Dean Rittenberg (ENG)	13.05.1996	4	(1)	
Cody Ruberto (ITA)	29.10.1990	15	(3)	7

Connah's Quay Nomads Football Club

Founded: 1946
Stadium: Deeside Stadium, Connah's Quay (1,500)
Trainer: Andrew Morrison (SCO) — 30.07.1970

Goalkeepers:	DOB	M	(s)	G
Lewis Brass	26.08.1996	25		
Eric Merner	17.09.2001	1		
Defenders:	**DOB**	**M**	**(s)**	**G**
John Disney	15.05.1992	16	(6)	1
Priestley Farquharson	15.03.1997	18	(3)	2
Danny Holmes	06.01.1989	26		1
George Horan (ENG)	18.02.1982	17	(1)	2
Kris Owens	07.12.1998	7	(8)	
Callum Roberts	16.10.1998	18	(3)	
Midfielders:	**DOB**	**M**	**(s)**	**G**
Sameron Dool	07.06.1999	6	(5)	
Danny Harrison (ENG)	04.11.1982	18	(1)	
Max Moore			(1)	
Callum Morris (ENG)	01.09.1992	21	(1)	3
Jay Owen	14.01.1991	16	(2)	
Declan Poole (ENG)	05.09.1995	21	(4)	3
Ryan Wignall (ENG)	12.03.1989	5	(4)	1
Aron Williams	08.11.1995		(1)	
Sam Williams			(1)	
Forwards:	**DOB**	**M**	**(s)**	**G**
Michael Bakare (ENG)	01.12.1986	15	(9)	8
Craig Curran (ENG)	23.08.1989	4		2
Connor Harwood	02.02.2000	1	(7)	
Jamie Insall (ENG)	01.03.1992	23	(2)	14
Michael Wilde	27.08.1983	24		9
Nathan Woolfe (ENG)	06.10.1988	4	(4)	

Newtown Association Football Club

Founded: 1875
Stadium: Latham Park, Newtown (5,000)
Trainer: Chris Hughes (SCO) — 21.04.1979

Goalkeepers:	DOB	M	(s)	G
David Jones	03.02.1990	25		
Khamran Steventon	15.09.2001		(1)	
Defenders:	**DOB**	**M**	**(s)**	**G**
Sam Barnes (ENG)	16.10.1991	14	(2)	1
Ryan Edwards (ENG)	07.10.1993	1		
Jack Kelly (ENG)	01.01.1996	24		
Kieran Mills-Evans	11.10.1992	25		1
Alun Morris	13.04.1989		(1)	
Craig T. Williams	21.12.1987	21	(1)	
Midfielders:	**DOB**	**M**	**(s)**	**G**
Jay Denny (USA)	06.01.1986	4	(1)	
Ryan Edwards	25.05.1994	2		
Alex Fletcher (ENG)	17.11.1996	20		2
Niall Flint (ENG)	15.08.1997	16	(4)	2
Tom Goodwin	12.01.1990		(2)	
Joe Kenton	19.05.1998	19	(4)	3
Sean McAllister (ENG)	15.08.1987	23		1
Sam Phillips	24.02.1999	1	(3)	
Jack Thorn	22.03.2001	9	(6)	
Forwards:	**DOB**	**M**	**(s)**	**G**
George Harry	07.06.1999	11	(10)	3
Neil Mitchell (ENG)	01.04.1988	15	(3)	
Lifumpa Mwandwe (ENG)	29.12.2000	13	(9)	3
Nicky Rushton	03.02.1992	19	(1)	4
Ian Sheridan (ENG)	12.03.1989	11	(7)	4
Matthew Williams	05.11.1982	2	(6)	

Pen-y-Bont Football Club

Founded: 2013 (as merger of Bridgend Town AFC and Bryntirion Athletic FC)
Stadium: Kymco Stadium, Bridgend (3,000)
Trainer: Rhys Griffiths — 01.03.1980

Goalkeepers:	DOB	M	(s)	G
Ashley Morris	31.07.1984	6		
Rhys Wilson	11.06.1992	19		
Defenders:	**DOB**	**M**	**(s)**	**G**
Billy Borge	22.05.1998	11	(5)	1
Oliver Dalton		9	(1)	
Dan Jefferies	30.01.1999	23		2
Kane Owen	22.10.1994	24		4
Daniel Summerfield		5		
Midfielders:	**DOB**	**M**	**(s)**	**G**
Ashley Evans	18.07.1989	6		
Michael George	12.06.1999	20	(3)	
Lewis Harling	11.06.1992	3	(1)	2
Matthew Harris (ENG)	16.01.1994	19	(3)	2
Kieran Howard	17.01.1991	1	(3)	1
Cullen Kinsella		5	(10)	
Keenan Patten	07.04.2001	11	(1)	1
James Saddler	11.01.1992	22	(1)	
Owain Warlow	25.10.1987	20	(5)	
Forwards:	**DOB**	**M**	**(s)**	**G**
Luke Borrelli	28.03.1991	5	(9)	1
Adam Carpenter			(2)	
Kostya Georgievsky	28.06.1996	8	(12)	3
Dan Griffiths	16.01.2001	13	(8)	5
Curtis Jay Jemmett-Hutson	14.08.1994	20	(3)	5
Eli Phipps	29.07.1997	2	(1)	
Nathan Daniel Wood	23.04.1997	21	(2)	1

The New Saints of Oswestry Town & Llansantffraid Football Club

Founded:	1959	
Stadium:	Park Hall Stadium, Oswestry (2,034)	
Trainer:	Scott Ruscoe (ENG)	15.12.1977

Goalkeepers:	DOB	M	(s)	G
Paul Harrison (ENG)	18.12.1984	26		
Defenders:	**DOB**	**M**	**(s)**	**G**
Keston Davies	02.10.1996	20		2
Ryan Harrington	03.10.1998	16	(5)	
Blaine Hudson (ENG)	28.10.1991	22		1
Adam Hughes (ENG)	29.11.1996		(1)	1
Kane Lewis (ENG)	17.03.1998	4		
Chris Marriott (ENG)	24.09.1989	20		1
Simon Spender	15.11.1985	13	(2)	1
Midfielders:	**DOB**	**M**	**(s)**	**G**
Joshua Bailey			(1)	
Ryan Brobbel (NIR)	05.03.1993	24		8

	DOB	M	(s)	G
Aeron Edwards	16.02.1988	20	(1)	6
Tom Holland (IRL)	22.04.1997	3		
Daniel Redmond (ENG)	02.03.1991	21	(1)	1
Jon Routledge (ENG)	23.11.1989	20	(1)	2
Ethan Short			(1)	
Billy Whitehouse (ENG)	13.06.1996	5	(8)	3
Forwards:	**DOB**	**M**	**(s)**	**G**
Kurtis Byrne (IRL)	09.04.1990	3	(18)	5
Adrian Cieslewicz (POL)	16.11.1990	19	(5)	7
Gregory Alexander Draper (NZL)	13.08.1989	11	(13)	18
Dean Ebbe (IRL)	16.07.1994	17	(5)	11
Jamie Mullan (ENG)	10.02.1988	9	(6)	1

SECOND LEVEL
2019/2020

<u>Please note</u>: the league was suspended on 13.03.2020 due to Covid-19 pandemic. Later, on 19.05.2020 the league was cancelled, standings being decided by a points by game average..

	Cymru North									
1.	Prestatyn Town FC	24	21	2	1	84	-	18	65	(2.71)
2.	Flint Town United FC (*Promoted*)	22	15	4	3	59	-	22	49	(2.23)
3.	Guilsfield FC	21	13	4	4	44	-	26	43	(2.05)
4.	Colwyn Bay FC	24	14	5	5	44	-	30	47	(1.96)
5.	Bangor City FC	22	10	7	5	27	-	25	37	(1.68)
6.	Conwy Borough FC	23	9	6	8	43	-	44	33	(1.43)
7.	Llanrhaeadr FC	21	9	3	9	35	-	34	30	(1.43)
8.	Penrhyncoch FC	23	10	2	11	29	-	35	32	(1.39)
9.	Ruthin Town FC	23	7	7	9	29	-	34	28	(1.22)
10.	Buckley Town FC	20	7	3	10	24	-	41	24	(1.20)
11.	Gresford Athletic FC	22	7	5	10	34	-	34	26	(1.18)
12.	Llandudno FC	21	6	4	11	32	-	38	22	(1.05)
13.	Llangefni Town FC	24	5	6	13	22	-	47	21	(0.88)
14.	Porthmadog FC (*Relegated*)	23	4	6	13	28	-	46	18	(0.78)
15.	Corwen FC (*Relegated*)	22	3	5	14	26	-	51	14	(0.64)
16.	Llanfair United FC (*Relegated*)	21	2	3	16	23	-	58	9	(0.43)

Rhyl FC were excluded in April 2020 for financial reasons, all their results were annulled.
Prestatyn Town FC failed to obtain a first level license, as result Flint Town United FC promoted to the Cymru Premier League 2020/2021.

	Cymru North									
1.	Swansea University FC	25	17	5	3	56	-	31	56	(2.24)
2.	Haverfordwest County AFC (*Promoted*)	25	17	4	4	58	-	26	55	(2.20)
3.	Briton Ferry Llansawel AFC	24	15	2	7	65	-	36	47	(1.96)
4.	STM Sports AFC Cardiff	22	12	3	7	51	-	34	39	(1.77)
5.	Cambrian & Clydach Vale Boys & Girls Club	23	11	7	5	41	-	31	40	(1.74)
6.	Llanelli Town AFC	26	12	4	10	47	-	51	40	(1.54)
7.	Ammanford AFC	25	12	1	12	44	-	47	37	(1.48)
8.	Goytre United FC	25	10	6	9	40	-	41	36	(1.44)
9.	Pontypridd Town AFC Cardiff	25	9	8	8	52	-	41	35	(1.40)
10.	Afan Lido FC Port Talbot	25	10	4	11	47	-	47	34	(1.36)
11.	Llantwit Major FC	24	7	6	11	34	-	39	27	(1.13)
12.	Undy Athletic FC	21	7	2	12	29	-	38	23	(1.10)
13.	Cwmbran Celtic FC	22	6	4	12	29	-	44	22	(1.00)
14.	Taff's Well AFC (*Relegated*)	25	6	3	16	40	-	64	21	(0.84)
15.	Cwmamman United FC Glanaman(*Relegated*)	22	5	2	15	22	-	55	17	(0.77)
16.	Caerau (Ely) AFC Cardiff (*Relegated*)	21	1	5	15	22	-	52	8	(0.38)

Swansea University FC failed to obtain a first level license, as result Haverfordwest County AFC promoted to the Cymru Premier League 2020/2021.

INTERNATIONAL MATCHES
(16.07.2019 – 15.07.2020)

Date	Venue	Match	Score	
06.09.2019	Cardiff	Wales - Azerbaijan	2-1(1-0)	(ECQ)
09.09.2019	Cardiff	Wales - Belarus	1-0(1-0)	(F)
10.10.2019	Trnava	Slovakia - Wales	1-1(0-1)	(ECQ)
13.10.2019	Cardiff	Wales - Croatia	1-1(1-1)	(ECQ)
16.11.2019	Bakı	Azerbaijan - Wales	0-2(0-2)	(ECQ)
19.11.2019	Cardiff	Wales - Hungary	2-0(1-0)	(ECQ)

06.09.2019   **WALES - AZERBAIJAN**   **2-1(1-0)**   16th EC. Qualifiers

Cardiff City Stadium, Cardiff; Referee: Trustin Farrugia Cann (Malta); Attendance: 28,385

WAL: Wayne Robert Hennessey, Neil John Taylor (80.Benjamin Thomas Davies), Joseph Peter Rodon, Ethan Kwame Colm Raymond Ampadu (75.Samuel Michael Vokes), Christopher James Mepham, Joseph Michael Allen, Thomas Morris Lawrence, Daniel Owen James, Harry Wilson (63.Jonathan Peter Williams), Connor Richard John Roberts, Gareth Frank Bale (Cap). Trainer: Ryan Joseph Giggs.

Goals: Pavel Vaqif Paşayev (28 own goal), Gareth Frank Bale (84).

09.09.2019   **WALES - BELARUS**   **1-0(1-0)**   Friendly International

Cardiff City Stadium, Cardiff; Referee: William Collum (Scotland); Attendance: 7,666

WAL: Daniel Ward, Benjamin Thomas Davies (90+1.Christopher Ross Gunter), Joseph Peter Rodon, Christopher James Mepham (77.Thomas Alun Lockyer), Joseph Michael Allen (Cap), Jonathan Peter Williams, Daniel Owen James (50.Gareth Frank Bale), Joseff John Morrell, Harry Wilson (89.William Robert Vaulks), Connor Richard John Roberts, Kieffer Roberto Francisco Moore (75.Samuel Michael Vokes). Trainer: Ryan Joseph Giggs.

Goal: Daniel Owen James (17).

10.10.2019   **SLOVAKIA - WALES**   **1-1(0-1)**   16th EC. Qualifiers

Štadión "Antona Malatinského", Trnava; Referee: Carlos del Cerro Grande (Spain); Attendance: 18,071

WAL: Wayne Robert Hennessey, Benjamin Thomas Davies, Thomas Alun Lockyer, Joseph Peter Rodon, Ethan Kwame Colm Raymond Ampadu (58.Joseff John Morrell), Joseph Michael Allen, Jonathan Peter Williams (66.Harry Wilson), Daniel Owen James, Connor Richard John Roberts, Gareth Frank Bale (Cap), Kieffer Roberto Francisco Moore. Trainer: Ryan Joseph Giggs.

Goal: Kieffer Roberto Francisco Moore (25).

13.10.2019   **WALES - CROATIA**   **1-1(1-1)**   16th EC. Qualifiers

Cardiff City Stadium, Cardiff; Referee: Björn Kuipers (Netherlands); Attendance: 31,745

WAL: Wayne Robert Hennessey, Benjamin Thomas Davies, Thomas Alun Lockyer, Joseph Peter Rodon, Ethan Kwame Colm Raymond Ampadu (50.Joseff John Morrell), Joseph Michael Allen, Jonathan Peter Williams (68.Harry Wilson), Daniel Owen James, Connor Richard John Roberts, Gareth Frank Bale (Cap), Kieffer Roberto Francisco Moore (86.Tyler D'Whyte Roberts). Trainer: Ryan Joseph Giggs.

Goal: Gareth Frank Bale (45+3).

16.11.2019   **AZERBAIJAN - WALES**   **0-2(0-2)**   16th EC. Qualifiers

Bakcell Arena, Bakı; Referee: Deniz Aytekin (Germany); Attendance: 8,622

WAL: Wayne Robert Hennessey, Benjamin Thomas Davies, Thomas Alun Lockyer, Ethan Kwame Colm Raymond Ampadu (88.William Robert Vaulks), Christopher James Mepham, Daniel Owen James (82.Rabbi Matondo), Joseff John Morrell, Harry Wilson, Connor Richard John Roberts, Gareth Frank Bale (Cap) (60.Joseff John Morrell), Kieffer Roberto Francisco Moore. Trainer: Ryan Joseph Giggs.

Goals: Kieffer Roberto Francisco Moore (10), Harry Wilson (34).

19.11.2019   **WALES - HUNGARY**   **2-0(1-0)**   16th EC. Qualifiers

Cardiff City Stadium, Cardiff; Referee: Ovidiu Alin Haţegan (Romania); Attendance: 31,762

WAL: Wayne Robert Hennessey, Benjamin Thomas Davies, Thomas Alun Lockyer, Christopher James Mepham, Joseph Michael Allen, Joseff John Morrell, Daniel Owen James, Joseff John Morrell (50.Ethan Kwame Colm Raymond Ampadu), Connor Richard John Roberts, Gareth Frank Bale (Cap) (88.Harry Wilson), Kieffer Roberto Francisco Moore. Trainer: Ryan Joseph Giggs.

Goals: Aaron James Ramsey (15, 47).